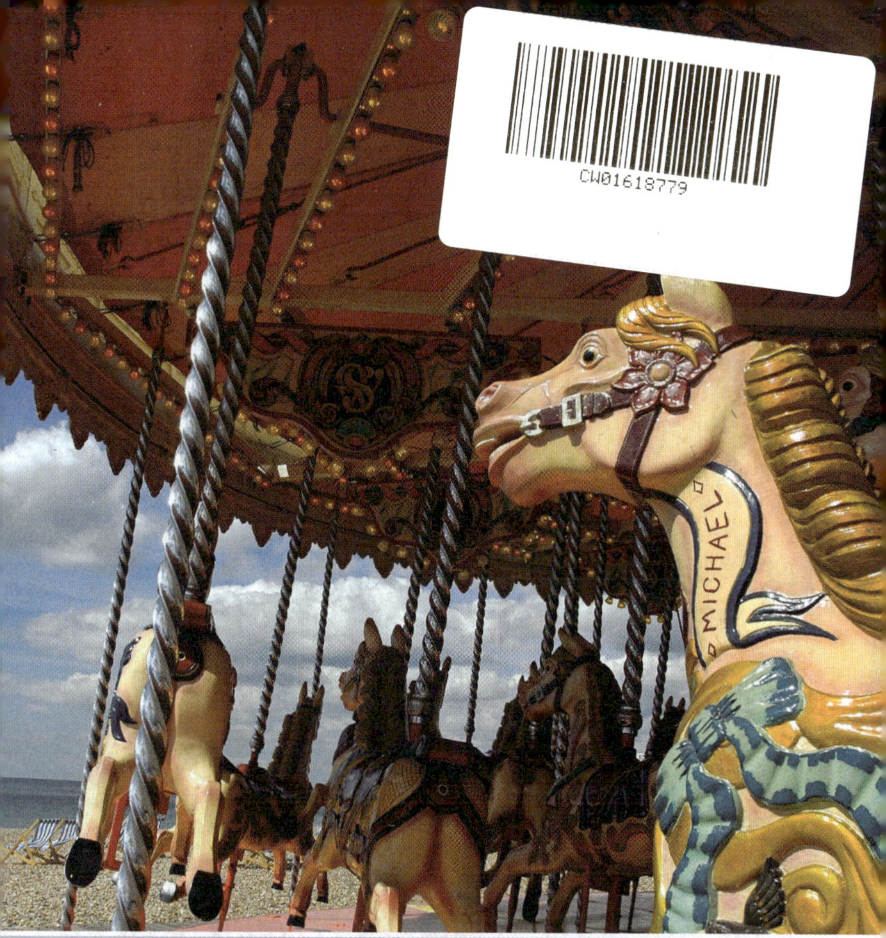

THE ROUGH GUIDE TO

Britain

written and researched by

Rob Andrews, Jules Brown, Tim Burford, Matthew Hancock, Dan Hodgkinson, Rob Humphreys, Phil Lee, Norm Longley, Donald Reid, Claire Saunders, Jos Simon, Helena Smith, Gavin Thomas, Amanda Tomlin, Lucy White and Paul Whitfield

ROUGH GUIDES

roughguides.com

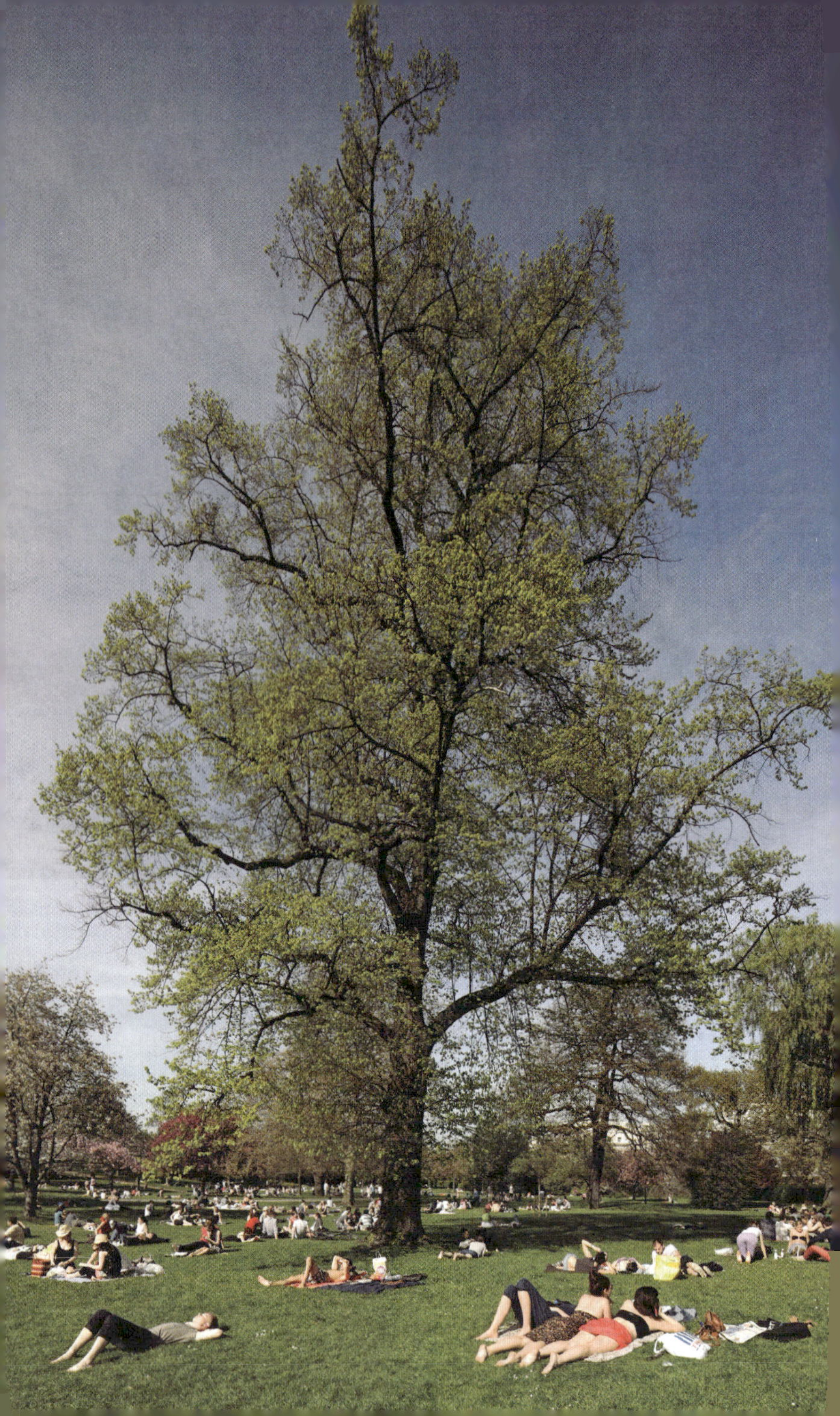

Contents

INTRODUCTION 4

Where to go 5
When to go 14
Things not to miss 16

BASICS 28

Getting there 29
Getting around 31
Accommodation 34
Food and drink 36
The media 39
Festivals and events 40
Sports and outdoor activities 42
Travel essentials 45

GUIDE 52

1 London 52
2 The Southeast 132
3 Hampshire, Dorset and Wiltshire 174
4 Oxfordshire, the Cotswolds and around 218
5 Bristol, Bath and Somerset 254
6 Devon and Cornwall 284
7 East Anglia 336
8 The West Midlands and the Peak District 374
9 The East Midlands 414
10 The Northwest 442
11 Cumbria and the Lakes 482
12 Yorkshire 508
13 The Northeast 558
14 South Wales 598
15 Mid-Wales 644
16 North Wales 678
17 Edinburgh and the Lothians 710
18 Southern Scotland 748
19 Glasgow and the Clyde 770
20 Central Scotland 796
21 Argyll 826
22 Northeast Scotland 850
23 The Highland region 874
24 Skye and the Western Isles 912
25 Orkney and Shetland 936

CONTEXTS 960

History 961
Books 978
Film 983

SMALL PRINT & INDEX 987

OPPOSITE REGENT'S PARK, LONDON **PREVIOUS PAGE** BRIGHTON BEACH

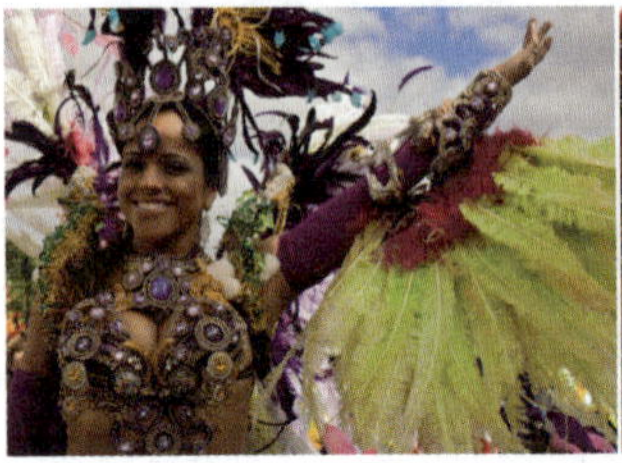
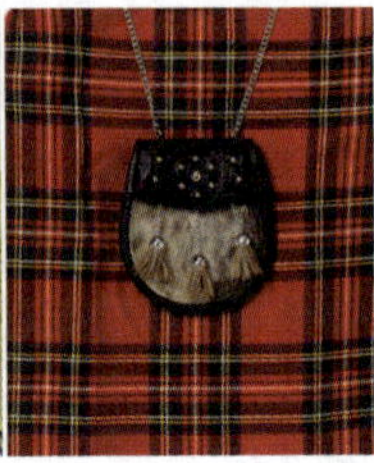
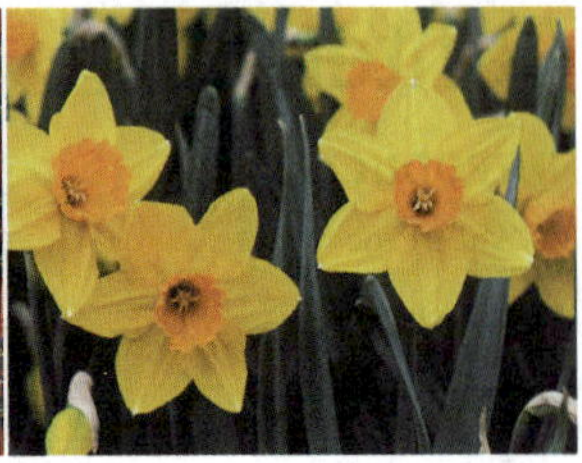

Introduction to **Britain**

If you didn't know that the "Great" in Great Britain was strictly a geographical term (it refers to the largest island – containing England, Scotland and Wales – of the British Isles), you'd be tempted to give Britain the accolade anyway. It's hard to think of another country that's given so much to the world – railways to royalty, shipbuilding to Shakespeare, football to fish and chips – and there are few holiday destinations suffused with as much history, based on more than five thousand years of settlement and a proud record of stability, democracy and invention. From dynamic London to misty Scottish mountains, fishing villages to futuristic cityscapes – and whether you're looking for urban adventures, pagan festivals, cutting-edge galleries, world-class museums, wilderness hikes or majestic buildings – Britain is undoubtedly best.

Of course, the kind of time you have here depends on which Britain you visit – which sounds odd until you take on board that we're talking about three different countries and three distinct national identities, all wrapped up in a relatively modest-sized "United Kingdom" on the western edge of Europe. England, Scotland and Wales have had centuries to get used to each other, but even so there are sharp reminders of past conflicts and present politics at every turn – from mighty border castles to proud, devolved parliaments – while you'll find separate "national" cultural collections in the three very different capital cities of London, Cardiff and Edinburgh. You're not walking into any kind of vicious separatist clamour – though Scotland may well vote on disengaging itself from the Union – but it's as well to remember that England (by far the dominant country) is not the same thing as Britain (even if the English sometimes act that way).

As well as the national variations that spice up any visit, there's also huge regional diversity in Britain – from the myriad accents and dialects that puzzle foreigners to the dramatically diverse landscapes. Bucolic Britain is still easy to find, be it in gentle

ABOVE NOTTING HILL CARNIVAL; TARTAN; DAFFODILS **RIGHT** WORCESTER AND BIRMINGHAM CANAL

rolling farmland or alpine peaks and lakes, and tradition and heritage still underpins much that is unique about the great British countryside. But increasingly it's Britain's urban culture – innovative arts and music, challenging architecture, trend-setting nightlife – that the tourist authorities choose to promote. Locals might eschew the marketing label "Cool Britannia" (there's something very un-British about that brash bravado) but there's no denying that times have changed when British museums, galleries, restaurants and clubs increasingly influence what goes on in the rest of the world.

The Empire may be long gone, and Britain might be uncertain about its political role in the modern world, but it's no longer bashful about its successes. The long build-up to London's 2012 Olympics, and Glasgow's 2014 Commonwealth Games, has put Britain centre stage again, and visitors – whether first-time tourists, or life-long residents – have lots to look forward to.

Where to go

There's enough to see and do in Britain to swallow up months of travel. The rundown of country-by-country highlights over the following pages will help you plan an itinerary – or remind you of how much you've yet to see.

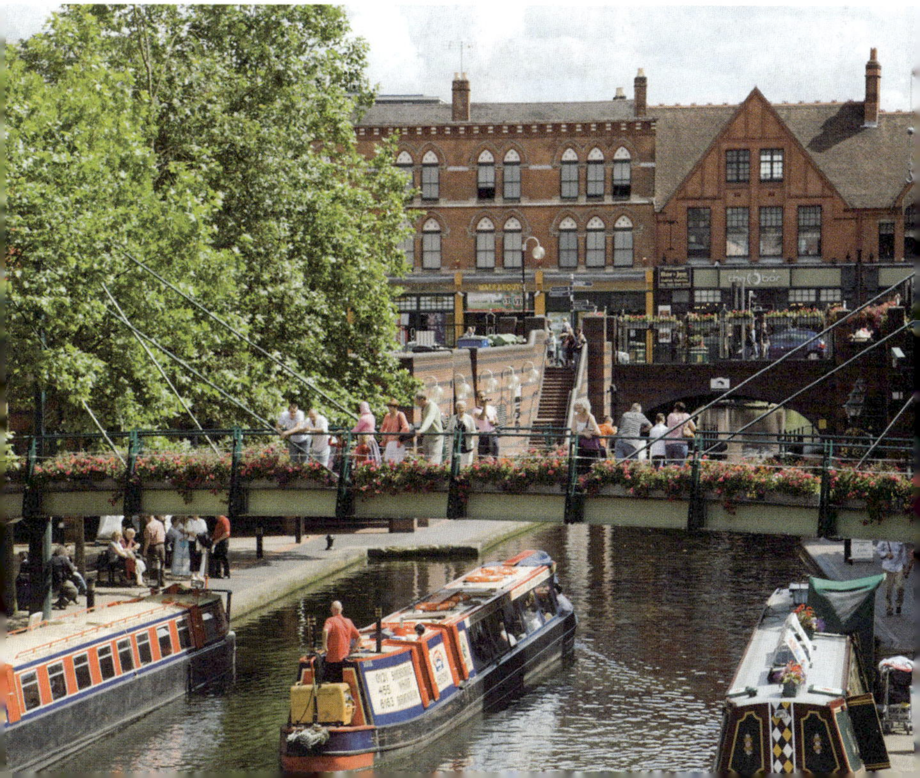

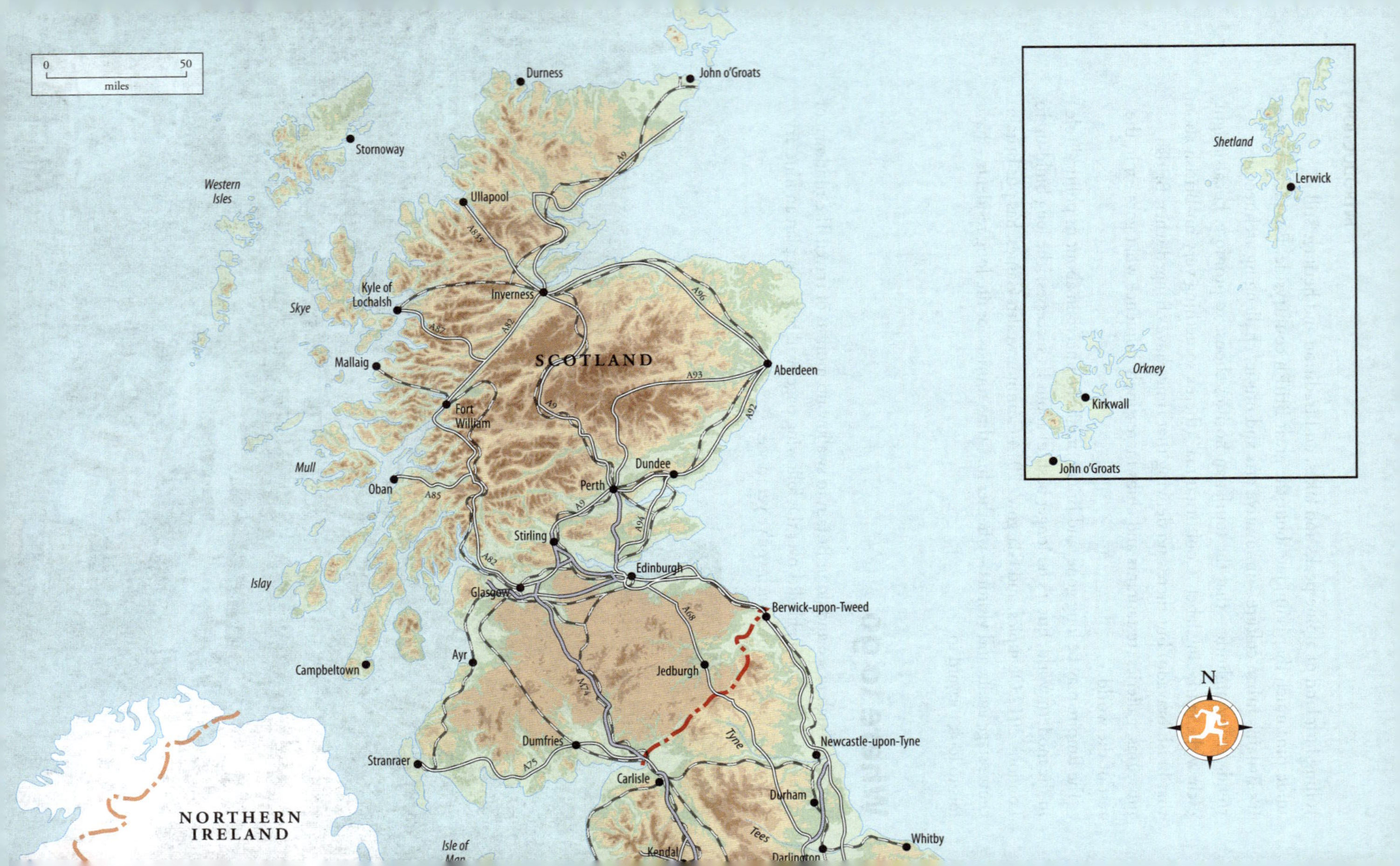

0
50
miles
Durness
John o'Groats
Stornoway
Western Isles
Ullapool
A835
A9
Kyle of Lochalsh
Inverness
Skye
A87
A82
A96
SCOTLAND
Mallaig
Aberdeen
A93
Fort William
A9
A92
Mull
Oban
A85
Dundee
Perth
A9
A94
Stirling
A82
Edinburgh
Islay
Glasgow
Berwick-upon-Tweed
A68
Ayr
Campbeltown
Jedburgh
M74
Tyne
Dumfries
Newcastle-upon-Tyne
Stranraer
A75
Carlisle
Durham
NORTHERN IRELAND
Tees
Whitby
Isle of Man
Kendal
Darlington
Shetland
Lerwick
Orkney
Kirkwall
John o'Groats
N

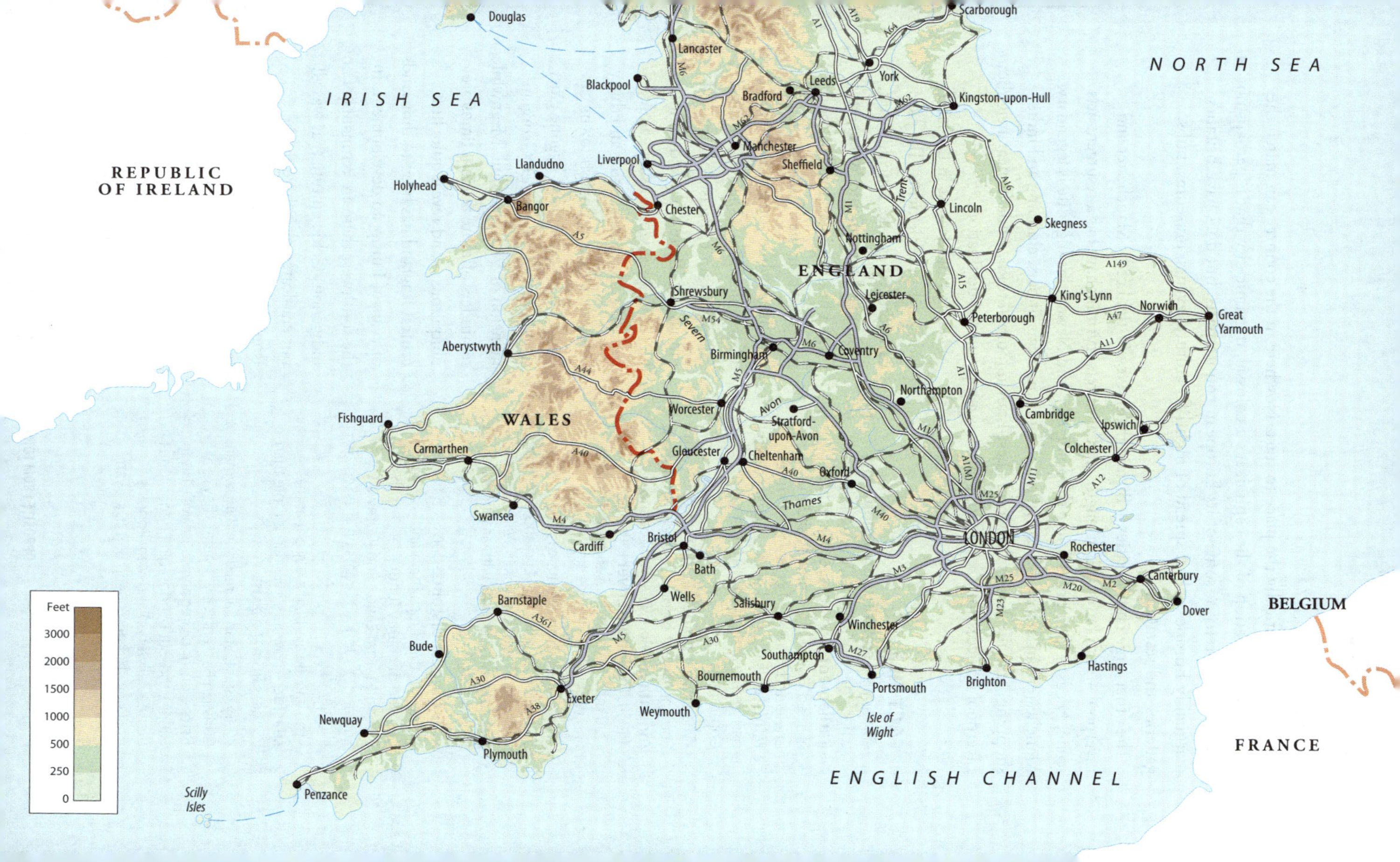
NORTH SEA
IRISH SEA
REPUBLIC OF IRELAND
ENGLAND
WALES
BELGIUM
FRANCE
ENGLISH CHANNEL
Douglas
Lancaster
Blackpool
Leeds
York
Bradford
Scarborough
Kingston-upon-Hull
Manchester
Liverpool
Sheffield
Llandudno
Holyhead
Bangor
Chester
Lincoln
Skegness
Nottingham
Leicester
Shrewsbury
King's Lynn
Norwich
Great Yarmouth
Peterborough
Aberystwyth
Birmingham
Coventry
Northampton
Fishguard
Worcester
Stratford-upon-Avon
Cambridge
Ipswich
Carmarthen
Gloucester
Cheltenham
Colchester
Oxford
Swansea
Cardiff
Bristol
LONDON
Rochester
Bath
Canterbury
Wells
Salisbury
Dover
Barnstaple
Winchester
Bude
Southampton
Hastings
Bournemouth
Portsmouth
Brighton
Exeter
Weymouth
Newquay
Isle of Wight
Plymouth
Scilly Isles
Penzance
Severn
Trent
Avon
Thames
A1
A19
A64
M6
M62
M1
A16
A5
M54
A15
A149
A47
A6
M6
A11
M5
A1
A44
M1
A40
A40
A1(M)
M11
M25
A12
M40
M4
M4
M3
M25
M20
M2
M23
A361
M5
A30
M27
A30
A38
Feet
3000
2000
1500
1000
500
250
0

England

London is emphatically the place to start. Nowhere in the country can match the scope and innovation of the capital. It's a colossal, dynamic city that is perhaps not as immediately pretty as some of its European counterparts, but does have Britain's – arguably Europe's – best spread of nightlife, cultural events, museums, pubs, galleries and restaurants.

The other large **English cities** – Birmingham, Newcastle, Leeds, Manchester and Liverpool – each have their strengths and admirers. Birmingham has a resurgent arts scene, Leeds is the north's prime shopping city, and Newcastle's nightlife is legendary. Manchester can match the capital for glamour in terms of bars, clubbing and indie shopping, and also boasts the world's best-known football team, while its near-neighbour Liverpool is successfully reinventing itself as a top cultural destination.

History runs deepest in England's oldest urban settlements. The glorious **cathedral cities**, like Lincoln, York, Salisbury, Durham and Winchester, form a beautiful national backbone of preserved churches, houses and buildings, while you're never more than a few miles from a spectacular castle, a majestic country house, or a ruined monastery. There are world-famous, UNESCO-recognized sites galore, from Blenheim Palace to Canterbury Cathedral, but all English towns can rustle up an example of bygone glory, whether medieval chapel, Georgian mansion or Victorian mill. Meanwhile, reminders of more **ancient times** are ubiquitous – and reveal quite how central England has been to thousands of years of European development. In the southwest there are remnants of an indigenous Celtic culture that was all but eradicated elsewhere by the Romans, who in turn left their mark from Hadrian's Wall in the north to Colchester in the south. Even more dramatic are the surviving traces of the very earliest **prehistoric** settlers – most famously the megalithic circles of Stonehenge and Avebury.

FACT FILE

- Britain is a **constitutional monarchy**, whose head of state is Queen Elizabeth II. **Parliament** is composed of the directly elected House of Commons and the unelected House of Lords – the **Prime Minister** is the head of the largest political party represented in the House of Commons.
- The **lowest point** is in the Fens of eastern England, at 13ft below sea level; the **highest mountain** is Ben Nevis, in Scotland, at 4406ft. The **longest river** is the Severn (220 miles), which flows through England and Wales.
- The **population** of Britain is about 59 million: 51 million in England, 5 million in Scotland and 3 million in Wales. The biggest city is London, with around 8 million inhabitants.
- The **longest distance** between two points on the British mainland – a journey beloved of charity fundraisers – is the 874 miles from Land's End (Cornwall, England) to John O'Groats (in the Scottish Highlands).
- You can always plan a day out at the **seaside** – nowhere in Britain is more than 75 miles from the coast.
- Cary Grant, Stan Laurel, John Barrowman, Christian Bale and Guy Pearce? They're all **Brits** – oh, and Gregory House, MD (Hugh Laurie), too. But London-girl Bridget Jones (Renée Zellweger) and Mary Poppins' Cockney chimney sweep Bert (Dick van Dyke)? Definitely not.

OPPOSITE FROM TOP LEFT CUILLIN HILLS, SKYE; A PINT DOWN THE PUB; THE CITY OF LONDON

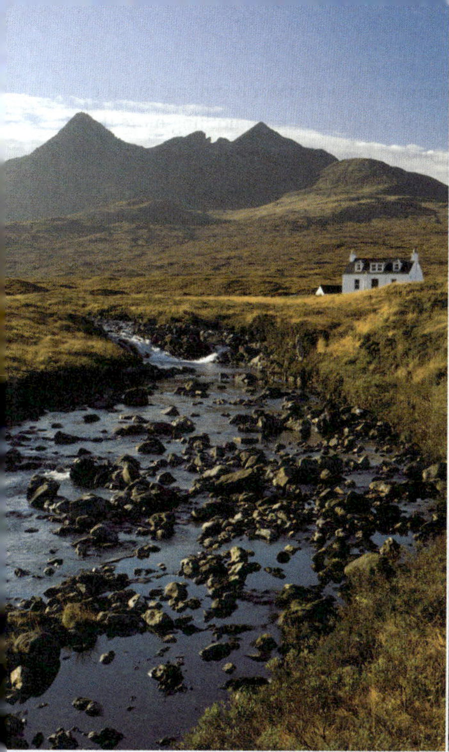

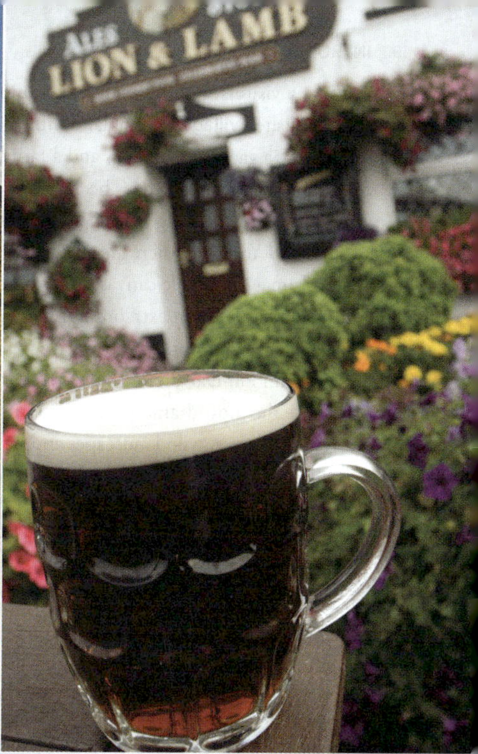
ALES
LION & LAMB

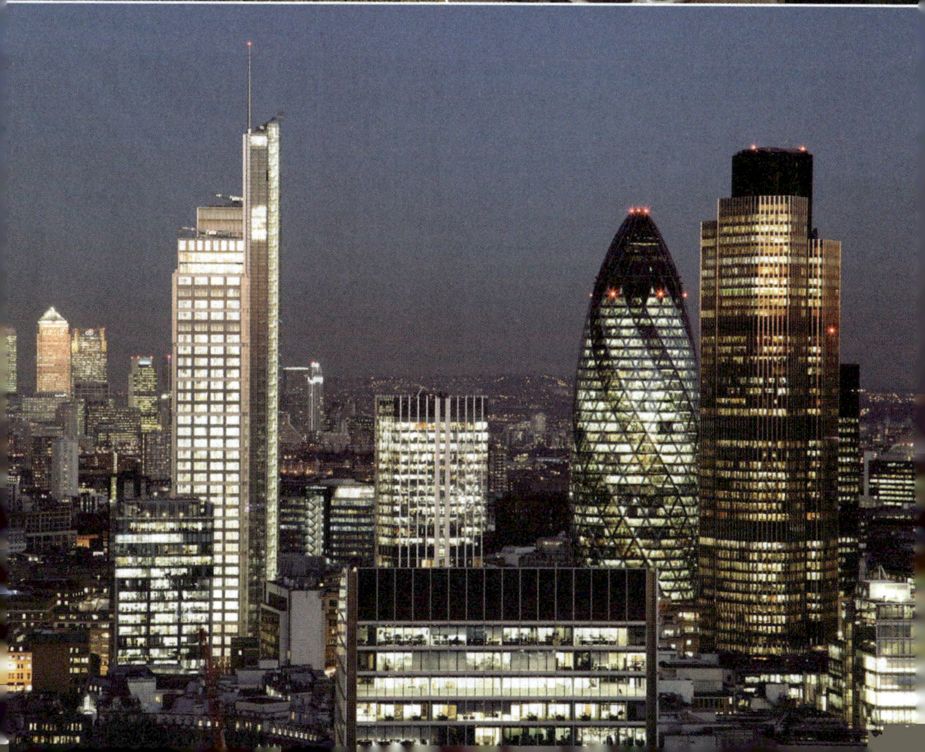

For many visitors, it's not the towns or monuments that are most beguiling, but the long-established **villages** of England, hundreds of which amount to nothing more than a pub, a shop, a gaggle of cottages and a farmhouse or two. Traditional rural life may well be on the wane – though that's been said of England since the Industrial Revolution, over two hundred years ago – but in places like Devon, Cornwall, the Cotswolds, Cumbria and Yorkshire there are still villages, traditions and festivals that seem to spring straight from a Constable canvas or a Wordsworth poem. Indeed, the English **countryside** has been an extraordinarily fecund source of inspiration for writers and artists, and the English themselves have gone to great length to protect their natural heritage. Exmoor, Dartmoor, the North York Moors, the Lake District and the Peak District are the most dramatic of the country's ten **national parks**, each offering a mix of picturesque villages, wild landscapes and wonderful walks.

Scotland

The Scottish capital, **Edinburgh**, is – whisper it to the English – a far more handsome city than London, famous for its magnificent setting, majestic castle and ancient royal quarter of Holyrood, not to mention an acclaimed international arts festival and some excellent museums. A short journey west is the larger city of **Glasgow**, a sprawling post-industrial metropolis on the banks of the River Clyde that's an upbeat destination with great bars, clubs and restaurants. Its museums and galleries are some of the best in Britain, while the city's impressive architecture reflects the wealth of its eighteenth- and nineteenth-century heyday.

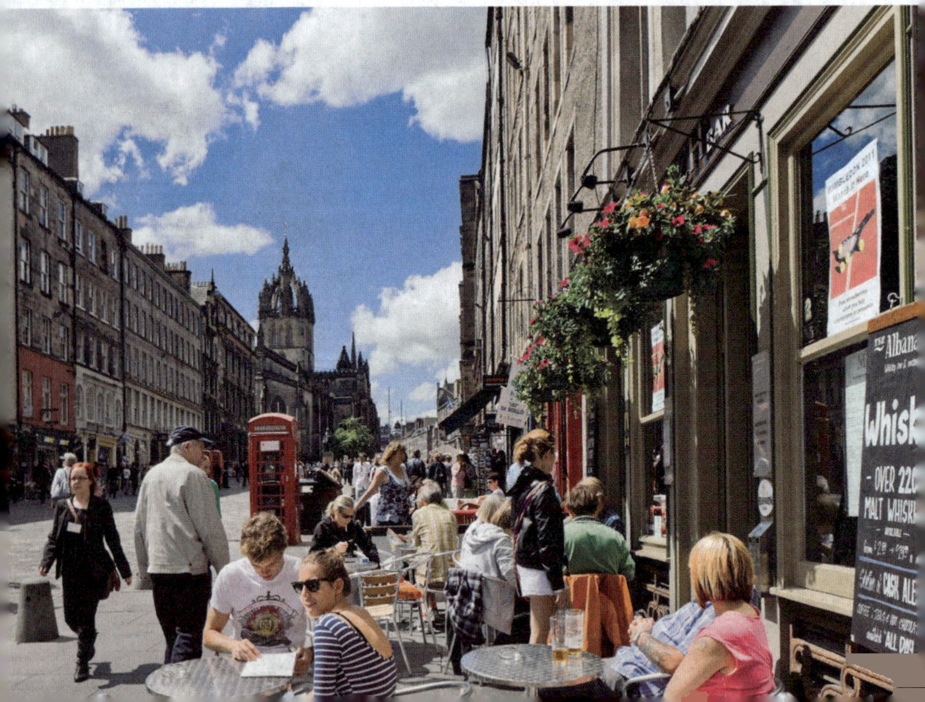

Author picks

Our indefatigable authors are always on the lookout for the best in Britain – start here for some truly wonderful British travel experiences…

Glorious gardens No one tends their gardens like the British, whether it's the Lost Gardens of Heligan in Cornwall (p.316), the intriguing "poison garden" at Alnwick in Northumberland (p.592), or the recently discovered historic walled gardens at Aberglasney (p.630).

Remote beaches Head to the extremities: to Par Beach, Isles of Scilly (p.326), the lonely beaches of North Uist (p.931) or Barafundle Bay, Pembrokeshire (p.635).

Wacky festivals The Welsh "capital of wackiness", Llanwrtyd Wells (p.657), combines festive fun and British idiosyncrasy, as does Hastings' Jack in the Green shindig (p.155).

Best views We simply can't choose – London from the London Eye (p.88), dramatic Hartland Point in Devon (p.311), the stunning Scottish coast from Wester Ross (p.898) or the River Wye at Tintern Abbey (p.604).

Incredible industry From Ironbridge (p.392) to Manchester (p.446), Rhondda (p.610) to the Clyde (p.792), Britain invented the stuff the world wanted.

Living history Step back in time at Beamish Museum in County Durham (p.568), the Culloden battle site in the Scottish Highlands (p.882) or Cregneash Village Folk Museum on Isle of Man (p.480).

Classic journeys The Settle to Carlisle Railway (p.529) and the West Highland Railway (p.880) take some beating, and Wales's Ffestiniog Railway (p.694) is simply splendid; walkers, meanwhile, should make for the South West Coast Path (p.289), Britain's longest footpath.

Boutique beds Britain does boutique beautifully, from London lavish *Hazlitt's* (p.112) via offbeat and arty *Wallace's Arthouse* in Edinburgh (p.737) to country-house chic at *Randy Pike* in The Lake District (p.492).

Our author recommendations don't end here. We've flagged up our favourite places – a perfectly sited hotel, an atmospheric café, a special restaurant – throughout the guide, highlighted with the ★ symbol.

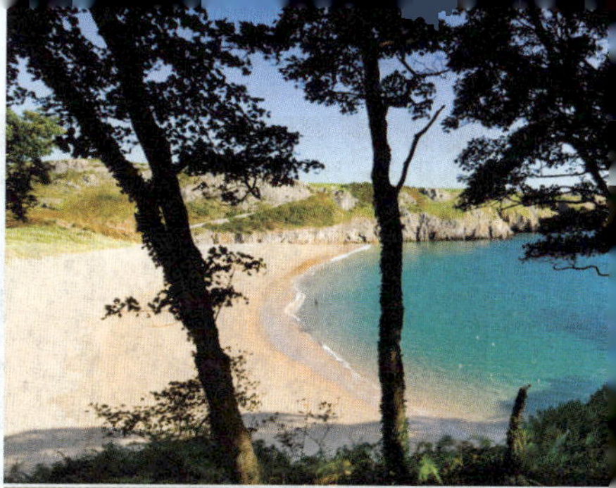

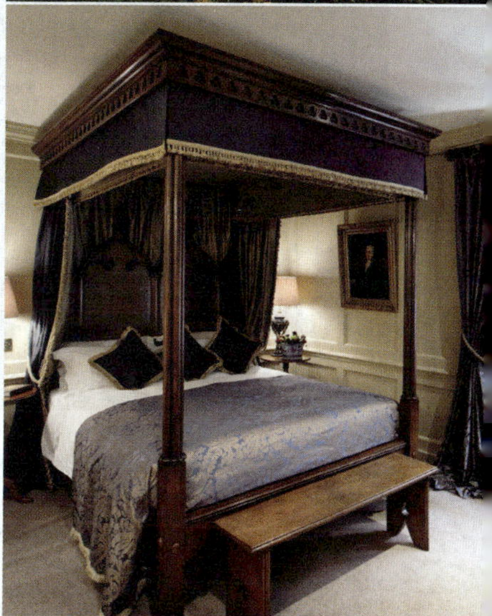

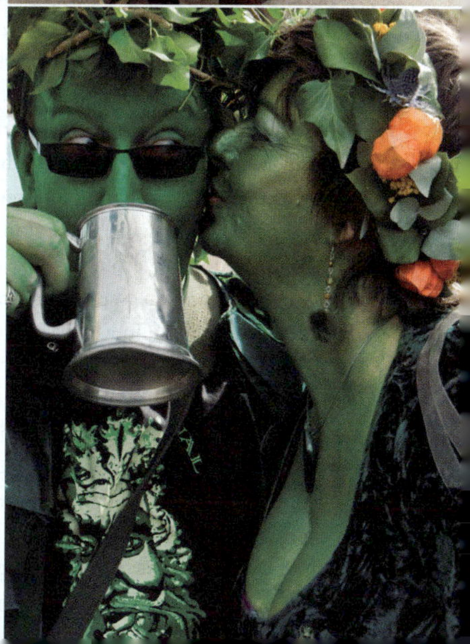

OPPOSITE THE ROYAL MILE, EDINBURGH **FROM TOP** BARAFUNDLE BAY; HAZLITT'S; JACK IN THE GREEN

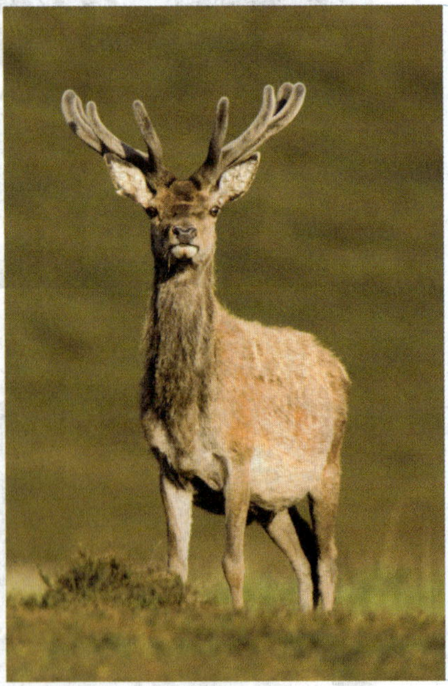

THE CALL OF THE WILD

Despite the crowded motorways and urban sprawl, Britain can still be an astonishingly wild place. Natural habitats are zealously guarded in fifteen national parks, from the far southwest to the distant north – a jaw-dropping number of protected areas for a nation of Britain's size.

Even in the most popular parks – the almost Alpine **Lake District** (pp.484–504), say, or the rugged **Peak District** (pp.406–413) – it's never a problem to escape the day-tripper crowds, while true wilderness awaits in the **Cairngorms** of Scotland (p.886) or **Snowdonia** in Wales (pp.685–693).

Outside the parks, too, every corner of Britain has its own wild charm – whether it's tracking Northumberland's **wild cattle** (p.590), seal-spotting at **Blakeney Point** (p.359), dolphin-watching on the **Moray Firth** (p.885) or hiking across windswept **Lundy Island** (p.309) to see its famous puffins.

Scotland's other towns and cities are only fitfully enticing, though central destinations like **Stirling, Perth** and **Dundee**, and **Aberdeen** in the northeast, make a valiant tilt at tourists, and, in the university town of **St Andrew's** (Prince William and Kate Middleton's alma mater) Scotland has a college town to rank with Oxford and Cambridge. However, what usually resonates most with visitors is Scotland's great outdoors, whether it's the well-walked hills of the **Trossachs** in central Scotland – home of Loch Lomond – or the **Highlands**, whose mountains, sea cliffs, shadowy glens and deep lochs cover the entire northern two-thirds of the country. In Highland Scotland in particular, famous destinations trip off the tongue – Loch Ness, Culloden, Cape Wrath and John O'Groats – while Ben Nevis has Britain's highest mountain.

Some of the most fascinating journeys are to be had on the **Scottish islands**, the most accessible of which extend in a long rocky chain off the Atlantic coast. Whether it's mooching around Mull, investigating the early Christian heritage of Iona, whisky-tasting on Islay, or touring the Isle of Arran – the most visited of the Hebrides – there are unique experiences on every inch of the Inner Hebridean archipelago. The outer Western Isles, meanwhile – from Lewis and Harris in the north to Barra in the south – feature some of Britain's most dramatic scenery, from towering sea cliffs to sweeping sandy beaches.

At Britain's northern extreme lie the sea- and wind-buffeted **Orkney** and **Shetland** islands, whose rich Norse heritage makes them distinct in dialect and culture from mainland Scotland, while their wild scenery offers some of Britain's finest birdwatching and some stunning Stone Age archeological remains.

ABOVE RED DEER STAG, CAIRNGORMS **OPPOSITE** MICHELDEVER FOREST, HAMPSHIRE

Wales

It's **Cardiff**, of course, the vibrant capital, that boasts most of Wales's major institutions – the National Assembly, Millennium Stadium, Millennium Centre, National Museum and Gallery – and is the best place to get the feel of an increasingly confident country. Second city, **Swansea**, is grittier by far, a handy base for the sandy bays, high cliffs and pretty villages of the wonderful **Gower peninsula**. Meanwhile, in the post-industrial **Valleys** – once a byword for coal mining – a superb sequence of heritage parks, memorials and museums illuminates the period when South Wales produced a third of the world's coal.

Castles are everywhere in Wales, from the little stone keeps of the early Welsh princes to Edward I's ring of doughty fortresses, including Beaumaris, Conwy and Harlech. Religion played its part too – the cathedral at **St Davids** was founded as early as the sixth century AD, and the quiet charms of the later, medieval monastic houses, like ruined **Tintern Abbey**, are richly rewarding. Much older relics also loom large – **stone circles** offer a link to the pre-Roman era when the priestly order of Druids ruled over early Celtic peoples.

If England glories in its villages, perhaps it's the **small towns** of Wales that appeal most – New Age Machynlleth and lively Llangollen, the foodie centre of Abergavenny and festival-fuelled Llanwrtyd Wells. You could concoct a delightful tour that went from one

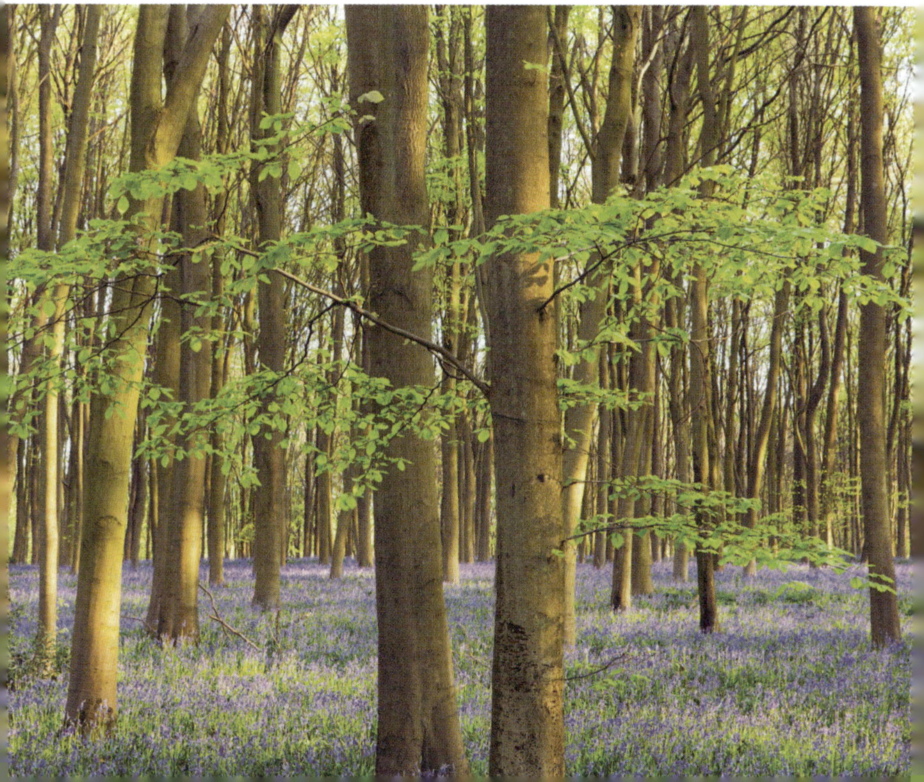

BRITAIN ON A PLATE

You might think of roast beef or fish and chips – but, only half-jokingly, Britain's national dish was recently proclaimed to be **chicken tikka masala**, a reflection of the extent to which Britain's postwar immigrant communities have contributed to the country's dining scene. Even the smallest town will have an Indian restaurant (more properly, Bangladeshi or Pakistani), with Chinese (largely Cantonese) and Thai restaurants common too – not to mention countless Italian trattorias and pizza places and Spanish tapas bars. For the most authentic food, there are a few ethnic enclaves you need to know about – **Chinatown** in London (p.118) and Manchester's "curry mile" in **Rusholme** (p.455) are probably the best-known, but there are all kinds of treats in store in the lesser-touristed parts of the country. Pakistani grills, Turkish meze or Polish pierogi in London's unheralded suburbs, a Kashmiri balti in **Birmingham** (pp.399–405) or **Bradford** (pp.523–524), or south Indian snacks in **Leicester** (pp.425–428) – all are as British as can be.

attractive, idiosyncractic town to another, but even so, you wouldn't want to miss Wales's other great glory – the wild countryside. The Cambrian mountains form the country's backbone, between the soaring peaks of **Snowdonia National Park** and the angular ridges of the **Brecon Beacons**. These are the two best places for a walking holiday – though you can get up Snowdon, Wales's highest mountain, by railway if you prefer. Mountainous Wales also offers world-class mountain biking – Coed-y-Brenin in Mid-Wales is the name that all bikers know. As for the Welsh seaside, don't miss the magnificent cliff-tops of the rippling **Pembrokeshire** coast or the sandy beaches of the western **Cambrian** shore. Most of the coast remains unspoiled, and even where the long sweeps of sand have been developed they are often backed by enjoyable, traditional **seaside resorts**, such as Llandudno in the north, Aberystwyth in the west or Tenby in the south.

When to go

Considering the temperate nature of the **British climate** (see p.45), it's amazing how much mileage the locals get out of the subject: a two-day cold snap is discussed as if it were the onset of a new Ice Age, and a week in the upper 70s starts rumours of a drought. The fact is that summers rarely get very hot and the winters don't get very cold, except in the north of Scotland and the highest points of the English, Welsh and Scottish uplands. **Rainfall** is fairly even, though again mountainous areas get higher quantities throughout the year (the west coast of Scotland is especially damp, and Llanberis, at the foot of Snowdon, gets more than twice as much rainfall as Caernarfon, seven miles away).

In general, the south is warmer and sunnier than the north, but the bottom line is that it's impossible to say with any degree of certainty what the weather will be like when you visit. May might be wet and grey one year and gloriously sunny the next; November stands an equal chance of being crisp and clear or foggy and grim. If you're planning to lie on a beach, or camp in the dry, you'll want to visit **between June and September** – though don't blame us if it pours down all August, as it might well do. Otherwise, if you're balancing the clemency of the weather against the density of the crowds, the best months to explore are April, May, September and October.

OPPOSITE FROM TOP LEFT CLEY WINDMILL, NORFOLK; ON THE SEAFRONT AT WESTON-SUPER-MARE; GLOUCESTER CATHEDRAL; PERFORMANCE OF *TWELFTH NIGHT* IN STRATFORD-UPON-AVON

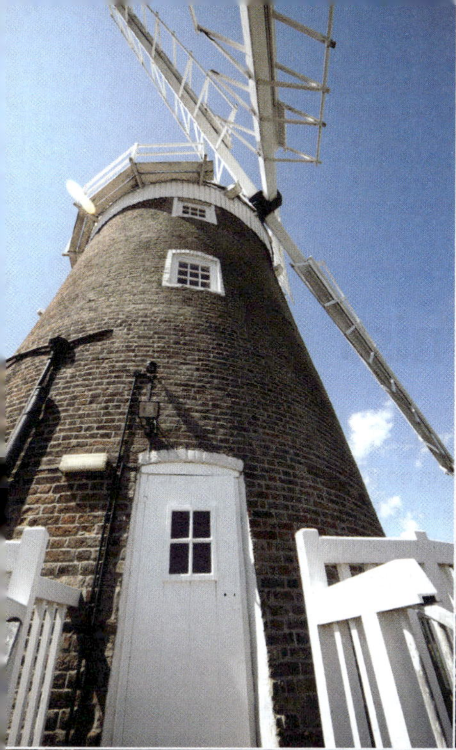

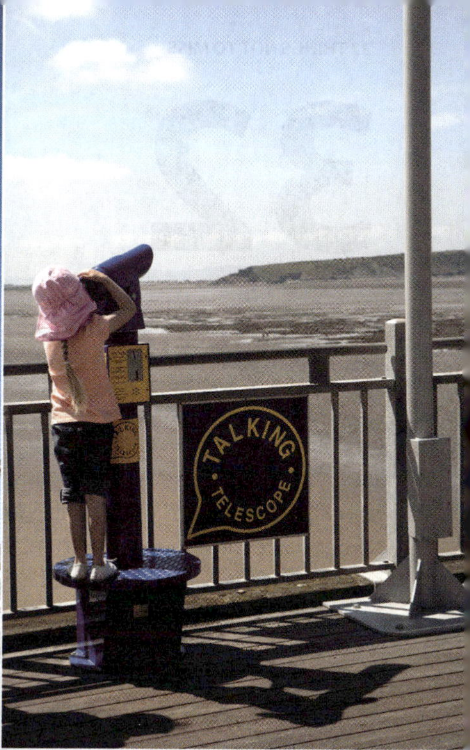
TALKING
TELESCOPE

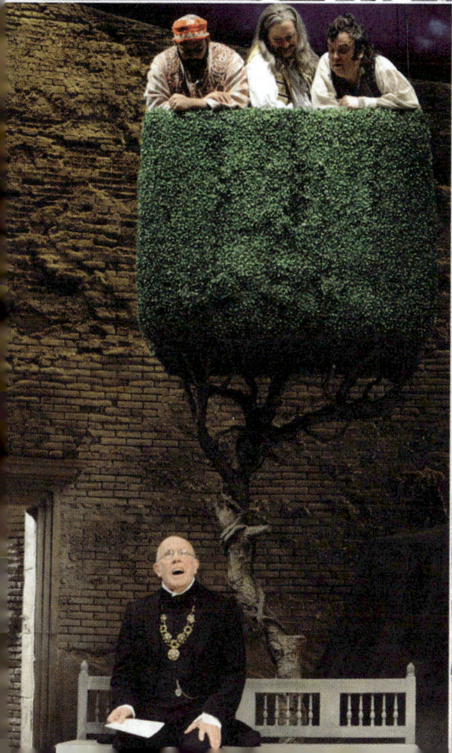

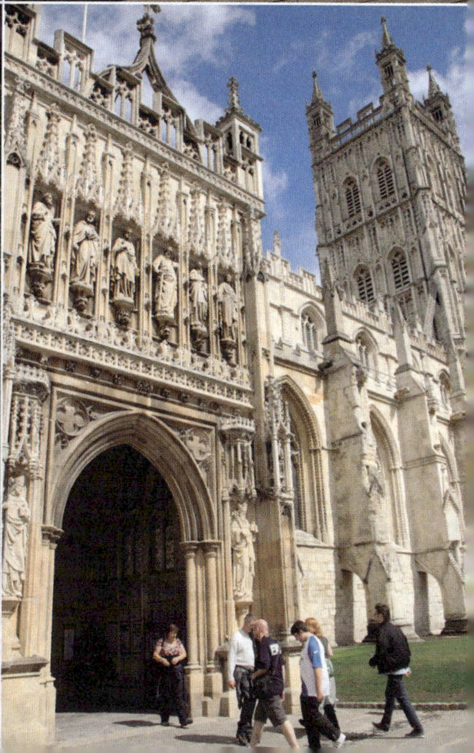

32

things not to miss

It's not possible to see everything that Britain has to offer in one trip – and we don't suggest you try. What follows, in no particular order, is a selective taste of the highlights of England, Wales and Scotland, including stunning scenery, awe-inspiring architecture, thrilling activities and incomparable urban experiences. Each entry has a page reference that will take you straight to the Guide where you can find out more.

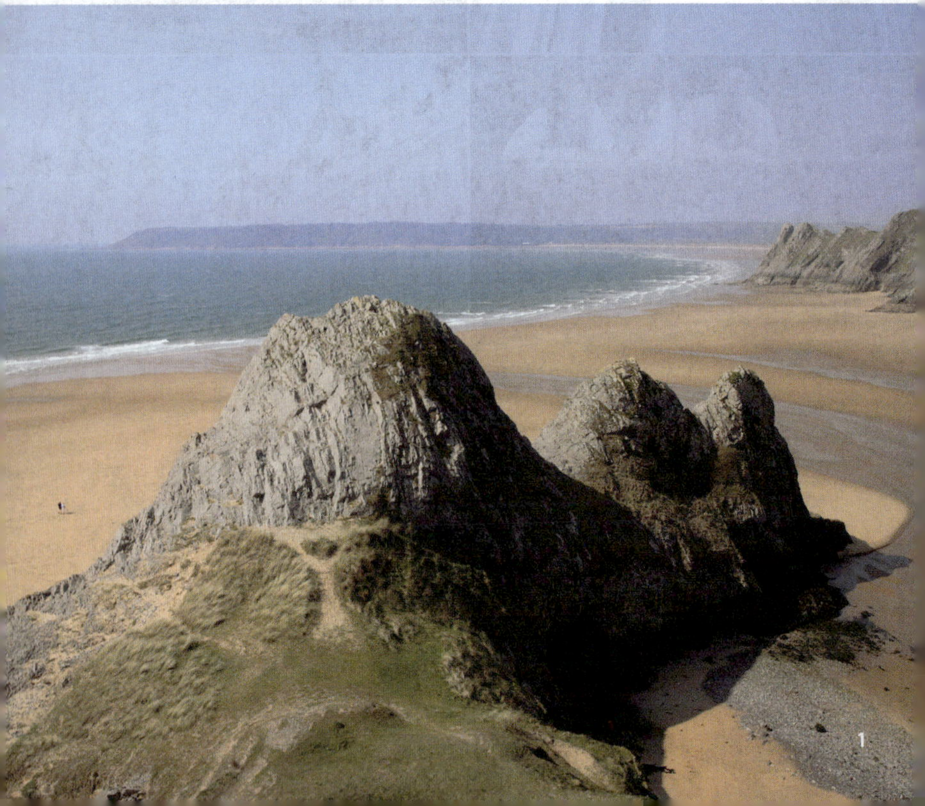

1

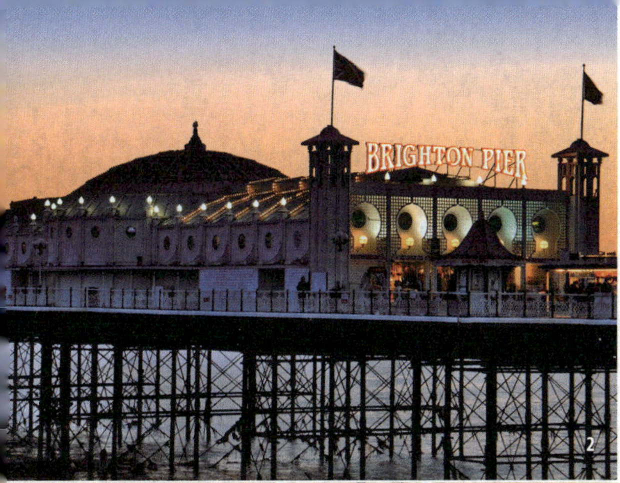

2

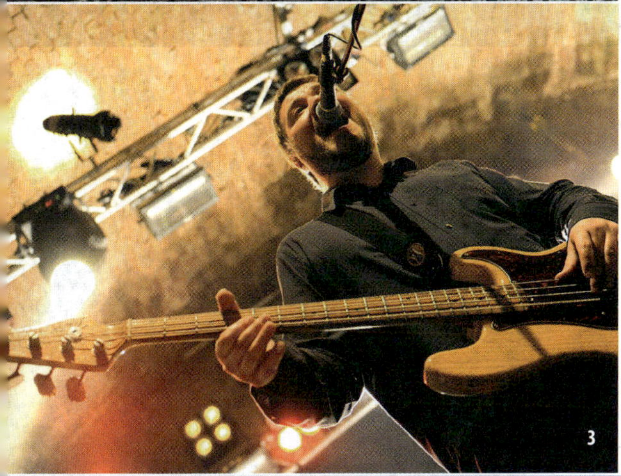
3

1 THE GOWER PENINSULA

Pages 626–628

A stunning stretch, fringed by glorious bays and dramatic cliffs, and dotted with prehistoric remains and castle ruins.

2 BRIGHTON

Pages 164–170

Bohemian Brighton, southern England's favourite seaside town, has it all, from the cheery pier to George IV's Royal Pavilion to its thriving gay scene.

3 MANCHESTER'S NIGHTLIFE

Pages 446–458

The Northwest's premier nightlife destination can't be bettered for its wonderfully vibrant music venues, clubs and bars.

4 THE LAKE DISTRICT

Pages 484–504

England's largest national park is also one of its favourites, with sixteen lakes and scores of mountains.

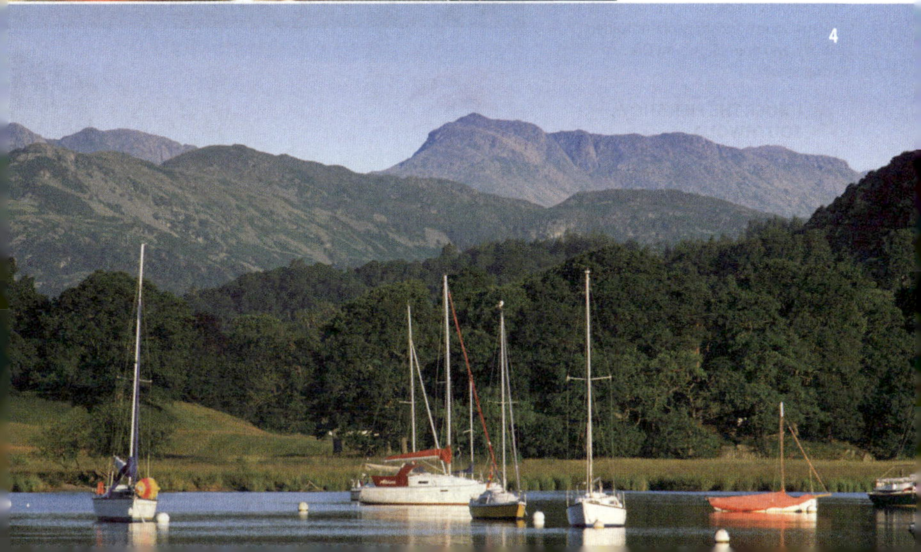
4

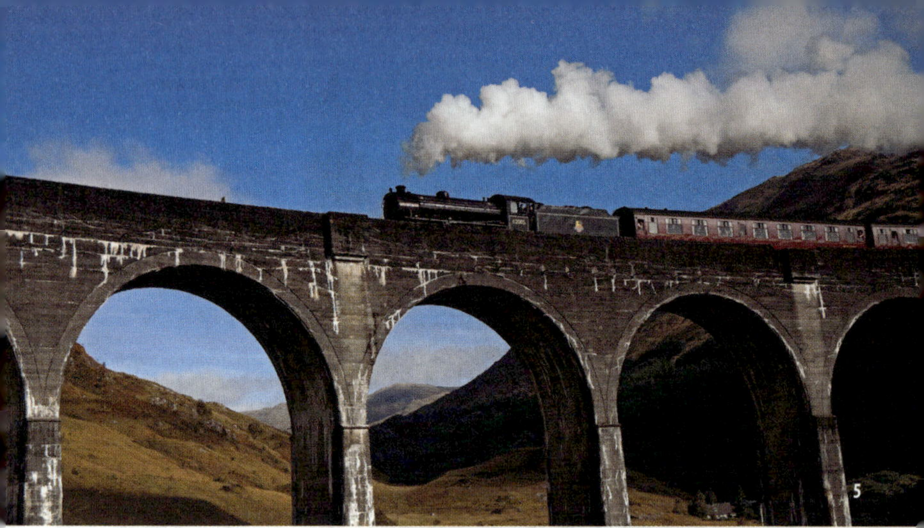
5

5 WEST HIGHLAND RAILWAY
Page 692
Take one of the great railway journeys of the world.

6 WHALE- AND DOLPHIN-WATCHING
Page 908
Boat trips in the Cromarty Firth get you a great view of these beautiful marine creatures.

7 AVEBURY
Page 216
Avebury's stone circle rivals Stonehenge, and is even more mysterious.

8 WHITBY
Pages 554–557
Irresistible seaside town with a picturesque port, atmospheric ruined abbey, and dramatic Count Dracula connections.

9 UNDER THE PIER SHOW, SOUTHWOLD
Pages 351–352
Odd mechanical toys and offbeat whimsical humour in this appealing seaside town.

10 THE BRITISH MUSEUM
Page 76
In parts controversial, and generally not British, the collections of the BM are still the greatest in the world.

11 EDINBURGH FESTIVAL
Pages 734–735
One of the world's great arts festivals – in fact, several festivals – transforms the handsome old city each year into a swirling cultural maelstrom.

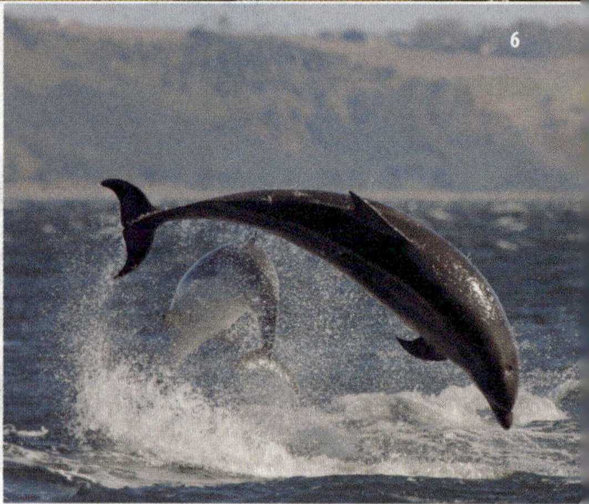
6

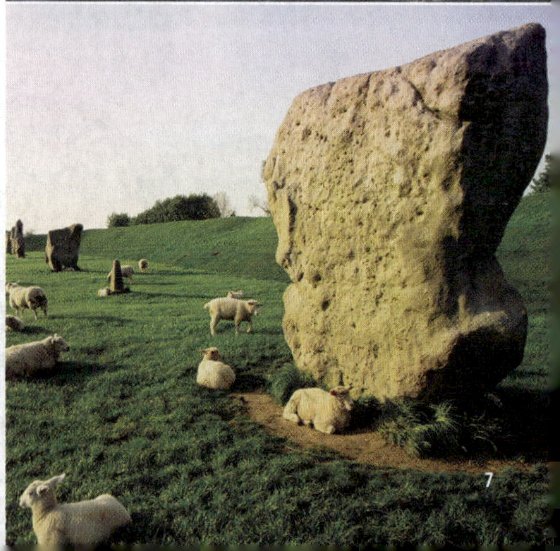
7

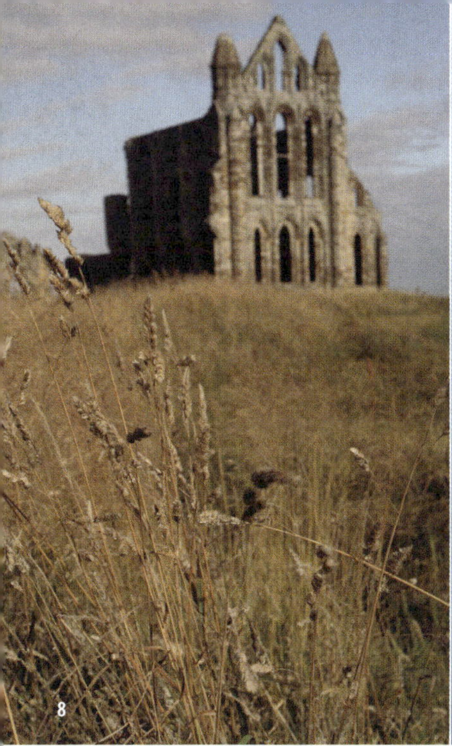
8

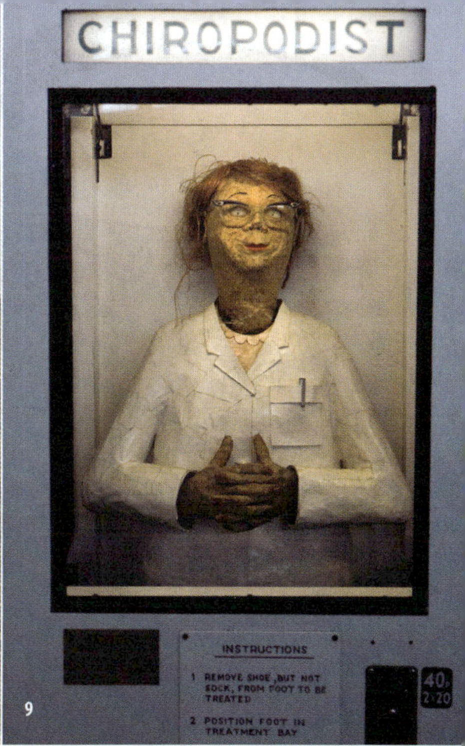
CHIROPODIST
INSTRUCTIONS
1 REMOVE SHOE, BUT NOT SOCK, FROM FOOT TO BE TREATED
2 POSITION FOOT IN TREATMENT BAY
40p
2×20
9

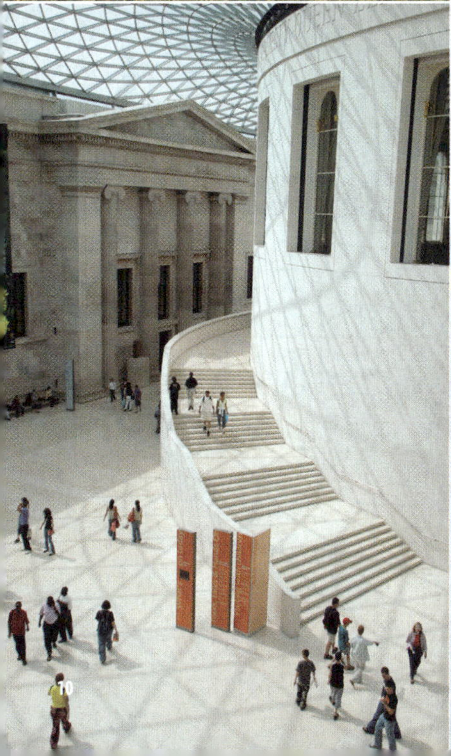
10

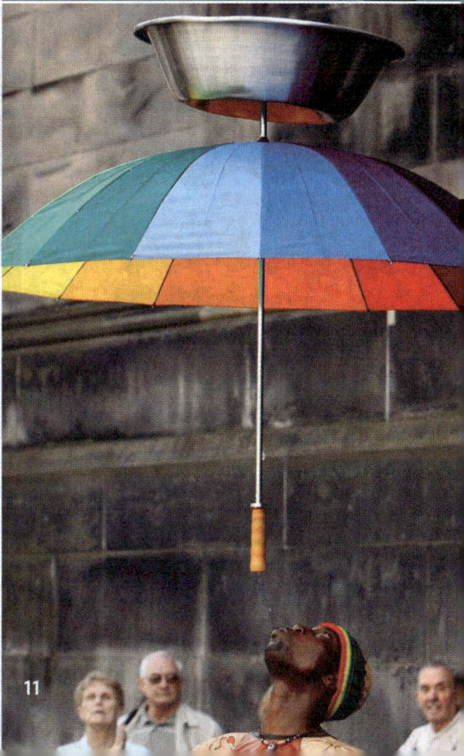
11

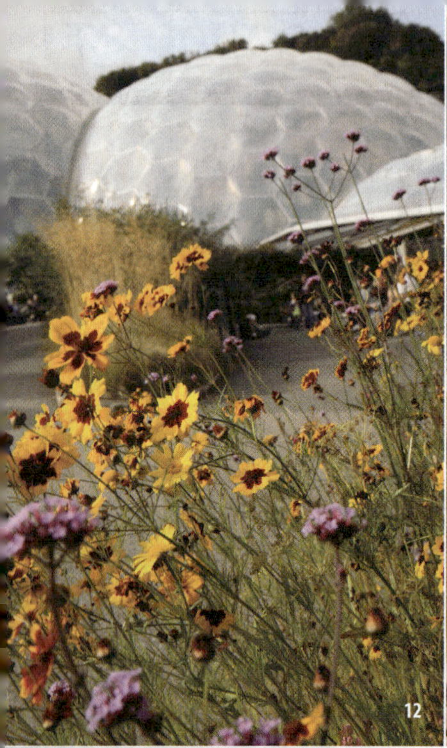
12

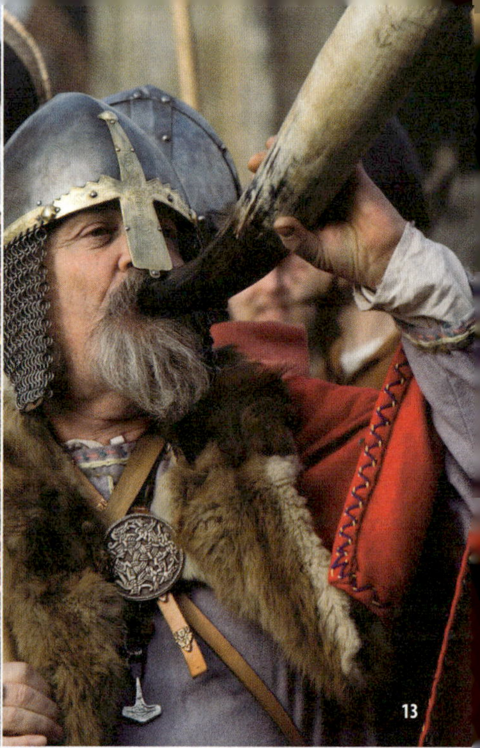
13

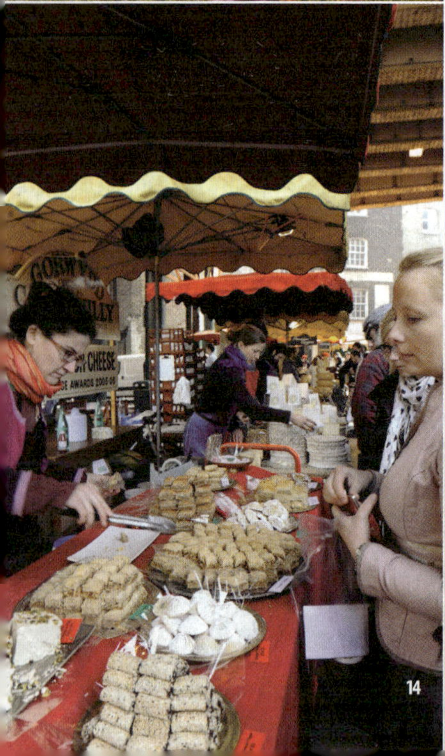
14

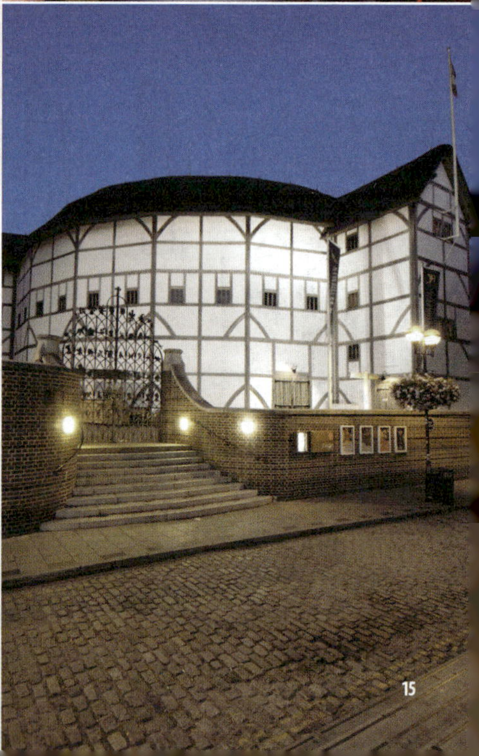
15

16

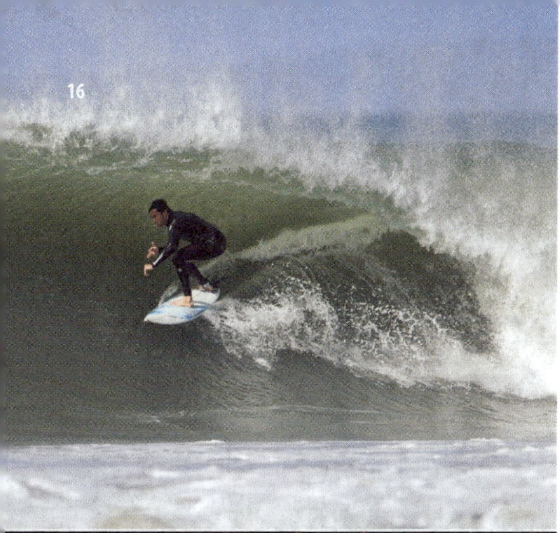

17

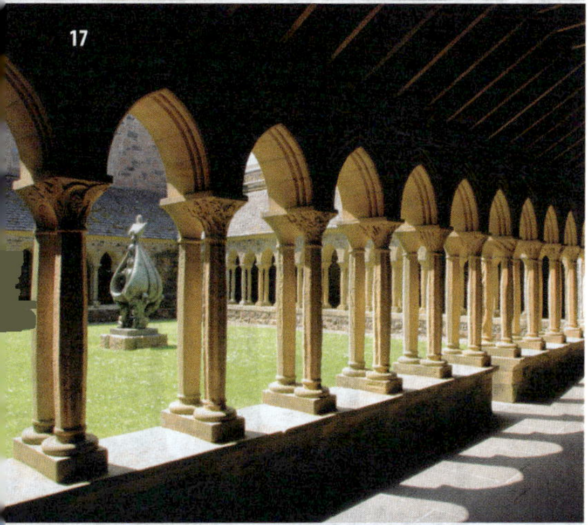

12 EDEN PROJECT, CORNWALL
Page 316

Spectacular and ungimmicky display of the planet's plant life, housed in vast geometric biodomes.

13 JORVIK, YORK
Page 540

Travel back in time to experience life in Viking York.

14 LONDON'S MARKETS
Page 131

From foodie treats in Borough to flowers in Columbia Road, London's markets have something for everyone.

15 SHAKESPEARE'S GLOBE THEATRE, LONDON
Page 89

It's a genuine thrill to watch Shakespeare performed in this reconstruction of the famous Elizabethan theatre.

16 SURFING IN NORTH DEVON
Page 310

The beaches along the north coast of Devon offer some truly great breaks.

17 IONA, ARGYLL
Pages 837–838

The home of Celtic Christian spirituality, and an island of pilgrimage since antiquity.

18 WALKING THE PENNINE WAY
Page 441

One of the most popular walks in Britain, this long-distance footpath stretches from the Peak District through Yorkshire and the Northumberland National Park into Scotland.

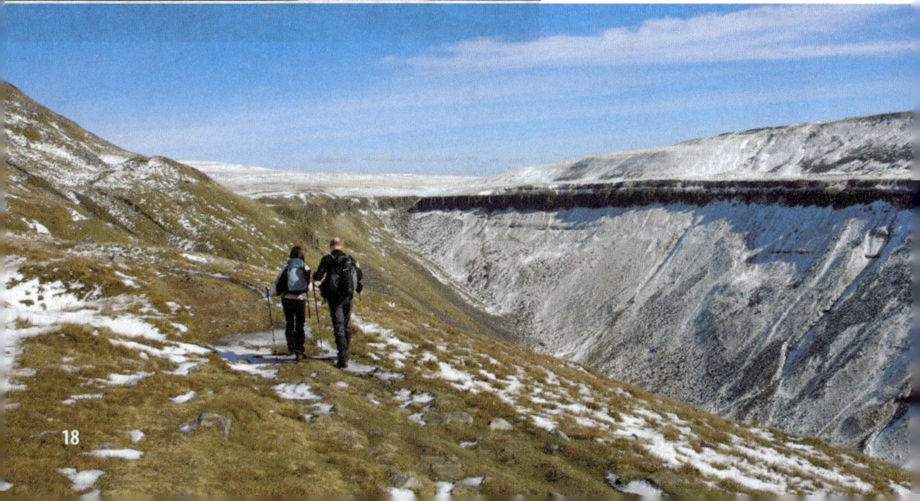

18

19 STATELY HOMES AND PALACES

Page 413

Britain's fine castles, stately homes and palaces – among them the splendid Chatsworth House – simply can't be bettered.

20 WHISKY IN SCOTLAND

Page 869

Sip a wee dram in Northeast Scotland's "whisky triangle", where the Malt Whisky Trail showcases the best distilleries.

21 HADRIAN'S WALL PATH, NORTHUMBERLAND

Pages 584–587

You can walk or cycle the length of this atmospheric Roman wall, once the frontier against Britain's northern tribes.

22 CURRY IN BRADFORD

Pages 523–524

Bradford's famed curry houses offer everything from cheap-and-cheerful baltis to slick contemporary dining.

23 KINLOCH CASTLE, RÙM

Page 924

Spend the night in a Scottish island hideaway – either in the old servants' quarters or in a four-poster bed.

24 OXFORD

Pages 226–237

One of the world's finest academic cities glories in its dreaming spires, honey-coloured stone and neat quadrangles.

25 HAY-ON-WYE LITERARY FESTIVAL

Page 656

The prestigious literary festival at this bibliophile border town brings in all the bookish great and good.

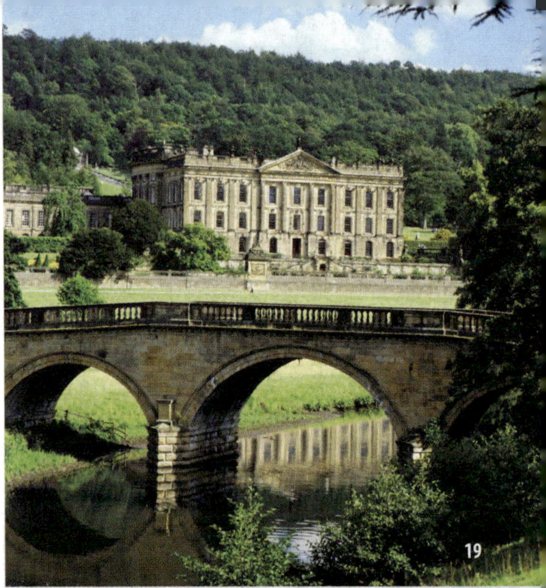

19

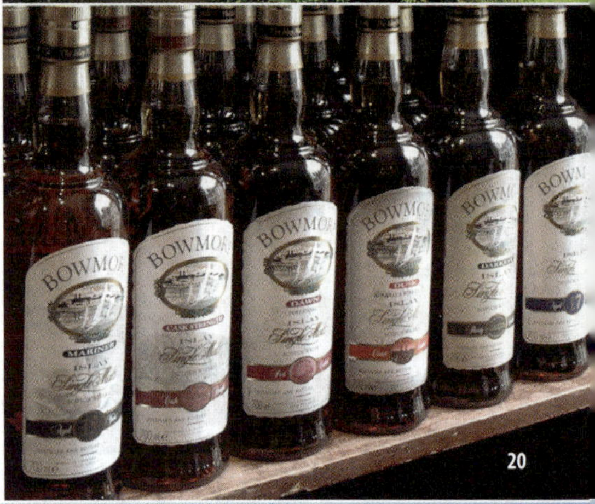

20

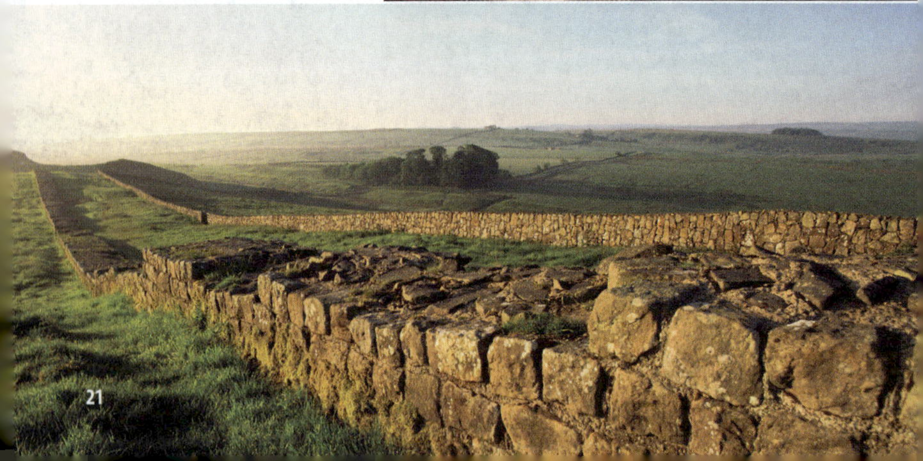

21

22

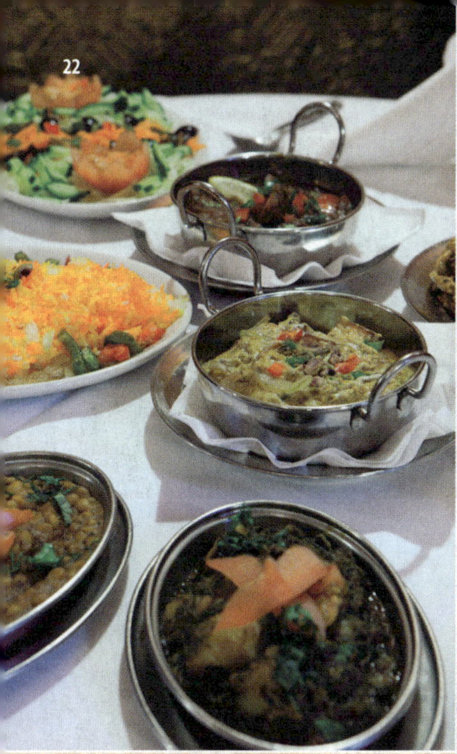

23

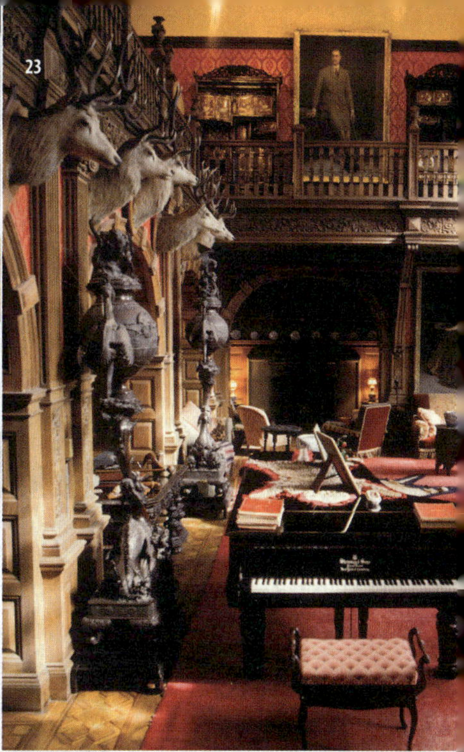

24

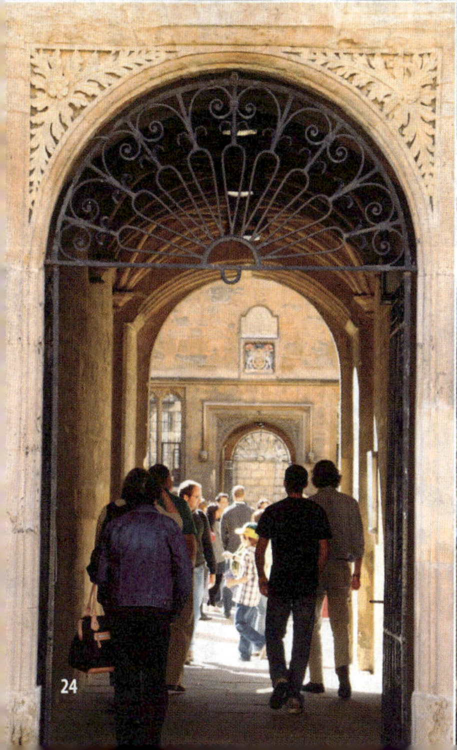

25

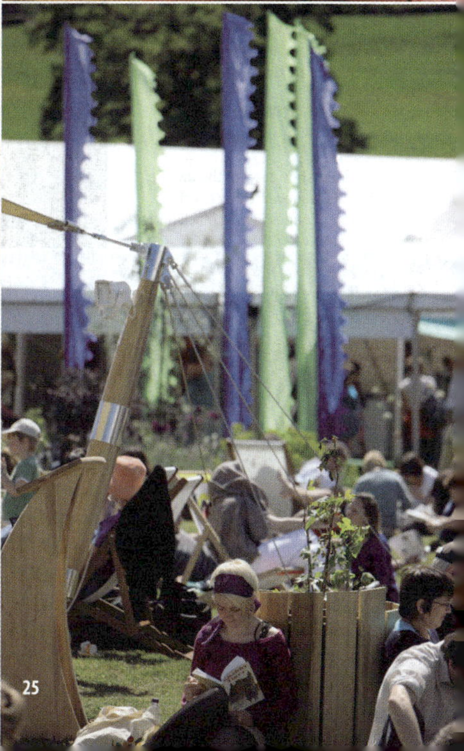

26 BLAENAFON
Pages 607–608

Head down a mine, if you dare, in this fascinating Welsh ironworks town.

27 EDWARD I'S IRON RING
Page 680

Edward's fearsome Iron Ring of fortresses, built across North Wales in the thirteenth century, include Conwy, Caernarfon, Harlech and Beaumaris.

28 BATH
Pages 265–271

From the Roman baths to England's most elegant Georgian terrace, Bath is one of the loveliest cities in Britain.

29 SEAFOOD IN CORNWALL
Pages 329–330

Feast on the fresh catch in Padstow, where chef Rick Stein rules the roost.

30 DURHAM CATHEDRAL
Pages 564–568

Arguably England's greatest Norman building, an imposing cathedral perched on a peninsula overlooking Durham's lovely old town.

31 PORTMEIRION
Page 696

Decidedly un-Welsh architecture makes this odd Italianate village a unique attraction.

32 GLASGOW SCHOOL OF ART
Page 779

The finest showcase for the unique style of Glasgow architect and designer Charles Rennie Mackintosh.

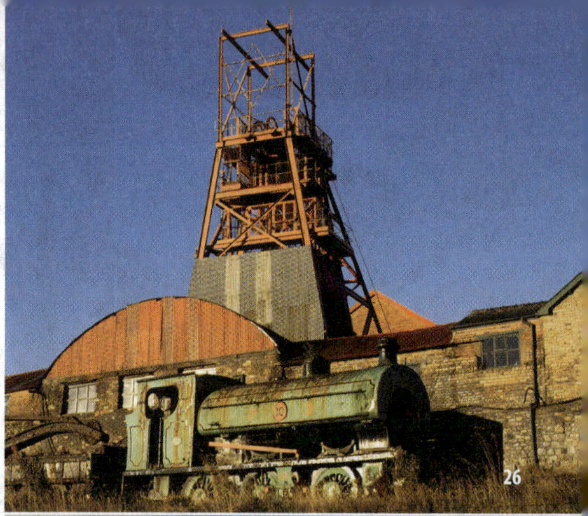

26

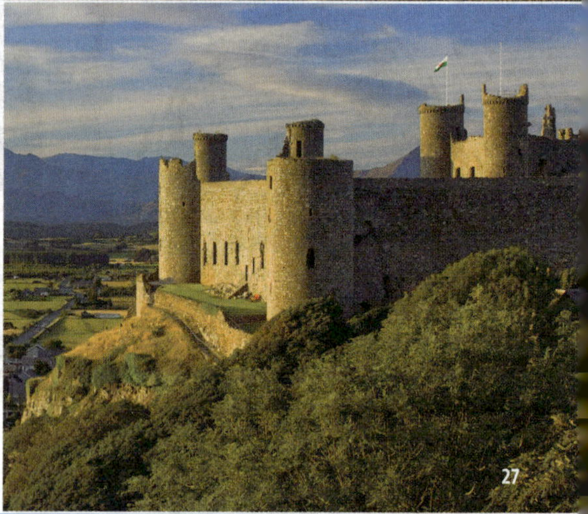

27

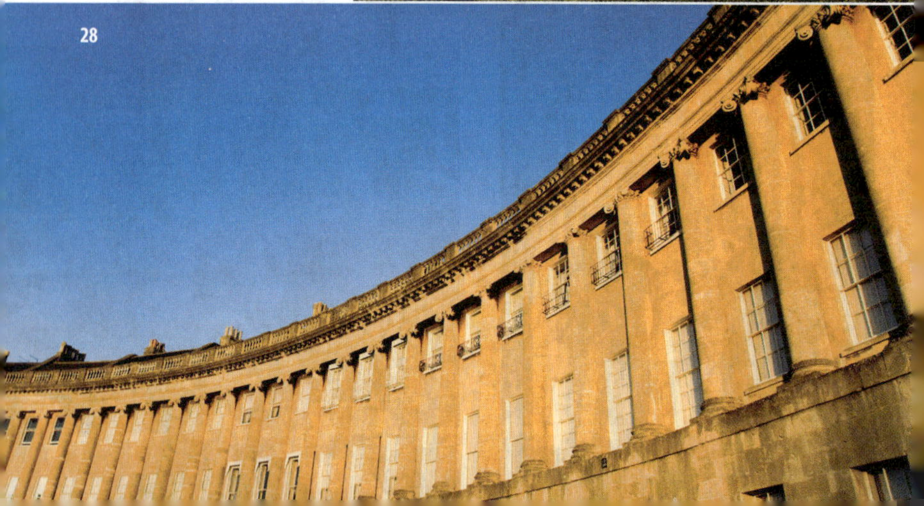

28

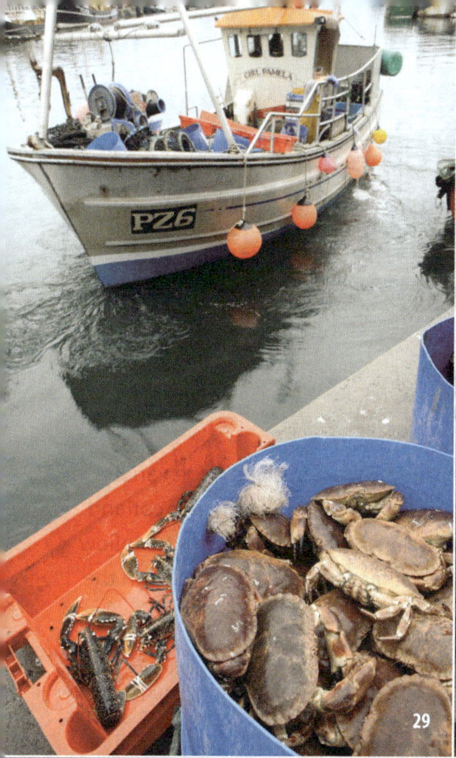

29

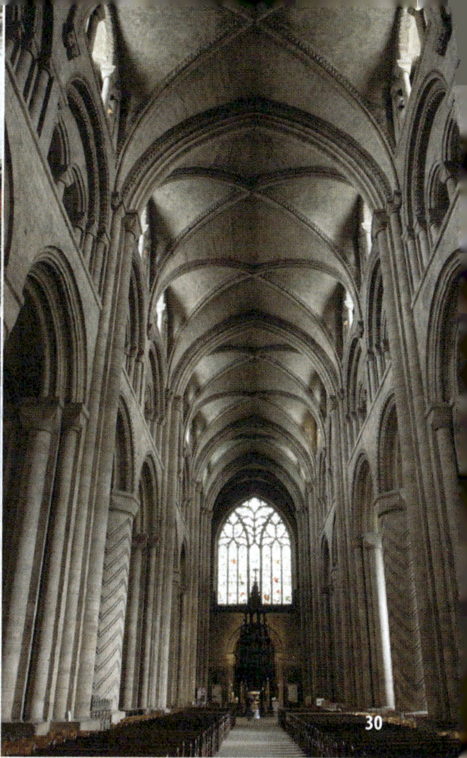

30

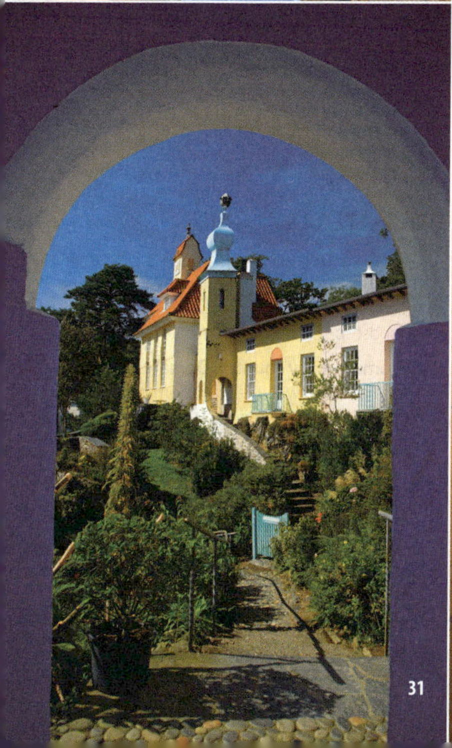

31

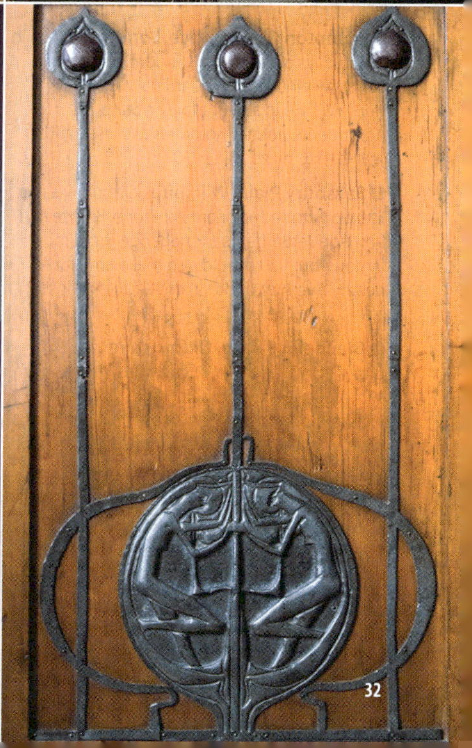

32

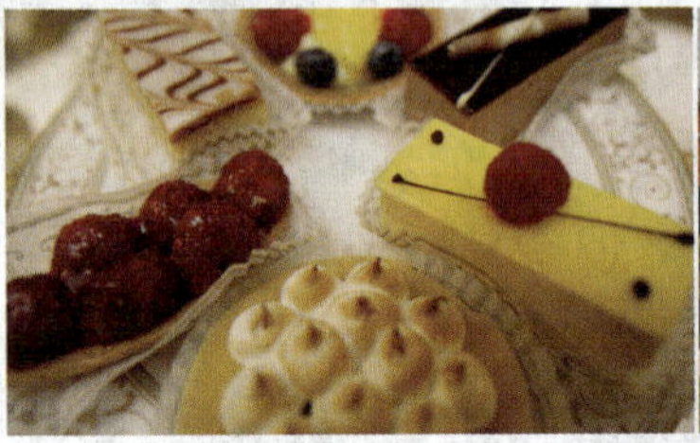

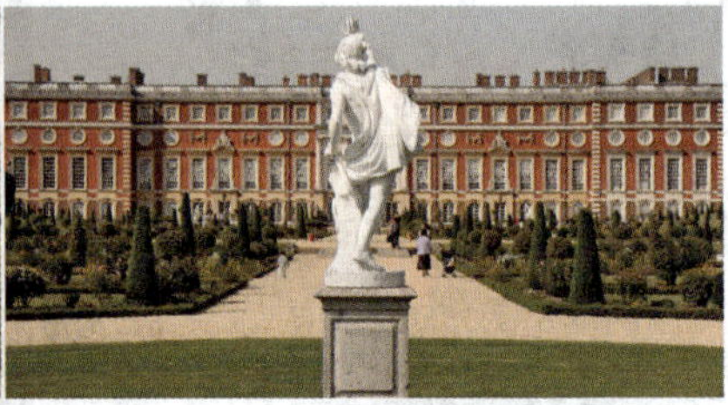

Itineraries

The following itineraries plan routes through Britain in all its huge variety, from the wave-lashed Cornish coast to the misty hills of northern Scotland. Whether you want to survey the remnants of ancient cultures in situ, follow in the footsteps of some of the world's most famous writers, or feast on the best of British dining, these will point the way.

A HERITAGE TOUR

If there's one thing the Brits do brilliantly, it's heritage. Take a couple of weeks to travel back through the millennia.

❶ **Hampton Court Palace, London** You could spend days exploring this Tudor palace, famously pinched from Cardinal Wolsey by Henry VIII. Head straight for the State Apartments, and try not to lose yourself in the yew-hedge maze. **See p.107**

❷ **Salisbury Plain, Wiltshire** Salisbury Plain is littered with the remnants of Stone, Bronze and Iron Age settlements. Stonehenge is the most famous, but you should also make time for nearby Avebury, another stone circle built soon after 2500 BC. **See p.214**

❸ **Blenheim Palace, Oxfordshire** In the picture-postcard-pretty Cotswolds, this sumptuous residence is England's grandest example of Baroque civic architecture, more a monument than a house. **See p.238**

❹ **Ironbridge Gorge, Shropshire** The gorge, home to the world's first iron bridge (1781) is now a UNESCO World Heritage Site, with an array of fascinating museums and industrial attractions. **See pp.392–396**

❺ **Conwy Castle, North Wales** The most spectacular of Edward I's Iron Ring of monumental fortresses is in a lovely town on the Conwy Estuary. **See pp.705–707**

❻ **Chatsworth House, Derbyshire** Chatsworth House, built in the seventeenth century, is one of Britain's finest – and most familiar – stately homes, in a lovely Peak District location. **See p.413**

❼ **Holy Island, Northumberland** Atmospheric tidal island where the illuminated Lindisfarne Gospels were created. **See p.595**

❽ **Edinburgh Castle** Perched imposingly atop an extinct volcanic crag, Edinburgh Castle dominates not only the city but the history of Scotland itself. **See p.718**

THE LITERARY TRAIL

You could spend two or three weeks on this tour, which takes in visits to birth- and burial places and dedicated museums, and allows you to explore the landscapes that inspired so many great books.

❶ **Thomas Hardy country, Dorset** Dorset will be forever linked with the wildly romantic works of Thomas Hardy. The town of Dorchester (or "Casterbridge") is the obvious focus, but the surrounding countryside and the coast to the south feature heavily in his novels too. **See p.204**

❷ **Chawton, Hampshire** The modest but elegant home where Jane Austen lived and wrote her most celebrated works is a delight; you can also visit her brother's house, which now holds a library of women's writing. **See p.192**

❸ **Stratford-upon-Avon, the Midlands** Britain's most celebrated playwright defines this

ABOVE AFTERNOON TEA AT THE RITZ; HAMPTON COURT

otherwise unextraordinary market town; don't miss Anne Hathaway's Cottage, and be sure to catch a RSC performance. **See pp.379–383**

❹ **Laugharne, South Wales** Laugharne is saturated with the spirit of Welsh poet, Dylan Thomas; visit his boathouse and his grave, and have a drink in his favourite boozer, *Brown's Hotel*. **See p.631**

❺ **Hay-on-Wye, Mid-Wales** Browse antiquarian bookshops and join fellow bibliophiles at the literary festival at this appealing Welsh/English border town. **See p.656**

❻ **Haworth, Yorkshire** Get a glimpse of the Brontë sisters' lives in the pretty Yorkshire village of Haworth, and take a romantic Wuthering Heights-style stroll on the wild surrounding moors. **See p.524**

❼ **The Lake District** The Lake District has had a huge influence on writers as diverse as Beatrix Potter, William Wordsworth and John Ruskin – tour their homes, but be sure to explore the stunning natural surroundings that inspired them, too. **See pp.484–504**

❽ **Dumfries and Alloway, Southern Scotland** Born in Alloway and laid to rest in Dumfries, Robert Burns is Scotland's most treasured poet. Both towns have a number of Burns-related sights. **See p.761 & p.767**

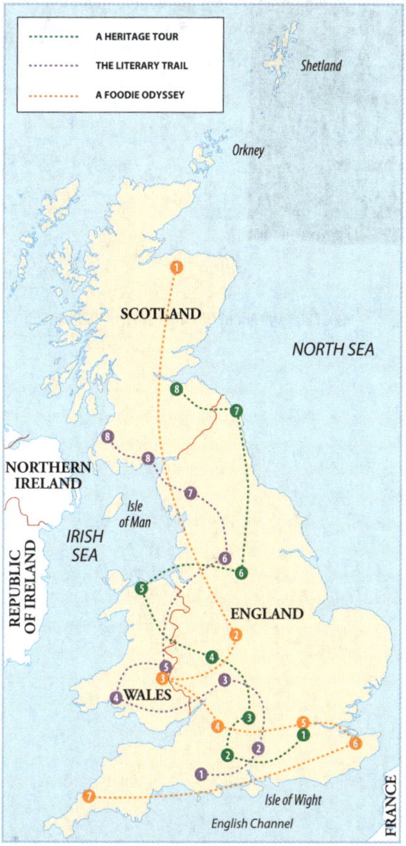

A FOODIE ODYSSEY

Long having lurked in the shadow of its more flamboyant European neighbours, British food is no longer the poor relation – this two-week-long trail focuses on offbeat destinations that offer memorable gastronomic experiences.

❶ **Speyside's Malt Whisky Trail, Northeast Scotland** Sample a wee dram and get behind the scenes at Scotland's "water of life" distilleries. **See p.869**

❷ **Baltis in Brum** This delicious sizzling curry, which travelled with Pakistani immigrants to Birmingham, is an umissable Brummy treat. **See p.404**

❸ **Abergavenny, Mid-Wales** Some of Britain's finest restaurants are to be found in and around the appealing market town of Abergavenny, along with a mouthwatering food festival in mid-September. **See p.654**

❹ **Michelin-starred dining in the Cotswolds** Splash out on a gastronomic experience at one of the Michelin-starred restaurants in the Cotswolds – among them *The Dining Room* near Malmesbury and *Le Champignon Sauvage* in Cheltenham. **See pp.240–248**

❺ **Afternoon tea in London** Dress up in your Sunday best for this quintessentially English treat, best enjoyed in the capital's posh hotels and fancy department stores. **See p.116**

❻ **Oysters in Whitstable, Kent** Kent's most bohemian seaside town has been farming oysters since classical times. July's Oyster Festival is a grand time to come, but you can tuck into freshly shucked bi-valves for most of the year. **See p.139**

❼ **Seafood feasts in Padstow, Cornwall** A stay on the Cornish coast warrants a fresh seafood extravaganza. Head to one of Rick Stein's restaurants for the very best in fish suppers. **See pp.329–330**

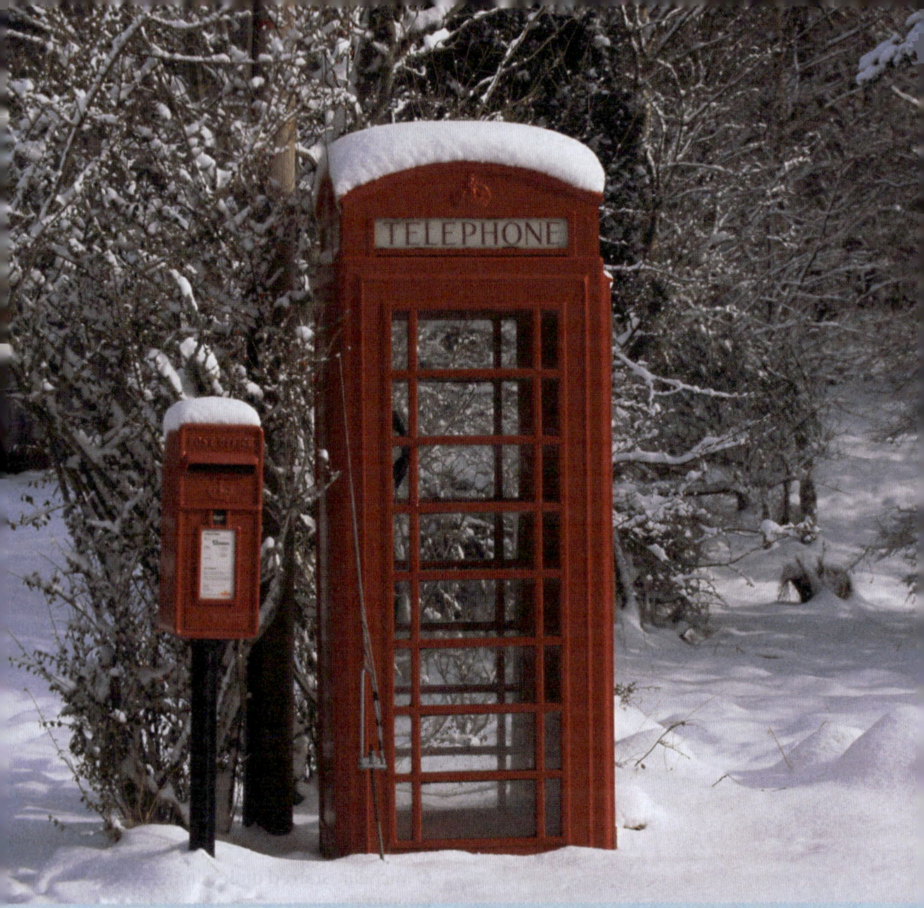

POST BOX AND PHONE BOX, THE SCOTTISH HIGHLANDS

Basics

29 Getting there

31 Getting around

34 Accommodation

36 Food and drink

39 The media

40 Festivals and events

42 Sports and outdoor activities

45 Travel essentials

Getting there

London is one of the world's busiest transport hubs, and there are good deals from around the world on flights into the British capital. However, if you're planning to tour the north of England, north Wales or Scotland, consider flying directly instead to more convenient international airports like Manchester or Glasgow.

London's biggest and best-known airports – **Heathrow** and **Gatwick** – take the bulk of transatlantic and long-haul flights into the UK, though there are also three smaller London airports – **Stansted**, **Luton** and **City** – and a host of useful regional British airports, many of which are served by low-cost flights from mainland Europe and Ireland. Principally, these are **Manchester** and **Liverpool** in England's northwest, **Birmingham** in the West Midlands, **Bristol,** Newquay and Exeter in the West Country, **Leeds-Bradford** and Doncaster-Sheffield in Yorkshire, **Newcastle** and Durham Tees Valley in the northeast, **East Midlands,** and Bournemouth and Southampton in the south, plus **Edinburgh**, **Glasgow** and **Aberdeen** in Scotland, and **Cardiff** and **Swansea** in Wales. The cheapest flight deals on all routes tend to have little or no flexibility, and taxes and fees can add significantly to any seemingly bargain quoted price.

Overland routes from Europe include high-speed trains into London (with onward connections) through the Channel Tunnel – either passenger-only Eurostar services or the drive-on drive-off **Eurotunnel** shuttle train. There's also a range of useful ferry routes offering direct access to various regions of England, Scotland and Wales.

Flights from the US and Canada

Many airlines fly nonstop to London, Manchester and some other British airports – flight time from the east coast is around seven hours, more like ten hours from the west. Flights on European airlines might be cheaper but tend to route through their respective European hubs, adding to your journey time.

From the **US**, New York has the most nonstop services, though there are also regular flights from Washington DC, Boston, Chicago, Atlanta, Miami, Las Vegas, San Francisco, Los Angeles and others. Straightforward standard-class tickets start at around $800 return, but can cost a lot more depending on the time of year and the airline.

From **Canada**, nonstop routes to London and Manchester start mainly from Toronto, Montréal and Vancouver, with return fares starting at around Can$900 or Can$1200.

Flights from Australia, New Zealand and South Africa

The route **from Australia and New Zealand** to London is highly competitive, with the lowest return fares usually in the range of Aus$1500–2500 from Sydney, Melbourne or Perth, NZ$2000–3000 from Auckland. The quickest and most convenient routes tend to be with the obvious major airlines, like Qantas, British Airways, Air New Zealand or Singapore Airlines. Some of the cheaper flights on Asian and Middle Eastern airlines involve a stop, while most New Zealand flights require a connection, whether in Asia or the US; there's little to choose between the two routes in terms of journey time. You're looking at a travel time from Australia or New Zealand of over twenty hours, even with the best connections, so you might want to consider a stopover in any case – most airlines will let you do this for no extra charge.

Flights from Johannesburg in **South Africa** take eleven hours nonstop, though some of the cheapest, operated by Emirates, involve lengthy connections in Dubai. There are fewer direct flights from Cape Town, and they take slightly longer and cost a bit more.

Flights from Ireland

Stiff competition on routes between **Ireland** and England means it's easy to find a one-way flight for

A BETTER KIND OF TRAVEL

At Rough Guides we are passionately committed to travel. We feel that travelling is the best way to understand the world we live in and the people we share it with – plus tourism has brought a great deal of benefit to developing economies around the world over the last few decades. But the growth in tourism has also damaged some places irreparably, and climate change is exacerbated by most forms of transport, especially flying. All Rough Guides' trips are carbon-offset, and every year we donate money to a variety of charities devoted to combating the effects of climate change.

around €30–50. There are routes out of Dublin, Cork, Knock, Kerry and Shannon to more than a dozen English, Scottish and Welsh airports, with airlines like Aer Arran, Ryanair, bmibaby, Aer Lingus and British Airways. The cheapest options **from Belfast** and Derry are usually easyJet, flybe and Ryanair, again, to a wide range of British regional airports.

Ferries

There are lots of ferry routes from mainland Europe and Ireland to Britain. The quickest, cheapest services to England are on the traditional cross-Channel routes **from the French ports of** Calais, Boulogne and Dunkerque to **Dover** in the southeast. However, there are many other routes from elsewhere in France, plus Belgium, the Netherlands, Spain, Denmark, Norway and Sweden into ports ranged around the southern, eastern and northeastern coasts of England, from Plymouth to Newcastle.

Ferry services from **Ireland** are mainly to England's northwest (Liverpool, Fleetwood, and Douglas on the Isle of Man) and to **Wales** (Holyhead in north Wales, Fishguard and Pembroke in south Wales). From Northern Ireland, there are regular services to **Scotland's southeast coast** (Stranraer, Troon and Cairnryan).

Fares on all routes vary considerably, according to time of year, and time and type of crossing – some high-speed ferry services can cut journey times on the same route by up to half – while accommodation is often obligatory on night crossings from the continent. Note that there are some really good ferry-plus-train deals available for foot passengers from Ireland – see "By train" below. For up-to-date and comprehensive **information** on routes, schedules and costs, contact Ⓦ directferries.com.

Trains

Direct **Eurostar trains** (Ⓦ eurostar.com) run roughly hourly to London St Pancras International from Lille (1hr 20min), Paris (2hr 15min) and Brussels (2hr), with connections into those cities from across Europe. Fares start from around €89 return, though these special rates come with restrictions and you'll have to book well in advance. There are discounts on standard fares for travellers under 26 and over 60.

For drivers, the fastest and most convenient cross-Channel option is the Eurotunnel (Ⓦ eurotunnel .com) drive-on-drive-off shuttle train from Calais to Folkestone, which runs 24 hours a day and takes 35 minutes. Although you can just turn up, booking is advised, especially at weekends, or if you want the best deals. Short-stay (under 5-day) returns start at €59 each way per car (including passengers), or from €77 for longer stays.

Irish Ferries (Ⓦ irishferries.com) offer a very good "Sail Rail" deal from Ireland, where you can book integrated train and ferry services from almost any station in Ireland to almost any station in Britain. Dublin to London, for example, takes under seven hours, with one-way fares starting at €40, plus another €10–20 for the connecting journey from your local Irish mainline station.

Buses

Eurolines (Ⓦ eurolines.com) coordinates international bus services to London (with connections onwards) from dozens of **European cities**, with fares very similar to those of a low-cost airline. However, you really do have to ask yourself how long you want to spend cooped up in a bus – only routes from nearby cities like Paris, for example (total journey time around 6hr), are anything like bearable.

Tours and organized holidays

Package tours of Britain, where all flights, accommodation and ground transport are arranged for you, can sometimes be cheaper than organizing things yourself. Many companies, for example, offer **coach tours** of Britain's historic highlights, or help you explore some aspect of the country's heritage, such as art and architecture, or gardens and stately homes. Other operators specialize in **activity holidays**, either escorted (ie, guide-led) or self-guided, the latter usually slightly cheaper. Some companies offer budget versions of their holidays, staying in hostels or B&Bs, as well as hotel packages.

GENERAL AND CULTURAL

Abercrombie & Kent US Ⓣ 1800 554 7016, Ⓦ **abercrombiekent .com.** Classy travel specialist, with no-expense-spared escorted and independent trips, from a 7-night River Thames cruise to tailor-made tours of Britain.

English Experience US Ⓣ 215 699 6863, Ⓦ **english-experience .com.** Small-group, customized tours in B&Bs or hotels (prices vary), covering the historic sights in Sussex, Kent, the Cotswolds, Devon and Cornwall, East Anglia, the Lake District, Yorkshire Dales, and Scotland.

Martin Randall Travel UK Ⓣ 020 8742 3355, Ⓦ **martinrandall .com.** Wide-ranging all-inclusive historical and cultural tours led by experts – for example, 7-day tours of Hadrian's Wall, or 10 days visiting the stately homes and gardens of northern England.

Maupintour US Ⓣ 1800 255 4266, Ⓦ **maupintour.com.** Quality, all-inclusive, themed escorted tours – from Scottish week-long barge cruises to a Great Britain Journey that takes in all the highlights.

ADVENTURE AND ACTIVITY TOURS

Contiki Holidays UK ⓣ **0845 075 0990,** ⓦ **contiki.com.** Lively, reasonably priced, budget-accommodation adventure tours for 18–35s, including 5-day London trips or a 9-day England and Scotland trip.

Outward Bound UK ⓣ **01931 740000,** ⓦ **outwardbound.org.uk.** Residential courses and activity holidays in Snowdonia, the Scottish Highlands and the Lake District, including climbing, caving, sailing and canoeing – they're geared towards under-25s, but family weekends are also available.

Road Trip UK ⓣ **0208 133 8375,** ⓦ **roadtrip.co.uk.** Inclusive, activity-filled budget bus tours, using mainly hostel accommodation – from Loch Ness Monster tours to Heart-of-England castles and mansions.

YHA UK ⓣ **01629 592700,** ⓦ **yha.org.uk.** Huge range of good-value hostel-based activity weekends and holidays, from walking, climbing and biking to surfing, kayaking and caving.

BOATING AND SAILING

Blakes Holiday Boating UK ⓣ **0844 856 7060,** ⓦ **blakes.co.uk.** Cruisers, yachts and narrowboats on the Norfolk Broads, the River Thames and various English and Scottish canals.

Classic Sailing UK ⓣ **01872 580022,** ⓦ **classic-sailing.co.uk.** Hands-on sailing holidays on traditional wooden boats and tall ships, including Devon, Cornwall and the Isles of Scilly.

CYCLING

Capital Sport UK ⓣ **01296 631671,** ⓦ **capital-sport.co.uk.** Gentle self-guided cycling tours, mainly in Kent, Oxford and the Cotswolds, in either B&B or "fine" accommodation.

Saddle Skedaddle UK ⓣ **0191 265 1110,** ⓦ **skedaddle.co.uk.** Biking adventures and classic road rides – including guided and self-guided tours in Cornwall, the Cotswolds, Northumberland, the New Forest, Wales and Scotland, lasting from a weekend to a week.

SURFING

Big Friday UK ⓣ **01637 872512,** ⓦ **bigfriday.com.** Surf weekend packages from London to Newquay, with accommodation, travel and tuition laid on.

Surfers World UK ⓣ **01271 871224,** ⓦ **surfersworld.co.uk.** Short breaks with surfing courses in Woolacombe, north Devon, and on the north Cornwall coast.

WALKING

Classic Journeys US ⓣ **1800 200 3887,** ⓦ **classicjourneys.com.** Upmarket guided "cultural walking adventures" in classic English and Scottish destinations, including the Cotswolds, the Cornish coast, Edinburgh and the Highlands.

Contours Walking Holidays UK ⓣ **01629 821900,** ⓦ **contours.co.uk.** Short breaks or longer walking holidays and self-guided hikes in every region of England, Scotland and Wales, from famous trails to little-known local routes.

English Lakeland Ramblers US ⓣ **1800 724 8801,** ⓦ **ramblers.com.** Escorted walking tours in the Lake District and the Cotswolds, as well as the Welsh Borders and the Scottish Highlands and islands, either inn-to-inn or based in a country hotel.

Ramblers Worldwide Holidays UK ⓣ **01707 331133,** ⓦ **ramblersholidays.co.uk.** Sociable guided walking tours (scenic, themed or special interest) all over the UK, graded from "leisurely" to "challenging".

Walkabout Scotland UK ⓣ **0845 686 1344,** ⓦ **walkaboutscotland.com.** A great way to get a taste of hiking in Scotland, with guided hillwalking holidays, tours and day-trips with all transport included.

Getting around

Almost every town and village in Britain can be reached by train or bus, but public transport costs are among the highest in Europe and travel can eat up a large part of your budget. It pays to investigate all the special deals and passes, some of which are only available outside Britain and must be bought before you arrive. It's sometimes cheaper to drive yourself around, though fuel and car rental rates are expensive – and traffic congestion can be pretty bad.

By air

For longer journeys across the country such as London–Inverness or Manchester–Newquay, you might consider **flying**, on airlines such as British Airways, easyJet, Ryanair, flybe and bmibaby, and – in Scotland – Loganair. Prices can often be lower than the equivalent train fares, though – given travel out to the airport and check-in procedures – you won't always save much on total door-to-door journey time. That said, flights to places like the Isle of Man, or the Scottish islands, can save a day of travel by local bus and ferry. The more remote parts of Scotland have numerous minor airports – some little more than gravel strips – and fares are pretty reasonable.

By train

Despite grumbles about the rail network, and the high cost of travel compared to other European rail systems, getting around Britain by train is still the best, most scenic and – usually – most painless way to travel. Few major towns in **England** lack rail links, and mainline routes out of London in particular are fast and frequent – the 200-mile trips to York and Exeter, for instance, are covered in two hours. The fastest journeys head north from London on east- and west-coast mainline routes (to Birmingham, Manchester, Leeds, Newcastle, among others); other journeys, however, can be more complicated, particularly if you're travelling east–west across the

TOP 5 TRAIN JOURNEYS

North York Moors Railway See p.551
Ravenglass and Eskdale Railway See p.502
Settle to Carlisle Railway See p.529
Snowdon Mountain Railway See p.690
West Highland Line See p.692

country, which might involve a train change or two. **Scotland** has a more modest rail network, at its densest in the central belt between Edinburgh and Glasgow, and at its most skeletal in the Highlands. In **Wales**, there are only two main lines, one in the north from Chester to Holyhead, the other in the south running from Newport to Fishguard.

In all instances, the **National Rail Enquiries** information line or website is an essential first call for timetable, route and fare information; it lists all the regional operators and offers ticket-buying links from its journey planner.

Aside from the national network, Britain's railway heritage is celebrated by scores of small, private railways converted to tourist use, often narrow-gauge and many with steam services.

Buying train tickets

As a rule, the earlier you book, the cheaper your ticket will be, though you should always look out for **online offers** with sites like The Train Line or Megatrain – the latter, in particular, offers a limited number of budget fares on certain popular routes, and you could travel from London to Birmingham, for example, for as little as £3. Just turning up and buying a ticket at the station is always the most expensive way to go (sometimes phenomenally so). Cheapest are advance fares, which are only available several weeks in advance – limited numbers are issued, and they sell out quickly. They are restricted to use only on the specified train – miss it, and you pay a surcharge or have to buy another ticket. Off-peak fares can be bought in advance or on the day of travel, but are only valid for travel at quieter times (generally after 9.30am Mon–Fri, and all day at weekends). Most expensive are Anytime tickets, which permit travel on any train. Price variations can be extraordinary – from London to Manchester, for example, advance fares start at £11.50, though you could pay well over £100 if you just turn up at the station.

A **seat reservation** is usually included with the ticket, while on many trains you can upgrade your ticket by buying a **first-class supplement** for around £15, worth it if you're facing a long journey on a popular route. If the station's ticket office is closed or does not have a ticket machine, you may buy your ticket on the train. Otherwise, **boarding without a ticket** will render you liable to paying the most expensive fare to your destination.

Rail passes

For overseas visitors planning to travel widely by train, a **BritRail pass** could be a wise investment. It gives unlimited travel throughout England, Scotland and Wales (there are also separate England and Scotland passes) and is valid for varied periods of up to one month (consecutive days travel) or two months (flexi-travel). The pass comes in many different varieties, with first- and second-class versions, discounted Youth Passes and Senior Passes (first-class only), while other BritRail combo passes are tailored to families or small groups. Note that BritRail passes have to be bought before you enter the UK.

Eurail passes are not valid in the UK, though they do provide discounts on Eurostar trains to England and on some ferry routes. However, if you've been resident in Europe for at least six months you can buy an **InterRail** pass from Rail Europe and other providers – you can't use it to travel in your own country of residence, so it's no good for Brits, but everyone else can get unlimited train travel in the UK (for 3, 4, 6 or 8 days within one month), as well as discounts on Eurostar and certain cross-Channel ferries.

In Britain itself, a huge variety of **regional rail "Ranger" and "Rover" passes** can be bought by both locals and visitors (see the National Rail website), offering unlimited travel in multi-day or flexi-day formats – typically, around £70 for four days' unlimited regional train travel.

Alternatively, for discounted fares nationwide, people aged between 16 and 25 (and students of an age) qualify for the 16–25 Railcard; those over 60 can get a **Senior Railcard**; while groups of up to four adults and four children travelling together (they don't have to be related) can get a **Family & Friends Railcard**. Each of these passes costs £28 for the year and gives up to a third off most adult fares in Britain (more for children's fares). You can buy the passes at stations or online.

RAIL CONTACTS

BritRail W britrail.com
Megatrain W megatrain.com
National Rail Enquiries UK T 0845 748 4950, W nationalrail.co.uk
Rail Europe W raileurope.co.uk, W raileurope.com
The Train Line W thetrainline.com

By bus

Travel by bus – long-distance services are known as "coaches" – is usually much cheaper than by train, though traffic congestion can make the same journey much longer.

The biggest inter-city bus operators in England and Wales are **National Express** (Ⓦnationalexpress.com), Stagecoach (Ⓦstagecoachbus.com) and Megabus (a Stagecoach subsidiary; Ⓦmegabus.com); north of the border, routes are largely covered by Megabus and **Scottish Citylink** (Ⓦcitylink.co.uk). On busy routes, and on any route at weekends and during holidays, it's advisable to book ahead, rather than just turn up. Fares are very reasonable, with big discounts for under-26s, over-60s and families, while advance-purchase fares and special deals are common – London or Glasgow to nearby cities for just £1, for example. Booking in advance always gets you the best deal.

Regional and urban bus services are run by a huge array of companies. In many cases, timetables and routes are well integrated, but operators tend to duplicate the busiest routes, leaving the more remote spots neglected. As a rule, the further away from urban areas you get, the less frequent and more expensive bus services become. However, there are very few rural areas in Britain that aren't served by at least an occasional bus.

Between Easter and the end of September, many national park areas support a network of **weekend and bank holiday buses**, taking visitors to beauty spots, villages and hiking trailheads.

For impartial, up-to-date information, the official service **Traveline** (Ⓦtraveline.org.uk) has full details of every route in the UK.

By car

Your British driving experience will depend very much on where you drive. Slogging through the traffic from major city to major city is rarely an illuminating way to see the nation – motorways ("M" roads) and main "A" roads may have up to four lanes in each direction, but even these can get very congested, with long tailbacks a regular occurrence, especially at peak travel times and on public holidays. Driving in the countryside, on the other hand, is far more agreeable, though on "B" roads and minor roads there might only be one lane (single track) for both directions. Keep your speed down, and be prepared for abrupt encounters with tractors, sheep and other hazards in remote spots.

Don't underestimate the British **weather**. Snow, ice, fog and wind cause havoc every year, and driving conditions – on motorways as much as in rural areas – can deteriorate quickly. BBC Radio Five Live (693 or 909 AM nationwide) and local stations feature regularly updated traffic bulletins, as does the Highways Agency.

Fuel is pricey – unleaded petrol (gasoline) and diesel can cost three times more than in the US. Out-of-town supermarkets usually have the lowest prices, while the highest prices are charged by motorway service stations.

Britain has so far resisted toll roads (apart from one or two examples), but the principle has been broached by the success of **congestion charging** in London – if you intend to drive a car into central London, it will cost you (see p.111 for more).

Rules and regulations

Drive on the left. You need a current full **driving licence**, to show on demand (an international licence is not necessary). If you're bringing your own vehicle into the country you should also carry your vehicle registration, ownership and insurance documents. **Seatbelts** must be worn by everyone in the vehicle, front and back. Motorbikers and their passengers must wear a helmet.

Speed limits are 20mph in many residential streets, 30mph or 40mph in built-up areas, 60mph on out-of-town single-carriageway roads (often signed by a white circle with a black diagonal stripe), 70mph on dual carriageways and motorways (freeways). As a rule, assume that in any area with street lighting the speed limit is 30mph unless otherwise stated.

The AA (Ⓦtheaa.com), RAC (Ⓦrac.co.uk) and Green Flag (Ⓦgreenflag.co.uk) all operate **24-hour emergency breakdown** services, and offer useful online route planners. You may be entitled to free assistance through a reciprocal arrangement with a motoring organization in your home country – check before setting out. You can make use of these emergency services if you are not a member of the organization, but you will need to join at the roadside and will incur a hefty surcharge too.

Parking

Car parking in towns, cities and popular tourist spots can be a nightmare and often costs a small fortune. A yellow line along the edge of the road indicates **parking restrictions**; check the nearest sign to see exactly what they are. A double-yellow line means no parking at any time, though you can stop briefly to unload or pick up people or goods, while a red line signifies no stopping at all. Fines for parking illegally are high – as much as £60 – and if you're wheel-clamped it will cost you £200 or so to have your vehicle released.

If you're in a tourist city for a day, look out for **park-and-ride schemes** in which you park on the outskirts and take a cheap or free bus to the centre. Parking in towns in the well-signposted "pay-and-display" **car parks** will be cheaper than using on-street meters, which often restrict parking time to one or two hours at the most.

Some towns operate free **disc-zone parking**, which allows limited-hours town-centre parking in designated areas: if that's what roadside signs indicate, you need to pick up a cardboard disc from any local shop and display it in your car.

Vehicle rental

Car rental is usually cheaper arranged in advance from home through one of the large multinational chains (Avis, Budget, easycar, Hertz or National, for example) or through your tour operator as part of a package.

If you rent a car from a company in the UK, expect to pay around £30 per day, £50 for a weekend, or from £120 per week. You can sometimes find deals of under £20 per day, though you'll need to book well in advance for the cheapest rates and be prepared for extra charges (like cleaning fees or additional driver charges). Few companies will rent to drivers with less than one year's experience and most will only rent to people between 21 and 75 years of age. Rental cars will be manual (stick shift) unless you specify otherwise.

By bike

No one would choose to get around Britain by **cycling** on the main "A" roads – there's simply too much traffic. It's far better to stick to the quieter "B" roads and country lanes – or, best of all, follow one of the **traffic-free trails** of the extensive National Cycle Network (see p.43).

Cycle helmets are not compulsory – but if you're hell-bent on tackling the congestion, pollution and aggression of city traffic, you're well advised to wear one. You do have to have a **rear reflector** and front and back **lights** when riding at night, and you are not allowed to carry children without a special **child seat**. It is also illegal to cycle on pavements and in most public parks, while **off-road** cyclists must stick to bridleways and by-ways designated for their use.

Bike rental is available at cycle shops in most large towns, and at villages within national parks and other scenic areas. Expect to pay around £15–20 per day, with discounts for longer periods; you may need to provide credit card details, or leave a passport as a deposit.

Accommodation

Accommodation in Britain ranges from motorway lodges to country retreats, and from budget guesthouses and hostels to chic boutique hotels. Characterful old buildings – former coaching inns, converted mansions and manor houses – also offer heaps of historic atmosphere.

Many tourist offices will **reserve rooms** for you. In some areas you pay a deposit that's deducted from your first night's bill (usually ten percent); in others the office will take a percentage or flat-rate commission – usually around £3.

A nationwide **grading system** awards stars to hotels, guesthouses and B&Bs. There's no hard and fast correlation between rank and price, but the grading system does lay down minimum levels of standards and service. On the whole, British people don't tend to insist on **seeing a room before taking it**, but you shouldn't be afraid to ask – any place worth its salt, be it designer hotel or humble B&B, should have no objection.

Hotels

British hotels vary wildly in size, style, comfort and price. The starting price for a regular hotel is around £70 per night for a double or twin room, breakfast usually included; anything more upmarket, or with a bit of boutique styling, can easily cost £100 a night, while top-end four- and five-star properties may charge around £200 a night, often considerably more in London or in resort or country-house hotels. Many city hotels in particular charge a room rate only – breakfast can be another whopping £10 or £15 on top.

Budget hotel chains – including Premier Inn (Ⓦ premierinn.com), Holiday Inn Express (Ⓦ hiexpress.com), Jurys Inn (Ⓦ jurysinns.com), Travelodge (Ⓦ travelodge.co.uk), Ibis (Ⓦ ibishotel.com) and

TOP 5 QUIRKY HOTELS

Belle Tout Beachy Head. See p.161
Cley Mill B&B Norfolk. See p.359
Hotel Portmeirion North Wales. See p.696
Kinloch Castle Hostel Rùm. See p.925
Rough Luxe London. See p.113

Comfort/Quality/Sleep Inn (ⓦchoicehotelsuk.co.uk) – have properties usefully located in city centres across the country. Their style tends towards the no-frills (with breakfast charged extra), but they're a good deal for families and small groups, while special offers can bring room rates down to a bargain £20–30 per night if booked in advance.

B&Bs and guesthouses

At its most basic, the typical British **bed-and-breakfast** (**B&B**) is an ordinary private house with a couple of bedrooms set aside for paying guests. Larger establishments with more rooms, particularly in resorts, style themselves **guesthouses**, but they are pretty much the same thing. They are great options for travellers looking for character and a local experience.

At the extreme budget end of the scale – basic B&Bs under £60 a night – you'll normally experience small rooms, fairly spartan facilities and shared bathrooms (though there are some fantastic exceptions). You'll pay a few pounds more for en-suite shower and toilet facilities, while at the top end of the range you can expect things like fancy furnishings, fresh flowers, gourmet breakfasts, king-sized beds and quality bathrooms. Many top-notch B&Bs – say around £90 and up – offer more luxury and better value pound for pound than more impersonal hotels.

Single travellers tend not to get a great deal, since many B&Bs and guesthouses don't have single rooms – establishments often charge well over half the room rate for sole occupancy of a double/twin room. Finally, don't assume that a B&B is no good if it's ungraded: many places choose not to enter into a grading scheme, and in the rural backwaters some of the best accommodation is to be found in **farmhouses** and other properties whose facilities may technically fall short of official standards.

ACCOMMODATION PRICES

Throughout this guide we give a headline price for every accommodation reviewed, which indicates the lowest price you could expect to pay per night for a **double or twin room in high season** (basically, from Easter to the end of September, though local variations apply). We also give the high-season price for **dorm accommodation** in youth and backpackers' hostels, and per pitch or per person prices for **campsites**.

USEFUL CONTACTS

Bed & Fed ⓦ**bedandfed.co.uk.** Directory of informal home-from-home overnight experiences – seaside cottages to farmhouses, city pads to Scottish castles.

Distinctly Different ⓦ**distinctlydifferent.co.uk.** Stay the night in converted buildings across the country, from old brothel to Baptist chapel, windmill to lighthouse.

Farm Stay ⓦ**farmstay.co.uk.** The UK's largest network of farm-based accommodation.

LateRooms.com ⓦ**laterooms.com.** Thousands of rooms across Britain – cottages to castles – available at up to fifty percent discounts.

Wolsey Lodges ⓦ**wolseylodges.com wolseylodges.com.** Superior B&B in properties across England, from Elizabethan manor houses to Victorian rectories.

Hostels

Between them, the **Youth Hostels Association** (ⓦyha.org.uk) of England and Wales, and the **Scottish Youth Hostels Association** (ⓦsyha.org.uk), have around 300 hostels across Britain, ranging from lakeside mansions to thatched country cottages. There are still shared bathrooms and traditional single-sex bunk-bed dormitories in most, though there's been a concerted move towards offering smaller rooms (sometimes en-suite) of two to six beds for couples, families and groups. Some hostels have been purpose-built, or have had expensive refurbishments, and in cities, resorts and national park areas the facilities are often every bit as good as budget hotels. Most hostels also offer self-catering kitchens, laundry facilities and lounges, while wi-fi access, cafés, bars, tour bookings and bike rental are common. The hostel will usually provide bed linen, pillows and duvet; towels and other necessities can often be rented.

YHA and SHYA hostels are affiliated to the global **Hostelling International** network, which you can join online or at any hostel when you arrive. However, you don't have to be a member to use the British hostels, though you get a £3 discount per night if you are. There are joint-member and family deals, and members qualify for discounts from various UK travel providers.

Prices are calculated according to season, location and demand, with adult dorm beds costing from £15–30 per night – it's most expensive in London and at peak holiday periods (school summer holidays, bank holidays etc). A private twin room in a hostel goes for around £40–60, and family rooms sleeping four from around £70. Hostel **meals** are good value – breakfast or a packed lunch for around £5, or £10–13 for dinner.

TOP 5 HOSTELS

Goofy's, Newquay. See p.328
Grasmere Independent Hostel See p.494
Lazy Crofter Bunkhouse, Scottish Highlands. See p.904
Nos Da Cardiff. See p.618
Whitby YHA See p.556

A large number of **independent hostels** offer similar facilities and prices, though they often attract a more youthful, backpacker crowd. The main source of information for these is **Independent Hostels UK** (ⓦindependenthostelsuk.co.uk), whose annually updated *Independent Hostel Guide* reviews around 300 such establishments across Britain.

University rooms

In university towns – from Brighton to St Andrew's – **student halls of residence** can offer great value, generally in single rooms or self-catering apartments that are available over the summer (July–Sept), plus at Easter and Christmas. Check ⓦbudgetstayuk.com and ⓦuniversityrooms.co.uk for details.

Camping

British camping is cool – the travel mags and newspapers all say so – and there are hundreds of **campsites**, ranging from small, family-run places to large sites with laundries, shops and sports facilities. Costs start at around £5 per adult in the simplest sites, though at larger, more popular locations you can pay twice as much, and sometimes there are separate charges too per car and tent. Many campsites also have accommodation in permanently fixed, fully equipped caravans, or in wooden cabins or similar. Meanwhile, "glamping" (that's glamorous camping) is all the rage, and tipis, yurts, bell tents and camping "pods" are an accepted part of the camping repertoire these days. Some of these are fairly lavish (with futons and wood-burners) and are priced accordingly.

Farmers may offer field-and-tap pitches for around £5 per night, but setting up a tent without asking first will not be well received. **Camping wild** is illegal in most national parks and nature reserves.

The wilder parts of England, Wales and Scotland offer **camping barns** and **bunkhouses** (known as bothies in Scotland), many administered by the YHA and SHYA, though with plenty of others operated by individual farmers and families. They are pretty basic – often in converted agricultural buildings, old crofters' cottages and the like – but they are weatherproof and cheap (from around £8–10 a night); check the hostel websites and ⓦcampingbarns.net for listings.

The Rough Guide to Camping in Britain has detailed **reviews** of the best campsites in the country, while ⓦcampingandcaravanningclub.co.uk and ⓦukcampsite.co.uk are useful resources.

Self-catering accommodation

Holiday self-catering properties range from city penthouses to secluded cottages. **Studios and apartments**, available by the night in an increasing number of British cities, offer an attractive alternative to hotel stays, with prices from around £90 a night (more in London). Rural **cottages and houses** work out cheaper, though the minimum rental period is usually a week. Depending on the season and location, expect to pay from around £300 for a week in a small cottage, though perhaps three or four times that for a larger property in a popular tourist spot.

RENTAL AGENCIES

Cornish Cottage Holidays ⓣ01326 573808, ⓦcornishcottageholidays.co.uk. Thatched cottages and seaside places.

Cottages 4You ⓣ0845 268 0760, ⓦcottages4you.co.uk. A wide range of properties all over the UK.

Heart of the Lakes ⓣ015394 32321, ⓦheartofthelakes.co.uk. Excellent choice of more than 350 quality properties in the Lake District.

Helpful Holidays ⓣ01647 433593, ⓦhelpfulholidays.com. Everything from cottage rentals to a castle, throughout the West Country.

Landmark Trust ⓣ01628 825925, ⓦlandmarktrust.org.uk. A preservation charity which lists more than 180 historic properties, ranging from restored forts and towers to a tiny radio shack used in World War II.

National Trust ⓣ0844 800 2070, ⓦnationaltrustcottages.co.uk. The NT owns 350 cottages, houses and farmhouses in England and Wales, most set in their own gardens or grounds.

Rural Retreats ⓣ01386 701177, ⓦruralretreats.co.uk. Upmarket accommodation in restored historic buildings from Cornwall to Scotland.

Scottish Country Cottages ⓣ0845 268 0801, ⓦscottish-country-cottages.co.uk. Superior cottages with lots of character scattered across Scotland.

Wales Holidays ⓣ01686 628200, ⓦwales-holidays.co.uk. A varied selection of 500 properties all over Wales.

Food and drink

You know times have changed when Britain is now seen as a gourmet destination. Over the last twenty years, changing popular tastes have transformed both supermarket shelves and restaurant menus, while there's an

increasing importance placed on "ethical" eating – not only sourcing products locally, but also using free-range, organic, humanely produced ingredients. London continues to be the main destination for all things foodie and fashionable, though great restaurants and "gastropubs" can be found right across Britain, often in surprisingly out-of-the-way places. Meanwhile, the old-fashioned British pub remains an enduring social institution, and is often the best introduction to town or village life.

Breakfast

The traditional British breakfast (aka the "Full English, "Full Scottish", etc) is many visitors' introduction to the local cuisine, and will keep you going all day. It kicks off with a choice of cereals, followed by any combination of eggs, bacon, sausage, tomatoes, mushrooms, baked beans and toast. Especially in northern England, it may also include "black pudding" (ie, blood sausage). Veggie alternatives are commonly available. A traditional **Scottish breakfast** includes oatmeal porridge (eaten with salt or sugar) and oatcakes (plain savoury biscuits). Anywhere in Britain, you may also be served kippers (smoked herring), haddock with a poached egg on top, omelettes and, increasingly, things like home-made muesli and yoghurt, fresh fruit salad, and pancakes. A "continental" breakfast usually means cereal, toast and preserves, though often croissants, fruit and yoghurt too.

British cuisine

For most overseas visitors the quintessential British meal is **fish and chips** (known in Scotland as a "fish supper", even at lunchtime), a dish that can vary from the succulently fresh to the indigestibly greasy: local knowledge is the key, as most towns, cities and resorts have at least one first-rate fish-and-chip shop or restaurant.

Other **traditional British dishes** – steak and kidney pie, liver and onions, lamb chops, roast beef and roast chicken – figure on menu after menu, though regional specialities are increasingly easy to find. Quality varies, of course, but for every dismal meal served, there's a café or restaurant somewhere providing excellent local food at reasonable prices, from Cornish pasty to Lancashire hotpot, seasonal soup to home-made ice cream. On your way, you may have to learn a whole lexicon to figure out what you're eating – from faggots (offal meatballs) to haggis (stuffed sheep's stomach), bubble-and-squeak (fried leftover potato and cabbage) to spotted dick (suet-pudding dessert). Even the basics aren't always straightforward – a simple bread roll, for example, is referred to as a roll, cob, bap, barmcake, teacake or bread-bun, depending on which part of Britain you're in.

Many hitherto neglected or previously unfashionable dishes – from brawn to brains – are finding their way into top-end restaurants these days, as inventive restaurateurs – keen on using cheap, seasonal produce – reinvent the classics. There's also a definite **Modern British** style of cuisine that marries local produce with ingredients and techniques from the Mediterranean, Southeast Asia or Pacific Rim. At worst, this can mean terrible crimes committed in the name of "fusion" food; at best, it results in dishes that rely on great taste and local sourcing, from hedgerow herbs to fish landed from local boats.

Cafés and tearooms

Every town, city and resort has a plethora of cheap **cafés**, characteristically unassuming places offering non-alcoholic drinks, all-day breakfasts, snacks and meals. Most are only open during the daytime, and tend to be cash-only establishments with few airs and graces. **Teashops** or **tearooms** tend to be more genteel, and serve sandwiches, cakes and light meals throughout the day, as well, of course, as tea.

Old-fashioned chrome-and-formica **coffee bars** – almost always Italian in origin – still cling on in London and a few other towns. Most, however, have been replaced by chain outlets, such as *Starbucks*, *Costa* and *Caffè Nero*.

Café-bars, pubs and gastropubs

Licensed (ie, alcohol-serving) **café-bars** on the European model are commonplace, and stay open day and night. Although primarily places to drink, many serve reasonably priced food. In some places, the pub might be your only choice for food and – in many places – it might be terrible, heavily reliant on

TOP 5 CAFÉS

Badger's Hall Chipping Camden. See p.247
Bar Italia London. See p.115
Betty's York. See p.536
Madame Fromage Cardiff. See p.619
Willow Tea Rooms Glasgow. See p.779

VEGGIE BRITAIN

Vegetarians are fairly well catered for in Britain. Away from London and the big cities, specialist vegetarian places are thin on the ground, but most restaurants and pubs have at least one vegetarian option on their menus, while Italian, Indian and Chinese restaurants usually provide a decent choice of meat-free dishes. For a list of vegetarian establishments across the UK, check the **Veg Dining** website (Ⓦvegdining.com).

the microwave and deep-fat fryer. However, many pubs have embraced the change in British tastes and these so-called **gastropubs** serve restaurant-quality food in country inns and city pubs alike. Some are really excellent – and just as expensive as a regular restaurant, though usually with a more informal feel.

Restaurants

It goes without saying that London has the best selection of **top-class restaurants**, and the widest choice of cuisines, but visitors to all other major cities hardly suffer these days. Indeed, wherever you are in the UK you're rarely more than half an hour's drive from a really good meal – and some of the very best dining experiences are just as likely to be found in a suburban back street or quiet village than a metropolitan hotspot. Heston Blumenthal's Michelin-starred *Fat Duck*, for example – often touted as one of the world's best restaurants – is in the small Berkshire village of Bray, while the best Indian food outside the Asian subcontinent is found in unsung cities like Bradford and Leicester.

While a great curry in Birmingham's Balti Triangle or a Cantonese feast in Manchester's Chinatown might **cost** you just £15 a head, the going rate for a meal with drinks in most modest restaurants is more like £25 per person. If a restaurant has any sort of reputation, you can expect to be spending £40–50 each, and much, much more for the services of a top chef – tasting menus (excluding drinks) at the best-known Michelin-starred restaurants cost upwards of £80 per person. However, set meals can be a steal, even at the poshest of **restaurants**, where a limited-choice two- or three-course lunch or a "pre-theatre" menu might cost less than half the usual price.

TOP 5 DESTINATION RESTAURANTS

Dinner by Heston Blumenthal London. See p.120
L'Enclume Cartmel. See p.488
The Kitchin Edinburgh. See p.740
The Foxhunter Nr Abergavenny. See p.655
Waterside Inn Bray. See p.225

Pubs and bars

Originating as wayfarers' hostelries and coaching inns, **pubs** – "public houses" – have outlived the church and marketplace as the focal points of many a British town and village. They are as varied as the townscapes: in larger market towns you'll find huge oak-beamed inns with open fires and polished brass fittings; in remoter upland villages there are stone-built pubs no larger than a two-bedroomed cottage. Otherwise, in towns and cities, you'll find plenty of chain bars, often aimed at a youth and student crowd, with cheap drinks to lure in raucous punters.

Opening hours in most pubs are 11am to 11pm, though cities and resorts all have a growing number of places with extended licenses, especially at weekends. The legal **drinking age** is 18 and unless there's a special family room or a beer garden, children are not always welcome.

Beer

Ask simply for a "beer" and you'll cause no end of confusion. Britain's unique glory is its **real ale**, a refreshing, uncarbonated beer brewed with traditional ingredients, pumped by hand from a cask and served at cellar temperature (not "warm", as foreign jibes have it). If it comes out of an electric pump (and especially if it's labelled "smoothflow" or similar), it isn't the real thing. The most common ale is known as **bitter**, with a colour ranging from straw-yellow to dark brown, depending on the brew. Other real ales include golden or **pale ales**, plus darker and maltier milds, stouts and porters. Controversy exists over the head of foam on top: in southern England, people prefer their pint without a head, and brimming to the top of the glass; in the north and Scotland, flat beer is frowned on and drinkers prefer a short head of foam. Traditional Scottish beer is a thick, dark ale known as **heavy**, graded by a shilling mark (/-) and served with a full head.

You'll also find "real" cider, made from fermented apple juice, and – particularly in England's West Country and Shropshire – **scrumpy**, a potent and cloudy beverage, usually flat, dry and very apple-y.

Many pubs are owned by large breweries who favour their own beers, though there should also be one or two "guest ales" available. For the best choice, however, you generally need to find a **free house** – an independently run pub that can sell whichever beer it pleases. There are some fantastic choices, since Britain's small- and medium-sized microbreweries are flourishing – each region has its own independent outfits, brewing beers that are confined to one particular area or even just one pub. For more on British beer and pubs, check the website of the influential **Campaign for Real Ale** (Ⓦcamra.org.uk). Armed with its annual *Good Beer Guide*, you'll never be stuck for a decent place to drink.

Whisky

Scotland's national drink is **whisky** – *uisge beatha*, the "water of life" in Gaelic (and almost never referred to as "scotch") – traditionally drunk in pubs with a half-pint of beer on the side, a combination known as a "nip and a hauf". There are two types of whisky: **single malt**, made from malted barley, and **grain whisky**, which is made from maize and a little malted barley in a continuous still. **Blended whisky**, which accounts for more than ninety percent of all sales, is a mixture of the two types, with each brand's distinctive flavour coming from the malt whisky which is added to the grain in different quantities: the more expensive the blend, the higher the proportion of malts that have gone into it. All are drunk neat or with water, sometimes with mixers such as soda or lemonade (though these additions may horrify your fellow drinkers).

Single malt whisky is infinitely superior, and, as a result, a great deal more expensive. It is best drunk neat or with a splash of water to release its distinctive flavours. Single malts vary enormously depending on the amount of peat used for drying the barley, the water used for mashing, and the type of oak cask used in the maturing process. The two most important whisky regions are **Speyside**, which produces famous varieties such as Glenlivet, Glenfiddich and Macallan, and **Islay**, which produces distinctively peaty whiskies such as Laphroaig, Lagavulin and Ardbeg.

The media

The British are fond of their newspapers, from national dailies to local weeklies, while there are hundreds of TV and radio stations, both terrestrial and digital.

Newspapers and magazines

From Monday to Saturday, four **daily newspapers** occupy the "quality" end of the English market: the Rupert Murdoch-owned *Times*, the staunchly Conservative *Daily Telegraph*, and the left-of-centre *Independent* and *Guardian*. Among the high-selling **tabloid titles**, the most popular is the *Sun*, a muck-raking right-wing Murdoch paper whose chief rival is the traditionally left-leaning *Daily Mirror*. The middlebrow daily tabloids – the *Daily Mail* and the *Daily Express* – are noticeably xenophobic and right-wing. England's oldest **Sunday newspaper** is *The Observer*, in the same stable as the *Guardian* and with a similar stance, while most other major papers publish their own Sunday editions.

In **Scotland**, the principal English papers are widely available, often as specific Scottish editions. The Scottish press produces two major daily papers, the liberal-left *Scotsman* and the slightly less-so *Herald*. Scotland's best-selling daily paper is the downmarket *Daily Record*. Scotland's own Sunday "quality" is *Scotland on Sunday*, though far more fun is the tabloid *Sunday Post*. In **Wales**, where again English papers are widely available, the only quality Welsh daily is the *Western Mail*, a mix of local, Welsh, British and international news. There is also one quality Sunday offering, *Wales on Sunday*.

Of the range of **specialist magazines and periodicals** covering just about every subject, *The Economist* is a sober business magazine that's essential reading in many a boardroom; the left-wing *New Statesman* concentrates on social issues, while the satirical bi-weekly *Private Eye* prides itself on printing the stories the rest of the press won't touch – and on riding the consequent stream of libel suits.

Television

UK **terrestrial television channels** are divided between the state-funded BBC (Ⓦbbc.co.uk), and the commercial channels ITV (Ⓦitv.com), Channel 4 (Ⓦchannel4.com) and Channel 5 (Ⓦchannel5.com). Despite periodic mutterings about the licence fee (paid by all British viewers), there's still more than enough quality to keep the **BBC** in good repute both at home and abroad. The commercial channels are united by a more tabloid approach to programme-making – necessarily so, because if they don't get the advertising they don't survive.

The UK's **satellite** and **cable** TV companies are mounting a strong challenge to the erstwhile dominance of the terrestrial channels. Live sport, in particular, is increasingly in the hands of Rupert

Murdoch's Sky, the major satellite provider, whose 24-hour rolling Sky News programme rivals that of CNN.

Most British homes and hotels get around 40 "freeview" channels spread across the networks, including dedicated news, film, sports, arts and entertainment channels from the BBC, ITV, Channel 4 and 5. You'll get a wider choice of channels if you have access to a subscription cable or satellite service.

Radio

The BBC's **radio network** (ⓦ bbc.co.uk/radio) has five nationwide stations. These are **Radio 1**, which is almost exclusively devoted to new chart music and specialist DJs; **Radio 2** (Britain's most listened-to radio station), a combination of light pop and specialist music, with a sprinkling of arts programmes and documentaries; **Radio 3**, which focuses on classical music; the speech-based **Radio 4**, a blend of current affairs, arts and drama; and **Five Live**, a 24-hour rolling sports and news channel. **Digital-only** BBC stations include the alternative-music station 6 Music, and the BBC Asian Network, while Scotland, Wales, Shetland and Orkney have their own dedicated BBC news, music, talk and sport stations.

There are other national stations – like TalkSport and Classic FM – as well as a whole host of local stations in each area, both BBC and commercial.

Festivals and events

Many of the showpiece events marketed to tourists – from the military pageant of the Trooping of the Colour to the displays at the Royal Tournament – say little about the country's folk history and even less about contemporary Britain. For a more instructive idea of what makes the British tick, you'd do better to catch some grassroots festivities, like London's exuberant Notting Hill Carnival or a wacky village celebration.

Many British festivals date back centuries, while others are more recent concoctions – from ancient agricultural shows and revived medieval jousting to contemporary performing arts. The May and August bank holiday weekends, and the summer school holidays (July and Aug) are the favoured times for events to be held.

A festival calendar

JANUARY

London Parade (Jan 1) **ⓦ londonparade.co.uk.** Floats, marching bands, clowns, cheerleaders and classic cars wend their way through the centre of London.

Celtic Connections (last 2 weeks Jan) **ⓦ celticconnections.com.** A major celebration of Celtic and folk music held in venues across Glasgow.

Burns Night (Jan 25). Scots worldwide get stuck into haggis, whisky and vowel-grinding poetry to commemorate Scotland's greatest poet.

FEBRUARY

Chinese New Year (Feb 10, 2013; Jan 31, 2014; Feb 19, 2015). Processions, fireworks and festivities in the country's three main Chinatowns in London, Liverpool and Manchester.

Shrove Tuesday (47 days before Easter Sunday, so 12 Feb, 2013; 4 March, 2014; 17 Feb, 2015). The last day before Lent is also known as "Pancake Day" – it's traditional to eat pancakes and, famously, in Olney (Buckinghamshire, ⓦ visitolney.com), to race with them.

Shrovetide Football (Shrove Tuesday & Ash Wednesday) **ⓦ ashbourne-town.com.** The world's oldest, largest, longest, maddest football game takes place in and around Ashbourne, Derbyshire.

MARCH

St David's Day (March 1). Parades and Celebrations all over Wales to honour the patron saint of Wales – the biggest events are in Cardiff.

EASTER

Easter Parade (Easter Monday). One of England's largest parades (since 1885) is held in London's Battersea Park.

APRIL

St George's Day (April 23) **ⓦ stgeorgesholiday.com.** England's national day – also, by chance, the birthday of William Shakespeare, so as well as traditional Morris dancing and other festivities in towns and villages, there are also Bard-related events at Stratford-upon-Avon (ⓦ shakespearesbirthday.ork.uk).

MAY

Padstow Obby Oss (May 1). Processions, music and dancing in Padstow, Cornwall See p.329.

Helston Furry Dance (May 8). A courtly procession and dance through the Cornish town. See p.319.

Glyndebourne Opera Festival (mid-May to end Aug) **ⓦ glyndebourne.com.** One of the classiest arts festivals in the country, in East Sussex. See p.164.

Bath International Music Festival (end of May, for 10 days) **ⓦ bathmusicfest.org.uk.** Arts and music jamboree, with a concurrent fringe festival. See p.271.

Chelsea Flower Show (3rd or 4th week) **ⓦ rhs.org.uk.** Essential event for England's green-fingered legions at Chelsea, in London.

Hay Festival of Literature and the Arts (last week) **ⓦ hayfestival.com.** The nation's literary types descend on this Welsh border town for a big bookish shindig. See p.656.

WEIRD AND WONDERFUL FESTIVALS

National nuttiness and general British barminess? You bet there is, on display at dozens of local festivals every year, starting with **Whuppity Scourie** (March 1), when local children race round Lanark church in Scotland beating each other with home-made paper weapons – a representation (it's thought) of the chasing away of winter or the warding off of evil spirits. **Easter** is also big on eccentricity, from the blacked-up Lancashire clog dancers doing the **Bacup Nutters Dance** (Easter Saturday) to the **Hare Pie Scramble** and **Bottle-Kicking** (Easter Monday), a chaotic village bottle-kicking contest at Hallaton, Leicestershire. Meanwhile, Gawthorpe, near Ossett, West Yorkshire sees the **World Coal-Carrying Championship** (Easter Monday), an annual race to carry 50kg of coal a mile through the village and be crowned "King of the Coil Humpers". There's more really odd racing at the **Brockworth Cheese Rolling** (late May, bank holiday Mon, Ⓦcheese-rolling.co.uk) – namely, the pursuit of a cheese wheel down a murderous Gloucestershire incline. Local sport in Wales tends to involve negotiating muddy swamps, as in the **World Bog Snorkelling Championships** (August bank holiday Mon) held in Llanwrtyd Wells – there's also a mountain-bike bog-leaping contest.

Meanwhile, thousands flock to Ashton, Northamptonshire, to watch modern-day gladiators fight for glory armed only with a nut and twelve inches of string, in the **World Conker Championship** (Oct, second Sun). Finally, if you ever doubted that the British are a nation of animal-lovers, the proof is at the **World Worm-Charming Championships** (end June, Ⓦwormcharming.com), held at Willaston, Cheshire.

Highland Games (starts end May, runs until September) Ⓦ **shga.co.uk.** Celebrating a tradition dating back over a thousand years, more than sixty separate events take place across the Scottish Highlands, the northeast and Argyll – all including traditional sports, cycling, running and wrestling, plus piping and Highland dance.

JUNE

Appleby Horse Fair (1st week, Thurs to following Wed) Ⓦ **applebyfair.org.** England's most important Gypsy and Travellers' gathering at Appleby-in-Westmorland, Cumbria, held since 1750 – culminates in showpiece trotting races.

Trooping the Colour (2nd Sat) Ⓦ **royal.gov.uk.** Massed bands, equestrian pageantry, gun salutes and fly-pasts for the Queen's Official Birthday on Horse Guards Parade, London. See p.63.

Aldeburgh Festival (June) Ⓦ **aldeburgh.co.uk.** Suffolk jamboree of classical music, established by Benjamin Britten. See p.348.

Beating Retreat (mid June) Ⓦ **guardsbeatingretreat.com.** Soldiers on foot and horseback provide a colourful, very British ceremony on Horse Guards Parade in London over three evenings, marking the old military custom of drumming and piping the troops back to base at dusk.

Cardiff Singer of the World (3rd week, next competitions 2013, 2015) Ⓦ **bbc.co.uk/wales/cardiffsinger.** The world's biggest singing competition for new international opera and concert singers.

JULY

Llangollen International Eisteddfod (early July) Ⓦ **international-eisteddfod.co.uk.** "The world's greatest folk festival" attracts more than 5000 international participants, including choirs, dancers, folk singers, groups and instrumentalists. See p.683.

Great Yorkshire Show (2nd week) Ⓦ **greatyorkshireshow.com.** England's biggest region celebrates its heritage, culture and cuisine at Harrogate, North Yorkshire.

Pride London (mid July) Ⓦ **pridelondon.org.** Britain's biggest LGBT rally, with parades, music and general gaiety. London-by-the-seaside (aka Brighton) also has a Big Gay Pride Bash of its own in August.

The Proms (mid-July to early Sept) Ⓦ **bbc.co.uk/proms.** Top-flight international classical music festival at the Royal Albert Hall, London, ending in the famously patriotic Last Night of the Proms. See p.129.

Swan Upping (3rd week) Ⓦ **royal.gov.uk.** Ceremonial counting of the swan population on River Thames, dating back to the twelfth century. At Windsor, liveried oarsmen stand to attention in their boats and salute the Queen.

Whitstable Oyster Festival (last week) Ⓦ **whitstableoysterfestival.com.** Oysters, champagne, Guinness, parades and music. See p.139.

WOMAD (late July) Ⓦ **womad.org.** Renowned three-day world music festival at Charlton Park, outside Malmesbury, Wiltshire.

AUGUST

Edinburgh Festival (Aug) Ⓦ **eif.co.uk,** Ⓦ **edfringe.com.** One of the world's great arts festivals, with an "official" festival and a "fringe" that runs for a month combined. See pp.734–735.

Eisteddfod Genedlaethol Cymry (1st week) Ⓦ **eisteddfod.org.uk.** The "National Eisteddfod of Wales" is Wales's leading festival and the largest travelling cultural festival in Europe – a week-long annual culture, music and arts bash that alternates between North and South Wales.

Lammas Fair (early Aug). The annual fair at St Andrews is the oldest medieval market in the country.

Cowes Week (2nd week) Ⓦ **cowesweek.co.uk.** Sailing extravaganza in the Isle of Wight, with partying and star-studded entertainment. See p.188.

Grasmere Sports and Show (bank holiday Sun) Ⓦ **grasmeresportsandshow.co.uk.** Wrestling, fell-running, ferret-racing and other curious Lake District pastimes.

Notting Hill Carnival (last Sun & bank holiday Mon). Vivacious celebration led by London's Caribbean community but including

TOP 5 MUSIC FESTIVALS

Green Man Crickhowell, Wales. See p.653
Melrose Music Festival, Southern Scotland. See p.753
Glastonbury See p.276
Cambridge Folk Festival See p.373
Latitude Southwold. See p.351

everything from Punjabi drummers to Brazilian salsa, plus music, food and floats. See p.125.

Whitby Folk Week (last week) Ⓦ **whitbyfolk.co.uk.** A week's worth of morris and sword dancing, finger-in-your-ear singing, storytelling and more. See pp.554–557.

SEPTEMBER

Blackpool Illuminations (early Sept to early Nov). Five miles of extravagantly kitsch light displays on the Blackpool seafront. See p.470.

Abbots Bromley Horn Dance (early Sept) Ⓦ **abbotsbromley.com.** Vaguely pagan mass dance in mock-medieval costume – one of the most famous of England's ancient customs, at Abbots Bromley, Staffordshire.

Heritage Open Days (2nd week) Ⓦ **heritageopendays.org.uk.** A once-a-year opportunity to peek inside hundreds of buildings in England that don't normally open their doors to the public, from factories to Buddhist temples.

St Ives September Festival (2 weeks mid-Sept) Ⓦ **stivesseptemberfestival.co.uk.** Eclectic Cornish festival of art, poetry, literature, jazz, folk, rock and world music.

Abergavenny Food Festival (2 days, mid-Sept) Ⓦ **abergavennyfoodfestival.com.** A weekend of tastings, tours, foraging, quaffing and general guzzling at Wales's pre-eminent foodie town.

Wigtown Book Festival (last week) Ⓦ **wigtownbookfestival.com.** Scotland's "national book town" celebrates its literary leanings with a ten-day book fest.

OCTOBER

Swansea Festival of Music and the Arts (early to mid-Oct) Ⓦ **swanseafestival.org.** Concerts, drama, opera, ballet and art events throughout the Welsh city over two weeks.

Glenfiddich Piping Championships (late Oct) Ⓦ **blairatholl.co.uk.** Held at Blair Atholl for the world's top ten solo pipers.

State Opening of Parliament (late Oct) Ⓦ **parliament.uk.** The Queen arrives in a fancy coach amid much pageantry to give a speech and officially open Parliament. It also takes place whenever a new government is sworn in after an election.

Halloween (Oct 31). Last day of the Celtic calendar and All Hallows Eve: pumpkins, plus a lot of ghoulish dressing-up, trick-or-treating and parties.

NOVEMBER

London to Brighton Veteran Car Rally (1st Sun) Ⓦ **veterancarrun.com.** Ancient machines lumbering the 57 miles down the A23 to the seafront.

Guy Fawkes Night/Bonfire Night (Nov 5). Nationwide fireworks and bonfires commemorating the foiling of the Gunpowder Plot in 1605 – atop every bonfire is hoisted an effigy known as the "guy" after Guy Fawkes, one of the conspirators. Most notable events are at York (Fawkes' birthplace), Ottery St Mary in Devon, and at Lewes, East Sussex (see p.162).

Lord Mayor's Show (2nd Sat) Ⓦ **lordmayorsshow.org.** Held annually in the City of London since 1215, and featuring a daytime cavalcade and night-time fireworks to mark the inauguration of the new Lord Mayor.

DECEMBER

Tar Barrels Parade (Dec 31). Locals in Allendale Town, Northumberland turn up with trays of burning pitch on their heads to parade round a large communal bonfire.

Hogmanay and Ne'er Day (Dec 31 & Jan 1). Traditionally more important to the Scots than Christmas and known for the custom of "first-footing", when groups of revellers troop into neighbours' houses at midnight bearing gifts. More popular these days are huge and highly organized street parties, most notably in Edinburgh, but also in Aberdeen, Glasgow and other Scottish cities.

New Year's Eve (Dec 31). In London, there's a massive fireworks display over the Thames, and thousands of inebriates in Trafalgar Square; also a huge bash on Newcastle's Quayside.

Sports and outdoor activities

As the birthplace of football, cricket, rugby and tennis, Britain can boast a series of sporting events that attract a world audience. If you prefer participating to spectating, the UK caters for just about every outdoor activity, too: we've concentrated below on walking, cycling and watersports, but there are also opportunities for anything from rock climbing to pony trekking.

Spectator sports

Football (soccer) is the national game in both Scotland and England, with a wide programme of professional league matches taking place every Saturday afternoon from early August to early May, with plenty of Sunday and midweek fixtures too. It's very difficult to get tickets to Premier League matches involving the most famous teams (Chelsea, Arsenal, Manchester United, Liverpool, Rangers and Celtic), but tours of their grounds are feasible or you can try one of the lower-league games.

Rugby comes in two codes – 15-a-side **Rugby Union** and 13-a-side **Rugby League**, both fearsomely brutal contact sports that can make entertaining viewing even if you don't understand the rules. In England, rugby is much less popular than football, but Rugby League has a loyal and dedicated fan base in the north – especially Yorkshire and Lancashire – while Union has traditionally been popular with the English middle class. Rugby League has never taken off in Wales and Scotland, but Rugby Union is popular in the Scottish Borders and is effectively the **national sport in Wales**. Key Rugby Union and League games are sold out months in advance, but ordinary fixtures present few ticketing problems. The Rugby Union season runs from September to May, Rugby League February to September.

The game of **cricket** is British idiosyncrasy at its finest. Foreigners – and most Britons for that matter – marvel at a game that can last several days and still end in a draw, while many people are unfamiliar with its rules. International, five-day "Test" matches, pitting the English national side against visiting countries, are played most summers at grounds around the country, and tickets are usually fairly easy to come by. The domestic game traditionally centres on four-day County Championship matches between English county teams, though there's far bigger interest – certainly for casual watchers – in the "Twenty20" format, designed to encourage flamboyant, decisive play in short, three-hour matches.

Finally, if you're in England at the end of June and early July, you won't be able to miss the country's annual fixation with **tennis** in the shape of the Wimbledon championships. No one gives a hoot about the sport for the other fifty weeks of the year, but as long as one plucky Brit endures, the entire country gets caught up with tennis fever.

Walking

Walking routes track across many of Britain's wilder areas, amid landscapes varied enough to suit any taste. Turn up in any national park area and local information offices will be able to advise on anything from a family stroll to a full day out on the mountains. It goes without saying that even for short hikes you need to be **properly equipped**, follow local advice and listen out for local weather reports – British weather is notoriously changeable. Excellent guidebooks to all England's and Wales's **national trails** are published by Aurum Press (Ⓦ aurumpress.co.uk); you will also need a good **map** (see p.49).

Hiking trails

England's finest **walking areas** are the granite moorlands and spectacular coastlines of Devon and Cornwall in the southwest, and the highlands of the north – notably the Yorkshire Dales, the North York Moors, and the Lake District. Keen hikers might want to tackle one of England's dozen **National Trails** (Ⓦ nationaltrail.co.uk), which amount to some 2500 miles of waymarked path and track. The most famous – certainly the toughest – is the **Pennine Way** (268 miles; usual walking time 16 days; see p.411), stretching from the Derbyshire Peak District to the Scottish Borders, while the challenging **South West Coast Path** (630 miles; 56 days; p.281) through Cornwall, Devon, Somerset and Dorset tends to be tackled in shorter sections. Other English trails are less gung-ho in character, like the **South Downs Way** (101 miles; 8 days; p.161) or the fascinating **Hadrian's Wall Path** (84 miles; 7 days).

Scotland has four official "**Long Distance Routes**", each of which takes days to walk, though you can of course just cover sections of them. The **Southern Upland Way** crosses Scotland from coast to coast in the south, and is the country's longest at 212 miles (12–20 days); the best known is the **West Highland Way** (p.807), a 95-mile hike from Glasgow to Fort William via Loch Lomond and Glen Coe (7–10 days).

The best long-distance walk in Wales is the spectacular **Pembrokeshire Coast Path** (186 miles, 10–15 days; p.635), one of Wales's three **National Trails** – the other two are the 177-mile-long **Offa's Dyke Path** (12 days; p.660) that traces the England–Wales border and **Glyndŵr's Way**, which weaves through mid-Wales for 135 miles (9 days).

Cycling

The **National Cycle Network** is made up of 12,500 miles of signed cycle route, a third on traffic-free paths (including disused railways and canal towpaths), the rest mainly on country roads. You're never very far from one of the numbered routes, all of which are detailed on the **Sustrans** website (Ⓦ sustrans.org.uk), a charitable trust devoted to the development of environmentally sustainable transport. Sustrans also publishes an excellent series of waterproof cycle maps (1:100,000) and guides.

Major routes include the **C2C** (Sea-to-Sea), 140 miles between Whitehaven/Workington on the English northwest coast and Newcastle/Sunderland on the northeast. There's also the **Cornish Way** (123 miles), from Bude to Land's End, and routes that cut through the very heart of England, such as from Derby to York (154 miles) or along the rivers Severn and Thames (128 miles; Gloucester to Reading). The classic cross-Britain route, however, is from Land's End, in the far southwest of England, to John O'Groats, on the northeast tip of Scotland – roughly

BRITAIN'S NATIONAL PARKS

Britain has fifteen national parks, ranging from Dartmoor in the southwest to the Cairngorms in the north. Check out the round-up below for the best things to do and see in each park, and visit nationalparks.gov.uk for more information and links.

- **Brecon Beacons** See pp.650–654. In southern Wales, this low-profile range of grassy hills covers 520 square miles, with a striking sandstone scarp at the head of the South Wales coalfield, and lush, cave-riddled limestone valleys to the south. Don't miss: the climb up Pen y Fan (p.651).
- **The Broads** See p.357. The best place for a boating holiday – the rivers, marshes, fens and canals of Norfolk and Suffolk make up one of the important wetlands in Europe, and are also ideal for birdwatching. It's the one park where a car isn't much use – cyclists and walkers have the best of it. Don't miss: a wildlife-viewing trip on the Electric Eel (p.357).
- **Cairngorms** See p.886. In the Scottish Highlands, this is Britain's biggest national park, which includes its highest mountain massif. It includes some marvellous walking around Aviemore, and a gamut of sports and recreational facilities, not least skiing. Don't miss: the RSPB Reserve at Loch Garten (p.886).
- **Dartmoor** See pp.302–307. England's largest wilderness attracts back-to-nature hikers and tripped-out stone-chasers to Devon in equal measure – the open moorland walking can be pretty hardcore, and Dartmoor is famous for its standing stones, Stone Age hut circles and hill forts. Don't miss: Grimspound Bronze Age village (p.304).
- **Exmoor** See pp.279–283. Exmoor straddles the Somerset/Devon border and on its northern edge overlooks the sea from high, hogback hills. Crisscrossed by trails and also accessible from the South West Coast Path, it's ideal for walking and pony trekking. Don't miss: the four-mile hike to Dunkery Beacon, Exmoor's highest point (p.280).
- **Lake District** See pp.484–504. Many people's favourite national park, the Lake District (in Cumbria, in northwest England) is an almost alpine landscape of glacial lakes and rugged mountains. It's great for hiking, rock climbing and watersports, but also has strong literary connections and thriving cultural traditions. Don't miss: Honister's hard-hat mine tour and mountain traverse (p.500).
- **Loch Lomond and the Trossachs** See pp.806–810. Scotland's first national park incorporates a stretch of the West Highland Way along the loch itself, the park's centrepiece. The wild glens of the Trossach range – a sort of miniature Highlands – are also highly scenic. Don't miss: the ascent of Ben Lomond (p.809).

a thousand miles, which can be covered in two to three weeks, depending on which of the three CTC-recommended routes you choose.

Watersports

Sailing and **windsurfing** are especially popular along the south coast (particularly the Isle of Wight and Solent) and in the southwest (around Falmouth in Cornwall, and around Salcombe and Dartmouth in Devon). Here, and in the northwest, in the Lake District, you'll be able to rent boards, dinghies and boats, either by the hour or for longer periods of instruction – from around £25 for a couple of hours of kayaking to around £140 for a two-day non-residential sailing course. The **UK Sailing Academy** (uk-sail.org.uk) in Cowes on the Isle of Wight is England's finest instruction centre for windsurfing, dinghy sailing, kayaking and kitesurfing.

Newquay in Cornwall is the country's undisputed **surfing** centre, whose main break, Fistral, regularly hosts international contests. But there are quieter spots all along the north coast of Cornwall and Devon, as well as a growing scene on the more isolated northeast coast from Yorkshire to Northumberland. There are plenty of places where you can rent or buy equipment, which means that prices are kept down to reasonable levels, around £10 per day each for board and wetsuit.

Surfing in **Wales** tends to be concentrated on the south coast, around the Gower Peninsula, which boasts a good variety of beach and reef breaks, but the most consistent surf beach in Wales is Freshwater West in Pembrokeshire. **Scotland** is fast gaining a reputation for the high quality of its

- **New Forest** See pp.193–196. In the predominantly domesticated landscape of Hampshire, the country's best surviving example of a medieval hunting forest can be surprisingly wild. The majestic woodland is interspersed by tracts of heath, and a good network of paths and bridleways offers plenty of scope for biking and pony rides. Don't miss: an off-road bike ride from Brockenhurst (p.196).
- **Northumberland** See pp.588–591. Where England meets Scotland, remote Northumberland in England's northeast is adventure country. The long-distance Pennine Way runs the length of the park, and the Romans left their mark in the shape of Hadrian's Wall, along which you can hike or bike. Don't miss: the Chillingham cattle wildlife safari (p.590).
- **North York Moors** See pp.547–551. A stunning mix of heather moorland, gentle valleys, ruined abbeys and wild coastline. Walking and mountain biking are the big outdoor activities here, but you can also tour the picturesque stone villages or hang out with Goths in Whitby. Don't miss: a day out at Ryedale Folk Museum (p.550).
- **Peak District** See pp.406–413. England's first national park (1951) is also the most visited, because it sits between the major population centres of the Midlands and the northwest. It's rugged outdoors country, with some dramatic underground caverns, tempered by stately homes and spa and market towns. Don't miss: a trip down Treck Cliff Cavern (p.411).
- **Pembrokeshire Coast** See p.635. One hundred and seventy miles of Wales's southwestern peninsula make up this park, best explored along the Pembrokeshire Coast Path that traverses the cliff-tops, frequently dipping down into secluded coves. Don't miss: the hike round St Bride's Bay (p.635).
- **Snowdonia National Park** See pp.685–693. Occupying almost the whole of the northwestern corner of Wales, this park incorporates a dozen of the country's highest peaks separated by dramatic glacial valleys and laced with hundreds of miles of ridge and moorland paths. Don't miss: a ride on the Snowdon Mountain Railway (p.690).
- **South Downs** See p.161. Britain's newest national park (established 2010) might not be as wild as the others – about 85 percent is farmland – but it offers a rural escape into West and East Sussex from one of the most densely populated parts of the country. Don't miss: a walk along the South Downs Way, which covers over 100 miles of the chalk uplands between Winchester and Beachy Head (p.161).
- **Yorkshire Dales** See pp.525–533. The best choice for walking, cycling and pony trekking, Yorkshire's second national park spreads across twenty dales, or valleys, at the heart of the Pennines. England's most scenic railway – the Settle to Carlisle line – is another great draw, while caves, waterfalls and castles provide the backdrop. Don't miss: the walk to dramatic Malham Cove (p.528).

breaks with the number-one spot being Thurso on the north coast. Many other good breaks lie within easy reach of large cities (eg Pease Bay, near Edinburgh, and Fraserburgh, near Aberdeen), while the spectacular west coast has numerous possibilities: try Sandwood Bay, the most isolated beach in Britain, or the waves of the Outer Hebrides.

Travel essentials

Climate

Britain has a generally temperate, maritime climate, which means largely moderate temperatures and a decent chance of at least some rain whenever you visit. If you're balancing the clemency of the weather against the density of the crowds, the best months to come to Britain are April, May, September and October.

Costs

Faced with another £4 pint, a £30 theatre ticket and a £20 taxi ride back to your £100-a-night hotel, Britain might seem like the most expensive place in Europe. Even if you're camping or hostelling, using public transport, buying picnic lunches and eating in pubs and cafés your minimum expenditure will be around £40 per person per day. Couples staying in B&Bs, eating at unpretentious restaurants and visiting tourist attractions should expect to spend £70 per person, while if you're renting a car, staying in hotels and eating well, budget for at least £120 each. Double that last figure if you choose to stay in stylish city or grand country-house hotels, while on any visit

AVERAGE DAILY MAXIMUM TEMPERATURES

BIRMINGHAM

	Jan	Feb	Mar	Apr	May	Jun	Jul	Aug	Sep	Oct	Nov	Dec
°F	42	43	48	54	61	66	68	68	63	55	48	44
°C	5	6	9	12	16	19	20	20	17	13	9	7

CARDIFF

	Jan	Feb	Mar	Apr	May	Jun	Jul	Aug	Sep	Oct	Nov	Dec
°F	45	45	50	56	60	68	69	69	64	58	51	46
°C	7	7	10	13	16	20	21	21	18	14	11	8

EDINBURGH

	Jan	Feb	Mar	Apr	May	Jun	Jul	Aug	Sep	Oct	Nov	Dec
°F	42	43	46	51	56	64	65	64	61	54	48	44
°C	5	6	8	11	13	18	18	18	16	12	9	7

FORT WILLIAM

	Jan	Feb	Mar	Apr	May	Jun	Jul	Aug	Sep	Oct	Nov	Dec
°F	43	44	48	52	58	61	62	63	61	54	49	45
°C	6	7	9	11	14	16	17	17	16	12	9	7

LONDON

	Jan	Feb	Mar	Apr	May	Jun	Jul	Aug	Sep	Oct	Nov	Dec
°F	43	44	50	56	62	69	71	71	65	58	50	45
°C	6	7	10	13	17	21	22	22	19	14	10	7

PLYMOUTH

	Jan	Feb	Mar	Apr	May	Jun	Jul	Aug	Sep	Oct	Nov	Dec
°F	47	47	50	54	59	64	66	67	64	58	52	49
°C	8	8	10	12	15	18	19	19	18	14	11	9

YORK

	Jan	Feb	Mar	Apr	May	Jun	Jul	Aug	Sep	Oct	Nov	Dec
°F	43	44	49	55	61	67	70	69	64	57	49	45
°C	6	7	10	13	16	19	21	21	18	14	9	7

to London work on the basis that you'll need an extra £30 per day to get the best out of the city.

Discounts and admission charges

Many of Britain's **historic attractions** – from castles to stately homes – are owned and/or operated by either the **National Trust** (Ⓦ nationaltrust.org.uk; denoted as NT in the guide), covering England and Wales, or the **National Trust for Scotland** (Ⓦ nts.org.uk; NTS). Many other historic sites are operated by **English Heritage** (Ⓦ english-heritage.org.uk; EH), **Historic Scotland** (Ⓦ historic-scotland.gov.uk; HS), and **CADW Welsh Historic Monuments** (Ⓦ cadw.wales.gov.uk; CADW). All these organizations usually charge entry fees (roughly £4–10), though some sites are free. If you plan to visit more than half a dozen places owned by any of them, it's worth considering an annual membership (around £40) – you can join on your first visit to any attraction.

US members of the Royal Oak Foundation (Ⓦ royal-oak.org) get free admission to all National Trust properties. Any non-UK resident can also buy a **Great British Heritage Pass** (Ⓦ britishheritagepass.com; valid for 3, 7, 15 or 30 days), which gives free entry to more than 400 cultural and historic attractions, including NT, NTS, EH and CADW sites. You can buy it online, from travel agents in your own country, or from major UK tourist offices.

Municipal art galleries and museums across the UK often have free admission, as do the world-class **state museums** in London, Cardiff, Edinburgh and elsewhere, from the British Museum (London) and the National Gallery of Scotland (Edinburgh) to York's National Railway Museum. Private and municipal museums and other collections rarely charge more than £6 admission. Most **cathedrals** and churches either charge admission – of around £4 – or ask for voluntary donations.

The admission charges given in the Guide are the full adult rate, unless otherwise stated. Concessionary rates – **generally half-price** – for **senior citizens** (over 60), under-26s and **children** (from 5 to 17) apply almost everywhere, from tourist attractions to public transport; you'll need official identification as proof of age. Children under 5 are rarely charged.

Full-time students can benefit from an International Student ID Card (ISIC), and those under 26 from an International Youth Travel Card (IYTC), while teachers qualify for the **International Teacher Identity Card (ITIC)**. All are valid for special air, rail and bus fares, and discounts at museums and other attractions – see Ⓦ isic.org for full details.

Crime and personal safety

Terrorist attacks and street riots in Britain may have changed the general perception of how safe the country feels, but it's still extremely unlikely that you'll be at any risk as you travel around. There's heightened **security** in place at airports and major train stations, and as a holiday-maker you won't be visiting the toughest urban estates where crime flourishes. You can walk more or less anywhere without fear of harassment, though all the big cities have their edgy districts and it's always better to err on the side of caution, especially late at night. Leave your passport and valuables in a hotel or hostel safe (carrying **ID** is not compulsory), and exercise the usual caution on public transport. If you're taking a taxi, make sure it's officially licensed – bar or restaurant staff can usually provide a reliable recommendation. If you are robbed, report it straight away to the police; your insurance company will require a **crime report number**.

Other than asking for directions, most visitors rarely come into contact with the British **police**, who as a rule are approachable and helpful – though they can get tetchy at football matches, demonstrations and in the evenings when pubs close and clubs open. Most wear chest guards and carry batons, though street officers do not normally carry guns.

Finally, making "jokes" about bombs or **suspicious packages** while in check-in queues or at security barriers is not advised, and can result in serious trouble, heavy delays and possibly prosecution.

Electricity

In the UK, the **current** is 240V AC. North American appliances will need a transformer and adaptor; those from Europe, South Africa, Australia and New Zealand only need an adaptor.

Entry requirements

EU citizens can travel to – and stay in – the UK with just a passport or identity card. US, Canadian, South African, Australian and New Zealand citizens can stay in the country for up to six months without a visa, provided they have a valid passport. Many other nationalities require a visa, obtainable from the British consular office where you live. Check with the **UK Border Agency** (Ⓦ ukvisas.gov.uk) for up-to-date information about visa applications, visa extensions and all other aspects of residency.

BRITISH EMBASSIES AND HIGH COMMISSIONS ABROAD

Australia Ⓦ ukinaustralia.fco.gov.uk
Canada Ⓦ ukincanada.fco.gov.uk
Ireland Ⓦ britishembassyinireland.fco.gov.uk
New Zealand Ⓦ ukinnewzealand.fco.gov.uk
South Africa Ⓦ ukinsouthafrica.fco.gov.uk
USA Ⓦ ukinusa.fco.gov.uk

Gay and lesbian travellers

Britain offers one of the most diverse and accessible **lesbian** and **gay** scenes anywhere in Europe. Nearly

TIPPING

Although there are no fixed rules for **tipping**, a ten to fifteen percent tip is anticipated by restaurant waiters. Tipping taxi drivers is purely optional. Some restaurants levy a "discretionary" or "optional" **service charge** of 10 or 12.5 percent, which must be clearly stated on the menu and on the bill. However, you are not obliged to pay it, and certainly not if the food or service wasn't what you expected. It is not normal to leave tips in pubs, but the bar staff are sometimes offered drinks, which they may accept in the form of money. The only other occasions when you'll be expected to tip are at the hairdressers, and in upmarket hotels where porters, bell boys and table waiters expect and usually get a pound or two.

every sizeable town has some kind of organized gay life – from bars and clubs to community groups – with the major scenes found in London, Manchester, Brighton, Edinburgh, Glasgow, Cardiff, Swansea and Newport. Listings, news and reviews can be found at Ⓦpinkpaper.com and in the glossy magazine *Gay Times* (Ⓦgaytimes.co.uk). For more information and useful links go to Ⓦgaybritain.co.uk and Ⓦgaytravel.co.uk. The age of consent in England, Scotland and Wales is 16.

Health

No vaccinations are required for entry into Britain. Citizens of all EU and EEA countries are entitled to reciprocal medical treatment within the UK's National Health Service (NHS), which includes the vast majority of hospitals and doctors, on production of their **European Health Insurance Card** (EHIC) or, in extremis, their passport or national identity card. The same applies to those Commonwealth countries that have reciprocal healthcare arrangements with the UK – for example Australia and New Zealand. If you don't fall into either of these categories, you will be charged for all medical services, so health insurance is strongly advised.

Pharmacists (known as **chemists** in Britain) can dispense a limited range of drugs without a doctor's prescription. Most are open standard shop hours, though check in the window (or in local newspapers) for which local chemists are due to stay open late and/or at the weekend. For generic pain-relief tablets, cold remedies and the like, the local supermarket is usually the cheapest option.

Minor complaints and injuries can be dealt with at a **doctor's (GP's) surgery** – any tourist office or hotel can point you in the right direction. For serious injuries, go to the 24-hour casualty (A&E, that is, accident and emergency) department of the nearest **hospital**. In an **emergency**, call an ambulance on Ⓣ999 or Ⓣ112.

For medical advice 24 hours a day, call **NHS Direct** (Ⓣ0845 4647, Ⓦnhsdirect.nhs.uk). The website is packed with useful information, and also has directories of doctors' surgeries and walk-in centres nationwide.

Insurance

Always take out an **insurance policy** before travelling to cover against theft, loss and illness or injury. A typical policy will provide cover for loss of baggage, tickets and – up to a certain limit – cash or travellers' cheques, as well as cancellation or curtailment of your journey. Most exclude so-called dangerous sports unless an extra premium is paid: in Britain this can mean most watersports, rock climbing and mountaineering, though hiking, kayaking and jeep safaris would probably be covered.

Medical coverage is strongly advised, though you should always ascertain beforehand whether benefits will be paid as treatment proceeds or only after you return home, and whether there is a 24-hour medical emergency number. When securing **baggage cover**, make sure that the per-article limit will cover your most valuable possession. Keep receipts for medicines and medical treatment, and in the event you have anything stolen you must obtain an official statement from the police.

Mail

Virtually all **post offices** (Ⓦpostoffice.co.uk) are open Monday to Friday from 9am to 5.30pm, and on Saturdays from 9am to 12.30pm. Small branches sometimes close at lunchtimes or on Wednesday afternoons, while main city offices stay open all day Saturday. In villages, there's often a post office counter in general stores, though post office facilities are only available during the hours given above even if the shop itself is open for longer.

Stamps are sold at post offices, as well as some supermarkets, newsagents and other stores. Postage

ROUGH GUIDES TRAVEL INSURANCE

Rough Guides has teamed up with WorldNomads.com to offer great travel insurance deals. Policies are available to residents of more than 150 countries, with cover for a wide range of adventure sports, 24hr emergency assistance, high levels of medical and evacuation cover and a stream of travel safety information. Roughguides.com users can take advantage of their policies online 24/7, from anywhere in the world – even if you're already travelling. And since plans often change when you're on the road, you can extend your policy and even claim online. Roughguides.com users who buy travel insurance with WorldNomads.com can also leave a positive footprint and donate to a community development project. For more information go to Ⓦroughguides.com/shop.

DISTANCES, WEIGHTS AND MEASURES

Distances (and speeds) on British signposts are in miles, and beer is still served in pints. For everything else – money, weights and measures – a confusing mixture of metric and imperial systems is used: fuel is dispensed by the litre, while meat, milk and vegetables may be sold in either or both systems.

rates depend on the size and weight of the item, as well as delivery speed. "First class" is theoretically for next-day UK delivery; "second class" for delivery within three working days. Airmail to European destinations should arrive within three working days, and to countries outside Europe within five.

Maps

For an overview of the **whole of Britain** on one (double-sided) map, Collins' 1:550,000 and Ordnance Survey's 1:625,000 maps are probably the best; both include some city plans. Ordnance Survey (OS; Ⓦ ordnancesurvey.co.uk) and Michelin also produce useful regional maps at a scale of 1:250,000 and 1:400,000 respectively, while Philips, in conjunction with OS, produce detailed county maps at a scale of 1:18,000. Otherwise, for general route-finding the most useful resources are the road atlases sold at any service station, at a scale of around 1:250,000.

The maps in Ordnance Survey's 1:50,000 (pink) Landranger series show enough detail to be useful for most walkers and cyclists, and there's more detail still in the full-colour 1:25,000 (orange) Explorer series – both cover the whole of Britain.

Most of these maps are widely available from specialist bookshops or **travel stores** in your own country, or online from the likes of Ⓦ randmcnally.com or Ⓦ stanfords.co.uk, the latter England's premier map and travel specialist.

Money

Britain's currency is the **pound sterling** (£), divided into 100 pence (p). Coins come in denominations of 1p, 2p, 5p, 10p, 20p, 50p and £1 and £2. Notes are in denominations of £5, £10, £20 and £50. Scottish and Northern Irish banknotes are legal tender throughout Britain, though some traders may be unwilling to accept them. For current **exchange rates**, consult Ⓦ xe.com.

The easiest way to get hold of cash is to use your **debit card** in an **ATM**; there's usually a daily withdrawal limit of £250. You'll find ATMs outside banks, at all major points of arrival and motorway service areas, at large supermarkets, petrol stations and even inside some pubs, rural post offices and village shops (though a charge may be levied on cash withdrawals at small, stand-alone ATMs – the screen will tell you and give you an option to cancel the operation). Depending on your bank and your debit card, you may also be able to ask for "cash back" when you shop at supermarkets.

Credit cards are widely accepted in hotels, shops and restaurants – MasterCard and Visa are almost universal, charge cards like American Express and Diners Club less so. Smaller establishments, such as B&Bs, may accept cash only. Remember that cash advances from ATMs using your credit card are treated as loans, with interest accruing daily from the date of withdrawal.

Paying by plastic – whether using your credit or debit card – involves inserting your card into a "chip-and-pin" terminal beside the till and then keying in your PIN to authorize the transaction; the only person handling your card is you. Many restaurants use wireless chip-and-pin handsets; your waiter will bring it to your table when it's time to pay. At establishments with an older "swipe" system, never let your card leave your sight; take it yourself to the till and watch while the staff do the swiping.

Some overseas travellers still prefer sterling **travellers' cheques**, at least as a backup. The most commonly accepted are issued by American Express, followed by Visa. American Express will not charge commission if you exchange cheques at their own offices, nor will some banks – otherwise you will be charged 2–3 percent commission. Note that in the UK you cannot use travellers' cheques as cash – you'll always have to cash them first, making them an unreliable source of funds in remote areas.

Outside banking hours, you can change cheques or cash at **post offices** and **bureaux de change** – the latter tend to be open longer hours and are found in most city centres, and at major airports and train stations. Avoid changing cash or cheques in hotels, where the rates are normally poor.

Opening hours and public holidays

We have given full **opening hours** for museums, galleries and tourist attractions, and cafés, restaurants and pubs, in the Guide.

PUBLIC HOLIDAYS

January 1
January 2 (Scotland only)
Good Friday
Easter Monday (not Scotland)
First Monday in May
Last Monday in May
Last Monday in August
November 30 (or nearest Mon if weekend; Scotland only)
December 25
December 26

Note that if January 1, December 25 or December 26 falls on a Saturday or Sunday, the next weekday becomes a public holiday.

As a rule of thumb, most businesses, shops and offices open from Monday to Saturday between 9am and 5.30 or 6pm, with many shops also open on Sundays from 10 or 11am to around 4pm. Larger **supermarkets** have longer hours (except on Sundays), sometimes staying open around the clock. **Banks** are usually open Monday to Friday from 9am to 4pm, with some branches also open on Saturday mornings. You can usually get **fuel** any time of the day or night in larger towns and cities.

Banks, businesses and most shops close on **public holidays**, though large supermarkets, small corner shops and many tourist attractions don't. However, nearly all museums, galleries and other attractions are closed on Christmas Day and New Year's Day, with many also closed on Boxing Day (Dec 26). Confusingly, several of Britain's public holidays are usually referred to as **bank holidays** (though it's not just the banks who have a day off).

Phones

Every British landline number has a prefix, which, if beginning ⓣ01 or 02 represents an **area code**. The prefix ⓣ07 is for mobile phones/cellphones; while a variety of ⓣ08 prefixes relate to the cost of calls – some, like ⓣ0800, are free to call from a landline, others (like ⓣ0845 and ⓣ0870) are increasingly more expensive depending on your phone or phone operator. Beware, particularly, **premium-rate ⓣ09 numbers**, common for pre-recorded information services (including some tourist authorities), which can be charged at anything up to £1.50 a minute.

Most public pay phones take coins and credit cards. You can make direct-dial **international calls** from any telephone box, though it's usually cheaper to buy a **phonecard**, available from many newsagents in denominations of £5, £10 and upwards. You dial the company's local access number, key in the pin number on the card and then make your call. Most hotel rooms have telephones, but there is almost always an exorbitant surcharge for their use.

Mobile phone access is universal in towns and cities, and rural areas are well served too, though coverage can get patchy. To use your own mobile phone, check with your provider before you leave home that international roaming is activated – and that your phone will work in the UK (phones bought for use in the US, for example, rarely work outside the States). If you do bring your own phone, note that you are likely to be charged extra for incoming calls or texts when abroad. If you're staying in Britain for any length of time, it's often easiest to **buy a mobile** and local SIM card in the UK – basic pre-pay ("pay as you go") models start at around £30, usually including some calling credit.

Phoning UK **directory enquiries is expensive**. You can look up numbers online at ⓦbt.com and ⓦyell.com.

In Britain, dial ⓣ100 for the **operator**, ⓣ155 for the international operator. To call Britain **from abroad**, dial your international access code, then ⓣ44, then the area code minus its initial zero, and finally the number.

CALLING ABROAD FROM BRITAIN

Note that the initial zero is omitted from the area code when dialling from abroad.

Australia 0061 + area code + number.
New Zealand 0064 + area code + number.
US and Canada 001 + area code + number.
Republic of Ireland 00353 + area code + number.
South Africa 0027 + area code + number.

Shopping

Although it is now one of the chief leisure activities of the Brits, shopping can be a rather soulless experience in towns and cities. High streets up and down the country feature the same bland chain stores selling very similar ranges of mass-produced items. But while out-of-town shopping centres and supermarkets have sucked much of the life out of town centres, it is still possible to track down neighbourhoods, stores and the occasional oddity that make for a more enjoyable retail experience.

Most places, for example, have a **market** at least once a week, which may vary from a sprawling sea of stalls to sedate local village affairs. Street markets or covered markets are often the best places to pick up craft items, though you may have to wade among a proliferation of candles, T-shirts and twee bric-a-brac to find anything truly original. Markets are also the only places (apart from antique shops and some secondhand shops) where **haggling** is acceptable. Look on Ⓦcountry-markets.co.uk to find where and when a market takes place close to you. Many towns also have a weekly or monthly **farmers' market** (see Ⓦfarmersmarkets.net), where local foodstuffs and artisan products are offered – the biggest of these is in Winchester, with more than 90 producers. You'll also find similarly authentic local items in rural **farmshops**, usually signposted by the side of the road.

Smoking

Smoking is banned outright in all public buildings and offices, restaurants and pubs, and on all public transport. In addition, the vast majority of hotels and B&Bs no longer allow it.

Time

Greenwich Mean Time (GMT) is used from late October to late March, when the clocks go forward an hour for British Summer Time (BST). Britain is five hours ahead of the US Eastern Standard Time, one hour behind most of Europe, and ten hours behind Australian Eastern Standard Time. Full details are at Ⓦtimeanddate.com.

Tourist information

Britain's tourism authority, VisitBritain (Ⓦvisitbritain.com), has offices worldwide, while regional tourism boards within the UK concentrate on particular areas. The official national websites, Ⓦenjoyengland.com, Ⓦvisitscotland.com and Ⓦvisitwales.com are particularly useful, covering everything from local accommodation to festival dates, and there is a large number of regional and other specialist websites dedicated to the UK that are worth consulting.

Tourist offices (also called Tourist Information Centres, or "TICs") exist in virtually every British town. They tend to follow standard shop hours (Mon–Sat 9am–5.30pm), though are sometimes also open on Sundays, with hours curtailed during the winter season (Nov–Easter). We've listed opening hours in the Guide. Staff will nearly always be able to book accommodation, reserve space on guided tours, and sell guidebooks, maps and walk leaflets. They can also provide lists of local cafés, restaurants and pubs, though they aren't supposed to recommend particular places.

The **national parks** usually have their own dedicated information centres, which offer similar services to tourist offices but can also provide expert guidance on local walks and outdoor pursuits.

Travellers with disabilities

On the whole, the UK has good facilities for travellers with disabilities. All new public buildings – including museums, galleries and cinemas – are obliged to provide **wheelchair access**; train stations and airports are fully accessible; many buses have easy-access boarding ramps; while dropped kerbs and signalled crossings are the rule in every city and town. The number of accessible hotels and restaurants is also growing, and reserved parking bays are available almost everywhere, from shopping malls to museums. If you have specific requirements, it's always best to talk first to your travel agent, chosen hotel or tour operator.

USEFUL CONTACTS

Access-Able Ⓦaccess-able.com. US-based resource for travellers with disabilities, with links to UK operators and organizations.

RADAR Ⓦradar.org.uk. The UK's largest disability rights campaigning network, with links to holiday and travel services in the UK.

Tourism For All Ⓦwtourismforall.org.uk. Excellent resource with advice, listings and useful information.

Travelling with children

Facilities in the UK for travellers with children are similar to those in the rest of Europe. Breast-feeding is legal in all public places, including restaurants and cafés, and **baby-changing** rooms are widely available, including in shopping centres and train stations. Children aren't allowed in certain **licensed (ie, alcohol-serving) premises**, though this doesn't apply to restaurants, and many pubs and inns have family rooms or beer gardens where children are welcome. Some **B&Bs and hotels** won't accept children under a certain age (usually 12). Under-5s generally travel free on public transport and get in free to attractions; 5–16-year-olds are usually entitled to concessionary rates of up to half the adult rate/fare.

The **websites** Ⓦtravellingwithchildren.co.uk and Ⓦbabygoes2.com are useful for tips and ideas.

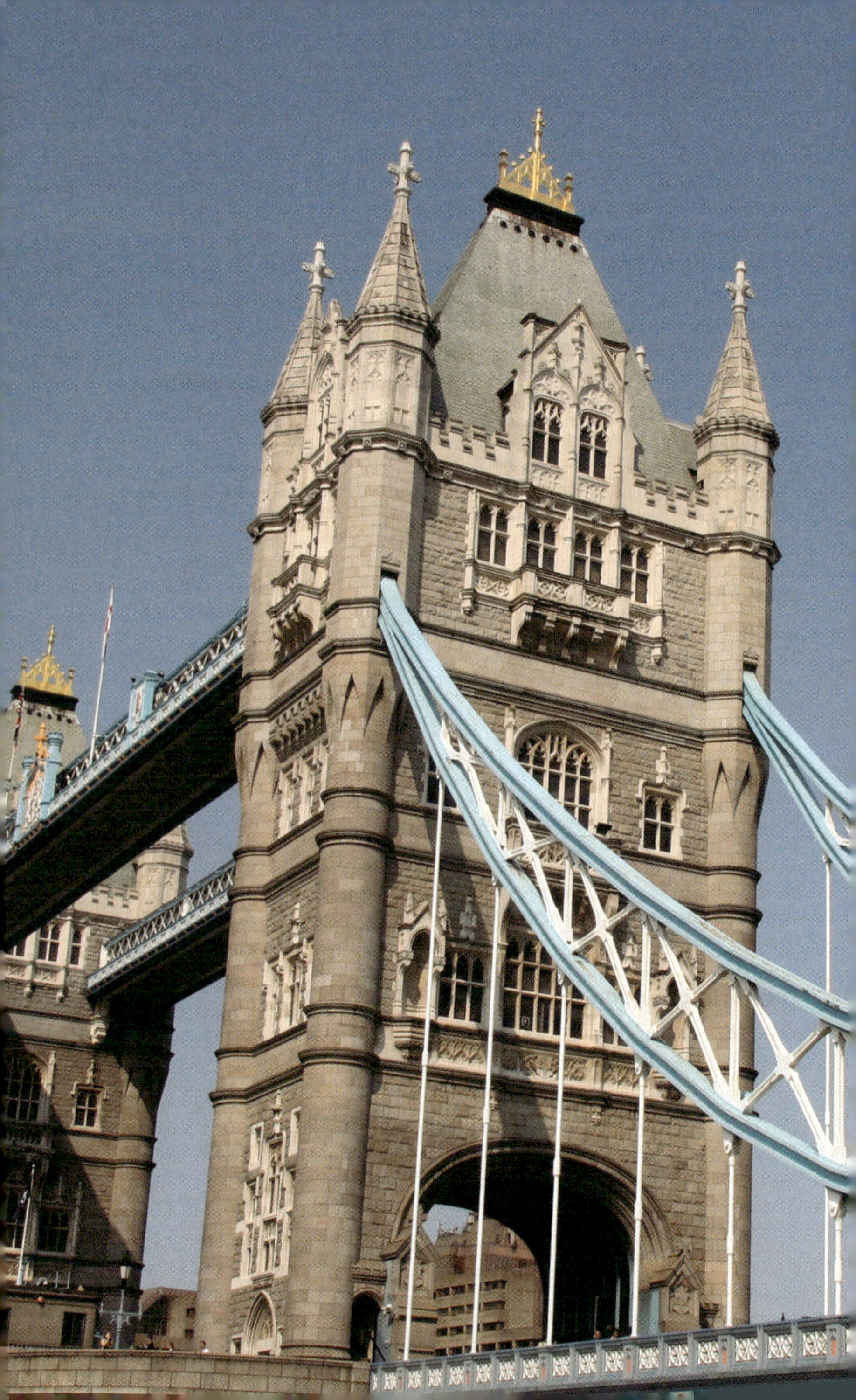

London

58 Westminster

67 St James's

69 Mayfair

71 Marylebone

71 Soho

72 Covent Garden

74 Strand

74 Bloomsbury

77 Holborn

78 The City

85 The East End

87 The South Bank

89 Southwark

92 Kensington and Chelsea

98 North London

102 South London

104 West London

107 Hampton Court

107 Windsor

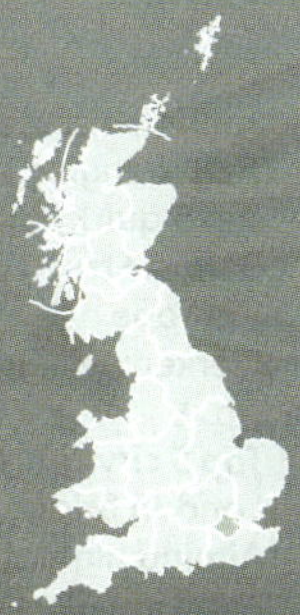

TOWER BRIDGE

1

London

For the visitor, London is a thrilling place. Monuments from the capital's glorious past are everywhere, from medieval banqueting halls and the great churches of Christopher Wren to the eclectic Victorian architecture of the triumphalist British Empire. You can relax in the city's quiet Georgian squares, explore the narrow alleyways of the City of London, wander along the riverside walks, and uncover the quirks of what is still identifiably a collection of villages. The largest capital in the European Union, stretching for more than thirty miles from east to west, and with a population of just under eight million, London is also incredibly diverse, ethnically and linguistically, offering cultural and culinary delights from right across the globe.

The capital's great historical **landmarks** – Big Ben, Westminster Abbey, Buckingham Palace, St Paul's Cathedral, the Tower of London and so on – draw in millions of tourists every year. This isn't a city that rests on its laurels, however. Since the turn of the millennium, all of London's world-class **museums**, **galleries** and institutions have been reinvented, from the Royal Opera House to the British Museum. With Tate Modern and the London Eye, the city boasts the world's largest modern art museum and Europe's largest Ferris wheel. And thanks to the 2012 Olympics, even the East End – not an area previously on most tourists' radar – has been given an overhaul.

You could spend days just **shopping** in London, mixing with the upper classes in the "tiara triangle" around Harrods, or sampling the offbeat weekend markets of Portobello Road, Brick Lane and Camden. The city's **pubs** have always had heaps of atmosphere, and **food** is now a major attraction too, with more than fifty Michelin-starred restaurants and the widest choice of cuisines on the planet. The **music**, **clubbing** and **gay and lesbian** scenes are second to none, and mainstream **arts** are no less exciting, with regular opportunities to catch outstanding theatre companies, dance troupes, exhibitions and opera.

London's special atmosphere comes mostly, however, from the life on its streets. A cosmopolitan city since at least the seventeenth century, when it was a haven for Huguenot immigrants escaping persecution in Louis XIV's France, today it is truly **multicultural**, with over a third of its permanent population originating from overseas. The last hundred years has seen the arrival of thousands from the Caribbean, the Indian subcontinent, the Mediterranean, the Far East and Eastern Europe, all of whom play an integral part in defining a metropolis that is unmatched in its sheer diversity.

London orientation: where to go p.58
The Changing of the Guard p.63
Top 5 quirky museums p.68
Oxford Street: the busiest street in Europe p.70
Clerkenwell, Hoxton and Shoreditch p.78
Top 5 city churches p.79
London Bridge p.83
Aiming high: city skyscrapers p.84
Thinking big: Olympic Park p.86
Regent's Canal by boat p.100
River transport: heading west p.104
Getting about: oyster cards and passes p.110
The congestion charge p.111
London postcodes p.112
Top 5 cheap London eats p.115
More than just a cuppa: afternoon tea p.116
Notting Hill Carnival p.125
The Proms p.129

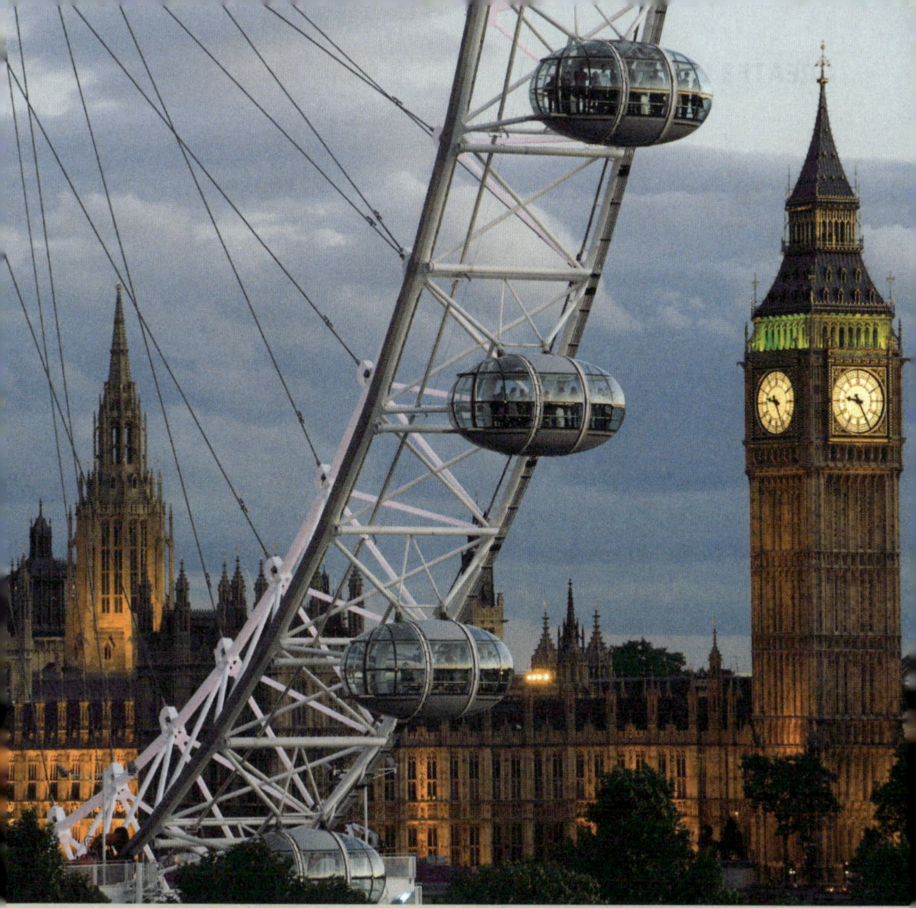

THE LONDON EYE AND HOUSES OF PARLIAMENT

Highlights

❶ **British Museum** Quite simply one of the world's greatest museums. **See p.76**

❷ **London Eye** The universally loved observation wheel is now a key London landmark. **See p.88**

❸ **Tate Modern** London's huge modern art gallery is housed in a spectacularly converted power station. **See p.89**

❹ **Shakespeare's Globe Theatre** Catch a show in this amazing reconstructed Elizabethan theatre. **See p.89**

❺ **Highgate Cemetery** The steeply sloping terraces of the West Cemetery's overgrown graves are the last word in Victorian Gothic gloom. **See p.101**

❻ **Greenwich** Picturesque riverside spot, with a weekend market, the National Maritime Museum and old Royal Observatory. **See p.102**

❼ **Kew Gardens** Stroll amid the exotic trees and shrubs, or head for the steamy glasshouses. **See p.106**

❽ **Hampton Court Palace** Tudor interiors, architecture by Wren and vast gardens make this a great day out. **See p.107**

❾ **Shopping at Liberty** London's most beautiful department store, opened as a retail outlet for the Victorian Arts and Crafts movement, and still the place to go for gorgeous fabrics and decorative household goods. **See p.130**

HIGHLIGHTS ARE MARKED ON THE MAP ON PP.56–57

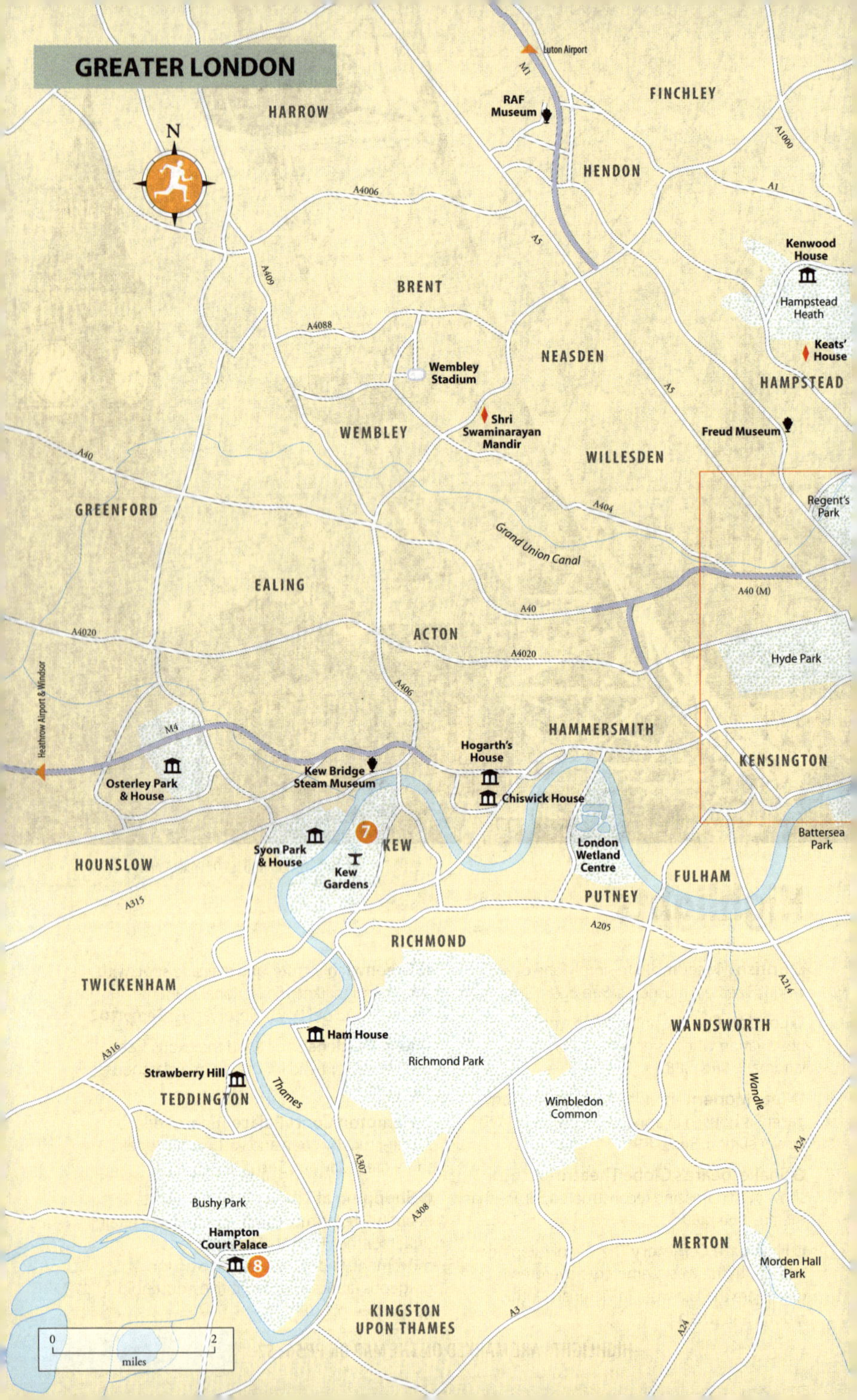
GREATER LONDON
N
Luton Airport
M1
RAF Museum
FINCHLEY
HARROW
HENDON
A1000
A1
A4006
A5
A409
Kenwood House
Hampstead Heath
Keats' House
BRENT
A4088
NEASDEN
Wembley Stadium
HAMPSTEAD
Shri Swaminarayan Mandir
WEMBLEY
Freud Museum
WILLESDEN
A40
GREENFORD
A404
Regent's Park
Grand Union Canal
EALING
A40 (M)
A40
A4020
ACTON
A4020
Hyde Park
Heathrow Airport & Windsor
A406
M4
HAMMERSMITH
Hogarth's House
KENSINGTON
Kew Bridge Steam Museum
Osterley Park & House
Chiswick House
7
Battersea Park
Syon Park & House
KEW
London Wetland Centre
HOUNSLOW
Kew Gardens
FULHAM
PUTNEY
A315
A205
RICHMOND
A214
TWICKENHAM
WANDSWORTH
Ham House
A316
Richmond Park
Strawberry Hill
Wandle
TEDDINGTON
Thames
Wimbledon Common
A24
A307
Bushy Park
A308
Hampton Court Palace
8
MERTON
Morden Hall Park
A3
KINGSTON UPON THAMES
A24
0
2
miles

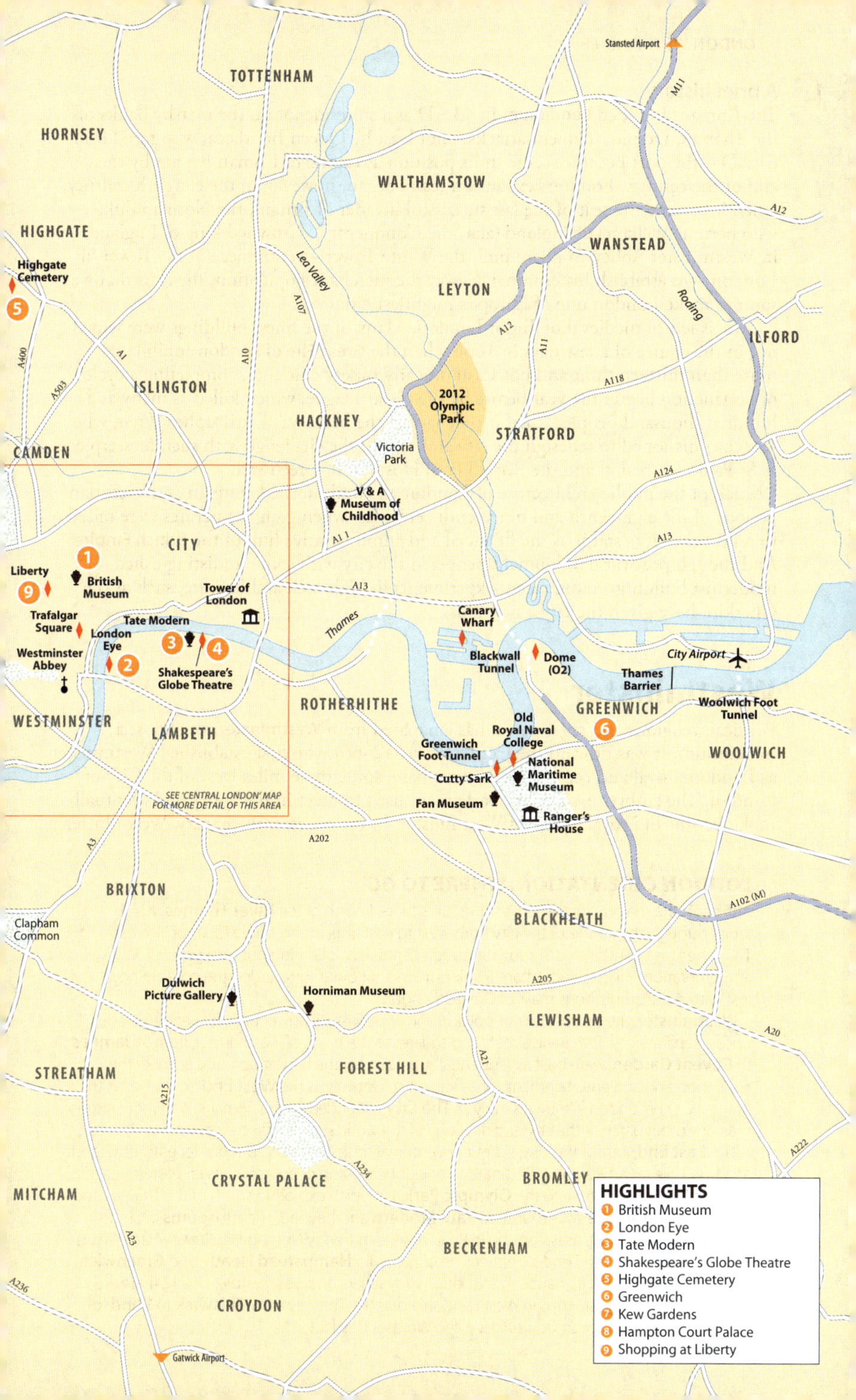

Stansted Airport
TOTTENHAM
HORNSEY
WALTHAMSTOW
HIGHGATE
Highgate Cemetery
WANSTEAD
LEYTON
ILFORD
ISLINGTON
2012 Olympic Park
HACKNEY
STRATFORD
CAMDEN
Victoria Park
V & A Museum of Childhood
CITY
Liberty
British Museum
Tower of London
Trafalgar Square
Tate Modern
London Eye
Westminster Abbey
Shakespeare's Globe Theatre
Canary Wharf
Blackwall Tunnel
Dome (O2)
City Airport
Thames Barrier
Thames
ROTHERHITHE
GREENWICH
Woolwich Foot Tunnel
WESTMINSTER
LAMBETH
Old Royal Naval College
Greenwich Foot Tunnel
WOOLWICH
National Maritime Museum
Cutty Sark
Fan Museum
Ranger's House
SEE 'CENTRAL LONDON' MAP FOR MORE DETAIL OF THIS AREA
BRIXTON
Clapham Common
BLACKHEATH
Dulwich Picture Gallery
Horniman Museum
LEWISHAM
STREATHAM
FOREST HILL
CRYSTAL PALACE
BROMLEY
MITCHAM
BECKENHAM
CROYDON
Gatwick Airport
HIGHLIGHTS
1 British Museum
2 London Eye
3 Tate Modern
4 Shakespeare's Globe Theatre
5 Highgate Cemetery
6 Greenwich
7 Kew Gardens
8 Hampton Court Palace
9 Shopping at Liberty

1

A brief history

The Romans founded **Londinium** in 43 AD as a stores depot on the marshy banks of the Thames. Despite frequent attacks – not least by Queen Boudicca, who razed it in 61 AD – the port became secure in its position as capital of Roman Britain by the end of the century. London's expansion really began, however, in the eleventh century, when it became the seat of the last successful invader of Britain, the Norman duke who became **William I of England** (aka "the Conqueror"). Crowned king of England in Westminster Abbey, William built the White Tower – centrepiece of the Tower of London – to establish his dominance over the merchant population, the class that was soon to make London one of Europe's mightiest cities.

Little is left of medieval or Tudor London. Many of the finest buildings were wiped out in the course of a few days in 1666 when the **Great Fire of London** annihilated more than thirteen thousand houses and nearly ninety churches, completing a cycle of destruction begun the year before by the Great Plague, which killed as many as a hundred thousand people. Chief beneficiary of the blaze was Christopher Wren, who was commissioned to redesign the city and rose to the challenge with such masterpieces as St Paul's Cathedral and the Royal Naval Hospital in Greenwich.

Much of the public architecture of London was built in the Georgian and Victorian periods of the eighteenth and nineteenth centuries, when grand structures were raised to reflect the city's status as the financial and administrative hub of the **British Empire**. And though postwar development peppered the city with some undistinguished modernist buildings, more recent experiments in high-tech architecture, such as the Gherkin, have given the city a new gloss.

Westminster

Political, religious and regal power has emanated from **Westminster** for almost a millennium. It was Edward the Confessor (1042–66) who first established Westminster as London's royal and ecclesiastical power base, some three miles west of the City of London. The embryonic English parliament used to meet in the abbey and eventually took over the old royal palace of Westminster. In the nineteenth century, Westminster

LONDON ORIENTATION: WHERE TO GO

Although the majority of the city's sights are situated north of the **River Thames**, which loops through the centre of the city from west to east, there is no single focus of interest. That's because London hasn't grown through centralized planning but by a process of agglomeration. Villages and urban developments that once surrounded the core are now lost within the amorphous mass of Greater London.

Westminster, the country's royal, political and ecclesiastical power base for centuries, was once a separate city. The grand streets and squares to the north of Westminster, from **St James's** to **Covent Garden**, were built as residential suburbs after the Restoration, and are now the city's shopping and entertainment zones known collectively as the **West End**. To the east is the original City of London – known simply as **The City** – founded by the Romans, with more history than any other patch of the city, and now one of the world's great financial centres.

The **East End**, east of the City, is not conventional tourist territory, but has recently emerged as a bolt hole for artists and a destination for clubbers – and of course, in its far eastern reaches, the East End is now home to the **Olympic Park**. It's worth exploring south of the Thames, too, from the **London Eye**, in the west, to **Tate Modern** and beyond. The **museums** of South Kensington are a must, as is Portobello Road market in trendy Notting Hill, literary Hampstead and Highgate, in North London, either side of half-wild **Hampstead Heath**, and **Greenwich**, in South London, with its nautical associations, royal park and observatory. Finally, there are plenty of rewarding day-trips in West London along the Thames from **Chiswick** to **Windsor**, most notably to Hampton Court Palace and Windsor Castle.

– and Whitehall in particular – became the "heart of the Empire", its ministries ruling over a quarter of the world's population. Even now, though the UK's world status has diminished, the institutions that run the country inhabit roughly the same geographical area: Westminster for the politicians, Whitehall for the civil servants.

The monuments and buildings in and around Westminster also span the millennium, and include some of London's most famous landmarks – **Nelson's Column**, **Big Ben** and the **Houses of Parliament**, **Westminster Abbey**, plus two of the city's finest permanent art collections, the **National Gallery** and **Tate Britain**. This is a well-trodden tourist circuit since it's also one of the easiest parts of London to walk round, with all the major sights within a mere half-mile of each other, linked by one of London's most majestic streets, **Whitehall.**

Trafalgar Square

Despite the persistent noise of traffic, **Trafalgar Square** is still one of London's grandest architectural set pieces. John Nash designed the basic layout in the 1820s, but died long before the square took its present form. The Neoclassical National Gallery filled up the northern side of the square in 1838, followed five years later by the central focal point, **Nelson's Column**, topped by the famous admiral; the very large bronze lions didn't arrive until 1868, and the fountains – a real rarity in a London square – didn't take their present shape until the late 1930s.

As one of the few large public squares in London, Trafalgar Square has been both a tourist attraction and a focus for **political demonstrations** since the Chartists assembled here in 1848 before marching to Kennington Common. Since then countless demos and rallies have taken place, and nowadays various free events, commemorations and celebrations are staged here.

Stranded on a traffic island to the south of the column, and pre-dating the entire square, is an **equestrian statue of Charles I**, erected shortly after the Restoration on the very spot where eight of those who had signed the king's death warrant were disembowelled. Charles's statue also marks the original site of the thirteenth-century **Charing Cross**, from where all distances from the capital are measured – a Victorian imitation now stands outside Charing Cross train station.

St Martin-in-the-Fields

Trafalgar Square • Mon, Tues & Fri 8.30am–1pm & 2–6pm, Wed 8.30am–1.15pm & 2–5pm, Thurs 8.30am–1.15pm & 2–6pm, Sat 9.30am–6pm, Sun 3.30–5pm; concerts Mon, Tues & Fri lunchtime • Free • T 020 7766 1100, W stmartin-in-the-fields.org • ⊖ Charing Cross

The northeastern corner of Trafalgar Square is occupied by James Gibbs's church of **St Martin-in-the-Fields**, fronted by a magnificent Corinthian portico. Designed in 1721, the interior is purposefully simple, though the Italian plasterwork on the barrel vaulting is exceptionally rich; it's best appreciated while listening to one of the church's free lunchtime **concerts**. There's a licensed café (see p.115) in the roomy **crypt**, along with a shop, gallery and brass-rubbing centre.

National Gallery

Trafalgar Square • Daily 10am–6pm, Fri 10am–9pm • Guided tours daily 11.30am & 2.30pm, plus Fri 7pm • Free • T 020 7747 2885, W nationalgallery.org.uk • ⊖ Charing Cross

The **National Gallery** was begun in 1824 by the British government. The gallery's canny acquisition policy has resulted in more than 2300 paintings, but the collection's virtue is not so much its size, but its range, depth and sheer quality. To view the collection chronologically, begin with the **Sainsbury Wing**, to the west. With more than 1000 paintings on permanent display in the main galleries, you'll need real stamina to see everything in one day, so if time is tight your best bet is to home in on your areas of special interest, having picked up a gallery plan at one of the information desks. **Audioguides**, with a brief audio commentary on each of the paintings on display are

1

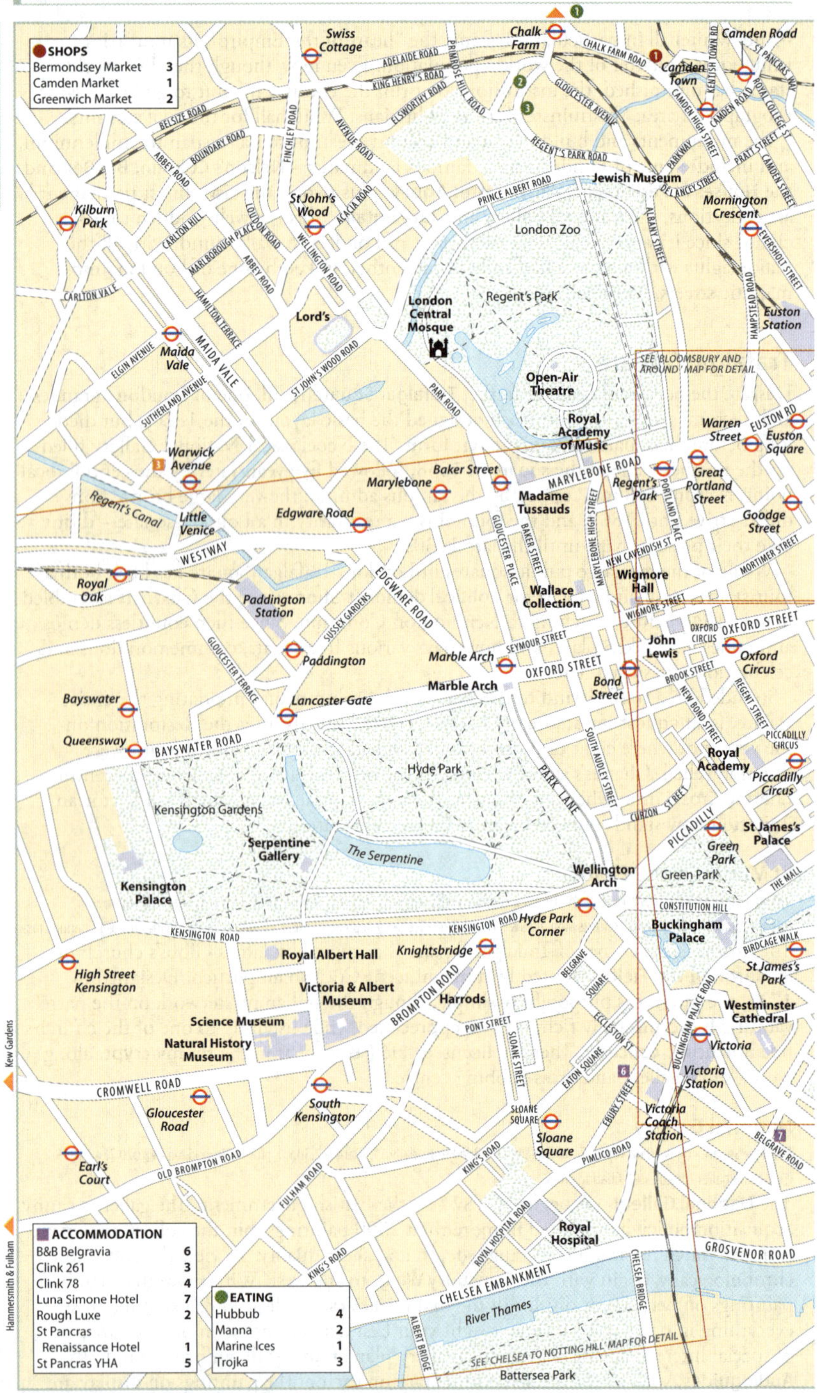
SHOPS
Bermondsey Market 3
Camden Market 1
Greenwich Market 2
ACCOMMODATION
B&B Belgravia 6
Clink 261 3
Clink 78 4
Luna Simone Hotel 7
Rough Luxe 2
St Pancras Renaissance Hotel 1
St Pancras YHA 5
EATING
Hubbub 4
Manna 2
Marine Ices 1
Trojka 3
Swiss Cottage
Chalk Farm
Camden Road
Camden Town
Kilburn Park
St John's Wood
Jewish Museum
Mornington Crescent
London Zoo
Regent's Park
London Central Mosque
Lord's
Euston Station
Maida Vale
SEE 'BLOOMSBURY AND AROUND' MAP FOR DETAIL
Open-Air Theatre
Royal Academy of Music
Warren Street
Euston Square
Warwick Avenue
Baker Street
Marylebone
Regent's Park
Great Portland Street
Madame Tussauds
Goodge Street
Regent's Canal
Little Venice
Edgware Road
Royal Oak
Paddington Station
Wigmore Hall
Wallace Collection
John Lewis
Oxford Circus
Paddington
Marble Arch
Bond Street
Bayswater
Lancaster Gate
Queensway
Royal Academy
Piccadilly Circus
Hyde Park
Kensington Gardens
Serpentine Gallery
The Serpentine
St James's Palace
Green Park
Kensington Palace
Wellington Arch
Buckingham Palace
Hyde Park Corner
Royal Albert Hall
Knightsbridge
High Street Kensington
St James's Park
Victoria & Albert Museum
Harrods
Westminster Cathedral
Science Museum
Natural History Museum
Victoria
Victoria Station
South Kensington
Gloucester Road
Victoria Coach Station
Sloane Square
Earl's Court
Royal Hospital
River Thames
SEE 'CHELSEA TO NOTTING HILL' MAP FOR DETAIL
Battersea Park
ADELAIDE ROAD
KING HENRY'S ROAD
ELSWORTHY ROAD
PRIMROSE HILL ROAD
CHALK FARM ROAD
GLOUCESTER AVENUE
REGENT'S PARK ROAD
KENTISH TOWN ROAD
CAMDEN HIGH STREET
CAMDEN ROAD
ST PANCRAS WAY
ROYAL COLLEGE ST
PRATT STREET
CAMDEN STREET
PARKWAY
DELANCEY STREET
PRINCE ALBERT ROAD
ALBANY STREET
EVERSHOLT STREET
HAMPSTEAD ROAD
BELSIZE ROAD
BOUNDARY ROAD
ABBEY ROAD
FINCHLEY ROAD
AVENUE ROAD
ACACIA ROAD
WELLINGTON ROAD
LOUDON ROAD
MARLBOROUGH PLACE
CARLTON HILL
HAMILTON TERRACE
CARLTON VALE
MAIDA VALE
ELGIN AVENUE
SUTHERLAND AVENUE
ST JOHN'S WOOD ROAD
PARK ROAD
EUSTON RD
MARYLEBONE ROAD
PORTLAND PLACE
NEW CAVENDISH ST
MARYLEBONE HIGH STREET
GLOUCESTER PLACE
BAKER STREET
MORTIMER STREET
WESTWAY
EDGWARE ROAD
SUSSEX GARDENS
GLOUCESTER TERRACE
WIGMORE STREET
OXFORD CIRCUS
OXFORD STREET
SEYMOUR STREET
BROOK STREET
NEW BOND STREET
REGENT STREET
BAYSWATER ROAD
PICCADILLY CIRCUS
PARK LANE
SOUTH AUDLEY STREET
CURZON ST
PICCADILLY
THE MALL
CONSTITUTION HILL
BIRDCAGE WALK
KENSINGTON ROAD
BELGRAVE SQUARE
BUCKINGHAM PALACE ROAD
BROMPTON ROAD
PONT STREET
SLOANE STREET
ECCLESTON ST
EATON SQUARE
CROMWELL ROAD
EBURY STREET
SLOANE SQUARE
OLD BROMPTON ROAD
KING'S ROAD
PIMLICO ROAD
BELGRAVE ROAD
FULHAM ROAD
ROYAL HOSPITAL ROAD
GROSVENOR ROAD
CHELSEA BRIDGE
CHELSEA EMBANKMENT
ALBERT BRIDGE
Kew Gardens
Hammersmith & Fulham

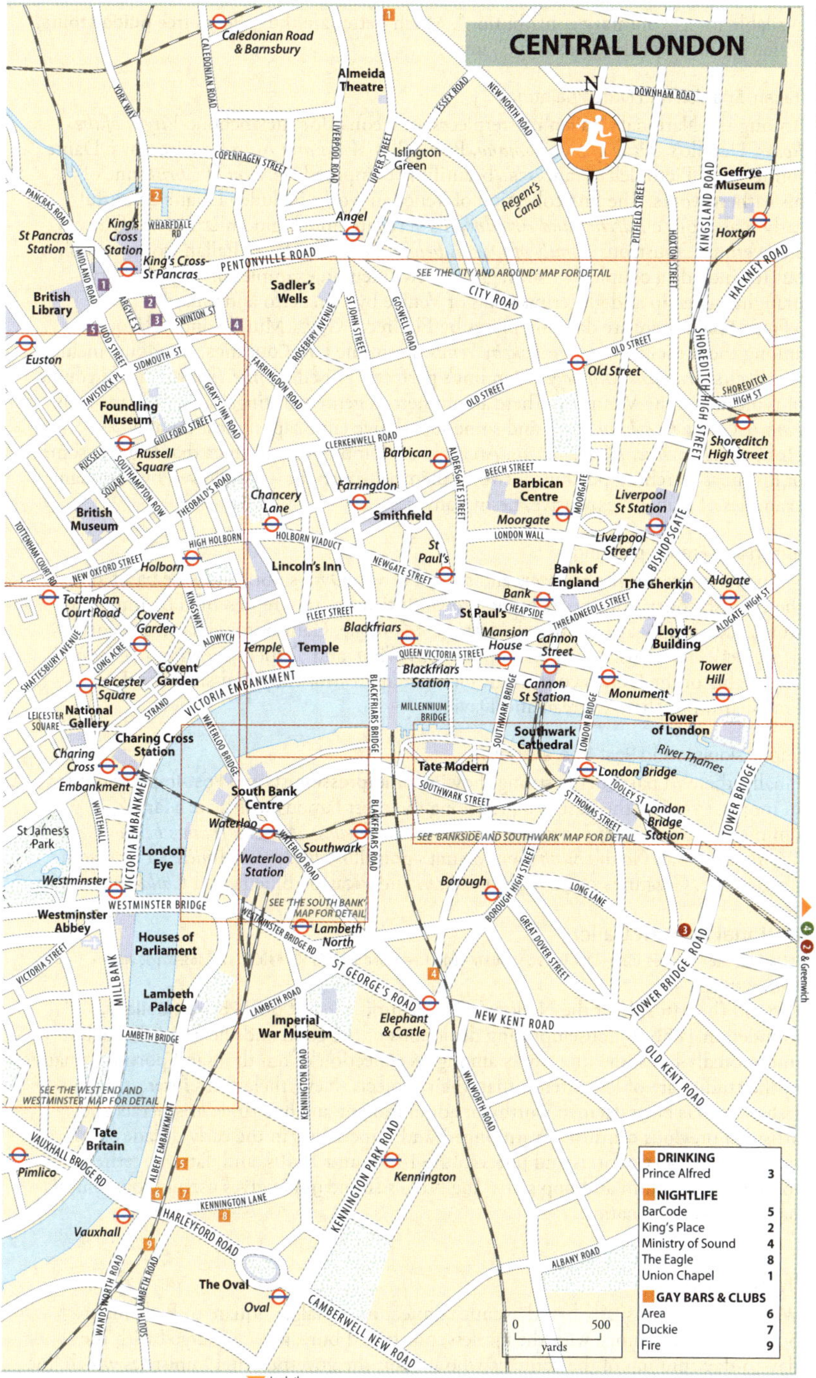
CENTRAL LONDON
N
Caledonian Road & Barnsbury
CALEDONIAN ROAD
Almeida Theatre
DOWNHAM ROAD
ESSEX ROAD
NEW NORTH ROAD
YORK WAY
LIVERPOOL ROAD
UPPER STREET
Islington Green
COPENHAGEN STREET
Regent's Canal
Geffrye Museum
KINGSLAND ROAD
PITFIELD STREET
HOXTON STREET
Hoxton
PANCRAS ROAD
King's Cross Station
WHARFDALE RD
Angel
St Pancras Station
MIDLAND ROAD
King's Cross-St Pancras
PENTONVILLE ROAD
SEE 'THE CITY AND AROUND' MAP FOR DETAIL
HACKNEY ROAD
British Library
ARGYLE ST
SWINTON ST
Sadler's Wells
ROSEBERY AVENUE
ST JOHN STREET
GOSWELL ROAD
CITY ROAD
JUDD STREET
Euston
SIDMOUTH ST
TAVISTOCK PL.
FARRINGDON ROAD
OLD STREET
Old Street
SHOREDITCH HIGH STREET
SHOREDITCH HIGH ST
GRAY'S INN ROAD
Foundling Museum
GUILFORD STREET
CLERKENWELL ROAD
Shoreditch High Street
Russell Square
RUSSELL SQUARE
SOUTHAMPTON ROW
Barbican
ALDERSGATE STREET
BEECH STREET
Barbican Centre
MOORGATE
Liverpool St Station
THEOBALD'S ROAD
Chancery Lane
Farringdon
Smithfield
Moorgate
BISHOPSGATE
British Museum
LONDON WALL
Liverpool Street
TOTTENHAM COURT ROAD
HOLBORN VIADUCT
St Paul's
HIGH HOLBORN
NEW OXFORD STREET
Holborn
Lincoln's Inn
NEWGATE STREET
Bank of England
The Gherkin
Aldgate
Tottenham Court Road
Covent Garden
KINGSWAY
FLEET STREET
Bank
CHEAPSIDE
THREADNEEDLE STREET
ALDGATE HIGH ST
St Paul's
Blackfriars
Mansion House
Cannon Street
Lloyd's Building
ALDWYCH
Temple
Temple
QUEEN VICTORIA STREET
SHAFTESBURY AVENUE
LONG ACRE
Covent Garden
Blackfriars Station
Tower Hill
Leicester Square
VICTORIA EMBANKMENT
Cannon St Station
Monument
BLACKFRIARS BRIDGE
MILLENNIUM BRIDGE
SOUTHWARK BRIDGE
LONDON BRIDGE
LEICESTER SQUARE
National Gallery
STRAND
Tower of London
Southwark Cathedral
Charing Cross Station
WATERLOO BRIDGE
River Thames
Charing Cross
Tate Modern
London Bridge
Embankment
South Bank Centre
SOUTHWARK STREET
TOOLEY ST
London Bridge Station
TOWER BRIDGE
VICTORIA EMBANKMENT
ST THOMAS STREET
St James's Park
WHITEHALL
Waterloo
WATERLOO ROAD
BLACKFRIARS ROAD
SEE 'BANKSIDE AND SOUTHWARK' MAP FOR DETAIL
London Eye
Southwark
Waterloo Station
BOROUGH HIGH STREET
Westminster
Borough
LONG LANE
WESTMINSTER BRIDGE
SEE 'THE SOUTH BANK' MAP FOR DETAIL
Westminster Abbey
Lambeth North
WESTMINSTER BRIDGE RD
GREAT DOVER STREET
TOWER BRIDGE ROAD
& Greenwich
Houses of Parliament
VICTORIA STREET
ST GEORGE'S ROAD
MILLBANK
Lambeth Palace
LAMBETH ROAD
Elephant & Castle
NEW KENT ROAD
Imperial War Museum
LAMBETH BRIDGE
OLD KENT ROAD
SEE 'THE WEST END AND WESTMINSTER' MAP FOR DETAIL
KENNINGTON ROAD
WALWORTH ROAD
Tate Britain
ALBERT EMBANKMENT
KENNINGTON PARK ROAD
VAUXHALL BRIDGE RD
Pimlico
Kennington
KENNINGTON LANE
Vauxhall
HARLEYFORD ROAD
ALBANY ROAD
WANDSWORTH ROAD
SOUTH LAMBETH ROAD
The Oval
Oval
CAMBERWELL NEW ROAD
0
500
yards
DRINKING
Prince Alfred 3
NIGHTLIFE
BarCode 5
King's Place 2
Ministry of Sound 4
The Eagle 8
Union Chapel 1
GAY BARS & CLUBS
Area 6
Duckie 7
Fire 9
Lambeth

available for a "voluntary contribution". Much better are the gallery's free **guided tours**, which set off from the Sainsbury Wing.

Italian, Spanish and Dutch paintings

Among the National's **Italian** masterpieces are Leonardo's melancholic *Virgin of the Rocks*, Uccello's *Battle of San Romano*, Botticelli's *Venus and Mars* (inspired by a Dante sonnet) and Piero della Francesca's beautifully composed *Baptism of Christ*, one of his earliest works. The fine collection of Venetian works includes Titian's colourful early masterpiece *Bacchus and Ariadne*, his very late, much gloomier *Death of Acteon*, and Veronese's lustrous *Family of Darius before Alexander*. Later Italian works to look out for include a couple by Caravaggio, a few splendid examples of Tiepolo's airy draughtsmanship and glittering vistas of Venice by Canaletto and Guardi.

From **Spain** there are dazzling pieces by El Greco, Goya, Murillo and Velázquez, among them the provocative *Rokeby Venus*. From the **Low Countries**, standouts include van Eyck's *Arnolfini Marriage*, Memlinc's perfectly poised *Donne Triptych*, and a couple of typically serene Vermeers. There are numerous genre paintings, such as Frans Hals' *Family Group in a Landscape*, and some superlative landscapes, most notably Hobbema's *Avenue, Middleharnis*. An array of Rembrandt paintings that features some of his most searching portraits – two of them self-portraits – is followed by abundant examples of Rubens' expansive, fleshy canvases.

British and French paintings

Holbein's masterful *Ambassadors* and several of van Dyck's portraits were painted for the English court; and there's home-grown **British** art, too, represented by important works such as Hogarth's satirical *Marriage à la Mode*, Gainsborough's translucent *Morning Walk*, Constable's ever-popular *Hay Wain*, and Turner's *Fighting Téméraire*. Highlights of the **French** contingent include superb works by Poussin, Claude, Fragonard, Boucher, Watteau and David.

Impressionism and Post-Impressionism

Finally, there's a particularly strong showing of **Impressionists** and **Post-Impressionists** in rooms 43–46 of the East Wing. Among the most famous works are Manet's unfinished *Execution of Maximilian*, Renoir's *Umbrellas*, Monet's *Thames below Westminster*, Van Gogh's *Sunflowers*, Seurat's pointillist *Bathers at Asnières*, a Rousseau junglescape, Cézanne's proto-Cubist *Bathers* and Picasso's Blue Period *Child with a Dove*.

National Portrait Gallery

St Martin's Place • Sat–Wed 10am–6pm, Thurs & Fri 10am–9pm • Free; sound guide £3.50 • T 020 7312 2463, W npg.org.uk • ⊖ Leicester Square

Around the east side of the National Gallery lurks the **National Portrait Gallery**, founded in 1856 to house uplifting depictions of the good and the great. Though it undoubtedly has some fine works among its collection of ten thousand portraits, many of the studies are of less interest than their subjects. Nevertheless, it's interesting to trace who has been deemed worthy of admiration at any one time: aristocrats and artists in previous centuries, warmongers and imperialists in the early decades of the twentieth century, writers and poets in the 1930s and 1940s, and, latterly, retired footballers, and film and pop stars. The NPG's **sound guide** gives useful biographical background information.

Whitehall

Whitehall, the unusually broad avenue connecting Trafalgar Square to Parliament Square, is synonymous with the faceless, pinstriped bureaucracy charged with the day-to-day running of the country, who inhabit the governmental ministries which line the street. During the sixteenth and seventeenth centuries, however, Whitehall was the permanent residence of the kings and queens of England, and was actually synonymous with royalty.

The statues dotted about recall the days when Whitehall stood at the centre of an empire on which the sun never set. Halfway down, in the middle of the road, stands Edwin Lutyens' **Cenotaph**, a memorial to the dead of World War I and the centre piece of the Remembrance Sunday ceremony in November. Close by are the locked gates of Downing Street, home to London's most famous address, **Number 10 Downing Street**, the seventeenth-century terraced house that has been the residence of the prime minister since it was presented to Sir Robert Walpole, Britain's first PM, by George II in 1732.

Banqueting House

Whitehall • Mon–Sat 10am–5pm • £5 • Ⓣ 020 3166 6154, Ⓦ hrp.org.uk • ⊖ Charing Cross

The original **Whitehall Palace** was the London seat of the Archbishop of York, confiscated and greatly extended by Henry VIII after a fire at Westminster forced him to find alternative accommodation. The chief section of the old palace to survive the fire of 1698 was the **Banqueting House** begun by Inigo Jones in 1619 and the first Palladian building to be built in England. The one room open to the public has no original furnishings, but is well worth seeing for the superlative Rubens ceiling paintings glorifying the Stuart dynasty, commissioned by Charles I in the 1630s. Charles himself walked through the room for the last time in 1649 when he stepped onto the executioner's scaffold from one of its windows.

Horse Guards: Household Cavalry Museum

Whitehall • Daily: March–Sept 10am–6pm; Oct–Feb 10am–5pm • £6 • Ⓣ 020 7930 3070, Ⓦ householdcavalrymuseum.org.uk • ⊖ Charing Cross or Westminster

Two mounted sentries of the Queen's Household Cavalry and two horseless colleagues are posted to protect **Horse Guards**, originally the main gateway to St James's Park and Buckingham Palace. Round the back of the building, you'll find the **Household Cavalry Museum** where you can try on a trooper's elaborate uniform, complete a horse quiz and learn about the regiments' history. With the stables immediately adjacent, it's a sweet-smelling place, and – horse-lovers will be pleased to know – you can see the beasts in their stalls through a glass screen. Don't miss the pocket riot act on display, which ends with the wise warning: "must read correctly: variance fatal".

Churchill War Rooms

King Charles St • Daily 9.30am–6pm • £14.50 • Ⓣ 020 7930 6961, Ⓦ cwr.iwm.org.uk • ⊖ Westminster

In 1938, in anticipation of Nazi air raids, the basements of the civil service buildings on the south side of King Charles Street, south of Downing Street, were converted into the **Cabinet War Rooms**. It was here that Winston Churchill directed operations and held Cabinet meetings for the duration of World War II and the rooms have been left pretty much as they were when they were finally abandoned on VJ Day 1945, making for an

THE CHANGING OF THE GUARD

The Queen is colonel-in-chief of the seven **Household Regiments**: the Life Guards (who dress in red and white) and the Blues and Royals (who dress in blue and white) are the two Household Cavalry regiments; while the Grenadier, Coldstream, Scots, Irish and Welsh Guards make up the Foot Guards.

The **Changing of the Guard** takes place at two London locations: the two Household Cavalry regiments take it in turns to stand guard at Horse Guards on Whitehall (Mon–Sat 11am, Sun 10am, with inspection daily at 4pm), while the Foot Guards take care of Buckingham Palace (April–Aug daily 11.30am; Sept–March alternate days; no ceremony if it rains). A ceremony also takes place regularly at Windsor Castle (see p.108).

1

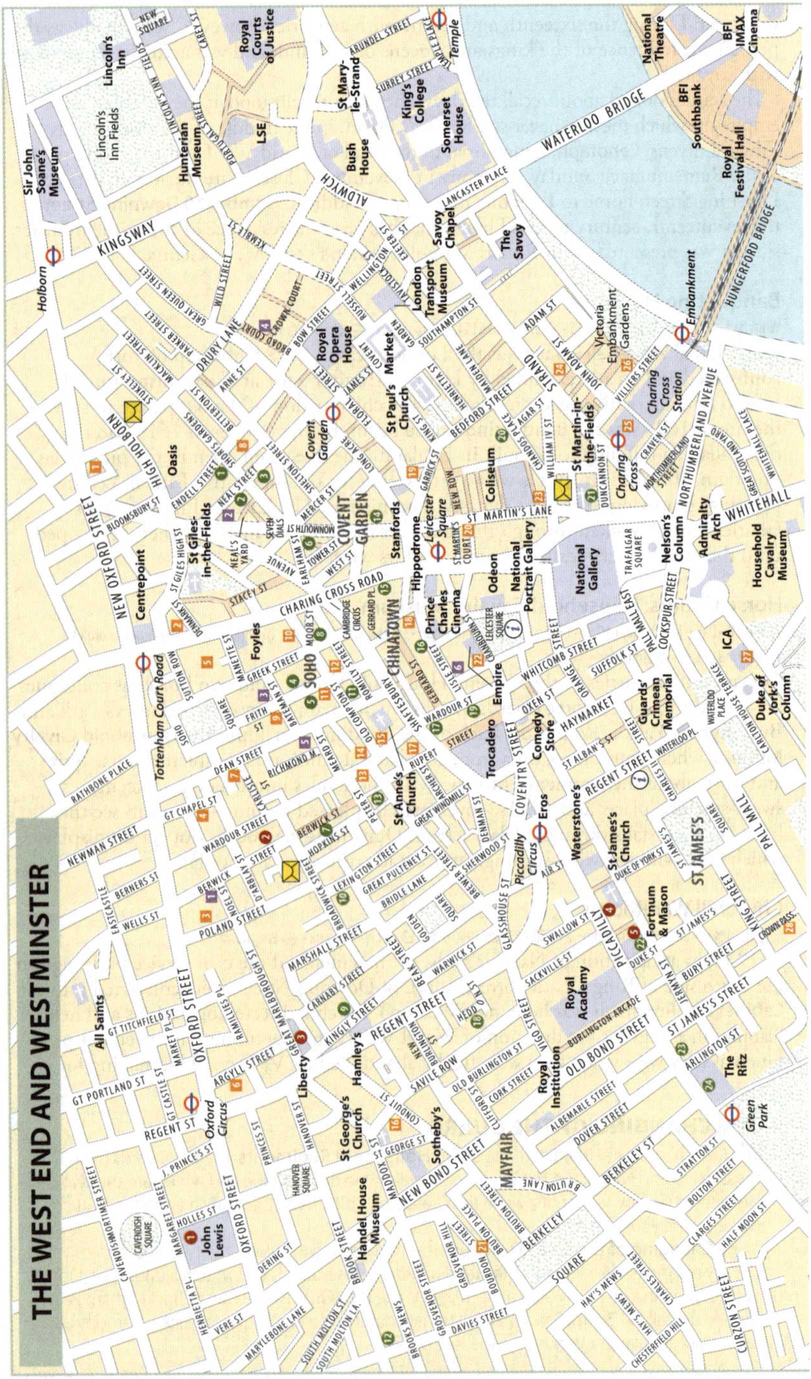
THE WEST END AND WESTMINSTER
Sir John Soane's Museum
Lincoln's Inn Fields
Lincoln's Inn
Hunterian Museum
LSE
Royal Courts of Justice
St Mary-le-Strand
Bush House
King's College
Somerset House
Temple
WATERLOO BRIDGE
National Theatre
BFI IMAX Cinema
BFI Southbank
Royal Festival Hall
HUNGERFORD BRIDGE
Embankment
Victoria Embankment Gardens
Charing Cross Station
Holborn
KINGSWAY
ALDWYCH
Savoy Chapel
The Savoy
London Transport Museum
Royal Opera House
Market
St Paul's Church
Covent Garden
COVENT GARDEN
STRAND
St Martin-in-the-Fields
Charing Cross
NORTHUMBERLAND AVENUE
WHITEHALL
Admiralty Arch
Nelson's Column
TRAFALGAR SQUARE
National Gallery
National Portrait Gallery
Household Cavalry Museum
Coliseum
Stanfords
Hippodrome
Leicester Square
Odeon
Prince Charles Cinema
Empire
CHINATOWN
CHARING CROSS ROAD
SEVEN DIALS
NEAL'S YARD
St Giles-in-the-Fields
Oasis
HIGH HOLBORN
NEW OXFORD STREET
Centrepoint
Tottenham Court Road
Foyles
SOHO
SHAFTESBURY AVENUE
St Anne's Church
Trocadero
Comedy Store
HAYMARKET
ICA
Guards' Crimean Memorial
Duke of York's Column
PALL MALL
Eros
Piccadilly Circus
Waterstone's
St James's Church
ST JAMES'S
Fortnum & Mason
PICCADILLY
Royal Academy
Royal Institution
OLD BOND STREET
The Ritz
Green Park
MAYFAIR
BERKELEY SQUARE
Sotheby's
NEW BOND STREET
St George's Church
Hamley's
Liberty
REGENT STREET
Oxford Circus
OXFORD STREET
All Saints
John Lewis
Handel House Museum
CAVENDISH SQUARE
HANOVER SQUARE
CURZON STREET

1

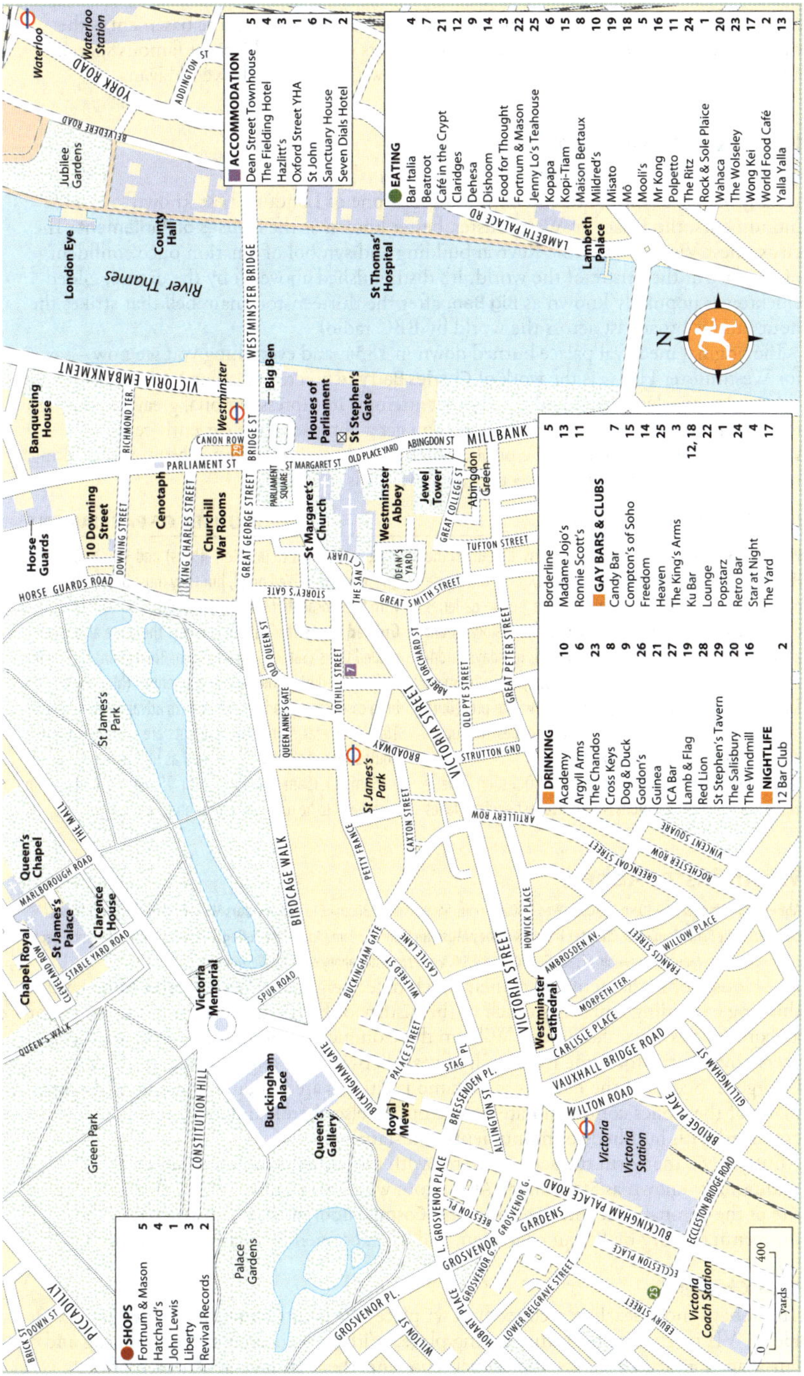
ACCOMMODATION
Dean Street Townhouse 5
The Fielding Hotel 4
Hazlitt's 3
Oxford Street YHA 1
St John 6
Sanctuary House 7
Seven Dials Hotel 2
EATING
Bar Italia 4
Beatroot 7
Café in the Crypt 21
Claridges 12
Dehesa 9
Dishoom 14
Food for Thought 3
Fortnum & Mason 22
Jenny Lo's Teahouse 25
Kopapa 6
Kopi-Tiam 15
Maison Bertaux 8
Mildred's 10
Misato 19
Mô 18
Mooli's 5
Mr Kong 16
Polpetto 11
The Ritz 24
Rock & Sole Plaice 1
Wahaca 20
The Wolseley 23
Wong Kei 17
World Food Café 2
Yalla Yalla 13
DRINKING
Academy 10
Argyll Arms 6
The Chandos 23
Cross Keys 8
Dog & Duck 9
Gordon's 26
Guinea 21
ICA Bar 27
Lamb & Flag 19
Red Lion 28
St Stephen's Tavern 29
The Salisbury 20
The Windmill 16
NIGHTLIFE
12 Bar Club 2
Borderline 5
Madame Jojo's 13
Ronnie Scott's 11
GAY BARS & CLUBS
Candy Bar 7
Compton's of Soho 15
Freedom 14
Heaven 25
The King's Arms 3
Ku Bar 12, 18
Lounge 22
Popstarz 1
Retro Bar 24
Star at Night 4
The Yard 17
SHOPS
Fortnum & Mason 5
Hatchard's 4
John Lewis 1
Liberty 3
Revival Records 2
0 400 yards

atmospheric underground trot through wartime London. Also in the basement is the excellent **Churchill Museum**. You can hear snippets of Churchill's most famous speeches and check out his trademark bowler, spotted bow tie and half-chewed Havana.

Houses of Parliament

Parliament Square • ⓣ 020 7219 4272, Ⓦ parliament.uk • ⊖ Westminster

Clearly visible at the south end of Whitehall is one of London's best-known monuments, the Palace of Westminster, better known as the **Houses of Parliament.** The city's finest Victorian Gothic Revival building and symbol of a nation once confident of its place at the centre of the world, it's distinguished above all by the ornate, gilded clocktower popularly known as **Big Ben**, after the thirteen-ton main bell that strikes the hour (and is broadcast across the world by BBC radio).

The original medieval palace burned down in 1834, and everything you see now – save for Westminster Hall – is the work of **Charles Barry**, who created an orgy of honey-coloured pinnacles, turrets and tracery that attempts to express national greatness through the use of Gothic and Elizabethan styles. You get a glimpse of the eleventh-century **Westminster Hall** en route to the public galleries, its huge oak hammer-beam roof making it one of the most magnificent secular medieval halls in Europe.

INFORMATION AND TOURS — HOUSES OF PARLIAMENT

Public galleries To watch proceedings in either the House of Commons – the livelier of the two – or the House of Lords, simply join the queue for the public galleries outside St Stephen's Gate. The public are let in slowly from about 4pm onwards on Mondays and Tuesdays, from around 1pm Wednesdays, noon on Thursdays, and 10am on Sitting Fridays. Security is tight and the whole procedure can take an hour or more, so to avoid the queues, turn up an hour or so later or on a Sitting Friday.

Question Time UK citizens can attend Question Time – when the House of Commons is at its liveliest – which takes place in the first hour (Mon–Thurs) and Prime Minister's Question Time (Wed only), but they must book in advance with their local MP (ⓣ 020 7219 3000).

Guided tours Throughout the year there are also weekly guided tours (Sat 9.15am–4.30pm; 1hr 15min; £15), with daily ones during the summer opening (Mon–Sat) – in both cases it's a good idea to book in advance (ⓣ 0844 847 1672). All year round, UK residents are entitled to a free guided tour of the palace, as well as up Big Ben (Mon–Fri 9.15am, 11.15am & 2.15pm; 1hr 15min; no under-11s); both need to be organized through your local MP.

Westminster Abbey

Abbey Mon–Thurs & Fri 9.30am–4.30pm, Wed 9.30am–6pm, Sat 9.30am–2.30pm • £16 **Verger tours** Mon–Fri times vary • £3 **Great Cloisters** Daily 8am–6pm • Free **Chapter House & Abbey Museum** Daily 10.30am–4pm • Free **College Garden** Tues–Thurs: April–Sept 10am–6pm; Oct–March 10am–4pm • Free • ⓣ 020 7654 4900, Ⓦ westminster-abbey.org • ⊖ Westminster

The Houses of Parliament dwarf their much older neighbour, **Westminster Abbey**, yet this single building embodies much of the history of England: it has been the venue for all coronations since the time of William the Conqueror, and the site of more or less every royal burial for some five hundred years between the reigns of Henry III and George II. Scores of the nation's most famous citizens are honoured here, too (though many of the stones commemorate people buried elsewhere), and the interior is crammed with hundreds of monuments and statues.

Entry is via the north transept, cluttered with monuments to politicians and traditionally known as **Statesmen's Aisle**, from which you can view the central sanctuary, site of the coronations, and the wonderful **Cosmati floor mosaic**, constructed in the thirteenth century by Italian craftsmen, and often covered by a carpet to protect it.

Lady Chapel

The abbey's most dazzling architectural set piece, the **Lady Chapel**, was added by Henry VII in 1503 as his future resting place. With its intricately carved vaulting and fan-shaped gilded pendants, the chapel represents the final spectacular gasp of the

English Perpendicular style. Look out for Edward I's **Coronation Chair**, a decrepit oak throne dating from around 1300 and still used for coronations.

Poets' Corner

Nowadays, the abbey's royal tombs are upstaged by **Poets' Corner**, in the south transept, though the first occupant, Geoffrey Chaucer, was in fact buried here not because he was a poet, but because he lived nearby. By the eighteenth century this zone had become an artistic pantheon, and since then, the transept has been filled with tributes to all shades of talent.

Great Cloisters and Nave

Doors in the south choir aisle (plus a separate entrance from Dean's Yard) lead to the **Great Cloisters**, rebuilt after a fire in 1298. On the east side lies the octagonal Chapter House, where the House of Commons met from 1257, boasting thirteenth-century apocalyptic wall paintings. Also worth a look is the Abbey Museum, filled with generations of lifelike (but bald) royal funereal effigies.

It's only after exploring the cloisters that you get to see the **nave** itself: narrow, light and, at over a hundred feet in height, by far the tallest in the country. The most famous monument in this section is the **Tomb of the Unknown Soldier**, by the west door, which now serves as the main exit.

Tate Britain

Millbank • Daily 10am–6pm; first Fri of month until 10pm • Free • T 020 7887 8888, W tate.org.uk • ⊖ Pimlico

A purpose-built gallery half a mile south of parliament, founded in 1897 with money from Henry Tate, inventor of the sugar cube, **Tate Britain** is devoted to British art. As well as the collection covering 1500 to the present, the gallery also puts on large-scale temporary exhibitions (for which there is a charge) that showcase British artists.

The pictures are rehung more or less annually, but always include a fair selection of works by British artists such as Hogarth, Constable, Gainsborough, Reynolds and Blake, plus foreign artists like Van Dyck who spent much of their career in Britain. The ever-popular **Pre-Raphaelites** are always well represented, as are established twentieth-century greats such as Stanley Spencer and Francis Bacon alongside living artists such as David Hockney and Lucian Freud. Lastly, don't miss the Tate's outstanding **Turner collection**, displayed in the Clore Gallery.

Westminster Cathedral

Off Victoria St • **Cathedral** Mon–Fri 7am–7pm, Sat 8am–7pm, Sun 8am–8pm • Free **Campanile** Mon–Fri 9.30am–5pm, Sat & Sun 9.30am–6pm • £3 • T 020 7798 9055, W westminstercathedral.org.uk • ⊖ Victoria

Begun in 1895, the stripey neo-Byzantine concoction of the Roman Catholic **Westminster Cathedral** was one of the last and wildest monuments to the Victorian era. It's constructed from more than twelve million terracotta-coloured bricks, decorated with hoops of Portland stone, and culminates in a magnificent tapered campanile which rises to 274ft, served by a lift. The **interior** is only half finished, so to get an idea of what the place will look like when it's finally completed, explore the series of **side chapels** whose rich, multicoloured decor makes use of more than one hundred different marbles from around the world.

St James's

St James's, the exclusive little enclave sandwiched between St James's Park and Piccadilly, was laid out in the 1670s close to St James's Palace. Regal and aristocratic residences

1

TOP 5 QUIRKY MUSEUMS

Dennis Severs' House East End. See p.86
Hunterian Museum Holborn. See p.78
Old Operating Theatre and Herb Garret Southwark. See p.91
Sir John Soane's Museum Holborn. See p.78
Wellcome Collection Bloomsbury. See p.77

overlook Green Park, gentlemen's clubs cluster along Pall Mall and St James's Street, while jacket-and-tie restaurants and expense-account gentlemen's outfitters line Jermyn Street. Hardly surprising then that most Londoners rarely stray into this area. Plenty of folk, however, frequent **St James's Park**, with large numbers heading for the Queen's chief residence, **Buckingham Palace**, and the adjacent Queen's Gallery and Royal Mews.

The Mall

Laid out as a memorial to Queen Victoria, the tree-lined sweep of **The Mall** is at its best on Sundays, when it's closed to traffic. The bombastic **Admiralty Arch** was erected to mark the entrance at the Trafalgar Square end of The Mall, while at the Buckingham Palace end stands the ludicrous **Victoria Memorial**, Edward VII's overblown 2300-ton marble tribute to his mother, which is topped by a gilded statue of Victory. Six outlying allegorical groups in bronze confidently proclaim the great achievements of her reign.

St James's Park

Flanking nearly the whole length of the Mall, **St James's Park** is the oldest of the royal parks, having been drained and enclosed for hunting purposes by Henry VIII. It was landscaped by Nash in the 1820s, and today its lake is a favourite picnic spot. Pelicans can still be seen at the eastern end of the lake, and there are exotic ducks, swans and geese aplenty.

Buckingham Palace

Late July to early Oct daily 9.45am–6.30pm • £17.50, advance booking fee £1.25 • ⓣ 020 7766 7300, ⓦ royalcollection.org.uk • ⊖ Green Park

The graceless colossus of **Buckingham Palace**, popularly known as "Buck House", has served as the monarch's permanent London residence only since the accession of Victoria. Bought by George III in 1762, the building was overhauled in the late 1820s by Nash and again in 1913, producing a palace that's as bland as it's possible to be.

For two months of the year, the hallowed portals are grudgingly nudged open. The interior, however, is a bit of an anticlimax: of the palace's 660 rooms you're permitted to see twenty or so, and there's little sign of life, as the Queen decamps to Scotland every summer. For the other ten months there's little to do here – not that this deters the crowds who mill around the railings, and gather in some force to watch the **Changing of the Guard** (see p.63), in which a detachment of the Queen's Foot Guards marches to appropriate martial music from St James's Palace (unless it rains, that is).

Queen's Gallery

Buckingham Palace Rd • Daily 10am–5.30pm • £9 • ⓣ 020 7766 7301, ⓦ royalcollection.org.uk • ⊖ Victoria

A Doric portico on the south side of Buckingham Palace forms the entrance to the **Queen's Gallery**, which puts on temporary exhibitions drawn from the **Royal Collection**, a superlative array of art that includes works by Michelangelo, Raphael, Holbein, Reynolds, Gainsborough, Vermeer, Van Dyck, Rubens, Rembrandt and Canaletto, as well as the world's largest collection of Leonardo drawings, the odd Fabergé egg and heaps of Sèvres china.

Royal Mews

Buckingham Palace Rd • Jan–March Mon–Fri 11am–4pm; April–Oct daily 10am–5pm; Nov & Dec 10am–4pm • £8 • 020 7766 7302, royalcollection.org.uk • Victoria

Royal carriages are the main attraction at the Nash-built **Royal Mews**, in particular the Gold Carriage, made for George III in 1762, smothered in 22-carat gilding and weighing four tons, its axles supporting four life-size figures.

St James's Palace

Chapel Royal Oct to Easter Sun services 8.30am & 11.15am **Queen's Chapel** Easter–July Sun 8.30am & 11.15am • Green Park

St James's Palace's main red-brick gate-tower is pretty much all that remains of the Tudor palace erected here by Henry VIII. When Whitehall Palace burned down in 1698, St James's became the principal royal residence and, in keeping with tradition, an ambassador to the UK is still accredited to the "Court of St James's", even though the court has since moved down the road to Buckingham Palace. The modest, rambling, crenellated complex is off-limits to the public, with the exception of the **Chapel Royal**, situated within the palace, and the **Queen's Chapel**, on the other side of Marlborough Road; both are open for services only.

Clarence House

Stable Yard Rd • Aug Mon–Fri 10am–4pm, Sat & Sun 10am–5.30pm; visits (by guided tour) must be booked in advance • £8.50 • 020 7766 7303, royalcollection.org.uk • Green Park

Clarence House, connected to the palace's southwest wing, was home to the Queen Mother, and now serves as the official London home of Charles and his second wife Camilla, but a handful of rooms can be visited over the summer when the royals are in Scotland. The rooms are pretty unremarkable, so apart from a peek behind the scenes in a working royal palace, or a few mementoes of the Queen Mum, the main draw is the twentieth-century British paintings on display by the likes of Walter Sickert and Augustus John.

Mayfair

Piccadilly, which forms the southern border of swanky **Mayfair**, may not be the fashionable promenade it started out as in the eighteenth century, but a whiff of exclusivity still pervades **Bond Street** and its tributaries, where designer clothes emporia jostle for space with jewellers, bespoke tailors and fine art dealers. **Regent Street** and **Oxford Street**, meanwhile, are home to the flagship branches of the country's most popular chain stores.

Piccadilly Circus

Anonymous and congested it may be, but **Piccadilly Circus** is, for many Londoners, the nearest their city comes to having a centre. A much-altered product of Nash's grand 1812 Regent Street plan and now a major traffic interchange, it may not be a picturesque place, but thanks to its celebrated aluminium statue, popularly known as **Eros**, it's prime tourist territory.

The fountain's archer is one of the city's top attractions, a status that baffles all who live here. Despite the bow and arrow, it's not the god of love at all but his lesser-known brother, Anteros, god of unrequited love, commemorating the selfless philanthropic love of the Earl of Shaftesbury, a Bible-thumping social reformer who campaigned against child labour.

1

OXFORD STREET: THE BUSIEST STREET IN EUROPE

As wealthy Londoners began to move out of the City in the eighteenth century in favour of the newly developed West End, so **Oxford Street** – the old Roman road to Oxford – gradually became London's main shopping thoroughfare. Today, despite successive recessions and sky-high rents, Oxford Street remains Europe's busiest street, simply because this two-mile hotchpotch of shops is home to (often several) flagship branches of Britain's major retailers. The street's only real landmark store is **Selfridges** (see p.130) opened in 1909 with a facade featuring the Queen of Time riding the ship of commerce and supporting an Art Deco clock.

Regent Street

Regent Street, drawn up by John Nash in 1812 as both a luxury shopping street and a triumphal way between George IV's Carlton House and Regent's Park, was the city's earliest attempt at dealing with traffic congestion, slum clearance and planned social segregation, something that would later be perfected by the Victorians. The increase in the purchasing power of the city's middle classes in the last century brought the tone of the street "down" and heavyweight stores now predominate. Among the best known are **Hamley's**, reputedly the world's largest toyshop, and **Liberty**, the upmarket department store that popularized Arts and Crafts designs.

Piccadilly

Piccadilly apparently got its name from the ruffs or "pickadills" worn by the dandies who used to promenade here in the late seventeenth century. It's no place for promenading in its current state, however, with traffic careering down it nose to tail most of the day and night. Infinitely more pleasant places to window-shop are the various **nineteenth-century arcades** that shoot off to the north, originally built to protect shoppers from the mud and horse dung on the streets, but now equally useful for escaping exhaust fumes.

Royal Academy of Arts

Piccadilly • Sat–Thurs 10am–6pm, Fri 10am–10pm • £10–12 • ⓣ 020 7300 8000, ⓦ royalacademy.org.uk • ⊖ Green Park

The **Royal Academy of Arts** occupies one of the few surviving aristocratic mansions that once lined the north side of Piccadilly. The country's first-ever formal art school, founded in 1768, the RA hosts a wide range of art exhibitions, and an annual **Summer Exhibition** that remains an essential stop on the social calendar of upper-middle-class England. Anyone can enter paintings in any style, and the lucky winners get hung, in rather close proximity, and sold. RA "Academicians" are allowed to display six of their own works – no matter how awful. The result is a bewildering display, which gets panned annually by highbrow critics.

Bond Street

While Oxford Street, Regent Street and Piccadilly have all gone downmarket, **Bond Street**, which runs parallel with Regent Street, has carefully maintained its exclusivity. It is, in fact, two streets rolled into one: the southern half, laid out in the 1680s, is known as Old Bond Street; its northern extension, which followed less than fifty years later, is known as New Bond Street. They are both pretty unassuming streets architecturally, yet the shops that line them are among the flashiest in London, dominated by perfumeries, jewellers and designer clothing stores. In addition to fashion, Bond Street is also renowned for its fine art galleries and its **auction houses**, the oldest of which is Sotheby's, 34–35 New Bond St, whose viewing galleries are open free of charge.

Marylebone

Marylebone, which lies to the north of Oxford Street, is, like Mayfair, another grid-plan Georgian development – a couple of social and real-estate leagues below its neighbour, but a wealthy area nevertheless. It boasts a very fine art gallery, the **Wallace Collection**, and, in its northern fringes, one of London's biggest tourist attractions, **Madame Tussauds**, the oldest and largest wax museum in the world.

Wallace Collection

Manchester Square • Daily 10am–5pm • Free • ⓣ 020 7563 9500, ⓦ wallacecollection.org • ⊖ Bond Street

Housed in a miniature eighteenth-century chateau, the splendid **Wallace Collection** is best known for its eighteenth-century French paintings, Franz Hals' *Laughing Cavalier*, Titian's *Perseus and Andromeda*, Velázquez's *Lady with a Fan* and Rembrandt's affectionate portrait of his teenage son, Titus. The museum has preserved the feel of a grand stately home, its exhibits piled high in glass cabinets, and paintings covering every inch of wall space. The fact that these exhibits are set amid period fittings – and a bloody great armoury – makes the place even more remarkable.

Madame Tussauds

Marylebone Rd • Mon–Fri 9.30am–5.30pm, Sat & Sun 9am–6pm • Online tickets from £26 • ⓣ 0871 894 3000, ⓦ madametussauds.com • ⊖ Baker Street

Madame Tussauds has been pulling in the crowds ever since the good lady arrived in London from Paris in 1802 bearing the sculpted heads of guillotined aristocrats. The entrance fee might be extortionate, the waxwork likenesses of the famous occasionally dubious and the attempts to relieve you of yet more cash relentless, but you can still rely on finding London's biggest queues here (book online to avoid waiting). You can choose to opt out of the Chamber of Horrors Live show, a piece of hokum designed to frighten the living daylights out of tourists.

Soho

Bounded by Regent Street to the west, Oxford Street to the north and Charing Cross Road to the east, **Soho** is very much the heart of the West End. It's been the city's premier red-light district for centuries and retains an unorthodox and slightly raffish air that's unique for central London. It has an immigrant history as rich as that of the East End and a louche nightlife that has attracted writers and revellers of every sexual persuasion since the eighteenth century. Today it's a very upfront gay enclave, especially around **Old Compton Street**. Conventional sights in Soho are few, yet there's probably more street life here than anywhere in the city centre, whatever the hour. Most folk head to Soho to go the cinema or theatre, and to have a drink or a bite to eat in the innumerable bars, cafés and restaurants that pepper the area, which includes **Chinatown** in the south.

Leicester Square

When the big cinemas and discos are doing good business, and the buskers are entertaining the crowds, **Leicester Square** is one of the most crowded places in London, particularly on a Friday or Saturday when huge numbers of tourists and half the youth of the suburbs seem to congregate here. It wasn't until the mid-nineteenth century that the square actually began to emerge as an entertainment zone; cinema moved in during the 1930s, a golden age evoked by the sleek black lines of the Odeon on the east side.

Chinatown

Chinatown, hemmed in between Leicester Square and Shaftesbury Avenue, is a self-contained jumble of shops, cafés and restaurants. Only a minority of London's Chinese live in these three small blocks, but it remains a focus for the community, a place to do business or the weekly shop, celebrate a wedding, or just meet up for meals, particularly on Sundays, when the restaurants overflow with Chinese families tucking into dim sum. **Gerrard Street** is the main drag, with telephone kiosks rigged out as pagodas and fake oriental gates or *paifang*.

Old Compton Street

If Soho has a main road, it has to be **Old Compton Street**, which runs parallel with Shaftesbury Avenue. The corner shops, peep shows, boutiques and trendy cafés here are typical of the area and a good barometer of the latest fads. Soho has been a permanent fixture on the **gay scene** for the better part of a century, and you'll find a profusion of gay bars, clubs and cafés jostling for position here and round the corner in Wardour Street.

Covent Garden

More sanitized and commercial than neighbouring Soho, the shops and restaurants of **Covent Garden** today are a far cry from the district's heyday when the piazza was the great playground (and red-light district) of eighteenth-century London. The buskers in front of St Paul's Church, the theatres round about, and the **Royal Opera House** on Bow Street are survivors of this tradition, and on a balmy summer evening, **Covent Garden Piazza** is still an undeniably lively place to be.

Covent Garden Piazza

London's oldest planned square, laid out in the 1630s by Inigo Jones, **Covent Garden Piazza** was initially a great success, its novelty value alone attracting a rich and aristocratic clientele, but over the next century the tone of the place fell as the fruit and vegetable market expanded, and theatres and coffee houses began to take over the peripheral buildings. When the market closed in 1974, the piazza narrowly survived being turned into an office development. Instead, the elegant Victorian market hall and its environs were restored to house shops, restaurants and arts-and-crafts stalls. Of Jones's original piazza, the only remaining parts are the two rebuilt sections of north-side arcading, and **St Paul's Church**, to the west.

London Transport Museum

Covent Garden Piazza • Sat–Wed 10am–6pm, Fri 11am–6pm • Adults £13.50, under-16s free • ☎ 020 7379 6344, 🌐 ltmuseum.co.uk • ⊖ Covent Garden

A former flower-market shed on Covent Garden Piazza's east side is home to the **London Transport Museum**, a sure-fire hit for families with kids under 10. To follow the displays chronologically, head for Level 2, where you'll find a reconstructed 1829 Shillibeer's Horse Omnibus, which provided the city's first regular horse-bus service. Level 1 tells the story of the world's first underground system and contains a lovely 1920s Metropolitan Line carriage in burgundy and green with pretty, drooping lamps. On the ground floor, one double-decker **tram** is all that's left to pay tribute to the world's largest tram system, dismantled in 1952. Look out, too, for the first **tube** train, from the 1890s, whose lack of windows earned it the nickname "the padded cell".

CLOCKWISE FROM TOP LEFT NEAL'S YARD, COVENT GARDEN (P.116); BALLERINA STATUE, BROAD COURT; LIBERTY (P.130); THE NATURAL HISTORY MUSEUM (P.97) >

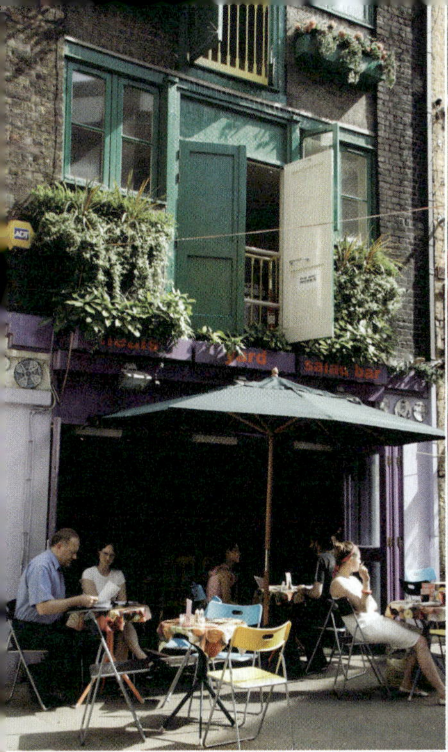

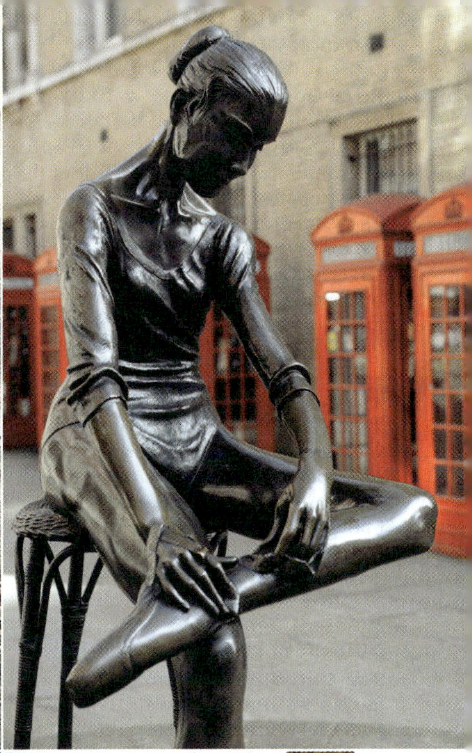

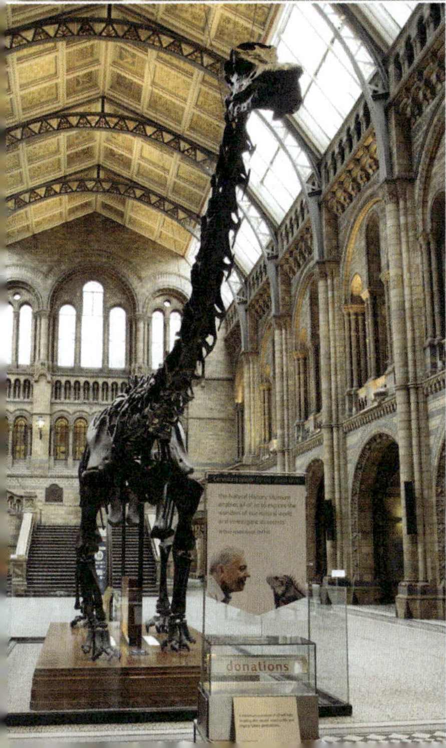
donations

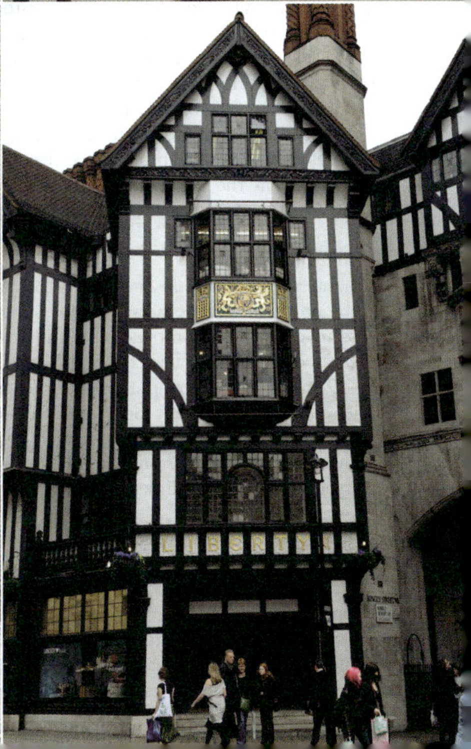
LIBERTY

Royal Opera House

Bow St • **Floral Hall** Daily 10am–3.30pm • Free **Backstage tours** Mon–Fri 10.30am, 12.30pm & 2.30pm, Sat 10.30am, 11.30am, 12.30pm & 1.30pm • £10 • T 020 7212 9389, W royaloperahouse.org • Covent Garden

The arcading on the northeast side of the piazza was rebuilt as part of the redevelopment of the **Royal Opera House**, whose main Neoclassical facade dates from 1811 and opens onto Bow Street. Now, however, you can reach the opera house from a passageway in the corner of the arcading. The spectacular wrought-iron **Floral Hall** serves as the opera house's main foyer, and is open to the public, as is the *Amphitheatre* bar/restaurant (from 90min before performance to the end of the last interval), which has a glorious terrace overlooking the piazza.

Strand

Once famous for its riverside mansions, and later its music halls, the **Strand** – the main road connecting Westminster to the City – is a shadow of its former self. One of the few vestiges of glamour is **The Savoy**, London's grandest hotel, built in 1889 on the site of the medieval Savoy Palace on the south side of the street. As its name suggests, the Strand once lay along the riverbank until the Victorians shored up the banks of the Thames to create the Embankment.

Somerset House

Strand • **Courtyard** Daily 7.30am–11pm • Free **Riverside terrace** Daily 8am–6pm • Free **Embankment galleries** Daily 10am–6pm • £6 • T 020 7845 4600, W somersethouse.org.uk • Temple or Covent Garden

Somerset House is the sole survivor of the grandiose river palaces that once lined the Strand. Although it looks like an old aristocratic mansion, the present building was purpose-built in 1776 to house government offices. Nowadays, Somerset House's granite-paved courtyard, which has a 55-jet **fountain** that spouts little syncopated dances straight from the cobbles, is used for open-air performances, concerts, installations and, in winter, an ice rink.

The south wing has a lovely riverside terrace with a café-restaurant and the **Embankment Galleries**, which host innovative special exhibitions on contemporary art and design. You can also admire the Royal Naval Commissioners' superb gilded eighteenth-century barge in the **King's Barge House**, below ground level in the south wing.

Courtauld Gallery

Daily 10am–6pm • £6, free Mon 10am–2pm • T 020 7848 2526, W courtauld.ac.uk • Temple or Covent Garden

In the north wing of Somerset House is the **Courtauld Gallery**, chiefly known for its dazzling collection of Impressionist and Post-Impressionist paintings. Among the most celebrated is a small-scale version of Manet's *Déjeuner sur l'herbe*, Renoir's *La Loge*, and Degas' *Two Dancers*, plus a whole heap of Cézanne's canvases, including one of his series of *Card Players*. The Courtauld also boasts a fine selection of works by the likes of Rubens, Van Dyck, Tiepolo and Cranach the Elder, and has recently been augmented by the long-term loan of a hundred top-notch twentieth-century paintings and sculptures by, among others, Kandinksy, Matisse, Dufy, Derain, Rodin and Henry Moore.

Bloomsbury

Bloomsbury was built over in grid-plan style from the 1660s onwards, and the formal bourgeois Georgian squares laid out then remain the area's main distinguishing feature. In the twentieth century, Bloomsbury acquired a reputation as the city's most learned quarter, dominated by the dual institutions of the **British Museum** and **London**

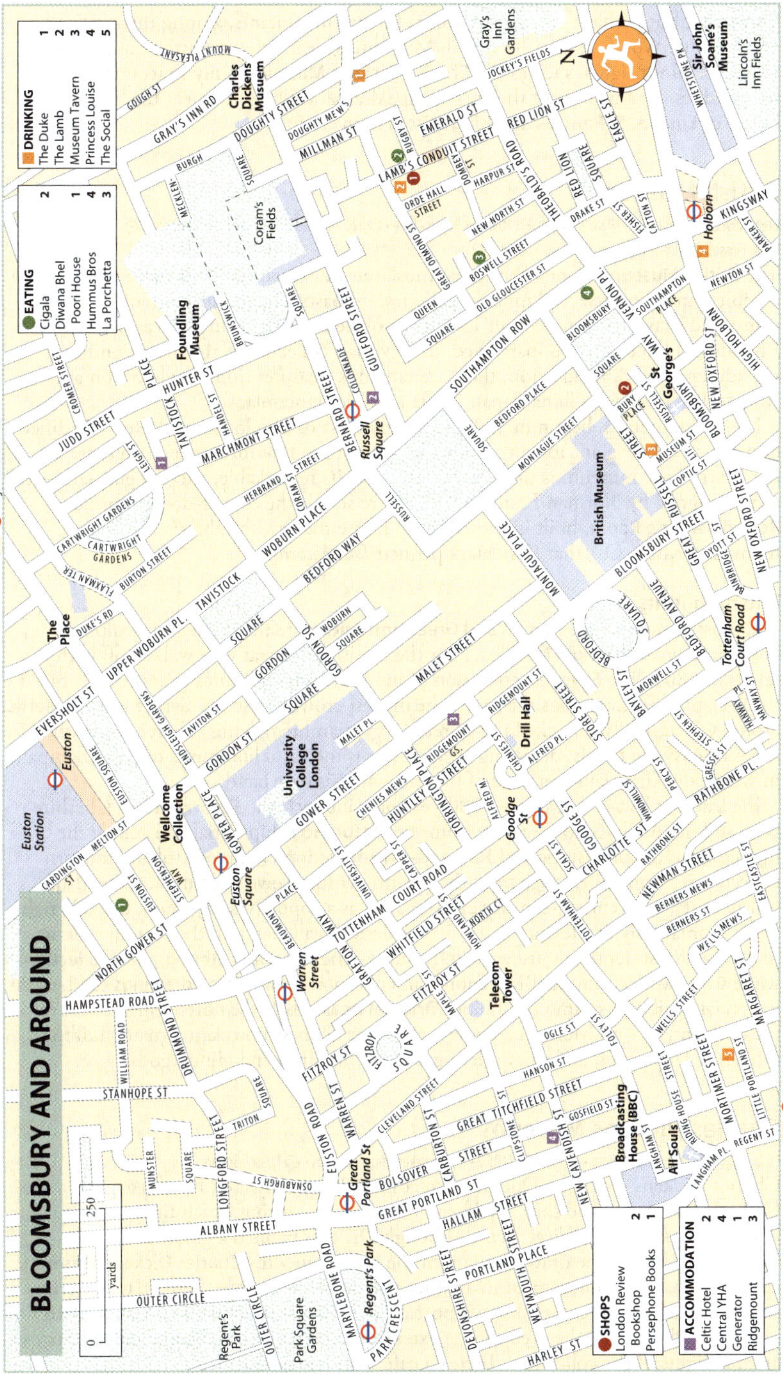
BLOOMSBURY AND AROUND
EATING
Cigala 2
Diwana Bhel 1
Poori House 4
Hummus Bros 3
La Porchetta
DRINKING
The Duke 1
The Lamb 2
Museum Tavern 3
Princess Louise 4
The Social 5
SHOPS
London Review Bookshop 2
Persephone Books 1
ACCOMMODATION
Celtic Hotel 2
Central YHA 4
Generator 1
Ridgemount 3
0 250 yards
British Museum
University College London
Euston Station
Wellcome Collection
Foundling Museum
Charles Dickens Museum
Sir John Soane's Museum
Telecom Tower
Broadcasting House (BBC)
All Souls
King's Cross & St Pancras
Oxford Circus

1

University, but perhaps best known for its literary inhabitants, among them T.S. Eliot and Virginia Woolf. Today, the British Museum is clearly the star attraction, but there are other minor sights, such as the **Charles Dickens Museum**. Only in its northern fringes does the character of the area change dramatically, as you near the hustle and bustle of **Euston**, **St Pancras** and **King's Cross** train stations.

British Museum

Great Russell St • Sat–Thurs 10am–5.30pm, Fri 10am–8.30pm • Free • ⓣ 020 7323 8000, ⓦ britishmuseum.org • ⊖ Tottenham Court Road, Russell Square or Holborn

The **British Museum** is one of the great museums of the world. With more than 70,000 exhibits ranged over several miles of galleries, it boasts a huge collection of antiquities, prints and drawings – more than 13 million objects (and growing). Its assortment of Roman and Greek art is unparalleled, its Egyptian collection is the most significant outside Egypt and, in addition, there are fabulous treasures from Anglo-Saxon and Roman Britain, from China, Japan, India and Mesopotamia.

The building itself, begun in 1823, is the grandest of London's Greek Revival edifices, dominated by the giant Ionian colonnade and portico that forms the main entrance. At the heart of the museum is the **Great Court**, with its remarkable, curving glass-and-steel roof, designed by Norman Foster. At the centre stands the copper-domed former **Round Reading Room**, built in the 1850s to house the British Library. It was here, reputedly at desk O7, that Karl Marx penned *Das Kapital*.

The highlights

The most famous of the **Roman and Greek antiquities** are the Parthenon sculptures, better known as the **Elgin Marbles**, after the British aristocrat who walked off with the reliefs in 1801. The **Egyptian collection** of monumental sculptures is impressive, but it's the ever-popular **mummies** that draw the biggest crowds. Also on display is the **Rosetta Stone**, which finally unlocked the secret of Egyptian hieroglyphs. There's a splendid series of **Assyrian reliefs**, depicting events such as the royal lion hunts of Ashurbanipal, in which the king slaughters one of the cats with his bare hands.

The leathery half-corpse of the 2000-year-old **Lindow Man**, discovered in a Cheshire bog, and the Anglo-Saxon treasure from the **Sutton Hoo** ship burial, are among the highlights of the prehistoric and Romano-British section. The medieval and modern collections, meanwhile, range from the twelfth-century **Lewis chessmen**, carved from walrus ivory, to twentieth-century exhibits such as a copper vase by Frank Lloyd Wright.

The dramatically lit Mexican and North American galleries, plus the African galleries in the basement, represent just a small fraction of the museum's **ethnographic collection**, while select works from the BM's enormous collection of **prints and drawings** can be seen in special exhibitions. Among fabulous **Oriental treasures** in the north wing, closest to the back entrance on Montague Place, are ancient Chinese porcelain, ornate snuffboxes, miniature landscapes, and a bewildering array of Buddhist and Hindu gods.

Charles Dickens Museum

48 Doughty St • Daily 10am–5pm • £7 • ⓣ 020 7405 2127, ⓦ dickensmuseum.com • ⊖ Russell Square

Charles Dickens moved to Doughty Street in 1837, shortly after his marriage to Catherine Hogarth, and they lived here for two years, during which time he wrote *Nicholas Nickleby* and *Oliver Twist*. Although Dickens painted a gloomy Victorian world in his books, the drawing room in the house, now the **Charles Dickens Museum**, appears to have been decorated in a rather upbeat Regency style. Letters, manuscripts and first editions, his earliest known portrait (a miniature painted by his aunt in 1830) and the reading copies he used during extensive lecture tours in Britain and the States are highlights of the collection. There's a café with free wi-fi.

Wellcome Collection

183 Euston Rd • Tues–Sat 10am–6pm, Thurs until 8pm, Sun 11am–6pm • Free • 020 7611 2222, wellcomecollection.org • Euston or Euston Square

The **Wellcome Collection** puts on thought-provoking exhibitions on topical scientific issues on the ground floor, where you'll also find an excellent café and bookshop. On the first floor, the permanent collection begins with **Medicine Now**, which focuses on contemporary medical concerns such as genomes, obesity and malaria. The unmissable **Medicine Man** exhibit, meanwhile, showcases the weird and wonderful collection of artefacts amassed by the American-born pharmaceutical magnate Henry Wellcome (1853–1936) – from Florence Nightingale's moccasins to a sign for a Chinese doctor's which is hung with human teeth.

British Library

96 Euston Rd • Mon & Wed–Fri 9.30am–6pm, Tues 9.30am–8pm, Sat 9.30am–5pm, Sun 11am–5pm • Free • 020 7412 7332, bl.uk • King's Cross

As one of the country's most expensive public buildings, the **British Library** took flak from all sides during its protracted construction. Yet while it's true that the building's red-brick brutalism is horribly unfashionable, and compares unfavourably with its cathedralesque Victorian neighbour, the *St Pancras Renaissance Hotel* (see p.113) the library's interior has met with general approval, and the exhibition galleries are superb.

With the exception of the reading rooms, the library is open to the public and puts on a wide variety of exhibitions and events, and has several cafés, a restaurant and free wi-fi. In the John Ritblat Gallery a selection of the BL's ancient manuscripts, maps, documents and precious books, including the richly illustrated Lindisfarne Gospels, is on display. You can also turn the pages of various texts – from the Mercator's 1570s atlas of Europe to Leonardo da Vinci's notebook – on touch-screen computers.

Holborn

Holborn, on the periphery of the financial district of the City, has long been associated with the law, and its **Inns of Court** make for an interesting stroll, their archaic, cobbled precincts exuding the rarefied atmosphere of an Oxbridge college, and sheltering one of the city's oldest churches, the twelfth-century **Temple Church**. Close by the Inns is the **Sir John Soane's Museum**, one of the most memorable and enjoyable of London's small museums, packed with architectural illusions and an eclectic array of curios.

Temple

Temple is the largest and most complex of the Inns of Court, where every barrister in England must study before being called to the Bar. A few very old buildings survive here and the maze of courtyards and passageways is fun to explore.

Middle Temple Hall

Mon–Fri 10–11.30am & 3–4pm, phone to check access • Free • 020 7427 4800 • Temple or Blackfriars

Medieval students ate, attended lectures and slept in the **Middle Temple Hall**, across the courtyard, still the Inn's main dining room. The present building, constructed in the 1560s, provided the setting for many great Elizabethan masques and plays – probably including Shakespeare's *Twelfth Night*, which is believed to have been premiered here in 1602. The hall is worth a visit for its fine hammer-beam roof, wooden panelling and decorative Elizabethan screen.

1

Temple Church

Usually Mon–Fri 2–4pm, but times vary • £3 • ⓣ 020 7353 3470, ⓦ templechurch.com • ⊖ Temple or Blackfriars

The complex's oldest building is **Temple Church**, built in 1185 by the Knights Templar, and modelled on the Church of the Holy Sepulchre in Jerusalem. The interior features striking Purbeck marble piers, recumbent marble effigies of medieval knights and tortured grotesques grimacing in the spandrels of the blind arcading. The church makes an appearance in both the book and the film of Dan Brown's *The Da Vinci Code*.

Hunterian Museum

35–43 Lincoln Inn Fields • Tues–Sat 10am–5pm • Free • ⓣ 020 7869 6560, ⓦ rcseng.ac.uk • ⊖ Holborn

The **Hunterian Museum**, on the first floor of the imposing Royal College of Surgeons building, contains the unique specimen collection of the surgeon-scientist John Hunter (1728–93). The centrepiece is the Crystal Gallery, a wall of jars of pickled skeletons and body pieces – from the gall bladder of a puffer fish to the thyroid of a dromedary – prepared by Hunter himself. Among the most prized exhibits are the skeleton of the "Irish giant", Charles Byrne (1761–83), who was 7ft 10 inches tall, and the Sicilian dwarf Caroline Crachami (1815–24), who stood at just over 1ft 10 1/2 inches when she died at the age of nine.

Sir John Soane's Museum

13 Lincoln's Inn Fields • Tues–Sat 10am–5pm, first Tues of the month candlelit 6–9pm • Free • Guided tour Sat 11am • £3 • ⓣ 020 7405 2107, ⓦ soane.org • ⊖ Holborn

A group of buildings on the north side of Lincoln's Inn Fields houses the fascinating **Sir John Soane's Museum**. Soane (1753–1837), a bricklayer's son who rose to be architect of the Bank of England, was an avid collector who designed this house not only as a home and office, but also as a place to stash his large collection of art and antiquities. Arranged much as it was in his lifetime, the ingeniously planned house has an informal, treasure-hunt atmosphere, with surprises in every alcove. Note that the museum is very popular and you may have to queue to get in – and get here early if you want to go on a guided tour or on a candlelit evening.

The City

The City is where London began. Long established as the financial district, it stretches from Temple Bar in the west to the Tower of London in the east – administrative boundaries that are only slightly larger than those marked by the Roman walls and their medieval successors. However, in this Square Mile (as the City is sometimes referred to), you'll find few leftovers of London's early days, since four-fifths of the area burnt down in the Great Fire of 1666. Rebuilt in brick and stone, the City gradually lost its centrality as London swelled westwards, though it has maintained its position as Britain's financial

CLERKENWELL, HOXTON AND SHOREDITCH

Since the 1990s, the northern fringe of the City has been colonized by artists, designers and architects and transformed itself into the city's most vibrant artistic enclave, peppered with contemporary art galleries and a whole host of very cool bars, restaurants and clubs. **Clerkenwell**, to the west, is the most thoroughly gentrified, whereas **Hoxton** (to the north of Old Street), and to a lesser extent **Shoreditch** (to the south), have a grittier side to them. There are few conventional sights as such in all three areas, though Hoxton and Shoreditch are stuffed full of art galleries (most famously the White Cube on Hoxton Square), but their hip nightlife and shopping scenes keep them lively.

heartland. What you see now is mostly the product of three fairly recent building phases: the Victorian construction boom; the overzealous postwar reconstruction following the Blitz; and the building frenzy that began in the 1980s and has continued ever since.

When you consider what has happened here, it's amazing that so much has survived to pay witness to the City's 2000-year history. Wren's spires still punctuate the skyline and his masterpiece, **St Paul's Cathedral**, remains one of London's geographical pivots. At the City's eastern edge, the **Tower of London** still boasts some of the best-preserved medieval fortifications in Europe. Other relics, such as Wren's **Monument** to the Great Fire and London's oldest synagogue and church, are less conspicuous, and even locals have problems finding modern attractions like the **Museum of London** and the **Barbican** arts complex.

Fleet Street

Fleet Street's associations with the printed press began in 1500, when Wynkyn de Worde, William Caxton's apprentice, moved the Caxton presses here from Westminster to be close to the lawyers of the Inns of Court (his best customers) and to the clergy of St Paul's. In 1702, the world's first daily newspaper, the now defunct **Daily Courant**, began publishing here, and by the nineteenth century, all the major national and provincial dailies had moved their presses to the area. Then in 1985, Britain's first colour tabloid, *Today*, appeared, using computer technology that rendered the Fleet Street presses obsolete. It was left to media tycoon Rupert Murdoch to take on the printers' unions in a bitter year-long dispute that changed the newspaper industry for ever. The press headquarters that once dominated the area have all now relocated, leaving just a handful of small publications and a few architectural landmarks to testify to 500 years of printing history.

St Bride's Church

Fleet St • Mon–Fri 8am–6pm, Sat 11am–3pm, Sun 10am–6.30pm • Free • Ⓣ 020 7427 0133, Ⓦ stbrides.com • ⊖ St Paul's

To find out more about Fleet Street's history, check out the exhibition in the crypt of **St Bride's Church**, the "journalists' and printers' cathedral", situated behind the former Reuters building. The church also features Wren's tallest, and most exquisite, spire (said to be the inspiration for the traditional tiered wedding cake).

St Paul's Cathedral

Mon–Sat 8.30am–4.30pm • £14.50 • Ⓣ 020 7236 4128, Ⓦ stpauls.co.uk • ⊖ St Paul's

Designed by Christopher Wren and completed in 1711, **St Paul's Cathedral** remains a dominating presence in the City, despite the encroaching tower blocks. Topped by an enormous lead-covered dome, its showpiece west facade is particularly magnificent.

TOP 5 CITY CHURCHES

The City of London is crowded with **churches** (Ⓦ london-city-churches.org.uk), the majority of them built or rebuilt by Wren after the Great Fire. Weekday lunchtimes are a good time to visit, when many put on free lunchtime concerts of classical and chamber music.

St Bartholomew-the-Great Cloth Fair; ⊖ Barbican. The oldest surviving pre-Fire church in the City and by far the most atmospheric.

St Mary Abchurch Abchurch Lane; ⊖ Cannon Street or Bank. Unique among Wren's City churches for its huge, painted, domed ceiling, plus the only authenticated reredos by Grinling Gibbons.

St Mary Aldermary Queen Victoria St; ⊖ Mansion House. Wren's most successful stab at Gothic, with fan vaulting in the aisles and a panelled ceiling in the nave.

St Mary Woolnoth Lombard St; ⊖ Bank. Hawksmoor's only City church, sporting an unusually broad, bulky tower and a Baroque clerestory that floods the church with light from its semicircular windows.

St Stephen Walbrook Walbrook; ⊖ Bank. Wren's dress rehearsal for St Paul's, with a wonderful central dome and plenty of original woodcarving.

1

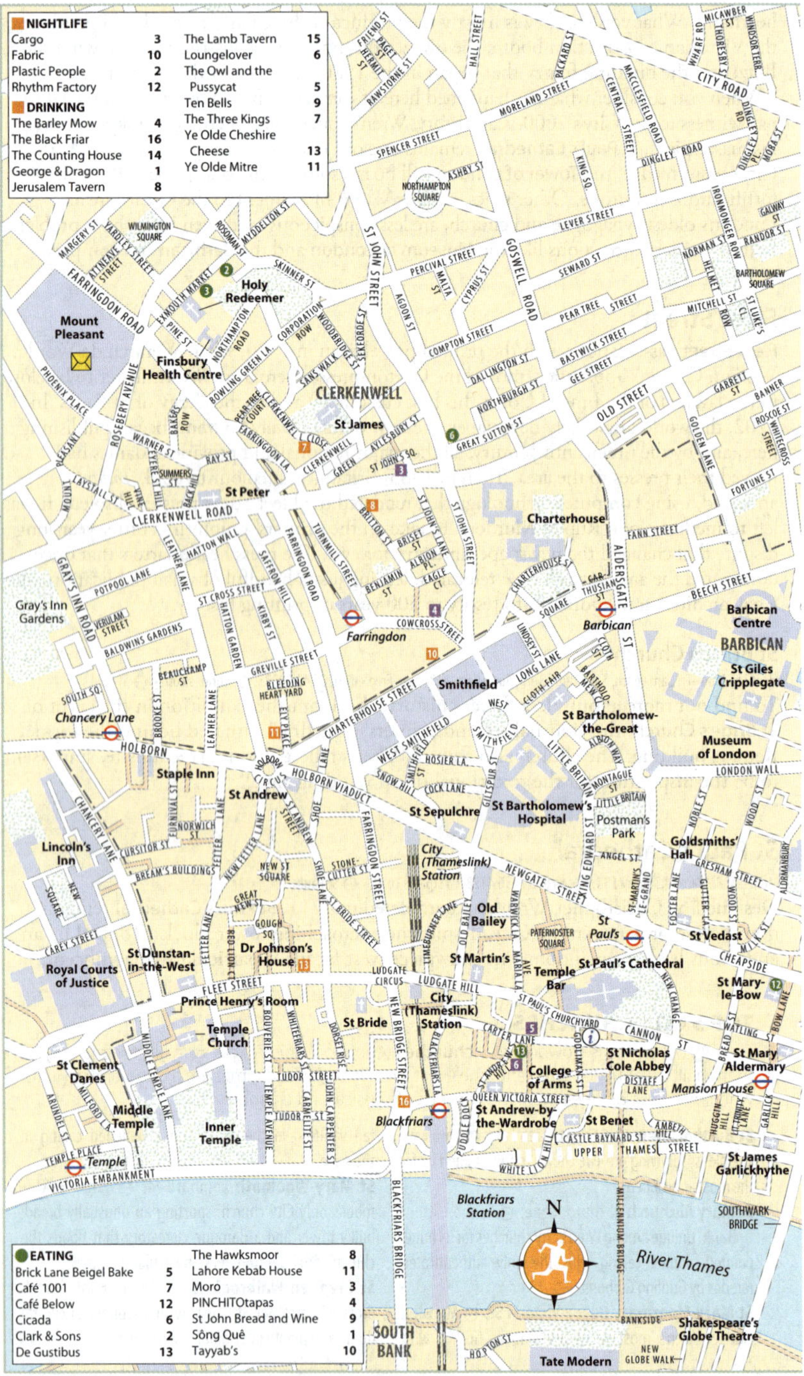
NIGHTLIFE
Cargo 3
Fabric 10
Plastic People 2
Rhythm Factory 12
DRINKING
The Barley Mow 4
The Black Friar 16
The Counting House 14
George & Dragon 1
Jerusalem Tavern 8
The Lamb Tavern 15
Loungelover 6
The Owl and the Pussycat 5
Ten Bells 9
The Three Kings 7
Ye Olde Cheshire Cheese 13
Ye Olde Mitre 11
EATING
Brick Lane Beigel Bake 5
Café 1001 7
Café Below 12
Cicada 6
Clark & Sons 2
De Gustibus 13
The Hawksmoor 8
Lahore Kebab House 11
Moro 3
PINCHITOtapas 4
St John Bread and Wine 9
Sông Quê 1
Tayyab's 10
CLERKENWELL
BARBICAN
Mount Pleasant
Holy Redeemer
Finsbury Health Centre
St James
St Peter
Charterhouse
Barbican Centre
St Giles Cripplegate
Museum of London
Smithfield
St Bartholomew-the-Great
St Bartholomew's Hospital
Postman's Park
Goldsmiths' Hall
St Sepulchre
Staple Inn
St Andrew
Gray's Inn Gardens
Lincoln's Inn
Old Bailey
St Martin's
Temple Bar
St Paul's Cathedral
St Vedast
St Mary-le-Bow
St Mary Aldermary
St Nicholas Cole Abbey
College of Arms
St Andrew-by-the-Wardrobe
St Benet
St James Garlickhythe
Dr Johnson's House
St Dunstan-in-the-West
Royal Courts of Justice
Prince Henry's Room
Temple Church
St Bride
St Clement Danes
Middle Temple
Inner Temple
City (Thameslink) Station
Blackfriars Station
Shakespeare's Globe Theatre
Tate Modern
SOUTH BANK
River Thames
Farringdon
Barbican
Chancery Lane
St Paul's
Mansion House
Blackfriars
Temple
Bloomsbury
FARRINGDON ROAD
CLERKENWELL ROAD
ST JOHN STREET
GOSWELL ROAD
OLD STREET
CITY ROAD
ALDERSGATE ST
HOLBORN
HOLBORN VIADUCT
NEWGATE STREET
CHEAPSIDE
FLEET STREET
LUDGATE HILL
QUEEN VICTORIA STREET
UPPER THAMES STREET
VICTORIA EMBANKMENT
BLACKFRIARS BRIDGE
MILLENNIUM BRIDGE
SOUTHWARK BRIDGE
LONDON WALL
BEECH STREET
CHARTERHOUSE STREET
GRAY'S INN ROAD
CHANCERY LANE
NEW BRIDGE STREET
FARRINGDON STREET
CANNON ST
N

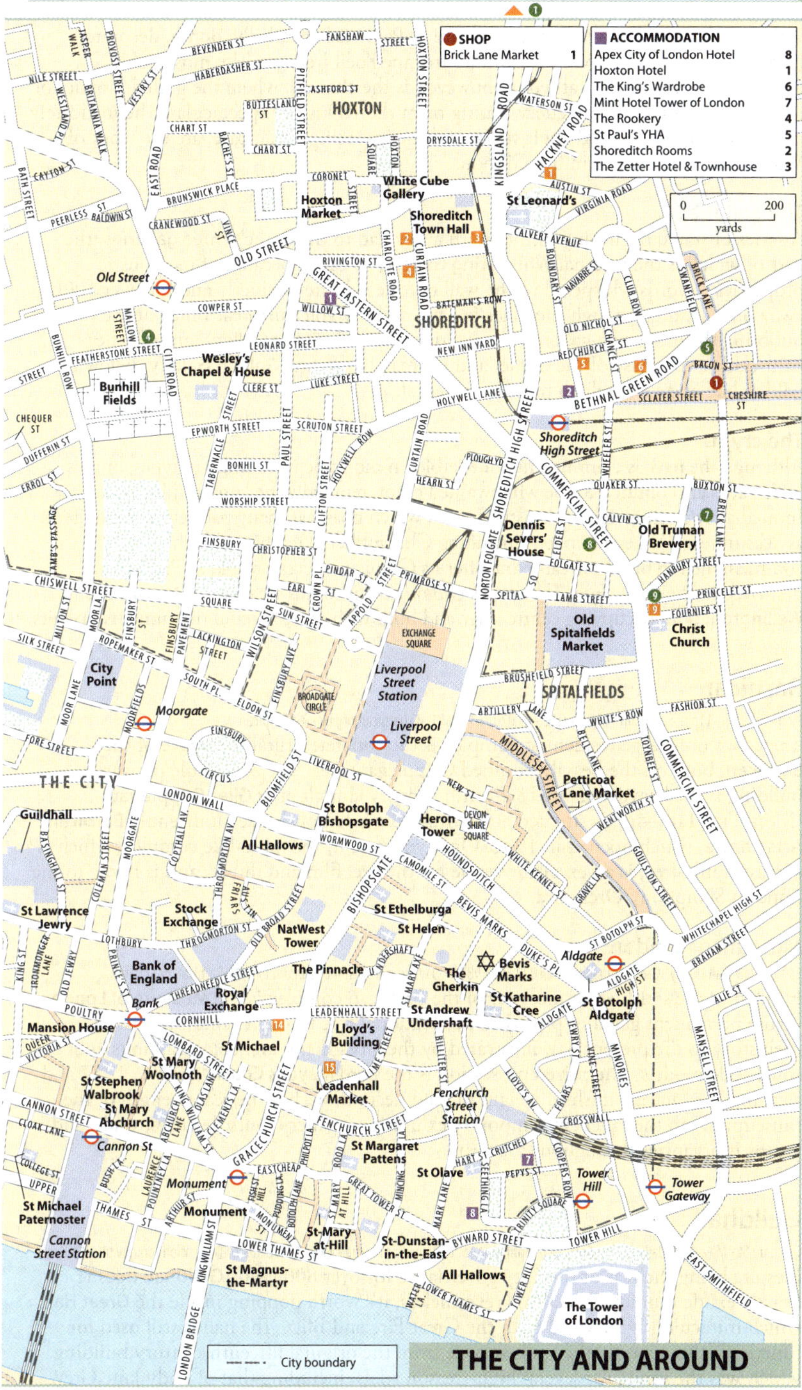
THE CITY AND AROUND
SHOP
Brick Lane Market 1
ACCOMMODATION
Apex City of London Hotel 8
Hoxton Hotel 1
The King's Wardrobe 6
Mint Hotel Tower of London 7
The Rookery 4
St Paul's YHA 5
Shoreditch Rooms 2
The Zetter Hotel & Townhouse 3
0 200
yards
City boundary
HOXTON
SHOREDITCH
SPITALFIELDS
THE CITY
White Cube Gallery
Hoxton Market
Shoreditch Town Hall
St Leonard's
Old Street
Wesley's Chapel & House
Bunhill Fields
Shoreditch High Street
Dennis Severs' House
Old Truman Brewery
Old Spitalfields Market
Christ Church
Liverpool Street Station
Liverpool Street
Exchange Square
Broadgate Circle
City Point
Moorgate
Petticoat Lane Market
Guildhall
St Botolph Bishopsgate
Heron Tower
All Hallows
St Lawrence Jewry
Stock Exchange
NatWest Tower
St Ethelburga
St Helen
The Pinnacle
The Gherkin
Bevis Marks
Aldgate
St Katharine Cree
St Botolph Aldgate
Bank of England
Royal Exchange
Bank
Mansion House
St Andrew Undershaft
Lloyd's Building
St Michael
St Mary Woolnoth
St Stephen Walbrook
St Mary Abchurch
Leadenhall Market
Fenchurch Street Station
Cannon St
St Margaret Pattens
St Olave
Tower Hill
Tower Gateway
Monument
St Michael Paternoster
Cannon Street Station
St-Mary-at-Hill
St-Dunstan-in-the-East
St Magnus-the-Martyr
All Hallows
The Tower of London
London Bridge
Old Street
City Road
Great Eastern Street
Commercial Street
Bethnal Green Road
Shoreditch High Street
Bishopsgate
Middlesex Street
London Wall
Cornhill
Leadenhall Street
Fenchurch Street
Cannon Street
Gracechurch Street
King William Street
Lombard Street
Threadneedle Street
Lower Thames St
Byward Street
Tower Hill
Minories
Whitechapel High St
Mansell Street
East Smithfield
Brick Lane
Hackney Road
Kingsland Road
Curtain Road
Worship Street
Finsbury Square
Finsbury Circus
Liverpool St
Houndsditch
Aldgate High St
Moorgate
Chiswell Street
Moor Lane
Fore Street
Poultry
Queen Victoria St
Upper Thames St
Eastcheap
Great Tower St
Hoxton Street
Pitfield Street
Old Nichol St
Redchurch St
Sclater Street
Cheshire St
Bacon St
Quaker St
Buxton St
Hanbury Street
Princelet St
Fournier St
Folgate St
Lamb Street
Brushfield Street
Artillery Lane
Fashion St
White's Row
Wentworth St
Goulston Street
Braham Street
Alie St
Crosswall
Pepys St
Hart St
Crutched
Trinity Square
10, 11 & 12

The best place from which to appreciate St Paul's is beneath the **dome**, decorated (against Wren's wishes) with Thornhill's trompe l'oeil frescoes. The most richly decorated section of the cathedral, however, is the **chancel**, where the gilded mosaics of birds, fish, animals and greenery, dating from the 1890s, are spectacular. The intricately carved oak and limewood **choir stalls**, and the imposing organ case, are the work of Wren's master carver, Grinling Gibbons.

The galleries

A series of stairs, beginning in the south aisle, lead to the dome's three **galleries**, the first of which is the internal **Whispering Gallery**, so called because of its acoustic properties – words whispered to the wall on one side are distinctly audible over 100ft away on the other, though the place is often so busy you can't hear much above the hubbub. The other two galleries are exterior: the wide **Stone Gallery**, around the balustrade at the base of the dome, and ultimately the tiny **Golden Gallery**, below the golden ball and cross which top the cathedral.

The crypt

Although the nave is crammed full of overblown monuments to military types, burials in St Paul's are confined to the whitewashed **crypt**, reputedly the largest in Europe. Immediately to your right is Artists' Corner, which boasts as many painters and architects as Westminster Abbey has poets, including Christopher Wren himself, who was commissioned to build the cathedral after its Gothic predecessor, Old St Paul's, was destroyed in the Great Fire. The crypt's two other star tombs are those of **Nelson** and **Wellington**, both occupying centre stage and both with more fanciful monuments upstairs.

Barbican

Mon–Sat 9am–11pm, Sun noon–11pm • Free • T 020 7638 8891, W barbican.org.uk • ⊖ Barbican

The City's only large residential complex is the concrete brutalist enclave of the **Barbican**, built on the heavily bombed Cripplegate area. The zone's sole prewar building is the heavily restored sixteenth-century church of **St Giles Cripplegate** (Mon–Fri 11am–4pm), situated across from the infamously user-unfriendly **Barbican Arts Centre**, which opened in 1982. Once you find it, the maze-like complex, which is at least traffic-free, is an excellent venue for theatre, film and music, and is home to the London Symphony Orchestra.

Museum of London

150 London Wall • Daily 10am–6pm • Free • T 020 7001 9844, W www.museumoflondon.org.uk • ⊖ Barbican or St Paul's

Hidden in the southwestern corner of the Barbican complex is the **Museum of London,** whose permanent galleries provide an educational trot through London's past, from prehistory to the present day, illustrated by the city's major archeological finds and some scale models. The prized possession is the **Lord Mayor's Coach**, built in 1757 and rivalling the Queen's in sheer weight of gold decoration, but the real strength of the museum lies in the excellent temporary exhibitions, gallery tours, lectures, walks and videos it organizes throughout the year.

Guildhall

Gresham St • May–Sept daily 10am–5pm; Oct–April Mon–Sat 10am–5pm • Free • T 020 7606 3030, W cityoflondon.gov.uk • ⊖ Bank

Despite being the seat of the City governance for over 800 years, **Guildhall** doesn't exactly exude municipal wealth. Nevertheless, it's worth popping inside the **Great Hall**, which miraculously survived both the Great Fire and Blitz. The hall is still used for functions, though only the walls survive from the original fifteenth-century building, which was the venue for several high-treason trials, including that of Lady Jane Grey.

Guildhall Art Gallery

Mon–Sat 10am–5pm, Sun noon–4pm • Free • ⊖ Bank

The purpose-built **Guildhall Art Gallery** contains one or two exceptional works, such as Rossetti's *La Ghirlandata*, and Holman Hunt's *The Eve of St Agnes*, plus a massive painting depicting the 1782 Siege of Gibraltar, commissioned by the Corporation, and a marble statue of Margaret Thatcher. In the basement, you can view the remains of a **Roman amphitheatre**, dating from around 120 AD, which was discovered when the gallery was built in 1988.

Clockmakers' Museum

Aldermanbury • Mon–Sat 9.30am–4.45pm • Free • Ⓣ 0207332 1868, Ⓦ clockmakers.org • ⊖ Bank

The **Clockmakers' Museum** has a collection of more than 600 timepieces, from Tudor pocket watches to grandfather clocks, which ring out in unison on the hour. Of particular interest is H5, a marine chronometer that looks like an oversized pocket watch, was tested by George III himself at Richmond observatory, and won John Harrison the Longitude Prize (see p.103).

Bank

Bank is the finest architectural arena in the City. Heart of the finance sector and the busy meeting point of eight streets, it's overlooked by a handsome collection of Neoclassical buildings – among them, the **Bank of England**, the **Royal Exchange** and **Mansion House** (the Lord Mayor's official residence) – each one faced in Portland Stone.

Bank of England

Threadneedle St • Mon–Fri 10am–5pm • Free • Ⓣ 020 7601 5545, Ⓦ bankofengland.co.uk • ⊖ Bank

Established in 1694 by William III to raise funds for the war against France, the **Bank of England** wasn't erected on its present site until 1734. All that remains of the building on which Sir John Soane spent the best part of his career from 1788 onwards is the windowless, outer curtain wall. However, you can view a reconstruction of Soane's Bank Stock Office, with its characteristic domed skylight, in the **museum**, which has its entrance on Bartholomew Lane.

Bevis Marks Synagogue

4 Heneage Lane • Mon, Wed & Thurs 10.30am–2pm, Tues & Fri 10.30am–1pm, Sun 10.30am–12.30pm • Guided tours Wed & Fri noon, Sun 11am • £4 • Ⓣ 020 7626 1274, Ⓦ bevismarks.org.uk • ⊖ Aldgate

Hidden away behind a red-brick office block in a little courtyard off Bevis Marks is the **Bevis Marks Synagogue**. Built in 1701 by Sephardic Jews who had fled the Inquisition in Spain and Portugal, this is the country's oldest surviving synagogue, and its roomy, rich interior gives an idea of just how wealthy the community was at the time. Nowadays, the Sephardic community has dispersed across London and the congregation has dwindled, though the magnificent array of chandeliers makes it popular for candlelit Jewish weddings.

LONDON BRIDGE

Until 1750, **London Bridge** was the only bridge across the Thames. The medieval bridge achieved world fame: built of stone and crowded with timber-framed houses, it became one of the great attractions of London – there's a model in the nearby church of **St Magnus the Martyr** (Tues–Fri 9.30am–4pm, Sun 10am–1pm). The houses were finally removed in the mid-eighteenth century, and a new stone bridge erected in 1831; that one now stands in the Arizona desert, having been bought in the 1960s by a man who, so the story goes, thought he'd purchased Tower Bridge. The present concrete structure, without doubt the ugliest yet, dates from 1972.

1

AIMING HIGH: CITY SKYSCRAPERS

Economic recession notwithstanding, the City skyline is sprouting a whole new generation of **skyscrapers**. From 1980, for thirty years, the City's tallest building was the 600ft-high Tower 42, designed as the **NatWest Tower** by Richard Seifert (in the shape of the bank's logo). Richard Rogers' **Lloyd's Building**, on Leadenhall Street, completed in 1984, was more remarkable for its inside-out design than its modest height – even with Norman Foster's 590ft-high **Gherkin**, it was the shape, not its height, that drew attention. In 2010, the NatWest Tower was finally topped by the **Heron Tower**, a fairly undistinguished 660-ft skyscraper, at 110 Bishopsgate, designed by Kohn Pedersen Fox – on the plus side, public access means you can check out the shark aquarium in the atrium, and pop into the bar-restaurant on the 40th floor. More are planned: Rafael Viñoly's 525-ft **Walkie Talkie**, 20 Fenchurch St, so-called because it will get wider as it gets bigger, will include a public "sky garden" on the roof; **The Pinnacle**, 22–24 Bishopsgate, also by Kohn Pedersen Fox, will be a swirling 945-ft helter-skelter of a tower (with a restaurant on the top floor); and **The Cheesegrater**, Richard Rogers' 737-ft triangular-shaped office block at 122 Leadenhall St, is due for completion in 2013.

Monument

Daily 9.30am–5.30pm • £2

The **Monument** was designed by Wren to commemorate the Great Fire of 1666. Crowned with spiky gilded flames, this plain Doric column stands 202ft high; if it were laid out flat it would touch the bakery where the Fire started, east of Monument. The bas-relief on the base, now in very bad shape, depicts Charles II and the Duke of York in Roman garb conducting the emergency relief operation. Views from the gallery, accessed by 311 steps, are somewhat dwarfed nowadays by the buildings springing up around it.

Tower of London

March–Oct Sun & Mon 10am–5.30pm, Tues–Sat 9am–5.30pm; Nov–Feb closes 4.30pm • £18, less online; free guided tours every 30min • ⓣ 020 3166 6000, ⓦ hrp.org.uk • ⊖ Tower Hill

One of Britain's main tourist attractions, the **Tower of London** overlooks the river at the eastern boundary of the old city walls. Despite all the hype, it remains one of London's most remarkable buildings, site of some of the goriest events in the nation's history, and somewhere all visitors and Londoners should explore at least once. Chiefly famous as a place of imprisonment and death, it has variously been used as a royal residence, armoury, mint, menagerie, observatory and – a function it still serves – a safe-deposit box for the Crown Jewels.

The lively free **guided tours** given by the Tower's **Beefeaters** (officially known as Yeoman Warders) are useful for getting your bearings. Visitors today enter the Tower along Water Lane, but in times gone by most prisoners were delivered through **Traitors' Gate**, on the waterfront. Immediately, they would have come to the **Bloody Tower**, which forms the main entrance to the Inner Ward, and which is where the 12-year-old Edward V and his 10-year-old brother were accommodated "for their own safety" in 1483 by their uncle, the future Richard III, and later murdered. It's also where **Walter Raleigh** was imprisoned on three separate occasions, including a thirteen-year stretch.

Tower Green

At the centre of the Inner Ward is **Tower Green**, where ten highly placed but unlucky individuals were beheaded, among them Anne Boleyn and her cousin Catherine Howard (Henry VIII's second and fifth wives). The **White Tower**, which overlooks the Green, is the original "Tower", begun in 1076, and now home to displays from the **Royal Armouries**. Even if you've no interest in military paraphernalia, you should at least pay a visit to the **Chapel of St John**, a beautiful Norman structure on the second floor that was completed in 1080 – making it the oldest intact church building in London.

Crown Jewels

The **Waterloo Barracks**, to the north of the White Tower, hold the **Crown Jewels**; queues can be painfully long, however, and you only get to view the rocks from moving walkways. The vast majority of exhibits post-date the Commonwealth (1649–60), when many of the royal riches were melted down for coinage or sold off. Among the jewels are the three largest cut diamonds in the world, including the legendary **Koh-i-Noor**, which was set into the Queen Mother's Crown in 1937.

Tower Bridge

Daily: April–Sept 10am–6.30pm; Oct–March 9.30am–6pm • £8 • T 020 7403 3761, W towerbridge.org.uk • ⊖ Tower Hill

Tower Bridge ranks with Big Ben as the most famous of all London landmarks. Completed in 1894, its neo-Gothic towers are clad in Cornish granite and Portland stone, but conceal a steel frame, which, at the time, represented a considerable engineering achievement, allowing a road crossing that could be raised to give tall ships access to the upper reaches of the Thames. The raising of the bascules (from the French for "see-saw") remains an impressive sight – phone ahead to find out when the bridge is opening. If you buy a ticket, you get to walk across the elevated walkways linking the summits of the towers and visit the Tower's Engine Room, on the south side of the bridge, where you can see the now defunct giant coal-fired boilers which drove the hydraulic system until 1976, and play some interactive engineering games.

The East End

Few places in London have engendered so many myths as the **East End** (a catch-all title which covers just about everywhere east of the City). Its name is synonymous with slums, sweatshops and crime, as epitomized by figures such as Jack the Ripper and the Kray Twins, but also with the rags-to-riches success stories of a whole generations of Jews who were born in these cholera-ridden quarters and then moved to wealthier pastures.

As the area is not an obvious place for sightseeing, and certainly no beauty spot – despite all the fanfare around the 2012 **Olympic Village** – most visitors to the East End come for its famous **Sunday markets**: cheap clothes on Petticoat Lane (Middlesex Street), clothes and crafts in trendy Spitalfields, hip vintage gear around Brick Lane and flowers on Columbia Road. As for the East End **Docklands**, including the vast and awesome **Canary Wharf** redevelopment, most of it can be gawped at from the overhead **light railway**.

Spitalfields

Spitalfields, within sight of the sleek tower blocks of the financial sector, lies at the old heart of the East End, where the French Huguenots settled in the seventeenth century, where the Jewish community was at its strongest in the late nineteenth century, and where today's Bengali community eats, sleeps, works and prays. If you visit just one area in the East End, it should be this, which preserves mementos from each wave of immigration. The focal point of the area is **Spitalfields Market**, the red-brick and green-gabled market hall built in 1893, which is busiest on Sundays.

THINKING BIG: OLYMPIC PARK

Focus of the 2012 Olympics, London's **Olympic Park** is situated in a most unlikely East End backwater, on a series of islands formed by the River Lea and various tributaries and canals. The centrepiece of the park is the **Olympic Stadium**, surrounded on three sides by rivers, and earmarked to become home to West Ham United football club. Standing close to the stadium, with a bird's-eye view of the whole site from its public observation deck, is the **Orbit** tower, a 377ft-high continuous loop of red recycled steel designed by Anish Kapoor, and dubbed the Helter Skelter. The most eye-catching venue, however, is Zaha Hadid's wave-like **Aquatics Centre**, to the east, which may have cost four times its original, but at least it looks good. The other truly sexy building is the curvy **Velodrome**, with its banked, Siberian pine track and adjacent BMX circuit. The nearest **tube** is Stratford; you can also approach from Hackney Wick Overground or Pudding Mill Lane DLR station.

Dennis Severs' House

18 Folgate St • Mon 6–9pm, Sun noon–4pm, also Mon following the 1st & 3rd Sun of the month noon–2pm • Mon lunchtime £5, Mon eve £12, Sun £8 • ⓣ 020 7247 4013, ⓦ dennisseversshouse.co.uk • ⊖ Liverpool Street

You can visit one of Spitalfields' characteristic eighteenth-century terraced houses at 18 Folgate St, where the American artist **Dennis Severs** lived until 1999. Eschewing all modern conveniences, Severs lived under candlelight, decorating his house as it would have been two hundred years ago. The public were invited to share in the experience that he described as like "passing through a frame into a painting". Today visitors are free to explore the cluttered, candlelit rooms, which resonate with the distinct impression that the resident Huguenot family has just popped out: not least due to the smell of cooked food and the sound of horses' hooves on the cobbles outside.

V&A Museum of Childhood

Cambridge Heath Rd • Daily 10am–5.45pm • Free • ⓣ 020 8983 5200, ⓦ vam.ac.uk • ⊖ Bethnal Green

The East End's most popular museum is the **V&A Museum of Childhood**. The open-plan, wrought-iron hall, originally part of (and still a branch of) the V&A (see p.96), was transported here in the 1860s to bring art to the East End. On the ground floor you'll see clockwork **toys** – everything from classic robots to a fully functioning model railway – marionettes and puppets, teddies and Smurfs and even Inuit dolls. The most famous exhibits are the remarkable antique **dolls' houses** dating back to 1673, now displayed upstairs, where you'll also find a play area for very small kids and the museum's special exhibitions.

Docklands

Built in the nineteenth century to cope with the huge volume of goods shipped along the Thames from all over the Empire, **Docklands** was once the largest enclosed cargo-dock system in the world. When the docks closed in the 1960s the area was generally regarded as having died forever, but regeneration in the 1980s brought luxury flats and, on the Isle of Dogs, a huge high-rise office development. Here, at **Canary Wharf**, Cesar Pelli's landmark stainless steel tower **One Canada Square** remains an icon on the city's skyline. The excellent **Museum of London Docklands** (daily 10am–6pm; free), in an old warehouse in Canary Wharf, charts the history of the area from Roman times to the present day.

The best way to view Docklands is either from one of the boats that course up and down the Thames, or from the driverless, overhead **Docklands Light Railway** or DLR, which sets off from Bank, or from Tower Gateway, close to Tower Hill tube. The train, which cuts right through the middle of the office buildings under a parabolic steel-and-glass canopy, is also a great way to get to Greenwich (see p.102).

1

The South Bank

The **South Bank** has a lot going for it. As well as the massive waterside **Southbank Centre**, it's home to a host of tourist attractions including the enormously popular **London Eye**. With most of London sitting on the north bank of the Thames, the views from here are the best on the river, and thanks to the wide, traffic-free riverside boulevard, the whole area can be happily explored on foot. Just a short walk away lies the absorbing **Imperial War Museum**, which contains the country's only permanent exhibition devoted to the Holocaust.

Southbank Centre

southbankcentre.co.uk • Waterloo or Embankment

In 1951, the South Bank Exhibition, on derelict land south of the Thames, formed the centrepiece of the national **Festival of Britain**, an attempt to revive morale postwar by celebrating the centenary of the Great Exhibition (when Britain really did rule over half the world). The most striking features of the site were the Ferris wheel (now reincarnated as the London Eye), the saucer-shaped Dome of Discovery (inspiration for the Millennium Dome), the Royal Festival Hall (which still stands) and the cigar-shaped steel-and-aluminium Skylon tower.

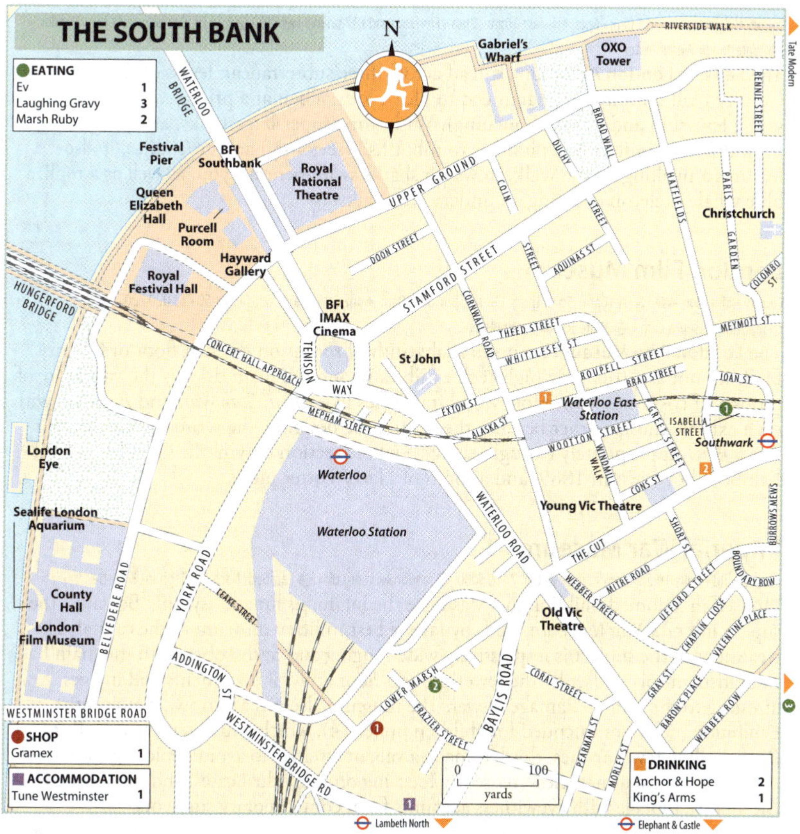

1

The Festival of Britain's success provided the impetus for the creation of the **Southbank Centre**, home to artistic institutions such as the Royal Festival Hall, the Hayward Gallery, the arts cinema BFI Southbank, and the National Theatre (see p.128). Its unprepossessing concrete appearance is softened by its riverside location, its avenue of trees, its buskers and skateboarders, and the busy secondhand bookstalls outside the BFI Southbank.

London Eye

Daily: April–June 10am–9pm; July & Aug 10am–9.30pm; Sept–March 10am–8.30pm • From £17 online • T 0871 781 3000, W londoneye.com • Waterloo or Westminster

Despite being little more than ten years old, the **London Eye** is one of the city's most famous landmarks. Standing an impressive 443ft high, it's the largest Ferris wheel in Europe, weighing over 2000 tons, yet as simple and delicate as a bicycle wheel. It's constantly in slow motion, which means a full-circle "flight" in one of its 32 pods (one for each of the city's boroughs) should take around thirty minutes: that may seem a long time but in fact it passes incredibly quickly. Book online (to save money), but note that unless you've paid extra you'll still have to queue to get on. Tickets are also sold from the box office at the eastern end of County Hall.

London Aquarium

County Hall • Mon–Thurs 10am–6pm, Fri–Sun 10am–7pm • From around £17 online • T 0871 663 1679, W visitsealife.com/London • Waterloo or Westminster

The **Sea Life London Aquarium,** spread across three subterranean levels of the old County Hall building, is guaranteed to please kids, albeit at a price (book online to save a few quid and to avoid queuing). With some super-large tanks, and everything from dog-face puffers and piranhas to robot fish (seriously) and crocodiles, it also features a thrilling Shark Walk, in which sharks swim beneath you, as well as a replica blue whale skeleton encasing an underwater walkway.

London Film Museum

County Hall • Mon–Wed & Fri 10am–5pm, Thurs 11am–5pm, Sat 10am–6pm, Sun 11am–6pm • £13.50 • T 020 7202 7043, W londfilmmuseum.com • Waterloo or Westminster

The **London Film Museum** occupies a labyrinth of rooms on the first floor of County Hall. It's not a particularly high-tech exhibition, and the main draw is the vast array of props and costumes from Hollywood franchises like *Alien*, *Star Wars* and *Batman*, with each exhibit chosen either because the studio, the designer, the writer or the director was a Brit. Appropriately enough, there's a whole section on Charlie Chaplin, a local Lambeth boy born in 1889, and a room of Harry Potter props.

Imperial War Museum

Lambeth Rd • Daily 10am–6pm • Free • T 020 7416 5000, W london.iwm.org.uk • Lambeth North or Elephant & Castle

Housed in a domed building that was once the infamous lunatic asylum "Bedlam", the superb **Imperial War Museum** holds by far the best military museum in the capital. The treatment of the subject is impressively wide-ranging and fairly sober, with the main hall's militaristic display offset by the lower-ground-floor array of documents and images attesting to the human damage of war. The museum also has a harrowing **Holocaust Exhibition** (not recommended for children under 14), which you enter from the third floor. Pulling few punches, this has made a valiant attempt to avoid depicting the victims of the Holocaust as nameless masses by focusing on individual cases, and interspersing the archive footage with eyewitness accounts from contemporary survivors.

Southwark

In Tudor and Stuart London, the chief reason for crossing the Thames to what is now **Southwark** was to visit the disreputable Bankside entertainment district around the south end of London Bridge. Four hundred years on, Londoners are heading to the area once more, thanks to a wealth of top attractions – led by the mighty **Tate Modern** – that pepper the traffic-free riverside path between Blackfriars Bridge and Tower Bridge. The area is conveniently linked to St Paul's and the City by the fabulous Norman Foster-designed **Millennium Bridge**, London's first pedestrian-only bridge.

Tate Modern

Bankside • Sun–Thurs 10am–6pm, Fri & Sat 10am–10pm; free guided tours daily 11am, noon, 2pm & 3pm • Free; multimedia guides £3.50 • T 020 7887 8888, W tate.org.uk • ⊖ Southwark

Bankside is dominated nowadays by the awesome **Tate Modern**. Originally designed as an oil-fired power station by Giles Gilbert Scott, this austere, brick-built "cathedral of power" was converted into a splendid modern art gallery in 2000. The best way to enter is down the ramp from the west so that you get the full effect of the stupendously large turbine hall. It's easy enough to find your way around the galleries, with levels 3 and 5 displaying the permanent collection, level 4 used for fee-paying special exhibitions, and level 7 home to a café with a great view over the Thames. Along with the free guided tours and multimedia guides, various apps are available (Tate has free wi-fi).

Works are grouped thematically. Although the displays change every year or so, you're still pretty much guaranteed to see works by **Monet** and Bonnard, Cubist pioneers **Picasso** and Braque, Surrealists such as **Dalí**, abstract artists like **Mondrian**, Bridget Riley and Pollock, and Pop supremos **Warhol** and Lichtenstein. And such is the space here that several artists get whole rooms to themselves, among them Joseph Beuys, with his shamanistic wax and furs, and **Mark Rothko**, whose abstract "Seagram Murals", originally destined for a posh restaurant in New York, have their own shrine-like room in the heart of the collection.

Shakespeare's Globe

21 New Globe Walk • Exhibition mid-April to mid-Sept Mon–Sat 9am–12.30pm & 1–5pm, Sun 9–11.30am & noon–5pm; mid-Oct to mid-April daily 9am–5.30pm • £11.50 • T 020 7902 1500, W shakespearesglobe.com • ⊖ Southwark or London Bridge

Dwarfed by Tate Modern, but equally remarkable in its own way, **Shakespeare's Globe Theatre** is a more or less faithful reconstruction of the polygonal playhouse where most of the Bard's later works were first performed. The theatre, which boasts the first new thatched roof in central London since the Great Fire, puts on plays by Shakespeare and his contemporaries, using only natural light and the minimum of scenery. To find out more about Shakespeare and the history of Bankside, the Globe's stylish **exhibition** is well worth a visit. You can have a virtual play on medieval instruments such as the crumhorn or sackbut, prepare your own edition of Shakespeare, and feel the thatch, hazelnut-shell and daub used to build the theatre. There's also an informative **guided tour** round the theatre itself; during the summer season, you get to visit the exhibition and the remains of the nearby Rose Theatre instead.

Golden Hinde

1 & 2 Pickfords Wharf • Mon–Sat 10am–5.30pm, Sun 10am–5pm, but phone ahead • £6 • T 020 7403 0123, W goldenhinde.com • ⊖ London Bridge

An exact replica of the **Golden Hinde**, the galleon in which Francis Drake sailed around the world from 1577 to 1580, nestles in St Mary Overie Dock, at the eastern end of Clink Street. The ship is surprisingly small, and its original crew of eighty-plus must

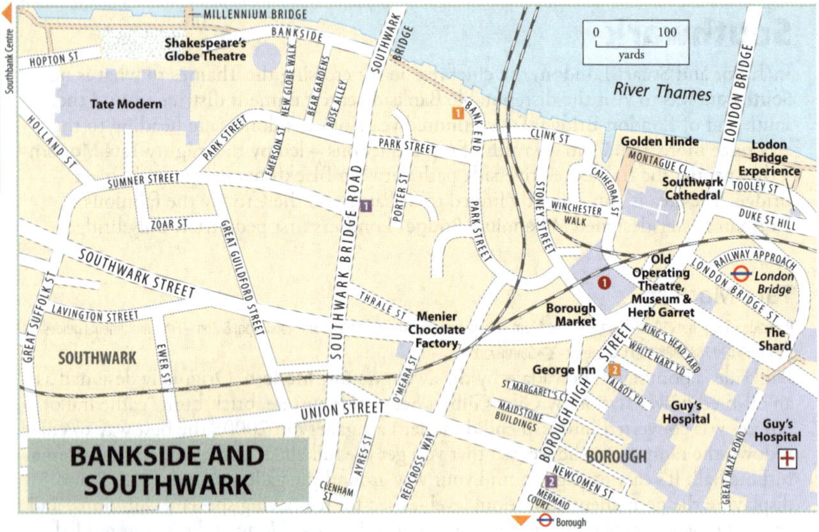

have been cramped to say the least. There's a lack of interpretive panels, so it's worth paying the little bit extra and getting a guided tour from one of the folk in period costume – ring ahead to check that a group hasn't booked the place up.

Southwark Cathedral

Mon–Fri 8am–6pm, Sat & Sun 8.30am–6pm • Free • Ⓦ cathedral.southwark.anglican.org • ⊖ London Bridge

Close by the *Golden Hinde* stands **Southwark Cathedral**, built as the medieval Augustinian priory church of St Mary Overie, and given cathedral status only in 1905. Of the original thirteenth-century church, only the choir and retrochoir now remain, separated by a tall and beautiful stone Tudor screen, making them probably the oldest Gothic structures left in London. The nave was entirely rebuilt in the nineteenth century, but the cathedral contains numerous interesting monuments, from a thirteenth-century oak effigy of a knight to an early twentieth-century memorial to Shakespeare.

Borough Market

8 Southwark St • Thurs 11am–5pm, Fri noon–6pm, Sat 9am–4pm • Ⓣ 020 7407 1002, Ⓦ boroughmarket.org.uk • ⊖ London Bridge

Borough Market is tucked beneath the railway arches between Borough High Street and Soutwark cathedral. The early-morning wholesale fruit and vegetable market winds up around 8am and is one of the few still trading under its original Victorian wrought-iron shed. But the market is best known nowadays for its busy specialist food market, with stalls selling top-quality and pricey produce from around the world.

The Shard

Ⓦ the-shard.com • ⊖ London Bridge

London's – and the EU's – tallest building, **the Shard** is squeezed in beside London Bridge Station. While there's a case to be made for the City's skyscrapers, and for those at Canary Wharf, it's hard to justify such a hubristic (Qatari-funded) enterprise south of the river. That said, Renzo Piano's tapered, glass-clad tower block does at least have a public viewing platform on the top (72nd) floor, from which, of course, there are terrific views over London, and – thankfully – no view of the Shard itself.

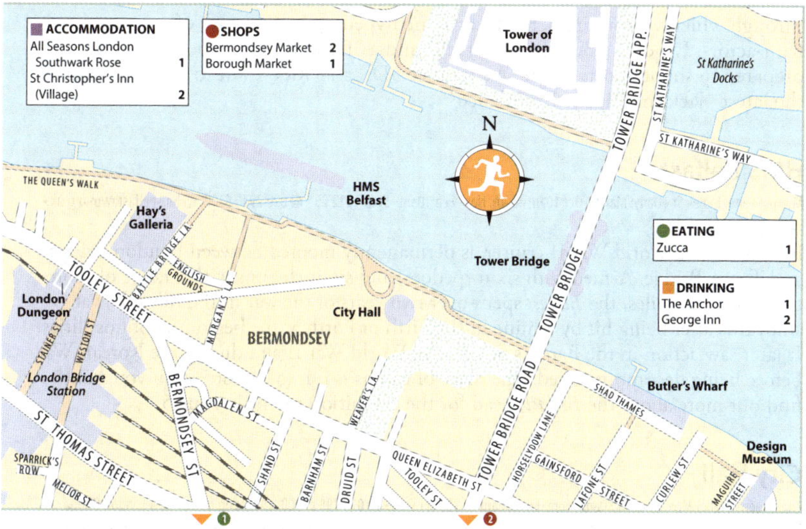

Old Operating Theatre Museum and Herb Garret

St Thomas St • Daily 10.30am–5pm; closed mid-Dec to early Jan • £5.90 • ☎ 020 7188 2679, ⓦ thegarret.org.uk • ⊖ London Bridge

The most educative and the strangest of Southwark's museums is the **Old Operating Theatre Museum and Herb Garret**. Built in 1821 up a spiral staircase at the top of a church tower, where the hospital apothecary's herbs were stored, this women's operating theatre was once adjacent to the women's ward of St Thomas' Hospital (now in Lambeth). Despite being gore-free, the museum is as stomach-churning as the nearby London Dungeon (see below). The surgeons who used this room would have concentrated on speed and accuracy (most amputations took less than a minute), but there was still a thirty percent mortality rate, with many patients simply dying of shock, and many more from bacterial infection.

London Bridge Experience

2 Tooley St • Mon–Fri 10am–5pm, Sat & Sun 10am–6pm • £23, from £11 online • ☎ 0844 847 2287, ⓦ thelondonbridgeexperience.com • ⊖ London Bridge

Inspired by the popular Hammer Horror mayhem of the nearby London Dungeons, some bright sparks have created the rival **London Bridge Experience** in the railway vaults on the north side of Tooley Street. First of all you're led on a theatrical trot through the history of London Bridge, with guides in period garb hamming up the gory bits. Then, in case, you're not scared enough, in the **London Tombs** section (no under-11s), more actors, dressed as zombies and murderers, leap out of the foggy gloom to frighten the wits out of you. Finally, in peace and quiet, you get to peruse some artefacts from (and a model of) old London Bridge.

London Dungeon

28–34 Tooley St • Daily: April–July, Sept & Oct 10am–5.30pm; Aug 9.30am–7pm; Nov–March 10am–5pm; longer hours in school holidays • £23, or £16 online • ☎ 020 7403 7221, ⓦ thedungeons.com • ⊖ London Bridge

Housed beneath the railway arches of London Bridge Station, the **London Dungeon** is an orgy of Gothic horror and one of the city's major crowd-pleasers – to avoid queuing (and save money), buy your ticket online. Young teenagers and the credulous probably get the most out of the various ludicrous live-action scenarios

1 through which visitors are herded, each one hyped up by the team of costumed ham-actors. Expect a "Boat Ride to Hell" and a "Drop Ride to Doom", and be prepared to shoot ghosts in the "Vengeance 5D Lasar Ride", not to mention endure the latest "Jack the Ripper Experience".

HMS Belfast

Morgan Lane, Tooley St • Daily: March–Oct 10am–6pm; Nov–Feb 10am–5pm • £12.25 • ⓣ 020 7940 6300, ⓦ hmsbelfast.iwm.org.uk • ⊖ London Bridge

HMS Belfast, a World War II cruiser, is permanently moored between London Bridge and Tower Bridge. Armed with six torpedoes, and six-inch guns with a range of more than fourteen miles, the *Belfast* spent over two years of the war in the Royal Naval shipyards after being hit by a mine in the Firth of Forth at the beginning of hostilities. It later saw action in the Barents Sea during World War II and during the Korean War, before being decommissioned. The maze of cabins is fun to explore but if you want to find out more about the *Belfast*, head for the exhibition rooms in zone 5.

City Hall

The Queen's Walk • Mon–Thurs 8.30am–6pm, Fri 8.30am–5.30pm • Free • ⓣ 020 7983 4000, ⓦ london.gov.uk • ⊖ London Bridge

East of the *Belfast*, overlooking the river, Norman Foster's startling glass-encased **City Hall** looks like a giant car headlight or fencing mask, and serves as the headquarters for the Greater London Authority and the Mayor of London. Visitors are welcome to stroll up the helical walkway, visit the café and watch proceedings from the second floor.

Butler's Wharf

In contrast to the brash offices on Tooley Street, **Butler's Wharf**, east of Tower Bridge, has retained its historical character. **Shad Thames**, the narrow street at the back of Butler's Wharf, has kept the wrought-iron overhead gangways by which the porters used to transport goods from the wharves to the warehouses further back from the river, and is one of the most atmospheric alleyways in the whole of the district.

Design Museum

Shad Thames • Daily 10am–5.45pm • £7 • ⓣ 0870 833 9955, ⓦ designmuseum.org • ⊖ Tower Hill

The chief attraction of Butler's Wharf is the superb riverside **Design Museum**, a stylish, Bauhaus-like conversion of a 1950s warehouse. The museum hosts a series of special exhibitions (up to four at once) on important designers, movements or single products. The shop is great for design classics and innovations, and the small coffee bar in the foyer serves delicious cakes. There's a pricier restaurant on the top floor.

Kensington and Chelsea

Hyde Park and Kensington Gardens cover a distance of two miles from Oxford Street in the northeast to Kensington Palace, set in the Royal Borough of **Kensington** and **Chelsea**. Other districts go in and out of fashion, but this area has been in vogue ever since royalty moved into **Kensington Palace** in the late seventeenth century.

The most popular tourist attractions lie in **South Kensington**, where three of London's top **museums** – the Victoria and Albert, Natural History and Science museums – stand on land bought with the proceeds of the 1851 Great Exhibition. Chelsea, to the south, has a slightly more bohemian pedigree. In the 1960s, the **King's Road** carved out its reputation as London's catwalk, while in the late 1970s it was the epicentre of the punk explosion. Nothing so rebellious goes on in Chelsea now, though its residents like to think of themselves as rather more artistic and intellectual than the purely moneyed types of Kensington.

Hyde Park and Kensington Gardens

Hyde Park Daily 5am–midnight **Kensington Gardens** Daily 6am–dusk • ☎ 020 7298 2100, royalparks.gov.uk • ⊖ Hyde Park Corner, Marble Arch, Knightsbridge or Lancaster Gate

Hangings, muggings, duels and the 1851 Great Exhibition are just some of the public events that have taken place in **Hyde Park**, which remains a popular spot for political demonstrations. For most of the time, however, the park is simply a lazy leisure ground – a wonderful open space that allows you to lose all sight of the city beyond a few persistent tower blocks.

The park is divided in two by the **Serpentine Lake**, which has a popular **Lido** (mid-June to mid-Sept daily 10am–6pm; £3.75) on its south bank and a pretty upper section known as the **Long Water**, which narrows until it reaches a group of four fountains. The western half of the park is, in fact, officially known as **Kensington Gardens**; its two most popular attractions are the **Serpentine Gallery** (daily 10am–6pm; free), which puts on contemporary art exhibitions, and the overblown **Albert Memorial**.

Marble Arch

At Hyde Park's treeless northeastern corner is **Marble Arch**, erected in 1828 as a triumphal entry to Buckingham Palace, but now stranded on a busy traffic island at the west end of Oxford Street. This is a historically charged piece of land, as it marks the site of **Tyburn gallows**, the city's main public execution spot until 1783. It's also the location of **Speakers' Corner**, a peculiarly English Sunday morning tradition, featuring an assembly of ranters and hecklers.

Wellington Arch

Hyde Park Corner • Wed–Sun: April–Oct 10am–5pm; Nov–March 10am–4pm • EH • £3.90 • ⊖ Hyde Park Corner

At the southeast corner of Hyde Park, around **Hyde Park Corner**, the **Wellington Arch** stands in the midst of one of London's busiest traffic interchanges. Erected in 1828, the arch was originally topped by an equestrian statue of the Duke himself, later replaced by Peace driving a four-horse chariot. Inside, you can view an exhibition on the history of the arch, and of London's outdoor sculpture, and take a lift to the top of the monument where the exterior balconies offer a bird's-eye view of the swirling traffic.

Apsley House

149 Piccadilly • Wed–Sun: April–Oct 11am–5pm; Nov–March 11am–4pm • EH • £6.30 • ⊖ Hyde Park Corner

Overlooking the traffic whizzing round Hyde Park Corner is **Apsley House**, Wellington's London residence and now a museum to the "Iron Duke". The highlight is the **art collection**, much of which used to belong to the King of Spain. Among the best pieces, displayed in the Waterloo Gallery on the first floor, are works by de Hooch, Van Dyck, Velázquez, Goya, Rubens and Correggio. The famous, more than twice life-size, nude statue of Napoleon by Antonio Canova stands at the foot of the main staircase.

Albert Memorial

Guided tours March–Dec first Sun of month 2pm & 3pm; 45min; £6 • ⊖ South Kensington

Erected in 1876, the richly decorated, High Gothic **Albert Memorial** is as much a hymn to the glorious achievements of Britain as to its subject, Queen Victoria's husband, who died of typhoid in 1861. Albert occupies the central canopy, gilded from head to toe and clutching a catalogue for the 1851 Great Exhibition that he helped to organize.

1

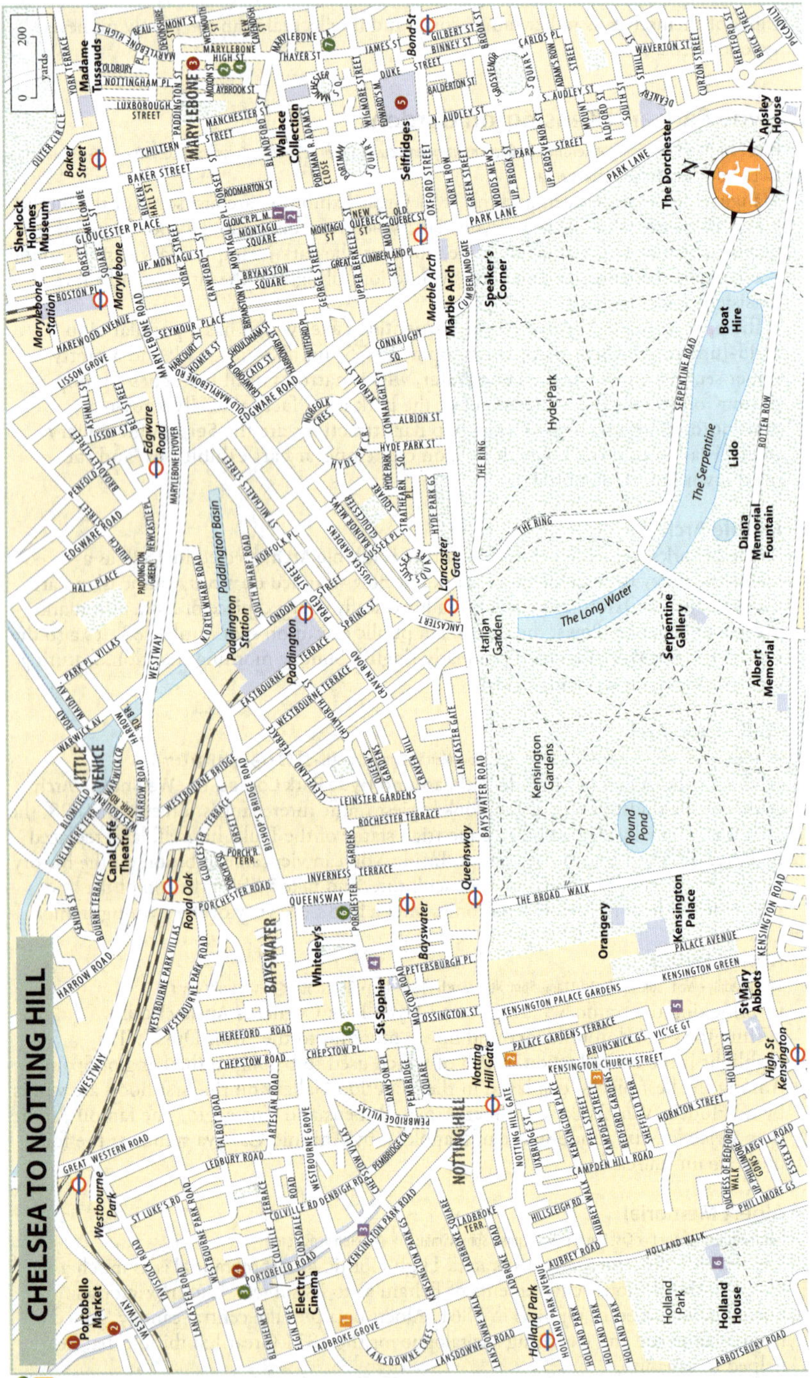
CHELSEA TO NOTTING HILL
0
200
yards
Madame Tussauds
Baker Street
Sherlock Holmes Museum
Marylebone
Marylebone Station
MARYLEBONE
Wallace Collection
Selfridges
Bond St
Marble Arch
Speaker's Corner
The Dorchester
Apsley House
Hyde Park
Boat Hire
The Serpentine
Lido
Diana Memorial Fountain
The Long Water
Serpentine Gallery
Albert Memorial
Italian Garden
Lancaster Gate
Edgware Road
Paddington
Paddington Station
Paddington Basin
LITTLE VENICE
Canal Café Theatre
Royal Oak
Kensington Gardens
Round Pond
Queensway
Bayswater
BAYSWATER
Whiteley's
St Sophia
Kensington Palace
Orangery
St Mary Abbots
High St Kensington
Notting Hill Gate
NOTTING HILL
Westbourne Park
Portobello Market
Electric Cinema
Holland Park
Holland House
PARK LANE
OXFORD STREET
BAKER STREET
EDGWARE ROAD
BAYSWATER ROAD
WESTWAY
KENSINGTON CHURCH STREET
HOLLAND PARK AVENUE
LADBROKE GROVE
PORTOBELLO ROAD
THE BROAD WALK
THE RING
SERPENTINE ROAD
KENSINGTON ROAD
PICCADILLY

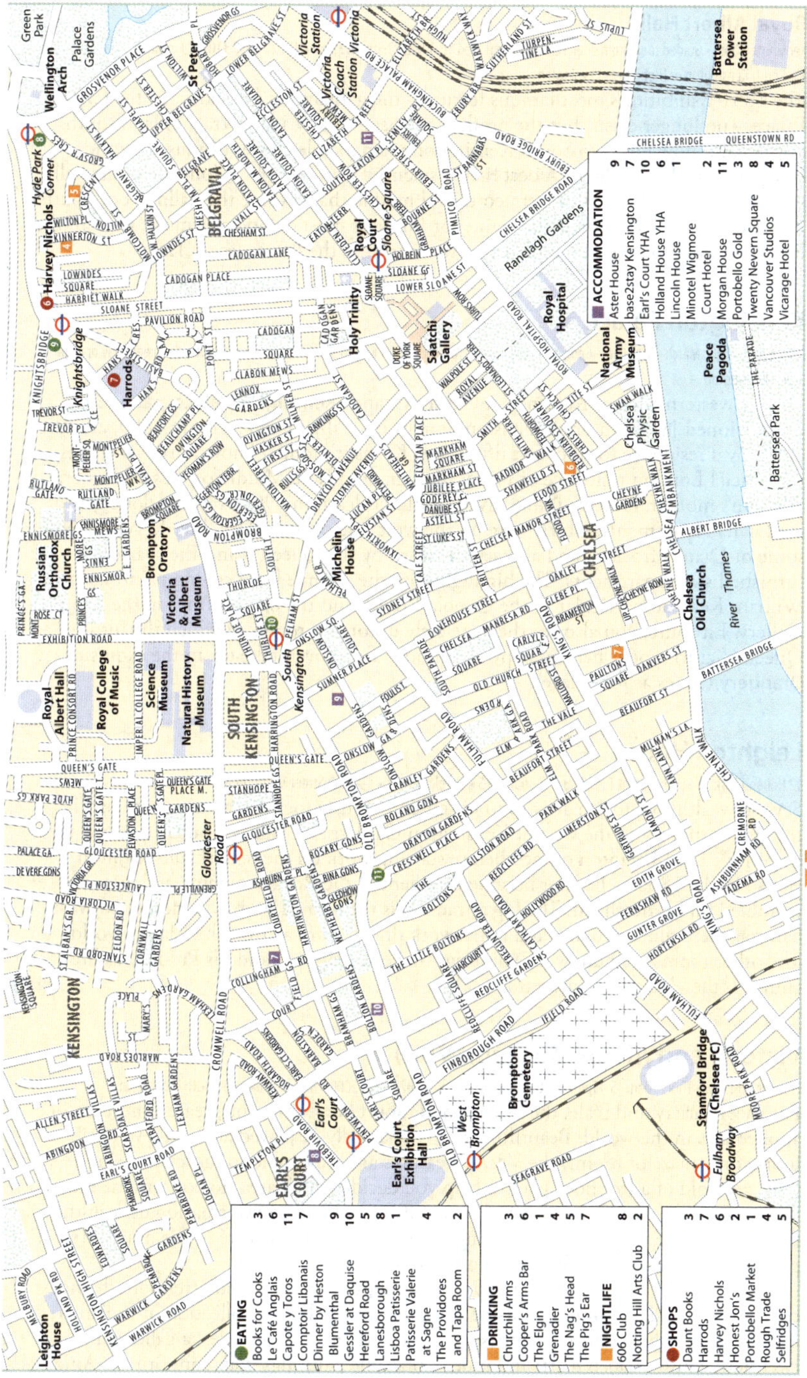
EATING
Books for Cooks 3
Le Café Anglais 6
Capote y Toros 11
Comptoir Libanais 7
Dinner by Heston Blumenthal 9
Gessler at Daquise 10
Hereford Road 5
Lanesborough 8
Lisboa Patisserie 1
Patisserie Valerie at Sagne 4
The Providores and Tapa Room 2
DRINKING
Churchill Arms 3
Cooper's Arms Bar 6
The Elgin 1
Grenadier 4
The Nag's Head 5
The Pig's Ear 7
NIGHTLIFE
606 Club 8
Notting Hill Arts Club 2
SHOPS
Daunt Books 3
Harrods 7
Harvey Nichols 6
Honest Jon's 2
Portobello Market 1
Rough Trade 4
Selfridges 5
ACCOMMODATION
Aster House 9
base2stay Kensington 7
Earl's Court YHA 10
Holland House YHA 6
Lincoln House 1
Minotel Wigmore Court Hotel 2
Morgan House 11
Portobello Gold 3
Twenty Nevern Square 8
Vancouver Studios 4
Vicarage Hotel 5
BELGRAVIA
CHELSEA
SOUTH KENSINGTON
KENSINGTON
EARL'S COURT
Victoria Station
Victoria Coach Station
Battersea Power Station
Battersea Park
River Thames
Royal Hospital
Ranelagh Gardens
National Army Museum
Chelsea Physic Garden
Peace Pagoda
Chelsea Old Church
Saatchi Gallery
Holy Trinity
Michelin House
Victoria & Albert Museum
Brompton Oratory
Natural History Museum
Science Museum
Royal College of Music
Royal Albert Hall
Russian Orthodox Church
Harrods
Harvey Nichols
Wellington Arch
Green Park
Palace Gardens
St Peter
Brompton Cemetery
Earl's Court Exhibition Hall
Stamford Bridge (Chelsea FC)
Leighton House

1

Royal Albert Hall

Kensington Gore • Guided tours from door 12 daily except Wed 10.30am–3.30pm; £8.50 • T 020 7838 3105, W royalalberthall.com • ⊖ South Kensington or High Street Kensington

The 1851 Exhibition's most famous feature – the gargantuan glasshouse of the Crystal Palace – no longer exists, but the profits were used to buy a large tract of land south of the park, now home to South Kensington's remarkable cluster of museums and colleges, plus the vast **Royal Albert Hall**, a splendid iron-and-glass-domed concert hall with an exterior of red brick, terracotta and marble that became the hallmark of South Ken architecture. The hall is the venue for Europe's most democratic music festival, the Henry Wood Promenade Concerts, better known as the **Proms** (see p.129).

Kensington Palace

Palace Ave • Daily: March–Oct 10am–6pm; Nov–Feb 10am–5pm • £12.50 • T 020 3166 6000, W hrp.org.uk • ⊖ Queensway or High Street Kensington

On the western edge of Kensington Gardens stands **Kensington Palace**, a modestly proportioned Jacobean brick mansion bought by William and Mary in 1689, and the chief royal residence for the next fifty years. KP, as it's fondly known in royal circles, is the official London residence of Prince William and Kate Middleton. It's also where William's mother, **Princess Diana**, lived until her death in 1997. Visitors don't get to see Diana's apartments, which were on the west side of the palace, but do get to view some of Diana's frocks – and also several worn by the Queen – and the sparsely furnished state apartments. The highlights are the trompe l'oeil ceiling paintings by William Kent, in particular in the Cupola Room, and the oil paintings in the King's Gallery. En route, you also see the tastelessly decorated rooms in which the future Queen Victoria spent her unhappy childhood. To recover, take tea in the exquisite **Orangery** (times as for palace).

Leighton House

12 Holland Park Rd • Daily except Tues 10am–5.30pm • £5 • W rbkc.gov.uk • ⊖ High Street Kensington

Several wealthy Victorian artists rather self-consciously founded an artists' colony in the streets that lay to the west of Kensington Gardens. "It will be opulence, it will be sincerity", Lord Leighton opined before starting work on the remarkable **Leighton House** in the 1860s – he later became President of the Royal Academy and was ennobled on his deathbed. The big attraction is the domed **Arab Hall**, decorated with Saracen tiles, gilded mosaics and latticework drawn from all over the Islamic world. The other rooms are hung with paintings by Lord Leighton and his Pre-Raphaelite chums – there's even a Tintoretto.

Victoria and Albert Museum (V&A)

Cromwell Rd • Sat–Thurs 10am–5.45pm, Fri 10am–10pm • Free • T 020 7942 2000, W vam.ac.uk • ⊖ South Kensington

For sheer variety and scale, the **Victoria and Albert Museum** is the greatest museum of applied arts in the world. Beautifully but haphazardly displayed across a seven-mile, four-storey maze of rooms, the V&A's treasures are impossible to survey in a single visit; get hold of a free floor plan to help you decide which areas to concentrate on, and look out for the various free tours that set off from the main information desk in the Grand Entrance. And if you're flagging, head for the edifying café in the museum's period-piece Morris, Gamble & Poynter Rooms.

Whatever your taste, there's bound to be something to grab your attention: the finest collection of Italian sculpture outside Italy, the world's largest collection of Indian art outside India, plus extensive Chinese, Islamic and Japanese galleries; a gallery of twentieth-century *objets d'art;* and more Constable paintings than Tate Britain. Among the other highlights are the justifiably popular Jewellery section, the beautifully designed British Galleries, the Costume rooms and the fascinating Theatre & Performance rooms which house the collection of the former Covent Garden Theatre Museum. In addition, the V&A's temporary shows on art, photography and fashion – some of which you have to pay for – are among the best in Britain.

Science Museum

Exhibition Rd • Daily 10am–6pm • Free • ☎ 0870 870 4868, Ⓦ sciencemuseum.org.uk • ⊖ South Kensington

Established as a technological counterpart to the V&A, the **Science Museum** is undeniably impressive, filling seven floors with items drawn from every conceivable area of science, with hands-on galleries that appeal to adults and kids.

Stop first at the **information desk**, pick up a museum plan and check the daily events schedule; you can also sign up for a free **guided tour** on a specific subject. Most people will want to head for the **Wellcome Wing**, full of state-of-the-art interactive computers and an IMAX cinema, and geared to appeal to even the most museum-phobic teenager. To get there, you must pass through the Making of the Modern World, a display of iconic inventions from Robert Stephenson's *Rocket* train of 1829 to the Ford Model T, the world's first mass-produced car.

Those with kids should head for the popular Launchpad, the museum's busiest interactive gallery on Floor 3. The Materials gallery, on Floor 1, is aimed more at adults, and is an extremely stylish exhibition covering the use of materials ranging from aluminium to zerodur (used for making laser gyroscopes), while Energy, on Floor 2, has a great "do not touch" electric-shock machine that absolutely fascinates kids.

Natural History Museum

Cromwell Rd • Daily 10am–5.50pm • Free • ☎ 020 7942 5000, Ⓦ nhm.ac.uk • ⊖ South Kensington

Alfred Waterhouse's purpose-built mock-Romanesque colossus ensures the status of the **Natural History Museum** as London's most handsome museum, both an important resource for serious zoologists and a major tourist attraction.

The main entrance leads to the **Blue Zone**, which includes the ever-popular Dinosaur gallery, with its grisly life-sized **animatronic dinosaurs.** Popular sections over in the **Green Zone** include the Creepy-Crawlies, and the excellent **Investigate** gallery, where children aged 7 to 14 get to play at being scientists (you need to obtain a timed ticket).

Little visited, compared to the rest of the museum, the **Darwin Centre** – also known as the **Orange Zone** – is dominated by the giant concrete **Cocoon**, home to more than 20 million specimens. Visitors can take the lift to the seventh floor and enter the Cocoon to learn more about the history of the collection, about taxonomy and the research and field trips the museum funds. In the nearby **Zoology spirit building**, you can view a small selection of bits and bobs pickled in glass jars, but if you want to join one of the **guided tours** that take you behind the scenes, you need to need to book on the day.

If the queues for the museum are long (as they can be at weekends and during school holidays), head for the side entrance on Exhibition Road, which leads into the former Geology Museum, now known as the **Red Zone**, a visually exciting romp through the earth's evolution. The most popular sections are the slightly tasteless Kobe earthquake simulator, and the spectacular display of gems and crystals in the Earth's Treasury.

Chelsea

From the Swinging Sixties up until the era of Punk, **Chelsea** had a slightly bohemian pedigree; these days, it's just another wealthy west London suburb. Among the most nattily attired of all those parading down the King's Road nowadays are the scarlet- or navy-blue-clad Chelsea Pensioners, army veterans from the nearby **Royal Hospital**.

1

Saatchi Gallery

King's Rd • Daily 10am–6pm • Free • 020 7823 2363, saatchi-gallery.co.uk • Sloane Square

Set back from the King's Road, a short stroll from Sloane Square, the former **Duke of York's HQ**, built in 1801 is now the unlikely home of the **Saatchi Gallery**, which puts on changing exhibitions of contemporary art in its fifteen whitewashed rooms. Charles Saatchi, the collector behind the gallery, was the man who introduced Young British Artists (YBAs) like Damien Hirst, Sarah Lucas, Tracey Emin and Rachel Whiteread to the world in the 1990s.

Royal Hospital

Royal Hospital Rd • April–Sept Mon–Sat 10am–noon & 2–4pm, Sun 2–4pm; Oct–March Mon–Sat 10am–noon & 2–4pm • Free • 020 7881 5200, chelsea-pensioners.co.uk • Sloane Square

Founded by Charles II in 1682, and designed by Christopher Wren, the **Royal Hospital**'s majestic red-brick wings and grassy courtyards became a blueprint for institutional and collegiate architecture all over the English-speaking world. The public are welcome to view the austere hospital chapel, and the equally grand, wood-panelled dining hall, opposite, where 300 or so Pensioners still eat under the royal portraits and the vast allegorical mural of Charles II. On the east side of the hospital, a small **museum** displays Pensioners' uniforms, medals and two German bombs.

National Army Museum

Royal Hospital Rd • Daily 10am–5.30pm • Free • 020 7730 0717, national-army-museum.ac.uk • Sloane Square

The concrete bunker next door to the Royal Hospital, on Royal Hospital Road, houses the **National Army Museum**. There are plenty of interesting historical artefacts, a top-class art gallery, plus an impressive array of uniforms and medals, a model of Waterloo and the skeleton of Napoleon's horse, Marengo, but for a more nuanced exploration of war, you're better off visiting the Imperial War Museum (see p.88).

North London

Almost all of **North London**'s suburbs are easily accessible by tube from the centre, though just a handful of these satellite villages, now subsumed into the general mass of the city, are worth bothering with. First off is one of London's finest parks, **Regent's Park**, home to London Zoo; **Camden Town**, famous for its huge weekend market, is nearby. The highlights, however, are the village-like suburbs of **Hampstead** and **Highgate**, on the edge of London's wildest patch of greenery, **Hampstead Heath**.

Regent's Park

Daily 5am to dusk • royalparks.org.uk • Regent's Park, Baker Street, Great Portland Street, St John's Wood or Camden Town

Regent's Park is one of London's smartest parks, with a boating lake, ornamental ponds, waterfalls and some lovely gardens. Under the reign of the Prince Regent (later George IV), the park was to be girded by a continuous belt of terraces, and sprinkled with a total of 56 villas, including a magnificent royal palace. Inevitably, the plan was never fully realized, but enough was built to create something of the idealized garden city that Nash and the Prince Regent had envisaged. Within the Inner Circle, the **Queen Mary's Gardens** are by far the prettiest section of the park.

Prominent on the skyline is the shiny copper dome of **London Central Mosque** at 146 Park Rd, an entirely appropriate addition given the Prince Regent's taste for the Orient.

CLOCKWISE FROM TOP LEFT MILLENNIUM BRIDGE AND ST PAUL'S CATHEDRAL (P.79); LITTLE VENICE (P.100); THE GREAT COURT, BRITISH MUSEUM (P.76) >

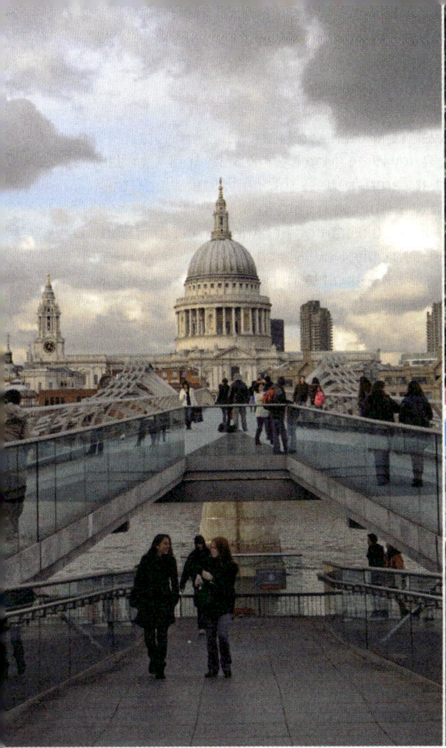
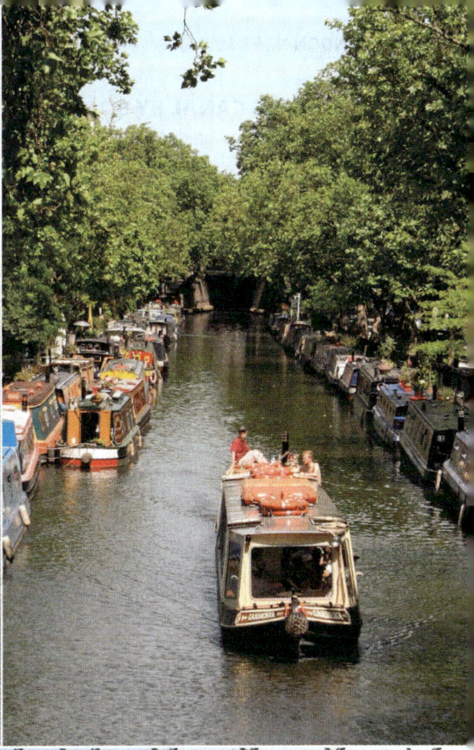
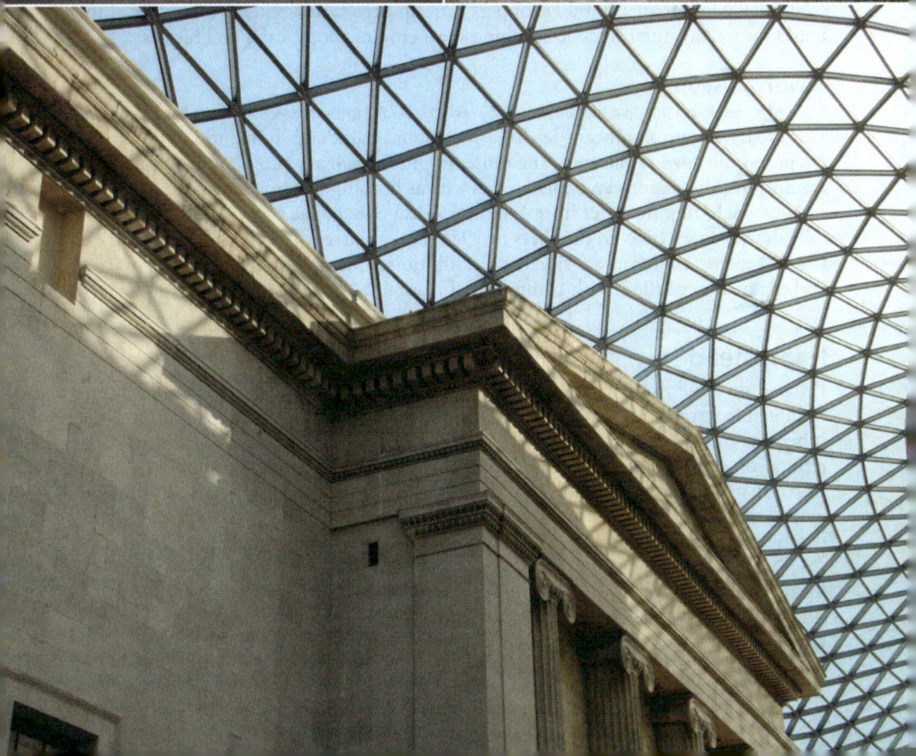

1

REGENT'S CANAL BY BOAT

Three companies run daily **boat services** between Camden and Little Venice, passing through the Maida Hill tunnel. The narrowboat *Jenny Wren* (March Sat & Sun; April–Oct daily; T 020 7485 4433, W walkersquay.com) starts off at Camden, goes through a canal lock (the only company to do so) and heads for Little Venice (with live commentary), while *Jason's* narrowboats (April–Oct; T 020 7286 3428, W jasons.co.uk) start off at Little Venice; the London Waterbus Company (April–Sept daily; Oct Thurs–Sun only; Nov–March Sat & Sun only, weather permitting; T 020 7482 2660, W londonwaterbus.com) sets off from both places and calls at London Zoo. Whichever you choose, you can board at either end; **tickets** cost around £10 return, and journey time is 50 minutes one-way.

London Zoo

Daily: March–Oct 10am–5.30pm; Nov–Feb 10am–4pm • £18 depending on season, book online to avoid queues • T 020 7722 3333, W zsl.org/zsl-london-zoo • ⊖ Camden Town

The northeastern corner of the park is occupied by **London Zoo**. Founded in 1826 with the remnants of the royal menagerie, the enclosures here are as humane as any inner-city zoo could make them, and kids usually enjoy themselves. Guaranteed winners are the regular "Animals in Action" live shows, Gorilla Kingdom, the invertebrate house – BUGS – and the walk-through Rainforest Life and Meet the Monkeys enclosures.

Camden Town

For all its tourist popularity, **Camden Market** remains a genuinely offbeat place. The sheer variety of what's on offer – from cheap CDs to furniture, along with a mass of street fashion and clubwear, and plenty of food stalls – is what makes **Camden Town** so special. More than 100,000 shoppers turn up here each weekend, and parts of the market now stay open week-long, alongside a crop of shops, cafés and bistros.

Jewish Museum

129 Albert St • Sat–Thurs 10am–5pm, Fri 10am–2pm • £7.50 • T 020 7284 7384, W jewishmuseum.org.uk • ⊖ Camden Town

Despite having no significant Jewish associations, Camden is home to London's purpose-built **Jewish Museum.** The museum puts on a lively programme of special exhibitions, discussions and concerts, as well as housing a permanent display of Judaica, including treasures from London's Great Synagogue on Duke's Place in the City, burnt down by Nazi bombers in 1941, and a sixteenth-century Venetian Ark of the Covenant. There's also a video and exhibition explaining Jewish religious practices and the history of the Jewish community in Britain.

Hampstead

Perched on a hill to the west of Hampstead Heath, **Hampstead** village developed into a fashionable spa in the eighteenth century, and was not much altered thereafter. Later, it became one of the city's most celebrated literary *quartiers* and even now it retains its reputation as a bolt hole of the high-profile intelligentsia and discerning pop stars. Proximity to **Hampstead Heath** is, of course, the real joy of Hampstead; this mixture of woodland, smooth pasture and landscaped garden is quite simply the most exhilarating patch of greenery in London.

Keats' House

Keats Grove • May–Oct Tues–Sun 1–5pm; Nov–April Fri–Sun 1–5pm • £5 • T 020 7332 3868, W keatshouse.cityoflondon.gov.uk • ⊖ Hampstead

Hampstead's most illustrious figure is celebrated at **Keats' House**, an elegant, whitewashed Regency double villa off Downshire Hill at the bottom of the High

Street. Inspired by the tranquillity of Hampstead and by his passion for girl-next-door Fanny Brawne (whose house is also part of the museum), Keats wrote some of his most famous works here before leaving for Rome, where he died of consumption in 1821. The neat, rather staid interior contains books and letters, Fanny's engagement ring and the four-poster bed in which the poet first coughed up blood, confiding to his companion, Charles Brown, "that drop of blood is my death warrant".

Freud Museum

20 Maresfield Gardens • Wed–Sun noon–5pm • £5 • Ⓦ freud.org.uk • ⊖ Finchley Road

The **Freud Museum** is one of the most poignant of London's house museums. Having lived in Vienna for his entire adult life, the psychotherapist, by now semi-disabled and with only a year to live, was forced to flee the Nazis, arriving in London in the summer of 1938. The ground-floor study and library look exactly as they did when Freud lived here; the collection of erotic antiquities and the famous couch, sumptuously draped in Persian rugs, were all brought here from Vienna. Upstairs, home movies of family life are shown continually, and a small room is dedicated to his daughter, Anna, herself an influential child analyst, who lived in the house until her death in 1982.

Hampstead Heath

Hampstead Heath may not have much of its original heathland left, but it packs a wonderful variety of bucolic scenery into its 800 acres. At its southern end are the rolling green pastures of **Parliament Hill**, north London's premier spot for kite flying. On either side are numerous ponds, three of which – one for men, one for women and one mixed – you can swim in. The thickest woodland is to be found in the **West Heath**, beyond Whitestone Pond, also the site of the most formal section, **Hill Garden**, a secretive and romantic little gem with eccentric balustraded terraces and a ruined pergola. Beyond lies **Golders Hill Park**, where you can gaze at pygmy goats and fallow deer, and inspect the impeccably maintained aviaries, home to flamingos, cranes and other exotic birds.

Kenwood House

Daily 11.30am–4pm • Free • Ⓣ 020 8348 1286 • Bus #210 from ⊖ Archway or Golders Green

Don't miss the landscaped grounds of **Kenwood**, in the north of the Heath, which are focused on the whitewashed Neoclassical mansion of **Kenwood House**. The house is now home to a collection of seventeenth- and eighteenth-century art, including a handful of real masterpieces by Vermeer, Rembrandt, Boucher, Gainsborough and Reynolds. Of the period interiors, the most spectacular is Robert Adam's sky-blue and gold library.

Highgate Cemetery

Swain's Lane • **East Cemetery** April–Oct Mon–Fri 10am–5pm, Sat & Sun 11am–5pm; Nov–March closes 4pm • £2 **West Cemetery** March–Nov Mon–Fri 2pm, Sat & Sun hourly 11am–4pm; Dec–Feb Sat & Sun hourly 11am–3pm • £7 • No under-8s • Ⓣ 020 8340 1834, Ⓦ highgate-cemetery.org • ⊖ Highgate

Highgate Cemetery, ranged on both sides of Swain's Lane, is London's best-known graveyard. The most illustrious incumbent of the **East Cemetery** is **Karl Marx**. Marx himself asked for a simple grave topped by a headstone, but by 1954 the Communist movement decided to move his grave to a more prominent position and erect the hulking bronze bust that now surmounts a granite plinth. To visit the more atmospheric and overgrown **West Cemetery**, with its spooky Egyptian Avenue and sunken catacombs, you must take a guided tour. Among the prominent graves usually visited are those of artist Dante Gabriel Rossetti, and lesbian novelist Radclyffe Hall.

1

RAF Museum

Grahame Park Way • Daily 10am–6pm • Free • 020 8205 2266, rafmuseum.org.uk • Colindale

A world-class assembly of historic military aircraft can be seen at the **RAF Museum**, in the former Hendon Aerodrome beside the M1 motorway. Enthusiasts won't be disappointed, but anyone looking for a balanced account of modern aerial warfare should probably go to the Imperial War Museum (see p.88). Those with children should head for the hands-on Aeronauts gallery; those without might prefer to explore the often overlooked display galleries, ranged around the edge of the Main Aircraft Hall, which contain an art gallery and an exhibition on the history of flight, accompanied by replicas of some of the deathtraps of early aviation.

Shri Swaminarayan Mandir

Daily 9am–6pm • Free, exhibition £2 • 020 8965 2651, mandir.org • Neasden

Perhaps the most remarkable building in the whole of London lies just off the North Circular, in the glum suburb of Neasden. Here, rising majestically above the surrounding semi-detached houses, is the **Shri Swaminarayan Mandir**, a traditional Hindu temple topped with domes and *shikharas*, erected in 1995 in a style and scale unseen outside of India for over a millennium. You enter through the Haveli (cultural complex) and, after taking off your shoes, proceed to the Mandir (temple) itself, carved entirely out of Carrara marble, with every possible surface transformed into a honeycomb of arabesques, flowers and seated gods. Beneath the Mandir, an **exhibition** explains the basic tenets of Hinduism and details the life of Lord Swaminarayan, and includes a video about the history of the building.

South London

Now largely built up into a patchwork of Victorian terraces, **South London** nevertheless includes one outstanding area for sightseeing, and that is **Greenwich**, with its fantastic ensemble of the Royal Naval College and the Queen's House, the National Maritime Museum, the Royal Observatory, and the beautifully landscaped royal park. The Sunday **market** is also a popular draw.

The only other suburban sights that stand out are the **Dulwich Picture Gallery**, a public art gallery even older than the National Gallery, and the eclectic **Horniman Museum**, in neighbouring Forest Hill.

Greenwich

Greenwich draws tourists out from the centre in considerable numbers. At its heart is the outstanding architectural set piece of the **Old Royal Naval College** and the **Queen's House**, courtesy of Christopher Wren and Inigo Jones respectively. Most visitors, however, come to see the **National Maritime Museum** and Greenwich Park's **Royal Observatory**. With the added attractions of its riverside pubs and walks – plus startling views across to Canary Wharf and Docklands – it makes for one of the best weekend trips in the capital. To reach Greenwich, you can take a **train** from London Bridge (every 30min), a **boat** from one of the piers in central London (every 20–30min), or the **DLR** to Cutty Sark station (every 4–10min).

Cutty Sark

020 8858 2698, cuttysark.org.uk • Cutty Sark DLR

Wedged in a dry dock by the river is the majestic **Cutty Sark**, the world's last surviving tea clipper. Launched in 1869, the *Cutty Sark* was actually more famous in its day as a wool clipper, returning from Australia in just 72 days. The vessel's name comes from

Robert Burns' *Tam O'Shanter*, in which Tam, a drunken farmer, is chased by Nannie, an angry witch in a short Paisley linen dress, or "cutty sark"; the clipper's figurehead shows her clutching the hair from the tail of Tam's horse. The ship closed for restoration and repairs following a fire in 2007, but is due to reopen in 2012.

Old Royal Naval College

Daily 10am–5pm • Free • ⓣ 020 8269 4747, ⓦ oldroyalnavalcollege.org • Cutty Sark DLR

It's appropriate that the one London building that makes the most of its riverbank location should be the **Old Royal Naval College**, a majestic Baroque ensemble designed, for the most part, by Wren. Initially built as a royal palace, but eventually converted into the Royal Hospital for Seamen, the complex was later home to the Royal Naval College, but now houses the University of Greenwich and the Trinity College of Music. The two grandest rooms, situated underneath Wren's twin domes, are open to the public and well worth visiting. The **Chapel**, in the east wing, has exquisite pastel-shaded plasterwork and spectacular, decorative detailing on the ceiling, all designed by James "Athenian" Stuart after a fire in 1799 destroyed the original interior. Opposite the chapel is the magnificent **Painted Hall** in the west wing, which is dominated by James Thornhill's gargantuan allegorical ceiling painting, and his trompe l'oeil fluted pilasters. Over in the Pepys Building, you can get a good overview of Greenwich's history in **Discover Greenwich**. The building also contains a tourist information office and the Royal Hospital's old brewhouse, which used to supply a ration of three pints to each seaman, and has now been revived and turned into a café/microbrewery.

National Maritime Museum

Romney Rd • Daily 10am–5pm • Free • ⓣ 020 8858 4422, ⓦ nmm.ac.uk • Cutty Sark DLR

The main building of the excellent **National Maritime Museum** is centred on a spectacular glass-roofed courtyard, which houses the museum's largest artefacts, among them the splendid 63ft-long gilded **Royal Barge**, designed in Rococo style by William Kent for Prince Frederick, the much unloved eldest son of George II. The various themed galleries are superbly designed to appeal to visitors of all ages. Level 3 has two hands-on galleries: **The Bridge**, where you can attempt to navigate a catamaran, a paddle steamer and a rowing boat to shore; and **All Hands**, where children can have a go at radio transmission, loading miniature cargo and firing a cannon.

Inigo Jones's **Queen's House**, originally built amidst a rambling Tudor royal palace, is now the focal point of the Greenwich ensemble, and is an integral part of the Maritime Museum. As royal residences go, it's an unassuming country house, but as the first Neoclassical building in the country, it has enormous architectural significance. The interior currently houses the museum's **art collection** including works by painters as diverse as Reynolds and Lowry. Off the Great Hall, a perfect cube, lies the beautiful **Tulip Staircase**, Britain's earliest cantilevered spiral staircase – its name derives from the floral patterning in the wrought-iron balustrade.

Royal Observatory

Blackheath Ave • **Astronomy Centre** Daily 10am–5pm • Free **Flamsteed House** Daily 10am–5pm • £10 **Planetarium** Mon–Fri 12.45–3.45pm; Sat & Sun & school holidays 11am–4pm • £6.50 • ⓣ 020 8858 4422, ⓦ nmm.ac.uk • Greenwich DLR/train station

Perched on the crest of Greenwich Park's highest hill, the **Royal Observatory** was established by Charles II in 1675. It's housed in a rather dinky Wren-built red-brick building, whose northeastern turret sports a bright-red time-ball that climbs the mast at 12.58pm and drops at 1pm GMT precisely; it was added in 1833 to allow ships to set their clocks.

Greenwich's greatest claim to fame, of course, is as the home of **Greenwich Mean Time** (GMT) and the **Prime Meridian**. Since 1884, Greenwich has occupied zero longitude – hence the world sets its clocks by GMT. The observatory housed the first Astronomer Royal, John Flamsteed, whose chief task was to study the night sky in order to discover an astronomical method of finding the longitude of a ship at sea. Beyond the Octagon Room, where the king used to show off to his guests, are the Time galleries, which display four of the clocks designed by **John Harrison**, including "H4", which helped win the Longitude Prize in 1763.

The **Astronomy Centre** houses high-tech galleries giving a brief rundown of the Big Bang theory of the universe and invites you to consider the big questions of astronomy today. You can also watch one of the thirty-minute presentations in the state-of-the-art **Planetarium**, introduced by a Royal Observatory astronomer.

Dulwich Picture Gallery

Gallery Rd • Tues–Sun 10am–5pm • £5 • T 020 8693 5254, W dulwichpicturegallery.org.uk • West Dulwich (from Victoria) or North Dulwich (from London Bridge) train stations

Dulwich Picture Gallery, the nation's oldest public art gallery, was designed by John Soane in 1814. Soane created a beautifully spacious building, awash with natural light and crammed with superb paintings – elegiac landscapes by Cuyp, one of the world's finest Poussin series, and splendid works by Hogarth, Gainsborough, Van Dyck, Canaletto and Rubens, plus **Rembrandt**'s tiny *Portrait of a Young Man*, a top-class portrait of poet, playwright and Royalist, the future Earl of Bristol. At the centre of the museum is a tiny mausoleum designed by Soane for the sarcophagi of the gallery's founders.

Horniman Museum

100 London Rd • Daily 10.30am–5.30pm • Free, aquarium £6 • T 020 8699 1872, W horniman.ac.uk • Forest Hill train station from Victoria or London Bridge

The wonderful **Horniman Museum** was purpose-built in 1901 by Frederick Horniman, a tea trader with a passion for collecting. In addition to the museum's natural history collection of stuffed birds and animals, there's an eclectic ethnographic collection, and a music gallery with more than 1500 instruments from Chinese gongs to electric guitars. Don't miss the state-of-the-art aquarium in the basement.

West London

Most visitors experience **West London** en route to or from Heathrow Airport, either from the confines of the train or tube (which runs overground at this point), or the motorway. The city and its satellites seem to continue unabated, with only fleeting glimpses of the countryside. However, in the five-mile stretch from Chiswick to Osterley there are several former country retreats, now surrounded by suburbia.

The Palladian villa of **Chiswick House** is perhaps the best known. However, it draws nothing like as many visitors as **Syon House**, most of whom come for the gardening centre rather than for the house itself, a showcase for the talents of Robert Adam, who also worked at **Osterley House**, another Elizabethan conversion.

Running through much of the area is the **River Thames**, once the "Great Highway of London" and still the most pleasant way to travel in these parts during summer. Boats

RIVER TRANSPORT: HEADING WEST

From April to October **Westminster Passenger Services** run a scheduled service from Westminster Pier to Kew, Richmond and Hampton Court (3hr one-way; £15 single, £22.50 return; T 020 7930 2062, W wpsa.co.uk). In addition, **Turks** runs a regular service from Richmond to Hampton Court (April to mid-Sept Tues–Sun; £6.80 single, £8.40 return; T 020 8546 2434, W turks.co.uk). For the latest on boat services on the Thames, see W tfl.gov.uk.

plough up the Thames all the way from central London via the **Royal Botanic Gardens** at **Kew** and the picturesque riverside at **Richmond**, as far as Hampton Court (see p.107).

Chiswick House

Great Chertsey Rd • **House** April–Oct Mon–Wed & Sun 10am–5pm • EH • £5.50 **Gardens** Daily 7am–dusk • Free • T 020 8995 0508, W chgt.org.uk • Chiswick train station from Waterloo or ⊖ Turnham Green

Chiswick House is a perfect little Neoclassical villa, designed in the 1720s by the Earl of Burlington, and set in one of the most beautifully landscaped gardens in London. Like its prototype, Palladio's Villa Rotonda near Vicenza, the house was created as a "temple to the arts" where, amid his fine art collection, Burlington could entertain artistic friends such as Swift, Handel and Pope. Entertaining took place on the **upper floor**, a series of cleverly interconnecting rooms, each enjoying a wonderful view out onto the gardens – all, that is, except the Tribunal, the domed octagonal hall at the centre of the villa, where the earl's finest paintings and sculptures would have been displayed.

Kew Bridge Steam Museum

Green Dragon Lane • Tues–Sun 11am–4pm • £9.50 • T 020 8568 4757, W kbsm.org • Bus #237 or #267 from ⊖ Gunnersbury or Kew Bridge train station from Waterloo

Difficult to miss, thanks to its stylish Italianate standpipe tower, **Kew Bridge Steam Museum** occupies a former Victorian pumping station on the corner of Kew Bridge Road and Green Dragon Lane, 100m west of the bridge itself. At the heart of the museum is the Steam Hall, which contains a triple expansion steam engine and four gigantic nineteenth-century Cornish beam engines. The museum also has a hands-on **Water for Life** gallery in the basement, devoted to the history of the capital's water supply. The best time to visit is at weekends, when each of the museum's industrial dinosaurs is put through its paces, and the small **narrow-gauge steam railway** runs back and forth round the yard (April–Oct Sun).

Syon House

London Rd • Mid-March to Oct Wed, Thurs & Sun 11am–5pm • £10 • T 020 8560 0881, W syonpark.co.uk • Bus #237 or #267 from ⊖ Gunnersbury or Kew Bridge train station

From its rather plain castellated exterior, you'd never guess that **Syon House** contains the most opulent eighteenth-century interiors in London. The splendour of Robert Adam's refurbishment is immediately revealed, however, in the pristine **Great Hall**, an apsed double cube with a screen of Doric columns at one end and classical statuary dotted around the edges. There are several more Adam-designed rooms to admire in the house, in particular the **Long Gallery** – 136ft by just 14ft – plus a smattering of works by Lely, Van Dyck and others.

While Adam beautified Syon House, Capability Brown laid out its **gardens** around an artificial lake, surrounding it with oaks, beeches, limes and cedars. The gardens' chief focus now, however, is the crescent-shaped **Great Conservatory**, an early nineteenth-century addition which is said to have inspired Joseph Paxton, architect of the Crystal Palace.

Osterley House

Jersey Rd • March Wed–Sun noon–3.30pm; April–Oct Wed–Sun noon–4.30pm; Nov & Dec Sat & Sun noon–3.30pm • NT • £8.25 • T 020 8232 5050, W nationaltrust.org.uk • ⊖ Osterley

Robert Adam redesigned another colossal Elizabethan mansion three miles northwest of Syon at **Osterley**, in one of London's largest surviving estate parks, which still gives the impression of being in the countryside, despite the M4 motorway to the north.

1

Osterley House boasts a characteristically cool **Entrance Hall**, followed by the so-called State Rooms of the south wing. Highlights include the **Drawing Room**, with Reynolds portraits on the damask walls and a coffered ceiling centred on a giant marigold, and the **Etruscan Dressing Room**, in which every surface is covered in delicate painted trelliswork, sphinxes and urns; Adam (and Wedgwood) dubbed the style "Etruscan", though it is in fact derived from Greek vases found at Pompeii.

Kew Gardens

Kew Rd • Daily 9.30am–6.30pm or dusk • £13.90 • ⓣ 020 8332 5000, ⓦ kew.org • ⊖ Kew Gardens

Established in 1759, Kew's **Royal Botanic Gardens** manage the extremely difficult task of being both a world leader in botanic research and an extraordinarily beautiful and popular public park. There's always something to see, whatever the season, but to get the most out of the place come sometime between spring and autumn, bring a picnic and stay for the day.

Of all the glasshouses, by far the most celebrated is the **Palm House**, a curvaceous mound of glass and wrought iron, designed by Decimus Burton in the 1840s. Its drippingly humid atmosphere nurtures most of the known palm species, while in the basement there's a small, excellent tropical aquarium.

Kew Palace

April–Sept Mon 11am–5pm, Tues–Sun 10am–5pm • £5.30 • ⓣ 0844 482 7777, ⓦ hrp.org • ⊖ Kew Gardens

The three-storey red-brick mansion of **Kew Palace**, to the northwest of the Palm House, was bought by George II as a nursery and schoolhouse for his umpteen children. Later, George III was confined to the palace and subjected to the dubious attentions of doctors who attempted to find a cure for his "madness". There are one or two bits and bobs belonging to the royals, like the much-loved dolls' house, on the ground floor, which belonged to George III's daughters. Upstairs, you can view the chair in which Queen Charlotte passed away in 1818, while the top floor has been left pretty much untouched since those days.

Richmond

Richmond, upriver from Kew, basked for centuries in the glow of royal patronage, with Plantagenet kings and Tudor monarchs frequenting the riverside palace. Although most of the courtiers and aristocrats have gone, it is still a wealthy district, with two theatres and highbrow pretensions.

Richmond Park

Daily: March–Sept 7am–dusk; Oct–Feb 7.30am–dusk • Free • ⓦ royalparks.gov.uk • Bus #371 or #65 from ⊖ Richmond to Petersham Gate

Richmond's greatest attraction is the enormous **Richmond Park**, at the top of Richmond Hill – 2500 acres of undulating grassland and bracken, dotted with coppiced woodland and as wild as anything in London. Eight miles across at its widest point, this is Europe's largest city park, famed for its red and fallow deer, which roam freely, and for its ancient oaks. For the most part untamed, the park does have a couple of deliberately landscaped plantations that feature splendid springtime azaleas and rhododendrons.

Ham House

Ham St • April–Oct Sat–Thurs noon–4pm • Guided tours: Feb & March daily except Fri 11.30am–3.30pm; Nov Mon, Tues, Sat & Sun 11.30am–3pm • NT • £9.90 • ⓣ 020 8940 1950 • Bus #371 or #65 from ⊖ Richmond

Leave the rest of London far behind at **Ham House**, home to the earls of Dysart for nearly three hundred years. Expensively furnished in the seventeenth century, but little altered since then, the house is blessed with one of the finest Stuart interiors in the country, from the stupendously ornate Great Staircase to the Long Gallery, featuring six "Court Beauties" by Peter Lely. Elsewhere, there are several fine Verrio ceiling paintings, some exquisite parquet flooring and works by Van Dyck and Reynolds. Also glorious are the formal seventeenth-century **gardens**, especially the Cherry Garden, laid out with a pungent lavender parterre. The Orangery, overlooking the original kitchen garden, currently serves as a tearoom.

Strawberry Hill

268 Waldegrave Rd • Mon–Wed 2–6pm, Sat & Sun noon–6pm (last admission 4.20pm) • £8 • ⓣ 020 8744 1241, ⓦ strawberryhillhouse.org.uk • Strawberry Hill train station from Waterloo

In 1747 writer, wit and fashion queen Horace Walpole, youngest son of former prime minister Robert Walpole, bought this "little play-thing house…the prettiest bauble you ever saw…set in enamelled meadows, with filigree hedges", renamed it **Strawberry Hill** and set about inventing the most influential building in the Gothic Revival. Walpole appointed a "Committee of Taste" to embellish his project with details from other Gothic buildings: screens from Old St Paul's and Rouen cathedrals, and fan vaulting from Henry VII's Chapel in Westminster Abbey. Walpole wanted visits of Strawberry Hill to be a theatrical experience, and, with its eccentric Gothic decor, it remains so to this day.

Hampton Court

Daily: April–Oct 10am–6pm; Nov–March 10am–4.30pm • Palace, gardens & maze £14.50, free guided tours available (45min); gardens only £5.30; maze only £3.85 • ⓣ 020 3166 6000, ⓦ hrp.org.uk • Hampton Court train station from Waterloo

Hampton Court Palace, a sprawling red-brick ensemble on the banks of the Thames thirteen miles southwest of London, is the finest of England's royal abodes. Built in 1516 by the upwardly mobile **Cardinal Wolsey**, Henry VIII's Lord Chancellor, it was purloined by Henry himself after Wolsey fell from favour. In the second half of the seventeenth century, Charles II laid out the gardens, inspired by what he had seen at Versailles, while William and Mary had large sections of the palace remodelled by Wren a few years later.

The **Royal Apartments** are divided into six thematic walking tours. There's not a lot of information in any of the rooms, but audioguides are available and free guided tours are led by period-costumed historians who bring the place to life. If your energy is lacking – and Hampton Court is huge – the most rewarding sections are: **Henry VIII's State Apartments**, which feature the glorious double-hammer-beamed Great Hall; **William III's Apartments**; and **Henry VIII's Kitchens**.

Tickets to the Royal Apartments cover entry to the rest of the sites in the grounds. Those who don't wish to visit the apartments are free to wander around the gardens and visit the curious **Royal Tennis Courts** (April–Oct), but have to pay to try out the palace's famously tricky yew-hedge **Maze**, and visit the **Privy Garden**, where you can view Andrea Mantegna's colourful, heroic canvases, *The Triumphs of Caesar*, housed in the Lower Orangery, and the celebrated **Great Vine**, whose grapes are sold at the palace each year in September.

Windsor

Every weekend trains from Waterloo and Paddington are packed with people heading for **WINDSOR**, the royal enclave 21 miles west of London, where they join the human conveyor belt round **Windsor Castle**. If you've got the energy or inclination, it's possible to cross the river to visit **Eton College**, which grew from a fifteenth-century free school for impoverished scholars and choristers to become one of the most elitest schools in the world (guided tours April–Sept daily 2pm & 3.15pm; term time Wed & Fri–Sun only; £6.50; ⓦ etoncollege.com).

Windsor Castle

Daily: March–Oct 9.45am–5.15pm; Nov–Feb 9.45am–4.15pm • £17 • ⓣ 020 7766 7304, ⓦ royalcollection.org.uk • Paddington to Windsor & Eton Central station via Slough, or Waterloo to Windsor & Eton Riverside station

Towering above the town on a steep chalk bluff, **Windsor Castle** is an undeniably imposing sight, its chilly grey walls, punctuated by mighty medieval bastions, continuing as far as the eye can see. Inside, most visitors just gape in awe at the monotonous, gilded grandeur of the **State Apartments**, while the real highlights – the paintings from the Royal Collection that line the walls – are rarely given a second glance. More impressive is **St George's Chapel**, a glorious Perpendicular structure ranking with Henry VII's chapel in Westminster Abbey (see p.66), and the second most important resting place for royal corpses after the Abbey. On a fine day, put aside some time for exploring **Windsor Great Park**, which stretches for several miles to the south of the castle.

ARRIVAL AND DEPARTURE — LONDON

BY PLANE

The capital's five **international airports** – Heathrow, Gatwick, Stansted, Luton and City Airport – are all less than an hour from the city centre.

HEATHROW

Fifteen miles west of central London, **Heathrow** (ⓦ heathrowairport.com), has five terminals and three train/tube stations: one for terminals 1, 2 and 3, and separate ones for terminals 4 and 5.

Heathrow Express High-speed (ⓦ heathrowexpress.com) trains travel non-stop to Paddington Station (every 15min; 15–23min; online tickets £16.50 single/£32 return, more if you buy your ticket at the ticket office or on the train).

Heathrow Connect Less pricey trains (ⓦ heathrow connect.com) travel to Paddington with several stops on the way (every 30min; 25–30min; £8.50 single/£16.50 return).

Underground An even cheaper alternative is to take the tube (Piccadilly line) into central London (every 5–9min; 50min; £5 single/£8 for a One Day Off-Peak Travelcard.

National Express National Express bus services (ⓦ nationalexpress.com) run direct to Victoria Coach Station (daily every 15–30min; 40–55min; £5 single, £9 return).

Night buses From midnight, you can take night bus #N9 (every 20min; 1hr; £2.20) from Heathrow to Trafalgar Square.

GATWICK

Around 30 miles south of London, **Gatwick** Airport (ⓦ baa .co.uk) has good transport connections with the city.

Gatwick Express The non-stop Gatwick Express (ⓦ gatwickexpress.com) runs between the airport's South Terminal and Victoria Station (every 15min; 30–35min; £30 return, less online).

Overground trains Other train options include Southern services to Victoria (every 15min; 35min) or First Capital Connect services to various stations (every 15–30min; journey 30–45min), including London Bridge and St Pancras; tickets for either cost around £12 single.

Buses easyBus (ⓦ easybus.co.uk) runs buses to West Brompton tube (every 20min; 1hr 10min), with online tickets from £2 single (£10 if you buy on board). National Express buses run from Gatwick direct to central London (hourly; 1hr 30min); tickets cost around £7 single, £12.50 return.

STANSTED

Roughly 35 miles northeast of the capital, **Stansted** (ⓦ stanstedairport.com) is commonly used by the budget airlines.

Stansted Express The most convenient way to get into town is on the Stansted Express (ⓦ stanstedexpress.com) to Liverpool Street (every 15–30min; 45min; £27 return).

Buses All year round, 24 hours a day, easyBus runs buses to Baker Street tube (every 20–30min; 1hr 15min; online tickets from £2 single, £10 if you buy on board). National Express runs buses to Victoria Coach Station (24hr; every 30min; 1hr 30min–1hr 45min; £10 single, £17 return).

LUTON

Around 30 miles north of London, **Luton** (ⓦ london -luton.co.uk) handles mostly charter flights.

Luton Airport Parkway A free shuttle bus (every 10min; 5min) transports passengers to Luton Airport Parkway train station, connected to St Pancras (every 15–30min; 25–35min; £12.50 single, £21.50 return) and other central London stations.

Buses All year round, 24 hours a day, Green Line and easyBus run the #757 coach from Luton Airport to Victoria Coach Station (every 20–30min; 1hr 20min; from £2 online, or as much as £10).

CITY AIRPORT

London's smallest airport, used primarily by business people, **City Airport** (ⓦ londoncityairport.com) is in Docklands, 10 miles east of central London. Docklands Light Railway (DLR) will take you straight to Bank in the City (20min; around £4), where you can change to the tube.

BY TRAIN

From Europe Eurostar (eurostar.com) trains arrive at St Pancras International, next door to King's Cross.

From Britain Arriving by train from elsewhere in Britain, you'll come into one of London's numerous mainline stations, all of which have adjacent Underground stations linking into the city centre's tube network.

Stations As a rough guide, Charing Cross handles services to Kent; Euston to the Midlands, northwest England and Glasgow; Fenchurch Street to south Essex; King's Cross to northeast England and Scotland; Liverpool Street to eastern England; Marylebone to the Midlands; Paddington to southwest England; St Pancras for Eurostar and the southeast, plus trains to East Midlands and South Yorkshire; and Victoria and Waterloo to southeast England.

Information National Rail Enquiries (08457 484 950, nationalrail.co.uk).

DESTINATIONS

London Charing Cross to: Canterbury West (hourly; 1hr 40min); Dover Priory (Mon–Sat every 30min; 1hr 40min–1hr 50min); Hastings (2 hourly; 1hr 30min); Rochester (every 30min; 1hr 10min).

London Euston to: Birmingham New Street (every 20min; 1hr 25min); Carlisle (every 2hr; 3hr 15min); Lancaster (hourly; 2hr 30min); Liverpool Lime St (hourly; 2hr 10min); Manchester Piccadilly (every 20min; 2hr 10min).

London King's Cross to: Brighton (Mon–Sat 4 hourly, Sun 2 hourly; 1hr); Cambridge (every 30min; 45min); Durham (hourly; 2hr 40min–3hr); Leeds (hourly; 2hr 25min); Newcastle (every 30min; 3hr); Peterborough (every 30min; 45min); York (every 30min; 2hr).

London Liverpool Street to: Cambridge (every 30min; 1hr 15min); Norwich (every 30min; 1hr 55min).

London Paddington to: Bath (every 30min–hourly; 1hr 30min); Bristol (every 30–45min; 1hr 40min); Cheltenham (every 2hr; 2hr 15min); Exeter (hourly; 2hr 15min); Gloucester (every 2hr; 2hr); Oxford (every 30min; 55min); Penzance (every 1–2hr; 5hr 30min); Plymouth (hourly; 3hr 15min–3hr 40min); Windsor (change at Slough; Mon–Fri every 20min; Sat & Sun every 30min; 30–40min); Worcester (hourly; 2hr 20min).

London St Pancras to: Brighton (every 20min; 1hr 20min); Canterbury (every 30min; 1hr); Dover Priory (hourly; 1hr 5min); Leicester (every 30min; 1hr 10min); Nottingham (every 30min; 1hr 40min–2hr); Rochester (every 30min; 40min); Sheffield (every 30min; 2hr 10min–2hr 30min).

London Victoria to: Arundel (Mon–Sat every 30min, Sun hourly; 1hr 30min); Brighton (every 30min; 50min); Canterbury East (every 30min–hourly; 1hr 25min); Chichester (Mon–Sat 2 hourly; 1hr 35min); Dover Priory (Mon–Sat every 30min; 1hr 40min–1hr 55min); Lewes (Mon–Sat every 30min, Sun hourly; 1hr 10min); Rochester (every 30min; 45min).

London Waterloo to: Portsmouth Harbour (every 30min; 1hr 35min); Southampton Central (every 30min; 1hr 15min); Winchester (every 30min; 1hr); Windsor (Mon–Sat every 30min, Sun hourly; 50min).

BY BUS

Victoria Coach Station Coming into London by coach (0870 580 8080, nationalexpress.com), you're most likely to arrive at Victoria Coach Station, a couple of hundred yards south down Buckingham Palace Road from the train and Underground stations of the same name.

Information Traveline (0871 200 2233, traveline.info).

Destinations Bath (hourly to every 1hr 30min; 3hr 30min); Birmingham (every 30min–hourly; 2hr 35min); Brighton (hourly; 2hr 10min); Bristol (hourly; 2hr 30min); Cambridge (hourly; 2hr); Canterbury (hourly; 2hr); Dover (hourly; 2hr 30min–3hr); Exeter (every 2hr; 4hr 15min); Gloucester (hourly; 3hr 20min); Liverpool (6 daily; 4hr 50min–5hr 30min); Manchester (9 daily; 4hr 50min–5hr 30min); Newcastle (5 daily; 6hr 25min–7hr 55min); Oxford (every 15min; 1hr 50min); Plymouth (6 daily; 5hr 20min); Stratford (4 daily; 3hr).

GETTING AROUND

London's **transport network** is among the most complex and expensive in the world, but on the bright side you should be able to get to wherever you want, most hours of the day or night, simply by arming yourself with a tube map. Avoid travelling during the **rush hour** (Mon–Fri 8–9.30am & 5–7pm), when tubes become unbearably crowded, and some buses get so full that they won't let you on.

Information Transport for London (TfL) provides excellent free maps and details of bus and tube services from its six Travel Information Centres: the most central is at Piccadilly Circus tube station (daily 9.15am–7pm); there are other desks at the arrivals at Heathrow (terminals 1, 2 & 3) and various tube/train stations. There's also a 24-hour helpline and website for information on all bus and tube services (0843 222 1234, tfl.gov.uk).

BY TUBE

Except for very short journeys, the Underground – or tube – is by far the quickest way to get about.

Tube lines Eleven different lines cross much of the metropolis, although London south of the river is not very well covered. Each line has its own colour and name – all you need to know is which direction you're travelling in: northbound, eastbound, southbound or westbound, and the final destination.

1

Zones London is divided into six concentric zones, with the vast majority of the city's accommodation, pubs, restaurants and sights in zones 1 and 2.

Services Services are frequent (Mon–Sat 5.30am–12.30am, Sun 7.30am–11.30pm), and you rarely have to wait more than five minutes for a train between central stations.

Fares Single fares are expensive – a journey in the central zone costs £4 – so if you're intending to make more than one journey, an Oyster card or a Travelcard is by far your best option (see below).

BY BUS

London's red buses – some of them, but not all, double-deckers – tend to get stuck in traffic jams, which prevents their running to a regular timetable. You must signal to get the bus to stop, and press the bell in order to get off.

Services Some buses run a 24-hour service, but most run between about 5am and midnight, with a network of Night Buses (prefixed with the letter "N") operating outside this period (every 20–30min).

Fares The standard walk-on fare is £2.20, but passes are available (see below).

BY TRAIN

Large areas of London's outskirts are best reached by the suburban (overground) train network. Wherever a sight can only be reached by overground train, we've indicated in the guide the nearest train station and the central terminus from which you can depart.

BY BOAT

Unfortunately, **boat services** on the Thames are not fully integrated into the public transport system. If you have a valid Travelcard (either in paper or Oyster form), you're entitled to a third off, but if you have a pay-as-you-go Oyster card, you get just ten percent off.

Services Timetables and services are complex, and there are numerous companies and small charter operators – for a full list pick up a booklet from a TfL information centre (see p.109) or visit tfl.gov.uk. One of the largest companies is Thames Clippers (thamesclippers.com), who run a regular commuter service (every 20–30min; around £5.50 single) between Waterloo and Greenwich; an off-peak hop-on, hop-off River Roamer on their services costs £12.60.

BY TAXI

Black cabs Compared to most capital cities, London's metered black cabs are an expensive option unless there are three or more of you. The minimum fare is £2.20, and a ride from Euston to Victoria, for example, costs around £12–15 (Mon–Fri 6am–8pm). After 8pm on weekdays and all day during the weekend, a higher tariff applies, and after 10pm it's higher still. A yellow light over the windscreen tells you if the cab is available – just stick your arm out to hail it. To order a black cab in advance, phone 0871 871 8710, and be prepared to pay an extra £2.

Minicabs Private minicabs are considerably cheaper than black cabs, but they cannot be hailed from the street. All minicabs should be licensed and able to produce a TfL ID on demand, but the best way to pick a company is to take the advice of the place you're at, unless you want to be certain of a woman driver, in which case call Ladycabs (020 7272 3300), or a gay/lesbian-friendly driver, in which case call Freedom Cars (020 7739 9080).

BY BIKE

Boris bikes The easiest way to cycle round London is to use the city's cycle hire scheme – or Boris bikes, as they're

GETTING ABOUT: OYSTER CARDS AND PASSES

The cheapest, easiest way to get about London is to use an **Oyster card**, a smartcard that's valid on the entire transport network. You can buy the card from tube stations, some newsagents and Travel Information Centres, and use it either to store a weekly/monthly/yearly **Travelcard**, or as a pay-as-you-go deal; you can top it up at all tube stations and many newsagents. As you enter the tube or bus, simply touch in your card at the card reader – if you're using pay-as-you-go, the fare will be taken off. If you're using the tube or train, you need to touch out again, or a maximum cash fare of up to £7.40 will be deducted. A pay-as-you-go Oyster operates daily price-capping; you will stop being charged when you've paid the equivalent of a Day Travelcard, but you still need to touch in (and out). Oyster cards are free for those buying monthly or yearly tickets; everyone else needs to hand over a £5 refundable deposit. Visitors can order a pay-as-you-go Oyster card in advance for just £3.

Children under 11 travel for free; children aged 11–15 travel free on all buses and at child-rate on the tube; children aged 16 or 17 can travel at half the adult rate on all forms of transport. However, all children over 10 must have an Oyster photocard to be eligible for the discounts – these should be applied for in advance online and will cost £10.

Various other travelcards and bus passes are available, too; check tfl.gov.uk for details.

THE CONGESTION CHARGE

All vehicles entering central London on weekdays between 7am and 6pm are liable to a **congestion charge** of £10 per vehicle. Drivers can pay the charge online, over the phone and at garages and shops, and must do so before midnight the same day or incur a £2 surcharge – 24 hours later, you'll be liable for a £120 Penalty Charge Notice (reduced to £60 if you pay within 14 days). Disabled travellers, motorcycles, minibuses and some alternative-fuel vehicles are exempt from the charge, and local residents get a 90 percent discount, but you must register in order to qualify. For more details, visit Ⓦ tfl.gov.uk.

universally known, after Boris Johnson, the Mayor of London at the time they were introduced. There are hundreds of docking stations across central London. With a credit or debit card, you can buy 24 hours' access to the bikes for just £1, after which you get the first half-hour free, so if you hop from station to station, you don't pay another penny. Otherwise, it's £1 for the first hour, increasing rapidly after that to £15 for three hours. If you're going to use the scheme a lot, you may be best off becoming a member and getting a key – for more details see Ⓦ tfl.gov.uk.

INFORMATION

Britain & London Visitor Centre London's main tourist office, at 1 Regent St (April–Sept Mon 9.30am–6.30pm, Tues–Fri 9am–6.30pm, Sat 9am–5pm, Sun 10am–4pm; Oct–March Mon 9.30am–6pm, Tues 9am–6pm, Sat & Sun 10am–4pm; Ⓣ 0870 156 6366, Ⓦ visitlondon.com; ⊖ Piccadilly Circus).

London Information Centre This tiny window in the tkts kiosk on Leicester Square (daily 8am–midnight; Ⓣ 020 7292 2333, Ⓦ londoninformationcentre.com; ⊖ Leicester Square) offers general tourist information.

City of London Information Centre The City has its own information office on the south side of St Paul's Cathedral (Mon–Sat 9.30am–5.30pm, Sun 10am–4pm; Ⓣ 020 7332 1456, Ⓦ visitthecity.co.uk; ⊖ St Paul's).

Maps If you want to find your way around every nook and cranny of the city you'll need to invest in either an *A–Z Atlas* or a *Nicholson Streetfinder*, both of which have a street index covering every street in the capital. You can get them at most bookshops and newsagents for around £5. Stanfords, in Covent Garden at 12–14 Long Acre, WC2 (Ⓣ 020 7836 1321, Ⓦ stanfords.co.uk) is a good map shop.

Listings magazines The most useful listings magazine for visitors, on the newsstands every Tuesday, is *Time Out*. It carries news and consumer features, along with critical appraisals of all the week's theatre, film, music, exhibitions, children's events and more; listings themselves are even more comprehensive on its website (Ⓦ timeout.com).

ACCOMMODATION

London **accommodation** is expensive. The city's hostels are among the most costly in the world, while venerable institutions such as the *Ritz*, the *Dorchester* and the *Savoy* charge guests the very top international prices – from £300 per luxurious night. For a decent **hotel** room, you shouldn't expect much change out of £100 a night, and even the most basic **B&Bs** struggle to bring their tariffs down to £70 for a double with shared facilities. If you're not bothered about atmosphere or local flavour then the **chain hotels** are a safe bet – but offer far less character than the family-owned places that we've reviewed below. *Premier Inn* (Ⓦ premierinn.com), *Travelodge* (Ⓦ travelodge.com), *easyHotel* (Ⓦ easyhotel.com) and *Yotel* (Ⓦ yotel.com) all have hotels in central locations. Whatever the time of year, you should phone as far in advance as you can if you want to stay within a couple of tube stops of the West End.

BOOKING

British Hotel Reservation Centre (BHRC). With desks at Heathrow, Gatwick and Stansted airports, and Paddington, St Pancras and Victoria train stations, BHRC offices (Ⓣ 020 7592 3055, Ⓦ bhrc.co.uk) are open daily from early till very late, and there's no booking fee – they can also get big discounts at the more upmarket hotels.

Useful websites You can book accommodation for free online at Ⓦ londontown.com; payment is made directly to the hotel and they offer good discounts. Ⓦ londonbb.com sources B&B options, while Ⓦ couchsurfing.com puts young travellers in touch with people to stay or hang out with for free, and Ⓦ crashpadder.com offers a similar service for people who want to rent a room in a private house.

HOTELS

When choosing your **area**, bear in mind that as a rule the West End – Soho, Covent Garden, St James's, Mayfair and Marylebone – and the western districts of Knightsbridge and Kensington are dominated by expensive, upmarket hotels, whereas Bloomsbury is both inexpensive and very central. For rock-bottom rooms, the widest choice is close to the main train termini of Victoria and Paddington, and among the budget B&Bs of Earl's Court.

1

LONDON POSTCODES

A brief word on **London postcodes**: the name of each street is followed by a letter giving the geographical location (E for "east", WC for "west central" and so on) and a number that specifies the postal area. However, this is not a reliable indication of the remoteness of the locale – W5, for example, lies beyond the more remote sounding NW10 – so it's always best to check a map before taking a room in what may sound like a fairly central area.

VICTORIA

B&B Belgravia 64–66 Ebury St, SW1 020 7259 8570, bb-belgravia.com; Victoria; map pp.60–61. A B&B with flair, close to the train and bus stations. The 17 rooms are boutique-style, with original cornicing, large sash windows and modern touches; those on the ground floor can be noisy. They also have nearby studios from £135. Free wi-fi and bike loan. **£129**

Luna Simone Hotel 47–49 Belgrave Rd, SW1 020 7834 5897, lunasimonehotel.com; Victoria; map pp.60–61. Good-value family-run B&B with friendly staff and well-maintained en-suite rooms, including triples (£130) and quads (£150). Big English breakfasts are included, and there's free wi-fi on the ground floor and in the lobby. **£95**

★ **Morgan House** 120 Ebury St, SW1 020 7730 2384, morganhouse.co.uk; Victoria; map pp.94–95. A well above-average B&B in a comfortable Georgian building in a pretty street on the Chelsea/Victoria borders. Rooms are mostly en suite; the family room (£148) crams in a double and a bunk bed. Full breakfasts, and free wi-fi in the lobby. **£78**

WESTMINSTER

Sanctuary House 33 Tothill St, SW1 020 7799 4044, fullershotels.com; St James's Park; map pp.64–65. Run by Fuller's Brewery, above a Fuller's pub, with uncontroversial sub-Victorian decor. Breakfast is extra, and served in the pub, but the location, right by St James's Park, is terrific. Ask about weekend deals. Free wi-fi. **£120**

MARYLEBONE

Lincoln House 33 Gloucester Place, W1 020 7486 7630, lincoln-house-hotel.co.uk; Marble Arch or Baker Street; map pp.94–95. Dark wood panelling and nautical paraphernalia give this Georgian guesthouse a quirky feel, but the rooms are en suite and comfortable, with tea and coffee facilities. Rates vary according to the size of the bed and length of stay; there are good online discounts. Breakfast costs extra. Free laundry facilities and wi-fi. **£75**

Minotel Wigmore Court Hotel 23 Gloucester Place, W1 020 7935 0928, wigmore-hotel.co.uk; Marble Arch or Baker Street; map pp.94–95. The decor may not be to everyone's taste, but this eighteenth-century townhouse is a better than average B&B, with lots of return customers, and the en-suite rooms, including family rooms, are comfortable. Free wi-fi, but it's patchy. **£110**

SOHO

★ **Dean Street Townhouse** 69–71 Dean St W1 0207/434 1775, deanstreettownhouse.com; Tottenham Court Road or Leicester Square; map pp.64–65. One of a chic set of hotels owned by the trendy Soho House members' club, this 1730s house offers a "broom cupboard" and a few "tiny" rooms (from £120) – OK for solo travellers, or if you're just staying one night. The "small" (from £160) rooms are ample, and "medium" and "bigger" (from £270) have plenty of space. Luxury details include handpainted wallpaper, funky toiletries, fresh milk and cookies, and clawfoot tubs, some of them in the bedrooms themselves. Free wi-fi. **£120**

★ **Hazlitt's** 6 Frith St, W1 020 7434 1771, hazlittshotel.com; Tottenham Court Road; map pp.64–65. An early eighteenth-century building hiding a quirky hotel of real character and charm, with en-suite rooms decorated and furnished as close to period style as convenience and comfort allow. Breakfast (served in the rooms) is not included. **£230**

St John Hotel 1 Leicester St, WC2 020 3301 8069, stjohnhotellondon.com; Leicester Square; map pp.64–65. A restaurant with rooms in the heart of Chinatown, providing diners at the newest *St John* (see p.120) restaurant an opportunity to sleep off their pig's trotters and tripe. Rooms, pared-down and modern, with a vaguely nautical feel, are lovely but pricey for the size. **£200**

COVENT GARDEN

The Fielding Hotel 4 Broad Court, Bow St, WC2 020 7836 8305, thefieldinghotel.co.uk; Covent Garden; map pp.64–65. Quietly situated on a pedestrianized, gas-lit court, this hotel is a hidden gem. Its en-suite rooms are a firm favourite with visiting performers, since it's just a few yards from the Royal Opera House. Breakfast is extra. Free wi-fi. **£140**

Seven Dials Hotel 7 Monmouth St, WC2 020 7681 0791, sevendialshotellondon.com; Covent Garden; map pp.64–65. Pleasant, family-run B&B in the heart of the West End. Rooms (singles to quads) are small, but all are clean, simple and en suite. Free wi-fi. **£105**

BLOOMSBURY AND KING'S CROSS

Celtic Hotel 61–63 Guilford St, WC1 020 7837 6737; Russell Square; map p.75. No frills in this simple, clean hotel just off Russell Square, with well-equipped rooms and two comfy lounges; the cheapest rooms have shared facilities. Rates include full English breakfast. **£73**

★ **Ridgemount** 65–67 Gower St, WC1 ⊕020 7636 1141, ⓦridgemounthotel.co.uk; ⊖Goodge Street; map p.75. Old-fashioned, cosy, family-run B&B, with very clean rooms (15 of the 32 have shared facilities – which are spotless). A reliable, basic Bloomsbury bargain. Full breakfast and free wi-fi. **£66**

Rough Luxe 1 Birkenhead St, WC1 ⊕020 7837 5338, ⓦroughluxe.co.uk; ⊖King's Cross; map pp.60–61. This funky nine-room hotel offers comfort and shabby chic opulence. Each room is different, but the aesthetic – peeling plaster, original artworks – is consistent. Free wi-fi. **£200**

St Pancras Renaissance Hotel Euston Rd, NW1 ⊕020 7841 3540, ⓦmarriott.co.uk/hotels/travel/lonpr-st-pancras; ⊖King's Cross; map pp.60–61. The old St Pancras station, George Gilbert Scott's Gothic Revival masterpiece, finally reopened in 2011 as a glamorous *Marriott*. The lofty public spaces and colossal lobby evoke the golden era of railway travel, but fewer than fifty of the total 245 rooms are actually in the main building. The others, in an annexe, aren't worth the price. There's an atmospheric bar, a restaurant and a spa. Online deals can halve the rack rates. **£385**

CLERKENWELL AND THE CITY

Apex City of London Hotel 1 Seething Lane, EC3 ⊕020 7977 9593, ⓦapexhotels.co.uk; ⊖Tower Hill; map pp.80–81. Swish business hotel on a secluded street near the Tower of London. The cheapest rooms have no windows, while the priciest have great views – rates vary according to availability, so book early. Free gym, sauna and steam room, and free wi-fi. The nearby *Apex London Wall* (7–9 Copthall Ave, EC2; Moorgate tube) has more of a boutique feel but the same rates. **£120**

The King's Wardrobe 6 Wardrobe Place, Carter Lane, EC4 ⊕020 7792 2222, ⓦbridgestreet.com; ⊖St Paul's; map pp.80–81. In a quiet courtyard just behind St Paul's Cathedral, this place is part of an international chain that caters largely for a business clientele – the apartments offer fully equipped kitchens and workstations, concierge service and housekeeping. Though housed in a fourteenth-century building that once contained Edward III's royal regalia, the interior is modern. **£133**

★ **Mint Hotel Tower of London** 7 Pepys St, EC3 ⊕0207 709 1000, ⓦminthotel.com; ⊖Tower Hill; map pp.80–81. Though it's geared towards business travellers, this large, modern hotel is a good option for all. Rooms – nearly 600 of them – are clean, bright and comfortable, with iMacs, and some face a verdant living wall. Look out for excellent online promotions. Free wi-fi. **£140**

The Rookery 12 Peter's Lane, Cowcross St, EC1 ⊕020 7336 0931, ⓦrookeryhotel.com; ⊖Farringdon; map pp.80–81. Rambling Georgian townhouse on the edge of the City, in trendy Clerkenwell, that makes a delightful little hideaway. Rooms offer faded Baroque glam, with antique fittings, characterful bathrooms and creaky floorboards. **£230**

The Zetter Hotel & Townhouse 86–88 Clerkenwell Rd, EC1 ⊕020 7324 4444, ⓦthezetter.com; ⊖Farringdon; map pp.80–81. Glamorous, in a warehouse conversion, but with a laidback edge, the *Zetter* fits in just right in Clerkenwell. The simple rooms are colourful, with lots of eco touches; the bar and bistro, and the open atrium, mean some rooms can be noisy. The Georgian *Townhouse*, across the square, is more whimsical, with thirteen boudoirish rooms and a cosy cocktail bar. Free wi-fi. **£220**

THE EAST END

Hoxton Hotel 81 Great Eastern St, EC2 ⊕020 7550 1000, ⓦhoxtonhotels.com; ⊖Old Street; map pp.80–81. "The Hox" has found its niche in this trendy neighbourhood, with exposed brick and burnished metal in the public spaces, and simple, modern rooms. Rates include a light Pret à Manger breakfast, free wi-fi and an hour's local calls a day, and there's a bar and restaurant. The cost – as little as £90 or as much as £199 – depends on availability; every so often they hold an online competition selling off around fifty rooms for £1. **£90**

Shoreditch Rooms Shoreditch House, Ebor St E1 ⊕020 7739 5040, ⓦshoreditchrooms.com; Shoreditch High Street Overground; map pp.80–81. From the same stable as the *Dean Street Townhouse* (see p.112) this hip little place has the same no-nonsense room-naming policy, with 26 options from "Tiny" up to "Small-plus". Rooms may be small but they're lovely, with lots of fresh, sun-bleached colours and vintage style. Staying here also allows you to hang out with the beautiful people in the members' club next door. Free wi-fi. **£150**

SOUTH BANK AND SOUTHWARK

All Seasons London Southwark Rose 43–47 Southwark Bridge Rd, SE1 ⊕020 7015 1480, ⓦall-seasons-hotels.com; ⊖London Bridge; map pp.90–91. The Southwark Rose has enough style to put it several notches above the bland chain hotels in the area. Giant aluminium lamps hover over the lobby, which is lined with colourful photographs, while the penthouse restaurant offers an all-you-can-eat breakfast with a rooftop view. Rates vary widely depending on availability. Free wi-fi. **£130**

★ **Tune Westminster** 118–120 Westminster Bridge Rd, London SE1 ⓦtunehotels.com; ⊖Lambeth North or Waterloo; map p.87. Doing away with fuss like tables, chairs and closets keeps rates low at this London outpost of a Malaysian cheapie chain. The pricing policy is smart – simply opt to pay for extras, including towels, TV, hairdryers or wi-fi, on the easy-to-use booking

1

site. Rooms are small and modern, with comfy beds and spotless showers. **£75**

KENSINGTON AND EARL'S COURT

★ **Aster House** 3 Sumner Place, SW7 ⓣ 020 7581 5888, ⓦ asterhouse.com; ⊖ South Kensington; map pp.94–95. Pleasant, award-winning B&B, in a luxurious South Ken white-stuccoed street; one of the thirteen rooms opens out onto the lovely garden, and there's a large conservatory where a buffet breakfast is served. **£180**

base2stay Kensington 25 Courtfield Gardens, SW5 ⓣ 020 7244 2255, ⓦ base2stay.com; ⊖ Earl's Court; map pp.94–95. Self-catering accommodation, with superb eco credentials and no fussy extras. Rooms vary in size but all are comfortable, clean and quiet, with mini-kitchens and free wi-fi. **£111**

Twenty Nevern Square 20 Nevern Square, SW5 ⓣ 020 7565 9555, ⓦ 20nevernsquare.co.uk; ⊖ Earl's Court; map pp.94–95. In an area of bog-standard B&Bs, this is a winner, a boutique hotel with considerable style. Rooms are en suite; some, however, are teensy. Buffet breakfast included. Free wi-fi. **£80**

Vicarage Hotel 10 Vicarage Gate, W8 ⓣ 020 7229 4030, ⓦ londonvicaragehotel.com; ⊖ Notting Hill Gate or High Street Kensington; map pp.94–95. Nicely located B&B on a residential street a step away from Kensington Gardens. Clean and smart floral rooms; some have shared facilities, and quads are available. A full English breakfast included. Rates are around £15 lower in winter. Free wi-fi (in the lounge). **£102**

PADDINGTON, BAYSWATER AND NOTTING HILL

Portobello Gold 95–97 Portobello Rd, W1 ⓣ 020 7460 4910, ⓦ portobellogold.com; ⊖ Notting Hill Gate or Holland Park; map pp.94–95. A fun and friendly option with six basic rooms and a small apartment above a funky pub. Rooms are plain, and some are tiny, with miniature en suites; the homely apartment sleeps six – at a pinch – and has a little roof terrace. Breakfast not included. Free wi-fi. **£75**

Vancouver Studios 30 Prince's Square, W2 ⓣ 020 7243 1270, ⓦ vancouverstudios.co.uk; ⊖ Bayswater; map pp.94–95. Self-contained self-catering studios in a grand old Victorian townhouse with maid service and a pretty walled garden. They also have a good-value apartment that costs £250 per night for four people. Free wi-fi. **£130**

NORTH LONDON

Hampstead Village Guesthouse 2 Kemplay Rd, NW3 ⓣ 020 7435 8679, ⓦ hampsteadguesthouse.com; ⊖ Hampstead. Prettily located on a quiet backstreet between Hampstead Village and the Heath, this is a quirky guesthouse in a family home. Rooms (most en suite) are full of character, crammed with books, pictures, and personal mementos. Free wi-fi. **£90**

HOSTELS

London's official **Youth Hostel Association (YHA) hostels** (ⓦ yha.org.uk) are generally the cleanest, most efficiently run in the capital. However, they charge more than private hostels, and tend to get booked up months in advance. **Independent hostels** are cheaper and more relaxed, but can be less reliable in terms of facilities. A good **website** for booking independent places online is ⓦ hostellondon.com.

YHA HOSTELS

★ **Central** 104 Bolsover St, W1 ⓣ 0845 371 9154, ⓔ londoncentral@yha.org.uk; ⊖ Great Portland Street; map p.75. Excellent, friendly and clean hostel, in a quiet location that's walking distance from Oxford Street. Free wi-fi, kitchen and a 24hr café-bar. No groups. Dorms only (4–8 beds).

Earl's Court 38 Bolton Gardens, SW5 ⓣ 0845 371 9114, ⓔ earlscourt@yha.org.uk; ⊖ Earl's Court; map pp.94–95. Better than a lot of accommodation in Earl's Court, this 186-bed hostel has a kitchen and café and patio garden. Single-sex dorms (4–10 beds), triples and doubles/twins.

Holland House Holland Walk, W8 ⓣ 0845 371 9122, ⓔ hollandhouse@yha.org.uk; ⊖ Holland Park or High Street Kensington; map pp.94–95. Idyllically situated in Holland Park and fairly convenient for the centre. Kitchen and café. Popular with groups. Dorms (4–10+ beds), plus a single, a double and a triple.

Oxford Street 14 Noel St, W1 ⓣ 0845 371 9133, ⓔ oxfordst@yha.org.uk; ⊖ Oxford Circus or Tottenham Court Road; map pp.64–65. This small, central backpacker hostel tends to be full year-round. Dorms (4 beds) and doubles/twins and triples.

St Pancras 79–81 Euston Rd, NW1 ⓣ 0845 371 9344, ⓔ stpancras@yha.org.uk; ⊖ King's Cross St Pancras; map pp.60–61. Popular with families. Rooms are clean, bright, double-glazed and en suite. No kitchen, but there is a café. No groups. Dorms (3–6 beds) and doubles/twins.

St Paul's 36 Carter Lane, EC4 ⓣ 0845 371 9012, ⓔ stpauls@yha.org.uk; ⊖ St Paul's; map pp.80–81. A 210-bed hostel in a superb location opposite St Paul's Cathedral. No kitchen, but it has a café for dinner. Small groups only. Breakfast included. Dorms (3–11 beds), singles and twins.

INDEPENDENT HOSTELS

Clink 261 261–265 Gray's Inn Rd, WC1 ⓣ 020 7833 9400, ⓦ ashleehouse.co.uk; ⊖ King's Cross; map pp.60–61. Stylish, smallish hostel in a converted office block near King's Cross Station, with laundry and kitchen facilities. Mostly 4–10 beds, with some budget 18-bed options, and private rooms, sleeping up to three, with shared facilities. Breakfast included. Dorm **£9**, double **£50**

★ **Clink 78** 78 King's Cross Rd, WC1 ⓣ 020 7183 9400, ⓦ clinkhostel.com; ⊖ King's Cross; map pp.60–61. This

1

appealing place is run by the same folk as *Clink 261*, with funky decor, a hip bar, and plenty of features from the days when it was a Victorian courthouse – you can even stay in an old cell. Dorms (4–16 beds) can be cramped, though partitions on the "pod" bunks increase privacy; special girls-only dorms include mirrors and hangers. Plus singles, doubles twins and triples, some en-suite. Kitchen. Breakfast included. Dorm £10, double £50

Generator 37 Tavistock Place, WC1 ☎020 7388 7666, generatorhostels.com; Russell Square or Euston; map p.75. A huge, funky hostel, with more than 870 beds and post-industrial decor. Dorms (some women-only) have 4–12 beds, and there are singles, twins, triples and quads – none en suite. There's a party atmosphere and a late-night bar. Café, but no kitchen; breakfast included. Laundry. Free wi-fi. Groups welcome. Dorm £15, double £50

St Christopher's Inns ☎020 8600 7500, st-christophers.co.uk map pp.90–91. St Christopher's run seven hostels across London, with three – including the flagship *Village* – on Borough High St, near London Bridge, plus branches in Camden, Greenwich, Shepherd's Bush and Hammersmith. The decor is upbeat, and there's a party-animal ambience fuelled by the hostel bars. Free breakfast and laundry but no kitchens. Dorm £17, double £55

EATING

You can pretty much sample any kind of **cuisine** in London, from Georgian to Peruvian, from Modern British to fusion – you can even get yourself some Cockney pie and mash. And it needn't be expensive – even in the fanciest restaurants, set menus (most often served at lunch) can be a great deal, and the small "sharing plates" that are currently all the rage are a godsend if you want to cut costs.

CAFÉS AND SNACKS

While the old-fashioned London **caffs** are a dying breed, the city has plenty of great little places where you can get quick, filling and inexpensive meals – especially good at lunchtime, most of them are open in the evenings too. Bear in mind also that many **pubs** (which are covered in the following section) serve food, from simple pub grub to haute cuisine.

WESTMINSTER

Café in the Crypt St Martin-in-the-Fields, Duncannon St, WC2 ☎020 7766 1158, stmartin-in-the-fields.org; Charing Cross; map pp.64–65. The buffet is nothing special, but there are lots of veggie dishes, and it's a handy (and atmospheric) location – below the church in the eighteenth-century crypt. Mon & Tues 8am–8pm, Wed 8am–10.30pm (live jazz after 8pm), Thurs–Sat 8am–9pm, Sun 11am–6pm.

Jenny Lo's Teahouse 14 Ecclestone St, SW1 ☎020 7259 0399, jennylo.co.uk; Victoria; map pp.64–65. Bright and bare, Jenny Lo's serves cheap Chinese noodles and soups, along with a few Thai and Vietnamese options. No credit cards. Mains £5–10. Mon–Fri noon–3pm & 6–10pm.

MAYFAIR AND MARYLEBONE

★ **Comptoir Libanais** 65 Wigmore St, W1 ☎020 7935 1110, lecomptoir.co.uk; Marble Arch; map pp.94–95. This cheap and cheerful, kitsch and stylish Middle Eastern deli/diner serves crunchy falafels, herby Lavosh breads, tagines and patisserie. It's BYOB, but the home-made lemonades are delicious. Main around £6. Mon–Fri 8am–10pm, Sat & Sun 10am–10pm.

Mô 25 Heddon St, W1 ☎020 7434 4040, momoresto.com; Piccadilly Circus; map pp.64–65. Reasonably priced, tasty snacks, honey-soaked pastries and aromatic mint tea in a wonderful Arabic tearoom/terrace stuffed with Moroccan memorabila. The attached restaurant is good fun, too. Daily noon–1am.

Patisserie Valerie at Sagne 105 Marylebone High St, W1 ☎020 7935 6240; Bond Street; map pp.94–95. With its glorious 1920s decor, this café is Marylebone's finest. You can get light lunches and snacks, but it's the cakes that are to die for. There's another splendid branch on Old Compton Street in Soho, and various others around town. Mon–Fri 7.30am–7pm, Sat 8am–7pm, Sun 9am–6pm.

★ **The Wolseley** 160 Piccadilly, W1 ☎020 7499 6996, thewolseley.com; Green Park; map pp.64–65. The Viennese-inspired food is delicious, though pricey – come for breakfast or afternoon tea – in this grand old café-restaurant with a stunning 1920s interior. Mon–Fri 7am–midnight, Sat 8am–midnight, Sun 8am–11pm.

SOHO AND CHINATOWN

★ **Bar Italia** 22 Frith St, W1 ☎020 7437 4520, baritaliasoho.co.uk; Leicester Square; map pp.64–65. Tiny espresso bar that's been a Soho institution since the 50s, keeping many of its original features (including the Gaggia coffee machine) and its iconic neon sign. Closed Mon–Fri 4–6am.

Beatroot 92 Berwick St, W1 ☎020 7437 8591, beatroot.org.uk; Piccadilly Circus, Oxford Circus or Tottenham Court Road; map pp.64–65. Great little veggie/vegan café by the market, doling out savoury

TOP 5 CHEAP LONDON EATS

Books for Cooks Notting Hill. See p.117
Diwana Bhel Poori Bloomsbury. See p.116
Hummus Brothers Soho. See p.116
Mr Kong Chinatown. See p.118
PINCHITOtapas Clerkenwell. See p.116

1

bakes, stews and salads (plus good cakes) in boxes of varying sizes. Mon–Fri 9am–9pm, Sat 11am–9pm.

Kopi-Tiam 67 Charing Cross Rd, WC2 020 7287 1113, malaysiakopitiam.co.uk; Leicester Square; map pp.64–65. Local Malays flock to this cheap Malaysian café for curries, coconut rice, juices and "herbal soups", all for around a fiver. There's Thai food, too, and a karaoke room upstairs. Daily noon–11pm.

★ **Maison Bertaux** 28 Greek St, W1 020 7437 6007, maisonbertaux.com; Leicester Square; map pp.64–65. Long-standing, old-fashioned and *très* French patisserie, with two floors and some outdoor seating. The decor is simple but the cakes are fabulous, and a loyal clientele keeps the place busy. Daily 8.30am–8pm.

Misato 11 Wardour St, W1 020 7734 0808; Leicester Square; map pp.64–65. Modern, canteen-style Japanese place serving filling rice and noodle dishes, plus hearty bento boxes and sushi. Mains £4–8. Daily noon–midnight.

Mooli's 50 Frith St, W1 020 7494 9075, moolis.com; Leicester Square; map pp.64–65. Bright, funky little place dishing up freshly made rotis with amazingly tasty, zingy fillings – Punjabi goat, cumin potatoes; paneer – for less than a fiver. Mon–Wed noon–10pm, Thurs–Sat noon–11.30pm.

COVENT GARDEN

★ **Food for Thought** 31 Neal St, WC2 020 7836 9072, foodforthought-london.co.uk; Covent Garden; map pp.64–65. This minuscule veggie restaurant and takeaway has been dishing up hearty veggie/vegan soups, salads, hot dishes and desserts for some forty years, from a menu that changes twice daily. It's a crush at peak times. Mon–Sat noon–8.30pm, Sun noon–5pm.

Rock & Sole Plaice 47 Endell St, WC2 020 7836 3785; Covent Garden; map pp.64–65. A rare survivor; a traditional fish-and-chip shop in central London. Eat in or at a pavement table, or take away. Mon–Sat 11.30am–11pm, Sat & Sun noon–10pm.

World Food Café 14 Neal's Yard, WC2 020 7379 0298; Covent Garden; map pp.64–65. First-floor veggie café that comes into its own in the summer when the windows are flung open and you can gaze down upon the pedestrianized square below. Dishes come from all over the globe: tortillas, thalis, tagines or meze. Mon–Fri 11.30am–4.30pm, Sat 11.30am–5pm.

BLOOMSBURY

★ **Diwana Bhel Poori House** 121–123 Drummond St, NW1 0207 387 5556; Euston; map p.75. On a street lined with good Indian restaurants, this South Indian vegetarian diner wins for its scrumptious all-you-can-eat lunchtime buffets (£7) and huge, deliciously fresh thalis (£8). Daily noon–11pm.

Hummus Bros 37–63 Southampton Row, WC1 020 7404 7079, hbros.co.uk; Holborn; map p.75. Hummus and toppings – chicken, falafels, guacamole – with pitta, feta cheese and salads on the side, all from £5. The mint and ginger lemonade is delicious. Also takeaway. Branches on Wardour St in Soho and on Cheapside in the City. Mon–Fri 11am–9pm.

CLERKENWELL AND HOXTON

Clark & Sons 46 Exmouth Market, EC1 020 7837 1974; Angel or Farringdon; map pp.80–81. This authentic old pie-and-mash shop is still going strong in gentrifying Exmouth Market – it's the most central spot in the capital to fill up on meat pies, mash with liquor (parsley sauce) and a side of eels. Mon–Thurs 10.30am–4pm, Fri & Sat 10.30am–5pm.

★ **PINCHITOtapas** 32 Featherstone St, EC1 020 7490 0121, pinchito.co.uk; Old Street; map pp.80–81.

MORE THAN JUST A CUPPA: AFTERNOON TEA

The classic English **afternoon tea** – assorted sandwiches, scones and cream, cakes and tarts, and, of course, lashings of tea – is available all over London. The best venues are the capital's top hotels and most fashionable department stores; a selection of the best is given below. To avoid disappointment it's essential to book ahead. Expect to spend £20–40 a head, and bear in mind that most hotels will expect "smart casual attire"; only *The Ritz* insists on jacket and tie.

Claridges Brook St, W1 020 7409 6307, claridges.co.uk; Bond Street. Daily 3pm, 3.30pm, 5pm & 5.30pm. £35.

Fortnum & Mason 181 Piccadilly, W1 0845 602 5694, fortnumandmason.com; Green Park. Mon–Sat noon–6.30pm, Sun noon–4.30pm. £34.

Lanesborough Hyde Park Corner, SW1 020 7259 5599, lanesborough.com; Hyde Park Corner. Daily 4pm, 4.30pm & 5pm. £35.

The Ritz Piccadilly, W1 020 7493 8181, theritzlondon.com; Green Park. Daily 11.30am, 1.30pm, 3.30pm, 5.30pm & 7.30pm. £40.

The Wolseley 160 Piccadilly, W1 020 7499 6996, thewolseley.com; Green Park; see p.115. Mon–Fri noon–3pm, Sat & Sun noon–3.30pm. £21.

From simple tapas to more elaborate Basque pintxos, this buzzy little place – all industrial steel and bare brick walls – does everything Spanish supremely well, and prices are astonishingly low. Takeaway available. Tapas £1.50–6.50. Mon–Fri 10am–midnight, Sat 5pm–midnight.

THE CITY, DOCKLANDS AND THE EAST END

Brick Lane Beigel Bake 159 Brick Lane, E1 ⓣ020 7729 0616; Shoreditch High Street Overground; map pp.80–81. Classic bagel takeaway in the heart of the East End – very cheap, even for your top-end filling, smoked salmon and cream cheese. Daily 24hr.

Café 1001 1 Dray Walk, E1 ⓣ020 7247 9679, ⓦcafe1001.co.uk; ⊖Whitechapel or Shoreditch High Street Overground; map pp.80–81. Just off Brick Lane, this café/bar is classic East End hip, with a beaten-up studenty look, sofas to crash on, used books to read and simple snacks and fattening cakes to sample. Frequent DJ sets and live music. Mon–Sat 6am–midnight, Sun 6am–11.30pm.

★ **Café Below** Church of St Mary-le-Bow, Cheapside, EC2 ⓣ020 7329 0789, ⓦcafebelow.co.uk; ⊖St Paul's or Bank; map pp.80–81. A City gem: a cosy, good-value café-restaurant, in a Norman church crypt, serving modern Mediterranean food, with lots of veggie choices, and sticky breakfast pastries. Mains from £6.50 at lunch, more in the evening. Mon–Fri 7.30am–9pm.

De Gustibus 53–55 Carter Lane, EC4 ⓣ020 7236 0056, ⓦdegustibus.co.uk; ⊖St Paul's or Blackfriars; map pp.80–81. Award-winning artisan bakery that creates sandwiches, bruschette, croques-monsieurs and quiche to eat in or take away. There's another branch in Borough Market. Mon–Fri 8am–5pm.

Hubbub 269 Westferry Rd, E14 ⓣ020 7515 5577, ⓦhubbubcafebar.com; Mudchute DLR; map pp.60–61. A real find in the otherwise drab Docklands eating scene, this café-bar is housed in a former Victorian church, now arts centre, and does decent fry-ups, sandwiches and tapas. Mon–Wed noon–11pm, Thurs & Fri noon–midnight, Sat 10am–midnight, Sun 10am–10.30pm.

THE SOUTH BANK

★ **Ev** 97–99 Isabella St, SE1 ⓣ020 7620 6191, ⓦtasrestaurant.com; ⊖Southwark or Waterloo; map p.87. An organic Middle Eastern deli/café in a pretty spot tucked under a railway arch. Genuinely relaxing, with a lofty barrel-vaulted ceiling, rustic wooden seats, hanging plants and a leafy terrace on a pedestrianized street. Great breads, salads and sweets, with an array of Turkish delight. The attached restaurant is good, too. Mon–Sat noon–11.30pm, Sun noon–10.30pm.

Marsh Ruby 30 Lower Marsh, SE1 ⓣ020 7620 0593, ⓦmarshruby.com; ⊖Waterloo; map p.87. Terrific filling lunchtime curries for around a fiver: the food, on seasonally changing menus, is organic/free range and the communal dining is basic but cheery. Mon–Fri 11.30am–3pm, Thurs & Fri 6.30–10.30pm.

KENSINGTON, CHELSEA AND NOTTING HILL

★ **Books for Cooks** 4 Blenheim Crescent, W11 ⓣ020 7221 1992, ⓦbooksforcooks.com; ⊖Ladbroke Grove or Notting Hill Gate; map pp.94–95. Tiny café within London's top cookery bookshop. Just wander in and have a coffee while browsing, or get there in time to grab a table for the set-menu lunch (noon–1.30pm). Tues–Sat 10am–6pm.

Capote y Toros 157 Old Brompton Rd, SW5 ⓣ020 7373 0567, ⓦcambiodetercio.co.uk; ⊖Gloucester Rd or South Kensington; map pp.94–95. The emphasis at this sunny bar is on Spain's wonderful sherries, with more than 40 available by the glass, and interesting tapas (£4–7) cooked with the stuff. Tues–Sat 5–11.30pm.

★ **Lisboa Patisserie** 57 Golborne Rd, W10 ⓣ020 8968 5242; ⊖Westbourne Park; map pp.94–95. Portuguese pastelaria, with the best custard tarts this side of Lisbon – also coffee, cakes and a friendly, crowded atmosphere. Café O'porto at 62a Golborne Rd is a good fallback if this place is full. Daily 8am–7pm.

NORTH LONDON

★ **Brew House** Kenwood House, Hampstead Lane, NW3 ⓣ020 8341 5384; ⊖Highgate. Splendid café serving everything from full English breakfasts to gourmet sandwiches, cakes and teas, either in the house's old servants' wing or in the huge, sunny garden courtyard. Daily 9am–6pm.

★ **Louis Patisserie** 32 Heath St, NW3 ⓣ020 7435 9908; ⊖Hampstead. For some fifty years now this tiny, understated, and gloriously old-fashioned Hungarian tearoom/patisserie has been serving sticky cakes, tea and coffee to Heath-bound hordes and elderly locals. Daily 9am–6pm.

Marine Ices 8 Haverstock Hill, NW3 ⓣ020 7482 9003, ⓦmarineices.co.uk; ⊖Chalk Farm; map pp.60–61. Midway between Camden and Hampstead, this is a splendid and justly famous old-fashioned Italian ice-cream parlour; pizza and pasta are served in the cheery, kiddie-friendly restaurant. Ice cream parlour: Tues–Sat noon–11pm, Sun noon–10pm; restaurant: Tues–Fri noon–3pm & 6–11pm, Sat noon–11pm, Sun noon–10pm.

WEST LONDON

Pembroke Lodge Richmond Park, Richmond TW10 ⓣ020 8940 8207; ⊖Richmond. In a gorgeous Georgian mansion in Richmond Park, this café has one of the best views in London and nice outdoor seating – food is limited to snacks, sandwiches and cakes. Daily 10am–5.30pm or dusk.

1

RESTAURANTS

MAYFAIR AND MARYLEBONE

Dehesa 25 Ganton St, W1 020 7494 4170, dehesa.co.uk; Oxford Circus or Piccadilly Circus; map pp.64–65. Spanish-Italian charcuterie/restaurant serving really excellent tapas (£3–10) – try deep-fried courgette flowers with goat's cheese and honey, or salt cod croquettes, or just enjoy a plate of melt-in-the-mouth jamón Iberico and a glass of Albariño. Mon–Fri noon–3pm & 5–11pm, Sat noon–11pm, Sun noon–5pm.

★ **The Providores and Tapa Room** 109 Marylebone High St, W1 020 7935 6175, theprovidores.co.uk; Baker Street or Bond Street; map pp.94–95. Outstanding fusion restaurant, run by the New Zealand chef Peter Gordon, with the more casual, cheaper *Tapa Room* downstairs. Mon–Fri 9am–11pm, Sat 10am–11pm, Sun 10am–10pm.

SOHO AND CHINATOWN

Mildred's 45 Lexington St, W1 020 7494 1634, mildreds.co.uk; Oxford Circus or Piccadilly Circus; map pp.64–65. Mildred's has a fresher and more contemporary feel than many veggie restaurants, and serves creative global cuisine. It's tiny, and can get very busy, but takes no bookings. Mains £8–10. Mon–Sat noon–11pm.

★ **Mr Kong** 21 Lisle St, WC2 020 7437 7341, mrkongrestaurant.com; Leicester Square; map pp.64–65. Chinatown stalwart, with a very long menu of Cantonese food – don't miss the mussels in black bean sauce – and a good range of veggie dishes. Dishes £4–25. Mon–Sat noon–2.45am, Sun noon–1.45am.

★ **Polpetto** 49 Dean St, W1 0207 734 1969, www.polpetto.co.uk; Leicester Square; map pp.64–65. Cosy, hugely popular and rather hip hideaway above the beloved Soho boozer *The French House*. The food, hearty Italian tapas and Venetian-style bar snacks, is great value. Reservations for lunch only. Mon–Sat noon–3pm & 5.30–11pm.

Wong Kei 41–43 Wardour St, W1 020 7437 8408; Leicester Square; map pp.64–65. Beloved four-storey Chinatown staple, seating around 500. It's as notorious for brusque service – though this is largely for show nowadays – as for the huge portions of cheap, hearty (but not gourmet) food. Mon–Sat noon–11.30pm, Sun noon–10.30pm.

Yalla Yalla 1 Greens Court, W1 020 70287 7663, yalla-yalla.co.uk; Piccadilly Circus; map pp.64–65. The name is Lebanese for "hurry, hurry!", and the ambience in this sleek hole-in-the-wall is buzzy and fast. Good-value veggie meze from £3 – baba ganoush, halloumi, spinach pies, tabbouleh and so on – and plenty of nicely spiced kebabs. Mon–Fri 10am–11.30pm, Sat11am–11pm.

COVENT GARDEN

★ **Dishoom** 12 Upper St Martin's Lane, WC2 020 7420 9320, dishoom.com; Leicester Square or Covent Garden; map pp.64–65. Recreating the atmosphere of the Persian cafés of Old Bombay, *Dishoom* is witty and stylish, but most importantly, serves delicious food – don't miss the black dhal. Mains from £6.50, small dishes for less. Mon–Thurs 8am–11pm, Fri 8am–midnight, Sat 10am–midnight, Sun 10am–10pm.

Kopapa 32–34 Monmouth St, WC2 020 7240 6076, kopapa.co.uk; Covent Garden; map pp.64–65. Fusion food from the Kiwi chef behind *Providores* (see opposite), in a casual café where the plain setting belies the complex flavours of dishes like shichimi-crusted baked tofu with shiitake, carrot and miso mustard. Mains from £11. Mon–Fri 8.30–11.30am & noon–10.45pm, Sat 10am–3pm & 3.30–10.45pm, Sun 10am–3pm & 3.30–9.45pm.

Wahaca 66 Chandos Place, WC2 0207 240 1883, wahaca.co.uk; Charing Cross, Leicester Square or Covent Garden; map pp.64–65. No bookings are taken at this big, brash modern Mexican restaurant, so everyone ends up getting merry on Margaritas at the bar before being ushered to shared tables and tucking into hearty, inexpensive food. Dishes from £3. Mon–Sat noon–11pm, Sun noon–10.30pm.

BLOOMSBURY

Cigala 54 Lamb's Conduit St, WC1 020 7405 1717, cigala.co.uk; Russell Square; map p.75. Simple dishes, robust flavours and Spanish flair at this sophisticated Iberian restaurant with seasonally changing menus. Mains from £8; two- and three-course set lunch menus £16/£18; tapas from £4. Mon–Fri noon–10.30pm, Sat 12.30–10.30pm, Sun noon–9.30pm.

La Porchetta 33 Boswell St, WC1 020 7242 2434, laporchetta.net; Holborn or Russell Square; map p.75. Tiny, cramped, noisy and cheery Italian restaurant that dishes up huge pizzas and great pasta dishes. Branches in Clerkenwell, Camden, Islington and Finsbury Park. Mains from £6.50. Mon–Thurs noon–3pm & 6–11pm, Fri noon–3pm & 6pm–midnight, Sat 6–11pm.

CLERKENWELL AND HOXTON

Cicada 132 St John St, EC1 020 7608 1550, rickerrestaurants.com/cicada; Farringdon; map pp.80–81. Pan-Asian bar-restaurant that serves everything from dim sum to Malaysian curries and sushi. Dishes £3–30. Mon–Fri noon–3pm & 6–11pm, Sat 6–11pm.

The Hawksmoor 157 Commercial St, E1 020 7247 7392, thehawksmoor.co.uk; Liverpool Street or Shoreditch High Street Overground; map pp.80–81. Carnivore heaven, dishing up succulent charcoal-grilled

CLOCKWISE FROM TOP LEFT AFTERNOON TEA AT THE RITZ (P.116); PORTOBELLO ROAD MARKET (P.131); THE LAMB PUB (P.122); BAR ITALIA, SOHO (P.115) >

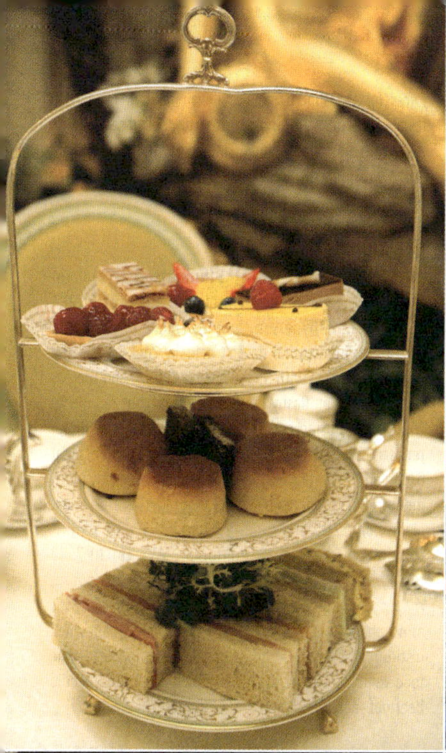

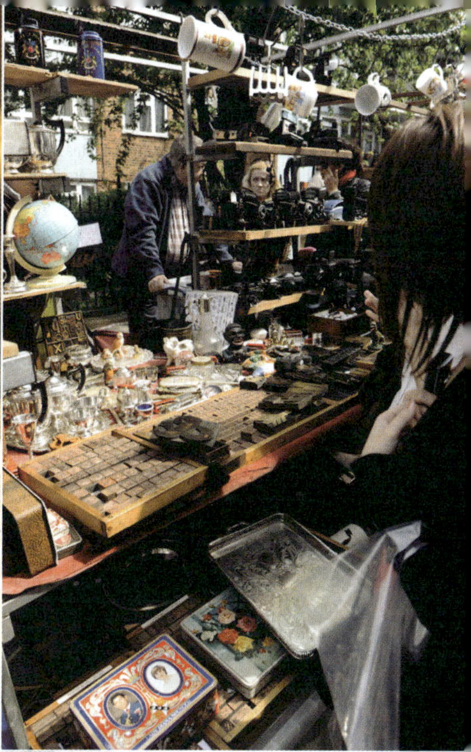

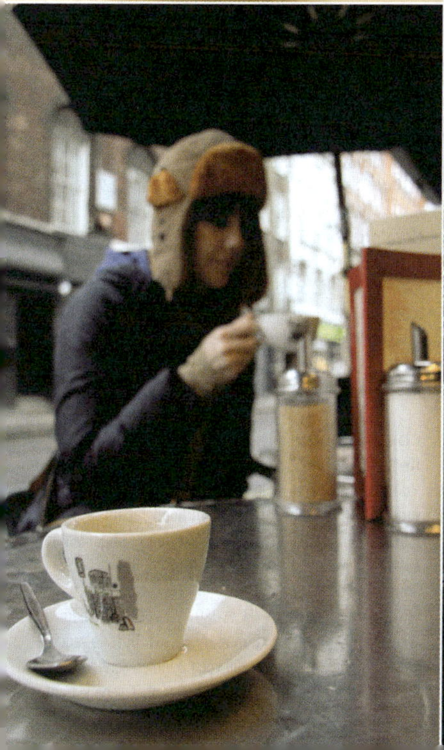

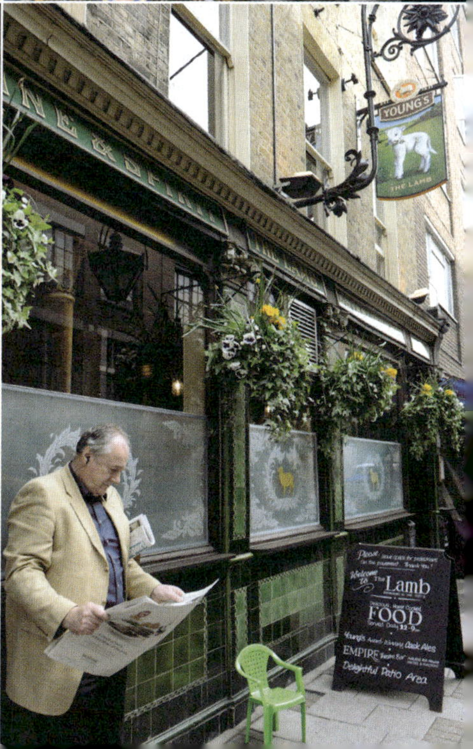

YOUNG'S
THE LAMB
Welcome to The Lamb
FOOD
Cask Ales
EMPIRE
Delightful Patio Area

1

cuts of meat sourced from the famed Yorkshire suppliers Ginger Pig. The Sunday roasts are a hit, while the blowout breakfasts (£35 for two) include dripping toast, black pudding and grilled bone marrow. Full meals around £40. Mon–Fri noon–3pm & 6–10.30pm, Sat 11am–4pm & 6–10.30pm, Sun 11am–5pm.

★ **Moro** 34–36 Exmouth Market, EC1 ☎ 020 7833 8336, @ moro.co.uk; ⊖ Farringdon or Angel; map pp.80–81. Gorgeous, welcoming restaurant that's a place of pilgrimage for disciples of Sam and Sam Clark's Moorish/Iberian cookbooks. The lamb dishes and the yoghurt cake are perennial hits, but all of it is good, prepared with lots of unusual ingredients. Booking essential. Tapas (around £5) are served all day, and they have a simpler tapas bar, *Morito*, next door (where no reservations are taken). Mains £16–19. Mon–Sat 12.30–10.30pm.

St John Bread and Wine 94–96 Commercial St, E1 ☎ 020 3301 8069, @ stjohnbreadandwine.com; ⊖ Liverpool Street; map pp.80–81. A simpler offshoot of the more expensive *St John*, with the same old-school British cuisine. It's a hit for breakfasts, puds and buns; later on, the small sharing plates won't break the bank. Dishes £6–15. Mon–Fri 9–11am, noon–4pm & 6–10.30pm, Sat 10–11am, noon–4pm & 6–10.30pm, Sun 10–11am, noon–4pm & 6–9.30pm.

Sông Quê 134 Kingsland Rd, E2 ☎ 020 7613 3222, @ songque.co.uk; Hoxton station; map pp.80–81. In a street crammed with budget Vietnamese restaurants, this simple place consistently has the edge, with very good *phô* (£3.60–7) and spicy seafood dishes. Mon–Sat noon–3pm & 5.30–11pm, Sun noon–11pm.

THE EAST END

Lahore Kebab House 2–10 Umberston St, E1 ☎ 020 7481 9737, @ lahore-kebabhouse.com; ⊖ Aldgate East; map pp.80–81. Bargain Punjabi kebab house, just off Commercial Rd. Go for the lamb cutlets and roti, and go hungry. BYOB. Mains £7–11. Daily noon–midnight.

★ **Tayyab's** 83–89 Fieldgate St, E1 ☎ 020 7247 9543, @ tayyabs.co.uk; ⊖ Whitechapel; map pp.80–81. For more than thirty years *Tayyab's* has been offering straightforward Pakistani food: good, freshly cooked and served without pretension. Prices (mains from £6) have remained low, and booking is essential. Daily 5–11.30pm.

SOUTHBANK AND SOUTHWARK

★ **Laughing Gravy** 154 Blackfriars Rd, SE1 ☎ 020 7998 1701, @ thelaughinggravy.co.uk; ⊖ Southwark; map p.87. Welcoming, cosy brasserie serving robust modern English and Mediterranean food in a brick-lined dining room; a great find in this neck of the woods. Mon–Fri 11am–11pm, Sat 5.30–11pm, Sun noon–6pm.

★ **Zucca** 184 Bermondsey St, SE1 ☎ 020 7378 6809, @ zuccalondon.com; ⊖ London Bridge; map pp.90–91. Prices for the superb modern Italian food in this lovely restaurant – fresh pasta, creamy risottos, grilled shellfish, all made with the freshest, simplest ingredients – are surprisingly low. Mains from £9. Tues–Sat 12.30–3pm & 6.30–10pm, Sun 12.30–3pm.

KENSINGTON AND CHELSEA

★ **Dinner by Heston Blumenthal** Mandarin Oriental Hotel, 66 Knightsbridge, SW1 ☎ 020 7201 3833, @ dinnerbyheston.com; ⊖ Knightsbridge; map pp.94–95. Blumenthal doesn't actually cook here – the head chef worked with him at the *Fat Duck* – and there is less emphasis on flashy molecular cuisine, but the quirky English food, using recipes from as far back as medieval times, is as wonderful as you would expect – try the "meat fruit" and the taffety tart. The three-course weekday lunch menu (£28) is a bargain– that's if you get a reservation. Mains from £25. Daily noon–2.30pm & 6.30–10.30pm.

Gessler at Daquise 20 Thurloe St, SW7 ☎ 020 7589 6117, @ gesslerlondon.com; ⊖ South Kensington; map pp.94–95. While it has kept some of its old, rustic atmosphere, this old-fashioned Polish café, a South Ken institution since 1947, has gone rather upmarket – the food remains superb, with tasty pierogi and a splendid beetroot soup. Daily noon until "the last guests leave".

BAYSWATER AND NOTTING HILL

Le Café Anglais 8 Porchester Gardens, W2 ☎ 020 7221 1415, @ lecafeanglais.co.uk; ⊖ Bayswater; map pp.94–95. Splendid modern British/European brasserie and oyster bar in an airy, vaguely Art Deco space – hard to believe you're in the bland Whiteley's shopping mall. Mains £14–28; set lunch menus (2/3 courses) from £18.50. Mon–Thurs noon–3.30 pm & 6.30–10.30pm, Fri & Sat noon–3.30 pm & 6.30–11pm, Sun noon–3.30pm & 6.30–10pm.

Hereford Road 3 Hereford Rd, W2 ☎ 020 7727 1144, @ herefordroad.org; ⊖ Queensway/Notting Hill Gate; map pp.94–95. *St John* alumni Tom Pemberton brings robust English cooking to West London, with the focus on simple, old-fashioned excellence. Set meals, from £13, are a bargain, and they do an express lunch for £9.50. Daily noon–3pm & 6–10.30pm, till 10pm Sun.

NORTH LONDON

Jin Kichi 73 Heath St, NW3 ☎ 020 7794 6158, @ jinkichi.com; ⊖ Hampstead. Jin Kichi is a cramped, homely and very busy (book ahead) neighbourhood Japanese place that specializes in charcoal-grilled skewers of meat. Mains £8–12. Tues–Sat 12.30–2pm & 6–10.45pm, Sun 12.30–2pm & 6–10.45pm.

Manna 4 Erskine Rd, NW3 ☎ 020 7722 8028, @ manna-veg.com; ⊖ Chalk Farm; map pp.60–61. Upscale veggie restaurant, full of Primrose Hill yoga bunnies, serving large portions of mostly organic food, much of it vegan, from

1

around the world. Mains £11–14, less at lunch. Tues–Fri 6.30–10.30pm, Sat & Sun noon–3pm & 6.30–10.30pm.

Trojka 101 Regent's Park Rd, NW1 020 7483 3765, trojka.co.uk; Chalk Farm; map pp.60–61. The Eastern European food, from pierogi to schnitzel, is wonderfully authentic, and there's live Russian music on Friday and Saturday evenings. Mains £6–9; two-course lunch menu £7.95/£9.95. Daily 9am–10.30pm.

SOUTH LONDON

★ **Old Brewery** Pepys Building, The Old Royal Naval College, SE10 0203 327 1280, oldbrewerygreenwich.com; Cutty Sark DLR. During the day, this warm, historic dining room serves breakfasts and light deli lunches to tourists, and then transforms into a relaxed neighbourhood brasserie/brewpub at night. Mon–Sat 10am–11pm, Sun 10am–10.30pm.

WEST LONDON

Chez Lindsay 11 Hill Rise, Richmond TW10 020 8948 7473, chezlindsay.co.uk; Richmond. Small, bright, riverside Breton restaurant, serving galettes, crepes and more formal French main courses, including lots of fresh fish and shellfish. Galettes from £5, mains £10–19. Mon–Sat noon–11pm, Sun noon–10pm.

DRINKING

WESTMINSTER

The Chandos 29 St Martin's Lane, W1 020 7836 1401; Charing Cross; map pp.64–65. If you can get one of the booths downstairs, or the leather sofas upstairs in the more relaxed Opera Room Bar, then you'll find it difficult to leave, especially given the cheap Sam Smith's beer. Mon–Sat 11am–11pm, Sun noon–10.30pm.

★ **St Stephen's Tavern** 10 Bridge St, SW1 020 7925 2286 Westminster; map pp.64–65. A beautifully restored, opulent Victorian pub, built in 1867, wall to wall with civil servants and MPs (there's a division bell), and serving good real ales. Mon–Fri 11am–11pm, Sat 11am–8pm, Sun noon–6pm.

ST JAMES'S, MAYFAIR & MARYLEBONE

Guinea 30 Bruton Place, W1 020 7409 1728, theguinea.co.uk; Bond Street or Oxford Circus; map pp.64–65. Pretty, old-fashioned, flower-strewn mews pub, serving good Young's bitter and excellent steak-and-kidney pies. Invariably packed to its tiny rafters. Closed Sun.

ICA Bar The Mall, SW1 020 7930 3647, ica.org.uk; Piccadilly Circus or Charing Cross; map pp.64–65. Cool late-opening drinking venue, popular with an arty crowd. Wed noon–11pm, Thurs–Sat noon–1am, Sun noon–9pm.

Red Lion 23 Crown Passage, SW1 020 7930 4141; Green Park; map pp.64–65. Hidden away in a passageway off Pall Mall, this is a genuinely warm and cosy local, with super-friendly bar staff, well-kept beer and excellent sandwiches. Mon–Sat 11.30am–11pm.

The Windmill 6–8 Mill St, W1 020 7491 8050; Oxford Circus; map pp.64–65. Convivial pub just off Regent St, a perfect retreat for exhausted shoppers. The Young's beers are top-notch, as are the steak-and-kidney pies, for which the pub has won numerous awards. Mon–Fri 11am–midnight, Sat noon–4pm.

SOHO

Academy 12 Old Compton St, W1 020 7437 7820, labbaruk.com; Leicester Square; map pp.64–65. Two-floor retro bar where cocktail-school graduates serve up classics and new concoctions. DJs on various nights. Mon–Sat 4pm–midnight, Sun 4–10.30pm.

Argyll Arms 18 Argyll St, W1 020 7734 6117; Oxford Circus; map pp.64–65. Mobbed by shoppers and tourists alike, but this Victorian pub has preserved many features of its traditional interior and offers a good range of real ales. Mon–Sat 11am–11.30pm, Sun noon–10.30pm.

Dog & Duck 18 Bateman St, W1 020 7494 0697; Tottenham Court Road; map pp.64–65. Tiny Soho pub that retains much of its old character, beautiful Victorian tiling and mosaics, a good range of real ales and a loyal clientele. If it gets too busy downstairs, head upstairs to the George Orwell Bar (he used to drink here). Mon–Sat 11am–11pm, Sun noon–10.30pm.

★ **The Social** 5 Little Portland St, W1 020 7636 4992, thesocial.com; Oxford Circus; map p.75. Industrial club-bar and diner, with great DJs playing everything from rock to rap, and a genuinely hedonistic-cum-alcoholic crowd. Sun & Mon 5pm–midnight, Tues &Wed noon–midnight, Thurs & Fri noon–1am, Sat 5pm–1am.

COVENT GARDEN AND STRAND

★ **Cross Keys** 31 Endell St, WC2 020 7836 5185; Covent Garden; map pp.64–65. Stuffed with copper pots, brass instruments, paintings and memorabilia, this most welcoming of West End pubs attracts an appealing blend of older Covent Garden residents, young workers and tourists. Mon–Sat 11am–11pm, Sun noon–10.30pm.

★ **Gordon's** 47 Villiers St, WC2 020 7930 1408, gordonswinebar.com; Charing Cross or Embankment; map pp.64–65. Cavernous, shabby, atmospheric wine bar specializing in ports, sherries and Madeiras. The genial atmosphere makes this a favourite with local office workers, who spill outdoors in the summer. Mon–Sat 11am–11pm, Sun noon–10pm.

Lamb & Flag 33 Rose St, WC2 020 7497 9504; Leicester Square; map pp.64–65. Over 300 years old, this agreeably tatty pub, tucked away down an alley

1

between Garrick and Floral streets, was where John Dryden was attacked in 1679. Mon–Sat 11am–11pm, Sun noon–10.30pm.

★ **The Salisbury** 90 St Martin's Lane, WC2 ⓣ020 7836 5863; ⊖Leicester Square; map pp.64–65. One of the capital's most beautifully preserved Victorian pubs, with etched and engraved windows, bronze figures and Art Nouveau light fittings. Mon–Fri 11am–11pm, Sat noon–midnight, Sun noon–10.30pm.

BLOOMSBURY

The Duke 7 Roger St, WC1 ⓣ020 7242 7230, ⓦdukepub.co.uk; ⊖Russell Square; map p.75. Lovely little neighbourhood gastropub, without the pretensions often associated with the breed, and an unusual Art Deco bent to the decor. Its discreet location keeps the crowd in the small bar manageable. Mon–Sat noon–11pm, Sun noon–10.30pm.

The Lamb 94 Lamb's Conduit St, WC1 ⓣ020 7405 0713; ⊖Russell Square; map p.75. Marvellously well-preserved Victorian pub, with mirrors, polished wood and etched glass "snob" screens. Deep green leather banquettes and small circular tables with dinky brass balustrades round things off splendidly. Mon–Sat 11am–midnight, Sun noon–10.30pm.

Museum Tavern 49 Great Russell St, WC1 ⓣ020 7242 8987; ⊖Tottenham Court Road or Russell Square; map p.75. Karl Marx's erstwhile drinking hole is a handsome old pub opposite the main entrance to the British Museum. Mon–Sat 11am–11pm, Sun noon–10.30pm.

HOLBORN

Princess Louise 208 High Holborn, WC1 ⓣ020 7405 8816; ⊖Holborn; map p.75. Architecturally, one of London's most impressive Victorian pubs, featuring gold-trimmed mirrors, gorgeous mosaics and a fine moulded ceiling. Even the toilets are listed for their historic features. Mon–Fri 11am–11pm, Sat noon–11pm.

★ **Ye Olde Mitre** 1 Ely Court, EC1 ⓣ020 7405 4751; ⊖Farringdon; map pp.80–81. Hidden down a tiny alleyway off Hatton Garden, this wonderfully atmospheric pub dates back to 1546; the low-ceilinged, wood-panelled rooms are packed with history and the real ales are excellent. Mon–Fri 11am–11pm.

CLERKENWELL

★ **Jerusalem Tavern** 55 Britton St, EC1 ⓣ020 7490 4281; ⊖Farringdon; map pp.80–81. Something special: a tiny, converted Georgian coffee house – the frontage dates from 1810 – that has retained much of its original character. Better still, the excellent draught beers are from St Peter's Brewery in Suffolk. Mon–Fri 11am–11pm.

The Three Kings 7 Clerkenwell Close, EC1 ⓣ020 7253 0483; ⊖Farringdon; map pp.80–81. This Clerkenwell favourite is tucked away just north of Clerkenwell Green, with a delightful eclectic interior and two small rooms upstairs perfect for long occupation. Right next to *The Crown*, on Clerkenwell Green itself, which is also well worth a trip, particularly on summer evenings. Mon–Sat noon–11pm.

HOXTON & SHOREDITCH

The Barley Mow 127 Curtain Rd, EC2 ⓣ020 7729 3910; ⊖Old Street; map pp.80–81. There are lots of fashionably down-at-heel pubs in Hoxton and Shoreditch (with the *Bricklayer's Arms* next door a real stalwart) but this is one of the best. The *Reliance*, close by on Old Street, is another reliable Shoreditch pub with a good range of beers. Mon–Sat 11am–11pm, Sun noon–10.30pm.

Loungelover 1 Whitby St, E1 ⓣ020 7012 1234, ⓦloungelover.co.uk; Shoreditch High Street Overground; map pp.80–81. Behind the unprepossessing facade of this former meat-packing factory lies a bizarre array of opulently camp bric-a-brac, expertly slung together to create an extraordinary-looking and unique cocktail bar. Mon–Thurs & Sun 6pm–midnight, Fri 5.30pm–1am, Sat 6pm–1am.

The Owl and the Pussycat 34 Redchurch St, E2 ⓣ020 3487 0088, ⓦowlandpussycatshoreditch.com; Shoreditch High Street Overground; map pp.80–81. Carefully dishevelled and appealing – but extremely popular, so approach with care on the busiest evenings. There are plenty of alternatives on its doorstep – try the American-style *Redchurch* bar with its excellent Sierra Nevada beer. Daily noon–late.

THE CITY

★ **The Black Friar** 174 Queen Victoria St, EC4 ⓣ020 7236 5474; ⊖Blackfriars; map pp.80–81. Utterly original place with Art Nouveau marble friezes of boozy monks and a highly decorated alcove – all original, dating from 1905. A lovely fireplace, and an unhurried atmosphere make this a relaxing place to drink. Mon–Fri 11am–11pm, Sat 11am–11.30pm, Sun noon–10.30pm.

The Counting House 50 Cornhill, EC2; ⓣ020 7283 7123; ⊖Bank; map pp.80–81. One of Fuller's inspired conversions, this one is in a bank, with a magnificent interior featuring high ceilings, marble walls, mosaic flooring and a large, oval island bar. Mon–Fri 11am–9pm.

The Lamb Tavern 10–12 Leadenhall Market, EC3 ⓣ020 7626 2454; ⊖Monument; map pp.80–81. In the middle of beautiful Leadenhall Market, this super Young's pub offers almost exclusively standing room only (both inside and out). Excellent roast beef, pork and sausage sandwiches at lunchtime. Mon–Fri 11am–11pm.

★ **Ye Olde Cheshire Cheese** Wine Office Court, 145 Fleet St, EC4 ⓣ020 7353 6170; ⊖Temple or Blackfriars; map pp.80–81. A famous seventeenth-century watering hole – chiefly because of patrons such as Dickens and Dr Johnson – with several snug, dark-panelled bars and real fires. Popular with tourists, but by no means exclusively so. Mon–Fri 11am–11pm, Sat noon–11pm, Sun noon–5pm.

EAST END & DOCKLANDS

The Gun 27 Coldharbour, E14 ⊕020 7515 5222, ⊛thegundocklands.com; ⊖Canary Wharf, South Quay or Blackwall DLR. Legendary dockers' pub, once the haunt of Lord Nelson, *The Gun* is now a classy gastropub, with unrivalled views over to the Dome. Mon–Sat 11am–midnight, Sun 11am–11pm.

Ten Bells 84 Commercial St, E1 ⊕020 7366 1721; ⊖Shoreditch High Street Overground; map pp.80–81. Stripped-down, pleasantly ramshackle pub, with some great Victorian tiling. Attracts a relentlessly hip and young crowd these days. Mon–Thurs & Sun noon–midnight, Fri & Sat noon–1am.

Town of Ramsgate 62 Wapping High St, E1 ⊕020 7264 0001; ⊖Wapping. Dark, narrow, medieval pub near what used to be Execution Dock. Captain Blood was discovered here with the Crown Jewels under his cloak, "Hanging" Judge Jeffreys was arrested here trying to flee, and Admiral Bligh and Fletcher Christian were regulars. Mon–Sat noon–midnight, Sun noon–10.30pm.

SOUTH BANK AND SOUTHWARK

Anchor & Hope 36 The Cut, SE1 ⊕020 7928 9898; ⊖Southwark; map p.87. The *Anchor* gastropub dishes up excellent, simple grub: soups, salads and mains such as slow-cooked pork with choucroute, as well as mouth-watering puds. You can't book a table, so the bar is basically the waiting room. Mon 5–11pm, Tues–Sat 11am–11pm, Sun 12.30–5pm.

The Anchor 34 Park St, SE1 ⊕020 7407 1577; ⊖London Bridge; map pp.90–91. Built in 1770, this sprawling pub retains only a few vestiges of the past, but has one of the few riverside terraces – inevitably it's often crowded with tourists. Mon–Sat 11am–11pm, Sun noon–10.30pm.

George Inn 77 Borough High St, SE1 ⊕020 7407 2056; ⊖Borough or London Bridge; map pp.90–91. London's only surviving galleried coaching inn, dating from the seventeenth century and now owned by the National Trust; mobbed by tourists, but it does serve a good range of real ales. Mon–Thurs 11am–11pm, Fri & Sat 11am–midnight, Sun noon–10.30pm.

★ **King's Arms** 25 Roupell St, SE1 ⊕020 7207 0784; ⊖Waterloo; map p.87. Terrific local divided into two sections; a traditional drinking area in the front, with a tastefully cluttered, conservatory-style dining space at the rear, where good Thai food is served at long wooden tables. Mon–Sat 11am–11pm, Sun noon–10.30pm.

KENSINGTON AND CHELSEA

Churchill Arms 119 Kensington Church St, W8 ⊕020 7229 4242; ⊖Notting Hill Gate; map pp.94–95. Justifiably popular, flower-festooned pub serving Fuller's beers, superb Guinness, and good Thai food. Mon–Wed 11am–11pm, Thurs–Sat 11am–midnight, Sun noon–10.30pm.

★ **Cooper's Arms Bar** 87 Flood St, SW3 ⊕020 7376 3120; ⊖Sloane Square; map pp.94–95. Decent, spacious neighbourhood pub, which may not be more than the sum of its parts – reasonable food, a good range of beers, plenty of spots to choose from – but is still a good find so close to the King's Road. Mon–Sat 11am–11pm, Sun noon–10pm.

The Elgin 96 Ladbroke Grove, W11 ⊕020 7229 5663; ⊖Ladbroke Grove; map pp.94–95. Enormous pub on Ladbroke Grove where the buzzy vibe, lovely original features and funky decor bring in the cool Portobello crowd. Mon–Sat 11am–11pm, Sun noon–10.30pm.

Grenadier 18 Wilton Row, SW1 ⊕020 7235 3074; ⊖Hyde Park Corner or Knightsbridge; map pp.94–95. Located in a private mews, this quaint little pub was Wellington's local (his horse block survives outside) and his officers' mess; the original pewter bar survives, and there's plenty of military paraphernalia. Classy but pricey bar food. Mon–Sat noon–11pm, Sun noon–10.30pm.

The Nag's Head 53 Kinnerton St, SW1 ⊕020 7235 1135; ⊖Hyde Park Corner or Knightsbridge; map pp.94–95. A convivial, quirky and down-to-earth little pub in a posh cobbled mews, with dark wood panelling, china handpumps and old prints on hunting, shooting and fishing. The unusual sunken back room has a flagstone floor and fires in winter. The pub grub's good. The landlord doesn't like mobiles and insists that all coats are hung up on pegs. Mon–Sat 11am–11pm, Sun noon–10.30pm.

The Pig's Ear 35 Old Church St, SW3 ⊕020 7352 2908, ⊛thepigsear.info; ⊖Sloane Square; map pp.94–95. Genuinely charming despite its moneyed milieu, *The Pig's Ear* has a busy and beguiling interior and is treasured by those fortunate enough to call it their local. Mon–Sat noon–11pm, Sun noon–10.30pm.

NORTH LONDON

Edinboro Castle 57 Mornington Terrace, NW1 ⊕020 7255 9651, ⊛edinborocastlepub.co.uk; ⊖Camden Town; map pp.60–61. A large, high-ceilinged pub with an attractively glammed-up interior. The main draw, though, is the large, leafy beer garden which hosts summer weekend barbecues. Above-average selection of draught continental lagers and a couple of real ales. Mon–Sat noon–11pm, Sun noon–10.30pm.

Lock Tavern 35 Chalk Farm Rd, NW1 ⊕020 7482 7163, ⊛lock-tavern.co.uk; ⊖Chalk Farm; map pp.60–61. Rambling pub with large, battered wooden tables, comfy sofas, a leafy upstairs terrace and beer garden down

1

below, as well as posh pub grub and DJs playing anything from punk funk and electro to rock. Mon–Thurs noon–midnight, Fri & Sat noon–1am, Sun noon–11pm.

Prince Alfred 5a Formosa St, W9 ⓣ 020 7286 3027; ⊖ Warwick Avenue; map pp.60–61. A Victorian pub with all its original 1862 fittings intact, right down to the glazed "snob screens" that divide the bar into a series of "snugs". Along with the heritage, the pub also runs a pricey Modern European restaurant at the back. Daily noon–11pm.

The Flask 77 Highgate West Hill, N6 ⓣ 020 8348 7346; bus #210 from ⊖ Archway. Ideally situated at the heart of Highgate village green – with a rambling, low-ceilinged interior and a summer terrace – and, as a result, very, very popular at the weekend. Mon–Sat noon–11pm, Sun noon–10.30pm.

The Holly Bush 22 Holly Mount, off Holly Hill, NW3 ⓣ 020 7435 2892; ⊖ Hampstead. A lovely old pub, with a real fire in winter, tucked away in the steep backstreets of Hampstead village. Some fine real ales on offer, as well as decent food (particularly the sausages and pies), though it can get mobbed at weekends. Mon–Sat noon–11pm, Sun noon–10.30pm.

SOUTH LONDON

Crown & Greyhound 73 Dulwich Village, SE21 ⓣ 020 8299 4976; North Dulwich station from London Bridge. Grandiose Victorian pub, convenient for the Picture Gallery, with an ornate plasterwork ceiling and lots of polished wood and stained glass. The two-tiered beer garden is perfect for summer barbecues. Mon–Wed 11am–11pm, Thurs–Sat 11am–midnight, Sun noon–10.30pm.

Cutty Sark Ballast Quay, off Lassell St, SE10 ⓣ 020 8858 3146; Cutty Sark DLR or Maze Hill station from Charing Cross. This Georgian pub is a good place for a riverside pint and much less touristy than the waterfront Trafalgar Tavern. Mon–Sat 11am–11pm, Sun noon–10.30pm.

WEST LONDON

★ **Dove** 19 Upper Mall, W6 ⓣ 020 8748 5405; ⊖ Ravenscourt Park. Wonderful low-beamed, old riverside pub with the smallest bar in the UK (4ft by 7ft), and very popular Sunday roast dinners. Mon–Sat 11am–11pm, Sun noon–10.30pm.

White Cross Hotel Water Lane, Richmond, TW9 1TJ ⓣ 020 8940 6844; ⊖ Richmond. With a longer pedigree and more character than its rivals, the *White Cross* has a very popular, large garden overlooking the river. In winter, you can decamp to the lovely upstairs lounge with its big bay windows and open fire. Mon–Sat 11am–midnight, Sun noon–10.30pm.

NIGHTLIFE

LIVE MUSIC VENUES

London's live music scene is extremely diverse, encompassing all variations of rock, blues, roots and world music, and, along with impressive homegrown talent, the city's media spotlight makes it pretty much the place for young bands to break into the global mainstream.

GENERAL VENUES

★ **Academy Brixton** 211 Stockwell Rd, SW9 ⓣ 020 7771 3000, ⓦ o2academybrixton.co.uk; ⊖ Brixton. The Academy has seen them all, from mods and rockers to Chase and Status. The 4000-capacity Victorian hall doesn't always deliver perfect sound quality, but remains a cracking place to see mid-level bands.

★ **Cargo** 83 Rivington St, EC2 ⓣ 020 7749 7840, ⓦ cargo-london.com; ⊖ Old Street or Shoreditch High Street Overground; map pp.80–81. Small, groovy venue in what was once a railway arch, with an attached restaurant and chilled garden area. Hosts a variety of live acts, including jazz, hip-hop, indie and folk, and excellent club nights.

Forum 9–17 Highgate Rd, NW5 ⓣ 020 7428 4099, ⓦ meanfiddler.com; ⊖ Kentish Town. Decent mid-sized venue, with a large stage hosting a mix of successful new acts and groups inching their way onto the nostalgia circuit.

★ **King's Place** 90 York Way, N1 ⓣ 020 7520 1490, ⓦ kingsplace.co.uk; ⊖ King's Cross; map pp.60–61. Two halls host good classical, jazz and world music gigs at this rather swish development, with great acoustics, beside the *Guardian* newspaper's offices.

Hammersmith Apollo 45 Queen Caroline St, W6 ⓣ 020 8563 3800, ⓦ hammersmithapollo.net; ⊖ Hammersmith. The former *Hammersmith Odeon* is a cavernous, theatre-style space (downstairs is seating or standing, depending on the occasion), featuring everyone from Lou Reed to Olly Murs, plus stand-up and popular theatre.

Roundhouse Chalk Farm Rd, NW1 ⓣ 0844 482 8008, ⓦ roundhouse.org.uk; ⊖ Chalk Farm. Dating from 1846, this magnificent Grade II-listed building is one of London's premier performing arts centres; alongside community work and theatre, its programme includes regular appearances by artier rock acts and world music stars.

★ **Shepherds Bush Empire** Shepherd's Bush Green, W12 ⓣ 0844 477 2000, ⓦ shepherds-bush-empire.co.uk; ⊖ Shepherd's Bush. Yet another grand old theatre, the *Empire* now plays host to a fine cross-section of mid-league UK and US bands. There's often a great atmosphere downstairs, while the vertigo-inducing upstairs balconies provide great stage views.

1

NOTTING HILL CARNIVAL

The two-day free **festival** (ⓦthenottinghillcarnival.com) in Notting Hill is the longest-running, best-known and biggest street party in Europe. Dating back more than forty years, the Caribbean carnival is a tumult of imaginatively decorated parade floats, eye-catching costumes, thumping sound systems, live bands, irresistible food and huge crowds. It takes place on the Sunday and Monday of the last weekend of August.

ROCK, BLUES, INDIE AND FOLK

★ **12 Bar Club** Denmark St, WC2 ⓣ020 7240 2622, ⓦ12barclub.com; ⊖Tottenham Court Road; map pp.64–65. Tiny, atmospheric bar and venue offering up-and-coming, cheap and often pleasantly eccentric indie gigs as well as blues and folk.

Borderline Orange Yard, Manette St, W1 ⓣ020 7734 5547, ⓦmeanfiddler.com; ⊖Tottenham Court Road; map pp.64–65. Small and slightly ramshackle basement joint with awkward pillars but good sound and a diverse musical policy.

KOKO 1a Camden High St, NW1 ⓣ0870 432 5527, ⓦkoko.uk.com; ⊖Mornington Crescent. An institution since its days as the *Camden Palace*, this venue's grand interior hosts clubs (Fri & Sat) and gigs (the rest of the time), with a hip assortment of indie-pop types dominating proceedings.

Underworld 174 Camden High St, NW1 ⓣ020 7482 1932, ⓦtheunderworldcamden.co.uk; ⊖Camden Town. Shouty, scruffy warren under the *World's End* pub – a great place to check out metal, hardcore and heavy-rock bands.

★ **Union Chapel** Compton Terrace, N1 ⓣ020 7226 1686, ⓦunionchapel.org.uk; ⊖Highbury & Islington; map pp.60–61. Intimate venue that doubles as a church, hence the pews; the array of acts ranges from contemporary folk to world-music legends, and there are regular Saturday lunchtime sessions.

JAZZ AND WORLD MUSIC

606 Club 90 Lots Rd, SW10 ⓣ020 7352 5953, ⓦ606club.co.uk; ⊖Fulham Broadway; map pp.94–95. Near the King's Rd, this basement jazz venue and restaurant has a particular focus on home-bred talent. It's open to all, but alcohol can only be served to non-members if they have a meal.

Jazz Cafe 5 Parkway, NW1 ⓣ020 7485 6834, ⓦjazzcafelive.com; ⊖Camden Town; map pp.60–61. There's the odd cheesy pop night here, but a combination of big names (at big prices) and acts from the clubbier end of jazz keep the dancefloor and balcony buzzing. You can dine, too, if you book in advance – though the service gets mixed reports.

Ronnie Scott's 47 Frith St, W1 ⓣ020 7439 0747, ⓦronniescotts.co.uk; ⊖Leicester Square; map pp.64–65. The most famous jazz club in London, this small and atmospheric Soho stalwart features all the jazz greats. Many people opt for the dinner package, but you don't have to.

★ **The Vortex** 11 Gillett Square, N16 ⓣ020 7254 4097, ⓦvortexjazz.co.uk; Dalston Kingsland or Dalston Junction Overground. Set in the snazzy Dalston Cultural House, this small venue is a serious player on the live jazz scene, managing to combine a touch of urban style with a cosy, friendly atmosphere.

CLUBS

London remains *the* place to come if you want to party after dark. This is the world's dance capital, bursting with home-grown talent, and a regular stop-off for DJs from around the globe. Many clubs keep going until 6am or later; some are open all week, others sporadically; and very often a venue will host a different club each night of the week. Admission charges vary enormously, with small midweek nights starting at around £3–5 and large weekend events charging as much as £30; around £10–15 is the average. For the latest, check flyers in the Soho record stores, and pick up a copy of *Time Out* (see p.111).

★ **Fabric** 77a Charterhouse St, EC1 ⓣ020 7336 8898, ⓦfabriclondon.com; ⊖Farringdon; map pp.80–81. Despite big queues (arrive early or late) and a confusing layout that means you may take hours to find friends, jackets and some of its numerous rooms, this 1600-capacity club remains one of the world's finest, playing drum'n'bass and dubstep (usually Fri), techno and house (usually Sat & Sun), live bands and quality DJ line-ups. Some Thurs 9pm–4am, Fri & Sun 10pm–6am, Sat 11pm–8am.

Madame JoJo's 8–10 Brewer St, W1 ⓣ020 7734 3040, ⓦmadamejojos.com; ⊖Piccadilly Circus; map pp.64–65. Louche, enjoyable and ever-so-slightly battered Soho institution. Alongside burlesque and magic shows, you'll find electronica, disco and rock – the big nights include funk (Fri), and indie (Tues). Usually Tues–Sun 10pm–3am, with shows earlier in the evening.

Ministry of Sound 103 Gaunt St, SE1 ⓣ020 7378 6528, ⓦministryofsound.com; ⊖Elephant & Castle; map pp.60–61. The vast headquarters of the brand may sometimes seem peopled largely by corporate clubbers and gawping visitors, but the sound system is exceptional and it gets the pick of visiting house and trance DJs. Usually Thurs 10pm–4am, Fri–Sat 11pm–6am.

★ **Notting Hill Arts Club** 21 Notting Hill Gate, W11 ⓣ020 7460 4459, ⓦnottinghillartsclub.com; ⊖Notting Hill Gate; map pp.94–95. Groovy, arty, dressed-down basement club/bar that's popular for everything from

1

Latin-inspired funk, jazz and hip-hop through to soul, house and indie; Saturday afternoon has free gigs courtesy of Rough Trade records. Usually Wed–Sun 7pm–2am.

★ **Plastic People** 147–149 Curtain Rd, EC2 ⓣ 020 7739 6471, ⓦ plasticpeople.co.uk; ⊖ Old Street; map pp.80–81. Thumping basement club whose broad booking policy stretches through techno, rock'n'roll, Afro-pop and splendid dubstep night FWD>>. Usually Thurs 10pm–2am, Fri & Sat 10pm–4am.

Rhythm Factory 16–18 Whitechapel Rd ⓣ 020 7375 3774, ⓦ rhythmfactory.co.uk; ⊖ Aldgate East or Whitechapel; map pp.80–81. This textile-factory-turned-cutting-edge club houses a bar and separate, often fairly packed, dancefloor. Live bands appear fairly regularly during the week; drum'n'bass and techno dominate the weekends. Mon–Thurs usually 7–11pm when open; Fri & Sat 10pm–6am.

Proud Camden Stables Market, Chalk Farm Rd, NW1 ⓣ 0207 482 3867, ⓦ proudcamden.com; ⊖ Camden Town; map pp.60–61. Indie, rave, live bands, costume parties, exhibitions and more – *Proud Camden* is as mixed up as you'd expect a former horse hospital to be, with decent food early on and an outdoor terrace in summer. Hours vary – clubs usually till 2.30am.

GAY AND LESBIAN NIGHTLIFE

London's **lesbian and gay scene** is so huge, diverse and well established that it's easy to forget just how much – and how fast – it has grown over the last couple of decades. **Soho** remains its spiritual heart, with a mix of traditional gay pubs, designer café-bars and a range of gay-run services. Details of most events appear in *Time Out*, while another excellent source of information is the London **Lesbian and Gay Switchboard** (ⓣ 020 7837 7324, ⓦ llgs.org.uk). The **outdoor event** of the year is **Pride London** (ⓦ pridelondon.org) in late June/early July, a colourful, noisy march through the city streets followed at the end of the month by a huge, ticketed party in a central London park.

BARS AND CLUBS

There are loads of lesbian and gay eating and watering holes in London, many of them operating as cafés by day and transforming into drinking dens by night. Lots have cabaret or disco nights and are open until the early hours, making them a fine (and affordable) alternative to the big clubs. Most have free admission, though a few levy a charge after 10.30pm (expect to pay about £5) if there's music, cabaret or a disco.

MIXED BARS

The Black Cap 171 Camden High St, NW1 ⓣ 020 7485 0538, ⓦ theblackcap.com; ⊖ Camden Town; map pp.60–61. Venerable north London establishment offering cabaret and dancing almost every night. The upstairs *Shufflewick* bar is in a quieter pub style, and opens onto the *Fong Terrace* in the summer. Mon–Thurs noon–2am, Fri noon–3am, Sun noon–1am.

Freedom 66 Wardour St, W1 ⓣ 020 7734 0071, ⓦ freedombarsoho.com; ⊖ Piccadilly Circus; map pp.64–65. Hip metrosexual place, popular with a straight/gay Soho crowd. The basement becomes an intimate club at night, complete with pink banquettes and glitter balls, that plays home to cabaret and comedy. Mon–Thurs 4pm–3am, Fri & Sat 2pm–3am, Sun 2pm–10.30pm.

George & Dragon 2–4 Hackney Rd, E2 ⓣ 020 7012 1100; ⊖ Old Street; map pp.60–61. Dandies, fashionistas and locals meet in this lively, often rammed East End hangout. The interior setup is traditional, but the attitudes are not. Daily 6pm–midnight.

★ **Ku Bar** 30 Lisle St, WC2, ⓣ 020 7437 4303, ⓦ ku-bar.co.uk; ⊖ Leicester Square; map pp.64–65. The Lisle St original, with a downstairs club open late, is one of Soho's largest and best-loved gay bars, serving a scene-conscious yet low-on-attitude clientele. It has a stylish sibling bar on Frith St. Lisle St Mon–Sat noon–3am, Sun noon–10.30pm.

★ **Retro Bar** 2 George Court (off Strand), WC2 ⓣ 020 7839 8760; ⊖ Charing Cross; map pp.64–65. Friendly, indie/retro bar playing 1970s, 80s, rock, pop, goth and alternative sounds, and featuring regular DIY DJ nights. Mon–Fri noon–11pm, Sat 2–11pm, Sun 2–10.30pm.

The Yard 57 Rupert St, W1 ⓣ 020 7437 2652, ⓦ yardbar.co.uk; ⊖ Piccadilly Circus; map pp.64–65. The courtyard and loft areas often heave with a varied post-work crowd at this laidback, sociable bar – in fine weather it's one of the best spots in Soho for alfresco drinking. Mon–Thurs & Sun noon–11.30pm, Fri & Sat noon–midnight.

LESBIAN BARS

Candy Bar 4 Carlisle St, WC2 ⓣ 020 7287 5041, ⓦ candybarsoho.com; ⊖ Tottenham Court Road; map pp.64–65. Now part of the *Ku* group of gay bars, this Sapphic magnet has been operating since 1996 and still has the same crucial, cruisey vibe that makes it the hottest girl bar in central London. Mon, Wed & Thurs 5pm–3am, Tues 7pm–3am, Fri & Sat 4pm–3am, Sun 5pm–12.30am.

Lounge Penthouse, 1 Leicester Square, WC2 ⓣ 020 734 0900, ⓦ lounge.uk.net; ⊖ Leicester Square; map pp.64–65. Bar, restaurant and club night, the monthly *Lounge* offers classy drinks and dressier vibes than you'll find elsewhere in town. From 9pm every third Thursday.

Star at Night 22 Great Chapel St, W1 ⓣ 020 7494 2488, ⓦ thestaratnight.com; ⊖ Tottenham Court Road; map pp.64–65. Comfortable, mixed but female-led, venue. It's popular with a slightly older crowd who want somewhere to sit, a decent glass of wine and good conversation. Tues–Sat 6–11.30pm.

GAY MEN'S BARS

★ **BarCode** Arch 69, Albert Embankment, SE11 ⓣ020 7582 4180, ⓦbar-code.co.uk; ⊖Vauxhall; map pp.60–61. Slick, spacious cruisey gay men's bar in the heart of Vauxhall's clubbing quarter, convenient for the clubs *Area* and *Fire* (see below). Mon–Wed 4pm–1am, Thurs 4pm–2am, Fri 4pm–5am, Sat 4pm–7am, Sun 5pm–1am.

Comptons of Soho 51–53 Old Compton St, W1; ⊖Leicester Square or Piccadilly Circus; map pp.64–65. This large, traditional-style pub attracts a butch, cruising yet relaxed 25-plus crowd. Upstairs is more chilled and draws younger folks. Mon–Fri noon–11pm, Sat 11am–11pm, Sun noon–10.30pm.

The King's Arms 23 Poland St, W1 ⓣ020 7734 5907; ⊖Oxford Circus; map pp.64–65. London's best-known and perennially popular bear bar, with a traditional London pub atmosphere, with a karaoke night on Sundays. Mon & Tues noon–11pm, Wed & Thurs noon–11.30pm, Fri & Sat noon–midnight, Sun 1pm–10.30pm.

CLUBS

Area 67–68 Albert Embankment, SE1 ⓣ020 3242 0040, ⓦareaclublondon.com; ⊖Vauxhall; map pp.60–61. With two dancefloors, chic decor and impressive laser and light displays, *Area* hosts big-name international DJs and the after-hours club *Beyond* on Sunday mornings. Sun 10pm–6am.

★ **Duckie** Royal Vauxhall Tavern, 372 Kennington Lane, SE11 ⓣ020 7737 4043, ⓦduckie.co.uk; ⊖Vauxhall; map pp.60–61. *Duckie*'s mix of regular live art performances and theme nights, as well as cult DJs The Readers Wifes playing everything from Kim Wilde to the Velvet Underground, has kept this splendid night going strong for 15 years.

★ **The Eagle** 349 Kennington Lane, SE11 ⓣ020 7793 0903, ⓦeaglelondon.com; ⊖Vauxhall; map pp.60–61. Home to the excellent disco Sunday-nighter Horse Meat Disco, the vibe here is a loose, friendly re-creation of late 1970s New York, complete with facial hair, checked shirts and a pool table. Mon–Thurs 9pm–2am, Fri & Sat 9pm–4am, Sun 9pm–3am.

Fire South Lambeth Rd, SW8 ⓣ020 3242 0040, ⓦfireclub.co.uk; ⊖Vauxhall; map pp.60–61. *Fire* is London's superclub of choice for a mixed though mostly male crowd of disco bunnies and hardboyz. The party runs from Saturday morning to Monday morning. Sat 3–11am, Sun noon–7pm & 11pm–9am.

Heaven Villiers St, WC2 ⓣ020 7930 2020, ⓦheaven nightclub-london.com; ⊖Charing Cross or Embankment; map pp.64–65. Said to be the UK's most popular gay club, this 2000-capacity venue is now home to G-A-Y (Thurs–Sat), the queen of London's scene nights, with big-name DJs, PAs and shows. More Muscle Mary than Diesel Doris. Thurs–Sat.

Popstarz The Den, 18a West Central St, WC1, ⓦpopstarz.org; ⊖Tottenham Court Road; map pp.64–65. The original Friday-night indie club's still-winning formula of alternative tunes, 1970s and 80s trash, cheap beer and no attitude attracts a mixed, studenty crowd. Fri 10pm–6am.

★ **Sink the Pink** Bethnal Green Working Men's Club, 42 Pollard Row, E2 ⓣ020 7739 7170, ⓦsinkthepink london.com; ⊖Bethnal Green. Silly, young and stupidly fun – attracting a handsome, mixed and inclusive crowd. Also keep an eye out for Sink the Pink events elsewhere, including *Dalston Superstore*, a trendy bar on Kingsland High St. Every second Sat 9pm–2am.

THEATRE

London has enjoyed a reputation for quality **theatre** since the time of Shakespeare and, despite the continuing dominance of blockbuster musicals and revenue-spinning star vehicles, still provides platforms for innovation and new writing. The **West End** is the heart of "Theatreland", with Shaftesbury Avenue its most congested drag, but the term is more of a conceptual pigeon-hole than a geographical term. Some of the most exciting work is performed in what have become known as the **Off-West End** theatres,while further down the financial ladder still are the **fringe** theatres, more often than not pub venues, where ticket prices are lower, and quality more variable.

COSTS

Prices Tickets for £10 are restricted to the fringe; the box-office average is closer to £20–30, with £50–70 the usual top price. The cheapest way to get a ticket is to go to the theatre box office in person; you will probably be charged a booking fee if you buy over the phone or online. Keep an eye on the websites, however, for special deals including cheap Monday seats, or standby "on-the-day" tickets – even for the big musicals and well-reviewed plays. Students, senior citizens and the unemployed can get concessionary rates for most shows, and many theatres offer reductions on standbys to these groups. Whatever you do, avoid the touts and the unofficial ticket agencies that abound in the West End – there's no guarantee that the tickets are genuine.

Discount tickets The Society of London Theatre (ⓦofficiallondontheatre.co.uk) runs a useful booth, tkts (Mon–Sat 10am–7pm, Sun 11am–4pm; ⓦtkts.co.uk), in Leicester Square, which sells on-the-day tickets for all the West End shows at discounts of up to fifty percent, though they tend to be in the top end of the price range, are limited to four per person, and carry a service charge of £3 per ticket. Tkts also sells some advance tickets, with no booking fee, for a smaller selection of shows.

1

THEATRES

Almeida Almeida St, N1 020 7359 4404, almeida.co.uk; Angel or Highbury & Islington. Popular little Islington venue that premieres excellent new plays and excitingly reworked classics, and has attracted some big Hollywood names.

Arcola Theatre 24 Ashwin St, E8 020 7503 1646, arcolatheatre.com; Dalston Junction Overground. Exciting fringe theatre in an old factory opposite Dalston Junction station. Challenging plays – classics and modern works – include shows from young, international companies. Some nights have a "Pay what you can" policy.

Barbican Centre Silk St, EC2 020 7638 8891, barbican.org.uk; Barbican or Moorgate. The Barbican's two venues – the splendid Barbican Theatre and the much smaller Pit – put on a wide variety of spectacles from puppetry and musicals to new drama.

Battersea Arts Centre 176 Lavender Hill, SW11 020 7223 2223, bac.org.uk; Clapham Junction train station from Victoria or Waterloo. A multi-stage building, housed in an old town hall, known for excellent contemporary drama, physical theatre, comedy and cabaret.

Bush Shepherd's Bush Green, W12 020 8743 5050, bushtheatre.co.uk; Shepherd's Bush. This minuscule above-pub theatre is one of London's most reliable venues for quality new writing.

Donmar Warehouse 41 Earlham St, WC2 0844 871 7624, donmarwarehouse.com; Covent Garden. A small, central performance space, noted for new writing and interesting reappraisals of the classics.

Menier Chocolate Factory 51–53 Southwark St, SE1 020 7378 1713, menierchocolatefactory.com; London Bridge. Great fringe venue in a former Victorian factory, with a decent bar and restaurant attached; the shows are consistently good.

National Theatre Southbank Centre, South Bank, SE1 020 7452 3000, nationaltheatre.org.uk; Waterloo. The country's top actors and directors produce shows ranging from Greek tragedies via experimental new writing to Broadway musicals in three separate theatres. Some productions sell out months in advance, but day tickets, for the lowest-priced seats available, go on sale on the morning of each performance – get there by 8am (two tickets per person only). Look out, too, for special "Travelex" performances, when half the seats go for £12.

Open Air Theatre Regent's Park, Inner Circle, NW1 0844 826 4242, openairtheatre.org; Baker Street. Lovely alfresco space in Regent's Park hosting a tourist-friendly summer programme of Shakespeare, musicals, plays and concerts, some of which are geared especially towards children.

Roundhouse Chalk Farm Rd, NW1 0844 482 8008, roundhouse.org.uk; Chalk Farm. Camden's exciting cultural venue, in an old – round – engine repairs shed, puts on cutting-edge theatre, circus and cabaret, with regular shows from the RSC (Royal Shakespeare Company).

Royal Court Sloane Square, SW1 020 7565 5000, royalcourttheatre.com; Sloane Square. The Royal Court is one of the best places in London to catch radical new writing, either in the proscenium arch Theatre Downstairs, or the smaller Theatre Upstairs. All tickets £10 on Mon.

Shakespeare's Globe New Globe Walk, SE1 020 7401 9919, shakespeares-globe.com; London Bridge, Blackfriars or Southwark. This open-roofed replica Elizabethan theatre uses only natural light and the minimum of scenery, and puts on fun Shakespearean shows – along with works from the Bard's contemporaries, including Christopher Marlowe, and modern works on Elizabethan themes – from April to mid-September. Seats are around £15, with "Yard" tickets (standing-room only) for around a fiver.

Soho Theatre 21 Dean St, W1 020 7478 0100, sohotheatre.com; Tottenham Court Road. Great, central theatre that specializes in new writing from around the globe, as well as regular comedy and cabaret.

Tricycle Theatre 269 Kilburn High Rd, NW6 020 7328 1000, tricycle.co.uk; Kilburn. One of London's most dynamic venues, showcasing a mixed bag of new plays, often with a multicultural bent, and usually with a sharp political focus.

COMEDY

From the big-name, big-theatre, big-ticket shows, to old favourites like the Comedy Store – at the heart of the alternative comedy movement of the 1980s – and neighbourhood pubs hosting new young hopefuls, you're never far in London from a **comedy gig**: Soho and Camden Town in particular both have a very healthy crop. Full listings appear on chortle.co.uk and in *Time Out*. Note that many venues only operate on Friday and Saturday nights, and that August can be a lean month, as much of London's talent heads north for the Edinburgh Fringe.

CINEMA

There are a lot of cinemas in London, especially the **West End**, with the biggest on and around Leicester Square. A few classy independent chains show more offbeat screenings, in various locations – check out the **Picturehouse** (picturehouses.co.uk), **Curzon** (curzoncinemas.com) and **Everyman** (everymancinema.com) – and there even exist a number of one-off arthouse cinemas. **Tickets** at the major screens cost at least £11, although afternoon shows are usually discounted, and concessionary rates are offered for some shows at virtually all cinemas, usually all day Monday or at other off-peak times. Anyone with an Orange phone can make use of the half-price "Orange Wednesday" tickets.

BFI Southbank Belvedere Rd, South Bank, SE1 ☎020 7928 3232, ⓦbfi.org.uk; ⊖Waterloo. Splendid themed seasons, showing between seven and fourteen films daily on four screens. The BFI also runs the IMAX (☎020 7199 6000, ⓦbfi.org.uk/imax), a huge glazed drum in the middle of Waterloo roundabout. The colossal screen is not recommended for anyone with vertigo.

Electric 191 Portobello Rd, W11 ☎020 7908 9696, ⓦthe-electric.co.uk; ⊖Notting Hill Gate or Ladbroke Grove. One of the oldest cinemas in the country (opened 1910), the Electric keeps much of its lovely old interior, but has added trendy leather armchairs, footstools and two-seater sofas. The programme concentrates on mainstream hits, with more offbeat offerings on Sundays.

ICA Cinema Nash House, The Mall, SW1 ☎020 7930 3647, ⓦica.org.uk; ⊖Piccadilly Circus or Charing Cross. One of the capital's most cutting-edge programmes – offering world, documentary and underground movies on two tiny screens (no armchairs here!) in the avant-garde HQ of the Institute of Contemporary Arts.

Prince Charles 7 Leicester Place, WC2 ☎020 7494 3654, ⓦprincecharlescinema.com; ⊖Leicester Square or Piccadilly Circus. Two screens in the heart of the West End, with good prices (starting at just £5.50) and a daily changing programme of newish movies, classics and cult favourites, plus participatory "singalong" romps.

Roxy 128 Borough High St, SE1 ☎020 7407 4057, ⓦroxybarandscreen.com; ⊖Borough. Excellent output – midnight screenings, indie releases, shorts – in a swish space with sofas, a big screen, and surroundsound. Sun–Wed only; members (£30, with various perks) can reserve a sofa or a table, otherwise it's first-come, first-served.

CLASSICAL MUSIC

On most days you should be able to catch a concert by one of the five major **orchestras** based in the capital or one of the more specialized ensembles. Unless a glamorous guest conductor is wielding the baton, or one of the world's high-profile orchestras is giving a performance, full houses are a rarity, so even at the biggest concert halls you should be able to pick up a ticket for around £15 (the usual range is about £12–50). During the week there are also numerous **free concerts**, often at lunchtimes, in London's churches (ⓦcityevents.co.uk), or given by the city's two leading conservatoires, the Royal College of Music (ⓦrcm.ac.uk) and Royal Academy of Music (ⓦram.ac.uk).

CONCERT VENUES

Barbican Centre Silk St, EC2 ☎020 7638 8891, ⓦbarbican.org.uk; ⊖Barbican or Moorgate. With the outstanding resident London Symphony Orchestra (ⓦlso.co.uk), the BBC Symphony Orchestra (ⓦbbc.co.uk/orchestras) as associate orchestra, and top foreign orchestras and big-name soloists in regular attendance, the Barbican is an outstanding venue.

Southbank Centre Belvedere Rd, South Bank, SE1 ☎0844 875 0073, ⓦsouthbankcentre.co.uk; ⊖Waterloo or Embankment. The SBC has three spaces, none of which is exclusively used for classical music. The 3000-seat Royal Festival Hall (RFH), home to the Philharmonia (ⓦphilharmonia.co.uk) and the London Philharmonic (ⓦlpo.co.uk), is tailor-made for large-scale choral and orchestral works, while the Queen Elizabeth Hall (QEH) and intimate Purcell Room are used for chamber concerts, solo recitals, opera and choirs.

Wigmore Hall 36 Wigmore St, W1 ☎020 7935 2141, ⓦwigmore-hall.org.uk; ⊖Bond Street or Oxford Circus. With its near-perfect acoustics, the Wigmore Hall – built in 1901 as a hall for the adjacent Bechstein piano showroom – is a firm favourite, so book well in advance. Piano recitals and chamber music are superb, as are the song recitals by some of the world's greatest singers.

OPERA

English National Opera Coliseum, St Martin's Lane, WC2 ☎0871 911 0200, ⓦeno.org; ⊖Leicester Square or Charing Cross. Operas sung in English, an adventurous repertoire, modern productions and reasonable pricing (£26–99, with day seats at £10–15 and standbys for concessions from £15).

THE PROMS

The London **Proms** (Royal Albert Hall, ☎0845 401 5045, ⓦbbc.co.uk/proms; ⊖South Kensington), provide a feast of classical music at bargain-basement prices. Uniquely, there are more than five hundred **standing places** – £5, even on the famed last night – which must be bought on the door, on the day; seated **tickets** cost between £7.50 and £90; last-night tickets start at £55. The acoustics may not be the world's best, but the calibre of the performers is unbeatable, the atmosphere superb, and the programme a creative mix of standards and new or obscure works. And the hall is so vast that even if you turn up an hour or so before the show starts you are unlikely to be turned away.

1

London's Little Opera House King's Head, 115 Upper St, N1 020 7478 0160, kingsheadtheatre.com; Angel or Highbury & Islington. Old pub theatre that reinvented itself in 2010 as an opera house. The small space – just 100 bench seats – now hosts an exciting programme of new writing, experimental pieces and classics with a twist from resident company Opera Up Close.

Royal Opera House Bow St, WC2 020 7304 4000, roh.org.uk; Covent Garden. Lavish operas, with some experimental productions. All are performed in the original language with surtitles. Ticket prices reach £900, though there is restricted-view seating (or standing room) from around £15, and some of the Linley Studio shows are less expensive. In summer, some performances are relayed live to screens in Trafalgar Square and Canary Wharf, for free.

DANCE

The biggest dance festival is **Dance Umbrella** (danceumbrella.co.uk), a season (Oct–Nov) of new and cutting-edge work. For a **roundup** of all the major dance events in town, check londondance.com.

The Place 17 Duke's Rd, WC1 020 7121 1100, theplace.org.uk; Euston. A small theatre that presents the work of contemporary choreographers and student performers.

Royal Opera House Bow St, WC2 020 7304 4000, roh.org.uk; Covent Garden. Based at the Opera House, the Royal Ballet is a world-renowned classical company with some outstanding principals. Tickets for the main house are cheaper than for opera (£7–400), and there are two smaller performing spaces, the Linbury Studio Theatre (£8–20) and the Clore Studio (£10–15). Sell-outs are frequent so book early.

Sadler's Wells Theatre Rosebery Ave, EC1 0844 412 4300, sadlerswells.com; Angel. Sadler's Wells hosts Britain's best contemporary dance companies, including the Rambert, and many of the finest international companies are regular visitors. The Lillian Baylis Theatre, tucked around the back, puts on smaller-scale shows, while the Peacock Theatre near Covent Garden adds some populist shows, including street dance, to the mix.

SHOPPING

DEPARTMENT STORES

Fortnum & Mason 181 Piccadilly, W1 020 7734 8040, fortnumandmason.com; Green Park or Piccadilly Circus; map pp.64–65. Beautiful 300-year-old store with murals, cherubs, chandeliers and fountains as a backdrop to its perfectly English offerings. Famous for its fabulous, pricey food, it also specializes in upmarket designer clothes, furniture, luggage and stationery. Mon–Sat 10am–8pm, Sun noon–6pm.

Harrods 87–135 Brompton Rd, Knightsbridge, SW1 020 7730 1234, harrods.com; Knightsbridge; map pp.94–95. Harrods has everything, including pretension in spades – a "clean and presentable" dress code is enforced, and backpacks either have to be carried or placed in the store's left luggage (£3). Check out the life-size bronze statue of Diana and Dodi Al Fayed, who was the son of previous owner Mohamed Al Fayed, dancing on a beach. Shopping-wise, it is most notable for its huge toy department, designer labels and glorious food hall, with exquisite Arts and Crafts tiling. Mon–Sat 10am–8pm, Sun noon–6pm.

Harvey Nichols 109–125 Knightsbridge, SW1 020 7235 5000, harveynichols.com; Knightsbridge; map pp.94–95. "Harvey Nicks" has all the latest designer collections, shop assistants who look like models, and a food hall offering frivolous goodies at high prices. Mon–Sat 10am–8pm, Sun noon–6pm.

John Lewis 300 Oxford St, W1 020 7629 7711, johnlewis.co.uk; Oxford Circus; map pp.64–65. Famous for being "never knowingly undersold", this much loved institution can't be beaten for basics, including well-made clothes, furniture and household goods. Mon–Sat 9.30am–8pm, Sun noon–6pm.

★ **Liberty** 210–220 Regent St, W1 020 7734 1234, liberty.co.uk; Oxford Circus; map pp.64–65. A fabulous emporium of luxury, this exquisite store, with its mock-Tudor exterior, is most famous for its fabrics, design and accessories, but is also great for mainstream and high fashion. Mon–Sat 10am–9pm, Sun noon–6pm.

★ **Selfridges** 400 Oxford St, W1 0800 123 400, selfridges.com; Bond Street; map pp.94–95. This huge, airy palace of clothes, food and furnishings was London's first great department store. The vast mens- and womenswear departments offer mainstream designers and casual lines alongside hipper, younger labels. The food hall is superb, too. Mon–Sat 9.30am–9pm, Sun noon–6pm.

BOOKS

Daunt Books 83 Marylebone High St, W1 020 7224 2295, dauntbooks.co.uk; Bond Street or Baker Street; map pp.94–95. Inspirational range of travel literature and guidebooks in a beautiful, galleried interior. Other branches. Mon–Sat 9am–7.30pm, Sun 11am–6pm.

Hatchards 187 Piccadilly, W1 020 7439 9921, hatchards.co.uk; Piccadilly Circus; map pp.64–65. A little overshadowed by the colossal Waterstone's down the road, and actually part of the Waterstone's group, the venerable Hatchards holds its own when it comes to quality fiction, biography, history and travel. Mon–Sat 9.30am–7pm, Sun noon–6pm.

★ **London Review Bookshop** 14 Bury Place, WC1 020 7269 9030, lrbshop.co.uk; Tottenham Court Road; map p.75. All the books reviewed in the august literary journal and many, many more in this superb, tranquil Bloomsbury bookstore. Mon–Sat 10am–6.30pm, Sun noon–6pm.

Persephone Books 59 Lamb's Conduit St, WC1 020 7242 9292, persephonebooks.co.uk; Russell Square or Holborn; map p.75. Lovely offspring of a publishing house that specializes in neglected twentieth-century writing by women. Mon–Fri 10am–6pm, Sat noon–5pm.

MUSIC

★ **Gramex** 25 Lower Marsh, SE1 020 7401 3830; Lambeth North; map p.87. A splendid find for classical-music and jazz-lovers, this new and secondhand record store features CDs and vinyl, and comfy leather armchairs. Mon–Sat 11am–7pm.

Honest Jon's 278 Portobello Rd, W10 020 8969 9822, honestjons.com; Ladbroke Grove; map pp.94–95. Jazz, soul, funk, R&B, rare groove, reggae, world music and more in this West London stalwart, with current releases, secondhand finds and reissues. Mon–Sat 10am–6pm, Sun 11am–5pm.

Revival Records 30 Berwick St, W1 020 7437 4271, revivalrecords.uk.com; Tottenham Court Road; map pp.64–65. Soho store for new, used and rare vinyl and CDs, specializing in rock, soul, jazz, dance, punk and reggae. Mon–Sat 10am–7pm.

Rough Trade 130 Talbot Rd, W11 020 7229 8541, roughtrade.com; Ladbroke Grove; map pp.94–95. The musos' favourite, this historic indie specialist has knowledgeable, friendly staff and a dizzying array from electronica to hardcore and beyond. Newer branch in East London, in the Old Truman Brewery (91 Brick Lane, E1). Mon–Sat 10am–6.30pm, Sun 11am–5pm.

MARKETS

Bermondsey (New Caledonian) Bermondsey St and Long Lane, SE1 bermondseysquare.co.uk/antiques.html; London Bridge; map pp.60–61. Huge antique market offering everything from obscure nautical instruments to pricey furniture. Fri 4am–1pm.

★ **Borough Market** 8 Southwark St, SE1 020 7407 1002, boroughmarket.org.uk; London Bridge or Borough; map pp.90–91. Foodie heaven with suppliers from all over the UK converging to sell pricey, delicious goodies. Thurs 11am–5pm, Fri noon–6pm, Sat 8am–5pm.

Brick Lane Brick Lane, Cygnet and Sclater streets, E1; Bacon, Cheshire and Chilton streets, E2; Aldgate East or Liverpool Street; map pp.80–81. Huge, sprawling, cheap and frenzied, this famous East End market has become a fixture on the hipster circuit. It would be hard to say what you *can't* find here. Sun 9am–5pm.

Camden Market Camden High St to Chalk Farm Rd, NW1 camdenlock.net; Camden Town; map pp.60–61. Once beloved of hippies, punks and Goths, and now a firm favourite with European tourists, Camden is actually a gaggle of markets, segueing into each other and supplemented by lively stores and restaurants in the surrounding streets. Daily 9.30am–6.30pm, but most action Thurs–Sun.

Greenwich Market Greenwich High Rd, SE10 shopgreenwich.co.uk/market/ and clocktowermarket.co.uk; Greenwich train station from Charing Cross or Cutty Sark DLR; map pp.60–61. Sprawling flea markets with some 150 stalls. Wednesday is mainly food; antiques are the speciality on Thursday and Friday, with Thursday the best for unusual and distinctive collectibles. Wed–Sun 10am–5.30pm.

Portobello Road Market Portobello and Golborne rds, W10 and W11 portobelloroad.co.uk; Ladbroke Grove or Notting Hill Gate; map pp.94–95. Approach from the Notting Hill end, work your way through the antiques and bric-a-brac down to the fruit and veg stalls, and then head under the Westway to hip new and secondhand clothes stalls. The Golborne Rd market is cheaper and less crowded, with some attractive antique and retro furniture. Antique market Sat 4am–6pm.

Spitalfields Commercial St, E1 visitspitalfields.com; Liverpool St; map pp.80–81. The East End's historic Victorian fruit and veg hall now houses a fashionable organic food, crafts and secondhand goods market. Thurs (antiques & vintage) & Fri (fashion & art) 10am–4pm; Sun (all stalls) 9am–5pm.

DIRECTORY

Hospitals For 24hr accident and emergency: St Mary's Hospital, Praed St, W2 (020 3312 6330; Paddington); University College London Hospital, 235 Euston Rd, NW1 (0845 155 5000; Euston Square or Warren Street).

Left luggage Left luggage is available at all airports and major train terminals (see p.108).

Police Phone 999 in emergencies, otherwise 0101 (met.police.uk). Central police stations include: Charing Cross, Agar St, WC2 (Charing Cross); Holborn, 10 Lambs Conduit St, WC1 (Holborn); Marylebone, 1–9 Seymour St W1 (Marble Arch); and West End Central, 27 Savile Row, W1 (Oxford Circus). The City of London has its own police force, 182 Bishopsgate, EC2 (020 7601 2222, cityoflondon.police.uk; Liverpool Street).

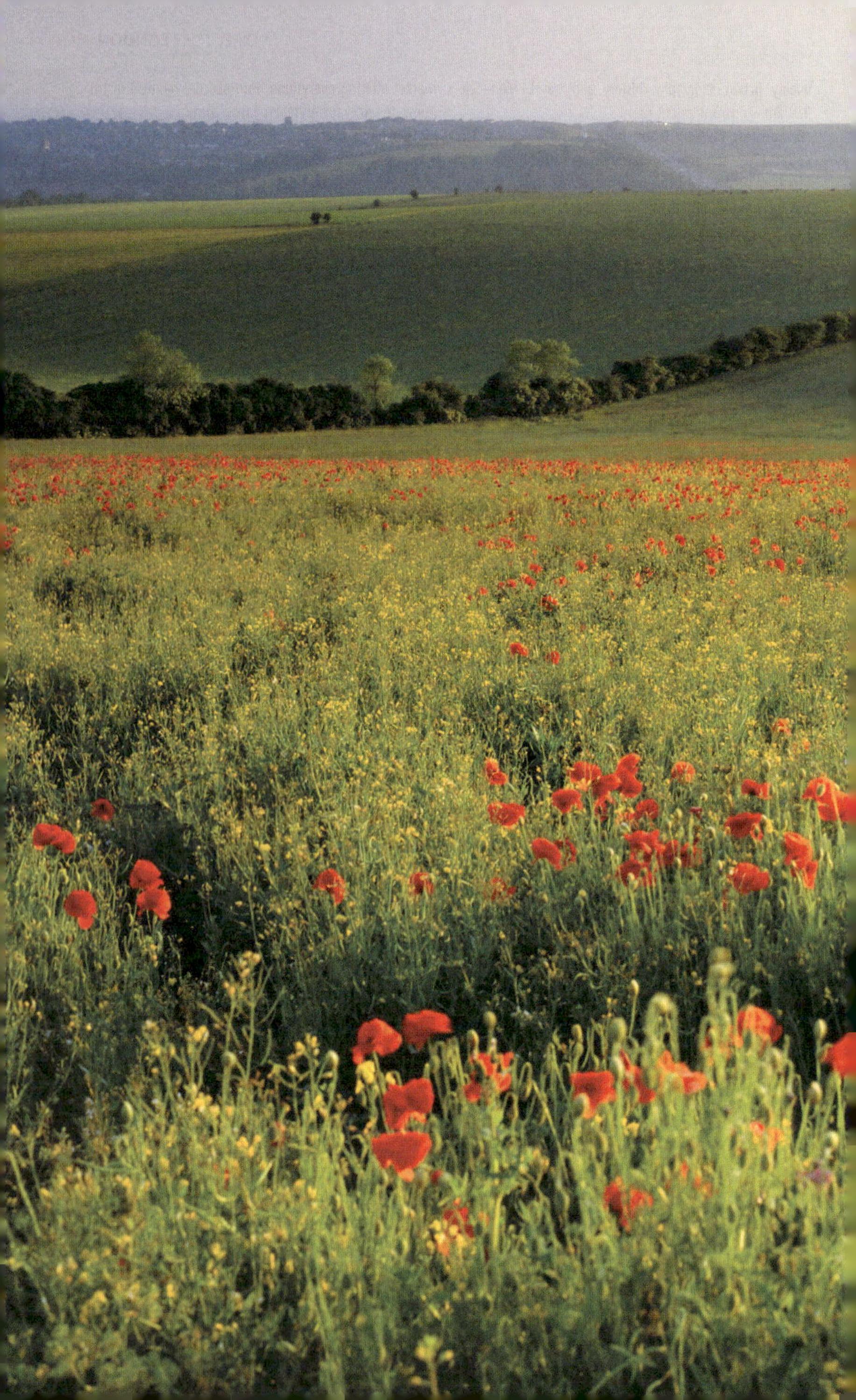

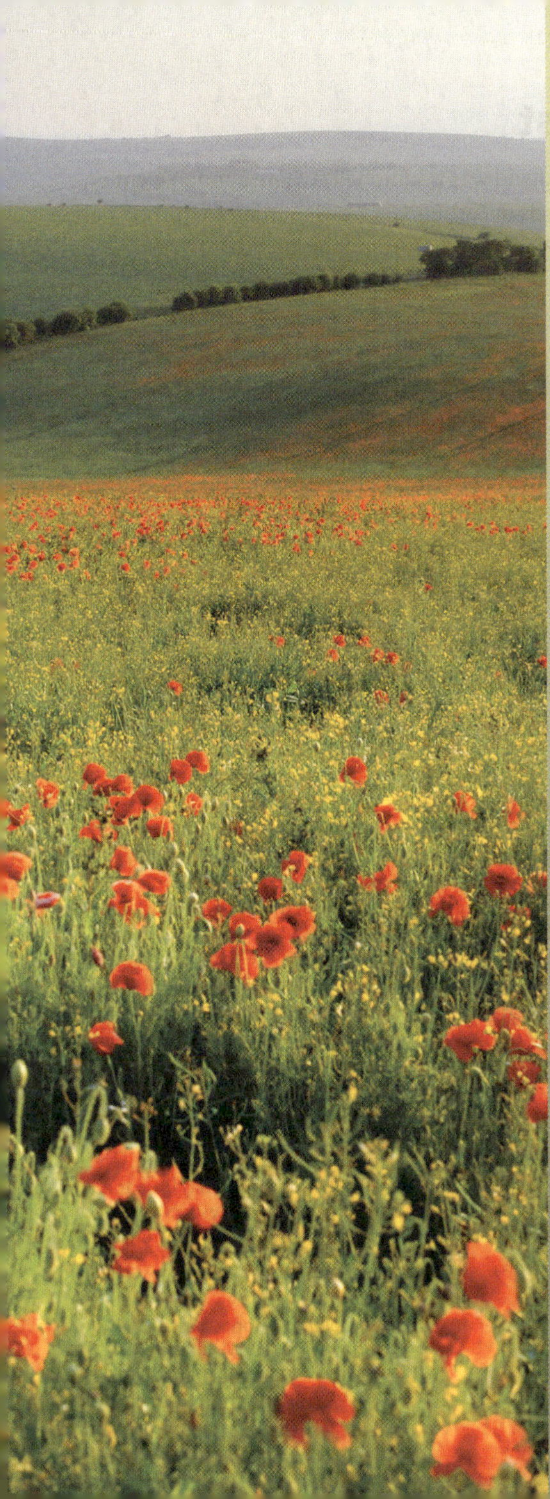

The Southeast

136 The North Kent coast
142 Canterbury
147 Sandwich
149 Deal
150 Dover
152 Romney and Denge marshes
152 The Kent Weald
155 Hastings and around
158 Rye
160 Eastbourne and around
162 Lewes and around
164 Brighton
170 Arundel and around
172 Chichester and around

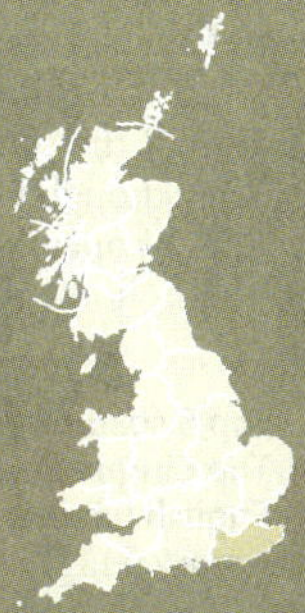

POPPIES ON THE SOUTH DOWNS, SUSSEX

2

The Southeast

The southeast corner of England was traditionally where London went on holiday. In the past, trainloads of East Enders were shuttled to the hop fields and orchards of Kent for a working break from the city; boats ferried people down the Thames to the beaches of north Kent; while everyone from royalty to cuckolding couples enjoyed the seaside at Brighton, a blot of decadence in the otherwise sedate county of Sussex. Although many of the old seaside resorts have struggled to keep their tourist custom in the face of ever more accessible foreign destinations, the region still has considerable charm, its narrow country lanes and verdant meadows appearing, in places, almost untouched by modern life.

The proximity of Kent and Sussex to the continent has dictated the history of this region, which has served as a gateway for an array of invaders. **Roman** remains dot the coastal area – most spectacularly at **Bignor** in Sussex and Lullingstone in Kent – and many roads, including the main A2 London to Dover, follow the arrow-straight tracks laid by the legionaries. When **Christianity** spread through Europe, it arrived in Britain on the **Isle of Thanet** – the northeast tip of Kent, since rejoined to the mainland by silting and subsiding sea levels. In 597 AD Augustine moved inland and established a monastery at **Canterbury**, still the home of the Church of England and the county's prime historic attraction.

The last successful invasion of England took place in 1066, when the **Normans** overran King Harold's army near **Hastings**, on a site now marked by **Battle Abbey**. The Normans left their mark all over this corner of the kingdom, and Kent remains unmatched in its profusion of medieval castles, among them **Dover**'s sprawling cliff-top fortress guarding against continental invasion and **Rochester**'s huge, box-like citadel, close to the old dockyards of **Chatham**, power base of the formerly invincible British navy.

Away from the great historic sites, you can spend unhurried days in elegant old towns such as **Royal Tunbridge Wells**, **Rye** and **Lewes**, or enjoy the less elevated charms of the traditional resorts, of which fashionable **Brighton** is by far the best, combining the buzz of a university town with a good-time atmosphere and excellent restaurants. The picturesque **South Downs Way** – which winds its way through the South Downs National Park – offers an expanse of rolling chalk uplands that, as much as anywhere can in the crowded southeast, gets you away from it all. Kent and Sussex also harbour some of the country's finest **gardens**, ranging from the lush flowerbeds of **Sissinghurst** to the great landscaped estate of **Petworth House.**

The home of wealthy metropolitan commuters, **Surrey** is the least pastoral and historically significant of the three southeastern counties surrounding London. The portion of the county within and around the M25 orbital motorway has little for tourists, though beyond the ring road it takes on a more countrified aspect, with swathes of open heathland along its western borders and the sleepy market town of Farnham, home to a twelfth-century castle.

Top 5 seafood restaurants p.140
The Cinque Ports p.148
English wine: a sparkling success story p.155
South Downs National Park and the South Downs Way p.161
Lewes: the bonfire societies p.162
Glyndebourne p.164

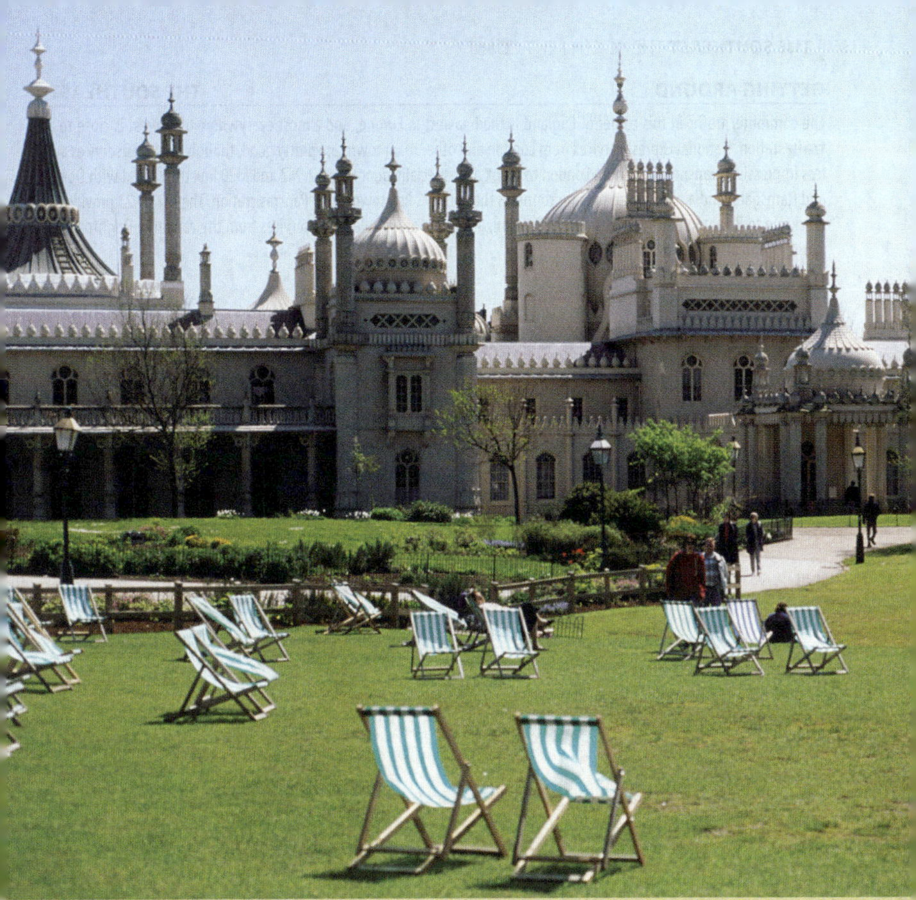

BRIGHTON'S ROYAL PAVILION

Highlights

❶ **Whitstable** Arty seaside retreat of weathered clapboard houses and beach huts, famous for its oysters, and with a clutch of top-notch restaurants. **See p.139**

❷ **Canterbury Cathedral** The destination of the pilgrims in Chaucer's *Canterbury Tales*, with a magnificent sixteenth-century interior that includes a shrine to the murdered Thomas à Becket. **See p.144**

❸ **The White Cliffs of Dover** Immortalized in song, art and literature, the famed chalky cliffs offer walks and vistas over the Channel. **See p.150**

❹ **Rye** Ancient hilltop town of picturesque cobbled streets offering some of the best places to stay and eat in Sussex. **See p.158**

❺ **Walking the South Downs Way** Experience the best walking in the southeast – and some fantastic views – on this national trail, which spans England's newest national park. **See p.161**

❻ **The Royal Pavilion, Brighton** The extraordinary palace of the decadent Prince Regent is the must-see sight in the south's favourite seaside town. **See p.166**

❼ **Petworth House** One of the country's most attractive stately homes also boasts a splendid art collection. **See p.171**

HIGHLIGHTS ARE MARKED ON THE MAP ON PP.136–137

GETTING AROUND — THE SOUTHEAST

The commuter traffic in this corner of England is the heaviest in Europe, and almost everywhere of interest is close to a **train** station. National Express services from London and other main towns are pretty good, though local **bus** services are less impressive. Transport links from London to **Kent** are especially good: the A2, M2 and M20 link the capital with Dover and Ramsgate, and a high-speed rail line connects the county's key towns to St Pancras station. The M23/A23 provides a quick run to Brighton on the south coast of **Sussex**, and there are regular train services from the capital to Brighton and Arundel, and along the coast.

The North Kent coast

Although commonly perceived as something of a wasteland, raced through on the way to or from the Channel ports, northern Kent has its fair share of attractions, all easily

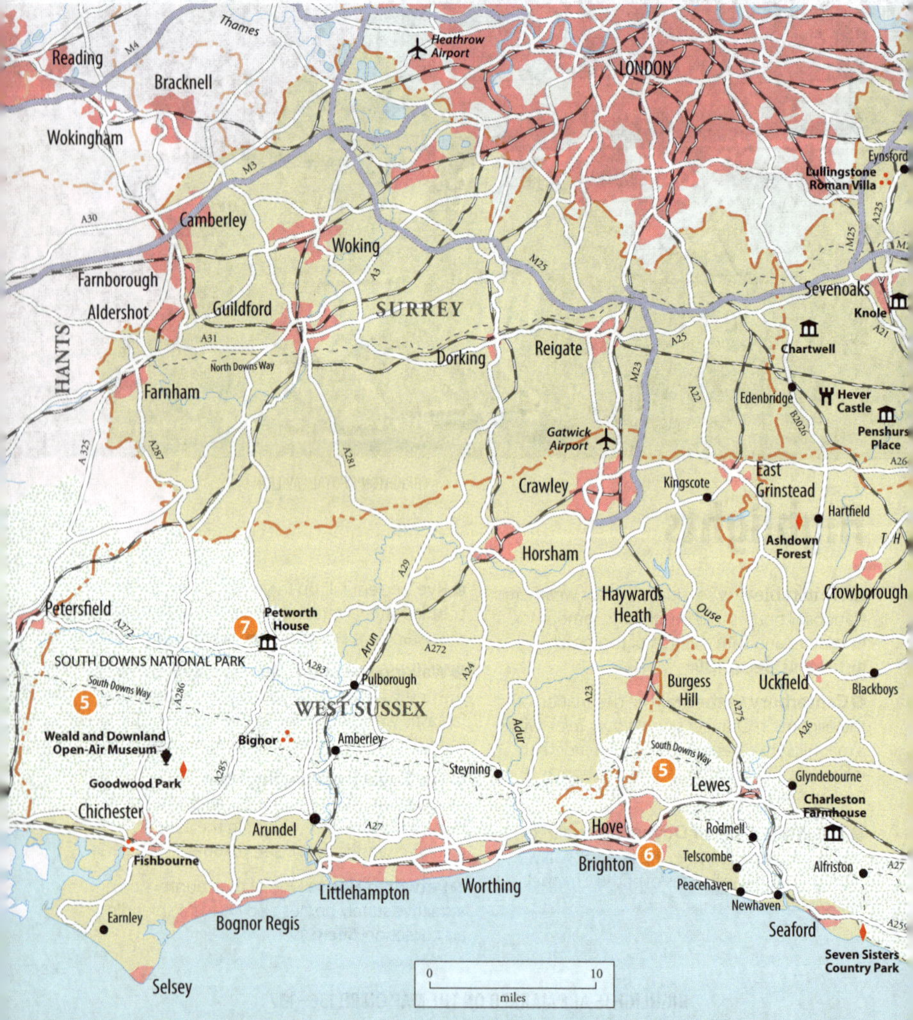

accessible from London. **Rochester** boasts both historic and literary interest, while the old-fashioned seaside resorts of **Whitstable** and **Broadstairs** have a growing cachet among weekenders from the capital.

Rochester and around

The handsome Medway town of **ROCHESTER** was first settled by the Romans, who built a fortress on the site of the present castle; some kind of fortification has remained here ever since. The town's most famous son is **Charles Dickens**, who spent his youth here but would seem to have been less than impressed by the place – it appears as "Mudfog" in *The Mudfog Papers*, and "Dullborough" in *The Uncommercial Traveller*. Many of the buildings feature in his novels: the *Royal Victoria and Bull Hotel*, at the top of the High Street, became the *Bull* in *Pickwick Papers* and the *Blue*

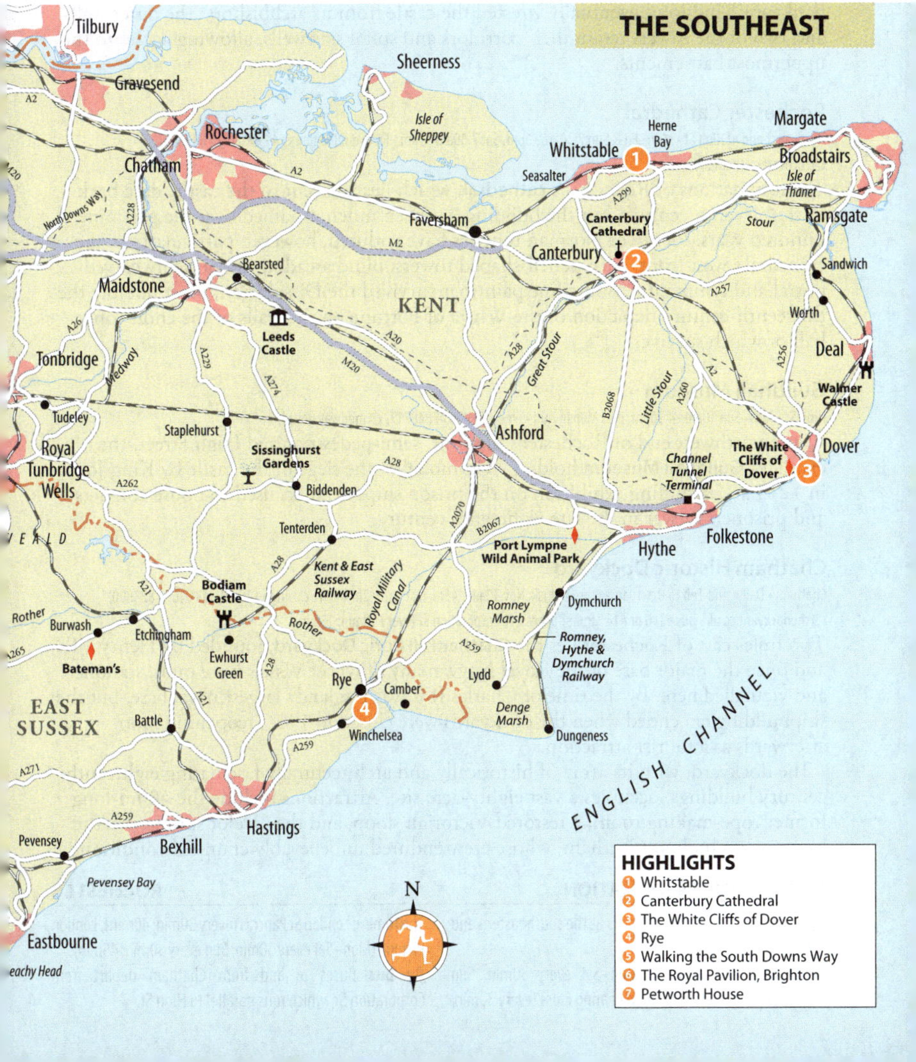

Boar in *Great Expectations*, while most of his last book, the unfinished *The Mystery of Edwin Drood*, was set in the town.

Two miles away in neighbouring Chatham, there's more historic architecture at the **Chatham Historic Dockyard**, which records more than 400 years of British maritime history.

Rochester castle

Northwest end of High St • Daily: April–Sept 10am–6pm; Oct–March 10am-4pm• EH • £5.50

In 1077, William I gave Gundulf – architect of the White Tower at the Tower of London – the job of improving defences on the River Medway's northernmost bridge on Watling Street. The resulting **Rochester castle** remains one of the best-preserved examples of a Norman fortress in England, with the stark 100ft-high keep glowering over the town, while the interior is all the better for having lost its floors, allowing clear views up and down the dank interior. It has four towers, three square and one cylindrical, the last rebuilt following its collapse during the siege of 1215, when the bankrupt King John eventually wrested the castle from its archbishop. The outer walls and two of the towers retain their corridors and spiral stairwells, allowing access to the uppermost battlements.

Rochester Cathedral

Northwest end of High St • Mon–Fri & Sun 7.30am–6pm, Sat 7.30am–5pm • Free, guided tours £4 • T 01634 843366, W rochestercathedral.org

The foundations of Rochester's **cathedral**, which lies adjacent to the castle, date back to the eleventh century, but the building has been much modified over the past nine hundred years. Plenty of Norman touches have endured, however, particularly in the cathedral's west front, with pencil-shaped towers, blind arcading and a richly carved portal and tympanum. Some fine paintings survived the Dissolution, most notably the thirteenth-century depiction of the Wheel of Fortune on the walls of the choir (only half of which survives).

Guildhall Museum

High St • Tues–Sun 10am–4.30pm, plus Mon in Aug • Free • T 01634 848717, W medway.gov.uk

At the northwest end of Rochester's pleasant, semi-pedestrianized High Street, the excellent **Guildhall Museum** holds a vivid model of the siege of the castle by King John in 1215 and a chilling exhibition on the prison ships or hulks used to house convicts and prisoners of war in the late eighteenth century.

Chatham Historic Dockyard

Chatham • Daily: mid-Feb to Oct 10am–6pm or dusk; Nov 10am–4pm; last entry 2hr before closing • £15.50 • T 01634 823800, W thedockyard.co.uk • Bus #140 or #141 from Rochester's Corporation St (every 10min; 15min)

Two miles east of Rochester lies the **Chatham Historic Dockyard**, founded by Henry VIII, and once the major base of the Royal Navy, many of whose vessels were built, stationed and victualled here. By the time of Charles II it was England's largest naval base, but the shipbuilding era ended when the dockyards were closed in 1984, reopening soon afterwards as a tourist attraction.

The dockyard, with its array of historically and architecturally fascinating eighteenth-century buildings, occupies a vast eighty-acre site. Attractions include the 400m-long former rope-making room, a restored Victorian sloop, and the Ocelot submarine, the last warship built at Chatham, whose crew endured unbelievably cramped conditions.

ARRIVAL AND INFORMATION — ROCHESTER

By train Rochester train station is at the southeastern end of High St.

Destinations Dover Priory (Mon–Sat every 30min, Sun hourly; 1hr–1hr 15min); London Charing Cross (every 30min; 1hr 10min); London St Pancras (every 30min; 40min); London Victoria (Mon–Sat every 30min, Sun every 30min; 45min).

By bus Buses to and from Chatham depart from Corporation St, which runs parallel to High St.

Tourist office 95 High St, opposite the cathedral (Mon–Fri 9am–5pm, Sat 10am–5pm, Sun 10.30am–5pm; ⓣ01634 843666, ⓦmedway.gov.uk).

ACCOMMODATION

Medway YHA hostel 351 Capstone Rd, Gillingham, 3 miles east of Chatham ⓣ0845 371 9649, ⓔemedway@yha.org.uk; bus #114. Rochester's nearest hostel is 3 miles away, set in a traditional Kent oast house in a lovely spot opposite a country park. Dorm **£18.40**, double **£46**

Salisbury House 29 Watts Ave ⓣ01634 400182. Pleasant Victorian guesthouse with two spotless rooms, friendly owners and a great location on a quiet leafy street, just a five-minute walk up the hill behind the castle. **£65**

2

EATING AND DRINKING

Coopers Arms 11 St Margaret's St ⓣ01634 404298. Friendly, atmospheric pub in a central spot between the castle and the cathedral, offering real ales and good lunches in its small beer garden. Mon–Thurs noon–midnight, Fri & Sat noon–1am, Sun noon–11.30pm.

Topes 60 High St ⓣ01634 845270, ⓦtopesrestaurant.com. Rochester's nicest restaurant serves inventive dishes such as sea bass with cardamom jam (£16.50) in a lovely wood-panelled room with sloping ceilings. Wed–Sat noon–2.30pm & 6.30–9.30pm, Sun noon–2.30pm.

Whitstable

One of the most agreeable spots along the north Kent coast and a popular day-trip destination for Londoners, pretty, bohemian **WHITSTABLE** has been farming the oysters for which it is famed since classical times, when the Romans feasted on the region's marine delicacies. Oysters are still farmed in the area today, but Whitstable is nowadays more dependent on its commercial port, fishing and seaside tourism. The annual **Oyster Festival** (last two weeks of July) sees the town come alive with parades, performances and a raucous oyster-eating competition.

Follow the signs at the top of the vibrant High Street, with its delis, restaurants and gift stores, to reach the **seafront**, a quiet shingle beach backed by pretty weatherboard cottages and a line of colourful beach huts.

Whitstable Museum and Gallery

Oxford St • Daily 10am–4pm • £3 • ⓣ01227 276998, ⓦcanterbury.gov.uk

Local maritime history is illustrated in the **Whitstable Museum and Gallery**, with displays on diving and some good photographs and old film footage of the town's heyday. The art gallery puts on regularly changing exhibitions.

ARRIVAL AND INFORMATION — WHITSTABLE

By train From the train station it's a 15min walk to the centre, along Cromwell Rd to Harbour St, the northern continuation of High St.

Destinations Broadstairs (every 30min; 25min); London Victoria (Mon–Sat every 30min; 1hr 20min); Ramsgate (every 30min; 35min).

By bus Buses #4 and #6 shuttle between Whitstable town centre and Canterbury (every 10min).

Useful website ⓦseewhitstable.com.

GETTING AROUND

Bike rental Whitstable Cycle Hire, 56 Harbour St (ⓣ01227 275156, ⓦwhitstablecyclehire.com) rents bikes for £15/day. Local cycle routes include the picturesque Crab and Winkle Way, a disused railway line linking the town to Canterbury, 6 miles away, and the coastal Oyster Bay Trail, which follows the coast round to Herne Bay (3 miles) and Reculver (5 miles).

ACCOMMODATION

Copeland House 4 Island Wall ⓣ01227 266207, ⓦcopelandhouse.co.uk. Handsome Georgian house, packed with seaside charm, just minutes from High St with a garden that backs onto the beach. The simple rooms – two with sea views – are bright and comfortable. No credit cards. **£75**

Victoria Villa 1 Victoria St ⓣ01227 779191, ⓦvictoria-villa.co.uk. Just set back from Harbour St, the northern

TOP 5 SEAFOOD RESTAURANTS

Eddie Gilbert's Ramsgate. See p.142
English's Oyster Bar Brighton. See p.169
Maggie's Hastings. See p.157
Riddle and Finns Brighton. See p.169
Wheeler's Oyster Bar Whitstable. See p.140

continuation of High St, this lovely Victorian B&B is in a great spot, and offers stylish rooms, superb breakfasts and civilized touches such as a free morning paper delivered to your room before breakfast. **£105**

EATING AND DRINKING

Old Neptune Marine Terrace 01227 272262, neppy.co.uk. Standing alone in its white weatherboards on the beach, this atmospheric pub is the perfect spot to enjoy a sundowner, or to hunker down with a pint after a bracing winter walk along the beach. July & Aug Mon–Sat 11am–late, Sun noon–10.30pm; rest of year noon–late. Simple pub fare served daily noon–4pm.

The Sportsman Seasalter, 4 miles west 01227 273370, thesportsmanseasalter.co.uk. Highly rated gastropub that draws foodies from far and wide for its faultless, locally sourced food; the owners even make their own salt from the seawater by the pub. Splash out if you can on the memorable £65 tasting menu (book in advance); the cheaper, daily-changing menu is great, too, with mains from £15. Tues–Sat noon–2pm & 7–9pm, Sun noon–2.30pm.

★ **Wheeler's Oyster Bar** 8 High St 01227 273311. A Whitstable institution, dating back to 1856. It has just four tables and a few stools at the counter, so you'll need to book well in advance, but the inventive seafood is the best around (mains from £18, half a dozen local oysters £9.75). BYOB; no cards. Mon, Tues & Thurs–Sat 1–7.30pm, Sun 1–7pm.

Margate

The tatty, down-at-heel seaside town of **MARGATE** is certainly not the prettiest on the Kent coast, but its fortunes are set to change with the recent opening of a spectacular new contemporary art gallery. With a cluster of funky little cafés, retro shops and hip galleries in the old town, and some excellent places to eat and stay, a stopover in Margate has plenty to recommend it.

Turner Contemporary

The seafront • Tues–Thurs, Sat & Sun 10am–7pm, Fri 10am–10pm • Free • 01843 233000, turnercontemporary.org

Rearing up on the east side of the harbour, on the site of the lodging house where J.M.W. Turner painted some of his famous seascapes, the stunning new **Turner Contemporary** gallery dominates the seafront. Inside, the light-flooded space hosts regularly changing displays of contemporary art, and there's a lovely café with views across the harbour and out to sea.

Shell Grotto

Grotto Hill, off Northdown Rd • Easter–Oct daily 10am–5pm; Nov–Easter Sat & Sun 11am–4pm • £3 • 01843 220008, shellgrotto.co.uk

Discovered by chance in 1835, Margate's bizarre **Shell Grotto** has been captivating visitors ever since. Accessed via a short, dark passageway, the walls of the grotto are decorated with fabulous mosaics made entirely from shells, more than 4.5 million of them. The origins and purpose of the grotto remain a mystery – some believe it to be an ancient sun temple, others a more recent Regency folly – which only adds to its offbeat charm.

ARRIVAL AND INFORMATION — MARGATE

By train The station is right by the seafront on Station Rd. Destinations Canterbury West (Mon–Sat hourly, Sun hourly; 30min); London St Pancras (Mon–Sat hourly; 1hr 30min); London Victoria (Mon–Sat every 30min, Sun hourly; 1hr 45min).

By bus Buses pull into Cecil Square, a few minutes away from the train station. Destinations Broadstairs (every 5–15min; 25min); Canterbury (Mon–Sat every 20min, Sun every 30min; 50min); London Victoria (4 daily; 2hr 30min); Ramsgate (every 5–15min; 30min).

Tourist office The Droit House, The Harbour Arm (April–Sept daily 10am–5pm; Oct–March Tues–Sat 10am–5pm; 01843 577577, visitthanet.co.uk).

ACCOMMODATION

Reading Rooms 31 Hawley Square ⓣ01843 225166, ⓦthereadingroomsmargate.co.uk. Uber-stylish boutique B&B in a handsome Georgian townhouse with artfully distressed walls, gorgeous furnishings and huge, luxurious bathrooms. **£150**

Walpole Bay Hotel Fifth Ave, Cliftonville, a few minutes' walk east of the centre ⓣ01843 221703, ⓦwalpolebayhotel.co.uk. This historic Margate hotel, complete with 1920s ballroom, Edwardian-style restaurant and gated lifts, styles itself as a "living museum" and prides itself on its old-fashioned charm. **£85**

2

EATING AND DRINKING

The Ambrette 44 King St ⓣ01843 231504, ⓦtheambrette.co.uk. Margate's finest restaurant doesn't look like much from the outside, but promises superlative Indian food (mains £13–19). Tues–Thurs 11.30am–2.30pm & 6–9.30pm, Fri–Sun 11.30am–2.30pm & 5.30–10pm.

BeBeached Harbour Arm ⓣ01843 226008, ⓦbebeached.co.uk. For brunch with a sea view you can't do better than an outside seat at this lovely café, in an unbeatable location on the harbour wall. Wed, Thurs & Sun 11am–4.30pm, Fri & Sat 11am–4.30pm & 7.30–9.30pm.

Broadstairs

Overlooking pretty little Viking Bay from its cliff-top setting, **BROADSTAIRS** is the smallest, quietest and most pleasant of the resort towns on the northeast tip of Kent. Its main claim to fame is as Dickens' holiday retreat: throughout his most productive years he stayed in various hostelries here, and eventually rented an "airy nest" overlooking Viking Bay, where he finished writing *David Copperfield*. In June, the **Dickens Festival** (ⓦbroadstairsdickensfestival.co.uk) features lectures, dramatizations and a nightly Victorian music hall.

Dickens House Museum

2 Victoria Parade • Daily: Easter–June & Sept-Oct 2–5pm; July & Aug 10am–5pm • £3.60 • ⓣ01843 863453

The building that now houses the **Dickens House Museum** was once the home of Miss Mary Pearson Strong, on whom Dickens based the character of Miss Betsey Trotwood in *David Copperfield* – his favourite of his own novels. Inside you'll find Victorian posters, photography and costumes, as well as letters written by the author, illustrations from the original novels, a reconstruction of Betsey Trotwood's parlour, and Dickens' old desk, which he modified to include a rack for six bottles of wine.

ARRIVAL AND DEPARTURE — BROADSTAIRS

By train It's a 10min walk from the train station along the High Street to Broadstairs' seafront.

Destinations London Victoria (Mon–Sat every 30min, Sun hourly; 1hr 50min); Ramsgate (every 20min; 5min); Whitstable (every 30min; 25min).

By bus Buses stop along the High Street.

Destinations Canterbury (Mon–Sat every 20min, Sun every 30min; 1hr 30min); Margate (every 5–15min; 25min); Ramsgate (every 10–20min; 10min).

ACCOMMODATION

★ **Belvidere Place** Belvedere Rd ⓣ01843 579850, ⓦbelvidereplace.co.uk. This stylish, quirky boutique B&B earns extra points for its warm, friendly management. The five lovely rooms feature sleek bathrooms, contemporary art and one-off vintage furniture finds. **£125**

East Horndon Hotel 4 Eastern Esplanade ⓣ01843 868306, ⓦeasthorndonhotel.com. Friendly, comfortable B&B in a fine Victorian house in a prime spot overlooking the sea, just a 5min stroll from the centre of Broadstairs. Most rooms have sea views, and there's access to the sandy beach of Stone Bay directly opposite the house. **£76**

EATING AND DRINKING

There are plenty of fish-and-chip outlets and **cafés** along Albion Street and Harbour Street.

Oscar's Festival Café 15 Oscar Rd ⓣ07595 750091, ⓦoscarsfestivalcafe.co.uk. This diminutive café, decked out in pastels and bunting, serves up such old-fashioned delights as potted shrimps, crab sandwiches and Kentish pork pies, alongside fabulous cakes. May–Aug Wed–Sun 10.30am–5pm; Sept–April Thurs–Sun 10.30am–5pm.

Restaurant 54 54 Albion St ⓣ01843 867150, ⓦrestaurant54.co.uk. Relaxed restaurant serving modern British cuisine in an elegant candlelit dining room. Mains might include roasted duck with a mango and papaya salad (£15), or the restaurant's own take on traditional fish and chips: tiger prawns, monkfish, plaice and scallops in a lemon and coriander batter (£16). Mon–Sat 6–9pm, Sun noon–3pm & 6–9pm.

Ramsgate

2

The handsome resort of **RAMSGATE**, rich in robust Victorian red brick, is mostly set high on a cliff linked to the seafront and harbour by broad, sweeping ramps. Down by the Georgian harbour a collection of cosmopolitan cafés and bars overlooks the bobbing yachts, while the town's small, pleasant beach lies just a short stroll away.

Ramsgate Maritime Museum

Inside the Clock House on the quayside • Easter–Sept Tues–Sun 10am–5pm; Oct–Easter Thurs–Sun 11am–4.30pm • £1.50 • ⓣ01843 570662, ⓦramsgatemaritimemuseum.org.uk

The **Ramsgate Maritime Museum** chronicles municipal life from Roman times onwards; its most illuminating section focuses on the Goodwin Sands sandbanks, six miles southeast of Ramsgate – the occasional playing field of the eccentric Goodwin Sands Cricket Club.

ARRIVAL AND DEPARTURE — RAMSGATE

By train Ramsgate's train station lies about a mile northwest of the centre, at the end of Wilfred Rd, at the top of the High St.
Destinations Broadstairs (every 20min; 5min); London St Pancras (Mon–Sat hourly; 1hr 15min); London Victoria (Mon–Sat hourly; 1hr 45min); Whitstable (every 30min; 35min).

By bus Buses pull in at Ramsgate's harbour.
Destinations Broadstairs (every 10–20min; 10min); Canterbury (Mon–Sat hourly; 45min); Margate (every 5–15min; 30min); London Victoria (4 daily; 3hr).

ACCOMMODATION

Royal Harbour Hotel 10–12 Nelson Crescent ⓣ01843 591514, ⓦroyalharbourhotel.co.uk. Two interconnecting Georgian townhouses with stylish rooms, from tiny "cabins" to four-posters with sea views, and a cosy lounge with real fires, newspapers and an honesty bar. **£108**

EATING AND DRINKING

Age & Sons Charlotte Court ⓣ01843 851515, ⓦageandsons.co.uk. No foodie should leave Ramsgate without a visit to this place, housed in an old Victorian warehouse. There's a relaxed café on the ground floor, a restaurant serving incredibly good-value cuisine with a Kentish twist (mains from £10.50) on the first floor, and a sleek and stylish bar in the basement. Café: Tues–Sun 9am–5pm; Restaurant Tues–Sat noon–3.30pm & 7–9.30pm, Sun noon–3.30pm; Bar: Tues–Sat 7pm–late.

Churchill Tavern 19–22 Paragon ⓣ01843 587862, ⓦchurchilltavern.co.uk. Atmospheric pub in a prime seafront location, with harbour views, weekly live music and a good monthly selection of real ales. Mon–Thurs 11.30am–11pm, Fri & Sat 11.30am–1am, Sun noon–11pm.

Eddie Gilbert's 32 King St ⓣ01843 852123, ⓦeddiegilberts.com. The best place in town for fish and seafood, serving everything from fish and chips (from £6.50) to more imaginative creations such as crispy smoked eel soldiers with soft-boiled duck egg. Downstairs there's an excellent fish and chip takeaway (Thurs–Sun only) and attached fishmonger. Mon–Sat 11.30am–2.30pm & 5.30–9.30pm, Sun 11.30am–3.30pm.

Canterbury

One of England's most venerable cities, **CANTERBURY** offers a rich slice through two thousand years of history, with Roman and early Christian ruins, a Norman castle and a famous cathedral that dominates a medieval warren of time-skewed Tudor dwellings. Its compact centre, partly ringed by ancient **walls**, is virtually car-free, but this doesn't stop the High Street seizing up all too frequently with the milling crowds.

Brief history

The city that began as a Belgic settlement was known as **Durovernum** to the Romans, who established a garrison and supply base here, and renamed **Cantwarabyrig** by the Saxons. In 597 the Saxon King Ethelbert welcomed Augustine, despatched by the pope to convert the British Isles to Christianity; one of the two Benedictine monasteries founded by Augustine – Christ Church, raised on the site of the Roman basilica – was to become England's first cathedral.

At the turn of the first millennium Canterbury suffered repeated sackings by the Danes, and Christ Church was eventually destroyed by fire a year before the Norman invasion. A struggle for power later developed between the archbishops, the abbots from the nearby Benedictine abbey and King Henry II, culminating in the assassination of Archbishop Thomas à Becket in 1170, a martyrdom that established this as one of Christendom's greatest shrines. Geoffrey Chaucer's **Canterbury Tales**, written towards the end of the fourteenth century, portrays the unexpectedly festive nature of pilgrimages to Becket's tomb, which was later plundered and destroyed on the orders of Henry VIII.

In 1830 a pioneering passenger railway service linked Canterbury to the sea and prosperity grew until the city suffered extensive German bombing on June 1, 1942, in

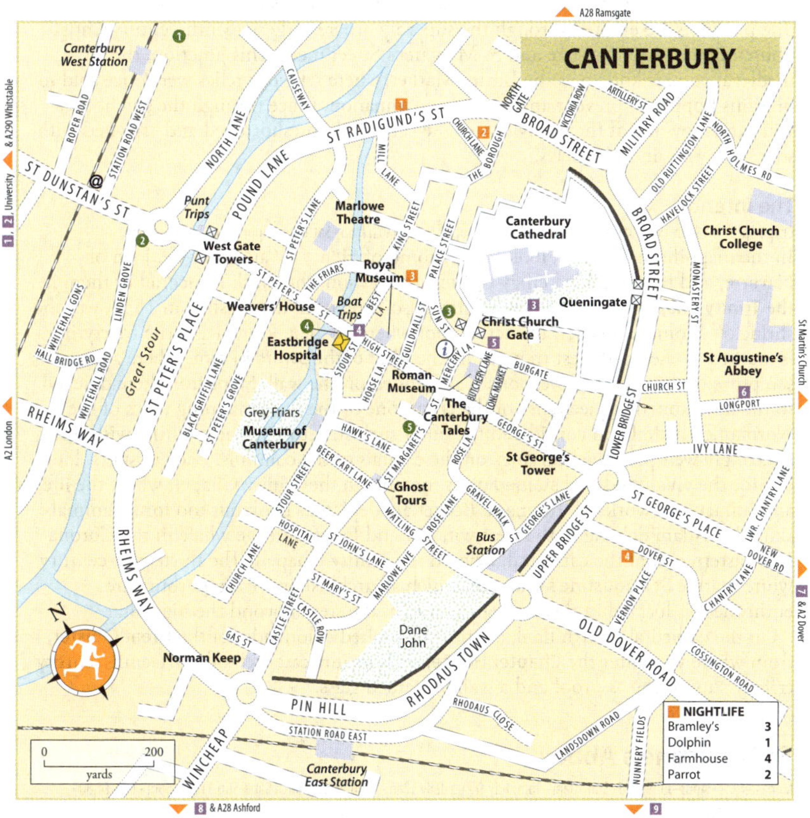

ACCOMMODATION

Abode	4	Canterbury Cathedral Lodge	3	Kipps	9
Arthouse B&B	1	Canterbury YHA	7	Neals Place Farm	2
Bluebells Guest House	8	Cathedral Gate	5	No. 7 Longport	6

EATING

Boho Café	4	The Goods Shed	1
Café des Amis	2	Tiny Tim's Tearoom	5
Deeson's	3		

one of the notorious **Baedeker Raids** – the Nazi plan to destroy Britain's most treasured historic sites as described in the eponymous German travel guides.

The cathedral

Christ Church Gate • April–Oct Mon–Sat 9am–5.30pm, Sun 12.30–2.30pm; Nov–March Mon–Sat 9am–5pm, Sun 12.30–2.30pm; closed on some days in mid-July for university graduation ceremonies • £9 • T 01227 762862, W canterbury-cathedral.org

Mother Church of the Church of England and seat of the Primate of All England – the Archbishop of Canterbury – **Canterbury Cathedral** fills the northeast quadrant of the city with a sense of authority, even if architecturally it's not the country's most impressive. A cathedral has stood here since 602, but in 1070 the first Norman archbishop, Lanfranc, levelled the original Saxon structure to build a new cathedral. Over successive centuries the masterpiece was heavily modified, and with the puritanical lines of the Perpendicular style gaining ascendancy in late medieval times, the cathedral now derives its distinctiveness from the thrust of the 235ft-high Bell Harry Tower, completed in 1505.

The precincts

Daily 7am–9pm • Free after 5pm Mon–Sat, and after 2.15pm on Sun; otherwise normal cathedral entry fee applies

The precincts are entered through the superbly ornate early sixteenth-century **Christ Church Gate**, where Burgate and St Margaret's Street meet. This junction, the city's medieval core, is known as the Butter Market, where religious relics were once sold to pilgrims hoping to prevent an eternity in damnation. Once through the gatehouse, you can enjoy one of the best views of the cathedral, foreshortened and crowned with soaring towers and pinnacles.

The interior

Crypt April–Oct Mon–Sat 10am–5.50pm, Sun 12.30–2.30pm; Nov–March Mon–Sat 10am–5pm, Sun 12.30–2.30pm

In the magnificent interior, look for the tomb of Henry IV and his wife, Joan of Navarre, and for the gilded effigy of Edward III's son, the Black Prince, all of them in the **Trinity Chapel** behind the main altar. Also here, until demolished in 1538, was the shrine of Thomas à Becket; the actual spot where he died, known as "The Martyrdom", is marked in the northwest transept by the **Altar of the Sword's Point**, where a jagged sculpture of the assassins' weapons is suspended on the wall. Steps from here descend to the low, Romanesque arches of the **crypt**, one of the few remaining relics of the Norman cathedral and considered the finest such structure in the country, with some amazingly well-preserved carvings on the capitals of the columns. Back upstairs, look out for the vivid medieval **stained glass**, notably in the Trinity Chapel, where the life and miraculous works of Thomas à Becket are depicted. Look out too for an animal-skin-clad Adam delving in the west window and Jonah and the whale in the Corona (the eastern end of the cathedral, beyond the Trinity Chapel). The thirteenth-century white marble **St Augustine's Chair**, on which all archbishops of Canterbury are enthroned, is located in the choir at the top of the steps beyond the high altar.

On the cathedral's north flank are the fan-vaulted colonnades of the **Great Cloister**, from where you enter the **Chapter House**, with its intricate web of fourteenth-century tracery supporting the roof and a wall of stained glass.

St Augustine's Abbey

Monastery St • April–June Wed–Sun 10am–5pm; July & Aug daily 10am–6pm; Sept–March Sat & Sun 11am–5pm • EH • £4.80 • T 01227 378100

The vestigial remains of **St Augustine's Abbey** occupy the site of the church founded by Augustine in 598. Built outside the city because of a Christian tradition forbidding burials within the walls, it became the final resting place of Augustine, Ethelbert and successive archbishops and kings of Kent, although no trace remains either of them or of the original Saxon church. Shortly after the Normans arrived, the church was demolished and replaced by a much larger abbey, most of which was destroyed in the Dissolution so that today only the ruins and foundations remain.

St Martin's Church

Corner of North Holmes Rd and St Martin's Lane • Tues, Thurs & Sat 10am–3pm, Sun 9.50–10.30am • Free • Ⓦ martinpaul.org

One of England's oldest churches, **St Martin's Church** was built on the site of a Roman villa or temple and used by the earliest Christians. Although medieval additions obscure the original Saxon structure, this is perhaps the earliest Christian site in Canterbury – it was here that Queen Bertha welcomed St Augustine in 597, and her husband King Ethelbert was baptized.

2

The Roman Museum

Butchery Lane • Daily 10am–5pm • £6 • Ⓣ 01227 785575

The redevelopment of the Longmarket area between Burgate and the High Street in the early 1990s exposed Roman foundations and mosaics that are now part of the **Roman Museum**. The display of recovered artefacts and general design of the museum are tasteful, with re-created Roman domestic scenes and a computer-generated view of Durovernum.

The Canterbury Tales

St Margaret's St • Daily: March–June, Sept & Oct 10am–5pm; July & Aug 9.30am–5pm; Nov–Feb 10am–4.30pm • £7.95 • Ⓣ 01227 454888, Ⓦ canterburytales.org.uk

Based on Geoffrey Chaucer's book, **The Canterbury Tales** is a quasi-educational, fun, show. Visitors follow a route through odour-enhanced galleries depicting a series of idealized fourteenth-century tableaux, in which mannequins recount five of Chaucer's famous tales.

Museum of Canterbury

Stour St • Daily 10am–5pm • £8 • Ⓣ 01227 475202

The exhibits in the interactive **Museum of Canterbury** provide an excellent jaunt through local history, from the splendour of Durovernum and the mystery surrounding the death of local-born Elizabethan playwright Christopher Marlowe, through to the more recent literary figures of Joseph Conrad and Oliver Postgate, originator, in the 1970s, of *Bagpuss* and *The Clangers*. The check-trousered philanthropist Rupert Bear has a museum all to himself within the main museum.

The High Street

Off the top of Stour Street on the High Street, the **Royal Museum and Art Gallery** (Ⓣ 01227 452747) is housed on the first floor of a superbly preserved mock-Tudor building. The museum is closed for refurbishment; once reopened, in 2012 it will house natural history displays, military memorabilia and an art collection that includes works by Henry Moore and Walter Sickert, as well as the city's library.

Eastbridge Hospital, standing where the High Street passes over a branch of the River Stour (Mon–Sat 10am–5pm; £1; Ⓣ 01227 471688, Ⓦ eastbridgehospital.org.uk), was founded in the twelfth century to provide poor pilgrims with shelter. Inside you can visit a refectory, a gallery showing the history of the hospital and sleeping quarters restored to their original medieval state. Over the road is the wonky, half-timbered **Weavers' House**, built around 1500 – once inhabited by Huguenot textile workers, it's now a restaurant.

2

Westgate Towers

St Peter's St • Daily 10am–4.30pm • £4 • ❶ 01227 789576, ⓦ canterburywestgatetowers.com

St Peter's Street – the western continuation of High Street – terminates at the massive crenellated towers of the medieval **West Gate**, the only one of the town's seven city gates to have survived intact. Inside you can climb the battlements for sweeping views over the city, and explore the cramped medieval prison cells – a stark contrast to those in the adjoining former 1830s gaol, which bears witness to the enlightened approach of the Victorian prison reform movement.

ARRIVAL AND INFORMATION — CANTERBURY

By train Canterbury has two train stations: Canterbury East and Canterbury West, each a 10min walk from the cathedral.

Destinations from Canterbury East Dover Priory (Mon–Sat every 30min, Sun hourly; 30min); London Victoria (Mon–Sat every 30min; 1hr 35min).

Destinations from Canterbury West Broadstairs (Mon–Sat every 30min, Sun hourly; 25min); London Charing Cross (Mon–Sat every 30min, Sun hourly; 1hr 45min); London St Pancras (hourly; 55min); Margate (Mon–Sat every 30min, Sun hourly; 30min); Ramsgate (Mon–Sat every 30min, Sun hourly; 25min); Whitstable (Mon–Sat every 30min, Sun hourly; 25–55min).

By bus The bus station is just inside the city walls on St George's Lane.

Destinations Broadstairs (Mon–Sat every 20min, Sun every 30min; 1hr 30min); Deal (Mon–Fri 1–3 hourly, Sat hourly, Sun 5 daily; 1hr 5min); Dover (Mon–Sat 1–every 30min, Sun 6 daily; 35min); London Victoria (hourly; 1hr 50min); Margate (Mon–Sat every 20min, Sun every 30min; 50min); Ramsgate (hourly; 45min); Sandwich (Mon–Sat 1–3 hourly, Sun 5 daily; 40min); Whitstable (every 5–15min; 30min).

Tourist office 12–13 Sun St, opposite the main entrance to the cathedral (Mon–Sat 9.30am–5pm, Sun 9.30am–4.30pm; ❶ 01227 378100, ⓦ canterbury.co.uk).

ACCOMMODATION

Canterbury accommodation consists mostly of B&Bs and small hotels and can be difficult to secure in July and August – book well in advance if possible.

HOTELS AND B&BS

Abode 30 High St ❶ 01227 766266, ⓦ abodehotels.co.uk/canterbury. The standard rooms are very ordinary at this boutique hotel, but special offers make a stay more reasonable. The priciest rooms come with balconies overlooking the cathedral, and there's also a top-notch restaurant and champagne bar. **£155**

★ **Arthouse B&B** 24 London Rd ❶ 01227 453032, ⓦ arthousebandb.com. Quirky, artist-owned B&B situated in the old fire station, a 5min walk from West Gate. Two stylish double rooms (each with private bathroom) share a lounge and kitchen – or you can rent both rooms and have the building to yourself. **£55**

Bluebells Guest House 248 Wincheap ❶ 01227 478842, ⓦ canterburybluebells.co.uk. Lovely Victorian B&B, fifteen minutes' walk from the centre, with lots of original features, stylish rooms, and nice touches like robes and fresh flowers in the rooms. **£65**

Canterbury Cathedral Lodge The Precincts ❶ 01227 865350, ⓦ canterburycathedrallodge.org. Modern hotel with unfussy rooms and an unbeatable location in the cathedral complex. Rates vary depending on availablilty, and can be as much as £30 more than quoted here. **£85**

Cathedral Gate 36 Burgate ❶ 01227 464381, ⓦ cathgate.co.uk. Built in 1438 and set in the city's medieval heart, this old pilgrims' hostelry features crooked floors and exposed timber beams along with modern amenities and fine views of the cathedral. The cheapest rooms share bathrooms. **£78.50**

No. 7 Longport 7 Longport ❶ 01227 455367, ⓦ 7longport.co.uk. This fabulous little hideaway – a tiny, beautifully presented cottage with a double bedroom, wet room and lounge – is situated in the courtyard of the friendly owner's home, just opposite St Augustine's Abbey. The same people also offer Love Lane, a three-bedroom Victorian cottage, which can be rented on a self-catering or B&B basis (£800 a week or £520 for 3 nights in high season). Both places are deservedly popular, and get booked up quickly. **£90**

HOSTELS

Canterbury YHA 54 New Dover Rd ❶ 0845 371 9010, ⓔ canterbury@yha.org.uk. Half a mile out of town, and 15min on foot from Canterbury East Station, this friendly hostel is set in a Victorian villa. Dorm **£18.40**, double **£46**

Kipps 40 Nunnery Fields ❶ 01227 786121, ⓦ kipps-hostel.com. Popular self-catering hostel close to Canterbury East Station, with a nice garden, plenty of homely touches and weekly events. Dorm **£20.50**, double **£55**

CAMPSITE

Neals Place Farm Neals Place Rd, off the A290 ❶ 01227 765632. Lovely campsite with just 18 pitches in the middle of an orchard, a mere 20min walk from the city. Closed Oct–March.

2

EATING

Boho Café 27 High St ⊕01227 458931. This hip, relaxed little hangout, with its quirky decor, delicious home-cooked food and friendly vibe, is deservedly popular. Mon 9am–4.30pm, Tues–Sat 9am–9pm, Sun 10am–4.30pm.

Café des Amis 93–95 St Dunstan's St ⊕01227 464390, ⓦcafedez.com. Very popular, authentic Mexican place close to West Gate, with eclectic decor featuring papier mâché creations by two local artists. Try the delicious paella (£26.50 for two) followed by a bubbling chocolate fundido. Mon–Thurs noon–10pm, Fri noon–10.30pm, Sat 10am–10.30pm, Sun 9am–9.30pm.

Deeson's 25–26 Sun St ⊕01227 767854, ⓦdeesonsrestaurant.co.uk. Delicious, modern British cooking and a stylish interior featuring linocuts by the owner's wife, are a winning combination at this popular little restaurant. Mains such as pork with pan haggerty and smoked crackling, or roast chicken in a local cider sauce will set you back £14–18. Daily noon–4pm & 6–10pm.

★ **The Goods Shed** Station Rd West ⊕01227 459153, ⓦthegoodsshed.co.uk. Buzzing restaurant set on a raised platform overlooking a bustling food hall in a converted goods shed. The menu features dishes such as local lamb roasted with anchovies or Kentish Ranger chicken with wild garlic pesto (both £16), with ingredients super-fresh from the adjacent produce market. Tues–Fri 8–10.30am, noon–2.30pm & 6–9.30pm, Sat 8–10.30am, noon–3pm & 6–9.30pm, Sun 9–10.30am & noon–3pm.

Tiny Tim's 34 St Margaret's St ⊕01227 450793, ⓦtinytimstearoom.com. Despite the name there's nothing twee about this elegant, 1930s-inspired tearoom, which offers more than thirty different blends of tea as well as hearty breakfasts, good-value lunches and a splendid afternoon tea. Tues–Sat 9.30am–5pm, Sun 10.30am–4pm.

DRINKING

Bramley's 15 Orange St ⊕01227 379933, ⓦbramleysbar.com. Cool, eclectic bar decked out with mismatched furniture, squishy armchairs and knick-knacks. They also serve good bar food. Mon–Thurs 6–11.30pm, Fri & Sat 6pm–12.30am.

Dolphin 17 St Radigund's St ⊕01227 455963, ⓦthedolphincanterbury.co.uk. Nice old pub with a good selection of real ales, a log fire in winter and a popular beer garden in summer. Tasty food, too. Daily noon–late.

Farmhouse 11 Dover St ⊕01227 456118, ⓦthefarmhousecanterbury.co.uk. Popular bar, live music (and occasionally theatre) venue and restaurant, just outside the city walls. Great food served Tues–Sat (breakfast, lunch & dinner), and Sun (lunch only). Tues–Thurs 9am–11pm, Fri & Sat 9am–2am, Sun 11am–5pm.

Parrot Radigund's Hall, 1–9 Church Lane ⊕01227 762355, ⓦtheparrotcanterbury.com. Ancient hostelry – the oldest in Canterbury – with loads of character, good food and a decent selection of ales. Daily noon–late.

NIGHTLIFE AND ENTERTAINMENT

The *Farmhouse* (see above) puts on **gigs**, as does the university on the other side of town. Taking place over two weeks in October, the **Canterbury Festival** (ⓦcanterburyfestival.co.uk) has an international mix of music, theatre and arts. For all events, see the free *What, Where and When* **listings magazine** available at the tourist office.

Gulbenkian Theatre Kent University ⊕01227 769075, ⓦkent.ac.uk/gulbenkian. Various cultural events, including drama, dance, comedy and film, are hosted at this excellent theatre-cum-cinema.

Marlowe Theatre The Friars ⊕01227 787787, ⓦmarlowetheatre.org.uk. This new theatre, named after the sixteenth-century Canterbury-born playwright, is the city's main venue for music, drama and shows.

Sandwich

One of the best-preserved medieval towns in the country, **SANDWICH** is best known nowadays for giving rise to England's favourite culinary contribution when, in 1762, the Fourth Earl of Sandwich, passionately absorbed in a game of cards, ate his meat between two bits of bread for a quick snack. Today it's a sleepy, picturesque town, with some fine half-timbered buildings and a lovely location on the willow-lined banks of the River Stour. It also boasts one of England's best golf courses, the **Royal St George Golf Course** (ⓦroyalstgeorges.com), just outside town. A frequent venue of the British Open tournament, it is open to all-comers on weekdays.

2

THE CINQUE PORTS

In 1278 Edward I formalized the unofficial confederation of defensive coastal settlements – Dover, Hythe, Sandwich, New Romney and Hastings – as the **Cinque Ports** (pronounced "sink", despite its French origin). In return for providing England with maritime support, chiefly in the transportation of troops and supplies during times of war, the five ports were granted trading privileges and other liberties. Later, Rye, Winchelsea and a few other "limb" ports on the southeast coast were added to the confederation. The ports' privileges were revoked in 1685; their maritime services had become increasingly unnecessary after Henry VIII had founded a professional navy and, due to a shifting coastline, several of the ports' harbours had silted up anyway, leaving some of them several miles inland. Nowadays, only Dover is still a major working port.

The waterfront

Until the River Stour began to silt up, the town was chief among the Cinque Ports (see above). By the bridge over the Stour stands Sandwich's best-known feature, the sixteenth-century **Barbican**, a stone gateway where tolls were once collected. Popular **boat trips** run from here up and down the river (£6–20; ❶07958 376183, ⓦsandwichriverbus.co.uk).

At the far corner of the quay you'll find the entrance to the **Secret Gardens of Sandwich** (daily: April–Sept 10am–5pm; Oct–March 10am–4pm; £6.50; ❶01304 619919, ⓦthe-secretgardens.co.uk), designed by Sir Edward Lutyens and planted by his famous gardening partner Gertrude Jekyll, and recently restored after being lost to the wilderness for 25 years.

The Guildhall

Guildhall Museum Cattle Market • April–Nov Tues, Wed, Fri & Sat 10.30am–12.30pm & 2–4pm, Thurs & Sun 2–4pm • £1

In the town centre, a fine sixteenth-century edifice, the **Guildhall**, houses both the tourist office (see below) and a small **museum** recounting the town's history as an influential Cinque port.

ARRIVAL AND INFORMATION — SANDWICH

By train The train station is on St George's Rd, a 5min walk from the centre.

Destinations Dover Priory (hourly; 25min); London Charing Cross (Mon–Sat every 30min, Sun hourly; 2hr 20min); London St Pancras (Mon–Sat every 30min, Sun hourly; 1hr 50min); Ramsgate (hourly; 15min).

By bus Buses pull in and depart from outside the tourist office.

Destinations Canterbury (Mon–Sat every 30min, Sun 6 daily; 45min); Deal (Mon–Sat every 30min, Sun 5 daily; 25min); Dover (Mon–Sat hourly, Sun every 2hr; 55min); Ramsgate (hourly; 30min).

Tourist office In the Guildhall (April–Oct Mon–Sat 10am–4pm; ❶01304 613565, ⓦwhitecliffscountry.org.uk).

ACCOMMODATION

Bell Hotel The Quay ❶01304 613388, ⓦbellhotelsandwich.co.uk. Rambling nineteenth-century hostelry that's been converted in sleek, modern style. Some rooms have balconies overlooking the grassy banks of the Stour, and there's an excellent in-house restaurant. **£110**

EATING AND DRINKING

George and Dragon 24 Fisher St ❶01304 613106, ⓦgeorgeanddragon-sandwich.co.uk. Popular pub in a quiet backstreet, with roaring real fires in winter and a courtyard garden for alfresco summer dining. Upmarket pub grub might include pork chops with cauliflower champ (£12) or lamb and chickpea curry (£15). Mon–Fri 11am–3pm & 6–11pm, Sat 11am–11pm, Sun 11am–4.30pm.

Secret Gardens Tearooms Quayside ❶01304 619919, ⓦthe-secretgardens.co.uk. This elegant tearoom features crisp white tablecloths and loose-leaf teas, and occupies a prime spot just inside the entrance to the Secret Gardens of Sandwich, with a fine outlook over Lutyens' handsome manor house. May–Sept daily 11am–5pm; Oct–April Sat–Wed 11am–5pm.

Deal

The old-fashioned resort of **DEAL**, six miles southeast of Sandwich, was the site of Julius Caesar's first successful landfall in Britain in 55 BC. Today it's a pleasant if unexciting spot, with a shingle beach backed by a jumble of Georgian townhouses, and a striking 1950s concrete pier that gives great views back across the town. Two seafront **castles**, built during the reign of King Henry VIII, are the town's biggest draw.

Deal Castle

Marine Rd • April–Oct daily 10am–6pm; Nov–March Sat & Sun 10am–4pm • EH • £4.80 • ⓣ 01304 372762

Diminutive **Deal Castle,** situated off The Strand at the south end of town, is one of the most unusual of Henry VIII's forts. It owes its unusual shape – viewed from the air it looks like a Tudor rose – to the premise that the rounded walls would be better at deflecting missiles. Inside, the comprehensive display on the other similar forts built during Henry VIII's reign is well worth a visit.

Walmer Castle

A mile south of Deal, Kingsdown Rd • March–Oct daily 10am–6pm • EH • £6.50 • ⓣ 01304 364288 • Hourly buses from Deal; also accessible on foot along the seafront

Walmer Castle is another rotund Tudor-rose-shaped affair, commissioned when the castle became the official residence of the Lord Warden of the Cinque Ports in 1730. Now it resembles a heavily fortified stately home more than a military stronghold. The best-known resident was the Duke of Wellington, who died here in 1842, and, not surprisingly, the house is devoted primarily to his life and times. Busts and portraits of the Iron Duke crowd the rooms and corridors, where you'll also find the armchair in which he expired and the original Wellington boots in which he triumphed at Waterloo.

ARRIVAL AND INFORMATION — DEAL

By train The train station is on Queen St, a 5min walk from the High St.

Destinations Canterbury (every 30min; 50min–1hr 10min); Dover (every 30min; 1hr 10min); London St Pancras (hourly; 1hr 40min); Ramsgate (Mon–Sat every 30min, Sun hourly; 20min); Sandwich (Mon–Sat every 30min, Sun hourly; 6min).

By bus Buses run from South Street in the town centre.

Destinations Canterbury (1–3 hourly; 1hr 10min); Dover (Mon–Sat hourly, Sun every 2hr; 40min); London Victoria (2 daily; 2hr 35min); Sandwich (Mon–Sat every 30min–1hr, Sun every 2hr; 30min).

Tourist office Landmark Centre, High St (Mon–Fri 10am–4pm, Sat 10am–2pm; ⓣ 01304 369576, ⓦ whitecliffscountry.org.uk).

ACCOMMODATION

★ **Number 1 B&B** 1 Ranelagh Rd ⓣ 01304 364459, ⓦ numberonebandb.co.uk. This friendly, popular B&B is the nicest place to stay in town. The handsome Victorian townhouse is in a great spot, just a few minutes' walk from Deal Castle and the beach, and the rooms are stylish and contemporary. **£75**

EATING

Black Douglas Coffee House 82 Beach St ⓣ 01304 365486, ⓦ blackdouglas.co.uk. Cosy hideaway on the blustery seafront, with scrubbed wooden tables, local art on the walls, newspapers and books for browsing, and a focus on top-quality, locally sourced home-made food. Mon–Wed 9am–5pm, Thurs–Sat 9am–5pm & 7–10pm, Sun 10am–4pm.

81 Beach St 81 Beach St ⓣ 01304 368136, ⓦ 81beachstreet.co.uk. Unfussy, top-notch beachfront brasserie. Mains might include slow-cooked pork belly (£16) or baked skate with saffron rice (£15.50); lunch is better value (two courses for £12.50). Mon–Sat noon–3pm & 6–10pm, Sun noon–4pm.

Dover

Badly bombed during World War II, **DOVER**'s town centre and seafront just don't have what it takes to induce many travellers to linger. **Dover Castle** is still by far the most interesting of the port's attractions, and you also shouldn't miss a walk along the legendary **White Cliffs**, which dominate the town and have long been a source of inspiration for lovers, travellers and soldiers sailing off to war.

2

Dover Castle

Castle Hill • Feb & March daily 10am–4pm; April–July & Sept daily 10am–6pm; Aug daily 9.30am–6pm; Oct daily 10am–5pm; Nov–Jan Mon & Thurs–Sun 10am–4pm • EH • £16

It was in 1168, a century after the Conquest, that the Normans constructed the keep that now presides over the bulk of **Dover Castle**, a superbly positioned defensive complex that was in continuous use as a military installation until the 1980s. Much earlier, the Romans had put Dover on the map when they chose the harbour as the base for their northern fleet, and erected a **lighthouse** (*pharos)* here to guide the ships into the river mouth. Beside the chunky hexagonal remains of this stands a Saxon-built church, **St Mary-in-Castro**, dating from the seventh century, with motifs graffitied by irreverent Crusaders still visible near the pulpit.

Further up the hill is the impressive, well-preserved **Great Tower**, built by Henry II as a palace. Inside, Henry's opulent royal court has been painstakingly re-created; everything from the pots and pans in the kitchen to the tapestries in the Kings Chamber has been meticulously researched and reproduced using, where possible, the materials and methods of the time. Audiovisual effects and costumed characters complete the experience.

The castle's other main attraction is its network of **Secret Wartime Tunnels** dug during the Napoleonic Wars and extended during World War II; free fifty-minute guided tours leave every twenty minutes.

The White Cliffs of Dover

There are some superb **walks** along Dover's cliffs: to reach Shakespeare Cliff, catch bus #D2A from Worthington Street towards Aycliff; alternatively, there's a steep two-and-a-half-mile climb from North Military Road, off York Street, taking you by the **Western Heights**, a series of defensive battlements built into the cliff in the nineteenth century.

ARRIVAL AND INFORMATION — DOVER

By train Dover Priory train station is situated off Folkestone Rd, a 10min walk west of the centre; there are regular shuttle buses to the Eastern and Western docks.

Destinations London Charing Cross (Mon–Sat every 30min; 1hr 40min); London St Pancras (hourly; 1hr 5min); London Victoria (Mon–Sat every 30min, Sun hourly; 1hr 50min).

By bus Buses from London run to the Eastern Docks and the town centre bus station on Pencester Rd.

Destinations Canterbury (Mon–Sat hourly, Sun every 2hr; 35min); Deal (Mon–Sat hourly, Sun every 2hr; 40min); Hastings (Mon–Sat hourly, Sun every 2hr; 2hr 40min); London Victoria (every 30min; 2hr 30min–3hr); Sandwich (Mon–Sat hourly, Sun every 2hr; 55min).

Tourist office In the Old Town Gaol, Biggin St (April, May & Sept Mon–Fri 9am–5.30pm, Sat & Sun 10am–4pm; June–Aug daily 9am–5.30pm; Oct–March Mon–Fri 9am–5.30pm, Sat 10am–4pm; ⓣ01304 205108, ⓦwhitecliffscountry.org.uk).

ACCOMMODATION

Maison Dieu 89 Maison Dieu Rd ⓣ01304 204033, ⓦmaisondieu.com. Warm and friendly B&B in a central location, with helpful on-site parking, family rooms and wi-fi. Some rooms have good views over Dover Castle. **£65**

Marquis at Alkham Alkham ⓣ01304 873410, ⓦthemarquisatalkham.co.uk. The best upmarket option in these parts, this restaurant-with-rooms is housed in a 200-year-old inn in a picturesque village 10min from Dover. The five chic rooms have perfect views across the downs, and the award-winning restaurant is superb. **£135**

CLOCKWISE FROM TOP LEFT LEEDS CASTLE (P.154); OYSTERS AT WHITSTABLE (P.139); BEACHY HEAD (P.160) >

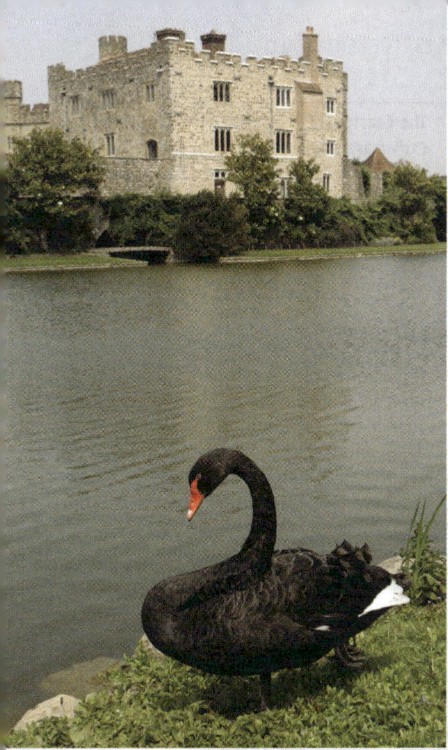

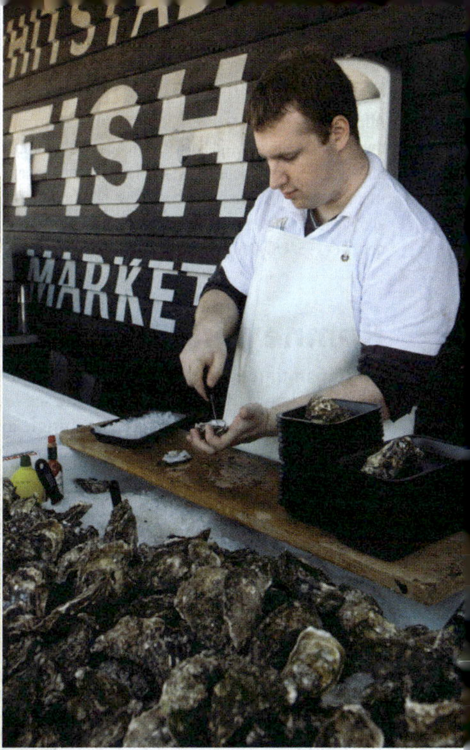
FISH
MARKET

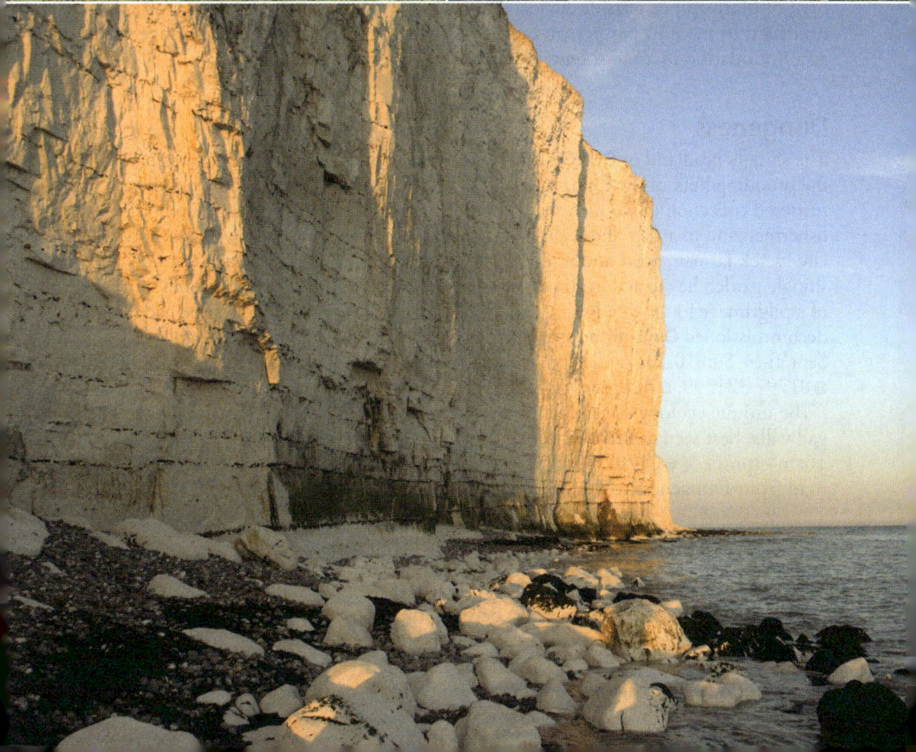

EATING AND DRINKING

Allotment 9 High St ⓣ01304 214467, ⓦtheallotmentdover.co.uk. This light-filled oasis on the shabby High Street serves up delicious breakfasts, lunches and dinners using ingredients sourced where possible from local allotments. In a town short of decent places to eat, this is a gem. Tues–Sat 8.30am–11pm.

The Coastguard St Margaret's Bay ⓣ01304 851019, ⓦthecoastguard.co.uk. Four miles east of Dover in the pretty cove of St Margaret's Bay, this pub is a perfect spot for lunch on a summer's day, with a terrace and beer garden that goes right down to the shingle. Daily 10.30am–11pm; food served 12.30–2.45pm & 6.30–8.45pm.

Romney and Denge marshes

In Roman times, what is now the southernmost part of Kent was submerged beneath the English Channel. The lowering of the sea levels in the Middle Ages and later reclamation created a forty-square-mile area of shingle and marshland, the **Romney and Denge marshes**, which today is populated mainly by sheep and has an eerie, forlorn appearance.

You can take in the marshes on the **Romney, Hythe and Dymchurch Railway** (April–Oct daily; Nov–March Sat & Sun, plus school hols; £14 return; ⓣ01797 362353, ⓦrhdr.org.uk), a fifteen-inch-gauge line which runs between Dungeness (see below) and the ancient town of **Hythe** on the marsh's western edge.

Port Lympne Wild Animal Park

Five miles west of Hythe and 17 miles from Dungeness • Daily: April–Oct 9.30am–6.30pm, last admission 3pm; Nov–March 10am–5pm, last admission 1pm • £23 • ⓦtotallywild.net

The **Port Lympne Wild Animal Park** is home to more than 650 beasts, including gorillas, African elephants, Barbary lions, Siberian and Indian tigers and the largest breeding herd of black rhinos outside Africa. The park offers fun **overnight safaris** (April to mid-Oct; from £115 per person), with game drives led by Zimbabwean rangers, and accommodation in a safari tent overlooking a watering hole.

Dungeness

The shingly headland of **DUNGENESS**, at the marsh's southernmost tip, is dominated by the brooding hulk of the Dungeness nuclear power station. In its shadow huddle a scattered collection of wooden shacks and disused railway carriages, home to both fishermen and to artists and recluses drawn to the area's bleak, otherworldly beauty. The late Derek Jarman, artist and filmmaker, made his home here at **Prospect Cottage**, and the shingle garden he created from beachcombed treasures and plants has become something of a pilgrimage for garden lovers. Panoramic views over the headland can be had from the decommissioned **Old Lighthouse** (April & Oct Sat & Sun 10.30am–4.30pm; May, June & Sept Tues–Sun 10.30am–4.30pm; July, Aug & school hols daily 10.30am–4.30pm; £3.50; ⓣ01797 321399, ⓦdungenesslighthouse.com), built in 1904.

The unique ecology at Dungeness attracts huge colonies of gulls, terns, smews and gadwalls, best seen at **RSPB visitor centre** (daily: March–Oct 10am–5pm; Nov–Feb 10am–4pm; £3; ⓣ01797 320558, ⓦrspb.org.uk), three miles from Dungeness, off the road from Dungeness to Lydd.

The Kent Weald

The Weald stretches across a large area between the North and South Downs and includes parts of both Kent and Sussex. The central part, the High Weald, is epitomized by gentle hills, sunken country lanes and somnolent villages as well as some of England's most beautiful gardens – **Sissinghurst** being the best known – and ancient heathland at

Ashdown Forest. The Weald also offers a wealth of highly picturesque historical sites, foremost among them **Leeds Castle** and **Hever Castle**, as well as stately homes at **Penshurst** and **Knole**, a well-preserved Roman villa at Lullingstone and the fascinating home of wartime leader Winston Churchill at **Chartwell**. The pleasant spa town of **Tunbridge Wells**, set in the heart of the beautiful High Weald countryside, makes an excellent base.

2

Royal Tunbridge Wells

The handsome spa town of **ROYAL TUNBRIDGE WELLS** was established after a bubbling spring discovered here in 1606 was claimed to have curative properties, and reached its height of popularity during the Regency period when such restorative cures were in vogue. It remains an elegant place, and with plenty of excellent places to stay and eat it's a good base for day-trips into the Weald.

The Pantiles

Hidden away at the southernmost end of the High Street, the **Pantiles** is an elegant colonnaded parade of shops and cafés, where the fashionable once gathered to promenade and take the waters. Hub of the Pantiles is the original **Chalybeate Spring** (pronounced with the emphasis on the "be") in the Bath House (Easter–Sept daily 10am–5pm), where a "dipper" has been employed since the late eighteenth century to serve the waters (40p).

ARRIVAL AND INFORMATION — ROYAL TUNBRIDGE WELLS

By train The train station is located where High St becomes Mount Pleasant Rd. There are frequent connections with London's Charing Cross (every 15min; 46–54min) and Hastings (38min).

By bus Buses set down and pick up along High St and its continuation, Mount Pleasant Rd.

Destinations Brighton (Mon–Sat every 30min, Sun hourly; 1hr 40min); Lewes (Mon–Sat every 30min, Sun hourly; 1hr 10min); London Victoria (1 daily; 1hr 30min); Sevenoaks (Mon–Sat every 30min, Sun every 2hr; 40–50min).

Tourist office In the Old Fish Market in the Pantiles (Mon–Sat 9am–5pm, Sun 10am–4/5pm; T 01892 515675, W visittunbridgewells.com).

ACCOMMODATION

40 York Rd B&B 40 York Rd T 01892 531342, W yorkroad.co.uk. Warm and friendly Regency-style B&B on a quiet street in the centre, with just two spacious rooms, a pretty courtyard garden and wi-fi. **£80**

Brew House Hotel 1 Warwick Park T 01892 520587, W thebrewhousehotel.net. Sleek boutique hotel in a great location near The Pantiles, with an excellent restaurant and bar attached. Some of the modern, luxurious rooms have fun "smart glass" bathrooms. **£155**

EATING AND DRINKING

Sankey's 39 Mount Ephraim T 01892 511422, W sankeys.co.uk. Cosy basement seafood brasserie and oyster bar serving top-notch, good-value seafood (fishcakes £10.50, bouillabaisse £16.50). Upstairs is a lovely pub decked out with enamel signs and brewery mirrors, with an open fire, secluded decked garden and great selection of specialist beers. Tues–Sat noon–3pm & 6–10pm.

Thackeray's House 85 London Rd T 01892 511921, W thackerays-restaurant.co.uk. One-time home of the writer, this ancient weatherboarded building is the finest restaurant in town: it's expensive (mains such as roast sloe-encrusted venison cost £20–30, while the tasting menu is £65), but the three-course lunch (Tues–Sat only) is a bargain at £16.95. Tues–Sun 12.30–4pm & 6–10pm.

Sissinghurst

Biddenden Rd, near Cranbrook, 14 miles east of Tunbridge Wells • Mid-March to Oct Mon, Tues & Fri–Sun 10.30am–5pm • NT • £10 • T 01580 710701 • Bus #5 stops in Sissinghurst village on its run between Maidstone and Hastings

When she and her husband took it over in the 1920s, **Sissinghurst** was described by Vita Sackville-West as "a garden crying out for rescue". Spread over the site of a medieval moated manor (which was rebuilt into an Elizabethan mansion of which only one wing remains today), the five-acre gardens were designed around the linear pattern of the former buildings' walls. The major appeal derives from the way that the flowers are allowed to spill over onto the narrow walkways, defying the classical formality of the great gardens that came before. The brick tower that Vita had restored and used as her study acts as a focal point and offers the best views of the walled gardens. Most impressive are the **White Garden**, composed solely of white flowers and silvery-grey foliage, and the **Cottage Garden**, featuring flora in shades of orange, yellow and red.

2

Leeds Castle

Thirty miles northeast of Tunbridge Wells • Daily 10am–5pm, last admission 4.30pm • Castle & grounds £18.50 for an annual pass • ⓣ 01622 765400, ⓦ leeds-castle.com • Trains from London Victoria to Bearsted station, then a coach shuttle service from the station (March–Oct)

Leeds Castle more closely resembles a fairy-tale palace than a defensively efficient fortress. Work on the castle began around 1120, half on an island in the middle of a lake and half on the mainland surrounded by landscaped parkland. Following centuries of regal and noble ownership (and, less glamorously, service as a prison) the castle now hosts conferences and sporting and cultural events. Its interior fails to match the stunning external appearance and, in places, modern renovations have quashed its historical charm. The most unusual feature inside is the dog-collar museum in the gatehouse, while the grounds hold a fine aviary with some superb and colourful exotic specimens, as well as manicured gardens and a mildly challenging maze.

Penshurst Place

Penshurst village, 5 miles northwest of Tunbridge Wells • April–Oct daily noon–4pm, grounds 10.30am–6pm • £9.80, grounds only £7.80 • ⓣ 01892 870307, ⓦ penshurstplace.com • Bus #231 or #233 from Tunbridge Wells (Mon–Sat only)

Tudor timber-framed houses and shops line the high street of the attractive village of **PENSHURST**. The main reason for coming here is to visit **Penshurst Place**, home to the Sidney family since 1552 and birthplace of the Elizabethan soldier and poet, Sir Philip Sidney. The fourteenth-century Barons Hall, built for Sir John de Pulteney, four times Mayor of London, is the glory of the interior, with its 60ft-high chestnut roof still in place.

Hever Castle

Eight miles northwest of Tunbridge Wells • March, Nov & Dec Wed–Sun 10.30am–5pm; April–Oct daily 10.30am–6pm; last entry 1hr before closing • £14, gardens only £11.50 • ⓣ 01732 865224, ⓦ hevercastle.co.uk • Trains from London Victoria to Edenbridge (3 miles from castle; taxis available), or to Hever (1 mile from castle; no taxis)

The moated **Hever Castle** is the childhood home of Anne Boleyn, second wife of Henry VIII, and where Anne of Cleves, Henry's fourth wife, lived after their divorce. In 1903, having fallen into disrepair, the castle was bought by William Waldorf-Astor, American millionaire-owner of *The Times*, who had the house assiduously restored. In the Inner Hall hangs a fine portrait of Henry VIII by Holbein; a Holbein painting of Elizabeth I hangs on the middle floor. Upstairs, Anne of Cleves' room holds an unusually well-preserved tapestry illustrating the marriage of Henry's sister to King Louis XII of France, with Anne Boleyn as one of the ladies-in-waiting.

Outside in the grounds is Waldorf-Astor's beautiful **Italian Garden**, built on reclaimed marshland and decorated with Roman statuary, as well as an adventure playground and a water maze.

Chartwell

Mapleton Rd, Westerham, 15 miles northwest of Tunbridge Wells • Mid-March to Oct Wed–Sun 11am–5pm; July & Aug also Tues • NT • £11.80 • ⓣ 01732 868381

Chartwell was the residence of Winston Churchill from 1924 until his death in 1965. It's an unremarkable, heavily restored Tudor building whose main appeal is the wartime

ENGLISH WINE: A SPARKLING SUCCESS STORY

No longer is English wine regarded with derision. Today there are around four hundred English vineyards producing around two million bottles a year (more than eighty percent of it white), and the best of the harvest more than rivals the more famous names over the Channel. Sparkling wine is the biggest success story, with some English wines beating the best Champagnes in blind tasting competitions.

With almost identical soil and geology to the Champagne region, and a helping hand from global warming, the southeast is home to many of the country's best vineyards, several of which now offer tours and tastings. In the Kent Weald, these include:

Biddenden Gribble Bridge Lane, Biddenden ⓣ01580 291726, ⓦbiddendenvineyards.com. Kent's oldest commercial vineyard, producing wines from nine varieties of grape, as well as traditional Kentish ciders. Free vineyard tours run once or twice a month, and there are free tastings daily. Mon–Sat 10am–5pm, Sun 11am–5pm. Closed Sun in Jan & Feb.

Chapel Down Small Hythe, Tenterden ⓣ01580 763033, ⓦenglishwinesgroup.com. Multi-award-winning winemaker, with a wine and English produce store on site, as well as a lovely terrace restaurant overlooking the vines. Guided tours and tastings (£9) daily June–Sept, weekends only in May & Oct.

See ⓦenglishwineproducers.com for details of more vineyards around the country.

premier's memorabilia, including his paintings, which show an unexpectedly contemplative side to the famously gruff statesman. Entry to the house is by timed ticket at peak times – expect long queues.

Knole

Sevenoaks, entered from the south end of Sevenoaks High St • **House** Mid-March to Oct Wed–Sun noon–4pm **Garden** Late April–Sept Tues 11am–4pm • NT • £10.40, garden £5 • ⓣ01732 450608 • Trains from London Charing Cross or Tunbridge Wells to Sevenoaks station, then a 30min walk

Numerically designed to match the calendar – with 365 rooms, 7 courtyards and 52 staircases – **Knole** palace, in the commuter town of Sevenoaks, was created in 1456 as a residence for the archbishops of Canterbury. It was later appropriated by Henry VIII, who lavished further expense on it and hunted in the thousand acres of **parkland** (free access throughout the year), still home to several hundred deer. Henry's daughter, Elizabeth I, passed the estate on to her cousin, Thomas Sackville, who remodelled the house in 1605; it has remained in the family's hands ever since, with its Jacobean exterior preserved. Vita Sackville-West was brought up here, and her one-time lover Virginia Woolf derived inspiration for her novel *Orlando* from her frequent visits. An array of fine, if well-worn, furnishings and tapestries are on display, together with paintings by Gainsborough, Reynolds and Van Dyck.

Hastings and around

Once an influential Cinque Port (see p.148), **HASTINGS** is a curious mixture of unpretentious fishing port, tatty seaside resort and bohemian retreat popular with artists. The town is best known, however, for the eponymous **battle** which took place nearby; in 1066, William, Duke of Normandy, landed at Pevensey Bay, a few miles west of town, and made Hastings his base, before his forces met Harold's army at nearby Battle (see p.157).

Old town

Hastings **old town**, east of the pier, holds most of the appeal of this part-tacky, part-pretty resort. **All Saints Street** is by far the most evocative thoroughfare, punctuated with the odd, rickety, timber-framed dwelling from the fifteenth century. In the parallel High Street, the thirteenth-century **St Clement's Church** displays, at the top of its tower, a cannonball lodged by a Dutch galleon in the 1600s – its poignancy rather dispelled by a companion fitted in the eighteenth century for the sake of symmetry.

The Stade

Down by the seafront, the area known as **The Stade** is characterized by its tall, black weatherboard **net shops**, most dating from the mid-nineteenth century (and still in use), but which first appeared here in Tudor times. Many of them sell fresh fish.

Jerwood Gallery

W jerwoodgallery.org

Adjacent to the fishing quarter, the **Jerwood Gallery**, scheduled to open in spring 2012, will provide a fabulous contemporary home for the Jerwood Foundation's modern art collection, which includes works by Stanley Spencer, Walter Sickert and Augustus John. The sleek new building, covered in shimmering dark-glazed tiles, will also contain a temporary exhibition space, a sculpture courtyard and a first-floor café overlooking the beach.

Castle Hill

Castle Hill, separating the old town from the less interesting modern quarter, can be ascended by the **West Hill Cliff Railway**, from George Street, off Marine Parade. It's one of two Victorian funicular railways in Hastings, the other being the **East Cliff Railway**, on Rock-a-Nore Road, which ascends to the cliff-top Hastings Country Park (both daily: March–Sept 10am–5.30pm; Oct–March 11am–4pm; £2.20).

The castle

The 1066 Story Mid-Feb to Easter Sat & Sun 10am–4pm; Easter–Aug daily 10am–5pm; Sept & Oct daily 10am–4pm • £4.25 • W discoverhastings.co.uk

Castle Hill is where William the Conqueror erected his first **castle** in 1066, built on the site of an existing fort, probably of Saxon origins. It was soon replaced by a more permanent stone structure, but in the thirteenth century storms caused the cliffs to subside, tipping most of the castle into the sea; the surviving ruins, however, offer an excellent prospect of the town. The castle is home to **The 1066 Story**, in which the events of the last successful invasion of the British mainland are described inside a mock-up of a siege tent.

ARRIVAL AND INFORMATION — HASTINGS

By train The train station is a 10min walk from the seafront along Havelock Rd.

Destinations Battle (every 30min; 15min); Brighton (every 30min; 1hr 5min); Eastbourne (every 20min; 25min); Lewes (every 30min; 55min); London Bridge (hourly; 1hr 24min); Rye (hourly; 20min).

By bus National Express bus services operate from the station at the junction of Havelock and Queen's roads.

Destinations Battle (Mon–Sat hourly, Sun 1 daily; 15min); Dover (Mon–Sat hourly, Sun 6 daily; 2hr 50min); Eastbourne (Mon–Sat every 20–30min, Sun hourly; 1hr 15min); London Victoria (2 daily; 2hr 35min–3hr 55min); Rye (Mon–Sat every 30min, Sun 6 daily; 40min).

Tourist office In the Town Hall on Queen's Square (May–Oct Mon–Fri 8.30am–6.15pm, Sat 9am–5pm, Sun 10.30am–4pm; T 01424 451111, W visit1066country.com). There's a smaller office in the old town, in the Old Town Hall Museum on High St (May–Oct daily 10am–4.30pm; Nov–April Sat & Sun 10am–4.30pm).

ACCOMMODATION

Senlac Guesthouse 46–47 Cambridge Gardens T 01424 430080, W senlacguesthouse.co.uk. Stylish yet affordable, this friendly B&B near the station is fantastic value. The cheapest rooms share bathrooms; self-contained apartments are also available. **£50**

★ **Swan House** 1 Hill St ⓣ01892 430014, ⓦswanhousehastings.co.uk. Simply beautiful B&B in a half-timbered fifteenth-century building on one of the old town's most picturesque streets. Rooms are luxurious and tasteful, and there's a pretty decked patio garden in which to enjoy the gourmet breakfast on sunny days. The owners also run the similarly elegant *Old Rectory*, around the corner on All Saints St. Minimum two-night stay at weekends. **£115**

EATING AND DRINKING

Dragon 71 George St ⓣ01424 423688. Great little retro-styled hangout – part restaurant, part lounge bar – with tasty food (the locally sourced menu changes almost daily), art exhibitions and a nice assortment of squishy sofas. Mon–Sat noon–11pm, Sun noon–10.30pm.

First In, Last Out 15 High St ⓣ01424 425079, ⓦthefilo.co.uk. Tiny, ever-popular traditional pub with snug booths, a huge roaring fire in winter, no jukeboxes or fruit machines, and its own microbrewery. Tasty food is served Mon–Sat lunchtimes. Mon–Sat 11am–midnight, Sun noon–midnight.

Maggies Above Hastings fish market, Rock-a-Nore ⓣ01424 430205. The best fish and chips in town can be found at this first-floor café, right on the beach. It's open for lunch only, and is very popular, so you'll need to book ahead. Mon–Sat noon–3pm.

Webbes 1 Rock-a-Nore Rd ⓣ01424 721650, ⓦwebbesrestaurants.co.uk. Top-notch seafood restaurant opposite the Jerwood Gallery, with plenty of outside seating in summer. Mains such as steamed panache of fish cost around £14, or you can pick and choose from tasting dishes at £3.50 each. Mon–Fri noon–2.30pm & 6–9.30pm, Sat & Sun noon–9.30pm.

NIGHTLIFE AND ENTERTAINMENT

There's a thriving live music scene in Hastings; pick up the *Ultimate Alternative* listings magazine (ⓦua1066.co.uk), available in pubs and clubs throughout town, for a comprehensive guide to what's on. Hastings' **May Day Jack-in-the-Green Festival** (end April/beginning May; ⓦhastingsjack.co.uk) is a weekend of festivities culminating in a riotous parade of dancers, drummers and leaf-bedecked revellers through the streets of the old town up to Hastings' hilltop castle, where "the Jack" – a garlanded leaf-covered figure whose origins date back to the eighteenth century – is ritually slain and the spirit of summer released.

Porter's Wine Bar 56 High St ⓣ01424 427000, ⓦporterswinebar.com. Friendly, family-run wine bar, with jazz and acoustic music on Wednesday and Thursday nights and Sunday afternoon, including a regular spot by acclaimed jazz pianist and local resident Lianne Carroll. Good, home-cooked, bistro-style food is on offer too. Mon–Fri noon–3pm & 7pm–midnight, Sat noon–midnight, Sun 12.30–11pm.

Battle

The town of **BATTLE**, six miles inland from Hastings, occupies the site of the most famous land battle in British history. Here, on October 14, 1066, the invading Normans swarmed up the hillside from Senlac Moor and overcame the Anglo-Saxon army of King Harold, who is thought to have been killed not by an arrow through the eye – a myth resulting from the misinterpretation of the Bayeux Tapestry – but by a workaday clubbing about the head. Before the battle took place, William vowed that, should he win the engagement, he would build a religious foundation on the very spot of Harold's slaying to atone for the bloodshed, and, true to his word, **Battle Abbey** was built four years later and subsequently occupied by a fraternity of Benedictines.

Battle Abbey

At the south end of High St • Daily: April–Sept 10am–6pm; Oct–March 10am–4pm • EH • £7.30 • ⓣ01424 775705

The magnificent structure of **Battle Abbey**, though partially destroyed in the Dissolution and much rebuilt and revised over the centuries, still dominates the town. You can wander through the ruins of the abbey to the spot where Harold was killed – the site of the high altar of William's abbey, now marked by a memorial stone – while a visitor centre holds an interactive exhibition and an auditorium showing a dramatic re-enactment of the battle using film and computer simulations.

2

ARRIVAL AND INFORMATION — BATTLE

By train The train station is a well-signposted 10min walk from the High St.

Destinations Hastings (every 30min; 15min); London Charing Cross (every 30min; 1hr 30min); Tunbridge Wells (every 30min; 30min).

By bus Buses #304 and #305 run from Hastings to Battle High St (Mon–Sat only; hourly; 15min).

Tourist office In the Gatehouse at Battle Abbey (April–Sept daily 10am–6pm; Oct–March check opening days, 10am–4pm; 01424 776789, visit1066country.com).

ACCOMMODATION

19 Upper Lake 19 Upper Lake 01424 773104, 19upperlake.co.uk. Lovely B&B in a characterful fifteenth-century house, complete with beams, flagstoned floor and sloping ceilings. Rooms are pretty and stylish, the breakfast earns top marks and there are even afternoon teas on offer, served in the cosy sitting room. **£85**

EATING

Nobles 17 High St 01424 774422, noblesrestaurant.co.uk. Highly rated restaurant serving delicious seasonal, local food, and with a walled garden for alfresco dining in summer. Mains such as saddle of Romney Marsh lamb will set you back around £16, or there's an excellent-value £10.66 set menu at lunchtimes (Mon–Sat only). Mon–Sat noon–3pm & 6.30pm–late, Sun noon–3pm.

Bodiam Castle

Nine miles north of Hastings • Mid-Feb to Oct daily 10am–6pm; Nov to mid-Dec Wed–Sun 11am–4pm; mid-Jan to mid-Feb Sat & Sun 11am–4pm • NT • £6.10 • 01580 830196 • Bus #349 from Hastings

Bodiam Castle is a classically stout square block with rounded corner turrets, battlements and a wide moat. When it was built in 1385 to guard what were the lower reaches of the River Rother, Bodiam was state-of-the-art military architecture, but during the Civil War, a company of Roundheads breached the fortress and removed its roof to reduce its effectiveness as a possible stronghold for the king. Over the next 250 years Bodiam fell into neglect until restoration in the last century by Lord Curzon. The extremely steep spiral staircases, leading to the crenellated battlements, will test all but the strongest of thighs.

ARRIVAL AND DEPARTURE — BODIAM CASTLE

The nicest way to arrive is on a **steam train** run by the **Kent & East Sussex Railway** (April–Oct only; £12.80 all day; 01580 765155, kesr.org.uk); full-scale steam trains and diesels chug their way along a picturesque route from **Tenterden**, 10 miles northeast, several times a day.

Bateman's

Bateman's Lane, Burwash, off the A265 15 miles northwest of Hastings • House and garden: mid-March to Oct Mon–Wed, Sat & Sun 11am–5pm; house also open 2 weeks in Dec, Sat & Sun 11.30am–3.30pm; garden only also open Nov & Dec, Mon–Wed, Sat & Sun 11am–4pm • NT • £7.80, garden free in Nov & Dec • 01435 882302 • Regular trains from Hastings to Etchingham station, then a 3-mile walk

Half a mile south of the picturesque village of Burwich, **Bateman's** was the idyllic home of the writer and journalist Rudyard Kipling from 1902 until his death in 1936. Built by a local ironmaster in the seventeenth century and set amid attractive gardens, it features a working watermill converted by Kipling to generate electricity. Inside, the house displays Kipling's letters, early editions of his work and mementos from his travels.

Rye

Ten miles northeast of Hastings, perched on a hill overlooking the Romney Marshes, the pretty, ancient town of **RYE** was added as a "limb" to the original Cinque Ports (see p.148), but was subsequently marooned two miles inland by the retreat of the sea and the silting-up of the River Rother. It is now one of the most visited places in East Sussex – half-timbered, skew-roofed and quintessentially English, but also very commercialized.

Rye's most picturesque street – and the most photographed – is the sloping cobbled **Mermaid Street**, the town's main thoroughfare in the sixteenth century. At the top of Mermaid Street, just around the corner in West Street, lies **Lamb House** (mid-March to mid-Oct Tues & Sat 2–6pm; NT; £4.30; ⓣ01580 762334), home of the authors Henry James and (subsequently) E.F. Benson.

Just a few cobbled yards away is the peaceful oasis of Church Square, where **St Mary's Church** boasts the oldest functioning pendulum clock in the country; the ascent of the church tower offers fine views over the clay-tiled roofs.

2

Rye Castle Museum

Ypres Tower Daily 10.30am–5pm • £3, joint ticket with Rye Castle Museum £5 **Rye Castle Museum** Sat & Sun 10.30am–5pm • £2.50, joint ticket with Ypres Tower £5 • ⓣ01797 226728, ⓦryemuseum.co.uk

In the far corner of Church Square stands the **Ypres Tower**, formerly used to keep watch for cross-Channel invaders, and now a part of the **Rye Castle Museum** on nearby East Street at no. 3. Both places house a number of relics from Rye's past, including an eighteenth-century fire engine.

Camber Sands

Around three miles east of Rye, on the other side of the River Rother estuary, **Camber Sands** is a two-mile stretch of dune-backed sandy beach that has become a renowned centre of wind- and watersports. The nicest way to reach it from Rye is by bike, on the three-mile dedicated cycle path.

ARRIVAL AND DEPARTURE — RYE

By train Rye's train station is at the bottom of Station Approach, off Cinque Ports St; it's a 5min walk up to the High Street. Regular trains run to Hastings (hourly; 20min) and London St Pancras (hourly; 1hr 5min–1hr 25min).

By bus Bus #100 runs into the centre of town from Hastings (Mon–Sat hourly, Sun every 2hr; 40min).

GETTING AROUND

You can rent **bicycles** from Rye Hire, 1 Cyprus Place (£14/day; ⓣ01797 223033).

INFORMATION

Tourist office 4–5 Lion St (daily: April–Sept 10am–5pm; Oct–March 10am–4pm; ⓣ01797 229049, ⓦvisitrye.co.uk).

Heritage and Information Centre Strand Quay (daily: April–Oct 10am–5pm; Nov–March 10am–4pm; ⓣ01797 226696, ⓦryeheritage.co.uk). Provides tourist information and audioguides (£4).

ACCOMMODATION

★ **The George** 98 High St ⓣ01797 222144, ⓦthegeorgeinrye.com. Very popular, this luxurious small hotel manages to get everything right, from the tasteful, individually furnished rooms (complete with cashmere covered hot-water bottles in winter), to the cosy, atmospheric bar and excellent restaurant. **£135**

Haydens 108 High St ⓣ01797 224501, ⓦhaydensinrye.co.uk. Friendly boutique B&B with elegant, contemporary rooms set above a popular café in the heart of town. **£85**

Strand House Tanyards Lane, Winchelsea, 2 miles southwest of Rye ⓣ01797 226276, ⓦthestrandhouse.co.uk. This pretty-as-a-picture Tudor hotel in the pretty, very quiet village of Winchelsea features oak-beamed ceilings, inglenook fireplaces and leaded windows, as well as a tranquil two-acre woodland garden which links the hotel with Winchelsea above. **£70**

EATING AND DRINKING

There's no shortage of excellent **places to eat** in Rye, including the restaurant at *The George* and café at *Haydens* (see above).

Apothecary 1 East St ⓣ 01797 229157, ⓦ apothecaryrye.co.uk. Leather armchairs, book-lined walls, scrubbed wooden tables and a wealth of original features make this lovely, atmospheric coffee shop, housed in Rye's old apothecary, the best in town. Daily 9am–5pm.

Mermaid Inn Mermaid St ⓣ 01797 223065, ⓦ mermaidinn.com. This fifteenth-century, half-timbered hotel simply oozes character and charm, and a meal at its in-house restaurant is an excellent way to soak up the atmosphere without breaking the bank. Three courses will set you back £25 at lunch, £37.50 at dinner. Daily noon–2.30pm & 7–9pm.

Tuscan Kitchen 8 Lion St ⓣ 01797 223269, ⓦ tuscankitchenrye.co.uk. The delicious, authentic Tuscan cuisine on offer at this beamed, low-ceilinged restaurant has won it a lot of fans, and is excellent value too. Tues–Thurs 6–10pm, Fri–Sun noon–3pm & 6–10pm.

Ypres Castle Gun Gardens, down the steps behind the Ypres Tower ⓣ 01797 223248, ⓦ yprescastleinn.co.uk. An unspoiled spot, with real ales, a beer garden with views over Romney Marsh, and live music on Friday nights. Decent food too (mains average £10–13). Daily 11am–late; food served Mon–Sat noon–3pm & 6–9pm (8pm on Fri), Sun noon–3pm.

Eastbourne and around

Like so many of the southeast's seaside resorts, **EASTBOURNE** was kick-started into life in the 1840s, when the Brighton, Lewes and Hastings Rail Company built a branch line from Lewes to the sea. Nowadays Eastbourne has a solid reputation as a retirement town by the sea, and though the relocated state-of-the-art **Towner Gallery** has introduced a welcome splash of modernity, the town's charms remain for the most part sedate and old-fashioned. The focus of the elegant seafront is the **pier**, one of the grandest on the south coast, jutting out from its long promenade. The real draw, however, is the stunning coastal scenery of the nearby **South Downs**, just a short walk away.

Towner Art Gallery and Museum

Devonshire Park • Tues–Sun 10am–6pm • Free • ⓣ 01323 415470, ⓦ townereastbourne.org.uk

First opened in 1923, the venerable **Towner Art Gallery and Museum** was in 2009 relocated to a glamorous new home in Devonshire Park, just a few minutes' walk inland from the Wish Tower, one of two Martello towers on the promenade. The gallery building – a sleek modern edifice of glass and smooth white curves – houses changing exhibitions of modern and contemporary art from the permanent Towner collection, as well as temporary special exhibitions. On the second floor there's a café-bar with a small terrace overlooking the rooftops of Eastbourne to the South Downs beyond.

Museum of Shops

20 Cornfield Terrace • Daily 10am–5.30pm • £5 • ⓣ 01323 737143, ⓦ howwelivedthen@btconnect.com

Over one hundred years of consumerism are recorded at the fascinating **"How We Lived Then" Museum of Shops**, where a range of artefacts from 1850 to 1950 – more than 100,000 in total, everything from old packages to coronation cups, toys, clothes and signs – is crammed into mock-up shops spread over several floors.

Seven Sisters Country Park

Beachy Head Visitor Centre Daily: April–Oct 10am–4pm; Nov, Dec & March Sat & Sun 11am–3.30pm • ⓣ 01323 737273, ⓦ beachyhead.org.uk • An open-top bus runs at least hourly (April–Oct; £5 return) from Eastbourne Pier to the top of Beachy Head Seven Sisters County Park Visitor Centre Easter–Oct daily 10.30am–4.30pm • ⓣ 01323 870280, ⓦ sevensisters.org.uk

A short walk west from Eastbourne – or an open-top bus ride – takes you out along the most dramatic stretch of coastline in Sussex, where the chalk uplands are cut by the sea into a sequence of splendid cliffs. The most spectacular of all, **Beachy Head**, is 575ft

SOUTH DOWNS NATIONAL PARK AND THE SOUTH DOWNS WAY

The fifteenth and newest member of Britain's national park family, the **South Downs National Park** came into being in 2010. Covering over six hundred square miles, it stretches for seventy miles from eastern Hampshire through the hills of West Sussex to the white chalk cliffs of East Sussex. The park is located in one of the most densely populated parts of the country, and in contrast to other "wilder" national parks, it contains a high proportion of farmland – about 85 percent of the park.

There are **visitor centres** in East Sussex at the Seven Sisters County Park and at Beachy Head (see opposite for both), and in Hampshire at the Queen Elizabeth County Park. The **South Downs National Park Authority** website (Ⓦ southdowns.gov.uk) is another useful source of information about the area.

THE SOUTH DOWNS WAY

One of the best ways to explore the park is to strike off into the countryside on the **South Downs Way**, which rises and dips over one hundred miles along the chalk uplands between the city of Winchester and the spectacular cliffs at Beachy Head, and offers the southeast's finest walks. If undertaken in its entirety, the bridle path is best traversed from west to east, taking advantage of the prevailing wind, Eastbourne's better transport services and accommodation, and the psychological appeal of ending at the sea. **Steyning**, the halfway point, marks a transition between predominantly wooded sections and more exposed chalk uplands.

The OS *Landranger* **maps** #198 and #199 cover the eastern end of the route; you'll need #185 and #197 as well to cover the lot. A **guidebook** is advised, and several are available, the best being by Kev Reynolds (written for following the route in either direction; published by Cicerone Press). You can also check out the **website** Ⓦ nationaltrail.co.uk/southdowns.

high, and a popular suicide spot. West of the headland the scenery softens into a diminishing series of chalk cliffs, a landmark known as the **Seven Sisters**. The eponymous country park provides some of the most impressive walks in the county, taking in the cliff-top path and the lower valley of the meandering River Cuckmere, into which the Seven Sisters subside. Head up to Seaford Head, on the western side of the Cuckmere estuary, for the iconic view of the cliffs you'll see on every postcard, with the picturesque coastguard's cottages in the foreground.

ARRIVAL AND INFORMATION — EASTBOURNE

By train Eastbourne's train station is a splendid Italianate terminus, just a 10min walk from the seafront up Terminus Rd.

Destinations Brighton (every 30min; 35min); Hastings (every 20–30min; 30min); Lewes (every 20–30min; 20–30min); London Victoria (Mon–Sat every 30min, Sun hourly; 1hr 35min).

By bus The bus station is on Cavendish Place right by the pier.

Destinations Brighton (every 20–30min; 1hr 15min); Hastings (Mon–Sat every 20min, Sun hourly; 1hr 10min); London Victoria (2 daily; 3–4hr).

Tourist office 3 Cornfield Rd, just off Terminus Rd (March–May & Oct Mon–Fri 9.15am–5.30pm, Sat 9.15am–4pm; June–Sept Mon–Fri 9.15am–5.30pm, Sat 9.15am–5pm; Nov–Feb Mon–Fri 9.15am–4.30pm, Sat 9.15am–1pm; Ⓣ 0871 663 0031, Ⓦ visiteastbourne.com).

ACCOMMODATION

★ **Belle Tout** Beachy Head Ⓣ 01323 423185, Ⓦ belletout.co.uk. For a real treat book into this fabulous lighthouse, perched high up on the dramatic cliffs just west of Beachy Head. The cosy rooms boast stupendous views, there's a snug residents' lounge and – best of all – there's unrestricted access to the lamproom at the top of the lighthouse, where you can sit and watch the sun go down. **£160**

The Guesthouse East 13 Hartington Place Ⓣ 01323 722774, Ⓦ heguesthouseeastbourne.co.uk. Boutique guesthouse just moments from the pier with six stylish self-catering suites, the larger ones great for families. Breakfasts are available for an extra charge (£5–9). **£84**

YHA hostel East Dean Rd Ⓣ 0845 371 9316, Ⓔ eastbourne@yha.org.uk. Modern hostel up on the South Downs, just a mile from the centre. Dorm **£16.40**, double **£43**

EATING AND DRINKING

Dolphin 14 South St ⓣ01323 746622, ⓦthedolphineastbourne.co.uk. One of the town's nicest pubs, this relaxed hangout has locally brewed beers on tap and serves good home-cooked food including burgers (£8.50). Mon–Fri 11am–11pm, Sat 11am–midnight, Sun noon–10.30pm.

Fusciardi's 30 Marine Parade ⓣ01323 722128. This fabulous ice-cream parlour is an Eastbourne institution, with piled-high sundaes that are a work of art. Light meals also available. No cards. Mon–Thurs 9am–8.30pm, Fri–Sun 9am–9pm.

2

Lewes and around

LEWES, the county town of East Sussex, straddles the River Ouse as it carves a gap through the South Downs on its final stretch to the sea. Though there's been some rebuilding, the core of Lewes remains remarkably good-looking: replete with crooked older dwellings, narrow lanes – or "twittens" – and Georgian houses. With numerous traces of its long history still visible, some of England's most appealing chalkland on its doorstep and the Bloomsbury Group's country home at **Charleston** close by, Lewes is a worthwhile stopover on any tour of the southeast – and an easy one, with good rail connections with London and along the coast.

Lewes Castle

169 High St • Tues–Sat 10am–5.30pm (or dusk in winter), Sun & Mon 11am–5.30pm (dusk in winter); closed Mon in Jan • £6.40, combined ticket with Anne of Cleves House £9.20 • ⓣ01273 486290, ⓦsussexpast.co.uk

Both **Lewes Castle** and St Pancras Priory (see opposite) were the work of William de Warenne, who was given the land by his father-in-law, William I, following the Norman Conquest. Inside the castle complex – unusual for being built on two mottes, or mounds – the shell of the eleventh-century keep remains, and both the towers can be climbed for excellent views over the town to the surrounding Downs. Tickets for the castle include admission to the **museum** (same hours as castle), by the castle entrance, where exhibits include archeological artefacts and a town model.

Southover

From the High Street, the steep, cobbled and much photographed **Keere Street** – down which the reckless Prince Regent is alleged to have driven his carriage – leads to

LEWES: THE BONFIRE SOCIETIES

Each November 5, while the rest of Britain lights small domestic bonfires or attends municipal firework displays to commemorate the 1605 foiling of a Catholic plot to blow up the Houses of Parliament, Lewes puts on a more dramatic show, whose origins lie in the deaths of the Lewes Martyrs, the seventeen Protestants burned here in 1556 at the height of Mary Tudor's militant revival of Catholicism. By the end of the eighteenth century, Lewes's **Bonfire Boys** had become notorious for the boisterousness of their anti-Catholic demonstrations, in which they set off fireworks indiscriminately and dragged rolling tar barrels through the streets – a tradition still practised today, although with a little more caution. In 1845 events came to a head when the incorrigible pyromaniacs of Lewes had to be read the Riot Act, instigating a night of violence between the police and Bonfire Boys. Lewes's first **bonfire societies** were established soon afterwards to instil some discipline into the proceedings, and in the early twentieth century they were persuaded to move their street fires to the town's perimeters.

Today's tightly knit bonfire societies spend much of the year organizing the Bonfire Night shenanigans, when their members dress up in traditional costumes and parade through the town carrying flaming torches, before marching off onto the Downs for their society's big fire. At each of the fires, effigies of Guy Fawkes and the pope are burned alongside contemporary, but equally reviled, figures – chancellors of the exchequer and prime ministers are popular choices.

Southover, the southern part of town. At the foot of Keere Street lies **Southover Grange** (daily dawn–dusk; free), built in 1572 from the remains of nearby St Pancras Priory, and once the childhood home of the diarist John Evelyn. Today the lovely gardens are a favourite picnic spot with Lewes locals.

Anne of Cleves House

52 Southover High St • March–Oct Tues–Sat 10am–5pm, Mon & Sun 11am–5pm • £4.40, combined ticket with the castle £9.20 • ⓣ 01273 474610, ⓦ sussexpast.org.uk

Though it was given to her in settlement after her divorce from Henry VIII, Anne never actually lived in the Tudor-built timber-framed **Anne of Cleves House**. The magnificent oak-beamed Tudor bedroom is impressive, with a 400-year-old Flemish four-poster and a cumbersome "bed wagon", a bed-warming brazier that would fail the slackest of fire regulations.

2

St Pancras Priory

Access via Cockshut Lane or Mountfield Road • Free • ⓦ lewespriory.org.uk

South of Southover High Street sprawl the evocative ruins of de Warenne's **St Pancras Priory**, recently reopened to the public. Interpretive boards help to form an impression of what the crumbling stones would have looked like in the priory's heyday, when it was one of Europe's principal Cluniac institutions, with a church the size of Westminster Abbey.

Cliffe

At the east end of the High Street, School Hill descends towards **Cliffe Bridge**, built in 1727 and entrance to the commercial centre of the medieval settlement. On the far side of the bridge rises the Victorian Gothic tower of **Harveys Brewery**, the oldest brewery in Sussex, dating back to 1790. A path leads up onto the Downs from the end of Cliffe High Street.

Charleston Farmhouse

Six miles east of Lewes, off the A27 • April–June, Sept & Oct Wed–Sat 1–6pm, Sun & bank holiday Mon 1–5.30pm; July & Aug Wed–Sat noon–6pm, Sun & bank holiday Mon noon–5.30pm; last entry 1hr before closing • £9, garden only £3 • Guided tours only Wed–Sat • ⓣ 01323 811265, ⓦ charlston.org.uk

Charleston Farmhouse was the country home and gathering place of the writers, intellectuals and artists known as the Bloomsbury Group. Virginia Woolf's sister Vanessa Bell, Vanessa's husband, Clive Bell, and her lover, Duncan Grant, moved here during World War I so that the men, both conscientious objectors, could work on local farms (farm labourers were exempted from military service). Almost every surface of the farmhouse interior is painted and the walls are hung with paintings by Picasso, Renoir and Augustus John, alongside the work of the markedly less talented residents.

ARRIVAL AND INFORMATION — LEWES

By train The train station lies south of High St down Station Rd.

Destinations Brighton (every 10–20min; 15min); Eastbourne (every 20–30min; 20–30min); London Victoria (Mon–Sat every 30min, Sun hourly; 1hr 10min).

By bus The bus station is on Eastgate St, near the foot of School Hill.

Destinations Brighton (Mon–Sat every 15min, Sun hourly; 30min); Tunbridge Wells (Mon–Sat every 30min, Sun hourly; 1hr 10min).

Tourist office At the junction of High St and Fisher St (April–Sept Mon–Fri 9am–5pm, Sat 9.30am–5.30pm, Sun 10am–2pm; Oct–March Mon–Fri 9am–5pm, Sat 10am–2pm; ⓣ 01273 483448, ⓦ lewes.gov.uk); they hold copies of the free monthly magazine *Viva Lewes* (ⓦ vivalewes .co.uk).

2

GLYNDEBOURNE

Founded in 1934, **Glyndebourne**, three miles east of Lewes, off the A27 (01273 813813, glyndebourne.com), is Britain's only unsubsidized opera house, and the Glyndebourne season (mid-May to Aug) an indispensable part of the high-society calendar. It's undeniably exclusive – and expensive – but the musical values are the highest in the country, using young talent rather than expensive star names, and taking the sort of risks Covent Garden wouldn't dream of. An award-winning theatre (seating 1200) has broadened this exclusive venue to a wider audience, and there are tickets available at reduced prices for dress rehearsals or for standing-room-only.

ACCOMMODATION

Castle Banks Cottage 4 Castle Banks 01273 476291, castlebankscottage.co.uk. Beamed period house with great views, tucked away off West Street just behind the castle. On warm summer mornings breakfast is served in the tiny flower-filled garden. No credit cards. **£75**

Monty's 4 Albion St 01273 474095, montysaccommodation.co.uk. Lovely self-contained basement flat with its own entrance and a stylish bedroom, lounge and shower room; nice little touches such as a DVD library and plenty of books and magazines add to the charm. **£100**

YHA hostel Telscombe village, 6 miles south of Lewes 0870 770 6062; bus #123 from Lewes. The nearest hostel to Lewes, offering simple accommodation in 200-year-old cottages. Dorm **£16.40**, double **£36**

EATING AND DRINKING

★ **Bills** 56 Cliffe High St 01273 476918, billsproducestore.co.uk. No visit to Lewes would be complete without a pit-stop at this always buzzing café-cum-produce store, whether for a leisurely weekend brunch or a fabulous flower-festooned cake. Mon–Wed 8am–6pm, Thurs–Sat 8am–10pm, Sun 9am–5pm.

Buttercup Café 15 Malling St, within Pastorale Antiques 01273 477664. Tucked away at the end of Cliffe High Street, this cosy, quirky café is something of a hidden gem, with plenty of outdoor seating in a tranquil sun-trap courtyard, and a simple daily-changing seasonal menu. The salad plates (£5.50) are amazing. Mon–Sat 9am–5pm, Sun 10.30am–4pm.

Lewes Arms Mount Place 01273 473252, lewesarms.co.uk. This characterful local is a good spot to sample a pint of Sussex Best, produced down the road at Harveys brewery. Good-value food is on offer too (burgers and sandwiches both £4.50). Mon–Thurs 11am–11pm, Fri & Sat 11am–midnight, Sun noon–11pm.

Pelham House St Andrew's Lane 01273 488600, pelhamhouse.com. The best place in town to treat yourself, this hotel restaurant is set in a beautiful sixteenth-century townhouse, with more tables outside on a lovely terrace with far-reaching views across to the South Downs. Mains might include lamb with carrot and vanilla puree, or mullet with herb blinis and fennel; two courses will set you back £17.95, three courses £22.95. Turn up early for cocktails at the stylish little bar. Mon–Sat noon–3pm & 6–9.30pm, Sun noon–3pm & 6–9pm.

Brighton

Recorded as the tiny fishing village of Brithelmeston in the Domesday Book, **BRIGHTON** seems to have slipped unnoticed through history until the mid-eighteenth century, when the new trend for sea-bathing established it as a resort. The fad received royal approval in the 1780s, after the decadent Prince of Wales (the future George IV) began patronizing the town in the company of his mistress, thus setting a precedent for the "dirty weekend". Trying to shake off this blowsy reputation, Brighton – which was granted city status in 2000 – now highlights its Georgian charm, its upmarket shops and classy restaurants, and its thriving conference industry. Despite these efforts, however, the essence of Brighton's appeal remains its faintly bohemian vitality, a buzz that comes from a mix of English holiday-makers, foreign-language students, a thriving gay community and an energetic local student population from the art college and two universities.

Any trip to Brighton inevitably begins with a visit to its two most famous landmarks – the exuberant **Royal Pavilion** and the wonderfully tacky **Brighton Pier**, a few minutes away – followed by a stroll along the seafront promenade or the pebbly beach. Just as interesting, though, is an exploration of Brighton's car-free **Lanes** – the maze of narrow

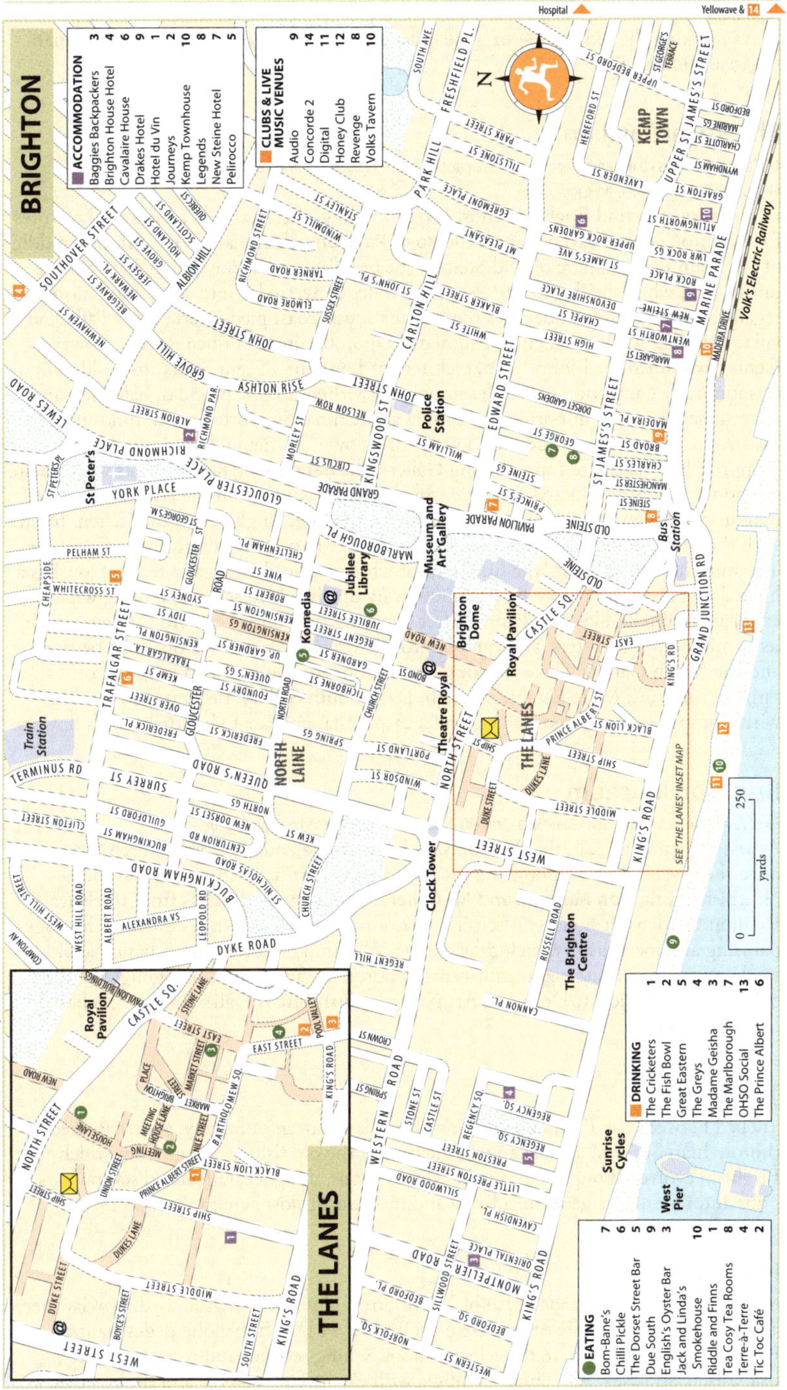
BRIGHTON
ACCOMMODATION
Baggies Backpackers 3
Brighton House Hotel 4
Cavalaire House 6
Drakes Hotel 9
Hotel du Vin 1
Journeys 2
Kemp Townhouse 10
Legends 8
New Steine Hotel 7
Pelirocco 5
CLUBS & LIVE MUSIC VENUES
Audio 9
Concorde 2 14
Digital 11
Honey Club 12
Revenge 8
Volks Tavern 10
EATING
Bom-Bane's 7
Chilli Pickle 6
The Dorset Street Bar 5
Due South 9
English's Oyster Bar 3
Jack and Linda's Smokehouse 10
Riddle and Finns 1
Tea Cosy Tea Rooms 8
Terre-à-Terre 4
Tic Toc Café 2
DRINKING
The Cricketers 1
The Fish Bowl 2
Great Eastern 5
The Greys 4
Madame Geisha 3
The Marlborough 7
OHSO Social 13
The Prince Albert 6
THE LANES
Hospital
Yellowave & 14
Duke of York's Picturehouse
Booth Museum of Natural History
Hove
KEMP TOWN
NORTH LAINE
THE LANES
Train Station
St Peter's
Police Station
Museum and Art Gallery
Jubilee Library
Komedia
Brighton Dome
Royal Pavilion
Theatre Royal
Clock Tower
The Brighton Centre
Bus Station
Sunrise Cycles
West Pier
Volk's Electric Railway
SEE 'THE LANES' INSET MAP
0 250 yards

alleys marking the old town – or a meander through the quaint, but more bohemian streets of **North Laine**.

The Royal Pavilion

4/5 Pavilion Buildings • Daily: April–Sept 9.30am–5.45pm; Oct–March 10am–5.15pm; last entry 45min before closing • £9.80 • Ⓣ 0300 290900, Ⓦ brighton-hove.rpml.org.uk

2

In any survey to find England's most loved building, there's always a bucketful of votes for Brighton's exotic extravaganza, the **Royal Pavilion**, which flaunts itself in the middle of the main thoroughfare of Old Steine. The building was a conventional farmhouse until 1787, when the fun-loving Prince of Wales converted it into something more regal, and for a couple of decades the prince's south-coast pied-à-terre was a Palladian villa, with mildly Oriental embellishments. Upon becoming Prince Regent, however, George commissioned John Nash, architect of London's Regent Street, to build an extraordinary confection of slender minarets, twirling domes, pagodas, balconies and miscellaneous motifs imported from India and China. Supported on an innovative cast-iron frame, the result defined a genre of its own – Oriental Gothic.

Approached via the restrained Long Gallery, the **Banqueting Room** erupts with ornate splendour and is dominated by a one-ton chandelier hung from the jaws of a massive dragon cowering in a plantain tree. Next door, the huge, high-ceilinged kitchen, fitted with the most modern appliances of its time, has iron columns disguised as palm trees. The stunning **Music Room**, the first sight of which reduced George to tears of joy, has a huge dome lined with more than 26,000 individually gilded scales and hung with exquisite umbrella-like glass lamps. After climbing the famous cast-iron staircase with its bamboo-look banisters, you can go into Victoria's sober and seldom-used bedroom and the North Gallery where the king's portrait hangs, along with a selection of satirical cartoons. More notable, though, is the **South Gallery**, decorated in sky-blue with trompe l'oeil bamboo trellises and a carpet that appears to be strewn with flowers.

Brighton Museum

Royal Pavilion Gardens • Tues–Sun 10am–5pm • Free • Ⓣ 0300 290900, Ⓦ brighton-hove.rpmp.org.uk

Across the gardens from the Pavilion stands the **Dome** entered from Church Street, once the royal stables and now the town's main concert hall. Adjoining it is the refurbished **Brighton Museum and Art Gallery**, entrance for which is from the Royal Pavilion Gardens. It houses an eclectic mix of modern fashion and design, archeology, painting and local history, including a large collection of pottery from basic Neolithic earthenware to delicate eighteenth-century porcelain figurines. The highlight of the collection of classic Art Deco and Art Nouveau furniture is Dalí's famous sofa based on Mae West's lips.

The Lanes

Tucked between the Pavilion and the seafront is a warren of narrow, pedestrianized thoroughfares known as **the Lanes** – the core of the old fishing village from which Brighton evolved. Long-established antiques shops, designer outlets and several bars, pubs and restaurants generate a lively and intimate atmosphere in this part of town.

North Laine

North Laine, which spreads north of North Street along Kensington, Sydney, Gardner and Bond streets, is more offbeat than the Lanes, with its hub along pedestrianized Kensington Gardens. Here the eclectic shops, selling secondhand records, clothes, bric-a-brac and New Age objects, mingle with earthy coffee shops and funky cafés.

The piers

Much of Brighton's **seafront** is an ugly mix of shops, entertainment complexes and hotels. To soak up the tackier side of Brighton, take a stroll along **Brighton Pier**, completed in 1899, its every inch devoted to cacophonous fun and money-making. Just east of the pier, the 165ft **Brighton Wheel** (daily 10am–11pm; £8; Ⓦbrightonwheel .com) offers panoramic views; it will remain in place until 2016. Half a mile west along the seafront, the **West Pier**, dating from 1866, has been virtually destroyed by storms and fires. A 600ft-tall viewing mast, the **i360** (Ⓦbrightoni360.co.uk) is scheduled to open at the seafront here in 2013.

2

Volks Railway

East of Brighton Pier • Easter to mid-Sept Mon–Fri 10.15am–5pm, Sat & Sun 10.15am–6pm • £2.80 return • Ⓦ volkselectricrailway.co.uk

Just east of Brighton Pier, the antiquated locomotives of **Volk's Electric Railway** – the first electric train in the country – run eastward towards the Marina and the nudist beach, usually the preserve of just a few thick-skinned souls.

Yellowave

299 Madeira Drive • May–Sept Mon–Fri 10am–10pm, Sat & Sun 10am–8pm; Oct–April Tues–Thurs 11am–9pm, Fri 11am–5pm, Sat & Sun 10am–5pm • Court hire £20/hr • Ⓣ 01273 672222, Ⓦ yellowave.co.uk

A fifteen-minute walk along Marine Parade from Brighton pier, or a quick hop on the Volks Railway – get off at the station at the halfway point – is the excellent **Yellowave Beach Sports Venue**, the perfect spot for a taster of beach volleyball on a sunny day, with six courts, plus a bouldering wall, a sandpit for youngsters and an excellent café.

Booth Museum of Natural History

194 Dyke Rd, 1 mile from the centre of town • Mon–Wed, Fri & Sat 10am–5pm, Sun 2–5pm • Free • Ⓣ 0300 290900, Ⓦ brighton-hove .rpml.org.uk • Bus #27, #27A or #27B from North St, Queen's Rd or Brighton station

In Brighton's northern suburbs, the **Booth Museum of Natural History** is worth seeking out – a wonderfully fusty old Victorian museum stuffed with beetles, butterflies and animal skeletons galore, as well as some imaginative temporary exhibitions.

ARRIVAL AND DEPARTURE — BRIGHTON

By train Brighton train station is at the head of Queen's Rd, which descends to the Clocktower and then becomes West St, eventually leading to the seafront, a 10min walk away.

Destinations Chichester (Mon–Sat every 30min, Sun hourly; 50min); Eastbourne (every 30min; 35min); Hastings (every 30min; 1hr–1hr 20min); Lewes (every 10–20min; 15min); London Bridge (Mon–Sat every 15min, Sun every 30min; 1hr); London Victoria (every 30min; 55min–1hr 20min); Portsmouth Harbour (Mon–Sat every 30min, Sun hourly; 1hr 30min).

By bus The long-distance bus station is just in from the seafront on the south side of the Old Steine.

Destinations Arundel (Mon–Sat every 30min, Sun 1 daily; 50min–2hr); Chichester (Mon–Sat every 30min, Sun hourly; 2hr 30min); Eastbourne (2–3 hourly; 1hr 15min); Lewes (Mon–Sat every 15min, Sun hourly; 25–30min); London Victoria (hourly; 2hr 20min); Portsmouth (Mon–Sat every 30min, Sun hourly; 3hr 30min); Tunbridge Wells (Mon–Sat every 30min, Sun hourly; 1hr 35min).

GETTING AROUND

Most of Brighton's sights are within easy walking distance of each other.

By bus Almost all local buses travel via the north side of the Old Steine. A one-day CitySaver ticket (£3.70) allows you unlimited travel on the city bus network.

By bike You can rent bikes at Sunrise Cycles, West Pier, King's Rd Arches (Ⓣ 01273 748881).

By taxi For a city taxi, call Ⓣ 01273 205205, Ⓣ 01273 204060 or Ⓣ 01273 747474.

2

INFORMATION

Tourist office Accessed through the Royal Pavilion shop at 4–5 Pavilion Buildings (daily 9.30am–5.15pm; 01273 290337, visitbrighton.com).

Internet There is free internet access at Jubilee Library just off North Rd.

ACCOMMODATION

Brighton's **accommodation** is pricey, with rates often rising substantially at weekends. The listings below quote weekday rates; unless otherwise stated, you should count on weekend rates being between £25 and £30 higher, and note that at weekends there's often a two-night-minimum stay. Some hotels and B&Bs may lower their rates out of season, but this is not the norm.

HOTELS AND B&BS

Brighton House Hotel 52 Regency Square 01273 323282, brighton-house.co.uk. Understated eco-friendly guesthouse with elegant, contemporary rooms and an all-organic breakfast buffet. Excellent value, and no increase at weekends. **£95**

Cavalaire House 34 Upper Rock Gardens 01273 696899, cavalaire.co.uk. Warm and welcoming B&B, with artwork from Brighton artists on the walls, fresh flowers in the cheery breakfast room, and a friendly resident dog. Rooms are clean and contemporary, though the cheapest double rooms lack the charm of the others. **£75**

Drakes Hotel 33–34 Marine Parade 01273 696934, drakesofbrighton.com. The unbeatable seafront location is the big draw at this chic, minimalist boutique hotel. All the luxuries you'd expect are here, and the most expensive rooms come with freestanding baths by floor-to-ceiling windows. The excellent in-house restaurant is one of Brighton's best. **£115**

Hotel du Vin Ship St 01273 718588, hotelduvin.com. A Gothic Revival building in a contemporary style, luxuriously furnished in subtle seaside colours, with an excellent bar and bistro. **£210**

Kemp Townhouse 21 Atlingworth St 01273 681400, kemptownhouse.com. Regency townhouse hotel with excellent service, chic rooms and great breakfasts. Sea-view rooms come with binoculars for gazing out to sea. **£95**

Legends 31–34 Marine Parade 01273 624462, legendsbrighton.com. Large, buzzing, gay hotel on the seafront, with a late bar for residents and their guests, and regular cabaret nights. Rates increase by around £10 at the weekend. **£75**

New Steine Hotel 10–11 New Steine 01273 681546, newsteinehotel.com. During the week, the stylish, modern rooms at this townhouse hotel are excellent value – rates increase by around £40 at the weekends. There's a small in-house bistro too, and exhibitions of local art. **£77.50**

Pelirocco 10 Regency Square 01273 327055, hotelpelirocco.co.uk. Self-styled rock'n'roll hangout with extravagantly themed rooms inspired by pop culture and pin-ups, a bohemian atmosphere and a late-opening bar. Rates increase by £15 at the weekends. **£90**

HOSTELS

Baggies Backpackers 33 Oriental Place 01273 733740, baggiesbackpackers.com. Spacious house a little west of the West Pier with private rooms and large bright dorms, decent showers and a relaxed, friendly vibe. No credit cards. Dorm **£13**, double **£40**

Journeys 33 Richmond Place 01273 695866, visitjourneys.com. Friendly, modern hostel in a great central location close to North Laine. Free wi-fi and breakfasts, and a small bar. Rates increase by around £10 at the weekend. **£14**

EATING

Brighton has the greatest concentration of **restaurants** in the southeast after London. Around North Laine are some great, inexpensive **cafés**, while for classier establishments head to the Lanes and out towards Hove.

CAFÉS

The Dorset Street Bar Corner of Gardner St and North Rd 01273 605423, thedorset.co.uk. Bar, café and restaurant rolled into one, this always-bustling place is a Brighton institution. Outside tables are great for people-watching, and the menu covers everything from moules (£9) to full English breakfasts. Daily 9am–late.

★ **Jack and Linda's Smokehouse** 197 Kings Arches. This tiny beachfront smokehouse is run by a lovely couple who've been traditionally smoking fish here for over a decade. Grab a fresh crab sandwich or hot mackerel roll (£2.80) to eat on the beach outside for a perfect summer lunch. Daily 9am–5pm, closed Jan & Feb.

Tea Cosy Tea Rooms 3 George St theteacosy.co.uk. Kitsch tearoom decked from head to foot in royal memorabilia. Cream teas are named after members of the royal family, and a strict code of etiquette forbids the dunking of biscuits in tea on pain of removal from the premises. Wed–Fri & Sun noon–5pm, Sat noon–6pm.

Tic Toc Café 53 Meeting House Lane 01273 770115, tictoc-cafe.co.uk. Quirky little café in the heart of the Lanes, decked out with vintage wallpaper, yellow leather banquettes, formica tables and fairy lights. Excellent coffee, tasty food and a few tables outside. Mon–Fri 8.30am–6.30pm, Sat 10am–6pm, Sun 10am–5pm.

RESTAURANTS

★ **Bom-Bane's** 24 George St ⓣ01273 606400, ⓦbom-banes.co.uk. Loveable café-restaurant run by two professional musicians. The decor is homely and decidedly eccentric – each of the individually designed tables holds a surprise in store – and the hearty Belgium-influenced food is delicious (stoemp and sausage £9.75). There are weekly live music (Tues) and film (Wed) nights, and a monthly musical night (£25), where dinner is interspersed with songs performed by the staff. Tues & Wed 5–11pm, Thurs–Sat 12.30–11.30pm.

Chilli Pickle 17 Jubilee St ⓣ01273 900383, ⓦthechillipickle.com. Stylish, buzzing restaurant in the North Laine serving sophisticated, authentic Indian food – everything from masala dosas to Tandoori sea bass (£14.50). At lunchtimes they offer a range of thalis as well as small portions of "street food" for sharing (each £3.50–7). Daily noon–3pm & 6–10.30pm.

Due South 139 Kings Rd Arches ⓣ01273 821218, ⓦduesouth.co.uk. Laidback seafront restaurant right on the beach, with an emphasis on locally sourced, sustainable produce. Tables outside make the most of the sea views. Daily noon–3.30pm & 6–9.45pm.

English's Oyster Bar 29–31 East St ⓣ01273 327980, ⓦenglishs.co.uk. Three fishermen's cottages knocked together to house a marble-and-brass oyster bar and a red velvet dining room. Seafood's the speciality, and better value than you might expect, especially the set menus (2 courses £15). Daily noon–10pm.

Riddle and Finns 12b Meeting House Lane ⓣ01273 328008, ⓦriddleandfinns.co.uk. Friendly, bustling champagne and oyster bar where you can tuck into a huge range of shellfish and fish (mains £13–18) at communal marble-topped tables in a white-tiled, candlelit dining room. It's very popular, and they don't take bookings, so expect to wait at busy times. Mon–Thurs & Sun noon–10pm, Fri & Sat noon–11pm, plus Sat & Sun 9–11.30am.

★ **Terre-à-Terre** 71 East St ⓣ01273 729051, ⓦterreaterre.co.uk. Fabulous, inventive global veggie cuisine (mains around £13) in a modern arty setting. The taster plate for two (£20) is a good place to start if you're befuddled by the weird and wonderful creations on offer. Mon–Fri noon–10.30pm, Sat noon–11pm, Sun noon–10pm.

2

DRINKING

The Cricketers 15 Black Lion St ⓣ01273 329472, ⓦgoldenliongroup.co.uk. Brighton's oldest pub, immortalized by Graham Greene in *Brighton Rock*, has a traditional feel, with good daytime pub grub, real ales and a cosy courtyard bar. Mon, Wed & Sun 11am–11pm, Tues & Thurs 11am–midnight, Fri & Sat 11am–1am.

The Fish Bowl 74 East St ⓣ01273 777505. Popular pre-club choice for its range of music; DJs five nights a week and free entry. Also a relaxing spot during the day, with a local, organic menu. Mon–Wed & Sun noon–2am, Fri & Sat noon–3am.

Great Eastern 74 East St ⓣ01273 685681. Small, mellow pub with bare boards and bookshelves, lots of real ale and malt whiskies, and no fruit machines or TV. Daily noon–late.

The Greys 105 Southover High St ⓣ01273 680734, ⓦgreyspub.com. Friendly pub with an open fire and a great menu. Frequent live music and Belgian beer nights. Mon–Wed 4–11pm, Thurs 4–11.30pm, Fri 4pm–12.30am, Sat noon–12.30am, Sun noon–11pm.

Madame Geisha 75 East St ⓣ01273 770847, ⓦmadamegeisha.com. Lavishly decked-out bar, restaurant and lounge with karaoke booths, exotic cocktails and Asian tapas. Mon–Wed 9pm–3am, Thurs 10pm–3am, Fri & Sat 6pm–3am.

The Marlborough 4 Princes St ⓣ01273 570028, ⓦdrinkinbrighton.co.uk/marlborough. Friendly pub, just off Old Steine, popular with Brighton's gay and lesbian communities. The small theatre upstairs hosts readings and other performances. Daily noon–late.

OHSO Social 250a Kings Road Arches ⓣ01273 746067, ⓦohsosocial.co.uk. Get the full Brighton experience on the terrace of this late-night beachfront bar, with great cocktails and uninterrupted views of Brighton pier. Mon–Thurs & Sun 10am–midnight, Fri & Sat 10am–2am.

The Prince Albert 48 Trafalgar St ⓣ01273 730499. By the train station, this place is often crowded with students drawn to the real ales and big-screen football. Also one of the best venues for gigs and live music in Brighton. Mon–Thurs & Sun noon–midnight, Fri & Sat noon–12.30am.

NIGHTLIFE AND ENTERTAINMENT

As well as its mainstream **theatre** and **concert** venues, Brighton has myriad **clubs**, lots of **live music** and plenty of **cinemas**. It also boasts one of Britain's longest-established and most thriving **gay communities**, with a variety of lively clubs and bars, and a number of gay events including the annual fortnight-long **Gay Pride Festival** at the beginning of July – check out ⓦgay.brighton.co.uk. In May, the three-week-long **Brighton Festival** (ⓣ01273 709709, ⓦbrightonfestival.org) includes funfairs, exhibitions, street theatre and concerts from classical to jazz.

For up-to-date details of **what's on**, there's an array of free listings magazines available from the tourist office, or check out the websites ⓦbrighton.co.uk, ⓦwhatson.brighton.co.uk and ⓦmagazine.brighton.co.uk.

2

CLUBS AND LIVE MUSIC VENUES

Audio 10 Marine Parade ⓣ01273 606906, ⓦaudiobrighton.com. Trendy hangout that boasts a terrace with sea views and a large bar on the first floor. The basement club is always packed, playing everything from indie to funky house and drum'n'bass. Bar: Mon–Thurs 4pm–midnight, Fri & Sat 2pm–3am. Club: Wed–Sat 11pm–4/4.30am.

Concorde 2 Madeira Shelter, Madeira Drive ⓣ01273 673311, ⓦconcorde2.co.uk. A Victorian tearoom in a former life, Brighton's trendiest live music venue has featured everyone from The White Stripes to Jarvis Cocker; it also hosts weekend club nights (11pm–4am) and the popular Silent Disco.

Digital 187–193 King's Rd Arches ⓣ01273 227767, ⓦyourfutureisdigital.com. Stylish venue where DJs spin a range of sounds from breaks to rock/indie, and there are regular live bands. You'll get laser shows and a great sound system. Tues & Wed 11pm–3.30am, Fri & Sat 10.30/11pm–4am.

Honey Club 214 King's Rd Arches ⓣ01273 202807, ⓦthehoneyclub.co.uk. One of Brighton's most popular beachfront venues, attracting a stylish crowd. Expect funky house, R&B, hip-hop and big-name DJs. Thurs–Sun around 11pm–3/4am.

Revenge 32 Old Steine ⓣ01273 606064, ⓦrevenge.co.uk. The south's largest gay club, with cheesy pop, upfront dance and retro boogie on two floors. Tues 10.30pm–3am, Thurs & Fri 10.30pm–5am, Sat 10.30pm–6am.

Volks Tavern 3 The Colonnade, Madeira Drive ⓣ01273 682828, ⓦvolksclub.co.uk. Under the arches on Marine Parade you'll find two rooms hosting live bands, reggae revival nights, hip-hop and breakbeats, attracting an eclectic crowd. Daily 10.30am–7pm & 11pm–early morning (9am at weekends).

ARTS CENTRES, THEATRES AND CINEMAS

Brighton Dome 29 New Rd ⓣ01273 709709, ⓦbrightondome.org. Home to three venues – Pavilion Theatre, Concert Hall and Corn Exchange – offering mainstream theatre, concerts, dance and performance.

Duke of Yorks Picturehouse Preston Circus ⓣ0871 7042056, ⓦpicturehouses.co.uk. Grade II-listed cinema with a licensed bar showing art-house, independent and classic films.

Komedia Gardner St, North Laine ⓣ01273 647100, ⓦkomedia.co.uk. Popular and highly regarded theatre-café showing stand-up comedy, live music and caberet.

Theatre Royal New Rd ⓣ01273 764400, ⓦambassadortickets.com/theatreroyal. One of the oldest working theatres in the country, offering predominantly mainstream plays, opera and musicals.

Arundel and around

The hilltop town of **ARUNDEL**, eighteen miles west of Brighton, has for seven centuries been the seat of the dukes of Norfolk, whose fine **castle** looks over the valley of the River Arun. The medieval town's well-preserved appearance and picturesque setting draws in the crowds on summer weekends, but at any other time a visit reveals one of West Sussex's least spoilt old towns. The two main attractions are the castle and the towering Gothic **cathedral**, but the rest of Arundel is pleasant to wander round – especially the antique-shop-lined Maltravers and Arun streets. North of Arundel lie a couple more attractions: **Bignor Roman Villa**, with some outstanding Roman mosaics; and the grand, seventeenth-century **Petworth House**, which has a notable art collection.

In the last week in August, Arundel's **festival** (ⓦarundelfestival.co.uk) features everything from open-air theatre to salsa bands.

Arundel Castle

Mill Rd • April–Oct Tues–Sun noon–5pm • Castle, keep, grounds & chapel £16; keep, grounds & chapel only £9 • ⓣ01903 882173, ⓦarundelcastle.org

Despite its medieval appearance, most of what you see of **Arundel Castle** is little more than a century old, the result of a lavish reconstruction from 1718 onwards, following the original Norman structure that was destroyed during the Civil War. From the top of the keep, you can see the current duke's spacious residence and the pristine castle grounds. Inside the castle, the renovated quarters include the impressive **Barons Hall** and the **library**, which has paintings by Gainsborough, Holbein and Van Dyck. On the edge of the castle grounds, the fourteenth-century **Fitzalan Chapel** houses tombs of past dukes of Norfolk including twin effigies of the seventh duke – one as he looked when he died and, underneath, one of his emaciated corpse. In the castle grounds, a new formal garden, the **Collector Earl's Garden**, is a playfully theatrical take on a Jacobean garden, with exotic planting, and pavilions, obelisks and urns made from green oak rather than stone.

Arundel Cathedral

Corner Parson's Hill and London Rd • Daily 9am–6pm or dusk • Free • ⓣ 01903 882297, ⓦ arundelcathedral.org

The flamboyant **Arundel Cathedral** was constructed in the 1870s by the fifteenth duke of Norfolk over the town's former Catholic church; its spire was designed by John Hansom, inventor of the hansom cab, the earliest taxi. Inside are the enshrined remains of St Philip Howard, the fourth duke's canonized son, who was sentenced to death in 1585 when he was caught fleeing overseas after praying for Catholic Spanish victory against the Protestant English.

Bignor Roman Villa

Bignor, 6 miles north of Arundel • Daily: March–May, Sept & Oct 10am–5pm; June–Aug 10am–6pm • £6 • ⓣ 01798 869259, ⓦ bigorromanvilla.co.uk

The excavated second-century ruins of the **Bignor Roman Villa**, just six miles north of town, have some of the best Roman mosaics in the country – the one showing Ganymede being carried by an eagle from Mount Ida is the most outstanding. The site is superbly situated at the base of the South Downs and features the longest extant section of mosaic in England, as well as the remains of a hypocaust, the underfloor heating system developed by the Romans.

Petworth House

Eleven miles north of Arundel • **House** mid-March to Oct Mon–Wed, Sat & Sun 11am–5pm **Park** Daily 8am–dusk • NT • £10.40, park free • ⓣ 01798 343929 • Train to Pulborough station, then Stagecoach Coastline #1 bus (Mon–Sat hourly, Sun every 2hr)

Petworth House, adjoining the pretty little village of **PETWORTH**, is one of the southeast's most impressive stately homes. Built in the late seventeenth century, the house contains an outstanding art collection, with paintings by Van Dyck, Titian, Gainsborough, Bosch, Reynolds, Blake and Turner – the last a frequent guest here. The extensive **Servants' Quarters**, connected by a tunnel to the main house, contain an impressive series of kitchens bearing the latest technological kitchenware of the 1870s, while the 700-acre grounds were landscaped by Capability Brown and are considered one of his finest achievements.

ARRIVAL AND INFORMATION — ARUNDEL

By train Arundel's train station is half a mile south of the town centre over the river on the A27.

Destinations Chichester (Mon–Sat every 30min, Sun hourly; 20min); London Victoria (Mon–Sat every 30min, Sun hourly; 1hr 30min); Portsmouth Harbour (every 30min; 55min); Pulborough (Mon–Sat every 30min, Sun hourly; 10min).

By bus Buses pull in either on High Street or River Road.

Destinations Brighton (Mon–Sat every 30min, 1 on Sun; 50min–2hr 10min); Chichester (Mon–Sat hourly, 1 on Sun; 35min).

Useful website ⓦ arundel.org.uk.

ACCOMMODATION

Amberley Castle Amberley, 4 miles north of Arundel ⓣ 01798 831992, ⓦ amberleycastle.co.uk. For a real splurge, indulge in an overnight stay at this 600-year-old castle, complete with portcullis, 60ft curtain walls, gardens, lakes, croquet lawn and nineteen luxurious bedrooms, many with four-poster beds. **£230**

Arundel House 11 High St ⓣ 01903 882136, ⓦ arundelhouseonline.com. Stylish boutique hotel in a nineteenth-century merchant's house in a prime location opposite the castle, with a great restaurant downstairs (see p.172). Excellent value. **£75**

Arundel YHA Warningcamp ⓣ0845 371 9002, ⓔarundel@yha.org.uk. Elegant Georgian mansion with a lovely garden, just over a mile northeast of Arundel and connected to town by a riverside path. Dorm **£16.40**, double **£43**

Billycan Camping Manor Farm ⓣ01903 882103, ⓦbillycancamping.co.uk. Luxurious campsite, a 15min walk from town, where pre-pitched bell tents come decked out with bunting and fresh flowers, and campers are welcomed with a communal stew around the campsite on a Friday night. Two-night minimum stay including breakfast hamper. **£195**

EATING AND DRINKING

2

Arundel House 11 High St ⓣ01903 882136, ⓦarundelhouseonline.com. Excellent hotel restaurant with a locally sourced, seasonally changing menu; mains might include confit belly of Sussex pork, or roast loin of venison. Two-course set-price menus cost £18 for lunch, £24 for dinner. Tues–Sat 12.30–2pm & 7–9pm.

The Bay Tree 21 Tarrant St ⓣ01903 883679, ⓦthebaytreearundel.co.uk. Cosy and relaxed little restaurant squeezed into three low-beamed rooms, with a small terrace out the back. Mains such as pheasant breast wrapped in bacon cost £14–18 at dinner; lunch features simpler dishes. Mon–Fri 11.30am–2.45pm & 6.45–9.15pm, Sat 10.30am–4pm & 6.45–9.30pm, Sun 10.30am–4pm & 6.45–9.15pm.

Black Rabbit Mill Rd, Offham ⓣ01903 882828, ⓦtheblackrabbitarundel.co.uk. A pleasant 30min walk from town will bring you to this lovely spot, overlooking the river, castle and surrounding wetlands. The pub grub is nothing special, but the idyllic setting still makes it well worth a visit, if only for a drink. Mon–Sat 11am–11pm, Sun 11am–10.30pm.

Chichester and around

The handsome market town of **CHICHESTER** has plenty to recommend it: a splendid twelfth-century **cathedral**, a thriving cultural scene and one of the finest collections of modern British art in the country on show at the **Pallant House Gallery**. The town began life as a Roman settlement, and its Roman cruciform street plan is still evident in the four-quadrant symmetry of the town centre. The main streets lead off from the Gothic **Market Cross**, a bulky octagonal rotunda topped by ornate finials and a crown lantern spire, built in 1501 to provide shelter for the market traders. The big attraction outside Chichester is **Fishbourne Roman Palace**, the largest excavated Roman site in Britain.

Chichester Cathedral

West St • Daily: June–Oct 7.15am–7pm; Nov–May 7.15am–6pm • Free • ⓣ01243 782595, ⓦchichestercathedral.org.uk

Chichester's chief attraction is its fine Gothic **Cathedral**. Building began in the 1070s, but the church was extensively rebuilt following a fire a century later and has been only minimally modified since about 1300, except for the slender spire and the unique, freestanding fifteenth-century bell tower. The **interior** is renowned for its contemporary devotional art, which includes a stained-glass window by Marc Chagall; there's also a sixteenth-century painting in the north transept of the past bishops of Chichester, and the fourteenth-century Fitzalan tomb that inspired Philip Larkin to write *An Arundel Tomb*. However, the highlight is a pair of reliefs in the south aisle, close to the tapestry – created around 1140, they show the raising of Lazarus and Christ at the gate of Bethany. Originally highly coloured, with semiprecious stones set in the figures' eyes, the reliefs are among the finest Romanesque stone carvings in England.

Pallant House Gallery

9 North Pallant • Tues, Wed, Fri & Sat 10am–5pm, Thurs 10am–8pm, Sun 11am–5pm • £7.50 • ⓣ01243 774557, ⓦpallant.org.uk

Off South Street, in the well-preserved Georgian quadrant of the city known as the Pallants, you'll find **Pallant House Gallery**, a superlative collection of twentieth-century British art – the best in the country – housed in a Queen Anne townhouse and award-winning contemporary extension. Artists on display from the permanent collection include Henry Moore, Lucian Freud, Walter Sickert, Barbara Hepworth and Peter Blake, and there are also excellent temporary exhibitions.

Fishbourne Roman Palace

Salthill Rd, Fishbourne, 2 miles west of Chichester • March–Oct daily 10am–5pm; Nov to mid-Dec & Feb daily 10am–4pm • £7.90 • T 01243 789829, W sussexpast.co.uk • Train from Chichester to Fishbourne Station

Fishbourne is the largest and best-preserved Roman palace in the country. Roman relics have long been turning up hereabouts, and in 1960 a workman unearthed their source – the site of a depot used by the invading Romans in 43 AD, which is thought later to have become the vast, hundred-room palace of a Romanized Celtic aristocrat. The north wing of the remains displays floor mosaics depicting Fishbourne's famous dolphin-riding cupid as well as the more usual geometric patterns. An audiovisual programme portrays the palace as it would have been in Roman times, and the extensive gardens attempt to re-create the palace grounds.

2

ARRIVAL AND INFORMATION — CHICHESTER

By train Chichester's train station lies on Stockbridge Rd; it's a 10min walk north to the Market Cross.

Destinations Arundel (Mon–Sat every 30min, Sun hourly; 20min); London Victoria (Mon–Sat every 30min, Sun hourly; 1hr 35min); Portsmouth Harbour (Mon–Sat every 30min, Sun hourly; 30–50min).

By bus The bus station is across the road from the train station at South St. It's a 10min walk north to the Market Cross.

Destinations Arundel (Mon–Sat hourly, Sun 1 daily; 35min); Brighton (Mon–Sat every 30min, Sun hourly; 2hr 30min); Portsmouth (hourly; 55min).

Tourist office 29a South St (April–Oct Mon 10.15am–5.15pm, Tues–Sat 9.15am–5.15pm, Sun 10.30am–3pm; Nov–March closed Sun; T 01243 775888, W visitchichester.org).

ACCOMMODATION

Richmond House 230 Oving Rd T 01243 771464, W richmondhousechichester.co.uk. Lovely boutique B&B, just a 20min walk from the centre, with three stylish rooms and fabulous breakfasts featuring home-baked bread and muffins. **£80**

Ship Hotel North St T 01243 778000, W theshiphotel.net. Handsome Grade II-listed Georgian townhouse with a grand sweeping staircase, contemporary rooms and a great location right in the centre of Chichester. There's a good in-house bistro and bar, too. **£110**

EATING AND DRINKING

Field and Fork Pallant House Gallery, 9 North Pallant T 01243 770827, W fieldandfork.co.uk. Small but perfectly formed café-restaurant serving up imaginative, locally sourced food, with fruit and veg supplied from their own glasshouse. Mains such as roast suckling pig or roasted pollock with chorizo and grilled squid cost £13–17, and delicious afternoon teas are on offer too (3–5pm). Tues, Wed & Sun 11.30am–5pm, Thurs–Sat 11.30am–5pm & 6–10pm.

Royal Oak East Lavant, 3 miles from Chichester T 01243 427434, W royaloakeastlavant.co.uk. Two-hundred-year-old coaching inn in a pretty village just outside Chichester, with great food (mains £15 and up) and a lovely terrace for alfresco dining. Mon–Fri noon–2pm & 6–9pm, Sat noon–2.30pm & 6–9.30pm, Sun noon–3pm & 6.30–9pm.

Swallow Bakery 81 North St T 01243 533008, W swallowbakery.com. Candy-coloured bakery-cum-café, popular for its fabulous cupcake creations, baked on site daily. Mon–Sat 9am–5.30pm, Sun 10am–5pm.

ENTERTAINMENT

Chichester is one of southern England's major cultural centres, well known for its **Festival Theatre** in Oaklands Park (T 01243 781312, W cft.org.uk), with a season running roughly between Easter and October. **Chichester Festivities** (T 01243 528356, W chifest.org.uk), taking place at a range of venues over two weeks in late June and early July, features music from blues to classical, plus talks and other events.

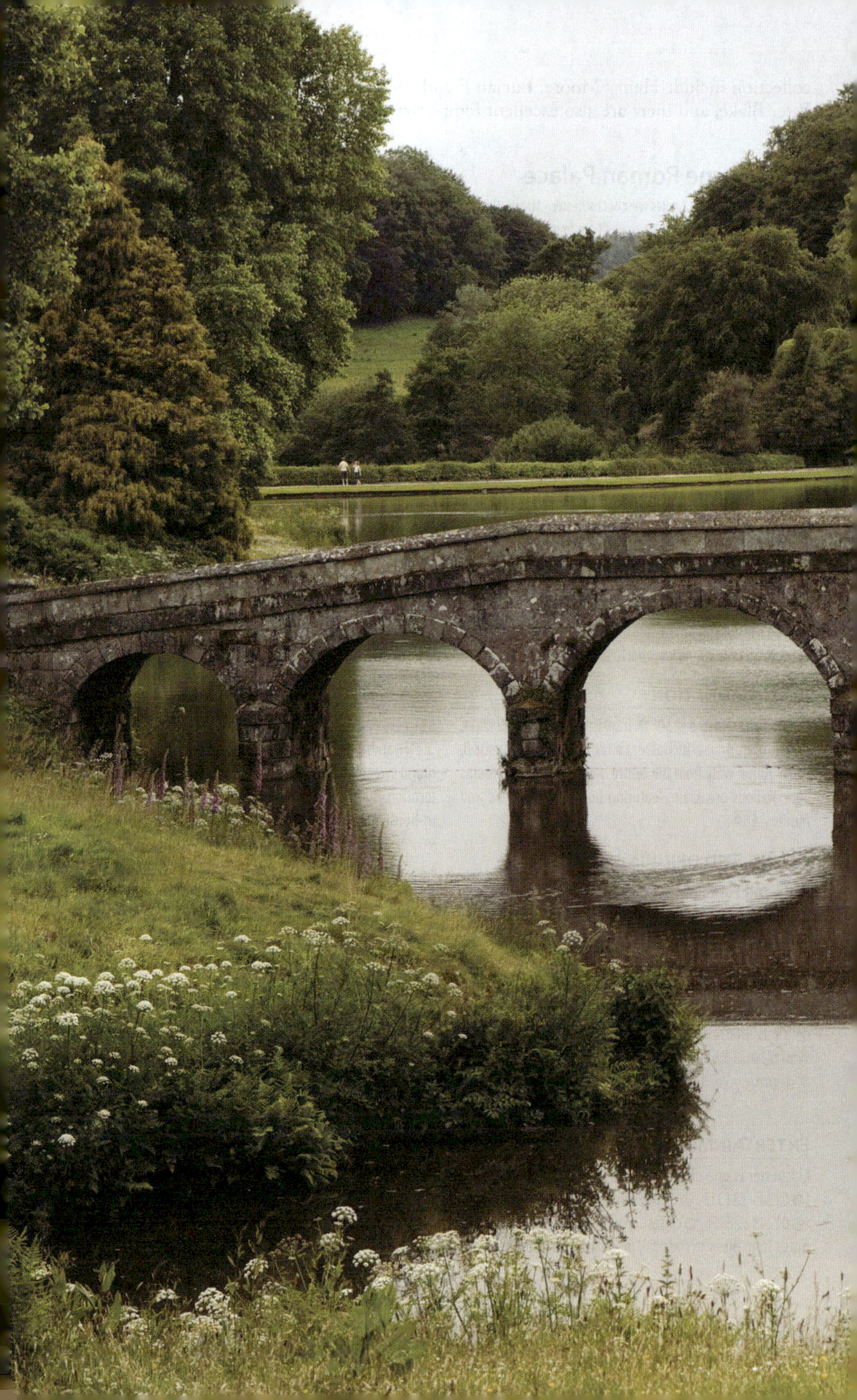

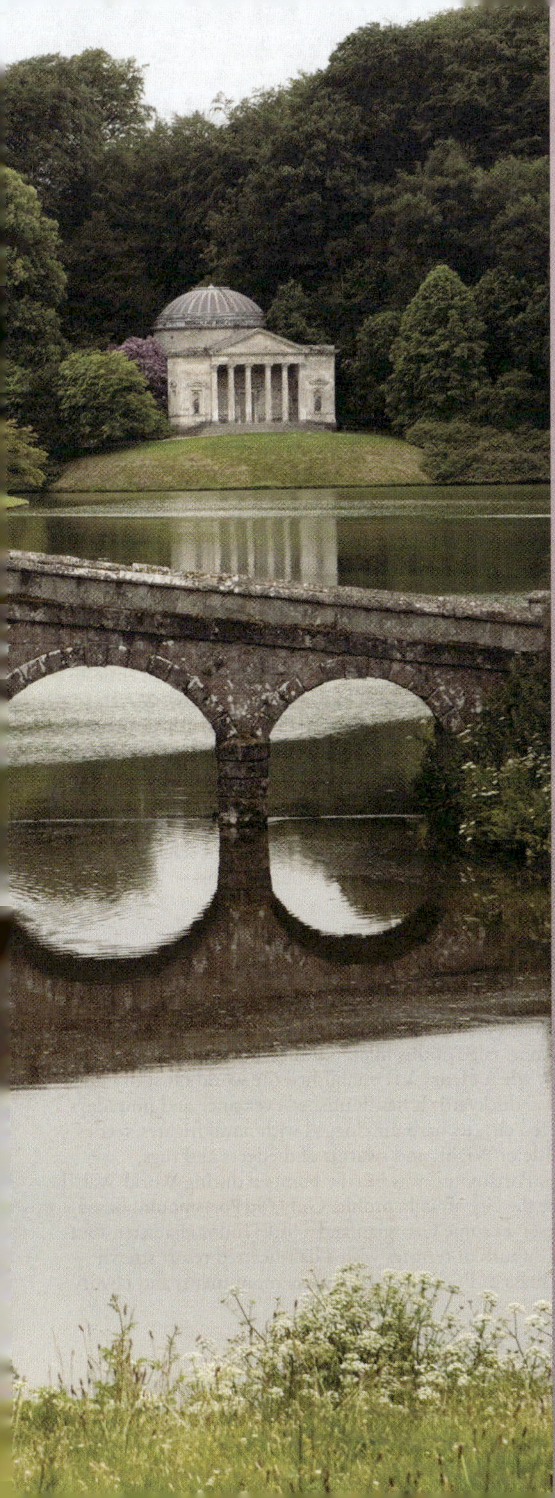

Hampshire, Dorset and Wiltshire

176 Portsmouth

183 Southampton

184 The Isle of Wight

189 Winchester

193 The New Forest

196 Bournemouth and around

201 The Isle of Purbeck

204 Dorchester and around

206 Sherborne

207 Shaftesbury

208 Weymouth and around

210 Bridport

210 Lyme Regis

212 Salisbury

214 Around Salisbury

216 Avebury and around

217 Stourhead and around

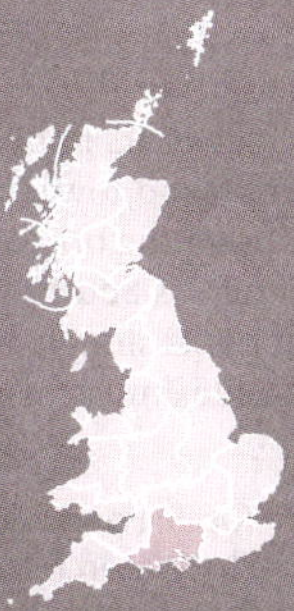

STOURHEAD, WILTSHIRE

Hampshire, Dorset and Wiltshire

The distant past is perhaps more tangible in Hampshire (often abbreviated to "Hants"), Dorset and Wiltshire than in any other part of England. Predominantly rural, these three counties overlap substantially with the ancient kingdom of Wessex, whose most famous ruler, Alfred, repulsed the Danes in the ninth century and came close to establishing the first unified state in England. And even before Wessex came into being, many earlier civilizations had left their stamp on the region. The chalky uplands of Wiltshire boast several of Europe's greatest Neolithic sites, including Stonehenge and Avebury, while in Dorset you'll find Maiden Castle, the most striking Iron Age hill fort in the country, and the Cerne Abbas Giant, source of many a legend.

The Romans tramped all over these southern counties, leaving the most conspicuous signs of their occupation at the amphitheatre of **Dorchester** – though that town is more closely associated with the novels of Thomas Hardy and his distinctively gloomy vision of Wessex. None of the landscapes of this region could be described as grand or wild, but the countryside is consistently seductive, not least the crumbling fossil-bearing cliffs around **Lyme Regis**, the managed woodlands of the **New Forest** and the gentle, open curves of **Salisbury Plain**. Its towns are also generally modest and slow-paced, with the notable exceptions of the two great maritime bases of **Portsmouth** and **Southampton**, a fair proportion of whose visitors are simply passing through on their way to the more genteel pleasures of the **Isle of Wight**. The two great cathedral cities in these parts, **Salisbury** and **Winchester**, and the seaside resort of **Bournemouth** see most tourist traffic, and the great houses of **Wilton**, **Stourhead**, **Longleat** and **Kingston Lacy** also attract the crowds; but you don't have to wander far off the beaten track to encounter medieval churches, manor houses and unspoilt country inns.

Portsmouth

Britain's foremost naval station, **PORTSMOUTH** occupies the bulbous peninsula of Portsea Island, on the eastern flank of a huge, easily defended harbour. The ancient Romans raised a fortress on the northernmost edge of this inlet, but this strategic location wasn't fully exploited until Tudor times, when Henry VII established the world's first dry dock here and made Portsmouth a royal dockyard. It has flourished ever since and nowadays Portsmouth is a large industrialized city, its harbour clogged with naval frigates, ferries bound for the continent or the Isle of Wight, and swarms of dredgers and tugs.

Due to its military importance, Portsmouth was heavily bombed during World War II, and bland tower blocks now give the city an ugly profile. Only **Old Portsmouth**, based around the original harbour, preserves some Georgian and a little Tudor character. East of here is **Southsea**, a residential suburb of terraces with a half-hearted resort strewn along its shingle beach, where a mass of B&Bs face stoic naval monuments and tawdry seaside amusements.

Top 5: Food with a view p.184
The Watercress Line p.191
Jane Austen in Chawton p.192
Chesil Beach p.209
Lyme's Jurassic coast p.211
Stonehenge: the site p.215

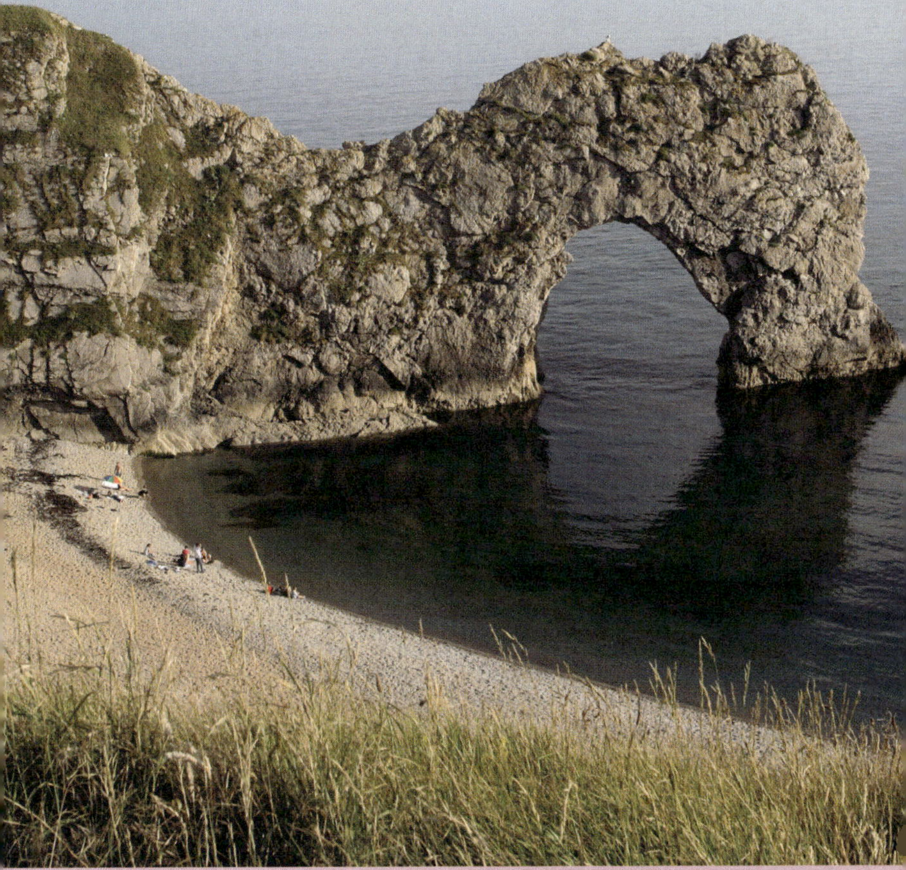

DURDLE DOOR, DORSET

Highlights

❶ **Osborne House** Wander around the stunning gardens and get an insight into royal family life at Queen Victoria's former seaside home. **See p.188**

❷ **The New Forest** William the Conqueror's old hunting ground, home to wild ponies and deer, is ideal for walking, biking and riding. **See pp.193–196**

❸ **Sea kayaking in Studland** View the rugged Old Harry Rocks up close on a guided kayak tour through sea arches and below towering chalk cliffs. **See p.203**

❹ **Durdle Door** Iconic natural arch at the end of a splendid beach, accessed by a steep cliff path – a great place for walkers and swimmers alike. **See p.204**

❺ **Hive Beach Café, Burton Bradstock** Sit right on the beach and sample some of Dorset's freshest local seafood, washed down with an ice-cold glass of wine. **See p.210**

❻ **Avebury** This crude stone circle has a more powerful appeal than nearby Stonehenge, not least for its great size and easy accessibility, in a peaceful village setting. **See p.216**

HIGHLIGHTS ARE MARKED ON THE MAP ON P.178

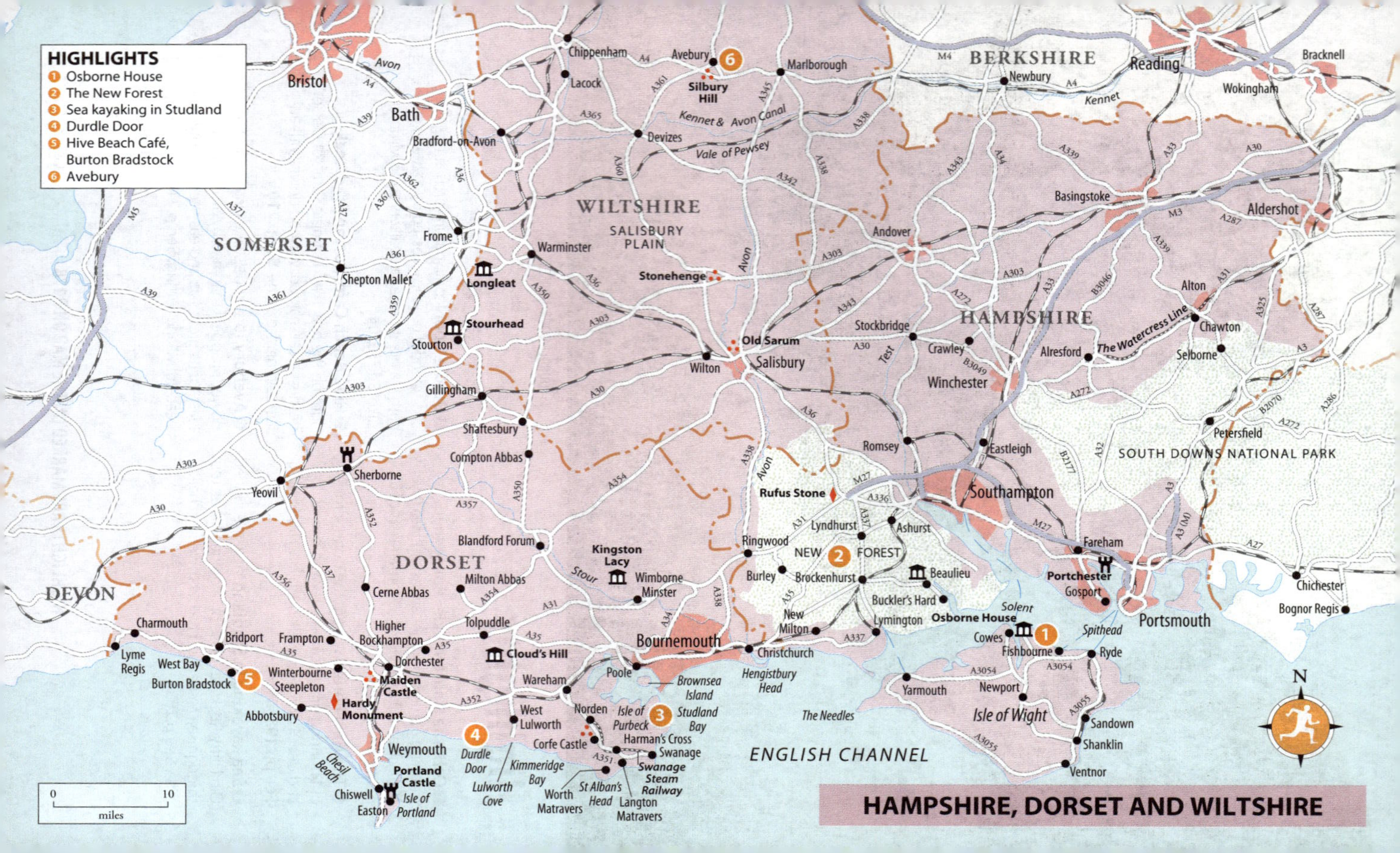

HAMPSHIRE, DORSET AND WILTSHIRE
HIGHLIGHTS
1 Osborne House
2 The New Forest
3 Sea kayaking in Studland
4 Durdle Door
5 Hive Beach Café, Burton Bradstock
6 Avebury
BERKSHIRE
WILTSHIRE
SALISBURY PLAIN
HAMPSHIRE
SOMERSET
DORSET
DEVON
SOUTH DOWNS NATIONAL PARK
NEW FOREST
ENGLISH CHANNEL
Isle of Wight
Isle of Purbeck
Isle of Portland
Bristol
Bath
Bradford-on-Avon
Chippenham
Lacock
Avebury
Silbury Hill
Marlborough
Newbury
Reading
Wokingham
Bracknell
Devizes
Kennet & Avon Canal
Vale of Pewsey
Frome
Warminster
Shepton Mallet
Longleat
Stourhead
Stourton
Stonehenge
Old Sarum
Salisbury
Wilton
Andover
Basingstoke
Aldershot
Alton
Chawton
Selborne
The Watercress Line
Alresford
Stockbridge
Crawley
Winchester
Petersfield
Romsey
Eastleigh
Southampton
Rufus Stone
Lyndhurst
Ashurst
Ringwood
Burley
Brockenhurst
Beaulieu
Buckler's Hard
Lymington
New Milton
Christchurch
Hengistbury Head
Fareham
Portchester
Gosport
Portsmouth
Chichester
Bognor Regis
Solent
Spithead
Osborne House
Cowes
Fishbourne
Ryde
Yarmouth
Newport
Sandown
Shanklin
Ventnor
The Needles
Gillingham
Shaftesbury
Compton Abbas
Sherborne
Yeovil
Blandford Forum
Kingston Lacy
Wimborne Minster
Stour
Milton Abbas
Cerne Abbas
Tolpuddle
Cloud's Hill
Bournemouth
Poole
Brownsea Island
Studland Bay
Wareham
Norden
Corfe Castle
Harman's Cross
Swanage
Swanage Steam Railway
St Alban's Head
Langton Matravers
Worth Matravers
Kimmeridge Bay
West Lulworth
Lulworth Cove
Durdle Door
Higher Bockhampton
Dorchester
Maiden Castle
Frampton
Hardy Monument
Winterbourne Steepleton
Weymouth
Portland Castle
Chiswell
Easton
Chesil Beach
Abbotsbury
Burton Bradstock
West Bay
Bridport
Charmouth
Lyme Regis
0 10 miles

Portsmouth Historic Dockyard

Queen St • Daily: April–Oct 10am–6pm; Nov–March 10am–5.30pm; last entry 90min before closing • All-inclusive ticket £19.90, valid for a year for one visit to HMS *Victory* and the Mary Rose Museum plus a harbour tour, as well as unlimited visits to the other attractions • ⓦ historicdockyard.co.uk

For most visitors, a trip to Portsmouth begins and ends at the **Historic Dockyard**, in the **Royal Naval Base** at the end of Queen Street. The complex comprises three ships and several museums, with the main attractions being HMS *Victory*, HMS *Warrior*, the National Museum of the Royal Navy, the Mary Rose Museum, and a boat tour around the harbour. In addition, the Dockyard Apprentice exhibition gives insights into the working of the docks in the early twentieth century, while Action Stations provides interactive activities and simulators, plus the UK's tallest indoor climbing tower.

HMS Warrior

Portsmouth Historic Dockyard's youngest ship, **HMS Warrior**, dates from 1860. It was Britain's first armoured (iron-clad) battleship, complete with sails and steam engines, and was the pride of the fleet in its day. The ship displays a wealth of weaponry, including rifles, pistols and sabres, though the *Warrior* was never challenged nor even fired a cannon in her 22 years at sea.

3

Mary Rose Museum

Just beyond HMS Warrior, the **Mary Rose Museum** houses thousands of objects retrieved from or near the wreck of Henry VIII's flagship, the **Mary Rose**, including guns, gold and the crew's personal effects. The ship capsized before the king's eyes off Spithead in 1545 while engaging French intruders, sinking swiftly with almost all her seven-hundred-strong crew. In 1982 a massive conservation project successfully raised the remains of the hull, which silt had preserved beneath the seabed. The ship itself is currently undergoing restoration and preservation work, so is not on display, but should be back in 2012 in a purpose-built museum (check the Historic Dockyard website).

HMS Victory

HMS Victory was already forty years old when she set sail from Portsmouth for Trafalgar on September 14, 1805, returning in triumph three months later, but bearing the corpse of Admiral Nelson. Shot by a sniper from a French ship at the height of the battle, Nelson expired below deck three hours later, having been assured that victory was in sight. A plaque on the deck marks the spot where Nelson was fatally wounded and you can also see the wooden cask where his body was preserved in brandy for the return trip to Britain. Although badly damaged during the battle, the *Victory* continued in service for a further twenty years, before being retired to the dry dock where she rests today.

National Museum of the Royal Navy

Opposite the *Victory*, various buildings house the exhaustive **National Museum of the Royal Navy**. Tracing naval history from Alfred the Great's fleet to the present day, the collection includes some jolly figureheads, Nelson memorabilia, including the only surviving sail from HMS Victory, and nautical models, though coverage of more recent conflicts is scantily treated. The Trafalgar Experience is a noisy, vivid recreation of the battle itself, with gory bits to thrill the kids.

Gosport

Portsmouth's naval theme persists throughout otherwise humdrum **Gosport**, which can be reached by taking the **passenger ferry** from Harbour train station jetty between the historic dockyard and Gunwharf Quays (daily every 7–15min 5.30am–midnight; 10–15min; £2.40 return; ⓦgosportferry.co.uk).

Royal Submarine Museum

Haslar Jetty • Daily: April–Oct 10am–5.30pm; Nov–March 10am–4.30pm, last tour 1hr before closing • £10, joint ticket with Explosion! £12.50 • ⓦsubmarine-museum.co.uk

As you might well guess from the name, the **Royal Submarine Museum** displays submarines – six of them, some of which you can enter. Allow a couple of hours to explore these slightly creepy vessels – a guided tour inside HMS *Alliance* gives you a gloomy insight into how cramped life was on board, and the museum elaborates evocatively on the history of submersible craft.

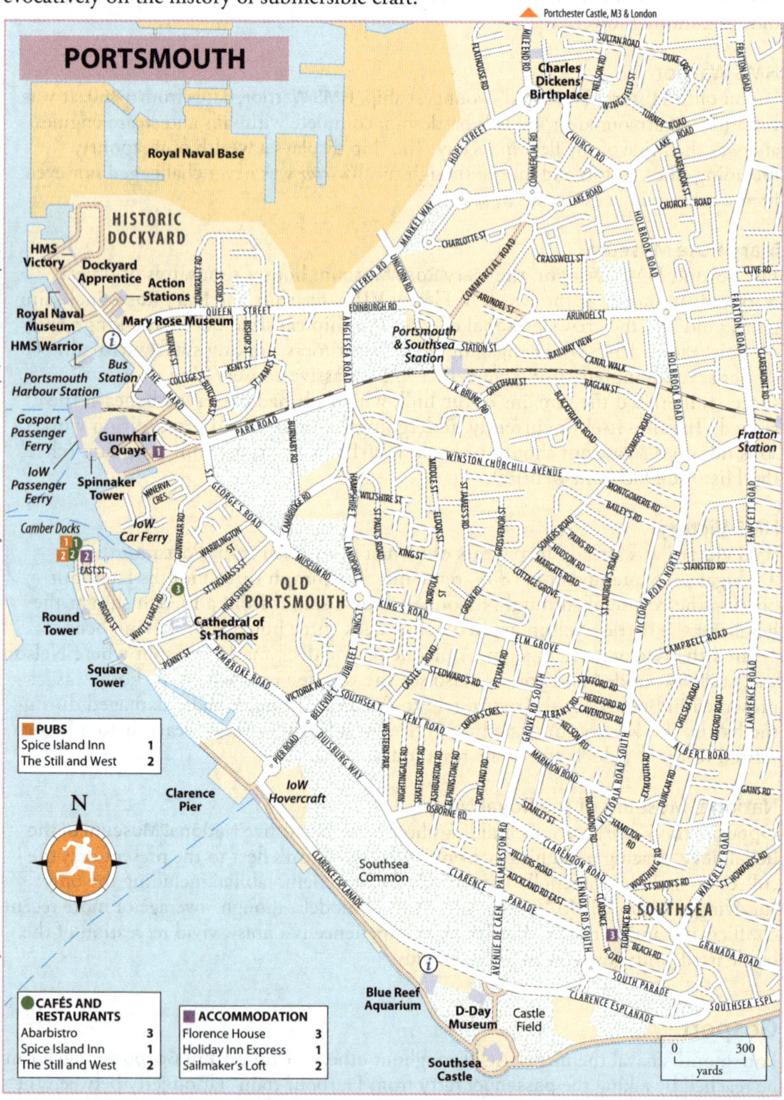

Explosion! The Museum of Naval Firepower

Priddy's Hard • April–Oct daily 10am–5pm; Nov–March Sat & Sun 10am–4pm, last entry 1hr before closing • £10, joint ticket with Submarine Museum £12.50 • Ⓦ explosion.org.uk

Near the Royal Submarine Museum, housed in an old armaments depot, **Explosion!** tells the story of naval warfare from the days of gunpowder to the present, with weapons of all descriptions, including mines, big guns and torpedoes, all backed up by vivid computer animations.

The Spinnaker Tower

Gunwharf Quays • Sept–July daily 10am–6pm; Aug Mon–Fri 10am–6pm, Sat & Sun 10am–7pm • £7.55 • Ⓦ spinnakertower.co.uk

From Portsmouth Harbour train station, it's a short walk along the historic waterfront to the sleek modern **Gunwharf Quays** development, with a myriad of cafés, restaurants, nightspots and shops. Here you'll find, the **Spinnaker Tower**, an elegant, 557ft-high sail-like structure, offering views of up to twenty miles over land and sea. Its three viewing decks can be reached by a high-speed lift, the highest one being open to the elements, though most people stick to View Deck 1, which has one of Europe's largest glass floors.

Old Portsmouth

It's a well-signposted fifteen-minute walk south of Gunwharf Quays to what remains of **Old Portsmouth**. Along the way, you pass the simple **Cathedral of St Thomas** on the High Street, whose original twelfth-century features have been obscured by rebuilding after the Civil War and again in the twentieth century. The High Street ends at a maze of cobbled Georgian streets huddling behind a fifteenth-century wall protecting the **Camber**, or old port, where Walter Raleigh landed the first potatoes and tobacco from the New World. Nearby, the Round and Square towers, which punctuate the Tudor fortifications, are popular vantage points for observing the comings and goings of the boats.

D-Day Museum

Clarence Esplanade, Southsea • Daily: April–Sept 10am–5.30pm; Oct–March 10am–5pm; last entry 30min before closing • £6.50 • Ⓦ ddaymuseum.co.uk

In the suburb of **Southsea**, south and west of Old Portsmouth, the **D-Day Museum** focuses on Portsmouth's role as the principal assembly point for the Normandy beach landings in World War II, code-named "Operation Overlord". The museum's most striking exhibit is the 295ft-long Overlord Embroidery, a sort of twentieth-century equivalent of the Bayeux Tapestry, which took five years to complete.

Southsea Castle

Clarence Esplanade, Southsea • May–Oct Tues–Sun & Bank Holiday Mon 10am–5pm • Free • Ⓦ southseacastle.co.uk

Next door to the D-Day Museum, Southsea's most historic building, marked by a little lighthouse, is the squat **Southsea Castle**, built from the remains of Beaulieu Abbey (see p.194). You can go inside the keep and learn about Portsmouth's military history, and can climb up to the spot from where Henry VIII is said to have watched the Mary Rose sink in 1545 (see p.179), though in fact you can get just as good views by climbing along the adjacent seafront ramparts.

Charles Dickens' Birthplace

393 Old Commercial Rd • April–Sept daily 10am–5.30pm • £4 • Ⓦ charlesdickensbirthplace.co.uk

Just over a mile northeast of Old Portsmouth, **Charles Dickens' Birthplace** is set up to look much as it would have looked when the famous novelist was born here in 1812.

Charles's father, John, moved to Portsmouth in 1809 to work for the Navy Pay Office before he was recalled to London in 1815, so Charles was only here for three years, but nevertheless he is said to have returned often and set parts of Nicholas Nickleby in the city. The modest house not only contains period furniture but also a wealth of information about the period in which Dickens lived here.

Portchester Castle

Six miles northwest of the centre, just past the marina development at Port Solent • Daily: April–Sept 10am–6pm • Oct–March 10am–4pm • EH • £4.80

Portchester Castle, northwest of the centre, was built by the Romans in the third century and boasts the finest surviving example of Roman walls in northern Europe – still over 20ft high and incorporating some twenty bastions. The Normans felt no need to make any substantial alterations when they moved in, but a castle was later built within Portchester's precincts by Henry II, which Richard II extended and Henry V used as his garrison when assembling the army that was to fight the Battle of Agincourt.

ARRIVAL AND INFORMATION — PORTSMOUTH

By train Portsmouth's main train station is in the city centre, but the line continues to Harbour Station, the most convenient stop for the main sights and old town.

Destinations Direct trains serve Brighton (hourly; 1hr 20min–1hr 30min); London Waterloo (3–4 hourly; 1hr 35min–2hr 10min); Salisbury (hourly; 1hr 20min); Southampton (every 20min; 45min–1hr) and Winchester (hourly; 55min).

By bus Buses stop at The Hard Interchange, right by Harbour Station.

Destinations Greyhound services to London Victoria (5 daily; 2hr); National Express buses to London Victoria (hourly; 2hr–2hr 20min) and Southampton (hourly; 40–50min).

By ferry Passenger ferries leave from the jetty at Harbour Station for Ryde, on the Isle of Wight (see p.184), and Gosport, on the other side of Portsmouth Harbour (see p.179). Wightlink car ferries depart from the ferry port off Gunwharf Road, just south of Gunwharf Quays, for Fishbourne on the Isle of Wight (see p.184), while hovercraft link Southsea with Ryde.

Tourist offices The Hard (daily: Sept–July 9.30am–5.15pm; Aug 9.30am– 5.45pm); also on Southsea's seafront, next to the aquarium (March–Oct daily 9.30am–5.15pm; Aug daily 9.30am–5.45pm; Nov–Feb Fri–Wed 9.30am–4.30pm; ☎ 023 9282 6722, ⓦ visitportsmouth.co.uk).

ACCOMMODATION

Florence House 2 Malvern Rd, Southsea ☎ 023 9275 1666, ⓦ florencehousehotel.co.uk. Very tasteful, boutique B&B in an Edwardian townhouse on a pleasant backstreet close to Southsea's waterfront. A range of rooms over three floors, all spick and span and with flatscreen TVs. There's a tiny downstairs bar and communal lounge, and parking permits can be provided. **£75**

Holiday Inn Express The Plaza, Gunwharf Quays ☎ 023 9289 4240, ⓦ hiexpress.co.uk. It may be part of a chain, but it's clean and contemporary, and Portsmouth's most central option. Rooms are compact, but its location, right on Gunwharf Quays, can't be faulted. There's a large, airy breakfast room and bar too. **£97**

Sailmaker's Loft 5 Bath Square ☎ 023 9282 3045, ⓦ sailmakersloft.org.uk. This modern B&B is just back from the waterfront, right opposite *The Still* pub, with top-floor rooms overlooking the water. It's worth paying the extra £5 to have your own bathroom. **£65**

EATING AND DRINKING

Abarbistro 58 White Hart Rd ☎ 023 9281 1585, ⓦ abarbistro.co.uk. Lively bar-restaurant with an outside terrace on the edge of Old Portsmouth. The menu features bistro-style classics such as *moules* (£12) and fishcakes (£10), as well as generous steaks (£18), plus a daily-changing menu of fish and pasta dishes. Mon–Sat 11am–midnight, Sun noon–11pm.

Spice Island Inn 1 Bath Square, Old Portsmouth ☎ 023 9287 0543. Traditional pub in the old town with a lovely seafront terrace, wooden floors inside and good views from the upstairs rooms. It serves decent pub grub, such as beef and ale pie (£9), and also does takeaway fish and chips, which you can eat outside sitting on the harbour walls. Mon–Sat 11am–11pm, Sun 11am–10.30pm.

The Still and West 2 Bath Square, Old Portsmouth ☎ 023 9282 1567. A waterfront terrace and cosy interior with views over the harbour make this pub worth stopping by: the food ranges from the traditional fish and chips (£10) to home-made game pie (£11) and fish stew (£12). Mon–Sat 10am–11pm, Sun 11am–10.30pm.

Southampton

A glance at the map gives some idea of the strategic maritime importance of **SOUTHAMPTON**, which stands on a triangular peninsula formed at the place where the rivers Itchen and Test flow into Southampton Water, an eight-mile inlet from the Solent. Sure enough, Southampton has figured in numerous stirring events: it witnessed the exodus of Henry V's Agincourt-bound army, the Pilgrim Fathers' departure in the *Mayflower* in 1620 and the maiden voyages of such ships as the *Queen Mary* and the *Titanic*. Despite its pummelling by the Luftwaffe and some disastrous postwar urban sprawl, the thousand-year-old city has retained some of its medieval charm in parts and reinvented itself as a twenty-first century shopping centre in others, with the giant glass-and-steel **West Quay** as its focus.

The Cultural Quarter

Core of the modern town is the **Civic Centre**, a short walk east of the train station and home to the excellent **Southampton City Art Gallery** that's particularly strong on contemporary British artists with works by Gilbert and George and Anthony Gormley: older paintings by, among others Gainsborough, Joshua Reynolds and the Impressionists – Monet and Corot – are also on show (Mon–Fri 10am–4pm, Sat & Sun 11am–4pm; free). The Civic Centre is at the heart of Southampton's new **Cultural Quarter**, where a **Sea City Museum** is currently being built to house a permanent exhibition on the *Titanic*, along with exhibits that used to be held in the Museum of Archeology and the Maritime Museum.

The city walls

The **Western Esplanade**, curving southward from the station, runs alongside the best remaining bits of the old city **walls.** Rebuilt after a French attack in 1338, they incorporate **God's House Tower**, at the southern end of the old town in Winkle Street, which currently houses the **Museum of Archeology** (Sat & Sun 11am–5pm; £2.50), though its exhibits are due to move into new Sea City Museum (see above). Best preserved of the city's seven gates is **Bargate**, at the opposite end of the old town, at the head of the High Street; it's an elaborate structure, cluttered with lions, classical figures and defensive apertures.

ARRIVAL AND INFORMATION — SOUTHAMPTON

By train Southampton's central station is in Blechynden Terrace, west of the Civic Centre.

Destinations Bournemouth (every 20min; 30min); London Waterloo (every 20min; 1hr 20min); Portsmouth (every 30min; 50min–1hr); Salisbury (every 20min; 30min); Weymouth (every 30min; 1hr 20–1hr 35min); Winchester (4 hourly; 15–30min).

By bus Greyhound buses leave from Town Quay, while National Express buses run from the coach station on Harbour Parade.

Destinations Greyhound to London Victoria (3 daily; 2hr–2hr 30min); National Express to Bournemouth (12 daily; 45min–1hr); London Victoria (15 daily; 2hr–2hr 30min); Portsmouth (13 daily; 40min–1hr); Salisbury (1 daily; 40min); Weymouth (2 daily; 2hr 40min) and Winchester (every 30min–hourly; 25–45min).

Tourist office 9 Civic Centre Rd (Mon–Sat 9.30am–5pm, Sun & bank hols 10am–3.30pm; T 023 8083 3333, W visit-southampton.co.uk).

ACCOMMODATION

Mercure Dolphin 34–35 High St T 023 8038 6460, W dolphin-southampton.com. Centrally located, this fifteenth-century coaching inn hosted Jane Austen's eighteenth birthday party. Completely renovated in 2010, its rooms are a comfortable blend of historic and contemporary, with flatscreen TVs and wi-fi. **£70**

White Star 28 Oxford St T 023 8082 1990, W whitestartavern.co.uk. Boutique-style rooms with comfortable beds, trendy toiletries, free wi-fi and modern decor, in this lively hotel above a highly regarded bar-restaurant. **£95**

EATING AND DRINKING

The Arthouse Gallery Café 178 Above Bar St ☎023 8023 8582, ⓦthearthousesouthampton.co.uk. Friendly community-run café, opposite the City Art Gallery, where you can get delicious home-made vegan and vegetarian dishes, as well as organic ciders and beers. Tues & Thurs 11am–5pm, Wed & Fri 11am–8pm, Sat & Sun noon–5pm.

Kuti's Royal Thai Gate House, Royal Pier ☎023 8033 9211, ⓦkutisroyalthaipier.co.uk. Choose from the à la carte menu or an excellent all-you-can-eat Thai buffet (Mon–Thurs £16, Fri & Sat £20) at this superbly ornate waterside restaurant that was once the terminal for ocean liners including the *Titanic*. There are fine views over the water from the upstairs restaurant, as well as an outside deck for summer evenings. Daily noon–2.30pm & 6pm–midnight.

Red Lion 55 High St ☎023 8033 3595. One of the oldest and most atmospheric pubs in Southampton, dating from the twelfth century, complete with its own minstrels' gallery. They serve fine real ales and traditional British dishes. Mon–Sat 11am–11pm, Sun noon–10.30pm.

The Isle of Wight

3

The lozenge-shaped **ISLE OF WIGHT** has begun to shake off its old-fashioned image and attract a younger, livelier crowd, with a couple of major annual rock **festivals** and a scattering of fashionable hotels. Despite measuring less than 23 miles at its widest point, the island packs in a surprising variety of landscapes and coastal scenery. Its beaches have long attracted holiday-makers, and the island was a favourite of such eminent Victorians as Tennyson, Dickens, Swinburne, Julia Margaret Cameron and Queen Victoria herself, who made **Osborne House**, near Cowes, her permanent home after Albert died.

ARRIVAL AND DEPARTURE — ISLE OF WIGHT

There are three **ferry** departure points from the mainland to the Isle of Wight – Portsmouth, Southampton and Lymington. **Wightlink** (ⓦwightlink.co.uk) runs car ferries from Lymington to Yarmouth (30min) and from Gunwharf Terminal in Portsmouth to Fishbourne (40min), as well as a high-speed catamaran from Portsmouth Harbour to Ryde Pier (passengers only; 20min). **Hovertravel** (ⓦhovertravel.co.uk), meanwhile, runs hovercrafts from Clarence Esplanade in Southsea to Ryde (passengers only; 10min). From Southampton, **Red Funnel** (ⓦredfunnel.co.uk) operates a high-speed catamaran to West Cowes (passengers only; 25min) and a car ferry to East Cowes (55min). **Fare** structures and **schedules** on all routes are labyrinthine, from £8 for a day-return foot passenger ticket on the Southampton to West Cowes route in low season to £160 for a high-season return for a car and four passengers on the Lymington to Yarmouth route.

GETTING AROUND

By bus Local buses are run by Southern Vectis (☎0871 200 2233, ⓦislandbuses.info). Good-value tickets give unlimited travel on the network (£10/day, £22/week).

By train There are two train lines on the island: the seasonal Isle of Wight Steam Railway (ⓦiwsteamrailway.co.uk) runs from Wootton Bridge to Smallbrook Junction, where it connects with the east-coast Island line from Ryde to Shanklin (every 20–40min; 25min; ⓦislandlinetrains.co.uk).

Cycling is a popular way of getting around the island, though in summer the narrow lanes can get very busy. For bike rental, contact Wight Cycle Hire (☎01983 761800, ⓦwightcyclehire.co.uk): it has offices in Yarmouth, Brading and Bembridge, and can deliver bikes anywhere on the island (£8/half-day, £14/day).

Ryde

As a major ferry terminal, **RYDE** is the first landfall many visitors make on the island, but one where few choose to linger, despite some grand nineteenth-century architecture and a fine sandy town beach.

TOP 5: FOOD WITH A VIEW

Hive Beach Café Burton Bradstock. See p.210
Kuti's Royal Thai Southampton. See p.184
The Salt Cellar Shaftesbury. See p.208
Urban Reef Boscombe. See p.198
Wheelers Crab Shed Isle of Wight. See p.187

Postcard Museum

15 Union St • March–Oct daily 10am–4.15pm • £3.50, free to Wightlink foot passengers on day-return tickets • Ⓦ donaldmcgill.info

Ryde's quirky little **Postcard Museum** crams in a good proportion of the 12,000 saucy postcards created by artist Donald McGill. The cards, produced throughout the first half of the twentieth century, reached their peak of popularity in the 1930s. Packed wtih daft double entendres – bookish man to pretty girl: "Do you like Kipling?" Girl: "I don't know, I've never kippled" – McGill's work also takes some slightly surreal turns, with lots of sly plays on language and English mores.

ARRIVAL AND DEPARTURE — RYDE

The **bus station**, **Hovercraft terminal** and **Esplanade train station** are all near the base of the pier, while **catamarans** from Portsmouth dock at the Pier Head.

ACCOMMODATION AND EATING

The Boathouse Springvale Rd, Seaview, 2 miles east of Ryde Ⓣ 01983 810616, Ⓦ theboathouseiow.co.uk. Accessible by foot along the coast from Ryde, this stylish gastropub – fresh fish, baguettes, prawn dishes – also offers spacious en-suite rooms decorated in a contemporary style with iPod docks: superior rooms have sea views. Food served daily 9am–11pm. **£100**

Kasbah 76 Union St Ⓣ 01983 810088, Ⓦ kas-bah.co.uk. Lively Moroccan-themed bar and restaurant where you can chill out to world music and play chess. Reasonably priced home-made dishes include a vegetable tajine for £6.65. Upstairs, the stylish rooms have sea views – it can be noisy at weekends, but is great value. Food served Mon & Tues 11.30am–11pm, Wed–Sat 11.30am–2am, Sun noon–12.30am. **£65**

Liberty's 12 Union St Ⓣ 01983 811007, Ⓦ libertyscafebar.co.uk. A big, stylish continental-style café-bar with great salads, sandwiches and main meals (pasta from around £9 and fish and meat dishes around £13) in the upstairs dining room. Food served Mon–Thurs noon–3pm & 6–9pm, Fri & Sat noon–9.30pm, Sun noon–4pm.

★ **The Priory Bay Hotel** Priory Drive, Seaview, 3 miles east of Ryde Ⓣ 01983 613146, Ⓦ priorybay.com. This elegant country house hotel has a wonderful setting with lawns leading down to the sands of Priory Bay. It's smart but unstuffy and child-friendly, and has a great restaurant. There's also an outdoor pool and self-catering cottages in the grounds. **£200**

3

Brading Roman Villa

Morton Old Road • Daily 9.30am–5pm • £6.50 • Ⓦ bradingromanvilla.org.uk

Just south of the ancient village of **Brading**, on the busy Ryde to Sandown A3055 (bus #3 from Ryde or Sandown), the remains of **Brading Roman Villa** are renowned for their mosaics. This is the more impressive of two such villas on the island, both of which were probably sites of bacchanalian worship. The Brading site is housed in an attractive modern museum and its superbly preserved mosaics include intact images of Medusa and depictions of Orpheus.

Sandown

The traditional seaside resort of **SANDOWN** merges with its neighbour Shanklin across the sandy reach of Sandown Bay, representing the island's holiday-making epicentre. Sandown, a traditional 1960s bucket-and-spade resort, appropriately enough possesses the island's only surviving pleasure **pier**, bedecked with various traditional amusements and a large theatre with nightly entertainment in season.

ARRIVAL AND DEPARTURE — SANDOWN

The Island Line **train** station, served by trains from Ryde and Shanklin, is on Station Ave, about a 10min walk inland from the pier.

ACCOMMODATION AND EATING

The Lawns 72 Broadway Ⓣ 01983 402549, Ⓦ lawnshotelisleofwight.co.uk. Friendly, comfortable, non-smoking guesthouse with attractive gardens, a bar and free wi-fi; the plush rooms have flatscreen TVs, and the breakfasts are good. Minimum stay of three nights in the summer. **£80**

The Reef The Esplanade ⓣ01983 403219, ⓦthereefsandown.co.uk. A bright bar-restaurant right on the seafront with great views. It serves up a range of mid-priced dishes including pizzas, pasta, steaks and fresh fish: prices start at around £8 for a pizza, ranging up to £20 for a 10oz fillet steak, with a big bowl of mussels and chips at £11. Food served summer daily 11am–10pm; winter Sun–Thurs 11am–9pm, Fri & Sat 11am–9.30pm.

Shanklin

SHANKLIN, with its auburn cliffs, Old Village and scenic Chine, has a marginally more sophisticated aura than its northern neighbour. The rose-clad, thatched **Old Village** may be syrupy, but the adjacent **Shanklin Chine** (daily: April to late May & mid-Sept to Oct 10am–5pm; late May to mid-Sept 10am–10pm; £3.90), a twisting pathway descending a mossy ravine and decorated on summer nights with fairy lights, is undeniably picturesque; local resident John Keats once drew inspiration from the environs.

ARRIVAL AND DEPARTURE — SHANKLIN

By train The final stop on the Island Line from Ryde, Shanklin train station is about half a mile inland at the top of Regent St.

By bus The bus station (buses #2 & #3 from Ryde and Newport) is a little south of the train station.

ACCOMMODATION

Pink Beach Hotel 20 The Esplanade ⓣ01983 862501, ⓦpink-beach-hotel.co.uk. In a great location right on the beach, this Victorian building has its own garden and simple rooms. It is worth paying a little extra (about £8) for sea views. **£72**

EATING AND DRINKING

Fisherman's Cottage At the southern end of the Esplanade, and at the bottom of Shanklin Chine ⓣ01983 863882, ⓦshanklinchine.co.uk/index.php/fishermans-cottage-welcome. An atmospheric thatched pub right on the seafront, with outside tables: it 's child-friendly and serves wholesome pub food, such as seafood pancake (£13) and leek and mushroom pie (£9). March–Oct food served daily 11am–2pm & 6–8pm.

★ **Old Thatch Teashop** 4 Church Rd ⓣ01983 865587, ⓦoldthatchteashop.co.uk. There are a warren of rooms in this friendly and efficient teahouse, with pretty gardens at the back. It serves lunches – soup and sandwiches – and is highly regarded for its delicious home-made scones and cakes. Mon–Sat 10am–5pm, Sun 10.30am–5pm.

Ventnor and around

The seaside resort of **VENTNOR** and its two village suburbs of **Bonchurch** and **St Lawrence** sit at the foot of St Boniface Down, the island's highest point at 787ft. The Down periodically disintegrates into landslides, creating the jumbled terraces known locally as the **Undercliff**, whose sheltered, south-facing aspect, mild winter temperatures and thick carpet of undergrowth have contributed to the former fishing village becoming a fashionable health spa. Thanks to these unique factors, the town possesses rather more character than the island's other resorts, its Gothic Revival buildings clinging dizzily to zigzagging bends.

The floral terraces of the Cascade curve down to the slender Esplanade and narrow beach, where some of the former boat-builders' cottages now house shops, cafés and restaurants. From the Esplanade, it's a pleasant mile-long stroll to Ventnor's **Botanical Gardens**.

ACCOMMODATION — VENTNOR

Hambrough Hotel Hambrough Rd, Ventnor ⓣ01983 856333, ⓦthehambrough.com. Small, stylish, modern hotel above a Michelin-starred restaurant, run by chef Robert Thompson. The minimalist rooms come with all the luxuries, including flatscreen TV and Molton Brown toiletries; most have sea views, and some have balconies. **£170**

Horseshoebay House Shore Rd, Bonchurch ⓣ01983 856800, ⓦhorseshoebayhouse.co.uk. A lovely B&B right on the beach below Bonchurch at Horseshoe Bay. All the comfortable rooms have sea views, wi-fi and flatscreen TVs and there's a lovely garden with a sunny terrace overlooking the beach. **£80**

St Augustine Villa The Esplanade, Ventnor ⓣ01983 852289, ⓦharbourviewhotel.co.uk. Large Victorian mansion in a great location facing the beach with period fittings in the lounge. The rooms come in various sizes, but it's worth paying the extra (generally less than £10) for sea views. Non-smoking, no pets or children. **£88**

EATING AND DRINKING

El Toro Contento 2 Pier St, Ventnor ⓣ01983 857600, ⓦeltorocontento.co.uk. A cosy restaurant dishing up home-made tapas, such as chorizo in cider, and spicy mussels, most for under a fiver. Also serves Spanish hams and cheeses and will cook paella for £10.40 a head (min 4 people) with 24hr notice. Daily 1–8pm.

★ **The Pond Café** Bonchurch Village Rd, Bonchurch ⓣ01983 855666, ⓦrobert-thompson.com/pond-cafe. Small and smart, this well-regarded restaurant overlooking the village pond is run by Robert Thompson, but is cheaper and less formal than its sister restaurant in Ventnor, *The Hambrough*. It has a short menu of good-value dishes, such as local mackerel (£12) and Isle of Wight rib-eye beef (£19). Daily 10am–9.30pm.

★ **Wheelers Crab Shed** Steephill Cove ⓣ01983 852177. Delicious home-made crab pasties, sandwiches and ciabattas served from a pretty shack on the seashore. Also tasty local lobster salads and daily fish specials. April–Nov, plus weekends and holidays the rest of the year 11am–3.30pm.

The southwest coast

The western Undercliff begins to recede at the village of Niton, where a footpath continues to the most southerly tip of the island, **St Catherine's Point**, marked by a modern lighthouse. A prominent landmark on the downs behind is **St Catherine's Oratory**, known locally as the "Pepper Pot", and originally a lighthouse, reputedly built in 1325.

Seven miles northwest along the coast, Military Road ascends the flank of Compton Down before descending into Freshwater Bay. If you're walking this way, you might stop off at the National Trust-owned **Compton Bay**, a splendid spot for a swim or a picnic, frequented by local surfers and accessed by a steep path leading down from the dark red cliffs.

Dimbola Lodge

Freshwater Bay • Tues–Sun plus Bank Hol Mons & Mon in school summer hols: March–Oct 10am–5pm; Nov–Feb 10am–4pm • £4 • ⓦdimbola.co.uk

On the coastal road at Freshwater Bay, **Dimbola Lodge** was the home of pioneer photographer Julia Margaret Cameron, who settled here after visiting local resident Tennyson in 1860. The building now houses a gallery of her work and changing exhibitions, as well as a room devoted to memorabilia from the Isle of Wight festival. There's also a bookshop and tearoom/restaurant.

The Needles and Alum Bay

The breezy four-mile ridge of **Tennyson Down** running from Freshwater Bay to **The Needles** is one of the island's most satisfying walks, with vistas onto rolling downs and vales. On top of the Down, there's a monument to the eponymous poet, who lived on the island for forty years from 1853 until his death. At its western tip sits the **Needles Old Battery**, a gun emplacement built 250ft above the sea in 1863 (mid-March to Oct daily 10.30am–5pm; NT; £5; fort may be closed in bad weather, check on ⓣ01983 754772). There are fabulous views from here over the three tall chalk stacks known as **The Needles**, which jut out into the English Channel. **Boat trips** round the Needles (April–Oct; Needles Pleasure Cruises; ⓣ01983 761587; £4) leave from **Alum Bay**, a twenty-minute walk away. To catch the boat, you can walk down the cliff path or take a chairlift (£4 return) which descends the polychrome cliffs to ochre-hued sands.

Yarmouth

Four miles east of the Needles and linked to Lymington in the New Forest by car ferry, the pleasant town of **YARMOUTH**, on the northern coast of the Isle of Wight, makes a lovely entrance to the island and is the best base for exploring its western tip. Although razed by the French in 1377, the port prospered after **Yarmouth Castle** (Easter–Sept Mon–Thurs & Sun 11am–4pm; EH; £3.50), tucked between the quay and the pier, was commissioned by Henry VIII. Inside, some of the rooms have re-created life in a sixteenth-century castle, and there's also a display on the many wrecks that floundered here in the Solent, while the battlements afford superb views over the estuary. Yarmouth's only other real sight is the Grade II listed **pier**, England's longest wooden pier still in use.

ACCOMMODATION — YARMOUTH

3

The George Hotel Quay St ⊙01983 760331, ⊛thegeorge.co.uk. In a great position right by the ferry dock, with a lovely garden looking out onto the Solent, this seventeenth-century hotel has comfortable, elegantly furnished rooms, some with balconies overlooking the water. Charles II once styaed here. It also has an excellent restaurant, specializing in local and organic produce. **£190**

EATING AND DRINKING

The Blue Crab High St ⊙01983 760014. A simply decorated restaurant, with cosy booths, offering fish and shellfish dishes such as salmon with samphire and fennel (£16). Also top-quality fresh fish and chips to take away for £5. Tues–Sat 11am–3pm & 6–11pm, Sun noon–3pm & 6–11pm.

The Wheatsheaf Bridge Rd ⊙01983 760456, ⊛wheatsheafyarmouth.co.uk. This no-nonsense pub with a pool table and patio garden also serves some of the best-value evening meals in town (mains £8–11), including chicken curry, king prawn linguine, Singapore noodles and pizzas. Mon–Sat 11am–11pm, Sun noon–10.30pm.

Cowes

COWES, at the island's northern tip, is associated with sailing craft and boat building: Henry VIII installed a castle to defend the Solent's expanding naval dockyards from the French and Spanish, and in the 1950s the world's first hovercraft made its test runs here. In 1820 the Prince Regent's patronage of the yacht club gave the port its cachet with the Royal Yacht Squadron, now one of the world's most exclusive sailing clubs. The first week of August sees the international yachting festival **Cowes Week** (⊛aamcowesweek.co.uk), where serious sailors mingle with visiting royalty; most summer weekends see some form of nautical event taking place in or around town.

The town is bisected by the River Medina, with West Cowes being the older, more interesting half. At the bottom of the meandering High Street, **boat trips** around the harbour and the Solent leave from Thetis Wharf, near the Parade (⊙01983/564602, ⊛solentcruises.co.uk). The more industrial **East Cowes**, where you'll find **Osborne House**, is connected to West Cowes by a "floating bridge", or chain ferry (pedestrians free, cars £1.80).

Osborne House

East Cowes • April–Sept daily 10am–6pm; Oct daily 10am–4pm; Nov–March Wed–Sun 10am–4pm • EH • £11.50 • Bus #4 from Ryde or #5 from Newport, or either from East Cowes

The only place of interest in East Cowes is Queen Victoria's family home, **Osborne House**, signposted one mile southeast of town. The house was built in the late 1840s by Prince Albert and Thomas Cubitt in the style of an Italianate villa, with balconies and large terraces overlooking the landscaped gardens towards the Solent. The state rooms, used for entertaining visiting dignitaries, exude formality as one would expect, while the private apartments feel homely in a manner appropriate to an affluent family holiday residence that Osborne was. Following Albert's death, the desolate Victoria spent much of her time here, and it's where she eventually died in 1901. Since then, according to her wishes, the house has remained virtually unaltered, allowing an intimate glimpse into Victoria's family life.

ACCOMMODATION — COWES

Albert Cottage York Ave, East Cowes ⓣ01983 299309, ⓦalbertcottagehotel.com. Adjacent to and once part of the Osborne estate, this lovely mansion, set in its own grounds, has a country house feel to it. Rooms are very comfortable, and have flatscreen TVs; it has its own highly rated restaurant, too. **£140**

The Fountain Inn High St, West Cowes ⓣ01983 292397, ⓦfountaininn-cowes.com. The best budget option in town, with tastefully furnished rooms, the nicest ones overlooking the waterside, all above a fine old inn serving good-value pub food. **£100**

EATING AND DRINKING

The Coast Bar & Dining Room 15 Shooters Hill ⓣ01983 298574, ⓦthecoastbar.co.uk. Light airy bar/restaurant with wooden floors and lively, informal vibe. The menu features dishes such as king prawns in garlic with chips (£13), asparagus and broad bean risotto (£10) and a good selection of steaks and burgers. Bar/café daily 11am–midnight. Food served Mon–Sat noon–3pm & 6–9pm, Sun noon–8.30pm.

Corries Cabin 17 Shooters Hill ⓣ01983 293733. Something of an institution, with queues out of the door for the takeaway fish and chips. There's also a restaurant serving good-value, freshly caught fish, such as mackerel baps. Restaurant Mon–Thurs 11.45am–8pm, Fri & Sat 11.45am–9pm.

Mojac's 10a Shooters Hill ⓣ01983 281118, ⓦmojacs.co.uk. Upmarket restaurant serving inexpensive lunches such as burgers and smoked salmon omelettes (£6.40). The good-value set menus – two courses £16, three courses £20 – include a bottle of wine between two; à la carte mains such as beef en croute cost around £14. Mon–Sat 11.45am–1.30pm & from 5.45pm.

3

Carisbrooke Castle

Southwest of Newport • Daily: April–Sept 10am–5pm; Oct–Easter 10am–4pm • EH • £7.30 • Bus #6, #7 or #12 from Newport

NEWPORT, the capital of the Isle of Wight, sits at the centre of the island at a point where the River Medina's commercial navigability ends. The town isn't particularly engaging, though is worth a visit for the hilltop fortress of **Carisbrooke Castle.** The most famous resident of this austere Norman pile was Charles I, detained here (and caught one night ignominiously jammed between his room's bars while attempting escape) before his execution in London. The **museum** features relics from his incarceration, as well as those of the last royal resident, Princess Beatrice, Queen Victoria's youngest daughter. There's also a sixteenth-century well-house, where you can watch donkeys trudge around a huge treadmill to raise a barrel 160ft up the well shaft.

Winchester

Nowadays a tranquil, handsome market town, **WINCHESTER** was once one of the mightiest settlements in England. Under the Romans it was Venta Belgarum, the fifth largest town in Britain, but it was **Alfred the Great** who really put Winchester on the map when he made it the capital of his Wessex kingdom in the ninth century. For the next two hundred years or so Winchester ranked alongside London, its status affirmed by William the Conqueror's coronation in both cities and by his commissioning of the local monks to prepare the **Domesday Book**. It wasn't until after the Battle of Naseby in 1645, when Cromwell took the city, that Winchester began its decline into provinciality.

Hampshire's county town now has a scholarly and slightly anachronistic air, embodied by the ancient almshouses that still provide shelter for senior citizens of "noble poverty" – the pensioners can be seen walking round the town in medieval black or mulberry-coloured gowns with silver badges.

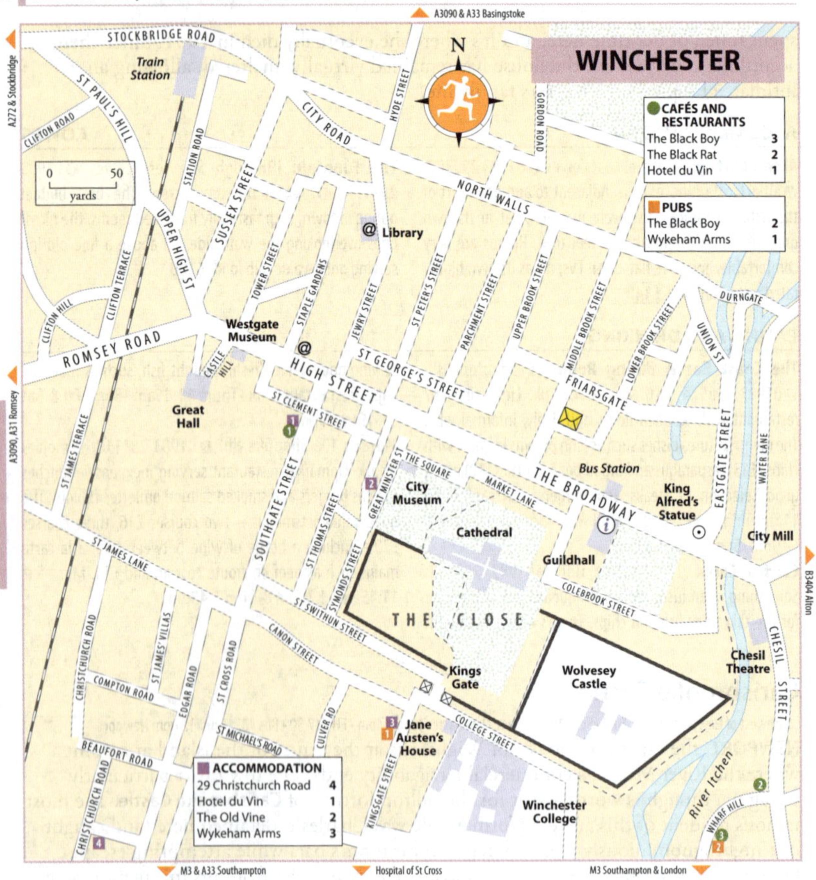

Winchester Cathedral

Cathedral Close • Mon–Sat 9.30am–5pm, Sun 12.30am–3pm • £6.75, including a guided tour; tower tour £6, £9 for both cathedral and tower • ⓦ winchester-cathedral.org.uk

The first minster to be built in Winchester was raised by Cenwalh, the Saxon king of Wessex in the mid-seventh century, and traces of this building have been unearthed near the present **cathedral**, which was begun in 1079 and completed some three hundred years later. The exterior is not its best feature – squat and massive, it crouches stumpily over the tidy lawns of the Cathedral Close. The interior is rich and complex, however, and its 556ft **nave** makes this Europe's longest medieval church. Outstanding features include the carved Norman font of black Tournai marble, the fourteenth-century misericords (the choir stalls are the oldest complete set in the country) and some amazing monuments – **William of Wykeham's Chantry**, halfway down the nave on the right, is one of the most ornate. **Jane Austen**, who died in Winchester, is commemorated close to the font by a memorial brass and slab beneath which she's interred, though she's recorded simply as the daughter of a local clergyman. Above the high altar lie the mortuary chests of pre-Conquest kings, including **Canute** (though the bones were mixed up after Cromwell's Roundheads broke up the chests in 1645); **William Rufus**, killed while hunting in the New Forest in 1100, lies in the presbytery. Behind the impressive Victorian screen at the end of the presbytery, look out for the memorial shrine to **St Swithun**. Originally buried outside in the churchyard, his remains were later interred inside where the "rain of heaven" could no longer fall on him, whereupon he took revenge and the heavens opened for forty days – hence the legend that if it rains on St Swithun's Day (July 15) it will do so for another forty. His exact burial place is unknown.

Accessible from the north transept, the Norman **crypt** – often flooded – is home to Anthony Gormley's contemplative figure *Sound II,* reflected in the waters. The cathedral's original foundations were dug in marshy ground, and at the beginning of last century a steadfast diver, William Walker, spent five years replacing the rotten timber foundations with concrete.

Great Hall

At the top of the High St on Castle Ave • Daily 10am–5pm • Free • ⓦ hants.gov.uk/greathall

The **Great Hall** is all that remains of a thirteenth-century castle destroyed by Cromwell. Sir Walter Raleigh heard his death sentence here in 1603, though he wasn't finally dispatched until 1618, and Judge Jeffreys held one of his Bloody Assizes (see p.204) in the castle after Monmouth's rebellion in 1685. The main interest now is a large, brightly painted disc slung on one wall like some curious antique dartboard. This is alleged to be King Arthur's Round Table, but the woodwork is probably fourteenth-century, later repainted as a PR exercise for the Tudor dynasty – the portrait of Arthur at the top of the table bears an uncanny resemblance to Henry VIII.

College Street

College Street is home to the buildings of **Winchester College**, the oldest public school in England – established in 1382 by William of Wykeham for "poor scholars", it now educates few but the wealthy and privileged. You can look round the medieval college buildings, its cloisters and Gothic chapel on a **guided tour** (Mon, Wed, Fri & Sat 10.45am, noon, 2.15pm & 3.30pm; Tues & Thurs 10.45am & noon; Sun 2.15pm & 3.30pm; £6; ⓦ winchestercollege.org).

At no.8 College Street stands the house where **Jane Austen** moved from Chawton in 1817 (see p.192), when she was already ill with Addison's Disease, dying there later the same year. It's privately owned, so you can't look round. At the top of the street, the thirteenth-century **Kings Gate** is one of the city's original medieval gateways, housing the tiny St Swithun's Church.

Wolvesey Castle

Entrance off College St • April–Oct daily 10am–5pm • EH • Free

East of the cathedral, the remains of Winchester's Saxon walls bracket the ruins of the twelfth-century **Wolvesey Castle** – actually the palace for the Bishops of Winchester, who once wielded great clout over England's religious and political affairs. As a result, this was once one of the most important buildings in Winchester, encompassing its own stables, prison, chapel and gardens. Today, the castle ruins remain impressive, dwarfing the current dwelling place of the Bishop of Winchester, a relatively modest house built in 1680, which sits alongside it.

THE WATERCRESS LINE

ALRESFORD, six miles east of Winchester, is the departure-point for the **Mid-Hants Watercress Line** (Jan–March, Oct & Dec Sat & Sun plus school hols; April–Sept daily; £14; ⓣ 01962 733810, ⓦ watercressline.co.uk), a steam-powered train so named because it passes through the former watercress beds that once flourished here. The train chuffs ten miles to **Alton**, with gourmet dinners served on board on Saturday evenings, plus real ales from local breweries and traditional Sunday lunches.

ARRIVAL AND INFORMATION — WINCHESTER

By train Winchester train station is about a mile northwest of the cathedral on Stockbridge Rd.

Destinations Bournemouth (every 20min; 45min–55min); London Waterloo (3–4 hourly; 1hr–1hr 15min); Portsmouth (hourly; 1hr); Southampton (every 15min; 15–20min).

By bus National Express and Greyhound buses pull in and depart from the conveniently located bus station on the Broadway, opposite the tourist office.

Destinations Bournemouth (4 daily; 1hr 15min–1hr 35min); London (National Express 9 daily; 1hr 30min–2hr; Greyhound 2 daily; 2hr); Southampton (approx hourly; 25–45min).

Tourist office In the imposing Guildhall (May–Sept Mon–Sat 10am–5pm, Sun & Bank hols 11am–4pm; Oct–April Mon–Sat 10am–5pm; T 01962 840500, W visit winchester.co.uk).

ACCOMMODATION

3

29 Christchurch Road 29 Christchurch Rd T 01962 868 661, W fetherstondilke.com. Well-furnished, comfortable B&B in a charming Regency house located in a quiet residential part of town. No smoking. **£80**

★ **Hotel du Vin** Southgate St T 01962 841414, W hotelduvin.com. The first in the classy hotel chain, this lovely Georgian townhouse has been given a stylish makeover and now comprises plush rooms – some cottage-style, with their own private entrances and terraces – a lovely patio garden, chic bar and great restaurant (see below). This is the first choice for accommodation in Winchester, especially if you can bag one of their periodic special offers. **£155**

The Old Vine 8 Great Minster St T 01962 854616, W oldvinewinchester.com. Lovely, big rooms that combine period decor with modern touches such as widescreen TVs, above a fine bar-restaurant, and right opposite the cathedral. The street can be noisy at night. **£100**

EATING AND DRINKING

The Black Boy Wharf Hill T 01962 861754, W theblack boypub.com. Fantastic old pub with log fires in winter, walls lined with books and low ceilings hung with old coins and miniature bottles. Good cask ales from local breweries are on draught and there's reasonable pub grub from £8.50, as well as a small outdoor terrace. Mon–Thurs noon–11pm, Fri & Sat noon–midnight, Sun noon–11.30pm.

The Black Rat 88 Chesil St T 01962 844465, W theblack rat.co.uk. Awarded a Michelin star in 2011, this cosy former pub serves top-quality modern British cuisine. Ingredients are locally sourced (including veg from their own allotment) with dishes such as Weymouth crab, home-made black pudding, local pork loin and English cheeses: the weekend set lunch menu is surprisingly reasonable for food of this quality, at £23.30 for three courses. Reservations advised. Mon–Fri 7–9.30pm, Sat & Sun noon–2.30pm & 7–9.30pm.

★ **Hotel du Vin** Southgate St T 01962 841414, W hotelduvin.com. Buzzy bistro-style restaurant in a series of attractive dining rooms, some with open fireplaces. The food is excellent, much of it locally sourced, and reasonably priced, with main courses such as roast pheasant (£19), and starters such as squid, chickpea and chorizo salad for £6.50. The wine list, as you would expect, is impressive, with many wines available by the half bottle. Mon–Fri noon–9.45pm, Sat & Sun 12.30pm–10.15pm.

Wykeham Arms 75 Kingsgate St T 01962 853834, W fullershotels.com. This highly atmospheric eighteenth-century pub has a warren of cosy rooms, with open fireplaces, good bar snacks and decent beers. Mon–Sat 11am–11pm, Sun noon–10.30pm.

JANE AUSTEN IN CHAWTON

A mile southwest of Alton – accessible on the "Watercress line" steam train, see p.191 – lies the village of **CHAWTON**, where Jane Austen lived from 1809 to 1817, during the last and most prolific years of her life, and where she wrote or revised almost all of her six books, including *Sense and Sensibility* and *Pride and Prejudice*. A plain red-brick building in the centre of the village, **Jane Austen's House** (Jan & Feb Sat & Sun 10am–5pm; March–May & Sept–Dec daily 10.30am–4.30pm; June–Aug daily 10am–5pm; £7) contains first editions of some of her greatest works and provides a fascinating insight into the daily life of the author. A short walk from the house is **Chawton House**, which belonged to Jane's brother, Edward Austen Knight. It remained in the Austen family until 1987, when it was bought by American IT millionairess Sandy Lerner who opened the **Chawton House Library**, containing an impressive collection of women's writing in English from 1600–1830. The house, which has now been fully restored, can be visited on a guided **tour** (book on T 01420 541010 as places are limited; Jan & Feb Tues 2.30pm; March–Dec Tues & Thurs 2.30pm; £6), or you can look round the **gardens** independently (Mon–Fri 10am–4pm; £3). The **library** is open by appointment only (Mon–Fri 10am–5pm).

The New Forest

Covering about 220 square miles, the **NEW FOREST** is one of southern England's favourite rural playgrounds, attracting some 13.5 million day-visits annually. The forest was requisitioned by William the Conqueror in 1079 as a game reserve, and the rights of its inhabitants soon became subservient to those of his precious deer. Fences to impede their progress were forbidden and terrible punishments were meted out to those who disturbed the animals – hands were lopped off, eyes put out. Later monarchs less passionate about hunting than the Normans gradually restored the forest-dwellers' rights, and today the New Forest enjoys a unique patchwork of ancient laws and privileges alongside the regulations applying to its National Park status.

The **trees** of the forest are now much more varied than they were in pre-Norman times, with birch, holly, yew, Scots pine and other conifers interspersed with the ancient oaks and beeches. One of the most venerable trees is the much-visited **Knightwood Oak**, just a few hundred yards north of the A35 three miles southwest of Lyndhurst, which measures about 22ft in circumference at shoulder height. The most conspicuous species of New Forest **fauna** is the New Forest **pony** – you'll see them grazing nonchalantly by the roadsides and ambling through some villages. The local deer are less visible now that some of the faster roads are fenced, although several species still roam the woods, including the tiny **sika deer**, descendants of a pair that escaped from nearby Beaulieu in 1904.

ARRIVAL AND DEPARTURE — THE NEW FOREST

By train The main London to Weymouth train line passes through the New Forest, with fast trains stopping at Brockenhurst (see p.196): slower trains also stop at Ashurst, Sway and New Milton. From Brockenhurst a branch line runs to Lymington (every 30min; 10min) to link with the Isle of Wight ferry.

By bus The southern forest stretches have a reasonably efficient bus network.

GETTING AROUND

Though bus services are good, to get the best from the New Forest, you need to walk or ride through it, avoiding the places cars can reach.

By bus Useful routes through the forest include the #56 and #6 from Southampton to Lymington via Lyndhurst and Brockenhurst; the coastal route #X1 from Christchurch to Lymington; and in summer the hop-on hop-off open-top New Forest Tour bus which runs a circular route around the main settlements (mid-June to mid-Sept; £9; ⓦ thenewforesttour.info). Services are run by Wilts and Dorset buses (ⓣ 01983 827005, ⓦ wdbus.co.uk) and Blue Star (ⓣ 01280 618233, ⓦ bluestarbus.co.uk).

By bike There are 150 miles of car-free gravel roads in the forest, making cycling an appealing prospect – pick up a book of route maps from tourist offices or bike rental shops. Bikes can be rented at AA Bike Hire in Gosport Lane, Lyndhurst (ⓣ 023 8028 3349, ⓦ aabikehirenewforest.co.uk) and at Cycle Experience, by the level crossing in Brockenhurst (ⓣ 01590 624204, ⓦ newforestcyclehire.co.uk).

INFORMATION

Information offices There are two information centres in the forest, one in Lyndhurst (see p.194), in the New Forest Museum and Visitor Centre, off the High St, and the other in Lymington (see p.195), on New St, off the High St (Mon–Sat: Sept–June 10am–4pm; July & Aug 10am–5pm; ⓣ 01590 689000, ⓦ lymington.org).

Maps The Ordnance Survey *Leisure Map 22* of the New Forest is best for exploring. Shopes in Lyndhurst sell numerous specialist walking books and natural history guides.

ACCOMMODATION

Forest Holiday campsites ⓣ 0845 130 8224, ⓦ camping.forestholidays.co.uk. In addition to numerous hotels and guesthouses, the best of which are reviewed below, there are ten campsites throughout the forest run by Forest Holidays. All are open from mid-April to early Sept, some are open year-round.

Lyndhurst

LYNDHURST, its town centre skewered by an agonizing one-way system, isn't a particularly interesting place, though the brick **parish church** is worth a glance for its William Morris glass and the grave of Mrs Reginald Hargreaves, better known as Alice Liddell, Lewis Carroll's model for Alice. The town is of most interest to visitors for the **New Forest Museum and Visitor Centre** in the central car park off the High Street (daily 10am–5pm; T 023 8028 2269, W thenewforest.co.uk), and the adjoining **museum** (£3.50), which focuses on the history, wildlife and industries of the forest.

The forest's most visited site, the **Rufus Stone**, stands three miles northwest of Lyndhurst. Erected in 1745, it marks the putative spot where the Conqueror's son and heir, **William II** – aka William Rufus after his ruddy complexion – was killed by a crossbow bolt in 1100.

ACCOMMODATION — LYNDHURST

3

Forest Cottage High St T 02380 283461, W forestcottage.co.uk. On a busy road, but decent enough rooms in an eighteenth-century townhouse with a well-stocked natural history library and attractive cottage garden. No credit cards; no smoking. **£60**

Limewood Hotel A mile outside Lyndhurst, Beaulieu Rd T 02380 287199, W limewoodhotel.co.uk. Luxurious hotel with spacious designer-style rooms in a country-house atmosphere. The grounds are beautiful and the Herb House spa with outdoor hot tub is great. **£245**

EATING AND DRINKING

★ **The Oak Inn** Pinkney Lane, Bank T 02380 282350. Fantastic little country pub a mile out of Lyndhurst, with low wooden ceilings and a roaring fire in winter and a garden for the summer. It's popular with walkers and cyclists and there's good, if pricey food, featuring local ingredients such as river fish and venison – it's best to book in advance. Mon–Fri 11.30am–3.30pm & 6–11.30pm, Sat 11.30am–11.30pm, Sun noon–11pm.

La Pergola Southampton Rd T 02380 284184, W la-pergola.co.uk. Lively Italian restaurant in an attractive building with its own garden. Sizzling meat dishes from around £17, tasty pasta and pizza from £9 and superb home-made desserts, as well as daily specials. Tues–Sun & Bank Hol Mon 11am–2.30pm & 6–10.30pm.

Beaulieu

The village of **BEAULIEU** (pronounced "Bewley"), in the southeast corner of the New Forest, was the site of one of England's most influential monasteries, a Cistercian house founded in 1204 by King John – in remorse, it is said, for ordering a group of supplicating monks to be trampled to death. Built using stone ferried from Caen in northern France and Quarr on the Isle of Wight, the **abbey** managed a self-sufficient estate of ten thousand acres, but was dismantled soon after the Dissolution. Its refectory now forms the parish church, which, like everything else in Beaulieu, has been subsumed by the Montagu family who have owned a large chunk of the New Forest since one of Charles II's illegitimate progeny was created duke of the estate.

The Beaulieu Estate

Daily: June–Sept 10am–6pm; Oct–May 10am–5pm • £16.75 includes all attractions • W beaulieu.co.uk

Beaulieu estate comprises **Palace House**, the attractive if unexceptional family home of the Montagus, a ruined Cistercian **Abbey** and the main attraction, the **National Motor Museum** – whose collection of 250 vehicles includes spindly antiques, Formula I cars and a Sinclair C5 – all set in fine grounds. The house, formerly the abbey's gatehouse, contains masses of Montagu-related memorabilia, and the undercroft of the abbey houses an exhibition depicting medieval monastic life.

EATING AND DRINKING — BEAULIEU

The Terrace, The Montagu Arms Lyndhurst Rd T 01590 612324, W montaguarmshotel.co.uk. The New Forest's only Michelin-starred restaurant, in an attractive dining room overlooking a pretty garden where you can eat in the summer. The menu uses local, seasonal ingredients, some grown in the hotel's own kitchen garden, and features dishes such as saddle of venison (£35) and wild sea bass (£32), though to get the full experience, the seven-course tasting menu will set you back £75 a head. Tues 7–9.30pm, Wed–Sun noon–2.30pm & 7–9.30pm.

Buckler's Hard

Daily: March–June, Sept & Oct 10am–5pm; July & Aug 10am–5.30pm; Nov–Feb 10am–4.30pm • £5.95, includes entrance to the museum and parking • ⓦ bucklershard.co.uk

The hamlet of **BUCKLER'S HARD**, a couple of miles downstream from Beaulieu, has a wonderful setting. A row of picturesque thatched shipwrights' cottages, some of which are inhabited, leads down to the Beaulieu River; it doesn't look much like a shipyard now, but from Elizabethan times onwards dozens of men o' war were assembled here from giant New Forest oaks. Several of Nelson's ships were launched here, to be towed carefully by rowing boats past the sandbanks and across the Solent to Portsmouth. The largest house in the hamlet, which forms part of the Montagu estate, belonged to Henry Adams, the master builder responsible for most of the Trafalgar fleet; it's now a hotel, pub and restaurant (see below). At the top of the village is the **Maritime Museum** which traces the history of the great ships and incorporates buildings preserved in their eighteenth-century form.

3

ACCOMMODATION — BUCKLERS HARD

Master Builders Hotel ⓣ 0844 815 3399, ⓦ themasterbuilders.co.uk. Picturesque and peaceful, this wonderful quirky hotel is in a sixteenth-century building with open fires and a superb location overlooking the river: the rooms are a mixed bunch, some quite simple, others newly refurbished with oriental flourishes and individually designed furniture. There's also a decent restaurant and pub – you can take your drink outside onto the lawns in nice weather. **£120**

Lymington

The most pleasant point of access for ferries to the Isle of Wight (see p.184) is **LYMINGTON**, a sheltered haven that's become one of the busiest leisure harbours on the south coast. Rising from the quay area, the old town is full of cobbled streets and Georgian houses and has one unusual building – the partly thirteenth-century church of **St Thomas the Apostle**, with a cupola-topped tower built in 1670.

ARRIVAL AND DEPARTURE — LYMINGTON

By train A branch line runs from the main line at Brockenhurst to Lymington (every 30min; 10min). Trains call first at Lymington Town station, a short walk from the high street, then run onto Lymington Pier to link with the Isle of Wight ferry.

By bus Buses #56 and #6 run from Southampton to Lymington via Lyndhurst and Brockenhurst; the coastal route #X1 arrives here from Christchurch.

ACCOMMODATION

Britannia House Mill Lane ⓣ 01590 672091, ⓦ britannia-house.com. A well-kept, friendly and central B&B, right by the train station. The comfortable rooms are on the small side but there's a fine sitting room commanding views over the waterfront. **£85**

Stanwell House High St ⓣ 01590 677123, ⓦ stanwellhouse.com. The most upmarket choice in town, this handsome boutique-style hotel has an array of individually designed rooms boasting rolltop baths, flatscreen TVs and the like. It also has a superb restaurant (see p.196). **£140**

EATING AND DRINKING

★ **Graze** 9 Gosport St ⓣ 01590 675595. Lymington's liveliest spot for dining, where the fusion-style food includes sumptuous courgette fritters, coconut shrimp and fried mixed fish for around £20 per person; the £7 set menu (two dishes) is great value. It also has a trendy bar, serving great cocktails, and a small garden area. Tues–Thurs noon–midnight, Fri & Sat noon–1am.

The Ship Inn The Quay ⓣ 01590 676903, ⓦ theshiplymington.co.uk. With a terrace facing the water, this classy, friendly pub has a stylish nautical interior of bleached wood and chrome. It also offers a superior restaurant menu featuring modern British seasonal dishes such as venison steak (£15.50), along with pub classics like beef and Guinness pie (£12). Food served Mon–Sat noon–10pm, Sun noon–9.30pm.

Stanwell House Restaurant High St ☎01590 677123, @stanwellhouse.com. The seafood restaurant at this classy hotel is Lymington's top spot to eat, in a dining room with a distinctly colonial feel (mains from around £17); there is also a less formal bistro serving modern European cuisine. Daily noon–9.30pm.

Brockenhurst

You'll frequently find New Forest ponies strolling down the high street of **BROCKENHURST**, undoubtedly the most attractive and liveliest town in the forest. Surrounded by idyllic heath and woodland and with a ford at one end, it's a picturesque spot and a useful travel hub.

ARRIVAL AND DEPARTURE — BROCKENHURST

3

By train The train station is on the eastern edge of town – from here, turn left and left again into the main Brookley Rd, where you'll find the bulk of shops, banks and places to eat and drink.

Destinations London Waterloo (every 20min; 1hr 30min); Southampton (every 15min; 15–20min); Winchester (every 20min; 30min). A branch line runs to Lymington (every 30min; 10min) to link with the Isle of Wight ferry.

ACCOMMODATION

Careys Manor Lyndhurst Rd ☎01590 623551, @careysmanor.com. This Victorian country house and former home of Charles II forester, John Carey, has a range of rooms, from traditional four-posters in the manor house to contemporary options with a terrace or balcony in the modern wing. There's a highly regarded Thai spa – though guests have to pay to use it – and three restaurants. **£140**

Thatched Cottage Hotel 16 Brookley Rd ☎01590 623090, @thatched-cottage.co.uk. Dating from 1627, this is indeed an ancient thatched cottage, its tiny, low-beamed rooms as crammed with character as they are with furniture. There are just five rooms, one with a small outdoor terrace, as well as an attached restaurant with its own garden. The cream teas are divine, too. **£80**

EATING AND DRINKING

The Buttery 25 Brookley Rd @thebuttery.org. Bear-themed tearoom which attracts a steady stream of regulars for its inexpensive lunches, superior cream teas and delicious home-made cakes – the sugar-free, wheat-free fruit cake is much nicer than it sounds – with tea served in giant teapots. Mon–Fri 9am–5pm, Sun 9am–6pm.

Rose and Crown Lyndhurst Rd @rosecrownpubbrockenhurst.co.uk. A traditional forest inn dating from the thirteenth century with a pleasant garden and a skittle alley. A selection of real ales, and large portions of good-value pub grub featuring local meat and cheese – try the New Forest beef stew (£10). Mon–Sat 11am–11pm, Sun noon–10pm.

Bournemouth and around

Renowned for its pristine white beach (one of southern England's cleanest) and its gardens, the resort of **BOURNEMOUTH** dates from 1811, when a local squire, Louis Tregonwell, built a summerhouse on the wild, unpopulated heathland that once occupied this stretch of coast, and planted the first of the pine trees that now characterize the area. The mild climate, sheltered site and glorious sandy beach encouraged the rapid growth of a full-scale family-holiday resort, complete with piers, cliff railways and boat trips. Today Bournemouth has a rather genteel, slightly geriatric image, counterbalanced by burgeoning numbers of language students, clubbers and **surfers**, attracted by Britain's only artificial reef in the neighbouring suburb of **Boscombe**.

In the centre of town, on Hinton Road, the graveyard of **St Peter's** church is where Mary Shelley, author of the Gothic horror tale *Frankenstein*, is buried, together with the heart belonging to her husband, the Romantic poet Percy Bysshe Shelley. The tombs of Mary's parents – radical thinker William Godwin and early feminist Mary Wollstonecraft – are also here.

CLOCKWISE FROM TOP STONEHENGE (P.215), BOURNEMOUTH (P.196), SALISBURY CATHEDRAL (P.212) >

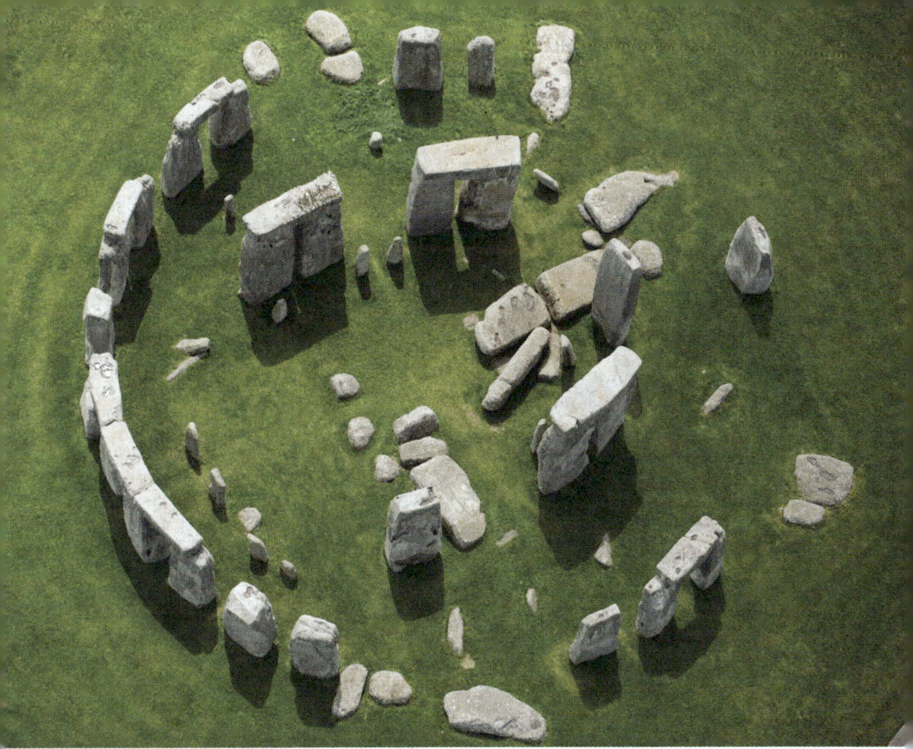
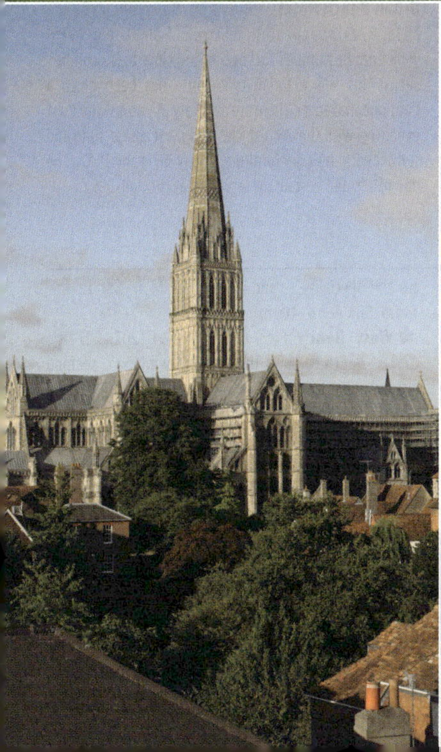
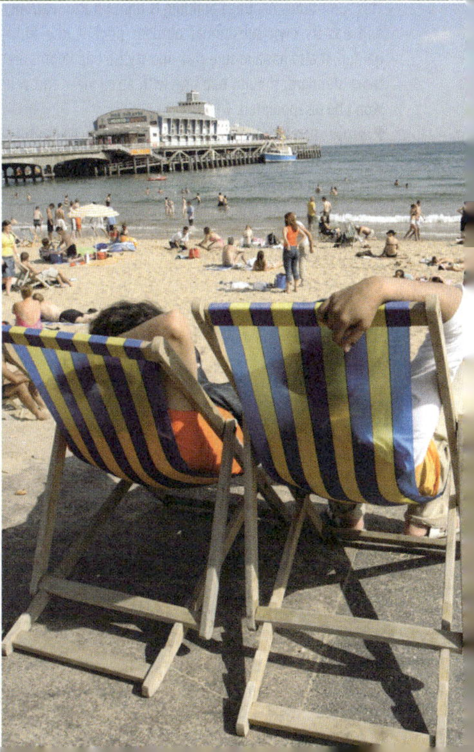

Russell-Cotes Art Gallery and Museum

East Cliff Promenade • Tues–Sun & Bank Hol Mon 10am–5pm • Free • ⓦ russell-cotes.bournemouth.gov.uk

Surrounded by lovely gardens on a cliff-top, the **Russell-Cotes Art Gallery and Museum** has one of the UK's best collections of Victoriana, collected from around the world by the wealthy Russell-Cotes family. The quirky assortment of artworks, Oriental souvenirs and curios, such as the axe that allegedly beheaded Mary Queen of Scots, are displayed in an ornately decorated mansion, once the family home. Highlights of the collection are Rossetti's *Venus Verticordia* (1864) and England's most important collection of Victorian nudes, which scandalized much of society at the time.

ARRIVAL AND INFORMATION — BOURNEMOUTH

The **train station** and **bus station** lie opposite each other about a mile inland. They're connected to the town centre and seafront by frequent buses, or you can walk there in around 15–20min.

3

By train Destinations Brockenhurst (3–4 hourly; 15–25min); Dorchester (every 30min–hourly; 45min); London Waterloo (every 30min; 2hr); Poole (every 20min; 10min); Southampton (every 20min; 30–50min); Weymouth (hourly; 55min); Winchester (every 20–30min; 45min–1hr).

By bus Destinations Direct National Express buses run to London (hourly; 2hr 30min); Salisbury (Mon–Sat every 30min, Sun 7 daily; 1hr 10min); Southampton (10 daily; 45min–1hr); Weymouth (4 daily; 1hr 15min–1hr 30min) and Winchester (5 daily; 1hr 15min–1hr 45min), while Greyhound buses also run to London (1–3 daily; 2hr 30min).

Tourist office Westover Rd (June to mid-Sept Mon–Sat 9.30am–5pm; July & Aug Mon–Sat 9.30am–5pm, Sun 11am–3pm; mid-Sept to May Mon–Sat 10am–4pm; ⓣ 0845 051 1701, ⓦ bournemouth.co.uk).

ACCOMMODATION

The Cumberland East Overcliff Drive, East Cliff ⓣ 01202 290722, ⓦ cumberlandbournemouth.co.uk. This sumptuous Art Deco building is right on the seafront, and has its own substantial outdoor pool in the front garden. It also has a leisure club and stylish bar. Rooms are more standard, though bag one with a sea view and you won't be disappointed. **£140**

Premier Inn Westover Rd ⓣ 0871 527 8124, ⓦ premierinn.com. In a 1930s Art Deco building where the cover of a Beatles album, *With the Beatles*, was shot, this chain hotel is very central and offers good-value rooms – all of them, including family options, are the same price, so request one with sea views. **£83**

Urban Beach Hotel 23 Argyll Rd, Boscombe ⓣ 01202 301509, ⓦ urbanbeachhotel.co.uk. A short (but steep) walk from Boscombe's surf beach, and close to Boscombe's shops, this old Victorian townhouse has been given a boutique makeover. There are a variety of rooms, the least expensive with shower cubicles, but most are en-suite and stylish with designer furniture, comfy beds and DVDs. The downstairs bar-restaurant serves great cocktails. **£97**

EATING AND DRINKING

Chez Fred 10 Seamoor Rd, Westbourne ⓣ 01202 761023, ⓦ chezfred.co.uk. Top-quality fish and chips at this sit-down restaurant and takeaway, which regularly wins awards and is popular with locals and visiting celebs – hence the queues at peak times. Mon–Fri 11.30am–2pm & 5–10pm, Sat 11.30am–2.30pm & 5–10pm, Sun 5–9pm.

Dosa World 280 Old Christchurch Rd ⓣ 01202 318535, ⓦ dosaworld.net. Excellent-value authentic South Indian and Sri Lankan dishes at this popular restaurant. It's mostly veggie, though there are a few non-veg dishes, such as squid masala (£5.75), but it's the huge, delicious dosas that are the speciality – and just £3.50. Mon–Sat noon–11pm, Sun noon–10pm.

★ **West Beach** Pier Approach ⓣ 01202 587785, ⓦ west-beach.co.uk. This award-winning seafood restaurant has a prime position on the beach, with decking out on the promenade. It's smart and stylish, and you can watch the chefs work in the open kitchen, or admire the sea views through huge floor-to-ceiling windows. Fish and seafood feature strongly, with main courses £15–20 – look out for the locally caught daily specials. Mon–Fri 9.30am–3pm & 6–11pm, Sat & Sun 9.30am–5pm & 6–11pm.

NIGHTLIFE AND ENTERTAINMENT

Aruba Bar Pier Approach ⓣ 01202 554211, ⓦ aruba-bournemouth.co.uk. A stylish Caribbean-themed bar sitting above the entrance to Bournemouth pier: its outdoor terrace has comfy swing seats and overlooks the beach. Inside, its soaring ceilings, palm trees, resident parrot, giant central bar area and various alcoves make it a great place to hang out, play scrabble or watch the beach activity below. Mon–Thurs 9am–midnight, Fri & Sat 9am–3am, Sun 9am–10.30pm.

★ **Sixty Million Postcards** 19 Exeter Rd ⊤01202 292697, Ⓦsixtymillionpostcards.com. One of Bournemouth's best bars, attracting a trendy but unpretentious student crowd. There are board games, various alcoves for cosy chats and lounge areas for larger groups. Offers a good range of beers, drinks and inexpensive snacks and occasional live music. Mon–Thurs & Sun noon–midnight, Fri noon–1am, Sat noon–2pm.

Minster of St Cuthberga

High St, Wimborne Minster, a few mins' drive north of the Bournemouth suburbs • Mon–Sat 9.30am–5.30pm, Sun 2.30–5.30pm • **Chained Library** Easter–Oct daily 10.30am–12.30pm & 2–4pm; Nov–Easter Sat 10am–12.30pm • Free

Built on the site of an eighth-century monastery, the **Minster of St Cuthberga**'s massive twin towers of mottled grey and tawny stone dwarf the rest of town. (At one time the church was even more imposing – its spire crashed down during morning service in 1602.) What remains today is basically Norman with later additions, such as the Perpendicular west tower; this bears a figure dressed as a grenadier of the Napoleonic era, who strikes every quarter-hour with a hammer. The **Chained Library** above the choir vestry, dating from 1686, is Wimborne's most prized possession and one of the oldest public libraries in the country. Its collection of ancient books includes a manuscript written on lambskin dating from 1343.

3

Kingston Lacy

Two miles northwest of Wimborne Minster • **House** Mid-March to Oct Wed–Sun 11am–5pm **Grounds** Daily: Jan to mid-March 10.30am–4pm; mid-March to Oct 10.30am–6pm; Nov & Dec 10.30am–4pm • NT • House & grounds £12, grounds only £6

The glorious seventeenth-century mansion of **Kingston Lacy** stands in 250 acres of parkland grazed by a herd of Red Devon cattle. Designed for the Bankes family, who were exiled from Corfe Castle (see p.202) after the Roundheads reduced it to rubble, the brick building was clad in grey stone during the nineteenth century by Sir Charles Barry, co-architect of the Houses of Parliament. William Bankes, then owner of the house, was a great traveller and collector, and the **Spanish Room** is a superb scrapbook of his Grand Tour souvenirs, lined with gilded leather and surmounted by a Venetian ceiling. Kingston Lacy's **picture collection** is also outstanding, featuring Titian, Rubens, Velázquez and many other old masters.

Christchurch

CHRISTCHURCH, five miles east of Bournemouth, is best known for **Christchurch Priory** (Mon–Sat 9.30am–5pm, Sun 2.15–5.30pm; £3 donation requested), which, at 311ft, is England's longest parish church. The oldest parts of the current church date back to 1094, and its fan-vaulted North Porch is the country's biggest. Fine **views** can be gained from the top of the 120ft-high tower (book on ⊤01202 485804; £2.50).

The area round the old town quay has a carefully preserved charm, with the **Red House Museum and Gardens** on Quay Road (Tues–Sat 10am–5pm, Sun 2–5pm; free) containing an affectionate collection of local memorabilia. Relaxing **boat trips** (Easter–Oct daily; ⊤01202 429119) leave from the grassy banks of the riverside quay east to the sandspit at Mudeford (30min; £6.50 return) or upriver to Tuckton (15min; £2.50 return).

ARRIVAL AND INFORMATION — CHRISTCHURCH

By train Christchurch is on the main Weymouth to London line; the train station is about a mile north of the centre.

By bus Local buses from Bournemouth in the east, Lymington in the west and Ringwood in the north, pull up at the bus stop close to the tourist information centre right on the high street.

Tourist office 49 High St (Mon–Fri 9.30am–5pm, Sat 9.30am–4.30pm; ⊤01202 471780, Ⓦvisitchristchurch.info).

ACCOMMODATION

Kings Hotel 18 Castle St ⓣ01202 483434, ⓦthekings-chirstchurch.co.uk. A decent place in the centre of town right opposite the castle ruins. The sixteen rooms are well furnished in boutique style, with Egyptian cotton sheets, flatscreen TVs and free wi-fi, and some have views over the castle at the front. **£115**

Mill Stream House 6 Ducking Stool Walk ⓣ01202 480114, ⓦchristchurchbedandbreakfast.co.uk. Just two en-suite rooms with all mod cons in this modern mews house overlooking the millstream. The location is quiet, but wonderfully central, a mere stone's throw from the *King's Hotel* and a short walk from the high street. **£70**

EATING AND DRINKING

The Jetty Christchurch Harbour Hotel, 95 Mudeford ⓣ01202 400950, ⓦthejetty.co.uk. Michelin-starred chef Alex Aitken uses local seasonal produce in this contemporary wooden restaurant with stunning views of Christchurch harbour. Interesting main courses include Mudeford paella using local seafood (£23): the set lunch/early evening menu is good value at £22 for three courses. Mon–Sat noon–2.30pm & 6.30–10pm, Sun noon–8pm.

3

★ **The Rising Sun** 123 Purewell ⓣ01202 486122, ⓦrisingpubs.com. Excellent-quality Thai food, much of it organic and MSG-free, served at this pleasant pub, with comfortable garden seating at the back. Prices are reasonable, particularly the two-course lunch menu (£8). Food served noon–2.15pm & 6.45–9.30pm.

Thomas Tripp 10 Wick Lane ⓣ01202 490498. Christchurch's liveliest pub defies the town's reputation for being full of retired people – a good-time, young crowd enjoy a great outdoor terrace, frequent live music and DJ sessions. Good value tapas-style dishes too – four for £10. Tues–Sat 10am–11pm, Sun noon–10.30pm.

Poole

West of Bournemouth, **POOLE** is an ancient seaport on a huge, almost landlocked harbour. The town developed in the thirteenth century and was successively colonized by pirates, fishermen and timber traders. The old quarter by the quayside contains more than one hundred historic buildings, as well as the contemporary **Poole Museum.**

Poole Museum

Old High St • Easter–Oct Mon–Sat 10am–5pm, Sun noon–5pm; Nov–Easter Tues–Sat 10am–4pm, Sun noon–4pm • Free • ⓦboroughofpoole.com/museums

Poole Museum traces the town's development through the centuries, with displays of local ceramics and tiles and a rare Iron Age log boat that was dug out of the harbour in 1964: carved out of a single tree trunk, the 33ft-long boat dates from around 300 BC. Look out, too, for the fascinating footage of the Poole flying boats that took off from the harbour during the 1940s for the Far East and Australia.

Brownsea Island

Mid-Feb to March Sat & Sun 10am–4pm (boats from Sandbanks only; £5; book on ⓣ01202 492161); April–Oct daily 10am–5pm (boats from Sandbanks and Poole Quay; £9; book on ⓣ01929 462383) • NT • £5.80

Brownsea Island is famed for its red squirrels, wading birds and other wildlife, which you can spot along themed trails. The landscape is surprisingly diverse for such a small island – much of it is heavily wooded, though there are also areas of heath and marsh, and narrow, shingly beaches – and it's pretty easy to escape from the boat-trippers and find a peaceful corner to picnic.

Compton Acres

Daily: April–Oct 10am–6pm; Nov–March 10am–4pm; last entry 1hr before closing • £6.95 • ⓦcomptonacres.co.uk

One of the area's best-known gardens, **Compton Acres**, lies on the outskirts of Poole, signposted off the A35 Poole Road towards Bournemouth (bus #50 from Bournemouth and #52 from Poole). Spectacularly sited over ten acres on steep slopes above Poole Harbour, each of the seven gardens here has a different international theme, including a formal Italian garden and the elegantly understated Japanese Garden, its meandering streams crossed by stone steps and wooden bridges.

ARRIVAL AND INFORMATION **POOLE**

By train Poole's train station is on Serpentine Lane, about a 15min walk from the waterfront along the high street.
Destinations Bournemouth (every 20min; 10min); London (every 30min; 2hr–2hr 10min); Weymouth (every 30min; 35–45min).

By bus The bus station is in front of the Dolphin Centre on Kingland Rd.
Destinations There are regular National Express (12 daily; 2hr 35min–3hr 30min) and Greyhound services (1–3 daily; 3hr) to London.

Tourist office Poole Quay (April–June, Sept & Oct daily 10am–5pm; July & Aug daily 10am–6pm; Nov–March Mon–Fri 10am–5pm, Sat 10am–4pm; ⓣ01202 253253, ⓦpooletourism.com).

ACCOMMODATION

Corkers 1 High St ⓣ01202 681393, ⓦcorkers.co.uk. Above a lively café-restaurant, this B&B offers some of the best-value rooms in town – the two superb front rooms, one of which sleeps three, have harbour-facing balconies. Parking offered for a small fee. **£80**

★ **Hotel du Vin** Thames St ⓣ01202 685666, ⓦhotelduvin.com. Inside a fine old mansion house with a double staircase, this stylish hotel has plush, comfortable, rooms, an atmospheric restaurant and wine cellar, and a very cosy bar with its own log fire – great in winter. The location is great, in the pretty old town a minute's walk from the Quay. **£155**

3

EATING AND DRINKING

★ **Deli on the Quay** D17 Dolphin Quays, The Quay ⓣ01202 660022. Bright, light harbourfront café-deli with floor-to-ceiling shelves stacked with delicious preserves, wines and the like. The café is a great breakfast or lunch stop, serving fresh croissants and sandwiches and decent coffee. Mon, Wed & Thurs 9am–5pm, Tues & Fri 9am–8.30pm, Sat & Sun 10am–5pm.

Poole Arms The Quay ⓣ01202 673450. Completely covered with green tiles, this wonderfully atmospheric historic pub is reassuringly old-fashioned, with prints of old Poole on the walls, decent beers and fresh fish daily. There's outdoor seating on the waterfront too. Mon–Sat 11am–11pm, Sun noon–11pm.

★ **Storm** 16 High St ⓣ01202 674970. Owned by a chef/fisherman, this restaurant, unsurprisingly, specializes in locally caught seafood. The menu changes daily according to what is available, but expect such delights as local bream (£18) and local crab and oysters (£7 for a starter). May–Oct Mon–Sat noon–2.30pm & 5.30pm–late; Nov–April Tues–Sat 7–9.30pm, phone for lunch hours.

The Isle of Purbeck

Though not actually an island, the **ISLE OF PURBECK** – a promontory of low hills and heathland jutting out beyond Poole Harbour – does have an insular and distinctive feel. Reached from the east by the **ferry from Sandbanks** (every 20min 7am–11pm; pedestrians £1, bikes 90p, cars £3.20), at the narrow mouth of Poole Harbour, or by a long and congested landward journey via the bottleneck of **Wareham**, Purbeck can be a difficult destination to reach, but its villages are immensely pretty, none more so than **Corfe Castle**, with its majestic ruins. From **Swanage**, a low-key seaside resort, the Dorset Coast Path provides access to the oily shales of Kimmeridge Bay, the spectacular cove at **Lulworth** and the much-photographed natural arch of **Durdle Door**.

The whole coast from Purbeck to Exmouth in Devon – dubbed the **Jurassic Coast** (ⓦjurassiccoast.com; see p.211) – is a World Heritage Site on account of its geological significance and fossil remains; walkers can access it along the South West Coast Path.

GETTING AROUND **ISLE OF PURBECK**

By bike Cycling is a great way to get round the Purbecks, though be prepared for some steep hills; bikes can be rented from Cycle Experience at Wareham Station (ⓣ01929 556601, ⓦpurbeckcyclehire.co.uk) and *The Globe Inn*, 3 Bell St, in Swanage (ⓣ07944 405350, ⓦtheglobeswanage.co.uk).

By bus The Purbeck Breezer runs two services around the Purbecks – route #40 from Poole to Swanage via Wareham and Corfe Castle, and route #50 from Bournemouth to Swanage via the Sandbanks ferry and Studland. In summer, some services are open-top.

By train Wareham is the only place served by mainline trains.

3

Wareham

The grid pattern of its streets indicates the Saxon origins of **WAREHAM**, and the town is surrounded by even older earth ramparts known as the Walls. A riverside setting adds greatly to its charms, though the place gets fairly overrun in summer. Nearby lies an enclave of quaint houses around **Lady St Mary's Church**, which contains the marble coffin of Edward the Martyr, murdered at Corfe Castle in 978 by his stepmother, to make way for her son Ethelred. **St Martin's Church**, at the north end of town, dates from Saxon times and holds a faded twelfth-century mural of St Martin offering his cloak to a beggar. The church's most striking feature, however, is a romantic effigy of T.E. Lawrence in Arab dress, which was originally destined for Salisbury Cathedral, but was rejected by the dean there who disapproved of Lawrence's sexual proclivities. Lawrence was killed in 1935 in a motorbike accident on the road from Bovington (six miles west); his simply furnished cottage is at **Clouds Hill**, seven miles northwest of Wareham (mid-March to Oct Wed–Sun 11am–5pm or dusk; NT; £4.50). The small **museum** next to Wareham's town hall in East Street (Easter–Oct Mon–Sat 10am–4pm; free) focuses on local history and Lawrence memorabilia.

ARRIVAL AND INFORMATION — WAREHAM

By train Wareham station, a 15min walk north of the town, sees regular trains from London (every 30min; 2hr 20min) and Weymouth (every 20–40min; 25–35min).

Tourist office Holy Trinity Church, South St (Easter–Oct Mon–Sat 9.30am–5pm; Nov–Easter Mon–Sat 9.30am–4pm; ⊕01929 552740, ⊕purbeck.gov.uk).

Corfe Castle

Daily: March & Oct 10am–5pm; April–Sept 10am–6pm; Nov–Feb 10am–4pm • NT • £6.50

The romantic ruins crowning the hill behind the village of **CORFE CASTLE** are perhaps the most evocative in England. The family seat of Sir John Bankes, Attorney General to Charles I, this Royalist stronghold withstood a Cromwellian siege for six weeks, gallantly defended by Lady Bankes. One of her own men, Colonel Pitman, eventually betrayed the castle to the Roundheads, after which it was reduced to its present gap-toothed state by gunpowder. Apparently the victorious Roundheads were so impressed by Lady Bankes' courage that they allowed her to take the keys to the castle with her – they can still be seen in the library at the Bankes' subsequent home, Kingston Lacy (see p.199).

ACCOMMODATION — CORFE CASTLE

★ **Purbeck Vineyard** Valley Rd, Harman's Cross, 2 miles southeast of Corfe Castle ⊕01929 481525, ⊕vineyard.uk.com. Plush, contemporary rooms with wi-fi, flatscreen TVs and terraces overlooking a working vineyard – and the Swanage steam railway in the distance. If you're here in the autumn, you can join the local villagers and help out with the grape harvest. There's a good restaurant on site, too, where you can sample their wines with your meal. **£110**

EATING AND DRINKING

The Greyhound The Square ⊕01929 480205, ⊕greyhoundcorfe.co.uk. One of England's oldest coaching inns, with a pleasant garden at the back boasting fine views of the castle. The food features local specialities such as venison casserole (£12.50), as well as a good range of hearty sandwiches – the steak sandwich in garlic butter comes with chips and salad for £7. Food served 10.30am–9.30pm.

Mortons House Restaurant East St ⊕01929 480988, ⊕mortonshouse.co.uk. Linked to a lovely small hotel, this fine dining restaurant offers three superb courses for £37.50, featuring dishes such as seared scallops with spice pork belly, and fennel and watercress risotto. Open daily.

National Trust Tearooms The Square ⊕01929 48133. Delicious cream teas, sandwiches, lunches and cakes served in a pretty garden overlooking the castle. Daily 10am–4/5/5.30pm.

Swanage

Purbeck's largest town, **SWANAGE**, is a traditional seaside resort with a pleasant sandy beach and an ornate town hall. The town's station is the southern terminus of the

Swanage Steam Railway (April–Oct daily; Nov– March Sat & Sun plus school hols; £9 return; ⓣ01929 425800, ⓦswanagerailway.co.uk), which runs for six miles to Norden, just north of Corfe Castle. West of Swanage, you can pick up the coastal path to **Durlston Country Park**, around a mile out of town. Set in 280 acres of coastal woodland and crisscrossed with cliff-top paths, it is a great place for a picnic or for wind-blown walks.

ACCOMMODATION — SWANAGE

The Swanage Haven 3 Victoria Rd ⓣ01929 423088, ⓦswanagehaven.com. Good-value boutique-style guesthouse: the smart rooms have flatscreen TVs and the decked garden has a great outdoor hot tub. Breakfasts are good, made from locally sourced ingredients. **£60**

★ **Tom's Field Campsite** Langton Matravers, a couple of miles west of Swanage ⓣ01929 427110, ⓦtomsfieldcamping.co.uk. Wonderfully sited and well-run, this is the best campsite in the region, with sea views from some of the pitches and direct access to the coast path. It also lets out bunks in a converted Nissen hut – The Walker's Barn (£10 per person) – or a converted pigsty called The Stone Room (£25 for the room). The campsite has a well-stocked shop, but only takes reservations for longer stays – for short stays, especially on sunny weekends, you'll need to turn up early to bag a pitch. **£14** for a small tent, car and 2 people.

3

EATING AND DRINKING

Gee Whites The Old Stone Quay, 1 High St ⓣ01929 425720, ⓦgeewhites.co.uk. Open-air seafood bar right on the quay serving a daily changing menu of local lobster, crabs, mussels and oysters. A great spot to enjoy reasonably priced, fresh seafood on a summer evening, washed down with a glass of ice-cold cava. April–Oct daily noon–9pm; Nov–March Sat & Sun only, weather permitting.

Ocean Bay 2 Ulwell Rd ⓣ01929 422222, ⓦoceanbayswanage.com. In an enviable position facing the beach, with outdoor tables on a narrow terrace, this is the best place for a top-quality meal. Dishes, such as Swanage Bay crab risotto and chargrilled Purbeck venison, use mostly local produce. Three courses cost £28 at dinner. Daily 9am–3pm & 6.30–9.15pm.

Studland

East of Swanage, you can follow the Southwest Coast path over Ballard Down to descend into the pretty village of **STUDLAND** at the southern end of **Studland Bay**. The most northerly stretch of the beach, **Shell Bay**, is a magnificent strand of icing-sugar sand backed by a remarkable heathland ecosystem that's home to all six British species of reptile – adders are quite common, so be careful. On Middle Beach, you can **hire kayaks** from the **Studland Sea School** (ⓣ01929 450430, ⓦstudlandseaschool.co.uk) or take one of their excellent guided kayak tours round Old Harry Rocks, through cliff arches and sea caves.

EATING AND DRINKING — STUDLAND

★ **Bankes Arms** Manor Rd ⓣ01929 450225, ⓦbankesarms.com. Lovely location, good food, and a great range of real ales, some from local independent breweries and others from its own on-site Isle of Purbeck Brewery. The pub food costs slightly more than average, but the portions are big, and frankly it's worth it for the joy of sitting in the grassy front garden with fantastic bay views, or by the roaring log fire in the cosy Purbeck stone interior. Daily 11am–11pm.

Lulworth Cove

The quaint thatch-and-stone villages of **EAST LULWORTH** and **WEST LULWORTH** form a prelude to **LULWORTH COVE**, a perfect shell-shaped bite formed when the sea broke through a weakness in the cliffs and then gnawed away at them from behind, forming a circular cave that eventually collapsed to leave a bay enclosed by sandstone cliffs. West of the cove, **Stair Hole** is a roofless sea cave riddled with arches that will eventually collapse to form another Lulworth Cove. The mysteries of local geology are explained at the **Lulworth Heritage Centre** (daily 10am–4/6pm; free) by the car park at the top of the lane leading down to the cove.

Durdle Door

A mile west of Lulworth Cove the iconic limestone arch of **Durdle Door** can be reached via the steep uphill path that starts from Lulworth Cove's car park. The arch itself sits at the end of a long shingle beach (which can be accessed via steep steps), a lovely place for catching the sun and swimming in fresh, clear water. There are other steps to a bay just east of Durdle Door, **St Oswald's Bay**, with another shingle beach and offshore rocks that you can swim out to.

ACCOMMODATION — LULWORTH COVE

The Beach House T 01929 400404, W lulworthbeachhouse.com. Great location right on the main street leading down to the cove and overlooking the duck pond. The first choice in Lulworth itself, especially if you can bag one of the front rooms that come with their own cove-view terraces (around £50 more than standard rooms). It's simple but with contemporary decor and a good restaurant. **£75**

Durdle Door Holiday Park T 01929 400200, W lulworth.com. Superbly positioned up on the cliffs above Durdle Door, this campsite has fabulous views from its touring field, while tents can be pitched in the more sheltered wooded field. It's a twenty-minute walk across fields to Lulworth Cove and there's also a shop and café/bar on site. **£32** for a tent plus car.

3

EATING AND DRINKING

Castle Inn Main Rd, West Lulworth T 01929 400311. Up in the village, this sixteenth-century thatched pub has a lovely terraced garden, a good range of local real ales and a selection of traditional pub games. High-quality pub grub features home-made steak and ale pie and beef bourguignon. It's also very dog-friendly. Food served Mon–Thurs noon–2.30pm & 7–11pm, Fri & Sat noon–2.30pm & 6–11pm, Sun noon–3pm & 7–10.30pm.

Lulworth Cove Inn Main Rd, Lulworth Cove T 01929 400333. Decent pub food, local Blandford ales, real fires and a pleasant garden with outdoor seating. They specialize in local seafood and game, with dishes such as wild boar and apple faggots (£11.50) and seafood paella (£12). Food served daily noon–9pm.

Dorchester and around

For many, **DORCHESTER,** county town of Dorset, is essentially **Thomas Hardy**'s town; he was born at Higher Bockhampton, three miles east, his heart is buried in Stinsford, a couple of miles northeast (the rest of him is in Westminster Abbey), and he spent much of his life in Dorchester itself, where his statue now stands on High West Street. The town appears in his novels as Casterbridge, and the local countryside is evocatively depicted, notably the wild heathland of the east (Egdon Heath) and the eerie yew forest of Cranborne Chase.

The real Dorchester – liveliest on Wednesday, market day – has a pleasant central core of mostly seventeenth-century and Georgian buildings, though the town's origins go back to the Romans, who founded "Durnovaria" in about 70 AD. The Roman walls were replaced in the eighteenth century by tree-lined avenues called "Walks", but some traces of the Roman period have survived. On the southeast edge of town, **Maumbury Rings** is where the Romans held vast gladiatorial combats in an amphitheatre adapted from a Stone Age site.

Antelope Hotel

In addition to its Hardy connections, Dorchester is also associated with the notorious **Judge Jeffreys**, who, after the ill-fated rebellion of the Duke of Monmouth (one of Charles II's illegitimate offspring) against James II, held his "Bloody Assizes" in the Oak Room of the **Antelope Hotel** on Cornhill in 1685. A total of 292 men were sentenced to death, though most got away with a flogging and transportation to the West Indies, while 74 were hung, drawn and quartered, their heads stuck on pikes throughout Dorset and Somerset. Judge Jeffreys lodged just round the corner from the *Antelope* in High West Street, in what is now a half-timbered Italian restaurant.

Old Crown Courts

High West St • Mon–Fri 10am–noon & 2–4pm • Free

The **Old Crown Courts**, also known as Shire Hall, are of interest principally as the place where six men from the nearby village of Tolpuddle, now known as the **Tolpuddle Martyrs** (see below), were sentenced to transportation for forming what was in effect Britain's first trade union. Although the council buildings are still in use, the room in which the Martyrs were tried has been preserved as a memorial; you can sit behind the judge's desk and bang his gavel, or ponder their fate from the jurors' bench.

Dorset County Museum

High West St • Jan–Oct Mon–Sat 10am–4/5pm; Nov & Dec Tues–Sat 10am–4pm • £6.50 • ⓦ dorsetcountymuseum.org

The best place to find out about Dorchester's history is the engrossing **Dorset County Museum**, where archeological and geological displays trace Celtic and Roman history, including a section on the nearby Maiden Castle (see below). Pride of place goes to the re-creation of Thomas Hardy's study, where his pens are inscribed with the names of the books he wrote with them.

3

Maiden Castle

Around 2 miles southwest of Dorchester • Free

One of southern England's finest prehistoric sites, **MAIDEN CASTLE** stands on a hill southwest of Dorchester. Covering about 115 acres, it was first developed around 3000 BC by a Stone Age farming community and then used during the Bronze Age as a funeral mound. Iron Age dwellers expanded it into a populous settlement and fortified it with a daunting series of ramparts and ditches, just in time for the arrival of Vespasian's Second Legion. The ancient Britons' slingstones were no match for the more sophisticated weapons of the Roman invaders, however, and Maiden Castle was stormed in a massacre in 43 AD.

What you see today is a massive series of grassy concentric ridges about 60ft high, creasing the surface of the hill. The main finds from the site are displayed in the Dorset County Museum (see above).

Cerne Abbas giant

Cerne Abbas, 7 miles north of Dorchester just off the A352 • NT • Free

The village of **CERNE ABBAS** has bags of charm, with gorgeous Tudor cottages and abbey ruins, but its main attraction is the enormously priapic **giant** carved in the chalk hillside just north of the village, standing 180ft high and flourishing a club over his disproportionately small head. The age of the monument is disputed, some believing it to be pre-Roman, others thinking it might be a Romano-British figure of Hercules. Either way, in view of his prominent feature it's probable that the giant originated as some primeval fertility symbol. Folklore has it that lying on the outsize member will induce conception, but the National Trust, who now own the site, do their best to stop people wandering over it and eroding the 2ft-deep trenches that form the outlines.

Tolpuddle Martyrs Museum

Tolpuddle, 8 miles east of Dorchester, off the A3 • April–Oct Tues–Sat 10am–5pm, Sun 11am–5pm; Nov–March Thurs–Sat 10am–4pm, Sun 11am–4pm • Free • ⓣ 0131 584 8237, ⓦ tolpuddlemartyrs.org.uk

The delightful Dorset village of **TOLPUDDLE** is of interest principally because of the **Tolpuddle Martyrs**. In 1834, six villagers, George and James Loveless, Thomas and John Standfield, John Brine and James Hammett, were sentenced to transportation for banding together to form the Friendly Society of Agricultural Labourers, in order to petition for a small wage increase on the grounds that their families were starving. After a public outcry the men were pardoned, and the Martyrs passed into history as founders of the trade union movement. Six memorial cottages were built in 1934 to commemorate the centenary of the Martyrs' conviction. The middle one has been turned into the little **Tolpuddle Martyrs Museum**, which charts the story of the men, from their harsh rural lives before their conviction to the horrors of transportation in a convict ship and the brutal conditions of the penal colonies in Australia.

ARRIVAL AND INFORMATION — DORCHESTER

By train Dorchester has two train stations, Dorchester South and Dorchester West, both south of the centre.
Destinations Dorchester South: Bournemouth (every 30min; 45min); London (every 30min; 2hr 40min); Weymouth (3–4 hourly; 10–15min). Dorchester West: Bath (7 daily; 2hr); Bristol (7 daily; 2hr 20min).
By bus Most local buses stop around the car park on Acland Rd, to the east of South St, though long-distance buses pull in next to Dorchester South train station.
Destinations Bournemouth (4 daily; 1hr–1hr 40min); London (4 daily; 4–5hr); Weymouth (frequently; 30min).
Tourist office Antelope Walk (April–Oct Mon–Sat 9am–5pm; Nov–March Mon–Sat 9am–4pm; T 01305 267992, W westdorset.com).

ACCOMMODATION

The Old Rectory Winterbourne Steepleton, 4 miles west T 01305 889468, W theoldrectorybandb.co.uk. A lovely former rectory in a tiny, pretty village. Dating from 1850, the B&B has four comfortable en-suite rooms, one with a four-poster, and attractive well-kept gardens. £70

Westwood House 29 High West St T 01305 268018, W westwoodhouse.co.uk. Comfortable townhouse on the busy high street, with well-furnished rooms, all with wi-fi and flatscreen TVs. The breakfasts are great, and include options such as poached haddock with poached egg. £70

EATING AND DRINKING

★ **Café Jagos** 8 High West St T 01305 266056, W cafe-jagos.co.uk. Good-value salads and sandwiches come in large portions at this pleasant café with contemporary decor – the fresh tuna salad, paninis and grills are all tasty, and there are some fine veggie options such as brie, courgette and potato crumble. Mon–Sat 10am–4pm.

King's Arms 30 High East St T 01305 265353, W kingsarmsdorchester.com. This eighteenth-century coaching house has its own restaurant area and bar with a selection of moderately priced pub food and daily specials, most made from locally sourced ingredients. Main courses include dishes such as Portland crab and squid ink spaghetti (£13), or steaks for around £20. Food served Mon–Sat noon–2pm & 6–9.30pm, Sun noon–2pm.

Sienna 36 High West St T 01305 250022, W siennarestaurant.co.uk. Dorset's only Michelin-starred restaurant, this tiny, upmarket place specializes in locally sourced modern British cuisine such as chargrilled Jurassic Coast veal with white bean casserole. Prices start at around £25 for the two-course lunch menu, up to £55 a head for the evening tasting menu. Tues–Sun noon–2pm & 7–9pm.

Sherborne

Tucked away in the northwest corner of Dorset, ten miles north of Cerne Abbas, the pretty town of **SHERBORNE** was once the capital of Wessex, its church having cathedral status until Old Sarum (see p.214) usurped the bishopric in 1075.

Abbey Church

Abbey Close • Daily: April–Oct 8am–6pm; Nov–March 8am–4pm • Suggested donation £3.50

Sherborne's former historical glory is embodied by the magnificent **Abbey Church** founded in 705 and later becoming a Benedictine abbey. Most of its extant parts date from a rebuilding in the fifteenth century. Among the abbey church's many tombs are those of Alfred the Great's two brothers, Ethelred and Ethelbert, and the Elizabethan poet Thomas Wyatt, all in the northeast corner.

The castles

Old Castle Castletom • April–June & Sept daily 10am–5pm; July & Aug daily 10am–6pm; Oct daily 10am–4pm • EH • £3.40 **Sherborne Castle and gardens** New Rd • April–Oct Tues–Thurs, Sat & Sun 11am–4.30pm; castle interior closed on Sat until 2pm • Castle & gardens £9.50, gardens only £5 • ⓦ sherbornecastle.com

Sherborne boasts no fewer than two "castles", both associated with Sir Walter Raleigh. Queen Elizabeth I first leased, then gave, Raleigh the twelfth-century **Old Castle**, but it seems that he despaired of feudal accommodation and built himself a more comfortably domesticated house, **Sherborne Castle**, in adjacent parkland. When Sir Walter fell from the queen's favour by seducing her maid of honour, the Digby family acquired the house and have lived there ever since. The Old Castle fared less happily, and was pulverized by Cromwellian cannon fire for the obstinately Royalist leanings of its occupants.

ARRIVAL AND INFORMATION — SHERBORNE

By train The station is in the south of the town, about a 5min walk from the centre, and is served by hourly trains between London and Exeter, with some services continuing on to Plymouth.

By bus Buses from Dorchester, Yeovil and Blandford Forum pull in outside the train station.

Tourist office Digby Rd (Mon–Sat: April–Oct 9am–5pm; Oct & Nov 9.30am–4pm; Dec–March 10am–3pm; ⓣ 01935 815341, ⓦ westdorset.com).

3

ACCOMMODATION AND EATING

The Eastbury Long St ⓣ 01935 813131, ⓦ theeastburyhotel.co.uk. Sited in a fine Georgian house, this is the smartest choice in town, with lovely walled gardens complete with a croquet lawn. The front rooms are small so it's worth paying extra for an executive room, which are spacious and nicely appointed and overlook the gardens. It also has a good restaurant specializing in dishes made from seasonal and locally sourced ingredients, and a bar. **£140**

★ **Oliver's** 19 Cheap St ⓣ 01935 815005. With long wooden benches laid out in a former butcher's, adorned with the original tiles, this friendly café-deli serves great cakes and coffee, accompanied by oodles of atmosphere. Mon–Sat 9.30am–5pm, Sun 10am–4pm.

Shaftesbury

Fifteen miles east of Sherborne on the A30, **SHAFTESBURY** perches on a spur of lumpy hills, with severe gradients on three sides of the town. On a clear day, views from the town are terrific – one of the best vantage points is **Gold Hill**, quaint, cobbled and very steep. At its crest, the local history **museum** (April–Oct daily 10.30am–4pm; free) displays items ranging from locally made buttons, for which the area was once renowned, to a mummified cat.

Pilgrims used to flock to Shaftesbury to pay homage to the bones of Edward the Martyr, which were brought to the **Abbey** in 978, though now only the footings of the abbey church survive, just off the main street (April–Oct daily 10am–5pm; £2.50). **St Peter's Church** on the marketplace is one of the few reminders of Shaftesbury's medieval grandeur, when it boasted a castle, twelve churches and four market crosses.

ARRIVAL AND INFORMATION — SHAFTESBURY

By bus Shaftesbury has limited services from Salisbury (Mon–Sat 3 daily) and Blandford Forum (Mon–Sat 6 daily).

Tourist office 8 Bell St (April–Sept Mon–Sat 10am–5pm; Oct–March Mon–Sat 10am–3pm; ⓣ 01747 853514, ⓦ ruraldorset.com).

ACCOMMODATION

La Fleur de Lys Bleke St ⓣ 01747 853717, ⓦ lafleurdelys.co.uk. The best option in town, with a range of stylish rooms above a highly rated if pricey restaurant; the back rooms have the best views, while those at the front are on a busy through-road. **£125**

The Retreat 47 Bell St ⓣ 01747 850372, ⓦ the-retreat.co.uk. A friendly, good-value B&B with several large, comfortable rooms on two floors in a Georgian former schoolhouse. **£82**

EATING AND DRINKING

The Mitre 23 High St ☎01747 853002, Ⓦyoungs.co.uk. A traditional pub with a terrace at the back giving lovely views; inside, there's a cosy dining room with a wood-burning stove and reasonably priced pub grub including steak and ale pie (£8). Mon–Thurs 10.30am–11pm, Fri & Sat 10.30am–midnight, Sun noon–10.30pm.

★ **The Salt Cellar** Gold Hill ☎01747 851838. Right at the top of the hill itself and with great views, this place serves inexpensive snacks and daily specials from around £7, including home-made pies, in the pillar-lined interior or at outdoor tables on the cobbles. Mon–Sat 9am–5pm, Sun 10am–5pm.

Weymouth and around

3

Whether George III's passion for sea bathing was a symptom of his eventual madness is uncertain, but it was at **WEYMOUTH** that in 1789 he became the first reigning monarch to follow the craze. Sycophantic gentry rushed into the waves behind him, and soon the town, formerly a busy port, took on the elegant Georgian stamp that it bears today.

A lively family holiday destination in summer, Weymouth reverts to a more sedate rhythm out of season. The highlight, of course, is its long sandy beach, but there are also a number of "all-weather" attractions in town. A few buildings survive from pre-Georgian times: the restored **Tudor House** on Trinity Street (May to mid-Oct Tues–Fri 1–3.45pm; Nov, Dec & Feb–April first Sun of month 2–4pm; £4) and the ruins of **Sandsfoot Castle** (free access), built by Henry VIII, overlooking Portland Harbour. But Weymouth's most imposing architectural heritage stands along the **Esplanade**, a dignified range of bow-fronted and porticoed buildings gazing out across the graceful bay. The more intimate quayside of the **Old Harbour** is linked to the Esplanade by the pedestrianized **St Mary's Street**. In Lodmoor Country Park, at the eastern end of the promenade, the excellent **Sea Life Park** (daily 10am–4/6pm; £18 or £14.60 online; Ⓦvisitsealife.com/Weymouth) is a splendid family attraction.

Just south of the town stretch the giant arms of Portland Harbour, and a long causeway links Weymouth to the **Isle of Portland**. The causeway stands on the easternmost section of the eighteen-mile bank of pebbles known as **Chesil Beach**, running northwest towards the fishing port of **West Bay**.

ARRIVAL AND INFORMATION — WEYMOUTH

By train Weymouth is served by trains from London, Southampton, Bournemouth and Poole (at least hourly), with less regular services from Bristol and Bath, which arrive at the station on King St, a couple of minutes' walk back from the seafront.

By bus Buses from Dorchester (every 30min or so) pull in at the stops by King George III's statue.

Tourist office The Esplanade (daily: April–Oct 9.30am–5pm; Nov–March 9.30am–4pm; ☎01305 785747, Ⓦvisitweymouth.co.uk).

ACCOMMODATION

★ **Bay View House** 35 The Esplanade ☎01305 782083, Ⓦbayview-weymouth.co.uk. Clean, friendly and well-kept guesthouse. A comfortable room at the front with a bay window overlooking the sea is great value, (it's just a little bit costlier than the others). Also has family rooms and free private garage parking. **£55**

Chatsworth Hotel 14 The Esplanade ☎01305 785012, Ⓦthechatsworth.co.uk. Lovely guesthouse in a great location. The furnishings are modern and all the rooms have either harbour or sea views. On fine days breakfast is served on a terrace overlooking the harbour: they also do meals here, specializing in local fish caught daily by the friendly owner's brother. **£88**

Old Harbour View 12 Trinity Rd ☎01305 774633, Ⓦoldharbourview.co.uk. Cosy guesthouse in a great location right on the harbourfront. It consists of just two rooms in a Georgian townhouse, but it's worth paying a few pounds extra for the one at the front with a harbour view. The breakfasts are great, using locally sourced and free-range ingredients. **£86**

EATING AND DRINKING

Floods Bistro 19 Custom House Quay ☎01305 772270, Ⓦfloodsrestaurant.co.uk. Small harbourfront restaurant with a few outside tables, serving top-quality fresh fish – try the skate wing with mussels and herb sauce (£13)

– they may even have lobster or John Dory depending on the catch of the day. Daily noon–2.30pm & 7–11pm.

Lanes 19 Trinity Rd ⓣ01305 772023, ⓦlanesweymouth.co.uk. Lively bar-restaurant with harbour views. Reasonably priced main courses include garlic mushroom linguine (£10.50), and there are tasty daily specials. The set lunch is good value at £11 for two courses, and there's occasional live music, including Spanish guitar. Summer daily noon–2.30pm & 6–9pm; rest of year Tues–Sat only.

Time for Tea 8 Cove St ⓣ01305 777500. Small, French-style tearooms/café, serving good-value meals, such as duck cassoulet (£10), as well as lighter lunches, including eggs Florentine (£5) and croque monsieur with salad (£5.20), plus home-made cakes and delicious cream teas. Some tables outside. Daily 9.30am–5pm.

Isle of Portland

A long causeway links Weymouth to the odd excrescence of the **Isle of Portland**. Stark, wind-battered and treeless, the isle is famed above all for its hard white limestone, which has been quarried here for centuries – Wren used it for St Paul's Cathedral, and it clads the UN headquarters in New York. It was also used for the 6000ft breakwater that protects Portland Harbour – the largest artificial harbour in Britain, built by convicts in the nineteenth century and still surveyed by **Portland Castle** (daily: April–June & Sept 10am–5pm; July & Aug 10am–6pm; Oct 10am–4pm; £4.30; EH), which was commissioned by Henry VIII. Southeast of here, the craggy limestone of the Isle rises to 496ft at Verne Hill. At **Portland Bill**, the southern tip of the island, you can climb the 153 steps of **Portland Lighthouse** (Easter–June Sun–Thurs 11am–5pm; July–Sept Sun–Fri 11am–5pm; £3), which dates from 1906, for superb views.

3

ARRIVAL AND INFORMATION — PORTLAND

By bus First Bus (ⓦfirstgroup.com) runs bus #1 every 10 min from Commercial Rd in Weymouth to Portland, plus an open-top bus #501 (May to Sept; approx hourly) from Weymouth Esplanade to Portland Bill.

Tourist office In the Portland Lighthouse (Easter–Sept & Oct half-term daily 11am–5pm; Oct–Easter Sun 11am–4pm; ⓣ01305 861233).

EATING AND DRINKING

Cove House Inn 91 Chiswell ⓣ01305 820895, ⓦthecovehouseinn.co.uk. A good spot for food or a quick drink on the island, with pub staples as well as a daily local fish menu, such as mackerel with salad (£6.50) and scallops with new potatoes (£11). It's cosy inside with a wood-burner and big windows with sea views, while the outside tables look over Chesil Beach. Mon–Sat 11am–11pm, Sun noon–10.30pm.

Crab House Café Ferrymans Way, Portland Rd, at the entrance to the Portland causeway ⓣ01305 788867, ⓦcrabhousecafe.co.uk. In a great location overlooking Chesil Beach, this upmarket beach shack is renowned for its superb, locally caught fish and seafood, including oysters from its own beds. Wed & Thurs noon–2pm & 6–8.30pm, Fri & Sat noon–2.30pm & 6–9pm, Sun noon–3.30pm.

Abbotsbury

At the point where Chesil Beach attaches itself to the shore is the pretty village of **ABBOTSBURY**, all tawny ironstone and thatch, which has three main attractions

CHESIL BEACH

Chesil Beach is the strangest feature of the Dorset coast, a 200-yard-wide, 50ft-high bank of pebbles that extends for eighteen miles, its component stones gradually decreasing in size from fist-like pebbles at Portland to "pea gravel" at Burton Bradstock in the west. This sorting is an effect of the powerful coastal currents, which make this one of the most dangerous beaches in Europe – churchyards in the local villages display plenty of evidence of wrecks and drownings. Though not a swimming beach, Chesil is popular with sea anglers, and its wild, uncommercialized atmosphere makes an appealing antidote to the south-coast resorts. Behind the beach, **The Fleet**, a brackish lagoon, was the setting for J. Meade Faulkner's classic smuggling tale, *Moonfleet*.

(**passport ticket** for all three £16). The most absorbing is the village **Swannery** (daily mid-March to Oct 10am–5/6pm; £9.95), a wetland reserve for mute swans dating back to medieval times, when presumably it formed part of the abbot's larder. If you visit in late May or June, you'll see baby cygnets waddling around and squabbling at your feet. The eel-grass reeds through which the swans paddle were once harvested to thatch roofs throughout the region. One example can be seen on the fifteenth-century Tithe Barn, the last remnant of the abbey and today housing the **Children's Farm** (mid-March to Aug & Oct half-term daily 10am–5/6pm; Sept & Oct Sat & Sun 10am–5pm; £8.50), whose highlights include goat-racing and pony rides. Lastly, in the **Subtropical Gardens** (daily 10am–4/5/6pm, closed over Christmas; £9.95), delicate species thrive in the microclimate created by Chesil's stones, which act as a giant radiator to deter all but the worst frosts.

Bridport

Ten miles west of Abbotsbury is the pretty town of **BRIDPORT**, mentioned in the Domesday Book of 1086 and an important port before the rivers silted up in the early 1700s, leaving it stranded a mile or so inland today. It's a pleasant old town of solid brick buildings with very wide streets, a hangover from its days as a major rope-making centre when cords were stretched between the houses to be twisted and dyed. Today, it's a lively **market** town (Wed and Sat) with an arty, alternative vibe. The town's harbour lies a mile or so south at **West Bay**, which has a fine sandy beach sheltered below majestic red cliffs – the sheer East Cliffs are a tempting challenge for intrepid walkers.

ACCOMMODATION AND EATING — BRIDPORT

The Bull 34 East St ⓣ 01308 422878, ⓦ thebullhotel.co.uk. Friendly, boutique-style hotel in a former seventeenth-century coaching inn in the centre of town. The rooms are comfortable and modern, with Neal's Yard toiletries: there are some family rooms. The restaurant and bar are good, too: try the West Bay crab cakes (£7.50) to start, followed by a 12oz rib-eye steak (£20). **£100**

★ **Hive Beach Café** Beach Rd, Burton Bradstock, 3 miles east of Bridport ⓣ 01308 897070, ⓦ hivebeachcafe.co.uk. Laidback café/restaurant on the beach, serving top-quality seafood, such as local wild bass (£24) and Lyme Bay mackerel (£10.50). If your budget can stretch to it, splash out on the fabulous seafood platter featuring local lobster, crab and scallops (£60 for two). Also delicious home-made cakes, excellent coffee, good breakfasts and very friendly service. Hours vary, but if it's a nice day they will almost certainly be open.

The Riverside West Bay ⓣ 01308 422011, ⓦ thefishrestaurant-westbay.co.uk. Reservations are recommended for this renowned restaurant which offers fresh sumptuous fish and seafood and fine river views. There is a daily changing menu, but expect the likes of Lyme Bay lemon sole and local lobster. The two-course midweek lunch menu is good value at £18.25. April–Sept Tues–Sun noon–2.30pm & Tues–Sat 6.30–9pm; Oct–March Tues–Sun noon–2.30pm & Fri & Sat 6.30–9pm.

Lyme Regis

LYME REGIS, Dorset's most westerly town, shelters snugly between steep, fossil-filled cliffs. Its intimate size and photogenic qualities make this a popular and congested spot in high summer, with some upmarket literary associations – Jane Austen summered in a seafront cottage and set part of *Persuasion* in Lyme (the town appears in the 1995 film version), while novelist John Fowles lived here until his death in 2005 (the film adaptation of his book, *The French Lieutenant's Woman*, was shot here).

Colourwashed cottages and elegant Regency and Victorian villas line its seafront and flanking streets, but Lyme's best-known feature is a practical reminder of its commercial origins: **the Cobb**, a curving harbour wall originally built in the thirteenth century. It has suffered many alterations since, most notably in the nineteenth century, when its

LYME'S JURASSIC COAST

The cliffs around Lyme are made up of a complex layer of limestone, greensand and unstable clay, a perfect medium for preserving **fossils**, which are exposed by landslips of the waterlogged clays. In 1811, after a fierce storm caused parts of the cliffs to collapse, 12-year-old Mary Anning, a keen fossil-hunter, discovered an almost complete dinosaur skeleton, a 30ft ichthyosaurus now displayed in London's Natural History Museum.

Hands-off inspection of the area's complex **geology** can be enjoyed all around the town: as you walk along the seafront and out towards The Cobb, look for the outlines of ammonites in the walls and paving stones. To the west of Lyme, the **Undercliff** is a fascinating jumble of overgrown landslips, now a nature reserve, where a great path wends its way through the undergrowth for around seven miles to neighbouring Seaton in Devon. East of Lyme, a huge landslip in 2008 closed the Dorset Coast Path to **Charmouth** (Jane Austen's favourite resort), as well as blocking the two-mile beach route to the resort, which was previously walkable at low tide. At Charmouth, you can rejoin the coastal path leading to the headland of **Golden Cap**, whose brilliant outcrop of auburn sandstone is crowned with gorse.

3

massive boulders were clad in neater blocks of Portland stone. On Bridge Street, the excellent **Lyme Regis Museum** (Easter–Oct Mon–Sat 10am–5pm, Sun 11am–5pm; Nov–Easter Wed–Sun11am–4pm; £3.50; ⓦlymeregismuseum.co.uk) displays artefacts related to the town's literary connections, including John Fowles' office chair, and provides a crash course in local history and geology, while **Dinosaurland** on Coombe Street (late Feb–late Oct daily 10am–4pm; sporadic openings at other times; £5; ⓦdinosaurland.co.uk), fills out the story of ammonites and other local fossils. Foodies should head to the **Town Mill Complex** (ⓦtownmill.org.uk) in Mill Lane, just off Coombe Street, where as well as a working mill, pottery and art gallery there's a fantastic cheese shop, local brewery and café/tearoom (see below).

ARRIVAL AND INFORMATION — LYME REGIS

By train Lyme's nearest station is in Axminster, 5 miles north: bus #31 runs from the station to Lyme, then onto Weymouth.
By bus First buses runs a daily bus service from Exeter, Bridport, Weymouth and Poole every couple of hours (ⓦfirstgroup.com).
Tourist office Church St (April–Oct Mon–Sat 10am–5am, Sun 10am–4pm; Nov–March Mon–Sat 10am–3pm; ⓣ01297 442138, ⓦlymeregistourism.co.uk).

ACCOMMODATION

1 Lyme Townhouse 1 Pound St ⓣ01297 442499, ⓦ1lymetownhouse.co.uk. This boutique-style B&B has a variety of contemporary rooms in a Grade II listed townhouse. The best are on the top floor with great sea views. Breakfast is delivered to your room in picnic hampers. Two-night minimum stay during high season. **£95**

Alexandra Hotel Pound St ⓣ01297 442010, ⓦhotelalexandra.co.uk. Popular with honeymooners, this is the town's top hotel, located inside an eighteenth-century manor house with bleached wood floors and lovely gardens overlooking the sea. Many of the comfortable rooms have sea views, and there is also a highly rated restaurant. Two-night minimum stay at weekends. **£125**

Royal Lion Broad St ⓣ01297 445622, ⓦroyallionhotel.com. Welcoming seventeenth-century coaching inn on the main street, complete with chandeliers in the dining room. There's off-street parking and a small indoor pool. Rooms in the modern extension have balconies facing the sea, those in the main building overlook the high street. **£110**

EATING AND DRINKING

Lyme Regis is something of a foodie destination, with lots of superb **fish restaurants** and good pubs.

Hix Oyster and Fish House Cobb Rd ⓣ01297 446910, ⓦhixoysterandfishhouse.co.uk. In a lovely location overlooking the town and sea, this airy restaurant, owned by acclaimed chef Mark Hix, specializes in local fish and seafood: main courses such as sea bass with fennel can be pricey at £24, though there are cheaper options, like fish pie (£14). April–Oct daily noon–3pm & 5–11pm; Nov–March Wed–Sun only.

The Mill Tea and Dining Room Town Mill, Mill Lane, ⓣ01297 445757, ⓦteaanddiningroom.co.uk. A tiny dining space in the mill complex with a few outdoor tables, specializing in authentic English recipes. The daily changing menu features such traditional dishes as grilled ling with braised oxtail (£17.50) or baked egg custard tart (£5.75). The cream teas are heavenly, with tea served in bone china cups, and home-made soft drinks – it's a cola-free zone! Tues 6.30–10pm, Wed–Sat 11am–4pm & 6.30–10pm, Sun noon–3pm.

Pilot Boat Inn Bridge St ⊕01297 443157. A lively pub that also serves some of the best-value food in town. Its extensive menu includes fresh fish, fine steaks and a good range of vegetarian options; you may have to wait for a table in high season. Daily 11am–11pm.

Town Mill Bakery 2 Coombe St ⊕01297 444754, ⊕townmillbakery.com. A wonderful bakery and restaurant that uses local and largely organic ingredients. Sublime breakfasts include home-made jam, boiled eggs and local honey – choose your bread and toast it yourself, then eat at the communal wooden tables. Daily 8.30am–7pm, until 8pm in summer; closed Mon–Fri eve in winter.

Salisbury

SALISBURY, huddled below Wiltshire's chalky plain in the converging valleys of the
3 Avon and Nadder, sprang into existence in the early thirteenth century, when the bishopric was moved from nearby **Old Sarum** (see p.214). Today, it looks from a distance very much as it did when Constable painted his celebrated view of it, and though traffic may clog its centre, this prosperous and well-kept city is designed on a pleasantly human scale, with no sprawling suburbs or high-rise buildings to challenge the supremacy of the cathedral's immense spire. The city's inspiring silhouette is best admired by taking a twenty-minute walk through the water meadows southwest of the centre to the suburb of **Harnham**.

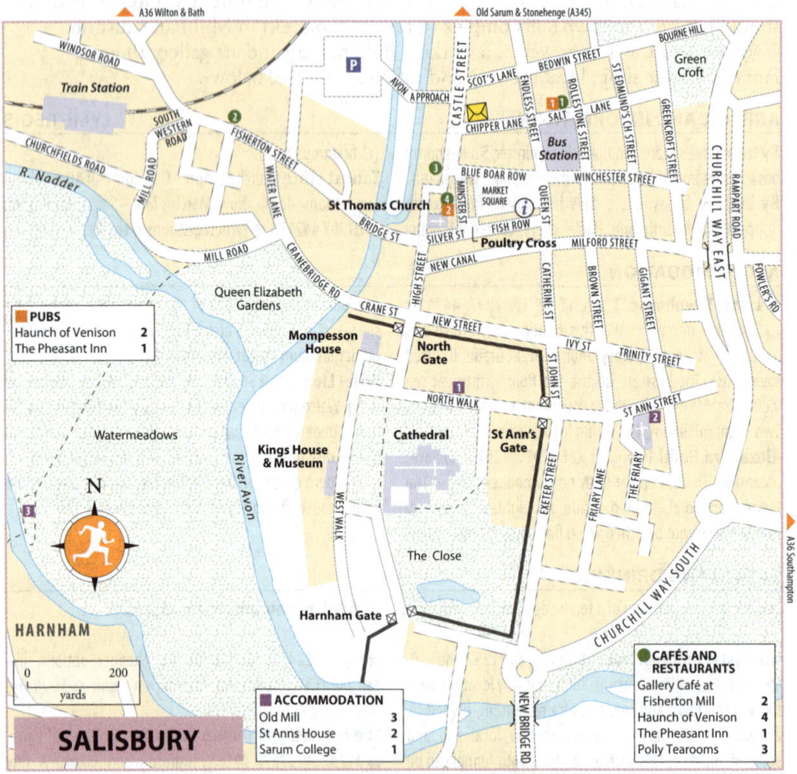

Salisbury Cathedral

Daily 7.15am–6.15pm; chapter house April–Oct Mon–Sat 9.30am–5.30pm, Sun 12.45am–5.30pm; Nov–March Mon–Sat 10am–4.30pm, Sun 12.45am–4.30pm • £5.50 suggested donation **Tower tours** Mon–Sat at least 1 daily, usually at 1.15pm, up to 5 daily at busy times (April–Sept); booking recommended • £8.50 • ⓣ 01722 55515

Begun in 1220, **Salisbury Cathedral** was mostly completed within forty years and is thus unusually consistent in its style, with one prominent exception – the **spire**, which was added a century later and, at 404ft, is the highest in England. Its survival is something of a miracle, for the foundations penetrate only about 6ft into marshy ground, and when Christopher Wren surveyed it he found the spire to be leaning almost 2.5ft out of true. He added further tie rods, which finally arrested the movement.

The interior is over-austere, but there's an amazing sense of space and light in its high nave, despite the sombre pillars of grey Purbeck marble, which are visibly bowing beneath the weight they bear. Monuments and carved tombs line the walls. Don't miss the octagonal **chapter house,** which displays a rare original copy of the Magna Carta, and whose walls are decorated with a frieze of scenes from the Old Testament.

3

The Close

Surrounding the cathedral is the **Close**, a peaceful precinct of lawns and mellow old buildings. Most of the houses have seemly Georgian facades, though some, like the Bishop's Palace and the deanery, date from the thirteenth century. **Mompesson House** (mid-March to Oct Mon–Wed, Sat & Sun 11am–5pm; NT; £5.75, garden only £1), built by a wealthy merchant in 1701, contains some beautifully furnished eighteenth-century rooms and a superbly carved staircase. Also in the Close is the **King's House**, home to the **Salisbury and South Wiltshire Museum** (Oct–May Mon–Sat 10am–5pm; June–Sept Mon–Sat 10am–5pm, Sun noon–5pm; £6) – an absorbing account of local history.

Around the Market Square

The Close's **North Gate** opens onto the centre's older streets, where narrow pedestrianized alleyways bear names like Fish Row and Salt Lane, indicative of their trading origin. Many half-timbered houses and inns have survived, and the last of four market crosses, **Poultry Cross**, stands on stilts in Silver Street, near the Market Square (markets Tues & Sat). Nearby, the church of **St Thomas** – named after Thomas à Becket – is worth a look inside for its carved timber roof and "Doom painting" over the chancel arch, depicting Christ presiding over the Last Judgment. Dating from 1475, it's the largest of its kind in England.

ARRIVAL AND INFORMATION — SALISBURY

By train Trains from London arrive half a mile west of Salisbury's centre, on South Western Rd.

Destinations Bath (hourly; 55min); Bristol (hourly; 1hr 10min); London Waterloo (every 30min; 1hr 30min); Portsmouth (hourly; 1hr 20min); Southampton (every 30min; 35min–1hr).

By bus The bus station is on Endless St.

Destinations Bournemouth (Mon–Sat every 30min, Sun hourly; 1hr 10min); London (2 daily; 3hr 5min); Southampton (Mon–Sat hourly, Sun 3 daily; 1hr 5min).

Tourist office Fish Row, just off Market Square (Mon, Tues & Thurs–Sat 9.30am–5.30pm; Wed 10am–5.30pm; June–Aug also Sun 11am–3pm; ⓣ 01722 334956, ⓦ visitsalisbury.com).

ACCOMMODATION

★ **Old Mill** Town Path, Harnham ⓣ 01722 327517, ⓦ signature-hospitality.com. The fully equipped rooms of this riverside pub have great views across the meadows to the cathedral. The location feels really rural but is just a short walk from the city centre. Real ales are on tap in the bar, and there's an adjoining restaurant serving good local food. **£90**

St Anns House 32–34 St Ann St ⓣ 01722 335657, ⓦ stanneshouse.co.uk. A well-restored Georgian townhouse with stylish, comfortable rooms in a quiet street a short walk from the cathedral. **£85**

★ **Sarum College** 19 The Close ⓣ 01722 424800, ⓦ sarum.ac.uk. By no means luxurious but in the best location in Salisbury, this friendly ecumenical college rents out simple en-suite doubles with views over The Close and cathedral, plus others without private facilities. There's also a decent common room, and breakfast is included. **£70**

EATING AND DRINKING

★ **Gallery Café at Fisherton Mill** 108 Fisherton St ⓣ01722 500200, ⓦfishertonmill.co.uk. Great café within a renovated mill/art gallery serving delicious soups (£4), sandwiches on stone-baked bread (£5) and main courses such as sausage with lentils (£10). Upstairs, you can watch artists at work in their studios, weaving and making jewellery. Tues–Fri 10am–5pm, Sat 9.30am–5pm. Also open for dinner one Fri & Sat a month, plus the odd Sunday brunch.

★ **Haunch of Venison** 1 Minster St ⓣ01722 411313, ⓦhaunchofvenison.uk.com. One of the city's most atmospheric and historic pubs, with a wonderful warren of rooms. Star attraction is the mummified hand of a nineteenth-century card player still clutching his cards: stolen from the pub in March 2010, it was subsequently returned in the post. The quirky, sloping-floored restaurant serves interesting dishes such as wild boar steak with treacle and cider sauce (£15) and game pie (£13). Mon–Sat 11.30am–11pm, Sun noon–10.30pm.

The Pheasant Inn 19 Salt St ⓣ01722 322866, ⓦrestaurant-salisbury.com. Local beers and good-value food at this traditional pub. Well-executed pub staples include home-made steak and ale pie (£10) and the Sunday roasts are a treat. Mon–Sat 11am–11pm, Sun noon–6pm.

Polly Tearooms 8 St Thomas's Square ⓣ01722 336037, ⓦthepolly.com. Lovely old-fashioned tearooms and patisserie right outside St Thomas' church, with outdoor tables. Mon–Fri 8.30am–5pm, Sat 8am–5pm, Sun 10am–4pm.

Around Salisbury

North of Salisbury stretches a hundred thousand acres of chalky upland, known as **Salisbury Plain**; it's managed by the Ministry of Defence whose presence has protected it from development and intensive farming, thereby preserving species that are all but extinct elsewhere in England. Its empty expanses are home to the country's only colony of **Great Bustards**, the world's heaviest flying bird, which became extinct in the UK in the 1840s. Chicks were re-introduced from Russia in 2004 to a secret location on Salisbury Plain, and the first Great Bustard to be born in the UK in nearly two hundred years appeared in 2009.

Though now largely deserted, in previous times Salisbury Plain positively throbbed with communities. Stone Age, Bronze Age and Iron Age settlements left hundreds of burial mounds scattered over the chalklands, as well as major complexes at Danebury, Badbury, Figsbury, **Old Sarum**, and, of course, the great circle of **Stonehenge**, England's most famous historial monument. To the west, Salisbury's hinterland also includes one of Wiltshire's great country mansions, **Wilton House**.

Wilton House

Five miles west of Salisbury • **House** Mid-April to Aug Sun–Thurs, & Bank Holiday Sat & Mon 11.30am–4.30pm **Grounds** Sun–Thurs, Bank Holiday Sat & Mon 11am–5pm; Sept Sat–Thurs 11am–5pm • House & grounds £14, grounds only £6

The splendid **Wilton House** dominates the village of Wilton, renowned for its carpet industry. The original Tudor house, built for the First Earl of Pembroke on the site of a dissolved Benedictine abbey, was ruined by fire in 1647 and rebuilt by Inigo Jones, whose classic hallmarks can be seen in the sumptuous Single Cube and Double Cube rooms, so called because of their precise dimensions.

The easel **paintings** are what makes Wilton really special, however – the collection includes works by Van Dyck, Rembrandt, two of the Brueghel family, Poussin, Andrea del Sarto and Tintoretto. In the grounds, the famous **Palladian Bridge** has been joined by various ancillary attractions including an adventure playground and an audiovisual show on the colourful earls of Pembroke.

Old Sarum

Two miles north of Salisbury • Daily: Feb 11am–4pm; March & Oct 10am–4pm; April–June & Sept 10am–5pm; July & Aug 9am–6pm; Nov–Jan 11am–3pm • EH • £3.70

The ruins of **Old Sarum** occupy a bleak hilltop site. Possibly occupied up to five thousand years ago, then developed as an Iron Age fort whose double protective ditches remain, it was settled by Romans and Saxons before the Norman bishopric of Sherborne was moved here in the 1070s. Within a couple of decades a new cathedral had been consecrated at Old Sarum, and a large religious community was living alongside the soldiers in the central castle. Old Sarum was an uncomfortable place, parched and windswept, and in 1220 the dissatisfied clergy – additionally at loggerheads with the castle's occupants – appealed to the pope for permission to decamp to Salisbury (still known officially as New Sarum). When permission was granted, the stone from the cathedral was commandeered for Salisbury's gateways, and once the church had gone the population waned. By the nineteenth century Old Sarum was deserted, and today the dominant features of the site are huge earthworks, banks and ditches, with a broad trench encircling the rudimentary remains of the Norman palace, castle and cathedral.

Stonehenge

Nine miles north of Salisbury • Daily: mid-March to May & Sept to mid-Oct 9.30am–6pm; June–Aug 9am–7pm; mid-Oct to mid-March 9.30am–4pm • EH • £7.50 includes audioguide • ☎ 01722 343834

No ancient structure in England arouses more controversy than **Stonehenge**, a mysterious ring of monoliths. While archeologists argue over whether it was a place of ritual sacrifice and sun-worship, an astronomical calculator or a royal palace, the guardians of the site struggle to accommodate its year-round crowds. Conservation of Stonehenge is an urgent priority, and unless you arrange for special access (book by phone or online), or come

STONEHENGE: THE SITE

Some people may find **Stonehenge** underwhelming, but understanding a little of its history and ancient significance gives an insight into its mystical appeal. What exists today is only a small part of the original prehistoric complex, as many of the outlying stones were probably plundered by medieval and later farmers for building materials. The **construction** of Stonehenge is thought to have taken place in several stages. In about 3000 BC the outer circular bank and ditch were built, just inside which was dug a ring of 56 pits, which at a later date were filled with a mixture of earth and human ash. Around 2500 BC the first stones were raised within the earthworks, comprising approximately forty great blocks of dolerite (bluestone), whose ultimate source was Preseli in Wales. Some archeologists have suggested that these monoliths were found lying on Salisbury Plain, having been borne down from the Welsh mountains by a glacier in the last Ice Age, but the lack of any other glacial debris on the plain would seem to disprove this theory. It really does seem to be the case that the stones were cut from quarries in Preseli and dragged or floated here on rafts, a prodigious task that has defeated recent attempts to emulate it.

The crucial phase in the creation of the site came during the next six hundred years, when the incomplete bluestone circle was transformed by the construction of a circle of 25 **trilithons** (two uprights crossed by a lintel) and an inner horseshoe formation of five trilithons. Hewn from Marlborough Downs sandstone, these colossal stones (called sarsens), ranging from 13ft to 21ft in height and weighing up to thirty tons, were carefully dressed and worked – for example, to compensate for perspectival distortion the uprights have a slight swelling in the middle, the same trick as the builders of the Parthenon were to employ hundreds of years later. More bluestones were arranged in various patterns within the outer circle over this period. The purpose of all this work remains baffling, however. The symmetry and location of the site (a slight rise in a flat valley with even views of the horizon in all directions) as well as its alignment towards the points of sunrise and sunset on the summer and winter solstices tend to support the supposition that it was some sort of observatory or time-measuring device. The site ceased to be used at around 1600 BC, and by the Middle Ages it had become a "landmark". Recent excavations have revealed the existence of a much larger settlement here than had previously been thought – the most substantial Neolithic village of this period to be found on the British mainland in fact – covering a wide area. Nothing is to be seen of the new finds as yet, though there are plans to re-create a part of the ancient complex.

during the summer **solstice** – when crowds of 35,000 or more gather to watch the sunrise – you must be content with walking around, rather than among, the stones.

Avebury and around

The village of **AVEBURY** stands in the midst of a **stone circle** (free access) that rivals Stonehenge – the individual stones are generally smaller, but the circle itself is much wider and more complex. A massive earthwork 20ft high and 1400ft across encloses the main circle, which is approached by four causeways across the inner ditch, two of them leading into wide avenues stretching over a mile beyond the circle. The best guess is that it was built soon after 2500 BC, and presumably had a similar ritual or religious function to Stonehenge. The structure of Avebury's diffuse circle is quite difficult to grasp, but there are plans on the site, and you can get an excellent overview at the **Alexander Keiller Museum**, at the western entrance (daily: April–Oct 10am–6pm or dusk; Nov–March 10am–4pm; NT & EH; £4.90, including Barn Gallery). The nearby **Barn Gallery** has an exhibition on Avebury and the surrounding country.

Silbury Hill and West Kennet Long Barrow

Just outside Avebury, the neat green mound of **Silbury Hill** is disregarded by the majority of drivers whizzing by on the A4. At 130ft it's no great height, but when you realize it's the largest prehistoric artificial mound in Europe, and was made using nothing more than primitive spades, it commands more respect. It was probably constructed around 2600 BC, and though no one knows quite what it was for, the likelihood is that it was a burial mound. You can't actually walk on the hill – having admired it briefly from the car park, cross the road to the footpath that leads half a mile to the **West Kennet Long Barrow** (free access; NT & EH). Dating from about 3250 BC, this was definitely a chamber tomb – nearly fifty burials have been discovered here.

INFORMATION — AVEBURY

Tourist office Avebury Chapel Centre, Green St (Tues–Sun: Feb–Oct 9.30am–5pm; Nov–Jan 9.30am–4.30pm; ⓣ01672 539179, ⓦvisitwiltshire.co.uk).

ACCOMMODATION AND EATING

Circles Next to the Barn Gallery ⓣ01672 539250. This National Trust café is your best bet for lunch, offering good meals and snacks, with plenty of veggie options. Daily: April–Oct 10am–5.30pm; Nov–March 10.30am–4pm.

Manor Farm High St ⓣ01672 539294, ⓦmanorfarmavebury.com. A comfortable B&B right in the village, where you can wake up to views of the stones. It's also a working farm and there's a private guests' sitting room. **£85**

Lacock

LACOCK, twelve miles west of Avebury, is the perfect English feudal village, albeit one gentrified by the National Trust and besieged by tourists all summer, partly due to its fame as a location for several films and TV series –the recent *Harry Potter* films among others. The village's most famous son is photography pioneer **Henry Fox Talbot**, a member of the dynasty that has lived in the local abbey since it passed to Sir William Sharington on the Dissolution of the Monasteries in 1539.

Fox Talbot was the first person to produce a photographic negative, and the **Fox Talbot Museum**, in a sixteenth-century barn by the abbey gates (daily: Jan to mid-Feb, Nov & Dec 11am–4pm; mid-Feb to Oct 10.30am–5.30pm; NT; £8.50 including abbey garden and cloisters, £11.50 including abbey, abbey garden and cloisters), captures something of the excitement he must have experienced as the dim outline of an oriel window in the abbey imprinted itself on a piece of silver nitrate paper.

The **abbey** itself (Jan to mid-Feb, Nov & Dec Sat & Sun noon–4pm; mid-Feb to Oct Wed–Mon 11am–5pm; cloisters and grounds same hours as Fox Talbot museum; NT; £11.50 including museum) preserves a few monastic fragments amid the eighteenth-century Gothic, while the church of **St Cyriac** (free access) contains the opulent tomb of Sir William Sharington himself, buried beneath a splendid barrel-vaulted roof.

ARRIVAL AND DEPARTURE — LACOCK

The #234 **bus** runs approximately hourly from Chippenham and Frome, stopping outside the *George Inn* (firstgroup.com).

ACCOMMODATION AND EATING

At the Sign of the Angel Church St 01249 730230, lacock.co.uk. The village's delightfully Chaucerian-sounding hostelry is a good, characterful hotel with its own restaurant, specializing in local and home-grown produce. Rooms are quirky, some with creaky floorboards and low doorways, but all have modern bathrooms and free wi-fi. There's a lovely garden at the back. **£130**

George Inn 4 West St 01249 730263. A rambling, attractive pub with roaring fires and a dog-wheel (the dog powered the wheel to turn a spit over the fire). Good for a drink or decent pub food, including a good range of steaks (£11–16.50). Daily 10am–11pm.

Lacock Pottery The Tanyard, Church St 01249 730266, lacockbedandbreakfast.com. Three comfortable B&B rooms in a lovely old building overlooking the church and the village. Breakfasts are good, featuring home-made bread and jams. **£84**

3

Stourhead and around

25 miles west of Salisbury • **House** Mid-Feb to mid-March Sat & Sun 11am–3pm; mid-March to mid-July & mid-Sept to mid-Oct Mon, Tues & Fri–Sun 11am–5pm; mid-July to mid-Sept & mid-Oct to early Nov daily 11am–5pm; Dec Fri–Sun 11am–3pm • NT • £8.10, £13.40 with garden **Garden** Daily 9am–6pm • £8.10, £13.40 with house **King Alfred's Tower** Mid-March to Oct daily 10am–5pm • £3.20

Landscape gardening was a favoured mode of display among the grandest eighteenth-century landowners, and **Stourhead** is one of the most accomplished examples of the genre. The Stourton estate was bought in 1717 by Henry Hoare, who commissioned Colen Campbell to build a new villa in the Palladian style. Hoare's heir, another Henry, returned from his Grand Tour in 1741 with his head full of the paintings of Claude and Poussin, and determined to translate their images of well-ordered, wistful classicism into real life. He dammed the Stour to create a lake, then planted the terrain with blocks of trees, domed temples, stone bridges, grottoes and statues, all mirrored vividly in the water. In 1772 the folly of **King Alfred's Tower** was added and today affords fine views across the estate and into neighbouring counties. The house is less interesting, though it has some good Chippendale furniture.

Longleat

Eight miles north of Stourhead • Feb half-term & April to early Nov daily 10am–5pm/6pm/7.30pm; March Sat & Sun 10am–5pm; check website for exact closing times each day • House and grounds only £12.90, all attractions £26 • longleat.co.uk

If Stourhead is an unexpected outcrop of Italy in Wiltshire, the African savannah intrudes even more bizarrely at **Longleat**. In 1946 the sixth marquess of Bath became the first stately-home owner to open his house to the paying public on a regular basis, and in 1966 he caused even more amazement when Longleat's Capability Brown landscapes were turned into England's first drive-through **safari park,** with lions, tigers, giraffes and rhinos on show, plus monkeys clambering all over your car. Other attractions followed, including a large hedge maze, a Doctor Who exhibition, high-tech simulators, and the seventh marquess's saucy murals (children not admitted). Beyond the razzmatazz, there's an exquisitely furnished Elizabethan house, built for Sir John Thynne, Elizabeth's High Treasurer, with an enormous library and a fine collection of pictures, including Titian's *Holy Family*.

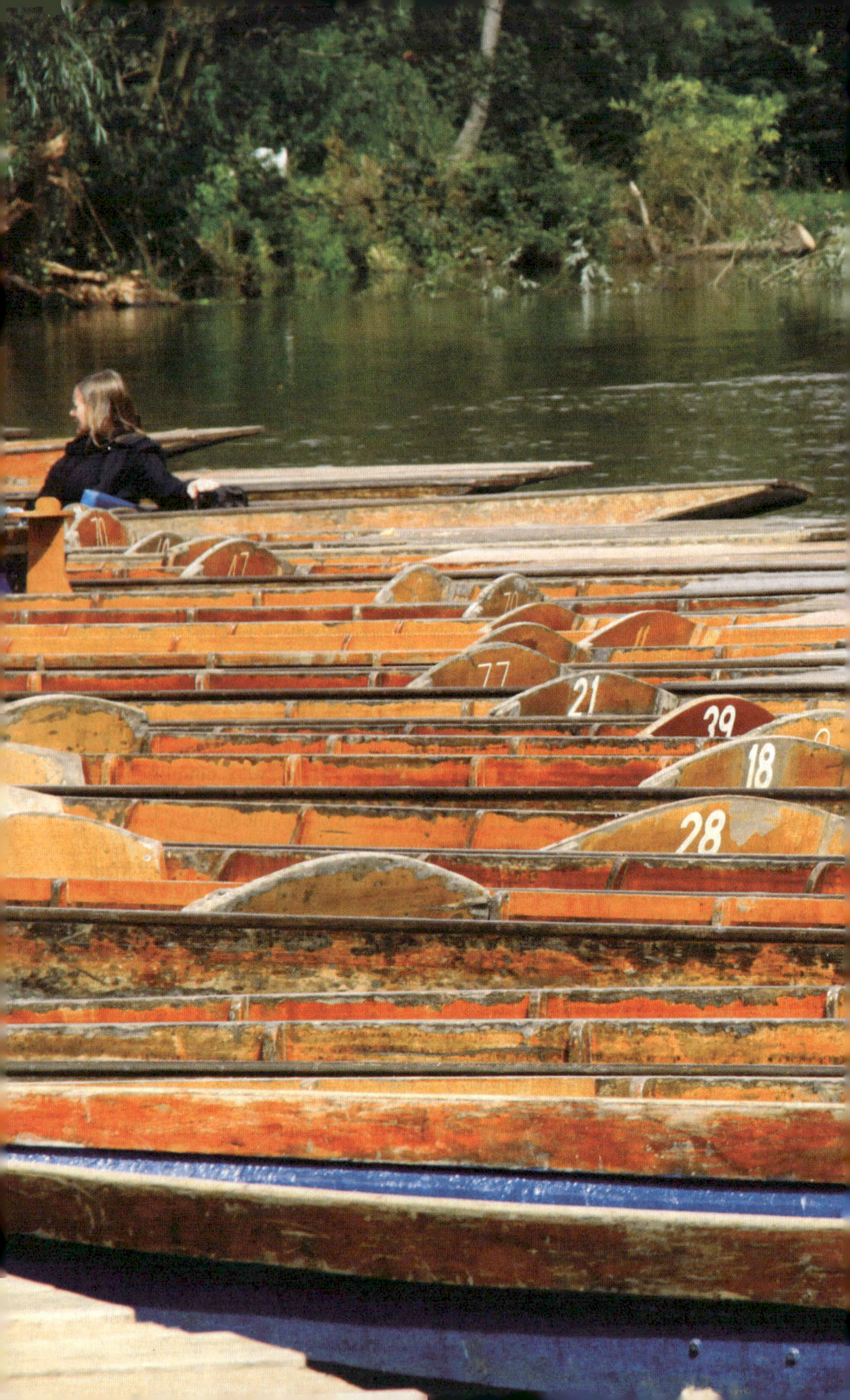

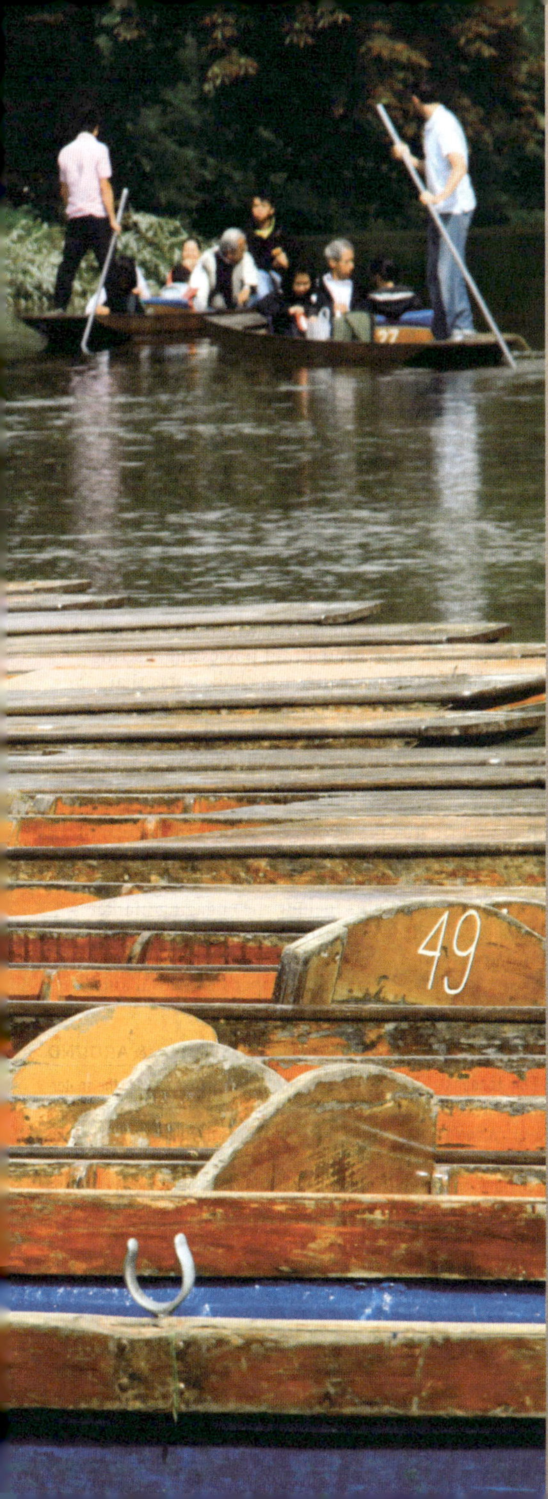

Oxfordshire, the Cotswolds and around

223 The Chiltern Hills
225 The Vale of White Horse
226 Oxford
237 Around Oxford
240 The Cotswolds
251 Gloucester

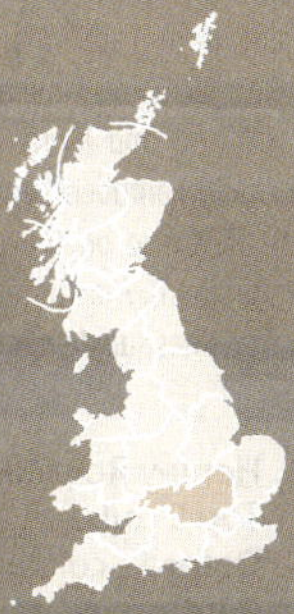

PUNTING IN OXFORD

Oxfordshire, the Cotswolds and around

Arching around the peripheries of London, beyond the orbital M25, the "Home Counties" of England form London's commuter belt. Beyond the suburban sprawl, however, there is plenty to entice. The northwestern Home Counties – Berkshire, Buckinghamshire and Hertfordshire – are at their most appealing amidst the Chiltern Hills, a picturesque band of chalk uplands whose wooded ridges rise near Luton, beside the M1, and stretch southwest. The hills provide an exclusive setting for many of the capital's wealthiest commuters, but for the casual visitor the obvious target is Henley-on-Thames, an attractive old town famous for its Regatta; it's a handy base for further explorations, with the village of Cookham – and its Stanley Spencer gallery – leading the way.

Striking west from the Chilterns across the North Wessex Downs is the 85-mile-long **Ridgeway**, a prehistoric track – and now a national trail possessing a string of prehistoric sites, the most extraordinary being the gigantic chalk horse that gives the **Vale of White Horse** its name. The Vale is dotted with pleasant little villages, though the star is the nearby university city of **Oxford**, with its superb architecture, museums and lively student population. Nearby is **Woodstock**, the handsome little town abutting one of England's most imposing country homes, **Blenheim Palace.**

Beyond Oxford lie the rolling hills and ridges of the **Cotswolds.** Covering much of **Oxfordshire** and **Gloucestershire**, this picture-postcard region is dotted with glorious honey-coloured villages, old churches and handsome stone mansions, and features some nice walking on the Cotswolds Way. Highlights include the engaging market town of **Chipping Campden**, the delightful village of **Northleach** and bustling **Cirencester**. To the west is **Cheltenham**, an appealing Regency spa town famous for its horse racing. It's a good base for visits to **Gloucester**, with its superb cathedral and rejuvenated docks area.

GETTING AROUND OXFORDSHIRE, THE COTSWOLDS & AROUND

By train There are mainline train services from London's Paddington Station to Oxford, Cheltenham and Gloucester; trains from Paddington also stop at several Cotswold towns, including Kingham (midway between Burford and Stow) and and Moreton in Marsh (between Stow and Chipping Campden), en route to Worcester and Hereford. Oxford is also on the main cross-country line between Birmingham, Winchester, Southampton and Bournemouth. Branch lines supplement the main routes.

By bus Long-distance buses stick mostly to the motorways, providing an efficient service to all the larger towns, but local services between the villages are patchy, sometimes nonexistent.

By car The Cotswolds are enclosed by the M5, M4 and M40, which, along with the M1 and AI(M) to the east provide easy access.

Henley Royal Regatta p.223
Top 5 pubs p.225
Oxford's colleges p.226
Punting in Oxford p.230
The Bodleian Library p.232
Top 5 churches p.240
Cheltenham Races p.249

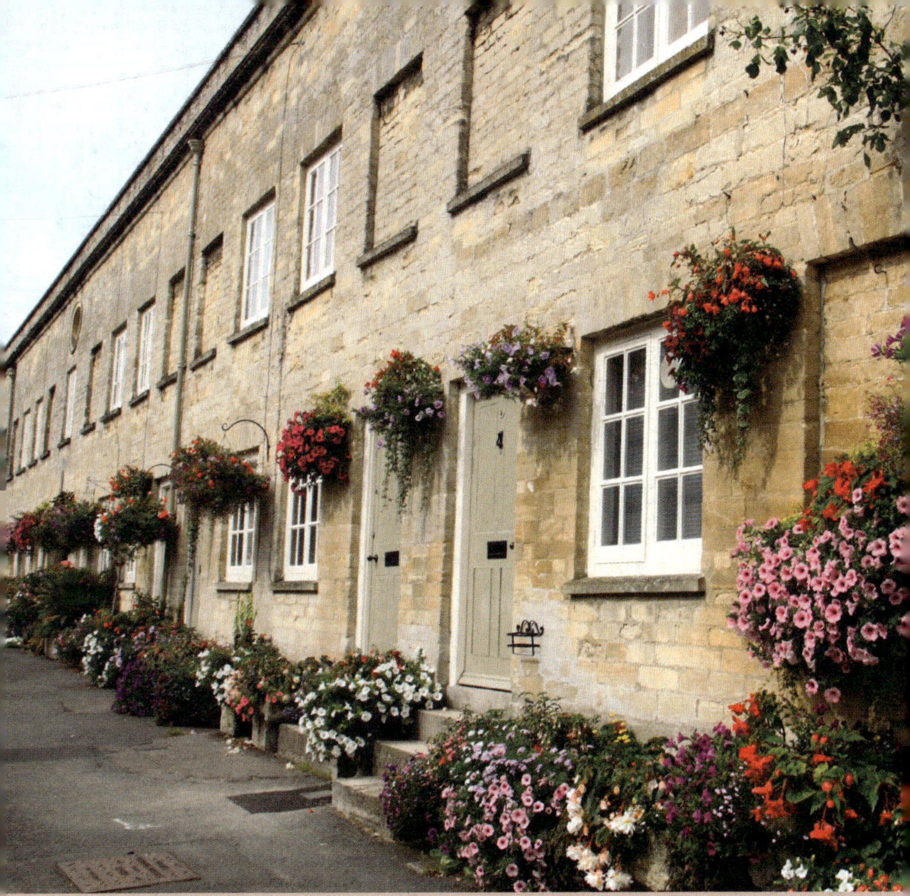

STONE COTTAGES, CIRENCESTER

Highlights

❶ **The Vale of White Horse** The vale takes its name from the huge, prehistoric horse cut into the chalk of the Berkshire Downs. **See p.225**

❷ **Oxford** One of Britain's most captivating cities, with dozens of historic colleges, memorable museums and an enjoyably lively undergraduate atmosphere. **See pp.226–237**

❸ **Cirencester** Self-styled "Capital of the Cotswolds", with a bustling marketplace overlooked by the superb Gothic church of St John the Baptist. **See p.241**

❹ **Chipping Campden** Perfectly preserved medieval wool town, with honey-coloured houses lining its historic main street. **See p.246**

❺ **Festivals in Cheltenham** Cheltenham's three-day National Hunt Festival is one of the highlights of the British racing calendar, while the town also boasts lively festivals dedicated to folk, jazz, classical music, literature and science. **See p.248 & p.249**

❻ **Gloucester Cathedral** The earliest – and one of the finest – examples of English Perpendicular architecture, topped by a magnificent tower. **See p.251**

HIGHLIGHTS ARE MARKED ON THE MAP ON P.222

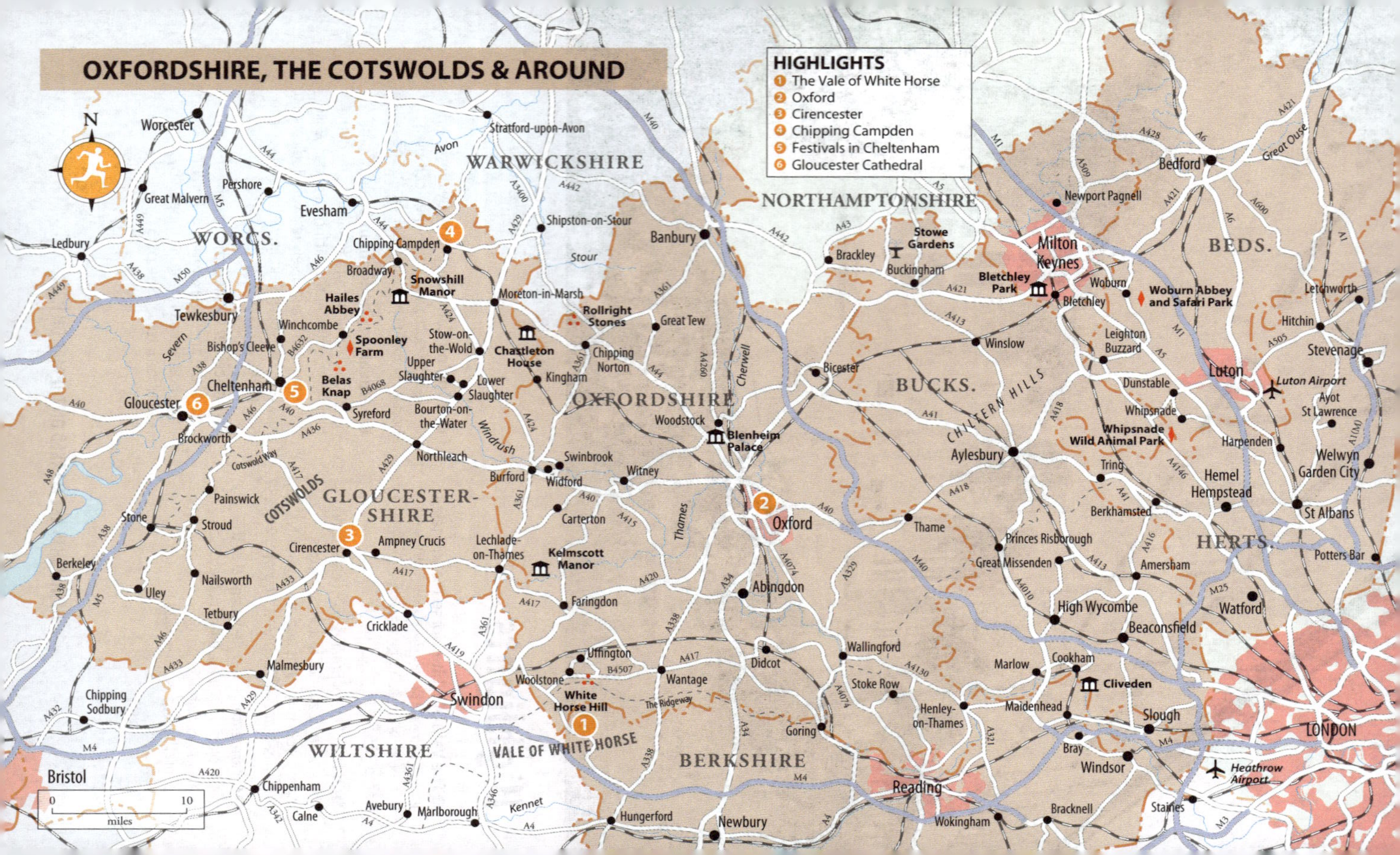
OXFORDSHIRE, THE COTSWOLDS & AROUND
HIGHLIGHTS
1 The Vale of White Horse
2 Oxford
3 Cirencester
4 Chipping Campden
5 Festivals in Cheltenham
6 Gloucester Cathedral
N
WARWICKSHIRE
NORTHAMPTONSHIRE
BEDS.
WORCS.
BUCKS.
OXFORDSHIRE
GLOUCESTERSHIRE
COTSWOLDS
CHILTERN HILLS
HERTS.
WILTSHIRE
VALE OF WHITE HORSE
BERKSHIRE
LONDON
Worcester
Great Malvern
Pershore
Evesham
Ledbury
Stratford-upon-Avon
Shipston-on-Stour
Banbury
Brackley
Stowe Gardens
Buckingham
Milton Keynes
Bletchley Park
Bletchley
Woburn
Woburn Abbey and Safari Park
Newport Pagnell
Bedford
Letchworth
Hitchin
Stevenage
Luton
Luton Airport
Ayot St Lawrence
Harpenden
Welwyn Garden City
St Albans
Hemel Hempstead
Potters Bar
Watford
Chipping Campden
Broadway
Snowshill Manor
Hailes Abbey
Moreton-in-Marsh
Rollright Stones
Great Tew
Tewkesbury
Winchcombe
Spooney Farm
Stow-on-the-Wold
Chastleton House
Chipping Norton
Bishop's Cleeve
Upper Slaughter
Lower Slaughter
Kingham
Cheltenham
Belas Knap
Bicester
Winslow
Leighton Buzzard
Dunstable
Whipsnade
Whipsnade Wild Animal Park
Gloucester
Syreford
Bourton-on-the-Water
Woodstock
Blenheim Palace
Aylesbury
Tring
Brockworth
Northleach
Swinbrook
Burford
Widford
Witney
Berkhamsted
Painswick
Stone
Stroud
Cirencester
Ampney Crucis
Lechlade-on-Thames
Kelmscott Manor
Carterton
Oxford
Thame
Princes Risborough
Great Missenden
Amersham
Berkeley
Nailsworth
Uley
Tetbury
Faringdon
Abingdon
High Wycombe
Beaconsfield
Cricklade
Malmesbury
Uffington
Woolstone
White Horse Hill
Wantage
Didcot
Wallingford
Stoke Row
Marlow
Cookham
Cliveden
Swindon
The Ridgeway
Chipping Sodbury
Henley-on-Thames
Maidenhead
Slough
Goring
Bray
Windsor
Heathrow Airport
Bristol
Chippenham
Calne
Avebury
Marlborough
Kennet
Hungerford
Newbury
Reading
Wokingham
Bracknell
Staines
Avon
Stour
Severn
Windrush
Thames
Cherwell
Great Ouse
Cotswold Way
M1
M3
M4
M5
M25
M40
M50
A1
A1(M)
A4
A5
A6
A34
A38
A40
A41
A43
A44
A46
A48
A321
A329
A338
A342
A346
A361
A415
A416
A417
A418
A419
A420
A421
A424
A428
A429
A432
A433
A436
A438
A442
A449
A505
A509
A600
A3400
A4010
A4074
A4130
A4146
A4260
A4361
B4068
B4507
B4632
0
10
miles

The Chiltern Hills

The **Chiltern Hills** extend southwest from the workaday town of Luton, beside the M1, bumping across Buckinghamshire and Oxfordshire as far as the River Thames. At their best, the hills offer handsome countryside, comprising a band of forested chalk hills with steep ridges and deep valleys interrupted by easy, rolling farmland. **Henley-on-Thames** is the draw, a pleasant riverside town within easy striking distance of the area's key attractions and with a reasonable range of accommodation. Nearby highlights include the village of **Cookham**, home to the fascinating Stanley Spencer Gallery. West of the Chilterns, the **Ridgeway National Trail** offers splendid hiking amongst the more open scenery of the Berkshire and Oxfordshire downs, especially in the **Vale of White Horse** (see p.225).

Henley-on-Thames

Three counties – Oxfordshire, Berkshire and Buckinghamshire – meet at **HENLEY-ON-THAMES**, long a favourite stopping place for travellers between London and Oxford. Nowadays, Henley is a good-looking, affluent commuter town at its prettiest among the old brick and stone buildings that flank the short main drag, **Hart Street**. At one end of Hart Street is the Market Place and its fetching **Town Hall**, at the other stand the easy Georgian curves of **Henley Bridge**. Overlooking the bridge is the parish church of **St Mary**, whose sturdy square tower sports a set of little turrets worked in chequerboard flint and stone.

River and Rowing Museum

Mill Meadows • Daily: Oct–April 10am–5pm; May–Sept 10am–5.30pm • £8 (ticket valid for one year's unlimited entry) • Ⓦ rrm.co.uk

A five-minute walk south along the riverbank from the foot of Hart Street lies Henley's imaginative **River and Rowing Museum**. Three galleries explore the wildlife and ecology of the Thames along with the history of rowing and the regatta, from ancient triremes through to the modern Olympics. A fourth gallery is devoted to models illustrating scenes from the children's classic *Wind in the Willows* by Kenneth Grahame (1859–1932). The book was set near Henley, where Grahame was sent to live with his grandmother after his mother died from scarlet fever.

ARRIVAL AND DEPARTURE — HENLEY ON THAMES

By train There are regular trains between Henley and London (every 30min with 1 or 2 changes; 1hr). From the train station, it's a 5min walk north to Hart Street, along Station Road and its continuation, Thames Side.

By bus All buses, including services to Oxford (hourly; 50min) and London (every 30min; 45min direct or 1hr, changing at Twyford) stop on either Hart St or Bell St, right in the middle of town.

INFORMATION AND TOURS

Tourist office In the basement of the Town Hall (Mon–Sat 10am–4pm, Oct–March 10.30am–3.30pm; Ⓣ 01491 578034, Ⓦ visithenley-on-thames.co.uk).

Boat trips Just south of the bridge, Hobbs of Henley offer boat trips along the Thames (April–Sept; 1hr; £8; Ⓣ 01491 572035, Ⓦ hobbsofhenley.com), and have rowing boats and motor-launches for rent.

HENLEY ROYAL REGATTA

Henley is best known for its **Royal Regatta**, established in 1839 and now the world's most important amateur rowing tournament. The regatta, featuring past and potential Olympic rowers, begins on the Wednesday before the first weekend in July and runs for five days. Further information is available from the Regatta Headquarters on the east side of Henley Bridge (Ⓣ 01491 572153, Ⓦ hrr.co.uk).

ACCOMMODATION

★ **Hotel du Vin** New St ⓣ01491 848400, ⓦhoteldu vin.com. Right in the centre of town, this is Henley's top hotel, occupying the creatively revamped old Brakspears Brewery. Rooms are kitted out in slick modern style; a few on the top floor have fine river views. The restaurant (see below) is top-notch. **£120**

EATING

The Angel Thame Side ⓣ01491 410678, ⓦtheangel henley.com. Of the many pubs in Henley, this one stands out thanks to its prime location right next to the Thames, with a fine outside deck overlooking the river below. Decent food, too. Mon–Thurs 11am–11pm, Fri & Sat 11am–midnight, Sun 11am–10pm.

★ **Hotel du Vin** New St ⓣ01491 848400, ⓦhoteldu vin.com. Henley's finest hotel is also the best restaurant in town, with sumptuous modern European cuisine using local produce, a huge wine list, a humidor and cosy "cigar-shack". Mains £11–16. Food served daily noon–2.30pm & 6.30–10pm (Sat & Sun lunch from 12.30am).

Maison Blanc Hart St ⓣ01491 577294, ⓦmaisonblanc .co.uk. Part of local celebrity chef Raymond Blanc's expanding culinary empire, this busy little café does good coffee along with fancy cakes, sandwiches and freshly baked bread – perfect for a picnic. Mon–Sat 8am–6.30pm, Sun 9am–5.30pm.

Cookham and around

Tiny **COOKHAM**, a prosperous Berkshire village eleven miles east of Henley near the border with Buckinghamshire, was the former home of **Stanley Spencer** (1891–1959), one of Britain's greatest – and most eccentric – artists.

4

About 5km south of Cookham, on the banks of the Thames south of Maidenhead, the even smaller village of **Bray** has the unlikely distinction of hosting two of just four triple-Michelin-starred restaurants in the UK (the other two are in London) – including, famously, Heston Blumenthal's *Fat Duck*.

Stanley Spencer Gallery

High St, Cookham • Easter–Oct daily 10.30am–5.30pm; Nov–Easter Thurs–Sun 11am–4.30pm • £5 • ⓦstanleyspencer.org.uk

The son of a local music teacher, Stanley Spencer spent much of his life in Cookham, which he once famously described as "a village in Heaven". Much of his work was inspired by the Bible, and many of his paintings depict biblical tales transposed into his Cookham surroundings. Much of Spencer's most acclaimed work is displayed in London's Tate Britain, but there's a fine sample here at the **Stanley Spencer Gallery**, which occupies the old Methodist Chapel on the High Street. Three prime exhibits are *View from Cookham Bridge*, the unsettling *Sarah Tubb and the Heavenly Visitors*, and the wonderful (unfinished) *Christ Preaching at Cookham Regatta*. The permanent collection is enhanced by regular exhibitions of Spencer's paintings and the gallery also contains incidental Spencer letters, documents and memorabilia. The gallery has a leaflet (£2.95, or print for free from the website) detailing an hour-long walk round Cookham, visiting places with which Spencer is associated.

ARRIVAL AND DEPARTURE — COOKHAM

By train Cookham train station is on the branch line between Marlow, 3 miles west, and Maidenhead (which is on the London Paddington to Reading line). From Henley, you have to change trains twice to reach Marlow (at Twycross and Maidenhead). It's a 15min walk east from the station along High St to the gallery.

EATING AND DRINKING

Bel & The Dragon High St ⓣ01628 521263, ⓦbeland thedragon-cookham.co.uk. Just across the street from the Spencer Gallery, this historic half-timbered pub is a nice place for a pint, while the airy modern restaurant around the back offers excellent modern British cuisine (mains £12–20) backed by an extensive but very reasonably priced wine list. Mon–Fri noon–2.30pm & 6–10pm, Sat noon–10.30pm, Sun noon–9pm.

BRAY

★ **Fat Duck** High St ⓣ01628 580333, ⓦthefat duck.co.uk. Regularly voted one of the world's top restaurants, showcasing chef Heston Blumenthal's uniquely inventive culinary style, with tasting menus (£180) featuring classic creations like snail porridge and egg-and-bacon ice cream, with whiskey wine gums to finish. Reservations (bookable up to two months in advance) are like gold dust. Tues–Sat noon–2pm & 7–9pm, Sun noon–2pm.

Waterside Inn Ferry Rd ⊤01628 620691, ⓦwaterside-inn.co.uk. Part of the Roux family's culinary empire, the lovely Thamesside *Waterside Inn* has been wowing diners with its exceptional – and idiosyncratic – take on classical French cuisine since 1972; in 2010 it became the first restaurant outside France to retain three Michelin stars for twenty-five years in a row. Signature dishes include the sumptuous soufflé Suissesse (cheese souffle with double cream) and tronçonnette de homard (pan-fried lobster with white port sauce). Expect to spend at least £100 per head and reserve well in advance. Wed–Sun noon–2pm & 7–10pm (also open Tues eve in summer).

TOP 5 PUBS

Eight Bells Inn Chipping Campden. See p.247
The New Inn Gloucester. See p.253
The Queen's Head Stow-on-the-Wold. See p.245
Royal Oak Painswick. See p.243
The Turf Tavern Oxford. See p.236

The Vale of White Horse

West of the Chilterns, beyond the large town of Reading, lies the pretty **Vale of White Horse**, a shallow valley whose fertile farmland is studded with tiny villages and dotted with a striking collection of prehistoric remains. The **Ridgeway National Trail**, running along – or near – the top of the downs, links several of these ancient sites and offers wonderful, breezy views. The Vale is easily visited as a day-trip from Oxford or elsewhere, but you might opt to stay locally in one of the Vale's quaint villages – tiny **Woolstone** is perhaps the most appealing.

White Horse Hill and around

White Horse Hill, overlooking the B4507 six miles west of the unexciting market town of Wantage, follows close behind Stonehenge (see p.215) and Avebury (see p.216) in the hierarchy of Britain's ancient sites, though it attracts nothing like the same number of visitors. Carved into the north-facing slope of the downs, the 374ft-long **horse** looks like something created with a few swift strokes of an immense brush. The first written record of the horse's existence dates from the time of Henry II, but it was cut much earlier, probably in the first century BC, making it one of the oldest chalk figures in Britain. There's no lack of weird and wonderful theories concerning its origins, but burial sites excavated in the surrounding area point to the horse having some kind of sacred function, though no one knows quite what.

Just below the horse is **Dragon Hill**, a small flat-topped hillock that has its own legend. Locals long asserted that this was where St George killed and buried the dragon, a theory proved, so they argued, by the bare patch at the top and the channel down the side, where blood trickled from the creature's wounds. Here also, at the top of the hill, is the Iron Age earthwork of **Uffington Castle**, which provides wonderful views over the Vale.

To reach the white horse, follow the B4507 and then turn left (south) at the signed side-turning to the National Trust car park, from where it's a ten-minute walk across the top of the downs to the White Horse. There are no regular buses.

Wayland Smithy

The Ridgeway runs alongside the horse and continues west to reach, after one and a half miles, **Wayland's Smithy**, a 5000-year-old burial mound encircled by trees. It is one of the best Neolithic remains along the Ridgeway, though heavy restoration has rather detracted from its mystery. In ignorance of its original function, the invading Saxons named it after Weland (hence Wayland), an invisible smith who, according to their legends, made invincible armour and shod horses without ever being seen.

ACCOMMODATION AND EATING **THE VALE OF WHITE HORSE**

★ **The Craven** Fernham Rd, Uffington, a couple of miles north of the White Horse, ⓣ 01367 820449, ⓦ thecraven.co.uk. Outstanding B&B in a delightful thatched cottage, featuring seven cosy guest rooms (some with shared bathroom), with breakfast served in the old farmhouse kitchen. £65

White Horse Inn Woolstone, about a mile north of the White Horse ⓣ 01367 820726, ⓦ whitehorsewoolstone.co.uk. In the minuscule hamlet of Woolstone, this half-timbered, partly thatched old building offers straightforward accommodation, mostly in a modern annexe, and good pub food. £75

Oxford

When they think of **OXFORD**, visitors almost always imagine its **university**, revered as one of the world's great academic institutions. But, although the university dominates central Oxford both physically and mentally, the wider city has an entirely different character, its economy built on the **car plants** of Cowley to the south of the centre. It was here that Britain's first mass-produced cars were produced in the 1920s and, although there have been more downs than ups in recent years, the plants are still vitally important to the area.

Oxford should be high on anyone's itinerary, and can keep you occupied for several days. The **colleges** include some of England's finest architecture, and the city also has some excellent **museums** and a good range of bars and restaurants.

Christ Church College

St Aldates • Mon–Sat 9am–5pm, Sun 2–5pm • £7.50 • ⓣ 01865 286573, ⓦ chch.ox.ac.uk

Stretching along the east side of St Aldates is the main facade of **Christ Church College**, whose distinctive Tom Tower was added by Christopher Wren in 1681 to house the weighty "Great Tom" bell. The tower lords it over the main entrance of what is

OXFORD'S COLLEGES

The origins of the university are obscure, but it seems that the reputation of **Henry I**, the so-called "Scholar King", helped attract students in the early twelfth century. The first **colleges**, founded mostly by rich bishops, were essentially ecclesiastical institutions and this was reflected in collegiate rules and regulations – until 1877 lecturers were not allowed to marry, and women were not granted degrees until 1920. There are common **architectural features** among the 39 colleges, with the private student rooms and most of the communal rooms – chapels, halls (dining rooms) and libraries – arranged around quadrangles (quads). Each, however, has its own **character** and often a label, whether it's the richest (St John's), most left-wing (Wadham) or most public-school-dominated (Christ Church). Collegiate rivalries are long established, usually revolving around sports, and tension between the university and the city – "Town" and Gown" – has existed as long as the university itself.

EXPLORING THE COLLEGES

All the more popular colleges have restricted **opening hours** – and may close totally during academic functions. Most now also impose an **admission charge**, while some (such as University and Queens) are out of bounds to outsiders.

One nice way to get to see the university buildings (including those that are otherwise closed to outsiders) is to attend choral evensong, held during term time and offering the chance to enjoy superb music in historic surroundings for free. New College Choir is generally reckoned to be the best, while Queens College and Merton are also good. Some colleges also **rent out student rooms** in the vacations (see p.235).

Oxford's largest and arguably most prestigious college, but visitors have to enter from the south, a signed five-minute walk away – just beyond the tiny War Memorial Garden and at the top of Christ Church Meadow. Don't be surprised if you have to queue to get in. This is the most touristy of all the Oxford Colleges, particularly popular nowadays thanks to its Harry Potter connections – many scenes from the films were shot here, while a studio recreation of the college's Great Hall provided the set of Hogwarts Hall.

Entering the college from the south, it's a short step to the striking **Tom Quad**, the largest quad in Oxford – so large in fact that the Royalists penned up their mobile larder of cattle here during the Civil War. Guarded by the Tom Tower, the Quad's soft, honey-coloured stone makes a harmonious whole, but it was actually built in two main phases with the southern side dating back to Wolsey, the north finally finished in the 1660s. A wide stone staircase in the southeast corner of the Quad leads up to the **Dining Hall**, the grandest refectory in Oxford with a fanciful hammer-beam roof and a set of stern portraits of past scholars by a roll call of famous artists, including Reynolds, Gainsborough and Millais. Albert Einstein, William Gladstone and no fewer than twelve other British prime ministers were educated here.

Christ Church Picture Gallery

Canterbury Quad, reached via Canterbury Gate, off Oriel Square, if you're not visiting the rest of Christ Church • May–Sept Mon–Sat 10.30am–5pm, Sun 2–5pm; Oct–April Mon–Sat 10.30am–1pm & 2–4.30pm • £3 • Ⓦ chch.ox.ac.uk/gallery

Hidden away in Christ Church's pocket-sized Canterbury Quad is the college's **Picture Gallery**. The extensive collection comprises around 300 paintings and 2000 drawings, with fine works by artists from Italy and the Netherlands including paintings by Tintoretto, Van Dyck and Frans Hals and drawings by da Vinci, Dürer, Raphael and Michelangelo.

4

Christ Church Meadow

Christ Church Meadow fills in the tapering gap between the rivers Cherwell and Thames. If you decide to delay visiting Christ Church College, you can take a stroll east along Broad Walk for the Cherwell or keep straight down tree-lined (and more appealing) New Walk for the Thames.

The Cathedral

Behind Christ Church's Tom Quad • Usually Mon–Sat 9am–4.30pm, Sun 1–4.30pm, although times vary • Ⓦ chch.ox.ac.uk/cathedral

The Anglo-Saxons built a church on this site in the seventh century as part of the priory of St Frideswide (Oxford's patron saint), although the present building dates mainly from 1120–80. The priory was suppressed in 1524, but the church survived, becoming a cathedral twenty years later (while continuing to function as the college chapel). It's an unusually discordant church, with all sorts of bits and bobs from different periods, but it's fascinating all the same. The dominant features are the sturdy circular columns and rounded arches of the Normans, but there are also early Gothic pointed arches and the chancel ceiling is a particularly fine example of fifteenth-century stone vaulting. You can visit for evensong (Tues–Sun at 6pm) during term.

Merton College

Merton St • Mon–Fri 2–4pm, Sat & Sun 10am–5pm • £2 • Ⓣ 01865 276310, Ⓦ merton.ox.ac.uk

Merton College is historically the city's most important. Balliol and University colleges may have been founded earlier, but it was Merton – opened in 1264 – which set the model for colleges in both Oxford and Cambridge, being the first to gather its students and tutors together in one place. Furthermore, unlike the other two, Merton retains some of its original medieval buildings, with the best of the thirteenth-century architecture clustered around **Mob Quad**, a charming courtyard with mullioned windows and Gothic doorways to the right of the Front Quad. From the Mob Quad, an archway

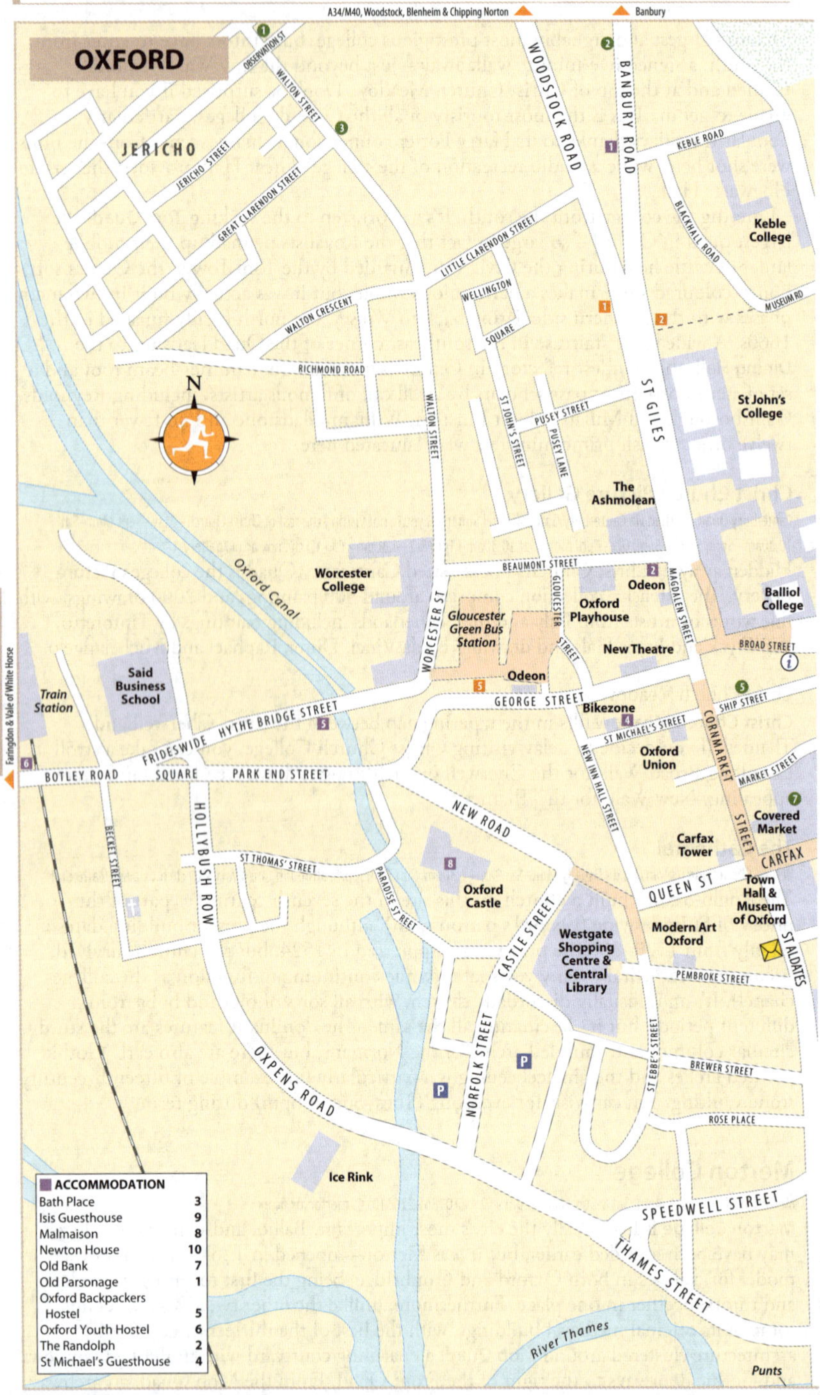
OXFORD
A34/M40, Woodstock, Blenheim & Chipping Norton
Banbury
Faringdon & Vale of White Horse
JERICHO
N
ACCOMMODATION
Bath Place 3
Isis Guesthouse 9
Malmaison 8
Newton House 10
Old Bank 7
Old Parsonage 1
Oxford Backpackers Hostel 5
Oxford Youth Hostel 6
The Randolph 2
St Michael's Guesthouse 4
OBSERVATION ST
WALTON STREET
JERICHO STREET
GREAT CLARENDON STREET
LITTLE CLARENDON STREET
WALTON CRESCENT
RICHMOND ROAD
WELLINGTON SQUARE
WOODSTOCK ROAD
BANBURY ROAD
KEBLE ROAD
BLACKHALL ROAD
MUSEUM RD
ST GILES
ST JOHN'S STREET
PUSEY STREET
PUSEY LANE
BEAUMONT STREET
GLOUCESTER STREET
MAGDALEN STREET
BROAD STREET
WORCESTER ST
GEORGE STREET
SHIP STREET
ST MICHAEL'S STREET
NEW INN HALL STREET
CORNMARKET STREET
MARKET STREET
CARFAX
QUEEN ST
ST ALDATES
PEMBROKE STREET
BREWER STREET
ROSE PLACE
ST EBBE'S STREET
HYTHE BRIDGE STREET
FRIDESWIDE SQUARE
BOTLEY ROAD
PARK END STREET
BECKET STREET
HOLLYBUSH ROW
ST THOMAS' STREET
PARADISE STREET
NEW ROAD
CASTLE STREET
NORFOLK STREET
OXPENS ROAD
SPEEDWELL STREET
THAMES STREET
River Thames
Oxford Canal
Keble College
St John's College
The Ashmolean
Worcester College
Odeon
Oxford Playhouse
Balliol College
Gloucester Green Bus Station
New Theatre
Bikezone
Oxford Union
Covered Market
Carfax Tower
Town Hall & Museum of Oxford
Oxford Castle
Westgate Shopping Centre & Central Library
Modern Art Oxford
Said Business School
Train Station
Ice Rink
Punts
P

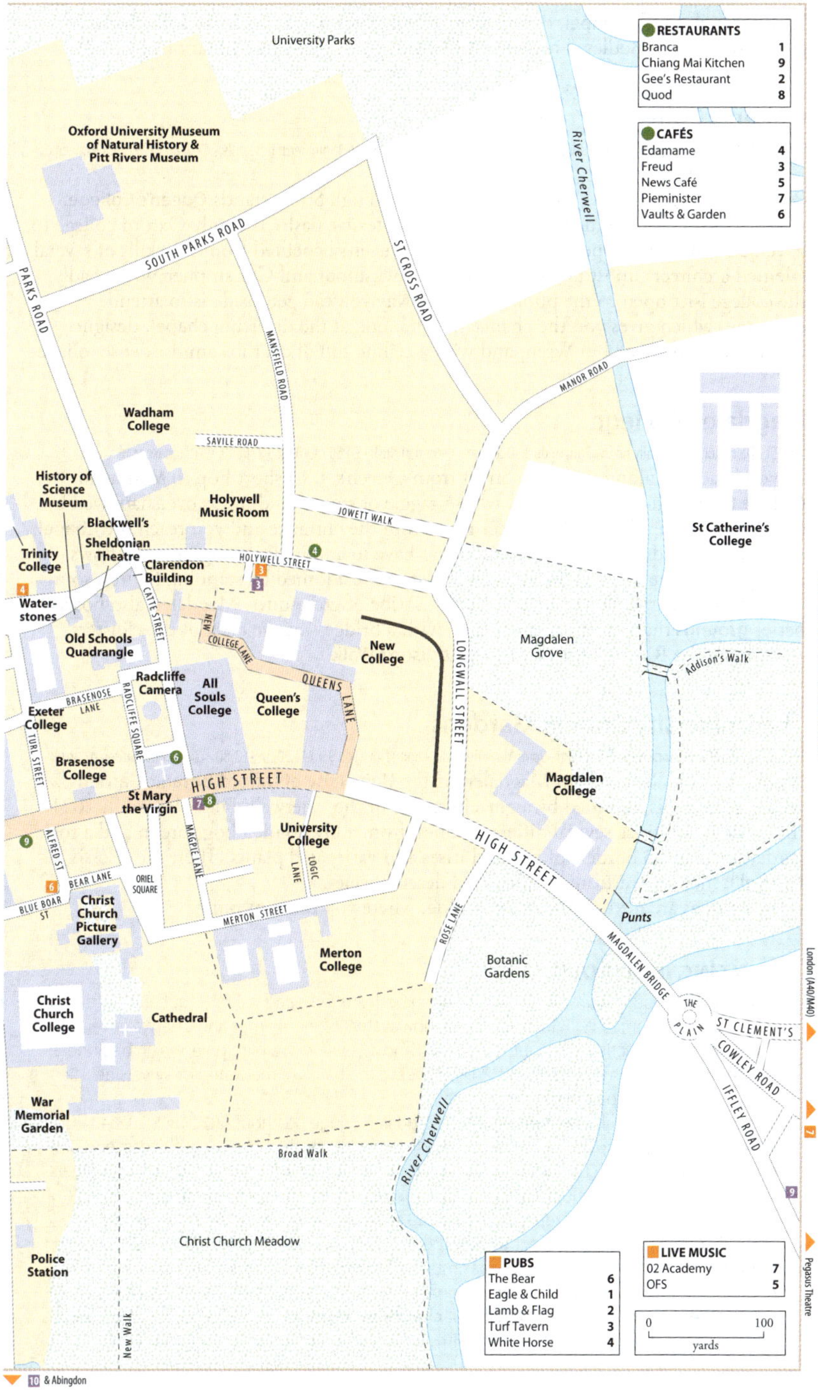

RESTAURANTS
Branca 1
Chiang Mai Kitchen 9
Gee's Restaurant 2
Quod 8
CAFÉS
Edamame 4
Freud 3
News Café 5
Pieminister 7
Vaults & Garden 6
PUBS
The Bear 6
Eagle & Child 1
Lamb & Flag 2
Turf Tavern 3
White Horse 4
LIVE MUSIC
02 Academy 7
OFS 5
0
100
yards
University Parks
Oxford University Museum of Natural History & Pitt Rivers Museum
River Cherwell
SOUTH PARKS ROAD
PARKS ROAD
ST CROSS ROAD
MANSFIELD ROAD
MANOR ROAD
Wadham College
SAVILE ROAD
History of Science Museum
Holywell Music Room
JOWETT WALK
St Catherine's College
Blackwell's
Sheldonian Theatre
Trinity College
Clarendon Building
HOLYWELL STREET
Water-stones
CATTE STREET
NEW COLLEGE LANE
QUEENS LANE
New College
LONGWALL STREET
Magdalen Grove
Addison's Walk
Old Schools Quadrangle
Radcliffe Camera
All Souls College
Queen's College
Exeter College
BRASENOSE LANE
RADCLIFFE SQUARE
TURL STREET
Brasenose College
HIGH STREET
Magdalen College
St Mary the Virgin
University College
ALFRED ST
MAGPIE LANE
LOGIC LANE
BEAR LANE
ORIEL SQUARE
BLUE BOAR ST
Christ Church Picture Gallery
MERTON STREET
ROSE LANE
Punts
Merton College
Botanic Gardens
MAGDALEN BRIDGE
THE PLAIN
ST CLEMENT'S
London (A40/M40)
COWLEY ROAD
IFFLEY ROAD
Christ Church College
Cathedral
War Memorial Garden
River Cherwell
Broad Walk
Christ Church Meadow
Police Station
New Walk
Pegasus Theatre
& Abingdon

leads through to the **Chapel**, dating from 1290, inside which you'll find the funerary plaque of Thomas Bodley – founder of Oxford's most important library (see p.232).

Queen's College

High St • Not open to the public except during evensong, Wed & Fri 6.30pm, Sun 6.15pm, term time only • T 01865 279120, W queens.ox.ac.uk

Rising impressively above the eastern end of the High Street stands **Queen's College**, whose handsome Baroque buildings cut an impressive dash. The only Oxford college to have been built in one period (1682–1765), Queen's benefited from the skills of several talented architects, most notably Nicholas Hawksmoor and Christopher Wren. Sadly, the college isn't open to the public; the only way you can get inside is to attend evensong, which gives you the chance to get a look at the diverting **chapel**, designed (or at least influenced by) Wren, and with a ceiling full of cherubs amidst dense foliage.

Magdalen College

High St • Daily: July–Sept daily noon–7pm or dusk; Oct–June 1–6pm or dusk • £4.50 • T 01865 276000, W magd.ox.ac.uk

As you head east along the High Street from Queen's, it's a short hop to **Magdalen College** (pronounced "Maudlin"), whose gaggle of stone buildings is overshadowed by its chunky medieval bell tower. Steer right from the entrance and you reach the **Chapel**, which has a handsome reredos, though you have to admire it through the windows of an ungainly stone screen. The adjacent **cloisters** are adorned by standing figures, some biblical and others folkloric, most notably a tribe of grotesques. Magdalen also boasts better **grounds** than most other colleges, with a bridge – at the back of the cloisters – spanning the River Cherwell to join **Addison's Walk**.

The University Botanic Gardens

High St • Daily: March, April, Sept & Oct 9am–5pm; May–Aug 9am–6pm; Nov–Feb 9am–4.30pm • £3.80 • W botanic-garden.ox.ac.uk

Across the High Street from Magdalen lie the **University of Oxford Botanic Gardens**, whose greenery is bounded by a graceful curve of the Cherwell. First planted in 1621, the gardens comprise several different zones, from a lily pond, a bog garden and a rock garden through to borders of bearded irises and variegated plants. There are also six large **glasshouses** featuring tropical and desert species.

The gardens are next to **Magdalen Bridge**, where you can rent punts.

PUNTING IN OXFORD

Punting is a favourite summer pastime among both students and visitors, but handling a punt – a flat-bottomed boat ideal for the shallow waters of the Thames and Cherwell rivers – requires some practise. The punt is propelled and steered with a long pole, which beginners inevitably get stuck in riverbed mud. Pulling over to the banks of the water for a riverside picnic is an essential part of the experience.

There are two central **boat rental** places: Magdalen Bridge boathouse (T 01865 202643, W oxfordpunting.co.uk; March–Oct daily 9.30am–9pm), beside the Cherwell at the east end of the High Street; and the Thames boat station at Folly Bridge (T 01865 243421, W salterssteamers.co.uk/punting.htm; May–Sept/Oct daily 10am–5pm), a short stroll south of the centre along St Aldates. In summer, the queues soon build up at both, so try to get there early – at around 10am. At both boathouses, expect **to pay** about £16–20 per hour for a boat plus a £30 deposit; ID may be required. Punts can take a maximum of five passengers – four sitting and one punting. Call the boathouses for opening times – which vary – or if there are any doubts about the weather. Both boathouses also rent out **chauffeured punts** (from £23/30min). You'll also find rowing boats and pedaloes for rent, although these aren't nearly as much fun.

New College

New College Lane • Daily: Easter to mid-Oct 11am–5pm; mid-Oct to Easter 2–4pm • Easter to early Oct £2; mid-Oct to Easter free • ⓣ 01865 279555, ⓦ new.ox.ac.uk

Founded in 1379, **New College** is entered via the large but rather plain **Front Quad**. On the left side of the quad rises the magnificent Perpendicular **Chapel**, arguably the finest in Oxford. The ante-chapel contains some superb fourteenth-century stained glass and the west window – of 1778 – holds an intriguing Nativity scene based on a design by Sir Joshua Reynolds. Beneath it stands the wonderful *Lazarus* by Jacob Epstein. Immediately past the chapel lies the college's peaceful **cloisters**.

An archway on the east side of the Front Quad leads through to the modest **Garden Quad**, with the thick flowerbeds of the **College Garden** beckoning beyond. The north side of the garden is flanked by the largest and best-preserved section of Oxford's medieval **city wall**, but the conspicuous earthen **mound** in the middle is a later decorative addition and not, disappointingly, medieval at all.

The Sheldonian Theatre

Broad St • Mon–Sat 10am–12.30pm & 2–4.30pm; Nov–Feb closes 3.30pm • £2.50 • ⓦ sheldon.ox.ac.uk

The east end of Broad Street abuts much of Oxford's most monumental architecture, beginning with the **Sheldonian Theatre**, ringed by a series of glum-looking, pop-eyed classical heads. The Sheldonian was Christopher Wren's first major work, a reworking of the Theatre of Marcellus in Rome, semicircular at the back and rectangular at the front. It was conceived in 1663, when the 31-year-old Wren's main job was as professor of astronomy. Designed as a stage for university ceremonies, nowadays it also functions as a concert hall, but the interior lacks any sense of drama, and even the views from the cupola are disappointing.

The Clarendon Building

Broad St • Not open to the public

Wren's colleague, Nicholas Hawksmoor, designed the **Clarendon Building**, a domineering, solidly symmetrical edifice topped by allegorical figures that is set at right angles to – and lies immediately east of – the Sheldonian. The Clarendon was erected to house the University Press, but is now part of the **Bodleian Library** (see p.232).

The Old Schools Quadrangle

Catte St • **Divinity School** Mon–Fri 9am–4.45pm, Sat 9.15am–3.45pm, Sun 11am–4.45pm • £1 **Duke Humfrey's Library** Not open to the public except on special Bodleian Library tours; see p.232

Immediately south of the Clarendon Building lies the venerable **Old Schools Quadrangle** (sometimes described, not quite accurately, as the Bodleian Library). The history of the quadrangle is rather convoluted. The complex began with the **Divinity School**, occupying the lower floor of the west wing. Built between 1427 and 1483, the school originally served as a venue for theological lectures and boasts an extravagant vaulted ceiling, a riot of pendants and decorative bosses – Oxford Gothic at its most memorable. From here, steps lead up to the atmospheric **Duke Humfrey's Library**, completed shortly after the Divinity School in 1488, with its magnificent beamed ceiling and antique books.

The remaining three wings of the quadrangle were constructed in ornate Jacobean style between 1613 and 1618 to house the expanding Bodleian Library and a sequence of lecture rooms, still signed in gold letters above the various doors. On the quad's east side rises the handsome **Tower of the Five Orders**, with tiers of columns built according to the five classical styles – Tuscan, Doric, Ionic, Corinthian and Composite.

THE BODLEIAN LIBRARY

The UK's largest after the British Library in London, the **Bodleian Library** stores some 11 million book stacked up along almost 120 miles of shelves and growing fast – as one of the UK's six legal deposit libraries, the Bodleian receives a copy of every work published in Britain.

The origins of the Bodleian go back to **Duke Humfrey's Library** of 1488 (see p.231). The Bodleian proper was founded in 1602 by Thomas Bodley, initially occupying Duke Humfrey's original library, although it grew so rapidly that the **Old Schools Quadrangle** (see p.231) was constructed between 1613 and 1618 to house the expanding collection. The library subsequently spread steadily outwards, occupying the Clarendon Building (see p.231), Radcliffe Camera (see below) and finally the New Bodleian Library on Broad Street, built in the 1930s.

TOURS OF THE BODLEIAN LIBRARY

There are a variety of **tours** (T 01865 277224, W bodleian.ox.ac.uk/about/visitors) of the library, most centred on the **Old Schools Quadrangle** (including the Divinity School – see p.231). **Sixty-minute guided tours** (usually 4 daily; £6.50) cover the Divinity School, Duke Humfrey's Library and other parts of the Old Schools Quad, while there are also **30min tours** (usually 2 daily; £4.50) visiting the Divinity School and Duke Humfrey's Library. An **extended tour** (Sat 10am & Wed 9.30am; 90min) adds visits to the Radcliffe Camera (the only way to get into the building for non-scholars) and the small medieval library of chained books in the Church of St Mary the Virgin. Tours are very popular, so it's a good idea to arrive early on the day to reserve. Alternatively, there's an **audioguide** (£2.50) that covers the quad and Divinity School.

The Radcliffe Camera

Catte St • Not open to the public except on special Bodleian Library tours; see above

Behind the Old Schools Quadrangle rises Oxford's most imposing – or vainglorious – building, the Bodleian's **Radcliffe Camera** (formerly the Radcliffe Library; no public access), a mighty rotunda, built between 1737 and 1748 by James Gibbs, architect of London's St Martin-in-the-Fields church. There's no false modesty here. Dr John Radcliffe was, according to a contemporary diarist, "very ambitious of glory" and when he died in 1714 he bequeathed a mountain of money for the construction of a library – the "Radcliffe Mausoleum" as one wag termed it. Gibbs was one of the few British architects of the period to have been trained in Rome and his rotunda is thoroughly Italian in style, its limestone columns ascending to a delicate balustrade, decorated with urns and encircling a lead-sheathed dome.

St Mary the Virgin

High St • Mon–Sat 9am–5pm, Sun 11.30am–5pm • £2 suggested donation, tower £3

Flanking the High Street just behind the Radcliffe Camera, **St Mary the Virgin** is a hotchpotch of architectural styles, but mostly dates from the fifteenth century. The church's saving graces are its elaborate, thirteenth-century pinnacled spire and its distinctive Baroque **porch**, flanked by chunky corkscrewed pillars. The interior is disappointingly mundane, though the carved poppy heads on the choir stalls are of some historical interest: the tips were brusquely flattened off when a platform was installed here in 1554 to stage the heresy trial of Cranmer, Latimer and Ridley, leading Protestants who had run foul of Queen Mary. The church's other diversion is the **tower**, with wonderful views across to the Radcliffe Camera and east over **All Souls College**.

All Souls College

High St • Mon–Fri 2–4pm during term only • Free • T 01865 279379, W all-souls.ox.ac.uk

One of the cluster of dramatic buildings flanking Catte Street, **All Souls** is the most memorably theatrical of all the Oxford colleges. Entrance is from the High Street, although the rather plain neo-Gothic street-facing facade and modest First Quadrangle give little hint of the extravagant scale and style of the **Great Quad** beyond. This is one of the finest architectural ensembles in the city, dominated by the two great mock-Gothic towers designed by Hawksmoor in his characteristically angular and chunky style and providing a striking visual counterpart to the Radcliffe Camera opposite. The south side of the quad is bounded by the fine college hall and late Gothic chapel; opposite, the north wing houses the Codrington Library (not open to the public), which sports an extravagant sundial designed by Wren.

History of Science Museum

Broad St • Tues–Fri noon–5pm, Sat 10am–5pm, Sun 2–5pm • Free • Ⓦ mhs.ox.ac.uk

The classical heads that shield the Sheldonian (see p.231) continue along the front of the **History of Science Museum**, whose two floors display an amazing clutter of antique microscopes and astrolabes, sundials, quadrants and sextants. The highlights are Elizabeth I's own astrolabe and a blackboard that belonged to Einstein.

Trinity College

Broad St • During term Mon–Fri 10am–noon & 2–4pm, Sat & Sun 2–4pm; outside term Sat & Sun 10am–noon & 2–4pm • £2 • Ⓣ 01865 279900, Ⓦ trinity.ox.ac.uk

Trinity College is fronted by three dinky lodge-cottages. Behind them the manicured lawn of the Front Quad stretches back to the richly decorated **Chapel**, awash with Baroque stucco work. Its high altar is flanked by an exquisite example of the work of Grinling Gibbons – a distinctive performance, with cherubs' heads peering out from delicate foliage. Behind the chapel stands **Durham Quad**, an attractive ensemble of old stone buildings begun at the end of the seventeenth century.

4

Exeter College

Turl St • Daily 2–5pm • Free • Ⓣ 01865 279600, Ⓦ exeter.ox.ac.uk

Today's **Exeter College** is another medieval foundation whose original buildings were chopped about in the nineteenth century. On this occasion, however, the Victorians did create something of interest in the richly decorated neo-Gothic **chapel**, designed by Gilbert Scott in the 1850s. The chapel contains a fine set of stained-glass windows illustrating scores of biblical stories – St Paul on the Road to Damascus and Samson bringing down the pillars of the Philistine temple for example – but their deep colours put the nave in permanent shade. The chapel also holds a superb Pre-Raphaelite tapestry, the **Adoration of the Magi**, a fine collaboration between William Morris and Edward Burne-Jones, who both studied at Exeter College.

The Ashmolean

Beaumont St • Tues–Sun 10am–6pm • Free • Ⓦ ashmolean.org

One of the country's finest museums, **The Ashmolean** occupies a mammoth Neoclassical building on the corner of Beaumont Street and St Giles. The museum grew from the collections of the magpie-like **John Tradescant**, gardener to Charles I, and an energetic traveller, and today it possesses a vast and far-reaching collection covering everything from Minoan vases to Stradivarius violins.

The Ashmolean boasts a series of light and airy modern galleries spread over four floors (pick up a **plan** at reception). The "orientation" gallery in the basement provides a thematic overview of the museum, while the ground floor houses the museum's "ancient world" exhibits, including its superb Egyptology collection and an imposing room full of Greek sculptures. Floor 1 is dedicated to Mediterranean, Indian and Islamic artefacts (Hindu bronzes, Iranian pottery and so on) while floor 2 is mainly

European, including the museum's wide-ranging collection of Dutch, Flemish and Italian paintings. Floor 3 focuses on European art since 1800, including works by Sickert, Pissarro and the Pre-Raphaelites.

Oxford University Museum of Natural History

Parks Rd • Daily 10am–5pm • Free • oum.ox.ac.uk

North of the centre lies the **University Museum of Natural History** occupying a grand neo-Gothic building illuminated with a huge glass roof. The wide-ranging exhibits include impressive casts of dinosaur skeletons (plus a couple of elephants for good measure), considerable quantities of stuffed animals and displays of local finds, including the remains of the "Oxford Brontosaurus", unearthed near Chipping Norton in 1825. Look out too for the well-preserved head and foot of a dodo, said to have been the inspiration for the dodo in Alice in Wonderland – Lewis Carroll was a regular visitor to the museum.

Pitt-Rivers museum

Parks Rd, entered via a door at the back of the Natural History Museum • Tues–Sun 10am–4.30pm, Mon noon–4.30pm • Free • prm.ox.ac.uk

Founded in 1884, the **Pitt-Rivers Museum** is one of the world's finest ethnographic museums and an extraordinary relic of the Victorian Age, arranged like an exotic junk shop with each bulging cabinet labelled meticulously by hand. The exhibits, brought to England by several explorers, Captain Cook among them, range from totem poles and mummified crocodiles to African fetishes and gruesome shrunken heads.

Carfax

Tower Daily: April–Sept 10am–5.30pm; Oct 10am–4.30pm; Nov–March 10am–3.30pm • £2.20; no under-7s

Too busy to be comfortable and too modern to be pretty, the **Carfax** crossroads is not a place to hang around, but it is overlooked by an interesting remnant of the medieval town. The chunky fourteenth-century **tower**, adorned by a pair of clocktower jacks dressed in vaguely Roman attire, is all that remains of St Martin's church, where legend asserts that William Shakespeare stood sponsor at the baptism of one of his friends' children. You can climb it for wide views over the centre, though other vantage points – principally St Mary's church (see p.232) – have the edge.

Modern Art Oxford

Pembroke St • Tues & Wed 10am–5pm, Thurs–Sat 10am–7pm, Sun noon–5pm (although may be closed for periods between exhibitions) • modernartoxford.org.uk

Just south of Carfax is the city's best contemporary art gallery, **Modern Art Oxford**. The gallery has an excellent programme of temporary exhibitions, featuring international contemporary art in a wide variety of media, along with lectures, films, workshops and multimedia performances (not all of which are free).

ARRIVAL AND DEPARTURE — OXFORD

By train The train station is on the west side of the city centre, a 10min walk from Carfax along Hythe Bridge St.

Destinations Bath (2 hourly; 1hr 20min–1hr 40min); Birmingham (2 hourly; 1hr 10min); Bristol (hourly; 1hr 40min); Cheltenham (every 30min; 2hr–2hr 15min); Gloucester (every 30min; 1hr 40min–2hr 20min); London (2–3 hourly; 1hr); Winchester (2 hourly; 1hr 10min–1hr 30min); Worcester (2 hourly; 1hr 15min–1hr 35min).

By bus Long-distance and many county-wide buses terminate at the Gloucester Green bus station, in the city centre adjoining George St. Most local and city buses terminate on the High Street and St Giles. There are fast and frequent services to London Gatwick and Heathrow airports, while the Oxford tube (oxfordtube.com) runs every 10–30min between Gloucester Green and Victoria Station in central London. Other local services are mostly in the hands of Stagecoach (T 01865 772250, W stagecoach-oxford.co.uk). For the Cotswolds, Swanbrook (T 01452 712386, W swanbrook.co.uk) operates a particularly useful bus service linking Oxford with Gloucester via Burford, Northleach and Cheltenham (Mon–Sat 3 daily, Sun 1 daily).

GETTING AROUND

By car Parking in central Oxford is limited and expensive, although there's an extensive Park-and-Ride scheme, with five large and clearly signed car parks on the main approach roads into the city from where buses (daily Mon–Sat 6am–11pm, Sun 9am–7pm) travel into the centre every 10 to 15min. Parking is free; the bus fare is around £2 return.

By bike Bikezone, 28–32 St Michael's St (T 01865 728877, W bike-zone.co.uk) rents bikes from £18/day.

By taxi Taxi ranks are liberally distributed across the city centre, with taxis lining up at the train station and on the High St. Alternatively, call Radio Taxis (T 01865 242424).

INFORMATION AND TOURS

Tourist office 15 Broad St (Mon–Sat 9.30am–5pm, Sun 10am–4pm; T 01865 252200, W visitoxfordandoxfordshire.com).

Listings information For local listings, pick up a copy of the free *In Oxford* from the tourist office or check out W inoxfordmag.co.uk or W dailyinfo.co.uk.

Guided tours The tourist office offers excellent guided walking tours of the city centre (10.45am & 2pm; £8). Further along Broad St, the main Blackwell's bookshop (T 01865 333606) also runs several literary-themed walking tours a week (£7). Advance booking for both is recommended.

ACCOMMODATION

As well as the places listed below, another good source of accommodation in Oxford is the **university** itself. Outside term time, many colleges (including Queen's, Trinity and Magdalen) let out rooms, offering the chance to stay in historic surroundings at often bargain rates (although the rooms themselves are unlikely to be particularly luxurious). For more information, visit W oxfordrooms.co.uk.

HOTELS

Bath Place 4 Bath Place T 01865 791 812, W bathplace.co.uk. This unusual, pink-and-blue hotel is tucked away down an old cobbled courtyard flanked by ancient buildings in an unbeatable central location. The sixteen rooms are each individually decorated in attractive antique style with canopied beds and bare stone walls. **£118**

Malmaison Oxford Castle, 3 New Rd T 01865 268400, W malmaison.com/hotels. Unusual lodgings in an old Victorian prison in the old Oxford Castle complex, now given a stylish makeover, with very chic modern rooms (some in former cells, others in the former House of Corrections). There's also an excellent restaurant with alfresco terrace ("The Exercise Yard"). **£125**

Old Bank 92 High St T 01865 799599, W oldbank-hotel.co.uk. Great location for a slick hotel in a glistening conversion of an old bank. More than forty bedrooms decorated in crisp, modern style, and some of them with great views over All Souls College. **£180**

Old Parsonage 1 Banbury Rd T 01865 310210, W oldparsonage-hotel.co.uk. Lovely hotel set in a charming, wisteria-clad old stone building of 1660, with thirty-odd bright, modern rooms. **£175**

★ **The Randolph** 1 Beaumont St T 0870 400 8200, W randolph-hotel.com. The most famous hotel in the city, long the favoured choice of the great and the good, the *Randolph* occupies a large and well-proportioned brick building with a distinctive neo-Gothic interior. Rooms are modern and comfortable – those on the top floor are the quietest. Rates fluctuate. **£175**

GUESTHOUSES AND B&BS

Isis Guesthouse 45–53 Iffley Rd T 01865 613700, W isisguesthouse.com. From July to September, this college hall – within easy walking distance of Magdalen Bridge – becomes a guesthouse with 37 single and double rooms (about half en suite), decorated in a brisk if frugal modern style. Excellent value. **£40**

Newton House 82–84 Abingdon Rd T 01865 240561, W oxfordcity.co.uk/accom/newton. Appealing, family-run guesthouse with thirteen smart rooms in two good-looking Victorian townhouses about 10min walk south of the centre – well placed for evening strolls along the Thames. **£70**

St Michael's Guesthouse 26 St Michael's St T 01865 242101. Friendly B&B in a cosy three-storey terrace house. Rooms (shared bathroom only) are fairly basic, although the central location and bargain prices can't be beat. **£56**

HOSTELS

Oxford Backpackers Hostel 9a Hythe Bridge St T 01865 721761, W funkyhostels.co.uk. Refurbished independent hostel with bright, modern quads and dorms, plus fully equipped kitchen, laundry, free wi-fi and bar. 24-hour access. **£16**

Oxford Youth Hostel 2a Botley Rd ☎01865 727275, ⓦyha.org.uk. In a modern block next to the train station, this popular YHA hostel has 187 beds divided into two-, four- and six-bedded rooms, plus doubles, some en suite. There's 24-hour access, laundry, wi-fi, and an inexpensive café. Open daily all year. Dorm **£17**, double **£43**

EATING

Touristy tea-shops and chain restaurants apart, central Oxford is somewhat lacking in good places to eat – with a few notable exceptions. The best restaurants and cafés can be found on the edge of the city centre, either in arty **Jericho**, northwest of the centre, or down grungy **Cowley Road** to the east.

CAFÉS

★ **Edamame** 15 Holywell St ☎01865 246916, ⓦedamame.co.uk. This minuscule but consistently packed backstreet café provides an unlikely setting for some of the region's finest Japanese cooking, featuring scrumptious versions of classics like pork/chicken katsu, chicken kara-agé and shoyu ramen. Reservations aren't accepted, so you'll probably have to queue (and perhaps share a table as well). Thursday is sushi night. Mains £7.50–9. Wed 11.30am–2.30pm, Thurs–Sat 11.30am–2.30pm & 5–8.30pm, Sun noon–3.30pm.

Freud 119 Walton St ☎01865 311171. Dramatically located inside a grand old converted Victorian church, this fashionable café-bar serves straightforward Italian/Mediterranean food, with mains from £6. Live music some nights. Daily 11am till late.

News Café 1 Ship St ☎01865 242317. Cheaper, less touristed and generally more peaceful than the cafés along the High Street, dishing up bagels, salads and soups plus more substantial mains and daily specials, plus beer and wine. Daily 9am–6pm.

Pieminister Covered Market, High St ☎01865 241613, ⓦpieminister.co.uk. Entertaining update of the classic pie-and-mash shop, with gourmet beef, chicken and veg pies (£2.95/£3.95) served in an array of international flavours ranging from Thai chook to the feisty Spanish "matador" – with mashed potatoes and mushy peas added on request. Mon–Sat 10am–5pm, Sun 10am–4pm.

Vaults & Garden Radcliffe Square. In an atmospheric stone-vaulted room attached to the church of St Mary the Virgin, this café serves up good coffee and cakes, as well as light lunches, with seating either indoors or on the attractive outdoor terrace. Daily 10am–5pm.

RESTAURANTS

★ **Branca** 111 Walton St ☎01865 556 111, ⓦbranca-restaurants.com. Large, buzzy bar-brasserie dishing up well-prepared Italian food, from simple pastas, pizzas and risottos through to more elaborate meat and fish *secondi* (£11–15). Daily 11am–11pm.

Chiang Mai Kitchen 130a High St ☎01865 202233, ⓦchiangmaikitchen.co.uk. An authentically spicy blast of Thai cooking in a homely little timber-framed medieval building tucked down an alleyway off the High Street. All the traditional classics are done well, including a good vegetarian selection. Mains £7–10. Reservations advised. Daily noon–2.30pm & 6–10.30pm.

Gee's Restaurant 61 Banbury Rd ☎01865 553540, ⓦgees-restaurant.co.uk. Popular, upmarket restaurant in an airy Victorian conservatory, with inventive, seasonally changing modern European food (mains £17–22) – lobster linguine, for example, or Gressingham duck breast with "Oxford sauce". Cheaper lunch and early dinner deals are available. Live jazz on Sun eve. Daily noon–2.30pm & 6–10pm (Fri & Sat until 10.30pm).

Quod Old Bank Hotel, 92 High St ☎01865 799599, ⓦoldbank-hotel.co.uk. Lively modern restaurant, with seating in the airy interior and on the outdoor terrace. The good, seasonal modern bistro food ranges from fish 'n' chips and New York-style burgers through to tasty pizzas and more substantial steaks. Most mains £9–15, plus good-value lunch and early dinner set menus. Daily 7am–11pm.

DRINKING

The Bear 6 Alfred St ☎01865 728164, ⓦfullers.co.uk. Tucked away down a narrow side street, this intimate and low-key little pub is one of the nicest city-centre drinking holes, with a decent range of beers, good food and glass cases full of old college (and other) ties. Mon–Sat 11am–11pm, Sun 11am–10.30pm.

Eagle & Child 49 St Giles ☎01865 302925. Known variously as the "Bird & Baby", "Bird & Brat" or "Fowl & Foetus", complete with low-beamed ceilings and a series of cramped, cosy rooms. Once the haunt of J.R.R. Tolkien and C.S. Lewis, it still attracts an interesting crowd. Mon–Thurs 11am–11pm, Fri & Sat 11am–11.30pm, Sun 11am–10.30pm.

Lamb & Flag St Giles ☎01865 515787. An old favourite with generations of university students and others – Thomas Hardy is said to have written much of Jude the Obscure here. It lacks the olde-worlde atmospheric of the *Eagle & Child* opposite, but has more space to swing a cat and one of the city's best selections of real ales. Mon–Sat noon–11pm, Sun noon–10.30pm.

★ **Turf Tavern** Bath Place, off Holywell St ☎01865 243235, ⓦtheturftavern.co.uk. Small, atmospheric seventeenth-century pub with a fine range of beers, and mulled wine in winter. Abundant seating in the attractive garden outside. Mon–11am–11pm, Sun noon–10.30pm.

4

White Horse 52 Broad St ⊤01865 204801, ⓦwhitehorseoxford.co.uk. A tiny old pub with snug rooms, pictures of old university sports teams on the walls and real ales. It was used as a set for the *Inspector Morse* TV series. Daily 11am–midnight.

ENTERTAINMENT AND NIGHTLIFE

For classical music and theatre **listings**, consult *In Oxford* (see p.235). The website ⓦoxfordplayhouse.com/ticketsoxford lists many upcoming classical music concerts, while the daily *Oxford Mail* newspaper also carries information on gigs and events. In addition to the classical music venues listed below, aficionados of choral music should take in evensong (see p.226) at one of the college chapels.

LIVE MUSIC AND CLUBS

OFS 40 George St ⊤01865 297170, ⓦoldfirestation.org.uk. The OFS (Old Fire Station) is a multipurpose venue hosting musicals and theatre, plus a separate café-bar featuring one-off DJ club nights.

02 Academy 190 Cowley Rd ⊤01865 813500, ⓦo2academyoxford.co.uk. Oxford's liveliest indie and dance venue, with a fast-moving programme of live bands and guest DJs.

CLASSICAL MUSIC AND THEATRE

Holywell Music Room 32 Holywell St ⊤01865 305305, ⓦoxfordplayhouse.com. This small, plain, Georgian building was opened in 1748 as the first public music hall in England. It offers a varied programme, from straight classical to experimental, with occasional bouts of jazz. Details are posted outside and are available at the Oxford Playhouse (see below), which also sells its tickets.

Oxford Playhouse 11 Beaumont St ⊤01865 305305, ⓦoxfordplayhouse.com. The city's top theatre, hosting professional touring companies and a mixture of plays, opera and concerts.

Pegasus Theatre Magdalen Rd ⊤01865 812150, ⓦpegasustheatre.org.uk. Low-budget, avant-garde productions dominate the programme of this adventurous theatre.

Sheldonian Theatre Broad St ⊤01865 277299, ⓦox.ac.uk/sheldonian. Oxford's top concert hall, and home to the resident Oxford Philomusica symphony orchestra (ⓦoxfordphil.com) and Oxford Bach Choir (ⓦoxfordbachchoir.org).

CINEMA

Phoenix Picture House 57 Walton St ⊤0871 9025736, ⓦpicturehouses.co.uk. Mainstream and art-house films, including occasional foreign-language works.

Ultimate Picture Palace Jeune St, off Cowley Rd ⊤01865 245288, ⓦultimatepicturepalace.co.uk. Very good art-house cinema, with screenings of contemporary and classic works of world cinema plus special events and talks.

4

DIRECTORY

Bookshops The leading university bookshop is Blackwells (ⓦblackwell.co.uk). Outlets include three shops on Broad St: Blackwells Music, Blackwells Art & Posters, and the main store, 48–51 Broad St (⊤01865 792 792).

Left luggage The only place to leave luggage is the *Oxford Backpackers* (see p.235), who charge £4 per item.

Around Oxford

From Oxford, it's a short trip west to the Cotswolds (see pp.240–248) and a brief haul south to both the Vale of White Horse (see p.225) and the Chiltern Hills (see p.223). Nearer still – a brief bus ride north – is the charming little town of **Woodstock** and its imperious neighbour, **Blenheim Palace**, birthplace of Winston Churchill.

Woodstock

WOODSTOCK, eight miles north of Oxford, has royal associations going back to Saxon times, with a string of kings attracted by its excellent hunting. The Royalists used Woodstock as a base during the Civil War, but, after their defeat, Cromwell never got round to destroying either the town or the palace: the latter was ultimately given to (and flattened by) the Duke of Marlborough in 1704 when work started on the building you see today. Long dependent on royal and then ducal patronage, Woodstock is now both a well-heeled commuter town for Oxford and a base for visitors to Blenheim. It is also an extremely pretty little place, its handsome stone buildings gathered around the main square, at the junction of Market and High streets.

Oxfordshire Museum

Fletcher's House, Park St • Tues–Sat 10am–5pm, Sun 2–5pm • Free • oxfordshire.gov.uk/museums

The town's one sight is the low-key **Oxfordshire Museum**, in the historic Fletcher's House, with eleven galleries offering a well-composed overview of the county's archeology, social history and industry, from Roman artefacts through to contemporary arts and crafts.

ARRIVAL AND INFORMATION — WOODSTOCK

By bus Stagecoach bus #S3 leaves Oxford bus station bound for Woodstock every 30min or so (hourly on Sun).

Tourist office In the Oxfordshire Museum (Mon–Sat: March–Oct 9.30am–5.30pm; Nov–Feb Mon–Sat 10am–5pm; 01993 813276, oxfordshirecotswolds.org).

ACCOMMODATION AND EATING

The Bear Park St 0844 879 9143, bearhotelwoodstock.co.uk. A creaky old thirteenth-century coaching inn with rooms kitted out in attractive, country-house style and a quality restaurant. The bar is also the most atmospheric place in the village for a drink, with low-beamed ceilings and an open fire in winter. Food served daily 12.30–2.30pm & 7–9/9.30pm. **£110**

King's Arms 19 Market St 01993 813636, kings-hotel-woodstock.co.uk. Fifteen chic rooms in an attractively updated Georgian house. The fine restaurant (mains £12–16) specializes in classic and modern British cuisine, with hearty creations like pot roasted leg of lamb or organic Shetland salmon with horseradish mash. Food served Mon–Fri noon–2.30pm & 6.30–9.30pm, Sat & Sun noon–9am. **£140**

Blenheim Palace

Mid-Feb to Oct daily 10.30am–5.30pm, last admission 4.45pm (park & gardens from 9am); Nov to mid-Dec Wed–Sun same hours • £19, or £11 for park & gardens only • blenheimpalace.com

In 1704, as a thank-you for his victory over the French at the Battle of Blenheim, Queen Anne gave **John Churchill, Duke of Marlborough** (1650–1722) the royal estate of Woodstock, along with the promise of enough cash to build himself a gargantuan palace.

Work started promptly on **Blenheim Palace** with Sir John Vanbrugh, who was also responsible for Castle Howard in Yorkshire (see p.541) as principal architect. However, the duke's formidable wife, Sarah Jennings, who had wanted Christopher Wren, was soon at loggerheads with Vanbrugh, while Queen Anne had second thoughts, stifling the flow of money. Construction work was halted and the house was only finished after the duke's death at the instigation of his widow, who ended up paying most of the bills and designing much of the interior herself. The end result is the country's grandest example of Baroque civic architecture, an Italianate palace of finely worked yellow stone that is more a monument than a house – just as Vanbrugh intended.

The **interior** of the main house is stuffed with paintings and tapestries, plus all manner of objets d'art, including furniture from Versailles and carvings by Grinling Gibbons. Those interested in Winston Churchill may prefer the **Churchill Exhibition**, which provides a brief introduction to the man, accompanied by live recordings of some of his more famous speeches. Born here at Blenheim, Churchill (1874–1965), grandson of the seventh Duke of Marlborough, now lies buried alongside his wife in the graveyard of Bladon church just outside the estate.

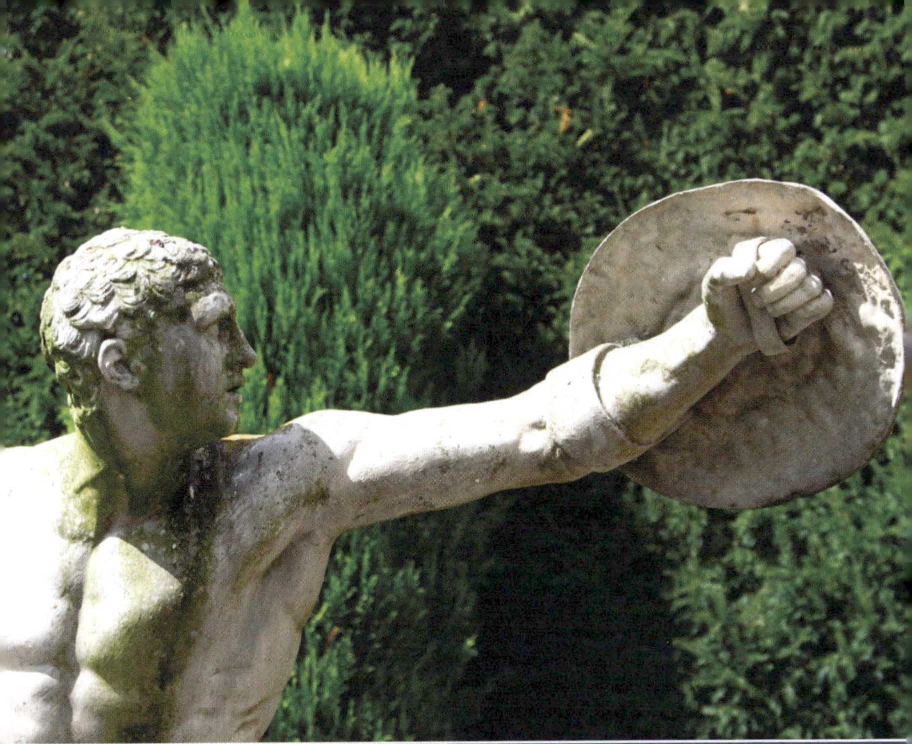
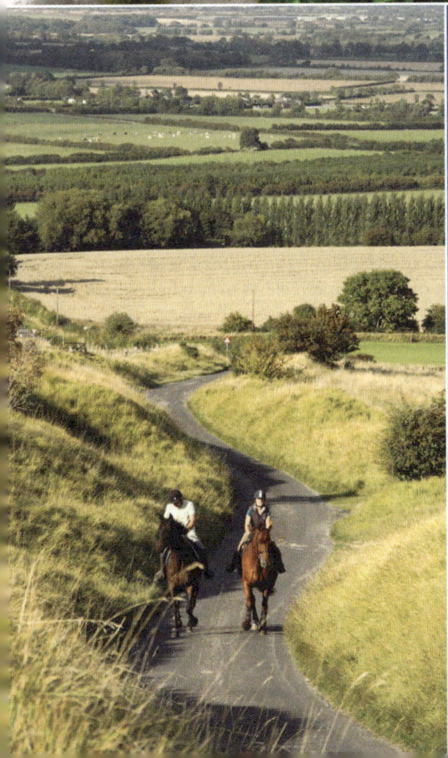
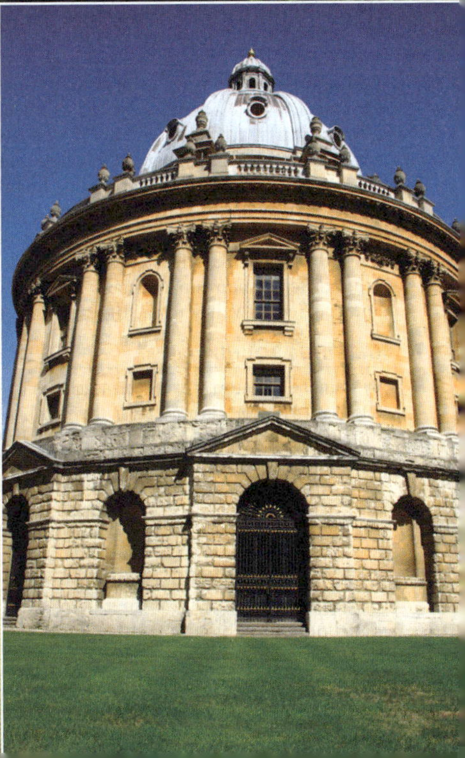

Blenheim Gardens

Blenheim's formal **gardens**, to the rear of the house, are divided into several distinct areas, including a rose garden and an arboretum, though the open **parkland** is more enticing, leading from the front of the house down to an artificial lake, **Queen Pool**. Vanbrugh's splendid Grand Bridge crosses the lake to the **Column of Victory**, erected by Sarah Jennings and topped by a statue of her husband posing heroically in a toga.

ARRIVAL AND DEPARTURE — BLENHEIM PALACE

There are two **entrances** to Blenheim, one just south of Woodstock on the Oxford road and another through the Triumphal Arch at the end of Park Street in Woodstock itself. Stagecoach **bus** #S3 runs to Blenheim Palace from Oxford's train station and Gloucester Green Bus Station every 30min (hourly on Sun).

The Cotswolds

4

The limestone hills that make up the **Cotswolds** are preposterously photogenic, dotted with a string of picture-book villages, many of them built by wealthy cloth merchants between the fourteenth and sixteenth centuries. Largely bypassed by the Industrial Revolution, which heralded the area's commercial decline, much of the Cotswolds is technically speaking a relic, its architecture beautifully preserved. Numerous churches are decorated with beautiful carving, for which the local limestone was ideal: soft and easy to carve when first quarried, but hardening after long exposure to the sunlight.

The Cotswolds have become one of the country's main tourist attractions, with many towns afflicted by plagues of tearooms and souvenir and antiques shops – this is Morris Dancing country. To see the Cotswolds at their best, you should visit off season or perhaps avoid the most popular towns and instead escape into the hills themselves, though even in high season the charms of towns like **Chipping Campden** – "Chipping'"as in *ceapen*, the Old English for market – Burford and Northleach are evident.

As for walking, this might be a tamed landscape, but there's good scope for exploring the byways, either in the gentler valleys that are most typical of the Cotswolds or along the dramatic escarpment that marks the boundary with the Severn Valley. The **Cotswold Way** national trail runs for a hundred miles along the edge of the Cotswold escarpment from Chipping Campden in the northeast to Bath in the southwest, with a number of prehistoric sites providing added interest along the route. The section around **Belas Knap** is particularly rewarding, offering superb views over Cheltenham and the Severn Valley to the distant Malverns.

GETTING AROUND — THE COTSWOLDS

By train The train network comes close to ignoring the Cotswolds, the main exception being the Oxford to Worcester service on which the slower trains stop at half a dozen of the region's villages and the town of Moreton-in-Marsh – though none of these are prime targets.

By bus As for the rest of the Cotswolds, you'll be reliant on the bus network, which does a good job connecting all the larger towns and villages, but not the smaller, more isolated places and nothing much at all on Sundays. All the region's tourist offices carry bus timetables and will be able to assist with travel plans.

TOP 5 CHURCHES

St James Chipping Campden. See p.246
St John the Baptist Burford. See p.241
St John the Baptist Cirencester. See p.242
St Mary the Virgin Oxford. See p.232
St Peter and St Paul Northleach. See p.244

Burford

Twenty miles west of Oxford you get your first real taste of the Cotswolds at **BURFORD**, where the long and wide High Street, which slopes down to the bridge over the River Windrush, is simply magnificent – despite all the traffic. The street is flanked by a remarkable line of old buildings that exhibit almost every type of classic Cotswolds feature, from wonky mullioned windows and half-timbered facades with bendy beams, through to spiky brick chimneys, fancy bow-fronted, stone houses and grand horse and carriage gateways.

St John the Baptist

By the river • Ⓦ burfordchurch.org

Of all the Cotswold churches, **St John the Baptist** has the most historical resonance, with architectural bits and pieces surviving from every phase of its construction, beginning with the Normans and ending in the wool boom of the seventeenth century – the soaring gothic spire built atop the old Norman tower is particularly eye-catching. Thereafter, it was pretty much left alone and, most unusually, its clutter of mausoleums, chapels and chantries survived the Reformation. A plaque outside commemorates the three "Levellers" (a loose coalition of free-thinking radicals that blossomed during the English Civil War) who were executed here in 1649 and whose aims are commemorated during the village's annual **Levellers Day** (Ⓦ levellers.org.uk).

ARRIVAL AND INFORMATION — BURFORD

By bus Buses pull in along High St. Swanbrook buses (Ⓣ 01452 712386, Ⓦ swanbrook.co.uk) run a useful service linking Burford with Oxford, Gloucester and Northleach (Mon–Sat 3 daily, Sun 1 daily).

Tourist office Towards the bottom of High St opposite the end of Priory Lane (Mon–Sat 9.30am–5pm, Sun 10am–4pm; Ⓣ 01993 823558, Ⓦ oxfordshirecotswolds.org).

4

ACCOMMODATION AND EATING

The Bay Tree Sheep St Ⓣ 01993 822791, Ⓦ cotswold-inns-hotels.co.uk. Characterful lodgings in a seventeenth-century wisteria-clad stone house. Rooms are either in the main house or in a couple of annexes. For dining, choose between the upmarket restaurant, with three-course meals for around £32, or excellent bar meals (from £12) featuring anything from oriental-style duck confit through to local pork and leek sausages. Food served daily noon–2pm & 7–9.30pm. **£120**

The Bull High St Ⓣ 01993 822220, Ⓦ bullatburford.co.uk. Historic coaching inn occupying a rather grand townhouse-style Georgian building. Rooms are simple but comfortable and good value; note that rates increase by around £20 at weekends. The restaurant is Burford's best, featuring superb modern British cuisine with international influences – think chilled asparagus mousse or soy-poached fillet of pork – and a good wine list. Mains £13–16. Food served daily noon–2.30pm & 7–9.30pm. **£70**

The Lamb Inn Sheep St Ⓣ 01993 823155, Ⓦ cotswold-inns-hotels.co.uk. Very similar to the adjacent Bay Tree, in a venerable old stone building with a pleasantly homely interior complete with rambling lounges, cosy rooms and a good in-house restaurant. Rates increase by around £50 at weekends. **£130**

Cirencester

Self-styled "Capital of the Cotswolds", the affluent town of **CIRENCESTER** lies on the southern fringes of the region, midway between Oxford and Bristol. As Corinium, it became a provincial capital and a centre of trade under the **Romans**. The town flourished for three centuries, and even had one of the largest forums north of the Alps, but the Saxons destroyed almost all of the Roman city, and the town only revived with the wool boom of the Middle Ages. Few medieval buildings other than the **St John the Baptist** church have survived, however, and the houses along the town's most handsome streets – Park, Thomas and Coxwell – date mostly from the seventeenth and eighteenth centuries. Today Cirencester's heart is the delightful, swirling **Market Place**, packed with traders' stalls on Mondays and Fridays.

St John the Baptist

Market Place • Daily: summer 10am–5pm; winter 10am–4pm • £2 suggested donation

Cirencester's Market Place is dominated by the magnificent parish church of **St John the Baptist**, built in stages during the fifteenth century. The church's most notable feature is its huge **porch**– so big that it once served as the local town hall. The extraordinary flying buttresses that support the tower had to be added when it transpired that the church had been constructed over a filled-in ditch. Inside the church sits a colourful wineglass **pulpit**, carved in stone around 1450 and one of the few pre-Reformation pulpits to have survived in Britain.

Corinium Museum

Park St • Mon–Sat 10am–5pm, Sun 2–5pm • £4.80

West of the Market Place, the sleek **Corinium Museum** is devoted to the history of the town from Roman to Victorian times. The collection of Romano-British antiquities is particularly fine, including several wonderful **mosaic pavements**. Other highlights include artefacts recovered from the Anglo-Saxon burial site at Butlers Field in nearby Lechlade and archeological finds from the town's now vanished Abbey of St Mary, once one of the wealthiest Augustinian monasteries in Britain.

New Brewery Arts Centre

Brewery Court, off Cricklade St • Mon–Sat 9am–5pm, Sun 10am–4pm • Free • T 01285 657181, W newbreweryarts.org.uk

Just south of the Market Place, the **New Brewery Arts Centre** is occupied by more than a dozen resident artists whose studios you can visit and whose work you can buy in the shop. The centre's theatre hosts high-calibre plays and concerts (from jazz to classical), and there's a busy café on the first floor.

4

ARRIVAL AND INFORMATION — CIRENCESTER

By bus Local buses stop in the Market Place; National Express services terminate at the Beeches Car Park on London Rd, on the edge of the centre.

Destinations Cheltenham (Mon–Sat hourly; 45min); Gloucester (Mon–Sat 5 daily; 40min–1hr); Moreton-in-Marsh (Mon–Sat every 2–3hr; 1hr); Northleach (Mon–Sat every 2–3hr).

Tourist office In the Corinium Museum, Park St (Mon 9.45am–5.30pm, Tues–Sat 9.30am–5.30pm; Dec closes 5pm; T 01285 654180, W cotswold.gov.uk).

ACCOMMODATION

Corinium Hotel 12 Gloucester St T 01285 659711, W coriniumhotel.com. In a handsome Georgian townhouse just west of the centre, this appealling little hotel has bags of character, with rustic stone walls, narrow staircases and neat little beamed rooms (no two exactly alike). There's also a cosy bar and a good restaurant. **£90**

The Ivy House 2 Victoria Rd T 01285 656626, W ivyhousecotswolds.com. One of a number of B&Bs along this road, a short walk east of the Market Place, occupying a high-gabled, ivy-covered Victorian house with four simple, comfy rooms. **£65**

EATING AND DRINKING

Jesse's The Stableyard, Black Jack St T 01285 641497, W jessesbistro.co.uk. Cirencester's top restaurant, in an elegantly updated old stone building around the back of the time-warped Jesse Smith Family Butchers. All food is local and seasonal, with hearty dishes like Cornish fish pie and sticky-toffee date pudding combining old-school home-cooking with a dash of French flair. Mains around £18. Tues–Sat noon–2.30pm & 7–9.30pm, Mon noon–2.30pm.

Keith's Coffee Shop 2 Black Jack St T 01285 654717. Neat little café at the back of a cute old-fashioned deli stacked high with jars and tins of coffee, tea, jam and pickles. Good range of inexpensive sandwiches, light meals and cakes, plus the best coffee in town. Mon–Sat 9am–5pm.

New Brewery Arts Café New Brewery Arts Centre, Brewery Court, off Cricklade St T 01285 657181, W newbreweryarts.org.uk. Overlooking the entrance to the arts centre, this lively café is a good choice for tasty, inexpensive food using fresh local ingredients, with interesting sandwiches, salads, cakes and coffee, plus daily specials and Sunday brunch. Mon–Sat 9am–5pm, Sun 10am–4pm.

Painswick

PAINSWICK is a congenial old Cotswolds wool town easily accessible from Cheltenham or Gloucester. The fame of Painswick's **church** stems not so much from the building itself as from the surrounding **graveyard**, where 99 yew trees, cut into bizarre bulbous shapes resembling lollipops, surround a collection of eighteenth-century table tombs unrivalled in the Cotswolds. However, it's the **Rococo Garden**, about half a mile north up the Gloucester road – and attached to Painswick House (no access) – that ranks as the town's main attraction.

Rococo Garden

Half a mile north of Painswick off the Gloucester Rd (B4073) • Mid-Jan to Oct daily 11am–5pm • £6 • ⓦ rococogarden.co.uk

Created in the early eighteenth century and later abandoned, the **Rococo Garden** has been restored to its original form with the aid of a painting dated 1748. It's a beautiful – and the country's only – example of Rococo garden design, a short-lived fashion typified by a mix of formal geometrical shapes and more naturalistic, curving lines. With a vegetable patch as an unusual centrepiece, the Painswick garden spreads across a sheltered gully – for the best vistas, walk around anticlockwise.

ARRIVAL AND INFORMATION — PAINSWICK

By bus Bus #256 links Painswick with Gloucester (2 on Wed), while #46 (Mon–Sat hourly, Sun 6 daily) runs from Cheltenham.

Tourist office Upstairs in the Town Hall, on Victoria St just off the main road through the village (April–Oct Mon–Fri 10am–4pm, Sat 10am–1pm; ⓣ 0750 351 6924, ⓦ painswick-pc.gov.uk).

ACCOMMODATION AND EATING

Cardynham House Tibbiwell St ⓣ 01452 814006, ⓦ cardynham.co.uk. Occupying an old stone fifteenth-century house, with themed rooms sporting four-poster or half-tester beds and plenty of period character. **£87**

★ **Royal Oak** St Mary's St ⓣ 01452 813129, ⓦ theroyaloakpainswick.co.uk. This homely old stone pub serves quality pub grub and afternoon teas either in its cosy interior or the flowery courtyard. Also has an excellent selection of local real ales and ciders. Daily 10am–midnight (Fri & Sat until 1am).

4

Malmesbury

The sleepy hilltown of **MALMESBURY,** twelve miles south of Cirencester, lies well off the main tourist trails. The town is lined up along a pretty High Street, which runs from the old silk mills by the river, up past a line of crooked ancient cottages before reaching the octagonal **Market Cross** of 1490. From here's it's just a few steps to Malmesbury's ruined Norman **abbey**, a majestic structure boasting some of the finest Romanesque sculpture in the country.

Malmesbury's local celebrities include **Elmer the Monk**, who in 1005 attempted to fly from the abbey tower with the aid of wings: he limped for the rest of his life, but won immortal fame as the "flying monk".

The abbey

Daily: summer 10am–5pm; winter 10am–4pm • Suggested donation £2

Approached via the eighteenth-century **Tolsey Gate** close to the Market Cross lies the once rich and powerful **Malmesbury Abbey**. The original abbey burned down in about 1050 and the second was roughed up during the Dissolution, but the beautiful Norman **nave of the abbey church** has survived, its south porch sporting a multitude of exquisite, if badly worn, figures. To the left of the high altar, the pulpit virtually hides the **tomb of King Athelstan**, grandson of Alfred the Great and the first Saxon to be recognized as king of England; the tomb, however, is empty and the location of the king's body is unknown. The abbey's greatest surviving treasures are housed in the *parvis* (room above the porch), reached via a narrow spiral staircase right of the main doorway, where pride of place is given to four Flemish **medieval bibles**, written on parchment and sumptuously illuminated with gilt ink and exquisite miniature paintings.

ARRIVAL AND INFORMATION — MALMESBURY

By bus Buses to Malmesbury pull into Cross Hayes, a small side street in the middle of the village where you'll also find the tourist office.

Tourist office Town Hall, Cross Hayes (Mon–Thurs 9am–4.50pm, Fri 9am–4.20pm, Easter–Sept also Sat 10am–4pm; ⓣ01666 823748, ⓦvisitwiltshire.co.uk).

Useful website ⓦmalmesbury.gov.uk.

ACCOMMODATION AND EATING

★ **The Dining Room** Whatley Manor, Easton Grey ⓣ01666 822888, ⓦwww.whatleymanor.com. A couple of miles west of Malmesbury, the rambling old Whatley Manor provides a memorable home for the Cotswolds' top restaurant, under chef Martin Burge, which has two Michelin stars. Dishes are modern Anglo-French, full of inventive ingredients and flavour combinations, while many are such works of art – chocolate mousse with fennel meringue designed to look like a miniature train, for example –that it seems almost a shame to eat them. Reckon on £100 per head with wine. Wed–Sun 7–10pm.

Old Bell Abbey Row ⓣ01666 822344, ⓦoldbellhotel.com. Originally built as a guesthouse for the abbey, this fine old hotel has bags of atmosphere, pleasantly appointed rooms, and a good restaurant/brasserie Food served Tues–Sat 12.30–2pm & 7–9.30pm, Sun & Mon 12.30–2pm. **£115**

Northleach

4

Secluded in a shallow depression some ten miles north of Cirencester, **NORTHLEACH** is one of the most appealing and least developed villages in the Cotswolds – a great base to explore the area. Rows of immaculate late medieval cottages cluster around the village's **Market Place** with more of the same framing the adjoining Green; the most outstanding feature is the handsome church of **St Peter and St Paul**, erected at the height of the wool boom.

Church of St Peter and St Paul

Daily 9am–5pm • Suggested donation £2

One of the finest of the Cotswolds wool churches, **St Peter and St Paul** is a classic example of the fifteenth-century Perpendicular style, with a soaring tower and beautifully proportioned nave lit by wide clerestory windows. The floors of the aisles are inlaid with an exceptional collection of memorial brasses, marking the tombs of the merchants whose endowments paid for the church. On several, you can make out the woolsacks laid out beneath the corpse's feet – a symbol of wealth and power that features to this day in the House of Lords, where a woolsack is placed on the Lord Chancellor's seat.

Keith Harding's World of Mechanical Music

High St • Daily 10am–5pm (last admission 4pm) • £8 • ⓦmechanicalmusic.co.uk

Two minutes' walk up along the High Street from the Market Place, the lively **Keith Harding's World of Mechanical Music** holds a bewildering collection of antique musical boxes, automata, barrel organs and mechanical instruments, all stuffed into one room. The entrance fee includes an hour-long tour.

ARRIVAL AND DEPARTURE — NORTHLEACH

By bus Buses pull into the centre of the village beside the green. Swanbrook buses (ⓣ01452 712386, ⓦswanbrook.co.uk) run to Northleach from Oxford, Gloucester and Burford (Mon–Sat 3 daily, Sun 1 daily).

ACCOMMODATION AND EATING

★ **Wheatsheaf Hotel** West End ⓣ01451 860244, ⓦcotswoldswheatsheaf.com. Lovely little hotel in a former coaching inn just steps from the Market Place. The old stone exterior has been left intact, but the fourteen en-suite rooms have been remodelled in an appealing modern style. There's a great in-house restaurant, with a daily-changing menu of top-notch British cuisine, all locally sourced (mains around £15–17). Food served Mon–Fri noon–3pm & 6–10pm, Sat & Sun 10am–4pm & 6–10pm. £120

Bourton-on-the-Water

If anywhere can be described as the epicentre of Cotswold tourism, it has to be **BOURTON-ON-THE-WATER**, some six miles northeast of Northleach. However, picturesque as it is, with five mini-bridges straddling the River Windrush as it courses between the old stone houses, the whole place has been destroyed by tourism and, sadly, retains all the charm of an international airport terminal. There's no reason to stay or, indeed, go anywhere near it, unless you have **kids** to entertain, in which case the various family-oriented attractions might appeal. These include the **Cotswold Motoring Museum and Toy Collection** (ⓦcotswoldmotormuseum.co.uk), the **Model Village** (ⓦtheoldnewinn.co.uk), **Model Railway** (ⓦbourtonmodelrailway.co.uk) and **Birdland Park and Gardens** (ⓦbirdland.co.uk).

Stow-on-the-Wold

Ambling over a steep hill some ten miles north of Northleach, **STOW-ON-THE-WOLD** draws in a number of visitors disproportionate to its size and attractions, which essentially comprise an old **marketplace** surrounded by pubs, antique and souvenir shops, and an inordinate number of tearooms. The narrow walled alleyways, or "tunes", running into the square were designed for funnelling sheep into the market, which is itself dominated by an imposing Victorian hall – but architecturally, that's pretty much it.

4

ARRIVAL AND INFORMATION — STOW-ON-THE-WOLD

By bus Buses pull in on the High St, just off the main square. There are regular services to Cheltenham, Cirencester and Stratford.

Tourist office The privately run Go Stow on Sheep St (Mon–Sat 10am–5pm, Sun 11am–4pm; ⓣ01451 870150, ⓦgo-stow.co.uk) carries oodles of local information and will also book accommodation for a small fee.

ACCOMMODATION

Number Four at Stow Fosseway, a mile or so south ⓣ01451 830297, ⓦhotelnumberfour.co.uk. Stylish modern rooms and classic English food given a classy continental twist in the attached *Cutler's Restaurant* (Mon–Sat noon–2pm & 7–9pm, Sun noon–3.30pm). £125

Number Nine 9 Park St ⓣ01451 870333, ⓦnumber-nine.info. In a classic old Cotswolds stone building (a former coaching inn) close to the village centre, this attractive place has just three rooms and offers very low rates, so it is essential to reserve in advance. £60

Youth Hostel The Square ⓣ0845 371 9540, ⓦyha.org.uk. The only YHA hostel in the Cotswolds, located in a good-looking Georgian townhouse on the main square. There are 48 beds in four- to eight-bed rooms (no double rooms available) and it's open throughout the year. £16

EATING AND DRINKING

Digbeths Digbeth St ⓣ01451 831609, ⓦdigbeths.com. The best of the innumerable tearooms dotted around town, with Lavazza coffee and speciality teas, soups, sandwiches and daily specials. It converts into a bistro after 6pm, serving quality local food (mains around £10–12). Teashop: daily except Wed 11am–4pm; bistro: Mon, Tues & Thurs–Sat 6–8.45pm.

★ **Queen's Head** The Square ⓣ01451 830563. Classic Cotswolds pub, in an old stone building on the square, with good Doningtons beer, a great local atmosphere, and tasty, unreconstituted pub grub – lasagne, gammon with fried egg, steak-and-kidney pie – all served in huge portions. Mains around £10. Daily noon–11.30pm; food Mon–Sat noon–2.30pm & 6–9pm, Sun noon–9pm.

The Royalist Hotel Just off the square on the corner of Park and Digbeth streets ⓣ01451 830670, ⓦtheroyalisthotel.com. Stow's oldest inn offers a range of eating options, including light meals in its *Eagle & Child* bar or more formal modern British dining in the chic *947 AD* restaurant (mains around £14). Food served Mon–Sat noon–2.30pm & 7–9.30pm, Sun noon–3pm & 7–9pm.

Chipping Campden

On the northern edge of the Cotswolds, **CHIPPING CAMPDEN** gives a better idea than anywhere else in the Cotswolds as to how a prosperous wool town might have looked in the Middle Ages. The short High Street is hemmed in by ancient houses, with an undulating line of weather-beaten roofs above and twisted beams and mullioned windows below. The seventeenth-century **Market Hall** has survived too, an open-sided pavilion propped up on sturdy stone piers in the middle of the High Street, where farmers once gathered to sell their produce. The town also served as a crucible for the burgeoning Cotswolds **Arts and Crafts** movement, largely thanks to the pioneering work of C. R. Ashbee.

Court Barn Museum

Church St • Tues–Sun 10am–4pm (April–Sept until 5pm) • £4 • Ⓦ courtbarn.org.uk

Just north of the High Street next to the church, the lovely little **Court Barn Museum** is devoted to the various members of the Arts and Crafts movement who worked in the town and surrounding area. Pride of place goes to **C. R. Ashbee**, who moved his pioneering Guild of Handicraft workshops from London's East End to the old Silk Mills (see below) in 1902, introducing the Arts and Crafts movement to the Cotswolds, where it continues to flourish to this day. Other featured include the works beautiful bookbindings of Katherine Adams, silverwork from the Hart Workshop and examples of furniture by Gordon Russell (see opposite).

4

Church of St James

Church St • April–Oct Mon–Fri 10am–5pm, Sat 11am–5pm & Sun 2–5.45pm; Nov–March Mon–Fri 11am–3pm, Sat 11am–4pm, Sun 2–4pm • Free

Immediately north of Court Barn Museum rises the imperious **Church of St James**, the archetypal Cotswold wool church built in the fifteenth century. Inside, the airy nave is bathed in light from the clerestory windows, while below some fine fifteenth-century brasses can be seen in the chancel floor along with the impressive canopied tomb of Sir Thomas Smyth (d.1593), first governor of the East India Company.

Silk Mills

Sheep St • Daily 10am–5pm • Ⓦ chippingcampden.co.uk

C. R. Ashbee (see above) established his original Guild of Handicraft in 1902 in the old **Silk Mills** on Sheep Street, off the high road. The old factory buildings now house various galleries of local artisans, many of them still producing work heavily influenced by the Arts and Crafts movement – piled with weighty hammers, mallets and chisels, Hart's silver workshop (Ⓦ hartsilversmiths.co.uk) upstairs can hardly have changed since Ashbee's time.

ARRIVAL AND INFORMATION — CHIPPING CAMPDEN

By bus Regular buses connect Chipping Campden with Cheltenham, Moreton-in-Marsh (for Oxford) and Stratford-upon-Avon.

Tourist office In the middle of town on the High St opposite the Market Hall (summer daily 9.30am–5.30pm; winter Mon–Thurs 9.30am–1pm, Fri–Sun 9.30am–4pm; Ⓣ 01386 841206, Ⓦ campdenonline.org). They can book accommodation for a small fee.

ACCOMMODATION

★ **Badgers Hall** High St Ⓣ 01386 840839, Ⓦ badgershall.com. Chipping Campden's best B&B, in an old stone house in the heart of the town. All the guest rooms are en suite and come complete with period detail – beamed ceilings and so forth. The tearoom downstairs is fabulous, too (see below). **£90**

EATING AND DRINKING

Badgers Hall High St Ⓣ 01386 840839, Ⓦ badgershall.com. This archetypal Cotswold teashop is by far the best in Chipping Campden, a cosy little spot serving fabulous cheese scones, cream teas and home-made cakes, along with light lunches and snacks. Mon–Sat 10am–4.30pm, Sun noon–4.30pm.

★ **Eight Bells Inn** Church St 01386 840371, eightbellsinn.co.uk. The pick of Chipping Campden's pubs, this is a cosy spot in a charming old stone building on the way to the church. The restaurant here is first-rate, using local, seasonal produce to create superior versions of pub classics like fish 'n' chips, toad-in-the-hole and chicken pie, plus fancier continental-style dishes. Reservations recommended for food. Mains around £13. Pub: daily noon–11pm; food served daily noon–2pm & 6.30–9pm.

Broadway

BROADWAY, five miles west of Chipping Campden, is a particularly handsome little village at the foot of the steep escarpment that rolls along the western edge of the Cotswolds. It seems likely that the Romans were the first to settle here, but Broadway's high times were as a stagecoach stop on the route from London to Worcester. It's this former function that has defined much of its present appearance – its long and wide main street framed by stone cottages and shaded by chestnut trees. The village attracts more visitors than is good for it, but things do quieten down in the evening.

Gordon Russell Design Museum

15 Russell Square • Tues–Sun: March–Oct 11am–5pm; Nov–Feb 11am–4pm • £4 • gordonrussellmuseum.org

Just off the green in the centre of the village, the absorbing **Gordon Russell Design Museum** is dedicated to the work of local furniture-maker Gordon Russell (1892–1980), whose factory formerly stood next door. Influenced both by the Arts and Crafts movement but also by modern technology, Russell's stated aim was to "make decent furniture for ordinary people" through "a blend of hand and machine". The museum showcases many of his classic furniture designs, alongside other period artefacts ranging from metalware to mirrors. 4

ARRIVAL AND DEPARTURE — BROADWAY

By bus Broadway has good bus connections, with services to and from Cheltenham, Stratford, Chipping Campden and other destinations. Services peter out on Sunday, however.

INFORMATION

Tourist office In the same building as the Gordon Russell Design Museum, 15 Russell Square (mid-Feb to Dec Mon–Sat 10am–5pm, Sun 2–5pm; 01386 852937, visitbroadway.co.uk).

ACCOMMODATION

The Olive Branch 78 High St 01386 853440, theolivebranch-broadway.com. Extremely pleasant B&B in an old stone house and with eight homely guest rooms. £95

EATING

Russell's 20 High St 01386 853555, russellsofbroadway.co.uk. In the former factory offices of Gordon Russell (see above), this stylish restaurant offers upmarket modern European dining, with mains for £11–23, plus good-value set menus. Mon–Fri noon–2.30pm & 6–9.30pm, Sat noon–2.30pm & 6.30–9.30pm.

The Workshop 20a High St 01386 858435, workshopbroadway.co.uk. Sister establishment to the adjacent Russell's but offering more casual and inexpensive food, including retro classics like fish-finger baps, prawn cocktails, and black pudding with fried egg. Daily noon–2.30pm, 3–5pm & 6–9pm.

Belas Knap

Up on the ridge around 10km southwest of Broadway, near the town of **Winchcombe** (and around 6km northeast of Cheltenham), the Neolithic long barrow of **Belas Knap** occupies one of the wildest spots in the Cotswolds. Dating from around 3000 BC, this is the best-preserved burial chamber in England, stretching out like a strange sleeping beast cloaked in green velvet.

ARRIVAL AND DEPARTURE — **BELAS KNAP**

The best way to get to Belas Knap is to **walk**, undertaking the two-mile climb up the Cotswold Way from **Winchcombe**. The path strikes off to the right near the entrance to Sudeley Castle; when you reach the country lane at the top, turn right and then left for the 10min hike to the barrow. It's also possible to drive along this same country lane; just follow the signs to the roadside pull-in where you can park before setting off for the briefest of hikes. If you continue south past Belas Knap, the lane scuttles over the hills and through dense woods bound for Syreford with the A40 (for Northleach, see p.244) a little further on.

Cheltenham

Prior to the eighteenth century **CHELTENHAM** was like any other small-time Gloucestershire town, until the discovery of a spring in 1716 transformed it into Britain's most popular **spa**. During Cheltenham's heyday, a century or so later, the royal, the rich and the famous descended in droves to take the waters, which were said to cure anything from constipation to worms. These days, the town has a lively, bustling atmosphere, lots of good restaurants and some of England's best-preserved Regency architecture.

The town is also a thriving arts centre, famous for its festivals of **folk** (Feb), **jazz** (April/May), **science** (June), **classical music** (July) and **literature** (Oct) – see Ⓦ cheltenhamfestivals.co.uk – and, of course, the races (see box opposite).

The Promenade

The focus of Cheltenham, the broad **Promenade**, sweeps majestically south from the High Street, lined with some of the town's grandest houses and smartest shops. It

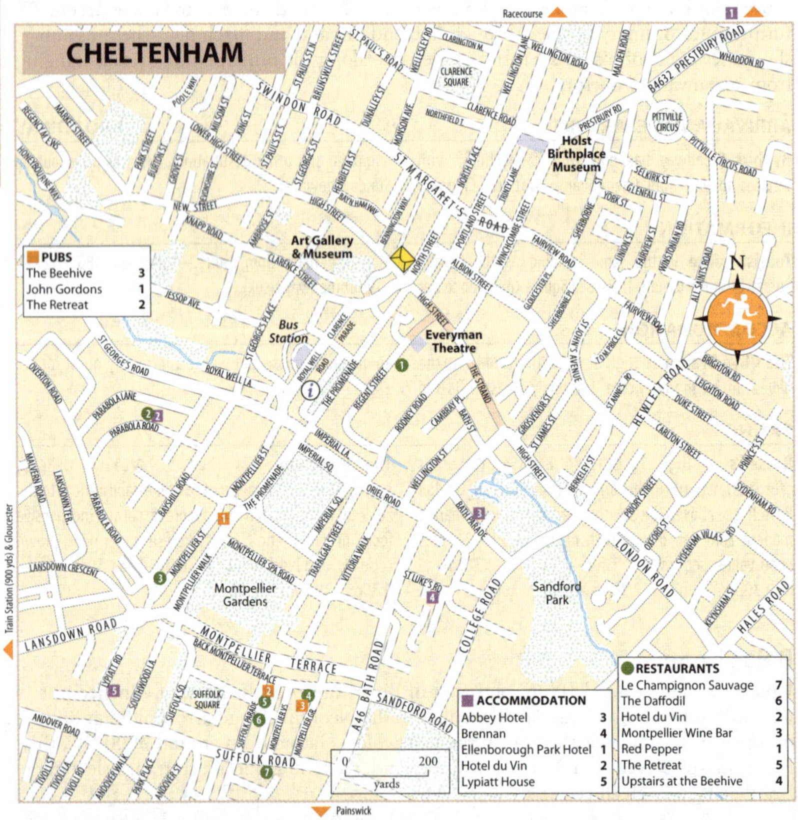

CHELTENHAM RACES

Cheltenham racecourse, on the north side of town, a ten-minute walk from Pittville Park at the foot of Cleeve Hill, is Britain's main steeplechasing venue. The principal event of the season, the three-day **National Hunt Festival** in March, attracts 40,000 people a day; it's essential to buy tickets in advance. Other meetings take place in January, April, October, November and December: a list of fixtures is posted at the tourist office. For the cheapest but arguably the best view, pay £8 (rising to £15 during the Festival, £25 on Gold Cup Day) for entry to the Best Mate Enclosure, as the pen in the middle is known. For schedules and other information, call T 0844 579 3003 or visit W cheltenham.co.uk.

leads into Imperial Square, whose greenery is surrounded by proud Regency terraces that herald the handsome and harmonious terraces and squares of the Montpellier district, which stretches south in a narrow block to Suffolk Road, making a delightful detour.

Cheltenham Art Gallery and Museum

Clarence St • W cheltenhammuseum.org.uk

Just to the north of the Promenade, the enjoyable **Cheltenham Art Gallery and Museum** is closed for major redevelopment until early 2013 while a brand new museum building is constructed next door to the existing gallery. This will eventually house works from the Arts and Crafts Movement plus paintings by twentieth-century British artists such as Stanley Spencer and Vanessa Bell, among other excellent exhibits.

4

Holst Birthplace Museum

4 Clarence Rd • Feb to mid-Dec Tues–Sat 10am–4pm • £4.50 • W holstmuseum.org.uk

The **Holst Birthplace Museum** is the former home of Gustav Holst, the composer of *The Planets*, who was born here in 1874 and spent much of his childhood in this neat little Regency terrace house. Inside, the intimate rooms retain much of their period character, giving a good insight into Victorian family life as well as showcasing plenty of Holst memorabilia – including his piano.

Pittville Pump Room

Pittville • Mon & Wed–Sun 10am–4pm (unless there is a function in progress)

It's about fifteen minutes' walk north from the centre of Cheltenham to the **Pittville** district, where a certain Joseph Pitt planned to build his own spa. Work began on his grand scheme in the 1820s, but he went bust before he could complete it. Most of Pittville is now parkland, but he did manage to complete the domed **Pump Room** before he hit the skids. A lovely classical structure with an imposing colonnaded facade, the Pump Room is now used as a venue for concerts, weddings and other functions. You can still sample the **spa waters** from the marble fountain in the main auditorium for free – and very pungent they are too.

ARRIVAL AND INFORMATION — CHELTENHAM

By train Cheltenham Spa train station is on Queen's Rd, southwest of the centre; local buses run into town every 10min, otherwise it's a 20min walk.

Destinations Bristol (every 20–30min; 35–50min); Gloucester (2–3 hourly; 10min–15min); London (every 30min; 2hr 10–2hr 40min).

By bus All long-distance buses at the station in Royal Well Rd, just west off the Promenade.

Destinations Gloucester (Mon–Sat every 15min, Sun every 30min; 15–40min); London (11–13 daily; 2hr 35min–3hr 20min); Painswick (Mon–Sat hourly; Sun 6 daily; 30min). Swanbrook (T 01452 712386, W swanbrook.co.uk) operates a handy bus service to Oxford via Gloucester , Burford and Northleach (Mon–Sat 3 daily, Sun 1 daily).

Tourist office 77 Promenade (Mon, Tues & Thurs–Sat 9.30am–5.15pm, Wed 10am–5.15pm; T 01242 522878, W visitcheltenham.com).

ACCOMMODATION

Cheltenham has plenty of **hotels** and **guesthouses**, many of them in fine Regency houses, but you should book well in advance during the races and festivals.

Abbey Hotel 14–16 Bath Parade ⊕01242 516053, ⊕abbeyhotel-cheltenham.com. Friendly B&B, with attractively furnished rooms and wholesome breakfasts served overlooking the garden. £80

Brennan 21 St Luke's Rd ⊕01242 525904, ⊕brennanguesthouse.co.uk. Excellent-value B&B in a small Regency building on a quiet square. Rooms are neat and spotless, although with shared bathroom only. No credit cards. £50

Ellenborough Park Hotel Southam Rd, Prestbury ⊕01242 545454, ⊕ellenboroughpark.com. On the northern edge of Cheltenham, a couple of miles from the city centre, this country house-style five-star occupies a wonderful rambling fifteenth-century stone manor house, with accommodation in the main building itself and in a range of outbuildings. There's an excellent restaurant and fine spa, with a superb Great Hall and magnificent gardens. £210

Hotel du Vin Parabola Rd ⊕01242 588450, ⊕hotelduvin.com. Occupying a splendid old Regency mansion, this swanky establishment is easily the nicest place to stay in the city centre. Rooms have been stylishly upgraded, while facilities include a soothing spa and excellent restaurant (see below). £150

Lypiatt House Lypiatt Rd ⊕01242 224994, ⊕lypiatt.co.uk. Upmarket B&B in a fine old Victorian villa set in its own grounds, with open fires and a conservatory with a small bar. £95

EATING

4

★ **Le Champignon Sauvage** Suffolk Rd ⊕01242 573449, ⊕lechampignonsauvage.co.uk. The modest facade belies one of the Cotswolds' top restaurants, boasting two Michelin stars and consistently excellent food – top-notch local ingredients prepared using classic French cooking techniques and a dash of pizzazz (such as wood pigeon with carrot tagine, or loin of pork with lapsang souchong). Two-course menus start at just £26. Book well ahead. Tues–Sat lunch from 12.30pm, dinner from 7.30pm.

★ **The Daffodil** 18–20 Suffolk Parade ⊕01242 700055, ⊕thedaffodil.co.uk. Eat in the circle bar or auditorium of this former cinema, where the screen has been replaced with a hubbub of chefs. Vibrant atmosphere and great modern British food, with mains around £16–18. Mon–Fri noon–2pm & 6.30–10pm, Sat noon–2pm & 6–10.30pm.

Hotel du Vin Parabola Rd ⊕01242 588450, ⊕hotelduvin.com. The stylish modern restaurant at this swanky hotel (see above) dishes up a lively atmosphere and some of the best food in town. Daily changing menus focus on local seasonal produce served with flair – pork osso bucco, pollack peperonata and so on. There's also a fine wine cellar and cigar shack. Mains around £15. Daily: lunch from 12.30pm, dinner from 6.30pm.

Montpellier Wine Bar Bayshill Lodge, Montpellier St ⊕01242 527774, ⊕montpellierwinebar.com. In a gracious old Regency building with lovely bow-fronted windows, this place combines a lively ground-floor wine bar with a more sedate restaurant below. Daily changing menus feature market-fresh produce, with offerings ranging from bubble-and-squeak to Thai green chicken curry. Mains £9–16. Bar: Mon–Wed 10am–11pm, Thurs–Sat 10am–midnight, Sun 11am–10.30pm. Brunch: daily 10am–noon; bistro: Mon–Thurs noon–3pm & 6–9.30pm, Fri–Sun noon–9.30pm.

Red Pepper 13 Regent St ⊕01242 253900, ⊕redpeppercheltenham.co.uk. Lively establishment combining a daytime café and deli downstairs (mains £6–8) and a more formal evening bistro upstairs (mains £11–13), both serving a range of tasty and good-value British and international dishes. Café daily 9am–6pm; bistro Tues–Fri 6–9.30pm, Sat & Sun noon–3pm & 6–9.30pm.

DRINKING AND NIGHTLIFE

The Beehive 1–3 Montpellier Villas ⊕01242 702270, ⊕thebeehivemontpellier.com. This easy-going little pub is a Cheltenham institution, with small courtyard garden, cosy snug and a good restaurant, *Upstairs* (reservations advised) serving great modern British food. Food served Wed–Sat 6–9.30pm, Sun noon–3pm.

John Gordons 11 Montpellier Arcade ⊕01242 245985, ⊕johngordons.co.uk. Sociable little bar-café stacked high with wine and whisky bottles. Drinks include 150-odd wines, 100 whiskies by the glass and many other tipples, while there's also a good selection of sandwiches, salads and bar snacks, plus good coffee. Mon–Wed 11am–10pm, Thurs–Sat 10am–11pm, Sun 11am–9pm.

The Retreat 10–11 Suffolk Parade ⊕01242 235436, ⊕theretreatwinebar.com. Sociable bar-cafe that caters to the business fraternity at lunchtimes and a lively younger crowd in the evenings. Good lunches too (around £5–8). Mon–Sat noon–midnight (lunch noon–3pm).

Gloucester

For centuries life was good for **GLOUCESTER**, just ten miles west of Cheltenham. The Romans chose this spot for a garrison to guard the River Severn, while in Saxon and Norman times the Severn developed into one of the busiest trade routes in Europe. The city became a major religious centre too, but from the fifteenth century onwards a combination of fire, plague, civil war and increasing competition from rival towns sent Gloucester into a decline from which it never recovered – even the opening of a new canal in 1827 between Gloucester and Sharpness to the south failed to revive the town's dwindling fortunes.

Today, the **canal** is busy once again, though this time with pleasure boats, and the Victorian **docks** have undergone a facelift, offering a fascinating glimpse into the region's industrial past. The main reason for a visit, however, remains Gloucester's magnificent **cathedral**, one of the finest in the country.

The Cathedral

College Green • Daily 7.30am–6pm • Suggested donation £5 • Ⓦ gloucestercathedral.org.uk

The superb condition of Gloucester **Cathedral** is striking in a city that has bulldozed so much of its history. The Saxons founded an abbey here, but four centuries later, in 1089, Benedictine monks arrived intent on building their own church; work began in 1089. As a place of worship it shot to importance after the murder of King Edward II in 1327: Bristol and Malmesbury supposedly refused to take his body, but Gloucester did, and the king's shrine became a major place of pilgrimage. The money generated helped finance the conversion of the church into the country's first and greatest example of the **Perpendicular style**: the magnificent 225ft tower crowns the achievement.

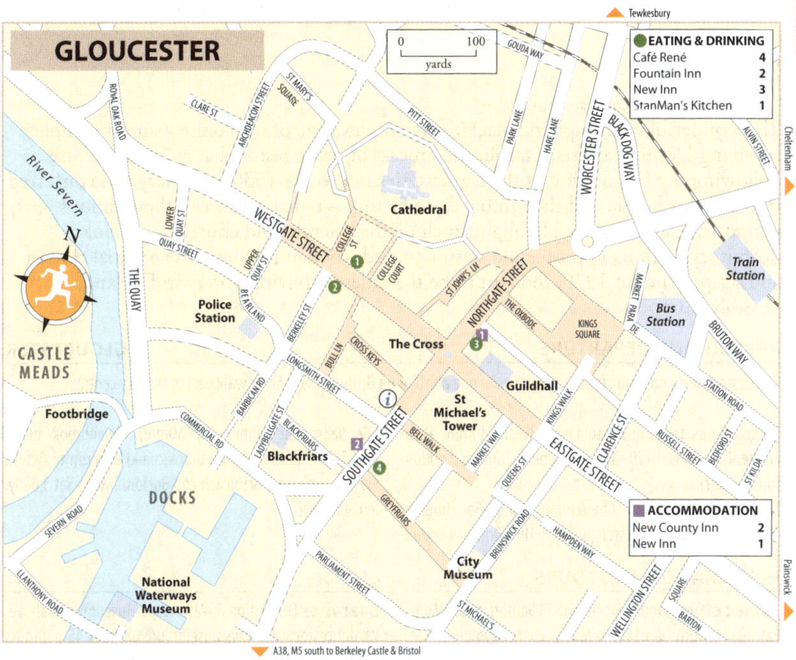

Beneath the reconstructions of the fourteenth and fifteenth centuries, some Norman aspects remain, best seen in the **nave**, which is flanked by sturdy pillars and arches adorned with immaculate zigzag carvings. The **choir** provides the best vantage point for admiring the **east window** completed in around 1350 and – at almost 80ft tall – the largest medieval window in Britain, a stunning cliff face of stained glass. Beneath it, to the left (as you're facing the east window) is the **tomb of Edward II**, immortalized in alabaster and marble. Below the east window lies the **Lady Chapel**, whose delicate carved tracery holds a staggering patchwork of windows. The innovative nature of the cathedral's design can also be appreciated in the beautiful **cloisters**, completed in 1367 and featuring the first fan vaulting in the country –used to represent the corridors of Hogwart's School in the *Harry Potter* films.

The docks

From the cathedral, it's about 600 yards to the Gloucester **docks**, whose fourteen capacious **warehouses** were built for storing grain following the opening of the Sharpness canal to the River Severn in 1827. Most of these warehouses have been turned into offices and apartments, while the swanky new **Gloucester Quays** complex (ⓦgloucesterquays.co.uk) holds more than fifty shops selling discounted high-street and designer fashions.

National Waterways Museum

Llanthony Warehouse • April–Oct Mon–Fri 10.30am–4.30pm, Sat & Sun 10am–5pm; Nov–March daily 11am–4pm • £4.75 • ⓦgloucesterwaterwaysmuseum.org.uk

The **National Waterways Museum** sports a range of entertaining interactive exhibits and displays on life along the canals alongside a miscellany of old machinery – engines, winches and pulleys – plus model boats and (outside) a couple of traditional narrowboats and a fine old dredger. They also run **boat trips** along the canal (see below).

Blackfriars

Ladybellgate St • EH • ⓦthecityofgloucester.co.uk

The wonderfully atmospheric **Blackfriars** complex, one of the country's most complete surviving Dominican friaries, is in the process of being restored as a cultural centre. Following the Dissolution of the Monasteries in the late 1530s the friary was converted into a Tudor house, and then into a cloth factory – remains from all these various periods can still be seen. Highlights include the splendid old church and monk's dormitory, with its imposing old scissor-braced wooden roof, and the original cloister and scriptorium of 1239, thought to be the oldest surviving library in England, possibly Europe.

ARRIVAL AND DEPARTURE — GLOUCESTER

Gloucester's bus and train stations are opposite one another on Bruton Way, a 5min walk east of the city centre.

By train Destinations Bristol (every 30min; 40min–1hr); Cheltenham (every 20–30min; 10min–15min); London (hourly; 2hr).

By bus Destinations Cheltenham (Mon–Sat hourly; 15min–40min); Cirencester (6 daily; 1hr 40min); London (12 daily; 3hr 20min–3hr 50min). Swanbrook buses (ⓣ01452 712386, ⓦswanbrook.co.uk) also run to Oxford via Cheltenham, Northleach and Burford (Mon–Sat 3 daily, Sun 1 daily).

INFORMATION AND TOURS

Tourist office Handily located at 28 Southgate St (Mon–Sat 10am–5pm; ⓣ01452 396572, ⓦthecityofgloucester.co.uk).

Boat trips The National Waterways Museum (see above; ⓦgloucesterwaterwaysmuseum.org.uk) runs 45min tours (£4.95) down the canal towards Sharpness.

ACCOMMODATION

New County Hotel 44 Southgate St ⓣ01452 307000, ⓦthenewcountyhotel.co.uk. Bang in the city centre, with spacious and comfortable – albeit functional – modern rooms. There's also a cosy downstairs bar and chic in-house restaurant serving good international food. **£90**

New Inn 16 Northgate St ⓣ01452 522177, ⓦnewinn-hotel.co.uk. One of the most perfectly preserved medieval inns in the country, built in 1455 and little changed since – previous visitors are said to have included William Shakespeare and Lady Jane Grey. The half-timbered courtyard is a perfect period piece, while accommodation is arranged around the balcony upstairs, with lopsided floors, oddly shaped doors and the occasional ghost. Rooms have been thoroughly modernized and are comfortable enough, albeit lacking the atmosphere of the public areas – although for pure atmosphere the whole place can't be beat. Check online for discounts. **£60**

EATING AND DRINKING

★ **Café René** Greyfriars, 31 Southgate St ⓣ01452 309340, ⓦcaferene.co.uk. Characterful bar-cum-restaurant-cum-live-music venue, with walls and ceilings covered with empty bottles and a buzzing atmosphere. House speciality is the lipsmackin' Desperate Dan Burger – available in three sizes from the merely enormous ("mini") to the humungous ("very desperate") – plus a range of other good bistro staples at bargain prices (mostly £7–8). Sun–Thurs 11am–midnight, Fri & Sat 11am–3am; food noon–9pm.

Fountain Inn Down a narrow alley off Westgate St ⓣ01452 522562. Another historic inn, said to have been founded in 1216, with a good selection of real ales, wholesome British pub meals and sunny outdoor seating in the attractive courtyard. Mon–Thurs 11am–11pm, Fri & Sat 11am–midnight, Sun noon–11pm.

★ **New Inn** 16 Northgate St ⓣ01452 522177, ⓦnewinn-hotel.co.uk. Marvellous medieval inn (see above) with bags of character and atmosphere – the splendid galleried courtyard is a great place for a pint, and inexpensive meals are available in the downstairs restaurant. Daily 11am–11pm.

StanMan's Kitchen 42–44 Westgate St ⓣ01452 412237, ⓦstanmanskitchen.co.uk. Cheery little local deli-café, stuffed with local cheeses, charcuterie and other Gloucestershire produce and serving cheap and tasty lunches (£4–5) plus good coffee and cream teas, with seating inside and out. Mon & Tues 9.30am–4.30pm, Wed–Sat 8.30am–5pm.

NIGHTLIFE

Café René Greyfriars 31 Southgate St ⓣ01452 309340, ⓦcaferene.co.uk. This lively bar-restaurant (see above) hosts a wide range of live music performances most Wednesdays and Fridays in its cellar bar. Sun–Thurs 11am–midnight, Fri & Sat 11am–3am.

Guildhall 23 Eastgate ⓣ01452 503050, ⓦgloucester.gov.uk/Freetime/Guildhall. The city's premier live music venue, hosting an eclectic range of acts (including occasional big names) with a good atmosphere and what is claimed to be the best-sprung dancefloor in the country.

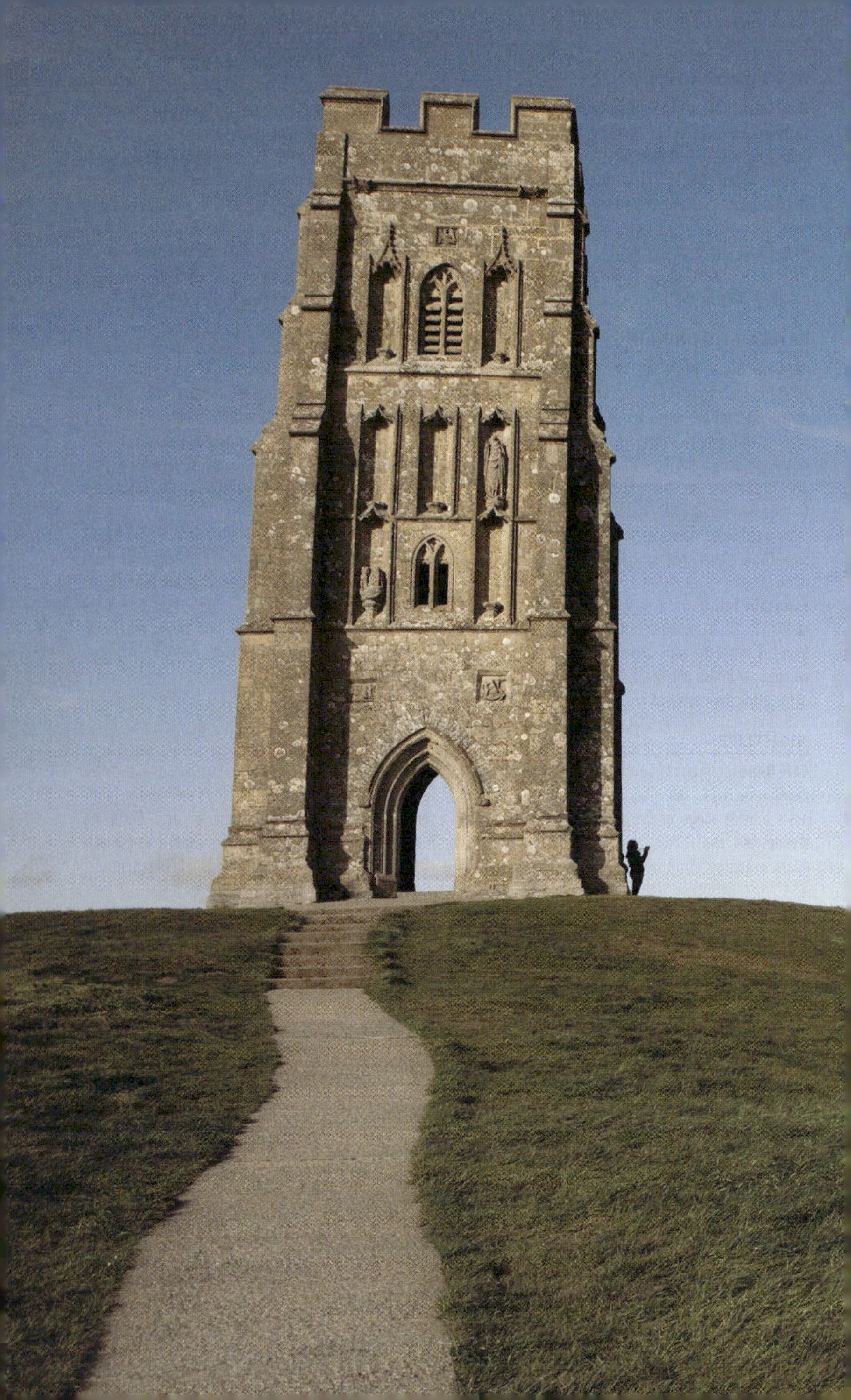

Bristol, Bath and Somerset

256 Bristol

265 Bath

271 Wells

273 The Mendips

274 Glastonbury

277 Taunton

277 The Quantock Hills

279 Exmoor

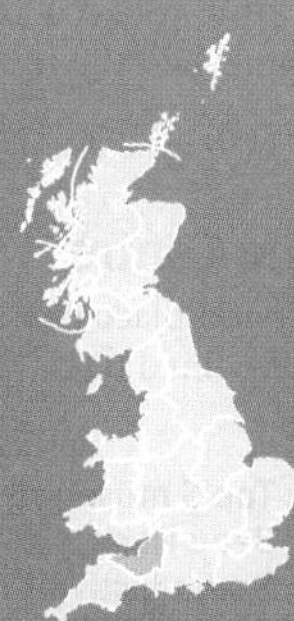

GLASTONBURY TOR

5

Bristol, Bath and Somerset

The undulating green swards of Somerset encapsulate rural England at its best. The landscape is always varied, with tidy cricket greens and well-kept country pubs contrasting with wilder, more dramatic landscapes. A world away from this bucolic charm, the main city hereabouts is Bristol, one of the most dynamic and cosmopolitan centres outside London. The dense traffic and some hideous postwar architecture are more than compensated for by the surviving traces of its long maritime history, along with a great range of pubs, clubs and restaurants. Just a few miles away, the graceful, Georgian, honey-toned terraces of Bath combine with beautifully preserved Roman baths and a mellow café culture to make it an unmissable stop.

Within easy reach to the south lie the exquisite cathedral city of **Wells** and the ancient town of **Glastonbury**, a site steeped in Christian lore, Arthurian legend and New Age mysticism. The nearby **Mendip Hills** are pocked by cave systems, as at **Wookey Hole** and **Cheddar Gorge**, while to the west, **Taunton** makes a useful base for exploring the Quantocks. Straddling the border between Somerset and Devon, the heathery slopes of **Exmoor** offer a range of hikes, with wonderful views from its cliffy seaboard.

GETTING AROUND — **BRISTOL, BATH AND SOMERSET**

Bristol, Bath and Taunton are connected to London Paddington by **train**. From these centres, a network of **bus routes** connects with nearly all the places covered in this chapter – though the Mendip and **Quantock hills** are more easily explored with your own transport. For First, the major operator in these parts, see ⓦ firstgroup.com or check ⓦ travelinesw.com for all services.

Bristol

On the borders of Gloucestershire and Somerset, **BRISTOL** has harmoniously blended its mercantile roots with an innovative, modern culture, fuelled by technology-based industries, a large student population and a lively arts and media community. As well as its vibrant **nightlife**, the city's sights range from medieval churches to cutting-edge attractions highlighting its scientific achievements.

Weaving through its centre, the River Avon forms part of a system of waterways that made Bristol a great inland port, in later years booming on the transatlantic trafficking of rum, tobacco and slaves. In the nineteenth century the illustrious **Isambard Kingdom Brunel** laid the foundations of a tradition of engineering, creating two of Bristol's greatest monuments – the SS *Great Britain* and the lofty Clifton Suspension Bridge.

The Centre

A good place to start exploring, where most local buses stop, **the Centre** was once a quay-lined dock but is now the traffic-ridden nucleus of the city. Just a few steps away

Top 5 museums p.261
Beau Nash p.267
Bath's festivals p.271
Glastonbury tales p.275
Glastonbury festival p.276
The West Somerset railway p.278
The South West Coast Path p.281

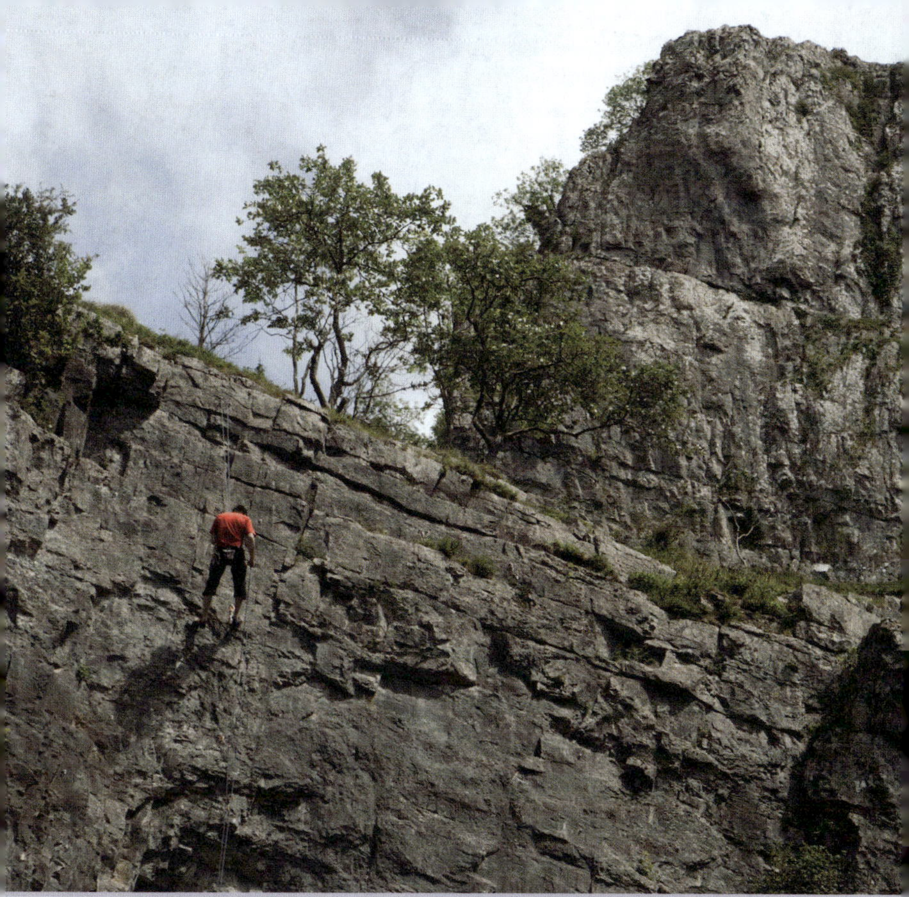

CLIMBING IN THE CHEDDAR GORGE

Highlights

❶ **M-Shed, Bristol** Bristol's flagship museum is dedicated to the city, taking in everything from the transatlantic slave trade to edgy street art. **See p.261**

❷ **Royal Crescent, Bath** In a city famous for its graceful arcs of Georgian terraces, this is the granddaddy of all crescents, an architectural tour de force with a magnificent vista. **See p.268**

❸ **Wells Cathedral** A gem of medieval masonry, not least for its richly ornamented west front, this Gothic monument is the centrepiece of England's smallest city. **See p.271**

❹ **Cheddar Gorge** Impressive rockscape with a network of illuminated caves at its base; it's an excellent starting point for wild walks in the Mendip Hills. **See p.273**

❺ **Glastonbury Abbey** These evocative and picturesque ruins are a fitting setting for a complexity of Christian legends and Arthurian myths. **See p.274**

❻ **Exploring Exmoor** Whether you choose to ride it, bike it or hike it, the rolling wilderness of Exmoor offers fine opportunities to experience the great outdoors. It's dotted with beauty spots and offers terrific views from its cliffy coastline. **See p.280**

HIGHLIGHTS ARE MARKED ON THE MAP ON P.258

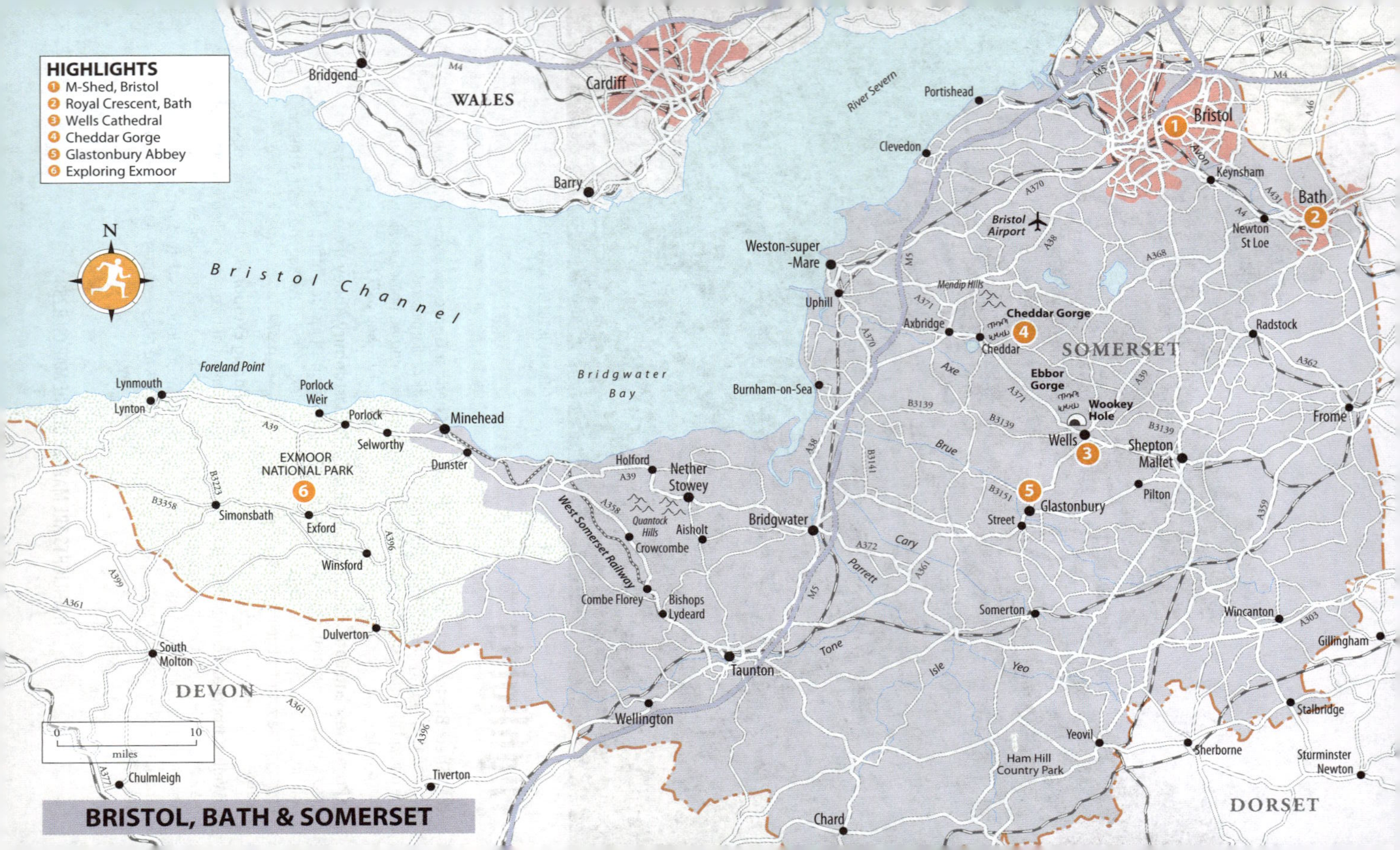
BRISTOL, BATH & SOMERSET
HIGHLIGHTS
1 M-Shed, Bristol
2 Royal Crescent, Bath
3 Wells Cathedral
4 Cheddar Gorge
5 Glastonbury Abbey
6 Exploring Exmoor
N
Bristol Channel
Bridgwater Bay
River Severn
WALES
SOMERSET
DEVON
DORSET
Bridgend
Cardiff
Barry
Portishead
Clevedon
Bristol
Avon
Keynsham
Bath
Newton St Loe
Bristol Airport
Weston-super -Mare
Uphill
Mendip Hills
Cheddar Gorge
Axbridge
Cheddar
Radstock
Frome
Ebbor Gorge
Wookey Hole
Wells
Shepton Mallet
Pilton
Glastonbury
Street
Burnham-on-Sea
Axe
Brue
Cary
Parrett
Tone
Isle
Yeo
Bridgwater
Holford
Nether Stowey
Quantock Hills
Aisholt
Crowcombe
West Somerset Railway
Combe Florey
Bishops Lydeard
Taunton
Wellington
Somerton
Wincanton
Gillingham
Stalbridge
Sherborne
Sturminster Newton
Yeovil
Ham Hill Country Park
Chard
Foreland Point
Lynmouth
Lynton
Porlock Weir
Porlock
Selworthy
Minehead
Dunster
EXMOOR NATIONAL PARK
Simonsbath
Exford
Winsford
Dulverton
South Molton
Chulmleigh
Tiverton
M4
M5
A46
A4
A431
A370
A38
A368
A371
A39
A362
B3139
B3141
B3151
A372
A361
A359
A303
A358
B3223
B3358
A396
A399
A377
0
10
miles

are the oldest quarter of town and the cathedral, while the nearby **Quayhead** is linked by water-taxi to the sights around the **Floating Harbour**, the waterway network that runs through town and connects with the River Avon.

Bristol Cathedral

College Green • Daily 8am–6pm • Free • ⓦ bristol-cathedral.co.uk

The grassy expanse of College Green is dominated by the crescent-shaped Council House and by the contrastingly medieval lines of **Bristol Cathedral**. This venerable building was founded as an abbey around 1140 on the supposed spot of St Augustine's convocation with Celtic Christians in 603, becoming a cathedral church with the Dissolution of the Monasteries. The two towers on the west front were erected in the nineteenth century in a faithful act of homage to Edmund Knowle, architect and abbot at the start of the fourteenth century. The interior offers a unique example among Britain's cathedrals of a German-style hall church, in which the aisles, nave and choir rise to the same height. Abbot Knowle's **choir** offers one of the country's most exquisite illustrations of the early Decorated style of Gothic, while the adjoining **Elder Lady Chapel**, from the early thirteenth century, contains fine tombs and eccentric carvings of animals, including a monkey playing the bagpipes accompanied by a ram on the violin. The **Eastern Lady Chapel** has some of England's finest examples of heraldic glass. From the south transept, a door leads to the **Chapter House**, a richly carved piece of late Norman architecture.

City Museum and Art Gallery

Queen's Rd, at the top of Park St • Mon–Fri 10am–5pm, Sat & Sun 10am–6pm • Free • ⓣ 0117 922 3571

Housed in a grandiose, Edwardian-Baroque building, the **City Museum and Art Gallery** has sections on local archeology, geology and natural history, as well as an important collection of Chinese porcelain, glassware, stoneware and ivory, and some magnificent eighth-century BC Assyrian reliefs. Art works by English Pre-Raphaelites and French Impressionists are mixed in with some choice older pieces, including a portrait of Martin Luther by Cranach and Giovanni Bellini's unusual *Descent into Limbo*.

St Stephen's

St Stephen's St, off Corn St • Daily 9.30am–4pm • ⓣ 0117 927 7977, ⓦ saint-stephens.com

Surrounded by characterless modern buildings just east of the Centre, **St Stephen's** is one of Bristol's oldest and most graceful churches. It dates from the thirteenth century, was rebuilt in the fifteenth, and was thoroughly restored with plenty of neo-Gothic trimmings in 1875. The church has some flamboyant tombs inside, mainly of various members of the merchant class who were the church's main patrons.

Corn Exchange

The Georgian **Corn Exchange** was designed by John Wood of Bath and now contains the covered **St Nicholas markets**, a lively spot for a wander or a bite to eat. The four engraved bronze pillars outside the entrance date from the sixteenth and seventeenth centuries and originally served as trading tables – thought to be the "nails" which gave rise to the expression "pay on the nail".

The New Room

Broadmead shopping centre • Mon–Sat 10am–4pm • Free • ⓣ 0117 926 4740, ⓦ newroombristol.org.uk

Hidden inside the **Broadmead** shopping centre is England's first Methodist chapel, the **New Room**. Established by John Wesley in 1739, it looks very much as he left it, with a

5

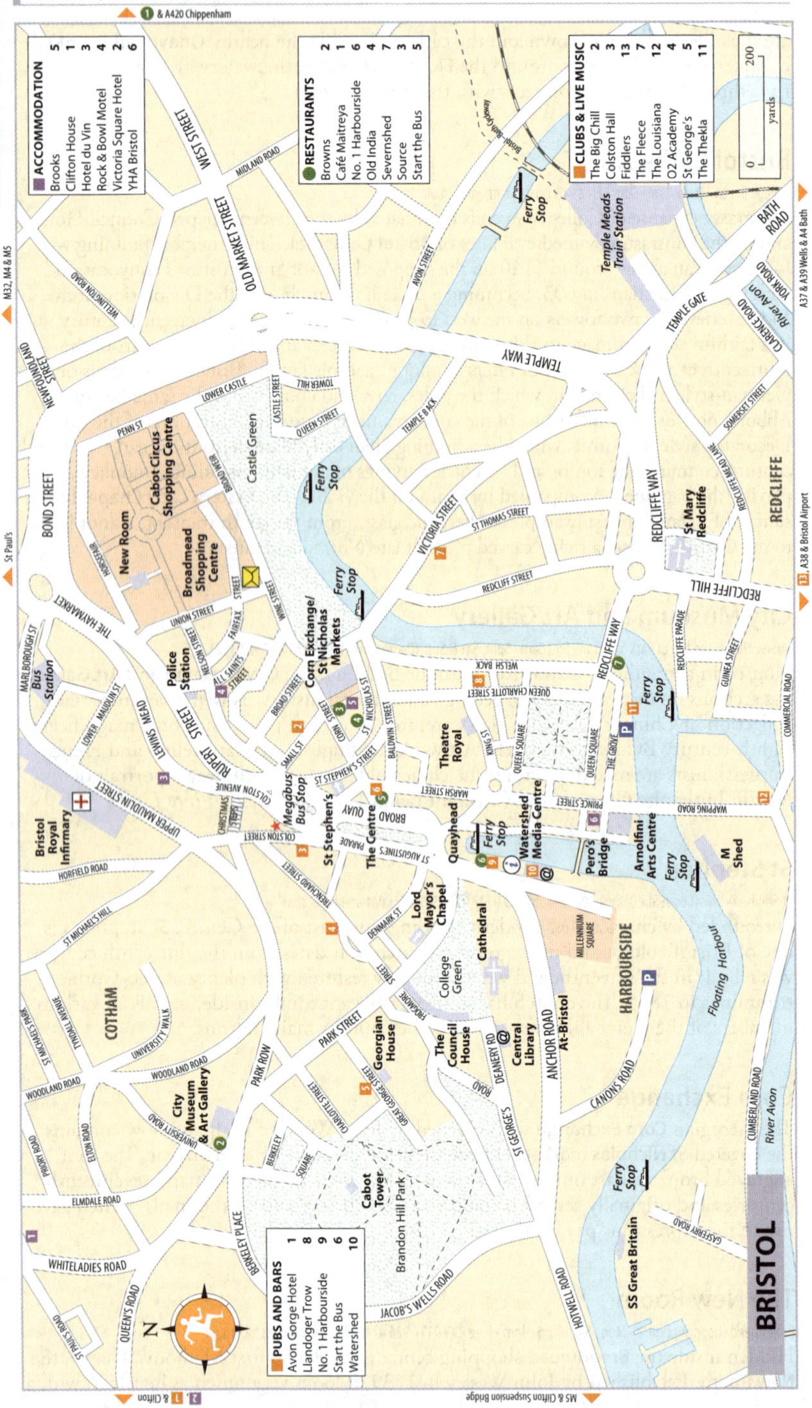
BRISTOL
ACCOMMODATION
Brooks 5
Clifton House 1
Hotel du Vin 3
Rock & Bowl Motel 4
Victoria Square Hotel 2
YHA Bristol 6
RESTAURANTS
Browns 2
Café Maitreya 1
No. 1 Harbourside 6
Old India 4
Severnshed 7
Source 3
Start the Bus 5
CLUBS & LIVE MUSIC
The Big Chill 2
Colston Hall 3
Fiddlers 13
The Fleece 7
The Louisiana 12
O2 Academy 4
St George's 5
The Thekla 11
PUBS AND BARS
Avon Gorge Hotel 1
Llandoger Trow 8
No. 1 Harbourside 9
Start the Bus 6
Watershed 10
0 200 yards
N
& A420 Chippenham
M32, M4 & M5
St Paul's
A38 & Bristol Airport
A37 & A39 Wells & A4 Bath
M5 & Clifton Suspension Bridge
& Clifton
Temple Meads Train Station
Ferry Stop
Cabot Circus Shopping Centre
Broadmead Shopping Centre
New Room
Castle Green
Corn Exchange/ St Nicholas Markets
Police Station
Bus Station
Bristol Royal Infirmary
Megabus Bus Stop
St Stephen's
The Centre
Theatre Royal
Quayhead
Watershed Media Centre
Pero's Bridge
Arnolfini Arts Centre
M Shed
St Mary Redcliffe
REDCLIFFE
Lord Mayor's Chapel
Cathedral
College Green
Millennium Square
HARBOURSIDE
Floating Harbour
At-Bristol
Central Library
The Council House
Georgian House
City Museum & Art Gallery
COTHAM
Cabot Tower
Brandon Hill Park
SS Great Britain
River Avon
TEMPLE WAY
VICTORIA STREET
REDCLIFFE WAY
REDCLIFFE HILL
BOND STREET
OLD MARKET STREET
WEST STREET
RUPERT STREET
PARK ROW
PARK STREET
ANCHOR ROAD
CANONS ROAD
HOTWELL ROAD
JACOB'S WELLS ROAD
BERKELEY PLACE
WHITELADIES ROAD
QUEEN'S ROAD
UPPER MAUDLIN STREET
THE HAYMARKET
BROAD QUAY
WAPPING ROAD
BATH ROAD
TEMPLE GATE

double-deck pulpit in the chapel, beneath a hidden upstairs window from which the evangelist could observe the progress of his trainee preachers.

King Street and around

King Street, a short walk southeast from the Centre, was laid out in 1633 and still holds a cluster of historic buildings, among them the **Theatre Royal**, the oldest working theatre in the country, opened in 1766 and preserving many of its original Georgian features. Further down, and in a very different architectural style, stands the timber-framed **Llandoger Trow** pub (see p.264), once the haunt of seafarers, and reputed to have been the meeting place of Daniel Defoe and Alexander Selkirk, the model for Robinson Crusoe. South of King Street is the elegant, grassy **Queen Square**.

St Mary Redcliffe

Redcliffe Way • Mon–Sat 9am–5pm in summer, 9am–4pm in winter, Sun 8am–7.30pm • T 0117 929 1487, W stmaryredcliffe.co.uk

Across Redcliffe Bridge from the Centre, the tall spire of **St Mary Redcliffe** is a distinctive feature on the city's skyline. Described by Elizabeth I as "the goodliest, fairest, and most famous parish church in England", St Mary was largely paid for and used by merchants and mariners. The present building was begun at the end of the thirteenth century, though it was added to in subsequent centuries and the spire dates from 1872. Inside, memorials and tombs recall figures associated with the building, including the Handel Window, installed in 1859 on the centenary of the death of Handel, who composed on the organ here.

Above the church's north porch is the muniment room, where **Thomas Chatterton** claimed to have found a trove of medieval manuscripts; the poems, distributed as the work of a fifteenth-century monk named Thomas Rowley, were in fact dazzling fakes. The young poet committed suicide after his forgery was exposed, supplying English literature with one of its most glamorous stories of self-destructive genius. The "Marvellous Boy" is remembered by a memorial stone in the south transept.

M-Shed

Princes Wharf • Tues–Fri 10am–5pm, Sat & Sun 10am–6pm • Free • T 0117 352 6600, W mshed.org

Opened in 2011, the superb **M-Shed**, housed in an old harbourside transit shed, is Bristol's first museum dedicated to itself, past and present. It's an enjoyable, unashamedly populist survey, full of memorabilia and anecdotes and casting light on everything from the city's mercantile history and its role in the transatlantic slave trade to its festivals and street-life. Head out to the long terrace for fantastic harbour views.

At-Bristol

Millennium Square • Daily: Mon–Fri during school terms 10am–5pm; Sat, Sun & school hols 10am–6pm; last entry 1hr before closing • £11.25, planetarium £1 • T 0845 345 1235, W at-bristol.org.uk

At one corner of the sleekly modern **Millennium Square**, marked out by the spherical, stainless-steel planetarium attached to one side, **At-Bristol** deals with all things science. It's chiefly aimed at children, but there's enough interactive wizardry here to entertain

TOP 5 MUSEUMS

Holburne Museum Bath. See p.269
M-Shed Bristol. See above
Museum of Somerset Taunton. See p.277
Roman Baths Museum Bath. See p.267
Somerset Rural Life Museum Glastonbury. See p.275

5

and inform everyone, with opportunities to view the blood in your veins, freeze your shadow and create animations (including input from Aardman Animations). The planetarium has 5–10 shows daily, which should be booked when you buy your tickets.

SS Great Britain

Gas Ferry Rd • Daily: April–Oct 10am–5.30pm; Nov–March 10am–4.30pm; last entry 1hr before closing • £12.50 • T 0117 926 0680, W ssgreatbritain.org

The major attraction on the Harbour, and one of Bristol's iconic sights, is the **SS Great Britain**, the first propeller-driven, ocean-going iron ship, built in 1843 by Brunel. She initially ran between Liverpool and New York, then between Liverpool and Melbourne, circumnavigating the globe 32 times over a period of 26 years. Her ocean-going days ended in 1886 when she was caught in a storm off Cape Horn, and she was eventually recovered and returned to Bristol in 1968. On board you can see restored cabins and peer into the immense engine room. The adjoining museum gives the background of the vessel and of Bristol's long shipbuilding history.

Clifton

On the western side of the city, **Clifton**, once an aloof spa resort, is now Bristol's stateliest neighbourhood. At the top of Blackboy Hill, the wide green expanse of **Durdham Down** and **Clifton Down** stretches right up to the edge of the Avon Gorge, a popular spot for picnickers, joggers and kite-flyers. On the southern edge of the Downs is the select enclave of Clifton Village, centred on the Mall, where **Royal York Crescent**, the longest Georgian crescent in the country, offers splendid views over the steep drop to the River Avon below.

Clifton Suspension Bridge

Visitor Centre daily 10am–5pm • Free

A few minutes' walk from Clifton Village is Bristol's most famous symbol, **Clifton Suspension Bridge**, 702ft long and poised 245ft above high water. Money was first put forward for a bridge to span the Avon Gorge by a Bristol wine merchant in 1753, though it was not until 1829 that a competition was held for a design, won by Isambard Brunel on a second round, and not until 1864 that the bridge was completed, five years after Brunel's death. Hampered by financial difficulties, the bridge never quite matched the engineer's original ambitious design, which included Egyptian-style towers topped by sphinxes at each end. You can see copies of his plans in the **Visitor Centre** at the far side of the bridge, alongside designs proposed by Brunel's rivals, some of them frankly bizarre.

ARRIVAL AND INFORMATION — BRISTOL

By train Temple Meads train station is a 20min walk east of the city centre.

Destinations Bath (every 15–30min; 15min); Birmingham (every 30min–1hr; 1hr 25min); Bridgwater (every 30min–1hr; 50min); Cheltenham (every 30min–1hr; 40min–1hr 30min); Exeter (every 30min–1hr; 1hr); Gloucester (every 30min–1hr; 40min–1hr); London (every 30min–1hr; 1hr 45min).

By bus Bristol's bus station is centrally located off Marlborough Street; Megabus services to and from London stop opposite Colston Hall, off the Centre.

Destinations Bath (Mon–Sat every 15min, Sun every 30min; 50min); Glastonbury (hourly; 1hr 25min); London (every 30min–1hr; 2hr 30min); Wells (every 30min–1hr; 1hr 10min).

Tourist office E-Shed, Canon's Rd (Daily: April–Sept 10am–6pm; Oct–March 10am–5pm; T 0906 711 2191, W visitbristol.co.uk).

GETTING AROUND

By ferry A ferry, setting off from the Quayhead, just south of the Centre, connects various parts of the Floating Harbour, including Temple Meads station, *SS Great Britain* and a few riverside pubs (every 40min; 10.30am–5.50pm;

CLOCKWISE FROM TOP LEFT AT-BRISTOL (P.261), LLANDOGER TROW PUB (P.264), BANKSY MURAL >

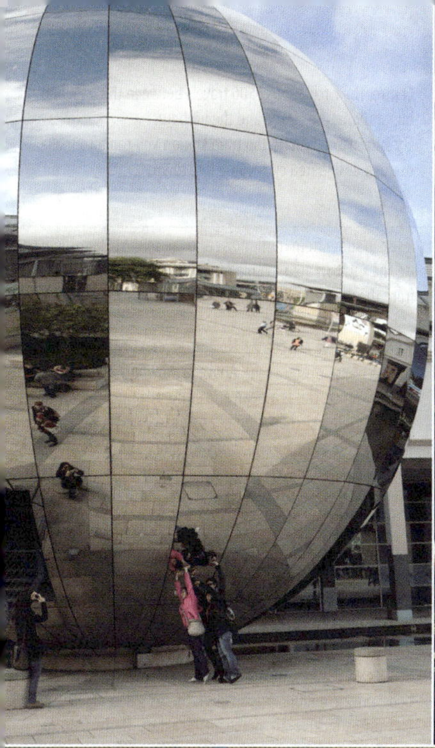

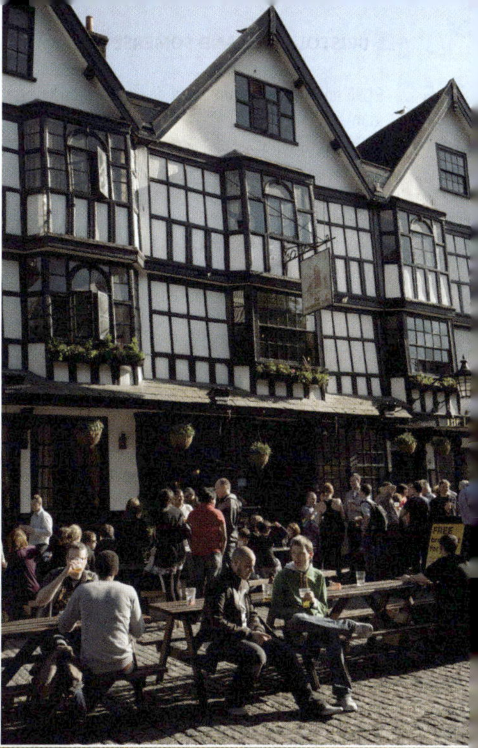

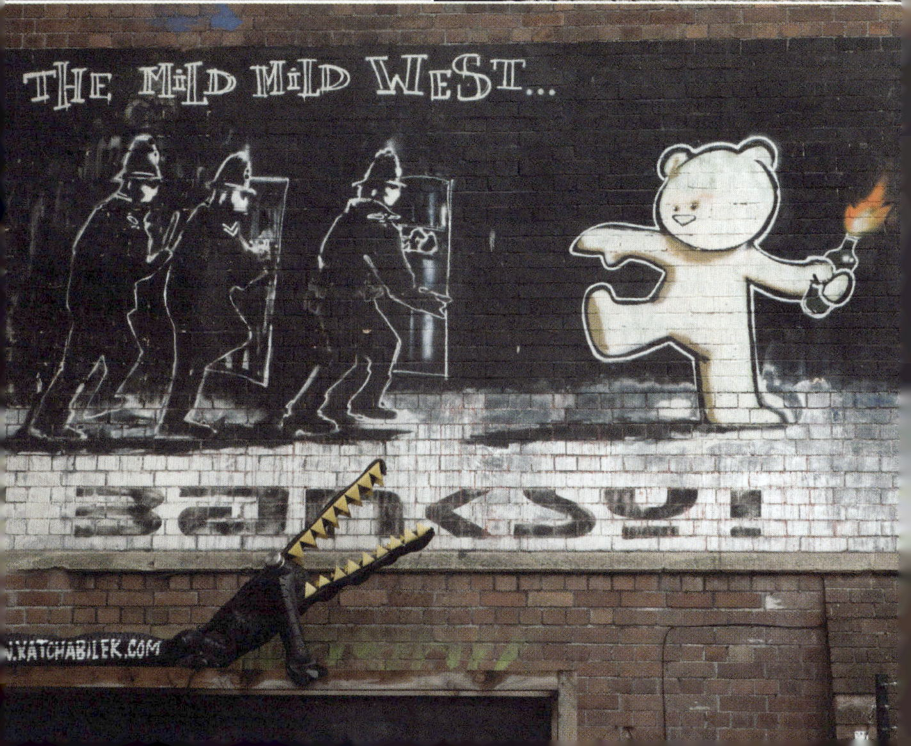
THE MILD MILD WEST...
KATCHABILEK.COM

5

£1.90 single; £4.90 return; £7 all-day ticket; Ⓦ bristolferry.com).

By bus Local buses are useful for getting to Clifton's upper reaches; take #8 or #9 from Temple Meads station or the Centre. The circular bus #500 travels between the train and bus stations, the Centre and the harbour.

By bike From behind the train station you can also make use of a designated cycle route into town.

ACCOMMODATION

Bristol has a range of **hotels** and **B&Bs** in the centre, though these can suffer from traffic noise and the sound of late-night revellers. For quieter and more traditional-style lodgings, choose the **Clifton** area, with a range of pubs and restaurants on the main axis of Whiteladies Road, an easy walk or bus ride from the centre.

★ **Brooks** Exchange Ave Ⓣ 0117 930 0066, Ⓦ brooksguesthousebristol.com. Bang next door to St Nicholas Market, this smart, functional B&B has small but clean and comfortable rooms that come with iPod dock, DVD and free wi-fi. The airy modern breakfast room gives onto a spacious courtyard for relaxing with a book or a drink. A couple of the rooms get street noise at weekends; rates vary. **£70**

Clifton House 4 Tyndall's Park Rd Ⓣ 0117 973 5407, Ⓦ cliftonhousebristol.com. This handily sited B&B at the bottom of Clifton and near the centre offers fairly plush rooms with big windows, modern bathrooms and plenty of space – superior rooms, costing £20 extra, are huge. There's free wi-fi and parking. **£65**

Hotel du Vin Narrow Lewins Mead Ⓣ 0117 925 5577, Ⓦ hotelduvin.co.uk. Chic conversion of an old dockside sugar warehouse, centrally located, with dark, contemporary decor. Rooms have big beds and lush bathrooms, and there's an excellent restaurant. **£140**

Rock & Bowl Motel 22 Nelson St Ⓣ 0117 325 1980, Ⓦ rocknbowlmotel.com. Above a bowling alley in an ex-dole office, this is a clean and efficiently run hostel with a self-catering kitchen, single- and mixed-sex dorms and a few en-suite doubles and twins. Laundry and wi-fi. Dorm **£13**, double **£48**

Victoria Square Hotel Victoria Square Ⓣ 0843 357 1490, Ⓦ victoriasquarehotel.co.uk. Some of the rooms in this Georgian hotel are on the small side, but the location is great, on a leafy square near Clifton Village, in the heart of the student district. Rates vary. **£89**

YHA Bristol 14 Narrow Quay Ⓣ 0845 371 9726, Ⓔ bristol@yha.org.uk. In a refurbished warehouse on the quayside, this is clean, warm, friendly and safe. Most dorms have four beds; private doubles are smallish. There's a decent kitchen, and prices include an abundant breakfast. Dorm **£18.50**, double **£46**

EATING

Browns 38 Queen's Rd Ⓣ 0117 930 4777, Ⓦ browns-restaurants.co.uk. Spacious and relaxed place for a salad, hamburger or fisherman's pie (£9–14), housed in the Venetian-style former university refectory. Brunch is served until noon, and the terrace makes a pleasant spot for a morning coffee or evening cocktail. Mon–Sat 9am–11pm, Sun 10am–10pm.

★ **Café Maitreya** 89 St Mark's Rd Ⓣ 0117 951 0100, Ⓦ cafemaitreya.co.uk. Tucked away in the multicultural Easton neighbourhood (bus #48/49 from the centre), this smart but easy-going place serves delicious, inventive vegetarian dishes – sweetcorn and cashew nuts in roast pepper, for example, or warm samphire salad. Set menus £20/£23. Tues–Sat 6.30–9.45pm.

Old India 34 St Nicholas St Ⓣ 0117 922 1136, Ⓦ oldindia.co.uk. In sumptuous surroundings in the old Stock Exchange building, this place has classy curries and unusual dishes – try the Anari Chops, lamb chops cooked with pomegranate juice. Mains £8.50–12. Mon–Sat 6–11.30pm.

Severnshed The Grove Ⓣ 0117 925 1212, Ⓦ severnshedrestaurant.co.uk. With a waterside terrace, *Severnshed* serves pastas and pizzas (£9–13) and grills, including firesticks – skewers of meat and fish (£15–18). DJs provide the soundtrack on Fri and Sat evenings, and there's live jazz on Sun from 2.30pm. Mon–Thurs & Sun 9am–midnight, Fri & Sat 9am–1am.

Source 1–3 Exchange Ave, off St Nicholas St Ⓣ 0117 927 2998, Ⓦ source-food.co.uk. Almost all the food in this canteen next to the market is from the West Country, and much of it is organic and can be bought to take away – Cornish crab cakes, steamed Exmouth mussels and polenta (all £9), for example. Mon–Sat 8am–6pm, first Sun of month 10am–4pm.

DRINKING

Avon Gorge Hotel Sion Hill Ⓣ 0117 973 8955, Ⓦ theavongorge.com. On the edge of the Gorge in Clifton Village, the modern bar attached to this hotel has magnificent views of the suspension bridge from its broad terrace. Coffees and meals available. Mon–Sat 11am–11pm, Sun 11am–10.30pm.

Llandoger Trow King St Ⓣ 0870 990 6424, Ⓦ brewersfayre.co.uk. Seventeenth-century tavern bursting with historical associations (see p.261), with cosy nooks and armchairs, and benches outside. Snacks and full meals are available, and there's a separate restaurant upstairs (eves only). Gets very busy on summer evenings. Mon–Sat noon–late.

No. 1 Harbourside Canons Rd ⓣ0117 929 1100, ⓦno1harbourside.co.uk. Laidback lounge bar for drinks and snacks all day until late, and live music every evening (at 10pm), or DJs on Fri & Sat. Meals (fish pie, sausages and veggie options) are accompanied by free soup. Mon–Wed 10am–midnight, Thurs 10am–1am, Fri & Sat 10am–2am, Sun 10am–10pm.

Start the Bus 7–9 Baldwin St ⓣ0117 930 4370, ⓦstartthebus.tv. Mellow, slightly grungy bar-restaurant by day, buzzing music venue at night, with live bands most evenings and a quirky quiz night on Mon. Food served until 10pm. Mon–Wed 10am–1am, Thurs–Sat 10am–3am, Sun 11am–1am.

★ **Watershed** Canons Rd ⓣ0117 927 5101, ⓦwatershed.co.uk. Café-bar overlooking the boats in one of Bristol's longest-established arts complexes. There are good coffees, local beers, good food, free internet terminals and a small (non-smoking) terrace. Mon 10.30am–11pm, Tues–Thurs 9.30am–11pm, Fri & Sat 9.30am–midnight, Sun 10am–10.30pm.

NIGHTLIFE AND ENTERTAINMENT

The Big Chill 15 Small St ⓣ0117 930 4217, ⓦbigchill.net. Cool lounge and club for late-night drinking and dancing, connected to the festival and London venue of the same name. It's got old records on the walls, burgers and tapas to nibble and a small roof terrace. Mon–Wed & Sun noon–midnight, Thurs noon–1am, Fri & Sat noon–3am.

Colston Hall Colston St ⓣ0117 922 3686, ⓦcolstonhall.org. Major names in the classical, jazz, rock and world genres appear in this stalwart mainstream venue. Hosts Bristol Folk Festival in April/May, among other events. Talks and smaller shows are held in Hall 2.

Fiddlers Willway St, Bedminster ⓣ0117 987 3403, ⓦfiddlers.co.uk. A great range of acts, from folk and world music to tribute bands, play at this relaxed, mid-size venue (formerly a prison). It's south of the river, off Bedminster Parade.

The Fleece 12 St Thomas St ⓣ0117 945 0996, ⓦthefleece.co.uk. Stone-flagged ex-wool warehouse, now a loud, sweaty pub owned by legendary Bristol art-rockers The Blue Aeroplanes, and staging everything from acoustic blues and alt-country to punk and deathcore.

The Louisiana Bathurst Terrace, Wapping Rd ⓣ0117 926 5978, ⓦthelouisiana.net. Above a pub, this is a great place to catch up on new and local bands. It's a mite cramped, but the acoustics and atmosphere are excellent.

02 Academy Frogmore St ⓣ0844 477 2000, ⓦ02academybristol.co.uk. Near the Centre, this spacious, multilevel place stages almost nightly live gigs as well as club nights, featuring big-name old and new acts. Friday night's Ramshackle offers indie, punk and metalcore.

★ **St George's** Great George St ⓣ0845 402 4001, ⓦstgeorgesbristol.co.uk. Lunchtime and evening concerts of classical, world and jazz music are staged in this elegant Georgian church with near perfect acoustics and atmosphere. There's a café-bar in the crypt.

The Thekla The Grove ⓣ0845/413 4444, ⓦtheklabristol.co.uk. Studenty riverboat venue, staging regular live bands plus dubstep, dub and indie club nights. Look out for the Banksy stencil of the Grim Reaper on the hull.

Bath

Just twelve miles from Bristol, **BATH** has a very different feel from its neighbour – more harmonious, compact, leisurely and complacent. The city's elegant crescents and Georgian buildings are studded with plaques naming Bath's eminent inhabitants from its heyday as a spa resort; it was here that Jane Austen set *Persuasion* and *Northanger Abbey*, and where Gainsborough established himself as a portraitist and landscape painter.

Bath owes its name and fame to its **hot springs** – the only ones in the country – which made it a place of reverence for the local Celtic population, though it took Roman technology to turn it into a fully fledged bathing establishment. The baths fell into decline with the departure of the Romans, but the town later regained its importance under the Saxons, its abbey seeing the coronation of the **first king of all England**, Edgar, in 973. A new bathing complex was built in the sixteenth century, popularized by the visit of Elizabeth I in 1574, and the city reached its fashionable zenith in the eighteenth century, when **Beau Nash** ruled the town's social scene (see p.267). It was at this time that Bath acquired its ranks of Palladian mansions and Regency townhouses, all of them built in the local **Bath stone**.

Although Bath could easily be seen on a day-trip from Bristol, it really deserves a stay of a couple of days. There's a rich concentration of museums to take in, but some of the

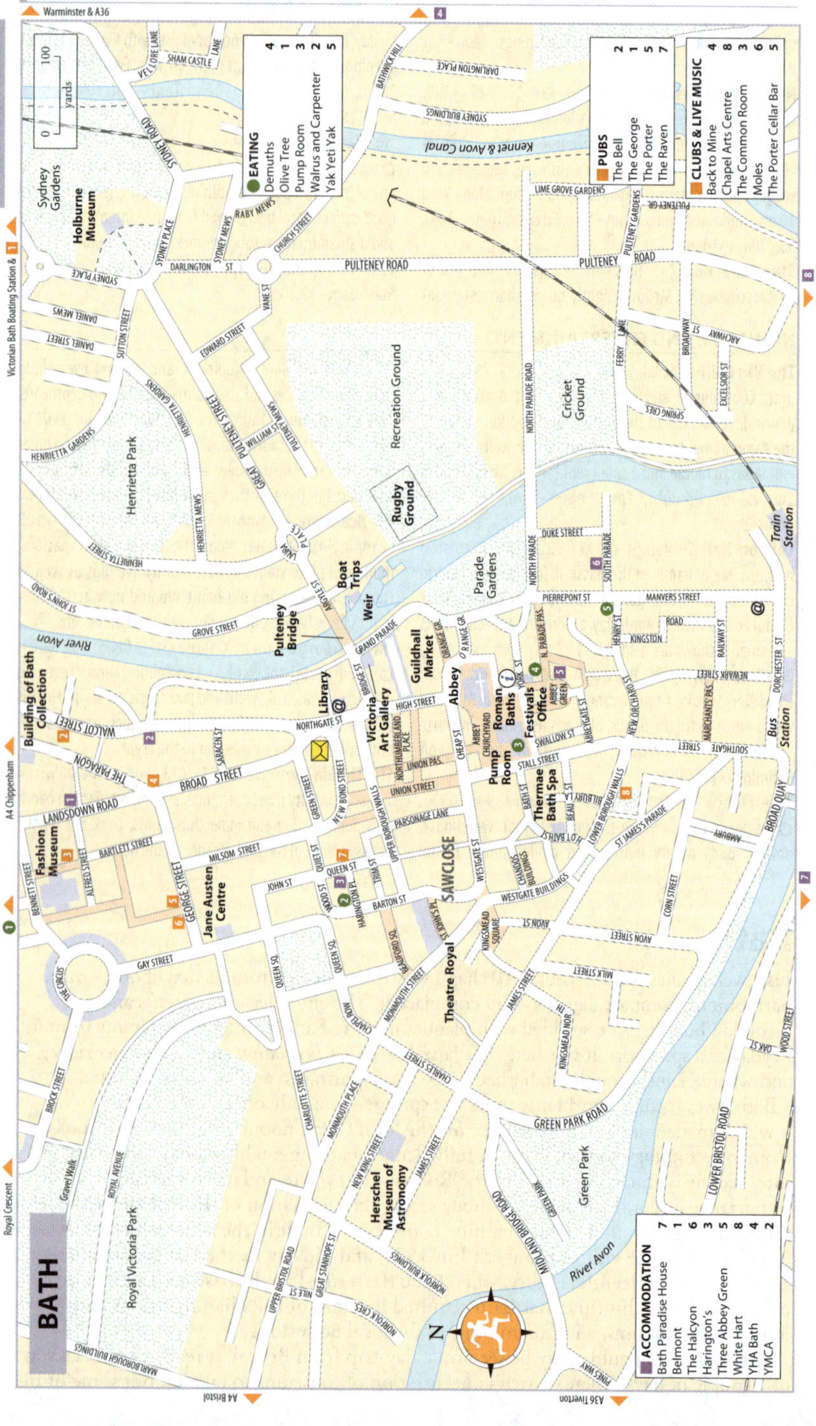
5
BATH
EATING
Demuths 4
Olive Tree 1
Pump Room 3
Walrus and Carpenter 2
Yak Yeti Yak 5
PUBS
The Bell 2
The George 1
The Porter 5
The Raven 7
CLUBS & LIVE MUSIC
Back to Mine 4
Chapel Arts Centre 8
The Common Room 3
Moles 6
The Porter Cellar Bar 5
ACCOMMODATION
Bath Paradise House 7
Belmont 1
The Halcyon 6
Harington's 3
Three Abbey Green 5
White Hart 8
YHA Bath 4
YMCA 2
Warminster & A36
Victorian Bath Boating Station & Sydney Gardens
A4 Chippenham
Royal Crescent
A4 Bristol
A36 Tiverton
Train Station
Bus Station
Kennet & Avon Canal
River Avon
Holburne Museum
Recreation Ground
Rugby Ground
Cricket Ground
Henrietta Park
Pulteney Bridge
Boat Trips
Weir
Parade Gardens
Guildhall Market
Abbey
Roman Baths
Pump Room
Festivals Office
Thermae Bath Spa
Library
Victoria Art Gallery
Building of Bath Collection
Fashion Museum
Jane Austen Centre
Theatre Royal
SAWCLOSE
Herschel Museum of Astronomy
Royal Victoria Park
Green Park
The Circus

BEAU NASH

Richard "Beau" Nash was an ex-army officer, ex-lawyer, dandy and gambler, who became Bath's Master of Ceremonies in 1704, conducting public balls of an unprecedented splendour. Wielding dictatorial powers over dress and behaviour, Nash orchestrated the social manners of the city and even extended his influence to cover road improvements and the design of buildings. In an early example of health awareness, he banned smoking in Bath's public rooms at a time when pipe-smoking was generally enjoyed among men, women and children. Less philanthropically, he also encouraged gambling and even took a percentage of the bank's takings. According to his rules, balls were always to begin at 6pm and end at 11pm and each one had to open with a minuet "danced by two persons of the highest distinction present". White aprons were banned, gossipers and scandalmongers were shunned, and, most radical of all, the wearing of swords in public places was forbidden.

greatest enjoyment comes simply from wandering the streets, with their pale gold architecture and sweeping vistas.

The Roman Baths

Abbey Churchyard • Daily: March–June, Sept & Oct 9am–6pm; July & Aug 9am–10pm; Nov–Feb 9.30am–5.30pm; last entry 1hr before closing • £12, £12.50 in July & Aug, £15.50 combined ticket with Fashion Museum • T 0225 477785, W romanbaths.co.uk

There are hours' worth of entertainment in Bath's premier attraction, the **Roman Baths**, with commentary provided by hourly guided tours and audioguides (both free). **Highlights** include the Sacred Spring, part of the temple of the local deity Sulis Minerva, where water still bubbles up at a constant 46.5°C; the open-air (but originally covered) Great Bath, its vaporous waters surrounded by nineteenth-century pillars, terraces and statues of famous Romans; the Circular Bath, where bathers cooled off, and the Norman King's Bath.

Among a quantity of coins, jewellery and sculpture exhibited are the gilt bronze head of Sulis Minerva and a grand, Celtic-inspired gorgon's head from the temple's pediment. Models of the complex at its greatest extent give some idea of the awe which it must have inspired, while the graffiti salvaged from the Roman era – mainly curses and boasts – offer a personal slant on this antique leisure centre.

You can get a free glimpse into the baths from the next door **Pump Room**, the social hub of the Georgian spa community and still redolent of that era, which houses a formal tearoom and restaurant (see p.270).

Bath Abbey

Abbey Churchyard • April–Oct Mon–Sat 9am–6pm, Sun 1–2.30pm & 4.30–5.30pm; Nov–March Mon–Sat 9am–4.30pm, Sun 1–2.30pm • Requested donation £2.50 • W bathabbey.org

Although there has been a church on the site since the seventh century, **Bath Abbey** did not take its present form until the end of the fifteenth century, when Bishop Oliver King began work on the ruins of the previous Norman building, some of which were incorporated into the new church. The bishop was said to have been inspired by a vision of angels ascending and descending a ladder to heaven, which the present facade recalls on the turrets flanking the central window. The west front also features the founder's signature in the form of carvings of olive trees surmounted by crowns, a play on his name.

The **interior** is in a restrained Perpendicular style, and boasts splendid fan vaulting on the ceiling, which was not completed until the nineteenth century. The floor and walls are crammed with elaborate monuments and memorials, and traces of the grander Norman building are visible in the Norman Chapel.

5

Thermae Bath Spa

Bath St • **Baths** Daily 9am–10pm, last entry 7.30pm • £25 (2hr) to £50 (full day) **Visitor centre** April–Oct Mon–Sat 10am–5pm, Sun 11am–4pm • Free • ⓣ 0844 888 0844, ⓦ thermaebathspa.com

At the bottom of the elegantly colonnaded Bath Street, **Thermae Bath Spa** allows you to take the waters in much the same way that visitors to Bath have done throughout the ages, but with state-of-the-art spa facilities. Heated by the city's thermal waters, the spa includes two open-air pools, one on the roof of its centrepiece, the New Royal Bath, Nicholas Grimshaw's sleekly futuristic "glass cube". Various treatments are offered, from massages to dry flotation, and a small **visitor centre** has displays relating to Bath's thermal waters.

Queen Square and around

North of Hot Bath Street, Sawclose is presided over by the **Theatre Royal**, opened in 1805 and one of the country's finest surviving Georgian theatres. Next door is the house where Beau Nash spent his last years (now a restaurant). Barton Street leads north of Sawclose to **Queen Square**, the first Bath venture of the architect **John Wood the Elder** (1704–54), champion of Neoclassical Palladianism, who lived at no. 15 (not no. 24 as a tablet there asserts). East of the square, the wide shopping strand of **Milsom Street** was designed by Wood as the main thoroughfare of Georgian Bath.

Herschel Museum of Astronomy

19 New King St • Feb to mid-Dec Mon, Tues, Thurs & Fri 1–5pm, Sat & Sun 11am–5pm • £5 • ⓦ bath-preservation-trust.org.uk

A few minutes west of the centre is the small **Herschel Museum of Astronomy**, the former home of the musician and astronomer Sir William Herschel and his sister Caroline, who together discovered the planet Uranus in 1781. Among the furnishings, musical instruments and knick-knacks from the Herschels' era, you can see a replica of the telescope with which Uranus was identified.

Jane Austen Centre

40 Gay St • Late March to June, Sept & Oct daily 9.45am–5.30pm; July & Aug Sun–Wed 9.45am–5.30pm, Thurs–Sat 9.45am–7pm; Nov to late March Mon–Fri & Sun 11am–4.30pm, Sat 9.45am–5.30pm • £7.45 • ⓣ 01225 443000, ⓦ janeausten.co.uk

The **Jane Austen Centre** provides a superficial overview of the author's connections with Bath, illustrated by extracts from her writings, contemporary costumes, furnishings and household items. Austen herself, who wasn't entirely enamoured of the city, lived just down the road at 25 Gay St – one of a number of places the author inhabited while in Bath.

The Royal Crescent and around

No. 1 Royal Crescent Tues–Sun: mid-Feb to late Oct 10.30am–5pm; late Oct to mid-Dec 10.30am–4pm • £6.50 • ⓦ bath-preservation-trust.org.uk

At the top of Gay Street, the elder John Wood's masterpiece, **the Circus**, consists of three crescents arranged in a tight circle of three-storey houses, with a carved frieze running round the entire circle. Wood died soon after laying the foundation stone for this enterprise, and the job was finished by his son, **John Wood the Younger** (1727–81), who was as instrumental as his father in defining Bath's elegant Georgian appearance. The painter Thomas Gainsborough lived at no. 17 from 1760 to 1774.

The Circus is connected by Brock Street to the **Royal Crescent**, grandest of Bath's crescents, begun by the younger John Wood in 1767. The stately arc of thirty houses is set off by a spacious sloping lawn from which a magnificent vista extends to green hills and distant ribbons of honey-coloured stone. The interior of **No. 1 Royal Crescent**, on the corner with Brock Street, has been restored to reflect as nearly as possible its original Georgian appearance.

At the bottom of the Crescent, Royal Avenue leads onto **Royal Victoria Park**, the city's largest open space, containing an aviary and botanical gardens.

The Fashion Museum

Bennett St • Daily: March–Oct 10.30am–5pm; Nov–Feb 10.30am–4pm • £7.25, or £15.50 with the Roman Baths • ⓣ 01225 477789, ⓦ museumofcostume.co.uk

The younger John Wood's **Assembly Rooms**, east of the Circus, were, with the Pump Room, the centre of Bath's social scene. A fire virtually destroyed the building in 1942, but it has since been perfectly restored and houses a **Fashion Museum**, an entertaining collection of clothing from the Stuart era to modern Milanese designs.

Building of Bath Collection

The Paragon • Mid-Feb to Nov Sat–Mon 10.30am–5pm • £4 • ⓦ bath-preservation-trust.org.uk

The Georgian-Gothic Countess of Huntingdon's Chapel, accessed from the raised pavement on the Paragon, houses the **Building of Bath Collection**, a fascinating exploration of the construction and architecture of the city. Everything is covered, from the kind of facades associated with the two John Woods to door designs, sash windows and such aspects of interior ornamentation as marbling, stencilling and japanning.

Holburne Museum

Sydney Place • Mon–Sat 10am–5pm, Sun 11am–5pm • Free • ⓦ holburne.org

The River Avon is crossed by the graceful, shop-lined **Pulteney Bridge**, an Italianate structure designed by Robert Adam. From the other side a lengthy vista stretches along Great Pulteney Street to the imposing classical facade of the **Holburne Museum**. The building, with a modern extension at the back, holds an impressive range of decorative and fine art, mostly furniture, silverware, porcelain and paintings, including several works by Gainsborough, notably the famous *Byam Family*, his largest portrait. Look out too for works by Constable, Stubbs, Turner, Angelika Kauffman and Pieter Brueghel the Younger.

ARRIVAL AND INFORMATION — BATH

By train Bath Spa train station is a short walk south of the centre on Dorchester St.

Destinations Bristol (2–4 hourly; 15min); London (every 30min–1hr; 1hr 40min); Salisbury (every 30min–1hr; 1hr–1hr 50min).

By bus The bus station lies next to the train station on Dorchester St.

Destinations Bristol (Mon–Sat every 12min, Sun every 30min; 55min); London (10 daily; 3–4hr); Salisbury (Mon–Sat every 30min with change, Sun 1 daily; 1hr 25min–2hr 30min); Wells (Mon–Sat hourly, Sun 6 daily; 1hr 20min).

By bike If you're coming from Bristol, you can cycle all the way along a cycle-path that follows the route of a disused railway line and the course of the Avon.

Tourist office Next to the abbey in Abbey Churchyard (June–Sept Mon–Sat 9.30am–6pm, Sun 10am–4pm; Oct–May Mon–Sat 9.30am–5pm, Sun 10am–4pm; ⓣ 0906 711 2000, ⓦ visitbath.co.uk).

GETTING AROUND

Walking or biking are the best ways to enjoy Bath's Georgian terraces – cars are a hindrance and parking is expensive; drivers should use one of the **Park-and-Ride** car parks on the periphery of town.

Bike rental Bath Bike Hire, Bath Narrowboats, Sydney Wharf, Bathwick Hill (£13/half-day, £19/day; ⓣ 01225 44727, ⓦ bathbikehire.com). They also rent narrowboats (£60–100 /half-day, £90–165/day).

ACCOMMODATION

Bath is chock-full of **hotels** and **B&Bs**, but most of the latter are small, and it's always worth booking early, especially at weekends, when most places demand a two-night minimum and prices rise. Rates quoted below are midweek. There are

5

also good-value, central **hostels**, though the nearest campsites are some distance outside town. Note that the centre can get noisy at night, so choose a room away from the street for an undisturbed sleep.

HOTELS AND B&BS

★ **Bath Paradise House** 88 Holloway ⓣ 01225 317723, ⓦ paradise-house.co.uk. Georgian villa an uphill trudge from the centre, but with wonderful views. Open fires in winter, four-posters in some of the rooms and three rooms opening straight onto the lush garden. **£120**

Belmont 7 Belmont, Lansdown Rd ⓣ 01225 423082, ⓦ belmontbath.co.uk. Large doubles, some with tiny, clean, modern en-suite bathrooms, in a centrally located B&B in a house designed by John Wood. No credit cards. **£50**

The Halcyon 2–3 South Parade ⓣ 01225 444100, ⓦ thehalcyon.com. Boutique-type hotel with small, smart rooms, some with cooking facilities. Breakfast is extra, at £6.50 per person (or £12 for a cooked option at weekends). The basement bar provides great cocktails and has pavement seating, and there's wi-fi in the bar/reception area. **£125**

Harington's Queen St ⓣ 01225 461728, ⓦ haringtons hotel.co.uk. Central hotel in a converted townhouse with modern, well-equipped rooms, mostly quite small, and some at the top of steep steps. Breakfasts are superlative, food is available throughout the day, service is friendly and there's wi-fi. **£145**

★ **Three Abbey Green** 3 Abbey Green ⓣ 01225 428558, ⓦ threeabbeygreen.com. Top-notch B&B in a beautifully renovated Georgian house just steps from the abbey. The airy, spotless rooms are wi-fi-enabled; the larger ones overlooking a peaceful square are more expensive. **£110**

HOSTELS

★ **White Hart** Widcombe Hill ⓣ 01225 313985, ⓦ whitehartbath.co.uk. The comfiest of Bath's hostels has a kitchen, a first-class bar/restaurant and a spacious courtyard. There are clean doubles and twins available, some en suite. Midnight curfew. Dorm **£15**, double **£50**

YHA Bath Bathwick Hill ⓣ 0845/371 9303, ⓔ bath@yha .org.uk. An Italianate mansion a mile from the centre, with gardens and panoramic views. Dorm beds (more expensive in summer) and doubles available, and evening meals. Bus #18 or #U18. Dorm **£16.50**, double **£36**

YMCA International House, Broad St ⓣ 01225 325900, ⓦ bathymca.co.uk. Clean, central and spacious, this place has dorms, singles and doubles, with reductions for weekly stays; all rates include breakfast (but there's no kitchen). Dorm **£18**, double **£53**

EATING

★ **Demuths** 2 North Parade Passage ⓣ 01225 446059, ⓦ demuths.co.uk. Bath's favourite veggie and vegan restaurant offers original and delicious dishes in an unruffled, arty environment. Choices range from "quick bites" at lunchtime (2 for £12.50) to more substantial "world food" concoctions (£10–15). Beers and wines are organic. Mon–Fri & Sun from noon & 5pm, Sat from 11.30am & 5pm.

Olive Tree Russel St ⓣ 01225 447928, ⓦ thequeensberry .co.uk. In the basement of the *Queensberry* hotel, this is one of Bath's top restaurants, offering French-inspired dishes, a contemporary ambience and discreetly attentive service. The menu might feature crab risotto, squab pigeon and roast venison, and the desserts are delectable. Set-price lunches £16–20, otherwise count on £40–60 per head. Mon 7–10pm, Tues–Sat noon–2pm & 7–10pm, Sun 12.30–2pm & 7–10pm.

Pump Room Abbey Churchyard ⓣ 01225 444477, ⓦ romanbaths.co.uk. Splash out on a Champagne breakfast, sample the excellent lunchtime menu or succumb to a Bath bun or a range of cream teas, all accompanied by a pianist or classical trio. It's a bit hammy and overpriced, and you may have to queue, but you get a good view of the Baths. Daily 9.30am–4.30pm; July, Aug & Dec and during major festivals 9.30am–9pm.

★ **Walrus and Carpenter** 28 Barton St ⓣ 01225 314864, ⓦ walrusandcarpenter.com. This warren of small, candlelit rooms near the Theatre Royal is friendly, relaxed and plastered with posters. There's an extensive vegetarian menu, and organic steaks and burgers are also available (£10–15). Mon–Sat noon–2.30pm & 6–11pm, Sun noon–11pm.

★ **Yak Yeti Yak** 12 Pierrepont St ⓣ 01225 442299. Nepalese restaurant in a series of cellar rooms with a choice of chairs or floor cushions. Meat dishes are stir-fried or spicily marinated, and there's a good vegetarian selection, all £5.50–9. Mon–Sat noon–2.30pm & 5–10.30pm, Sun noon–2.30pm & 5–10pm.

DRINKING

★ **The Bell** 103 Walcot St ⓣ 01225 460426, ⓦ walcot street.com. Easy-going, slightly grungy tavern with a great juke box, live music (Mon & Wed eve, plus Sun lunchtime) and DJs (Fri, Sat & Sun). There's bar billiards and a beer garden with table footy. Mon–Sat 11.30am–11pm, Sun noon–10.30pm.

The George Mill Lane, Bathampton ⓣ 01225 425079, ⓦ chefandbrewer.com. Popular canal-side pub a 20min walk from the centre, with local ales and better than average bar food. There's plenty of outside seating. By car, it's off the Warminster road, at the bottom of Bathampton Lane. Mon–Sat 11am–11pm, Sun noon–10.30pm.

BATH'S FESTIVALS

There's a great range of festivals throughout the year, notably the **Bath International Music Festival** (Ⓦbathmusicfest.org.uk), held between mid-May and June and featuring jazz, classical and world music; the **Bath Fringe Festival** (late May to early June; Ⓦbathfringe.co.uk), with the accent on art and performance; and **Bath Literature Festival** (ten days in Feb/March; Ⓦbathlitfest.org.uk). For further information on these and other festivals, contact the festivals office at 2 Church St, Abbey Green (Ⓣ01225 463362, Ⓦbathfestivals.org.uk).

The Porter 2 Miles Buildings, George St Ⓣ01225 424104, Ⓦtheporter.co.uk. Very relaxed café/pub serving good beer, coffees and all-veggie food until 9pm, with free wi-fi. There are tables outside and nightly music and comedy events in the *Cellar Bar* (see below). Mon–Wed noon–midnight, Thurs noon–2am, Fri & Sat noon–3am, Sun noon–11.30pm.

The Raven 7 Queen St Ⓣ01225 425045, Ⓦtheravenofbath.co.uk. Civilized watering hole with first-rate local ales (try the Raven Gold), served both downstairs and in the less crowded upstairs room (unless one of the regular readings and talks are being held there). Food available, including renowned pies. Mon–Thurs 11.30am–11pm, Fri & Sat 11.30am–midnight, Sun noon–10.30pm.

NIGHTLIFE AND ENTERTAINMENT

The two or three **theatres** in town often stage productions before or after their London run, but most are fairly mainstream. Bath's **music** scene is lively, especially during the festival (see above), while its small (and relaxed) clubbing scene, overshadowed by the proximity of Bristol, takes place mostly in unventilated basements.

Back to Mine The Paragon Ⓣ01225 425677, Ⓦbacktomineclub.co.uk. For a slightly older, more laidback crowd – there's even a back room for real conversation – this club plays everything from retro to reggae (and has poker too). Mon–Sat 10pm–2am.

Chapel Arts Centre St James Memorial Hall, Lower Borough Walls Ⓣ01225 461700, Ⓦchapelarts.org. Nice little venue for all kinds of performing arts, with an emphasis on jazz, blues and folk. Arrive early to get one of the cabaret-style tables.

The Common Room 2 Saville Row Ⓣ01225 425550. Intimate spot for late-night chat and chilled sounds, though things get a bit more raucous at the weekends. There's a small dancefloor and a quieter room upstairs. Sun–Thurs 8pm–2am, Fri & Sat 8pm–3am.

★ **Moles** George St Ⓣ01225 404445, Ⓦmoles.co.uk. This Bath institution features a mix of live music and DJs. The cramped basement can get pretty hot and sweaty though – not for claustrophobes. Sun & Mon 11am–midnight, Tues & Wed 11am–2am, Thurs 11am–3am, Fri & Sat 11am–4am.

The Porter Cellar Bar 2 Miles Buildings, George St Ⓣ01225 424104, Ⓦtheporter.co.uk. Below The *Porter* pub (see above), the *Cellar Bar* has free live music (Mon–Thurs) and DJs (Fri & Sat). Comedy nights (Sun) cost £7. Mon–Wed noon–midnight, Thurs noon–2am, Fri & Sat noon–3am, Sun noon–11.30pm.

Theatre Royal Sawclose Ⓣ01225 448844, Ⓦtheatreroyal.org.uk. Theatre and ballet fans should check out what's showing at this historic venue, if only for the atmosphere. More experimental productions are staged in its Ustinov Studio. Book as early as you can.

Wells

WELLS, twenty miles south of Bristol across the Somerset border and the same distance southwest from Bath, is a miniature cathedral city that has not significantly altered in eight hundred years.

Wells Cathedral

Cathedral Green • Daily: April–Sept 7am–7pm; Oct–March 7am–6pm • £6 • Ⓣ01749 674483, Ⓦwellscathedral.org.uk

Hidden from sight until you pass into its spacious close from the central Market Place, **Wells Cathedral** presents a majestic spectacle, the broad lawn of the former graveyard providing a perfect foreground. The west front teems with some three hundred thirteenth-century figures of saints and kings, once brightly painted and gilded, though

5

their present honey tint has a subtle splendour of its own. The facade was constructed about fifty years after work on the main building was begun in 1180.

The **interior** is a supreme example of early English Gothic, the long nave punctuated by a dramatic "scissor arch", one of three that were constructed in 1338 to take the extra weight of the newly built tower. Beyond the arch, there are some gnarled old tombs to be seen in the aisles of the **Quire**, at the end of which is the richly coloured stained glass of the fourteenth-century **Lady Chapel**. The **capitals and corbels** of the transepts hold some amusing narrative carvings – look out for the men with toothache and an old man caught pilfering an orchard – and, in the north transept, there's a 24-hour astronomical clock dating from 1390. From his seat high up on the right of the clock, a figure known as Jack Blandiver kicks a couple of bells every quarter-hour, heralding the appearance of a pair of jousting knights charging at each other, and on the hour he strikes the bell in front of him.

Wells & Mendip Museum

8 Cathedral Green • Easter–Oct Mon–Sat 10am–5pm, Sun 1.30–4pm; Nov–Easter Mon–Sat 11am–4pm, Sun 1.30–4pm • £3 • T 01749 673477, W wellsmuseum.org.uk

The row of clerical houses on the north side of Cathedral Green mainly dates from the seventeenth and eighteenth centuries (though one of the houses, the **Old Deanery**, shows traces of its fifteenth-century origins). The chancellor's house is now the **Wells & Mendip Museum**, displaying some of the cathedral's original statuary as well as a good geological section with fossils from the Mendip area.

Bishop's Palace

Daily: April–Oct 10.30am–6pm, occasionally closed Sat from 2pm for functions; last entry at 5pm • £5.45 • T 01749 988111, W bishopspalacewells.co.uk

The tranquil grounds of the **Bishop's Palace**, residence of the Bishop of Bath and Wells, are reachable through the Bishop's Eye archway from Market Place. The palace was walled and moated as a result of a rift with the borough in the fourteenth century, and the imposing gatehouse still displays the grooves of the portcullis and a chute for pouring oil and molten lead on would-be assailants. The gardens contain the springs from which the city takes its name and the scanty but impressive remains of the **Great Hall**, built at the end of the thirteenth century and despoiled during the Reformation. Across the lawn stands the square **Bishop's Chapel**, a few state rooms holding displays relating to the history of the site and the **Undercroft** café.

ARRIVAL AND INFORMATION — WELLS

By bus Wells' bus station is off Market St.

Destinations Bath (Mon–Sat hourly, Sun 6 daily; 1hr 20min); Bridgwater (Mon–Sat hourly; 1hr 30min); Bristol (every 30min–1hr; 1hr 15min); Glastonbury (1–4 hourly; 20min); Wookey Hole (Mon–Sat every 30min–1hr, Sun 4 daily; 30min).

Tourist office There's an info desk in the Wells & Mendip Museum, 8 Cathedral Green (Easter–Sept Mon–Sat 10am–5pm, Sun 1.30am–4pm; Oct–Easter Sun 1.30am–4pm; T 01749 671770, W wellssomerset.com).

ACCOMMODATION

★ **Canon Grange** Cathedral Green T 01749 671800, W canongrange.co.uk. Parts of this B&B date back to 1450. Three of the traditionally furnished rooms face the west front of the cathedral, and breakfast, which can cover various dietary requirements, is taken overlooking the green. **£72**

The Crown Market Place T 01749 673457, W crownatwells.co.uk. Fifteenth-century coaching inn where William Penn was arrested in 1695 for illegal preaching. It's got a suitably old-fashioned flavour that verges on the fusty and faded. Can be noisy from the bar and bistro below or the Saturday market. **£95**

Swan Hotel Sadler St T 01749 836300, W swanhotelwells.co.uk. A swankier choice than *The Crown*, this rambling inn has plenty of antique character and a rated restaurant (for which booking is essential). Pricier rooms have cathedral views. **£120**

EATING AND DRINKING

City Arms Cuthbert St ⓣ01749 673916, ⓦthecityarmsatwells.com. Formerly the city jail, this is a good place to taste the local beers or take a full meal in the restaurant (most dishes around £8, steaks £15). There's also seating in the plant-filled courtyard. Daily 10am–11pm.

★ **Good Earth** Priory Rd ⓣ01749 678600. Excellent organic produce is served at this inexpensive vegetarian café near the bus station, with pizzas, stews and salads as well as delicious takeaway goodies. Expect queues at lunchtime. Mon–Sat 9am–5pm.

Old Spot 12 Sadler St ⓣ01749 689099, ⓦtheoldspot.co.uk. Spacious, easy-going place with Old Spot pork among other items on the eclectic set-price two- and three-course menus (lunch £19.50/£22.50, dinner £23.50/£28.50). Tues 7–10.30pm, Wed–Sat 12.30–2.30pm & 7–10.30pm, Sun 12.30–2.30pm.

The Mendips

Northwest of Wells, the **Mendip Hills** are chiefly famous for **Wookey Hole** – the most impressive of many caves in this narrow limestone chain – and for **Cheddar Gorge**, where a walk through the narrow cleft makes a starting point for more adventurous trips across the Mendips. Both can be reached on regular buses from Wells.

Wookey Hole

Two miles northwest of Wells • Daily: April–Oct 10am–6pm; Nov–March 10am–5pm; last tour 1hr before closing • £16 • ⓣ01749 672243, ⓦwookey.co.uk

It's folklore rather than geology that takes precedence at **Wookey Hole**, a stunning cave complex of deep pools and intricate rock formations hollowed out by the River Axe. Highlight of the hour-long tour is the alleged petrified remains of the Witch of Wookey, a "blear-eyed hag" who was said to turn her evil eye on crops, young lovers and local farmers. To finish off, there's a functioning Victorian paper mill, rooms containing speleological exhibits, and a collection of Edwardian fairground pieces.

ARRIVAL AND DEPARTURE **WOOKEY HOLE**

Regular **buses** run to Wookey Hole from Wells (Mon–Sat every 30min–1hr, Sun 4 daily; 30min).

ACCOMMODATION AND EATING

Wookey Hole Inn ⓣ01749 676677, ⓦwookeyholeinn.com. Very close to the caves, this is a great place to stay the night, with funky, fully equipped guest rooms. The bar serves a range of Belgian beers, while the restaurant (booking essential) offers a range of ambitious, expensive dishes (£9–15 at lunch, £14–24 eves). Bar Mon–Sat noon–2.30pm & 7–11pm, Sun noon–6pm; restaurant Mon–Sat noon–2.30pm & 7–9.30pm, Sun noon–3pm. **£90**

Cheddar Gorge

Six miles west of Wookey on the A371, the nondescript village of **Cheddar** has given its name to Britain's best-known cheese – most of it now mass-produced far from here – and is also renowned for the **Cheddar Gorge**, lying beyond the neighbourhood of Tweentown about a mile to the north.

Cutting a jagged gash across the Mendip Hills, the limestone gorge is an amazing geological phenomenon, though its natural beauty is rather compromised by the minor road running through it and by the Lower Gorge's mile of shops and parking areas. Few trippers venture further than the first few curves of the gorge, which holds its most dramatic scenery, though each turn of the two-mile length presents new, sometimes startling vistas.

At its narrowest the road squeezes between cliffs towering almost 500ft above. Those in a state of honed fitness can climb the 274 steps of **Jacob's Ladder** to a cliff-top viewpoint looking towards Glastonbury Tor, with occasional glimpses of Exmoor and the sea (daily: 10am–5.30pm; winter 10.30am–4.30pm; £4.80, free to Cheddar Caves

5

ticket-holders) – or you can reach the same spot more easily via the narrow lane winding up behind the cliffs. There's a circular three-mile cliff-top Gorge Walk, and you can branch off along marked paths to such secluded spots as **Black Rock**, just two miles from Cheddar, or **Black Down**, at 1067ft the Mendips' highest point.

Cheddar Caves

Daily: July, Aug & school hols 10am–5.30pm; Sept–June 10.30am–5pm • £17.80 • Ⓦ visitcheddar.co.uk

Beneath the towering Cheddar Gorge, the **Cheddar Caves** were scooped out by underground rivers in the wake of the Ice Age, and subsequently occupied by primitive communities. Today the caves are floodlit to pick out the subtle tones of the rock, and the array of rock formations that resemble organ pipes, waterfalls and giant birds. Tickets include a trip through the Gorge on an **open-top bus** (mid Feb to March & Oct Sat & Sun; daily April–Sept; no service in rainy weather).

ARRIVAL AND DEPARTURE — CHEDDAR GORGE

The #126 **bus** runs to and from Wells (Mon–Sat hourly, 4 on Sun; 35min).

ACCOMMODATION

Cheddar Bridge Park Draycott Rd, off Wells Rd Ⓣ 01934 743048, Ⓦ cheddarbridge.co.uk. Most central of the local campsites, with the River Yeo running through, this adult-only campsite has spotless facilities and wi-fi. There are also apartments to rent (**£60** daily) and static caravans. No under-18s. Closed Dec to early March. From **£10**

Chedwell Cottage 59–61 Redcliffe St, off Cliff St and Union St Ⓣ 01934/743268, Ⓔ info@chedwellcottage.co.uk. In a quiet lane a 10min walk from the gorge, this B&B has three simply furnished en-suite rooms, and fresh fruit salad, yoghurt and free-range eggs for breakfast. No credit cards. **£60**

YHA Cheddar Hillfield, off The Hayes Ⓣ 0845 371 9730, Ⓔ cheddar@yha.org.uk. A 10min walk from the gorge, this modernized Victorian house offers basic but clean and warm facilities; call to check winter opening. **£10**

Glastonbury

On the southern edge of the Mendips and six miles south of Wells, **GLASTONBURY**, famed for its annual music festival, is built around the evocative set of ruins belonging to its former abbey. The town lies at the heart of the so-called **Isle of Avalon**, a region rich with mystical associations, and for centuries it has been one of the main Arthurian sites of the West Country – today it's an enthusiastic centre for all manner of New Age cults.

Glastonbury Abbey

Daily: March–May 9am–6pm; June–Aug 9am–9pm; Sept–Nov 9am–5pm; Dec–Feb 9am–4pm • £6 • Ⓣ 01458 832267, Ⓦ glastonburyabbey.com

Aside from its mythological origins, **Glastonbury Abbey** can claim to be the country's oldest Christian foundation, dating back to the seventh century and possibly earlier. Enlarged by St Dunstan in the tenth century, it became the richest Benedictine abbey in the country; three Anglo-Saxon kings (Edmund, Edgar and Edmund Ironside) were buried here, and the library had a far-reaching fame. Further expansion took place under the Normans, though most of the additions were destroyed by fire in 1184. Rebuilt, the abbey was later a casualty of the Dissolution of the Monasteries in the 1530s, and the ruins, now hidden behind walls and nestled among grassy parkland, can only hint at its former extent. The most prominent remains are the transept piers and the shell of the Lady Chapel, with its carved figures of the Annunciation, the Magi and Herod.

The abbey's **choir** holds what is alleged to be the tomb of **Arthur and Guinevere.** The discovery of two bodies in an ancient cemetery outside the abbey in 1191 was taken to confirm that here was, indeed, the mystic Avalon, and they were transferred here in 1278. Elsewhere in the grounds, the fourteenth-century **abbot's kitchen** is the only

GLASTONBURY TALES

At the heart of the complex web of **myths surrounding Glastonbury** is the early Christian legend that the young Jesus once visited this site, a story that is not as far-fetched as it sounds. The Romans had a heavy presence in the area, mining lead in the Mendips, and one of these mines was owned by **Joseph of Arimathea**, a well-to-do merchant said to have been related to Mary. It's not completely impossible that the merchant took his kinsman on one of his many visits to his property, in a period of Christ's life of which nothing is recorded. It was this possibility to which William Blake referred in his *Glastonbury Hymn*, better known as *Jerusalem*: – "And did those feet in ancient times/Walk upon England's mountains green?"

Another legend relates how Joseph was imprisoned for twelve years after the Crucifixion, miraculously kept alive by the **Holy Grail**, the chalice of the Last Supper, in which the blood was gathered from the wound in Christ's side. The Grail, along with the spear which had caused the wound, were later taken by Joseph to Glastonbury, where he founded the abbey and commenced the conversion of Britain.

Glastonbury is also popularly identified with the mythical **Avalon**; the story goes that King Arthur, having been mortally wounded in battle, sailed to Avalon where he was buried alongside his queen – somehow Glastonbury was taken to be the best candidate for the place.

monastic building to survive intact, with four huge corner fireplaces and a great central lantern above. Behind the main entrance to the grounds, look out for the thorn tree that is supposedly a descendant of the original **Glastonbury Thorn** said to have sprouted from the staff of Joseph of Arimathea. Big-name **concerts and drama productions** take place in the abbey grounds in summer – check the website for details.

Glastonbury Lake Village Museum

Glastonbury High St • Mon–Sat 10am–4pm • EH • £2.50

Abbots once presided over legal cases in the fourteenth-century **Tribunal**; it later became a hotel for pilgrims, and now holds the tourist office and the small **Glastonbury Lake Village Museum**, which displays finds from the Iron Age villages that fringed the former marshland below the Tor.

Somerset Rural Life Museum

Chilkwell St • April–Oct Tues–Sat 10am–5pm • Free • ⓣ 01458 831197

On the southeastern edge of the abbey grounds, the fourteenth-century Abbey Barn is centrepiece of the excellent **Somerset Rural Life Museum**, which focuses on local rural occupations from cheese- and cider-making to peat-digging, thatching and farming.

Chalice Well

Chilkwell St • Daily: April–Oct 10am–6pm; Nov–March 10am–4.30pm • £3.60 • ⓣ 01458 831154, ⓦ chalicewell.org.uk

The **Chalice Well** stands amid a lush garden intended for quiet contemplation at the foot of Glastonbury Tor. The iron-red waters of the well – which is fondly supposed to be the hiding place of the Holy Grail – were considered to have curative properties, making the town a spa for a brief period in the eighteenth century, and they are still prized (there's a tap in Wellhouse Lane).

Glastonbury Tor

From Chilkwell Street, turn left into Wellhouse Lane and immediately right for the footpath that leads up to **Glastonbury Tor**, at 521ft a landmark for miles around. The conical hill – topped by the dilapidated **St Michael's Tower**, sole remnant of a

5

GLASTONBURY FESTIVAL

Glastonbury is, of course, best known for its **music festival** (glastonburyfestivals.co.uk), which takes place most years over four days at the end of June outside the nearby village of Pilton. Having started as a small hippy affair in the 1970s, the festival has become one of the biggest in the country, without shedding too much of its alternative feel. Bands range from huge acts such as Elbow to up-and-coming indie groups, via old hands such as U2, while performance art, circus, club nights and all manner of shenanigans take place around the sprawling complex. Though **tickets** cost around £200, they are snapped up almost immediately after going on sale in October.

fourteenth-century church – commands stupendous views. Pilgrims once embarked on the stiff climb here with hard peas in their shoes as penance – nowadays people come to feel the vibrations of crossing ley lines.

ARRIVAL AND INFORMATION — GLASTONBURY

By bus Frequent buses #29, #376 and #377 connect Glastonbury with Wells; #376 also goes to Bristol and #29 goes to Taunton.

Destinations Bristol (Mon–Sat hourly, Sun 6 daily; 1hr 35min); Taunton (Mon–Sat hourly; 1hr 10min); Wells (Mon–Sat 4 hourly, Sun every 30min–1hr; 20–30min).

Tourist office In the Tribunal on the High St (Mon–Sat 10am–4pm; 01458 832954, glastonburytic.co.uk).

Internet There's internet access in the tourist office, and a relaxed internet café in Glastonbury's Assembly Rooms (Tues–Sat noon–6pm; assemblyrooms.org.uk), reached through a courtyard off the High St.

GETTING AROUND

By bus You can save some legwork by using the Glastonbury Tor Bus (April–Sept daily 9.30am–7pm; £3 valid all day), which runs from the abbey car park to the base of the Tor, and stops at the Rural Life Museum and Chalice Well.

By bike The *Hundred Monkeys* café (see below) rents bikes for £5–10/half-day.

ACCOMMODATION

George & Pilgrim Hotel 1 High St 01458 831146, relaxinnz.co.uk. This fifteenth-century oak-panelled inn with mullioned windows brims with medieval atmosphere. Some of the rooms are a bit ordinary, though – go for one of the older ones, which include four-posters. **£100**

Glastonbury Backpackers 4 Market Place 01458 833353, glastonburybackpackers.com. Above *The Crown* inn (see below), this is a bit scuffed, but clean enough, with a kitchen, a games room, wi-fi access and no curfew. Can get noisy from the lively bar. Dorm **£16.50**, double **£60**

Mapleleaf Middlewick Cottages Wick Lane 01458 832351, middlewickholidaycottages.co.uk. A mile and a half north of town, this Canadian-run place offers self-catering cottages in rural surroundings. There's a steam room, indoor pool, barbecue and pizza oven. Minimum one-week stay in July & Aug. **£85**

★ **White House 21** Manor House Rd 01458 830886, theglastonburywhitehouse.com. Lovely eco-friendly B&B with two en-suite rooms. An optional organic breakfast (£7.50–10) can be served in your room. They offer aromatherapy and reflexology, and free internet. No credit cards. **£55**

EATING AND DRINKING

Blue Note Café 4 High St 01458 832907. A relaxed place to hang out over coffees and cakes with some courtyard seating. It's vegetarian and mostly organic, with nourishing soups, salads and schnitzels (around £8). Mon–Sat 9.30am–5pm.

The Crown Market Place 01458 833353. A convivial spot for drinks and snacks at all hours, with TVs showing live sport. In the evenings you can sample acoustic music (Thurs), DJs (Fri), bands (Sat) and jazz (Sun).

★ **Hundred Monkeys** 52 High St 01458 833386. Mellow café-restaurant with a courtyard. Wholesome snacks and full meals include a renowned seafood soup. Mains £9–12. Mon, Tues & Thurs 10am–8pm, Wed 10am–4pm, Fri & Sat 10am–9pm, Sun 11am–4pm.

Who'd a Thought It 17 Northload St 01458 834460, whodathoughtit.co.uk. Quirkily decorated inn with a patio, serving real ales alongside well-executed meals such as Cornish mussels (£5.50), home-made pies (£9.50), vegetarian dishes (£10.50) and local lamb and beef (£14–17). Evening meals should be booked. Food served Mon–Thurs noon–2pm & 6–9pm, Fri & Sat noon–2pm & 6–9.30pm, Sun noon–2pm & 6.30–9pm; bar Mon–Sat 11am–11pm, Sun 11.45am–10.30pm.

Taunton

Travelling west from Glastonbury, your route could take you through Bridgwater and **Taunton,** Somerset's county town. Either would make a handy starting point for excursions into the Quantock Hills (see below), but Taunton, home to the new **Museum of Somerset**, is of more interest. While in town, take a look at the pinnacled and battlemented towers of its two most important churches – **St James** on Coal Orchard and **St Mary Magdalene** on Church Square – both fifteenth-century structures remodelled by the Victorians.

Museum of Somerset

Taunton Castle, Castle Green • Tues–Sat 10am–5pm • Free • ⓣ 01823 278805

Taunton Castle, started in the twelfth century, staged the trial of royal claimant Perkin Warbeck, who in 1490 declared himself to be the Duke of York, the younger of the "Princes in the Tower" – the sons of Edward IV, who had been murdered seven years earlier. Most of the structure was pulled down in 1662 and much of the rest has been altered, and it now houses the **Museum of Somerset**, a wide-ranging display that includes finds from Somerset's Lake Villages; the "Frome Hoard" – the second largest collection of Roman coins ever discovered in Britain – and a superb fragment of Roman mosaic found near Langport. Part of the castle houses the Great Hall where Judge Jeffreys held one of his "Bloody Assizes" following the Monmouth Rebellion of 1685 – his portrait is on display, alongside a few bits of personal memorabilia.

ARRIVAL AND INFORMATION — TAUNTON

By train The train station lies a 20min walk north of town. For the West Somerset Railway, whose terminus lies at Bishop's Lydeard, see p.278.

Destinations Bristol (every 20–30min; 55min); Exeter (every 30–30min; 30min).

By bus Taunton's bus station is off Castle Green.

Destinations Bishop's Lydeard (Mon–Sat every 20–30min, Sun hourly; 30min); Exeter (3 daily; 45min–1hr); Glastonbury (5–6 daily; 50min); Minehead (Mon–Sat every 30min, Sun hourly; 1hr 30min); Wells (Mon–Sat 1hr 25min; 1hr 20min).

Tourist office In the library building, Paul St (Mon–Sat 9.30am–4.30pm; ⓣ 01823 336344, ⓦ heartofsomerset.com). Provides information and publications on the whole area, including the Quantocks.

ACCOMMODATION

The Castle Castle Green ⓣ 01823 272671, ⓦ the-castle-hotel.com. The town's most atmospheric hotel is an upmarket choice, a wisteria-clad, three-hundred-year-old mansion next to Taunton Castle, exuding an appropriately old-fashioned baronial style. Breakfast costs £15.50 on top of room rates. **£190**

★ **The Old Mill** Netherclay, Bishop's Hull ⓣ 01823 289732, ⓦ bandbtaunton.co.uk. Right on the River Tone, this peaceful B&B in a village 2 miles west of town only has a couple of rooms; the larger one is worth the slightly higher price for its river views. Restored pieces of the old mill machinery lend the place the air of a small museum. No credit cards. **£65**

EATING AND DRINKING

The Brewhouse Coal Orchard ⓣ 01823 283244, ⓦ thebrewhouse.net. This arts centre by the river has a snack bar and a more formal restaurant, *Edwardo's* (set menus £14 for two courses, £18 for three before 7pm, otherwise £18/£22). There are tables inside and out. Mon–Sat 10am–11pm, or 6pm on nights with no performances.

The Cosy Club Hunts Court, Corporation St ⓣ 01803 253476, ⓦ cosyclub.co.uk. In a converted ex-art college, this bar has several rooms on two floors, with comfy chairs and quirky decor. Coffees, teas and snacks are available; tapas are £8 for three, burgers £8–9. Sun–Wed 9am–11pm, Thurs–Sat 9am–2.30am; food served till 10pm.

The Quantock Hills

Extending for some twelve miles north of Taunton and rising to 1260ft, the **Quantock Hills** are fairly off the beaten track, enclosed by a triangle of roads leading coastwards from

5

Bridgwater and Taunton. Steep, narrow lanes connect the snug villages set in scenic wooded valleys or "combes" that are watered by clear streams and grazed by red deer.

Nether Stowey and around

Eight miles west of Bridgwater on the A39, on the edge of the hills, the pretty village of **NETHER STOWEY** is best known for its association with **Samuel Taylor Coleridge**, who in 1796 walked here from Bristol to join his wife and child at their new home. Soon afterwards William Wordsworth and his sister Dorothy moved into the grander Alfoxden House, a couple of miles down the road near Holford. The year that Coleridge and Wordsworth spent as neighbours was extraordinarily productive – Coleridge composed some of his best poetry at this time, including *The Rime of the Ancient Mariner* and *Kubla Khan*, and the two poets collaborated on the *Lyrical Ballads*, the poetic manifesto of early English Romanticism.

Coleridge Cottage

35 Lime St • April–Sept Thurs–Sun 2–5pm • NT • £4 • ⓣ 01643 821314

At this "miserable cottage", as Sara Coleridge called what is now **Coleridge Cottage**, you can see the poet's parlour and reading room, and, upstairs, his bedroom and an exhibition room containing various letters and first editions. Rooms, including the kitchen, are laid out as they would have been in the eighteenth century, filled with the family's personal belongings and mementos.

Pick up leaflets at the Coleridge cottage (or consult ⓦ coleridgeway.co.uk) about the **Coleridge Way**, a walking route that supposedly follows the poet's footsteps between Nether Stowey and Porlock (see p.281) on the Exmoor coast; waymarked with quill signs, the 36-mile hike passes through some of the most scenic parts of the Quantocks and Exmoor.

The western Quantocks

On the southwestern edge of the Quantocks, the village of **BISHOPS LYDEARD**, terminus of the West Somerset Railway, is worth a wander, not least for **St Mary's** church, with a splendid tower and carved bench ends inside. A couple of miles north, **COMBE FLOREY** is almost exclusively built of the pink-red sandstone characteristic of Quantock villages. For over fifteen years (1829–45), the local rector was the unconventional cleric Sydney Smith, called "the greatest master of ridicule since Swift" by Macaulay; more recently it was home to Evelyn Waugh.

A little over three miles further north along the A358, **CROWCOMBE** is another typical cob-and-thatch Quantock village, with a well-preserved Church House from 1515 and a lovely old church with a superb collection of pagan-looking carved bench-ends. A minor road from here winds up to Triscombe Stone, in the heart of the Quantocks, from where a footpath leads to the range's highest point at **Wills Neck** (1260ft), about a mile distant.

THE WEST SOMERSET RAILWAY

Fringing the western side of the Quantocks, the **West Somerset Railway** (ⓣ 01643 704996, ⓦ west-somerset-railway.co.uk) is a restored branch line that runs some twenty miles between the station outside the village of Bishops Lydeard, five miles out of Taunton, to Minehead on the Somerset coast (see p.280; 1hr 15min; £10.40 one way, £15.60 return). Between late March and October (plus some winter dates), up to eight steam and diesel trains depart daily from Bishops Lydeard, stopping at renovated stations on the way. Rover tickets, allowing multiple journeys, cost £15.60/day, £29/two days, and bikes travel at 25 percent of the adult rate. Bus #28 goes to Bishops Lydeard station from Taunton's centre and train station.

Stretching between Wills Neck and the village of Aisholt, the moorland plateau of **Aisholt Common** is best explored from **West Bagborough**, where a five-mile path starts at Birches Corner. Lower down the slopes, outside Aisholt, the banks of **Hawkridge Reservoir** make a lovely picnic stop.

GETTING AROUND — THE QUANTOCK HILLS

Public transport is minimal. The **West Somerset Railway** (see opposite) stops near some of the villages along the west flank of the range, though you'll need your own transport or foot-power to reach the best spots.

ACCOMMODATION

★ **The Blue Ball Inn** Triscombe ⓣ01984 618242, ⓦblueballinn.info. This secluded inn below Wills Neck has two tastefully decorated B&B rooms and a self-catering cottage accommodating up to four. Meals, good ales and a nice pub garden are on hand. **£75**

Mill Farm Caravan and Camping Park Fiddington, a couple of miles east of Nether Stowey ⓣ01278 732286, ⓦmillfarm.biz. Signposted outside the village of Fiddington, this family-friendly site has indoor and outdoor pools, a boating lake, a gym and pony rides. Advance booking essential at peak times.

★ **The Old House** Nether Stowey ⓣ01278 732392, ⓦtheoldhouse-quantocks.co.uk. This large house in the centre of the village once accommodated Coleridge. The two rooms – Sarah's Room and the huge Coleridge Suite – are period-furnished, and there's an acre of garden. Self-catering cottages also available. **£70**

★ **Parsonage Farm** Over Stowey, a mile south of Nether Stowey ⓣ01278 733237, ⓦparsonfarm.co.uk. Next to a lovely old Quantock church, this homely B&B with its own orchard and walled kitchen garden has stone floors, brick fireplaces and heaps of character. Run organically and sustainably by a native of Vermont, it offers a Vermont breakfast among other options, and simple candlelit suppers (£10). No credit cards. **£60**

Quantock Orchard Caravan Park Flaxpool, Crowcombe ⓣ01984 618618, ⓦquantock-orchard.co.uk. Just off the A358 and a few minutes' walk from the West Somerset Railway stop at Crowcombe Heathfield, this small, neat site is convenient for walks around Wills Neck. It offers a gym and heated outdoor pool (May–Sept), and has static caravans to rent (£55/night or £385/week in high season). There's a small shop but no restaurant. Bike hire available.

EATING AND DRINKING

Carew Arms Crowcombe ⓣ01984 618631, ⓦthecarewarms.co.uk. Don't be put off by the stags' heads covering the walls and the riding boots by the fire – this is a delightful rustic pub with a skittles alley and a spacious garden. Local ales complement the top-notch nosh (£12–17). Rooms also available. Bar daily noon–11pm; food served Tues–Sat noon–2pm & 7–9pm, Sun & Mon noon–2pm.

Farmers Arms Combe Florey ⓣ01823 432267, ⓦfarmersarmsatcombeflorey.co.uk. Signposted off the A39 just south of the village, this tidily thatched old pub has log fires, a garden and a menu strong on lamb and poultry (mains £8.50–9.50 at lunchtime, £14–16 in the evening). Booking advisable at peak times. Bar daily noon–11pm; food served noon–2.30pm & 7–9pm.

Rose and Crown St Mary's St, Nether Stowey ⓣ01278 732265, ⓦroseandcrown-netherstowey.co.uk. Good local ales and excellent bar meals at this cosy village inn (en-suite rooms are available), and there's a nice walled garden. The menu includes curries and steaks, mostly £7–9. Bar Mon–Sat noon–11pm, Sun noon–10.30pm; food served daily noon–2pm & 6–8.30pm.

Exmoor

A high bare plateau sliced by wooded combes and splashing rills, **EXMOOR** can present one of the most forbidding landscapes in England, especially when shrouded in a sea mist. When it's clear, though, the moorland of this National Park reveals rich swathes of colour and an amazing diversity of wildlife, from buzzards to the unique **Exmoor ponies**, a breed closely related to prehistoric horses and now on the endangered breeds list. In the treeless heartland of the moor in particular, it's not difficult to spot these short and stocky animals, though fewer than twelve hundred are registered, and of these only about 150 are free-living on the moor. Much more elusive are the **red deer**, England's largest native wild animal, of which Exmoor supports the country's only wild population, currently around three thousand.

5

Endless **walking routes** are possible along a network of some six hundred miles of footpaths and bridleways, and **horseback riding** is another option for getting the most out of Exmoor's desolate beauty – visitor centres can supply details of guided walks and local stables. Whether walking or riding, bear in mind that over seventy percent of the National Park is privately owned and that access is theoretically restricted to public rights of way; special permission should certainly be sought before camping, canoeing, fishing or similar. Check the website ⓦactiveexmoor.com for **organized activity** operators on Exmoor.

Inland, there are four obvious bases for walks, all on the Somerset side of the county border: **Dulverton** in the southeast, site of the main information facilities; **Simonsbath** in the centre; **Exford**, near Exmoor's highest point of Dunkery Beacon; and the attractive village of **Winsford**, close to the A396 on the east of the moor. Exmoor's coastline offers an alluring alternative to the open moorland, all of it accessible via the **South West Coast Path**, which embarks on its long coastal journey at **Minehead**, though there is more charm to be found further west at the sister villages of **Lynmouth** and **Lynton**, just over the Devon border.

Dulverton and the eastern moor

The village of **DULVERTON**, on the southern edge of the National Park, is the Park Authority's headquarters and, with its cafés and shops, makes a good entry point to Exmoor. Five miles north, just west of the A396, **WINSFORD** lays justified claim to being the moor's prettiest hamlet. A scattering of thatched cottages ranged around a sleepy green, it is watered by a confluence of streams and rivers – including the Exe – giving it no fewer than seven bridges.

Four miles northwest of Winsford, the village of **EXFORD**, an ancient crossing point on the River Exe, is popular with hunting folk as well as with walkers for the four-mile hike to **Dunkery Beacon**, Exmoor's highest point at 1700ft.

Exmoor Forest and Simonsbath

At the heart of the National Park lies **Exmoor Forest**, the barest part of the moor, scarcely populated except by roaming sheep and a few red deer – the word "forest" denotes simply that it was a hunting reserve. In the middle of it stands the village of **SIMONSBATH** (pronounced "Simmonsbath"), once home to the Knight family, who bought the forest in 1818 and, by introducing tenant farmers, building roads and importing sheep, brought systematic agriculture to an area that had never before produced any income. Little more than a pub and a hotel, the village makes a useful base for exploring the Barle Valley.

Minehead

The Somerset port of **MINEHEAD** quickly became a favourite Victorian watering hole with the arrival of the railway, and it has preserved an upbeat holiday-town atmosphere ever since. Steep lanes link the two quarters of **Higher Town**, on North Hill, containing some of the oldest houses, and **Quay Town**, the harbour area. The town is a terminus for the **West Somerset Railway**, which curves eastwards into the Quantocks as far as Bishops Lydeard (see p.278), and also for the South West Coast Path (see opposite), signposted beyond the harbour.

Dunster

Three miles southeast of Minehead, the old village of **DUNSTER** is the area's major attraction. Its impressive castle rears above its well-preserved High Street, where the octagonal **Yarn Market**, dating from 1609, recalls Dunster's wool-making heyday.

THE SOUTH WEST COAST PATH

Britain's longest trail, the **South West Coast Path**, starts at Minehead and tracks the coastline along the northern seaboard of Devon and Somerset, round Cornwall, back into Devon, and on to Dorset, where it finishes close to the entrance to Poole Harbour. Much of the **630-mile route** runs on land owned by the National Trust, and all of it is well signposted.

The relevant Ordnance Survey **maps** can be found at most village shops en route, while Aurum Press (Ⓦ aurumpress.co.uk) publishes four *National Trail Guides* covering the route. The National Trail website Ⓦ southwestcoastpath.com also suggests some itineraries, while the **South West Coast Path Association** (Ⓣ 01752 896237, Ⓦ southwestcoastpath.org.uk) publishes an annual guide to the whole path, including accommodation lists, ferry timetables and transport details.

Dunster Water Mill

Mill Lane, off West St • April–Oct daily 11am–4.30pm • £3.25 • Ⓣ 01643 821759, Ⓦ dunsterwatermill.co.uk

The three-hundred-year-old **Dunster Water Mill** is still used commercially, milling the various grains which go to make the flour and muesli sold in the shop – the **café**, overlooking its riverside garden, is a good spot for lunch.

Dunster Castle

Castle: Mid-March to early April, late April to mid-July & late Aug to Oct Mon–Wed & Fri–Sun 11am–5pm; April & mid-July to late Aug daily 11am–5pm; grounds daily: mid-March to Oct 10am–5pm; Nov to mid-March 11am–4pm • NT • £8.50, grounds only £4.70 • Ⓣ 01643 821314

A landmark for miles around with its towers and turrets, **Dunster Castle** has parts dating back to the fourteenth century, but most of its fortifications were demolished following the Civil War. The structure was subjected to a thorough Victorian restoration in 1868–72, from which it emerged as something of an architectural showpiece, though its interior preserves much from its earlier incarnations. Tours take in a bedroom once occupied by Charles I, a fine seventeenth-century carved staircase, a richly decorated banqueting hall and various portraits of the Luttrells, owners of the house for six hundred years. The grounds include terraced gardens and riverside walks, all overlooked by a hilltop folly, **Conygar Tower**, dating from 1776.

Porlock

Six miles west of Minehead and cupped on three sides by the hogbacked hills of Exmoor, the thatch-and-cob houses and distinctive charm of **PORLOCK** draw armies of tourists. Many come in search of the village's literary links: according to Coleridge's own less-than-reliable testimony, it was a "man from Porlock" who broke the opium trance in which he was composing *Kubla Khan*, while the High Street's beamed *Ship Inn* features prominently in the Exmoor romance *Lorna Doone* and, in real life, sheltered the poet Robert Southey. Two miles west over reclaimed marshland, the tiny harbour of **PORLOCK WEIR** is a tranquil spot for a breath of sea air and a drink.

Lynton

Nine miles west of Porlock, just inside Devon, the Victorian resort of **LYNTON** perches above a lofty gorge with splendid views over the sea. Almost completely cut off from the rest of the country for most of its history, the village struck lucky during the Napoleonic Wars, when frustrated Grand Tourists – unable to visit their usual continental haunts – discovered in Lynton a domestic piece of Swiss landscape. Coleridge and Hazlitt trudged over to Lynton from the Quantocks, but the greatest spur to the village's popularity came with the publication in 1869 of R.D. Blackmore's Exmoor melodrama *Lorna Doone*, based on the outlaw clans who inhabited these parts in the seventeenth century.

5

Lynmouth

Some 500ft below Lynton, at the junction and estuary of the East and West Lyn rivers, **LYNMOUTH** – joined to Lynton by an ingenious **cliff railway** (mid-Feb to early Nov; £3 return; cliffrailwaylynton.co.uk), or walkable along an adjacent path – was where the poet Shelley spent nine weeks with his 16-year-old bride Harriet Westbrook, writing his polemical *Queen Mab*. At the top of the village, you can explore the walks, waterfalls and an exhibition on the uses of waterpower in the wooded **Glen Lyn Gorge** (daily: Easter–Oct 10am–6pm; Nov–Easter 10am–3pm; £5). **Boat trips** (Easter–Sept; £10; 01598 753207) depart from the harbour for Woody Bay and back – a great opportunity to view the cliffs and the birdlife that thrives on them.

ARRIVAL AND DEPARTURE — EXMOOR

By bus In addition to the bus services listed below, the Moor Rover provides a service to and from anywhere within the national park (and along the Coleridge Way, see p.278) for walkers and bikers – bikes are hitched on the back; call to book a ride at least 24hr in advance (01643 709701, atwest.org.uk).

Destinations from Dulverton: Minehead (Mon–Sat 6 daily; 1hr 25min).

Destinations from Lynmouth/Lynton: Barnstaple (Mon–Sat hourly; 1hr); Ilfracombe (April to late May & late Sept to Oct Sat & Sun 2 daily; late May to mid-Sept 3 daily; 1hr 20min); Minehead (April–Oct 3–4 daily; 50min); Porlock (April–Oct 3–4 daily; 35min).

Destinations from Minehead: Porlock (Mon–Sat every 30min–1hr, plus 3 on Sun April–Oct; 20min).

INFORMATION

NATIONAL PARK VISITOR CENTRES

Dulverton Information on the whole moor is available at the National Park Visitor Centre on Fore St (daily: April–Oct 10am–1.15pm & 1.45–5pm; Nov–March 10.30am–3pm; 01398 323841, exmoor-nationalpark.gov.uk).

Dunster At the top of Dunster Steep by the main car park (Easter–Oct daily 10am–5pm; Nov & Feb–Easter Sat & Sun 10.30am–3pm; 01643 821835, exmoor-nationalpark.gov.uk).

Lynmouth Lyndale car park by the bridge (Easter–Oct daily 10am–5pm, Nov & mid-Feb to Easter Sat & Sun 10.30am–3pm; 01598 752509, exmoor-nationalpark.gov.uk).

TOURIST OFFICES

Minehead On the seafront, close to the West Somerset Railway station on Warren Rd (01643 702624, visit-exmoor.co.uk).

Porlock West End, High St (Tues–Fri 10am–12.30pm, Sat 10am–2pm; 01643 863150, porlock.co.uk); internet access available.

Lynton Local information and internet access is available in the town hall, Lee Rd (Easter–Sept Mon–Sat 10am–5pm, Oct–Easter 10am–4pm, Sun 10am–2pm; 0845 6603232, www.lynton-lynmouth-tourism.co.uk).

ACCOMMODATION AND EATING

In addition to the options listed below, there are **YHA hostels** at Exford and Minehead, YHA-affiliated **camping barns** outside Dulverton (woodsdulverton.co.uk), and a good **campsite** near Exford (exmoorcamping.co.uk).

Andrew's on the Weir Porlock Weir 01643 863300, andrewsontheweir.co.uk. This "restaurant with rooms" offers superb, locally sourced dishes and swanky but unfussy bedrooms with magnificent sea views. Open daily 10am–7pm (last orders). Closed late Dec to late Jan. **£90**

★ **Baytree** 29 Blenheim Rd, Minehead 01643 703374, derekcole@onetel.com. Victorian B&B with spacious rooms with private bathrooms, including a family suite. The science fiction author Arthur C. Clarke was born a few doors along at no. 13. No credit cards. Closed Nov–March. **£60**

Exmoor Forest Inn Simonsbath 01643 831341, exmoorforestinn.co.uk. A friendly moorland lodge with plain but clean and comfortable rooms. The bar is good for Exmoor ales and snacks, while the restaurant serves classic English dishes (£9–15). There's a field for camping but no camping facilities. Bar daily 11am–11pm; food served daily noon–2.30pm & 6.30–9pm. **£95**

Exmoor Lodge Chapel St, Exford 01643 831694, exmoor-lodge.co.uk. Small, plain and friendly B&B, with most rooms en suite, and lots of local information on hand. Packed lunches and evening meals can be arranged. No credit cards. **£50**

★ **Glen Lodge** Hawkcombe 01643 863371, glenlodge.net. Beautifully furnished Victorian B&B offering perfect seclusion, comfort and character. There are distant sea views from the rooms and access to the moor right behind. No credit cards. **£90**

Hillside House 22 Watersmeet Rd ⓣ01598 753836, ⓦhillside-lynmouth.co.uk. Apart from the bears, this simple B&B is refreshingly free of the tweeness that affects most of the B&Bs hereabouts. Most rooms are spacious, and all but one enjoy views over the East Lyn River. Free wi-fi. **£56**

Lorna Doone Hotel High St, Porlock ⓣ01643 862404, ⓦlornadoonehotel.co.uk. This thoroughly Victorian lodging offers three sizes of rooms of varying prices, all clean, comfortable and en suite, with wi-fi access. The restaurant concentrates on local dishes for around £13–15, though there are set-price midweek menus for under £10. It's also a snug spot for snacks and teas. Food served daily 5.30–8.15pm. **£48**

Luttrell Arms 25–31 High St, Dunster ⓣ01643 821555, ⓦluttrellarms.co.uk. Traditional, atmospheric fifteenth-century inn with open fires and beamed rooms, some with four-posters. Standard rooms are more ordinary and lack views. The bar and more formal restaurant (mains £14–19) offer decent food, and there's a garden. Bar daily 10am–11pm; restaurant daily 7–9.30pm. **£100**

North Walk House North Walk, Lynton ⓣ01598 753372, ⓦnorthwalkhouse.co.uk. Top-quality B&B in a panoramic position overlooking the sea, and convenient for the coast path. The spacious, stylish rooms have rugs, wooden floors and free wi-fi. Breakfasts are filling and delicious and great organic dinners are available to guests for £24 per person. **£106**

Rising Sun Harbourside, Lynmouth ⓣ01598 753223, ⓦrisingsunlynmouth.co.uk. Rooms in this fourteenth-century inn have all the requisite beams and sloping floors. The pub and restaurant too are full of atmosphere, and attract crowds for their classic English dishes of lamb, duck and seafood (around £15) – there are few vegetarian options. Bar Mon–Sat 11am–11pm, Sun 11am–10.30pm; food served daily noon–2.30pm & 6.30–9pm in bar, 7–8.30pm in restaurant.

Royal Oak Winsford ⓣ01643 851455, ⓦroyaloak-somerset.co.uk. This thatched and rambling old inn dominates the centre of the hamlet. It offers Exmoor ales, snacks and full restaurant meals (most mains £10–14). The accommodation is plush but rooms vary, so check first. Bar Mon–Sat noon–midnight, Sun noon–11pm; food served daily noon–2.30pm & 6.30–9.30pm. **£80**

★ **St Vincent House** Castle Hill, Lynton ⓣ01598 752244, ⓦst-vincent-hotel.co.uk. This whitewashed, Georgian guesthouse has elegantly furnished, light and airy rooms, all en suite. Breakfast includes home-made yoghurt and fruit compotes, and packed lunches and Belgian beers are also available. No under-16s. Closed Nov–March. **£75**

Shelley's 8 Watersmeet Rd, Lynmouth ⓣ01598 753219, ⓦshelleyshotel.co.uk. Right next to the Glen Lyn Gorge, this traditional hotel/B&B has friendly owners, a great location and literary credentials. You can sleep in the room supposed to have been occupied by the poet Shelley when he honeymooned here. **£149**

★ **Simonsbath House** Simonsbath ⓣ01643 831259, ⓦsimonsbathhouse.co.uk. Cosy bolt hole offering spacious and plush rooms with glorious moorland views and a quality restaurant (three-course meals £35). Self-catering cottages in a converted barn are also available. **£110**

Tongdam 26 High St, Dulverton ⓣ01398 323397, ⓦtongdamthai.co.uk. Take a break from English country cooking at this Thai outpost (most dishes £10–15). There's also excellent, modern and tastefully furnished accommodation: two doubles with shared bathroom and a suite with a separate sitting room and a balcony. Food served daily noon–3pm & 6–10.30pm. **£56**

Vanilla Pod 10–12 Queens St, Lynton ⓣ01598 753706. Good wholesome meals are served at this friendly, modern restaurant, with a large choice of daily specials. Evening mains such as duck cassoulet and steak entrecôte are £10–16. Daily 10.30am–9.30pm.

Woods 4 Bank Square, Dulverton ⓣ01398 324007, ⓦwoodsdulverton.co.uk. Decorated wth a scattering of antlers, boots and riding whips, this gastropub offers traditional dishes such as grilled sole, slow-roast shoulder of pork and guinea fowl (lunch mostly £9–14, evening £14–17). Coffees and cakes are served during the day. Camping barns available. Daily noon–2.30pm & 6–9.30pm (7–9.30pm on Sun).

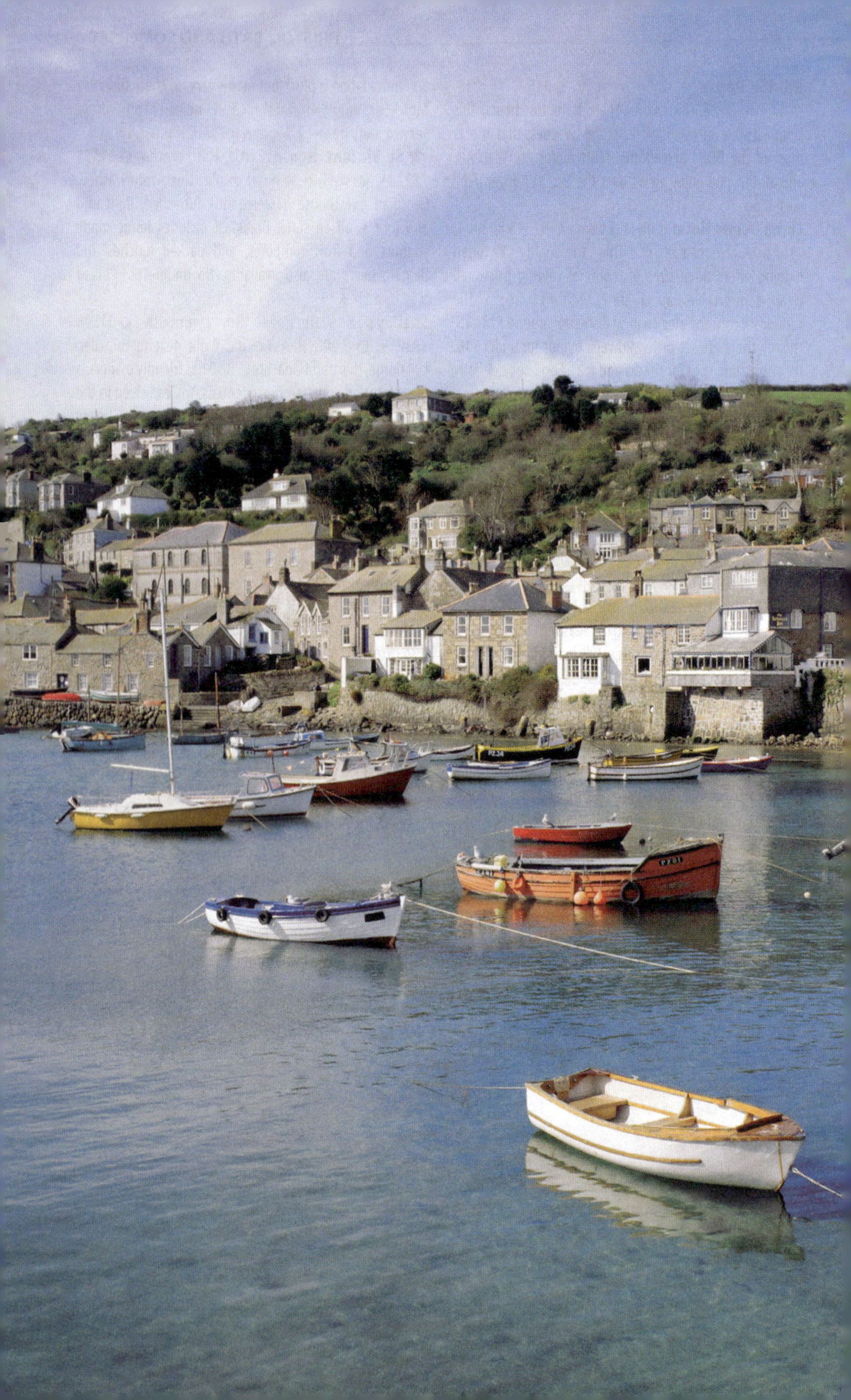

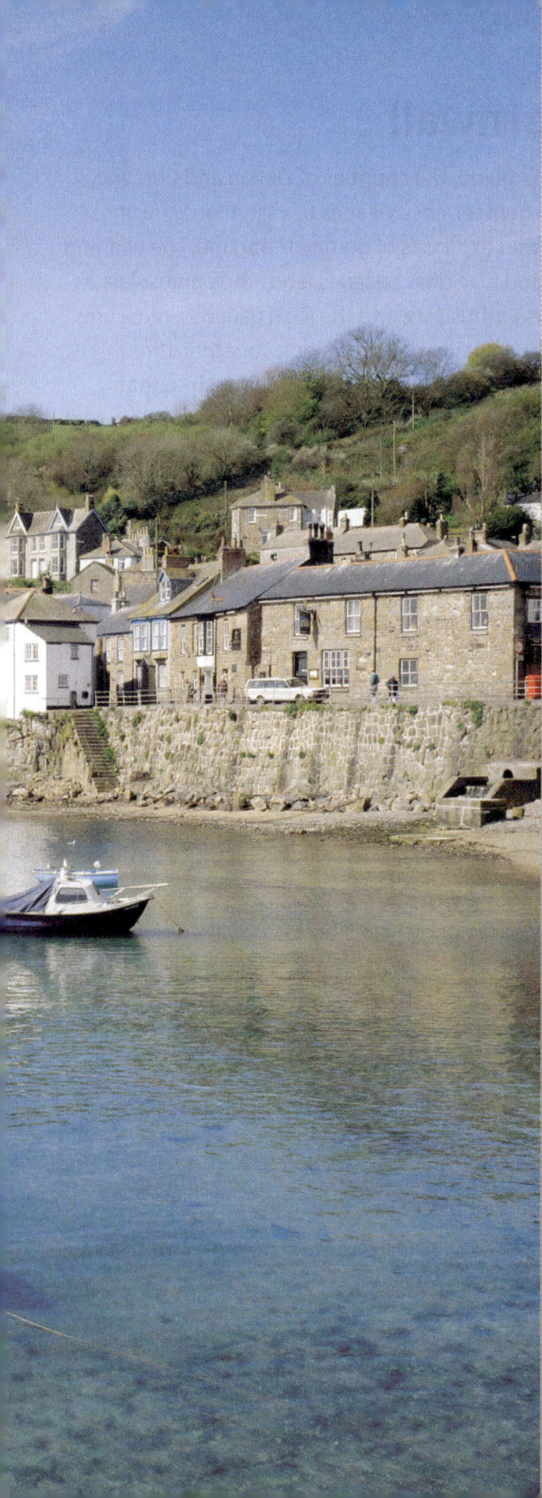

Devon and Cornwall

289 Exeter

294 Torquay

295 Paignton

297 Dartmouth and around

299 Plymouth and around

302 Dartmoor

307 Barnstaple

316 The Eden Project

317 Truro

318 Falmouth

319 The Lizard peninsula

321 The Penwith peninsula

326 The Isles of Scilly

327 Cornwall's Atlantic coast

332 Bodmin Moor

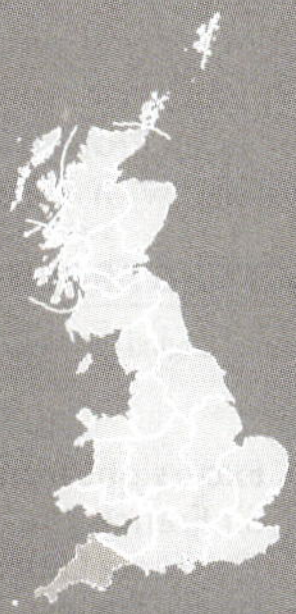

MOUSEHOLE, CORNWALL

Devon and Cornwall

At the western extremity of England, the counties of Devon and Cornwall encompass everything from genteel, cosy villages to vast Atlantic-facing strands of golden sand and wild expanses of granite moorland. The winning combination of rural peace and first-class beaches lends the peninsula a particular appeal to outdoors enthusiasts, and the local galleries, museums and restaurants provide plenty of rainy-day diversions. Together, these attractions have made the region perennially popular, so much so that tourism has replaced the traditional occupations of fishing and farming as the main source of employment and income. The authentic character of Devon and Cornwall may be obscured during the summer season, but avoid the peak periods and you can't fail to be seduced by their considerable charms.

If it's wilderness you're after, nothing can beat the remoter tracts of **Dartmoor**, the greatest of the West Country's granite massifs, much of which retains its solitude despite its proximity to the region's two major cities. Of these, **Exeter** is by far the more interesting, dominated by the twin towers of its medieval cathedral and offering a rich selection of restaurants and nightlife. As for **Plymouth**, much of this great naval port was destroyed by bombing during World War II, though some of the city's Elizabethan core has survived.

The coastline on either side of Exeter and Plymouth enjoys more hours of sunshine than anywhere else on the British mainland, and there is some justification in Devon's principal resort, **Torquay**, styling itself the capital of the "English Riviera". St Tropez it ain't, but there's no denying a certain glamour, alloyed with an old-fashioned charm that the seaside towns of **East Devon** and the cliff-backed resorts of the county's northern littoral share.

Cornwall too has its pockets of concentrated tourist development – chiefly at **Falmouth** and **Newquay**, the first of these a sailing centre, the second a major draw for surfers due to its fine west-facing beaches. **St Ives** is another crowd-puller, though the town has a separate identity as an arts centre. Further up Cornwall's long northern coast, the fortified site of **Tintagel** and the rock-walled harbour of **Boscastle** have an almost embattled character in the face of the turbulent Atlantic. However, the full elemental power of the ocean can best be appreciated on the western headlands of **Lizard Point** and **Land's End**, where the cliffs resound to the constant thunder of the waves, or, offshore, on **Lundy Island**, in the Bristol Channel, and the **Isles of Scilly**, 28 miles west of Land's End.

Inland, the mild climate has enabled a slew of gardens to flourish, none quirkier than the **Eden Project**, which imaginatively highlights the diversity of the earth's plant systems with the help of science-fiction-style "biomes".

GETTING AROUND **DEVON AND CORNWALL**

Getting around the West Country by public transport can be a convoluted and lengthy process, especially in remoter areas.

Excursions from Totnes p.297
Sir Francis Drake p.299
The Tarka Line and the Tarka Trail p.307
Lundy Island p.309
Surfing in North Devon p.310
Top 5 surf spots p.328
King Arthur in Cornwall p.331
Top 5 gardens p.333

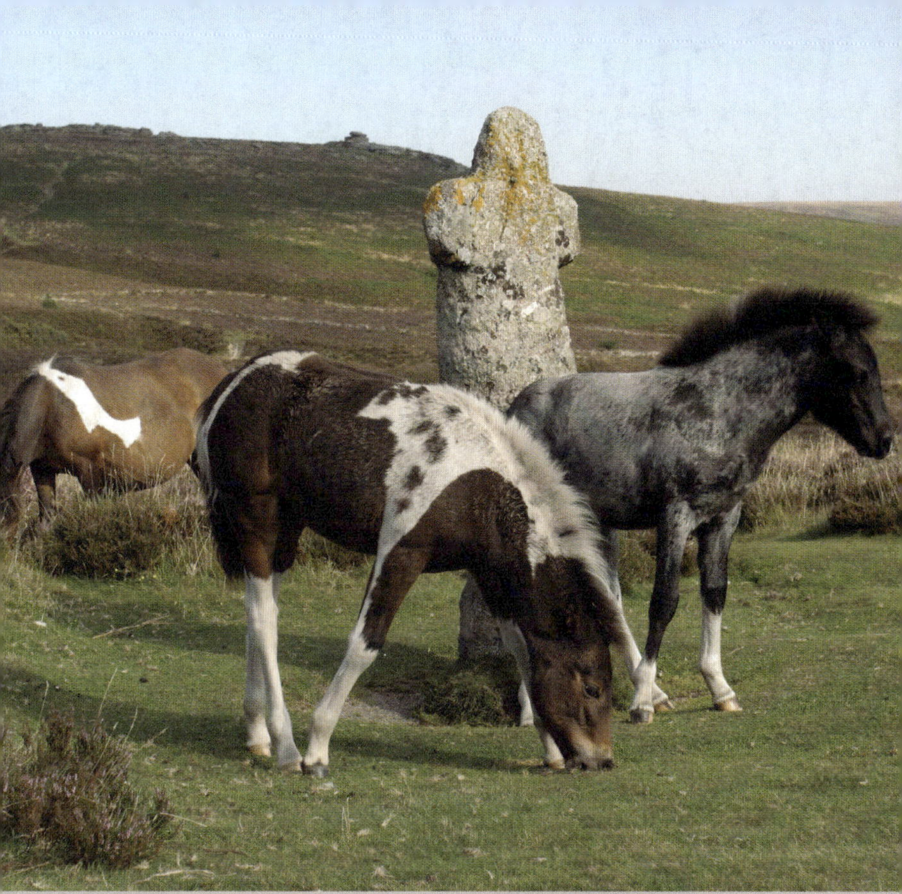

DARTMOOR PONIES

Highlights

❶ **Hiking on Dartmoor** Experience this bleakly beautiful landscape along a good network of paths. **See p.302**

❷ **Surfing in North Devon** Devon's west-facing northern coast – above all Woolacombe, Croyde and Saunton – and its endless ranks of rollers draw surfers of every ability. **See p.310**

❸ **Eden Project, Cornwall** Embark on a voyage of discovery around the planet's ecosystems at this disused clay pit, now home to a fantastic array of exotic plants and crops. **See p.316**

❹ **Cornish beaches** Cornwall has some of the country's best beaches, most of them in fabulous settings. Beauties include Newquay, Whitesand Bay, the Isles of Scilly and Bude; and Porthcurno, overlooked by dramatic black crags. **See p.323**

❺ **St Ives** Fine-sand beaches, a brace of renowned galleries and a maze of tiny lanes give this bustling harbour town a feel-good vibe. **See p.325**

❻ **Seafood restaurants** The local catch goes straight into the excellent restaurants of the southwestern peninsula. Culinary hotspots include Newquay, St Ives and, most famously Padstow, where celebrity chef Rick Stein owns a number of places. **See p.330**

HIGHLIGHTS ARE MARKED ON THE MAP ON P.288

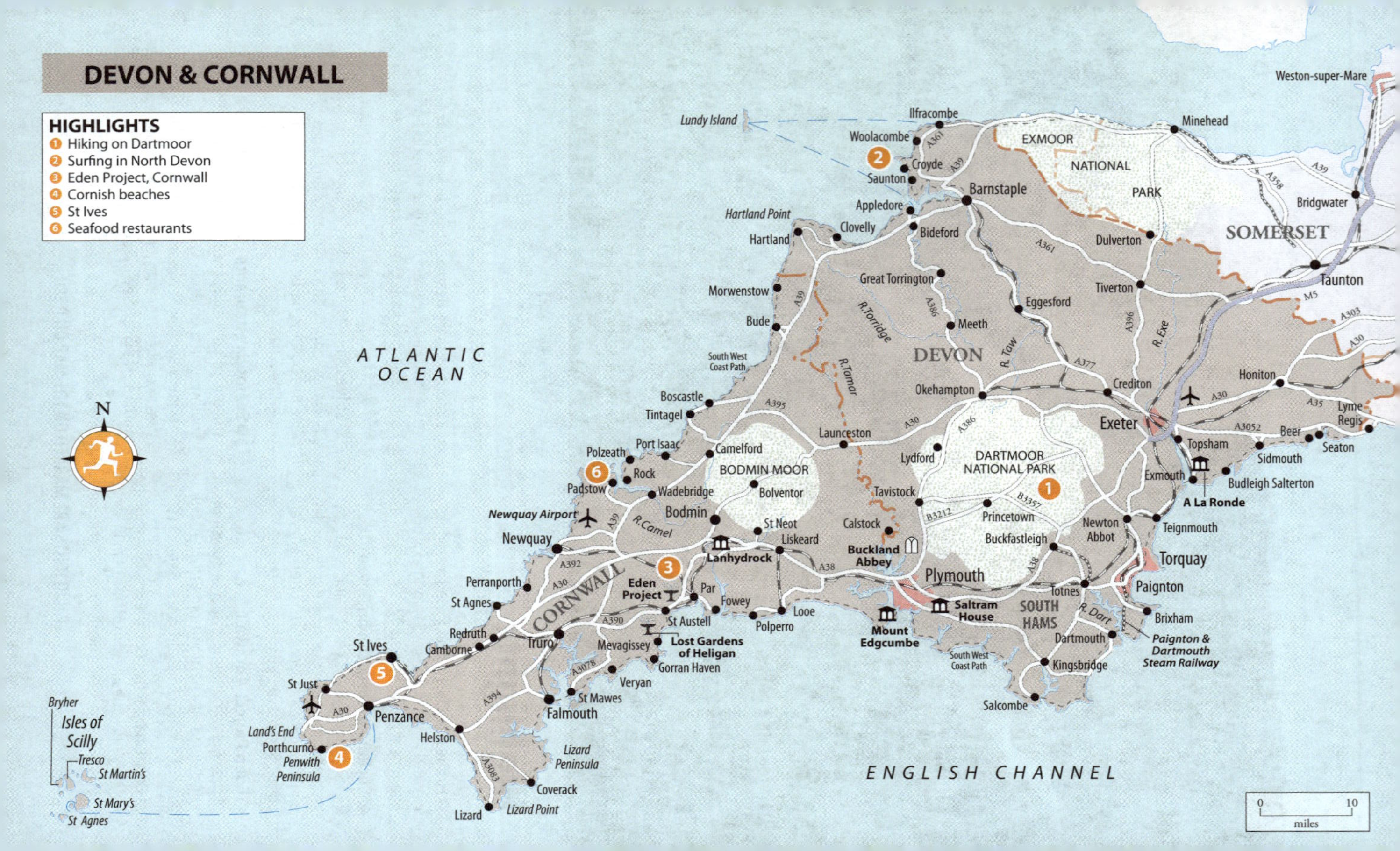
DEVON & CORNWALL
HIGHLIGHTS
1 Hiking on Dartmoor
2 Surfing in North Devon
3 Eden Project, Cornwall
4 Cornish beaches
5 St Ives
6 Seafood restaurants
ATLANTIC OCEAN
ENGLISH CHANNEL
N
DEVON
CORNWALL
SOMERSET
EXMOOR NATIONAL PARK
DARTMOOR NATIONAL PARK
BODMIN MOOR
SOUTH HAMS
Lundy Island
Ilfracombe
Woolacombe
Croyde
Saunton
Barnstaple
Appledore
Bideford
Hartland Point
Hartland
Clovelly
Great Torrington
Morwenstow
Bude
South West Coast Path
Boscastle
Tintagel
Port Isaac
Polzeath
Rock
Padstow
Wadebridge
Camelford
Bolventor
Bodmin
St Neot
Liskeard
Lanhydrock
Newquay Airport
Newquay
Perranporth
St Agnes
Redruth
Camborne
Truro
St Ives
St Just
Penzance
Land's End
Porthcurno
Penwith Peninsula
Helston
Lizard Peninsula
Coverack
Lizard
Lizard Point
Falmouth
St Mawes
Veryan
Gorran Haven
Mevagissey
Lost Gardens of Heligan
St Austell
Eden Project
Par
Fowey
Polperro
Looe
Launceston
Calstock
Buckland Abbey
Tavistock
Lydford
Okehampton
Meeth
Eggesford
Minehead
Dulverton
Tiverton
Crediton
Exeter
Topsham
Exmouth
A La Ronde
Budleigh Salterton
Sidmouth
Beer
Seaton
Lyme Regis
Honiton
Taunton
Bridgwater
Weston-super-Mare
Princetown
Buckfastleigh
Newton Abbot
Teignmouth
Torquay
Paignton
Brixham
Paignton & Dartmouth Steam Railway
Totnes
Dartmouth
Kingsbridge
Salcombe
Plymouth
Saltram House
Mount Edgcumbe
R.Torridge
R.Tamar
R. Taw
R. Exe
R.Camel
R. Dart
Isles of Scilly
Bryher
Tresco
St Martin's
St Mary's
St Agnes
0 10 miles

By train You can reach Exeter, Plymouth, Bodmin, Truro and Penzance by train on the main rail lines from London and the Midlands, with branch lines linking Falmouth (from Truro), Newquay (from Par) and St Ives (from St Erth).

By bus Buses from the chief towns fan out along the coasts and into the interior, though the service can be rudimentary or nonexistent for the smaller villages.

South West Coast Path The best way of exploring the coast of Devon and Cornwall is on foot along the South West Coast Path, Britain's longest waymarked trail.

Devon

With its verdant meadows, winding country lanes and cosy thatched cottages, **Devon** has long been idealized as a vision of a pre-industrial, "authentic" England. In fact much of the county is now inhabited largely by retired folk and urban refugees, but there is still tranquillity and sugar-free charm to be found here, from moorland villages to quiet coves on the cliff-hung coastline.

Reminders of Devon's leading role in the country's **maritime history** are never far away, particularly in the two cities of **Exeter** and **Plymouth**. These days it's the yachties who take advantage of the numerous creeks and bays, especially on Devon's southern coast, where ports such as **Dartmouth** and **Salcombe** are awash with amateur sailors. Landlubbers flock to the sandy beaches and seaside resorts, of which **Torquay**, on the south coast, and **Ilfracombe**, on the north, are the busiest. The most attractive are those which have preserved traces of their nineteenth-century elegance, such as **Sidmouth**, in east Devon. Inland, the county is characterized by swards of lush pasture and a scattering of sheltered villages, the population dropping to almost zero on **Dartmoor**, the wildest and bleakest of the West's moors.

Exeter

EXETER boasts more historical sights than any other town in Devon or Cornwall, legacies of an eventful existence dating from its Celtic foundation and the establishment here of the most westerly Roman outpost. After the Roman withdrawal, Exeter was refounded by Alfred the Great and by the time of the Norman Conquest had become one of the largest towns in England, profiting from its position on the banks of the River Exe. The expansion of the wool trade in the Tudor period sustained the city until the eighteenth century, since when Exeter has maintained its status as Devon's commercial and cultural hub, despite having much of its ancient centre gutted by World War II bombing.

St Peter's Cathedral

Cathedral Close • Mon–Sat 9am–4.45pm, Sun open for services only • £5 • ⓦ exeter-cathedral.org.uk

The most distinctive feature of Exeter's skyline, **St Peter's Cathedral** is a stately monument with two great Norman towers flanking the nave. Close up, it's the facade's ornate Gothic screen that commands attention: its three tiers of sculpted (and very weathered) figures – including Alfred, Athelstan, Canute, William the Conqueror and Richard II – were begun around 1360, part of a rebuilding programme which left only the towers from the original construction.

Entering the cathedral, you're confronted by the longest unbroken **Gothic ceiling** in the world, its **bosses** vividly painted – one, towards the west front, shows the murder of Thomas à Becket. The **Lady Chapel** and **Chapter House** – at the far end of the building and off the right transept respectively – are thirteenth-century, but the main part of the nave, including the lavish rib vaulting, dates from a century later. There are many fine examples of sculpture from this period, including, in the minstrels' gallery high up on the left side, angels playing musical instruments, and, below them, figures of Edward III and Queen Philippa. In the **Choir** don't miss the 60ft **bishop's throne** or the **misericords** – decorated with mythological figures and dating from around 1260, they are thought to be the oldest in the country. Outside, a graceful statue of the theologian Richard Hooker surveys the

6

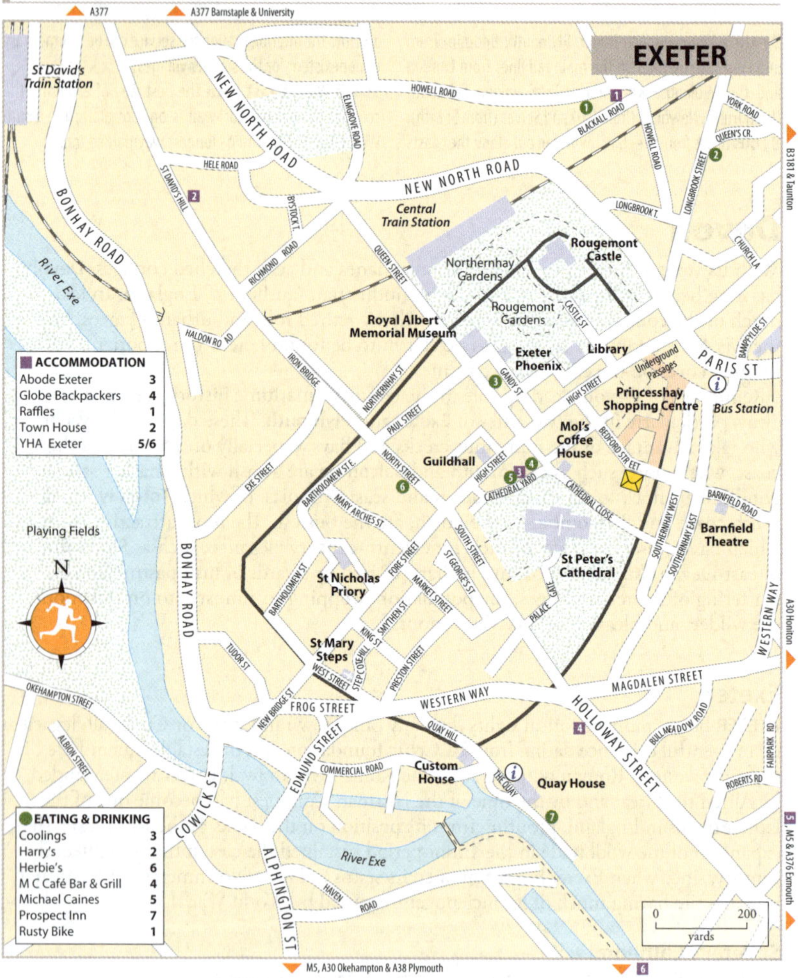

Cathedral Close, a motley mixture of architectural styles from Tudor to Regency, though most display Exeter's trademark red brickwork.

Guildhall

High St • Mon–Fri 10.30am–1pm & 1.30–4pm, Sat 10.30am–12.30pm; sometimes closed for functions • Free

Some older structures still stand amid the banal concrete of the modern town centre, including, on the pedestrianized High Street, Exeter's finest civic building, the fourteenth-century **Guildhall**, claimed to be England's oldest municipal building in regular use. It's fronted by an elegant Renaissance portico, and merits a glance inside for its main chamber, whose arched roof timbers rest on carved bears holding staves, symbols of the Yorkist cause during the Wars of the Roses.

Royal Albert Memorial Museum

Queen St • Mon–Sat 10am–5pm • Free • ⓦ rammuseum.org.uk

The **Royal Albert Memorial Museum** is the closest thing in Devon to a county museum. Exuding the Victorian spirit of wide-ranging curiosity, it includes everything from a menagerie of stuffed animals to mock-ups of the various building styles used at different periods in the city. The collections of silverware, watches and clocks contrast nicely with the colourful ethnography section, and the picture gallery has some good specimens of West Country art.

Underground passages

Paris St • June–Sept & school hols Mon–Sat 9.30am–5.30pm, Sun 10.30am–4pm; Oct–May Tues–Fri 11.30am–5.30pm, Sat 9.30am–5.30pm, Sun 11.30am–4pm • £5.50 • ⓦ exeter.gov.uk

Off the top end of the High Street, the Princesshay shopping precinct holds the entrance to a network of **underground passages**, first excavated in the thirteenth century to bring water to the cathedral precincts, and now visitable on a guided **tour** – not recommended to claustrophobes.

Around the River Exe

The **River Exe** marks the old city's southwestern boundary; today, the **Quayside** is mostly devoted to leisure activities. Pubs, shops and cafés share space with handsomely restored nineteenth-century warehouses and the smart **Custom House**, built in 1681, its opulence reflecting the former importance of the cloth trade.

The area comes into its own at night, but is worth a wander at any time; you can rent bikes and canoes here, too (see below).

ARRIVAL AND INFORMATION — EXETER

By train Exeter has two train stations, Exeter Central and St David's, the latter a little further out from the centre of town, and connected by frequent city buses. South West trains from Salisbury stop at both, as do trains on the branch lines to Barnstaple and Exmouth, but most long-distance trains stop at St David's only.

Destinations Barnstaple (Mon–Sat hourly, Sun 6 daily; 1hr–1hr 30min); Bodmin (every 30min–1hr; 1hr 45min); Liskeard (every 1–2hr; 1hr 30min); London (every 30min–1hr; 2–3hr); Par (hourly; 2hr); Penzance (every 1–2hr; 3hr 10min); Plymouth (every 30min–1hr; 1hr); Torquay (every 30min–1hr; 30–50min); Totnes (every 30min–1hr; 40min); Truro (every 1–2hr; 2hr 15min).

By bus The bus station is on Paris St, opposite the main tourist office.

Destinations Newquay (3–5 daily; 3hr 10min–4hr); Penzance (3–4 daily; 4–6hr); Plymouth (Mon–Sat hourly, Sun every 1–2hr; 1hr 15min–1hr 40min); Sidmouth (Mon–Sat every 20–30min, Sun every 30min–1hr; 40–50min); Torquay (Mon–Sat hourly, Sun 11 daily; 1hr–1hr 25min); Truro (3–4 daily; 3hr 20min–4hr 30min).

Tourist office Dix's Field, off Princesshay (April–Sept Mon–Sat 9am–5pm; Oct–March 9.30am–4.30pm; ⓣ 01392 665700, ⓦ heartofdevon.com).

GETTING AROUND

Saddles & Paddles On the quayside (daily 9.30am–5.30pm; ⓣ 01392 424241, ⓦ sadpad.com). You can rent bikes here; they also have canoes, should you wish to explore the Exeter Canal, which runs 5 miles to Topsham and beyond.

ACCOMMODATION

Abode Exeter Cathedral Yard ⓣ 01392 319955, ⓦ abodehotels.co.uk. Built in 1769 and reputedly the first inn in England to be described as a "hotel", the former *Royal Clarence* is now part of an upmarket chain. It boasts a superb location, with contemporary bedrooms (some small) and a swanky restaurant (see p.292). **£125**

Globe Backpackers 71 Holloway St ⓣ 01392 215521, ⓦ exeterbackpackers.co.uk. Clean and central (though a bit of a hike from the stations), this hostel has a kitchen and free wi-fi. Dorms have six to ten beds and there's a spacious double. Closed noon–3.30pm. Dorm **£17.50**, double **£45**

Raffles 11 Blackall Rd ⓣ 01392 270200, ⓦ raffles-exeter.co.uk. The rooms in this elegant Victorian B&B are furnished with Pre-Raphaelite etchings and other items from the owners' antique business. Breakfasts make use of the organic garden produce. Free wi-fi. **£78**

Town House 54 St David's Hill ⓣ 01392 494994, ⓦ townhouseexeter.co.uk. This Edwardian guesthouse midway between the train stations backs onto a churchyard and has a garden, wi-fi access and abundant breakfasts. Rooms are modern but some bathrooms are small. **£72**

YHA Exeter 47 Countess Wear Rd ⓣ 0845 371 9516, ⓔ exeter@yha.org.uk. A country house 3 miles southeast of the centre (take minibus #K or #T, or bus #57 or #85, or walk along the Exe). Closed during the day. **£18.40**

6

EATING

Coolings 11 Gandy St ⓣ01392 434184, ⓦcoolingsbar.co.uk. Popular wine bar and bistro serving tasty meals (most dishes around £8), with a cellar bar open for late cocktails on Wed, Fri & Sat. Mon–Thurs & Sun 10.30am–11pm, Fri & Sat 10.30am–12.30am; food served Mon–Thurs until 9pm, Fri & Sat until 6pm.

Harry's 86 Longbrook St ⓣ01392 202234, ⓦharrys-exeter.co.uk. In a converted Victorian stonemason's workshop, this place attracts a cheery crowd with its good-value Mexican, Italian and American staples (most around £10). Daily 8.30–10am, noon–2pm & 6–11pm.

★ **Herbie's** 15 North St ⓣ01392 258473. Friendly, dimly lit place serving up great vegan, vegetarian and wholefood dishes (average £9.50) and organic beers, wines and ice cream. Mon 11am–2.30pm, Tues–Fri 11am–2.30pm & 6–9.30pm, Sat 10.30am–4pm & 6–9.30pm.

MC Café Bar & Grill Cathedral Yard ⓣ01392 223626, ⓦmichaelcaines.com. Opposite the cathedral, this is a modish spot for a coffee, a salad or burger for lunch, or a full evening meal (mains £10–18). There's live music on alternate Fridays, when booking is advised. Mon–Sat 9am–10pm, Sun 10am–10pm.

Michael Caines Abode Exeter Hotel, Cathedral Yard ⓣ01392 223638, ⓦmichaelcaines.com. Exeter's classiest restaurant offers sophisticated modern European cuisine in sleek surroundings. Prices are fairly high (mains around £24) but there are reasonable fixed-price lunchtime and early evening menus (£13.50 and £17). Mon–Sat noon–2.30pm & 6–9.45pm (last orders).

DRINKING

Prospect Inn The Quay ⓣ01392 273152, ⓦheavitreebrewery.co.uk. You can eat and drink sitting outside at this seventeenth-century riverside pub, which was the setting for TV drama *The Onedin Line*. Mon–Thurs & Sun 10am–11pm, Fri & Sat 10am–midnight.

★ **Rusty Bike** 67 Howell Rd ⓣ01392 214440, ⓦrustybike-exeter.co.uk. There's an excellent vibe at this pub with vintage table-football and a range of malt whiskeys and tequilas as well as local beers and ciders. Plus good bar meals, a garden and occasional live music. Mon–Wed 6–11pm, Thurs–Sun noon–3pm & 6–11pm.

NIGHTLIFE AND ENTERTAINMENT

Cavern Club 83 Queen St ⓣ01392 495370, ⓦexetercavern.com. A long-established hub of Exeter's music scene, this subterranean haunt is best known for its live bands, mainly post-punk, dub, electro and indie, but it also has club nights and is open for daytime snacks. Mon–Sat 11am–5pm & 8pm–late (sometimes open Sun eve).

Exeter Phoenix Bradlynch Place, Gandy St ⓣ01392 667080, ⓦexeterphoenix.org.uk. Live music and comedy are among the cultural offerings at this arts centre, which also hosts films, exhibitions and readings and has a nice café-bar. Mon–Sat 10am–11pm.

Timepiece Little Castle St ⓣ01392 493096, ⓦtimepiecenightclub.co.uk. Occupying a former prison, this bar, club and performance venue hosts student bands (Mon in term time), Latin music (Tues), students' night (Wed), r'n'b (Thurs), dance mixes (Fri & Sat) and world music (Sun in term time). Tues–Sat 7.30pm–1.30/2am, also Sun & Mon in term time.

A La Ronde

Easter–June, Sept & Oct Mon–Wed, Sat & Sun 11am–5pm; July & Aug Mon–Wed & Fri–Sun • NT • £7 • Bus #57 or #58

Five miles south of Exeter off the A376, the Gothic folly of **A La Ronde** was the creation of two cousins, Jane and Mary Parminter, who in the 1790s were inspired by their European Grand Tour to build a sixteen-sided house, possibly based on the Byzantine basilica of San Vitale in Ravenna. The end product is filled with mementos of the Parminters' travels as well as a number of their more offbeat creations, such as a frieze made of feathers culled from game birds and chickens. In the upper rooms are a gallery and staircase completely covered in shells, too fragile to be visited, though part can be glimpsed from the completely enclosed octagonal room on the first floor. Superb views over the Exe estuary extend from the dormer windows on the second floor.

Sidmouth

Set amid a shelf of crumbling red sandstone, **SIDMOUTH** is the stately queen of east Devon's resorts. The cream-and-white town boasts nearly five hundred buildings listed as having special historic or architectural interest, among them the grand Georgian homes of **York Terrace** behind the Esplanade. Both the mile-long main town beach and **Jacob's Ladder**, a cliff-backed shingle and sand strip to the west of town, are easily accessible and well tended. To the east, the coast path climbs steep Salcombe Hill to follow cliffs that give sanctuary to a range of birdlife including yellowhammers, green woodpeckers and the rarer grasshopper warbler. Further on, the path descends to meet one of the most isolated and attractive beaches in the area, **Weston Mouth**.

ARRIVAL AND INFORMATION — SIDMOUTH

By bus Sidmouth can be reached on bus #52A or #52B from Exeter.

Tourist office Ham Lane, off the eastern end of the Esplanade (March & April Mon–Thurs 10am–4pm, Fri & Sat 10am–5pm, Sun 10am–1pm; May–July, Sept & Oct Mon–Sat 10am–5pm, Sun 10am–4pm; Aug Mon–Sat 10am–6pm, Sun 10am–5pm; Nov–Feb Mon 10am–4pm, Tues–Sat 10am–1.30pm; T 01395 516441, W visitsidmouth.co.uk).

ACCOMMODATION

The Hollies Salcombe Rd T 01395 514580, W holliesguesthouse.co.uk. Rooms in this Regency building blend contemporary and traditional, with the owner's watercolours on the walls. The seafront is less than a 10min walk away. No credit cards. **£70**

The Longhouse Salcombe Hill Rd T 01395 577973, W holidaysinsidmouth.co.uk. It's about a mile from the seafront, but the hilltop views from this B&B – once part of the Norman Lockyer Observatory – compensate. The two rooms are large and comfortable, and there's a nice patio-garden. No credit cards. **£65**

EATING AND DRINKING

Brown's Wine Bar & Bistro 33 Fore St T 01395 516724. Locally sourced dishes, including polenta and grilled seafood (mains around £14), with coffee and snacks available during the day. Early-evening menus prove good value at £16–19. Mon–Sat 10am–3pm, also Tues–Thurs 5–8.30pm, Fri & Sat 5–9.30pm. Reduced winter opening.

Swan Inn 37 York St T 01395 512849, W youngs.co.uk. Close to the tourist office, this convivial pub with a garden serves real ales, baguettes and fresh fish (around £8.50). Mon–Fri 11am–2.30pm & 5.30–11pm, Sat & Sun noon–3pm & 7–11pm.

Beer

Eight miles east of Sidmouth, the largely unspoiled fishing village of **BEER** lies huddled within a small sheltered cove between gleaming white headlands. A stream rushes along a deep channel dug into Beer's main street, and if you can ignore the crowds in high summer much of the village looks unchanged since the time when it was a smugglers' eyrie.

Beer Quarry Caves

Quarry Lane, a mile or so west of the village • Mid-April to Sept 10am–6pm; Oct 11am–5pm; last tour 1hr before closing • £5.50 • W beerquarrycaves.fsnet.co.uk

The area around Beer is best known for its quarries, which were worked from Roman times until the nineteenth century: **Beer stone** was used in many of Devon's churches and houses, and as far afield as London. You can visit the underground **Beer Quarry Caves**, about a mile west of the village, including an exhibition of pieces carved by medieval masons.

ARRIVAL AND DEPARTURE — BEER

Beer is connected to Sidmouth by **bus** #899 (Mon–Sat 3–5 daily; 25–50min). From Exeter take #X53 (every 2hr; 1hr).

ACCOMMODATION AND EATING

Barrel o' Beer Fore St T 01297 20099, W barrelobeer.co.uk. Traditional pub on the main street serving local delicacies such as home-smoked fish and Devon oysters (£12–17.50). Mon–Fri noon–2.30pm & 6–11pm, Sat & Sun noon–11pm (in winter noon–2.30pm & 6–11pm).

Bay View Fore St ⓣ01297 20489, ⓦbayviewbeer.com. Close to the beach and harbour, most of the rooms in this B&B overlook the sea. Abundant breakfasts include smoked haddock and waffles with maple syrup. No credit cards. Closed Nov–Easter. **£62**

Torquay

6

Sporting a mini-corniche and promenades landscaped with flowerbeds, **TORQUAY** comes closest to living up to the self-styled "English Riviera" sobriquet. The much-vaunted palm trees and the coloured lights that festoon the harbour by night contribute to the town's unique flavour, a blend of the mildly exotic with classic English provincialism. Torquay's transformation from a fishing village began with its establishment as a fashionable haven for invalids, among them the consumptive Elizabeth Barrett Browning, who spent three years here.

The town centres on the small **harbour** and marina, separated by limestone cliffs from Torquay's main beach, **Abbey Sands**, which takes its name from **Torre Abbey**, sited in ornamental gardens behind the beachside road.

Torre Abbey

King's Drive • March–Oct daily 10am–5pm • £5.85 • ⓦtorre-abbey.org.uk

The Norman church that once stood here was razed by Henry VIII, though a gatehouse, tithe barn, chapter house and tower escaped demolition. **Torre Abbey** now contains a good museum, with collections of silver and glass, window designs by Edward Burne-Jones, illustrations by William Blake, and nineteenth-century and contemporary works of art.

Living Coasts

Beacon Quay • Daily: Easter–Sept 10am–6pm; Oct–Easter 10am–5pm; last entry 1hr before closing • £9.05, or £18.85 with Paignton Zoo (see p.295) • ⓦlivingcoasts.org.uk

At the northern end of Torquay harbour, **Living Coasts** is home to a variety of fauna and flora found on British shores, including puffins, penguins and seals. There are reconstructed beaches, cliff faces and an estuary, as well as underwater viewing areas and a huge meshed aviary. The rooftop café and restaurant have splendid panoramic views.

Beaches

East of Torquay's harbour, you can follow the shore round to some good sand beaches. **Meadfoot Beach**, one of the busiest, is reached by crossing Daddyhole Plain, named after a large chasm in the adjacent cliff caused by a landslide, but locally attributed to the devil ("Daddy"). North of the Hope's Nose promontory, the coast path leads to a string of less crowded beaches, including **Babbacombe Beach** and, beyond, **Watcombe** and **Maidencombe**.

ARRIVAL AND INFORMATION — TORQUAY

By train Torquay's main train station is off Rathmore Rd, southwest of Torre Abbey Gardens. Destinations include Exeter (every 30min–1hr; 45min).

By bus Most buses stop on The Strand, close to the marina. Destinations include Exeter (Mon–Sat 8–11 daily, Sun 3 daily; 50min) and Plymouth (Mon–Sat hourly, Sun 6 daily; 1hr 50min–2hr 10min).

Tourist office Vaughan Parade, by the harbour (April–Oct Mon–Sat 9.30am–5.30pm, also July & Sept Sun 10am–4pm; Oct–March Mon–Sat 10am–4pm; ⓣ0844 474 2233, ⓦenglishriviera.co.uk).

ACCOMMODATION

Allerdale Hotel 21 Croft Rd ⓣ01803 292667, ⓦallerdalehotel.co.uk. For glorious views and stately surroundings, head for this Victorian villa, a pleasingly old-fashioned place with a long garden and spacious rooms. Meals are available, and there's a bar, snooker and free wi-fi. **£90**

Exton House 12 Bridge Rd ⓣ01803 293561, ⓦextonhotel.co.uk. Small, clean and quiet B&B a 10min walk from the train station (free pick-up is offered), and just 15min from the centre. The guests' lounge has a balcony, and there's free wi-fi. £62

Torquay Backpackers 119 Abbey Rd ⓣ01803 299924, ⓦtorquaybackpackers.co.uk. Clean and friendly hostel a 10min walk from the station, with free tea and coffee, nice common areas and free internet facilities. Dorm £16, double £36

EATING AND DRINKING

Hole in the Wall Park Lane ⓣ01803 200755. This pub is supposed to be one of Torquay's oldest, and was Irish playwright Sean O'Casey's boozer when he lived here. There's a good range of beers, a separate restaurant (with mains around £10) and live music nights. Daily noon–midnight.

Number 7 Fish Bistro Beacon Terrace ⓣ01803 295055, ⓦno7-fish.com. Just above the harbour, this place is a must for seafood fans, covering everything from fresh whole crab to grilled turbot – or whatever else the boats have brought in. Most mains cost around £18. July–Sept daily 12.15–1.45pm & 6.30–9.45pm; Oct & June Mon–Sat 12.15–1.45pm & 6.30–9.45pm; Nov–May Tues–Sat 12.15–1.45pm & 6.30–9.45pm.

Sea Spray 8 Victoria Parade ⓣ01803 293734, ⓦsearayrestaurant.co.uk. Informal harbourside restaurant specializing in fresh fish, though meat dishes are also available. Main courses are £6–8 for lunch, £9–15 in the evening. Daily noon–9pm.

6

Paignton

Lacking Torquay's gloss, **PAIGNTON** is the least attractive of the Riviera's resorts, though it is home to **Paignton Zoo** (daily: summer 10am–6pm; winter 10am–4.30pm or dusk; last entry 1hr before closing; £11.90, or £18.85 with Living Coasts in Torquay; ⓦpaigntonzoo.org.uk), a mile out on Totnes Road.

Near the seafront, Paignton's Queen's Park train station is also the terminus of the **Dartmouth Steam Railway** (April–Oct, plus a few dates in Dec; ⓣ01803 555872, ⓦdartmouthrailriver.co.uk), which connects with **Goodrington Sands** beach before following the Dart to Kingswear, seven miles south. You could make a day of it by taking the ferry from Kingswear to Dartmouth (see p.297), then taking a riverboat up the Dart to Totnes, from where you can take any bus back to Paignton – a "Round Robin" ticket (£21) lets you do this.

ARRIVAL AND DEPARTURE — PAIGNTON

By train Paignton's train station is off Sands Rd, 5min west of the harbour.
Destinations Exeter (every 30min–1hr; 5min); Torquay (every 30min–1hr; 40min–1hr).

By bus The bus station is next to the train station, off Sands Road.
Destinations Brixham (every 10–20min; 25min); Exeter (every 30min–1hr; 1hr 15min–1hr 30min); Torquay (every 5–10min; 25min).

Brixham

BRIXHAM is a major fishing port and the prettiest of the Torbay towns. Among the trawlers on the quayside is moored a full-size reconstruction of the **Golden Hind** (Feb–Oct daily 10am–4pm, longer hours in Aug; £4; ⓦgoldenhind.co.uk), the surprisingly small vessel in which Francis Drake circumnavigated the world. The harbour is overlooked by an unflattering statue of William III, who landed in Brixham to claim the crown of England in 1688.

From the harbour, climb King Street and follow Berry Head Road to reach the promontory at the southern limit of Torbay, **Berry Head**, now a conservation area attracting colonies of nesting seabirds. There are fabulous views, and you can see the remains of fortifications built during the Napoleonic Wars.

ARRIVAL AND INFORMATION — BRIXHAM

By bus Most buses arrive in and depart from Town Square and Bank Lane, in the upper town.
Destinations Exeter (2 daily; 1hr 45min); Paignton (every 10–20min; 25min); Torquay (every 10–20min; 50min).

Tourist office 19 The Quay (Easter–June & Sept Mon–Sat 9.30am–1pm & 2–5pm; July & Aug Mon–Sat 9.30am–1pm & 2–5.30pm, Sun 10am–1.30pm & 2–4pm; ⓣ 0844 474 2233, ⓦ englishriviera.co.uk).

ACCOMMODATION

Harbour View King St ⓣ 01803 853052, ⓦ harbourviewbrixhambandb.co.uk. As the name implies, its position is the best asset of this B&B, which has small but clean and modern en-suite rooms. A self-catering cottage is also available. **£70**

Quayside Hotel King St ⓣ 01803 855751, ⓦ quaysidehotel.co.uk. Classy hotel with superb harbour views, two bars and a good restaurant where meat and seafood dishes are £17–20. It's worth paying extra for a harbour-facing room. **£96**

6

EATING AND DRINKING

Blue Anchor 83 Fore St ⓣ 01803 859373. A great spot for a relaxed pint of local ale, with open fires and low beams. They also offer a full menu of (rather mediocre) bar food. Mon–Sat 11am–midnight, Sun 11am–11.30pm; food served daily noon–2.30pm & 6–9.30pm.

Poopdeck 14 The Quay ⓣ 01803 858681, ⓦ poopdeckrestaurant.com. You'll find all manner of cockles, whelks and crab sticks at Brixham's harbourside stalls, but for a top-class seafood feast try this place, where a plate of grilled local fish costs £15 and a hot shellfish platter is £22 – book early for a table overlooking the harbour. Mon–Thurs 6.30–9.30pm, Fri–Sun noon–2.30pm & 6–10pm, July & Aug open daily for lunch.

Greenway

Galmpton • Early March to Oct Wed–Sun 10.30am–5pm, also Tues 10.30am–5pm during Easter and summer school hols • NT • £8.75, or £7.80 if arriving by river, by bike or on foot

The birthplace of Walter Raleigh's three seafaring half-brothers, the Gilberts, and later rebuilt for Agatha Christie, **Greenway** stands high above the Dart amid steep wooded grounds (the ascent from the river landing is challenging). The house today contains a low-key collection of memorabilia belonging to the Christie family, including archeological scraps, silverware, ceramics and books, while the grounds afford lovely views over the river.

ARRIVAL AND DEPARTURE — GREENWAY

By car If you drive, note that parking at Greenway must be booked at least one day in advance, either online at ⓦ greenwayhouse.org.uk or by calling ⓣ 01803 842382.

By foot You can reach the house on foot on the waymarked "Greenway walk" from Brixham or via the Dart Valley Trail from Dartmouth or Kingswear (Dartmouth's tourist office can supply route maps; see p.298).

By ferry The easiest approach to Greenway is by river from Dartmouth (£8 return) or Totnes (£12 return); call ⓣ 01803 882811 or see ⓦ greenwayferry.co.uk for details. Ferries from Brixham and Torquay, via Dartmouth, cost £19.50 return.

Totnes

On the west bank of the River Dart, **TOTNES** has an ancient pedigree, its period of greatest prosperity occurring in the sixteenth century when this inland port exported cloth to France and brought back wine. Some handsome sixteenth-century buildings survive from that era, and there is still a working port down on the river, but these days Totnes has mellowed into a residential market town, popular with the alternative and New Age crowd.

The town centres on the long main street that changes its name from Fore Street to the High Street at the **East Gate**, a much retouched medieval arch. On Fore Street, the town **museum**, occupying a four-storey Elizabethan house, illustrates how wealthy clothiers lived at the peak of Totnes's fortunes (mid-March to Oct Mon–Fri 10.30am–5pm; £2; ⓣ 01803 863821). From the East Gate, **Ramparts Walk** trails off along the old city walls, curving round the fifteenth-century church of **St Mary**, a red sandstone building containing an exquisitely carved rood screen. Looming over the High Street, the town's oldest monument, **Totnes Castle**, is a classic Norman structure

EXCURSIONS FROM TOTNES

The highest navigable point on the **River Dart** for seagoing vessels, Totnes is the starting point for **cruises to Dartmouth**, leaving from Steamer Quay (Feb–Oct 1–4 daily; 1hr 15min; £14 return; ⓣ01803 555872, ⓦdartmouthrailriver.co.uk). **Riverside walks** in either direction pass some congenial pubs and, near the railway bridge at Littlehempston, the station of the **South Devon Railway**, where you can board a steam train running along the Dart to Buckfastleigh, on the edge of Dartmoor (late March to Oct 4–9 daily; 30min; £10 return; ⓣ0845 345 1420, ⓦsouthdevonrailway.org).

of the motte and bailey design (daily: April–Sept 10am–5/6pm; Oct 10am–4pm; EH; £3.40).

ARRIVAL AND INFORMATION — TOTNES

By train Totnes train station lies north of the centre off Station Rd, a 10min walk from the centre.

Destinations Exeter (every 20min–1hr; 30min); Plymouth (every 20min–1hr; 30min).

By bus Most buses stop on or around The Plains.

Destinations Exeter (Mon–Sat 10 daily, Sun 6 daily; 1hr 15min–1hr 35min); Paignton (Mon–Sat every 20min, Sun every 2hr; 25min); Plymouth (Mon–Sat every 30min–1hr, Sun 7 daily; 1hr–1hr 15min); Torquay (Mon–Sat every 30min, Sun 5 daily; 50min).

Tourist office Town Mill, near the Morrisons car park (April–Oct Mon–Fri 9.30am–5pm, Sat 10am–4pm; Nov–March Mon–Fri 10am–4pm, Sat 10am–1pm; ⓣ01803 863168, ⓦtotnesinformation.co.uk).

ACCOMMODATION

3 Plymouth Rd Off the High St ⓣ01803 866917, ⓦmlfen.freeserve.co.uk. Central, great-value B&B run by a former tourist guide, with three simple rooms, one of them en suite. Wi-fi available. No credit cards. Closed Nov–Feb. **£50**

Great Grubb Fallowfields, Plymouth Rd ⓣ01803 849071, ⓦthegreatgrubb.co.uk. Leather sofas, restful colours, healthy breakfasts and a patio are the main appeal of this friendly B&B a short walk from the centre, where work by local artists is displayed in the rooms. Free wi-fi. **£70**

Royal Seven Stars Hotel The Plains ⓣ01803 862125, ⓦroyalsevenstars.co.uk. This seventeenth-century coaching inn has had a modern makeover, giving it contemporary bedrooms and a stylish bar alongside the traditional Saloon Bar and brasserie. Non-guests can stop by for a drink or meal. Free wi-fi. **£119**

EATING AND DRINKING

The Barrel House 59 High St ⓣ01803 863000, ⓦbarrelhousetotnes.co.uk. There's a café at street level and a former ballroom upstairs where you can eat salads, burgers and more for under £10. Occasional DJs, live music and comedy nights. Mon–Sat 9am–5pm, Sun 10am–5pm; shows usually Wed–Sat from 8pm.

Steampacket St Peter's Quay ⓣ01803 863880, ⓦsteampacketinn.co.uk. This family-friendly inn reached by walking south along The Plains makes an excellent spot for a riverside drink or bite to eat. There's a range of local ales, bar snacks and meals in the conservatory restaurant (mains £10–14). Mon–Sat 11am–11pm, Sun noon–10.30pm.

Willow 87 High St ⓣ01803 862605. Inexpensive vegetarian snacks, evening meals and organic drinks are served at this mellow café-restaurant. Main dishes are less than £10. There's a courtyard, and live acoustic music on Fridays. No credit cards. Mon–Sat 10am–5pm, also Wed, Fri & Sat 6.30–9pm.

Dartmouth and around

South of Torbay, and eight miles downstream from Totnes, **DARTMOUTH** has thrived since the Normans recognized the trading potential of this deep-water port. Today its activities embrace fishing, freight and a booming leisure industry, as well as the education of the senior service's officer class at the Royal Naval College, on a hill overlooking the port.

Regular ferries shuttle across the River Dart between Dartmouth and **Kingswear**, terminus of the Dartmouth Steam Railway (see p.295). **Boat cruises** from Dartmouth are the best way to view the deep creeks and grand houses overlooking the river, among them the **Royal Naval College** and **Greenway** (see p.296).

Dartmouth Museum

April–Oct Tues–Sat 10am–4pm, Sun & Mon 1–4pm; Nov–March daily noon–3pm • £2

Behind the enclosed boat basin at the heart of town, the four-storey **Butterwalk** at the top of Duke Street was built in the seventeenth century for a local merchant. The timber-framed construction, richly decorated with woodcarvings, was restored after bombing in World War II though still looks precarious as it overhangs the street on eleven granite columns. This arcade now holds shops and Dartmouth's small **museum**, mainly devoted to maritime curios, including old maps, prints and models of ships.

6

Dartmouth Castle

Late March to June & Sept daily 10am–5pm; July & Aug daily 10am–6pm; Oct daily 10am–4pm; Nov–March Sat & Sun 10am–4pm • EH • £4.70

A twenty-minute riverside walk from **Bayard's Cove** – a short cobbled quay lined with eighteenth-century houses, where the Pilgrim Fathers stopped en route to the New World – brings you to **Dartmouth Castle**, one of two fortifications on opposite sides of the estuary dating from the fifteenth century. The castle was the first in England to be constructed specifically to withstand artillery, though was never tested in action, and consequently is excellently preserved.

If you don't relish the walk back, you can take a **ferry** back to Dartmouth Quay (Easter–Oct continuous service 10am–4/5pm; £2).

Blackpool Sands

Continuing southwest from Dartmouth Castle, the coastal path brings you through the pretty hilltop village of **Stoke Fleming** to **Blackpool Sands**, the best beach in the area. The unspoilt cove, flanked by steep, wooded cliffs, was the site of a battle in 1404 in which Devon archers repulsed a Breton invasion force sent to punish the privateers of Dartmouth for their cross-Channel raiding.

ARRIVAL AND INFORMATION — DARTMOUTH

By ferry Coming from Torbay, visitors to Dartmouth can save time and a long detour through Totnes by using the frequent Higher Ferry or Lower ferry across the Dart from Kingswear (50p–£1.10 foot passengers; £4–4.50 for cars); the last ones are at around 10.45pm.

Tourist office Mayor's Ave (Easter–Oct Mon–Sat 10am–5pm, Sun 10am–2pm; Nov–Easter Mon, Tues & Thurs–Sat 10am–4pm, Wed 10am–1pm; T 01803 834224, W discoverdartmouth.com).

ACCOMMODATION

Avondale 5 Vicarage Hill T 01803 835831, W avondaledartmouth.co.uk. On a steep hill, this is a friendly, spacious and elegantly furnished B&B with terrific views over the town and river. Free wi-fi. No credit cards. **£75**

Browns 27–29 Victoria Rd T 01803 832572, W brownshoteldartmouth.co.uk. Boutique-style hotel, with small, stylish rooms, contemporary paintings and an up-to-the-minute feel. Good Mediterranean dishes are served in the bar and restaurant. Two-night minimum stay at weekends. **£95**

EATING AND DRINKING

Café Alf Resco Lower St T 01803 835880, W cafealfresco.co.uk. Funky, wi-fi-enabled snack bar that's good for all-day breakfasts, steaming coffees and occasional live music in summer. Good accommodation is also available. No credit cards. Daily 7am–2pm.

The Seahorse 5 South Embankment T 01803 835147, W seahorserestaurant.co.uk. Seafood restaurant facing the river, offering such Italian-inspired dishes as lobster spaghetti and flame-grilled sea bass. It's pricey, with mains around £18, but there's a £15 lunch menu, and the same team also runs *Rockfish*, which serves a couple of doors down, first-class fish and chips (open all day). Tues 6–10pm, Wed–Sat noon–3pm & 6–10pm, Sun 12.30–2.30pm.

Salcombe

The area between the Dart and Plym estuaries, the **South Hams**, holds some of Devon's comeliest villages and most striking coastline. The "capital" of the region, **Kingsbridge**, is a useful transport hub but lacks the appeal of **SALCOMBE**, reachable on a summer ferry from Kingsbridge. Once a nondescript fishing village, Devon's southernmost resort is now a full-blown sailing and holiday centre, its calm waters strewn with small pleasure-craft.

You can swot up on boating and local history at **Salcombe Maritime Museum** on Market Street, off the north end of the central Fore Street (Easter–Oct 10.30am–12.30pm & 2.30–4.30pm; £1.50), or take a ferry down to South Sands and climb up to the intriguing **Overbeck's Museum** at Sharpitor (NT; £7), which focuses on the area's natural history and nineteenth-century curiosities.

INFORMATION — SALCOMBE

Tourist office Market St (Easter to late July and early Sept to Oct daily 10am–5pm; mid-July to early Sept Mon–Sat 9am–6pm, Sun 10am–5pm; Nov–March Mon–Sat 10am–3pm; T 01548 843927, W salcombeinformation.co.uk).

ACCOMMODATION

Waverley Devon Rd T 01548 842633, W waverleybandb.co.uk. Rooms in this B&B are clean and wi-fi-enabled, and breakfasts are excellent, with lots of choice. It's less than a 10min walk to the centre. Self-catering also available. **£76**

YHA Salcombe Sharpitor T 0845 371 9341, E salcombe@yha.org.uk. Occupying part of Overbeck's Museum (see above), this hostel is idyllically sited with lovely views. There's a kitchen and restaurant. Call to check winter opening. **£18.40**

EATING AND DRINKING

Captain Flint's 82 Fore St T 01548 842357. For a lively evening, try this family-friendly place which specializes in salads, steaks, pastas and pizzas (£7–10). Bookings aren't taken, so be prepared to queue. Easter–Oct daily 5.30–9.30pm.

Winking Prawn North Sands T 01548 842326, W winkingprawn.co.uk. Right on the beach, this is an alluring stop for a cappuccino, baguette or ice cream by day, or a steak or chargrilled chicken in the evening, from around 6pm, when booking is advised (mains £16–22). You don't need to book for the summer barbecues (from 4pm; £17). Daily 8am–8.30pm.

Plymouth and around

PLYMOUTH's predominantly bland and modern face belies its great historic role as a naval base and, in the sixteenth century, the stamping ground of such national heroes as John Hawkins and Francis Drake. It was from here that Drake sailed to defeat the Spanish Armada in 1588, and 32 years later the port was the last embarkation point for

SIR FRANCIS DRAKE

Born around 1540 near Tavistock, **Francis Drake** worked in the domestic coastal trade from the age of 13, but was soon taking part in the first English slaving expeditions between Africa and the West Indies, led by his Plymouth kinsman John Hawkins. Later, Drake was active in the secret war against Spain, raiding and looting merchant ships in actions unofficially sanctioned by Elizabeth I. In 1572 he became the first Englishman to sight the Pacific, and soon afterwards, on board the *Golden Hind*, became the first to **circumnavigate the world**, for which he received a knighthood on his return in 1580. The following year Drake was made mayor of Plymouth, settling in Buckland Abbey (see p.301), but was back in action before long – in 1587 he "singed the king of Spain's beard" by entering Cadiz harbour and destroying 33 vessels that were to have formed part of Philip II's **armada**. When the replacement invasion fleet appeared in the English Channel in 1588, Drake – along with Raleigh, Hawkins and Frobisher – played a leading role in wrecking it. The following year he set off on an unsuccessful expedition to help the Portuguese against Spain, but otherwise most of the next decade was spent in relative inactivity in Plymouth, Exeter and London. Finally, in 1596 Drake left with Hawkins for a raid on Panama, a venture that cost the lives of both captains.

the Pilgrim Fathers, whose New Plymouth colony became the nucleus for the English settlement of North America. The importance of the city's Devonport dockyards made the city a target in World War II, when the Luftwaffe reduced most of the old centre to rubble. Subsequent reconstruction has done little to improve the place, though it would be difficult to spoil the glorious vista over **Plymouth Sound**, the basin of calm water at the mouth of the combined Plym, Tavy and Tamar estuaries, largely unchanged since Drake played his famous game of bowls on the Hoe before joining battle with the Armada.

One of the best local excursions from Plymouth is to **Mount Edgcumbe**, where woods and meadows provide a welcome antidote to the urban bustle. East of Plymouth, the aristocratic opulence of **Saltram House** includes fine art and furniture, while to the north you can visit Francis Drake's old home at **Buckland Abbey**.

Plymouth Hoe

A good place to start a tour of the city is **Plymouth Hoe**, an immense esplanade with glorious views over the water. Here, alongside various war memorials stands a rather portly statue of Sir Francis Drake, gazing grandly out to the sea. Appropriately, there's a bowling green back from the brow.

Smeaton's Tower

April–Sept Tues–Fri 10am–noon & 1–4.30pm, Sat 10am–noon; Oct–March Tues–Sat 10am–noon & 1–3pm • £2.50 • Ⓦ plymouth .gov.uk

In front of the memorials on Plymouth Hoe, the red-and-white-striped **Smeaton's Tower** was erected in 1759 by John Smeaton on the treacherous Eddystone Rocks, fourteen miles out to sea. When replaced by a larger lighthouse in 1882, it was reassembled here, where it gives lofty views across Plymouth Sound.

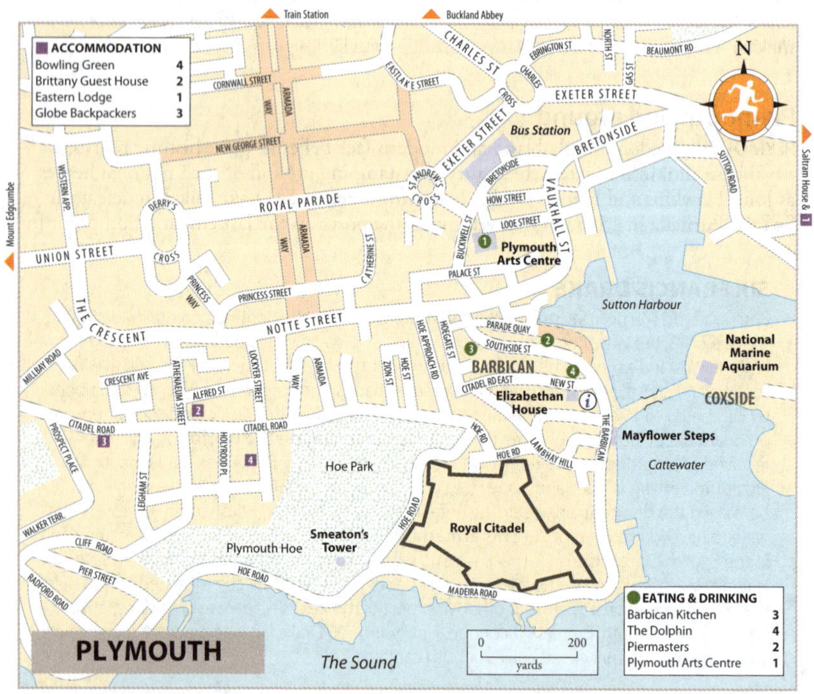

Around the Barbican

At the old town's quay at **Sutton Harbour**, the **Mayflower Steps** commemorate the sailing of the Pilgrim Fathers, with a plaque listing the names and professions of the 102 Puritans on board. Edging the harbour, the **Barbican** district is the heart of old Plymouth: most of the buildings are now shops and restaurants.

Elizabethan House

32 New St • April–Sept Tues–Sat 10am–noon & 1–5pm • £2.50 • Ⓦ plymouth.gov.uk

New Street, which was off the quayside, holds some of Plymouth's oldest buildings, among them the **Elizabethan House**, a captain's dwelling retaining most of the original architectural features, including a spiral staircase around what was probably a disused ship's mast. The three floors are crammed with fine sixteenth- and seventeenth-century furniture and textiles.

National Marine Aquarium

Daily 10am–5/6pm; last entry 1hr before closing • £9.50 • Ⓦ national-aquarium.co.uk

Across the footbridge from Sutton Harbour, the **National Marine Aquarium** has re-created a range of marine environments, from moorland stream to coral reef and deep-sea ocean. The most popular exhibits are the seahorses, the colourful reefs and the sharks, though some of the smaller tanks hold equally compelling exhibits – the anemones, for example. At the top of the building, Explorocean highlights the technological aspects of oceanography.

Mount Edgcumbe

Easter–Sept Mon–Thurs & Sun 11am–4.30pm • £7.20 • Ⓦ plymouth.gov.uk • Bus #34 from Royal Parade to Stonehouse, then passenger ferry to Cremyll from Admiral's Hard (at least hourly; Ⓦ cremyll-ferry.co.uk); alternatively, in summer take the direct motor-launch from the Mayflower Steps to Cawsand (Ⓦ cawsandferry.co.uk), then 2hr walk to house

Lying on the Cornish side of Plymouth Sound and visible from the Hoe is **MOUNT EDGCUMBE** house, a reconstruction of the bomb-damaged Tudor original, though inside the predominant note is eighteenth-century, the rooms elegantly restored with authentic Regency furniture. Far more enticing are the impeccable **gardens** divided into French, Italian and English sections – the first two a blaze of flowerbeds adorned with classical statuary, the last an acre of sweeping lawn shaded by exotic trees. The **park**, which is free and open all year, gives access to the coastal path and the huge **Whitsand Bay**, the best bathing beach for miles around, though subject to dangerous shifting sands and fierce currents.

Saltram House

Near Plympton, 2 miles east of Plymouth off the A38 • **House** Mid-March to Oct daily except Fri noon–4.30pm • £9.10 including garden **Garden** Jan to mid-March daily except Fri 11am–4pm; mid-March to Oct daily 11am–5pm; Nov & Dec daily 11am–4pm • NT • £4.70, £9.10 including house • Buses #19, #21 or #51 from Royal Parade to Cot Hill, from where it is a walk of a mile or so (signposted)

The remodelled Tudor **Saltram House** is Devon's largest country house, featuring work by architect Robert Adam and fourteen portraits by **Joshua Reynolds**, who was born in nearby Plympton. The showpiece is the Saloon, a fussy but exquisitely furnished room dripping with gilt and plaster, and set off by a huge Axminster carpet especially woven for it in 1770. Saltram's landscaped **garden** provides a breather from this riot of interior design.

Buckland Abbey

Six miles north of Plymouth • Late Feb to early March & early Nov to mid-Dec Fri–Sun 11am–4.30pm; mid-March to Oct daily 10.30am–5.30pm • NT • £8.05, grounds only £4.05 • Bus #83 to Tavistock, changing at Yelverton for #55

Close to the River Tavy and on the edge of Dartmoor, **Buckland Abbey** was once the most westerly of England's Cistercian abbeys. After its dissolution, Buckland was converted to a family home by the privateer Richard Grenville (cousin of Walter

Raleigh), from whom the estate was acquired by Francis Drake in 1582, the year after he became mayor of Plymouth. It remained Drake's home until his death, though the house reveals few traces of his residence. There are, however, numerous maps, portraits and mementos of his buccaneering exploits on show, most famous of which is Drake's Drum, which was said to beat a supernatural warning of impending danger to the country. More eye-catching are the oak-panelled **Great Hall**, previously the nave of the abbey, and, in the majestic grounds, a fine fourteenth-century **monastic barn**.

ARRIVAL AND INFORMATION — PLYMOUTH

By train Plymouth's train station is a mile north of The Hoe off Saltash Rd (bus #25 to the centre from Mayflower St, a 5min walk).

Destinations Bodmin (every 30min–1hr; 40min); Exeter (every 20min–1hr; 1hr); Liskeard (every 30min–1hr; 30min); Par (every 30min–1hr; 50min); Penzance (hourly; 2hr); Truro (hourly; 1hr 15min).

By bus Buses pull in at Bretonside, just over St Andrew's Cross from Royal Parade.

Destinations Bodmin (3 daily; 1hr 10min); Exeter (every 1–2hr; 1hr 15min–1hr 50min); Falmouth (2 daily; 2hr 30min); Newquay (3–4 daily; 1hr 50min); Penzance (5–6 daily; 3hr–3hr 30min); St Austell (4 daily; 1hr 20min); St Ives (3 daily; 3hr–3hr 30min); Torquay (Mon–Sat hourly, Sun 4 daily; 2hr–3hr 50min); Truro (5 daily; 2hr).

Tourist office Off Sutton Harbour at 3 The Barbican (April–Oct Mon–Sat 9am–5pm, Sun 10am–4pm; Nov–March Mon–Fri 9am–5pm, Sat 10am–4pm; ⓣ01752 306330, ⓦvisitplymouth.co.uk).

ACCOMMODATION

Bowling Green 9–10 Osborne Place, Lockyer St ⓣ01752 209090, ⓦthebowlinggreenplymouth.com. Smart establishment with bright rooms overlooking Francis Drake's fabled haunt on the Hoe. There's a conservatory and garden, limited parking and free wi-fi. £75

Brittany Guest House 28 Athenaeum St ⓣ01752 262247, ⓦbrittanyguesthouse.co.uk. A good choice on this row close to the Barbican, with all rooms en suite. The easy-going owners offer a choice of breakfasts, and there's even a car park (a definite bonus in these parts). No under-5s. £46

★ **Eastern Lodge** Membland, near Newton Ferrers ⓣ01752 871450, ⓦeasternlodge.co.uk. Ten miles southeast of town off the A379, this beautiful old gatehouse sits right by the coast path and has terrific views. Dinners available, and German and Spanish spoken. No credit cards. £80

Globe Backpackers 172 Citadel Rd ⓣ01752 225158, ⓦplymouthbackpackers.co.uk. Relaxed hostel west of the Hoe, with kitchen, free tea and coffee, free wi-fi and a courtyard garden. It's a bit run-down, but clean enough. Book ahead. Dorm £16, double £36

EATING AND DRINKING

Barbican Kitchen 60 Southside St ⓣ01752 604448, ⓦbarbicankitchen.com. Modern decor, tasty food and a casual ambience draw the crowds at this bistro, housed in the ancient Black Friars Distillery. Choose from a range of dishes, from sausage and mash to beef medallions (£10–14). Mon–Sat noon–3pm & 5–10pm, Sun noon–3pm & 6–10pm.

The Dolphin 14 The Barbican ⓣ01752 660876. A local institution, this harbourside pub has an authentic atmosphere and Tribute and Bass ales straight from the barrel. Look out for the pictures by Beryl Cook, who used to drink here. Mon–Sat 10am–11pm, Sun noon–11pm.

Piermasters 3 Southside St ⓣ01752 229345, ⓦpiermastersrestaurant.com. The raw material for this seafood restaurant comes straight from the harbour. There are fixed-price lunchtime and evening menus (£12–20), or choose à la carte. Mon–Sat noon–2.30pm & 5–10pm.

Plymouth Arts Centre 38 Looe St ⓣ01752 206114, ⓦplymouthartscentre.org. Exhibitions, films and performances are held here, and there's a quiet café-restaurant, the *Green Room*, open for snacks and dishes such as red lentil curry (£7.25). Café Tues–Sat 11am–8.30pm.

Dartmoor

Occupying the main part of the county between Exeter and Plymouth, **DARTMOOR** is southern England's greatest expanse of wilderness, some 365 square miles of raw granite, barren bogland, sparse grass and heather-grown moor. It was not always so desolate, as testified by the remnants of scattered Stone Age settlements and the ruined relics of the area's nineteenth-century tin-mining industry. Today desultory flocks of sheep and groups of ponies are virtually the only living creatures to be seen wandering

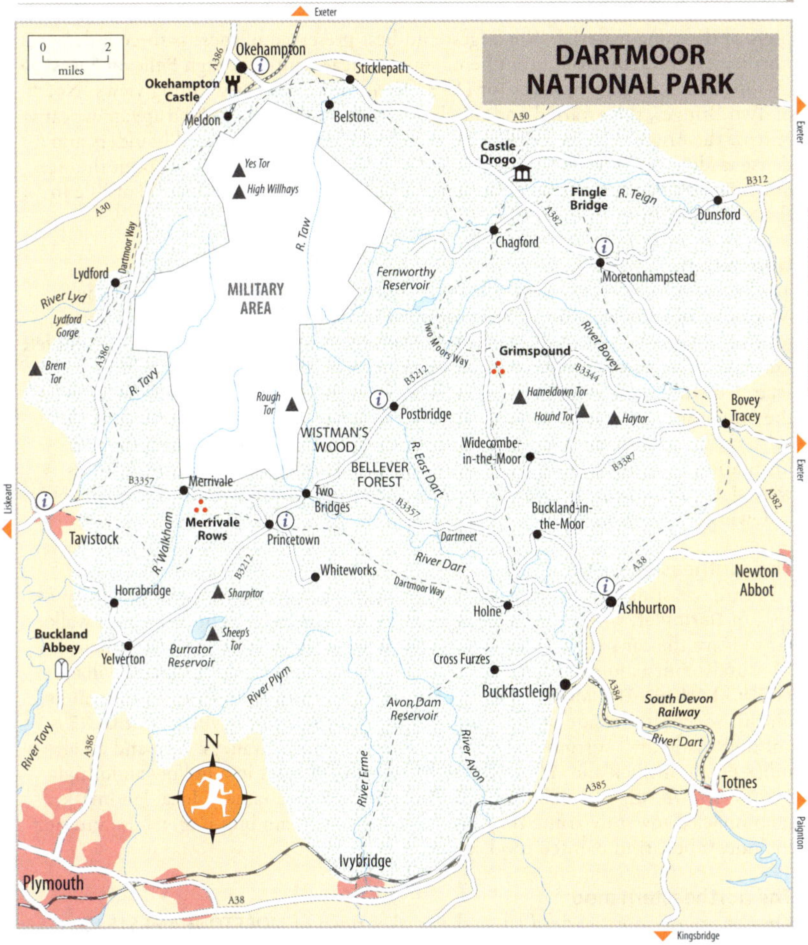

over the central fastnesses of the National Park, with solitary birds – buzzards, kestrels, pipits, stonechats and wagtails – wheeling and hovering high above.

The core of Dartmoor, characterized by tumbling streams and high tors chiselled by the elements, is **Dartmoor Forest**, which has belonged to the Duchy of Cornwall since 1307, though there is almost unlimited public access. Networks of signposts or painted stones exist to guide **walkers**, but map-reading abilities are a prerequisite for any but the shortest walks, and considerable experience is essential for longer distances. Overnight parking is only allowed in authorized places, and no vehicles are permitted beyond fifteen yards from the road; camping should be out of sight of houses and roads, and fires are strictly forbidden. Information on **guided walks** and riding facilities is available from National Park visitor centres and tourist offices in Dartmoor's major towns and villages.

Postbridge and around

Northeast of Princetown, two miles north of the crossroads at **Two Bridges**, you can see one of Dartmoor's **clapper bridges**: used by tin miners and farmers since medieval times, these simple structures consist of huge slabs of granite supported by piers of the same material. The largest and best preserved of these is three miles northeast at **POSTBRIDGE**. From here, you can head south through **Bellever Forest** to the open moor, where **Bellever Tor** (1453ft/443m) affords outstanding views. North of Two Bridges, the dwarfed and misshapen oaks of **Wistman's Wood** are an evocative relic of the original Dartmoor Forest, cluttered with lichen-covered boulders and a dense undergrowth of ferns. The gnarled old trees are alleged to have been the site of druidic gatherings, a story unsupported by any evidence but quite plausible in this solitary spot.

Grimspound

To the east of the B3212, reachable on a right turn towards Widecombe-in-the-Moor, the Bronze Age village of **Grimspound** lies below Hameldown Tor, about a mile off the road. Inhabited some three thousand years ago, this is the most complete example of Dartmoor's prehistoric settlements, consisting of 24 circular huts scattered within a four-acre enclosure. The site is thought to have been the model for the Stone Age settlement in which Sherlock Holmes camped in *The Hound of the Baskervilles*; while **Hound Tor**, an outcrop three miles to the southwest, provided inspiration for Conan Doyle's tale – according to local legend, phantom hounds were sighted racing across the moor to hurl themselves on the tomb of a hated squire following his death in 1677.

The southeastern moor

Four miles east of the crossroads at Two Bridges, crowds home in on the beauty spot of **Dartmeet**, where the valley is memorably lush and you don't need to walk far to leave the car park and ice-cream vans behind. From here the Dart pursues a leisurely course, joined by the River Webburn near the pretty moorland village of **BUCKLAND-IN-THE-MOOR**, one of a cluster of moorstone-and-thatched hamlets on this southeastern side of the moor. South of Buckland, the village of **HOLNE** is another rustic idyll surrounded on three sides by wooded valleys. Two and a half miles north of Buckland, **WIDECOMBE-IN-THE-MOOR** is set in a hollow amid high granite-strewn ridges. Its church of **St Pancras** provides a famous local landmark, its pinnacled tower dwarfing the fourteenth-century main building, whose interior includes a beautiful painted rood screen.

The northeastern moor

On Dartmoor's northeastern edge, the market town of **MORETONHAMPSTEAD** makes an attractive entry point from Exeter. Moretonhampstead has a historic rivalry with neighbouring **CHAGFORD**, a Stannary town (a chartered centre of the tin trade) that also flourished from the local wool industry. It stands on a hillside overlooking the River Teign, and has a fine fifteenth-century church and some good accommodation and eating options. Numerous **walks** can be made along the Teign and elsewhere in the vicinity.

Castle Drogo

Northeast of Chagford across the A382, near Drewsteignton • **House** Late Feb daily 11am–4pm; mid-March to Oct daily 11am–5pm; early Nov to mid-Dec Sat & Sun noon–4.30pm • £8.20 including grounds **Grounds** Daily: Jan to mid-March 11am–4pm; mid-March to Oct 9am–5.30pm; Nov & Dec 11am–5pm • £5.10, £8.20 with house • NT

The twentieth-century extravaganza of **Castle Drogo** is stupendously sited above the Teign gorge northeast of Chagford. Having retired at the age of 33, grocery magnate Julius Drewe unearthed a link that suggested his descent from a Norman baron, and set about creating a castle befitting his pedigree. Begun in 1910, to a design by **Edwin Lutyens**, it was not completed until 1930, but the result was an unsurpassed synthesis of medieval and modern elements. Paths lead from Drogo east to **Fingle Bridge**, a lovely spot, where shaded green pools shelter trout and the occasional salmon.

6

Okehampton

The main centre on the northern fringes of Dartmoor, **OKEHAMPTON** grew prosperous as a market town for the medieval wool trade, and some fine old buildings survive between the two branches of the River Okement that meet here, among them the prominent fifteenth-century tower of the **Chapel of St James**. Across the road from the seventeenth-century town hall, a granite archway leads into the **Museum of Dartmoor Life** (April–Oct Mon–Fri 10.15am–4.15pm; £3.50), which offers an excellent overview of habitation on the moor since earliest times.

Okehampton Castle

Daily: April–June & Sept 10am–5pm, July & Aug 10am–6pm • EH • £3.70

Perched above the West Okement a mile southwest of the centre, **Okehampton Castle** is the shattered hulk of a stronghold laid waste by Henry VIII. The tottering ruins include a gatehouse, Norman keep, and the remains of the Great Hall, buttery and kitchens. Woodland walks and riverside picnic tables invite a gentle exploration of what was once the deer park of the earls of Devon.

Lydford

Five miles southwest of Okehampton, the village of **LYDFORD** preserves the sturdy but small-scale **Lydford Castle**, a Saxon outpost, then a Norman keep and later used as a prison. The chief attraction here, though – apart from the hotels and restaurants – are the one-and-a-half-mile **Lydford Gorge** (NT; £5.80, free in winter) – overgrown with thick woods and alive with butterflies, spotted woodpeckers, dippers and herons.

Tavistock and around

The main town of the western moor, **TAVISTOCK** owes its distinctive Victorian appearance to the building boom that followed the discovery of copper deposits here in 1844. Originally, however, this market and Stannary town on the River Tavy grew around what was once the West Country's most important Benedictine abbey, established in the eleventh century. Some scant remnants survive in the churchyard of **St Eustace**, a mainly fifteenth-century building with stained glass from William Morris's studio in the south aisle.

North of Tavistock, a four-mile lane wanders up to **Brent Tor**, 1130ft high and dominating Dartmoor's western fringes. Access to its conical summit is easiest along a path gently ascending through gorse on its southwestern side, leading to the small church of St Michael at the top.

ARRIVAL AND DEPARTURE — DARTMOOR

BY TRAIN

Between mid-May and mid-September, Okehampton sees a useful Sunday rail connection with Exeter (Sun 4 daily; 40min–1hr). The station is a 15min walk up Station Rd from Fore St.

BY BUS

Destinations from Princetown Exeter (late May to mid-Sept Sun 5 daily; 1hr 35min); Moretonhampstead (late May to mid-Sept Sun 5 daily; 45min); Plymouth (late May to mid-Sept Sun 5 daily; 50min); Tavistock (Mon–Sat 1 daily; 30min).

Destinations from Moretonhampstead Chagford (Mon–Sat 3 daily; 15min); Exeter (5–7 daily; 50min); Okehampton (Mon–Sat 1 daily; 1hr); Princetown (late May to mid-Sept Sun 5 daily; 40min).

Destinations from Chagford Exeter (Mon–Sat 5 daily; 1hr); Moretonhampstead (Mon–Sat 3 daily; 15min); Okehampton (Mon–Sat 5 daily; 50min).

Destinations from Okehampton Exeter (every 30min–1hr; 1hr–1hr 15min); Moretonhampstead (Mon–Sat 1 daily; 1hr); Tavistock (7–8 daily; 45–50min).

Destinations from Tavistock Okehampton (7 daily; 45–55min); Plymouth (Mon–Sat every 30min, 1 on Sun; 1hr) and Princetown (Mon–Sat 1 daily; 30min).

GETTING AROUND

By bus Public transport is good to the main centres on the periphery of the moor – Okehampton, Tavistock, Moretonhampstead – but extremely sketchy for the heart of the moor. The best bets are the #82 "Transmoor Link" (June to mid-Sept Sun only), between Plymouth and Exeter, taking in Princetown, Two Bridges, Postbridge and Moretonhampstead en route, and the #98 connecting Tavistock, Princetown, Two Bridges and Postbridge (not Sun).

INFORMATION

A significant portion of northern Dartmoor, containing the moor's highest tors and some of its most famous beauty spots, is run by the **Ministry of Defence**, whose **firing ranges** are marked by red-and-white posts; when firing is in progress, red flags or red lights signify that entry is prohibited. Generally, if no warning flags are flying by 9am between April and September, or by 10am from October to March, there will be no firing on that day; alternatively, check at T 0800 458 4868 or W mod.uk/access.

6

Princetown National Park Visitor Centre Tavistock Rd (March & Oct daily 10am–4pm; April–Sept daily 10am–5pm; Nov–Feb Thurs–Sun 10.30am–3.30pm; T 01822 890414, W dartmoor-npa.gov.uk).

Postbridge National Park Visitor Centre Main car park (daily: April–Sept 10am–5pm; Oct 10am–4pm; T 01822 880272, W dartmoor-npa.gov.uk).

Morehampton tourist office New St (April–Oct daily 9.30am–5pm; Nov–Easter Thurs–Sat 10am–4pm, Sun 11am–3pm; T 01647 440043, W moretonhampstead.com).

Okehampton tourist office Fore St (Mon–Sat 10am–5pm; reduced days and hours in winter; T 01837 53020, W okehamptondevon.co.uk).

Tavistock tourist office Bedford Square (April–Oct Mon–Sat 10am–5pm; reduced hours in winter; T 01822 612938, W dartmoor.co.uk).

ACCOMMODATION AND EATING

Scattered **accommodation** options include several **camping barns**, which it's always wise to book ahead, particularly at weekends: call the numbers given in our reviews, or else the YHA, which administers them (T 01629 592700, E campingbarns@yha.org.uk).

22 Mill Street Chigford T 01647 432244, W 22millst.com. This smart country restaurant offers top-quality modern European cuisine: two- and three-course menus cost £17/£22 for lunch, £36/£42 for dinner. They also have two luxury guestrooms. Food served Tues–Sat noon–2.30pm & 7–10.30pm.

Castle Inn Next to Lydford Castle T 01822 820241, W castleinndartmoor.co.uk. Sixteenth-century inn where one of the en-suite rooms has its own roof terrace looking onto the castle; there are also little cottage rooms and one with a four-poster. Free wi-fi. The oak-beamed, fire-lit bar provides good drinks and there's a beer garden and a restaurant. Food served daily until 10pm. **£65**

Cyprian's Cot 47 New St, Chigford T 01647 432256, W cyprianscot.co.uk. Comfy, sixteenth-century cottage where you can warm your bones by an inglenook fireplace and in fine weather breakfast and take tea in the garden. No credit cards. **£60**

Dartmoor Inn A386 opposite Lydford turning T 01822 820221, W dartmoorinn.com. Three spacious guest rooms available above a popular gastropub, each furnished with antiques. The restaurant menu features tasty options like fish casserole and pork belly. Set-price menus £16.50/£20.50; à la carte mains £15–19. Booking advised. They also have a simpler bar menu (not Fri or Sat eves; dishes £10–15). Food served Mon 6.30–9.15pm (last orders), Tues–Sat noon–2.30pm & 6.30–9.15pm, Sun noon–3.15pm. **£95**

Duchy House Tavistock Rd, Princetown T 01822 890552, W duchyhouse.co.uk. Just 250m from the centre of Princetown, this Victorian B&B offers staid but reliable accommodation in traditionally furnished rooms – one with its own bathroom – and a guests' lounge. **£70**

Great Houndtor camping barn Near Manaton T 01629 592700. This YHA-managed former farmhouse offers a cooking area and hot water for showers, and there's an open fire. **£6.50**

Higher Venton Farm Half a mile south of Widecombe T 01364 621235, W ventonfarm.com. A peaceful sixteenth-century thatched longhouse that was once home to the Dartmoor writer Beatrice Chase. The bedrooms are fine, and it's close to a couple of good pubs. **£70**

Kestor Inn Manaton T 01647 221626, W www.kestorinn.com. A popular pub with walkers, serving hot food as well as local ales and ciders, and selling maps, provisions and walking guides. Daily 11am–11pm.

Meadowlea 65 Station Rd, Okehampton T 01837 53200, W meadowleaguesthouse.co.uk. A short walk south of the centre, below the train station and within 500m of the Granite Way cycling route, this B&B has seven rooms (most en suite), wi-fi access and cycle storage. **£60**

★ **Mount Tavy Cottage** Half a mile east of Tavistock, B3357 Princetown road T 01822 614253, W mounttavy.co.uk. Set in a lush garden with a lake, this B&B has comfortable rooms, organic breakfasts, evening meals and a self-catering option. **£75**

Plume of Feathers The Square, Princetown T 01822 890240. B&B, bunkhouse dorms and a campsite right in the centre of Princetown. Bar meals are available here and from the neighbouring *Railway Inn*, under the same management. Dorm **£15**, double **£75**

Sparrowhawk Backpackers 45 Ford St, Moretonhampstead 01647 440318, sparrowhawkbackpackers.co.uk. Excellent, eco-friendly hostel, with fourteen beds in a light and spacious bunkroom and a private room sleeping up to four. Good kitchen for self-catering. Dorm £16, double £36

Warren House Inn 2 miles northeast of Postbridge 01822 880208, warrenhouseinn.co.uk. In a bleak tract of moorland north of Postbridge, this solitary pub offers firelit comfort and meals (around £9.50). Easter–Nov Mon–Sat 11am–11pm, Sun 11am–10.30pm; Nov–Easter Mon & Tues 11am–5pm, Wed–Sat 11am–11pm, Sun noon–10.30pm.

YHA Bellever Near Postbridge 0845 371 9622, bellever@yha.org.uk. One of Dartmoor's two YHA hostels lies a mile or so south of Postbridge on the edge of the forest and on the banks of the East Dart River. By bus, take the daily #98 from Tavistock or Princetown (not Sun) or #82 from Princetown, Plymouth or Exeter (summer Sun only) to Postbridge and walk a mile. £20.40

YHA Okehampton Klondyke Rd, Okehampton 0845 371 9651, okehampton@yha.org.uk. Housed in a converted goods shed at the station, and offers a range of outdoor activities as well as bike rental. Camping also available. Dorm £23, double £60

6

Barnstaple

BARNSTAPLE, at the head of the Taw estuary, makes an excellent North Devon base, well connected to the resorts of Bideford Bay, Ilfracombe and Woolacombe, as well as to the western fringes of Exmoor. The town's centuries-old role as a marketplace is perpetuated in the daily bustle around the huge timber-framed **Pannier Market** off the High Street, alongside which runs **Butchers Row**, its 33 archways now converted to a variety of uses. At the end of Boutport Street, the **Museum of North Devon** (Mon–Sat 9.30am–4/5pm; free) holds a lively miscellany that includes a collection of the eighteenth-century pottery for which the region was famous. The museum lies alongside the Taw, where footpaths make for a pleasant riverside stroll, with the colonnaded eighteenth-century **Queen Anne's Walk** – built as a merchants' exchange – providing some architectural interest. It houses the **Barnstaple Heritage Centre** (April–Oct Tues–Sat 10am–5pm, also Mon in school hols; Nov–March Tues–Fri 10am–4.30pm, Sat 10am–3.30pm; £3.50), which traces the town's social history by means of reconstructions and touch-screen computers.

ARRIVAL AND INFORMATION — BARNSTAPLE

By train Barnstaple's train station is on the south side of the Taw, a 5min walk from the centre. There are good connections with Exeter on the Tarka Line (Mon–Sat hourly, Sun 7 daily; 1hr 10min).

By bus The bus station is centrally located between Silver St and Belle Meadow Rd.

Tourist office Museum of North Devon, Boutport St (Mon–Sat 9.30am–4/5pm; 01271 375000, staynorthdevon.co.uk).

THE TARKA LINE AND THE TARKA TRAIL

North Devon is closely associated with Henry Williamson's *Tarka the Otter* (1927), which relates the travels and travails of a young otter, and is one of the finest pieces of nature writing in the English language. With parts of the book set in the Taw valley, it was perhaps inevitable that the Exeter to Barnstaple rail route – which follows the Taw for half of its length – should be dubbed the **Tarka Line**. Barnstaple itself forms the centre of the figure-of-eight traced by the **Tarka Trail**, which tracks the otter's wanderings for a distance of more than 180 miles. To the north, the trail penetrates Exmoor (see p.279) then follows the coast back, passing through Williamson's home village of **Georgeham** on its return to Barnstaple. South, the path takes in Bideford (see p.310), and continues as far as Okehampton (see p.305).

Twenty-three miles of the trail follow a former rail line that's ideally suited to **bicycles**, and there are bike rental shops at Barnstaple and Bideford. You can pick up a *Tarka Trail* booklet and free leaflets on individual sections of the trail from tourist offices.

ACCOMMODATION

Broomhill Art Hotel Muddiford, 2 miles north of Barnstaple off the A39 ⓣ01271 850262, ⓦbroomhillart.co.uk. Striking combination of gallery, restaurant and hotel where the rooms look onto a sculpture garden. Half-board only at weekends. £75

Mount Sandford Landkey Rd ⓣ01271 342354. A couple of miles southeast of the centre, this elegant, porticoed Regency building offers spacious en-suite rooms overlooking a lovely garden. From the museum, follow Taw Vale, New Rd and Newport Rd to Landkey Rd. No credit cards. £50

The Old Post Office 22 Pilton St ⓣ01271 859439, ⓦtheoldpostoffice-pilton.co.uk. Quality B&B half a mile north of the centre, with tasteful, period furnishings and a garden. Breakfasts are mainly free range and organic. No credit cards. £85

6

EATING AND DRINKING

Old School Coffee House 6 Church Lane ⓣ01271 372793. This well-preserved building from 1659 now houses a no-frills café-restaurant – nothing fancy, but brimming with atmosphere – where you can spin out a coffee or tea, or tuck into a dish of Persian lamb (around £6). Mon & Wed 9.15am–3pm, Tues & Thurs–Sat 9.15am–4pm.

Terra Madre Broomhill Art Hotel, Muddiford ⓣ01271 850262, ⓦbroomhillart.co.uk. Bar meals and delicious, Mediterranean-style fixed-price lunches (Wed–Sun; £15) and dinners (Wed–Sat, but may close Wed & Thurs; £25) are served at this restaurant attached to a hotel and gallery. Mon–Sat 12.30–2pm & 7.30–8.30pm (last orders), Sun 12.30–2pm.

Ilfracombe and around

The most popular resort on Devon's northern coast, **ILFRACOMBE** is essentially little changed since its evolution into a Victorian and Edwardian tourist centre. In summer, if the crowds of holiday-makers become oppressive, you can escape on a coastal tour, a fishing trip or the fifteen-mile cruise to Lundy Island (see opposite), all available at the small harbour. On foot, you can explore the attractive stretch of coast running east out of Ilfracombe and beyond the grassy cliffs of Hillsborough, where a succession of undeveloped coves and inlets is surrounded by jagged slanting rocks and heather-covered hills.

There are sandy **beaches** here, though many prefer those beyond **Morte Point**, five miles west of Ilfracombe, from where the view takes in Lundy. Below the promontory, the pocket-sized **Barricane Beach** is famous for the tropical shells washed up by Atlantic currents from the Caribbean. It's a popular swimming spot, though there's more space just south of here on the two miles of **Woolacombe Sands**, a broad, west-facing expanse much favoured by surfers and families alike.

INFORMATION — ILFRACOMBE

Tourist office Landmark Theatre, on the seafront (Easter–Oct Mon–Fri 10am–5pm, Sat 10am–5pm; reduced hours in winter; ⓣ01271 863001, ⓦvisitilfracombe.co.uk).

ACCOMMODATION

Ocean Backpackers 29 St James Place ⓣ01271 867835, ⓦoceanbackpackers.co.uk. Excellent, central hostel that's popular with surfing folk. Dorms are mostly six-bed, there are doubles available, and there's a well-equipped kitchen and free wi-fi. Dorm £13.50, double £38

Westwood Torrs Park ⓣ01271 867443, ⓦwest-wood.co.uk. In a quiet area a 10min walk from the centre (and just 5min from the coast path), this B&B is more like a boutique hotel, with boldly decorated rooms and terrific views. £90

EATING AND DRINKING

The Quay 11 The Quay ⓣ01271 868091, ⓦ11thequay.co.uk. By the harbour, Ilfracombe's most famous restaurant (co-owned by artist Damien Hirst, whose works are displayed) offers a Mediterranean menu using local ingredients– risotto nero with cuttlefish tempura, for example, or roasted fillet of cod with chorizo. Most mains are around £15, and there are good-value set-price deals. Drinks and snacks are available daily in the relaxed ground-floor bar. Daily 10am–late, restaurant noon–2.30pm & 6–9.30pm; reduced hours in winter.

6

LUNDY ISLAND

There are fewer than twenty full-time residents on **Lundy**, a tiny windswept island twelve miles north of Hartland Point. Now a refuge for thousands of marine birds, Lundy has no cars, just one pub and one shop – indeed little has changed since the Marisco family established itself here in the twelfth century, making use of the shingle beaches and coves to terrorize shipping along the Bristol Channel. The family's fortunes only fell in 1242 when one of their number, William de Marisco, was found to be plotting against the king, whereupon he was hung, drawn and quartered at Tower Hill in London. The castle erected by Henry III on Lundy's southern end dates from this time.

Today the island is managed by the Landmark Trust. Unless you're on a specially arranged diving or climbing expedition, **walking** along the interweaving tracks and footpaths is really the only thing to do here. The shores – mainly cliffy on the west, softer and undulating on the east – shelter a rich variety of **birdlife**, including kittiwakes, fulmars, shags and Manx shearwaters, which often nest in rabbit burrows. The most famous birds, though, are the **puffins** after which Lundy is named – from the Norse *Lunde* (puffin) and *ey* (island). They can only be sighted in April and May, when they come ashore to mate. Offshore, **grey seals** can be seen all the year round.

ARRIVAL AND INFORMATION

By boat Between April and October, the *MS Oldenburg* sails to Lundy up to four times a week from Ilfracombe, less frequently from Bideford (around 2hr from both places; day returns £33.50, open returns £58). To reserve a place, call ⓣ 01271 863636 (day returns can also be booked from the local tourist offices).

Useful website ⓦ lundyisland.co.uk.

ACCOMMODATION

Self-catering A number of idiosyncratic Landmark Trust properties are available for self-catering by the week. These range from eighteenth-century hideaways for two in a castle keep to weathered fishermen's cottages. They're hugely popular, so book well in advance through the Landmark Trust (ⓣ 01628 825925, ⓦ landmarktrust.org.uk).

B&B Availability for nightly B&B is very limited, with bookings only possible within one week of the proposed visit. Outside the holiday season, however, it's still possible to find a double room for around £60 per night. Contact ⓣ 01271 863636.

Camping Lundy also has a campsite (closed Nov–March; book two weeks ahead at ⓣ 01271 863636).

Woolacombe and around

At the more crowded northern end of **Woolacombe Sands**, a cluster of hotels, villas and retirement homes makes up the summer resort of **WOOLACOMBE**. At the quieter southern end lies the choice swimming spot of **Putsborough Sands** and the promontory of **Baggy Point**, where gannets, shags, cormorants and shearwaters gather from September to November.

South of here is **Croyde Bay**, another surfers' delight, more compact than Woolacombe, with stalls on the sand renting surfboards and wet suits, and **Saunton Sands**, a magnificent long stretch of coast pummelled by endless ranks of classic breakers.

INFORMATION — WOOLACOMBE

Tourist office The Esplanade (April–Oct daily 10am–5pm; Nov–March Mon–Sat 10am–1pm; ⓣ 01271 870553, ⓦ woolacombetourism.co.uk).

ACCOMMODATION

North Morte Farm Mortehoe, a mile north ⓣ 01271 870381, ⓦ northmortefarm.co.uk. More peaceful than many of the campsites around here, this has panoramic sea views and access to Rockham Beach, though not much shelter. Mortehoe's pubs are a short walk away. Closed Nov–March. £9.25 per person

Rocks Hotel Beach Rd ⓣ 01271 870361, ⓦ therockshotel.co.uk. Woolacombe's top accommodation choice is a surfer-friendly place close to the beach, with smallish but smart high-spec bedrooms and bathrooms, and a breakfast room styled like a 1950s American diner. £79

6

SURFING IN NORTH DEVON

Devon's premier surfing sites are on the west-facing coast between Morte Point and the Taw estuary. The two extensive fine-sand beaches of **Woolacombe Sands**, to the north, and **Saunton Sands**, south, are long enough to accommodate any number of surfers, but smaller **Croyde Bay**, sandwiched between them, can get congested in summer. **Equipment** is available to rent from numerous places in the villages of Woolacombe and Croyde or from stalls on the beach (around £8–12 for 4hr or £10–15 per day for a board, £8 for 4hr or £10 per day for a wet suit). Check the local surf reports and webcams at Ⓦsurfstation.co.uk.

EATING AND DRINKING

Bar Electric Beach Rd Ⓣ01271 870429. Friendly hangout that stays buzzing till late, with a range of drinks and meals, including pizzas and pastas (all £8–10). Easter–May, Nov & Dec Fri 5pm–midnight, Sat noon–midnight, Sun noon–3pm; June, July, Sept & Oct Wed–Fri 5pm–midnight, Sat noon–midnight, Sun noon–11pm; Aug daily noon–midnight. Food served until 3pm & 9pm.

Blue Groove 2 Hobbs Hill, Croyde Ⓣ01271 890111, Ⓦblue-groove.co.uk. As well as burgers, steaks and seafood, this modern village restaurant-bar offers global dishes from Basque chicken to Thai mussels and Goan fish curry (£11–16). In the evening, settle down with a cocktail, absinthe or Japanese saki. Easter–Dec daily 9/10am–late.

Bideford and around

Like Barnstaple, nine miles to the east, the estuary town of **BIDEFORD** formed an important link in north Devon's trade network in the Middle Ages, mainly due to its **bridge**, which still straddles the River Torridge. A couple of miles downstream, the old shipbuilding port of **APPLEDORE**, lined with pastel-coloured Georgian houses, is worth a wander and a drink in one of its cosy **pubs**.

INFORMATION — BIDEFORD

Tourist office in the Burton Art Gallery and Museum, Kingsley Rd (Mon–Sat 10am–4pm, Sun 11am–4pm; Ⓣ01237 477676, Ⓦtorridge.gov.uk).

ACCOMMODATION AND EATING

The Mount Northdown Rd Ⓣ01237 473748, Ⓦthemountbideford.co.uk. Set in its own walled garden, with elegant rooms, this Georgian B&B has a guests' lounge, free wi-fi, and evening meals. It's linked to the centre by a footpath. **£80**

Serendipity 26 Mill St Ⓣ01237 473007. This lively café/bistro is good for daytime snacks or Italian-style evening meals – the menu includes pizzas and pastas as well as steaks and burgers (all £10–14) – and there's a small courtyard. Closed Mon eve & Sun.

Velvet & Vanilla 12 Cooper St Ⓣ01237 420444, Ⓦvelvetandvanilla.co.uk. Small and snug spot for soups and toasties or, in the evening, mezes and stonebaked pizzas (£7.50–9.50, or £20 for three mezes and a bottle of wine). Mon–Thurs 10am–4pm, Fri & Sat 10am–4pm & 7pm–noon.

Clovelly

West along Bideford Bay, picturesque **CLOVELLY** was put on the map in the second half of the nineteenth century by two books: Charles Dickens' *A Message From the Sea* and *Westward Ho!* by Charles Kingsley, whose father was rector here for six years. The picture-postcard tone of the village has been preserved by strict regulations, but its excessive quaintness and the streams of visitors on summer days can make it hard to see beyond the artifice.

Beyond the **visitor centre**, where an entrance fee to the village is charged, the cobbled, traffic-free main street plunges down past neat, flower-smothered cottages. The tethered sledges here are used for transporting goods, the only way to carry supplies up and down the hill since they stopped using donkeys. At the bottom, Clovelly's stony beach and tiny harbour snuggle under a cleft in the cliff wall.

GETTING AROUND AND INFORMATION — CLOVELLY

Land Rover service If you can't face the return climb to the top of the village, make use of the Land Rover service that leaves from behind the *Red Lion* on the quayside (Easter–Oct 9.30am–5.30pm; every 15min; £2.50).

Visitor centre At the top of the village (daily 10am–4pm, summer school hols 9am–6pm; clovelly.co.uk); an entrance fee to the village is payable here (£5.95).

ACCOMMODATION AND EATING

East Dyke Farmhouse Higher Clovelly, near the A39 junction 01237 431216, bedbreakfastclovelly.co.uk. Away from the old village, this two-hundred-year-old building with a beamed and flagstoned dining room has guest rooms with fridges and private bathrooms. No credit cards. **£60**

Red Lion The Quay 01237 431237, clovelly.co.uk. Of the village's two luxurious and pricey hotels, this one enjoys the best position, right on the harbourside. It's got a congenial bar and a formal restaurant specializing in super-fresh seafood (two courses £24.50, three courses £29.50). **£142**

Hartland and around

Three miles west of Clovelly, the inland village of **HARTLAND** holds little appeal, but the coast around is among Devon's most spectacular. You could arrive at **Hartland Point** along minor roads, but the best approach is on foot along the coast path. The jagged black rocks of the dramatic headland are battered by the sea and overlooked by a solitary lighthouse 350ft up. South of Hartland Point, the saw-toothed rocks and near-vertical escarpments defiantly confront the waves, with spectacular waterfalls tumbling over the cliffs.

Hartland Abbey

Mansion Easter to late May Wed, Thurs & Sun 2–5pm; late May to early Oct Mon–Thurs & Sun 2–5pm • £10 with grounds **Grounds** Easter to early Oct Sun–Fri noon–5pm • £5, £10 with mansion • hartlandabbey.com

Surrounded by gardens and lush woodland, **Hartland Abbey** is an eighteenth-century mansion incorporating the ruins of an abbey dissolved in 1539. The Regency library has portraits by Gainsborough and Reynolds, George Gilbert Scott designed the vaulted Alhambra Corridor and outer hall, and fine furniture, old photographs and frescoes are everywhere. A path leads a mile from the house to cliffs and a small, sandy bay.

ACCOMMODATION AND EATING — HARTLAND

★ **2 Harton Manor** The Square, off Fore St 01237 441670, twohartonmanor.co.uk. Small, friendly B&B offering two rooms above an artist's studio – one en-suite with a four-poster. Organic, locally sourced and Aga-cooked breakfasts are eaten in the flagstoned kitchen. No credit cards. **£72**

Stoke Barton Farm Stoke, half a mile west of Hartland Abbey 01237 441238, westcountry-camping.co.uk. Right by the fourteenth-century church of St Nectan's, this working farm offers basic camping (March–Oct) as well as teas, fresh scones and home-baked cakes. Tearoom May & June Sat & Sun 2–5.30pm; July & Aug Wed–Sun 2–5.30pm. **£6.50** per person

Cornwall

When D.H. Lawrence wrote that being in **Cornwall** was "like being at a window and looking out of England", he wasn't just thinking of its geographical extremity. Virtually unaffected by the Roman conquest, Cornwall was for centuries the last haven for a **Celtic culture** elsewhere eradicated by the Saxons. Primitive granite crosses and a crop of Celtic saints remain as traces of this formative period, and the Cornish language is present in place names that in many cases have grown more exotic as they have mutated over time.

Cornwall's formerly thriving **industrial economy** is far more conspicuous than in neighbouring Devon. Its more westerly stretches in particular are littered with the derelict stacks and castle-like ruins of the engine houses that once powered the region's

6

copper and **tin mines**, while deposits of **china clay** continue to be mined in the area around St Austell, as witnessed by the conical spoil heaps thereabouts. Also prominent throughout the county are the grey nonconformist chapels that reflect the impact of Methodism on Cornwall's mining communities. Nowadays, of course, Cornwall's most flourishing industry is tourism. The impact of the holiday business has been uneven, for instance cluttering **Land's End** with a tacky leisure complex but leaving Cornwall's other great headland, **Lizard Point**, undeveloped. The thronged resorts of **Falmouth**, site of the National Maritime Museum, and **Newquay**, the West's chief surfing centre, have adapted to the demands of mass tourism, but its effects have been more destructive in smaller, quainter places, such as **Mevagissey**, **Polperro** and **Padstow**, whose genuine charms can be hard to make out in full season. Other villages, such as **Fowey** and **Boscastle**, still preserve an authentic feel, however, while you couldn't wish for anything more remote than **Bodmin Moor**, a tract of wilderness in the heart of Cornwall, or the **Isles of Scilly**, idyllically free of development. It would be hard to compromise the sense of desolation surrounding **Tintagel**, site of what is fondly known as King Arthur's Castle, or the appeal of the seaside resorts of **St Ives** and **Bude** – both with great surfing beaches – while, near **St Austell**, the spectacular **Eden Project** celebrates environmental diversity with visionary style.

Looe

The southeast strip of the Cornish coast holds a string of compact harbour towns interspersed with long stretches of magnificent coastline. The first of these towns, **LOOE**, was drawing crowds as early as 1800, when the first "bathing-machines" were wheeled out; it was the arrival of the railway in 1879, though, that really packed its beaches. Though the river-divided town now touts itself as something of a shark-fishing centre, most people come here for the sand, the handiest stretch being the beach in front of East Looe. Away from the river mouth, you'll find cleaner water a mile eastwards at **Millendreath**.

ARRIVAL AND INFORMATION — LOOE

By train There's a rail link from Liskeard to Looe (hourly, not Sun in winter; 30min).

By bus Looe has bus connections with Liskeard (Mon–Sat hourly, Sun every 2hr; 25min); Plymouth (Mon–Sat 9 daily, Sun 2 daily; 1hr 10min–1hr 35min); Polperro (Mon–Sat every 20min–1hr, Sun hourly; 20min).

Tourist office New Guildhall, Fore St (Easter–Oct daily 10am–5pm; reduced hours in winter; ⓣ01503 262072, ⓦvisit-southeastcornwall.co.uk).

ACCOMMODATION AND EATING

Old Sail Loft The Quay ⓣ01503 262131, ⓦtheoldsailloftrestaurant.com. This oak-beamed former warehouse offers the freshest seafood as well as meat-based dishes, such as a trio of local fish (£17) or a grilled steak (£18–20). Mon & Wed–Sat noon–2pm & 6–8.45pm (last orders), Tues & Sun 6–8.45pm, closed Tues eve in winter.

Schooner Point 1 Trelawney Terrace, West Looe ⓣ01503 262670, ⓦschoonerpoint.co.uk. Just 100m from Looe Bridge, this family-run guesthouse has great river views from most of its good-value rooms, which include a single. No credit cards. £65

Shutta House Shutta Rd ⓣ01503 264233, ⓦshuttahouse.co.uk. A short walk outside the centre and just across from the station, this neo-Gothic ex-vicarage has clean, airy en-suite rooms, some with garden views, and free wi-fi. £75

Polperro

Linked to Looe by frequent buses, **POLPERRO** is smaller and quainter than its neighbour, but has a similar feel. From the bus stop and car park at the top of the village, it's a five- or ten-minute walk alongside the River Pol to the pretty harbour. The surrounding cliffs and the tightly packed houses rising on each side of the stream have an undeniable

CLOCKWISE FROM TOP LEFT PORTHCURNO (P.323); CREAM TEA; GODREVY BEACH, NEAR ST IVES; CORNISH PASTIES >

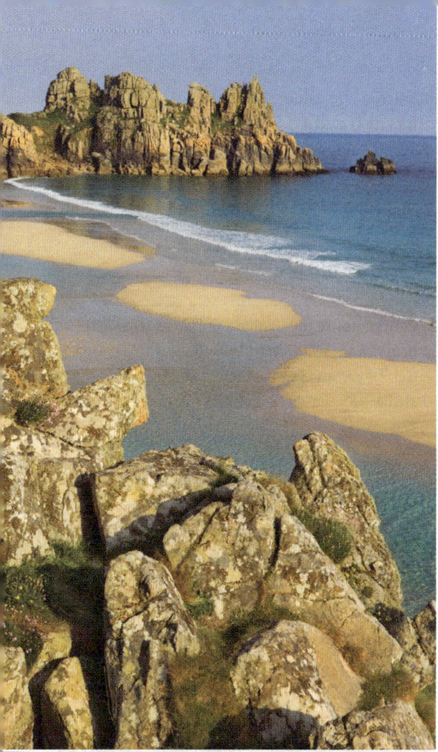

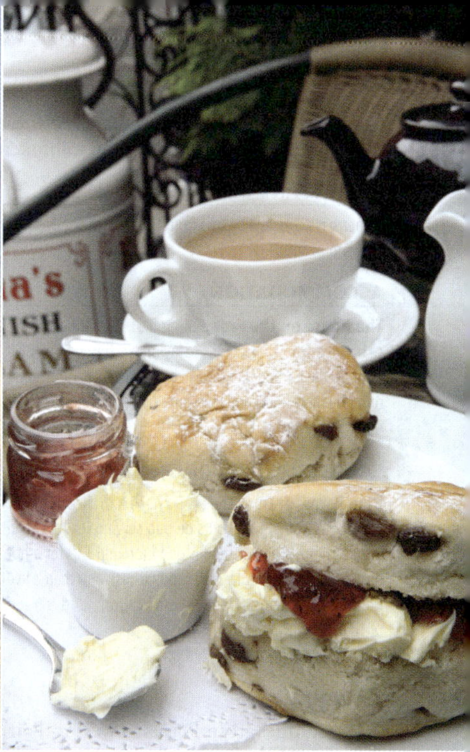

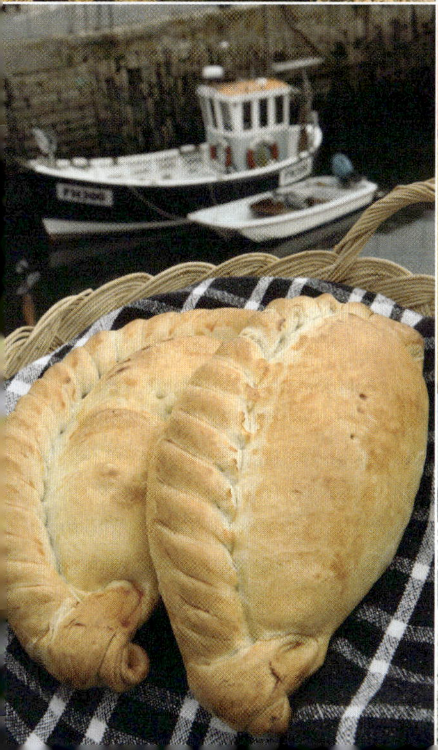

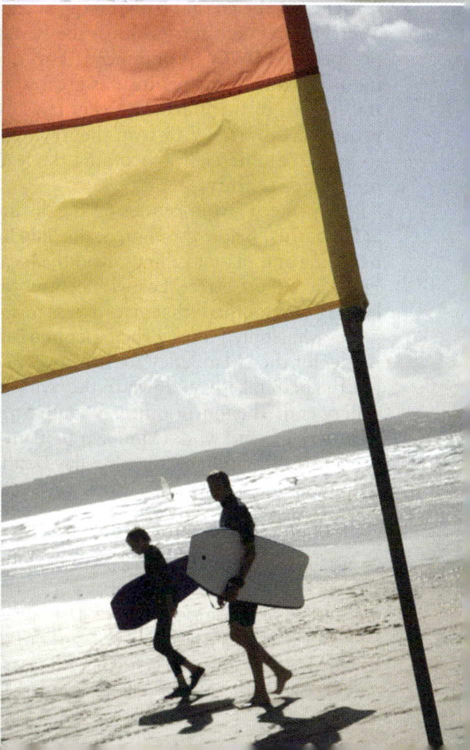

charm, and the tangle of lanes is little changed since the village's heyday of pilchard fishing and smuggling, but the tourist stream has also ruined it, and its straggling main street – the Coombes – is now an unbroken row of tacky shops and food outlets.

ARRIVAL AND DEPARTURE — POLPERRO

Polperro is accessible by **bus** from Looe (Mon–Sat every 20min–1hr, Sun hourly; 20min) and Plymouth (1 daily; Mon–Sat 1hr 15min, Sun 2hr).

ACCOMMODATION

The House on the Props Talland St ⓣ01503 272310, ⓦhouseontheprops.co.uk. Staying at this quirky B&B right on the harbour is a bit like being on a boat, with snug rooms, wonky floors and awesome views; there's also a tea-room and restaurant on board. **£80**

Penryn House The Coombes ⓣ01503 272157, ⓦpenrynhouse.co.uk. Relaxed and friendly B&B with a country-house feel. The immaculately clean rooms are small but cosy – those at the back are quietest, though have no view. Parking available. **£72**

EATING AND DRINKING

Blue Peter The Quay ⓣ01503 272743, ⓦthebluepeter.co.uk. Welcoming harbourside pub serving real ales and local scrumpy. The bar food is good (around £10 for a hot dish or £8.20 for chunky crab sandwiches), and there's live music at weekends. Daily 11am–11pm; food served until 8.30/9pm.

Old Mill House Mill Hill ⓣ01503 272362, ⓦoldmillhouseinn.co.uk. Central but relatively secluded, this is an agreeable pub with a separate restaurant. Accommodation also available. Daily 9am–midnight; food served noon–2pm & 5.30–8.45pm.

Fowey

The ten miles from Polperro west to Polruan are among south Cornwall's finest stretches of the coastal path, giving access to some beautiful secluded **sand beaches**. There are frequent ferries across the River Fowey from Polruan, affording a fine prospect of **FOWEY** (pronounced "Foy"), a cascade of neat, pale terraces at the mouth of one of the peninsula's greatest rivers. The major port on the county's south coast in the fourteenth century, Fowey finally became so ambitious that it provoked Edward IV to strip the town of its military capability, though it continued to thrive commercially, becoming the leading port for china clay shipments in the nineteenth century.

Fowey's steep layout centres on the distinctive fifteenth-century church of **St Fimbarrus**. Below the church, the **Ship Inn**, which sports some fine Elizabethan panelling and plaster ceilings, held the local Roundhead HQ during the Civil War. From here, Fore Street, Lostwithiel Street and the Esplanade fan out, the **Esplanade** leading to a footpath that gives access to some splendid **coastal walks**. One of these passes Menabilly House, where **Daphne Du Maurier** lived for 24 years – it was the model for the "Manderley" of her novel *Rebecca*. The house is not open to the public, but the path takes you down to the twin coves of **Polridmouth**, where Rebecca met her watery end. The tourist office, 5 South Street, houses a small exhibition of Du Maurier's life and work (Mon–Sat 9.30am–5pm, Sun 10am–4pm; free), and can provide information on the nine-day **Daphne Du Maurier Festival** (ⓣ01726 833847, ⓦdumaurierfestival.co.uk), which takes place each May.

ARRIVAL AND INFORMATION — FOWEY

By bus Fowey is easily accessible from the west by #25, #524 and #525 buses from the train stations at St Austell (Mon–Sat 2–3 hourly, Sun hourly; 45min) and Par (Mon–Sat 2–3 hourly, Sun hourly; 10min).

By ferry Fowey can be reached by ferry across the river every 10–15min daily from Bodinnick (foot passengers and vehicles) and Polruan (foot passengers only); tickets cost around £1.50 for a foot passenger, £3.50–4.50 for a car and passengers (ⓦctomsandson.co.uk).

Tourist office 5 South St (Mon–Sat 9.30am–5pm, Sun 10am–4pm; ⓣ01726 833616, ⓦfowey.co.uk).

ACCOMMODATION

Coombe Farm Off B3269 ⓣ 01726 833123, ⓦ coombefarmbb.co.uk. A 20min walk from town, this place provides perfect rural isolation – and there's a bathing area just 300m away. No credit cards. £65

YHA Golant Three miles north of Fowey, outside Golant ⓣ 0845 371 9019, ⓔ golant@yha.org.uk. There are great views over the valley from this Georgian mansion, and good food available. To get there, take bus #25 to Castle Dore, then walk 1.5 miles. Dorm £20.40, double £51

EATING AND DRINKING

The Other Place 41 Fore St ⓣ 01726 833636, ⓦ otherplacefowey.co.uk. If you don't fancy sitting down to a plate of fresh fish (around £10) or steak and chips (£12.50), order breakfast or pick up a takeaway. Takeaway daily 8am–8/9pm; restaurant summer daily 5.30–9pm (last orders); winter Thurs–Sat 5.30–9pm (last orders).

Sam's 20 Fore St ⓣ 01726 832273, ⓦ samsfowey.co.uk. With a menu ranging from burgers (£9–12) to seafood (£10–15), this place has 1960s rock'n'roll decor and friendly service. It doesn't take bookings, so arrive early or be prepared to wait. There's a late-closing lounge bar upstairs. Daily noon–9pm (last orders).

6

St Austell Bay

It was the discovery of china clay, or kaolin, in the downs to the north of **St Austell Bay** that spurred the area's growth in the eighteenth century. An essential ingredient in the production of porcelain, kaolin had until then only been produced in northern China. Still a vital part of Cornwall's economy, the clay is now mostly exported for use in the manufacture of paper, as well as paint and medicines. The conical spoil heaps left by the mines are a feature of the local landscape, the great green and white mounds making an eerie sight.

The town of **ST AUSTELL** itself is fairly unexciting, but makes a useful stop for trips in the surrounding area. Its nearest link to the sea is at **CHARLESTOWN**, an easy downhill walk from the centre of town. This unspoilt port is still used for china clay shipments, and provides a backdrop for the location filming that frequently takes place here. Behind the harbour, the **Shipwreck & Heritage Centre** (March–Oct daily 10am–5.30pm; £5.95; ⓦ shipwreckcharlestown.com) is entered through tunnels once used to convey the clay to the docks, and shows a good collection of photos and relics as well as tableaux of historical scenes.

On either side of the dock, the coarse sand and stone **beaches** have small rock pools, above which cliff walks lead around the bay.

ARRIVAL AND DEPARTURE — ST AUSTELL BAY

By train St Austell is the main rail stop in southeast Cornwall; the station is off High Cross St.

Destinations Bodmin (every 30min–1hr; 20min); Truro (hourly; 20min).

By bus Buses pull in next to St Austell's train station, off High Cross St.

Destinations Bodmin (Mon–Sat hourly, Sun 5 daily; 35min); Charlestown (Mon–Sat 4 hourly, Sun 1–2 hourly; 15–30min); Falmouth (2 daily; 1hr); Newquay (hourly; 45min–1hr); Plymouth (4 daily; 1hr 20min); Truro (Mon–Sat every 30min–1hr, Sun every 2hr; 1hr).

ACCOMMODATION

The most attractive place to stay hereabouts is **Charlestown**.

Broad Meadow House Quay Rd, behind the Shipwreck Centre, Charlestown ⓣ 01726 76636, ⓦ broadmeadowhouse.com. A lovely, intimate campsite offering "tent and breakfast" glamping in family-size tents (three-night minimum stay); breakfast (including a fresh smoothie) is brought to your tent in the morning. A couple of pitches are available for people bringing their own tents (£10). No credit cards. Closed mid-Sept to April. £30 per person

T'Gallants Charlestown ⓣ 01726 70203, ⓦ t-gallants.co.uk. Elegantly furnished Georgian B&B at the back of the harbour with a variety of en-suite rooms. Those at the front, including one with a four-poster, have sea views and cost more than the others. Tasty cream teas are served in the garden. £75

The Eden Project

Four miles northeast of St Austell • Daily: April–Oct 9.30am–6pm; Nov–March 9.30am–3pm, closes later some dates late July to early Sept, Nov & Dec; last entry 90min before closing • £22, or £18.70–19.80 online, £18 if arriving by bus, by bike or on foot; tickets are valid for a year when registered as a donation • Ⓦ edenproject.com

Occupying a 160ft-deep crater whose awesome scale only reveals itself once you have passed the entrance at its lip, the **Eden Project** showcases the diversity of the planet's plant life in an imaginative style. Centre stage are the geodesic "biomes" – vast conservatories made up of eco-friendly Teflon-coated, hexagonal panels. One holds groves of olive and citrus trees, cacti and other plants usually found in the warm, temperate zones of the Mediterranean, southern Africa and southwestern USA, while the larger one contains plants from the tropics, including teak and mahogany trees, with a waterfall and river gushing through. Equally impressive are the grounds, where plantations of bamboo, tea, hops, hemp and tobacco are interspersed with brilliant swathes of flowers. In summer, the grassy arena sees **performances** of a range of music – from Peter Gabriel to Fleet Foxes – and in winter they set up a skating rink.

ARRIVAL AND DEPARTURE — THE EDEN PROJECT

Allow at least half a day for a full exploration, but arrive early to avoid congestion. Drivers will find the site signposted on most roads in the area, and there's a useful network of routes for walkers and cyclists. The most useful buses are #101 from St Austell train station, #527 from Newquay and St Austell and #X5 from Plymouth and Truro (not Sun).

Mevagissey and around

MEVAGISSEY was once known for the construction of fast vessels, used for carrying contraband as well as pilchards. Today the tiny port might display a few stacks of lobster pots, but the real business is tourism, and in summer the maze of backstreets is saturated with day-trippers, converging on the inner harbour and overflowing onto the large sand beach at **Pentewan** a mile to the north.

Four miles south of Mevagissey juts the striking headland of **Dodman Point**, cause of many a wreck and topped by a stark granite cross built by a local parson as a seamark in 1896. The promontory holds the substantial remains of an Iron Age fort, with an earthwork bulwark cutting right across the point. Curving away to the west, elegant **Veryan Bay** holds a string of exquisite inlets and coves, such as **Hemmick Beach**, a fine place for a dip with rocky outcrops affording a measure of privacy, and **Porthluney Cove**, a crescent of sand whose centrepiece is the battlemented **Caerhays Castle** (mid-March to May Mon–Fri noon–4pm; gardens mid-Feb to May daily 10am–5pm; last entry 1hr before closing; house £7.50, garden £7.50, combined ticket £12.50), built in 1808 by John Nash and surrounded by beautiful gardens. A little further on is minuscule and whitewashed **Portloe**, fronted by jagged black rocks that throw up fountains of seaspray, giving it a good, end-of-the-road feel.

Lost Gardens of Heligan

Pentewan • Daily: April–Sept 10am–6pm; Oct–March 10am–5pm; last entry 90min before closing • £10 • Ⓦ heligan.com

A couple of miles north of Mevagissey lie the **Lost Gardens of Heligan**, a fascinating Victorian garden which had fallen into neglect and was resurrected by Tim Smit, the visionary instigator of the Eden Project (see above). A boardwalk takes you through a jungle and under a canopy of bamboo and ferns down to the Lost Valley, where there are lakes, woods and wild-flower meadows.

ARRIVAL AND INFORMATION — MEVAGISSEY

By bus From St Austell's bus and train station, #26 and #526 leave for Mevagissey (Mon–Sat every 20min, Sun hourly; 25min) and #526 goes to Heligan (hourly; 30min). For Portloe take #27 to Probus, then #551 (not Sun).

Tourist office St George's Square (April–Oct Mon–Fri & Sun 10am–5pm; Nov–March Mon–Fri 11am–2pm; Ⓣ 01726 844440, Ⓦ mevagissey-cornwall.co.uk).

ACCOMMODATION AND EATING

Alvorada 17 Church St 01726 842055. Small, family-run Portuguese restaurant offering tapas (about £6) and such dishes as caldeirada (fish stew) and rojoes (pork stew), costing around £15. July & Aug daily 6.30pm–late; March–June & Sept Tues–Sat only; Oct–Feb Thurs–Sat only.

Wild Air Polkirt Hill, Mevagissey 01726 843302, wildair.co.uk. Away from the harbour crowds, this wi-fi-enabled B&B has three tastefully furnished rooms, all with en-suite or private bathrooms, and all enjoying lofty views over the harbour and coast. No children. £80

YHA Boswinger Boswinger, half a mile from Hemmick Beach 0845 371 9107, boswinger@yha.org.uk. Set in a former farmhouse, this is a remote spot a mile from the bus stop at Gorran Churchtown (#526 from St Austell and Mevagissey). Kitchen and meals available. Groups only Nov–March. Dorm £20.40, double £51

6

Truro

Cornwall's capital, **TRURO**, presents a mixture of different styles, from the graceful Georgian architecture that came with the tin-mining boom of the 1800s to its neo-Gothic cathedral and its modern shopping centre. It's an attractive place, not overwhelmed by tourism and with a range of good-value facilities.

Truro Cathedral

Pydar St • Mon–Sat 7.30am–6pm, Sun 9am–7pm • £5 suggested donation • trurocathedral.org.uk

Truro's dominant feature is its faux-medieval **cathedral**, completed in 1910 and incorporating part of the fabric of the old parish church that previously occupied the site. In the airy interior, the neo-Gothic baptistry commands attention, complete with emphatically pointed arches and elaborate roof vaulting. Free **tours** take place daily between April and October.

Royal Cornwall Museum

River St • Tues–Sat 10am–4.45pm • Free • royalcornwallmuseum.org.uk

Truro's **Royal Cornwall Museum** offers a rich and wide-ranging hoard that takes in everything from the region's natural history to Celtic inscriptions. If time is tight you could confine yourself to the renowned collection of minerals on the ground floor and the upstairs galleries holding works by Cornish artists including members of the Newlyn School.

ARRIVAL AND INFORMATION — TRURO

By train The train station is on Richmond Hill, a 10min walk west of the centre.

Destinations Exeter (hourly; 2hr 20min); Falmouth (every 30min; 20min); Liskeard (every 30min–1hr; 50min); Penzance (every 1–2hr; 45min); Plymouth (hourly; 1hr 20min).

By bus Buses stop centrally at Lemon Quay or near the train station.

Destinations Falmouth (Mon–Sat every 15–20min, Sun hourly; 35–50min); Newquay (Mon–Sat every 15min, Sun every 30min; 50min–1hr 25min); Penzance (Mon–Sat every 30min–1hr, Sun 3 daily; 1hr 10min–1hr 45min); Plymouth (hourly; 1hr 45min); St Austell (Mon–Sat every 30min, Sun hourly; 50min–1hr 15min); St Ives (Mon–Sat hourly, Sun 1 daily; 1hr–1hr 35min); St Mawes (Mon–Sat 8 daily, Sun 4 daily; 1hr).

Tourist office Boscawen St (Easter–Oct Mon–Fri 9am–5.30pm, Sat 9am–4pm; Nov–Easter Mon–Fri 9am–5pm 01872 274555, tourism.truro.gov.uk).

ACCOMMODATION

Bay Tree 28 Ferris Town 01872 240274, baytree-guesthouse.co.uk. Homely, restored Georgian house halfway between the train station and the town centre, with a friendly owner and shared bathrooms. Singles available. Advance booking recommended. No credit cards. £55

Mannings Lemon St 01872 270345, manningshotels.co.uk. This city-centre hotel has a bright, contemporary feel and a good, informal brasserie. Rooms are compact and over-heated – ask for one at the back for the most peace and quiet. £99

Truro Lodge 10 The Parade 01872 260857 or 0781 375 5210, trurobackpackers.co.uk. Relaxed hostel in a large Georgian terrace house near the centre. There's a self-catering kitchen, a lounge and a nice veranda. Dorm £18, double £38

EATING AND DRINKING

The Olive 15 Kenwyn St ⓣ01872 278258. This Mediterranean-style café/restaurant with a small garden is the place for light, healthy lunches and a choice of organic coffees and Belgian beers. A tagine or deli platter costs around £8, and there's a takeaway option. Mon–Sat 10am–4pm.

One Eyed Cat 116 Kenwyn St ⓣ01872 222122, ⓦoneeyedcat.co.uk. In a converted chapel, this bar and brasserie has an incongruous setting, but the food, either tapas or more substantial meat and seafood dishes (£9–16), is good. Reservations essential at weekends. Mon–Thurs & Sun 10am–midnight, Fri & Sat 10am–2am.

Wig & Pen 1 Frances St ⓣ01872 273208, ⓦstaustellbrewery.co.uk. The pick of Truro's pubs serves St Austell ales and bar food, as well as brunches and cream teas, with some tables outside. Dishes such as braised pork belly and rib-eye steak are around £12. Food served Mon–Fri noon–2.30pm & 6–9.30pm, Sat 11am–3.30pm & 6–9.30pm, Sun 11am–3.30pm.

6

Falmouth

Amid the lush tranquillity of the **Carrick Roads** estuary basin, the major resort of **FALMOUTH** is the site of one of Cornwall's mightiest castles, **Pendennis Castle**, and of one of the country's foremost collections of boats in the **National Maritime Museum Cornwall**. The town sits at the mouth of the Fal estuary, at the end of a rail branch line from Truro and connected by ferry to Truro and St Mawes. Round Pendennis Point, south of the centre, a long sandy bay holds a succession of sheltered **beaches**: from the popular **Gyllyngvase Beach**, you can reach the more attractive **Swanpool Beach** by cliff path, or walk a couple of miles further on to **Maenporth**, from where there are some fine cliff-top walks.

National Maritime Museum Cornwall

Discovery Quay • Daily 10am–5pm • £9.50 • ⓦnmmc.co.uk

Vessels from all around the world are exhibited in Falmouth's **National Maritime Museum Cornwall**. Of every size and shape, the craft are arranged on three levels, many of them suspended in mid-air in the cavernous Flotilla Gallery. Smaller galleries examine specific aspects of boat-building, seafaring history and Falmouth's packet ships, and a lighthouse-like lookout tower offers excellent views over the harbour and estuary.

Pendennis Castle

Pendennis Head • April–June & Sept Mon–Fri & Sun 10am–5pm, Sat 10am–4pm; July & Aug Mon–Fri & Sun 10am–6pm, Sat 10am–4pm; Oct–March daily 10am–4pm • EH • £6.30

A few minutes' walk west of the National Maritime Museum, **Pendennis Castle** stands sentinel at the tip of the promontory that separates the Carrick Roads estuary from Falmouth Bay. The extensive fortification shows little evidence of its five-month siege by the Parliamentarians during the Civil War, which ended only when half its defenders had died and the rest had been starved into submission. Though this is a less-refined contemporary of the castle at St Mawes (see opposite), its site wins hands down, the stout ramparts offering the best all-round views of Carrick Roads and Falmouth Bay.

ARRIVAL AND INFORMATION — FALMOUTH

By train The branch rail line from Truro (Mon–Sat every 30min, Sun 10 daily; 30min) stops at Falmouth Town, best for the centre, and Falmouth Docks, 2min away, near Pendennis Castle.

By bus Most buses stop on The Moor, close to the Prince of Wales Pier, a 20min walk from the train stations.

Destinations Helston (Mon–Sat every 2hr, Sun 2–4 daily; 25min–1hr 10min); Penzance (Mon–Sat every 2hr, Sun 1 daily; 1–2hr); St Austell (2 daily; 1hr 10min); Truro (Mon–Sat every 15–20min, Sun hourly; 35–50min).

Tourist office Prince of Wales Pier (April–Oct daily 10am–5pm; Nov–March Mon–Fri 10am–5pm; ⓣ01326 312300, ⓦdiscoverfalmouth.co.uk).

ACCOMMODATION

Arwenack Hotel 27 Arwenack St ⓣ01326 311185, ⓦfalmouthtownhotels.co.uk. It's basic and desperately old-fashioned, but this place offers clean, central and good-value en-suite accommodation, including two rooms at the top with great views. No credit cards. **£58**

Falmouth Lodge 9 Gyllyngvase Terrace ⓣ01326

319996, ⓦfalmouthbackpackers.co.uk. Clean and friendly backpackers' hostel located a couple of minutes' walk from the beach, with a sociable lounge and kitchen and free wi-fi. Dorm £19, double £42

Falmouth Townhouse Grove Place ⓣ01326 312009, ⓦfalmouthtownhouse.co.uk. Chic boutique hotel in a Georgian building just across from the Maritime Museum. It's all highly designed, with a buzzing bar, spacious guestrooms and quirky bathrooms, though some rooms suffer from street noise at night. £85

EATING AND DRINKING

Café Cinnamon Old Brewery Yard ⓣ01326 211457. Wholefood, vegetarian and vegan café that offers lunchtime snacks and organic wines. Try the chickpea and spinach pie, and leave room for tasty desserts. Stays open late for live music Sat in Aug, when they serve "evening bites" (£5–8). Usually Tues–Sat 10am–3pm.

Chain Locker Quay St ⓣ01326 311085. This harbourside drinker festooned with nautical bits and pieces offers real ales and standard bar meals (£7.50–10.50), but its main asset is the outdoor seating – the perfect spot to while away an evening. Mon–Thurs & Sun 11am–11pm, Fri & Sat 11am–midnight.

Gylly Beach Café Gyllyngvase Beach ⓣ01326 312884, ⓦgyllybeach.com. Cool beachside hangout serving everything from nachos to buckets of prawns. Breakfast is served until noon, lunch dishes cost £7–9, evening mains £11–17. There are barbecues in summer and live music Sun eves. Daily 9am–late, reduced hours in winter.

6

St Mawes and around

Situated on the east side of the Carrick Roads estuary, the two-pronged **Roseland peninsula** is a luxuriant backwater of woods and sheltered creeks. The main settlement is **ST MAWES**, a tranquil old fishing port easily reached on ferries from Falmouth.

St Mawes Castle

April–June & Sept Mon–Fri & Sun 10am–5pm; July & Aug Mon–Fri & Sun 10am–6pm; Oct daily 10am–4pm; Nov–March Fri–Mon 10am–4pm • EH • £4.30

At the end of the walled seafront of St Mawes stands the sister fort of Pendennis Castle, the small and pristine **St Mawes Castle**, built during the reign of Henry VIII to a clover-leaf design. The castle owes its excellent condition to its early surrender to Parliamentary forces during the Civil War in 1646. The dungeons and gun installations contain various artillery exhibits as well as some background on local social history.

ARRIVAL AND DEPARTURE — ST MAWES

St Mawes can be reached on frequent **ferries** from Falmouth's Prince of Wales Pier and Custom House Quay (£8 return).

ACCOMMODATION AND EATING

Lowen Meadow St Mawes ⓣ01326 270036. This smart guesthouse in the higher part of the village has spacious, en-suite rooms, friendly hosts and sea views. If there are no vacancies, the owners can put you in touch with family members who also run B&Bs nearby. No credit cards. £80

Tresanton Hotel St Mawes ⓣ01326 270055, ⓦtresanton.com. Cornwall doesn't get much ritzier than this, a slice of Mediterranean-style luxury with bright, sunny colours and a yacht and speedboat available in summer to guests. There's a fabulous restaurant too, where you can have a snack lunch or full meal (fixed-price lunch £26.50 or £35, dinner £43.50). Food served daily 12.30–2.30pm & 7.30–9.30pm. £245

The Lizard peninsula

The **Lizard peninsula** – from the Celtic *lys ardh*, or "high point" – is mercifully undeveloped. If this flat and treeless expanse can be said to have a centre, it's **Helston**, a junction for **buses** running from Falmouth and Truro and for services to the spartan villages of the peninsula's interior and coast.

Helston

HELSTON is best known for its **Furry Dance** (or Flora Dance), which dates from the seventeenth century. Held on May 8 (unless this falls on Sun or Mon, when the procession takes place on the preceding Sat), it's a stately procession of top-hatted men and summer-frocked women performing a solemn dance through the town's streets and gardens. You can learn something about it and absorb plenty of other local history in the eclectic **Helston Folk Museum** (Mon–Sat 10am–1pm, closes 4pm school hols; free), housed in former market buildings behind the Guildhall on Church Street.

Porthleven and around

Two and a half miles southwest of Helston, tin ore from inland mines was once shipped from **PORTHLEVEN**. Good **beaches** lie to either side: the best for swimming are around **Rinsey Head**, three miles north along the coast, including the sheltered **Praa Sands**. One and a quarter miles south of Porthleven, strong currents make it unsafe to swim at **Loe Bar**, a strip of shingle which separates the freshwater **Loe Pool** from the sea. The elongated Pool is one of two sites which claim to be the place where the sword Excalibur was restored to its watery source (the other is on Bodmin Moor). The path running along the western edge of Loe Pool makes a fine walking route between here and Helston.

Mullion and around

The inland village of **MULLION**, five miles south of Porthleven, has a fifteenth- to sixteenth-century church dedicated to the Breton **St Mellane** (or Malo), with a dog-door for canine churchgoers. A lane leads a mile and a quarter west to **Mullion Cove**, where a tiny beach is sheltered behind harbour walls and rock stacks, though the neighbouring sands at **Polurrian** and **Poldhu**, to the north, are better and attract surfers.

Lizard Point and around

Four miles south of Mullion, the peninsula's best-known beach, **Kynance Cove**, has sheer 100ft cliffs, stacks and arches of serpentine rock and offshore outcrops. The water quality here is excellent – but take care not to be stranded by the tide. A little more than a mile southeast, **Lizard Point**, the southern tip of the promontory and mainland Britain's southernmost point, is marked by a plain lighthouse above a tiny cove and a restless, churning sea. If you're not following the coast path, you can reach the point via the road and footpath leading a mile south from the nondescript village called simply **THE LIZARD**, where you'll find several places to stay and eat.

The east coast

In the north of the peninsula, the snug hamlets dotted around the **River Helford** are a complete contrast to the rugged character of most of the Lizard. On the river's south side, **Frenchman's Creek**, one of a splay of serene inlets, was the inspiration for Daphne Du Maurier's novel of the same name. From Helford Passage you can take a ferry (April–Oct; £5.50 return) to reach **Helford**, an agreeable old smugglers' haunt on the south bank.

South of here, on the B3293, the broad, windswept plateau of Goonhilly Downs is interrupted by the futuristic saucers of Goonhilly Satellite Station and the nearby ranks of wind turbines. Heading east, the road splits: left to **ST KEVERNE**, an inland village whose tidy square is flanked by two inns and a church, right to **COVERACK**, a fishing port in a sheltered bay. Following the coast path or negotiating minor roads south will bring you to the safe and clean swimming spot of **Kennack Sands**.

GETTING AROUND — THE LIZARD PENINSULA

From Helston, **buses** #2 and #2A go to Porthleven, #537 goes to Mullion and The Lizard, and #538 goes to St Keverne and Coverack (not Sun).

ACCOMMODATION AND EATING

Blue Anchor 50 Coinagehall St, Helston ⓣ01326 562821, ⓦspingoales.com. Deeply traditional West Country pub, once a fifteenth-century monastery rest house, now brewing its own Spingo beer on the premises. Four B&B

rooms are available in an adjacent building. Pub Mon–Thurs & Sun 10am–midnight, Fri & Sat 10am–1am. £55

Mounts Bay Inn Mullion 01326 240221, mountsbaymullion.co.uk. Mullion's best place for Cornish ales and pub meals (£10–15) with views over Mounts Bay and steps down to a beer garden. Live bands every fortnight and Cornish songs on the last Sun of the month. Mon–Thurs 11am–2.30pm & 6–11pm, Fri & Sat 11am–midnight, Sun noon–10.30pm.

Old Lifeboat House The Cove, Coverack 01326 281212, lifeboathouse.com. This place by the harbour serves superb fresh seafood, with main dishes around £16, with first-class fish and chips from the attached takeaway. April, May, Sept & Oct Tues–Sat noon–2pm & 6–9pm (last orders); June–Aug daily; takeaway noon–9pm.

Old Vicarage Nansmellyon Rd, Mullion 01326 240898, bandbmullion@hotmail.com. Facing an enclosed garden, this charming guesthouse once provided accommodation to Arthur Conan Doyle. Rooms are elegant with period furnishings and en-suite or private facilities. No credit cards. £80

★ **Penmenner House** Penmenner Rd, The Lizard 01326 290370, penmennerhouse.com. The poet Rupert Brooke once stayed in this lovely house, which has richly coloured rooms, sea views from its spacious guests' lounge and interesting knick-knacks from around the world. No credit cards. £65

Poldhu Beach Café Poldhu Cove, near Mullion 01326 240530, poldhu.net. The perfect beach café, with energizing breakfasts, burgers (£6) good coffee and hot chocolate, and locally produced ice cream. Daily 9.30am–5.30pm, summer school hols 9am–9pm.

YHA Lizard Lizard Point 0845 371 9550, lizard@yha.org.uk. This hostel occupies a former Victorian hotel right on the coast, with majestic views. It gets booked up quickly. Groups only Nov–March. Dorm £22.40, double £51

6

The Penwith peninsula

Though more densely populated than the Lizard, the **Penwith peninsula** is a more rugged landscape, with a raw appeal that is still encapsulated by **Land's End**, despite the commercialization of that headland. The seascapes, the quality of the light and the slow tempo of the local fishing communities made this area a hotbed of artistic activity from the late nineteenth century onwards, when the painters of Newlyn, near **Penzance**, established a distinctive school of painting. More innovative figures – among them Ben Nicholson, Barbara Hepworth and Naum Gabo – were soon afterwards to make **St Ives** one of England's liveliest cultural communities, and their enduring influence is illustrated in the St Ives branch of the **Tate Gallery**, which showcases the modern artists associated with the locality.

GETTING AROUND — THE PENWITH PENINSULA

Penwith is far more easily toured than the Lizard, with a road circling its coastline and a better network of **public transport** from the two main towns, St Ives and Penzance, which also have most of the accommodation.

Penzance and around

Occupying a sheltered position at the northwest corner of Mount's Bay, **PENZANCE** has always been a major port, but most traces of the medieval town were obliterated at the end of the sixteenth century by a Spanish raiding party. From the top of **Market Jew Street** (from *Marghas Jew*, meaning "Thursday Market"), which climbs from the harbour and the train and bus stations, turn left into **Chapel Street** to see some of the town's finest buildings, including the flamboyant **Egyptian House**, built in 1835 to contain a geological museum but subsequently abandoned until its restoration thirty years ago. Across the street, the seventeenth-century **Union Hotel** originally held the town's assembly rooms, where news of Admiral Nelson's victory at Trafalgar and the death of Nelson himself was first announced in 1805.

Penlee House Gallery and Museum

Morrab Rd, west of Chapel St • Mon–Sat: Easter–Sept 10am–5pm; Oct–April 10.30am–4.30pm • £4.50, free on Sat • penleehouse.org.uk

Long a centre of the local art movements, **Penlee House Gallery and Museum** holds an important collection of Cornish art, notably works of the Newlyn School – impressionistic harbour scenes, frequently sentimentalized but often bathed in an evocatively luminous light. There are also displays on local archeology and history, and frequent exhibitions.

6

St Michael's Mount

Off Marazion, 5 miles east of Penzance • **House** April–June, Sept & Oct Mon–Fri & Sun 10.30am–5pm; July & Aug 10.30am–5.30pm; Nov–March guided tours Tues & Fri at 11am & 2pm, book on ⓣ 01736 710507 • £7, £8.75 with garden **Garden** Mid-April to June Mon–Fri 10.30am–5pm; July to late Aug Thurs & Fri 10.30am–5.30pm; Sept Thurs & Fri 10.30am–5pm • £3.50, £8.75 with house • NT • At low tide the promontory can be approached on foot via a cobbled causeway; at high tide there are boats from Marazion (£1.50)

Frequent buses from Penzance leave for Marazion, five miles east, the access point to **St Michael's Mount**, a couple of hundred yards offshore. A vision of the archangel Michael led to the building of a church on this granite pile around the fifth century, and within three centuries a Celtic monastery had been founded here. The present building derives from a chapel raised in the eleventh century by Edward the Confessor, who handed it over to the Benedictine monks of Brittany's Mont St Michel, whose island abbey was the model for this one. Following the Civil War, it became the residence of the St Aubyn family, who still inhabit the castle. Some of the buildings date from the twelfth century, but the later additions are more interesting, such as the battlemented **chapel** and the seventeenth-century decorations of the **Chevy Chase Room**, the former refectory.

ARRIVAL AND DEPARTURE — PENZANCE

By air Helicopters for the Isles of Scilly take off from the heliport a mile east of Penzance (ⓦ islesofscillyhelicopter.com; see p.326).

By train Penzance's train station lies on the seafront.
Destinations Bodmin (hourly; 1hr 20min); Exeter (hourly; 3hr); Plymouth (hourly; 2hr); St Ives (most via St Erth; hourly; 25–45min); Truro (hourly; 40min).

By bus The bus station is next to the train station on the seafront.
Destinations Falmouth (Mon–Sat 7–8 daily, Sun 1 daily; 1hr–1hr 45); Helston (Mon–Sat hourly, Sun 7 daily; 1hr); Plymouth (7 daily; 2hr 50min–3hr 45min); St Austell (2–3 daily; 1hr 45min–2hr 15min); St Ives (Mon–Sat 3–5 hourly, Sun every 30min–1hr; 30–50min); Truro (Mon–Sat every 30min–1hr, Sun 4 daily; 1hr 10min–1hr 45min).

By boat From Easter to October boats depart from Penzance Quay for St Mary's on the Isles of Scilly (Mon–Sat 4–6 weekly; 2hr 40min; ⓦ islesofscilly-travel.co.uk; see p.326).

ACCOMMODATION

Abbey Hotel Abbey St, off Chapel St ⓣ 01736 366906, ⓦ theabbeyonline.co.uk. Pamper yourself at this homely, seventeenth-century hotel owned by 1960s model Jean Shrimpton and her husband. Lashings of old-fashioned comfort, books and antiques everywhere, and great views. **£150**

Penzance Arts Club Chapel St ⓣ 01736 363761, ⓦ penzanceartsclub.co.uk. Formerly the Portuguese consulate, this has a cheerful bohemian ambience and rooms that combine modern art, antique furnishings and great views. There's wi-fi, a good café/restaurant in the basement, plus cabaret, music and poetry nights. **£90**

Penzance Backpackers Alexandra Rd, parallel to Morrab Rd ⓣ 01736 363836, ⓦ pzbackpack.com. One of the region's tidiest and most welcoming hostels, with en-suite dorms, a kitchen, lounge and laundry, and wi-fi. Dorm **£16**, double **£36**

EATING AND DRINKING

Admiral Benbow 46 Chapel St ⓣ 01736 363448. Characterful pub crammed with gaudy ships' figureheads and other nautical items. The bar meals are pretty standard (most dishes around £11), but the atmosphere compensates. Daily 11am–11pm.

Archie Browns Bread St ⓣ 01736 362828, ⓦ archiebrowns.co.uk. Vegans, vegetarians and wholefoodies will be happy in this café above a health shop, with its relaxed, friendly vibe and local art on the walls. Dishes include quiches, curries, stews and homity pie (£5–8). Mon–Sat 9am–5pm.

The Boatshed Wharf Rd ⓣ 01736 368845, ⓦ boatshed.org.uk. A relaxed snack stop during the day, this café-bar with granite walls, ships' timbers and tables outside also offers tasty vegetarian, meat and seafood dishes (£9–14) as well as pizzas (around £7.50). Daily 11am–9/9.30pm.

Harris's 46 New St ⓣ 01736 364408, ⓦ harrissrestaurant.co.uk. Traditional fine dining at this formal restaurant, with the accent on seafood. Choose between the main menu (dishes around £20) or the less expensive brasserie menu (mains £11–16), leaving room for a memorable dessert. July–Oct Mon–Sat noon–2pm & 7–9.30pm; Nov–June Tues–Sat noon–2pm & 7–9.30pm.

Mousehole

Accounts vary as to the derivation of the name of **MOUSEHOLE** (pronounced "Mowzle"), though it may be from a smugglers' cave just to the south. In any case, the name evokes perfectly this minuscule fishing port cradled in the arms of a granite breakwater, three miles south of Penzance. The village attracts more visitors than it can handle, so hang around until the crowds have departed before exploring its tight tangle of lanes, where you'll come across Mousehole's oldest house, the fourteenth-century **Keigwin House**, a survivor of the sacking of the village by Spaniards in 1595.

ACCOMMODATION AND EATING — MOUSEHOLE

Ship Inn Harbourside 01736 731234, shipmousehole.co.uk. Overlooking the boats, this is a perfect spot for a pint or a Ploughman's Lunch (£6.75) or Cornish fish pie (£11). Accommodation is available in surprisingly modern en-suite rooms, some in an annexe (those with a view cost extra). Daily 11am–midnight; food served noon–9pm. **£80**

Porthcurno

Eight miles west of Mousehole, one of Penwith's best beaches lies at **PORTHCURNO**, sandwiched between cliffs. On the shore to the east, a white pyramid marks the spot where the first transatlantic cables were laid in 1880. On the headland beyond lies an Iron Age fort, **Treryn Dinas**, close to the famous rocking stone called **Logan Rock**, a seventy-ton monster that was knocked off its perch in 1824 by a gang of sailors, among them a nephew of writer and poet Oliver Goldsmith. Somehow they replaced the stone, but it never rocked again.

Minack Theatre

Exhibition Centre Daily: April–Oct 9.30am–5.30pm; Nov–March 10am–4pm • £4 **Theatre** From late May to September, a range of plays, operas and musicals are presented; bring a cushion and a rug (or hire one at the theatre) • £8–9.50 • 01736 810181, minack.com

Steep steps lead up from the beach of tiny white shells to the **Minack Theatre**, hewn out of the cliff in the 1930s and since enlarged to hold 750 seats, though retaining the basic Greek-inspired design. In summer, the spectacular backdrop of Porthcurno Bay makes this one of the country's most inspiring theatres – providing the weather holds. The attached **Exhibition Centre** gives access to the theatre during the day and explains the story of its creation.

Land's End

The extreme western tip of England, **Land's End**, lies four miles west of Porthcurno. Best approached on foot along the coastal path, the 60ft turf-covered cliffs provide a platform to view the Irish Lady, the Armed Knight, Dr Syntax Head and the rest of the Land's End outcrops, beyond which you can spot the Longships lighthouse, a mile and a half out to sea, and sometimes the Wolf Rock lighthouse, nine miles southwest, or even the **Isles of Scilly**, 28 miles away (see p.326).

Whitesand Bay

To the north of Land's End the rounded granite cliffs fall away at **Whitesand Bay** to reveal a glistening mile-long shelf of beach that offers the best swimming on the Penwith peninsula. The rollers make for good surfing and boards can be rented at **Sennen Cove**, the more popular southern end of the beach.

ACCOMMODATION AND EATING — WHITESAND BAY

Pengelly House Sennen Cove 01736 871866, pengellyhouse.com. Guesthouse near the beach, offering three rooms (including a single) with mini-fridges, a large shared bathroom and wi-fi access, but no breakfast (nearby breakfast places are plentiful). No credit cards. **£65**

Whitesands Sennen, inland on the A30 01736 871776, whitesandshotel.co.uk. This place offers various accommodation options: themed en-suite guestrooms, bunkrooms with a self-catering kitchen (£21 per person) and tipis and yurts (£64 for four), with a minimum two-night stay. The café/restaurant, with outdoor seating and regular barbecues in summer, is open to all and has excellent pizzas, curries, and grilled meat and seafood (£8–15). Food served 8.30am–8.30pm; the bar stays open until 11pm. **£70**

St Just-in-Penwith and around

Three miles north of Sennen Cove, the highly scenic headland of **Cape Cornwall** is dominated by the chimney of the Cape Cornwall Mine, which closed in 1870. Half a mile inland is the grimly grey village of **ST JUST-IN-PENWITH** formerly a centre of the tin and copper industry, with rows of cottages radiating out from Bank Square. The tone is somewhat lightened by **Plen-an-Gwary**, a grassy open-air theatre where miracle plays were once staged, later used by Methodist preachers and Cornish wrestlers.

ARRIVAL AND DEPARTURE — ST JUST-IN-PENWITH

By plane Land's End Airport, around 1.5 miles south of St Just, sees flights from St Mary's on the Isles of Scilly (Mon–Sat 4–10 daily; 15min).

ACCOMMODATION AND EATING

Kegen Teg 12 Market Square ⓣ01736 788562. Organic, local and mainly vegetarian food – try the falafel (£9.80) or Welsh rarebit (£7.20) – with tasty breakfasts, cakes, smoothies and organic ice cream. Summer Mon–Sat 9am–5pm, Sun 10am–5pm; reduced hours in winter.

Kelynack Caravan and Camping Park Kelynack ⓣ01736 787633, ⓦkelynackcaravans.co.uk. Secluded campsite, one of the few sheltered ones on Penwith, about a mile south of St Just. There are also B&B rooms and a self-catering option (£58). **£70**

★ **Old Fire Station** Nancherrow Terrace, near Market Square ⓣ01736 786463, ⓦoldfirestationstjust.co.uk. Central, modern B&B with an open-plan lounge and breakfast room, and three smallish but airy en-suite bedrooms, the top two with distant sea views. **£65**

YHA Land's End ⓣ0845 371 9643, ⓔlandsend@yha.org.uk. Less than a mile south of St Just and a convenient half-mile from the coast path, this has camping facilities, a kitchen and cooked meals. Take the left fork past the post office to find it. **£20.40**

Zennor and around

Eight miles northeast of St Just, set in a landscape of rolling granite moorland, **ZENNOR** is where D.H. Lawrence came to live with his wife Frieda in 1916. "It is a most beautiful place," he wrote, "lovelier even than the Mediterranean". The Lawrences stayed a year and a half in the village – long enough for him to write *Women in Love* – before being given notice to quit by the local constabulary, who suspected them of unpatriotic sympathies (their Cornish experiences were later described in *Kangaroo*). Zennor's fascinating **Wayside Museum** is dedicated to Cornish life from prehistoric times (Easter–Oct daily 10.30/11am–5/5.30pm; £3.75). At the top of the lane, the church of **St Sennen** displays a sixteenth-century bench-carving of a mermaid who, according to local legend, was so entranced by the singing of a chorister that she lured him down to the sea, from where he never returned – though his song can still occasionally be heard.

Chysauster

Daily: April–June & Sept 10am–5pm; July & Aug 10am–6pm; Oct 10am–4pm • EH • £3.40

On a windy hillside a couple of miles inland from Zennor, the Iron Age village of **Chysauster** is the best-preserved ancient settlement in the Southwest. Dating from about the first century BC, it contains two rows of four buildings, each consisting of a courtyard with small chambers leading off it, and a garden that was presumably used for growing vegetables.

ACCOMMODATION AND EATING — ZENNOR

Gurnard's Head Treen ⓣ01736 796928, ⓦgurnardshead.co.uk. A mile or so west of Zennor, this relaxed gastropub serves delicious Mediterranean-inspired meals (mains around £16; booking advised). Smallish B&B rooms are also available. Food served daily noon/12.30–2.30pm & 6/6.30–9pm; bar closes 11pm. **£95**

Old Chapel ⓣ01736 798307, ⓦzennorbackpackers.net. Excellent backpackers' hostel in a former Wesleyan chapel, with six-bedded dorms, a couple of family rooms sleeping four and a small kitchen. The café provides snacks (10am–5pm). Dorm **£18.50**, family room **£70**

St Ives

East of Zennor, the road runs four hilly miles on to the steeply built town of **ST IVES**. By the time the pilchard reserves dried up around the early 1900s, the town was beginning to attract a vibrant **artists' colony**, precursors of the wave later headed by Ben Nicholson, Barbara Hepworth, Naum Gabo and the potter Bernard Leach, who in the 1960s were followed by a third wave including Peter Lanyon and Patrick Heron.

Tate St Ives

Porthmeor Beach • March–Oct daily 10am–5.20pm; Nov–Feb Tues–Sun 10am–4.20pm; closes two or three times a year for about ten days • £6.25, £9.75 with Hepworth Museum • ⓣ 01736 796226, ⓦ tate.org.uk

The place to view the best work created in St Ives is the **Tate St Ives**, overlooking Porthmeor Beach on the north side of town. Most of the paintings, sculptures and ceramics displayed within the airy, gleaming-white building date from 1925 to 1975, with specially commissioned contemporary works also on view as well as exhibitions. The gallery's rooftop **café** is a splendid spot for a coffee.

Barbara Hepworth Museum

Barnoon Hill • March–Oct daily 10am–5.20pm; Nov–Feb Tues–Sun 10am–4.20pm • £5.20, or £9.75 with the Tate • ⓦ tate.org.uk

Not far from the Tate St Ives, the **Barbara Hepworth Museum** provides further insight into the local arts scene. One of the foremost nonfigurative sculptors of her time, Hepworth lived in the building from 1949 until her death in a studio fire in 1975. Apart from the sculptures, which are arranged in positions chosen by Hepworth in the house and garden, the museum has background on her art, from photos and letters to catalogues and reviews.

Beaches

Porthmeor Beach dominates the northern side of St Ives, its excellent water quality and surfer-friendly rollers drawing a regular crowd, while the broader **Porthminster Beach**, south of the station, is usually less busy. A third town beach, the small and sheltered **Porthgwidden**, lies in the lee of the prong of land separating Porthmeor and Porthminster, while east of town a string of magnificent golden beaches lines **St Ives Bay** on either side of the Hayle estuary.

ARRIVAL AND INFORMATION — ST IVES

By train St Ives train station is off Porthminster Beach.
Destinations Penzance (most via St Erth; every 30min–1hr; 30–50min).

By bus The station is on Station Hill.
Destinations Penzance (Mon–Sat 3–5 hourly, Sun every 20min–1hr; 30–50min); Plymouth (3 daily; 3hr 20min–3hr 45min); Truro (Mon–Sat every 30min, Sun 1 daily; 1hr 10min–1hr 40min).

Tourist office Street-an-Pol, a 5min walk from the bus station (Mon–Fri 10am–5pm, Sat & Sun 10am–4pm; reduced hours in winter; ⓣ 01736 796297, ⓦ stivesvisitorinfo.co.uk).

ACCOMMODATION

Cornerways The Square ⓣ 01736 796706, ⓦ cornerwaysstives.com. Daphne du Maurier once stayed here; its now a modern cottage conversion with friendly management and small, bright rooms. Ask about complementary tickets for the Tate and Hepworth galleries. No credit cards. **£80**

★ **Little Leaf** 16 Park Ave ⓣ 01736 795427, ⓦ littleleafguesthouse.co.uk. With friendly young hosts and local art on the walls, this guesthouse has five en-suite rooms; one a family suite and two with fantastic views. Breakfasts are fresh and local. Free wi-fi and use of iPad in the communal lounge. **£70**

Primrose Valley Porthminster Beach ⓣ 01736 794939, ⓦ primroseonline.co.uk. Convenient for the bus and train stations and Porthminster Beach, this Edwardian villa has fresh, contemporary rooms, some sea-facing with balconies. Three- or four-day minimum stay in July & Aug. **£125**

St Ives Backpackers The Stennack ⓣ 01736 799444, ⓦ backpackers.co.uk/st-ives. Centrally located hostel in an old Wesleyan chapel school from 1845. Dorms have 4–8 beds, and a kitchen, games and wi-fi are on hand. Dorm **£18**, double **£40**

EATING

Alba Wharf Rd ⓣ01736 797222, ⓦthealbarestaurant.com. Sleekly modern harbourfront restaurant with top-class seafood, including a superb fish soup. Set-price menus (£15.50 & £18.50) are available until 7.30pm, otherwise mains are £13–17. Sit upstairs for the best view. Daily noon–2.30pm & 5–10pm.

6

★ **Blas Burgerworks** The Warren ⓣ01736 797272, ⓦblasburgerworks.co.uk. This "alternative burger bar" doles out probably the best burgers you'll ever taste, using local ingredients (£7.50–10). There's just one small room with four communal tables made from found or reclaimed wood. No reservations. Easter–Sept & school hols daily noon–10pm, Oct & mid-Feb to Easter Tues–Sun 6–10pm.

Porthminster Café Porthminster Beach ⓣ01736 795352, ⓦporthminstercafe.co.uk. With its sun deck and beach location, this is an appealing venue for coffees, snack lunches and sophisticated seafood dinners (mains around £17; book ahead). April–Sept daily 9am–10pm; Oct–April Tues–Sun 11am–9pm.

St Andrews Street Bistro 16 St Andrews St ⓣ01736 797074. Rugs and tall white walls filled with quirky objects set the mood here. The creative menu features such dishes as seafood linguini and scallop risotto, with most mains around £15. June–Sept daily 6pm–late, Oct–May Tues–Sat 6pm–late.

The Isles of Scilly

The **Isles of Scilly** are a compact archipelago of about a hundred islands, 28 miles southwest of Land's End. None is bigger than three miles across, and only five of them are inhabited – **St Mary's**, **Tresco**, **Bryher**, **St Martin's** and **St Agnes**. In the annals of folklore, the Scillies are the peaks of the submerged land of Lyonnesse, a fertile plain that extended west from Penwith before the ocean broke in, drowning the land and leaving only one survivor to tell the tale. In fact they form part of the same granite mass as Land's End, Bodmin Moor and Dartmoor, and despite rarely rising above 100ft, they possess a remarkable variety of landscape. Points of interest include irresistible **beaches**, such as Par Beach on St Martin's; the Southwest's greatest concentration of **prehistoric remains**; some fabulous **rock formations**, and the exuberant **Tresco Abbey Gardens** (daily 10am–4pm; £9). Along with tourism, the main source of income is flower-growing, for which the equable climate and the long hours of sunshine – their name means "Sun Isles" – make the islands ideal. The profusion of **wild flowers** is even more noticeable than the fields of narcissi and daffodils, and the heaths and pathways are often dense with marigolds, gorse, sea thrift, trefoil and poppies, not to mention a host of more exotic varieties introduced by visiting foreign vessels. The waters hereabouts are held to be among the country's best for **diving**, while between May and September, on a Wednesday or Friday evening, islanders gather for **gig races**, performed by six-oared vessels – some of them more than a hundred years old and 30ft long.

Free of traffic, theme parks and amusement arcades, the islands are a welcome respite from the tourist trail, the main drawbacks being the high cost of reaching them and the shortage of **accommodation**, most of which is on the main isle of St Mary's.

ARRIVAL AND INFORMATION — THE ISLES OF SCILLY

The islands are accessible by sea or air. Launches link each of the inhabited islands, though these are sporadic in winter.

By plane For most of the year, the main departure points for flights (run by Isles of Scilly Travel; ⓣ0845 710 5555, ⓦislesofscilly-travel.co.uk) are Land's End Airport, near St Just; Newquay; Exeter; Bristol and Southampton. In winter, there are departures only from Land's End and Newquay. British International (ⓣ01736 363871, ⓦislesofscillyhelicopter.com) also runs helicopter flights (20min) to St Mary's and Tresco from the heliport a mile east of Penzance.

By boat Boats to St Mary's, operated by Isles of Scilly Travel (ⓣ0845 710 5555, ⓦislesofscilly-travel.co.uk), depart from Penzance's South Pier between Easter and October (2hr 45min).

Tourist office Hugh St, Hugh Town, St Mary's (April–Oct Mon–Sat 8.30am–5.30pm, Sun 9am–2pm; Nov–March Mon–Fri 9am–5pm; ⓣ01720 424031, ⓦsimplyscilly.co.uk).

ACCOMMODATION AND EATING

St Mary's has the great majority of the **accommodation** on the islands; the smaller isles (excepting Tresco) each have two or three B&Bs only, and these are booked up early. Two of the islands – Tresco and St Martin's – have luxury hotels, and all the islands except Tresco have **campsites**, which usually close in winter (camping rough is not allowed). See ⓦ simplyscilly.co.uk for complete accommodation lists. St Mary's also has most of the **restaurants** and **pubs**. Each of the other inhabited islands has a pub serving food and one or two cafés, while all hotels and some B&Bs also provide meals.

Cornwall's Atlantic coast

The north Cornish coast is punctuated by some of the finest beaches in England, the most popular of which are to be found around **Newquay**, the surfers' capital, and **Padstow**, also renowned for its gourmet seafood restaurants. North of the Camel estuary, the coast features an almost unbroken line of cliffs as far as the Devon border; this gaunt, exposed terrain makes a melodramatic setting for **Tintagel Castle**. There are more good beaches at **Bude**.

Newquay

In a superb position on a knuckle of cliffs overlooking fine golden sands and Atlantic rollers, its glorious natural advantages have made **NEWQUAY** the premier resort of north Cornwall. It is difficult to imagine a lineage for the place that extends more than a few decades, but the "new quay" was built in the fifteenth century in what was already a long-established fishing port, up to then more colourfully known as Towan Blistra. The town was given a boost in the nineteenth century when a railway was constructed across the peninsula for china clay shipments; with the trains came a swelling stream of seasonal visitors.

The centre of town is a somewhat tacky parade of shops and restaurants from which lanes lead to ornamental gardens and cliff-top lawns. The main attraction is the **beaches. Surfing competitions** and festivals run through the summer, when the town can get very crowded.

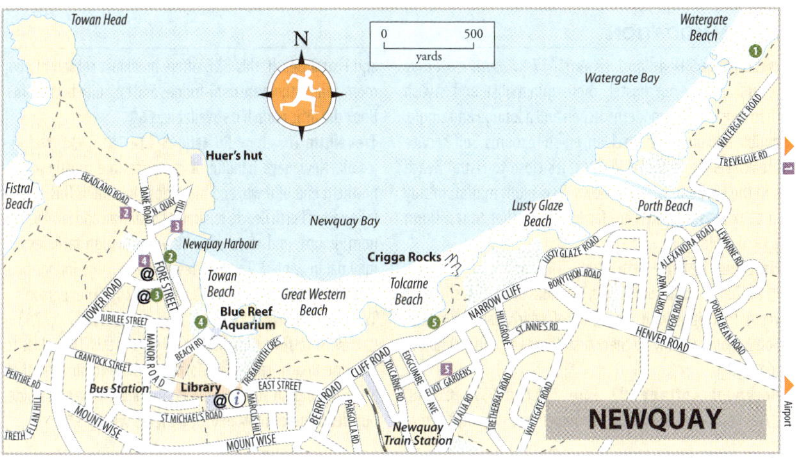

■ ACCOMMODATION				● EATING AND DRINKING			
Goofys	2	Trevelgue	1	The Boat House	2	Fifteen Cornwall	1
Harbour Hotel	3	Trewinda Lodge	5	Café Irie	3	Kahuna	5
Rockpool Cottage	4			The Chy	4		

TOP 5 SURF SPOTS

Croyde Bay See p.310
Fistral See p.328
Polzeath See p.329
Watergate Bay See p.328
Whitesands Bay See p.323

6

Beaches

All Newquay's beaches can be reached fairly easily on foot, otherwise take bus #556 for Porth Beach and Watergate Bay, #585 and #587 for Fistral and Crantock; take #587 for Holywell Bay

In the crook of Towan Head, **Towan Beach** is the most central of the seven miles of firm sandy beaches that line the coast around Newquay. Town beaches such as this and **Porth Beach**, with its grassy headland, can get very busy with families in high season, and are popular with surfers all year, though the latter are more partial to **Watergate Bay** to the north, and **Fistral Bay**, west of Towan Head.

On the other side of East Pentire Head from Fistral, **Crantock Beach** – reachable over the Gannel River by ferry or upstream footbridge – is usually less crowded, and has a lovely backdrop of dunes and undulating grassland. South of Crantock, **Holywell Bay** and the three-mile expanse of **Perran Beach**, enhanced by caves and natural rock arches, are also very popular with surfers.

ARRIVAL AND INFORMATION — NEWQUAY

By plane Newquay's airport is at St Mawgan, 5 miles northeast of town, with connections to major British and Irish cities, and linked to town by local buses.
Destinations St Mary's, Isles of Scilly (Mon–Sat 2–4 daily, 1 on Sat in winter; 30min).

By train Newquay's train station is off Cliff Rd.
Destinations Par (4–8 daily, not Sun in winter; 50min).

By bus The bus station is on Manor Rd, near the tourist office.
Destinations Bodmin (4 daily; 50min–1hr 10min); Padstow (Mon–Sat hourly, Sun 5 daily; 1hr 20min); Plymouth (5 daily; 1hr 45min–2hr); St Austell (Mon–Sat every 30min–1hr, Sun every 1–2hr; 50min); Truro (2–3 hourly; 50min–1hr 25min).

Tourist office Marcus Hill (April–Oct Mon–Fri 9.15am–5.30pm, Sat & Sun 10am–4pm; Nov–March Mon–Fri 10am–4pm, Sat & Sun 10am–3pm; ⓣ01637 854020, ⓦvisitnewquay.org).

ACCOMMODATION

★ **Goofys** 5 Headland Rd ⓣ01637 872684, ⓦgoofys .co.uk. Family-run hostel, more minimalist and stylish than most, with a modern kitchen and a lounge and single, double and bunk beds in clean, en-suite rooms. Self-service breakfasts are included in rates. It's close to Fistral Beach and the harbour, with sea views. Two-night minimum stay in peak season; prices are far lower at other times. Dorm £39, double £88

Harbour Hotel North Quay Hill ⓣ01637 873040, ⓦtheharbour.uk.com. Small, luxurious hotel with stunning views from its stylish rooms, all of which have balconies. Some rooms are tiny, so check first. There's a good restaurant, too. £130

Rockpool Cottage 92 Fore St ⓣ01637 870848, ⓦrockpoolcottage.co.uk. Convenient for the town centre and Fistral Beach, this B&B offers breakfast served in your room, where there are mini-fridges and en-suite bathrooms. Book the attic room if it's available. £60

Trevelgue Trevelgue Rd ⓣ0845 130 1515, ⓦtrevelgue .co.uk. Newquay's handful of campsites are mostly at the northern end of town, and most close in winter. This one's a mile east of Porth Beach, separates its caravan and family sites from groups, and stays open all year (though facilities are minimal in winter). There's a restaurant, a large indoor pool and nightly entertainment in summer. £10.40 per person

Trewinda Lodge 17 Eliot Gardens ⓣ01637 877533, ⓦtrewinda-lodge.co.uk. The owners of this B&B, close to Tolcarne Beach, can give informed advice to surfers (they also run Dolphin Surf School). Rooms are on the small side, but clean and comfortable, and there's wi-fi. £56

EATING AND DRINKING

The Boat House Newquay Harbour ⓣ01637 874062. The most atmospheric place in town sits right by the old harbour. Inevitably, seafood is the main event: locally caught monkfish, skate and turbot (£13–18), and whatever else appears on the daily specials board. Summer daily 10am–11pm, food served noon–3pm & 6.30–9.30pm; winter Fri & Sat only.

★ **Café Irie** 38 Fore St ⓣ01637 859200, ⓦcafeirie.co .uk. Laidback haven away from Newquay's bustle, offering abundant breakfasts, salads and sandwiches (£6–8) and delicious fruit smoothies. Organic ciders and beers are available, and there's occasional live music in summer. No credit cards. Easter–Nov daily 10am–5pm, 10am–11pm during summer school hols; Dec–Easter Fri–Sun 10am–5pm.

The Chy 12 Beach Rd ⓣ01637 873415, ⓦthekoola.com. Contemporary bar/restaurant with a spacious terrace and upper deck where you can order everything from breakfasts and sandwiches to burgers and seafood dishes (around £10). In the evening, you can sip cocktails and listen to DJs. Easter–Sept daily 10am–late; Oct–Easter Fri–Mon 10am–late.

Fifteen Cornwall Watergate Bay ⓣ01637 861000, ⓦfifteencornwall.co.uk. Overlooking the beach, this contemporary restaurant set up by TV chef Jamie Oliver showcases the culinary talents of trainee chefs. The Italian-inspired but locally sourced dishes are inventive and delicious; set menus are £27 at lunchtime, £58 (£102 including select wines) in the evening, and breakfasts are also worth tucking into. Daily 8.30–10am, noon–4.30pm & 6.15pm–midnight.

Kahuna Tolcarne Beach ⓣ01637 850440, ⓦkahunatolcarne.co.uk. The perfect hangout after a day in the surf, for an evening drink or meal of seafood or local lamb (£10–18), with great views. You can also come here for breakfast and lunch snacks. Easter–Dec daily 10am–late, Jan–Easter Fri–Sun 10am–late.

Padstow and around

PADSTOW attracts nearly as many holiday-makers as Newquay, but has a very different feel. Enclosed within the estuary of the Camel – the only river outlet of any size on Cornwall's north coast – the town has long retained its position as North Cornwall's principal fishing port, and can boast some of the county's best seafood **restaurants**. The **harbour** is jammed with launches and boats offering cruises in the bay, while a regular **ferry** (daily: April–Sept 8am–5.30/7.30pm; Nov–March 8am–4.30pm; £3 return) carries people across the river to **ROCK** – close to the isolated church of **St Enodoc** (John Betjeman's burial place) and to the good beaches around Polzeath. Padstow is also known for its annual **Obby Oss** festival, a May Day romp when a local in horse costume prances through the town preceded by a masked and club-wielding "teaser", in a spirited re-enactment of an old fertility rite.

Church of St Petroc

Church Lane

On the hill overlooking Padstow, the **church of St Petroc** is dedicated to Cornwall's most important saint, a Welsh or Irish monk who landed here in the sixth century, died in the area and gave his name to the town – "Petrock's Stow". The building has a fine fifteenth-century font, an Elizabethan pulpit and some amusing carved bench ends – seek out the one to the right of the altar depicting a fox preaching to a congregation of geese.

Prideaux Place

Easter & early May to early Oct Mon–Thurs & Sun 1.30–5pm, last tour at 4pm; grounds open from 12.30pm • £8, grounds only £3.50 • ⓦprideauxplace.co.uk

Padstow's ancient Prideaux family – whose Cornish origins date back to the Normans – still occupy **Prideaux Place**, an Elizabethan manor house with grand staircases, richly furnished rooms full of portraits, fantastically ornate ceilings and formal gardens. You might recognize some parts of the house, which is used extensively for location filming and has appeared in a plethora of films, including *Oscar and Lucinda*.

Padstow Bay beaches

Padstow Bay has a fine choice of **beaches** within a short walk or drive. On the **east side** of the Camel estuary, you can follow the coast north from Rock to the family-friendly **Daymer Bay** and the beaches around **POLZEATH**, pelted by rollers and – inevitably – a favourite with surfers (tuition and gear to rent are available from stalls and shops). On the **west side** of the estuary, round **Stepper Point**, you can reach the sandy and secluded **Harlyn Bay** and, turning the corner southwards, **Constantine Bay**, the best surfing beach hereabouts. The dunes backing the beach and the rock pools skirting it make this one of the most appealing bays on this coast, though the tides can be treacherous and bathing hazardous near the rocks. Three or four miles further south, the slate outcrops of **Bedruthan Steps** were traditionally held to be the stepping-stones of a giant; they can be readily viewed from the cliff-top path and the B3276, with steps descending to the broad beach below (not safe for swimming).

ARRIVAL AND INFORMATION — PADSTOW

By bus Buses #556 from Newquay and #555 from Bodmin pull in on Station Rd, above the harbour.

Destinations Bodmin (Mon–Sat hourly, Sun 6 daily; 55min); Newquay (Mon–Sat hourly, Sun 6 daily; 1hr 20min).

Tourist office North Quay, by the harbour (Easter–Oct Mon–Fri 9am–5.30pm, Sat & Sun 10am–4pm; Nov–Easter Mon–Fri 10am–4pm, Sat 10am–2pm; T 01841 533449, W padstowlive.com).

ACCOMMODATION

St Petroc's Hotel Treverbyn Rd T 01841 532700, W rickstein.com. Restaurateur Rick Stein has extended his Padstow empire to include classy accommodation, including this chic little lodging away from the harbour, with modernist decor and outstanding breakfasts. £150

Treverbyn House Treverbyn Rd T 01841 532855, W treverbynhouse.com. A short walk up from the harbour, this elegant Edwardian B&B has large, beautifully furnished rooms with wi-fi. Breakfast is served in your room or on a terrace in the garden with river views. No credit cards. £85

YHA Treyarnon Treyarnon Bay, 4.5 miles west T 0845 371 9664, E treyarnon@yha.org.uk. Beautifully sited hostel in a 1930s summer villa right by the beach. Bus #556 from Padstow or Newquay to Constantine, then walk half a mile. Surf packages available. Dorm £20.40, double £46

EATING AND DRINKING

Foodies know Padstow for its high-class restaurants, particularly those associated with star chef **Rick Stein**; the waiting list for a table at one of his establishments can be months long, though a weekday reservation out of season can mean booking only a day or two ahead. For something a little cheaper, try Stein's fish and chip shop or his deli, both on South Quay.

★ **Rick Stein's Café** 10 Middle St T 01841 532700, W rickstein.com. More casual and less pricey than the flagship restaurant (see below), serving breakfasts, light lunches and suppers – cod fishcakes, hot smoked salmon salad, oven-roasted hake and the like. Mains £10–12. Reservations for dinner only. Daily 8–10.30am, noon–4pm & 5–9.30pm.

The Seafood Restaurant Riverside T 01841 532700, W rickstein.com. The core of Rick Stein's culinary empire, this is one of Britain's top places for fish, with most mains –Singapore chilli crab, Padstow lobster, chargrilled sea bass with tomato, butter and vanilla vinaigrette – costing £25–35. Daily noon–2.30pm & 6.30–10pm.

Shipwrights Inn North Quay T 01841 532451, W staustellbrewery.co.uk. Family-friendly St Austell pub opposite the tourist office, offering ploughman's lunches and other snacks, or hot pies, scampi and meat dishes for £7–15. There are tables downstairs, upstairs and outside. Mon–Sat 11am–11pm, Sun noon–10.30pm, food served until 9.30pm.

Tintagel

Despite its romantic name and its famous **castle** standing aloof on a promontory to the north, the village of **TINTAGEL** is for the most part a dreary collection of cafés and B&Bs.

Tintagel Castle

Daily: April–Sept 10am–6pm; Oct 10am–5pm; Nov–March 10am–4pm • EH • £5.50

The wild and unspoiled coast around Tintagel provides an appropriate backdrop for the forsaken ruins of **Tintagel Castle**. It was the twelfth-century chronicler Geoffrey of Monmouth who first popularized the notion that this was the **birthplace of King Arthur**, son of Uther Pendragon and Ygrayne, though the visible ruins in fact belong to a Norman stronghold occupied by the earls of Cornwall. After sporadic spurts of rebuilding, the castle was allowed to decay, and most of it had been washed into the sea by the sixteenth century. The remains of a sixth-century **Celtic monastery** on the headland have provided important insights into how the country's earliest monastic houses were organized.

ARRIVAL AND INFORMATION — TINTAGEL

By bus Buses pull in on Bossiney Rd.

Destinations Boscastle (Mon–Sat hourly, Sun 4 daily; 10min); Camelford (Mon–Sat hourly, Sun 4 daily; 20min).

Tourist office Bossiney Rd (Mon–Sat: April–Sept 10am–5pm; Oct–March 11am–3pm; T 01840 779084, W visitboscastleandtintagel).

ACCOMMODATION AND EATING

Bosayne Atlantic Rd T 01840 770514, W bosayne.co.uk. In a quiet spot a few minutes' walk from Tintagel's centre, this eco-friendly B&B has en-suite doubles and singles with shared bathrooms, all with mini-fridges and free wi-fi, and some rooms have sea views. **£65**

Wyldes Bossiney Rd T 01840 770007, W wyldestogo.co.uk. The options in this small, friendly café-restaurant range from breakfasts to panini, pies, fried halloumi and afternoon tea. It's mainly locally sourced, and wheat- and dairy-free items are available. No credit cards. Easter–Oct daily 9am–5pm.

YHA Tintagel Dunderhole Point T 0845 371 9145, E tintagel@yha.org.uk. Three-quarters of a mile south of Tintagel, the offices of a former slate quarry now house this hostel with great coastal views. There's a kitchen but no restaurant. **£20.40**

6

Boscastle

Three miles east of Tintagel, the port of **BOSCASTLE** lies compressed within a narrow ravine drilled by the rivers Jordan and Valency, and ending in a twisty harbour. The tidy riverfront bordered by thatched and lime-washed cottages was the scene of a devastating flash flood in 2004, but most of the damage has now been repaired. Above and behind, you can see more seventeenth- and eighteenth-century cottages on a circular walk that traces the valley of the Valency for about a mile to reach Boscastle's graceful parish church of **St Juliot**, tucked away in a peaceful glen, where Thomas Hardy once worked as a young architect.

ARRIVAL AND INFORMATION — BOSCASTLE

By bus There are bus stops at the car park and Boscastle Bridge, at the top of the harbour.

Destinations Bude (4–6 daily; 55min); Camelford (Mon–Sat hourly, Sun 4 daily; 30min); Tintagel (Mon–Sat hourly,

KING ARTHUR IN CORNWALL

Did **King Arthur** really exist? If he did, it's likely that he was an amalgam of two people: a sixth-century Celtic warlord who united the local tribes in a series of successful battles against the invading Anglo-Saxons, and a local Cornish saint. Whatever his origins, his role was recounted and inflated by poets and troubadours in later centuries. The Arthurian legends were elaborated by the medieval chroniclers Geoffrey of Monmouth and William of Malmesbury and in Thomas Malory's epic, *Morte d'Arthur* (1485), further romanticized in Tennyson's *Idylls of the King* (1859) and resurrected in T.H. White's saga, *The Once and Future King* (1958).

Although there are places throughout Britain and Europe that claim some association with Arthur, it's England's West Country, and **Cornwall** in particular, that has the greatest concentration of places boasting a link. Here, the myths, enriched by fellow Celts from Brittany and Wales, have established deep roots, so that, for example, the spirit of Arthur is said to be embodied in the Cornish chough – a bird now almost extinct. Cornwall's most famous Arthurian site is his supposed birthplace, **Tintagel**, where Merlin apparently lived in a cave under the castle (he also resided on a rock near Mousehole, south of Penzance, according to some sources). Nearby **Bodmin Moor** is littered with places with names such as "King Arthur's Bed" and "King Arthur's Downs", while Camlan, the battlefield where Arthur was mortally wounded fighting against his nephew Mordred, is associated with Slaughterbridge, on the northern reaches of the moor near **Camelford** (which is also sometimes identified as Camelot itself). At **Dozmary Pool**, the knight Bedivere was dispatched by the dying Arthur to return the sword Excalibur to the mysterious hand emerging from the water – though Loe Pool in Mount's Bay also claims this honour. Arthur's body, it is claimed, was carried after the battle to **Boscastle**, on Cornwall's northern coast, from where a funeral barge transported it to Avalon (identified with Glastonbury in Somerset; see p.275).

Sun 4 daily; 10min).

Tourist office The Harbour (Mon–Sat: April–Sept 10am–5pm; Oct–March 11am–3pm; 01840 250010, visitboscastleandtintagel).

ACCOMMODATION AND EATING

Napoleon Inn High St 01840 250204, napoleoninn.co.uk. Among Boscastle's excellent pubs, this one in the upper town has tankards hanging off the ceiling, shove ha'penny and great food (mains around £10). Live music evenings Fri and, in summer, Wed in the garden. Daily 11am–11pm, food served 12.30–9pm.

6

Old Rectory St Juliot, 1.5 miles above Boscastle 01840 250225, stjuliot.com. For a real Thomas Hardy experience, head for this luxurious Victorian B&B, where you can stay in the author's bedroom and roam the extensive grounds. Closed mid-Nov to mid-Feb. £90

★ **YHA Boscastle** Harbourside 0845 371 9006, boscastle@yha.org.uk. Fine old hostel in a former stables right by the river. Rooms have 3–6 beds and there's a self-catering kitchen and a comfy lounge. Groups only Dec–March. £20.40

Bude and around

Just four miles from the Devon border, Cornwall's northernmost town of **BUDE** is built around an estuary surrounded by a fine expanse of sands. The town has sprouted a crop of hotels and holiday homes, though these have not unduly spoilt the place nor the magnificent cliffy coast surrounding it.

Of the excellent beaches hereabouts, the central **Summerleaze** is clean and spacious, but the mile-long **Widemouth Bay**, south of town, is the main focus of the holiday crowds (though bathing can be dangerous near the rocks at low tide). Surfers also congregate five miles down the coast at **Crackington Haven**, wonderfully situated between 430ft crags at the mouth of a lush valley. To the **north** of Bude, acres-wide **Crooklets** is the scene of **surfing** and life-saving demonstrations and competitions. A couple of miles further on, **Sandy Mouth** holds a pristine expanse of sand with rock pools beneath the encircling cliffs. It's a short walk from here to another surfers' delight, **Duckpool**, a tiny sandy cove flanked by jagged reefs at low tide, and dominated by the three-hundred-foot **Steeple Point**.

ARRIVAL AND INFORMATION — BUDE

By bus Buses stop on The Strand.

Destinations Boscastle (4–6 daily; 1hr); Exeter (Mon–Sat 5 daily, Sun 2 daily; 2hr); Hartland (Mon–Sat 4 daily; 45min).

Tourist office In the car park off the Crescent (April–Sept Mon–Sat 10am–5/6pm, Sun 10am–4pm; Oct–March daily 10am–4pm; 01288 354240, visitbude.info).

ACCOMMODATION AND EATING

Brendon Arms Falcon Terrace 01288 354542, brendonarms.co.uk. Large, agreeable old inn with tables on the front lawn, good for a pint of real ale and a snack or bar meal for under £10. Accommodation available. Bar daily 11am/noon–midnight, food served noon–9pm. £80

Life's a Beach Summerleaze Beach 01288 355222, lifesabeach.info. Right on the beach, this is a café by day, offering baguettes, burgers and drinks, and a romantic bistro strong on seafood in the evening (mains £15–19). Mon–Sat 10.30am–8.45pm (last orders), Sun 10.30am–3.30pm; Christmas–Easter Thurs–Sat only.

North Shore 57 Killerton Rd 01288 354256, northshorebude.com. Friendly backpackers' hostel 5min from the centre of town, with clean and spacious rooms – including en-suite doubles – a large garden, a kitchen and internet access. Dorm £14, double £45

Upper Lynstone Lynstone 01288 352017, upperlynstone.co.uk. This clean, basic campsite lies some three quarters of a mile south of town, linked by a panoramic cliff-top walk. There's a shop on site, and electric hook-ups. Closed Oct–Easter. Pitches £19

Bodmin Moor

Bodmin Moor, the smallest of the West Country's great moors, has some beautiful tors, torrents and rock formations, but much of its fascination lies in the strong human imprint, particularly the wealth of relics left behind by its **Bronze Age** population. Separated from these by some three millennia, the churches in the villages of **St Neot**,

Blisland and **Altarnun** are among the region's finest examples of fifteenth-century art and architecture.

Bodmin

BODMIN's position on the western edge of Bodmin Moor, equidistant from the north and south Cornish coasts and the Fowey and Camel rivers, encouraged its growth as a trading town. It was also an important ecclesiastical centre after the establishment of a priory by St Petroc, who moved here from Padstow in the sixth century.

Church of St Petroc

Priory Rd • Open for services & April–Sept Mon–Sat 11am–3pm; at other times call to check • Free • ⓣ 01208 73867

After Bodmin's priory had disappeared, the town retained its prestige through its **church of St Petroc**, built in the fifteenth century and still Cornwall's largest parish church. Inside, there's an extravagantly carved twelfth-century font and an ivory casket that once held the bones of the saint. The southwest corner of the churchyard holds a sacred well.

Bodmin Jail

Berrycoombe Rd • Daily 10am–dusk • £6.50 • ⓦ bodminjail.org

The notorious **Bodmin Jail** is redolent of the public executions that were guaranteed crowd-pullers until 1862, though it didn't finally close until 1927. You can visit part of the original eighteenth-century structure, including the condemned cell and "execution pit", and some grisly exhibits chronicling the lives of the inmates. *The Warder's Room*, a café-restaurant, stays open until late.

Lanhydrock

Three miles southeast of Bodmin • **House** Tues–Sun: March & Oct 11am–5pm; April–Sept 11am–5.30pm; also open Mon in school hols • £10.40 including grounds and gardens **Gardens** Daily 10am–6pm or dusk • £6.10 • NT • A walk of less than 2 miles from Bodmin Parkway station

One of Cornwall's most celebrated country houses, **Lanhydrock** originally dates from the seventeenth century but was totally rebuilt after a fire in 1881. Much remains of its Jacobean past within the granite exterior, however; the 50 rooms include a long picture gallery with a plaster ceiling depicting scenes from the Old Testament, while the servants' quarters fascinatingly reveal the daily workings of a Victorian manor house. The grounds have magnificent **gardens** with lush beds of magnolias, azaleas and rhododendrons, and a huge area of wooded parkland bordering onto the River Fowey.

Blisland

BLISLAND stands in the Camel valley on the western slopes of Bodmin Moor, three miles northeast of Bodmin. Georgian and Victorian houses cluster around a village green and a church whose well-restored interior has an Italianate altar and a startlingly painted screen.

The western moor

On **Pendrift Common** above Blisland, the gigantic **Jubilee Rock** is inscribed with various patriotic insignia commemorating the jubilee of George III's coronation in 1809. From this 700ft vantage point you look eastward over the De Lank gorge and

TOP 5 GARDENS

Eden Project See p.316
Lanhydrock See p.333
Lost Gardens of Heligan See p.316
Mount Edgcumbe See p.301
Tresco Abbey Gardens See p.326

the boulder-crowned knoll of **Hawk's Tor**, three miles away. On the shoulder of the tor stand the Neolithic **Stripple Stones**, a circular platform once holding 28 standing stones, of which just four are still upright.

Camelford

The northern half of Bodmin Moor is dominated by its two highest tors, both of them easily accessible from **CAMELFORD**, an unassuming local centre where the **North Cornwall Museum** (April–Sept Mon–Sat 10am–5pm; £3) displays domestic items and exhibits relating to the local slate industry.

The northern tors

Four miles southeast of Camelford, **Rough Tor** is the second highest peak on Bodmin Moor at 1311ft. A short distance to the east stand **Little Rough Tor**, where there are the remains of an Iron Age camp, and **Showery Tor**, capped by a prominent formation of piled rocks. Easily visible to the southeast, **Brown Willy** is, at 1378ft, the highest peak in Cornwall, as its original name signified – Bronewhella, or "highest hill". Like Rough Tor, Brown Willy shows various faces, its sugarloaf appearance from the north sharpening into a long multi-peaked crest as you approach. The tor is accessible by continuing from the summit of Rough Tor across the valley of the De Lank, or, from the south, by footpath from Bolventor.

Bolventor and around

The village of **BOLVENTOR**, lying at the centre of the moor midway between Bodmin and Launceston, is an uninspiring place close to one of the moor's chief focuses for walkers and literary sightseers alike – **Jamaica Inn**.

Jamaica Inn

Smugglers Museum Daily: Feb, March, Nov & Dec 11am–4pm; April–Oct 10am–5/6pm • £3.95 • T 01566 86250, W jamaicainn.co.uk

A staging post even before the precursor of the A30 road was laid here in 1769, the inn was described as being "alone in glory, four square to the winds" by **Daphne Du Maurier**, who stayed here in 1930, soaking up inspiration for her smugglers' yarn, *Jamaica Inn*. There's a room inside devoted to the author, and the hotel also has an attached **Smugglers Museum**, illustrating the diverse ruses used for concealing contraband.

Dozmary Pool

A mile south of Bolventor

The car park at *Jamaica Inn* makes a useful place to leave your vehicle and venture forth on foot. Just a mile south, **Dozmary Pool** is another link in the West Country's Arthurian mythologies – after Arthur's death Sir Bedivere hurled Excalibur, the king's sword, into the pool, where it was seized by an arm raised from the depths. Despite its proximity to the A30, the diamond-shaped lake usually preserves an ethereal air, though it's been known to run dry in summer, dealing a bit of a blow to the legend that it is bottomless.

Altarnun

Four miles northeast of Bolventor, **ALTARNUN** is a pleasant, granite-grey village snugly sheltered beneath the eastern heights of the moor. Its prominent **church**, St Nonna's, contains a fine Norman font and 79 bench ends carved at the beginning of the sixteenth century, depicting saints, musicians and clowns.

The southeastern moor

Approached through a lush wooded valley, **ST NEOT** is one of the moor's prettiest villages. Its fifteenth-century **church** contains some of the most impressive stained-glass windows of any parish church in the country, the oldest glass being the fifteenth-century **Creation Window**, at the east end of the south aisle.

One of the moor's most attractive spots lies a couple of miles east, below Draynes Bridge, where the Fowey tumbles through the **Golitha Falls**, less a waterfall than a series of rapids. Dippers and wagtails flit through the trees, and there's a pleasant woodland walk to Siblyback Lake reservoir just over a mile away. North and east of Siblyback Lake are some of Bodmin Moor's grandest landscapes. The quite modest elevations of Hawk's Tor (1079ft) and the lower Trewartha Tor appear enormous from the north, though they are overtopped by **Kilmar**, highest of the hills on the moor's eastern flank at 1280ft. **Stowe's Hill** is the site of the moor's most famous stone pile, **The Cheesewring**, a precarious pillar of balancing granite slabs, marvellously eroded by the wind. A mile or so south down Stowe's Hill stands an artificial rock phenomenon, **The Hurlers**, a wide complex of three circles dating from about 1500 BC. The purpose of these stark upright stones is not known, though they owe their name to the legend that they were men turned to stone for playing the Celtic game of hurling on the Sabbath.

The Hurlers are easily accessible just outside **MINIONS**, Cornwall's highest village, three miles south of which stands another Stone Age survival, **Trethevy Quoit**, a chamber tomb nearly nine feet high, surmounted by a massive capstone. Originally enclosed in earth, the stones have been stripped by centuries of weathering to create Cornwall's most impressive megalithic monument.

ARRIVAL AND INFORMATION — BODMIN MOOR

By train Three miles outside Bodmin itself, Bodmin Parkway train station has a regular bus connection to the centre of Bodmin.

Destinations Exeter (every 30min–1hr; 1hr 40min); Penzance (every 30min–1hr; 1hr 20min); Plymouth (every 30min–1hr; 45min).

By bus All buses to Bodmin stop on Mount Folly, near the tourist office.

Destinations Newquay (4 daily; 1hr); Padstow (Mon–Sat hourly, Sun 6 daily; 50min); Plymouth (4 daily; 1hr 10min); St Austell (Mon–Sat hourly, Sun 5 daily; 50min).

Tourist offices Mount Folly, Bodmin (Easter–Oct Mon–Sat 10am–5pm; Nov–Easter Mon–Fri 10am–5pm; T 01208 76616, W bodminlive.com), and North Cornwall Museum, The Cleese, Camelford (April–Sept Mon–Sat 10am–5pm; T 01840 212954).

ACCOMMODATION AND EATING

★ **Bedknobs** Polgwyn, Castle St, Bodmin T 01208 77553, W bedknobs.co.uk. Victorian villa in an acre of wooded garden, with three spacious and luxurious rooms, the priciest with its own en-suite Airbath and the cheapest with a separate bathroom that includes a spa bath. Friendly, eco-aware hosts and lots of extras. No under-12s. **£85**

Blisland Inn The Green, Blisland T 01208 850739. Traditional moorland pub, serving eight real ales on tap (and one from the barrel), Cornish fruit wine, bar snacks (£5–7) and full meals (£8–15). It has outdoor tables and hosts live music most Saturdays. Mon–Sat 11am–11pm, Sun noon–11pm, food served noon–2pm & 6.30–9pm.

Chapel an Gansblydhen Fore St, Bodmin T 01208 261730, W jdwetherspoon.co.uk. Bodmin has a poor choice of places to eat, but this Wetherspoons pub in a former Methodist chapel from 1840 is fine, with an atmospheric setting, outdoor tables and cheap food and beer all day. Daily 8am–midnight.

Jamaica Inn Bolventor T 01566 86250, W jamaicainn.co.uk. Despite its fame, this inn immortalized by Daphne du Maurier has lost any trace of romance since its development into a bland hotel and restaurant complex. It occupies a grand site, though, ideal for excursions onto the moor. Food served daily noon–9pm. **£105**

Mason's Arms Fore St, Camelford T 01840 213309, W jdwetherspoon.co.uk. Traditional, rather poky pub with St Austell ales and some of the best nosh around (mains around £10). Daily 11am–11pm; food served noon–2.30pm & 6–9pm.

Roscrea 18 St Nicholas Rd, Bodmin T 01208 74400, W roscrea.co.uk. Central, friendly B&B with tasteful Victorian rooms. Breakfasts include eggs laid in the garden, and you can request a great two-course dinner for £18.50 – a good option. No credit cards. **£78**

Warmington House 32 Market Place, Fore St, Camelford T 01840 214961, W warmingtonhouse.co.uk. Elegant Queen Anne building in the heart of the village, with light and airy rooms (one single), period furnishings and modern comforts. No credit cards. **£90**

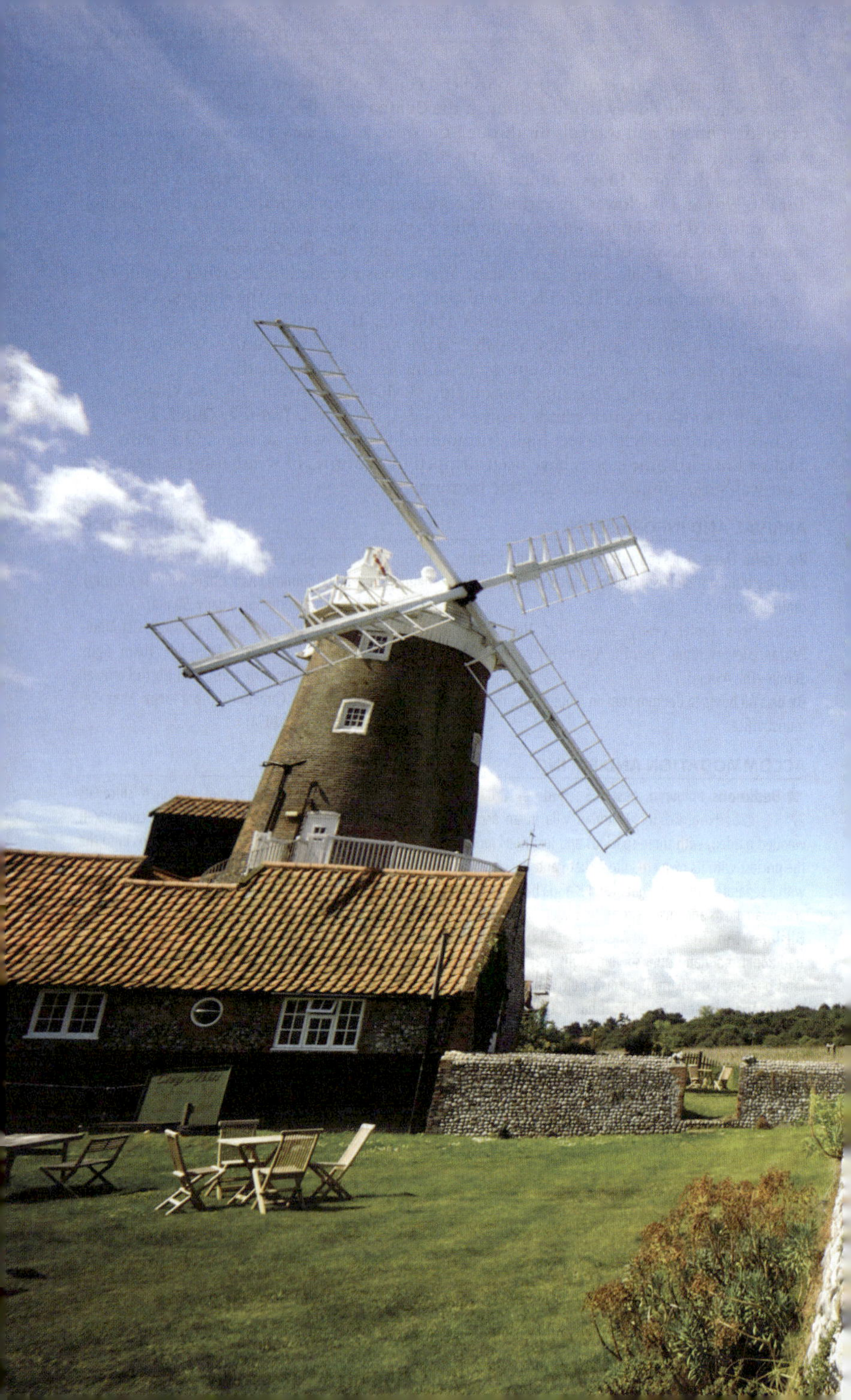

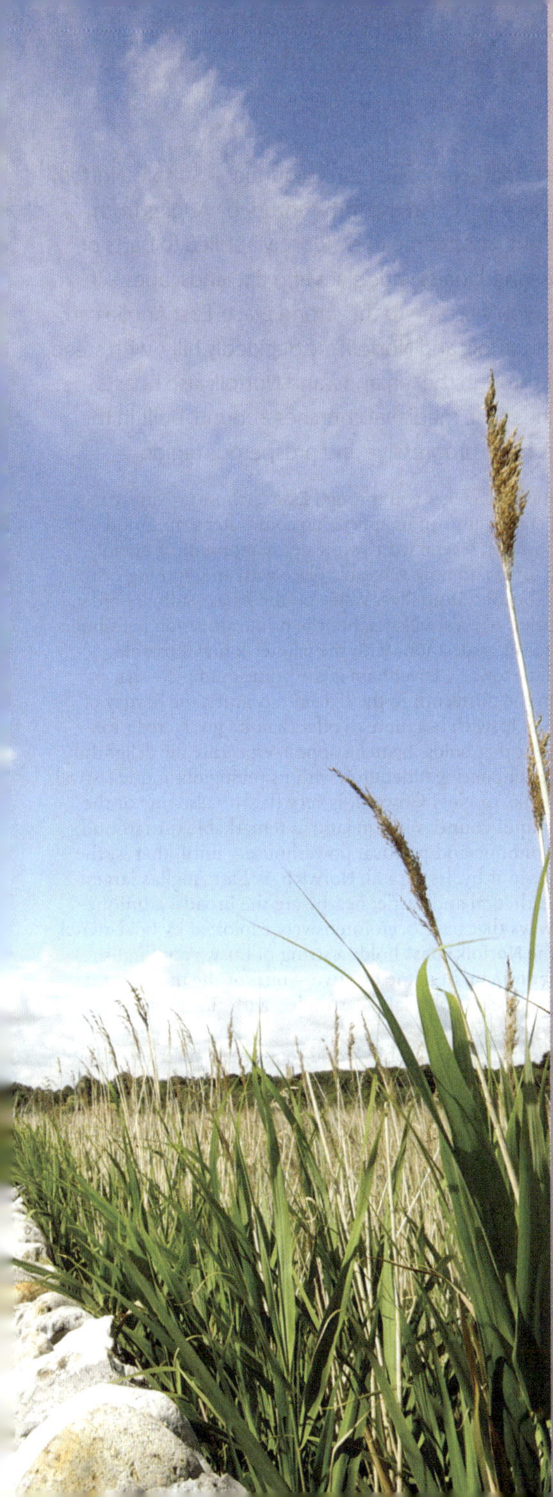

East Anglia

340 Colchester

342 The Stour Valley

345 Ipswich

346 The Suffolk coast

352 Norwich

356 The north Norfolk coast

363 King's Lynn

364 Ely

366 Cambridge

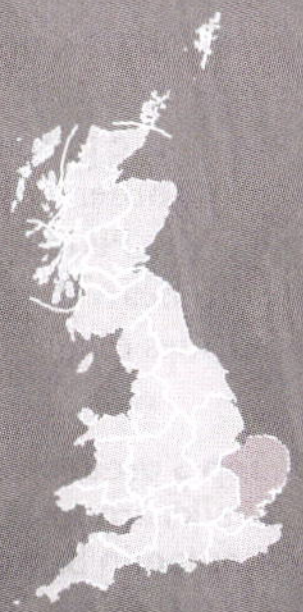

CLEY WINDMILL, NORFOLK

East Anglia

Strictly speaking, East Anglia is made up of just three counties – Suffolk, Norfolk and Cambridgeshire, which were settled in the fifth century by Angles from today's Schleswig-Holstein – but it has come to be loosely applied to parts of Essex too. As a region it's renowned for its wide skies and flat landscapes – if you're looking for mountains, you've come to the wrong place. East Anglia can surprise, nonetheless: parts of Suffolk and Norfolk are decidedly hilly, with steep coastal cliffs; broad rivers cut through the fenlands; and Norfolk also boasts some wonderful sandy beaches. Fine medieval churches abound, built in the days when this was England's most progressive and prosperous region.

Heading into East Anglia from the south takes you through **Essex**, whose proximity to London has turned much of the county into an unappetizing commuter strip. Amid the suburban gloom, there are, however, several worthwhile destinations, most notably **Colchester**, once a major Roman town and now a likeable place with an imposing castle, and the handsome hamlets of the bucolic **Stour River Valley** on the Essex–Suffolk border. Essex's **Dedham** is one of the prettiest of these villages, but the prime attraction hereabouts is Suffolk's **Flatford Mill**, famous for its associations with the painter John Constable.

Suffolk boasts a string of pretty little towns – **Lavenham** is the prime example – that enjoyed immense prosperity from the thirteenth to the sixteenth century, the heyday of the wool trade. The county town of **Ipswich** has more to offer than it's given credit for, but really it's the north Suffolk coast that holds the main appeal, especially the delightful seaside resort of **Southwold** and neighbouring **Aldeburgh** with its prestigious music festival.

Norfolk, as everyone knows thanks to Noël Coward, is very flat. It's also one of the most sparsely populated and tranquil counties in England, a remarkable turnaround from the days when it was an economic and political powerhouse – until, that is, the Industrial Revolution simply passed it by. Its capital, **Norwich**, is East Anglia's largest city, renowned for its Norman cathedral and castle; nearby are the **Broads**, a unique landscape of reed-ridden waterways that have been intensively exploited by boat-rental companies. Similarly popular, the **Norfolk coast** holds a string of busy, very English seaside resorts – **Cromer** and **Sheringham** to name but two – but for the most part it's charmingly unspoilt, its marshes, creeks and tidal fats studded with tiny flintstone villages, most enjoyably **Blakeney** and **Cley**.

Cambridge is much visited, principally because of its world-renowned university, whose ancient colleges boast some of the finest medieval and early-modern architecture in the country. The rest of Cambridgeshire is pancake-flat **fenland**, for centuries an inhospitable marshland, but now rich alluvial farming land. The cathedral town of **Ely**, settled on one of the few areas of raised ground in the fens, is an easy and popular day-trip from Cambridge.

Given the prevailing flatness of the terrain, **hiking** in East Anglia is less strenuous than in most other English regions, and there are several long-distance footpaths. The main one is the **Peddars Way** (Ⓦ nationaltrail.co.uk), which runs north from Knettishall Heath, near Thetford, to the coast at Holme-next-the-Sea, near Hunstanton, where it continues east as the **Norfolk Coast Path** to Cromer – 93 miles in total.

Top 5 great places to stay p.342
Walks around Constable country p.343
Benjamin Britten and the Aldeburgh Festival p.348
The Norfolk Broads p.357
Blakeney boat trips p.360
Cambridge: taking a punt p.366

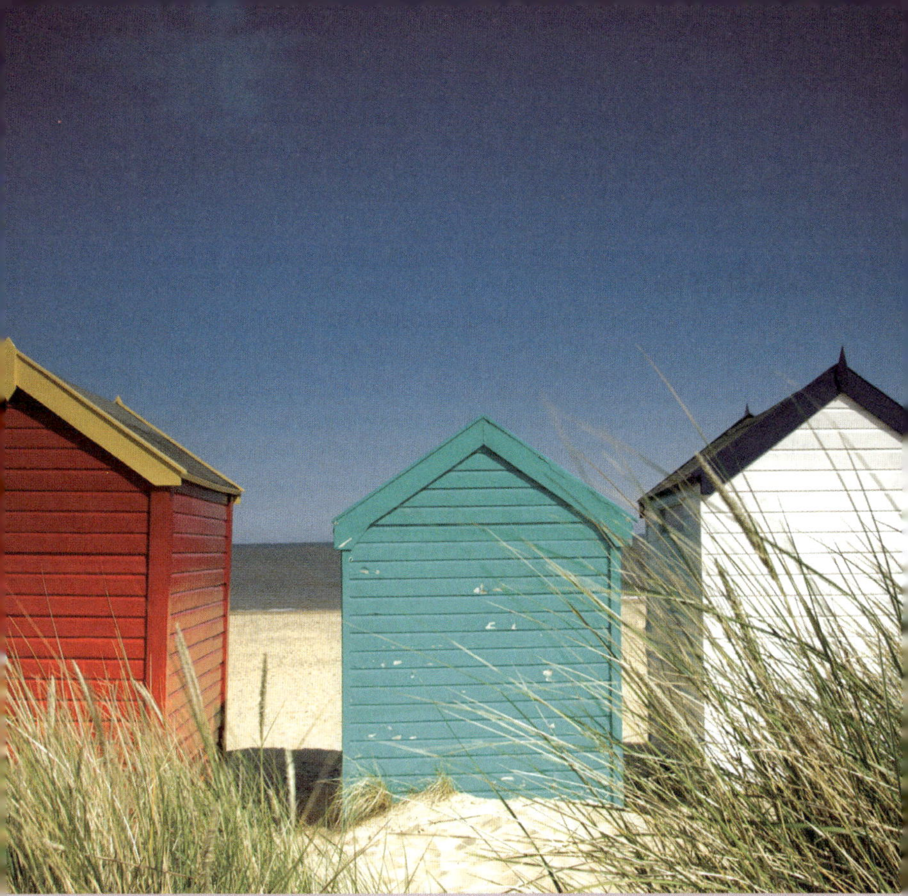

BEACH HUTS, SOUTHWOLD

Highlights

❶ **Orford** Solitary hamlet with a splendid coastal setting that makes for a wonderful weekend away. **See p.347**

❷ **The Aldeburgh Festival** The region's prime classical music festival takes place every June. **See p.348**

❸ **Southwold** Extraordinarily pretty, genteel seaside town that is perfect for walking and bathing – with the added incentive of the most inventive Under the Pier Show in the country. **See p.351**

❹ **Norwich Market** This open-air market is the region's biggest and best for everything from whelks to wellies. **See p.354**

❺ **Holkham Bay and beach** Wide bay holding Norfolk's finest beach – acres of golden sand set against hilly, pine-dusted dunes. **See p.361**

❻ **Ely** Isolated Cambridgeshire town, with a true fenland flavour and a magnificent cathedral. **See p.364**

❼ **Cambridge** With some of the finest late medieval architecture in Europe, Cambridge is a must-see, its compact centre graced by dignified old colleges and their neatly manicured quadrangles. **See pp.366–373**

HIGHLIGHTS ARE MARKED ON THE MAP ON P.340

GETTING AROUND **EAST ANGLIA**

By train Trains from London are fast and frequent: one main line links Colchester, Ipswich and Norwich, another Cambridge and Ely. One useful cross-country branch line links Petersborough, Ely, Norwich and Ipswich.

By bus Beyond the major towns you'll have to rely on local buses. Services are patchy, except on the north Norfolk coast, which is well served by the Norfolk Coasthopper bus (Ⓦ coasthopper.co.uk).

Colchester

If you visit anywhere in Essex, it should be **COLCHESTER**, a busy sort of place with a **castle**, a university and an army base, fifty miles or so northeast of London. Colchester prides itself on being England's oldest town, and there is indeed documentary evidence of a settlement here as early as the fifth century BC. Today, Colchester makes a potential base for explorations of the surrounding countryside – particularly the **Stour valley** towns of Constable country, within easy reach a few miles to the north.

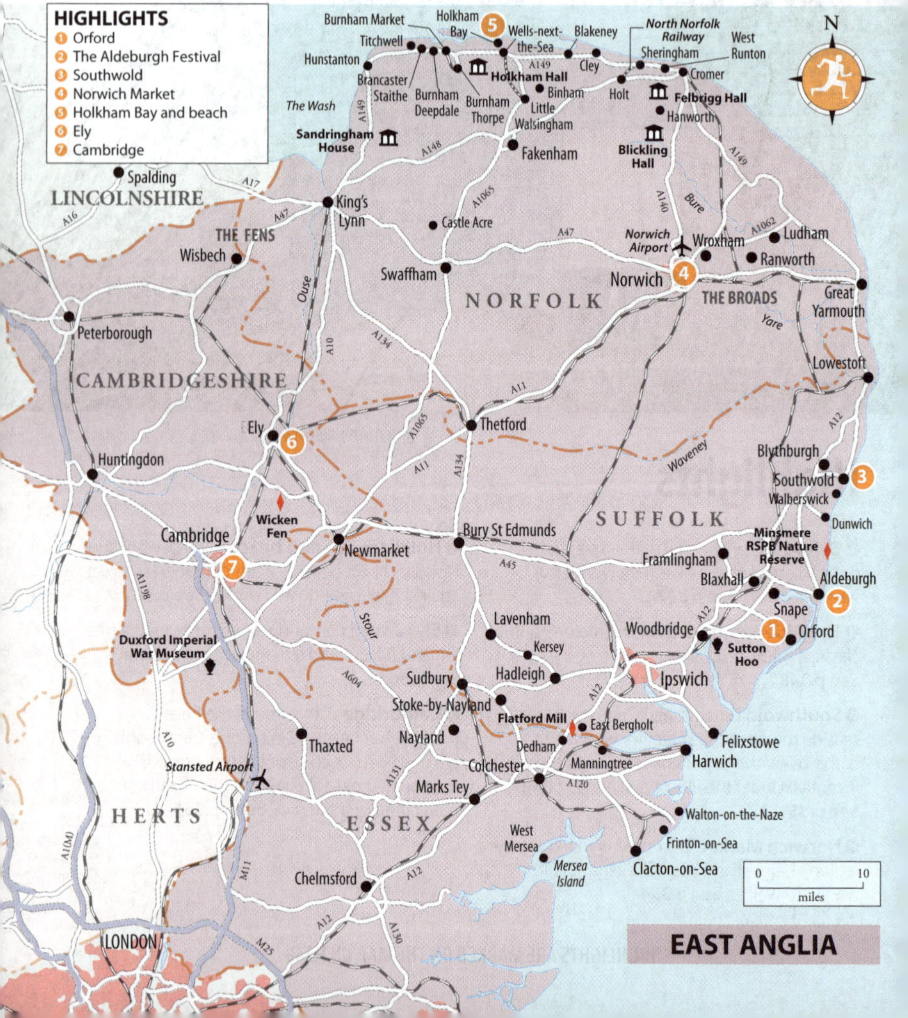

Brief history

By the first century AD, the town was the region's capital under **King Cunobelin** – better known as Shakespeare's Cymbeline – and when the **Romans** invaded Britain in 43 AD they chose Colchester (Camulodunum) as their new capital, though it was soon eclipsed by London. Later, the conquering Normans built one of their mightiest strongholds in Colchester, but the conflict that most marked the town was the **Civil War**. In 1648, Colchester was subjected to a gruelling siege by the Parliamentarian army; after three months, during which the population ate every living creature within the walls, the town finally surrendered and the Royalist leaders were promptly executed for their pains.

The castle

Mon–Sat 10am–5pm, Sun 11–5pm • £6 • Guided tours 45min; £2.50 • ⓣ 01206 282939, ⓦ colchestermuseums.org.uk/castle

At the heart of Colchester are the remains of its **castle**, a ruggedly imposing, honey-coloured keep, set in attractive parkland stretching down to the River Colne. Begun less than ten years after the Battle of Hastings, the keep was the largest in Europe at the time, built on the site of the Temple of Claudius. Inside the keep, a **museum** holds an excellent collection of Romano-British archeological finds, notably a miscellany of coins and tombstones. The museum also runs regular **guided tours**, giving access to the Roman vaults, the Norman chapel and the castle roof, which are otherwise out of bounds. Outside, down towards the river in Castle Park, is a section of the old **Roman walls**, whose battered remains are still visible around much of the town centre. They were erected after Boudicca had sacked the city and, as such, are a case of too little too late.

The Town Hall

High St

The castle stands at the eastern end of the wide and largely pedestrianized **High Street**, which follows pretty much the same route as it did in Roman times. The most arresting building here is the flamboyant **Town Hall**, built in 1902 and topped by a statue of St Helena, mother of Constantine the Great and daughter of "Old King Cole" of nursery-rhyme fame – after whom, some say, the town was named.

Balkerne Gate

High St

Looming above the western end of the High Street is the town landmark, "**Jumbo**", a disused nineteenth-century water tower, considerably more imposing than the nearby **Balkerne Gate**, which marked the western entrance to Roman Colchester. Built in 50 AD, this is the largest surviving Roman gateway in the country, though with the remains at only a touch over 6ft high, it's far from spectacular.

ARRIVAL AND INFORMATION — COLCHESTER

By train Colchester has two train stations, one for local services and the other, Colchester North, for mainline trains. From this mainline station, it's a 15min walk south into town – follow the signs.

Destinations Mainline services to Harwich ferry port (hourly; 30min); Ipswich (every 20min; 20min); London Liverpool Street (every 15min; 1hr); Norwich (every 30min; 1hr).

By bus The bus station is off Queen St, a couple of minutes' walk from High St and yards from both the castle and the tourist office.

Tourist office 1 Queen St (Mon–Sat 10am–5pm; ⓣ 01206 282920, ⓦ visitcolchester.com).

ACCOMMODATION

Charlie Browns B&B 60 East St ⓣ 01206 517541, ⓦ charliebrownsbedandbreakfast.co.uk. Chic three-bedroomed B&B in a tastefully converted former shop in a handy central location. Lots of original features – like the exposed half-timbered walls – with deluxe additions in soothing, comfortable rooms. £55

Old Manse 15 Roman Rd 01206 545154, theoldmanse.uk.com. One of the best of the town's B&Bs, with three pleasant, en-suite guest rooms in a well-maintained, bay-windowed Victorian house on a quiet cul-de-sac; it's on the east side of the castle, a couple of minutes' walk from the tourist office. £68

EATING

Colchester's **oysters** have been highly prized since Roman times and today are at their best among the oyster fisheries of **Mersea Island**, about 6 miles south of Colchester; the season runs from September to May.

The Company Shed 129 Coast Rd, West Mersea 01206 382700. The freshest of oysters served simply at rickety tables in, to quote their own PR, a "romantically weatherbeaten shed". Romantic or not, the oysters are indeed delicious. Tues–Sat 9am–5pm, Sun 10am–5pm. Last orders for eating in 4pm.

7

The Lemon Tree Bistro 48 St John's St 01206 767337, the-lemon-tree.com. In antique premises in the heart of town, this popular restaurant has a creative, pan-European menu – try the marinated chicken with aubergine. Mains hover around £15. Mon–Sat 10.30am–10.30pm.

The Stour Valley

Six miles or so north of Colchester, the **Stour River Valley** forms the border between Essex and Suffolk, and signals the beginning of East Anglia proper. The valley is dotted with lovely little villages, where rickety, half-timbered Tudor houses and elegant Georgian dwellings cluster around medieval churches, proud buildings with square, self-confident towers. The Stour's prettiest villages are concentrated along its lower reaches – to the east of the A134 – in Dedham Vale, with **Dedham** the most appealing of them all. The vale is also known as "**Constable Country**", as it was the home of John Constable, one of England's greatest artists, and the subject of his most famous paintings. Inevitably, there's a Constable shrine – the much-visited complex of old buildings down by the river at **Flatford Mill**. Elsewhere, the best-preserved of the old south Suffolk wool towns is **Lavenham**; nearby **Sudbury** has a fine museum, devoted to the work of another talented English artist, Thomas Gainsborough.

Brief history

The villages along the River Stour and its tributaries were once busy little places at the heart of East Anglia's medieval weaving trade. By the 1490s, the region produced more cloth than any other part of the country, but in Tudor times production shifted to Colchester, Ipswich and Norwich and, although most of the smaller settlements continued spinning cloth for the next three hundred years or so, their importance slowly dwindled. Bypassed by the Industrial Revolution, **south Suffolk** had, by the late nineteenth century, become a remote rural backwater, an impoverished area whose decline had one unforeseen consequence: with few exceptions, the towns and villages were never prosperous enough to modernize, and the architectural legacy of medieval and Tudor times survived.

GETTING AROUND — THE STOUR VALLEY

Seeing the Stour Valley by **public transport** is problematic – distances are small (Dedham Vale is only about ten miles long), but **buses** between the villages are infrequent and you'll find it difficult to get away from the towns. Several **rail** lines cross south Suffolk, the most useful being the London Liverpool Street to Colchester and Marks Tey to Sudbury routes.

TOP FIVE GREAT PLACES TO STAY

Cley Mill B&B Cley. See p.359
Crown & Castle Orford. See p.347
Gothic House Norwich. See p.355
Great House Hotel Lavenham. See p.345
Ocean House B&B Aldeburgh. See p.348

Flatford Mill

"I associate my careless boyhood with all that lies on the banks of the Stour," wrote **John Constable**, who was born in **East Bergholt**, nine miles northeast of Colchester in 1776. The house in which he was born has long since disappeared, so it has been left to **FLATFORD MILL**, a mile or so to the south, to take up the painter's cause. The mill was owned by his father and was where Constable painted his most celebrated canvas, *The Hay Wain* (now in London's National Gallery), which created a sensation when it was exhibited in Paris in 1824. To the chagrin of many of his contemporaries, Constable turned away from the landscape painting conventions of the day, rendering his scenery with a realistic directness that harked back to the Dutch landscape painters of the seventeenth century.

The mill itself – not the one he painted, but a Victorian replacement – is not open to the public and neither is neighbouring **Willy Lott's Cottage**, which does actually feature in *The Hay Wain*, but the National Trust has colonized several local buildings, principally **Bridge Cottage**.

7

Bridge Cottage

Flatford Mill • Jan & Feb Sat & Sun 11am–3.30pm; March Wed–Sun 11am–4pm; April daily 11am–5pm; May–Sept daily 10.30am–5.30pm; Oct daily 11am–4.30pm; Nov & Dec Wed–Sun 11am–3.30pm • NT • Free, except for parking • ☎ 01206 298260 • The nearest train station is at Manningtree, 2 miles away

Although it was familiar to Constable, none of the artist's paintings is displayed in the gorgeous, thatched **Bridge Cottage**. It is, however, packed with memorabilia and an exhibition on the artist, and provides a fulcrum for the Constable tourism in the area. The cottage also has a very pleasant riverside tearoom where you can take in the view.

ACCOMMODATION — **FLATFORD MILL**

The Granary B&B Flatford Mill ☎ 01206 298111, granaryflatford.co.uk. In the annexe of the old granary that was once owned by Constable's father, this appealing B&B has a real cottagey feel with its beamed ceilings and antique furniture. There are two ground-floor guest rooms, both en suite. **£58**

Dedham

Constable went to school in **DEDHAM**, just upriver from Flatford Mill and one of the region's prettiest villages, its wide and lazy main street graced by a handsome medley of old timber-framed houses and Georgian villas. Day-trippers arrive here by the coach load throughout the summer.

Church of St Mary

Dedham's main sight is the **Church of St Mary**, a large, well-proportioned structure with a sweeping, sixteenth-century nave that is adorned by some attractive Victorian stained glass. Constable painted the church on several occasions, and today it holds one of the artist's rare religious paintings, *The Ascension* – frankly, it's a good job Constable concentrated on landscapes.

ARRIVAL AND DEPARTURE — **DEDHAM**

There is a reasonably frequent **bus** service from Colchester to Dedham (Mon–Sat 3–4 daily; 40min).

WALKS AROUND CONSTABLE COUNTRY

Many visitors are keen to see the sites associated with Constable's paintings and, although there is something a tad futile about this – so much has changed – the National Trust does organize **guided walks** to these locations; the nearest are the remains of the Dry Dock next to Bridge Cottage and the Hay Wain view itself.

ACCOMMODATION AND EATING

The Sun Inn High St ⓣ01206 323351, ⓦthesuninndedham.com. Among Dedham's several pubs, the pick is *The Sun*, an ancient place that has been sympathetically modernized. The menu is strong on local ingredients and offers tasty Italian and British dishes, all washed down by real ales; mains average around £13. They also have five attractive en-suite rooms; rates increase considerably at the weekend. Food served Mon–Fri noon–2.30pm & 6.30–9.30pm, Sat & Sun noon–3pm & 6.30–10pm. £105

Sudbury

7

SUDBURY is by far the most important town in this part of the Stour Valley. A handful of timber-framed houses recalls its days of wool-trade prosperity, but its salad days were underwritten by another local industry, **silk weaving**. The town's most famous export, however, is **Thomas Gainsborough**, the leading English portraitist of the eighteenth century. Although he left Sudbury when he was just 13, moving to London where he was apprenticed to an engraver, the artist is still very much identified with the town: his statue, with brush and palette, stands on Market Hill, the predominantly Victorian marketplace, while a superb collection of his work is on display a few yards away at **Gainsborough's House**.

Gainsborough's House

46 Gainsborough St • Mon–Sat 10am–5pm • £4.50, free on Tues afternoons (1–5pm) • ⓣ01787 372958, ⓦgainsborough.org.

Among the many highlights of **Gainsborough's House** – where Thomas Gainsborough (1727–88) was born – is the earliest of his surviving portrait paintings, *Boy and Girl*, a remarkably self-assured work dated to 1744. In 1752, Gainsborough moved on from London to Ipswich, where he quickly established himself as a portrait painter, with one of his specialities being wonderful "**conversation pieces**", so called because the sitters engage in polite chitchat – or genteel activity – with a landscape as the backdrop. Stints in Bath and London followed, and it was during these years that Gainsborough developed his distinctively fluid style. Examples of his later work on display include the *Portrait of Harriet, Viscountess Tracy* and the particularly striking *Portrait of Abel Moysey, MP*.

ARRIVAL AND INFORMATION — SUDBURY

By train With hourly services to and from Marks Tey, on the London to Colchester line, Sudbury train station is a 5- to 10min walk from the centre via Station Rd.

By bus Sudbury bus station is on Hamilton Rd, just south of Market Hill. The main local bus company is H.C. Chambers (ⓣ01787 227233, ⓦchamberscoaches.co.uk), who – among a batch of services – link Sudbury with Colchester.

Tourist office At the back of the Town Hall on Gaol Lane, just off Market Hill (April–Sept Mon–Fri 9am–5pm, Sat 10am–4.45pm; Oct–March Mon–Fri 9am–5pm, Sat 10am–2.45pm; ⓣ01787 881320, ⓦsudburytowncouncil.co.uk).

EATING AND DRINKING

Black Adder Brewery Tap 21 East St ⓣ01787 370876, ⓦblackaddertap.co.uk. Not much in the way of finesse here, but who cares when the big deal is the beer – a rotating selection of eight real ales on draught, but always including something from Mauldons, a local brewer. There's a courtyard patio and pub grub. Mon–Thurs 11am–11pm, Fri & Sat 11am–midnight, Sun noon–10.30pm.

The Secret Garden 21 Friars St ⓣ01787 372030, ⓦtsg.uk.net. Cosy local tearoom in a very old building, where the sophisticated menu has lots of French flourishes and they do their best to source locally. For lunch, try their ham, spinach and cheddar cheese on focaccia for just under £10; dinner might include a seared sea bass fillet or grilled duck breast. Mon–Thurs 9am–5pm, Fri & Sat 9am–5pm & 7–9.30pm.

Lavenham

LAVENHAM, eight miles northeast of Sudbury, was once a centre of the region's wool trade and is now one of the most visited villages in Suffolk, thanks to its unrivalled ensemble of perfectly preserved half-timbered houses. In outward appearance at least, the whole place has changed little since the demise of the wool industry, owing in part to a zealous local preservation society, which has carefully maintained the village's antique appearance. Lavenham is at its most beguiling in the triangular **Market Place**, an airy spot flanked by pastel-painted, medieval dwellings whose beams have been warped into all sorts of wonky angles by the passing of the years.

Guildhall of Corpus Christi

Market Place • March Wed–Sun 11am–4pm; April–Oct daily 11am–5pm; Nov Sat & Sun 11am–4pm • NT • £4 • ⓣ01787 247646

On Market Place you'll find the village's most celebrated building, the lime-washed, timber-framed **Guildhall of Corpus Christi**, erected in the sixteenth century as the headquarters of one of Lavenham's four guilds. In the much-altered interior (used successively as a prison and workhouse), there are modest exhibitions on timber-framed buildings, medieval guilds, village life and the wool industry, though most visitors soon end up in the walled garden or the teashop next door.

ARRIVAL AND INFORMATION — LAVENHAM

By bus Buses pull in at the corner of Water and Church streets, a 5min walk from the Market Place. Among several services, Chambers bus #753 (Mon–Sat hourly; ⓦchamberscoaches.co.uk) links Lavenham with Sudbury, Bury St Edmunds and Colchester.

Tourist office Lady St, just south of Market Place (mid-March to Oct daily 10am–4.45pm; Nov to mid-Dec daily 11am–3pm; Jan to mid-March Sat & Sun 11am–3pm; ⓣ01787 248207, ⓦsouthandheartofsuffolk.org.uk).

ACCOMMODATION AND EATING

Angel Hotel Market Place ⓣ01787 247388, ⓦwheelersangel.com. The *Angel*, owned by chef Marco Pierre White, has just eight, spick and span modern guest rooms. Some are enlivened by period flourishes – exposed beams, old open fires and so forth. The popular bar-restaurant cooks up a good range of English dishes and prices are reasonable for the excellent quality. Food served daily noon–2pm & 6–9.30pm. **£110**

★ **Great House Hotel & Restaurant** Market Place ⓣ01787 247431, ⓦgreathouse.co.uk. Delightful, family-run hotel bang in the centre of the village. Each of the five guest rooms is decorated in a thoughtful and tasteful manner, amalgamating the original features of the old – very old – house with the new. Deeply comfortable beds and a great breakfast round it all off. The hotel restaurant specializes in classic French cuisine, with three-course set meals (£21 at lunch, £32 at night), and à la carte. Food served Wed–Sun noon–2.30pm, Tues–Sat 7–10.30pm. **£95**

★ **Swan Hotel** High St ⓣ01787 247477, ⓦtheswanatlavenham.co.uk. This excellent hotel is a veritable rabbit warren of a place, its nooks and crannies dating back several hundred years. There's a lovely, very traditional, lounge to snooze in, a courtyard garden, an authentic Elizabethan Wool Hall, and a wood-panelled bar, and most of the comfy guest rooms abound in original features. The restaurant is first-rate too, serving imaginative British-based cuisine – roasted wood pigeon and puy lentils for example – with mains starting at around £13. Restaurant daily 7–9pm; brasserie daily noon–2.30pm & 5.30–9.30pm. **£180**

Ipswich

IPSWICH, situated at the head of the Orwell estuary, was a rich trading port in the Middle Ages, but its appearance today is mainly the result of a revival of fortunes in the Victorian era – give or take some clumsy postwar development. The two surviving reminders of old Ipswich – **Christchurch Mansion** and the splendid **Ancient House** – plus the recently renovated **quayside** are all reason enough to spend at least an afternoon here, and there's also the **Cornhill**, the ancient Saxon marketplace and still the town's focal point, an agreeable urban space flanked by a bevy of imposing Victorian edifices – the Italianate town hall, the old Neoclassical Post Office and the grandiose pseudo-Jacobean Lloyds building.

The Ancient House

Buttermarket

From Cornhill, it's just a couple of minutes' walk southeast to Ipswich's most famous building, the **Ancient House**, whose exterior was decorated around 1670 in extravagant style, a riot of pargeting and stucco work that together make it one of the finest examples of Restoration artistry in the country.

Christchurch Mansion

Soane St • Tues–Sun 10am–5pm • Free • ⓣ 01473 433554, ⓦ ipswich.gov.uk

Christchurch Mansion is a handsome, if much-restored Tudor building, sporting seventeenth-century Dutch-style gables and set in 65 acres of parkland – an area larger than the town centre itself. The labyrinthine interior is worth exploring, with period furnishings and a good assortment of paintings by Constable and Gainsborough.

The Wet Dock

Half a mile south of Cornhill

The **Wet Dock** was the largest dock in Europe when it opened in 1845. Today, after an imaginative refurbishment, it's flanked by apartments and offices, pubs, hotels and restaurants, many converted from the old marine warehouses. Walking around the Wet Dock is a pleasant way to pass an hour or so – look out, in particular, for the proud Neoclassical **Customs House**.

ARRIVAL AND INFORMATION — IPSWICH

By train Ipswich train station is on the south bank of the River Orwell, about a 10min walk from Cornhill along Princes St.

Destinations Cambridge (hourly; 1hr 20min); Colchester (every 15min; 20min); Ely (every 2hr; 1hr); London Liverpool St (every 30min; 1hr); Norwich (every 30min; 40min).

By bus The bus station is on Turret Lane, a short walk south of Cornhill.

Tourist office St Stephens Lane, in what used to be St Stephen's Church (Mon–Sat 9am–5pm; ⓣ 01473 258070, ⓦ visit-suffolk.com).

ACCOMMODATION

Salthouse Harbour Neptune Quay ⓣ 01473 226789, ⓦ salthouseharbour.co.uk. Housed in an imaginatively converted old warehouse down on the quayside, this is the city's best choice, with 70 large, modern and minimalist-style rooms whose floor-to-ceiling windows look out over Ipswich's harbour. Rates can go up to more than £200. **£125**

EATING AND DRINKING

Aqua Eight 8 Lion St ⓣ 01473 218994, ⓦ aquaeight.com. Cool Asian fusion restaurant right in the heart of town. Most mains go for £10–12 but you can't go wrong with the superb Alaskan black cod with miso sauce for £18.50. It also has a great bar serving good oriental-style meze and finger food. Tues–Thurs noon–2.30pm & 7–10pm, Fri & Sat noon–2.30pm & 5.30–11pm, Sun 5.30–10pm.

The Eaterie Salthouse Harbour hotel ⓣ 01473 226789, ⓦ salthouseharbour.co.uk. The restaurant lives up to the hotel's high standards, with curvy banquettes and a low-lit, warehousey feel. The food is hearty rather than healthy, but served with a flourish and a good eye to detail. There are usually a few specials on the board too; generally starters go for £5.95–8.95, mains £12.95–16.95. Daily noon–10pm.

The Suffolk coast

The **Suffolk coast** feels detached from the rest of the county: the road and rail lines from Ipswich to the seaport of Lowestoft funnel traffic a few miles inland for most of the way, and patches of marsh and woodland make the separation still more complete. The coast has long been plagued by erosion and this has contributed to the virtual extinction of the local fishing industry, and, in the case of **Dunwich**, almost destroyed the whole town. What is left, however, is undoubtedly one of the most unspoilt shorelines in the country – if, that is, you set aside the Sizewell nuclear power station. Highlights include the sleepy isolation of minuscule **Orford** and several genteel resorts, most notably **Southwold** and Aldeburgh, which have both evaded the lurid fate of so many English seaside towns. There are scores of delightful **walks** around here too, easy routes along the coast that are best followed with either the appropriate OS *Explorer Map* or the simplified footpath maps available at most tourist offices. The Suffolk coast is also host to East Anglia's most compelling cultural gathering, the three-week-long **Aldeburgh Festival**, which takes place every June.

GETTING AROUND **THE SUFFOLK COAST**

Getting around the Suffolk coast by **public transport** requires planning; work out your route in advance on Ⓦtravelineeastanglia.org.uk. Some journeys are straightforward – there is, for example, a regular bus from Ipswich to Aldeburgh – but some are more complicated: to get from Southwold to Aldeburgh, for instance, you catch the bus to Halesworth, the train from Halesworth to Saxmundham and then another bus to Aldeburgh, which all in all takes at least a couple of hours.

7

Orford

Some twenty miles from Ipswich, on the far side of Tunstall Forest, two medieval buildings dominate the tiny, eminently appealing village of **ORFORD**. The more impressive is the twelfth-century **castle** (April–Sept daily 10am–5pm; Oct–March Thurs–Mon 10am–4pm; EH; £5.60; Ⓦenglish-heritage.org.uk), built on high ground by Henry II, and under siege within months of its completion from Henry's rebellious sons. Most of the castle disappeared centuries ago, but the lofty keep remains, its striking stature hinting at the scale of the original fortifications. Orford's other medieval edifice is **St Bartholomew's church**, where Benjamin Britten premiered his most successful children's work, *Noye's Fludde*, as part of the 1958 Aldeburgh Festival (see p.348).

Orford Ness National Nature Reserve

Boat trips Late April to late June & Oct Sat only; late June to Sept Tues–Sat; outward boats 10am–2pm, last boat 5pm • NT • £7.50 • Ⓣ01728 648024

From the top of the castle keep, there's a great view across **Orford Ness National Nature Reserve**, a six-mile-long shingle spit that has all but blocked Orford from the sea since Tudor times. The National Trust offers **boat trips** across to the Ness from Orford Quay, 400yds down the road from the church – and a five-mile hiking trail threads its way along the spit.

ACCOMMODATION AND EATING **ORFORD**

Butley Orford Oysterage Market Square Ⓣ01394 450277, Ⓦbutleyorfordoysterage.co.uk. A local institution, dishing up great fish and seafood, much of it caught and smoked locally by the family themselves and served in a simple café-restaurant. Mon–Fri 10am–4.30pm, Sat 9am–4.30pm & Sun 10am–4pm.

★ **Crown & Castle** Market Hill Ⓣ01394 450205, Ⓦcrownandcastlehotel.co.uk. Orford's gentle, unhurried air is best experienced by staying overnight at this outstanding hotel, with eighteen stylish guest rooms and an excellent restaurant. Local, seasonal ingredients are the focus – rump of Suffolk lamb with broad-bean cream sauce for example – with mains around £20. Food served 12.15–2pm & 6.45–9pm. **£175**

Aldeburgh

Well-heeled **ALDEBURGH**, just along the coast from Orford, is best known for its annual **arts festival**, the brainchild of composer **Benjamin Britten** (1913–76), who is buried in the village churchyard alongside the tenor Peter Pears, his lover and musical collaborator. They lived by the seafront in Crag House on Crabbe Street – named after the poet, George Crabbe, who provided Britten with his greatest inspiration (see p.348) – before moving to a large house a few miles away.

7

BENJAMIN BRITTEN AND THE ALDEBURGH FESTIVAL

Born in Lowestoft in 1913, **Benjamin Britten** was closely associated with Suffolk for most of his life. The main break was during World War II when, as a conscientious objector, Britten exiled himself to the USA. Ironically enough, it was here that Britten first read the work of the nineteenth-century Suffolk poet, George Crabbe, whose *The Borough*, a grisly portrait of the life of the fishermen of Aldeburgh, was the basis of the libretto of Britten's best-known opera, *Peter Grimes*, which was premiered in London in 1945 to great acclaim. In 1948, Britten launched the **Aldeburgh Festival** as a showpiece for his own works and those of his contemporaries. He lived in the village for the next ten years, during which time he completed much of his finest work as a conductor and pianist. For the rest of his life he composed many works specifically for the festival, including his masterpiece for children, *Noye's Fludde*, and the last of his fifteen operas, *Death in Venice*.

By the mid-1960s, the festival had outgrown the parish churches in which it began, and moved into a collection of disused malthouses, five miles west of Aldeburgh on the River Alde, just south of the small village of **Snape**. The complex, the **Snape Maltings** (ⓦ snapemaltings.co.uk) were subsequently converted into one of the finest concert venues in the country and, in addition to the concert hall, there are now recording studios, galleries, a tearoom, and a pub, the *Plough & Sail*.

The Aldeburgh Festival takes place every June for two and a half weeks. Core performances are still held at the Maltings, but a string of other local venues are pressed into service as well. Throughout the rest of the year, the Maltings hosts a wide-ranging programme of musical and theatrical events, including the three-day Britten Festival in October. For more information, contact **Aldeburgh Music** (ⓣ 01728 687110, ⓦ aldeburgh.co.uk), which operates two box offices, one at Snape Maltings, the other on Aldeburgh High Street in premises it shares with the tourist office. **Tickets** for the Aldeburgh Festival usually go on sale to the public towards the end of March, and sell out fast for the big-name recitals.

Outside of June, Aldeburgh is a relaxed and low-key coastal resort, with a small fishing fleet selling its daily catch from wooden shacks along the pebbled shore. Aldeburgh's slightly old-fashioned/local shop appearance is fiercely defended by its citizens, who caused an almighty rumpus – Barbours at dawn – when Maggi Hambling's 13ft-high *Scallop* sculpture appeared on the beach in 2003. Hambling described the sculpture as a conversation with the sea and a suitable memorial to Britten; many disgruntled locals compared it to a mantelpiece ornament gone wrong.

Aldeburgh's wide **High Street** and its narrow side streets run close to the beach, but this was not always the case – hence their quixotic appearance. The sea swallowed much of what was once an extensive medieval town long ago and today Aldeburgh's oldest remaining building, the sixteenth-century, red-brick, flint and timber **Moot Hall**, which began its days in the centre of town, now finds itself on the seashore. Several **footpaths** radiate out from Aldeburgh, with the most obvious trail leading north along the coast to Thorpeness, and others going southwest to the winding estuary of the **River Alde**.

ARRIVAL AND INFORMATION — ALDEBURGH

By bus Buses to Aldeburgh pull in along the High St. One particularly useful service is First Group's (ⓦ firstgroup.com) bus #64 linking Aldeburgh with Ipswich (Mon–Sat hourly; 1hr 30min)

Tourist office 152 High St (Mon–Sat 9am–5pm, plus June–Sept Sun 10am–4pm; ⓣ 01728 453637, ⓦ suffolkcoastal.gov.uk/tourism); the festival box office (see above) is in the same office.

ACCOMMODATION

Brudenell The Parade ⓣ 01728 452071, ⓦ brudenellhotel.co.uk. Recently refurbished, this seafront hotel has a New England feel that sits very comfortably here in Aldeburgh. There's a pleasant sitting room downstairs with sea views and the bedrooms are thoughtfully furnished in contemporary style. £170

★ **Ocean House B&B** 25 Crag Path ⓣ 01728 452094, ⓦ oceanhousealdeburgh.co.uk. In an immaculately maintained Victorian dwelling right on the seafront in the centre of town, the *Ocean House* has just three traditional, en-suite guest rooms including a top-floor suite. The full English breakfasts, with home-made bread, are delicious. £90

FROM TOP ALDEBURGH BEACH (P.348); FLATFORD MILL (P.343) >

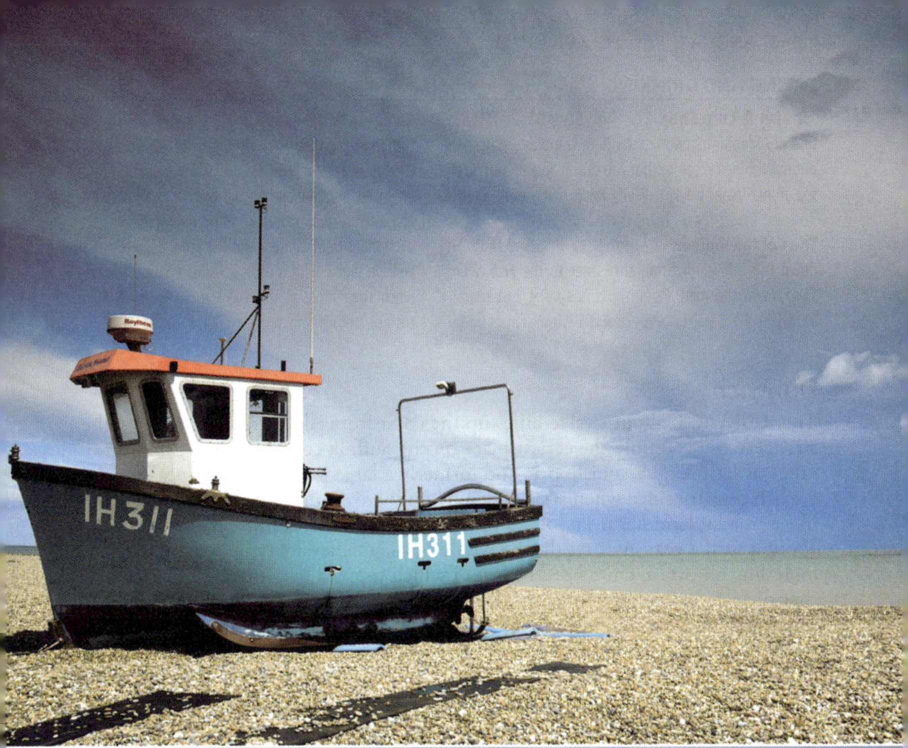
IH311
IH311

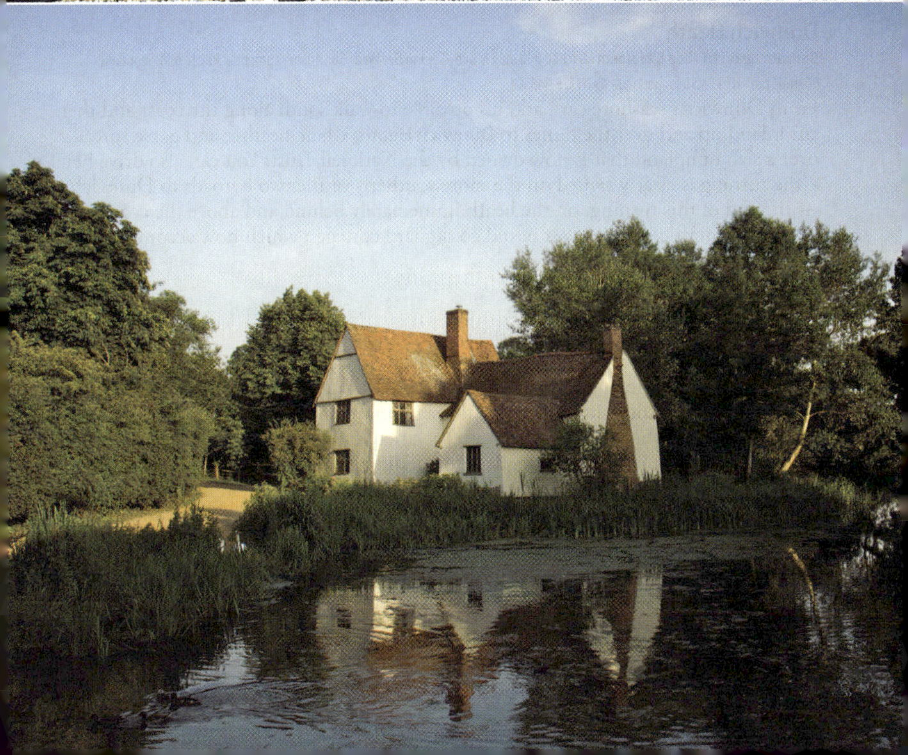

EATING AND DRINKING

★ **Fish & Chip Shop** 226 High St ⓣ01728 454685. One of Aldeburgh's two outstanding chippies – this is the original, doing takeaway that you can sit and eat out on the sea front. Usually Mon–Wed, Fri & Sat noon–2pm & 5–8pm, Thurs noon–2pm, Sun noon–7pm.

The Golden Galleon 137 High St ⓣ01728 454685. Sit-down fish-and-chip restaurant, sister to the *Fish & Chip Shop* down the road. Opening times vary, but usually Mon–Wed, Fri & Sat noon–2pm & 5–8pm, Thurs noon–2pm, Sun noon–7pm.

★ **The Lighthouse** 77 High St ⓣ01728 453377, ⓦlighthouserestaurant.co.uk. Aldeburgh's best restaurant, a relaxed, informal and always busy place in cosy premises. The menu favours locally sourced ingredients, featuring everything from burgers and fish and chips to the likes of venison tagine with couscous. Mains average around £12 at lunchtimes, more in the evening. Daily from 10am (for coffee), noon–2pm, dinner 6.30pm–late.

Dunwich

7

Tiny **DUNWICH**, about twelve miles up the coast from Aldeburgh, is probably the strangest and certainly the eeriest place on the Suffolk coast. The one-time seat of the kings of East Anglia, a bishopric and formerly a large port, Dunwich peaked in the twelfth century since when it's all been downhill: over the last millennium something like a mile of land has been lost to the sea, a process that continues at the rate of about a yard a year. As a result, the whole of the medieval city now lies under water, including all twelve churches, the last of which toppled over the cliffs in 1919. All that survives today are fragments of the Greyfriars monastery, which originally lay to the west of the city and now dangles near the sea's edge. For a potted history of the lost city, head for the **museum** (daily: April–Sept 11.30am–4.30pm; Oct noon–4pm; £1 donation; ⓣ01728 648796, ⓦdunwichmuseum.org.uk) in what's left of Dunwich – little more than one small street of terraced houses built by the local landowner in the nineteenth century.

Dunwich Heath

Dunwich Heath NT shop & tearoom March to mid-July & mid–Sept to Dec Wed–Sun 10am–4pm; mid-July to mid-Sept daily 10am–5pm • NT • £4.50 for parking • ⓣ01728 648501

From Dunwich's seashore car park, it's possible to walk south along the coast and then cut inland up and over the dunes to **Dunwich Heath**, where heather and gorse spread over a slab of upland that is now owned by the National Trust. You can also drive here – the turning is clearly signed on the more southerly of the two byroads to Dunwich. At the end of this turning, on the heath immediately behind and above the coast – the views are fantastic – stand a set of old coastguard cottages, which now accommodate a National Trust shop and tearoom.

Minsmere RSPB Nature Reserve

Reserve Daily 9am–9pm or dusk• £5 **Visitor centre** Daily 9am–5pm, 4pm in the depths of winter

From the coastguard cottages at Dunwich Heath, it's a twenty-minute walk south along the dunes and then inland to the **Minsmere RSPB Nature Reserve visitor centre**, though there's a road here too – just watch for the sign on the more southerly of the two byroads into Dunwich. The reserve covers a varied terrain of marsh, scrub and beach and in the autumn it's a gathering place for wading birds and waterfowl, which arrive here by the hundred. The reserve is also home to a small population of bitterns, one of England's rarest birds. You can rent binoculars from the visitor centre and strike out on the trails to the birdwatching hides.

EATING AND DRINKING — DUNWICH

Flora Tea Rooms Dunwich beach ⓣ01728 648433. Right on the beach, this extremely popular café is a large hut-like affair, where they serve steaming cups of tea and piping hot fish and chips to an assortment of birdwatchers, hikers and anglers. Daily 11am–4pm.

Southwold

Perched on robust cliffs just to the north of the River Blyth, **SOUTHWOLD** had become, by the sixteenth century, Suffolk's busiest fishing port. Eventually, however, it lost most of its fishery to neighbouring Lowestoft and today, although a small fleet still brings in herring, sprats and cod, the town is primarily a seaside resort, a genteel and eminently appealing little place with none of the crassness of many of its competitors. There are fine Georgian buildings, a long sandy beach, open heathland, a dinky harbour and even a little industry – in the shape of the Adnams brewery – but no burger bars and certainly no amusement arcades. This gentility was not to the liking of **George Orwell**, who lived for a time at his parents' house at 36 High St (a plaque marks the spot); who knows what he might have made of Southwold's major music festival, **Latitude** (ⓦlatitudefestival.co.uk), which spreads over four days in the middle of July with happy campers grubbing down in Henham Park beside the A12 about five miles west of town.

Sailors' Reading Room

East Cliff • Daily: April–Sept 9am–5pm; Oct–March 9am–3.30pm • Free

A short stroll along East Street from the pocket-sized Market Place brings you to a cliff-top vantage point, which offers a grand view over the beach. Also on the cliff is the curious **Sailors' Reading Room**, where pensioners gather to shoot the breeze in the mornings amid a room full of model ships, seafaring texts and vintage photos of local tars, all beards and sea boots.

Under the Pier Show

Southwold pier • Daily 9am–7pm • Free • ⓦ underthepier.com

Southwold pier is the latest incarnation of a structure that dates back to 1899. Recently revamped and renovated, the pier houses the usual – if rather more polite than usual – cafés and souvenir shops, but it's star turn is the **Under the Pier Show**, where a series of knowingly playful machines, handmade by Tim Hunkin, provide all sorts of arcade-style sensory surprises, from the "Autofrisk" to the "Rent-a-Dog" and the mischievous "Whack-a-banker".

The harbour

Ferry Early April & June–Sept daily 10am–12.30pm & 2–5pm; late April, May & Oct Sat & Sun 10am–5pm • 90p

The **harbour**, at the mouth of the River Blyth, is an idyllic spot, where fishing smacks rest against old wooden jetties and nets are spread out along the banks to dry. From the mouth of the river, a footpath leads west to a tiny passenger **ferry**, which shuffles across the river to Walberswick. If you're heading back towards Southwold, however, keep going along the river until you pass the *Harbour Inn* and then take the path that leads back into town across **Southwold Common**. The whole circular walk takes about thirty minutes.

East Green and around

From the Market Place, it's a couple of hundred yards north along Church Street to East Green, with **Adnams Brewery** on one side and a stumpy old lighthouse on another. Close by is Southwold's architectural pride and joy, the **Church of St Edmund**, a handsome fifteenth-century structure whose solid symmetries are balanced by its long and elegantly carved windows.

ARRIVAL AND INFORMATION — SOUTHWOLD

By bus Buses to Southwold pull in on High St.

Tourist office 69 High St (April–Oct Mon–Fri 10am–5pm, Sat 10am–5.30pm, Sun 11am–4pm; Nov–March Mon–Fri 10.30am–3pm, Sat 10am–4.30pm; ⓣ01502 724729, ⓦvisit-sunrisecoast.co.uk).

ACCOMMODATION

The Crown High St ❶01502 722186, ⓦhotels.adnams.co.uk. Adnams the brewers owns two hotels in Southwold and this one offers fourteen rooms above a bar-restaurant. Some of the guest rooms are large and decorated in a pleasant contemporary style, others are a tad poky. **£150**

Home@21 21 North Parade ❶01502 722573, ⓦhomeat21northparade.co.uk. Near the pier, this seafront guesthouse occupies a well-maintained Victorian terrace house. There are three sympathetically updated guest rooms, two of which are en suite and two sea-facing. **£95**

★ **The Swan** Market Place ❶01502 722186, ⓦhotels.adnams.co.uk. Delightful hotel occupying a splendid Georgian building right at the heart of Southwold. The main building is a real period piece, its nooks and crannies holding all manner of Georgian details. Some of the guest rooms are here, others (the "Lighthouse Rooms") are in the more modern garden annexe at the back. **£140**

EATING AND DRINKING

★ **The Crown** 90 High St ❶01502 722186, ⓦhotels.adnams.co.uk. Deluxe bar food featuring local, seasonal ingredients, all washed down with Adnams ales. Mains average around £16 and tables are allocated on a first-come, first-served basis. Food served daily noon–2pm & 6–9pm, drinks till 11pm.

Lord Nelson East St ❶01502 722079, ⓦthelordnelsonsouthwold.co.uk. This lively neighbourhood pub, with its low, beamed ceilings, has a first-rate locally inspired menu. Try, for example, the herring, Nelson smokes' (smoked haddock and cod in sauce) or the dressed crab. Food daily noon–2pm & 7–9pm.

★ **Tilly's** 51 High St ❶01502 725677. The pick of Southwold's several teashops, serving a great line in sandwiches and home-made cakes both inside and outside in the walled garden. Daily 9am–7pm.

7

Norwich

One of the five largest cities in Norman England, **NORWICH** once served a vast hinterland of East Anglian **cloth producers**, whose work was brought here by river and then exported elsewhere. Its isolated position beyond the Fens meant that it enjoyed closer links with the Low Countries than with the rest of England and, by 1700, Norwich was the second richest city in the country after London. With the onset of the Industrial Revolution, however, Norwich lost ground to the northern manufacturing towns – the city's famous mustard company, Colman's, is one of its few industrial success stories – and this has helped preserve much of the ancient street plan and many of the city's older buildings. Pride of place goes to the beautiful **cathedral** and the sterling **castle**, but the city's hallmark is its medieval **churches**, thirty or so squat flintstone structures with sturdy towers and sinuous stone tracery round the windows. Many are no longer in regular use and are now in the care of the **Norwich Historic Churches Trust** (ⓦnorwich-churches.org), whose website describes each church in precise detail.

Norwich's relative isolation has also meant that the population has never swelled to any great extent and today, with just 140,000 inhabitants, it remains an easy and enjoyable city. Yet Norwich is no provincial backwater. In the 1960s, the foundation of the **University of East Anglia** (UEA) made it more **cosmopolitan** and bolstered its arts scene, while in the 1980s it attracted new high-tech companies, who created something of a mini-boom, making the city one of England's wealthiest. As East Anglia's unofficial capital, Norwich also lies at the hub of the region's **transport** network, serving as a useful base for visiting the Broads and as a springboard for the north Norfolk coast.

The Cathedral

Tombland • Daily 7.30am–6.30pm • Free, but £5 donation requested • ❶01603 218300, ⓦcathedral.org.uk

Of all the medieval buildings in **Norwich**, it's the **Cathedral** that fires the imagination: a mighty, sand-coloured structure finessed by its prickly octagonal spire, it rises to a height of 315ft, second only to Salisbury Cathedral in Wiltshire. Entered via the Hostry, a glassy, well-proportioned visitor centre, the **interior** is pleasantly light thanks

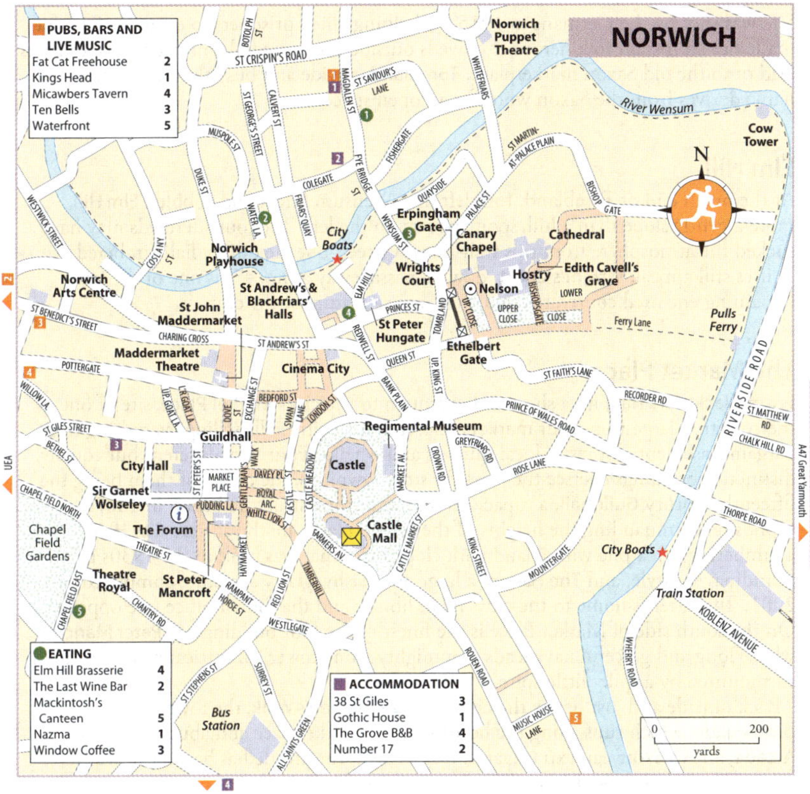

to a creamy tint in the stone and the clear glass windows of much of the **nave**, where the thick pillars are a powerful legacy of the Norman builders who began the cathedral in 1096. The nave's architectural highlight is the ceiling, a finely crafted affair whose delicate and geometrically precise fan vaulting is adorned by several dozen roof **bosses**. Pushing on down the south (right) side of the ambulatory, you soon reach **St Luke's Chapel** and the cathedral's finest work of art, the *Despenser Reredos*, a superb painted panel commissioned to celebrate the crushing of the Peasants' Revolt of 1381. Accessible from the south aisle of the nave are the cathedral's unique **cloisters**. Built between 1297 and 1450, and the only two-storey cloisters left standing in England, they contain a remarkable set of sculpted **bosses**, similar to the ones in the main nave, but here they are close enough to be scrutinized without binoculars. The dominant theme of the fabulously intricate carving is the **Apocalypse**, but look out also for the bosses depicting green men, originally pagan fertility symbols.

The cathedral precincts

Outside, in front of the main entrance, stands the medieval **Canary Chapel**. This is the original building of Norwich School, whose blue-blazered pupils are often visible during term time – the rambling school buildings are adjacent. A statue of the school's most famous boy, **Horatio Nelson**, faces the chapel, standing on the green of the **Upper Close**, which is guarded by two ornate and imposing medieval gates, **Erpingham** and, a few yards to the south, **Ethelbert**. Beside the Erpingham gate is a memorial to **Edith Cavell**, a local woman who was a nurse in occupied Brussels during World War I.

She was shot by the Germans in 1915 for helping allied prisoners to escape, a fate that made her an instant folk hero; her grave is outside the cathedral ambulatory. Both gates lead onto the old Saxon marketplace, **Tombland**, a wide and busy thoroughfare whose name derives from the Saxon word for an open space.

Elm Hill

At the north end of Tombland, fork left into Wensum Street and cobbled **Elm Hill**, more a gentle slope than a hill, soon appears on the left. The tourist crowds may have sucked the atmosphere from this well-known street, but the quirky half-timbered houses still appeal; **Wright's Court**, down a passageway at no. 43, is one of the few remaining enclosed courtyards that were once a feature of the city.

The Market Place

From **Blackfriars Hall**, it's a short walk through to the city's **Market Place**, site of one of the country's largest open-air **markets** (closed Sun), with stalls selling everything from bargain-basement clothes to local mussels and whelks. Four very different but equally distinctive buildings oversee the market's stripy awnings, the oldest of them being the fifteenth-century **Guildhall**, a capacious flint and stone structure begun in 1407. Opposite, commanding the heights of the marketplace, are the austere **City Hall**, a lumbering brick pile with a landmark clocktower that was built in the 1930s in a Scandinavian style, and **The Forum**, a large and flashy, glassy structure completed in 2001. The latter is home to the city's main library and the tourist office (see opposite). On the south side of Market Place is the finest of the four buildings, **St Peter Mancroft**, whose long and graceful nave leads to a mighty stone tower, an intricately carved affair surmounted by a spiky little spire.

Back outside and just below the church is **Gentlemen's Walk**, the town's main promenade, which runs along the bottom of the marketplace and abuts the **Royal Arcade**, an Art Nouveau extravagance from 1899. The arcade has been beautifully restored to reveal the swirling tiling, ironwork and stained glass.

The Castle Museum and Art Gallery

Castle Meadow • Oct–June Mon–Sat 10am–4.30pm, Sun 1–4.30pm; July–Sept Mon–Sat 10am–5pm, Sun 1–5pm • £6.20 • Ⓣ 01603 493625, Ⓦ museums.norfolk.gov.uk

Perched high on a grassy mound in the centre of town – and with a modern shopping mall drilled into its side – stern **Norwich Castle** dates from the twelfth century. Formerly a reminder of Norman power and then a prison, the castle now holds the **Castle Museum and Art Gallery**, which is divided into three zones. The **Art and Exhibitions** zone is the pick, scoring well with its temporary displays and the outstanding selection of work by the **Norwich School**. Founded in 1803, and in existence for just thirty years, this school of landscape painters produced – for the most part – richly coloured, formally composed land- and seascapes in oil and watercolour, paintings whose realism harked back to the Dutch landscape painters of the seventeenth century. The leading figures were **John Crome** (1768–1821) – aka "Old Crome" – and **John Sell Cotman** (1782–1842), each of whom has a gallery devoted to their work.

The **castle keep** itself is no more than a shell, its gloomy walls towering above a scattering of local archeological finds and some gory examples of traditional forms of punishment. More unusual is a bloated model **dragon**, known as Snap, which was paraded round town on the annual guilds' day procession – a folkloric hand-me-down from the dragon St George had so much trouble finishing off. To see more of the keep, join one of the regular **guided tours** that explore the battlements and the dungeons.

The University

UEA Campus Earlham Rd • Open access • Free • ⓣ 01603 456161, ⓦ uea.ac.uk **Sainsbury Centre for Visual Arts** Tues–Sun 10am–5pm • Free, but admission charged for some exhibitions • ⓣ 01603 593199, ⓦ scva.org.uk • To get to the UEA campus by bus from the city centre, take #22, #25 or #35 from Castle Meadow, or #25 from the train station

The **University of East Anglia** (UEA) occupies a sprawling campus on the western outskirts of the city beside the B1108. Its buildings are resolutely modern, an assortment of concrete-and-glass blocks of varying designs, some quite ordinary, others like the prize-winning "ziggurat" halls of residence, designed by Denys Lasdun, eminently memorable. The main reason to visit is the **Sainsbury Centre for Visual Arts,** which occupies a large, shed-like building designed by Norman Foster. Well-lit and beautifully presented, the body of the permanent collection spreads out over the main floor, beginning with a substantial selection of non-European – particularly Asian and African – artefacts positioned close to some of the European paintings and sculptures they influenced and/or inspired.

ARRIVAL AND INFORMATION — NORWICH

7

By plane Norwich Airport (ⓦ norwichairport.co.uk) is about 4 miles northwest of the city centre along the A140. There are regular buses to the city centre (20min) from the airport's Park and Ride; the taxi fare is around £6.

By train Norwich train station is on the east bank of the River Wensum, a 10min walk from the city centre along Prince of Wales Rd.

Destinations Cambridge (hourly; 1hr 20min); Colchester (every 30min; 1hr); Ely (every 30min; 1hr), London Liverpool St (every 30min; 2hr).

By bus Long-distance buses mostly terminate at the Surrey Street Station, from where it's about a 10min walk north to the town centre, though some services also stop in the centre on Castle Meadow.

Tourist office In the glassy Forum building overlooking the Market Place (April–Oct Mon–Sat 9.30am–6pm, Sun 10.30am–4.30pm; Nov–March Mon–Sat 9.30am–5.30pm; ⓣ 01603 213999, ⓦ visitnorwich.co.uk).

ACCOMMODATION

38 St Giles 38 St Giles St ⓣ 01603 662944, ⓦ 38stgiles.co.uk. Billing itself as a cross between a B&B and a hotel, this deluxe establishment has five en-suite guest rooms of varying size and description. Breakfasts feature home-made bread, freshly baked croissants, fresh fruit and cereals – with the option of a "full English"' instead. It's in a handy location too, a few yards from the Market Place, on the first floor above other premises. **£140**

★ **Gothic House** King's Head Yard, Magdalen St ⓣ 01603 631879, ⓦ gothic-house-norwich.com. This particularly charming B&B occupies a slender, three-storey Georgian house down a little courtyard off Magdalen Street. The interior has been meticulously renovated in a period style, the two, salon-style bedrooms reached via the most charming of spiral staircases. The guest rooms are not attached to the bathroom facilities, but this really is no inconvenience. **£95**

★ **The Grove B&B** 59 Bracondale ⓣ 01603 622053, ⓦ thegrovenorwich.co.uk. In a large Victorian villa, this outstanding – and outstandingly friendly – B&B has three rooms, each decorated in an extremely attractive version of period style, complete with comfy brass beds and a scattering of antiques and bygones. All the guest rooms are en suite, but the toilet is in an adjoining room, not squeezed into the bedroom – hurrah for that. Tasty breakfasts are cooked to order. **£85**

Number 17 17 Colegate ⓣ 01603 764486, ⓦ number17norwich.co.uk. Family-run guest house with eight, en-suite guest rooms decorated in a brisk, modern style with solid oak flooring; there are two larger family rooms as well. Good location, in one of the nicest parts of the centre. **£78**

EATING

★ **Elm Hill Brasserie** 2 Elm Hill ⓣ 01603 624847. This intimate, one-room bistro-brasserie, housed in an old shop, offers a creative menu with a full flourish of French flair. Daily specials, written on a blackboard, are reasonably priced at around £14 per main. Mon–Sat 12.30–2.30pm & 5.45–10.30pm, Sun noon–6pm.

★ **The Last Wine Bar** 76 St George's St ⓣ 01603 626626, ⓦ lastwinebar.co.uk. Imaginatively converted old shoe factory, a couple of minutes' walk north of the river, holding a relaxed and very amenable wine bar in one section and an excellent restaurant in the other. The food is firmly Modern British, with the likes of braised lamb shank with carrots and parsnips in a rosemary jus (around £14). Mon–Fri noon–2.30pm & 5pm–12.30am, Sat noon–2.30pm & 6pm–12.30am; kitchen closes 10.30pm.

Mackintosh's Canteen Unit 410, Chapelfield Plain ⓣ 01603 305280, ⓦ thewildebeest.co.uk. This busy, bustling café and restaurant is named after the old chocolate factory – Mackintosh's – that stood here for decades. Decorated in sharp, modern style, both dining rooms serve fresh, resolutely British food with the emphasis on local, seasonal products. Try the delicious home-made hamburger. Mains around £12. Mon–Fri 10am–midnight, Sat & Sun 9am–midnight.

Nazma 15 Magdalen St 01603 618701, nazmabrasseries.co.uk. The menu at this splendid modern Indian restaurant covers all the classics, each prepared from scratch with the freshest of ingredients, but it's particularly strong on Bangladeshi cuisine. Mains around £9; takeaway available. Daily noon–2.30pm & 6pm–midnight.

Window Coffee 25 Wensum St 07913 672491, thewindowcoffee.com. Odd little place – "little" being the operative word as it's billed as the smallest coffee shop in the world. It occupies the window of what was once a shop, and sells excellent coffee and cakes with a smile. Tues–Fri 8am–3pm & Sat 9am–3pm.

DRINKING

Fat Cat Freehouse 49 West End St 01603 624364, fatcatpub.co.uk. Award-winning pub with a friendly atmosphere and a fantastic range of well-kept, top-quality draught ales. Also a great range of bottled beers, ciders and perries, and takeaway if you don't want to hang around. It's northwest of the city centre off the Dereham Road. Mon–Wed & Sun noon–11pm, Thurs–Sat noon–midnight.

7

★ **Kings Head** 42 Magdalen St kingsheadnorwich.com. The perfect drinkers' pub with precious little in the way of distraction – there are certainly no one-armed bandits here. The outstanding selection of real ales is supplemented by an equally impressive, international range of bottled beers, most notably Belgian. The pub has just two smallish rooms, so you may need to be assertive to get served. Daily 11am–11pm.

Micawbers Tavern 92 Pottergate 01603 626627, micawberstavern.com. Lodged in an old beamed building on one of the city's prettiest streets, this friendly, busy pub is a local par excellence, featuring an outstanding range of guest ales on draft. There's home-cooked food and Sports TV too. Daily 4pm till late.

Ten Bells 74 St Benedict's St at Ten Bells Lane 01603 667833. Weird and wonderful place that attracts a weird and wonderful clientele, who hunker down among the crusty old sofas and the rickety chairs with barely a light to illuminate proceedings. As you might expect, lots of students. Daily 11am–11pm.

NIGHTLIFE AND ENTERTAINMENT

Cinema City Suckling House, St Andrew's St 0871 902 5724, picturehouses.co.uk. By far the finest cinema in town, featuring the best new releases plus themed evenings and cult and classic films. Also live feeds from, for example, the New York Met, a Kids' Club and regular late-night horror films, billed as Friday frighteners.

Norwich Arts Centre St Benedict's St 01603 660352, norwichartscentre.co.uk. Popular rendezvous featuring everything from kids' theatre to world music.

Norwich Puppet Theatre Church of St James, Whitefriars 01603 629921, puppettheatre.co.uk. Housed in a deconsecrated medieval church beside the busy Whitefriars roundabout, this long-established puppet theatre company has an outstanding reputation for the quality of its puppets and the excellence of its shows. Some performances are aimed at young children (£5) – who are simply enraptured – others are for adults (£7).

Theatre Royal Theatre St 01603 630000, theatreroyalnorwich.co.uk. The city's major performance venue, in a revamped 1300-seater Art Deco theatre. It casts its artistic net wide, but for the most part it's mainstream stuff and classical music predominates.

Waterfront 139–141 King St 01603 508050, waterfrontnorwich.com.This happening club and alternative music venue, which occupies what was once an old beer bottling plant, showcases some great bands, both big names and local talent, and offers club and DJ nights too. Run by the University of East Anglia's student union. Fri & Sat from 9pm, plus additional gigs.

The north Norfolk coast

The first place of any note on the **north Norfolk coast** is **Cromer**, a seaside town whose steep and blustery cliffs have drawn tourists for over a century. A few miles to the west is another well-established resort, **Sheringham**, but thereafter the shoreline becomes a ragged patchwork of salt marshes, dunes and shingle spits which form a series of nature reserves, supporting a fascinating range of flora and fauna. It's a lovely stretch of coast and the villages bordering it, principally **Cley**, **Blakeney** and **Wells-next-the-Sea**, are prime targets for an overnight stay.

THE NORFOLK BROADS

Three **rivers** – the Yare, Waveney and Bure – meander across the flatlands to the east of Norwich, converging on Breydon Water before flowing into the sea at Great Yarmouth. In places these rivers swell into wide expanses of water known as "**broads**", which for years were thought to be natural lakes. In fact they're the result of extensive peat cutting, several centuries of accumulated diggings made in a region where wood was scarce and peat a valuable source of energy. The pits flooded when sea levels rose in the thirteenth and fourteenth centuries to create these **Norfolk Broads** (Ⓦ enjoythebroads.com), now one of the most important wetlands in Europe – a haven for many birds such as kingfishers, grebes and warblers – and one of the county's major tourist attractions. Looking after the Broads, the **Broads Authority** (Ⓦ broads-authority.gov.uk) maintains a series of information centres throughout the region.

The Norfolk Broads are crisscrossed by roads and rail lines, but the best – really the only – way to see them is **by boat**, and you could happily spend a week or so exploring the 125 miles of lock-free navigable waterways, visiting the various churches, pubs and windmills en route. Of the many **boat rental** companies, Blakes (Ⓣ 0844 8567060, Ⓦ blakes.co.uk) and Norfolk Broads Boating Holidays (Ⓣ 01603 782207, Ⓦ norfolkbroadsdirect.co.uk), are both well established and have rental outlets at **Wroxham**, seven miles northeast of Norwich – and easy to reach by train, bus and car. Prices for cruisers start at around £700 a week for four people in peak season, but less expensive, short-term rentals are widely available too. **Houseboats** are much cheaper than cruisers, but they are, of course, static.

Trying to explore the Broads by car is pretty much a waste of time, but cyclists and walkers can take advantage of the region's network of footpaths and cycle trails. There are Broads Authority **bike rental** points dotted around the region and **walkers** might consider the 56-mile Weavers' Way, a long-distance footpath that winds through the best parts of the Broads on its way from Cromer to Great Yarmouth. There are many shorter options too. As for **specific sights** for landlubbers and boaters alike, one prime target is **Toad Hole Cottage** (June–Sept daily 9.30am–5pm; April, May & Oct Mon–Fri 10.30am–1pm & 1.30–5pm, Sat & Sun 10.30am–5pm; free), an old eel-catcher's cottage holding a small exhibit on the history of the trade, which was common in the area until the 1940s. The cottage is at How Hill, close to the hamlet of **Ludham**, six miles east of Wroxham on the A1062. Behind the cottage is the narrow River Ant, where there are hour-long, wildlife-viewing **boat trips** in the *Electric Eel* (June–Sept daily 10am–4pm, April, May & Oct daily 11am–3pm; every hour; £5; Ⓣ 01603 756096).

GETTING AROUND — THE NORTH NORFOLK COAST

There's a regular **train** service on the Bittern Line (Ⓣ 08457 484950, Ⓦ bitternline.com) from Norwich to Cromer and Sheringham (Mon–Sat hourly; Sun every 2hr). A battery of local **buses** fills in (most of) the gaps, but easily the most useful is the **Norfolk Coasthopper** (Ⓣ 01553 776980, Ⓦ coasthopper.co.uk), which runs along the coast between Cromer and King's Lynn via a whole gaggle of coastal towns and villages, including Blakeney, Sheringham, Wells and the Burnhams. Frequencies vary on different stretches of the route and there are more services in the summer than in the winter, but on the more popular stretches buses appear every thirty minutes or hourly, less frequently on Sundays. There are lots of different tickets and **discounts**; perhaps the most useful is the Coasthopper Rover, which provides unlimited travel on the whole of the route for either one-day (£7), three days (£15) or seven days (£30); tickets can be bought from the driver.

Cromer

Dramatically poised on a high bluff, **CROMER** should be the most memorable of the Norfolk coastal resorts, but its fine aspect has long been undermined by a certain shabbiness in its narrow streets and alleys. Things are at last on the mend, with new businesses arriving to add a touch of flair, while the town council keeps a string of cliff-top mini-parks and gardens in immaculate condition.

It's no more than the place deserves: Cromer has a long history, first as a prosperous medieval port – witness the tower of **St Peter and St Paul**, at 160ft the tallest in Norfolk

– and then as a fashionable watering hole after the advent of the railway in the 1880s. There are three things you must do here: take a walk on the beach, stroll out onto the **pier**, and, of course, grab a **crab:** Cromer crabs are famous right across England and several places sell them, reliably fresh, and cooked and stuffed every which way.

ARRIVAL AND INFORMATION — CROMER

By train Somewhat miraculously, Cromer has managed to retain its rail link with Norwich – and from the train station it's a 5min walk northeast into the centre.

Destinations Norwich (hourly; 45min); Sheringham (hourly; 10min).

By bus Buses to Cromer, including the Norfolk Coasthopper (see p.357) stop outside *Julio's Café*, on Cadogan Rd, on the western side of the town centre.

North Norfolk Information Centre Louden Rd, on the south side of the town centre (Jan to late May & Sept–Dec daily 10am–4pm; late May to Aug Mon–Sat 10am–5pm, Sun 10am–4pm; T 0871 200 3071, W visitnorfolk.co.uk).

ACCOMMODATION

7

Cambridge House B&B East Cliff T 01263 512085, W cambridgecromer.co.uk. In a hard-to-beat location, with wide views out to sea, this B&B occupies a classic, Victorian terrace house on the cliff-top in the centre of Cromer. There are six nicely decorated bedrooms, most of them en suite (those with shared facilities are £10 or so cheaper), and each with high ceilings. No cards. **£76**

Cliftonville Hotel 29 Runton Rd T 01263 512543, W cliftonvillehotel.co.uk. Among the big old mansions that line Runton Road just west of the town centre facing out to sea, this is the smartest, its grand Edwardian foyer equipped with an impressive double staircase and oodles of wood panelling. After the foyer, the rooms beyond can't help but seem a tad mundane, but they are large and they all have sea views. **£150**

Virginia Court Hotel Cliff Ave T 01263 512398, W virginiacourt.co.uk. The new owners of this medium-sized hotel are in the process of a major upgrade – and have started with what's most important: the beds are super comfy, the towels super thick, the duvets super warm and there's free wi-fi. The hotel dates back to Edwardian times, hence the capacious foyer with its wide, sweeping staircase, and the atmosphere is very much that of a traditional seaside hotel, friendly and relaxed. Dinner for two costs £40 extra per room. **£140**

EATING AND DRINKING

Mary Jane's Fish & Chip Shop 27 Garden St T 01263 511208. Norfolk tourists are fastidious about their fish and chips, with allegiances strongly argued and felt. This basic, family-owned place is especially popular, for the lightness of the batter and the freshness of the fish. Eat in or take away. Open daily.

Red Lion Brook St T 01263 514964, W redlion-cromer.co.uk. Right in the centre of old Cromer, on the ridge facing out to sea, this lively pub has a splendid old bar with enough liquors to destroy the average liver, a good supply of real ales and above-average pub grub too. Daily 11am–11pm.

Rocket House Café RNLI building, The Gangway T 01263 519126, W rockethousecafe.co.uk. Offering sparkling views over the beach, pier and ocean from its giant windows – and from its blustery terrace – this café has the best location in town, though the food lacks subtlety – stick to the crabs and the salads. Salads start at just £4.50. Mon–Fri 9am–5pm, Sat 10am–5pm & 6–9pm, Sun 10am–5pm.

Salthouse

Travelling west from Cromer, it's about ten miles along the coast to the tiny hamlet of **SALTHOUSE**, whose flocks of sheep once provided a rich living for the lord of the manor. Today, the main evidence of this past wealth is the **church of St Nicholas**, an imposing and strikingly beautiful edifice stuck on top of a grassy knoll, its prominent position both a reminder to the faithful and a landmark for those at sea.

EATING AND DRINKING — SALTHOUSE

Cookies Crab Shack The Green T 01263 740352, W salthouse.org.uk. *Cookies* has something of a cult following, certainly not for the decor, which is simple in the extreme, but for the freshness and variety of the seafood. Crabs, prawns and smoked fish lead the way, but there's lots more to choose from including samphire, a local delicacy harvested from the surrounding mud flats and salt marshes from late June to mid-September. Daily: Oct–March 10am–4pm; April–Sept 9am–7pm.

Cley and around

CLEY (more formally **Cley-next-the-Sea**), once a busy wool port, is now little more than a row of flint cottages and Georgian mansions set beside a narrow, marshy inlet that (just) gives access to the sea. The sea once dipped further inland, which explains why Cley's fine medieval **church of St Margaret** is located half a mile to the south, at the very edge of the current village, overlooking the green. You're near a couple of splendid **nature reserves** here, both excellent destinations for birdwatchers – and don't miss the **Cley Smoke House** for superb locally smoked fish.

Cley Marshes Nature Reserve

A149 • Daily: April–Oct 10am–5pm; Nov–March 10am–4pm • £4 • ⓣ 01263 740008, ⓦ norfolkwildlifetrust.org.uk

Less than a mile from Cley village, it's a hop, skip and a jump east along the A149 to **Cley Marshes Nature Reserve**, whose conspicuous, roadside visitor centre attracts birdwatchers like bees to a honey-pot. Owned and operated by the Norfolk Wildlife Trust (NWT), the visitor centre issues permits for entering the reserve, whose saltwater and freshwater marshes, reed beds and coastal shingle ridge are accessed on several footpaths and overseen by half a dozen hides.

Blakeney Point

Blakeney Point National Trust information centre April–Sept dawn to dusk • NT • Free

On the west side of the Cley Marshes Nature Reserve – and about 400 yards east of Cley village – is the mile-long byroad that leads to the shingle mounds of **Cley beach**. This is the starting point for the four-mile hike west out along the spit to **Blakeney Point**, a nature reserve famed for its colonies of terns and seals. The seal colony is made up of several hundred common and grey seals, and the old lifeboat house, at the end of the spit, is now a National Trust **information centre**. The shifting shingle can make walking difficult, so keep to the low-water mark. The easier alternative is to take one of the **boat trips** to the point from Blakeney or Morston (see p.360).

Wiveton Hall Fruit Farm, Café & Farm Shop

Daily 9.30am–4.30pm • ⓣ 01263 740525, ⓦ wivetonhall.co.uk

In between Cley and Blakeney, signposted from the A149, **Wiveton Hall Fruit Farm, Café & Farm Shop** casts its gastronomic net as widely as possible. Visitors can pick their own fruit and vegetable in the fields and buy super-fresh local produce (including honey and eggs); there is also a splendid café (see below).

ARRIVAL AND DEPARTURE — CLEY

The Norfolk Coasthopper **bus** (see p.357) stops outside the Picnic Fayre deli on Cley's main street (which is also the A149).

ACCOMMODATION

★ **Cley Mill B&B** Cley ⓣ 01263 740209, ⓦ cleymill.co.uk. This outstanding B&B occupies a converted windmill offering wonderful views over the surrounding marshes. The guest rooms, both in the windmill and the adjoining outhouses, are decorated in attractive period style and the best, like the Stone Room, have splendid beamed ceilings; self-catering arrangements are possible as well. At peak times, there's a minimum two-night stay. **£129**

EATING AND DRINKING

Cley Smokehouse High St, Cley ⓣ 01263 740282, ⓦ cleysmokehouse.com. Excellent, famed little place in an old forge on the main street, where they prepare delicious local oak-smoked fish – among other delicacies – to take away. Mon–Sat 8.30am–5pm, Sun 9.30am–4.30pm.

Wiveton Farm Café A149 between Cley and Blakeney ⓣ 01263 740515, ⓦ wivetonhall.co.uk The café of this lovely deli/farm is a delightfully rustic place with a homely feel, offering excellent home-made snacks and meals that use the farm's produce whenever possible. April to early Nov daily 9.30am–4.30pm.

Blakeney

A mile or so west of Cley, delightful **BLAKENEY** was once a bustling port exporting fish, corn and salt, and is now a lovely little place of pebble-covered cottages sloping up from a narrow harbour. Crab sandwiches are sold from stalls at the quayside, the meandering high street is flanked by family-run shops, and footpaths stretch out along the sea wall to east and west, allowing long, lingering looks over the salt marshes.

Blakeney **harbour** is linked to the sea by a narrow channel that wriggles its way through the salt marshes and is only navigable for a few hours at high tide. At low tide the harbour is no more than a muddy creek (ideal for a bit of quayside crabbing and mud sliding).

ARRIVAL AND DEPARTURE — BLAKENEY

Buses to Blakeney, including the Norfolk **Coasthopper** (see p.357) pull in at the Westgate bus shelter, a couple of minutes' walk from the harbour.

ACCOMMODATION AND EATING

Blakeney White Horse 4 High St ⓣ01263 740574, ⓦblakeneywhitehorse.co.uk. Recently revamped, this long-established inn holds nine guest rooms kitted out in a bright and cheerful version of country-house style. Rates increase at weekends. The *White Horse* is also noted for its food. Great play is made of local ingredients, the bread is baked here daily, and they offer lunchtime snacks and à la carte suppers. Mains £16 or less. Food served daily noon–2pm & 6–9pm. **£80**

King's Arms Westgate St ⓣ01263 740341, ⓦblakeneykingsarms.co.uk. The best pub in Blakeney by far, this traditional boozer, with its low, beamed ceilings and rabbit-warren rooms, offers top-ranking bar food, largely English but with an international zip. They also have seven, modest en-suite bedrooms. Food served daily, lunch and dinner. **£70**

The Moorings High St ⓣ01263 740054. Informal, cheerful little bistro where the creative menu is particularly strong on Norfolk fish and shellfish. A typical main course might be sautéed lamb kidneys with pancetta and rosemary with a white bean ragout (£16.50). Tues–Sat 10.30am–9.30pm, July & Aug also Mon.

Wells-next-the-Sea

Despite its name, **WELLS-NEXT-THE-SEA**, some eight miles west of Blakeney, is actually a good mile or so from open water. In Tudor times, before the harbour silted up, this was one of the great ports of eastern England, a major player in the trade with the Netherlands. Today it's the only commercially viable port on the north Norfolk coast, but more importantly Wells is now a popular coastal resort.

The town divides into three areas, starting with **The Buttlands**, a broad rectangular green on the south side of town, lined with oak and beech trees and framed by a string of fine Georgian houses. North from here, across Station Road, lie the narrow lanes of the town centre with **Staithe Street**, the minuscule main drag, flanked by old-fashioned shops. Staithe Street leads down to the **quay**, a somewhat forlorn affair inhabited by a couple of amusement arcades and fish-and-chip shops, and the mile-long byroad that scuttles north to the **beach**, a handsome sandy tract backed by pine-clad dunes. The beach road is shadowed by a high flood defence and a tiny narrow-gauge **railway** that scoots down to the beach (Easter to October every 20min or so from 10.30am; £1.30 each way).

BLAKENEY BOAT TRIPS

Depending on the tides, there are **boat trips** from either Blakeney or **Morston quay**, a mile or so to the west, to both Blakeney Point (see p.359) – where passengers have a couple of hours at the point before being ferried back – and to the seal colony just off the point (both trips £9). The main **operators** advertise departure times on blackboards by the quayside; you can reserve in advance with Beans Boats (ⓣ01263 740505, ⓦbeansboattrips.co.uk) or Bishop's Boats (ⓣ01263 740753, ⓦbishopsboats.co.uk).

Holkham Hall

Three miles west of Wells on the A149 • **Hall** April–Oct Sun, Mon & Thurs noon–4pm • £9; parking £2.50 **Park** Vehicle access as per house; pedestrian access April–Oct daily 7am–7pm; Nov–March Mon, Wed & Fri 7am–7pm or dusk, Tues & Thurs 9.30am–7pm or dusk • Free • ⓣ 01328 710227, ⓦ holkham.co.uk • The Norfolk Coasthopper bus (see p.357) stops at the north entrance of the Holkham estate, about a mile from Holkham Hall

One of the most popular outings from Wells is to **Holkham Hall**, three miles to the west and a stop on the Coasthopper bus (see p.357). This grand, self-assured (or vainglorious) stately home was designed by the eighteenth-century architect William Kent for the first earl of Leicester and is still owned by the family. The severe sandy-coloured Palladian exterior belies the warmth and richness of the interior, which retains much of its original decoration, notably the much-admired marble hall, with its fluted columns and intricate reliefs. The rich colours of the state rooms are an appropriate backdrop for a fabulous selection of **paintings**, including canvases by Van Dyck, Rubens, Gainsborough and Gaspar Poussin.

The **grounds** are laid out on sandy, saline land, much of it originally salt marsh. The focal point is an 80ft-high obelisk, atop a grassy knoll, from where you can view both the hall to the north and the triumphal arch to the south. In common with the rest of the north Norfolk coast, there's plenty of **birdlife** to observe – Holkham's lake attracts Canada geese, herons and grebes and several hundred deer graze the open pastures.

Holkham Bay

The **footpaths** latticing the Holkham estate stretch as far as the A149, from where a half-mile byroad – Lady Anne's Drive – leads north across the marshes from opposite the *Victoria Hotel* to **Holkham Bay**, which boasts one of the finest beaches on this stretch of coast, with golden sand and pine-studded sand dunes. Warblers, flycatchers and redstarts inhabit the drier coastal reaches, while waders paddle about the mud and salt flats.

ARRIVAL AND INFORMATION — WELLS-NEXT-THE-SEA

By bus Buses to Wells stop on Station Rd, in between Staithe St and the Buttlands, and some also travel down to The Quay. The town is on the route of the Norfolk Coasthopper bus (see p.357).

Tourist office The seasonal tourist office is a few yards from The Quay on Staithe St (late March to mid-May & early Sept to Oct daily 10am–2pm; mid–May to early Sept Mon–Sat 10am–5pm & Sun 10am–4pm; ⓣ 0871 200 3071, ⓦ visitnorthnorfolk.com).

ACCOMMODATION

★ **The Crown** The Buttlands ⓣ 01328 710209, ⓦ crownhotelnorfolk.co.uk. An attractive, three-storey former coaching inn with several cosy and quaint public rooms, all low ceilings and stone-flagged floors. The dozen guest rooms are decorated in a soothing country-house style (though opinions are divided on the – very colourful – toilet seats). **£145**

The Merchant's House 47 Freeman St ⓣ 01328 711877, ⓦ the-merchants-house.co.uk. Occupying one of the oldest houses in Wells, parts of which date back to the fifteenth century, this deluxe B&B has just two, en-suite guest rooms. It's handily located, just a couple of minutes' walk from the quayside and holds a wide supply of information on local sights and walks. **£80**

Pinewoods Holiday Park Beach Rd; about 15min walk from The Quay ⓣ 01328 710439, ⓦ pinewoods.co.uk. Behind a long line of pine-clad sand dunes that abut a splendid stretch of sandy beach, and accessible on the narrow-gauge railway (see opposite), Pinewoods has been welcoming holiday-makers for over sixty years. It's a sprawling complex that holds touring and static caravans, beach huts, camping pitches and cosy wooden lodges. The camp and caravan pitches are open from mid-March to late October, the lodges from mid-March to December. Tariffs vary widely, but in high season a three-bed (six berth) lodge costs around **£750** per week.

EATING

★ **The Crown** The Buttlands ⓣ 01328 710209, ⓦ crownhotelnorfolk.co.uk. *The Crown* hotel (see above) prides itself on its food, with splendid takes on traditional British dishes. Mains average around £15. Daily noon–2.30pm & 6.30–9.30pm.

7

Burnham Market

As you head west from Wells, it's about five miles to the pretty little village of **BURNHAM MARKET**, where a medley of Georgian and Victorian houses surrounds a dinky little green. The village attracts a well-heeled, north London crowd, most of them here to enjoy the comforts of the *Hoste Arms*.

ARRIVAL AND DEPARTURE — BURNHAM MARKET

The Norfolk Coasthopper **bus** (see p.357) stops beside the green on Market Place.

ACCOMMODATION AND EATING

Hoste Arms Market Place 01328 738777, hostearms.co.uk. One of the most fashionable spots on the Norfolk coast, this former coaching inn has been modernized and extended with style and flair. The menu is a well-balanced mixture of land and sea, with main courses ranging from £15 to £20 in the evening, slightly less at lunch. The hotel's 35 guest rooms are at the back and range from the small (verging on the cramped) to the much more expansive (and expensive). Food served daily noon–2pm & 6–9pm, with cream teas 9am–noon & 3–5.30pm. £150

Burnham Deepdale and around

From Burnham Market, it's a couple of miles west to **BURNHAM DEEPDALE**, which leads seamlessly into **BRANCASTER STAITHE** and then **BRANCASTER**, all three of which spread along the main coastal road, the A149. Behind them, to the north, lies pristine coastline, a tract of lagoon, sandspit and creek that pokes its head out into the ocean, attracting thousands of wildfowl. This is prime **walking** territory and it's best explored along the Norfolk Coast Path (see p.338) as it nudges its way through the marshes that back up towards the ocean. Pushing on west from Brancaster, it's a mile or so more to minuscule **TITCHWELL**, with its bird reserve; from here it's just six miles more to Hunstanton, a kiss-me-quick resort at the west end of the north Norfolk coast.

Titchwell Marsh RSPB Nature Reserve

Titchwell • Daily dawn to dusk • Free, but £4 parking • **Shop & information centre** Daily : April–Oct 9.30am–5pm; Nov–March 9.30am–4pm • 01485 210779, wrspb.org.uk/titchwell

The RSPB's **Titchwell Marsh Nature Reserve** comprises a mix of marsh, reed bed, mud flat, lagoon and sandy beach. A series of footpaths explore this varied terrain, which attracts a wide variety of birds, and there are several well-positioned bird hides.

ARRIVAL AND DEPARTURE — BURNHAM DEEPDALE

The Norfolk Coasthopper **bus** (see p.357) sticks to the main coastal road, the A149, as it travels through Burnham Deepdale, Brancaster Staithe, Brancaster and Titchwell.

ACCOMMODATION AND EATING

Deepdale Backpackers & Camping Deepdale Farm, Burnham Deepdale 01485 210256, deepdalefarm.co.uk. Full marks for ingenuity go to this lively, youthful and very amiable setup, where they operate a combined campsite, info centre, café and eco-friendly backpackers' hostel in creatively renovated former stables. They also have tipis (£70-80/night) and yurts (£85–95/night). Dorm £13, double £45

★ **Titchwell Manor Hotel** Titchwell 01485 210221, titchwellmanor.com. One of the nicest hotels on the Norfolk coast, facing the salt marshes. The outstanding restaurant, and a couple of simpler eating spaces, serve superb, very British food. There are nine guest rooms in the main building and more in a contemporary courtyard complex – everything, from the top-quality duvets to the bespoke furniture, is top-notch. Rates increase at the weekend. Food served daily noon–2.30pm & 6.30–9.30pm, plus snacks and light meals all day. £110

★ **White Horse** Brancaster Staithe 01485 210262, whitehorsebrancaster.co.uk. This restaurant, pub and hotel backs straight onto the coastal marshes – and is right on the North Norfolk Coast Path. Brancaster is famous for its mussels and oysters, and this is a good place to try them, though the restaurant has many other temptations (mains average around £16). There are seven en-suite rooms in the main building and eight more, with grass roofs, at the back. The decor is light and airy, with a few nautical bits and bobs thrown in for good measure. Food served daily noon–2pm & 6.30–9pm; bar menu daily 11am–9pm. £70

King's Lynn

Straddling the canalized mouth of the River Great Ouse a mile or so before it slides into The Wash, **King's Lynn** is an ancient port whose merchants grew rich importing fish from Scandinavia, timber from the Baltic and wine from France, while exporting wool, salt and corn. The good times came to an end when the focus of maritime trade moved to the Atlantic seaboard, but its port struggled on until it was reinvigorated in the 1970s by the burgeoning trade between the UK and the EU. Much of the old centre was demolished during the 1960s and as a result most of Lynn – as it's known locally – is not especially enticing, but it does have a cluster of handsome old **riverside buildings**, and its lively, open-air **markets** attract large fenland crowds.

Saturday Market Place and around

Behind the Kings Lynn waterfront, the **Saturday Market Place,** the older and smaller of the town's two marketplaces, is a focal point of the old town. In addition to the Saturday market, it's home to Lynn's main parish church, **St Margaret's**, and the striking **Trinity Guildhall**, which has a wonderful, chequered flint-and-stone facade dating to 1421. 7

Church of St Margaret

Saturday Market Place • Ⓦ stmargaretskingslynn.org.uk

The hybrid **Church of St Margaret** dominates the Saturday Market Place. A large and dignified building, it features an eighteenth-century organ and choir stalls covered with images of the Black Prince and Edward III – a monarch further remembered by two extravagant medieval bronzes in the south aisle, the Walsoken brass and the Braunche brass.

Custom House

Purfleet Quay • April–Sept Mon–Sat 10am–4.30pm, Sun noon–4.30pm; Oct–March closes 3.30pm • £1 • Ⓣ 01553 763044

A couple of minutes' north of the Saturday Market Place along Georgian Queen Street, Lynn's finest building, the riverside **Custom House**, was erected in 1683 in a style clearly influenced by the Dutch, with classical pilasters, petite dormer windows and a rooftop balustrade, but it's the dinky little cupola that catches the eye. Inside, a small exhibition illustrates Lynn's maritime and mercantile history; the tourist office (see p.364) is also based here.

King Street and around

Beyond the Custom House, **King Street** continues where Queen Street leaves off, and is perhaps the town's most elegant thoroughfare, lined with beautifully proportioned Georgian buildings. On the left, just after Ferry Lane, **St George's Guildhall** is one of the oldest surviving guildhalls in England. It was a theatre in Elizabethan times and is now part of the popular King's Lynn Arts Centre (see p.364). At the end of King Street, the **Tuesday Market Place**, a handsome square surrounded by Georgian buildings and the plodding Neoclassical **Corn Exchange** (now a theatre), hosts Kings Lynn's main market on Fridays and, yes, Tuesdays.

Lynn Museum

Market St • Tues–Sat 10am–5pm • £3.50, free Oct–March • Ⓣ 01553 775001, Ⓦ museums.norfolk.gov.uk

Housed in the old Union Chapel, much of **Lynn Museum** is given over to "Seahenge", a prehistoric timber circle whose 556 posts were spotted on the Norfolk coast in 1998 and relocated here a few years later. The rest of the museum has displays on every aspect of life in Lynn from medieval times onwards.

7

ARRIVAL AND INFORMATION — KING'S LYNN

By train Kings Lynn's train station is a short walk east of the town centre across Railway Rd, the principal north–south thoroughfare.

Destinations Cambridge (hourly; 45min); Ely (hourly; 30min); London King's Cross (hourly; 2hr); Norwich (hourly 2hr).

By bus The bus station is right in the centre, in the main shopping area west of Railway Rd. The Norfolk Coasthopper (see p.357) begins (and ends) its journey at King's Lynn, putting a whole range of Norfolk destinations within easy reach.

Tourist office Custom House, Purfleet Quay (Mon–Sat 10am–5pm, Sun noon–5pm; ⓣ01553 763044, ⓦvisitwestnorfolk.com).

ACCOMMODATION

Bank House Hotel King's Staithe Square ⓣ01553 660492, ⓦthebankhouse.co.uk. A riverside boutique hotel in a fantastic Georgian house in the heart of Kings Lynn's historic district. The eleven rooms are lovely, and its great bar and restaurant (see below) make it almost a destination in itself. Rooms and rates vary, but almost all rooms enjoy river views. **£100**

The Old Rectory 33 Goodwins Rd, east off London Rd, a southerly extension of Railway Rd ⓣ01553 768544, ⓦtheoldrectory-kingslynn.com. Small, agreeable B&B on the southern side of town; bedrooms are decorated in a reassuringly modern/cosy style. **£60**

EATING AND DRINKING

Bank House Hotel King's Staithe Square ⓣ01553 660492, ⓦthebankhouse.co.uk. Wonderfully inviting bar and restaurant, whose modern British menu features such dishes as Lowestoft plaice, guinea fowl with bacon and cabbage. Mains from £10. Daily noon–2.30pm & 6.30–9.30pm.

Crofters Coffee Shop 29 Lynn St ⓣ01553 765565. Part of the arts centre complex, this café serves as good a breakfast or light lunch as you'll find in central Lynn, with sandwiches, salads and quiches. Mon–Sat 9.30am–5pm.

Market Bistro 11 Saturday Market Place ⓣ01553 771483, ⓦmarketbistro.co.uk. Superb food in a stripped-down bistro using locally sourced ingredients – specials include seared scallops with home-made black pudding. Mains from £13. Tues–Sat noon–2pm & 6.30–9.30pm.

NIGHTLIFE AND ENTERTAINMENT

King's Lynn Arts Centre 29 King St ⓣ01553 764864, ⓦkingslynnarts.co.uk. A wide range of performances and exhibitions held both on this site and in several other downtown venues, including the old Corn Exchange on Tuesday Market Place.

Ely

Perched on a mound of clay above the River Great Ouse about thirty miles south of King's Lynn, the attractive little town of **ELY** – literally "eel island" – was to all intents and purposes a true island until the draining of the fens in the seventeenth century. Until then, the town was encircled by treacherous marshland, which could only be crossed with the help of the local "fen-slodgers" who knew the firm tussock paths. In 1070, **Hereward the Wake** turned this inaccessibility to military advantage, holding out against the Normans and forcing William the Conqueror to undertake a prolonged siege – and finally to build an improvised road floated on bundles of sticks. Centuries later, the Victorian writer Charles Kingsley resurrected this obscure conflict in his novel *Hereward the Wake*. He presented the protagonist as the Last of the English who "never really bent their necks to the Norman yoke and … kept alive those free institutions which were the germs of our British liberty" – a heady mixture of nationalism and historical poppycock that went down a storm.

Since then, Ely has been associated with Hereward, which is a little ridiculous as Ely is, above all else, a Norman town. The Normans built the **cathedral**, a towering structure visible for miles across the flat fenland landscape and Ely's main sight. The rest of Ely is pretty enough: to the immediate north of the church is the **High Street**, a slender thoroughfare lined with old-fashioned shops, and the **river** is a relaxing spot with a riverside footpath, a tearoom or two, a small art gallery and an entertainment complex.

Ely Cathedral

June–Sept daily 7am–7pm; Oct–May Mon–Sat 7am–6.30pm, Sun 7am–5pm • Mon–Sat £6.50, Sun free; Mon–Sat fee includes a ground-floor tour, but octagon tours cost an extra £5.50 (reserve ahead); no tours on Sun • ⓣ 01353 667735, ⓦ elycathedral.org/visitors
Stained Glass Museum Easter–Oct Mon–Sat 10.30am–5pm, Sun noon–6pm; Nov–Easter Mon–Sat 10.30am–5pm, Sun noon–4.30pm • £4 • ⓦ stainedglassmuseum.com

Ely Cathedral is one of the most impressive churches in England, but the west facade, where visitors enter, has been an oddly lopsided affair ever since one of the transepts collapsed in a storm in 1701. Nonetheless, the remaining transept, which was completed in the 1180s, is an imposing structure, its dog-tooth windows, castellated towers and blind arcading possessing all the rough, almost brutal charm of the Normans.

The first things to strike you as you enter the **nave** are the sheer length of the building and the lively nineteenth-century painted ceiling, largely the work of amateur volunteers. The nave's procession of plain late Norman arches leads to the architectural feature that makes Ely so special, the **octagon** – the only one of its kind in England – built in 1322 to replace the collapsed central tower. Its construction, employing the largest oaks available in England to support some four hundred tons of glass and lead, remains one of the wonders of the medieval world, and the effect, as you look up into this Gothic dome, is simply breathtaking. When the central tower collapsed, it fell eastwards onto the **choir**, the first three bays of which were rebuilt at the same time as the octagon in the Decorated style – in contrast to the plainer Early English of the choir bays beyond. The other marvel is the **Lady Chapel**, a separate building accessible via the north transept. It lost its sculpture and its stained glass during the Reformation, but its fan vaulting remains, an exquisite example of English Gothic. The south triforium near the main entrance holds the **Stained Glass Museum**, an Anglican money-spinner that exhibits examples of this applied art from 1200 to the 1970s.

Oliver Cromwell's House

29 St Mary's St • April–Oct daily 10am–5pm; Nov–March Mon–Fri & Sun 11am–4pm, Sat 10am–5pm • £4.50

Northwest of the cathedral is **Oliver Cromwell's House**, a timber-framed former vicarage that holds a small exhibition on the Protector's ten-year sojourn in Ely, when he was employed as a tithe collector. The tourist office (see below) is here as well.

ARRIVAL AND INFORMATION — ELY

By train Ely lies on a major rail intersection, receiving direct trains from as far afield as Liverpool, Norwich and London, as well as from Cambridge, just 20min to the south. From the train station, it's a 10min walk to the cathedral, straight up Station Rd and then Back Hill before veering right along The Gallery.

Destinations Cambridge (every 30min; 20min); Ipswich (every 2hr; 1hr); London Kings Cross (every 30min; 1hr); Norwich (every 30min; 1hr).

By bus Buses, including regular services from King's Lynn, stop on Market St immediately north of the cathedral.

Tourist office 29 St Mary's St, in what was once Oliver Cromwell's House, a couple of minutes' walk northwest of the cathedral (April–Oct daily 10am–5pm; Nov–March Mon–Fri & Sun 11am–4pm, Sat 10am–5pm; ⓣ 01353 662062, ⓦ visitely.eastcambs.gov.uk).

ACCOMMODATION

29 Waterside B&B 29 Waterside ⓣ 01353 614329, ⓔ info@29waterside.org.uk. Down near the river, this cosy B&B occupies a pair of pretty little brick cottages dating back to the 1750s. Several original features have been preserved, including the beamed ceilings, and the remainder has been sympathetically modernized. If the sun is out, breakfast can be taken in the garden. **£66**

Riverside Inn 8 Annesdale ⓣ 01353 661677, ⓦ riverside inn-ely.co.uk. Ely is noticeably short on hotels, but the *Riverside* does its best to remedy matters, its three guest rooms decorated in a pleasing version of country-house-meets-boutique style. All overlook the marina and are competitively priced. **£90**

EATING AND DRINKING

The Almonry 36 High St ⓣ 01353 666360. The *Almonry* has the nicest location of all Ely's cafés, with lovely views of the cathedral from a pleasant outside area. The food, however, comprises a pretty routine bunch of sandwiches and snacks. Daily 10am–5pm.

The Boathouse 5 Annesdale ⓣ 01353 664388. This modern, bistro-style place right down by the river is Ely's finest restaurant. The menu is firmly British with the likes of pheasant and skate, mutton and – the house speciality – sausages and mash; mains average £14. Mon–Thurs noon–2.30pm & 6.30–9pm, Fri & Sat noon–2.30pm & 6.30–9.30pm, Sun noon–2.30pm & 6.30–8.30pm.

★ **Peacocks Tearoom** 65 Waterside ⓣ 01353 661100, ⓦ peacockstearoom.co.uk. Down by the river, this popular tearoom – easily the best in town – serves a delicious range of cream teas, salads, sandwiches, soups and lunches with the odd surprise: try, for example, the chocolate zucchini cake. Also an enormous choice of teas from around the world. Wed–Sun 10.30am–5pm.

Cambridge

7

On the whole, **CAMBRIDGE** is a much quieter and more secluded place than Oxford, though for the visitor what really sets it apart from its scholarly rival is "**The Backs**" – the green sward of land that straddles the languid River Cam, providing exquisite views over the backs of the old colleges. At the front, the handsome facades of these same colleges dominate the layout of the town centre, lining up along the main streets. Most of the older colleges date back to the late thirteenth and early fourteenth centuries and are designed to a **similar plan**, with the main gate leading through to a series of "courts," typically a carefully manicured slab of lawn surrounded on all four sides by college residences or offices. Many of the buildings are extraordinarily beautiful, but the most famous is **King's College**, whose magnificent **King's College Chapel** is one of the great statements of late Gothic architecture. There are 31 university colleges in total, each an independent, self-governing body, proud of its achievements and attracting – for the most part at least – a close loyalty from its students.

Note that most colleges have restricted **opening times** and some impose admission charges; during the exam period (late April to early June) most of them close their doors to the public at least some of the time.

King's College

King's Parade • Term time: Mon–Fri 9.30am–3.30pm, Sat 9.30am–3.15pm, Sun 1.15–2.15pm; rest of year: Mon–Sat 9.30am–4.30pm, Sun 10am–5pm • £6.50 including chapel • ⓣ 01223 331100, ⓦ kings.cam.ac.uk

Henry VI founded **King's College** in 1441, but he was disappointed with his initial efforts. So, four years later he cleared away half of medieval Cambridge to make room for a much grander foundation. His plans were ambitious, but the Wars of the Roses – and bouts of royal insanity – intervened and by the time of his death in 1471 very little had been finished and work on what was intended to be Henry's **Great Court** hadn't even started. This part of the site remained empty for no less than three hundred years and the Great Court complex of today – facing King's Parade from behind a long stone screen – is largely neo-Gothic, built in the 1820s to a design by William Wilkins.

CAMBRIDGE: TAKING A PUNT

Punting is the quintessential Cambridge activity, though it is, in fact, a good deal harder than it looks. First-timers find themselves zigzagging across the water and "punt jams" are very common on the stretch of the River Cam beside The Backs in summer. **Punt rental** is available at several points, including the boatyard at Mill Lane (beside the Silver Street bridge), at Magdalene Bridge, and at the Garret Hostel Lane bridge at the back of Trinity College. It costs around £16/hr per person (and most places charge a deposit), with up to six people in each punt. Alternatively, you can hire a **chauffeured punt** from any of the rental places for about £12/hr per person.

Henry's workmen did, however, start on the college's finest building, the much-celebrated **King's College Chapel,** on the north side of today's Great Court and reached – depending on the season – from either the main gatehouse on King's Parade or the North Gate beyond the Senate House at the end of Senate House Passage (see p.368).

King's once enjoyed an exclusive supply of students from Eton and until 1851 claimed the right to award its students degrees without taking any examinations. The

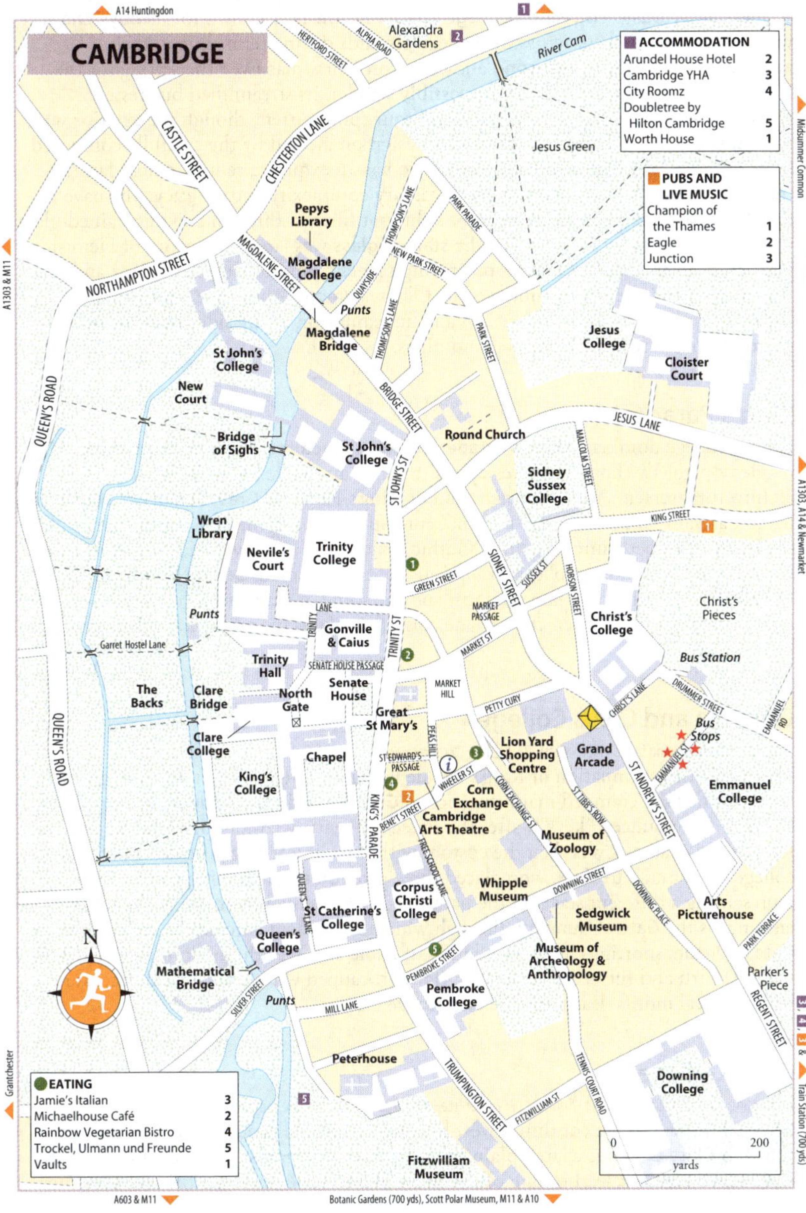

first non-Etonians were only accepted in 1873. Times have changed, however, and, if anything, King's is now one of the more progressive colleges, having been one of the first to admit women in 1972.

King's College Chapel

Evensong Mon–Sat at 5.30pm, Sun 6.30pm

Committed to canvas by Turner and Canaletto, and eulogized in no fewer than three sonnets by Wordsworth, **King's College Chapel** is now best known for its **boys' choir**, whose members process across the college grounds during term time in their antiquated garb to sing **evensong** and carols on Christmas Eve. The setting for the choristers is supreme, the chapel impossibly slender, its streamlined buttresses channelling up to a dainty balustrade and four spiky turrets, though the exterior was, in a sense at least, a happy accident – its design predicated by the carefully composed interior. Here, the high and handsome **nave** has an exquisite ceiling, whose fan-tail tracery is a complex geometry of extraordinary complexity and delicacy. The nave is flooded with kaleidoscopic patterns of light that filter in through copious stained-glass windows. Paid for by Henry VIII, the **stained glass** was largely the work of Flemish glaziers, with the lower windows portraying scenes from the New Testament and the Apocrypha, and the upper windows the Old Testament. Above the **altar** hangs Rubens' tender *Adoration of the Magi* and an exhibition in the side **chantries** puts more historical flesh on Henry's grand plans.

King's Parade

King's College dominates **King's Parade**, the town's medieval High Street, but the higgledy-piggledy shops and cafés opposite are an attractive foil to Wilkins's architectural screen. At the northern end of King's Parade is **Great St Mary's** (May–Aug Mon–Sat 9am–5pm, Sun 12.30–5pm; Sept–April closes 4pm; free; Ⓦgsm.cam.ac.uk), the university's pet church, a sturdy Gothic structure whose tower (£3.50) offers a good view of the surrounding colleges. Opposite the church stands **Senate House**, an exercise in Palladian classicism by James Gibbs, and the scene of graduation ceremonies on the last Saturday in June, when champagne corks fly around the rabbit-fur collars and black gowns.

Gonville and Caius College

Trinity St • No set opening hours • Free • Ⓣ01223 332400, Ⓦcai.cam.ac.uk

The northern continuation of King's Parade is Trinity Street, a short way along which, on the left, is the cramped main entrance to **Gonville and Caius College**, known simply as Caius (pronounced "keys"), after the sixteenth-century co-founder John Keys, who latinized his name as was then the custom with men of learning. The design of the college owes much to Keys, who placed three gates on two adjoining courts, each representing a different stage on the path to academic enlightenment: at the main entrance is the **Gate of Humility**, through which the student entered the college; the **Gate of Virtue**, sporting the female figures of Fame and Wealth, marks the entrance to Caius Court; and the exquisite **Gate of Honour**, capped with sundials and decorated with classical motifs, leads onto Senate House Passage.

Clare College

Trinity Lane • Daily 10.45am–4.30pm • Summer £2; winter free • Ⓣ01223 333200, Ⓦclare.cam.ac.uk

Senate House Passage continues west beyond Caius College's Gate of Honour en route to **Clare College**. Clare's plain period-piece courtyards, completed in the early eighteenth century, lead to one of the most picturesque of all the bridges over the

Cam, **Clare Bridge**. Beyond lies the **Fellows' Garden**, one of the loveliest college gardens open to the public (times as college). Back at the entrance to Clare, it's a few steps more to the North Gate of King's College, beside King's College Chapel (see opposite).

Trinity College

Trinity St • Daily 9am–4pm • £1 • ⓣ 01223 338400, ⓦ trin.cam.ac.uk **Wren Library** Mon–Fri noon–2pm, plus Sat during term 10.30am–12.30pm • Free

Trinity College is the largest of the Cambridge colleges, and its list of famous alumni, probably longer than any of its rivals, includes John Dryden and Vladimir Nabokov; the Cambridge spies Blunt, Burgess and Philby; Alasteir Crowley and Enoch Powell; Pandit Nehru, Bertrand Russell and Prince Charles.

A statue of Henry VIII, who founded the college in 1546, sits in majesty over Trinity's **Great Gate**, his sceptre replaced long ago with a chair leg by a student wag. Beyond lies the vast asymmetrical expanse of **Great Court**, which displays a superb range of Tudor buildings, the oldest of which is the fifteenth-century clocktower. The centrepiece of the court is a delicate fountain, in which, legend has it, Lord Byron used to bathe naked with his pet bear – the college forbade students from keeping dogs.

On the far side of the Great Court, walk through "**the screens**" – the narrow passage separating the Hall from the kitchens – to reach **Nevile's Court**, where Newton first calculated the speed of sound. The west end of Nevile's Court is enclosed by one of the university's most famous buildings, the **Wren Library**. Viewed from the outside, it's impossible to appreciate the scale of the interior thanks to Wren's clever device of concealing the internal floor level by means of two rows of stone columns. Natural light pours into the white stuccoed interior, which contrasts wonderfully with the dark lime-wood bookcases, also Wren-designed.

St John's College

St John's St • Daily: March–Oct 10am–5.30pm; Nov–Feb 10am–3.30pm • £3.20 • ⓣ 01223 338600, ⓦ www.joh.cam.ac.uk

Next door to Trinity, **St John's College** sports a grandiloquent Tudor gatehouse, which is distinguished by the coat of arms of the founder, Lady Margaret Beaufort, the mother of Henry VII, which is held aloft by two spotted, mythical beasts. Beyond, three successive courts lead to the river, but there's an excess of dull reddish brickwork here – enough for Wordsworth, who lived above the kitchens on F staircase, to describe the place as "gloomy". The arcade on the far side of Third Court leads through to the **Bridge of Sighs**, a chunky, covered bridge built in 1831 but in most respects very unlike its Venetian namesake. The bridge is best viewed from the much older – and much more stylish – Wren-designed bridge a few yards to the south. The Bridge of Sighs links the old college with the fanciful nineteenth-century **New Court**, a crenellated neo-Gothic extravaganza topped by a feast of dinky stone chimneys and pinnacles.

Magdalene College

Magdalene St • Daily 10am–6pm • Free • ⓣ 01223 332100, ⓦ magd.cam.ac.uk **Pepys Library** Mid-Jan to mid-March, Oct & Nov Mon–Sat 2.30–3.30pm; late April to Aug Mon–Sat 11.30am–12.30pm & 2.30–3.30pm • Free

Founded as a hostel by the Benedictines, **Magdalene College** – pronounced "maudlin" – became a university college in 1542; it was also the last of the colleges to admit women, finally succumbing in 1988. The main focus of attention here is the **Pepys Library**, in the second of the college's ancient courtyards. Samuel Pepys, a Magdalene student, bequeathed his entire library to the college, where it has been displayed ever since in its original red-oak bookshelves. His famous diary is also parked here.

7

Jesus College

Jesus Lane • Daily 10am–5pm • Free • ⓣ 01223 339339, ⓦ jesus.cam.ac.uk

The intimate cloisters of **Jesus College** are reminiscent of a monastery – appropriately, as the Bishop of Ely founded the college on the grounds of a suppressed Benedictine nunnery in 1496. The main red-brick gateway is approached via a distinctive walled walkway that is commonly known as "the Chimney". Beyond, much of the ground plan of the nunnery has been preserved, especially around **Cloister Court**, the first court on the right after the entrance and the prettiest part of the college, dripping with ivy and, in summer, overflowing with hanging baskets. Entered from the Cloister Court, the college **chapel** occupies the former priory chancel and looks like a medieval parish church, though in fact it was imaginatively restored in the nineteenth century, using ceiling designs by William Morris and Pre-Raphaelite stained glass. The poet Samuel Taylor Coleridge was the college's most famously bad student, absconding in his first year to join the Light Dragoons, and returning only to be kicked out for a combination of bad debts and unconventional opinions.

Sidney Sussex College

Sidney St • No set opening times • Free • ⓣ 01223 338800, ⓦ sid.cam.ac.uk

Leading off **Hobson Street** – named after the owner of a Cambridge livery stable, who would only allow customers to take the horse nearest the door, hence "Hobson's choice" – a pleasant shopping **arcade** occupies the Victorian red bricks of tiny Sussex Street. The arcade leads through to **Sidney Sussex College**, whose sombre, mostly mock-Gothic facade glowers over Sidney Street. The interior is fairly unexciting too, though the long, slender **chapel** is noteworthy for its fancy marble floor, hooped roof and Baroque wood panelling, as well as for being the last resting place of the skull of its most famous alumnus, Oliver Cromwell – though the exact location remains a closely guarded secret.

Christ's College

St Andrew's St • Daily 9.30am–4.30pm • Free • ⓣ 01223 334900, ⓦ www.christs.cam.ac.uk

At the hub of the hustle and bustle of Cambridge's central shopping area, the turreted gateway of **Christ's College** features the coat of arms of the founder, Lady Margaret Beaufort, who also founded St John's. Passing through First Court you come to the Fellows' Building, attributed to Inigo Jones, whose central arch gives access to the **Fellows' Garden**. The poet John Milton is said to have either painted or composed here, though there's no definite proof that he did either; another of Christ's famous undergraduates was Charles Darwin, who showed little academic promise and spent most of his time hunting.

Queens' College

Daily: mid-March to mid-May & late June to Sept 10am–4.30pm; Oct to mid-March 2–4pm • £2.50 in summer, otherwise free • ⓣ 01223 335511, ⓦ queens.cam.ac.uk

Queens' College is accessed through the visitors' gate on Queens' Lane. This is one of the most popular colleges with university applicants, and it's not difficult to see why. In the **Old Court** and the **Cloister Court**, Queens' possesses two fairy-tale Tudor courtyards; the first of the two a perfect illustration of the original collegiate ideal, with kitchens, library, chapel, hall and rooms all set around a tiny green. Flanking Cloister Court is the Long Gallery of the President's Lodge, the last remaining half-timbered building in the university, and the tower where Erasmus is thought to have beavered away during his four years here, probably from 1510 to 1514. Equally eye-catching is the wooden **Mathematical Bridge** over the River Cam (visible for free from the Silver Street Bridge), a copy of the mid-eighteenth-century original, which – so it was claimed – would stay in place even if the nuts and bolts were removed.

The Fitzwilliam Museum

Trumpington St • Tues–Sat 10am–5pm, Sun noon–5pm • Free • T 01223 332900, W fitzmuseum.cam.ac.uk

The **Fitzwilliam Museum** displays the city's premier fine and applied art collection in a grandiloquent Neoclassical edifice, which was built to house the vast hoard bequeathed by Viscount Fitzwilliam in 1816. Since then, the museum has been gifted a string of private collections, most of which follow a particular specialism. The **Lower Galleries,** on the ground floor, contain a wealth of antiquities including Egyptian sarcophagi and mummies, fifth-century BC Greek vases, plus a bewildering display of early European and Asian ceramics and sections dedicated to armour, glass and pewterware.

The **Upper Galleries** contain an eclectic assortment of mostly eighteenth-, nineteenth- and early twentieth-century European paintings and sculptures. There are two rooms of French paintings, with works by Picasso, Matisse, Monet, Renoir, Delacroix, Cézanne and Degas, and two rooms of Italian works including paintings by Fra Filippo Lippi, Simone Martini, Titian and Veronese. Two further rooms feature British paintings, with canvases by William Blake, Constable and Turner, Hogarth, Reynolds, Gainsborough and Stubbs, and one is devoted to Dutch art, displaying paintings by Frans Hals, Steen and Ruisdael. Among the more modern works, there are pieces by Lucian Freud, David Hockney, Henry Moore, Ben Nicholson, Jacob Epstein and Barbara Hepworth.

Scott Polar Museum

Lensfield Rd • Tues–Sat 10am–4pm • Free • T 01223 336540, W spri.cam.ac.uk

Founded in the 1920s in memory of the explorer, Captain Robert Falcon Scott (1868–1912), the revamped **Scott Polar Museum** has extensive displays on the various expeditions that have ventured out into both the Arctic and the Antarctic as well as galleries devoted to climate – and climate change – and polar native cultures.

Cambridge University Botanic Garden

Main entrance: the Brookside Gate, corner of Trumpington Rd and Bateman St • Daily: Feb, March & Oct 10am–5pm; April–Sept 10am–6pm; Nov–Jan 10am–4pm • £4 • W botanic.cam.ac.uk

Founded in 1760 and covering forty acres, the **Cambridge University Botanic Garden** has several glasshouses as well as bountiful outdoor displays. The outdoor beds are mostly arranged by natural order, but there's also a particularly interesting series of chronological beds, showing when different plants were introduced into Britain.

Duxford Imperial War Museum

Duxford, Jct 10 off the M11 • Daily: mid-March to late Oct 10am–6pm; late Oct to mid-March 10am–4pm • £16.50 • T 01223 835000, W duxford.iwm.org.uk

Eight miles south of Cambridge, the giant hangars of the **Duxford Imperial War Museum** dominate the eponymous airfield. Throughout World War II, East Anglia was a centre of operations for the RAF and the USAF, with the region's flat, unobstructed landscape dotted by dozens of airfields, among which Duxford was one of the more important. In total, the museum holds more than 150 historic aircraft, a wide-ranging collection of civil and military planes from the Sunderland flying boat to Concorde and the Vulcan B2 bombers, which were used for the first and last time in the 1982 Falklands conflict; the Spitfires, however, remain the most enduringly popular. Most of the planes are kept in full working order and are taken out for a spin several times a year at **Duxford Air Shows**, which attract thousands of visitors. There are usually half a dozen air shows a year and advance bookings are strongly recommended – call ahead or consult the museum website.

ARRIVAL AND INFORMATION — CAMBRIDGE

By plane Cambridge is just 30 miles north of London Stansted Airport, from where there are hourly trains to the city (35min).

By train Cambridge train station is a mile or so southeast of the city centre, off Hills Rd. You can walk from here into the centre (an easy but tedious 20min), or take local Citi bus #1, #3, or #7 to the bus stops on Emmanuel Street.

Destinations Bury St Edmunds (hourly; 40min); Ely (every 30min; 15min); Ipswich (hourly; 1hr 20min); King's Lynn (hourly; 45min); London Kings Cross (every 30min; 50min); London Stansted Airport (hourly; 35min); Norwich (hourly; 1hr 20min).

By bus The long-distance bus station is near the city centre on Drummer St.

By car Arriving by car, you'll find much of the city centre closed to traffic and on-street parking well-nigh impossible to find; for a day-trip, at least, the best option is a park-and-ride car park; they are signposted on all major approaches.

Tourist office Right in the centre of town on Peas Hill, just off King's Parade (Oct–March Mon–Sat 10am–5pm; April–Sept Mon–Sat 10am–5pm, Sun 11am–3pm; T 0871 226 8006, W visitcambridge.org). They sell city maps and coordinate a wide range of guided walking tours (reservations required).

GETTING AROUND

Popular with locals and students alike, **cycling** is an enjoyable way to get around the city. There are bike rental outlets all over town with one of the biggest concerns being Station Cycles (W stationcycles.co.uk), which has stores down near the train station on Station Rd (T 01223 307125) and in the city centre on Corn Exchange St (T 01223 307655). Wherever you leave your bike, padlock it to something immovable as bike theft is not infrequent.

ACCOMMODATION

Cambridge is light on central accommodation and those few **hotels** and **guesthouses** that do occupy prime locations are expensive. That said, there is a cluster of less pricey places, including a YHA hostel, around the train station and another on Chesterton Lane and its continuation, Chesterton Rd, the busy street running east from the top of Magdalene St. In high season, when vacant rooms are often thin on the ground, the tourist office's **accommodation-booking service** can be very useful.

Arundel House Hotel 53 Chesterton Rd T 01223 367701, W arundelhousehotels.co.uk. One of the better mid-range hotel choices, in a converted row of late Victorian houses overlooking the river and Jesus Green. Neat and tidy rooms, but mundane modern furnishings. **£95**

Cambridge YHA 97 Tenison Rd T 0845 3719728, E cambridge@yha.org.uk. This long-established hostel occupies a rambling Victorian house near the train station – Tenison Rd is a right turn a couple of hundred yards down Station Rd. Facilities include a laundry and self-catering, a cycle store, a games room and a small courtyard garden. There are one hundred beds in two- to eight-bedded rooms and advance reservations are advised. Dorm **£18.40**, double **£46**

City Roomz Station Rd T 01223 304050, W cityroomz.com. This bargain-basement, hostel-style hotel is in a converted granary warehouse right outside the train station. Most of the rooms are kitted out with bunks, though there are a few doubles and twins too. All are en suite, but space is in short supply. **£59**

★ **Doubletree by Hilton Cambridge** Granta Place, Mill Lane T 01223 259988, W doubletree.hilton.co.uk. This is the city's most appealing hotel by a long chalk, occupying a modern 1960s building a couple of minutes' walk from the centre. The best rooms have balconies overlooking the river (though the views are hardly riveting); breakfasts are first-rate. **£120**

Worth House 152 Chesterton Rd T 01223 316074, W worth-house.co.uk. Very recommendable B&B in a pleasantly upgraded Victorian house a 20min walk from the centre. All the bedrooms have large en-suite bathrooms and facilities are immaculate. Great breakfasts too. **£55**

EATING

With most Cambridge students eating at their college dining halls, good-quality restaurants are thin on the ground, whereas the **takeaway** and **café** scene is on a roll.

Jamie's Italian The Old Library, 2 Wheeler St T 01223 654094, W jamieoliver.com/italian/cambridge. OK, celebrity chef Jamie Oliver may not be everyone's cup of tea, but this large city-centre restaurant has a real buzz about it, and the food – which is largely but not exclusively Italian – is undeniably very tasty. Mains from £11. Mon–Sat noon–11pm, Sun noon–10.30pm.

Michaelhouse Café Trinity St ⓣ01223 309147 ⓦmichaelhouse.org.uk. Good-quality café food – snacks, salads and so forth – in an attractively renovated medieval church. Great, central location too. Mon–Sat 8am–5pm.

Rainbow Vegetarian Bistro 9A King's Parade ⓣ01223 321551, ⓦrainbowcafe.co.uk. Cramped but agreeable vegetarian restaurant with main courses – ranging from couscous to lasagne and North African tagine, and specializing in vegan and gluten-free food – for around £9. Organic wines served with meals. Handy location, opposite King's College. Tues–Sat 10am–10pm, Sun 10am–4pm.

Trockel, Ulmann und Freunde 13 Pembroke St ⓣ01223 460923. Café food at its best in bright, creatively decorated premises. The baguettes have imaginative fillings – hummus and avocado, for example; the soups are hot and tasty; and the cakes are simply delicious. Tends to get jam-packed during term time. Mon–Fri 9am–5pm, Sat 10am–5pm.

Vaults 14 Trinity St ⓣ01223 506090, ⓦthevaults.biz. Cosy, basement restaurant with a lively, varied and inexpensive menu, some of it designed for sharing. Asian and British main courses from £11. The adjacent bar has live bands. Mon–Fri noon–2.30pm & 5.30–10pm, Sat & Sun noon–4pm & 5.30–10pm.

7

DRINKING

★ **Champion of the Thames** 68 King St ⓣ01223 352043. Gratifyingly old-fashioned central pub with decent beer and a student/academic crowd. Sun–Thurs noon–11pm, Fri & Sat 11am–11pm.

Eagle 8 Bene't St ⓣ01223 505020. An ancient if somewhat careworn inn with a cobbled courtyard, the *Eagle* is associated with Crick and Watson who discovered DNA in 1953. It's been tarted up since and gets horribly crowded, but is still worth a pint of anyone's time. Mon–Sat 11am–11pm, Sun noon–10.30pm.

NIGHTLIFE AND ENTERTAINMENT

The **performing arts** scene is at its busiest and best during term time with numerous student **drama** productions, **classical concerts** and **gigs** culminating in the traditional whizzerama of excess following the exam season. The most celebrated concerts are those given by **King's College choir** (see p.368), though the choral scholars who perform at the chapels of St John's College and Trinity are also exceptionally good. The four-day **Cambridge Folk Festival** (ⓦcambridgefolkfestival.co.uk), one of the longest-running folk festivals in the world, takes place in neighbouring Cherry Hinton at the end of July. For upcoming events, the tourist office (see opposite) issues various free **listings** leaflets and brochures.

Arts Picturehouse 38–39 St Andrew's St ⓣ0871 9025720, ⓦpicturehouses.co.uk. Art-house cinema with an excellent, wide-ranging programme.

Cambridge Arts Theatre 6 St Edward's Passage, off King's Parade ⓣ01223 503333, ⓦcambridgeartstheatre.com. The city's main rep theatre, founded by John Maynard Keynes, and launch pad of a thousand-and-one famous careers; offers a top-notch range of cutting-edge and classic productions.

Cambridge Corn Exchange Wheeler St ⓣ01223 357851, ⓦcornex.co.uk. Revamped nineteenth-century trading hall, now the main city-centre venue for opera, ballet, musicals and comedy as well as regular rock and folk gigs.

Junction Clifton Rd ⓣ01223 511511, ⓦjunction.co.uk. Rock, indie, jazz, reggae or soul gigs, plus theatre, comedy and dance at this popular arts venue.

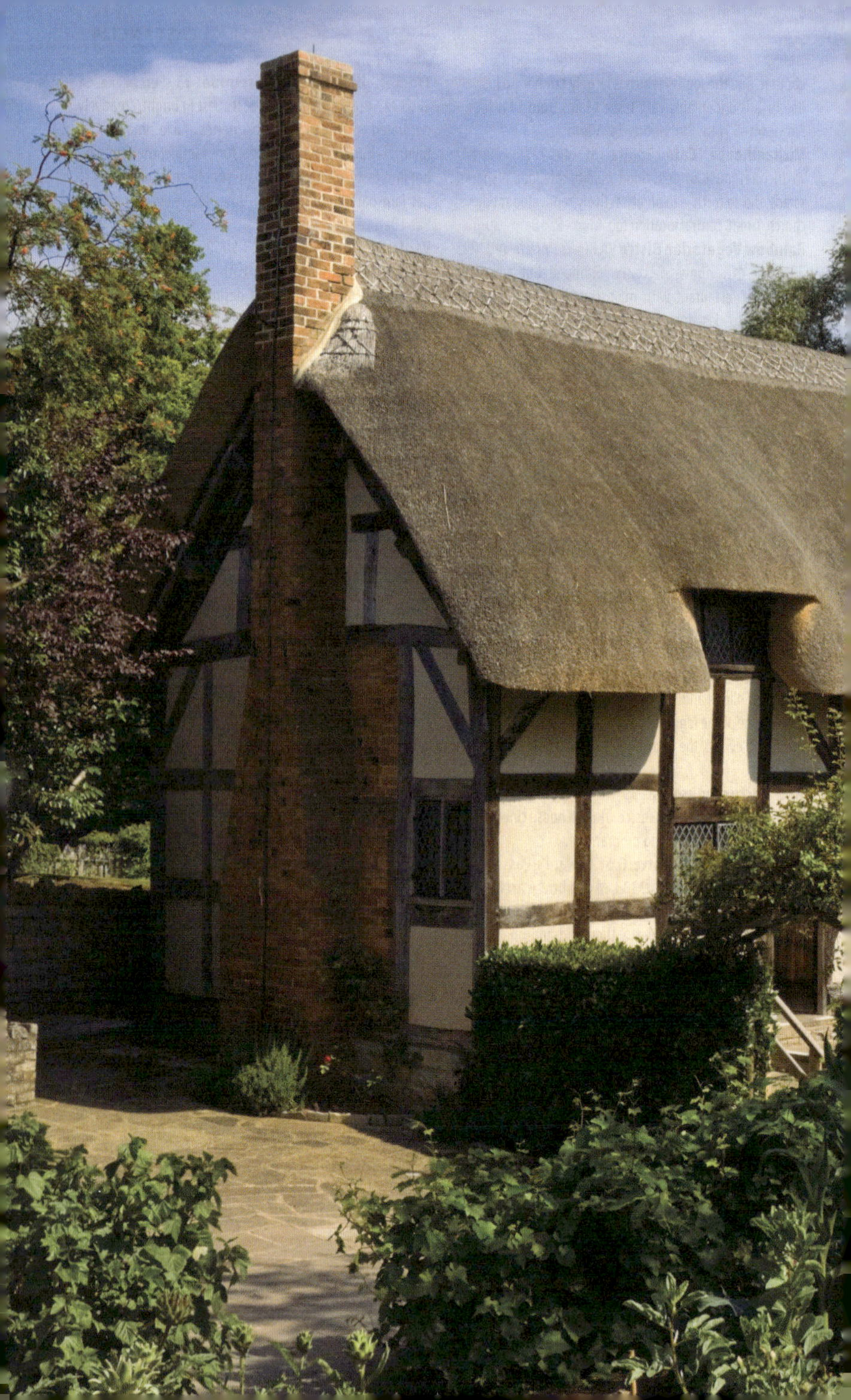

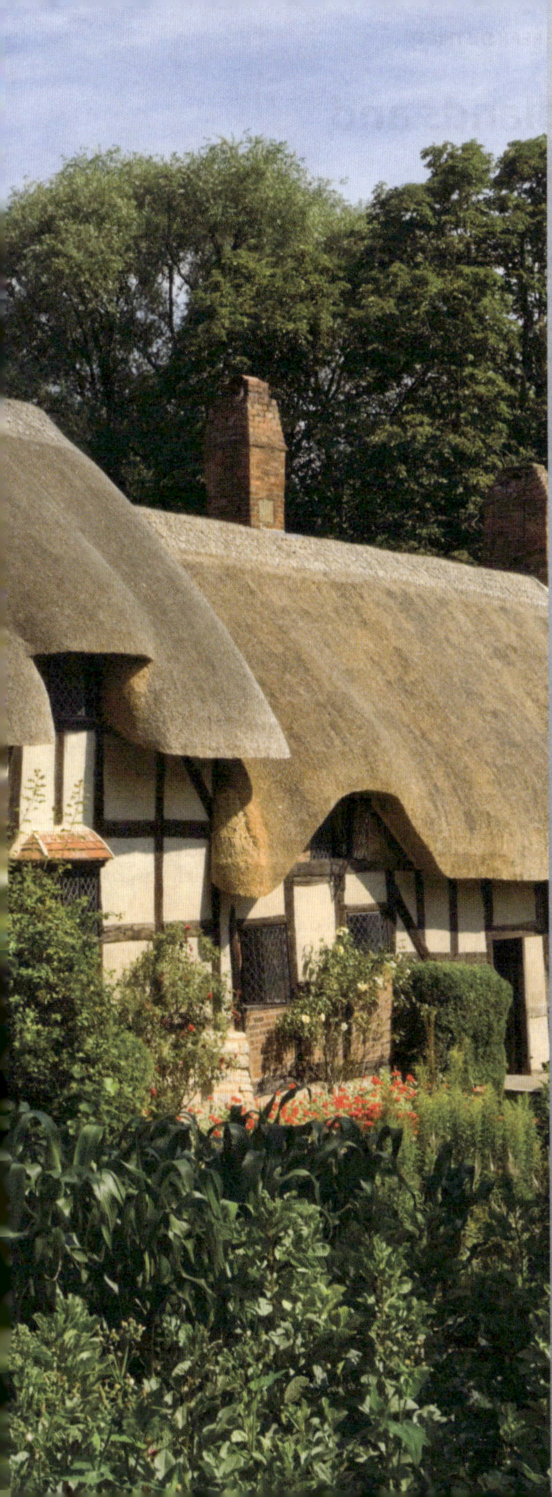

The West Midlands and the Peak District

379 Stratford-upon-Avon

383 Warwick

385 Worcester

387 The Malvern Hills

388 Herefordshire

391 Shropshire

399 Birmingham

406 The Peak District

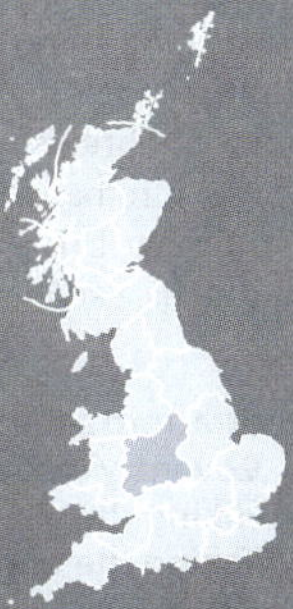

ANNE HATHAWAY'S COTTAGE

The West Midlands and the Peak District

Birmingham, the urban epicentre of the West Midlands, is Britain's second city and was once the world's greatest industrial metropolis, its slew of factories powering the Industrial Revolution. Long saddled with a reputation as a culture-hating, car-loving backwater, Birmingham has redefined its image in recent years, initiating some ambitious architectural and environmental schemes and jazzing up its museums and industrial heritage sites. Within easy striking distance are the rural shires that stretch out towards Wales, with the bumpy Malvern Hills, one of the region's scenic highlights in between; you could also drift north to the rugged scenery of the Peak District, whose surly, stirring landscapes stretch out beyond the attractive little spa town of Buxton.

Change was forced on Birmingham by the drastic decline in its manufacturing base during the 1970s; things were even worse in the **Black Country**, that knot of industrial towns clinging to the western side of the city, where de-industrialization has proved particularly painful. The counties to the south and west of Birmingham and beyond the Black Country – **Warwickshire**, **Worcestershire**, **Herefordshire** and **Shropshire** – comprise a rural stronghold that maintains an emotional and political distance from the conurbation. Of the four counties, **Warwickshire** is the least obviously scenic, but draws by far the largest number of visitors, for – as the road signs declare at every entry point – this is "Shakespeare Country". The prime target is, of course, **Stratford-upon-Avon**, with its handful of Shakespeare-related sites and world-class theatre, but spare time also for the town of **Warwick**, which has a superb church and a whopping castle.

Neighbouring **Worcestershire**, which stretches southwest from the urban fringes of the West Midlands, holds two principal places of interest, **Worcester**, which is graced by a mighty cathedral, and **Great Malvern**, a mannered inland resort spread along the rolling contours of the **Malvern Hills** – prime walking territory. From here, it's west again for **Herefordshire**, a large and sparsely populated county that's home to several amenable market towns, most notably **Hereford**, where the remarkable medieval Mappa Mundi map is displayed in the cathedral, and pocket-sized **Ross-on-Wye**, which is within easy striking distance of an especially scenic stretch of the **Wye River Valley**. Next door, to the north, is rural **Shropshire** which has **Ludlow**, one of the region's prettiest towns, awash with antique half-timbered buildings, and the amiable county town of **Shrewsbury**, which is also close to the hiking trails of the **Long Mynd**. Shropshire has a fascinating industrial history, too, for it was here in the **Ironbridge Gorge** that British industrialists built the world's first iron bridge and pioneered the use of coal as a smelting fuel.

Stratford's theatres p.381
Coventry cathedral p.385
Hiking the Malvern Hills p.387
Taking the Great Malvern waters p.388
Birmingham orientation p.399
Buxton festivals p.408
The Pennine Way p.411
Hiking around Bakewell p.413

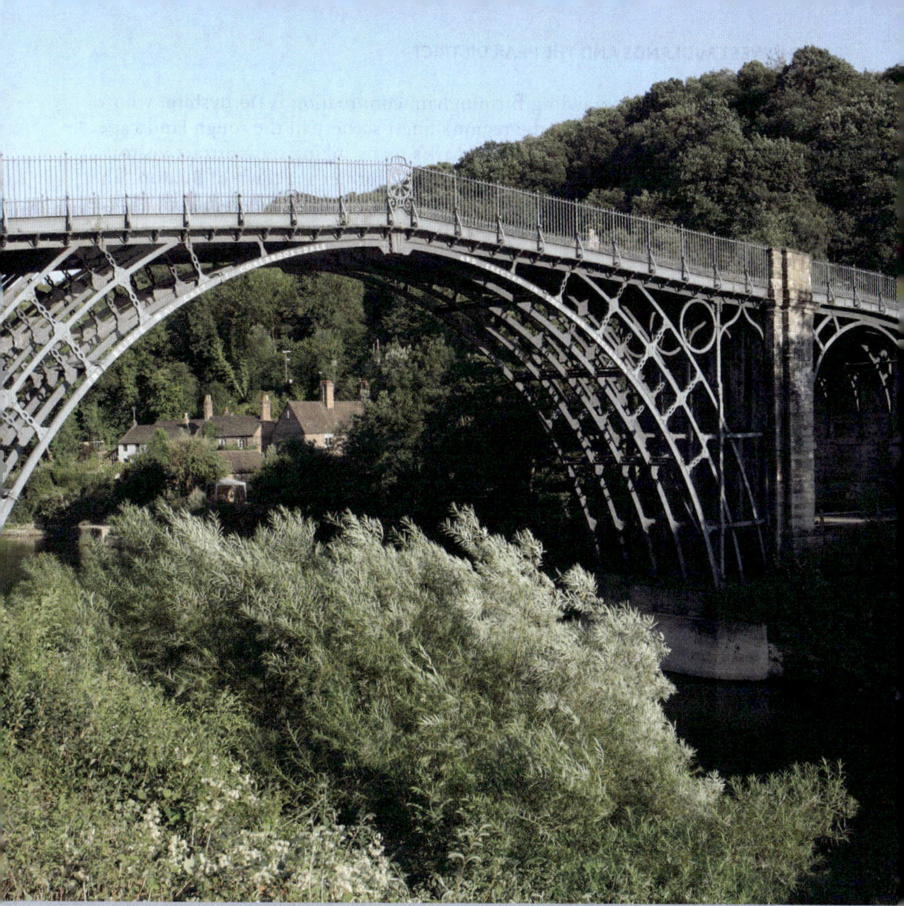

IRONBRIDGE, SHROPSHIRE

Highlights

❶ RSC theatres, Stratford-upon-Avon Shakespeare's birthplace is quite simply the best place in the world to see the great man's plays, performed by the pre-eminent Royal Shakespeare Company. **See p.381 & p.383**

❷ Mappa Mundi, Hereford Cathedral This glorious antique map, dating to around 1000 AD, provides a riveting insight into the medieval sensibility. **See p.389**

❸ Ironbridge Gorge The first iron bridge ever constructed arches high above the River Severn – industrial poetry in motion. **See pp.392–396**

❹ Ludlow A postcard-pretty country town with a herd of half-timbered houses and a sprawling castle – and some wonderful restaurants, too. **See p.398**

❺ Staying Cool, Birmingham Stay Cool and be cool by renting an apartment at the top of the Rotunda, one of Birmingham's landmark buildings. Enjoy the views – they are fabulous. **See p.404**

❻ Buxton Good-looking and relaxed former spa town with good hotels and restaurants –an ideal base for exploring the Peak District. **See p.408**

HIGHLIGHTS ARE MARKED ON THE MAP ON P.378

To the north of the sprawling Birmingham conurbation is **Derbyshire**, whose northern reaches incorporate the region's finest scenery in the rough landscapes of the **Peak District National Park**. The park's many hiking trails attract visitors by the thousand; the best base is the appealing former spa town of **Buxton**. The Peaks are also home to the limestone caverns of **Castleton**, the so-called "Plague Village" of **Eyam** and the grandiose stately pile of **Chatsworth House**, a real favourite hereabouts.

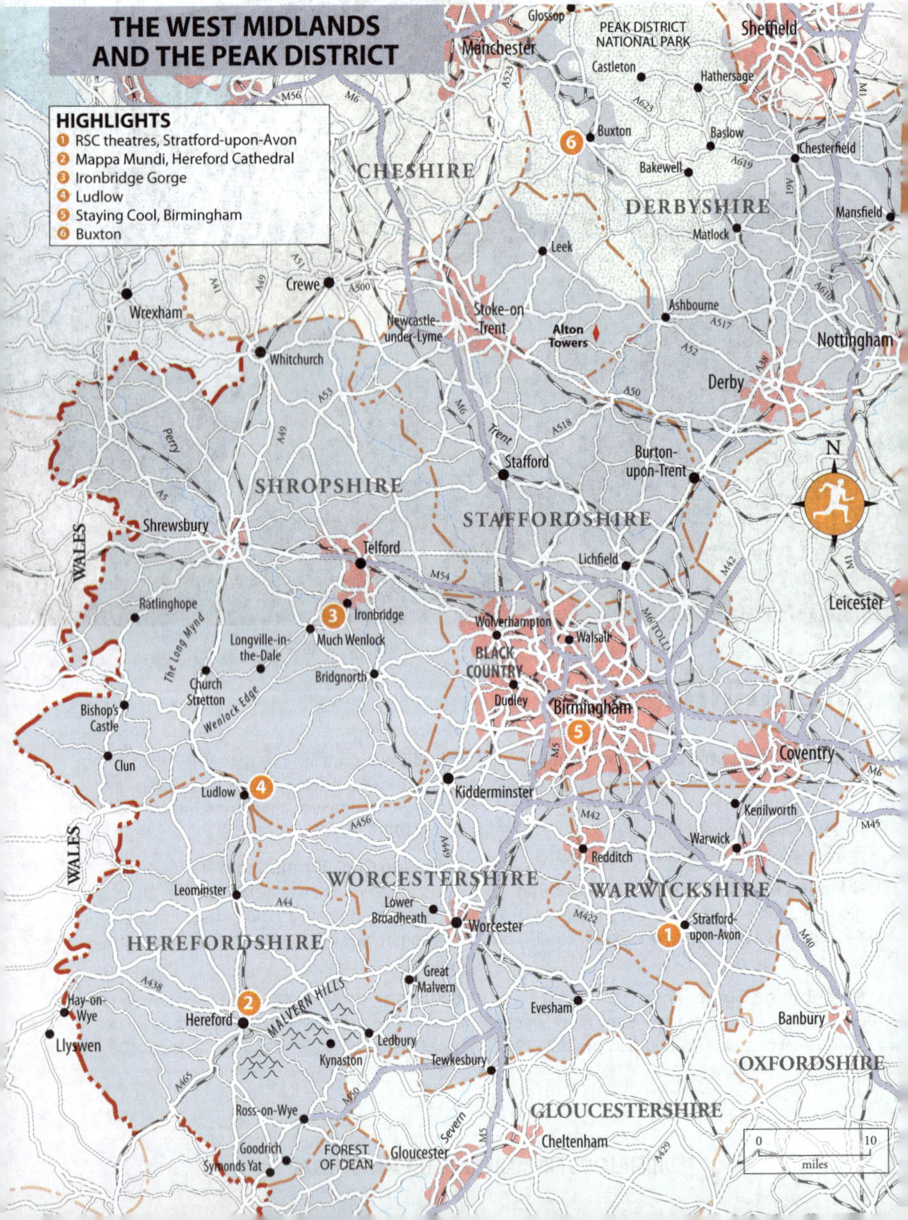

GETTING AROUND **THE WEST MIDLANDS AND THE PEAK DISTRICT**

The region's public transport hub, **Birmingham**, has a major international **airport** and is easily accessible by **train** from London Euston, Liverpool, Manchester, Leeds, York and a score of other towns. It is also well served by the National Express **bus** network, with dozens of buses leaving every hour for destinations all over Britain. Local bus services are excellent around the West Midlands conurbation and very good in the Peak District, but fade away badly in amongst the villages of Worcestershire, Herefordshire and Shropshire.

Stratford-upon-Avon

Despite its worldwide fame, **STRATFORD-UPON-AVON** is at heart an unassuming market town with an unexceptional pedigree. A charter for Stratford's weekly market was granted in the twelfth century and the town later became an important stopping-off point for stagecoaches between London, Oxford and the north. Like all such places, Stratford had its clearly defined class system and within this typical milieu John and Mary **Shakespeare** occupied the middle rank, and would have been forgotten long ago had their first son, William, not turned out to be the greatest writer ever to use the English language. Nowadays this ordinary little town is all but smothered by package-tourist hype and, in the summer at least, its central streets groan under the weight of thousands of tourists. Don't let that deter you: the **Royal Shakespeare Company** offers superb theatre and if you are willing to forego the busiest attractions – principally **Shakespeare's Birthplace** – you can avoid the crush. All Stratford's key attractions – many of them owned and run by the **Shakespeare Birthplace Trust** (see p.382) – are dotted around the centre, a flat and compact slice of land spreading back from the River Avon.

8

Shakespeare's Birthplace

Henley St • April, May, Sept & Oct daily 9am–5pm; June–Aug daily 9am–6pm; Nov–March daily 10am–4pm • Shakespeare Birthplace Trust combination ticket £12.50/£19.50 (see p.382) • ⓣ 01789 204016, ⓦ shakespeare.org.uk

Top of everyone's bardic itinerary is **Shakespeare's Birthplace**, comprising a modern visitor centre and the heavily restored, half-timbered building where the great man was born – or rather, where it is generally believed he was born. The visitor centre pokes into every corner of Shakespeare's life and times, making the most of what little hard evidence there is. Next door, the half-timbered birthplace dwelling is actually two buildings knocked into one. The northern, much smaller and later part was the house of Joan, Shakespeare's sister; adjoining it is the main family home, bought by John Shakespeare in 1556 and now returned to something like its original appearance. It includes a glover's workshop, where Shakespeare's father beavered away, though some argue that he was a wool merchant or a butcher. Despite the many historical uncertainties, the house has been attracting visitors for centuries. One of the old mullioned windows upstairs, now displayed in a glass cabinet, bears the scratch-mark signatures of some of them, including Thomas Carlyle and Walter Scott.

Nash's House and New Place

Chapel St • Daily: April–June, Sept & Oct 10am–5pm; July & Aug 10am–6pm; Nov–March 11am–4pm • Shakespeare Birthplace Trust combination ticket £12.50/£19.50 (see p.382) • ⓣ 01789 204016, ⓦ shakespeare.org.uk

Nash's House, a Birthplace Trust property, was once owned by Thomas Nash, the first husband of Shakespeare's granddaughter, Elizabeth Hall. The ground floor is kitted out with a pleasant assortment of period furnishings, while upstairs, one display provides a potted history of Stratford and a second focuses on the house itself. One cabinet holds woodcarvings made from the **mulberry tree** that once stood outside and was reputedly planted by Shakespeare.

The gardens adjacent to Nash's House contain the foundations of **New Place**, Shakespeare's last residence, which was demolished long ago. The foundations have prompted all sorts of speculation, queries and questions that may be resolved by the **archeological dig** that is currently burrowing into the site.

Hall's Croft

Old Town • Daily: April–Oct 10am–5pm; Nov–March 11am–4pm • Shakespeare Birthplace Trust combination ticket £12.50/£19.50 (see p.382) • Ⓣ 01789 204016, Ⓦ shakespeare.org.uk

Stratford's most impressive medieval house is **Hall's Croft**, the former home of Shakespeare's elder daughter, Susanna, and her doctor husband, John Hall. The immaculately maintained house, with its beamed ceilings and rickety rooms, holds a good-looking medley of period furniture and – mostly upstairs – a fascinating display on **Elizabethan medicine.** Hall established something of a reputation for his medical know-how and after his death some of his case notes were published in a volume entitled *Select Observations on English Bodies*.

Holy Trinity Church

Old Town • March & Oct Mon–Sat 9am–5pm, Sun 12.30–5pm; April–Sept Mon–Sat 8.30am–6pm, Sun 12.30–5pm; Nov–Feb Mon–Sat 9am–4pm, Sun 12.30–5pm • Free, but chancel £1.50 • Ⓣ 01789 266316

The mellow, honey-coloured stonework of **Holy Trinity Church** dates from the thirteenth century. Enhanced by its riverside setting, the dignified proportions of this quintessentially English church are the result, however, of several centuries of chopping and changing, culminating in the replacement of the original wooden spire with today's stone version in 1763. Inside, the nave is flanked by a fine set of stained-glass windows, some of which are medieval, and bathed in light from the clerestory windows up above. William Shakespeare lies buried in the **chancel**, his remains overseen by a sedate and studious memorial plaque and effigy added just seven years after his death.

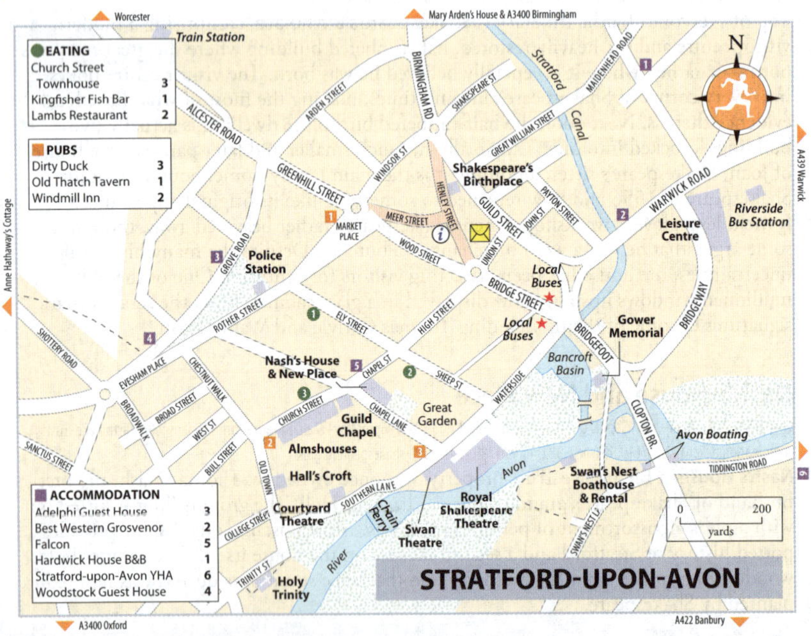

STRATFORD'S THEATRES

Passing through a narrow breach in the wall of Holy Trinity Church graveyard brings you onto a footpath; this runs along the riverbank, with the RSC's Courtyard Theatre to the left on Southern Lane and the dinky little **chain ferry** (50p) across the Avon to the right. After a short walk you emerge beside the Royal Shakespeare Company's two main **theatres**, the Swan and the Royal Shakespeare. There was no theatre in Stratford in Shakespeare's day and indeed the first home-town festival in his honour was only held in 1769 at the behest of London-based David Garrick. Thereafter, the idea of building a permanent home in which to perform Shakespeare's works slowly gained momentum, and finally, in 1879, the first Memorial Theatre was opened on land donated by local beer baron Charles Flower. A fire in 1926 necessitated the construction of a new theatre, and the ensuing architectural competition, won by Elisabeth Scott, produced the **Royal Shakespeare Theatre**, a red-brick edifice that has recently been remodelled and extended, its proscenium stage replaced by a thrust stage – to the horror of many and the delight of some. Attached to the main theatre is the **Swan Theatre**, a replica "in-the-round" Elizabethan stage that has also been refurbished.

Bancroft Basin

In front of the Royal Shakespeare Theatre, the manicured lawns of a small riverside park stretch north as far as **Bancroft Basin**, where the Stratford Canal meets the river, and which is usually packed with narrowboats. In the small park on the far side, over either of two pedestrian bridges, the finely sculpted **Gower Memorial** of 1888 shows a seated Shakespeare surrounded by characters from his plays.

8

Anne Hathaway's Cottage

Shottery • Daily: April–Oct 9am–5pm; Nov–March 10am–4pm • £7.50, or combined Birthplace Trust ticket £19.50 (see p.382) • T 01789 204016, W shakespeare.org.uk

Anne Hathaway's Cottage, a Birthplace Trust property, is just over a mile west of the centre in the well-heeled suburb of **Shottery**. The cottage – actually an old farmhouse – is an immaculately maintained, half-timbered affair with a thatched roof and dinky little chimneys. This was the home of Anne Hathaway before she married Shakespeare in 1582, and the interior holds a comely combination of period furniture, including a superb, finely carved four-poster bed. The garden is splendid too, bursting with blooms in the summertime. The adjacent orchard features a scattering of modern sculptures and more than forty types of tree, shrub and rose mentioned in the plays, with each bearing the appropriate quotation inscribed on a plaque. The nicest way to get to the cottage from the centre is on the signposted **footpath** from Evesham Place, at the south end of Rother Street.

Mary Arden's Farm

Three miles northwest of Stratford, Station Rd, Wilmcote • Daily April–Oct 10am–5pm • £9.50, or combined Birthplace Trust ticket £19.50 (see p.382) • T 01789 293455, W shakespeare.org.uk

The Birthplace Trust also owns **Mary Arden's Farm**, three miles northwest of the town centre in the village of **Wilmcote**. Mary was Shakespeare's mother and the only unmarried daughter of her father, Robert, at the time of his death in 1556. Unusually for the period, Mary inherited the house and land, thus becoming one of the neighbourhood's most eligible women – John Shakespeare, eager for self-improvement, married her within a year. The house is a well-furnished example of an Elizabethan farmhouse and, though the labelling is rather scant, a platoon of guides fills in the details of family life and traditions. There's a farmyard here too.

ARRIVAL AND DEPARTURE STRATFORD-UPON-AVON

By train Stratford train station on the northwest edge of town, a 10min walk from the centre. London Midland operates hourly services here from Birmingham (Moor Street and Snow Hill stations; 1hr 10min/55min), while Chiltern Railways runs a direct train every two to three hours from London Marylebone (2hr 10min); Stratford is at the end of the line for both services.

By bus Local buses arrive and depart from the east end of Bridge St; National Express services and most other long-distance buses pull into Riverside bus station on the east side of the town centre, off Bridgeway.

INFORMATION

Tourist office 62 Henley St (daily: March–Oct 10am–5pm, Nov–Feb 10am–4pm; T 01789 264293, W discover-stratford.com). Among many other useful things, they offer a last-minute accommodation booking service that can be especially handy at the height of the summer.

Shakespeare Birthplace Trust The Shakespeare Birthplace Trust (T 01789 204016, W shakespeare.org.uk) owns five properties – three in the town centre (Shakespeare's Birthplace, Nash's House and Hall's Croft) and two on the outskirts (Anne Hathaway's Cottage and Mary Arden's Farm). Tickets are not available for the three individual properties in the town centre – instead you have to buy a combined ticket for £12.50 or a ticket for all five at £19.50. Alternatively, you can also purchase an individual ticket at the two outlying attractions. Tickets are on sale at all five.

ACCOMMODATION

In peak months and during the **Shakespeare birthday celebrations** around April 23, it's pretty much essential to book accommodation well ahead. The town has a dozen or so **hotels**, the pick of which occupy old half-timbered buildings right in the centre, but most visitors choose to stay in a **B&B**; there's a particular concentration to the west of the centre around Grove Road and Evesham Place.

8

Adelphi Guest House 39 Grove Rd T 01789 204469, W adelphi-guesthouse.com. Extremely cosy B&B in a good-looking Victorian townhouse a short walk from the centre. The owners have accumulated all sorts of interesting curios – from vintage theatrical posters to ornate chandeliers – and the five double guest rooms are all en suite. The best room, which has a four-poster, is in the attic and offers pleasing views. Top-ranking, home-cooked breakfasts too. **£70**

Best Western Grosvenor Warwick Rd T 01789 269213, W bwgh.co.uk. Close to the canal, just a couple of minutes' walk from the town centre, the *Grosvenor* occupies a row of pleasant, two-storey Georgian houses. The interior is crisp and modern and there's ample parking at the back. **£80**

Falcon Chapel St T 0844 411 9005, W legacy-hotels.co.uk. Handily situated in the middle of town, this chain hotel is a rambling affair whose front section, with its half-timbered facade and stone-flagged bar, dates from the sixteenth century. A corridor connects this part of the hotel to the modern block behind, where the rooms are neat, trim and really rather well designed. **£95**

Hardwick House B&B 1 Avenue Rd T 01789 204307, W hardwickstratford.co.uk. Particularly pleasant B&B with a handful of smartly decorated modern rooms in a large Victorian red-brick on the north side of the town centre. **£65**

Stratford-upon-Avon YHA Hemmingford House, Alveston, two miles east of the town centre on the B4086 T 0845 371 9661, E stratford@yha.org.uk. Occupying a rambling Georgian mansion on the edge of the pretty village of Alveston, this hostel has dorms, double and family rooms, some of which are en suite, plus a laundry, cycle hire, internet access, car parking and self-catering facilities. Breakfasts and evening meals are on offer, too. Served by local buses #18, #18A and #15 from Bridge St. Open all year. Dorm **£10**, double **£20**

Woodstock Guest House 30 Grove Rd T 01789 299881, W woodstock-house.co.uk. A smart, neatly kept B&B just a 5min walk from the centre, by the start of the path to Anne Hathaway's Cottage (see p.381). The five extremely comfortable bedrooms are all en suite, decorated in a frilly modern style. No credit cards. **£55**

EATING

Stratford is accustomed to feeding and watering thousands of visitors, but most places are geared up for the day-trippers and, as a result, there are surprisingly few good **restaurants**.

Church Street Townhouse 16 Church St T 01789 262222, W churchstreettownhouse.com. Smart, appealing bar and restaurant in one of the town's oldest premises. The menu is creative with due emphasis on local ingredients – try, for example, the steak, Guinness & mushroom pie with mash and crushed peas for £11.50. Daily 8am–10pm.

Kingfisher Fish Bar 13 Ely St T 01789 292513. The best fish-and-chip shop in town, a 5min walk from the theatres. Takeaway and sit-down available. Mon–Sat 11.30am–1.45pm & 5–9.30pm.

★ **Lambs Restaurant** 12 Sheep St ⊕01789 292554, ⓦlambsrestaurant.co.uk. A mouthwatering range of stylish English and continental dishes – slow-roasted lamb shank, for example –dished up in a smart restaurant with lots of period features including beamed ceilings and modern art on the walls. Daily specials around £9, other main courses £14–16. Mon 5–9pm, Tues–Sat noon–2pm & 5–9pm, Sun noon–2pm & 6–9pm.

DRINKING

Stratford's **pubs** are rather better than its restaurants, with several convivial spots.

Dirty Duck 53 Waterside ⊕01789 297312, ⓦdirtyduck-pub-stratford-upon-avon.co.uk. The archetypal actors' pub, stuffed to the gunwales every night with a vocal entourage of RSC thesps and admirers. Traditional beers in somewhat spartan premises plus a terrace for hot-weather drinking. Daily 11am till late.

Old Thatch Tavern Market Place ⊕01789 295216. Ancient pub with a convivial atmosphere and a good range of beers that attracts a mixed crew of tourists and locals. Daily 11am till late.

Windmill Inn Church St ⊕01789 297687. Popular pub with a rabbit-warren of rooms and low-beamed ceilings. Flowers beers too. Daily 11am till late.

NIGHTLIFE AND ENTERTAINMENT

The Royal Shakespeare Company ⊕0844 800 1110, ⓦrsc.org.uk. As the RSC works on a repertory system, you could stay in Stratford for a few days and see three or four different plays, and not necessarily by Shakespeare: though the RSC does indeed focus on the great man's plays, it offers other productions too, from new modern writing through to works by Shakespeare's contemporaries. With the Courtyard Theatre closed for a revamp, the RSC is currently confined to two venues – the Royal Shakespeare and the Swan. Tickets start from as little as £14 and can be bought online, by phone, and in person at the Royal Shakespeare box office. However, many performances are sold out months in advance and although there's always the off-chance of a last-minute return or stand-by ticket (for unsold seats), don't bet on it.

Warwick

Pocket-sized **WARWICK**, just eight miles northeast of Stratford and easily reached by bus and train, is famous for its massive **castle**, but it also possesses several charming streetscapes erected in the aftermath of a great fire in 1694. An hour or two is quite enough time to nose around the town centre, though you'll need the whole day if, braving the crowds and the medieval musicians, you're also set on exploring the castle and its extensive grounds: either way, Warwick is the perfect day-trip from Stratford.

Warwick Castle

Daily: April–Sept 10am–6pm; Oct–March 10am–5pm • Various ticketing options from £20.64 in advance (£24.60 on the day); parking £4 • ⊕0871 265 2000, ⓦwarwick-castle.co.uk

Towering above the River Avon at the foot of the town centre, **Warwick Castle** is often proclaimed the "greatest medieval castle in Britain". This claim is valid enough if bulk equals greatness, but actually much of the existing structure is the result of extensive nineteenth-century tinkering. It's likely that the Saxons raised the first fortress on this site, though things really took off with the Normans, who built a large motte and bailey here towards the end of the eleventh century. Almost three hundred years later, the eleventh Earl of Warwick turned the stronghold into a formidable stone castle, complete with elaborate gatehouses, multiple turrets and a keep.

The **entrance** to the castle is through the old stable block at the foot of Castle Street. Beyond, a footpath leads round to the imposing moated and mounded **East Gate**. Over the footbridge – and beyond the protective towers – is the main **courtyard**. You can stroll along the ramparts and climb the towers, but most visitors head straight for one or other of the special, very touristy displays installed inside the castle's many chambers and towers. The **grounds** are perhaps much more enjoyable, acres of woodland and lawn inhabited by peacocks and including a large glass **conservatory**. A footbridge leads over the River Avon to **River Island**, the site of jousting tournaments and other such medieval hoopla.

Lord Leycester Hospital

60 High St • Tues–Sun: April–Oct 10am–5pm; Nov–March 10am–4.30pm • £4.90 • ⓣ 01926 491422, ⓦ lordleycester.com

The remarkable **Lord Leycester Hospital**, a tangle of half-timbered buildings leaning at fairy-tale angles against the old West Gate, represents one of Britain's best-preserved examples of domestic Elizabethan architecture. It was established as a hostel for old soldiers by Robert Dudley, Earl of Leicester – a favourite of Queen Elizabeth I – and incorporates several beamed buildings, principally the Great Hall and the Guildhall, as well as a wonderful galleried courtyard and an intimate chantry chapel. There's a **tearoom** too, plus a modest regimental museum – appropriately enough as retired servicemen (and their wives) still live here.

St Mary's Church

Old Square • Daily: April–Oct 10am–6pm; Nov–March 10am–4.30pm • £2 donation suggested • ⓦ stmaryswarwick.org.uk

8

Near Castle Street is **St Mary's Church**, which was rebuilt in a weird Gothic-Renaissance amalgam after the fire of 1694. Most of the chancel, however, remained untouched – and it's a simply glorious illustration of the Perpendicular style with a splendid vaulted ceiling of flying and fronded ribs. On the right-hand side of the chancel is the **Beauchamp Chantry Chapel**, which contains the equally beautiful tomb of Richard Beauchamp, Earl of Warwick, who is depicted in an elaborate, gilded-bronze suit of armour of Italian design from the tip of his swan helmet down to his mailed feet. A griffin and a bear guard Richard, who lies with his hands half joined in prayer so that, on the Resurrection, his first sight would be of Christ triumphant at the Second Coming. The adjacent tomb of Ambrose Dudley is of finely carved and painted alabaster, as is that of Robert Dudley and his wife – the same Dudley who founded the **Lord Leycester Hospital** (see above).

ARRIVAL AND INFORMATION — WARWICK

By train From Warwick train station, at the northern edge of town, it's about a 15min walk to the centre via Station and Coventry roads.

Destinations Birmingham Snow Hill (every 30min; 30min); Stratford-upon-Avon (every 2hr; 30min).

By bus Buses stop on Market St, close to the Market Place, from where it's a couple of minutes' walk east to St Mary's Church.

Tourist office In the old Courthouse, on the corner of Castle and Jury streets (Mon–Fri 9.30am–4.30pm, Sat 10am–4.30pm, Sun 10am–3.30pm; ⓣ 01926 492212, ⓦ visitwarwick.co.uk).

ACCOMMODATION

Although, with Stratford so near and easy to reach, there's no special reason to stay, the town does have one particularly good accommodation option.

Rose and Crown 30 Market Place ⓣ 01926 411117, ⓦ www.roseandcrownwarwick.co.uk. Part of a small and well-regarded pub chain, the *Rose and Crown* has five attractive guest rooms, all en suite, and each decorated in a bright and breezy contemporary style. They also serve good-quality bar food, which you can wash down with a prime selection of guest beers; mains cost anywhere between £10 and £16. **£80**

EATING

Catalan 6 Jury St ⓣ 01926 498930, ⓦ cafecatalan.com. This slick and modern café-restaurant, which offers tasty tapas and light lunches during the day, and Mediterranean-inspired food at night, is the cream of Warwick's gastronomic crop. Tapas (at lunch and until 7.30pm), like the chorizo sausage cooked in red wine, average around £5, à la carte main courses £17. Mon–Fri noon–3pm & 6–10.30pm, Sat noon–10.30pm.

COVENTRY CATHEDRAL

At the outbreak of World War II, **COVENTRY**, eleven miles north of Warwick, was a major engineering centre and its factories attracted the attentions of the Luftwaffe, who well-nigh levelled the town in a huge bombing raid on November 14, 1940. Out of the ashes arose what is now Coventry's one sight of note, Basil Spence's **St Michael's Cathedral** (Mon–Sat 9am–5pm, Sun noon–3.45pm; £4.50, free on Sun; ⓦ coventrycathedral.org.uk), raised alongside the burnt-out shell of the old cathedral right in the centre of town and dedicated with a performance of Benjamin Britten's specially written *War Requiem* in 1962. One of the country's most successful postwar buildings, the cathedral's pink sandstone is light and graceful, the main entrance adorned by a stunningly forceful *St Michael Defeating the Devil* by Jacob Epstein. Inside, Spence's high and slender nave is bathed in light from the soaring stained-glass windows, a perfect setting for the magnificent and immense **tapestry** of *Christ in Glory* by **Graham Sutherland**. The choice of artist could not have been more appropriate. A painter, graphic artist and designer, Sutherland (1903–80) had been one of Britain's official war artists, his particular job being to record the effects of German bombing. A canopied walkway links the new cathedral with the old, whose shattered nave flanks the church tower and spire that somehow eluded the bombs.

Worcester

8

In geographical terms, **Worcestershire** can be compared to a huge saucer, with the low-lying plains of the Severn Valley and the Vale of Evesham, Britain's foremost fruit-growing area, rising to a lip of hills, principally the Malverns in the west and the Cotswolds (see pp.240–248) to the south. In character, the county divides into two broad belts. To the north lie the industrial and overspill towns – Droitwich and Redditch for instance – that have much in common with the Birmingham conurbation, while the south is predominantly rural. Bang at the geographical heart of the county is **WORCESTER**, an amenable county town where a liberal helping of half-timbered Tudor and handsome Georgian buildings stand cheek by jowl with some fairly charmless modern developments. The biggest single influence on the city has always been the **River Severn**, which flows along Worcester's west flank. It was the river that made the city an important settlement as early as Saxon times, though its propensity to breach its banks has prompted the construction of a battery of defences which tumble down the slope from the mighty bulk of the **cathedral**, easily the town's star turn. Worcester's centre is small and compact – and, handily, all the key sights plus the best restaurants are clustered within the immediate vicinity of the cathedral.

Worcester Cathedral

Daily 7.30am–6pm • Free • ⓣ 01905 732900, ⓦ worcestercathedral.co.uk

Towering above the River Severn, the soaring sandstone of **Worcester Cathedral** comprises a rich stew of architectural styles dating from 1084. The bulk of the church is firmly medieval, from the Norman transepts through to the late Gothic cloister, though the Victorians did have a good old hack at the exterior. Inside, the highlight is the thirteenth-century **choir**, a beautiful illustration of the Early English style, with a forest of slender pillars rising above the intricately worked choir stalls. Here also, in front of the high altar, is the **table tomb** of England's most reviled monarch, **King John** (1167–1216), who certainly would not have appreciated the lion that lies at his feet biting the end of his sword – a reference to the curbing of his power by the barons when they obliged him to sign the Magna Carta. Just beyond the tomb – on the right – is **Prince Arthur's Chantry**, a delicate lacy confection of carved stonework erected in 1504 to commemorate Arthur, King Henry VII's son, who died at the age of 15. He was on his honeymoon with Catherine of Aragon, who was soon passed on – with such momentous consequences – to his younger brother, Henry. A doorway on the south side of the nave leads to the **cloisters**, with their delightful roof bosses, and the circular, largely Norman **chapter house**, which has the distinction of being the first such building constructed with the use of a central supporting pillar.

Worcester Porcelain Museum

Severn St • Easter to Oct Mon–Sat 10am–5pm; Oct–Easter Tues–Sat 10.30am–4pm • £6 • ⊕ 01905 21247, ⊕ worcesterporcelainmuseum.org

There was a time when Severn Street, tucked away just to the south of the cathedral, hummed with the activity of one of England's largest porcelain factories, **Royal Worcester**. Those days ended, however, when the company hit the skids and was finally rolled up in 2008 after more than one hundred and fifty years in production. The old factory complex is currently being turned into apartments, but the **Worcester Porcelain Museum** has survived, exhibiting a comprehensive collection of the ornate, indeed fancifully ornate, porcelain for which Royal Worcester was famous.

The Commandery

Sidbury • Easter–Oct Mon–Sat 10am–5pm, Sun 1.30–5pm; Nov to Easter closed Fri • £5.40 • ⊕ worcestercitymuseums.org.uk

Occupying Worcester's oldest building, a rambling, half-timbered structure dating from the early sixteenth century, the **Commandery**, on the far side of the busy Sidbury dual carriageway, is the town's main history museum. The building itself is historically important: **King Charles II** used it as his headquarters during the battle-cum-siege of Worcester in 1651, the end game of his unsuccessful attempt to regain the throne from Cromwell and the Parliamentarians, who had executed his father – King Charles I – in 1649. The high point inside is the **painted chamber**, whose walls are covered with intriguing cameos recalling the building's original use as a monastery hospital. Each relates to a saint with healing powers – for example St Thomas à Becket is shown being stabbed in the head by a group of knights, which was enough to make him the patron saint for headaches.

Greyfriars

Friar St • March to mid-Dec Tues–Sat 1–5pm • NT • £4.35 • ⊕ 01905 23571, ⊕ nationaltrust.org.uk

From the Commandery, it's a short step northwest along Sidbury to narrow **Friar Street**, whose hotchpotch of half-timbered houses and small, independent shops make it Worcester's prettiest thoroughfare. Among the buildings is **Greyfriars**, a largely fifteenth-century townhouse whose wonky timbers and dark-stained panelling shelter a charming collection of antiques. There's an attractive walled garden here too. From Greyfriars, it's a couple of minutes' walk west to the High Street, a couple more back to the cathedral.

ARRIVAL AND INFORMATION — WORCESTER

By train Worcester has two main train stations. The handiest for the city centre is Foregate Street, from where it's about half a mile south to the cathedral along Foregate St and its continuation The Cross and then High St. The other train station, Shrub Hill, is further out, about a mile to the northeast of the cathedral.

Destinations Worcester Foregate to: Birmingham Moor St (every 30min; 1hr); Hereford (hourly; 50min).

By bus The bus station at the back of the sprawling Crowngate shopping mall on The Butts, about six hundred yards northwest of the cathedral.

Tourist office Guildhall, towards the cathedral end of the High St (Mon–Sat 9.30am–5pm; ⊕ 01905 726311, ⊕ visitworcester.com).

ACCOMMODATION

Barrington House B&B 204 Henwick Rd ⊕ 01905 422965, ⊕ barringtonhouse.eu. Occupying an immaculately restored Georgian property right by the river about a mile north of the centre along the A443 – and across the river from Worcester Racecourse – this is the best B&B in town. It comes with a large garden and has three en-suite guest rooms decorated in a broadly period style. Tasty breakfasts too. **£80**

Diglis House Hotel Severn St ⓣ01905 353518, ⓦdiglishousehotel.co.uk. Family-owned hotel in an attractive Georgian villa beside the river, about 5min walk south of the cathedral at the end of Severn St. Most of the 28 guest rooms have been revamped in a pleasant version of country-house style, but the hotel's prime feature is the large conservatory overlooking the river. **£110**

EATING AND DRINKING

Browns South Quay St ⓣ01905 26263, ⓦwww.brownsrestaurant.co.uk. Worcester's best restaurant, a smart, modern place in a handsomely converted old grain mill down by the river just west of High St. The menu is Modern British, featuring the likes of lamb with pea and mint risotto, and main courses cost around £15 at night, much less at lunch, when they also do sandwiches (noon–5.30pm). You can drink here too – the bar is open daily from 10am till late. Food served daily noon–2.30pm & 6–10pm.

The Glasshouse 55 Sidbury ⓣ01905 611120, ⓦtheglasshouse.co.uk. Informal, brasserie-style place in a glass and steel block in between the cathedral and The Commandery. They probably try to cover too many gastronomic bases, but the deluxe fish and chips, for one, are very good. Doubles up as a lounge bar too. Food served Mon–Sat noon–3pm & 5.30–11pm, last orders 8.45pm.

The Malvern Hills

One of the more prosperous parts of the West Midlands, **The Malverns** is the generic name for a string of towns and villages stretched along the eastern lower slopes of the **Malvern Hills**, which rise spectacularly out of the flatlands a few miles to the southwest of Worcester. About nine miles from north to south – between the A44 and the M50 – and never more than five miles wide, the hills straddle the Worcestershire–Herefordshire boundary. Of ancient granite rock, they are punctuated by over twenty summits, mostly around 1000ft high, and in between lie innumerable dips and hollows. It's easy, if energetic, walking country, with great views, and there's an excellent network of **hiking trails**, most of which can be completed in a day or half-day with **Great Malvern** being the obvious base.

8

Great Malvern

Of all the towns in the Malverns, it's **GREAT MALVERN** that grabs the attention, its pocket-sized centre clambering up the hillside with the crags of North Hill beckoning beyond. The grand but often rather faded old houses, which congregate on and around the top of the main drag, **Church Street**, mostly date from Great Malvern's nineteenth-century heyday as a spa town when the local **spring waters** drew the Victorians here by the train load. You can still sample the waters today (see p.388), but the town's principal sight is its splendid **Priory Church**, close to the top of Church Street (daily 9am–5pm; free; ⓦgreatmalvernpriory.org.uk). The Benedictines built one of their abbeys here at Great Malvern and, although Henry VIII closed the place down in 1538, the elaborate decoration witnesses the priory's former wealth. Inside, the Norman nave sweeps down to the chancel, which came later, a fine example of Perpendicular Gothic, its sinuous tracery serving to frame a simply fabulous set of late medieval **stained-glass windows**.

HIKING THE MALVERN HILLS

Great Malvern tourist office (see p.388) sells hiking maps and issues half a dozen free **Trail Guide leaflets**, which describe circular routes up to and along the hills that rise behind the town. The shortest trail is just one and a half miles, the longest four. One of the most appealing is the 2.5-mile hoof up to the top – and back – of **North Hill** (1307ft), from where there are panoramic views over the surrounding countryside; this hike also takes in *St Ann's Well Café*, where you can taste the local spring water (see p.388).

TAKING THE GREAT MALVERN WATERS

The gushing **Malvhina spring** in the mini-park at the top of Church Street is the obvious and certainly the most convenient way to taste Great Malvern's waters. There's also a spring at **St Ann's Well Café**, a sweet little café in an attractive Georgian building a steep 25-minute walk up the wooded hillside from town (normally Easter to June & Sept Tues–Sun 10am–4pm; July & Aug daily 10am–4pm; Oct to Easter Fri 11.30am–3.30pm, Sat & Sun 10am–4pm; but call ⓣ01684 560285 or go to ⓦhillsarts.co.uk/stannswell to check opening times); the signposted path begins beside the *Mount Pleasant Hotel*, on Belle Vue Terrace, just to the left (south) of the top of Church Street.

ARRIVAL AND INFORMATION — GREAT MALVERN

By train From Great Malvern's rustic train station, with its dainty ironwork and quaint chimneys, it's about half a mile to the town centre – take Avenue Rd, which leads to Church St, the steeply sloping main drag.

Tourist office At the top of Church St, across from the Priory Church (daily 10am–5pm; ⓣ01684 892289, ⓦvisitthemalverns.org).

ACCOMMODATION

The Abbey Abbey Rd ⓣ01684 892332, ⓦsarova.com. Easily the most conspicuous hotel in Great Malvern, a few yards from the tourist office, much of it occupying a rambling, creeper-clad Victorian building executed in a sort of neo-Baronial style. It's part of a small chain, and the guest rooms, especially in the hotel's lumpy modern wing, can be a little characterless – they are comfortable enough, though, and some have attractive views back over town. £90

The Copper Beech House 32 Avenue Rd ⓣ01684 565013, ⓦcopperbeechhouse.co.uk. The best of the town's several B&Bs, in a large Victorian family home near the train station. The eight en-suite guest rooms range from large and plush to small and slightly plain. £50

EATING AND DRINKING

Great Malvern Deli 11 Abbey Rd ⓣ01684 899091. A combined shop and café just a few paces from the top of Church St, where they serve, among many other things, great ham salad sandwiches, fresh soup and delicious home-made cakes. Mon 9.30am–3pm, Tues–Sat 9.30am–5pm (food served till 4.30pm only).

The Morgan 52 Clarence Rd ⓣ01684 578575, ⓦwyevalleybrewery.co.uk. Near the train station, this is the best pub in town, where you can sample the assorted brews of Herefordshire's much-praised Wye Valley Brewery. Drink outside on the terrace if the sun is out, or inside in the wood-panelled bar. Mon–Sat noon–3pm & 5–11.30pm, Sun noon–3pm & 6.30–11.30pm.

Pepper & Oz 23 Abbey Rd ⓣ01684 562676, ⓦpepperandoz.co.uk. Lively, informal place, just a few yards up from the priory, which does a tasty line in Italian dishes and more than fifty wines by the glass. Mains average out at about £11. Tues–Sat noon–3.30pm & 5.30–11pm.

Herefordshire

Over the Malvern Hills from Worcestershire, the rolling agricultural landscapes of **Herefordshire** have an easy-going charm, but the finest scenery hereabouts is along the banks of the **River Wye**, which wriggles and worms its way across the county. Plonked in the middle of Herefordshire on the Wye is the county town, **Hereford**, a sleepy, rather old-fashioned place whose proudest possession, the cathedral's remarkable **Mappa Mundi** map, was almost flogged off in a round of ecclesiastical budget cuts back in the 1980s. Beyond Hereford, the southeast corner of the county has one especially attractive town, **Ross-on-Wye**, a genial little place with a picturesque setting that also serves as a convenient gateway to one of the wilder portions of the **Wye River Valley**, around **Symonds Yat**, where canoeists gather in their droves.

GETTING AROUND — HEREFORDSHIRE

By train Herefordshire possesses one rail line, linking Ledbury and Hereford with points north to Shrewsbury and east to Great Malvern and Worcester.

By bus The county's buses provide a reasonable service

between the villages and towns, except on Sundays when there's very little at all. All the local tourist offices have bus timetables and there's local bus information on ⓣ 0870 608 2608 and ⓦ herefordshire-buses.tbctimes.co.uk.

Hereford

The low-key county town of **HEREFORD** was long a border garrison town held against the Welsh, its military importance guaranteed by its strategic position beside the River Wye. Today, with the fortifications that once girdled the city all but vanished, it's the **cathedral** – and its extraordinary medieval **Mappa Mundi** – that catches the attention, lying just to the north of the river and at the heart of the city centre, whose compact tangle of narrow streets and squares is clumsily boxed in by the ring road. Taken as a whole, Hereford makes for a pleasant overnight stay, especially as it possesses a particularly fine hotel.

Hereford Cathedral

Daily 9.15am–5.30pm • £5 donation suggested • ⓣ 01432 374202, ⓦ herefordcathedral.org

Hereford Cathedral is a curious building, an uncomfortable amalgamation of styles, with bits and pieces added to the eleventh-century original by a string of bishops and culminating in an extensive – and not especially sympathetic – Victorian refit. From the outside, the sandstone **tower** is the dominant feature, constructed in the early fourteenth century to eclipse the Norman western tower, which subsequently collapsed under its own weight in 1786. The crashing masonry mauled the **nave** and its replacement lacks the grandeur of most other English cathedrals, though the forceful symmetries of the long rank of surviving Norman arches and piers more than hint at what went before. The **north transept** is, however, a flawless exercise in thirteenth-century taste, its soaring windows a classic example of Early English architecture.

8

The Mappa Mundi

Mon–Sat: Easter–Oct 10am–5pm; Nov–Easter 10am–4pm, but some closures for maintenance in Jan • £6

In the 1980s, the cathedral's finances were so parlous that a plan was drawn up to sell its most treasured possession, the **Mappa Mundi**. Luckily, the government and John Paul Getty Jr rode to the rescue, with the oil tycoon stumping up a million pounds to keep the map here and install it in a new building, the New Library, which blends in seamlessly with the older buildings it adjoins at the west end of the cloisters.

The exhibit sets off with a series of interpretative panels explaining the historical background to – and the composition of – the Mappa. Included is a copy of the Mappa in English, which is particularly helpful as the original, which is displayed in a dimly lit room just beyond, is in Latin. Measuring 64 by 52 inches and dating to about 1300, the Mappa provides an extraordinary insight into medieval society. It is indeed a map (as we know it) in so far as it suggests the general geography of the world – with Asia at the top and Europe and Africa below, to left and right respectively – but it also squeezes in history, mythology and theology.

In the same building as the Mappa Mundi is the **Chained Library**, a remarkably extensive collection of books and manuscripts dating from the eighth to the eighteenth century. A selection is always open on display.

Hereford Museum and Art Gallery

Broad St • Tues–Fri 10am–5pm, Sat 10am–4pm • Free • ⓣ 01432 260692, ⓦ herefordshire.gov.uk

After the Mappa, Hereford's other attractions can't help but seem rather pedestrian. Nonetheless, the **Hereford Museum and Art Gallery**, in a flamboyant Victorian building opposite the cathedral on Broad Street, does hold a mildly diverting collection of geological remains and local memorabilia spruced up by temporary art exhibitions.

ARRIVAL AND INFORMATION — HEREFORD

By train From Hereford train station, it's about half a mile southwest to the main square, High Town, via Station Approach, Commercial Rd and its continuation Commercial St.

Destinations Birmingham (hourly; 1hr 30min); Great Malvern (hourly; 30min); Ludlow (every 30min; 30min); Shrewsbury (every 30min; 1hr); Worcester (hourly; 40min).

By bus The long-distance bus station is on the northeast side of the town centre, just off Commercial Rd. There's a reasonably good bus service from here to Ross-on-Wye (Mon–Sat hourly, Sun 5 daily; 45min).

Tourist office 1 King St, opposite the cathedral (April–Sept daily 9.30am–4.30pm, Oct–March Mon–Fri 10am–4.30pm; T 01432 268430, W visitherefordshire.co.uk).

ACCOMMODATION AND EATING

Cafe@allsaints Broad St T 01432 370415. Near the cathedral, in the old church at the top of Broad Street, this excellent café serves a range of well-conceived and tasty veggie dishes – ricotta pie with salad leaves for instance – at around £8. Mon–Sat 8am–5pm.

★ **Castle House** Castle St T 01432 356321, W castlehse.co.uk. Occupying an immaculately refurbished Georgian mansion not far from the cathedral, it's hard to praise this hotel too highly: the staff are very obliging; the rooms are delightful, with all sorts of period details; and the breakfast room has a lovely outside terrace beside what was originally the town moat. It is also the smartest restaurant in town, with an emphasis on local ingredients – Hereford beef and Gloucestershire pork for instance – and main courses start at £15. You can also eat in a more relaxed fashion in the bar. Food served daily noon–2pm & 6.30–9.30pm (9pm on Sun). £190

Charades 34 Southbank Rd T 01432 269444, W charadeshereford.co.uk. One of Hereford's best B&Bs, with fifteen comfortable, en-suite guest rooms in a large Victorian house a 10- to 15min walk northeast from the centre. £70

8

DRINKING

Don't leave Hereford without sampling the favourite local tipple, **cider**; every pub in town serves it.

The Barrels 69 St Owen's St T 01432 274968, W wyevalleybrewery.co.uk. A popular local just five minutes' walk southeast of High Town, *The Barrels* is the home pub of the local Wye Valley Brewery, whose trademark bitters are much acclaimed. Mon–Thurs 11am–11.30pm, Fri & Sat 11am–midnight, Sun noon–11.30pm.

Ross-on-Wye

The small market town of **ROSS-ON-WYE**, nestling above a loop in the river sixteen miles southeast of Hereford, is a relaxed and easy-going place with an artsy/New Age undertow. Ross's jumble of narrow streets converges on the **Market Place**, which is shadowed by the seventeenth-century **Market House**, a sturdy two-storey sandstone structure that sports a medallion bust of a bewigged Charles II. Veer right at the top of the Market Place, then turn left up Church Street to reach Ross's other noteworthy building, the mostly thirteenth-century **St Mary's Church**, whose sturdy stonework culminates in a slender, tapering spire. In front of the church, at the foot of the graveyard, is a plain but rare **Plague Cross**, commemorating the three hundred or so townsfolk who were buried here by night without coffins during a savage outbreak of the plague in 1637.

ARRIVAL AND INFORMATION — ROSS-ON-WYE

By bus There are no trains to Ross, but the bus station is handily located on Cantilupe Rd, from where it's a couple of minutes' walk west to the Market Place.

Tourist office Market House, on the Market Place, right in the centre of town (Wed–Mon: April–Sept 10.30am–4.30pm; Oct–March 10.30am–4pm; T 01432 260675, W visitherefordshire.co.uk).

ACCOMMODATION

★ **Linden House** 14 Church St T 01989 565373, W lindenguesthouse.com. In a fetching, three-storey Georgian building opposite St Mary's Church, this B&B has three, en-suite guest rooms, each of which is cosily decorated, and a self-catering holiday apartment on the top floor. The breakfasts are delicious too – both traditional and vegetarian. £66

Old Court House B&B 53 High St T 01989 762275,

Ⓦwyenot.com. An unusual B&B in so far as it occupies a rabbit warren of an old stone building, complete with open fires and exposed wooden beams. Handily located in the centre of the town. **£80**

EATING

Nature's Choice 17 Broad St Ⓣ01989 763454. Just north of the Market Place, this pleasant little café-restaurant sells a tasty range of snacks and light meals during the day, and more substantial dinners on Saturday nights. The emphasis is on health foods, locally sourced. Be sure to leave room for the home-made cakes. Mon–Fri 9.30am–5pm, Sat 9.30am–10pm, Sun 10am–4pm.

Yaks N Yetis 1 Brookend St Ⓣ01989 564963. Not the prettiest of restaurants perhaps, but this is genuine Nepalese (Ghurkha) cuisine, make no mistake – and the staff are more than willing to help explain its intricacies. It's delicious and, with mains from around £7, economically priced too. Brookend is a continuation of Broad Street, which runs north from the Market Place. Tues–Sun noon–2.30pm & 6–11pm.

The Wye River Valley

Travelling south from Ross along the B4234, it's just five miles to the sullen sandstone mass of **Goodrich Castle** (April–June, Sept & Oct daily 10am–5pm; July & Aug daily 10am–6pm; Nov–March Wed–Sun 10am–4pm; EH; £5.80; Ⓦenglish-heritage.org.uk), which commands wide views over the hills and woods of the **Wye River Valley**. The castle's strategic location guaranteed its importance as a border stronghold from the twelfth century onwards and today the substantial ruins incorporate a Norman keep, a maze of later rooms and passageways and walkable ramparts. The castle stands next to the tiny village of **GOODRICH**, from where it's around a mile and half southeast along narrow country lanes to the solitary *Welsh Bicknor Hostel* (see below), which, with the **Wye Valley Walk** running past the front door, makes a great base (in a no-frills sort of way) for **hikers**.

8

From Goodrich, it's a couple of miles south along narrow country lanes to a fork in the road – veer right for Symonds Yat East, or keep straight for the wriggly road up to the top of **Symonds Yat Rock**, one of the region's most celebrated viewpoints, rising high above a wooded, hilly loop in the River Wye. Down below is **SYMONDS YAT EAST**, a pretty little hamlet that straggles along the east bank of the river. It's a popular spot and one that offers canoe rental and regular **river trips** (40min) – and there's a good hotel here too (see below).

The road to the village is a dead end, so you have to double back to regain Goodrich (or Symonds Yat Rock), though you can cross the river to **Symonds Yat West** by means of a hand-pulled rope **ferry** (£1), which leaves from outside the *Saracen's Head Inn* (see below).

ACCOMMODATION AND EATING — THE WYE RIVER VALLEY

Camping There's a riverside caravan and camping park at Symonds Yat West (Ⓣ07969 078436, Ⓦriverwyecamping.com), and another rather more attractive campsite, the Doward Park Campsite (Ⓣ01600 890438 , Ⓦdowardpark.co.uk), in a wooded location a mile or two to the west.

Saracens Head Inn Symonds Yat East Ⓣ01600 890345, Ⓦsaracensheadinn.co.uk. There are ten en-suite guest rooms in this village hotel beside the River Wye, each decorated in pleasant modern style with wooden floors and pastel-painted walls. You can eat well both in the restaurant and in the bar, with the menu featuring English and Italian favourites with mains averaging £15. Food served daily noon–2.30pm & 6.30–9pm. **£89**

Welsh Bicknor YHA Hostel Near Goodrich Ⓣ0845 3719666, Ⓔwelshbicknor@yha.org.uk. If you're after a remote location, this is the hostel to head for – in a Victorian rectory in its own grounds above the River Wye. There are 76 beds, in anything from two- to ten-bed dorms, as well as camping facilities, and evening meals are provided on request. Open Easter to Oct. **£16.40**

Shropshire

One of England's largest and least populated counties, **Shropshire** (Ⓦshropshiretourism.co.uk) stretches from its long and winding border with Wales to the very edge of the urban Black Country. The Industrial Revolution made a huge stride forward here, with the spanning of the River Severn by the very first **iron bridge** and, although the assorted industries that subsequently squeezed into the **Ironbridge Gorge** are long gone, a series of **museums** celebrates their craftsmanship – from tiles through to iron. The River Severn also flows through the county town of **Shrewsbury**, whose antique centre holds dozens of old half-timbered buildings, though **Ludlow**, further south, has the edge when it comes to handsome Tudor and Jacobean architecture. In between the two lie some of the most beautiful parts of Shropshire, primarily the **Long Mynd**, a prime hiking area that is readily explored from the attractive little town of **Church Stretton**.

GETTING AROUND — SHROPSHIRE

By train There are frequent trains from Birmingham to Telford and Shrewsbury, which is also linked to Church Stretton and Ludlow on the Hereford line.

By bus Bus services are patchy, but one small step forward has been the creation of the Shropshire Hills Shuttle bus service (mid-April to Sept Sat & Sun only; every 1–2hr; ⓦ shropshirehillsshuttles.co.uk) aimed at the tourist market. The shuttle noses round the Long Mynd as well as the Stiperstones and drops by Church Stretton. An adult Day Rover ticket, valid on the whole route, costs just £7. Timetables are available at most Shropshire tourist offices and on the website.

Ironbridge Gorge

Ironbridge Gorge was the crucible of the Industrial Revolution, a process encapsulated by its famous span across the Severn – the world's first **iron bridge**, engineered by **Abraham Darby** and opened on New Year's Day, 1781. Darby was the third innovative industrialist of that name – the first Abraham Darby started iron-smelting here back in 1709 and the second invented the forging process that made it possible to produce massive single beams in iron. Under the guidance of such creative figures as the Darbys and Thomas Telford, the area's factories once churned out engines, rails, wheels and other heavy-duty iron pieces in quantities unmatched anywhere else in the world. Manufacturing has now all but vanished, but the surviving monuments make the Gorge the most extensive **industrial heritage site** in England – and one that has been granted World Heritage Site status by UNESCO.

The Gorge contains several museums and an assortment of other industrial attractions spread along a five-mile stretch of the Severn Valley just to the south of new-town Telford. A thorough exploration takes a couple of days, but the highlights – the **Iron**

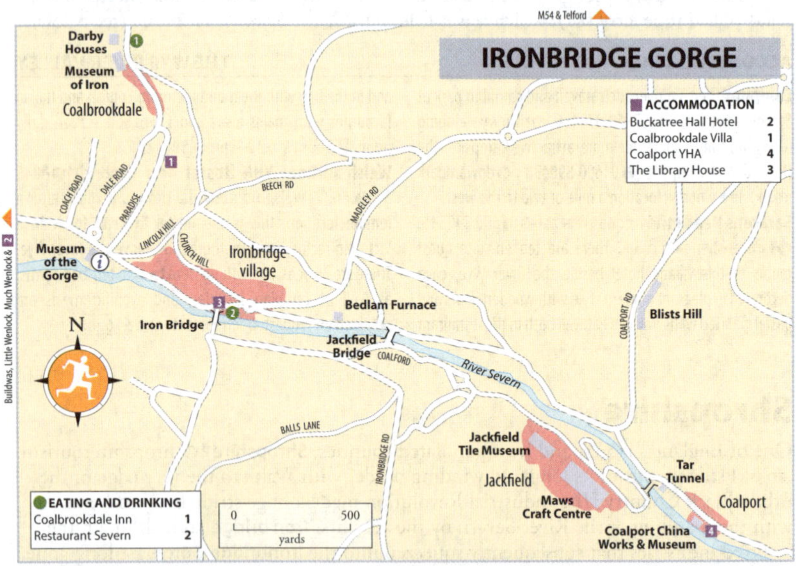

Bridge itself, the **Museum of Iron** and the **Jackfield Tile Museum** – are easily manageable on a day-trip.

Ironbridge village

There must have been an awful lot of nail-biting during the construction of the **iron bridge** over the River Severn in the late 1770s. No one was quite sure how the new material would wear and although the single-span design looked sound, many feared the bridge would simply tumble into the river. To compensate, Abraham Darby used more iron than was strictly necessary, but the end result still manages to appear stunningly graceful, arching between the steep banks with the river far below. The settlement at the north end of the span was promptly renamed **IRONBRIDGE**, and today its brown-brick houses climb prettily up the hill from the bridge.

The Museum of the Gorge

Daily 10am–5pm • £3.75, but covered by Passport Ticket (see p.394) • Ⓦ ironbridge.org.uk

Ironbridge village is also home to the **Museum of the Gorge**, in a church-like, neo-Gothic old riverside warehouse about 700 yards west of the bridge along the main road. This provides an introduction to the Gorge's industrial history and gives a few environmental pointers too; it also houses the main visitor centre (see p.394).

Coalbrookdale Museum of Iron

Coalbrookdale • Daily 10am–5pm • £7.60, but covered by Passport Ticket (see p.394) • Ⓦ ironbridge.org.uk

At the roundabout just to the **west** of the Museum of the Gorge, turn right for the half-mile trip up to what was once the Gorge's big industrial deal, the **Coalbrookdale iron foundry**, which boomed throughout the eighteenth and early nineteenth century, employing up to four thousand men and boys. The foundry has been imaginatively converted into the **Museum of Iron**, with a wide range of displays on iron-making in general and the history of the company in particular. There are superb examples of Victorian and Edwardian ironwork here, including the intricate castings – stags, dogs and even camels – that became the house speciality. Also in the complex, across from the foundry beneath a protective canopy, are the ruins of the **furnace** where Abraham Darby pioneered the use of coke as a smelting fuel in place of charcoal.

The Bedlam Furnace

As you head **east** from the Iron Bridge, it's a third of a mile along the river to the battered brick-and-stone remains of the **Bedlam furnace** (open access; free), one of the first furnaces to use coke rather than charcoal. It was kept alight around the clock, and at night its fiery silhouette was said to have scared passers-by out of their wits – hence the name.

Tar Tunnel

April–Oct daily 10.30am–4pm • £2.60, but covered by Passport Ticket (see p.394) • Ⓦ ironbridge.org.uk

From the Bedlam furnace, it's a mile to the turning for Blists Hill Victorian Town (see p.394) and another 500 yards or so to the **Tar Tunnel**, built to transport coal from one part of the Gorge to another, but named for the bitumen that oozes naturally from its walls.

Jackfield

Beside the Tar Tunnel, a **footbridge** crosses the Severn to reach the brown-brick cottages that make up the old centre of **JACKFIELD**, now a sleepy little village which strings along the river, but once a sooty, grimy place that hummed to the tune of two large tile factories, Maws and Craven Dunnill. Both were built in the middle of the nineteenth century to the latest industrial design, a fully integrated manufacturing system that produced literally thousands of tiles at breakneck speed. From the footbridge, it's a couple of minutes' walk west to the first of the two, now the **Maws Craft Centre** (Ⓦ mawscraftcentre.co.uk), which holds more than twenty arts, craft and specialist shops.

Jackfield Tile Museum

Jackfield • Daily 10am–5pm • £7.60, but covered by Passport Ticket (see below) • ironbridge.org.uk

From the Maws Craft Centre, it's about half a mile west to the former Craven Dunnill factory complex, a small part of which still produces Craven Dunnill tiles (cravendunnill.co.uk).

The complex is also home to the excellent **Jackfield Tile Museum**, whose exhibits include the superb "Style Gallery" and "Tiles Everywhere Galleries", where room after room illustrates many different types of tile, by style – Art Deco and Art Nouveau through to Arts and Crafts and the Aesthetic Movement – and location, from a London underground station to a butcher's shop.

Coalport China Museum

Coalport • Daily 10am–5pm • £7.60, but covered by Passport Ticket (see below) • ironbridge.org.uk

From the Tar Tunnel, a canal towpath leads east in a couple of minutes to **Coalport China works**, a large brick complex holding the **Coalport China Museum**, packed with gaudy Coalport wares. There's also a workshop, where potters demonstrate their skills, and two **bottle-kilns**, those distinctive conical structures that were long the hallmark of the pottery industry. In the base of one is a small display of Coalport pieces, whilst the other explains how the kilns worked – though quite how the firers survived the conditions defies the imagination.

Blists Hill Victorian Town

8

Daily 10am–5pm • £14.95, but covered by Passport Ticket (see below) • ironbridge.org.uk

Doubling back along the river, it's a third of a mile west from Coalport to the clearly signed, mile-long side road that cuts up to the Gorge's most popular attraction, the rambling **Blists Hill Victorian Town**. This encloses a substantial number of reconstructed Victorian buildings, most notably a school, a candle-maker's, a doctor's surgery, a pub, and wrought-iron works. Jam-packed on most summer days, it's especially popular with school parties, who keep the period-dressed employees busy.

ARRIVAL AND DEPARTURE — IRONBRIDGE GORGE

By bus Arriva bus #96 (arrivabus.co.uk) connects both Shrewsbury (30min) and Telford (15min) bus stations with Ironbridge village (Mon–Sat every 2hr).

GETTING AROUND

By bus The only connecting buses along the Gorge run at the weekend and on Bank Holidays (April–Oct only), when the Gorge Connect bus shuttles from Coalbrookdale in the west to Coalport in the east, taking in Ironbridge village and Blists Hill on the way (every 30min 9.30am–5pm). A day ticket costs £3; Passport Ticket holders (see below) travel free.

By bike You can rent bikes from the Bicycle Hub (Mon–Wed & Fri 10am–5pm, Thurs 10am–7pm, Sat 9am–6pm; 01952 883249, thebicyclehub.co.uk) in the same complex as the Jackfield Tile Museum (see above).

INFORMATION

Tourist office The Ironbridge Gorge Visitor Information Centre (Mon–Fri 9am–5pm, Sat & Sun 10am–5pm; 01952 884391, ironbridge.org.uk) is in the Museum of the Gorge, approximately 700 yards west of the bridge along the main road. In addition to local maps and information, the centre sells attraction passes.

Admissions and passes Each museum and attraction charges its own admission fee, but if you're intending to visit several, then buy a Passport Ticket (£22.50), which allows access to each of them once in any calendar year. Passport Tickets are available at all the main sights and at the Visitor Information Centre. An extra £1.50 buys you a ticket covering all the museum car parks for a day.

ACCOMMODATION

Most visitors to the Gorge come for the day, but there are a couple of pleasant **B&Bs** in Ironbridge village, which is where you want to be, and a number of interesting options nearby.

FROM TOP DAVID TENNANT AS HAMLET IN STRATFORD; MOORLANDS AROUND DERWENT, THE PEAK DISTRICT >

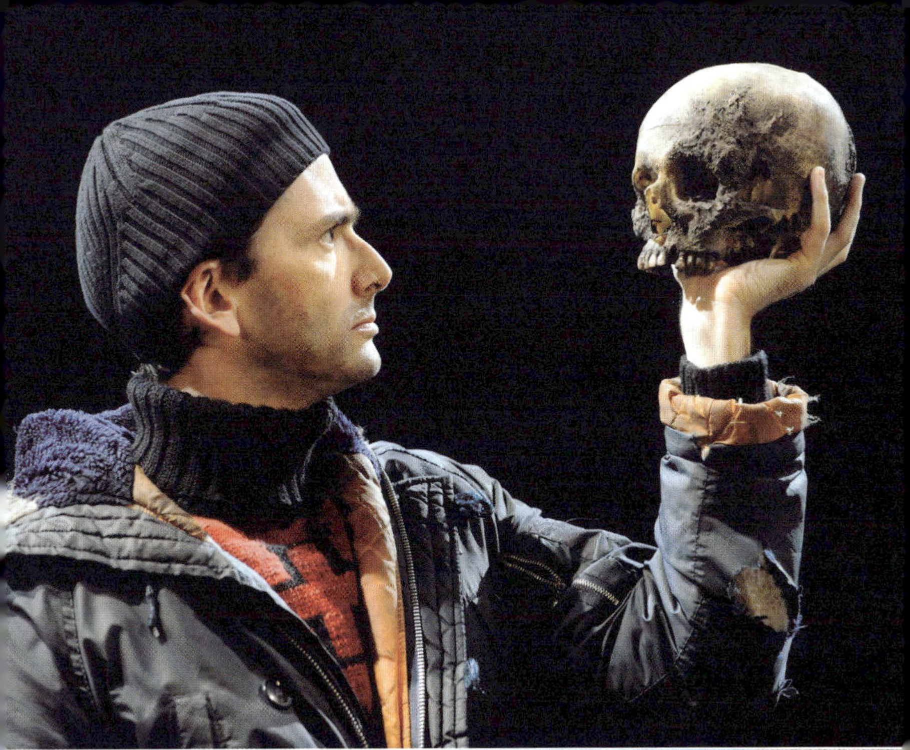

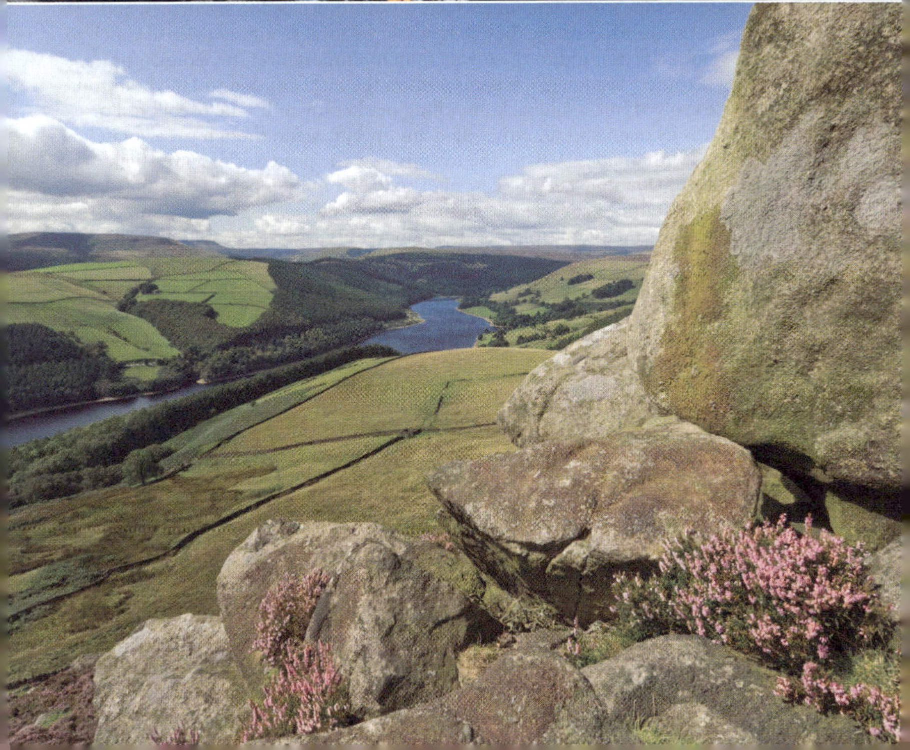

Buckatree Hall Hotel The Wrekin, Telford, just south of the M54 and Wellington T 01952 641821, W buckatreehallhotel.co.uk. In a pleasant rural setting near the wooded slopes of The Wrekin, the distinctive 1334ft peak that rises high above its surroundings, the *Buckatree* comprises the original Edwardian house and a modern annexe-wing. Most of the comfortable rooms have balconies. £90

Coalbrookdale Villa 17 Paradise, Coalbrookdale T 01952 433450, W coalbrookdalevilla.co.uk. This B&B occupies an attractive Victorian ironmaster's house set in its own grounds about half a mile up the hill from Ironbridge village in the tiny hamlet of Paradise. Sedately decorated, country-house-style, en-suite bedrooms. £70

Coalport YHA Coalport T 0845 3719325, E ironbridge@yha.org.uk. At the east end of the Gorge in the former Coalport China factory, this YHA hostel has 80 beds in two- to ten-bedded rooms, self-catering facilities, laundry, a shop and a café. Dorm £10, double £20

The Library House 11 Severn Bank, Ironbridge village T 01952 432299, W libraryhouse.com. Enjoyable B&B, the best in the village, in a charming Georgian villa just yards from the Iron Bridge. Four doubles, decorated in a modern rendition of period style. £80

EATING AND DRINKING

Coalbrookdale Inn Wellington Rd T 01952 433953, W coalbrookdaleinn.co.uk. On the main road across from the Coalbrookdale iron foundry, this traditional pub offers a top-notch selection of real ales plus filling pub grub, both in the bar and in its restaurant (mains from about £14). Mon–Thurs noon–2pm & 5–11.30pm, Fri–Sun noon–11.30pm; food served Mon–Sat noon–2pm & 6–9pm, Sun noon–2pm.

Restaurant Severn 33 High St T 01952 432233, W restaurantseven.co.uk. This smart little place, just a few yards from the bridge, offers an inventive menu with main courses such as venison in a cognac and cranberry sauce. In the evening, a two-course set meal costs around £25. Wed–Sat 6.30–8.30pm, Sun noon–1.30pm.

Shrewsbury

SHREWSBURY, the county town of Shropshire, sits in a tight and narrow loop of the River Severn. It would be difficult to design a better defensive site and predictably the Normans built a stone castle here, one which Edward I decided to strengthen and expand in the thirteenth century, though by then the local economy owed as much to the Welsh wool trade as it did to the town's military importance. In Georgian times, Shrewsbury became a fashionable staging post on the busy London to Holyhead route and has since evolved into a laidback, middling market town. It's the overall feel of the place that is its main appeal, rather than any specific sight, though to celebrate its associations with **Charles Darwin**, the town is now the possessor of a 40ft-high sculpture entitled **Quantum Leap**: it cost nigh-on half a million pounds, so most locals are ruing the cost rather than celebrating the artistic vision.

The logical place to start an exploration of Shrewsbury is the **train station**, built in a fetching combination of styles, neo-Baronial meets country house, in the 1840s. Poking up above the train station are the battered ramparts of the **castle**, a pale reminder of the mighty medieval fortress that once dominated the town – the illustrious Thomas Telford turned the castle into the private home of a local bigwig in the 1780s. **Castle Gates** and its continuation **Castle Street/Pride Hill** cuts up from the station into the heart of the river loop where the medieval town took root. Turn left off Castle Street onto St Mary's Street and you soon reach Shrewsbury's most interesting church, **St Mary's**, whose architecturally jumbled interior is redeemed by a magnificent east window. From St Mary's, it's a couple of minutes walk to **St Alkmund's Church**, from where there's a charming view of the fine old buildings of **Fish Street**, which weaves its way down to the High Street. Turn right here to get to The Square which is at the very heart of the city; its narrow confines are inhabited by the **Old Market Hall**, a heavy-duty stone structure dating from 1596.

ARRIVAL AND INFORMATION — SHREWSBURY

By train Shrewsbury train station stands at the northeast end of the town centre.

Destinations Birmingham (every 30min; 1hr); Church Stretton (every 30min; 15min); Hereford (hourly; 1hr); Ludlow (hourly; 30min); Telford (every 30min; 20min).

By bus Long-distance buses pull into the Raven Meadows

bus station, off the Smithfield Rd, a 5min walk north of The Square.

Tourist office The permanent home of the tourist office is right in the centre of town on The Square, but until 2012, when its premises will have been converted into an information centre and museum, it has been moved to Rowley's House, on Barker St (Oct–April Mon–Sat 10am–5pm; May–Sept Mon–Sat 10am–5pm, Sun 10am–4pm; T 01743 281200, W visitshrewsbury.com).

ACCOMMODATION AND EATING

Good Life Wholefood Restaurant Barracks Passage, just off 73 Wyle Cop T 01743 350455. The best café in town, specializing in salads and vegetarian dishes. Mains around £7. Mon–Sat 9.30am–4pm.

Mad Jack's 15 St Mary's St T 01743 358870, W madjacks.uk.com. There are just four en-suite guest rooms here, each decorated in a slick, modern style. It's also home to Shrewsbury's finest restaurant, a smart little place with an outside terrace serving a wide range of English dishes, from lamb to mussels, with due emphasis on local, seasonal ingredients. Mains around £13. Food served daily 10am–10pm. **£80**

Prince Rupert Hotel Butcher Row, off Pride Hill T 01743 499955, W prince-rupert-hotel.co.uk. Probably the smartest hotel in Shrewsbury, the *Rupert* occupies a cannily converted old building in the middle of the town centre. There are seventy bedrooms and although some are a tad fussy – ornate canopies and so forth – they are undeniably comfortable. **£105**

Tudor House B&B 2 Fish St T 01743 351735, W tudorhouseshrewsbury.com. Cosy B&B with a handful of rooms in an ancient half-timbered house in the heart of the town. The rooms are small, but kitted out with care and attention to detail. **£79**

The Long Mynd

8

Beginning about nine miles south of Shrewsbury, the upland heaths of the **Long Mynd**, some ten miles long and between two and four miles wide, run parallel to and just to the west of the A49. This is prime **walking** territory and the heathlands are latticed with footpaths, the pick of which offer sweeping views over the border to the Black Mountains of Wales. Also popular with hikers, if even more remote, are the **Stiperstones**, a clot of boggy heather dotted with ancient cairns and earthworks that lies to the west of the Long Mynd.

Church Stretton

Nestled at the foot of the Mynd beside the A49 is **CHURCH STRETTON**, a tidy little village that makes an ideal base for hiking the area. The village also possesses the dinky parish **church of St Laurence**, parts of which – especially the nave and transepts – are Norman. Look out also for the (badly weathered) fertility symbol over the side door, just to the left of the entrance – it's a genital-splaying **sheela-na-gig**, whose sheer explicitness comes as something of a surprise.

ARRIVAL AND INFORMATION — **CHURCH STRETTON**

By train Church Stretton train station is beside the A49 about 600 yards east of High St, which is the heart of the village.

Destinations Hereford (every 1hr–1hr 30min; 40min); Ludlow (every 1hr–1hr 30min; 15min); Shrewsbury (every 1hr–1hr 30min; 15min).

By bus Most buses pull in beside the train station, but some also continue on to High St. See p.392 for information on the Shropshire Hills Shuttle bus service.

Tourist office Church St, immediately west of High St (April–Sept Mon–Sat 9.30am–5pm; Oct–March Mon–Sat 9.30am–12.30pm & 1.30–5pm; T 01694 723133, W churchstretton.co.uk).

ACCOMMODATION

Bridges Long Mynd Youth Hostel 5 miles west of Church Stretton on the edge of Ratlinghope T 01588 650656. On the edge of a tiny village, this hostel occupies a converted village school, has 37 beds in two- to ten-bedded rooms, a café, camping and a self-catering kitchen. It's a great base for hiking to the Long Mynd or the Stiperstones. **£13**

Victoria House 48 High St T 01694 723823, W bedandbreakfast-shropshire.co.uk. There are several excellent B&Bs in and around Church Stretton, but this is the most central, an extraordinarily cosy little place with six guest rooms above the owners' teashop. The rooms are kitted out with heavy drapes, thick carpets and iron beds; the breakfasts are simply delicious too. **£55**

EATING

Berry's Coffee House 17 High St ⓣ01694 7224452, ⓦberryscoffeehouse.co.uk. This is the dinkiest of (licensed) cafés, squeezed into antique premises in the centre of the village. They serve delicious salads and light meals during the daytime, diversifying into full dinners on Friday and Saturday nights. Mon–Thurs 9am–5pm, Fri & Sat 9am–8.30pm, last orders 7.30pm.

The Studio 59 High St ⓣ01694 722672. The menu here at this intimate, family-run restaurant, Church Stretton's best, is a canny mix of French and English dishes with a two-course set menu costing £24. Reservations are well-nigh essential. Wed–Fri 7–8.30pm, Sat 6.30–9pm.

Ludlow

LUDLOW, perched on a hill in a loop of the River Teme nearly thirty miles south of Shrewsbury, is one of the most picturesque towns in the West Midlands, if not in England – a gaggle of beautifully preserved black-and-white half-timbered buildings packed around a craggy stone castle, with rural Shropshire forming a drowsy backdrop.

These are strong recommendations in themselves, but Ludlow scores even more by being something of a gastronomic hidey-hole with a clutch of outstanding **restaurants**, whose chefs and sous-chefs gather at the much-vaunted **Ludlow Food Festival** (ⓦfoodfestival.co.uk), held over three days every September. The other leading event is the Ludlow Festival (ⓣ01584 872150, ⓦludlowfestival.co.uk), two weeks of musical and theatrical fun running from the end of June to early July.

8

Ludlow Castle

Castle Square • Jan Sat & Sun 10am–4pm; Feb–July & Sept–Dec daily 10am–4/5pm; Aug daily 10am–7pm • £5 • ⓣ01584 873355, ⓦludlowcastle.com

Ludlow's large and imposing **castle** dates mostly from Norman times, its rambling remains incorporating towers and turrets, gatehouses and concentric walls as well as the remains of the 110ft Norman **keep** and an unusual **Round Chapel** built in 1120. With its spectacular setting high above the river, the castle also makes a fine open-air auditorium during the Ludlow Festival (see above).

Castle Square and around

The castle entrance abuts **Castle Square**, an airy rectangle whose eastern side breaks into several short and narrow lanes, with the one on the left leading through to the gracefully proportioned **Church of St Laurence**, whose interior is distinguished by its stained-glass windows. From the church, it's a few paces to the **Butter Cross**, a Neoclassical extravagance from 1744, and a few more to the **Bull Ring**, home of the **Feathers Hotel**, a fine Jacobean building with the fanciest wooden facade imaginable.

Broad Street

To the south of Castle Square, the gridiron of streets laid out by the Normans has survived intact, though most of the buildings date from the eighteenth century. It's the general appearance that appeals rather than any special sight, but steeply sloping **Broad Street** is particularly attractive, flanked by many of Ludlow's five hundred half-timbered Tudor and red-brick Georgian listed buildings. At the foot of Broad Street is Ludlow's only surviving **medieval gate**, which was turned into a house in the eighteenth century.

ARRIVAL AND INFORMATION — LUDLOW

By train From Ludlow train station, which is on the Shrewsbury–Hereford line, it's a 15min walk southwest to the castle – just follow the signs.

Destinations Church Stretton (every 1hr–1hr 30min; 15min); Hereford (every 1hr–1hr 30min; 30min); Shrewsbury (every 30min–hourly; 30min).

By bus Most buses stop on Mill St, just off Castle Square.

Tourist office Castle Square (April–Sept Mon–Sat 10am–5pm, Sun 10.30am–5pm; Oct–March Mon–Sat 10am–5pm; ⓣ01584 875053, ⓦludlow.org.uk).

ACCOMMODATION

Dinham Hall Hotel Dinham 01584 876464, dinhamhall.co.uk. Handily located close to the castle, this deluxe hotel, with thirteen appealing guest rooms, occupies a rambling, bow-windowed eighteenth-century stone mansion, which has previously seen service as a boarding house for Ludlow School. **£145**

Ludlow Bed & Breakfast 35 Lower Broad St 01584 876912, ludlowbedandbreakfast.blogspot.com. Cosy B&B with just two doubles in a pair of old terrace cottages that have been carefully knocked into one. Great breakfasts. It's a 5- to 10min walk from the castle; they can pick you up from the train station if you call in advance. **£70**

EATING

DeGreys 5 Broad St 01584 872764, degreys.co.uk. This is the best tearoom in town, where uniformed staff bustle around a long, narrow and very old beamed room with assorted sandwiches and snacks; the prices, though, are a little high – the toasties, for one, cost £6. Daily 9am–5.30pm.

La Bécasse 17 Corve St 01584 872325, labecasse .co.uk. Michelin-starred restaurant with a strong French influence, where a two-course menu du jour costs a reasonable £25. Try, for example, the boned and rolled local rabbit saddle with smoked bacon and caramelized celery. Tues 7–10pm, Wed–Sat noon–2.30pm & 7–10pm, Sun noon–2.30pm.

★ **Mr Underhill's** Dinham Weir 01584 874431, mr-underhills.co.uk. One of the very best of Ludlow's top-flight restaurants, with a menu skillfully crafted from local ingredients, and some superb, creative vegetarian options (try the open ravioli of spiced beetroot). The eight-course daily market menu costs £60 per person. Reservations essential. They have luxurious rooms, too. Wed–Sun evenings only.

Birmingham

8

If anywhere can be described as the first purely industrial conurbation, it has to be **BIRMINGHAM**. Unlike the more specialist industrial towns that grew up across the north and the Midlands, "Brum" – and its "Brummies" – turned its hand to every kind of manufacturing, gaining the epithet "the city of 1001 trades". It was here also that the pioneers of the Industrial Revolution – James Watt, Matthew Boulton, Josiah Wedgwood, Joseph Priestley and Erasmus Darwin (grandfather of Charles) – formed the **Lunar Society**, an extraordinary melting-pot of scientific and industrial ideas. They conceived the world's first purpose-built factory, invented gas lighting and pioneered both the distillation of oxygen and the mass production of the steam engine. Thus, a modest Midlands market town mushroomed into the nation's economic dynamo with the population to match: in 1841 there were 180,000 inhabitants; just fifty years later that number had trebled.

BIRMINGHAM ORIENTATION

Many visitors get their first taste of central Birmingham at **New Street Station**, whose unreconstructed ugliness – piles of modern concrete – makes a dispiriting start, though there are plans afoot to give the place a thoroughgoing face-lift. Things soon improve if you cut up east from the station to the newly developed **Bull Ring**, once a 1960s eyesore, but now a gleaming new shopping mall distinguished by the startling design of its leading store, **Selfridges**. Head west along pedestrianized **New Street** from here and it's a brief stroll to the elegantly revamped **Victoria Square** and the adjacent **Chamberlain Square**, where pride of place goes to the **Birmingham Museum and Art Gallery**, the city's finest museum, complete with a stunning collection of Pre-Raphaelite art. Beyond, further west still, is the glossy **International Convention Centre**, from where it's another short hop to the **Gas Street Basin**, the prettiest part of the city's serpentine canal system. Close by is canalside **Brindleyplace**, a smart, brick-and-glass complex sprinkled with slick cafés and bars and holding the enterprising **Ikon Gallery** of contemporary art. From Brindleyplace, it's a short walk southeast to **The Mailbox**, the immaculately rehabilitated former postal sorting office with yet more chic bars and restaurants, or you can head north along the old towpath of the **Birmingham and Fazeley Canal** as far as **Newhall Street**. The latter is within easy walking distance of the Georgian **St Philip's Cathedral**.

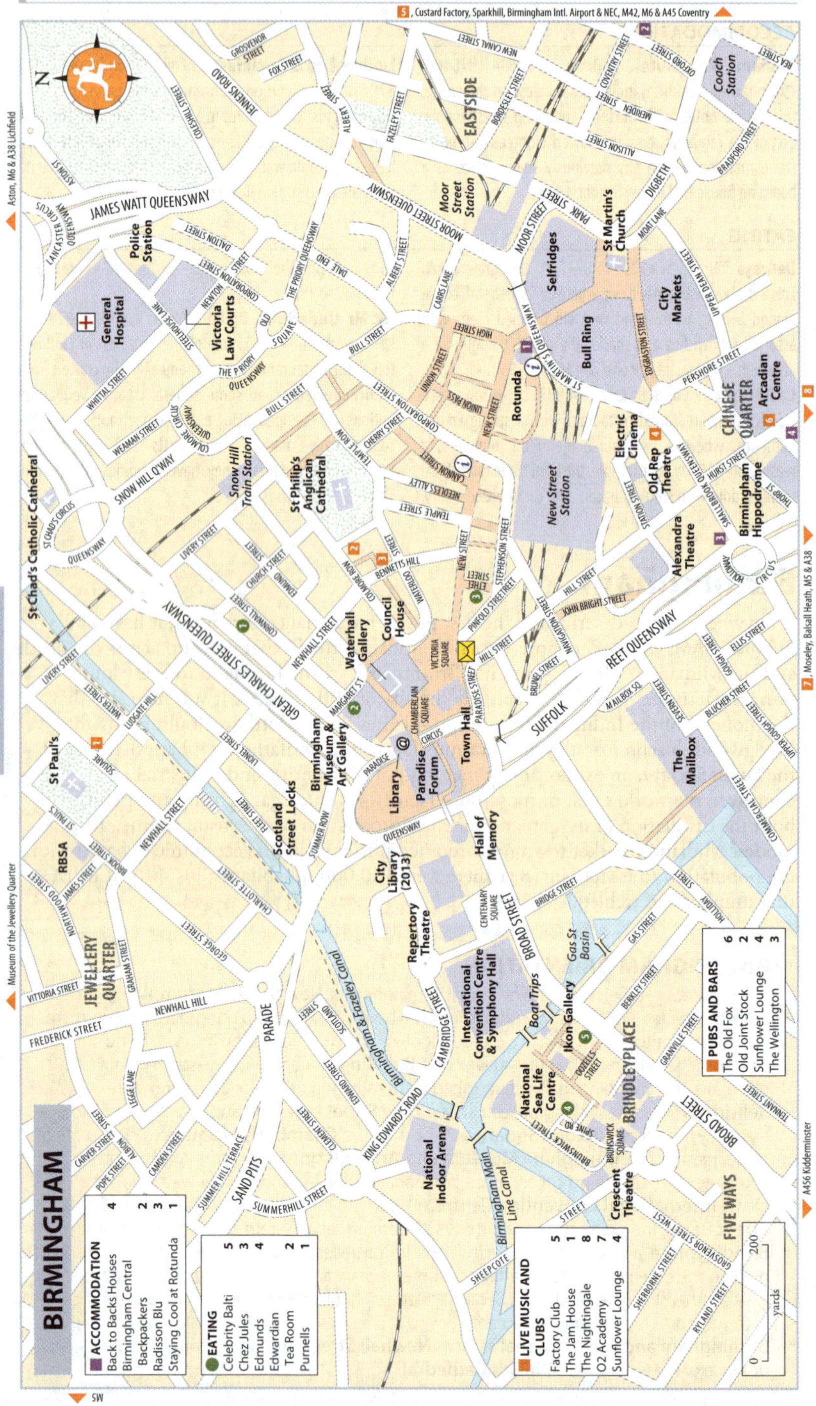
5, Custard Factory, Sparkhill, Birmingham Intl. Airport & NEC, M42, M6 & A45 Coventry
Aston, M6 & A38 Lichfield
Museum of the Jewellery Quarter
M5
A456 Kidderminster
7, Moseley, Balsall Heath, M5 & A38
8
BIRMINGHAM
ACCOMMODATION
Back to Backs Houses 4
Birmingham Central Backpackers 2
Radisson Blu 3
Staying Cool at Rotunda 1
EATING
Celebrity Balti 5
Chez Jules 3
Edmunds 4
Edwardian Tea Room 2
Purnells 1
LIVE MUSIC AND CLUBS
Factory Club 5
The Jam House 1
The Nightingale 8
O2 Academy 7
Sunflower Lounge 4
PUBS AND BARS
The Old Fox 6
Old Joint Stock 2
Sunflower Lounge 4
The Wellington 3
0 200 yards
EASTSIDE
Moor Street Station
Police Station
General Hospital
Victoria Law Courts
St Martin's Church
Selfridges
Bull Ring
City Markets
Rotunda
CHINESE QUARTER
Arcadian Centre
Coach Station
Electric Cinema
Old Rep Theatre
New Street Station
Birmingham Hippodrome
Alexandra Theatre
Snow Hill Train Station
St Philip's Anglican Cathedral
St Chad's Catholic Cathedral
Council House
Waterhall Gallery
Birmingham Museum & Art Gallery
Library
Paradise Forum
Town Hall
Scotland Street Locks
St Paul's
RBSA
JEWELLERY QUARTER
City Library (2013)
Hall of Memory
Repertory Theatre
International Convention Centre & Symphony Hall
The Mailbox
Gas St Basin
Boat Trips
Ikon Gallery
National Sea Life Centre
BRINDLEYPLACE
National Indoor Arena
Crescent Theatre
FIVE WAYS
Birmingham & Fazeley Canal
Birmingham Main Line Canal

Britain's second-largest city, with a population of over one million, Birmingham has long outgrown the squalor and misery of its boom years and today its industrial supremacy is recalled – but only recalled – by a crop of **recycled buildings**, from warehouses to an old custard factory, and an extensive network of **canals**. With a revamped city centre, and a vibrant cultural life, Birmingham also boasts a thoroughly multiracial population – this is one of Britain's most cosmopolitan cities. Nevertheless, there's no pretending that Birmingham is packed with interesting sights – it isn't – but, along with its first-rate restaurant scene and nightlife, it's well worth at least a couple of days.

The Bull Ring

A few steps from New Street Station, Rotunda Square which marks the intersection of New and High streets, takes its name from the soaring **Rotunda**, a handsome and distinctive cylindrical tower that is the sole survivor of the notorious **Bull Ring** shopping centre, which fulfilled every miserable cliché of 1960s town planning until its demolition in 2001. The new Bull Ring shopping centre, opened in 2003, has two strokes of real invention. Firstly, the architects split the shops into two separate sections, providing an uninterrupted view of the medieval spire of St Martin's in the gap – an obvious contrast between the old and the new perhaps, but still extraordinarily effective. The second coup was the design of **Selfridges**' store.

Selfridges

Mon–Fri 10am–8pm, Sat 9am–8pm, Sun 11am–5.30pm • ⓣ 0800 123400, ⓦ selfridges.com

Birmingham's **Selfridges** is an extraordinary sight – a billowing organic swell protruding from the Bull Ring's east side, and seen to good advantage from the wide stone stairway that descends from Rotunda Square to St Martin's. Reminiscent of an inside-out octopus, Selfridges shimmers with an architectural chain mail of thousands of spun aluminium discs, an altogether bold and hugely successful attempt to create a popular city landmark.

Victoria Square

Stretching west from the Bull Ring, **New Street** is a busy pedestrianized thoroughfare lined with shops. At its west end, it opens out into the handsomely refurbished **Victoria Square**, whose centrepiece is a large and particularly engaging **water fountain** designed by Dhruva Mistry. The waterfall outdoes poor old Queen Victoria, whose statue is glum and uninspired, though the thrusting self-confidence of her bourgeoisie is very apparent in the flamboyant **Council House** behind her, completed in 1879. Across the square, and very different, is the **Town Hall** of 1834, whose classical design – by Joseph Hansom, who went on to design Hansom cabs – was based on the Roman temple in Nîmes. The building's simple, flowing lines contrast with much of its surroundings, but it's an appealing structure all the same, and now houses a performing arts venue.

The Birmingham Museum and Art Gallery

Chamberlain Square • Mon–Thurs & Sat 10am–5pm, Fri 10.30am–5pm, Sun 12.30–5pm • Free • ⓣ 0121 303 1966, ⓦ bmag.org.uk

The **Birmingham Museum and Art Gallery** (BM&AG), which occupies a rambling, Edwardian building on **Chamberlain Square**, possesses a multifaceted collection divided into several sections. The bulk is spread over one long floor – Floor 2 – which is where you'll find the fine art, which attracts most attention. In 2009, the museum also part-purchased the **Staffordshire Hoard**, the largest collection of Anglo-Saxon gold ever found with more than 1500 pieces mostly related to warfare. The museum's collection is too large for it all to be exhibited at any one time, and artworks are regularly rotated; be sure to pick up a **plan** at reception. There's a good **café** (see p.404) for when you need a break.

The Pre-Raphaelites

The BM&AG holds a significant sample of **European** paintings and an excellent collection of eighteenth- and nineteenth-century British art, most notably a supreme muster of **Pre-Raphaelite** work. Founded in 1848, the Pre-Raphaelite Brotherhood consisted of seven young artists, of whom Rossetti, Holman Hunt, Millais and Madox Brown are the best known. The name of the group was selected to express their commitment to honest observation, which they thought had been lost with the Renaissance. Two seminal Pre-Raphaelite paintings here are **Dante Gabriel Rossetti**'s stirring *Beata Beatrix* (1870) and **Ford Madox Brown**'s powerful image of emigration, *The Last of England* (1855). The Brotherhood disbanded in the 1850s, but a second wave of artists carried on in its footsteps, most notably **Edward Burne-Jones**, whose *Star of Bethlehem* – in Room 14 – is one of the largest watercolours ever painted, a mysterious, almost magical piece with earnest Magi and a film-star-like Virgin Mary.

The Industrial Gallery, Gas Hall and the Waterhall Gallery

Sharing Floor 2 is the **Industrial Gallery**, which is set around an expansive atrium whose wrought-iron columns and balconies clamber up towards fancy skylights. The gallery holds a choice selection of ceramics, jewellery and stained glass retrieved from defunct churches all over Birmingham. Here also is the *Edwardian Tea Room*, one of the city's more pleasant places for a cuppa (see p.404). Floor 1's cavernous **Gas Hall** is an impressive venue for touring art exhibitions, while the **Waterhall Gallery** (same times), inside the Council House, just across Edmund Street from the main museum building, showcases temporary exhibitions of modern and contemporary art.

Centenary Square

The dominant feature of **Centenary Square** is its unusual World War I war memorial, the **Hall of Memory** (Mon–Sat 10am–4pm; free). Erected in 1923 to commemorate those 13,000 Brummies who died in World War I, the memorial is an architectural hybrid, a delightful mix of Art Deco and Neoclassical features, whose centrepiece is a domed Remembrance chamber. From the memorial, it's a brief walk west past the site where the new city library will eventually appear (in 2013) to the showpiece **International Convention Centre** (ICC) and **Symphony Hall** with the **Birmingham Repertory Theatre** on the right.

Gas Street Basin

Gas Street Basin is the hub of Birmingham's intricate canal system. There are eight canals within the city's boundaries, comprising 32 miles of canal, and although much of Birmingham's surviving canal network slices through the city's grimy, industrial bowels, certain sections have been immaculately restored with Gas Street Basin leading the way. At the junction of the Worcester and Birmingham and Birmingham Main Line canals, the Basin, with its herd of brightly painted narrowboats, is edged by a delightful medley of old brick buildings.

The Mailbox

Following the towpath along the canal southeast from the Gas Street Basin soon brings you to **The Mailbox**, a talented reinvention of Birmingham's old postal sorting office complete with restaurants, hotels, and some of the snazziest shops in the city – including Jaeger and Harvey Nichols.

Brindleyplace

Southwest of Centenary Square, the waterside **Brindleyplace** is named after James Brindley, the eighteenth-century engineer responsible for many of Britain's early canals. In this aesthetically pleasing development of bars, shops and offices, you'll also find the city's much-lauded **Ikon Gallery**.

Ikon Gallery

1 Oozells Square, Brindleyplace • Tues–Sun 11am–6pm • Free • T 0121 248 0708, W ikon-gallery.co.uk

Housed in a rambling Victorian building in the attractive Brindleyplace complex, the splendid **Ikon Gallery** is one of the country's most imaginative venues for touring exhibitions of contemporary art, with workshops, family days and a little café to boot.

National Sea Life Centre

Brindleyplace • Mon–Fri 10am–5pm, Sat & Sun 10am–6pm • £18, children £14.40 • T 0121 643 6777, W visitsealife.com

Just beyond Brindleyplace, in front of the huge dome of the National Indoor Arena (NIA), the canal forks: the Birmingham & Fazeley leads northeast (to the right) and the Birmingham Main Line Canal cuts west (to the left). Also beside the main canal junction is the shell-like **National Sea Life Centre**, an educational venture offering Birmingham's landlubbers an opportunity to view and even touch many unusual varieties of fish and sea life.

Birmingham & Fazeley Canal

8

Beyond the main canal fork, the first part of the **Birmingham & Fazeley Canal** has been attractively restored, its antique brick buildings cleaned of accumulated grime as far as the quaint **Scotland Street Locks**. Further on, the canal cuts past a string of new apartment blocks as well as the (unsigned) flight of steps that leads up to Newhall Street, about half a mile from the main canal junction – and a few minutes' walk from **St Paul's Square**, where a good-looking ensemble of old houses flank the comely Neoclassical **church of St Paul's**.

St Philip's Cathedral

Colmore Row • Sept–June Mon–Fri 7.30am–6.30pm, Sat & Sun 8.30am–5pm; July to early Sept Mon–Fri 7.30am–5pm, Sat & Sun 8.30am–5pm • Free • T 0121 262 1840, W birminghamcathedral.com

The string of fancily carved, High Victorian stone buildings on Colmore Row provide a suitable backdrop for **St Philip's Anglican Cathedral**, a bijou example of English Baroque. Consecrated in 1715, the church is a handsome affair, its graceful, galleried interior all balance and poise, its harmonies unruffled by the Victorians, who enlarged the original church in the 1880s, when four stained-glass windows were commissioned from local boy **Edward Burne-Jones**, a leading light of the Pre-Raphaelite movement.

ARRIVAL AND DEPARTURE — BIRMINGHAM

By plane Birmingham's International Airport is 8 miles east of the city centre off the A45 and near the M42 (Junction 6); the terminal is beside Birmingham International train station, from where there are regular services into New Street train station.

By train New Street train station, right in the heart of the city, is where all inter-city and the vast majority of local services go, though trains on the Stratford-upon-Avon, Warwick and Worcester lines mostly use Snow Hill and Moor Street stations, both about 10min signposted walk from New Street to the north and east respectively.

Destinations from New Street Birmingham International (every 15–30min; 15min); Coventry (3–5 hourly; 25min); Derby (every 30min; 45min); Great Malvern (hourly; 1hr); Hereford (hourly; 1hr 30min); Shrewsbury (every 30min; 1hr); Telford (Mon–Sat every 30min, Sun hourly; 40min).

Destinations from Moor Street Station Stratford-upon-Avon (hourly; 50min); Warwick (hourly; 30min); Worcester (hourly; 50min).

Destinations from Snow Hill Station Stratford-upon-Avon (hourly; 1hr); Warwick (hourly; 40min).

By bus National Express long-distance buses arrive at the Digbeth coach station, from where it's a 10min walk northwest to the Bull Ring.

GETTING AROUND

Birmingham has an excellent **public transport system**, whose trains, metro and buses delve into almost every urban nook and cranny. Various companies provide these services, but they are all co-ordinated by Centro (T 0121 200 2787, W centro.org.uk).

INFORMATION

Tourist offices The main office is at 150 New St, beside the Bull Ring at the back of the Rotunda (Mon–Sat 9.30am–5.30pm, Sun 10.30am–4.30pm; T 0844 888 3883, W visitbirmingham.com). There's a smaller kiosk in front of New Street station, at the junction of New Street and Corporation St (Mon–Sat 9am–5pm, Sun 10am–4pm; same number).

ACCOMMODATION

To see Birmingham at its best, you really need to stay in the centre, preferably in the vicinity of **Centenary Square**, though chain hotels do monopolize the downtown scene. The Rotunda tourist office (see above) operates a free **room-booking** service.

Back to Backs Houses 52 Inge St T 0844 800 2070, W nationaltrustcottages.co.uk. The most distinctive place to stay in town: the National Trust has refurbished a small block of nineteenth-century back-to-back workers' houses conveniently located just to the south of the city centre along Hurst Street. Part of the complex now holds two small "cottages" – really terraced houses – kitted out in Victorian period style, but with the addition of en-suite and self-catering facilities. Each accommodates two guests and can be rented out for two nights or longer with costs varying with the season: a two-night stay costs £165 in January, rising to £246 in July.

Birmingham Central Backpackers 58 Coventry St T 0121 643 0033, W birminghamcentralbackpackers.com. Welcoming hostel with self-catering facilities, a large sociable lounge, a small garden and a café and bar. Dorms have four to eight bunks per room. A short walk from Digbeth bus station. £14.50

Radisson Blu 12 Holloway Circus T 0121 654 6000, W birmingham.radissonblu.co.uk. Smart hotel in a tall, sleek skyrise within a few minutes' walk of the centre. The interior is designed in routine modern-minimalist style, but the floor-to-ceiling windows of many of the bedrooms add élan. £100

★ **Staying Cool at Rotunda** The Rotunda, New St T 0121 643 0815, W stayingcool.com. The top three floors of the Rotunda, right at the heart of Birmingham, have been converted into fully furnished, serviced apartments, from small to extra-large. All are modern and spotless, and those on the top floor – Floor 20 – come with a balcony from where there are panoramic views over the city. The apartments can be rented for one night – no problem. £150

EATING

Central Birmingham has a bevy of first-rate restaurants with a string of smart new venues springing up in the slipstream of the burgeoning conference and trade-fair business. Birmingham's gastronomic speciality is the **balti**, a delicious Kashmiri stew cooked and served in a small wok-like dish called a karahi, with naan bread instead of cutlery. The original balti houses are concentrated out in the **suburbs** of Balsall Heath, Moseley and Sparkhill to the south of the centre, but there are a couple of prime balti houses in the centre too.

Celebrity Balti 44 Broad St T 0121 643 8969. The days when you had to venture out into the suburbs for a top-ranking balti are over now that this city-centre restaurant is in full swing: the decor may be old-fashioned, but there's little argument about the quality of the food. Baltis cost around £8. Daily 6pm till late.

Chez Jules 5a Ethel St, off New St T 0121 633 4664. Cosy, mid-priced, first-floor French restaurant in the city centre, with especially good lunchtime deals. Try the coq au vin; mains average £13 at night, less at lunchtimes. Sept–June Mon–Sat noon–3pm & 5–11pm Sun noon–3pm; July & Aug Mon–Sat noon–3pm & 5–11pm.

Edmunds 6 Central Square, Brindleyplace T 0121 633 4944, W edmundsrestaurant.co.uk. High-style dining in smart, contemporary premises. The menu features seasonal ingredients – baked turbot with buttered spinach, mussels and Burgundy sauce is typical. A two-course, à la carte meal will set you back about £40, but they also have a two-/three-course pre-theatre menu on Fri and Sat for £18/£20. Tues–Thurs noon–2pm & 7–10pm, Fri noon–2pm & 5.30–10pm, Sat 5.30–10pm.

Edwardian Tea Room BM&AG, Chamberlain Square T 0121 303 1966, W bmag.org.uk. This café-cum-canteen has a great setting in one of the large and fancily decorated halls of the museum's industrial section – check out all those handsome cast-iron columns – your surroundings outshine the food, which is run-of-the-mill. Mon–Sat 11am–4pm & Sun 12.30–4pm.

★ **Purnells** 55 Cornwall St ⓣ0121 212 9799, ⓦpurnellsrestaurant.com. Smooth and polished restaurant housed in a Victorian red-brick, though the interior is all soft colours and modern paintings – prestige dining from Michelin-starred chef Glynn Purnell, with a three-course à la carte meal costing £45. A typical dish might be brill cooked in coconut milk with Indian red lentils, or piglet confit with vanilla. Reservations essential. Tues–Fri noon–4.30pm & 7pm–1am, Sat 7pm–1am, last orders 9.30pm.

DRINKING

The Old Fox 54 Hurst St ⓣ08721 077077. Over-modernized but popular pub, with an excellent selection of beers and a boisterous atmosphere. At least the great long windows (of 1891) have survived the updaters. Daily 11am–11pm.

★ **Old Joint Stock** 4 Temple Row West ⓣ0121 200 1892, ⓦoldjointstocktheatre.co.uk. This delightful pub has the fanciest decor in town – with busts and a balustrade, a balcony and chandeliers, all dating from its days as a bank. Occasional jazz and theatre upstairs. Daily 11am–11pm.

Sunflower Lounge 76 Smallbrook Queensway ⓣ0121 632 6756, ⓦthesunflowerlounge.co.uk. Quirky pub-cum-bar in modern premises on the inner ring road near New Street station that attracts an indie/student crowd. It covers many bases, with quizzes and big-screen TV plus resident DJs and live gigs. It really is cool without being pretentious – just as they say on their website. Daily hours vary depending on event.

The Wellington 37 Bennetts Hill ⓣ0121 200 3115, ⓦthewellingtonrealale.co.uk. Specialist real ale pub with a top-notch range of local brews, including those of the much-proclaimed Black Country Brewery, and a good selection of ciders, too. Daily 11am–11pm.

NIGHTLIFE AND ENTERTAINMENT

Birmingham's **club scene** is one of Britain's best, spanning everything from word-of-mouth underground parties to meat-market mainstream clubs. **Live music** is strong, too, with big-name concerts at several major venues and other (often local) bands appearing at some clubs and pubs. Birmingham's showpiece **Symphony Orchestra** and **Royal Ballet** are the spearheads of the city's **classical scene**. Top-ranking **festivals** include the **Jazz Festival** (ⓦbirminghamjazzfestival.com) held for two weeks in July and the three-day **Artsfest** (ⓣ0121 464 5678, ⓦartsfest.org.uk) of film, dance, theatre and music in September. For current **information** on all events, performances and exhibitions, ask at the tourist office (see opposite) or consult either ⓦbirminghammail.net or ⓦlivebrum.co.uk.

8

LIVE MUSIC AND CLUBS

Factory Club Custard Factory, Gibb Square, off Digbeth ⓣ0121 772 2094, ⓦfactoryclub.co.uk. Bar-cum-club in a laidback, extremely groovy arts complex that was once a custard factory. They have an eclectic, impeccable music policy, plus a whole raft of juicy live events – come here for one of Birmingham's best nights out.

★ **The Jam House** 3 St Paul's Square ⓣ0121 200 3030, ⓦthejamhouse.com. Jazz, funk, blues and swing joint pulling in artists from every corner of the globe under the eye of the musical director, Jools Holland. Tues–Sat from 6pm.

The Nightingale 18 Kent St ⓣ0121 622 1718, ⓦnightingaleclub.co.uk. The king of Brum's gay clubs, popular with straights as well. Five bars, three levels, two discos, a café-bar and even a garden. Just south of the Hippodrome (see opposite).

O2 Academy 16–18 Horsefair, Bristol St Ticket line: ⓣ0844 477 2000, ⓦo2academybirmingham.co.uk. State-of-the-art venue with three rooms hosting either gigs or club nights, though the big deal are the top-ranking artists – Katey P, Paloma Faith, The Kooks and so forth.

CLASSICAL MUSIC, THEATRE, DANCE AND CINEMA

Birmingham Hippodrome Hurst St ⓣ0844 338 5000, ⓦbirminghamhippodrome.com. Lavishly refurbished, the Hippodrome is home to the Birmingham Royal Ballet. Also features touring plays and big pre- and post-West End productions, plus a splendiferous Christmas pantomime.

Birmingham Repertory Theatre Centenary Square, Broad St ⓣ0121 236 4455, ⓦbirmingham-rep.co.uk. Mixed diet of classics and new work featuring local and experimental writing.

Electric Cinema 47 Station St ⓣ0121 6437879, ⓦtheelectric.co.uk. Britain's oldest working cinema, housed in a handsome Art Deco building, with an inventive programme of mainstream and art-house films. Sofas and waiter service also.

Symphony Hall International Convention Centre, Broad St ⓣ0121 780 3333, ⓦthsh.co.uk. Acoustically one of the most advanced concert halls in Europe, home of the acclaimed City of Birmingham Symphony Orchestra (CBSO; ⓦcbso.co.uk), as well as a venue for touring music and opera.

Town Hall Broad St ⓣ0121 780 3333, ⓦthsh.co.uk. Recently refitted and refurbished, the old Town Hall offers a varied programme of pop, classical and jazz music through to modern dance and ballet.

The Peak District

In 1951, the hills and dales of the **Peak District**, at the southern tip of the Pennine range, became Britain's first national park. Wedged between **Derby**, Manchester and Sheffield, it is effectively the back garden for the fifteen million people who live within an hour's drive of its boundaries, though somehow it accommodates the huge influx with minimum fuss.

Landscapes in the Peak District come in two forms. The brooding high moorland tops of **Dark Peak**, to the east of Manchester, take their name from the underlying gritstone, known as millstone grit for its former use – a function commemorated in the millstones demarcating the park boundary. Windswept, mist-shrouded and inhospitable, the flat tops of these peaks are nevertheless a firm favourite with walkers on the **Pennine Way**, which meanders north from the tiny village of **Edale** to the Scottish border (see p.411). Altogether more forgiving, the southern limestone hills of the **White Peak** have been eroded into deep forested dales populated by small stone villages and often threaded by walking trails, some of which follow former rail routes. The limestone is riddled with complex cave systems around **Castleton** and on the periphery of **Buxton**, a charming former spa town lying just outside the park's boundaries and at the end of an industrialized corridor that reaches out from Manchester. Elsewhere, one of the country's most distinctive manorial piles, **Chatsworth House**, stands near **Bakewell**, a town famed locally not just for its cakes but also for its **well-dressing**, a possibly pagan ritual of thanksgiving for fresh water that takes place in about thirty local villages each summer. The well-dressing season starts in May and continues through to mid-September; get exact dates and details on Ⓦwelldressing.com.

As for a **base**, Buxton is your best bet by a (fairly) long chalk, though if you're after hiking and cycling you'll probably prefer one of the area's villages – Edale and Castleton will do nicely.

ARRIVAL AND DEPARTURE — THE PEAK DISTRICT

By train There are frequent trains south from Manchester to end-of-the-line Buxton, and Manchester–Sheffield trains cut through Edale.

By bus The main bus access is via the Trent Barton bus company's TransPeak (Ⓦtranspeak.co.uk) service from Nottingham to Manchester via Derby, Bakewell and Buxton (daily every 1–2hr; 3hr 30min). Otherwise, First (Ⓦfirstgroup.com) bus #272 runs regularly from Sheffield to Castleton, via Hathersage and Hope, and TM Travel (Ⓦtmtravel.co.uk) bus #65 connects Sheffield to Buxton.

GETTING AROUND

By bus Once you've reached the Peak District, you'll find that local bus services are really rather good, though less so on Sundays and in the depths of winter. Local tourist offices almost always have bus and train timetables, including the encyclopedic Peak District Bus Timetable; you can also check online at Ⓦderbysbus.info.

By bike The Peak District has a good network of dedicated cycle lanes and trails, sometimes along former railway lines, and the Peak District National Park Authority (see below) operates three cycle rental outlets: at Ashbourne (Ⓣ01335 343156); Derwent, Bamford (Ⓣ01433 651261); and Parsley Hay, Buxton (Ⓣ01298 84493).

INFORMATION

Visitor centres The Peak District National Park Authority (Ⓣ01629 816200, Ⓦpeakdistrict.gov.uk) operates four visitor centres, one of which is in Castleton; these supplement a host of town and village tourist offices.

Maps and guides A variety of maps and trail guides is widely available across the Peaks, but for the non-specialist it's hard to beat the *Grate Little Guides* (£2.50) a series of leaflets that provide hiking suggestions and trail descriptions for a dozen or so localities in a clear and straightforward style. They cost £2.50 each and are on sale at most tourist offices and information centres. Note that the maps printed on the leaflets are best used in conjunction with an OS map.

Useful website Ⓦvisitpeakdistrict.com.

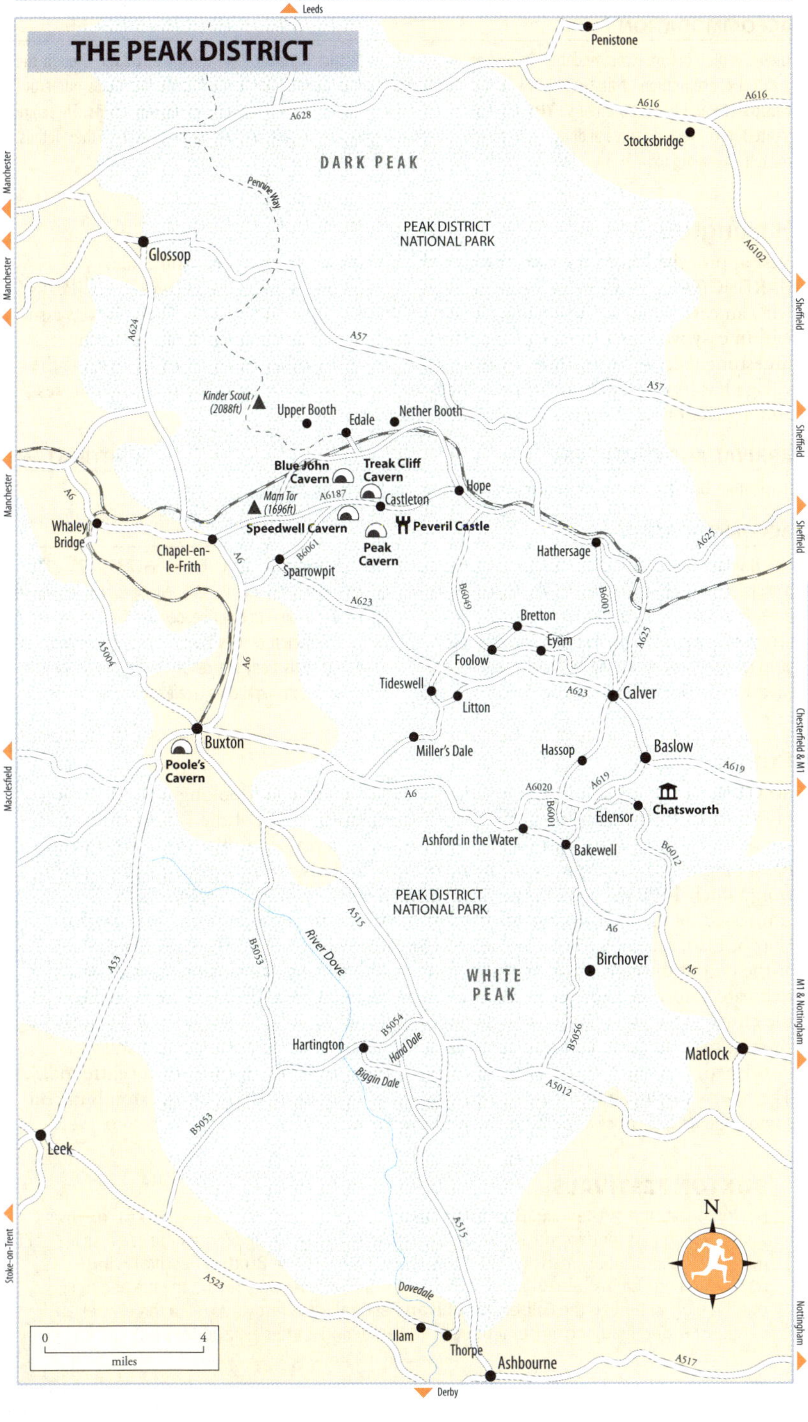
THE PEAK DISTRICT
Leeds
Penistone
A616
A628
Stocksbridge
DARK PEAK
Pennine Way
PEAK DISTRICT NATIONAL PARK
A6102
Manchester
Glossop
Sheffield
A624
A57
Kinder Scout (2088ft)
Upper Booth
Edale
Nether Booth
Blue John Cavern
Treak Cliff Cavern
Mam Tor (1696ft)
A6187
Castleton
Hope
Whaley Bridge
Speedwell Cavern
Peveril Castle
Chapel-en-le-Frith
A6
B6061
Sparrowpit
Peak Cavern
Hathersage
A625
B6049
B6001
A623
Bretton
Eyam
A5004
Foolow
Tideswell
Litton
Calver
Buxton
Poole's Cavern
Miller's Dale
Hassop
Baslow
A619
Chesterfield & M1
Macclesfield
A6020
Chatsworth
Edensor
Ashford in the Water
Bakewell
B6012
PEAK DISTRICT NATIONAL PARK
A515
River Dove
B5053
WHITE PEAK
Birchover
A53
B5054
Hand Dale
Hartington
B5056
Matlock
M1 & Nottingham
Biggin Dale
A5012
Leek
Stoke-on-Trent
A523
Dovedale
N
Nottingham
0
4
miles
Ilam
Thorpe
Ashbourne
A517
Derby

8

ACCOMMODATION

There's a plethora of accommodation in and around the Peak District National Park, mostly in **B&Bs**, though the greatest concentration of first-rate B&Bs is just outside the park in Buxton. The Peak District also holds numerous **campsites** and half a dozen or so **YHA hostels** as well as a network of YHA-operated **camping barns**. These are located in converted farm buildings and provide simple and inexpensive self-catering facilities. For further details, consult Ⓦyha.org.uk.

Hartington

Best approached from the east, through the boisterous scenery of Hand Dale, **HARTINGTON**, 25 miles northwest of Derby, is one of the prettiest villages in the Peaks, with an easy ramble of stone houses centred in on a tiny duck pond. The village is also within easy walking distance of the River Dove as well as a sequence of handsome limestone dales – **Biggin Dale** is perhaps the pick. The other excitement is cheese – the village has its own specialist **cheese shop** with a raft of local and international cheeses and a selection of chutneys to lighten the gastronomic load.

ARRIVAL AND DEPARTURE — HARTINGTON

Hartington's **bus** stop is in the centre of the village, a few yards from the duck pond.

ACCOMMODATION

The Hayloft Church St Ⓣ01298 84358, Ⓦhartingtonhayloft.co.uk. Perhaps the best of Hartington's several B&Bs, in a recently converted barn a few yards from the duck pond and part of a working farm. There are just four guest rooms – two upstairs and two down below – each of which is decorated in a straightforward modern style. **£60**

YHA Hartington Hall Bank Ⓣ0845 371 9740, Ⓔhartington@yha.org.uk. Well-equipped hostel whose 130 beds – in one- to eight-bedded rooms – are squeezed into a seventeenth-century manor house, Hartington Hall, about 300 yards from the centre of the village. Facilities include a self-catering kitchen, a café and internet access. **£23**

Buxton

BUXTON, twelve miles north of Hartington, is a stylish, good-looking place. Its string of excellent B&Bs make it a perfect base for exploring much of the Peaks, while its handful of splendid **festivals** (see below) has added a real zip to the town. Buxton also has a long history as a **spa**, beginning with the Romans, who happened upon a spring from which 1500 gallons of pure water gushed every hour at a constant 28°C. Impressed by the recuperative qualities of the water, the Romans came here by the chariot load, setting a trend that was to last hundreds of years. The spa's hay day came at the end of the eighteenth century with the **fifth Duke of Devonshire**'s grand design to create a northern answer to Bath or Cheltenham, a plan ultimately thwarted by the climate, but not before some distinguished buildings had been erected. Victorian Buxton may not have had quite the élan of its more southerly rivals but it still flourished, creating the raft of handsome stone houses that edge the town centre today. The town's **thermal baths** were closed for lack of custom in 1972, but Buxton hung on to emerge as the most appealing town in the Peaks.

BUXTON FESTIVALS

Buxton boasts the outstanding **Buxton Festival** (box office Ⓣ0845 127 2190, Ⓦbuxtonfestival.co.uk), which runs for two and a half weeks in July and features a full programme of classical music, opera and literary readings. This has spawned the first-rate **Buxton Festival Fringe** (Ⓦbuxtonfringe.org.uk), also in July, which focuses on contemporary music, theatre and film, but the biggest fiesta is the **Gilbert & Sullivan Festival** (Ⓦgs-festival.co.uk), a three-week affair in August mainly featuring amateur troupes and attracting enthusiastic audiences.

The Crescent and around

The centrepiece of Buxton's hilly, compact centre is **The Crescent**, a broad sweep of Georgian stonework commissioned by the fifth Duke of Devonshire in 1780 and modelled on the Royal Crescent in Bath. It was cleaned and scrubbed a few years ago, but has lain idle ever since, though work will soon start on turning it into a five-star hotel complete with thermal baths. Facing The Crescent, and also currently empty, is the old **Pump Room**, an attractive Victorian building where visitors once sampled the local waters; next to it is a **water fountain**, supplied by St Ann's Well and still used to fill many a local water bottle. For a better view of The Crescent and the town centre, clamber up **The Slopes**, a narrow slice of park that rises behind the Pump Room dotted with decorative urns. From here, it's impossible to miss the enormous **dome** of what was originally the Duke of Devonshire's stables and riding school, erected in 1789 and now part of Derby University.

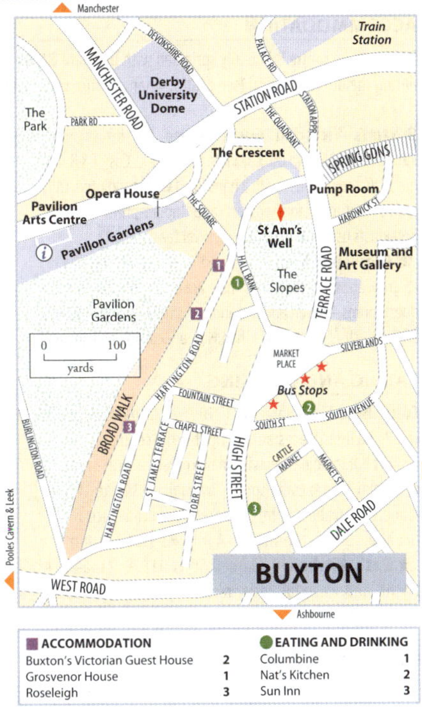

Pavilion Gardens and around

Next to The Crescent, the appealing old stone buildings of **The Square** – though square it isn't – nudge up to the grandly refurbished **Buxton Opera House**, an Edwardian extravagance whose twin towers date from 1903. Stretching back from the Opera House are the **Pavilion Gardens**, a slender string of connected buildings distinguished by their wrought-iron work and culminating in a large and glassy dome, the **Octagon**, which was originally a music hall, and the **Pavilion Arts Centre**. The adjoining **park**, also known as the Pavilion Gardens and cut across by the River Wye, is particularly pleasant, its immaculate lawns and neat borders graced by a bandstand, ponds, dinky little footbridges and fountains.

Poole's Cavern

A mile southwest of central Buxton, just off Green Lane • Daily 9.30am–5pm • £8 • ⓣ 01298 26978, ⓦ poolescavern.co.uk • Take the A53 road towards Macclesfield and Leek and watch for the sign

The Peaks are riddled with cave systems and around half a dozen have become popular tourist attractions. One is **Poole's Cavern** whose impressively large chambers are home to a host of orange and blue-grey stalactites and stalagmites.

ARRIVAL AND INFORMATION — BUXTON

By train Hourly trains (1hr) from Manchester Piccadilly pull into Buxton train station, a 3min walk from the town centre.

By bus Buses, including the TransPeak (see p.406), stop in the Market Place, a 4min walk from the Opera House.

Tourist office Pavilion Gardens, behind the Opera House (daily: April–Oct 9.30am–5pm; Nov–March 10am–4pm; ⓣ 01298 25106, ⓦ visitbuxton.co.uk). It operates an accommodation-booking service and has plentiful information on the town in particular and the Peaks in general.

ACCOMMODATION

Buxton town centre is liberally sprinkled with first-rate **B&Bs** and finding somewhere to stay is rarely a problem, except during the Buxton Festival (see p.408), when advance reservations are essential.

Buxton's Victorian Guest House 3a Broad Walk ⊕01298 78759, ⓦbuxtonvictorian.co.uk. Cosy B&B in a grand Victorian house with a handful of well-appointed, frilly rooms featuring four-posters and Indian-print cushions. Breakfasts use local produce wherever feasible. **£82**

★ **Grosvenor House** 1 Broad Walk ⊕01298 72439, ⓦgrosvenorbuxton.co.uk. There are eight unfussy, en-suite guest rooms – seven doubles and one single – in this friendly B&B, which is located in a handsome Victorian townhouse. The best rooms offer gentle views over the gardens. Delicious home-made breakfasts, too. **£65**

Roseleigh 19 Broad Walk ⊕01298 24904, ⓦroseleighhotel.co.uk. This classic, three-storey gritstone Victorian townhouse, overlooking Pavilion Gardens, is an excellent place to stay. The trim public rooms are decorated in attractive Victorian style, and the en-suite bedrooms are well appointed. Family-run and competitively priced. **£75**

EATING AND DRINKING

Columbine 7 Hall Bank ⊕01298 78752. The menu at this small and intimate restaurant, right in the centre of Buxton, is short but imaginative, with main courses – such as saddle of monkfish with crab risotto – averaging £14. Pre-theatre dinners, from about 5pm, can be reserved in advance. May–Oct Mon–Sat 7–10pm; Nov–April Tues–Sat 7–10pm.

★ **Nat's Kitchen** 9 Market St ⊕01298 214642. A bright and cheerful little restaurant with a laidback atmosphere and an ambitious menu – calves liver with bacon sauce for example. Mains average around £12. Tues–Sat noon–2.30pm & 5–9pm, Sun noon–4pm.

Sun Inn 33 High St ⊕01298 23452. This fine old pub, with its maze of antique beamed rooms, is just south of the Market Place. It's a good spot for a fine range of real ales and above-average bar food. Daily noon–11pm.

Castleton and around

The agreeable little village of **CASTLETON**, ten miles northeast of Buxton, lies on the northern edge of the White Peak, its huddle of old stone cottages ringed by hills and set beside a babbling brook. As a starting point for local walks, the place is hard to beat and hikers regularly prepare for the off in the **Market Place**, yards from the main drag, just behind the church.

Peveril Castle

Market Place • April–Oct daily 10am–5pm; Nov–March Mon & Thurs–Sun 10am–4pm • EH • £4.30

Overseeing Castleton is **Peveril Castle**, from which the village takes its name. William the Conqueror's illegitimate son William Peveril raised the first fortifications here to protect the king's rights to the forest that then covered the district, but most of the remains – principally the ruinous square keep – date to the 1170s. After a stiff climb up to the keep, you can trace much of the surviving curtain wall, which commands great views over the Hope Valley down below.

Caves around Castleton

The limestone hills pressing in on Castleton are riddled with water-worn **cave systems**, four of which have been developed as tourist attractions. Each can be reached by car or on foot, though most visitors settle for just one set of caves – the Peak Cavern and the Treak Cliff Cavern are particularly recommended.

The Peak Cavern

April–Oct daily 10am–5pm; Nov–March Sat & Sun 10am–5pm • £8.25 • ⊕01433 620285, ⓦpeakcavern.co.uk

Peak Cavern is the handiest of Castleton's four cave systems, tucked into a gully at the back of the village, its gaping mouth once providing shelter for a rope factory and a small village. Daniel Defoe, visiting in the eighteenth century, noted the cavern's colourful local name, the **Devil's Arse**, a reference to the fiendish fashion in which its interior contours twisted and turned.

The Treak Cliff Cavern

Daily 10am–5pm • £7.95 • ⓣ 01433 621487, ⓦ bluejohnstone.com

Treak Cliff Cavern, about 800 yards west of Castleton up off a minor road, is a major source of a rare sparkling fluorspar known as **Blue John**. Highly prized for ornaments and jewellery since Georgian times, this semi-precious stone comes in a multitude of hues from blue through deep red to yellow, depending on its hydrocarbon impurities. The Treak Cliff contains the best examples of the stone in situ and is also the best cave to visit in its own right, dripping – literally – with ancient stalactites, flowstone and bizarre rock formations, all visible on an entertaining forty-minute walking tour through the main cave system.

ARRIVAL AND INFORMATION — CASTLETON

By train There are no trains to Castleton – the nearest you'll get is Hope, a couple of miles or so to the east along the valley on the Manchester Piccadilly–Sheffield line. Buses connect Hope with Castleton (see below).

By bus The most scenic approach to Castleton is from Sparrowpit, about 5 miles to the west on the A623, from where the road wiggles through the dramatic Winnats Pass, but the principal bus service arrives from the east – from Sheffield, Hathersage and Hope (South Yorkshire First bus #272; hourly). There's also a daily bus from Buxton (1hr) with Hulleys bus company (ⓦ hulleys-of-baslow.co.uk).

Tourist office The Castleton Visitor Centre (daily: April–Oct 10am–5.30pm; Nov–March 10.30am–4.30pm; ⓣ 01629 816572, ⓦ peakdistrict.gov.uk), a combined museum, community centre and tourist office, stands beside the car park on the west side of the village, just off the main street (also the A6187).

Maps The visitor centre sells hiking leaflets and maps, which are invaluable for a string of walking routes that take you up to the swollen hilltops that rise in every direction.

8

ACCOMMODATION AND EATING

You should book **accommodation** in advance at holiday times. There's nowhere outstanding to **eat**, though several of Castleton's **pubs** offer bar food, including *The George*, on Castle St, yards from the Market Place.

Bargate Cottage Market Place ⓣ 01433 620201, ⓦ bargatecottage.co.uk. In an old cottage at the heart of the village, this friendly B&B has a handful of en-suite rooms decorated in a cosy, traditional style. The home-made breakfasts are delicious. **£65**

Causeway House Back St ⓣ 01433 623291, ⓦ causewayhouse.co.uk. The cream of the crop, this B&B occupies an old and well-tended stone cottage just north of the Market Place. There are five guest rooms, three en suite, all tastefully kitted out to make the most of the cottage's original features. **£65**

YHA Castleton Market Place ⓣ 0845 371 9628, ⓔ castleton@yha.org.uk. Occupying Castleton Hall, a capacious if somewhat careworn old stone mansion in the centre of the village, this hostel is well equipped with a self-catering kitchen, a café, cycle store and drying room. Its 135 beds are parcelled up into two- to six-bedded rooms, many of which are en suite. **£16.40**

THE PENNINE WAY

The 268-mile-long **Pennine Way** (ⓦ nationaltrail.co.uk) was the country's first official long-distance footpath, opened in 1965. It stretches north from the boggy plateau of the Peak District's Kinder Scout, proceeds through the Yorkshire Dales and Teesdale, and then crosses Hadrian's Wall and the Northumberland National Park, before entering Scotland to fizzle out at the village of Kirk Yetholm. One of the most popular walks in the country, either taken in sections or completed in two to three weeks, depending on your level of fitness and experience, the Pennine Way is a challenge in the best of weather, since it passes through some of the wildest countryside in Britain. You must certainly be properly equipped and able to use a map and compass. The **National Trail Guides** *Pennine Way: South* and *Pennine Way: North*, are essential, though some still prefer to stick to Wainwright's *Pennine Way Companion*. Information centres along the route – like the one at Edale village (see p.412) – stock a selection of guides and associated trail leaflets and can offer advice.

Edale village

There's almost nothing to **EDALE village**, about five miles northwest of Castleton, except for a slender, half-mile trail of stone houses, which march up the main street from the train station with a couple of pubs, an old stone church and a scattering of B&Bs on the way – and it's this somnambulant air that is its immediate appeal. The village is also extremely popular with walkers, who arrive in droves throughout the year to set off on the **Pennine Way** (see box, p.411) – the route's starting point is signposted from outside the *Old Nag's Head* at the head of the village. If that sounds too daunting, note that there are lots of more manageable alternatives, including an excellent **circular walk** (9 miles; 5hr) that takes in the first part of the Pennine Way, leading up onto the bleak gritstone, table-top of **Kinder Scout** (2088ft), below which Edale cowers.

ARRIVAL AND INFORMATION — EDALE VILLAGE

By train With hourly trains in both directions, Edale village train station is on the Sheffield–Manchester line.

Moorland Centre From Edale train station, it's 400 yards or so up the road to the Moorland Centre (April–Sept Mon–Fri 9.30am–5pm, Sat & Sun 9.30am–5.30pm; Oct–March Mon–Fri 10am–3pm, Sat & Sun 9.30am–4.30pm; T 01433 670207, W peakdistrict.gov.uk), who sell all manner of trail leaflets and hiking guides and can advise on local accommodation.

ACCOMMODATION

Stonecroft Edale T 01433 670262, W stonecroftguesthouse.co.uk. The pick of several B&Bs in Edale village, this detached Edwardian house offers two comfortable guest rooms decorated in an unfussy traditional style. £80

8

Upper Booth Farm & Campsite West of Edale village on the way to Kinder Scout T 01433 670250, W upperboothcamping.co.uk. This conveniently located campsite and camping barn is a popular spot for walkers on the Pennine Way. Camping £5, £6 in the camping barn.

YHA Edale Rowland Cote, Nether Booth, about 2 miles east of Edale train station T 0845 371 9514, E edale@yha.org.uk. With 157 beds in two- to ten-bedded rooms, plus good facilities including a laundry, café and self-catering kitchen, this YHA also offers an extensive range of outdoor activities. These must be booked in advance – as must accommodation. The hostel is signed from the road into Edale, or you can hoof it there across the fields from near the Moorland Centre (see above). £18.40

Bakewell

BAKEWELL, flanking the banks of the River Wye about thirty miles southeast of Edale, is famous for both its **Bakewell Pudding** and its **Bakewell Tart**. The former is much more distinctive (and less commonplace), being a sweet and slippery, almond-flavoured confection – now with a dab of jam – invented here around 1860 when a cook botched a recipe for strawberry tart. Almost a century before this fortuitous mishap, the Duke of Rutland set out to turn what was then a remote village into a prestigious spa, thereby trumping the work of his rival, the Duke of Devonshire, in Buxton. The frigidity of the water made failure inevitable, leaving only the prettiness of **Bath Gardens** at the heart of the town centre as a reminder of the venture. Worth an hour or two of anyone's time, Bakewell is within easy striking distance of the big tourist attraction hereabouts, **Chatsworth House** (see opposite).

ARRIVAL AND INFORMATION — BAKEWELL

By bus Buses to Bakewell stop on – or very close to – central Rutland Square; there are no trains.

Tourist office Bridge St, right in the centre of town (daily: April–Oct 9.30am–5pm; Nov–Easter 10am–5pm; T 01629 816558, W peakdistrict.gov.uk).

EATING

Old Original Bakewell Pudding Shop The Square T 01629 812193, W bakewellpuddingshop.co.uk. Bakeries over town claim to make Bakewell Pudding to the original recipe, but the most authentic are served up here. They sell the pudding in several sizes, from the small and handy to the gargantuan, enough to keep the average family going for a whole day. Mon–Sat 8.30am–6pm, Sun 9am–6pm.

HIKING AROUND BAKEWELL

Bakewell is a popular starting point for short hikes out into the easy landscapes that make up the town's surroundings, with one of the most relaxing excursions being a four-mile loop along the banks of the **River Wye** to the south of the centre. Chatsworth (see below) is within easy hiking distance, too – about seven miles there and back – or you could venture out onto one of the best-known hikes in the national park – **Monsal Trail**, which cuts eight miles north and then west through some of Derbyshire's finest limestone dales using part of the old Midland Railway line. The trail begins at Coombs viaduct, one mile southeast of Bakewell, and ends at Blackwell Mill Junction, three miles east of Buxton.

Chatsworth House

East of Bakewell • Mid-March to late Dec daily 11am–5.30pm, last admission 4.30pm; gardens till 6pm, last admission 5pm • House & gardens £12, gardens only £7.75 • ⓣ 01246 565300, ⓦ chatsworth.org

Fantastically popular, and certainly one of the finest stately homes in Britain, **Chatsworth House**, just to the east of Bakewell, was built in the seventeenth century by the first Duke of Devonshire. It has been owned by the family ever since and several of them have done a fair bit of tinkering – the sixth duke, for instance, added the north wing in the 1820s – but the end result is remarkably harmonious. The property is seen to best advantage from the B6012, which meanders across the estate to the west of the house, giving a full view of its vast Palladian frontage, whose clean lines are perfectly balanced by the undulating partly wooded **parkland**, which rolls in from the south and west.

Many visitors forego the **house** altogether, concentrating on the gardens instead – an understandable decision given the predictability of the assorted baubles accumulated by the family over the centuries. Nonetheless, amongst the maze of grandiose rooms and staircases, there are several noteworthy highlights, including the ornate ceilings of the **State Apartments** and, in the State Bedroom, the four-poster bed in which George II breathed his last. And then there are the **paintings**. Amongst many, Frans Hals, Tintoretto, Veronese and Van Dyck all have a showing and there's even a Rembrandt – *A Portrait of an Old Man* – hanging in the chapel.

Back outside, the **gardens** are a real treat and owe much to the combined efforts of Capability Brown, who designed them in the 1750s, and Joseph Paxton (designer of London's Crystal Palace), who had a bash seventy years later. Amongst all sorts of fripperies, there are water fountains, a rock garden, an artificial waterfall, a grotto and a folly as well as a nursery and greenhouses. Afterwards, you can wend your way to the **café** in the handsomely converted former stables.

ARRIVAL AND DEPARTURE — CHATSWORTH HOUSE

By bus There are buses to Chatsworth House from Sheffield, Bakewell and several other Peak District villages with TM Travel (see p.406).

By foot The best way to get to Chatsworth is by walking one of the footpaths that network the estate, the most obvious departure point being Baslow on the northern edge of the estate. It's easy walking, and The *Grate Little Guide to Chatsworth* (see p.406) describes an especially pleasant four-mile loop that begins and ends in the village, taking in the house on the way.

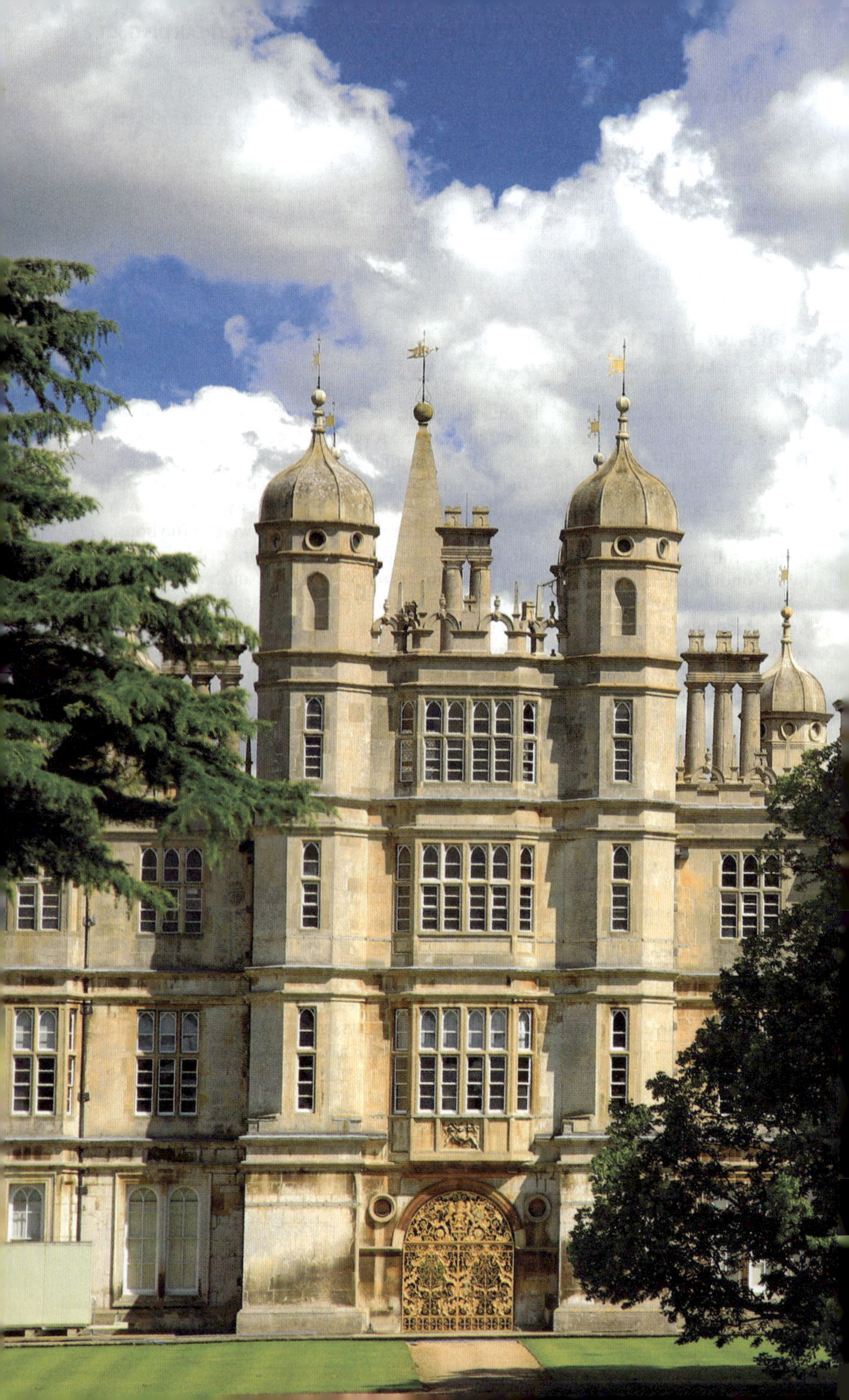

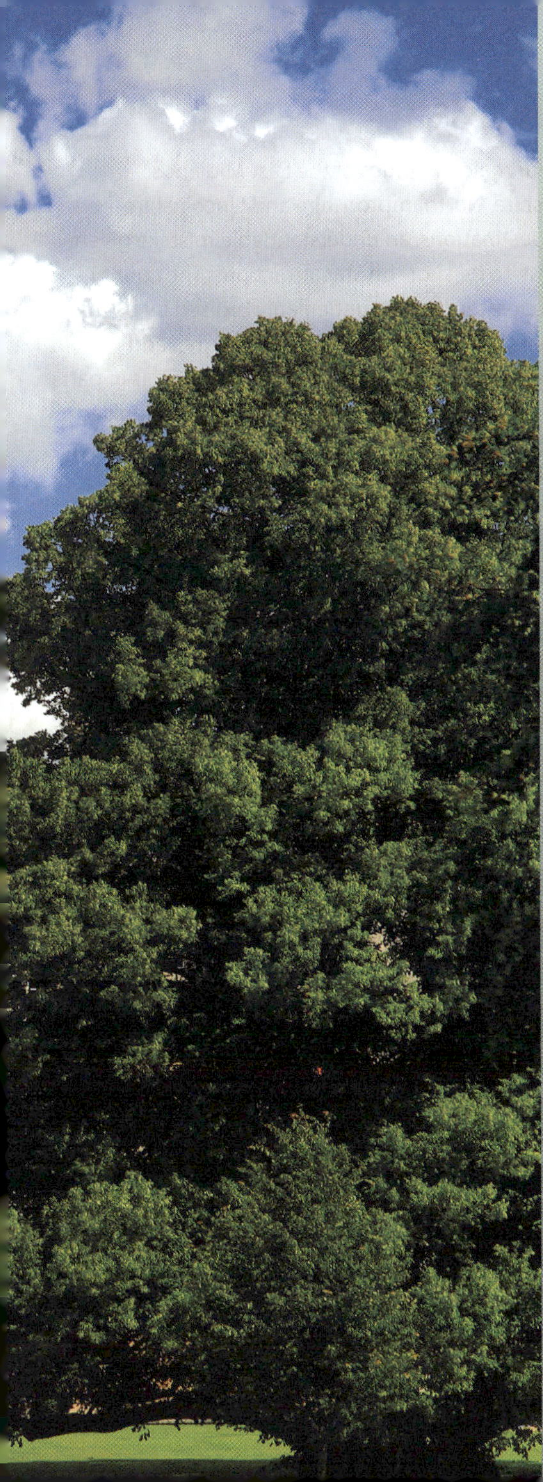

The East Midlands

419 Nottingham and around

424 Northern Nottinghamshire

425 Leicester

428 Market Bosworth and around

429 Ashby-de-la-Zouch and around

430 Rutland

431 Northampton

432 Around Northampton

434 Lincoln

438 The Lincolnshire coast

438 The Lincolnshire Fens

439 Stamford

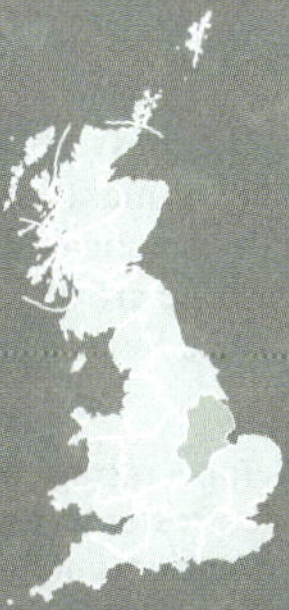

BURGHLEY HOUSE

9

The East Midlands

Many tourists bypass the four major counties of the East Midlands – Nottinghamshire, Leicestershire, Northamptonshire and Lincolnshire – on their way to more obvious destinations, an understandable mistake given that the region seems, at first, to be short on star attractions. The county towns of Nottingham and Leicester, though undeniably bruised by postwar town planning and industrial development, have enough sights and character to give them appeal, and Lincoln, with its fine cathedral, is in parts at least a dignified old city, but it's the surrounding countryside, sprinkled with prestigious country homes, pretty villages and historic market towns that provides the real draw in this region.

In **Nottinghamshire**, Byron's **Newstead Abbey** is intriguing; the Elizabethan **Hardwick Hall** (just over the border in Derbyshire but covered in this chapter) is even better. **Leicestershire** offers Market Bosworth, an amiable country town famous as the site of the battle of Bosworth Field, and a particularly intriguing church at Breedon-on-the-Hill. The county also lies adjacent to the easy countryside of **Rutland**, the region's smallest county, where you'll find another pleasant country town, **Oakham**. Rutland and **Northamptonshire** benefit from the use of limestone as the traditional building material and rural Northamptonshire is studded with handsome stone villages and towns – most notably **Fotheringhay** – as well as a battery of country estates, the best known of which is **Althorp**, the final resting place of Princess Diana.

Lincolnshire is very different in character from the rest of the region, an agricultural backwater that remains surprisingly remote – locals sometimes call it the "forgotten county". This was not always the case: throughout medieval times the county flourished as a centre of the wool trade with Flanders, its merchants and landowners becoming some of the wealthiest in England. Reminders of the high times are legion, beginning with the majestic cathedral that graces the county town of **Lincoln**. Equally enticing is the splendidly intact stone town of **Stamford**, while out in the sticks, Lincolnshire's most distinctive feature is **The Fens**, whose pancake-flat fields, filling out much of the south of the county and extending deep into Cambridgeshire, have been regained from the marshes and the sea. Fenland villages are generally short of charm, but their **parish churches**, whose spires regularly interrupt the wide-skied landscape, are simply stunning; two of the finest – at Gedney and Long Sutton – are set beside the A17 as it slices across the fens on its way to Norfolk. Very different again is the Lincolnshire **coast**, whose long sandy beach extends, with a few marshy interruptions, from Mablethorpe to **Skegness**, the region's main resort. The coast has long attracted thousands of holiday-makers from the big cities of the East Midlands and Yorkshire, hence its trail of bungalows, campsites and caravan parks, though significant chunks of the seashore are now protected as **nature reserves**, with the Gibraltar Point National Nature Reserve being the pick.

Top 5 restaurants p.422
Leicester festivals p.426
Outdoors at Rutland Water p.431
The Nene Way p.433
Guided tours of Lincoln Cathedral p.436
The Lincoln imp p.437
Shakespeare in the Park p.441

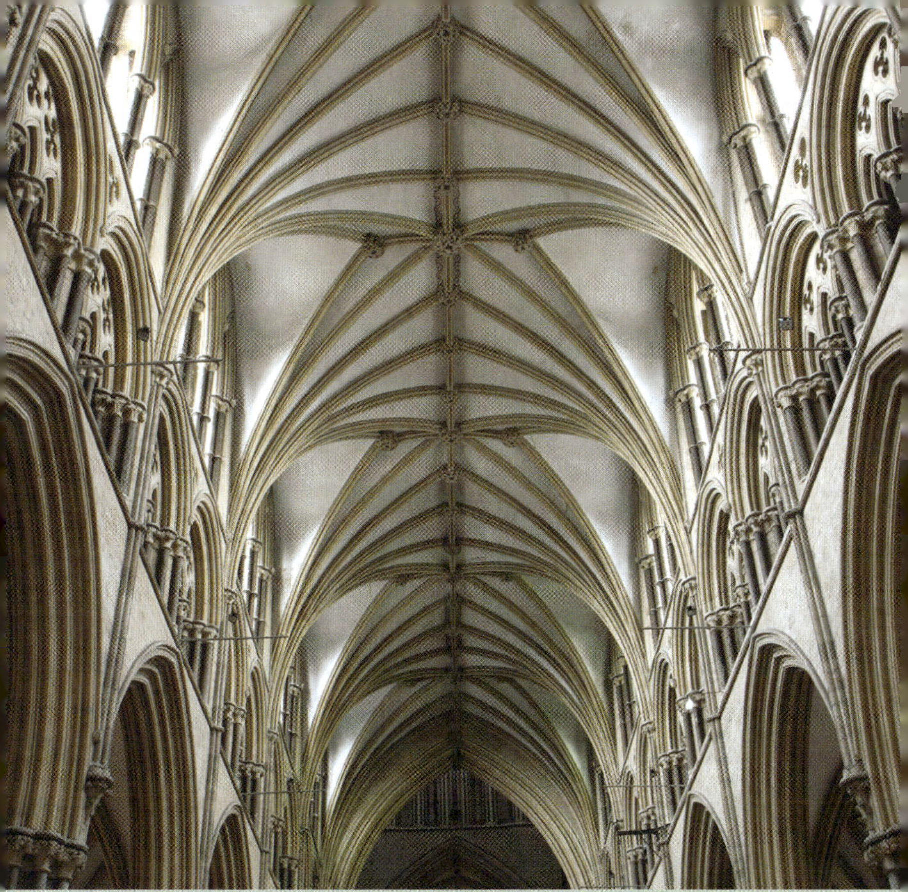

LINCOLN CATHEDRAL

Highlights

❶ **Memsaab Restaurant, Nottingham** This hard-to-beat Indian restaurant brings sophisticated style and oodles of gastronomic flair to Nottingham's dining scene. Everything's good, but try the Amritsari Machli (fried cod) for a fail-safe bet. **See p.423**

❷ **Newstead Abbey** One-time home of Lord Byron, this intriguing old mansion has superb period rooms, lots of Byron memorabilia, and lovely gardens. **See p.424**

❸ **Hardwick Hall** A beautifully preserved Elizabethan mansion that was home to the formidable Bess of Hardwick, one of the leading businesspeople of the sixteenth century. The gardens and surrounding parkland are wonderful, too. **See p.425**

❹ **Lincoln Cathedral** One of the finest medieval cathedrals in the land, dominating this fine old city and seen to best advantage on a rooftop guided tour. Watch out for the Lincoln imp! **See p.435**

❺ **Stamford** Lincolnshire's prettiest town, with its cobbled lanes, lovely old churches, and ancient limestone buildings, well deserves an overnight stay – and you can eat in style here too. **See p.439**

HIGHLIGHTS ARE MARKED ON THE MAP ON P.418

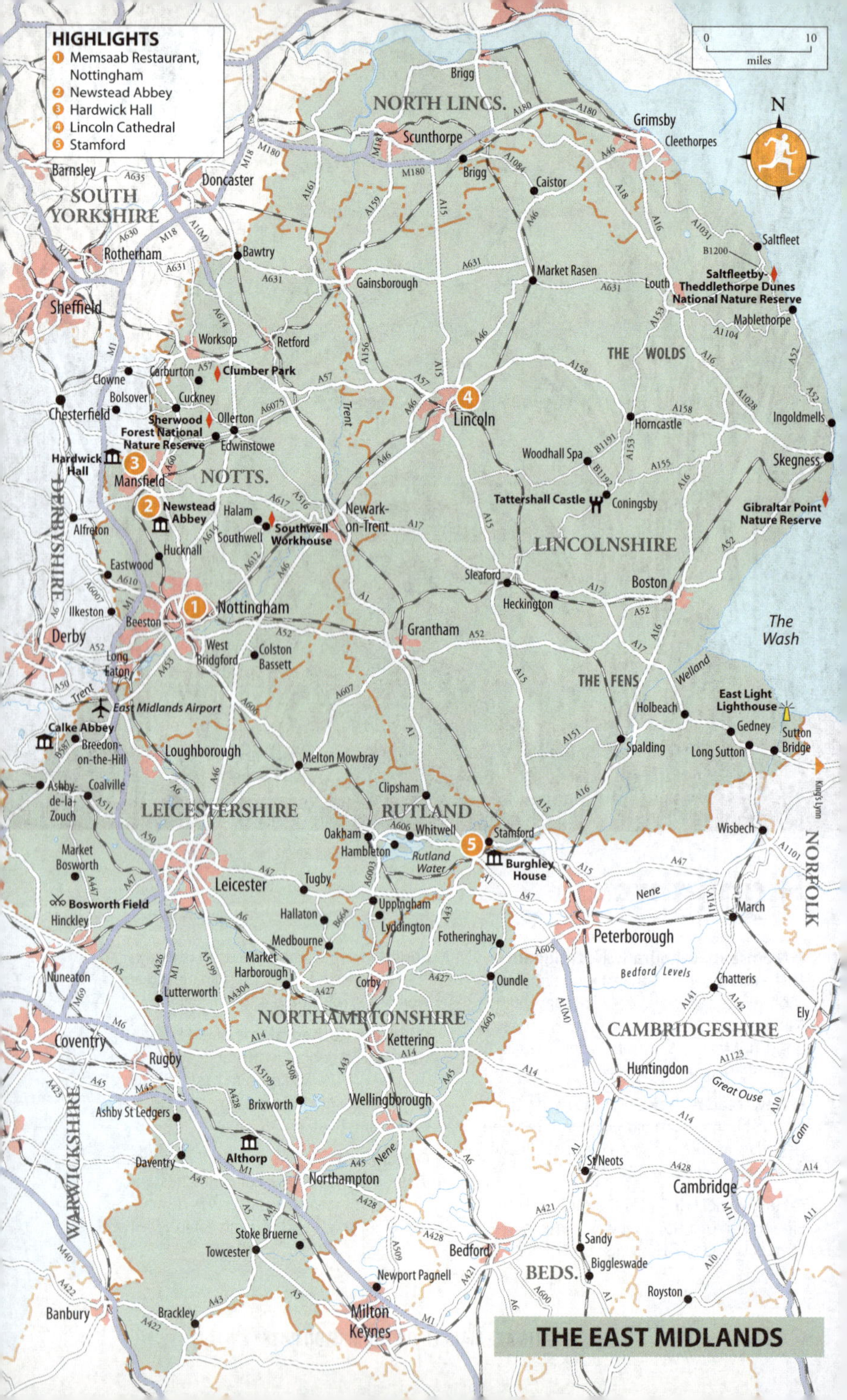

HIGHLIGHTS
1 Memsaab Restaurant, Nottingham
2 Newstead Abbey
3 Hardwick Hall
4 Lincoln Cathedral
5 Stamford
0
10
miles
N
THE EAST MIDLANDS
NORTH LINCS.
SOUTH YORKSHIRE
NOTTS.
DERBYSHIRE
LINCOLNSHIRE
LEICESTERSHIRE
RUTLAND
NORTHAMPTONSHIRE
CAMBRIDGESHIRE
WARWICKSHIRE
NORFOLK
BEDS.
THE WOLDS
THE FENS
The Wash
Brigg
Scunthorpe
Grimsby
Cleethorpes
Barnsley
Doncaster
Caistor
Saltfleet
Saltfleetby-Theddlethorpe Dunes National Nature Reserve
Mablethorpe
Rotherham
Bawtry
Gainsborough
Market Rasen
Louth
Sheffield
Worksop
Retford
Clumber Park
Carburton
Clowne
Bolsover
Cuckney
Chesterfield
Sherwood Forest National Nature Reserve
Ollerton
Edwinstowe
Lincoln
Horncastle
Ingoldmells
Skegness
Woodhall Spa
Hardwick Hall
Mansfield
Newstead Abbey
Halam
Southwell Workhouse
Southwell
Newark-on-Trent
Tattershall Castle
Coningsby
Gibraltar Point Nature Reserve
Alfreton
Hucknall
Eastwood
Sleaford
Boston
Heckington
Ilkeston
Nottingham
Beeston
Derby
West Bridgford
Colston Bassett
Grantham
Long Eaton
East Midlands Airport
Trent
Welland
East Light Lighthouse
Holbeach
Gedney
Sutton Bridge
Long Sutton
Spalding
Calke Abbey
Breedon-on-the-Hill
Loughborough
Melton Mowbray
King's Lynn
Ashby-de-la-Zouch
Coalville
Clipsham
Oakham
Whitwell
Hambleton
Rutland Water
Stamford
Burghley House
Wisbech
Market Bosworth
Leicester
Tugby
Bosworth Field
Hinckley
Hallaton
Uppingham
Lyddington
Medbourne
Fotheringhay
Peterborough
March
Nene
Market Harborough
Corby
Oundle
Bedford Levels
Chatteris
Nuneaton
Lutterworth
Coventry
Kettering
Ely
Rugby
Huntingdon
Great Ouse
Ashby St Ledgers
Brixworth
Wellingborough
Daventry
Althorp
Northampton
St Neots
Cambridge
Cam
Stoke Bruerne
Towcester
Bedford
Sandy
Biggleswade
Newport Pagnell
Royston
Banbury
Brackley
Milton Keynes

GETTING AROUND **THE EAST MIDLANDS**

Travelling between the cities of the East Midlands by **train** or **bus** is simple and most of the larger towns have good regional links, too. Things are very different in the country, however, where bus services are distinctly patchy. The region has one international **airport**, East Midlands (ⓦ eastmidlandsairport.com), just off the M1 between Derby, Nottingham and Leicester.

Nottingham and around

With a population of around 290,000, **NOTTINGHAM** is one of England's big cities. A one-time lace manufacturing and pharmaceutical centre (the Boots chain is from here), today it is still famous for its association with **Robin Hood**, the legendary thirteenth-century outlaw. Hood's bitter enemy was, of course, the **Sheriff of Nottingham**, but unfortunately his home and lair – the city's imposing medieval castle – is long gone, replaced by a handsome Palladian mansion that is still called, somewhat confusingly, Nottingham Castle. Nowadays, Nottingham is at its most diverting in and around both the castle and the handsome **Market Square**, which is also the centre of a heaving, teeming nightlife every weekend. Within easy striking distance of the city is the former coal-mining village of **Eastwood**, home of the **D.H. Lawrence Birthplace Museum**.

Brief history

Controlling a strategic crossing point over the River Trent, the Saxon town of **Nottingham** was built on one of a pair of sandstone hills whose 130ft cliffs looked out over the river valley. In 1068, William the Conqueror built a castle on the other hill, and the Saxons and Normans traded on the low ground in between, the Market Square. The castle was a military stronghold and royal palace, the equal of the great castles of Windsor and Dover, and every medieval king of England paid regular visits. In August 1642, Charles I stayed here too, riding out of the castle to raise his standard and start the Civil War – not that the locals were overly sympathetic. Hardly anyone joined up, even though the king had the ceremony repeated on the next three days.

After the Civil War, the Parliamentarians slighted the castle and, in the 1670s, the ruins were cleared by the Duke of Newcastle to make way for a palace, whose continental – and, in English terms, novel – design he chose from a pattern book, probably by Rubens. Beneath the castle lay a handsome, well-kept market town until the second half of the eighteenth century, when the city was transformed by the expansion of the lace and hosiery industries. Within the space of fifty years, Nottingham's population increased from ten thousand to fifty thousand, the resulting slum becoming a hotbed of radicalism.

The worst of Nottingham's slums were cleared in the early twentieth century, when the city centre assumed its present structure, with the main commercial area ringed by alternating industrial and residential districts. Thereafter, crass postwar development, adding tower blocks, shopping centres and a ring road, ensconced and embalmed the remnants of the city's past.

The Market Square

One of the best-looking central squares in England, Nottingham's **Market Square** is still the heart of the city, an airy open plaza whose shops, offices and fountains are overseen and overlooked by the grand neo-Baroque **Council House**, completed as part of a make-work scheme in 1928. Also on the square is a statue honouring one of the city's heroes, the former manager of Nottingham Forest FC, **Brian Clough** (1935–2004), shown in his characteristic trainers and tracksuit. Clough won two

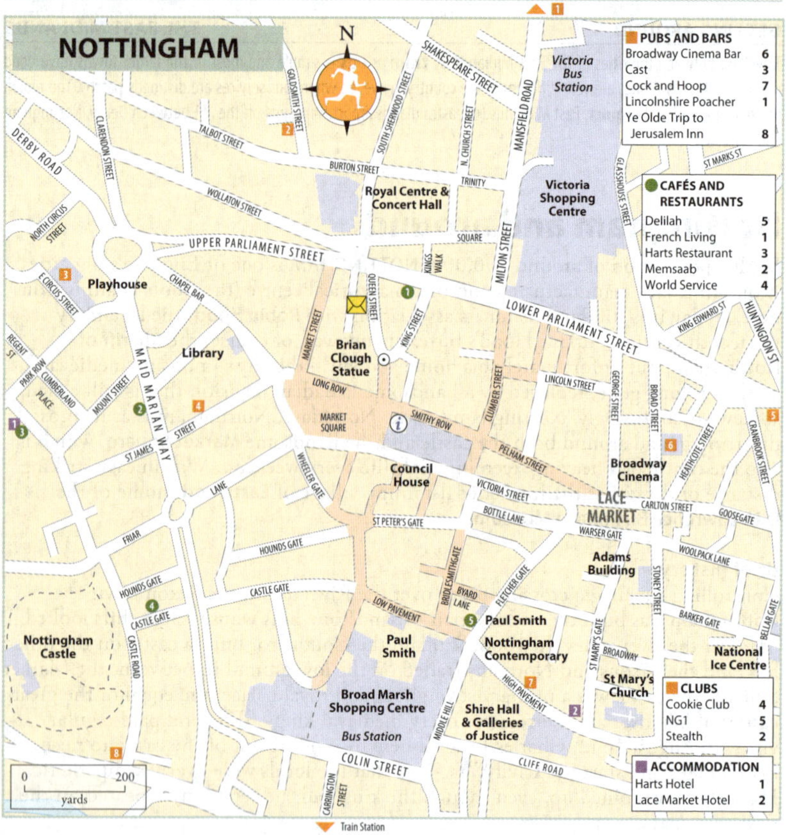

European cups with Forest, a remarkable achievement by any standards, but his popularity came as much from his forthright personality and idiosyncratic utterances. Two quotes suffice to show the mettle of the man: "I wouldn't say I was the best manager in the business, but I was in the top one", and, on the subject of hoofing the football into the air, "If God had wanted us to play football in the sky, He'd have put grass up there".

Nottingham Castle

Friar Lane • Tues–Sun: March–Sept 10am–5pm; Oct-Feb 10am–4pm • £5.50 • Ⓦ nottinghamcity.gov.uk **Caves** 2–3 1hr guided tours daily • £2.50 • Ⓣ 0115 915 3700

From the Market Square, it's a five-minute walk west up Friar Lane to **Nottingham Castle**, whose heavily restored medieval gateway leads into the gardens, which slope up to the squat, seventeenth-century ducal **palace**.

Inside, in the **Castle Museum and Art Gallery**, a particular highlight is the "Story of Nottingham", a lively, well-presented account of the city's development. Look out, too, for a small but exquisite collection of late medieval **alabaster carvings**, an art form for which Nottingham once had an international reputation. It's worth walking up to the top floor for a turn around the main **picture gallery**, a handsome and spacious room, which displays a curious assortment of mostly English nineteenth-century Romantic paintings.

Just outside the main entrance to the palace, two sets of steps lead down into the maze of ancient **caves** that honeycomb the cliff beneath. One set is open for guided tours, and this leads into **Mortimer's Hole**, a 300ft shaft along which, so the story goes, the young Edward III and his chums crept in October 1330 to capture the queen mother, Isabella, and her lover, Roger Mortimer. The couple had already polished off Edward III's father, the hapless Edward II, and were intent on usurping the crown, but the young Edward proved too shrewd for them and Mortimer came to a sticky end.

The Lace Market

The narrow lanes and alleys of the **Lace Market**, beginning a couple of minutes' walk east of the Market Square, are flanked by large and imposing Victorian factories and warehouses. **Stoney Street** is the Lace Market at its most striking, its star turn being the **Adams Building**, whose beautiful stone-and-brick facade combines both neo-Georgian and neo-Renaissance features. Neighbouring **Broadway** doesn't lag far **behind**, with a line of neat red-brick and sandstone-trimmed buildings performing a neat swerve halfway along the street. Sitting ugly on the edge of the Lace Market, there's also the spaceship-like **National Ice Centre** skating rink (Ⓦ national-ice-centre.com).

Galleries of Justice

High Pavement • Mon–Fri 9am–5pm, tours 10.30am–4pm; Sat & Sun 10.30am–5pm, tours 10.30am–4pm • Mon & Tues £5.95, Wed–Sun £8.95 • Ⓣ 0115 952 0555, Ⓦ galleriesofjustice.org.uk

The Lace Market abuts **High Pavement**, the administrative centre of Nottingham in Georgian times, and it's here you'll find **Shire Hall**, whose Neoclassical columns, pilasters and dome date from 1770. The facade also bears the marks of a real Georgian cock-up: to the left of the entrance, at street level, the mason carved the word "Goal" onto an arch and then had to have a second bash, turning it into "Gaol"; both versions are clearly visible. The hall now houses the **Galleries of Justice**, whose child-friendly "Crime and Punishment" tour involves lots of role play. The building is actually much more interesting than the hoopla, incorporating two superbly preserved Victorian courtrooms, an Edwardian police station, some spectacularly unpleasant old cells, a women's prison with bath house and a prisoners' exercise yard.

Nottingham Contemporary

Weekday Cross • Tues–Fri 10am–7pm, Sat 10am–6pm, Sun 11am–5pm • Free • Ⓣ 0115 948 9750, Ⓦ nottinghamcontemporary.org

Just along the street from the Galleries of Justice is the city's new art gallery, **Nottingham Contemporary**, which – despite the grand assurances of the architects – looks like something assembled from a giant IKEA flat pack. That said, the gallery's temporary exhibitions are consistently strong; hit shows have included the early paintings of David Hockney and the sculptures and installations of Klaus Weber.

Paul Smith

10 Byard Lane Mon–Sat 10am–6pm, Sun 11am–5pm • Ⓣ 0115 950 6712 **20 Low Pavement** Mon–Sat 10am–6pm, Sun 11am–5pm • Ⓣ 0115 968 5990, Ⓦ paulsmith.co.uk

Local lad Paul Smith (b.1946) worked in a clothing factory as a young man, but only developed a passion for art and design after a bike accident left him incapacitated for six months. He opened his first small shop on Byard Lane in 1970, since when he has gone on to become one of the major success stories of contemporary British fashion, his trademark multicoloured stripes proving popular on every continent. He also has a much larger, flagship store just around the corner at 20 Low Pavement.

9

D.H. Lawrence Birthplace Museum

8a Victoria St, Eastwood, off Nottingham Rd • Guided tours by advance booking only • £5 • ⓣ 01773 717353, ⓦ broxtowe.gov.uk • There is a good bus service from Nottingham's Victoria bus station to Eastwood (every 20min; 30min); ask the driver to put you off at the nearest stop

D.H. Lawrence (1885–1930) was born in the pit village of **Eastwood**, about six miles west of Nottingham. The mine closed years ago, and Eastwood is something of a post-industrial eyesore, but Lawrence's childhood home has survived, a tiny, red-brick terraced house refurbished as the **D.H. Lawrence Birthplace Museum**. None of the furnishings and fittings are Lawrence originals, which isn't too surprising considering the family moved out when he was two, but it's an appealing evocation of the period, interlaced with biographical insights into the author's early life. Afterwards, enthusiasts can follow the three-mile Blue Line Walk round those parts of Eastwood with Lawrence associations: the walk takes an hour or so, and a brochure is available at the museum. Interestingly, few locals thought well of Lawrence – and the sexual scandals hardly helped. Famously, he ran off with Frieda, the wife of a Nottingham professor, and then there was the *Lady Chatterley's Lover* obscenity trial, but much of his local unpopularity was caused by the author's move to the political right until, eventually, he espoused a cranky and unpleasant form of (Nietzschean) elitism.

ARRIVAL AND INFORMATION — NOTTINGHAM

By plane East Midlands Airport is 18 miles southwest of the city; Skylink buses (ⓦ eastmidlandsairport.com) run into town, pulling in at the bus stop opposite the train station.

By train Nottingham train station is on the south side of the city centre, a 5- to 10min walk (just follow the signs), or a tram ride, from the Market Square.

Destinations Birmingham (every 20–30min; 1hr 20min); Leicester (every 30min; 20min); Lincoln (hourly; 1hr 10min); London (hourly; 1hr 40min); Newark (hourly; 30min); Oakham (hourly; 1hr, change at Leicester).

By bus Most long-distance buses arrive at the Broad Marsh bus station, down the street from the train station on the way to the centre, but some – including services to north Nottinghamshire (see p.424) – pull in at the Victoria bus station, a 5min walk north of the Market Square.

Tourist office Market Square, on the ground floor of the Council House, 1 Smithy Row (Mon–Fri 9am–5.30pm, Sat 9.30am–5pm; ⓣ 0844 477 5678, ⓦ visitnottingham.com).

ACCOMMODATION

Almost all of Nottingham's central hotels are standard-issue chains; the best located is the *Jury's Inn*, in a large tower block near the train station on Station St.

★ **Harts Hotel** Standard Hill, Park Row ⓣ 0115 988 1900, ⓦ hartsnottingham.co.uk. Chic hotel, with lots of style – ultramodern fixtures and fittings, Egyptian cotton bed linen and so forth. It also has a first-rate location, near both the castle and the Market Square. The restaurant is excellent, too (see below). **£125**

Lace Market Hotel 29 High Pavement ⓣ 0115 852 3232, ⓦ thefinessecollection.com. Great location, footsteps from Nottingham Contemporary, this smart hotel has just over forty slick, modern rooms decorated in sharp minimalist style – and all within a tastefully modernized Georgian building. **£70**

EATING

Delilah 15 Middle Pavement ⓣ 0115 948 4461, ⓦ delilahfinefoods.co.uk. The best deli in town, with more cooked meats and cheeses than you can shake a stick at plus a café-counter for tasty lunches and light meals, though finding a seat can be difficult. Mon–Fri 8am–7pm, Sat 9am–7pm & Sun 11am–5pm.

TOP 5 RESTAURANTS

George Hotel Stamford. See p.441
Maiyango Leicester. See p.428
Memsaab Nottingham. See p.423
Old Bakery Lincoln. See p.437
World Service Nottingham. See p.423

French Living 27 King St ⓣ 0115 958 5885, ⓦ frenchliving.co.uk. Authentic French cuisine served in an intimate, candlelit basement. Daytime snacks and baguettes in the ground-floor café too. Evening main courses from £12. Mon–Sat noon–10pm.

Harts Restaurant Standard Court, Park Row ⓣ 0115 911 0666, ⓦ hartsnottingham.co.uk. One of the city's most acclaimed restaurants, occupying part of the old general hospital and serving an international menu of carefully presented meals. Attractive modernist decor and attentive service; reservations are recommended. Mains from about £17. For something rather less expensive, go next door to the bar of *Harts Hotel* (see opposite), where – among much else – they serve great fish and chips with mushy peas. Restaurant daily noon–2pm & 7–10.30pm, Sun till 9pm.

★ **Memsaab** 12 Maid Marian Way ⓣ0115 957 0009, ⓦmem-saab.co.uk. One of a new breed of Indian restaurants (to Nottingham at least) – no burgundy flock wallpaper here, but crisp modern decor and bags of space. The food – canny amalgamations of different Indian cooking styles from different regions – is exquisite. The large and imaginative menu has main courses starting from as little as £10. Try the fried cod, Goan fish curry or the slow-cooked lamb flavoured with cardamom. Mon–Sat 5.30–10.30pm, Sun 5.30–10pm.

★ **World Service** Newdigate House, Castle Gate ⓣ0115 847 5587, ⓦworldservicerestaurant.com. Chic restaurant with bags of decorative flair in charming premises up near the castle. A Modern British menu, featuring such offerings as pork cutlets with onion marmalade and rack of lamb with butternut squash tarte tatin, is prepared with imagination and close attention to detail. In the evenings, main courses start at around £17, but there are great deals at lunchtimes with two-course set meals costing £13, or £18 for three courses. Daily noon–2pm & 7–10pm, Sun till 9pm.

DRINKING

Central Nottingham's **pubs** literally heave on the weekend and are not for the faint-hearted. Anyone over thirty years old (or even twenty) may well prefer the quieter pubs a few minutes' walk out of the centre.

★ **Broadway Cinema Bar** Broadway Cinema, 14 Broad St in the Lace Market ⓣ0115 9526611, ⓦbroadway.org.uk. Informal, fashionable (in an arty sort of way) bar serving an eclectic assortment of bottled beers to a cinema-keen clientele. Filling, inexpensive bar food too. Daily breakfast 9am–noon; bar food noon–9pm.

★ **Cast** Nottingham Playhouse, Wellington Circus ⓣ0115 941 9419, ⓦnottinghamplayhouse.co.uk. The bar of the Nottingham Playhouse is a popular, easy-going spot with courtyard seating on summer nights. Patrons have the advantage of being able to gaze at a piece of modern art too – Anish Kapoor's whopping, reflective *Sky Mirror*. Daily noon–late.

Cock and Hoop 25 High Pavement, Lace Market ⓣ0115 852 3231. Smart and small, well-behaved city-centre pub with thick carpets and comfortable chairs. Superior bar food is served in the main bar at the front and in the cellar-like room at the back. Real ales, too. Very different from almost every other pub in the centre. Daily noon–11pm; food served Mon–Sat noon–3pm & 6–10pm, Sun noon–6pm.

Lincolnshire Poacher 161 Mansfield Rd ⓣ0115 941 1584. Very popular and relaxed pub, where the decor is pleasantly traditional and the customers take their (real) ales fairly seriously. Attracts an older clientele. About half a mile from the Market Square. Mon–Wed 11am–11pm, Thurs–Sat 11am–midnight, Sun noon–11pm.

★ **Ye Olde Trip to Jerusalem Inn** Brewhouse Yard, below the castle ⓣ0115 947 3171, ⓦtriptojerusalem.com. Carved into the castle rock, this ancient inn – said to be the oldest in England – may well have been a meeting point for soldiers gathering for the Third Crusade. Its cave-like bars, with their rough sandstone ceilings, are delightfully secretive and there's a good range of ales too. Sun–Thurs 11am–11pm, Fri & Sat 11am–midnight.

NIGHTLIFE

Cookie Club 22 James St ⓣ0115 988 1912, ⓦcookieclub.co.uk. Central nightspot casting a wide musical net, from indie/student favourites to goth and retro. Wed, Fri & Sat 10.30pm–3am.

NG1 76 Lower Parliament St ⓣ0115 958 8440, ⓦng1club.co.uk. Nottingham's leading gay club with four ambiences, three sound systems, two dancefloors and a capacity of 800. Wed & Sun 11pm–4am, Fri 10pm–5am Sat 10pm–6am.

Stealth Masonic Place, Goldsmith St ⓣ0115 828 3174, ⓦstealthattack.co.uk. The biggest club in Nottingham hosts live music, wild club nights and a battery of leading DJs.

ENTERTAINMENT

The Broadway 14 Broad St in the Lace Market ⓣ0115 9526611, ⓦbroadway.org.uk. The best cinema in the city, featuring a mixed bag of mainstream and avant-garde films.

Nottingham Playhouse Wellington Circus ⓣ0115 941 9419, ⓦnottinghamplayhouse.co.uk. Long-established theatre offering a wide-ranging programme of plays – Shakespeare through to Ayckbourn – plus dance, music and comedy, often with a local twist or theme.

Royal Centre Concert Hall South Sherwood St ⓣ0115 989 5555, ⓦroyalcentre-nottingham.co.uk. All the big names in live music, both popular and classical, play at this large auditorium.

9

Northern Nottinghamshire

Rural **northern Nottinghamshire**, with its gentle rolling landscapes and large ducal estates, was transformed in the nineteenth century by **coal** – deep, wide seams of the stuff that spawned dozens of collieries, and colliery towns, stretching north across the county and on into Yorkshire. Almost without exception, the mines have closed, their passing marked only by the occasional pithead winding wheel, left to commemorate the thousands of men who laboured here. The suddenness of the pit closure programme imposed by the Conservative government in the 1980s knocked the stuffing out of the area, but one prop of its slow revival has been the tourist industry: the countryside in between these former mining communities holds several enjoyable attractions, the best-known of which is **Sherwood Forest** – or at least the patchy remains of it – with one chunk of woodland preserved in the Sherwood Forest National Nature Reserve, supposedly where Robin Hood did some canoodling with Maid Marian. Byron is a pipsqueak in the celebrity stakes by comparison, but his family home – **Newstead Abbey** – is here too, as is **Hardwick Hall**, a handsome Elizabethan mansion built at the behest of one of the most powerful women of her day, Bess of Hardwick (1521–1608).

With the exception of Hardwick Hall, all these attractions are easy to reach by **bus** from Nottingham.

Newstead Abbey

Ten miles north of Nottingham on the A60 • **House** April–Sept Sun guided tours 1pm, 2pm & 3pm; 45min **Gardens** Daily 9am–6pm or dusk • House & gardens £10; gardens only £4 • ⓦ newsteadabbey.org.uk

In 1539, **Newstead Abbey** was granted by Henry VIII to Sir John Byron, who demolished most of the church and converted the monastic buildings into a family home. **Lord Byron (1788–1824)** inherited the estate, which was by then little more than a ruin, in 1798; he restored part of the complex during his six-year residence (1808–14), but most of the present structure actually dates from later renovations, which maintained much of the shape and feel of the medieval original while creating the warren-like mansion that exists today. Inside, a string of intriguing period rooms begins with the neo-Gothic Great Hall and Byron's bedroom, one of the few rooms to look pretty much like it did when he lived here, and then continues on into the Library, which holds a collection of the poet's possessions, from letters and an inkstand through to his pistols and boxing gloves. A further room contains a set of satirical, cartoon-like watercolours entitled *The Wonderful History of Lord Byron & His Dog* by his friend Elizabeth Pigot – there's a portrait of the self-same dog, Boatswain, in the south gallery, and a conspicuous memorial bearing an absurdly extravagant inscription to the mutt in the delightful walled garden. Beyond lie the main gardens, a secretive and subtle combination of lake, Gothic waterfalls, yew tunnels and Japanese-style rockeries, complete with idiosyncratic pagodas.

ARRIVAL AND DEPARTURE — NEWSTEAD ABBEY

A fast and frequent Pronto **bus** (every 20min; 25min; ⓣ 0845 606 0605, ⓦ prontobus.co.uk) leaves Nottingham's Victoria bus station bound for Mansfield; it stops at the gates of Newstead Abbey, a mile from the house.

Sherwood Forest

Edwinstowe • Daily dawn–dusk • Free, but weekend parking fee £3 • ⓣ 01623 823202, ⓦ nottinghamshire.gov.uk

Most of **Sherwood Forest**, once a vast royal woodland of oak, birch and bracken covering all of northern Nottinghamshire, was cleared in the eighteenth century. It's difficult today to imagine the protection all the greenery provided for generations of outlaws, the most famous of whom was of course **Robin Hood**. There's no "true story" of Robin's life – the earliest reference to him, in Langland's *Piers Plowman* of 1377, treats him as a fiction – but to the balladeers of fifteenth-century England, who invented most of Hood's folklore, this was hardly the point. For them, Robin was a symbol of yeoman decency, a semi-mythological opponent of corrupt clergymen and evil officers of the law; in the early tales, Robin may show sympathy for the peasant, but he has rather more respect for the decent nobleman, and he's never credited with robbing the rich to give to the poor. This and other parts of the legend, such as Maid Marian and Friar Tuck, were added later. Robin Hood may lack historical authenticity, but it hasn't discouraged the county council from spending thousands of pounds sustaining the **Major Oak**, the creaky tree where Maid Marian and Robin are supposed to have plighted their troth. The Major Oak is on a pleasant one-mile woodland walk that begins beside the visitor centre at the main entrance to **Sherwood Forest National Nature Reserve**, which comprises 450 acres of oak and silver birch crisscrossed with footpaths.

ARRIVAL AND INFORMATION — SHERWOOD FOREST

Stagecoach's Sherwood Arrow **bus** (W stagecoachbus.com) links Nottingham's Victoria bus station with Worksop via the visitor centre (4 daily; 1hr). The Sherwood Forest National Nature Reserve **visitor centre** is half a mile north of the village of Edwinstowe, which is itself about 20 miles north of Nottingham via the A614.

Hardwick Hall

Doe Lea, Derbyshire • **Hardwick Hall & gardens** Mid-Feb to Oct Wed–Sun 11am–4.30pm • NT • Hall & gardens £10; gardens £5; combined ticket Hardwick Hall, gardens and Hardwick Old Hall £12 **Parkland** Daily 8.30am–6pm or dusk • NT • Free • T 01246 850430 **Hardwick Old Hall** April–Oct Wed–Sun 10am–5pm • EH • £4.50, car parking £2; combined ticket with Hardwick Hall and Gardens £12 • T 01246 850431

Born the daughter of a minor Derbyshire squire, Elizabeth, Countess of Shrewsbury (1527–1608) – aka **Bess of Hardwick** – became one of the leading figures of Elizabethan England, renowned for her political and business acumen. She also had a penchant for building and her major achievement, **Hardwick Hall,** begun when she was 62, has survived in amazingly good condition. The house was the epitome of fashionable taste, a balance of symmetry and ingenious detail in which the rectangular lines of the building are offset by line upon line of windows – there's actually more glass than stone – while up above, her giant-sized initials (E.S.) hog every roof line. Inside on the top floor, the **High Great Chamber**, where Bess received her most distinguished guests, boasts an extraordinary plaster frieze, a brightly painted, finely worked affair celebrating the goddess Diana, the virgin huntress – it was, of course, designed to please the Virgin Queen herself. Next door, the breathtaking **Long Gallery** features exquisite furnishings and fittings from splendid chimneypieces and tapestries through to a set of portraits, including one each of the queen and Bess. Bess could exercise here while keeping out of the sun – at a time when any hint of a tan was considered decidedly plebeian.

Outside, the **garden** makes for a pleasant wander and, beyond the ha-ha (the animal-excluding low wall and ditch), rare breeds of cattle and sheep graze the surrounding **parkland.** Finally – and rather confusingly – Hardwick Hall is next to **Hardwick Old Hall**, Bess's previous home, but now little more than a broken-down if substantial ruin.

ARRIVAL AND DEPARTURE — HARDWICK HALL

The easiest way to reach Hardwick is via the M1: come off at Junction 29 and follow the signs from the roundabout at the top of the slip road ; it's a 3-mile trip. There are no buses.

Leicester

At first glance, **LEICESTER**, some 25 miles south of Nottingham, seems a resolutely modern city, but further inspection reveals traces of its medieval and Roman past, situated immediately to the west of the downtown shopping area near the River Soar.

9

It's probably fair to say that Leicester has a reputation for looking rather glum, but the centre is very much on the move, with the addition of Highcross, a brand new shopping centre, and the creation of a Cultural Quarter equipped with a flashy performance venue, **Curve Theatre**. The star turn, however, is the **New Walk Museum and Art Gallery**, which includes an exemplary collection of German Expressionist paintings. About a third of Leicester's population is **Asian** – the city elected England's first Asian MP, Keith Vaz, in 1987. The focus of the Asian community is the **Belgrave Road** and its environs, an area of terraced houses about a mile to the northeast of the city centre beyond the flyover, where people come from miles around to eat at the splendid **Indian restaurants**.

Brief history

The Romans chose this site to keep an eye on the rebellious Corieltauvi, constructing a fortified town beside the Fosse Way (now the A46), the military road running from Lincoln to Cirencester. Later, the Emperor Hadrian kitted the place out with huge public buildings, though the Danes, who overran the area in the eighth century, were not overly impressed and didn't even bother to pilfer much of the stone. Later still, the town's medieval castle became the base of the earls of Leicester, the most distinguished of whom was **Simon de Montfort**, who forced Henry III to convene the first English Parliament in 1265. Since the late seventeenth century, Leicester has been a centre of the **hosiery trade** and it was this industry that attracted hundreds of Asian immigrants to settle here in the 1950s and 1960s.

The city centre

The most conspicuous buildings in Leicester's crowded centre are two large shopping centres, the ultramodern Highcross and the clumpy **Haymarket**, but the proper landmark is the Victorian **clocktower** of 1868, standing in front of the Haymarket and marking the spot where seven streets meet. One of the seven is Cheapside, which leads to Leicester's open-air **market** (Mon–Sat), one of the best of its type in the country and the place where the young **Gary Lineker**, now the UK's best-known football pundit, worked on the family stall. Good-hearted Gary remains a popular figure hereabouts and has been made a freeman of the city, which, among other things, gives him the right to graze his sheep in front of the town hall. East of the clocktower is Leicester's nascent **Cultural Quarter**, whose two main attractions are the **Curve Theatre** and the Phoenix cinema (see p.428).

The Lanes and around

One of the seven streets beginning at Leicester's clocktower is Silver Street (subsequently Guildhall Lane), which passes through **The Lanes**, where a medley of small, independent shops gives this part of the centre real character. Just south is **Leicester Cathedral** (Mon–Sat 8am–6pm, Sun 7am–5pm; free; Ⓦcathedral.leicester.anglican.org), a much-modified eleventh-century structure incorporating two finely carved porches – a stone one at the front and an earlier timber version at the rear.

LEICESTER FESTIVALS

Belgrave is the hub for two major Hindu festivals – **Diwali**, the Festival of Light, held in October or November, when six thousand lamps are strung out along Belgrave Road, and **Navratri**, a nine-day celebration in October held in honour of the goddess Durga. In addition, the city's sizeable Afro-Caribbean community holds England's second biggest street festival after the Notting Hill Carnival (see p.125), the **Leicester Caribbean Carnival** (Ⓦleicestercarnival.com), on the first weekend in August.

The Guildhall

Guildhall Lane • Feb–Nov Mon–Wed & Sat 11am–4.30pm, Sun 1–4.30pm • Free • ⓣ 0116 253 2569, ⓦ leicester.gov.uk

Next door to the Cathedral is the **Guildhall**, a half-timbered building that has served, variously, as the town hall, prison and police station. The most interesting part of a visit is the rickety Great Hall, its beams bent with age, but there are a couple of old cells too, plus the town gibbet on which the bodies of the hanged were publicly displayed until the 1840s.

The Jewry Wall

Beside St Nicholas Circle, a large roundabout that is part of the ring road, you'll spot the conspicuous **church of St Nicholas**; beside that, in a little dell, lie the foundations of the Emperor Hadrian's public baths, which culminate in the **Jewry Wall**, a substantial chunk of Roman masonry some 18ft high and 73ft long. The baths were a real irritation to the emperor: the grand scheme was spoilt by the engineers, who miscalculated the line of the aqueduct that was to pipe in the water, and so bathers had to rely on a hand-filled cistern replenished from the river – which wasn't what he had in mind at all.

Castle Gardens and around

Castle Gardens, a narrow strip of a park that runs alongside a canalized portion of the River Soar, is a pleasant spot, incorporating the overgrown mound where Leicester's Norman castle motte once stood.

St Mary de Castro

At the far end of Castle Gardens, you emerge on The Newarke; turn left and follow the road round, and in a jiffy you'll reach **Castle View**, a narrow lane spanned by the Turret Gateway, a rare survivor of the city's medieval castle. Just beyond the gateway is **St Mary de Castro**, a dignified old church with a dainty crocketed spire where Chaucer may well have got married.

New Walk Museum and Art Gallery

55 New Walk • Mon–Sat 10am–5pm, Sun 11am–5pm • Free • ⓣ 0116 225 4900, ⓦ leicester.gov.uk

The **New Walk** is a long and pleasant pedestrianized promenade that's home to the city's best museum, the **New Walk Museum and Art Gallery**. The museum covers a lot of ground, from the natural world to geology and beyond, but one highlight is its extensive collection of Ancient Egyptian artefacts, featuring mummies and hieroglyphic tablets brought back to Leicester in the 1880s. The museum also holds an enjoyable collection of paintings and, although these are rotated regularly, you're likely to see a good range of works by British artists as well as an outstanding collection of German Expressionist works, mostly sketches, woodcuts and lithographs by artists such as Otto Dix and George Grosz.

ARRIVAL AND INFORMATION — LEICESTER

By train Leicester train station is on London Rd, from where it's a 10min walk northwest to the city centre.

Destinations Birmingham (every 30min; 1hr); Lincoln (hourly; 1hr 40min); London (every 30min; 1hr 30min); Nottingham (every 30min; 30min); Oakham (hourly; 30min); Stamford (hourly; 50min).

By bus St Margaret's bus station is on the north side of the centre, just off Gravel St – to get to the Haymarket, just follow the signs.

Tourist office A short walk south of the Haymarket at 7–9 Every St, on Town Hall Square (Mon–Fri 10am–5.30pm, Sat 10am–5pm; ⓣ 0844 888 5181, ⓦ goleicestershire.com).

ACCOMMODATION

Leicester has a good crop of business **hotels**, mostly within walking distance of the train station. The tourist office (see above) will help fix you up with somewhere to stay, but things rarely get tight except during the Navrati and Diwali festivals (see opposite).

9

Belmont Hotel De Montfort St 0116 254 4773, belmonthotel.co.uk. Proficient hotel in a modernized and extended Georgian property about 300 yards south of the train station via London Rd. It's popular with business folk, though they have family rooms too. £79

Maiyango 13–21 St Nicholas Place 0116 251 8898, maiyango.com. The new kid on the accommodation block, this hotel – the best in town – has fourteen slick modern rooms with wooden floors, plasma TVs, subdued lighting and wide, low-slung beds. It also has a handy location, a brief walk from the principal sights and Leicester's main shopping centres, the Haymarket and Highcross. There's a first-rate restaurant on site too (see below). £90

Spindle Lodge Hotel 2 West Walk 0116 233 8801, spindlelodge.com. Well-maintained, family-run hotel in a pleasantly converted, three-storey, ivy-clad Victorian town house. The public rooms have period touches and the bed rooms beyond are decorated in plain, unfussy style. On a quiet residential street, a 10min walk south of the train station. £60

EATING AND DRINKING

Visitors to Leicester should have at least one meal in one of the **Indian restaurants** along **Belgrave Road**, which begins just beyond the flyover, a mile or so northeast of the centre. There are top-notch restaurants in the city centre too and a battery of **bars**, though most of these are chains.

Bobby's 154 Belgrave Rd 0116 266 0106, eatatbobbys.com. This bright, modern Gujarati restaurant – and takeaway – is strictly vegetarian. A mind-blowing menu covers almost every pure veg option you can think of, and then some. Mains from as little as £5. Daily 11am–10pm.

Chaat House 108 Belgrave Rd 0116 266 0513. Going for more than thirty years, the *Chaat House* is something of a local institution, serving satisfying mounds of vegetarian food to its many customers – the masala dosas are wonderful. £20 will cover a meal for two. Daily noon–8pm.

Globe 43 Silver St 0116 262 9819, everards.co.uk/pubs/globe_70. Traditional pub in an attractive old building at the heart of the city. Smashing range of real ales and filling bar food too. Mon–Thurs 11am–11pm, Fri & Sat 11am–midnight, Sun noon–10.30pm; food served Mon–Sat noon–7pm, Sun noon–5pm.

★ **Maiyango** 13–21 St Nicholas Place 0116 251 8898, maiyango.com. Chi-chi lounge-bar and restaurant beneath the hotel of the same name (see above). The restaurant mostly uses local, seasonal ingredients and the menu is wide-ranging – try the soy-scented guinea fowl breast in a sweet and sour plum jus, for example, or the courgette flowers with crab and lobster. Mains average £16. Mon & Tues noon–11pm, Wed noon–11.30pm, Thurs noon–midnight, Fri noon–1am, Sat noon–1.30am, Sun 6.30–10.30pm.

Taps 10 Guildhall Lane 0116 253 0904, tapsleicester.com. Inventive bar and restaurant, whose claim to fame is the beer taps at many of the tables – help yourself and pay later (yes, the taps are monitored as they dispense). Excellent range of bottled beers too, plus vaulted cellars that date back yonks, and an above-average menu – chicken breast stuffed with apples and stilton in a creamy leek sauce, for example, for just £12. Mon–Sat from noon.

NIGHTLIFE AND ENTERTAINMENT

Curve 60 Rutland St 0116 242 3595, curveonline.co.uk. At the heart of the Cultural Quarter, Curve is Leicester's leading performing arts venue, offering a varied programme from behind its startling glass facade.

Phoenix 4 Midland St 0116 242 2800, phoenix.org.uk. Just a couple of minutes' walk from Curve in the Cultural Quarter, the Phoenix is an outstanding art-house cinema, one of the best in the East Midlands.

Market Bosworth and around

The thatched cottages and Georgian houses of tiny **MARKET BOSWORTH**, some eleven miles west of Leicester, fan out from a dinky **Market Place**, which was an important trading centre throughout the Middle Ages. From the sixteenth to the nineteenth century, the dominant family hereabouts were the Dixies, merchant-landlords who mostly ended up at the **church of St Peter**.

The Dixies were not universally admired, however, and the young Samuel Johnson, who taught at the **Dixie Grammar School** – its elongated facade still abuts the Market Place – disliked the founder, Sir Wolstan Dixie, so much that he recalled his time there "with the strongest aversion and even a sense of horror".

Church of St Peter

Church St • Daily 8.30am–dusk • Free • T 01455 290239

The **church of St Peter**, a three-minute walk north of the Market Place, is a good-looking edifice with a castellated nave and a sturdy square tower. Heavily revamped by the Victorians, the church's interior is fairly routine, but the chancel does hold the early eighteenth-century **tomb** of John Dixie, one-time rector, who is honoured by a long hagiographic plaque and the effigy of his weeping sister.

Bosworth Field

Market Bosworth is best known for the **Battle of Bosworth Field**, which was fought on hilly countryside near the village in 1485. This was the last and most decisive battle of the Wars of the Roses, an interminably long-winded and bitterly violent conflict among the nobility for control of the English Crown. The victor was Henry Tudor, subsequently Henry VII; he defeated Richard III, who famously died on the battlefield. In desperation, Shakespeare's villainous Richard cried out "A horse, a horse, my kingdom for a horse," but in fact the defeated king seems to have been a much more phlegmatic character. Taking a glass of water before the fighting started, he actually said, "I live a king: if I die, I die a king".

Bosworth Battlefield Heritage Centre

Sutton Cheney, a couple of miles south of Market Bosworth • Daily: April–Oct 10am–5pm; Nov–March 10am–4pm • £7, plus £1.50 parking • T 01455 290429, W bosworthbattlefield.com

The **Bosworth Battlefield Heritage Centre** features a workmanlike description of the battle and explains its historical context, though the less said about the ersatz medieval village that is beginning to take shape next door the better. The Heritage Centre also has a separate section on recent archeological efforts to find the actual site of the battle: unfortunately, it turns out that the battlefield was a couple of miles further west on what is now private land, which leaves the centre, never mind the adjoining circular two-mile **Battle Trail**, which identifies where tradition had the protagonists meet, somewhat marooned. Nevertheless, the ramble along the trail is pleasant enough and on the way you'll pass **King Richard's Well**, a rough cairn where the king was supposed to have had his final drink.

ARRIVAL AND DEPARTURE — MARKET BOSWORTH

There are hourly **buses** from Leicester to Market Bosworth's Market Place.

ACCOMMODATION AND EATING

Softleys Market Place T 01455 290464, W softleys.com. Right in the centre of the village, this first-rate, family-run hotel has three well-appointed bedrooms decorated in a homely, informal style. The rooms are really run as an adjunct to the restaurant, where the menu is lively and creative – the lamb is especially good. Mains average around £17. Food served Tues–Sat noon–2pm & 7–10.30pm, last orders 9.45pm; Sun noon–3.15pm, last orders 2.30pm. **£85**

Ashby-de-la-Zouch and around

ASHBY-DE-LA-ZOUCH, fourteen miles northwest of Leicester, takes its fanciful name from two sources – the town's first Norman overlord was Alain de Parrhoet la Souche and the rest means "place by the ash trees". Nowadays, Ashby is far from rustic, but it's still an amiable little place with one main attraction, its **castle**.

Just a few miles away, **Breedon-on-the-Hill** is well worth a trip for its good walking and great views, and some fascinating Anglo-Saxon carvings at the Church of St Mary and St Hardulph.

9

Ashby Castle

South St, off the town's main drag, Market St • April–June & Sept–Oct Thurs–Mon 10am–5pm; July–Aug daily 10am–5pm; Nov–March Thurs–Mon 10am–4pm • EH • £4.30 • Buses to Market St from Leicester (every 30min; 1hr).

Originally a Norman manor house, Ashby's **castle** was the work of Edward IV's chancellor, Lord Hastings, who received his "licence to crenellate" in 1474. But Hastings didn't enjoy his new home for long. Just nine years later, he was dragged from a Privy Council meeting to have his head hacked off on a log by the order of Richard III, his crime being his lacklustre support for the Yorkist cause. Today, the rambling ruins include substantial leftovers from the old fortifications, as well as the shattered remains of the great hall, solar and chapel, but the star turn is the 100ft-high **Hastings Tower**, a self-contained four-storey stronghold which has survived in good nick. This tower house represented the latest thinking in castle design. It provided much better accommodation than was previously available, improved living quarters that reflected the power and pride of a burgeoning landowning class.

ARRIVAL AND DEPARTURE **ASHBY-DE-LA-ZOUCH**

Regular Arriva **buses** run from Leicester to Ashby's Market Place.

Breedon-on-the-Hill

It's five miles northeast from Ashby to the village of **BREEDON-ON-THE-HILL**, which sits in the shadow of the large, partly quarried hill from which it takes its name. A steep footpath and a winding, half-mile by-road lead up from the village to the summit, from where there are smashing views over the surrounding countryside.

Church of St Mary and St Hardulph

Daily 9.30am–4pm, sometimes later in summer • Free

Breedon is also the site of the fascinating **church of St Mary and St Hardulph**, which occupies the site of an Iron Age hill fort and an eighth-century Anglo-Saxon monastery. Mostly dating from the thirteenth century, the church is kitted out with a Georgian pulpit and pews as well as a large and distinctly rickety box pew. Much more rare are a number of **Anglo-Saxon carvings** that include individual saints and prophets and wall friezes, where a dense foliage of vines is inhabited by a tangle of animals and humans. The friezes are quite extraordinary, and the fact that the figures look Byzantine rather than Anglo-Saxon has fuelled much academic debate.

Rutland

To the east of Leicestershire lies England's smallest county, **Rutland**, reinstated in its own right in 1997 following 23 unpopular years of merger with its larger neighbour. Rutland has one real place of note, **Oakham**, a pocket-sized county town with a scattering of elegant Georgian buildings.

Oakham

The prosperity of well-heeled **OAKHAM**, 23 miles east of Leicester, is bolstered by Oakham School, one of the region's more exclusive private schools, and by its proximity to **Rutland Water**, a large reservoir whose assorted facilities attract cyclists, ramblers, sailors and birdwatchers by the hundred. Oakham's stone terraces and Georgian villas are too often interrupted to assume much grace, but the town does have its architectural moments, particularly in the L-shaped **Market Place**, where a brace of sturdy awnings shelter the old water pump and town stocks, and where **Oakham School** is housed in a series of impressive ironstone buildings.

OUTDOORS AT RUTLAND WATER

The gentle waters and easy, green hills of **Rutland Water** have made it a major centre for outdoor pursuits. There's sailing at Rutland Sailing Club (W rutlandsc.co.uk); cycle hire with Rutland Water Cycling (W rutlandcycling.com); and a Watersports Centre at Whitwell on the north shore (W anglianwater.co.uk). Rutland Water also attracts a wide range of waterfowl, which prompted the establishment of a **nature reserve** with no fewer than 27 hides and two visitor centres at its west end. The reserve is home to a successful Osprey breeding project (W ospreys.org.uk).

Oakham Castle

Market Place • Tues–Fri 10am–5pm, Sat 10am–4pm • Free • W rutland.gov.uk

A few steps from the north side of the Market Place stands **Oakham Castle**, a large banqueting hall that was once part of a twelfth-century fortified house. The hall is a good example of Norman domestic architecture and surrounding the building are the grassy banks that once served to protect it. Inside, the whitewashed walls are covered with **horseshoes**, the result of an ancient custom by which every lord or lady, king or queen, is obliged to present an ornamental horseshoe when they first set foot in the town.

All Saints' Church

On the right-hand side of Oakham School on the Market Place, a narrow lane leads to **All Saints' Church**, whose heavy tower and spire rise high above the town. Dating from the thirteenth century, the church is an architectural hybrid, but the airy interior is distinguished by the intense medieval carvings along the columns of the nave and choir, with Christian scenes and symbols set alongside dragons, grotesques, devils and demons.

ARRIVAL AND DEPARTURE — OAKHAM

By train Trains from Leicester pull into Oakham train station, on the northwest side of town, a 10min walk from the Market Place.

By bus Buses, which connect Oakham with Leicester, Nottingham and Melton Mowbray, arrive on John St, just west of the Market Place.

ACCOMMODATION AND EATING

Finch's Arms Oakham Rd, Hambleton T 01572 756575, W finchsarms.co.uk. Inhabiting old stone premises in the tiny hamlet of Hambleton, just outside Oakham, this country inn has been attractively modernized and its bar and restaurant serve good English dishes with local, seasonal ingredients; mains hover around £16. They also have a few smart, modern bedrooms. Food served Mon–Sat noon–2.30pm & 6.30–9.30pm, Sun noon–9.30pm. £115

Hambleton Hall Hambleton T 01572 756991, W hambletonhall.com. Just a couple of miles southeast of Oakham, overlooking Rutland Water in Hambleton, this opulent hotel occupies an imposing Baronial-Gothic mansion set in its own immaculate grounds. Part of the Relais & Châteaux group, it's seriously expensive – and seriously luxurious. £265

Northampton

Spreading north from the banks of the River Nene, **NORTHAMPTON** is a workaday town whose modern appearance largely belies its ancient past. Throughout the Middle Ages, this was one of central England's most important towns, a flourishing commercial hub whose now demolished castle was a popular stopping-off point for travelling royalty. A fire in 1675 burnt most of the medieval city to a cinder, and the Georgian town that grew up in its stead was itself swamped by the Industrial Revolution, when Northampton swarmed with boot- and shoemakers, whose products shod almost everyone in the British Empire. Errol Flynn kitted himself out with several pairs of Northampton shoes and boots when he was in repertory here in 1933, but he

9

annoyed the city's tailors no end by hightailing it out of town after a year, leaving a whopping tailors' debt behind him.

Church of All Saints

3 George Row • Mon–Sat 10am–5pm • Free • ⓣ 01604 632194, ⓦ allsaintsnorthampton.co.uk

From Northampton's expansive Market Square, it's just a short walk to the town's ecclesiastical pride and joy, the **Church of All Saints**, whose unusually secular appearance stems from its finely proportioned, pillared portico and towered cupola. A statue of a bewigged Charles II in Roman attire surmounts the portico, a (flattering) thank you for his donation of a thousand tons of timber after the Great Fire of 1675 had incinerated the earlier church. Inside, the handsome interior holds a sweeping timber gallery and a batch of Neoclassical pillars, which lead the eye up to the fancy plasterwork that decorates the ceiling.

Northampton Museum and Art Gallery

4–6 Guildhall Rd • Tues–Sat 10am–5pm, Sun 2–5pm • Free • ⓣ 01604 838111, ⓦ northampton.gov.uk

The **Northampton Museum and Art Gallery**, just a couple of minutes' walk from the church of All Saints, celebrates the town's industrial heritage with a wonderful collection of **shoes and boots**. Along with silk slippers, clogs and high-heeled nineteenth-century court shoes, there's one of the four boots worn by an elephant during the British Expedition of 1959, which retraced Hannibal's putative route over the Alps into Italy. There's celebrity footwear too, such as the giant DMs Elton John wore in *Tommy*, plus whole cabinets of heavy-duty riding boots, pearl-inlaid raised wooden sandals from Ottoman Turkey, and a couple of cabinets showing just how long high heels have been in fashion.

ARRIVAL AND INFORMATION — NORTHAMPTON

By train From Northampton train station, it's a 10min walk east to the Market Square.

Destinations Birmingham (every 30min; 1hr); London Euston (every 30min; 1hr 15min).

By bus Buses pull into the bus station on Greyfriars, behind the over-large Grosvenor Shopping Centre, immediately north of the Market Square.

Tourist office In the former county courthouse across from All Saints on George Row (Mon–Fri 8.30am–5.30pm; ⓣ 01604 622677, ⓦ explorenorthamptonshire.co.uk).

EATING

The Vineyard 7 Derngate ⓣ 01604 633978. This pleasantly turned-out, family-run little place, right in the centre of town, yards from the Guildhall, is strong on both seafood and Italian dishes. Mains from as little as £10. Mon–Sat noon–2.15pm & 6–10.30pm.

Around Northampton

A few miles outside town, in opposite directions, both **Althorp**, family home of the Spencers and the burial place of Diana, Princess of Wales, and **Stoke Bruerne**, an intriguing canalside village, make good stop-offs. Further out is the delightful village of **Fotheringhay**, where Mary, Queen of Scots was imprisoned and executed.

Althorp

Six miles northwest of Northampton off the A428 • July & Aug daily 11am–5pm, last admission 4pm • £12.50 • ⓣ 01604 770107, ⓦ althorp.com • There are no scheduled buses from Northampton to Althorp

The Spencer family lived at the lavish country home and estate of **Althorp** for centuries, which was of little interest to anyone else until one of the tribe, **Diana**,

THE NENE WAY

Northamptonshire has one notable long-distance footpath, the **Nene Way**, which follows the looping course of the river right across the county from Badby in the west to Wansford in the east, passing through Oundle and Fotheringhay on the way; beyond Wansford it continues east, following the river to its mouth at Sutton Bridge (see p.439) on the Lincolnshire coast, a total distance of 110 miles. For the most part it's easy, if sometimes muddy, and in Northamptonshire the path weaves through a verdant landscape. Brochures are available from Northampton's tourist office or consult ⓦldwa.org.uk.

married Prince Charles in 1981. The disintegration of the marriage and Diana's elevation to sainthood is a story known to millions, and the public outpouring of grief following Diana's death in 1997 was quite astounding. Momentarily, Althorp became the focus of massive media attention as the coffin was brought up the M1 motorway from London to be buried on an island in the grounds of the family estate. Today, visitors still troop round the grandiloquent rooms of Althorp house, drop by the **Diana exhibition** in the old stable block, and then take the footpath that leads round a lake in the middle of which is the islet (no access) where Diana is buried.

Stoke Bruerne

Heading south out of Northampton on the A508, it's about eight miles to the village of **STOKE BRUERNE**, which sits beside a flight of seven locks on the Grand Union Canal. By water at least, the village is very close to England's longest navigable tunnel, the one-and-three-quarter-miles-long **Blisworth Tunnel**, constructed at the beginning of the nineteenth century. Before the advent of steam tugs in the 1870s, boats were pushed through the tunnel by "legging" – two or more men would push with their legs against the tunnel walls until they emerged to hand over to waiting teams of horses.

Over the canal bridge, the *Boat Inn* **pub**, jam-packed with narrowboat trinkets, operates **narrowboat cruises** to the tunnel (Easter–Sept most days; 30min; £3) as well as longer canal trips (call to book, as sailings don't take place every day; ⓣ01604 862428, ⓦboatinn.co.uk).

Stoke Bruerne Canal Museum

Chapel Lane • April–Oct daily 10am–5pm; Nov–March Wed–Fri 11am–3pm, Sat & Sun 11am–4pm • £4.75 • ⓣ01604 862229, ⓦstokebruernecanalmuseum.org.uk • Buses run from Northampton to Stoke Bruerne (Mon–Sat 4 daily; 40min)

The exhausting task of "legging" (see above) is fully explained in the village's folksy **canal museum**, which is housed in a converted canalside corn mill. The museum delves into two hundred years of canal history with models, exhibits of canal art and spit-and-polish engines.

Fotheringhay

Hard to believe today, but pocket-sized **FOTHERINGHAY**, a delightful hamlet nestling by the River Nene about thirty miles northeast of Northampton, is where **Mary, Queen of Scots** came to her untimely end. The castle where she was imprisoned and died has long gone, and the village has been left to its own devices for centuries, but its medieval heyday is recalled by the magnificent **church of St Mary and All Saints**, which rises mirage-like above the green riverine meadows.

Church of St Mary and All Saints

Daily dawn–dusk • Free

Begun in 1411 and a hundred and fifty years in the making, Fotheringay's **Church of St Mary and All Saints** is a paradigm of the Perpendicular, its exterior sporting wonderful

9 arching buttresses, its nave lit by soaring windows and the whole caboodle topped by a splendid octagonal lantern tower. The interior is a tad bare, but there are two fancily carved medieval pieces to inspect – a painted pulpit and a sturdy stone font.

Fotheringhay Castle ruins

Signposted down a short and narrow lane on the bend of the road as you come into the village from Oundle • Open access • Free

Precious little remains of **Fotheringhay Castle** today, but the stronghold witnessed two key events – the birth of Richard III in 1452 and the beheading of Mary, Queen of Scots, in 1587. On the orders of Elizabeth I, Mary – who had been imprisoned for nearly twenty years – was beheaded in the castle's Great Hall with no one to stand in her defence, apart, that is, from her dog, which is said to have rushed from beneath her skirts as her head hit the deck. Thereafter, the castle fell into disrepair and nowadays only a grassy mound and ditch remain to mark where it once stood.

EATING AND DRINKING — FOTHERINGHAY

The Falcon ⓣ01832 226254, ⓦthefalcon-inn.co.uk. This excellent pub-restaurant, which occupies a neat stone building with a modern patio, offers an imaginative menu – lamb shank and artichoke for example – with delicious main courses costing around £15. Mon–Sat noon–2.15pm & 6.15–9.15pm, Sun noon–3pm & 6.15–8.30pm.

Lincoln

Reaching high into the sky from the top of a steep hill, the triple towers of **LINCOLN**'s mighty **cathedral** are visible for miles across the surrounding flatlands. The cathedral, along with the **castle**, are the city's main tourist draws – although Lindum Colonia was an important **Roman** city, few fragments of this era survive.

For visitors, almost everything of interest is confined to the **Uphill** part of town, within easy walking distance of both castle and cathedral. In addition to the major sights, this part of town also features a number of historic remains, notably several chunks of Roman wall, the most prominent of which is the second-century **Newport Arch** straddling Bailgate and once the main north gate into the city. There are also several well-preserved medieval stone houses, notably on and around the aptly named **Steep Hill** as it cuts down from the cathedral to the city centre.

The key sights can be seen in about half a day, though Lincoln does make for a pleasant overnight stop, particularly in December during its lively open-air **Christmas market**.

Brief history

High ground is in short supply in Lincolnshire, so it's no surprise that the steep hill that is today surmounted by Lincoln Cathedral was fortified early, firstly by the **Celts**, who called their settlement Lindon, "hillfort by the lake", a reference to the pools formed by the River Witham in the marshy ground below. In 47 AD the **Romans** occupied Lindon and built a fortified town, which subsequently became **Lindum Colonia**, one of the four regional capitals of Roman Britain. During the reign of William the Conqueror the construction of the **castle** and **cathedral** initiated Lincoln's medieval heyday – the town boomed, first as a Norman power base and then as a centre of the wool trade with Flanders, until 1369 when the wool market was transferred to neighbouring Boston. It was almost five hundred years before Lincoln could revive, its recovery based upon the manufacture of agricultural machinery and drainage equipment for the neighbouring fenlands. As the nineteenth-century town spread south down the hill and out along the old Roman road – the Fosse Way – so Lincoln became a place of precise class distinctions: the **Uphill** area, spreading north from the cathedral, became synonymous with middle-class respectability, **Downhill** with the proletariat.

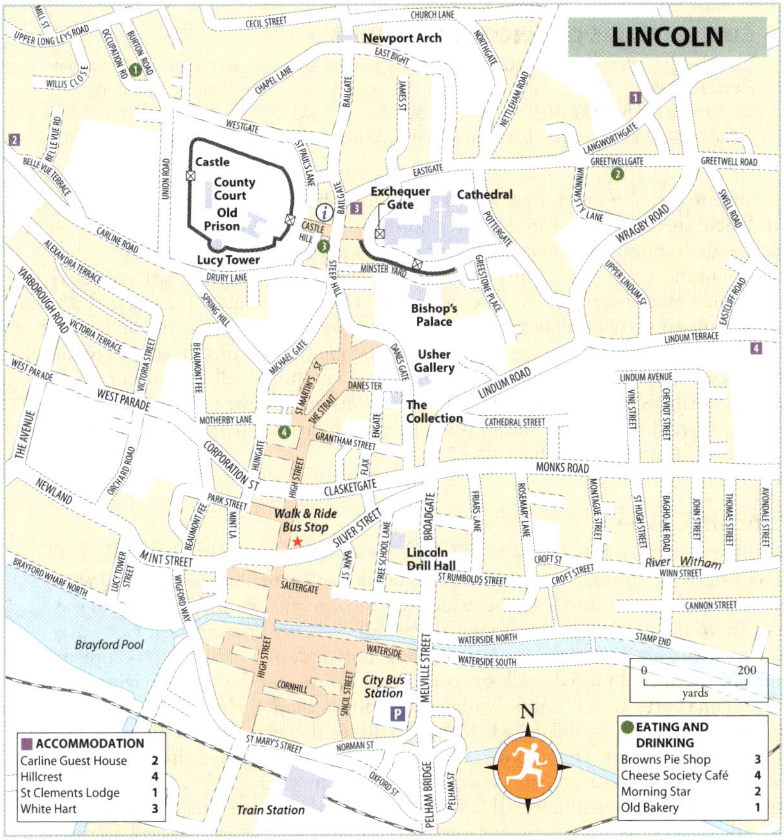

Lincoln Cathedral

Castle Hill • July & Aug Mon–Fri 7.15am–8pm, Sat & Sun 7.15am–6pm; Sept–June Mon–Sat 7.15am–6pm, Sun 7.15am–5pm; access restricted during services • £6 including guided tour (see p.436) • ⓣ 01522 561600, ⓦ lincolncathedral.com

Not a hill at all, **Castle Hill** is in fact a wide, short and level cobbled street that links Lincoln's castle and cathedral. It's a charming spot and its east end is marked by the arches of the medieval **Exchequergate**, beyond which soars the glorious west front of **Lincoln Cathedral**, a veritable cliff-face of blind arcading mobbed by decorative carving. The west front's apparent homogeneity is, however, deceptive, and further inspection reveals two phases of construction – the small stones and thick mortar of much of the facade belong to the original church, completed in 1092, whereas the longer stones and finer courses date from the early thirteenth century. These were enforced works: in 1185, an earthquake shattered much of the Norman church, which was then rebuilt under the auspices of **Bishop Hugh of Avalon**, the man responsible for most of the present cathedral, with the notable exception of the (largely) fourteenth-century central tower.

The cavernous **interior** is a fine example of Early English architecture, with the nave's pillars conforming to the same general design yet differing slightly, their varied columns and bands of dark Purbeck marble contrasting with the oolitic limestone that is the building's main material. Looking back up the nave from beneath the **central tower**, you can also observe a major medieval cock-up: Bishop Hugh's roof is out of alignment with the earlier west front, and the point where they meet has all the wrong angles. It's

9

GUIDED TOURS OF LINCOLN CATHEDRAL

The cathedral offers two **guided tours**, both free with the price of admission. The first – the **Floor Tour** (Mon–Sat 2–3 daily) – is a quick trot around the cathedral's defining features, while the second, the **Roof Tour** (Mon–Sat 1–2 daily; 90min), takes in parts of the church otherwise out of bounds. Both are very popular, so it's a good idea to book in advance on ❶01522 561600.

possible to pick out other irregularities, too – the pillars have bases of different heights, and there are ten windows in the nave's north wall and nine in the south – but these are deliberate features, reflecting a medieval aversion to the vanity of symmetry.

Beyond the nave lies **St Hugh's Choir**, whose fourteenth-century misericords carry an eccentric range of carvings, with scenes from the life of Alexander the Great and King Arthur mixed up with biblical characters and folkloric parables. Further on is the open and airy **Angel Choir**, completed in 1280 and famous for the tiny, finely carved **Lincoln Imp** (see opposite), which embellishes one of its columns. Finally, a corridor off the choir's north aisle leads to the wooden-roofed **cloisters** and the polygonal **chapter house**, where Edward I and Edward II convened gatherings that pre-figured the creation of the English Parliament.

Lincoln Castle

Castle Hill • Daily: April & Sept 10am–5pm; May–Aug 10am–6pm; Oct–March 10am–4pm • £6 • ❶01522 511068, ⓦlincolnshire.gov.uk

From the west front of the cathedral, it's a quick stroll across Castle Hill to **Lincoln Castle**. Intact and forbidding, the castle walls incorporate bits and pieces from the twelfth to the nineteenth centuries with the wall walkway offering great views over town. The castle wall encloses a large central courtyard, part of which is occupied by the old prison, a dour red-brick structure that holds one of the four surviving copies of the **Magna Carta** as well as a truly remarkable **prison chapel**. Here, the prisoners were locked in high-sided cubicles, where they could see the preacher and his pulpit but not their fellow inmates. This approach was not just applied to chapel visits: the prisoners were kept in perpetual solitary confinement, and were compelled to wear masks when they took to the exercise yard. This system was founded on the pseudo-scientific theory that defined crime as a contagious disease, but unfortunately for the theorists, their so-called Pentonville System of "Separation and Silence", which was introduced here in 1846, drove so many prisoners crazy that it had to be abandoned thirty years later; nobody ever bothered to dismantle the chapel.

The Collection

Danes Terrace • Daily 10am–4pm • Free • ❶01522 55099, ⓦthecollectionlincoln.org

Occupying two contrasting buildings – a striking modern structure and a really rather grand 1920s edifice close by – **The Collection** is Lincoln's prime museum. Pride of place in the more modern building is the city's extensive collection of archeological artefacts, from prehistoric times onwards; the older building, or the **Usher Gallery**, focuses on fine art. The Usher's permanent collection also includes an eclectic collection of coins, porcelain, watches and clocks. The timepieces were given to the gallery by its benefactor, James Ward Usher, a local jeweller and watchmaker who made a fortune on the back of the **Lincoln Imp** (see opposite).

ARRIVAL AND INFORMATION — LINCOLN

By train Lincoln train station is on St Mary's St, "Downhill" in the city centre.

Destinations Leicester (hourly; 2hr); Newark (hourly; 25min); Nottingham (hourly; 1hr); Peterborough (every 2hr; 1hr 30min); Stamford (hourly; 1hr 40 min–2hr 20min).

By bus The bus station, just north of the train station on Melville St, is also "Downhill".

Tourist office 9 Castle Hill, between the cathedral and the castle (Mon–Sat April–Sept 10.30am–4pm, Oct–March 11am–3pm; 01522 545458, visitlincolnshire.com). They have lots of local information and can book accommodation.

GETTING AROUND

From both the train and bus stations, it's a very steep, 15min walk up to the cathedral, or you can take the **Walk & Ride minibus** (Mon–Sat 10am–5pm, Sun noon–5pm; every 20min; £1.30 each way). This leaves from the train station as well as from the designated bus stop on Silver St, just off High St.

ACCOMMODATION

Carline Guest House 1–3 Carline Rd 01522 530422, carlineguesthouse.co.uk. One of the best B&Bs in the city, *Carline* occupies a neat and trim Edwardian house about a 10min walk down from the cathedral – take Drury Lane from in front of the castle and keep going. Breakfasts are very good, and the rooms are large and pleasantly furnished in a traditional style. No credit cards. £60

Hillcrest 15 Lindum Terrace 01522 510182, hillcrest-hotel.com. Traditional, very English hotel in a large red-brick house that was originally a Victorian rectory. Sixteen comfortable rooms with all mod cons plus a large, sloping garden. About a 10min walk from the cathedral. £95

St Clements Lodge 21 Langworthgate 01522 521532, stclementslodge.co.uk. In a modest, modern house a short walk from the cathedral, this comfortable, very friendly B&B has three unassuming, en-suite rooms. Homemade breakfasts too – try the haddock or the kippers. £68

White Hart Bailgate 01522 526222, whitehart-lincoln.co.uk. Antique former coaching inn, whose public rooms still have all sorts of hidden nooks and crannies despite a fairly humdrum modern revamp. The bedrooms are in a more traditional, country-house style and the pick overlook the cathedral. Great location. £99

EATING AND DRINKING

Browns Pie Shop 33 Steep Hill 01522 527330, brownspieshop.co.uk. Not a pie shop at all, *Browns* is a first-rate restaurant in ancient premises yards from the cathedral. The creative menu puts the emphasis on local ingredients and prices are very reasonable with main courses costing about £12. Save room for the earth-shattering puddings. Mon–Sat noon–2.30pm & 5pm till late, Sun noon–8pm.

Cheese Society Café 1 St Martin's Lane 01522 511003, thecheesesociety.co.uk. Bright and breezy little café attached to a specialist cheese shop, selling every sort of cheese you can think of and then some. As you would expect, the café menu does fine rarebits, raclettes and baked halloumi dishes – but there are non-cheesy options, too, including a good steak-frites. No children under 10. Mon–Sat 10am–4.30pm.

Morning Star 11 Greetwellgate 01522 527079. Old-fashioned and friendly locals' pub with a good range of ales. A couple of minutes' walk from the cathedral – if you want something livelier, head for the bars on Bailgate. Daily noon–2.30pm & 6–11pm.

★ **Old Bakery** 26 Burton Rd 01522 576057, theold-bakery.co.uk. Cosy, award-winning restaurant, where the menu is both well considered and inventive – try, for example, the grilled corn polenta and cherry tomatoes with Gorgonzola and green olive purée. Reservations recommended. Mains from £14. Tues–Sat noon–2pm & 6.30–9pm, Sun noon–2pm.

NIGHTLIFE AND ENTERTAINMENT

Lincoln Drill Hall Free School Lane 01522 873894, lincolndrillhall.com. Lincoln's prime arts and entertainment venue, featuring everything from stand-up and theatre to classical concerts, rock and pop.

THE LINCOLN IMP

Legends had abounded for centuries about the **Lincoln imp**, carved high on a column in Lincoln cathedral, but it was the entrepreneurial James Ward Usher in the 1880s who turned the wee beastie into a tidy profit, selling Lincoln imp tie-pins, cuff-links, spoons, brooches and beads. Usher also popularized the traditional legend of the imp, a tall tale in which a couple of imps are blown to Lincoln by a playful wind. They then proceed to hop around the cathedral, until one of them is turned to stone for trying to talk to the angels carved into the roof of the Angel Choir. His chum makes a hasty exit on the back of a witch, but the wind is still supposed to haunt the cathedral, awaiting its opportunity to be mischievous again.

9

The Lincolnshire coast

Heading east from Lincoln on the A158, it's about forty miles to **Skegness**, the county's biggest – and brightest – resort. From here, a thick band of bungalows, campsites and caravans marches up along the seashore beside and behind a sandy beach that extends, with a few marshy interruptions, north to **Mablethorpe** and ultimately **Cleethorpes**. All this bucket-and-spade and amusement-arcade commercialism is not to everyone's taste, but small portions of the coast have been preserved and protected, most notably in the **Gibraltar Point Natural Nature Reserve** south of Skegness.

Skegness

SKEGNESS has been a busy resort ever since the railways reached the Lincolnshire coast in 1875. Its heyday was pre-1960s, when the Brits began to take themselves off to sunnier climes, but it still attracts tens of thousands of city-dwellers who come for the wide, sandy beaches and for a host of attractions ranging from nightclubs to bowling greens. Every inch the traditional English seaside town, Skegness outdoes its rivals by keeping its beaches sparklingly clean and its parks spick-and-span. That said, the seafront, with its rows of souvenir shops and amusement arcades, can be dismal, especially on rainy days, and you may well decide to sidestep the whole caboodle by heading south along the coastal road to the **Gibraltar Point National Nature Reserve**.

Gibraltar Point National Nature Reserve

Gibraltar Rd • **Reserve** Daily dawn–dusk • Free, but parking from £1 **Visitor Centre** April–Oct daily 10am–4pm; Nov–March Mon–Fri 11am–3pm, Sat & Sun 11am–4pm • ⓣ 01754 898079, ⓦ lincstrust.org.uk/reserves/gib/

At the **Gibraltar Point National Nature Reserve**, three miles south of Skegness, a network of clearly signed footpaths patterns a narrow strip of salt- and freshwater marsh, sand dune and beach that attracts an inordinate number of birds, both resident and migratory. The reserve's smart-looking **Visitor Centre** has an observation deck equipped with binoculars and a telescope – which are free to use.

ARRIVAL AND INFORMATION — SKEGNESS

By bus and train Skegness bus and train stations are next door to each other, about 10min walk from the seashore – cut across Lumley Square and head straight up the High St to the landmark clocktower.

Tourist office Just a few yards from the clocktower on Grand Parade in the Embassy Theatre (core hours Mon–Fri 9.30am–4pm; ⓣ 0845 674 0505, ⓦ visitlincolnshire.com).

ACCOMMODATION AND EATING

If it's **fish and chips** you're after, you've come to the right place – line up and fill up at any of the dozen or so chippies on and around the High St.

Best Western Vine Hotel Vine Rd ⓣ 01754 610611, ⓦ bw-vinehotel.co.uk. One of the more appealing of Skegness's scores of bargain-basement hotels, B&Bs and guesthouses. On a quiet residential street about three-quarters of a mile from the clocktower on the road to Gibraltar Point, the building itself is a rambling old house – though the decor is uninspiringly modern. **£70**

The Lincolnshire Fens

The Fens, that great chunk of eastern England extending from Boston in Lincolnshire right down to Cambridge, encompass some of the most productive farmland in Europe. Give or take the occasional hillock, this pancake-flat, treeless terrain has been painstakingly reclaimed from the marshes and swamps which once drained into the intrusive stump of **The Wash**, a process that has taken almost two thousand years. In earlier times, outsiders were often amazed by the dreadful conditions hereabouts, but they did spawn the distinctive culture of the so-called **fen-slodgers**, who embanked small portions of marsh to create pastureland and fields, supplementing their diets by catching fish and fowl and gathering reed and sedge for thatching and fuel. This local economy was threatened by the large-scale land reclamation schemes of the late fifteenth and sixteenth centuries, and time and again the fenlanders sabotaged progress by breaking down new banks and dams. But the odds were stacked against the saboteurs, and a succession of great landowners eventually drained huge tracts of the fenland – and by the 1790s the fen slodgers' way of life had all but disappeared. Nonetheless, the **Lincolnshire Fens** remain a distinctive area, with a scattering of introverted little villages spread across the flatlands within easy striking distance of the A17. Several of these villages are distinguished by their imposing **medieval churches** – St Mary Magdalene's in **Gedney** and St Mary's in **Long Sutton** for example – and their soaring spires are seen to best advantage in the pale, watery sunlight and wide skies of the fenland evening.

Gedney

Heading south from Lincoln, it's about seventeen miles to the A17, which runs east across the Lincolnshire Fens bound for King's Lynn (see p.363). En route, it slips past the scattered hamlet of **GEDNEY**, where the massive tower of **St Mary Magdalene** (daily dawn–dusk; free) intercepts the fenland landscape. Seen from a distance, the church seems almost magical, or at least mystical, its imposing lines so much in contrast with its fen-flat surroundings. Close up, the three-aisled nave is simply beautiful, its battery of windows lighting the exquisite Renaissance alabaster effigies of Adlard and Cassandra Welby, who, in death, face each other on the south wall near the chancel.

Long Sutton

There's more ecclesiastical excitement just a mile or two to the east of Gedney in **LONG SUTTON**, a modest farming centre that limps along the road until it reaches its trim Market Place. Here, the **church of St Mary** (daily dawn–dusk; free) has preserved many of its Norman features, with its arcaded tower supporting the oldest lead spire in the country, dating from around 1200. Look out also for the striking stained-glass windows. Long Sutton once lay on the edge of the five-mile-wide mouth of the **River Nene**, where it emptied into The Wash. This was the most treacherous part of the road from Lincoln to Norfolk, and locals had to guide travellers across the mud flats and marshes on horseback. In 1831, the River Nene was embanked and then spanned with a wooden bridge at **Sutton Bridge**, a hamlet just two miles east of Long Sutton – and a few miles from King's Lynn (see p.363). The present swing bridge, with its nifty central tower, was completed in 1894.

Stamford

Delightful **STAMFORD**, in the southwest corner of Lincolnshire, is a handsome little limestone town of yellow-grey seventeenth- and eighteenth-century buildings edging narrow streets that slope up from the River Welland. The town's salad days were as a centre of the medieval wool and cloth trade, when wealthy merchants built its medley of stone churches and houses. Stamford was also the home of **William Cecil**, Elizabeth I's chief minister, who built his splendid mansion, **Burghley House**, close by.

The town survived the collapse of the wool trade, prospering as an inland port after the Welland was made navigable to the sea in 1570, and, in the eighteenth century, as a staging point on the Great North Road from London. More recently, Stamford escaped the three main threats to old English towns – the Industrial Revolution, wartime bombing and postwar development – and was designated the country's first Conservation Area in 1967. Thanks to this, its unspoilt streets readily lend themselves to period drama- and filmmaking, and although it's the harmony of Stamford's architecture that pleases rather than any specific sight, there are still a handful of buildings of some special interest.

Church of St Mary

St Mary's St • No regular opening hours • Free

A convenient place to start an exploration of Stamford is the **Church of St Mary**, sitting pretty just above the main bridge on St Mary's Street. The church has a splendid spire and a small but airy interior, which incorporates the **Corpus Christi chapel**, whose intricately embossed, painted and panelled ceiling dates from the 1480s.

Browne's Hospital

Broad St • May–Sept Sat 11am–4pm, Sun 2–4.30pm • £2.50

Across the street from the Church of St Mary, several lanes thread up to the carefully preserved **High Street**, from where Ironmonger Street leads north again to the wide and handsome Broad Street, the site of **Browne's Hospital**, the most extensive of the town's almshouses, dating from the late fifteenth century. Not all of the complex is open to the public, but it's still worth visiting; the first room – the old dormitory – is capped by a splendid wood-panelled ceiling. The adjacent chapel holds some delightfully folksy misericords and then it's upstairs for the audit room, which is illuminated by a handsome set of stained-glass windows.

Church of All Saints

Red Lion Square • Daily dawn–dusk • Free

Red Lion Square is overlooked by the **Church of All Saints**, a stone's throw from Browne's Hospital. Entry is via the south porch, an ornate structure with a fine – if badly weathered – crocketted gable, and, although much of the interior is routinely Victorian, the carved capitals are of great delicacy. There's also an engaging folkloric carving of the Last Supper behind the high altar.

High Street St Martin's

Down the slope from St Mary's, across the reedy River Welland on High Street St Martin's, is the **George Hotel**, a splendid old coaching inn whose Georgian facade supports one end of the gallows that span the street – not a warning to criminals, but a traditional advertising hoarding.

Church of St Martin

High St St Martin's • Daily 9.30am–4pm • Free

The sombre, late fifteenth-century **Church of St Martin** shelters the magnificent tombs of the lords Burghley, with a recumbent William Cecil carved beneath twin canopies, holding his rod of office and with a lion at his feet. Immediately behind, the early eighteenth-century effigies of John Cecil and his wife show the couple as Roman aristocrats, propped up on their elbows, she to gaze at him, John to stare across the nave commandingly.

SHAKESPEARE IN THE PARK

One of the most enjoyable of Stamford's several festivals is the **Stamford Shakespeare Company**'s (Ⓣ01780 756133, Ⓦstamfordshakespeare.co.uk) open-air performances of the bard's works in the grounds of **Tolethorpe Hall**, an Elizabethan mansion just outside town. The season lasts from June to August with the audience protected from the elements by a vast canopy.

Burghley House

A mile and a half east of Stamford along the Barnack Rd • Mid-March to late Oct Sat–Thurs 11am–5pm • £12.20, including gardens • Ⓣ01780 752451, Ⓦburghley.co.uk

Burghley House, an extravagant Elizabethan mansion standing in parkland landscaped by Capability Brown, is just outside Stamford. Completed in 1587 after 22 years' work, the house sports a mellow yellow ragstone exterior, embellished by dainty cupolas, a pyramidal clocktower and skeletal balustrading, all to a plan by **William Cecil**, the long-serving adviser to Elizabeth I. However, with the notable exception of the Tudor kitchen, little remains of Burghley's Elizabethan interior and, instead, the house bears the heavy hand of John, fifth Lord Burghley, who toured France and Italy in the late seventeenth century, buying paintings and commissioning furniture, statuary and tapestries. To provide a suitable setting for his old masters, John brought in Antonio Verrio and his assistant Louis Laguerre, who between them covered many of Burghley's walls and ceilings with frolicking gods and goddesses. These gaudy and gargantuan murals are at their most engulfing in the **Heaven Room**, an artfully painted classical temple that adjoins the **Hell Staircase**, where the entrance to the inferno is through the gaping mouth of a cat.

The grounds of Burghley House are at their busiest during the prestigious **Burghley Horse Trials** (Ⓦburghley-horse.co.uk), held over four days in late August and early September.

ARRIVAL AND INFORMATION — STAMFORD

By train It's a 5- to 10min walk north from Stamford train station to the town centre, on the other side of the River Welland.

Destinations Cambridge (hourly; 1hr 10min); Leicester (hourly; 40min); Oakham (hourly; 15min).

By bus The bus station is in the town centre, on Sheepmarket, off All Saints' St.

Tourist office Right in the centre of town, in the Stamford Arts Centre, 27 St Mary's St (April–Oct Mon–Sat 9.30am–5pm, Sun 10.30am–4pm; Nov–March Mon–Sat 9.30am–5pm; Ⓣ01780 755611, Ⓦsouthwestlincs.com).

ACCOMMODATION

Elm Guest House New Cross Rd Ⓣ01780 764210, Ⓦelmguesthouse.co.uk. In a large modern house a 10min walk north of the centre of Stamford, this upmarket B&B has four very well-appointed en-suite bedrooms, each decorated in a bright and breezy, appealingly modern style. **£70**

George Hotel 71 High St St Martin's Ⓣ01780 750750, Ⓦgeorgehotelofstamford.com. Stamford's most celebrated hotel by a mile, *The George* is a sympathetically renovated old coaching inn, which comes complete with flagstone floors and antique furnishings; the most appealing of the plush rooms overlook a cobbled courtyard. There's a good restaurant, too (see below). **£150**

EATING

George Hotel 71 High St St Martin's Ⓣ01780 750750, Ⓦgeorgehotelofstamford.com. The food at this excellent hotel (see above) is as classy as the rooms. There are several eating areas, but perhaps the best is the moderately priced and informal *Garden Room* where the emphasis is on British ingredients served in imaginative ways. Main courses here average around £15; you'll pay less if you eat in the hotel's delightfully antiquated *York Bar*. Garden Room daily noon–10.30pm.

Hambleton Bakery 1 Ironmonger St Ⓣ01572 812995, Ⓦhambletonbakery.co.uk. If you're after a sandwich, this is the best spot in town, selling a wide range of freshly baked breads with a suitably wide selection of fillings. Mon–Sat 9am–5pm.

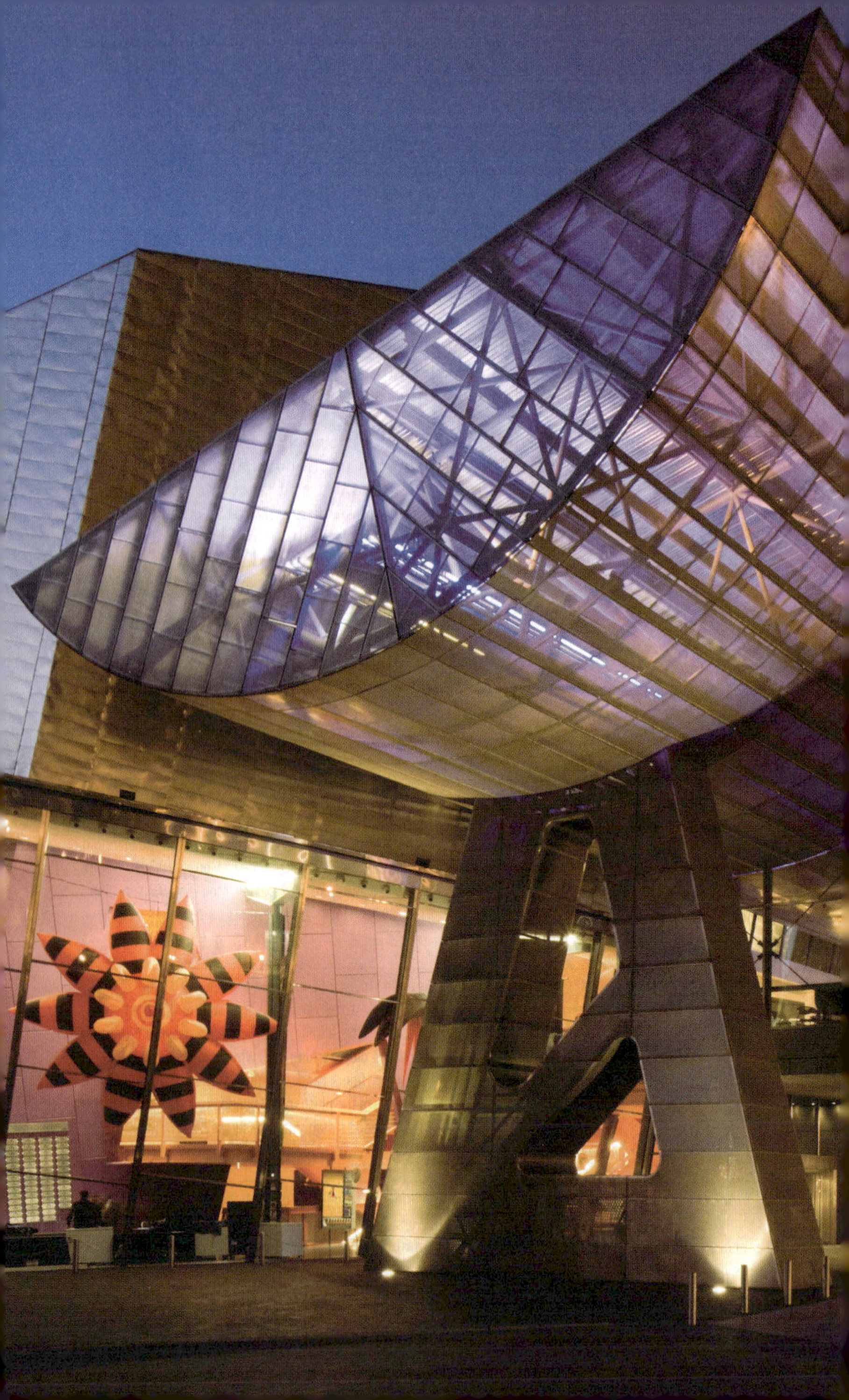

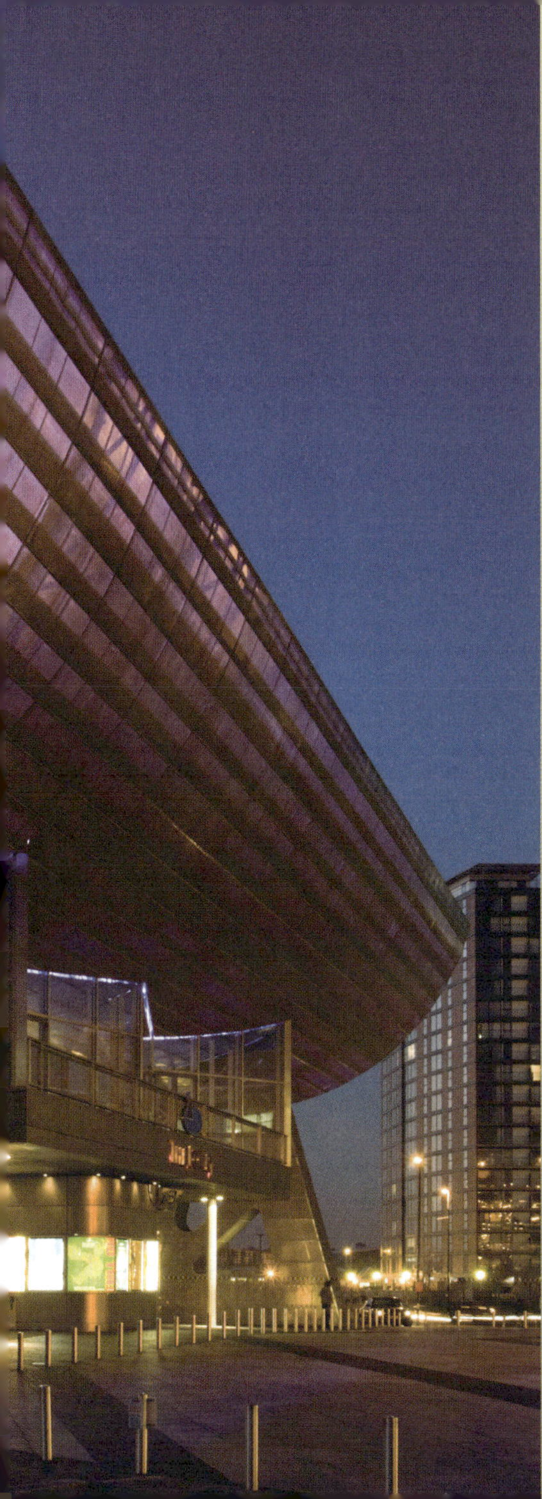

The Northwest

446 Manchester

458 Chester

462 Liverpool

470 Blackpool

473 Lancaster and around

475 The Isle of Man

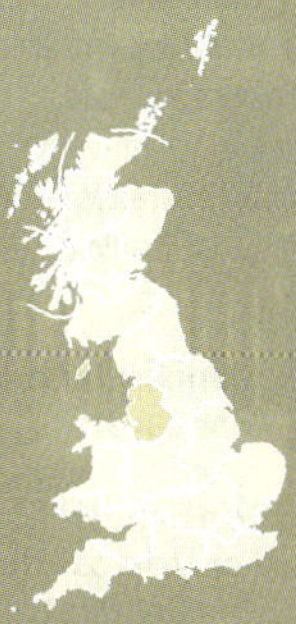

THE LOWRY, SALFORD QUAYS

The Northwest

10

Ask most Brits about northwest England and they'll probably mention football and rain. Beyond the stereotypes, however, this is one of the most exciting corners of the country, its dynamic urban centres, pretty countryside, iconic seaside resorts and historic towns offering considerable appeal. One of the world's great industrial cities, Manchester has transformed its cityscape in recent decades to place itself firmly in the vanguard of modern British urban design, and complements its top-class visitor attractions with lively cafés and an exciting music scene. Just thirty miles west, revitalized Liverpool has kept apace of the "northern renaissance", too, and is a city of great energy and charm.

The southern suburbs of Manchester bump into the steep hills of the **Pennine range**, and to the southwest the city slides into pastoral **Cheshire**, a county of rolling green countryside whose dairy farms churn out the famed crumbly white cheese. The county town, **Chester**, with its complete circuit of town walls and partly Tudor centre, is as alluring as any of the country's northern towns, capturing the essence of one of England's wealthiest counties.

The historical county of **Lancashire** reached industrial prominence in the nineteenth century primarily due to the cotton-mill towns around Manchester and the thriving port of Liverpool. Today, neither city is part of the county, and Lancashire's oldest town, and major commercial and administrative centre, is **Preston**, though tourists are perhaps more inclined to linger in the charming towns and villages of the nearby **Ribble Valley**. Along the coast to the west and north of the major cities stretches a line of **resorts** – from Southport to **Morecambe** – which once formed the mainstay of the northern British holiday. Only **Blackpool** is really worth visiting for its own sake, a rip-roaring resort which has stayed at the top of its game by supplying undemanding entertainment with more panache than its neighbours. For anything more culturally invigorating you'll have to continue north to the historically important city of **Lancaster**, with its Tudor castle. Finally, the Crown Dependency of the **Isle of Man**, just 25 miles off the coast, provides a rugged terrain almost as rewarding as that of the Lake District, but without the seasonal overcrowding.

GETTING AROUND — THE NORTHWEST

By train Both Manchester and Liverpool are well served by trains, with regular high-speed connections to the Midlands and London, and up the west coast to Scotland. The major east–west rail lines in the region are the direct routes between Manchester, Leeds and York, and between Blackpool, Bradford, Leeds and York. The Lancaster–Leeds line slips through the Yorkshire Dales and further south, the Manchester–Sheffield line provides a rail approach to the Peak District.

By bus The major cities, as well as Chester, are connected by frequent bus services.

Manchester orientation p.447
Manchester's Gay Village and Gay Pride p.452
Top 5 music nights p.457
Ferry across the Mersey p.465
The Beatles trail p.466
Blackpool – behind the scenes p.471
On Your Bike p.473
The Forest of Bowland p.474
Tynwald Day p.478
The Calf of Man p.479

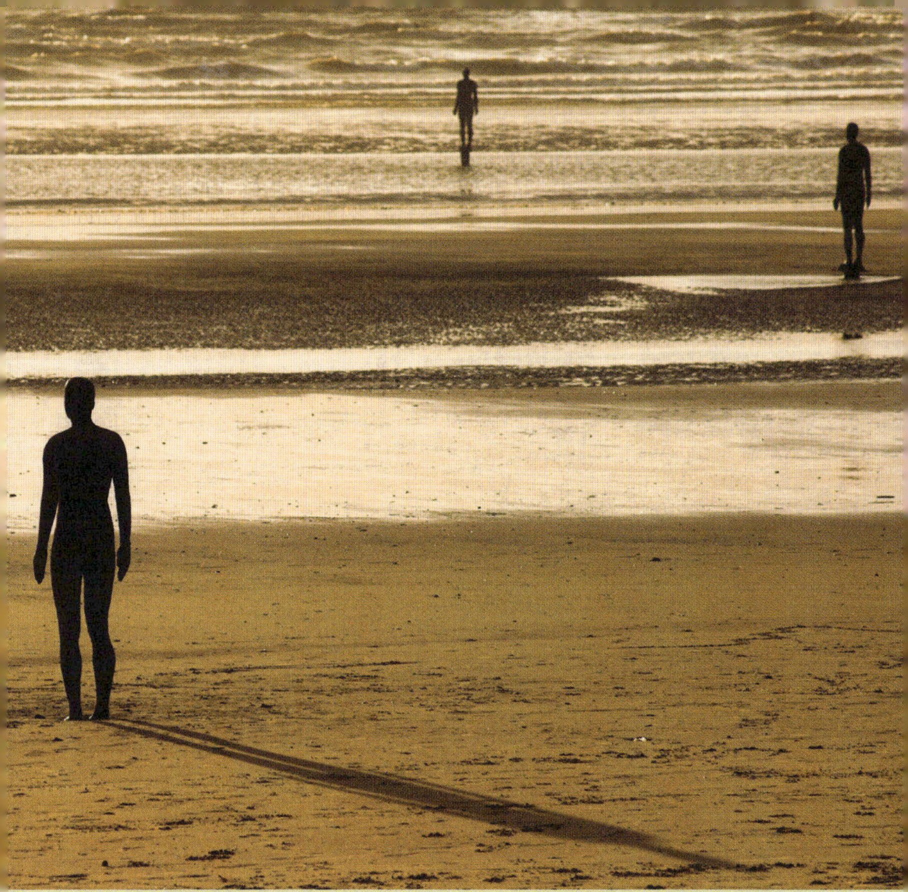

CROSBY BEACH

Highlights

❶ **People's History Museum** Manchester's national museum tells the story behind the forces that have shaped human history and the modern world. **See p.450**

❷ **Manchester's Northern Quarter** Lose yourself in chic shops, café-bars and happening music venues in this vibrant warehouse district. **See p.451**

❸ **City walls, Chester** The handsome old town of Chester is best surveyed from the heights of its Roman walls. **See p.459**

❹ **Crosby Beach, Liverpool** Home to Antony Gormley's eerie life-size cast iron statues, which disappear at high tide. **See p.467**

❺ **Blackpool Pleasure Beach** Bright, bawdy and brash, Britain's cheekiest resort is constantly reinventing itself. **See p.471**

❻ **Lancaster Castle** From the dungeons to the ornate courtrooms, the castle is a historical tour-de-force. **See p.473**

❼ **Sunset across Morecambe Bay** Drink in one of the country's finest sunsets at the bar in the Art Deco Midland Hotel. **See p.475**

❽ **Sea-kayaking, the Calf of Man** Taking to the water in a kayak allows you to view local seal colonies, seabirds, and the Isle of Man's stunning rugged coast from a unique perspective. **See p.479**

HIGHLIGHTS ARE MARKED ON THE MAP ON P.446

Manchester

MANCHESTER has had a global profile for more than 150 years, since the dawn of the industrial revolution. But today's elegant core of converted warehouses and glass skyscrapers is a far cry from the smoke-covered sprawl George Orwell once described as "the belly and guts of the nation". Its renewed pre-eminence expresses itself in various ways, most swaggeringly in its **football**, as home to the world's most famous and

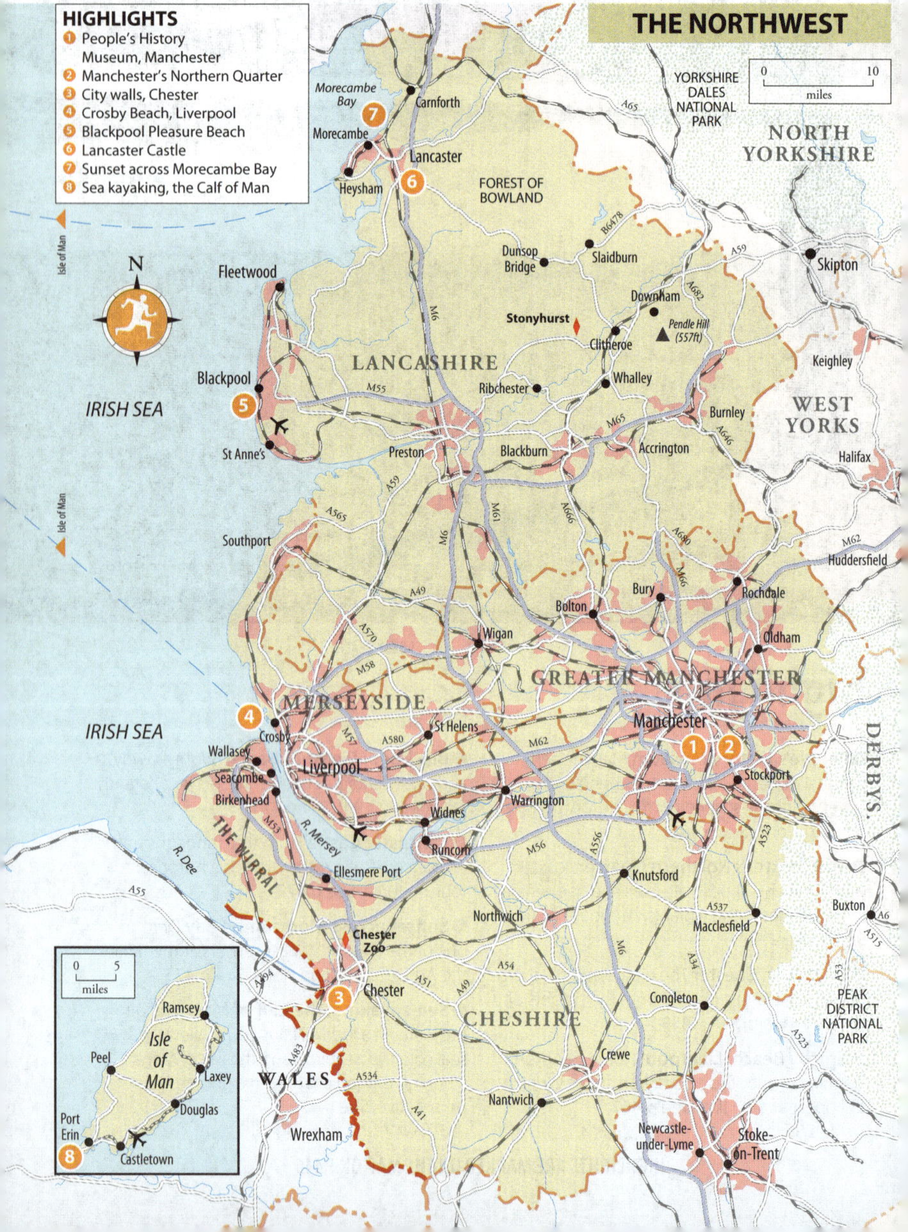

MANCHESTER ORIENTATION

If Manchester can be said to have a centre, it's **Albert Square** and the cluster of buildings surrounding it – the Town Hall, the Central Library and the *Midland Hotel*, originally built in the railway age to host visitors to Britain's greatest industrial city. South of here, the former Central Station now functions as the **Manchester Central** convention centre, with the Hallé Orchestra's home, **Bridgewater Hall**, just opposite. **Chinatown** and the **Gay Village** are just a short walk to the east, while to the northeast, the revamped **Piccadilly Gardens** provides access to the funky **Northern Quarter**. To the southwest is the **Castlefield** district, site of the **Museum of Science and Industry**. The central spine of the city is **Deansgate**, which runs from Castlefield to the cathedral and, in its northern environs, displays the most dramatic core of urban regeneration in the country, centred on the unalloyed modernity of **Exchange Square**.

wealthiest clubs – Manchester United and Manchester City, respectively – but also in a thriving **music scene** that has given birth to world-beaters as diverse as the Hallé Orchestra and Oasis. Its cultural significance is epitomized by the bi-annual **Manchester International Festival** that features upwards of twenty world premiers of new, creative talent. Moreover, the city's celebrated concert halls, theatres, clubs and cafés feed off the cosmopolitan drive provided by the country's largest **student** population outside London and a blooming, proud **gay** community.

There are plenty of sights, too: the centre possesses the **Manchester Art Gallery**, the **National Football Museum** and the fantastic **People's History Museum** as well as the **Museum of Science and Industry**, while further out, to the west, the revamped **Salford Quays** are home to the prestigious **Lowry arts centre**, complete with a handsome selection of L.S. Lowry paintings, and the stirring and stunning **Imperial War Museum North**.

Brief history

Despite a **history** stretching back to Roman times, and pockets of surviving medieval and Georgian architecture, Manchester is first and foremost a **Victorian manufacturing city**. Its rapid growth set the pace for the flowering of the Industrial Revolution elsewhere – transforming itself in just a hundred years from little more than a village to the world's major cotton centre. The spectacular rise of **Cottonopolis**, as it became known, arose from the manufacture of vast quantities of competitively priced imitations of expensive Indian calicoes, using water and then steam-driven machines developed in the late eighteenth and nineteenth centuries. This rapid industrialization brought immense wealth for a few but a life of misery for the majority. The discontent this came to a head in 1819 when eleven people were killed at **Peterloo**, in what began as a peaceful demonstration against the oppressive **Corn Laws**. Things were, however, even worse when the 23-year-old Friedrich Engels came here in 1842 to work in his father's cotton plant: the grinding poverty he recorded in his *Condition of the Working Class in England* was a seminal influence on his later collaboration with **Karl Marx** in the *Communist Manifesto*.

The **Manchester Ship Canal**, constructed in 1894 to entice ocean-going vessels into Manchester and away from burgeoning Liverpool, played a crucial part in sustaining Manchester's competitiveness. From the late 1950s, however, the docks, mills, warehouses and canals were in dangerous decline. The main engine of change turned out to be the devastating **IRA bomb**, which exploded outside the Arndale shopping centre in June 1996, wiping out a fair slice of the city's commercial infrastructure. Rather than simply patching things up, the city council embarked on an ambitious rebuilding scheme, which transformed the face of the city forever.

Albert Square

Most of Manchester's panoply of **neo-Gothic** buildings and monuments date from the city's heyday in the second half of the nineteenth century. One of the more fanciful is

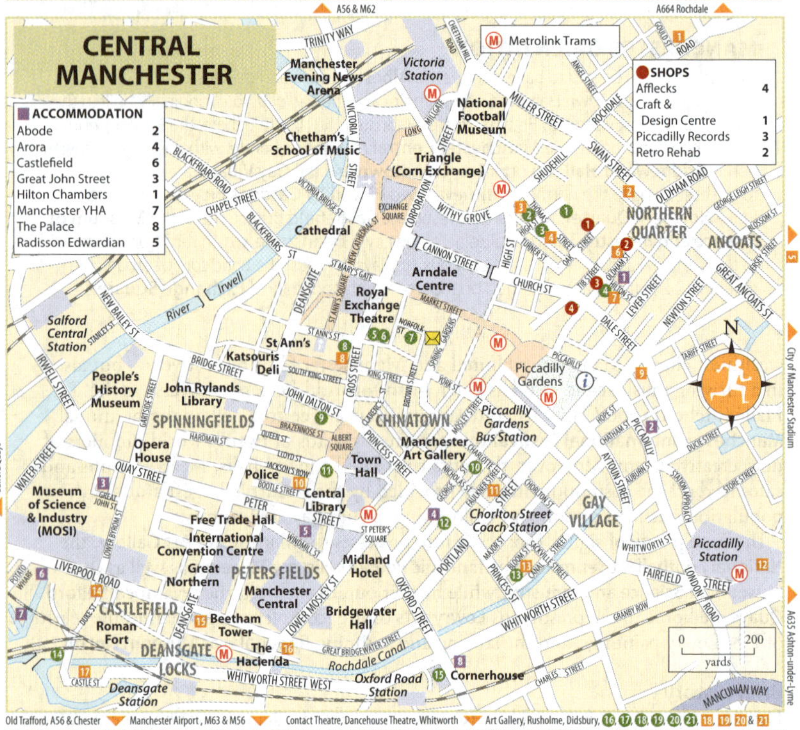

RESTAURANTS	
Chaophraya	5
Jaffa	18
Lime Tree	21
Little Yang Sing	10
Mr Thomas' Chop House	8
The Market Restaurant	1
Punjab Tandoori	19
Royal Suite Darbar	20
Sam's Chop House	6
Stock	7
Tampopo	11
Vertigo	9
Yang Sing	12

CAFÉS	
Barça Bar	14
Cornerhouse	15
Dry Bar	4
Eighth Day	16
The Gallery Café	17
Manto	13
Odd	3
Trof Central	2

PUBS AND BARS	
Big Hands	20
Britons Protection	16
Circus Tavern	11
Cloud 23	15
Dry Bar	7
Dukes '92	17
Mr Thomas' Chop House	8
Manto	13
Marble Arch	1
Odd	4
The Ox	14
Sand Bar	18
Trof Central	3

CLUBS & LIVE MUSIC	
42nd Street	10
Band on the Wall	2
The Deaf Institute	19
Manchester Academy	21
Manto	13
Matt and Phreds	6
Odd	4
Roadhouse	9
Sankey's Soap	5
Trof Central	3
Warehouse Project	12

the shrine-like, canopied **monument** to Prince Albert, Queen Victoria's husband, perched prettily in the middle of the trim little square that bears his name – **Albert Square**. The monument was erected in 1867, six years after Albert's death, supposedly because the prince had always shown an interest in industry, but perhaps more to curry favour with the grieving queen. Overlooking the prince is Alfred Waterhouse's magnificent, neo-Gothic **Town Hall** (Mon–Fri 9am–5pm; free), whose mighty clocktower, completed in 1877, pokes a sturdy finger into the sky, soaring high above its gables, columns and arcaded windows.

St Peter's Square and around

Just south of the Town Hall, facing **St Peter's Square**, the circular **Central Library** (due to reopen in 2013) was built in 1934 as the largest municipal library in the world, a self-consciously elegant, classical construction with a domed reading room. Footsteps away, over on Peter Street, the **Free Trade Hall** was the home of the city's

Hallé Orchestra for more than a century – until Bridgewater Hall was completed in 1996. The Italianate facade survived intense wartime bombing and is now a protected part of the *Radisson Edwardian Hotel*, whose modern tower block rises up behind at a (fairly) discreet distance.

Manchester Art Gallery

Mosley St • Tues–Sun 10am–5pm • Free • ⓦ manchestergalleries.org • St Peter's Square Metrolink

Manchester Art Gallery, as well as attracting big-name exhibitions by contemporary artists, holds an invigorating collection of eighteenth- and nineteenth-century art. Spread across **Floor 1**, these works are divided by theme – Face and Place, Expressing Passion and so on – rather than by artist (or indeed school of artists), which makes it difficult to appreciate the strength of the collection, especially when it comes to its forte, the Pre-Raphaelites. There's much else – views of Victorian Manchester, a Turner or two, a pair of Gainsboroughs, and Stubbs' famous *Cheetah and Stag with Two Indians* to name but a few. **Floor 2** features temporary exhibitions and crafts, while the **Ground Floor**'s Manchester Gallery is devoted to a visual history of the city.

Deansgate Locks and around

South of St Peter's Square, on **Lower Mosley Street**, stands Britain's finest concert hall, **Bridgewater Hall**, balanced on shock-absorbing springs to guarantee the clarity of the sound. The apartment block at the corner of Lower Mosley Street and Whitworth Street West bears the name of the site's previous occupant, the infamous **Hacienda Club**, the spiritual home of Factory Records, an independent label that defined a generation of music through such bands as Joy Division, New Order and the Happy Mondays before closing down in 1997.

Turn right along Whitworth Street West and you'll spot the string of café-bars and restaurants that have been shoehorned along the Rochdale canal's **Deansgate Locks**, a pattern repeated along and across the street in the old railway arches abutting Deansgate Station. Look up and you'll see the striking **Beetham Tower**, easily the tallest skyscraper in Manchester and home to a glitzy hotel.

MOSI: The Museum of Science and Industry

Liverpool Rd • Daily 10am–5pm • Free, but admission charge for special exhibitions • ⓣ 0161 832 2244, ⓦ msim.org.uk • Deansgate Metrolink

One of the most impressive museums of its type in the country, the **Museum of Science and Industry** mixes technological displays and blockbuster exhibitions with trenchant analysis of the social impact of industrialization. Key points of interest include the **Power Hall**, which trumpets the region's remarkable technological contribution to the Industrial Revolution by means of a hall full of steam engines, some of which are fired up daily. There's more steam in the shape of a working replica of Robert Stephenson's *Planet*, whose original design was based on the *Rocket*, the work of Robert's father George. Built in 1830, the *Planet* reliably attained a scorching 30mph but had no brakes; the museum's version does, however, and it's used at weekends (noon–4pm), dropping passengers a couple of hundred yards away at the **Station Building**, the world's oldest passenger railway station. It was here that the *Rocket* arrived on a rainy September 15, 1830, after fatally injuring Liverpool MP William Huskisson at the start of the inaugural passenger journey from Liverpool.

The **1830 Warehouse** features a sound-and-light show that delves into the history of the city's immense warehouses, and the **Air and Space Hall**, which barely touches on Manchester at all, features vintage planes, cutaway engines and space exploration displays.

People's History Museum

Bridge St • Daily 10am–5pm • Free • ⓣ 0161 838 9190, ⓦ phm.org.uk • Deansgate Metrolink

The superb **People's History Museum** explores Britain's rich history of radicalism and the struggles of marginalized people to acquire rights and extend suffrage – ideas that developed out of the workers' associations and religious movements of the industrial city and which helped to shape the modern world. Housed in a former pump house and an ultramodern, four-storey extension, the galleries use interactive displays – including coffins and top hats – to trace a compelling narrative from the Peterloo Massacre of 1819 onwards. As the gallery shows, this moment became the catalyst for agitation that led to the 1832 Reform Act, and subsequent rise of the egalitarian Chartist movement. The galleries go on to explore the struggle for female suffrage, the Communist party in Britain, Oswald Mosely's fascists, and the working-class origins of football and pop music, and include the finest collection of trade union banners in the country.

Deansgate

Deansgate cuts through the city centre from the Rochdale canal to the cathedral, its architectural reference points ranging from Victorian industrialism to post-millennium posturing. One landmark is the **Great Northern** mall, flanking Deansgate between Great Bridgewater and Peter streets. This was once the **Great Northern Railway Company's Goods Warehouse**, a great sweep of brickwork dating back to the 1890s, originally an integral part of a large and ambitious trading depot with road and rail links on street level and subterranean canals down below.

John Rylands Library

Deansgate • **Library** Tues–Sat 10am–5pm, Sun & Mon noon–5pm **Close-up public viewings** Rare books can be seen close up on one Thurs a month at 12.15pm (booking required) • Library free; viewings £3 • ⓣ 0161 306 0555, ⓦ library.manchester.ac.uk • Deansgate Metrolink

Nestling between the modern Spinningfields financial district and the north end of Deansgate, **John Rylands Library** is the city's supreme example of Victorian Gothic – notwithstanding the presence of an unbecoming modern entrance wing. The architect who won the original commission, Basil Champneys, opted for a cloistered neo-Gothicism of narrow stone corridors, delicately crafted stonework, stained-glass windows and burnished wooden panelling. The library, which has survived in superb condition, now houses specialist collections of rare books and manuscripts.

St Ann's Square

Slender **St Ann's Square** is tucked away off the eastern side of Deansgate, a couple of blocks up from the Rylands Library. Flanking the square's southern side is **St Ann's Church** (daily 9.45am–4.45pm; free), a trim sandstone structure whose Neoclassical symmetries date from 1709, though the stained-glass windows are firmly Victorian. At the other end of the square is the **Royal Exchange**, which houses the much-lauded **Royal Exchange Theatre**. Formerly the Cotton Exchange, this building employed seven thousand people until trading finished on December 31, 1968 – the old trading board still shows the last day's prices for American and Egyptian cotton.

Exchange Square

A pedestrian high street – **New Cathedral Street** – runs north from St Ann's Square to **Exchange Square**, with its water features, public sculptures and massive department stores (primarily Selfridges and Harvey Nichols). On the southeast side of the square stands the whopping **Arndale Centre**, once a real Sixties eyesore, but now a modern shopping precinct, clad in glass.

Manchester Cathedral and around

Exchange Station Approach, Victoria St • Mon–Fri 8.30am–6.30pm, Sat 8.30am–5pm, Sun 8.30am–7pm • Free • Ⓦ manchestercathedral.org • Victoria Metrolink

Manchester's **Cathedral** dates back to the fifteenth century, though its Gothic lines have been hacked about too much to have any real architectural coherence. Actually, it's surprising it's still here at all: in 1940, a 1000lb bomb all but destroyed the interior, knocking out most of the stained glass, which is why it's so light inside today.

Chetham's School of Music

Long Millgate • Library Mon–Fri 9am–12.30pm & 1.30–4.30pm • Free • Ⓣ 0161 834 7961, Ⓦ chethams.org.uk • Victoria Metrolink

The choristers in Manchester cathedral are trained at **Chetham's School of Music**. This fifteenth-century manor house became a school and a free public library in 1653 and was turned into a music school in 1969. There are free recitals during term time and, although there's no public access to most of the complex, you can visit the oak-panelled **Library** with its handsome carved eighteenth-century bookcases. Along the side corridor is the main **Reading Room**, where Marx and Engels beavered away on the square table that still stands in the windowed alcove.

National Football Museum

Cathedral Gardens • Sun–Wed 10am–6pm, Thurs–Sat 10am–8pm • Free except for special exhibitions • Ⓦ nationalfootballmuseum.com Metrolink • Victoria Metrolink

Manchester's **National Football Museum**, housed in a suitably spectacular structure – the sloping, six-storey glass Urbis building near Victoria station – houses some true treasures of the world's most popular game. Here you can see the 1966 World Cup Final ball, Maradona's "Hand of God" shirt, and the only surviving version of the Jules Rimet world cup trophy. They also display the personal collection of Sir Stanley Matthews, considered one of the greatest English footballers of all time.

Victoria Train Station

Station Approach, behind the cathedral • Victoria Metrolink

With its long, gently curving stone facade, **Victoria Station** is the most likeable of the city's several stations. Pop inside for a look at the Art Deco ticket booths and the immaculate tiled map of the Lancashire and Yorkshire Railway network as it was in the 1920s.

Piccadilly Gardens

Off Portland St and Oldham St • Piccadilly Gardens Metrolink

Next to the busy Piccadilly bus interchange and east of the Arndale Centre, **Piccadilly Gardens,** historically the largest green space in the city, was re-landscaped in 2002 as a family-friendly space with shady trees, green carpeted lawns, a fountain and water jets, and a pavilion at one end to screen off the traffic. Regular events keep the gardens lively, including weekend food **markets** selling local produce and gourmet goodies, so it's always worth popping by to see what's going on.

The Northern Quarter

Oldham Street, which shoots off northeast from Piccadilly Gardens, is the shabby gateway to the hip **Northern Quarter.** Traditionally, this is Manchester's garment district and you'll still find old-fashioned shops and wholesalers selling clothes, shop fittings, mannequins and hosiery alongside the more recent designer shops, music stores and trendy café-bars. **Thomas Street** is at the heart of the area; for details of some of the best **shops** around here, see p.458.

10

MANCHESTER'S GAY VILLAGE AND GAY PRIDE

The side roads off Portland Street lead down to the Rochdale canal, where **Canal Street** forms the heart of Manchester's thriving **Gay Village**: the pink pound has filled this area of the city with canalside cafés, clubs, bars and businesses. Always lively, the village is packed to bursting point during Manchester's huge **Gay Pride** festival (manchesterpride.com), which usually occurs on the last weekend of August. The village is closed off as thousands of revellers descend for music – big-name performers have included Beth Ditto and Boy George – comedy, theatre and exhibitions, all celebrating lesbian, gay, bi, and trans-gendered sexuality (weekend tickets £20, day tickets £12.50; book online).

Chinatown

From Piccadilly Gardens, it's a short walk south to **Chinatown**, whose grid of narrow streets stretch north–south from Charlotte to Princess Street between Portland and Mosley streets, with the inevitable **Dragon Arch**, at Faulkner and Nicolas, providing the focus for the annual Chinese New Year celebrations.

Cornerhouse

Junction of Oxford Rd and Whitworth St • 0161 200 1500, cornerhouse.org • St Peter's Square Metrolink

One block west of the Gay Village, the **Cornerhouse** is the dynamo of the Manchester arts scene. In addition to screening art-house films (see p.457), it has three floors of gallery space devoted to contemporary and local artists' work, along with a popular café and bar (see p.455).

Salford Quays

After the Manchester Ship Canal opened in 1894, **Salford docks** played a pivotal role in turning the city into one of Britain's busiest seaports. Following their closure in 1982, which left a post-industrial mess just a couple of miles to the west of the city centre, an extraordinarily ambitious redevelopment transformed **Salford Quays**, as it was rebranded, into a hugely popular waterfront complex with its own gleaming apartment blocks, shopping mall and arts centre, **The Lowry**. Also on the quays is the **Imperial War Museum North**, with its splendidly thoughtful displays on war in general and its effects on the individual in particular.

The Lowry

Pier 8, Salford Quays • **Galleries** Sun–Fri 11am–5pm, Sat 10am–5pm • Free, but donation requested • 0870 787 5780, thelowry.com • Harbour City Metrolink

Perched on the water's edge, **The Lowry** is the quays' shiny steel arts centre. The **Galleries**, which host sixteen different exhibitions each year, are largely devoted to the paintings of **Lawrence Stephen Lowry** (1887–1976), the artist most closely associated with Salford. The earlier paintings – those somewhat desolate, melancholic portrayals of Manchester mill workers – are the most familiar, while later works, repeating earlier paintings but changing the greys and sullen browns for lively reds and pinks, can come as a surprise. Lowry also expanded his repertoire as he grew older, capturing mountain scenes and seascapes in broad sweeps, and painting full-bodied realistic portraits that mark a surprising move away from his internationally famous matchstick crowds.

Imperial War Museum North

The Quays, Trafford Wharf North • Daily: March–Oct 10am–6pm; Nov–Feb 10am–5pm • Free • north.iwm.org.uk • Harbour City Metrolink

A footbridge spans the Manchester Ship Canal to link The Lowry with the startling **Imperial War Museum North**, which raises a giant steel fin into the air, is a building designed by the architect Daniel Libeskind. The interior is just as striking, its angular lines serving as a dramatic backdrop to the displays, which kick off with the Big Picture, when the walls of the main hall are transformed into giant screens to show regularly rotated, fifteen-minute, surround-sound films. Superb themed displays fill six separate exhibition areas – the "Silos" – focusing on everything from women's work in the World Wars to war reporting (you can see the very bullet that landed in Kate Adie's leg) and the suicide bomb attacks on Al Matanabbi Street that shook Baghdad in 2007.

Old Trafford

Sir Matt Busby Way, off Warwick Rd • Tours daily 9am–5pm, advance booking essential • £15 • ⓣ 0161 868 8000, ⓦ manutd.com • Old Trafford Metrolink

Old Trafford, the self-styled "Theatre of Dreams", is the home of **Manchester United**, arguably the most famous football team in the world. The club's following is such that only season-ticket holders ever get to attend a game, but **guided tours** of the grounds and museum placate out-of-town fans who want to gawp at the silverware and sit in the dug-out.

The City of Manchester Stadium

Sport City, off Alan Turing Way • Tours daily 9am–5pm, advanced booking advised • £10 • ⓣ 0161 444 1894, ⓦ mcfc.co.uk

Across the other side of town from Old Trafford, United's long-suffering local rivals, **Manchester City**, became the world's richest club in a dramatic twist of fate one night in 2008 after being bought by the royal family of Abu Dhabi. They play at the **City of Manchester Stadium**, occupying the Commonwealth Games site, a thirty-minute walk east of the city centre. It's easier to get tickets for City games than for United's.

ARRIVAL AND DEPARTURE — MANCHESTER

By plane Manchester Airport (ⓣ 0161 489 3000, ⓦ manchesterairport.co.uk) is 10 miles south of the city centre. There's an excellent train service to Manchester Piccadilly (£4.10 single); the taxi fare is around £22.

By train Of Manchester's three stations, Piccadilly, facing London Rd on the east side of the centre, sees the largest number of long-distance services, some of which continue on to Oxford Road, just south of the centre. On the north side of the city, Victoria Station mainly sees services to Lancashire and Yorkshire. All three stations are connected to the centre via a free Metroshuttle bus service (see p.454); Piccadilly and Victoria are also on the Metrolink tram line (see p.454).

Destinations from Manchester Piccadilly Barrow-in-Furness (Mon–Sat 7 daily, Sun 3 daily; 2hr 15min); Birmingham (hourly; 1hr 30min); Blackpool (hourly; 1hr 10min); Buxton (hourly; 1hr); Carlisle (8 daily; 1hr 50min); Chester (every 30min; 1hr–1hr 20min); Lancaster (hourly; 1hr); Leeds (hourly; 1hr); Liverpool (every 30min; 50min); London (hourly; 2hr 20min); Newcastle (10 daily; 3hr); Oxenholme (4–6 daily; 40min–1hr 10min); Penrith (2–4 daily; 1hr 40min); Preston (every 20min; 50min); Sheffield (hourly; 1hr); York (every 30min; 1hr 30min).

Destinations from Manchester Oxford Road Blackpool (hourly; 1hr 15min); Carlisle (8 daily; 1hr 50min); Chester (hourly; 1hr); Lancaster (8 daily; 1hr); Leeds (10 daily; 1hr); Liverpool (every 30min; 50min); Oxenholme (8 daily; 1hr 10min); Penrith (8 daily; 1hr 40min); Preston (every 30min; 45min); Sheffield (hourly; 1hr); York (hourly; 1hr 30min).

Destinations from Manchester Victoria Blackpool (6 daily; 1hr 30min); Leeds (every 30min; 1hr 20min); Liverpool (10 daily; 1hr); Preston (hourly; 55min).

By bus Most long-distance buses use Chorlton Street Coach Station, about half-way between Piccadilly train station and Albert Square, though some regional buses also leave from Shudehill Bus Station, between the Arndale Centre and the Northern Quarter.

Destinations Birmingham (6 daily; 3hr); Blackpool (5 daily; 1hr 40min); Chester (3 daily; 1hr); Leeds (6 daily; 2hr); Liverpool (hourly; 40min); London (every 1–2hr; 4hr 30min–6hr 45min); Newcastle (6 daily; 5hr); Sheffield (4 daily; 2hr 40min).

Travel information For information on train and bus services, contact TFGM (ⓣ 0871 200 2233, ⓦ tfgm.com).

GETTING AROUND

About a 30min walk from top to bottom, central Manchester is compact enough to cover on foot, though most visitors take to the bus or tram as soon as it starts raining.

By bus A free Metroshuttle bus service (every 5–10min) weaves its way across the centre of town, connecting all the major points of interest.

By tram Metrolink trams (metrolink.co.uk) whisk through the city centre bound for the suburbs. There are two routes: one links central Manchester with Bury in the north and Altrincham in the south, the other travels west to Eccles via Salford Quays, the location of the Imperial War Museum North.

By taxi Mantax (0161 230 3333) and Taxifone (0161 232 3333) are two reliable taxi firms.

10

INFORMATION

Tourist office Manchester Visitor Centre, 45–50 Piccadilly Plaza, on the corner of Portland St (Mon–Sat 9.30am–5.30pm, Sun 10.30am–4.30pm; 0871 222 8223, visitmanchester.com).

Listings information The weekly *Time Out Manchester* (timeout.com/manchester) is particularly good for music and event information, while the *Manchester Evening News* (manchestereveningnews.co.uk) is reliable for popular events.

Useful website manchesterconfidential.com

ACCOMMODATION

There are many city-centre **hotels**, especially budget chains, which means you have a good chance of finding a smart, albeit formulaic, en-suite room in central Manchester for around £60–70 at almost any time of the year – except when United are playing at home. Less expensive **guesthouses** and **B&Bs** are concentrated some way out of the centre, mainly on the southern routes into the city.

Abode 107 Piccadilly 0161 247 7744, abodehotels .co.uk/Manchester; Piccadilly Gardens Metrolink. Part of a small chain of boutique hotels, this gem occupies a former cotton warehouse a stone's throw from Piccadilly Station. Rooms are light and elegant, with high ceilings and polished wooden floors. **£210**

Arora 18–24 Princess St 0161 236 8999, manchester .arorahotels.com; Piccadilly Gardens Metrolink. Four-star with more than 100 neat, modern rooms – five of them with themes relating to part-owner Cliff Richard – in a listed building opposite the Manchester Art Gallery. Good online discounts. **£190**

Castlefield Liverpool Rd 0161 832 7073, castlefield-hotel.co.uk; Deansgate-Castlefield Metrolink. Large, very modern, red-brick, warehouse-style hotel handily located opposite the Museum of Science and Industry. Nicely appointed rooms, and a gym and pool (free to guests). **£80**

★ **Great John Street** Great John St 0161 831 3211, greatjohnst.co.uk; Deansgate-Castlefield Metrolink. Deluxe hotel in an imaginatively refurbished old school building not far from Deansgate, with thirty individual, spacious and comfortable suites, some split-level. The on-site bar-cum-restaurant has an open fire and deep sofas, with a gallery breakfast room up above. Nice rooftop garden, too. **£240**

★ **Hilton Chambers** 15 Hilton St 0161 236 4414 hattersgroup.com/Hilton; Piccadilly Gardens Metrolink. Part of a small chain operating in the northwest, this newish hostel is right in the heart of the Northern Quarter, and a great location for exploring the city's nightlife. A range of different rooms (room rates increase considerably at the weekend) and some great communal spaces, including an outdoor deck. Dorm **£19**, double **£55**

Manchester YHA Potato Wharf, Castlefield 0161 839 9960, yha.org.uk; Deansgate-Castlefield Metrolink. Excellent hostel overlooking the canal that runs close to the Museum of Science and Industry, with 35 rooms (thirty four-bunk, two five-bunk, and three doubles). Facilities include wi-fi access, laundry, self-catering and a café. Dorm **£25**, double **£45**

★ **The Palace** Oxford Rd 0161 288 1111, principal-hotels.com; St Peter's Square Metrolink. Occupying one of the city's grandest Victorian buildings, a terracotta-clad extravagance built to a design by Alfred Waterhouse in 1891, the *Palace* is part of a small deluxe chain. The public rooms have all the stately grandeur you might expect, complete with ersatz Roman pillars and columns, and there are 250 plush rooms and suites. **£230**

Radisson Edwardian Peter St 0161 835 9929, radissonedwardian.com; St Peter's Square Metrolink. The Neoclassical facade is all that's left of the Free Trade Hall; inside, this five-star luxury hotel has a sleek modern interior full of natural light, tasteful rooms, and all the extras you'd expect – spa, gym and the trendy *Opus One* bar. **£120**

EATING

Rivalling London in the breadth and scope of its **cafés** and **restaurants**, Manchester has something to suit everyone. The bulk of Manchester's eating and drinking places are scattered around the **city centre**, but the **Rusholme** district, a couple of miles south, possesses the city's widest and best selection of Asian restaurants. From Rusholme, it's another couple of miles along Wilmslow Road to **Didsbury**, a leafy suburb with several excellent places to eat.

CAFES AND CAFÉ-BARS

Most city-centre pubs dish up something filling at lunchtime, but for a more modish snack or drink, European-style café-bars are everywhere, especially in the Northern Quarter, and in the Gay Village on the Rochdale canal.

Barça Bar Arches 8 & 9, Catalan Square ⊕0161 839 7099, ⓦbarca-manchester.co.uk; Deansgate-Castlefield Metrolink. Ideal for a drink on a sunny afternoon, this trendy Castlefield café-bar does have a great location, tucked into the old railway arches off Castle St, a stone's throw from the Rochdale Canal. Best on the weekend. Sun–Thurs noon–11pm, Fri & Sat noon–1am.

Cornerhouse 70 Oxford St ⊕0161 200 1500, ⓦcornerhouse.org; St Peter's Square Metrolink. Slick ground-floor bar and first-floor café-bar in Manchester's premier arts centre. Tasty, inexpensive snacks and light meals – from around £5 – and a good beer and wine menu. Mon–Thurs 11am–11pm, Fri & Sat 11am–midnight, Sun 11am–10.30pm.

Dry Bar 28–30 Oldham St, Northern Quarter ⊕0161 236 9840; Piccadilly Metrolink. The first designer café-bar on the scene, started by Factory Records and the catalyst for much of what has happened since in the Northern Quarter. Still as cool (though not always easy) as they come. Sun–Thurs 11am–2am, Fri & Sat 11am–4am.

Eighth Day 107–111 Oxford Rd ⊕0161 273 4878, ⓦeighth-day.co.uk. Manchester's oldest organic vegetarian café has a shop, takeaway and juice bar upstairs, with a great-value café/restaurant downstairs. Mon–Fri 9am–7pm, Sat 10am–4.30pm.

★ **The Gallery Café** Whitworth Art Gallery, Oxford Rd ⊕0161 275 7450. Just inside the gallery's elegant entrance, this lovely café serves locally sourced breakfasts, posh sandwiches and light lunches for no more than £6. Mon–Sat 10am–5pm, Sun noon–4pm.

Manto 46 Canal St, Gay Village ⊕0161 236 2667; Piccadilly Gardens Metrolink. Probably the most iconic and oldest bar in the Gay Village, constantly reinventing itself since it was established in 1990. It attracts a chic crowd, who lap up the cool sounds and club nights. Inexpensive fusion dishes served. Daily noon–8pm.

★ **Odd** 30–32 Thomas St, Northern Quarter ⊕0161 833 0070, ⓦoddbar.co.uk; Shude Hill Metrolink. Oozes Manchester's cosmopolitan pride in kitsch surroundings. Great food follows the quirky theme – the NYPD (New York Pastrami Doorstep), for instance. DJ nights most weekends, and a three-page drinks menu. Mon–Wed 11am–midnight, Thurs 11am–1am, Fri & Sat 11am–1.30am, Sun noon–midnight.

Trof Central 6–8 Thomas St, Northern Quarter ⓦtrof.co.uk, ⊕0161 833 3197; Shude Hill Metrolink. The epitome of new Manchester: three storeys of cool, relaxed café-bar populated by trendy young things. It's ideal for a late breakfast or early afternoon drink, and hosts open-mic nights, poetry readings and DJ sets. Sun–Wed 10am–midnight, Thurs 10am–1am, Fri & Sat 10am–3am.

RESTAURANTS

Chaophraya Chapel Walks, off Cross St ⊕0161 832 8342, ⓦchaophraya.co.uk/manchester; Deansgate-Castlefield Metrolink. A Manchester institution that serves great, generous Thai classics for around £10. Try the *Gaeng Kiew Wan* – green curry with aubergine, bamboo shoot and Thai sweet basil. Daily noon–midnight.

Jaffa 185 Wilmslow Rd, Rusholme ⊕0161 225 0800. More Lebanese canteen than curry house, this cheap and cheerful Rusholme place is a superb spot for meze, lamb kebabs, and *shawarma* (no more than £6) and very popular with local Asian families. Daily 10am–9pm.

Lime Tree 8 Lapwing Lane, West Didsbury ⊕0161 445 1217, ⓦthelimetreerestaurant.co.uk. The finest local food, with a menu that chargrills and oven-roasts as if its life depended on it – the Hardingland suckling pig is a joy. Main courses cost £14 and up in the evening, less at lunchtime. It's fashionable, so reservations are recommended. Tues–Fri noon–2.30pm & 5.30pm–late, Sat–Mon 5.30pm–late.

Mr Thomas' Chop House 52 Cross St ⊕0161 832 2245, ⓦtomsmanchester.thevictorianchophousecompany.com; Market St Metrolink. Good traditional English "chop-house" food (oysters, bubble and squeak and the like) served in the ornate dining-and-drinking room at the rear of a lovely old pub (see p.456). Mon–Sat 11.30am–11pm, Sun noon–9pm.

The Market Restaurant 104 High St, Northern Quarter ⊕0161 834 3743, ⓦmarket-restaurant.com; Piccadilly Gardens Metrolink. A Northern Quarter institution with a regularly changing menu that puts together contemporary British dishes in adventurous, eclectic combinations. Main courses around £13–18. Reservations essential. Tues–Thurs 5–9.30pm, Fri & Sat noon–10pm.

Punjab Tandoori 177 Wilmslow Rd, Rusholme ⊕0161 225 2960. Despite the name, this is the only distinctively southern Indian – as opposed to Pakistani – restaurant on Rusholme's "Curry Mile" strip. The special dosa starters are great, and prices very reasonable – a full meal should cost no more than £15. A local favourite without pretensions. Daily 3pm till very late.

Royal Suite Darbar 65–67 Wilmslow Rd ⊕0161 224 4392. Award-winning South Asian food in plain, friendly surroundings. The house speciality is *nihari*, a slow-cooked lamb dish, while other home-style choices appear on Sunday; the *karahi gosht* is particularly good. Take your own booze. Mains from £9. Daily 3pm till very late.

★ **Sam's Chop House** Chapel Walks, off Cross St ⊕0161 834 3210, ⓦsamschophouse.co.uk; Market St Metrolink. The restaurant attached to this wonderful old-world pub is a hidden gem. It has a Victorian gas-lit feel and a delightful menu of English food (mains £14–16) – and

10

they really know their wine, too. Mon–Sat noon–3pm & 5.30–11pm, Sun noon–8pm.

Stock 4 Norfolk St 0161 839 6644, stockrestaurant.co.uk; Market St Metrolink. Superior Italian cooking – the fish is renowned – and a serious wine list. It's housed in the city's old stock exchange, hence the name. You'll need to dress up to fit in. Mains around £18, less at lunch and 5–7pm. Mon–Sat noon–2.30pm & 5.30pm till late.

Tampopo 16 Albert Square 0161 819 1966, tampopo.co.uk; St Peter's Square Metrolink. One of a small chain, this casual basement noodle bar – Japanese, Thai, Malaysian or Indonesian – serves dishes under £7 to a quick in-and-out crowd. Mon–Sat noon–11pm, Sun noon–10pm.

Vertigo 36 John Dalton St 0161 839 9907, vertigomanchester.co.uk; St Peter's Square Metrolink. The ostentatious decor of this confident new restaurant mirrors their dishes to wonderful effect – try the black pudding with apple foam or lobster ravioli. Mains around £20. Mon–Sat noon–11pm.

★ **Yang Sing** 34 Princess St 0161 236 2200, yang-sing.com; St Peter's Square Metrolink. One of the best Cantonese restaurants in the country, with authentic dishes ranging from a quick fried noodle plate to the full works. For the most interesting food you should stray from the printed menu; ask the friendly staff for advice. Its sister restaurant, the *Little Yang Sing* on George St, slightly cheaper, is also worth stopping by. Mains from £11. Daily noon–10.45pm.

DRINKING

★ **Big Hands** 296 Oxford Rd 0161 272 7779. In front of the Contact Theatre, this intimate, über-cool bar is popular with trendy students, usually post-gig as it has a late licence. Mon–Thurs 11am–2am, Fri & Sat 11am–3am.

Britons Protection 50 Great Bridgewater St 0161 236 5895, britonsprotection.co.uk; Deansgate-Castlefield Metrolink. Cosy old pub with a couple of small rooms, a backyard beer garden and all sorts of Victorian detail – most splendidly the tiles and the open fires in winter. Daily 11am–11pm.

Circus Tavern 86 Portland St 0161 236 5818; Piccadilly Gardens Metrolink. Manchester's smallest pub, this Victorian drinking hole is a favourite city-centre pit-stop. You may have to knock to get in; once you do, you're confronted by the landlord in the corridor pulling pints. Daily 11am–11pm.

Cloud 23 Beetham Tower, 301 Deansgate 0161 870 1688, cloud23bar.com; Deansgate-Castlefield Metrolink. Manchester's highest and most popular cocktail bar, with a 23rd-floor glass overhang. Expensive, but worth it for the view of the city and Pennines beyond. Mon–Thurs 5pm–1am, Fri 5pm–2am, Sat 4.30pm–2am, Sun 5pm–midnight.

Dukes '92 Castle St 0161 839 8646, dukes92.com; Deansgate-Castlefield Metrolink. Classily revamped former stable block with art on the walls, terrace seating and a good selection of beers – an ideal spot for a sunny afternoon pint by the picturesque canal lock. Serves great-value food too, including a wide range of patés and cheeses. Mon–Sat 11.30am–11pm, Sun noon–10.30pm.

★ **Mr Thomas' Chop House** 52 Cross St 0161 832 2245, tomsmanchester.thevictorianchophousecompany.com; Market St Metrolink. Victorian classic with Dickensian nooks and crannies. Office workers, daytime drinkers, old goats and students all call it home. They serve good-value, traditional food, too (see p.455). Mon–Sat 11am–11pm, Sun noon–9pm.

Marble Arch 73 Rochdale Rd, Northern Quarter 0161 832 5914, marblebeers.co.uk. A little way out of the centre, but don't be put off by the surroundings. The interior has beautiful, ornate Victorian tiling and a wooden bar, and they serve beers from their own microbrewery – including a highly popular ginger beer. Mon–Fri 11.30am–11pm, Sat noon–11pm, Sun 7–10.30pm.

The Ox 71 Liverpool Rd 0161 839 7740, theox.co.uk; Deansgate-Castlefield Metrolink. Pleasant, popular old boozer that dates back to Victorian times – as does some of the tilework. You can choose from a good range of cask ales here, and they do superior bar food, too. Sun–Thurs 11.30am–midnight, Fri & Sat 11.30am–1am.

Sand Bar 120–122 Grosvenor St 0161 273 1552. Between the university and the city centre, this is a brilliant modern take on the traditional pub, where students, lecturers and workers shoot the breeze. There's a great selection of beers and wines. Mon–Wed & Sun noon–midnight, Thurs noon–1am, Fri & Sat noon–2am.

NIGHTLIFE AND ENTERTAINMENT

Manchester's musical heritage and whopping student population keep things lively and interesting. **Clubs** change styles depending on the night of the week, and frequently change names; in addition, many of the city's hip **café-bars** (see p.455) host regular club nights. There is also an excellent **live music** scene, of course, with tickets for local bands usually under £5, perhaps £10–15 for bigger names. Check ubiquitous fly-posters, and the websites listed below, to see what's on. The bi-annual artist-led **Manchester International Festival** (mif.co.uk; next taking place in 2013) has included upwards of twenty world premiers of shows by names such as Damon Albarn and Björk.

As for **classical music**, the city is blessed with the North's most highly prized **orchestra**, the Hallé, which is resident at Bridgewater Hall. Other acclaimed names include the **BBC Philharmonic** and the **Manchester Camerata** chamber

TOP 5 MUSIC NIGHTS

Cavern Club Liverpool. See p.469
The Deaf Institute Manchester. See below
Liverpool Philharmonic Liverpool. See p.469
Matt and Phred's Manchester. See below
Warehouse Project Manchester. See below

orchestra (ⓦmanchestercamerata.com), who perform at a variety of venues. The Cornerhouse is the local **alternative arts** mainstay, while a range of mainstream and fringe **theatres** produce a lively, year-round programme.

Information *Time Out Manchester* (see p.454) has the broadest coverage of Manchester's nightlife and entertainment listings. For music, club, and art events look to Good for the Soul, a Manchester-based music cooperative that produces an excellent listings website (ⓦgoodforthesoul.net).

LIVE MUSIC AND CLUBS

42nd Street 2 Bootle St ⓣ0161 831 7108, ⓦ42ndstreetnightclub.co.uk; St Peter's Square Metrolink. An unashamedly Manc-focused indie club that will guarantee you a fun night of Stone Roses, Oasis and The Smiths – though you shouldn't expect much else. Tues–Sat 10pm–2.30am.

★ **Band on the Wall** 25 Swan St, Northern Quarter ⓣ0161 834 1786, ⓦbandonthewall.org. This legendary Northern Quarter joint remains true to its commitment to "real music": it's one of the city's best venues to see live bands – from world and folk to jazz and reggae – and it hosts club nights to boot. Mon–Thurs 9am–1am, Fri & Sat 9am–3am, Sun noon–5pm.

The Deaf Institute 135 Grosvenor St ⓣ0161 276 9350 ⓦthedeafinstitute.co.uk. A mile down Oxford Rd, south of the centre, this bar and music hall sits in a funky makeover of the elegant Victorian former deaf institute. Mostly folk, indie and r'n'b, with lots of up-and-coming talent. Sun–Wed 9am–midnight, Thurs–Sat 9am–4am.

Manchester Academy Oxford Rd ⓣ0161 275 2930, ⓦmanchesteracademy.net. All three locations – Academy 1 is on the university campus, opposite the medical school; Academy 2 & 3 are inside the Students' Union building on Oxford Rd – are popular student venues featuring new and established bands.

Matt and Phreds 64 Tib St, Northern Quarter ⓣ0161 831 7002, ⓦmattandphreds.com; Shudehill Metrolink. The city's finest jazz bar, offering everything from swing to gritty New Orleans blues. Mon–Thurs 5pm–2am, Fri & Sat 5pm–3am.

Roadhouse 8 Newton St, Northern Quarter, ⓣ0161 237 9789, ⓦtheroadhouselive.co.uk; Piccadilly Gardens Metrolink. Regular and varied gigs by local bands plus a succession of club nights. Daily 8pm–2am.

Sankey's Soap Beehive Mill, Jersey St, Ancoats ⓣ0161 236 5444, ⓦsankeys.info; Shudehill Metrolink. A Manchester classic, especially during the superb nights brought to you by the legendary Tribal Gathering crew, popular for their sleazy house music. There are other club night specials too. Thurs 10.30pm–3am, Fri & Sat 10.30pm–6am.

★ **Warehouse Project** Underneath Piccadilly Station ⓦthewarehouseproject.com; Piccadilly Metrolink. An internationally acclaimed three-month season of the country's best dance and house acts – 2manydjs, Annie Mac, La Roux – smashing out sessions in a warehouse below the station. Tickets (£20) are like gold dust, so book well in advance. Oct–Dec Fri & Sat.

STADIUMS

Manchester Apollo Stockport Rd, Ardwick Green ⓣ08709 913913, ⓦalive.co.uk/apollo. Huge theatre auditorium for all kinds of concerts.

Manchester Central Petersfield ⓣ0161 834 2700, ⓦmanchestercentral.co.uk; Deansgate-Castlefield Metrolink. Mid-sized city-centre indoor stadium.

Manchester Evening News Arena 21 Hunt's Bank, beside Victoria Station ⓣ0844 847 8000, ⓦmenarena.com; Victoria Metrolink. Indoor stadium seating 20,000 and hosting all the big names.

CLASSICAL MUSIC

Bridgewater Hall Lower Mosley St ⓣ0161 907 9000, ⓦbridgewater-hall.co.uk; Deansgate-Castlefield Metrolink. Home of the Hallé Orchestra and the Manchester Camerata; also a full programme of chamber, pop, classical and jazz concerts.

Royal Northern College of Music (RNCM) 124 Oxford Rd ⓣ0161 907 5555, ⓦrncm.ac.uk. Top-quality classical and modern jazz concerts, including performances by Manchester Camerata.

THEATRE, CINEMA AND DANCE

★ **Cornerhouse** 70 Oxford St ⓣ0161 200 1500, ⓦcornerhouse.org; St Peter's Square Metrolink. Engaging centre for contemporary arts, with three cinema screens, changing art exhibitions, recitals and talks, plus a bookshop, café and bar.

Dancehouse Theatre 10 Oxford Rd ⓣ0161 237 9753, ⓦthedancehouse.co.uk. Home to the Northern Ballet School and the eponymous theatre troupe; venue for dance, drama and comedy.

Opera House Quay St ⊤0161 828 1700, ⓦticketmaster.co.uk; Deansgate-Castlefield Metrolink. Major venue for touring West End musicals, drama, comedy and concerts.

Royal Exchange Theatre St Ann's Square ⊤0161 833 9833, ⓦroyalexchange.co.uk; Market St Metrolink. The theatre-in-the-round in the Royal Exchange is the most famous stage in the city, with a Studio Theatre (for works by new writers) alongside.

SHOPPING

Aside from the high-end boutiques on **King Street**, and the **department stores** around Market Street and Exchange Square, the city has a plethora of smaller independent stores catering for all tastes. If you're around between mid-November and the week before Christmas, it's well worth making for the city's **German Christmas Market**, which sees Albert Square transformed into a Bavarian picture postcard.

Afflecks 52 Church St, Northern Quarter ⊤0161 839 0718, ⓦafflecks.com; Piccadilly Gardens Metrolink. A Manchester institution, where more than fifty independent stalls are spread over four floors mixing everything from goth outfits to retro cocktail dresses and quirky footwear. Mon–Fri 10.30am–6pm, Sat 10am–6pm, Sun 11am–5pm (ground floor only).

Craft & Design Centre 17 Oak St, Northern Quarter ⊤0161 832 4274, ⓦcraftanddesign.com; Shudehill Metrolink. The city's best place to pick up ceramics, fabrics, earthenware, jewellery and decorative art – there's also a good little café. Mon–Sat 10am–5.30pm.

Piccadilly Records 53 Oldham St, Northern Quarter ⊤0161 839 8008, ⓦpiccadillyrecords.com; Piccadilly Gardens Metrolink. The enthusiastic staff, many of them DJs themselves, are more than willing to navigate you through the shelves of collectibles and vinyl towards some special gem, whatever your taste. Open daily.

Retro Rehab 91 Oldham St, Northern Quarter ⊤0161 839 2050; Piccadilly Gardens Metrolink. Gorgeously feminine dresses abound, be they reworked vintage styles or genuine 1950s pieces, in this wonderful little boutique that prides itself on the range of its fashions from across several decades. Mon–Sat 10am–5.30pm.

Chester

CHESTER, forty miles southwest of Manchester across the Cheshire Plain, is home to a glorious two-mile ring of medieval and Roman **walls** that encircles a kernel of Tudor and Victorian buildings, all overhanging eaves, mini-courtyards, and narrow cobbled lanes, which culminate in the raised arcades called the "**Rows**". The centre of the city is full of easy charms that can be explored on foot, and taken altogether, Chester has enough in the way of sights, restaurants and atmosphere to make it an enjoyable base for a day or two.

The Rows

Intersecting at **The Cross**, the four main thoroughfares of central Chester are lined by **The Rows**, galleried shopping arcades that run along the first floor of a wonderful set of half-timbered buildings with another set of shops down below at street level. This engaging tableau, which extends for the first 200 or 300 yards of each of the four main streets, is a blend of genuine Tudor houses and Victorian imitations. There's no clear explanation of the origin of The Rows – they were first recorded shortly after a fire wrecked Chester in 1278 – but it seems likely that the hard bedrock that lies underneath the town centre prevented its shopkeepers and merchants from constructing the cellars they required, so they built upwards instead. The finest Tudor buildings are on **Watergate Street**, though **Bridge Street** is perhaps more picturesque. From The Cross, it's also a brief walk along **Eastgate Street** to one of the old town gates, above which is perched the filigree **Eastgate Clock**, raised in honour of Queen Victoria's Diamond Jubilee.

The Cathedral

Northgate St • Mon–Sat 9am–5pm, Sun 12.30–4pm • £4 • ⓦchestercathedral.com

North of The Cross, along **Northgate Street**, rises the neo-Gothic **Town Hall**, whose acres of red and grey sandstone look over to the **Cathedral**, a much modified red sandstone

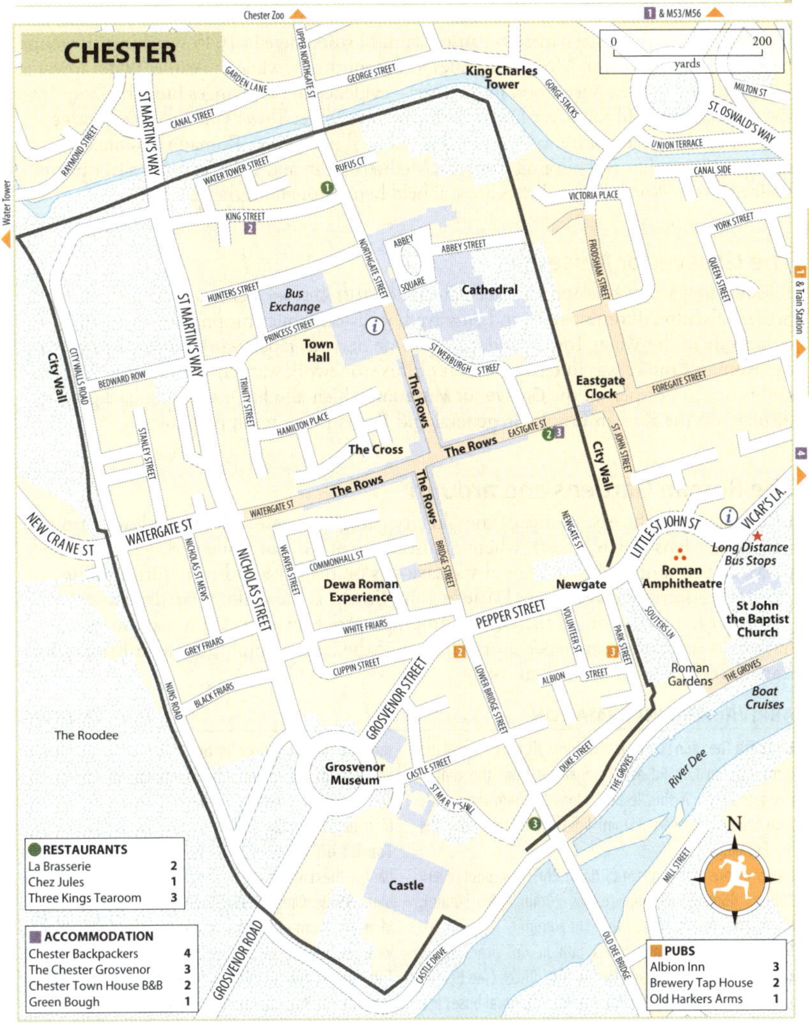

structure dating back to the Normans. The **nave**, with its massive medieval pillars, is suitably imposing, and on one side it sports a splendid sequence of Victorian Pre-Raphaelite mosaic panels that illustrate Old Testament stories in melodramatic style. Close by, the **north transept** is the oldest and most Norman part of the church – hence the round-headed arch and arcade – and the adjoining **choir** holds an intricately carved set of fourteenth-century choir stalls with some especially beastly misericords.

Around the city walls

East of the cathedral, steps provide access to the top of the **city walls** – a two-mile girdle of medieval and Roman handiwork that's the most complete in Britain, though in places the wall is barely above street level. You can walk past all its towers, turrets and gateways in an hour or so, and most have a tale or two to tell. The fifteenth-century **King Charles Tower** in the northeast corner is so named because Charles I stood here in 1645 watching his troops being beaten on Rowton Moor, two miles to the southeast, while the earlier **Water Tower** at the northwest corner, once stood in the river – evidence of the changes brought about by the gradual silting of the River Dee. South from the Water Tower you'll see the **Roodee**, England's oldest racecourse, laid out on a silted tidal pool where Roman ships once unloaded wine, figs and olive oil from the Mediterranean and slate, lead and silver from their mines in North Wales. Races are still held here throughout the year.

The Grosvenor Museum

27 Grosvenor St • Mon–Sat 10.30am–5pm, Sun 1–4pm • Free • T 01244 402033, W grosvenormuseum.co.uk

Scores of sculpted tomb panels and engraved headstones once propped up the wall to either side of the Water Tower, evidence of some nervous repair work undertaken when the Roman Empire was in retreat. Much of this stonework was retrieved by the Victorians and is now on display at the **Grosvenor Museum**, which also has interesting background displays on the Roman Empire in general and Roman Chester in particular.

The Roman Gardens and around

Immediately to the east of one of the old city gates, **Newgate**, a footpath leads into the **Roman Gardens** (open access), where a miscellany of Roman stonework – odd bits of pillar, coping stones and incidental statuary – is on display amidst the surrounding greenery. Footsteps away, along Little St John Street, is the shallow, partly excavated bowl that marks the site of the **Roman Amphitheatre** (open access); it is estimated to have held seven thousand spectators, making it the largest amphitheatre in Britain, but frankly it's not much to look at today.

ARRIVAL AND INFORMATION — CHESTER

By train The train station is a 10min walk northeast of the centre, down City Rd and Foregate St from the central Eastgate Clock. A shuttle bus (Mon–Sat 8am–6pm, free with rail ticket; every 15min) links the station with the Bus Exchange.

Destinations Birmingham (5 daily; 2hr); Liverpool (every 30min; 45min); London (every 20min; 3hr 30min); Manchester (every 30min; 1hr–1hr 20min).

By bus Long-distance buses pull in on Vicar's Lane, opposite one of the town's two tourist offices (see below) and a 5min walk from the city centre, while local buses use the Bus Exchange right in the centre of town, between Princess and Hunter streets, off Northgate St.

Destinations Liverpool (every 20min; 1hr 20min); Manchester (3 daily; 1hr).

Tourist offices Chester has two information offices: one bang in the centre, in the Town Hall, Northgate St (April–Sept Mon–Sat 9.30am–5.30pm, Sun 10am–4pm; Oct–March Mon–Fri 10am–4pm, Sat 10am–5pm) and the other on Vicar's Lane (same hours, plus Oct–March Sun 10am–4pm). They share the same telephone number and website (T 01244 351609, W visitchester.com).

ACCOMMODATION

Chester is a popular tourist destination and although most of its visitors are day-trippers, enough of them stay overnight to sustain dozens of **B&Bs** and a slew of **hotels**. At the height of the summer and on high days and holidays – like Chester Races – advance booking is strongly recommended, either direct or via the tourist office.

Chester Backpackers 67 Boughton T 01244 400185, W chesterbackpackers.co.uk. Close to the city walls and a 5min walk from the train station, in a typically Chester mock-Tudor building. En-suite doubles and 18-bed dorms. Dorm £17, double £45

The Chester Grosvenor Eastgate St T 01244 324024, W chestergrosvenor.co.uk. Superb luxury hotel in an immaculately maintained Victorian building in the centre of town. Extremely comfortable bedrooms and a whole host of facilities, not least a full-blown spa. Discounts common at the weekend. £240

Chester Town House B&B 23 King St T 01244 350021, W chestertownhouse.co.uk. High-standard B&B in a comfortable seventeenth-century townhouse on a cobbled central street off Northgate St. Five en-suite rooms and private parking. £75

CLOCKWISE FROM TOP LEFT BLACKPOOL BEACH (P.471); BEATLES GRAFFITI, LIVERPOOL; COAST NEAR DOUGLAS, ISLE OF MAN (P.476) >

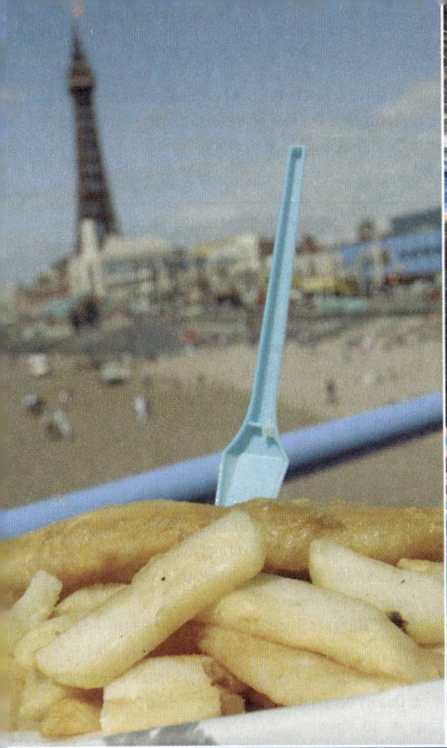

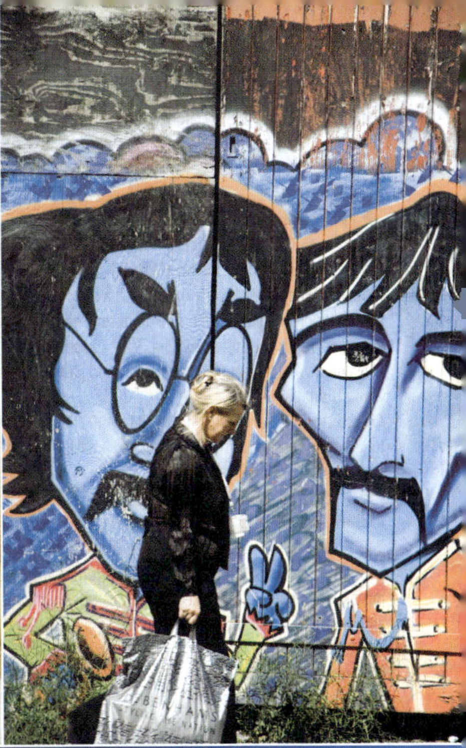

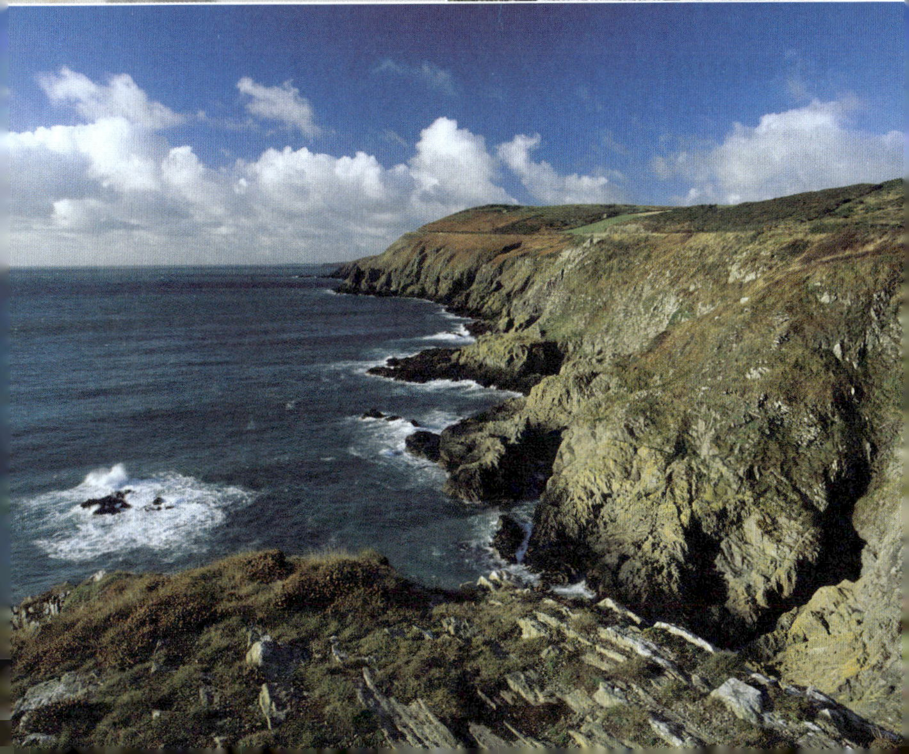

★ **Green Bough** 60 Hoole Rd ⓣ 01244 326241, ⓦ greenbough.co.uk. Small, friendly family-run hotel with all sorts of thoughtful details and very comfortable beds. Great breakfasts too, plus three-course evening meals for £45 and a rooftop garden. One mile northeast of the city centre en route to the M53/M56. **£175**

EATING

10

★ **La Brasserie** Chester Grosvenor, Eastgate St ⓣ 01244 324024, ⓦ chestergrosvenor.com/chester-brasserie. In the same hotel as *Simon Radley's*, a Michelin-starred gourmet restaurant where the à la carte menu sits at a cool £69, this is a much more affordable yet smart brasserie that serves inventive French and fusion cooking. Main courses average £16, and it's also a great place for a coffee and pastry. Daily 7am–10pm.

Chez Jules 71 Northgate St ⓣ 01244 400014, ⓦ chezjules.com. There's a classic brasserie menu – salade nicoise to vegetable cassoulet, Toulouse sausage to rib-eye steak – at this popular spot in an attractive half-timbered building. In the evenings, main courses begin at about £10, but they also do a terrific-value, two-course lunch for £7.90. Mon–Sat noon–3pm & 6–10.30pm, Sun noon–4.30pm.

Three Kings Tearoom 90 Lower Bridge St ⓣ 01244 317717, ⓦ threekingstearooms.com. Behind the cutest of antique shops, an amenable little tearoom with pleasantly fuddy-duddy decor and tasty food – a filling salad and sandwich combo costs about £4. Tues–Sun 10am–4pm.

DRINKING

Albion Inn Corner of Albion and Park Sts ⓣ 01244 340345, ⓦ albioninnchester.co.uk. A Victorian terraced pub in the shadow of the city wall – no fruit machines or muzak, and good old-fashioned decor, plus tasty bar food and a great range of ales. Mon–Sat noon–3pm & 5–11pm, Sun noon–2.30pm & 7–10.30pm.

Brewery Tap House 52–54 Lower Bridge St ⓣ 01244 340999, ⓦ the-tap.co.uk. Up the cobbled ramp, this converted medieval hall, owned by the royalist Gamul family and confiscated by Parliament after the English Civil War, serves a good selection of ales from a local brewery in a tall barn-like room with whitewashed walls. Mon–Sat noon–11pm, Sun noon–10.30pm.

★ **Old Harkers Arms** 1 Russell St, below the City Rd bridge. Canalside real-ale pub imaginatively sited in a former warehouse about 500 yards northeast of Foregate St. Quality bar food too. Mon–Sat 11.30am–11pm, Sun noon–10.30pm.

Liverpool

Standing proud in the 1700s as the empire's second city, **LIVERPOOL** faced a dramatic change in fortune in the twentieth century, suffering a series of harsh economic blows and ongoing urban deprivation. The postwar years were particularly tough, with the battered city becoming a byword for British economic malaise, but the outlook changed again at the turn of the millennium, as economic and social regeneration brightened the centre and old docks, and the city's stint as European Capital of Culture in 2008 transformed the view from outside. Today Liverpool is a dynamic, exciting place: it's a vibrant city with a Tate Gallery of its own, a series of innovative museums and a fascinating social history. And of course it also makes great play of its musical heritage – as well it should, considering that this is the place that gave the world The Beatles.

The main sights are scattered throughout the centre of town, but you can easily walk between most of them. The **River Mersey** provides one focus, whether crossing on the famous ferry to the **Wirral** peninsula or taking a tour of the Albert Dock. **Beatles** sights could easily occupy another day. If you want a cathedral, they've "got one to spare" as the song goes; plus there's a fine showing of British art in the celebrated **Walker Art Gallery** and **Tate Liverpool**, a multitude of exhibits in the terrific **World Museum Liverpool**, and a revitalized arts and nightlife urban quarter centred on **FACT**, Liverpool's showcase for film and the media arts.

Brief history

Liverpool gained its charter from King John in 1207, but remained a humble fishing village for half a millennium until the booming slave trade prompted the building of the first dock in 1715. From then until the abolition of slavery in Britain in 1807,

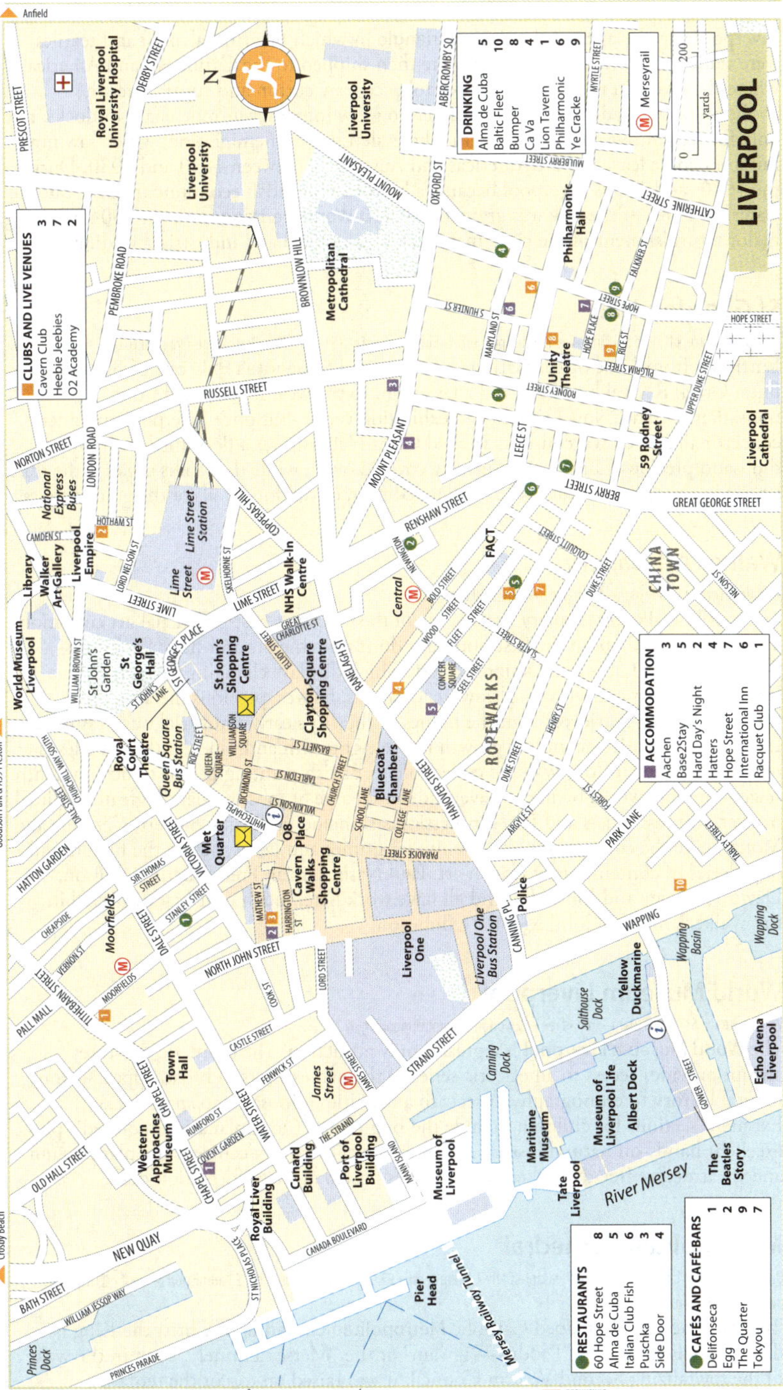
LIVERPOOL
Anfield
A562 Widnes
Sefton Park, John Lennon Airport & Speke Hall
Queen's Dock
Birkenhead
Wallasey
Douglas (Isle of Man)
Crosby Beach
Goodison Park & A59 Preston
0
200
yards
Merseyrail
CLUBS AND LIVE VENUES
Cavern Club 3
Heebie Jeebies 7
O2 Academy 2
DRINKING
Alma de Cuba 5
Baltic Fleet 10
Bumper 8
Ca Va 4
Lion Tavern 1
Philharmonic 6
Ye Cracke 9
ACCOMMODATION
Aachen 3
Base2Stay 5
Hard Day's Night 2
Hatters 4
Hope Street 7
International Inn 6
Racquet Club 1
RESTAURANTS
60 Hope Street 8
Alma de Cuba 5
Italian Club Fish 6
Puschka 3
Side Door 4
CAFÉS AND CAFÉ-BARS
Delifonseca 1
Egg 2
The Quarter 9
Tokyou 7
Royal Liverpool University Hospital
Liverpool University
Metropolitan Cathedral
Philharmonic Hall
Unity Theatre
59 Rodney Street
Liverpool Cathedral
CHINA TOWN
ROPEWALKS
FACT
Central
Concert Square
Bluecoat Chambers
Clayton Square Shopping Centre
St John's Shopping Centre
NHS Walk-In Centre
Lime Street Station
Lime Street
Liverpool Empire
National Express Buses
Library
Walker Art Gallery
World Museum Liverpool
St John's Garden
St George's Hall
Royal Court Theatre
Queen Square Bus Station
Met Quarter
08 Place
Cavern Walks Shopping Centre
Liverpool One
Liverpool One Bus Station
Police
Moorfields
Town Hall
Western Approaches Museum
James Street
Cunard Building
Port of Liverpool Building
Royal Liver Building
Museum of Liverpool
Pier Head
Mersey Railway Tunnel
Tate Liverpool
Maritime Museum
Museum of Liverpool Life
Albert Dock
Canning Dock
Salthouse Dock
Yellow Duckmarine
Wapping Basin
Wapping Dock
Echo Arena Liverpool
The Beatles Story
River Mersey
Princes Dock
PRINCES PARADE
WILLIAM JESSOP WAY
BATH STREET
NEW QUAY
OLD HALL STREET
PALL MALL
TITHEBARN STREET
HATTON GARDEN
DALE STREET
VICTORIA STREET
NORTH JOHN STREET
CASTLE STREET
WATER STREET
STRAND STREET
CANADA BOULEVARD
WAPPING
PARK LANE
HANOVER STREET
PARADISE STREET
CHURCH STREET
BOLD STREET
SEEL STREET
DUKE STREET
RANELAGH ST
LIME STREET
RENSHAW STREET
BERRY STREET
GREAT GEORGE STREET
LEECE ST
RODNEY STREET
HOPE STREET
MOUNT PLEASANT
BROWNLOW HILL
OXFORD ST
CATHERINE STREET
RUSSELL STREET
LONDON ROAD
PEMBROKE ROAD
NORTON STREET
COPPERAS HILL
PRESCOT STREET
DERBY STREET
ABERCROMBY SQ
MULBERRY STREET
MYRTLE STREET
FALKNER ST
UPPER DUKE STREET
NELSON ST
TABLEY STREET
FOREST ST
GOWER STREET

10

Liverpool was the apex of the **slaving triangle** in which firearms, alcohol and textiles were traded for African slaves, who were then shipped to the Caribbean and America where they were in turn exchanged for tobacco, raw cotton and sugar. After the abolition of the trade, the port continued to grow into a seven-mile chain of docks, not only for freight but also to cope with wholesale European emigration, which saw nine million people leave for the Americas and Australasia between 1830 and 1930. During the 1970s and 1980s Liverpool became a byword for British economic malaise, but the waterfront area of the city was granted **UNESCO World Heritage** status in 2004, spurring major refurbishment of the city's magnificent municipal and industrial buildings.

St George's Hall

St George's Place, off Lime St • Tues–Sat 10am–5pm, Sun 1–5pm • Free • ⓣ 0151 225 6909, ⓦ stgeorgesliverpool.co.uk

Emerging from Lime Street Station, you can't miss **St George's Hall**, one of Britain's finest Greek Revival buildings and a testament to the wealth generated from transatlantic trade. Now primarily an exhibition venue, but once Liverpool's premier concert hall and crown court, its vaulted Great Hall features a floor tiled with thirty thousand precious Minton tiles (usually covered over), while the Willis organ is the third largest in Europe. You can take a self-guided tour, or call for details of the guided tours.

Walker Art Gallery

William Brown St • Daily 10am–5pm • Free • ⓦ thewalker.org.uk

Liverpool's **Walker Art Gallery** houses one of the country's best provincial art collections. The paintings are up on the first floor, but don't miss the ground-floor Sculpture Gallery, nor the Craft and Design Gallery, which displays changing exhibits from a large applied arts collection – glassware, ceramics, fabrics, precious metals and furniture, largely retrieved from the homes of the city's early industrial businessmen. Liverpool's explosive economic growth in the eighteenth and nineteenth centuries is reflected in much of the Walker's collection, as British painting begins to occupy centre stage – notably works by native Liverpudlian George Stubbs, England's greatest animal painter. Impressionists and Post-Impressionists, including Degas, Sickert, Cézanne and Monet, take the collection into more modern times and tastes, before the final round of galleries of contemporary British art. Paul Nash, Lucian Freud, Ben Nicholson, David Hockney and John Hoyland all have work here, much of it first displayed in the Walker's biennial John Moores Exhibition.

World Museum Liverpool

William Brown St • Daily 10am–5pm • Free • ⓦ worldmuseumliverpool.org.uk

The **World Museum Liverpool** is a great family attraction. The dramatic six-storey atrium provides access to an eclectic series of themed exhibits of broad appeal – from natural history to ethnography, insects to antiquities, dinosaurs to space rockets. Excellent sections for children include the Bug House (no explanation required), plus excellent hands-on natural history and archeology discovery centres. The planetarium and theatre have free daily shows, with times posted at the information desk.

Metropolitan Cathedral

On the hill behind Lime St, off Mount Pleasant • Daily 7.30am–6pm • £2.50 suggested donation, £3 admission to crypt • ⓦ liverpoolmetrocathedral.org.uk

The idiosyncratically shaped Catholic **Metropolitan Cathedral** of Christ the King is denigratingly known as "Paddy's Wigwam" or the "Mersey Funnel". Built in the wake of the revitalizing Second Vatican Council, it was raised on top of the tentative beginnings of Sir Edwin Lutyens' grandiose project to outdo St Peter's in Rome. The present building, to Sir Frederick Gibberd's spectacular Modernist design, is anchored by sixteen concrete ribs supporting the landmark stained-glass lantern, and was consecrated in 1967. Ceremonial steps mark the approach from Mount Pleasant/ Hope Street, with a café-bar at the bottom and four huge bells at the top.

Liverpool Cathedral

Hope St • Daily 8am–6pm • Donation requested **Tower and audiotour** Mon–Wed, Fri & Sat 10am–4.30pm, Thurs 10.30am–7.30pm, Sun 11.45am–3.30pm • £5 • Ⓦ liverpoolcathedral.org.uk

The Anglican **Liverpool Cathedral** looks much more ancient than the Metropolitan Cathedral, but was actually completed eleven years later, in 1978, after 74 years in construction. The last of the great British neo-Gothic structures, Sir Giles Gilbert Scott's masterwork claims a smattering of superlatives: Britain's largest and the world's fifth-largest cathedral, the world's tallest Gothic arches and the highest and heaviest bells. On a clear day, a trip up the 330ft tower is rewarded by views to the Welsh hills.

Ropewalks and around

At the heart of Liverpool's regenerating city centre, **Ropewalks**, the former warehouse and factory district between Bold Street and Duke Street, is anchored by **FACT**, 88 Wood St (Ⓦ fact.co.uk) – that's Film, Art and Creative Technology – with its galleries for art, video and new media exhibitions (Tues–Sun 11am–6pm; free), community projects, cinema screens, café and bar. The beautifully proportioned Bluecoat Chambers, built in 1717 as an Anglican boarding school for orphans, is in nearby School Lane. An integral part of Liverpool's cultural life for years, **The Bluecoat** (Ⓦ thebluecoat.org.uk), includes artists' studios, exhibitions, courses and performances, as well as a fantastic **Display Centre** (Ⓦ bluecoatdisplaycentre.com) where contemporary crafts are for sale. Further southwest is the massive new development of the **Liverpool One** shopping precinct.

Western Approaches Museum

1 Rumford St, off Chapel St • Mon–Thurs & Sat 10.30am–4.30pm • £6 • Ⓦ liverpoolwarmuseum.co.uk

En route to Pier Head, the **Western Approaches Museum** reveals an underground labyrinth of rooms, formerly headquarters for the Battle of the Atlantic during World War II. The massive Operations Room vividly displays all the technology of a 1940s nerve centre – wooden pushers and model boats, chalkboards and ladders.

The waterfront

Dominating the waterfront are the so-called **Three Graces** – namely the Port of Liverpool Building (1907), Cunard Building (1913) and, most prominently, the 322ft-high Royal Liver Building (1910), topped by the "Liver Birds", a couple of cormorants that have become the symbol of the city. As the waterfront has developed

FERRY ACROSS THE MERSEY

Though the tumult of shipping which once fought the current in Liverpool has gone, the **Pier Head** landing stage remains the embarkation point for the Mersey Ferry (Ⓣ 0151 330 1444, Ⓦ merseyferries.co.uk) to Woodside (for Birkenhead) and Seacombe (Wallasey). Straightforward ferry shuttles (£2.50–3.50 return) operate during the morning and evening rush hours. At other times the boats run circular fifty-minute "river explorer" **cruises** (hourly: Mon–Fri 10am–3pm, Sat & Sun 10am–6pm; £6.70), which you can combine with a visit to the **Spaceport** space exploration visitor attraction at Seacombe (Tues–Sun 10.30am–4.30pm; £8, with ferry £11; Ⓦ spaceport.org.uk).

in the last decade or so, it has sprouted a number of attractions, including **Tate Liverpool**, the excellent **Maritime Museum**, the **Beatles Story** and the impressive new **Museum of Liverpool**.

Museum of Liverpool

Pier Head • Daily 10am–5pm • Free • T 0151 478 4545, W liverpoolmuseums.org.uk/mol

Huge and flashy, in a show-stopping Danish-designed building, the **Museum of Liverpool** opened in 2011. Spread over three floors, the galleries play on Liverpool's historic status as the "second city of Empire", exploring the complex political and life histories that have unfolded in a community whose wealth and social fabric were built on international trade. The ground-floor Global City gallery is particularly good, unravelling the history of local families as well as exhibiting some dubiously acquired antiquarian treasures including a brass Buddha taken in 1886 from King Thibaw's palace in Burma. Anyone with kids in tow should take a look at "Little Liverpool", a gallery where very small children can design and build their own city.

Albert Dock

Five minutes' walk south of Pier Head is **Albert Dock,** built in 1846 when Liverpool's port was a world leader. Its decline began at the beginning of the twentieth century, as the new deep-draught ships were unable to berth here, and the dock last saw service in 1972. A decade later the site was given a complete refit, and it is now one of the city's most popular areas, full of **attractions** – including the **Beatles Story** (see below) – bars and restaurants.

THE BEATLES TRAIL

Mathew Street, ten minutes' walk west of Lime Street Station, is now a little enclave of Beatles nostalgia, most of it bogus and typified by the **Cavern Walks Shopping Centre**, with a bronze statue of the boys in the atrium. **The Cavern** club, where the band was first spotted by Brian Epstein, saw 275 Beatles' gigs between 1961 and 1963; it closed in 1966 and was partly demolished in 1973, though a latter-day successor, the *Cavern Club* at 10 Mathew St, complete with souvenir shop, was rebuilt on the original site. The *Cavern Pub*, across the way, boasts a coiffed Lennon mannequin lounging against the wall and an exterior "Wall of Fame" highlighting the names of all the bands who appeared at the club between 1957 and 1973 as well as brass discs commemorating every Liverpool chart-topper since 1952 – the city has produced more UK No. 1 singles than any other. There's more Beatlemania at **The Beatles Shop**, 31 Mathew St (W thebeatleshop.co.uk), which claims to have the largest range of Beatles gear in the world.

For a personal and social history, head to the Albert Dock for **The Beatles Story** (daily 10am–6pm; £12.95; W beatlesstory.com), which traces the band's rise from the early days to their disparate solo careers. Then it's on to the two houses where John Lennon and Paul McCartney grew up. Both **20 Forthlin Rd**, home to the McCartney family from 1955 to 1964, and the rather more genteel **Mendips**, where Lennon lived with his Aunt Mimi and Uncle George between 1945 and 1963, are only accessible on pre-booked **National Trust** minibus tours (£20, NT members £8.30; T 0151 427 7231 or 0844 800 4791), which run from both the city centre (mid-March to Oct Wed–Sun 10am & 10.50am; Feb to mid-March & Nov 10am, 12.30pm & 3pm) and Speke Hall, seven miles south (mid-March to Oct 2.30pm & 3.20pm). The experience is disarmingly intimate, whether you're sitting in John Lennon's bedroom – which has its original wallpaper – on a replica bed looking out, as he would have done, onto his front lawn, or simply entering Paul's tiny room and gazing at pictures of his childhood.

BEATLES TOURS

Phil Hughes T 0151 228 4565 or 07961 511223, W **tourliverpool.co.uk**. Small (8-seater) minibus tours run daily on demand with a guide well versed in The Beatles and Liverpool life (3hr 30min; £14; private tour £70). Includes city-centre pick-ups/drop-offs and refreshments.

Magical Mystery Tour T 0151 236 9091, W **cavernclub.org; or book at tourist offices.** Tours on the multicoloured Mystery Bus (daily; 2hr; £15.95) leave from The 08 Place and Albert Dock.

Merseyside Maritime Museum

Albert Dock • Daily 10am–5pm • Free • ⓦ liverpoolmuseums.org.uk/maritime

The **Merseyside Maritime Museum** fills one wing of the Dock; allow at least two hours to see it all. The basement houses **Seized**, giving the lowdown on smuggling and revenue collection, along with **Emigrants to a New World**, an illuminating display detailing Liverpool's pivotal role as a springboard for more than nine million emigrants. Other galleries tell the story of the Battle of the Atlantic and of the three ill-fated liners – the *Titanic*, *Lusitania* and *Empress of Ireland*. Finally, the unmissable **International Slavery Museum** on the third floor manages to be both challenging and chilling, as it tells dehumanizing stories of slavery while examining contemporary issues of equality, freedom and racial injustice.

Tate Liverpool

Albert Dock • June–Aug daily 10am–5.50pm; Sept–May Tues–Sun 10am–5.50pm • Free, special exhibitions usually £5 • ⓦ tate.org.uk/liverpool

The country's national collection of modern art from the north, **Tate Liverpool** holds popular retrospectives of artists such as Mondrian, Dalì, Magritte, and Calder, along with an ever-changing display from its vast collection, and temporary exhibitions of artists of international standing. There's also a full programme of events, talks and tours.

Crosby Beach

Cambridge Rd or Mariners Rd/Hall Rd West, Crosby • Trains from Lime Street to Hall Road Station; every 30min; 20min

Seven miles north of Liverpool city centre, **Crosby Beach** was an innocuous, if picturesque, spot until the arrival in 2005 of Antony Gormley's haunting **Another Place** installation, spread along more than 1000 yards of the shore. An eerie set of a hundred life-size cast-iron statues, each cast from Gormley's own body, are buried at different levels in the sand, all gazing out to sea and slowly becoming submerged as high tide rolls in.

ARRIVAL AND DEPARTURE — LIVERPOOL

By plane Liverpool John Lennon Airport (ⓣ 0870 129 8484, ⓦ liverpooljohnlennonairport.com) is 8 miles southeast of the city centre; it has an information desk (daily 5.30am–8.30pm; ⓣ 0151 233 2008). The Airlink #500 bus (5.10am–midnight; every 20–30min; £2) runs from outside the main entrance into the city. A taxi to Lime Street costs around £14.

By train Mainline trains pull in to Lime Street Station, northeast of the city centre.

Destinations from Lime Street Birmingham (hourly; 1hr 40min); Chester (every 30min; 45min); Leeds (hourly; 1hr 40min); London Euston (hourly; 2hr 20min); Manchester (hourly; 50min); Preston (14 daily; 1hr); Sheffield (hourly; 1hr 45min); York (11daily; 2hr 15min).

By bus National Express buses use the station on Norton St, just northeast of Lime Street train station.

Destinations Chester (12 daily; 1hr); London (9 daily; 5hr 10min–6hr 40min); Manchester (hourly; 1hr).

By ferry Ferries to and from the Isle of Man, run by the Isle of Man Steam Packet Company (ⓣ 0871 222 1333, ⓦ steam-packet.com), dock at the terminals just north of Pier Head, not far from James Street Merseyrail station. From Belfast, Lagan Seaways or Mersey Seaways (ⓣ 0870 600 4321; ⓦ norfolkline.com) pull in over the water on the Wirral at Twelve Quays, near Woodside ferry terminal (ferry or Merseyrail to Liverpool). To cross the Mersey, Mersey Ferries (ⓣ 0151 330 1444, ⓦ merseyferries.co.uk) leave from the angular modern Pier Head terminal. For more on ferries across the Mersey, see p.465.

GETTING AROUND

By bus Local buses depart from Queen Square and Liverpool One bus station.

By train The suburban Merseyrail system (trains from Chester) calls at four underground stations, including Lime Street and James Street (for Pier Head and the Albert Dock).

Information Merseytravel (ⓣ 0871 200 2233, ⓦ mersey travel.gov.uk) has travel centres at Queen Square and the Liverpool One Interchange.

INFORMATION AND TOURS

Tourist office 08 Place, 36–38 Whitechapel (Mon–Sat 10am–6pm; ⓣ 0151 233 2008, ⓦ visitliverpool.com).

Albert Dock Visitors Centre Anchor Courtyard (daily 10am–5/5.30pm; ⓣ 0151 233 2008, ⓦ albertdock.com).

Visitor passes If you're here for any length of time, consider buying a "Your Ticket for Liverpool" visitor card (from £24.99; ⓣ0870 055 3471, ⓦyourticketforliverpool.com), which gives free and discounted entry into attractions and on buses for between one and three days.

Useful websites ⓦliverpoolmuseums.org.uk, ⓦartinliverpool.com and ⓦliverpool.com.

Walking tours ⓦvisitliverpool.com has details of local guides (most Easter–Sept; from £3).

10

Yellow Duckmarine A fantastic tour on an amphibious World War II landing vehicle, which departs from Gower St, in front of Albert Dock (daily 10.30/11am; 1hr; peak time £12.95, off-peak £9.95; ⓣ0151 708 7799, ⓦtheyellowduckmarine.co.uk).

Football tours You're unlikely to get a ticket for a Liverpool game, but there are daily tours (not on match days) around the museum, trophy room and dressing rooms (museum and tour £14; museum only £6; ⓦliverpoolfc.tv). Everton, the city's less glamorous side, also offers tours (Mon, Wed, Fri & Sun 11am & 1pm; ⓣ0151 530 5212; £8.50; ⓦevertonfc.com).

Beatles tours See p.466

ACCOMMODATION

Budget chains are well represented in Liverpool, with *Premier*, *Travel Inn*, *Ibis*, *Express by Holiday Inn* and others all with convenient city-centre locations, including down by Albert Dock and near Mount Pleasant.

Aachen 89–91 Mount Pleasant ⓣ0151 709 3477, ⓦaachenhotel.co.uk. The best of the Mount Pleasant budget choices, with a range of good-value rooms (with and without en-suite showers), big "eat-as-much-as-you-like" breakfasts, and a late bar. **£65**

Base2Stay 29 Seel St, ⓣ0151 705 2626, ⓦbase2stay.com/liverpool. Smack in the heart of the RopeWalks is this converted warehouse, with more than 100 minimalist rooms that complement the building's original brickwork and well-appointed modern art pieces. **£89**

Hard Day's Night North John St ⓣ0151 236 1964, ⓦharddaysnighthotel.com. Up-to-the-minute four-star close to Mathew St. Splashes of vibrant colour and artful lighting enhance the elegant decor. The Lennon and McCartney suites (more than £700) are the tops. Breakfast not included. **£150**

Hatters 56–60 Mount Pleasant ⓣ0151 709 5570, ⓦhattersgroup.com/Liverpool. Though it's housed in the former YMCA building – with an institutional feel and gymnasium-size dining hall – *Hatters* has clean rooms, friendly staff and a great location. Standard facilities, including internet. Dorm **£19**, double **£70**

★ **Hope Street** 40 Hope St (entrance on Hope Place) ⓣ0151 709 3000, ⓦhopestreethotel.co.uk. This former Victorian warehouse still retains its original elegant brickwork and cast-iron columns but now comes with hardwood floors, huge beds, TVs and luxurious bathrooms. Breakfast not included. **£180**

★ **International Inn** 4 South Hunter St, off Hardman St ⓣ0151 709 8135, ⓦinternationalinn.co.uk. Converted Victorian warehouse in a great location, with modern en-suite rooms sleeping two to ten people. Dorm **£15**, double **£36**

★ **Racquet Club** 5 Chapel St ⓣ0151 236 6676, ⓦracquetclub.org.uk. Boutique-style townhouse hotel with just eight rooms, each mixing fine linens and traditional furniture with contemporary art and modern fittings. Breakfast is not in the price, but is available courtesy of *Ziba*, the hotel's cutting-edge restaurant. **£80**

EATING, DRINKING AND NIGHTLIFE

Most **eating** choices are in three distinct areas – at Albert Dock, around Hardman and Hope streets, and along Berry and Nelson streets, the heart of Liverpool's Chinatown. Alternatively, take a short taxi ride out to Lark Lane in Aigburth, close to Sefton Park, where a dozen eating and drinking spots pack into one short street. The **Heritage Market** at Stanley Dock attracts around 200 stalls, including delicious food (along with retro clothing and antiques) every Sunday. In the RopeWalks area, most action is centred on Concert Square.

★ **60 Hope Street** 60 Hope St ⓣ0151 707 6060, ⓦ60hopestreet.com. The star of the Liverpool gastronomic scene, set in a Georgian terrace, serves British cuisine with creative flourishes – Cumbrian venison with pancetta purée or cod with red-lentil dhal, for example – as well as a vegetarian menu and extensive wine list. Mains around £20. Mon–Fri noon–2.30pm & 7–10.30pm, Sun noon–2.30pm & 5–8pm.

★ **Delifonseca** 12 Stanley St ⓣ0151 255 0808, ⓦdelifonseca.co.uk. Upstairs from the deli, this bistro's changing menu offers Italian and British delights, including Welsh black beef salad, or spiced mutton and apricot pie. Mains around £10. Mon–Sat 8am–9pm.

Egg 16 Newington ⓣ0151 707 2755, ⓦeggcafe.co.uk. Up on the third floor, this plant-strewn bohemian café serves excellent vegan and vegetarian food with good set-meal deals. Also a nice place for a chai. Mon–Fri 9am–10.30pm, Sat & Sun 10am–10pm.

Italian Club Fish 128 Bold St ⓣ0151 707 2110, ⓦtheitalianclubfish.co.uk. Proper Italian seafood place with a menu that adapts to what's fresh – try the *saute di Maurizio*. There are also a few token meat and vegetarian dishes, all around £13. Mon 5–10pm, Tues–Sat noon–10pm, Sun noon–9pm.

Puschka 16 Rodney St 0151 708 8698, puschka.co.uk. Contemporary, if pricey, English dining from a seasonally changing menu – locals like its relaxed, funky atmosphere and there's usually a good vegetarian choice. Tues–Sat 5–10pm, Sun 5–9pm.

The Quarter 7 Falkner St 0151 707 1965, thequarteruk.com. Between the two cathedrals, this wonderful bistro-deli serves pasta, posh pies and gourmet pizza. Alternatively, you can stop by for coffee and excellent pastries outside on the Georgian terrace. Mon–Fri 8–11pm, Sat 10am–11pm, Sun 10am–10.30pm.

Side Door 29a Hope St 0151 707 7888, thesidedoor.co.uk. The intimate Georgian townhouse bistro has a winning combination of Mediterranean food and reasonable prices – with a bargain pre-theatre menu of £14.95. Mon–Sat noon–2.30pm & 5.30–10.30pm.

Tokyou 7 Berry St 0871/963 2891. Great-value noodle bar offering a selection of Japanese, Korean and Chinese – a meal shouldn't cost more than £10. Daily 12.30–11.30pm.

10

DRINKING

The business district's **Victoria Street** is a fast-developing area for bars and nightlife, as is **Albert Dock**.

★ **Alma de Cuba** St Peter's Church, Seel St 0151 702 7394, www.alma-de-cuba.com. It may have far more candles now than when it was a church – and even more in the mezzanine restaurant – but the mirrored altar is still the focus of this bar's rich, dark Cuban-themed interior. Daily 11am–2am.

Baltic Fleet 33a Wapping 0151 709 3116. Restored, no-nonsense, quiet pub with age-old shipping connections and an open fire, just south of the Albert Dock. Good pub grub on offer. Sun–Fri noon–midnight, Sat 11am–midnight.

★ **Bumper** 18 Hardman St 0151 707 9902, bumperliverpool.co.uk. For Liverpool's hip young things, no night is complete without a drink in this cool Americana-strewn indie bar. Club nights on weekends. Mon & Tues 5pm–2am, Wed–Sun 5pm–4am.

Ca Va 4A Wood St 0151 709 9300. Masses of hip students crowd into this fun-time, dark, loud bar for nights of tequila shots and Mexican beer. Mon–Sat noon–2am, Sun noon–12.30am.

Lion Tavern 67 Moorfields 0151 236 1734, www.liontavern.com. Real ale in superbly restored Victorian surroundings, beautifully embellished with decorative tiles and a stained-glass rotunda. They also serve excellent cheese and paté lunches (Mon–Fri). Daily 11am–11pm.

★ **Philharmonic** 36 Hope St 0151 707 2837. Liverpool's finest traditional watering hole where the main attractions – beer aside – are the mosaic floors, tiling, gilded wrought-iron gates and the marble decor in the gents. Daily 10am–midnight.

Ye Cracke 13 Rice St 0151 709 4171. Crusty backstreet pub off Hope St, much loved by the young Lennon, and with a great jukebox, and cheap-as-chips food (daytime only). Sun–Thurs noon–11.30pm, Fri & Sat noon–midnight.

NIGHTLIFE AND ENTERTAINMENT

Liverpool's **club scene** is famously unpretentious, with posing playing second fiddle to drinking and dancing. Popular annual **festivals** include Beatles Week (last week of Aug) and the Mathew Street Festival (Aug Bank Hol; mathewstreetfestival.co.uk), with half a million visitors dancing to hundreds of local, national and tribute bands. As for the classical music scene, the **Royal Liverpool Philharmonic Orchestra**, ranked with Manchester's Hallé as the northwest's best, dominates. The evening paper, the *Liverpool Echo* and liverpool.com have events listings.

LIVE MUSIC AND CLUBS

Cavern Club 10 Mathew St 0151 236 1965, cavernclub.org. The self-styled "most famous club in the world" has live bands, from Beatles tribute acts to indie pop and rock, at the weekends, along with occasional backstage tours and special events. The atmosphere is always high-spirited, and even though this is not the very same *Cavern* club of the Beatles' days (see p.466), there's a certain thrill to it all. Open daily from 12.30pm.

Heebie Jeebies 80–82 Seel St 0151 708 7001. Student favourite in a huge brick-vaulted room. Mainly indie and soul, with some live bands. Thurs–Sat 10pm–2am.

02 Academy 11–13 Hotham St 0151 707 3200, liverpool-academy.co.uk. A good roster of contemporary indie and rock gigs.

CLASSICAL MUSIC, THEATRE AND CINEMA

Liverpool Empire Lime St 0870 606 3536, liverpool-empire.co.uk. The city's largest theatre, a venue for touring West End shows and large-scale opera and ballet productions – Welsh National Opera and English National Ballet both perform regularly.

Philharmonic Hall Hope St 0151 709 3789, liverpoolphil.com. Home to the Royal Liverpool Philharmonic Orchestra, and with a full programme of other concerts. They also show classic films once a month.

Picturehouse at FACT Wood St 0871 704 2063, picturehouses.co.uk. The city's only independent cinema screens new films, re-runs, cult classics and festivals.

Royal Court Theatre Roe St ⓣ 0870 787 1866, ⓦ royalcourtliverpool.co.uk. Art Deco theatre and concert hall, which sees regular plays, music and comedy acts.

DIRECTORY

Football Liverpool FC, Anfield (ⓣ 0844 844 0844, ⓦ liverpoolfc.tv); Everton FC, Goodison Park (ⓣ 0871 663 1878, ⓦ evertonfc.com). See p.468 for details of tours.

Hospital Royal Liverpool University Hospital, Prescot St (ⓣ 0151 706 2000); NHS Walk-in Centre 52 Great Charlotte Row (ⓣ 0151 285 3535).

Police Canning Place (ⓣ 0151 709 6010).

10

Blackpool

Shamelessly brash **BLACKPOOL** is the archetypal British seaside resort, its "Golden Mile" of piers, amusement arcades, tram and donkey rides, fish-and-chip shops, candyfloss stalls, fun pubs and bingo halls making no concessions to anything but lowbrow fun of the finest kind. It was the coming of the railway in 1846 that made Blackpool what it is today: Blackpool's own "Eiffel Tower" on the seafront and other refined diversions were built to cater to the tastes of the first influx of visitors, but it was the Central Pier's "open-air dancing for the working classes" that heralded the crucial change of accent. Suddenly Blackpool was favoured destination for the "Wakes Weeks", when whole Lancashire mill towns descended for their annual holiday.

With seven miles of beach – the tide ebb is half a mile, leaving plenty of sand at low tide – a revamped **prom** and an increasingly attractive, gentrified centre, there is more to Blackpool than just amusements. Where other British holiday resorts have suffered from the rivalry of cheap foreign packages, Blackpool has gone from strength to strength. Underneath the populist veneer there's a sophisticated marketing approach, which balances ever more elaborate rides and public art installations with well-grounded traditional entertainment. And when other resorts begin to close up for the winter, Blackpool's main season is just beginning, as more than half a million light bulbs create the **Illuminations** that decorate the prom from the beginning of September to early November.

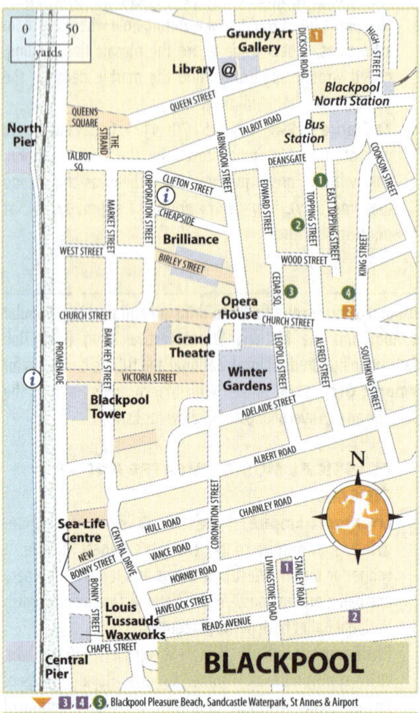

RESTAURANTS		ACCOMMODATION		BARS AND CLUBS	
AJ's	2	The Big Blue	3	Funny Girls	1
Blues Brasserie	5	FouRooms	2	The Syndicate	2
Kwizeen	4	Number One	4		
The Lounge	3	Raffles	1		
Yorkshire Fisheries	1				

Blackpool Tower

Tower Mon–Fri 10am–4pm, Sat & Sun 10am–5pm • £12
Circus 2 shows daily; 2hr • Fee included in tower ticket • ⓦ theblackpooltower.co.uk

Between Central and North piers stands the 518ft-high **Blackpool Tower**, erected in 1894 when it was thought that the northwest really ought not to be outdone by Paris. Ride up to the top for the stunning view and an

BLACKPOOL – BEHIND THE SCENES

There is, after all, an alternative Blackpool – one of history, heritage and even a spot of culture. Scene of party political conferences over the decades, the **Winter Gardens** (Coronation Street) opened to fanfares in 1878. Among the motley array of cafés, bars and amusements, seek out the extraordinary **Spanish Hall Suite** (in the form of a carved galleon), and the **Opera House** honours board – Lillie Langtry, George Formby and Vera Lynn are all present. From in front of the Opera House, follow Abingdon Street to Queen Street and the porticoed Central Library, next to which the **Grundy Art Gallery** (Mon–Sat 10am–5pm; free) might tempt you in to see its Victorian oils and watercolours, contemporary art and special exhibitions. **North Pier**, the first pier to be opened (1863) on the Blackpool seafront, is now a listed building. Head northbound from here on the tram to the **Imperial Hotel**, whose wood-panelled No. 10 Bar is covered with photographs and mementos of every British prime minister since Lloyd George.

unnerving walk on the see-through glass floor. The all-day ticket covers all the other tower attractions, including the gilt Edwardian ballroom, with its Wurlitzer organ tea dances and big band evenings, plus dungeon, children's entertainers, Lost City adventure playground, cafés and amusements. From the earliest days, there's also been a Moorish-inspired **circus** held between the tower's legs.

Blackpool Pleasure Beach

March–Oct daily from 10am • Free, though individual rides cost; wristband £27, cheaper if booked online • ⓦ blackpoolpleasurebeach.com

The major draw in town is **Blackpool Pleasure Beach** on the South Promenade, just south of South Pier. Entrance to the amusement park is free, but you'll have to fork out for the superb array of white-knuckle rides including the 235ft-high "Big One". The wonderful antique wooden roller coasters ("woodies" to aficionados) may seem like kids' stuff, but each is unique – the original "Big Dipper" was invented at Blackpool in 1923 and still thrills, as does the "Grand National" (1935). Recuperate in the park's champagne and oyster bar, which adds a bit of class to the otherwise relentless barrage of fairground noise, shrieking, jangling and fast food.

Great Promenade Show

South from the Pleasure Beach, from the Sandcastle Waterpark down to Squire's Gate • Free

Perhaps nowhere sums up the "new" Blackpool better than the **Great Promenade Show**, a set of ambitious outdoor sculptures, installations and soundscapes set along a mile or so of the new promenade. All relating to some aspect of Blackpool's history or its natural environment, these include the mighty **High Tide Organ**, which gives off haunting music when "played" by the swell of the waves, a set of sculptures of circus characters by **Sir Peter Blake**, and the world's largest **disco ball**, named, for some mysterious reason, "They Shoot Horses, Don't They".

ARRIVAL AND INFORMATION — BLACKPOOL

By plane Blackpool's airport (ⓦ blackpoolinternational.com) – which handles regular flights to more than 25 European destinations – lies 2 miles south of the centre; there are buses from the bus station, or it's a £6 taxi ride.

By train The town's main train station, Blackpool North, is a few minutes' walk west of the town centre on Talbot Rd, with a smaller terminus, Blackpool South, just north of the Pleasure Beach on Waterloo Rd.

Destinations Manchester (hourly; 1hr 10min); Preston (hourly; 30min); another service (on the Blackpool South Line) also departs hourly from Blackpool Pleasure Beach to Preston.

By bus The bus station is just a few steps away from the train station down Talbot Rd.

Tourist office 1 Clifton St on the corner of Corporation St (Mon–Sat 9am–5pm; ⓣ 01253 478222, ⓦ visitblackpool.com). They sell discounted admission tickets for all major Blackpool attractions (except the Pleasure Beach), and travel passes.

GETTING AROUND

By tram You'll want to jump on and off the electric trams (blackpooltransport.com) if you plan to get up and down much between the piers. Covering the length of the promenade, they travel from Fleetwood, north of Blackpool, to Starr Gate, south of the Pleasure Beach. Prices vary; you can buy a ticket on board from a conductor, or use a travel pass – the tourist office (see p.471) sells travel cards (1/3/5/7-day, £5.50/13.50/18.60/20.70) for local buses and trams.

By bike You can whizz up and down the seafront using Blackpool's Rent-a-Bike scheme – stations are dotted around the front (£10/day; 01253 320094, hourbike.com).

10

ACCOMMODATION

Bed-and-breakfast **prices** are generally low (from £25 per person, even less on a room-only basis or out of season), but rise at weekends and during the Illuminations. To avoid the noisy crowds in peak season, make for the peace and quiet (an unusual request in Blackpool, it has to be said) along the North Shore, beyond North Pier (the grid west of Warbreck Hill Road has hundreds of options).

The Big Blue Ocean Blvd, Blackpool Pleasure Beach 0845 367 3333, bigbluehotel.com. Spacious family rooms with games consoles and separate children's area, plus boutique-style, dark-wood executive rooms. There's a bar and brasserie, parking and a gym. It's next to the Pleasure Beach (and Blackpool South train station), and most rooms look out on the rides. Parking available. £130

★ **FouRooms** 60 Reads Ave 01253 752171, fourroomsblackpool.co.uk. One of Blackpool's best boutique hotels, a tastefully converted Victorian townhouse with airy rooms and original dark wood fittings. The four suites are individually furnished, and staff are keen to help. £90

★ **Number One** 1 St Luke's Rd 01253 343901, numberoneblackpool.com. There's no other B&B quite like this – an extraordinarily lavish boutique experience hosted by the ultra-amiable Mark and Claire. There are just three extravagantly appointed rooms here, with more at *Number One South Beach* nearby. Parking available. £70

Raffles 73–77 Hornby Rd 01253 294713, raffleshotelblackpool.co.uk. Nice place back from Central Pier and away from the bustle, with well-kept rooms, a bar, and traditional tearooms attached. Winter rates are a good deal. £72

EATING

AJ's 65 Topping St 01253 626111, ajs-bistro.co.uk. A festival of meat, this unpretentious restaurant is at its best with steaks and grills, though it makes some concessions to vegetarians. Non-steak mains around £10. Mon–Fri 5.30pm till late, Sat noon–11pm, Sun 3pm till late.

Blues Brasserie Ocean Blvd, Blackpool Pleasure Beach 0845 367 3333, bigbluehotel.com/dining. Looking out onto the roller coasters of the Pleasure Beach, with a good choice of light and main meals, as well as a Sunday carvery. Reasonable prices, with mains under a tenner. Daily 10am–9.30pm.

★ **Kwizeen** 49 King St 01253 290045, kwizeenrestaurant.co.uk. This friendly, contemporary bistro is the best restaurant in town, with a seasonally changing menu that emphasizes local produce, from Blackpool tomatoes and Lancashire cheese to Fylde farm ostriches. Mains around £13, though there's a bargain two-course weekday lunch. Mon–Fri lunch & dinner, Sat dinner only; closed 2 weeks in Feb & a week in Aug.

The Lounge 10a Cedar Square 01253 291112. Typical of Blackpool's newfound love affair with café culture, where you can enjoy a posh sandwich and espresso from a moulded plastic chair, looking out over cobbled Cedar Square and St John's church. Also a selection of light lunches. Closed weekday eves, except Fri.

Yorkshire Fisheries 14–16 Topping St 01253 627739. Behind the Winter Gardens, this sit-down and takeaway fish and chip shop is commonly agreed to be the best in the centre of town. Mon–Sat 11.30am–7pm.

NIGHTLIFE AND ENTERTAINMENT

Blackpool has a plethora of **theme bars** and any number of places for **karaoke** or **dancing**. Family-orientated fun revolves around musicals, veteran TV comedians, magicians, ice dance, tribute bands, crooners and stage spectaculars put on at a variety of end-of-pier and historic venues.

Funny Girls 5 Dickson Rd, off Talbot Rd 0870 350 2665, funnygirlsshowbar.co.uk. A Blackpool institution – a transvestite-run bar with nightly cabaret shows that attract long (gay and straight) queues. It's a hen party favourite and not to everyone's tastes, but the best place in town if you fancy some unabashedly bawdy Blackpool fun.

The Grand Theatre Church St 01253 290190, blackpoolgrand.co.uk. Built in 1894 for the town's more refined audiences, the Grand has a tradition of distinguishing itself from other amusements, putting on performances of Shakespeare as well as more popular variety shows.

Opera House Church St ⓣ 0870 380111, ⓦ blackpoollive.com. Set in the Winter Gardens, the Opera House has a star-studded history that includes such populist greats as Charlie Chaplin, George Formby and Vera Lynn. These days you'll find a variety of shows on offer, including West End hits.

Pleasure Beach Theatre Pleasure Beach ⓣ 0871 222 9090, ⓦ blackpoolpleasurebeach.com. Spectacular stuff: huge choreographed dance shows, dramatic stunts and blood-pumping musical accompaniment.

The Syndicate 120–140 Church St ⓦ thesyndicate.com. The Northwest's biggest club, specializing in themed nights plus star DJ sets throughout the year.

Lancaster and around

LANCASTER, Lancashire's county town, dates back at least as long ago as the Roman occupation, though only scant remains survive from that period. A Saxon church was later built within the ruined Roman walls as Lancaster became a strategic trading centre, and by medieval times a **castle** had been built on the heights above the river. Lancaster became an important port on the slave trade triangle, and it's the **Georgian buildings** from that time – especially those around the castle – that give the town much of its character. Many people choose to stay here on the way to the Lakes or Dales to the north; and it's an easy side-trip the few miles west to the resort of **Morecambe** and to neighbouring **Heysham village**, with its ancient churches, or east through the **Forest of Bowland**.

Lancaster Castle

Daily: tours every 30min 10.30am–4pm • £5 • ⓦ lancastercastle.com

The site of **Lancaster Castle** has been the city's focal point since Roman times. The Normans built the first defences here, at the end of the eleventh century – two hundred years later it became a **crown court**, a role it maintains today. Currently, about a quarter of the battlemented building can be visited on an entertaining hour-long tour, though court sittings sometimes affect the schedules.

Judges' Lodgings

15 Castle Hill • Easter–June & Oct Mon–Fri 1–4pm, Sat & Sun noon–4pm; July–Sept Mon–Fri 10am–4pm, Sat & Sun noon–4pm • £3

A two-minute walk down the steps between the castle and the neighbouring **Priory Church of St Mary** brings you to the seventeenth-century **Judges' Lodgings**, once used by visiting magistrates. The top floor is given over to a Museum of Childhood, with memory-jogging displays of toys and games, and a period (1900) schoolroom.

Maritime Museum

Daily: April–Oct 11am–5pm; Nov–March 12.30pm–4pm • £3

Down on the banks of the River Lune – which lent Lancaster its name – one of the eighteenth-century quayside warehouses is taken up by part of the **Maritime Museum**. The museum amply covers life on the sea and inland waterways of Lancashire, including the role of Lancaster's residents in the highly profitable slave trade.

ON YOUR BIKE

Lancaster promotes itself as a **cycling centre**, and miles of canal towpaths, old railway tracks and riverside paths provide excellent traffic-free routes around the Lune estuary, Lancaster Canal and Ribble Valley. Typical is the easy riverside path to the **Crook O'Lune** beauty spot, where you can reward yourself with a bacon buttie and an Eccles cake at *Woodies'* famous snack bar.

Williamson Park

Daily: April–Sept 10am–5pm; Oct–March 10am–4pm • Free • ⓦ williamsonpark.com

For a panorama of the town, Morecambe Bay and the Cumbrian fells, take a steep 25-minute walk up Moor Lane (or a taxi from the bus station) to **Williamson Park**, Lancaster's highest point. Funded by local statesman and lino magnate Lord Ashton, the park's centrepiece is the 220ft-high Ashton Memorial, a Baroque folly raised by his son in memory of his second wife.

ARRIVAL AND DEPARTURE — LANCASTER

By train Trains pull in at Meeting House Lane, a 5min walk from the town centre.

Destinations Carlisle (every 30min–1hr; 50min); Manchester (every 30min–1hr; 1hr); Morecambe (every 30min–1hr; 10min); Preston (every 20–30min; 20min).

By bus The bus station is on Cable St, a 5min walk from the tourist office.

Destinations Carlisle (4–5 daily; 1hr 20min); Kendal (hourly; 1hr); Manchester (2 daily; 2hr); Windermere (hourly; 1hr 45min).

INFORMATION AND TOURS

Tourist office Meeting House Lane, off Castle Hill (Mon–Sat 9.30am–5pm; ⓣ 01524 582394, ⓦ citycoastcountryside.co.uk).

Canal cruises For canal cruises, contact Lancaster Canal Packet Boats (ⓣ 01524 389410, ⓦ budgietransport.co.uk).

ACCOMMODATION

Penny Street Bridge Penny St ⓣ 01524 599900, ⓦ pennystreetbridge.co.uk. Overlooking the river, this elegantly restored listed townhouse has 28 oddly shaped rooms, all with airy high ceilings and flatscreen TVs. It's worth popping in the bar for a pint of good local ale too. £85

Shakespeare 96 St Leonard's Gate ⓣ 01524 841041. Seven cosy en-suite rooms (including two singles) in this popular townhouse B&B on a central street near several long-stay car parks. No credit cards. £55

★ **Sun** 63 Church St ⓣ 01524 66006, ⓦ thesunhotelandbar.co.uk. The city centre's only four-star hotel has eight handsome rooms (some with king-sized beds, all with fine bathrooms) above a contemporary bar fashioned from a 300-year-old building. Breakfast and meals available in the bar. £82

EATING AND DRINKING

1725 Bar 28 Market St ⓣ 01524 66898, ⓦ bar1725.co.uk. A tasteful modern conversion joining two of Lancaster's ancient buildings, which serves good-value tapas and meals – try their home-made bean pot. You shouldn't need to spend more than £15 all in. Daily 11am–11pm.

★ **The Borough** 3 Dalton Square ⓣ 01524 64170, ⓦ theboroughlancaster.co.uk. Great for informal dining, this roomy gastropub – in a refurbished 1824 building – has a rigorously sourced local and organic menu. Moderately priced tapas-style platters offer smoked fish, Lancashire cheese and the like, while mains range from ostrich to salmon. Food served Sun–Thurs 9am–9pm, Fri & Sat noon–9.30pm.

Water Witch Canal towpath, Aldcliffe Lane ⓣ 01524 63828, ⓦ thewaterwitch.co.uk. Relaxing canalside pub named after an old canal packet boat. A youthful crowd munches burgers, shoots pool and hogs the canal-side tables, and there is an impressive range of real ales and continental lagers. Daily.

Whale Tail 78a Penny St ⓣ 01524 845133, ⓣ whale

THE FOREST OF BOWLAND

The remote **Forest of Bowland** (ⓦ forestofbowland.com), designated an Area of Outstanding Natural Beauty, is a picturesque drive east from Lancaster. The name forest is used here in its traditional sense of "a royal hunting ground" – it's a captivating landscape of remote fells and farmland with plenty of walks and populated by rare birds like the golden plover, short-eared owl, snipe and merlin. Head east on the A683, turning off towards High Bentham; once at the village turn right at the sign for the station and you begin the fifteen-mile slog down an old drovers' track (now a very minor road) known as the **Trough of Bowland.** This winds through heather- and bracken-clad hills before ending up at the compact village of Slaidburn. If you've got time, it's worth pushing ahead to **Clitheroe**, a tidy little market town overlooked by a Norman keep.

tailcafe.co.uk. Tucked away in a yard and up on the first floor, this cheery veggie and wholefood café serves good breakfasts, quiche, moussaka and baked potatoes. Mon–Fri 10am–4pm, Sat 10am–5pm, Sun 10am–3pm.

NIGHTLIFE AND ENTERTAINMENT

Dukes Moor Lane ⊕01524 598500, ⊕dukes-lancaster.org. Lancaster's arts centre is the main cultural destination in town, with cinemas and stages for all manner of theatre and dance performances, exhibition space and a café-bar.

10

Morecambe and around

The seaside resort of **MORECAMBE** lies five miles west of Lancaster – there's a pleasant cycle path between the two, and bus and train services that can whizz you there in ten minutes. The sweep of the bay is the major attraction, with the Lake District fells visible beyond, while the **Stone Jetty** features bird motifs and sculptures – recognizing Morecambe Bay as Britain's most important wintering site for wildfowl and wading birds. A little way along the prom stands the statue of one of Britain's most treasured comedians – Eric Bartholomew, who took the stage name **Eric Morecambe** when he met his comedy partner, Ernie Wise.

Heysham Village

Three miles southwest of Morecambe – you can walk here along the promenade – the shoreside **HEYSHAM VILLAGE** is centred on a group of charming seventeenth-century cottages and barns. Proudest relic is the well-preserved Viking hog's-back tombstone in Saxon **St Peter's Church**, set in a romantic churchyard below the headland. Don't miss the local **nettle beer**, dating from Victorian times, and served in the village tearooms.

ACCOMMODATION — MORECAMBE

Midland Hotel ⊕08458 503502, ⊕elh.co.uk/hotels/midland. Lovely four-star Art Deco hotel whose comfortable rooms extend the modernist theme. Even if you're not staying it's worth popping into electric-blue bar, and taking a drink onto the terrace to watch the sunset. **£90**

The Isle of Man

The **Isle of Man**, almost equidistant from Ireland, England, Wales and Scotland, is one of the most beautiful spots in Britain, a mountainous, cliff-fringed island just 33 miles by thirteen. There's peace and quiet in abundance, walks around the unspoilt hundred-mile coastline, rural villages and steam trains straight out of a 1950s picture book – a yesteryear ensemble if ever there was one.

Many true Manx inhabitants, who comprise a shade under fifty percent of its 80,000 population, insist that the Isle of Man is not part of England, nor even of the UK. Indeed, although a Crown dependency, the island has its own government, **Tynwald**, arguably the world's oldest democratic parliament, which has run continuously since 979 AD. To further complicate matters, the island maintains a unique associate status in the EU, and also has its own sterling currency (worth the same as the mainland currency), its own laws, an independent postal service, and a Gaelic-based language which is taught in schools and seen on dual-language road signs.

All roads lead to the capital, **Douglas**, the only town of any size. From the summit of **Snaefell**, the island's highest peak, you get an idea of the island's varied scenery, the finest parts of which are to be found in the seventeen officially designated National Glens. Most of these are linked by the 100-mile **Raad Ny Foillan** (Road of the Gull) coastal footpath, which passes several of the island's numerous hill forts, Viking ship burials and Celtic crosses. Scenery aside, the main tourist draw is the **TT (Tourist Trophy) motorcycle races** (held in the two weeks around the late May bank holiday), a frenzy of speed and burning rubber that's shattered the island's peace annually since 1907.

ARRIVAL AND DEPARTURE — THE ISLE OF MAN

By plane The cheapest way to get to the Isle is by air, with several budget airlines – among them Aer Arran (aerarann.com); Flybe (flybe.com); and Manx2 (manx2.com) – offering flights from many British and Irish regional airports.

By ferry Ferries or the quicker fastcraft (Sea Cats), both run by the Isle of Man Steam Packet Company (0872 299 2992, steam-packet.com), leave from Heysham (ferries; 2 or 3 daily; 3hr 30min) and Liverpool (fastcraft; 1 or 2 daily most of the year, 1 daily Sat & Sun in Dec; 2hr 30min).

GETTING AROUND

Travel passes "Island Explorer" tickets – sold at Douglas' Welcome Centre (see opposite) – give one (£16), three (£30), or seven (£45) days' unlimited travel on all buses and trains on the island.

Useful website iombusandrail.info.

INFORMATION

Manx National Heritage (gov.im/mnh) run thirteen heritage sites and museums around the Isle of Man including the Old House of Keys, the House of Manannan, Castle Rushen and the Laxey Wheel. They also offer money-saving passes including a 10-Day Heritage Explorer pass (£16, available from any attraction).

Douglas

Dubbed "the Naples of the North" by John Betjeman, **DOUGLAS** has developed since its 1950s heyday of seaside holiday-making into a major offshore financial centre. The seafront vista has changed little since Victorian times, and is still trodden by heavy-footed carthorses pulling trams (May–Sept, from 9am; £2 return). On Harris Promenade the opulent Edwardian **Gaiety Theatre** sports a lush interior that can be seen on fascinating tours (April–Sept Sat 10am; 90min; £7.50; 01624 694500, villagaiety.com).

Further up Harris Promenade, approaching Broadway, the **Villa Marina gardens** display classic Victorian elegance with their colonnade walk, lawns and bandstand. The main sight, however, is the **Manx Museum**, on the corner of Kingswood Grove and Crellin's Hill (Mon–Sat 10am–5pm; free), which helps the visitor get to grips with Manx culture and heritage. Finally, out on **Douglas Head** – the point looming above the southern bay – the town's Victorian camera obscura has been restored for visits (Easter week, plus May–Sept Sat 1–4pm, Sun & bank hols 11am–4pm, weather permitting; £2).

ARRIVAL AND DEPARTURE — DOUGLAS

By plane Ronaldsway Airport (01624 821600, iom-airport.com) is 10 miles south of Douglas, close to Castletown. A regular bus runs into town, while a taxi costs around £20.

By ferry The Isle of Man Steam Packet Company (steam-packet.com) ferries from Liverpool, Heysham, Dublin, and Belfast arrive at the 1960s Sea Terminal (April–Oct 7am–8pm; Nov–March 8am–6/8pm), close to the centre of town, at the south end of the promenade.

By train The Steam Railway (April–Oct 10.15am–4.15pm; £4.80–11.60 return) extends for 15 miles and connects Douglas to Port Soderick, Santon, Castletown, Port St Mary and Port Erin. The Douglas station is alongside the river and fishing port, at the top end of the North Quay. Meanwhile, the Manx Electric Railway (April–Oct daily 9.40am–4.40pm; some later departures in summer; £4–12 return), which runs for 17 miles from Douglas to Snaefell, departs from the northern end of the seafront at Derby Castle Station.

By bus The Lord Street terminal, the hub of the island's dozen or so bus routes, is 50 yards west of the Sea Terminal's forecourt taxi rank.

GETTING AROUND

By bus Buses #24, #24a, #26 and #26a run along Douglas' promenade from North Quay; you can also take a horse-drawn tram.

By bike Eurocycles, 8a Victoria Rd, off Broadway (Mon–Sat; 01624 624909, eurocycles.iofm.net) rent bikes.

By car Most rental outfits have offices at the airport or can deliver cars to the Sea Terminal. Contact Athol (01624 822481, athol.co.im); Mylchreests (01624 823533, mylchreests.com); or Ocean Ford (01624 820830, oceanford.com).

INFORMATION AND TOURS

Tourist office The Welcome Centre in the Sea Terminal building (Mon–Sat 8am–6pm, Sun 10am–2pm; ⓣ 01624 686766 or 01624 662525) is a great starting point and the best place for island-wide information.

Useful websites ⓦ gov.im, ⓦ visitisleofman.com and ⓦ iomguide.com.

Cruises Seasonal cruises on the MV *Karina* head out to Port Soderick or Laxey from Villier steps by the Sea Terminal (daily April–Sept, weather permitting; ⓣ 01624 861724 or 07624 493592).

ACCOMMODATION

Admiral House Loch Promenade ⓣ 01624 629551, ⓦ admiralhouse.com. At the ferry terminal end of the prom, this retreat features rooms in bold colours and equipped with elegant bathrooms. The town's most expensive restaurant, *Ciapelli's* (closed Sun) is on the ground floor. **£70**

★ **Birchfield House** York Rd ⓣ 01624 673000, ⓦ birchfieldhouse.com. The most distinctive of Douglas's guesthouses offers sunny spacious rooms loaded with antiques, all creature comforts, and luxurious bathrooms. It's run by celebrity chef Kevin Woodford, who will offer cookery lessons. **£175**

Dreem Ard Ballanard Rd, 2 miles west of the centre ⓣ 01624 621491. Tranquil, out-of-town B&B with three en-suite rooms, including a family room and large garden suite with its own dressing room and sitting area. No credit cards. **£60**

Mereside 1 Empire Terrace, just off the Central Promenade ⓣ 01624 676355, ⓦ hqbar.im. Small, family-owned B&B with elegant modern fittings and very well maintained modern rooms. There's a good bar/restaurant downstairs. **£80**

Sefton Harris Promenade ⓣ 01624 645500, ⓦ seftonhotel.co.im. Next to the Gaiety Theatre, this four-star has sleek, spacious rooms offering either a sea view or a balcony overlooking the impressive internal water garden. Facilities include pool, gym, internet access, free bikes, a bar and restaurant. **£65**

Welbeck Mona Drive, off Central Promenade ⓣ 01624 675663, ⓦ welbeckhotel.com. A traditional mid-sized family-run seaside hotel, with comfortable rooms and friendly service. It lies 100yd from the seafront, up the hill. **£49**

EATING

★ **The Bay Room** Manx Museum, Kingswood Grove ⓣ 01624 612211. Enclosed by the Manx National Heritage Sculpture collection with wonderful views across the bay, this café serves a selection of soups, sandwiches and pastries. Mon–Sat 10am–5pm.

★ **Café Tanroagan** 9 Ridgeway St ⓣ 07624 472411, ⓦ tanroagan.co.uk. The best fish and seafood on the island, straight off the boat, served simply or with an assured Mediterranean twist in a relaxed, contemporary setting. Dinner reservations essential. Mains around £17. Tues–Fri noon–2pm & 6.30–9.30pm, Sat 6.30–9.30pm.

L'Experience Queen's Promenade ⓣ 01624 623103, ⓦ lex.co.im. This seemingly innocuous whitewashed shack is in fact a long-standing French bistro that has good meat dishes as well as daily caught fish specials, and good lunchtime dishes. £15 average for a main. Mon & Wed–Sat noon–2pm & 7–11pm.

Greens Douglas Station, North Quay. A very handy and pleasant plant-filled vegetarian café in the ticket office, serving drinks and snacks until 5pm, with hot lunches and a veggie buffet between noon and 2.30pm. Mon–Sat 10am–5pm.

Spill the Beans 1 Market Hill ⓣ 01624 614167. Douglas's best coffee house, with a choice of brews plus muffins, croissants, cakes and pastries. Mon–Sat 9am–5pm.

DRINKING

Bar George Hill St ⓣ 01624 617799, ⓦ bargeorge.net. A fashionable haunt housed in a converted Sunday School, opposite St George's church. Mon–Sat till late.

Queen's Hotel Queen's Promenade ⓣ 01624 674438. This old seafront pub at the top end of the promenade is the best place for alfresco drinks, with picnic tables looking out over the sweeping bay. Daily 11am–11pm.

Rovers Return 11 Church St ⓣ 01624 611101. Cosy old local where you can try the local Manx beers, including "Old Bushy Tail". Daily 11am–11pm.

Laxey

Filling a narrow valley, the straggling village of **LAXEY**, seven miles north of Douglas, spills down from its train station to a small harbour and long, pebbly beach, squeezed between two bulky headlands. The Manx Electric Railway from Douglas drops you at the station used by the Snaefell Mountain Railway (see p.478). Passengers disembark and then head inland and uphill to Laxey's pride, the **"Lady Isabella" Great Laxey Wheel**

TYNWALD DAY

The trans-island A1 (hourly buses #5 or #6 from Douglas) follows a deep twelve-mile-long furrow between the northern and southern ranges from Douglas to Peel. A hill at the crossroads settlement of **ST JOHN'S**, nine miles along, is the original site of **Tynwald**, the ancient Manx government, which derives its name from the Norse *Thing Völlr*, meaning "Assembly Field". Nowadays the word refers to the Douglas-based House of Keys and Legislative Council, but acts passed in the capital only become law once they have been proclaimed here on **July 5** (ancient Midsummer's Day) in an annual open-air parliament that also hears the grievances of the islanders.

Until the nineteenth century the local people arrived with their livestock and stayed a week or more – in true Viking fashion – to thrash out local issues, play sports, make marriages and hold a fair. Now **Tynwald Day** begins with a service in the chapel, followed by a procession, a fair and concerts.

(April–Oct daily 10am–5pm; £4; @laxeywheel.co.uk), smartly painted in red and white. With a diameter of more than 72ft it's said to be the largest working water wheel in the world. In **Old Laxey**, around the harbour, half a mile below the station, large car parks attest to the popularity of the beach and river.

Snaefell

Every thirty minutes, the tramcars of the **Snaefell Mountain Railway** (May–Oct daily 10.15am–3.45pm; £10 return) begin their 30min wind from Laxey through increasingly denuded moorland to the island's highest point, the top of **Snaefell** (2036ft) – the Vikings' "Snow Mountain" – from where, on a clear day, you can see England, Wales, Scotland and Ireland. At the summit, most people are content to pop into the café and bar and then soak up the views for the few minutes until the return journey. But with a decent map and good weather, you could walk back instead, following trails down to Laxey (the easiest and most direct route), Sulby Glen or the Peel–Ramsey road.

Maughold

Bus #16 direct from Ramsey (not Sun)

The Manx Electric Railway trains stop within a mile and a half of **MAUGHOLD**, seven miles northeast of Laxey, a tiny hamlet just inland from the cliff-side lighthouse at Maughold Head. The isolation adds to the attraction of its **parish church**, with its outstanding collection of early Christian and Norse carved crosses – 44 pieces, dating from the sixth to the thirteenth century, and ranging from fragments of runic carving to a 6ft-high rectangular slab.

Peel

The main settlement on the west coast, **PEEL** (bus #5 or #6 hourly from Douglas) is one of the most Manx of all the island's towns, with an imposing medieval **castle** rising across the harbour and a popular sandy **beach** running the length of its eastern promenade.

Peel Castle

April–Oct daily 10am–5pm • £4

What probably started out as a flint-working village on a naturally protected spot gained significance with the foundation of a **monastery** in the seventh or eighth century, parts of which remain inside the ramparts of the red sandstone **Peel Castle**. The site became the residence of the Kings of Mann until 1220, when they moved to

Castle Rushen in Castletown. It's a fifteen-minute walk from the town around the river harbour and over the bridge to the castle.

House of Manannan

Daily 10am–5pm • £6, combined ticket with Peel Castle £8.50

On the way to the castle, you'll pass the excellent harbourside **House of Manannan** heritage centre named after the island's ancient sea god. You should allow at least two hours to get around this splendid participatory museum, where you can listen to Celtic legends in a replica roundhouse, wander through a replica kipper factory and even examine the contents and occupants of a life-sized Viking ship.

EATING AND DRINKING — PEEL

Creek Inn The Quayside ⓣ01624 842216, ⓦthecreekinn.co.uk. Popular quayside pub opposite the House of Manannan, serving real ale, with monthly guest beers, and a delicious array of specials. Live music at the weekends. Daily from 10am; food served noon–10pm.

Marine Hotel Shore Rd ⓣ01624 842337, ⓦmarinehotelpeel.co.uk. Seafront pub, popular with locals, serving Manx ales, guest beers and bar meals. Daily noon–midnight; food served noon–9pm.

Port Erin

The small, time-warped resort of **PORT ERIN**, at the southwestern tip of the island, 75 minutes' train ride from Douglas, has a wide, fine sand beach backing a deeply indented bay sitting beneath green hills. For a stretch of the legs, head up the promenade past the golf club to the entrance of Bradda Glen, where you can follow the path out along the headland to Bradda Head.

ARRIVAL AND DEPARTURE — PORT ERIN

By train Trains pull in on Station Rd, a couple of hundred yards above and back from the beach.

By bus Buses #1 and #2 from Douglas/Castletown, and #8 from Peel/St John's, stop on Bridson St, across Station Rd and opposite the *Cherry Orchard* hotel.

ACCOMMODATION

Rowany Cottier Spaldrick ⓣ01624 832287, ⓦrowanycottier.com. Port Erin's best B&B, in a detached house overlooking the bay, opposite the entrance to Bradda Glen. No credit cards. **£72**

Port St Mary and around

Two miles east of Port Erin, the fishing harbour still dominates little **PORT ST MARY**, with its houses strung out in a chain above the busy dockside. The best beach is away to the northeast, reached from the harbour along a well-worked Victorian path that clings to the bay's rocky edge.

THE CALF OF MAN

It is worth making the effort to visit the **Calf of Man**, a craggy, heath-lined nature reserve lying off the southwest tip of the Isle of Man, where resident wardens monitor the seasonal populations of kittiwakes, puffins, choughs, razorbills, shags, guillemots and others, and grey seals can be seen all year round basking on the rocks.

Charter boats leave from Port St Mary, but the most reliable scheduled service (weather permitting) is from Port Erin pier (Easter–Sept daily; £13; 10am; ⓣ01624 832339); call in advance as numbers are limited and weather conditions affect schedules. You can also **sea kayak** around this spectacular coast. **Adventurous Experiences** (ⓣ01624 843034, ⓦadventurousexperiences.com) run trips from evening paddles (£45) to full-day excursions (£85) – no experience is required.

From Port St Mary, a minor road runs out along the Meayll peninsula towards **CREGNEASH**, the oldest village on the island. The **Cregneash Village Folk Museum** (April–Oct daily 10am–5pm; £4) is a picturesque cluster of nineteenth-century thatched crofts populated by craftspeople in period costume; there's a café and information centre. Local views are stunning, and it's just a short walk south to **The Chasms**, a headland of gaping rock cliffs swarming with gulls and razorbills.

The footpath continues around Spanish Head to the turf-roofed **Sound Visitor Centre** (daily 10/11am–4/5pm; free), which also marks the end of the road from Port St Mary. There's an excellent café, with windows looking out across The Sound to the **Calf of Man**.

ARRIVAL AND DEPARTURE — PORT ST MARY

By train Regular steam trains run to Port Erin or back to Douglas from Port St Mary. The station is a 10min walk from the harbour along High St, Bay View Rd and Station Rd.

By bus Hourly buses from the harbour serve the same destinations.

ACCOMMODATION

★ **Aaron House** The Promenade ⊕01624 835702, ⊕aaronhouse.co.uk. High up on The Promenade, this guesthouse lovingly recreates a Victorian experience and features brass beds and clawfoot baths in the rooms, with home-made scones and jam in the parlour and splendid breakfasts. The bay views from the front are superb. **£75**

EATING

Harbour Lights 1 Queen St ⊕01624 832064, ⊕harbour-lights.net. In a sea-salty old boathouse next to the harbour, this cheery restaurant serves fresh fish and local produce, as well as cream teas, hot toasted crumpets and light snacks. Wed–Sat 10am–late, Sun 10am–5pm.

Castletown and around

From the twelfth century until 1869, **CASTLETOWN** was the island's capital, but then the influx of tourists and the increase in trade required a bigger harbour and Douglas took over. Its sleepy harbour and low-roofed cottages are dominated by **Castle Rushen** (April–Oct daily 10am–5pm; £5.50), formerly home to the island's legislature and still the site of the investiture of new lieutenant-governors.

Old House of Keys

Parliament Square • April–Oct daily 11am & 3pm • £4 • ⊕01624 648017

Across the central Market Square and down Castle Street in tiny Parliament Square you'll find the **Old House of Keys**. Built in 1821, this was the site of the Manx parliament, the Keys, until 1874 when it was moved to Douglas. The frock-coated Secretary of the House meets you at the door and shows you into the restored debating chamber, where visitors are included in a highly entertaining participatory session of the House, guided by a hologram Speaker.

Rushen Abbey

Ballasalla, 2 miles north of Castletown • Daily: June–Aug 10am–6pm; April, May, Sept & Oct 11am–4pm • £4 • Buses #1, 1C, 2, 8 or X2 from Castletown or steam railway

The island's most important medieval religious site, **Rushen Abbey** lies two miles north of Castletown at Ballasalla ("place of the willows"). A Cistercian foundation of 1134, it was abandoned by its "White Monks" in the 1540s and was subsequently used as a school. The excavated remains themselves – low walls, grass-covered banks and a sole church tower from the fifteenth century – would hold only specialist appeal were it not for the excellent interpretation centre, which explains much about daily life in a Cistercian abbey.

ARRIVAL AND DEPARTURE — CASTLETOWN

By train Castletown Station is a 5min walk from the centre, out along Victoria Rd from the harbour.

By bus Buses #8 (from Peel/Port Erin) and #1 (from Douglas) stop in the main square.

EATING AND DRINKING

The Garrison 5 Castle St ⊕01624 824885, ⓦgarrison.co.im. This so-called tapas bar isn't a tapas bar in the traditional sense, but rather serves small plates of tasty food from goat's cheese tart to salt cod fritters. It's the best place for food in the village, and has a sunny courtyard. Mon–Thurs 9.30am–11pm, Fri & Sat 9.30am–midnight, Sun 10.30am–5pm.

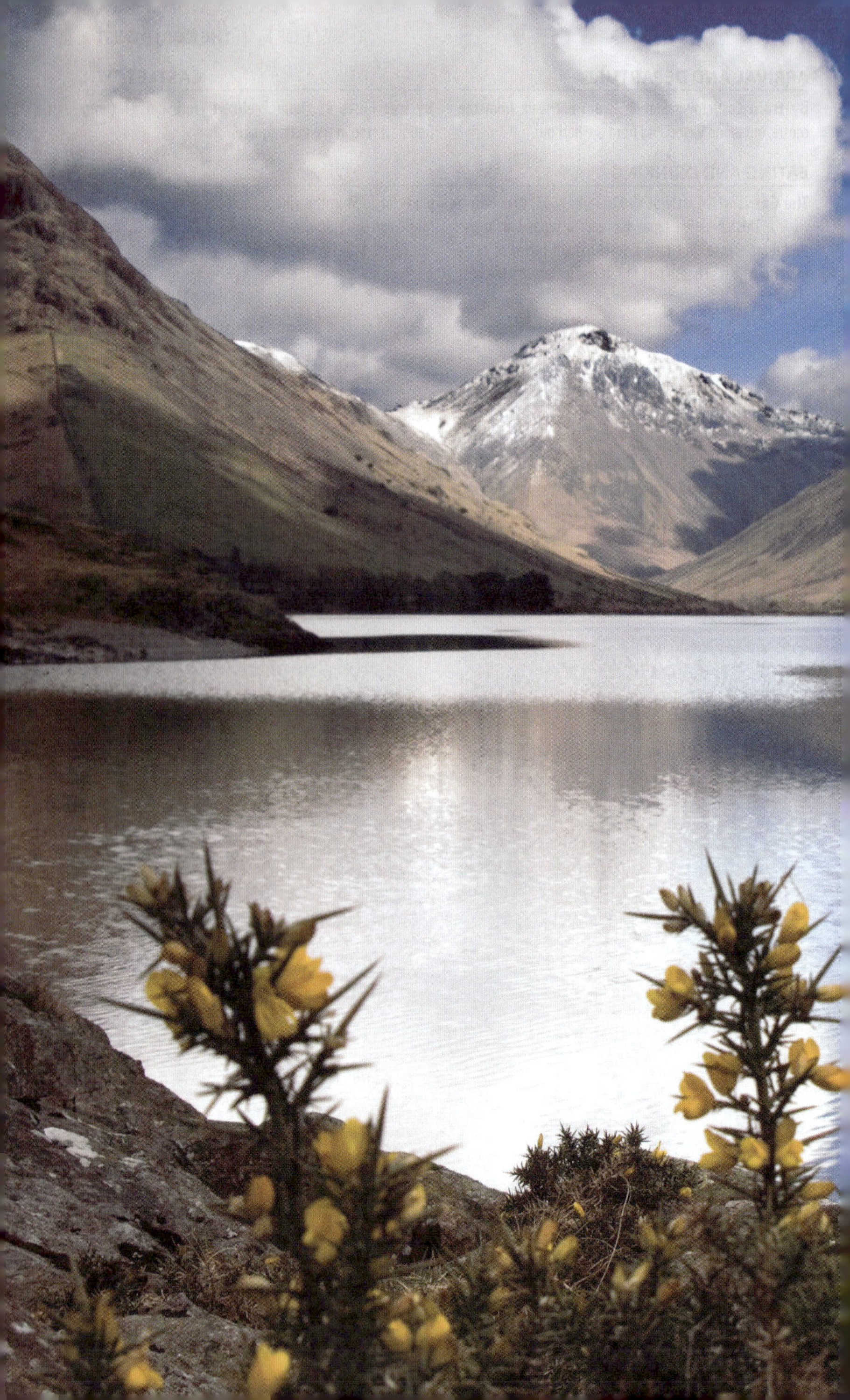

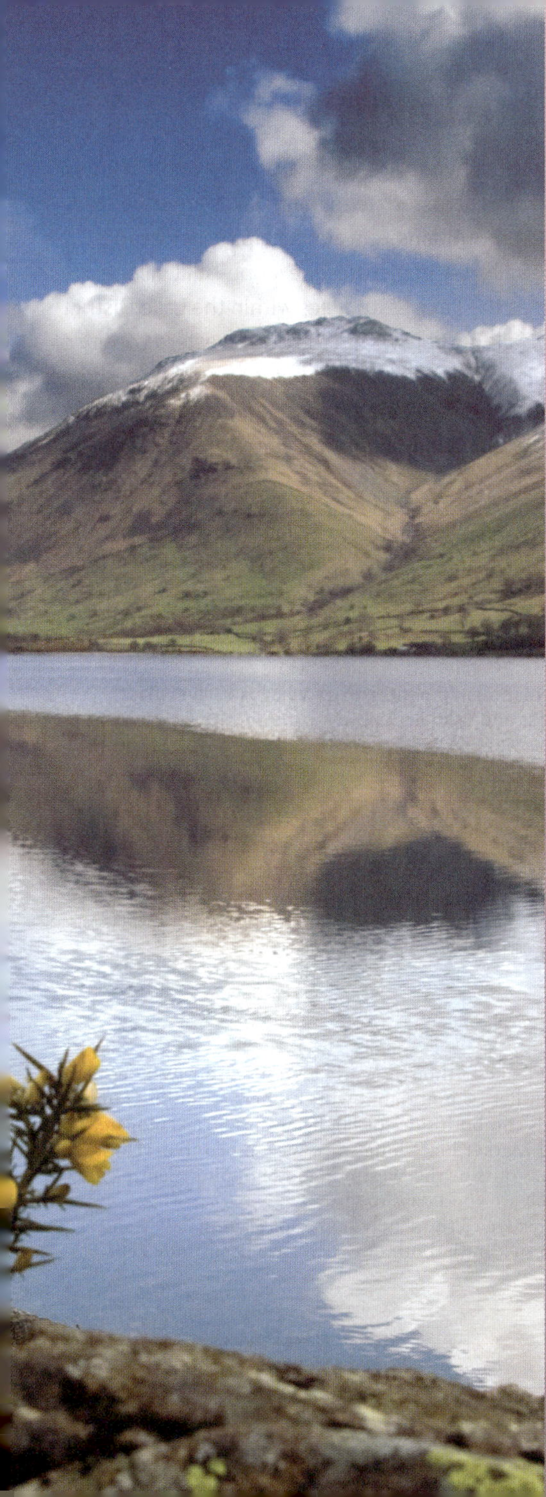

Cumbria and the Lakes

484 Kendal and around
488 Cartmel
488 Windermere town
490 Bowness and the lake
491 Ambleside
493 Great Langdale
493 Grasmere and around
494 Coniston and around
496 Hawkshead and around
498 Keswick and around
500 Honister Pass
501 Buttermere
501 Eskdale
501 Ravenglass and around
502 Whitehaven and around
503 Cockermouth
504 Ullswater
504 Penrith and around
505 Carlisle and around

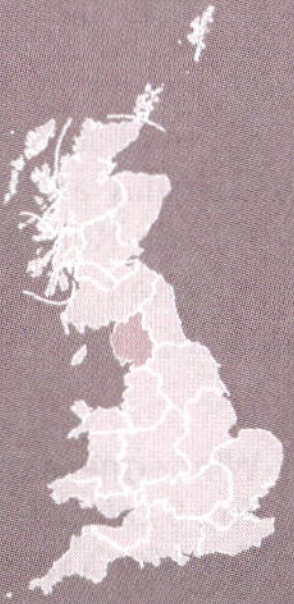

GREAT GABLE, SEEN FROM WAST WATER

Cumbria and the Lakes

The Lake District is England's most hyped scenic area, and for good reasons. Within an area a mere thirty miles across, sixteen major lakes are squeezed between the country's highest mountains – an almost alpine landscape of glistening water, dramatic valleys and picturesque stone-built villages. Most of what people refer to as the Lake District lies within the Lake District National Park, which, in turn, falls entirely within the northwestern county of Cumbria. The county capital is Carlisle, a place that bears traces of a pedigree that stretches back to Roman times, while both the isolated western coast and eastern market towns like Kendal and Penrith counter the notion that Cumbria is all about its lakes.

Given a week you could easily see most of the famous settlements and lakes – a circuit taking in the towns of Ambleside, Windermere and Bowness, all on **Windermere**, the Wordsworth houses in **Grasmere**, and the more dramatic northern scenery near **Keswick** and **Ullswater** would give you a fair sample of the whole. But it's away from the crowds that the Lakes really begin to pay dividends, in the dramatic valleys of **Langdale** and **Eskdale**, for example, while over on the coast are more off-the-beaten-track destinations, like the estuary village of **Ravenglass** – access point for the **Ravenglass and Eskdale Railway** – and the attractive Georgian port of **Whitehaven**.

GETTING AROUND AND INFORMATION — CUMBRIA AND THE LAKES

By bus National Express coaches connect London and Manchester with Windermere, Ambleside, Grasmere and Keswick. The one-day Stagecoach Explorer Ticket (£9.75; Ⓦ stagecoachbus.com) is valid on the entire local bus network.

By train Trains leave the West Coast main line at Oxenholme, north of Lancaster, for the branch line service to Kendal and Windermere. The only other places directly accessible by train are Penrith, further north on the West Coast line, and the towns along the Cumbrian coast.

Useful websites Ⓦ golakes.co.uk and, for the national park, Ⓦ lake-district.gov.uk.

Kendal and around

The self-billed "Gateway to the Lakes" (though nearly ten miles from Windermere), **KENDAL** is the largest of the southern Cumbrian towns. It offers rewarding rambles around the "yards" and "ginnels" on both sides of Highgate and Stricklandgate, the main streets, and while the old Market Place long since succumbed to development, traditional stalls still do business outside the Westmorland Shopping Centre every Wednesday and Saturday, which are good days to visit.

Outside Kendal, the main trips are to the stately homes of **Sizergh Castle** and **Levens Hall**, just a few miles to the south, both of which have beautifully kept gardens.

Windermere cruises p.489
Top 5 Lake District views p.491
Coniston's speed king p.495
Ullswater lake services p.504
Potty Penrith p.505

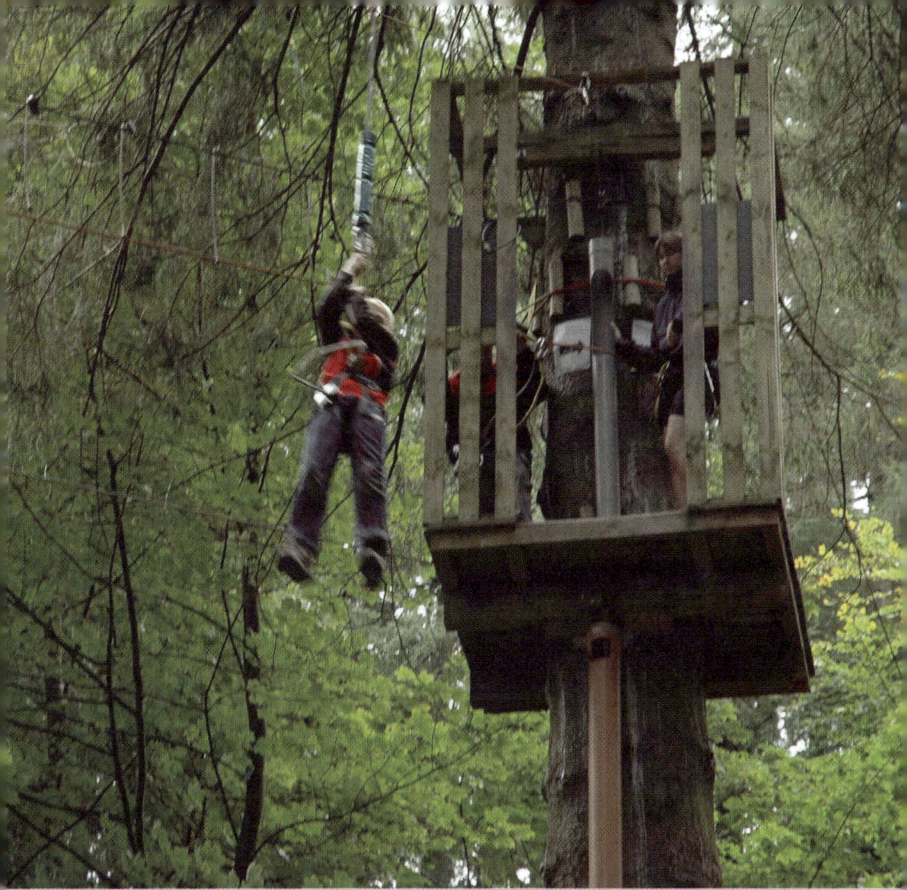

GOING APE IN GRIZEDALE FOREST

Highlights

❶ **Lake Windermere** Enjoy the changing seasons and serene views with a cruise on England's largest lake. **See p.489**

❷ **Old Dungeon Ghyll Hotel, Langdale** The hikers' favourite inn – cosy rooms, stone-flagged floors and open fires – has England's most famous mountains on the doorstep. **See p.493**

❸ **Brantwood, Coniston Water** John Ruskin's elegant home and inspiring garden is beautifully sited on Coniston Water. **See p.495**

❹ **Go Ape, Grizedale Forest** Swing through the trees on an exciting aerial high-ropes adventure course. **See p.497**

❺ **Via Ferrata, Honister Pass** The Lake District's biggest thrill sees you scrambling, climbing and hanging on for dear life along the old miners' route up Fleetwith Pike. **See p.500**

❻ **Ravenglass and Eskdale Railway, Ravenglass** It's a great day out on the narrow-gauge railway from coast to mountains. **See p.502**

❼ **Wordsworth House, Cockermouth** Costumed staff and authentic surroundings bring the eighteenth century back to life at the birthplace of William Wordsworth. **See p.503**

❽ **Carlisle Castle** Cumbria's mightiest castle dominates the county town. **See p.507**

HIGHLIGHTS ARE MARKED ON THE MAP ON P.486

Kendal Museum

Station Rd • Thurs–Sat 10.30am–5pm; closed Christmas week • Free • ⓣ 01539 815597, ⓦ kendalmuseum.org.uk

The **Kendal Museum** holds the district's natural history and archeological finds, and town history displays. These are bolstered by the reconstructed office, pen-and-ink drawings and personal effects of **Alfred Wainwright** (1907–91), Kendal's former borough treasurer (and honorary clerk at the museum). Wainwright moved to Kendal in 1941, and by 1952, dissatisfied with the accuracy of existing maps, he embarked on his series of highly personal walking guides, painstakingly handwritten with mapped routes and delicately drawn views. They have been hugely popular

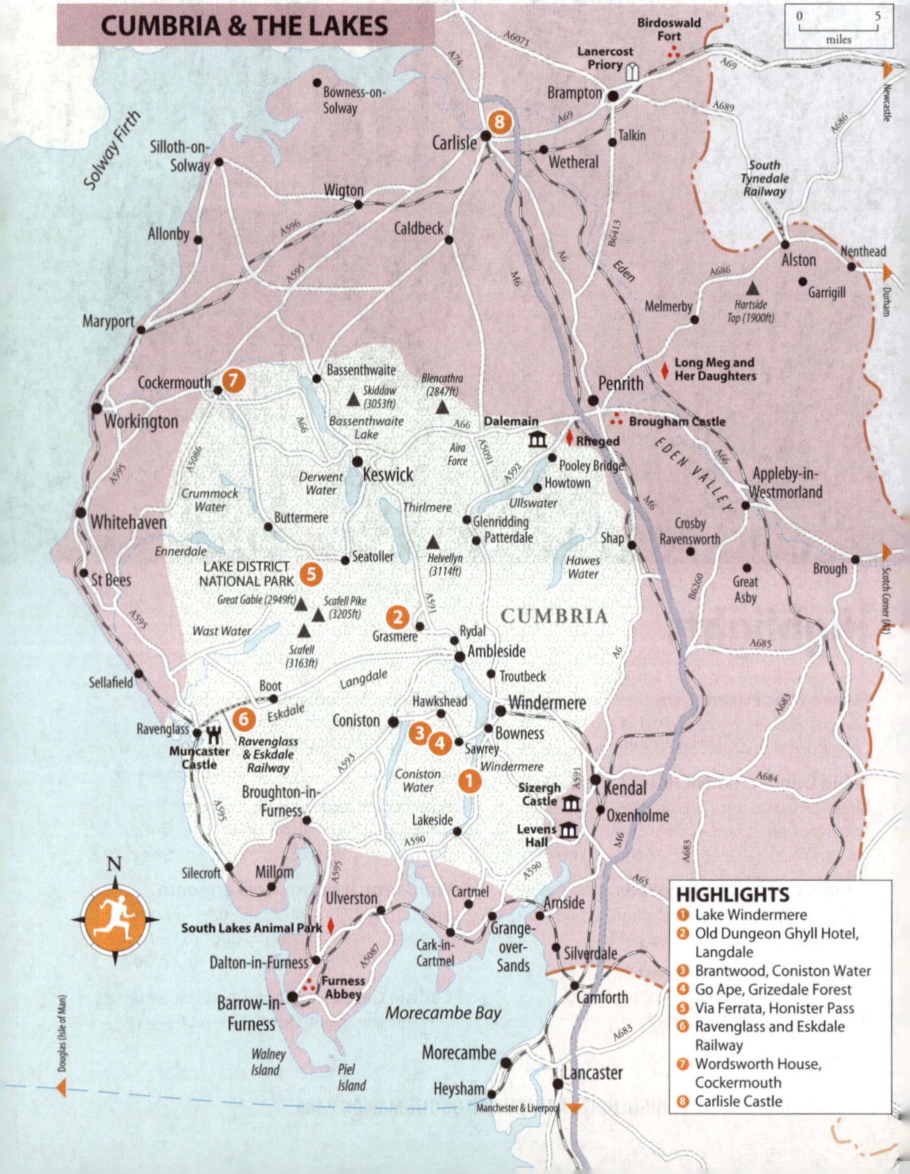

guidebooks ever since, which many treat as gospel in their attempts to "bag" ascents of the 214 fells he recorded.

Abbot Hall

Mon–Sat 10.30am–5pm (Nov–March closes at 4pm); closed mid-Dec to mid-Jan **Abbot Hall Art Gallery** £6, combined ticket with museum £8 • T 01539 722464, W abbothall.org.uk **Museum of Lakeland Life and Industry** £5, combined ticket with gallery £8 • T 01539 722464, W lakelandmuseum.org.uk

The town's two main museums are at the Georgian **Abbot Hall**, by the river near the parish church. The principal hall houses the **Art Gallery**, concentrating in particular on the works of the eighteenth-century "Kendal School" of portrait painters, most famously George Romney. Across the way, the former stables contain the **Museum of Lakeland Life and Industry**, where reconstructed seventeenth-, eighteenth- and nineteenth-century house interiors stand alongside workshops which exhibit rural trades and crafts, from spinning and weaving to shoe-making and tanning.

Sizergh Castle

Off A591, 3 miles south of Kendal • Easter–Oct Mon–Thurs & Sun noon–5pm; guided tours noon–1pm; gardens Easter–Oct daily 11am–5pm, Nov & Dec 11am–4pm • NT • £8.45, gardens only £5.50 • T 015395 60951 • Bus #555 from Kendal

Sizergh Castle owes its "castle" epithet to the fourteenth-century peel tower at its core, one of the best examples of the towers built as safe havens during the region's protracted medieval border raids. There are guided tours of the rooms – largely Elizabethan – between noon and 1pm; thereafter, you can wander around at will.

Levens Hall

Off A6, 6 miles south of Kendal • Easter to mid-Oct Mon–Thurs & Sun noon–4.30pm, last entry at 4pm; gardens Easter to mid-Oct Mon–Thurs & Sun 10am–5pm • £11.50, gardens only £8.50 • T 015395 60321, W www.levenshall.co.uk • Bus #555 from Kendal

Levens Hall was refurbished in the classic Elizabethan manner between 1570 and 1640. House stewards are on hand to point out the oddities and curios – for example, the dining room is panelled not with oak but with goat's leather, printed with a deep-green floral design. Outside are beautifully trimmed topiary gardens, where yews in the shape of pyramids, peacocks and top hats stand between colourful bedding plants and apple orchards.

ARRIVAL AND INFORMATION — KENDAL

By train Trains leave the West Coast main line at Oxenholme, north of Lancaster, for the hourly branch line service to Kendal (5min) and on to Windermere (20min). Kendal's train station's a 10min walk from the centre.

By bus The bus station is on Blackhall Rd (off Stramongate), with main routes including the #599 (to Windermere, Ambleside and Grasmere) or #555 (to Keswick, Lancaster or Carlisle).

Destinations Ambleside (hourly; 40min); Grasmere (hourly; 1hr); Keswick (hourly; 1hr 30min); Lancaster (hourly; 1hr); Windermere/Bowness (hourly; 30min).

Tourist office Made in Cumbria, Kendal TIC, 25 Stramongate (Mon–Sat: April–Oct 10am–5pm; Nov–March 10am–4pm; T 01539 725758).

Useful website W kendaltowncouncil.org.uk.

ACCOMMODATION

Standard B&Bs are ranged along Milnthorpe Rd, a few minutes south of the centre – walk straight down Highgate and Kirkland. There's a youth hostel in town, but better ones await in the nearby Lakes.

Beech House 40 Greenside T 01539 720385, W beechhouse-kendal.co.uk. Boutique B&B with a keen sense of decorative design – think swagged curtains, plumped pillows, richly coloured fabrics, and black-and-white bathrooms with gleaming roll-top baths. **£80**

★ **Punch Bowl Inn** Crosthwaite, 5 miles west of Kendal T 015395 68237, W the-punchbowl.co.uk. A super-stylish country inn – the earth-toned rooms have exposed beams and superb bathrooms, while the restaurant serves scrumptious, locally sourced food (from pot-roast wood pigeon to local lamb). Rooms are individually priced, going up to £225, and are more expensive still at weekends and holidays. **£120**

EATING AND DRINKING

★ **Grain Store** Brewery Arts Centre, 122 Highgate ⓣ01539 725133, ⓦbreweryarts.co.uk. The easy-going arts centre café-restaurant has a good-value lunch menu of sandwiches, salads and gourmet pizzas – there's also pizza at dinner as well as bistro favourites, from sea bass to fellbred Cumbrian steak (lunch for a fiver, pizzas £6–8, other dishes £9–15). Mon–Fri noon–2.30pm & 5.30–11pm, Sat noon–11pm, Sun noon–2.30pm.

Waterside Wholefood Gulfs Rd, bottom of Lowther St ⓣ01539 729743, ⓦwatersidewholefood.co.uk. A great place by the river for veggie and vegan wholefood snacks or meals (£3.50–7) – you can eat outside or grab a table in one of the homely little interior rooms. Mon–Sat 8.30am–4.30pm.

NIGHTLIFE AND ENTERTAINMENT

Brewery Arts Centre 122 Highgate ⓣ01539 725133, ⓦbreweryarts.co.uk. Hub of everything that's happening in town, with cinema, theatre, galleries and concert hall, not to mention café-bar, restaurant (see above) and lively pub.

11

Cartmel

Around eighteen miles southwest of Kendal, and sheltered several miles inland from Morecambe Bay, the pretty village of **CARTMEL** is something of an upmarket getaway, with its Michelin-starred restaurant-with-rooms, winding country lanes and cobbled market square brimming with inns and antique shops. You're in luck if you're looking to buy a handmade dolls' house or embroidered footstool, while in the **Cartmel Village Shop** on the square they sell the finest sticky-toffee pudding known to humanity. Quite what the original monks of Cartmel would have made of all this is anyone's guess – the village first grew up around its twelfth-century Augustinian priory and is still dominated by the proud **Church of St Mary and St Michael**.

Holker Hall

Cark-in-Cartmel, 2 miles west of Cartmel • Easter–Oct Mon–Fri & Sun, house 11am–4pm, gardens 10.30am–5.30pm • £11.50, gardens only £7.50 • ⓣ015395 58328, ⓦholker.co.uk

A couple of miles west of Cartmel, one of Cumbria's most interesting country estates, **Holker Hall**, is still in use by the Cavendish family who've owned it since the late seventeenth century. The highly impressive 23-acre **gardens**, both formal and woodland, are the highlight for many, and a celebrated annual garden festival (June) is held here, as well as spring and winter markets.

ACCOMMODATION AND EATING — CARTMEL

L'Enclume Cavendish St ⓣ015395/36362, ⓦlenclume.co.uk. One of England's most critically acclaimed dining experiences – a succession of artfully constructed dishes accompanied by intensely flavoured jellied cubes, mousses or foams, or suffused with wild herbs, hedgerow flowers and exotic roots. There are menus at £69 and £89, while a dozen highly individual rooms and suites (up to £199, depending on location and size) mix French antique furniture and designer fabrics. Closed first two weeks Jan. Food served Mon & Tues 6.30–9pm, Wed–Sun noon–1.30pm & 6.30–9pm. **£99**

Windermere town

For many, the Lakes proper begin with Windermere, though **WINDERMERE** town was all but non-existent until 1847 when a railway terminal was built here, making England's longest lake (after which the town is named) an easily accessible resort. Windermere remains the transport hub for the southern lakes, but there's precious little else to keep

WINDERMERE CRUISES

Windermere Lake Cruises (windermere-lakecruises.co.uk) operates services to Lakeside at the southern tip (£9.80 return) or to Waterhead (for Ambleside) at the northern end (£9.50 return). There's also a direct service from Ambleside to the Lake District Visitor Centre at Brockhole (£7 return), and a shuttle service across the lake between Pier 3 at Bowness and Ferry House, Sawrey (£2.50 each way). An enjoyable circular **cruise around the islands** departs several times daily from Bowness (£7; 45min), while a 24-hour **Freedom-of-the-Lake** ticket costs £17.25. Services on all routes are frequent between Easter and October (every 30min–1hr at peak times), and reduced during the winter – but there are sailings daily except Christmas Day.

you in the slate-grey streets. All the traffic pours a mile downhill to Windermere's older twin town, Bowness, actually on the lake, but you should at least stay long enough to make the twenty-minute stroll up through the woods to **Orrest Head** (784ft), from where you get a 360 degree panorama from the Yorkshire fells to Morecambe Bay. The path begins by the Windermere Hotel on the A591, across from Windermere train station.

Lake District Visitor Centre at Brockhole

Brockhole, A591, 3 miles northwest of Windermere town • Easter–Oct daily 10am–5pm; grounds & gardens same times all year • Free, parking fee charged • 015394 46601, lake-district.gov.uk • Buses between Windermere and Ambleside run past the visitor centre, or you can take the cruise launch from Waterhead, near Ambleside (see p.492)

The Lake District National Park Authority has its main visitor centre at **Brockhole**, a late Victorian mansion set in lush grounds on the shores of Windermere, northwest of Windermere town. It's the single best place to get to grips with what there is to see and do in the Lakes and, besides the permanent natural history and geological displays, the centre hosts a full programme of walks and activities. The gardens are a treat, too.

ARRIVAL AND INFORMATION — WINDERMERE TOWN

By train Windermere is as far into the Lakes as you can get by train, on the branch line from Oxenholme, via Kendal.
Destinations Kendal (hourly; 15min) and Oxenholme (hourly; 20min), for onward services to Lancaster and Manchester, or Penrith and Carlisle.

By bus All buses (including National Express coaches from London and Manchester) stop outside Windermere train station.
Destinations Ambleside (hourly; 15min); Bowness (every 20–30min; 15min); Brockhole Visitor Centre (every 20–30min; 7min); Carlisle (3 daily; 2hr 20min); Grasmere (every 20–30min; 30min); Kendal (hourly; 25min); Keswick (hourly; 1hr).

Tourist office Victoria St (Mon–Sat 9am–5pm, Sun 10am–5pm; 015394 46499, lakelandgateway.info), 100 yards away from the train station at the top of town.

Tours Mountain Goat, near the tourist office on Victoria St (015394 45161, mountain-goat.com) offers minibus tours (half-day from £26, full-day £36) that get off the beaten track, departing daily from Windermere and other towns.

Bike rental Country Lanes at the train station (015394 44544, countrylaneslakedistrict.co.uk) provides bikes (£20–32/day), plus route maps for local rides.

ACCOMMODATION

★ **Archway** 13 College Rd 015394 45613, the-archway.com. Four trim rooms in a Victorian house known for its breakfasts – either the traditional Full English or American pancakes, kippers, home-made yoghurt and granola, smoked haddock and the like. **£65**

Brendan Chase 1–3 College Rd 015394 45638, placetostaywindermere.co.uk. Popular place with overseas travellers, providing a friendly welcome, a good breakfast and eight comfortable rooms (some en suite). No cards. **£60**

Holbeck Ghyll Holbeck Lane, off A591, 3 miles north of Windermere town 015394 32375, holbeckghyll.com. Stalwart of the lakeland country-house hotel scene, with luxurious rooms either in the main house or in the lodge or suites in the grounds – there's a sherry decanter in every room, seven acres of gardens, and Michelin-starred food of great refinement (dinner included in the price). **£250**

Lake District Backpackers' Lodge High St, across from the tourist office 015394 46374, lakedistrictbackpackers.co.uk. Twenty basic backpackers' beds in small dorms (available as private rooms on request, £16.50 per person). The price includes a tea-and-toast breakfast. No credit cards. **£14.50**

YHA Windermere High Cross, Bridge Lane, 1 mile north of Troutbeck Bridge ⓣ0845 371 9352, ⓔwindermere@yha.org.uk. The local YHA hostel is a revamped old mansion with magnificent lake views. Rates are usually £2 higher at weekends, but drop in winter. Dorm beds **£16.65**

EATING

Francine's 27 Main Rd ⓣ015394 44088, ⓦfrancinesrestaurantwindermere.co.uk. During the day you can drop into this easy-going café-restaurant for anything from a pain au chocolat to a big bowl of mussels. Dinner sees the lights dimmed for a wide-ranging continental menu of pork belly confit to seafood marinara, with most mains from £9 to £14. Tues 10am–3pm, Wed–Sat 10am–3pm & 6–11pm, Sun 10am–3pm.

Hooked Ellerthwaite Square ⓣ015394 48443, ⓦhookedwindermere.co.uk. Contemporary seafood place serving fish straight from the Fleetwood boats. Typical dishes include hake with chorizo, fava beans and garlic, or Thai-style sea bass. Starters are £6–7, mains £15–21. Tues–Sun 5.30–10pm.

Bowness and the lake

BOWNESS-ON-WINDERMERE – to give it its full title – spills back from its lakeside piers in a series of terraces lined with guesthouses and hotels. There's been a village here since the fifteenth century and a ferry service across the lake for almost as long – these days, however, you could be forgiven for thinking that Bowness begins and ends with its best-known attraction, the **World of Beatrix Potter**. At ten and a half miles long, a mile wide in parts and a shade over 200ft deep, the **lake** itself – **Windermere**, incidentally, never "Lake" Windermere – is the heavyweight of Lake District waters. On a busy summer's day, crowds swirl around the trinket shops, cafés, ice-cream stalls and lakeside seats, but you can easily escape out on to the water or into the hills, and there are attractions around town to fill a rainy day.

The World of Beatrix Potter

Old Laundry, Crag Brow • Daily: Easter–Sept 10am–5.30pm; Oct–Easter 10am–4.30pm; closed 2 weeks in Jan • £6.75, all-year family Freedom Pass £30 • ⓣ0844 504 1233, ⓦhop-skip-jump.com

You either like Beatrix Potter or you don't, but it's safe to say that the elaborate 3D story scenes, audiovisual "virtual walks", themed tearoom and gift shop here at the interactive **World of Beatrix Potter** find more favour with children than the more formal Potter attractions at Hill Top and Hawkshead.

Blackwell

1.5 miles south of Bowness, off A5074 • Daily: April–Oct 10.30am–5pm; Nov–March 10.30am–4pm; closed 2 weeks Jan • £7 • ⓣ015394 46139, ⓦblackwell.org.uk

Mackay Hugh Baillie Scott's **Blackwell** was built in 1900 as a lakeside holiday home, and today you can see some of the rooms in its superbly restored Arts and Crafts interior. Lakeland motifs – trees, flowers, birds and berries – abound, while temporary exhibits focus on furniture and decoration. There's an informative introductory talk (usually weekdays at 2.30pm), plus a tearoom, craft shop and gardens. Parking is available; alternatively, you can walk from Bowness in about 25 minutes.

Lakeside and Haverthwaite Railway

Easter–Oct 6–7 departures daily • £6.20 return, or £14.50 including cruise boat from Bowness • ⓣ015395 31594, ⓦlakesiderailway.co.uk

From Bowness piers, boats head to the southern reaches of Windermere at Lakeside, which is also the terminus of the **Lakeside and Haverthwaite Railway**, whose steam-powered engines puff gently along four miles of track along the River Leven and through the woods of Backbarrow Gorge. Boat arrivals from Bowness connect with train departures throughout the day, and as well as the boat-and-train combination there are also joint tickets for Lakeside's Aquarium and the nearby Lakeland Motor Museum.

ARRIVAL AND DEPARTURE — BOWNESS

By bus The open-top #599 bus from Windermere train station stops at the lakeside piers (£3.25 return). For onward routes to Ambleside and Grasmere you have to return first to Windermere station.

By ferry The traditional ferry service is the chain-guided contraption from Ferry Nab on the Bowness side (10min walk from the cruise piers) to Ferry House, Sawrey (every 20min; Mon–Sat 7am–10pm, Sun 9am–10pm; 50p, bike and cyclist £1, cars £3.50), providing access to Beatrix Potter's former home at Hill Top and to Hawkshead beyond. There's also a useful pedestrian launch service between Bowness piers and Ferry House, Sawrey (see p.489), saving you the walk down to the car ferry.

Cross Lakes Experience A connecting boat-and-minibus shuttle service (up to 10 daily; mid-Feb to Easter Sat & Sun; Easter–Oct daily; Ⓣ015394 48600, Ⓦlake-district.gov.uk/crosslakes) runs from Bowness pier 3 to Beatrix Potter's house at Hill Top (£9.20 return), and then to Hawkshead (£10.70) and Coniston Water (£18.60).

11

ACCOMMODATION

There are lots of B&B possibilities on **Kendal Rd**, but be warned that a lake view doesn't come cheap – most places in town with even a glimpse of the water set their prices accordingly.

Angel Inn Helm Rd Ⓣ015394 44080, Ⓦthe-angelinn.com. A dozen chic rooms – all burnished wood and black leather – above a smooth bar bring a bit of metropolitan style to Bowness. Snacks, wraps and sandwiches and posh pub food are served in the contemporary bar, back restaurant or terraced garden. **£80**

Linthwaite House Crook Rd, B5284, 1 mile south of Bowness Ⓣ015394 88600, Ⓦlinthwaite.com. Contemporary boutique style grafted on to an ivy-covered country house set high above Windermere. A conservatory and terrace offer grandstand lake and fell views, and you can work up an appetite for dinner with a walk in the extensive gardens to the hotel's private tarn. Rates vary according to outlook and size, but run up to £400, suites up to £600, dinner included. **£275**

★ **Number 80** 80 Craig Walk Ⓣ015394 43584, Ⓦnumber80bed.co.uk. Colin and Mandy's quiet townhouse offers quirky, stylish B&B in four rather dramatic, earth-toned double rooms – a grown-up space for couples (no pets, no children). **£80**

EATING AND DRINKING

Bowness has plenty of places offering pizza, fish and chips, a Chinese stir-fry or a budget café meal – a stroll along pedestrianized **Ash Street** and up **Lake Road** shows you most of the possibilities.

★ **Hole in't Wall** Fallbarrow Rd Ⓣ015394 43488. For a drink and a bar meal (£9–12) you can't beat the town's oldest hostelry, with stone-flagged floors, open fires and real ales, plus a terrace-style beer garden that's a popular spot on summer evenings. Mon–Sat 11am–11pm, Sun noon–11pm.

Ambleside

Five miles northwest of Windermere, **AMBLESIDE** is a first-class base for walkers, who are catered for by a large number of outdoors shops. The town centre consists of a cluster of grey-green stone houses, shops, pubs and B&Bs hugging a circular one-way system, which loops round just south of the narrow gully of stony Stock Ghyll. Huge car parks

TOP 5 LAKE DISTRICT VIEWS

Castlerigg Stone Circle Keswick. See p.498
Cat Bells Derwent Water. See p.499
Hardknott Roman Fort Eskdale. See p.501
Loughrigg Terrace Grasmere. See p.493
Orrest Head Windermere. See p.489

soak up the day-trip trade, but actually Ambleside improves the longer you spend here, with some enjoyable local walks and also the best selection of accommodation and restaurants in the area. The rest of town lies a mile south at **Waterhead**, where the cruise boats dock, overlooked by the grass banks and spreading trees of Borrans Park.

Armitt Collection

Rydal Rd • Mon–Sat 10am–4.30pm • £3.50 • T 015394 31212, W armitt.com

For some background on Ambleside's history, stroll a couple of minutes from the centre along Rydal Road to the **Armitt Collection**, which catalogues the very distinct contribution to Lakeland society made by writers and artists from John Ruskin to Beatrix Potter.

ARRIVAL AND INFORMATION — AMBLESIDE

11

By bus All buses in town on Kelsick Rd, opposite the library, with regular local services to Windermere, Grasmere and Keswick, plus services to Hawkshead and Coniston (#505), and Elterwater and Langdale (#516).

By ferry There are ferry services from Bowness and Lakeside; it's a 15min walk into Ambleside from the piers at Waterhead.

Tourist office "Hub of Ambleside", Central Buildings, Market Cross (daily 9am–5.30pm; T 015394 32582, W lakeland gateway.info).

GETTING AROUND

Bike rental Biketreks, Rydal Rd (daily 9.30am–5pm; T 015394 31245, W biketreks.net); and Ghyllside Cycles, The Slack (Easter–Oct daily 9.30am–5.30pm; Nov–Easter closed Wed; T 015394 33592, W ghyllside.co.uk) rent bikes at £20/day, with maps for day rides included in the price.

ACCOMMODATION

Lake Rd, running between Waterhead and Ambleside, is lined with straightforward **B&Bs**, as are Church St and Compston Rd.

Compston House Compston Rd T 015394 32305, W compstonhouse.co.uk. There's a breezy New York vibe in this traditional Lakeland house, where the American style extends from the rooms to the breakfasts – home-made pancakes and maple syrup, fluffy omelettes and the like. £80

Low Wray Campsite Low Wray, off B5286 (Hawkshead road), 3 miles south; bus #505 T 015394 63862, W ntlakescampsites.org.uk or W 4windslakelandtipis.co.uk or W long-valley-yurts.co.uk. The beautiful National Trust site on the western shore of the lake is a glampers' haven – as well as tent pitches (£8–12 per night), there are wooden camping "pods" for couples and families (£30–45), tipis (part-week rental from £180, weekends from £210) and bell tents (part-week from £235, full week from £355). Closed Nov–Easter. Tents from £8

★ **Randy Pike** B5286 (Hawkshead road), 3 miles south, just past Low Wray turn-off T 015394 36088, W randypike.co.uk. Two amazing, boutique B&B suites open out on to the gardens of what was once a Victorian gentleman's hunting lodge. It's a grown-up, romantic retreat, and you can either stay put with the snack larder, terrace and gardens, or be whizzed down to the owners' *Jumble Room* restaurant in Grasmere (see p.494) for dinner. £200

Riverside Under Loughrigg T 015394 32395, W riverside-at-ambleside.co.uk. Charming guesthouse, half a mile (10min walk) from Ambleside across Rothay Park. Six large, light country-pine-style rooms available, including a river-facing four-poster (£116). £98

YHA Ambleside Waterhead, A591, 1 mile south T 0845 371 9620, E ambleside@yha.org.uk. The YHA's flagship regional hostel has an impressive lakeside location (most rooms have a water view), and 260 beds divided amongst neatly furnished small dorms, twins, doubles and family rooms. Facilities are first-rate too – private jetty, tour- and activity-bookings, and licensed bar and restaurant. Dorm £25, twin £42

EATING AND DRINKING

★ **Lucy's On A Plate** Church St T 015394 31191, W lucysofambleside.co.uk. Quirky, hugely enjoyable, informal bistro – if they know you're coming, you'll probably find yourself namechecked on the daily changing menu. Daytime café dishes (breakfasts, dips, pastas, salads, soup and sandwiches, £4–10) give way to a dinner menu (mains £14–19) that is "sourced locally, cooked globally". Daily 10am–9pm.

Zeffirelli's Compston Rd T 015394 33845, W zeffirellis.com. *Zeffirelli's* arty, independent cinema has five screens at three locations in town; this restaurant, attached to the Compston Rd screens, is well known for its wholemeal-base pizzas, plus Italian-with-a-twist pastas and salads, all vegetarian (pizzas and mains £8–10). The menu's available at lunch and dinner, but *Zeff's* is also open from 10am as a café. There's a great music-bar upstairs, too, as well as an associated fine-dining veggie restaurant (*Fellini's*) elsewhere in town. Daily 10am–10pm.

Great Langdale

Three miles west of Ambleside along the A593, Skelwith Bridge marks the start of **Great Langdale**, a U-shaped glacial valley overlooked by the prominent rocky summits of the **Langdale Pikes**, the most popular of the central Lakeland fells. You can get to the pretty village of **Elterwater** – where there's a tiny village green overlooked by the excellent *Britannia Inn* (see below) – by bus (17min); the bus then continues on to the *Old Dungeon Ghyll* hotel at the head of the valley (30min). Three miles from Elterwater, at **Stickle Ghyll** car park, Harrison Stickle (2414ft), Pike of Stickle (2326ft) and Pavey Ark (2297ft) form a dramatic backdrop, though many walkers go no further than the hour-long climb to **Stickle Tarn** from Stickle Ghyll. Another car park, a mile further west up the valley road by the **Old Dungeon Ghyll Hotel**, is the starting point for a series of more hardcore hikes to resonant Lakeland peaks like Crinkle Crags (2816ft) or Bowfell (2960ft).

ARRIVAL AND DEPARTURE — GREAT LANGDALE

The #516 Langdale Rambler **bus** from Ambleside runs to Elterwater and the *Old Dungeon Ghyll* (5–6 daily).

ACCOMMODATION AND EATING

Britannia Inn Elterwater ⓣ015394 37210, ⓦbritinn.co.uk. The popular pub on Elterwater's green has nine charming, cosy rooms – cosy being the operative word, since there's not a lot of space in a 500-year-old inn. Rates are £30 higher at weekends. They offer a wide range of beers and good-value food – from home-made pies and Cumberland sausage to seared scallops and Hawkshead trout (mains £11–14) served either in the dining room (booking advised) or front bar. Food served daily: lunch noon–2pm, snacks & bar food 2–5.30pm, evening meals 6.30–9.30pm. **£90**

Great Langdale ⓣ015394 63862, ⓦntlakescampsites.org.uk or ⓦlong-valley-yurts.co.uk. The National Trust's stupendously sited Langdale campsite has gone stellar since camping pods (£30–45 per night) and yurts (part-week from £285/full week £385, school and bank hols £325/460) were added into the mix. The bar at the *Old Dungeon Ghyll* is a 5min walk away. Pods from **£30**

★ **Old Dungeon Ghyll** ⓣ015394 37272, ⓦodg.co.uk. The Lakes' most famous inn is decidedly old-school – well-worn oak, floral decor, vintage furniture – but walkers can't resist its unrivalled location. Of the rooms, the en-suite ones offer the best value; weekend prices are £10 higher. Dinner (£25, reservations essential) is served at 7.30pm in the dining room, though all the action is in the stone-flagged *Hikers' Bar*, which has real ales and hearty meals (from £9). Bar meals noon–2pm & 6–9pm. **£105**

Grasmere and around

Four miles northwest of Ambleside, the village of **GRASMERE** consists of an intimate cluster of grey-stone houses on the old packhorse road that runs beside the babbling River Rothay. Pretty it certainly is, but it loses some of its charm in high summer thanks to the hordes who descend on the trail of the village's most famous former resident, **William Wordsworth** (1770–1850). The poet, his wife Mary, sister Dorothy and other members of his family are buried beneath the yews in **St Oswald's churchyard**, around which the river makes a sinuous curl. There's little else to the village, save its gift shops, galleries, tearooms and hotels, though the **lake** is just a ten-minute walk away, down Redbank; tremendous views unfold from **Loughrigg Terrace**, on its southern reaches. A four-mile circuit of Grasmere and adjacent **Rydal Water** takes around two hours, with the route passing Wordsworth haunts **Rydal Mount** and **Dove Cottage**.

Dove Cottage

Town End, just outside Grasmere on A591 • Daily: March–Oct 9.30am–5.30pm; Nov–early Jan & Feb 9.30am–4.30pm • £7.50 • T 015394 35544, W wordsworth.org.uk • Buses #555 and #599

Dove Cottage, home to William and Dorothy Wordsworth from 1799 to 1808, was the place where Wordsworth wrote some of his best poetry. Guides, bursting with anecdotes, lead you around the cottage rooms, little changed now but for the addition of electricity and internal plumbing. In the adjacent **museum** are paintings, manuscripts (including that of "Daffodils") and mementos of the so-called "Lake Poets", Robert Southey and Samuel Taylor Coleridge, as well as "opium-eater" Thomas De Quincey who also lived in the cottage for several years.

Rydal Mount

Two miles southeast of Grasmere, A591 • March–Oct daily 9.30am–5pm; Nov–Feb Wed–Sun 11am–4pm; closed for 3 weeks in Jan • £6.50, gardens only £4 • T 015394 33002, W rydalmount.co.uk • Buses #555 and #599

11

At Dove Cottage Wordsworth had been a largely unknown poet of straitened means, but by 1813 he'd written several of his greatest works (though not all had yet been published) and had been appointed Westmorland's Distributor of Stamps, a salaried position which allowed him to take up the rent of a comfortable family house. **Rydal Mount** remained Wordsworth's home from 1813 until his death in 1850, and the house is owned by descendants of the poet. You're free to wander around what is essentially still a family home, as well as explore Wordworth's cherished garden.

ARRIVAL AND DEPARTURE — GRASMERE

The #555 **bus** (between Kendal and Keswick) and the #599 (from Kendal, Bowness, Windermere and Ambleside) stop on the village green.

ACCOMMODATION

You should book well in advance for accommodation in any budget, at any time of year.

★ **Grasmere Independent Hostel** Broadrayne Farm, A591, 0.5 miles north T 015394 35055, W www.grasmerehostel.co.uk. A stylish gem of a backpackers' hostel, with 24 beds, all in small, carpeted en-suite rooms – the price goes up a quid at weekends and two on bank holidays. There's an impressively equipped kitchen, and even a sauna, with the local pub just a few hundred yards away for meals. Dorm **£19.50**

How Foot Lodge Town End, 0.5 miles southeast T 015394 35366, W howfoot.co.uk. You won't get a better deal on good-quality B&B accommodation in Grasmere than in this light-filled Victorian villa just a few yards from Dove Cottage. **£72**

Moss Grove Organic Grasmere T 015394 35251, W mossgrove.com. Stunning, revamped Victorian-era hotel that's been designed along organic, low-impact lines – thus, handmade beds of reclaimed timber, wallpaper coloured with natural inks, and windows screened by natural wood blinds. It's feels less like a hotel than a private house party – you're encouraged to forage in the kitchen for a buffet-style breakfast. Add £40 per night for a weekend visit. **£129**

EATING AND DRINKING

★ **Jumble Room** Langdale Rd T 015394 35188, W thejumbleroom.co.uk. Funky, relaxed dining spot, where the menu roams the world – Tuscan crostini, Thai salmon salad, or fish in organic beer batter – and, once ensconced, no one's in any hurry to leave. Most mains £14–20. Wed–Sun 5.30–10pm, plus weekend lunches in summer; closed 2 weeks in Dec.

Coniston and around

Coniston Water is not one of the most immediately imposing of the lakes, yet it has a quiet beauty that sets it apart from the more popular destinations. The nineteenth-century art critic and social reformer John Ruskin made the lake his home, and today

CONISTON'S SPEED KING

On January 4, 1967, **Donald Campbell** set out to better his own world water-speed record (276mph, set three years earlier in Australia) on the glass-like surface of Coniston Water. Just as his jet-powered *Bluebird* hit an estimated 320mph, however, a patch of turbulence sent it into a somersault. Campbell was killed immediately and his body and boat lay undisturbed at the bottom of the lake until both were retrieved in 2001. Campbell's grave is in the small village cemetery behind the *Crown Hotel*, while the reconstructed *Bluebird* is displayed in a purpose-built gallery at the local museum, where you can find out more about Campbell and that fateful day.

his isolated house, **Brantwood**, on the northeastern shore, provides the most obvious target for a day-trip. **Arthur Ransome** was also a frequent visitor, his local memories and experiences providing much of the detail in his famous *Swallows and Amazons* children's books.

Coniston village

The small, slate-grey village of **CONISTON** hunkers below the craggy and coppermine-riddled bulk of **The Old Man of Coniston** (2628ft), which most fit walkers can climb in under two hours. In the village itself, **John Ruskin's grave** lies in St Andrew's original churchyard beneath a beautifully worked Celtic cross, while just up the road is the highly entertaining local **museum** – named after its most famous resident but devoted to all aspects of local life and work.

Ruskin Museum

Yewdale Rd • Easter to mid-Nov daily 10am–5.30pm; mid-Nov to Easter Wed–Sun 10.30am–3.30pm • £5.25 • ⓣ 015394 41164, ⓦ ruskinmuseum.com

The **Ruskin Museum** is first port of call for anyone interested in the life, ideas and theories of this hugely influential writer and artist – not to mention his socks, matriculation certificate from Oxford, and a mixed bag of letters, manuscripts, sketchbooks and watercolours.

Coniston Water

Steam Yacht Gondola Easter–Oct roughly hourly 10.30am–4.15pm, weather permitting • NT • £9.90 return • ⓣ 015394 41288

Coniston Launch Easter–Oct hourly 10.15am–5pm; Nov–Easter up to 5 daily • £9.50 return (north route) or £13.50 (south) • ⓣ 017687 75753, ⓦ conistonlaunch.co.uk

Coniston Water is hidden out of sight, half a mile southeast of the village. As well as boat and kayak rental from the pier, there are two lake cruise services, which both call at Ruskin's Brantwood (on the opposite shore) as well as various other points around the lake. The National Trust's restored **Steam Yacht Gondola** is the historic choice, while the **Coniston Launch** runs the solar-powered wooden vessels "Ruskin" and "Ransome" on two routes around the lake, north and south. You can stop off at any pier en route, and local walking leaflets are available, as well as special cruises throughout the year.

Brantwood

2.5 miles southeast of Coniston, off B5285 • Mid-March to mid-Nov daily 11am–5.30pm; mid-Nov to mid-March Wed–Sun 11am–4.30pm • £6.95, gardens only £4.95 • ⓣ 015394 41396, ⓦ brantwood.org.uk

Sited on a hillside above the eastern shore of Coniston Water, **Brantwood** was home to John Ruskin from 1872 until his death in 1900. Ruskin was the champion of J.M.W. Turner and the Pre-Raphaelites and foremost Victorian proponent of the supremacy of Gothic architecture. His **study** and **dining room** boast superlative lake views, bettered only by those from the **Turret Room** where he used to sit in later life in his bathchair. The surviving Turners from Ruskin's own art collection are on show, and other exhibition rooms and galleries display Ruskin-related arts and crafts, while the excellent *Jumping Jenny Tearooms* – named after Ruskin's boat – has an outdoor terrace with lake views. Meanwhile, paths wind through the lakeside meadows and into the various **gardens**, some based on Ruskin's own plans – his slate seat is sited in the Professor's Garden.

ARRIVAL AND DEPARTURE — CONISTON

By bus The #505 "Coniston Rambler" bus (from Kendal, Windermere, Ambleside or Hawkshead) stops on the main road through Coniston village. The good-value "Ruskin Explorer" ticket (available on the bus) includes return travel on the #505 from Windermere, a return trip on the Coniston Launch to Brantwood and entry to Brantwood itself (from £16.40).

Cross Lakes Experience The boat-and-minibus service from Bowness (mid-Feb to Easter Sat & Sun; Easter–Oct daily; 015394 48600, lake-district.gov.uk/crosslakes) runs as far as the *Waterhead Hotel* pier (for Brantwood and lake services), at the head of Coniston Water, half a mile out of the village.

ACCOMMODATION AND EATING

Bank Ground Farm Coniston Water, east side, north of Brantwood 015394 41264, bankground.com. The beautifully set shoreside farmhouse was the original model for Holly Howe Farm in *Swallows and Amazons* and later used in the 1970s film. Seven traditionally furnished rooms have oak beams and carved beds (room 8 has the best views), and there's also a farmhouse tearoom. Tearoom Easter–Oct Thurs–Sun, or Thurs–Tues in school summer holidays. **£90**

Black Bull Inn Coppermines Rd, by the bridge 015394 41335, blackbullconiston.co.uk. The village's best pub has a variety of reasonably spacious B&B rooms (£10 cheaper during the week). It also brews it own beer, while local lamb, sausage and trout are menu mainstays (bar meals £9–15). Food served daily noon–9pm. **£100**

Church House Inn Torver, 2 miles south 015394 41282, churchhouseinntorver.com. The five B&B rooms are small but charming, while excellent food is served in the snug real-ale bar or dining room – locally sourced and strong on the classics (potted shrimps, local "tattie" hotpot, steak and ale pudding, fish pie). Mains £13–19. Food served daily noon–3pm & 6–9pm. **£70**

★ **Yew Tree Farm** A593, 2 miles north 015394 41433, yewtree-farm.com. The classiest farmhouse B&B in the Lakes, where three hugely atmospheric rooms are tucked away under mind-your-head oak beams. There's an excellent breakfast sourced from the farm, walks straight from the gates (Tarn Hows is only half a mile away), and a decanter of port waiting for you in front of the fire. **£105**

Hawkshead and around

HAWKSHEAD, midway between Coniston and Ambleside, wears its beauty well, its patchwork of cottages and cobbles backed by woods and fells and barely affected by modern intrusions. Huge car parks at the village edge take the strain, and when the crowds of day-trippers leave, Hawkshead regains its natural tranquillity. It's a major stop on both the **Beatrix Potter** and **Wordsworth** trails (Potter's house, Hill Top, is nearby, while William and his brother went to school here), and makes a handy base for days out in **Grizedale Forest**.

The best local **walk** is to lovely **Tarn Hows**, a body of water surrounded by spruce and pine and circled by paths and picnic spots. It's two miles from Hawkshead on country lanes and paths; it takes about an hour to walk around the tarn.

Beatrix Potter Gallery

Main St • Sat–Thurs: Feb half-term to Easter 11am–3.30pm; Easter–Oct 11am–5pm • NT • £4.60, discount available for Hill Top visitors • 015394 36355

Hawkshead's **Beatrix Potter Gallery** occupies rooms once used by Potter's solicitor husband, William Heelis, and contains an annually changing selection of her original sketchbooks, drawings, watercolours, letters and manuscripts. Those less devoted to the "Tales" will find displays on Potter's life as a keen naturalist, conservationist and early supporter of the National Trust more diverting.

Hill Top

Near Sawrey, 2 miles southeast of Hawkshead • Sat–Thurs: Feb half-term to Easter 10.30am–3.30pm; Easter–Oct 10.30am–4.30pm • NT • £7; garden free during opening hours • T 015394 36269

Beatrix Potter's beloved house, **Hill Top**, lies close to Hawkshead in the gorgeous hamlet of Near Sawrey. A Londoner by birth, Potter bought the farmhouse here with the proceeds from her first book, *The Tale of Peter Rabbit*, and retained it as her study long after she moved out following her marriage in 1913. Bear in mind that entry is by timed ticket, you'll probably have to wait in line to enter the small house, and sell-outs are possible, especially in school holidays (and you can't book in advance).

Grizedale Forest

2.5 miles southwest of Hawkshead • Free, parking fee charged • #X30 bus from Hawkshead, connects with Cross Lakes Experience
Grizedale Forest Centre Daily: Easter–Oct 10am–5pm; Nov–Easter 10am–4pm • T 01229 860010, W forestry.gov.uk/grizedale

Grizedale Forest extends over the fells separating Coniston Water and Hawkshead from Windermere, and the picnic spots, open-air sculptures, children's activities, cycle trails and tree-top adventure course make for a great day out away from the main lakes. The best starting point is the **Grizedale Forest Centre**, where there's a café and information point.

Go Ape

Easter–Oct Wed–Mon in term time, daily in school holidays; Nov Sat & Sun • adults £30, kids £20, advance booking essential, online or by phone • T 0845 643 9215, W goape.co.uk

Go Ape, a high-ropes adventure course in the thick of Grizedale Forest, has you frolicking in the tree canopy for a couple of hours. You get a quick safety briefing and then make your own way around the fixed-ropes course – fantastic fun involving zip-wires, Tarzan-swings and aerial walkways.

ARRIVAL — HAWKSHEAD

The main **bus** service to Hawkshead is the #505 Coniston Rambler between Windermere, Ambleside and Coniston.

GETTING AROUND

Cross Lakes Experience The bus shuttle service (mid-Feb to Easter Sat & Sun; Easter–Oct daily; T 015394 48600, W lake-district.gov.uk/crosslakes) runs from Hawkshead down to the Beatrix Potter house at Hill Top and on to Sawrey for boat connections back to Bowness.

Bike rental W grizedalemountainbikes.co.uk.

ACCOMMODATION AND EATING

Ann Tyson's Cottage Wordsworth St T 015394 36405, W anntysons.co.uk. Wordsworth briefly boarded here, on a quaint cobbled street, and now you can too. There are three B&B rooms in the main house (one with an antique carved bed from Ruskin's house at Brantwood), and three slightly more spacious ones to the side. **£74**

★ **Drunken Duck Inn** Barngates crossroads, 2 miles north, off B5285 T 015394 36347, W drunkenduckinn.co.uk. Superb, stylish restaurant-with-rooms in a beautifully located 400-year-old inn with divine local views. Rooms and rates vary considerably – smallish standard rooms (midweek rates) in the inn itself are cheapest, weekend stays cost at least £140, and there's more deluxe accommodation too (up to £295 a night). Bar meals at lunch (dishes, from belly pork to roast cod, £9–14) give way to more elaborate dishes at dinner, with local sourcing a priority (mains £14–25; reservations essential). And don't miss the beer from the on-site brewery. Daily noon–4pm & 6–9pm. **£95**

Yewfield Hawkshead Hill, 2 miles northwest off B5285 T 015394 36765, W yewfield.co.uk. Splendid vegetarian guesthouse set amongst organic vegetable gardens and wild-flower meadows. The house is a Victorian Gothic beauty, filled with Oriental artefacts and art from the owners' travels. Closed Dec & Jan. **£98**

Keswick and around

Standing on the shores of **Derwent Water**, the market town of **KESWICK** makes a good base for exploring the northern Lake District, particularly delightful Borrowdale to the south of town or the heights of Skiddaw (3053ft) and Blencathra (2847ft), which loom over Keswick to the north. Granted its market charter by Edward I in 1276 – **market day** is Saturday – Keswick was an important wool and leather centre until around 1500, when these trades were supplanted by the discovery of local graphite. Keswick went on to become an important pencil-making town; the entertaining **Cumberland Pencil Museum**, across the river (daily 9.30am–5pm; £3.75; ⓦpencilmuseum.co.uk) tells the whole story.

Castlerigg Stone Circle

Don't miss Keswick's most mysterious landmark, **Castlerigg Stone Circle**, where 38 hunks of volcanic stone, the largest almost 8ft tall, form a circle 100ft in diameter, set against a magnificent mountain backdrop. Take the Threlkeld rail line path (signposted by the *Keswick Country House Hotel*) and follow the signs for around a mile and a half all told.

Derwent Water

Keswick Launch departures: Easter–Nov daily, Dec–Easter Sat & Sun only • £9 return, £1.95 per stage; 1hr summer evening cruise £9.20 • ⓣ017687 72263, ⓦkeswick-launch.co.uk

The shores of **Derwent Water** lie five minutes' walk south of the town centre. It's among the most attractive of the lakes, ringed by crags and studded with islets, and is most

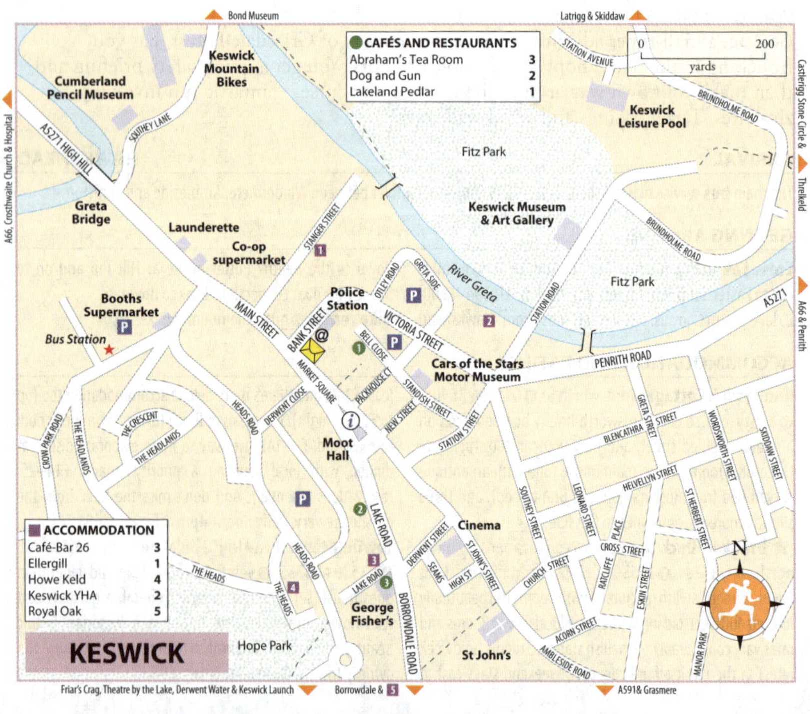

easily seen by hopping on the **Keswick Launch**, which runs around the lake calling at several points en route. You can jump off the launch at any of the half a dozen piers on Derwent Water for a stroll, but if you've only got time for one hike, make it up **Cat Bells** (take the launch to Hawes End), a superb vantage point (1481ft) above the lake's western shore – allow two and a half hours for the scramble to the top and a return to the pier along the wooded shore.

Borrowdale

It is difficult to overstate the beauty of **Borrowdale**, with its river flats and yew trees, lying at the head of Derwent Water and overshadowed by Scafell Pike, the highest mountain in England, and Great Gable, reckoned as one of the finest looking. At the straggling hamlet of **Rosthwaite**, seven miles south of Keswick, there are a couple of hotels with public bars, while another mile up the valley, eight from Keswick, the #78 bus route ends its run at Seatoller, where there's also a café and a car park. From here, it's twenty minutes' walk down the minor road to the hamlet of **Seathwaite**, the base for walks up **Scafell Pike** (3205ft): the classic ascent is up the thrilling Corridor Route, then descending via Esk Hause, a tough, eight-mile (6hr) loop walk in all from Seathwaite.

ARRIVAL AND DEPARTURE — KESWICK

By bus Buses (including National Express services from Manchester and London) use the terminal in front of the large Booths supermarket, off Main St. Local services include the #77A (down the west side of Derwent Water, via access point for Cat Bells) and the scenic #78 "Borrowdale Rambler", which runs south down B5289 to Seatoller. You can use either service all day with the "Honister and Borrowdale Day Rider" ticket (from £6.50).

Destinations Ambleside (hourly; 45min); Buttermere (2 daily; 30min); Carlisle (3 daily; 1hr 10min); Cockermouth (every 30min–1hr; 30min); Grasmere (hourly; 40min); Honister (Easter–Oct 4 daily; 40min); Kendal (hourly; 1hr 30min); Rosthwaite (every 30min–1hr; 25min); Seatoller (every 30min–1hr; 30min); Windermere (hourly; 1hr).

GETTING AROUND

Bike rental Keswick Mountain Bikes, Southey Hill, Greta Bridge (daily 9am–5pm; T 017687 75202, W keswickmountainbikes.co.uk), rents bikes from £15/day.

INFORMATION AND TOURS

National Park Information Centre Moot Hall, Market Square (daily: April–Oct 9.30am–5.30pm; Nov–March 9.30am–4.30pm; T 017687 72645, W lake-district.gov.uk).

Guided walks For a good walk in company – lakeside rambles to mountain climbs – just turn up with a packed lunch at the Moot Hall (Easter–Oct daily 10.15am; £10, some longer walks £12).

ACCOMMODATION

B&Bs and **guesthouses** cluster around Southey, Blencathra, Church and Eskin streets, in the grid off the A591 (Penrith road). Smarter guesthouses and **hotels** line The Heads, overlooking Hope Park, a couple of minutes south of the centre on the way to the lake, while nearby **Borrowdale** has several fine old inns and country-house hotels.

Café-Bar 26 26 Lake Rd T 017687 80863, W cafebar26.co.uk. Four stylishly decorated rooms on the first floor offer a chintz-free base right in the town centre, while downstairs is a funky café-bar. Weekend rates are £15 higher. £60

★ **Ellergill** 22 Stanger St T 017687 73347, W ellergill.co.uk. Owners Robin and Clare have grafted a chic European feel onto their restored Victorian house, and offer classy B&B in five rooms. £65

★ **Howe Keld** 5–7 The Heads T 017687 72417, W howekeld.co.uk. The Fishers' boutique guesthouse puts local crafts and materials centre stage, with furniture and floors handcrafted from Lake District trees, plus green-slate bathrooms and carpets of Herdwick wool. Breakfast is terrific, from the daily home-baked organic bread to veggie rissoles and other specialities. £96

Keswick YHA Station Rd T 0845 371 9746, E keswick@yha.org.uk. Once a riverside woollen mill, Keswick's YHA has a more contemporary look after a major overhaul. It's big (84 beds in 21 rooms) but you're still advised to book, especially if you want one of the twin-bedded or family rooms. Dorm £23, double £57

Royal Oak Rosthwaite, Borrowdale, B5289, 7 miles south ⓣ017687 77214, ⓦroyaloakhotel.co.uk. The hikers' favourite – B&B rooms in a traditional inn with stone-flagged bar, where a hearty lakeland dinner (you get no choice, but a vegetarian alternative is always available) is served promptly at 7pm, and a bacon-and-eggs breakfast at 8.30am. Weather conditions are posted daily, packed lunches and filled flasks supplied. Rates include dinner. **£116**

EATING AND DRINKING

Abraham's Tea Room George Fisher's, 2 Borrowdale Rd ⓣ017687 72178, ⓦgeorgefisher.co.uk. Keswick's celebrated outdoors store has a fine top-floor tearoom for warming mugs of *Glühwein*, home-made soups, big breakfasts, open sandwiches and other daily specials (£4–6.50). Mon–Fri 10am–5pm, Sat 9.30am–5pm, Sun 10.30am–4.30pm.

★ **Dog and Gun** 2 Lake Rd ⓣ017687 73463. The most welcoming pub in town is a real ale, open fire, dog-friendly kind of place. Local beers aside, the house special is the Hungarian goulash (£8.50), made every day to a recipe handed down over the years. Daily noon–11pm.

11

Lakeland Pedlar Henderson's Yard, Bell Close, off Main St ⓣ017687 74492, ⓦlakelandpedlar.co.uk. Keswick's best café serves tasty veggie food – from breakfast burritos to falafel wraps or spicy chilli (£4–8). The bread's home-made and organic, the cakes are great, while a few outdoor tables soak up the sun. Daily 9am–5pm, plus Thurs–Sat 5–9pm in school hols.

ENTERTAINMENT

There's a fair amount going on in Keswick throughout the year, including the **jazz festival** and **mountain festival** (ⓦkeswickmountainfestival.co.uk), both in May, a **beer festival** in June, and the **Keswick Agricultural Show** (Aug bank holiday).

Theatre by the Lake Lake Rd ⓣ017687 74411, ⓦtheatrebythelake.com. England's loveliest theatre hosts a full programme of drama, concerts, exhibitions, readings and talks. "Words By The Water", a literature festival, takes place here in the spring.

Honister Pass

Near the head of Borrowdale at Seatoller, the B5289 road cuts west, snaking up and over the dramatic **Honister Pass**, en route to Buttermere. At the top lie the unassuming buildings of **Honister Slate Mine** – an unexpectedly great place for daredevil adventurers with its deep mine tours and mountain activities. Come suitably clothed – it's either wet or windy up here at the best of times.

Honister Slate Mine

Honister Pass • **Visitor centre, shop and café** Daily 9am–5pm • Free **Tours** Daily 10.30am, 12.30pm & 3.30pm • £9.95, reservations essential • ⓣ017687 77230, ⓦhonister-slate-mine.co.uk • Bus #77A from Keswick

Slate has been quarried on Honister since the eighteenth century. **Honister Slate Mine**, the last remaining working slate mine in England, was rescued by local entrepreneurs in 1996 and is now operating again as a sustainable, commercial enterprise. To get an idea of what traditional mining entailed, you can don a hard hat and lamp to join one of the hugely informative guided tours, which lead you through narrow tunnels into illuminated, dripping caverns.

Via Ferrata

Daily departures from Honister Slate Mine, reservations essential • £30, £35 including zip-wire option; all-day pass including mine tour £42 or £48 including zip-wire • ⓣ017687 77714, ⓦhonister-slate-mine.co.uk • Bus #77A from Keswick

Honister features England's first **Via Ferrata** – a dramatic Alpine-style three-hour mountain climb using a fixed cableway and harness, which allows visitors to follow the old miners' route up the exposed face of Fleetwith Pike (2126ft), the peak that's right above the mines. It's terrifying and exhilarating in equal measure – though you don't need climbing experience to do it, you should check out the photos and videos on the website first to see what you're in for.

Buttermere

Ringed by peaks and crags, the tranquil waters and lakeside paths of **Buttermere** make a popular day-trip from Keswick, with the best approach being the sweeping descent into the valley from Honister Pass. There's no real village here – just a few houses and farms, a couple of hotels and a youth hostel, a café and large car park. The four-mile, round-lake stroll circling Buttermere shouldn't take more than a couple of hours; you can always detour up Scarth Gap to the peak known as **Haystacks** (1900ft) if you want more of a climb and views.

ARRIVAL AND DEPARTURE — BUTTERMERE

The direct **bus** is the #77 from Keswick via Whinlatter Pass; the #77A comes the long way around through Borrowdale via Honister Pass.

Eskdale

Eskdale is perhaps the prettiest of the unsung Lake District valleys, reached on a long and twisting drive from Ambleside, over the dramatic Hardknott Pass. It can also be accessed from the Cumbrian coast by the Ravenglass and Eskdale Railway (see p.502) – either route ends up in the heart of superb walking country around the dead-end hamlet of **BOOT**. Here, there's an old mill to explore and several local hikes, not to mention the three-mile walk or drive back out of the valley to the superbly sited **Hardknott Roman Fort** (always open; free), which commands a strategic and panoramic position. There's plenty of rustic, hideaway accommodation in Eskdale, including a great selection of old inns – if you're looking for an off-the-beaten-track stay in the rural western Lakes, with walks off the doorstep, you won't find better.

ACCOMMODATION AND EATING — ESKDALE

Boot Inn Boot ⓣ019467 23224, ⓦbootinn.co.uk. Families like the beer garden and children's areas at this cosy, traditional pub right in the middle of the hamlet, and there are also nine straightforward rooms plus bar meals (mains around £10). **£90**

Hollins Farm Eskdale, Hardknott Pass road, 200 yards east of Boot ⓣ019467 23253, ⓦhollinsfarmcampsite.co.uk. Small campsite, beautifully sited in the Esk valley, just a short walk from the railway and the valley's pubs. For camping without canvas they also have ten heated "pods" per night. Closed 2 weeks Jan, & Feb. Tent pitch from **£9**, pods **£41**

★ **Woolpack Inn** Eskdale, Hardknott Pass road, 1 mile east of Boot ⓣ019467 23230, ⓦwoolpack.co.uk. Friendly country inn, just up the road from Boot, that's had a real facelift – eight assorted B&B rooms are slowly being freshened up, while downstairs the bar has a classy urban feel, complete with leather sofas and wood-fired pizza oven. It's still strong on Cumbrian real ales, and the beer garden has lovely fell views, or you can buy local produce and a bottle of wine from their "Rainy Day Shop" and head for the hills. **£80**

Ravenglass and around

A sleepy coastal village at the estuary of three rivers, the Esk, Mite and Irt, **RAVENGLASS** is best known for being the starting point for the wonderful narrow-gauge **Ravenglass and Eskdale Railway**. It's worth taking some time to look around, though, before hopping on the train or heading out to **Muncaster Castle**, the other main local attraction. The single main street preserves a row of characterful nineteenth-century cottages facing out across the estuarine mud flats and dunes – the northern section, across the Esk, is a **nature reserve** where black-headed gulls and terns are often seen (get there by crossing over the mainline railway footbridge).

Ravenglass and Eskdale Railway

March–Oct, at least 5 trains daily (up to 15 daily in school summer hols); trains also most winter weekends, plus Christmas, New Year and Feb half-term hols • £12 return • T 01229 717171, W ravenglass-railway.co.uk

Opened in 1875 to carry ore from the Eskdale mines to the coastal railway, the 15-inch-gauge track of the **Ravenglass and Eskdale Railway** winds seven miles up through the Eskdale Valley to Dalegarth Station near Boot. The ticket lets you break your journey and get off and take a walk from one of the half-dozen stations en route; the full return journey, without a break, takes an hour and forty minutes. Another really good day out is to take your bike up on the train and cycle back from Dalegarth down the traffic-free **Eskdale Trail** (8.5 miles, 2hr; route guide available from Ravenglass or Dalegarth stations).

Muncaster Castle

A595, 1 mile east of Ravenglass • Feb half-term hols to first week of Nov; castle Mon–Fri & Sun noon–4.30pm; gardens and owl centre daily 10.30am–6pm or dusk; bird displays daily 2.30pm • £12, £9.50 without castle entrance • T 01229 717614, W muncaster.co.uk • There's a footpath (30min) from Ravenglass and parking at the castle

The **Muncaster Castle** estate, a mile east of Ravenglass, provides one of the region's best days out. Apart from the ghost-ridden rooms of the castle itself, there are also seventy acres of well-kept **grounds and gardens**, at their best in spring and autumn, as well as an entertaining **owl centre** where they breed endangered species (including England's own barn owl).

Whitehaven and around

Around twenty miles up the coast from Ravenglass, some fine Georgian houses mark out the centre of **WHITEHAVEN** – one of the few grid-planned towns in England and easily the most interesting destination on Cumbria's west coast. Whitehaven had long had a trade in coal, but its rapid economic expansion was largely due to the booming slave trade – the town spent a brief period during the eighteenth century as one of Britain's busiest ports, importing sugar, rum, spices, tea, timber and tobacco.

The Beacon

West Strand, on the harbour • Tues–Sun 10am–4.30pm • £5 • T 01946 592302, W thebeacon-whitehaven.co.uk

The best place to swot up on Whitehaven's local history is **The Beacon**, an enterprising museum on the harbour with interactive exhibitions covering a variety of themes from slaving to smuggling. You could easily spend a couple of hours here, teaching yourself how to build a ship, tie a sailor's knot or dress like a Roman centurion.

Rum Story

Lowther St • Daily 10am–4.30pm; closed 3rd week in Jan • £5.45 • T 01946 592933, W rumstory.co.uk

Housed in the eighteenth-century shop, courtyard and warehouses of the Jefferson family, the **Rum Story** museum is where you can learn about rum, the Navy, temperance and the hideousness of the slaves' Middle Passage, amongst other matters.

St Bees

Five miles south of Whitehaven, long sands lie a few hundred yards west of the coastal village of **St Bees**. The steep, sandstone cliffs of **St Bees Head** to the north are good for windy walks and birdwatching, while the headland's lighthouse marks the start of Alfred Wainwright's 190-mile **Coast-to-Coast Walk** to Robin Hood's Bay.

ARRIVAL AND DEPARTURE — WHITEHAVEN

By train From Whitehaven's train station (services to St Bees and Ravenglass, or north to Carlisle) you can walk around the harbour to The Beacon in less than 10min.

By bike Whitehaven is the start of the 140-mile C2C cycle route to Sunderland/Newcastle – a metal cut-out at the harbour marks the spot.

ACCOMMODATION

★ **Lowther House** 13 Inkerman Terrace ⓣ 01946 63169, ⓦ lowtherhouse-whitehaven.com. A highly personal, period restoration of an old Whitehaven house – there are three charming rooms (one with harbour and sea views), you're welcomed with tea and cake, and breakfast is a chatty affair around your host's kitchen table. **£90**

11

Cockermouth

There's a lot to admire about the attractive small town and market centre of **COCKERMOUTH** – impressive Georgian facades, tree-lined streets and riverside setting – and there's no shortage of local attractions, not least the logical first stop on the **Wordsworth** trail, namely the house where the future poet was born. In the smartened up Market Place (now with monthly farmers' **markets**) there are more reminders of bygone days, including a pavement plaque teaching you the basics of talking Cumbrian.

Wordsworth House

Main St • Easter–Oct Sat–Thurs 11am–5pm • £6.50, admission by timed ticket on busy days • ⓣ 01900 820884, ⓦ wordsworthhouse.org.uk

The **Wordsworth House**, where William and sister Dorothy spent their first few years, is presented as a functioning eighteenth-century home – with a costumed cook sharing recipes in the kitchen and a clerk completing the ledger with quill and ink. It's an education, in the best sense, and a really excellent visit.

Jennings Brewery

Brewery Lane • Tours July & Aug 2 daily; March–June, Sept & Oct Mon–Sat 2 daily; Nov–Feb Mon–Fri 1 daily, Sat 2 daily • £6.50 • ⓣ 0845 129 7190, ⓦ jenningsbrewery.co.uk

Follow your nose in town, after the heady smell of hops, and you're likely to stumble upon **Jennings Brewery**, near the river. Jennings have been brewers in Cockermouth since 1874 and you don't have to step far to sample their product, available in any local pub. Or you can take the ninety-minute brewery tour, which ends with a free tasting in the bar.

ACCOMMODATION — COCKERMOUTH

Old Homestead Byresteads Farm, Hundrith Hill Rd, off B5292, 2 miles southeast ⓣ 01900 822223, ⓦ byresteads .co.uk. Serious country-chic in an original farmhouse (from 1624) that's been authentically restored using traditional lime plaster, cobbles, oak and stone. Breakfast is eaten in the space where the animals were once kept, and there's a huge inglenook fireplace in the lounge. **£80**

★ **Six Castlegate** 6 Castlegate ⓣ 01900 826786, ⓦ sixcastlegate.co.uk. Period-piece house that retains its lofty Georgian proportions, impressive carved staircase and oak panelling, though the half-dozen B&B rooms are contemporary country in style. **£65**

EATING AND DRINKING

★ **Bitter End** 15 Kirkgate ⓣ 01900 828993, ⓦ bitterend.co.uk. The cosiest pub in town also contains Cumbria's smallest brewery, producing ales like "Farmers", "Cockersnoot" and "Cuddy Lugs". Food ranges from bangers

ULLSWATER LAKE SERVICES

Ullswater steamer services started in 1859, and the lake still has a year-round ferry and cruise service. The **Ullswater Navigation & Transit Company** (T 017684 82229, W ullswater-steamers.co.uk) runs boats from Glenridding to Howtown on the eastern shore (40min) and on to Pooley Bridge (20min) at the northern tip, and back again. Any one stage costs £5.80 one-way, £9.30 return, though there's also a one-day "Freedom of the Lake Pass" (£12.70). In school and summer holidays there are up to nine **daily departures** from Glenridding (basically an hourly service), down to between three and six a day at other times of the year – only Christmas Eve and Christmas Day have no sailings.

and mash to peppered tuna (most dishes £9–15). Mon–Fri & Sun noon–2.30pm & 6–11.30pm, Sat noon–11.30pm.

Merienda 7A Station St T 01900 822790, W merienda.co.uk. Bright and breezy café-bar offering breakfasts, soups, sandwiches and meze plates (£2–6). Also open Friday nights for tapas and music. Mon–Thurs & Sat 9am–5pm, Fri 9am–midnight, Sun 10am–4pm.

11

Ullswater

Wordsworth declared **Ullswater** "the happiest combination of beauty and grandeur, which any of the Lakes affords", a judgement that still holds good. At almost eight miles, it's the second longest lake in the national park, with a dramatic serpentine shape that's overlooked by soaring fells, none higher than the challenging reaches of **Helvellyn** (3114ft), the most popular of the four 3000ft mountains in Cumbria. Cruises depart from the tiny village of **Glenridding**, at the southern foot of the lake. Meanwhile, at **Gowbarrow Park**, three miles north of Glenridding, the hillside still blazes green and gold in spring, as it was doing when the Wordsworths visited in April 1802; it's thought that Dorothy's recollections of the visit in her diary inspired William to write his famous "Daffodils" poem. The car park and tearooms here mark the start of a walk up to the 70ft falls of **Aira Force** (40min return).

ARRIVAL AND INFORMATION — GLENRIDDING

By bus Buses from Penrith, Keswick and Bowness/Windermere) stop on the main road (the A592) through the village. The steamer pier is just 5min walk away on the lakeside.

National Park Information Centre In the main car park at Glenridding (daily 9.30am–5.30pm; T 017684 82414, W lake-district.gov.uk).

ACCOMMODATION AND EATING

Sharrow Bay 2 miles south of Pooley Bridge, on the Howtown road T 017684 86301, W sharrowbay.co.uk. The special-occasion place par excellence, England's first country-house hotel (in business since 1948) offers a breathtaking setting, personal service and highly refined Michelin-starred food. Needless to say, it's London prices in the country (rooms up to £310 a night, suites up to £700) but there are few places anywhere in England that compare. **£200**

Penrith and around

The nearest town to Ullswater – just four miles from the head of the lake – is **PENRITH,** whose brisk streets actually have more in common with the towns of the North Pennines than the stone villages of south Cumbria. The local building materials emphasize the geographic shift, with its deep-red buildings erected from the same rust-red sandstone used to construct **Penrith Castle** in the fourteenth century; this is now a romantic, crumbling ruin, opposite the train station. The town itself is at its best in the narrow streets, arcades and alleys off **Market Square**, and around **St Andrew's churchyard**, where the so-called "Giant's Grave" is actually a collection of pre-Norman crosses and "hogback" tombstones.

Dalemain

A592, 2 miles north of Pooley Bridge • Mon–Thurs & Sun: Easter–Oct 11.15am–4pm, gardens & tearoom 10.30am–5pm; Nov to mid-Dec & Feb–Easter gardens & tearoom only 11am–3pm • £9.50, gardens only £6.50 • ⓣ 017684 86450, ⓦ dalemain.com

Residence to the same family since 1679, the country house of **Dalemain** started life in the twelfth century as a fortified tower, but has been added to by successive generations, culminating with a Georgian facade grafted on to a largely Elizabethan house. Its grounds are gorgeous, and while there are guided tours of the house in the mornings, in the afternoon, rather remarkably, you're given the run of the public rooms, which the Hasell family still use.

Rheged

Redhills, A66, half a mile west of the M6 (junction 40) • Daily 10am–5.30pm • General admission and parking free; admission to one film £6.50, each extra film £3.50 • ⓣ 01768 868000, ⓦ rheged.com • Bus #X4/X5 from Penrith or Keswick/Cockermouth

Rheged – a Cumbrian "visitor experience", just outside Penrith – is billed as Europe's largest earth-covered building, and blends in admirably with the surrounding fells – from the main road you wouldn't know it was there. An impressive atrium-lit underground visitor centre fills you in on the region's history, and you'll also find souvenir shops, food outlets, galleries, workshops, demonstrations and play areas. The staple visit, though, is for the big-screen 3D cinema, showing family-friendly movies.

11

ARRIVAL AND DEPARTURE — PENRITH

By train Penrith train station (services from Manchester, London, Glasgow and Edinburgh) is 5min walk south of Market Square and the main street, Middlegate.

By bus The bus station is on Albert St, behind Middlegate, and has regular services to Ullswater, Keswick, Cockermouth and Carlisle.

ACCOMMODATION

Brooklands 2 Portland Place St ⓣ 01768 863395, ⓦ brooklandsguesthouse.com. A very handsome 1870s townhouse whose colour-coordinated B&B rooms have country pine furniture and small but snazzy bathrooms. **£75**

Crake Trees Manor Crosby Ravensworth, 15 miles southeast of Penrith, A6 via Shap or M6 junction 39 ⓣ 01931 715205, ⓦ craketreesmanor.co.uk. A gorgeous barn conversion B&B in the nearby Eden Valley. Rooms have slate floors, antique beds, serious showers and fluffy wrap-me-up towels; you could also consider a night in the cosy Shepherds' Hut (£70, £80 in July & Aug) in the grounds. **£95**

★ **George and Dragon Clifton** A6, 3 miles northeast of Askham ⓣ 01768 865381, ⓦ georgeanddragonclifton.co.uk. This revamped eighteenth-century inn is a class act – country-chic rooms feature big beds with brocade headboards and slate-floor bathrooms, and the informal downstairs bar and restaurant (around £25 for 3 courses) sources pretty much everything from the adjacent Lowther Estate, whether it's organic meat, farmhouse cheese, kitchen-garden veg or wild fish. **£90**

Carlisle and around

The county capital of Cumbria and its only city, **CARLISLE** is also the repository of much of the region's history, its strategic location having been fought over for more than 2000 years, since the construction of Hadrian's Wall – part of which survives at

POTTY PENRITH

Potfest (ⓦ potfest.co.uk), Europe's biggest ceramics show, takes place in Penrith over two consecutive weekends (late July/early Aug). The first is **Potfest in the Park**, with ceramics on display in marquees in front of Hutton-in-the-Forest country house, as well as larger sculptural works laid out in the lovely grounds. This is followed by the highly unusual **Potfest in the Pens**, which sees potters displaying their creations in the unlikely setting of the covered pens at Penrith's cattle market, just outside town on the A66. Here, the public can talk to the artists, learn about what inspires them and even sign up for free classes.

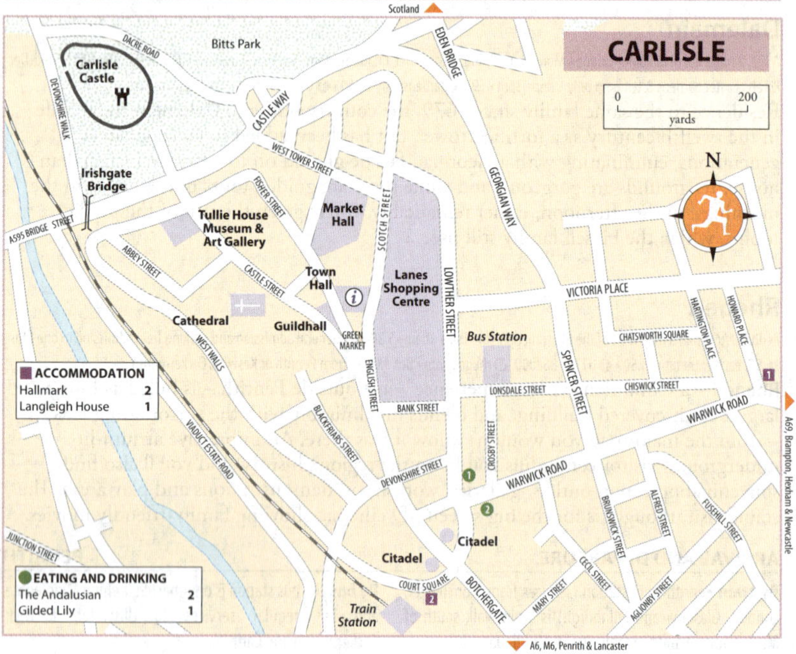

nearby **Birdoswald Fort**. The later struggle with the Scots defined the very nature of Carlisle as a border city: William Wallace was repelled in 1297 and Robert the Bruce eighteen years later, but Bonnie Prince Charlie's troops took Carlisle in 1745 after a six-day siege, holding it for six weeks before surrendering to the Duke of Cumberland. It's not surprising, then, that the city trumpets itself as "historic Carlisle", and is well worth a night's stop. Edinburgh is under two hours north, and Carlisle is also the terminus of the historic Settle to Carlisle Railway (see p.529).

Carlisle Cathedral

Castle St • Mon–Sat 7.30am–6.15pm, Sun 7.30am–5pm • Free, donation requested • ⓣ 01228 548151, ⓦ carlislecathedral.org.uk

Carlisle Cathedral which dominates the city, was founded in 1122 but embraces a considerably older heritage. Christianity was established in sixth-century Carlisle by St Kentigern (often known as St Mungo), who became the first bishop and patron saint of Glasgow. Parliamentarian troops during the Civil War caused much destruction, but there's still much to admire in the ornate fifteenth-century choir stalls and the glorious **East Window**, which features some of the finest pieces of fourteenth-century stained glass in the country.

Tullie House Museum and Art Gallery

Castle St • Mon–Sat 10am–5pm, Sun 11am–5pm (Nov–March Sun noon–5pm) • £5.20 • ⓣ 01228 618718, ⓦ tulliehouse.co.uk

The wonderful **Tullie House Museum and Art Gallery** takes an imaginative approach to Carlisle's turbulent past, with special emphasis put on life on the edge of the Roman Empire. Climbing a reconstruction of part of Hadrian's Wall, you learn about catapults and stone-throwers, while other sections elaborate on domestic life, work and burial practices.

Carlisle Castle

Bridge St • April–Sept daily 9.30am–5pm; Oct daily 10am–4pm; Nov–March Sat & Sun 10am–4pm • EH • £5 • Guided tours Easter–Oct daily; ask at the entrance • T 01228 591922

A public walkway from outside Tullie House crosses to **Carlisle Castle**. With a thousand years of military occupation of the site, it's loaded with significance – not least as the place where, in 1568, Elizabeth I kept Mary Queen of Scots as her "guest". Guided tours help bring the history to life; don't leave without climbing to the battlements for a view of the Carlisle rooftops.

Birdoswald Fort

Fifteen miles northeast of Carlisle, signposted from A69 • April–Sept daily 9.30am–5pm; Oct daily 10am–4pm; Nov–March Sat & Sun 10am–4pm • EH • £5 • T 016977 47602

One of sixteen major fortifications along Hadrian's Wall, **Birdoswald Fort** has all tiers of the Roman structure intact, while a drill hall and other buildings have been excavated. There's a tearoom and picnic area at the fort.

11

ARRIVAL AND INFORMATION — CARLISLE

By train Carlisle is on the West Coast mainline (for London–Manchester–Scotland services); there are also Cumbrian coastal services to Whitehaven, and cross-country trains to Newcastle. From the train station, it's a 5min walk to the tourist office in the city centre. The Settle to Carlisle Railway, the magnificent scenic railway through the Yorkshire Dales (W settle-carlisle.co.uk), ends its run at Carlisle – see p.505.

Destinations Lancaster (every 30min–1hr; 1hr); Newcastle (hourly; 1hr 20min–1hr 40min); Whitehaven (hourly; 1hr 10min).

Hadrian's Wall Bus The seasonal Hadrian's Wall Bus, #AD122 (see p.586) connects Carlisle with Birdoswald Fort (40min), before running on to the rest of the Hadrian's Wall sights.

Tourist office Old Town Hall, Green Market (March, April, Sept & Oct Mon–Sat 9.30am–5pm; May–Aug Mon–Sat 9.30am–5pm, Sun 10.30am–4pm; Nov–Feb Mon–Sat 10am–4pm; T 01228 625600, W discovercarlisle.co.uk).

ACCOMMODATION

Most of Carlisle's **budget rooms** are concentrated in a conservation area in the streets between Victoria Place and Warwick Road. There's also summer-only YHA accommodation in a university hall of residence near the castle.

Hallmark Court Square T 01228 531951, W hallmarkhotels.co.uk. Right outside the train station, the boutique-style *Hallmark* has a chic look, sleek rooms with big beds and a contemporary bar and brasserie. **£89**

Langleigh House 6 Howard Place T 01228 530440, W langleighhouse.co.uk. Nicely presented Victorian townhouse B&B – furnishings reflect the period, and original features abound. **£72**

EATING AND DRINKING

The Andalusian Warwick Rd T 01228 539665, W theandalusianbar.co.uk. The gorgeous tile work, carved oak bar, squishy sofas and big fireplaces make for a relaxed meet-and-greet bar, with tapas (£3–7) to share over drinks. Daily noon–midnight.

Gilded Lily 6 Lowther St T 01228 593600, W gildedlily.info. Fabulous-looking restaurant and lounge-bar serving cosmopolitan food at lunch and dinner, noodles to local lamb, burgers to piri-piri prawns (£8–15). Mon–Thurs 9am–midnight, Fri & Sat 9am–1am, Sun noon–midnight.

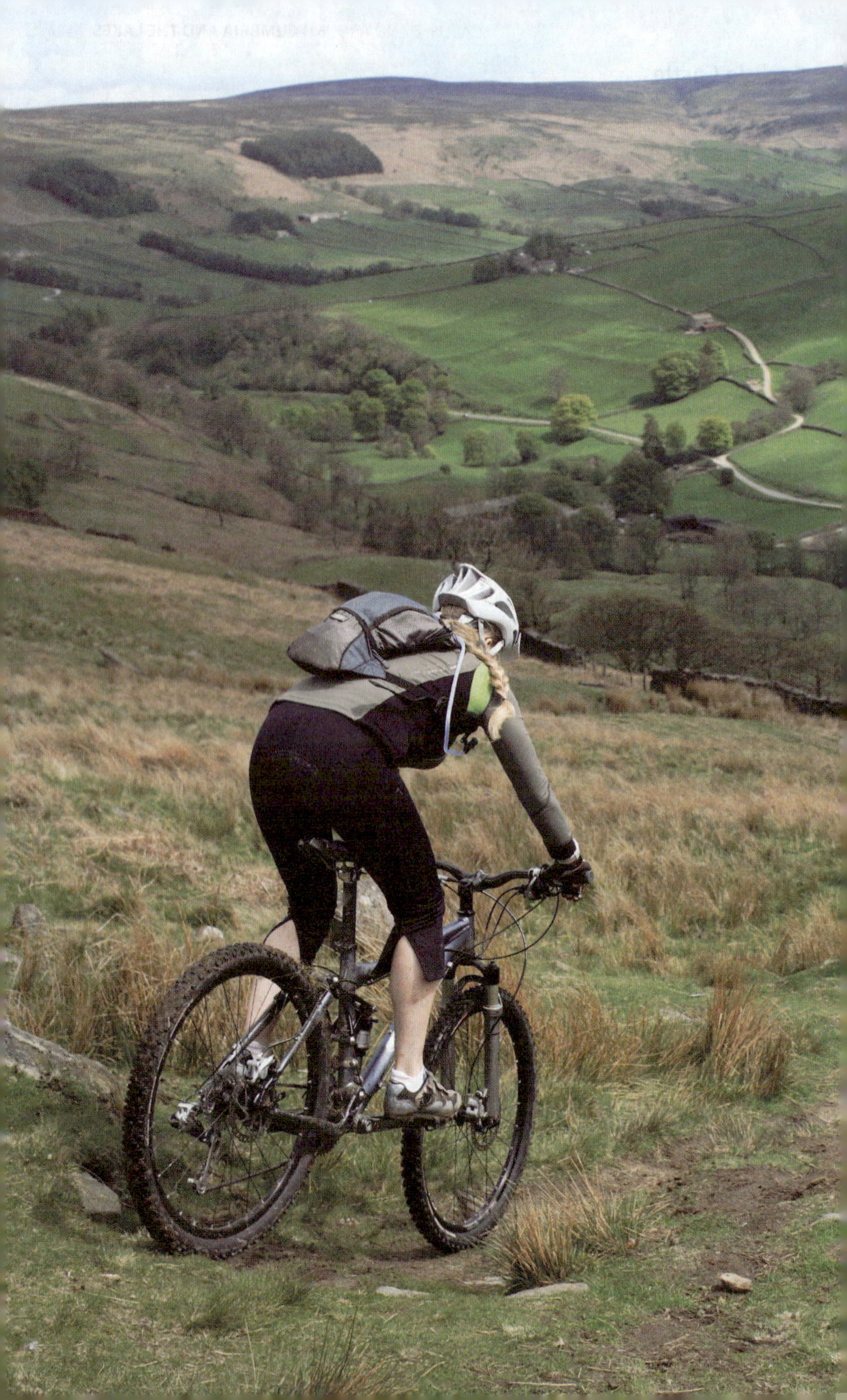

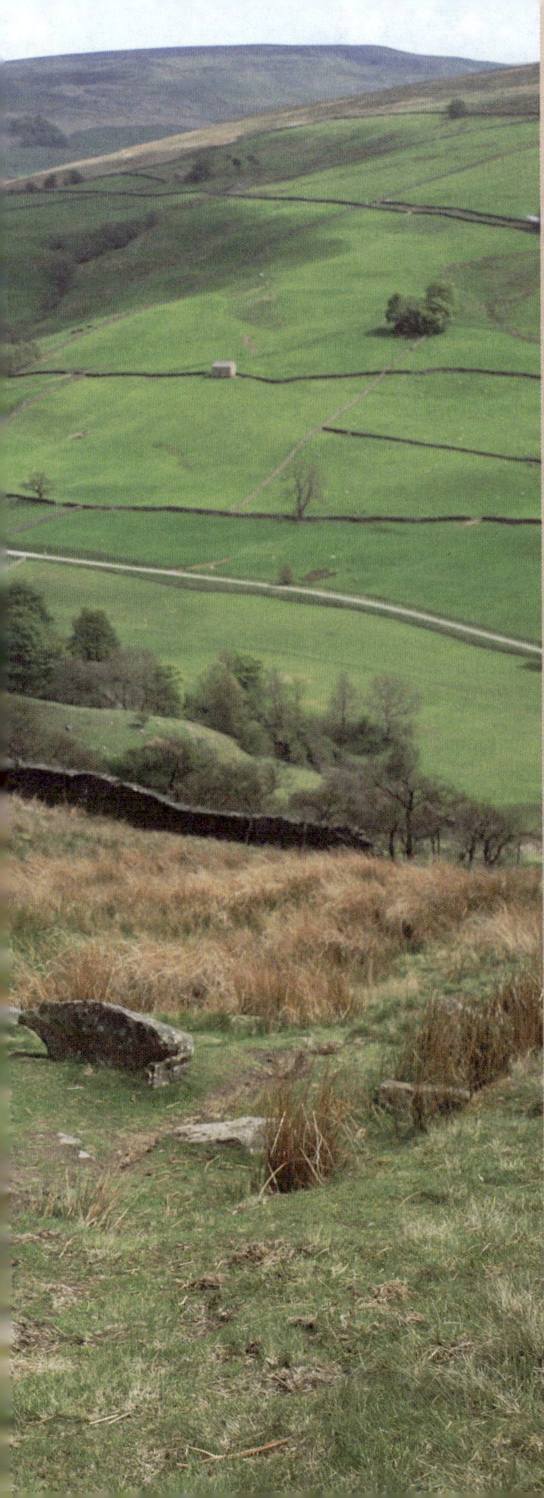

Yorkshire

514 Sheffield and around

517 Leeds and around

523 Bradford and around

524 Haworth

525 The Yorkshire Dales

533 Ripon and around

534 Harrogate

536 York and around

543 Hull

545 Beverley

546 The East Yorkshire coast

547 The North York Moors

551 The North Yorkshire coast

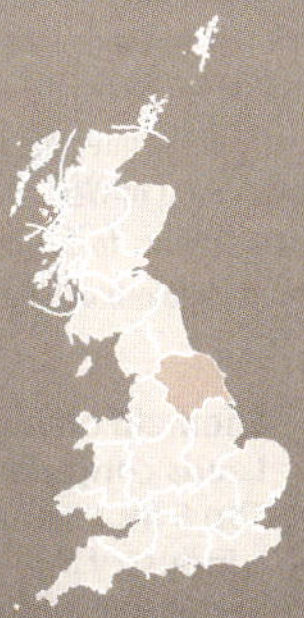

MOUNTAIN BIKING IN THE YORKSHIRE DALES

Yorkshire

It's easy to be glib about Yorkshire – to outsiders it's the archetypal "up North" with all the clichés that implies, from flat caps to grim factories. For their part, many Yorkshire locals are happy to play up to these prejudices, while nursing a secret conviction that there really is no better place in the world to live. In some respects, it's a world apart, its most distinctive characteristics – from the broad dialect to the breathtaking landscapes – deriving from a long history of settlement, invention and independence. As for Yorkshire's other boasts (the beer's better, the air's cleaner, the people are friendlier) – anyone who spends any time here will find it hard to argue with those.

The number-one destination is undoubtedly **York**, for centuries England's second city, until the Industrial Revolution created new centres of power and influence. York's mixture of medieval, Georgian and Victorian architecture is repeated in towns such as **Beverley**, **Ripon** and **Richmond**, while the Yorkshire coast, too, retains something of its erstwhile grandeur – **Bridlington** and **Scarborough** boomed in the nineteenth century and again in the postwar period, though it's in smaller resorts like **Whitby** and **Robin Hood's Bay** that the best of the coast is to be found today.

The engine of growth during the Industrial Revolution was not in the north of the county, but in the south and west, where Leeds, Bradford, Sheffield and their satellites were once the world's mightiest producers of textiles and steel. Ruthless economic logic devastated the area in the twentieth century, but a new vigour has infused South and West Yorkshire during the last decade. The city-centre transformations of **Leeds** and **Sheffield** in particular have been remarkable, while **Bradford** is a fine diversion on the way to **Haworth**, home of the Brontë sisters.

The **Yorkshire Dales**, to the northwest, form a patchwork of stone-built villages, limestone hills, serene valleys and majestic heights. The county's other National Park, the **North York Moors**, is divided into bleak upland moors and a tremendous rugged coastline between Robin Hood's Bay and Staithes.

GETTING AROUND — YORKSHIRE

By train Fast train services on the East Coast main line link York to London, Newcastle and Edinburgh. Leeds is also served by regular trains from London, and is at the centre of the integrated Metro bus and train system that covers most of West and South Yorkshire. There are also train services to Scarborough (from York) and Whitby (from Middlesbrough), while the Settle to Carlisle line, to the southern and western Yorkshire Dales, can be accessed from Leeds.

Transport passes The North Country Rover ticket (£76 for any four days in eight) covers unlimited train travel north of Leeds, Bradford and Hull and south of Newcastle and Carlisle.

Sheffield orientation p.515
Leeds concerts and festivals p.522
Top 5 museums of science and industry p.524
Settle to Carlisle railway p.529
Here for the beer p.531
Top 5 Yorkshire pubs p.549
The North York Moors railway p.551
Bram Stoker and Dracula see p.554

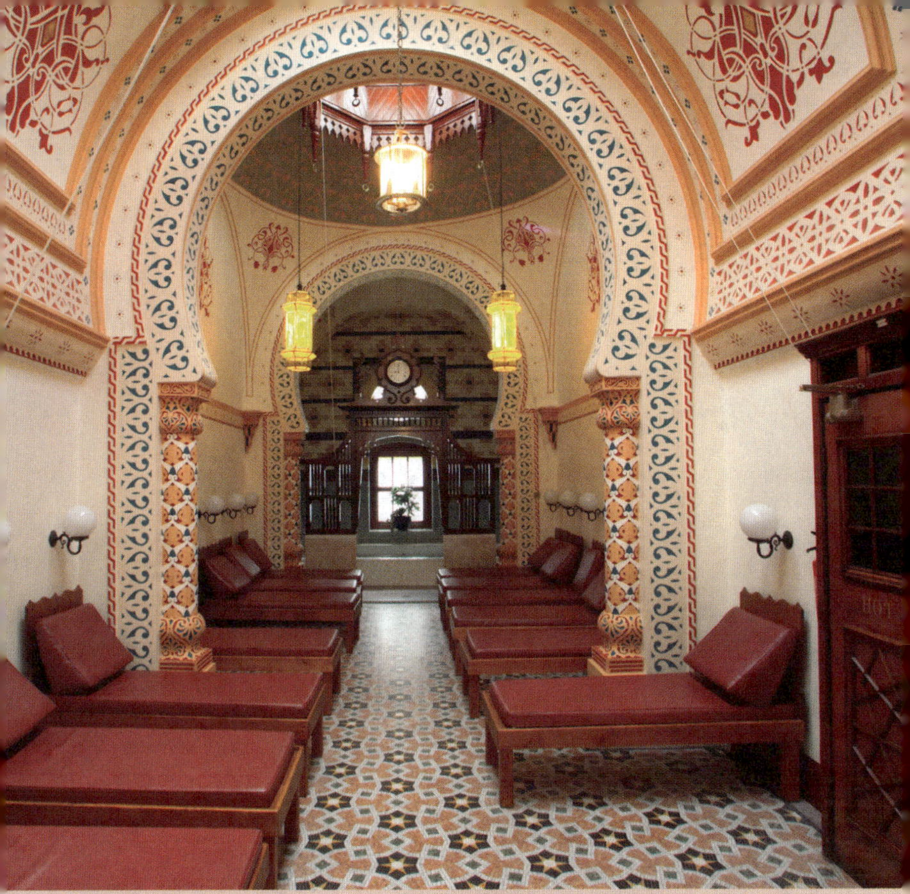

HARROGATE TURKISH BATHS

Highlights

❶ **National Coal Mining Museum** A working coal mine until the mid-1980s, now a museum; you can even head underground, if you're brave enough. **See p.520**

❷ **Bradford curry houses** Bradford's Indian restaurants provide wonderful opportunities for gastronomic exploration. **See p.524**

❸ **Haworth** Visiting the moorland home of the talented and ultimately tragic Brontë sisters is an affecting experience, despite the crowds. **See p.524**

❹ **Malham** It's a breathtaking hike from Malham village to the glorious natural amphitheatre of Malham Cove. **See p.528**

❺ **Fountains Abbey** Enjoy views of the atmospheric ruins of Fountains Abbey set in spectacular Studley Water Gardens. **See p.534**

❻ **Harrogate Turkish Baths** The late Victorian opulence of Harrogate's magnificently restored Turkish baths is a great place to get pampered. **See p.534**

❼ **Jorvik/Dig!, York** Travel through time to Viking York, then seek out new discoveries at Dig! **See p.540**

❽ **Whitby** Follow in the footsteps of Count Dracula and Captain James Cook in this spectacularly pretty former whaling port. **See p.554**

HIGHLIGHTS ARE MARKED ON THE MAP ON PP.512–513

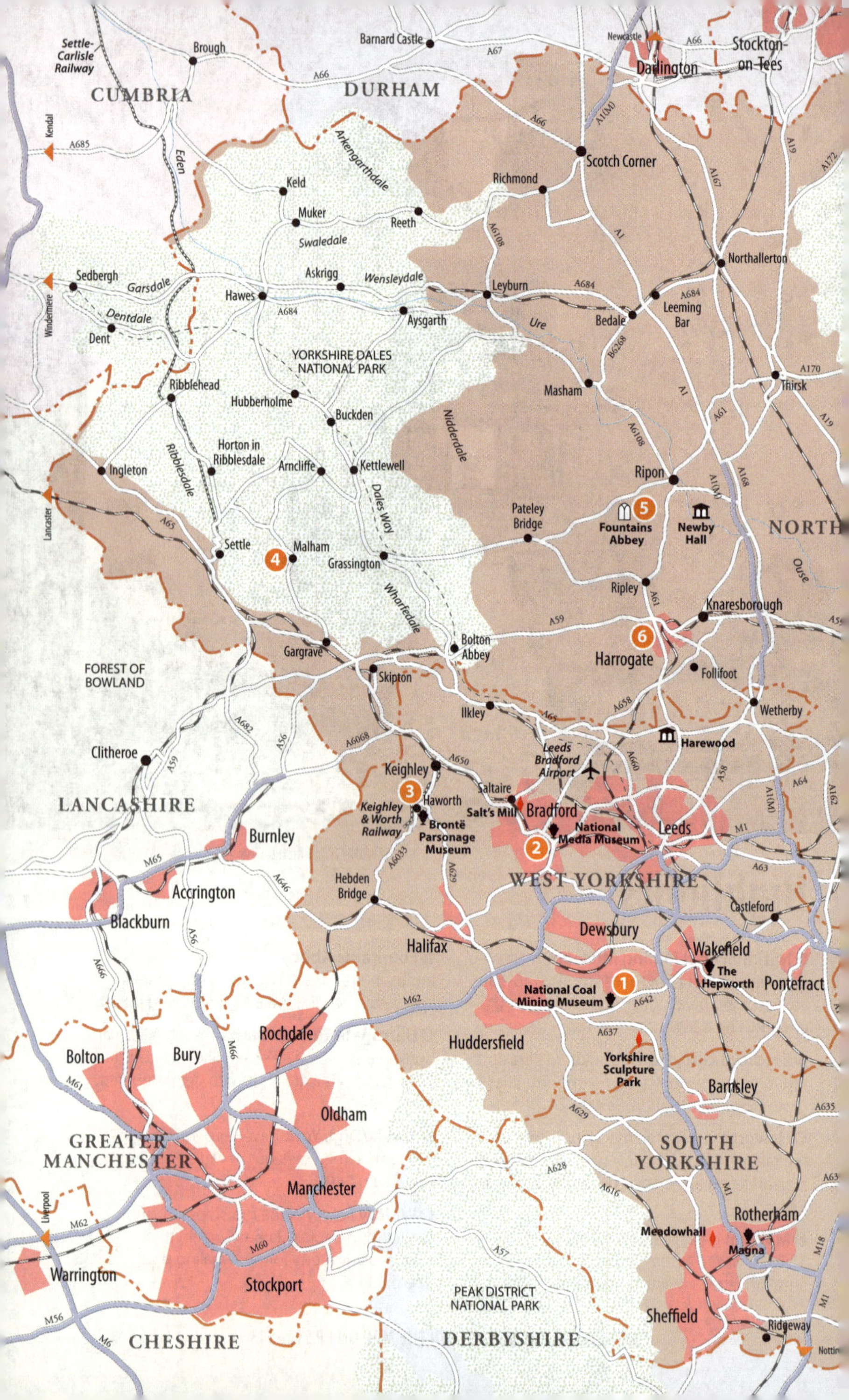

CUMBRIA
DURHAM
NORTH
LANCASHIRE
WEST YORKSHIRE
SOUTH YORKSHIRE
GREATER MANCHESTER
CHESHIRE
DERBYSHIRE
YORKSHIRE DALES NATIONAL PARK
PEAK DISTRICT NATIONAL PARK
FOREST OF BOWLAND
Settle-Carlisle Railway
Brough
Barnard Castle
Darlington
Stockton-on-Tees
Newcastle
Kendal
Windermere
Lancaster
Liverpool
Scotch Corner
Richmond
Keld
Muker
Reeth
Swaledale
Arkengarthdale
Eden
Sedbergh
Garsdale
Dentdale
Dent
Hawes
Askrigg
Wensleydale
Aysgarth
Leyburn
Ure
Bedale
Leeming Bar
Northallerton
Thirsk
Masham
Ribblehead
Hubberholme
Buckden
Nidderdale
Ingleton
Ribblesdale
Horton in Ribblesdale
Arncliffe
Kettlewell
Dales Way
Ripon
Fountains Abbey
Newby Hall
Pateley Bridge
Ouse
Settle
Malham
Grassington
Wharfedale
Ripley
Knaresborough
Harrogate
Follifoot
Bolton Abbey
Gargrave
Skipton
Ilkley
Wetherby
Harewood
Leeds Bradford Airport
Clitheroe
Keighley
Haworth
Keighley & Worth Railway
Brontë Parsonage Museum
Saltaire
Salt's Mill
Bradford
National Media Museum
Leeds
Burnley
Accrington
Blackburn
Hebden Bridge
Halifax
Dewsbury
Castleford
Wakefield
The Hepworth
Pontefract
National Coal Mining Museum
Huddersfield
Yorkshire Sculpture Park
Barnsley
Bolton
Bury
Rochdale
Oldham
Manchester
Stockport
Warrington
Rotherham
Meadowhall
Magna
Sheffield
Ridgeway
1
2
3
4
5
6

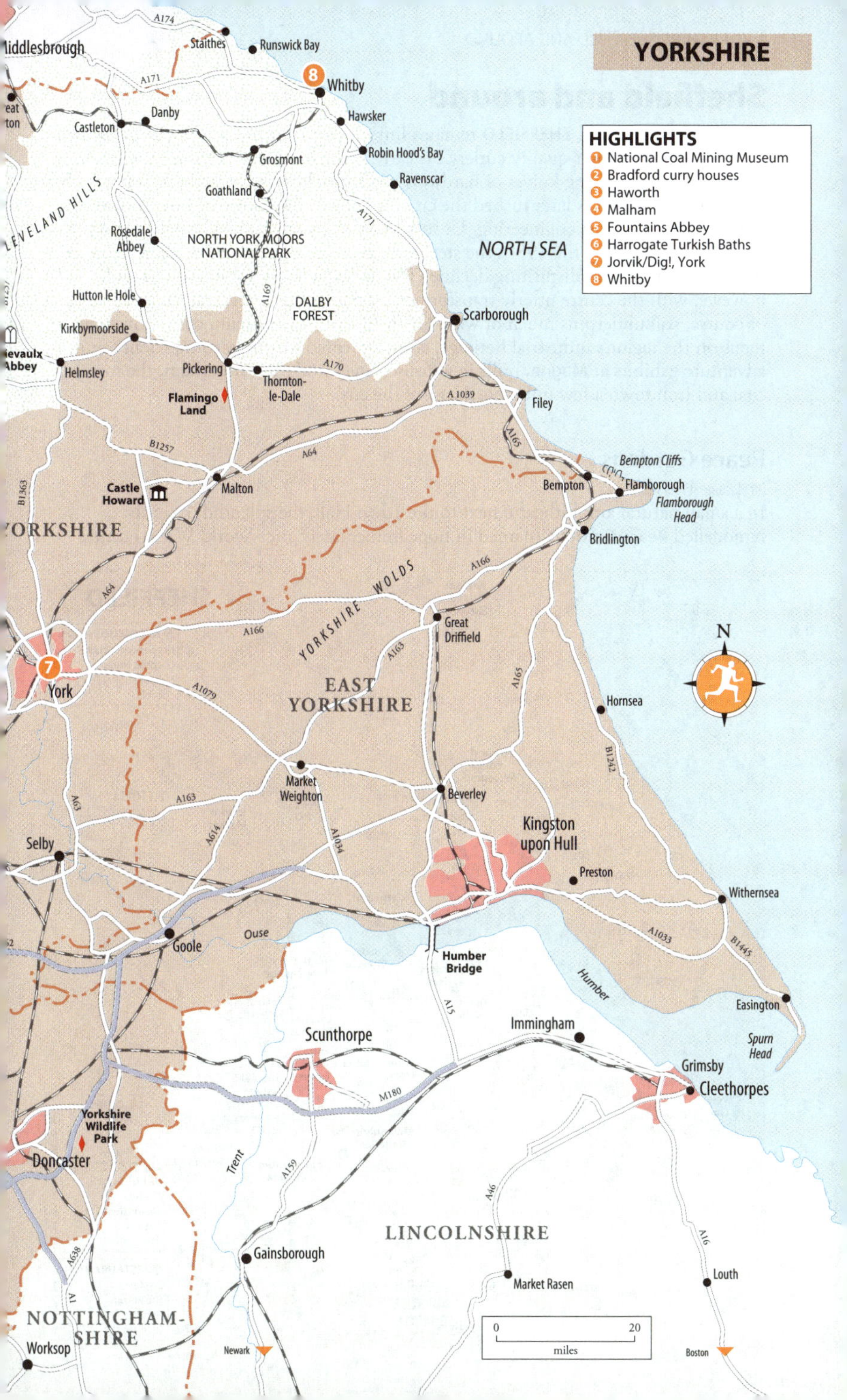
YORKSHIRE
HIGHLIGHTS
1 National Coal Mining Museum
2 Bradford curry houses
3 Haworth
4 Malham
5 Fountains Abbey
6 Harrogate Turkish Baths
7 Jorvik/Dig!, York
8 Whitby
NORTH SEA
Middlesbrough
Staithes
Runswick Bay
Whitby
Hawsker
Robin Hood's Bay
Ravenscar
Danby
Castleton
Grosmont
Goathland
CLEVELAND HILLS
Rosedale Abbey
NORTH YORK MOORS NATIONAL PARK
Hutton le Hole
DALBY FOREST
Scarborough
Kirkbymoorside
Helmsley
Pickering
Thornton-le-Dale
Flamingo Land
Filey
Castle Howard
Malton
Bempton Cliffs
Bempton
Flamborough
Flamborough Head
Bridlington
YORKSHIRE WOLDS
Great Driffield
York
EAST YORKSHIRE
Hornsea
Market Weighton
Beverley
Kingston upon Hull
Preston
Withernsea
Selby
Goole
Ouse
Humber Bridge
Humber
Easington
Spurn Head
Scunthorpe
Immingham
Grimsby
Cleethorpes
Yorkshire Wildlife Park
Doncaster
Trent
LINCOLNSHIRE
Gainsborough
Market Rasen
Louth
NOTTINGHAMSHIRE
Worksop
Newark
Boston
A174
A171
A169
A170
A1039
A165
A64
B1257
B1363
A166
A163
A1079
A63
A614
A1034
B1242
A1033
B1445
A15
M180
A159
A46
A16
A638
A1
0
20
miles
N

Sheffield and around

Yorkshire's second city, **SHEFFIELD** remains linked with its steel industry, in particular the production of high-quality cutlery. As early as the fourteenth century the carefully fashioned, hard-wearing knives of hardworking Sheffield enjoyed national repute, while technological advances later turned the city into one of the country's foremost centres of heavy and specialist engineering. Unsurprisingly, it was bombed heavily during World War II, and by the 1980s the steel industry's subsequent downturn had tipped parts of Sheffield into dispiriting decline. The subsequent revival has been rapid, however, with the centre utterly transformed by flagship architectural projects. Steel, of course, still underpins much of what Sheffield is about: museum collections tend to focus on the region's industrial heritage, complemented by the startling science-and-adventure exhibits at **Magna**, built in a disused steel works at **Rotherham**, the former coal and iron town a few miles northeast of the city.

Peace Gardens

Off Pinstone St • All year • Free

In a small natural amphitheatre next to the Town Hall, the splendid, recently remodelled **Peace Gardens** (named in hope immediately after World War II) centre

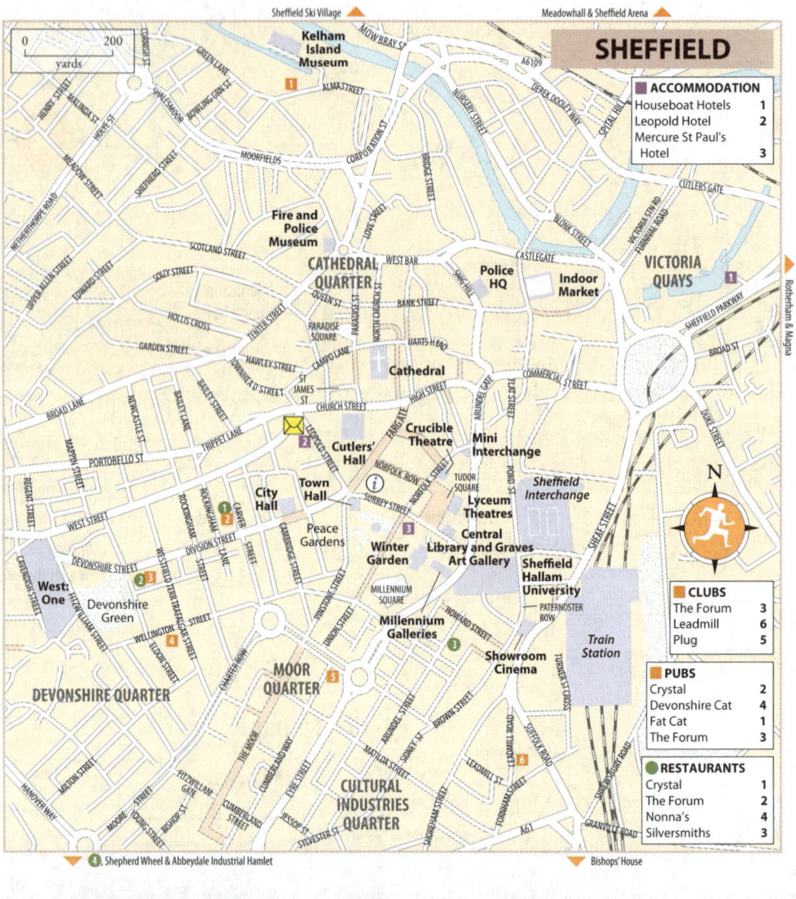

SHEFFIELD ORIENTATION

Sheffield's city centre is very compact and easily explored on foot. Southeast of the Winter Garden/Peace Gardens hub, clubs and galleries exist alongside arts and media businesses in the **Cultural Industries Quarter**. North of the stations, near the River Don, **Castlegate** has a traditional indoor **market** (closed Sun) while spruced-up warehouses and cobbled towpaths line the neighbouring canal basin, **Victoria Quays**. South of here, down Fargate and across Peace Gardens, the pedestrianized **Moor Quarter** draws in shoppers, though it's the **Devonshire Quarter**, east of the gardens and centred on Division Street, that is the trendiest shopping area. A little further out, to the northeast of the city centre and easily accessible by bus or tram, lies the huge **Meadowhall Shopping Complex**, built on the site of one of Sheffield's most famous steelworks.

on huge bronze water features inspired by Bessemer converters. It's a lively spot, especially on sunny days, when delighted kids dash in and out of the pavement-level fountains, or float paper boats down the converging ceramic-lined rills representing the rivers that gave Sheffield steel mills their power.

Winter Garden

Surrey St • Daily 8am–6pm • Free

A minute's walk east of the Peace Gardens, the stunning **Winter Garden** is a potent symbol of the city's regeneration. A twenty-first-century version of a Victorian conservatory on a huge scale (230ft feet long, and around 70ft high and wide), it's created from unvarnished, slowly weathering wood and polished glass, and filled with more than 2000 seasonally changing plants and towering trees.

Millennium Galleries

Arundel Gate • Daily 10am–4pm • Free; visiting exhibitions £4 • W sheffieldgalleries.org.uk

Backing onto the Winter Garden, the **Millennium Galleries** consist of the Metalwork Gallery, devoted to the city's world-famous cutlery industry, including an introduction to the processes involved and a collection of fine silver and stainless steel cutlery, and the diverting Ruskin Gallery. Based on the cultural collection founded by John Ruskin in 1875 to "improve" the working people of Sheffield, this includes manuscripts, minerals, watercolours and drawings all relating in some way to the natural world.

Sheffield Cathedral

Church St • W sheffield-cathedral.co.uk

The **Cathedral Church of St Peter and St Paul**, to give **Sheffield Cathedral** its full title, was a simple parish church before 1914, and subsequent attempts to give it a more dignified bearing have frankly failed. It's a mishmash of styles and changes of direction, and you'd need a PhD in ecclesiastical architecture to make any sense of it. That said, the magnificent **Shrewsbury Chapel**, at the east end of the south aisle, is worth a look. Built around 1520, it contains the tombs of the fourth and sixth Earls of Shrewsbury, whose alabaster effigies adorn their tombs.

Kelham Island Museum

Alma St • Mon–Thurs 10am–4pm, Sun 11am–4.45pm • £4 • T 0114 272 2106, W simt.co.uk

Fifteen minutes' walk north of the cathedral, the **Kelham Island Museum** reveals the breadth of the city's industrial output – cutlery, of course, but also Barnes Wallis's

22ft-long Grand Slam bomb, the Sheffield Simplex roadster, and the gigantic River Don steam engine. Many of the old machines are still working, arranged in period workshops where craftspeople show how they were used.

Weston Park Museum

Weston Bank • Mon–Fri 10am–3pm, Sat & Sun 11am–4pm • Free • T 0114 278 2600, W sheffieldgalleries.org.uk • Bus #51 or #52 from city centre, or Sheffield University tram

You can put the city's life and times into perspective a mile or so west of the centre at the **Weston Park Museum**. Here the imaginatively themed and family-friendly galleries draw together the city's extensive archeology, natural history, art and social history collections.

Magna

Sheffield Rd (A6178), Templeborough, Rotherham, just off the M1 a mile from the Meadowhall Shopping Complex • Daily 10am–5pm • £10.95, family ticket from £27.95 • T 01709 720002, W visitmagna.co.uk • Bus #69 from either Sheffield or Rotherham Interchanges, or a 15min taxi ride from Sheffield

Housed in a former steelworks building in **ROTHERHAM**, about six miles northeast of Sheffield, **Magna** is the UK's best science adventure centre. The vast internal space comfortably holds four gadget-packed **pavilions**, themed on the elements of earth, air, fire and water. You're encouraged to get your hands on a huge variety of interactive exhibits, games and machines – operating a real JCB, filling diggers and barrows, blasting a rock face or investigating a twister, for example. On the hour, everyone decamps to the main hall for the **Big Melt**, when the original arc furnace is used in a bone-shaking light and sound show that has visitors gripping the railings.

ARRIVAL AND INFORMATION — SHEFFIELD

By train Sheffield's train station is on the eastern edge of the city centre.

Destinations Leeds (every 30min; 40min–1hr 25min); London (hourly; 2hr 20min); York (every 30–60min; 1hr).

By bus Sheffield Interchange bus and coach station lies about 200 yards north of the train station.

Destinations Buses run to and from most regional and national centres – including all the main South Yorkshire towns, London, Birmingham, Liverpool and Manchester.

Tourist office 14 Norfolk Row (Mon–Fri 10am–5pm, Sat 10am–4pm; T 0114 221 1900, W sheffieldtourism.co.uk, W spinsheffield.com).

GETTING AROUND

Most local buses depart from High Street or Arundel Gate, while the **Supertram** system (W supertram.com) connects the city centre with the flagship shopping mall at Meadowhall. For fare and timetable **information**, visit the Mini Interchange travel centre on Arundel Gate, behind the Crucible Theatre (Mon–Sat 7am–7pm; T 01709 515151 or 0114 201 2675, W sypte.co.uk).

ACCOMMODATION

Houseboat Hotels Victoria Quays T 0114 232 6556 or 07974 590264, W houseboathotels.com. Something different – three moored houseboats, available by the night, with en-suite bathrooms and kitchens. You get exclusive use of your own boat, from £59 to £150 per night for one to four people. **£59**

Leopold Hotel 2 Leopold St T 0114 252 4000, W leopoldhotel.co.uk. Once a boys' grammar school, this is immaculately modernized but retains some original features. Centrally located, the hotel backs onto remodelled Leopold Square, which has no fewer than eight places to eat. **£96**

Mercure St Paul's Hotel 119 Norfolk St T 0114 278 2000, W mercure.com. Sandwiched between the Peace Gardens and Tudor Square, this modern hotel couldn't be more central. Comfortable rather than innovative, with understated (if a little anodyne) decor and fine views over the city the higher you go. **£104**

University of Sheffield T 0114 289 3500, W victoriahall.com. Self-catering student rooms (late June to mid-Sept) can be booked through the university; from **£25**

EATING

★ **The Forum** 127–129 Devonshire St ⓣ0114 272 0569, ⓦforumsheffield.co.uk. A vibrant mixture of bar, café, music venue and boutique mall, with a lively clientele who use it as a breakfast stop, lunch spot, after-work bar, dinner venue, comedy club and night club. Mon–Thurs & Sun 10am–1am, Fri & Sat 10am–2am.

★ **Nonna's** 535–541 Ecclesall Rd ⓣ0114 268 6166, ⓦnonnas.co.uk. Italian bar/restaurant with a great reputation. Restaurant reservations advised. The deli and ice-cream parlour around the corner in Hickmott Rd (closed Mon & Tues) are worth a visit, too. Mains £12–18. Mon–Thurs noon–3.30pm & 6–9.30pm, Fri & Sat noon–3.30pm & 6–10pm, Sun noon–3.30pm.

Silversmiths 111 Arundel St ⓣ0114 270 6160, ⓦsilversmiths-restaurant.com. A "kitchen nightmare" turned around in 2008 by Gordon Ramsay in his eponymous TV show, city-centre *Silversmiths* supplies top-notch Yorkshire food from locally sourced ingredients – venison sausages and pies, spinach tart with Yorkshire Blue cheese – in a 200-year-old silversmith's workshop. Tuesday is pie night (£8.50) and there's a three-course set menu from Wednesday to Saturday (£15). Reservations recommended. Tues–Thurs 5.30–11.30pm, Fri & Sat 5.30pm–midnight.

DRINKING

For the best insight into what makes Sheffield tick as a party destination take a night-time walk along **Division Street** and **West Street** where competing theme and retro bars go in and out of fashion. Locals and students also frequent the bars and pubs of **Ecclesall Road** (the so-called "golden mile"), out of the centre to the southwest.

Crystal 23–32 Carver St ⓣ0114 272 5926, ⓦcrystalbar.uk.com. A former scissor factory provides stunning premises for this airy bar-restaurant, good for drinks, food and great for a night out, with a bar until 1.30am and a patio. Tues 10.30pm–3am, Fri & Sat 9.30pm–3am.

★ **Devonshire Cat** 49 Wellington St, Devonshire Green ⓣ01142 796700, ⓦwww.devonshirecat.co.uk. Renowned ale house with wide variety of domestic and imported beers. Good pub food (£6.50–13) with drinks matched to every selection. Mon–Thurs 11.30am–11pm, Fri & St 11.30am–1am, Sun noon–10.30pm.

★ **Fat Cat** Alma St ⓣ0114 249 4801, ⓦthefatcat.co.uk. Bought by real ale enthusiasts in 1981 after a brewery sell-off, the *Fat Cat* is now a Sheffield institution offering a wide range of bottled and draft beers, ciders and country wines, and a hearty pub-grub menu (meals around £4.50). With its open fires, polished mahogany bar and etched mirrors, and its total absence of flashing gaming machines and piped music, this is pub-going as it used to be. Mon–Sat noon–midnight, Sun noon–3pm & 7–11pm.

12

NIGHTLIFE AND ENTERTAINMENT

Crucible, Lyceum and Studio Tudor Square ⓣ0114 249 6000, ⓦsheffieldtheatres.co.uk. Sheffield's theatres put on a full programme of theatre, dance, comedy and concerts. The Crucible, of course, has hosted the World Snooker Championships for thirty years. It also presents the annual Music in the Round festival of chamber music (May), and the Sheffield Children's Festival (late June or July).

Leadmill 6–7 Leadmill Rd ⓣ0114 221 2828, ⓦleadmill.co.uk. In the Cultural Industries Quarter, this place hosts live bands and DJs most nights of the week.

Plug 14 Matilda St ⓣ0114 241 3040, ⓦthe-plug.com. Mid-sized music venue featuring everything from live acoustic folk to diverse club nights, including the award-winning "Jump Around".

Sheffield City Hall Barker's Pool ⓣ0114 278 9789, ⓦsheffieldcityhall.com. Year-round programme of classical music, opera, mainstream concerts, comedy and club nights, in a magnificent, renovated concert hall. There's a bar, and dining is possible with pre-arranged VIP packages.

The Showroom 7 Paternoster Row ⓣ0114 275 7727, ⓦshowroom.org.uk. The biggest independent cinema outside London, and also a popular meeting place, with a relaxed café-restaurant on one side and a great bar on the other.

Leeds and around

Yorkshire's commercial capital, and one of the fastest-growing cities in the country, **LEEDS** has undergone a radical transformation in recent years. There's still a true northern grit to its character, and in many of its dilapidated suburbs, but the grime has been removed from the impressive Victorian buildings and the city is revelling in its new persona as a booming financial, commercial and cultural centre. The renowned **shops, restaurants, bars** and **clubs** provide one focus of a visit to contemporary Leeds – it's certainly Yorkshire's top destination for a day or two of conspicuous consumption

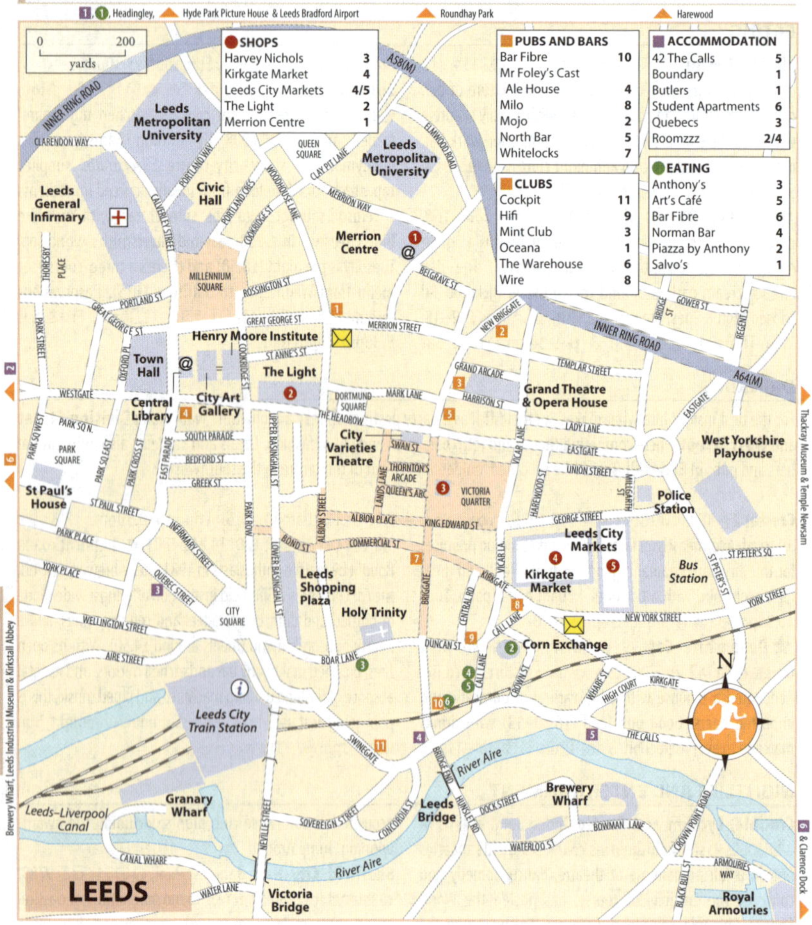

and indulgence. Museums include the impressive **Royal Armouries**, which hold the national arms and armour collection, while the **City Art Gallery** has one of the best collections of British twentieth-century art outside London. Beyond the city, a number of major attractions are accessible by bus or train, from the stately home **Harewood House** and the gritty **National Coal Mining Museum** to the stunning new **Hepworth Gallery** and the **Yorkshire Sculpture Park**.

City Art Gallery

The Headrow • Mon & Tues 10am–5pm, Wed noon–5pm, Thurs–Sat 10am–5pm, Sun 1–5pm • Free • ⓣ 0113 247 8256, ⓦ leeds.gov.uk/artgallery

Sharing a building with the Central Library, the **City Art Gallery** has an important collection of largely nineteenth- and twentieth-century paintings, prints, drawings and sculptures, some on permanent display, others rotated. There's an understandable bias towards pieces by Henry Moore and Barbara Hepworth, both former students at the Leeds School of Art; Moore's Reclining Woman lounges at the top of the steps outside the gallery.

Henry Moore Institute

The Headrow • Sun–Tues 10am–5.30pm, Wed 10am–9pm • Free • ⓦ henry-moore-fdn.co.uk

The City Art Gallery connects with the adjacent **Henry Moore Institute**, which, despite its misleading name, is devoted not to Moore himself but to temporary exhibitions of sculpture from all periods and nationalities.

Royal Armouries

Armouries Drive • Daily 10am–5pm • Free • ⓣ 0113 220 1999, ⓦ armouries.org.uk • Bus #28 from city centre

On the south side of the riverbank beckons the spectacular glass turret and gunmetal grey bulk of the **Royal Armouries**, purpose-built to house the arms and armour collection from the Tower of London. One of the best museums of its type in the world, its five enormous galleries hold beautifully displayed weapons for war, tournaments and hunting, armour and other artefacts dating from Roman times onwards. Particularly spectacular are the reconstruction of a tiger hunt; the Indian elephant armour (the heaviest armour in the world) consisting of 8500 iron plates; fabulously decorated ceremonial suits of full plate armour; a Sikh "quoit turban" which carried a blood-curdling array of throwing quoits; garrotting wires and knives; Samurai, Mongol and Indian armour and weapons; and many ornate guns, from a reconstruction of an enormously long Essex punt gun to an exquisite Tiffany-decorated Smith and Wesson .44 Magnum.

12

Thackray Museum

Beckett St • Daily 10am–5pm, last admission 3pm • £7 • ⓣ 0113 244 4343, ⓦ thackraymuseum.org • Bus #42 or #50 from the Headrow, or #4 or #49 from Kirkgate (all around 15min)

Essentially a medical history museum, and a hugely entertaining one, the **Thackray Museum**, next to St James' Hospital, has displays on subjects as diverse as the history of the hearing aid and the workings of the human intestine. It's gruesome, too, with a film of a Victorian limb amputation in a gallery called "Pain, pus and blood". Needless to say, children love it.

Temple Newsam

Off Selby Rd, 4 miles east of Leeds **House** Tues–Sun: summer 10.30am–5pm; winter 10.30am–4pm • £3.70 **Rare breeds farm** Tues–Sun: summer 10am–5pm; winter 10am–4pm • £3.30 • ⓣ 0113 264 7321, ⓦ leeds.gov.uk/templenewsam • On Sun bus #63a runs to the house from central Leeds; during the rest of the week #19 and #19a run to Colton, from where it is less than a mile's walk

The Tudor-Jacobean house of **Temple Newsam** shows many of the paintings and much of the decorative art owned by Leeds City Art Gallery. Arranged in thirty tasteful interiors, there are paintings from the sixteenth to the nineteenth centuries, furniture (including a number of Chippendale pieces), textiles and tapestries, silver, porcelain and pottery. There are over 1500 acres on the estate, which also contains Europe's largest **rare breeds farm**, where you can see four breeds of pigs, six of sheep, eight of poultry and no fewer than nine of cattle.

Harewood House

Harewood, 7 miles north of Leeds • Opening hours vary widely according to day and season; check website for full details • Freedom ticket, covering all parts of house and gardens £13, £7.50 in winter • ⓦ harewood.org • Frequent buses run to Harewood from Leeds, including the #36 (every 20min, every 30min on Sun)

Harewood House – still the home of the Earl and Countess of Harewood – is one of the UK's greatest country mansions. It was created in the mid-eighteenth century by an all-star team: designed by John Carr of York, with interiors by Robert Adam, furniture by Thomas Chippendale and paintings by Turner, Reynolds, Titian and El Greco, all sitting in beautiful grounds landscaped by Capability Brown. Tours take in the below-stairs kitchen and servants' quarters as well as innumerable galleries, halls, reception rooms and staircases, dripping with antiques and priceless art treasures, while added attractions include an adventure playground and gardens – including the famous bird garden. Numerous special-interest tours and talks on things like bee-keeping, photography and food keep things lively, with frequent special events and a number of refreshment areas. Incidentally, the village is pronounced "Harewood" as it is spelt, while the house is pronounced "Harwood".

Hepworth Gallery

Gallery Walk, Wakefield • Tues–Sat 10am–6pm, Sun 11am–5pm • Free • T 01924 247360, W hepworthwakefield.org • Train from Leeds to Wakefield Westgate (about 25min), then within walking distance of Wakefield's two railway stations, with numerous buses stopping at Doncaster Rd (5min walk) or Bridge St (next to the gallery)

Opened in May 2011, the £35million **Hepworth** is the largest new gallery to open outside London for decades. A cuboid concrete riverside building designed by Sir David Chipperfield, it has ten display areas housing a wonderful collection of Dame Barbara Hepworth's work – not only finished sculptures, but also working models in plaster and aluminium, lithographs and screen prints. You can even see her original workbench and tools. Other contemporary artists are represented, too, and a flow of new exhibits are assured by close cooperation with the Tate. There's a café and shop, and a children's playground within its pleasant surroundings.

National Coal Mining Museum

Caphouse Colliery, Overton, about 10 miles south of Leeds, halfway between Wakefield and Huddersfield (on the A642, signposted from M1) • Daily 10am–5pm; last tour 3.15pm • Free • W ncm.org.uk • Trains from Leeds to Wakefield Westgate; from the station #128 goes right past the museum, while #232 passes nearby

While the gentry enjoyed the comforts of life in grand houses like Harewood (see p.519), just a few miles away generations of Yorkshiremen sweated out a living underground. Mining is now little more than a memory in most parts of Yorkshire, but visitors can get all too vivid an idea of pit life through the ages at the excellent **National Coal Mining Museum**. Based in a former pit, Caphouse Colliery, the highlight is an underground mine tour (90min, warm clothes required; arrive early in school hols) with a former miner as your guide.

Yorkshire Sculpture Park

West Bretton, outside Wakefield, a mile from the M1 (junction 38) • Daily: summer 10am–6pm; winter 10am–5pm • Free, parking £4 • T 01924 832631, W ysp.co.uk • Train from Leeds to Wakefield Westgate, then bus #96 (Sun #435/436) – a fair bit of walking is necessary

The Yorkshire country estate at West Bretton now serves as the **Yorkshire Sculpture Park**. Trails and paths run across 500 acres of eighteenth-century parkland, past open-air "gallery spaces" for some of Britain's most famous sculptors. The two big local names represented here are Henry Moore (1898–1986), born in nearby Castleford, and his contemporary Barbara Hepworth (1903–75), from Wakefield. The **visitor centre** is the place to check on current exhibitions and pick up a map – the restaurant has great views over Moore's monumental pieces.

ARRIVAL AND INFORMATION — LEEDS

By train National and local Metro trains use Leeds Station. Destinations Bradford (every 15min; 20min); Carlisle (3–7 daily; 2hr 40min); Harrogate (every 30min; 35min); Hull (hourly; 1hr); Knaresborough (every 30min; 45min); Lancaster (4 daily; 2hr); Liverpool (hourly; 1hr 50min); London (every 30min; 2hr 20min); Manchester (every 15min; 1hr); Scarborough (every 30min–1hr; 1hr 20min); Settle (3–8 daily; 1hr); Sheffield (every 30min; 40min–1hr); Skipton (hourly; 45min); York (every 10–15min; 25min).

By bus The bus station occupies a site to the east, behind Kirkgate Market, on St Peter's St, though there's a comprehensive set of bus stops outside the rail station as well. Buses run from here to all parts of the city, the outer suburbs, the rest of West Yorkshire and, via National Express, the rest of the country.

Travel information The Metro Travel Centres at the bus and train stations have up-to-date service details for local transport; you can also call Metroline (daily 7am–10pm; T 0113 245 7676, W wymetro.com).

Leeds Visitor Centre The Arcade (Mon 10am–5.30pm, Tues–Sat 9am–5.30pm, Sun 10am–4pm; T 0113 242 5242, W leeds.gov.uk or W leedsliveitloveit.com). Good range of published material and gifts, and an accommodation booking service (T 0800 808050).

ACCOMMODATION

There's a good mix of **accommodation** in Leeds. Cheaper lodgings lie out to the northwest in the student area of Headingley, though these are a bus or taxi ride away. For **short breaks** and weekends contact the tourist office's special booking line on T 0800 808050.

42 The Calls 42 The Calls T 0113 244 0099, W 42thecalls.co.uk. Converted riverside grain mill, where rooms come with great beds and sharp bathrooms. Being next to the Centenary footbridge, it can sometimes suffer from noisy passers-by. £85

★ **Boundary** Cardigan Rd, Headingley, 1.5 miles northwest T 0113 275 7700, W boundaryhotel.co.uk. Associated with *Butlers* (see below) but slightly cheaper; some rooms have shared bath. £54

★ **Butlers** Cardigan Rd, Headingley, 1.5 miles northwest T 0113 274 4755, W butlershotel.co.uk. This hotel offers cosy, smart, traditionally furnished rooms on a suburban street; it is next to and associated with *Boundary* (see above). £69

★ **Quebecs** 9 Quebec St T 0113 244 8989, W theetoncollection.com. The ultimate city-boutique lodgings, boasting glorious Victorian oak panelling and stained glass, offset by chic rooms. Online deals can cut costs considerably. £170

Roomzzz 12 Swine Gate; also at 2 & 361 Burley Rd, T 0113 233 0400, W roomzzz.co.uk. Self-catering, one- and two-bedroom apartments in contemporary style, at three locations – Swine Gate is the most central. All come with great kitchens and widescreen TVs. Reduced rates if you book more than a week in advance. £88

Student apartments Clarence Dock T 0113 343 6100, W universallyleeds.co.uk. Self-catering rooms near the Royal Armouries, available every summer holiday (mid-July to mid-Sept). Two-night minimum stay £48, £21 a night thereafter.

12

EATING

Anthony's 19 Boar Lane T 0113 245 5922, W anthonysrestaurant.co.uk. Earthy flavours and ingredients dominate in the city's hottest restaurant, so expect monkfish ceviche, sous-vide mackerel and country-style combinations, immaculately presented. Set menus £21–45. Tues–Thurs noon–4pm & 7–9pm, Fri & Sat 7–10pm.

★ **Art's Café** 42 Call Lane T 0113 243 8243, W artscafebar.co.uk. A relaxed hangout for drinks, dinner or a lazy Sunday brunch. Mediterranean flavours dominate the well-priced menu, and the wine list is excellent. Lunch plates £6.50, à la carte £12.50 (two courses) or £15 (three courses). Mon–Fri & Sun noon–11pm, later on Sat.

Norman Bar 36 Call Lane T 0113 234 3988, W normanbar.co.uk. A boho-chic interior – from the cast-iron girders to the cuckoo clock – with a juice bar, Asian noodle/stir-fry/dim sum menu, and varied club nights. Most mains £7–10. Daily noon–late, and even later on Fri (3am) & Sat (4am).

Piazza by Anthony Corn Exchange T 0113 247 0995, W anthonysrestaurant.co.uk. Not just a restaurant – there's a bakery, patisserie, chocolatier, wine shop and cheese shop as well, all in the magnificent Corn Exchange building. Food is tasty, mainly English, with a range of unpretentious meat and fish dishes at reasonable prices. Mon–Thurs 10am–10pm, Fri & Sat 10am–10.30pm, Sun 10am–9pm.

Salvo's 115 Otley Rd, Headingley T 0113 275 5017, W salvos.co.uk. Mention pizza to Leeds locals and they'll think of *Salvo's*, though there's a classy Italian menu as well – mains from £10 – and a choice list of daily specials. It really is worth the trek out from the centre. Mon–Thurs noon–2pm & 6–10.30pm, Fri & Sat noon–2pm & 5.30–11pm.

DRINKING

The best of the city's **pubs** are the ornate Victorian ale houses in which Leeds specializes.

Bar Fibre 168 Lower Briggate T 0870 120 0888, W barfibre.com. Leeds' finest gay bar comes with plenty of attitude and an outside balcony. There's food during the day at *Café Mafiosa*, and regular alfresco parties in the courtyard outside. Mon–Wed noon–midnight, Thurs & Fri noon–5am, Sat noon–3am, Sun noon–midnight.

Mr Foley's Cask Ale House 159 The Headrow T 0113 242 9674, W mrfoleyscaskalehouse.co.uk. Super Victorian pub near the Town Hall, with several bars on different levels, draught beers listed on a blackboard with strengths and tasting notes, and bottled beers from around the world. Food is served, too, for around a fiver. Sun–Thurs 11am–11pm, Fri & Sat 11am–1am.

Milo 10–12 Call Lane ⓣ0113 245 7101. Unpretentious, intimate and offbeat bar, with DJs most evenings, ringing the changes from old soul and reggae to indie and electronica. Tues 5–11pm, Wed & Thurs 5pm–1am, Fri 5pm–2am, Sat noon–2am.

★ **Mojo** 18 Merrion St ⓣ0113 244 6387, ⓦmojobar.co.uk. A great bar with classic tunes ("music for the people" – an eclectic mix with a swerve towards soul) – and a classy drinks menu with lots of cocktails. Mon–Thurs 5pm–2am, Fri–Sun 5pm–3am.

North Bar 24 New Briggate ⓣ0113 242 4540, ⓦnorthbar.com. The city's beer specialist has a massive selection of guest beers (more Belgian than bitter) plus cold meats and cheeses to nibble on. Mon & Tues noon–1am, Wed–Sat noon–2am, Sun noon–midnight.

★ **Whitelocks** Turk's Head Yard, off Briggate ⓣ0113 245 3950. Leeds' oldest and most atmospheric pub retains its traditional decor and a good choice of beers. Mon–Sat 11am–11pm, Sun noon–6pm.

NIGHTLIFE

When the pubs close you can move on to one of the city's DJ bars or **clubs**, many of which have a nationwide reputation – not least because Leeds lets you dance until 5am or 6am most weekends. For information about **what's on**, your best bets are the fortnightly listings magazine *The Leeds Guide* (ⓦleedsguide.co.uk) or the daily *Yorkshire Evening Post*.

Cockpit Bridge House, Swinegate ⓣ0113 244 1573, ⓦthecockpit.co.uk. The city's best live music venue, plus assorted indie/new wave club nights.

Hifi 2 Central Rd ⓣ0113 242 7353, ⓦthehificlub.co.uk. Small club playing everything from Stax and Motown to hip-hop or drum 'n' bass.

12

Mint Club 8 Harrison St ⓣ0113 244 3168, ⓦthemintclub.com. Up-to-the-minute beats (there's a "no-cheese" policy), and the best chill-out space in the city.

Oceana 16–18 Woodhouse Lane ⓣ0113 243 8229, ⓦoceanaclubs.com. Choose between dance, chart, r'n'b and indie in the Venetian Grand Ballroom; 1970s and 1980s disco on Europe's largest illuminated dance floor; or bars decked out like a Parisian boudoir or ski lodge. Some comedy nights.

The Warehouse 19–21 Somers St ⓣ0113 246 8287. Recently refurbished, with a completely new sound system. House, electro and techno bring in clubbers from all over the country, especially for Saturday's Technique night.

Wire 2–8 Call Lane ⓣ0113 243 1481, ⓦwireclub.co.uk. A good indie/alternative dance/rock/electronic club associated with *Hifi* (see above) with weekly club nights and individual events.

ENTERTAINMENT

City Varieties Swan St, Briggate ⓣ0845 644 1881, ⓦcityvarieties.co.uk. One of the country's last surviving music halls, currently closed for refurbishment.

Grand Theatre and Opera House 46 New Briggate ⓣ0870 121 4901, ⓦleeds.gov.uk/grandtheatre. The regular base of Opera North (ⓦoperanorth.co.uk) and Northern Ballet (ⓦnorthernballettheatre.co.uk) also puts on a full range of theatrical productions.

Hyde Park Picture House Brudenell Rd, Headingley ⓣ0113 275 2045, ⓦhydeparkpicturehouse.co.uk. The place to come for classic cinema with independent and art-house shows alongside more mainstream films; get there on bus #56.

West Yorkshire Playhouse Quarry Hill ⓣ0113 213 7700, ⓦwyp.org.uk. The city's most innovative theatre has two stages, plus a bar, restaurant and café.

SHOPPING

Leeds is one of the best cities in which to shop outside the capital. In addition to the usual high street chains, it also has numerous independent shops, a throng of classy emporia in the beautifully restored **Victoria Quarter** (ⓦv-q.co.uk) – the "Knightsbridge of the North" – and other arcades that open off **Briggate**. Other options include the shopping and

LEEDS CONCERTS AND FESTIVALS

Temple Newsam, four miles east of the centre (see p.519) hosts numerous concerts and events, from plays to rock gigs and opera, and at Kirkstall Abbey every summer there's a **Shakespeare Festival** (ⓦbritishshakespearecompany.com/leeds) with open-air productions of the Bard's works. Roundhay Park is the other large outdoor venue for concerts, while Bramham Park, ten miles east of the city, hosts the annual **Leeds Carling Festival** (ⓦleedsfestival.com) at the end of August with rock/indie music on five stages. August bank holiday weekend heralds the **West Indian Carnival** in the Chapeltown area of Leeds.

entertainment complex of **The Light** (www.thelightleeds.co.uk), the malls that crowd the city centre – such as the **Merrion Centre** (merrioncentre.co.uk), off Merrion St – and the eight hundred traders housed in the Edwardian **Leeds City Markets** in Kirkgate.

Harvey Nichols 107–11 Briggate 0113 204 8888, harveynichols.com/leeds. Harvey Nicks, who opened their first branch outside London here in the Victoria Quarter in 1996, are the lodestone for this chi-chi shopping district. Mon–Wed 10am–6pm, Thurs 10am–8pm, Fri & Sat 10am–7pm, Sun 11am–5pm.

Kirkgate Market leedsmarket.com. The largest covered market in the north of England, housed in a superb Edwardian building. If you're after tripe, haberdashery or big knickers, this is the place to come. Mon–Sat 9am–5pm.

Bradford and around

BRADFORD has always been a working town, booming in tandem with the Industrial Revolution, when just a few decades saw it transform from a rural seat of woollen manufacture to a polluted metropolis. In its Victorian heyday it was the world's biggest producer of worsted cloth, its skyline etched black with mill chimneys, and its hills clogged with some of the foulest back-to-back houses of any northern city. A look at the Venetian-Gothic **Wool Exchange** building on Market Street, or a walk through **Little Germany**, northeast of the city centre (named for the German wool merchants who populated the area in the second half of the 1800s) provides ample evidence of the wealth of nineteenth-century Bradford.

Contemporary Bradford, perhaps the most multicultural centre in the UK outside London, is valiantly rinsing away its associations with urban decrepitude, and while it can hardly yet be compared with neighbouring Leeds as a visitor attraction, it has two must-see attractions in the **National Media Museum** and the industrial heritage site of **Saltaire**. The major annual event is the **Bradford Mela** (www.bradfordmela.org.uk), a one-day celebration of the arts, culture and food of the Indian subcontinent, held in June or July.

National Media Museum

Pictureville • Tues–Sun 10am–6pm • Free, screenings £6.95 • 0870 701 0200, nationalmediamuseum.org.uk

The main interest in the centre of Bradford is provided by the superb **National Media Museum**, which wraps itself around one of Britain's largest cinema screens showing daily **IMAX** and 3D film screenings. Exhibitions are devoted to every nuance of film and television, including topics like digital imaging, light and optics, and computer animation, with fascinating detours into the mechanics of advertising and news-gathering.

Saltaire

Three miles northwest of Bradford towards Keighley • **1853 Gallery** Mon–Fri 10am–5.30pm, Sat & Sun 10am–6pm • Free • saltsmill.org.uk • Trains run from Bradford Forster Square, or take bus #679 from the Interchange

The city's extraordinary outlying attraction of **Saltaire** was a model industrial village built by the industrialist Sir Titus Salt. Still inhabited today, the village was constructed between 1851 and 1876, and centred on **Salt's Mill**, which, larger than London's St Paul's Cathedral, was the biggest factory in the world when it opened in 1853. The mill was surrounded by schools, hospitals, parks, almshouses and some 850 homes, yet for all Salt's philanthropic vigour the scheme was highly paternalistic: of the village's 22 streets, for example, all – bar Victoria and Albert streets – were named after members of his family, and although Salt's workers and their families benefitted from far better living conditions than their contemporaries elsewhere, they certainly were expected to toe the management line. Salt's Mill remains the fulcrum of the village, the focus of which is the **1853 Gallery**, three floors given over to the world's largest retrospective collection of the works of Bradford-born **David Hockney**.

TOP 5 MUSEUMS OF SCIENCE AND INDUSTRY

Kelham Island Museum Sheffield. See p.515
Magna Rotherham. See p.516
National Coal Mining Museum Wakefield. See p.520
National Media Museum Bradford. See p.523
National Railway Museum York. See p.540

ARRIVAL AND INFORMATION — BRADFORD

By train Bradford has two train stations: Bradford Forster Square, off Forster Square, just north of the city centre, offers routes to suburbs, towns and cities to the north and west of the city, while Bradford Interchange, off Bridge St south of the city centre, serves destinations broadly south and west of the city. The two stations, and the city centre, are linked by a free city bus service (every 10min; Mon–Fri 7am–7pm, Sat 8am–5.30pm).

Destinations from Bradford Forster Square Carlisle (every 30min–1hr; 2hr 45min with changes); Ilkley (every 30min; 31min); Keighley (every 30min; 28min); Lancaster (hourly; 2hr with changes); Leeds (every 30min; 22min); Morecambe (every 30min; 2hr 24min with changes); Skipton (every 30min; 48min).

Destinations from Bradford Interchange Blackpool (hourly; 1hr 50min); Burnley (hourly; 43min); Halifax (every 15min; 12min); Leeds (every 15min; 23min); Manchester (every 30min; 1hr 20min); Todmorden (hourly; 40min).

By bus Buses, which centre on the Bradford Interchange, run to all parts of the city and the rest of West Yorkshire (Ⓦ firstgroup.com). The Interchange also has a National Express coach station.

Tourist office City Hall, Centenary Square, a 3min signposted walk from Bradford Interchange (Mon 10am–5pm, Tues–Sat 9am–5pm; Ⓣ 01274 433678, Ⓦ visitbradford.com).

12

ACCOMMODATION AND EATING

As Haworth, York and the Yorkshire Dales are all only an hour away, few visitors stay the night, but Bradford does have its share of **chain hotels**. Meanwhile, with nearly a quarter of its population having roots in south Asia, Bradford is renowned for its south Asian food shops and restaurants, and was crowned "Curry Capital of England" in 2011. The city boasts literally hundreds of **Indian** restaurants.

Akbar's 1276 Leeds Rd, Thornbury Ⓣ 01274 773311, Ⓦ akbars.co.uk. The original in a chain that now has branches across the north of England (and one in Birmingham). It's famed for the quality of its south Asian cuisine, offering a wide range of chicken, lamb and prawn curries and is hugely popular, so at weekends you may end up waiting, even when you've booked. Most dishes well under £10. Mon–Sat 5pm–midnight, Sun 2–11.30pm.

Mumtaz 386–410 Great Horton Rd Ⓣ 01274 522533, Ⓦ mumtaz.co.uk. *Mumtaz* is probably even more well regarded than *Akbar's* (and there's now another one at Clarence Dock in Leeds), with plaudits from everyone from Dawn French and Amir Khan, through Shilpa Shetty and Frank Bruno, to Queen Elizabeth II herself (or so its website claims). With its delicious Kashmiri food – a range of karahi and biryani dishes, with meat, fish and vegetarian options – and smart decor it's always busy with locals and visitors from all over the country. Remember, though – no alcohol. Expect to pay around £30 per person. Sun–Thurs 11am–midnight, Fri & Sat 11am–1am.

Haworth

Of English literary shrines, probably only Stratford sees more visitors than the quarter of a million who swarm annually into the village of **HAWORTH**, eight miles north of Bradford, to tramp the cobbles once trodden by the Brontë sisters. In summer the village's steep Main Street is lost under huge crowds, herded by multilingual signs around the various stations on the **Brontë trail**. The most popular local walk runs to **Brontë Falls** and **Bridge**, reached via West Lane (a continuation of Main Street) and a track from the village, signposted "Bronte Falls", and to **Top Withens**, a mile beyond, a ruin fancifully (and erroneously) thought to be the model for the manor, Wuthering Heights (allow 3hr for the round trip). The moorland setting beautifully evokes the flavour of the book, and to enjoy it further you could walk on another two and a half miles to **Ponden Hall**, claimed by some to be Thrushcross Grange is *Wuthering Heights*.

Brontë Parsonage Museum

Church St • Daily: summer 10am–5.30pm; winter 11am–5pm • £6.80 • ⓣ 01535 642323, ⓦ bronte.info

First stop in Haworth should be the **Brontë Parsonage Museum**, a modest Georgian house bought by Patrick Brontë in 1820 and in which he planned to bring up his family. After the tragic early loss of his wife and two eldest daughters, the surviving four children – Anne, Emily, Charlotte and their dissipated brother, Branwell – spent most of their short lives in the place, which is furnished as it was in their day, and filled with the sisters' pictures, books, manuscripts and personal treasures. The **parish church** in front of the parsonage contains the family vault; Charlotte was married here in 1854.

ARRIVAL AND INFORMATION — HAWORTH

By train The nicest way of getting to Haworth is on the steam trains of the Keighley and Worth Valley Railway (Easter week, school hols, July & Aug daily; rest of the year Sat & Sun; day rover ticket £14; ⓣ 01535 645214, ⓦ kwvr.co.uk); regular trains from Leeds or from Bradford's Forster Square Station run to Keighley, from where the steam train takes 15min to Haworth.

By bus Bus #662 from Bradford Interchange runs to Keighley (every 10min); change there for the #663, #664 (not Sun) or #665 (every 20–30min).

Tourist office Main St, on the West St fork (daily: May–Aug 9.30am–5.30pm, Wed from 10am; Sept–April 9.30am–5pm; ⓣ 01535 642329, ⓦ haworth-village.org.uk).

ACCOMMODATION AND EATING

Apothecary 86 Main St ⓣ 01535 643642, ⓦ theapothecaryguesthouse.co.uk. Traditional guesthouse opposite the church, in a seventeenth-century building with oak beams, millstone grit walls and quaint passages. The rear rooms, breakfast room and attached café have moorland views. **£55**

Weaver's 15 West Lane ⓣ 01535 643822, ⓦ weaversmallhotel.co.uk. A renowned restaurant-with-rooms, with three bedrooms in a converted row of weavers' cottages. Meals – good modern Northern cuisine using local ingredients – will set you back around £25 a head in the evening. Food served Tues–Sat noon–2pm & 6.30–9pm. **£90**

YHA Haworth A mile from the centre at Longlands Hall, Lees Lane, off the Keighley road ⓣ 0870 770 5858, ⓔ haworth@yha.org.uk. YHA hostel overlooking the village; Bradford buses stop on the main road nearby. Closed Mon–Fri Nov to mid-Feb. **£16.40**

12

The Yorkshire Dales

The **Yorkshire Dales** – "dales" from the Viking word *dalr* (valley) – form a varied upland area of limestone hills and pastoral valleys at the heart of the Pennines. Protected as a National Park, (or, in the case of Nidderdale, as an Area of Outstanding Natural Beauty), there are more than twenty main dales covering 680 square miles, crammed with opportunities for outdoor activities. Most approaches are from the south, via the superbly engineered **Settle to Carlisle Railway**, or along the main A65 road from towns such as **Skipton**, **Settle** and **Ingleton**. Southern dales like **Wharfedale** are the most visited, while neighbouring **Malhamdale** is also immensely popular due to the fascinating scenery squeezed into its narrow confines around **Malham** village. **Ribblesdale** is more sombre, its villages popular with hikers intent on tackling the famous **Three Peaks** – the mountains of Pen-y-ghent, Ingleborough and Whernside. To the northwest lies the more remote **Dentdale**, one of the least known but most beautiful of the valleys, and further north still **Wensleydale** and **Swaledale**, the latter of which rivals Dentdale as the most rewarding overall target. Both flow east, with Swaledale's lower stretches encompassing the appealing historic town of **Richmond**.

INFORMATION — THE YORKSHIRE DALES

There are useful **National Park Centres** (ⓦ yorkshiredales.org.uk) at Grassington, Aysgarth Falls, Malham, Reeth and Hawes (April–Oct daily10am–5pm; for winter hours, check with centre). For the three peaks area, a useful source of local knowledge is the **Pen-y-ghent Café** (see p.529).

GETTING AROUND

Walking The Pennine Way cuts right through the heart of the Dales, and the region is crossed by the Coast-to-Coast Walk, but the principal local route is the 84-mile Dales Way (Ⓦ dalesway.org.uk). Shorter guided walks (5–13 miles; April–Oct Sun & Bank Hol Mon) are organized by the National Park Authority and Dalesbus Ramblers (Ⓦ dalesbusramblers.org.uk).

By bike The Dales also has a network of over 500 miles of bridleways, byways and other routes for mountain bikers (Ⓦ mtbthedales.org.uk). The main touring cycle route is the circular 130-mile Yorkshire Dales Cycle Way (Ⓦ cyclethedales .org.uk), which starts and finishes in Skipton.

Public transport timetables Bus timetables (Ⓦ dalesbus .org) are available at tourist offices across the region, as are *Dales Explorer* timetable booklets, or consult Ⓦ traveldales .org.uk.

Skipton

Skipton (Anglo-Saxon for "sheep town"), the gateway to the Dales, sits on their southern edge, at the intersection of the two routes that between them cradle the National Park and Area of Outstanding Natural Beauty – the A65 to the western and the A59/61 to the eastern dales. A pleasant market town with a long history, it is defined by its **castle** and **church**, by its long, wide and sloping **High Street**, and by a **water system** that includes the Leeds and Liverpool Canal, its spur the Springs Canal and the Eller Beck.

ARRIVAL AND INFORMATION — SKIPTON

12

By train Skipton has rail services to Leeds and Bradford (every 30min–2hr), and a daily service to London. The train is by far the best way of getting to Ribblesdale/Dentdale, but it can involve a lot of walking.

By bus Buses run from Skipton up Wharfedale towards Buckden (#72, #72R and, via Bolton Abbey, #884; every 2hr), to Malhamdale (#210/211 and #883/884 and #890; every 2–3hr) and Settle (#580; hourly). Links to the rest of the Dales are more difficult, and usually involve using trains and/or changing buses.

Tourist office Coach St (Easter–Oct Mon–Sat 10am–5pm, Sun 11am–3pm; Nov–Easter Mon–Sat 10am–4pm; Ⓣ 01756 792809, Ⓦ skiptononline.co.uk.

ACCOMMODATION AND EATING

Herriot's Hotel Broughton Rd Ⓣ 01756 792781, Ⓦ herriotsforleisure.co.uk. A short walk along the canal towpath from the centre of Skipton, in a Victorian listed building, the boutique-style hotel and its restaurant, *Rhubarb*, both offer cheerful decor and lots of original features. Rooms vary in size and price, and there are frequent packages available. £85

The Woolly Sheep Inn 38 Sheep St Ⓣ 01756 700966, Ⓦ woollysheepinn.co.uk. Pleasant town centre Timothy Taylor tavern which offers a good range of pub food (from £8) along with sandwiches, steaks and pasta dishes. The nine rooms are comfortable and well furnished, though some are small. Convivial, but can be noisy. £75

Wharfedale

The River Wharfe runs south from just below Wensleydale, eventually joining the Ouse south of York. The best of **Wharfedale** starts just east of Skipton at **Bolton Abbey**, and then continues north in a broad, pastoral sweep scattered with villages as picture-perfect as any in northern England. The popular walking centre of **Grassington** is the main village.

Bolton Abbey

BOLTON ABBEY, five miles east of Skipton, is the name of a whole village rather than an abbey, a confusion compounded by the fact that the place's main monastic ruin is known as **Bolton Priory** (daily 9am–dusk; free). The priory is the starting point for several popular riverside **walks**, including a section of the **Dales Way** footpath that follows the river's west bank to take in Bolton Woods and the **Strid** (from "stride"), an extraordinary piece of white water two miles north of the abbey, where softer rock has allowed the river to funnel into a cleft just a few feet wide. Beyond the Strid, the path emerges at **Barden Bridge**, four miles from the priory, where **Barden Tower** shelters a tearoom.

ARRIVAL AND INFORMATION — BOLTON ABBEY

For the loveliest approach to Bolton Abbey, take the **Embsay and Bolton Abbey Steam Railway** – the station is a mile and a half by footpath from the priory ruins. The trains (roughly hourly in summer; rest of year Sat & Sun at least; ⊕01756 710614 or 795189, ⊕embsayboltonabbeyrailway.org.uk; £7 return) start from Embsay, 2 miles east of Skipton. Local **information** is available from the estate office (⊕01756 18009, ⊕boltonabbey.com) and an information point at **Cavendish Pavilion**, a mile north of the priory, where there's also a riverside restaurant and café.

ACCOMMODATION

Cavendish Pavilion ⊕01756 710245, ⊕cavendishpavilion.co.uk. A riverside restaurant and café a mile north of Bolton Priory serving roasts, casseroles and the like at good prices. March–Nov daily 10am–5pm; Nov–March Mon–Fri 10am–3.30pm, Sat & Sun10am–5pm.

Grassington

GRASSINGTON is the Wharfedale's main village, nine miles from Bolton Abbey. The cobbled Market Square is home to several inns, a few gift shops and, in a converted lead miner's cottage, a small **Folk Museum** (Easter–Oct Tues–Sun 2–4.30pm) filled with domestic equipment and artefacts relating to local crafts and farming.

ARRIVAL AND INFORMATION — GRASSINGTON

By bus Buses to Grassington run roughly hourly (not Sun in winter) from Skipton, and then, six times a day, on up the B6160 to Kettlewell, Starbotton and Buckden in upper Wharfedale.

National Park Centre Hebden Rd, across from the bus stop (April–Oct daily 10am–5pm; for winter hours, check with centre; ⊕01756 751690, ⊕yorkshiredales.org.uk).

12

ACCOMMODATION AND EATING

★ **Angel Barn Lodgings/Angel Inn** Hetton, 4 miles southwest of Grassington ⊕01756 730263, ⊕angelhetton.co.uk. The Dales' gastropub par excellence has five immaculate rooms and suites. Over the road in the inn, Modern British food is served either in the bar-brasserie or more formal restaurant. Brasserie: daily noon–1.45pm & 6–9.30pm; restaurant: Mon–Sat 6–9.30pm, Sun noon–1.45pm. **£140**

Ashfield House Summers Fold ⊕01756 752584, ⊕ashfieldhouse.co.uk. Lovely seventeenth-century house, off the square, with a walled garden. The owner is very knowledgeable about the area. Special room rate offers are often available. Dinner is served, mainly to guests, for £36 per person. **£96**

★ **Grassington Lodge** 8 Wood Lane ⊕01756 752518, ⊕grassingtonlodge.co.uk. A splash of contemporary style – co-ordinated fabrics, hardwood floors, Dales photographs – together with a pleasant front terrace enhance this comfortable village guesthouse. **£75**

Upper Wharfedale

KETTLEWELL (Norse for "bubbling spring") is the main centre for **upper Wharfedale**, with plenty of local B&B accommodation plus a youth hostel. It was also one of the major locations for *Calendar Girls*, the based-on-a-true-story film of doughty Yorkshire ladies who bared all for a charity calendar.

ARRIVAL AND DEPARTURE — UPPER WHARFEDALE

There are summer weekend and bank holiday **bus** services connecting the top end of Wharfedale with Hawes in Wensleydale (#800/805).

ACCOMMODATION AND EATING

Blue Bell Inn Kettlewell ⊕01756 760230 ⊕bluebellkettlewell.co.uk. Pretty seventeenth-century coaching inn that's very much a traditional pub and serves good, no-nonsense pub grub (lasagne, meat and potato pie and the like; main courses £9–14). Food served noon–5pm & 6–9pm. **£80**

Racehorses Hotel Kettlewell ⊕01756 760233 ⊕racehorseshotel.co.uk. Comfortable, recently refurbished hotel in what was once the *Blue Bell Inn*'s stables. The food is a cut above your standard bar food (gentleman's paté, for example, or rare breed belly pork); main courses start at £9. Food served noon–2pm & 6–9pm. **£80**

Malhamdale

A few miles west of Wharfedale lies **Malhamdale** (malhamdale.com), one of the National Park's most heavily visited regions, thanks to its three outstanding natural features of **Malham Cove**, **Malham Tarn** and **Gordale Scar**. All three attractions are within easy hiking distance of **Malham village**.

Malham

MALHAM village is home to barely a couple of hundred people who inhabit the huddled stone houses on either side of a bubbling river. Appearing in spectacular fashion a mile to the north, the white-walled limestone amphitheatre of **Malham Cove** rises 300ft above its surroundings. After a breath-sapping haul to the top, you are rewarded with fine views and the famous limestone pavement, an expanse of clints (slabs) and grykes (clefts) created by water seeping through weaker lines in the limestone rock. A simple walk (or summer shuttle bus ride) over the moors abruptly brings **Malham Tarn** into sight, its waterfowl protected by a nature reserve on the west bank. Meanwhile, at **Gordale Scar** (also easily approached direct from Malham village), the cliffs are if anything more spectacular than at Malham Cove. The classic circuit takes in cove, tarn and scar in a clockwise **walk from Malham** (8 miles; 3hr 30min), but you can also do it on horseback – the **Yorkshire Dales Trekking Centre** at Holme Farm in the village centre is the place to enquire about saddling up (01729 830352, ydtc.net; rides from £12).

ARRIVAL AND INFORMATION — MALHAM

12

By bus Malham village is reached by bus from Skipton (Mon–Fri year-round) or on the seasonal Malham Tarn shuttle which runs between Settle (Easter–Oct Sun & bank hols) and the National Park Centre (see below).

National Park Centre At the southern edge of the village (April–Oct daily 10am–5pm; for winter hours, check with centre; 01969 652380, yorkshiredales .org.uk).

ACCOMMODATION AND EATING

Buck Inn 01729 830 317, buckinnmalham.co.uk. Pleasant pub popular with walkers. With good, locally sourced food – especially sausages, pies and steaks (main courses £9–22) – comfortable rooms, and a relaxed attitude to muddy boots, this is the ideal base for a walking holiday. Food served daily noon–3pm & 6–9pm. **£45**

Miresfield Farm 01729 830414, miresfield-farm .com. The first house in the village, by the river, with lovely rural views. The country-pine-bedecked rooms vary in size, and there's a small campsite with toilet and shower. Breakfast available. **£64**

YHA 0845 371 9529, yha.org.uk. A purpose-built hostel that's a good bet for families and serious walkers. Open all year. Office open 7–10am & 5–10.30pm. **£18.40**

Ribblesdale

The river Ribble runs south along the western edges of the Yorkshire Dales, starting in the bleak uplands near the Ribblehead Viaduct, flowing between two of Yorkshire's highest mountains, **Ingleborough** and **Pen-y-ghent**, and through the village of **Horton in Ribblesdale** and on to **Settle**, the upper dale's principal town.

Settle

Ribblesdale, west of Malhamdale, is entered from **SETTLE**, starting point of the **Settle to Carlisle Railway** (see opposite). The small town has a typical seventeenth-century market square (market day Tues), still sporting its split-level arcaded shambles, which once housed butchers' shops, and the **Museum of North Craven Life** (Tues, Sat & Sun 10am–4.30pm; £1.80; 01524 251 388) housed in the eccentric Folly.

ARRIVAL AND INFORMATION — SETTLE

By train The train station is less than 5min walk from Market Place, down Station Rd.

By bus Regular buses connect Skipton with Settle, from where there are services (3 or 4 daily; Mon–Sat) north to

THE SETTLE TO CARLISLE RAILWAY

The 72-mile **Settle to Carlisle** line is a feat of Victorian engineering that has few equals in Britain. In particular, between Horton and Ribblehead, "**England's most scenic railway**" climbs 200ft in five miles, before crossing the famous 24-arched **Ribblehead viaduct** and disappearing into the 2629 yards of the Blea Tunnel. Meanwhile, the station at **Dent Head** is the highest, and bleakest, mainline station in England.The journey from Settle to Carlisle takes 1hr 40min, so it's easy to do the full **return trip** in one day (£18). If your time is short, ride the most dramatic section between Settle and Garsdale (30min). There are connections to Settle from Skipton (20min) and Leeds (1hr); full **timetable** details are available from National Rail Enquiries, T 0845 748 4950, or W settle-carlisle.co.uk.

Horton, and northwest to Ingleton in the western Dales. The Malham Tarn shuttle (6 daily; Easter–Oct Sat, Sun & bank hols) also runs over the tops to Malham in an hour.

Tourist office In the town hall, just off Market Place (daily 9.30am–4.30pm; T 01729 825192). They can provide hiking maps and pamphlets.

ACCOMMODATION AND EATING

The Lion Duke St T 01729 822203, W thelionsettle.co.uk. Recently refurbished throughout, the *Lion* (until recently the *Golden Lion*) has comfortable rooms (which cost around £20 more at weekends) and a wide range of locally sourced fish, meats, pies and sausages, with a fine choice of cheeses (£8.50–20). Food served daily 8am–9pm. **£80**

Ye Olde Naked Man Café Market Place T 01729 823230. For non-alcoholic drinks and good plain food this café is the best bet. Don't be put off by the twee name – the building was once an undertaker's, and the name is a reference to the old Yorkshire saying, "you bring now't into't world and you take now't out". Daily 9am–5pm (4pm on Wed).

12

Horton in Ribblesdale

The valley's only village of any size is **HORTON IN RIBBLESDALE**, a noted walking centre which is the usual starting point for the famous **Three Peaks Walk** – namely the 25-mile, 12-hour circuit of Pen-y-ghent (2273ft), Whernside (2416ft) – Yorkshire's highest point – and Ingleborough (2373ft).

INFORMATION — HORTON IN RIBBLESDALE

The *Pen-y-ghent Café* (see below) doubles as a **tourist office** and an unofficial headquarters for the **Three Peaks walk**. They operate a clocking in/clocking out system; walkers who complete the route within a 12-hr period become eligible to join the Three Peaks of Yorkshire Club. They no longer provide automatic back-up should walkers fail to return, but are happy to do so ad hoc on request. Opening hours are complicated, so phone to check.

EATING

Pen-y-ghent Café T 01729 860333. A local institution for more than forty years, not only supplying much-needed hot drinks, snacks and meals, but also local information and advice (see above). Roughly Feb half-term hols to mid-Oct Mon & Wed–Fri 9am–5.30pm, Sat 8am–6pm, Sun 8.30am–5.30pm; closed mid-Oct to Boxing Day; Jan & Feb hours vary.

The western Dales

The **western Dales** is a term of convenience for a couple of tiny dales running north from **Ingleton**, and for **Dentdale**, one of the loveliest valleys in the National Park. Ingleton has the most accommodation, but **Dent** is by far the best target for a quiet night's retreat, with a cobbled centre barely altered in centuries.

Ingleton and around

The straggling slate-grey village of **INGLETON** sits upon a ridge at the confluence of two streams, the Twiss and the Doe, whose beautifully wooded valleys are easily the area's best features. The 4.5-mile **Falls' Walk** (daily 9am–dusk; entrance fee £4; 01524 241930, ingletonwaterfallswalk.co.uk) is a lovely circular walk (2hr 30min) taking in both valleys, and providing viewing points over its waterfalls.

Just 1.5 miles out of Ingleton on the Ribblehead/Hawes road (B6255) is the entrance to the **White Scar Caves** (Feb–Oct daily 10am–5pm; Nov–Jan Sat & Sun only, weather permitting; £8.50; 01524 241244, whitescarcave.co.uk). It's worth every penny for the eighty-minute tour of dank underground chambers, contorted cave formations and glistening stalactites.

ARRIVAL AND INFORMATION — INGLETON

By bus Buses run from the tourist information centre to Lancaster in the west and Settle in the east.

Tourist information centre Community Centre car park, Main St (Easter–Sept 10am–4.30pm; 01524 241049).

ACCOMMODATION AND EATING

The Inglesport Café Main St 01524 241146. On the first floor of a hiking supplies store, this café dishes up hearty soups, and potatoes with everything. Daily, café and shop 9am–6pm.

Riverside Lodge 24 Main St 01524 241359, riversideingleton.co.uk. Clean and tidy, with eight bedrooms decorated individually (if a little fussily) and named after flowers. There's a small sauna and play room, and an optional evening meal at £16.50. **£64**

Youth Hostel Sammy Lane 0870 770 5880, ingleton@yha.org.uk. This hostel is in an attractively restored Victorian stone house, set in its own gardens, close to the village centre. Reception 7–10am & 5–11pm. **£18.50**

12

Dentdale

In the seventeenth and eighteenth centuries, **Dentdale** (dentdale.com) supported a flourishing hand-knitting industry, later ruined by mechanization. These days, the hill-farming community supplements its income through tourism and craft ventures, and in **DENT** village itself the main road soon gives way to grassy cobbles.

ARRIVAL AND DEPARTURE — DENTDALE

By train While the famous Settle to Carlisle railway (see p.529) might seem a good alternative to the bus, be warned that Dent station is over 4 miles from the village itself.

By bus Most of Dent's bus connections are with towns outside Yorkshire – Sedbergh, Kirkby Stephen and Kendal – though there is a service to Settle.

ACCOMMODATION AND EATING

George & Dragon Dent centre 01539 625256, thegeorgeanddragondent.co.uk. Opposite the fountain in the centre of the village, the *George & Dragon* is bigger and more expensive than the nearby *Sun*. Ten comfortable rooms (though some are small), good service and a convivial bar. There's an extensive menu of traditional pub food with a twist (try, for example, the "steak and t'owd tup pie") – mains cost around £10. **£85**

Wensleydale

The best known of the Dales, if only for its cheese, **Wensleydale** (wensleydale.org) is also the largest. With numerous towns and villages, the biggest and busiest being **Hawes**, it has plenty of appeal to non-walkers, too; many of its rural attractions will be familiar to devotees of the **James Herriott** books and TV series.

Hawes

HAWES is Wensleydale's chief town, main hiking centre, and home to its tourism, cheese and rope-making industries. It also claims to be Yorkshire's highest market town; it received its market charter in 1699, and the weekly Tuesday market is still going strong. Attractions include the **Dales Countryside Museum**, in the same building as the **National Park Centre** (April–Oct daily 10am–5pm; for winter hours, check with centre, see opposite; £3.50), which focuses on local trades and handicrafts, and the **Wensleydale Creamery** (daily 9am–5pm, winter hours may

HERE FOR THE BEER

If you're a beer fan, the handsome Wensleydale market town of **Masham** (pronounced Mass'm) is an essential point of pilgrimage. At **Theakston brewery** (tours daily 11am–3pm; reservations advised; ⓣ01765 680000; £6.25, ⓦtheakstons.co.uk), sited here since 1827, you can learn the arcane intricacies of the brewer's art and become familiar with the legendary Old Peculier ale. The **Black Sheep Brewery**, set up in the early 1990s by one of the Theakston family brewing team, also offers tours (daily 11am–4pm, but call for availability; £5.95; ⓣ01765 680100, ⓦblacksheepbrewery.com). Both are just a few minutes' signposted walk out of the centre.

vary; £2.50; ⓣ01969 667664, ⓦwensleydale.co.uk) on Gayle Lane, a little way south of the town centre. The first cheese in Wensleydale was made by medieval Cistercian monks from ewes' milk; after the Dissolution local farmers made a version from cows' milk which, by the 1840s, was being marketed as "Wensleydale" cheese. The Creamery doesn't make cheese every day, so call first.

ARRIVAL AND INFORMATION — HAWES

By bus Year-round public transport is provided by a combination of post and service buses from Hawes on varied routes via Bainbridge, Askrigg, Aysgarth and Castle Bolton to Leyburn (for Richmond). There are also summer weekend and bank holiday services connecting Hawes to Wharfedale (#800/805).

National Park Centre (April–Oct daily 10am–5pm; for winter hours, check with centre; ⓣ01969 666210).

12

ACCOMMODATION

There are plenty of **B&Bs** in Hawes, while all the **pubs** on and around the market square – the *Board*, *Crown*, *Fountain*, *Bull's Head* and *White Hart* – have rooms, too.

Herriot's Main St ⓣ01969 667536, ⓦherriotsinhawes.co.uk. Small, friendly hotel in an eighteenth-century building off the market square. Just six rooms – some of which have fell views. Good hearty breakfasts are cooked to order. **£75**

The Old Dairy Farm Widdale, 3 miles west of Hawes ⓣ01969 667070, ⓦolddairyfarm.com. Once the home of the original Wensleydale dairy herd, this farm offers luxurious and contemporary accommodation, with fine dining available (main courses around £15). While non-residents are welcome to dine, there are no fixed opening hours – it is essential to phone first. **£130**

EATING

Chaste Market Place ⓣ01969 667145, ⓦchastehawes.co.uk. Nice restaurant that offers good, largely locally sourced food in a relaxed atmosphere. Prices from around £8.50 (bar menu) and £12 (dinner menu). Daily 9am until late.

Herriot's Kitchen Main St ⓣ01969 667536, ⓦherriotsinhawes.co.uk. Light lunches, Yorkshire cream teas and a variety of cakes, along with tasty suppers (for which advance booking is essential) most evenings except Sunday. Daily except Mon.

Askrigg

The mantle of "Herriot country" lies heavy on **ASKRIGG**, six miles east of Hawes, as the TV series *All Creatures Great and Small* was filmed in and around the village. Nip into the *King's Arms* – a cosy old haunt with wood panelling, good beer and bar meals – and you can see stills from the TV series.

Aysgarth

The ribbon-village of **AYSGARTH**, straggling along and off the A684, sucks in Wensleydale's largest number of visitors due to its proximity to the **Aysgarth Falls**, half a mile below. A marked nature trail runs through the surrounding woodlands and there's a big car park and excellent **National Park Centre** on the north bank of the River Ure (April–Oct daily 10am–5pm; for winter hours check with centre; ⓣ01969 662910).

Bolton Castle

Feb–Oct daily 11am–5pm; restricted winter opening, call for details • £8.50, gardens only £4 • T 01969 623981, W boltoncastle.co.uk

A superb circular **walk** heads northeast from Aysgarth via the village of Castle Bolton (6 miles; 4hr), starting at Aysgarth Falls and climbing up through Thoresby, with the foursquare battlements of **Bolton Castle** visible from miles away. Completed in 1399, its Great Chamber, a few adjacent rooms and the castle gardens have been restored, and there's also a café that's a welcome spot if you've trudged up from Aysgarth.

Swaledale

Narrow and steep-sided in its upper reaches beyond the tiny village of Keld, **Swaledale** emerges rocky and rugged in its central tract around Thwaite and Muker before more typically pastoral scenery cuts in at **REETH**, the dale's main village and market centre (market day is Friday). Its desirable cottages sit around a triangular green, where you'll find a couple of pubs, a hotel, a **National Park Centre** and the **Swaledale Museum** (April–Oct daily 10.30am–5.30pm; T 01748 884118, W swaledalemuseum.org.) Downriver, the dale opens out into broad countryside and the splendid historic town of **Richmond**.

Richmond

RICHMOND is the Dales' single most tempting destination, thanks mainly to its magnificent **castle**, whose extensive walls and colossal keep cling to a precipice above the River Swale. Indeed, the entire town is an absolute gem, centred on a huge cobbled market square backed by Georgian buildings, hidden alleys and gardens. Market day is Saturday, augmented by a farmers' market on the third Saturday of the month.

12

Richmond Castle

Riverside Rd • April–Sept daily 10am–6pm; Oct–March Mon & Thurs–Sun 10am–4pm • EH • £4.60

Most of medieval Richmond sprouted around its **castle**, which, dating from around 1071, is one of the oldest Norman stone fortresses in Britain. The star turn is, without doubt, the massive **keep** – which was built between 1150 and 1180 – with its stone staircases, spacious main rooms and fine battlements. From the top, the views down into the town, across the turbulent Swale and out across the gentle countryside, are out of this world. For more splendid views, with the river roaring below, take a stroll along Castle Walk, around the outside of the curtain walls.

Richmondshire Museum

Ryder's Wynd, off the Victoria Rd roundabout at the top of King St • April–Oct daily 10.30am–4.30pm • £2.50 • W richmondshiremuseum.org.uk

For a fascinating chunk of Richmond history, visit the charming **Richmondshire Museum**, off the northern side of the market square. It's full of local treasures, covering subjects as varied as lead mining and toys through the ages, with reconstructed houses and shops recreating village life, and even the set from the TV series *All Creatures Great and Small.*

Theatre Royal

Victoria Rd • Tours mid-Feb to mid-Dec Mon–Sat 10am–4pm, on the hour • £3.50 • W georgiantheatreroyal.co.uk

Richmond's Georgian **Theatre Royal** (1788) is one of England's oldest extant theatres. It's open for both performances and tours, with a gift shop and a little bar. The theatre seats 214 people in the main body of the pit, with boxes on three sides and a gallery.

Easby Abbey

A mile southeast of the town • Daily dawn to dusk • EH • Free

A signposted walk runs along the north bank of the River Swale out to the golden stone walls of **Easby Abbey**. The evocative ruins are extensive, and in places – notably the thirteenth-century refectory – still remarkably intact.

ARRIVAL AND DEPARTURE — SWALEDALE

RICHMOND

By bus Buses stop in the market square. Bus #159 runs between Masham, Leyburn and Richmond, while bus #30 (not Sun) runs up the valley along the B6270 as far as Keld, 8 miles north of Hawes and at the crossroads of the Pennine Way and the Coast-to-Coast path.

Destinations Leyburn (hourly; 25 min); Masham (Mon–Sat hourly; 55min); Ripon (Mon–Sat hourly; 1hr 15min).

By train There are regular services into Wensleydale and Swaledale, and to Darlington, 10 miles to the northeast, on the main east-coast train line.

INFORMATION AND TOURS

RICHMOND

Tourist office Friary Gardens, Victoria Rd (summer daily 9.30am–5.30pm; winter Mon–Sat 9.30am–5.30pm; ⓣ01748 50252, ⓦrichmond.org.uk).

REETH

National Park Centre (April–Oct daily 10am–5pm; call for winter hours; ⓣ01748 84059).

ACCOMMODATION AND EATING

RICHMOND

Frenchgate Hotel 59–61 Frenchgate ⓣ01748 822087, ⓦthefrenchgate.co.uk. Georgian townhouse hotel with eight rooms and walled gardens. Its food (set menu £34) has an excellent reputation – spiced loin of Yorkshire rabbit, for example, or breast of Goosnargh duck. Restaurant closed Mon. **£118**

Frenchgate House 66 Frenchgate ⓣ01748 823421, ⓦ66frenchgate.co.uk. Three immaculately presented rooms, plus breakfast with the best – panoramic – view in town. **£82**

★ **Millgate House** Millgate ⓣ01748 823571, ⓦmillgatehouse.com. Shut the big green door of this Georgian house and enter a world of books, antiques, embroidered sheets, handmade toiletries, scrumptious breakfasts and the finest (and least precious) hosts you could wish for. No credit cards. **£110**

Rustique Finkle St ⓣ01748 821565, ⓦrustiqueyork.co.uk. The clue to *Rustique*'s ambience lies in its name – it concentrates on rustic French food and wine in a bistro setting. The atmosphere is busy and cheerful, and the food's lovely, and very reasonably priced (two courses £11.95, three for £13.95). Mon–Sat 10am–9pm.

★ **Whashton Springs** Near Whashton, 3 miles north, Ravensworth Rd ⓣ01748 822884, ⓦwhashtonsprings.co.uk. This working Dales farm offers a peaceful night in the country in rooms (in the main house or round the courtyard) filled with family furniture. **£70**

REETH

King's Arms ⓣ01748 884259, ⓦthekingsarms.com. Attractive eighteenth-century inn on the green, offering a range of meals and snacks and rooms (2-night min at the weekend). **£70**

STONESDALE MOOR

Tan Hill Inn ⓣ01833 628246, ⓦtanhillinn.com. Reputedly the highest inn in Britain (1732ft above sea level), and claims to be the highest wi-fi hotspot. It's certainly one of the most rural – you might well find sheep in the bar. The seven rooms are comfortable, and the menu covers all the old pub favourites (mains £6.50–10.50). Food served Sept–June Mon–Fri noon–2.30pm & 6.30–9.45pm, Sat & Sun noon–3pm & 6.30–9.45pm; July & Aug daily noon–9.45pm. Dorm **£25**, double **£70**

12

Ripon and around

The attractive market town of **RIPON**, eleven miles north of Harrogate, is centred upon its small **cathedral** (daily 8am–6.30pm; donation requested, ⓦriponcathedral.org.uk), which can trace its ancestry back to its foundation by St Wilfrid in 672; the original crypt below the central tower can still be reached down a stone passage. The town's other focus is its **Market Place**, linked by narrow Kirkgate to the cathedral (market day is Thursday, with a farmers' market on the third Sunday of the month). Meanwhile, three restored buildings – prison, courthouse and workhouse – show a different side of the local heritage, under the banner of the **Yorkshire Law and Order Museums** (all daily: July, Aug & school hols 11am–4pm; April–June & Oct 1–4pm; combined ticket £6; ⓦriponmuseums.co.uk). Just four miles away lies **Fountains Abbey**, the one Yorkshire monastic ruin you must see.

Fountains Abbey and Studley Royal

Four miles southwest of Ripon off the B6265 • April–Sept daily 10am–5pm; Oct, Feb & March daily 10am–4pm; Nov–Jan Sat–Thurs 10am–4pm; free guided tours of abbey April–Oct daily • NT & EH • £9 • ⓣ 01765 608888, ⓦ fountainsabbey.org.uk

It's tantalizing to imagine how the English landscape might have appeared had Henry VIII not dissolved the monasteries: **Fountains Abbey** gives a good idea of what might have been. The abbey was founded in 1133 by thirteen dissident Benedictine monks and formally adopted by the Cistercian order two years later. Within a hundred years, Fountains had become the wealthiest Cistercian foundation in England, supporting a magnificent **abbey church**. The **Perpendicular Tower**, almost 180ft high, looms over the whole ensemble, while equally grandiose in scale is the undercroft of the **Lay Brothers' Dormitory** off the cloister, a stunningly vaulted space over 300ft long that was used to store the monastery's annual harvest of fleeces. Its sheer size gives some idea of the abbey's entrepreneurial scope; some thirteen tons of wool a year were turned over, most of it sold to Venetian and Florentine merchants who toured the monasteries.

A riverside walk, marked from the visitor centre car park, takes you through Fountains Abbey to a series of ponds and ornamental gardens, harbingers of **Studley Royal** (same times as the abbey), which can also be entered via the village of Studley Roger, where there's a separate car park. This lush medley of lawns, lake, woodland and **Deer Park** was laid out in 1720 to form a setting for the abbey, and there are some scintillating views from the gardens, though it's the cascades and water gardens that command most attention.

ARRIVAL AND INFORMATION — RIPON

12

By bus The bus station (#36 from Harrogate, or Leeds) is just off Market Place.

Tourist information centre Minster Rd, opposite the cathedral (April–Oct Mon–Sat 10am–5pm, Sun 10am–1pm; Nov–March Thurs & Sat 10am–4pm; ⓣ 0845 389 0178, ⓦ visitripon.org).

ACCOMMODATION AND EATING

The Old Deanery Minster Rd ⓣ 01765 600003, ⓦ theolddeanery.co.uk. Luxurious contemporary hotel opposite the cathedral. The innovative menu (main courses from £15) features dishes such as belly of pork or pumpkin tortellini. Mon–Sat noon–2pm & 7–9pm, Sun 12.30–2.30pm. £125

Harrogate

HARROGATE – the very picture of genteel Yorkshire respectability – owes its landscaped appearance and early prosperity to the discovery of Tewit Well in 1571. This was the first of more than eighty ferrous and sulphurous springs that, by the nineteenth century, were to turn the town into one of the country's leading spas. Tours of the town should begin with the **Royal Baths**, facing Crescent Road, first opened in 1897 and now restored to their late Victorian finery. You can experience the beautiful Moorish-style interior during a session at the **Turkish Baths and Health Spa** (separate sessions for men and women; from £14; ⓣ 01423 556746). Just along Crescent Road from the Royal Baths stands the **Royal Pump Room**, built in 1842 over the sulphur well that feeds the baths. The town's earliest surviving spa building, the old Promenade Room of 1806, is just 100 yards from the Pump Room on Swan Road – now housing the **Mercer Art Gallery** (Tues–Sat 10am–5pm, Sun 2–5pm; free) and its changing fine art exhibitions.

To the southwest (entrance opposite the Royal Pump Room), the 120-acre **Valley Gardens** are a delight, while many visitors also make for the botanical gardens at **Harlow Carr** (daily 9.30am–4/6pm; £6; ⓦ rhs.org.uk), the northern showpiece of the Royal Horticultural Society. These lie 1.5 miles out, on the town's western edge – the nicest approach is to walk (30min) through the Valley Gardens and pine woods, though bus #106 (every 20min) will get you there as well.

CLOCKWISE FROM TOP LEFT LEEDS CORN EXCHANGE (P.521); CASTLE HOWARD (P.541); BEVERLEY MINSTER (P.545); WORLD OF JAMES HERRIOTT, THIRSK (P.547) >

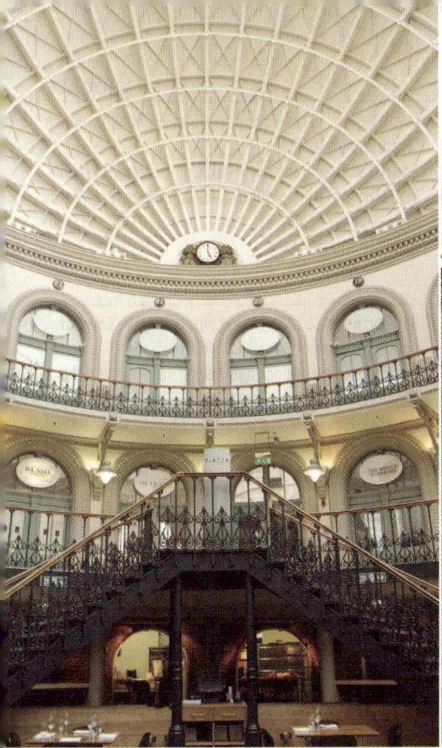
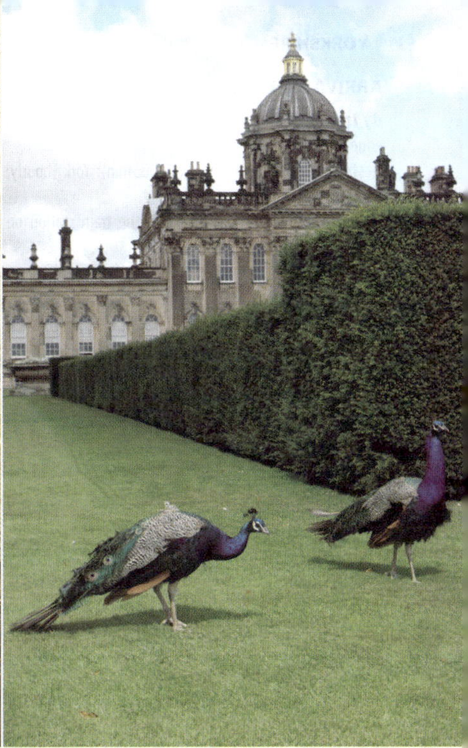
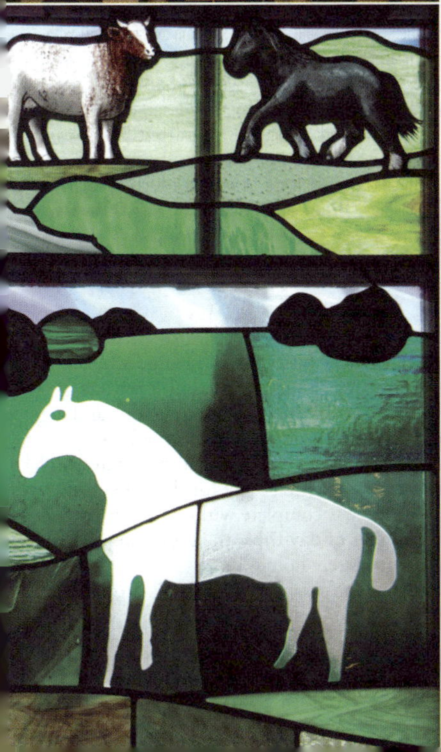
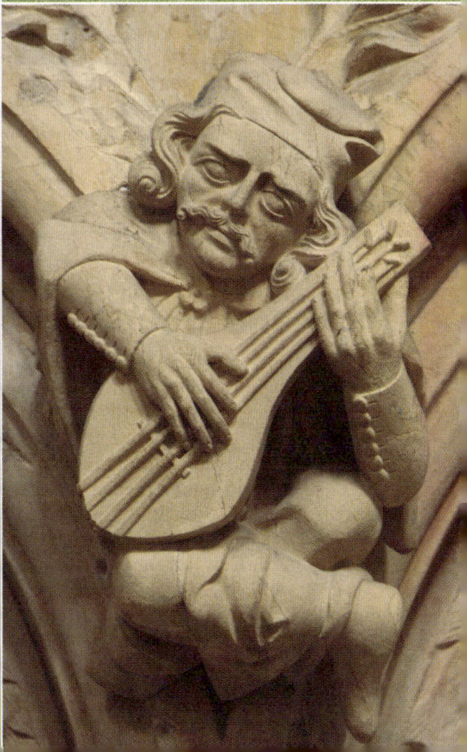

ARRIVAL AND INFORMATION — HARROGATE

By train The station is on Station Parade, on the eastern edge of the town centre.

Destinations Leeds (every 30min; 35min); York (hourly; 40min).

By bus The bus station is next to the train station on Station Parade.

Destinations Leeds (every 20–60min; 40min); Ripon (every 20min; 30min).

Tourist office In the Royal Baths on Crescent Rd (April–Sept Mon–Sat 9am–5.30pm, Sun 10am–1pm; Oct–March Mon–Fri 9am–5pm, Sat 9am–4pm; ⓣ01423 537300, ⓦenjoyharrogate.com).

ACCOMMODATION

Acorn Lodge Studley Rd ⓣ01423 525630, ⓦacornlodgeharrogate.co.uk. A guesthouse with big-hotel aspirations (luxury fittings, individual decor, jacuzzi, in-room massages) but B&B friendliness (and tariffs). Well placed for the town centre (5min). **£57**

Applewood House St George's Rd ⓣ01423 544549, ⓦapplewoodhouse.co.uk. Imposing Victorian house south of the Stray, with light, airy, spotless rooms and wonderfully personal service. A gem. **£89**

Balmoral Hotel Franklin Mount ⓣ01423 508208, ⓦbalmoralhotel.co.uk. Recently refurbished boutique hotel occupying a rather grand terrace of three Edwardian houses a few minutes' walk from the town centre. Spacious rooms, luxurious fittings and helpful service make this a winner. **£155**

Studley Hotel Swan Rd ⓣ01423 560425, ⓦstudleyhotel.co.uk. Mid-sized independent hotel with attached Thai restaurant. The attractive rooms vary in size and cost, and service is good, though the restaurant can get very busy. You can find surprisingly good rates if you shop around online. **£115**

EATING AND DRINKING

12

Betty's 1 Parliament St ⓣ01423 502746, ⓦbettys.co.uk. A Yorkshire institution with branches in several North Yorkshire towns (they've refused to open any outside the county), *Betty's* has a uniquely old-fashioned air, with a wrought-iron canopy, large bowed windows, a light airy room, waiting staff in starched linen, and baking that harks back to the past. While they are known for cakes, speciality teas and coffees, they also offer delicious breakfasts and mains – summer vegetable pancakes, for instance, or garlic and thyme chicken. No reservations, so you may have to wait. Daily 9am–9pm.

Le D2 Bower Rd ⓣ01423 502700, ⓦled2.co.uk. Quality French food and excellent service in unpretentious surroundings, and at affordable prices – two courses for £9.95 at lunch and £14.95 in the evening. Closed Sun & Mon.

The Tannin Level 5 Raglan St ⓣ01423 560595. Popular brasserie, smartly understated, with a Michelin-trained cook, super locally sourced food and an admirably simple dinner menu – starters and sweets all £5, main courses all £10, with cheaper lunch and early bird deals. Tues–Thurs noon–2pm & 5.30pm–9pm, Fri & Sat noon–2pm & 5.30pm–9.30pm.

Winter Gardens Royal Baths, Parliament St ⓣ01423 877010. For rock-bottom prices, you can't beat *Wetherspoon's*, a pub chain renowned for revitalizing interesting buildings. This is one of their best – all wrought iron, glass and ornate staircases. Mon–Wed 7am–midnight, Thurs 7am–1am, Fri & Sat 7am–2am, Sun 7am–midnight.

York and around

YORK is the North's most compelling city, a place whose history, said George VI, "is the history of England". This is perhaps overstating things a little, but it reflects the significance of a metropolis that stood at the heart of the country's religious and political life for centuries, and until the Industrial Revolution was second only to London in population and importance. These days a more provincial air hangs over the city, except in summer when it comes to feel like a heritage site for the benefit of tourists. That said, no trip to this part of the country is complete without a visit to York, and the city is also well placed for any number of **day-trips**, the most essential being to **Castle Howard**, the gem amongst English stately homes.

The **Minster** is the obvious place to start, and you won't want to miss a walk around the walls. The medieval city is at its most evocative around the streets known as Stonegate and the **Shambles**, while the earlier Viking city is entertainingly presented at **Jorvik**, perhaps the city's favourite family attraction. Standout historic buildings include the Minster's Treasurer's House, Georgian Fairfax House, the Merchant Adventurers'

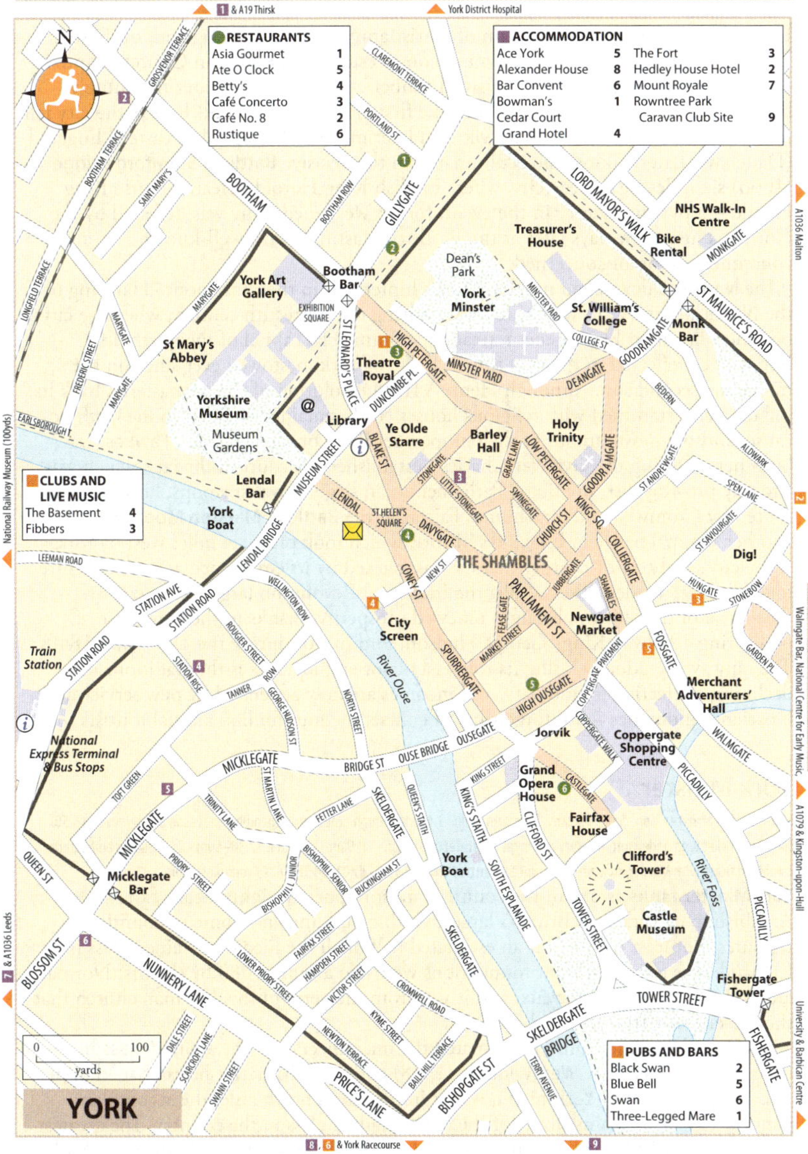

Hall, and the stark remnants of York's **Castle**. The two major museum collections are the incomparable **Castle Museum** and the **National Railway Museum** (where the appeal goes way beyond railway memorabilia), while the evocative ruins and gardens of **St Mary's Abbey** house the family-friendly **Yorkshire Museum**. Just fifteen miles away from town, and accessible by bus, **Castle Howard** is one of the nation's finest stately homes.

Brief history

An early Roman fortress of 71 AD in time became a city – Eboracum, capital of the empire's northern European territories and the base for Hadrian's northern campaigns.

Later, the city became the fulcrum of Christianity in northern England: on Easter Day in 627, Bishop Paulinus, on a mission to establish the Roman Church, baptized King Edwin of Northumbria in a small timber chapel. Six years later the church became the first minster and Paulinus the first archbishop of York. In 867 the city fell to the **Danes**, who renamed it **Jorvik**, and later made it the capital of eastern England (Danelaw). Later Viking raids culminated in the decisive **Battle of Stamford Bridge** (1066) six miles east of the city, where English King Harold defeated Norse King Harald – a pyrrhic victory in the event, for his weakened army was defeated by the Normans just a few days later at the Battle of Hastings, with well-known consequences for all concerned.

The **Normans** devastated much of York's hinterland in their infamous "Harrying of the North". Stone walls were thrown up during the thirteenth century, when the city became a favoured Plantagenet retreat and commercial capital of the north, its importance reflected in the new title of Duke of York, bestowed ever since on the monarch's second son. Although Henry VIII's Dissolution of the Monasteries took its toll on a city crammed with religious houses, York remained wedded to the Cathoic cause, and the most famous of the Gunpowder Plot conspirators, **Guy Fawkes**, was born here. During the **Civil War** Charles I established his court in the city, which was strongly pro-Royalist, inviting a Parliamentarian siege. Royalist troops, however, were routed by Cromwell and Sir Thomas Fairfax at the **Battle of Marston Moor** in 1644, another seminal battle in England's history, which took place six miles west of York.

The city's eighteenth-century history was marked by its emergence as a social centre for Yorkshire's landed elite. Whilst the Industrial Revolution largely passed it by, the arrival of the **railways** brought renewed prosperity, thanks to the enterprise of pioneering "Railway King" George Hudson, lord mayor during the 1830s and 1840s. The railway is gradually losing its role as a major employer, as is the traditional but declining confectionery industry, and incomes are now generated by new service and bioscience industries – not forgetting, of course, the four million annual tourists.

York Minster

Minster Yard • **Minster** Mon–Sat 9/9.30am–5pm, Sun noon–3.45pm, though times vary depending on season and services • £5.50, combined ticket with undercroft, treasury and crypt £9 **Undercroft** Mon–Sat 9am–5pm, Sun 12.30–5pm • £4 including audioguide, combined ticket with Minster, treasury and crypt £9 **Central tower** £5.50 • T 01904 57216, W yorkminster.org

York Minster ranks as one of the country's most important sights. Seat of the Archbishop of York, it is Britain's largest Gothic building and home to countless treasures, not least of which is an estimated half of all the medieval stained glass in England. The first significant foundations were laid around 1080 by the first Norman archbishop, Thomas of Bayeux, and it was from the germ of this Norman church that the present structure emerged.

Nothing else in the Minster can match the magnificence of the **stained glass** in the nave and transepts. The **West Window** (1338) contains distinctive heart-shaped upper tracery (the "Heart of Yorkshire"), whilst in the nave's north aisle, the second bay window (1155) contains slivers of the oldest stained glass in the country. The greatest of the church's 128 windows, however, is the majestic **East Window** (1405), at 78ft by 31ft the world's largest area of medieval stained glass in a single window.

The foundations, or **undercroft,** have been turned into a museum, while amongst precious relics in the adjoining **treasury** is the eleventh-century *Horn of Ulf*, presented to the Minster by a relative of the tide-turning King Canute. There's also access from the undercroft to the **crypt**, the spot that transmits the most powerful sense of antiquity, as it contains sections of the original eleventh-century church, including pillars with fine Romanesque capitals. Access to the undercroft, treasury and crypt is from the south transept, which is also the entrance to the **central tower**, which you can climb for rooftop views over the city.

Around the walls

The city's superb **walls** date mainly from the fourteenth century, though fragments of Norman work survive, particularly in the gates (known as "bars"), and the northern sections still follow the line of the Roman ramparts. **Monk Bar** is as good a point of access as any, tallest of the city's four main gates and host to a small **Richard III Museum** (daily: March–Oct 9am–5pm; Nov–Feb 9.30am–4pm; £2.50; ⓦrichardiiimuseum.co.uk), where you're invited to decide on the guilt or innocence of England's most maligned king. For just a taste of the walls' best section – with great views of the Minster and acres of idyllic-looking gardens – take the ten-minute stroll west from Monk Bar to Exhibition Square and **Bootham Bar**, the only gate on the site of a Roman gateway and marking the traditional northern entrance to the city. A stroll round the walls' entire two-and-a-half-mile length will also take you past the southwestern **Micklegate Bar**, long considered the most important of the gates since it marked the start of the road to London.

York Art Gallery

Exhibition Square • Daily 10am–5pm • Free • ⓦyorkartgallery.org.uk

York Art Gallery houses an extensive collection of early Italian, British and northern European paintings. The gallery puts on a year-round series of special exhibitions and events, and is noted for its collections of British studio pottery and twentieth-century British painters.

The Yorkshire Museum

12

Museum Gardens • Daily 10am–5pm • £7.50 • ⓣ01904 687687, ⓦyorkshiremuseum.org.uk

In the beautiful Museum Gardens between Exhibition Square and the river, next to the romantic ruins of St Mary's Abbey, sits the majestic Grade I listed building of the **Yorkshire Museum**, reopened in August 2010 after a nine-month, £2 million makeover. Five exciting, hands-on galleries comprise the "History of York", a multiscreen, audiovisual display; "Extinct", which covers dinosaurs and more recently extinct creatures; "Meet the People of the Empire" (Roman York); the "Power and the Glory" (Medieval York); and "Enquiry", about how archeology and science can uncover the past.

Stonegate

Stonegate is as ancient as the city itself: originally the Via Praetoria of Roman York, it's now paved with thick flags of York stone, which were once carried along here to build the Minster (hence the name). The Tudor buildings that line it retain their considerable charm – **Ye Olde Starre** at no. 40, one of York's original inns, is on every tourist itinerary (you can't miss the sign straddling the street).

Barley Hall

Off Stonegate • Daily 10am–5pm (4pm In winter) • £4.95 • ⓦbarleyhall.org.uk

Step through an alley known as Coffee Yard (by the *Olde Starre*) to find **Barley Hall**, a fine restoration of a late medieval townhouse with a lively museum where you can learn about fifteenth-century life by, among other things, playing period games and trying on costumes.

The Shambles

The **Shambles** could be taken as the epitome of medieval York. Almost impossibly narrow and lined with perilously leaning timber-framed houses, it was the home of York's butchers (the word "shambles" derives from the Old English for slaughterhouse) – old meat hooks still adorn the odd house.

Jorvik

Coppergate • Daily: Easter–Oct 10am–5pm; Nov–Easter 10am–4pm • £9.25, joint ticket with Dig! £11.20 • ⓣ 01904 43402, ⓦ vikingjorvik.com

The city's blockbuster historic exhibit is **Jorvik**, located by the Coppergate shopping centre. Propelling visitors in "time capsules" on a ride through the tenth-century city of York, the museum presents not only the sights but also the sounds and even the smells of a riverside Viking city. Excavations of Coppergate in 1976 uncovered a real Viking settlement, now largely buried beneath the shopping centre outside. But at Jorvik you can see how the unearthed artefacts were used, and watch live-action domestic scenes on actual Viking-age streets, with constipated villagers, axe-fighting and other singular attractions.

Dig!

St Saviourgate • Daily 10am–5pm • £5.50, joint ticket with Jorvik £11.20; pre-booking advised • ⓦ vikingjorvik.com

Where Jorvik shows what was unearthed at Coppergate, the associated attraction that is **Dig!** illustrates the science involved. Housed five minutes' walk away from the museum, in the medieval church of St Saviour, on St Savioursgate, a simulated dig allows you to take part in a range of excavations in the company of archeologists, using authentic tools and methods. Tours (£1) to visit **Dig Hungate**, York's latest major archeological excavation, start from here.

12

Clifford's Tower

Tower St • Daily 10am–6pm • EH • £3.90 • ⓦ cliffordstower.com

There's precious little left of **York Castle**, one of two established by William the Conqueror. Only the perilously leaning **Clifford's Tower** remains, a stark stone keep built between 1245 and 1262.

Castle Museum

Eye of York • Daily 9.30–5pm • £8.50 • ⓦ yorkcastlemuseum.org.uk

Housed in what was once a couple of prisons, displays in the **Castle Museum** begin with a series of period rooms from the seventeenth century to the 1980s. There's a large room devoted to Victorian attitudes to birth, marriage and death, followed by a wonderful reconstruction of the sights and sounds of York's Kirkgate during the final years of the nineteenth century, often staffed by people dressed in authentic costume. There are displays, too, of period kitchens – who'd have thought that state-of-the-art equipment from the 1980s could look quite so out-of-date – hygiene, costume through the ages, toys and World War II. There's also a superb re-creation of the fashion, music and news stories of the 1960s. Finally, the cells in the basement of the prison building contain an affecting series of real-life stories, told by video recordings of actors projected onto cell walls, gleaned from the prison's records.

The National Railway Museum

Leeman Rd, a 10min walk from the train station • Daily 10am–6pm • Free • ⓦ nrm.org.uk • Tourist "train" (Easter–Oct; every 30min 11.15am–4.15pm) from Duncombe Place, near the Minster

The **National Railway Museum** is a must if you have even the slightest interest in railways, history, engineering or Victoriana. The Great Hall alone features some fifty restored locomotives dating from 1829 onwards, among them the *Mallard*, at 126mph the world's fastest steam engine. The museum has one of the world's great engines – the *Flying Scotsman* – which, after a seemingly interminable overhaul, should be on display in the Great Hall from 2012 (check for updates at the museum or consult ⓦ nrm.org.uk/flyingscotsman).

Castle Howard

Fifteen miles northeast of York off the A64 • Late March to late Oct & late Nov to mid-Dec; house daily 11am–4pm, grounds 10am–5.30pm; grounds also open Jan to late March, Nov & mid-Dec • £13; grounds only £8.50 • Ⓣ 01653 648333, Ⓦ castlehoward.co.uk • The summer Moorsbus (see p.547) comes out here from Helmsley, while some Yorkshire Coastliner buses run from York, Malton or Pickering. You can also take a bus tour from York

Immersed in the deep countryside of the Howardian Hills, **Castle Howard** is the seat of one of England's leading aristocratic families and among the country's grandest stately homes. The grounds especially are worth visiting, and you could easily spend the best part of a day here. The colossal main house was designed by **Sir John Vanbrugh** in 1699 and was almost forty years in the making – remarkable enough, even were it not for the fact that Vanbrugh was, at the start of the commission at least, best known as a playwright and had no formal architectural training. Shrewdly, Vanbrugh recognized his limitations and called upon **Nicholas Hawksmoor**, who had a major part in the house's structural design – the pair later worked successfully together on Blenheim Palace.

Vanbrugh also turned his attention to the estate's thousand-acre **grounds**, where he could indulge his playful inclinations – the formal gardens, clipped parkland, towers, obelisks and blunt sandstone follies stretch in all directions, sloping gently to two artificial lakes. The whole is a charming artifice of grand, manicured views – an example of what three centuries, skilled gardeners and pots of money can produce.

ARRIVAL AND DEPARTURE — YORK

By train Trains arrive at York Station, just outside the city walls, a 10min walk from the historic core.

Destinations Bradford (hourly; 1hr); Durham (every 30min; 50min); Harrogate (hourly; 30min); Hull (9 daily; 1hr); Leeds (every 30min; 30min); London (every 30min; 2hr 15min); Manchester (hourly; 1hr 5min); Newcastle (every 30min; 1hr); Scarborough (hourly; 50min); Sheffield (every 30–60min; 1hr).

By bus National Express buses (Ⓣ 0870 580 8080) and most other regional bus services drop off and pick up on Rougier St, 200 yards north of the train station, just before Lendal Bridge. Companies include East Yorkshire (for Hull, Beverley and Bridlington; Ⓣ 01482 222222) and Yorkshire Coastliner (for Leeds, Castle Howard, Pickering, Scarborough and Whitby; Ⓣ 01653 692556).

Destinations Beverley (Mon–Sat hourly, Sun 7 daily; 30min); Hull (Mon–Sat hourly, Sun 7 daily; 1hr 45min); Pickering (hourly; 1hr 15min); Scarborough (hourly; 1hr 35min); Whitby (4–6 daily; 2hr).

12

GETTING AROUND

There are **taxi** ranks at Rougier St, Duncombe Place, Exhibition Square and the train station; or call Station Taxis Ⓣ 01904 623332.

INFORMATION AND TOURS

Tourist information centre 1 Museum St, on the corner with Blake St (summer Mon–Sat 9am–6pm, Sun 10am–5pm; winter Mon–Sat 9am–5pm, Sun 10am–4pm; Ⓣ 01904 550099, Ⓦ visityork.org). There is also a smaller tourist office at the train station.

Listings information *The Evening Press* (Ⓦ thisisyork .co.uk), and the monthly *What's On York* (Ⓦ whatsonyork .com).

Bus tours City tours by bus – pick up details at the tourist office – cost around £10. York Pullman offers day-trips to Castle Howard (£17.50; Ⓣ 01904 622992, Ⓦ yorkpullmanbus .co.uk), along with several routes to the Dales.

Walking tours There are various guided walks (around £5.50) available, including evening ghost walks. There's not much to choose between them, though one is free – the York Association of Voluntary Guides (Ⓣ 01904 640780, Ⓦ york.touristguides.btinternet.co.uk) offers a guided tour year round (daily 10.15am; 2hr), plus additional tours in summer (April, May & Sept 2.15pm; June–Aug 2.15pm & 6.45pm), from outside the York Art Gallery – just turn up.

River cruises The best river operator is YorkBoat (Ⓣ 01904 628324, Ⓦ yorkboat.co.uk), whose one-hour "cruise on the Ouse" sails daily from King's Staith and Lendal Bridge (Feb–Dec; cruises from £7.50, families £20).

ACCOMMODATION

The main **B&B** concentration is in the side streets off Bootham (immediately west of Exhibition Square), with nothing much more than a 10min walk from the centre.

12

Ace York Micklegate House, 88–90 Micklegate 01904 627720, acehotelyork.co.uk. In a handsome 1752 building in the centre of the city, with many impressive features. Dorms (sleeping 4 to 14) and private rooms, all en suite; prices rise at weekends and drop for multi-night stays. Continental breakfast included. Dorm £16, double £80

Alexander House 94 Bishopthorpe Rd 01904 625016, alexanderhouseyork.co.uk. Small, friendly B&B in a lovely Victorian townhouse renovation, a 10min walk south of the city centre. Clean and comfortable, with excellent service and lots of free parking. £42.50

Bar Convent 17 Blossom St 01904 643238, bar-convent.org.uk. Unique opportunity to stay in a convent. The grand Georgian building houses a museum and café as well as nine single rooms (£33–37 each), twins, doubles and a family room, self-catering kitchen and guest lounge. Continental breakfast included. £76

Bowman's 33 Grosvenor Terrace 01904 622204, bowmansguesthouse.co.uk. Six spotless rooms in a friendly renovated Victorian terrace B&B off Bootham, within easy reach of the city centre. They provide a permit for free on-street parking. £40

Cedar Court Grand Hotel Station Rise 0845 409 6430, cedarcourtgrand.co.uk. York's new (and only) five-star hotel, a 2min walk from the train station, housed in what was the 1906 headquarters of the North Eastern Railway. Bags of character, with wonderful views of the walls and the Minster, luxurious rooms, a fine-dining restaurant and relaxing bar. £130

The Fort Little Stonegate 01904 620222, thefortyork.co.uk. An interesting idea – a "boutique hostel" in the city centre, offering rooms and dorms decorated on themes (log cabin, deep sea creatures) at a knock-down price. Dorm £22, double £52

Hedley House Hotel 3 Bootham Terrace 01904 637404, hedleyhouse.com. Friendly, comfortable small hotel that is at its best in summer – when the outdoor area with sauna/aqua spa comes into its own. Rooms can be a little chilly in winter – especially in the (separate) annexe. Free car parking on first-come, first-served basis. £80

Mount Royale The Mount 01904 628 856, mountroyale.co.uk. Lots of antiques, super garden suites (and cheaper rooms), and a heated outdoor pool in summer. Plus a hot tub, sauna and steam room, and a well-regarded restaurant. £105

Rowntree Park Caravan Club Site Terry Ave 01904 658 997, caravanclub.co.uk. A wonderful site, the best-located in the city, 10min walk from the centre, with a back gate that opens onto a street of takeaways, pubs and shops. Open to non-members. Mainly for caravans and motorhomes, but with a small tent enclosure – those with tents must arrive on foot. Advance booking essential, especially at weekends. £11.80

EATING

Asia Gourmet 61 Gillygate 01904 622728. Small, cheerful restaurant in the city centre with prompt service. Mainly Japanese food (sushi a specialty) though other Asian cuisines are available. Tues–Sun 5.30–10.30pm.

Ate O Clock 13a High Ousegate 01904 644080, ateoclock.co.uk. The name is dreadful, but the – largely Mediterranean – food is excellent, and there's attentive service and a relaxed atmosphere. Two-course lunch £8.80, main dishes £13.50–22. Tues–Fri noon–2pm & 6–9.30pm, Sat noon–2.30pm & 5.30–9.30pm.

Betty's 6–8 St Helen's Square 01904 659142, bettys.co.uk. Famous across Yorkshire, *Betty's* specializes in cakes and pastries like granny used to make (or not) – try the pikelets or the Yorkshire fat rascals – plus hot dishes and puddings to die for. No reservations. In the basement there's a mirror with the signatures of the hundreds of Allied airmen who used *Betty's* as an unofficial mess during World War II. Daily 9am–9pm.

Café Concerto 21 High Petergate 01904 610478, cafecocerto.biz. Relaxed, Belle Epoque-style bistro facing the Minster, with sheet-music-papered-walls and waiting staff in robust aprons. Food is modern European; there are papers to browse. Daily 8.30am–10pm.

Café No. 8 8 Gillygate 01904 653074, cafeno8.co.uk. Limited menu using excellent locally sourced produce (Masham sausages, Yorkshire beef and lamb, Ryedale ice cream, beer from Masham) in unpretentious surroundings. Mains around £10 during the day, £14–17 in the evening. Its heated garden is a popular spot. Mon–Fri noon–9.30pm, Sat & Sun 11am–late, last orders 9.30pm.

Rustique 28 Castlegate 01904 612744, rustiqueyork.co.uk. French-style bistro serving excellent-value Gallic food and wine. There are a couple of set menus (two courses £11.95, three £13.95); à la carte features all the classics, including steak frites, moules marinières, and confit de canard. Mon–Sat noon–10pm.

DRINKING

For a major eighteenth-century coaching town, the number of good **pubs** in York is disappointing: a lot of the old coaching inns have been demolished.

Black Swan Peasholme Green 01904 679131, blackswanyork.com. York's oldest pub is an imposing half-timbered, sixteenth-century tavern, with wonderful details – flagstones, period staircase, inglenook – good beer, and occasional jazz and folk nights (blackswanfolkclub.org.uk). Mon–Thurs noon–11pm, Fri & Sat noon–midnight, Sun noon–10.30pm.

Blue Bell Fossgate 01904 654904. Built in 1798, the *Blue Bell* is a tiny, friendly local with two rooms, oak-panelling and good real ales. No mobile phones. Mon–Sat 11am–11pm, Sun noon–10.30pm.

Swan 16 Bishopgate 01904 634968. Lovely local, a Tetley Heritage Inn that offers convivial surroundings, well-kept real ale and a really friendly atmosphere a few minutes from the city centre. Mon–Wed 4–11pm, Thurs 4–11.30pm, Fri 4pm–midnight, Sat noon–midnight, Sun noon–10.30pm.

Three-Legged Mare 15 High Petergate 01904 638246. A converted shop provides an airy outlet for York Brewery's own quality beer. No kids, no juke box, no video games. It's named after a three-legged gallows – it's there on the pub sign, with a replica in the beer garden. Mon–Sat noon–midnight, Sun noon–11pm.

NIGHTLIFE

The Basement 13–17 Coney St, below City Screen cinema 01904 612940, thebasementyork.co.uk. An intimate venue with a variety of nights – from music to comedy to arts events. The first Weds of every month is Café Scientifique – a free evening of discussion surrounding current issues in science, while Sunday night sees stand-up comedy. Live music events are scattered through the week, along with cabaret, burlesque and club nights.

Fibbers 8 The Stonebow 01904 651250, fibbers.co.uk. York's primary live music venue, *Fibbers* regularly puts on local and nationally known bands in a lively atmosphere. Club nights include Hammertime (90s) on Fridays and Melt (indie/electro) on Saturdays.

ENTERTAINMENT

York has its fair share of theatres and cinemas, and **classical music concerts** and recitals are often held in the city's churches and York Minster. Major annual events include the **Viking Festival** (vikingjorvik.com) every February and the **Early Music Festival** (ncem.co.uk), perhaps the best of its kind in the country, held in July. The city is also famous for its **Mystery Plays** (yorkmysteryplays.co.uk), traditionally held every four years – the next are planned for 2014.

12

City Screen 13–17 Coney St 0870 758 3219, picturehouses.co.uk. The city's independent cinema is the art-house choice, with three screens, a riverside café-bar, and the *Basement Bar*.

Grand Opera House Cumberland St at Clifford St 0870 606 3595, grandoperahouseyork.org.uk. Musicals, ballet, pop gigs and family entertainment in all its guises.

The National Centre for Early Music St Margaret's Church, Walmgate 01904 658338, ncem.co.uk. Not just early music, but also folk, world and jazz.

DIRECTORY

Hospital York District Hospital, Wigginton Rd (24hr emergency number 01904 31313); bus #2, #5 or #6. The NHS Walk-in Centre, 31 Monkgate (daily 7am–10pm) offers care, advice and treatment without an appointment.

Police Fulford Rd 0845 606 0247.

Hull

HULL – officially Kingston upon Hull – dates back to 1299, when it was laid out as a seaport by Edward I. It quickly became England's leading harbour, and was still a vital garrison when the gates were closed against Charles I in 1642, the first serious act of rebellion of what was to become the English Civil War. Fishing and **seafaring** have always been important here, and today's city maintains a firm grip on its heritage with a number of superb visitor attractions.

The Maritime Museum

Queen Victoria Square • Mon–Sat 10am–5pm, Sun 1.30–4.30pm • Free • 01482 300300

The city's maritime legacy is covered in the **Maritime Museum**, housed in the Neoclassical headquarters of the former Town Docks Offices. With displays on fishing, whaling and sailing, this provides a valuable record of centuries of skill and expertise, not to mention courage and fortitude, now fading into the past. Highlights include the whaling gallery, with whale skeletons, fearsome exploding harpoons, the sort of flimsy boats in which whalers of old used to chase the leviathans of the deep, a crow's nest made of a barrel, and oddities such as a whalebone seat, a blubber cauldron and a group of Narwhal tusks. An exhilarating and humbling experience.

The Museums Quarter

Between High St and the River Hull • All attractions Mon–Sat 10am–5pm, Sun 1.30–4.30pm • Free • T 01482 300300

Over towards the River Hull, you reach the **Museums Quarter** and **High Street**, which has been designated an "Old Town" conservation area thanks to its crop of former merchants' houses and narrow cobbled alleys. At its northern end stands **Wilberforce House**, the former home of William Wilberforce, which contains fascinating exhibits on slavery and its abolition, the cause to which he dedicated much of his life. Next door is **Streetlife**, devoted to the history of transport in the region and centred on a 1930s street scene. The adjoining **Hull and East Riding Museum** is even better, with showpiece attractions including vivid displays of Celtic burials and an impressive full-size model of a woolly mammoth.

The Deep

Tower St • Daily 10am–6pm, last entry 5pm • £9.95 • W thedeep.co.uk

12

Protruding from a promontory overlooking the River Humber, Hull's splendid aquarium, **The Deep**, is just ten minutes' walk from the old town. Its educational displays and videos wrap around an immense 30ft-deep, 2.3-million gallon viewing tank filled with sharks, rays and octopuses. There's an underwater tunnel along the bottom of the tank, together with a magical glass lift in which you can ascend or descend through the water while coming eye to eye with some of the more intriguing denizens of the deep.

ARRIVAL AND INFORMATION — HULL

Hull's train and bus **station** is situated in the Paragon Interchange off Ferensway.

By train There are direct trains from London to Hull, while the city is also linked to the main London–York line via Doncaster.

Destinations Beverley (Mon–Sat every 30min, Sun 6 daily; 15min); Leeds (hourly; 1hr); London (6 daily; 2hr 45min); Scarborough (every 2hr; 1hr 30min); York (9 daily; 1hr).

By bus Buses run to all parts of the region including Hornsea (hourly; 53min) and Scunthorpe (hourly; 1hr 16min).

Tourist office Paragon St at Queen Victoria Square (Mon–Sat 10am–5pm, Sun 11am–3pm; T 01482 223559, W hullcc.gov.uk/visithull). Here you can pick up the entertaining "Fish Trail" leaflet, a self-guided trail that kids will love.

ACCOMMODATION

Holiday Inn Hull Marina Castle St T 0870 400 9043, W holiday-inn.co.uk. Rooms at the city's best central hotel overlook the marina, and there's a restaurant and bar, plus indoor pool, gym and sauna. **£59**

Kingston Theatre Hotel 1–2 Kingston Square T 01482 225828, W kingstontheatrehotel.com. Straightforward, good-value hotel rooms on the city's prettiest square, across from *Hull New Theatre*. Street parking only. **£65**

EATING AND DRINKING

Cerutti's 10 Nelson St T 01482 328501, W ceruttis.co.uk. Facing the old site of the Victoria Pier (now replaced by a wooden deck overlooking the river), this Italian restaurant is especially good for fish dishes. The atmosphere is busy and friendly, and there are frequent special events including live jazz. Main courses £14–20, but look out for two- and three-course deals. Mon–Fri noon–2pm & 6.45–9.30pm, Sat 6.45–9.30pm.

The George The Land of Green Ginger T 01482 226373. Venerable pub on Hull's most curiously named street – see if you can find England's smallest window. Mon–Thurs noon–11.30pm, Fri–Sun noon–midnight.

Pave Café-Bar 16–20 Princes Ave T 01482 333181, W pavebar.co.uk. Nice laidback atmosphere with lots going on – live jazz/blues and comedy nights, and readings by the likes of Alexei Sayle, Will Self and Simon Armitage

– and a comprehensive menu of home-cooked food served till 7pm (most mains well under £10). Sun–Thurs 11am–11.30pm, Fri & Sat 11am–midnight.

Taman Ria Tropicana 45–47 Princes Ave 01482 345640, tropicana-hull.co.uk. Specifically Malay (rather than the more generic Malaysian) cuisine. All food is halal, and pork is never used. Check with staff regarding how spicy different dishes are. The "three dishes for £10.50" option is a good way to try things out. Tues–Sun 6–11pm.

Ye Olde White Harte 25 Silver St yeoldewhiteharte.co.uk. Dating back to the sixteenth century, this place has a pleasant courtyard garden, flagged floors, open brickwork and well-polished furniture, and serves traditional pub grub at good prices. Mon–Thurs 11am–midnight, Fri & Sat 11am–1am, Sun noon–midnight.

ENTERTAINMENT

Hull Truck Theatre Company 50 Ferensway 01482 323638, hulltruck.co.uk. Renowned theatre, where, among other high-profile works, many of the plays of award-winning John Godber see the light of day.

Beverley

With its tangle of old streets, cobbled lanes and elegant Georgian and Victorian terraces **BEVERLEY**, nine miles north of Hull, is the very picture of a traditional market town. More than 350 of its buildings are listed, and though you could see its first-rank offerings in a morning, it makes an appealing place to stay.

Beverley Minster

Minster Yard North • May–Aug Mon–Sat 9am–5.30pm, Sun noon–4.30pm; April, Sept & Oct Mon–Sat 9am–5pm, Sun noon–4.30pm; Nov–Feb Mon–Sat 9am–4pm, Sun noon–4pm; March Mon–Sat 9am–5pm, Sun noon–4pm • Free, but donations requested • beverleyminster.org

12

The town is dominated by the fine, Gothic twin towers of **Beverley Minster**. The **west front**, which crowned the work in 1420, is widely considered without equal, its survival due in large part to architect Nicholas Hawksmoor, who restored much of the church in the eighteenth century. The carving throughout is magnificent, particularly the 68 misericords of the oak **choir** (1520–24), one of the largest and most accomplished in England. Much of the decorative work here and elsewhere is on a musical theme. Beverley had a renowned guild of itinerant minstrels, which provided funds in the sixteenth century for the carvings on the transept aisle capitals, where you'll be able to pick out players of lutes, bagpipes, horns and tambourines.

St Mary's

Corner of North Bar Within and Hengate • April–Sept Mon–Fri 9.30am–4.30pm, Sat 10am–4pm, Sun 2–4pm; Oct–March Mon–Fri 9.30am–noon & 1–4pm, Sun before and after services only • Free • stmarysbeverley.org.uk

Cobbled Highgate runs from the Minster through town, along the pedestrianized shopping streets and past the main Market Square, to Beverley's other great church, **St Mary's**, which nestles alongside the **North Bar**, sole survivor of the town's five medieval gates. Inside, the chancel's painted panelled ceiling (1445) contains portraits of English kings from Sigebert (623–37) to Henry VI (1421–71), and among the carvings, the favourite novelty is the so-called "Pilgrim's Rabbit", said to have been the inspiration for the White Rabbit in Lewis Carroll's *Alice in Wonderland*.

ARRIVAL AND INFORMATION — BEVERLEY

By train Beverley's train station on Station Square is just a couple of minutes' walk from the town centre and the Minster. Destinations Bridlington (every 30min; 30min); Hull (every 20min; 15min); Sheffield (hourly; 1hr 43min).

By bus The bus station is at the junction of Walkergate and Sow Hill Rd, with the main street just a minute's walk away.

Tourist office 34 Butcher Row in the main shopping area (Mon–Fri 9.30am–5.15pm, Sat 10am–4.45pm, plus Sun in July & Aug 11am–3pm; 01482 391672, visiteastyorkshire.com).

ACCOMMODATION AND EATING

Beverley Arms Hotel North Bar Within ⓣ01482 870907, ⓦbrook-hotels.co.uk. A 1794 coach house (it appears in one of Anthony Trollope's novels) in a brilliant position directly opposite St Mary's. Nice ambience, with a stone-flagged bar and brick patio. Rooms are a little tired, but refurbishment is imminent. Jazz on Friday nights. £107

Cerutti 2 Station Square ⓣ01482 866700, ⓦceruttis.co.uk. Occupying what was once the station waiting rooms, *Cerutti 2*, run by the same family as *Cerutti's* in Hull, specializes in fish, though there are meat and vegetarian options too. Popular with locals, so it's as well to book, especially at weekends. Mains £10.95–20.95. Tues–Sat noon–2pm & 6.45–9.30pm.

Friary Youth Hostel Friar's Lane ⓣ0845 371 9004, ⓦyha.org.uk. Beautiful medieval monastic house in the shadow of the Minster. What it lacks in luxury it makes up for in atmosphere, location and, of course, economy. £14.40

King's Head Hotel 38 Saturday Market ⓣ01482 868103, ⓦkingsheadpubbeverley.co.uk. Tucked into a corner of busy Saturday Market, this period building has contemporary decor inside. It's a Marston's pub, with food from £7, and it can be noisy, especially at weekends, but the rear rooms are quieter, and ear plugs are provided. £80

The East Yorkshire coast

12

The **East Yorkshire coast** curves south in a gentle arc from the mighty cliffs of Flamborough Head to Spurn Head, a hook-shaped promontory formed by relentless erosion and shifting currents. There are few parts of the British coast as dangerous – indeed, the Humber lifeboat station at Spurn Point is the only one in Britain permanently staffed by a professional crew. Between the two points lie a handful of tranquil villages and miles of windswept dunes and mud flats. The two main resorts, **Bridlington** and **Filey**, couldn't be more different, but each has their own appeal.

GETTING AROUND — EAST YORKSHIRE COAST

By train Bridlington and Filey are linked by the regular service between Hull and Scarborough.

By bus There's an hourly bus service between Bridlington, Filey and Scarborough, while the seasonal Sunday Spurn Ranger service (Easter–Oct; ⓣ01482 222222) gives access to the isolated Spurn Head coastline.

Bridlington and around

The southernmost resort on the Yorkshire coast, **BRIDLINGTON** has maintained its harbour for almost a thousand years. The seafront promenade looks down upon the town's best asset – its sweeping sandy **beach**. It's an out-and-out family resort, which means plenty of candyfloss, fish and chips, rides, boat trips and amusement arcades. The historic core of town is a mile inland, where in the largely Georgian Bridlington Old Town the **Bayle Museum** (April–Sept Mon–Fri 10am–4pm, Sun 11am–4pm; £2) presents local history in a building that once served as the gateway to a fourteenth-century priory. Every November, Bridlington hosts a highly regarded World Music Festival, **Musicport** (ⓦmusicportfestival.com), which pulls in some very big names.

Around fourteen miles of precipitous 400ft-high cliffs gird **Flamborough Head**, just to the northeast of Bridlington. The best of the seascapes are visitable on the peninsula's north side, accessible by road from Flamborough village.

Bempton

From **BEMPTON**, two miles north of Bridlington, you can follow the cliff-top path all the way round to Flamborough Head or curtail the journey by cutting up paths to Flamborough village. The RSPB sanctuary at **Bempton Cliffs**, reached along a quiet lane from Bempton, is the best single place to see the area's thousands of cliff-nesting birds – it's the only mainland gannetry in England. Bempton also has the second-largest **puffin colony** in the country, with several thousand returning to the cliffs each year. Late March and April is the best time to see the puffins, but the **Visitor Centre** (daily

9.30am/10am–4/5pm; parking £3.50; ⓣ01262 851179, ⓦrspb.org.uk) can advise on other breeds' activities.

Filey

FILEY, half a dozen miles north up the coast from Bempton, is at the very edge of the Yorkshire Wolds (and technically in North Yorkshire). It has a good deal more class as a resort than Bridlington, retaining many of its Edwardian features, including some splendid panoramic gardens. It, too, claims miles of wide sandy beach, stretching most of the way south to Flamborough Head and north the mile or so to the jutting rocks of **Filey Brigg**, where a nature trail wends for a couple of miles through the surroundings.

The North York Moors

Virtually the whole of the **North York Moors** (ⓦmoors.uk.net), from the Hambleton and Cleveland hills in the west to the cliff-edged coastline to the east, is protected by one of the country's finest National Parks. The heather-covered, flat-topped hills are cut by deep, steep-sided valleys, and views here stretch for miles, interrupted only by giant cultivated forests. This is great walking country; footpaths include the superb **Cleveland Way**, one of England's premier long-distance National Trails, which embraces both wild moorland and the cliff scenery of the North Yorkshire coast. Barrows and ancient forts provide memorials of early settlers, mingling on the high moorland with the battered stone crosses of the first Christian inhabitants and the ruins of great monastic houses such as **Rievaulx Abbey**. 12

GETTING AROUND — THE NORTH YORK MOORS

By train The steam trains of the North York Moors Railway run between Pickering and Grosmont and on to Whitby (even more popular since being used as the Hogwarts Express in the *Harry Potter* films). At Grosmont you can connect with the regular trains on the Esk Valley line, running either 6 miles east to Whitby and the coast, or west through more remote country settlements (and ultimately to Middlesbrough).

By bus The main bus approaches to the moors are from Scarborough and York to the main towns of Helmsley and Pickering – pick up the free *Moors Explorer* timetable booklet from tourist offices and park information centres. There are also seasonal Moorsbus services (April–Oct; ⓣ01845 597000, ⓦmoors.uk.net/moorsbus), connecting Pickering and Helmsley to everywhere of interest in the National Park. There are several departures daily in the school summer holidays, fewer at other times (at least every Sun & Bank Hol Mon).

INFORMATION

National Park Visitor centres There are two National Park Visitor centres for the North York Moors, one in Danby (April–Oct daily 10am–5pm; for winter hours check with centre; ⓣ01439 772737), and the other in Sutton Bank (see p.548); both offer exhibitions, pamphlets and maps, a café and a shop.

Cleveland Way Project Maps and information about the route, including an annual, downloadable accommodation guide (ⓣ01439 770657, ⓦnationaltrail.co.uk/ClevelandWay).

Thirsk

The market town of **THIRSK**, 23 miles north of York, made the most of its strategic crossroads position on the ancient drove road between Scotland and York and on the historic east–west route from dales to coast. Its medieval prosperity is clear from the large, cobbled **Market Place** (markets Mon & Sat), while well-to-do citizens later endowed the town with fine Georgian houses and halls. However, Thirsk's main draw is its attachment to the legacy of local vet Alf Wight, better known as James Herriott. Thirsk was the "Darrowby" of the Herriott books, and the vet's former surgery, at 23 Kirkgate, is now the hugely popular **World of James Herriott** (daily 10am–5pm; £6.55; ⓦworldofjamesherriot.org), crammed with period pieces and Herriott memorabilia.

ARRIVAL AND INFORMATION — THIRSK

By train The train station is a mile west of town on the A61 (Ripon road); minibuses connect the station with the town centre.

Destinations Middlesborough (about every 90min; 40min); Manchester (every 40min; 1hr 50min); London (every 2hr; 2hr 30min).

By bus Buses stop in the Market Place.

By car Thirsk is just a 30min drive from York, making it an easy day-trip.

Tourist office 49 Market Place (Easter–Nov daily 10am–5pm; Dec–Easter Mon–Sat 10am–4pm; ⊕01845 522755, ⊛visit-thirsk.com).

ACCOMMODATION AND EATING

Charles' Bistro Bakers Alley, 27 Market Place ⊕01845 527444. Bistro food – they're known for their steak pie – in a friendly atmosphere and comfortable surroundings. Around £6–7 a dish, £9.95 for two courses, except on Saturday night, when it's more expensive. Tues–Sat 11.30am–3pm & 6.30–11pm.

Gallery 18 Kirkgate ⊕01845 523767, ⊛gallerybedandbreakfast.co.uk. An award-winning B&B with three comfortable rooms and excellent breakfasts in an eighteenth-century Grade II-listed building. It's on a main street, and can get noisy at closing time. **£65**

Golden Fleece Market Place ⊕01845 523108, ⊛goldenfleecehotel.com. Good rooms and a nice busy atmosphere in this charming old coaching inn nicely located on Thirsk's large cobbled square. They serve locally sourced food, too. Food served Mon–Sat noon–3pm & 6.30–9.15pm, Sun noon–2pm & 6.30–9pm. **£98**

The Poplars Carlton Miniott ⊕01845 522712, ⊛thepoplarsthirsk.com. Near the station and the racecourse, this B&B offers clean rooms and "cottages" (actually cabins; three-night minimum). All have their own access. **£65**

12

Osmotherley and around

Eleven miles north of Thirsk, the little village of **OSMOTHERLEY** huddles around its green. The pretty settlement gets by as a hiking centre, since it's a key stop on the **Cleveland Way** as well as starting point for the brutal 42-mile **Lyke Wake Walk** to Ravenscar, south of Robin Hood's Bay.

Mount Grace Priory

On the A19 • April–Sept Mon & Thurs–Sun 10am–6pm; Oct–March Thurs–Sun 10am–4pm • NT & EH • £5

An easy two-mile walk from Osmotherley via Chapel Wood Farm, the fourteenth-century **Mount Grace Priory** is the most important of England's nine Carthusian ruins. The Carthusians took a vow of silence and lived, ate and prayed alone in their two-storey cells, each separated from its neighbour by a privy, small garden and high walls. The foundations of the cells are still clearly visible, and one has been reconstructed to suggest its original layout.

Sutton Bank

The main A170 road enters the National Park from Thirsk as it climbs 500ft in half a mile to **Sutton Bank** (960ft), a phenomenal viewpoint from where the panorama extends across the Vale of York to the Pennines on the far horizon.

INFORMATION — SUTTON BANK

North York Moors National Park Visitor Centre At the top of Sutton Bank (April–Oct daily 10am–5pm; for winter hours check with centre; ⊕01845 597426, ⊛moors.uk.net). With leaflets, maps and exhibits, this visitor centre is particularly good on the short walks and off-road bike rides you can make from here.

Kilburn

To the south of the A170, the **White Horse Nature Trail** (2–3 miles; 1hr 30min) skirts the crags of Roulston Scar en route to the **Kilburn White Horse**, northern England's only turf-cut figure, 314ft long and 228ft high. You could make a real walk of it by dropping a couple of miles down to pretty **KILBURN** village (a minor

TOP 5 YORKSHIRE PUBS

Duke of York Whitby. See p.556
Fat Cat Sheffield. See p.517
Star Inn Harome. See p.550
The Swan York. See p.543
Whitelocks Leeds. See p.522

road also runs from the A170, passing the White Horse car park) which is synonymous with woodcarving since the days of "Mouseman" Robert Thompson (1876–1955), whose woodcarvings are marked by his distinctive mouse motif. The **Mouseman Visitor Centre** (Jan–Sept daily 10am–5pm; Oct Tues–Sun 10am–5pm; Nov & Dec Wed–Sun 11am–4pm; £4; Ⓦ robertthompsons.co.uk) displays examples of Thompson's personal furniture.

Coxwold

Most visitors to the attractive village of **COXWOLD** come to pay homage to the novelist **Laurence Sterne**, who is buried by the south wall (close to the porch) in the churchyard of **St Michael's**, where he was vicar from 1760 until his death in 1768. **Shandy Hall**, further up the road past the church (house May–Sept Wed 2–4.30pm, Sun 2.30–4.30pm; gardens May–Sept Sun–Fri 11am–4.30pm; also by appointment; house & gardens £4.50, gardens only £2.50; Ⓣ 01347 868465, Ⓦ shandean.org), was Sterne's home, now a museum crammed with literary memorabilia. It was here that he wrote *A Sentimental Journey through France and Italy* and the wonderfully eccentric *The Life and Opinions of Tristram Shandy, Gentleman*.

12

Helmsley and around

One of the moors' most appealing towns, **HELMSLEY** makes a perfect base for visiting the western moors and Rievaulx Abbey. Local life revolves around a large cobbled market square (market Fri), dominated by a boastful monument to the second earl of Feversham, whose family was responsible for rebuilding most of the village in the nineteenth century. The old **market cross** now marks the start of the 110-mile **Cleveland Way**. Signposted from the square, it's easy to find **Helmsley Castle** (daily: March–Oct 10am–6pm; Nov–Feb 10am–5pm; EH; £4.80), its unique twelfth-century D-shaped keep ringed by massive earthworks.

Rievaulx Abbey

Follow signposts left off the B1257 a couple of miles northwest of Helmsley • April–Sept daily 10am–6pm; Oct–March Mon & Thurs–Sun 10am–5pm • EH • £5.60

From Helmsley you can easily walk across country to **Rievaulx Abbey** on a signposted path (90min). Founded in 1132, the abbey became the mother church of the Cistercians in England, quickly developing into a flourishing community with interests in fishing, mining, agriculture and the woollen industry. At its height, 140 monks and up to 500 lay brothers lived and worked here, though numbers fell dramatically once the Black Death (1348–49) had done its worst. The end came with the Dissolution, when many of the walls were razed and the roof lead stripped – the beautiful ruins, however, still suggest the abbey's former splendour.

Rievaulx Terrace

On the B1257, a couple of miles northwest of Helmsley • Daily 11am–5pm • NT • £5

Although they form some sort of ensemble with the abbey, there's no access between the ruins and **Rievaulx Terrace**. This half-mile stretch of grass-covered terraces and woodland was laid out as part of Duncombe Park in the 1750s, and was engineered partly to enhance the views of the abbey. The resulting panorama over the ruins and the valley below is superb, and this makes a great spot for a picnic.

ARRIVAL AND INFORMATION — HELMSLEY

By bus Buses from Scarborough and York stop on or near the Market Place. In addition, seasonal Moorsbus services (April–Oct; T 01845 597000, W moors.uk.net/moorsbus), connect Helmsley to most places in the National Park.

Tourist office The castle visitor centre (April–Oct daily 10am–5pm; check winter hours with centre; T 01439 770173, W ryedale.gov.uk) has information on the Cleveland Way.

ACCOMMODATION AND EATING

Black Swan Market Place T 0870 400 8112, W blackswan-helmsley.co.uk. An interesting Tudor/Georgian ex-coaching inn right on the main square, with a comfortable bar, airy restaurant, award-winning tearoom and charming, attentive staff. The hotel is progressively refurbishing its rooms. Restaurant daily 7–9.30pm; brasserie Wed–Sun 6.30–9.30pm; tearoom daily 10am–5.30pm. **£99**

Feathers Hotel Market Place T 01439 770275, W feathershotelhelmsley.co.uk. Pub serving restaurant food – all the staples, from £10.50 – and with a surprisingly large choice of rooms, including a cheaper economy option honestly described as "unmodernized and occasionally noisy". Food served Mon–Fri noon–2.30pm & 5.30–9pm, Sat & Sun noon–3pm & 5.30–9pm. **£70**

Feversham Arms 1 High St T 01439 770766, W fevershamarmshotel.com. One of Yorkshire's top hotels, multi-award winning, luxurious yet unpretentious. It has a pool, underground car park, spa and a terrific fine-dining restaurant. Look out for special deals. Mon–Sat noon–2pm, Sun 12.30–2.30pm; daily afternoon tea 2.30–5.30pm, dinner 6.45–9.30pm. **£196**

Star Inn Harome, less than 3 miles southeast of Helmsley T 01439 770397, W thestaratharome.co.uk. The *Star* is not only a spectacularly beautiful thatched inn, but also one of Yorkshire's longest-standing Michelin-starred restaurants. Food is classic British and surprisingly affordable (main courses £15–24), and the atmosphere is blessedly unpretentious. Accommodation is available in a separate building, and there's an associated shop/deli across the road. Food served Mon 6–9.30pm, Tues–Sat 11.30am–2pm & 6–9.30pm, Sun noon–6pm. **£150**

Hutton le Hole

Eight miles northeast of Helmsley, one of Yorkshire's quaintest villages, **HUTTON LE HOLE**, has become so great a tourist attraction that you'll have to come off-season to get much pleasure from its stream-crossed village green and the sight of sheep wandering freely through the lanes. Apart from the sheer photogenic quality of the place, the big draw is the family-oriented **Ryedale Folk Museum** (mid-Jan to mid-Dec daily 10am–5.30pm; £5.50; W ryedalefolkmuseum.co.uk), where local life is explored in a series of reconstructed buildings, notably a sixteenth-century house, a glass furnace, a crofter's cottage and a nineteenth-century blacksmith's shop.

INFORMATION — HUTTON LE HOLE

National Park information centre Ryedale Folk Museum (mid-Jan to mid-Dec daily 10am–5.30pm; T 01751 417367). They have a list of local B&Bs.

ACCOMMODATION AND EATING

The Barn Hotel T 01751 417311, W thebarnhotel.info. Comfortable rooms and tearooms serving home-made cakes, scones, sandwiches and hot specials. Food served daily 10.30am–5pm. **£77**

The Crown T 01751 417343. Spacious real ale pub where you can sit outside and enjoy the peace of the village. They serve traditional, freshly cooked food, too; you can eat well for under a tenner. Mon & Tues 11.15am–2.30pm & 5–10.30pm, Wed–Sun 11.15am–10.30pm (though closing time varies according to how many customers are left, especially on Sat).

Pickering

The biggest centre for miles around, **PICKERING** takes for itself the title "Gateway to the Moors", which is pushing it a bit, though it's certainly a handy halt if you're touring the

THE NORTH YORKSHIRE MOORS RAILWAY

The **North Yorkshire Moors Railway** (NYMR; ⓣ01751 472508, ⓦnymr.co.uk) connects **Pickering** with the Esk Valley (Middlesbrough–Whitby) line at **Grosmont**, eighteen miles to the north. The line was completed by George Stephenson in 1835, just ten years after the opening of the Stockton and Darlington Railway. Scheduled **services** operate year-round (limited to weekend and school hol service Nov–Feb), and a **day-return ticket** costs £16. Part of the line's attraction are the **steam trains**, though be warned that diesels are pulled into service when the fire risk in the forests is high. Steam services have also been extended from the end of the NYMR line at Grosmont to the nearby seaside resort of Whitby – departures are usually during school and bank holidays, with a return fare from Pickering of £21.

villages and dales of the **eastern moors**. Its most attractive feature is its motte and bailey **castle** on the hill north of the Market Place (July & Aug daily 10am–5pm; April–June & Sept Thurs–Mon 10am–5pm; EH; £3.80), reputedly used by every English monarch up to 1400 as a base for hunting in nearby Blandsby Park. The other spot worth investigating is the **Beck Isle Museum of Rural Life** on Bridge Street (Feb–Oct daily 10am–5pm; £5; ⓦbeckislemuseum.co.uk), which has reconstructions of a gents' outfitters, and barber's shop, a case full of knickers, and a painting of two giant Welsh guardsmen produced by Rex Whistler for a children's party. **Market** day in town is Monday, and there's a farmers' market on the first Thursday of the month.

ARRIVAL AND INFORMATION — PICKERING

12

By train The steam trains of the North Yorkshire Moors Railway (even more popular since being used as the Hogwarts Express in the *Harry Potter* films) run between Pickering and Grosmont (April–Oct 5–8 daily; limited winter service; 1hr 5min) and then on to Whitby (Pickering–Whitby 1hr 35min). The NYMR train station (see above) is a 5min signposted walk from the main street.

By bus Buses stop outside the library and tourist office, opposite the Co-op in the centre of town.

Destinations Helmsley (hourly; 40min); Scarborough (hourly; 1hr); Whitby (4–6 daily; 55min); York (hourly; 1hr 15min).

Tourist office The Ropery (March–Oct Mon–Sat 9.30am–5pm, Sun 9.30am–4pm; Nov–Feb Mon–Sat 9.30am–4.30pm; ⓣ01751 473791, ⓦryedale.gov.uk).

ACCOMMODATION AND EATING

The tourist office can help with **B&Bs**, though Whitby, just a 20min drive away on the coast, is the better overnight destination (see p.554).

The White Swan Market Place ⓣ01751 472288, ⓦwhite-swan.co.uk. Delightful traditional coaching inn, fully refurbished and updated, with contemporary and traditional bedrooms, and fine Modern British food (mains from £13). Food served noon–2pm & 6.45–9pm. **£150**

The North Yorkshire coast

The **North Yorkshire coast** (ⓦdiscoveryorkshirecoast.com) is the southernmost stretch of a cliff-edged shore that stretches almost unbroken to the Scottish border. **Scarborough** is the biggest resort, with a full set of attractions and a terrific beach. Cute **Robin Hood's Bay** is the most popular of the coastal villages, with fishing and smuggling traditions, while bluff **Staithes** – a fishing harbour on the far edge of North Yorkshire – has yet to tip over into a full-blown tourist trap. **Whitby**, between the two, is the best stopover, with its fine sands, good facilities, abbey ruins, Georgian buildings and maritime heritage – more than any other local place Whitby celebrates Captain Cook as one of its own. Two of the best sections of the **Cleveland Way** start from Whitby: southeast to Robin Hood's Bay (six miles) and northwest to Staithes (eleven miles), both along thrilling high-cliff paths.

Scarborough

The oldest resort in the country, **SCARBOROUGH** first attracted early seventeenth-century visitors to its newly discovered mineral springs. To the Victorians it was "the Queen of the Watering Places", but Scarborough saw its biggest transformation after World War II, when it became a holiday haven for workers from the industrial heartlands. All the traditional ingredients of a beach resort are still here in force, from superb, clean sands and kitsch amusement arcades to the more refined pleasures of its tight-knit old-town streets and a genteel round of quiet parks and gardens. In addition to the sights detailed below, make sure to drop into the **Church of St Mary** (1180), below the castle on Castle Road, whose graveyard contains the tomb of Anne Brontë, who died here in 1849.

Rotunda Museum

Vernon Rd • Tues–Sun 10am–5pm • £4.50 • ⓣ 01723 353665, ⓦ rotundamuseum.co.uk

The second oldest purpose-built museum in the country (the oldest is in Oxford), the **Rotunda Museum** was constructed to the plans of William Smith, the founder of English geology, and opened in 1829. A fascinating building in its own right, it has recently been updated to include in its venerable shell some high-tech displays on geology and local history. The Dinosaur Coast Gallery is particularly child-friendly.

Art Gallery

The Crescent • Tues–Sun 10am–5pm • £2 • ⓦ scarboroughartgallery.co.uk

Scarborough's **Art Gallery**, housed in an Italianate villa, contains the town's permanent collection – largely the work of local artists, and including paintings, posters and photography – which gives an insight into the way the town has been depicted over the centuries.

Scarborough Castle

Castle Rd • April–Sept daily 10am–6pm; Oct–March Mon & Thurs–Sun 10am–4/5pm • EH • £4.80

There's no better place to acquaint yourself with the local layout than **Scarborough Castle**, mounted on a jutting headland between two golden-sanded bays. Bronze and Iron Age relics have been found on the wooded castle crag, together with fragments of a fourth-century Roman signalling station, Saxon and Norman chapels and a Viking camp, reputedly built by a Viking with the nickname of Scardi (or "harelip"), from which the town's name derives.

The bays

The miniature **North Bay Railway** (Easter–Sept daily) runs up to the **Sea Life Centre and Marine Sanctuary** on the North Bay at Scalby Mills (daily 10am–4.30/5.30pm; £11.95), distinguished by its white pyramids. From the harbourside, short **cruises** and **speedboat trips** shoot off throughout the day in the summer. For unique entertainment, head for Peasholm Park, where **naval warfare**, in the shape of miniature man-powered naval vessels, battle it out on the lake (July & Aug Mon, Thurs & Sat; details from the tourist office).

The **South Bay** is more refined, backed by the Valley Gardens and the Italianate meanderings of the South Cliff Gardens, and topped by an esplanade from which a **hydraulic lift** (April–Sept daily 10am–5pm) chugs down to the beach.

ARRIVAL AND INFORMATION — SCARBOROUGH

By train The train station is at the top of town facing Westborough.

Destinations Hull (every 2hr; 1hr 30min); Leeds (hourly; 1hr 20min); York (hourly; 50min).

By bus Buses pull up outside the train station or in the surrounding streets, though the National Express services (direct from London) stop in the car park behind the station.

Destinations Bridlington (hourly; 1hr 15min); Filey (hourly; 30min); Helmsley (hourly; 1hr 30min); Hull (hourly; 2hr 50min); Leeds (hourly; 2hr 40min); Pickering (hourly; 1hr); Robin Hood's Bay (hourly; 45min); Whitby (hourly; 1hr); York (hourly; 1hr 35min).

Tourist offices Scarborough has two tourist offices; one inside the Brunswick Shopping Centre on Westborough (April–June, Sept & Oct Mon–Sat 9.30am–5.30pm, Sun 11am–4.30pm; July & Aug Mon–Sat 9am–5.30pm, Sun 11am–4.30pm; check for winter hours; T 01723 83637), and the other on Sandside by the harbour (April–June, Sept & Oct daily 10am–5.30pm; check with the Brunswick Centre office for high summer and winter hours).

GETTING AROUND

By bus Open-top seafront buses (Easter–Sept daily from 9.30am, March Sat & Sun only; £1.60) run from North Bay to the Spa Complex in South Bay.

ACCOMMODATION

Alexandra House 21 West St T 01723 503205, W scarborough-alexandra.co.uk. One of the traditional guesthouses that Scarborough excels in. Just off the Esplanade, this is a particularly child-friendly hotel, with lots of baby equipment and books/toys/videos/games for older children available – you can even borrow buckets and spades. **£58**

Beiderbecke's 1–3 The Crescent T 01723 365766, W beiderbeckes.com. Boutique hotel in a sedate terrace (c.1832) on the South Cliff. Rooms are comfortable and the bar is old-fashioned (in a good way), with live jazz on Saturdays. Free parking. They have a stylish, reasonably priced brasserie, too. **£130**

Scarborough YHA Burniston Rd, two miles north of town T 0845 371 9657. In an early seventeenth-century water mill a 15min walk from the sea, this is a good hostel for families with kids. **£16.40**

EATING AND DRINKING

Café Fish 19 York Place, at the intersection with Somerset Terrace T 01723 500301. More of a top-end fish restaurant than a fish 'n' chip shop, where a two-course dinner with wine could feature fish curry, steamed mussels or Thai fishcakes, and will cost about £30. Gets very busy at weekends. Dinner only.

Café Italia 36 St Nicholas Cliff T 01723 501973. Enchanting, tiny Italian coffee bar. Good coffee, ice cream and cakes. Mon–Sat, closes 4pm.

Golden Grid 4 Sandside T 01723 360922, W goldengrid.co.uk. The harbourside's choicest fish-and-chip establishment, "catering for the promenader since 1883". Offers grilled fish, crab and lobster, a fruits-de-mer platter and a wine list alongside the standard crispy-battered fry-up. Decent portions of fish from £8.95. Daily: summer 10am–9.30pm (Sat "a bit later"); winter 11am–6.30pm.

NIGHTLIFE AND ENTERTAINMENT

Stephen Joseph Theatre Westborough T 01723 370541, W sjt.uk.com. Housed in a former Art Deco cinema, this premieres every new play of local playwright Alan Ayckbourn and promotes strong seasons of theatre and film. There's a good, moderately priced café/restaurant and a bar open daily except Sun.

Robin Hood's Bay

The most heavily visited spot on this stretch of coast, **ROBIN HOOD'S BAY** is made up of gorgeous narrow streets and pink-tiled cottages toppling down the cliff-edge site, evoking the romance of a time when this was both a hard-bitten fishing community and smugglers' den par excellence. From the upper village, lined with Victorian villas, now mostly B&Bs, it's a very steep walk down the hill to the harbour. The **Old Coastguard Station** (June–Sept Tues–Sun 10am–5pm; Oct–May Sat, Sun & school hols only; NT; free; T 01947 885900) has been turned into a visitor centre with displays relating to the area's geology and sealife. When the tide is out, the massive rock beds below are exposed, split by a geological fault line and studded with fossil remains. There's an easy circular walk (2.5 miles) to **Boggle Hole** and its youth hostel, a mile south, returning inland via the path along the old Scarborough–Whitby railway line.

12

ARRIVAL AND INFORMATION — ROBIN HOOD'S BAY

By bus Robin Hood's Bay is connected to Whitby on Arriva #19 buses (every 30min–1hr; 20min) and to Scarborough on Arriva #93 (every 40min; 40min).

Tourist office Though you can pick up a lot of information at the Old Coastguard Station (June–Sept Tues–Sun 10am–5pm; Oct–May Sat, Sun & school hols only; T 01947 885900), the nearest official tourist offices are in Whitby (see p.556) and Scarborough (see p.553).

GETTING AROUND

By bike A couple of miles northwest of Robin Hood's Bay at Hawsker, on the A171, Trailways (T 01947 820207, W trailways.fsnet.co.uk) is a bike rental outfit based in the old Hawsker train station, perfectly placed for day-trips in either direction along the disused railway line.

ACCOMMODATION AND EATING

Many people see Robin Hood's Bay as a day-trip from Whitby. You can ask about accommodation in Whitby's tourist office (see p.556), or simply stroll the streets of the old part of the village to see if any of the small cottage **B&Bs** has vacancies. There are three good **pubs** in the lower village, two of which offer rooms – food at the *Bay Hotel* is the best.

Bay Hotel On the harbour T 01947 880278. At the traditional start or end of the Coast-to-Coast Walk, this inn offers rooms and bar meals, with main courses at around £8. Mon–Sat 11am–11pm, Sun noon–11pm. **£80**

Swell Café Old Chapel, Chapel St T 01947 880180, W swell.org.uk. A gift shop, café and cinema in an old Wesleyan Chapel, built in 1779, where John Wesley himself once preached. They serve a good range of snacks, sandwiches, cakes, teas and coffees, and alcoholic drinks, and there are great coastal views from its terrace tables. Daily 10am–4.15pm or later if busy.

Youth hostel Boggle Hole. Fylingthorpe T 0870 770 5704, E bogglehole@yha.org.uk. In a former mill in a wooded ravine about a mile south of Robin Hood's Bay at Mill Beck, this hostel has a great location near the beach. **£18.40**

12

Whitby

If there's one essential stop on the North Yorkshire coast it's **WHITBY**, with its historical associations, atmospheric ruins, fishing harbour, lively music scene and intrinsic charm. The seventh-century cliff-top **abbey** here made Whitby one of the key foundations of the early Christian period, and a centre of great learning. Below, on the harbour banks of the River Esk, for a thousand years the local herring boats landed their catch until the great **whaling** boom of the eighteenth century transformed the fortunes of the town. Melville's *Moby Dick* makes much of Whitby whalers such as William Scoresby, and James Cook took his first seafaring steps from the town in 1746, on his way to becoming a national hero. All four of Captain Cook's ships of discovery – the *Endeavour*, *Resolution*, *Adventure* and *Discovery* – were built in this town.

Walking around Whitby is one of its great pleasures. Divided by the River Esk, the town splits into two halves joined by a swing bridge: the cobbled **old town** to the east,

BRAM STOKER AND DRACULA

The story of **Dracula** is well known, but it's the exact attention to the geographical detail of Whitby – little changed since Bram Stoker first wrote the words – which has proved a huge attraction to visitors. Using first-hand observation of a town he knew well – he stayed at a house on the West Cliff, now marked by a plaque – Stoker built a story which mixed real locations, legend and historical fact: the grounding of Count Dracula's ship on Tate Hill Sands was based on an actual event reported in the local papers.

It's hardly surprising that the town has cashed in on its **Dracula Trail**. The various sites – Tate Hill Sands, the abbey, church and steps, the graveyard, Stoker's house – can all be visited, while down on the harbourside the Dracula Experience attempts to pull in punters to its rather lame horror-show antics. Keen interest has also been sparked amongst the **Goth** fraternity, who now come to town en masse a couple of times a year (in late spring and around Halloween) for a vampire's ball, concerts and readings.

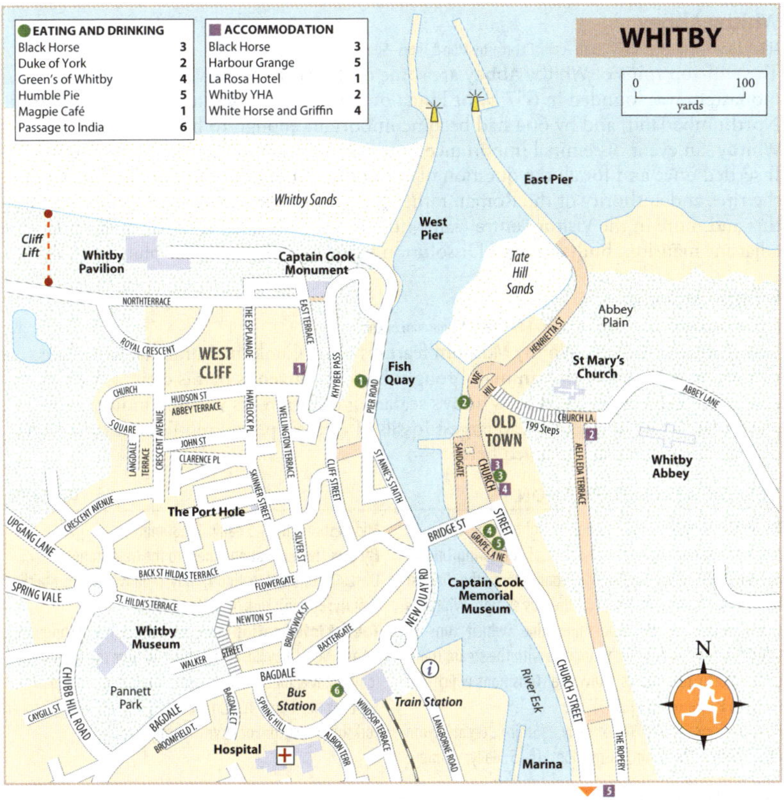

12

and the newer (mostly eighteenth- and nineteenth-century) town across the bridge, generally known as **West Cliff. Church Street** is the old town's main thoroughfare, barely changed in aspect since the eighteenth century, though now lined with tearooms and gift shops. Parallel **Sandgate** has more of the same, the two streets meeting at the small **marketplace** where souvenirs and trinkets are sold, and which hosts a farmer's market every Thursday.

Captain Cook Memorial Museum

Grape Lane • Daily: March 11am–3pm; April–Oct 9.45am–5pm • £4.50 • ⓦ cookmuseumwhitby.co.uk

Whitby, understandably, likes to make a fuss of Captain Cook, who served an apprenticeship here from 1746–49 under John Walker, a Quaker ship owner. The **Captain Cook Memorial Museum**, housed in Walker's rickety old house, contains an impressive amount of memorabilia, including ships' models, letters, and paintings by artists seconded to Cook's voyages.

Church of St Mary

At the north end of Church Street, you climb the famous **199 steps** of the Church Stairs – now paved, but originally a wide wooden staircase built for pall-bearers carrying coffins to the **Church of St Mary** above. This is an architectural amalgam dating back to 1110, boasting a Norman chancel arch, a profusion of eighteenth-century panelling, box pews unequalled in England and a triple-decker pulpit – note the built-in ear trumpets, added for the benefit of a nineteenth-century rector's deaf wife.

Whitby Abbey

Abbey Lane • April–Sept daily 10am–6pm; Oct–Easter Mon & Thurs–Sun 10am–4pm • EH • £6

The cliff-top ruins of **Whitby Abbey** are some of the most evocative in England. Its monastery was founded in 657 by St Hilda of Hartlepool, daughter of King Oswy of Northumberland, and by 664 had become important enough to host the **Synod of Whitby**, an event of seminal importance in the development of English Christianity. It settled once and for all the question of determining the date of Easter, and adopted the rites and authority of the Roman rather than the Celtic Church. You'll discover all this and more in the **Visitor Centre** (same hours), which is housed in the shell of the adjacent mansion, built after the Dissolution using material from the plundered abbey.

Whitby Museum

Pannett Park • Tues–Sun 9.30am–4.30pm • £4 • Ⓦ whitbymuseum.org.uk

The gloriously eclectic **Whitby Museum** features more Cook memorabilia, including various objects and stuffed animals brought back as souvenirs by his crew, as well as casefuls of exhibits devoted to Whitby's seafaring tradition, its whaling industry in particular. Some of the best and largest fossils of Jurassic period reptiles unearthed on the east coast are also preserved here.

ARRIVAL AND INFORMATION — WHITBY

12

By train Whitby's train station is right in the centre of town on Station Square, just south of the swing bridge, conveniently just across the road from the Tourist Information Centre and next to the bus station. Whitby is the terminus of the Esk Valley line, which runs to Middlesbrough (and which connects with the steam trains of the North York Moors Railway at Grosmont which run south to Pickering; see p.551).

Destinations Danby (4–5 daily; 35min); Great Ayton (4–5 daily; 1hr 5min); Grosmont (4–5 daily; 15min); Middlesbrough (4–5 daily; 1hr 30min).

By bus The bus station is next to the train station.

Destinations Robin Hood's Bay (hourly;19min); Staithes (hourly; 30min); York (4–6 daily; 2hr).

Tourist Information Centre On the corner of Langborne Rd and New Quay Rd, across the road from the train station (daily: May & June 9.30am–5pm; July & Aug 9.30am–7pm; Sept–April 10am–4.30pm; Ⓣ 01723 383637, Ⓦ discoveryorkshirecoast.com or Ⓦ visitwhitby.com).

ACCOMMODATION

For upmarket **self-catering**, check out the very chic boutique apartments (minimum stay two nights) offered by *Green's of Whitby* (see opposite).

Black Horse 91 Church St Ⓣ 01947 602906, Ⓦ the-black-horse.com. Four simple en-suite guest rooms above this fine old pub (see below), each named after one of Captain Cook's ships. Two-night minimum at weekends. **£60**

Harbour Grange Spital Bridge, Church St Ⓣ 01947 600817, Ⓦ whitbybackpackers.co.uk. Backpackers' hostel right on the river (eastern side) with 24 beds in five small dorms. Self-catering kitchen and lounge; 11.30pm curfew. **£17**

La Rosa Hotel 5 East Terrace Ⓣ 01947 606981, Ⓦ larosa.co.uk. Eccentric B&B with themed rooms done out in extravagantly individual style courtesy of auctions, eBay and car boot sales. Great fun, with terrific views of the harbour and the abbey. Breakfast picnic delivered in a basket to your door. Street parking. **£110**

Whitby YHA Abbey House, East Cliff Ⓣ 0845 371 9049, Ⓔ whitby@yha.org.uk. Flagship hostel in a Grade 1 listed building next to the Abbey Visitor Centre. Stunning views, good facilities, and a Victorian conservatory, tearoom and restaurant. Rates include breakfast and entry to the abbey. Dorm **£18.40**, double **£53**

White Horse and Griffin 87 Church St Ⓣ 01947 604857, Ⓦ whitehorseandgriffin.co.uk. In the centre of Whitby's old town, with wonderful views of the harbour. Nicely renovated rooms (and several cottages) with many original features. It's full of character, but can be noisy. **£65**

EATING AND DRINKING

Black Horse 91 Church St Ⓣ 01947 602906, Ⓦ the-black-horse.com. Lovely old pub (parts date from the seventeenth century) in the heart of the old town, with real ales, tapas, Yorkshire cheeses and local seafood. Mon–Sat 11am–11pm, Sun noon–11pm; food served all day.

Duke of York 124 Church St Ⓣ 01947 600324, Ⓦ dukeofyork.co.uk. In a great position at the bottom of the 199 steps, this is a warm and inviting pub, with beams, nautical memorabilia, church pews and views across to the harbour and West Cliff. Come for good real ales, modern pub food and music. Daily; food served noon–9pm.

Green's of Whitby 13 Bridge St 01947 600284, greensofwhitby.com. A few yards from the swing bridge, and reckoned by many to be the best restaurant in Whitby, friendly and unpretentious *Green's* has a lively bistro downstairs and a more formal dining room on the first floor, with the same menu and prices available in both. Ingredients are locally sourced, with lots of good fish and meat dishes. Mon–Fri noon–2pm & 6.30–9.30pm, Sat & Sun noon–10pm.

Humble Pie 163 Church St 07919 074954, humblepienmash.com. Tiny sixteenth-century building serving a range of pies, cooked fresh to order – steak, stout and leek; Romany; Homity; haggis and neep, and many more – with mash and peas. The decor is 1940s, with World War II background music. All pies £4.99; soft drinks only. Mon–Sat 12.30–8.30pm, Sun 12.30–5pm.

Magpie Café 14 Pier Rd 01947 602058, magpiecafe.co.uk. Said by Rick Stein to be one of the best fish-and-chip shops in the country, the *Magpie* has served food from its 1750-built premises since the start of World War II. To call it a fish-and-chip shop is a bit disingenuous – although it provides the normal takeaway service, it also serves lesser known fish like Woof and John Dory in its restaurant, and has an extensive wine list. Daily 11.30am–9pm.

Passage to India 30–31 Windsor Terrace 01947 606500, passagetoindia.eu. Stylish tandoori restaurant near the station, with bright red-and-black decor, great food, and friendly, efficient service. Main courses £8–12; look out for the Tandoori king prawn karahi, or the Lam Kam. Mon–Thurs 5.30pm–midnight, Fri 5.30pm–1am, Sat noon–1am, Sun noon–midnight.

NIGHTLIFE AND ENTERTAINMENT

Whitby has a strong **local music** scene, with an emphasis on folk and world music.

Whitby Folk Week During this annual festival (whitbyfolk.co.uk; held the week preceding the August bank holiday), the town is filled day and night with singers, bands, traditional dancers, storytellers and music workshops.

Information The best place to find out more is at *The Port Hole*, 16 Skinner St (01947 603475), a Fair Trade craft shop that's also the HQ of local collective Musicport (musicportfestival.com) who put on gigs from big names in the world/folk scene and hold a renowned annual World Music Festival in Bridlington in November.

Staithes

Beyond Whitby Sands, a fine coastal walk starts at Sandsend, leads through pretty Runswick Bay, and reaches, in around four hours, the fishing village of **STAITHES**. An improbably beautiful grouping of huddled stone houses around a small harbour, the village is backed by the severe outcrop of Cowbar Nab, a sheer cliff face that protects the northern flank of the village. James Cook worked here in a draper's shop before moving to Whitby, and he's remembered in the **Captain Cook and Staithes Heritage Centre**, on the High Street (March–Dec daily 10am–5pm; Jan & Feb Sat & Sun 10am–5pm; £2.75), which recreates an eighteenth-century street among other interesting exhibits. Other than this, you'll have to content yourself with pottering about the rocks near the harbour – there's no beach to speak of – or clambering the nearby cliffs for spectacular views. At **Boulby**, a mile and a half's trudge up the coastal path (45min), you're walking on the highest cliff (670ft) on England's east coast.

ACCOMMODATION — STAITHES

Endeavour House 1 High St 01947 841735, endeavour-restaurant.co.uk. Four lovely doubles in a two-centuries-old house by the harbour. The good news is that it has four dedicated parking spaces (like gold dust in Staithes), the bad news is that there's a four-night minimum. Prices start at £375 for four nights.

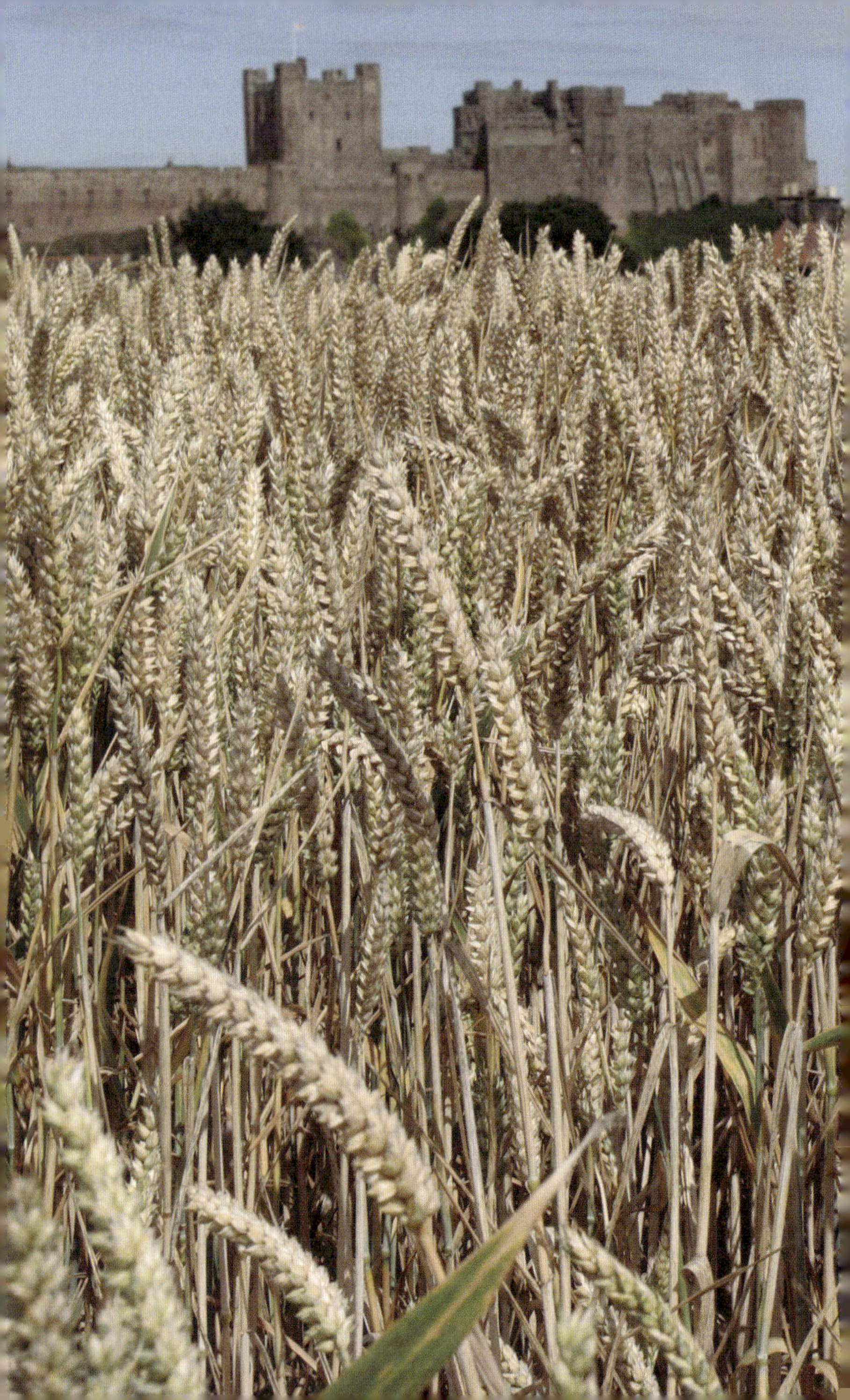

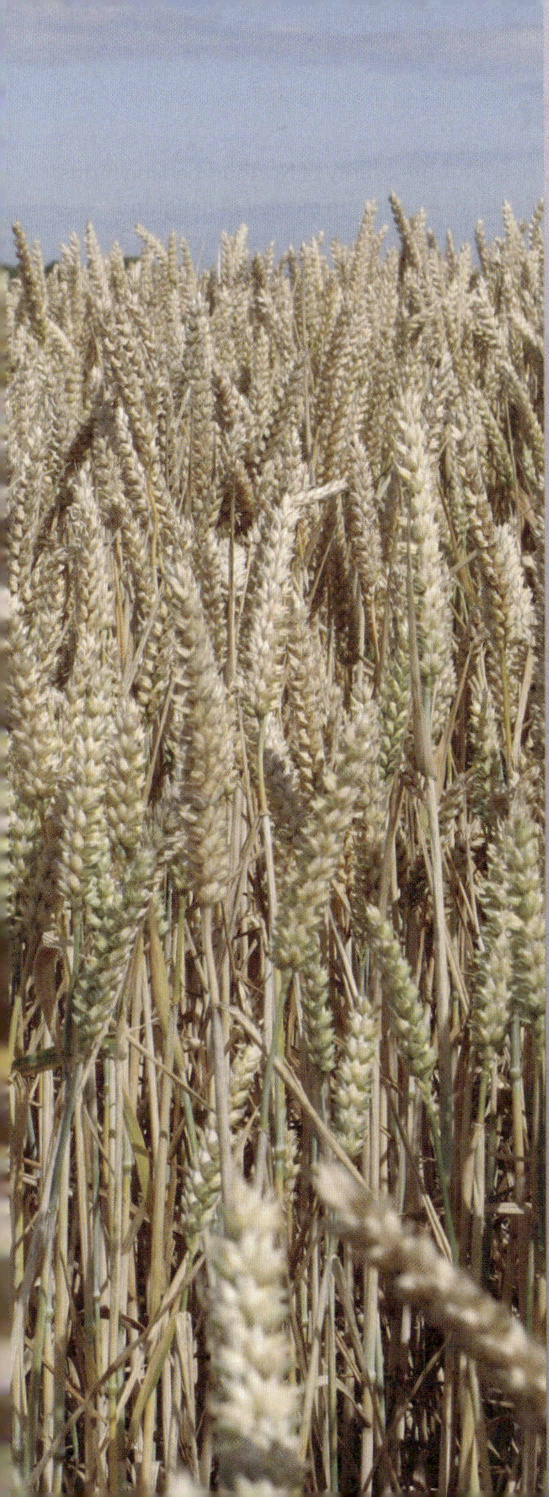

The Northeast

564 Durham

568 Around Durham

573 The Tees Valley

574 Newcastle upon Tyne

583 Around Newcastle

584 Hadrian's Wall

588 Northumberland National Park

591 The Northumberland coast

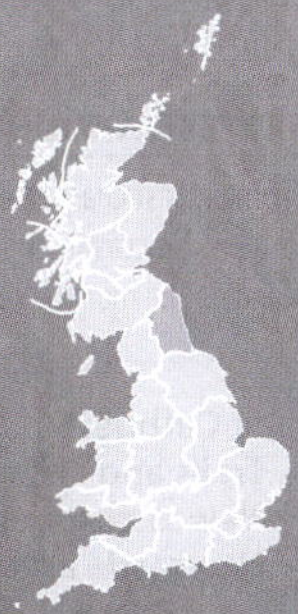

BAMBURGH CASTLE

13

The Northeast

Remote and breathtakingly beautiful, the county of Northumberland forms the bulk of the northeast of England. An enticing medley of delightful market towns, glorious golden beaches, wooded dells, wild uplands and an unsurpassed collection of historical monuments, it's undoubtedly the main draw in the Northeast, and where you should focus the majority of your time. South of Northumberland lies County Durham, famous for its lovely university town and magnificent twelfth-century cathedral, while to the southeast and edged by the North Sea is industrial Tyne and Wear. It's home to the busy and burgeoning metropolis of Newcastle-upon-Tyne, a dynamic and distinctive city crammed with cultural attractions, great shops and an exceptionally energetic nightlife.

While its most recent past is defined by industry and in particular post-industrial hardship, the Northeast has an eventful early history: Romans, Vikings and Normans have all left dramatic evidence of their colonization, none more cherished than the 84-mile-long **Hadrian's Wall**, built by the Romans in 122 AD to contain the troublesome tribes of the far north. Thousands come each year to walk along parts, or all, of the Wall, or to cycle the nearby National Route 72. Neighbouring Northumberland National Park also has plenty for outdoors enthusiasts, with its huge reservoir, **Kielder Water** and surrounding footpaths and cycleways.

As well as Roman ruins, medieval **castles** scatter the region, the best preserved being Alnwick, with its wonderful gardens, and stocky Bamburgh, on the coast. The shoreline round here, from Amble past Bamburgh to the Scottish border town of Berwick-upon-Tweed – and officially the end of Northumberland – is simply stunning, boasting miles of pancake-flat, dune-backed beach and a handful of off-shore islands. Reached by a tidal causeway, the lonely little islet of **Lindisfarne** – Holy Island – where early Christian monks created the Lindisfarne Gospels, is the most famous, while not far away to the south, near Seahouses, the **Farne Islands** are the perfect habitat for large colonies of seabirds including puffins, guillemots and kittiwakes.

South of Northumberland, **County Durham** and **Tyne and Wear** better illustrate the Northeast's industrial heritage. It was here in 1825 that the world's first railway opened – the Darlington and Stockton line – with local coal and ore fuelling the shipbuilding and heavy-engineering companies of Tyneside. Abandoned coalfields, train lines, quaysides and factories throughout the area have been transformed into superb, child-friendly tourist attractions.

GETTING AROUND — THE NORTHEAST

The main East Coast **train** line runs up and down the coast from London King's Cross to Edinburgh, calling at Darlington, Durham, Newcastle and Berwick-upon-Tweed, while cross-country trains and **buses** serve smaller towns and villages inland. In the more remote areas public transport is spotty, so it's best to have your own car or bike.

St Cuthbert p.565
Trails and cycleways p.568
Newcastle orientation p.574
Newcastle art galleries p.577
The Geordie Nation p.583
Along Hadrian's Wall p.584
Top 5 Northumbrian castles p.591

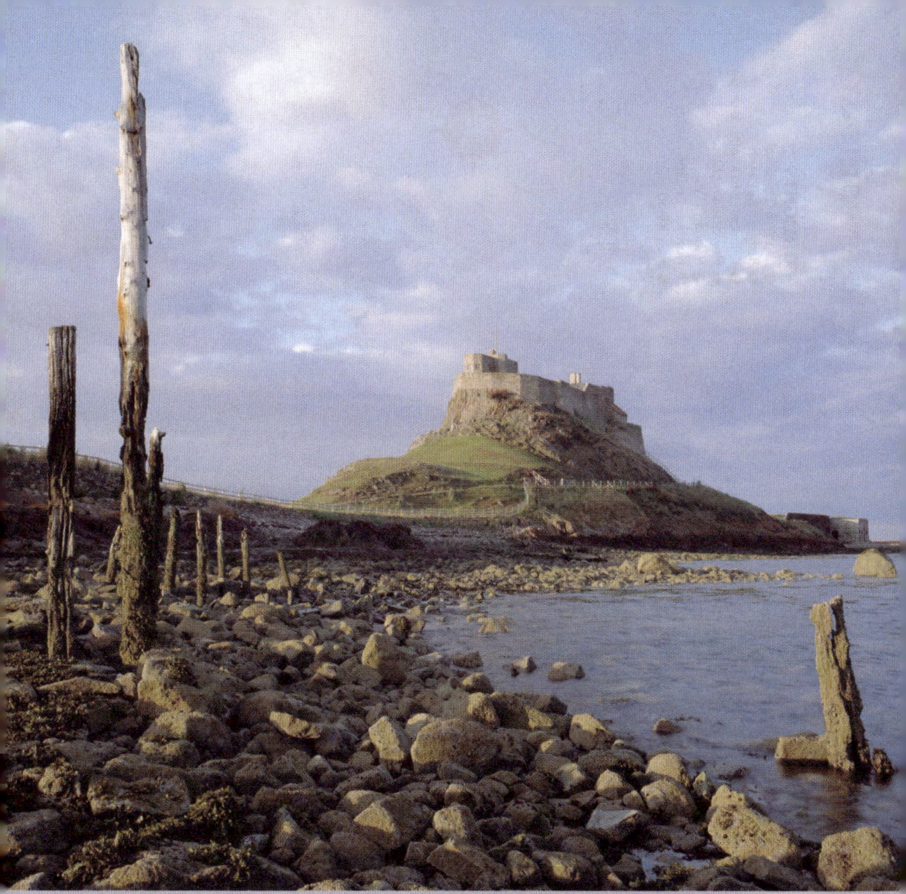

LINDISFARNE CASTLE, HOLY ISLAND

Highlights

❶ **Durham Cathedral** Said to be the finest Norman building in Europe, this awe-inspiring cathedral soars above the River Wear. **See p.565**

❷ **Beamish Museum** Exceptional open-air museum that recreates the Northeast's industrial past. **See p.568**

❸ **Killhope Lead Mining Museum** Put on a hard hat and get down the pit to see what life was really like for the Weardale coal miners. **See p.572**

❹ **Newcastle nightlife** From raucous clubs and chic wine bars to cosy boozers and chilled-out indie gigs, there's something for everybody. **See p.582**

❺ **Hadrian's Wall** Walk the length of the greatest Roman monument in England. **See p.584**

❻ **Northumberland castles** Northumberland is littered with beautiful castles, telling of a violent past ridden with ferocious battles and embittered family feuds. **See p.591**

❼ **Holy Island** A brooding lump of rock reached by a tidal causeway, this is a cradle of Christianity, where the splendid, illuminated Lindisfarne Gospels were created. **See p.595**

HIGHLIGHTS ARE MARKED ON THE MAP ON PP.562–563

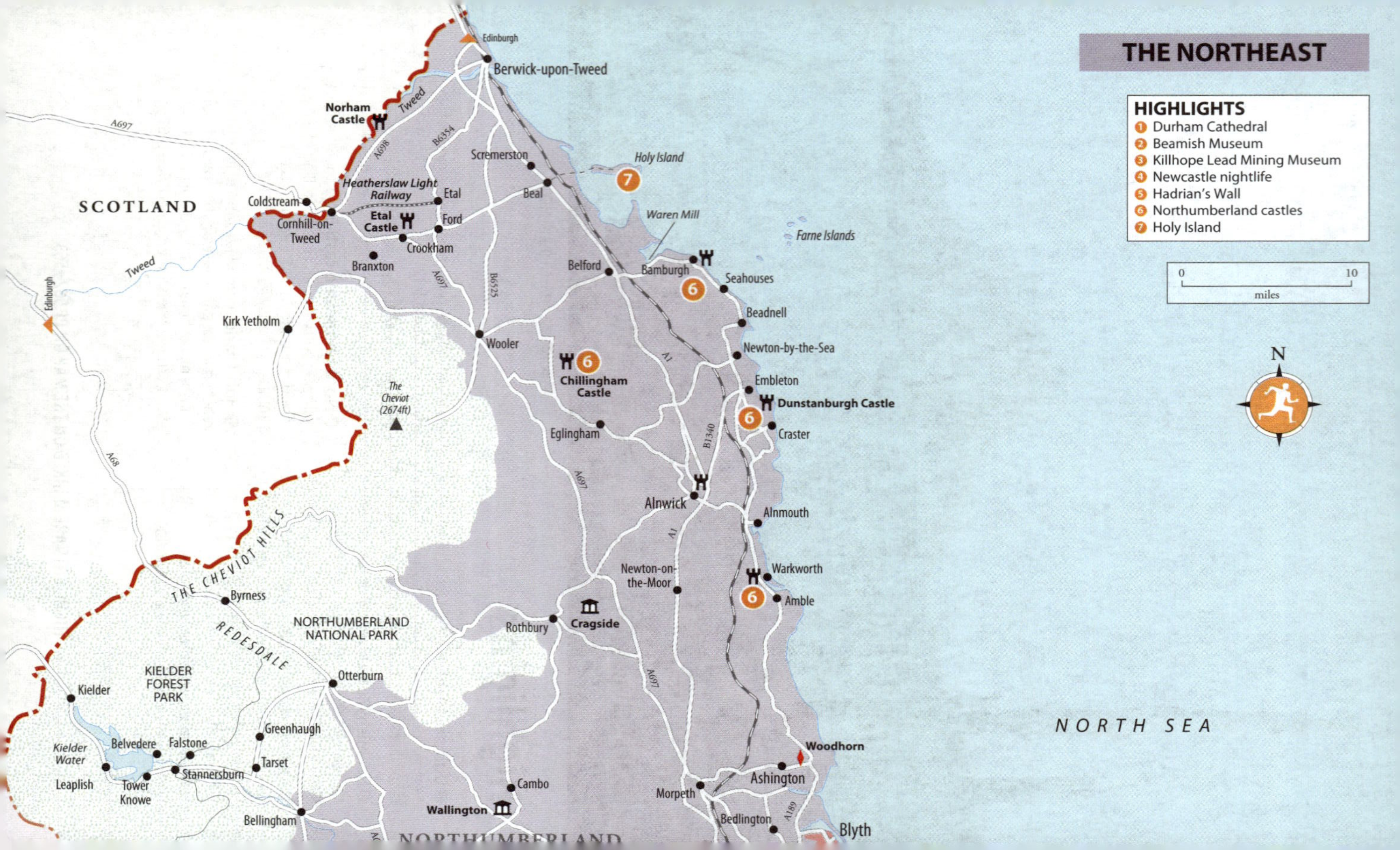
THE NORTHEAST
HIGHLIGHTS
1 Durham Cathedral
2 Beamish Museum
3 Killhope Lead Mining Museum
4 Newcastle nightlife
5 Hadrian's Wall
6 Northumberland castles
7 Holy Island
0
10
miles
N
NORTH SEA
SCOTLAND
NORTHUMBERLAND
Edinburgh
Berwick-upon-Tweed
Norham Castle
Tweed
A697
A698
B6354
Scremerston
Holy Island
Beal
Heatherslaw Light Railway
Etal
Etal Castle
Ford
Coldstream
Cornhill-on-Tweed
Crookham
Waren Mill
Farne Islands
Branxton
Belford
Bamburgh
Seahouses
Beadnell
B6525
Kirk Yetholm
Wooler
Chillingham Castle
A1
Newton-by-the-Sea
Embleton
Dunstanburgh Castle
Craster
The Cheviot (2674ft)
Eglingham
B1340
A68
Alnwick
Alnmouth
THE CHEVIOT HILLS
Newton-on-the-Moor
Warkworth
Amble
Byrness
Cragside
Rothbury
NORTHUMBERLAND NATIONAL PARK
REDESDALE
KIELDER FOREST PARK
Kielder
Otterburn
Greenhaugh
Falstone
Belvedere
Kielder Water
Tarset
Stannersburn
Leaplish
Tower Knowe
Cambo
Woodhorn
Ashington
Morpeth
Wallington
Bellingham
Bedlington
A189
Blyth

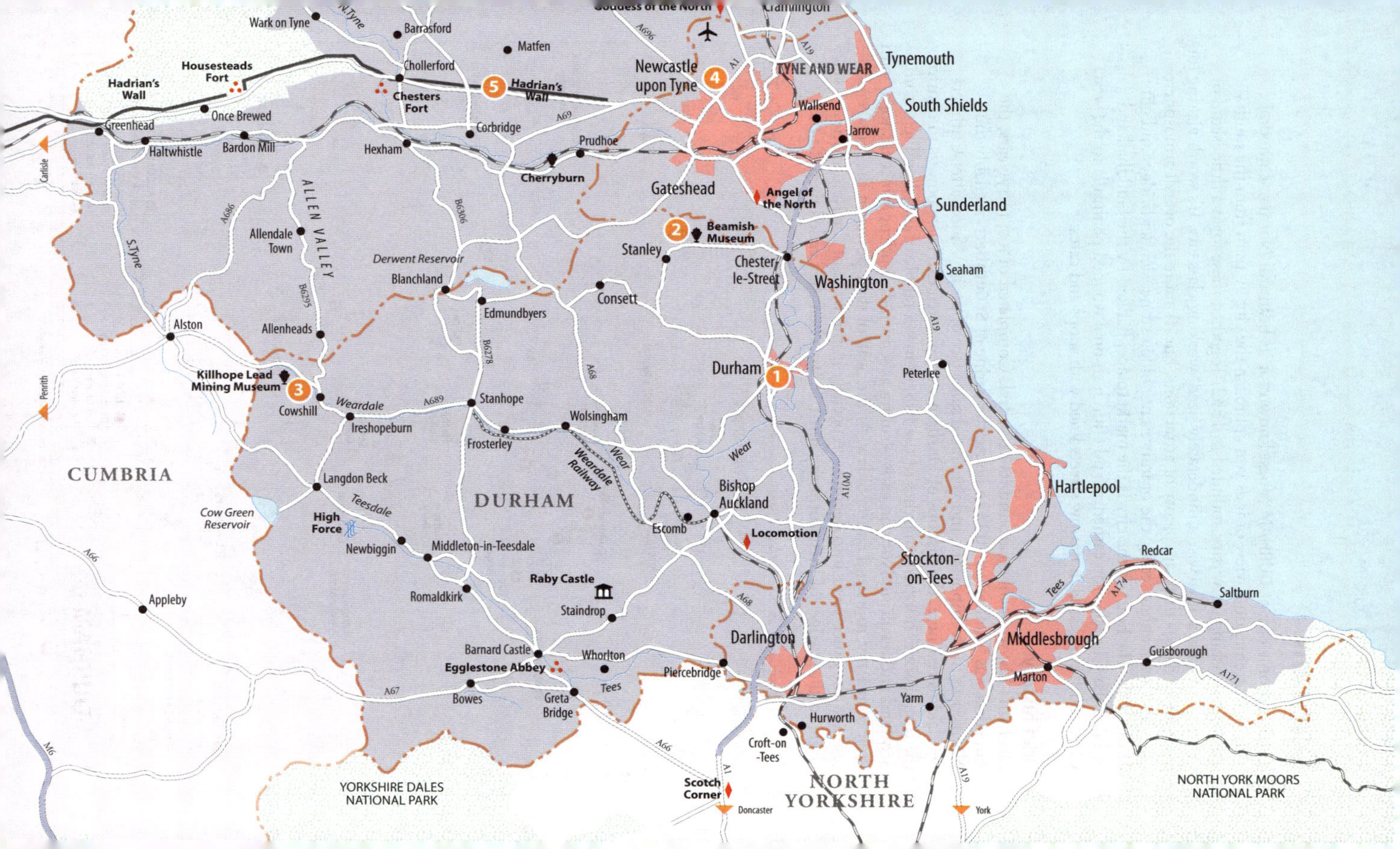

Tynemouth
South Shields
Sunderland
Seaham
Washington
Hartlepool
Redcar
Saltburn
Guisborough
Middlesbrough
Marton
Stockton-on-Tees
Yarm
Hurworth
Croft-on-Tees
Darlington
Scotch Corner
Doncaster
York
NORTH YORKSHIRE
NORTH YORK MOORS NATIONAL PARK
YORKSHIRE DALES NATIONAL PARK
CUMBRIA
DURHAM
TYNE AND WEAR
Newcastle upon Tyne
Gateshead
Wallsend
Jarrow
Angel of the North
Beamish Museum
Stanley
Chester-le-Street
Durham
Peterlee
Consett
Bishop Auckland
Escomb
Locomotion
Piercebridge
Raby Castle
Staindrop
Whorlton
Barnard Castle
Egglestone Abbey
Greta Bridge
Bowes
Romaldkirk
Middleton-in-Teesdale
Newbiggin
High Force
Teesdale
Langdon Beck
Cow Green Reservoir
Appleby
Alston
Killhope Lead Mining Museum
Cowshill
Weardale
Ireshopeburn
Stanhope
Frosterley
Wolsingham
Weardale Railway
Wear
Tees
Edmundbyers
Blanchland
Derwent Reservoir
Allenheads
Allendale Town
ALLEN VALLEY
Haltwhistle
Greenhead
Bardon Mill
Once Brewed
Housesteads Fort
Hadrian's Wall
Hexham
Corbridge
Prudhoe
Cherryburn
Chesters Fort
Chollerford
Barrasford
Matfen
Wark on Tyne
N.Tyne
S.Tyne
Carlisle
Penrith
A1
A1(M)
A19
A66
A67
A68
A69
A171
A174
A686
A689
A696
M6
B6278
B6295
B6306

13

Durham

The handsome city of **DURHAM** is best known for its beautiful Norman **cathedral** – there's a tremendous view of it as you approach the city by train from the south – and its flourishing university, founded in 1832. Together, these form a little island of privilege in what's otherwise a moderately sized, working-class city. It's worth visiting for a couple of days – there are plenty of attractions, but it's more the overall atmosphere that captivates, enhanced by the omnipresent golden stone, slender bridges and glint of the river. The heart of the city is the **marketplace**, flanked by the Guildhall and St Nicholas Church. The cathedral and church sit on a wooded peninsula to the west, while southwards stretch narrow streets lined with shops and cafés.

Brief history

Durham's history revolves around its cathedral. Completed in just forty years, the cathedral was founded in 1093 to house the shrine of **St Cuthbert**, arguably the Northeast's most important and venerated saint (see opposite). Soon after Cuthbert was laid to rest here, the bishops of Durham were granted extensive powers to control the troublesome northern marches of the Kingdom – a rabble of invading Picts from Scotland and revolting Norman earls – ruling as semi-independent **Prince Bishops**, with their own army, mint and courts of law. At the peak of their power in the fourteenth century, the office went into decline – especially in the wake of the Reformation – yet clung to the vestiges of their authority until 1836, when they ceded them to the

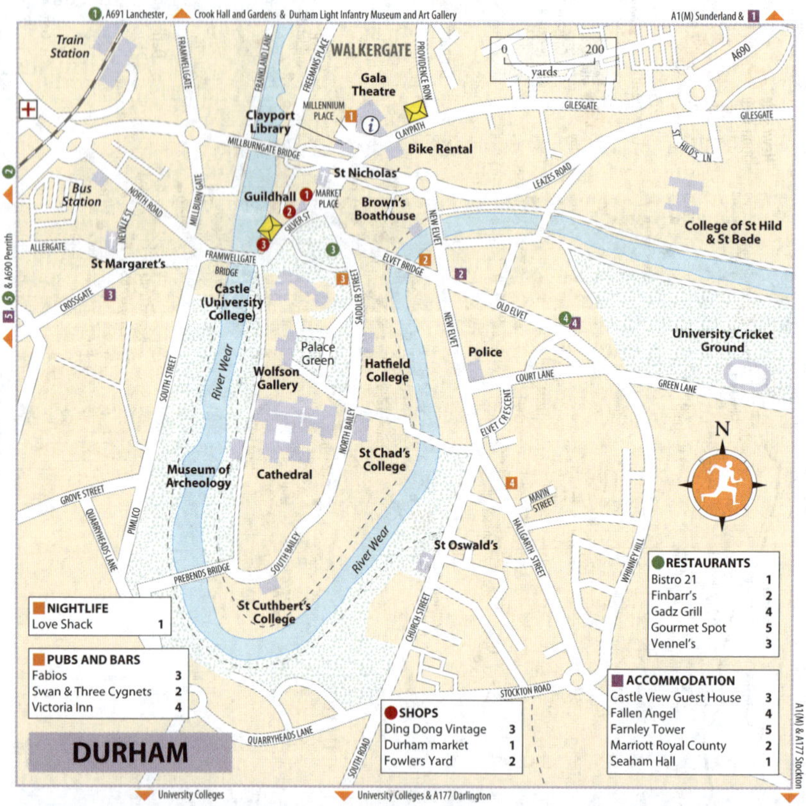

ST CUTHBERT

Born in North Northumbria in 653, **Cuthbert** spent most of his youth in Melrose Abbey (p.753) in Scotland, from where he moved briefly to Lindisfarne Island, which was at that time a well-known centre of religious endeavour. Preferring the peace and rugged solitude of the Farne Islands, he lived on Inner Farne for thirty years. News of his piety spread, however, and he was head-hunted to become Bishop of Lindisfarne, a position he accepted reluctantly. Uncomfortable in the limelight, he soon returned to Inner Farne, and when he died his remains were moved to Lindisfarne before being carted off to Durham Cathedral which soon became a pilgrimage site.

Crown. They abandoned Durham Castle for their palace in Bishop Auckland (see p.569) and transferred their old home to the fledgling Durham University, England's third-oldest seat of learning after Oxford and Cambridge.

Durham Cathedral

July & Aug Mon–Sat 9.30am–8pm, Sun 12.30–8pm; Sept–June Mon–Sat 9.30am–6pm, Sun 12.30–5.30pm • Donation requested; Cathedral Highlights Pass (£5) covers entry to the Monks' Dormitory, the Treasures of St Cuthbert and the audiovisual displays • Guided tours April–Oct 2–3 daily • **Tower** April–Sept Mon–Sat 10am–4pm; Oct–March Mon–Sat 10am–3pm; access sometimes restricted, call to check • £5 • T 0191 386 4266, W durhamcathedral.co.uk

From the marketplace, it's a five-minute walk up Saddler Street to **Durham Cathedral**, considered a supreme example of the Norman-Romanesque style. The awe-inspiring **nave** used pointed arches for the first time in England, raising the vaulted ceiling to new and dizzying heights. The weight of the stone is borne by massive pillars, their heaviness relieved by striking Moorish-influenced geometric patterns. A door on the western side gives access to the **tower**, from where there are beautiful views. Separated from the nave by a Victorian marble screen is the **choir**, where the dark Restoration stalls are overshadowed by the 13ft-high **bishop's throne**. Beyond, the **Chapel of the Nine Altars** dates from the thirteenth century. Here, and around the **Shrine of St Cuthbert**, much of the stonework is of local Weardale marble, each dark shaft bearing its own pattern of fossils. Cuthbert himself lies beneath a plain marble slab, his shrine having gained a reputation over the centuries for its curative powers. The legend was given credence in 1104, when the saint's body was exhumed in Chester-le-Street for reburial here, and was found to be completely uncorrupted, more than four hundred years after his death on Lindisfarne. Almost certainly, this was the result of his fellow monks having (unintentionally) preserved the body by laying it in sand containing salt crystals.

Back near the entrance, at the west end of the church is the **Galilee Chapel**; begun in the 1170s, its light and exotic decoration is in imitation of the Great Mosque of Córdoba. The chapel contains the simple tombstone of the **Venerable Bede** (see p.584), the Northumbrian monk credited with being England's first historian. Bede died at the monastery of Jarrow in 735, and his remains were first transferred to the cathedral in 1020.

The Monks' Dormitory and Treasures of St Cuthbert

Monks' Dormitory April–Oct Mon–Sat 10am–4pm, Sun 2–4.30pm • **Treasures of St Cuthbert** Mon–Sat 10am–4.30pm, Sun 2–4.30pm • Cathedral Highlights Pass (£5) covers entry to the Monks' Dormitory, the Treasures of St Cuthbert and the audiovisual displays

A large wooden doorway opposite the cathedral's main entrance leads into the spacious **cloisters**, flanked by what remains of the monastic buildings. On the right of the passage lies the **Monks' Dormitory** with its original twelfth-century oak roof – it now houses the cathedral library. At the end of the passage, in the undercroft, the **Treasures of St Cuthbert** exhibition displays some striking relics, including the cathedral's original twelfth-century lion-head Sanctuary Knocker (the one on the main door is a replica), and a splendid facsimile copy of the Lindisfarne Gospels (the originals are in the British Library in London). A couple of interesting **audiovisual displays** detail the history of the cathedral, too.

13

The Wolfson Gallery

Tues–Fri 10am–4.45pm, Sat & Sun noon–4.45pm • £3 • ☎ 0191 334 2972, Ⓦ dur.ac.uk

The **Wolfson Gallery**, housed in the Palace Green library between the cathedral and the castle, shows off a wonderful collection of the university's treasures, drawn from the city's various museums. The displays change regularly, but could feature anything from a series of illuminated medieval manuscripts to Chinese imperial textiles and ancient Egyptian relics.

Durham Castle

Easter & July–Sept daily tours 10am, 11am, noon & hourly 2–5pm; rest of the year daily 2pm, 3pm & 4pm • £5 • ☎ 0191 334 3800, Ⓦ dur.ac.uk

Durham Castle lost its medieval appearance long ago, and the university subsequently renovated the old keep as a hall of residence. It's only possible to visit the castle on a 45-minute guided tour, highlights of which include the fifteenth-century kitchen, a climb up the enormous hanging staircase and the Norman chapel, notable for its lively Romanesque carved capitals.

Crook Hall

Frankland Lane, Sidegate • Easter weekend to mid-Sept Sun–Thurs 11am–5pm • £6 • ☎ 0191 384 8028, Ⓦ crookhallgardens.co.uk

Crook Hall is a hidden gem in Durham, and well worth making the effort to find. A rare mix of medieval, Jacobean and Georgian architecture, with origins dating from the twelfth century, it's said to be one of the oldest inhabited houses in the area. You can explore its rambling rooms, complete with period furniture and rickety staircases, as well as a series of beautifully tended, themed gardens, including the ethereal Silver and White garden, the Shakespeare Garden, planted with herbs used in Elizabethan times, and the delightful Secret Walled Garden. The flower-swathed **coffeeshop** serves up delicious cream teas (£8.50 per person).

Durham Light Infantry Museum and Art Gallery

Aykley Heads • April–Oct daily 10am–5pm; Nov–March 10am–4pm • £3.50 • ☎ 0191 384 2214, Ⓦ durham.gov.uk/dli

Just north of the city centre and set in pleasant open parkland, the **Durham Light Infantry Museum and Art Gallery** tells the story of the DLI, one of the most famous county regiments in the British Army, from their beginnings in 1181, via World War I (when it lost 12,000 soldiers) to its last parade in 1968. Exhibits include splendid uniforms, a huge collection of more than three thousand medals and weapons, and personal items including letters and photographs. Upstairs, the art gallery features temporary exhibitions showcasing work from emerging and established artists.

ARRIVAL AND INFORMATION — DURHAM

By train Durham's train station is on North Rd, a 10min walk from the centre of the city.

Destinations Berwick-upon-Tweed (every 30min; 1hr 10min), Darlington (frequent; 20min); London (every 30–60min; 3hr); Newcastle (frequent; 15min); York (frequent; 50min).

By bus It's a 5min walk to the city centre from the bus station on North Road.

Destinations Bishop Auckland (frequent; 30min); Chester-le-Street (frequent; 20min); Darlington (every 20min; 1hr 10min); Middlesbrough (every 30min; 55min); Newcastle (Mon–Sat every 30min, Sun 4–6 daily; 50min); Stanhope (Mon–Fri 4 daily; 45min).

Tourist office 2 Millennium Place, off Claypath (Mon–Sat 9.30am–5.30pm, Sun 11am–4pm; ☎ 0191 384 3720, Ⓦ durhamtourism.co.uk).

GETTING AROUND

Cathedral Bus A minibus runs two routes round Durham serving the train station, the bus station, the marketplace and the cathedral. Tickets cost 50p and are valid all day.

ACCOMMODATION

Castle View Guest House 4 Crossgate ⓣ0191 386 8852, ⓦcastle-view.co.uk. Pretty terraced house near St Margaret's Church, with lovely views of the castle. The peaceful rooms are freshly decorated and extremely clean, and overlook a leafy courtyard garden. **£80**

★ **Fallen Angel** 34 Old Elvet ⓣ0191 384 1037, ⓦfallenangelhotel.com. Durham's first boutique hotel with ten quirky, themed rooms including the sumptuous Cruella, with Gothic black walls dripping with faux-diamonds, and the dreamy Russian Bride suite with bamboo flooring, fur quilts and velvet-soft bed. For families, there's the fun, stars-and-stripes decorated New York apartment. The Gadz Grill downstairs serves quality meat and seafood. **£125**

Farnley Tower The Avenue ⓣ0191 375 0011, ⓦfarnley-tower.co.uk. A 10min walk up a steep hill west from the centre, this fine stone Victorian house has thirteen comfortable rooms with bright, co-ordinated fabrics. The best rooms have sweeping city views. They also run a smart restaurant, *Gourmet Spot* (see below). **£95**

Marriott Hotel Royal County Old Elvet ⓣ0191 386 6821, ⓦmarriotthotels.com. Elegant and luxurious, the *Marriott* has long been regarded as Durham's top hotel. Rooms have huge beds, marble-trimmed bathrooms and comfortable sitting areas. There's a fitness centre and a swimming pool, as well as a selection of restaurants and bars. **£235**

Seaham Hall Lord Byron's Walk, Seaham, 10 miles northeast of Durham ⓣ0191 516 1400, ⓦseaham-hall.co.uk. Perched on a cliff-top overlooking the sea, this hip, exclusive hotel makes a great coastal base for city sightseeing – Durham is only a 20min drive away. It's known for its luxurious spa and pampering treatments and has a wonderful restaurant; spa, dinner, bed and breakfast packages are available. **£200**

EATING

Bistro 21 Aykley Heads ⓣ0191 384 4354, ⓦbistrotwentyone.co.uk. Housed in a lemon-yellow building a 10min walk from the DLI Museum and Art Gallery, Bistro 21 serves excellent, seasonal cuisine; mains start at £18 and could include fishcakes with a parsley cream and buttered spinach or a juicy sirloin steak with triple-cooked chips. The interior is fresh and pretty, with wooden tables, wicker chairs and whitewashed walls. Mon–Sat noon–2pm & 6–10pm.

Finbarrs Waddington St, Flass Vale ⓣ0191 370 9999, ⓦfinbarrsrestaurant.co.uk. This chic restaurant in leafy surroundings serves up anything from full English breakfasts and banana pancakes to dinners of Moroccan lamb with golden raisins; the sweet cherry and pistachio sundaes are delicious. Mains from £15. Mon–Sat 7–9.30am, noon–2.30pm & 6–9.30pm, Sun 7.30–10.30am & noon–9pm.

Gourmet Spot The Avenue ⓣ0191 384 6655, ⓦgourmet-spot.co.uk. Funky little restaurant with sleek black furniture, red and cream walls and a big glitter ball. There's as à la carte (two courses £30, three £38) and a seven-course tasting menu (£55 without wine, £75 with) featuring innovative dishes such as braised pigs' cheeks with grapefruit and pea shoots, and delectable puddings including coconut pannacotta with passion fruit jelly. Tues–Sun 5pm–late.

Vennel's Saddler's Yard, Saddler St ⓣ0191 375 0571. Named after the skinny alley or "vennel" where it stands – near the junction with Elvet Bridge – this café serves up generous sandwiches, salads, quiche and tasty cakes in its sixteenth-century courtyard. Daily 10am–5pm.

DRINKING

Walkergate is the area to head for if you're after loud, lively bars and mainstream nightclubs pumping out cheesy music, but there are also plenty of quieter establishments and more traditional, laidback pubs.

Fabios 66 Sadler St ⓣ0191 383 9290, ⓦfabiosdurham.com. Just above *La Spaghettata* pizzeria, *Fabios* occupies a series of rooms filled with comfy, rug-draped sofas and chalked-up blackboards offering drinks from around £3. The atmosphere is cool and relaxed, with music a melange of rap, r'n'b and dance. Jazz nights every Wednesday. Daily 6pm–2am.

Swan & Three Cygnets Elvet Bridge ⓣ0191 384 0242. Sitting proudly at the end of Elvet Bridge overlooking the River Wear, this loud and cheery pub serves cheap drinks and is filled with a mixed crowd of locals and students. Mon–Sat 11am–11pm, Sun noon–10.30pm.

Victoria Inn 86 Hallgarth St ⓣ0191 386 5269, ⓦvictoriainn-durhamcity.co.uk. With its three open fires and rickety wooden stools, this cosy, traditional pub specializes in local ales – try the creamy Tyneside Blonde or the hoppy Centurion Bitter – and stocks more than thirty Irish whiskeys. Mon–Sat noon–3pm & 6–11pm, Sun noon–3pm & 7–11pm.

NIGHTLIFE AND ENTERTAINMENT

Durham's **clubs**, frequented by students during the week and locals at the weekends are scattered through the city centre and in Walkergate. There's generally no dress code, but the locals tend to make an effort. In addition to shows at the Gala Theatre, you can catch regular **classical concerts** at venues around the city, including the cathedral. Ask the tourist office for more details.

13

Gala Theatre Millennium Place 0191 332 4041, galadurham.co.uk. Music of all kinds, plus theatre, cinema, dance and comedy.

Love Shack Walkergate 0191 384 5575, loveshackdurham.com. Large, popular club with two bars, snug booths and a sleek dancefloor. Music is an energetic mix of contemporary club tunes and cheesy classics. Admission £2–4; free for women on Fridays. Wed & Thurs 10pm–2am, Fri & Sat 8am–2pm.

SHOPPING

Durham Market Durham's Indoor Market holds a variety of stalls including a haberdashers, sweet shop and fishmongers. Mon–Sat from 9am.

★ **Ding Dong Vintage** 45 The Gates 07887 536409. A hectic jumble of wonderful vintage clothes, hats, bags, shoes and jewellery. The men's section includes an assortment of watches, medals and regimental uniforms. Mon–Sat 10am–5.30pm.

Farmers' Market Market Place durhammarkets.co.uk. Fresh local produce sold on the third Thursday of every month. 9am–3.30pm.

Fowlers Yard Silver St, behind the marketplace fowlersyarddurham.co.uk. A series of workshops showcasing local trades and crafts. Drop by to watch the craftspeople at work, commission a piece or buy off the cuff. Opening hours vary.

Around Durham

County Durham has shaken off its grimy reputation in recent years and recast itself as a thriving tourist area. The well-to-do market towns of **Bishop Auckland** and **Barnard Castle** make great day-trips from Durham, and there's plenty of excellent walking and cycling in the wilds of the two Pennine valleys, **Teesdale** and **Weardale**. You'll find some top-class museums in the area, too, including **Beamish**, **Locomotion** and the **Bowes Museum**.

Beamish Museum

Ten miles north of Durham, off the A693 • April–Oct daily 10am–5pm; Nov–March Tues–Thurs, Sat & Sun 10am–4pm; in winter, only the town, pit colliery and tramway are open • April–Oct £16; Nov–March Tues–Thurs £8, Sat & Sun £16; 20 percent discount if you get there by bus • 0191 370 4000, beamish.org.uk • Waggonway #28/28A runs from Newcastle (April–Oct daily, Nov–March Sat & Sun; every 30min; day returns from £2.40); bus #128 runs hourly from Durham (April–Oct Sat only)

The open-air **Beamish Museum** spreads out over 300 acres, with buildings taken from all over the region painstakingly reassembled in six main sections linked by restored trams and buses. Complete with costumed shopkeepers, workers and householders, four of the sections show life in 1913, before the upheavals of World War I, including a **colliery village** complete with drift mine (regular tours throughout the day) and a large-scale recreation of the High Street in a market **town**. Two areas date to 1825, at the beginning of the northeast's industrial development, including a **manor house**, with horse yard, formal gardens, vegetable plots and orchards. You can ride on the beautifully restored steam-powered carousel, the **Steam Galloper** – dating from the 1890s – and the **Pockerley Waggonway**, which is pulled along by a replica of George Stephenson's *Locomotion* (see opposite), the first passenger-carrying steam train in the world.

TRAILS AND CYCLEWAYS

Coast to Coast (C2C) c2c-guide.co.uk. This demanding cycle route runs 140 miles from Whitehaven to Sunderland.

Hadrian's Wall Path hadrians-wall.org. An 84-mile waymarked trail allowing you to walk the length of this atmospheric Roman monument.

National Route 72 cycle-routes.org/hadrianscycleway. Cycle path that runs the length of Hadrian's Wall.

Pennine Way thepennineway.co.uk. This 270-mile-long footpath starts in the Peak District National Park, runs along the Pennine ridge through the Yorkshire Dales, up into Northumberland, across the Cheviots, and finishes in the Scottish Borders.

Bishop Auckland

BISHOP AUCKLAND, a busy little market town eleven miles southwest of Durham, grew up slowly around its showpiece building, **Auckland Castle**, and became famous throughout England as the homeland of the mighty Prince Bishops. Today the town has paled into lesser significance but still offers enough for a pleasant hour or two's wander.

Auckland Castle

Castle Easter–June & Sept Sun & Mon 2–5pm; July & Aug Sun 2–5pm, Mon & Wed 11am–5pm • £4 **Deer park** Daily 7am–dusk • Free • ⓣ 01388 602576, ⓦ auckland-castle.co.uk

Looking more like a Gothic mansion than a traditional castellated castle, **Auckland Castle** has been the official residence of the Bishop of Durham since 1832, although its origins are in fact much older. Founded in 1183, the palace was established as a hunting lodge for the Prince Bishops and is set within acres of lush parkland. Most of the rooms are today rather sparsely furnished, save the splendid seventeenth-century marble-and-limestone chapel and the long dining room, with its thirteen paintings of Jacob and his sons by Francisco de Zurbarán, commissioned in the 1640s for a monastery in South America. After you've seen the castle, stroll around the parkland and into the adjacent **Bishop's Deer Park**, with its Deer House dating from 1760.

Binchester Roman Fort

Daily: Easter–June & Sept 11am–5pm; July & Aug 10am–5pm • £2.55 • ⓣ 0191 370 8712, ⓦ durham.gov.uk

From the town's marketplace, it's a pleasant twenty-minute walk along the banks of the River Wear to the remains of **Binchester Roman Fort**. While most of the stone fort and a civilian settlement that occupied the area remain hidden beneath surrounding fields, the bathhouse with its sophisticated underground heating system (hypocaust) is visible. Excavations are ongoing.

Locomotion (National Railway Museum Shildon)

Shildon, 5 miles southeast of Bishop Auckland • April–Oct daily 10am–5pm; Nov–March Wed–Sun 10am–4pm • Free • ⓣ 01388 777999, ⓦ nrm.org.uk • Regular trains from Darlington to Bishop Auckland stop at Shildon station, a 2min walk from the museum. Buses #1 and 1B (to Crook and Tow Law) run from Darlington (Mon–Sat every 30min), stopping at Dale Rd, a 15min walk from the museum.

The first passenger train in the world left from the station at Shildon in 1825 – making the small County Durham town the world's oldest railway town. It's a heritage explored in the magnificently realized **Locomotion** (also known as National Railway Museum Shildon), the regional outpost of York's National Railway Museum. It's less a museum and more an experience, spread out around a 1.5mile-long site, with the attractions linked by free bus from the reception building. Depots, sidings, junctions and coal drops lead ultimately to the heart of the museum, **Collection** – a gargantuan steel hangar containing an extraordinary array of seventy locomotives, dating from the very earliest days of steam. With interactive children's exhibits, summer steam rides, rallies and shows, it makes an excellent family day out.

Barnard Castle

Affectionately known as "Barney", the honey-coloured market town of **BARNARD CASTLE** lies fifteen miles southwest of Bishop Auckland. The middle of the town is dominated by the splendid octagonal **Market Cross**; built in 1747 and formerly functioning as a market for dairy and butter, it now serves a more mundane purpose as a roundabout.

The castle

Galgate • Daily: April–Sept 10am–6pm; Oct 10am–4pm; rest of the year limited opening hours • EH • £4.30 • ⓣ 01833 638212

The skeletal remains of the town's **castle** sit high on a rock overlooking the River Tees. It was founded in 1125 by the powerful Norman baron Bernard de Balliol – thus the

13

town's name – and later ended up in the hands of Richard III. Richard's crest, in the shape of a boar, is still visible carved above a window in the inner ward.

Bowes Museum

Half a mile east of the town centre • Daily 10am–5pm • £9 • ⓣ 01833 690606, ⓦ bowesmuseum.org.uk

Castle aside, the prime attraction in town is the grand French-style chateau that constitutes the **Bowes Museum**. Begun in 1869, the chateau was commissioned by John and Josephine Bowes, a local businessman and MP and his French actress wife, who spent much of their time in Paris collecting ostentatious treasures and antiques. Don't miss the beautiful Silver Swan, a life-size musical automaton dating from 1773 – every afternoon at 2pm he puts on an enchanting show, preening his shiny feathers while swimming along a river filled with jumping fish.

Egglestone Abbey

A mile southeast of Barnard Castle, off the B6277 • April–Oct 10am–6.30pm; rest of the year limited opening hours • EH • Free

It's a fine mile-long walk from the castle, southeast (downriver) through the fields above the banks of the Tees, to the lovely shattered ruins of **Egglestone Abbey,** a minor foundation dating from 1195. A succession of wars and the Dissolution destroyed most of it, but you can still see the skeleton of a thirteenth-century church and the remains of the monk's living quarters, including an ingenious latrine system.

ARRIVAL AND INFORMATION — BARNARD CASTLE

By bus Buses stop either side of Galgate.

Destinations Bishop Auckland (Mon–Sat 6 daily; 50min); Darlington (Mon–Sat every 30min; Sun hourly; 45min); Middleton-in-Teesdale (Mon–Sat hourly; 35min); Raby Castle (Mon–Sat hourly; 15min).

Tourist office Flatts Rd, at the end of Galgate by the castle (April–Oct Mon–Thurs & Sat 9.30am–5pm, Fri 9.30am–4.30pm, Sun 10am–4pm; Nov–March Mon–Sat 10am–3pm; ⓣ 01833 696356).

ACCOMMODATION

Crich House 94 Galgate ⓣ 01833 630357, ⓦ crich-house.co.uk. Spotless, homely rooms in a lovely Victorian house run by a warm, welcoming couple. The king-sized breakfasts have won local awards – expect an array of eggs, locally sourced meats, delicious cereals and yoghurts. £65

Homelands 85 Galgate ⓣ 01833 638757, ⓦ homelandsguesthouse.co.uk. An assortment of pretty rooms with lots of floral soft furnishings and comfortable beds. The owners are very knowledgeable about the area and can recommend plenty of good walks. Breakfast is great, featuring delicious fruit salads and generous cooked options. £70

EATING AND DRINKING

Blagraves House 30–32 The Bank ⓣ 01833 637668, ⓦ blagraves.com. Supposed to be the oldest house in Barnard Castle, dating back 500 years, this refined restaurant – oozing atmosphere, with its low oak wooden beams, open log fires and plush furnishings – specializes in traditional British cuisine. Tues–Sun 7–9.30pm.

The Bridge Inn Whorlton, 4 miles east ⓣ 01833 627341, ⓦ thebridgeinnwhorlton-village.com. Cosy country pub, with open fires and flagstone floors, in the picturesque village of Whorlton. The food is traditional pub grub – sausages and mash, chicken pie and the like. Closed Mon.

Riverside Bridge End ⓣ 01833 637576, ⓦ riverside-restaurant.co.uk. Overlooked by the castle, this small, snug restaurant has lovely wooden beams and is lit by flickering candles. The food is excellent – try the breast of local pheasant with parsnip crisps and merlot jus (£16.50) and don't miss the indulgent chocolate truffle pot with pistachio ice cream (£5.95). Their Sunday lunches are deservedly acclaimed. Tues–Sat from 6pm, Fri–Sun noon–2pm.

Teesdale

TEESDALE extends twenty-odd miles northwest from Barnard Castle, its pastoral landscapes on the lower reaches beginning calmly enough but soon replaced by wilder Pennine scenery. Picturesque little villages like **Middleton-in-Teesdale** and

Romaldkirk pepper the valley, while natural attractions include the stunning **Cow Green Reservoir** in Upper Teesdale, home to the indigenous Teesdale Violet and the blue Spring Gentian.

Raby Castle

Staindrop, 8 miles northeast of Barnard Castle • Easter week, May, June & Sept Sun–Wed 1–4.30pm; July & Aug Sun–Fri 1–4.30pm • Gardens same days 11am–5.30pm • £9.50, park & gardens only £6 • ⓣ 01833 660202, ⓦ rabycastle.com

Eight miles from Barnard Castle, up the A688, beckon the splendid, sprawling battlements of **Raby Castle**, reflecting the power of the Neville family, who ruled the local roost until 1569. The Neville estates were confiscated after the "Rising of the North", the abortive attempt to replace Elizabeth I with Mary Queen of Scots, with Raby subsequently passing to the Vane family in 1626, who still own it today. You can explore the interior, with its lavish bedrooms, dining room, kitchen and drawing rooms filled with furniture and artwork dating from the sixteenth and seventeenth centuries.

Middleton-in-Teesdale

Surrounded by magnificent, wild countryside laced with a myriad of public footpaths and cycling trails, the attractive town of **MIDDLETON-IN-TEESDALE** is a popular base for walkers and cyclists. A relaxed little place, it was once the archetypal "company town", owned lock, stock and barrel by the London Lead Company, which began mining here in 1753. Just a few miles out of town is a famous set of waterfalls, **Low Force** and **High Force**.

High Force

Daily 10am–5pm • £1.50, car park £2 • Minibuses from the town centre on Wed only (2 daily; 15min)

Heading on the B6277 northwest out of Middleton-in-Teesdale, you'll first pass the turning off to the rapids of **Low Force**. Another mile up the road is the altogether more spectacular **High Force** waterfall, a 70ft cascade that tumbles over an outcrop of the Whin Sill ridge and into a deep pool. The waterfall is on private Raby land (see above) and is reached by a short woodland walk.

ARRIVAL AND INFORMATION — MIDDLETON-IN-TEESDALE

By bus There are hourly bus services to Middleton-in-Teesdale from Barnard Castle (35min).

Tourist office Market Place (restricted hours, though usually daily 10am–1pm; ⓣ 01833 641001).

ACCOMMODATION AND EATING

The Old Barn 12 Market Place ⓣ 01833 640258, ⓦ theoldbarn-teesdale.co.uk. In a very central location next to the tourist office, this sympathetically converted barn has three attractive B&B rooms with rustic furniture, elegant iron beds and Egyptian cotton sheets. There's a little patio garden to chill out in after a hard day's walking. **£56**

★ **Rose & Crown** Romaldkirk, 4 miles southwest ⓣ 01833 650213, ⓦ rose-and-crown.co.uk. Beautiful ivy-clad eighteenth-century coaching inn set on the village green and next to a pretty Saxon church. Beneath the tastefully decorated rooms is a refined restaurant (four courses £32.50), serving accomplished dishes such as pan-fried woodpigeon with juniperberry sauce and grilled pancetta, a more relaxed brasserie (mains from £10), and a cosy bar with a wood fire. **£67.50**

Weardale

Sitting to the north of Teesdale, the valley of **WEARDALE** was once hunting ground reserved for the Prince Bishops, but was later transformed into a major centre for lead-mining and limestone quarrying; this industrial heritage is celebrated at the excellent **Killhope Iron Mining musueum** and the **Weardale Museum** in Irehopesburn. The main settlement is **Stanhope**, a small market town with a pleasant open-air heated swimming pool (ⓦ woaspa.co.uk), perfect for cooling off after a long walk in the hills.

13

Weardale Museum

Ireshopeburn, 9 miles west of Stanhope • Easter, May–July & Sept Wed–Sun 2–5pm; Aug daily 2–5pm • £3 • T 01388 517433, W weardalemuseum.co.uk

At Ireshopeburn, west of Stanhope, the **Weardale Museum** tells the story of the dale, in particular its lead mining and the importance of Methodism (the faith of most of County Durham's lead miners). There's a reconstructed miner's house as well as the "Wesley Room", dedicated to the founder of Methodism, John Wesley, and filled with his writings, books and belongings.

Killhope Lead Mining Museum

Five miles west of Ireshopeburn and 5 miles east of Alston • April–Oct daily 10.30am–5pm • £7 including mine visit • T 01388 537505, W killhope.org.uk • Request bus stop on bus #101 (see below)

If you're keen to learn about Weardale's mining past, a visit to **Killhope Lead Mining Museum**, five miles west of Ireshopeburn, is an absolute must. After many successful years as one of the richest mines in Britain, Killhope shut for good in 1910, and now houses a terrific, child-friendly museum that brings to life the difficulties and dangers of a mining life. The site is littered with preserved machinery and nineteenth-century buildings, including the Mine Shop where workers would spend the night after finishing a late shift. The highlight of the visit comes when you descend Park Level Mine – you'll be given wellies, a hard hat and a torch – in the company of a guide who expounds entertainingly about the realities of life underground, notably the perils of the "Black Spit", a lung disease which killed many men by their mid-forties.

ARRIVAL AND INFORMATION — WEARDALE

By bus Bus #101 runs roughly hourly between Bishop Auckland and Stanhope, calling at Wolsingham and Frosterley.

Durham Dales Centre On Stanhope's main road, the Dales Centre houses the tourist office (daily: April–Oct 10am–5pm; Nov–March 10am–4pm; T 01388 527650, W durhamdalescentre.co.uk) and a café.

GETTING AROUND

By bus Apart from #101, buses are relatively irregular and spotty round these parts. It's best to use the minibuses run by the Weardale Bus Company (T 01388 528235, W weardale-travel.co.uk).

Weardale Railway This volunteer-run steam railway chugs along from Bishop Auckland (see p.569) to Stanhope, stopping at Wolsingham and Frosterley on request; for up-to-date timetables and fares see W weardale-railway.org.uk.

ACCOMMODATION

Dowfold House Crook, 6 miles east of Wolsingham T 01388 762473, W dowfoldhouse.co.uk. Wonderful, relaxed B&B in a Victorian house surrounded by lush gardens and with splendid views out over Weardale. Breakfast, served in the elegant dining room, is the highlight, with free-range eggs, locally sourced sausages and bacon, home-made bread and jams – make sure you're hungry. **£70**

Lord Crewe Arms Hotel Blanchland, 10 miles north of Stanhope off the B6278 T 01434 675251, W lordcrewehotel.com. Formerly connected to Blanchland Abbey, and functioning as the Abbot's Headquarters, this atmospheric stone hotel has a selection of tranquil rooms, some with four-poster beds and one with a resident ghost (supposedly). There's also a comfortable restaurant serving good pub food, and a popular bar. **£90**

EATING AND DRINKING

★ **Black Bull** Frosterley T 01388 527784, W blackbullfrosterley.com. Hop off the Weardale Railway (see above) and into this charming, traditional pub with olde worlde beams, ranges, oak tables and flagstone floors. The ales are excellent, as is the food, which is hearty and delicious; mains, like herb-crusted lamb shoulder with apricot and walnut stuffing, start at £10.95. Wed–Sat 10.30am–11pm, Sun 10.30am–5pm; food served till 2.30pm on Sun.

The Tees Valley

Admittedly not much of a tourist hotspot in comparison to Northumberland or County Durham, the **TEES VALLEY** – once an industrial powerhouse and birthplace of one of the greatest developments in Britain, the public steam railway – nevertheless has some enjoyable attractions. **Darlington**, with its strong railway heritage, is a pleasant place to spend a day, while Middlesbrough's **MIMA** and Hartlepool's **Maritime Experience** (Daily: April–Oct 10am–5pm; Nov–March 11am–4pm; £8.25; **T** 01429 860077, **W** hartlepoolsmaritimeexperience.com) are extremely worthwhile, the latter particularly if you have children to entertain.

Darlington

Abbreviated to "Darlo" by the locals, the busy market town of **DARLINGTON** hit the big time in 1825, when George Stephenson's "Number 1 Engine", later called *Locomotion*, hurtled from here to nearby Stockton-on-Tees at the terrifying speed of fifteen miles per hour. The town subsequently grew into a rail-engineering centre, and didn't look back till the closure of the works in 1966. The origins of the rest of Darlington lie deep in Saxon times. The monks carrying St Cuthbert's body from Ripon to Durham (see p.564) stopped here, the saint lending his name to the graceful riverside church of **St Cuthbert**. The market square, one of England's largest, spreads beyond the church up to the restored and lively **Victorian covered market** (Mon–Sat 8am–5pm).

Head of Steam

North Rd Station, a 20min walk up Northgate from the marketplace • April–Sept 10am–4pm, Oct–March Wed–Sun 11am–3.30pm • £4.95 • **T** 01325 460532, **W** head-of-steam.co.uk

Darlington's railway history is celebrated at the wonderful little **Head of Steam** museum, which is actually the restored 1842 passenger station on the original Stockton and Darlington railway route. The highlight is Stephenson's *Locomotion No. 1*, a tiny wood-panelled steam engine, the first ever steam train to carry fare-paying passengers. Other locomotives jostle for space alongside, including the shiny, racing-green Derwent, the oldest surviving Darlington-built steam train. These, along with a collection of station and lineside signs, uniforms, luggage, a reconstructed ticket office and carriages, successfully bring to life the most important era in Darlington's existence.

ARRIVAL AND INFORMATION — DARLINGTON

By train The train station is on Bank Top, a 10min walk from the central marketplace: from the train station walk up Victoria Road to the roundabout and turn right down Feethams.

Destinations Bishop Auckland (frequent; 25min); Durham (frequent; 20min); Newcastle (frequent; 35min).

By bus Most buses stop outside the Town Hall on Feethams.

Destinations Barnard Castle (Mon–Sat every 30min, Sun hourly; 45min); Bishop Auckland (Mon–Sat every 30min, Sun hourly; 1hr); Durham (every 20min; 1hr 10 min).

Tourist office Leaflets about the town and surroundings are available at the library on Crown St (Mon & Tues 9am–6pm, Thurs 10am–6pm, Wed & Fri 9am–5pm, Sat 9am–4pm; **T** 01325 462034, **W** visitdarlington.com).

ACCOMMODATION

Clow Beck B&B Croft-on-Tees, 2 miles south **T** 01325 721075, **W** clowbeckhouse.co.uk. Very welcoming B&B with thirteen individually decorated rooms named after flowers and set round a pretty landscaped garden. The owner is also an accomplished chef, creating delicious breakfasts – the Skipton sausage is very tasty – and evening meals (mains from £15). **£135**

Rockliffe Hall Hurworth-on-Tees, 5 miles south **T** 01325 729999, **W** rockliffehall.com. Swanky new hotel between the villages of Croft-on-Tees and Hurworth, which lays claim to having the UK's longest golf course. The rooms are cool and luxurious, and there's a spa and three restaurants. Breakfast included. **£285**

13

EATING AND DRINKING

★ **Bay Horse** 45 The Green, Hurworth, 5 miles south ⊕01325 720663, ⊛thebayhorsehurworth.com. Proud owner of a Michelin star, this exquisite pub has a roaring fire, exposed wooden beams, comfy bar stools and chalked-up menus. Tuck into delicious meals such as venison sausage with fondant potatoes and Yorkshire gravy (£12.95) and make sure you leave room for their puds; the sticky toffee pudding with green apple ice cream (£5.95) is fabulous. Mon–Sat 11am–11pm, Sun noon–10.30pm; no food served Sun evening.

Oven 30 Duke St ⊕01325 466668, ⊛ovenrestaurant .co.uk. Pricey but great food served in a smart restaurant with white tablecloths and dark walls. Mains (lots of well-executed fish and meat dishes) cost around £18 in the evening. Tues–Fri 12.30–2.30pm & 5–9.30pm, Sat 12–2.30pm, Sun noon–4pm.

Middlesbrough Institute of Modern Art

Middlesbrough, 15 miles east of Darlington, on Centre Square, a 10min walk from the train station • Tues–Sat 10am–4.30pm, Sun noon–4pm • Free • ⊕01642 726720, ⊛visitmima.com

The stunning **Middlesbrough Institute of Modern Art (MIMA)** is one of the few tourist draws in the industrial town of Middlesbrough. Bringing together its municipal art collections for the first time, changing exhibitions concentrate on fine arts and crafts from the early twentieth century to the present day, with a heavy emphasis on ceramics and jewellery. The collection features work by David Hockney, L.S Lowry and Tracey Emin, among others.

Newcastle upon Tyne

Vibrant and handsome, **NEWCASTLE UPON TYNE** has emerged from its industrial heyday and its post-industrial difficulties with barely a smut on its face. Its reputation for lively nightlife is just the tip of the iceberg; with its collection of top-class art galleries, museums and flourishing theatre scene – not to mention the shopping – the city is up there among the most exciting in Britain.

The de facto capital of the area between Yorkshire and Scotland, the city was named for its "new castle" founded in 1080 and hit the limelight during the Industrial Revolution – Grainger Town in the city's centre is lined with elegant, listed classical buildings, indicating its past wealth and importance as one of Britain's biggest and most important exporters of coal, iron and machinery. The decline of industry damaged Newcastle badly, signalling decades of poverty and hardship – a period recalled by Antony Gormley's mighty statue the **Angel of the North**, which, since its appearance in 1998, has become both a poignant eulogy for the days of industry and a symbol of resurgence and regeneration.

NEWCASTLE ORIENTATION

Visitors are encouraged to think of the city as **Newcastle Gateshead**, an amalgamation of the two conurbations straddling the Tyne. On Gateshead Quays are the **BALTIC** contemporary arts centre and Norman Foster's **Sage** music centre, and on the opposite side, Newcastle's **Quayside** is scene of much of the city's contemporary nightlife. The city splits into several distinct areas, though it's only a matter of minutes to walk between them. The **castle** and **cathedral** occupy the heights immediately above the River Tyne, while north of here lies the city centre, **Grainger Town**. Chinatown and the two big draws of the **Discovery Museum** and the **Life Science Centre** are west of the centre, while east is the renowned **Laing Gallery**. In the north of the city, on the university campus, is the **Great North Museum: Hancock** and even further north, through the landscaped Exhibition Park, is the **Town Moor**, 1200 acres of common land where freemen of the city – including Jimmy Carter, Nelson Mandela and Bob Geldof – are entitled to graze their cattle. The old industrial **Ouseburn Valley**, home to an alternative cultural scene, interesting galleries, the excellent **Seven Stories** children's museum and some popular bars, is a short walk east along the river from the city centre.

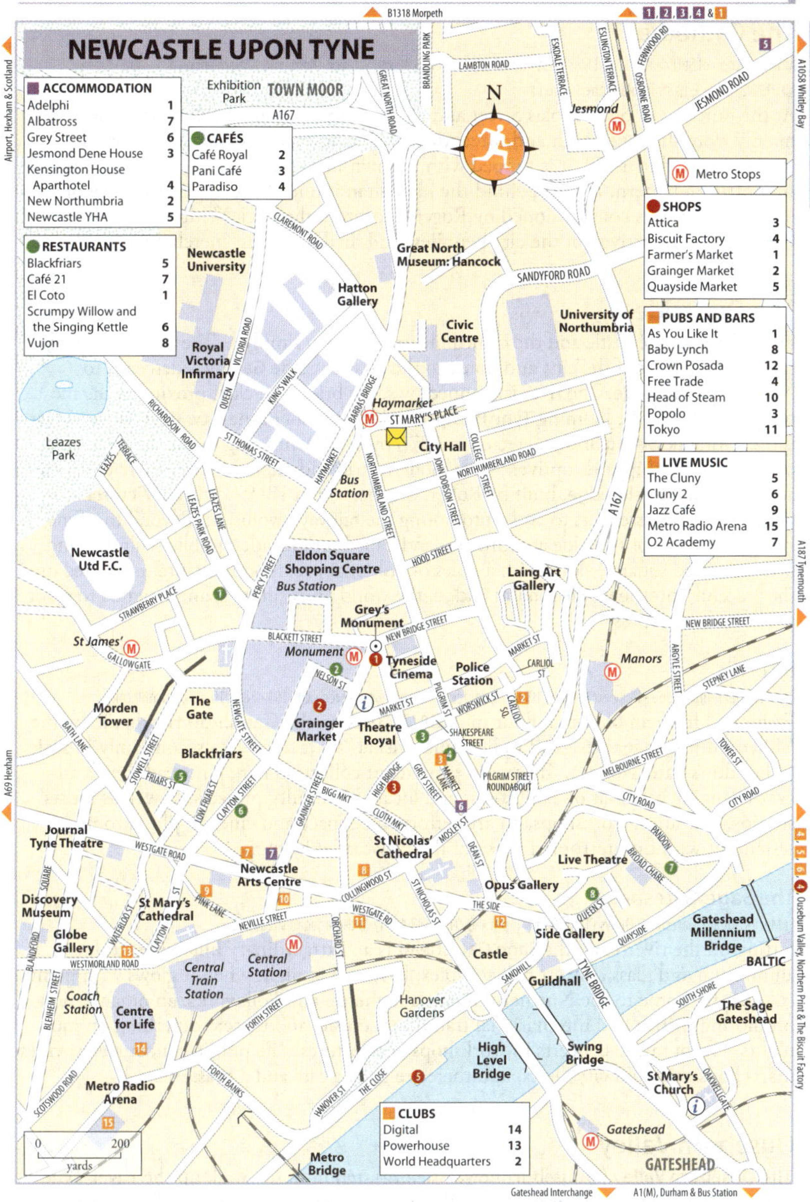

The Castle

Mon–Sat 10am–5pm, Sun noon–5pm • £4 • ⓣ 0191 233 1221, ⓦ castlekeep-newcastle.org.uk

Anyone arriving by train from the north will get a sneak preview of the **Castle**, as the rail line splits the keep from its gatehouse, the **Black Gate**, on St Nicholas Street. A wooden fort was built here over an Anglo-Saxon cemetery by Robert Curthose, illegitimate eldest son of William the Conqueror, but the present keep dates from the twelfth century. There's a great view from the rooftop over the river and city.

The Cathedral

At the junction of St Nicholas St and Mosley St • Mon–Fri 7.30am–6.30pm, Sat 8am–4pm, Sun 7.30am–noon & 4–7pm • Free • ⓣ 0191 232 1939, ⓦ stnicholascathedral.co.uk

At the junction of St Nicholas Street and Mosley Street stands the **Cathedral**, dating mainly from the fourteenth and fifteenth centuries and remarkable chiefly for its tower – erected in 1470, it is topped with a crown-like structure of turrets and arches supporting a lantern. Inside, behind the high altar, is one of the largest funerary brasses in England; it was commissioned by Roger Thornton, the Dick Whittington of Newcastle, who arrived in the city penniless and died its richest merchant in 1429.

The Quayside

From between the castle and the cathedral a road known simply as The Side – formerly the main road out of the city, and home to the excellent **Side Gallery** – descends to Newcastle's **Quayside**. The river is spanned by seven bridges in close proximity, the most prominent being the looming **Tyne Bridge** of 1928, symbol of the city. Immediately west is the hydraulic **Swing Bridge**, erected in 1876 by Lord Armstrong so that larger vessels could reach his shipyards upriver, while modern road and rail lines cross the river on the adjacent **High Level Bridge**, built by Robert Stephenson in 1849 – Queen Victoria was one of the first passengers to cross, promoting the railway revolution. Beyond the Tyne Bridge is an area of riverside apartments, landscaped promenades, public sculpture and pedestrianized squares, along with a series of fashionable bars and restaurants centred on the graceful **Gateshead Millennium Bridge**, the world's first tilting span, designed to pivot to allow ships to pass.

BALTIC

By the Millennium Bridge • Daily except Tues 10am–6pm, Tues 10.30am–6pm • Free • ⓣ 0191 478 1810, ⓦ balticmill.com

Fashioned from an old brick flour mill, **BALTIC** sits on the Gateshead riverbank, by the Millennium Bridge. Designed to be a huge visual "art factory", it's second only in scale to London's Tate Modern. There's no permanent collection here – instead there's an ever-changing calendar of exhibitions and local community projects, as well as artists' studios, education workshops, an art performance space and cinema, plus a rooftop restaurant with uninterrupted views of the Newcastle skyline.

The Sage Gateshead

St Mary's Square, Gateshead Quays • Daily 9am–11pm • ⓣ 0191 443 4661, ⓦ thesagegateshead.org

Sitting on the riverbank, the **Sage Gateshead** is an extraordinary billowing steel, aluminium and glass concert hall complex, best seen at night when it glows with many colours. It's home to the Northern Sinfonia orchestra and Folkworks, an organization promoting British and international traditional music, and there's something on most nights – from music concerts to workshops and lectures. The public concourse provides marvellous river and city views, and there are bars, a café and a brasserie.

Ouseburn Valley

The **Ouseburn Valley** (ⓦ ouseburnnewcastle.org), ten minutes' walk up the River Tyne from Millennium Bridge, was once at the heart of Newcastle's industrial activities but became a derelict backwater in the mid-twentieth century. A jumble of old Victorian mills and warehouses, the area has seen a remarkable rejuvenation, as artists, musicians, businesses and even residents move in. Lime Street, home to the quirky **Cluny** music bar (see p.582), artist's workshops and the nationally renowned **Seven Stories**, is the hub, but there are plenty of attractions nearby including Europe's biggest commercial art space – the **Biscuit Factory** – an art-house cinema, riding stables and a small working farm.

NEWCASTLE ART GALLERIES

Biscuit Factory 16 Stoddart St, Ouseburn ⊕0191 261 1103, ⊛thebiscuitfactory.com. Britain's largest commercial art gallery, displaying and selling anything from pendulum clocks and carved wooden tables to ceramic teapots and quirky necklaces. Free. Tues–Sat 11am–5pm, Sun & Mon 10am–6pm.

Globe Gallery 53–57 Blanford Sq ⊕0191 597 9377, ⊛globegallery.org. Contemporary arts space that supports local, up-and-coming artists; there's a variety of exhibitions and one-off events. Free. Wed–Fri 11.30am–5pm.

Northern Print Stepney Bank, Ouseburn ⊕0191 261 7000, ⊛northernprint.org.uk. Little gallery that sells affordable prints by local artists. You can also learn how to make prints at the studio's workshop. Free. Wed–Sat noon–4pm.

Opus Gallery Milburn House, Dean St ⊕0191 232 7389, ⊛opus-art.com. Original contemporary art, prints and photographs in a striking Art Nouveau building. By appointment daily 10am–5pm.

Seven Stories

30 Lime St • Daily 10am–5pm • £6 • ⊕0845 271 0777, ⊛sevenstories.org.uk

Housed in a beautifully converted Victorian riverside mill and spread over seven floors, **Seven Stories** celebrates the art of children's books through displays of original artwork, manuscripts and related documents. The bright, interactive exhibitions change regularly but highlights include original sketches taken from Noel Streatfield's *Ballet Shoes*, material from *Charlie and the Chocolate Factory* by Roald Dahl, Philip Pullman's early drafts, and the unpublished novel by Enid Blyton, *Mr Tumpy's Caravan*.

Grainger Town

The heart of the city is known as **Grainger Town**, one of the best-looking city centres in Britain. Thrown up in a few short mid-nineteenth-century years by businessmen-builders and architects such as Richard Grainger, Thomas Oliver and John Dobson, the area is known for its classical facades of stone lining splendid, wide streets, and in particular, **Grey Street**, named for the second Earl Grey (he of the tea), prime minister from 1830 to 1834. In 1832, Grey carried the Reform Act – which granted seats in the House of Commons to large cities that had developed during the Industrial Revolution, like Newcastle – through parliament, an act commemorated by **Grey's Monument** at the top of the street. The restored **Grainger Market** (Mon–Sat 8am–5pm), nearby, was Europe's largest covered market when built in the 1830s, and is today home to the smallest branch of Marks and Spencer, known as the Original Penny Bazaar.

Centre for Life

Times Square, off Westmorland Rd and Scotswood Rd • Mon–Sat 10am–6pm, Sun 11am–6pm; last admission 3.30pm • £9.95 • ⊕0191 243 8210, ⊛life.org.uk

A five-minute walk west of Central Station, the sleek buildings of the **Centre for Life** reach around the sweeping expanse of Times Square. This ambitious "science village" project combines bioscience and genetics research with a science visitor centre that aims to convey the secrets of life using the latest entertainment technology. Children find the whole thing enormously rewarding – from the sparkling Planetarium to the motion simulator – so expect to spend a good three hours here, if not more.

Discovery Museum

Blandford Square • Mon–Sat 10am–5pm, Sun 2–5pm • Free • ⊕0191 232 6789, ⊛twmuseums.org.uk

The **Discovery Museum** concentrates on the maritime history of Newcastle and Tyneside, as well as their role in Britain's scientific and technological developments. Highlights include the Tyneside-invented *Turbinia* – which dominates the entrance to the museum – the first ship to be powered by a steam turbine, as well as the Newcastle Story, a walk through the city's past with tales from animatronic characters along the way.

Laing Art Gallery

New Bridge St • Mon–Sat 10am–5pm, Sun 2–5pm • Free • ⓦ twmuseums.org.uk

The **Laing Art Gallery**, in the east of the city, is home to the northeast's premier art collection: the permanent display is a sweep through British art from the seventeenth century to today, featuring sculpture from Henry Moore and a large collection of John Martin's fiery landscapes, along with a smattering of Pre-Raphaelites, so admired by English industrial barons. Another permanent display highlights a superb collection of Newcastle silver dating from the seventeenth century and some colourful 1930s glassware by George Davidson.

Great North Museum: Hancock

Barras Bridge • **Hancock Museum** Mon–Sat 10am–5pm, Sun 2–5pm • Free; planetarium £2.50 • ⓣ 0191 222 6765, ⓦ twmuseums.org.uk • **Hatton Gallery** Mon–Sat 10am–5pm • Free • ⓣ 0191222 6059, ⓦ twmuseums.org.uk

A five-minute walk north from Haymarket Metro stop, the **Great North Museum: Hancock** is a clunkily named amalgamation of four museums, the best of which are the Great North Museum, housed in the Hancock building, and the nearby Hatton Gallery. The **Great North Museum** has an engaging mishmash of natural history exhibits – there's a knobbly T-Rex skeleton, some stuffed animals and an aquarium – historical artefacts such as the large-scale replica Hadrian's Wall, and a planetarium. The little **Hatton Gallery**, a two-minute walk away on the university's campus, is famous for housing the only surviving example of German Dadaist Kurt Schwitters' *Merzbau* (a sort of architectural collage); it also hosts a variety of temporary exhibitions.

Angel of the North

Six miles south of Newcastle-upon-Tyne, off the A167 (signposted Gateshead South) • ⓦ angelofthenorth.org.uk • Bus #21 or #22 from Eldon Shopping Centre; there's car parking at the site

Since 1998, Antony Gormley's 66ft-high **Angel of the North** has stood sentinel over the A1 at Gateshead. A startling steel colossus that greets anyone travelling up from the south by rail or road, it's sited on top of a former coal-mining site, thus acknowledging the area's hardest hit and most emotive industry. At the same time, with its wide-open, 175ft wingspan, inclining slightly forwards in an embrace, the angel expresses a forward-thinking, hopeful vision for the future.

The Angel is set to be rivalled by the new **Goddess of the North** (or Northumberlandia) nine miles north in Cramlington. Made out of 1.5 million tonnes of earth from Shotton mine and standing 111ft tall, the Goddess is due to be unveiled in 2013.

ARRIVAL AND DEPARTURE — NEWCASTLE UPON TYNE

By plane Newcastle International Airport is 6 miles north of the city (ⓣ 0871 882 1121, ⓦ newcastleairport.com). It is linked by the Metro to Central Station (every 7–15min 5.45am–11.58pm; 22min; £3) and beyond. You can also take a taxi into the centre (around £15).

By train Central Station is a 5min walk from the city centre or Quayside, and has a Metro station.

Destinations Alnmouth (hourly; 30min); Berwick-upon-Tweed (hourly; 45min); Carlisle (hourly; 1hr 30min); Darlington (frequent; 35min); Durham (frequent; 15min); Hexham (every 30min; 40min); London (frequent; 2hr 45min–3hr 15min); York (frequent; 1hr).

By bus National Express buses stop on St James's Boulevard, not far from Central Station, while regional buses stop at Haymarket bus station (Haymarket Metro). Gateshead Interchange is a big bus station served by local and national buses, linked by Metro to the city centre.

FROM TOP ANGEL OF THE NORTH (P.578); GATESHEAD MILLENNIUM BRIDGE (P.576) >

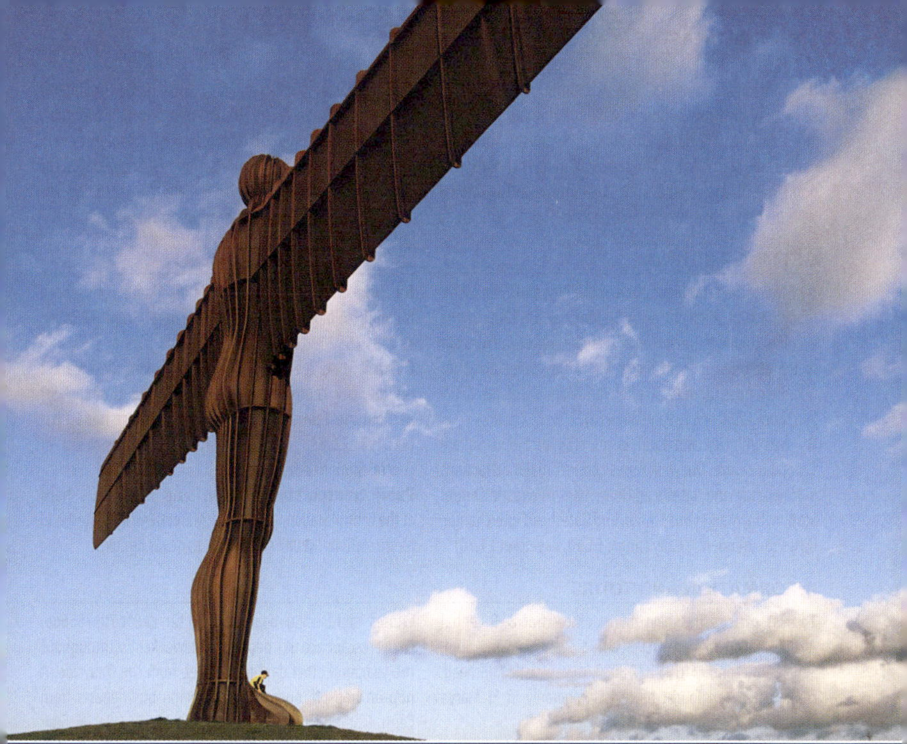

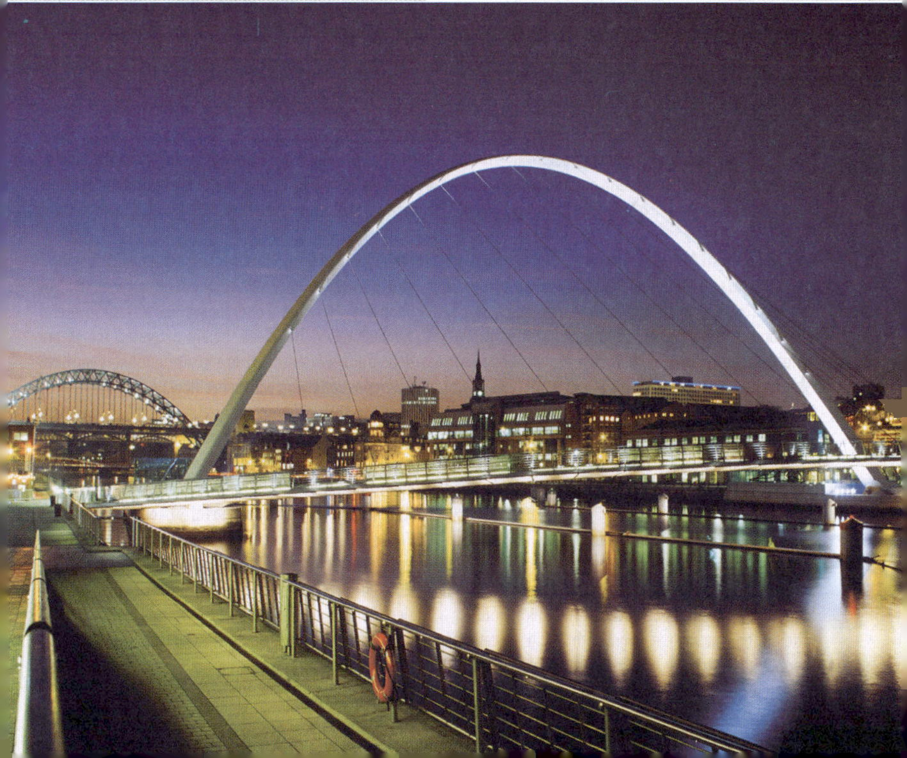

13

Destinations Alnmouth (every 30min; 1hr 30min); Alnwick (daily every 30min; 1hr 20min); Bamburgh (Mon–Sat 3 daily; Sun 2 daily; 2hr 30min); Beamish (April–Oct daily, Nov–March Sat & Sun; every 30min; 1hr); Berwick-upon-Tweed (Mon–Sat 8 daily; 2hr 30min); Carlisle (Mon–Sat hourly; 2hr 10min); Chester-le-Street (frequent; 45min); Craster (Mon–Sat 7 daily, Sun 4 daily; 1hr 50min); Durham (Mon–Sat every 30min, Sun 4–6 daily; 50min); Hexham (hourly; 50min); Middlesbrough (Mon–Sat every 30min; 1hr); Rothbury (Mon–Sat hourly, Sun 2 daily; 1hr 30min); Seahouses (Mon–Sat 3 daily, Sun 2 daily; 2hr 10min); Warkworth (daily every 30min; 1hr 20min).

GETTING AROUND

By Metro The convenient, easy-to-use Tyne and Wear Metro (daily 5.30am–midnight, every 5–10min or 10–20min in the evening) connects the city centre with the airport and runs out to the suburbs. You can buy a Metro Day Saver ticket for unlimited rides (from £2.10 after 9am Mon–Fri, all day Sat & Sun; from £2.50 before 9am Mon–Fri).

By bus All city and local buses stop at Eldon Square shopping centre. Quaylink buses connect major attractions in Newcastle and Gateshead Quays with Newcastle Central Station, Haymarket Bus Station and Gateshead Interchange. Buses run frequently daily (single £1.10, day ticket £1.70).

By bike Rent bikes at Saddle Skedaddle, Ouseburn Building, Albion Row (daily 9am–6pm; from £25/day; T 0191 265 1110, W skedaddle.co.uk).

By taxi There are taxi ranks at Haymarket, Bigg Market (in the city centre between Grey St and Grainger St) and outside Central Station. To book, contact Noda Taxis (T 0191 222888 or 232 7777, W noda-taxis.co.uk) at Central Station.

Public transport information Nexus Traveline has shops at the Central Station, Haymarket, Monument and Gateshead Metro stations (T 0871 200 2233, W nexus.org.uk).

INFORMATION AND TOURS

Tourist offices The main tourist office is at 8–9 Central Arcade, Market St (Mon–Fri 9.30am–5.30pm, Sat 9am–5pm, Sun 10am–4pm; T 0191 277 8000, W newcastlegateshead.com). Gateshead Tourist office is temporarily in St Mary's Church (daily 10am–4pm; T 0191 478 4222).

Tours City tours and various tours to Hadrian's Wall, Northumberland and Durham are run by Castle City Tours (from £40 per group of seven people max; T 07780 958679, W newcastlecitytours.co.uk) while River Escapes Cruises' sightseeing boats (£6/10/12; T 01670 785666, W riverescapes.co.uk) depart most weekends throughout the year, and other days in summer, from the Quayside. A hop-on hop-off, open-top sightseeing bus departs from Central Station (April–Oct daily, Nov & Dec Sat & Sun; every 30min–1hr; £8; T 01789 299123, W city-sightseeing.com). Saddle Skedaddle (see above) also organize C2C tours and trips to Hadrian's Wall.

ACCOMMODATION

Budget **hotel chains** offer plenty of good-value rooms in the city centre and down by the Quayside, while the biggest concentration of small hotels and guesthouses – and the YHA hostel – lies a mile north of the centre in popular, student-filled Jesmond, along and off Osborne Road: take bus #33 from Central Station or Haymarket.

Adelphi 63 Fern Ave, off Osborne Rd, Jesmond T 0191 281 3109, W adelphihotelnewcastle.co.uk. Good-value, family-run B&B in an attractive terraced house. Rooms are clean and comfortable and the cooked breakfast is pretty good. Five of the seven bedrooms are en suite. **£60**

★ **Albatross** 51 Grainger St T 0191 233 1330, W albatrossnewcastle.co.uk. This award-winning 170-bed backpackers' hostel has a variety of clean and modern dorms, from 2-bed to 12-bed, and isn't far from the town centre. There's towel hire, free tea-and-toast breakfasts, free wi-fi and a laundry service. From **£16.50**

Grey Street 2 Grey St T 0191 230 6777, W greystreethotel.com. This fashionable hotel in an elegant Georgian house couldn't be more central (triple-glazed windows block the night-time noise outside). The "chic rooms" are a little on the small side – upgrade to a suite to get more space. Designer touches like iPod docks and smart toiletries add to the boutique feel. Breakfast is extra. **£105**

★ **Jesmond Dene House** Jesmond Dene Rd, Jesmond T 0191 212 3000, W jesmonddenehouse.co.uk. An imposing Arts and Crafts house in a very peaceful wooded valley. The sleek, boldly decorated rooms are decked out in decadent velvet and silk furnishings and have enormous bathrooms with under-floor heating. There's fine dining in the garden-room restaurant and breakfasts are particularly luxurious, with smoked salmon, a range of cooked meats and champagne on offer. Rates vary; book well in advance. **£130**

Kensington House Aparthotel 5 Osborne Rd T 0191 281 8175, W kensingtonaparthotel.com. Twenty-three upmarket apartments of varying sizes, conveniently situated near Jesmond Metro. The decor is modern and sleek, with wood floors, cream carpets and marble kitchen surfaces. Beds are kitted out with luxurious Egyptian cotton sheets and feather down duvets. Six apartments have disabled access. **£95**

New Northumbria 61–69 Osborne Rd, Jesmond ⓣ0191 281 4961, ⓦthenewnorthumbria.com. In a prime position along Osborne Road among the popular, student-filled restaurants and bars, *New Northumbria* has 57 rooms, all with large beds and unfussy decor. There's a bar downstairs and an Italian restaurant attached. £69

EATING

Newcastle has a great variety of places to eat, from expensive, top-quality restaurants showcasing the talents of young and creative chefs, to fun, relaxed cafés and budget-friendly Chinese restaurants (mostly around Stowell Street in Chinatown). The popular chain restaurants are down by the Quayside.

★ **Blackfriars** Friars St ⓣ0191 615945, ⓦblackfriarsrestaurant.co.uk. Housed in a beautiful stone building dating back to 1239, *Blackfriars* offers superb traditional British dishes using local ingredients. Mains could include pork loin with a bacon and cheese Gateshead floddie (potato cakes, originating from Gateshead, and traditionally eaten for breakfast) or a Doddington cheese and onion Wellington with chive cream sauce (£11), and, for afters, dig into sticky toffee pudding with green grape ice cream and Brown Ale caramel (£6). Booking recommended. Mon–Sat noon–2.30pm & 5.30–late, Sun noon–4pm.

Café 21 Trinity Gardens ⓣ0191 222 0755, ⓦcafetwentyone.co.uk. Stylish Parisian-style bistro with crisp white tablecloths, leather banquettes, a classic French menu, and slick service. Expect dishes like confit of duck with Lyonnaise potatoes (£17.80) or wild mushrooms on toasted brioche and a poached egg (£11), and delicious desserts – the hot chocolate doughnut with pistachio ice cream (£8.60) is particularly good. Mon–Sat noon–2.30pm & 5.30–10.30pm, Sun 12.30–3.30pm & 6.30–10pm.

Café Royal 8 Nelson St. Bright and buzzy café with great smoothies, coffees and delectable home-made breads and cakes – try the raspberry scones with clotted cream (£1.95) or hazelnut twists (£1.75). Mon–Sat 8am–6pm.

El Coto 21 Leazes Park Rd ⓣ0191 261 0555, ⓦelcoto.co.uk. Cute and cosy, this great tapas place has an extensive, good-value menu featuring all the usuals, such as patatas bravas and marinated sardines – dishes cost around £4, though paella goes for £10 per person. Daily from noon.

Pani Café 61–65 High Bridge St, off Grey St ⓣ0191 232 4366, ⓦpaniscafe.co.uk. On a side street below the Theatre Royal, this lively Sardinian café has won a loyal clientele for its good-value sandwiches, pasta and salads. Mon–Sat 10am–10pm.

Paradiso 1 Market Lane ⓣ0191 221 1240, ⓦparadiso.co.uk. Mellow café-bar hidden down an alley off Pilgrim St – the snack food in the daytime becomes more substantial at night, with truffle risotto, salmon steaks and the like. There are set menus throughout the day (two courses from £9.95, three courses from £12.95) as well as à la carte. When the weather's good you can dine on the outdoor terrace. Mon–Thurs 11am–2.30pm & 5–10.30pm, Fri & Sat 11am–10.45pm.

Scrumpy Willow and the Singing Kettle 89 Clayton St ⓣ0191 221 2323, ⓦscrumpywillowandthesingingkettle.co.uk. Wonderful little organic café-restaurant with a relaxed atmosphere and pretty, shabby chic decor – think candles, mirrors and rickety wood furniture. It's great for vegetarians and vegans: pop in for a tasty brunch of eggs Benedict, porridge or pancakes. The evening menu features locally sourced meat and fish including a delicious Kielder lamb with farm vegetables and pearl barley. Mains from £6.95. Mon–Sat 10am–8pm, Sun 11am –4pm.

Vujon 29 Queen St ⓣ0191 221 0601, ⓦvujon.com. The city's classiest Indian restaurant, housed in an elegant building by the Quayside, serving dishes a cut above the ordinary, from venison Jaipur-style with chilli jam (£15.90) to the spicy duck *salan* (£14.90). Daily 5.30–11.30pm.

DRINKING

Newcastle's boisterous pubs, bars and clubs are concentrated in several areas: in the **Bigg Market** (between Grey St and Grainger St), around the **Quayside** and in the developing **Ouseburn** area, where bars tend to be quirkier and more sophisticated; in **Jesmond**, with its thriving student-filled strip of café/bars; and in the mainstream leisure-and-cinema complex known as **The Gate** (Newgate St). The **gay** area, known as the "Pink Triangle", focuses on the Centre for Life, spreading out to Waterloo Street and Westmorland and Scotswood roads. Top drinking brew is Newcastle Brown – an ale known locally as "Dog" – produced in this city since 1927.

★ **As You Like It** Archbold Terrace ⓣ0191 281 2277, ⓦasyoulikeitjesmond.com. The top bar in the Jesmond area, and part of the *Mr Lynch* chain (see below). Incongruously sitting beneath an ugly tower block, this funky bar-restaurant has a relaxed vibe, exposed brick walls and a mishmash of furniture. The Supper Club (ⓦwww.thesupperclubjesmond.com), a late-night club night on Fri–Sun (10pm–2am) features jazz, blues and soul. Sun–Thurs noon–midnight, Fri & Sat noon–2am.

Baby Lynch 26 Collingwood St ⓣ0191 261 8271, ⓦbabylynch.com. Part of a Newcastle-based chain (includes *As You Like It*, *Nancy Bordellos*, *Floritas*, *Madame Koo* and *Mr Lynch*), but still cool for it, *Baby Lynch* oozes 1970s chic with its retro wooden floorboards, cosy booths and bamboo

13

loungers. The cocktail menu is extensive and very tempting (cocktails from £4.95). It gets busy later on, with the overspill from next door *Floritas*. Fri–Sun 7pm–3am.

Crown Posada 31 The Side 0191 232 1269. A proper old man's boozer: local beers and guest ales in this small wood-and-glass-panelled Victorian pub. You might fancy the dark, malty Hadrian's Gladiator (£3.80) or opt for the golden, hoppy Tyneside Blonde (£3.80). Mon–Wed noon–11pm, Thurs 11am–11pm, Fri 11am–midnight, Sat noon–midnight, Sun 7–10.30pm.

★ **Free Trade** St Lawrence Rd 0191 265 5764. Walk along the Newcastle Quayside past the Millennium Bridge and look for the shabby pub on the hill, where you are invited to "drink beer, smoke tabs" with the city's pub cognoscenti. Cask beer from local microbreweries, a great free juke box and superb river views from the beer garden. Mon–Thurs 11am–11pm, Fri & Sat 11am–midnight, Sun noon–11pm.

Head of Steam 2 Neville St 0191 230 4236, theheadofsteam.co.uk. In an unpromising modern building (but a whole lot better-looking inside), this small, split-level drinking den has good sounds and big sofas. Usually live gigs in the basement from 8pm. Sun–Thurs noon–2am, Fri & Sat noon–3am.

Popolo 82–84 Pilgrim St 0191 232 8923, popolo.co.uk. This casual American-style bar is a firm city favourite, and is known for its huge cocktail menu, featuring masses of martinis, mojitos and shooters. Sun–Tues 11am–midnight, Wed–Sat 11am–1am.

Tokyo 17 Westgate Rd 0191 232 1122, tokyonewcastle.co.uk. The dark, sleek main bar's handsome enough, but follow the tealights up the stairs to the outdoor "garden" bar lined by plants and trees, giving the area a secret, exclusive feel. A pre-club favourite for Shindig (see below). Sun–Thurs 5pm–midnight & Fri & Sat 4pm–1am.

NIGHTLIFE

Newcastle's biggest club night is **Shindig**, taking place on Saturdays and switching locations around the city. See shindiguk.com for the latest. Gigs, club nights and the gay scene are reviewed exhaustively in *The Crack* (monthly; free; thecrackmagazine.com), available in shops, pubs and bars.

CLUBS

Digital International Centre for Life, Times Sq 0191 261 9755, www.yourfutureisdigital.com, lovesaturdays.com. The city's top club, with an amazing sound system pumping out a variety of musical genres. If you like cheesy classics, look out for Born in the Sixties nights, while house, funk and disco fans will get their fix on Saturday's Love nights. Cover £10–15 Fri & Sat, cheaper on Mon & Thurs. Mon & Thurs 10.30pm–2.30am, Fri & Sat 10.30pm–3.30am.

Powerhouse 7–19 Westmorland Rd 0191 261 5348, powerhouseclub.co.uk. Spread over four floors, each playing different music, *Powerhouse* is Newcastle's most popular gay club. It sometimes hosts X-Factor finalists nights. Entry fee from £3. Mon & Thurs 11pm–3.30am, Fri–Sun 11pm–4am.

World Headquarters Carliol Square, East Pilgrim St 0191 281 3445, welovewhq.com. Smallish and down-to-earth club that's always packed. Music is a medley of house, hip-hop, soul and r'n'b and reggae. Downstairs there's a comfy lounge area with squashy sofas and a pool table. Entry fee around £10. Fri & Sat 10.30pm–3am.

LIVE MUSIC VENUES

★ **The Cluny** 36 Lime St, Ouseburn Valley 0191 230 4474, theheadofsteam.co.uk. This is the best small music venue in the city, with something going on most nights, from quirky indie bands to contemporary punk-pop. *Cluny 2*, around the corner at 34 Lime St (same hours), is its spacious sister venue, with less frequent gigs. Sun–Thurs noon–11pm, Fri & Sat noon–1am.

Jazz Café 23–25 Pink Lane 0191 232 6505. Slick and intimate jazz club in inauspicious surroundings, hosting top-quality jazz from 9.30pm. The bar has a late licence and there 's a jam session on Sunday afternoons. Thurs–Sat 8.30pm–2am, Sun 4–10pm.

Metro Radio Arena Arena Way 0844 493 4567, metroradioarena.co.uk. The biggest concert and exhibition venue in the Northeast; big names have included Coldplay, Elton John and Tom Jones. Book popular gigs well in advance.

02 Academy Westgate Rd 0844 477 2000, o2academynewcastle.co.uk. Housed in the former bingo hall, this mainstream venue hosts a variety of big names and local talent.

ENTERTAINMENT

Journal Tyne Theatre 111 Westgate Rd 0844 493999, thejounaltynetheatre.co.uk. Beautifully restored Victorian theatre with a wide range of plays, comedy shows and gigs.

Live Theatre 27 Broad Chare 0191 232 1232, live.org.uk. Enterprising theatre company that aims to find and develop local, and particularly young, talent – the attached *Caffe Vivo* is good for coffee by day and pre-theatre meal deals by night.

Theatre Royal 100 Grey St 0844 811 2121, theatreroyal.co.uk. Drama, opera, dance, musicals and comedy; also hosts the annual RSC season in Nov.

Tyneside Cinema 10 Pilgrim St 0845 217 9909, thetynesidecinema.co.uk. The city's premier art-house cinema, with coffee, light meals and movie talk in the Art Deco cinema café.

SHOPPING

Attica 2 Old George Yard, off Highbridge 0191 261 4062, atticavintage.co.uk. Excellent vintage shop selling all sorts of clothing for men and women – there's a great selection of glamorous evening wear, jewellery and hats as well as some quirky furniture dating from the 1950s, 1960s and 1970s. Mon–Sat 10.30am–5.30pm.

Biscuit Factory 16 Stoddart St, Ouseburn 0191 261 1103, thebiscuitfactory.com. Airy art gallery (see p.577) packed with paintings, ceramics, sculptures, jewellery and furniture – all for sale. Prices range from £10 to over £2000. Tues–Sat 11am–5pm, Sun & Mon 10am–6pm.

Farmers' Market Grey's Monument. Central market selling wonderful locally sourced fruit and veg, jams, meats and fish. First Fri of each month.

Quayside Market Busy, popular market down on the quayside selling locally produced food, clothes and art and crafts including jewellery. Sun 9.30am–4pm.

DIRECTORY

Hospital Royal Victoria Infirmary, Queen Victoria Rd (0191 233 6161, newcastle-hospitals.org.uk) has 24hr A&E services and a Minor Injuries Unit (daily 8am–9pm). The Westgate Walk-in Centre at Newcastle General Hospital, Westgate Rd, is open daily (8am–8pm).

Police Corner of Market and Pilgrim Streets 0191 214 6555.

Around Newcastle

There are a number of attractions near Newcastle, all accessible by Metro. The train runs east towards **Wallsend**, where **Segendum** fort marks the beginning of Hadrian's Wall, while further east **Bede's World** pays homage to Christianity's most important historian. Further out, near Sunderland, is the splendid **Washington Wildfowl Centre**.

Segedunum

Budle St, Wallsend, 4 miles east of Newcastle • April–Sept daily 10am–5pm; Nov–March Mon–Fri 10am–3pm • £4.50 • 0191 236 9347, twmuseums.org.uk/segedunum • Newcastle Metro to Wallsend

Wallsend, four miles east of Newcastle, was the last outpost of Hadrian's great border defence. **Segedunum**, the "strong fort" a couple of minutes' signposted walk from the Metro station, has been admirably developed as one of the prime attractions along the Wall. The grounds contain a fully reconstructed bathhouse, complete with heated pools and colourful frescoes, while the "wall's end" itself is visible at the edge of the site, close to the river and Swan Hunter shipyard. From here, the **Hadrian's Wall Path** (see p.584) runs for 84 miles to Bowness-on-Solway in Cumbria; you can get your walk "passport" stamped inside the museum.

THE GEORDIE NATION

Tyneside and Newcastle's native inhabitants are known as **Geordies**, the word probably derived from a diminutive of the name "George". There are various explanations of who George was (King George II, railwayman George Stephenson), all plausible, none now verifiable. Geordies speak a highly distinctive dialect and accent, heavily derived from Old English. Phrases you're likely to come across include: haway man! (come on!), scran (food), a'reet (hello) and propa belta (really good) – and you can also expect to be widely referred to as "pet" or "flower".

13

Bede's World

On the edge of Jarrow, 5 miles east of Newcastle • April–Sept 10am–5.30pm, Sun noon–5.30pm; Oct–March closes 4.30pm • £5.50 • T 0191 489 2106, W bedesworld.co.uk • Newcastle Metro to Jarrow, from where it's a 20min walk through the industrial estate

Bede's World sits at the edge of the town of **JARROW** – ingrained on the national consciousness since the 1936 **Jarrow Crusade**, when 201 people marched 300 miles down to London to protest against the government's refusal to ease unemployment and poverty in the Northeast. The complex explores the life of Venerable Bede (673–735 AD), who lived here as a boy, growing to become one of Europe's greatest scholars and England's first historian – his *History of the English Church and People*, describing the struggles of the island's early Christians, was completed at Jarrow in 731. Exhibits include extracts from Bede's writings and various archeological finds, and outside there's a reconstructed monastic village; children will enjoy the small farmyard complete with pigs, goats and sheep.

Washington Wildfowl and Wetlands Centre

Pattinson, 4 miles from the A1(M) • Daily: April–Oct 9.30am–5.30pm; Nov–March 9.30am–4.30pm • £8.45 • T 0191 416 5454, W wwt.org.uk • Bus #8 from Sunderland stops at the Waterview Park, a short walk from the wildfowl centre

Taking up 100 acres of the north bank of the River Wear in Pattinson (formerly District 15), the popular **Washington Wildfowl and Wetlands Centre** is a lush conservation area of meadows, woods and wetlands that acts as a winter habitat for migratory birds, including geese, ducks, herons and flamingos. In summer, you can watch fluffy ducklings hatch in the Waterfowl Nursery.

Hadrian's Wall

Hadrian's Wall (W hadrians-wall.org) was constructed in 122 AD at the behest of the Roman Emperor Hadrian. Keen for peace and safety within his empire, fearing attacks from Pictish Scotland, Hadrian commissioned a long wall to act as a border, snaking its way from the Tyne to the Solway Firth. It was built up to a height of 15ft in places and was interspersed by milecastles, which functioned as gates, depots and mini-barracks. The best-preserved portions of the Wall are concentrated between **Chesters Roman Fort**, four miles north of Hexham, and Haltwhistle, sixteen miles to the west, which passes **Housesteads Roman Fort**, **Vindolanda** and the **Roman Army Museum**. Most people come to walk or cycle the length of the Wall. There are plenty of lovely places to stay and eat around and along the Wall; the handsome market towns of **Hexham** (see p.587), Haltwhistle and Corbridge also make good bases.

Chesters Roman Fort

Four miles north of Hexham • Daily: April–Sept 10am–6pm; Oct 10am–4pm, call for opening hours Nov–March • EH • £5 • T 01434 681379

Beautifully sited next to the gurgling River Tyne, **Chesters Roman Fort**, otherwise known as Cilurnum, was built to guard the Roman bridge over the river. Enough

ALONG HADRIAN'S WALL

The best way to visit the Wall is to walk or cycle the length of it. The **Hadrian's Wall Footpath** (W nationaltrail.co.uk/hadrianswall) runs for 84 miles alongside the Wall itself from Wallsend (see p.583) to Bowness-on-Solway. It takes on average seven days to complete and there's an optional Passport system (May–Oct) involving collecting a series of stamps to prove you've done it. The **National Route 72** (signposted NCN 72; W cycle-routes.org/hadrianscycleway), shares some of the same route as the Footpath, and runs from South Shields to Ravenglass in Cumbria. There's bike hire in Newcastle (see p.580).

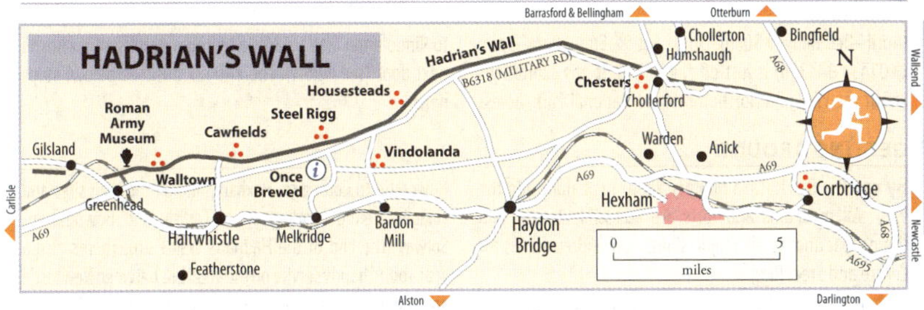

remains of the original structure to pick out the design of the fort, and each section has been clearly labelled, but the highlight is down by the river where the vestibule, changing room and steam range of the garrison's **bathhouse** are still visible, along with the furnace and the latrines.

Housesteads Roman Fort

Around 8 miles west of Chesters • Daily: April–Sept 10am–6pm; Oct–March 10am–4pm • EH & NT • £5 • ⓣ 01434 344525

Housesteads Roman Fort is one of the most popular sites on the Wall. The fort is of standard design but for one enforced modification – forts were supposed to straddle the line of the Wall, but here the original stonework follows the edge of the cliff, so Housesteads was built on the steeply sloping ridge to the south. Enter via the tiny **museum**, and walk across to the south gate; next to this lies the ruins of a garrison of up to 1000 infantrymen. It's not necessary to pay for entrance to the fort if you're simply walking along the Wall west from here; the three-mile hike takes in wonderful views as it meanders past **Crag Lough** and over to **Steel Rigg** (which has a car park).

Vindolanda

Access from behind Once Brewed Visitor Centre • Daily: mid- to end March & Oct 10am–5pm; April–Sept 10am–6pm; reduced hours in winter, call in advance • £6.25, joint admission with Roman Army Museum £9.50 • ⓣ 01434 344277, ⓦ vindolanda.com

The garrison fort of **Vindolanda** is believed to have been built and occupied before the construction of the Wall itself. Guarding the important central section of the east–west supply route across Britain, a series of early forts in this location were built of timber, eventually replaced with a stone construction during Hadrian's reign. Preserved beneath the remains of the stone fortress, these early forts are now being excavated – around 300 to 400 volunteers take part every day. The museum contains the largest collection of Roman leather items ever discovered on a single site – sandals, purses, an archer's thumb guard – and a fascinating series of **writing tablets** dating to 90 AD. The earliest written records found in Britain, they feature shopping lists, duty rotas and even a birthday party invitation from one Claudia Severa to Sulpicia Lepidina.

Roman Army Museum

Seven miles west of Vindolanda • Daily: mid- to end March & Oct 10am–5pm; April–Sept 10am–6pm; reduced hours in winter, call in advance • £5, joint admission with Vindolanda £9.50 • ⓣ 01434 344277, ⓦ vindolanda.com

The **Roman Army Museum** aims to illustrate how the Roman soldiers stationed here lived. There's everything from armour and weapons – including javelins, shields and swords – to a full-size chariot and a wagon. It's all very entertaining, and successfully brings to life the ruins you may just have seen at Vindolanda.

ARRIVAL AND INFORMATION — HADRIAN'S WALL

By train The nearest train stations are on the Newcastle–Carlisle line at Corbridge, Hexham, Bardon Mill and Haltwhistle.

Tourist information Once Brewed Visitor Centre

13

(April–Oct daily 9.30am–5pm, Sat & Sun 10am–3pm; 01434 344396) is just off the B6318. It has exhibitions about the Wall and Northumberland National Park, access to Vindolanda (see p.585), a tearoom, toilets and a hostel next door (see below). The #AD122 bus (see below) stops here.

GETTING AROUND

By car The B3618 (aka Military Road) runs alongside the Wall. All museums and forts are accessible by car and there's parking at all major sights, Once Brewed Visitor Centre and Steel Rigg.

By bus The little #AD122 (known as the "Hadrian's Wall bus"; Easter–Oct up to 5 times daily in each direction) runs from Newcastle to Corbridge, Hexham, and all the Wall sites and villages, before heading on to Carlisle and Bowness-on-Solway (the end of the Hadrian's Wall Path). There's also a year-round hourly service on the #685 bus between Newcastle and Carlisle, and other local services from Carlisle and Hexham, which provide access to various points on the Wall.

ACCOMMODATION

In addition to the B&Bs in the countryside around the Wall, Hexham (see p.587) has a good selection of accommodation.

★ **Carraw B&B** Military Rd, Humshaugh 01434 689857, carraw.co.uk. It's not often you can say "I've slept on Hadrian's Wall", but here you can – this beautiful B&B, run by a friendly couple, is built right next to Hadrian's masterpiece and boasts stunning views. Lovely homely touches, like home-made shortbread and cake on arrival, hot-water bottles and luxurious toiletries make this place really special. Delicious breakfasts – the nutty granola is a winner. Three-course evening meals £25. **£80**

Grindon Cartshed 4 miles north of Haydon Bridge 01434 684273, grindon-cartshed.co.uk. Wonderful views from this cosy B&B, which is complemented by a self-catering farmhouse barn (sleeps 6) next door. Evening meals (£19) are available on request. Suitable for wheelchair users – ask for details. Self-catering (1 week in high season £620). **£75**

Hadrian's Wall Camping and Caravan Site 2 miles north of Melkridge, just south of B6318 01434 320495, romanwallcamping.co.uk. Friendly, family-run site half a mile from the Wall, with showers, café, washing machine and dryer and bike storage; breakfast and evening meals (£6) available. There's also a heated bunk barn sleeping 10 people (£15 per person). Open all year. Tent for two **£12**, campervan **£16.50**

Langley Castle A686, 2 miles south of Haydon Bridge 01434 688888, langleycastle.com. Suitably regal rooms – four-poster beds, sumptuous furnishings and beautiful bathrooms with saunas and spa baths – in this turreted medieval castle. The cheaper rooms are in the grounds, looking onto the castle. There's also an atmospheric restaurant, cocktail bar, lounge and gardens. **£74.50**, castle rooms **£122.50**

Once Brewed YHA Military Rd Once Brewed 0845 371 9753, oncebrewed@yha.org.uk. Basic and welcoming youth hostel next to the visitor centre. They have plenty of walking leaflets, a restaurant and self-catering facilities. Dorm **£18.40**, family room s **£51**

Twice Brewed Inn Military Rd 01434 344534, twicebrewedinn.co.uk. Just 50 yards up from Once Brewed Visitor Centre and hostel, this friendly community pub has simple rooms, a beer garden, local beers on tap and perhaps the Northeast's largest selection of rums (54 of them). En-suites are slightly pricier. **£56**

★ **Willowford Farm** 01697 747962, willowford.co.uk. Strictly speaking just over the Northumbrian border in Cumbria, but this farmhouse B&B still makes a lovely, tranquil base to explore the Wall. Rooms are in converted farm buildings and decked out with pretty wooden beams and large beds. Three-course evening meals (£18) should be ordered in advance. No credit or debit cards. Closed Nov–March. **£75**

EATING AND DRINKING

★ **Barrasford Arms** Barrasford, 9 miles north of Hexham 01434 681237, barrasfordarms.co.uk. Endearingly ramshackle, welcoming and homely, this country pub serves great traditional British food with a French twist; dishes could include Cumbrian outdoor-reared chicken with haricot bean and tomato stew (£12) and for pudding sticky pistachio meringue with orange mascarpone (£5). Booking advisable. Food served Mon 6.30–11pm, Tues–Sat noon–2pm & 6.30–11pm, Sun noon–11pm.

Battlesteads Country Inn and Restaurant Wark-on-Tyne, 12 miles north of Hexham 01434 230209, battlesteads.com. In a charming little village by a trickling stream, this locally renowned restaurant with a lovely beer garden uses fresh produce sourced from within a 30-mile radius. Leave room for their famed whisky and marmalade bread and butter pudding (£5.75). Best to book. Food served daily noon–3pm & 6.30–9.30pm.

General Havelock Inn Haydon Bridge 01434 684376. Eighteenth-century inn that specializes in tasty Modern British food, from crab cakes and Cumberland sausages to chocolate brûlée and ice cream sundaes. Great locally brewed ales on offer, too. Main meals average around £17. Food served daily noon–3pm & 6–11pm.

Milecastle Inn Military Rd 01434 321372, milecastle-inn.co.uk. Just off the Wall, in a small, wind-battered white building, the *Milecastle Inn* is a snug and inexpensive pub specializing in pies (from £7.50) – fillings vary but could include wild boar and duckling, or turkey ham and chestnut. Food served daily: summer noon–8.45pm, winter noon–3pm & 6–8.45pm.

Hexham

HEXHAM is the only significant stop between Newcastle and Carlisle, and however keen you are on seeing the Wall, you'd do well to give this handsome market town a night – or even make it your base.

The focal point is the **abbey**, whose foundations were originally part of a fine Benedictine monastery founded by St Wilfrid in 671. Claimed, according to contemporaneous accounts, to be the finest this side of the Alps, the church – or rather its gold and silver – proved irresistible to the Vikings, who savaged the place in 876. It was rebuilt in the eleventh century as part of an Augustinian priory, and the town grew up in its shadow.

Hexham Abbey

Daily 9.30am–5pm • hexhamabbey.org.uk

The stately exterior of **Hexham Abbey** dominates the west side of the central marketplace. Entry is through the south transept, where there's a bruised but impressive first-century tombstone honouring Flavinus, a standard-bearer in the Roman cavalry, who's shown riding down his bearded enemy. The memorial lies at the foot of the broad, well-worn steps of the canons' **night stair**, one of the few such staircases – providing access from the monastery to the church – to have survived the Dissolution. The chancel, meanwhile, displays the inconsequential-looking **frith-stool**, an eighth-century stone chair that was once believed to have been used by St Wilfrid, rendering it holy enough to serve as the medieval sanctuary stool.

The Old Gaol

Hallgate • April–Sept Tues–Sat 11am–4.30pm; Oct–Nov & Feb–March Tues & Sat 11am–4.30pm • £3.95 • 01434 652349, tynedaleheritage.org

Britain's first purpose-built prison, **Hexham Old Gaol** occupies a solid sandstone building to the east of the abbey. It was commissioned by the powerful Archbishop of York in 1330, and constructed using stone plundered from the Roman ruins at Corbridge. Inside there's an entertaining museum extolling the virtues and pitfalls of medieval crime and punishment.

ARRIVAL AND INFORMATION — HEXHAM

By train The train station sits on the northeastern edge of the town centre, a 10min walk from the abbey.

Destinations Carlisle (hourly; 50min); Haltwhistle (hourly; 20min); Newcastle (hourly; 50min).

By bus The bus station is off Priestpopple, a few minutes' stroll east of the abbey.

Destinations Bellingham (Mon–Sat hourly; 45min); Newcastle (hourly; 50min).

Tourist office In the main Wentworth car park, near the supermarket (April–Oct Mon–Sat 9.30am–5pm, Sun 11am–4pm; Nov–March Mon–Sat 9.30am–4.30pm; 01434 652220, hadrians-wall.org).

ACCOMMODATION

Hallbank Hallgate, behind the Old Gaol 01434 605567, hallbankguesthouse.com. A restored house in a quiet town-centre location, with eight very comfortable rooms and an associated coffee shop/restaurant. Evening meals available on request. **£90**

Matfen Hall Matfen, 10 miles northeast of Hexham 01661 886500, primahotels.co.uk/matfen. Large, ritzy country hotel surrounded by swathes of green parkland harbouring a golf course and driving range. There's a spa and a good, fine dining restaurant. It's a popular spot for weddings. **£185**

13

EATING AND DRINKING

Bouchon Bistrot 4 Gilesgate ⓣ01434 609943, ⓦbouchonbistrot.co.uk. Very stylish restaurant in a handsome terraced townhouse, serving sophisticated French dishes such as lamb shank "de 5 heures" with sautéed potatoes (£15.50) and crème caramel with langues du chat (£4.95). Tues–Sat noon–2pm & 6–9.30pm.

Dipton Mill Inn Dipton Mill Rd, 2 miles south of Hexham ⓣ01434 606577, ⓦdiptonmill.co.uk. A lovely, traditional country pub covered in ivy. While the food is excellent – good pub grub like steak and kidney pie and vegetable casserole – it's most famous for the home-brewed ales, made at Hexhamshire Brewery. Try Old Humbug, named after the landlord. Mon–Sat noon–2.30pm & 6pm–11pm, Sun noon–3pm.

★ **Rat Inn** Anick, 2 miles northeast of Hexham ⓣ01434 602814, ⓦtheratinn.com. In a glorious hillside location overlooking Hexham, this quaint pub has a roaring fire in winter and a pretty summer garden. The food is all locally sourced – try the braised local beef in Allendale beer (£10.50). Booking essential for Sunday lunch. On Mondays in summer there are fresh sandwiches available for lunch (from £3.95). April–Sept daily noon–11pm; Oct–March Mon–Fri noon–3pm & 6–11pm.

Northumberland National Park

Northwest Northumberland, the great triangular chunk of land between Hadrian's Wall and the coastal plain, is dominated by the wide-skied landscapes of **Northumberland National Park** (ⓦnorthumberland-nationalpark.org.uk), whose four hundred windswept square miles rise to the Cheviot Hills on the Scottish border. The bulk of the Park is taken up by **Kielder Water and Forest nature reserve**, a superb destination for watersports and outdoor activities; the small town of Bellingham makes a good base for the reserve, as do **Rothbury** and **Wooler**, both of which also provide easy access to some superb walking in the craggy **Cheviot Hills**.

Kielder Water and Forest

Surrounded by 250 acres of dense, pine forest, **Kielder Water** is the largest reservoir in England. The road from Bellingham follows the North Tyne River west and skirts the forested edge of the lake, passing an assortment of visitor centres, waterside parks, picnic areas and anchorages that fringe its southern shore. Mountain biking, hiking, horseriding and fishing are some of the land-based activities on offer, and watersports like waterskiing, sailing, kayaking and windsurfing are hugely popular, too. The mass of woodlands and wetlands mean that **wildlife** is abundant – you might spot badgers, deer, otters, ospreys and red squirrels. **Leaplish Waterside Park**, on the western flank of the reservoir, is the best place to head if you're visiting for the first time and need to get your bearings.

Leaplish Waterside Park

Birds of Prey Centre daily from 10.30am • Flying demonstrations summer 1.30pm & 3pm, Oct–March 2pm • £7 • ⓣ01434 250400, ⓦkwbopc.com

The hub of the Park is **Leaplish Waterside Park**, a purpose-built collection of lodges (see opposite) with cafés and a restaurant, a visitor centre (see below) and a Birds of Prey Centre where you can see a variety of handsome, sharp-taloned beasts, from owls and falcons to vultures and some inscrutable ospreys.

ARRIVAL AND INFORMATION — KIELDER WATER

By bus The #880 from Hexham serves Tower Knowe Centre, Leaplish (by request) and Kielder Castle via Bellingham (2 daily Tues & Sat). The #714 from Newcastle-upon-Tyne runs on Sundays (1 daily) to Tower Knowe, Leaplish (by request) and Kielder Castle.

Visitor centres Tower Knowe: from Bellingham, the first visitor centre you come to as you head anti-clockwise round the reservoir (daily: April–June & Sept 10am–5pm; July & Aug 10am–6pm; Oct 10am–4pm; ⓣ0845 155 0236); Leaplish: western flank of the reservoir (Feb–Oct daily 9am–5pm; ⓣ01434 251000); Kielder Castle: at the northernmost point of the reservoir (daily 10am–5pm; ⓣ01434 250 2009).

GETTING AROUND

By bike Purple Mountain (April–Oct 9am–5pm; Nov–March Sat & Sun 9am–5pm; ⓣ 01434 250532, ⓦ purplemountain.co.uk) or the Bike Place (Mon–Sat 10am–6pm; ⓣ 0845 634 1895, ⓦ thebikeplace.co.uk), both near Kielder Castle Visitor Centre, both offer day rental from £20.

By car The nearest petrol station is in Bellingham (14 miles away; closed Sun), so check your tank. For parking, you can buy one ticket at your first stop (£4) that's valid for all other car parks throughout the day.

By ferry The 74-seater Osprey Ferry (ⓣ 01434 251000) sails round the reservoir, with stops at Leaplish, Tower Knowe and Belvedere. Tickets (day pass £6.75, short journeys from £4.40) are available at Tower Knowe or Leaplish; prior booking is necessary.

ACCOMMODATION AND EATING

Hollybush Inn Greenhaugh, 12 miles east of Kielder Water ⓣ 01434 240391, ⓦ hollybushinn.net. Super little pub in a remote village serving great ales and food, and with four simple and attractive bedrooms upstairs. **£65**

Kielder Lodges Leaplish Waterside Park ⓣ 0870 240 3549, or Hoseasons ⓣ 01502 502588, ⓦ hoseasons.co.uk. Scandinavian-style self-catering lodges, all with access to the park's pool, sauna, bar and restaurant. Bring plenty of midge repellent. Weekly rates from **£335**

★ **Pheasant Inn** Stannersburn ⓣ 01434 240382, ⓦ thepheasantinn.com. A traditional country pub on the road from Bellingham, the *Pheasant Inn* has eight very comfortable bedrooms (including one family room). The highlight is the food, though, served downstairs in the cosy restaurant; expect game pies, Northumbrian cheeses and plenty of fish (mains around £12 in the evening). Booking recommended. Restaurant daily 8–9am & 7–9pm; bar meals noon–2pm & 7–9pm. **£85**

YHA Kielder Butteryhaugh, Kielder village ⓣ 0845 371 9126, ⓔ kielder@yha.org.uk. Well-equipped activity-based hostel, with some two- and three-bedded rooms plus small dorms. Dorm **£16.40**, family room **£34.95**

Rothbury and around

ROTHBURY, straddling the River Coquet thirty miles northeast of Hexham, prospered as a late Victorian resort because it gave ready access to the forests, burns and ridges of the **Simonside Hills**. The small town remains a popular spot for walkers, with several of the best local trails beginning from the **Simonside Hills** car park, a couple of miles southwest of Rothbury. Nearby, the estates of **Cragside** and **Wallington** are good options if you want to take a break from hiking.

Cragside

A mile east of Rothbury • House: March–Oct Sat & Sun 11am–5pm, Tues & Fri 1–5pm; gardens: March–Oct 10am–7pm • NT • £13.20, gardens only £8.55 • ⓣ 01669 620333

Victorian Rothbury was dominated by Sir William, later the first Lord Armstrong, the wealthy nineteenth-century arms manufacturer, shipbuilder and engineer who built his country home at **Cragside**, a mile to the east of the village. He hired Richard Norman Shaw, one of the period's top architects, who produced a grandiose Tudor-style mansion entirely out of place in the Northumbrian countryside. Armstrong was an avid innovator, and in 1880 Cragside became the first house in the world to be lit by hydroelectric power. The surrounding **gardens**, complete with the remains of the original pumping system, are beautiful and there's a pleasant tearoom for a light snack.

Wallington

Thirteen miles south of Rothbury • House: March–Oct Mon & Wed–Fri 1–5pm, Sat & Sun 11am–5pm; gardens only daily 10am–7pm • NT • £9.70, gardens only £6.70 • ⓣ 01670 773967

South of Rothbury, thirteen miles down the B6342, stands **Wallington**, an ostentatious mansion rebuilt in the 1740s by Sir Walter Blackett, the coal- and lead-mine owner. The house is known for its Rococo plasterwork and William Bell Scott's Pre-Raphaelite murals of scenes from Northumbrian history. Children will love the collection of dolls' houses, one of which has thirty-six rooms and was originally fitted with running water and a working lift. However, it's the magnificent **gardens and grounds** that are the real delight, with lawns, woods and lakes laced with footpaths. There are events, concerts and activities throughout the year, as well as a café and farm shop on site.

13

ARRIVAL AND INFORMATION — ROTHBURY

By bus Buses from Newcastle stop outside the *Queen's Head* pub in the centre.

National Park Visitor Centre Near the cross on Church St (April–Oct daily 10am–5pm; Nov–March Sat & Sun 10am–3pm; ⓣ01669 620887, ⓦvisit-rothbury.co.uk).

ACCOMMODATION

★ **Hillcrest** 200yd from Rothbury centre ⓣ01669 621944, ⓦhillcrestbandb.co.uk. Superb B&B in a pretty Georgian house, with two beautifully decorated bedrooms – wooden floorboards, antique furniture, exposed walls and the like – with an intriguing past (the owner will explain). Wonderful breakfasts, too. **£75**

★ **Thistleyhaugh** Longframlington, 5 miles east of Rothbury ⓣ01665 570629, ⓦthistleyhaugh.co.uk. Gorgeous, ivy-smothered Georgian farmhouse with five luxurious, tasteful bedrooms. They serve delicious three-course dinners (7pm; £20) and hearty breakfasts. **£80**

Tosson Tower Great Tosson, 2 miles southwest of Rothbury ⓣ01669 620228, ⓦtossontowerfarm.com. Eight lovely rooms on this little working farm in a quiet hamlet with spectacular views out over the Cheviot Hills. Plus some charming self-catering cottages. **£80**

Wooler and around

Stone-terraced **WOOLER** – rebuilt after a terrible fire in the 1860s – is a one-street market town twenty miles north of Rothbury. It's the best base for climbs up **the Cheviot** (2674ft), seven miles to the southwest and the highest point in the Cheviot Hills. From *Wooler Youth Hostel* at 30 Cheviot St, it's four hours there and back; from Hawsen Burn, the nearest navigable point, it's two hours walking there and back. Wooler is also a staging-post on the Pennine Way and the lovely **St Cuthbert's Way** (from Melrose in Scotland to Lindisfarne).

Chillingham Castle

Six miles southeast of Wooler • April–Oct Sun–Fri noon–5pm • £8.50 • ⓣ01668 215359, ⓦchillingham-castle.com

Chillingham Castle started life as an eleventh-century tower. The castle was augmented at regular intervals until the nineteenth century, but from 1933 was largely left to the elements for fifty years, until the present owner set about restoring it in his own individualistic way: bedrooms, living rooms and even a grisly torture chamber (designed to "cause maximum shock") are decorated with all manner of historical paraphernalia to give an idea of how the place would have looked through the ages.

Chillingham Wild Cattle

Off the A697 between Alnwick and Belford, signposted The Wild White Cattle • April–Oct Mon–Fri tours 10am, 11am, noon, 2pm, 3pm & 4pm, Sun 2pm, 3pm & 4pm; winter by appointment • £6 • ⓦchillinghamwildcattle.org.uk, ⓔwild.cattle@btinternet.com

In 1220, Chillingham Castle's adjoining 365 acres of parkland were enclosed to protect the local wild cattle for hunting and food. And so the **Chillingham Wild Cattle** – a fierce, primeval herd with white coats, black muzzles and black tips to their horns – have remained to this day, cut off from mixing with domesticated breeds. It's possible to visit these unique relics, who number around ninety, but only in the company of a warden, as the animals are potentially dangerous and need to be protected from outside infection. The visit takes about two hours and involves a short country walk before viewing the cattle at a safe distance – the closest you're likely to get to big game viewing in England. Bring strong shoes or walking boots if it's wet.

ARRIVAL AND INFORMATION — WOOLER

By bus The bus station is set back off High St.

Destinations Alnwick (Mon–Sat 9 daily; 45min); Berwick-upon-Tweed (Mon–Sat 9 daily; 50min).

Tourist office Cheviot Centre, Padgepool Place (leaflets and accommodation information available Mon–Fri 9am–5pm; staffed desk Easter–Oct daily 10am–4.30pm; Nov–March Sat & Sun 10am–2pm; ⓣ01668 282123).

ACCOMMODATION AND EATING

Milan 2 High St, through the arch of the Black Bull hotel ⊤01668 283692, ⓦmilan-restaurant.co.uk. Good-value Italian restaurant with exposed brick walls and a jolly ambience, serving large pizzas (from £6.75), pasta dishes (from £7.95) and plenty of meat and fish options. It's a very popular place, so book ahead. Daily 5–10pm.

Tilldale House 34 High St ⊤01668 281450, ⓦtilldalehouse.co.uk. Snug seventeenth-century stone cottage in the middle of town with three en-suite bedrooms. With enormous, soft beds, deep-pile carpets, an open fire and great breakfasts, it makes a very cosy and enticing base after a long day hiking in the hills. **£58**

The Northumberland coast

Stretching 64 miles north of Newcastle up to the Scottish border, the low-lying **Northumberland coast** is the region's shining star, stunningly beautiful and packed with impressive sights. Here you'll find the mighty fortresses at **Warkworth**, **Alnwick** and **Bamburgh** and the magnificent Elizabethan ramparts surrounding **Berwick-upon-Tweed**, while in between there are glorious sandy beaches as well as the site of the Lindisfarne monastery on **Holy Island** and the seabird and nature reserve of the **Farne Islands**, reached by boat from Seahouses.

Warkworth

WARKWORTH, a peaceful coastal hamlet set in a loop of the River Coquet a couple of miles from Amble, is best seen from the north, from where the grey stone terraces of the long main street slope up towards the commanding remains of **Warkworth Castle**. From the castle, the main street sweeps down into the village, flattening out at Dial Place and the Church of St Lawrence before curving right to cross the River Coquet; just over the bridge, a signposted quarter-mile lane leads to the **beach**, which stretches for five miles from Amble to Alnmouth.

Warkworth Castle

April–Oct daily 10am–5pm; rest of the year limited opening hours, call before visiting; Duke's Rooms Wed, Sun & bank hols • EH • £4.80 • ⊤01665 711423

Ruined but well-preserved, **Warkworth Castle** has Norman origins, but was constructed using sandstone during the fourteenth and fifteenth centuries. Home to generations of the Percy family, the powerful earls of Northumberland, it appears as a backdrop in several scenes of Shakespeare's *Henry IV, Part II*. The cross-shaped keep contains a great hall, a chapel, kitchens, storerooms and the Duke's Rooms, which are kitted out in period furniture and furnishings.

Warkworth Hermitage

Weather permitting April–Sept Wed & Sun 11am–5pm; rest of the year limited opening hours, call before visiting • EH • £3.20 • ⊤01665 711423

A path from the churchyard heads along the right bank of the Coquet to the boat that shuttles visitors across to **Warkworth Hermitage**, a series of simple rooms and a claustrophobic chapel that were hewn out of the cliff above the river some time in the fourteenth century, but abandoned by 1567. The last resident hermit, one George Lancaster, was charged by the sixth earl of Northumberland to pray for his noble family, for which lonesome duty he received around £15 a year and a barrel of fish every Sunday.

TOP 5 NORTHUMBRIAN CASTLES

Alnwick See p.592
Bamburgh Castle See p.594
Chillingham Castle See p.590
Dunstanburgh Castle See p.593
Warkworth See p.591

13

Alnmouth

It's three miles north from Warkworth to the seaside resort of **ALNMOUTH**, whose narrow centre is strikingly situated on a steep spur of land between the sea and the estuary of the Aln. It's a lovely setting and has been a low-key holiday spot since Victorian times, and is particularly popular with golfers: the village's nine-hole course, right on the coast, was built in 1869 (it's claimed to be the second oldest in the country) and dune-strollers really do have to heed the "Danger – Flying Golf Balls" signs which adorn Marine Road.

ARRIVAL AND DEPARTURE — ALNMOUTH

There are local **bus** services from Alnwick and Warkworth, and the regular Newcastle–Alnwick bus also passes through Alnmouth and calls at its train station at Hipsburn, 1.5 miles west of the centre.

ACCOMMODATION AND EATING

Red Lion 22 Northumberland St ⓣ 01668 30584, ⓦ redlionalnmouth.com. Six spacious and modern rooms, with pine furniture, cream walls and fresh bathrooms, above a popular, traditional pub. The beer garden is perfect for sunny days, and the menu has everything from big open sandwiches (from £4.95) to sirloin steak (£17.50). **£85**

Alnwick

The appealing market town of **ALNWICK** (pronounced "Annick"), thirty miles north of Newcastle and four miles inland from Alnmouth, is renowned for its **castle** and gardens – seat of the dukes of Northumberland – which overlook the River Aln. It's worth spending a couple of days here, exploring the medieval maze of streets, the elegant gatehouses on Pottergatea and Bondgate and the best **bookshop** in the north.

Alnwick Castle

April–Oct daily 10am–6pm • £13; castle and garden £22 • ⓣ 01665 511100, ⓦ alnwickcastle.com

The Percys – who were raised to the dukedom of Northumberland in 1750 – have owned **Alnwick Castle** since 1309. In the eighteenth century, the first duke had the interior refurbished by Robert Adam in an extravagant Gothic style – which in turn was supplanted by the gaudy Italianate decoration preferred by the fourth duke in the 1850s. There's plenty to see inside, though the **interior** can be crowded at times – not least with families on the *Harry Potter* trail, since the castle doubled as Hogwarts School in the first two films.

Alnwick Garden

Daily 10am–6pm; Grand Cascade and Poison Garden closed in winter • £11; garden and castle £22 • ⓣ 01665 511350, ⓦ alnwickgarden.com

The grounds of the castle are taken up by the huge and beautiful **Alnwick Garden**, designed by an innovative Belgian team and full of quirky features such as a bamboo labyrinth maze, a serpent garden involving topiary snakes, and the popular **Poison Garden**, filled with the world's deadliest plants. The heart of the garden is the computerized Grand Cascade, which shoots water jets in a regular synchronized display, while to the west is Europe's largest treehouse with a restaurant within (see opposite).

Barter Books

Wagonway Rd • April–Sept daily 9am–7pm; Oct–March Mon–Wed & Fri–Sun 9am–5pm, Thurs 9am–7pm • ⓣ 01665 604888, ⓦ barterbooks.co.uk

Housed in the Victorian train station on Wagonway Road, and containing visible remnants of the ticket office, passenger waiting rooms and the outbound platform, the enchanting **Barter Books** is one of the largest secondhand bookshops in England. With its sofas, murals, open fire, coffee and biscuits – and, best of all, a model train that runs on top of the stacks – it is definitely worth a visit.

ARRIVAL AND INFORMATION — ALNWICK

By bus The station is on Clayport St, a couple of minutes' walk west of the marketplace.

Destinations Bamburgh (Mon–Sat 7 daily, Sun 4 daily; 1hr 15min); Berwick-upon-Tweed (Mon–Sat 6 daily, Sun 3 daily; 1hr); Craster (Mon–Fri 7 daily, Sat 4 daily; 35min); Wooler (Mon–Sat 9 daily; 45min).

Tourist office 2 The Shambles, off the marketplace (April–June & Sept–Oct Mon–Sat 9.30am–5pm, Sun 10am–4pm; July & Aug daily 9am–5pm; Nov–March Mon–Fri 9.30am–4.30pm, Sat 10am–4pm; ⓣ 01665 511 333, ⓦ visitalnwick.org.uk).

ACCOMMODATION

The Old School Newton-on-the-Moor, 6 miles south of Alnwick ⓣ 01665 575767, ⓦ northumberlandbedandbreakfast.co.uk. In a quaint little village just outside Alnwick, this superb B&B is housed in a venerable eighteenth-century building surrounded by tranquil gardens. The rooms – an attractive blend of country and modern decor – come complete with gloriously fluffy dressing gowns, delicious-smelling toiletries, flatscreen TVs and wi-fi. In the morning, wake up to a fantastic cooked breakfast. **£80**

Tate House 11 Bondgate Without ⓣ 01665 604661, ⓦ stayinalnwick.co.uk. In a pretty Victorian house opposite Alnwick Gardens, this B&B has three comfortable bedrooms with spotless bathrooms and nice little touches such as hot-water bottles, iPod docks and DVD players. **£75**

EATING

Alnwick Garden Treehouse Alnwick Gardens ⓣ 01665 511852, ⓦ alnwickgarden.com. Glorious restaurant in the enormous treehouse in Alnwick Gardens. There's an open fire in the middle of the room and even tree trunks growing through the floor. Simple meals (sandwiches, quiche and soup) for lunch and in the evening, expensive but tasty mains – honey-glazed duck with braised red cabbage (£18.50) for example, and a refreshing kirsch and blackcurrant sorbet (£4.95) for pudding. Mon–Wed 11.30am–2.45pm, Thurs–Sun 11.30am–2.45pm & 6.30pm–late.

Louis' Steakhouse Market Place ⓣ 01665 606947, ⓦ louis-steakhouse.co.uk. Chic little restaurant that does a great line in steaks (from £13), as well as breakfasts, paninis, omelettes and salads (all around £5). Breakfasts daily from 9am; evening meals Mon–Sat 5–11pm.

Craster and around

The tiny fishing village of **CRASTER** – known for its kippers – lies six miles northeast of Alnwick, right on the coast. It's a delightful little place, with its circular, barnacle-encrusted harbour walls fronting a cluster of tough, weather-battered little houses and the cheery *Jolly Fisherman* pub. Other villages worth visiting round here include **Newton-on-Sea** and **Beadnell**, both exuding wind-swept, salty charm. The **coastline** between Dunstanburgh and Beadnell is made up of the long sandy beaches Northumberland is famous for.

Dunstanburgh Castle

April–Sept daily 10am–5pm; Oct daily 10am–4pm; Nov–March Mon & Thurs–Sun 10am–4pm • NT & EH • £4 • ⓣ 01665 576231

Looming in the distance, about a thirty-minute walk northwards up the coast from Craster, is stunning **Dunstanburgh Castle**. Built in the fourteenth century, in the wake of civil war, its shattered remains occupy a magnificent promontory, bordered by sheer cliffs and crashing waves.

ACCOMMODATION — CRASTER

Old Rectory Howick, 2 miles south ⓣ 01665 577590, ⓦ oldrectoryhowick.co.uk. Just 400yds from the wind-whipped North Sea, this fantastic B&B sits in its own peaceful grounds and has extremely pretty bedrooms and comfortable sitting areas. Superb breakfasts feature plenty of cooked options, including Craster kippers. **£90**

EATING AND DRINKING

There's not much in the way of fine dining round these parts; most villages simply have a traditional pub serving decent meals. Craster's beloved **kippers** are smoked at L. Robson & Sons (ⓣ 01665 576223, ⓦ kipper.co.uk) in the centre of the village; they also sell salty oak-smoked salmon.

Jolly Fisherman 9 Haven Hill ☎01665 576461. Just above the harbour, this pub has sea views from its back window and a lovely summer beer garden. Not surprisingly for a pub opposite L. Robson & Sons, it serves plenty of fish – crab sandwiches, kipper pâté and a famously good crabmeat, whisky and cream soup. Mon–Fri 11am–3pm & 7–11pm, Sat & Sun 11am–11pm.

Ship Inn Low Newton-by-the-Sea, 5 miles north ☎01665 576262, Ⓦshipinnnewton.co.uk. Great, rustic pub in a coastal hamlet serving dishes using ingredients from local suppliers – there's plenty of L. Robson smoked fish on the menu. Mains from £7. Ales are supplied by their own brewery next door. Dinner reservations advised. Mon–Sat 11.30am–11pm, Sun 11am–11pm.

Seahouses and around

Around ten miles north from Craster, beyond the small village of Beadnell, lies the fishing port **SEAHOUSES**, the only place on the local coast that could remotely be described as a resort. It's the embarkation point for boat trips out to the windswept **Farne Islands**, a rocky archipelago lying a few miles offshore.

ACCOMMODATION — **SEAHOUSES**

★**St Cuthberts** Seahouses ☎01665 720456, Ⓦstcuthbertshouse.com. Award-winning B&B in a beautifully converted 200-year-old chapel. Rooms cleverly incorporate period features like the original arched windows with lovely modern touches such as wet rooms, flatscreen TVs, comfy dressing gowns and slippers. Breakfast is all locally sourced, from the sausages and the eggs to the kippers and the honey. **£105**

The Farne Islands

Owned by the National Trust and maintained as a nature reserve, the **Farne Islands** (Ⓦfarne-islands.com) are the summer home of hundreds of thousands of migrating sea birds, notably puffins, guillemots, terns, eider ducks and kittiwakes, and home to the only grey seal colony on the English coastline. A number of boat trips potter around the islands – the largest of which is Inner Farne – offering birdwatching tours, grey seal-watching tours and the Grace Darling tour, which takes visitors to the lighthouse on Longstone Island, where the famed local heroine (see opposite) lived.

ARRIVAL AND INFORMATION — **FARNE ISLANDS**

By boat Weather permitting, several operators in Seahouses run daily boat trips (2–3hr; from £13) from the quayside, usually starting at around 10am. You can just wander down and pick a departure, or contact either the National Trust Shop, 16 Main St (☎01665 721099), by the Seahouses traffic roundabout, or the tourist office in the main car park. During the breeding season (May–July) landings are restricted to morning trips to Staple Island and afternoons to Inner Farne. Landing fees for the islands are payable to the National Trust (£5–6).

Bamburgh

One-time capital of Northumbria, the little village of **BAMBURGH** (Ⓦbamburgh.org.uk), just three miles from Seahouses, lies in the lee of its magnificent **castle**. Attractive stone cottages – holding the village shop, a café, pubs and B&Bs – flank each side of the triangular green, and at the top of the village on Radcliffe Road is the diminutive **Grace Darling Museum**. From behind the castle it's a brisk, five-minute walk to two splendid sandy **beaches**, backed by rolling, tufted dunes.

Bamburgh Castle

April–Oct daily 11am–5pm • £6.50 • ☎01668 214515, Ⓦbamburghcastle.com

Solid and chunky, **Bamburgh Castle** is a spectacular sight, its elongated battlements crowning a formidable basalt crag high above the beach. Its origins lie in Anglo-Saxon times, but it suffered a centuries-long decline – rotted by sea spray and buffeted by winter storms, the castle was bought by Lord Armstrong (of Rothbury's Cragside) in 1894, who demolished most of the structure to replace it with a hybrid castle-mansion. Inside there's plenty to explore, including the sturdy keep that houses an unnerving armoury packed with vicious-looking pikes, halberds, helmets and muskets; the King's Hall, with its marvellous teak ceiling that was imported from Siam (Thailand) and carved in Victorian times; and a medieval kitchen complete with original jugs, pots and pans.

Grace Darling Museum

Radcliffe Rd • Easter–Oct daily 10am–5pm; Oct–Easter Tues–Sun 10am–4pm • £2.75 • ⓣ 01668 214910, ⓦ rnli.org.uk

The **Grace Darling Museum** celebrates the life of celebrated local heroine Grace Darling. In September 1838, a gale dashed the steamship *Forfarshire* against the rocks of the Farne Islands. Nine passengers struggled onto a reef where they were subsequently saved by Grace and her lighthouseman father, William, who left the safety of the Longstone lighthouse to row out to them. *The Times* trumpeted Grace's bravery, offers of marriage and requests for locks of her hair streamed into the Darlings' lighthouse home, and for the rest of her brief life Grace was plagued by unwanted visitors – she died of tuberculosis aged 26 in 1842, and was buried in Bamburgh, in the churchyard of the thirteenth-century St Aidan's.

ARRIVAL AND DEPARTURE — BAMBURGH

By bus A regular bus service links Alnwick and Berwick-upon-Tweed with Bamburgh, stopping on Front St by the green.
Destinations Alnwick (Mon–Sat 7 daily, Sun 5 daily; 1hr 15min); Berwick-upon-Tweed (Mon–Sat 3 daily, Sun 2 daily; 40min); Craster (Mon–Sat 7 daily, Sun 5 daily; 30–40min); Seahouses (Mon–Sat 7 daily, Sun 5 daily; 10min).

ACCOMMODATION AND EATING

Blacketts 2 Lucker Rd ⓣ 01668 214714, ⓦ blackettsofbamburgh.co.uk. Sunday lunches, lighter snacks and bigger mains (fish pie, pork steak and giant king prawns, for example) on offer at this cheerful little restaurant at the top of Bamburgh's main road. Mains from £9. Daily 10am–5pm & 6.30pm–close.

Copper Kettle 21 Front St ⓣ 01668 14315, ⓦ copperkettletearooms.com. Sweet little tearoom, with a sunny sitting area out the back, serving tasty cakes, teas and coffees – try the fruit loaf or the tempting carrot cake with icing. Also light meals such as sandwiches (£5), jacket potatoes (£6.50) and pies (£6). Daily 10am–6pm.

Victoria Hotel Front St ⓣ 01668 214431, ⓦ victoriahotel.net. This smart boutique hotel has elegant rooms in a variety of sizes – one with lovely castle views – a couple of relaxing bars and a more expensive brasserie (dinner only). Rates include breakfast. **£80**

Holy Island

It's a dramatic approach to **HOLY ISLAND** (**Lindisfarne**; ⓦ lindisfarne.org.uk), past the barnacle-encrusted marker poles that line the three-mile-long causeway. Topped with a stumpy **castle**, the island is small (just 1.5 miles by one), sandy and bare, and in winter it can be bleak, but come summer day-trippers clog the car parks as soon as the causeway is open. Even then, though, Lindisfarne has a distinctive and isolated atmosphere. Give the place time and, if you can, stay overnight, when you'll be able to see the historic remains without hundreds of others cluttering the views. The island's surrounding tidal mud flats, salt marshes and dunes have been designated a **nature reserve**.

Brief history

It was on Lindisfarne (as the island was once known) that St Aidan of Iona founded a monastery at the invitation of King Oswald of Northumbria in 634. The monks quickly established a reputation for scholarship and artistry, the latter exemplified by the **Lindisfarne Gospels**, the apotheosis of Celtic religious art, now kept in the British Library. The monastery had sixteen bishops in all, the most celebrated being the reluctant **St Cuthbert**, who never settled here – within two years, he was back in his hermit's cell on the Farne Islands, where he died in 687. His colleagues rowed the body back to Lindisfarne, which became a place of pilgrimage until 875, when the monks abandoned the island in fear of marauding Vikings, taking Cuthbert's remains with them.

13

Lindisfarne Priory

Priory & museum April–Sept daily 9.30am–5pm; Oct daily 9.30am–4pm; Nov–Jan Sat–Mon 10am–2pm; Feb & March limited opening hours • EH • £4.80 • 01289 389200

Just off the village green, the tranquil, pinkish sandstone ruins of **Lindisfarne Priory** date from the Benedictine foundation. The **museum** next door displays a collection of incised stones that constitute all that remains of the first monastery.

Lindisfarne Castle

March–Oct Tues–Sun, hours vary according to tide but always include noon–3pm; Jan & Feb Sat & Sun 10am–3pm • NT • £6.30 • 01289 389244

Stuck on a small pyramid of rock half a mile away from the village, **Lindisfarne Castle** was built in the middle of the sixteenth century to protect the island's harbour from the Scots. It was, however, merely a decaying shell when Edward Hudson, the founder of *Country Life* magazine, stumbled across it in 1901. He promptly commissioned Sir Edwin Lutyens to turn it into an Edwardian country house, and installed a charming walled garden in the castle's former vegetable gardens, to designs by Gertrude Jekyll.

ARRIVAL AND INFORMATION — HOLY ISLAND

By bus The #477 bus from Berwick-upon-Tweed to Holy Island (35min) is something of a law unto itself given the interfering tides, but basically service is daily in August and twice-weekly the rest of the year.

Crossing the causeway The island is cut off for about 5hr a day. Consult tide timetables at a tourist office, in the local paper or at lindisfarne.org.uk

Castle shuttle A minibus trundles the half a mile to the castle from the main car park, The Chare (every 20min 10.20am–4.20pm; £1).

ACCOMMODATION AND EATING

Due to the size of the island and the small number of B&Bs, it's imperative to **book in advance** if you're staying over.

Bamburgh View Fenkle St 01289 389212, bamburghview@btinternet.com. Sweet, friendly B&B very near the priory, with three airy, wood-floored rooms, good showers and generous breakfasts. **£85**

Café Beangoose Selby House 01289 389083, cafebeangoose.co.uk. Overlooking the green, this excellent restaurant is in a family home, its small rooms complete with knick-knacks and snoozing cats. Meals are hearty and locally sourced: braised beef, sea trout and the like for around £11. Holiday cottages available (£885/week). May–Oct daily dinner; hours depend on tides.

St Aidan's Winery In the modern building behind the green 01289 389230 lindisfarne-mead.co.uk. If you're keen to sample some of the world-famous Lindisfarne mead, this is the place to come. They also sell home-made chutneys, biscuits and jams. Hours depend on tides.

The Ship Marygate 01289 389311. The best pub on the island; friendly and traditional, with open fires and wood-panelled walls. The ales are good, as is the inexpensive pub grub. They have four cosy, en-suite rooms upstairs. **£104**

Berwick-upon-Tweed

Before the union of the English and Scottish crowns in 1603, **BERWICK-UPON-TWEED**, twelve miles north of Holy Island, was the quintessential frontier town, changing hands no fewer than fourteen times between 1174 and 1482, when the Scots finally ceded the stronghold to the English. Interminable cross-border warfare ruined Berwick's economy, turning the prosperous Scottish port of the thirteenth century into an impoverished English garrison town. By the late sixteenth century, Berwick's fortifications were in a dreadful state and Elizabeth I, fearing the resurgent alliance between France and Scotland, had the place rebuilt in line with the latest principles of military architecture. Berwick was reborn as an important seaport between 1750 and 1820, and is still peppered with elegant **Georgian mansions** dating from that period.

Berwick's **walls** – one and a half miles long and still in pristine condition – are no more than 20ft high but incredibly thick. They are now the town's major attraction; it's possible to walk the mile-long circuit (1hr) round them, allowing for wonderful views out to sea, across the Tweed and over the orange-tiled rooftops of the town. Protected by ditches on three sides and the Tweed on the fourth, the walls are strengthened by immense bastions.

Cell Block Museum

Marygate • Easter–Sept Mon–Fri tours 10.30am & 2pm • £2 • ⓣ 01289 330900

Within the ramparts, the Berwick skyline is punctured by the stumpy spire of the eighteenth-century Town Hall at the bottom of Marygate, right at the heart of the centre. Inside, the town's original jailhouse now houses the **Cell Block Museum**, where lively tours dwell on tales of crime and punishment in Berwick.

The Barracks

April–Sept Mon–Fri 10am–5pm; Oct–March limited opening hours • EH • £3.80 • ⓣ 01289 304493

The town's finely proportioned **Barracks**, designed by Nicholas Hawksmoor (1717) functioned as a garrison until 1964, when the King's Own Scottish Borderers regiment decamped. Inside there's the rather specialist **By the Beat of the Drum** exhibition, tracing the lives of British infantrymen from the Civil War to World War I, as well as the Kings Own Scottish Borderers Museum, the Berwick Borough Museum and the **Gymnasium Gallery** of contemporary art.

ARRIVAL AND INFORMATION — BERWICK-UPON-TWEED

By train From the train station it's a 10min walk down Castlegate and Marygate to the town centre.

Destinations Durham (every 30min; 1hr 10min); Edinburgh (hourly; 45min); Newcastle (hourly; 45min).

By bus Most regional buses stop on Golden Square (where Castlegate meets Marygate), though some may also stop in front of the train station.

Destinations Bamburgh (Mon–Sat 6 daily, Sun 2 daily; 40min); Holy Island (Aug 2 daily, rest of the year 2 weekly; 35min); Newcastle (Mon–Sat 7 daily; 2hr 15min); Wooler (Mon–Sat 9 daily; 50min).

Tourist office 106 Marygate (April, May & Oct Mon–Sat 10am–5pm; June–Sept Mon–Sat 10am–5pm & Sun 11am–3pm; Nov–March Mon–Sat 10am–4pm; ⓣ 01289 330733).

Tours The tourist office can book you onto a walking tour of town (Easter–Oct Mon–Fri 2 daily; £4.50; ⓦ explore-northumberland.co.uk) or onto the Hidden Berwick tour (April–Sept Sun–Fri, 1 daily; £6), which includes entry into an eighteenth-century gun bastion not usually open to the public.

ACCOMMODATION

Berwick Backpackers 56–58 Bridge St ⓣ 01289 331481, ⓦ berwickbackpackers.co.uk. This rambling place (once a factory) has simple but smartly decorated en-suite rooms, a kitchen/lounge, and wi-fi; rates include continental breakfast. Dorm £19.90, double £60

Clovelly House 58 West St ⓣ 01289 302337, ⓦ clovelly53.freeserve.co.uk. Central B&B on a steep cobbled street by the Arts Centre (free parking nearby). Smart rooms come with luxuries like dressing gowns, slippers and chocolate biscuits; breakfast is superb. No credit cards. £70

★ **No.1 Sallyport** Bridge St ⓣ 01289 308827, ⓦ sallyport.co.uk. Berwick's most luxurious B&B, with six sensational rooms in a seventeenth-century house. The two spacious doubles and four lavish suites (£40 more) are elegantly furnished. They also have a little café full of delicious goodies, and serve simple dinners in the evenings. £110

Queen's Head 6 Sandgate ⓣ 01289 307852, ⓦ queensheadberwick.co.uk. One of the best pubs in town has six snug rooms, including a family room. Great evening meals and breakfasts, too (mains around £15). £90

EATING AND DRINKING

Barrel's Ale 59 Bridge St ⓣ 01289 308013, ⓦ thebarrels.co.uk. Atmospheric pub specializing in (frequently changing) cask ales, lagers and stouts. It's also a great music venue, hosting an eclectic mix of jazz, blues, rock and indie bands. Mon–Thurs noon–11.30pm, Fri–Sat noon–1am, Sun noon–midnight.

★ **Café Curios** 52 Bridge St ⓣ 01289 302666. With its daily changing French-inspired menu, this little restaurant is run by a husband and wife team who are fans of the Slow Food movement. As well as à la carte, they serve a four-course "surprise menu" (£25) and wine comes by recommendation only (there's no list). The restaurant itself is beautiful, packed with flickering candles and antique china (it's all for sale). Mon–Sat 10.30am–4pm, plus Fri & Sat 7pm–close.

ENTERTAINMENT

The Maltings Eastern Lane ⓣ 01289 330999, ⓦ maltingsberwick.co.uk. Berwick's arts centre has a year-round programme of music, theatre, comedy, film and dance, and river views from its licensed café.

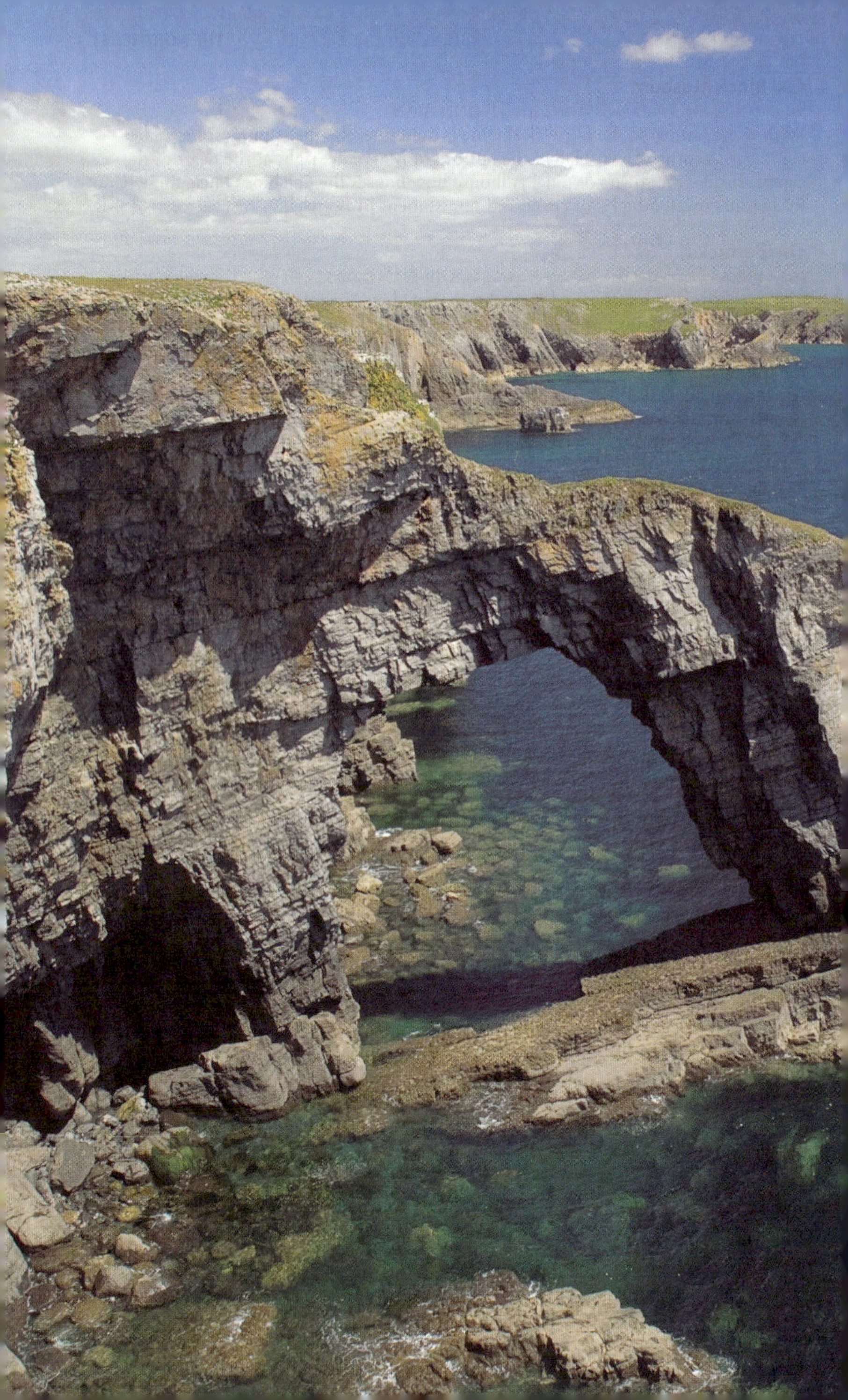

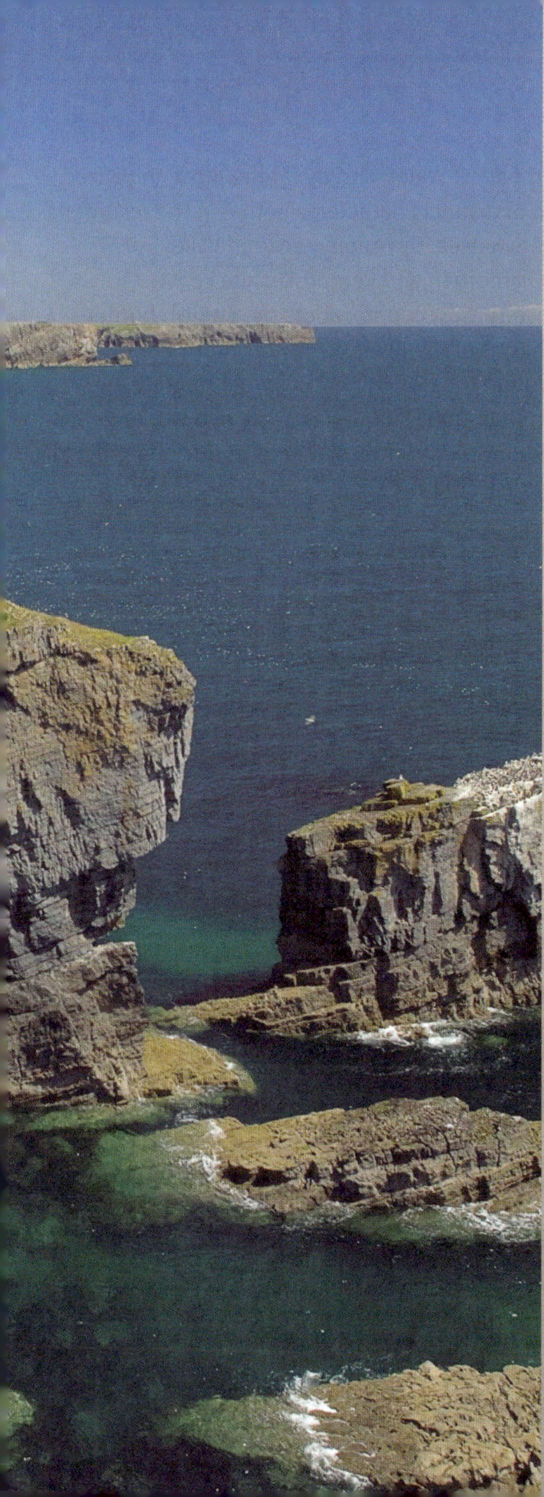

South Wales

602 The Wye Valley

607 The Valleys

611 Cardiff and around

621 Swansea

626 The Gower Peninsula

628 Carmarthenshire

634 Southern Pembrokeshire

637 Mid- and northern Pembrokeshire

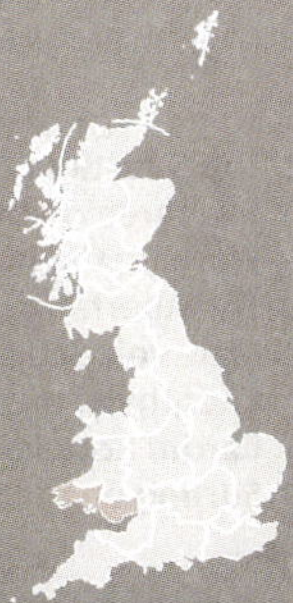

ST GOVAN'S HEADLAND, PEMBROKESHIRE

14

South Wales

The most heavily populated part of Wales, and by far the most anglicized, is the south. This is a region of distinct character, whether in the resurgent seaport cities of Cardiff and Swansea, the mining-scarred Valleys or the dramatically beautiful Glamorgan and Pembrokeshire coasts. Monmouthshire, Wales's easternmost county, abuts the English border and contains the bucolic charms of the River Wye and Tintern Abbey. To the west and north, although the coal mines no longer operate, the world-famous Valleys retain their tight-knit towns and a rich working-class heritage, and some excellent museums and colliery tours, including Big Pit at Blaenafon and the Rhondda Heritage Park in Trehafod.

The Valleys course down to the great ports of the coast, which once shipped Wales's products all over the world. The greatest of them all was **Cardiff**, now Wales's upbeat capital and an essential stop. Further west is Wales's second city, **Swansea** – rougher, tougher and less anglicized than Cardiff, it sits on an impressive arc of coast that shelves round to the delightful **Gower Peninsula**, replete with grand beaches, rocky headlands, bracken heaths and ruined castles.

Carmarthenshire, often missed out, is well worth visiting: of all the routes radiating from the county town of Carmarthen, the most glorious is the winding road to **Llandeilo** along the **Tywi Valley**, past ruined hilltop forts and two of the country's finest gardens. Immediately east sits Wales's most impressively sited castle at **Carreg Cennen**, high on a dizzy rock-plug on the edge of the Black Mountain. The wide sands fringing Carmarthen Bay stretch towards the popular seaside resort of **Tenby**, a major stop on the 186-mile **Pembrokeshire Coast Path**. The rutted coastline of **St Bride's Bay** is the most glorious part of the coastal walk, which leads north to brush past the impeccable mini-city of **St Davids**, whose exquisite cathedral shelters in a protective hollow. Nearby are plenty of opportunities for spectacular coast and hill walks, boat crossings to nearby islands, wildlife-watching and numerous outdoor activities.

GETTING AROUND — SOUTH WALES

Southeast Wales is by far the easiest part of the country to travel around, with the **M4** connecting to swift dual carriageways. South Wales is also the only part of the country with a half-decent **train** service, and most suburban and rural services interconnect with Cardiff, Newport or Swansea. **Bus** services fill in virtually all of the gaps left by trains, though often rather slowly.

Top 5 castles p.604
The three castles p.606
Working the black seam p.608
The Aberfan disaster p.609
Male voice choirs p.610
Caerphilly: the big cheese p.617
Cardiff Rocks p.620
Surfing on the Gower p.627
Dylan Thomas p.631
Caldey Island p.633
The Pembrokeshire Coast National Park and Coast Path p.635
Skomer, Skokholm and Grassholm islands p.638
Outdoor activities in St Davids p.640
Top 5 restaurants p.643

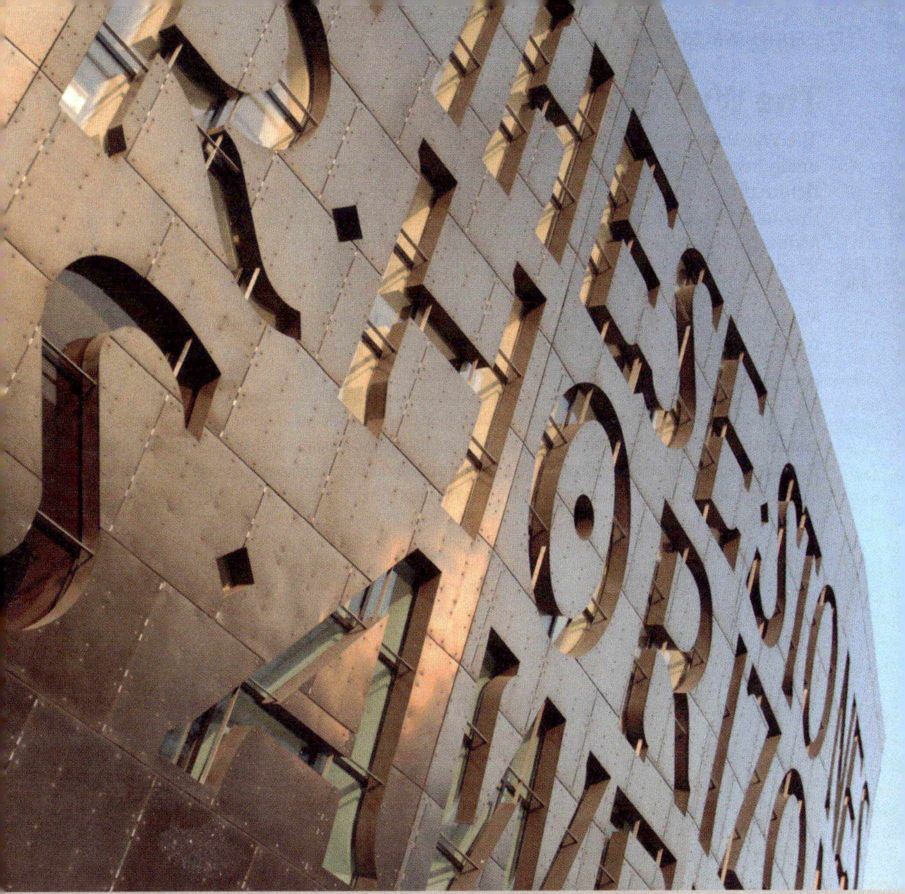

WALES MILLENNIUM CENTRE

Highlights

❶ **Blaenafon** Industrial heritage at its finest, thanks to a thrilling deep-mine museum and the fascinating ironworks town. **See p.608**

❷ **Wales Millennium Centre, Cardiff Bay** A symphony of opposites – industry and art, grandeur and intimacy – the WMC is a bold and brilliant asset to the capital. **See p.615**

❸ **National Waterfront Museum, Swansea** A celebration of Welsh innovation and industry – one of the best museums in Wales. **See p.623**

❹ **The Gower** Holding some of the country's most inspirational coastal and rural scenery, culminating in the stunning Rhossili Bay. **See p.626**

❺ **Carreg Cennen** The most magnificently sited castle in Wales, this fantasy fortress offers splendid views and endless possibilities for exploration. **See p.631**

❻ **The Pembrokeshire Coast Path** A narrow ribbon of mainly cliff-top footpath that winds its way through some magnificent coastal scenery. **See p.635**

❼ **St Davids** Inspirational city (little more than a village, in fact) with a splendid cathedral and heart-racing boat trips out to offshore islands. **See p.639**

HIGHLIGHTS ARE MARKED ON THE MAP ON PP.602–603

The Wye Valley

The **Wye Valley** (Ⓦvisitwyevalley.com), along with the rest of Monmouthshire, was finally recognized as part of Wales in the local government reorganization of 1974. Before then, the county was officially included as part of neither England nor Wales, so that maps were frequently headlined "Wales and Monmouthshire". Most of the rest of Monmouthshire is undoubtedly Welsh, but the woodlands and hills by the meandering River Wye have more in common with the landscape over the border. The two main centres are **Chepstow**, with its massive castle, and the spruce, old-fashioned town of **Monmouth**, sixteen miles upstream. Six miles north of Chepstow lie the atmospheric ruins of the Cistercian **Tintern Abbey**.

INFORMATION — THE WYE VALLEY

The excellent **Old Station Visitor Centre** (April–Oct daily 10.30am–5.30pm; Ⓣ01291 689566) is a mile or so along the road from Tintern Abbey to Monmouth in the former Tintern station; two refurbished carriages house an exhibition on the Wye Valley, and you can pick up leaflets on walks, including the surrounding wildflower meadows and cliff rambles above the meandering river. There's a lovely café here too. Bus #69 stops outside.

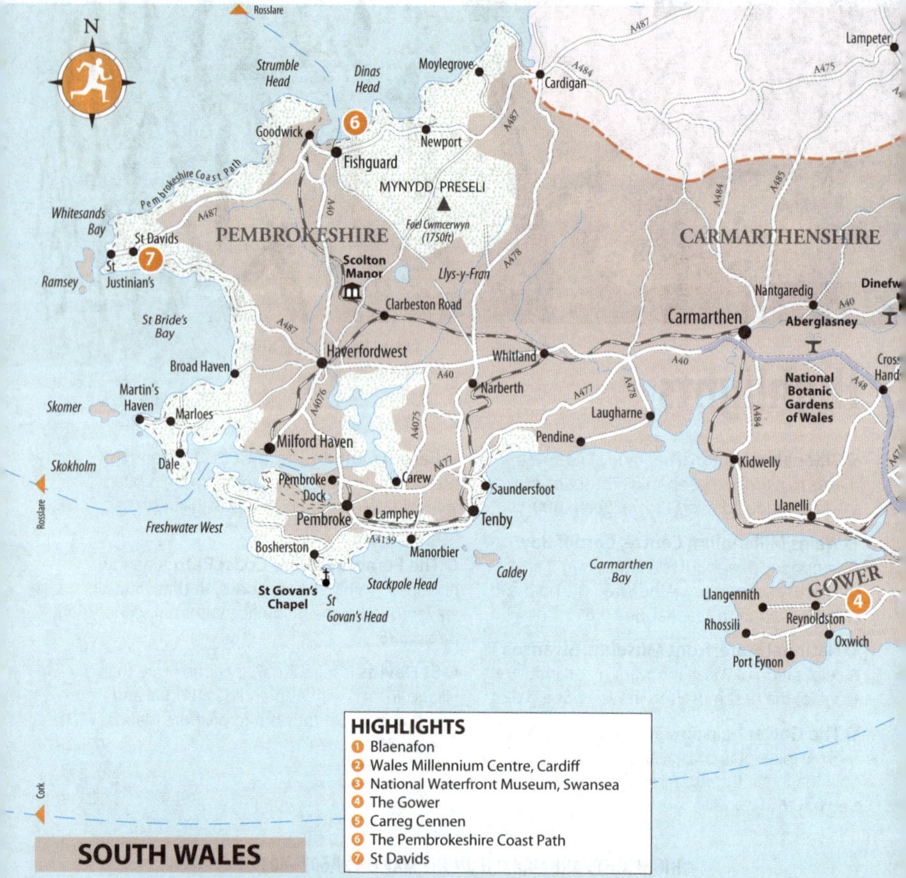

Chepstow

Of all the places that call themselves "the gateway to Wales", **CHEPSTOW** (Cas-Gwent), sitting on the western bank of the River Wye, has probably the best claim. Although lacking the immediate charm of many other Welsh market towns, there is, nonetheless, an identifiably medieval street plan hemmed in by the thirteenth-century **Port Wall**, which encases a tight loop of the River Wye and the strategically sited **Chepstow Castle.**

Chepstow Castle

March–Oct daily 9.30am–5pm; July & Aug daily 9.30am–6pm; Nov–Feb Mon–Sat 10am–4pm, Sun 11am–4pm • CADW • £4 • ⓣ 01291 624065

Guarding this key route into Wales, **Chepstow Castle** was the first stone castle to be built in Britain. The Lower Ward, dating mainly from the thirteenth century, was the largest of the three enclosures. Here you'll find the **Great Hall**, now colourfully recreated as the Earl's chamber. Twelfth-century defences separate the Lower Ward from the Middle Ward, dominated by the still-imposing ruins of the **Great Tower**, built in 1067. Beyond this, the far narrower Upper Ward leads up to the Barbican **watchtower** from where there are superb views down to the estuary.

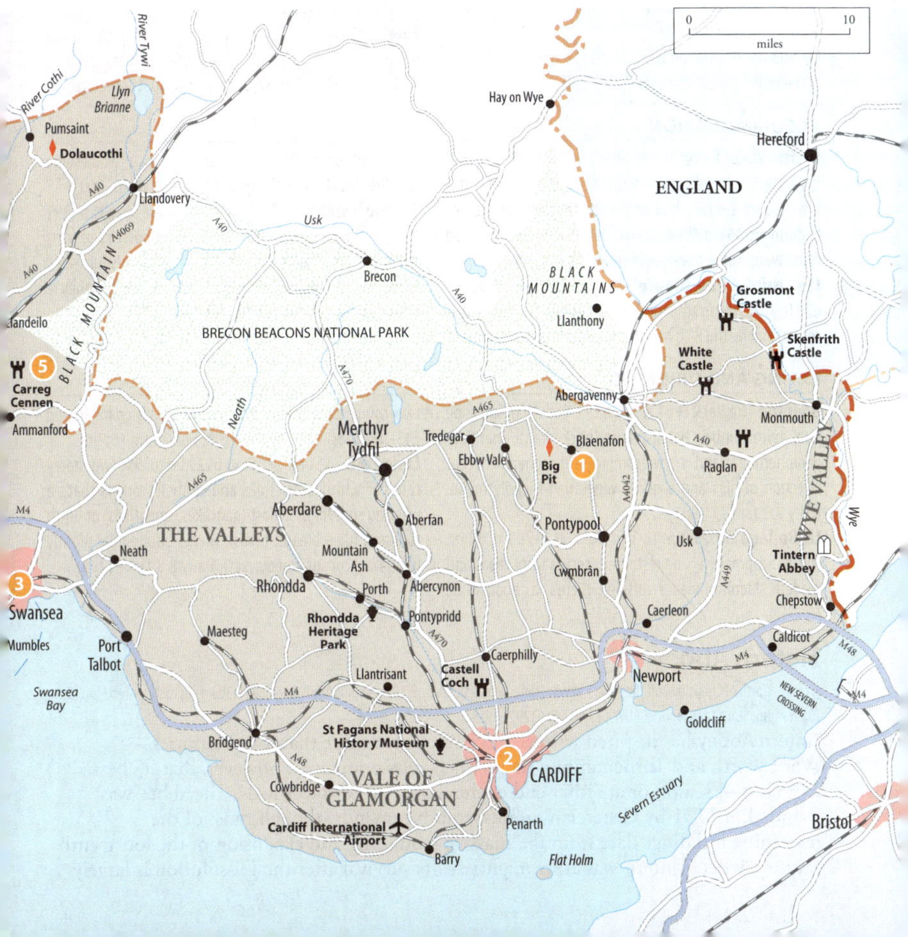

TOP 5 CASTLES

Caerphilly Castle See p.617
Carreg Cennen See p.631
Chepstow Castle See p.603
Pembroke Castle See p.635
Raglan Castle See p.606

Chepstow Museum

Bridge St • July–Sept Mon–Sat 10.30am–5.30pm, Sun 2–5.30pm; Oct & March–June Mon–Sat 11am–5pm, Sun 2–5pm; Nov–Feb Mon–Sat 11am–4pm, Sun 2–4pm • Free • 01291 626370

Housed in a handsome Georgian townhouse, **Chepstow Museum** contains a wealth of nostalgic photographs and paintings of the trades once supported by the River Wye, as well as records of Chepstow's brief life as a shipbuilding centre in the early twentieth century.

ARRIVAL AND INFORMATION — CHEPSTOW

By train Chepstow's train station is a 5min walk south of High St.

Destinations Cardiff (every 30–60min; 40min); Gloucester (every 30–60min; 30min); Newport, Monmouthshire (every 30–60min; 25min).

By bus The bus station is on Thomas St, a 5min walk west of the High St, just beyond the West Gate.

Destinations Bristol (hourly; 50min); Cardiff (every 30min–1hr, 1 change; 1hr 20min); Monmouth (hourly; 50min); Newport, Monmouthshire (every 30min; 50min); Tintern (8 daily; 20min).

Tourist office Castle car park, off Bridge St (daily: Easter–Oct 9.30am–1pm & 2–5pm; Nov–Easter 9.30am–1pm & 2–3.30pm; 01291 623772, chepstowtowncrier.org.uk).

ACCOMMODATION

Castle View Hotel 16 Bridge St 01291 620349, castleviewhotel.com. Bags of charm in this seventeenth-century building, with thirteen cosy rooms featuring crooked floors, thick oak beams and exposed stone walls; some have castle views. **£77**

First Hurdle Guesthouse 9 Upper Church St 01291 622189, thefirsthurdle.com. Rooms in this large, central and restful B&B have firm beds, attractive decor and shiny bathrooms; guests can indulge in a wholesome "English" breakfast in the quaint breakfast room. **£60**

George Hotel Moor St, next to the West Gate 01291 625363, thegeorgechepstow.com. A hostelry of sorts for several centuries, the *George* has large, simply furnished rooms above a ground-floor bar and restaurant – they're reasonably well insulated against noise. **£50**

EATING AND DRINKING

Boat Inn The Back 01291 628192. Convivial waterside pub, with timber beams, bare brick walls, maritime paraphernalia and a welcoming atmosphere; decent selection of ales and a good, vegetarian-friendly menu. Daily 9.30am–11pm.

La Bodega Susan'na 18 The Back 01291 626868. This handsome riverside restaurant serves tasty tapas and modern Mediterranean cuisine; there's a good-value two-course lunch menu, while mains usually go for around £15–18. Tues–Sat 10am–11pm, Sun 10am–6pm.

Lime Tree 24 St Mary's St 01291 620959. Two-storey café/bar with leather sofas and softly lit corners that's a cracking spot for breakfast (pancakes, smoothies) or lunch (burgers, filled breads, tapas); there's also regular nightly fun (jazz, acoustic and quizzes). Daily 8.30am–11pm.

Tintern Abbey

Six miles north of Chepstow, off the A466 • March–June, Sept & Oct daily 9.30am–5pm; July & Aug daily 9.30am–6pm; Nov–Feb Mon–Sat 10am–4pm, Sun 11am–4pm • CADW • £3.80 • 01291 689251

Tintern Abbey has inspired writers and painters for more than two centuries – Wordsworth and Turner among them. Such is its popularity, however, that it's best to go out of season or at either end of the day to avoid the crowds. The abbey was founded in 1131 by Cistercian monks from Normandy, though most of the remaining buildings date from the massive rebuilding and expansion of the fourteenth century, when Tintern was at its mightiest. Its survival after the Dissolution is largely due to its remoteness, as there were no nearby villages ready to use the abbey stone for rebuilding.

The centrepiece of the complex is the magnificent Gothic **church**, whose remarkable tracery and intricate stonework remain intact. Around the church are the less substantial ruins of the monks' domestic quarters and cloister, mostly reduced to one-storey rubble. The course of the abbey's waste-disposal system can be seen in the Great Drain, an irregular channel that links kitchens, toilets and the infirmary with the nearby Wye. The **Novices' Hall** lies handily close to the Warming House, which together with the kitchen and infirmary would have been the abbey's only heated areas, suggesting that novices might have gained a falsely favourable impression of monastic life before taking their final vows.

Monmouth

Enclosed on three sides by the rivers Wye and Monnow, **MONMOUTH** (Trefynwy), fifteen miles north of Chepstow, retains some of its quiet charm as an important border post and county town, and makes a good base for a drive – or a long hike – around the **Three Castles** of the pastoral border country to the north. The centre of the town is **Agincourt Square**, a handsome open space at the top of the wide, shop-lined Monnow Street. The street narrows to squeeze through the seven-hundred-year-old **Monnow Bridge**, crowned with its hulking stone gate of 1262.

Shire Hall

Agincourt Square • Mon–Fri 10am–5pm, Sat & Sun 10am–4pm • Self-guided tours £2, guided tours (Wed 2pm) £2.50 • ⓣ 01600 775257

The arched, Georgian **Shire Hall**, built in 1724 as a law court, was where, in 1839, the three ringleaders of the Chartists – Frost, Williams and Jones – were sentenced to death (though this was later commuted to transportation). The Chartists were responsible for drafting the 1838 People's Charter, which called for widespread political and social reform throughout the UK, and demanded, among other things, a vote for every man aged over 21 and secret ballots. The hall continued to function as a court until 1992, and you can still see the original courtrooms and the holding cells. Embedded in the facade is an eighteenth-century statue of the Monmouth-born King Henry V, victor of the Battle of Agincourt in 1415, and just in front is the pompous statue of another local, the Honourable Charles Stewart Rolls, co-founder of Rolls-Royce and, in 1910, the first man to pilot a double flight over the English Channel.

Castle Hill

Almost opposite Shire Hall is **Castle Hill**, which you can walk up to glimpse some of the scant ruins of the **castle**, founded in 1068. The neighbouring **Great Castle House** is the headquarters of the Royal Monmouthshire regiment, whose history is relayed in the small **regimental museum** (April–Oct daily 2–5pm; Nov–March Sat & Sun 2–4pm; free).

ARRIVAL AND INFORMATION — MONMOUTH

By bus The bus station is at the bottom of Monnow St.
Destinations Abergavenny (6 daily; 50min); Chepstow (hourly; 50min); Raglan (hourly; 20min); Tintern (9 daily; 35min).

Tourist office Shire Hall (Mon–Fri 10am–5pm, Sat & Sun 10am–4pm; ⓣ 01600 775257, ⓔ monmouth.tic@monmouthshire.gov.uk).

ACCOMMODATION AND EATING

Bistro Prego 7 Church St ⓣ 01600 712600, ⓦ pregomonmouth.co.uk. Eight tightly packed en-suite rooms in a cosy B&B located above the town's finest restaurant. There's also a comfortable lounge with widescreen TV. The restaurant has lunch and dinner menus, with imaginative Italian-influenced dishes like tagliatelle with rabbit ragu. Booking advised at weekends. Mains £12–15. Food served daily 11am–10pm. **£65**

Gate House Old Monnow Bridge ⓣ01600 713890. Occupying an enviable spot by the medieval bridge, and with a veranda perched over the water, the Gate House is one of the best spots in town for a pint on a sunny day. Daily 11am–11pm.

Monnow Bridge Campsite Drybridge St ⓣ01600 714004. Small and basic but tidy site in a handy central location; cross the Monnow Bridge, turn right, and it's behind the *Three Horseshoes* pub. Pitches **£10.50**

Punch House 4 Agincourt Square ⓣ01600 713855, ⓔpunchhouse@sabrain.com. Right next to the Shire Hall, the Tudor-looking Punch House is the town's most popular hostelry, a rambling, reputedly haunted, inn serving mainly Brains beers. The good-value rooms are simple but agreeable, with timber beams and uneven floors and doors. Breakfast costs extra. **£40**

Raglan Castle

March–June, Sept & Oct daily 9.30am–5pm; July & Aug daily 9.30am–6pm; Nov–Feb Mon–Sat 10am–4pm, Sun 11am–4pm • CADW • £3.50 • ⓣ01291 690228

Unassuming **RAGLAN** (Rhaglan), seven miles west of Monmouth, is known for its glorious **castle**, whose fussy and comparatively intact style distinguishes it from so many other crumbling Welsh fortresses. The last medieval fortification built in Britain, designed to combine practical strength with ostentatious style, Raglan was begun by Sir William ap Thomas in 1435 on the site of a Norman motte. The **gatehouse**, still the main entrance, houses fantastic examples of the castle's decoration in its heraldic shields, intricate stonework edging and gargoyles. In the mid-fifteenth century, ap Thomas's grandson, William Herbert II, built two courts around the original gatehouse, hall and keep: the cobbled **Pitched Stone Court** – designed to house functional rooms like the kitchen, with its two vast, double-flued chimneys, and the servants' quarters – and to the left, **Fountain Court**, a well-proportioned grassy space surrounded by opulent state rooms and grand apartments. Separating the two are the original hall, from 1435, the buttery, the remains of the chapel and the dank, cold cellars below.

White Castle

Eight miles northwest of Monmouth and 6 miles east of Abergavenny • April–Oct daily 10am–5pm • CADW • £2.80 (generally free access rest of the year) • ⓣ01600 780380

So named after the white rendering on its exterior, **White Castle** (Castell Gwyn), is the most awesome of the Three Castles, set in rolling countryside with superb views over to the hills surrounding the River Monnow. The grassy Outer Ward is enclosed by a curtain wall with four towers, divided by a moat from the brooding mass of the Inner Ward. A bridge leads to the dual-towered Inner Gatehouse, where you can climb the western tower for its sublime vantage point. At the back of the Inner Ward are the massive foundations of the Norman keep, demolished in about 1260.

THE THREE CASTLES

The fertile, low-lying land between the Monnow and Usk rivers was important for easy access into the agricultural lands of South Wales, and in the eleventh century the Norman invaders built a trio of strongholds here to protect their interests. In 1201, **Skenfrith**, **Grosmont** and **White** castles were presented by King John to Hubert de Burgh, who employed sophisticated new ideas on castle design to replace the earlier, square-keeped structures. In 1260, the advancing army of Llywelyn ap Gruffydd began to threaten the king's supremacy in South Wales, and the three castles were refortified in readiness. Gradually, the castles were adapted as living quarters and royal administration centres, and the only return to military usage came in 1404–05, when Owain Glyndŵr's army pressed down to Grosmont, only to be defeated by the future King Henry V. The castles slipped into disrepair and were finally sold separately in 1902, the first time since 1138 that the three had fallen out of single ownership.

Skenfrith Castle

Skenfrith (Ynysgynwraidd), 7 miles northeast of White Castle • Unrestricted access • NT • Free • Ⓣ 01874 625515

The thirteenth-century **Skenfrith Castle**, in the attractive border village of Skenfrith (Ynysgynwraidd), has an irregular rectangle of sturdy red sandstone walls. Dominating the site, atop a large earth mound, is a roofless circular keep that replaced an earlier Norman structure. Below are the vestiges of the great hall and private apartments; the domestic buildings alongside feature a thirteenth-century window with intact iron bars.

Grosmont Castle

Five miles upstream of Skenfrith • Unrestricted access • CADW • Free • Ⓣ 01600 780380

Right on the English border, the dilapidated **Grosmont Castle** sits on a small hill above its village. A wooden bridge above the dry moat brings you into the small central courtyard, dominated on the right-hand side by the ruins of a large Great Hall dating from the early thirteenth century.

The Valleys

No other part of Wales is as instantly recognizable as the **Valleys**, a generic name for the strings of settlements packed into the narrow gashes in the mountainous terrain to the north of Newport and Cardiff. Each of the Valleys depended almost solely on coal mining which, although nearly defunct as an industry, has left its mark on the staunchly working-class towns: row upon row of brightly painted terraced housing, tipped along the slopes at incredible angles, are broken only by austere chapels, the occasional remaining pithead and the dignified memorials to those who died underground.

This may not be traditional tourist country, but it's one of the most interesting and distinctive corners of Wales, with a rich social history. Some former mines have reopened as gutsy museums – **Big Pit** at Blaenafon and the **Rhondda Heritage Park** at Trehafod are the best – while other excellent civic museums include those at **Pontypridd** and **Aberdare**. Meanwhile, there's a more traditional visitor attraction in the form of **Llancaiach Fawr Manor.**

Blaenafon

Fourteen miles north of Newport, the valley of the Llwyd opens out at the airy iron and coal town of **BLAENAFON** (sometimes Blaenavon), whose population has shrunk to five thousand, a third of its size in the nineteenth century. It's a spirited and evocative place, a fact recognized by UNESCO, who granted it World Heritage Site status in 2000.

Blaenafon ironworks

North St • Easter–Oct Mon–Fri 9.30am–4.30pm, Sat 10am–5pm, Sun 10am–4.30pm • CADW • Free • Ⓣ 01495 792615

The town's boom kicked off at the **Blaenafon ironworks**, just off the Brynmawr road, founded in 1789. Limestone, coal and iron ore – ingredients for successful iron-smelting – were abundant locally, and the Blaenafon works was one of the largest in Britain until it closed in 1900. This remarkable site contains three of the five original Georgian blast furnaces, one with its cast house still attached, and the immense water-balance lift. Also here are the workers' cottages, some unchanged and others converted into a museum offering a thorough picture of the process and the lifestyle that went with it.

14

WORKING THE BLACK SEAM

The land beneath the inhospitable South Wales Valleys had some of the most abundant and accessible natural seams of **coal and iron ore** to be found, and were readily milked in the boom years of the nineteenth and early twentieth centuries. Wealthy, predominantly English capitalists came to Wales and ruthlessly stripped the land of its natural assets, while simultaneously exploiting those who risked life and limb underground. The mine owners were in a formidably strong position as thousands flocked to the Valleys in search of work and some sort of sustainable life. By the turn of the twentieth century, the Valleys became packed with pits, chapels and immigrant workers from Ireland, Scotland, Italy and all over Wales.

In 1920, there were 256,000 men working in the 620 mines of the South Wales coalfields, providing a third of the world's coal. Vast Miners' Institutes jostled for position with the Nonconformist chapels, whose muscular brand of Christianity was matched by the zeal of the region's politics – trade-union-led and avowedly left-wing. Great socialist orators rose to national prominence, cementing the Valleys' reputation as a world apart from the rest of Britain, let alone Wales. Even Britain's pioneering National Health Service, founded by a radical Labour government in the years following World War II, was based on a Valleys' community scheme devised by local politician Aneurin Bevan. More than half of the original pits closed in the harsh economic climate of the 1930s, as coal seams became exhausted and the political climate changed. In the 1980s, further closures threatened to bring the number of men employed in the South Wales coalfields down to four figures, and the miners went on strike from 1984–85. The last of the deep pits closed in 2008.

Big Pit National Mining Museum

A mile west of town off the B4246 • Feb–Nov daily 10am–3.30pm, 1hr tours; Dec & Jan call for times • Free • T 01495 790311, W museumwales.ac.uk • The X30 bus departs hourly from the High St for the museum

Guided tours at the evocative **Big Pit National Mining Museum** involve being kitted out with lamp, helmet and very heavy battery pack, and then lowered 300ft into the labyrinth of shafts and coalfaces. The guides – mostly ex-miners – lead you through explanations and examples of the different types of coal mining, while all the while streams of rust-coloured water flow by. The dank and chilly atmosphere must have terrified the small children who were once paid twopence – of which one penny was taken out for the cost of their candles – for a six-day week pulling the coal wagons along the tracks. Back on the surface, the old pithead baths – one of the last remaining in the country – now holds a compelling, and very moving, museum documenting the lives and times of the miners and their families.

INFORMATION — BLAENAFON

Tourist office The Blaenavon Heritage Centre, Church Rd (Tues–Sun: April–Sept 9am–5pm; Oct–March 9am–4pm; T 01495 742333, W visitblaenavon.co.uk) offers information, with a good exhibition on coal mining and ironworking, and a café.

The Taff and Cynon valleys

The River Taff flows into the Bristol Channel at Cardiff, after passing through a couple of dozen miles of industry and population. The first town in the Taff vale is **Pontypridd**, one of the cheeriest in the Valleys, and probably the best base. Continuing north, valleys meet at **Abercynon**, where the River Cynon flows in from **Aberdare**, site of the excellent **Cynon Valley Museum**. Just outside Abercynon is the enjoyable, sixteenth-century **Llancaiach Fawr** manor house.

Pontypridd

PONTYPRIDD, twelve miles north of Cardiff, is built up around its quirky arched **bridge** that was once the largest single-span stone bridge in Europe, built in 1775 by local amateur stonemason William Edwards. Across the river is **Ynysangharad Park**, where

Sir W. Goscombe John's cloying statue honours Pontypridd weaver Evan James, who composed the stirringly nationalistic song *Hen Wlad fy Nhadau* (*Land of My Fathers*), now the Welsh national anthem.

Pontypridd Museum

Taff St • Mon–Sat 10am–5pm • Free • T 01443 490748

By the bridge, a lovingly restored church houses the illuminating **Pontypridd Museum**, a treasure-trove of photographs, videos, models and exhibits that paints a warm picture of the town and its outlying valleys, as well as paying homage to the town's famous sons, singer Tom Jones and opera star Sir Geraint Evans.

14

ARRIVAL AND INFORMATION — PONTYPRIDD

By train The train station is a 10min walk south of the old bridge on The Graig.
Destinations Abercynon (every 15min; 10min); Aberdare (every 30min; 35min); Cardiff (every 20–30min; 30min).
By bus Pontypridd bus station is directly above the old bridge on the western bank of the river.
Destinations Abercynon (every 15min; 15min); Aberdare (every 15min; 45min); Cardiff (every 15min; 35min).
Tourist office Inside Pontypridd Museum on Taff St (Mon–Sat 10am–5pm; T 01443 490748).

ACCOMMODATION AND EATING

Blueberry Hotel Market St T 01443 485331, W blueberryhotel.com. Sparkling little hotel whose nine rooms are fashioned in one of two styles; cool, crisp white-on-white, or classic French. There are some nice touches, too, such as smart toiletries in the bathrooms, and fresh milk, Welsh cakes and bottled water in each room. £80

★ **Bunch of Grapes** Ynysangharad Rd T 01443 402934, W bunchofgrapes.org.uk. A terrific combination of restaurant/pub, whose imaginative menu (braised rabbit with chard and spinach, Breconshire ox cheek with tarragon mash) is the best for miles around. The beer's great too, with typically more than half a dozen real ales on at any one time. It's on a residential street beyond the park and A470 flyover. Mains £14–18. Daily 11am–11pm.

Llancaiach Fawr Manor

Two miles east of Abercynon • Tues–Sun 10am–5pm (last admission 4pm) • £6.50 • T 01443 412248, W llancaiachfawr.co.uk • Mon–Sat hourly bus #X38 from Pontypridd

Five miles north of Pontypridd at **Abercynon**, the Cynon River flows into the Taff from Aberdare in the northwest. Two miles east, just north of the village of **NELSON**, is **Llancaiach Fawr Manor**. A Tudor house, built around 1530, the manor has been transformed into a living history museum set in 1645, during the Civil War, with guides dressed as house servants and speaking the language of seventeenth-century Britain. Although potentially tacky, it is quite deftly done, with authentic period colour and numerous fascinating anecdotes. Special tours include seventeenth-century evenings, and, between October and March, candlelit and ghost tours, befitting the manor's status as, allegedly, one of the country's most haunted residences.

THE ABERFAN DISASTER

North of Abercynon, the Taff Valley contains one sight that's hard to forget. Two neat lines of distant arches mark the graves of 144 people killed in October 1966 by an unsecured slag heap collapsing on Pantglas primary school in the village of **Aberfan**. Thousands of people still make the pilgrimage to the village graveyard, to stand silent and bemused by the enormity of the disaster. Among the dead were 116 children, who died huddled in panic at the beginning of their school day. A humbling and beautiful valediction can be seen on one of the gravestones, that of a 10-year-old boy, who, it simply records, "loved light, freedom and animals". Official enquiries all told the sorry tale that this disaster was almost inevitable, given the cavalier approach to safety so often displayed by the coal bosses. Gwynfor Evans, then newly elected as the first Plaid Cymru (Welsh Nationalist) MP in Westminster, spoke with well-founded bitterness when he said: "Let us suppose that such a monstrous mountain had been built above Hampstead or Eton, where the children of the men of power and wealth are at school". But that, of course, would never have happened.

Aberdare

Eight miles northwest of Abercynon, towards the top of the Cynon Valley, is the spacious town of **ABERDARE** (Aberdâr), built on the local iron, brick and brewing industries. It's also home to one of the Valleys' best museums, the **Cynon Valley Museum & Gallery**, in an old tram depot next to the Tesco superstore.

Cynon Valley Museum & Gallery

Depot Rd • Mon–Sat 9am–4.30pm • Free • ⓣ 01685 886729, ⓦ cvmg.co.uk

Exhibits at the **Cynon Valley Museum & Gallery** portray the valley's social history, from the appalling conditions of the mid-nineteenth century, when nearly half of all children born here died by the age of 5, to stirring memories of the 1926 General Strike and the 1984–85 Miners' Strike. Alongside are some fun videos and exhibits on Victorian lantern slides, teenage life through the ages, the miners' jazz bands and Aberdare's role as a centre of early Welsh-language publishing. There's also a bright art gallery and decent café here.

The Rhondda

Pointing northwest from Pontypridd, the **Rhondda Fawr** – sixteen miles long and never as much as a mile wide – is undoubtedly the most famous of all the Welsh Valleys, as well as being the heart of the massive South Wales coal industry. For many it immediately conjures up Richard Llewellyn's 1939 book – and subsequent Oscar-winning weepie – *How Green Was My Valley*, although this was, strictly speaking, based on the author's early life in nearby Gilfach Goch, outside the valley. Between 1841 and 1924 the Rhondda's population grew from under a thousand to 167,000, squeezed into ranks of houses grouped around sixty or so pitheads. The Rhondda, more than any other of the Valleys, became a self-reliant, hard-living, chapel-going, poor and terrifically spirited breeding ground for radical religion and firebrand politics – for decades, the Communist Party ran the town of Maerdy (nicknamed "Little Moscow" by Fleet Street in the 1930s). The last pit in the Rhondda closed in 1990, but what was left behind was not some dispiriting ragbag of depressing towns, but a range of new attractions, cleaned-up hillsides and some of the friendliest pubs and communities to be found anywhere in Britain.

Rhondda Heritage Park

Coed Cae Rd, Trehafod • April–Sept daily 9am–6pm, last admission 4.30pm; Oct–March Tues–Sun 9am–6pm, last admission 4.30pm • Guided tours 10am, noon & 2pm • £5.60 • ⓣ 01443 682036, ⓦ rhonddaheritagepark.com • The park is a few minutes' walk from Trehafod train station

The best attraction hereabouts is the **Rhondda Heritage Park** at **TREHAFOD**. The site was opened in 1880 by William Lewis (later Lord Merthyr), and by 1900 some five thousand men were employed here, producing more than a million tons of coal a year. Wandering around the yard, you can see the 140ft-high chimney stack, which fronts two iconic latticed shafts, named Bertie and Trefor after Lewis's sons. **Guided tours** take you through the engine-winding houses, lamp room and fan house, and give you a

MALE VOICE CHOIRS

Fiercely protective of its reputation as a land of song, Wales demonstrates its fine voice most affectingly in its ranks of **male voice choirs**. Although found all over the country, it is in the southern, industrial heartland that they are loudest and strongest. Their roots lie in the Nonconformist religious traditions of the seventeenth and eighteenth centuries, when Methodism in particular swept the country, and singing was a free and potent way of cherishing the often persecuted faith. Classic hymns like *Cwm Rhondda* and the Welsh national anthem, *Hen Wlad Fy Nhadau* (*Land of My Fathers*), are synonymous with the choirs. Each Valleys town still has its own choir, most of whom welcome visitors to sit in on rehearsals. Ask at the local tourist office or library, and take the chance to hear one of the world's most distinctive choral traditions in full, roof-raising splendour.

simulated "trip underground", with stunning visuals and sound effects re-creating 1950s' life through the eyes of colliers.

ARRIVAL AND DEPARTURE **THE RHONDDA**

By train A train line from Cardiff, punctuated with stops every mile or so, runs the entire length of the Rhondda, stopping at Trehafod, a few minutes' walk from the Heritage Park.

By bus Buses cover the Rhondda, continuing up into the mountains and the Brecon Beacons.

Cardiff and around

Official capital of Wales since only 1955, buoyant **CARDIFF** (Caerdydd) grew swiftly into its new role. A number of massive developments, not least the shiny Welsh National Assembly and Millennium Centre on the rejuvenated Cardiff Bay waterfront, and a fabulous city-centre sports stadium, give the city the feel of an international capital, if not always with a very Welsh flavour.

Cardiff's sights are clustered in fairly small, distinct districts. The compact commercial centre is bounded by the **River Taff**, which flows past the tremendous **Millennium Stadium**; in this rugby-mad city, the atmosphere in the pubs and streets when Wales have a home match – particularly against the old enemy, England – is charged with good-natured, beery fervour. Just upstream, the Taff is flanked by the wall of Cardiff's extraordinary **castle**, an amalgam of Roman remains, Norman keep and Victorian fantasy. North of the castle is a series of white Edwardian buildings grouped around **Cathays Park**: the City Hall, Cardiff University and the superb **National Museum**. A mile south of the centre, **Cardiff Bay**, once a bustling port, now a classy waterside development, houses the stunning Welsh National Assembly and Millennium buildings, and a stack of bars and restaurants. North of the city, a number of sights warrant a visit: **Llandaff Cathedral**, with its strange clash of Norman and modern styles; the thirteenth-century fairy-tale castle of **Castell Coch**, on a hillside in the woods; and the massive **Caerphilly Castle**. To the west, there's the hugely popular **National History Museum** at St Fagans.

Brief history

The second Marquess of Bute built Cardiff's first dock in 1839, opening others in swift succession. The Butes owned massive swathes of the rapidly industrializing South Wales Valleys and insisted that all coal and iron exports use the family docks in Cardiff, which became one of the world's busiest ports. The twentieth century saw varying fortunes: the dock trade slumped in the 1930s and the city suffered heavy bombing in World War II, but with the creation of Cardiff as capital in 1955, optimism and confidence in the city blossomed. Many government and media institutions have moved here from London, and the development of the dock areas around the new Assembly building in Cardiff Bay has given a largely positive boost to the cityscape.

Central Cardiff

Cardiff **centre** forms a rough square bounded by the castle, Queen Street and Central stations and the Motorpoint Arena. Dominating the skyline is the magnificent **Millennium Stadium**.

Millennium Stadium

Westgate St • Daily tours, subject to events, hourly Mon–Sat 10am–5pm, Sun 10am–4pm • £6.65 • ⓣ 029 2082 2228, ⓦ millenniumstadium.com

Since opening in 1999, the **Millennium Stadium** has become an iconic symbol not only of Cardiff but also of Wales as a whole. With its trademark retractable roof, and seating for 74,500 people, it has hosted sporting matches of every description, as well as an

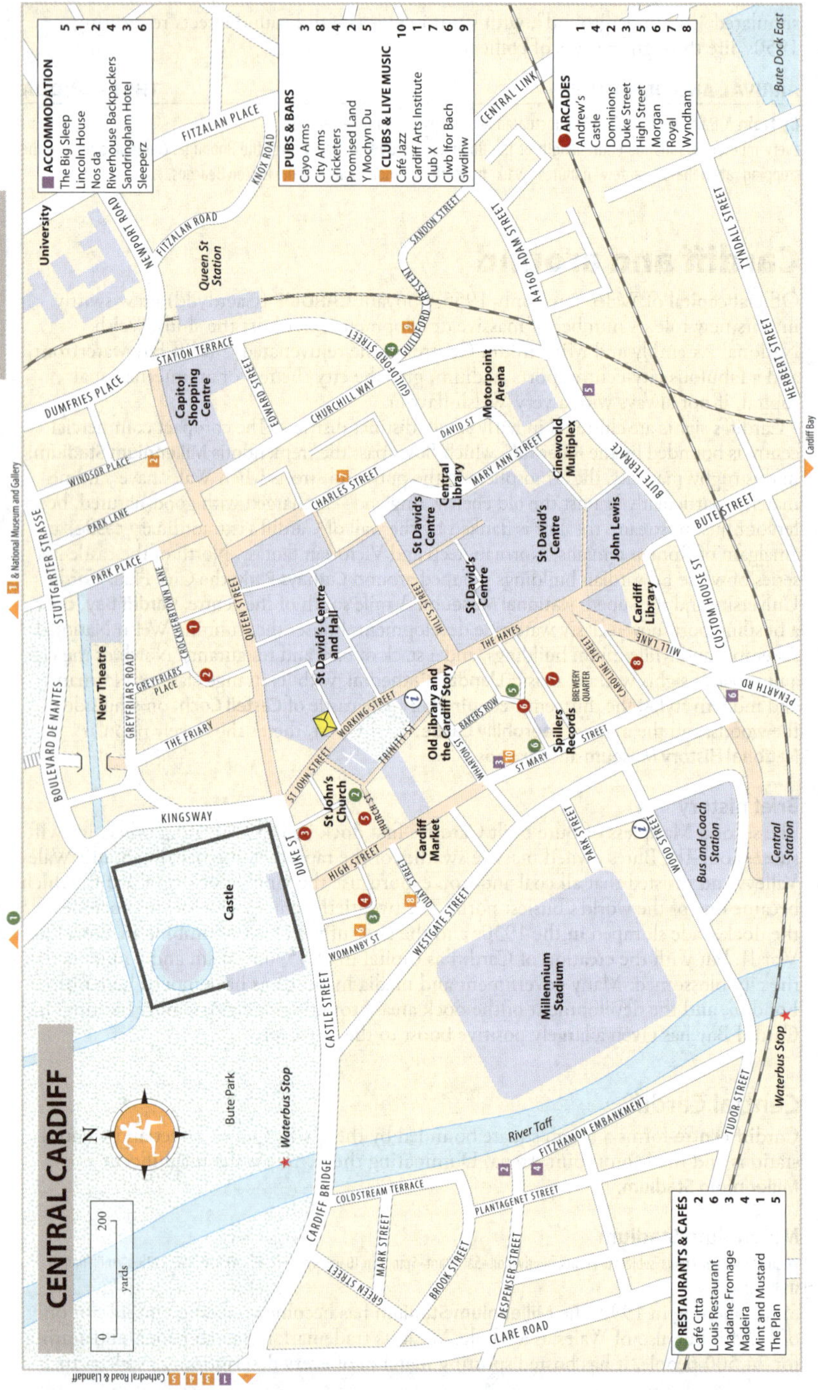
CENTRAL CARDIFF
0
200
yards
N
ACCOMMODATION
The Big Sleep 5
Lincoln House 1
Nos da 2
Riverhouse Backpackers 4
Sandringham Hotel 3
Sleeperz 6
PUBS & BARS
Cayo Arms 3
City Arms 8
Cricketers 4
Promised Land 2
Y Mochyn Du 5
CLUBS & LIVE MUSIC
Café Jazz 10
Cardiff Arts Institute 1
Club X 7
Clwb Ifor Bach 6
Gwdihŵ 9
ARCADES
Andrew's 1
Castle 4
Dominions 2
Duke Street 3
High Street 5
Morgan 6
Royal 7
Wyndham 8
RESTAURANTS & CAFÉS
Café Città 2
Louis Restaurant 6
Madame Fromage 3
Madeira 4
Mint and Mustard 1
The Plan 5
& National Museum and Gallery
Cardiff Bay
Cathedral Road & Llandaff
University
Queen St Station
Capitol Shopping Centre
Motorpoint Arena
Cineworld Multiplex
Central Library
St David's Centre
St David's Centre and Hall
John Lewis
Cardiff Library
New Theatre
Old Library and the Cardiff Story
Spillers Records
BREWERY QUARTER
St John's Church
Cardiff Market
Castle
Millennium Stadium
Bus and Coach Station
Central Station
Bute Park
Waterbus Stop
River Taff
Bute Dock East
FITZALAN PLACE
FITZALAN ROAD
KNOX ROAD
NEWPORT ROAD
CENTRAL LINK
SANDON STREET
GUILDFORD CRESCENT
GUILDFORD STREET
A4160 ADAM STREET
TYNDALL STREET
HERBERT STREET
STATION TERRACE
DUMFRIES PLACE
EDWARD STREET
CHURCHILL WAY
DAVID ST
WINDSOR PLACE
CHARLES STREET
MARY ANN STREET
BUTE TERRACE
BUTE STREET
PARK LANE
PARK PLACE
STUTTGARTER STRASSE
CROCKHERBTOWN LANE
QUEEN STREET
HILLS STREET
THE HAYES
CUSTOM HOUSE ST
MILL LANE
CAROLINE STREET
PENARTH RD
GREYFRIARS ROAD
GREYFRIARS PLACE
THE FRIARY
WORKING STREET
TRINITY ST
BAKERS ROW
WHARTON ST
ST MARY STREET
BOULEVARD DE NANTES
KINGSWAY
ST JOHN STREET
CHURCH ST
DUKE ST
HIGH STREET
QUAY STREET
WESTGATE STREET
WOMANBY ST
PARK STREET
WOOD STREET
CASTLE STREET
CARDIFF BRIDGE
COLDSTREAM TERRACE
FITZHAMON EMBANKMENT
TUDOR STREET
MARK STREET
PLANTAGENET STREET
GREEN STREET
BROOK STREET
DESPENSER STREET
CLARE ROAD

array of huge rock gigs and other spectaculars. **Stadium tours** start from the **Cardiff Arms Store** by Gate 3 on Westgate Street and take you into the press centre, dressing rooms, VIP areas, players' tunnel and pitchside. Afterwards, stroll the riverside walkway, cantilevered out over the water to accommodate the huge swell of the stadium walls.

Cardiff Arcades

Dominating the city centre east of the stadium is the **St David's Centre,** a gargantuan complex of predictable big-name chain stores. Far more interesting are the **Arcades**, a series of Victorian and Edwardian galleries where you'll find many alluring little independent shops and cafés – great for picking up flyers and information on gigs, club nights and other such events. Particularly impressive are the **High Street** and **Castle arcades**, either side of the High Street near the castle. A few yards further down towards Central Station is the elegant Edwardian **indoor market** and further still the **Royal** and **Morgan arcades**, linking St Mary Street with the lower end of The Hayes.

The Cardiff Story

Old Library, The Hayes • Mon–Sat 10am–5pm, Sun 11am–4pm • Free • T 029 2078 8334, W cardiffstory.com

On The Hayes, the beautifully colonnaded frontage of the **Old Library** houses both the city's tourist office and the eminently enjoyable **Cardiff Story.** Using old artefacts, hands-on gizmos and audiovisual displays, it's an enlightening romp through the city's colourful history, with particular emphasis on how it was shaped by the docks and the local coal industry. Don't miss the stunning **tiled corridor**; something of a hidden gem, this was the original library entrance, its ornate floor-to-ceiling tiles produced by Maw & Co in 1882.

Cardiff Castle

Daily: March–Oct 9am–6pm; Nov–Feb 9am–5pm • £11, premium ticket £14; admission includes an audioguide • T 029 2087 8100, W cardiffcastle.com

The political, geographical and historical heart of the city is **Cardiff Castle**. An intriguing hotchpotch, the fortress hides inside a vast walled yard corresponding roughly to the outline of the original fort built by the Romans. The neat Norman motte and **keep** look down onto the turrets and towers of the **Castle Apartments**, which date in part from the fourteenth and fifteenth centuries, but were much extended in Tudor times, when residential needs began to overtake military priorities. In the late nineteenth century, the third Marquess of Bute, one of the richest men in the world, lavished a fortune on upgrading his pile – although he only spent a few weeks a year here – commissioning architect and decorator William Burges to aid him. With their passion for the religious art and symbolism of the Middle Ages, they transformed the crumbling interiors into palaces of vivid colour and intricate design.

Guided tours (available on the premium ticket) take in the **Winter Smoking Room**, the **Nursery**, with hand-painted tiles and silhouette lanterns depicting contemporary nursery rhymes, the **Bachelor's Bedroom** and, above that, the **Summer Smoking Room**. From here, the tour enters several rooms that are also accessible to regular ticket holders, including the **Arab Room**, decorated by imported craftsmen, the grand **Banqueting Hall**, built in 1428 but transformed by Bute and Burges with the installation of a riotously kitsch fireplace, and the **library**, possessed of a similarly fanciful chimneypiece.

Cathays Park and around

On the northern edge of the city centre is **Cathays Park**, a large rectangle of lawns and flowerbeds that forms the focus for the impressive buildings of the **civic centre**.

Dating from the early twentieth century, the gleaming white buildings are arranged with pompous Edwardian precision, and speak volumes about Cardiff's self-confidence, a full half-century before it was officially declared capital of Wales. The dragon-topped, domed **City Hall** is the magnificent centrepiece, an exercise in every cliché of ostentatious civic self-glory, with a roll call of statues of male Welsh heroes including Llywelyn ap Gruffydd, St David, Giraldus Cambrensis and Owain Glyndŵr.

National Museum and Gallery

Cathays Park • Tues–Sun 10am–5pm • Free • ☎ 029 2039 7951, W museumwales.ac.uk

The fine **National Museum and Gallery** starts with the epic **Evolution of Wales** exhibition, a fabulous mix of high-tech gizmos and hugely detailed displays on the country's natural history. Next door, the even better **Origins archeology gallery** holds a dazzling assortment of mostly Bronze and Iron-age treasures. Pride of place goes to the **Red Lady of Paviland Cave**, a red-stained skeleton discovered in 1823 on the Gower which was later revealed to be that of a young man. It's around 26,000 years old, making it the earliest known burial in Britain.

The first floor is given over to the museum's extraordinary **art collection**. The great eighteenth-century Welsh artists, and in particular Richard Wilson, William Parry and Thomas Jones, are well represented; of the fine landscapes, look out for Wilson's *Caernarfon Castle* and *Dolbadarn Castle*, and Jones' *A View from Radnorshire*, and the memorable *The Bard*.

Galleries Eleven to Sixteen begin with nineteenth-century French Art and include Millet (the haunting, unfinished *Peasant Family* and lovely, pastoral *Goose Girl at Gruchy*), Boudin and Manet. Gallery Twelve concentrates on **modern art from the 1930s**, with some terrific pieces by Welsh supremo Ceri Richards, and surrealists such as Magritte.

Best of all, though, is Gallery Sixteen, which has a fabulous collection of **Impressionists** and **Post-impressionists**. Dominating the room are several pieces by Monet, including an uncharacteristically grey *Thames at London*, in addition to Cézanne, Sisley (with his views of Penarth and Langland Bay), Pissarro and Renoir (a chirpy portrait of *La Parisienne*). The centrepiece here, though, is Van Gogh's magnificent *Rain at Auvers*, painted just weeks before his suicide. Look out, too for the wonderful **sculpture collection** in the Rotunda, including many by the one-man Victorian Welsh statue industry, Goscombe John.

Cardiff Bay

Cardiff Bay has become one of the world's biggest regeneration projects, the downbeat dereliction of the old docks having been almost completely transformed into a designer heaven. In years gone by, when the docks were some of the busiest in the world, the area was better known by its evocative name of **Tiger Bay**, immortalized by local lass Shirley Bassey.

The Bay area now comprises three distinct parts, situated either side of **Roald Dahls Plass**, the main square named after the Cardiff-born children's author (1916–90): on the eastern side the civic precincts around the glorious **Wales Millennium Centre**, to the west the shiny **millennium waterfront**, including the **Mermaid Quay** retail and leisure complex, and, set back from the water's edge, the suburb of **Butetown**.

ARRIVAL AND DEPARTURE — **CARDIFF BAY**

Cardiff Bay is just a 30min stroll from the city centre along either endearingly tatty Bute St or the newer but sadly characterless "ceremonial boulevard", Lloyd George Ave. **Trains** run every 20min from Queen Street station and Baycar **bus** #6 leaves from Central Station. You can also take an hourly **waterbus** from Bute Park and Taff's Mead Embankment.

Wales Millennium Centre

Visitor centre daily 10am–6pm • Guided tours daily 11am & 2pm • £5.50 • ☎ 029 2063 6464, Ⓦ wmc.org.uk

The mesmerizing **Wales Millennium Centre** is a vibrant performance space built in 2004 for theatre and music. Likened by critics to a copper-plated armadillo or a great snail, the WMC soars gracefully over the Bay rooftops, its exterior swathed in Welsh building materials, topped with a stainless-steel shell tinted with a bronze oxide to resist salty air.

Guided tours of the building allow complete backstage access, as well as intimate views of the main auditorium, the acoustically sensational Donald Gordon Theatre. The ground floor houses a visitor centre, the main box office, a music shop, souvenir shop, bar and brasserie. Daily **free performances**, of anything from poetry to hip-hop, take place in the foyer, usually at lunchtime and 6pm.

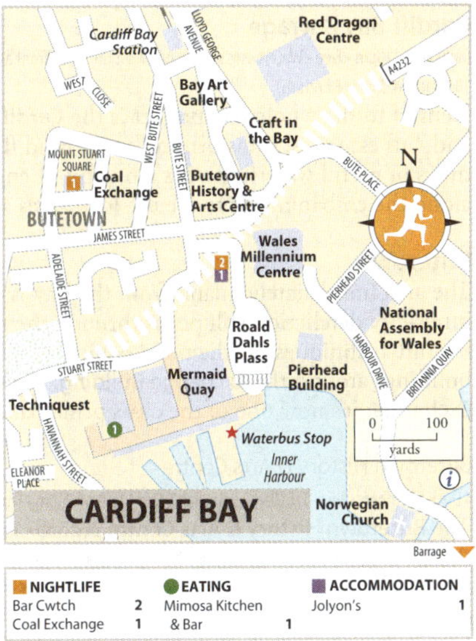

Pierhead Building

On the waterfront • Daily 10.30am–4.30pm • Free • ☎ 029 2089 8200, Ⓦ pierhead.org

Down by the water's edge is the magnificent red-brick **Pierhead Building**, a typically ornate neo-Gothic terracotta pile that was built for the Cardiff Railway Company, formerly the Bute Dock Company. It now houses an enjoyable **exhibition** documenting the rise and fall of the local coal-exporting industry, as well as the genesis of the nearby National Assembly for Wales.

National Assembly for Wales

On the waterfront • Free guided tours • ☎ 0845 010 5500, Ⓦ assemblywales.org

Adjacent to the Pierhead is the **Senedd** building (various times), a striking building designed by Richard Rogers, and inaugurated in 1999 for the **National Assembly for Wales**. It's possible to witness the decision-making in progress in the giant circular debating chamber, while guided tours give a more thorough insight into the assembly's workings.

Norwegian church

Harbour Drive • Sun–Thurs 9am–6pm, Fri & Sat 9am–8pm; opening hours can vary depending on special events • ☎ 029 2087 7959, Ⓦ norwegianchurchcardiff.com

The lovely white, stumpy-spired **Norwegian church** is an old seamen's chapel that once served the needs of thousands of Scandinavian sailors. It was also where Roald Dahl was christened (his parents were Norwegian), and is now an excellent café and performance and exhibition space.

Mermaid Quay and around

On the waterfront west of Roald Dahls Plass, **Mermaid Quay** is an airy jumble of shops, bars and restaurants that, on a warm day, makes a fine place to hang out and watch the world amble by. The city's waterbuses (see p.618) leave from here. Further west, **Techniquest**, on Stuart St (Mon–Fri 9.30am–4.30pm, Sat & Sun 10am–5pm; £7), is a fun, hands-on science gallery – perfect for kids.

Cardiff Bay Barrage

Daily 7am–10pm • Free • Waterbuses shuttle between the waterfront and the southern end of the barrage at Penarth (daily 10.30am–4.30pm; £4 return)

Central to the whole Bay project is the **Cardiff Bay Barrage**, built right across the Ely and Taff estuaries, transforming a vast mud flat into a freshwater lake and creating eight miles of useful waterfront. It's a fine bit of engineering, and it's well worth a wander along the embankment to see the lock gates and sluices.

Butetown

The area immediately inland from the Bay is the salty old district of **Butetown**, whose inner-city dereliction still peeps through the rampant gentrification. James Street, behind Techniquest, is the main commercial focus, while to its north are the old buildings around the **Exchange Building,** built in the 1880s as Britain's central **Coal Exchange**; it's now one of the city's principal concert venues.

Butetown History & Arts Centre

4 Dock Chambers • Tues–Fri 10am–5pm, Sat & Sun 11am–4.30pm • Free • ⓣ 029 2025 6757, ⓦ bhac.org

The **Butetown History & Arts Centre** records and celebrates the multicultural pedigree of the district, which is home, for example, to one of Britain's oldest black communities, many of whom settled here following the outbreak of World War I. Pop in to view the excellent archives or one of their consistently fine temporary exhibitions.

Craft in the Bay

Lloyd George Ave • Daily 10.30am–5.30pm • Free • ⓣ 029 2048 4611, ⓦ makersguildinwales.org.uk

Craft in the Bay, housed in a jazzily revamped old warehouse on Lloyd George Ave, showcases a wide range of contemporary applied art and craft from practitioners all over Wales, as well as overseas. In addition to exhibitions, they also have crafts for sale and run workshops; there's also a cute café.

Llandaff Cathedral

Llandaff, 2 miles northwest of the city centre along Cathedral Rd • Daily 10am–7pm • Free • ⓣ 029 2056 4554, ⓦ llandaffcathedral.org.uk • Bus #33 or #33A

The small, quiet suburb of **Llandaff** is home to a church that has now grown up into the city's **cathedral**. It's believed to have been founded in the sixth century by St Teilo, but was rebuilt in Norman style in around 1120, and worked on well into the thirteenth century. From the late fourteenth century on it fell into an advanced state of disrepair, and one of the twin towers and the nave roof eventually collapsed. Restoration only began in earnest in the 1840s, when **Pre-Raphaelite** artists such as Edward Burne-Jones, Dante Gabriel Rossetti and William Morris were commissioned to make colourful new windows and decorative panels. Their work is best seen in the south aisle.

The fusion of different styles and ages is evident from outside, especially in the mismatched western towers. Inside, the nave is dominated by Jacob Epstein's overwhelming *Christ in Majesty*, a concrete parabola topped with a soaring Christ figure. At the west end of the north aisle, the **St Illtyd Chapel** features Rossetti's cloying triptych *The Seed of David*. In the south presbytery is a tenth-century Celtic cross, the only survivor of the pre-Norman cathedral.

Castell Coch

Four miles north of Llandaff • April–Oct daily 9am–5pm, July & Aug till 6pm; Nov–March Mon–Sat 9.30am–4pm, Sun 11am–4pm • CADW • £3.80 • ⓣ 029 2081 0101 • Bus #26A from Cardiff bus station

The turreted **Castell Coch** was once a ruined thirteenth-century fortress. Like Cardiff Castle, it was rebuilt and transformed into a fantasy structure in the late 1870s by

CAERPHILLY: THE BIG CHEESE

In addition to its castle, Caerphilly is also known for its crumbly white cheese, which has inspired the vibrant **Big Cheese Festival**, held over three days in late July in the shadow of the castle. It's a hoot, with concerts, street theatre, historical re-enactments, a funfair, falconry and, naturally, a cheese race. See ⓦcaerphilly.gov.uk/bigcheese.

William Burges for the third Marquess of Bute. With its working portcullis and drawbridge, Castell Coch is pure medieval fantasy, isolated on its almost alpine hillside, yet only a few hundred yards from the motorway and Cardiff suburbs. There are many similarities with Cardiff Castle, notably the lavish decor, culled from religious and moral fables.

Caerphilly Castle

Caerphilly, 7 miles north of Cardiff • April–June, Sept & Oct daily 9.30am–5pm; July & Aug daily 9.30am–6pm; Nov–March Mon–Sat 10am–4pm, Sun 11am–4pm • CADW • £4 • ⓣ029 2088 3143 • Frequent trains and buses from Cardiff

Caerphilly (Caerffili), seven miles north of Cardiff, has a particularly staggering town-centre **castle**, the first in Britain built concentrically, with an inner system of defences overlooking the outer ring. Looming out of its vast surrounding moat, the medieval fortress with its cock-eyed tower occupies more than thirty acres, presenting an awesome promise not entirely fulfilled inside. The castle was begun in 1268 by Gilbert de Clare as a defence against Llywelyn the Last. For the next few centuries Caerphilly was little more than a decaying toy, given at whim by kings to their favourites. By the turn of the twentieth century, it was in a sorry state, sitting amidst a growing industrial town that saw fit to build in the then-dry moat and castle precincts. Houses and shops were demolished in order to allow the moat to be reflooded in 1958.

The most interesting section of the castle is the massive eastern gatehouse, which includes an impressive upper hall and oratory and, to its left, the wholly restored and re-roofed **Great Hall**.

St Fagans National History Museum

St Fagans, 4 miles west of Cardiff • Daily 10am–5pm • Free • ⓣ029 2057 3500, ⓦmuseumwales.ac.uk • Buses #320 and #322 from Cardiff bus station

St Fagans (Sain Ffagan) has a rural feel that is only partly disturbed by the busloads of tourists rolling in to visit the excellent **National History Museum**, built around **St Fagans Castle**, a country house erected in 1580 and now furnished in early nineteenth-century style.

Beyond the castle lies the **open-air museum**, an outstanding assemblage of buildings from all corners of Wales that have been carefully dismantled and rebuilt on this site. Highlights include the diminutive, whitewashed Pen-Rhiw Chapel, built in Dyfed in 1777; the pristine and evocative St Mary's Board School, built in Lampeter in Victorian times; and the stern mini-fortress of a toll house that once guarded the southern approach to Aberystwyth, from 1772. The superb Rhyd-y-car **ironworkers' cottages**, from Merthyr Tydfil, were originally built in around 1800; each of the six houses are furnished in the style of a different period, stretching from 1805 to 1985.

ARRIVAL AND DEPARTURE — CARDIFF

By plane Cardiff International Airport is out at Rhoose, near Barry (ⓣ01446 711111, ⓦcwlfly.co.uk). The quickest way into the centre is by Xpress bus #X91 (daily; every 2hr; £3.40). Alternatively, you can take a shuttle bus from the main terminal to Rhoose Cardiff International Airport train station and then a connecting train (Mon–Sat hourly, Sun every 2hr; £3.70 combined ticket). A taxi from the airport to Cardiff Central costs around £26.

14

By train Cardiff Central train station sees all intercity services as well as many suburban and Valley Line services. Queen Street station, at the eastern edge of the centre, is for local trains only.

Destinations from Cardiff Central Abergavenny (hourly; 40min); Bristol (every 30min; 50min); Caerphilly (every 15min; 20min); Carmarthen (hourly; 1hr 45min); Chepstow (hourly; 40min); Haverfordwest (10 daily; 2hr 30min); London (hourly; 2hr); Merthyr Tydfil (hourly; 1hr); Newport, Monmouthshire (every 15–30min; 10min); Pontypool (hourly; 30min); Swansea (every 30min; 1hr).

By bus The main bus station is off Wood St, on the southwestern side of the city centre near Cardiff Central.

Destinations Abergavenny (hourly; 1hr 20min); Aberystwyth (2 daily; 4hr); Blaenafon (hourly, 1 change; 1hr 30min); Brecon (5 daily; 1hr 25min); Caerphilly (every 30min; 40min); Chepstow (every 30min–1hr, 1 change; 1hr 20min); London (6 daily; 3hr 10min); Merthyr Tydfil (every 30min; 45min); Newport, Monmouthshire (every 30min; 30min); Swansea (every 30min; 1hr).

GETTING AROUND

Cardiff is compact enough to walk around, and even the bay area is just a 30min stroll from Central station. Once you're out of the centre, however, it's best to rely on local buses.

By bus Information and passes are available from the Cardiff Bus sales office in Wood St (Mon–Fri 8.30am–5.30pm, Sat 9am–4.30pm; ⓣ 029 2066 6444, ⓦ cardiffbus.com). A one-way trip anywhere in the city costs £1.50 (payable on the bus). Useful passes, which can also be bought on buses, include the "Day to Go" ticket (£3), giving a day's unlimited travel around Cardiff and Penarth, which can be extended to Barry, the Vale of Glamorgan, the Caerphilly district and Newport with the Network Dayrider ticket (£7). The "Weekly to Go" ticket (£14) is good for seven days' travel.

By waterbus A useful waterbus service (hourly; £3 single; ⓣ 07500 556556, ⓦ aquabus.com) operates daily between Mermaid Quay and the city centre at Taff's Mead Embankment, diagonally across from the Millennium Stadium.

INFORMATION

Tourist office In the Old Library on The Hayes (Mon–Sat 9.30am–5pm, Sun 10am–4pm; ⓣ 029 2087 3573, ⓦ visitcardiff.com). They have copies of *Buzz*, a free monthly guide to arts and events, and offer internet (£1/30min).

ACCOMMODATION

The Big Sleep Bute Terrace ⓣ 029 2063 6363, ⓦ thebigsleephotel.com; map p.612. Opposite the huge Motorpoint Arena, this hotel feels exactly like the old office block it once was, but is a fun budget option. Choose between budget rooms with simple pine furnishings, and standard rooms in vivid shades of blue. All have flatscreen TV. **£58**

★ **Jolyon's** 5 Bute Crescent, Cardiff Bay ⓣ 029 2048 8775, ⓦ jolyons.co.uk; map p.615. An exquisite boutique hotel in a former seaman's house . Six beautifully conceived rooms each has its own selling point, be it a wrought-iron or antique carved wooden bed, Indian teak fittings or slate-tiled bathroom walls. There's a delightful cellar bar too. **£65**

Lincoln House 118 Cathedral Rd, Pontcanna ⓣ 029 2039 5558, ⓦ lincolnhotel.co.uk; map p.612. Elegant small hotel restored in Victorian style: button-leather couches, heavy brocade and even a couple of four-poster beds. Classy lounge bar for residents. **£90**

★ **Nos da** 53–59 Despenser St ⓣ 029 2037 8866, ⓦ nosda.co.uk; map p.612. Hip hostel/budget hotel on the riverbank opposite the Millennium Stadium. Accommodation is in singles, doubles (some en-suite) and four- to ten-bed dorms, with quirky touches including fold-down beds disguised as modern art. Dorm **£19.50**, double **£44**

Riverhouse Backpackers 59 Fitzhamon Embankment ⓣ 029 2039 9810, ⓦ riverhousebackpackers.com; map p.612. Cosy, contemporary backpackers' hostel set in a Victorian villa with mixed and female-only dorms and twin rooms, as well as a self-catering kitchen, lovely dining/lounge area and a sunny terrace. Dorm **£18**, double **£44**

Sandringham Hotel 21 St Mary St ⓣ 029 2023 2161, ⓦ sandringham-hotel.com; map p.612. Pleasantly old-fashioned, family-run hotel offering plain but clean decor, good service and a friendly atmosphere. One of the better-value options. **£40**

★ **Sleeperz** Station Approach ⓣ 029 2047 8747, ⓦ sleeperz.com; map p.612. Cleverly utilizing the architectural space in between the rail line and two roads, this vibrant, funkily designed hotel has cool, light-filled rooms in breezy white/orange and black/grey colour schemes; the corner cabin bunk rooms are particularly neat, though there are some fabulous touches throughout. Terrific. **£55**

EATING

The city has a great mix of places serving innovative **Welsh cuisine** and ethnic food. There are a number of decent options in the centre, but you'll find the best a little further out; try around Pontcanna and on Mermaid Quay in Cardiff Bay.

Café Citta 4 Church St ⓣ 029 2022 4040; map p.612. A friendly, laidback pizzeria straight out of Italy, with a fine little log-burning oven, pizza dough and sauces made on the premises, and locally sourced ingredients. Mains £8–12. Tues–Sat 11am–11pm, Sun noon–6pm.

Louis Restaurant 32 St Mary St ⓣ 029 2022 5722; map p.612. Wondrously old-fashioned restaurant, serving huge helpings of well-cooked, good-value comfort food such as roast chicken and cottage pie. Mains £6–10. Mon–Sat 8.30am–8pm, Sun 9.30am–4.30pm.

★ **Madame Fromage** 21–25 Castle Arcade ⓣ 029 2064 4888, ⓦ madamefromage.co.uk; map p.612. A small slice of Paris at this delightful corner café-cum-deli where cheese is king – the menu offers a lot more, however, from quiche to lamb cawl and charcuterie platters. Afterwards, check out the shop's tempting stock of jams, pickles and chutneys. Mon–Fri 10am–5.30pm, Sat 9.30am–5.30pm, Sun noon–5pm.

Madeira 2 Guildford Crescent ⓣ 029 2066 7705, ⓦ madeirarestaurante.co.uk; map p.612. Rustically decorated Portuguese restaurant known for its great skewers of meat (espetadas), steaks and other carnivorous delights. There are some beautifully cooked fish dishes too, including caldeirada, a traditional Portugese fish broth. The two-course lunch menu (£9) is great value. Mains £12–20. Mon–Sat noon–2.30pm and 6–11pm.

★ **Mimosa Kitchen & Bar** Mermaid Quay, Cardiff Bay ⓣ 029 2049 1900, ⓦ mimosakitchen.co.uk; map p.615. Cardiff Bay's most rewarding restaurant, sporting a simple but striking design with a brushed steel bar, deep brown leather seating and slate flooring. The Welsh-oriented menu ranges from the simple (Gower lamb cutlets in mint oil) to the ambitious (roasted wild cod with chorizo), while the gut-busting gourmet burgers are a real standout. Mains £12–17. Mon–Thurs 10am–11pm, Fri & Sat til midnight, Sun til 10.30pm.

★ **Mint and Mustard** 134 Whitchurch Rd ⓣ 029 2060 0333, ⓦ mintandmustard.com; map p.612. Arguably the country's finest Indian restaurant, with a menu as brilliant as it is bold; try the Tiffin sea bass wrapped in banana leaves, the stir-fried lamb with coconut chips and curry leaves, or one of the many exceptional vegetarian dishes. Tasteful, modern surrounds and first-class service round things off to perfection. Mains £10–15. Mon–Sat 6–11pm.

The Plan 28–29 Morgan Arcade ⓣ 029 2039 8764; map p.612. Great-looking two-floored café with floor-to-ceiling windows, offering a super range of coffees and light meals (breakfasts, jackets, toasties and salads) derived from locally sourced organic produce. Mon–Sat 8.45am–5pm, Sun 10.30am–4pm.

14

DRINKING

The **pub** scene is lively, with some wonderful Edwardian palaces of etched, smoky glass and deep red wood, where you'll find Cardiff's very own Brains bitter.

Bar Cwtch Jolyon's Hotel, 5 Bute Crescent, Cardiff Bay ⓣ 029 2048 8775, ⓦ jolyons.co.uk/bar-cwtch; map p.615. This basement bar is very cosy indeed, with a wood-burning stove, squishy sofas and a terrific, friendly atmosphere. Mon–Thurs 5–11pm, Fri 5pm–1am, Sat 3pm–1am, Sun 3–11pm.

Cayo Arms Cathedral Rd, Pontcanna ⓣ 029 2039 1910; map p.612. Take a five-minute walk up Cathedral Road to find this proudly Welsh pub, in a building created from two conjoined Victorian townhouses. There's always a good crowd here, enjoying Tomos Watkin beers and decent food. Mon–Sat noon–11pm, Sun noon–10.30pm.

City Arms 10 Quay St ⓣ 029 2064 1913, ⓦ www.thecityarmscardiff.com; map p.612. Opposite the Millennium Stadium, this no-nonsense boozer is always popular, especially on international match days and before gigs at *Clwb Ifor Bach* just around the corner. They offer Brains beers as well as some choice guest ales. Mon–Thurs 11am–11pm, Fri & Sat 11am–2.30am, Sun noon–10.30pm.

★ **Cricketers** 66 Cathedral Rd ⓣ 029 2034 5102, ⓦ cricketerscardiff.co.uk; map p.612. Set in a gorgeous Victorian townhouse, the beautiful-looking *Cricketers* combines a sunny interior with lively beer gardens both front and back. The cask-conditioned Welsh beers are some of Cardiff's best and the food is very creditable too. Daily noon–11pm.

Promised Land 4 Windsor Place ⓣ 029 2039 8998, ⓦ www.thepromisedlanduk.com; map p.612. Welcoming, modestly sized two-floored venue with strong musical associations, as the many wall-mounted signed photographs and posters testify – it's not unknown for stars to pop in here and spin a tune or two post-gig. During the day it's a cracking spot to chill out with a drink and a bite to eat. Sun–Wed 10am–11pm, Thurs 10am–midnight, Fri & Sat till 2am.

★ **Y Mochyn Du** Sophia Close, off Cathedral Rd ⓣ 029 2037 1599, ⓦ ymochyndu.com; map p.612. In the shadow of the cricket ground, this old gatekeeper's lodge is a fine place to sup a pint of Welsh-brewed beer, either in the conservatory or outside among the greenery. It's particularly popular with Welsh-speakers, but everyone is very welcome. Mon–Fri noon–11pm, Sat noon–midnight, Sun noon–10.30pm.

CARDIFF ROCKS

Welsh music has a fantastically strong pedigree, and Cardiff has spawned its fair share of great **bands** in recent years, not least the wonderful Super Furry Animals, whose lead singer, Gruff Rhys, has also made several Welsh-language albums. Hailing from the nearby mining town of Blackwood, Indie/rock champions the Manic Street Preachers have been making thrilling records for the best part of twenty years, while bands such as Los Campesinos! and the Lostprophets (from Pontypridd) have recently taken up the baton.

Great places to catch live music include the Cardiff Arts Institute (see below) in Cathays, the venerable *Coal Exchange* (see below) down in Cardiff Bay, and the inimitable *Clwb Ifor Bach* (see below), which has long been a bastion for Welsh-language bands. Cardiff is also home to the world's oldest record shop, **Spillers**, founded in 1894; you could easily spend a couple of hours leafing through its hard-to-find tracks of all genres. You'll find it in Morgan's Arcade (Mon–Sat 9.30am–5.45pm).

NIGHTLIFE

Café Jazz 21 St Mary St ⓣ029 2066 5161, ⓦcafejazzcardiff.com; map p.612. Unassuming but popular venue, below the *Sandringham Hotel*, hosting a diverse range of jazz gigs; electric blues, funk, gypsy jazz and the like. Entrance typically £2–6. Tues–Fri.

Cardiff Arts Institute 29 Park Place ⓣ029 2023 1252, ⓦcardiffinstitute.org; map p.612. This anonymous red-brick building, opposite the National Museum, conceals a sociable bar and arts venue with a dynamic programme that encompasses everything from live bands and DJ sets to art and multimedia events. Daily noon–late.

Club X 39 Charles St ⓣ029 2064 5721, ⓦclub-x-cardiff.co.uk; map p.612. Cardiff's modest gay and lesbian scene is centred on Charles St, just off Queen St; this stylish and popular gay club is one of the stalwarts, managing to span both the cheesy and cutting-edge ends of the spectrum. There's a wonderful roof garden and a great atmosphere. Fri & Sat 10pm–6am.

Clwb Ifor Bach Womanby St ⓣ029 2023 2199, ⓦclwb.net; map p.612. Cardiff's premier venue for Welsh-language bands (hence the "Welsh Club" moniker), this is a sweaty and enjoyable live music venue and club with nightly gigs and sessions. A top evening is guaranteed. Tues–Sat 10pm–3am.

Coal Exchange Mount Stuart Square, Cardiff Bay ⓣ029 2049 4917, ⓦcoalexchange.co.uk; map p.615. A lovely Victorian building that has been well converted for all manner of musical events, notably some top-drawer rock and indie bands.

★ **Gwdihw** 6 Guildford Crescent ⓣ029 2039 7933, ⓦgwdihw.co.uk; map p.612. Pronounced "goody-hoo", the Owl is a wonderful little corner café/bar, its exterior painted bright orange and the interior decked out with stripped wood flooring, odd bits of furniture and retro bits and bobs. Daily happenings include alternative movies, poetry recitals, micro-festivals and regular bouts of live music on the dinky little stage. Mon–Thurs noon–midnight, Fri & Sat till 2am, Sun 4pm–midnight.

ENTERTAINMENT

Chapter Arts Centre Market Rd, Canton ⓣ029 2030 4400, ⓦchapter.org. Multifunctional arts complex that's home to fine British and touring theatre and dance companies, with an emphasis on the radical and alternative. It's also the best place for art-house movies.

St David's Hall The Hayes ⓣ029 2087 8444, ⓦstdavidshallcardiff.co.uk. Part of the massive St David's shopping centre, this large venue is home to visiting orchestras and musicians from jazz to opera to folk, and is frequently used by the excellent BBC National Orchestra of Wales.

Sherman Theatre Senghennydd Rd, Cathays ⓣ029 2064 6900, ⓦshermancymru.co.uk. Excellent two-auditorium rep theatre hosting a mixed bag of new and translated classic Welsh-language pieces, stand-up comedy, children's entertainment, drama, music and dance. Many plays on Welsh themes in both English and Welsh.

Wales Millennium Centre Roald Dahls Plass, Cardiff Bay ⓣ029 2063 6464, ⓦwmc.org.uk. Permanent home of the Welsh National Opera (ⓦwno.org.uk), together with a collection of other music and dance companies. Also the place to see West End spectaculars and other big touring shows.

DIRECTORY

Hospital The city's main hospital is the University Hospital of Wales, Heath Park (ⓣ029 2074 7747).

Police Cardiff Central Police Station, King Edward VII Ave, Cathays Park (ⓣ029 2022 2111); Cardiff Bay Police Station, James St (ⓣ029 2022 2111).

14

Swansea

Dylan Thomas called **SWANSEA** (Abertawe) – his birthplace – an "ugly, lovely town", which fellow poet Paul Durcan updated to "pretty, shitty city". Both ring true. Sprawling and boisterous, with around 200,000 people, Swansea may be only the second city of Wales, but it's the undoubted Welsh capital of attitude, coated in a layer of chunky bling. The city centre was massively rebuilt after devastating bomb attacks in World War II, and a jumble of tower blocks now dot the horizon. But closer inspection reveals Swansea's multifarious charms: some intact old corners of the city centre, the spacious and graceful suburb of **Uplands**, a wide **seafront** overlooking Swansea Bay and a bold marina development around the old docks. Spread throughout are some of the best-funded **museums** in the country, including the stunning National Waterfront Museum.

Brief history

Swansea's Welsh name, Abertawe, refers to the mouth of the **River Tawe**, a grimy ditch that is slowly recovering after centuries of abuse by heavy industry. The city itself dates back to 1099 when William the Conqueror's troops built a castle here. A settlement grew around this, later exploiting its location between the coalfields and the sea to become a shipbuilding centre, and then, by 1700, the largest coal port in Wales. Copper smelting took over as the area's dominant industry in the eighteenth century,

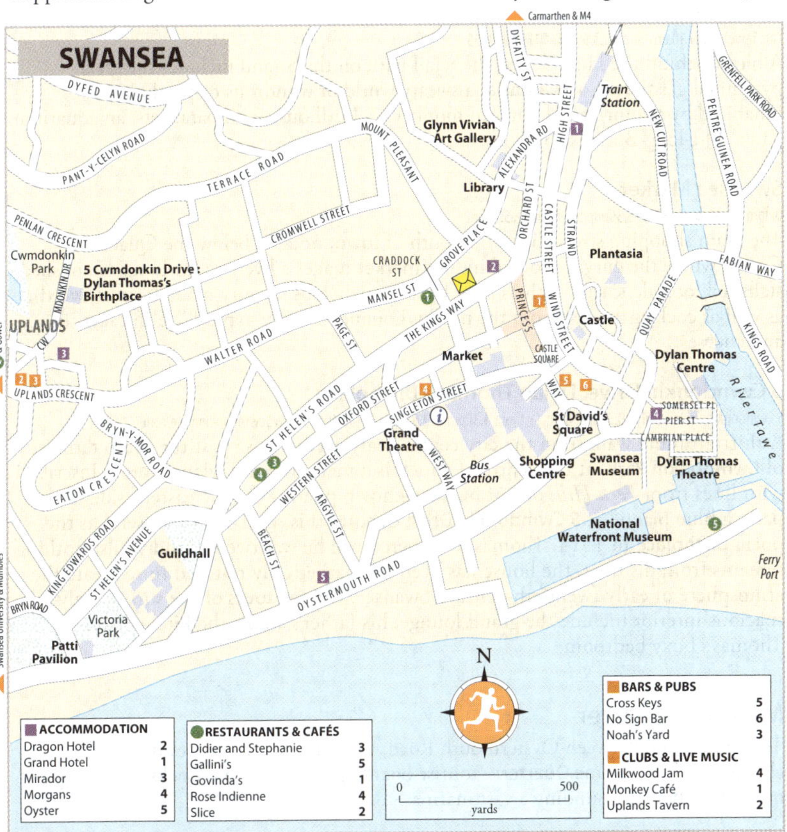

and this attracted other metal trades, developing the region into one of the world's most prolific metal-bashing centres.

The city centre

The train station faces out onto the High Street, which runs south into Castle Street and past the remains of the Norman **castle,** facing the revamped Castle Square. Continuing south from here, Wind Street (pronounced as in "whined") is nocturnal Swansea's main drag, chock-full of theme and chain bars, pubs and restaurants, with a few more unusual establishments sprinkled into the mix.

Glynn Vivian Art Gallery

Alexandra Rd • Tues–Sun 10am–5pm • Free • T 01792 516900

A few minutes' walk south of the train station is the **Glynn Vivian Art Gallery**, a delightful Edwardian showcase of inspiring Welsh art including the huge, frantic canvases of Ceri Richards, Wales's most respected postwar painter, and works by Gwen John and her brother Augustus, whose mesmerizing portrait of Caitlin Thomas, Dylan's wife, is a real highlight. The gallery also houses a large collection of fine porcelain – of which Swansea was a noted centre in the early nineteenth century.

Plantasia

Parc Tawe • Daily 10am–5pm • £3.95 • T 01792 474555

A block behind the High Street, the retail park on the Strand includes the great pyramidal glasshouse of **Plantasia**, a sweaty world of wondrous tropical plants inhabited by a mini-zoo of tamarin monkeys, a birdhouse with parakeets, an aquarium and a 20ft-long Burmese python.

Swansea Market

Oxford St • Mon–Fri 8am–5.30pm, Sat 7.30am–5.30pm

The main shopping streets lie to the south of town, notably below the Quadrant Centre where the curving-roofed indoor **market** makes a lively sight. Long-established stalls sell local delicacies such as laver bread (a delicious savoury made from seaweed), as well as cockles trawled from the nearby Loughor estuary, typical Welsh cakes, fish and cheeses.

5 Cwmdonkin Drive: Dylan Thomas's Birthplace

5 Cwmdonkin Drive • Daily 10.30am–6pm, last tour 4.30pm • £4.95 • T 01792 405331, W 5cwmdonkindrive.com

A thirty-minute walk from the city centre, leafy avenues rise past the sharp terraces of **Cwmdonkin Park**, at the centre of which is a memorial to Dylan Thomas inscribed with lines from *Fern Hill*, one of his best-known poems. On the eastern side of the park, a blue plaque at **5 Cwmdonkin Drive** denotes this solid Victorian semi as the poet's **birthplace** in 1914. Thomas lived here until he was twenty, and whilst nothing remains from his time, the house has been sympathetically restored to re-create the atmosphere of early twentieth-century Swansea. **Guided tours** of the surprisingly spacious interior include the grand lounge, his father's study, the kitchen and Thomas's boxy bedroom.

Maritime Quarter

The spit of land between Oystermouth Road, the sea and the Tawe estuary has been christened the **Maritime Quarter** – tourist-board-speak for the old docks – with legions of modern flats surrounding a vast marina.

Swansea Museum

Victoria Rd • Tues–Sun 10am–5pm • Free • ⓣ 01792 653763

The city's old South Dock features the enticingly old-fashioned **Swansea Museum**, whose highlight is the Cabinet of Curiosities, a roomful of glass cases stuffed with everything from offbeat household items and memento mori – miniature shrines containing photos and models of the deceased – to intriguing local photos, including several of Winston Churchill during his visit here in World War II. There's also a marble bust of a Gower boy, Edgar Evans, who perished with Scott in Antarctica in 1912.

Dylan Thomas Centre

Somerset Place • Daily 10am–4.30pm • Free • ⓣ 01792 463980, ⓦ dylanthomas.com

Wales's national literature centre, the airy **Dylan Thomas Centre** offers a superb exhibition on the life and times of the poet. There is some unique archive material on display here; original worksheets, bar tabs, the writer's only known painting, and the last photos of Thomas before his death, taken, appropriately enough, in a New York bar. The centre also has a theatre space, a café-cum-bookshop and two galleries.

National Waterfront Museum

Oystermouth Rd • Daily 10am–5pm • Free • ⓣ 01792 638950, ⓦ museumwales.ac.uk

On the marina, Swansea's sublime **National Waterfront Museum** was carved out of the shell of the old Industrial and Maritime Museum, which has been stunningly extended to house a breathtakingly varied set of exhibitions dealing with Wales's history of innovation and industry. The museum is divided into fifteen zones, looking at topics such as energy, landscape, coal, genealogy, networks and money, and each section is bursting with interactive technology. Within the complex, there are shops, a café and a lovely waterfront balcony.

ARRIVAL AND INFORMATION — SWANSEA

By train Swansea is the main interchange for trains out to the west of Wales, and for the slow line across to Shrewsbury in England. The station is at the top end of High St.

Destinations Cardiff (every 30min; 55min); Carmarthen (hourly; 50min); Haverfordwest (9 daily; 1hr 30min); Llandrindod Wells (3 daily; 2hr 20min); London (hourly; 3hr); Newport, Monmouthshire (every 30min; 1hr 20min); Pembroke (8 daily; 2hr 10min); Tenby (8 daily; 1hr 40min).

By bus The large bus station is sandwiched between the Quadrant shopping centre and the Grand Theatre.

Destinations Cardiff (every 30min; 1hr); Carmarthen (every 30min; 1hr 20min); Merthyr Tydfil (hourly; 1hr); Mumbles (every 10min; 15min); Oxwich (9 daily, 1 change; 1hr); Port Eynon (9 daily; 50min); Rhossili (Mon–Sat 10 daily, 3 on Sun; 1hr).

Tourist office Plymouth St, behind the Grand Theatre next to the bus station (Oct–May Mon–Sat 9.30am–5.30pm; June–Sept Mon–Sat 9.30am–5.30pm, Sun 10am–4pm; ⓣ 01792 468321, ⓦ visitswanseabay.com); there's stacks of material here on both the city and the Gower, and you can also pick up the comprehensive bi-monthly magazine *What's On*.

ACCOMMODATION

For a fairly large city, Swansea doesn't have a lot of great **accommodation**. That said, there are some inexpensive hotels and B&Bs lining the seafront Oystermouth Rd, with slightly pricier options in the leafy Uplands district. There are no hostels, and the nearest campsite is west of the city towards Mumbles.

Dragon Hotel Kingsway Circle ⓣ 01792 657100, ⓦ dragon-hotel.co.uk. Despite its officious-looking facade, this landmark central hotel is an elegant and modern establishment with plush, air-conditioned rooms coloured vivid red; the luxury amenities include a gym, indoor pool and beauty salon, and there's a lounge, piano bar and restaurant. **£89**

Grand Hotel Ivey Place, High St ⓣ 01792 645898, ⓦ thegrandhotelswansea.co.uk. Accomplished yet pleasingly informal hotel opposite the train station harbouring softly coloured, air conditioned rooms with flatscreen TV/DVD players, and sparkling bathrooms with fantastic showers. There's a basement spa with steam room and hot tub. **£75**

★ **Mirador** 14 Mirador Crescent ⓣ 01792 466976, ⓦ themirador.co.uk. Swansea's most inspirational accommodation, a family-run townhouse in the Uplands area with seven brilliant rooms, each themed on a particular part of the world. The attention to detail is extraordinary; it's not a place you'll forget in a hurry. £69

★ **Morgans** Somerset Place ⓣ01792 484848, ⓦmorganshotel.co.uk. Swansea's showpiece boutique hotel, split between the sumptuously converted old Port Authority HQ and the beautiful Regency terrace townhouse opposite. Superbly appointed rooms boast hardwood flooring, polished wood fittings and Egyptian cotton bed linen. Rates can go up to £200. £65

Oyster 262 Oystermouth Rd ⓣ01792 654345, ⓦoysterhotel.com. Small, cheap and friendly hotel overlooking the shore, with some en-suite and family rooms and a little guest lounge stocked with books and DVDs. £45

14

EATING

Didier and Stephanie 56 St Helen's Rd ⓣ01792 655603. Small, lovely, French restaurant with just ten tables in a beautiful Victorian house, with pastel painted walls and stripped wood flooring. The menu specializes in some fairly obscure regional Gallic surprises. Mains £16–19. Tues–Sat noon–2.30pm & 7pm–midnight.

Gallini's 3 Fishmarket Quay ⓣ01792 456285, ⓦgallinis restaurant.co.uk. This cheery Italian restaurant is the place in town for fresh pasta and seasonally caught fish – try the grey mullet in marinara sauce, or tiger prawns in ginger, garlic and white wine. Mains £10–15. Mon–Sat noon–2.30pm & 6pm–midnight.

Govinda's 8 Craddock St ⓣ01792 468469. Simple and clean vegetarian restaurant in the Hare Krishna tradition, selling ultra-cheap, wholesome meals, including excellent subji (mixed veg) dishes for around £4–5, and freshly pressed juices. Mon–Sat 11am–5pm.

★ **Rose Indienne** 73–74 St Helen's Rd, Uplands ⓣ01792 467000. The beautifully appointed Rose Indienne offers some genuinely exciting and unusual dishes, for example Goan duck curry, and salmon marinated in Masala with mint chutney, in addition to a dozen or so lentil and vegetable-based dishes. Charmingly staffed too. Mains £10–12. Mon–Sat noon–2.30pm & 5.30–11pm, Sun noon–4pm.

★ **Slice** 73–75 Everley Rd ⓣ01792 290929, ⓦslice swansea.co.uk. Out in the Sketty area, the diminutive Slice – so named because of the quirkily shaped building – offers a level of cuisine unmatched anywhere in the city, with confident contemporary dishes such as venison pie with parsnip purée and roast duck breast with Sichuan pepper. There are only a handful of tables, so booking is essential. Mains £15–20. Thurs–Sun noon–2pm & 6.30–11pm.

DRINKING

Swansea has a proliferation of **pubs** and **bars**; most of the action centres on Wind Street – not a place for the faint-hearted on a Friday or Saturday evening – though the Uplands area has its fair share of good-time party places.

Cross Keys 12 St Mary St ⓣ01792 630921, ⓦoxkeys .com. Dating from the 1700s, Swansea's oldest hostelry is a deceptively large affair, offering good ales, a sunny beer garden (BBQs in summer), and a loyal band of rugby followers. Mon–Sat 11am–11pm, Sun noon–10.30pm.

No Sign Bar 56 Wind St ⓣ01792 456110, ⓦnosignbar .co.uk. A narrow frontage leads into a long, warm pub interior, one of the oldest in town and easily the best on Wind St. The reason behind the name is explained in depth in the window. Daily 11am–1am.

Noah's Yard 38 Uplands Crescent. Classy wine bar with big bay windows, bare brick walls and Art Deco lighting, Chesterfield sofas and trunks for tables, as well as lots of postmodern artwork including a piece by legendary street artist Banksy. Live jazz on Mondays from the very accomplished house band. Mon–Thurs 4pm–midnight, Fri & Sat till 12.30am, Sun till 11pm.

NIGHTLIFE

The **club** scene is extremely diverse, and many places double up as live music venues, showcasing a varied and exciting range of bands and other entertainment.

Milkwood Jam 50 Plymouth St ⓦmilkwoodjam.co.uk. Cracking city centre club which packs them in for its regular programme of live music, typically rock and blues. The open-mic night every Wednesday is well attended, too. Daily 8pm–2am.

Monkey Café 13 Castle St ⓣ01792 480822, ⓦmonkey cafe.co.uk. Groovy, inexpensive, mosaic-floored café with a relaxed atmosphere that draws a pretty diverse crowd. Daily happenings include live music, DJs, burlesque, and tango and salsa classes. On a good night, it's the best place in town. Daily 11am–2am, Fri & Sat 11am–4.30am.

Uplands Tavern 42 Uplands Crescent ⓣ01792 458242. Next to Noah's Yard, this former haunt of Dylan Thomas – the walls of the Dylan snug corner are plastered with some fabulous photos – is a popular live music venue, especially for rock and blues. Daily 11am–11pm, Fri & Sat till midnight.

CLOCKWISE FROM TOP THREE CLIFFS BAY, GOWER (P.626); CASTELL COCH (P.616); CELTIC CROSS, CAREW (P.637) >

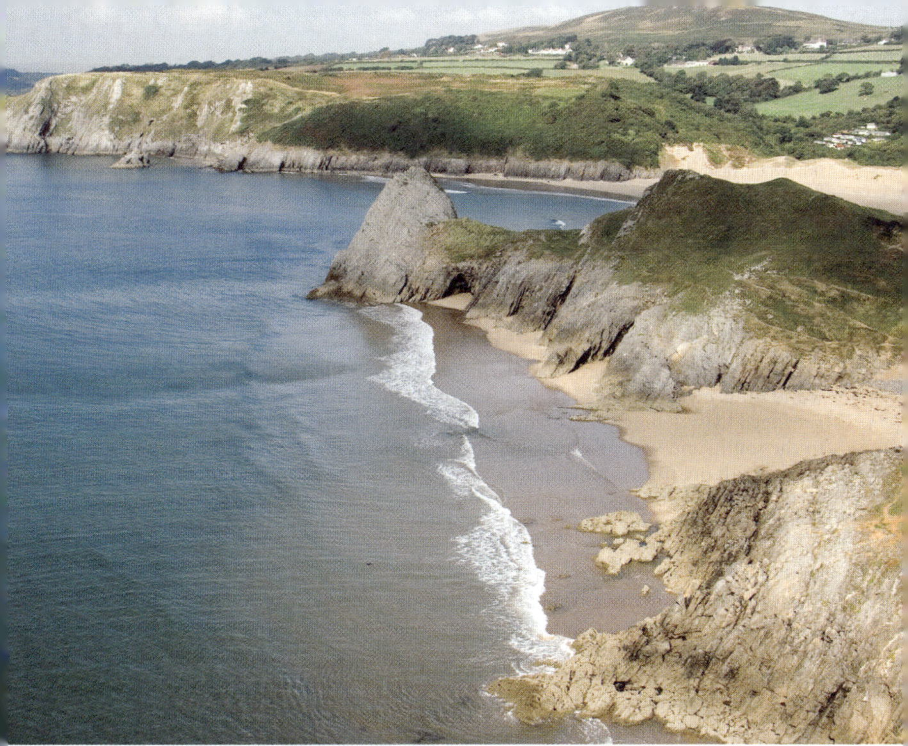

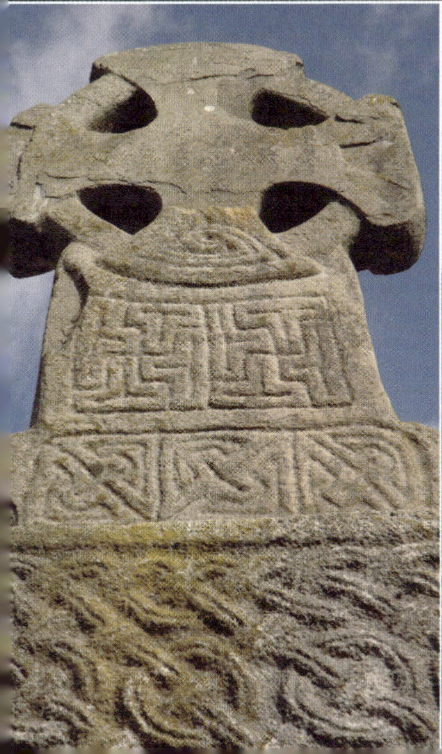

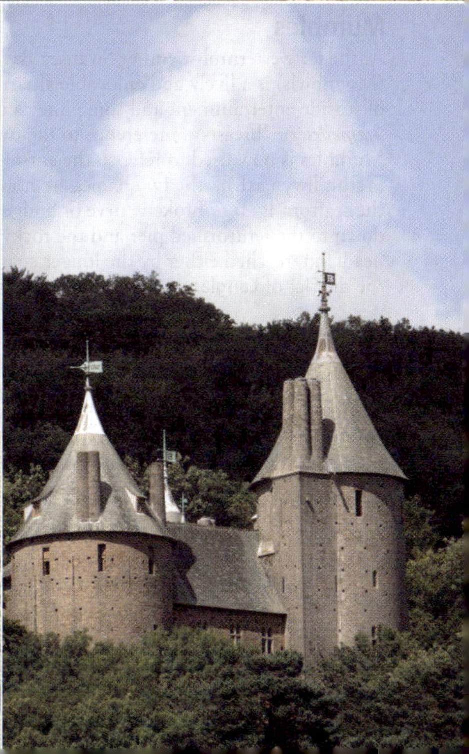

ENTERTAINMENT

Brangwyn Hall The Guildhall, Guildhall Rd South ⓣ01792 635432. Impressive music hall in the Art Deco civic centre which hosts regular concerts by the BBC National Orchestra of Wales and others.

Dylan Thomas Theatre Dylan Thomas Square ⓣ01792 473238, ⓦdylanthomastheatre.org.uk. Thriving community operation staging reruns of Thomas's classics and other modern works in the Little Theatre.

Taliesin Arts Centre Swansea University ⓣ01792 602060, ⓦtaliesinartscentre.co.uk. Welsh, English and international visiting theatre; film; dance and jazz and world music gigs, with an emphasis on the offbeat and alternative.

The Gower Peninsula

A fifteen-mile-long finger of undulating sandstone and limestone, **Gower** (Gqyr) is a world of its own, pointing into the Bristol Channel to the west of Swansea. The area is fringed by sweeping yellow bays and precipitous cliffs, with caves and blowholes to the south, and wide, flat marshes and cockle beds to the north. Bracken heaths dotted with prehistoric remains and tiny villages lie between, and there are numerous castle ruins and curious churches lurking about. Out of season, the winding lanes afford wonderful opportunities for exploration, but in high summer – July and August especially – they can be horribly congested. Frequent buses from Swansea serve the whole peninsula.

Gower starts in Swansea's western suburbs, following the curve of Swansea Bay to the pleasantly old-fashioned resort of **Mumbles** and finishing at **Rhossili Bay**. West of Port Eynon, the coast becomes a wild, frilly series of inlets and cliffs, topped by a five-mile path that stretches all the way to the peninsula's glorious westernmost point, **Worms Head**. The northern coast merges into the tidal flats of the Loughor estuary.

Mumbles

At the far westernmost end of Swansea Bay and on the cusp of Gower, **MUMBLES** (Mwmbwls) is a lively and enjoyable alternative base to Swansea, with a diverse range of seaside entertainment and some fine cafés and restaurants. Derived from the French *mamelles*, or "breasts" (a reference to the twin islets off the end of Mumbles Head), Mumbles is now used to refer to the entire loose sprawl of **OYSTERMOUTH** (Ystumllwynarth) – the two names are now used pretty much interchangeably. Here, the seafront is an unbroken curve of budget hotels, breezy pubs and cafés, leading down to the refurbished pier and the rocky plug of Mumbles Head. Around the headland, reached either by the longer coast road or by a short walk over the hill, is the district of **Langland Bay**, whose sandy beach is popular with surfers.

Oystermouth Castle

July–Sept daily 11am–5pm • £1.20

The hilltop above town is crowned by the ruins of **Oystermouth Castle**, founded as a Norman watchtower and strengthened to withstand attacks by the Welsh, before being converted for residential purposes during the fourteenth century. Today you can see the remains of a late thirteenth-century keep next to a more ornate three-storey ruin incorporating an impressive banqueting hall and state rooms. However, the castle is only partially open at present, owing to a major restoration which is scheduled to continue for several years.

ARRIVAL AND INFORMATION **MUMBLES**

By bus Regular buses from Swansea stop right in the centre at Oystermouth Square.

Tourist office In the Methodist church on Mumbles Rd, just beyond the Newton Rd junction (Easter–Sept Mon–Sat 10am–5pm, Oct–Easter 10am–4pm; ⓣ01792 361302, ⓦmumblesinfo.org.uk). Staff can advise on accommodation in Mumbles and around the Gower.

ACCOMMODATION

Coast House 708 Mumbles Rd ⓣ01792 368702, ⓦthecoasthouse.co.uk. Welcoming and very affordable seafront guesthouse with six fresh-looking rooms decorated predominantly in Laura Ashley-style floral tones. Closed Dec & Jan. **£65**

Patrick's with Rooms 638 Mumbles Rd ⓣ01792 360199, ⓦpatrickswithrooms.com. The lovely Patrick's has sixteen fantastically stylish en-suite rooms, individually furnished in bold colours and all with sea-facing views. **£115**

★ **Tides Reach** 388 Mumbles Rd ⓣ01792 404877, ⓦtidesreachguesthouse.co.uk. Seven spacious and immaculate rooms in this elegant, cheerfully run guesthouse, with a homely lounge and delightful courtyard garden bursting with roses and honeysuckle. **£60**

EATING AND DRINKING

Mumbles is one of Wales's culinary havens, with some superb **restaurants** and cafés.

Café 93 93 Newton Rd ⓣ01792 368793, ⓦcafe93.com. Cheery, two-storey pink-and-white café at the top of the road, with tea, coffee and cakes, plus pizzas and juicy burgers. Mon & Tues 9am–5pm, Wed–Sat 9am–11pm.

The Kitchen Table 626 Mumbles Rd ⓣ01792 367616. Comforting café-cum-restaurant, sporting kitchen-style tables and chairs and serving organic, home-made burgers and tasty veggie dishes. Mains £10. Tues & Wed 9.30am–5.30pm, Thurs–Sat 9.30am–5.30pm & 6.30–9.30pm.

★ **P.A.'s Wine Bar** 95 Newton Rd ⓣ01792 367723. Mumbles' most rewarding restaurant, whose myriad seafood possibilities complement perfectly its outstanding repertoire of wines. The vine-covered terrace is a lovely spot to eat in warmer weather. Mains £15–25. Mon–Sat noon–2.30pm & 6–11pm, Sun noon–2.30pm.

Verdi's Knab Rock ⓣ01792 369135, ⓦverdis-cafe.co.uk. Overlooking the sea near the pier, this Welsh-Italian institution is hugely well regarded for its superb pizzas and ice creams, sorbets and sundaes. Mon–Thurs 10am–6pm, Fri–Sun 10am–9pm.

Rhossili and around

The spectacularly sited village of **RHOSSILI** (Rhosili), at the western end of Gower, is a centre for walkers and beach loungers alike. Dylan Thomas wrote of the "rubbery, gull-limed grass, the sheep-pilled stones, the pieces of bones and feathers" to the west of the village, and you can follow his footsteps to **Worms Head**, an isolated string of rocks, accessible for only five hours at low tide.

Rhossili Bay

Below Rhossili, a great curve of white sand stretches into the distance, a dazzling coastline vast enough to absorb the crowds, especially if you are prepared to head north towards **Burry Holms**, an islet that is cut off at high tide. The northern end of the beach can also be reached by the small lane from Reynoldston, in the middle of the peninsula, to **Llangennith**, on the other side of the towering, 633ft **Rhossili Down**.

ARRIVAL AND INFORMATION — RHOSSILI AND AROUND

By bus Buses drop off in Rhossili by the car park near the Worm's Head Hotel.

Tourist office The National Trust Centre, at the head of the road beyond Rhossili, stocks plenty of literature and excellent walking maps (Jan–March & Nov–Dec Wed–Sun 11am–4pm; Easter–Oct daily 10.30am–5pm; ⓣ01792 390707).

SURFING ON THE GOWER

The Gower has some of Britain's finest **surf**, with the bays and beaches of Langland, Caswell, Oxwich, Rhossili and Llangennith offering the best and most consistent waves. Check ⓦgowerlive.com for live webcams and tide times. For **equipment rental**, the best place is PJ's Surfshop in Llangennith (ⓣ01792 386669, ⓦpjsurfshop.co.uk), which has a wide range of surfboards (£11/day), boogie boards (£6/day) and wet suits (£11/day). A mile away at the *Hillend* campsite, the Welsh Surfing Federation's Surf School (ⓣ01792 386426, ⓦwsfsurfschool.co.uk) runs half-day **surfing courses** (£25 for the first lesson; £20 for subsequent lessons).

14

ACCOMMODATION

Hillend Llangennith ⊕01792 386204, ⊕hillendcamping.com. Large, fabulously sited campsite behind the dunes and with direct access to the glorious beach. Closed Nov–March. £18–22 per pitch.

King Arthur Hotel Reynoldston ⊕01792 390775, ⊕kingarthurhotel.co.uk. The village's convivial pub has half a dozen comfortable en-suite rooms upstairs, though the annexe offers larger, more attractive rooms, with French windows and cast-iron beds and tables. £70

King's Head Llangennith ⊕01792 386212, ⊕kingsheadgower.co.uk. The most prominent accommodation in the village offers rooms of a high standard (some with sea views), both in the newer building up from the pub, and in an annexe attached to the pub itself. £65

Western House Llangennith, on the lane towards the beach ⊕01792 386620, ⊕westernhousebandb.co.uk. Three cool and wildly colourful rooms in this red limewashed B&B, whose remarkably chilled-out proprietors ensure a relaxing stay. £60

Worm's Head Hotel Rhossili ⊕01792 390512, ⊕thewormshead.co.uk. Spectacularly sited on the cliff-top, this small, welcoming hotel has fairly ordinary rooms, but the views are sensational. £86

YHA Port Eynon Port Eynon ⊕0870 770 5998, ⊕yha.org.uk. In a tremendous beachside location, this Victorian lifeboat station has been converted into a super hostel, with four- to eight-bedded dorms. Shared shower facilities, self-catering kitchen and lounge. Groups only Nov–March. £18

EATING AND DRINKING

Bay Bistro Rhossili ⊕01792 390519, ⊕thebaybistro.com. Easy-going café serving light meals (salads, sandwiches, burgers), home-made cakes, coffee and tea; park yourself inside on one of the sunken armchairs or out on the windy terrace for wonderful coastal views. Daily 10am–5.30pm & 7–9pm.

Carmarthenshire

Frequently overlooked in the stampede towards the resorts of Pembrokeshire, **Carmarthenshire** is a quiet part of the world. **Kidwelly**, with its dramatically sited castle, is the only reason to stop before **Carmarthen**, the unquestioned regional capital but one that fails to live up to the promise of its status. Better to press on up the bucolic Tywi Valley, visiting the **National Botanic Garden** and the more intimate grounds of **Aberglasney** on the way to **Llandeilo** and the wonderfully sited **Carreg Cennen** castle. On the coast, the village of **Laugharne** has become a place of pilgrimage for Dylan Thomas devotees, while **Tenby** is the quintessential British seaside resort, built high on cliffs and with views across to monastic **Caldey Island**.

Kidwelly

The sleepy little town of **KIDWELLY** (Cydweli) is dominated by its imposing **castle**, established around 1106 by the bishop of Salisbury as a satellite of Sherborne Abbey in Dorset.

Kidwelly Castle

March–Oct daily 9.30am–5pm; July & Aug daily 9.30am–6pm; Nov–Feb Mon–Sat 10am–4pm, Sun 11am–4pm • CADW • £3.50

Kidwelly Castle is situated at a strategic point overlooking the River Gwendraeth and vast tracts of coast. On entering through the massive gatehouse, completed in 1422, you can still see portcullis slats and the murder holes through which noxious substances could be tipped onto intruders. The gatehouse forms the centrepiece of the impressively intact outer-ward walls, which can be climbed for some great views over the grassy courtyard and rectangular inner ward to the river.

ARRIVAL AND DEPARTURE — KIDWELLY

Kidwelly **train** station, half a mile west of the town centre down Station Rd, is on the main line between Swansea (15 daily; 30min) and Carmarthen (15 daily; 15min).

ACCOMMODATION AND EATING

Carmarthen Bay Touring & Camp Site Tanylan Farm ⓣ01267 267306, ⓦtanylanfarmholidays.co.uk. A caravan-oriented campsite perched beside the estuary north of Kidwelly. Closed Oct to mid-March. Pitches £16–24

Penlan Isaf Farm ⓣ01554 890084, ⓦpenlanisaf.co.uk. Superb B&B on a dairy farm with great views over the town and coast. You'll receive a warm welcome and excellent food. £55

Time for Tea 7 Bridge St ⓣ01554 892908. Family-run place offering daytime meals, snacks, shakes and coffees, much of it using local produce. Daily 9am–5pm.

14

Carmarthen and around

In the early eighteenth century **CARMARTHEN** (Caerfyrddin) was the largest town in the country and it remains the regional hub, a solid, if hardly thrilling, place best known as the supposed birthplace of the wizard Merlin.

The most picturesque part of town is around Nott Square, where the handsome eighteenth-century **Guildhall** sits at the base of Edward I's uninspiring **castle**. From the top of Nott Square, King Street heads northeast towards the undistinguished **St Peter's Church** and the Victorian School of Art, which has metamorphosed into **Oriel Myrddin** (Mon–Sat 10am–5pm; free), a craft centre and excellent gallery that acts as an imaginative showcase for local artists.

Carmarthenshire County Museum

Abergwili, 2 miles east of central Carmarthen • Tues–Sat 10am–4.30pm • Free

The severe grey Bishop's Palace in Abergwili, the seat of the Bishop of St Davids between 1542 and 1974, now houses the **Carmarthenshire County Museum**. The interesting exhibitions include the history of Welsh translations of the New Testament and Book of Common Prayer – both first translated here, in 1567.

ARRIVAL AND INFORMATION **CARMARTHEN**

By train Trains between Swansea and Pembrokeshire stop at the station on the south side of the River Tywi.

Destinations Cardiff (20 daily; 1hr 45min–2hr); Fishguard (5 daily; 1hr); Haverfordwest (11 daily; 40min); Pembroke (9 daily; 1hr 10min); Swansea (26 daily; 50min); Tenby (9 daily; 50min).

By bus The bus station is on Blue St, north of the river.

Destinations Aberystwyth (hourly; 2hr 20min); Haverfordwest (3 daily; 1hr); Kidwelly (every 30min; 25min); Laugharne (6 daily; 30min); Llandeilo (10 daily; 40min); Swansea (every 30min; 1hr 20min); Tenby (1 daily; 1hr 10min).

Tourist office 113 Lammas St, near the Crimea Monument (July & Aug daily 10am–5pm; April–June, Sept & Oct Mon–Sat 10am–5pm; Nov–March Mon–Sat 10am–4pm; ⓣ01267 231557, ⓦcarmarthenshire.gov.uk).

ACCOMMODATION AND EATING

Caban y Dderwen 11 Mansel St ⓣ01267 238989. The best spot in town for snacks and light lunches, including pan-fried laverbread with cockles (£6). Mon–Wed, Fri & Sat 9am–5pm, Thurs 9am–3.30pm.

The Café at 4 Queen St 4 Queen St ⓣ0870 042 4176. A stylish café, serving good coffee, teas and cakes, and light lunches including club sandwiches and soups with home-made bread. Mon–Sat 9am–5pm.

Rose and Crown Lammas St ⓣ01267 232050, ⓦroseandcrowncarmarthen.co.uk. Ancient coaching inn well refurbished with chic rooms, DVD players, and full Welsh breakfasts in the bar downstairs. £60

Y Dderwen Fach 98 Priory St ⓣ01267 234193. The best of the central budget B&Bs, in a simple seventeenth-century house. Some rooms have bathtubs; others have shared showers. £50

The Tywi Valley

The **River Tywi** curves and darts its way east from Carmarthen through some of the most magical scenery in South Wales as well as through a couple of budding gardens: one, the **National Botanic Garden of Wales**, and the other a faithful reconstruction of walled gardens around the long-abandoned house of **Aberglasney**. The twenty-mile trip to Llandeilo is punctuated by gentle, impossibly green hills topped with ruined castles, notably the wonderful **Carreg Cennen**: it's not hard to see why the Merlin legend has taken such a hold in these parts.

The National Botanic Garden

Seven miles east of Carmarthen • Daily: April–Sept 10am–6pm; Oct–March 10am–4.30pm • £8.50, Nov–Feb £5, discounts for groups and those arriving by bike or public transport • gardenofwales.org.uk • Bus #166 runs twice daily from Carmarthen train station

Opened in 2000, the great glass "eye" of the **National Botanic Garden of Wales**, seven miles east of Carmarthen, quickly became the centrepiece of the Tywi Valley. Its central walkway leads past lakes, sculpture and geological outcrops from all over Wales, with walks down towards slate-bed plantings and wood and wetland habitats. A double-walled garden has been teased back to life (providing vegetables for the restaurant), and enhanced with the addition of a small, exquisite Japanese garden, a tropical house and a bee garden that's home to a million bees. At the top of the hill is Norman Foster's stunning oval **glasshouse**, packed with endangered plants from South Africa, Chile, California and the Mediterranean. The whole centre, including the excellent café, is sustainably managed, and the surrounding land has been turned over to either organic farming or the restoration of some typical Welsh habitat.

Aberglasney

Half a mile south of the A40 near Broad Oak • Daily: April–Sept 10am–6pm; Nov–March 10.30am–4pm • £7 • aberglasney.org

Five miles northeast of the National Botanic Garden, a much older garden can be found at **Aberglasney**. While a partly ruined manor house is the estate's centrepiece, interest is focused on the stunning **gardens** where archeological work has peeled back half a century of neglect to reveal a set of interlinking walled gardens mostly constructed between the sixteenth and eighteenth centuries. Once massively overgrown, they have already regained much of their original formal splendour, especially the kitchen garden and what is thought to be the only secular cloister garden in Britain. A walkway leads around the top of the cloister, giving access to a set of six Victorian aviaries from where there are great views over the Jacobean pool garden. One oddity is the **yew tunnel**, planted around three hundred years ago and trained over to root on the far side. The glassed-in atrium of the house is now being populated with subtropical plants.

Llandeilo

Fifteen miles east of Carmarthen, the handsome market town of **LLANDEILO** is in a state of transition, with a small kernel of chichi cafés and shops just off the main Rhosmaen Street.

There's little to see in town, but a mile west is the tumbledown shell of the largely thirteenth-century **Dinefwr Castle,** reached through the gorgeous parkland of **Dinefwr Park**. Set on a wooded bluff above the Tywi, the castle became ill suited to the needs of the Rhys family, who aspired to something a little more luxurious. The "new" castle, half a mile away, now named **Newton House**, was built in 1523, and is now arranged internally just as it was a hundred years ago (mid-March to Oct Mon & Thurs–Sun 11am–5pm; NT; £5.45).

ARRIVAL AND DEPARTURE — LLANDEILO

By train Llandeilo train station, on the scenic Heart of Wales line from Swansea to Shrewsbury, is a couple of blocks east of the centre.

Destinations Shrewsbury (4 daily; 2hr 50min); Swansea (4 daily; 1hr 10min).

By bus Buses stop on New Rd. Destinations include Carmarthen (10 daily; 40min)

ACCOMMODATION AND EATING

Angel Hotel 62 Rhosmaen St 01558 822765, angelbistro.co.uk. Convivial pub serving great food. The back room is a slightly more formal restaurant (mains £11–15). Mon–Wed two courses £10, three courses £12; Fri & Sat £12/14; Thurs features an internationally themed buffet. Mon–Sat 11.30am–3pm & 6–11pm.

Barita 139 Rhosmaen St ⓣ01558 823444. A great deli (for fine Welsh cheeses) and health-food shop, with seating upstairs where you can savour the coffee. Mon–Fri 9.30am–5.30pm, Sat 9.45am–5pm.

Cawdor Arms 70 Rhosmaen St ⓣ01558 823500, ⓦthecawdor.com. Llandeilo's focal point, this former coaching inn has been given a postmodern makeover with delightful, simply decorated rooms (all different) and stunning attic suites. Rates vary, going up to £200. **£65**

Fronlas 7 Thomas St ⓣ01558 824733, ⓦfronlas.com. This large terraced house has been creatively transformed into a modern three-room B&B, all bare boards, funky lighting, wild wallpapers and minimalist design. Breakfasts are largely organic and made with local ingredients. The lounge has an honesty bar and a good DVD collection. **£80**

Carreg Cennen

Four miles southeast of Llandeilo • Daily: April–Oct 9.30am–6.30pm; Nov to March 9.30am–4pm • CADW • £4

Isolated in rural hinterland in the far western extremes of the Brecon Beacons National Park (see p.650), **Carreg Cennen Castle** is one of the most magnificently sited castles in Wales. Urien, one of King Arthur's knights, is said to have built his fortress on the fearsome rocky outcrop, although the first known construction dates from 1248. Carreg Cennen fell to the English King Edward I in 1277, and was largely destroyed in 1462 by the Earl of Pembroke, who believed it to be a rebel base. The most astounding aspect of the castle is its commanding position, 300ft above a sheer drop down into the green valley of the small River Cennen. The highlights of a visit are the views down into the river valley and the long, damp descent into a pitch-black **cave** that is said to have served as a well. Torches are essential (£1 rental from the excellent tearoom near the car park) – continue as far as possible and then turn them off to experience spooky absolute darkness.

Laugharne

The village of **LAUGHARNE** (Talacharn), on the western side of the Taf estuary, is a delightful spot, with its ragged castle looming over the reeds and tidal flats, and narrow lanes snuggling in behind. Catch it in high season, though, and you're immediately aware that Laugharne is increasingly being taken over by the legend of the poet **Dylan Thomas.** The village plays its Thomas connections with curiously disgruntled aplomb – nowhere more so than his old boozing hole, **Brown's Hotel**, on the main street, where

DYLAN THOMAS

Dylan Thomas was the stereotypical Celt – fiery, verbose, richly talented and habitually drunk. Born in 1914 into a middle-class family in Swansea's Uplands district, Dylan's first glimmers of literary greatness came when he joined the *South Wales Evening Post* as a reporter. Some of his most popular tales in the *Portrait of the Artist as a Young Dog* were inspired during this period.

Rejecting what he perceived as the coarse provincialism of Swansea and Welsh life, Thomas arrived in London as a broke 20-year-old in 1934, weeks before the appearance of his first volume of poetry, which was published as the first prize in a *Sunday Referee* competition. Another volume followed shortly afterwards, cementing the engaging young Welshman's reputation in the British literary establishment. Having married in 1937, he returned to Wales and settled in the hushed, provincial backwater of Laugharne. Short stories – crackling with rich and melancholy humour – tumbled out as swiftly as poems, further widening his base of admirers, though, like so many other writers, Thomas only gained star status posthumously. Perhaps better than anyone, he wrote with an identifiably Welsh rhythmic wallow in the language.

Thomas, especially in public, liked to adopt the persona of what he perceived to be an archetypal stage Welshman: sonorous tones, loquacious, romantic and inclined towards a stiff tipple. This role was particularly popular in the United States, where he journeyed on lucrative lecture tours. It was on one of these that he died, in 1953, supposedly from a massive whisky overdose, although it now seems likely he was a victim of pneumonia or diabetes and incompetent doctors. Just one month earlier, he had put the finishing touches to what many regard as his masterpiece: *Under Milk Wood*, a "play for voices".

Thomas's cast-iron table still sits in a window alcove in the nicotine-crusted front bar. The poet is buried in the graveyard of the parish church just north of the centre, his grave marked by a simple white cross.

Dylan Thomas Boathouse

Dylan's Walk • Daily: May–Oct & Easter weekend 10am–5.30pm; Nov–April 10.30am–3.30pm • £4 • ⓦ dylanthomasboathouse.com

Down a narrow lane by the estuary is the **Dylan Thomas Boathouse**, the simple home of the Thomas family from 1949 until Dylan's death in 1953. It's an enchanting museum, with views of the peaceful, ever-changing water and light of the estuary and its "heron-priested shore". Along the narrow lane, you can peer into the green garage where he wrote: curled photographs of literary heroes, a pen collection and scrunched-up balls of paper suggest that he could return at any minute.

Laugharne Castle

South end of King St • April–Sept daily 10am–5pm • CADW • £3.20

At the bottom of the main street, the gloomy hulk of **Laugharne Castle** broods over the estuary. Built in the twelfth and thirteenth centuries, most of the original buildings were obliterated in Tudor times when it was transformed into a splendid mansion, largely destroyed in the Civil War. The Inner Ward is dominated by two original towers, one of which you can climb for sublime views from the domed roof over the huddled town. This is now surrounded by an attractive formal garden with fine mature trees.

ACCOMMODATION — LAUGHARNE

Tiny Laugharne has no tourist office and only limited **accommodation**, so book ahead in season.

Ants Hill Camping Park ⓣ 01994 427293, ⓦ antshill.co.uk. The nearest campsite to Laugharne lies a few hundred yards north. Closed Nov–Feb. **£20**

Boat House Inn 1 Gosport St ⓣ 01994 427263, ⓦ theboathousebnb.co.uk. Stylish, comfortable four-room B&B right in the centre. Great breakfasts might include vanilla waffles, or smoked salmon. **£70**

Swan Cottage 20 Gosport St ⓣ 01994 427409. Appealing one-room B&B with a nice garden and good rates for singles and extended stays. **£56**

EATING AND DRINKING

The Cors Newbridge Rd ⓣ 01994 427219, ⓦ thecors.co.uk. Open for excellent modern Welsh cuisine served casually by candlelight. The menu might include smoked haddock crème brûlée or grilled sewin (sea trout), with mains for around £20. Booking essential. Thurs–Sat evenings.

The Green Room 6 Grist Square ⓣ 01994 427870. Modern coffee shop doing espressos and bowls of cawl during the day and handmade pizzas at night (except Tues). Mon & Tues 10am–3pm & 5–9pm, Thurs–Sun 10am–9pm.

New Three Mariners Victoria St ⓣ 01994 427426. Cheery pub that offers the best drinking in town, coffees and decent bar meals except on Mondays (the *Old Three Mariners* across the road is now a roofless smoking area). Daily 11.30am–11pm.

Tenby

On a natural promontory of great strategic importance, beguilingly old-fashioned **TENBY** (Dinbych-y-Pysgod) is everything a seaside resort should be. Narrow streets wind down from the medieval centre to the harbour past miniature gardens fashioned to face the afternoon sun, and steps lead down the steeper slopes to dockside arches where fishmongers sell the morning's catch.

First mentioned in a ninth-century bardic poem, Tenby grew under the twelfth-century Normans, who erected a castle on the headland in their attempt to colonize South Pembrokeshire and create a "**Little England beyond Wales**". Three times in the twelfth and thirteenth centuries the town was ransacked by the Welsh. In response, the castle was refortified and the stout town walls – largely still intact – were built. Tenby prospered as a port between the fourteenth and sixteenth centuries, and although decline followed, the arrival of the railway renewed prosperity as the town became a fashionable resort.

Today, wandering the medieval streets is one of Tenby's delights. The town is triangle-shaped, with two sides formed by the coast meeting at Castle Hill, and the third by the remains of the 20ft-high town **walls**, built in the late thirteenth century and massively strengthened by Jasper Tudor in 1457. In the middle of the remaining stretch is the only town gate still standing, **Five Arches**, a semicircular barbican that combined practical day-to-day usage with hidden lookouts and angles acute enough to surprise invaders.

St Mary's Church

Between St George's St and Tudor Square • ⓣ 01834 845484, ⓦ stmaryschurchtenby.com

The centre's focal point is the 152ft-high spire of the largely fifteenth-century **St Mary's church**. Its pleasantly light interior shows the elaborate ceiling bosses in the chancel to good effect, and the tombs of local barons demonstrate Tenby's important mercantile tradition.

Tudor Merchant's House

Quay Hill • Mid-March to Oct Sun–Fri; Feb half-term & mid-July to end Aug daily; 11am–5pm • NT • £3 • ⓣ 01834 842279

Wedged in a corner of Quay Hill is the fifteenth-century **Tudor Merchant's House**. The compact house with its Flemish-style chimneypieces is on three floors, and has been filled with reproduction Tudor furniture that you are welcome to sit on. The rear herb garden gives a good view of the huge Flemish chimney.

ARRIVAL AND INFORMATION — TENBY

By train Tenby's station is at the western end of the town centre, at the bottom of Warren St.

Destinations Carmarthen (9 daily; 50min); Pembroke (9 daily; 20min); Swansea (8 daily; 1hr 45min).

By bus Some buses stop at South Parade, at the top of Trafalgar Rd, although most call at the bus shelter on Upper Park Rd.

Destinations Carmarthen (1 daily; 1hr); Haverfordwest (hourly; 1hr); Manorbier (hourly; 20min); Pembroke (hourly; 45min).

Tourist office Upper Park Rd (Easter–Oct Mon–Fri 9.30am–5pm, Sat & Sun 10am–4pm; Nov–Easter Mon–Sat 10am–4pm; ⓣ 01834 842402).

CALDEY ISLAND

Celtic monks first settled **Caldey Island** (Ynys Pyr), a couple of miles offshore from Tenby, in the sixth century. This community may have been wiped out in Viking raids, but in 1136 Benedictine monks founded a priory here. After the dissolution of the monasteries in 1536, the island was bought and sold until 1906, when it was again sold to a Benedictine order, and subsequently to Reformed Cistercians, who have run the place since then.

A short woodland walk from the island's jetty leads to its main settlement: a tiny post office, the popular Tea Gardens and a **perfume shop** selling the herbal fragrances distilled by the monks from Caldey's abundant flora. The narrow road to the left leads past the abbey to the heavily restored **chapel of St David**, whose most impressive feature is the round-arched Norman door.

A lane leads south from the village to the old **priory**, and the remarkable, twelfth-century **St Illtud's church**, which houses one of the most significant pre-Norman finds in Wales, the sandstone **Ogham Cross**, under the stained-glass window on the south side of the nave. It is carved with an inscription from the sixth century, which was added to, in Latin, during the ninth. The lane continues south, climbing up to the gleaming white island **lighthouse**, built in 1828, from where there are memorable views.

ARRIVAL AND DEPARTURE

Caldey Island is accessible by **boats** from Tenby Harbour, or Castle Beach when the tide is out (every 20–30min: Easter–Sept Mon–Sat, Oct Mon–Fri 10am–3pm, returning until 5pm; 20min; £10 return; ⓣ 01834 844453, ⓦ caldey-island.co.uk). Tickets (not for any specific sailing) are sold at the kiosk at the harbour.

ACCOMMODATION

14

Atlantic The Esplanade ⓣ01834 842881, ⓦatlantic-hotel.uk.com. The best hotel along the South Beach, with high-standard rooms (some with sea views), a good restaurant and a pool and spa. Rates include breakfast; watch out for good off-season specials. £128

Bay House 5 Picton Rd ⓣ01834 849015, ⓦbayhousetenby.co.uk. Considerable thought has gone into every aspect of this excellent three-room B&B, from the comfortable, restrained decor to the delicious breakfasts – especially the Glamorgan sausages. £85

Glenholme Picton Terrace ⓣ01834 843909, ⓦglenholmetenby.co.uk. Agreeable eight-room B&B near the town centre, with en-suite rooms and cycle storage. £52

Manorbier YHA hostel Skrinkle Haven ⓣ0845 371 9031, ⓔmanorbier@yha.org.uk. Modern hostel in an old MOD building overlooking the cliffs 5 miles west of Tenby, near the Manorbier bus route. Meals and camping facilities available. Closed Nov–Feb. Dorm £14, double £40

Meadow Farm Northcliff ⓣ01834 844829. Under a mile north of town on the coastal path, this campsite in a grassy field has limited facilities but long views over the town towards Caldey Island. Closed Nov–March. £7 per person.

EATING AND DRINKING

Caffè Vista 3 Crackwell St. Great little licensed Greek-Australian-run café with excellent panini, espresso and cakes, plus a small selection of dishes such as beef or butterbean stew. Good harbour views from the terrace and free wi-fi. Summer Sun–Wed 9am–5pm, Thurs–Sat 9am–10.30pm; rest of year daily 9am–5pm.

Coach and Horses Upper Frog St ⓣ01834 842704. Animated, wooden-beamed pub (said to be the oldest in Tenby) with good beer, well-prepared bar meals and some tasty Thai dishes. Food served noon–3pm & 6–9pm.

Lifeboat Tavern St Julian's St ⓣ01834 844948. Popular and enjoyable pub, with a youthful clientele and live music performances on Tues and Sun. Daily noon–midnight.

★ **The Plantagenet** Quay Hill ⓣ01834 842350. For a splurge, try this cosy and thoroughly enjoyable restaurant in one of the oldest houses in Tenby – ask for a table inside the massive tenth-century Flemish chimney. Dinner mains go for £18–23 (£15 for vegetarian), but lunch is cheaper (dishes £8). April–Oct & Christmas/New Year daily 10.30am–2.30pm & 5–10pm; Nov, Dec & March Fri dinner, Sat lunch & dinner, Sun lunch.

Southern Pembrokeshire

The southern zigzag of coast that darts west from Tenby is a strange mix of caravan parks, Ministry of Defence shooting ranges, spectacularly beautiful bays and gull-covered cliffs. From Tenby, the coastal road passes through **Penally**, with its wonderful beach, and continues past idyllic coves, the lily ponds at **Bosherston** and the remarkable and ancient **St Govan's Chapel**, squeezed into a rock cleft above the crashing waves. The ancient town of **Pembroke** really only warrants a visit to its impressive castle and the fine Bishop's Palace in neighbouring **Lamphey**. **Buses** to most corners of the peninsula radiate out from Tenby, Pembroke and Haverfordwest.

West of Tenby

The coastal path south and west of Tenby skirts the gorgeous long beach of **Penally**, then hugs the cliff-top for a couple of miles to **Lydstep Haven** (fee charged for the sands). A mile further west is the cove of Skrinkle Haven, and above it the excellent *Manorbier* hostel (see above). A couple of miles further on, the quaint village of **MANORBIER** (Maenorbŷr), pronounced "manner-beer", was birthplace in 1146 of the Welsh-Norman historian, writer and ecclesiastical reformist Giraldus Cambrensis.

Manorbier Castle

Easter–Sept & Oct half-term daily 10am–6pm • £4 • ⓦmanorbiercastle.co.uk

Founded in the early twelfth century as an impressive baronial residence, **Manorbier Castle** sits above the village and its beach on a hill of wild gorse. The strong Norman walls surround gardens and a grass courtyard in which the remains of chapel and staterooms jostle for position with the nineteenth-century domestic residence. Views from the ramparts are wonderful, taking in the corrugated coastline, bushy dunes,

THE PEMBROKESHIRE COAST NATIONAL PARK AND COAST PATH

The **Pembrokeshire Coast** is Britain's only predominantly sea-based national park (Ⓦ pcnpa.org.uk), hugging the rippled coast around the entire southwestern section of Wales. Established in 1952, the park is not one easily identifiable mass, rather a series of occasionally unconnected coastal and inland scenic patches.

Crawling around almost every wriggle of the coastline, the **Pembrokeshire Coast Path** winds 186 miles from Amroth, just east of Tenby, to its northern terminus at St Dogmael's near Cardigan. For the vast majority of the way, the path clings precariously to cliff-top routes, overlooking seal-basking rocks, craggy offshore islands, unexpected gashes of sand and shrieking clouds of seabirds. The most popular and ruggedly inspiring segments of the coast path are the stretch along the southern coast from the castle at Manorbier to the tiny cliff chapel at Bosherston; either side of St Bride's Bay, around St David's Head and the Marloes Peninsula; and the generally quieter northern coast either side of Fishguard, past undulating contours, massive cliffs, bays and old ports.

Spring is perhaps the finest season for walking: the crowds are yet to arrive and the cliff-top flora is at its most vivid. The best of the numerous publications available about the coast path is Brian John's *National Trail Guide* (£13), which includes 1:25,000 maps of the route. The national park publishes an accommodation list on Ⓦ pcnpa.org.uk.

deep-green fields and smoking chimneys of the tinted village houses. In the walls and buildings are a warren of dark passageways to explore, occasionally opening out into little cells populated by lacklustre wax figures, including Gerald himself.

The Stackpole Estate

The rocky little harbour at **Stackpole Quay**, reached by a small lane from East Trewent and part of the National Trust's Stackpole Estate, is a good starting point for walks along the breathtaking cliffs to the north. Another walk leads half a mile south to one of the finest beaches in Wales, **Barafundle Bay**, its soft sands fringed by wooded cliffs at either end. The path continues around the coast, through the dunes of **Stackpole Warren**, to **BROAD HAVEN**, where a pleasant small beach overlooks several rocky islets. Road access is through the village of **BOSHERSTON** where three artificial fingers of water known as **Bosherston Lakes** (NT; free) were beautifully landscaped in the late eighteenth century. The westernmost lake is the most scenic, especially in late spring and early summer when the lilies that form a carpet across its surface are in full bloom.

A lane from Bosherston (often closed Mon–Fri, due to military use) dips south across the MoD training grounds to a spot overlooking the cliffs where tiny **St Govan's Chapel** is wedged: it's a remarkable building, at least eight hundred years old. Steps descend straight into the sandy-floored chapel, now empty save for the simple stone altar.

Pembroke

The old county town of **PEMBROKE** (Penfro) and its fearsome castle sit on the southern side of Pembroke River. Despite its location, Pembroke is surprisingly dull, with one long main street of attractive Georgian and Victorian houses, some intact stretches of medieval town wall, but little else to catch the eye.

Pembroke Castle

Daily: April–Sept 9.30am–6pm; March & Oct 10am–5pm; Nov–Feb 10am–4pm • £5.25 • Ⓦ pembrokecastle.co.uk

Pembroke's history is inextricably bound up with that of its **castle**, founded by the Normans as the strongest link in their chain of fortresses across South Wales. During the Civil War, Pembroke was a Parliamentarian stronghold until its military governor suddenly switched allegiance to the king, whereupon Cromwell's troops sacked the castle after a 48-day siege. Yet despite this battering, and centuries of subsequent neglect, Pembroke Castle still inspires awe with its sheer, bloody-minded bulk. The soaring gatehouse, housing some excellent history displays, leads into the large, grassy courtyard around the vast, round Norman **keep**, 75ft high and with walls 18ft thick. Beyond this, steps lead far down into **Wogan Cavern**, a huge natural cave, dank and slimy, where light beams in through a barred hole in the wall facing out over the waterside path.

ARRIVAL AND INFORMATION — PEMBROKE

By train Pembroke's train station lies at the eastern end of Main St.
Destinations Lamphey (9 daily; 3min); Manorbier (9 daily; 12min); Pembroke Dock (9 daily; 10min); Tenby (9 daily; 20min).
By bus Buses follow the one-way system around town with stops on Main St and Commons Rd. The Coastal Cruiser is a hikers' bus that takes a loop from Pembroke to Angle via Bosherston and Stackpole; journey times depend on whether you take the #387 (anticlockwise) or #388 (clockwise).
Destinations Bosherston (Coastal Cruiser; May–Sept 6 daily; Oct–April Mon, Thurs & Sat 4 daily; 35min–1hr); Haverfordwest (hourly; 55min); Manorbier (every 30min; 20min); Pembroke Dock (every 20min; 10min); Stackpole (Coastal Cruiser; May–Sept 6 daily; Oct–April Mon, Thurs & Sat 4 daily; 30min–1hr 15min); Tenby (hourly; 40min).
By ferry Irish Ferries (T 0870 517 1717, W irishferries.com) operate two daily services from Rosslare in Ireland to Pembroke Dock, 2 miles northwest of Pembroke and starting point of trains to Carmarthen and Swansea.
Tourist office Commons Rd, parallel to Main St (Easter–Oct Mon–Fri 10am–4pm, Sat 10am–1pm; winter Tues–Sat 10am–1pm; T 01646 776499).

ACCOMMODATION

Beech House B&B 76–78 Main St T 01646 683740, W beechhousepembroke.com. Rooms here have shared bathrooms, but for comfort, style and hospitality it easily outdoes places charging twice as much. £40

Tregenna 7 Upper Lamphey Rd T 01646 621525, W tregennapembroke.co.uk. If *Beech House* is full, try one of the four en-suite rooms here, about 800m beyond the train station. £55

EATING AND DRINKING

The Cornstore North Quay T 01646 684290, W thecornstore.com/cafe. Down by the river, this little café, linked to an interior design shop, is a great spot for good espresso, scrumptious home-made cakes and light meals made from local produce. Mon–Sat 10am–5pm.

Old King's Arms 13 Main St T 01646 683611, W oldkingsarmshotel.co.uk. For something substantial try the traditional dining room at this historic inn. Most food is locally sourced, with meaty mains around £14–20 at dinner (cheaper for Sunday lunch); bar food is cheaper and lighter, and they do real ales, too. Food served daily noon–2.15pm & 6.30–10pm.

Waterman's Arms Northgate St, over the bridge T 01646 682718, W watermansarmspembroke.co.uk. It's hard to beat a summer evening here, where you can while away the hours on a veranda overlooking the mill pond. Daily 11.30am–11pm; snacks and meals throughout the day Easter–Oct; lunch and dinner only in winter.

Lamphey

The pleasant village of **LAMPHEY** (Llandyfai), two miles east of Pembroke and accessible on **buses** and **trains** between Tenby and Pembroke, is best known for the ruined **Bishop's Palace**, off a quiet lane to the north of the village. It also has a handful of good **places to stay** nearby.

Bishop's Palace

April–Oct daily 10am–5pm • CADW • £3.20 • T 01646 672224

A country retreat for the bishops of St Davids, Lamphey's **Bishop's Palace** dates from around the thirteenth century, but was abandoned following the Reformation. Stout walls surround the scattered ruins, and many of the palace buildings have long been lost under grassy banks. Most impressive are the remains of the Great Hall, at the eastern end of the complex, topped by fourteenth-century arcaded parapets.

ACCOMMODATION **LAMPHEY**

Lamphey Court Hotel & Spa ⓣ01646 672273, ⓦlampheycourt.co.uk. Grand if slightly over-the-top accommodation, with spa, opposite the palace ruins. **£134**

Portclew House B&B Two miles south of Lamphey, Freshwater East ⓣ01646 672800, ⓦportclewhouse.co.uk. Just half a mile from the superb beach of Freshwater East, this Grade II-listed Georgian house, in two acres of grounds, offers seven spacious rooms, plus self-catering units. **£56**

14

Carew

Tiny **CAREW**, four miles northeast of Pembroke, is a pretty place beside the River Carew. By the main road just south of the river crossing stands a 13ft **Celtic cross**, the graceful taper of the shaft covered in fine tracery of ancient Welsh designs.

Carew Castle and Tidal Mill

April–Oct daily 10am–5pm; Nov–March castle only Mon–Fri 11am–3pm • April–Oct £4.50, Nov–March £3 • ⓦcarewcastle.com

An Elizabethan walled garden houses the ticket office for **Carew Castle and Tidal Mill**. Little remains of the castle, a hybrid of defensive necessity (c.1100) and Elizabethan whimsy, but its large, impressive bare walls give a good sense of scale. A few hundred yards west is the **Tidal Mill**, used commercially until 1937 and now the only tide-powered mill in Wales. The impressive eighteenth-century exterior belies the pedestrian displays inside.

Mid- and northern Pembrokeshire

The most westerly point of Wales is one of the country's most enchanting. The chief town of the region, **Haverfordwest**, is rather soulless, but it's useful as a jumping-off point for the stunning **St Bride's Bay**. The coast here is broken into rocky outcrops, islands and broad, sweeping beaches curving between two headlands that sit like giant crab pincers facing out into the warm Gulf Stream. The southernmost headland winds around every conceivable angle, offering calm, east-facing sands at **Dale** and sunny expanses of south-facing beach at **Marloes**. At **Martin's Haven**, boats depart for the offshore islands of **Skomer**, **Skokholm** and **Grassholm**. To the north, there's spectacularly lacerated coast around **St Davids peninsula**, with towering cliffs interrupted only by occasional strips of sand. The tiny cathedral city of **St Davids** is most definitely a highlight: rooks and crows circle above the impressive ruins of the huge Bishop's Palace, sitting beneath the delicate bulk of the cathedral, the most impressive in Wales.

The north-facing coast that forms the very southern tip of Cardigan Bay is wild, rugged and breathtakingly beautiful. It's also noticeably less commercialized and far more Welsh than the touristy shores of south and mid-Pembrokeshire. From the crags and cairns above St David's Head, the coast path perches precariously on the cliffs where only the thousands of seabirds have access. Hidden coves and secluded beaches slice into the rocky headlands, which are at their most magnificent around **Strumble Head,** where a picturesque lighthouse flashes its warning from a tiny islet. From here, there's only wilderness to detain you en route to the charming town of **Newport** – unless you're heading for **Fishguard** and the ferries to Ireland.

Haverfordwest

In the seventeenth and eighteenth centuries, the town of **HAVERFORDWEST** (Hwlffordd), ten miles north of Pembroke, prospered as a port and trading centre. Despite its natural advantages, it is scarcely a place to linger, though as its the main transport hub and shopping centre for western Pembrokeshire, you are likely to pass through.

14

ARRIVAL AND INFORMATION — HAVERFORDWEST

By train Trains stop a10min walk east of the Old Bridge.
Destinations Cardiff (7 daily; 2hr 25min); Carmarthen (10 daily; 40min); Swansea (7 daily; 1hr 30min).

By bus The bus station is at the end of the Old Bridge.
Destinations Broad Haven (6 daily; 20min); Cardigan (hourly; 1hr 20min); Carmarthen (3 daily; 1hr); Fishguard (hourly; 40min); Manorbier (hourly; 1hr 10min); Newport, Pembrokeshire (hourly; 1hr); Pembroke (hourly; 55min); St Davids (hourly; 45min); Tenby (hourly; 1hr).

Tourist office Next to the bus terminus, at the end of the Old Bridge (April–Oct Mon–Fri 9.30am–5pm, Sat 10am–4pm; Nov–March Mon–Sat 10am–4pm; T 01437 763110).

GETTING AROUND

By bike Mike's Bikes 17 Prendergast, a quarter of a mile northeast of the bus station (Mon–Sat 9am–5.30pm; T 01437 760068, W mikes-bikes.co.uk). The best bike rental in the region, renting out mountain bikes and hybrid tourers (both £12/day) with panniers, lock and helmet, and tag-a-longs for kids.

ACCOMMODATION AND EATING

Black Sheep High St T 01437 767017, W blacksheeprestaurant.co.uk. This ambitious restaurant adds exotic flavours to local produce and indeed meat from its own farm. Main courses cost £6–8 at lunchtime or around £12 in the evening (£16–20 for duck or steak). Mon–Sat noon–3pm, Tues–Sat from 6pm.

Casa Maria 2 Castle Square T 01437 779194, W casamariadeli.co.uk. At the start of the walk up to the castle ruins, this classy deli sells Spanish, French and Welsh cheeses, meats and olives, with a café upstairs serving tapas with wine. Mon–Sat 10am–4pm.

College Guest House 93 Hill St T 01437 763710, W collegeguesthouse.com. One of several decent B&Bs near the Leisure Centre (free parking) at the top of Hill St. £70

East Hook Farmhouse Portfield Gate T 01437 762211, W easthookfarmhouse.co.uk. Delightful Georgian farmhouse 3 miles west of town, serving delicious breakfasts, plus dinner for around £20. £73

Dale

DALE, fourteen miles west of Haverfordwest, can be unbearably crowded in peak season; the sheltered east-facing shore makes it excellent for bathing and **watersports** in the lighter seas. West Wales Windsurf and Sailing (T 01646 636642, W surfdale.co.uk) gives instruction in power-boating, windsurfing, surfing, sailing and kayaking (around £65 per half-day), and rents gear. You can also take a cruise from Dale to Skokholm and Grassholm islands (see below).

ACCOMMODATION — DALE

Allenbrook T 01646 636254, W allenbrook-dale.co.uk. A luxurious, charming, richly furnished country house hotel close to the beach. All rooms look out over the garden and towards the sea. No children under 15. £70

Richmond House T 07974 925009, W richmond-house.com. On the waterfront (and next to the local pub), this is a comfortable B&B with nicely decorated, cabin-style rooms, all en suite. £90

SKOMER, SKOKHOLM AND GRASSHOLM ISLANDS

Weather permitting, **boats** (April–Oct Tues–Sun & bank hols 10am, 11am & noon; £18; no booking required) run from Martin's Haven to **Skomer Island**, a 722-acre flat-topped island whose rich birdlife and spectacular carpets of wild flowers make it perfect for birdwatching and walking.

Though no landings are permitted, fast cruises leave from Dale to loop around Skomer and **Skokholm Island** (daily 9.30am, 3.30pm & 6.30pm; 2hr 30min; £30; booking essential; T 0800 028 4090 or 01646 603110, W dale-sailing.co.uk), a couple of miles south of Skomer and far smaller, more rugged and remote, noted for its cliffs of warm red sandstone. Britain's first bird observatory was founded here in 1933, and there are still huge numbers of petrels, gulls, puffins, oystercatchers and Manx shearwaters.

The same company also offers cruises out to the tiny outpost of **Grassholm Island**, more than five miles west of Skomer (daily 12.30pm; 2hr 30min; £30). Some 80,000 or so screaming gannets nest here, and though they do not land, boats stop to watch the wildlife.

Marloes

MARLOES, a mile north of Dale, is an unexciting little place, but the broad, deserted beach is magnificent, and offers a safe place to swim, as well as fine views of the island of Skokholm. The coast path and a narrow road continue for two miles to the National Trust-owned headland of **Deer Park**, the grassy far tip of the southern peninsula of St Bride's Bay – and **Martin's Haven**, from where you can take a **boat** out to the islands of Skomer (where you can disembark), Skokholm and Grassholm.

ACCOMMODATION — MARLOES

YHA Marloes Sands Runwayskiln ⓣ 0845 371 9333. Converted farm buildings overlooking the northern end of Marloes Sands. 11pm curfew. Closed mid-Sept to April. **£18**

St Davids

ST DAVIDS (Tyddewi) is one of the most enchanting spots in Britain. This miniature city – really just a large village – sits at the very westernmost point of Wales in bleak, treeless countryside, above its purple- and gold-flecked **cathedral**, the spiritual heart of Wales. Traditionally founded by the Welsh patron saint himself in 550 AD, the shrine of St David has drawn pilgrims for a millennium and a half – William the Conqueror included – and by 1120, Pope Calixtus II decreed that two journeys to St Davids were the spiritual equivalent of one to Rome. Today, with so many historical sites, outdoor-pursuit centres, surf beaches, good cafés, superb walks, bathing and climbing, St Davids and its peninsula are a must.

From the central **Celtic cross**, the main street runs under the thirteenth-century **Tower Gate**, which forms the entrance to the serene **Cathedral Close**, backed by a windswept landscape of treeless heathland. The cathedral lies down to the right, hidden in a hollow by the River Alun. This apparent modesty is explained by reasons of defence, as a towering cathedral, visible from the sea on all sides, would have been vulnerable to attack. On the other side of the babbling Alun lie the ruins of the **Bishop's Palace**.

St Davids Cathedral

Daily 9am–5.30pm • £4 donation requested • ⓣ 01437 720202, ⓦ stdavidscathedral.org.uk

St Davids Cathedral's 125ft tower, topped by pert golden pinnacles, has clocks on only three sides – the people of the northern part of the parish couldn't raise enough money for one to be constructed facing them. You enter through the south side of the low, twelfth-century nave in full view of its most striking feature, the intricate latticed oak **roof**, added to hide emergency restoration work in the sixteenth century. The nave floor still has a pronounced slope and the support buttresses inserted in the northern aisle look incongruously new and temporary. At the back of the south choir stalls is a unique **monarch's stall**, complete with royal crest, for, unlike any other British cathedral, the Queen is an automatic member of the St Davids Cathedral Chapter.

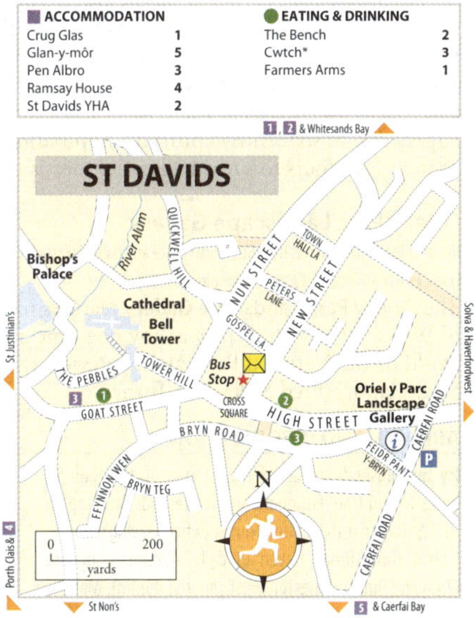

OUTDOOR ACTIVITIES IN ST DAVIDS

Several local companies run **boat trips** to the outlying islands (see p.638), and there are all manner of activities from **biking** to **rock climbing**.

Preseli Venture Halfway to Fishguard near Mathry ⊕01348 837709, ⓦpreseliventure.co.uk. Coasteering, sea kayaking, surfing, walking and biking.

Re-Cycles Bike Hire ⊕01437 711123, ⓦpembrokeshireonline.co.uk/re-cycle. Bike rental (£10/day); they'll deliver to any location.

TYF 1 High St ⊕01437 721611, ⓦtyf.com. TYF pioneered coasteering, an exhilarating multi-sport combination that involves scrambling over rocks, jumping off cliffs and swimming across the narrow bays of St Davids peninsula. Coasteering is possible for just about anyone (even non-swimmers) and is available all year, along with surfing, kayaking and rock climbing. Also multi-day sessions and courses.

Separating the choir and the presbytery is an unusual **parclose screen** of finely traced woodwork; beyond this is the tomb of Edmund Tudor, father of King Henry VII. The back wall of the **presbytery** was once the eastern extremity of the cathedral, as can be seen from the two lines of windows. The upper row has been left intact, while the lower three were blocked up and filled with delicate gold mosaics in the nineteenth century. The colourful fifteenth-century roof, a deceptively simple repeating medieval pattern, was restored by Sir George Gilbert Scott in the 1860s. On the south side are two thirteenth-century bishops' tombs, and opposite is the disappointingly plain tomb of St David, largely destroyed in the Reformation. Behind the filled-in lancets at the back of the presbytery is **Bishop Vaughan's chapel**, with an exquisite fan tracery roof built between 1508 and 1522. A peephole looks back into the presbytery, over a casket reputedly containing some of the intermingled bones of St David and his friend, St Justinian.

The Bishop's Palace

Across the River Arun from the cathedral • March–June, Sept & Oct daily 9am–5pm; July & Aug daily 9am–6pm; Nov–March Mon–Sat 10am–4pm, Sun 11am–4pm • CADW • £3.20

The splendid fourteenth-century **Bishop's Palace** has a huge central quadrangle fringed by a neat jigsaw of ruined buildings built in extraordinarily richly tinted stone. The **arched parapets** that run along the top of most of the walls were a favourite feature of the fourteenth-century Bishop Gower. Two ruined but still impressive halls – the **Bishop's Hall** and the enormous **Great Hall**, with its glorious rose window – lie off the main quadrangle, above and around a myriad of rooms adorned by some eerily eroded corbels. Beneath the Great Hall, dank vaults contain an interesting exhibition on the palace and the indulgent lifestyles of its occupants. The destruction of the palace is largely due to sixteenth-century Bishop Barlow, who supposedly stripped the buildings of their lead roofs to provide dowries for his five daughters' marriages to bishops.

Oriel y Parc Landscape Gallery

National Park tourist office, High St • Tourist office and gallery: Easter–Oct daily 9.30am–5.30pm; Nov–Easter Mon–Sat 10am–4.30pm • Free • ⊕01437 720392, ⓦpembrokeshirecoast.org.uk

The **Oriel y Park Landscape Gallery** features rotating loans from the National Museum of Wales. Works on display at any one time aim to interpret the landscape and natural world of the National Park; artists previously exhibited here have included Graham Sutherland, Alfred Sisley and Turner.

ARRIVAL AND INFORMATION — ST DAVIDS

By bus Buses from Haverfordwest stop on the High St; buses to and from Fishguard and Whitesands Bay stop on New St (when arriving) and Nun St (when leaving).

Destinations Broad Haven (3 daily; 45min); Fishguard (7 daily; 50min); Haverfordwest (hourly; 45min); Marloes (3 daily; 1hr 20min).

National Park tourist office On the main road from Haverfordwest, here called High St (Easter–Oct daily 9.30am–5.30pm; Nov–Easter Mon–Sat 10am–4.30pm; ⊕01437 720392, ⓦstdavids.co.uk).

ACCOMMODATION

★ **Crug Glas** Abereiddi, 4 miles northeast ⓣ 01348 831302, ⓦ crug-glas.co.uk. Luxurious country house on a working farm. Breakfasts are excellent (great bacon) and delicious four-course evening meals are available for around £25. **£90**

Glan-y-môr Caerfai Rd, half a mile south of town ⓣ 01437 721788, ⓦ glan-y-mor.co.uk. The nearest campsite to town, with a pub and restaurant on site. No bookings. Closed Oct–Feb. **£12** per double tent.

Pen Albro 18 Goat St ⓣ 01437 721865. More a Bed & Snack than a B&B, but it's the cheapest in town, with no en-suite rooms; right beside the *Farmers Arms* pub. **£40**

Ramsey House Lower Moor ⓣ 01437 720321, ⓦ ramseyhouse.co.uk. Quality B&B on the road to Porth Clais, with six boutique-style rooms and excellent breakfasts: expect the likes of home-made apple and sage sausages and fresh bread. They also do three-course evening meals for £35 and have a bar. Closed Nov–Feb. **£100**

St Davids YHA Hostel Llaethdy, 2 miles northwest near Whitesands Bay ⓣ 0870 770 6042. Large, renovated hostel in a former farmhouse and outbuildings. Daytime lockout and 11pm curfew. Closed Nov–March. Dorm **£18.40**, double **£60**

14

EATING AND DRINKING

★ **The Bench** 11 High St ⓣ 01437 721778, ⓦ bench-bar.co.uk. Versatile Italian bar-restaurant with a sunny conservatory and garden. Decent pizza and fresh pasta dishes (£7–9), plus good panini and espresso, and great Italian ice cream to take away (including alcoholic ices for over-18s). There's internet access, with free wi-fi and computer terminals. Spring and summer daily 9am–9pm; limited hours otherwise.

★ **Cwtch*** 22 High St ⓣ 01437 720491, ⓦ cwtchrestaurant.co.uk. Some of the finest dining in Pembrokeshire can be found at the award-winning *Cwtch** (pronounced "cutsh"), an intimate and easy-going restaurant that's all slate and wood and blackboard menus, featuring top-quality local ingredients. You'll pay £26/30 for two/three courses; booking recommended. April–Oct daily from 6pm; Nov–March Tues–Sat from 6pm.

Farmers Arms Goat St ⓦ farmersstdavids.co.uk. Lively and very friendly pub, with a terrace overlooking the cathedral – especially enjoyable on a summer's evening. Decent pub grub also available. Daily 11am–midnight.

St Davids peninsula

Surrounded on three sides by inlets, coves and rocky stacks, St Davids is an easy base for some excellent walking around the headland of the same name. A mile due south, the popular **Caerfai Bay** provides a sandy gash in the purple sandstone cliffs – rock which was used in the construction of the cathedral.

St Non's Bay

Immediately south of St Davids (reached by Goat St), the craggy indentation of **St Non's Bay** is where St Non reputedly gave birth to St David during a tumultuous storm around 500 AD. The bay has received pilgrims for centuries, resulting in the foundation of a tiny, isolated **chapel** in the pre-Norman age; the ruins of the subsequent thirteenth-century chapel now lie in a field near the sadly dingy well and coy shrine marking the birthplace of the nation's patron saint.

Porth Clais

Just west of St Non's, **Porth Clais** is supposedly where St David was baptized by a bishop with the unlikely name of St Elvis. This was the city's main harbour from Roman times, its spruced-up remains still visible at the bottom of the turquoise river creek. Today, commercial traffic has long gone, replaced by fishing boats and dinghies.

Whitesands Bay

From **St Justinians**, two miles west of St Davids, the coast path leads north over another lowly headland to the magnificent **Whitesands Bay** (Porth-mawr), a narrow arc of dune-backed sand that's popular with both surfers and families alike, and is also accessible by road from St Davids. From here though, there's no further road access to the coast for some distance, giving this section of the coast path a thoroughly wild feel, and making it perfect for wildlife-watching.

Ramsey Island

The harbour at St Justinians has a ticket hut for the boats over to **Ramsey Island**. This enchanting dual-humped plateau, less than two miles long, has been under the able stewardship of the RSPB since 1992. Birds of prey circle the skies above the island, but it's better known for the tens of thousands of seabirds that noisily crowd the sheer cliffs on its western side and the seals lazing sloppily about.

ARRIVAL AND DEPARTURE — RAMSEY ISLAND

Thousand Islands Expeditions **boat trips** (April–Oct daily; ⓣ01437 721721, ⓦthousandislands.co.uk; £15) allow up to six hours on Ramsey. During the springtime nesting season you actually see more from boats which circle the island but don't land: try Voyages of Discovery (daily; ⓣ01437 720285 or 0800 854367, ⓦramseyisland.co.uk; £25).

Fishguard

From St Davids peninsula the main road runs northeast, parallel to numerous small and less-commercialized bays, to the wild and windswept **Strumble Head**, perhaps the best place in Wales for watching seabirds. This protects **FISHGUARD** (Abergwaun), an attractive, hilltop town mainly of interest as the port for the **ferries** to and from Rosslare in Ireland.

In the centre of town is the **Royal Oak Inn**, where a bizarre Franco-Irish attempt to conquer Britain in 1797 at nearby Carregwastad Point is remembered. Having landed in the wrong place and then got hopelessly drunk, the hapless forces surrendered after two days. This is said to have been triggered by the sight of a hundred local women marching towards them. Due to their stovepipe hats and red flannel dresses they mistook them for British infantry and instantly capitulated. Even if this is not true, it is undisputed that 47-year-old cobbler's wife Jemima Nicholas, the "Welsh Heroine", single-handedly captured fourteen French soldiers with nothing but a pitchfork. Her grave can be seen next to the uninspiring Victorian church, **St Mary's**, behind the pub. The fabulous **Fishguard Tapestry**, telling the story of this ramshackle invasion, is on display in the town hall across the road (Mon–Wed, Fri & Sat 9.30pm–5pm, Thurs 9.30pm–6.30pm; Oct–March closes 1pm on Sat; free).

ARRIVAL AND INFORMATION — FISHGUARD

By train Fishguard train station is next to the ferry terminal on Quay Rd in Goodwick.

Destinations Cardiff (3 daily; 2hr 40min); Carmarthen (7 daily; 50min); Swansea (4 daily; 1hr 50min).

By bus Buses stop in the central Market Square, right outside Fishguard's tourist office, and on Station Hill in Goodwick, half a mile from the ferry terminal.

Destinations Cardigan (hourly; 40min); Haverfordwest (hourly; 40min); Newport, Pembrokeshire (hourly; 15min); St Davids (6–8 daily; 45min).

By ferry Stena Line ferries and fast catamarans (ⓣ08705 707070, ⓦstenaline.com) leave three times daily for Rosslare in Ireland. A taxi (ⓣ01348 872088) into town costs around £4.

Tourist offices The main office is in the town hall on the central Market Square (Easter–Oct Mon–Fri 9.30am–5pm, Sat 9.30am–4pm; Aug also Sun 10am–4pm; Nov–Easter Mon–Sat 10am–4pm; ⓣ01347 776636). There's a second office (daily: Easter–Oct 9.30am–5/6pm, Nov–Easter 10am–4pm; ⓣ01348 874737) on The Parrog on the Goodwick foreshore; it's in the Ocean Lab, an education centre with an exhibition on marine life and detailed information on the coastal path.

ACCCOMMODATION

Cefn-y-Dre ⓣ01348 875663, ⓦcefnydre.co.uk. Just a mile south of town along Hamilton St, there's a relaxed and understated elegance to this lovely country house. Just three rooms, attractive grounds, tasty breakfasts, and superb home-cooked meals (£25; reserve in advance) prepared by wonderful hosts. **£75**

Hamilton Lodge 21–23 Hamilton St ⓣ01348 874797, ⓦhamiltonbackpackers.co.uk. Cosy, very central and well set-up hostel with dorms, doubles and twins, and a free light breakfast. Bedding is provided. Dorm **£16**, double **£32**

EATING AND DRINKING

Café Celf 16 West St ⓦ westwalesartscentre.com. Arty café that's great for a restful cake and espresso or one of their lunch platters (£5–9). High season: Mon–Thurs 10am–4pm, Fri & Sat 10am–4pm & from 7pm; low season Mon–Thurs 10am–3pm, Fri & Sat 10am–3pm & from 7pm.

Royal Oak Market Square ⓣ 01348 872514. Historic pub with real ales and good pub meals (baguettes £4–5, mains £9) served in a separate dining area. Daily 10.30am–11pm; food noon–2pm & 6–9pm.

Ship Inn Lower Town ⓣ 01348 874033. Eccentric, unmissable pub with fine ales and lots of interesting clutter all over the walls and ceiling, including black-and-white photos of the filming of *Under Milk Wood* and *Moby Dick*. Daily noon–11pm.

Newport

Newport (Trefdraeth) is an ancient and proud little town set on a gentle slope leading down to the Nevern estuary. There's little to do except stroll around, but you'd be hard pressed to find a better place to do it. The footpath that runs along the river either side of the bridge is marked as the Pilgrims' Way; follow it eastwards for a delightful riverbank stroll to Nevern, a couple of miles away. Another popular local walk is up to the craggy and magical peak of **Carn Ingli**, the Hill of Angels, behind the town.

Newport's nearest beach, the **Parrog**, is complete with sandy stretches at low tide. On the other side of the estuary is the vast dune-backed **Traethmawr beach**. Newport also makes a good jumping-off point for **Pentre Ifan**, a couple of miles south, with its massive, four-thousand-year-old capstone.

ARRIVAL AND INFORMATION — NEWPORT

By bus Buses stop on Bridge St in the centre of town.

Destinations Cardigan (hourly; 20min); Fishguard (hourly; 15min); Haverfordwest (hourly; 1hr).

Tourist office Long St, just off the main road (Easter–Oct Mon–Sat 9am–5.30pm, plus mid-July to Aug Sun 10am–1.15pm; Nov–Easter Mon & Fri 10am–3pm, Tues, Wed, Thurs & Sat 10.30am–1pm; ⓣ 01239 820912).

ACCOMMODATION

The Globe B&B Upper St Mary St ⓣ 01239 820296, ⓦ theglobepembs.co.uk. About the cheapest around, with shared bathroom and continental breakfast included. **£60**

Morawelon The Parrog ⓣ 01239 820565. Seaside campsite about 300 yards from town, nicely set in pleasant gardens and with its own café overlooking the beach, and coin-op showers. Closed Nov–Feb. **£6–7.50** per person.

YHA Newport hostel Lower St Mary St ⓣ 0870 7706072. Tucked in behind the Eco Centre Wales, this classy conversion of an old school has dorms and a couple of private rooms. Dorm **£14.40**, double **£72**

EATING AND DRINKING

★ **Cnapan** East St ⓣ 01239 820575, ⓦ cnapan.co.uk. Fresh local produce informs the menu at this classic dinner-only restaurant with (comfortable) rooms, where spicy mussel chowder might be followed by guinea fowl with gooseberry and elderflower sauce. £26/32 for two/three courses. Booking essential. Easter–Oct Wed–Mon; call for hours at other times.

Golden Lion East St ⓣ 01239 820321, ⓦ goldenlionpembrokeshire.co.uk. Nice old pub with bare stone walls and timber beams; along with real ales, they serve a superb menu of carefully prepared pub food and fancier restaurant-style dishes, either in the bar or more formally out the back. Food served daily noon–2pm & 6–9pm.

★ **Llys Meddyg** East St ⓣ 01239 820008, ⓦ llysmeddyg.com. You can eat in the Georgian dining room, cellar bar or partly walled kitchen garden in this lovely restaurant with rooms; exquisitely prepared dinners might include local baby crab cakes with papaya mustard then wild bass with a sweet and sour mushroom broth. Lunches are no less appealing. Restaurant Mon–Sat & bank hol Sun 6.30–9pm; garden room Tues–Sun noon–3pm & 6–9pm; bar Mon–Sat.

TOP 5 RESTAURANTS

Cnapan Newport. See above
Cwtch* St Davids. See p.641
Mimosa Bar & Kitchen Cardiff. See p.619
Mint and Mustard Cardiff. See p.619
Slice Swansea. See p.624

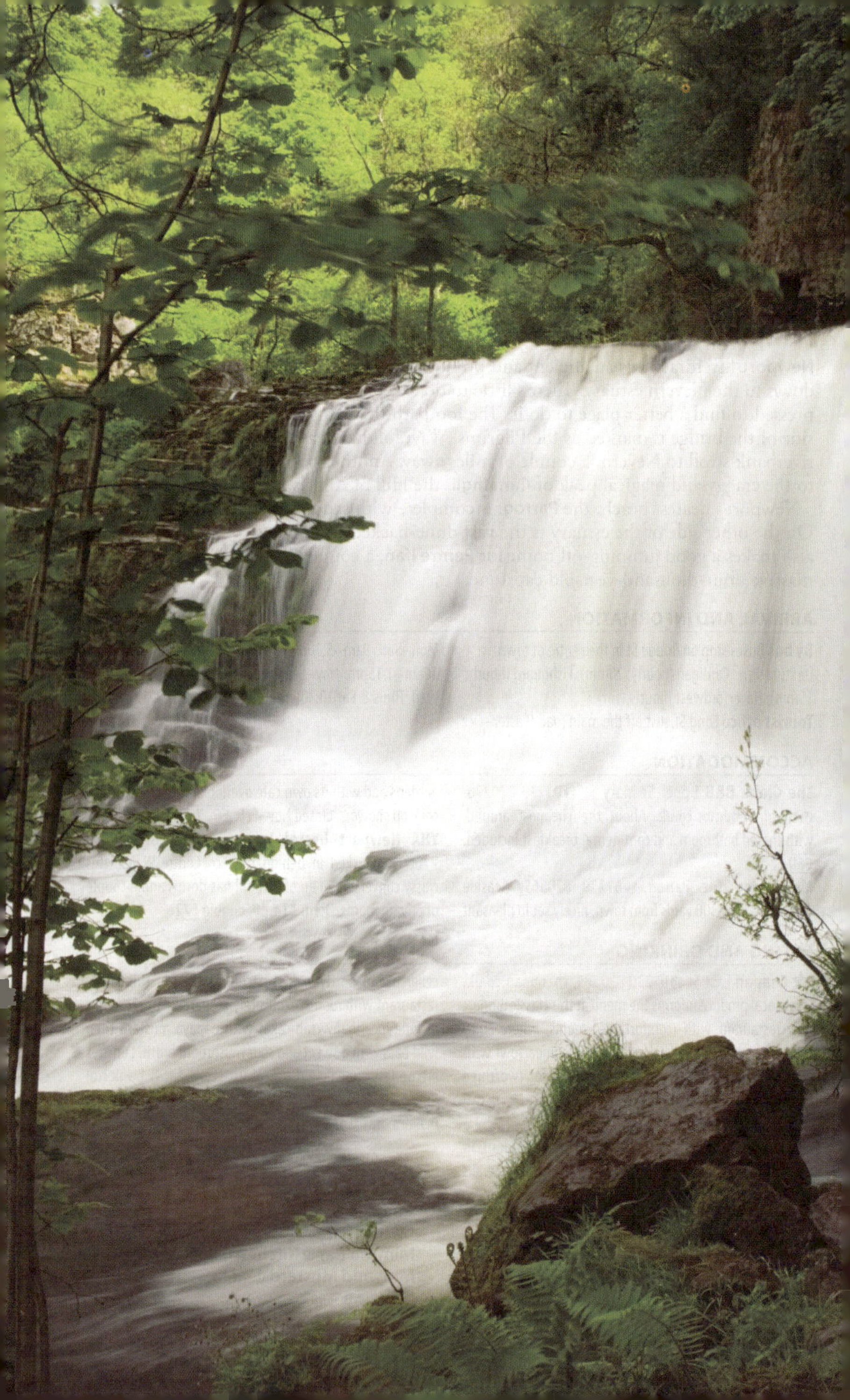

Mid-Wales

650 The Brecon Beacons National Park

657 The Wells towns

659 Elan Valley and around

660 Montgomeryshire

666 The Cambrian coast

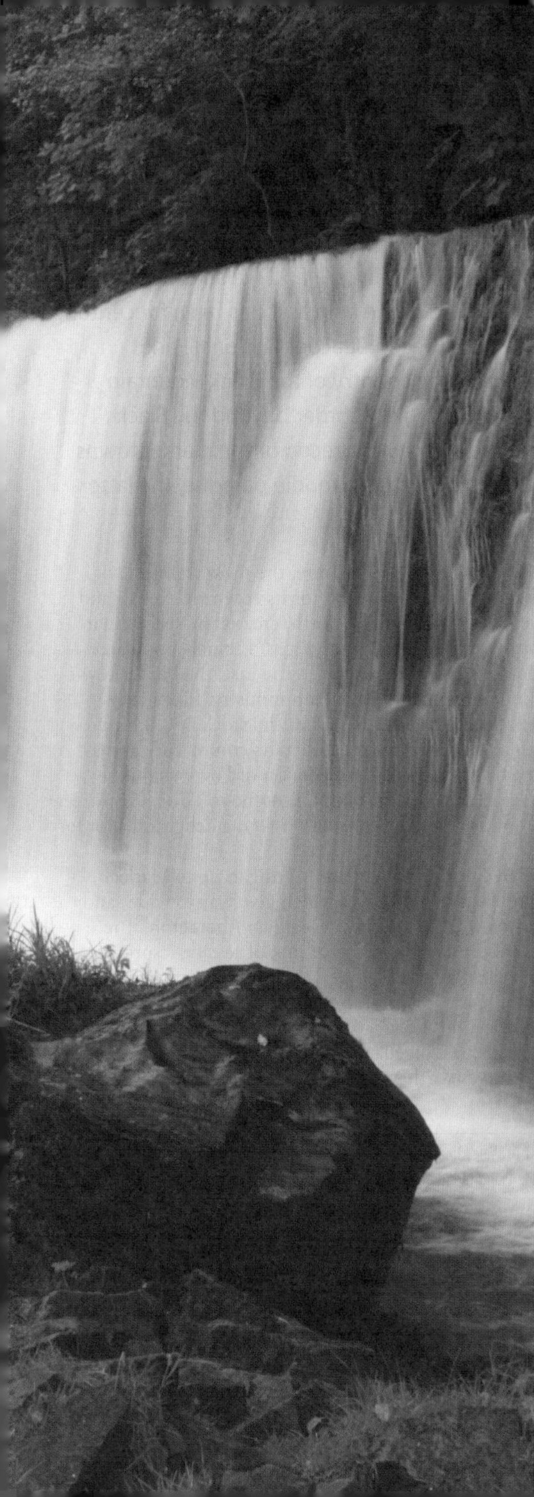

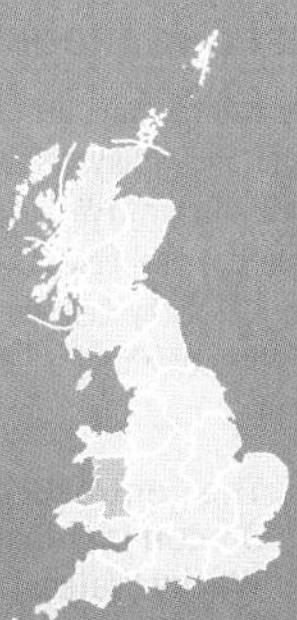

SGWD ISAF CLUN GWYN, BRECON BEACONS

Mid-Wales

Mid-Wales is a huge, beautiful region, crisscrossed by mountain passes, dotted with characterful little towns and never far from water – whether sparkling rivers, great lakes or the sea of the Cambrian coast. This is the least-known part of Wales, and it's here that you'll find Welsh culture at its most natural, folded into the contours of the land as it has been for centuries. By far the most popular attraction is Brecon Beacons National Park, stretching from the dramatic limestone country of the Black Mountain (singular) in the west through to the English border beyond the Black Mountains. The best bases are the tiny city of Brecon or the market towns of Abergavenny and Hay-on-Wye, the former a foodie paradise, the latter a must for bibliophiles.

15

North of the Beacons lie the old spa towns of Radnorshire, the most enjoyable of which are **Llanwrytd Wells**, known throughout the land for its eccentric events, and twee **Llandrindod Wells.** The quiet countryside to the north, crossed by spectacular mountain roads such as the **Abergwesyn Pass** from Llanwrtyd, is barely populated, dotted with ancient churches and introspective villages. In the east, the border town of **Knighton** is the home of the flourishing **Offa's Dyke Path** industry. Like many country towns in Mid-Wales, beautiful **Llanidloes** has a healthy stock of old hippies among its population, contributing to a thriving arts and crafts community and a relaxed atmosphere. **Montgomeryshire** is the northern portion of Powys, similarly underpopulated and remote. Its largest town, **Welshpool**, is home to Powis Castle, one of the country's finest fortresses, and is also close to **Lake Vyrnwy**, a delightful spot for rambling and nature watching.

The enduringly popular **Cambrian coast** stretches from Cardigan up to Harlech, starting off with cliff-top paths and small sandy coves which give way to wide sandy beaches around higgledy-piggledy **New Quay** and neat Georgian **Aberaeron**. The beguiling "capital" of Mid-Wales, **Aberystwyth**, is a great mix of seaside resort, university city and market town backed by the Vale of Rheidol Railway to **Devil's Bridge**. Further north, **Machynlleth** revels in beaches, mountains and the showpiece **Centre for Alternative Technology**. Beyond the great mountain massif of **Cadair Idris**, the beautiful **Mawddach Estuary** leads to Dolgellau, a base for mountain biking in **Coed-y-Brenin** and the first of the huge North Wales castles at **Harlech**.

GETTING AROUND MID-WALES

By train Services are restricted to the Heart of Wales line from Shrewsbury to Swansea via Knighton, Llandrindod Wells, Llanwrtyd Wells and smaller stops in between; and the Cambrian line, from Shrewsbury to Machynlleth via Welshpool. At Machynlleth, the line splits, with one heading south to Aberystwyth, the other going north along the coast to Llŷn.

By bus In the absence of a comprehensive train service, buses plug virtually all of the gaps, though you'll find just a few daily services between some towns, and sometimes none at all on Sundays. The #X50 and #X32, which jointly cover the coast between Cardigan and Dolgellau, are useful.

The Central Beacons near Brecon p.651
Brecon jazz festival p.652
Wacky Wales: Llanwrtyd Wells p.657
The Abergwesyn Pass p.658
Offa's Dyke p.660
Owain Glyndŵr, Welsh hero p.672
Walks around Dolgellau p.675

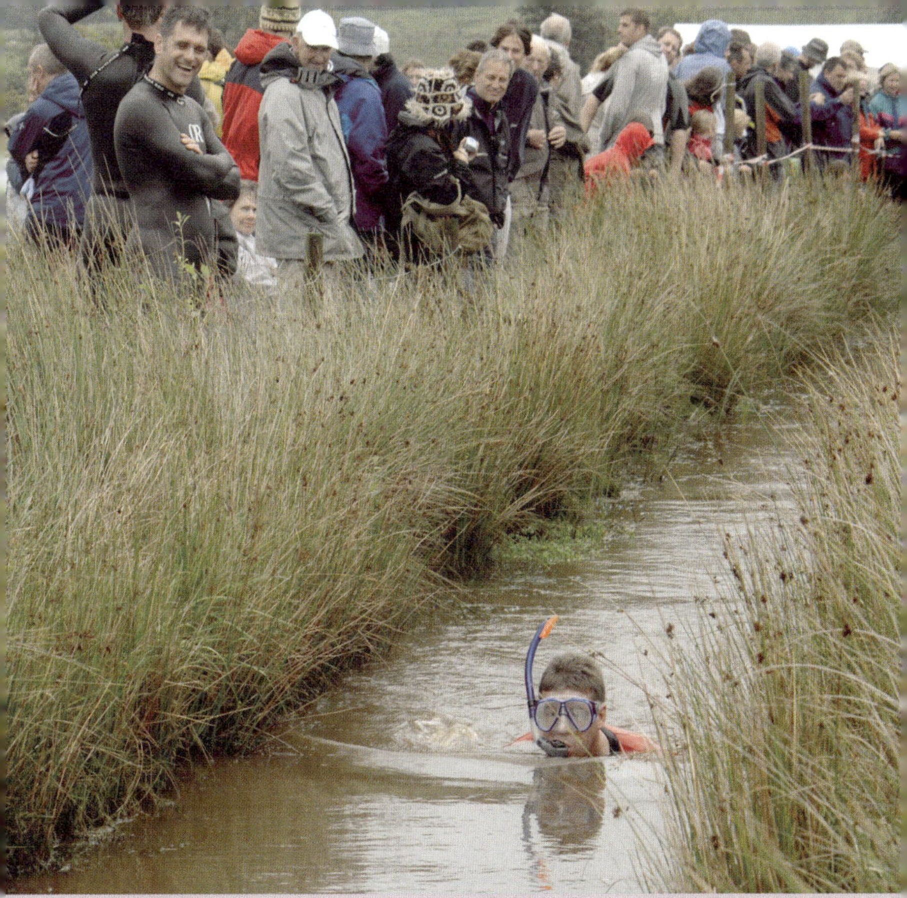

BOG SNORKELLING, LLANWRYTD WELLS

Highlights

❶ **Brecon Beacons National Park** Trek to your heart's content amongst these wild, rambling moors, with dozens of thundering waterfalls. **See pp.650–654**

❷ **Abergavenny Food** Some of Britain's finest restaurants, along with a lip-smacking food festival. **See pp.654–655**

❸ **Hay-on Wye** Britain's capital of books, spilling over with bookshops and hosting the year's biggest literary jamboree. **See p.656**

❹ **Llanwrytd Wells** Bizarre events galore, notably the Man versus Horse Marathon, the World Bog Snorkelling Championships and the Real Ale Wobble. **See p.657**

❺ **New Quay** Follow Dylan Thomas's footsteps through the salty seaside town that inspired *Under Milk Wood*. **See p.667**

❻ **Aberaeron** Even if you're not in town for Aberaeron's Seafood Festival, stroll around its colourful Georgian harbour lined by great places to sleep and eat. **See p.668**

❼ **Aberystwyth** A lively, seaside university town, steeped in Welsh culture. **See p.669**

❽ **Bwlch Nant yr Arian** Visit mid-afternoon to see dozens of red kites squabbling over ten kilos of beef and lamb; bring a mountain bike and combine that with some of the best singletrack in Wales. **See p.672**

HIGHLIGHTS ARE MARKED ON THE MAP ON PP.648–649

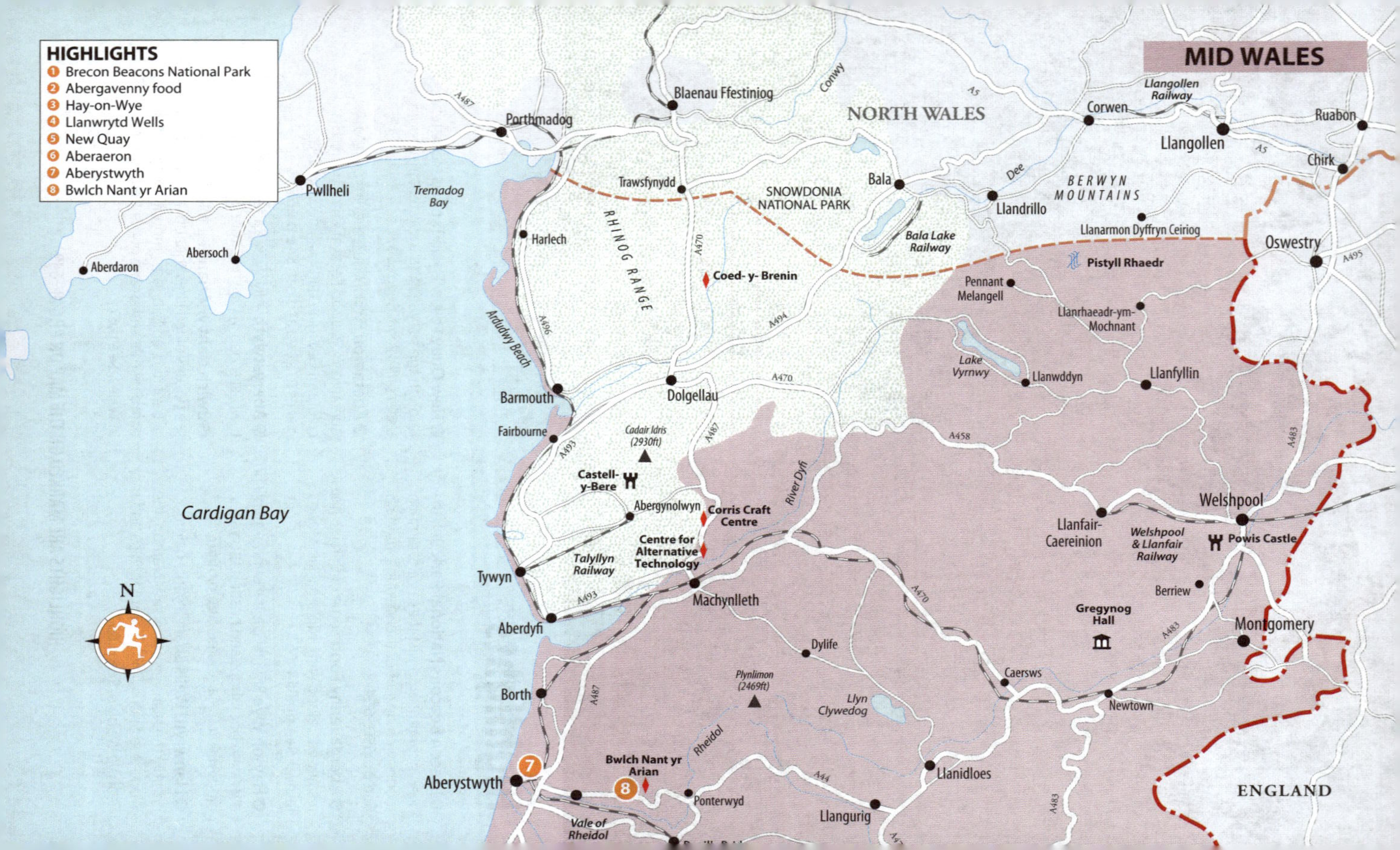

MID WALES
HIGHLIGHTS
1 Brecon Beacons National Park
2 Abergavenny food
3 Hay-on-Wye
4 Llanwrytd Wells
5 New Quay
6 Aberaeron
7 Aberystwyth
8 Bwlch Nant yr Arian
NORTH WALES
SNOWDONIA NATIONAL PARK
BERWYN MOUNTAINS
RHINOG RANGE
ENGLAND
Cardigan Bay
Tremadog Bay
Ardudwy Beach
Blaenau Ffestiniog
Porthmadog
Pwllheli
Abersoch
Aberdaron
Harlech
Trawsfynydd
Bala
Bala Lake Railway
Llandrillo
Corwen
Llangollen Railway
Llangollen
Ruabon
Chirk
Oswestry
Llanarmon Dyffryn Ceiriog
Pistyll Rhaedr
Pennant Melangell
Llanrhaeadr-ym-Mochnant
Lake Vyrnwy
Llanwddyn
Llanfyllin
Coed- y- Brenin
Dolgellau
Barmouth
Fairbourne
Cadair Idris (2930ft)
Castell-y-Bere
Abergynolwyn
Corris Craft Centre
Centre for Alternative Technology
Talyllyn Railway
Tywyn
Aberdyfi
Machynlleth
River Dyfi
Dylife
Plynlimon (2469ft)
Llyn Clywedog
Rheidol
Borth
Aberystwyth
Bwlch Nant yr Arian
Ponterwyd
Vale of Rheidol
Llangurig
Llanidloes
Caersws
Newtown
Gregynog Hall
Berriew
Llanfair-Caereinion
Welshpool & Llanfair Railway
Welshpool
Powis Castle
Montgomery
Conwy
Dee
N
A487
A5
A470
A494
A496
A493
A458
A483
A495
A44

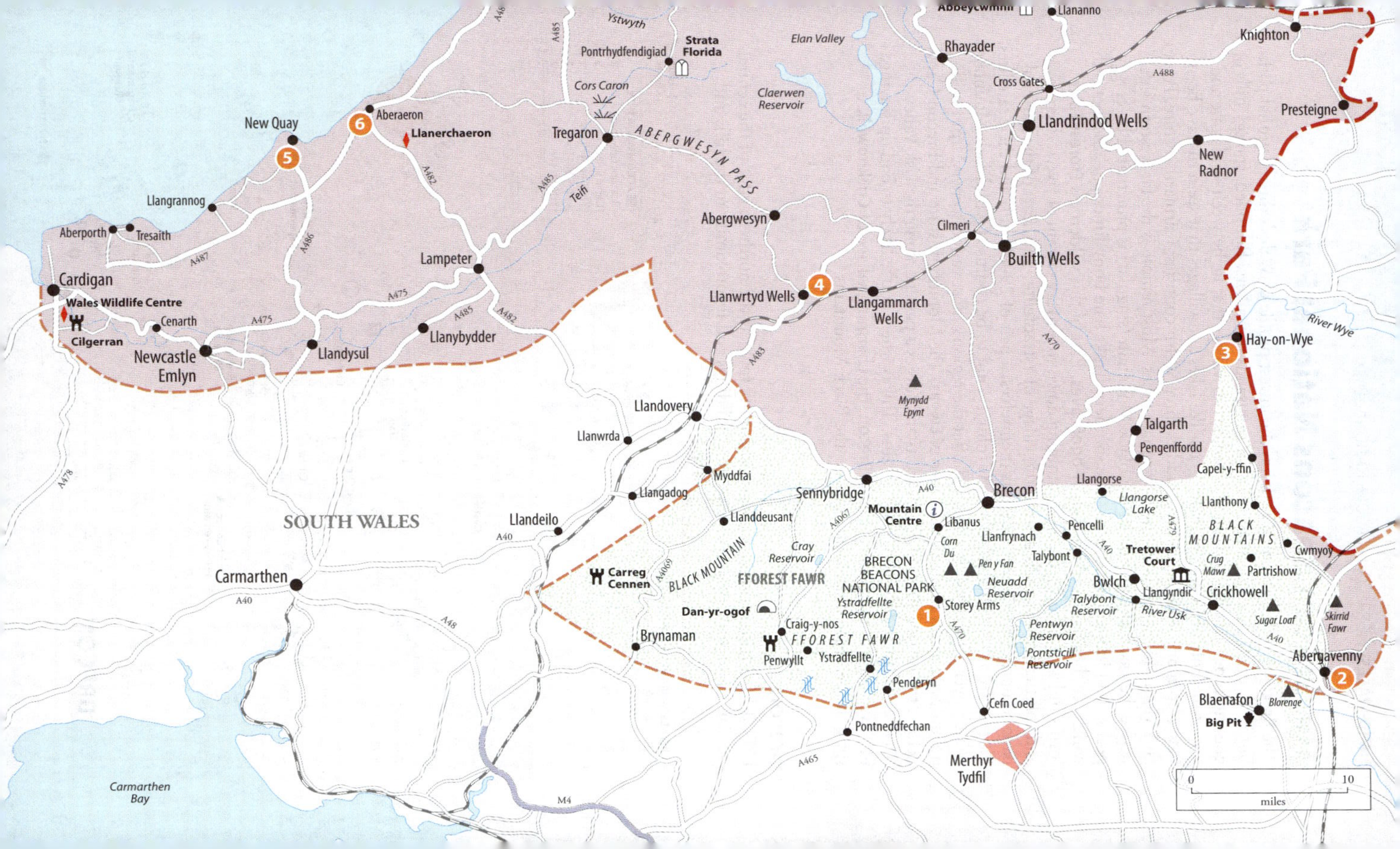

Llananno
Ystwyth
Strata Florida
Pontrhydfendigiad
Elan Valley
Rhayader
Knighton
Cross Gates
A488
Cors Caron
Claerwen Reservoir
Presteigne
Llandrindod Wells
New Quay
Aberaeron
Llanerchaeron
Tregaron
ABERGWESYN PASS
New Radnor
Llangrannog
A482
A485
Teifi
Aberporth
Tresaith
A486
Abergwesyn
Cilmeri
A487
Lampeter
Builth Wells
Cardigan
A475
Wales Wildlife Centre
Llanwrtyd Wells
Llangammarch Wells
Cenarth
A485
A482
River Wye
Hay-on-Wye
Cilgerran
Newcastle Emlyn
Llandysul
Llanybydder
A483
A470
Mynydd Epynt
Llandovery
Talgarth
Llanwrda
Pengenffordd
Capel-y-ffin
A478
Myddfai
Llangorse
Llangadog
Sennybridge
A40
Brecon
Llangorse Lake
Llanthony
SOUTH WALES
Llandeilo
Llanddeusant
Mountain Centre
Libanus
Pencelli
A4067
A479
BLACK MOUNTAINS
A40
Cray Reservoir
Corn Du
Llanfrynach
Talybont
Tretower Court
Cwmyoy
BRECON BEACONS NATIONAL PARK
Pen y Fan
Crug Mawr
Partrishow
Carreg Cennen
A4069
BLACK MOUNTAIN
FFOREST FAWR
Neuadd Reservoir
Bwlch
Carmarthen
A40
Ystradfellte Reservoir
Storey Arms
Talybont Reservoir
Llangynidr
Crickhowell
Dan-yr-ogof
River Usk
Sugar Loaf
Skirrid Fawr
A48
Craig-y-nos
A470
Pentwyn Reservoir
Brynaman
FFOREST FAWR
A40
Penwyllt
Ystradfellte
Pontsticill Reservoir
Abergavenny
Penderyn
Blaenafon
Blorenge
Cefn Coed
Big Pit
Pontneddfechan
A465
Merthyr Tydfil
0
10
miles
Carmarthen Bay
M4

The Brecon Beacons National Park

The **Brecon Beacons National Park** has the lowest profile of Wales's three national parks, but it is nonetheless the destination of thousands of walkers. Rounded, spongy hills of grass and rock tumble and climb around river valleys that lie between sandstone and limestone uplands, peppered with glass-like lakes and villages that seem to have been hewn from one rock. The park straddles three Welsh counties: Carmarthenshire, Powys and Monmouthshire, covering 520 square miles. Most remote is the far western side, where the vast, open terrain of the Black Mountain (singular) is punctuated by craggy peaks and hidden upland lakes. The southern flanks bare bony limestone ribs, beneath which are the chasms of the **Dan-yr-ogof caves**. East of this wilderness **Fforest Fawr** forms miles of tufted moorland tumbling down to a rocky terrain of rivers, deep caves and spluttering waterfalls around the village of **Ystradfellte**. The heart of the national park comprises the **Brecon Beacons** themselves, a pair of 2900ft hills and their satellites. East of Brecon, the **Black Mountains** (plural – not to be confused with Black Mountain) stretch over the English border, and offer the region's most varied scenery, from rolling upland wilderness to the gentler **Vale of Ewyas**. The Monmouthshire and Brecon Canal defines the eastern limit of the Beacons and forges a passage along the Usk Valley between them and the Black Mountains. This is where you're likely to end up staying, in towns such as the county seat of **Brecon**, the charming village of **Crickhowell**, or sprightly **Abergavenny**, nestled below the Black Mountains.

Brecon

BRECON (Aberhonddu) is a handsome county town at the northern edge of the central Beacons. The proliferation of Georgian buildings and its proximity to the hills and

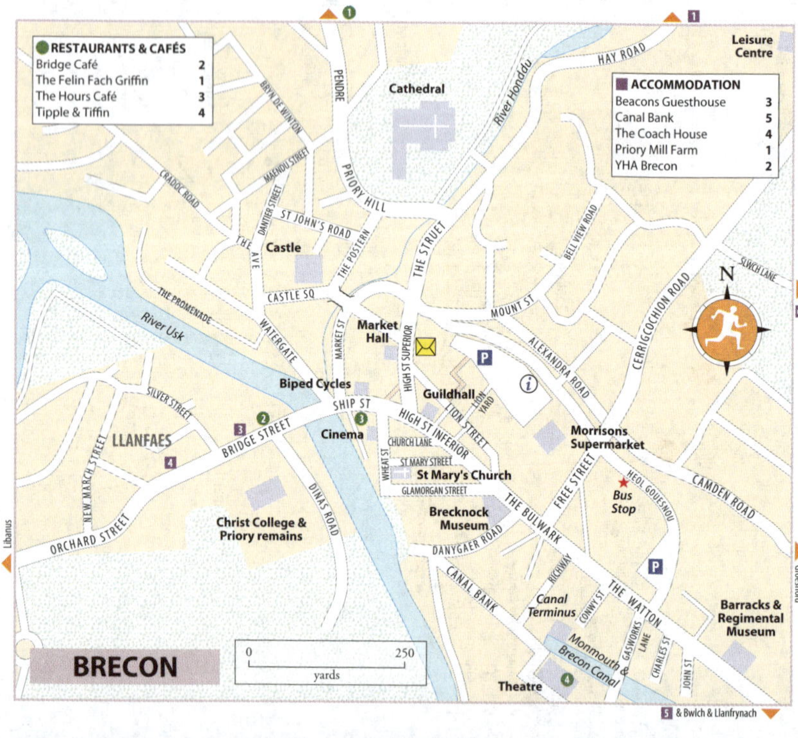

THE CENTRAL BEACONS NEAR BRECON

Popular for walking and pony trekking, the central **Brecon Beacons**, grouped around the two highest peaks in the national park, are easily accessible from Brecon, which lies just six miles to the north. The panorama fans out from the **Brecon Beacons Mountain Centre** (daily: March–June & Sept–Oct 9.30am–5pm; July & Aug 9.30am–5.30pm; Nov–Feb 9.30am–4.30pm; ⓣ01874 623366, ⓦbreconbeacons.org), on a windy ridge just off the A470 turn-off at Libanus, six miles southwest of Brecon. As well as a fantastic café, there are displays on the area and a well-stocked shop. **Pen y Fan** (2907ft) is the highest peak in the Beacons. Together with **Corn Du** (2863ft), half a mile to the west, they form the most popular ascents in the park.

lakes of the national park make it a popular stopping-off place and a good base for day-walks in the well-waymarked hills to the south.

Regimental Museum

The Watton • Easter–Sept Mon–Fri 10am–5pm, Sat 10am–4pm, plus certain Sun; Oct–March Mon–Fri 10am–5pm • £4 • ⓣ01874 613310, ⓦrrw.org.uk

Midway along the Watton is the foreboding frontage of the South Wales Borderers' **barracks**, which is also home to its **Regimental Museum**, packed with mementos from the regiment's three-hundred-year existence. As well as an extraordinary stash of guns and medals, there's comprehensive coverage of campaigns in Burma, the Napoleonic and Boer Wars, both World Wars and the ongoing mission in Afghanistan. There's even a piece of the Berlin Wall.

Brecon Cathedral

Priory Hill • ⓣ01874 623857, ⓦbreconcathedral.org.uk

From the town centre crossroads, High Street Superior goes north, becoming The Struet, running alongside the rushing waters of the Honddu. Off to the left, a footpath climbs up to the **cathedral**, whose lofty interior, framed by a magnificent timber roof, is graced with a few Norman features from the eleventh century, including a hulking font. More impressive is the **Cresset Stone,** a concrete boulder indented with thirty scoops in which to place oil or wax candles. The mid-sixteenth-century **Games Monument**, in the southern aisle, is made of oak and depicts a woman whose identity remains uncertain with hands clasped in prayer but whose arms and nose appear to have been unceremoniously hacked off.

ARRIVAL AND INFORMATION — BRECON

By bus Buses stop above the car park on Heol Gouesnou.

Destinations Abergavenny (hourly; 40min–1hr); Cardiff (6 daily; 1hr 30min); Craig-y-nos/Dan-yr-ogof (6 daily; 30min); Crickhowell (hourly 25–45min); Hay-on-Wye (7 daily; 45min); Libanus (every 30min–1hr; 20min); Llandrindod Wells (Mon–Sat 7 daily, 1hr); Merthyr Tydfil (every 30min–1hr; 40min).

Tourist office In the car park off Lion St (April–Oct Mon–Sat 9.30am–5.15pm, Sun 10am–4pm; Nov–March daily 10am–4pm; ⓣ01874 622485, ⓦbreconbeacons.org); its vast stock of material includes a good range of walking maps for the Brecons.

ACCOMMODATION

Beacons Guesthouse 16 Bridge St, Llanfaes ⓣ01874 623339, ⓦthebreconbeacons.co.uk. Rambling converted townhouse concealing a number of differently coloured rooms (some with shared showers and one with a four-poster), all leading off a central spiral staircase. Pleasant guest lounge and a dinky cellar bar with just two tables. **£58**

★ **Canal Bank** Ty Gardd ⓣ01874 623464, ⓦaccommodation-breconbeacons.co.uk. Picturesquely pitched right on the canal just five minutes' walk from town, this wonderful three-room guesthouse comes with lots of super home comforts, genial hospitality and a superb breakfast. **£90**

The Coach House 12/13 Orchard St, Llanfaes ⓣ01874 620043, ⓦcoachhousebrecon.com. High-class and very hospitable guesthouse with rooms painted in smooth creams and browns and furnished with designer accessories. Great Welsh breakfasts, including vegetarian options. **£70**

Priory Mill Farm Hay Rd ⓣ01874 611609, ⓦpriorymillfarm.co.uk. Lovely, low-key riverside campsite, with wooden cabins for showers and trays for log fires. It's on the

BRECON JAZZ FESTIVAL

Held over the second or third weekend of August, the **Brecon Jazz Festival** (@hayfestival.com/breconjazz) is one of Britain's most prestigious music gatherings. The line-up is invariably outstanding, with artists of the calibre of Femi Kuti, Zoe Rahman and the Matthew Herbert Big Band playing venues as diverse as Brecon Cathedral, Christ's College and the Market Hall. Tickets typically cost £8–15.

northern edge of town, reached by a 10min walk along the riverbank. Closed Nov–Feb. £7 per pitch.

YHA Brecon Groesfford, just over 2 miles east of Brecon ⊕0870 770 5718 or 0845 371 9506, @yha.org.uk. Large Victorian farmhouse close to Brecon, reached via the path (Slwch Lane) from Cerrigcochion Rd in town or a mile from bus stops at either Cefn Brynich lock (Brecon–Abergavenny buses) or Troedyrharn Farm (Brecon–Hereford buses). Dorm £16.40, double £48

EATING

15

Bridge Café 7 Bridge St ⊕01874 622024, @bridgecafe.co.uk. Good-looking café/bistro, by the bridge, featuring a homespun interior with oak flooring, kitchen-style tables and chairs, and fireside sofas. The menu changes monthly but expect a range of dishes like Welsh beef goulash and Catalan fish stew. Mains £11. Shame about the limited opening hours. Thurs–Sat 6.30–11pm, Sun 9–11am. Closed Nov–Feb.

★ **The Felin Fach Griffin** Felinfach, 3 miles northwest of town on the A470 ⊕01874 620111, @eatdrinksleep.ltd.uk. High-end gastropub that's well worth a visit for its superb modern Welsh cuisine; the meat is sourced locally (Bwlch venison with artichoke) and the fish is delivered from Cornwall (monkfish tail with chicory). Mains £15–20. Daily 11.30am–11pm.

The Hours Café 15 Ship St ⊕01874 622800. Cheerful daytime café-cum-bookshop with sloping floors and black timber beams, where you can enjoy warm salads and sandwiches, hearty soups, cakes and a good range of free-trade coffees. Tues–Sat 10am–5pm.

★ **Tipple & Tiffin** Theatr Brycheiniog, Canal Wharf ⊕01874 611866, @brycheiniog.co.uk/tipple.html. A fetching waterside setting and easy-going atmosphere mark this place out as Brecon's most inviting restaurant; tapas-style dishes designed for sharing, along with a few more substantial options chalked up daily on a blackboard. Tues–Sat 10am–10pm, Sun noon–4pm.

The Fforest Fawr

Covering a vast expanse west of the central Brecon Beacons, the **Fforest Fawr** (Great Forest) seems something of a misnomer for an area of largely unforested sandstone hills dropping down to a porous limestone belt in the south. The name, however, refers to its former status as a hunting area. The hills rise up to the south of the A40, west of Brecon, with the dramatic A4067 defining the western side of the range and the A470 dividing it from the central Beacons.

Ystradfellte and around

In the heart of the range, a twisting mountain road crosses a bleak plateau and descends into one of Britain's classic limestone landscapes. The hamlet of **YSTRADFELLTE** is hugely popular for its walks over great pavements of bone-white rock next to cradling potholes, disappearing rivers and crashing **waterfalls**. At **Sgwd Clun Gwyn** (White Meadow Fall), the river crashes 50ft over two large, angular steps of rock before hurtling down the course for a few hundred yards to two more falls – the impressive **Sgwd Isaf Clun Gwyn** (Lower White Meadow Fall) and, around the wooded corner, the **Sgwd y Pannwr** (Fall of the Fuller). A little further along the Hepste is **Sgwd yr Eira** (Fall of Snow), whose rock below the main tumble has eroded, allowing access behind a dramatic 20ft curtain of water.

Dan-yr-ogof Showcaves

April–Oct daily 10am–3pm • £13.50 • ⊕01639 730284, @showcaves.co.uk

Six miles of upland forest and grass-covered mountains lie between Ystradfellte and the **Dan-yr-ogof Showcaves** to the west. Discovered in 1912, they are claimed to form the largest system of subterranean caverns in northern Europe. The path leads you into the **Dan-yr-ogof** showcave, framed by stalactites and frothy limestone deposits, from where you'll be steered around a circular route of about a mile and a half. Back outside, you pass a recreated and rather downbeat Iron Age "village" to get to the **Cathedral Cave**, an impressive 150ft-long, 70ft-high cavern. Reached via a precarious path behind the tacky dinosaur park, the final viewable cavern, **Bone Cave** was inhabited by prehistoric tribes.

INFORMATION **THE FFOREST FAWR**

The Waterfalls Centre Pontneddfechan, a couple of miles south of Ystradfellte (Easter–Sept daily 9.30am–5pm (closed 1–1.30pm), Oct–Easter Sat & Sun 9.30am–3pm; ⓣ01639 721795) can provide lots of good information on walks to the many falls.

The Black Mountains

The easternmost section of the national park centres on the **Black Mountains**, far quieter than the central belt of the Brecon Beacons and skirted by the wide valley of the River Usk to the south and the Wye to the north. The only exception to the Black Mountains' unremitting sandstone is an isolated outcrop of limestone, long divorced from the southern belt, that peaks north of Crickhowell at Pen Cerrig-calch (2302ft). The Black Mountains have the feel of a landscape only partly tamed by human habitation: tiny villages, isolated churches and delightful lanes are folded into an undulating green landscape that levels out to the south around the village of **Crickhowell**.

15

Crickhowell

Compact **CRICKHOWELL** (Crug Hywel) lies on the northern bank of the wide and shallow Usk. Apart from a grand seventeenth-century **bridge**, with thirteen arches visible from the eastern end and only twelve from the west, spawning many a local myth, there's not much to see in town. That said, it is a hugely popular destination for walkers, especially in March when the annual **Walking Festival** (ⓦcrickhowellfestival.com) takes place here; it's also the setting for the country's premier music gathering, the **Green Man Festival** (ⓦgreenman.net).

Table Mountain (1481ft) provides a spectacular northern backdrop, topped by the remains of the 2500-year-old hill fort (*crug*) of Hywel, accessed on a path past The Wern, off Llanbedr Road. Many walkers follow a route north from Table Mountain, climbing two miles up to the plateau-topped limestone hump of **Pen Cerrig-calch** (2302ft) and on to Pen Allt-mawr from where a circular route can be completed.

ARRIVAL AND INFORMATION **CRICKHOWELL**

By bus Crickhowell is served by Regular Brecon–Abergavenny buses.

Tourist office The Crickhowell Resource and Information Centre on Beaufort St (daily 10am–5pm; ⓣ01873 811970, ⓦcrickhowellinfo.org.uk) also has a café, internet (£1.50/30min) and a local art gallery.

ACCOMMODATION AND EATING

Bear Hotel Beaufort St ⓣ01873 810408, ⓦbearhotel.co.uk. A grand old coaching inn whose architectural quirks have lent themselves to some highly idiosyncratic rooms; those in the hotel itself possess more character, while those in the old courtyard stables are a touch more polished. **£92**

Bridge End Bridge St ⓣ01873 810338, ⓦthebridgeendinn.com. Comprising part of the town's former toll house, this is a truly old-fashioned pub, with flagstone flooring, a stone fireplace and brass and copper pots hanging off the walls and ceilings. Daily 11am–11.30pm.

★ **Nantyffin Cider Mill** Brecon Rd ⓣ01873 810775, ⓦcidermill.co.uk. In a great stone barn a mile or so along the A40 towards Brecon, the old mill (with the cider press still intact) is now a tip-top restaurant serving such dishes as chicken liver and brandy parfait and home-smoked fish pie with spinach. There's a serious wine list too. Mains £15–18. Tues–Sat noon–3pm & 6–11pm, Sun noon–3pm.

Riverside Caravan Park New Rd ⓣ01873 810397, ⓦriversidecaravanscrickhowell.co.uk. A level, nicely manicured site with decent facilities. Over-18s only. Closed Nov–Feb. £6 per tent.

★ **Tt Gwyn** Brecon Rd ⓣ01873 811625, ⓦtygwyn.com. Handsome eighteenth-century house a 5min walk north of town, offering three warm and sunny rooms, each one on the theme of a Welsh writer (Dylan, Cordell, Vaughan) and stocked accordingly. Breakfast is taken in the delightful conservatory dining room. £65

Abergavenny and around

Flanking the Brecon Beacons National Park, **ABERGAVENNY** (Y Fenni), seven miles southeast of Crickhowell, is a busy and breezy market town which people flock to primarily for its outstanding cuisine – this reaches its zenith during the September **Food Festival**. The town is also a useful base for walkers bound for the local mountains: **Sugar Loaf**, **the Blorenge**, and the legend-infused **Skirrid Mountain** (Ysgyryd Fawr). Stretching north from town, the **Vale of Ewyas** runs along the foot of the Black Mountains, where the astounding churches at Partrishow and Cwmyoy are lost in rural isolation.

Abergavenny also makes a good base for visiting Monmouthshire's "Three Castles" (see p.606), set in the pastoral border country to the east.

The castle and town museum

Castle St • **Museum** March–Oct Mon–Sat 11am–1pm & 2–5pm, Sun 2–5pm; Nov–Feb Mon–Sat 11am–1pm & 2–4pm • Free • ⓣ01873 854282, ⓦabergavennymuseum.co.uk

From the train station, Monmouth Road rises gently, eventually becoming High Street, off which you'll find the fragmented remains of the medieval **castle**. Entrance is through the sturdy, though now roofless, gatehouse, to the right of which stands an extensive portion of the curtain wall. The old Victorian keep now houses the **town museum**, which displays ephemera from Abergavenny's history and a reconstruction of an old grocery shop. Glorious views aside, the grounds are a lovely spot for a picnic.

Church of St Mary

Monk St

Abergavenny's **Church of St Mary** contains some superb detail, not least the **Jesse Tree**, one of the finest late medieval sculptures in Britain. Tombs here span the entire medieval period, including those of Sir William ap Thomas, founder of Raglan Castle, and Dr David Lewis (died 1584), the first Principal of Jesus College, as well as effigies of members of the notorious de Braose family.

Tithe Barn

Monk St • Mon–Sat 10am–4pm • Free • ⓣ01873 858787

The wonderfully restored **Tithe Barn**, next door to the Church of St Mary, holds an exhibition on the town's history, though this is overshadowed by the Abergavenny Tapestry, a large, vibrant cloth stitched by more than fifty volunteers; it took four years and was completed just in time for the millennium. There's a fine café here, too.

ARRIVAL AND INFORMATION — ABERGAVENNY

By train The station is a 5min walk southeast of town on Station Rd.

Destinations Cardiff (every 30min–1hr; 45min); Hereford (every 45–60min; 25min); Newport (every 30min–1hr; 30min).

By bus The bus station, at the bottom of Cross St, is even closer to the centre than the train terminus.

Destinations Brecon (hourly; 40min–1hr); Cardiff (hourly; 2hr); Clydach (every 30min; 40min); Crickhowell (hourly; 15min); Llanfihangel Crucorney (7 daily; 15min); Merthyr Tydfil (hourly; 1hr 30min); Monmouth (6 daily; 45min); Raglan (6 daily; 20min).

Tourist office The TIC and the Brecon Beacons National Park office are in the same building, next to the bus station (daily: April–Oct 10am–5pm; Nov–March 10am–4pm; ⓣ01873 857588, ⓦvisitabergavenny.co.uk).

Bike rental Bike hire is available at Hopyard Cycles in Govilon, a couple of miles west of town (ⓣ01873 830219, ⓦhopyardcycles.co.uk; from £15/day); they can deliver bikes throughout the area.

ACCOMMODATION

Angel Hotel 15 Cross St ⓣ01873 857121, ⓦangelhotelabergavenny.com. Occupying an old coaching inn, Abergavenny's premier central hotel is a warren of corridors with a range of very classy rooms, most of which possess big comfy beds and large bathrooms with posh toiletries. £96

Black Sheep Backpackers 24 Station Rd ⓣ01873 859125, ⓦblacksheepbackpackers.com. A few paces down from the station, this converted railway hotel has twin, quad and dorm rooms, all with separate shower facilities. Continental breakfast included. Dorm £16, double £39

★ **The Guest House** 2 Oxford St ⓣ01873 854823, ⓦtheguesthouseabergavenny.co.uk. Fun, popular guesthouse whose six sunny rooms come with tea, coffee and water, plus a stack of books. Guest lounge with Sky Sports and a Wii console, a resident parrot in the dining room, and a backyard petting area with aviary. No credit cards. £70

Pyscodlyn Farm Llanwenarth Citra, 2 miles west of town off the A40 ⓣ01873 853271, ⓦpyscodlyncaravanpark.com. Primarily a caravan site, but with one grassy, sheltered field for campers. They sell day fishing licences. All Brecon and Crickhowell buses pass by. £8 per pitch.

EATING AND DRINKING

★ **The Foxhunter** Nantyderry, 6.6 miles southeast of Abergavenny ⓣ01873 881101, ⓦthefoxhunter.com. Award-winning modern British cuisine by TV chef Matt Tebbutt, served in a lovingly restored former stationmaster's house. Poached loin of rabbit with black pudding is typical of the terrific food on offer; there's also a fantastic wild food menu (£35), and you can partake in foraging trips. Mains £16–20. Tues–Sat noon–3pm & 7–11pm.

Greyhound Vaults Market St ⓣ01873 858549. Don't be fooled by the dull, pub-like exterior and earthy interior – this place serves a wide range of tasty, moderately priced Welsh and English specialities, such as Welsh Black steak with leeks, and topside of beef with Yorkshire pudding. Mains £10–15. Tues–Thurs & Sun lunch only, Fri & Sat lunch & dinner.

★ **The Hardwick** Old Raglan Rd, 2 miles east of town ⓣ01873 854220, ⓦthehardwick.co.uk. Headed up by TV chef Stephen Terry, this fabulous-looking pub offers a fantastic choice of dishes such as pan-fried sea bass with tomato and potato gnocchi and wild sea spinach. It's pricey, but well worth it. Mains £17–25. Daily noon–3pm & 6.30–10pm.

Hen and Chickens Flannel St, off High St ⓣ01873 853613. Timeless, traditional pub popular with locals and visitors alike, serving some of the best beer in town and putting on regular live music, including jazz most Sunday evenings. Daily 10.30am–11pm.

Kings Arms 29 Neville St ⓣ01873 855074. Handsome pub combining the old (stone fireplace and wonderful curving beams on the low ceiling) and the new (neat modern furnishings) to great effect. Good beer and some very creditable food, too. Daily 11am–11pm, Fri & Sat till 1am.

Trading Post 14 Neville St ⓣ01873 855448. Formerly the eighteenth-century *Cow Inn* – cast your eyes up to the row of cow's heads on the front of the building – this is now a classy coffee house and bistro, a great place to read the paper over a cappuccino or tucking into inexpensive mains ranging from tortillas to tortellini. Mon–Sat 9am–5pm.

15

The Vale of Ewyas

The main A465 Hereford road leads six miles north out of Abergavenny to Llanfihangel Crucorney, where the B4423 diverges off to the north into the enchanting **Vale of Ewyas** along the banks of the Honddu River. In Llanfihangel Crucorney, the reputedly haunted **Skirrid Inn** was first mentioned in 1110 and is thus thought to be the oldest pub in Wales. It's said that some 180 people were hanged here during the seventeenth century; you can still see the beam that bears the scorch marks of the rope. It's an atmospheric spot for a drink.

Llanthony Priory

Daily 10am–4pm • CADW • Free

Four miles from Llanfihangel Crucorney stand the wide-open ruins of **Llanthony Priory**. The priory was founded in around 1100 by the Norman knight William de Lacy, who, it is said, was so captivated by the spiritual beauty of the site that he renounced worldly living and founded a hermitage, attracting like-minded recluses and forming Wales's first Augustinian priory. The roofless church, with its pointed transitional arches and squat tower, was constructed in the latter half of the twelfth century and retains a real sense of spirituality and peace.

15

Hay-on-Wye

Straddling the Anglo-Welsh border some twenty miles west of Hereford, the hilly little town of **HAY-ON-WYE** has an attractive riverside **setting** and narrow, winding streets lined with an engaging assortment of old stone houses, but is known to most people for one thing – **books**. Hay saw its first bookshop open in 1961; today just about every inch of the town is given over to the trade, including the old cinema and the ramshackle stone castle. The prestigious **Hay Festival of literature and the arts** (ⓦhayfestival.com), is held over ten days at the end of May, when London's literary world decamps here en masse.

ARRIVAL AND INFORMATION — HAY-ON-WYE

By bus Buses stop on Oxford Rd, just along from the tourist office. Destinations include Hereford (4 daily; 1hr).

Tourist office In the craft centre on Oxford Rd, just along from the bus stop (daily: Easter–Oct 10am–5pm, closed 1–2pm Tues, Thurs & Sun; Nov–Easter 11am–1pm & 2–4pm; ⓣ01497 820144, ⓦhay-on-wye.co.uk). They publish a useful free booklet detailing the town's bookshops, galleries, restaurants and bars.

ACCOMMODATION

Hay has lots of accommodation, though prices are a little higher here than in places nearby, and there are no hostels. Just about everywhere gets booked up months in advance for the festival.

★ **Old Black Lion** Lion St ⓣ01497 820841, ⓦoldblacklion.co.uk. Very well-regarded thirteenth-century inn which has charming en-suite rooms both above the pub and in the neighbouring annexe (these are slightly more appealing). £90

Radnors End A 10min walk from town across the Hay-Bridge on the road to Clyro ⓣ01497 820780, ⓦhay-on-wye.co.uk/radnorsend. Small but neat field in a beautiful setting overlooking Hay, with on-site showers and laundry facilities. Closed Nov–Feb. Pitches £5

The Start Hay Bridge ⓣ01497 821391, ⓦthe-start.net. Neatly renovated Georgian house on the riverbank, with three rooms boasting antique furnishings and handmade quilts. The vegetable garden provides many of the ingredients for the scrummy breakfast. £70

★ **Tinto House** 13 Broad St ⓣ01497 821556, ⓦtinto-house.co.uk. Charming old house with three large, sumptuous rooms, each different, and a self-contained unit in the old stable block which has splendid garden views. £80

EATING AND DRINKING

Blue Boar Castle St ⓣ01497 820884. Tasteful, wood-panelled real ale pub centred around a gently curving bar and two stone fireplaces, with a separate dining area to one side. Daily 9am–11pm.

The Granary Broad St ⓣ01497 820790. This unpretentious café-bistro offers a wide range of excellent meals, with good veggie options. Save space for the wonderful desserts and espresso. Mains £10. Daily 9am–5.30pm, school holidays until 9pm.

★ **The Old Stables Tearooms** Bear St ⓣ07796 484766. Barely half a dozen tables are crammed into this delightful place, with chalked-up boards offering superb Welsh produce and a fantastic array of teas and home-made tarts. On a warm day, eat in the flower-filled yard. Tues–Sat 10.30am–4pm.

Shepherd's Ice Cream 9 High Town ⓣ01497 821898. Popular Georgian-style café/ice cream parlour doling out local ice cream made from sheep's milk; flavours include raspberry cheesecake and banana toffee crunch. Mon–Fri 9.30am–5.30pm, Sat 9.30am–6pm, Sun 10am–5.30pm.

SHOPPING

Hay has more than thirty **bookshops**, many of which are highly specialized, focusing on areas like travel, poetry or murder mystery.

Hay Castle Bookshop The castle ⓣ01497 820503, ⓦrichardbooth.demon.co.uk. Across the street from the tourist office, a signed footpath leads up the slope to the castle, a careworn Jacobean mansion built into the walls of an earlier medieval fortress. It's owned by bookseller Richard Booth, who has filled one wing with a large, ramshackle collection of titles with a particular focus on art and architecture, photography, transport, and Native American history. Honesty boxes are provided for payment. Daily 9.30am–6pm.

Richard Booth's Bookshop 44 Lion St ⓣ01497 820322. Just beyond the main square, High Town, this slicked-up, three-floored emporium (despite the name, no longer owned by Booth) offers unlimited browsing potential. Superb stock of first edition, rare and antiquarian books, mostly at a price. Mon–Sat 9am–5.30pm, Sun 11am–5pm.

The Wells towns

The **spa towns** of Mid-Wales, strung out along the Heart of Wales rail line between Swansea and Shrewsbury, were once all obscure villages, but with the arrival of the great craze for spas in the early eighteenth century, anywhere with a decent supply of apparently healing water joined in on the act. Royalty and nobility spearheaded the fashion, but the arrival of the railways opened them to all. Today, best of the bunch is undoubtedly the westernmost spa of **Llanwrtyd Wells**, hunkered down beneath stunning mountain scenery and renowned for its bizarre events. **Llandrindod Wells**, the most famous spa, attracted the international elite in its Victorian heyday, and has two excellent museums to enjoy. In between, the larger town of **Builth Wells** was very much the spa of the Welsh working classes and there's no real reason to stop, except in mid-July when it hosts the absorbing **Royal Welsh Show**, Britain's biggest rural jamboree.

Llanwrtyd Wells

Of the four spa towns, **LLANWRTYD WELLS**, twenty miles northwest of Brecon, is the most appealing. This was where the Welsh – Dyfed farmers along with Nonconformist middle classes from Glamorgan – flocked to the great eisteddfodau (festivals of Welsh music, dance and poetry) in the valley of the River Irfon; today, it's the Welsh capital of wacky events (see below).

In town, Dolecoed Road winds for half a mile along the river to the *Dolecoed Hotel*, built near the spa's original sulphurous spring. Although the distinctive aroma had been noted in the area for centuries, it was truly "discovered" in 1732 by the local priest, Theophilus Evans, who drank from an evil-smelling spring after seeing a rudely healthy frog pop out of it. The spring, named **Ffynnon Drewllyd** (Stinking Well), bubbles up amongst the dilapidated spa buildings a hundred yards behind the hotel.

ARRIVAL AND INFORMATION — LLANWRTYD WELLS

By train The station is a 5min walk east of town on Station Rd, and sees trains from Knighton (4 daily; 1hr 20min), Llandrindod Wells (4 daily; 30min), Shrewsbury (4 daily; 2hr) and Swansea (4 daily; 2hr).

By bus Buses stop on the main square. Destinations include Builth Wells (5 daily; 25min).

Tourist office Just off the main square (April–Dec Mon, Tues & Thurs–Sat; Jan–March Mon & Thurs–Sat 10am–5pm; ⓣ01591 610666, ⓦllanwrtyd.com). A welcoming place, it offers cheap internet access, sells local art and crafts and has a small café.

Bike rental and guided tours Green Dragon Activities, Victoria Rd (ⓣ01591 610508, ⓦgreendragonactivities.co.uk; £25/day bike rental).

ACCOMMODATION

Elenydd Wilderness Hostel Dolgoch and Ty'n Cornel ⓣ0870 7708868 or 01443 790720, ⓦelenydd-hostels.co.uk. Two converted farmhouses with nice, clean dorms, with camping space at both. Advance booking for both hostels is essential in winter. Camping £6 per pitch, dorm £12

★ **Lasswade Hotel** Station Rd ⓣ01591 610515, ⓦlasswadehotel.co.uk. A lovely Edwardian residence overlooking lush fields with eight tranquil, florally decorated rooms. There's a five percent discount for those arriving by train. £75

Stonecroft Inn Dolecoed Rd ⓣ01591 610332, ⓦstonecroft.co.uk. Self-catering, hostel-type place next to the pub; rooms, en-suite or with shared bath, have beds rather than bunks, and there's a kitchen. Bed £18

WACKY WALES: LLANWRTYD WELLS

Of Llanwrtyd Wells' various quirky events, three stand out: in mid-June, the **Man Versus Horse** marathon, a punishing 22-mile endurance test between man and beast over various types of terrain; at the end of August, the **world bog-snorkelling championships**, in which competitors must complete two lengths of a water-filled trench cut through a peat bog; and in November, the **Real Ale Wobble**, an event for the somewhat less serious-minded cyclist, that involves two days of combined mountain biking and beer drinking. See ⓦgreen-events.co.uk for full listings.

THE ABERGWESYN PASS

A lane from Llanwrtyd meets up with another road from Beulah at the riverside hamlet of **ABERGWESYN**, five miles north. From here, you can drive the quite magnificent winding thread of an ancient cattle-drovers' road – the **Abergwesyn Pass** – up the perilous **Devil's Staircase** and through dense conifer forests to miles of wide, desolate valleys where sheep graze unhurriedly. At the little bridge over the tiny Tywi River, a track heads south past an isolated, gas-lit hostel at **DOLGOCH**. Remote paths lead from the hostel through the forests and hillsides to the exquisitely isolated chapel at **Soar-y-Mynydd** and over the mountains to the next hostel at **TYNCORNEL**, five miles from Dolgoch.

EATING AND DRINKING

★ **Carlton Riverside** Irfon Crescent T 01591 610248, W carltonriverside.com. Modern British food at this well-regarded place, prepared with flair and imagination. The restaurant itself is lovely, with well-spaced, crisply laid tables offering river views. Two-course menu £19.50; à la carte £34. There's also a cool little cellar bar serving home-baked pizza. Mon–Sat 7–11pm.

Drover's Rest Riverside Restaurant The Square T 01591 610264, W food-food-food.co.uk. Bric-a-brac fills this warm, cottage-like restaurant, where wholesome traditional Welsh dishes are the order of the day; Brecon venison in red wine, Celtic pork tenderloin, and delicious cheese-based vegetarian dishes. They also run cookery and art classes. Mains £15–20. Tues & Thurs–Sun 10.30am–3.30pm & 7.30–10pm.

Neuadd Arms The Square T 01591 610236. Lively place, home to the Heart of Wales Brewery, which produces five fabulous ales that you can soak up with good bar food, including some great curries. Note the memorial top hat on the exterior wall, in honour of Screaming Lord Sutch, who performed here on several occasions. Daily 11am–midnight.

Llandrindod Wells

Once the most chichi spa resort in Wales, **LLANDRINDOD WELLS** (Llandrindod) is a pale imitation of its former self. That said, many of its fine Victorian buildings still stand, and there are two superb museums. It was the railway that made Llandrindod, arriving in 1864 and bringing carriages full of well-to-do Victorians to the fledgling spa. The town blossomed, new hotels were built, neat parks were laid out and it came to rival many of the more fashionable spas and resorts over the border. You can sample more than enough of the town's metallic, salty spa water in **Rock Park**, where a free chalybeate fountain stands in a glade to the front of the lavish **spa pump room** (restoration plans are afoot).

Radnorshire Museum

Temple St • April–Sept Tues–Fri 10am–4pm, Sat 10am–4pm; Oct–March Tues–Fri 10am–4pm, Sat 10am–1pm • £1 • T 01597 824513

The small but entertaining **Radnorshire museum** evokes the area's history with exhibits ranging from archeological finds to items from Victorian spa days. Among the pick of these is a Sheela-na-gig, a typically explicit and remarkably well-preserved carved relief of a figure displaying its vulva, which was found in the local parish church, and a log-boat dredged up from the Ifor River in 1929 and thought to date from around 1200 AD.

National Cycle Collection

Corner Temple St and Spa Rd • May–Oct Mon–Fri 10am–4pm; Nov–April Tues, Thurs & Sun 10am–4pm • £3.50 • T 01597 825531, W cyclemuseum.org.uk

The **National Cycle Collection** is a nostalgic collection of more than 280 bikes, ranging from a reproduction 1818 hobbyhorse to relatively modern folding bikes and choppers, including some contraptions that look far too uncomfortable to have been a success. The museum also holds some notable machinery, including the bike belonging to serial record-breaking time trialist Eileen Sheridan, and the reserve bike and racing skin belonging to 1992 Olympic gold medallist Chris Boardman.

ARRIVAL AND INFORMATION **LLANDRINDOD WELLS**

By train The station is a 5min walk east of town on Station Rd.

Destinations Knighton (4 daily; 40min); Llanwrtyd Wells (4 daily; 30min); Shrewsbury (4 daily; 1hr 30min); Swansea (4 daily; 2hr 30min).

By bus Buses pull in by the train station.

Destinations Aberystwyth (2 daily; 1hr 40min); Brecon (7 daily Mon–Sat; 1hr); Builth Wells (hourly; 20min); Disserth (16 daily; 45min); New Radnor (8 daily Mon–Sat; 30min); Newtown (6 daily; 55min); Rhayader (6 daily; 30min).

Tourist office In front of the Radnorshire museum on Temple St (Easter–Oct Mon–Fri 10am–4pm, Sat 10am–1pm; Nov–Easter Mon–Sat 10am–1pm; T 01597 822600, W llandrindod.co.uk).

ACCOMMODATION

The Cottage Spa Rd T 01597 825435, W thecottagebandb.co.uk. Handsome Edwardian property with seven differently configured rooms, all laden with period-style furnishings. No TVs in the rooms but guests are welcome to use the lounge. **£62**

Greylands High St T 01597 822253, W greylandsguesthouse.co.uk. Tall Victorian red-brick house in the town centre, near the station, with seven comfortable, good-value rooms. **£58**

15

EATING

Herb Garden Café 5 Spa Centre T 01597 823082. Fresh, organic salads and platters, juicy house burgers and a stack of sweet treats at this attractive, friendly diner; the big windows and squashy sofas make it a great venue in which to kick back. Mon–Sat 9.30am–5pm.

Llanerch Inn Llanerch Lane T 01597 822234. Opposite the train station, this sixteenth-century hostelry is central Llandrindod's only pub, and pre-dates most of the surrounding town by quite some time. Enjoy a pint in front of the stone fireplace or a well-cooked, classic pub meal. Daily 7am–11pm.

Elan Valley and around

From the workaday market town of **RHAYADER**, ten miles west of Llandrindod Wells, the B4518 heads southwest four miles to the gorgeous **Elan Valley**. It was here that the poet Shelley spent his honeymoon in buildings now submerged by the waters of the valley's reservoirs, a nine-mile-long string of four lakes built between 1892 and 1903 to supply water to the rapidly growing industrial city of Birmingham, 75 miles east.

Frequent guided **walks** head off from the valley's visitor centre, and a road tucks in along the first reservoir, Caban Coch, to the **Garreg Ddu** viaduct, where it winds along for four spectacular miles to the vast, rather chilling 1952 dam on **Claerwen Reservoir**. More remote and less popular than the Elan lakes, Claerwen is a good base for a serious **walk** from the far end of the dam across eight or so harsh but beautiful miles to the monastery of Strata Florida. Alternatively, you can follow the path that skirts around the northern shore of Claerwen to the lonely **Teifi Pools**, glacial lakes from which the River Teifi springs.

Back at the Garreg Ddu viaduct, a more popular road continues north along the long, glassy finger of Garreg Ddu reservoir, before doubling back on itself just below the awesome **Pen-y-garreg** dam and reservoir; if the dam is overflowing, the vast wall of foaming water is mesmerizing. At the top of Pen-y-garreg lake, it's possible to drive over the final dam on the system, at **Craig Goch**. Thanks to its gracious curve, elegant Edwardian arches and neat little green cupola, this is the most photographed of all the dams.

Gigrin Farm Red Kite Feeding Station

A quarter-mile south of Rhayader, just off the A470 • Daily: summer 1–5pm; winter 1–4pm • £4 • T 01597 810243, W gigrin.co.uk

Gigrin Farm is a working sheep farm that's become an official RSPB **red kite** feeding station. Every day at 2pm (3pm in summer), they put out meat scraps to attract hundreds of these beautiful birds that were once close to extinction in the UK. It's a breathtaking spectacle, with the huge animals, swooping down over a well-placed hide, displaying their aerial agility and magnificent wingspan.

OFFA'S DYKE

Offa's Dyke has provided a potent symbol of Welsh–English antipathy ever since it was created in the eighth century as a demarcation line by King Offa of Mercia, ruler of central England. George Borrow, in his classic book *Wild Wales*, notes that, once, "It was customary for the English to cut off the ears of every Welshman who was found to the east of the dyke, and for the Welsh to hang every Englishman whom they found to the west of it".

The earthwork – up to 20ft high and 60ft wide – made use of natural boundaries like rivers in its run north to south, and is best seen in the sections near **Knighton**. Today's England–Wales border crosses the dyke many times, although the basic boundary has changed little since Offa's day. A glorious, 177-mile **long-distance footpath** runs the length of the dyke from Prestatyn in the north to Chepstow, and is one of the most rewarding walks in Britain.

ARRIVAL AND INFORMATION — ELAN VALLEY

15

There is no **public transport** to the Elan valley, so you will require a car or a bike, or you can hike.

Tourist office Just below the dam of the first reservoir, Caban Coch, the Elan Valley visitor centre (mid-March to Oct daily 10am–5.30pm; T 01597 810898, W elanvalley.org.uk) has useful leaflets on walks around the valley, a permanent exhibition about the history and ecology of the area, and a tearoom.

Bike rental Clive Powell Mountain Bikes, West St, Rhayader (Fri–Wed 9am–5.30pm; T 01597 811343, W clivepowell-mtb.co.uk; £5/hr, £20/day); they also offer all-inclusive cycling packages.

ACCOMMODATION

Elan Valley Hotel Elan T 01597 810448, W elanvalleyhotel.co.uk. Delightful, privately run country house on the Rhayader side of Elan village, which offers eleven subtly decorated, individually styled rooms, good food in its well-regarded restaurant and a lively bar. £75

Ty Morgans East St, Rhayader T 01597 811666, W tymorgans.co.uk. Superb building housing nine effortlessly cool rooms, most of which still feature their original red or grey bare brick walls and oak-beamed ceilings. Thick carpets, low slung beds and numerous mod cons round things off in great style. £75

Wyeside A few hundred yards north of Rhayader off the A470 T 01597 810183, W wyesidecamping.co.uk. On the banks of the Wye, a smart site with separate camping and caravan areas and clean, modern amenities. Closed Dec & Jan. £3 per pitch plus £6.50 per adult.

EATING AND DRINKING

Crown Inn North St, Rhayader T 01597 811099. Most agreeable of the town's several boozers, with lots of small, dark wooden tables gathered around a large stone fireplace, and Brains beer. Daily noon–11pm.

Ty Morgans East St, Rhayader T 01597 811666, W tymorgans.co.uk. Great-looking bar/bistro (three-course menu £20), offering dishes from simple (fish and chips, sausage and mash) to sophisticated (ham hock roulade, pan-seared red sword fish). The bistro opens out into the bustling Strand coffee house, complete with a sweet little deli selling artisan chocs. Daily 8am–11pm.

Montgomeryshire

The northern part of Powys is made up of the old county of **Montgomeryshire** (Maldwyn), an area of enormously varying landscapes and few inhabitants. The solid little town of **Llanidloes** is a base for ageing hippies on the banks of the infant River Severn (Afon Hafren). To the east, the muted old county town of **Montgomery**, with its fine Georgian architecture, perches amid gentle, green hills above the border and Offa's Dyke. Further north, **Welshpool**, the only major settlement, is packed in above the wide flood plain of the Severn; with its good pubs and hotels it's a fair base for Montgomeryshire's one unmissable sight, the sumptuous **Powis Castle** and its exquisite terraced gardens.

CLOCKWISE FROM TOP HARLECH CASTLE (P.676); ABERAERON (P.668); SHEEP IN THE BRECON BEACONS >

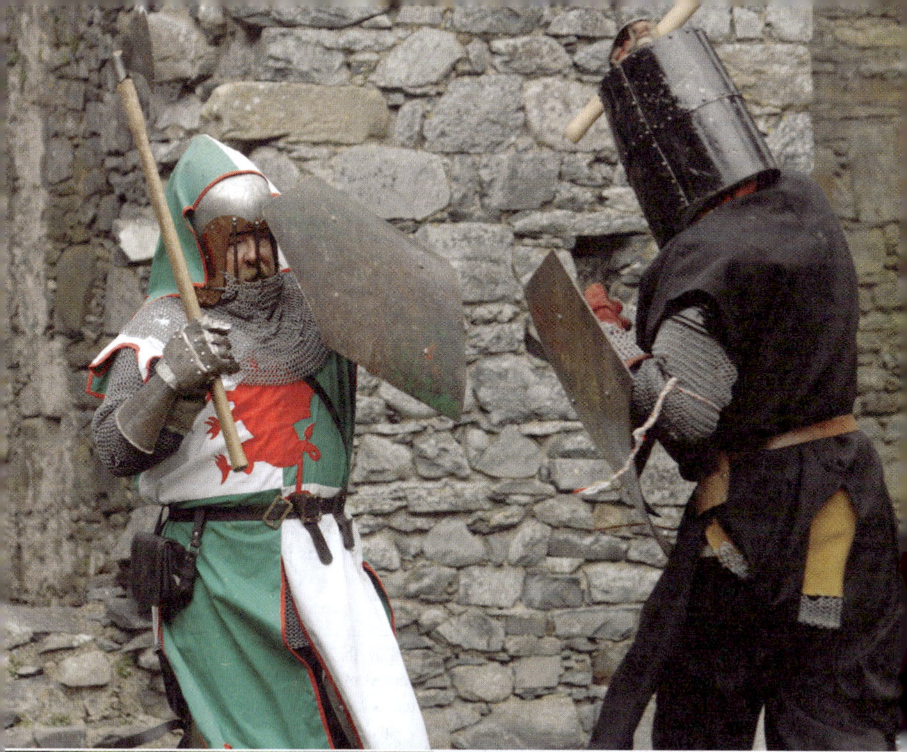

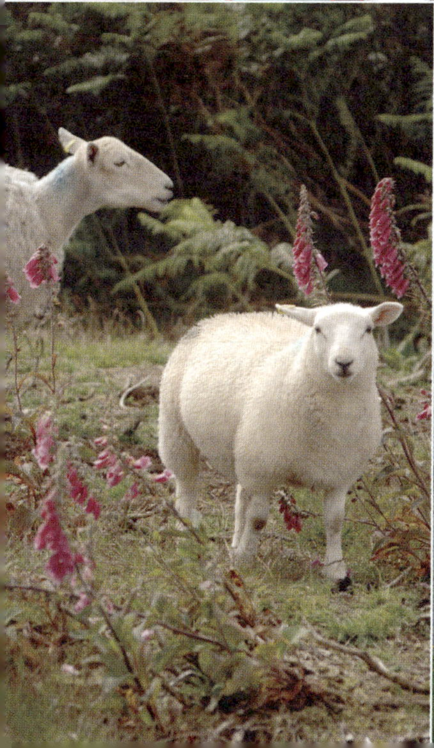

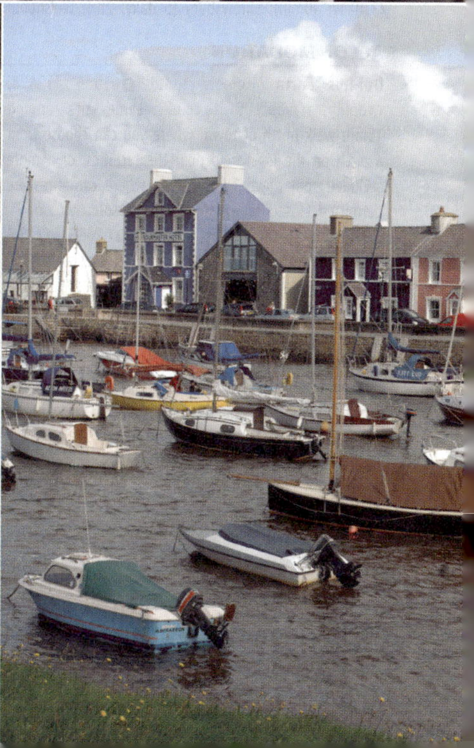

Llanidloes

The small market town of **LLANIDLOES**, twelve miles north of Rhayader, has developed from a rural village to a weaving town, and is now an arty, alternative-lifestyle kind of place. One of mid-Wales's prettiest towns, it has four main streets that meet at the black-and-white **market hall**, built on timber stilts in 1600. Running parallel with the length of the market hall are China Street and Long Bridge Street; the latter has some interesting little shops.

Town hall and museum

Great Oak St • June–Aug Tues, Thurs & Fri 11am–1pm & 2–4pm, Sat 10am–1pm & 2–5pm; Sept–May Tues, Thurs & Fri 11am–1pm & 2–4pm, Sat 11am–2pm • Donation requested • T 01686 413777

From the market hall, the broad Great Oak Street heads west to the **town hall**, originally built as a temperance hotel to challenge the boozy *Trewythen Arms* opposite. A plaque on the closed hotel commemorates Llanidloes as an unlikely-seeming place of industrial and political unrest, when, in April 1839, Chartists stormed the hotel, dragging out and beating up special constables who had been despatched to the town in a futile attempt to suppress political activism among the town's flannel-weavers. In the town hall, you'll also find the eclectic **museum**, where the diverting collection of old local prints and mementos pales beside the stuffed two-headed lamb, born locally in 1914.

ARRIVAL AND INFORMATION — LLANIDLOES

By bus China St curves down to the car park where all buses arrive and depart.

Destinations Aberystwyth (3 daily; 1hr); Dylife (1 postbus daily; 30min); Newtown (7 daily; 30min); Ponterwyd (3 daily; 40min); Shrewsbury (5 daily; 2hr); Welshpool (6 daily; 1hr 20min).

Tourist office The independently run visitor information centre is at 3 Long Bridge St (Mon–Sat 10am–1pm & 2–4pm; T 01686 412287, W llanidloes.com).

ACCOMMODATION

Dol-llys Farm Trefeglwys Rd T 01686 412694, W dolllyscaravancampsite.co.uk. Large site around 15min walk north of town, where you can choose from a pitch on the level field near the facilities, or a more secluded spot down by the river, where campfires are permitted. Closed Nov–Easter. £6 per person.

★ **Lloyds Hotel** Cambrian Place T 01686 412284, W lloydshotel.co.uk. Superbly run, idiosyncratic hotel with seven beautifully conceived rooms, each awash with colour and character. The personal touch is evident everywhere, right down to the wall-mounted sepia prints and watercolours. £76

Unicorn Hotel 4 Long Bridge St T 01686 411171, W unicornllanidloes.co.uk. A small hotel of considerable charm and quality, hosting six crisp, generous and impeccably clean rooms; there's a substantial breakfast to look forward to as well. £70

EATING AND DRINKING

★ **Lloyds Hotel** Cambrian Place T 01686 412284, W lloydshotel.co.uk. A unique dining experience. Pre-dinner drinks are served at 7.30pm, followed by a surprise five-course menu, finishing around 11pm – the food could be absolutely anything, so contact them in advance if there is anything you don't eat. Advance booking essential. £39.50. One sitting daily, 7.30pm

Red Lion 8 Long Bridge St T 01686 412270. The tatty, exposed brick frontage conceals the town's most agreeable pub; the main lounge bar has comfy leather seating huddled around an imposing stone fireplace, while the other room is principally for bar games. Daily 11am–midnight.

★ **Unicorn Hotel** 4 Long Bridge St T 01686 411171, W unicornllanidloes.co.uk. Fabulous restaurant offering a seductive, game-heavy menu (wild boar steak, pan-roasted guinea fowl) alongside some fishy treats (monkfish tail with scallop mousse). Mains £15–20. Tues–Sat 10.30am–2pm & 6.30–11pm, Sun noon–2pm.

Montgomery

Tiny **MONTGOMERY** (Trefaldwyn), around twenty miles northeast of Llanidloes, is Montgomeryshire at its most anglicized. From the mound of its **castle**, situated just on the Welsh side of Offa's Dyke, there are wonderful views over the lofty church tower and the handsome Georgian streets, notably the impressively symmetrical main road – appropriately named Broad Street – which swoops up to the little red-brick **town hall**, crowned by a pert clocktower. The rebuilt tower of Montgomery's parish **Church of St Nicholas** dominates the snug proportions of the buildings around it. Largely thirteenth-century, the highlights of its spacious interior include a 1600 monument to local landowner Sir Richard Herbert and his wife. Their eight children – who included prominent Elizabethan poet George Herbert – have been carved in beatific kneeling positions behind them.

Montgomery is within striking distance of one of the best-preserved sections of **Offa's Dyke** (see p.660), traced by the long-distance footpath that runs on either side of the B4386.

ARRIVAL AND DEPARTURE — MONTGOMERY

There are **bus** connections with Newtown (3 daily; 40min), Shrewsbury (4 daily; 50min) and Welshpool (3 daily Mon–Sat; 25min); the stop is on Broad St.

ACCOMMODATION AND EATING

Brynwylfa 4 Bishops Castle St **T** 01686 668555, **W** brynwylfa.co.uk. Just off the main square, there are just two rooms in this beautiful townhouse, one with exposed brick walls, the other with a gorgeous roll-top bath. **£60**

Castle Kitchen 8 Broad St **T** 01686 668795, **W** castlekitchen.org. Sociable café/restaurant doling out soups, quiches and tarts, and in the evenings, more substantial dishes like lamb and olive tagine with fruity couscous. The busy downstairs area extends to a vine-covered terrace; upstairs is all wonky flooring and stripey walls. Mon–Sat 9.30am–4.30pm, Sun 11am–4pm, plus Fri & Sat 7–9.15pm.

Dragon Hotel Next to the town hall **T** 01686 668359, **W** dragonhotel.com. The rambling *Dragon Hotel* is showing its age a little and is slightly overpriced, but the rooms are plentifully furnished (some have four-poster beds) and there is an indoor pool. **£96**

Ivy House Church Bank **T** 01686 668746, **W** ivyhousetearooms.com. Sweet, flowery tearoom serving veggie snacks, teas and cakes, as well as food to take away. Daily 9am–5pm.

Welshpool and around

Eastern Montgomeryshire's chief town of **WELSHPOOL** (Y Trallwng), seven miles north of Montgomery, was formerly known as just Pool, its prefix added in 1835 to distinguish it from the English seaside town of Poole in Dorset. Lying in the valley of the River Severn, just three miles from the English border, it's an attractive place, with fine Tudor, Georgian and Victorian buildings in the centre, and the fabulous **Powis Castle** nearby.

Powysland Museum

Canal Wharf • June–Aug Mon, Tues, Thurs & Fri 11am–1pm & 2–5pm, Sat & Sun opens 10am; Sept–May Mon, Tues, Thurs & Fri 11am–1pm & 2–5pm, Sat 11am–2pm • Free • **T** 01938 554656

A humpback bridge over the much-restored **Montgomery Canal** hides the canal wharf and a wharfside warehouse that has been carefully restored as the **Powysland Museum**. The impressive local history collection includes archeological nuggets such as those from an old local woodhenge, and displays medieval remains from the now-obliterated local Cistercian abbey of Strata Marcella. There's also a nostalgic look at the Welshpool and Llanfair railway.

Welshpool and Llanfair Light Railway

Raven Square • Generally 2–3 trains a day; June–Aug daily; April, May, Sept & Oct holidays & weekends only • £11.90 return • **T** 01938 810441, **W** wllr.org.uk

Broad Street changes name five times as it rises up the hill towards the tiny Raven Square station of the **Welshpool and Llanfair Light Railway**. The eight-mile narrow-gauge rail line was open to passengers for less than thirty years prior to its closure in 1931. Now, scaled-down engines once more chuff their way along to the peaceful little village of **Llanfair Caereinion**, a good base for daytime walks.

Powis Castle

A mile from Welshpool up Park Lane • April–Sept Mon & Wed–Sun castle 1–5pm, gardens 11am–5.30pm; March & Oct Mon & Wed–Sun castle 1–4pm, gardens 11am–4.30pm; Nov & Dec Fri–Sun castle noon–4pm, gardens 11am–4pm • NT • Castle and gardens £12.40, gardens only £9.10 • ☎ 01938 551944

In a land of ruined castles, the sheer scale and beauty of **Powis Castle** is quite staggering. On the site of an earlier Norman fort, the castle was started in the reign of Edward I by the Gwenwynwyn family; to qualify for the site and the barony of De la Pole, they had to renounce all claims to Welsh princedom.

In 1587, Sir Edward Herbert bought the castle and began to transform it into the Elizabethan palace that survives today. Inside, the **Clive Museum** – named after Edward Clive, son of Clive of India, who married into the family in 1784 – forms
15 a lively account of the British in India, through diaries, letters, paintings, tapestries, weapons and jewels. But it is the sumptuous period rooms that impress most, from the vast, kitsch frescoes by Lanscroon above the balustraded staircase, to the mahogany bed, brass-and-enamel toilets and decorative wall hangings of the state bedroom. The elegant **Long Gallery** has a rich sixteenth-century plasterwork ceiling overlooking winsome busts and marble statuettes of the four elements, placed between glowering family portraits.

The **gardens**, designed by Welsh architect William Winde, are spectacular. Dropping down from the castle in four huge, stepped terraces, the design has barely changed since the seventeenth century, with a charming orangery and trim topiary. In summer, there are outdoor **concerts**, frequently with fireworks.

ARRIVAL AND INFORMATION — WELSHPOOL

By train The station is at the bottom of Severn St, behind the neo-Gothic turrets of the old Victorian station.

Destinations Aberystwyth (8 daily; 1hr 30min); Birmingham (8 daily; 1hr 25min); Machynlleth (8 daily; 55min); Newtown (8 daily; 15min); Pwllheli (2 daily; 3hr 30min); Shrewsbury (8 daily; 25min).

By bus Buses use the Old Station on Severn Rd.

Destinations Berriew (8 daily Mon–Sat; 20min); Llanidloes (6 daily; 1hr 15min); Llanfyllin (5 daily Mon–Sat; 35min); Llanymynech (5 daily; 30min); Montgomery (3 daily Mon–Sat; 25min); Newtown (9 daily; 35min); Oswestry (4 daily; 45min); Shrewsbury (6 daily; 45min).

Tourist office Just off Church St in the Vicarage Gardens car park (Mon–Sat 9.30am–5pm, Sun 10am–4pm; ☎ 01938 552043, ⓦ welshpool.org). It's one of the few tourist offices in the region, with stacks of information.

ACCOMMODATION AND EATING

The Raven Inn Raven Square ☎ 01938 553070, ⓦ theravenwelshpool.co.uk. Up by the narrow-gauge train station, the perky Raven has a great reputation for its food. Its vast menu features a stack of carnivorous treats including fillet steak with blue stilton and spinach and great home-made burgers (pork and apple, for example). Mains £10–15. Tues–Sun noon–11pm.

Revells Berriew St ☎ 01938 559000, ⓦ revellsbistro.co.uk. Housed within a striking muddy-green Art Deco cinema building, this welcoming restaurant combines a simple early evening menu (5.30–7pm) with a more sophisticated main evening bistro menu where you can expect to see the likes of grilled sardines with sunblush tomatoes and artichoke bruschetta. Mains £12–16. Thurs–Sat 5.30–11pm, Sun noon–3pm.

Royal Oak The Cross ☎ 01938 552217, ⓦ royaloakhotel.info. Traditional Georgian coaching inn with a range of spruce rooms, which come in two categories; the standard rooms are fine, but the "contemporary" options are marginally more polished. **£89**

Trefnant Hall Farm Four miles southwest of Welshpool, beyond Powis Castle ☎ 01686 640262, ⓦ trefnanthall.co.uk. You'll need your own transport to get to this isolated Georgian farmhouse, whose three florally decorated rooms have delightful views of green sloping fields. Guests are free to use the lounge with its gorgeous fireplace. **£60**

Llanfyllin and around

The hills and plains of northern Montgomeryshire conceal a maze of deserted lanes along the contours that swell up towards the north and the foothills of the Berwyn mountains. The only town of any size is **Llanfyllin**, ten miles northwest of Welshpool, a handsome place with a Thursday market. Continuing west, you'll come to **Lake Vyrnwy**; pressing north there's **Pistyll Rhaeadr**, Wales's highest waterfall.

The Rhaeadr Valley

For a place so near the English border, **LLANRHAEADR-YM-MOCHNANT**, six miles north of Llanfyllin, is extremely Welsh. The small village is remembered as the serving parish of Bishop William Morgan, who translated the Bible into Welsh in 1588, but it's mostly visited as a base for **Pistyll Rhaeadr**, Wales's highest waterfall (240ft). The river tumbles down the crags in two stages, flowing under a natural stone arch known as the Fairy Bridge. Make sure to walk to the top of the fall, to enjoy vertiginous views down the valley and paths up into the moody Berwyns.

ACCOMMODATION AND EATING

Bron Heulog Waterfall St, Llanrhaeadr-Ym-Mochnant ⓣ01691 780521, ⓦbronheulog.co.uk. Grand Victorian house with three beautifully decorated rooms, each themed on a different flower: bluebell, sunflower and orchid. £70

Plough Inn Llanrhaeadr-Ym-Mochnant ⓣ01691 780654, ⓦploughcountryinn.com. Just two rooms (a twin and double, both en-suite) in this delightful country pub, which itself is a great spot for a pint or bite to eat. Mon–Thurs 4–11pm, Fri–Sun noon–11pm. £55

Tan-y-Pistyll Café Pistyll Rhaeadr ⓣ01691 780392, ⓦpistyllrhaeadr.co.uk. The owners of this easy-going café offer two en-suite rooms, a cottage sleeping five (£140) and a lovely campsite in the back field, where fires are allowed. They also run spiritual retreats. Café: summer 9.30am–6pm, winter 10am–4pm. Camping pitch £5.50 per person, double room £85

Lake Vyrnwy

A monument to the self-aggrandizement of the Victorian age, **Lake Vyrnwy** (Llyn Efyrnwy) combines its functional role as a water supply for Liverpool with a touch of architectural genius in the shape of the huge nineteenth-century dam at its southern end and the turreted straining-tower that edges out into the icy waters. It's a magnificent place, with a number of **nature trails**, and a popular spot for walking and **birdwatching**. The Coed-y-Capel hide, at the northern end of the lake, is dedicated to spotting peregrines (typically April–July), and in the small hide across the road from the RSPB Visitor Centre, you can sit and watch forest birds attacking the feeders outside the windows.

INFORMATION — LAKE VYRNWY

RSPB Visitor Centre On the western side of the dam, this excellent little centre (a shop, really) can advise on the best places to birdwatch, and offers free guided walks at 11.30am and 2pm on summer weekends (April–Oct daily 10.30am–5pm; Nov–March Sat & Sun 10.30am–4pm; ⓣ01691 870278, ⓦrspb.org.uk/lakevyrnwy).

ACCOMMODATION AND EATING

Artisans Coffee Shop Just below the visitor centre ⓣ01691 870317, ⓦartisans-lakevyrnwy.co.uk. Large, well-stocked café serving teas, coffees, cakes and snacks; they also offer bike rental (£5/hr, minimum 2hr). Daily 9.30am–4.30pm.

Lake Vyrnwy Hotel Southeastern shore ⓣ01691 870692, ⓦlakevyrnwy.com. The lake's most prominent accommodation, a lavish spa retreat overlooking the waters. Top-notch rooms have either hill or (more expensive) lake views. £130

Lakeview Tearoom On the lakeside road two miles beyond the Lake Vyrnwy Hotel ⓣ01691 870286. Daytime snacks and full evening meals are available at this sweet, mildly quirky tearoom. Mon–Fri noon–3pm, Sat & Sun 11.30am–4.30pm, restaurant daily from 7.30pm.

The Oaks ⓣ01691 870250, ⓦvyrnwyaccommodation.co.uk. An old-fashioned, very pleasant B&B just beyond the visitor centre offering three pastel-coloured rooms, two of which share bathrooms. Small TV and tea-making facilities in each. £70

The Cambrian coast

Cardigan Bay (Bae Ceredigion) takes a huge bite out of the west Wales coast, leaving behind the Pembrokeshire peninsula in the south and the Llŷn in the north. Between them lies the **Cambrian coast**, a loosely defined mountain-backed strip periodically split by tumbling rivers, which stretches from Cardigan up to Harlech. Large sand-fringed sections are peppered with low-key coastal resorts, peopled in the summer by families from the English Midlands.

The southern Ceredigion coast is broken by some spirited little ports, all soaked in a relaxed, upbeat and firmly Welsh culture: the old county town of **Cardigan** fringed by the lovely **Teifi Marshes** and **Cilgerran Castle**; higgledy-piggledy **New Quay**; and pretty Georgian **Aberaeron**. Ceredigion's main town is ebullient **Aberystwyth**, a great base for the waterfalls and woods of the **Vale of Rheidol** out towards **Devil's Bridge** and the red kites at **Bwlch Nant yr Arian**.

15

To the north, the flat river plain and rolling hills of the **Dyfi Valley** lay justifiable claim to being one of the greenest corners of Europe. Their focal point is the genial town of **Machynlleth**, a candidate for the Welsh capital in the 1950s and site of Owain Glyndŵr's embryonic fifteenth-century Welsh parliament. In the hills to the north lies the fascinating **Centre for Alternative Technology**. Machynlleth looks up at one of Wales's most inspirational mountains, **Cadair Idris** (2930ft), incised by the Talyllyn Valley (with its toy railway) and the delightful Dysynni Valley. On its northern flank, the beautiful **Mawddach estuary** snakes its way seaward from grey-stone **Dolgellau**, springboard for the mountain biking and forest pursuits at **Coed-y-Brenin**. The coast begins to feel more like north Wales at hilltop fortress of **Harlech** where the castle overlooks the dunes and the Llŷn.

Cardigan and around

An ancient former port of **CARDIGAN** (Aberteifi) was founded by the Norman lord Roger de Montgomery in 1093 around a castle (closed to the public). From the castle, Bridge Street sweeps up to the turreted oddity of the **Guildhall**, through which you access the town's **covered market**, a typically eclectic mix of fresh food, local crafts and secondhand stalls. Cardigan sits at the lowest bridging point of the **River Teifi**, one of Wales's most eulogized rivers, for its rich spawn of fresh fish, its meandering rural charm and the coracles that have been a regular feature since pre-Roman times.

Welsh Wildlife Centre

Marshes Open access • Free **Centre** Easter–Dec daily 10.30am–5pm; Nov to mid-Dec Wed–Sun 10.30am–4pm • Free, parking £3 • ☎ 01239 621600, welshwildlife.org • You can drive from Cardigan (a very roundabout route of about 4 miles) but the best approach is to walk (or cycle) the mile from Cardigan's river bridge along the bed of an old railway

A lovely walk from Cardigan, passing a couple of bird hides, brings you to the extensive **Teifi Marshes Nature Reserve**, an area of important reed beds, meadows and untouched oak woodland that's home to otters, badgers, butterflies and even a herd of **buffalo**, brought in to control invasive bulrushes. Two main walks head off from the **Welsh Wildlife Centre**, which houses informative displays and has an airy café with splendid views: one heads around the reed beds, while the other takes in an enticing gorge section of the Teifi, which you can also explore on **kayak** or **canoe trips** (£35; ask at centre).

Cilgerran Castle

Cilgerran, a couple of miles up the Teifi River from Cardigan • Daily: April–Oct 10am–5pm; Nov–March 10am–4pm • CADW • April–Oct £3.20; Nov–March free

The attractive village of **CILGERRAN** clusters behind the bulk of its **castle**, on a high wooded bluff above the river. This is the site of an attack in 1109 that culminated in the abduction of Nest (the "Welsh Helen of Troy") by a love-struck Prince Owain of Powys. Her husband, Gerald of Pembroke, escaped the attack by slithering down a toilet waste chute through the castle walls. The two massive drum towers still dominate the castle, and the outer walls are traced by vertiginously high walkways. The outer ward is a good example of the keepless castle that evolved in the thirteenth century.

Tresaith

The best destination on the lovely south Ceredigion coast is tiny **TRESAITH**, eight miles northeast of Cardigan, which staggers down impossibly narrow lanes to a delightful beach and the *Ship Inn*. A few yards around the rocks to the right, a refreshing small waterfall cascades right onto the beach.

Llangrannog

Four miles north of Tresaith, **LLANGRANOG** comes wedged between bracken and gorse-beaten hills, the streets winding to the tiny seafront. The beach can become horribly congested in midsummer, when it's better to follow the cliff path to **Cilborth Beach**, and on to the glorious NT-owned headland, **Ynys Lochtyn**.

ARRIVAL AND INFORMATION — CARDIGAN AND AROUND

By bus Buses to Cardigan stop on Finch Square.
Destinations Aberaeron (7 daily; 50min); Aberystwyth (12 daily; 1hr 30min–2hr); Cenarth (11 daily; 15min); Cilgerran (13 daily; 15min); Llangrannog (3 daily; 15min); New Quay (hourly; 1hr).

Tourist office The Cardigan tourist office is in Theatr Mwldan, Bath House Rd (July & Aug daily 10am–5pm; Sept–June Mon–Sat 10am–5pm; ⓣ01239 613230, ⓔcardigantic@ceredigion.gov.uk).

ACCOMMODATION

★ **Ffynnon Fendigaid** Rhydlewis, 3 miles south of Llangrannog ⓣ01239 851361, ⓦffynnonf.co.uk. Eclectically decorated rural B&B in six acres of semi-wild grounds – badgers have been spotted. Walkers are welcome (pick-ups possible) and the owners do a great breakfast. **£75**

Glandŵr At the top of Tresaith village on the road to Aberporth, ⓣ01239 811442, ⓦglandwrtresaith.co.uk. Three contemporary rooms in a rich Georgian country house that's just a 5min walk from the beach but feels a world away with its seven acres of woodland and gardens. **£90**

Llety Caravan Park Tresaith ⓣ01239 810354, ⓦlletycaravanpark.co.uk. Amid the static caravans there's a wonderful (if significantly sloping) cliff-top field for tents with a footpath straight to the beach. **£15–17** per pitch.

Llety Teifi Pendre, Cardigan ⓣ01239 615566, ⓦllety.co.uk. Ten contemporary rooms in a Victorian townhouse with its own restaurant/bar. The deluxe room (£10 more) has its own jacuzzi. **£75**

YHA Poppit Sands 4 miles northwest of Cardigan ⓣ0845 371 9037, ⓔpoppit@yha.org.uk. Remote hostel and the northern end of the Pembrokeshire Coast Path, with great views. The #407 bus stops within half a mile. Camping available. Closed Nov–Feb. **£16**

EATING AND DRINKING

Ferry Inn St Dogmael's, 1.5 miles west of Cardigan ⓣ01239 615172. A fine spot with loads of seating beside the Teifi, and a smart interior where they serve great beer and moderately priced, tasty meals (using lots of local ingredients). Mon–Sat 10am–11.30pm, Sun noon–11.30pm.

Fforest Café Castle St, Cardigan ⓣ01239 615286. Great little café run by the folks who operate the adjacent Fforest outdoor shop. Come for cream teas, smoothies and home-made cakes; free wi-fi, too. Mon–Sat 9am–5pm.

Shampan Far end of Quay St, Cardigan ⓣ01239 621444. This smart floating Indian restaurant, moored on the riverbank, serves the usual curries done to a very high standard. Mains £6–8. Daily 5–11pm.

New Quay and around

NEW QUAY (Cei Newydd) lays claim to being the original Llareggub in Dylan Thomas's *Under Milk Wood*. Certainly, it has the little tumbling streets, prim Victorian terraces, cobbled stone harbour and air of dreamy isolation that Thomas evoked in his play. Although there is a singular lack of excitement in town, it's a pleasant base for good beaches, dolphin-spotting and the rocky promontory of **New Quay Head**, where the invigorating coast path steers along the top of aptly named **Bird Rock**.

Cardigan Bay Marine Wildlife Centre

Centre April–Oct daily 9am–5pm • Donation requested **Boat trips** 2hr • £18 • T 01545 560032, W cbmwc.org

Tucked away down the slipway above New Quay's beach, the **Cardigan Bay Marine Wildlife Centre** has excellent interactive and interpretive displays on the dolphins, seals and seabirds of Cardigan Bay. They also organize (weather permitting) daily whale/dolphin-watching boat trips.

ARRIVAL AND INFORMATION — NEW QUAY

By bus Buses from Aberaeron (hourly; 20min), Aberystwyth (hourly; 1hr) and Cardigan (hourly; 1hr) stop at the south end of town on Park St.

Tourist office On the corner of Church St and Wellington Place (April–Sept Mon–Sat 10am–6pm; T 01545 560865, E newquay@ceredigion.gov.uk).

15

ACCOMMODATION AND EATING

Cambrian Hotel New Rd, 1 mile southeast T 01545 560295, E cambrianhotel@newquay.co.uk. Clean, well-presented and friendly hotel with beautiful, understated rooms and original features like stained-glass leadlight windows. Good restaurant too. **£70**

★ Crown Inn Llwyndafydd, 4 miles south T 01545 560396 W the-crown-inn.moonfruit.com. Excellent real ale pub famed for its hearty portions of straightforward food (burgers £6; most mains £9–12) and the Sunday carvery lunches (noon –2pm; £6). Daily noon–10pm or later.

Hungry Trout 2 South John St T 01545 560680, W thehungrytrout.co.uk. A couple of delightful rooms, both with sea views but only one en-suite (£10 more), above New Quay's finest seafood restaurant, where you might try monkfish wrapped in Carmarthen ham (£12). There's outside seating for those summer evenings. Food served daily 8am–10pm. **£85**

Seahorse Inn Margaret St T 01545 560736. This fine, traditional local, a world away from the holiday bustle down the street, is little more than one room with exposed stonework, fake beams, pool table and a limited range of good ales. Known to Dylan Thomas as the *Commercial*, it was the model for the *Sailor's Arms* in *Under Milk Wood*. Daily 11am–10pm or later.

Aberaeron and around

ABERAERON, seven miles northeast of New Quay, comes as something of a surprise. This little nugget of Georgian architecture was built by the Reverend Alban Gwynne, who spent his wife's inheritance dredging the Aeron Estuary and constructing a planned town around it as a new port for Mid-Wales. The colourful terraces of quoin-edged buildings around **Alban Square** and along **Quay Parade** are undoubtedly pretty, though the moneyed weekenders from Cardiff (and even London) are more interested in the excellent array of places to stay as well as the good restaurants.

Aberaeron's beach is unappealing, so head out along the coast path or just amble around the streets and waterfront and graze in its cafés and pubs.

Llanerchaeron

Three miles east of Aberaeron along the A482 **House & gardens** April–Oct daily 11am–5pm; reduced hours in winter • NT • £5.80 **Parkland** All year dawn–dusk • NT • Free • T 01545 570200

Aberaeron's one essential sight, **Llanerchaeron**, was once an integrated smallholding typical of this region. Today the estate boasts exquisite kitchen gardens and a pristine, Nash-designed main house.

ARRIVAL AND INFORMATION — ABERAERON

By bus Buses from Aberystwyth (every 30min; 40min), Cardigan (7 daily; 50min) and New Quay (hourly; 20min) stop on the A487/Bridge St.

Tourist office Pen Cei (July–Sept daily 10am–5pm; Oct–June Mon–Sat 10am–5pm; T 01545 570602, E aberaerontic@ceredigion.gov.uk). They lend visitors free "town trail" audioguides for a two-hour stroll around the notable buildings.

ACCOMMODATION AND EATING

Cadwgan 10 Market St ⓣ01545 570149. Unpretentious local that's like walking into someone's living room; someone who serves a rotating roster of real ales and a few bar snacks, that is. Daily 11am–10pm or later.

★ **Harbourmaster Hotel** 1 Pen Cei ⓣ01545 570755, ⓦharbour-master.com. Wonderful hotel with ultra-modern rooms all with crisp white linen softened by Welsh wool throws. Singles and suites are available. The convivial bistro/bar is great, too – perfect for sinking into a sofa with a real ale or one of the two dozen wines by the glass. There's no attempt to be flash, but what they do – the likes of cheeseburger, pepper steak, Moroccan lamb stew or classic pizza (all £10–14), plus delicious desserts – they do with aplomb. The more formal restaurant offers fancier dishes: pork belly with creamed celeriac, perhaps, or pan-fried scallops (mains £16–18). Daily: bistro 8–11.15am & noon–9pm; restaurant 6.30–9pm. **£110**

The Monachty Market St ⓣ01545 570389, ⓦsabrain.com. These seven modernized rooms over a Brains pub are the cheapest in town; some have great views. There's free wi-fi but breakfast is not included. **£55**

Naturally Scrumptious Market St ⓣ01545 574733 ⓦnaturallyscrumptious.co.uk. Excellent deli groaning with Welsh cheese, pies, posh sausages and panini. The cakes are best eaten with a coffee or one of their fine teas in the cute little café behind. Daily 9am–4pm.

Aberystwyth

The liveliest seaside resort in Wales, **ABERYSTWYTH** is an essential stop. With two long, gentle bays curving around between rocky heads, its position is hard to beat, and being rooted in all aspects of Welsh culture, it is possibly the most enjoyable and relaxed place to gain an insight into the national psyche. As the capital of sparsely populated

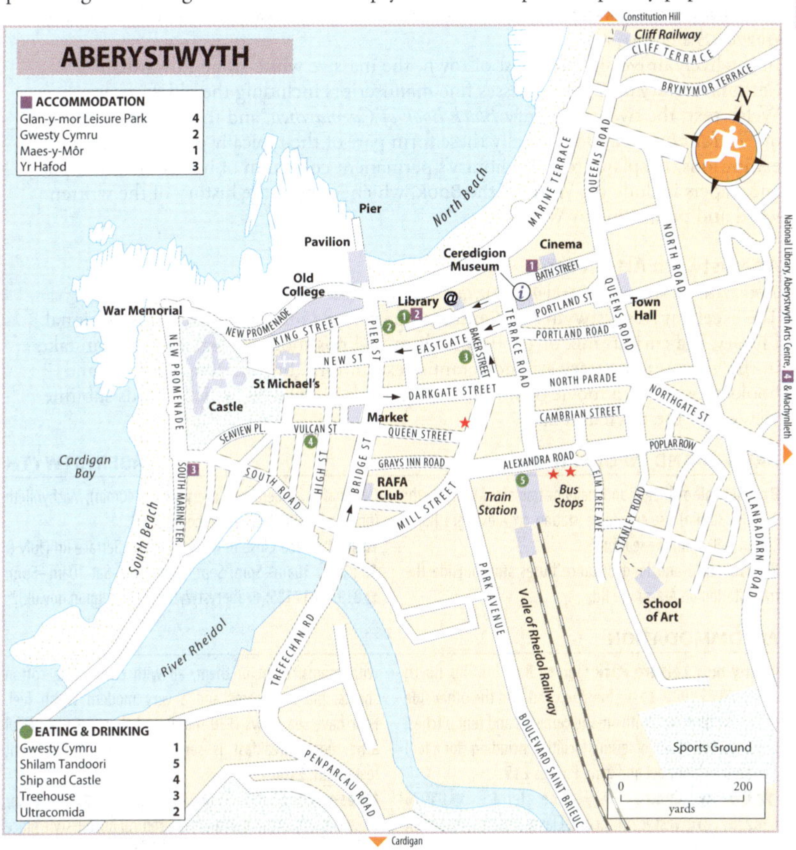

Mid-Wales, and with one of the most prestigious university colleges in the country, it offers plenty of things to do, and has a nice array of Victorian and Edwardian seaside trappings. Politics here are firmly radical Welsh – in a country that still struggles with its inherent conservatism, Aberystwyth is a blast of fresh air.

Marine Terrace and around

At the north end of **Marine Terrace**, Aberystwyth's long Promenade, **Constitution Hill** (430ft) rises from the rocky beach to a tatty jumble of amenities – café, picnic area, telescopes and an octagonal **camera obscura** (Easter–Oct daily 10am–5pm; free). You can walk/hike up, or take the clanking 1896 **cliff railway** (April–Oct daily 10am–6pm; Nov–March Wed–Sun 10.30am–4pm; £3.50 return; ⓦaberystwythcliffrailway.co.uk). The **Ceredigion Museum** (Easter–Oct Mon–Sat 10am–5pm; Nov–Easter Mon–Sat noon–4.30pm; free), just off Marine Terrace on Terrace Rd, houses reconstructed cottages, a dairy and a nineteenth-century pharmacy in the ornate Edwardian music hall, the Coliseum.

Marine Terrace continues past the spindly **pier** to the dazzling, John Nash-designed **Old College**, all turrets, friezes and mosaics. Originally a villa, it was converted to a hotel to soak up the anticipated masses arriving on the new railway. When the venture failed, the building was sold to the fledgling university.

National Library of Wales

University campus, off Penglais Rd • Mon–Fri 9.30am–6pm, Sat 9.30am–5pm; free guided tours Mon 11am & Wed 2.15pm • Free • ⓣ01970 632548, ⓦllgc.org.uk

In the lively university area, east of town, the massive white-stone Edwardian **National Library of Wales** possesses fine manuscripts including the oldest extant Welsh text, the twelfth-century *Black Book of Carmarthen*, and the earliest manuscript of *The Mabinogion*. Occasionally these form part of the typically excellent temporary exhibitions. Displays from the library's permanent collection of books, manuscripts and papers include the **World of the Book**, which looks at the history of the written word and publishing in Wales.

Aberystwyth Arts Centre

University campus, off Penglais Rd • ⓣ01970 623232, ⓦaberystwythartscentre.co.uk

The excellent **Aberystwyth Arts Centre**, a quarter of a mile uphill from the National Library, is a curious mix of 1960s brutalism and postmodern elegance. You can take in the various temporary art and ceramics exhibitions, browse designer crafts and bookshops, catch a movie or simply have a drink in the **café**, which affords sublime views over the town and bay.

ARRIVAL AND INFORMATION — ABERYSTWYTH

By train Vale of Rheidol and mainline trains (to Machynlleth: 9 daily; 30min) use the same station on Alexandra Rd, a 10min walk from the seafront.

By bus Local and long-distance buses stop outside the train station on Alexandra Rd.

Destinations Aberaeron (every 30min; 40min); Machynlleth (hourly; 45min); New Quay (hourly; 1hr).

Tourist office Close to the seafront on Terrace Rd (July & Aug daily 10am–5pm; Sept–June Mon–Sat 10am–5pm; ⓣ01970 612125; ⓔaberystwythtic@ceredigion.gov.uk).

ACCOMMODATION

Glan-y-mor Leisure Park Clarach Bay, 3 miles north ⓣ01970 828900, ⓦsunbourne.co.uk. On the other side of Constitution Hill, with on-site caravans and tent pitches, plus a superb range of leisure facilities including (for a fee) a heated indoor pool and gym. Pitches **£19**

★ **Gwesty Cymru** 19 Marine Terrace ⓣ01970 6122252, ⓦgwestycymru.com. Classy seafront restaurant with rooms: eight of them, all with crisp white cotton sheets, big bathrooms and a very modern Welsh feel. Four have sea views (£30 more) and there's a wonderful attic room. Breakfast is served in the half-basement restaurant. **£100**

Maes-y-Môr 25 Bath St ⓣ01970 639270, ⓦmaesymor.co.uk. Brightly painted and very central hostel-style place with two doubles, six twins and a family room, plus a good guest kitchen, laundry and free wi-fi. Each room has TV, tea and coffee. Breakfast not included. £55

★ **Yr Hafod** 1 South Marine Terrace ⓣ 01970 617579, ⓦ yrhafod.co.uk. Good-value seafront accommodation, with spacious, well-maintained and tastefully decorated rooms (some en-suite and several with sea views). £78

EATING AND DRINKING

Gwesty Cymru 19 Marine Terrace ⓣ 01970 6122252, ⓦ gwestycymru.com. This lovely slate-floored restaurant is one of the smartest places to eat in town. Expect the likes of crispy duck with mango and lychee salsa (£7) followed by mains such as hake florentine (£16). The £8 lunches (Mon–Fri) are excellent value and the sea-view terrace makes an ideal spot for a pre-dinner drink. Daily noon–3pm & 6–10pm.

Shilam Tandoori Alexandra Rd ⓣ 01970 615015, ⓦ shilam.co.uk. Superb restaurant in the train station with unusual specialities and good vegetarian choices such as shabjee khufta with vegetable balls. The daily buffet (noon–5pm) is great value at £5.50. Daily noon–11pm.

Ship and Castle Corner of Vulcan and High sts ⓣ 01970 612334, ⓦ shipandcastle.co.uk. Nicely refurbished, youthful pub with a pool table, a great jukebox and the best selection of real ales in town. Daily 11am–11pm.

★ **Treehouse** 14 Baker St ⓣ 01970 615791, ⓦ treehousewales.co.uk. Upbeat, mostly vegetarian café above a wholefood shop. Good veggie rissoles, pizza, salads and coffee, plus daily specials. They also bake their own breads and cakes. Mon–Fri 10am–5pm, Sat 9am–5pm.

★ **Ultracomida** 31 Pier St ⓣ 01970 630686, ⓦ ultracomida.co.uk. Spain comes to Aber in this fabulous deli, full of Iberian wines, French and Welsh cheeses, and olives. They do freshly made sandwiches to go, and a great Spanish breakfast (Serrano, manchego, OJ and strong coffee; 10–11.30am; £6). Also tapas-style dinners on Fri & Sat nights (£20). Mon–Thurs 10am–5pm, Fri & Sat 10am–9pm, Sun 1–3.30pm.

15

NIGHTLIFE AND ENTERTAINMENT

Aberystwyth Arts Centre University campus, off Penglais Rd ⓣ 01970 623232, ⓦ aberystwythartscentre.co.uk. The town's main venue for art-house cinema, touring theatre, classes and events.

Côr Meibion Aberystwyth RAFA Club, Bridge St ⓣ 01970 615320. Visitors are welcome to attend rehearsals of the Male Voice Choir here. Thurs 7–8.30pm.

Drwm National Library, University campus, off Penglais Rd ⓣ 01970 632800, ⓦ drwm.llgc.org.uk. There's always lots going on at this centre for film, lectures and concerts, housed in the National Library (see opposite).

The Vale of Rheidol

Inland from Aberystwyth, the River Rheidol winds its way up to a secluded, wooded valley, where old industrial workings have sometimes moulded themselves into the contours, rising up past waterfalls and hamlets to **Devil's Bridge**. The latter is best accessed by narrow-gauge railway; otherwise you need your own transport.

Vale of Rheidol Railway

April–Oct 2–4 trains most days • £14.50 return • ⓣ 01970 625819, ⓦ rheidolrailway.co.uk

Steam trains on the narrow-gauge **Vale of Rheidol Railway** wheeze their way along steep hillsides from the Aber terminus to Devil's Bridge. It was built in 1902, ostensibly for the valley's lead mines but with a canny eye on its tourist potential as well, and has run ever since.

Devil's Bridge

Twelve miles east of Aberystwyth, folk legend, picturesque scenery and travellers' lore combine at **DEVIL'S BRIDGE** (Pontarfynach), a tiny settlement built solely for the growing visitor trade of the last few hundred years.

The **bridge** spanning the chasm of the churning River Mynach is actually three stacked bridges – the eleventh-century original, a stone arch from 1753 and the modern road bridge. Enter the turnstile (£1) upstream of the bridge and head down slippery steps to the deep cleft for a remarkable view of the **Punch Bowl**, where the water pounds and hurtles through the gap crowned by the bridges.

Mynach Falls

Open all hours • Easter–Oct daily 9.45am–5pm • £3.50, at other times pay £2 in the turnstile

Across the road from the Punch Bowl the trails around the crashing **Mynach Falls** offer even more dramatic sights as the path tumbles down into the valley below the bridges. The scenery here is magnificent: sharp, wooded slopes rise away from the frothing river and distant mountain peaks surface on the horizon.

Bwlch Nant yr Arian

A44, 9 miles east of Aberystwyth • **Visitor Centre** daily: Easter–Sept 10am–5pm; Oct–Easter generally 10.30am to dusk • Free, parking £1.50 • ⓣ 01970 890453, ⓦ www.forestry.gov.uk/bwlchnantyrarian

Bwlch Nant yr Arian is famous for its red kites, easy walks and varied mountain biking (no rentals). From the **visitor centre**, which has a decent café with a lovely deck, three well-marked walking trails (30min, 1hr & 2hr) head out into the evergreen forest and among the abandoned lead-mining detritus. The easiest and shortest trail loops around a lake past the kite hide, a superb spot for watching the daily red kite feeding (3pm, 2pm in winter) when 20lb of beef and lamb lure up to two hundred kites.

Machynlleth and around

Eighteen miles northeast of Aberystwyth is **MACHYNLLETH** (pronounced "ma-hun-cthleth"), a bustling little place with a great vibe, as well being the undisputed centre of all things "New Age", thanks in large part to the nearby **Centre for Alternative Technology**. The wide main street, **Heol Maengwyn**, is busiest on Wednesdays, when a lively market springs up; **Heol Penrallt** intersects this at the fussy clocktower.

Owain Glyndŵr Centre

Heol Maengwyn • Mid-June to Aug daily 10am–5pm; March to mid-June & Sept Tues–Sat 10am–5pm; Oct–Dec Tues–Sat 11am–4pm • £2.50 • ⓣ 01654 702932, ⓦ canolfanglyndwr.org

The **Owain Glyndŵr Centre**, in the partly fifteenth-century **Parliament House,** charts Glyndŵr's life (see below), his military campaign, his downfall, and the 1404 parliament when he controlled almost all of what we now know as Wales.

Museum of Modern Art Wales

Heol Penrallt • Mon–Sat 10am–4pm • Free • ⓣ 01654 703355, ⓦ www.momawales.org.uk

The **Museum of Modern Art Wales**, housed in a beautifully serene old chapel, hosts an ongoing programme of temporary exhibitions. It also has a peaceful, arty **café**, and

OWAIN GLYNDŴR, WELSH HERO

Owain Glyndŵr has remained a potent figurehead of Welsh nationalism since he rose up against the occupying English in the early fifteenth century. He was born into an aristocratic family, and studied English in London, where he became a distinguished soldier of the English king. When he returned to Wales to take up his claim as Prince of Wales, he became the focus of a rebellion born of discontent with the English rulers.

Glyndŵr garnered four thousand supporters and attacked Ruthin, Denbigh, Rhuddlan, Flint and Oswestry, before finally encountering English resistance at Welshpool. In a vain attempt to break the spirit of the rebellion, England's Henry IV drew up severely punitive laws, even outlawing Welsh-language bards and singers. Even so, by the end of 1403, Glyndŵr controlled most of Wales. In 1404, he was crowned king of a free Wales and assembled a parliament at Machynlleth, where he drew up mutual recognition treaties with France and Spain. Glyndŵr made plans to carve up England and Wales into three as part of an alliance against the English king, but started to lose ground before eventually being forced into hiding (where he died). The anti-Welsh laws remained in place until the coronation of Henry VII, who had Welsh origins, in 1485, and Wales was subsequently subsumed into English custom and law.

hosts films, theatre, comedy and concerts, along with the **Gŵyl Machynlleth festival**, held in August, which combines classical and some folk music with theatre and debate.

Centre for Alternative Technology

A487, 3 miles north of Machynlleth • Daily: Easter–Oct 10am–5.30pm; Nov–Easter 10am–5pm • £8.50 summer, £6.50 winter, £1 discount for walkers, cyclists and bus users, 50 percent off for train arrivals • ⓣ 01654 705952, ⓦ cat.org.uk

After the oil crisis of 1974, seven acres of a once-derelict slate quarry were turned into the **Centre for Alternative Technology** (CAT), an almost entirely sustainable community. At one stage, eighty percent of the power was generated from wind, sun and water, but this is no back-to-the-land hippy commune. Much of the on-site technology was developed and built here, but with the rise of eco-consciousness the emphasis has shifted more towards promoting its application in urban situations. CAT's water-balanced **cliff railway** (Easter–Oct) whisks visitors 200ft up from the car park to the beautiful main site, sensitively landscaped using local slate and wood, and you can easily spend half a day sauntering around. There's plenty for kids, a good wholefood restaurant and an excellent shop. Check the website for summer residential **volunteer programmes**.

Corris Mine Explorers

Corris Craft Centre, A487, 6 miles north of Machynlleth • Tours all year on demand, book ahead • 1hr Taster £10, 2hr Explorer £16, 4hr Expedition £32 • ⓣ 01654 761244, ⓦ corrismineexplorers.co.uk

Corris Mine Explorers take you – sporting climbing harnesses and helmets – deep into a cool, dark disused slate mine that has been barely touched since it closed down in 1970. Ancient tallow candles are stuck to the walls, hand drills lies scattered along the passageways and winch flywheels still spin at the slightest touch. Adventurous parties might be clipped into safety wires in order to sidle along the steeply shelving walls of a vast slate cavern, while others might just want to hear fascinating stories about mining life. Wear something warm.

ARRIVAL AND DEPARTURE — MACHYNLLETH

By train The station is a 5min walk up Heol Penrallt from the town's central clocktower.

Destinations Aberdyfi (8 daily; 20min); Aberystwyth (9 daily; 30min); Harlech (8 daily; 1hr 20min); Porthmadog (8 daily; 1hr 50min).

By bus Buses stop close to the town's central clocktower, and many also call at the train station.

Destinations Aberdyfi (8 daily; 20min); Aberystwyth (hourly; 45min); Corris (hourly; 15min); Dolgellau (mostly hourly; 30min).

ACCOMMODATION AND EATING

Maenllwyd Newtown Rd ⓣ 01654 702928, ⓦ maenllwyd.co.uk. Comfortable eight-room B&B in a former manse. All is clean and well maintained and there's a large garden. **£65**

Quarry Café Heol Maengwyn ⓣ 01654 702624, ⓦ cat.org.uk/qsqc. This popular, CAT-run veggie café is like stepping back into the 1980s; it does cheesy vegetable bakes, wholesome salads and the "Big Mach" burger (with lentil patty and soya mayo). Mon–Sat 9am–4.30pm.

Reditreks Bunkhouse Off Heol Powys ⓣ 01654 702184, ⓦ reditreks.com. Deluxe bunkhouse in the heart of town with camping facilities, a drying room, bike wash, BBQ area and bike storage shed. Camping **£5**, bunks **£15**

Wynnstay Arms Heol Maengwyn ⓣ 01654 702941, ⓦ wynnstay-hotel.com. Some rooms in this former coaching inn have heavy beams, creaky floors and a four-poster, others are relatively modern. The hotel is at the heart of the town's social life, with a couple of good restaurants and cosy guest lounges where you can curl up with a book. For something casual head for the superb pizzeria out the back (closed Sun), or step up to the classic slate-floored restaurant with inventive Welsh dishes like duck with vegetable linguini and truffle gravy (mains £13–17). It's a fine place for a beer too. Daily noon–2.30pm & 6–11pm. **£90**

★ **Ynyshir Hall** A487, 6 miles southwest beside the Ynys-hir Nature Reserve ⓣ 01654 781209, ⓦ ynyshir-hall.co.uk. Sublime country-house hotel that ranks among Britain's finest. Set in fourteen acres of manicured grounds, it's gracious without being stuffy, and regularly attracts the glitterati. Its elegant Michelin-starred restaurant uses the finest local produce in Modern British dishes on a six-course à la carte menu (£72.50) and ten-course tasting menu (£90). You could also have Sunday lunch (three courses £25), and afternoon tea (£19.50) served in the grounds or any of the delightful public rooms. Daily noon–2pm, 3–5pm & 7–10pm. £315

Aberdyfi and around

The proud maritime heritage of **ABERDYFI** (Aberdovey) has largely been replaced by the life of a well-heeled resort. With its south-facing aspect across the Dyfi estuary, it's a lovely base for exploring the Talyllyn and Dysynni valleys to the north, but there's not much in the way of activities – though you can swim at Cemetery Beach, about a mile and a half north.

ARRIVAL AND INFORMATION — ABERDYFI

By train There are stations at both ends of town, with services from Machynlleth (8 daily; 20min) and Porthmadog (8 daily; 1hr 30min).

15

By bus Buses from Machynlleth (8 daily; 20min) and Tywyn (8 daily; 10min) stop in the centre of the resort.

Tourist office Wharf Gardens (Easter–Oct daily 9.30am–5.30pm; T 01654 767321, E tic.aberdyfi@eryri-npa.gov.uki).

ACCOMMODATION AND EATING

Britannia Inn 13 Seaview Terrace T 01654 767426, W britannia-aberdovey.co.uk. Three smart rooms, one with superb sea views (£10 more) above the town's best pub. In good weather, everyone piles onto the deck for the sunset with a pint of real ale. Meals (mostly £10–13) are a cut above the usual pub standard and might include Aberdyfi crab. Mon–Wed 11am–midnight, Thurs–Sat 11am–1am, Sun noon–midnight. £95

★ **Llety Bodfor** On the seafront T 01654 767475, W lletybodfor.co.uk. The eight contemporary rooms in this townhouse include a couple of singles, plus doubles and very spacious suites with sea views. Hang out in the lovely guest lounge equipped with a piano, games and a stack of old vinyl. Breakfast isn't included but there is a small self-catering kitchen. £75

Talyllyn Railway

Station Rd, Tywyn, 4 miles north of Aberdyfi • April–Oct 2–7 trains daily, plus some winter weekends • £13 unlimited one-day travel, first-class additional £2 each way • T 01654 710472, W talyllyn.co.uk

Experience the lower Talyllyn Valley aboard the cute 27-inch gauge **Talyllyn Railway**, the inspiration for Thomas the Tank Engine. The railway tootles seven miles inland from Tywyn through the delightful wooded valley to the old slate quarries at Nant Gwernol. From 1866 to 1946, the rail line hauled slate to Tywyn Wharf station. Five years after the quarry's closure, rail enthusiasts took over the running of services, making this the world's first volunteer-run railway. The round trip takes just over two hours, but you can get on and off as frequently as the schedule allows, taking in some fine broadleaf forest walks (best at Dolgoch Falls station), or the small village of **Abergynolwyn**.

The Dysynni Valley

The **Dysynni valley** has more sights than the Talyllyn valley, but limited public transport. A mile and a half northwest of Abergynolwyn, a side road cuts northeast to the hamlet of **Llanfihangel-y-Pennant** where the church contains a fabulous three-dimensional patchwork map of the Dysynni Valley. Nearby, visit the scant, moody ruins of **Castell-y-Bere** (CADW; free access), a fortress built by Llywelyn the Great in 1221 to protect the mountain passes. Three miles seaward stands the impressive **Craig y Deryn** (Birds' Rock), a 760ft-high cliff where breeding cormorants have remained loyal to the spot despite being left landlocked by the receding sea.

Dolgellau and around

The handsome former county town of **DOLGELLAU** still maintains an air of unhurried importance, never more so than when all the area's farmers pile into town for market.

WALKS AROUND DOLGELLAU

There some great **walks** and beautiful cycle trails around Dolgellau. Here are a couple of the best; the Dolgellau tourist office (see below) has details of many more.

Precipice Walk (3–4 miles; 2hr; negligible ascent). Easy-going loop with great views to the 1000ft ramparts of Cadair Idris and along the Mawddach Estuary – best in late afternoon or early morning sun.

Cadair Idris: Pony Path (9 miles; 4–5hr; 2800ft ascent). If the weather is fine, don't miss this classic and enjoyable ascent of Cadair Idris. Early views to the craggy flanks of the massif are tremendous, but they disappear as you climb steeply to the col, where you turn left on a rocky path to the summit shelter on Penygadair (2930ft).

With the lofty crags of **Cadair Idris** framing the grey squares and streets, Dolgellau feels as Welsh as it is possible to be.

Tŷ Siamas

Eldon Square • Tues–Fri 10am–4pm Sat 10am–1pm • £3.95 • T 01341 421800, W tysiamas.com

15

The National Centre for Welsh Folk Music is known as **Tŷ Siamas**, after the local creator of the Welsh triple harp. Modern examples can be seen alongside traditional instruments such as the pibgorn, the crwth and the pibacwd. Touch screens let you try your hand at playing instruments.

Coed-y-Brenin

A470, 7 miles north of Dolgellau • **Visitor Centre** April–Oct daily 9.30am–5pm; Nov–March Mon–Fri 9.30am–4.30pm, Sat & Sun 9.30am–5pm • Parking £4 • T 01341 440747, W www.forestry.gov.uk/coedybrenin

For years, mountain bikers from around Britain and beyond have been flocking to **Coed-y-Brenin** for some of Wales's finest mountain biking. With the addition of dedicated forest running and walking trails, a high ropes adventure, orienteering and Geocaching courses and a kids' play area, it has developed into one of the most popular spots in southern Snowdonia. At the visitor centre you can rent bikes (from £25 a day), buy a pack of trail maps (£2.50; or download free from the website), take a shower (£1) and recover in the good café.

ARRIVAL AND INFORMATION — DOLGELLAU

By bus Buses pull into Eldon Square. Most northbound services head inland past Coed-y-Brenin.

Destinations Bala (hourly; 35min); Machynlleth (mostly hourly; 30min); Porthmadog (6 daily; 50min).

Tourist office Eldon Square (Easter–Oct daily 9.30am–5.30pm; Nov–Easter Mon & Thurs–Sun 9.30am–4.30pm; T 01341 422888, E tic.dolgellau@eyri-npa.gov.uk). Lots of information on local walks (see above) along with displays on the town's Quaker heritage and on the southern reaches of Snowdonia.

Bike rental Dolgellau Cycles, Smithfield St (T 01341 423332, W dolgellaucycles.co.uk) rent bikes suitable for the Mawddach Trail (£13/half day, £20/day).

ACCOMMODATION

★ **Ffynnon** Love Lane T 01341 421774, W ffynnontownhouse.com. The area's most stylish accommodation, with five subtly decorated rooms offset by feature pieces. All rooms have separate sitting areas, large bathrooms (all with bathtub) and great views. Rates include afternoon tea on arrival, newspapers and honesty bar, and they will even send you out with a deluxe picnic lunch. **£135**

George III Hotel A493, Penmaenpool, 2.3 miles west of Dolgellau T 01341 422525, W georgethethird.co.uk. Superb seventeenth-century hotel right by the Mawddach Estuary (bus #28). The wood-beamed rooms (some in former train station buildings) have been smartly updated, and the restaurant (see p.676) is great. **£100**

Tan-y-Fron Arran Rd T 01341 422638, W tanyfron.co.uk. Well-appointed camping and caravan site handily sited a 5min walk from town. Countryside views and spotless facilities, including hot showers. Pitches **£17**

Tyddyn Mawr Farmhouse Islawrdref, 3 miles southwest of Dolgellau T 01341 422331, W wales-guesthouse.co.uk. Eighteenth-century farmhouse on the slopes of Cadair Idris at the foot of the Pony Path. Very welcoming and great value, with open fireplaces and just two large rooms. **£74**

YHA Kings Penmaenpool, 4.6 miles west of Dolgellau

T 0845 371 9327, E kings@yha.org.uk. Large country house a mile up a wooded valley off the #28 Tywyn bus route (last bus around 6pm), with six-bed rooms and a self-catering kitchen but no TV or even mobile reception. An ideal base for the Pony Path up Cadair Idris. Take food with you. £15

EATING AND DRINKING

★ **Dylanwad Da** 2 Smithfield St T 01341 422870, W dylanwad.co.uk. The best restaurant in town, with creative dishes – like Thai seafood soup and cumin-spiced salmon or Moroccan lamb stew (mains £14–19) – in simple surroundings. Good coffee and cakes during the day. March–Jan Thurs–Sat 10am–3pm & 7–9pm.

George III A493, Penmaenpool, 2.3 miles west of Dolgellau T 01341 422525, W georgethethird.co.uk. This hotel restaurant is a superb spot for a cream tea overlooking the Mawddach Estuary – you can also enjoy a sunset drink in the dark wood bar. Quality pub meals (mostly £9–12) might include lamb shank, fish and chips or bacon-wrapped chicken. Daily 11am–10.30pm.

★ **Mawddach** A496, 2 miles northwest T 01341 424020, W mawddach.com. Slate floors, exposed beams and great mountain and estuary views combine with simply prepared and beautifully cooked dishes (mains mostly £10–15), from hake with purple broccoli and caper sauce to butternut squash risotto. Wed–Sat 12.30–3pm & 6.30–10.30pm, Sun noon–4pm.

★ **Siop Coffi T.H.** Glyndŵr St T 01341 423 552. Great café in a former ironmongers, the glassed-in office now a snug where folk are usually tapping away on laptops (free wi-fi, naturally). Baguettes and panini are all freshly made and there are heaps of sumptuous cakes. Mon–Sat 9am–5pm, Sun 10am–4pm.

15

Harlech

Charming **HARLECH**, twenty miles northwest of Dolgellau, is one of the highlights of the Cambrian coast, with its time-worn castle dramatically clinging to its rocky outcrop and the town cloaking the ridge behind, commanding one of Wales's finest views over Cardigan Bay to the Llŷn.

Harlech Castle

March–June, Sept & Oct daily 9.30am–5pm; July & Aug daily 9.30am–6pm; Nov–Feb Mon–Sat 10am–4pm, Sun 11am–4pm • CADW • £3.80 • T 01766 780552

Harlech's substantially complete **castle** sits on its 200ft-high bluff, a site chosen by Edward I for one more link in his magnificent chain of fortresses. Begun in 1285, it was built of a hard Cambrian rock, known as Harlech grit, hewn from the moat. Harlech withstood a siege in 1295, but was taken by Owain Glyndŵr in 1404. The young Henry VII withstood a seven-year siege at the hands of the Yorkists until 1468, when the castle was again taken. It fell into ruin, but was put back into service for Charles I during the Civil War; in March 1647, it was the last Royalist castle to fall. The first defensive line comprised the three successive pairs of gates and portcullises built between the two massive half-round towers of the **gatehouse**, where an **exhibition** now outlines the castle's history. Much of the castle's outermost ring has been destroyed, leaving only the 12ft-thick curtain walls rising up 40ft to the exposed **battlements**. Only the towering gatehouse prevents you from walking the full circuit.

ARRIVAL AND INFORMATION — HARLECH

By train The train station is on the A496 below the castle.
Destinations Barmouth (8 daily; 25min); Machynlleth (8 daily; 1hr 20min); Porthmadog (8 daily; 20min).

By bus Buses generally call both at the train station and at the southern end of High St.
Destinations Barmouth (hourly; 30min); Blaenau Ffestiniog (3 daily; 35min).

Tourist office High St (Easter–Oct daily 9.30am–5.30pm; T 01766 780658, E ticharlech@eryri-npa.gov.uk). In 2013 or 2014 it may move to the former Castle Hotel, opposite the Castle entrance, which is set to become home to an interpretive centre.

ACCOMMODATION AND EATING

★ **Castle Cottage** Pen Llech, T 01766 780479, W castlecottageharlech.co.uk. Excellent restaurant with rooms, with a contemporary yet cosily informal feel. The seven rooms (including three fabulous suites) are each very different, many with massive weathered beams and slate floors, but they're all well appointed, decorated in lovely natural tones. People travel from miles around for the wonderful food at the unpretentious Modern British restaurant with Welsh art on the walls. There's just one price (£38); this gets you canapés and three courses which might include Cardigan Bay dressed crab followed by roasted porcetta and black pudding. Food served daily 7–10pm. **£126**

Castle Restaurant & Armoury Bar Twtil T 01766 780416, W caribbeancrabharlech.com. Harlech seems an unlikely place to find a restaurant specializing in contemporary Caribbean cuisine, but it makes a welcome change. Many of the dishes (mains £15–18) are Trinidadian in origin – spicy concoctions such as lamb shank with allspice and sweet potato, or butternut, chickpea and spinach curry, eaten to a background of calypso, jazz or reggae. March–Oct Tues–Thurs 6.30–10.30pm, Fri & Sat 6.30–11pm, Sun 6.30–10pm.

★ **Cemlyn** Stryd Fawr T 01766 780637. Upmarket café serving the best loose-leaf teas and espressos around, plus delicious afternoon teas (£6) and light lunches. The small terrace offers views of Harlech Castle. Mid-March to Nov Wed–Sun 10.30am–5pm.

Pen-y-Garth Old Llanfair Rd T 01766 781352, W pen-y-garth.co.uk. B&B of a high standard in a former YHA. Some rooms come with sea or castle views. Cyclists, walkers and vegetarians are particularly welcome – they even do packed lunches. **£60**

Shell Island T 01341 241453, W shellisland.co.uk. Massive 300-acre campsite with heaps of beachside sites. Campers must pitch tents at least 60ft from each other (unless agreed otherwise), guaranteeing relative solitude amid spectacular scenery, with simply stunning sunsets. No walk-ins; you must have a vehicle. Closed Nov–Feb. **£6** per person.

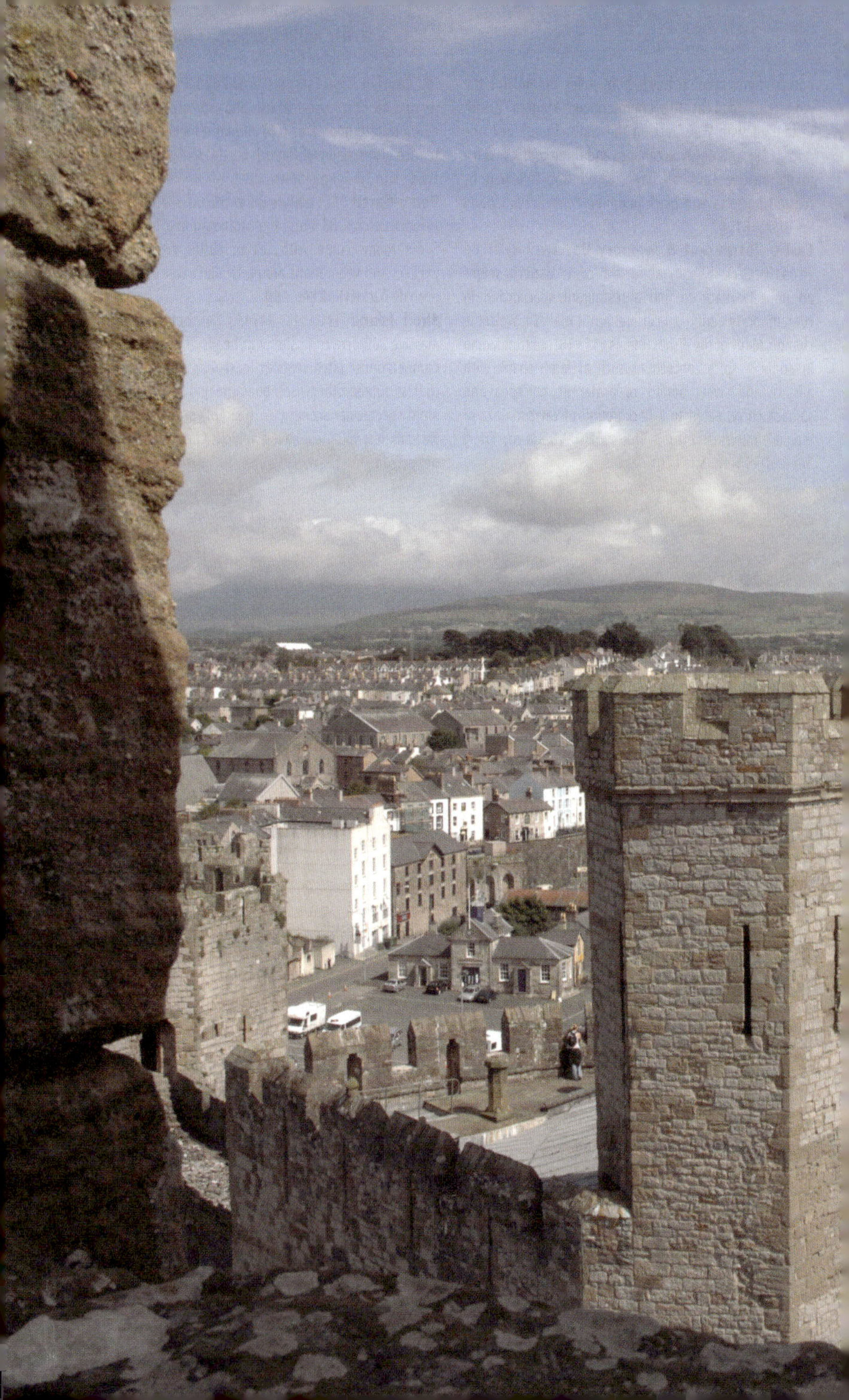

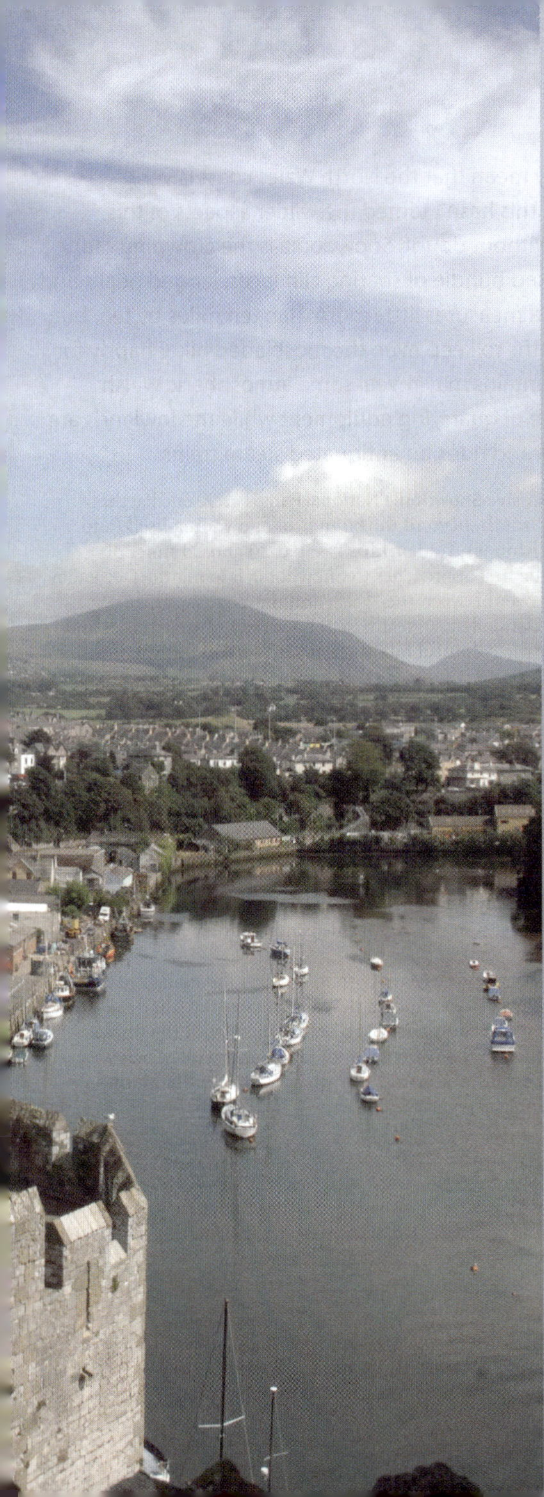

North Wales

683 Llangollen

685 Snowdonia

694 The Llŷn

700 Anglesey

703 The north coast

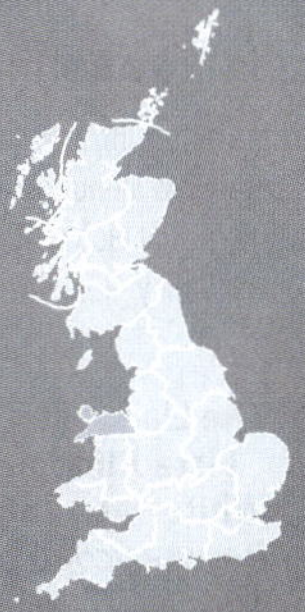

CAERNARFON

North Wales

The fast A55 motorway may mean that the North Wales coast is very accessible, but, fortunately, this hasn't tamed the wilder aspects of this stunningly beautiful area. Without doubt, Snowdonia is the crowning glory of the region. A tightly packed bundle of soaring cliff faces, jagged peaks and plunging waterfalls, the area measures little more than ten miles by ten, but packs enough mountain paths to keep even the most jaded hiker happy for weeks. The folds of the mountains may reveal some atmospheric Welsh castle ruin or decaying piece of quarrying equipment while the lowlands are perfect for lakeside rambles and rides on antiquated steam trains.

Snowdonia is the heart of the massive **Snowdonia National Park** (Parc Cenedlaethol Eryri), which extends north and south, beyond the bounds of Snowdonia itself (and this chapter), to encompass the Rhinogs, Cadair Idris (see p.675) and 23 miles of superb coastal scenery. One of the best approaches to Snowdonia is along the **Dee Valley**, a fertile landscape much fought over between the Welsh and the English. There's a tangibly Welsh feel to fabulous **Llangollen**, a great base for a variety of ruins, rides and rambles, as well as the venue for the colourful **International Eisteddfod** festival. Pressing on along the A5 – the region's second main road – you hit the fringes of Snowdonia at **Betws-y-Coed**, which is slightly twee but great for gentle walks and mountain biking. As you head deeper into the park, old mining and quarry towns such as **Beddgelert**, **Llanberis** and **Blaenau Ffestiniog** make arguably better bases, while on the eastern fringes of Snowdonia, **Bala** tempts with whitewater rafting down the Tryweryn.

16

To the west of Snowdonia, the former slate port of **Porthmadog** is home to the quirky "village" of **Portmeirion** and two superb narrow-gauge steam railways: the **Ffestiniog Railway** and **Welsh Highland Railway**. Beyond lies the gentle rockiness of the **Llŷn peninsula** where Wales ends in a flourish of small coves and seafaring villages. Roads loop back along the **Llŷn** to **Caernarfon**, which is overshadowed by its stupendous castle, the mightiest link in Edward I's Iron Ring of thirteenth-century fortresses across North Wales.

Two historic bridges span the picturesque Menai Strait between the mainland and the island of **Anglesey**, a gentle patchwork of beautiful beaches, ancient sites and Edward's final castle in the handsome town of **Beaumaris**. Back on the mainland, the university and cathedral city of **Bangor** is the area's most cosmopolitan haunt, while **Conwy**'s gritty castle and narrow streets huddle around a scenic quay. Victorian **Llandudno** is easily the best of the seaside resorts.

GETTING AROUND — NORTH WALES

By train Getting around North Wales by train is a pleasure. Fast services along the north coast run all the way to the Irish ferries at Holyhead on Anglesey, while the delightful Conwy Valley line threads inland to link up with the narrow-gauge Ffestiniog Railway at Blaenau Ffestiniog. This in turn meets the Porthmadog–Caernarfon Welsh Highland Railway through Beddgelert and across the southern flanks of Snowdon.

The Llangollen International Music Eisteddfod p.683
Whitewater rafting at Bala p.685
Betws-y-coed biking p.687
Top 5 outdoor activities p.688
Walks from the Ogwen Valley p.689
Ascending Snowdon p.690
The Welsh slate industry p.693
Watersports in Abersoch p.697

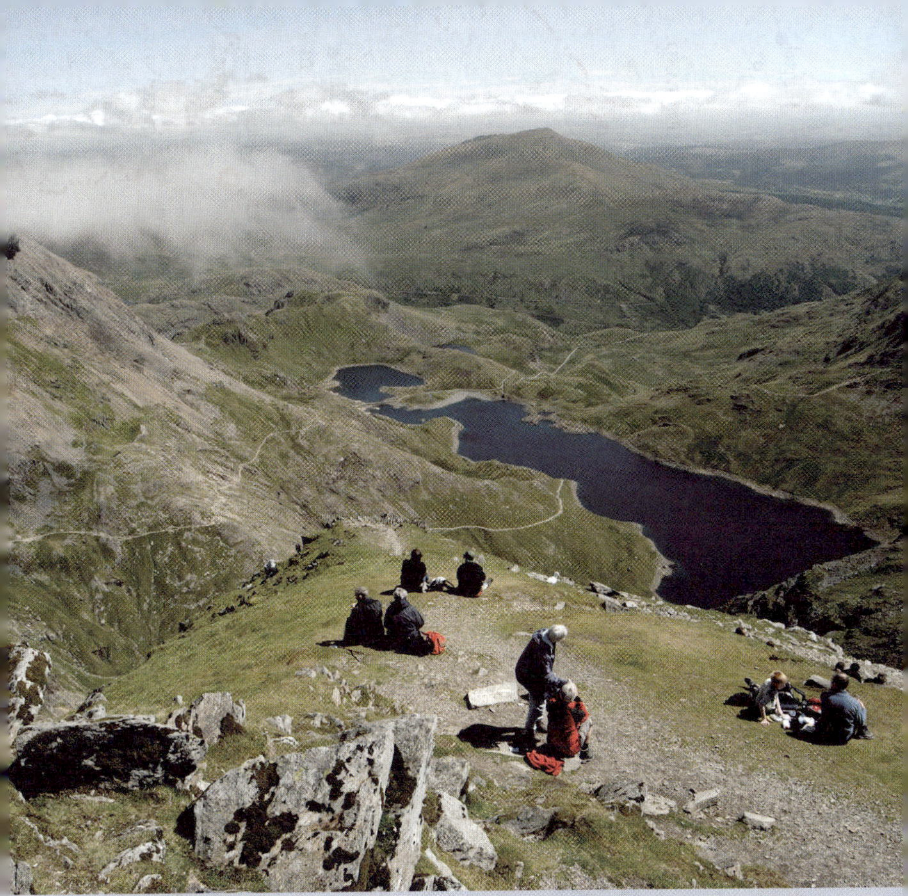

VIEW FROM SNOWDON

Highlights

❶ **Llangollen** Robust and enjoyable riverside town featuring a romantic house, impressive aqueduct and poetic castle ruins. **See p.683**

❷ **Snowdon** Scale Wales's highest mountain, the only one with half a dozen hiking paths and a cog railway converging on the summit-top café and bar. **See p.690**

❸ **Blaenau Ffestiniog** Atmospheric slate-mining town amid rugged mountains, best reached by the narrow-gauge Ffestiniog Railway. **See p.692**

❹ **Portmeirion** Spend the day at this surreal seaside "village" made from bits of rescued architecture, the setting for the cult TV series *The Prisoner*. **See p.696**

❺ **Caernarfon Castle** One of the greatest of Edward I's "Iron Ring" of thirteenth-century castles, with other superb examples at Beaumaris and Conwy. **See p.699**

❻ **Beaumaris** A fine castle and Georgian townscape make this a splendid base for exploring Anglesey's beaches and Neolithic remains. **See p.700**

❼ **Conwy** The pick of North Wales towns, with its imposing castle and intact ring of medieval walls enclosing a fascinating centre. **See p.705**

❽ **Llandudno** The town's gentility is nicely offset by the ruggedness of the neighbouring limestone hummock of the Great Orme, which is reached by cable car. **See p.707**

HIGHLIGHTS ARE MARKED ON THE MAP ON P.682

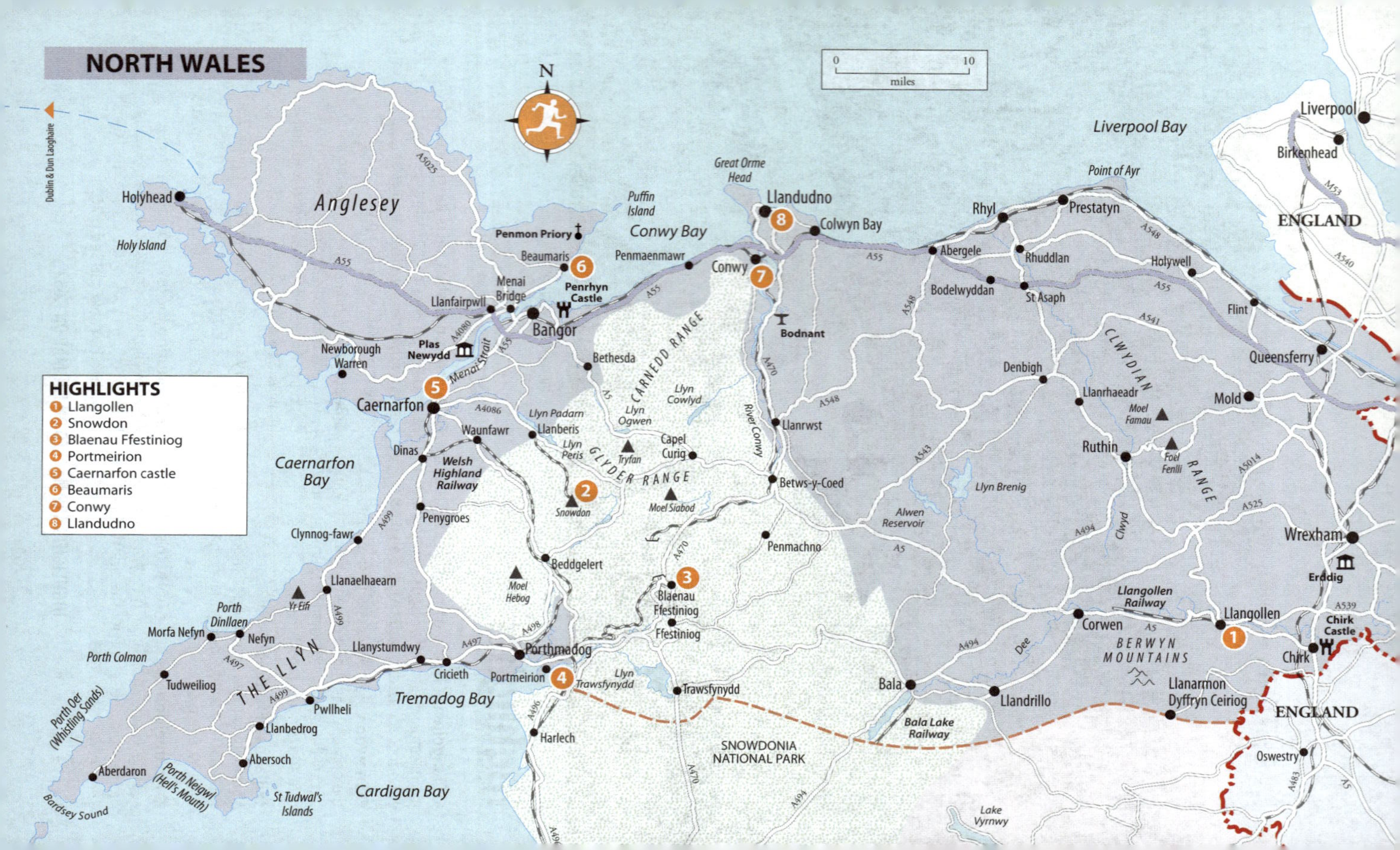
NORTH WALES
HIGHLIGHTS
1 Llangollen
2 Snowdon
3 Blaenau Ffestiniog
4 Portmeirion
5 Caernarfon castle
6 Beaumaris
7 Conwy
8 Llandudno
N
0 10 miles
Dublin & Dun Laoghaire
Holyhead
Holy Island
Anglesey
Penmon Priory
Beaumaris
Menai Bridge
Llanfairpwll
Penrhyn Castle
Bangor
Newborough Warren
Plas Newydd
Menai Strait
Caernarfon
Caernarfon Bay
Puffin Island
Conwy Bay
Penmaenmawr
Great Orme Head
Llandudno
Colwyn Bay
Conwy
Bodnant
Liverpool Bay
Point of Ayr
Rhyl
Prestatyn
Abergele
Rhuddlan
Bodelwyddan
St Asaph
Holywell
Flint
Queensferry
Liverpool
Birkenhead
ENGLAND
Bethesda
CARNEDD RANGE
Llyn Cowlyd
Llyn Ogwen
Llyn Padarn
Llanberis
Llyn Peris
Tryfan
Capel Curig
GLYDER RANGE
Moel Siabod
Snowdon
River Conwy
Llanrwst
Betws-y-Coed
Penmachno
Waunfawr
Dinas
Welsh Highland Railway
Penygroes
Clynnog-fawr
Beddgelert
Moel Hebog
Blaenau Ffestiniog
Ffestiniog
Llanaelhaearn
Yr Eifl
Porth Dinllaen
Morfa Nefyn
Nefyn
Porth Colmon
Tudweiliog
THE LLYN
Llanystumdwy
Cricieth
Porthmadog
Portmeirion
Llyn Trawsfynydd
Trawsfynydd
Tremadog Bay
Pwllheli
Llanbedrog
Abersoch
Harlech
Porth Oer (Whistling Sands)
Aberdaron
Porth Neigwl (Hell's Mouth)
St Tudwal's Islands
Bardsey Sound
Cardigan Bay
SNOWDONIA NATIONAL PARK
Bala
Bala Lake Railway
Lake Vyrnwy
Llandrillo
Denbigh
Llanrhaeadr
CLWYDIAN RANGE
Moel Famau
Foel Fenlli
Ruthin
Mold
Llyn Brenig
Alwen Reservoir
Clwyd
Dee
Wrexham
Erddig
Llangollen Railway
Corwen
Llangollen
Chirk Castle
Chirk
BERWYN MOUNTAINS
Llanarmon Dyffryn Ceiriog
Oswestry
A55
A5025
A4080
A4086
A499
A497
A498
A496
A470
A5
A548
A543
A541
A494
A5014
A525
A539
A540
M53
A483

By bus Buses plug the gaps, especially the Snowdon Sherpa services, which provide hiker access all around Snowdon and the Ogwen Valley. There is no useful bus or train service linking Llangollen with Snowdonia along the A5: instead head along the north coast to either Llandudno Junction or Bangor then inland from there.

Llangollen

LLANGOLLEN, just six miles from the English border, is the embodiment of a Welsh town, clasped tightly in the narrow Dee Valley where the river runs beneath the weighty, Gothic bridge. This was an important town long before the early Romantics arrived at the end of the eighteenth century. Turner came to paint the swollen river and the Cistercian ruin of **Valle Crucis**; John Ruskin found the town "entirely lovely in its gentle wildness"; and writer George Borrow made Llangollen his base for the early part of his 1854 tour detailed in *Wild Wales*. The rich and famous also came to visit the "Ladies of Llangollen" at **Plas Newydd**. But by this stage some of the town's rural charm had been eaten up by the works of one of the century's finest engineers, Thomas Telford, who squeezed both his London–Holyhead trunk road and the **Llangollen Canal** alongside the river.

Plas Newydd

Half a mile up Hill St from the southern end of Castle St • **House** April–Oct Wed–Sun 10am–5pm • £5.50 **Grounds** Open access • Free • Ⓣ 01978 862834

Standing in twelve acres of formal gardens, the two-storey mock-Tudor **Plas Newydd** was, for almost fifty years, home to the **Ladies of Llangollen**. Lady Eleanor Butler and Sarah Ponsonby were a lesbian couple from Anglo-Irish aristocratic backgrounds, who tried to elope at the end of the eighteenth century. After two botched attempts dressed in men's clothes, they were grudgingly allowed to leave their family seats in 1778 with enough allowance to settle in Llangollen, where they became celebrated hosts. Despite their desire for a "life of sweet and delicious retirement", they didn't seem to mind the constant stream of gentry who called on them. Walter Scott was well received, though he found them "a couple of hazy or crazy old sailors" in manner, and like "two respectable superannuated clergymen" in their mode of dress. Visitors' gifts of sculpted **wood panelling** formed the basis of the riotous friezes of woodwork that cover the walls of their modest house; this is set off by a mixed bag of furniture in a style similar to that owned by the ladies.

Llangollen Railway

April–Oct 3–7 services most days; call ahead at other times • £12 return • Ⓣ 01978 860979, Ⓦ llangollen-railway.co.uk

The hills around Llangollen echo to the shrill cry of steam engines easing along the **Llangollen Railway**, shoehorned into the north side of the valley. From Llangollen's

THE LLANGOLLEN INTERNATIONAL MUSIC EISTEDDFOD

Llangollen is heaving all summer, and never more so than in early July, when for six days the town explodes in a frenzy of music, dance, poetry and colour. Unlike the National Eisteddfod, which is a purely Welsh affair, the **International Music Eisteddfod** (Ⓣ 01978 862001, Ⓦ international-eisteddfod.co.uk) draws amateur performers from fifty countries, all competing for prizes inside the 6000-seat Royal International Pavilion, and at several other venues. The eisteddfod has been held in its present form since 1947 when forty choirs from fourteen countries performed. Today, more than 4000 participants lure up to 150,000 visitors, and there is an irresistible *joie de vivre* as brightly costumed dancers stroll the streets and fill the restaurants.

The eisteddfod is followed by the less frenetic **Llangollen Fringe** (Ⓣ 0800 145 5779, Ⓦ llangollenfringe.co.uk), with a number of more "alternative" acts – music, dance, comedy and so on – performing over the third week in July.

time-warped station ancient carriages proudly sporting the liveries of their erstwhile owners are hauled along eight miles of the old Ruabon–Barmouth line to Carrog. A two-mile extension to Corwen should be open by mid-2012.

Castell Dinas Brân

Follow signs to Offa's Dyke Path from Llangollen Wharf

The panoramic view, especially at sunset, justifies the 45-minute slog up to **Castell Dinas Brân** (Crow's Fortress Castle), a few evocative stumps of masonry perched on a hill 800ft above town. This was once the district's largest and most important Welsh fortress, built in the 1230s by the ruler of northern Powys, Prince Madog ap Gruffydd Maelor. Edward I captured it as part of his first campaign against Llywelyn ap Gruffydd, but the castle was left to decay.

Valle Crucis Abbey

A542, 1.6 miles west of Llangollen • April–Oct daily 10am–5pm; Nov–March open access • CADW • April–Oct £2.80; Nov–March free • ⓣ01978 860326

The gaunt ruin of **Valle Crucis Abbey** greets you with its largely intact west wall, pierced by the frame of a rose window. Though one of the last Cistercian foundations in Wales, and the first Gothic abbey in Britain, it is no match for Tintern Abbey (see p.604), but nevertheless stands majestically in a pastoral – and much less-visited – setting. After the Dissolution, in 1535, the church fell into disrepair and the monastic buildings were used as farm buildings. Now they hold displays on monastic life, reached by a detour through the mostly ruined cloister and past the weighty vaulting of the chapter house.

Llangollen Canal

When it was built in 1806, the **Llangollen Canal** was one of Britain's finest feats of canal engineering. Its architect, Thomas Telford, succeeded in building a canal without locks through fourteen miles of hilly terrain, most spectacularly by means of the 100ft-long **Pontcysyllte Aqueduct**, passing 127ft over the River Dee at Froncysyllte, four miles east. Both canal and aqueduct are now a UNESCO World Heritage Site. **Canal trips** (Easter–Oct daily; £12; ⓣ01978 860702, ⓦhorsedrawnboats.co.uk) across the aqueduct leave from Llangollen Wharf, almost opposite the train station.

Erddig

Off the A483, 10 miles northeast of Llangollen • Daily: mid-March to Oct 12.30–4.30pm; Nov & Dec 11am–3.30pm • NT • £9.90, outbuildings & gardens only £6.30 • ⓣ01978 355314

The ancestral home of the Yorke family, the seventeenth-century **Erddig Hall** has now been restored to its 1922 appearance: the family's State Rooms upstairs have their share of fine furniture and portraits, but the real interest lies in the quarters of the servants, whose lives were fully documented by their unusually benevolent masters. Eighteenth- and early nineteenth-century portraits of staff are still on display in the Servants' Hall, each of which has a verse written by one of the Yorkes. You can also see the blacksmith's shop, lime yard, stables, laundry, kitchen, still-used bakehouse and the lovely walled garden.

ARRIVAL AND INFORMATION — LLANGOLLEN

By train The nearest station is 5 miles away at Ruabon, reached by frequent buses on the Llangollen–Wrexham run.

By bus Buses from Bala (8 daily; 1hr) and Dolgellau (8 daily; 1hr 45min) stop on Parade St, as do daily National Express coaches on the Wrexham–Llangollen–Birmingham–London run: tickets are sold at the tourist office).

Tourist office Y Capel, Castle St (Daily: Easter–Oct 9.30am–5.30pm; Nov–Easter 9.30am–5pm; ⓣ01978 860828, ⓔllangollen@nwtic.com, ⓦllangollen.org.uk).

ACCOMMODATION

Cornerstones 15–19 Bridge St ⓣ01978 861569, ⓦcornerstones-guesthouse.co.uk. River views from three of the five rooms and over-the-top exuberance in this luxury sixteenth-century B&B. Amenities include DVD library, well-appointed guest lounges and an extensive breakfast. Midweek deals are available. **£80**

★ **Glasgwm** Abbey Rd ⓣ01978 861975, ⓦglasgwm-llangollen.co.uk. Relaxed B&B with plenty of books, a piano and engaging hosts whose tastes are reflected in the decor of the doubles, twin and single (which has its own deep bath). They'll do Offa's Dyke pick-ups and drop-offs, and can even make packed lunches and dinners. **£55**

Llangollen Hostel Berwyn St ⓣ01978 861773, ⓦllangollenhostel.co.uk. Neat bunks in modernized rooms (mostly en-suite with 4–6 bunks) in a Victorian townhouse plus a well-equipped kitchen, comfy lounge and free wi-fi. Bunks **£18**, en-suite room **£45**

★ **Tyddyn Llan Country House** Llandrillo, 15 miles southwest ⓣ01490 440264, ⓦtyddynllan.co.uk. Elegant Georgian restaurant with rooms, where the emphasis is on Bryan Webb's Modern British food (two courses £42, three for £50). The restaurant is open to non-guests for dinner and for lunch on Fri & Sat (£28/£35) and Sunday (£35, including roast Welsh beef). **£75**

Wern Isaf Farm ⓣ01978 860632, ⓦwernisaf.co.uk. Simple but lovely farmhouse campsite almost a mile up the steep (turn right over the canal on Wharf Hill). Closed Nov–March. Pitch **£14**

EATING, DRINKING AND ENTERTAINMENT

★ **The Corn Mill** Dee Lane ⓣ01978 869555. Superb conversion of a town-centre mill, with a sunny riverside deck. Good all day for coffee and well-prepared café-bar food such as beef and horseradish sandwiches (£6) and bistro mains (£10–16). The real ales are well kept. Mon–Sat noon–11pm, Sun noon–10.30pm.

★ **Gales Wine Bar** 18 Bridge St ⓣ01978 860089. Old church pews, wooden floors, a blackboard menu of delicious, bistro-style food (mains £9–13) and a good selection of wines from around the world make this long-standing, chilled-out place a Llangollen favourite. Mon–Sat noon–2pm & 6–10pm, Sun 11am–3pm.

Male voice choir Acrefair School Hall, just off the A539, 5 miles east ⓦfronchoircom. Visitors are welcome to attend the rehearsals of Côr Meibion Froncysyllte, one of Wales's most exalted male voice choirs. Directions are on their website. Mon & Thurs 7–9pm.

Sun Inn Regent St ⓣ01978 860079. Convivial, slate-floored locals' pub with basic meals for a fiver, a wide range of beers and live bands (of just about any stripe) every Fri & Sat night. Wednesday is open-mic night. Daily noon–10pm or later.

16

Snowdonia

The mountains of **Snowdonia** provide the most dramatic and alluring of all Welsh scenery, a compact, barren land of tortured ridges dividing glacial valleys, whose sheer faces belie the fact that the tallest peaks only just top 3000ft. It was to this mountain fastness that Llywelyn ap Gruffydd, the last true prince of Wales, retreated in 1277 after his first war with Edward I; it was also here that Owain Glyndŵr held on most tenaciously to his dream of regaining for the Welsh the title of Prince of Wales. Centuries later, the English came to remove the mountains: slate barons built huge fortunes from Welsh toil and reshaped the patterns of

WHITEWATER RAFTING AT BALA

The little watersports town of **BALA** (Y Bala), on the border of the park, twenty miles southwest of Llangollen, sits at the northern end of Wales's largest natural lake, **Llyn Tegid**. Nearby, waters crash down the Tryweryn River, perfect for **whitewater rafting**.

The National White Water Centre A4212, 4 miles west of Bala, ⓣ01678 521083, ⓦukrafting.co.uk Water is released on around 200 days a year at the National White Water Centre, crashing down a mile and a half of Grade III rapids where numerous rafting options include the Taster (40–60min; £32) involving two runs down the course: wet-suit hire extra. The two-hour session (£60) typically gives you four runs, or you can step up a notch to the Orca Adventure (half-day; £82) involving two runs down in a normal raft followed by a chance to tackle the rapids in a more challenging two-person inflatable. Dec to mid-Oct daily 9am–dusk.

Snowdonian life forever, as men looking for steady work in the quarries left the hills and became town dwellers.

Thousands of hikers arrive every weekend to hike up **Snowdon** massif (Eryri) over steep, exacting and constantly varying terrain. Several of the ascent routes are superb, and you can always take the cog railway up to the summit café from **Llanberis**. But the other mountains are as good, and far less busy, and give unsurpassed views of Snowdon. The **Glyderau** and **Tryfan** – best tackled from the **Ogwen Valley** – are particular favourites for more experienced walkers.

But Snowdonia isn't all about walking. Small settlements are dotted in the valleys, usually coinciding with some enormous mine or quarry. Foremost among these are **Blaenau Ffestiniog**, where a mine opens its slate caverns for underground tours, and **Beddgelert**, whose former copper mines are also open to the public. The only place of any size not associated with slate mining is **Betws-y-Coed**, a largely Victorian resort away from the higher peaks.

Betws-y-Coed and around

BETWS-Y-COED (pronounced "betoos-er-coyd"), sprawled out around the confluence of the Conwy, Llugwy and Lledr valleys, overlooked by the conifer-clad slopes of the **Gwydyr Forest Park**, and centred on the low cataract of **Pont-y-Pair Falls**, is almost totally devoted to the needs of visitors, particularly walkers – there are seven outdoor gear retailers but no decent grocery shop. The town has the best choice of accommodation in the region, but after an hour mooching around you'll soon want

ACCOMMODATION	
Bryn Elltyd	15
Bryn Tyrch Inn	6
Cae Gwyn	5
Cae'r Blaidd	16
Gwern Gôf Uchaf	2
Gwydir Castle	1
Llyn Gwynant Campsite	13
Pengwern	11
Pen-y-Gwryd Hotel	8
Plas Coch	4
Plas Curig	6
Rynys Farm	12
St Curig's Church	6
Sygun Fawr	14
The Vagabond	9
YHA Idwal Cottage	3
YHA Pen-y-Pass	7
YHA Snowdon Ranger	10

EATING & DRINKING	
Bryn Tyrch Inn	3
Caffi Caban	1
CeLL B	11
Conwy Falls Café	8
Glaslyn Ices/ Café Glyndŵr	10
Pen-y-Gwryd Hotel	6
Pete's Eats	2
Stables	5
Sygun Fawr	9
Tŷ Gwyn	7
Vaynol Arms	4

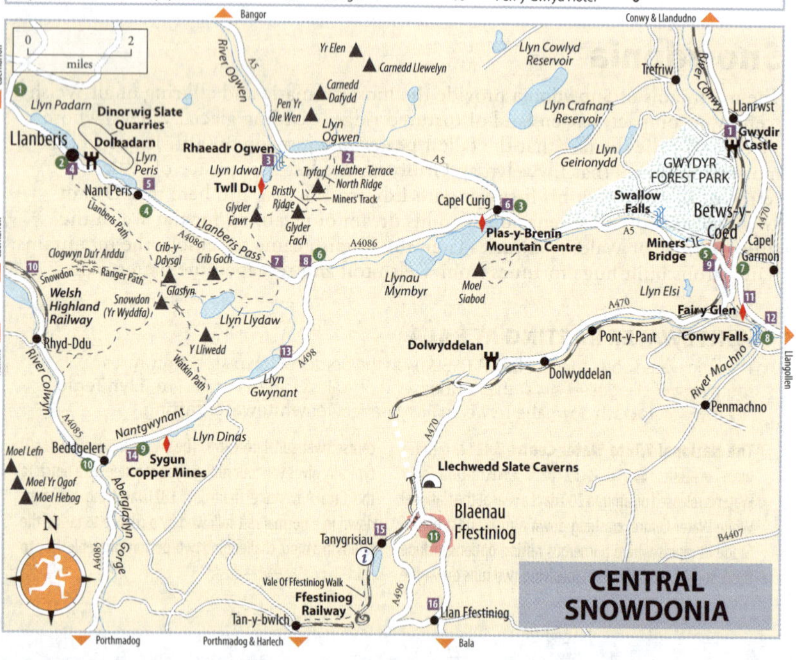

BETWS-Y-COED BIKING

Gwydyr Forest Park, just outside town, is one of the top trail-riding locales in Wales. The classic route is the **Marin Trail** (25km loop; 2–4hr) with mostly forest track ascents and numerous singletrack descents of varying difficulty. The scenery is great, with mountain views along the higher sections. For **rental**, contact Planet Fear, Holyhead Rd (hardtails £17/half-day, £25/day; full suspension £27/35; ⓣ 01690 710888, ⓦ planetfear.co.uk).

to head out into the hinterland. Serious mountain walkers should continue west, but for everyone else there are some delightful and popular easy strolls to the local beauty spots of the **Conwy** and **Swallow** falls.

Conwy Falls

A couple of miles southeast of Betws-y-Coed • Place £1 into the turnstile beside the Conwy Falls Café

East of Betws-y-Coed, the river plunges 50ft over the **Conwy Falls** into a deep pool. After paying the fee, you can view the falls on the right and a series of rock steps to the left; these were cut in 1863 as a kind of primitive fish ladder, now superseded by a tunnel through the rock on the far side.

Swallow Falls

Two miles west of Betws-y-Coed along the A5 towards Capel Curig • £1.50

Swallow Falls, west of town, is the region's most visited sight. You can pay to view this pretty cascade, or better still, catch a glimpse from the **Llugwy Valley Walk** (3 miles; 400ft ascent; 1hr 30min), a forested path from the north side of Pont-y-Pair Falls which follows the twisting and plunging river upstream towards Capel Curig. Along the way you pass the steeply sloping **Miners' Bridge** below which are a series of idyllic plunge pools, perfect for swimming.

16

Gwydir Castle

B5106, 3 miles north of Betws-y-Coed • March–Oct Tues–Fri & Sun 10am–4pm • £4 • ⓣ 01492 641687, ⓦ gwydir-castle.co.uk

Former home of the powerful Wynn family, **Gwydir Castle** is actually a low-slung manor house begun around 1490 with later additions. Its core is a three-storey solar tower, whose windows relieve the gloom of the great halls, each with enormous fireplaces and stone-flagged or heavy timber floors. Most of the original fittings and Tudor furniture were sold in 1921, and much of the rest of the house was ruined in a fire a few months later. The subsequent restoration was kept simple – tapestries cover the solid stone walls, a few tables and chairs are scattered about and you'll see some fine painted glass. Some of the original furnishings have been tracked down, including the magnificent **Dining Room** once shipped to America but now re-installed. Outside, the **Dutch Garden** has peacocks and a fine Cedar of Lebanon dating back to 1625.

Go Below

Meet at Conwy Falls Café, 2 miles southeast of Betws-y-Coed • £40, book a day or two in advance • ⓣ 01690 710108, ⓦ www.go-below.co.uk

Go Below allows you to head underground, exploring magical old **mine workings** with harness, helmet and headlamp. You'll get a nice balance between learning about the mine and getting active on zip-lines, abseiling and even paddling across a small subterranean lake.

Plas-y-Brenin: the National Mountaineering Centre

400 yards south of the junction of the A4086 and the A5 • **Climbing wall** Daily 10am–11pm • £5 **Dry ski slope** Daily 10am–4pm • £8/hr including ski rental, £30/hr for instruction; call for availability • ⓣ 01690 720214, ⓦ www.pyb.co.uk

As well as its internationally renowned residential courses, **Plas-y-Brenin** runs two-hour indoor climbing, lake canoeing and dry-slope skiing sessions during August and other

TOP 5 OUTDOOR ACTIVITIES

Mine Exploring with Go Below See p.687
Mountain biking Gwydir Forest See p.687
Rafting the Tryweryn See p.685
Rock climbing from Plas-y-Brenin See p.687
Summitting Snowdon See p.690

school holidays (£15). Kids who want a full-day taster of canoeing, skiing and abseiling can be left on the "3 in a Day" adventure session (£35), where adults are welcome too. There's also a good bar and talks on recent international expeditions (usually Mon, Wed & Sat 8pm; free).

ARRIVAL AND INFORMATION — BETWS-Y-COED

By train The train station serves the Conwy Valley Railway (conwy.gov.uk/cvr).
Destinations Blaenau Ffestiniog (6 daily; 30min); Llandudno Junction (6 daily; 30min).
By bus Buses fan out from near the train station.
Destinations Blaenau Ffestiniog (9 daily; 20min); Capel Curig (hourly; 10min); Idwal Cottage (5 daily; 20min); Llandudno (9 daily; 50min); Llanberis (7 daily; 30min).
Tourist office Royal Oak Stables (daily: Easter to mid-Oct 9.30am–5.30pm; mid-Oct to Easter 9.30am–4.30pm; 01690 710426, tic.byc@eryri-npa.gov.uk); they have displays and a movie giving an overview of Snowdonia.

ACCOMMODATION

16

★ **Bryn Tyrch Inn** A5 at Capel Curig, 6 miles west of Betws-y-Coed 01690 720223, bryntyrchinn.co.uk. Modernized twelve-room inn offering simple, tasteful rooms with well-appointed bathrooms and TV. Also four-bunk B&B dorm rooms (minimum 3 people). The warm and lively restaurant and bar has real ales, good meals (mains mostly £12–17) and a wonderful view of Snowdon. Food served daily noon–2.30pm & 6–9pm. Dorm £25, double £85

★ **Gwydir Castle** 3 miles north on the B5106 01492 641687, gwydir-castle.co.uk. Two splendid bedrooms have been fitted out in baronial style with four-poster beds, deep baths and elegantly eclectic decor in this authentic castle with the air of a family home. There's no TV but you can relax in the oak-panelled parlour, where a hearty breakfast is served. £85

★ **Pengwern** Allt Dinas, 1.5 miles east on the A5 01690 710480, snowdoniaaccommodation.com. Beautiful, welcoming and tastefully decorated country house set in two acres of woods with a guest lounge and just three rooms, two with valley views and one with a four-poster. There's also a self-catering cottage let from around £360 a week in summer. £78

Plas Curig A5 Capel Curig, 6 miles west of Betws-y-Coed 01690 720225, snowdoniahostel.co.uk. Deluxe backpackers' hostel in a revamped former YHA with bunks, doubles and family rooms (no en-suites). Closed Dec & Jan. Dorm £20, double £50

★ **Rynys Farm** 2 miles southeast of town on the A5 near the Conwy Falls 01690 710218, rynys-camping.co.uk. Charming, peaceful and clean farm campsite with great valley views and good facilities. Handy for the Conwy Falls Café. £7 per person.

★ **St Curig's Church** A5 at Capel Curig, 6 miles west of Betws-y-Coed 01690 720469, stcurigschurch.com. Great B&B fashioned from a former church with six lovely rooms, some en-suite, plus a recess off the lounge with bunks for four. Rates include breakfast. Dorm £20, double £75

The Vagabond Craiglan Rd 01690 710850, thevagabond.co.uk. Central independent hostel with 36 bunks (with sheets) in 4- to 8-bunk dorms and good facilities including free internet and wi-fi, secure bike lock-up and off-street parking. There's a self-catering kitchen but they also serve breakfasts (£5) and evening meals (£7) and have an inexpensive bar with patio seating. Bookings recommended at weekends when B&B is obligatory. £17

EATING AND DRINKING

★ **Conwy Falls Café** A5, 2 miles southeast of Betws-y-Coed 01690 710696, conwyfalls.com. High-quality food, an enormous range of teas and superb coffee at this relaxed café. There's free wi-fi and they open Fri & Sat evenings for great build-your-own pizza, and they occasionally host music events. Easter to mid-Oct Mon–Thurs & Sun 9am–4pm, Fri & Sat 9am–9pm; mid-Oct–Easter Fri & Sat 9am–9pm, Sun 9am–4pm.

The Stables Royal Oak Hotel, High St 01690 710219. The town's liveliest bar, with outdoor seating and sports TV. Their signature haddock, chips and mushy peas is good value at £8. Daily 11am–11pm.

★ **Tŷ Gwyn** A5, 0.5 miles southeast 01690 710383, tygwynhotel.co.uk. Superb wood-beamed former

WALKS FROM THE OGWEN VALLEY

Tourists hike up Snowdon (see p.690), but mountain connoisseurs prefer the sharply angled peaks of Tryfan and the Glyderau, with their challenging terrain, cantilevered rocks and fantastic views back to Snowdon. If you're going to attempt the walks, arm yourself with either the 1:50,000 OS *Landranger* #115 or the 1:25,000 OS *Outdoor Leisure* #17 map.

Cwm Idwal (1.5 miles return; 1hr; 200ft ascent). An easy hike on a well-graded path leading up to Llyn Idwal, nestled in the magnificent cirque of Cwm Idwal. The area was designated Wales's first nature reserve in 1954, after botanists discovered rare arctic-alpine plants growing here. Tackling the rough, rocky paths right around the lake can turn this into a half-day outing, partly beneath huge sloping cliffs – the Idwal Slabs.

Tryfan Miners' Track (5 miles; 4–6hr; 2000ft ascent). The standard route up Tryfan, from the car park at Idwal Cottage. You'll need to use your hands for the final section up the South Ridge of Tryfan, past the Far South Peak to the summit. You can then tackle the 5ft jump between Adam and Eve, the two chunks of rhyolitic lava which crown this regal mountain. Don't underestimate the seriousness of the leap: it's only when you see the mountain dropping away on all sides that it hits home quite how disastrous it would be to overshoot.

coaching inn with excellent bar meals (£10) and à la carte dining (mains around £15) served either in the wonderfully intimate low-roofed bar or the slightly more formal restaurant. Expect anything from wild mushroom stroganoff to lamb Wellington. Daily 11am–11pm.

The Ogwen Valley

Northwest of Capel Curig, the A5 forges through the **Ogwen Valley**, which separates the imposing Carneddau massif from the rock-peppered summits of the **Glyderau** range and distinctive triple-peaked **Tryfan**, perhaps Snowdonia's most demanding mountain. West of Tryfan, the road follows the shores of **Llyn Ogwen**, to the YHA hostel, the start of some of the UK's finest walks (see above).

16

ARRIVAL AND DEPARTURE — THE OGWEN VALLEY

Five **buses** a day run along the valley between Bethesda and Capel Curig, with connections to Betws-y-Coed and Bangor.

ACCOMMODATION

★ **Gwern Gôf Uchaf** A5, 4 miles west of Capel Curig ⓣ01690 720294, Wtryfanwales.co.uk. Superbly sited campsite at the base of Tryfan with a modern shower block, 14-berth bunkhouse, kitchen and a drying room: bring a sleeping bag and food. Camping £5, bunkhouse £10

YHA Idwal Cottage A5, 5 miles west of Capel Curig ⓣ0845 371 9744, ⓔidwal@yha.org.uk. Recently refurbished but traditional YHA with mostly 4-bunk dorms, a double, a single, family rooms and an alcohol license, but no meals. Opens 5pm. Closed Jan and weekdays in Nov, Dec & Feb. Dorm £18.40, double £48, camping £9.50

Llanberis

LLANBERIS, ten miles west of Capel Curig, is the nearest you'll get in Wales to an alpine climbing village, its main street thronged with weather-beaten walkers and climbers. At the same time, this is very much a Welsh rural community, albeit a depleted one now that slate is no longer being torn from the flanks of Elidir Fawr, the mountain across the town's twin lakes. The town is inextricably linked with **Snowdon**, the highest British mountain outside Scotland.

Snowdon

Hardened outdoor enthusiasts sometimes dismiss **Snowdon** (3560ft) as overused, and it can certainly be crowded in summer when a thousand visitors a day can be pressed into the postbox-red carriages of the **Snowdon Mountain Railway**, while another 1500 pound the well-maintained paths. But this fine mountain massif sports some of the finest walking and scrambling in the park: hike early, late or out of season if you want a bit more solitude.

The Snowdon Mountain Railway

Mid-March to Oct 6–25 trains daily • Summit return £25, one-way £18 • T 0870 720 0033, W snowdonrailway.co.uk

The **Snowdon Mountain Railway** is Britain's only rack-and-pinion railway, completed in 1896. Trains (sometimes pushed by seventy-year-old steam locos) still climb to the summit in just under an hour from the eastern end of Llanberis to the smart summit café (mid-May to Oct). Inside is a bar and a post office where, for a few pennies, you can enchant your friends with a "Summit of Snowdon – Copa'r Wyddfa" postmark. Times, type of locomotive and final destination vary with demand and ice conditions at the top: to avoid disappointment, buy your tickets early on clear summer days.

Dinorwig Power Station Underground Tour

Tours start from the Electric Mountain complex on the A4086 • Easter–Oct daily, plus selected winter days • £7.75 • T 01286 870636, W electricmountain.co.uk

Views north from Llanberis are dominated by the entrance to the **Dinorwig Pumped Storage Power Station**, hollowed out of the ground in the mid-1970s and visited on a bus tour. It actually consumes more electricity than it produces, but benefits the national grid by being able to instantly supply electricity to cope with the early evening surge in demand. This is one of Snowdonia's more popular rainy-day activities, so book ahead if the weather turns foul.

Padarn Country Park

Open access • Free

At **Padarn Country Park** lakeside oak woods are gradually recolonizing the discarded workings of the defunct **Dinorwig Slate Quarries**, formerly one of the largest slate

ASCENDING SNOWDON

The following are justifiably the most popular of the seven accepted **walking** routes up Snowdon. All are easy to follow in good weather but you should still carry the 1:25,000 *OS Explorer* #OL17 map.

Llanberis Path (5 miles to summit; 3200ft ascent; 3hr). The easiest and longest route up Snowdon, following the rail line, which gets gradually steeper, to the "Finger Stone" at Bwlch Glas (Green Pass). This marks the arrival of the routes coming up from Pen-y-Pass to join the Llanberis Path for the final ascent to Yr Wyddfa, the summit.

Miners' Track (4 miles to summit; 2400ft ascent; 2hr 30min). The easiest of the three routes up from Pen-y-Pass, a broad track leading south then west to the dilapidated remains of the former copper mines in Cwm Dyli. Skirting around the right of a lake, the path climbs more steeply to the lake-filled Cwm Glaslyn, then again to Upper Glaslyn, followed by a switchback ascent to the junction with the Llanberis Path.

Pig Track (3.5 miles to summit; 2400ft ascent; 2hr 30min). A steeper and stonier variation on the Miners' Track, leaving from the western end of the Pen-y-Pass car park and climbing up to Bwlch y Moch (the Pass of the Pigs) before meeting the Miners' Track prior to the zigzag up to the Llanberis Path.

GUIDES AND BIKES

If you're not equipped or confident enough to get out on the rock by yourself, there are various companies who will **guide** you. You could also consider **cycling** up the mountain: in addition to many easy rides, the Llanberis Path, Snowdon Ranger Path and Pitt's Head Track to Rhyd-Ddu are open to cyclists, although there's restricted cycle access to and from the summit between 10am and 5pm (May–Sept).

High Trek Snowdonia Tal y Waen, Deiniolen T 01286 871232, W climbing-wales.co.uk. High Trek guide everything from straightforward hillwalking to scrambling, rock climbing (all abilities), navigation and winter climbing.

Llanberis Bike Hire 34 High St T 01286 872787. Rental (£22/day; £15/half-day) and a good source of information about local rides.

quarries in the world. Equipment and engines that once hauled materials up inclined tramways have been partly restored and punctuate the paths which link the levels chiselled out of the hillside.

National Slate Museum

Easter–Oct daily 10am–5pm; Nov–Easter daily except Sat 10am–4pm • Free • T 01286 870630, W museumwales.ac.uk

The fort-like former quarry's maintenance workshops now house Wales's **National Slate Museum** where a 50ft-diameter water wheel that once powered cutting machines still turns. Most of the equipment was still in use until the quarries closed in 1969 and is quite familiar to the former quarry workers who demonstrate their skills at turning an inch-thick slab of slate into six, even eight, perfectly smooth slivers. The slate was delivered to the slate-dressing sheds by means of a maze of tramways, cranes and rope lifts, all kept in good order in the fitting and repair shops. Look out for the slate workers' cottages, furnished in the style of 1861, 1901 and 1969.

ARRIVAL AND INFORMATION — LLANBERIS

By bus Buses stop along High Street. Frequent Sherpa #S1 buses travel up daily to Pen-y-Pass, the recommended approach even if you have a car, since the Pen-y-Pass car park is expensive and almost always full. Use the "Park and Ride" car park at the bottom of the pass, near the *Vaynol Arms*.

Destinations Bangor (hourly; 45min); Betws-y-Coed (6 daily; 30min); Caernarfon (every 30min; 25min); Capel Curig (7 daily; 30min); Pen-y-Pass (at least hourly; 15min).

Tourist office Llanberis's tourist office (Easter–Oct Sat–Wed 9.30am–4.30pm; T 01286 870765, E llanberis.tic@gwynedd.gov.uk) is in the process of moving. Look for signs on arrival.

16

ACCOMMODATION

Cae Gwyn Nant Peris, 2 miles southeast of Llanberis T 01286 870718. Grassy field campsite and primitive bunkhouse (bring everything) with £1 coin-op showers, almost opposite the *Vaynol Arms* pub. Camping **£6**, bunkhouse **£11**

★ **Pen-y-Gwryd Hotel** A mile east of Pen-y-Pass T 01286 870211, W pyg.co.uk. Wonderfully rustic hotel, with magnificent Edwardian bathrooms, an outdoor sauna, and a lot of muddy boots in the bar. The 1953 Everest expedition stayed here while training, and signed the ceiling, and a piece of Everest sits in the "Smoke Room". Rooms (some en-suite) are priced per person. If you stay, expect lots of plain home cooking (three courses £25; five courses £30) and a congenial if regimented atmosphere; even if you don't stay or eat, make sure to pop in for a pint. Two-night minimum Sat & Sun. Closed Nov & Dec and from Mon–Fri in Jan & Feb. **£40** per person

★ **Plas Coch** High St T 01286 872122, W plas-coch.co.uk. Attractive B&B with seven en-suite rooms plus an extra bathroom with a tub for post-hike soaks. The new owners are going the extra mile, and offer packed lunches to hikers. **£65**

YHA Pen-y-Pass T 0845 371 9534, E penypass@yha.org.uk. The only accommodation at Pen-y-Pass, this fine hostel is usually full of walkers (there's another YHA hostel in Llanberis). There's 24hr access, limited free parking, a few two-bunk rooms, a bar licence and good meals. **£18.40**

EATING AND DRINKING

★ **Caffi Caban** Yr Hen Ysgol, Brynrefail, 2.3 miles northwest of Llanberis T 01286 685500, W caban-cyf.org. Relaxed, licensed daytime café, with big windows overlooking the woods and outdoor seating. Predominantly organic, local or fair-trade ingredients go into their breakfasts and lunches (mostly £4–7), and with free wi-fi it is a great place to hang out on a wet day. Daily 9am–4pm.

★ **Pete's Eats** 40 High St T 01286 870117. Hikers, climbers and bikers fortify themselves with Pete's large portions of top-value caff food and some more delicate dishes. Free jukebox, heaps of magazines and maps to browse. When the weather turns bad, everyone just orders another huge mug of tea. They have basic dorms and twin rooms upstairs, too, with self-catering facilities. Daily 8am–8pm or later.

Vaynol Arms Nant Peris, 2 miles east of Llanberis T 01286 872672. Slate-floored pub with good beer, hearty bar meals (£8) and mountain and slate-mining photos plastering the walls. It's alive with locals midweek, and climbers and campers at weekends. Daily 11am–3pm & 6–11pm.

Beddgelert

A huddle of grey houses, prodigiously brightened with floral displays in summer, makes up **BEDDGELERT**. A sentimental tale fabricated by a wily local publican to lure punters tells how the town got its name: **Gelert's Grave** (*bedd* means burial place), an enclosure just south of town, is supposedly the final resting place of Prince Llywelyn ap Iorwerth's faithful dog, Gelert, who was left in charge of the prince's infant son while he went hunting. On his return, the child was gone and the hound's muzzle was soaked in blood. Jumping to conclusions, the impetuous Llywelyn slew the dog, only to find the child safely asleep beneath its cot and a dead wolf beside him. Llywelyn hurried to his dog, which licked his hand as it died.

Aberglaslyn Gorge

A few hundred yards downstream from Beddgelert, the river crashes down the picturesque **Aberglaslyn Gorge** towards Porthmadog. You can walk past Gelert's Grave, then cross over the bridge onto a path which hugs the left bank for a mile, running parallel to the line of the Welsh Highland Railway and affording a closer look at the river's course through chutes and channels in sculpted rocks. Return the same way; the round trip takes around an hour.

Welsh Highland Railway

Late March to Oct 2–4 trains daily • £9.60 to Rhyd Ddu return; £14.50 to Porthmadog • T 01766 516000, W festrail.co.uk

Since 2011 Beddgelert has been linked to both Caernarfon and Porthmadog by the **Welsh Highland Railway**. You can travel to either town and explore or just ride the most exciting section through the Aberglaslyn Gorge to Nantmor (£3.50 one way) then walk back to Beddgelert along the Fisherman's Path (1hr). Alternatively, take the train over the steepest part of the route to Rhyd Ddu (1hr round trip) where there is almost always a train waiting on the other side of the platform for the return trip.

16

ARRIVAL AND DEPARTURE — BEDDGELERT

By bus Beddgelert is on two bus routes: the #S4 Snowdon Sherpa from Caernarfon and the #S97 between Pen-y-Pass and Porthmadog. Services stop on the main street.

Destinations Caernarfon (8 daily; 30min), Pen-y-Pass (5 daily; 20min) and Porthmadog (8 daily; 25min).

Tourist office On the A498 in the village centre (Easter–Oct daily 9.30am–5.30pm; Nov–Easter Fri–Sun 9.30am–4.30pm; T 01766 890615, W beddgelerttourism.com).

ACCOMMODATION AND EATING

Glaslyn Ices/Cafe Glyndŵr On the south side of the river bridge T 01766 890339, W glaslynices.co.uk. Great ice-cream shop with 36 flavours to take away, plus a family-style restaurant that's well above the usual standard. Baguettes are all super fresh and they do great pizzas and evening specials. Daily 10am–8pm or later.

Llyn Gwynant Campsite A498, 5 miles northeast T 01766 890853, W gwynant.com. Wonderful lakeside campsite with access to Snowdon's Watkin Path. There can be up to 400 tents here on busy weekends, but there are free hot showers, radios are banned, mobile phones don't work and you can rent kayaks and canoes (June–Sept). Closed Nov to mid-March. **£7** per person

★ **Sygun Fawr** 0.7 miles northeast off the A498 T 01766 890258, W sygunfawr.co.uk. This partly seventeenth-century country house in its own grounds is the pick of the local hotels. Some of its comfy rooms have views of Snowdon, and there are two- and three-night deals that include dinner in the snug dining room. Choose from beautifully prepared four-course evening meals (£26) or à la carte dining (mains £11–15). Bookings recommended; open to non-residents except Tues. Food served Tues–Sun 7–10pm. **£82**

YHA Snowdon Ranger Rhyd Ddu, 5 miles northwest of Beddgelert on the A498 T 0845 371 9659, E snowdon@yha.org.uk. A former inn, at the foot of the Snowdon Ranger Path. Bunks are mostly in two- and four-bed rooms, meals are available and the place is licensed. April–Aug; call for other times. Dorm **£16.40**, double **£41**

Blaenau Ffestiniog

BLAENAU FFESTINIOG sits at the head of the bucolic Vale of Ffestiniog, hemmed in by stark slopes strewn with heaps of splintered slate. When clouds hunker low in this great cwm and rain sheets the grey roofs, grey walls and grey paving slabs, it can be a terrifically gloomy place. Thousands of tons of slate were once hewn from the labyrinth

THE WELSH SLATE INDUSTRY

The Romans roofed their Welsh houses with **slate** and Edward I used it extensively in his Iron Ring of castles around Snowdonia, but it wasn't until the Industrial Revolution that the demand for Welsh roofing slates rocketed. For the 1862 London Exhibition, one skilled craftsman produced a sheet of slate 10ft long, 1ft wide and a sixteenth of an inch thick – so thin it could be flexed – firmly establishing Welsh slate as the finest in the world. By 1898, Snowdonia's quarries were producing half a million tons of dressed slate a year. At Penrhyn and Dinorwig quarries, mountains were hacked away. Workers often slept through the week in damp dormitories on the mountain, and tuberculosis was common, exacerbated by the slate dust. At **Blaenau Ffestiniog**, the seams required mining underground, with miners having to buy their own candles, the only light they had. In spite of this, thousands left their hillside smallholdings for the burgeoning quarry towns. Few workers were allowed to join Undeb Chwarelwyr Gogledd Cymru (the North Wales Quarrymen's Union), and in 1900 the workers in Lord Penrhyn's quarry at Bethesda went on strike. They stayed out for three years, but failed to win any concessions. Those who got their jobs back were forced to work for even less money as a recession took hold, and although the two World Wars heralded mini-booms as bombed houses were replaced, the industry never recovered its nineteenth-century prosperity, and most quarries and mines closed in the 1950s. What little slate is produced today mostly goes to make floor tiles, road aggregate, and an astonishing array of kitsch ashtrays and coasters etched with mountainscapes.

of underground caverns here each year, but these days the town is only kept alive by its extant slate-cavern tour, and by tourists who change from the Conwy Valley train line onto the wonderful, narrow-gauge **Ffestiniog Railway** (see p.694), which winds up from Porthmadog.

Llechwedd Slate Caverns

A470, a mile north of town • Daily: April–Sept 10am–6pm; Oct–March 10am–5pm; last tour 45min before closing • Single tour £10, both tours £16.30 • T 01766 830306, W llechwedd-slate-caverns.co.uk

For a real sense of what slate means to Blaenau Ffestinog, visit the **Llechwedd Slate Caverns**. On the **Miners' Tramway Tour**, a small train takes you a third of a mile along one of the oldest levels to the enormous Cathedral Cave and the open-air Chough's Cavern; more dramatic, the **Deep Mine Tour** uses a steeply inclined railway to descend to a labyrinth of tunnels through which you are guided by an irksome taped spiel of a Victorian miner. The long caverns angling back into the gloom are increasingly impressive, culminating in one softly lit, limpid pool.

ARRIVAL AND DEPARTURE — BLAENAU FFESTINIOG

By train The central train station serves both the Ffestiniog Railway and mainline services.

Destinations Betws-y-Coed (6 daily; 30min), Llandudno Junction (6 daily; 1hr); Llandudno (6 daily; 1hr 20min).

By bus Buses stop outside the train station.

Destinations Betws-y-Coed (9 daily; 20min); Harlech (3 daily; 40min); Llandudno (9 daily; 1hr 10min); Porthmadog (hourly; 30min).

ACCOMMODATION AND EATING

Bryn Elltyd 1 mile from Blaenau in Tanygrisiau T 01766 831356, W accommodation-snowdonia.com. An environmentally friendly option overlooking Llyn Ystradau and beside the Ffestiniog Railway, run by a mountain leader. Excellent evening meals (from £14) are available. **£70**

★ **Cae'r Blaidd** 3 miles south on the A470 T 01766 762765, W www.caerblaidd.fsnet.co.uk. Wonderfully spacious Victorian country house set in four acres of woodland with just three rooms, two with fabulous views of the Moelwyn mountains. Sustaining breakfasts and table d'hôte dinners (£20 for 3 courses) are excellent. **£80**

CeLL B Park Square T 01766 832001, W cellb.org. Fledgling arts centre in a former police station with gigs, cinema nights (featuring a different country each month) and a spruce café/bar with mountain views, good coffee and free wi-fi. Hours very flexible.

The Llŷn

The most westerly part of North Wales, **the Llŷn** forms a cliff- and cove-lined finger of land that juts out south and west from Snowdonia, separating Cardigan and Caernarfon bays. Its hills taper along its spine, carrying an ancient route to Aberdaron, where pilgrims once sailed for Ynys Enlli (Bardsey Island). Most come to the **Llŷn** for its beaches, especially those of the south coast family resorts of **Pwllheli** and **Abersoch**, but **Aberdaron** is the star around here.

Nowhere in Wales is more remote and staunchly Welsh: the term Stryd Fawr is used instead of High Street, and in most local shops you'll only hear Welsh spoken. The Llŷn is reached through one of the two gateway towns: **Porthmadog**, home to the private "dream village" of **Portmeirion** and terminus of the **Ffestiniog Railway**; or **Caernarfon**, where a magnificent fortress guards the mouth of the Menai Strait.

Porthmadog and around

In a region stuffed with wonderful views, **PORTHMADOG**, at the crook of the Cambrian Coast and the Llŷn, has some of the finest – up the Vale of Ffestiniog and across the estuary of the Glaslyn River to the mountains of Snowdonia. The bustling town itself makes little of its wonderful position, but it's a good base for exploring. Wales's heritage railway obsession reaches its apogee here with two fantastic lines – the peerless **Ffestiniog Railway** and the newly restored **Welsh Highland Railway** – and if steam trains don't blow your whistle, you can head for the strange but wonderful Italianate folly of **Portmeirion**.

Ffestiniog Railway

April–Oct 4–8 services daily; Nov–March services several days a week • Return to Blaenau Ffestiniog £19; £15.40 saver fare on 8.45am & 6.30pm trains; single fares are two-thirds of a return; under-16s travel free with an adult • T 01766 516024, W festrail.co.uk

The **Ffestiniog Railway** ranks as Wales's finest narrow-gauge rail line, twisting and looping up 650ft from the wharf at Porthmadog to the slate mines at Blaenau Ffestiniog, thirteen miles away. The gutsy little engines make light of the steep gradients and chug through stunning scenery, from broad estuarine expanses to the deep greens of the Vale of Ffestiniog, only fading to grey on the final approaches to the slate-bound upper terminus at Blaenau Ffestiniog. In the late nineteenth century the rail line was carrying 100,000 tons a year of Blaenau Ffestiniog slate, but after the collapse of the slate roofing industry the line was abandoned (in 1946) and fell into disrepair. Reconstruction of the tracks was complete by 1982.

Leaving Porthmadog, trains cross The Cob and then stop at **Minffordd**, a mile from Portmeirion.

Welsh Highland Railway

Late March to Oct 2–4 trains daily • £17.50 to Beddgelert; £32 to Caernarfon; single fares are two-thirds of a return; under-16s travel free with an adult • T 01766 516024, W festrail.co.uk

In 2011 the narrow-gauge Welsh Highland Railway once again connected Porthmadog with Caernarfon, 25 miles away. One of the most scenic lines in a land packed with charming railways, it rises from sea level to 650ft along the southern flank of Snowdon and passes a gorgeous river estuary, oak woods and the **Aberglaslyn Gorge**, where the line hugs the tumbling river.

The full Porthmadog–Caernarfon round trip gives you a full five hours on the train but only an hour in Caernarfon. Alternatively, ride to Beddgelert then walk down the Aberglaslyn Pass to Nantmor (1hr) and catch the train back to Porthmadog from there.

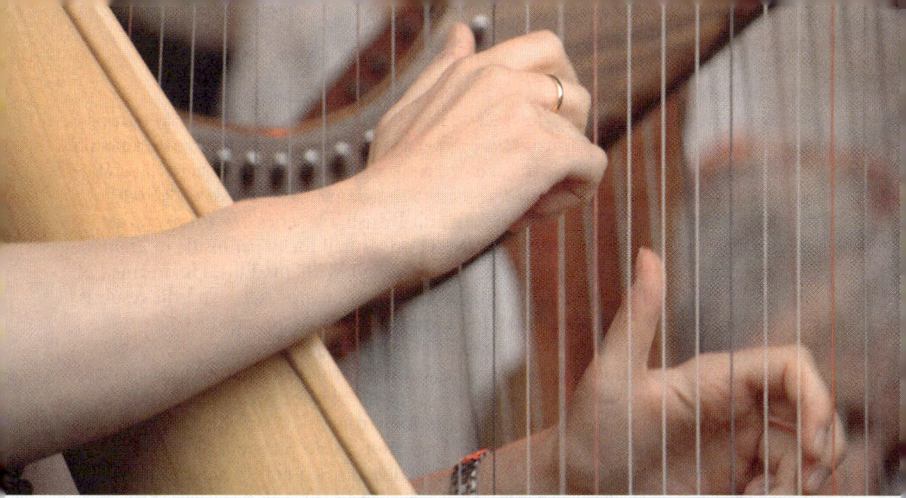

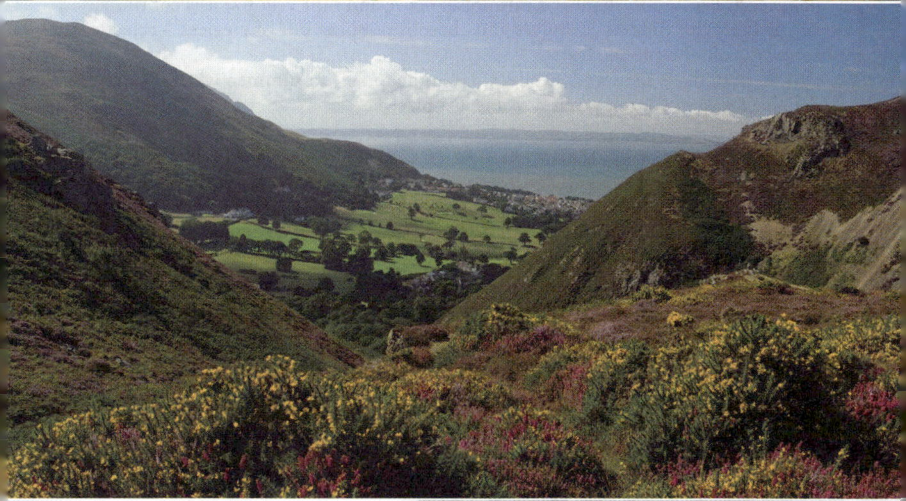

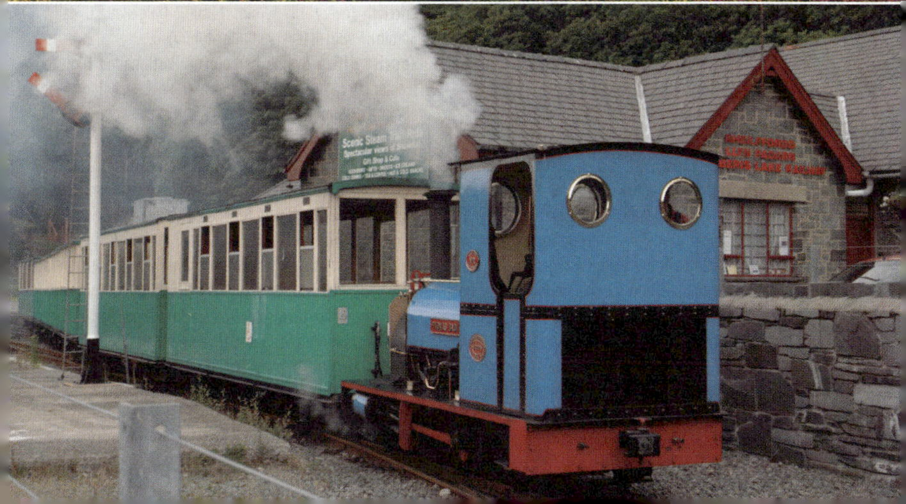
Scenic Steam

Portmeirion

Three miles east of Porthmadog near Minffordd • Daily 9.30am–7.30pm • £9, £4.50 after 3.30pm; free afternoon entry if you pre-book a meal at the *Portmeirion Hotel* or have lunch at *Castell Deudraeth*; free entry Nov–March with downloaded voucher • Guided tours daily 10.30am–3.30pm (20min; free) • Ⓦ portmeirion-village.com • Walk there in an hour from Porthmadog, or catch the #1b bus, which goes right to the gate. By train, take either the main line or Ffestiniog trains to Minffordd, from where it's a signposted 25min walk

Best known as "The Village" in the 1960s cult British TV series *The Prisoner*, the Italianate private village of **PORTMEIRION**, set on a small rocky peninsula in Tremadog Bay, was the brainchild of eccentric architect Clough Williams-Ellis. He dreamed of building an ideal village using a "gay, light-opera sort of approach", and the result is certainly theatrical: a stage set with a lucky dip of buildings arranged to distort perspectives and reveal tantalizing glimpses of the seascape behind.

In the 1920s, Williams-Ellis bought the site and turned an existing house into a hotel, the income from this providing funds for his "Home for Fallen Buildings". Endangered structures in every conceivable style from all over Britain and abroad were brought here and arranged around a Mediterranean piazza: a Neoclassical colonnade from Bristol, Siamese figures, a Jacobean town hall, a campanile and a pantheon. Painted in shades of turquoise, ochre and buff yellows, it is continually surprising, with hidden entrances and cherubs popping out of crevices – eclectic yet somehow all of a piece.

More than three thousand visitors a day come to ogle in summer, when it can be a delight; fewer in winter, when it seems just bizarre.

Criccieth Castle

Criccieth, 5 miles west of Porthmadog • April–Oct daily 10am–5pm; Nov–March Fri & Sat 9.30am–4pm, Sun 11am–4pm • CADW • April–Oct £3.20; Nov–March free • Ⓣ 01766 522227

Battle-worn **Criccieth Castle,** with its distinctive twin-towered gatehouse, was started by Llywelyn ap Iorwerth in 1230, strengthened by Edward I around 1283, and razed by Owain Glyndŵr in 1404. It's a great spot to sit and look over Cardigan Bay to Harlech, but leave time for the ticket office, where there's a wonderful animated cartoon about twelfth-century Wales.

ARRIVAL AND INFORMATION — PORTHMADOG AND AROUND

By train Porthmadog's mainline train station is at the north end of the high street, while the Ffestiniog and Welsh Highland station is by the harbour about half a mile to the south.

Destinations Barmouth (6 daily; 45min); Blaenau Ffestiniog by (Ffestiniog Railway; April–Oct 4–8 daily; Nov–March several weekly; 1hr); Harlech (8 daily; 30min); Machynlleth (8 daily; 2hr); Pwllheli (8 daily; 25min).

By bus National Express buses stop outside Tesco in between Porthmadog's two train stations; local buses stop near the tourist office.

Destinations Beddgelert (8 daily; 25min); Blaenau Ffestiniog (hourly; 30min); Caernarfon (7 daily; 40min); Criccieth (every 15–30min; 15min); Dolgellau (6 daily; 50min); Pwllheli (every 30min; 40min).

Tourist office By the harbour on Porthmadog High St (Easter–Oct daily 9.30am–5pm; Nov–Easter Mon–Sat 10am–3.30pm; Ⓣ 01766 512981, Ⓦ visitsnowdonia.info).

ACCOMMODATION

★ **Castell Deudraeth** Portmeirion Ⓣ 01766 772400, Ⓦ portmeirion-village.com. Chic designer hotel in a remodelled Victorian "castle" decorated in muted tones with the finest fittings. Just a 10min walk from Portmeirion village, where you're free to roam and use the outdoor heated pool. They have a good Modern British bistro on site, too. **£215**

★ **Hotel Portmeirion** Portmeirion Ⓣ 01766 770000, Ⓦ portmeirion-village.com. Though it has been stylishly upgraded with feature wallpapers and modern amenities, the spirit of Clough Williams-Ellis still shines through. Quirky architectural and decorative elements remain both in the main waterside hotel and in the cottages throughout Portmeirion village. Check for off-season web specials. **£215**

Tyddyn Llwyn Black Rock Rd Ⓣ 01766 512205, Ⓦ tyddynllwyn.com. A superior family campsite on a grassy hillside, with all facilities and a bar, a 15min walk along the road to Morfa Bychan following Bank Place southwest off High St. Closed Nov–Feb. **£14**

Yr Hen Fecws 16 Lombard St, Porthmadog Ⓣ 01766 514625, Ⓦ henfecws.com. Relaxed, pleasant B&B with comfy, uncluttered rooms, many with exposed stone walls. Breakfast is served in the owners' café next door. **£70**

EATING AND DRINKING

Moorings Bistro 4 Ivy Terrace, Borth-y-Gest, 1 mile south of Porthmadog ⓣ01766 513500, ⓦmooringsbistro borthygest.com. Great little spot specializing in local seafood, and also serving a great Sunday roast lunch (£10) and local ales. Mid-Feb to Dec Wed–Sat 6–10pm, Sun noon–2.30pm.

Y Llong (The Ship) 14 Lombard St, Porthmadog ⓣ01766 512990. Cosy pub with a stock of real ales and a lively atmosphere. Daily 11.30am–11pm.

★ **Y Sgwar** The Square, Tremadog T01766 515451. Well-prepared and presented meals at this simple but stylish restaurant – good for a steak-and-ale pie at lunch (£9), or dinner starting with Chinese duck pancakes (£16 for 2) then lamb shank with leeks (£16). The 3-course early-bird special (Mon–Fri 6–7pm) is excellent value at £18. Mon–Sat noon–3pm & 6–10pm.

Pwllheli

PWLLHELI (pronounced "poolth-heli") is the market town for the peninsula, a role it has maintained since 1355 when it gained its charter, though there's little sign of its history nowadays. Primarily useful as the final stop for Cambrian coast **trains** and the terminus for National Express **coaches**, it's a thoroughly Welsh place: even in the tourist season you'll hear far more Welsh spoken here than English.

ARRIVAL AND INFORMATION — PWLLHELI

By train The station is in the centre of town, on Station Square.

Destinations Criccieth (8 daily; 15min); Harlech (8 daily; 1hr); Porthmadog (8 daily; 25min).

By bus National Express and local buses pull in at Y Maes.

Destinations Aberdaron (6 daily; 40min); Abersoch (11 daily; 20–30min); Caernarfon (roughly hourly; 45min); Criccieth (every 30min; 25min); Porthmadog (every 30min; 40min).

Tourist office Station Square (April–Sept Mon–Thurs & Sat 9.30am–5pm; ⓣ01758 613000, ⓔpwllheli.tic@gwynedd .gov.uk)

16

ACCOMMODATION AND EATING

Bank Place 29 Stryd Fawr ⓣ01758 612103. Three rooms share two bathrooms at this simple but well-maintained B&B. They serve a full cooked breakfast. **£50**

Penlan Fawr 3 Penlan St ⓣ01758 612864. Tastefully updated four-hundred-year-old slate-floored pub, good for a beer, burgers, grills and vegetarian meals (mostly £5–10). It morphs into the liveliest place in town at weekends. Daily 11am–11pm.

★ **Plas Bodegroes** Efailnewydd, on the A497, 2 miles north of Pwllheli ⓣ01758 612363, ⓦbodegroes.co.uk. Wonderful restaurant with rooms; meals here have been ranked amongst Wales's finest for 25 years. Modern interpretations of traditional dishes are presented for lunch and dinner (£45 for three courses), the wine list is superb and Sunday lunch costs a modest £20. Hotel closed Sun & Mon. Restaurant Tues–Sat 7–10pm, Sun noon–3pm. **£130**

Abersoch

The former fishing village of **ABERSOCH**, pitched in the middle of two golden bays, is a largely anglicized resort, catering to affluent boat-owners and holidaying families. At high tide the harbour is an attractive spot to stroll. It is only five minutes' walk to the closest beach, **Abersoch Bay**, a long, clean strand lined by several dozen colourful beach huts. Surfers make for **Porth Neigwl** (Hell's Mouth), two miles to the southwest, which is one of the finest **surf** beaches in Wales – though beware of the undertow if you're swimming.

WATERSPORTS IN ABERSOCH

Abersoch Sailing School Main beach ⓣ01758 712963, ⓦabersochsailingschool.com. Sailing lessons (£160 for two lessons of 2hr 30min each) plus rental of Lasers, catamarans and other craft on the town's main beach (from £45/2hr). March–Oct.

Offaxis Centre of town ⓣ01758 713407, ⓦoffaxis .co.uk. Wakeboarding and surfing academy (£30 per lesson) and gear rental.

West Coast Surf Lôn Pen Cei ⓣ01758 713067, ⓦwww.westcoastsurf.co.uk. Surf gear rental (boards £10, wet suits £8) and lessons (£30/2hr) throughout the summer.

ARRIVAL AND INFORMATION — ABERSOCH

By bus Buses from Pwllheli (11 daily; 20–30min) loop through the middle of Abersoch, stopping on Lôn Pen Cei. To continue to Aberdaron by bus, you must take a Pwllheli-bound service as far as Llanbedrog, then change onto the #17.

Tourist office In The Vestry on Lôn Engan (June–Sept daily 10.30am–3.30pm; Oct–May Sat & Sun 11am–2pm; 01758 712929, abersochtouristinfo.co.uk).

ACCOMMODATION AND EATING

Angorfa Lôn Sarn Bach 01758 712967, angorfa.com. Bare boards and white linen characterize this superior budget B&B – the two attic rooms have the best view. Breakfast is served in the daytime café downstairs. **£70**

Coconut Kitchen Lôn Pont Morgan 01758 712250. The best Thai place for miles, with an open kitchen. Go for classics like beef Massaman or green chicken curry (around £11) or their exquisite Songkla dishes from south Thailand. (£15). Takeaways available. Daily 5.30–10pm.

★ **Goslings at the Carisbrooke** Lôn Sarn Bach 01758 712526, goslingsabersoch.co.uk. Friendly, central restaurant with rooms, including en-suite doubles, family rooms with DVD players and a couple of self-catering flats nearby. Delicious breakfasts, too. **£85**

★ **Venetia** Lôn Sarn Bach 01758 713354, venetiawales.com. Apart from the view from a couple of rooms, you barely know you're at the seaside at this urban chic boutique hotel with five individually styled rooms and plush bathrooms. Marco's Italian heritage influences the menu which is usually strong on fish and seafood (often straight from local boats). Sip a pre-dinner cocktail in the bar as you select from the seasonal Modern British menu. Most mains £14–17. Food served Wed–Sun 6.30–10pm. **£128**

Aberdaron and around

16

You really feel you're at the end of Wales at the lime-washed fishing hamlet of **ABERDARON**, two miles short of the tip of the Llŷn. For the best part of a thousand years up until the sixteenth century the inn and church here were the last stops on a pilgrim trail to Ynys Enlli, around the headland.

Ynys Enlli (Bardsey Island)

Bardsey Island or **Ynys Enlli** (The Island of the Currents) is separated from the tip of the Llŷn by two miles of churning, unpredictable water. This national nature reserve has been an important pilgrimage site since the sixth century: three visits were proclaimed equivalent to one pilgrimage to Rome. You can still see the ruins of the thirteenth-century abbey, but most visitors come to watch **birds** – Manx shearwaters, fulmars and guillemots, and an amazing number of vagrants – plus the **seals** slathered all over the rocks at low tide.

ARRIVAL AND DEPARTURE — ABERDARON

By bus The only public transport to Aberdaron is the #17 bus from Pwllheli (6 daily; 40min).

By boat Bardsey Boat Trips (£30 return; 07971 769895, bardseyboattrips.com) head to Ynys Enlli from Porth Meudwy, a tiny cove a mile south of Aberdaron. Sailings are dependent on sea conditions and a viable load of passengers.

ACCOMMODATION AND EATING

Bardsey Island Trust 0845 811 2233, bardsey.org. The island's owners rent eight spartan but substantial electricity-free houses by the week (mid-April to mid-Oct), mostly to birders. From **£210** a week.

Mynydd Mawr Llanllawen Fawr, 2 miles southwest 01758 760223. A couple of peaceful grassy fields right by the entrance to Mynydd Mawr and with views across to Ynys Enlli. Hot showers and electricity hook-up available. Closed Nov–Feb. **£10** per pitch

The Ship 01758 760204, theshiphotelaberdaron.co.uk. The cheaper of the village's two hotels, with an excellent array of ales and a restaurant serving the likes of local crab starter (£8) and a range of meat and veggie mains (£10–14). Food served daily noon–2pm & 6.30–9pm. **£89**

Y Gegin Fawr 01758 760359. The fourteenth-century stone "Big Kitchen" once served as the pilgrims' final gathering place before the treacherous crossing to Ynys Enlli. It's now a simple café serving clotted cream teas on the raised terrace, with glimpses of the sea. Summer daily 11am–4pm.

Caernarfon

CAERNARFON, superbly set at the southern entrance to the Menai Strait, has a lot going for it. Its distinctive polygonal-towered **castle** is an undoubted highlight, the **Welsh Highland Railway** connects the town with the slopes of Snowdon and Porthmadog (see p.692 & p.694), and the modern marina development adds **Galeri Caernarfon**, a modest but interesting arts centre. The town walls are no match for Conwy's, but there is some great accommodation nearby, making this a good base for exploring both sides of Snowdon, the Llŷn and even Anglesey.

Caernarfon Castle

July & Aug daily 9.30am–6pm; April–June, Sept & Oct daily 9.30am–5pm; Nov–Feb Mon–Sat 10am–4pm, Sun 11am–4pm • CADW • £5.25 • ⓣ 01286 677617

In 1283, Edward I started work on **Caernarfon Castle**, the strongest link in his Iron Ring, a decisive hammer-blow to any Welsh aspirations to autonomy and the ultimate symbol of Anglo-Norman military might – it withstood two sieges by Owain Glyndŵr with a garrison of only 28 men-at-arms. As you enter through the **King's Gate**, the castle's strength is immediately apparent. Embrasures and murder holes between the octagonal towers face in on no fewer than five gates and six portcullises, and that's once you have crossed the moat. Inside, the huge lawn gives a misleading impression as the wall dividing the two original wards, and all the buildings that filled them, crumbled away long ago. The towers are in a much better state, linked by an exhausting honeycomb of wall-walks and tunnels. The tallest is the **Eagle Tower** whose three slender turrets are adorned with eagle sculptures and give the best views of the town.

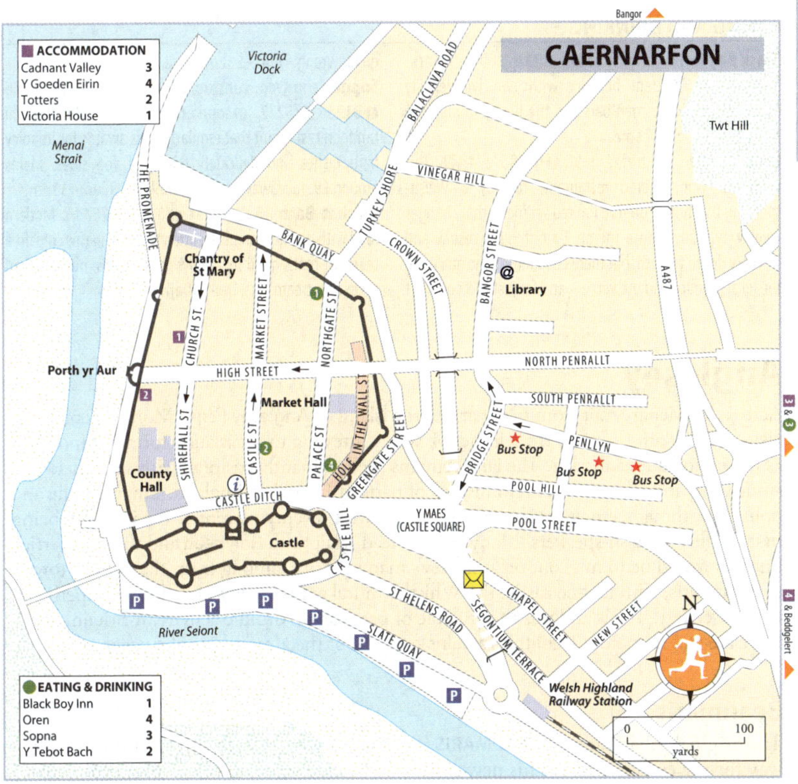

The Northeast Tower houses the **Prince of Wales Exhibition**, just outside which is the slate dais that was used for Charles's investiture in 1969.

ARRIVAL AND INFORMATION — CAERNARFON

By train The Welsh Highland Railway (see p.692 & p.694) operates from a small station on St Helen's Rd. Ride to Beddgelert and back, or just as far as Snowdon Ranger, from where you can explore the Snowdon Ranger Path (late March to Oct 2–4 trains daily; £23.60 to Beddgelert, £32 to Porthmadog; T 01286 677018, W festrail.co.uk).

By bus National Express and local buses stop on Penllyn, just steps from the central Y Maes (Castle Square).

Destinations Bangor (every 10min; 25min); Beddgelert (8 daily; 30min); Llanberis (every 30min; 25min); Porthmadog (7 daily; 40min); Pwllheli (roughly hourly; 45min).

Tourist office Castle St (Easter–Oct daily 9.30am–4.30pm; Nov–Easter Mon–Sat 10am–4pm; T 01286 672232, E caernarfon.tic@gwynedd.gov.uk).

ACCOMMODATION

Cadnant Valley T 01286 673196, W cwmcadnantvalley.co.uk. Pleasant wooded campsite a 10min walk east of town near the start of the A4086 to Llanberis. Closed Nov–Feb. **£11**

★ Totters Plas Porth Yr Aur, 2 High St T 01286 672963, W totters.co.uk. Excellent, central hostel with lovely communal spaces, including a fourteenth-century cellar kitchen. There's also a great attic en-suite double with sea views and *Over The Road*, a separate self-contained house sleeping six (£20–25 per person). Dorm **£16**, double **£50**

16

★ Victoria House 13 Church St T 01286 678263, W thevictoriahouse.co.uk. Very comfortable and good-value B&B within the town walls. Decor is Victorian-styled in rooms that come with flatscreen TV/DVD, free wi-fi and complimentary drinks. **£70**

★ Y Goeden Eirin Dolydd, 4 miles south of Caernarfon T 01286 830942, W ygoedeneirin.co.uk. Stylish and hospitable farmhouse B&B with eco credentials and an artistic sensibility. Dinner (£25 for 4 courses) is a relaxed affair served on oak tables; try the local red wine. **£80**

EATING AND DRINKING

Black Boy Inn Northgate St T 01286 673604, W black-boy-inn.com. Ancient hostelry with two wonderfully characterful low-beamed bars and the best pub meals in town. Daily 11am–11pm.

Oren 26 Hole in the Wall St T 01286 674343. This delightful wood-floored restaurant, run by a Welsh-speaking Dutchman, offers a limited set menu that changes weekly, typically with a theme. Everything is casual, and crockery doesn't match, but there's no faulting the quality of the local produce and the verve – and for just £15 you can't go far wrong. Thurs–Sat noon–2.30pm & 6.30–10pm.

Sopna Felin Wen, Pontrug, 2 miles east on the A4086 T 01286 675222, W sopna.co.uk. Quality Bangladeshi tandoori restaurant that regularly wins awards for its spicy balti dishes and delicately flavoured veg sides. Mains around £9. Takeaway available. Daily 11.30am–11pm.

Y Tebot Bach 13 Castle St T 01286 678444. Modern food with old-fashioned attention to detail in this chip-free tearoom that's good for sandwiches, salads, home-baked cakes and cream teas. Daily 10am–4.30pm.

Anglesey

Across the Menai Strait from Caernarfon, the island of **Anglesey** (Ynys Môn) welcomes visitors to "Mam Cymru", the Mother of Wales, attesting to the island's former importance as the national breadbasket. The land remains predominantly pastoral, with small fields, stone walls and white houses reminiscent of parts of Ireland or England. Linguistically and politically, though, Anglesey is intensely Welsh, with seventy percent of the islanders being first-language Welsh-speakers. Many people head straight to **Holyhead** and the Irish ferries, but this would be to miss out on Anglesey's many charms, among them the ancient town of **Beaumaris**, with its fine castle, the Whistler mural at **Plas Newydd** and some superb coastal scenery. The island was the crucible of pre-Roman druidic activity in Britain, and there are still numerous **Neolithic remains** redolent of the atmosphere of a pagan past.

Beaumaris

The original inhabitants of **BEAUMARIS** (Biwmares) were evicted by Edward I to make way for the construction of his new castle and bastide town, dubbed "beautiful marsh" in an attempt to attract English settlers. Today the place can still seem like the small English outpost Edward intended, with its elegant Georgian terrace along the front (designed by Joseph Hansom, of cab fame) and more plummy English accents than you'll have heard for a while.

Beaumaris Castle

Castle St • March–June, Sept & Oct daily 9.30am–5pm; July & Aug daily 9.30am–6pm; Nov–March Mon–Sat 10am–4pm, Sun 11am–4pm • CADW • £3.80 • ⓣ 01248 810361

Beaumaris Castle might never have been built had Madog ap Llywelyn not captured Caernarfon in 1294. When asked to build the new castle, James of St George abandoned the Caernarfon design in favour of a concentric plan, developing it into a highly evolved symmetrical octagon. Sited on flat land at the edge of town, the castle is denied the domineering majesty of Caernarfon or Harlech, its low outer walls appearing almost welcoming until you begin to appreciate the concentric layout of the defences protected by massive towers, a moat linked to the sea and the Arab-influenced staggered entries through the two gatehouses. Despite more than thirty years' work, the project was never quite finished, leaving the inner ward empty. You can explore a number of inner and outer **wall walks**, and wander through miles of internal passages in the walls.

Beaumaris Court

Castle St • April–Sept Sat–Thurs 10.30am–5pm • £3.50, £7 joint ticket with Beaumaris Gaol • ⓣ 01248 811691, ⓦ visitanglesey.co.uk

Almost opposite the castle stands the Jacobean **Beaumaris Court** , built in 1614 and used as an Assizes court until 1971. Take a look at *The Lawsuit*, a plaque in the magistrates' room depicting two farmers pulling the horns and tail of a cow while a lawyer milks it.

16

Beaumaris Gaol

Steeple Lane • April–Sept Sat–Thurs 10.30am–5pm • £4.25, £7 joint ticket with Beaumaris Court • ⓣ 01248 810921, ⓦ visitanglesey .co.uk

Many citizens were transported from Beaumaris Court to the colonies for their felonies; others wound up in the 1829 **Beaumaris Gaol**, which was considered a model prison, with running water and toilets in each cell, and an infirmary. Still, it's a gloomy place: witness the windowless punishment cell, the yard for stone-breaking and the treadmill water-pump operated by the prisoners.

Puffin Island Cruises

Beaumaris Pier • Easter–Sept daily 10am–5pm • £8 • ⓣ 01248 810251, ⓦ starida.co.uk

Interesting as Beaumaris is, a fine day might be better spent **cruising** to **Puffin Island**, five miles northeast. Numbers permitting, you can book an hour-long excursion around, but not onto, the island spotting nesting razorbills, guillemots and puffins, and also go fishing on cruises (from £25/3hr).

ARRIVAL AND DEPARTURE — BEAUMARIS

Regular **buses** (#53, #56, #57 and #58) to Beaumaris include services from Bangor (every 30min; 20–35min).

ACCOMMODATION

★ **Cleifiog** Townsend ⓣ 01248 811507, ⓦ cleifiogbandb.co.uk. Three lovely rooms in a Georgian townhouse with great views across Menai Strait to Snowdonia. A welcome tray with jars of biscuits and coffee, plus a great breakfast, round out the welcoming hospitality. **£85**

Victoria Cottage Victoria Terrace ⓣ 01248 810807, ⓦ victoriacottage.net. Good boutique B&B with two spacious en-suite rooms and two cheaper loft rooms that share a bathroom with a big bath. **£85**

Ye Olde Bull's Head Inn 18 Castle St ⓣ 01248 810329, ⓦ bullsheadinn.co.uk. This ancient coaching inn has accommodation in antique rooms in the main building and chic – more expensive – modern rooms in the adjacent *Townhouse*, all with an excellent breakfast. **£100**

EATING AND DRINKING

Red Boat Ice Cream Parlour 34 Castle St ⓦredboatgelato.com. Slip into one of the booths in this retro ice cream parlour with an ever-changing selection of superb made-on-the-premises gelati and sorbets. Daily 10am–6pm.

Sarah's Deli and The Coffee House 11 Church St ⓣ01248 811534. This licensed, daytime café and deli is good for melt-in-the-mouth cakes, welsh rarebit, tapas and meze platters and daily blackboard specials (mostly £6–9). Daily except Wed & Sun 9am–5pm.

★ **Ye Olde Bull's Head Inn** 18 Castle St ⓣ01248 810329, ⓦbullsheadinn.co.uk. Excellent combination: a cosy old-fashioned bar, bare-boards conservatory brasserie (mains around £12) and superb *Loft* restaurant, serving inventive modern dishes (£41 for 3 courses). Loft Tues–Thurs 7–9.30pm, Fri & Sat 6.30–9.30pm; Brasserie daily noon–2pm (Sun 3pm) & 6–9pm.

Llanfairpwllgwyngyllgogerychwyrndrobwllllandysiliogogogoch (Llanfairpwll) and around

In the 1880s a local tailor invented the longest place name in Britain in a successful attempt to draw tourists. Sadly, however, it is an utter disappointment to arrive at **Llanfairpwllgwyngyllgogerychwyrndrobwllllandysiliogogogoch**, which translates as "St Mary's Church in the hollow of white hazel near a rapid whirlpool and the Church of St Tysilio near the red cave" – commonly shortened to **LLANFAIRPWLL**. There's little here but a train station and Anglesey's main **tourist office**; the nearby house of **Plas Newydd**, however, is worth a visit.

16

Plas Newydd

A4080, 1.5 miles southwest of Llanfairpwll • Mid-March to Oct Sat–Wed 1–5pm plus 11.15am–1pm on free guided tours only; gardens open an hour earlier • NT • £9.30 • ⓣ01248 715272 or 01248 714795

The marquesses of Anglesey still live at **Plas Newydd**, a modest three-storey mansion with incongruous Tudor caps on slender octagonal turrets. Corridors of oil paintings and period rooms lead to the highlight, a 58ft-long wall consumed by a trompe l'oeil painting by **Rex Whistler**, who spent a couple of years here in the 1930s. Walking along his imaginary seascape, your position appears to shift by more than a mile as the mountains of Snowdonia and a whimsical composite of elements, culled from Italy as well as Britain, change perspective. Portmeirion is there, as is the Round Tower from Windsor Castle, and Whistler appears both as a gondolier and as a gardener in one of the two right-angled panels at either end. The prize exhibit in the **Cavalry Museum**, a few rooms further on, is the world's first articulated false leg, all wood, leather and springs, designed for the first marquess, who lost his leg at Waterloo.

ARRIVAL AND INFORMATION — LLANFAIRPWLL

There are **trains** and **buses** from Bangor (train 9 daily; 10min, bus every 30min; 15min) and Holyhead (train 9 daily; 30min, bus hourly; 1hr). The **tourist office** is on Holyhead Rd (April–Oct Mon–Sat 9.30am–5.30am, Sun 9.30am–4.30pm; Nov–March Mon–Sat 9.30am–5pm, Sun 9.30–4.30pm; ⓣ01248 713177; ⓦvisitanglesey.co.uk).

Holyhead and around

Drab **HOLYHEAD** (Caergybi; pronounced in English as "holly-head") is Anglesey's largest town and the terminus for ferry routes to Ireland. It isn't somewhere you'll want to spend much time, though it has some lovely coastline all about and the cliff-top delights of **South Stack** (Ynys Lawd), just over Holyhead Mountain, two miles to the west (no buses).

South Stack Lighthouse

Easter–Sept daily 10.30am–5.30pm • £4

A twisting path with more than four hundred steps leads down from the South Stack car park to a suspension bridge over the surging waves, once the keeper's only access to the now fully automated pepper-pot **lighthouse**, built in 1809. Views on to the cliffs are stupendous as you climb down to the island and, once there, you'll find exhibitions on local wildlife and you can take a tour of the lighthouse itself. Tickets are issued at the RSPB-run *South Stack Kitchen*, a café-cum-interpretive centre a hundred yards back along the lane.

Ellin's Tower Seabird Centre

Easter–Sept daily 10am–5.30pm • Free • ⓣ 01407 762100, ⓦ rspb.org.uk/wales

Views of the cliffs below the *South Stack Kitchen* are best from the RSPB-run **Ellin's Tower Seabird Centre**, where binoculars and closed-circuit TV give an unrivalled opportunity to watch up to 3000 birds – razorbills, guillemots and a few puffins – nesting on the nearby sea cliffs while choughs and peregrines wheel outside the tower's windows.

ARRIVAL AND DEPARTURE — HOLYHEAD

By train Local Arriva trains and long-distance Virgin trains arrive at the train station beside the ferry port.

Destinations Bangor (22 daily; 30–40min); Conwy (11 daily; 1hr); Llandudno (18 daily; 1hr 20min); Llanfairpwll (9 daily; 30min).

By bus Local and National Express buses stop by the passenger ferry terminal.

Destinations Bangor (hourly; 1hr 15min); Llanfairpwll (hourly; 1hr).

By ferry Irish Ferries (ⓦ irishferries.com) and Stena Line (ⓦ stenaline.com) run to Dublin and Dun Laoghaire using ferries (4hr) and fast catamarans (2hr).

ACCOMMODATION AND EATING

★ **Cleifiog Uchaf** Spenser Rd, Valley, 4 miles southeast ⓣ 01407 741888, ⓦ www.cleifioguchaf.co.uk. Outstanding eight-room hotel in a beautifully restored sixteenth-century farmhouse in peaceful grounds. The spirit is thoroughly Welsh, from the wool throws and slate flagstones to the ingredients in the superb restaurant (open to non-residents). There are usually just three choices for each course (one vegetarian); expect the likes of pan-fried cod with fennel (£17) followed by rhubarb tart with crème anglaise (£6). Food served Tues–Sat 6–9pm. **£95**

Harbourfront Bistro Newry Beach ⓣ 01407 763433, ⓦ harbourfrontbistro.co.uk. Sandwiches, toasted baguettes cakes and good coffee, plus dishes such as pan-seared tiger prawns (£9) and veggie pasta bake (£8) served in a bistro with good harbour views and some outdoor seating. Wed & Sun 11am–2.30pm, Thurs–Sat 11am–2.30pm & 6–9pm.

Yr Hendre Porth-y-Felin Rd ⓣ 01407 762929, ⓦ yr-hendre.net. Very comfy B&B with three floral rooms and a generous welcome, set in a charming ex-manse. **£65**

The north coast

Anglesey connects with the mainland at the university town of **Bangor**, a lively enough place that's best used as base for visiting **Penrhyn Castle** or as a springboard for Snowdonia. Heading east you encounter the **north coast** proper, where the castle town of **Conwy** and elegant **Llandudno** are the essential stops.

Bangor and around

BANGOR, across the bridge from Anglesey, is not big, but as the largest town in Gwynedd and home to Bangor University, it passes in these parts for cosmopolitan. Bangor is a hotbed of passionate Welsh nationalism, hardly surprising in such a staunchly Welsh-speaking area, and it's a dramatic contrast from the largely English-speaking north coast resorts.

Bangor Cathedral

Glanrafon • Daily 11am–5pm • Free

Bangor's thirteenth- to fifteenth-century **cathedral** boasts the longest continuous use of any cathedral in Britain, easily pre-dating the town. A hint of its ancient origins can be gleaned from the blocked-in window dating from the Norman rebuilding of 1071. Pop in if only to see the sixteenth-century wooden **Mostyn Christ**, depicted bound and seated on a rock.

Bangor Pier

Mon–Fri 8.30am–dusk, Sat & Sun 10am–dusk • 50p

For a good look down the Menai Strait to Telford's graceful bridge (the world's first large iron suspension bridge, completed in 1826), walk along Garth Road to Bangor's rejuvenated and pristine Victorian pier, which reaches halfway across to Anglesey.

Penrhyn Castle

A5 at Llandygai, 2 miles east of Bangor • Wed–Mon: Mid-March to June, Sept & Oct noon–5pm; July & Aug 11am–5pm • NT • £9, £6 for grounds & railway museum only • T 01248 363219 • Buses #5, #6, #67 and #75 run frequently from Bangor to the gates, from where it is a mile-long walk to the house

There can hardly be a more vulgar testament to the Anglo-Welsh landowning gentry's oppression of the rural Welsh than the compelling **Penrhyn Castle**. This monstrous, nineteenth-century neo-Norman fancy, with more than three hundred rooms dripping with luxurious fittings, was funded by the quarry's huge profits. The sugar and slate fortune built by anti-abolitionist Richard Pennant, first Baron Penrhyn, provided the means for his self-aggrandizing great-great-nephew George Dawkins to hire architect Thomas Hopper, who spent thirteen years from 1827 encasing the neo-Gothic hall in a Norman fortress complete with monumental five-storey keep.

16

Three-foot-thick oak doors separate the rooms, ebony is used to dramatic effect, and a slate bed was built for the visit of Queen Victoria. The decoration is glorious, and fairly true to the Romanesque style, with its deeply cut chevrons, billets and double-cone ornamentation. The family amassed Wales's largest private painting collection, including a Gainsborough landscape, Canaletto's *The Thames at Westminster* and a Rembrandt portrait. Also worth a visit are the Victorian kitchen and servants' quarters, something of an antidote to the opulence "above stairs".

ARRIVAL AND DEPARTURE — BANGOR

By train Bangor's train station lies at the south end of Holyhead Rd.

Destinations Chester (21 daily; 1hr); Conwy (11 daily; 20min); Holyhead (22 daily; 30–40min); Llandudno (18 daily; 40min).

By bus National Express and local buses stop in the centre of town.

Destinations Beaumaris (every 30min; 20–35min); Caernarfon (every 10min; 25min); Conwy (every 15min; 45min); Holyhead (hourly; 1hr 15min); Llanberis (hourly; 45min); Llandudno (every 15min; 1hr); Llanfairpwll (every 30min; 15min).

ACCOMMODATION

Eryl Môr Hotel 2 Upper Garth Rd T 01248 353789, W erylmorhotel.co.uk. Quiet, comfy, fully licensed hotel with Its own restaurant. The best rooms overlook Bangor's pier and the Menai Strait. **£75**

Treborth Hall Farm A487, 1.8 miles southwest of upper Bangor T 01248 364104, W www.treborthleisure.co.uk. The nearest campsite to town, well-kept with coin-op showers (£1). Bus #5 passes the entrance. **£12**

Y Garth Garth Rd T 01248 362277, W thegarthguesthouse.co.uk. There are en-suite rooms and full breakfasts in this guesthouse, the best in a row of three serviceable B&Bs. **£60**

EATING AND DRINKING

★ **Blue Sky** Rear of 236 High St T 01248 355444, W blueskybangor.co.uk. Airy, casual daytime café with mismatched tables, free wi-fi and delicious breakfasts, soups, sandwiches, burgers and platters (often organic; £5–7) plus great coffee. Check the website for evening gigs and movies. Mon–Sat 9.30am–5.30pm and occasional evenings.

Kyffin 129 High St T 01248 355161. Vegetarian and vegan café with excellent Fairtrade coffee and a warm atmosphere that makes you want to stick around for their light lunches (mostly under £6). Mon–Sat 9.30am–5pm.

Tap & Spile Garth Rd T 01248 370835. Popular students' and locals' pub with great views of the pier and Menai Strait, plus meals and real ales at good prices. Tues–Sun noon–11pm.

Conwy and around

CONWY, wonderfully set on the Conwy Estuary, twenty miles east of Bangor, is backed by a forested fold of Snowdonia. The town has a fine **castle** and a complete, three-quarter-mile-long belt of 30ft-high town **walls** encircling a compact core of medieval and Victorian buildings. This makes it extremely easy to potter around, and though you'll see everything you need to in a day, you may well find yourself wanting to stay longer.

Conwy Castle

April–June, Sept & Oct daily 9.30am–5pm; July & Aug daily 9.30am–6pm; Nov–March Mon–Sat 10am–4pm, Sun 11am–4pm • CADW • £4.80, joint ticket with Plas Mawr £7.30 • ⓣ 01492 592358

Conwy Castle is the toughest-looking link in Edward I's Iron Ring of fortresses around North Wales. With 1500 men, James of St George took just five years to construct eight massive **towers** in a rectangle around the two wards on a strategic knoll near the mouth of the river. The inner ward was separated from the outer by a **drawbridge** and **portcullis**, and further protected by turrets atop the four eastern towers, now the preserve of crows.

In 1401, on Good Friday, when the fifteen-strong castle guard were at church, two cousins of Owain Glyndŵr took the castle and razed the town for Glyndŵr's cause. It was re-fortified for the Civil War then subsequently stripped of all its iron, wood and lead, and was left substantially as it is today.

The outer ward's 130ft-long **Great Hall** and the **King's Apartments** are both well preserved, but the only part of the castle to have kept its roof is the **Chapel Tower**, named for the small room built into the wall whose semicircular apse still shows some heavily worn carving.

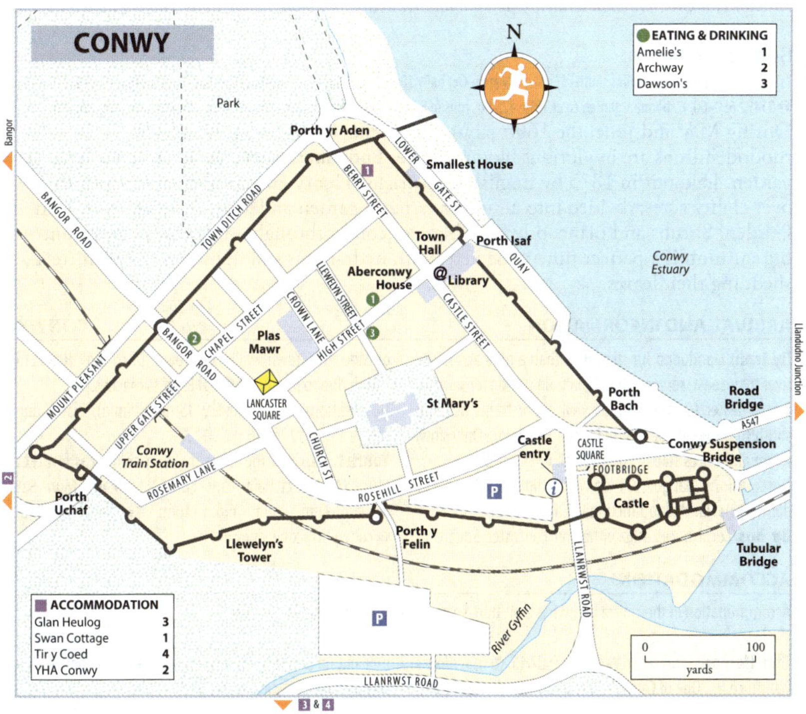

Conwy Suspension Bridge

Mid-March to Oct daily 11am–5pm • NT • £1 • ⓣ 01492 573282

Anchored to the castle walls, Telford's narrow **Conwy Suspension Bridge** was prompted by the need for better communications to Ireland after the Act of Union, and contemporary with Telford's far greater effort spanning the Menai Strait. Restored to its original state, it now operates as a footbridge.

Aberconwy House

Castle St • Mid-Feb to Oct daily 11am–5pm • NT • £3.40 • ⓣ 01492 592246

Aberconwy House is the oldest in Conwy, built about 1300 and variously used as a bakery, antique shop, sea captain's house and temperance hotel. Its incarnations are re-created in rooms furnished with a simple yet elegant collection of rural furniture.

Plas Mawr

20 High St • **House** Tues–Sun: April–Sept 9am–5pm; Oct 9.30am–4pm • £5.20, joint ticket with castle £7.30 **Evening tours** Mid-April to Oct Thurs 6pm & 7.30pm • CADW • £6 • ⓣ 01492 580167

The Dutch-style **Plas Mawr** is among the best-preserved Elizabethan townhouses in Britain, built in 1576 for Robert Wynn, one of the first Welsh people to live in the town. Much of the dressed stonework was replaced during renovations in the 1940s and 1950s, but the interior sports more original features, in particular the friezes and superb moulded plaster ceilings depicting fleurs-de-lis, griffons, owls and rams.

16

The smallest house in Great Britain

Conwy Quay • Easter to mid-Oct daily 10am–5pm • £1

The two tiny rooms of the **smallest house in Great Britain** are together only 9ft high and 6ft wide. You'll have to duck to get in, a problem that by all accounts vexed the last resident, a 6ft 3in fisherman, until he left in around 1900.

Bodnant Garden

Tal-y-Cafn, off the A470, 8 miles south of Conwy • March–Oct daily 10am–5pm; first two weeks of Nov daily 10am–4pm • NT • £7.70 • ⓣ 01492 650460, ⓦ bodnantgarden.co.uk • The #25 bus runs to Bodnant from Llandudno and Llandudno Junction (roughly hourly)

During May and June, the 160ft laburnum tunnel flourishes and banks of rhododendrons are in glorious bloom all over **Bodnant Garden**, Wales's finest formal garden. Laid out in 1875 by English industrialist Henry Pochin, the garden spreads over eighty acres, divided into an upper terraced garden and lower Pinetum and Wild Garden. Shrubs and plants provide a blaze of colour throughout the opening season, but autumn is a perfect time to be here, with hydrangeas still in bloom and fruit trees shedding their leaves.

ARRIVAL AND INFORMATION — CONWY

By train Llandudno Junction, less than a mile across the river to the east, serves as the main train station for services from Chester to Holyhead, as well as for trains heading south to Betws-y-Coed and Blaenau Ffestiniog. Only slow, regional services stop in Conwy itself (on request).

Destinations Bangor (11 daily; 20min); Holyhead (11 daily; 1hr); Llandudno Junction (11 daily; 4min).

By bus Local buses stop either on Lancaster Square or outside the town walls on Town Ditch Rd. Head to Llandudno to pick up National Express coaches.

Destinations Bangor (every 15min; 45min); Llandudno (every 15min; 20min).

Tourist office In the same building as the castle ticket office (April–Oct daily 9am–5pm; Nov–March Mon–Sat 9.30am–4pm, Sun 11am–4pm; ⓣ 01492 592248, ⓔ conwytic@conwy.gov.uk).

ACCOMMODATION

Accommodation in the centre of town is a bit thin, so you should book ahead in summer.

Glan Heulog Llanrwst Rd ⓣ 01492 593845, ⓦ snowdoniabandb.co.uk. One of Conwy's best small guesthouses, half a mile out on the B5106 Trefriw road in a Victorian house with seven, mostly en-suite rooms. **£58**

★**Swan Cottage** 18 Berry St ⓣ01492 596840, ⓦswancottage.net. Central B&B with small, attractive en-suite rooms, two with great estuary views, one tucked into the attic overlooking the town walls. **£50**

Tir y Coed Rowen, 4 mile south ⓣ01492 650219, ⓦtirycoed.com. Very peaceful country house with landscaped grounds and views of the Carneddau range from some of the eight bold and eclectically decorated rooms, most with bathtubs. Dining (table d'hôte; £37) is very much part of the experience. **£125**

★**YHA Conwy** Lark Hill ⓣ0845 371 9732, ⓔconwy@yha.org.uk. Spacious, modernized hostel a 10min walk from town up the Sychnant Pass Rd, open all day, with good meals and bike rental. **£18–22**

EATING AND DRINKING

Amelie's 10 High St ⓣ01492 583142. Lovely, cosy café that's perfect for soup, a light lunch or just coffee and cake. Evening meals have a French accent and include chicken cassoulet (£14) and baked cod on roasted ratatouille (£15). Mon–Wed & Sun 9.30am–4.30pm, Thurs–Sat 9.30am–9.30pm.

Archway 12 Bangor Rd ⓣ01492 592 458. Quality eat-in and take-out fish and chip restaurant also doing pizza and pies. On a fine evening take your haul to the quay and wash it down with a pint from the *Liverpool Arms*. Daily 11am–10pm or later.

Dawson's Castle Hotel, High St ⓣ01492 582800, ⓦcastlewales.co.uk. Smart bar and restaurant where the emphasis is on quality ingredients cooked well and served without too much fuss – though there's nothing sloppy here. Come for a pint or pre-dinner cocktail in the bar then something like local haddock and chorizo risotto (£8) followed by tandoori monkfish with vanilla mash (£16). Mon–Thurs & Sun 7.30am–9.30pm, Fri & Sat 7.30am–10pm.

Llandudno

16

The twin limestone hummocks of the 680ft **Great Orme** and its southern cousin the Little Orme provide a dramatic frame for the gently curving Victorian frontage of **LLANDUDNO**, four miles north of Conwy. Despite the arrival of more rumbustious fun-seekers to its seaside resort, Llandudno retains an undeniably dignified air, bolstered by its ever-improving selection of chic hotels and quality restaurants.

Llandudno's early history revolves around the **Great Orme**, where St Tudno, who brought Christianity to the region in the sixth century, built the monastic cell that gives the town its name. In the mid-nineteenth century, local landowner Edward Mostyn exploited the growing craze for sea-bathing and built a town for the upper-middle classes which quickly became synonymous with the Victorian ideal of a respectable seaside resort.

The pier

Daily: summer 9am–11pm; winter 9am–6pm • Free

At one time the embodiment of Llandudno's ornate Victoriana, the **pier**'s neat wooden deck is overrun in summer with kids clamouring to board the modest fairground rides, and deckchair denizens cocking an ear to the recorded sounds of a Wurlitzer maestro. Ice cream and candyfloss outlets abound, as a town ordinance bars the sale of such fripperies anywhere else on the waterfront.

The Oriel Mostyn

12 Vaughan St • Daily 10.30am–5pm • Free • ⓣ01492 87921, ⓦmostyn.org

The elaborate terracotta brick facade of the **Oriel Mostyn** gives little clue as to the raw interior spaces of this newly refurbished gallery – all rough-cast bare concrete – named after Lady Mostyn, for whom it was originally built in 1901. The five rooms are almost always showing something of interest, much of it by leading Welsh artists. There's also a good arts shop and the bare Café Lux.

The Great Orme

The view from the top of the **Great Orme** (Pen y Gogarth) ranks with those from the far loftier summits in Snowdonia, combining the seascapes east towards Rhyl and west over the sands of the Conwy Estuary with the brooding, quarry-chewed northern limit of the Carneddau range where Snowdonia crashes into the sea. This huge lump of carboniferous limestone was subject to some of the same stresses that folded Snowdonia, producing fissures filled by molten mineral-bearing rock.

Great Orme Tramway

Daily: Easter–Sept 10am–6pm; Oct 10am–5pm • £3.90 single, £5.80 return • ⓣ 01492 879306, ⓦ greatormetramway.co.uk

The base of the Great Orme is traditionally circumnavigated on **Marine Drive**, a five-mile anticlockwise circuit from just near Llandudno's pier. The best way to get to the copper mines and the grasslands on top of the Orme is by the San Francisco-style **Great Orme Tramway**, which creaks up from the bottom of Old Road, much as it has done since 1902.

Great Orme Ancient Mines

Mid-March to Oct daily 10am–5pm • £6.50 • ⓣ 01492 870447, ⓦ greatormemines.info

A Bronze Age settlement developed around what are now the **Great Orme Copper Mines**, accessed via the tramway. Hard hats and miners' lamps are provided for the self-guided **tour** through just a small portion of the tunnels, enough to give you a feel for the cramped working conditions and the dangers of falling rock.

ARRIVAL AND INFORMATION — LLANDUDNO

16

By train Direct services to Llandudno's forlorn train station arrive from Betws-y-Coed and Chester; for all other services change at Llandudno Junction, near Conwy.

Destinations Bangor (18 daily; 40min); Betws-y-Coed (4 daily; 40min); Blaenau Ffestiniog (6 daily; 1hr 20min); Chester (roughly hourly; 1hr 10min); Holyhead (18 daily; 1hr 20min); Llandudno Junction (every 30min; 10min).

By bus Local buses stop on either Mostyn St or Gloddaeth St, while National Express buses from Chester, Bangor and Pwllheli (bookings at the tourist office) stop at the Coach Park on Mostyn Broadway. Alpine run an open-top double-decker bus looping from Llandudno to Conwy and back (late May to mid-Sept every 30min 10am–4pm; £7.50; ⓣ 01492 879133) – perfect for a half-day visit to Conwy.

Destinations Bangor (every 15min; 1hr); Betws-y-Coed (9 daily; 50min); Blaenau Ffestiniog (9 daily; 1hr 10min); Conwy (every 15min; 20min).

Tourist office Library Building, Mostyn St (Easter–Sept Mon–Sat 9am–5pm, Sun 9.30am–4.30pm; Oct–Easter Mon–Sat 9am–5pm; ⓣ 01492 577577, ⓔ llandudnotic@conwy.gov.uk, ⓦ visitllandudno.org.uk); they stock a good free map of Great Orme footpaths.

ACCOMMODATION

Finding a place to stay is not usually a problem, though booking ahead is wise. Most of the budget places congregate along St David's Rd, just west of the station, and on Deganwy Ave. The nearest tent **camping** is at Conwy.

★ **The Cliffbury** 34 St David's Rd ⓣ 01492 877224, ⓦ thecliffbury.co.uk. Stylish wallpapers, sparkling white bathrooms and dedicated hosts define this classy B&B on a quiet street with six individually decorated rooms and free wi-fi. Superior rooms (£20 more) come with DVD player and robes. Two-night minimum. **£62**

★ **Escape** 48 Church Walks ⓣ 01492 877776, ⓦ escapebandb.co.uk. Chic boutique B&B with nine individually designed rooms combining clean-lined modernism with retro or antique touches. Aveda toiletries, wi-fi, classy breakfasts and a guest lounge with honesty bar complete the package. **£100**

Glenthorne 2 York Rd ⓣ 01492 879591, ⓔ rebrw@aol.com. Very good guesthouse with seven comfy rooms and a welcoming atmosphere, plus good-value three-course evening meals (£13). Single supplement just £5. **£54**

Plas Madoc 60 Church Walks ⓣ 01492 876514, ⓦ plasmadocguesthouse.co.uk. Comfortable five-room guesthouse with one superior room with bath and good views over the town. Full breakfasts include the option of soy or rice milk, vegan sausages and the like. Free wi-fi. **£65**

EATING AND DRINKING

Llandudno has the best choice of **restaurants** in north Wales. The liveliest **bars** are along Upper Mostyn St, which can be chaotically crowded at weekends.

The Albert 56 Madoc St ⓣ 01492 877188, ⓦ albertllandudno.co.uk. If all you want is quality pub food in gut-splitting portions then this is your spot. Excellent value, with most mains £10–12. Daily 11.30am–10pm or later.

★ **Bodysgallen Hall** A470, 3 miles south of town ⓣ 01492 584466, ⓦ bodysgallen.com. Oil paintings, heavy curtains and views across the parterre garden make a perfect setting for some of the finest dining around. Sip a sherry by the fire then embark on a three-course Modern British dinner (£49; smart dress required) or a sumptuous lunch (£10–23). The afternoon teas (£14.50) and Sunday lunches (£27.50) are superb. Alternatively, go for the more contemporary 1620 bistro in the former coach house (Mon–Fri two-course lunches £14 if booked in advance). Restaurant Tues–Sun 12.30–1.45pm & 7–9pm; bistro Mon–Sat 12.30–3pm & 5.30–9pm.

The Hambone Food Hall 3 Lloyd St ⓣ 01492 860084. Good deli producing made-to-order sandwiches along with a wide range of meat pies, pâtés and salads to go or eat in. Mon–Sat 9am–5pm, Sun 10am–4pm.

Osborne's 17 North Parade ⓣ 01492 860330. Lit by candles and chandeliers, this opulent café and grill serves modern dishes: go for the three-course deal (£19). Also an excellent spot for a full afternoon tea (£11) or a champagne afternoon tea for two (£45). Mon–Sat 10.30am–10pm, Sun 10.30am–9pm.

The Seahorse 7 Church Walks ⓣ 01492 875315, ⓦ the-seahorse.co.uk. Unusual two-in-one dinner-only restaurant with an intimate fine dining feel upstairs and a sociable cellar brasserie below. The predominantly fish and seafood menu is the same in both, however (£26 for 2 courses, £30 for 3) and the food reliably excellent. Expect dishes such as seafood linguini or monkfish wrapped in Parma ham. Daily 4.30–10pm.

Bodelwyddan Castle and around

Eighteen miles east of Conwy • Generally mid-April–Oct Wed–Sun plus Mon & Tues in school holidays 10am–5pm; Nov to mid-April Sat & Sun 11am–4pm • £6 including audio tour • ⓦ bodelwyddan-castle.co.uk

The finest art showcase in North Wales is **Bodelwyddan Castle**, an outpost of the National Portrait Gallery. The opulent Victorian interiors provide a suitable setting for hundreds of paintings by Millais, Rossetti, Browning, John Singer Sargent and Landseer, among others. Look out for two sensitive portraits highlighting the Pre-Raphaelite movement's support for social reform: William Holman Hunt's portrayal of the vociferous opponent of slavery and capital punishment, Stephen Lushington; Ford Madox Brown's double portrait of Henry Fawcett, prime mover in the passing of the 1867 Reform Bill, and suffragette Millicent Garrett.

St Asaph Cathedral

St Asaph (Llanelwy), 2 miles east of Bodelwyddan • Daily 9am–6.30pm • Free

ST ASAPH (Llanelwy) is home to Britain's smallest **cathedral**, founded around 570 by St Kentigern and no bigger than many village churches. From 1601 until his death in 1604, the bishopric was held by **William Morgan**, who was responsible for the translation of the first Welsh-language Bible, without which the language may have died out. A thousand Morgan Bibles were printed, of which only nineteen remain, one of them displayed in the south transept along with notable prayer books and psalters.

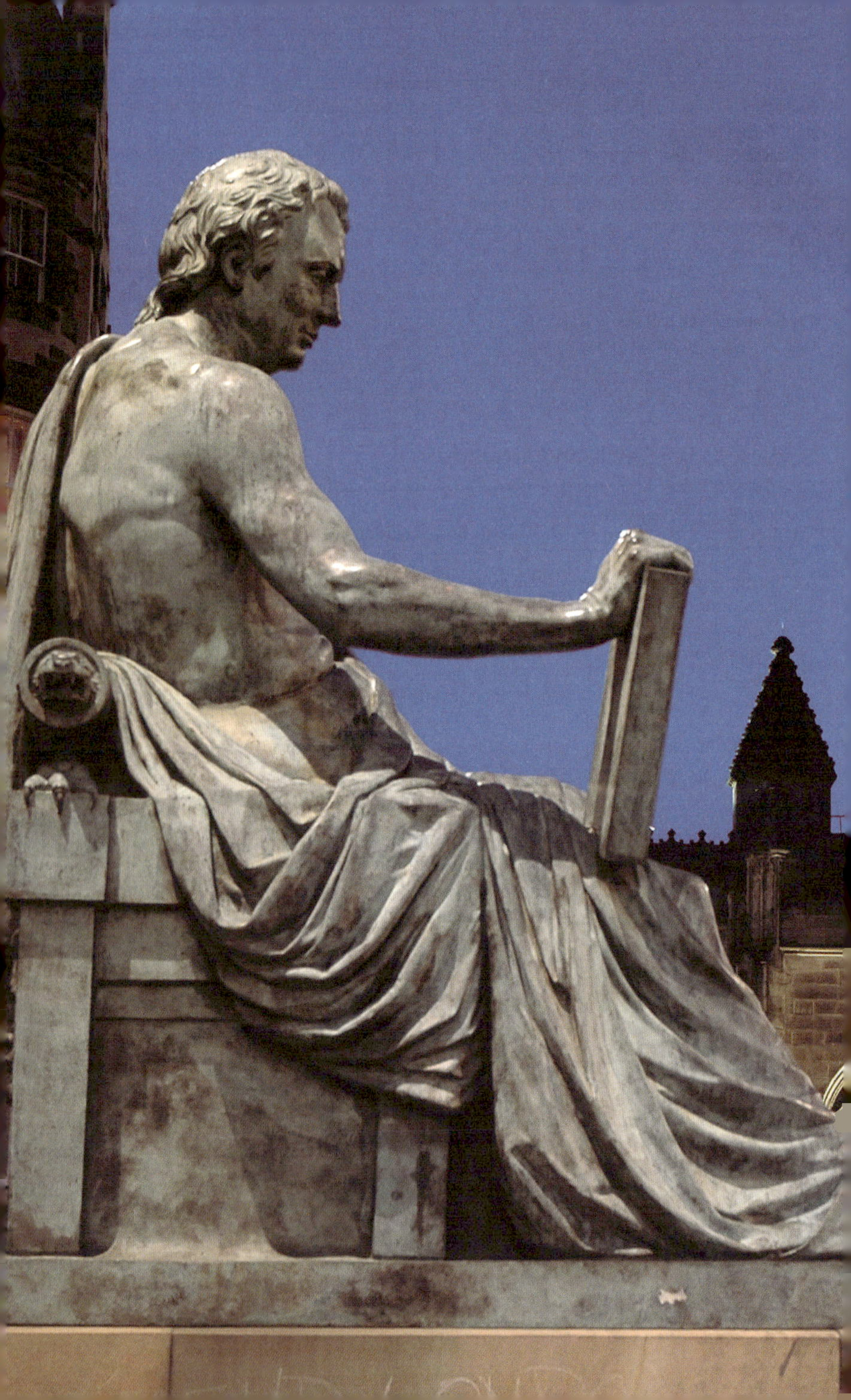

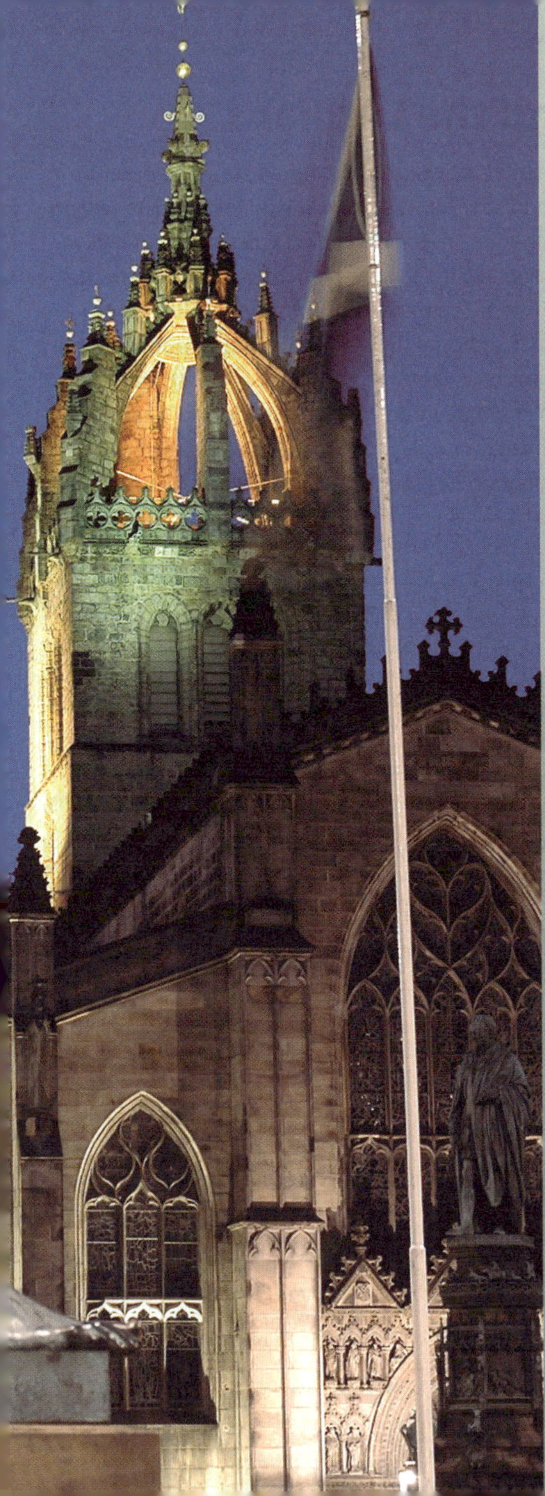

Edinburgh and the Lothians

718 The Old Town

727 The New Town

732 Out from the centre

743 East Lothian

745 Midlothian

745 West Lothian

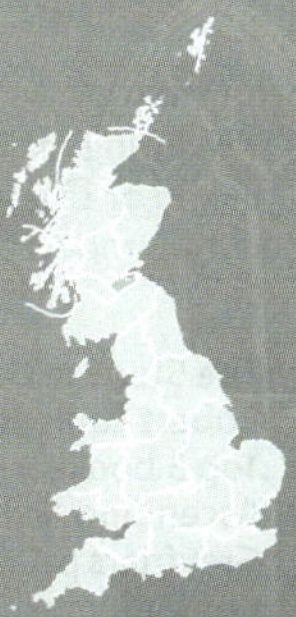

THE ROYAL MILE, EDINBURGH

17

Edinburgh and the Lothians

Edinburgh, the showcase capital of Scotland, is a venerable, cosmopolitan and cultured city famed worldwide for its superb annual festival. The setting is wonderfully striking: perched on a series of extinct volcanoes and rocky crags which rise from the generally flat landscape of the Lothians, with the sheltered shoreline of the Firth of Forth to the north. "My own Romantic town", Sir Walter Scott called it, although it was another native author, Robert Louis Stevenson, who perhaps best captured the feel of his "precipitous city", declaring that "No situation could be more commanding for the head of a kingdom; none better chosen for noble prospects". Edinburgh's ability to capture the literary imagination has seen it dubbed a "World City of Literature" by UNESCO, who have also conferred World Heritage Site status on much of the centre.

The area north of the castle, the dignified, Grecian-style **New Town** was laid out in the eighteenth century after the announcement of a plan to improve conditions in the city. The **Old Town**, on the other hand, with its tortuous alleys and tightly packed closes, is unrelentingly medieval, associated in popular imagination with the city's underworld lore of murderers Burke and Hare and of schizophrenic Deacon Brodie, inspiration for Stevenson's *Strange Case of Dr Jekyll and Mr Hyde*.

Set on the hill which sweeps down from the fairy-tale castle to the royal **Palace of Holyroodhouse**, the Old Town preserves all the key reminders of its role as a historic capital, augmented now by the dramatic and unusual new **Scottish Parliament building**, opposite the palace. A few hundred yards away, a tantalizing glimpse of the wild beauty of Scotland's scenery can be had in **Holyrood Park**, an extensive area of open countryside dominated by **Arthur's Seat**, the largest and most impressive of the volcanoes. Among Edinburgh's many museums, the exciting **National Museum of Scotland** houses 10,000 of Scotland's most precious artefacts, while the **National Gallery of Scotland** and its offshoot, the **Scottish National Gallery of Modern Art**, house two of Britain's finest collections of paintings.

Beyond the centre, Edinburgh's liveliest area is **Leith**, the city's medieval port, whose seedy edge is softened by a series of great bars and restaurants, along with the presence of the former royal yacht **Britannia**. The wider rural surroundings of Edinburgh, known as the **Lothians**, mix rolling countryside and attractive country towns with some impressive historic ruins.

Brief history

It was during the **Dark Ages** that the name Edinburgh – at least in its early forms of Dunedin or Din Eidyn ("fort of Eidyn") – first appeared. The strategic fort atop the Castle Rock volcano served as Scotland's **southernmost border post** until 1018, when King

The Stone of Destiny p.718
Robert Louis Stevenson p.721
Top 5 bookish sights p.723
Ascending Arthur's Seat p.725
Greyfriars p.726
Contemporary art in Edinburgh p.729
The Edinburgh Festival pp.734–735
City tours p.736
Shopping in Edinburgh p.742
Hogmanay p.743
Rosslyn's secrets p.745

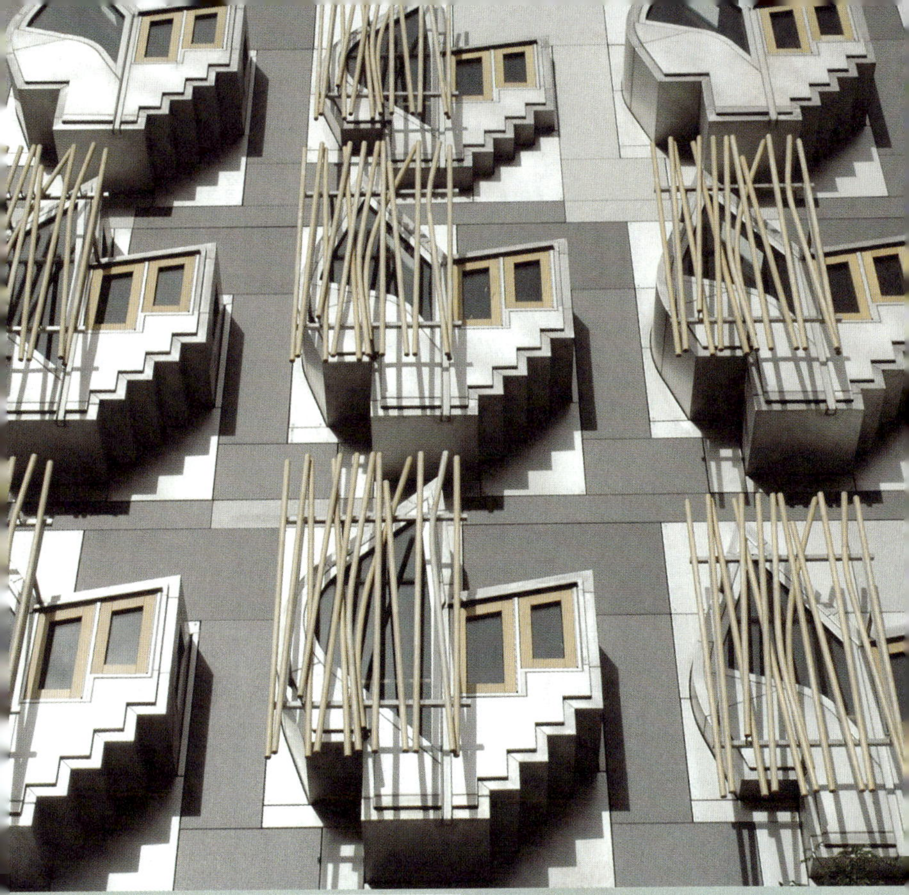

SCOTTISH PARLIAMENT, EDINBURGH

Highlights

❶ **The Old Town** The evocative heart of the historic city, with its tenements, closes, courtyards, ghosts and catacombs cheek-by-jowl with many of Scotland's most important buildings. **See p.718**

❷ **Edinburgh Castle** Perched on an imposing volcanic crag, the castle dominates Scotland's capital, its ancient battlements protecting the Crown Jewels. **See p.718**

❸ **Scottish Parliament** Enric Miralles' quirky design is a dynamic modern presence in Holyrood's historic royal precinct. **See p.724**

❹ **Holyrood Park** Wild moors, rocky crags and an 800ft peak (Arthur's Seat), all slap in the middle of the city. **See p.725**

❺ **National Museum of Scotland** The treasures of Scotland's past housed in a dynamic and superbly conceived building. **See p.726**

❻ **The Edinburgh Festival** In August and early September, around a million visitors flock to the world's biggest arts festival, which is in fact a series of separate festivals: bewildering, inspiring, exhausting and endlessly entertaining. **See pp.734–735**

❼ **Café Royal Circle Bar** There are few finer pubs in which to sample a pint of local 80 shilling beer, accompanied by six oysters (once the city's staple food). **See p.741**

HIGHLIGHTS ARE MARKED ON THE MAP ON P.714

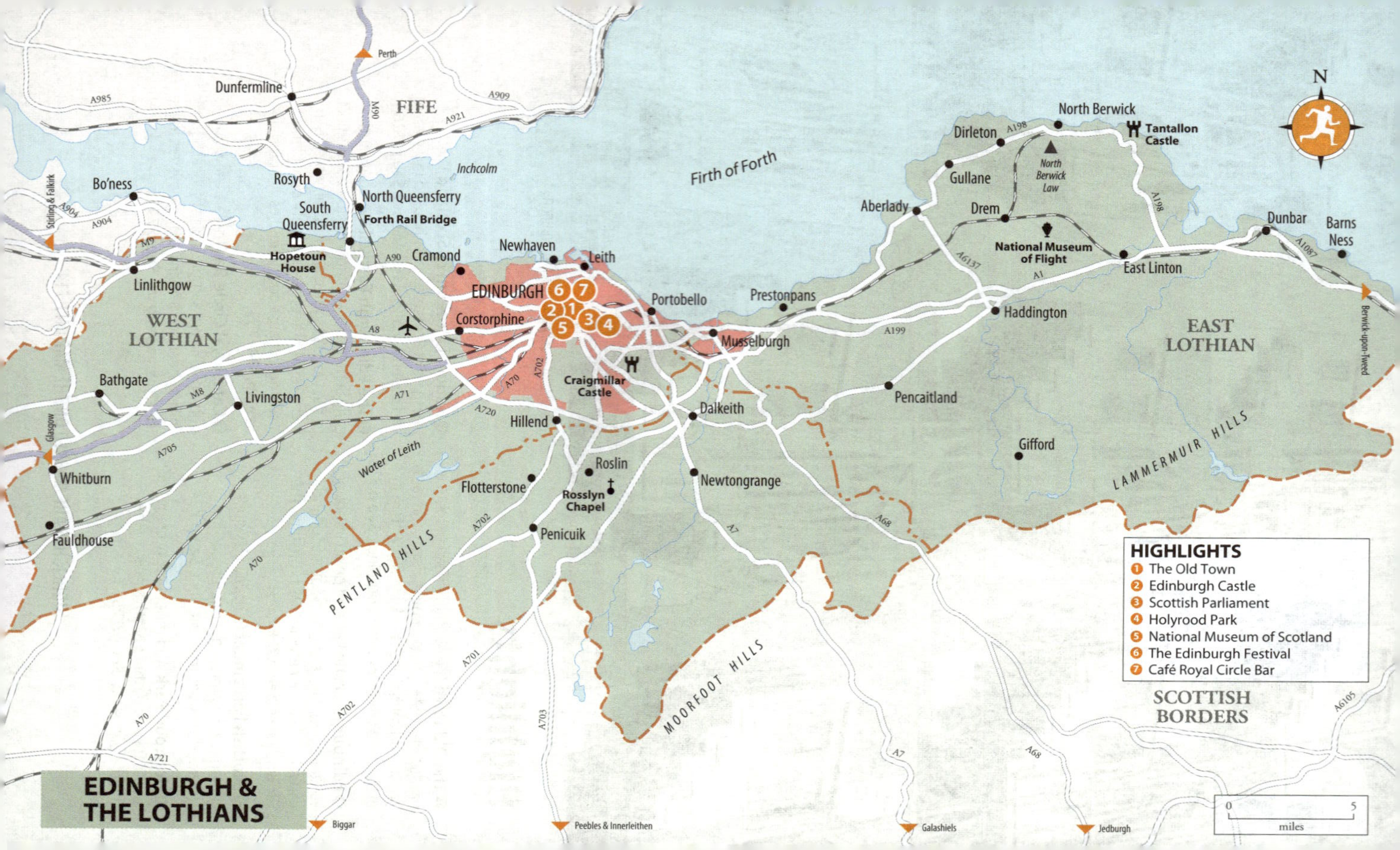

EDINBURGH &
THE LOTHIANS
HIGHLIGHTS
1 The Old Town
2 Edinburgh Castle
3 Scottish Parliament
4 Holyrood Park
5 National Museum of Scotland
6 The Edinburgh Festival
7 Café Royal Circle Bar
N
Perth
Dunfermline
FIFE
A985
A909
A921
M90
Rosyth
Inchcolm
Firth of Forth
Bo'ness
Stirling & Falkirk
A904
South Queensferry
North Queensferry
Forth Rail Bridge
Hopetoun House
M9
A90
Cramond
Newhaven
Leith
EDINBURGH
Corstorphine
Portobello
Prestonpans
Musselburgh
Linlithgow
WEST LOTHIAN
A8
Bathgate
M8
Livingston
A71
A720
A70
A702
Craigmillar Castle
Hillend
Dalkeith
Glasgow
Whitburn
A705
Water of Leith
Roslin
Rosslyn Chapel
Flotterstone
Newtongrange
Fauldhouse
Penicuik
PENTLAND HILLS
MOORFOOT HILLS
A701
A703
A721
A7
A68
North Berwick
Tantallon Castle
Dirleton
A198
Gullane
North Berwick Law
Aberlady
Drem
National Museum of Flight
A6137
A1
East Linton
Dunbar
Barns Ness
A1087
Haddington
A199
Pencaitland
EAST LOTHIAN
Berwick-upon-Tweed
Gifford
LAMMERMUIR HILLS
SCOTTISH BORDERS
A6105
Biggar
Peebles & Innerleithen
Galashiels
Jedburgh
0
5
miles

Malcolm I established the River Tweed as the permanent frontier. In the reign of Malcolm Canmore in the late eleventh century, the castle became one of the main seats of the court, and the town, which was given privileged status as a **royal burgh**, began to grow.

Turbulent Middle Ages

Under King James IV (1488–1513), the city enjoyed a short but brilliant **Renaissance era**, which saw not only the construction of a new palace alongside Holyrood Abbey, but also the granting of a **royal charter** to the College of Surgeons, the earliest in the city's long line of academic and professional bodies. This period came to an abrupt end in 1513 with the calamitous defeat by the English at the Battle of Flodden leading to several decades of political instability. In the 1540s, English king Henry VIII's attempt to force a royal union with Scotland led to the sack of Edinburgh, prompting the Scots to turn to France: French troops arrived to defend the city, while the young Scottish queen Mary was dispatched to Paris as the promised bride of the Dauphin, later Francois II of France. While the French occupiers succeeded in removing the English threat, they themselves antagonized the locals, who had become increasingly sympathetic to the ideals of the **Reformation**. When the radical preacher John Knox returned from exile in 1555, he quickly won over the city to his Calvinist message.

The Scottish Enlightenment

James VI's rule saw the foundation of the University of Edinburgh in 1582, but following the **Union of the Crowns** in 1603, when James assumed the throne of England in addition to that of Scotland, the city was totally upstaged by London: although James promised to visit every three years, it was not until 1617 that he made his only return trip. The **Union of the Parliaments** of 1707 dealt a further blow to Edinburgh's political prestige, though the guaranteed preservation of the national church and the legal and educational systems ensured that it was never relegated to a purely provincial role. On the contrary, it was in the second half of the eighteenth century that Edinburgh achieved the height of its intellectual influence, led by natives such as David Hume and Adam Smith. Around the same time, the city began to expand beyond its medieval boundaries, laying out the **New Town**, a masterpiece of the Neoclassical style and grand town planning.

The nineteenth century and beyond

Industrialization affected Edinburgh less than any other major city in the nation, and it never lost its white-collar character. Through the Victorian era Edinburgh cemented its role as a conservative bastion of the establishment, controlling Scotland's legal, ecclesiastical and education systems. Nonetheless, the city underwent an enormous **urban expansion** in the nineteenth century, annexing, among many other small burghs, the large port of **Leith**.

In 1947 Edinburgh was chosen to host the great **International Festival** which served as a symbol of the new peaceful European order; despite some hiccups, it has flourished ever since, in the process helping to make tourism a mainstay of the local economy. During the 1980s Glasgow, previously the poor relation but always a tenacious rival, began to challenge the city's status as a cultural centre, and it took the re-establishment of a devolved Scottish P**arliament** in 1999 for Edinburgh to reassert its status in a meaningful way. With debates and decisions about crucial aspects of the government of Scotland taking place in Edinburgh, there was a notable upturn in the city's standing, augmented by significant achievements in scientific research and the arts. The financial sector burgeoned, with the Royal Bank of Scotland becoming the second largest banking group in the UK in the early years of the new century. Its near collapse and subsequent bail-out by the government during the 2009 economic crisis dented not only the city's self-confidence, but also the arguments made by nationalist politicians that Scotland has the stability and economic prowess to prosper as an independent country.

17

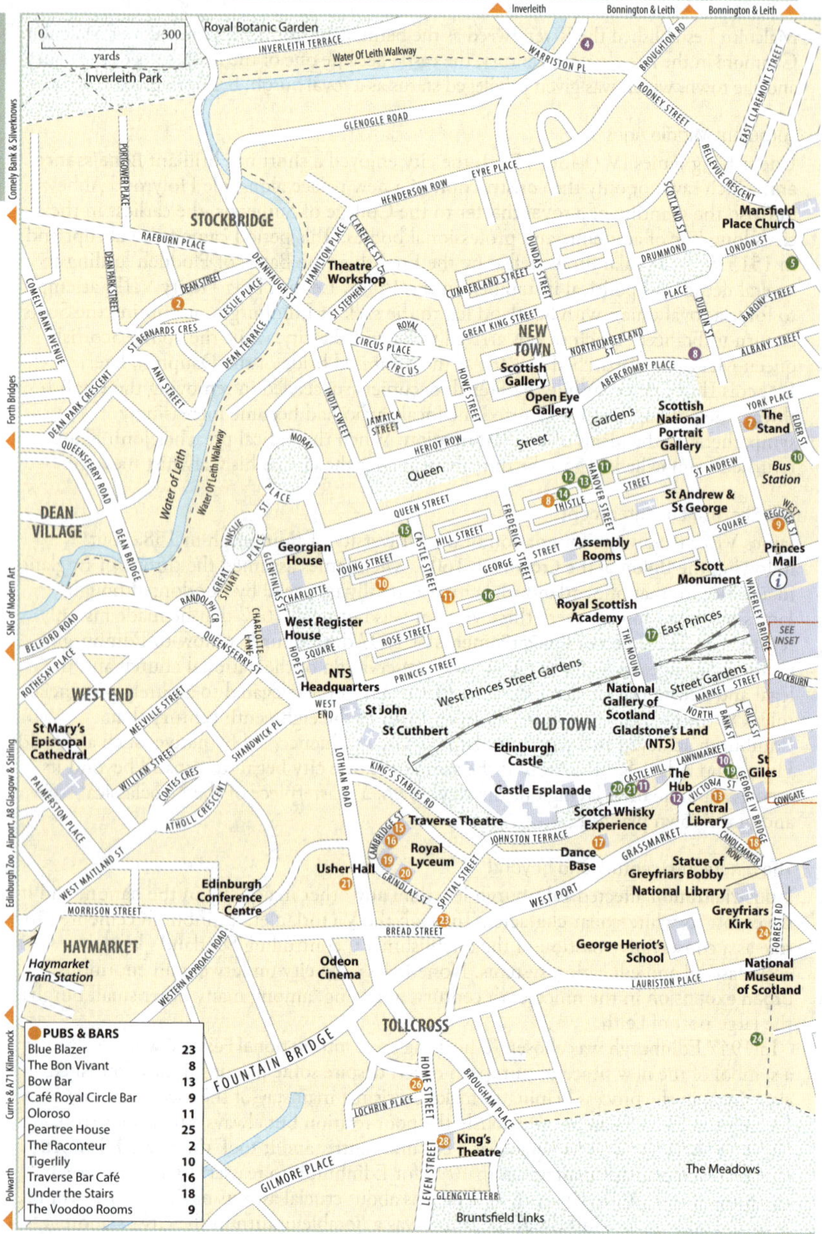

PUBS & BARS

Blue Blazer	23
The Bon Vivant	8
Bow Bar	13
Café Royal Circle Bar	9
Oloroso	11
Peartree House	25
The Raconteur	2
Tigerlily	10
Traverse Bar Café	16
Under the Stairs	18
The Voodoo Rooms	9

ACCOMMODATION

Brodies 1	1	The Glasshouse	9
Canon Court Apartments	4	Hotel Missoni	10
Castle Rock Hostel	12	Ibis Edinburgh Centre	2
Edinburgh Central SYHA	5	Ramsay's Bed and Breakfast	6
Express by Holiday Inn Edinburgh City Centre	7	Smart City Hostel	3
Gerald's Place	8	Ten Hill Place	13
		The Witchery Apartments	11

RESTAURANTS, CAFÉS & BISTROS

21212	9
Amber	20
Artisan Roast	7
David Bann's Vegetarian Restaurant	4
The Dining Room, Scotch Malt Whisky Society	12
The Dogs	13

17

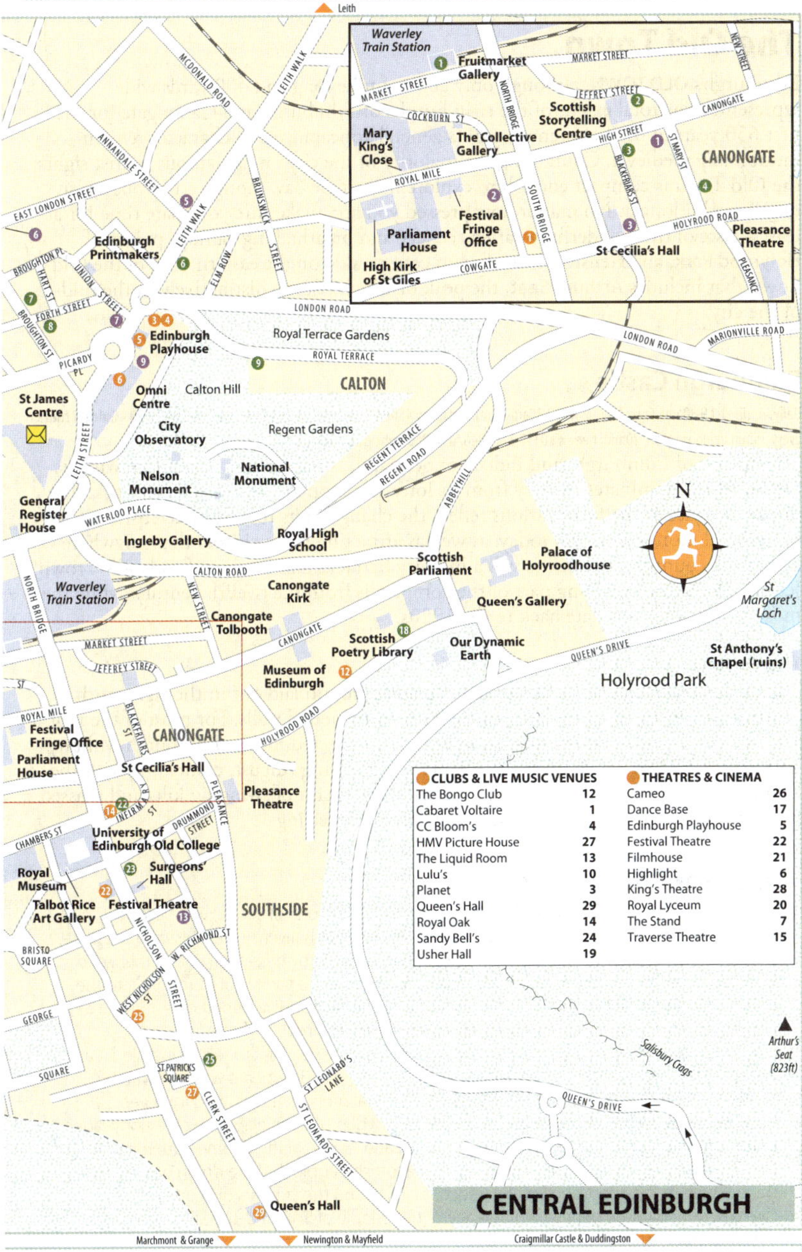

CLUBS & LIVE MUSIC VENUES	
The Bongo Club	12
Cabaret Voltaire	1
CC Bloom's	4
HMV Picture House	27
The Liquid Room	13
Lulu's	10
Planet	3
Queen's Hall	29
Royal Oak	14
Sandy Bell's	24
Usher Hall	19

THEATRES & CINEMA	
Cameo	26
Dance Base	17
Edinburgh Playhouse	5
Festival Theatre	22
Filmhouse	21
Highlight	6
King's Theatre	28
Royal Lyceum	20
The Stand	7
Traverse Theatre	15

Dusit	14
The Edinburgh Larder	3
L'Escargot Bleu	5
Foodies at Holyrood	18
Fruitmarket Gallery Café	1
La Garrigue	2
The Honours	15
Kalpna	25
Mother India's Café	22
Mussel Inn	16
Ondine	19
Peter's Yard	24
The Scottish Café and Restaurant	17
Spoon Café Bistro	23
Urban Angel	8/11
Valvona & Crolla	6
Valvona & Crolla Vincaffè	10
The Witchery by the Castle	21

17

The Old Town

Edinburgh's **OLD TOWN**, although only about a mile long and 400 yards wide, represented the total extent of the twin burghs of Edinburgh and Canongate for the first 650 years of their existence, and its general appearance and character remain indubitably medieval. Containing the majority of the city's most famous tourist sights, the Old Town is compact enough to explore in a single day, though a thorough visit requires a bit longer. No matter how pressed you are, make sure you spare time for at least a taste of the wonderfully varied scenery and breathtaking vantage points of **Holyrood Park**, an extensive tract of open countryside on the eastern edge of the Old Town that includes **Arthur's Seat**, the peak of which rises so distinctively in the midst of the city.

Edinburgh Castle

Daily: April–Oct 9.30am–6pm; Nov–March 9.30am–5pm, last entry 45min before closing • £14–15, audioguides £3.50 • **Guided tours** Every 15min in high season; 20min; free • T 0131 225 9846, W edinburghcastle.gov.uk

The history of Edinburgh, and indeed of Scotland, is indissolubly bound up with its **castle**, which dominates the city from its lofty seat atop an extinct volcanic rock. The disparate styles of the fortifications reflect the change in its role from defensive citadel to national monument, and today, as well as attracting more visitors than anywhere else in the country, the castle is still a military barracks and home to Scotland's Crown Jewels. The oldest surviving part of the complex is from the twelfth century, while the most recent additions date back to the 1920s.

The Esplanade

The castle is entered via the **Esplanade**, a parade ground laid out in the eighteenth century and enclosed a hundred years later by ornamental walls. For most of the year it acts as a coach park, though huge grandstands are erected for the Edinburgh Military Tattoo (see p.734), which takes place every night during August, coinciding with the Edinburgh Festival. A shameless and spectacular pageant of swinging kilts and massed pipe bands, the tattoo makes full use of its dramatic setting.

THE STONE OF DESTINY

Legend has it that the **Stone of Destiny** (also called the Stone of Scone) was "Jacob's Pillow", on which he dreamed of the ladder of angels from earth to heaven. Its real history is obscure, but it's known to have been moved from Ireland to Dunadd by missionaries, and thence to Dunstaffnage, from where Kenneth MacAlpine, king of the Dalriada Scots, brought it to the abbey at Scone, near Perth, in 838. There it remained for almost five hundred years, used as a coronation throne on which all kings of Scotland were crowned.

In 1296, an over-eager Edward I stole what he believed to be the Stone and installed it at Westminster Abbey, where, apart from a brief interlude in 1950 when it was removed by Scottish nationalists and hidden in Arbroath for several months, it remained for seven hundred years. All this changed in December 1996 when, after an elaborate ceremony-laden journey from London, the Stone returned to Scotland, in one of the doomed attempts by the Conservative government to convince the Scottish people that the Union was a good thing. Much to the annoyance of the people of Perth and the curators of Scone Palace (see p.819), and to the general indifference of the people of Scotland, the Stone was placed in Edinburgh Castle.

However, speculation surrounds the authenticity of the Stone, for the original is said to have been intricately carved, while the one seen today is a plain block of sandstone. Many believe that the canny monks at Scone palmed this off onto the English king (some say that it's nothing more sacred than the cover for a medieval septic tank), and that the real Stone of Destiny lies hidden in an underground chamber, its whereabouts a mystery to all but the chosen few.

The lower defences

Edinburgh Castle has a single entrance, a 10ft-wide opening in the **gatehouse**, one of many Romantic-style additions made in the 1880s. Rearing up behind is the most distinctive and impressive feature of the castle's silhouette, the sixteenth-century **Half Moon Battery**, which marks the outer limit of the actual defences. Once through the gatehouse, you'll find the main ticket office on your right, with an information centre alongside. Continue uphill along Lower Ward, showing your ticket at the **Portcullis Gate**, a handsome Renaissance gateway marred by the addition of a nineteenth-century upper storey with anachronistic arrow slits. Beyond this is the wide main path known as Middle Ward, with the six-gun **Argyle Battery** to the right. Further west on **Mill's Mount Battery**, a well-known Edinburgh ritual takes place – the daily firing of the **one o'clock gun**. Originally designed for the benefit of ships in the Firth of Forth, these days it's an enjoyable ceremony for visitors to watch and a useful time signal for city-centre office workers. Both batteries offer wonderful panoramas over Princes Street and the New Town to the coastal towns and hills of Fife across the Forth. There's an interesting little exhibition about the history of the firing of the gun in a room immediately below Mill's Mount Battery.

National War Museum

Located in the old hospital buildings, down a ramp between the restaurant immediately behind the one o'clock gun and the Governor's House, the **National War Museum** covers the last four hundred years of Scottish military history. Scots have been fighting for much longer than that, of course, but the slant of the museum is very definitely towards the soldiers who fought *for* the Union, rather than against it. The various rooms are packed with uniforms, medals and other interesting memorabilia, carefully avoiding favouritism towards any of the Scottish regiments, each of which has strong traditions more forcefully paraded in the various regimental museums found in different parts of Scotland – the Royal Scots and the Scots Dragoon Guards, for instance, both have displays in other parts of Edinburgh Castle.

St Margaret's Chapel

Near the highest point of the castle, **St Margaret's Chapel** is the oldest surviving building within it, and probably also in Edinburgh itself. Built by King David I as a memorial to his mother, and used as a powder magazine for three hundred years, this tiny Norman church was rediscovered in 1845 and eventually re-dedicated in 1934, after sympathetic restoration.

The battlements in front of the chapel offer the best of all the castle's extensive views. Here you'll see the famous fifteenth-century siege gun, **Mons Meg**, which could fire a 500-pound stone nearly two miles. Just below the battlements there's a small, immaculately kept **cemetery**, the last resting place of the **soldiers' pets**. Continuing eastwards, you skirt the top of the Forewall and Half Moon batteries, passing the 110ft-deep **Castle Well** en route to **Crown Square**, the highest, most important and secure section of the complex.

Crown Square

The eastern side of Crown Square is occupied by the **Palace**, a surprisingly unassuming edifice begun in the 1430s. The palace owes its Renaissance appearance to King James IV, though it was remodelled for Mary, Queen of Scots, and her consort Henry, Lord Darnley, whose entwined initials (MAH), together with the date 1566, can be seen above one of the doorways.

Another section of the Palace houses the nation's **Crown Jewels**, properly known as the **Honours of Scotland**; you get to see them by joining a slow-moving line that shuffles past a series of historical tableaux before reaching the Crown Room. One of the most potent images of Scotland's nationhood, the jewel-encrusted **crown** made for

17 James V by the Scottish goldsmith James Mosman, incorporates the gold circlet worn by Robert the Bruce and is topped by an enamelled orb and cross. Sitting alongside is the incongruously plain **Stone of Destiny** (see p.718).

On the south side of Crown Square is James IV's hammerbeam-ceilinged **Great Hall**, used for meetings of the Scottish Parliament until 1639; opposite, the serene Hall of Honour houses the **Scottish National War Memorial**, created in 1927 by the architect Sir Robert Lorimer and 200 Scottish artists and craftsmen.

The Royal Mile

The **Royal Mile**, the name given to the ridge linking the castle with Holyrood, was described by Daniel Defoe in 1724, as "the largest, longest and finest street for Buildings and Number of Inhabitants, not in Bretain only, but in the World". Almost exactly a mile in length, it is divided into four sections – Castlehill, Lawnmarket, High Street and Canongate. From these, branching out in a herringbone pattern, are a series of tightly packed closes and steep lanes entered via archways known as "pends". After the construction of the New Town much of the housing along the Royal Mile degenerated into a slum, but has since shaken off that reputation, with bijou flats, holiday apartments, student residences and offices now inhabiting the tightly packed buildings.

Scotch Whisky Experience

354 Castlehill • Daily: June–Aug 10am–6.30pm; Sept–May 10am–6pm, last tour 1hr before closing • £12 • T 0131 220 0441, W scotch-whisky-experience.co.uk

A short way downhill from the castle esplanade, the **Scotch Whisky Experience** mimics the kind of tours offered at distilleries in the Highlands, and while it can't match the authenticity of the real thing, the centre does offer a thorough introduction to the "water of life" (*uisge beatha* in Gaelic). On the ground floor, a well-stocked shop gives an idea of the sheer range and diversity of the drink, while downstairs there's a pleasant whisky bar and restaurant, *Amber* (see p.738).

The Hub

348 Castlehill • Daily 9.30am–5pm; extended hours in Festival • T 0131 473 2015, W thehub-edinburgh.com

The imposing black church at the foot of Castlehill is **The Hub**, also known as "Edinburgh's Festival Centre". It's open year-round, providing performance, rehearsal and exhibition space, a ticket centre and a café. The building itself was constructed in 1845 to designs by James Gillespie Graham and Augustus Pugin, one of the architects of the Houses of Parliament in London. Permanent works of art have been incorporated into parts of the centre, including over two hundred delightful 1ft-high sculptures depicting Festival performers and audiences.

Gladstone's Land

477b Lawnmarket • Daily: April–Oct 10am–5pm, July & Aug 10am–6.30pm • NTS • £5.50 • T 0844 493 2120

Doing its best to maintain its dignity among a sea of cheap tartan gifts and discounted woolly jumpers, **Gladstone's Land** is the Royal Mile's best surviving example of a typical seventeenth-century tenement. The tall, narrow building – not unlike a canalside house in Amsterdam – would have been home to various families living in cramped conditions. The arcaded and wooden-fronted ground floor is home to a reconstructed cloth shop; pass through this to encounter a warren of tight little staircases, tiny rooms, creaking floorboards and peek-hole windows.

Writers' Museum

Lady Stair's Close • Mon–Sat 10am–5pm; also Sun noon–5pm in Aug • Free • T 0131 529 4901, W edinburghmuseums.org.uk

The arched entranceway to Lady Stair's Close is one of a number of attractive courtyards just off the Royal Mile. Within the seventeenth-century Lady Stair's House

ROBERT LOUIS STEVENSON

Born in Edinburgh into a distinguished family of lighthouse engineers, **Robert Louis Stevenson** (1850–94) was a sickly child, with a solitary childhood dominated by his governess, Alison "Cummie" Cunningham, who regaled him with tales drawn from Calvinist folklore. Sent to the university to study engineering, Stevenson rebelled against his upbringing by spending much of his time in the lowlife howffs and brothels of the city.

Stevenson's early successes were two **travelogues**, *An Inland Voyage* and *Travels with a Donkey in the Cevennes*, kaleidoscopic jottings based on his journeys in France, where he went to escape Scotland's weather, which was damaging his health. It was there that he met Fanny Osbourne, an American ten years his senior. Having married the now-divorced Fanny, Stevenson began an elusive search for an agreeable climate that led to Switzerland, the French Riviera and the Scottish Highlands. He belatedly turned to the novel, achieving immediate acclaim in 1881 for **Treasure Island**, a moralistic adventure yarn that began as an entertainment for his stepson and future collaborator, Lloyd Osbourne. In 1886, his most famous short story, **Dr Jekyll and Mr Hyde**, despite its nominal London setting, offered a vivid evocation of Edinburgh's Old Town: an allegory of its dual personality of prosperity and squalor, and an analysis of its Calvinistic preoccupations with guilt and damnation. The same year saw the publication of the historical romance **Kidnapped**, an adventure novel that exemplified Stevenson's view that literature should seek above all to entertain. In 1887 Stevenson left Britain for good, travelling first to the United States. A year later, he set sail for the South Seas, and eventually settled in **Samoa**, where he died suddenly from a brain haemorrhage in 1894.

is the **Writers' Museum**, dedicated to Scotland's three greatest literary lions: Sir Walter Scott, Robert Louis Stevenson and Robert Burns. The house itself holds as much interest as the slightly lacklustre collection of portraits, manuscripts and knick-knacks, its tight, winding stairs and poky, wood-panelled rooms offering a flavour of the medieval Old Town. The open courtyard outside, known as the Makars' Court after the Scots word for the "maker" of poetry or prose, features a series of paving stones inscribed with quotations from Scotland's most famous writers.

The High Kirk of St Giles

High St • May–Sept Mon–Fri 9am–7pm, Sat 9am–5pm, Sun 1–5pm; Oct–April Mon–Sat 9am–5pm, Sun 1–5pm • Free • Ⓦ stgilescathedral.org.uk

The dominant building in the High Street, the central section of the Royal Mile, is the **Kirk of St Giles**, the original parish church of medieval Edinburgh, from where John Knox launched and directed the Scottish Reformation.

The resplendent **crown spire** of the kirk is formed from eight flying buttresses and dates back to 1485, while **inside**, the four massive piers supporting the tower were part of a Norman church built here around 1120. In the nineteenth century, St Giles was adorned with a whole series of funerary monuments on the model of London's Westminster Abbey; around the same time it acquired several attractive Pre-Raphaelite stained-glass windows designed by Edward Burne-Jones and William Morris.

At the southeastern corner of St Giles, the **Thistle Chapel** was built by Sir Robert Lorimer in 1911 as the private chapel of the sixteen knights of the Most Noble Order of the Thistle, the highest chivalric order in Scotland. Based on St George's Chapel in Windsor, it's an exquisite piece of craftsmanship, with an elaborate ribbed vault, huge drooping bosses and extravagantly ornate stalls showing off Lorimer's bold Arts and Crafts styling.

Mary King's Close

2 Warriston's Close, High St • Tours daily every 20min: April–Oct: daily 10am–9pm; Nov–March: Sun–Thurs 10am–5pm, Fri–Sat 10am–9pm; 1hr • £12.50 • Ⓣ 0845 070 6244, Ⓦ realmarykingsclose.com

Subterranean **Mary King's Close** is one of Edinburgh's most unusual attractions. When work on the chambers began in 1753, the tops of the existing houses on the site were

17 simply sliced through at the level of the High Street and the new building constructed on top of them. Because the tenements had been built on a steep hillside, this process left parts of the houses, together with the old streets (or closes) that ran alongside them, intact but entirely enclosed among the basement and cellars of the City Chambers. You can visit this rather spooky "lost city" on **tours** led by costumed actors.

Scottish Storytelling Centre

43–45 High St • Mon–Sat 10am–6pm, also Sun noon–6pm in July & Aug • £4.25 entry to John Knox House • Ⓣ 0131 556 9579, Ⓦ scottishstorytellingcentre.co.uk

There are two distinct parts to the **Scottish Storytelling Centre**: one half is a stylish contemporary development based around an airy Storytelling Court with a small permanent exhibition about Scottish stories from ancient folk tales to Harry Potter. By contrast, the **John Knox House** is a fifteenth-century stone-and-timber building that, with its distinctive external staircase, overhanging upper storeys and busy pantile roof, is a classic example of the Royal Mile in its medieval heyday. Regular performances and events, often aimed at a younger audience, take place in the centre.

Canongate

For over seven hundred years, the **Canongate** district, through which the eastern section of the Royal Mile runs, was a burgh in its own right, officially separate from the capital. A notorious slum area even into the 1960s, it has been the subject of some of the most ambitious **restoration** programmes in the Old Town, though the lack of harmony between the buildings renovated in different decades is fairly obvious. For such a central district, it's interesting to note that most of the buildings here are residential, and by no means are they all bijou apartments. The eclectic range of **shops** includes a gallery of historic maps and sea charts, an old-fashioned whisky bottler and a bagpipe-maker.

Canongate Kirk

153 Canongate • Mon–Sat 10.30am–4.30pm, Sun 12.30–4.30pm, depending on volunteer staff and church services • Free • Ⓣ 0131 556 3515, Ⓦ canongatekirk.org.uk

Built to house the congregation expelled from Holyrood Abbey when the latter was commandeered by James VII (James II in England), **Canongate Kirk** is the church used by the Queen when she's at Holyrood and was the location for Britain's "other royal wedding" of 2011, when Prince William's cousin Zara Philips married England rugby player Mike Tindall. The kirk has a modesty rarely seen in churches built in later centuries, with a graceful curved facade and a bow-shaped gable to the rear. The surrounding churchyard provides an attractive and tranquil stretch of green in the heart of the Old Town and affords fine views of Calton Hill; it also happens to be one of the city's most exclusive cemeteries – well-known internees include the political economist Adam Smith, Mrs Agnes McLehose (better known as Robert Burns's "Clarinda") and Robert Fergusson, regarded by some as Edinburgh's greatest poet, despite his death at the age of 24. Fergusson's headstone was donated by Burns, a fervent admirer, and a statue of the young poet can be seen just outside the kirk gates.

Museum of Edinburgh

142 Canongate • Mon–Sat 10am–5pm, also Sun noon–5pm in Aug• Free • Ⓦ edinburghmuseums.org.uk

The **Museum of Edinburgh** is the city's principal collection devoted to local history, and is as interesting for the labyrinthine network of wood-panelled rooms as for its rather quirky array of artefacts. These do, however, include a number of items of real historical significance, in particular the National Convention, the petition for religious freedom drawn up on a deerskin parchment in 1638, and the original plans for the layout of the New Town drawn by James Craig (see p.726), chosen by the city council after a competition in 1767.

TOP 5 BOOKISH SIGHTS

City tours See p.736
Rosslyn Chapel See p.745
The Scott Monument See p.728
Scottish Poetry Library See below
Writers' Museum See p.720

Scottish Poetry Library

5 Crichton's Close • Tues, Wed & Fri 10am–5pm, Thurs 10am–8pm, Sat 10am–4pm • Free • ☎ 0131 557 2876, 🌐 spl.org.uk

A sweet note of modern architectural eloquence amid a cacophony of large-scale developments, the **Scottish Poetry Library** incorporates a section of an old city wall, and the attractive, contemporary design harmoniously combines brick, oak, glass, Caithness stone and blue ceramic tiles. The library contains Scotland's most comprehensive collection of native poetry, and visitors are free to read the books, periodicals and leaflets found on the shelves, or listen to recordings of poetry in English, Scots and Gaelic.

Holyrood

At the foot of Canongate lies **Holyrood**, with its ruined thirteenth-century **abbey** and the **Palace of Holyroodhouse**, the residence of the Queen and other royals when they're in town. The area has been transformed by Enric Miralles' dazzling but highly controversial **Scottish Parliament**, which was deliberately landscaped to blend in with the cliffs and ridges of Edinburgh's most dramatic natural feature, the nearby **Holyrood Park** and its slumbering peak, Arthur's Seat.

The Palace of Holyroodhouse

Daily: April–Oct 9.30am–6pm; Nov–March 9.30am–4.30pm; last admission 1hr before closing • £10.75, £15.10 joint ticket with the Queen's Gallery • ☎ 0131 556 5100, 🌐 royalcollection.org.uk

The **Palace of Holyroodhouse** is largely a seventeenth-century creation, planned for Charles II. Tours of the palace move through a series of royal **reception rooms** featuring some outstanding encrusted plasterwork, each more impressive than the last – an idea Charles II had picked up from his cousin Louis XIV's Versailles – while on the northern side of the internal quadrangle, the **Great Gallery** extends almost the full length of the palace and is dominated by portraits of 96 Scottish kings, painted by Jacob de Wet in 1684 to illustrate the lineage of Stewart royalty: the result is unintentionally hilarious, as it's clear that the artist's imagination was taxed to bursting point in his commission to paint so many different facial types without having an inkling as to what the subjects actually looked like. Leading from this into the oldest part of the palace, known as James V's tower, the formal, ceremonial tone gives way to dark medieval history, with a tight spiral staircase leading to the chambers used by Mary, Queen of Scots. These contain various relics, including jewellery, associated with the queen, though the most compelling viewing is a tiny supper room, from where, in 1566, Mary's Italian secretary, David Rizzio, was dragged by conspirators, who included her jealous husband, Lord Darnley, to the outer chamber and stabbed 56 times; a brass plaque on the wall points out what are rather unconvincingly identified as the bloodstains on the wooden floor.

Holyrood Abbey

Immediately adjacent to the palace • Free as part of palace tour

The evocative ruins of **Holyrood Abbey**, some of which date from the thirteenth century, lie next to the palace. The roof tumbled down in 1768, but the melancholy scene has inspired artists down the years, among them Felix Mendelssohn, who in 1829 wrote "Everything is in ruins and mouldering …

17 I believe I have found the beginning of my Scottish Symphony there today". Next to the abbey are the formal palace gardens, open to visitors in summer and offering some pleasant strolls.

The Queen's Gallery

Daily: April–Oct 9.30am–6pm; Nov–March 9.30am–4.30pm; last admission 1hr before closing • £6 or £15.10 joint ticket with Holyroodhouse • Ⓦ royalcollection.org.uk

Essentially an adjunct to Holyrood palace, the **Queen's Gallery** is located in the shell of a former church directly between the palace and the parliament. It's a compact space with just two principal viewing rooms used to display changing exhibitions from the Royal Collection, a vast array of art treasures held by the Queen on behalf of the British nation. Because the pieces are otherwise exhibited only during the limited openings of Buckingham Palace and Windsor Castle, the exhibitions here tend to draw quite a lot of interest.

Scottish Parliament

Horse Wynd • April–Oct: Mon–Fri 10am–6pm, Sat & Sun 10am–4pm; Nov–March 10am–4pm • Free access; guided tours 1hr, free, bookings not essential • Ⓣ 0131 348 5200, Ⓦ scottish.parliament.uk

By far the most controversial public building to be erected in Scotland since World War II, the **Scottish Parliament** houses the country's directly elected assembly. A separate parliament to look after the running of internal Scottish affairs was reintroduced to the British constitution in 1999, nearly 200 years after the previous Scottish parliament had joined the English assembly at Westminster as part of the Union of the two nations in 1707. The home of the directly elected parliament was eventually opened in 2004, late and dramatically over-budget – initial estimates for the building's cost were tentatively put at £40 million; the final bill was over £400 million. Made up of various linked elements rather than one single building, the complex was designed by Catalan architect **Enric Miralles**, whose death in 2000, halfway through the building process, caused ripples of uncertainty as to whether he had in fact set down his final draft. However, the finished product is an impressive – if imperfect – testament to the ambition of Miralles, and it has won over the majority of the architectural community, scooping numerous awards including Britain's prestigious Royal Institute of British Architects (RIBA) Stirling Prize in 2005.

Visiting the parliament

There's free access into the entrance lobby of the Parliament, entered from Horse Wynd, opposite the palace, where you'll find a small exhibition providing some historical, political and architectural background. If parliament is in session, it's normally possible to watch proceedings in the debating chamber from the public gallery. To see the rest of the interior properly you'll need to join one of the regular **guided tours**, well worth doing to get a more detailed appreciation of the building's design.

Some of the most memorable features of the building are the fanciful motifs and odd architectural signatures running through the design, including the anvil-shaped cladding, and the extraordinary windows of the offices for MSPs (Members of the Scottish Parliament), said to have been inspired by a monk's contemplative cell. The stark concrete of the interior may not be to all tastes, though several of the staircases and passageways remain evocative of the country's medieval castles.

The main **debating chamber** is grand yet intimate, with light flooding in through high windows and a complex network of thick oak beams, lights and microphone wires. The European-style layout is a deliberate move away from the confrontational Westminster model, though some have been quick to point out that while the traditional inter-party insults still fly, the quality of the parliamentarians' rhetoric rarely matches that of the soaring new arena.

Our Dynamic Earth

Holyrood Rd • April–June & Sept–Oct daily 10am–5.30pm; July & Aug daily 10am–6pm; Nov–March Wed–Sun 10am–5.30pm; last entry 1hr 30min before closing • £10.80 • ⓣ 0131 550 7800, ⓦ dynamicearth.co.uk

Sitting beneath a miniature version of London's Millennium Dome, **Our Dynamic Earth** is a high-tech attraction aimed at children between 5 and 15. Galleries cover the formation of the earth and continents with crashing sound effects and a shaking floor, while the calmer grandeur of glaciers and oceans are explored through magnificent large-screen landscape footage; further on, the polar regions – complete with a real iceberg – and tropical jungles are imaginatively re-created, with interactive screens and special effects at every turn.

Holyrood Park

Information Centre Holyrood Lodge, Horse Wynd • Daily: summer 8/9am–5/6pm; winter 8/9am–3/4pm

Holyrood Park – or Queen's Park – a natural wilderness in the heart of the modern city, is one of Edinburgh's greatest assets. Packed into an area no more than five miles in diameter is an amazing variety of landscapes – hills, crags, moorland, marshes, glens, lochs and fields – representing a microcosm of Scotland's scenery. While old photographs of the park show crops growing and sheep grazing, it's now most used by walkers, joggers, cyclists and other outdoor enthusiasts. A single tarred road, **Queen's Drive**, loops through the park, but you need to get out and stroll around to appreciate it fully. You can pick up a map of suggested walks – including those to Salisbury Crags and Arthur's Seat – as well as details on the geology and flora of the park, from the Park Information Centre.

The University of Edinburgh and around

Founded as the "Tounis College" in 1583 by James VI (later James I of England), the University of Edinburgh is the largest in Scotland, with nearly 20,000 students. The earliest surviving part is the **Old College** on South Bridge, an imposing quadrangle designed by Robert Adam and finished in modified form by William Playfair (1789–1857), one of Edinburgh's greatest architects. These days the Old College houses only a few university departments as well as the small **Talbot Rice Art Gallery** (ⓦ trg.ed.ac.uk) displaying part of the University's art and bronze collection; the main campus colonizes the streets and squares to the south.

Surgeons' Hall Museum

Nicolson St • Mon–Fri noon–4pm, plus Sat & Sun noon–4pm in Aug • £5 • ⓣ 0131 527 1649, ⓦ www.rcsed.ac.uk

Inside the stately **Surgeons' Hall**, a handsome Ionic temple built by Playfair as the headquarters of the Royal College of Surgeons, is one of the city's most unusual and morbidly compelling **museums**. In the eighteenth and nineteenth centuries Edinburgh developed as a leading centre for medical and anatomical research, nurturing world-famous figures such as James Young Simpson, pioneer of anaesthesia, and Joseph Lister,

ASCENDING ARTHUR'S SEAT

The usual starting point for the ascent of **Arthur's Seat**, which at 823ft above sea level towers over Edinburgh's numerous high points, is Dunsapie Loch, reached by following the tarred Queen's Drive in a clockwise direction from the information centre in Holyrood Park (30–40min walk). Part of a volcano which last saw action 350 million years ago, its connections to the legendary king are fairly sketchy: the name is likely to be a corruption of the Gaelic **Ard-na-said**, or "height of arrows". From Dunsapie Loch it's a twenty-minute climb up grassy slopes to the rocky summit. On a clear day, the views might just stretch to the English border and the Atlantic Ocean; more realistically, the landmarks which dominate are Fife, a few Highland peaks and, of course, Edinburgh laid out on all sides.

the father of modern surgery. The intriguing exhibits range from early surgical tools to a pocketbook covered with the leathered skin of serial killer William Burke.

National Museum of Scotland

Chambers St • Mon–Sun 10am–5pm • Free • Ⓦ nms.ac.uk

The **National Museum of Scotland** fuses a grand Victorian building with an extension built in the 1990s. The recently refurbished older section is a traditional grand city museum covering natural history, indigenous cultures, science and crafts from around the world. Alongside it, the clean lines and imaginatively designed interior of the modern section offer a fresh perspective on Scottish history from earliest man to the present day, laid out in broadly chronological order over seven levels.

Scotland Galleries

The seven levels of the National Museum's modern extension make up Scotland's premier historical museum. The nation's beginnings and earliest peoples are covered in the basement, with artefacts including the **Cramond Lioness**, a sculpture from a Roman tombstone found recently in the Firth of Forth, along with carved stones and jewellery from Pictish times. Moving up through the museum, look out for the famous **Lewis chessmen**, idiosyncratic twelfth-century pieces carved from walrus ivory, along with pieces relating to the more significant periods of Scotland's past, including the Highland uprisings under Bonnie Prince Charlie (whose silver travelling canteen is on display). **Industry and Empire** covers the era of heavy industry and mass emigration, while **Scotland: A Changing Nation** traces the different experiences of people living and working in contemporary Scotland, through film, objects and personal stories.

From the small **roof garden**, accessed by a lift, sweeping views open out to the Firth of Forth, the Pentland hills and across to the Castle and Royal Mile skyline. Other fine views can be enjoyed from the museum's stylish *Tower* restaurant.

Elsewhere in the Museum

Centred on a soaring, three-storey atrium, the former **Royal Museum of Scotland**, a dignified Venetian-style palace with a cast-iron interior modelled on the Crystal Place in London, reopened in 2011 following a £47 million refurbishment. There's much to appreciate simply from the building itself, with the main **Grand Gallery** flooded by natural light and encircled by two levels of balcony. The main exhibits are found in rooms off the Grand Gallery, the most notable (particularly for younger visitors) being the **natural history** collection with stuffed animals, dinosaur skeletons and numerous sea creatures suspended from the ceiling among giant plasma screens showing wildlife

GREYFRIARS

The **statue of Greyfriars Bobby** at the southwestern corner of **George IV Bridge**, just across the road from the Museum of Scotland, must rank as Edinburgh's most sentimental tourist attraction. According to the legend – no doubt embellished down the years – Bobby was a Skye terrier acquired as a working dog by a police constable named John Gray. When Gray died in 1858, Bobby was found a few days later sitting on his grave, a vigil he maintained until his death fourteen years later. Bobby's legendary dedication was picked up by Disney, whose 1960 feature film of the story ensured that streams of tourists have paid their respects ever since.

The grave Bobby mourned over is in the **Greyfriars Kirkyard**, which has a fine collection of seventeenth-century gravestones and mausoleums, including one to the Adam family of architects. The kirkyard is visited regularly by ghost tours (see p.736) and was known for grave-robbing, when freshly interred bodies were exhumed and sold to the nearby medical school. Greyfriars Kirk itself was built in 1620 on land that had belonged to a Franciscan convent, though little of the original late Gothic-style building remains.

in action. An area dedicated to **science and technology** has everything from robots and space ships to a stuffed model of Dolly the sheep.

The Grassmarket

Tucked in below the castle's high southern ediface is an open, partly cobbled area known as the **Grassmarket**, which was used as the city's cattle market from 1477 to 1911 and was also the location of Edinburgh's public gallows – the spot is marked by a tiny garden. Despite the height of many of the surrounding buildings, Grassmarket offers an unexpected view up to the precipitous walls of the castle and, come springtime, it's sunny enough for cafés to put tables and chairs along the pavement. In the northwest corner is the award-winning modern architecture of **Dance Base** (0131 225 5525, dancebase.co.uk), Scotland's National Centre for Dance, which holds classes, workshops and shows.

The Grassmarket's pubs and restaurants are busy by night, while by day you can admire the architectural quirks and interesting shops, in particular the string of offbeat boutiques on curving **Victoria Street**, an unusual two-tier thoroughfare, with arcaded shops below and a pedestrian terrace above.

The New Town

The **NEW TOWN**, itself well over two hundred years old, stands in total contrast to the Old Town: the layout is symmetrical, the streets are broad and straight, and most of the buildings are Neoclassical. Originally intended to be residential, today the New Town is the bustling hub of the city's professional, commercial and business life, dominated by shops, banks and offices.

The existence of the New Town is chiefly due to the vision of **George Drummond**, who made schemes for the expansion of the city soon after becoming Lord Provost in 1725. Work began on the draining of the Nor' Loch below the castle in 1759, a job that took some sixty years. The North Bridge, linking the Old Town with the main road leading to the port of Leith, was built between 1763 and 1772 and, in 1766, following a public competition, a plan for the New Town by 22-year-old architect **James Craig** was chosen. Its gridiron pattern was perfectly matched to the site: central **George Street**, flanked by showpiece squares, was laid out along the main ridge, with parallel **Princes Street** and **Queen Street** on either side, built up on one side only, so as not to block the spectacular views of the Old Town and Fife.

The layout of the greater New Town is a remarkable grouping of squares, circuses, terraces, crescents and parks along with **Charlotte Square** and the assemblage of curiosities on and around **Calton Hill**. However, it also contains assorted Victorian additions, notably the **Scott Monument** on Princes Street, the **Royal Botanic Garden** on its northern fringe, as well as two of the city's most important public collections – the **National Gallery of Scotland** and, further afield, the **Scottish National Gallery of Modern Art**.

Princes Street

Although only allocated a subsidiary role in the original plan of the New Town, **Princes Street** had developed into Edinburgh's principal thoroughfare by the middle of the nineteenth century, a role it has retained ever since. Its unobstructed views across to the castle and the Old Town are undeniably magnificent. Indeed, without the views, Princes Street would lose much of its appeal; its northern side, dominated by large outlets of the familiar national chains, is almost always crowded with shoppers, and few of the original eighteenth-century buildings remain.

17

Princes Street Gardens

Dawn to dusk • Free **Ice rink** Late Nov to early Jan daily 10am–10pm • £8–9.50 **Ferris wheel** Late Nov to early Jan daily 10am–10pm • £4–5

It's hard to imagine that the **gardens** that flank nearly the entire length of Princes Street were once the stagnant, foul-smelling Nor' Loch, into which the effluent of the Old Town flowed for centuries. The railway has since replaced the water and today a sunken cutting carries the main lines out of Waverley Station to the west and north. The gardens, split into East and West sections, were originally the private domain of Princes Street residents and their well-placed acquaintances, only becoming a public park in 1876. The larger and more verdant western section has a floral clock and the Ross Bandstand, a popular Festival venue, while at Christmas the eastern section is home to an ice rink and a towering Ferris wheel.

The Scott Monument

East Princes Street Gardens • April–Sept daily 10am–7pm; Oct–March Mon–Sat 9am–4pm, Sun 10am–4pm • £3

The 200ft-high **Scott Monument** was erected in memory of prolific author and patriot Sir Walter Scott within a few years of his death. The architecture is closely modelled on Scott's beloved Melrose Abbey (see p.753), while the rich sculptural decoration shows sixteen Scottish writers and 64 characters from Scott's famous *Waverley* novels. On the central plinth at the base of the monument is a **statue** of Scott with his deerhound Maida, carved from a thirty-ton block of Carrara marble. Inside the memorial a tightly winding spiral staircase climbs 287 steps to a narrow platform near the top: from here, you can enjoy some inspiring – if vertiginous – vistas of the city below, and hills and firths beyond.

The National Gallery of Scotland

The Mound, Princes St • Daily 10am–5pm, Thurs till 7pm • Free, charge for some temporary exhibitions • ⓣ 0131 624 6200, ⓦ natgalscot.ac.uk

Princes Street Gardens are bisected by the **Mound**, one of only two direct road links between the Old and New Towns (the other is North Bridge), formed in the 1780s by dumping piles of earth and other waste brought from the New Town's building plots. At the foot of the mound on the Princes Street level are two grand Neoclassical buildings, the interlinked **National Gallery of Scotland** and the **Royal Scottish Academy**. Both were designed by William Henry Playfair (1790–1857), though the exterior of the National Gallery is considerably more austere than its bold Athenian counterpart.

Built as a "temple to the fine arts" in 1850, the National Gallery houses Scotland's finest array of European and Scottish art from the early 1300s to the late 1800s. Its modest size makes it a manageable place to visit in a couple of hours and affords a pleasantly unrushed atmosphere.

Early works

A gallery highlight is a superb painting by **Botticelli**, *The Virgin Adoring the Sleeping Christ Child* which, along with **Raphael**'s graceful tondo *The Holy Family with a Palm Tree*, has undergone careful restoration to reveal a striking luminosity and depth of colour. Of the four mythological scenes by **Titian**, the sensuous *Three Ages of Man* is one of his most accomplished early compositions. Alongside the Titians, **Bassano**'s *Adoration of the Kings* and a dramatic altarpiece, *The Deposition of Christ*, by **Tintoretto**, as well as several other works by **Veronese**, complete the fine **Venetian** section.

European highlights

Rubens' *The Feast of Herod* is an archetypal example of his sumptuously grand manner. Among the four canvases by **Rembrandt** are a poignant *Self-Portrait Aged 51* and the ripely suggestive *Woman in Bed. Christ in the House of Martha and Mary* is the largest and probably the earliest of the thirty or so surviving paintings by **Vermeer**.

Impressionist masters have a strong showing, including a collection of **Degas'** sketches, paintings and bronzes, **Monet's** *Haystacks* (*Snow*) and **Renoir's** *Woman Nursing Child*. Representing the Post-Impressionists are three exceptional works by **Gauguin**,

CONTEMPORARY ART IN EDINBURGH

In addition to the contemporary art collections in the city's National Galleries there are a number of smaller, independent galleries around the city.

The Collective Gallery 22–28 Cockburn St ⓣ 0131 220 1260, ⓦ collectivegallery.net. Tends to focus on young local artists, and doesn't flinch from showing experimental modern work. Tues–Sun 11am–5pm.

Edinburgh Printmakers 23 Union St ⓣ 0131 557 2479, ⓦ edinburgh-printmakers.co.uk. A highly respected studio and gallery dedicated to contemporary printmaking. Tues–Sat 10am–6pm.

Fruitmarket Gallery 45 Market St ⓣ 0131 225 2383, ⓦ fruitmarket.co.uk. The stylish modern design of this dynamic and much-admired art space is the capital's first port of call for top-grade international artists. Mon–Sat 11am–6pm, Sun noon–5pm.

Ingleby Gallery 15 Carlton Rd ⓣ 0131 556 4441, ⓦ inglebygallery.com. Ingleby's reputation for ambitious projects and innovative artists makes it one of the nation's foremost small private art galleries, often featuring Scotland's premier stars such as Alison Watt, Kenny Hunter and Callum Innes. Mon–Sat 10am–6pm, plus Sun noon–5pm in Aug.

Open Eye Gallery 34 Abercromby Place ⓣ 0131 557 1020, ⓦ openeyegallery.co.uk. One of the city's best commercial galleries, regularly featuring shows by Scotland's top contemporary artists.

Scottish Gallery 16 Dundas St ⓣ 0131 558 1200, ⓦ scottish-gallery.co.uk. The longest established of a number of small galleries on this New Town street; some of the most striking works are in the basement area, dedicated to applied art. Mon–Fri 10am–6pm, Sat 10am–4pm.

including *Vision After the Sermon*, set in Brittany, **Van Gogh's** *Olive Trees*, and **Cézanne's** *The Big Trees* – a clear forerunner of modern abstraction.

Scottish and English works

Of **Sir Henry Raeburn's** large portraits, the swaggering masculinity of *Sir John Sinclair in Highland Dress* shows the artist's technical mastery, though he was equally confident when working on a smaller scale, as seen in one of the gallery's most popular pictures, *The Rev Robert Walker Skating on Duddingston Loch*. The gallery also owns a brilliant array of watercolours by **Turner**, faithfully displayed each January when damaging sunlight is at its weakest; at other times two of his fine Roman views are displayed in a dim gallery.

George Street and around

Parallel to Princes Street, and originally designed as the central thoroughfare of the New Town, **George Street** leads along the crest of the hill that sweeps down to the Forth. At the western end is **Charlotte Square**, designed by Robert Adam in 1791, a year before his death. Generally regarded as the epitome of the New Town's elegant simplicity, the square was once the most exclusive residential address in Edinburgh, and though much of it is now occupied by offices, the imperious dignity of the architecture is still evident. Indeed, the north side is once again the city's premier address, with the official residence of the First Minister of the Scottish Executive at no. 6 (Bute House), the Edinburgh equivalent of 10 Downing Street. In August each year, the gardens in the centre of the square are colonized by the temporary tents of the Edinburgh Book Festival (see p.735).

The Georgian House

7 Charlotte Square • Daily: March & Nov–Dec 11am–3pm; April–June, Sept & Oct 10am–5pm; July & Aug 10am–7pm • NTS • £5 • ⓣ 0844 493 2117

The **Georgian House** provides a revealing sense of well-to-do New Town living in the early nineteenth century. Though a little stuffy, the rooms are impressively decked out in period furniture – look for the working barrel organ which plays a selection of Scottish airs – and hung with fine paintings, including portraits by Ramsay and Raeburn. In the basement are the original wine cellar, lined with roughly made bins, and a kitchen complete with an open fire for roasting and a separate oven for baking.

17

Scottish National Portrait Gallery

1 Queen St • Fri–Wed 10am–5pm, Thurs 10am–7pm • Free, entrance charge for some temporary exhibitions • ⓦ nationalgalleries.org

The recently refurbished **Scottish National Portrait Gallery** occupies a fantastic red sandstone Gothic palace, an 1889 building designed by Sir Robert Rowand Anderson that makes an extravagant contrast to the New Town's prevailing Neoclassicism. The exterior is encrusted with statues of famous national heroes, a theme reiterated by William Hole's frieze depicting notable figures from Scotland's past in the stunning two-storey entrance hall. Other galleries provide a star-studded romp through Scottish history with a few thematic cultural diversions along the way, all told through portraits – paintings and photographs – and complemented by changing exhibitions.

Calton Hill

Edinburgh's tag as the "Athens of the North" is nowhere better earned than on **Calton Hill**, the volcanic peak that rises up above the eastern end of Princes Street. The hill and its odd collection of grandiose buildings aren't just for looking *at*: this is also one of the best viewpoints from which to appreciate the whole city and the sea beyond – much closer to Edinburgh than many visitors expect.

Old Royal High School

Set majestically on the slopes of Calton Hill looking towards Arthur's Seat sits one of Edinburgh's greatest buildings, the **Old Royal High School**. With its bold central portico of Doric columns and graceful symmetrical colonnaded wings, Thomas Hamilton's elegant building of 1829 is regarded by many as the epitome of Edinburgh's Athenian aspirations. Once considered as a possible home for the Scottish Parliament, it's currently used as council offices, with plans to convert it into a hotel.

Nelson Monument

April–Sept Mon–Sat 10am–6pm, plus Sun noon–5pm in Aug; Oct–March Mon–Sat 10am–3pm • £3

Robert Louis Stevenson reckoned that Calton Hill was the best place to view Edinburgh, "since you can see the Castle, which you lose from the Castle, and Arthur's Seat, which you cannot see from Arthur's Seat". Though the panoramas from ground level are spectacular enough, those from the top of the **Nelson Monument**, perched near the summit, are even better.

National Monument

The **National Monument** is often referred to as "Edinburgh's Disgrace", yet many locals admire this unfinished and somewhat ungainly attempt to replicate the Parthenon atop Calton Hill. Begun as a memorial to the dead of the Napoleonic Wars, the project's shortage of funds led architect William Playfair to ensure that it would still serve as a striking landmark, despite having only twelve completed columns. With a bit of effort and care you can climb up and around the monument, sit and contemplate from one of the huge steps or meander around the base of the mighty pillars.

Mansfield Place Church

Mansfield Place • Viewing of the murals one Sun afternoon each month, more often during the Festival • ⓦ mansfieldtraquair.org.uk

The highlight of the Broughton Street area, northeast of the central New Town, is the neo-Norman **Mansfield Place Church**, by the corner of Broughton and East London streets. It contains a cycle of **murals** by the Dublin-born **Phoebe Anna Traquair**, a leading light in the Scottish Arts and Crafts movement. Covering vast areas of the walls and ceilings of the main nave and side chapels, the wonderfully luminous paintings depict biblical parables and texts, with rows of angels, cherubs flecked with gold and worshipping figures painted in delicate pastel colours.

The Royal Botanic Garden

Entrances on Inverleith Row and Arboretum Place • Daily: March & Oct 10am–6pm; April–Sept 10am–7pm; Nov–Feb 10am–4pm• Free; glasshouses £4; guided tours (April–Sept 11am & 2pm) £3 • Ⓦ rbge.org.uk

Just beyond the northern boundaries of the New Town, the seventy-acre **Royal Botanic Garden** is filled with mature trees and a huge variety of native and exotic plants and flowers. The "Botanics" (as they're commonly called) are most popular simply as a place to stroll and lounge around on the grass. The main entrance is the West Gate on Arboretum Place, through the contemporary, eco-designed **John Hope Gateway**, where you'll find interpretation areas, a shop and a restaurant. Towards the eastern side of the gardens, a series of ten **glasshouses**, including a soaring 1850s Palm House, shows off a steamy array of palms, ferns, orchids, cycads and aquatic plants. Scattered around are a number of outdoor sculptures, and some parts have fabulous vistas: the lawns near **Inverleith House**, a gallery showing changing exhibits of contemporary art, offer one of the city's best views of the castle and Old Town's steeples and monuments.

The Scottish National Gallery of Modern Art

Belford Rd • Daily 10am–5pm, till 6pm in Aug • Free, entrance charge for some temporary exhibitions • Ⓣ 0131 624 6200, Ⓦ natgalscot.ac.uk

At the far northwestern fringe of the New Town, the **Scottish National Gallery of Modern Art** was Britain's first collection devoted solely to twentieth-century painting and sculpture, and now covers two grand Neoclassical buildings on either side of Belford Road. The extensive wooded grounds serve as a **sculpture park**, featuring works by Jacob Epstein, Henry Moore, Barbara Hepworth and, most strikingly, Charles Jencks, whose *Landform*, a swirling mix of ponds and grassy mounds, dominates the area in front of the gallery.

Modern One

The gallery on the western side of Belford Road, **Modern One**, divides its display spaces between temporary exhibitions and selections from the gallery's own holdings; the latter are arranged thematically, but are almost constantly moved around. The collection starts with early twentieth-century Post-Impressionists, then moves through the Fauvists, German Expressionism, Cubism and Pop Art, with works by **Lichtenstein** and **Warhol** establishing a connection with the extensive holdings of Eduardo Paolozzi's work in the Modern Two. There's a strong section on living **British artists**, from Gilbert & George to **Britart** stars, while modern **Scottish** art ranges from the Colourists to the distinctive styles of contemporary Scots including John Bellany, a portraitist of striking originality, and the poet-artist-gardener Ian Hamilton Finlay.

Modern Two

Modern Two, also known as the **Dean Gallery**, was refurbished to make room for the huge collection of work of Edinburgh-born sculptor **Sir Eduardo Paolozzi**, described by some as the father of Pop Art. There's an awesome introduction to Paolozzi's work in the form of the huge *Vulcan*, a half-man, half-machine that squeezes into the Great Hall immediately opposite the main entrance – view it both from ground level and the head-height balcony to appreciate the sheer scale of the piece. In the rooms to the right of the main entrance Paolozzi's London studio has been expertly re-created, right down to the clutter of half-finished casts, toys and empty pots of glue.

The ground floor also holds a world-renowned collection of **Dada** and **Surrealist** art; Marcel Duchamp, Max Ernst and Man Ray are all represented. Look out also for Dali's *The Signal of Anguish* and Magritte's *Magic Mirror* along with work by Miró and Giacometti – all hung on crowded walls with an assortment of artefacts and ethnic souvenirs. Elsewhere, look out for 2009 Turner Prize winner Richard Wright's major wall-painting *The Stairwell Project*, his most complex and ambitious work to date in Britain.

17

Out from the centre

Just over a mile northeast of the city centre is **Leith**, a fascinating mix of cobbled streets and new developments, run-down housing and excellent restaurants, as well as Edinburgh's **zoo**, a perennial favourite with children.

Leith

Although **LEITH** is generally known as the port of Edinburgh, it developed independently of the city up the hill, its history bound up in the hard graft of fishing, shipbuilding and trade. The presence of sailors, merchants and continental traders also gave the place a cosmopolitan – if slightly rough – edge, which is still obvious today. While the stand-alone attractions are few, Leith is an intriguing place, not just for the contrasts to central Edinburgh, but also for its nautical air and its excellent cafés, pubs and restaurants.

Leith's initial revival from down-and-out port to des-res waterfront began in the 1980s around the area known as the **Shore**, the old harbour at the mouth of the Water of Leith. More recently, the massive dock areas beyond are being transformed at a rate of knots, with landmark developments including a vast building housing civil servants from the Scottish Government, and Ocean Terminal, a shopping and entertainment complex beside which the former royal yacht **Britannia** has settled into her retirement.

Britannia

Ocean Terminal • Daily: April–June & Oct 10am–4pm; July–Sept 9.30am–4.30pm; Nov–March 10am–3.30pm • £11.50 • ⓣ 0131 555 5566, ⓦ royalyachtbritannia.co.uk • Tour buses leave from Waverley Bridge; otherwise, take buses #11, #22 or #34 from Princes St, or #35 from the Royal Mile

Launched in 1953, *Britannia* was used by the royal family for 44 years for state visits, diplomatic functions and royal holidays. Video clips of the ship's most famous moments are shown in the **visitor centre** (within Ocean Terminal) along with royal holiday snaps, and you can roam around the yacht itself, which has been largely kept as she was while in service, with a well-preserved 1950s dowdiness – a far cry from the opulent splendour which many expect.

Edinburgh Zoo

Corstorphine Hill • Daily: April–Sept 9am–6pm; March & Oct 9am–5pm; Nov–Feb 9am–4.30pm • £15.50 **Penguin parade** April–Sept daily 2.15pm, plus sunny days in March & Oct • ⓣ 0131 334 9171, ⓦ edinburghzoo.org.uk • Buses #12, #26, #31 & #100 from town

A couple of miles west of the city centre, **Edinburgh Zoo**, established in 1913, has a reputation for preserving rare and endangered species. With its imaginatively designed habitats and viewing areas, the place is permanently packed with kids. Historically, the zoo's most famous attraction is its penguin parade, though a pair of pandas – the only ones in the UK – have nabbed the top spot since their arrival in 2011.

ARRIVAL AND DEPARTURE — EDINBURGH

By air Edinburgh International Airport (ⓣ 0844 481 8989, ⓦ edinburghairport.com) is at Turnhouse, 7 miles west of the city centre, close to the start of the M8 motorway to Glasgow. Airlink shuttle buses (#100; every 10–15min 4am–midnight; every 30min midnight–4am; 30min; £3.50) connect to Waverley Station in the centre of town. Taxis charge £15–20 for the same journey.

Destinations Belfast (Mon–Fri 8 daily; Sat & Sun 4 daily; 55min); Cardiff (1–2 daily; 1hr 10min); Dublin (4 daily; 1hr); Kirkwall (Mon–Fri 2 daily, Sat & Sun 1 daily; 1hr 55min); London City (Mon–Fri 8 daily, Sat 1, Sun 3 daily; 1hr 15min); London Gatwick (Mon–Fri 12 daily, Sat & Sun 5 daily; 1hr 15min); London Heathrow (Mon–Fri 15 daily, Sat & Sun 11–15 daily; 1hr); London Luton (Mon–Fri 7 daily, Sat & Sun 4 daily; 1hr 20min); London Stansted (Mon–Fri 6 daily, Sat & Sun 4–6 daily; 1hr 10min); Stornoway (Mon–Fri 3 daily, Sat 2, Sun 1; 1hr 10 min); Sumburgh (Shetland) (2 daily; 1hr 30min); Wick (Mon–Fri 1 daily; 1hr 10min).

By train Waverley Station (ⓣ 0845 748 4950) is the main arrival point for all mainline trains. The other mainline train

CLOCKWISE FROM TOP LEITH (P.732), FESTIVAL FRINGE OFFICE (P.735), PRINCES STREET GARDENS (P.728) >

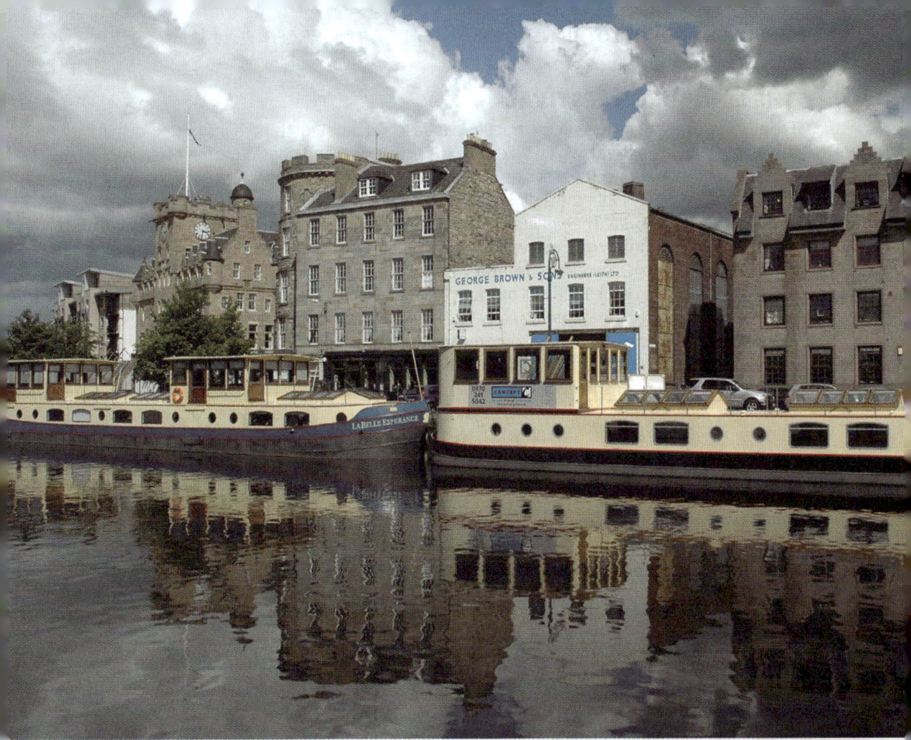
GEORGE BROWN & SONS
LA BELLE ESPERANCE

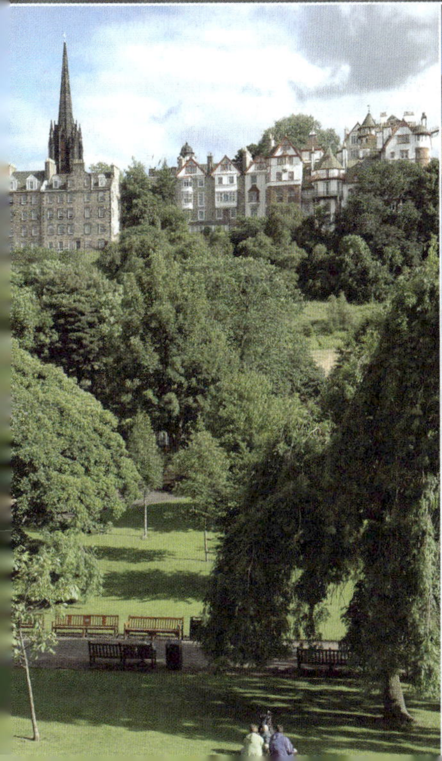

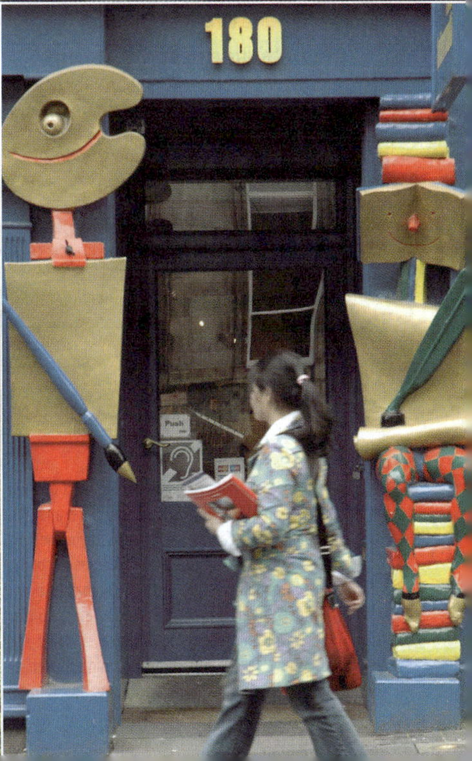
180

THE EDINBURGH FESTIVAL

For all its appeal as a historic and attractive capital city, Edinburgh is perhaps best known for its incredible annual **Festival**, which takes place every August and transforms the place into an overwhelming mass of cultural activity. To even attempt to get a handle on what's going on, it's worth appreciating that the "Edinburgh Festival" is an umbrella term that encompasses several different festivals. The principal events are the **Edinburgh International Festival** and the much larger **Edinburgh Festival Fringe**, but there are also **Book**, **Jazz and Blues** and **Art** festivals going on, as well as a **Military Tattoo** on the Castle Esplanade.

The sheer volume of the Festival's output can be bewildering: virtually every branch of arts and entertainment is represented, and world-famous stars mix with pub singers in the daily line-up. It can be a struggle to find **accommodation**, get hold of the **tickets** you want, book a table in a **restaurant** or simply get from one side of town to another; you can end up seeing something truly dire, or something mind-blowing; you'll inevitably try to do too much, stay out too late or spend too much – but then again, most Festival veterans will tell you that if you don't experience these things then you haven't really "done" the Festival.

Dates, venues, names, star acts, happening bars and burning issues change from one year to the next. This **unpredictability** is one of the Festival's greatest charms, so be prepared for – indeed, enjoy – the unexpected.

THE EDINBURGH INTERNATIONAL FESTIVAL

The **Edinburgh International Festival**, or the "Official Festival", was the original Edinburgh Festival, conceived in 1947 as a celebration of pan-European culture in the postwar era. Initially dominated by opera, other elements such as top-grade theatre, ballet, dance and classical music now carry as much weight, and it's still a highbrow event, its high production values and serious approach offering an antidote to the Fringe's slapdash vigour.

Performances take place at the city's larger venues such as the Usher Hall and the Festival Theatre and, while ticket prices run to over £60, it is possible to see shows for £10 or less if you're prepared to queue for the handful of tickets kept back until the day. The festival culminates in a **Fireworks Concert** beside the castle, visible from various points in the city.

THE EDINBURGH FESTIVAL FRINGE

Even standing alone from its sister festivals, the **Fringe** is easily the world's largest arts gathering. Each year sees more than 40,000 performances from more than 750 companies, with more than 21,000 participants from all over the world. There are something in the region of 1500 shows every day, round the clock, in 250 venues around the city. Much more than any other part of the Festival, it's the dynamism, spontaneity and sheer exuberance of the Fringe that dominate Edinburgh every August.

These days, the most prominent aspect of the Fringe is **comedy**, but you'll also find a wide range of theatre, musicals, dance, children's shows, exhibitions, lectures and music – and a decent range of free shows.

While the Fringe is famous for its tiny and unexpected auditoriums, five Fringe giants colonize clusters of different-sized spaces for the duration of the Festival. These are all safe bets for decent shows and a bit of star-spotting. And while it's nothing like as large as the venues reviewed below, you shouldn't ignore the programme put on at the Traverse Theatre (see p.743). Long a champion of new drama, the "Trav" combines the avant-garde with professional presentation and its plays are generally among the Fringe's most acclaimed.

stop, Haymarket Station is just under 2 miles west of town on the lines from Waverley to Glasgow, Fife and the Highlands, and is only really of use if you're staying nearby.

Destinations from Waverley Station Aberdeen (hourly; 2hr 20min); Birmingham (hourly; 5hr); Dunbar (8 daily; 30min); Dundee (hourly; 1hr 45min); Falkirk (every 15min; 25min); Fort William (change at Glasgow, 3 daily; 4hr 55min); Glasgow (every 15–30min; 50min); Inverness (6 daily direct; 3hr 50min); London (hourly; 4hr 30min); Manchester (3 daily; 4hr); Newcastle upon Tyne (hourly; 1hr 30min); North Berwick (hourly; 30min); Oban (2–3 daily, change at Glasgow; 4hr 10min); Perth (6 daily; 1hr 15min); Stirling (every 30min; 45min); York (hourly; 2hr 30min).

By bus The terminal for local and intercity services is on the east side of St Andrew Square, a 2min walk from Waverley Station.

Destinations Aberdeen (hourly; 3hr 50min); Birmingham

INFORMATION

Edinburgh International Festival office Main booking office at The Hub, Castlehill; mid-Aug to early Sept; ⓦ eif.co.uk.

Festival Fringe Office 180 High St; daily 10am–9pm. Fringe tickets (generally £5–15) available from here, online or at venues; ⓣ 0131 226 0000, ⓦ edfringe .com.

Useful website For up-to-date information any time of year, visit ⓦ edinburghfestivals.co.uk, which has links to the home pages of most of the main festivals.

Publications Each festival produces its own programme well in advance and during the Festival various publications are widely available. Local what's-on guide *The List* comes out weekly during the Festival and manages to combine comprehensive coverage with an on-the-pulse sense of what's hot. Of the local newspapers, *The Scotsman* carries a dedicated daily Festival supplement with an events diary and respected reviews, while various freebie newspapers are also available – the best is *Fest*, which mixes news with pithy reviews and yet more listings.

FRINGE VENUES

Assembly 50 George St ⓣ 0131 623 3000, ⓦ assemblyrooms.com. Long based in George Street's Assembly Rooms, Assembly has been on the move in recent years with its impressive line-up of top-of-the-range drama and big-name music and comedy acts.

C Various locations ⓣ 0870 701 5105, ⓦ cthefestival .com. The most varied programme of the big five, occasionally staging controversial productions that other venues might be too wary to promote.

Gilded Balloon Teviot Row House, Bristo Square ⓣ 0131 622 6555, ⓦ gildedballoon.co.uk. The comedy-focused Gilded Balloon bases its operations in a students' union, the gothic Teviot Row.

Pleasance Courtyard 60 The Pleasance ⓣ 0131 556 6550, ⓦ pleasance.co.uk. A slighty raucous atmosphere, thanks to its busy courtyard bar, with offbeat comedy and whimsical appearances by panellists on Radio 4 game shows. They organize events at a variety of external venues, too.

Underbelly 58 Cowgate ⓣ 0844 545 8252, ⓦ underbelly.co.uk. Operates eleven comedy and cabaret spaces, including the giant, inflatable upside-down cow, "the Udderbelly", on Bristo Square.

THE OTHER FESTIVALS

Edinburgh Art Festival ⓦ edinburghartfestival .com. A relative newcomer on the scene, held throughout August and including high-profile exhibitions by internationally renowned contemporary artists as well as retrospectives of work by pioneering twentieth-century artists. Virtually every art gallery in the city participates, from small private concerns to blockbuster shows at the National Galleries of Scotland's five venues.

Edinburgh International Book Festival ⓣ 0845 373 5888, ⓦ edbookfest.co.uk. Taking place in the last two weeks of August, this is the world's largest celebration of the written word. It's held in a tented village in Charlotte Square and offers talks, readings and signings by a star-studded line-up of visiting authors, as well as panel discussions and workshops.

Edinburgh Jazz and Blues Festival ⓣ 0131 473 2000, ⓦ edinburghjazzfestival.com. Immediately prior to the Fringe in the first week in August, easing the city into the festival spirit. Highlights include nightly jam sessions and a colourful New Orleans-style Mardi Gras and street parade.

The Military Tattoo ⓣ 0131 225 1188, ⓦ edin tattoo.co.uk. Staged in the spectacular stadium of the Edinburgh Castle Esplanade, the Tattoo is an unashamed display of pomp and military pride. The programme of choreographed drills, massed pipe bands, historical tableaux, energetic battle re-enactments, national dancing and pyrotechnics has been a feature of the Festival for over half a century, its emotional climax provided by a lone piper on the Castle battlements. Followed by a quick fireworks display, it's a successful formula barely tampered with over the years. Tickets (£16–50) should be booked well in advance.

(2–3 daily; 6hr 50min); Dundee (hourly; 1hr 45min–2hr); Glasgow (every 15min; 1hr 10min); Inverness (hourly; 3hr 30min–4hr 30min); London (10 daily; 7hr 50min); Newcastle upon Tyne (5 daily; 2hr 45min); Perth (hourly; 1hr 20min).

INFORMATION

Tourist office Edinburgh's main tourist office is on top of Princes Mall near the northern entrance to the train station (April & Oct Mon–Sat 9am–6pm, Sun 10am–6pm; May, June & Sept Mon–Sat 9am–7pm, Sun 10am–7pm; July & Aug Mon–Sat 9am–8pm, Sun 10am–8pm; Nov–March Mon–Wed 9am–5pm, Thurs–Sat 9am–6pm, Sun 10am–5pm; ⓣ 0845 225 5121, ⓦ edinburgh.org). The much smaller airport branch is in the main concourse, right beside international arrivals (daily: April–Oct 6.30am–10.30pm; Nov–March 7am–9pm).

17

CITY TOURS

Despite the compactness of the city centre, open-top **bus tours** are big business, with several companies taking slightly varying routes around the main sights. All cost much the same, depart from Waverley Bridge and allow you to get on and off at leisure. There are also several **walking tours**, many of which depart from the central section of the Royal Mile near the High Kirk of St Giles; ghost tours and specialist tours are also available. **Advance booking** is recommended for all the tours below, and for the specialist tours in particular.

City of the Dead Graveyard Tour ⓣ0131 225 9044, ⓦblackhart.uk.com. Spine-tingling night-time tours around the Old Town.

Edinburgh Literary Pub Tour ⓣ0131 226 6665, ⓦedinburghliterarypubtour.co.uk. Good specialist tour that mixes a pub crawl with extracts from local authors acted out along the way.

Geowalks ⓣ0131 555 5488, ⓦgeowalks.demon.co.uk. Guided walks up Arthur's Seat in the company of a qualified geologist.

MacTours ⓣ0131 220 0770, ⓦedinburghtour.com. The most engaging bus tours, using a fleet of vintage buses.

Mercat Tours ⓣ0131 225 5445, ⓦmercat-tours.com. Reliable operator for walking tours and Old Town ghost tours.

Rebustours ⓣ0131 553 7473, ⓦrebustours.com. Trace the footsteps of Inspector Rebus, hero of Ian Rankin's bestselling detective novels.

Trainspotting ⓣ0131 555 2500, ⓦleithwalks.co.uk. A tour that takes you to places made famous from Irvine Welsh's novels.

GETTING AROUND

Most places worth visiting lie within Edinburgh's compact centre, which is easily explored **on foot**. Edinburgh is a hilly city, however, so be prepared for some steep slopes and intimidating flights of steps.

By bus The city is generally well served by buses; the white-and-maroon Lothian Buses provide the most frequent and comprehensive coverage (timetables and passes from offices on Waverley Bridge, Shandwick Place or Hanover St; ⓣ0131 555 6363, ⓦlothianbuses.co.uk); all buses referred to in the text are run by Lothian unless otherwise stated.

By bike Although hilly, Edinburgh is a reasonably bike-friendly city, with several cycle paths. The local cycling action group, Spokes (ⓣ0131 313 2114, ⓦspokes.org.uk), publishes an excellent map of the city. For rental, try Biketrax, 13 Lochrin Place (ⓣ0131 228 6633, ⓦbiketrax.co.uk), in Tollcross, or Cycle Scotland & Rent-a-Bike, 29 Blackfriars St (ⓣ0131 556 5560, ⓦcyclescotland.co.uk), just off the Royal Mile.

By car It is a very bad idea to take a car into central Edinburgh; despite the presence of several expensive multistorey car parks, finding somewhere to park involves long and often fruitless searches, and illegally parked cars are very likely to be fined £30 by one of the swarms of inspectors who patrol day and night.

By taxi You can hail black cabs on the street, pick them up from a rank or phone for a booking. Try Central Radio Taxis (ⓣ0131 229 2468) or City Cabs (ⓣ0131 228 1211).

ACCOMMODATION

Edinburgh has a greater choice of accommodation than anywhere else in Britain outside London. **Hotels** (and large backpacker **hostels**) are essentially the only options you'll find right in the heart of the city, but within relatively easy reach of the centre the selection of **guesthouses**, **B&Bs**, **campus accommodation** and even **campsites** broadens considerably. Making **reservations** is worthwhile at any time of year, and is strongly recommended for stays during the Festival and around Hogmanay, when places can get booked out months in advance. VisitScotland operates a booking centre for accommodation all over the country, including Edinburgh (ⓣ0845 225 5121, ⓦvisitscotland.com; £3, or free if your book online).

HOTELS

Hotel **prices** are significantly higher than elsewhere in Scotland, with double rooms starting at £60 per night. Budget chains offer the best value if you want basic accommodation right in the centre, with rooms available for £60–80; £80–100 per night will get you something more stylish.

OLD TOWN

Ibis Edinburgh Centre 6 Hunter Square ⓣ0131 240 7000, ⓦaccorhotels.com. Probably the best-located chain hotel cheapie in the Old Town, within sight of the Royal Mile; rooms are modern and inexpensive, but there are few facilities other than a rather plain bar. £84

★ **Hotel Missoni** 1 George IV Bridge ⓣ0131 220

6666, hotelmissoni.com. Quite what this funky, sexy new tie-up between the Italian fashion house and *Rezidor* hotels is doing in the heart of prim Edinburgh is unclear, but the zigzag fabrics, wacky lighting and mosaic-like tiling are enticing, if a little headache-inducing. **£180**

Ten Hill Place 10 Hill Place 0131 662 2080, tenhillplace.com. A contemporary, efficient hotel linked to the historic Royal College of Surgeons, with 78 sleek and smartly styled bedrooms, all run according to an environmentally conscious policy. **£95**

The Witchery Apartments Castlehill, Royal Mile 0131 225 5613, thewitchery.com. Seven riotously indulgent suites grouped around this famously spooky restaurant just downhill from the castle; expect antique furniture, big leather armchairs, tapestry-draped beds, oak panelling and huge roll-top baths, as well as ultramodern sound systems and complementary bottles of champagne. **£325**

NEW TOWN

Express by Holiday Inn Edinburgh City Centre Picardy Place, Broughton 0131 558 2300, hieedinburgh.co.uk. It's by a busy roundabout, but otherwise in a good location in an elegant old Georgian tenement near the top of Broughton St, with 161 rooms featuring neat but predictable chain-hotel decor and facilities. **£99**

Gerald's Place 21b Abercromby Place 0131 558 7017, geraldsplace.com. A homely taste of New Town life at an upmarket but wonderfully hospitable and comfy basement B&B. **£119**

The Glasshouse 2 Greenside Place, Broughton 0131 525 8200, theetoncollection.co.uk. Incorporating the castellated facade of the former Lady Glenorchy's Church, this ultra-hip hotel has 65 chi-chi rooms with push-button curtains and sliding doors opening onto a huge, lush roof garden scattered with Philippe Starck furniture. Perfect if you're in town for a weekend of flash indulgence. **£200**

Ramsay's Bed and Breakfast 25 East London St, Broughton 0131 557 5917, ramsaysbedandbreakfastedinburgh.com. Well located just around the corner from Broughton St, this terraced townhouse has four simple and neat bedrooms, all with en-suite bathrooms. A full Scottish breakfast is served, and families are welcome. **£80**

LEITH AND NORTH EDINBURGH

Fraoch House 66 Pilrig St, Pilrig 0131 554 1353, fraochhouse.com. A relaxing nine-bedroom guesthouse with a slick, modern look created by its young owners. It's a 10–15min walk from both Broughton St and the heart of Leith. **£75**

The Inverleith Hotel 5 Inverleith Terrace, Inverleith 0131 556 2745, inverleithhotel.co.uk. Pleasant option near the Botanic Gardens, with ten rooms of various sizes in a Victorian terraced house; all are en suite and tastefully decorated with wooden floors, antiques and tapestries. **£89**

Malmaison 1 Tower Place 0131 468 5000, malmaison.com. Chic, modern hotel set in the grand old seamen's hostel just back from the wharf-side. Bright, bold original designs in each room, as well as CD players and cable TV. Also has a gym, room service, Parisian brasserie and café-bar serving lighter meals. A linked *Hotel du Vin* is located up in town near the university. **£110**

Wallace's Arthouse Scotland 41/4 Constitution St 07941 343714, wallacesarthousescotland.com. Fantastic boutique B&B in Leith owned and run by a fashion designer. With its kitsch surroundings and friendly service it's one of the city's finest recent additions. **£95**

SOUTH OF THE CENTRE

★ **94DR** 94 Dalkeith Rd, Newington 0131 662 9265, 94dr.com. A boutique guesthouse offering three different styles with its couture, bespoke and tailored rooms. Front-facing rooms have a view of Arthur's Seat. **£110**

Cluaran House 47 Leamington Terrace, Viewforth 0131 221 0047, cluaran-house-edinburgh.co.uk. Tasteful and welcoming B&B with original features and paintings. Serves good wholefood breakfasts. Close to the Meadows with bus links (including #11 & #23) from nearby Bruntsfield Place. **£90**

HOSTELS, SELF-CATERING AND CAMPUS ACCOMMODATION

Edinburgh is one of the UK's most popular backpacker destinations, and there are a large number of hostels in and around the centre, ranging in size, atmosphere and quality. Custom-built **self-catering serviced apartments** with no minimum let are popular, and make a viable if somewhat pricey alternative to guesthouses. **Campus accommodation** is available in summer, and while a good option for solo travellers, you can get better value on doubles elsewhere.

OLD TOWN

Brodies 1 93 High St 0131 556 6770, brodieshostels.co.uk. Tucked down a typical Old Town close, with four straightforward dorms sleeping up to a dozen and limited communal areas. It's smaller than many hostels, and a little bit more homely as a result. Dorm **£12**, double **£48**

Castle Rock Hostel 15 Johnston Terrace 0131 225 9666, castlerockedinburgh.com. Tucked below the Castle ramparts, with 200 or so beds arranged in large, bright dorms, as well as triple and quads and some doubles. The communal areas include a games room with pool and table tennis. Dorm **£14**, double **£40**

Smart City Hostel 50 Blackfriars St 0131 524 1989, smartcityhostels.com. A five-star hostel just off the Royal Mile, with 622 beds in twin rooms or dorms. Women-only rooms are available. A reasonable bar-bistro serves good-value food and breakfasts, and there's a late-night bar for residents. Dorm **£11**, double **£52**

17

NEW TOWN AND AROUND

Canon Court Apartments 20 Canonmills ☎0131 554 2721, 🌐canoncourt.co.uk. A block of smart, comfortable self-catering one- and two-bedroom apartments not far from Canonmills Bridge over the Water of Leith, at the northern edge of the New Town. Double apartments from £145

Edinburgh Central SYHA 9 Haddington Place, Leith ☎0131 524 2090, 🌐edinburghcentral.org. In a handy location at the top of Leith Walk, this five-star hostel has single, double and eight-bed rooms with en-suite facilities. There is a reasonably priced bistro and self-catering kitchen facilities. Dorm £18, double £65

SOUTH OF THE CENTRE

Argyle Backpackers 14 Argyle Place, Marchmont ☎0131 667 9991, 🌐argyle-backpackers.co.uk. Quiet, less intense version of the typical backpackers' hostel, pleasantly located in three adjoining townhouses near the Meadows in studenty Marchmont. It's walking distance to town, or you can get bus #41 from the door. The small dorms have single beds, and there are a dozen or so double/twin rooms, as well as a pleasant communal conservatory and garden at the back. Dorm £14, double £48

University of Edinburgh, Pollock Halls of Residence 18 Holyrood Park Rd, Newington ☎0131 651 2007, 🌐edinburghfirst.com. Unquestionably the best setting of any of the city's university accommodation, right beside Holyrood Park, and with a range of accommodation from single rooms (£32) and en-suite doubles to self-catering flats (from £400 per week). Mostly available Easter & June to mid-Sept, though some rooms available year-round. Double £79

EATING

Edinburgh's dining scene is a feather in the city's cap – with five restaurants holding **Michelin stars**, it can justifiably claim second place behind London in the UK's fine-dining pecking order. Under this level, small diners and bistros predominate, and Edinburgh is an excellent place if you like **fish** and shellfish. Plenty of tourist-oriented restaurants offer **haggis** and other classic clichés, mostly with little culinary merit; a better idea is to seek out the crop of places using locally sourced, quality ingredients available from small and **artisan producers** around Scotland. During the **Festival** the majority of restaurants keep longer hours than are given below, but they are also much busier.

ROYAL MILE AND AROUND

CAFÉS, BISTROS AND CASUAL DINING

★ **David Bann's Vegetarian Restaurant** 56–58 St Mary's St ☎0131 556 5888, 🌐davidbann.com. Thoroughly modern vegetarian restaurant, open long hours and offering a wide choice of interesting dishes such as chickpea koftas with home-made curd cheese or risotto of roasted tomato, peas and basil (£10.75). Prices are reasonable and the overall design is stylish and classy. Mon–Fri noon–10pm, Sat & Sun 11am–10pm.

The Edinburgh Larder 15 Blackfriars St ☎0131 556 6922, 🌐www.edinburghlarder.co.uk. Just 20yds off the Royal Mile, but acts like a neighbourhood café, with friendly staff, food that dares to depart from the norm, and almost all ingredients sourced from the smaller Scottish producers around Edinburgh, such as a Great Glen venison, pork and pepper salami and Anster cheese on a roll with seasonal salads (£5.95). Mon–Sat 8am–5pm, Sun 9am–5pm.

Foodies at Holyrood 67 Holyrood Rd ☎0131 557 6836, 🌐foodiesatholyrood.com. There's a dearth of decent eating places in Holyrood, and while cafés within the Parliament and Palace offer convenience, the food here is a step or two above, with freshly made sandwiches (£4), decent veggie options, hand-baked cakes and a pleasant if undistinguished setting. Mon–Fri 8am–6pm, Sat & Sun 10am–6pm.

Fruitmarket Gallery Café 45 Market St ☎0131 226 1843, 🌐fruitmarket.co.uk. This attractive café feels like an extension of the gallery space, its airy, reflective ambience enhanced by the wall of glass onto the street. Stop in for soups, coffees or a sizeably portioned roll with Dunbar smoked trout and salad (£6.95). Mon–Sat 11.30am–4pm, Sun noon–4pm.

Mother India's Cafe 3–5 Infirmary St ☎0131 524 9801, 🌐motherindiascafeedinburgh.co.uk. This Glasgow-based operation has a refreshing approach to Indian food, serving freshly prepared tapas-style dishes that allow you to eat well but also lightly, with disarmingly simple dishes such as ginger chicken and spinach leaf (£4.60). Old stone walls and original photos on the walls help maintain an informal but buzzy atmsophere. Mon–Thurs noon–2pm, 5–10.30pm; Fri & Sat noon–11pm; Sun noon–10pm.

★ **Spoon Café Bistro** 6a Nicholson St ☎0131 557 4567, 🌐spooncafebistro.co.uk. A lovely, large first-floor room opposite the Festival Theatre, with quirky retro fittings and a reliable menu of well-made rustic dishes with punchy flavours and good ingredients – try an open sandwich with grilled sardines, lamb's lettuce and grilled tomato (£7.50). They also make the best soup in town. Mon–Sat 10am–10pm.

FINE DINING

Amber Scotch Whisky Heritage Centre, 354 Castlehill ☎0131 477 8477, 🌐amber-restaurant.co.uk. Neat, contemporary place serving light food such as potted shrimp at lunchtime and more substantial dishes in the evenings, when a "whisky sommelier" will suggest the best drams to accompany your fillet of sea bream with creamed cabbage and crushed new potatoes (£17.95). Tues–Sat noon–3.45pm & 7–9pm, Sun & Mon noon–3.45pm.

La Garrigue 31 Jeffrey St ⓣ0131 557 3032, ⓦlagarrigue.co.uk. A place of genuine charm and quality, with a menu and wine list dedicated to the produce and traditions of the Languedoc region of France. The care and honesty of the cooking shine through in dishes such as blue cheese soufflé with artichoke salad, or shin of beef in red wine sauce with tomatoes, olives and pasta gratin, available as part of a set-price deal of £26.50 for two courses. Two other branches in the New Town and Leith. Daily noon–2.30pm & 6.30–9.30pm.

★ **Ondine** 2 George IV Bridge ⓣ0131 226 1888, ⓦondinerestaurant.co.uk. Tucked in next to the *Hotel Missoni*, this seafood restaurant from Edinburgh chef Roy Brett, once Rick Stein's main chef in Padstow, turns out some sublime dishes such as grilled lemon sole with brown shrimps and capers (£23.95), using native shellfish and fish from sustainable sources. Mon–Sat noon–10pm, Sun noon–4pm.

The Witchery by the Castle Castlehill ⓣ0131 225 5613, ⓦthewitchery.com. An upmarket restaurant set in magnificently over-the-top medieval surroundings full of Gothic panelling, tapestries and heavy stonework, all a mere broomstick-hop from the Castle. The rich fish and game dishes such as loin of Cairngorm venison with potato and turnip cake, squash purée, red cabbage and chocolate oil (£27) are pricey, but you can steal a sense of it all with a lunch or pre- or post-theatre set menu for under £16. Daily noon–4pm & 5.30–11.30pm.

NEW TOWN AND AROUND

CAFÉS

★ **Artisan Roast** 57 Broughton St ⓦartisanroast.co.uk. If you're into the black stuff, this is a must. A narrow, grungy shop lined with hessian, they roast on site, make coffee with skill and care, and delight in taking pops at mainstream coffee culture. Perch on a stool in the main shop or shuffle through to cushioned benches in "The Mooch". Other than pastries and cakes, they don't serve much food. Mon–Thurs 8am–7.30pm, Fri 8am–6.30pm, Sat 9am–6.30pm, Sun 10am–6.30pm.

The Gallery Café Scottish National Gallery of Modern Art, Belford Rd, Dean Village ⓣ0131 332 8600. The cultured setting (which includes a lovely outside eating area) and appealing, mid-priced menu of hearty soups, healthy salads and specials such as smoked haddock Florentine with roast tomatoes and mozzarella (£6.25) pull in reassuring numbers of locals. Mon–Fri 9am–4.30pm, Sat & Sun 10am–4.30pm.

The Scottish Café and Restaurant National Gallery of Scotland, The Mound ⓣ0131 226 6524, ⓦthescottishcafeandrestaurant.com. An admirable (and mostly successful) attempt to bring the best of Scottish food to a busy venue that celebrates the best of Scottish art. Choose luxury porridge or a buttery (the local equivalent of a croissant) for morning snack, or a starter portion of local haggis with neeps and tatties (£5.95) for lunch. Mon–Wed, Fri & Sat 8am–6pm; Thurs 8am–7pm; Sun 10am–6pm.

★ **Valvona & Crolla** 19 Elm Row, Leith Walk ⓣ0131 556 6066, ⓦvalvonacrolla.com. The café at the back of what is arguably Britain's finest Italian deli serves authentic and delicious breakfasts, lunches and daytime snacks including an antipasto plate of cured meats, roast vegetables and bruschetta (£11). *V&C* also has a wine bar and evening restaurant (*Vincaffè*) at 11 Multrees Walk, just off St Andrew Square. Mon–Sat 8.30am–5.30pm, Sun 10.30am–3.30pm.

BISTROS AND CASUAL DINING

The Dogs 110 Hanover St ⓣ0131 220 1208, ⓦthedogsonline.co.uk. Back-to-basics British cooking with offal, cheap cuts and cheaper fish served in well-cooked dishes for properly decent prices – braised lamb heart stuffed with prunes and bacon (£7.95) for example. There's an equally good-value wine list and unconventionally offhand but well-meaning service. Variations on the formula reappear almost next door at sister restaurants *Amore Dogs* (the Italian version) and *Seadogs* (the fishy version) at 43 Rose St. Daily noon–4pm & 5–10pm.

Dusit 49a Thistle St, West End ⓣ0131 220 6846, ⓦdusit.co.uk. The bold but effective blend of Thai flavours and well-sourced Scottish ingredients brings a bit of originality and refinement to the often predictable Thai dining scene. Specialities include Gaeng Phet red curry with chicken, bamboo shoots, aubergine, chilli and basil (£10.95). Mon–Sat noon–3pm & 6–11pm, Sun noon–11pm.

L'Escargot Bleu 56 Broughton St ⓣ0131 557 1600, ⓦlescargotbleu.co.uk. A nice step up from the rustic, no-frills French bistro that's still in evidence across Edinburgh. Here, classic French country cooking is brought to bear on a range of locally sourced produce, from rare-breed pork cooked in red wine to Trossachs pike with lobster sauce and Comté cheese (£13.80). Daily noon–3pm & 5.30–10pm (closed Sun in winter).

Mussel Inn 61–65 Rose St ⓣ0131 225 5979, ⓦmussel-inn.com. After feasting on a kilo of mussels and a basket of chips for under £15 you'll realize why there's a demand to get in here. They have close ties to west coast shellfish farmers, which helps ensure that the journey from sea to plate is short and swift. Mon–Thurs noon–3pm, 5.30–10pm; Fri–Sun noon–10pm.

Urban Angel 121 Hanover St ⓣ0131 225 6215, ⓦurban-angel.co.uk. Right-on and easy-going subterranean bistro with a diverse and adaptable blackboard menu using lots of organic and Fairtrade produce. They'll do you a home-made burger with Highland blue cheese, coleslaw and fries for £12. There's a second, equally attractive branch at 1 Forth St just off Broughton St. Mon–Fri 8am–10pm, Sat 9am–10pm, Sun 10am–5pm.

17

FINE DINING

21212 3 Royal Terrace, Calton Hill 0845 222 1212, 21212restaurant.co.uk. The most challenging and polarizing restaurant to arrive in Edinburgh in recent years; some (including the Michelin inspectors) love chef Paul Kitching's shopping-list style of cooking and whimsical concoctions, while others are convinced they've been had. As part of a £67, five-course dinner you might encounter a dish such as baked sea bass fillet with lemon and saffron pancakes, pink radish, shiitake mushrooms and cardamom ginger butter sauce. Tues–Sat lunch & dinner.

★ **The Dining Room, Scotch Malt Whisky Society** 28 Queen St 0131 220 2044 thediningroomedinburgh.co.uk. This stylish, relatively modern club isn't nearly as stuffy as you'd expect, and the classy ground-floor restaurant, open to non-members, is excellent, serving dishes such as halibut, scallops and langoustine with citrus risotto (£28.50). Lunch Mon–Sat, dinner Tues–Sat.

The Honours 58a Castle St 0131 220 2513, thehonours.co.uk. A brasserie in the grand New York style, but with chef Martin Wishart overseeing proceedings (but not cooking – his talented partner Paul Tamburrini does that here); standards and quality are high. Options range from soufflés to cottage pie with good seafood and offal in there too. Lunch Tues–Sun, dinner Tues–Sat.

SOUTHSIDE

CAFÉS, BISTROS AND CASUAL DINING

The Apartment Bistro 7–13 Barclay Place, Bruntsfield 0131 228 6456. A sultry, Parisian-style brasserie with dishes such as grilled hake with asparagus in mussel and almond vinaigrette (£13.20) showing off hearty cooking, good wines and plenty of stylish sophistication. Mon–Fri 5–11pm, Sat & Sun 11am–11pm.

Kalpna 2–3 St Patrick's Square, Newington 0131 667 9890, kalpnarestaurant.com. Outstanding vegetarian restaurant serving authentic Gujarati dishes. Four set meals (from £13.50), including a vegan option, and a good main menu. Mon–Sat lunch & dinner; also Sun dinner in summer.

Peter's Yard 27 Simpson Loan (Quartermile) 0131 228 5876, petersyard.com. A Swedish outfit with the bread ovens on view and baskets of delicious loaves out front. Set on the edge of The Meadows, it's popular with flush-feeling students and professionals drawn by the excellent soup (£4), coffee and bakery treats. Mon–Fri 7am–6pm; Sat & Sun 9am–6pm.

Sweet Melinda's 11 Roseneath St, Marchmont 0131 229 7953, wwwsweetmelindas.co.uk. A pleasant seafood restaurant in a timber-panelled room with a friendly neighbourhood feel. Two courses with dishes such as grilled sardines with garlic and rosemary, or red gurnard with king prawns, ginger, soy and toasted sesame oil, costs £22.50. Mon dinner, Tues–Sat lunch & dinner.

LEITH AND NEWHAVEN

With some of the city's top restaurants, great seafood places and well-worn, friendly pubs, **Leith** and its neighbouring harbour district of **Newhaven** are among the best places to eat and drink in Edinburgh.

CAFÉS, BISTROS AND CASUAL DINING

Chop Chop 76 Commercial Quay, Leith 0131 553 1818, chop-chop.co.uk. Second branch of a Chinese restaurant that specializes in northern Chinese cooking, with its dumplings a particular draw alongside intriguing dishes such as pork belly and sauerkraut broth (£9.95). Success on one of Gordon Ramsay's TV shows has seen it blossom. Mon–Fri noon–2pm, Sat & Sun 12.30–10pm.

Loch Fyne Restaurant 25 Pier Place, Newhaven Harbour 0131 559 3900, lochfyne.com. Fantastic location by the fish market and old stone harbour at Newhaven for this English-based chain with strong connections to Scotland's west coast. Best for simple oysters and fish with a glass of wine, though there are plenty of mains including Loch Fyne poached smoked haddock with spinach, peas and mashed potato (£11.95). Daily 10am–10pm.

Porto & Fi 47 Newhaven Main St 0131 551 1900, portofi.com. A bright daytime café not far from Newhaven's old stone harbour, with tempting cakes alongside serious daily specials, including the house fish pie topped with leek mash (£9.75), from an accomplished kitchen. Mon–Sat 8am–7.30pm, Sun 10am–6pm.

The Shore 3–4 The Shore, Leith 0131 553 5080, fishersbistros.co.uk/theshore. A well-lived-in bar/restaurant with huge mirrors, wood panelling and aproned waiters who'll do you snails in garlic (£5) or smart fish and chips with mushy peas (£9.50). Live jazz, folk and hubbub float through from the adjoining bar. Daily noon–1am.

The Water of Leith Café Bistro 52 Coburg St 0131 555 2613, thewaterofleithcafebistro.co.uk. A wee bit out on its own, but this welcoming, family-friendly spot is right beside the Water of Leith walkway. The French chef's wide experience shows in the quality of dishes such as smoked haddock and salmon fishcakes with home-made tartare sauce (£6.70). Tues–Sun 10am–5.30pm.

FINE DINING

★ **The Kitchin** 78 Commercial Quay, Leith 0131 555 1755, thekitchin.com. Opened in 2006 by young Scottish chef Tom Kitchin and the winner – less than six months later – of a Michelin star, this upwardly mobile operation puts itself at the more relaxed end of the fine-dining spectrum and offers some tantalizing dishes including rolled pig's head with crispy ear salad (£18), or razor clams with chorizo as well as tasting menus from £70. Tues–Sat lunch & dinner.

Restaurant Martin Wishart 52 The Shore, Leith ⓣ 0131 553 3557, ⓦ martin-wishart.co.uk. The eponymous chef is one of the leading lights of the Scottish culinary scene, and was the first Michelin-star holder in Edinburgh. Though relatively small and demure, his original restaurant (he also runs a brasserie, *The Honours*, in the New Town) wows the gourmets with highly accomplished and exquisitely presented dishes featuring Scottish-sourced fish and meat. A two-course lunch is £24.50, a six-course evening tasting menu £65. Tues–Sat lunch & dinner.

DRINKING

Many of Edinburgh's **pubs**, especially in the Old Town, have histories that stretch back centuries, while others, particularly in the New Town, are unaltered Victorian or Edwardian period pieces. Add a plentiful supply of trendy modern bars, and there's enough to cater for all tastes. Note that the **opening hours** quoted below may well be extended during Festival.

THE ROYAL MILE AND AROUND

★ **Bow Bar** 80 West Bow, Old Town ⓣ 0131 226 7667. Wonderful old wood-panelled bar and one of the most pleasant, convivial drinking spots in the city centre. Choose from among nearly 150 whiskies or a changing selection of first-rate Scottish and English cask beers. Mon–Thurs noon–11.30pm, Fri & Sat noon–midnight, Sun noon–11pm.

Peartree House 36 West Nicolson St, Newington ⓣ 0131 667 7533. Fine bar in an eighteenth-century house with old sofas and a large courtyard – one of central Edinburgh's very few beer gardens. Mon–Thurs 11am–11.45pm, Fri & Sat 11am–12.45am, Sun 12.30–11.45pm.

Under the Stairs 3a Merchant St, Old Town ⓣ 0131 466 8550, ⓦ underthestairs.org. Comfy, shabby-chic bar with great cocktails, popular with the pre-clubbing crowd. Food served late, with sharing plates available right up till closing time. Mon–Sat noon–1am, Sun noon–midnight.

NEW TOWN AND WEST END

Blue Blazer 2 Spittal St, Tollcross ⓣ 0131 229 5030. This traditional Edinburgh howff with an oak-clad bar and church pews serves good real ales and has a great choice of whiskies and rums. Mon–Sat 11am–1am; Sun 12.30pm–1am.

The Bon Vivant 55 Thistle St, New Town ⓣ 0131 225 3275, ⓦ bonvivantedinburgh.co.uk. Classy city-centre bar, with an excellent wine list and good choice of champagne by the glass, as well as interesting food available in tapas-sized portions. Daily noon–1am.

★ **Café Royal Circle Bar** 17 West Register St, New Town ⓣ 0131 556 1884, ⓦ caferoyal.org.uk. Worth a visit just for its Victorian decor, notably the huge elliptical island bar and tiled portraits of renowned inventors. The beer and food are good, too. The *Café* is a better bet than its equally venerable, but much more staid neighbouring *Oyster Bar* restaurant. Mon–Wed 11am–11pm, Thurs 11am–midnight, Fri/Sat 11am–1am, Sun 12.30pm–11pm.

Oloroso 33 Castle St, New Town ⓣ 0131 226 7614, ⓦ oloroso.co.uk. Though there's a glamorous upmarket dining space here, the rooftop bar with views of the castle and the Forth is a more convivial and cost-effective way to enjoy the setting. Daily noon–1am.

The Raconteur 50 Dean St, Stockbridge ⓣ 0131 343 3221, ⓦ theraconteuredinburgh.com. Relaxed and cosy neighbourhood pub, quietly tucked away in the cobbled streets of Stockbridge, which shakes up a mean cocktail or two. Daily 5pm–late.

Tigerlily 125 George St, New Town ⓣ 0131 777 8119, ⓦ tigerlilyedinburgh.co.uk. The daddy of all George Street's decadent destination bars, where the locals come to see and be seen. Can be tons of fun – but only if you're wearing the right clothes. Daily 8am–1am.

Traverse Bar Café Traverse Theatre, 10 Cambridge St, West End ⓣ 0131 228 5383, ⓦ traverse.co.uk/bar-café/. Much more than just a theatre bar, attracting a lively, sophisticated crowd who dispel any notion of a quiet interval drink. Good food available. One of the places to be during the Festival. Mon 10.30am–2am, Tues & Wed 9am–2am, Thurs–Sat 9am–3am, Sun 9am–1am.

The Voodoo Rooms 19a West Register St, New Town ⓣ 0131 556 7060, ⓦ thevoodoorooms.com. Glamorous gilt and plush booths attract a dressed-up crowd, especially at the weekend. Frequent live music, performance and club nights, including Edinburgh's legendary Vegas! Mon–Thurs 4pm–1am, Fri–Sun noon–1am.

LEITH

Kings Wark 36 The Shore ⓣ 0131 554 9260, ⓦ thekingswark.co.uk. Real ale in a restored eighteenth-century pub right in the heart of Leith. There's an attached restaurant, and great bar meals – check in at the bar for a table. Sun–Thurs noon–11pm, Fri & Sat noon–midnight.

The Roseleaf 23/24 Sandport Place ⓣ 0131 476 5268, ⓦ roseleaf.co.uk. Chintzy-cool local that's a little off the beaten track but worth the trip for the pot-tails alone – funky cocktails served in vintage teapots. Daily 10am–1am.

★ **The Shore** 3–4 The Shore ⓣ 0131 553 5080, ⓦ fishersbistros.co.uk/theshore. Atmospheric traditional bar with an adjacent restaurant (see opposite). There's regular live jazz or folk music as well as real ales and good bar snacks. Daily noon–1am.

17

NIGHTLIFE AND ENTERTAINMENT

Inevitably, Edinburgh's **nightlife** is at its best during the Festival (see p.734), which can make the other 49 weeks of the year seem like an anticlimax. However, at any time the city has plenty to offer, especially in the realm of **theatre** and **music**. The best way to find out **what's on** is to pick up a copy of *The List*, a fortnightly listings magazine covering both Edinburgh and Glasgow (£2.50).

CLUBS

The Bongo Club Moray House, 37 Holyrood Rd ⊕0131 558 7604, ⓦthebongoclub.co.uk. Legendary Edinburgh club and arts venue; its line-up is eclectic but always worth checking out. Look out for the monthly drum 'n' bass night Xplicit, or funk, jazz and Latin night Four Corners.

Cabaret Voltaire 36–38 Blair St ⊕0131 220 6176, ⓦthecabaretvoltaire.com. Atmospheric nightclub in the Old Town's underground vaults, hosting some of the city's best clubs, including house favourite Ultragroove.

The Liquid Room 9c Victoria St ⊕0131 225 2564, ⓦliquidroom.com. Recently refurbished, with a cutting-edge sound and light system. One of the best of the larger venues, with nights such as the indie Wednesday-nighter Indigo and irregular house night Musika, which always brings top-name guests. Also good for live music.

Lulu's 125b George St ⊕0131 225 5005, ⓦluluedinburgh.co.uk. Sultry subterranean nightspot beneath OTT bar and restaurant *Tigerlily*. A place to see and be seen, with its fair share of Travolta-wannabes striding to the sound-responsive disco lightfloor.

GAY CLUBS AND BARS

CC Bloom's 23–24 Greenside Place ⊕0131 556 9331. Edinburgh's most enduring gay club, with a big dancefloor, stonking rhythms and a young, friendly crowd.

Planet 6 Baxter's Place ⊕0131 556 5551. Loud and outrageous bar beside the Playhouse Theatre; a popular meeting point.

LIVE MUSIC VENUES

HMV Picture House 31 Lothian Rd ⊕0131 221 2280, ⓦedinburgh-picturehouse.co.uk. A 1500-capacity city-centre venue that still manages to feel intimate. The reasonably eclectic gig list includes local bands, breakthrough chart-toppers and the occasional tribute band.

Queen's Hall 85–89 Clerk St ⊕0131 668 2019, ⓦthequeenshall.net. Converted Georgian church which now operates as a concert hall; it's used principally by the Scottish Chamber Orchestra and Scottish Ensemble, and is much favoured by jazz, blues and folk groups.

Royal Oak 1 Infirmary St ⊕0131 557 2976, ⓦroyal-oak-folk.com. Traditional pub hosting regular informal folk sessions and the "Wee Folk Club" on Sun.

Sandy Bell's 25 Forrest Rd ⊕0131 225 2751. A friendly bar that's a good bet for folk music most nights of the week.

Usher Hall Cnr Lothian Rd & Grindlay St ⊕0131 228 1155, ⓦusherhall.co.uk. Edinburgh's main civic concert hall is excellent for choral and symphony concerts, but less suitable for solo vocalists. The upper circle seats are cheapest and have the best acoustics.

THEATRE AND DANCE

Dance Base 14–16 Grassmarket ⊕0131 225 5255, ⓦdancebase.co.uk. Scotland's sparkling new National Centre for Dance is used mostly for modern dance workshops and classes, but also hosts occasional performances.

Edinburgh Playhouse 18–22 Greenside Place ⊕0844 847 1660, ⓦedinburgh-playhouse.co.uk. The largest theatre in Britain, formerly a cinema. Used largely for extended runs of popular musicals and occasional rock concerts.

Festival Theatre Nicolson St ⊕0131 529 6000, ⓦfctt.org.uk. The largest stage in Britain, principally used for Scottish Opera and Scottish Ballet's appearances in the

SHOPPING IN EDINBURGH

Princes Street, one of Britain's most famous shopping streets, is all but dominated by standard chain outlets, though no serious shopper should miss out on a visit to Edinburgh's venerable department store, *Jenners*, opposite the Scott Monument. More fashionable upmarket shops are to be found on and around parallel **George Street**, including a street (Multrees Walk) of exclusive international fashion boutiques on the east side of St Andrew Square. There's nothing compelling about central Edinburgh's two big shopping malls, **Princes Mall** and the **St James Centre**, which are dominated by the big names.

For more original outlets, head for **Victoria Street** and the **Grassmarket** where you'll find an eclectic range of antique, crafts, food and book shops. Along and around the **Royal Mile**, meanwhile, several distinctly offbeat places sit among the tacky souvenir sellers. Edinburgh's only regular **market** is its impressive farmers' market, on Castle Terrace, immediately west of the castle, which draws around 35 local produce stalls from south and east Scotland (Sat 9am–1pm).

HOGMANAY

Edinburgh hosts one of the worlds' landmark **New Year's Eve street parties**, with around 100,000 people on the streets of the city seeing out the old year. For the street party, stages are set up in different parts of the city centre, with big-name rock groups and local ceilidh bands playing to the increasingly inebriated masses. The high point of the evening is, of course, midnight, when hundreds of tons of fireworks are let off into the night sky above the castle, and Edinburgh joins the rest of the world singing **"Auld Lang Syne"**, an old Scottish tune with lyrics by Robert Burns, Scotland's national poet. For information about celebrations in Edinburgh, and how to get hold of tickets for the street party, go to Ⓦedinburghshogmanay.org.

capital, but also for everything from the children's show "Singing Kettle" to Engelbert Humperdinck.

King's Theatre 2 Leven St Ⓣ0131 529 6000, Ⓦfctt.org.uk. Stately Edwardian civic theatre that majors in pantomime, touring West End plays and the occasional major drama or opera performance.

Royal Lyceum 30 Grindlay St Ⓣ0131 248 4848, Ⓦlyceum.org.uk. Fine Victorian civic theatre with a compact auditorium. The leading year-round venue for mainstream drama.

Traverse Theatre 10 Cambridge St Ⓣ0131 228 1404, Ⓦtraverse.co.uk. One of Britain's premier venues for new plays and avant-garde drama from around the world. Going from strength to strength in its custom-built home beside the Usher Hall, with a great bar downstairs.

COMEDY

Highlight Omni Centre, Greenside Place Ⓣ0131 524 9300, Ⓦthehighlight.co.uk.com. An Edinburgh link in a national chain located in a huge glass-fronted cinema complex at the foot of Calton Hill. Fairly reliable for a year-round chance to see big-name stand-up acts, with an after-party thrown in.

The Stand 5 York Place Ⓣ0131 558 7272, Ⓦthestand.co.uk. The city's top comedy spot, with a different act every night and some of the UK's top comics headlining at the weekends.

ART-HOUSE CINEMAS

Cameo 38 Home St, Tollcross Ⓣ0131 228 2800, Ⓦpicturehouses.co.uk. A treasure of an art-house cinema; screens the more challenging mainstream releases and cult late-nighters. Tarantino's been here and thinks it's great.

Filmhouse 88 Lothian Rd Ⓣ0131 228 2688, Ⓦfilmhousecinema.com. Three screens showing an eclectic programme of independent, art-house and classic films. The café is a hangout for the city's film buffs.

DIRECTORY

Hospital Royal Infirmary, Little France (Ⓣ0131 536 1000), has a 24hr casualty department. There's also a minor injuries clinic at the Western General, Crewe Rd North (8am–9pm; Ⓣ0131 537 1330), and a casualty department for children at Royal Hospital for Sick Children, Sciennes Rd (Ⓣ0131 536 0000). NHS24 (Ⓣ08454 242424) offers health advice and clinical assessment over the phone; it essentially covers periods when doctors' surgeries aren't open, but is available 24hr.

Left luggage Counter by platform 1 at Waverley Station (£5/ item; daily 7am–11pm; Ⓣ0131 558 3829).

Police In an emergency call 999. Otherwise contact Lothian and Borders Police HQ, Fettes Ave Ⓣ0131 311 3131.

East Lothian

East Lothian consists of the coastal strip and hinterland immediately east of Edinburgh, bounded by the Firth of Forth to the north and the Lammermuir Hills to the south. All of it is within easy day-trip range from the capital, though there are places you can stay overnight if you're keen to explore. Often mocked as the "home counties" of Edinburgh, there's no denying its well-ordered feel, with prosperous farms and large estate houses dominating the scenery. The main attractions are on or near the coast, with the trip east from Edinburgh taking you past wide sandy beaches by **Aberlady** and famous golf courses at **Gullane**. The town of **North Berwick** is the main focal point on the coast, with dramatic cliff-top ruins at **Tantallon** and the supersonic draw of **Concorde** at the Museum of Flight both within easy reach.

17

North Berwick and around

NORTH BERWICK has a great deal of charm and a somewhat faded, old-fashioned air, its guesthouses and hotels extending along the shore in all their Victorian and Edwardian sobriety. The town's small harbour is set on a headland which cleaves two crescents of sand, though it is the two nearby volcanic heaps, the offshore **Bass Rock** and 613ft-high **North Berwick Law**, which are the town's defining physical features.

Scottish Seabird Centre

By the harbour • April–Sept daily 10am–6pm; Nov–Jan Mon–Fri 10am–4pm, Sat & Sun 10am–5pm; Feb, March & Oct Mon–Fri 10am–5pm, Sat & Sun 10am–5.30pm • £7.15 • T 01620 890202, W seabird.org

Resembling a giant molar, the **Bass Rock** rises 350ft above the sea some three miles east of North Berwick and is home to around 100,000 nesting gannets in summer, as well as razorbills, terns, puffins, guillemots and fulmars. The best place to observe the rock and its inhabitants is North Berwick's principal attraction, the **Scottish Seabird Centre**. Among the interactive exhibits and child-oriented displays there's a live link from the centre to cameras mounted on the island. Weather permitting, **boat trips** are available.

ARRIVAL AND INFORMATION — NORTH BERWICK

By train North Berwick is served by a regular train from Edinburgh Waverley (30min), with discount deals for those heading for the Seabird Centre. From the station it's a 10min walk east to the town centre.

By bus Buses from Edinburgh (every 30min) run along the coast via Aberlady, Gullane and Dirleton and stop on High St, while the hourly services from Haddington and Dunbar terminate outside the tourist office.

Tourist office Quality St, by the eastern end of the main street (April & May Mon–Sat 9.30am–6pm; June Mon–Sat 9.30am–6pm, Sun 11am–4pm; July & Aug Mon–Sat 9.30am–7pm, Sun 11am–6pm; Sept Mon–Sat 9.30am–6pm, Sun 11am–6pm; Oct Mon–Sat 9.30am–5pm; Nov–March Thurs–Sat 9.30am–5pm; T 01620 892197).

ACCOMMODATION AND EATING

Beach Lodge 5 Beach Rd T 01620 892257, W beachlodge.co.uk. Located near the main street and harbour, this smartly turned out B&B has a nice maritime feel to it. Of the four rooms, two have balconies and another has sea views. **£80**

Lobstershack The Harbour T 07910 620480, W lobstershack.co.uk. Get lobster, langoustine and mackerel straight from the boats at this harbourside hut with a handful of outdoor tables and chairs. The menu's more sophisticated than you'd think and it's licensed. A whole lobster and chips comes in at under £20. June to mid-Sept daily 11am–6/8pm; May & mid-Sept to Oct Sat & Sun only.

Seabird Centre Café The Harbour T 01620 890202, W seabird.org. A great location with outdoor decking and panoramic views over the beach and Bass Rock. Some decent options such as hot quiche salad (£6.25) among a mainstream and kid-friendly menu. Daily 10am–4pm.

Tantallon Castle

Three miles east of North Berwick on the A198 • April–Sept daily 9.30am–5.30pm; Oct daily 9.30am–4.30pm; Nov–March Mon–Wed, Sat & Sun 9.30am–4.30pm • HS • £4.70 • T 01620 892727 • From North Berwick take the Dunbar bus (Eves Coaches #120; Mon–Sat 6 daily, Sun 2 daily; 15min), or walk along the cliffs in around 1hr

The melodramatic ruins of **Tantallon Castle** stand on precipitous cliffs facing the Bass Rock. With a sheer drop down to the sea on three sides and a sequence of moats and ditches on the fourth, the castle's desolate invincibility is daunting, especially when the wind howls over the remaining battlements and the surf crashes on the rocks far below.

National Museum of Flight

Five miles south of North Berwick • April–Oct daily 10am–5pm; Nov–March Sat & Sun 10am–4pm • £9 • T 0131 247 4238, W nms.ac.uk/flight • First Bus #121 from North Berwick or Haddington, both of which have connections from Edinburgh

Standing on an old military airfield by East Fortune, the **National Museum of Flight** is home to *Alpha Alpha*, British Airways' first **Concorde**. The supersonic passenger jet, one of only twenty such planes built, has been reassembled to show how she looked when decommissioned in 2003. A visit onboard is restricted to a slightly stooped wander through the forward half of the aircraft, while a display follows the Concorde project as a whole, from the early days of Anglo-French bickering to the tragic Paris crash of 2000. In and around the older hangars on the site, you can see more than fifty vintage aircraft including a Vulcan bomber, a Comet airliner, a Spitfire and a Tigermoth.

Midlothian

Immediately south of Edinburgh lies the old county of **MIDLOTHIAN**, once called Edinburghshire. It's one of the hilliest parts of the Central Lowlands, with the Pentland chain running down its western side, and the Moorfoots defining its boundary with the Borders to the south.

Roslin

The tranquil village of **ROSLIN**, seven miles south of the centre of Edinburgh, has two claims to fame: it was near here, at the Roslin Institute, that the world's first cloned sheep, Dolly, was created in 1997, and it's also home to the mysterious, richly decorated late Gothic **Rosslyn Chapel.**

Rosslyn Chapel

Chapel Loan • April–Sept Mon–Sat 9.30am–5.30pm, Sun noon–4.15pm; Oct–March Mon–Sat 9.30am–4.30pm, Sun noon–4.15pm • £7.50 • Ⓦ rosslynchapel.org.uk • Roslin can be reached by bus #15 from Edinburgh's St Andrew Square

After a long period of neglect, a massive restoration project is underway to preserve **Rosslyn Chapel**, most of which dates to the late fifteenth century. Rosslyn's exterior bristles with pinnacles, gargoyles, flying buttresses and canopies, while inside the stonework is, if anything, even more intricate. Among the carvings are representations of cacti and Indian corn, compounding the legend that the founder's grandfather, the daring sea adventurer Prince Henry of Orkney, did indeed set foot in the New World a century before Columbus. The greatest and most original carving of all is the extraordinary knotted **Apprentice Pillar** at the southeastern corner of the Lady Chapel. According to local legend, the pillar was made by an apprentice during the absence of the master mason, who killed him in a fit of jealousy on seeing the finished work.

West Lothian

To many, West Lothian is a poor relative to the rolling, rich farmland of East and Midlothian, with a landscape dominated by motorways, industrial estates and giant

ROSSLYN'S SECRETS

The imagery of certain carvings found in Rosslyn Chapel, together with the history of the family, the St Clairs, which owns the chapel, leave little doubt about its links to the **Knights Templar** and **Freemasonry**. The Masonic connection was said to have saved the chapel from the armies of Oliver Cromwell, himself a Freemason, which destroyed the surrounding area but spared Rosslyn. More intriguing still are claims that, because of such connections, Rosslyn Chapel has been the repository for items such as the lost Scrolls of Solomon's Temple in Jerusalem, the true Stone of Scone and, most famously, the Holy Grail. The chapel is regularly drawn into conspiracy theories on these themes, most famously in recent years through Dan Brown's bestseller *The Da Vinci Code*; the chapel's appearance in the film of the same name precipitated a huge surge in visitor numbers, which detracts a little from the mysterious air of the place.

hillocks of ochre-coloured mine waste called "bings". However, in the royal palace at **Linlithgow**, the area boasts one of Scotland's more magnificent ruins. Nearby, the village of **South Queensferry** lies under the considerable shadow of the **Forth rail and road bridges**, though it's an interesting enough place in its own right, with a historic high street and the stately home of **Hopetoun** nearby.

Linlithgow

Fifteen miles west of Edinburgh is the ancient royal burgh of **LINLITHGOW**. The town itself has largely kept its medieval layout, but development since the 1960s has, sadly, stripped it of some fine buildings, notably around the **Town Hall** and **Cross** – the former marketplace – on the long High Street.

Linlithgow Palace

Linlithgow Loch • Daily: April–Sept 9.30am–5.30pm; Oct–March 9.30am–4.30pm • HS • £5.20

Hidden from the main road, **Linlithgow Palace** is a splendid fifteenth-century ruin romantically set on the edge of Linlithgow Loch. The palace's royal connections are strong: from the top of the northwest tower, Queen Margaret looked out in vain for the return of James IV from the field of Flodden in 1513 (the views from her bower, six storeys up from the ground, are exceptional). The ornate octagonal **fountain** in the inner courtyard, with its intricate figures and medallion heads, flowed with wine for the wedding of James V and Mary of Guise; their daughter Mary was born here on 8 December 1542 and just six days later began her reign as the most famous Queen of Scots.

ARRIVAL AND INFORMATION — LINLITHGOW

By train Linlithgow is on the main train routes from Edinburgh to both Glasgow Queen Street and Stirling; the station lies at the southern end of town.

Tourist office In the Town Hall building at the Cross (April–Oct Sat & Sun 10am–6pm; Nov–March Sat 10am–4pm, Sun noon–4pm; T 01506 844600), between the Palace and High St.

ACCOMMODATION AND EATING

Belsyde Farm Belsyde T 01506 842098, W belsydehouse.co.uk. An upmarket, spacious and well-appointed late eighteenth-century house on a sheep and cattle farm beside the Union Canal on the outskirts of Linlithgow. **£66**

Champany Inn Champany T 01506 834532, W champany.com. The old-school restaurant, which serves seriously expensive steaks and seafood as well as top-notch South African wines, holds a Michelin star, though there's also a less formal chop and ale house as well as smart rooms. Restaurant closed Sun. **£100**

Taste 47 High St T 01506 844445, W taste-deli-cafe.co.uk. Decent deli with café attached: pick up a picnic to eat in the grounds of the palace or eat in on soup and a half sandwich (£5.95). Mon–Fri 8.30am–5.30pm, Sat 9am–5.30pm, Sun 10am–4.30pm.

EICA:Ratho

Five miles west of Edinburgh Airport, just beyond the Newbridge junction of the M8 and M9 • Mon–Fri 10am–10pm, Sat & Sun 10am–7pm • Free, times and charges for activities vary • T 0131 333 6333, W eica-ratho.com

EICA:Ratho, or Edinburgh International Climbing Arena, is the world's largest indoor climbing facility, incorporating a remarkable artificial climbing wall. The spectacular vision of its architect founders was to enclose (and roof) a disused quarry, creating a giant arena that's now used for international climbing competitions as well as classes (from £20 for an hour-long taster session) for climbers of all levels, including beginners and kids. Above the arena, just under the glass roof, is "Aerial Assault" (£9.50), a stomach-churning, suspended obstacle course 100ft off the ground – thankfully, you are safely attached via a sliding harness.

South Queensferry

Eight miles northwest of Edinburgh city centre is the small town of **SOUTH QUEENSFERRY**, located at the southern end of the two mighty Forth Bridges. It's an attractive old settlement, with a narrow, cobbled High Street lined with tightly packed buildings, most of which date from the seventeenth and eighteenth centuries. The small **museum**, 53 High St (Mon & Thurs–Sat 10am–1pm & 2.15–5pm, Sun noon–5pm; free), contains historical relics and information on the building of the two bridges that loom overhead.

ARRIVAL AND DEPARTURE — SOUTH QUEENSFERRY

By train It's an easy 20min trip to South Queensferry by train from Edinburgh – note that the local station is called Dalmeny, and that it's a 10min walk from the station down to the village.

By bus First bus #43 connects Edinburgh and South Queensferry.

ACCOMMODATION AND EATING

★ **The Boathouse** 19b High St ⓣ0131 331 5429, ⓦtheboathouse-sq.co.uk. A great location with views out above the water to the two Forth bridges. Excellent seafood options, such as Scottish halibut with an orange, ginger and pink peppercorn reduction (£20) in the main restaurant; the easy-going bistro and small wine bar offer simpler food. Daily noon–9/9.30pm.

Orocco Pier 17 High St ⓣ0870 118 1664, ⓦoroccopier.co.uk. A stylish contemporary drinking spot on South Queensferry's medieval high street, boasting unbeatable views over the water to the Forth Bridges and serving pleasant bistro food such as mussels or roast rump of lamb (£17). They also have smart guest rooms. Bistro Mon–Fri 7am–1am, Sat & Sun 8am–1am. **£110**

Hopetoun House

On the south shore of the Forth, just west of South Queensferry • April–Sept daily 10am–5pm • £8 house and grounds, £3.70 grounds only • ⓣ0131 331 2451, ⓦhopetounhouse.com

Hopetoun House ranks as one of the most impressive stately homes in Scotland. The original house was built at the turn of the eighteenth century for the first Earl of Hopetoun by Sir William Bruce, the architect of Holyroodhouse. A couple of decades later, William Adam carried out an enormous extension, engulfing the structure with a curvaceous main facade and two projecting wings – superb examples of Roman Baroque pomp and swagger. The **grounds** include a long, regal driveway and lovely walks along woodland trails and the banks of the Forth, as well as plenty of picnic spots.

Inchcolm

From South Queensferry's Hawes Pier, just west of the rail bridge, ferry services head out to the island of **Inchcolm**, about five miles northeast. The island is home to the best-preserved medieval **abbey** in Scotland, founded in 1235 after King Alexander I was stormbound here. Although the structure as a whole is half-ruined today, the tower, octagonal chapter house and echoing cloisters are intact and well worth exploring. The ninety minutes you're given ashore by the boat timetables also allows time for a picnic on the abbey's lawns or the chance to explore Inchcolm's old military fortifications.

If you're lucky, you might spot **dolphins** or porpoises from the boat crossing to the island.

ARRIVAL AND DEPARTURE — INCHCOLM

Ferries to Inchcolm (April–Oct) are run by *Maid of the Forth* (ⓣ0131 331 4857, ⓦmaidoftheforth.co.uk; £14.70 including landing fee) and *Forth Belle* (ⓣ0870/118 1866, ⓦforthtours.com; £22.70 including bus from Edinburgh and landing fee).

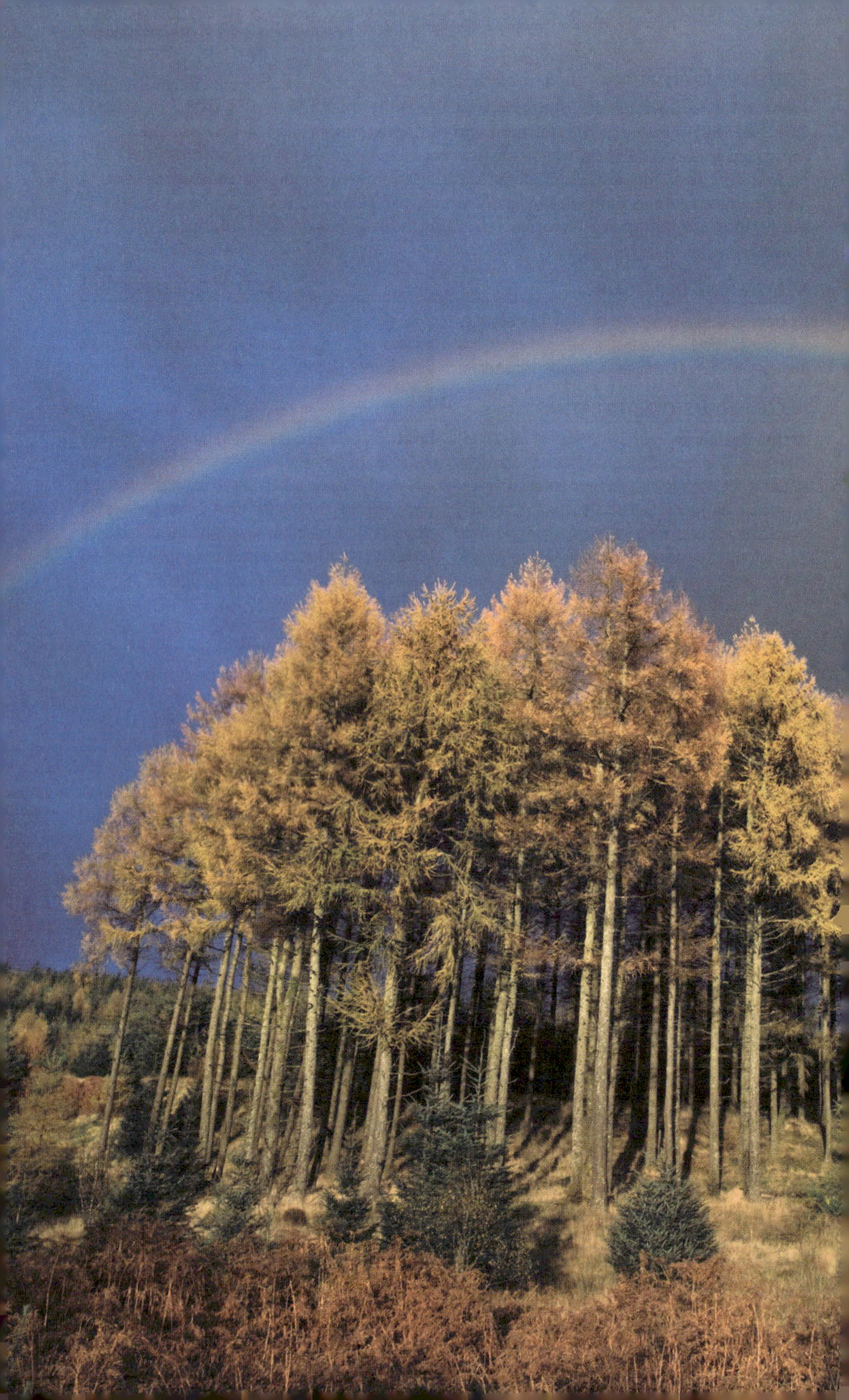

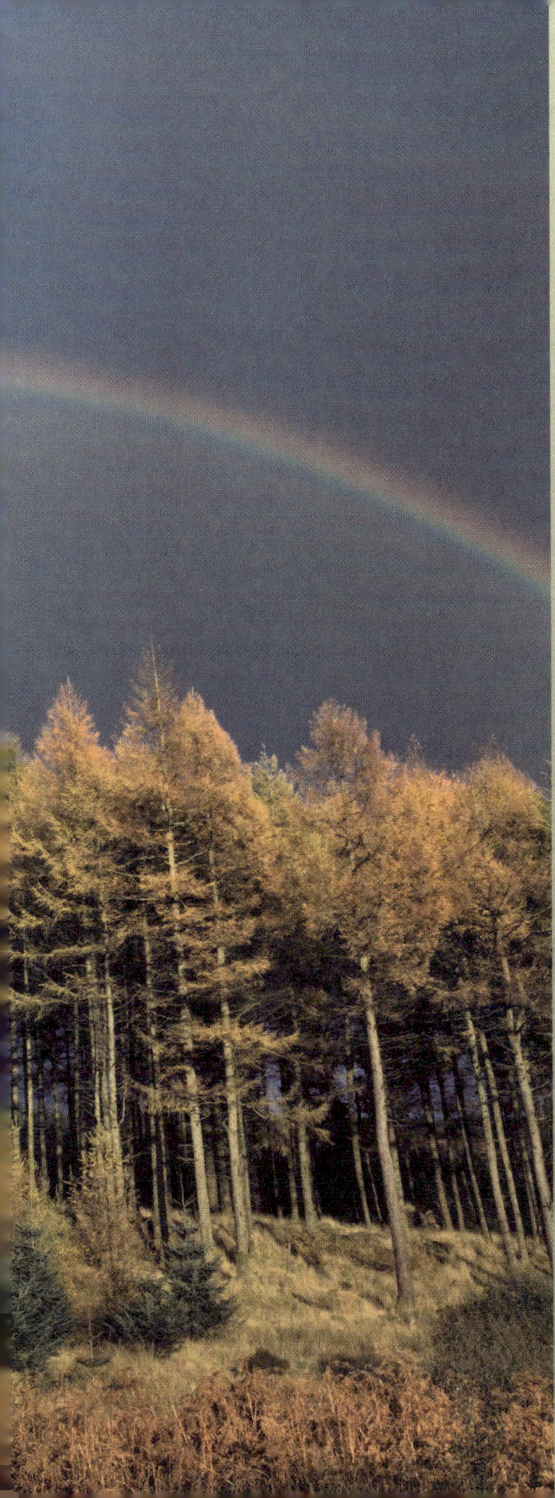

Southern Scotland

750 The Borders

759 Dumfries and Galloway

766 Ayrshire

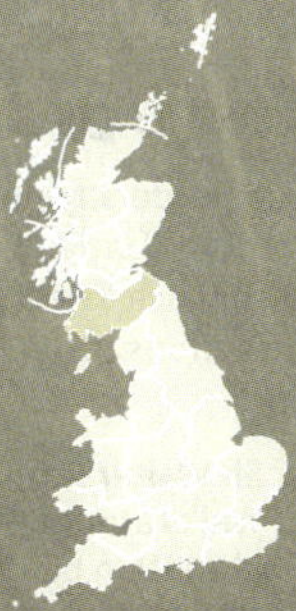

GALLOWAY FOREST PARK

Southern Scotland

18

Dominated by the Southern Uplands, a chain of bulging round-topped hills, Southern Scotland divides neatly into three regions: the Borders, Dumfries and Galloway, and Ayrshire. Although none of them has the highest of tourist profiles, those visitors who whizz past on their way north to Edinburgh, Glasgow or the Highlands are missing out on a huge swathe of Scotland that is in many ways the very heart of the country. Over the centuries, its inhabitants, particularly in the Borders, bore the brunt of long, brutal wars with the English, its farms have fed Scotland's cities since industrialization, and two of the country's greatest literary icons, Sir Walter Scott and Robbie Burns, lived and died here.

North of the inhospitable Cheviot Hills, which separate Scotland from England, the **Borders** region is dominated by the meanderings of the **River Tweed**. The towns here have provided inspiration for countless folkloric ballads telling of bloody battles with the English and clashes between the notorious warring families, the Border Reivers. The delightful small town of **Melrose** is the most obvious base, and has the most impressive of the four **Border abbeys** founded by the medieval Canmore kings, all of which are now reduced to romantic ruins.

Dumfries and Galloway, in the southwestern corner of Scotland, gets even more overlooked than the Borders. If you do make the effort to get off the main north–south highway to Glasgow, you'll find more ruined abbeys, medieval castles, forested hills and dramatic tidal flats and sea cliffs ideal for birdwatching. The key resort is the modest, charming town of **Kirkcudbright**, halfway along the Solway coast, indented by sandy coves.

Ayrshire is rich farming country, with fewer sights than its neighbours; almost everything of interest is confined to the coast. The **golf courses** along its gentle coastline are among the finest links courses in the country, while fans of **Robert Burns** could happily spend several days exploring the author's old haunts, especially at **Ayr**, the county town, and the nearby village of Alloway, the poet's birthplace.

GETTING AROUND **SOUTHERN SCOTLAND**

The Borders have limited **train** services, with a more comprehensive range in Dumfries and Galloway and a reasonable network in Ayrshire. **Buses** will get you practically everywhere mentioned in this chapter, although there is no link between the Borders and the rest of the region.

The Borders

The **Borders** region is sandwiched between the Cheviot Hills on the English border and the Pentland and Moorfoot ranges to the south of Edinburgh. The finest section of the lush **Tweed valley** lies between **Melrose** and **Peebles**, where you'll find a string of attractions, from Sir Walter Scott's eccentric mansion at **Abbotsford** to the ancient seat

Sir Walter Scott p.754
Walks around Peebles p.757
Mountain biking in Glentress p.758
On the Burns trail in Dumfries p.761
Galloway Forest Park p.764
Robert Burns p.768
Ailsa Craig p.769

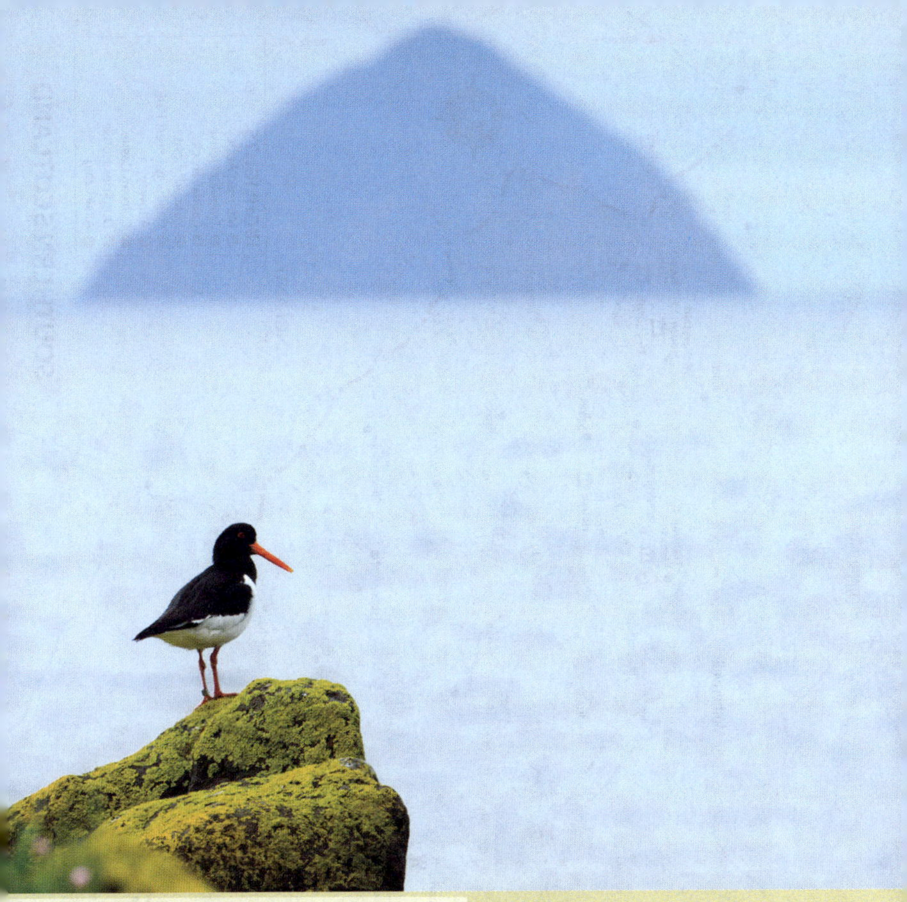

AILSA CRAIG

Highlights

❶ **Melrose Abbey** Border abbey with superbly preserved sculptural detail. **See p.753**

❷ **Traquair House** The oldest continuously inhabited house in Scotland, virtually unchanged since the fifteenth century. **See p.757**

❸ **Caerlaverock** One of Scotland's most photogenic moated castles, beside a superb site for waterfowl and waders. **See p.761**

❹ **Kirkcudbright** One-time artists' colony, and the best-looking town on the "Scottish Riviera". **See p.763**

❺ **Galloway Forest Park** Go mountain biking along remote forest tracks, or hiking on the Southern Upland Way. **See p.764**

❻ **Alloway** The village where poet Robert Burns was born, and the best of many Burns pilgrimage spots in the region. **See p.767**

❼ **Culzean Castle** Stately home with a fabulous cliff-edge setting, surrounded by acres of gardens and woods reaching down to the shore. **See p.768**

❽ **Dumfries House** An eighteenth-century architectural masterpiece, designed by the Adam brothers and decked out by Thomas Chippendale. **See p.769**

❾ **Ailsa Craig** Take a boat out to this volcanic lump and watch baby gannets learn the art of flying and diving for fish. **See p.769**

HIGHLIGHTS ARE MARKED ON THE MAP ON P.752

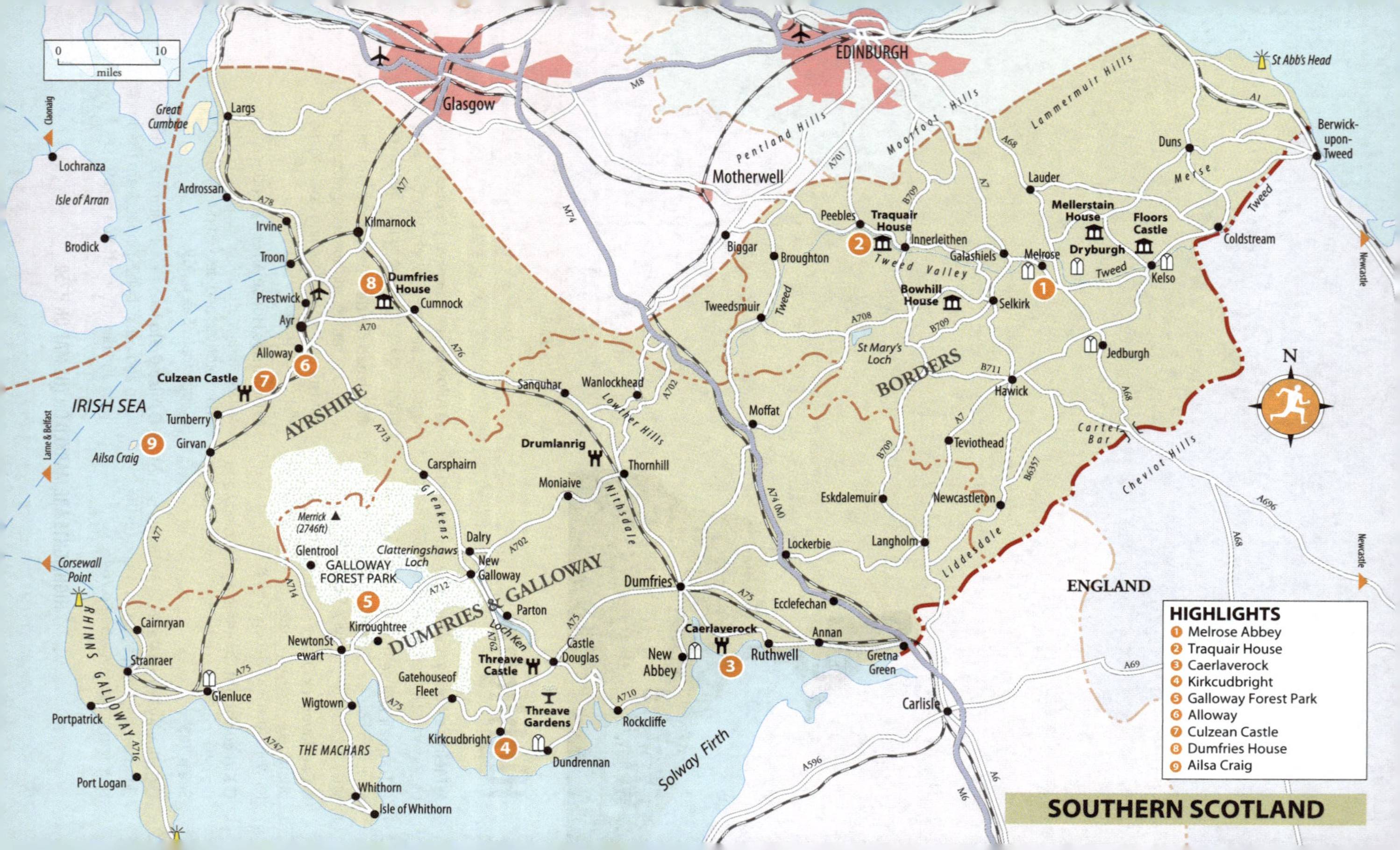
SOUTHERN SCOTLAND
HIGHLIGHTS
1 Melrose Abbey
2 Traquair House
3 Caerlaverock
4 Kirkcudbright
5 Galloway Forest Park
6 Alloway
7 Culzean Castle
8 Dumfries House
9 Ailsa Craig
Edinburgh
Glasgow
Motherwell
Borders
Ayrshire
Dumfries & Galloway
England
Irish Sea
Solway Firth
Galloway Forest Park
Rhinns Galloway
The Machars
Lammermuir Hills
Moorfoot Hills
Pentland Hills
Lowther Hills
Cheviot Hills
Tweed Valley
Merse
Nithsdale
Glenkens
Liddesdale
Carter Bar
Merrick (2746ft)
St Abb's Head
Berwick-upon-Tweed
Duns
Coldstream
Lauder
Mellerstain House
Floors Castle
Dryburgh
Kelso
Melrose
Galashiels
Innerleithen
Traquair House
Peebles
Selkirk
Bowhill House
Jedburgh
Hawick
Teviothead
Newcastleton
Langholm
Eskdalemuir
St Mary's Loch
Moffat
Tweedsmuir
Broughton
Biggar
Lockerbie
Ecclefechan
Annan
Gretna Green
Carlisle
Ruthwell
Caerlaverock
New Abbey
Dumfries
Rockcliffe
Dundrennan
Threave Gardens
Threave Castle
Castle Douglas
Parton
Loch Ken
Kirkcudbright
Gatehouse of Fleet
New Galloway
Dalry
Clatteringshaws Loch
Glentrool
Kirroughtree
Newton Stewart
Wigtown
Whithorn
Isle of Whithorn
Glenluce
Stranraer
Cairnryan
Portpatrick
Port Logan
Corsewall Point
Moniaive
Thornhill
Drumlanrig
Wanlockhead
Sanquhar
Carsphairn
Cumnock
Dumfries House
Kilmarnock
Ayr
Alloway
Prestwick
Troon
Irvine
Ardrossan
Largs
Great Cumbrae
Culzean Castle
Turnberry
Girvan
Ailsa Craig
Isle of Arran
Lochranza
Brodick
Claonaig
Larne & Belfast
Newcastle
Tweed
A1
A68
A7
A701
A702
A708
A709
B709
B711
B6357
A74 (M)
M74
M8
A77
A76
A70
A78
A713
A712
A714
A75
A762
A710
A747
A716
A69
A696
A6
A596
M6
0
10
miles

of **Traquair House**, along with the region's famous **abbeys**, founded in the reign of King David I (1124–53).

Melrose and around

Minuscule **MELROSE**, tucked in between the Tweed and the gorse-backed Eildon Hills, is the most beguiling of towns, its narrow streets trimmed by a harmonious ensemble of styles, from pretty little cottages and tweedy shops to high-standing Georgian and Victorian facades. Its chief draw is its ruined **abbey**, but it's also well positioned for exploring the Tweed Valley, with the Scott-related attractions of **Abbotsford** and **Dryburgh** nearby.

Melrose Abbey

Abbey St • Daily: April–Sept 9.30am–5.30pm; Oct–March 9.30am–4.30pm • HS • £5.50 • ⓣ 01896 822562

The pink- and red-tinted stone ruins of **Melrose Abbey** soar above their riverside surroundings. Founded in 1136, Melrose was the first Cistercian settlement in Scotland and grew rich selling wool and hides to Flanders. The English repeatedly razed the abbey, most viciously in 1385 and 1545, and most of the remains date from the intervening period. The site is dominated by the **Abbey Church**, which has lost its west front, and whose nave is reduced to the elegant window arches and chapels of the south aisle. Amazingly, however, the stone **pulpitum** (screen), separating the choir monks from their lay brothers, is preserved. Beyond, the **presbytery** has its magnificent perpendicular window, lierne vaulting and ceiling bosses intact, with the capitals of the surrounding columns sporting the most intricate of curly kale carving. In the **south transept**, another fine fifteenth-century window sprouts yet more delicate, foliate tracery and the adjacent cornice is enlivened by weathered angels playing musical instruments. Look out, too, for the Coronation of the Virgin on the east end gable, and the numerous mischievous **gargoyles**, such as the pig playing the bagpipes on the roof on the south side of the nave. The sculptural detailing at Melrose is easy to miss if you don't know where to look, so using the free audioguide, or buying yourself a guidebook, is a good idea.

Abbotsford

Three miles up the Tweed from Melrose • Mid-March to May Mon–Sat 9.30am–5pm, Sun 11am–4pm; June–Sept daily 9.30am–5pm • £7 • ⓣ 01896/752043, ⓦ scottsabbotsford.co.uk • The fast, frequent Melrose–Galashiels bus provides easy access to Abbotsford: ask for the Tweedbank island on the A6091, from where the house is a 10min walk

Abbotsford was designed to satisfy the Romantic inclinations of **Sir Walter Scott**, who lived here from 1812 until his death. The building took twelve years to evolve, with the fanciful turrets and castellations of the Scots Baronial exterior incorporating copies of medieval originals. Despite all the exterior pomp, the interior is surprisingly small and poky, with just six rooms open for viewing on the upper floor. Visitors start in the wood-panelled study, with its small writing desk made of salvage from the Spanish Armada, at which Scott banged out the Waverley novels at a furious rate. The wood-panelled library boasts his extraordinary assortment of memorabilia, including Napoleon's pen case and blotting book, Rob Roy's purse and *skene dhu* (knife), and the inlaid pearl crucifix that accompanied Mary, Queen of Scots, to the scaffold. Henry Raeburn's famous portrait of Scott hangs in the drawing room.

Dryburgh Abbey

Three miles southeast of Melrose • April–Sept daily 9.30am–5.30pm; Oct–Easter daily 9.30am–4.30pm • HS • £4 • ⓣ 01835 822381 • Dryburgh is not easy to reach by public transport, though it's just a mile's walk north of St Boswell's on the A68, and a pleasant 3 or 4 miles from Melrose. Drivers and cyclists should approach via Scott's View

Hidden away in a U-bend in the Tweed, the remains of **Dryburgh Abbey** occupy an idyllic position against a hilly backdrop. Founded in the twelfth century by the

18

SIR WALTER SCOTT

As a child, **Walter Scott** (1771–1832), disabled by polio, was sent to recuperate at his grandfather's farm in Smailholm, where his imagination was fuelled by his relative's tales of the old, violent troubles in the Borders. Throughout the 1790s he transcribed hundreds of old Border ballads, publishing a three-volume collection entitled *Minstrelsy of the Scottish Borders* in 1802. An instant success, *Minstrelsy* was followed by Scott's own *Lay of the Last Minstrel*, a narrative poem whose strong story and rose-tinted regionalism proved very popular. More **poetry** was to come, most successfully *Marmion* (1808) and *The Lady of the Lake* (1810).

However, despite having two paid jobs, his finances remained shaky. He had become a partner in a printing firm, which put him into debt, not helped by the enormous sums he spent on his mansion, Abbotsford. From 1813, writing to pay the bills, Scott thumped out a flood of historical novels, producing his best work within the space of ten years: *Waverley* (1814), *The Antiquary* (1816), *Rob Roy* and *The Heart of Midlothian* (both 1818), as well as two notable novels set in England, *Ivanhoe* (1819) and *Kenilworth* (1821).

In 1825 Scott's money problems reached crisis proportions after an economic crash bankrupted his printing business. Attempting to pay his creditors in full, he found the quality of his writing deteriorating with its increased speed. His last years were plagued by illness; in 1832 he died at Abbotsford and was buried within the ruins of Dryburgh Abbey.

Premonstratensians, virtually nothing survives of the nave of the **Abbey Church**, though the transepts have fared better, their chapels now serving as private burial grounds for, among others, Sir Walter Scott and Field Marshal Haig, the infamous World War I commander. The night stairs, down which the monks stumbled in the early hours of the morning, survive in the south transept, and lead even today to the monks' dormitory. Leaving the church via the east processional door in the south aisle, with its dog-tooth decoration, you enter the cloisters, the highlight of which is the barrel-vaulted **Chapter House**, complete with low stone benches and blind interlaced arcading.

ARRIVAL AND INFORMATION — MELROSE

By bus Buses stop in Market Square, from where it's a brief walk north to the abbey ruins.

Destinations Edinburgh (hourly; 2hr 15min); Jedburgh (Mon–Sat every 30min–1hr, 7 on Sun; 30min); Kelso (Mon–Sat 8–12 daily, 4 on Sun; 30min); Peebles (Mon–Sat hourly, 6 on Sun; 1hr 10min); Selkirk (Mon–Sat hourly, 2 on Sun; 20min).

Tourist office Opposite the abbey (April–Oct daily 9am–5pm; Nov–March Fri & Sat 10am–5pm; ⓣ01896 822283).

ACCOMMODATION

Gibson Caravan Park High St ⓣ01896 822969. A level, peaceful and immaculately run site (which welcomes tent campers) conveniently situated right in the centre opposite the Greenyards rugby grounds. Closed mid-Sept to mid-May. **£17.30**

★ **Old Bank House** 27 Buccleuch St ⓣ01896 823712, ⓦoldbankhousemelrose.co.uk. Solid Victorian town-house with charming hosts and three attractive, pristinely maintained en-suite rooms (two twins and a double). **£65**

SYHA hostel Priorwood ⓣ01896 822521, ⓦsyha.org.uk. Housed in a sprawling Georgian mansion with plenty of character, with good kitchen facilities and a lovely dining room overlooking the garden. April–Oct. **£17**

The Townhouse Market Square ⓣ01896 822645, ⓦthetownhousemelrose.co.uk. Small, smart hotel on the main square, with eleven stylishly renovated en-suite doubles, with contemporary furnishings, flatscreen TVs and an excellent brasserie plus a more formal restaurant. **£125**

EATING AND DRINKING

Marmion's Brasserie Buccleuch St ⓣ01896 822245, ⓦmarmionsbrasserie.co.uk. Pleasant brasserie that serves up everything from breakfast and simple lunches to three-course dinners. The menu is strong on classics such as beef stroganoff, venison steak and chicken supreme (mains £12–20). Daily 9am–9pm.

Russell's Market Square ⓣ01896 822335. For a light lunch or tea and cakes, join the locals in this small, popular, traditional tearoom. Tues–Thurs 9.30am–4.30pm, Fri & Sat 9.30am–5pm, Sun noon–5pm.

NIGHTLIFE AND ENTERTAINMENT

Ship Inn East Port ⓣ01896 822190. The liveliest pub town, especially during the Folk Festival and on Saturday afternoons when the Melrose rugby team have played at home. Mon–Wed 11am–11pm, Thurs 11am–midnight, Fri 11am–1am, Sat 11am–midnight, Sun 12.30–11pm.

The Wynd ⓣ01896 820028, ⓦthewynd.com. Melrose's pint-sized theatre, tucked away down an alleyway north of the main square, hosts films and gigs as well as drama.

Kelso and around

KELSO, ten miles or so downstream from Melrose, grew up in the shadow of its now-ruined Benedictine **abbey**, once the richest and most powerful of the Border abbeys. Sadly, very little survives today, although at first sight, it looks pretty impressive, with the heavy Norman west end of the abbey church almost entirely intact at the end of Abbey Row. Beyond, little remains, though it is possible to make out the two transepts and towers that gave the abbey the shape of a double cross, unique in Scotland.

Kelso town is centred on **The Square**, a large cobbled expanse presided over by the honey-hued Ionic columns, pediment and oversized clock bell tower of the elegant **Town Hall.** Leaving the Square along Roxburgh Street, take the alley down to the **Cobby Riverside Walk**, where a brief stroll leads to Floors Castle. En route, but hidden from view by the islet in the middle of the river, is the spot where the Teviot meets the Tweed. This bit of river, known as The Junction, has long been famous for its **salmon fishing**, with permits – costing thousands – booked years in advance.

Floors Castle

A mile northwest of Kelso • Easter–Oct daily guided tours 11am–5pm • £8, grounds & garden only £4.50 • ⓣ 01573 223333, ⓦroxburghe.net

If you stand on Kelso's handsome bridge over the Tweed, you can easily make out the pepperpot turrets and castellations of **Floors Castle**, a vast, pompous mansion to the northwest. The bulk of the building was designed by William Adam in the 1720s, and, picking through the Victorian modifications, the interior still demonstrates his uncluttered style. However, you won't see that much of it, as Floors is still privately owned and just ten rooms and a basement are open to the public. Highlights include paintings by Matisse, Augustus John and Odilon Redon, and some fine Brussels and Gobelin tapestries. There's an above-average café, and you can wander down to the Tweed and see the spot where James II was killed in 1460.

Mellerstain House

Six miles northwest of Kelso off the A6089 • Guided tours 12.30–5pm: Easter, May, June & Sept Wed & Sun; July & Aug Mon, Wed, Thurs & Sun; Oct Sun only • £8.50, gardens only £4 • ⓣ01573 410225, ⓦmellerstain.com

Mellerstain House represents the very best of the Adam brothers' work – William designed the wings in 1725, and his son Robert the castellated centre fifty years later. Robert's love of columns, roundels and friezes culminates in a stunning sequence of plaster-moulded, pastel-shaded ceilings: the **library** is the high-point of the tour for admirers of his work, with four unusual long panels in plaster relief of classical scenes that relegate the books to second place. The art collection, which includes works by Constable, Gainsborough, Ramsay and Veronese, is also noteworthy. After a visit you can wander the formal Edwardian gardens, which slope down to the lake.

ARRIVAL AND INFORMATION — **KELSO**

By bus Kelso bus station, on Roxburgh St, is a brief walk from The Square.

Destinations Edinburgh (4–6 daily; 2hr); Melrose (Mon–Sat 8–12 daily, 4 on Sun; 30min).

Tourist office Town Hall, The Square (April–Nov Mon–Sat 10am–5pm, Sun 10am–2pm; Jan–March Mon, Fri & Sat 10am–2pm; ⓣ01573 223464).

ACCOMMODATION AND EATING

Cobbles Inn 7 Bowmont St 01573 223548, thecobblesinn.co.uk. Restaurant and bar housed in a former pub just north of The Square – pub grub includes burgers and fish and chips for around £10, while the restaurant offers more elaborate two- and three-course menus featuring venison and duck from £20. Tues–Thurs 11.30am–3.30pm & 5–10pm, Fri & Sat 11.30am–late, Sun noon–10pm.

★ **The Old Priory** Woodmarket 01573 223030, theoldpriorykelso.com. A tasteful Georgian townhouse, just off The Square, with a very pretty garden. Rooms are spacious and light, with lovely wooden furniture. £75

Selkirk and around

Just five miles southwest of Melrose lies the royal burgh of **SELKIRK**. The old town sits high up above the river of Ettrick Water; down by the riverside, the imposing grey-stone woollen mills are mostly boarded up now, an eerie reminder of a once prosperous era. Situated on the edge of some lovely countryside, the town serves as the gateway to the picturesque, sparsely populated valleys to the west.

At the centre of Selkirk you'll find the tiny **Market Square**, overlooked by a statue of Sir Walter Scott; the former Town House, now dubbed **Sir Walter Scott's Courtroom** (April–Sept Mon–Fri 10am–4pm, Sat 11am–3pm; Oct Mon–Sat noon–3pm; free), is where he served as sheriff for 33 years. Just off Market Square to the south is **Halliwell's House Museum** (April–Oct Mon–Sat 11am–4pm, Sun noon–3pm; free), an old-style hardware shop with an informative exhibit on the industrialization of the Tweed valley.

Bowhill

Three miles west of Selkirk off the A708 • **House** July & Aug guided tours daily 11.30am–4.30pm • £8 **Country Estate** Easter daily 11am–4pm; April–June Sat & Sun 11am–4pm; July & Aug daily 10am–5pm • £3.50 • 01750 22204, bowhill.org • Walk (1hr) from Selkirk along the north bank of Ettrick Water and cross over General's Bridge and into the estate, or take a taxi from Selkirk (£8)

A pleasant three-mile walk from Selkirk, **Bowhill House** is the property of the seriously wealthy Duke of Buccleuch. Beyond the grandiose mid-nineteenth-century mansion's facade of dark whinstone is an outstanding collection of French antiques and European **paintings**: in the dining room, for example, there are portraits by Reynolds and Gainsborough, and a Canaletto cityscape, while the drawing room features Boulle furniture, Meissen tableware, paintings by Ruysdael, Leandro Bassano and Claude Lorraine, as well as two more family portraits by Reynolds. Look out also for the Scott Room, which features a splendid portrait of Sir Walter by Henry Raeburn, and the Duke of Monmouth's execution shirt.

The wooded hills of Bowhill's **Country Estate** are crisscrossed by scenic footpaths and cycle trails. The woods also shelter a 72-seat **Bowhill Theatre**, in the house's former game larder, which hosts the occasional production.

ARRIVAL AND INFORMATION — SELKIRK

By bus Regular buses arrive in the Market Square from Edinburgh (hourly; 1hr 40min) and Melrose (Mon–Sat hourly, 2 on Sun; 20min).

Tourist office Halliwell's House, off Market Square (April–Oct Mon–Sat 11am–4pm, Sun noon–3pm; 01750 20054).

ACCOMMODATION

Glen Hotel Yarrow Terrace 01750 20259, glenhotel.co.uk. An imposing hunting, shooting and fishing Victorian pile near the bridge, with nine clean rooms – including two family rooms and a four-poster – and friendly staff. £90

Heatherlie House Hotel Heatherlie Park 01750 721200, heatherliehouse.co.uk. A large Victorian mansion set in its own wooded grounds, a sharp left turn up from the road to Ettrick at Heatherlie Park. All but one of the seven rooms are en suite. £74

Peebles and around

Fast, wide, tree-lined and fringed with grassy banks, the Tweed looks at its best at **PEEBLES**, a handsome royal burgh that sits on the north bank, fifteen miles northwest of Selkirk. The town itself has a genteel, relaxed air, its wide, handsome High Street bordered by houses in a medley of architectural styles, mostly dating from Victorian times, and ending in the soaring crown spire of the **Old Parish Church** (daily 10am–4pm; free) at the western end.

Tweedale Museum & Gallery

High St • Mon–Fri 10.30am–12.30pm & 1–4pm, Sat 9.30am–12.30pm • Free • T 01721 724820

Halfway down the High Street is the **Tweedale Museum & Gallery**, stuffed with casts of the world's most famous sculptures. Although most were lost long ago, today's "Secret Room" has two handsome friezes: one a copy of the Elgin marbles taken from the Parthenon; the other of the **Triumph of Alexander**, originally cast in 1812 to honour Napoleon.

Traquair House

Six miles east of Peebles, a mile or so south of the A72 • Daily: April, May & Sept 11am–5pm; June–Aug 10.30am–5pm; Oct 11am–4pm; Nov Sat & Sun 11am–3pm • £7.60, grounds only £4 • T 01896 830323, W traquair.co.uk

The Maxwell Stuarts have lived in **Traquair House** since 1491, making it the oldest continuously inhabited house in Scotland. The whitewashed facade is strikingly handsome, with narrow windows and trim turrets surrounding the tiniest of front doors – in other words it's a welcome change from other grandiose stately homes. Inside, you can see original vaulted cellars, where locals once hid their cattle from raiders; the twisting main staircase as well as the earlier medieval version, later a secret escape route for persecuted Catholics; a carefully camouflaged priest's hole; and even a **priest's room** where a string of resident chaplains lived in hiding. In the **museum room** there is a wealth of treasures, including a fine example of a Jacobite Amen glass, a rosary and crucifix owned by Mary, Queen of Scots, and the cloak worn by the Earl of Nithsdale during his dramatic escape from the Tower of London.

Spare time for the surrounding **gardens**, where you'll find a **hedge maze**, several craft workshops and the **Traquair House Brewery**, the only British brewery that still ferments totally in oak. There's a café serving snacks in an estate cottage on the redundant avenue that leads to the locked **Bear Gates**; Bonnie Prince Charlie left the house through these gates, and the then-owner promised to keep them locked till a Stuart should ascend the throne.

ARRIVAL AND INFORMATION — PEEBLES

By bus Buses, including services from Edinburgh (hourly; 1hr) stop outside Peebles' post office, a few doors down from the tourist office.

Tourist office 23 High St (Jan–March Mon–Sat 9.30am–4pm; April–Dec Mon–Sat 9am–5pm, Sun 11am–4pm; T 01721 723159).

ACCOMMODATION

Rowanbrae Northgate T 01721 721630, E john@rowanbrae.freeserve.co.uk. A trim, semi-detached Victorian place with a lovely garden, on a quiet cul-de-sac off the east end of High St. £60

Traquair House Six miles east of Peebles, south of the A72 T 01896 830323, W traquair.co.uk. You can stay here in one of three spacious B&B rooms decked out with antiques and canopied beds. Breakfast is served in a

WALKS AROUND PEEBLES

Of the various walks through the hills surrounding Peebles, the five-mile **Sware Trail** is one of the easiest and most scenic, weaving west along the north bank of the river and looping back to the south. On the way, it passes **Neidpath Castle**, a gaunt medieval tower-house perched high above the river on a rocky bluff. The walk also goes by the splendid skew rail bridge, part of the defunct Glasgow line.

MOUNTAIN BIKING IN GLENTRESS

One of seven forest biking centres in southern Scotland – known collectively as the 7 Stanes (7stanes.gov.uk) – **Glentress Forest**, two miles east of Peebles on the A72, has some of the best mountain biking in Scotland. There are five superb, carefully crafted purpose-built trails, colour-coded for difficulty, and a fantastic bike hire centre,The Hub (01721 72136, thehubintheforest.co.uk).

suitably grand manner. **£180**

Winkston Farmhouse Edinburgh Rd 01721 721264, winkstonholidays.co.uk. Grand Georgian country house a mile and a half north of Peebles – rooms are spacious and smart, with pine furniture and wi-fi. **£70**

EATING AND DRINKING

Osso Innerleithen Rd 01721 724477, ossorestaurant.com. Sandwiches, tapas, meze and comfort food for under £10 for lunch, and a more imaginative evening menu featuring dishes like braised hare leg or coley, mussel and spelt risotto. Mon–Wed 10am–4.30pm, Thurs–Sat 10am–4.30pm & 6–9pm, Sun 11am–4.30pm.

The Sunflower 4 Bridgegate 01721 722420, sunflowerrestaurant.co.uk. A tiny, colourful restaurant, just off Northgate, which does everything from adventurous bruschetta and sandwiches to wild boar burger and lentil bake. Mon–Wed 10am–3pm, Thurs–Sat 10am–3pm & 6–9pm.

Jedburgh

Ten miles south of Melrose, **JEDBURGH** (jedburgh.org.uk) nestles in the lush valley of the Jed Water. During the interminable Anglo-Scottish Wars, this was the quintessential frontier town, a heavily garrisoned royal burgh incorporating a mighty castle and abbey. Though the castle was destroyed by the Scots in 1409 to keep it out of the hands of the English, the abbey survived, albeit in ruins. Today, Jedburgh is the first place of any size that you come to on the A68, having crossed over Carter Bar from England, and as such gets quite a bit of passing tourist trade.

Jedburgh Abbey

Daily: April–Sept 9.30am–5.30pm; Oct–March 9.30am–4.30pm • HS • £5.50 • 01835 863925

Founded in the twelfth century as an Augustinian priory, **Jedburgh Abbey** is the best preserved of all the Border abbeys, its vast church towering over a sloping site right in the centre of town, beside the Jed Water. Entry is through the **visitor centre** at the bottom of the hill, where you can view Jedburgh's most treasured archeological find, the **Jedburgh Comb**, carved around 1100 from walrus ivory and decorated with a griffin and a dragon. Enter the **Abbey Church** itself via the west door to appreciate fully the three-storey nave's perfectly proportioned parade of columns and arches.

Jedburgh Castle Jail

Castlegate • Easter–Oct Mon–Sat 10am–4.30pm, Sun 1–4pm • £2 • 01835 864750

At the top of Castlegate stands **Jedburgh Castle Jail**, an impressive castellated nineteenth-century pile built on the site of the old royal castle. As well as detailed information about Jedburgh's history, there's a fascinating insight into conditions in jail, deportation, crime and punishment. The cells themselves are, for the period, remarkably comfortable, reflecting the influence of reformer John Howard.

Mary, Queen of Scots' House

Queen St • March–Nov Mon–Sat 10am–4.30pm, Sun 11am–4pm • £3 • 01835 863331

At the Market Place, signs will guide you to **Mary, Queen of Scots' House**. Despite the name, it seems unlikely that Mary ever actually stayed in this particular sixteenth-century home, though she did visit the town in 1566. The highlights are a copy of Mary's death mask and one of the few surviving portraits of the Earl of Bothwell.

ARRIVAL AND INFORMATION — JEDBURGH

By bus Buses pick up and drop off at Canongate just east of the Market Place.

Destinations Edinburgh (Mon–Fri hourly, 9 on Sat, 5 on Sun; 1hr 40min); Kelso (Mon–Sat 8–12 daily; 30min); Melrose (Mon–Sat every 30min–1hr, 7 on Sun; 30min).

Tourist office Murray's Green (April–Oct daily 10am–5pm; Nov–March Mon–Sat 10am–5pm; T 01835 863170).

ACCOMMODATION AND EATING

There's a shortage of good eating places in Jedburgh, but do make sure to try the local speciality, **Jethart Snails**, sticky boiled sweets invented by a French POW in the 1700s and on sale everywhere.

18

Jedwater Caravan Park Five miles south of town on the A68 T 01835 840219, W jedwater.co.uk. The cheaper and more secluded of two campsites nearby, with a pleasant riverside site. Closed Nov–Feb. **£13–18**

Meadhon House 48 Castlegate T 01835 862504, W meadhon.com. Pronounced "mawn", this is the finest of several B&Bs among Castlegate's old houses, with a conservatory overlooking a pretty sloping garden. **£56**

Simply Scottish 6–8 High St T 01835 864696, W simplyscottish.co.uk. A smart but relaxed bistro-style café/restaurant serving the usual snacks at lunchtime, such as baked potatoes and sandwiches, and dishes such as pork tenderloin or rainbow trout in the evening. Mon–Thurs 10am–5.30pm, Fri & Sat 10am–8pm, Sun 11am–8pm.

Willow Court The Friars T 01835 863702, W willowcourtjedburgh.co.uk. The attention to detail and the luxuries – Egyptian cotton bed linen, flatscreen TVs – put this a cut above most of Jedburgh's B&Bs. **£75**

Dumfries and Galloway

The southwest corner of Scotland, **Dumfries and Galloway**, has stately homes, deserted hills and ruined abbeys to compete with the best of the Borders. It also has the **Solway coast**, a long, indented coastline of sheltered sandy coves that's been dubbed the "Scottish Riviera" – it's certainly Scotland's warmest, southernmost stretch of coastline.

Dumfries is the largest town in the region, and only really a must for those on the trail of **Robert Burns**. Further west is enticing **Kirkcudbright**, once a bustling port thronged with sailing ships, later an artists' retreat, and now a tranquil, well-preserved little town. Contrasting with the essentially gentle landscape of the Solway coast is the brooding presence of the **Galloway Hills** to the north, their beautiful moors, mountains, lakes and rivers centred on the **Galloway Forest Park**, a hillwalking and mountain-biking paradise.

Dumfries

On the wide banks of the River Nith a short way inland from the Solway Firth, **DUMFRIES** is the largest town in southwest Scotland. Long known as the "Queen of the South" (as is its football club), the town flourished as a medieval seaport and trading centre. Enough remains of the original, warm red sandstone buildings to distinguish Dumfries from other towns in the southwest, though its main appeal is its associations with **Robert Burns**.

Dumfries Museum

Rotchell Rd • April–Sept Mon–Sat 10am–5pm, Sun 2–5pm; Oct–March Tues–Sat 10am–1pm & 2–5pm • Free, camera obscura £2.30 • T 01387 253374

On the hill above the Robert Burns Centre stands the **Dumfries Museum**, from where there are great views over the town. The museum is housed partly in an eighteenth-century windmill, which was converted into the town's observatory in the 1830s, and features a **camera obscura** on its top floor.

Old Bridge House Museum

Mill Rd • April–Sept Mon–Sat 10am–5pm, Sun 2–5pm • Free • T 01387 256904

A little upstream from the RBC is the pedestrian **Devorgilla Bridge**, built in 1431 and one of the oldest bridges in Scotland. Attached to its southwestern end is the town's

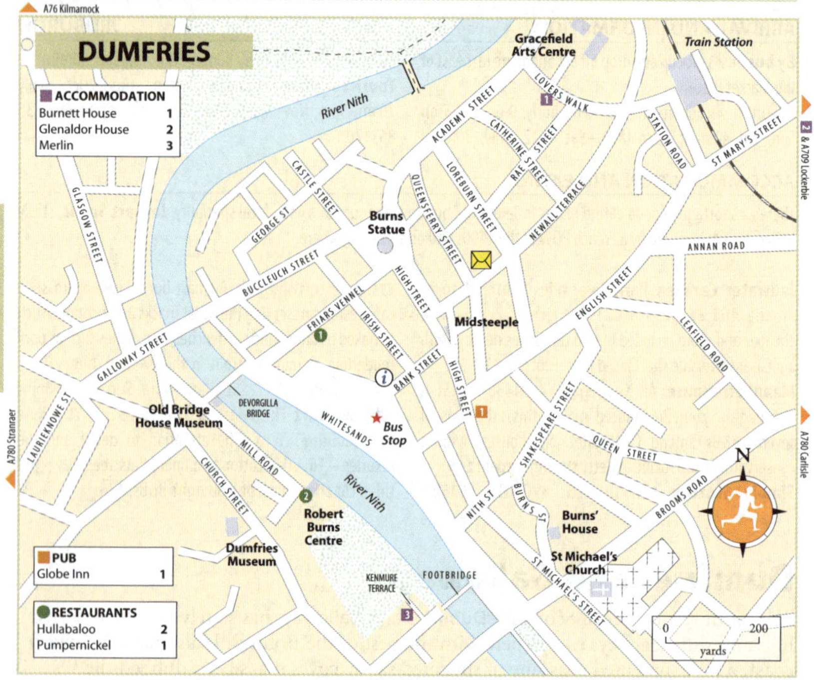

oldest house, built in 1660, now home to the tiny, quirky **Old Bridge House Museum**, stuffed full of Victorian bric-a-brac, including a teeth-chattering range of dental gear; the house was once an inn, which Burns would undoubtedly have visited.

ARRIVAL AND INFORMATION — DUMFRIES

By train The station is a 5min walk east of the town centre.
Destinations Carlisle (Mon–Sat 14 daily, 5 on Sun; 40min); Glasgow Central (Mon–Sat 8 daily, 2 on Sun; 1hr 50min); Stranraer (Mon–Sat 2 daily; 3hr).

By bus Buses stop at Whitesands beside the River Nith.
Destinations Ayr (Mon–Sat every 2hr; 2hr 10min); Caerlaverock (Mon–Sat every 2hr, 2 on Sun; 30min); Carlisle (Mon–Sat hourly, Sun every 2hr; 1hr 35min); Castle Douglas (Mon–Sat hourly, Sun every 2hr; 45min); Edinburgh (Mon–Sat 4 daily, 2 on Sun; 2hr 40min); Kirkcudbright (Mon–Sat hourly, 6 on Sun; 1hr 10min); New Abbey (Mon–Sat hourly, 4 on Sun; 15min); Newton Stewart (Mon–Sat every 2hr, 2 on Sun; 1hr 30min); Rockcliffe (5 daily; 1hr); Stranraer (Mon–Sat every 2hr, 2 on Sun; 2hr 10min).

Tourist office 64 Whitesands (Mon–Sat 9am–5.30pm; June–Sept also Sun 10am–3.30pm; T 01387 245550).

Bike rental Bikes are useful for reaching the nearby Solway coast; head for Grierson and Graham, 10 Academy St (T 01387 259483).

ACCOMMODATION

Burnett House 4 Lovers Walk T 01387 263164, W burnetthouse.co.uk. For value and convenience, you can't beat this very smartly maintained Victorian B&B near the station; cyclists are welcome. £27.50

Glenaldor House 5 Victoria Terrace T 01387 264248, W glenaldorhouse.co.uk. A light and bright Victorian house near the station with four en-suite bedrooms and bountiful breakfasts. £56

Merlin 2 Kenmure Terrace T 01387 261002. Terrace B&B in a distinctive setting, overlooking the suspension bridge over the Nith near the RBC. £52

EATING AND DRINKING

Globe Inn 56 High St T 01387 252335, W globeinndumfries.co.uk. This howff has a bit more atmosphere than other pubs in town. Its oak-panelled rooms, crammed with Burns memorabilia – he was a regular – have

ON THE BURNS TRAIL IN DUMFRIES

Burns' House Burns St ⓣ01387 255297. Simple sandstone building where the poet died of rheumatic heart disease in 1796, a few days before the birth of his last son, Maxwell. Inside, one of the bedroom windows bears his signature, scratched with his diamond ring. Free. April–Sept Mon–Sat 10am–5pm, Sun 2–5pm; Oct–March Tues–Sat 10am–1pm & 2–5pm.

Burns Statue Northern end of High St. Presiding over a roundabout, this sentimental piece of Victorian frippery in white Carrara marble features the great man holding a posy. His faithful hound, Luath, lies curled around his feet.

Midsteeple High St. Burns' body lay in state here, in Dumfries' most singular building, a wonky hotchpotch of a place built in 1707 to fulfil the multiple functions of prison, clocktower, courthouse and arsenal.

Robert Burns Centre (**RBC**) Mill Rd ⓣ01387 264808. A free exhibition on the poet's years in Dumfries plus an optional 20min slide show (£2). April–Sept Mon–Sat 10am–5pm, Sun 2–5pm; Oct–March Tues–Sat 10am–1pm & 2–5pm.

St Michael's Church 39 Cardoness St ⓦstmichaelschurchdumfries.org. Originally buried in a simple grave near St Michael's Church, in 1815 Burns was dug up and moved across the graveyard to a purpose-built mausoleum, a Neoclassical eyesore which houses a statue of him being accosted by the Poetic Muse. Mon–Fri 10am–4pm.

18

changed little since his time. Mon–Wed 10am–11pm, Thurs–Sun 10am–midnight.

Hullabaloo RBC, Mill Rd ⓣ01387 259679, ⓦhullabaloorestaurant.co.uk. A cosy restaurant on the top floor of the RBC, with a summer terrace overlooking the river. Wraps, bagels and ciabatta sandwiches are on offer for lunch, with more adventurous global dishes (mains from £10) for dinner. Easter–Sept Mon 11am–4pm, Tues–Sat 11am–4pm & 6–11pm, Sun 11am–3pm; Oct–Easter closed Sun.

Pumpernickel 60–62 Friars Vennel ⓣ01387 254475, ⓦpumpernickelcatering.co.uk. Simple place offering haggis and cheese toasties, lunch specials, and home-baked cakes. Closed Sun.

Around Dumfries

Notable sights around Dumfries include grand **Drumlanrig Castle** with its fine paintings, moated **Caerlaverock**, and the picturesque ruins of thirteenth-century **Sweetheart Abbey**; the **Caerlaverock Wetland Centre** is a good destination for twitchers.

Drumlanrig Castle

Seventeen miles north of Dumfries • **Castle** Mid-March to Aug daily 11am–5pm • £9 **Country park** April–Sept daily 11am–5pm • £5 • ⓣ01848 331555, ⓦdrumlanrig.co.uk

Drumlanrig Castle is not a castle at all, but the grandiose stately home of the Duke of Buccleuch and Queensberry. The highlights of the richly furnished interior are the **paintings**, in particular, Rembrandt's *Old Woman Reading* and Hans Holbein's formal portrait of Sir Nicholas Carew. As well as the house, Drumlanrig offers a host of other attractions, including formal **gardens** and a forested **country park**. The old stableyard beside the castle contains a visitor centre, a few shops, the inevitable tearoom, and also a useful **bike rental** outlet – the park is crisscrossed by footpaths and cycle routes. If you're heading here by bus from Dumfries or Ayr, bear in mind it's a 1.5-mile walk from the road to the house.

Caerlaverock Castle

Eight miles southeast of Dumfries • Daily: April–Sept 9.30am–5.30pm; Oct–March 9.30am–4.30pm • HS • £5.50 • ⓣ01387 770244 • Buses from Dumfries run to Caerlaverock along the B725

Caerlaverock Castle is a picture-perfect ruined castle, moated, built from rich local red sandstone, triangular in shape and with a mighty double-towered gatehouse. The most surprising addition, however, lies inside, where you're confronted by the ornate Renaissance facade of the **Nithsdale Lodging**, erected in the 1630s by the first earl of Nithsdale. The decorated tympana above the windows feature lively mythological and heraldic scenes. Sadly, six years later Nithsdale and his garrison were forced to surrender after a thirteen-week siege and bombardment by the Covenanters, who wrecked the place. It was never inhabited again.

Caerlaverock Wildfowl and Wetlands Trust

Eastpark • Daily 10am–5pm • £5.50 • 01387 770200, wwt.org.uk • Some buses from Dumfries to Caerlaverock stop at the start of the two-mile lane leading off the B725 to the centre

18

Three miles east of Caerlaverock Castle is the **Caerlaverock Wildfowl and Wetlands Trust (WWT) Centre**, 1400 acres of protected salt marsh and mud flat edging the Solway Firth. Famous for the 25,000 or so Svalbard barnacle geese that winter here between September and April, it also has wild whooper swans and offers free wildlife safaris; call for details.

ACCOMMODATION — CAERLAVEROCK

WWT Caerlaverock Wetland Centre Eastpark Farm, Caerlaverock 01387 770200, pam.mundy@wwt.org.uk. You can camp or stay in the centre's converted farmhouse, which has its own observation tower, plus a kitchen and washing machine for guests' use. Camping £5, double £50

Sweetheart Abbey

East of New Abbey • April–Sept daily 9.30am–5.30pm; Oct daily 9.30am–4.30pm; Nov–March Mon–Wed, Sat & Sun 9.30am–4.30pm • HS • £4 • 01387 850397

Sweetheart Abbey, lying romantically ruined to the east of the village of **NEW ABBEY**, takes its name from its founder, Devorgilla de Balliol, who carried the embalmed heart of her husband, John Balliol (of Oxford college fame) for the last 22 years of her life – she is buried with the casket, in the presbytery. The last of the Cistercian abbeys to be founded in Scotland – in 1273 – Sweetheart is dominated by the red sandstone abbey church, which remains intact, albeit minus its roof. Its grassy nave is flanked by giant compound piers supporting early Gothic arches, and above them a triforium. The other great survivor is the precinct wall, a massive structure made from rough granite boulders.

ACCOMMODATION AND EATING — SWEETHEART ABBEY

Abbey Arms 1 The Square, New Abbey 01387 850489, abbeyarmshotel.com. One of two pubs at the centre of the village, facing each other across a cobbled square. Rooms are plain but comfortable, and there's bar food, including pies and burgers as well as locally caught salmon. £60

Abbey Cottage Tearoom Near the abbey 01387 850377, abbeycottagetearoom.com. This delightful cottage tearoom is renowned for its good coffee, tiered teas and home-made cakes, and enjoys an unrivalled view over the abbey. There's a garden for sunny days. April–Oct 10am–5pm, Nov–March 11am–4pm.

The Colvend coast

The **Colvend coast**, twenty miles or so southwest of Dumfries, is one of the finest stretches of coastline along the so-called "Scottish Riviera". The best approach is via the A710, which heads south through New Abbey, before cutting across a handsome landscape of rolling farmland to **ROCKCLIFFE**, a beguiling little place of comfortable villas sheltered beneath wooded hills and around a rocky sand and shell bay.

For vehicles, Rockcliffe is a dead end, but it's the start of a pleasant half-hour's walk along the Jubilee Path to neighbouring **KIPPFORD**, a tiny, lively yachting centre strung out along the east bank of the Urr estuary. At low tide you can walk over the Rough Firth causeway from the shore below across the mud flats to **Rough Island**, a humpy twenty-acre bird sanctuary owned by the National Trust for Scotland – it's out of bounds in May and June during the nesting season.

ACCOMMODATION AND EATING — THE COLVEND COAST

Anchor Hotel Kippford 01556 620205, anchorkippford.co.uk. Right on Kippford's waterfront, the popular *Anchor Hotel* is a good reward for the gentle stroll required to get here from Rockcliffe. They serve local fish and ales, and there's a real fire in winter. Daily 11am–11pm.

Castle Point Caravan Site Rockcliffe 01556 630248. Secluded site just south of Rockcliffe village and a stone's throw from the seashore. Closed Nov–Feb. £20.50

Millbrae House Rockcliffe ⓣ 01556 630217, ⓦ millbraehouse.co.uk. Excellent B&B in a whitewashed cottage near the bay. Rooms are light and elegant, and breakfast is served in the conservatory. Closed Nov–Feb. **£64**

Rosemount Kippford ⓣ 01556 620214, ⓦ rosemountguesthouse.com. A very good guesthouse on the seafront, with a deluxe double, en-suite twin, and a chalet-style family room in the garden annexe. Closed Dec & Jan. **£80**

Castle Douglas and around

Most folk come to **CASTLE DOUGLAS**, eighteen miles southwest of Dumfries, in order to visit the nearby attractions of **Threave Garden** and **Threave Castle**.

18

Threave Garden

A mile south of Castle Douglas • Daily 9.30am–5.30pm • NTS • £6.50 • ⓣ 0844 4932245

Threave Garden is a pleasant mile or so's walk south of Castle Douglas along the shores of Loch Carlingwark. The garden features a magnificent spread of flowers and woodland, sixty acres divided into more than a dozen areas from the bright, old-fashioned blooms of the Rose Garden to the brilliant banks of rhododendrons in the Woodland Garden. In springtime, thousands of visitors turn up for the flowering of more than two hundred types of daffodil.

Threave Castle

A mile north of Threave Garden • April–Sept daily 9.30am–5pm • HS • £4.50 • ⓣ 07711 223101

The best way of reaching **Threave Castle**, a mile or so north of the gardens, is to walk through the estate. However you decide to get there, follow the signs to the Open Farm, from where it's a lovely fifteen-minute walk down to the River Dee. Here you ring a brass bell for the boat to take you over to the flat and grassy island on which the stern-looking tower house stands. Built for Archibald the Grim, the sturdy, rectangular fortress was completed shortly after the War of Independence, in around 1370. The rickety curtain-wall to the south and east is all that remains of the artillery fortifications, hurriedly constructed in the 1450s in a desperate – and unsuccessful – attempt to defend the castle against James II's newfangled cannon. The place was wrecked in 1640 after a siege, but enough remains to make it worth exploring.

ARRIVAL AND INFORMATION — CASTLE DOUGLAS

By bus Buses connect with Dumfries (Mon–Sat hourly, 4 on Sun; 45min) and Kirkcudbright (Mon–Sat hourly, Sun every 2hr; 20min).

Tourist office King St (April–June, Sept & Oct Mon–Sat 10am–4.30pm, Sun 11am–4pm; July & Aug Mon–Sat 10am–6pm, Sun 11am–5pm; ⓣ 01556 502611).

Bike rental Bikes, useful for getting out to Threave, are available from the Castle Douglas Cycle Centre, Church St (Mon–Sat 9am–5pm; ⓣ 01556 504542, ⓦ cdbikes.co.uk).

ACCOMMODATION AND EATING

Albion House 49 Ernespie Rd ⓣ 01556 502360, ⓦ albionhousecastledouglas.co.uk. One of a number of sturdy Victorian guesthouses in town, this one is plush and well equipped, with free wi-fi, complimentary coffee and bics and good cooked breakfasts. Closed Dec–Feb. **£75**

Designs 179 King St ⓣ 01556 504552, ⓦ designsgallery.co.uk. Nice daytime café at the back of a crafts gallery, serving great ciabattas and decent coffee and with a lovely conservatory and garden. Mon–Sat 9.30am–5.30pm.

Lochside Caravan and Camping Site Loch Carlingwark ⓣ 07824 528467. Well-maintained site, surrounded by trees, a short walk from the bottom of King St down Marle St. Closed Nov–Easter. **£20**

Kirkcudbright

KIRKCUDBRIGHT – pronounced "kir-coo-bree" – hugging the muddy banks of the River Dee ten miles southwest of Castle Douglas, is the only major town along the Solway coast to have retained a working harbour. In addition, it has a ruined **castle** and an attractive town centre, a charming medley of simple two-storey cottages and medieval pends, Georgian villas and Victorian townhouses, all brightly painted.

MacLellan's Castle

April–Sept daily 9.30am–5.30pm • HS • £3.50 • ⓣ 01557 331856

The most surprising sight in Kirkcudbright is **MacLellan's Castle**, a pink-flecked sixteenth-century tower house sitting at one end of the high street by the harbourside. Part fortified keep and part spacious mansion, the castle was built in the 1570s for the then Provost of Kirkcudbright, Sir Thomas MacLellan of Bombie. Its interior is well preserved, from the kitchen (complete with bread oven) to the spyhole known as the "**laird's lug**", behind the fireplace of the Great Hall.

Broughton House

High St • April–June, Sept & Oct Mon & Thurs–Sun noon–5pm; July & Aug daily noon–5pm; also Feb & March garden only daily 11am–4pm • NTS • £8 • ⓣ 0844 493 2246

Near the castle, on the L-shaped High Street, is **Broughton House**, a smart Georgian townhouse and former home of the artist **Edward Hornel** (1863–1933). Hornel, an important member of the late nineteenth-century Scottish art scene, spent his childhood a few doors down the street, and returned in 1900 to establish an artists' colony with some of the "Glasgow Boys" (see p.783). At the back of the house Hornel added a studio and a vast gallery, now filled with the mannered, vibrant paintings of girls at play, which he churned out in the latter part of his career. Hornel's trip to Japan in 1893 imbued him with a lifelong affection for the country, and his densely packed rambling **gardens** have a strong Japanese influence.

Tolbooth Art Centre

High St • May, June & Sept Mon–Sat 11am–5pm, Sun 2–5pm; July & Aug Mon–Sat 10am–5pm, Sun 2–5pm; Oct Mon–Sat 11am–4pm, Sun 2–5pm; Nov–April Mon–Sat 11am–4pm • Free • ⓣ 01557 331556

For background information on Kirkcudbright, visit the imposing, church-like **Tolbooth**, with its stone-built clocktower and spire. Built in the 1620s, the building now houses the **Tolbooth Art Centre**, which has a small display of paintings including Hornel's striking *Japanese Girl*, and S.J. Peploe's Colourist view of the Tolbooth.

GALLOWAY FOREST PARK

Galloway Forest Park (ⓦ www.forestry.gov.uk) is Britain's largest forest park, with a spectacularly varied landscape of mountain peaks, lochs, coast and moorland, cut through by the Southern Uplands Way. It has **visitor centres** (times vary but are basically April–Oct daily 10.30am–4.30pm) at Clatteringshaws Loch, Glentrool and Kirroughtree. Each has a tearoom, several waymarked walks and information on activities and events. The only **tarmacked road** to cross the park is the desolate twenty-mile stretch of the A712 between Newton Stewart and New Galloway, known as the **Queen's Way**. There's a **Wild Goat Park** on the Queen's Way in the heart of the park and, a mile or so further up the road, a **Red Deer Range**.

Both Glentrool and Kirroughtree visitor centres have **mountain bike trails**, which form part of southern Scotland's outstanding mountain-biking facilities, known as the 7 Stanes (ⓦ 7stanes.co.uk). Of the two, Kirroughtree, three miles east of the town of Newton Stewart, is by far the most varied and fun, with lots of exciting singletrack trails for all abilities and good bike-rental facilities.

About seven miles east of Newton Stewart, at the **Grey Mare's Tail Bridge**, various **hiking trails** delve into the pine forests beside the tarmacked road, crossing gorges, waterfalls and burns. **Clatteringshaws Loch**, meanwhile, a reservoir surrounded by pine forest at the southeastern edge of the park, has a fourteen-mile footpath running right around it. Serious hikers should head for **Glentrool**, at the western edge of the park, about ten miles north of Newton Stewart, where a narrow lane twists the five miles over to Loch Trool. From here, you can follow the Gariland Burn to Loch Neldricken and Loch Enoch, with their silver granite sands, and then on to the **Devil's Bowling Green**, strewn with hundreds of boulders left by the retreating glaciers. Alternatively, you can head for the **Range of the Awful Hand**, whose five peaks include the Merrick (2746ft).

ARRIVAL AND INFORMATION — KIRKCUDBRIGHT

By bus Buses stop by the harbour car park, next to the tourist office.

Tourist office Harbour Square (mid-Feb to March & Nov Mon–Sat 10am–4pm, Sun 11am–4pm; April–June, Sept & Oct Mon–Sat 10am–5pm, Sun 11am–4pm; July & Aug Mon–Sat 9.30am–6pm, Sun 11am–5pm; ⓣ 01557 330494).

ACCOMMODATION

Baytree House 110 High St ⓣ 01557 330824, ⓦ baytreekirkcudbright.co.uk. An imposing Georgian townhouse in the centre, with a friendly welcome and a fine breakfast. £72

The Greengate 46 High St ⓣ 01557 331895, ⓦ thegreengate.co.uk. Very pretty whitewashed terraced cottage – former home of "Glasgow Girl", Jessie King – with just one double bedroom. Jessie's studio is still used by the current owners. £70

EATING AND DRINKING

Castle Restaurant 5 Castle St ⓣ 01557 330569, ⓦ thecastlerestaurant.net. A smart little place offering Mediterranean cuisine, mostly made from local ingredients. Plus French house wines and whiskies from the Isle of Skye. Mon–Sat lunch & dinner, Sun lunch only.

Kirkpatrick's 29 St Cuthbert Place ⓣ 01557 330888, ⓦ kirkpatricksrestaurantkirkcudbright.co.uk. In a less appealing location than the Castle, but serving excellent Scottish food, some of it inspired by seventeenth- and eighteenth-century dishes, with an imaginative twist. Tues–Sat 6.30–9pm.

Solway Tide 16 St Cuthbert St ⓣ 01557 330735. An attractive tearoom which dishes up good coffee, smoothies, paninis, bagels and home-made scones. Mon–Sat 10.30am–4.30pm.

Wigtown

Seven miles south of Newton Stewart, **WIGTOWN** is a tiny place with a remarkable main square, a vast, triangular-shaped affair laid out as it was in medieval times. Overlooking and dominating the square and its central bowling green are the gargantuan **County Buildings**, built in French Gothic style, and now home to a CCTV link to a local osprey nest (May–Sept Mon, Thurs & Sat 10am–5pm, Tues, Wed & Fri 10am–7.30pm, Sun 2–5pm; free). Wigtown styles itself as "Scotland's National Book Town", with a highly rated **literary festival** in late September and more than twenty **bookshops** occupying some of the modest houses that line the square, and more elsewhere in the vicinity.

Whithorn and around

Fifteen miles south of Wigtown is **WHITHORN**, a one-street town where, in 397 AD, **St Ninian** is thought to have founded the first Christian church north of Hadrian's Wall. No one can be sure where Ninian's church actually stood, but his tomb at Whithorn soon became a popular place of pilgrimage. These days, it takes a serious leap of the imagination to envisage Whithorn as a medieval pilgrimage centre; start by watching the audiovisual show (Easter–Oct daily 10.30am–5pm; £3.50) at the **Whithorn Dig** on the main street. More compelling than the dig itself are the early Christian standing crosses and headstones housed in the on-site **Whithorn Museum**.

Isle of Whithorn

The pilgrims who crossed the Solway to visit St Ninian's shrine landed at the **ISLE OF WHITHORN**, four miles south of town; it's no longer an island, but an antique and picturesque little seaport. Walk down to the end of the harbour to pick up signs to the minuscule remains of the thirteenth-century **St Ninian's Chapel**, which some believe was the site of the original Candida Casa.

ACCOMMODATION AND EATING — ISLE OF WHITHORN

Steam Packet Inn Harbour Row ⓣ 01988 500334, ⓦ steampacketinn.biz. Right on the quayside, serving above-average pub grub and restaurant meals. The bar features a good range of guest beers and ales, and caters for the local fishermen, as well as visitors. £80

18

The Rhinns of Galloway

The hilly, hammer-shaped peninsula at the western end of the Solway coast is known as the **Rhinns of Galloway**. The main town is **STRANRAER** but unless you're heading to (or coming from) Northern Ireland, there's really no reason to go there. Stena Line still use Stranraer, which has rail links with Ayr and Glasgow, but they are threatening to move five miles north to **CAIRNRYAN**.

Portpatrick

The nicest place to stay on the peninsula is the old seafaring port of **PORTPATRICK**, with an attractive pastel-painted seafront that wraps itself round a small rocky bay sheltered by equally rocky cliffs.

ACCOMMODATION AND EATING — PORTPATRICK

★ **Campbell's Restaurant** 1 South Crescent ⊕01776 810314, ⊛campbellsrestaurant.co.uk. This modern, buzzy little place serves great local seafood; you'll often see the owner nipping out in his boat. They also have a self-catering holiday cottage nearby. Tues–Sun noon till late.

The Crown 9 North Crescent ⊕01776 810261, ⊛crownportpatrick.com. On the seafront, this is probably the cosiest drinking option in town (though the adjacent *Harbour House Hotel* has real ale), and there's plenty of seafood on the menu. Daily 11am–late.

Waterfront Hotel 7 North Crescent ⊕01776 810800, ⊛www.waterfronthotel.co.uk. The best accommodation option in town, lilac-painted *Waterfront Hotel* has an attractive terrace bar. Rooms have been recently refurbished, and there are annexe rooms in neighbouring cottages. **£66**

Mull of Galloway

It's twenty miles south from Portpatrick to the **Mull of Galloway**, but it's well worth the ride. This precipitous headland, crowned by a classic whitewashed Stevenson lighthouse, from which you can see the Isle of Man, really feels like the end of the road. It's the southernmost point in Scotland, and a favourite nesting spot for guillemots, razorbills and kittiwakes. The headland has a **lighthouse** that can be climbed on summer weekends (April–Sept Sat & Sun 10am–3.30pm; £2).

EATING AND DRINKING

★ **Gallie Craig café** Drummore ⊕01776 840558, ⊛galliecraig.co.uk. Just below the car park and perched on the cliff edge, this excellent coffee house/restaurant serves hot meals and tasty snacks. The terrace is a splendid spot for a little armchair birdwatching. April–Oct daily 10am–5.30pm, Nov & Feb–March Mon, Tues & Fri–Sun 11am–4pm.

Ayrshire

The rolling hills and rich soil of **Ayrshire** are not really at the top of most visitors' Scottish itinerary. **Ayr**, the county town and birthplace of Robert Burns, won't distract you for long. Most folk stick to the coastline, attracted by the wide, flat sandy **beaches** and the vast number of **golf** courses. South of Ayr, the most obvious points of interest are **Culzean Castle**, with its Robert Adam interior and extensive wooded grounds, and the offshore islands of **Ailsa Craig**, while to the east is fascinating **Dumfries House**. North of Ayr is **Irvine**, home to the Scottish Maritime Museum.

Ayr and around

AYR is by far the largest town on the Firth of Clyde coast. It was an important seaport and trading centre for many centuries, and rivalled Glasgow in size and significance right up until the late seventeenth century. Nowadays, it pulls in the crowds for the Scottish Grand National and the Scottish Derby (⊛ayr-racecourse.co.uk), and for the fact that Robbie Burns was born in the neighbouring village of **Alloway** (see opposite).

The town centre, wedged between Sandgate and the south bank of the River Ayr, is busy most days with shoppers from all over the county. East of the High Street, the medieval **Auld Brig** is one of the oldest stone bridges in Scotland, built during the reign of James IV (1488–1513). A short stroll upstream brings you to the much-restored **Auld Kirk**, the church funded by Cromwell as recompense for the one he incorporated into the town's fortress. The dark and gloomy interior retains the original pulpit (ask at the tourist office about access). All you can see of Cromwell's zigzag **Citadel**, built to the west of the town centre in the 1650s, is a small section of the old walls.

The opening of the Glasgow–Ayr train line in 1840 brought the first major influx of holiday-makers to the town, but today, only a few hardy visitors and local dog-walkers take a stroll along Ayr's bleak, long **Esplanade** and beach, which look out to the Isle of Arran.

ARRIVAL AND INFORMATION — AYR

By plane Ayr is the nearest large town to Glasgow Prestwick Airport (T 0871 223 0700, W gpia.co.uk), which lies 3 miles north of town and is connected by regular train to Ayr and Glasgow.

By train The station is a 10min walk southeast of the town centre.

Destinations Glasgow Central (every 30min; 50min); Irvine (every 30min; 15–20min); Prestwick Airport (every 30min; 7min); Stranraer (Mon–Sat 7 daily, 2 on Sun; 1hr 20min).

By bus The station is in the centre at the foot of Sandgate, near the tourist office.

Destinations Ardrossan (Mon–Sat every 30min, Sun every 2hr; 55min); Culzean Castle (Mon–Sat hourly, Sun every 2hr; 30min); Dumfries (Mon–Sat every 2hr; 2hr 10min); Glasgow (hourly; 55min); Portpatrick (Mon–Sat 6 daily; 2hr 25min); Stranraer (4–6 daily; 2hr).

Tourist office 22 Sandgate (July & Aug Mon–Sat 9am–6pm, Sun 10am–5pm; Oct–June Mon–Sat 9am–1pm & 2–5pm T 0845 225 5121).

ACCOMMODATION

Craggallan 8 Queen's Terrace T 01292 264998, W cragallan.com. A friendly little guesthouse – the best on the street – with modern furnishings, carpeted rooms and simple decor. **£65**

The Dunn Thing 13 Park Circus T 01292 284531, W thedunnthing.co.uk. Brightly decorated B&B that lets out rooms with or without breakfast. There's a cot available, and tea- and coffee-making facilities. **£55**

Heads of Ayr Dunure Rd T 01292 442269, W headsofayr.com. Three miles south of Ayr along the coastal A719, this caravan and campsite is located beside the popular Heads of Ayr Farm Park. Closed Nov–Feb. **£14**

EATING AND DRINKING

Rupee Room 26a Wellington Square T 01292 283002, W therupeeroom.com. A popular and welcoming inexpensive Indian restaurant, decked out with modern furnishings. Mon–Thurs & Sun 5–11pm, Fri & Sat noon–2.30pm, 4–11pm.

West Kirk 58A Sandgate T 01292 880 416. For a quiet pint of real ale, head for this music-free *Wetherspoon* church-to-pub conversion, its wooden balconies held up by pistachio-coloured fluted pillars. Mon–Thurs 8am–midnight, Fri & Sat 8am–12.30am, Sun 8am–midnight.

Alloway

ALLOWAY, formerly a small village but now on the southern outskirts of Ayr, is the birthplace of Robert Burns (1759–96), Scotland's national poet. The several places associated with him have been linked as the **Robert Burns Birthplace Museum** (W burnsmuseum.org.uk).

Burns Cottage and Museum

Murdoch's Lane • April–Sept 10am–5.30pm; Oct–March 10am–5pm • NTS • £8 • W burnsmuseum.org.uk

Burns was born in what is now the **Burns Cottage and Museum**: a low, whitewashed, single-room thatched cottage where animals and people lived under the same roof. The **museum** shows original manuscripts and personal belongings with a good dash of technology and interactive elements.

ROBERT BURNS

The eldest of seven, **Robert Burns** was born in Alloway on January 25, 1759. His tenant farmer father's bankruptcy had a profound effect on the boy, leaving him with an antipathy towards authority. After the death of his father, Robert, now head of the family, moved them to a farm at Mossgiel where he began to write in earnest: his first volume, *Poems Chiefly in the Scottish Dialect*, was published in 1786. The book proved immensely popular with ordinary Scots and Edinburgh literati alike, with *Holy Willie's Prayer* attracting particular attention. The object of Burns' poetic scorn was the kirk, whose ministers had condemned him for fornication.

18

Burns spent the winter of 1786–87 in the capital, but despite his success he felt financially trapped, unable to leave farming. His radical views also landed him in a political snare, his recourse being to play the unlettered ploughman-poet who might be excused impetuous outbursts and hectic womanizing. He made useful contacts in Edinburgh, however, and was recruited to write songs set to traditional Scottish tunes: works including *Auld Lang Syne* and *Green Grow the Rushes, O*. At this time, too, he produced *Tam o' Shanter* and a republican tract, *A Man's a Man for a' That*.

Burns fathered several illegitimate children, but in 1788 married **Jean Armour**, a stonemason's daughter with whom he already had two children, and moved to Ellisland Farm, near Dumfries. The following year he was appointed excise officer and could leave farming. But his years of labour, allied to a rheumatic fever, damaged his heart, and he died in Dumfries in 1796, aged 37.

Burns's work, inspired by romantic nationalism and tinged with wry wit, has made him a potent symbol of "Scottishness". Today, Burns Clubs all over the world mark the poet's birthday with the Burns' Supper, complete with haggis, piper and whisky – and a ritual recital of *Ode to a Haggis*.

Other Burns sights

Ten minutes' walk down the road from the cottage are the plain, roofless ruins of **Alloway Kirk**, where Robert's father William is buried, and where Burns set much of *Tam o' Shanter*. Down the road from the church, the **Brig o' Doon**, the picturesque thirteenth-century humpback bridge over which Tam is forced to flee for his life, still stands, curving gracefully over the river. High above the river and bridge, towers the **Burns Monument** (daily: April–Sept 9am–5pm; Oct–March 10am–4pm; free), a striking Neoclassical temple in a small, carefully manicured garden.

ARRIVAL AND DEPARTURE — ALLOWAY

To reach Alloway from Ayr town centre, take **bus** #1 or #57 from Sandgate (Mon–Sat hourly) to Burns Cottage, or #58 or #60 from the bus station.

Culzean Castle

Ten miles south of Ayr • **Castle** Easter–Oct daily 10.30am–5pm • £14 **Park** Daily 9.30am to dusk • NTS • £8 • Ⓦ culzeanexperience.org

Sitting on the edge of a sheer cliff, looking out over the Firth of Clyde to Arran, **Culzean Castle** (pronounced "Cullane") couldn't want for a more impressive situation. The current castle is actually a grand, late eighteenth-century stately home, designed by Scottish Neoclassical architect **Robert Adam**. Adam's most brilliantly conceived work is the Oval Staircase, where tiers of classical columns lead up to a huge glazed cupola. Other highlights include a portrait of Napoleon by Lefèvre, a superb Chippendale four-poster bed and a boat-shaped cradle. Many folk come here purely to stroll and picnic in the castle's 500-acre **country park**, mess about by the beach, or have tea and cakes.

ACCOMMODATION — CULZEAN CASTLE

Culzean Castle Ⓣ 01655 884455, Ⓦ culzeanexperience.org. You can stay at Culzean on the top floor, where six double rooms have been done out in a comfortable, genteel style. Closed Nov–March. **£175**

★ **Culzean Castle campsite** Ⓣ 01655 760627, Ⓦ culzeanexperience.org. This great little Camping and Caravanning Club-affiliated site is in the woods by the castle entrance, with lovely views across to Arran. Closed Nov–Feb.

Dumfries House

Just north of Cumnock, 15 miles east of Ayr • April–Oct 11am–4pm, pre-booked guided tour only • £8.50 • ⓣ 01290 425959, ⓦ dumfries-house.org.uk • From Ayr take the #46 bus

The handsome Palladian villa of **Dumfries House** is an essential stop for anyone with an interest in domestic architecture. Lively tours illuminate the beauty of the furnishings: the house was built and decked out swiftly – between 1756 and 1760 – meaning its Rococo decorative scheme is in perfect harmony with the graceful sandstone exterior. Chief among the treasures is a huge collection of **Chippendale furniture.** Throughout the house, the family symbols of the wyvern (small dragon) and the thistle recur in inventive and playful touches, and exotic Oriental motifs crop up in the fanciful plasterwork ceilings and gilded pierglasses.

Irvine

IRVINE, twelve miles north of Ayr, was once the principal port for trade between Glasgow and Ireland, and later for coal from Kilmarnock. Its halcyon days are recalled in an enjoyable living history **museum**, spread across several locations around the town's beautifully restored old harbour.

Scottish Maritime Museum

Various locations • April–Oct daily 10am–5pm • £3.50 • ⓦ scottishmaritimemuseum.org

The best place to start a tour of the **Scottish Martime Museum** sights is in the late nineteenth-century **Linthouse Engine Shop**, on Harbour Road, housing everything from old sailing dinghies and canoes to giant ship's turbines. Free guided tours set off regularly for the nearby **Shipyard Worker's Tenement Flat**, which has been restored to its appearance in 1910, when a family of six to eight plus a lodger would have occupied its two rooms and scullery. Moored at the **pontoons** on Harbour Street is an assortment of craft that you can board, including the oldest seagoing steam yacht in the country.

ARRIVAL AND DEPARTURE — IRVINE

Arriving at Irvine's adjacent **train** (trains from Glasgow every 30min; 35min) or **bus stations**, you'll find yourself exactly halfway between the harbour, to the west, and the Riverfront shopping complex and old town, to the east.

ACCOMMODATION AND EATING

Annfield House Hotel 6 Castle St ⓣ 01294 278903. A big Victorian mansion overlooking the river at the end of Sandgate, with nine spacious bedrooms. Friendly staff and a pretty good restaurant, too. **£60**

AILSA CRAIG

If the weather's half decent, it's impossible to miss **Ailsa Craig**, ten miles off the south Ayrshire coast in the middle of the Firth of Clyde. The island's name means "Fairy Rock" in Gaelic, though it actually looks more like an enormous muffin. It would certainly have been less than enchanting for the persecuted Catholics who escaped here during the Reformation. The island's granite has long been used for making curling stones, and in the late nineteenth century 29 people lived here, either working in the quarry or at the Stevenson lighthouse. With its volcanic, columnar cliffs and 1114ft summit, Ailsa Craig is now a **bird sanctuary** – home to some 40,000 gannets. The **best time** to make the trip is at the end of May and in June when the fledglings are learning to fly. Several companies in the town of **GIRVAN** offer **cruises** round the island, but only Mark McCrindle, who also organizes sea-angling trips, is licensed to land (May to late Sept 1–2 daily; ⓣ 01465 713219, ⓦ ailsacraig.org.uk). It takes about an hour to reach the island. Timings and prices depend on the length of trip, tides and weather; booking ahead is essential.

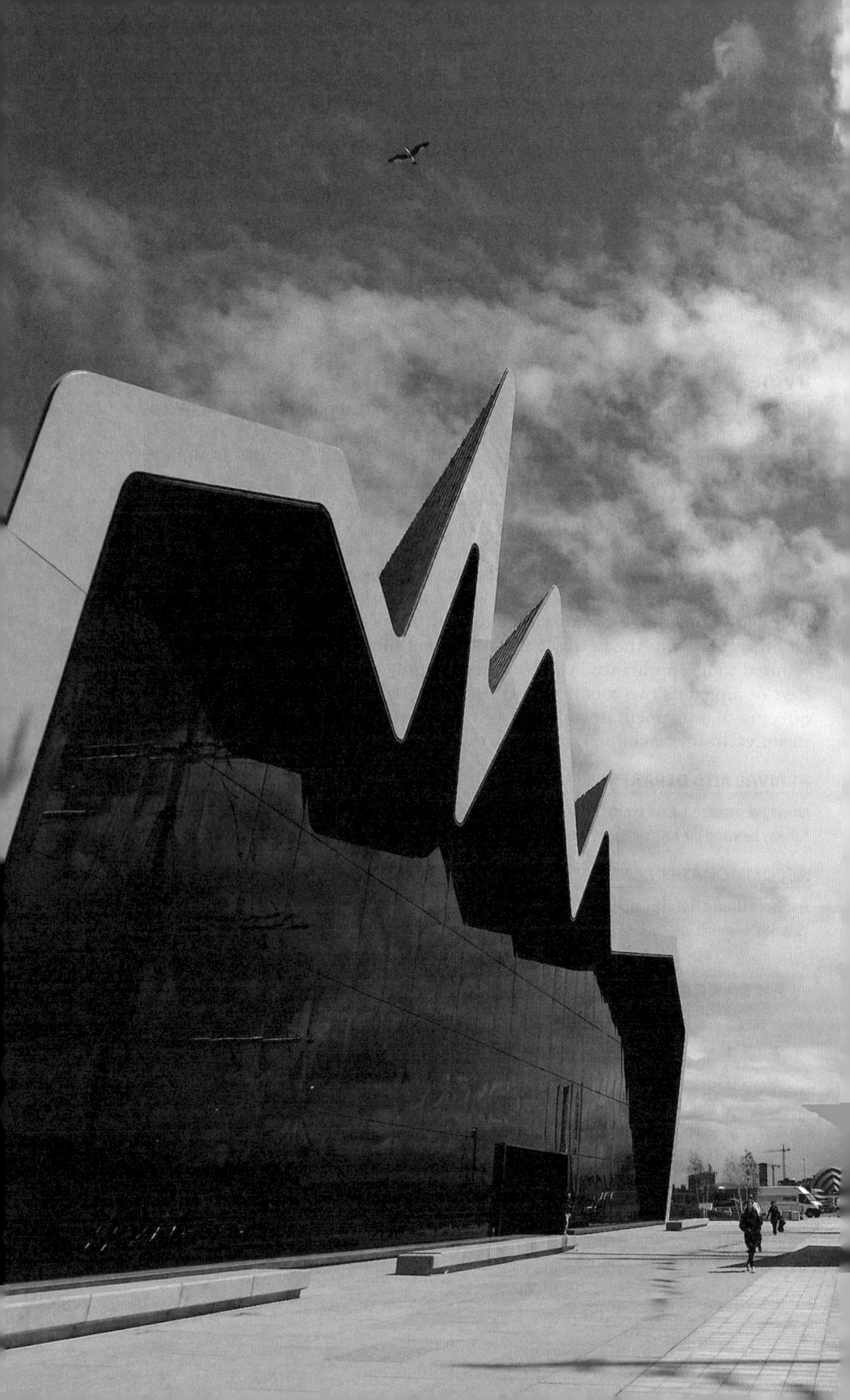

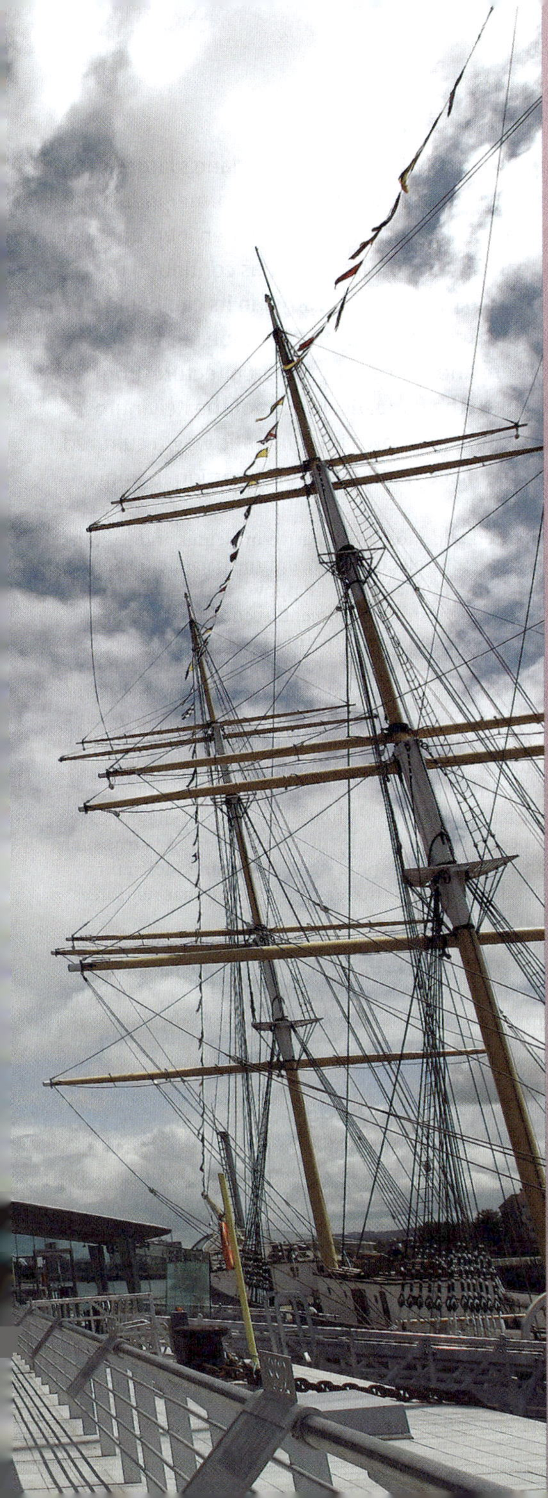

Glasgow and the Clyde

775 The city centre
780 The East End
782 The West End
784 Clydeside
785 The Southside
792 The Clyde

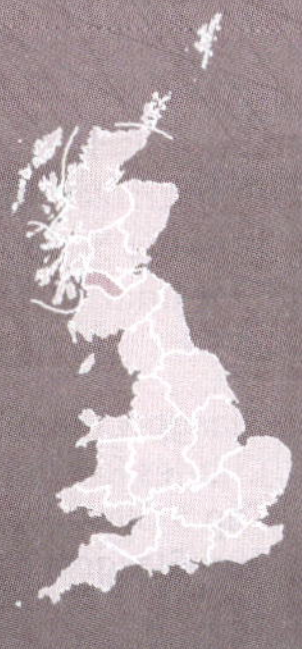

RIVERSIDE MUSEUM, GLASGOW

Glasgow and the Clyde

Set on the banks of the mighty River Clyde, Glasgow, Scotland's largest city, has not traditionally enjoyed the best of reputations. This former industrial giant changed its image irrevocably in 1990, however – when it energetically embraced its status as European City of Culture – and has continued to transform itself ever since, with the most recent feather in its cap being the hosting of the Commonwealth Games in 2014. The cityscape has been spruced up, and many visitors are knocked out by the architecture, from long rows of sandstone terraces to the fantastical spires of the Kelvingrove Museum. Glasgow is without doubt, in its own idiosyncratic way, a cultured, vibrant and irrepressibly sociable place that's well worth getting to know.

The city has some of the best-financed and most imaginative museums and galleries in Britain – among them the showcase **Burrell Collection** and the palatial **Kelvingrove Art Gallery and Museum** – nearly all of which are free. Glasgow's **architecture** is some of the most striking in the UK, from the restored eighteenth-century warehouses of the **Merchant City** to the hulking Victorian prosperity of George Square. Most distinctive of all is the work of local luminary Charles Rennie Mackintosh, whose elegantly Art Nouveau designs appear all over the city, reaching their apotheosis in the stunning **School of Art**. Development of the old shipyards of the Clyde, notably in the space-age shapes of the **Glasgow Science Centre** and the dynamic new **Riverside Museum**, hint at yet another string to the city's bow: combining design with innovation. The metropolis boasts thriving live-music venues, distinctive places to eat and drink, busy theatres, concert halls and an opera house. Despite all the upbeat hype, however, Glasgow's gentrification has passed by deprived inner-city areas such as the **East End**, home of the **Barras market** and some staunchly change-resistant pubs. Indeed, even in the more stylish quarters, there's a gritty edge that reinforces the city's peculiar mix of grime and glitz.

Glasgow makes an excellent base from which to explore the **Clyde valley and coast**, easily accessible by a reliable train service. Chief among the draws is the remarkable eighteenth-century **New Lanark** mills and workers' village, a World Heritage Site, while other day-trips might take you towards the scenic Argyll sea lochs, past the old shipbuilding centres on the Clyde estuary.

Brief history

Glasgow's earliest history, like so much else in this surprisingly romantic city, is obscured in a swirl of myth. Its name is said to derive from the Celtic *Glas-cu*, which loosely translates as "the dear, green place". It is generally agreed that the first settlers arrived in the sixth century to join Christian missionary **Kentigern** – later to become St Mungo – in his newly founded monastery on the banks of the tiny Molendinar Burn.

Glasgow tenements p.779
Charles Rennie Mackintosh pp.780–781
Top 5 Glasgow must-dos p.782
The Glasgow Boys and the Colourists p.783
The Waverley p.785
The Old Firm p.786
Glasgow shopping p.792
Ferries: Gourock and Wemyss Bay p.793

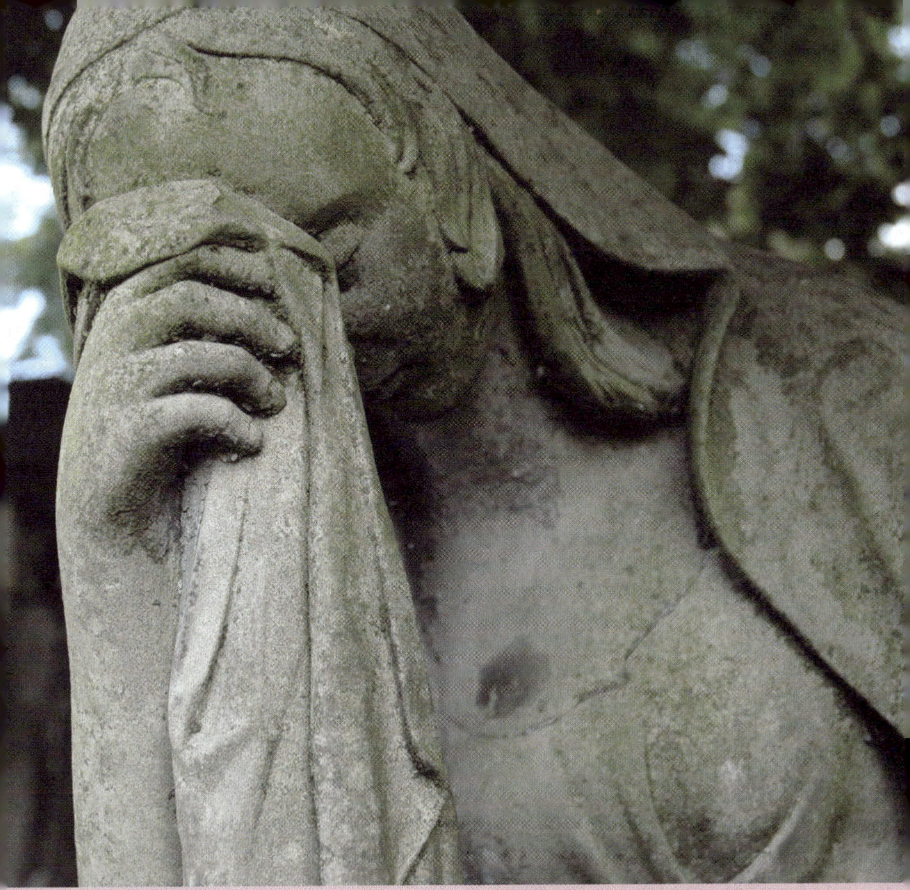

THE NECROPOLIS

Highlights

❶ **Glasgow School of Art** Take a student-led tour of Charles Rennie Mackintosh's architectural masterpiece, where his art is displayed in everything from the light-filled central stairwell to the delicate decorative details. **See p.779**

❷ **Necropolis** Elegantly crumbling graveyard on a city-centre hill behind the ancient cathedral, with great views giving a different perspective on the city. **See p.782**

❸ **Kelvingrove Art Gallery and Museum** Splendid civic collection in a magnificent red sandstone building in the West End; a regular Sunday outing for Glaswegians. **See p.782**

❹ **Clydeside** The river that made Glasgow: walk or cycle along it, take a boat on it, cross a bridge over it, or get a view of it from the absorbing new Riverside Museum. **See p.784**

❺ **Burrell Collection** An inspired and eclectic art collection displayed in a purpose-built museum in leafy Pollok Park. **See p.786**

❻ **New Lanark** Stay for next to nothing in the hostel at this lovely eighteenth-century planned village, where there's fascinating background on mill life, as well as superb woodland walks. **See p.794**

HIGHLIGHTS ARE MARKED ON THE MAP ON P.774

GLASGOW & THE CLYDE

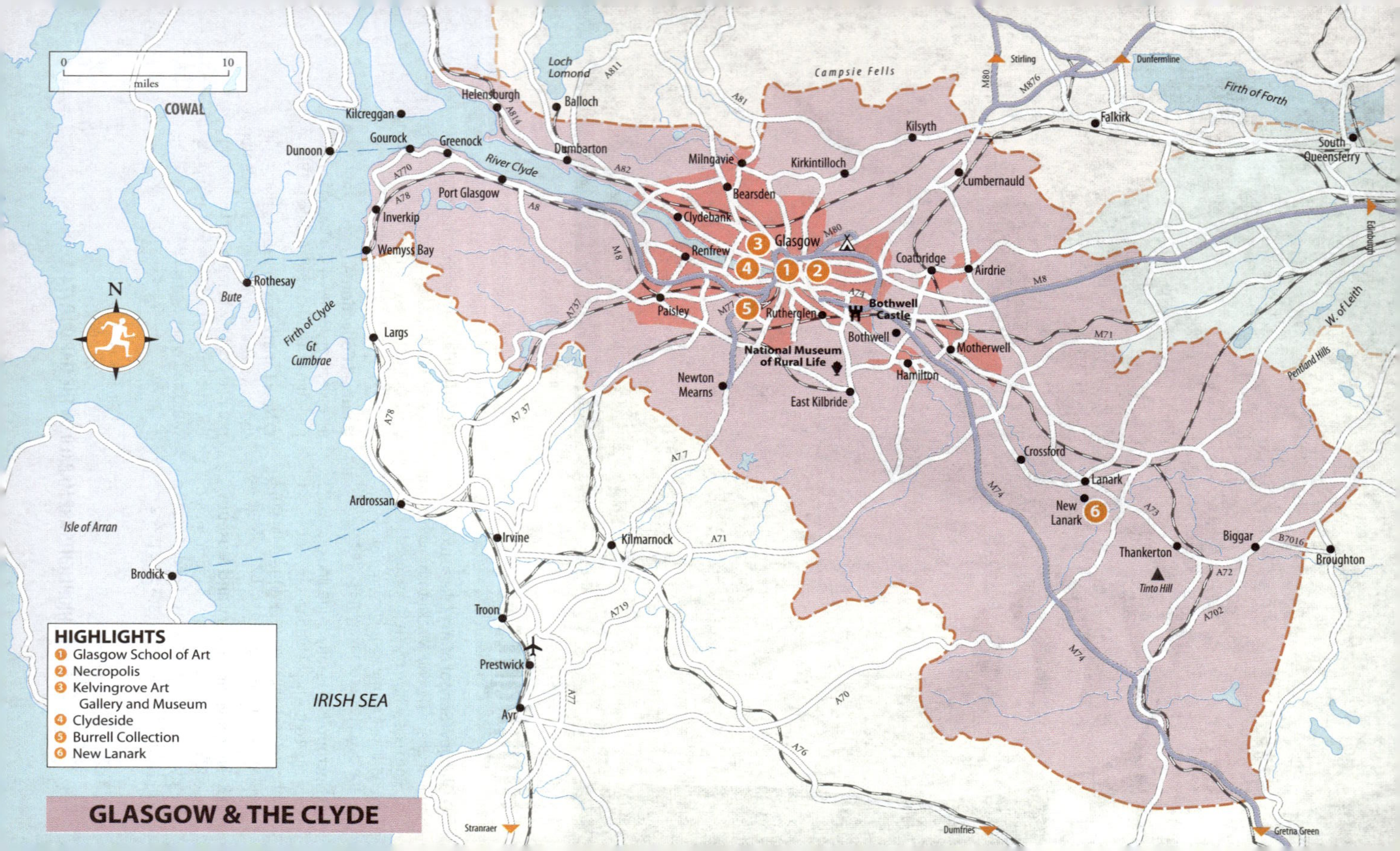

The university and the port

William the Lionheart granted the town an official charter in 1175, after which it continued to grow in importance, peaking in the mid-fifteenth century when the **university** was founded on Kentigern's site – the second in Scotland after St Andrews. This led to the establishment of an archbishopric, and hence city status, in 1492, and, due to its situation on a large, navigable river, Glasgow soon expanded into a major industrial **port**. The first cargo of tobacco from Virginia offloaded in Glasgow in 1674, and the 1707 Act of Union between Scotland and England – despite demonstrations against it in Glasgow – led to a boom in trade with the colonies. Following the **Industrial Revolution** and James Watt's innovations in steam power, coal from the abundant seams of Lanarkshire fuelled the ironworks all around the Clyde, worked by the cheap hands of the Highlanders and, later, those fleeing the Irish potato famine of the 1840s.

Shipbuilding and decline

The **Victorian** age transformed Glasgow beyond recognition. The population boomed from 77,000 in 1801 to nearly 800,000 at the end of the century, and new tenement blocks swept into the suburbs in an attempt to cope with the choking influxes of people. By the turn of the twentieth century, Glasgow's industries had been honed into one massive **shipbuilding** culture. Everything from tugboats to transatlantic liners were fashioned out of sheet metal in the yards that straddled the Clyde. In the 1930s, however, unemployment spiralled, and Glasgow could do little to counter its popular image as a city dominated by inebriate violence and (having absorbed vast numbers of Irish emigrants) sectarian tensions. The **Gorbals** area in particular became notorious as one of the worst slums in Europe. The city's image has never been helped by the depth of animosity between its two great rival football teams, Catholic **Celtic** and Protestant **Rangers**.

The city reinvented

Shipbuilding, and many associated industries, died away almost completely in the 1960s and 1970s, leaving the city depressed and directionless. Then, in the 1980s, the self-promotion campaign began, snowballing towards the year-long party as European City of Culture in 1990. Glasgow then beat off competition from Edinburgh and Liverpool to become **UK City of Architecture and Design** in 1999, and won the right to host the **Commonwealth Games** of 2014. These various titles have helped Glasgow break the industrial shackles of the past and evolve into a city of stature, confidence and style.

The city centre

Glasgow's large **city centre** is ranged across the north bank of the River Clyde. At its geographical heart is **George Square**, a nineteenth-century municipal showpiece crowned by the enormous **City Chambers** at its eastern end. Behind this lies the **Merchant City**, an area that blends magnificent Victorian architecture with yuppie conversions. The grand buildings and trendy cafés cling to the borders of the run-down **East End**, a strongly working-class district that chooses to ignore its rather showy neighbour. The oldest part of Glasgow, around the **Cathedral**, lies immediately north of the East End.

George Square

Now hemmed in by the city's grinding traffic, the imposing architecture of **George Square** reflects the confidence of Glasgow's Victorian age. The wide-open plaza

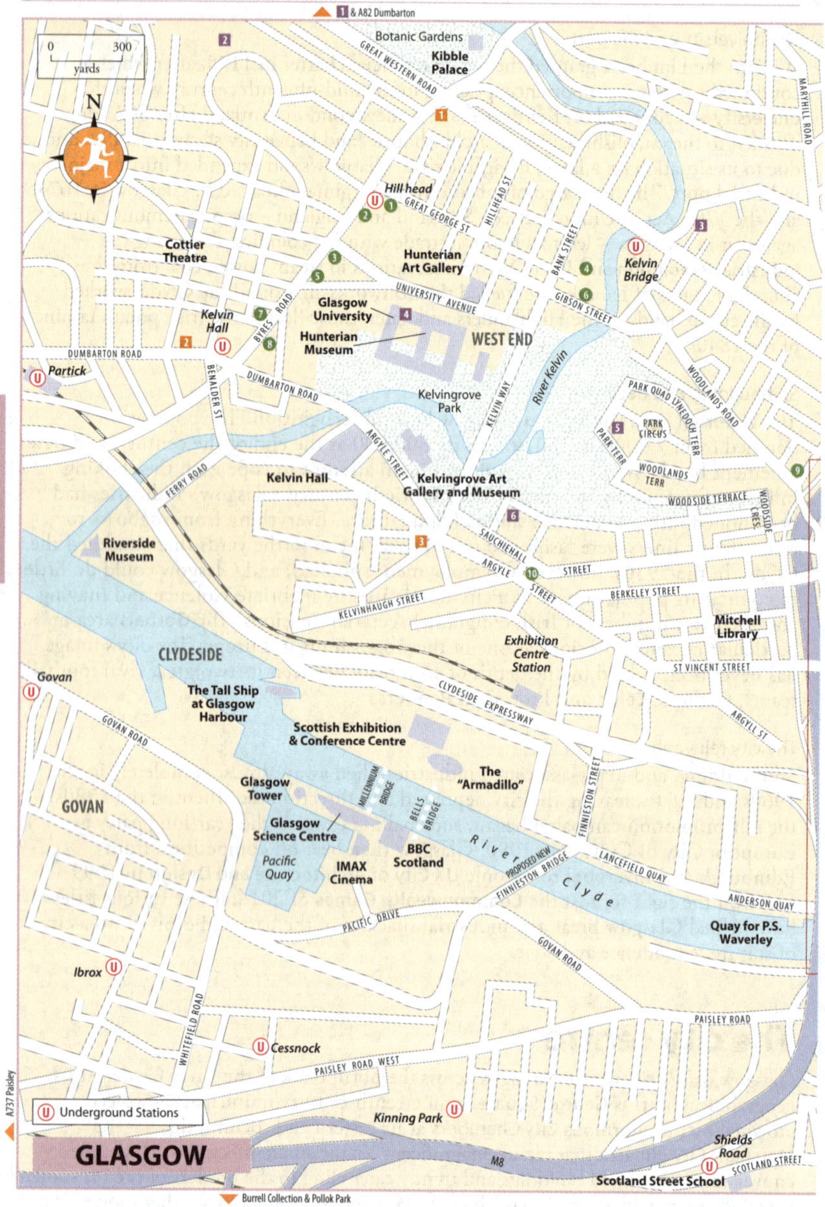

almost has a continental airiness about it, although there isn't much subtlety about the 80ft column rising up at its centre. It's topped by a statue of Sir Walter Scott, even though his links with Glasgow are, at best, sketchy. Haphazardly dotted around the great writer's plinth are a number of dignified statues of assorted luminaries, ranging from Queen Victoria to Scots heroes such as James Watt and wee Robbie Burns.

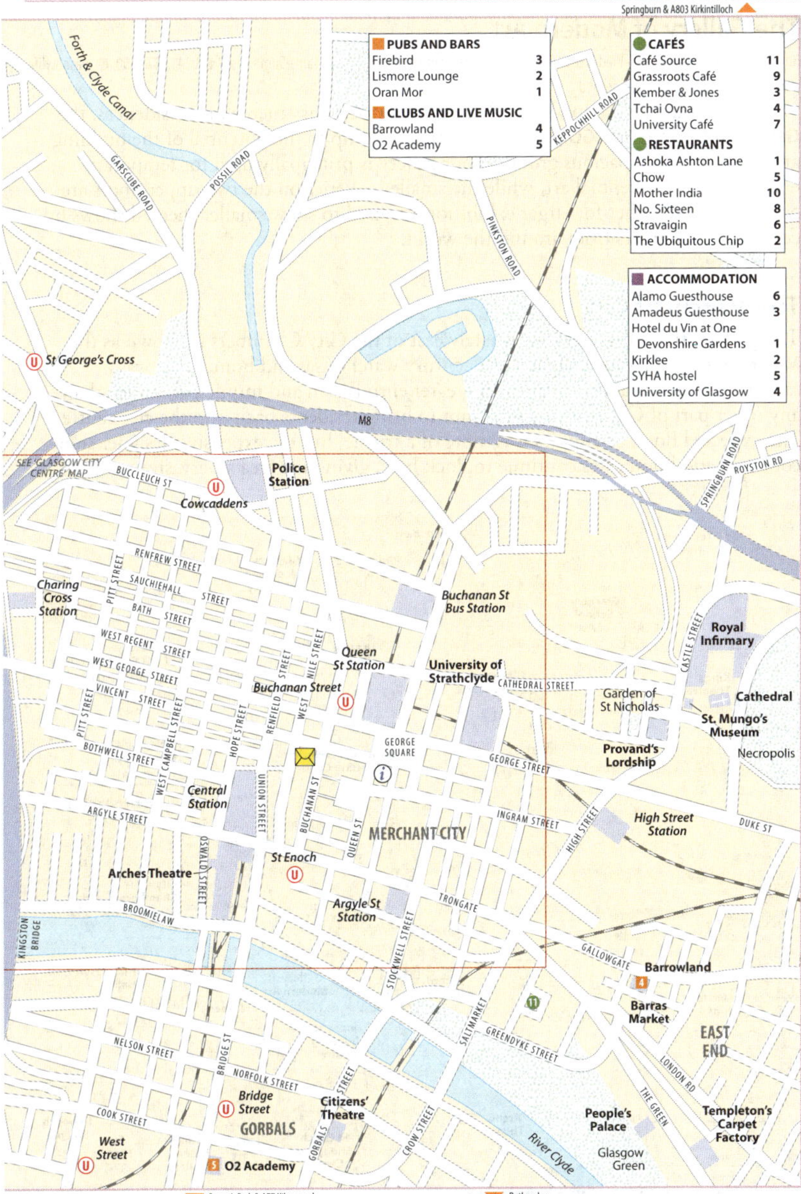

19

City Chambers

Mon–Fri 10.30am & 2.30pm • Free guided tours 10.30am & 2.30pm • ⓣ 0141 287 4018 • Buchanan Street underground

The florid splendour of the **City Chambers**, opened by Queen Victoria in 1888, occupies the entire eastern end of the square. Built from wealth gained by colonial trade and heavy industry, it epitomizes the aspirations and optimism of late Victorian city elders. Inside, you can wander around the ground floor, with its domed mosaic ceilings and two mighty Italian marble stairwells; free **guided tours** explore the labyrinthine interior.

The Gallery of Modern Art

Royal Exchange Square • Mon–Wed & Sat 10am–5pm, Thurs 10am–8pm, Fri & Sun 11am–5pm • Free • T 0141 287 3050, W glasgowlife.org.uk • Buchanan Street underground

Occupying one of Glasgow's grandest eighteenth-century merchant's residences, the **Gallery of Modern Art (GOMA)** has not quite lived up to the potential of the building and location. The spacious ground-floor gallery is principally used for temporary exhibitions of conceptual art, while the smaller galleries on the two upper floors are either linked together for larger exhibitions or used to show smaller themed shows by contemporary artists from around the world.

The Merchant City

19

The grid of streets that lies immediately east of the City Chambers is known as the **Merchant City**, an area of eighteenth-century warehouses and homes that was sandblasted and swabbed clean with greater enthusiasm and municipal money than any other part of Glasgow in an attempt to bring residents back into the city centre. The expected flood of yuppies was more of a trickle, but the expensive designer shops, cool bars and bijou cafés continue to flock here, giving the area a pervasive air of

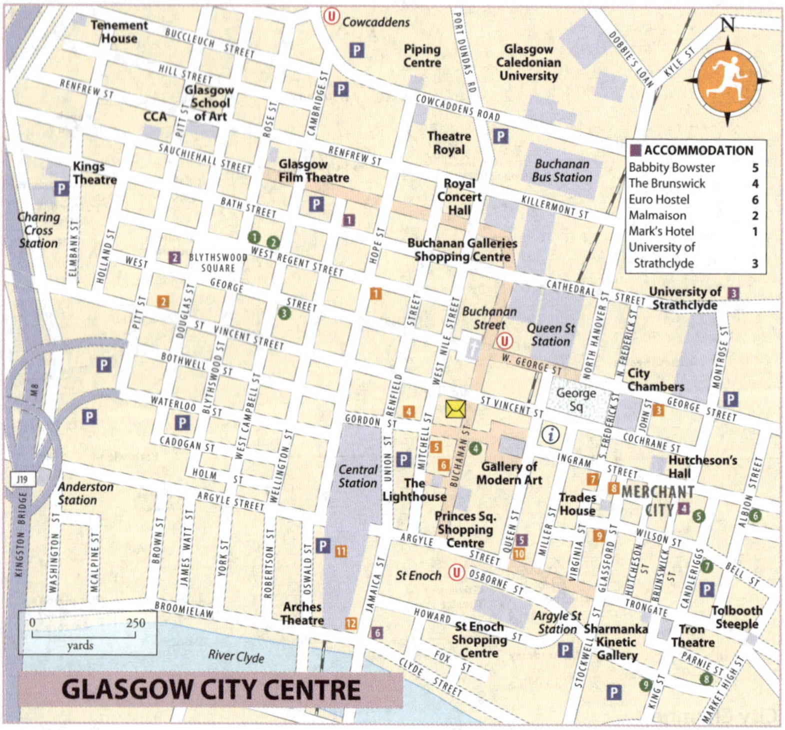

RESTAURANTS
- The 13th Note Café 9
- Brian Maule at Le Chardon d'Or 2
- City Merchant 5
- Dakhin 5
- The Dhabba 7
- Gamba 3
- Rogano 4

CAFÉS
- Café Gandolfi and Bar Gandolfi 6
- Trans Europe-Café 8
- Where the Monkey Sleeps 1

PUBS AND BARS
- The Arches 11
- Babbity Bowster 10
- Bar 10 6
- Corinthian 7
- Horseshoe Bar 4
- Pot Still 1
- Revolver 3

CLUBS AND LIVE MUSIC
- The Arches 11
- Bennets 8
- King Tut's Wah Wah Hut 2
- Polo Lounge 9
- Sub Club 12
- The Tunnel 5

sophistication. A Merchant City Trail leaflet, which guides you around a dozen of the most interesting buildings in the area, is available at the tourist office (see p.787).

Sharmanka Kinetic Gallery

Trongate 103 • Wed–Sun 3pm, Sat & Sun also 1pm; Thurs & Sun 7pm; 70min show • £5/8 • ⓣ 0141 552 7080, ⓦ sharmanka.com • St Enoch underground

Founded by Russian émigrés Eduard Bersudsky and Tatyana Jakovskaya, the **Sharmanka Kinetic Gallery** is like a mad inventor's magical workshop, with dozens of allegorical contraptions made from old wheels, levers, lights, carved wooden figures and scrap metal which spark into life during performances. A unique art form, Sharmanka (Russian for barrel organ or hurdy-gurdy) is at once hypnotic, playful and deeply poignant, with its mechanical sculptures, or "kinemats" imprisoned in their relentless routine.

Sauchiehall Street

Glasgow's most famous street, **Sauchiehall Street**, runs in a straight line west from the northern end of Buchanan Street, past some unexciting shopping malls to a few of the city's most interesting sights.

Willow Tea Rooms

217 Sauchiehall St • Mon–Sat 9am–5pm Sun 11am–5pm • ⓣ 0141 332 0521, ⓦ willowtearooms.co.uk • Cowcaddens underground

Enthusiasts of the work of **Charles Rennie Mackintosh** should head for the **Willow Tea Rooms**, above Henderson the Jeweller. This is a faithful reconstruction on the site of the 1904 original, which was created for Kate Cranston, one of Mackintosh's few contemporary supporters in the city. Taking inspiration from the word *Sauchiehall*, which means "avenue of willow", he chose the willow leaf as a theme to unify everything from the tables to the mirrors and the ironwork.

Glasgow School of Art

167 Renfrew St • Guided tours April–Sept daily on the hour 10am–4pm; Oct–March Mon–Sat 11am, 2pm & 3pm; booking advised • £8.75 • ⓣ 0141 353 4526, ⓦ gsa.ac.uk • Cowcaddens underground

Rising above Sauchiehall Street to the north is one of the city centre's steepest hills, with Dalhousie and Scott streets veering up to Renfrew Street, where you'll find Charles Rennie Mackintosh's **Glasgow School of Art**. Widely considered to be the pinnacle of Mackintosh's work, the school is a characteristically angular building of warm sandstone that, due to financial constraints, had to be constructed in two sections (1897–99 and 1907–09). There's a clear change in the architect's style from the earlier severity of the mock-Baronial east wing to the softer lines of the western half.

The only way to see the school is to take a student-led **guided tour**; these show off-key examples of Mackintosh's dynamic and inspired touch and a handful of the most impressive rooms. All over the school, from the roof to the stairwells, Mackintosh's

GLASGOW TENEMENTS

Originally conceived as a convenient way to house the influx of workers in the late 1800s, the **Glasgow tenement** design became more refined as the wealthy middle classes began to realize its potential. Mainly constructed between 1860 and 1910, these tenements, decked out with bay windows, turrets and domes, were home to the vast majority of Glaswegians for much of the twentieth century, and developed a culture and vocabulary all of their own: the "hurley", for example, was the bed on castors which was kept below the box bed in an alcove of the kitchen; a "single end" tenement comprised just one room; and the "dunny" was the secluded bottom end of the "close" (entrance way), the perfect spot for games of hide and seek as well as romantic and nefarious encounters.

CHARLES RENNIE MACKINTOSH

The work of the architect **Charles Rennie Mackintosh** (1868–1928) is synonymous with the image of Glasgow. Historians may disagree over whether his work was a forerunner of the Modernist movement or merely the sunset of Victorianism, but he undoubtedly created buildings of great beauty, idiosyncratically fusing Scots Baronial with Gothic, Art Nouveau and modern design. Though the bulk of his work was conceived at the turn of the twentieth century, since the postwar years Mackintosh's ideas have become particularly fashionable, giving rise to a certain amount of ersatz "**Mockintosh**" in his home city, with his distinctive lettering and design details used time and again by shops, pubs and businesses. Fortunately, there are also plenty of examples of the genuine article, making the city a pilgrimage centre for art and design students from all over the world.

Although his family did little to encourage his artistic ambitions, as a young child Mackintosh began to cultivate his interest in drawing from nature during walks in the countryside taken to improve his health. This talent was to flourish when he joined the **Glasgow School of Art** in 1884, whose vibrant new director, Francis Newberry, encouraged his pupils to create original and individual work. Here Mackintosh met Herbert MacNair and the sisters Margaret and Frances MacDonald, whose work seemed to be in sympathy with his, fusing the organic forms of nature with a linear, symbolic Art Nouveau style. Nicknamed "**The Spook School**", the four created a new artistic language, using extended vertical design, stylized abstract organic forms and muted colours, reflecting their interest in Japanese design and the work of Whistler and Beardsley. However, it was **architecture** that truly challenged Mackintosh, allowing him to use his creative artistic impulse in a three-dimensional manner.

His big break came in 1896, when he won the competition to design a new home for the **Glasgow School of Art** (see p.779). This is his most famous work, but a number of smaller buildings created during his tenure with the architects Honeyman and Keppie, which began in 1889, document the development of his style. In the 1890s Glasgow went wild for tearooms, where the middle classes could play billiards and chess, read in the library or merely chat. The imposing Miss Cranston, who dominated the Glasgow teashop scene and ran the most elegant establishments, gave Mackintosh great freedom of design, and in 1896 he started to plan the interiors for her growing business. Over the next twenty years he designed articles from teaspoons to furniture and, finally, as in the case of the **Willow Tea Rooms** (see p.779), the structure itself.

Despite his success, the spectre of limited budgets was to haunt Mackintosh throughout his career, and he never had the chance to design and construct with complete freedom. However, these constraints didn't manage to dull his creativity. His forceful personality and unique touches recur – Japanese lantern shapes, images of seeds and roses and stylized Celtic illuminations.

Tenement House

145 Buccleuch St • March–Oct daily 1–5pm • NTS • £6 • ⓣ 0844 493 2197 • Cowcaddens underground

On the first floor of a typical tenement block still inhabited today, the fascinating **Tenement House** holds the perfectly preserved home of one Agnes Toward, who moved here with her mother in 1911, changing nothing and throwing very little out until she was hospitalized in 1965. The flat gives every impression of still being lived in, with a cluttered hearth and range, kitchen utensils, recess beds, framed religious tracts and sewing machine all untouched.

The East End

East of Glasgow Cross, down Gallowgate beyond the train lines, lies the **East End**, the district that perhaps most closely corresponds to the old perception of Glasgow. Hemmed in by Glasgow Green to the south and the old university to the west, this densely packed industrial area essentially created the city's wealth. Today, isolated pubs, tatty shops and

originality did not endear him to construction workers, however: he would frequently change his mind or add details at the last minute, often over-stretching budgets. This lost him the support of local builders and architects, despite his being admired on the continent, and prompted him to move to Suffolk in 1914 to escape the "philistines" of Glasgow. World War I curtailed building projects and effectively ended Mackintosh's career; from 1923 he lived in the south of France where he gave up architectural work in favour of painting.

MACKINTOSH SIGHTS

The one-day **Mackintosh Trail Ticket** pass (£12) includes entry to twelve principal Mackintosh buildings as well as unlimited Underground and bus travel. It can be bought from the tourist office, from any of the attractions on the trail or from the Charles Rennie Mackintosh Society (W crmsociety.com).

The Lighthouse Mitchell Lane, off Argyle St. One of Mackintosh's earliest commissions, during his tenure with Honeyman and Keppie: a new building to house the Glasgow *Herald* constructed in 1894. A massive tower rises up from the corner, giving the building its popular name.

Queens Cross Church Junction of Garscube and Maryhill roads in the northwest of the city T 0141 946 6600, W crmsociety.com. Mackintosh designed few religious buildings: this church of 1896 is the only completed example standing. Hallmarks include a sturdy box-shaped tower and asymmetrical exterior with complex heart-shaped floral motifs in the large chancel window. To give height to the small and peaceful interior, Mackintosh used an open-arched timber ceiling, enhanced by carved detail and an oak pulpit decorated with tulip-form relief. It isn't the most unified of structures, but shows the flexibility of his distinctive style, and is now home to the Charles Rennie Mackintosh Society. March–Oct Mon–Fri 10am–5pm, Sun 2–5pm; Sept–Feb Mon–Fri 10am–5pm. £4; included in the Mackintosh Trail Ticket.

Scotland Street School Just south of the river opposite Shields Road underground. Dating from 1904, this is Mackintosh's most symmetrical work, with a whimsical nod to history in the Scots Baronial conical tower roofs and sandstone building material. Note the two main stairways that frame the entrance, lit by glass-filled bays that protrude from the building. Mon–Thurs & Sat 10am–5pm, Fri & Sun 11am–5pm. Free.

House for an Art Lover T 0141 353 4770, W houseforanartlover.co.uk. The building which arguably displays Mackintosh at his most flamboyant was one he never saw built, constructed in Bellahouston Park in 1996, 95 years after plans for it were submitted to a German architectural competition. The exterior is austere but dramatic, while the interior features a double-height entrance hall and galleries. April–Sept Mon–Wed 10am–4pm, Thurs–Sun 10am–1pm; Oct–March Sat & Sun 10am–1pm; call for weekday opening in winter. £4.50; included on the Mackintosh Trail Ticket.

19

cafés sit amid the dereliction, in sharp contrast to the gloss of the Merchant City just a few blocks west. You're definitely off the tourist trail here, though it's not as threatening as it may feel. Between London Road and the River Clyde are the wide and tree-lined spaces of **Glasgow Green**. Reputedly Britain's oldest public park, the Green has been common land since at least 1178, and has been a popular spot for Sunday afternoon strolls for centuries.

People's Palace

Glasgow Green • Mon–Thurs & Sat 10am–5pm, Fri & Sun 11am–5pm • Free • T 0141 276 0788, W glasgowlife.org.uk

A squat, red sandstone Victorian structure, built as a museum back in 1898, **People's Palace** offers a wonderfully haphazard evocation of the city's history. Many displays are designed to bring back a warm glow of nostalgia, and it's all refreshingly unpretentious, with visitors almost always outnumbered by Glaswegian families.

Glasgow Cathedral

Castle St • April–Sept Mon–Sat 9.30am–5.30pm, Sun 1–5pm; Oct–March Mon–Sat 9.30am–4pm, Sun 1–4pm • Free • T 0141 552 8198, W glasgowcathedral.org.uk • Buchanan Street underground

Built in 1136, destroyed in 1192 and rebuilt soon after, stumpy-spired **Glasgow Cathedral** was not completed until the late fifteenth century. Dedicated to the city's patron saint and reputed founder, St Mungo, the cathedral is effectively on two levels, the crypt being part of the lower church. On entering, you arrive in the impressively lofty nave of the **upper church**, with the lower church entirely hidden from view. Beyond the nave, the **choir** is concealed by the curtained stone pulpit, making the interior feel a great deal smaller than might be expected from outside. In the choir's northeastern corner, a small door leads into the gloomy **sacristy**, in which Glasgow University was first founded over five hundred years ago. Two sets of steps from the nave lead down into the **lower church**, where you'll find the dark and musty **chapel** surrounding the tomb of St Mungo. The saint's relics were removed in the late Middle Ages, although the tomb still forms the centrepiece. The chapel itself is one of the most glorious examples of medieval architecture in Scotland, best seen in the delicate fan vaulting rising up from the thicket of cool stone columns.

The Necropolis

Behind the Cathedral • ⓦ glasgownecropolis.org • Buchanan Street underground

Inspired by the Père Lachaise cemetery in Paris, the atmospheric **Necropolis** is a grassy mound covered in a fantastic assortment of crumbling and tumbling gravestones, ornate urns, gloomy catacombs and Neoclassical temples. Paths lead through the rows of eroding, neglected graves, and from the summit, next to the column topped with an indignant John Knox, there are superb **views** of the city and its trademark mix of grit and grace.

The West End

The urbane **West End** seems a world away from Glasgow's industrial image and the bustle of the centre. In the 1800s, wealthy merchants established huge estates here away from the soot and grime of city life, and in 1870 the ancient university was moved from its cramped home near the cathedral to a spacious new site overlooking the River Kelvin. Elegant housing swiftly followed, the Kelvingrove Art Gallery and Museum was built to house the 1888 International Exhibition and, in 1896, the Glasgow District Subway – today's underground – started its circuitous shuffle from here to the city centre.

The hub of life hereabouts is **Byres Road**, running between Great Western Road and Dumbarton Road past Hillhead underground station. Shops, restaurants, cafés, some enticing pubs and hordes of students give the area a sense of style and vitality, while glowing red sandstone tenements and graceful terraces provide a suitably upmarket backdrop.

The main sights straddle the banks of the cleaned-up River Kelvin, which meanders through the gracious acres of the **Botanic Gardens** and the slopes, trees and statues of **Kelvingrove Park**. Overlooked by the Gothic towers and turrets of **Glasgow University**, Kelvingrove Park is home to the pride of Glasgow's civic collection of art and artefacts, **Kelvingrove Art Gallery and Museum**, off Argyle Street.

Kelvingrove Art Gallery and Museum

Argyle St • Mon–Thurs & Sat 10am–5pm, Fri & Sun 11am–5pm • Free • ⓣ 0141 276 9599, ⓦ glasgowlife.org.uk • Kelvin Hall underground

Founded on donations from the city's Victorian industrialists and opened at an international fair held in 1901, the huge, red sandstone fantasy castle of **Kelvingrove**

TOP 5 GLASGOW MUST-DOS

Designer shopping see p.792
A movie at the GFT see p.792
A night out in the West End see p.790
Oysters at Rogano see p.789
A stroll in the Botanics see p.784

THE GLASGOW BOYS AND THE COLOURISTS

In the 1870s a group of Glasgow-based painters formed a loose association that was to imbue Scottish art with a contemporary European flavour far ahead of the rest of Britain. Dominated by five men – Guthrie, Lavery, Henry, Hornel and Crawhall – "**The Glasgow Boys**" came from very different backgrounds, but all rejected the eighteenth-century conservatism which spawned little other than sentimental, anecdotal renditions of Scottish history peopled by "poor but happy" families.

Sir James Guthrie, taking inspiration from the *plein air* painting of the Impressionists, spent his summers in the countryside, observing and painting everyday life. Instead of happy peasants, his work shows individuals staring out of the canvas, detached and unrepentant, painted with rich tones but without undue attention to detail or the play of light. Typical of his finest work during the 1880s, *A Highland Funeral* (in the Kelvingrove collection; see p.782) was hugely influential for the rest of the group, who found inspiration in its restrained emotional content, colour and unaffected realism. Seeing it persuaded **Sir John Lavery**, then studying in France, to return to Glasgow. Lavery was eventually to become an internationally popular society portraitist, his subtle use of paint revealing his debt to Whistler, but his earlier work, depicting the middle class at play, is filled with light and motion.

An interest in colour and decoration united the work of friends **George Henry** and **E.A. Hornel**. The predominance of pattern, colour and design in Henry's *Galloway Landscape*, for example, is remarkable, while their joint work *The Druids* (both part of the Kelvingrove collection; see p.782), in thickly applied impasto, is full of Celtic symbolism. In 1893 both artists set off for Japan, funded by Alexander Reid and later William Burrell, where their work used vibrant tone and texture for expressive effect and took Scottish painting to the forefront of European trends.

Newcastle-born **Joseph Crawhall** was a reserved and quiet individual who combined superb draughtsmanship and simplicity of line with a photographic memory to create watercolours of an outstanding naturalism and originality. Again, William Burrell was an important patron, and a number of Crawhall's works reside at the Burrell Collection (see p.786).

The Glasgow Boys school reached its height by 1900 and did not outlast World War I, but the influence of their work cannot be underestimated, shaking the foundations of the artistic elite and inspiring the next generation of Edinburgh painters, who became known as the "**Colourists**". Samuel John Peploe, John Duncan Fergusson, George Leslie Hunter and Francis Cadell shared an understanding that the manipulation of colour was the heart and soul of a good painting. All experienced and took inspiration from the avant-garde of late nineteenth-century Paris as well as the landscapes of southern France. **J.D. Fergusson**, in particular, immersed himself in the bohemian, progressive Parisian scene, rubbing shoulders with writers and artists including Picasso. Some of his most dynamic work, which can be seen in the Fergusson Gallery in Perth (see p.819), displays elements of Cubism, yet is still clearly in touch with the Celtic imagery of Henry, Hornel and, indeed, Charles Rennie Mackintosh. The work of the Scottish Colourists has become highly fashionable and valuable, with galleries and civic collections throughout the country featuring their work prominently.

Art Gallery and Museum is a brash statement of Glasgow's nineteenth-century self-confidence. Intricate and ambitious both in its riotous exterior detailing and within, Kelvingrove offers an impressive and inviting setting for its exhibits. The wide and sometimes bizarre range of objects on show, from a World War II Spitfire suspended from the roof of the West Court to suits of armour, ancient Egyptian relics and priceless paintings by Rembrandt, Whistler and Raeburn, form the basis of an undeniably rich and deliberately varied civic collection.

Most visitors will be drawn to the **paintings**, most famous of which is Salvador Dalí's stunning *St John of the Cross*. You can also acquaint yourself with significant **Scottish art** including works by the Glasgow Boys and the Scottish Colourists. There's a special section of paintings, furniture and murals devoted to Charles Rennie Mackintosh and the "**Glasgow Style**" he and his contemporaries inspired.

Glasgow University

University Visitor Centre & Shop Oct–May Mon–Sat 9.30am–5pm, June–Sept Mon–Sat 9.30am–5pm, Sun 11am–3pm **Guided tours** From the Visitor Centre, bookings advised • April– Sept Wed–Sat 11am • £3.50 • ⓣ 0141 330 5511, ⓦ gla.ac.uk • Kelvin Hall/ Hillhead underground

Dominating the West End skyline, the gloomy turreted tower of **Glasgow University**, designed by Sir George Gilbert Scott in the mid-nineteenth century, overlooks the glades edging the River Kelvin.

The Hunterian

University Ave • Mon–Sat 9.30am–5pm • Free • ⓣ 0141 330 5431, ⓦ hunterian.gla.ac.uk

Beside the Visitor Centre is the **Hunterian Museum**, Scotland's oldest public museum, dating back to 1807. Opposite, across University Avenue, is Hunter's more frequently visited bequest, the **Hunterian Art Gallery**, best known for its wonderful works by James Abbott McNeill Whistler: only Washington, DC, has a larger collection. The gallery's other major collection is of nineteenth- and twentieth-century Scottish art, including the quasi-Impressionist Scottish landscapes of William McTaggart, a forerunner of the Glasgow Boys movement, itself represented here by Guthrie and Hornel. Finally, the monumental dancing figures of J.D. Fergusson's *Les Eus* preside over a small collection of work by the Scottish Colourists.

Mackintosh House

Hillhead St • Mon–Sat 9.30am–5pm • £3, free after 2pm Wed • ⓣ 0141 330 5431, ⓦ hunterian.gla.ac.uk

A side gallery from the Hunterian Art Gallery leads to the **Mackintosh House**, a re-creation of the interior of the now-demolished Glasgow home of Margaret MacDonald and Charles Rennie Mackintosh. Its exquisitely cool interior contains more than sixty pieces of Mackintosh furniture on three floors. In addition, a permanent gallery shows a selection of his two-dimensional work, from watercolours to architectural drawings.

The Botanic Gardens

730 Great Western Rd • **Botanic Gardens** Daily 7am–dusk **Kibble Palace** 10am–4.45pm or 4.15pm in winter • Free • ⓣ 0141 276 1614 • Hillhead underground

At the northern, top end of Byres Road, where it meets the Great Western Road, is the main entrance to the **Botanic Gardens**. The best-known glasshouse here, the hulking, domed **Kibble Palace,** houses lush ferns, exotic blooms and swaying palms from around the world. Nearby, in the **Main Range Glasshouse**, stunning orchids, cacti, ferns and tropical fruit luxuriate in the humidity. In addition to the area around the main glasshouses, there are some beautifully remote paths in the gardens that weave along the closely wooded banks of the deep-set River Kelvin, linking up with the walkway running alongside the river all the way down to Dumbarton Road, near its confluence with the Clyde.

Clydeside

"The **Clyde** made Glasgow and Glasgow made the Clyde" runs an old saying, full of sentimentality for the days when the river was the world's premier shipbuilding centre, and when its industry lent an innovation and confidence that made Glasgow a major city of the British Empire. Despite the hardships heavy industry brought, every Glaswegian would follow the progress of the skeleton ships under construction in the riverside yards, cheering them on their way down the Clyde as they were launched. The last of the great liners to be built on **Clydeside** was the *QE2* in 1967. Such events are hard to visualize today: shipbuilding is restricted to a couple of barely viable yards.

THE WAVERLEY

One of Glasgow's best-loved treasures is the **Waverley** (T 0845 130 4647 or W waverley excursions.co.uk), the last seagoing paddle steamer in the world, which spends the summer cruising "doon the watter" to various ports on the Firth of Clyde and the Ayrshire coast from its base at Glasgow Science Centre. Built on Clydeside in 1947, she's an elegant vessel to look at, not least when she's thrashing away at full steam with the hills of Argyll or Arran in the background. Contact for sailing times and itinerary.

However the river is once again becoming a focus of attention, with striking new buildings including the titanium-clad **Armadillo** concert hall, **Glasgow Science Centre** and the Zaha Hadid-designed **Riverside Museum**.

The Glasgow Science Centre

19

50 Pacific Quay • Daily 10am–6pm • £9.95 • T 0141 420 5000, W www.gsc.org.uk • Govan underground

On the south bank of the river, linked to the SECC by pedestrian Bell's Bridge, are the three space age, titanium-clad constructions which make up the **Glasgow Science Centre**. Of the three buildings, the largest is the curvaceous, wedge-shaped **Science Mall**. Behind the vast glass wall facing the river, four floors of interactive exhibits range from lift-your-own-weight pulleys to thermograms. The centre covers almost every aspect of science, from simple optical illusions to cutting-edge computer technology, including a section on moral and environmental issues – all good fun, although weekends and school holidays are a scrum. Meanwhile, a bubble-like **IMAX theatre** shows science- and nature-based documentaries, while the 416ft-high **Glasgow Tower**, built with an aerofoil-like construction to allow it to rotate to face into the prevailing wind, has a viewing tower offering panoramic vistas of central Glasgow.

Riverside Museum

100 Pointhouse Place • Mon–Thurs & Sat 10am–5pm, Fri & Sun 11am–5pm • Free; Tall Ship £5 • T 0141 287 2720, W glasgowlife.org.uk • Govan underground

Just west of the Science Centre, on the other side of the river, the magnificent new **Riverside Museum** – Scotland's Museum of Transport and Travel – houses artefacts from Glasgow's old transport museum, and a lot more besides. The wave-like titanium-clad building by Zaha Hadid is an attraction in its own right, its cathedral-like interior home to a huge, dramatically displayed collection of trains, boats, trams, bike, cars and ships models. Interactive exhibits provide engaging background on the city's social fabric, with walk-through streets incorporating real interiors from Glasgow shops and cafés.

The Southside

The section of Glasgow south of the Clyde is generally described as the **Southside**, though within this area there are a number of recognizable districts, including the notoriously deprived **Gorbals** and Govan, which are sprinkled with new developments but still derelict and tatty in many parts. There's little reason to venture here unless you're making your way to the Clydeside museums (see above) and the famously innovative Citizens' Theatre (see p.791). Further south, inner-city decay fades into altogether gentler and more salubrious suburbs, including Queen's Park, home to Scotland's national football stadium, **Hampden Park**, Pollokshaws and the rural landscape of Pollok Park, which contains one of Glasgow's major museums, the **Burrell Collection**.

19

THE OLD FIRM

Football, or *fitba'* as it's pronounced locally, is one of Glasgow's great passions – and one of its great blights. While the city can claim to be one of Europe's premier footballing centres, it's known above all for one of the most bitter rivalries in any sport, that between **Celtic** and **Rangers**. Two of the largest clubs in Britain, with weekly crowds regularly topping 60,000, the Old Firm, as they're collectively known, have dominated Scottish football for a century; in the last twenty years they've lavished vast sums of money on foreign talent in an often frantic effort both to outdo each other and to stay in touch with the standards of the top English and European teams.

The roots of Celtic, who play at Celtic Park in the eastern district of Parkhead (T 0871 226 1888, W celticfc.net), lie in the city's immigrant Irish and **Catholic** population, while Rangers, based at Ibrox Park in Govan on the Southside (T 0871 702 1972, W rangers.co.uk), have traditionally drawn support from local **Protestants**: as a result, sporting rivalries have been enmeshed in a sectarian divide, and although Catholics do play for Rangers, and Protestants for Celtic, sections of supporters of both clubs seem intent on perpetuating the feud. While large-scale violence on the terraces and streets has not been seen for some time – thanks in large measure to canny policing – Old Firm matches often seethe with bitter passions, and sectarian-related assaults do still occur in parts of the city.

However, there is a less intense side to the game, found not just in the fun-loving "Tartan Army" which follows the (often rollercoaster) fortunes of the Scottish national team, but also in Glasgow's smaller clubs, who actively distance themselves from the distasteful aspects of the Old Firm and plod along with home-grown talent in the lower reaches of the Scottish league. All important reminders that it is, after all, only a game.

Scottish Football Museum

Hampden Park • Mon–Sat 10am–5pm, Sun 11am–5pm • £6 • T 0141 616 6139, W scottishfootballmuseum.org.uk • Trains from Central station to Mount Florida

Two and a half miles south of the city centre, just west of the tree-filled Queen's Park, the floodlights and giant stands of Scotland's national football stadium, **Hampden Park**, loom over the surrounding suburban tenements and terraces. It's home to the engaging **Scottish Football Museum**, with memorabilia, video clips and displays covering almost every aspect of the game. On view is the Scottish Cup, the world's oldest football trophy and a re-creation of the old changing room at Hampden, as well as a bizarre life-sized reconstruction of the most famous goal in Scottish footballing history, scored during the 1978 World Cup in Argentina.

The Burrell Collection

Pollok Park, 6 miles southwest of the city centre • Mon–Thurs & Sat 10am–5pm, Fri & Sun 11am–5pm • Free • From the centre take a train to Pollokshaws West station (not to be confused with Pollokshields West), or bus #45, #47, #48 or #57 to Pollokshaws Road, or a taxi (£10). A free minibus (every 30min 10am–4.30pm) runs from the park gates to the collection

The outstanding **Burrell Collection**, the lifetime collection of shipping magnate Sir William Burrell (1861–1958), is, for some, the principal reason for visiting Glasgow. Sir William's only real criterion for buying a piece was whether he liked it or not, enabling him to buy many unfashionable works that cost comparatively little but subsequently proved their worth.

The simplicity and clean lines of the Burrell building are superb, with large picture windows giving sweeping views over woodland and serving as a tranquil backdrop to the objects inside. An airy covered **courtyard** includes the **Warwick Vase**, a huge bowl containing fragments of a second-century AD vase from Emperor Hadrian's villa in Tivoli. On three sides of the courtyard, a trio of dark and sombre panelled rooms have been re-erected in faithful detail from the Burrells' Hutton Castle home, their tapestries, antique furniture and fireplaces displaying the same eclectic taste as the rest of the museum.

Elsewhere on the ground floor, Greek, Roman and earlier artefacts include an exquisite mosaic Roman cockerel from the first century BC and a 4000-year-old Mesopotamian lion's head. Nearby, also illuminated by enormous windows, the excellent **Oriental Art** collection forms nearly a quarter of the whole display, ranging from Neolithic jades through bronze vessels and Tang funerary horses to cloisonné. Burrell considered his **medieval and post-medieval European art**, which encompasses silverware, glass, textiles and sculpture, to be the most valuable part of his collection: these are ranged across a maze of small galleries.

Upstairs, the cramped and comparatively gloomy **mezzanine** is probably the least satisfactory section of the gallery, not the best setting for its sparkling array of paintings by artists that include Degas, Manet, Cézanne and Boudin.

ARRIVAL AND DEPARTURE GLASGOW

By plane Glasgow International Airport (T 0870 040 0008, W glasgowairport.com) is at Abbotsinch, 8 miles southwest of the city. From here, the 24-hour Glasgow Flyer bus (£3.95) runs from bus stop 1 into the central Buchanan Street bus station (every 10min during the day; 10min). Airport taxis charge £18–20. Glasgow's second airport, Prestwick (T 0871 223 0700, W gpia.co.uk), lies 30 miles south of Glasgow, near Ayr. The simplest way to get from here to Glasgow is by train to Central station (Mon–Sat every 30min, Sun hourly; 45min): there's a station right by the terminal (alight at the airport, not Prestwick Town).

Destinations from Glasgow International Barra (2 daily; 1hr 10min); Belfast (Mon–Fri 7 daily; Sat & Sun 3 daily; 45min); Benbecula (Mon–Sat 2 daily; Sun 1 daily; 1hr); Campbeltown (Mon–Fri 2 daily; 40min); Dublin (3 daily; 55min); Islay (Mon–Fri 2 daily, Sat 1 daily; 40min); Kirkwall (1 daily; 1hr 20min); London City (Mon–Fri 4 daily, Sun 1 daily; 1hr 35min); London Gatwick (Mon–Fri 11 daily, Sat & Sun 4 daily; 1hr 30min); London Heathrow (Mon–Fri 18 daily, Sat & Sun 10 daily; 1hr 20min); London Luton (Mon–Fri 5 daily, Sat 2 daily, Sun 3 daily; 1hr 15min); London Stansted (Mon–Fri 5 daily, Sat 3 daily, Sun 4 daily; 1hr 20min); Shetland (Mon–Fri 2 daily, Sat & Sun 1 daily; 1hr 30min); Stornoway (Mon–Fri 4 daily, Sat & Sun 2 daily; 1hr 10min); Tiree (Mon–Sat 1 daily; 50min).

Destinations from Glasgow Prestwick Dublin (Mon–Fri 3 daily, Sat & Sun 2 daily; 45min); London Stansted (4 daily; 1hr 10min).

By train Nearly all trains from England come into Central Station, which sits over Argyle St, one of the city's main shopping thoroughfares. Bus #398 from the front entrance on Gordon St (every 10min) shuttles to Queen Street station, at the corner of George Square, terminus for trains serving Edinburgh and the north. The walk between the two takes about 10min.

Destinations from Glasgow Central Ardrossan for Arran ferry (every 30min; 45min); Ayr (every 30min; 50min); East Kilbride (every 30min; 30min); Gourock (every 30min; 50min); Greenock (every 30min; 40min); Lanark (every 30min; 50min); London (hourly; 5–6hr); Paisley (every 10min; 10min); Queen's Park (every 15min; 6min); Stranraer (4 daily direct; 2hr 15min); Wemyss Bay (every 30min; 50min).

Destinations from Glasgow Queen Street Aberdeen (hourly; 2hr 30min); Balloch (every 30min; 45min); Dumbarton (every 20min; 30min); Dundee (hourly; 1hr 20min); Edinburgh (every 15min; 50min); Fort William (1–3 daily; 3hr 40min); Helensburgh (every 30min; 45min); Inverness (3 daily direct; 3hr 25min); Milngavie (every 30min; 25min); Oban (1–3 daily; 3hr); Perth (hourly; 1hr); Stirling (hourly; 30min).

By bus Buchanan Street bus station is the arrival point for regional and intercity coaches.

Destinations Aberdeen (hourly; 3hr 15min); Campbeltown (3 daily; 4–5hr); Dundee (every 30min; 1hr 50min); Edinburgh (every 15min; 1hr 10min); Fort William (4 daily; 3hr); Glen Coe (4 daily; 2hr 30min); Inverness (1 direct daily; 4–5hr); Kyle of Lochalsh (3 daily; 5–6hr); Loch Lomond (hourly; 45min); London (5 daily; 8–9hr); Oban (3 daily; 2hr 50min); Perth (hourly; 1hr 35min); Portree (3 daily; 6–7hr); Stirling (hourly; 45min).

INFORMATION

Tourist office 11 George Square (April & May Mon–Sat 9am–6pm, Sun 10am–6pm; June & Sept Mon–Sat 10am–7pm, Sun 10am–6pm; July & Aug Mon–Sat 9am–8pm, Sun 10am–6pm; Oct–March Mon–Sat 9am–6pm; T 0141 204 4400, W seeglasgow.com); there's another in Glasgow Airport's international arrivals hall (May–Sept daily 7.30am–5pm; Oct–April Mon–Sat 7.30am–5pm, Sun 8am–5pm; T 0141 848 4440).

Listings information The best resource for finding out what's on in the city is the comprehensive, lively and informative *The List* magazine (W list.co.uk), published fortnightly.

GETTING AROUND

Although it can be tough negotiating Glasgow's steep hills, walking is the best way to explore any one part of the city. However, as the main sights are scattered – the West End, for example, is a good 30min walk from the centre – you'll probably need to use the comprehensive public transport system. If you're travelling beyond the city centre or the West End, or to the main sights on the Southside, you may need to use the bus and train networks. The **Travel Centre** on St Enoch's Square has full details on transport in and around the city.

By underground The best way to get between the city centre and the West End is to use the underground (Mon–Sat 6.30am–11pm, Sun 10am–6.30pm), whose stations are marked with a large orange U.

By bus The array of different bus companies and the routes they take is perplexing even to locals; pick up individual timetables at the Travel Centre.

19

By train The suburban train network is swift and convenient. Suburbs south of the Clyde are connected to Central station, either at the mainline station or the subterranean low-level station. The trains are an excellent way to link to points west and northwest of Glasgow, including Milngavie (for the start of the West Highland Way), Balloch (for Loch Lomond) and Helensburgh.

By bike West End Cycles, 16 Chancellor St (0141 357 1344) has a good selection and is located close to the start of the Glasgow to Loch Lomond route, one of a number of cycle routes that radiate out from the city.

By taxi Glasgow Taxi Ltd (0141 429 7070); Glasgow Private Hire (0141 774 3000).

ACCOMMODATION

There's a good range of accommodation in Glasgow, from a large, well-run SYHA hostel through to some fashionable (and not overpriced) designer hotels in the centre. In general, **prices** are significantly lower than in Edinburgh, and given that many hotels are business-oriented, you can often negotiate good deals at weekends.

CITY CENTRE AND THE MERCHANT CITY

★ **Babbity Bowster** 16–18 Blackfriars St, off High St 0141 552 5055, babbitybowster.com; map p.778. Best known as a pub (see p.790), Babbity Bowster also features six plain, serviceable rooms in a great Merchant City location. No breakfast. £60

★ **The Brunswick** 106 Brunswick St 0141 552 0001, brunswickhotel.co.uk; map p.778. Small, independent designer hotel in the heart of the Merchant City; fashionable but good value with minimalist furniture and a smart bar and restaurant. £60

Euro Hostel 318 Clyde St 0141 222 2828, euro-hostels.co.uk; map p.778. Glasgow isn't short of bed space, thanks to this bright-pink liveried, seven-storey hostel smack in the centre. Its 360 beds are all bunks, but they're in smart en-suite rooms sleeping two, four, six or more – some have great views. Continental breakfast included. £15

Malmaison 278 West George St 0141 572 1000, malmaison.com; map p.778. Glasgow's version of the sleek, chic mini-chain, an austere Grecian-temple frontage masking a superbly comfortable designer hotel. Have a drink at their Cosmo bar. £100

Mark's Hotel 110 Bath St 0141 353 0800, markshotels.com; map p.778. Angular, glass-fronted central hotel, with rooftop views from the upper floors, 103 smartly appointed rooms and a chic bar and restaurant. Double, triple and family rooms available. £90

University of Strathclyde 0141 553 4148, rescat.strath.ac.uk; map p.778. Various sites, most of which are around the cathedral. B&B in single rooms is available near the main campus on Cathedral St. Closed mid-Sept to May. From £22.50 per person, four-bed rooms £60

WEST END

Alamo Guesthouse 46 Gray St 0141 339 2395, alamoguesthouse.com; map pp.776–777. Good-value, family-run boarding house next to Kelvingrove Park. The small but comfortable rooms are decorated in soft colours and with antique furnishings; some have chandeliers. £59

★ **Amadeus Guesthouse** 441 North Woodside Rd 0141 339 8257, amadeusguesthouse.co.uk; map pp.776–777. Handily located near Great Western Rd, but on a quiet street opposite the River Kelvin, this place offers stylish en-suite rooms in a welcoming Victorian townhouse. £48

Hotel du Vin at One Devonshire Gardens 1 Devonshire Gardens, Great Western Rd 0141 339 2001, hotelduvin.com; map pp.776–777. Glasgow's most exclusive and exquisite small hotel, a 10min walk up the Great Western Rd from the Botanic Gardens. £130

Kirklee 11 Kensington Gate 0141 334 5555, kirkleehotel.co.uk; map pp.776–777. Characterful West End B&B in an extravagant red sandstone Edwardian townhouse, with antique furniture and walls crammed with paintings and etchings. A panelled hallway and parquet floors add to the atmosphere. £80

Queensgate Apartments 0141 339 1615, queensgateapartments.com. A choice of attractive and cosy flats in traditional tenement buildings. Three apartments are within walking distance of the West End's vibrant Byres Road, and all have TVs and wi-fi. and other mod cons. A good option for families or groups. Around **£400** per week.

SYHA hostel 7–8 Park Terrace 0870 004 1119, syha.org.uk; map pp.776–777. This popular, well-equipped hostel occupies a wonderful townhouse in one of the West End's grandest terraces. It's a 10min walk south of Kelvinbridge underground station; bus #44 from the city centre leaves you with a short stroll west up Woodlands Rd. Dorm **£20**, double **£55**

University of Glasgow 0141 330 4116, cvso.co.uk; map pp.776–777. Low-priced self-catering rooms and flats, mostly in the West End. Closed mid-Sept to May. From **£16** per person per night.

EATING

Glasgow's **restaurant scene** is reasonably dynamic, with new places replacing old (and sometimes not very old) every year. Most places to eat are concentrated in the commercial hub and Merchant City district of the city centre, as well as in the trendy West End. Modern Scottish cuisine, combining excellent fresh local ingredients with Mediterranean-style cooking techniques, is on the menus of the city's best restaurants. And Glasgwegians have a particular fondness for Indian and Chinese food, too.

19

CITY CENTRE AND THE MERCHANT CITY

CAFÉS, DINERS AND CAFÉ-BARS

★ **Café Gandolfi and Bar Gandolfi** 64 Albion St 0141 552 6813, cafegandolfi.com; map p.778. *Gandolfi* was one of the first to test the waters in the revived Merchant City in the 1980s and today it's a landmark. Designed with distinctive wooden furniture, the café serves up Scottish staples (including great black pudding), soups, salads, fish and Continental cuisine (mains £12–18). The food's equally good in the contemporary bar upstairs. Daily 9am–11.30pm.

Café Source 1 St Andrew's Square 0141 548 6020, standrewsinthesquare.com; map pp.776–777. In the basement of St Andrew's, an eighteenth-century church, patterned on London's St Martin in the Fields, and now a folk music and Scottish dance centre. The café serves up inexpensive Scottish favourites featuring local produce. Frequent live jam sessions and a monthly jazz supper club. Daily 10am–11pm.

★ **Trans Europe-Café** 25 Parnie St 0141 552 7999, transeuropecafe.co.uk; map p.778. A fun railway-style diner which takes culinary inspiration from various European capitals and dishes up excellent soup and gourmet sandwiches at reasonable prices. Mon–Wed & Sun 10am–5pm Thurs– Sat 10am–10pm.

Where the Monkey Sleeps 182 West Regent St 0141 226 3406, monkeysleeps.com; map p.778. Owned by graduates of the nearby Glasgow School of Art who acquired their barista skills between classes, this hip homegrown café features freshly prepared sandwiches and salads, and the espresso is superb. Mon–Fri 10am–5pm.

RESTAURANTS

The 13th Note Café 50–60 King St 0141 553 1638, 13thnote.co.uk; map p.778. Inexpensive veggie and vegan food, with Greek and other Mediterranean influences, in a hip bar and experimental music venue on arty King St. Daily noon–midnight.

Brian Maule at Le Chardon d'Or 176 West Regent St 0141 248 3801, brianmaule.com; map p.778. Owner-chef Maule, who worked with the Roux brothers at *Le Gavroche* restaurant in London, turns out fancy but not pretentious French-influenced food along the lines of grilled sea bass with fennel and broad beans in a Pernod cream. Mains from £23. Mon–Fri noon–2.30pm, 6pm–10pm, Sat noon–10pm.

City Merchant 97 Candleriggs 0141 553 1577, citymerchant.co.uk; map p.778. Popular brasserie that blazed the Merchant City trail. Fresh Scottish produce from Ayrshire lamb to the house speciality: west coast seafood. Mains from £17.50. Mon–Sat noon–10.30pm, Sun 4.30–9.30pm.

★ **Dakhin** 89 Candleriggs 0141 553 2585, dakhin.com; map p.778. Owned by the same people as *The Dhabba* (see below), this first-floor restaurant (above *Bar 91*) specializes in reasonably priced South Indian cuisine. Be sure and try a rice dosa. Mon–Fri noon–2pm, 5–11pm, Sat & Sun 1 –11pm.

The Dhabba 44 Candleriggs 0141 553 1249, thedhabba.com; map p.778. Not your typical Glasgow curry house. Prices are higher and portions are smaller, but the menu has some truly interesting options and fresh ingredients that place it steps above most others. Mon–Fri noon–2pm, 5–11pm, Sat & Sun 1–11pm.

★ **Gamba** 225a West George St 0141 572 0899, gamba.co.uk; map p.778. This modern basement restaurant offers one of the best meals in Glasgow. Continental contemporary sophistication prevails, with dishes such as mussel and oyster stew or grilled halibut with scallop cream (£20–25). If you love fish, come here. Mon–Sat noon–2.30pm & 5–10pm, Sun 5–9pm.

Rogano 11 Exchange Place 0141 248 4055, roganoglasgow.com; map p.778. An Art Deco fish restaurant and Glasgow institution since 1935, decked out in the style of the *Queen Mary* ocean liner. Mains cost around £25; *Café Rogano*, in the basement, is cheaper. Or just have some oysters at the bar. Daily noon–10.30pm.

19

WEST END

CAFÉS, DINERS AND CAFÉ-BARS

Grassroots Café 93 St George's Rd 0141 333 0534, grassrootsorganic.co.uk; map pp.776–777. Although the competition is not especially stiff, this vegetarian health-food store and deli has the best reputation for meat-free food in Glasgow. Fresh, creative cooking, good prices and a relaxed atmosphere. Mon–Wed 8am–6pm, Thurs & Fri 8am–7pm, Sat 9am–6pm, Sun 11am–5pm.

★ **Kember & Jones** 134 Byres Rd 0141 337 3851, kemberandjones.co.uk; map pp.776–777. This café and deli is a popular spot in the competitive Byres Rd, serving freshly made salads and sandwiches from around £6 along with irresistible cakes and pastries. Mon–Fri 8am–1pm, Sat 9am–1pm, Sun 9am–6pm.

Tchai Ovna 42 Otago Lane 0141 357 4524, tchaiovna.com; map pp.776–777. A low-key bohemian hangout overlooking the Kelvin River, offering savoury vegetarian options (try the red dahl curry at £5.90), cakes, snacks and a selection of teas from around the world. Mon–Sun 11am–11pm.

★ **University Café** 87 Byres Rd 0141 339 5217; map pp.776–777. This institution dates back to the 1910s and has been adored by at least three generations of students and West End residents, with its formica tables in snug booths, glass counters and original architectural features. The favourites are fish'n'chips or mince'n'tatties rounded off with an ice-cream cone – you won't spend more than a tenner. Mon–Thurs 9am–10pm, Fri–Sat 9am–10.30pm, Sun 10am–10pm.

RESTAURANTS

Ashoka Ashton Lane 19 Ashton Lane 0141 337 1115, ashokarestaurants.com; map pp.776–777. Lively curry house with franchises across the west of Scotland; all offer consistent quality and reasonable prices. Mon–Thurs noon–midnight, Fri & Sat noon–1am, Sun 5pm–midnight.

Chow 98 Byres Rd 0141 334 9818, chowrestaurant.co.uk; map pp.776–777. This bijou diner with extra seating upstairs offers excellent-value meals – hot tossed shredded chicken, for example – in a sleek, modern setting. Mains from £8.90. Mon–Thurs noon–2pm, 5–11.30pm, Fri & Sat noon–2pm, 5pm–midnight, Sun 4.30–11.30pm.

Mother India 28 Westminster Terrace, off Sauchiehall St 0141 221 1663, motherindiaglasgow.co.uk; map pp.776–777. One of the best Indian restaurants in Glasgow, serving home cooking with original specials and affordable favourites in laidback surroundings. Mon–Thurs 5.30–10.30pm, Fri & Sat noon–11pm, Sun noon–10pm.

No. Sixteen 16 Byres Rd 0141 339 2544, number16.co.uk; map pp.776–777. A local favourite, with daily menus of modern seasonal Scottish cooking using produce from pigeon to sea bream. Mains from £15.50. Mon–Sat noon–2.30pm, 5.30–10pm, Sun 1–3pm & 5.30–9pm.

★ **Stravaigin** 28–30 Gibson St 0141 334 2665, stravaigin.com; map pp.776–777. Scottish meat and fish are given an international makeover using a host of unexpected ingredients, offering unusual combinations such as Thai-spiced Aberdeen Angus beef carpaccio or ham and pistachio terrine. Look out for the occasional "wild food" nights. There's exceptional-value food in the street-level bar-café, and adventurous fine dining in the pricier basement restaurant. Mains from £9.95. Daily 11am–10.30pm; restaurant closed Mon.

The Ubiquitous Chip 12 Ashton Lane 0141 334 5007, ubiquitouschip.co.uk; map pp.776–777. Opened in 1971, *The Chip* led the way in headlining upmarket modern Scottish cuisine. Some say it's living on its reputation, but it's still up there; come for organic salmon with lime and vanilla mash or wood pigeon in a wild mushroom sauce. Two-course menu with appetizer £35, three courses with appetizer £40; the brasserie upstairs has mains from £10. Mon–Sat noon–2.30pm, 5.30–11pm, Sun 12.30–3pm & 6.30–11pm.

DRINKING

Most drinking dens in the **city centre**, the **Merchant City** and the **West End** are places to experience real Glaswegian bonhomie, with a good selection of characterful pubs featuring folk music, as well as more upscale bar/clubs.

CITY CENTRE AND THE MERCHANT CITY

The Arches 253 Argyle St 0141 565 1035, thearches.co.uk; map p.778. The basement bar is a focal point in this contemporary arts centre beneath Central station. Decent pub grub and an arty clientele. Good club nights, too (see opposite). Mon–Sat 11am–midnight; Sun 12.30pm–midnight.

★ **Babbity Bowster** 16–18 Blackfriars St, off High St 0141 552 5055, babbitybowster.com; map p.778. Lively place with an unforced and kitsch-free Scottish feel that features spontaneous folk sessions at the weekend. Good beer and wine, tasty food and some outdoor seating. Mon–Sat 11am–midnight, Sun 12.30pm–midnight.

Bar 10 10 Mitchell St 0141 572 1448; map p.778. Across from the Lighthouse, and considered the granddaddy of Glasgow style bars. Still popular and suitably chic. Mon–Sat 10am–midnight, Sun noon–midnight.

Corinthian 191 Ingram St 0141 552 1101, thecorinthianclub.co.uk; map p.778. A remarkable renovation of a florid, early Victorian Italianate bank with bars, a restaurant and a casino: dress smartly. Daily 11am till late.

Horseshoe Bar 17 Drury St 0141 248 6368,

Ⓦhorseshoebar.co.uk; map p.778. A must for pub aficionados. An original "Gin Palace" with the longest continuous bar in the UK, this is reputedly Glasgow's busiest drinking hole; karaoke upstairs. Mon–Sat 10.30am–midnight, Sun 12.30pm–midnight.

Pot Still 154 Hope St Ⓣ0141 333 0980, Ⓦthepotstill.co.uk; map p.778. Whisky galore – at least 500 different single malts are found in this traditional pub, which has a decent ale selection as well. Daily 11am–midnight.

WEST END

Firebird 1321 Argyle St Ⓣ0141 334 0594, Ⓦfirebirdglasgow.com; map pp.776–777. Airy, modern drinking spot near the Kelvingrove Art Gallery, with a wood-stoked pizza oven producing tasty snacks, and DJs to keep the pre-clubbing crowd entertained. Mon–Thurs noon–midnight, Fri/Sat noon–1am, Sun noon–midnight.

Lismore Lounge 206 Dumbarton Rd Ⓣ0141 576 0103; map pp.776–777. Decorated with specially commissioned stained-glass panels depicting the Highland Clearances, this bar is a meeting point for the local Gaels, who come to chat, relax and enjoy impromptu music sessions. Daily 11am–midnight.

Oran Mor Byres Rd at corner of Great Western Rd Ⓣ0141 357 6200, Ⓦwww.oran-mor.co.uk; map pp.776–777. An impressive player on Glasgow's nightlife scene, with a big bar, club and performance space auditorium (plus two different dining rooms) all set within a beautifully – and expensively – restored Kelvinside parish church. Mon–Sat 9am–3am, Sun 12.30pm–3am.

19

NIGHTLIFE AND ENTERTAINMENT

Glasgow is a great place for **contemporary music**, with loads of new bands emerging every year, many of them making the big time, and the city's **clubs** are excellent, with a range of places for every dance taste as well as a small but thriving gay scene. Glasgow is no slouch when it comes to the **performing arts**, either: it's home to Scottish Opera, Scottish Ballet and the Royal Scottish National Orchestra. Most of the larger theatres, multiplexes and concert halls are in the city centre; the West End is home to just one or two venues, while the Southside can boast two theatres noted for cutting-edge drama, the *Citizens'* and *Tramway*. For detailed **listings**, check *The List* (Ⓦlist.co.uk), or consult Glasgow's *Herald* or *Evening Times* newspapers.

CLUBS

The Arches 253 Argyle St Ⓣ0141 565 1000, Ⓦthearches.co.uk; map p.778. In converted railway arches under Central station, the club portion of this huge arts venue offers an eclectic array of music: hard house, trance, techno and funk. One of *DJ* magazine's top 10 clubs in the world.

Sub Club 22 Jamaica St Ⓣ0141 248 4600, Ⓦsubclub.co.uk; map p.778. Near-legendary venue, home to quality underground house and techno nights, as well as the brilliantly entertaining Sun night mash-up Optimo (Espacio).

The Tunnel 84 Mitchell St Ⓣ0141 204 1000, Ⓦtunnelglasgow.co.uk; map p.778. Contemporary and progressive house club with arty decor (have a look at the gents' cascading waterfall walls) and fairly strict dress codes – leave your trainers at home.

GAY CLUBS AND BARS

Bennets 80 Glassford St, Merchant City Ⓣ0141 552 5761; map p.778. Glasgow's longest-running gay club: predominantly male and fairly traditional, with MOR music. Wed–Sun.

Polo Lounge 84 Wilson St, off Glassford St Ⓣ0141 553 1221; map p.778. Original Victorian decor – marble tiles and open fires – and gentleman's-club atmosphere upstairs, with dark, pounding nightclub downstairs; attracts a mixed gay and gay-friendly crowd.

Revolver 6a John St Ⓣ0141 553 2456, Ⓦrevolverglasgow.com; map p.778. Geared more towards the art of conversation than dance, although the (free) jukebox is fantastic; welcomes men and women.

LIVE MUSIC VENUES

Barrowland 244 Gallowgate Ⓣ0141 552 4601, Ⓦglasgow-barrowland.com; map pp.776–777. Legendary East End ballroom that hosts some of the sweatiest and best gigs you may ever encounter. With room for a couple of thousand, it mostly books bands securely on the rise but still hosts some big-time acts who return to it as their favourite venue in Scotland.

King Tut's Wah Wah Hut 272a St Vincent St Ⓣ0141 221 5279, Ⓦkingtuts.co.uk; map p.778. Famous as the place where Oasis were discovered, and still presenting one of the city's best live music programmes. Also a good bar, with an excellent jukebox.

02 Academy 121 Eglington St Ⓣ0870 771 2000, Ⓦglasgow-academy.co.uk; map pp.776–777. With a capacity of 2500, this is the city's principal mid-sized venue. Less atmosphere than the *Barrowland*, but gets reliably big names.

THEATRE

Arches Theatre 253 Argyle St Ⓣ0141 565 1000, Ⓦthearches.co.uk. Home to its own avant-garde theatre company, reviving old classics and introducing new talent in a hip subterranean venue.

Citizens' Theatre 119 Gorbals St Ⓣ0141 429 0022, Ⓦcitz.co.uk. The "Citz" has evolved from its 1960s working-class roots into one of Britain's most respected

SHOPPING IN GLASGOW

The main area for spending in the city centre is formed by the Z-shaped and mostly pedestrianized route of **Argyle**, **Buchanan** and **Sauchiehall** streets. Along the way you'll find **Princes Square**, a stylish and imaginative shopping centre hollowed out of the innards of a soft sandstone building. The interior, all recherché Art Deco and ornate ironwork, holds lots of pricey, fashionable shops. Otherwise, make for the **West End** or the **Merchant City**, which have more eccentric and individual offerings. The latter is the place for secondhand and antiquarian **bookshops** as well as quirky vintage and one-off fashion stores on the lanes off Byres Road.

and innovative contemporary theatres. Three stages, concessions for students and free preview nights.

Theatre Royal 282 Hope St ⓣ0141 332 9000, ⓦatgtickets.com/glasgow. This late nineteenth-century playhouse was revived in the mid-1970s as the opulent home of Scottish Opera, whose repertoire features large-scale and adventurous productions. It also hosts visiting theatre groups, including the Royal Shakespeare Company, and orchestras.

Tramway 25 Albert Drive, off Pollokshaws Rd ⓣ0845 330 3501, ⓦwww.tramway.org. Based in a converted tram terminus, whose lofty proportions make it a remarkable venue for experimental productions by directors such as Peter Brook and Robert Lepage. They've also played a significant role in promoting visual art by artists such as David Mach, Douglas Gordon and Christine Borland.

Tron Theatre 63 Trongate ⓣ0141 552 4267, ⓦtron .co.uk. Varied repertoire of mainstream and challenging productions from itinerant companies including Glasgow's Vanishing Point, and live folk music in the theatre bar.

CONCERT HALLS

City Halls Candleriggs ⓣ0141 353 8000, ⓦglasgow cityhalls.com. This Merchant City performance space, in a renovated old fruit market, is home to the BBC Scottish Symphony and hosts many of the annual Celtic Connections concerts.

Glasgow Royal Concert Hall 2 Sauchiehall St ⓣ0141 353 8000, ⓦglasgowconcerthalls.com. One of Glasgow's less memorable modern buildings, this is the venue for big-name touring orchestras and the home of the Royal Scottish National Orchestra. Also features major rock and R&B stars, and middle-of-the-road music-hall acts.

ART-HOUSE CINEMAS

Glasgow Film Theatre 12 Rose St ⓣ0141 332 8128, ⓦgft.org.uk. Dedicated art, independent and rep cinema house. *Café Cosmo* is an excellent place for pre-show drinks.

Grosvenor Ashton Lane ⓣ0141 339 8444, ⓦgrosvenor cinema.co.uk. Renovated two-screen neighbourhood film house with bar and sofas you can reserve for screenings of mostly mainstream films.

DIRECTORY

Hospital 24hr casualty department at the Royal Infirmary, 84 Castle St near Glasgow Cathedral (ⓣ0141 211 4000).

Left luggage Buchanan St bus station and lockers at Central or Queen St train stations.

Police Strathclyde Police HQ, Pitt St (ⓣ0141 532 2000).

Post office Main office at 47 St Vincent St (Mon–Fri 8.30am–5.45pm, Sat 9am–5.30pm); city centre office at 87–91 Bothwell St.

The Clyde

The **River Clyde** is the dominant physical feature of Glasgow and its environs, an area that comprises the largest urban concentration in Scotland, with almost two million people living in the city and satellite towns. Little of this hinterland can be described as beautiful, with crisscrossing motorways and grim housing estates dominating much of the landscape. Beyond the sprawl, however, rolling green hills, open expanses of water and attractive countryside eventually begin to dominate, holding promises of wilder country beyond.

West of the city, regular trains and the M8 motorway dip down from the southern bank of the Clyde to **Paisley**, where the distinctive cloth pattern gained its name, before heading back up to the edge of the river again as it broadens into the **Firth of Clyde**. North of Glasgow trains terminate at tiny Milngavie (pronounced "Mill-guy"), which acts as the start of Scotland's best-known long-distance footpath, the **West Highland Way** (see p.807).

Southeast of Glasgow, the industrial landscape of the **Clyde valley** eventually gives way to a far more attractive scenery of gorges and towering castles. Here lies the stoic town of **Lanark**, where eighteenth-century philanthropists built their model workers' community around the mills of **New Lanark**.

Paisley

Founded in the twelfth century as a monastic settlement around an abbey, **PAISLEY** expanded after the eighteenth century as a linen-manufacturing town, specializing in the production of highly fashionable imitation Kashmiri shawls. It quickly eclipsed other British centres producing the cloth, eventually lending its name to the swirling pine-cone design. Inside the **Museum and Art Gallery**, opposite the university (Tues–Sat 10am–5pm, Sun 2–5pm; free), the Shawl Gallery deals with the growth and development of the Paisley pattern.

Opposite the town hall is Paisley's **Abbey** (Mon–Sat 10am–3.30pm; free) which was built on the site of the town's original settlement and massively overhauled in the Victorian age. The unattractive, fat grey facade of the church does little justice to its renovated interior, which is tall, spacious and ornately decorated.

ARRIVAL AND INFORMATION — PAISLEY

By plane Glasgow International Airport lies 2 miles north of town; buses connect the airport with the train station (every 10min).

By train Regular trains from Glasgow Central connect with Paisley's Gilmour Street station in the centre of town.

Tourist office 9a Gilmour St (Mon–Sat 9am–5pm; ⓣ0141 889 0711).

Dumbarton Castle

Dumbarton • April–Sept daily 9.30am–5.30pm; Oct–March Sat–Wed 9.30am–4.30pm • HS • £4.50 • ⓣ01389 732167

Heading west out of Glasgow, the A82 road and the train tracks follow the north bank of the river, passing through Clydebank, another ex-shipbuilding centre, and Bowling, the western entry point of the Forth & Clyde canal. Three miles beyond Bowling, they reach the town of **DUMBARTON**, founded in the fifth century, but today for the most part a brutal concrete sprawl. Only **Dumbarton Castle**, which sits atop a twin outcrop of volcanic rock surrounded by water on three sides, is worth stopping to see. First founded as a Roman fort, the castle became a royal seat, from which Mary, Queen of Scots, sailed for France to marry Henri II's son in 1548. Since the 1600s, the castle has been used as a garrison and artillery fortress to guard the approaches to Glasgow; most of the current buildings date from this period.

FERRIES: GOUROCK AND WEMYSS BAY

Northwest of Glasgow on the coast lies the dowdy old resort of **GOUROCK**, once a holiday destination for generations of Glaswegians, but today only of real significance as a **ferry terminal**: both CalMac (ⓦcalmac.co.uk) and the more frequent Western Ferries (ⓦwww.western-ferries.co.uk) ply the route across the Firth of Clyde to Dunoon on the Cowal peninsula (20min), while a passenger ferry (ⓦspt.co.uk) runs year-round to Kilcreggan (15min) and Helensburgh (30min) on the north bank of the Clyde. Immediately south of Gourock, **WEMYSS BAY**, where thousands of Glaswegians used to alight for their steamer trip "doon the watter", is today of note only for its splendid 1903 train station and the CalMac **ferry** connection to Rothesay on Bute (see p.828).

Helensburgh

HELENSBURGH, twenty miles or so northwest of Glasgow, is a smart, Georgian grid-plan settlement overlooking the Clyde estuary. The inventor of TV, John Logie Baird, was born here, as was Charles Rennie Mackintosh (see pp.780–781), who in 1902 was commissioned by the Glaswegian publisher Walter Blackie to design **Hill House**.

Hill House

Upper Colquhoun St • April–Oct daily 1.30–5.30pm • NTS • £9 • T 0844 493 2208

Without doubt the best surviving example of Mackintosh's domestic architecture, **Hill House** is stamped with his very personal, elegant interpretation of Art Nouveau – right down to the light fittings and fire irons – characterized by his sparing use of colour and stylized floral patterns. Various upstairs rooms are given over to interpretative displays on the architect's use of light, colour, form and texture, while changing exhibitions on contemporary domestic design from around Britain are a testament to Mackintosh's ongoing influence and inspiration. After exploring the house, head for the **tearoom** in the kitchen quarters, or wander round the beautifully laid-out **gardens**.

The Clyde valley

Mostly following the course of the Clyde upstream, the journey southeast of Glasgow into Lanarkshire is dominated by endless suburbs, industrial parks and wide strips of concrete highway. The principal road here is the M74, though you'll have to get off the motorway to find the main points of interest, which tend to lie on or near the banks of the river. The **National Museum of Rural Life**, set on a historic farm, offers an in-depth look at the history of agriculture in Scotland, while further south lies the remarkable eighteenth-century planned village of **New Lanark**.

National Museum of Rural Life

East Kilbride, 7 miles southeast of Glasgow • Daily 10am–5pm • NTS • £5 • Transport isn't straightforward if you don't have your own vehicle. Bus #31 from Glasgow's St Enoch Centre to East Kilbride takes you past the museum (Stewartfield Way), or you can get the train from Glasgow Central, and then take a taxi for the final 3 miles

Situated on the edge of **EAST KILBRIDE** new town, the **National Museum of Rural Life** is an unexpected union of historic farm and modern museum. The 170-acre farm, **Kittochside**, avoided the intensive farming that came to dominate agriculture in Britain after World War II, and today showcases traditional methods. On its edge, the custom-built museum uses light and space extremely well to explore the Scots' relationship with the land over centuries. A tractor and trailer shuttles visitors the half-mile up to the eighteenth-century **farmhouse**, which is furnished much as it would have been in the 1950s, the crucial decade just before traditional methods using horses and hand-tools were replaced by tractors and mechanization.

New Lanark

25 miles southeast of Glasgow • Daily : April–Sept 10am–5pm, Oct–March 11am–5pm • Passport ticket £8.50 • T 01555 661345, W newlanark.org

A UNESCO-designated World Heritage Site, the eighteenth-century planned village of **NEW LANARK** lies a mile below the neat little market town of **Lanark**. The first sight of the place, hidden away down in the gorge, is unforgettable: large, broken, curving walls of honeyed warehouses and tenements, built in Palladian style, are lined up along the turbulent river's edge. The community was founded by David Dale and Richard Arkwright in 1785 to harness the power of the Clyde waterfalls in their cotton-spinning industry, but it was Dale's son-in-law, Robert Owen, who revolutionized the social side of the experiment in 1798, creating a "village of unity". Believing the welfare of the workers to be crucial to industrial success, Owen built adult educational facilities, the world's first day nursery and playground, and schools in which dancing and music were obligatory and there was no punishment or reward.

While you're free to wander around the village, which rather unexpectedly for such a historic site is still partially residential, you need to buy a passport ticket to get into any of the **exhibitions**. The Neoclassical building that now houses the visitor reception was opened by Owen in 1816 under the utopian title of **The Institute for the Formation of Character**. These days, it houses the **New Millennium Experience**, which whisks visitors on a chairlift through a social history of the village, conveying Robert Owen's vision not just for the idealized life at New Lanark, but also what he predicted for the year 2000.

Other parts of New Lanark village prove just as fascinating: everything, from the cooperative store to the workers' tenements and workshops, was built in an attempt to prove that industrialism need not be unaesthetic. Situated in the Old Dyeworks, the **Scottish Wildlife Trust Visitor Centre** (daily: Jan & Feb noon–4pm; March–Dec 11am–5pm; £2) provides information about the history and wildlife of the area. Beyond the visitor centre, a riverside path leads you the mile or so to the major **Falls of the Clyde**, where at the stunning tree-fringed Cora Linn the river plunges 90ft in three tumultuous stages.

ARRIVAL AND INFORMATION — NEW LANARK

By train You can catch a train from Glasgow Central to Lanark (every 30min; 50min); from there either walk (it's 1.5 miles away) or take a local bus or taxi from the station.

Tourist office In the Horsemarket, 100 yards west of the station (May–Sept daily 10am–5pm; Oct–April Mon–Sat 10am–5pm; T 01555 661661).

ACCOMMODATION

By far the most original places to stay in the area, at both ends of the market, make creative use of the village's reconstructed mill buildings.

New Lanark Mill T 01555 667200, W newlanarkhotel.co.uk. A four-star hotel converted from an eighteenth-century mill building, with good views and lots of character; the *Mill* restaurant serves decent food, and there's a swimming pool and sauna. £79

SYHA hostel Wee Row, Rosedale St T 0870 004 1143, W syha.org.uk. A very appealing hostel, with two-, four- and five-bed rooms in a restored millworkers' tenement row. Closed Nov–March. Dorm £20, double £55

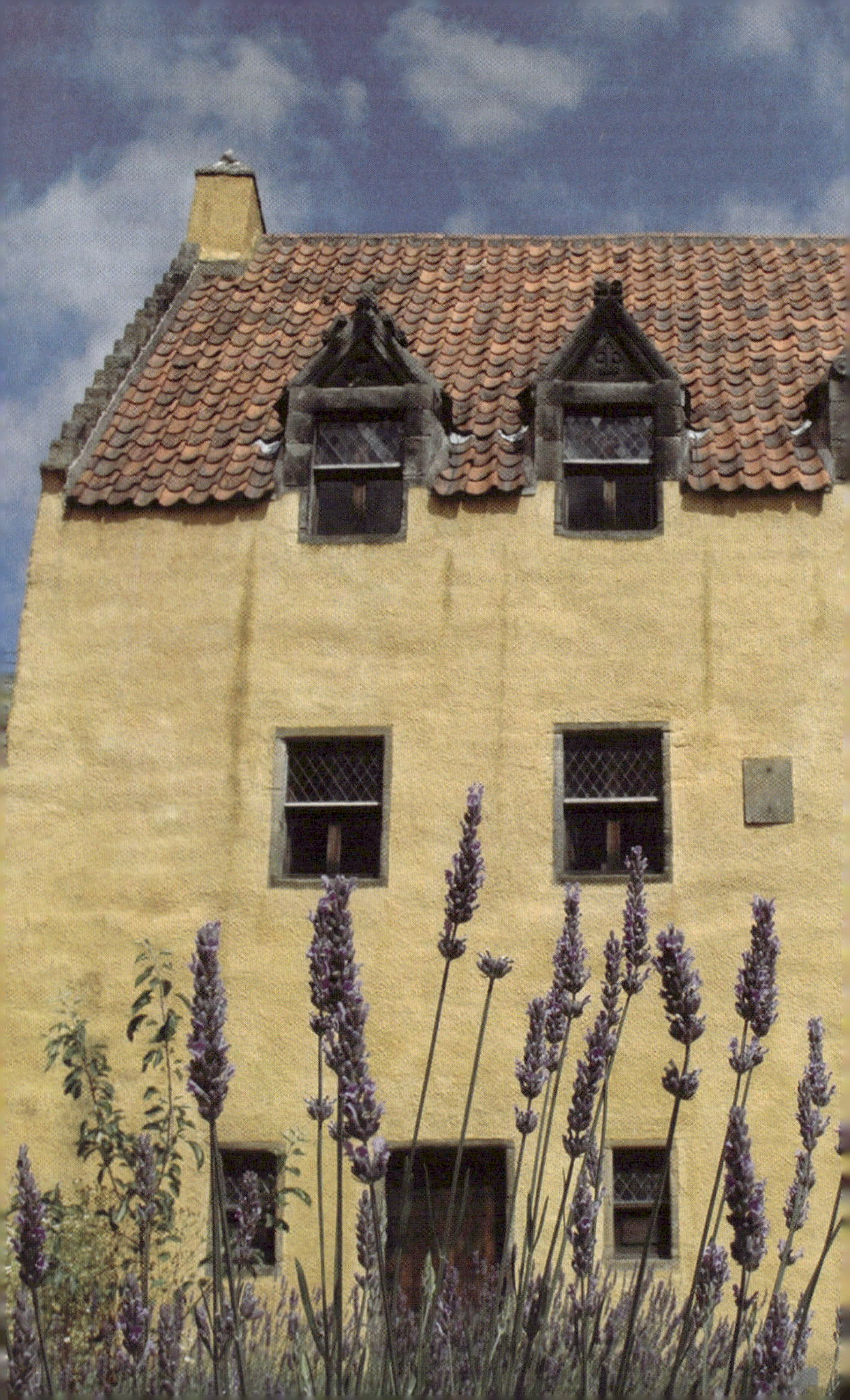

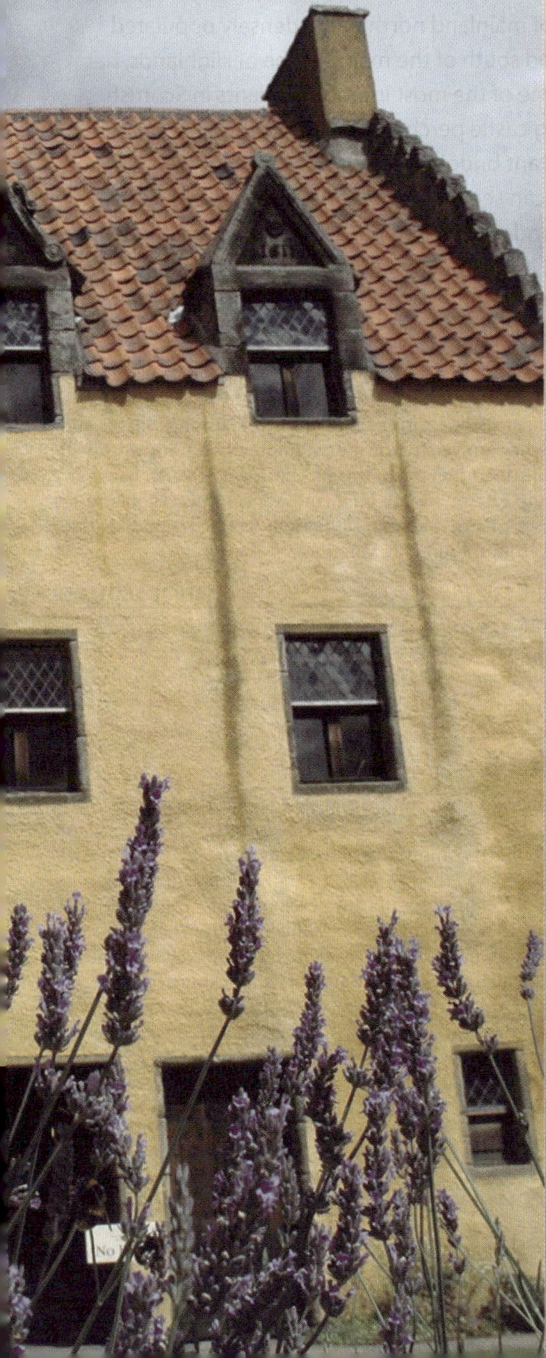

Central Scotland

798 Stirling and around

806 Loch Lomond

808 The Trossachs

810 Fife

818 Perthshire

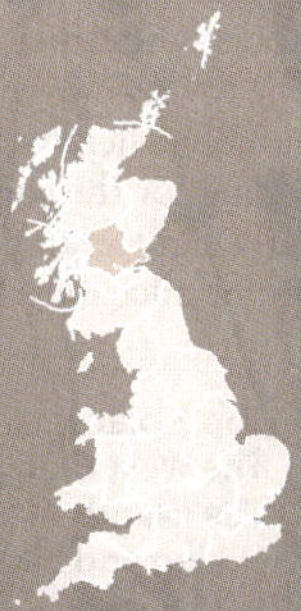

CULROSS PALACE

Central Scotland

Central Scotland, the strip of mainland north of the densely populated Glasgow–Edinburgh axis and south of the main swathe of Highlands, has been the main stage for some of the most important events in Scottish history. Stirling, its imposing castle perched high above the town, was historically the most important bridging point across the River Forth. From the castle battlements you can see the peaks of the forested Trossachs region, with its wild and wonderful archetypal Scottish scenery. Popular for walking and, in particular, cycling, much of the Trossachs, together with the attractive islands and "bonnie, bonnie banks" of Loch Lomond, form the core of Scotland's first national park.

To the east, between the firths of Forth and Tay, lies the county of **Fife**, a Pictish kingdom that boasts a fascinating coastline sprinkled with historic fishing villages and sandy beaches, as well as the historic university town of **St Andrews**, famous worldwide for its venerable golf courses. A little to the north, the ancient town of **Perth** has as much claim as anywhere to be the gateway to the Highlands. Spectacular **Highland Perthshire** begins north and west of Perth – an area of glorious wooded mountainsides and inviting walks, particularly around Rannoch Moor.

GETTING AROUND **CENTRAL SCOTLAND**

While Stirling, Falkirk and Perth are well served by **trains** from all over Scotland, the rest of the region is only accessible on sporadic local **bus** services so you may find it easier to have your own transport. Many people opt to explore the Trossachs by mountain bike.

Stirling and around

Straddling the River Forth a few miles upstream from the estuary at Kincardine, **STIRLING** appears, at first glance, like a smaller version of Edinburgh. With its crag-top castle, steep, cobbled streets and mixed community of locals, students and tourists, it's an appealing place.

Stirling was the scene of some of the most significant developments in the evolution of the Scottish nation. It was here that the Scots under William Wallace defeated the English at the **Battle of Stirling Bridge** in 1297, only to fight – and win again – under Robert the Bruce just a couple of miles away at the **Battle of Bannockburn** in 1314. The town enjoyed its golden age in the fifteenth to seventeenth centuries, most notably when its castle was the favoured residence of the Stuart monarchy and the setting for the coronation in 1543 of the young Mary, future Queen of Scots. By the early eighteenth century the town was again besieged, its location being of strategic importance during the Jacobite rebellions of 1715 and 1745. Today Stirling is known

Top 5 places to walk p.806
The West Highland Way p.807
The islands of Loch Lomond p.808
Hiking and biking in the Trossachs p.809
Golf in St Andrews p.813
Outdoor activities in Perthshire p.818
Rannoch Moor p.823

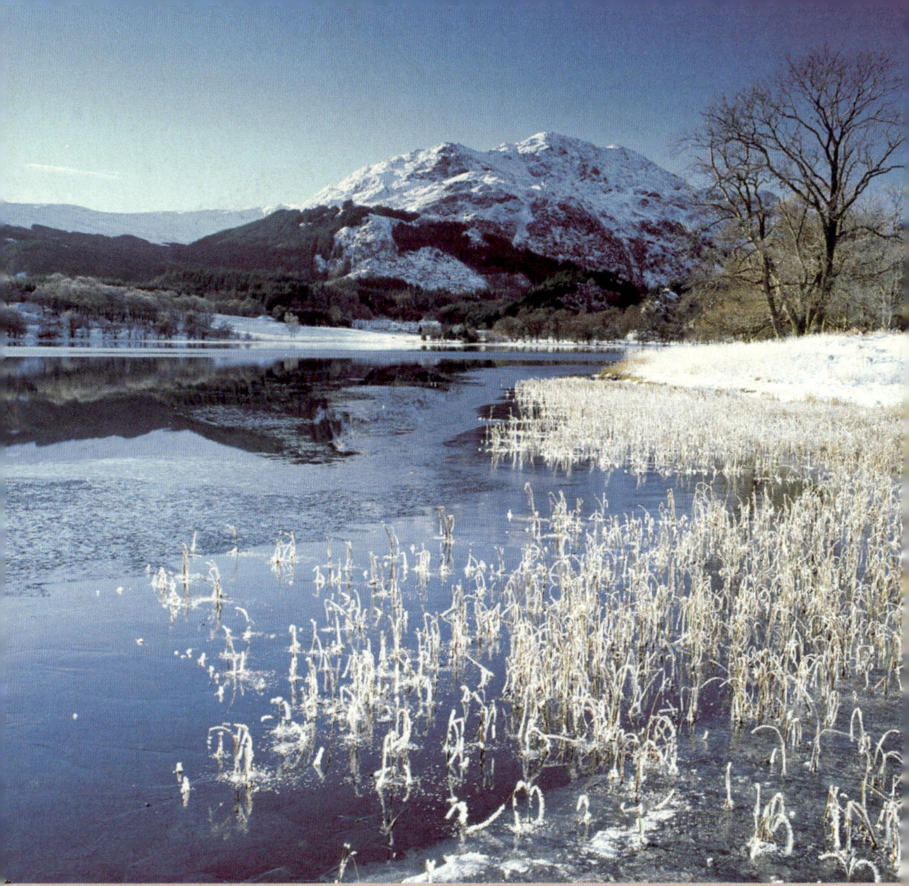

THE TROSSACHS

Highlights

❶ Stirling Castle Impregnable, impressive and resonant with history. If you see only one castle in Scotland, make it this. **See p.802**

❷ Falkirk Wheel The most remarkable piece of modern engineering in Britain, this fascinating contraption lifts boats 100ft between two canals. **See p.805**

❸ The Trossachs Pocket Highlands with shining lochs, wooded glens and noble peaks. Great for hiking and mountain biking. **See p.808**

❹ Himalayas putting green, St Andrews The world's finest putting course right beside the world's finest golf course; a snip at £1.50 a round. **See p.813**

❺ The East Neuk Buy freshly cooked lobster from the wooden shack at Crail's historic stone harbour or dine in style at *The Cellar* restaurant in the fishing town of Anstruther. **See p.814**

❻ Forth Rail Bridge An icon of Victorian engineering spanning the Firth of Forth, floodlit to stunning effect at night. **See p.817**

❼ The Fergusson Gallery, Perth A touch of Antibes in Perthshire: the gallery celebrates the vibrant work of J.D. Fergusson and his dancer wife Margaret Morris. **See p.819**

❽ Rannoch Moor One of the most inaccessible places in Scotland, where hikers can discover a true sense of remoteness. **See p.823**

HIGHLIGHTS ARE MARKED ON THE MAP ON PP.800–801

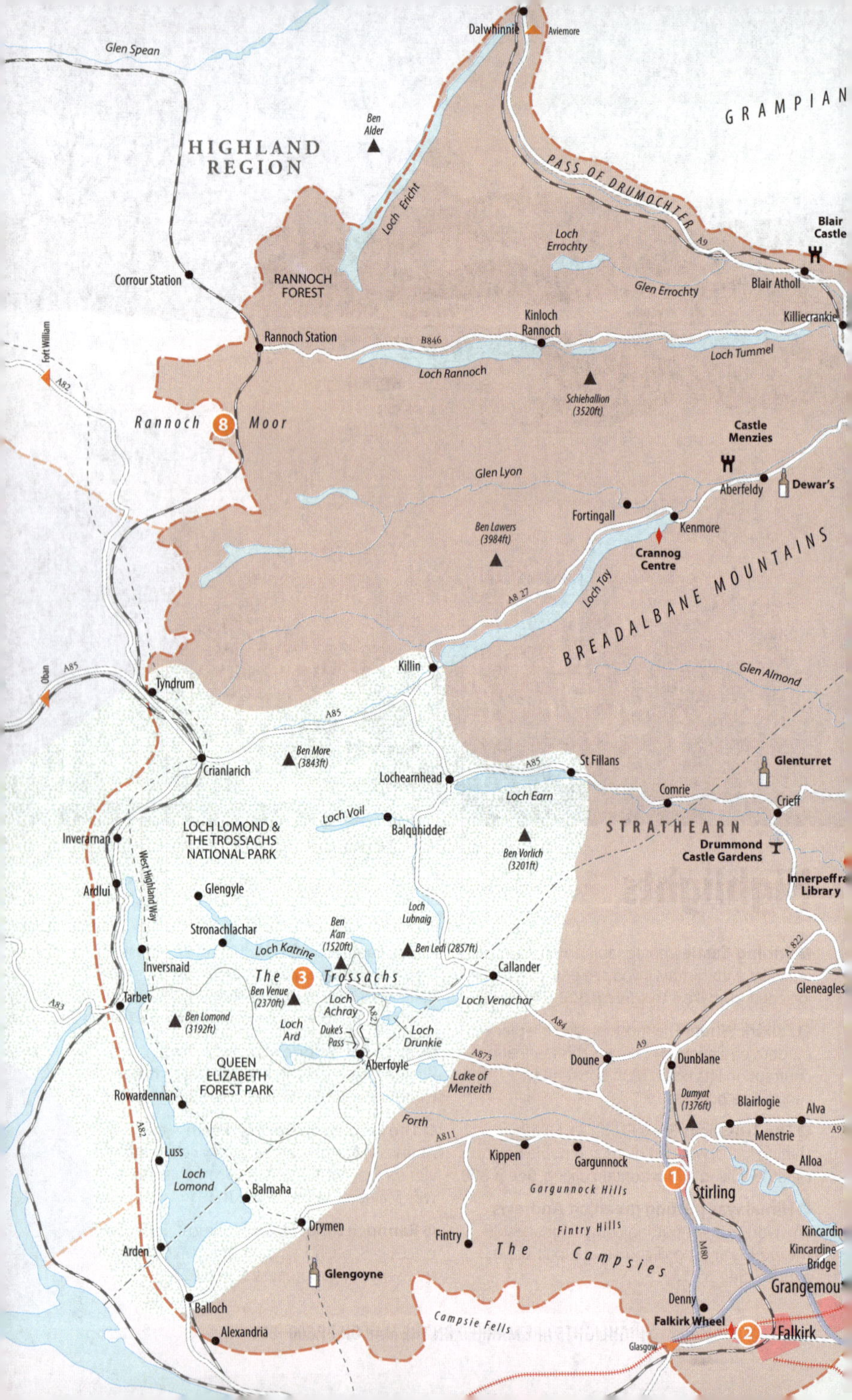
Glen Spean
Dalwhinnie
Aviemore
GRAMPIAN
HIGHLAND REGION
Ben Alder
Loch Ericht
PASS OF DRUMOCHTER
A9
Blair Castle
Loch Errochty
Glen Errochty
Blair Atholl
Corrour Station
RANNOCH FOREST
Killiecrankie
Kinloch Rannoch
Rannoch Station
B846
Loch Tummel
Loch Rannoch
Fort William
A82
Schiehallion (3520ft)
Rannoch 8 Moor
Castle Menzies
Glen Lyon
Aberfeldy
Dewar's
Fortingall
Kenmore
Ben Lawers (3984ft)
Crannog Centre
BREADALBANE MOUNTAINS
Loch Tay
A827
Killin
Glen Almond
Oban
A85
Tyndrum
Ben More (3843ft)
Crianlarich
St Fillans
Glenturret
Lochearnhead
Loch Earn
Comrie
Crieff
Loch Voil
Balquhidder
STRATHEARN
LOCH LOMOND & THE TROSSACHS NATIONAL PARK
Inverarnan
Ben Vorlich (3201ft)
Drummond Castle Gardens
West Highland Way
Ardlui
Innerpeffray Library
Glengyle
Loch Lubnaig
Ben A'an (1520ft)
Stronachlachar
Loch Katrine
Ben Ledi (2857ft)
Inversnaid
Callander
The 3 Trossachs
A822
Ben Venue (2370ft)
Gleneagles
Tarbet
Loch Achray
Loch Venachar
A83
Ben Lomond (3192ft)
A821
Loch Ard
Loch Drunkie
A84
Duke's Pass
A9
QUEEN ELIZABETH FOREST PARK
Aberfoyle
A873
Doune
Dunblane
Lake of Menteith
Rowardennan
Dumyat (1376ft)
Blairlogie
Alva
Forth
Menstrie
A811
Luss
Kippen
Gargunnock
Alloa
Loch Lomond
1 Stirling
Gargunnock Hills
Balmaha
Fintry Hills
Drymen
Fintry
The Campsies
Kincardine
Kincardine Bridge
M80
Arden
Glengoyne
Grangemouth
Balloch
Denny
Campsie Fells
Falkirk Wheel
2 Falkirk
Alexandria
Glasgow

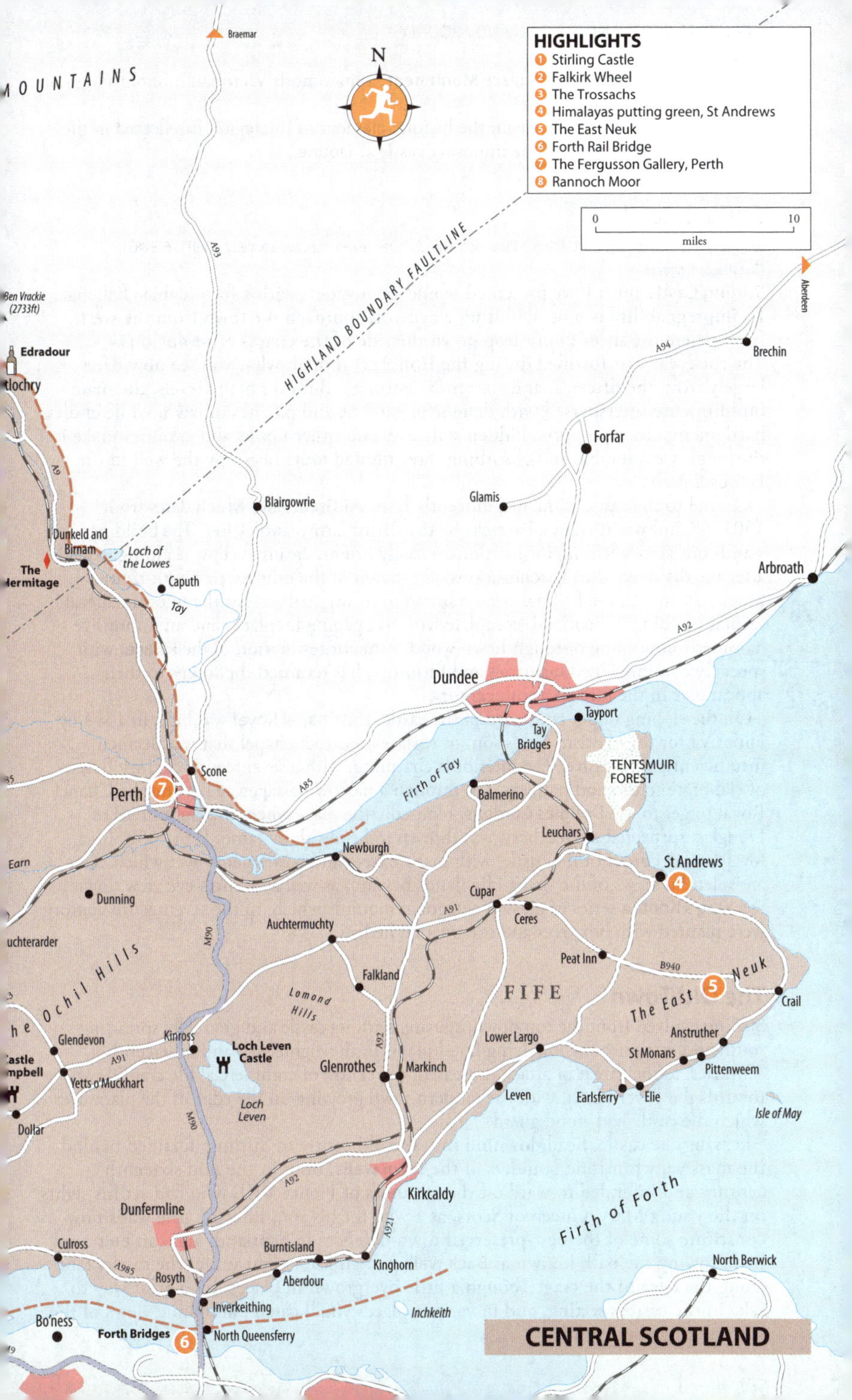
HIGHLIGHTS
1 Stirling Castle
2 Falkirk Wheel
3 The Trossachs
4 Himalayas putting green, St Andrews
5 The East Neuk
6 Forth Rail Bridge
7 The Fergusson Gallery, Perth
8 Rannoch Moor
0
10
miles
N
Braemar
MOUNTAINS
A93
HIGHLAND BOUNDARY FAULTLINE
Aberdeen
Ben Vrackie (2733ft)
Edradour
tlochry
A94
Brechin
Forfar
A9
Blairgowrie
Glamis
Dunkeld and Birnam
Loch of the Lowes
The Hermitage
Caputh
Tay
Arbroath
A92
Dundee
Tayport
Tay Bridges
TENTSMUIR FOREST
Scone
Perth
A85
Firth of Tay
Balmerino
Leuchars
Newburgh
Earn
St Andrews
Dunning
Cupar
A91
Ceres
M90
Auchtermuchty
uchterarder
Peat Inn
B940
Ochil Hills
Falkland
Lomond Hills
FIFE
The East Neuk
Crail
Glendevon
Kinross
Loch Leven Castle
Lower Largo
Anstruther
Castle Campbell
A91
Yetts o'Muckhart
Glenrothes
Markinch
St Monans
Pittenweem
Dollar
Loch Leven
Leven
Earlsferry
Elie
Isle of May
A92
Kirkcaldy
Firth of Forth
Dunfermline
A921
Culross
Burntisland
A985
Rosyth
Kinghorn
Aberdour
North Berwick
Inverkeithing
Inchkeith
Bo'ness
Forth Bridges
North Queensferry
CENTRAL SCOTLAND

for its **castle** and the lofty **Wallace Monument**, a mammoth Victorian monolith high on Abbey Craig to the northeast.

To the north and west of town, the historic element of the region is reflected in the cathedral at **Dunblane** and the imposing castle at **Doune**.

Stirling Castle

Daily: April–Sept 9.30am–6pm; Oct–March 9.30am–5pm • HS • £13; free guided tours, audioguide £2 • ☎ 0131 668 8831, Ⓦ stirlingcastle.gov.uk

Stirling Castle must have presented would-be invaders with a formidable challenge. Its impregnability is most daunting when you approach the town from the west, from where the sheer 250ft drop down the side of the crag is most obvious. The rock was first fortified during the Iron Age, though what you see now dates largely from the fifteenth and sixteenth centuries. Built on many levels, the main buildings are interspersed with delightful gardens and patches of lawn, while endless battlements, cannon ports, hidden staircases and other nooks and crannies make it thoroughly explorable and absorbing. Free **guided tours** begin by the well in the Lower Square.

Central to the castle is the magnificently restored **Great Hall**, which dates from 1501–03 and was used as a barracks by the British army until 1964. The building stands out across Stirling for its controversially bright, creamy yellow cladding, added after the discovery during renovations of a stretch of the original sixteenth-century limewash. Inside, the hall has been restored to its original state as the finest medieval secular building in Scotland, complete with five gaping fireplaces and an impressive hammerbeam ceiling of rough-hewn wood. A major restoration of the **Palace**, with specially commissioned tapestries and furniture, has returned the rooms to their appearance in the mid sixteenth century.

On the sloping upper courtyard of the castle, the **Chapel Royal** was built in 1594 by James VI for the baptism of his son, to replace an earlier chapel that was deemed insufficiently impressive. The interior is charming, with a seventeenth-century fresco of elaborate scrolls and patterns. Go through a narrow passageway beyond the Chapel Royal to get to the **Douglas Gardens**, reputedly the place where the eighth Earl of Douglas, suspected of treachery, was thrown to his death by James II in 1452. It's a lovely, quiet corner of the castle, with mature trees and battlements over which there are splendid views of the rising Highlands beyond, as well as a bird's-eye view down to the **King's Knot**, a series of grassed octagonal mounds which, in the seventeenth century, were planted with box trees and ornamental hedges.

The Old Town

Stirling evolved from the top down, starting with its castle and gradually spreading south and east onto the low-lying flood plain. In the eighteenth and nineteenth centuries, as the threat of attack decreased, the centre of commercial life crept down towards the River Forth, with the modern town growing on the edge of the plain over which the castle had stood guard.

Leaving the castle, head downhill into the old centre of Stirling, fortified behind the massive, whinstone boulders of the **town walls**, built in the mid sixteenth century and intended to ward off the advances of Henry VIII, who had set his sights on the young Mary, Queen of Scots, as a wife for his son, Edward. The walls now constitute some of the best-preserved town defences in Scotland, and can be traced by following the path known as **Back Walk**, which leads right under the castle, taut along the edge of the crag. Though a little overgrown in places, it's a great way to take in the castle's setting, and in various places you'll catch panoramic views of the surrounding countryside.

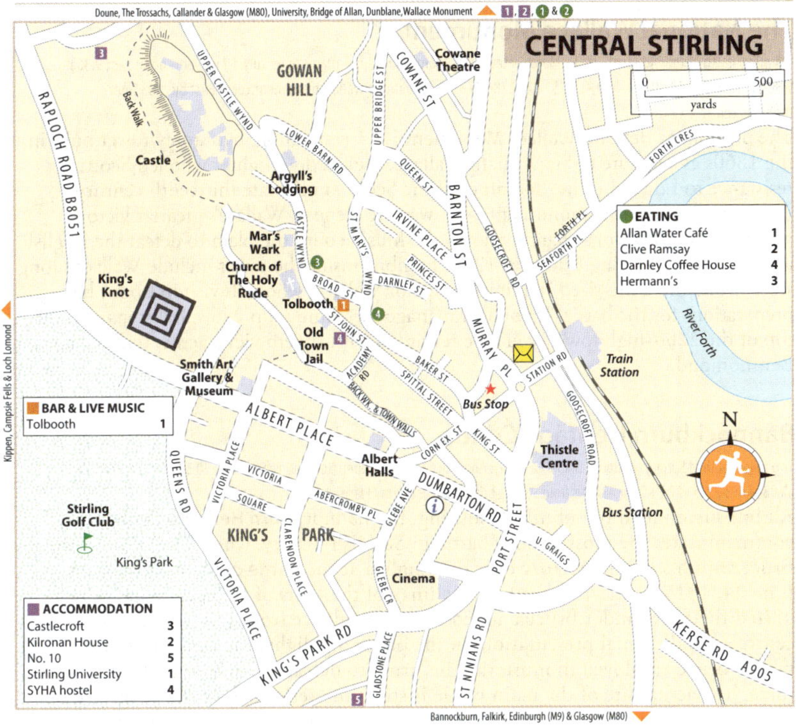

20

The Tolbooth

Jail Wynd • Daily from 9am • ⓣ 01786 274000, ⓦ www.stirling.gov.uk/tolbooth

Built on the site of Stirling's medieval prison, the **Tolbooth** is now an inspirational music and arts centre, a striking modern redevelopment of a 1705 structure. During renovations a secret staircase was discovered, along with a complete skeleton thought to have been that of the last man publicly hanged in Stirling. Inside, a top-floor viewing platform looks out over the Old Town rooftops. In addition to performances (see p.806) the Tolbooth hosts music workshops, summer ceilidhs and contemporary art shows.

Old Town Jail

St John St • End May–Oct daily 10am–5pm • £6.65 • ⓣ 01786 450050, ⓦ oldtownjail.com

A sweeping driveway leads up to the impressive **Old Town Jail**. Built by Victorian prison reformers, it was rescued from dereliction in 1994, with part of the building turned into offices and a substantial section used to create an entertaining visitor attraction. Telling the history of the building and prisons in general, tours are enthusiastically led by actors who change costumes and character a number of times. Take the glass lift up to the prison roof for spectacular views across Stirling and the Forth Valley.

Smith Art Gallery and Museum

Dumbarton Rd • Tues–Sat 10.30am–5pm, Sun 2–5pm • Free • ⓣ 01786 471917, ⓦ www.smithartgallery.demon.co.uk

The further downhill you go in Stirling's Lower Town, the newer the buildings become. The only sight of note is the **Smith Art Gallery and Museum**, which houses "The Stirling Story", a reasonably entertaining whirl through the history of the town, balancing out stories of kings and queens with social history.

The National Wallace Monument

1.5 miles north of the Old Town • Daily: March–May & Oct 10am–5pm; June 10am–6pm; July & Aug 9am–6pm; Sept 9.30am–5.30pm; Nov–Feb 10.30am–4pm • £7.75 • T 01786 472140, W nationalwallacemonument.com • First bus #63 from the town centre

The prominent **National Wallace Monument** is a freestanding, five-storey tower built in the 1860s as a tribute to Sir William Wallace, the freedom fighter who led Scottish resistance to Edward I, the "Hammer of the Scots", in the late thirteenth century. The crag on which the monument is set was the scene of Wallace's greatest victory, when he sent his troops charging down the hillside onto the plain to defeat the English at the Battle of Stirling Bridge in 1297. Exhibits inside the tower include Wallace's long steel sword and a life-sized "talking" model of Wallace, who tells visitors about his preparations for the battle. If you can manage the climb – up 246 spiral steps – to the top of the 220ft-high tower, you'll be rewarded with superb views across to Fife and Ben Lomond.

Bannockburn Heritage Centre

Two miles south of Stirling centre, on the A872 • Daily: April–Oct 10am–5.30pm; Nov, Dec, Feb & March 10.30am–4pm • NTS • £6 • T 0844 493 2139 • #24, #52 or #57 bus from Stirling bus station or Murray Place

All but surrounded by suburban housing, the **Bannockburn Heritage Centre** commemorates the most famous battle in Scottish history, when King Robert the Bruce won his mighty victory over the English at the **Battle of Bannockburn** on June 24, 1314. It was this battle, the climax of the Wars of Independence, which united the Scots under Bruce and led to independence from England. Inside the centre an audiovisual presentation on the battle highlights the brilliantly innovative tactics Bruce employed in mustering his army to defeat a much larger English force. The actual site of the main battle is still a matter of debate: most agree that it didn't take place near the present visitor centre, but on a boggy carse a mile or so to the west.

Dunblane Cathedral

The Cross, Dunblane, 5 miles north of Stirling • April–Sept Mon–Sat 9.30am–5pm, Sun 2–5pm; Oct–March Mon–Sat 9.30am–4pm, Sun 2–4pm • HS • Free • T 01786 825388, W dunblanecathedral.org.uk

The attractive small town of **DUNBLANE** has been an important ecclesiastical centre since the seventh century, when the Celts founded the Church of St Blane here. **Dunblane Cathedral** dates mainly from the thirteenth century, and restoration work carried out a century ago has returned it to its Gothic splendour. Inside, note the delicate blue-purple stained glass, and the exquisitely carved pews, screen and choir stalls, all crafted in the early twentieth century. Memorials within the cathedral include a tenth-century Celtic cross-slab standing stone and a modern, four-sided standing stone by Richard Kindersley commemorating the tragic shooting in 1996 of sixteen Dunblane schoolchildren and their teacher.

Doune Castle

Three miles west of Dunblane • April–Sept daily 9.30am–6.30pm; Oct–March Mon–Wed & Sat 9.30am–4.30pm, Sun 2–4.30pm • HS • £5 • T 01786 841742

Standing on a small hill in a bend of the River Teith in the sleepy village of **DOUNE**, the stern-looking, fourteenth-century **Doune Castle** is a marvellous semi-ruin. The castle's greatest claim to fame is as the setting for the 1970s movie *Monty Python and the Holy Grail*; the shop by the gatehouse keeps a scrapbook of stills from the film, as well as a selection of souvenirs including bottles of the locally brewed Holy Grail Ale.

The Falkirk Wheel

Lime Rd, 2 miles west of Falkirk, which is 10 miles southeast of Stirling on the M9 to Edinburgh • **Wheel** Daily: April–Oct every 30min 9.30am–4.30pm; Nov–March hourly 10am–3pm • £7.95 **Visitor Centre** Daily 9.30am–6pm • Free • T 08700 500208, W www.thefalkirkwheel.co.uk • Trains to Falkirk from Edinburgh (every 15–30min; 30min), Glasgow Queen St (every 15–30min; 25min) and Stirling (every 30min; 15min). Taxis can take you the short journey from the station to the wheel

The town of **FALKIRK** has a good deal of visible history, going right back to the remains of the Roman Antonine Wall. A massive transformation came in the eighteenth century with the construction of canals connecting Glasgow and Edinburgh; within a few years, however, the trains arrived, and the canals gradually fell into disuse. While Falkirk's canals were a very visible sign of the area's industrial heritage, it was only recently that their leisure potential was realized, thanks to British Waterway's £84.5 million **Millennium Link** project to restore them and re-establish a navigable link between east and west coasts.

The icon of this project is the remarkable **Falkirk Wheel**. The giant grey wheel, the world's first rotating boat-lift, scoops boats in two giant buckets, or caissons, and moves them the 79ft between the levels of the Forth & Clyde and Union canals linked to Glasgow and Edinburgh respectively. Beneath the wheel, the **visitor centre** sells tickets for a one hour **boat trip** from the lower basin into the wheel, along the Union Canal, and back again. If you want to simply see the wheel in action, walk around the basin and adjoining towpaths.

ARRIVAL AND INFORMATION — STIRLING

By train The train station is in the centre of town on Goosecroft Rd.

Destinations Aberdeen (hourly; 2hr 5min); Dundee (hourly; 55min); Edinburgh (every 30min; 1hr); Falkirk Grahamston (every 30min; 15min); Glasgow Queen St (every 20min; 30min); Inverness (3–5 daily; 2hr 55min); Perth (hourly; 30min).

By bus The station, on Goosecroft Rd, can be accessed from the Thistles shopping centre.

Destinations Aberfoyle (4 daily; 45min); Callander (1–2hr; 45min); Dollar (every 2hr; 30min); Doune (1–2hr; 25min); Dunblane (hourly; 20min); Dundee (hourly; 1hr 30min); Edinburgh (hourly; 1hr); Falkirk (hourly; 30min); Glasgow (hourly; 50min); Inverness (every 2hr; 3hr 20min); Perth (hourly; 40min); St Andrews (every 2hr; 1hr 55min).

Tourist office Near the town centre at 41 Dumbarton Rd (April & May Mon–Sat 9am–5pm; June & Sept Mon–Sat 9am–6pm, Sun 10am–4pm; July & Aug Mon–Sat 9am–7pm, Sun 9.30am–6pm; Oct Mon–Sat 9.30am–5pm; Nov–March Mon–Fri 10am–5pm, Sat 10am–4pm; T 01786 475019).

Useful website W visitstirling.org.

20

ACCOMMODATION

Castlecroft Ballengeich Rd T 01786 474933, W castlecroft-uk.com. Modern guesthouse with six en-suite rooms on the site of the King's Stables just beneath the castle rock, with terrific views north and west and a very friendly welcome. £55

Kilronan House 15 Kenilworth Rd, Bridge of Allan T 01786 831054, W kilronan.co.uk. A grand Victorian family house built in 1853 with spacious en-suite B&B rooms in the Bridge of Allan, a couple of miles north of Stirling and easily reached by regular buses. £60

No. 10 10 Gladstone Place T 01786 472681, W cameron-10.co.uk. Modernized Victorian home with neat, uncluttered decor providing friendly and pleasant B&B accommodation. It's close to the city centre, but on a quiet and elegant King's Park street. £60

Stirling University T 01786 467141, W www.stir.ac.uk/about/short-breaks-and-vacations. Campus accommodation in halls of residence and self-catering flats a couple of miles north of the town centre. The campus is served by regular buses from Murray Place in the town centre. Closed mid-Sept to May. From £18.90 shared, £27 en-suite

SYHA Hostel St John St T 01786 473442, W syha.org.uk. Located at the top of the town, a strenuous trek with a backpack, in a converted church with an impressive 1824 Palladian facade. All rooms have en-suite showers and toilets, and facilities include a games room and internet access. £17.75

EATING AND ENTERTAINMENT

Allan Water Café 15 Henderson St, Bridge of Allan T 01786 833060, W allanwatercafe.co.uk. Established in 1902, this traditional Italian café serves reasonably priced fish suppers with mushy peas and their very own ice cream, made to a secret family recipe. Mon–Sat 8am–8.30pm, Sun 9am–8.30pm.

Clive Ramsay 28 Henderson St, Bridge of Allan ☎01786 831616. This is not a deluxe dining experience, but a relaxed, friendly and fairly stylish option. The varied menu (mains from £12) uses good Scottish ingredients, with haggis a popular option. Daily 8am–late.

Darnley Coffee House Bow St ☎01786 474468, Ⓦdarnley.connectfree.co.uk. A bit old-fashioned but with plenty of Old Town atmosphere and serving reasonably priced lunches, teas and home-made cakes in an impressive barrel-vaulted interior.

Hermann's 58 Broad St ☎01786 450632, Ⓦhermanns.co.uk. Stirling's classiest option, set in the historic Mar Place House towards the top of the Old Town. It operates brasserie-style at lunchtime, offering upmarket Austrian-Scottish dining such as *jager schnitzel* (veal) or Scottish lamb with cheese potatoes in the evening (mains from £16).

★ **Tolbooth** Jail Wynd ☎01786 274000, Ⓦstirling.gov.uk/tolbooth. By far the best option for a night out, the Tolbooth (see p.803) has a glamorous high-ceilinged bar (open only when there's an event on) and eclectic live music programme. Look out for their boisterous ceilidhs in July & Aug. Open daily.

Loch Lomond

The largest stretch of fresh water in Britain (23 miles long and up to five miles wide), **Loch Lomond** is the epitome of Scottish scenic splendour, thanks in large part to the ballad that fondly recalls its "bonnie, bonnie banks". In reality, however, the peerless scenery of the loch can be tainted by the sheer numbers of tourists and day-trippers.

20

Designated Scotland's first national park in 2002, the **Loch Lomond and the Trossachs National Park** (Ⓦlochlomond-trossachs.org) covers a large stretch of scenic territory from the lochs of the Clyde Estuary to Loch Tay in Perthshire, with the centrepiece being Loch Lomond. The most popular gateway into the park is the town of **Balloch**, nineteen miles from Glasgow city centre. Both Balloch and the western side of the loch around Luss are often packed with day-trippers and tour coaches, though the loch's eastern side, abutting the Trossachs, is very different in tone, with wooden ferryboats puttering out to a scattering of tree-covered islands off the village of **Balmaha**.

Balloch

Little more than a suburb of the much larger factory-town of Alexandria, to the south, **BALLOCH**, the settlement in the southwestern corner of Loch Lomond, has few redeeming features. However, its road and train links with Glasgow ensured that it was chosen as the focal point of the national park: the location for the huge **Loch Lomond Shores** complex.

Loch Lomond Shores

National Park Gateway Centre Daily 9.30am–6pm, later in summer • ☎08707 200631 **Drumkinnon Tower** Daily 10am–5pm • £12 • ☎01389 721000 **Can You Experience** ☎01389 602576, Ⓦcanyouexperience.com • Ⓦlochlomondshores.com

Signposted from miles around, **Loch Lomond Shores** contains the **National Park Gateway Centre**, which has background, tourist information and a leaflet outlining all transport links within the park, as well as internet access and a "retail crescent" including a branch of Jenners. Alongside, **Drumkinnon Tower** is a striking cylindrical building housing an aquarium, and, next to that, Can You Experience organizes a number of **activities**, including nature walks and canoe-, bike- and pedalo-rental.

TOP 5 PLACES TO WALK

Ben Lawers See p.822
Loch Lomond See pp.806–808
Pass of Killiecrankie See p.824
Queen Elizabeth Forest Park See p.809
Rannoch Moor See p.823

THE WEST HIGHLAND WAY

Opened in 1980, the spectacular **West Highland Way** was Scotland's first long-distance footpath, stretching some 95 miles from Milngavie (pronounced "mill-guy") six miles north of central Glasgow, to Fort William, where it reaches the foot of Ben Nevis, Britain's highest mountain. Today, it is by far the most popular such footpath in Scotland, and while for many the range of scenery, relative ease of walking and nearby facilities make it a classic route, others find it a little too busy in high season.

The route runs along the eastern shores of Loch Lomond, over the Highland Boundary Fault Line, then round Crianlarich, crossing the open heather wilderness of **Rannoch Moor**. It passes close to **Glen Coe**, notorious for the massacre of the MacDonald clan, before reaching **Fort William**. Apart from one stretch halfway along when the path is within earshot of the main road, this is wild, remote country, and you should be well prepared for sudden and extreme weather changes.

Though this is emphatically not the most strenuous of Britain's long-distance walks, a moderate degree of fitness is required as there are some steep ascents. If you're looking for an added challenge, you could work in a climb of Ben Lomond or Ben Nevis. You might choose to walk individual sections of the Way (the eight-mile climb from Glen Coe up the Devil's Staircase is particularly spectacular), but to tackle the whole thing you need to set aside at least seven days; avoid a Saturday start from Milngavie and you'll be less likely to be walking with hordes of people, and there'll be less pressure on accommodation. Most walkers tackle the route from south to north, and manage between ten and fourteen miles a day, staying at hotels, B&Bs and bunkhouses en route. Camping is permitted at recognized sites.

Although the path is clearly waymarked, you may want to check one of the many maps or guidebooks published: the **official guide**, published by Mercat Press, includes a foldout map as well as descriptions of the route, with detailed cultural, historical, archeological and wildlife information. For further details on the Way, including a comprehensive accommodation list and various tour options, see Ⓦwest-highland-way.co.uk.

ARRIVAL AND DEPARTURE — BALLOCH

Balloch has good **train** connections with Glasgow (every 30min; 40min), while **buses** connect with Balmaha (every 2hr; 25min) and Luss (hourly; 15min).

ACCOMMODATION

Loch Lomond Hostel Arden, just off the A82, 2 miles northwest of the train station Ⓣ0870 004 1136, Ⓦsyha.org.uk. Few bother staying in Balloch: instead, head to one of Scotland's most impressive SYHA hostels – a grand country house with turrets, stained-glass windows and walled gardens. Dorms sleep five to ten. Closed Nov–March. **£17.75**

Balmaha

The tranquil **eastern shore** of Loch Lomond is far better for walking and appreciating the loch's natural beauty than the overcrowded western side. The dead-end B837 from Drymen will take you halfway up the east bank, as far as you can get by car or bus, while the West Highland Way (see above) sticks close to the shores for the entire length of the loch, beginning at the tiny lochside settlement of **BALMAHA**. The village stands on the Highland Boundary Fault, the geological fault that separates the Highlands from the Lowlands; if you stand on the viewpoint above the pier, you can see the fault line clearly marked by a series of woody islands that form giant stepping-stones across the loch.

ARRIVAL AND INFORMATION — BALMAHA

By bus The #309 bus from Balloch and Drymen runs to Balmaha every 2hr.

National Park Centre Next to the large car park (April–Sept daily 10am–5.30pm; Ⓣ01360 870470). They have good information on local forest walks.

THE ISLANDS OF LOCH LOMOND

Many of Loch Lomond's 37 **islands** are privately owned, and, rather quaintly, an old wooden mail-boat still delivers post to four of them. It's possible to join the **mail-boat cruise**, which is run by MacFarlane & Son from the jetty at Balmaha (May–Oct Mon, Thurs & Sat 11.30am returns 2pm; July & Aug daily 11.30am returns 2pm; Oct–April Mon & Thurs 10.50am returns 12.50pm; £9; ⓣ01360 870214, ⓦbalmahaboatyard.co.uk). In summer the timetable allows a one-hour stop on Inchmurrin Island, the largest and most southerly of the islands inhabited by just ten permanent residents; if you're looking for an island to explore, however, a better bet is **Inchailloch**, the closest to Balmaha. Owned by Scottish Natural Heritage, it has a two-mile, signposted nature trail. You can row here yourself using a boat hired from MacFarlane & Son (from £10/hr or £30/day), or use their on-demand ferry service (£5 return).

ACCOMMODATION

Cashel Rowardennan, 2 miles north of Balmaha ⓣ01360 870234. A lovely, secluded Forestry Commission campsite on the loch shore with a decent loo block. Campers can launch craft from here onto the loch, and Ben Lomond is just 4 miles away. Closed Nov–March. Basic pitch **£15**

Oak Tree Inn Balmaha ⓣ01360 870357, ⓦoak-tree-inn.co.uk. This well-run inn is set back from the boatyard, and offers en-suite doubles and bunk-bed quads. There's also a convivial pub, and food is served all day. **£75**

Passfoot Cottage B&B Balmaha ⓣ01360 870324, ⓦpassfoot.com. This friendly and appealing little option is housed in a whitewashed toll cottage, enjoying an idyllic location and lochside garden. Great for walks along the shore. **£75**

The Trossachs

Often described as the Highlands in miniature, the **Trossachs** area boasts a magnificent diversity of scenery, with dramatic peaks and mysterious, forest-covered slopes that live up to all the images ever produced of Scotland's wild land. It is country ripe for stirring tales of brave kilted clansmen, a role fulfilled by **Rob Roy Macgregor**, the seventeenth-century outlaw whose name seems to attach to every second waterfall, cave and barely discernible path. The Trossachs' high tourist profile was largely attributable in the early days to the novels of Sir Walter Scott, which are set in the area. Since then, neither the popularity nor beauty of the region have waned, and in high season the place is jam-packed with coaches full of tourists as well as walkers and mountain bikers taking advantage of the easily accessed scenery. Autumn is a better time to come, when the hills are blanketed in rich, rusty colours and the crowds are thinner.

Aberfoyle

Each summer the sleepy little town of **ABERFOYLE**, twenty miles west of Stirling, dusts itself down for its annual influx of tourists. Though of little appeal itself, Aberfoyle's position in the heart of the Trossachs is ideal. From here, the A821 road to **Loch Katrine** winds its way into the Queen Elizabeth Forest, snaking up **Duke's Pass** (so called because it once belonged to the Duke of Montrose).

The Lake of Menteith

About 4 miles east of Aberfoyle towards Doune

The **Lake of Menteith** is a superb fly-fishing centre and Scotland's only lake (as opposed to loch), so named due to a historic mix-up with the word *laigh*, Scots for "low-lying ground", which applied to the whole area. From the northern shore, you can take a little ferry out to the **Island of Inchmahome** in order to explore the lovely ruined Augustinian abbey.

Inchmahome Priory

Daily: April–Sept 10am–4.30pm; Oct 9.30am–3.30pm • HS • £5 including ferry • ⓣ 01877 385294

Founded in 1238, **Inchmahome Priory** is the most beautiful island monastery in Scotland, its remains rising tall and graceful above the trees. The masons employed to build the priory are thought to be those who built Dunblane Cathedral (see p.804); certainly the western entrance there resembles that at Inchmahome.

ARRIVAL AND INFORMATION — ABERFOYLE

By bus Buses connect with Callander (late June to mid-Oct 4 daily Thurs–Tues; 25min) and Port of Menteith (late June to mid-Oct 4 daily Thurs–Tues; 10min).

Queen Elizabeth Forest Park Visitor Centre Walk or drive from Aberfoyle the short way to this excellent visitor centre at the David Marshall Lodge. They have maps of the walks and cycle routes in the forest, information on the flora and fauna of the area, which includes roe deer and birds of prey, and a nice café with splendid views over the tree tops (Jan Sat & Sun 10am–4pm; Feb Thurs–Sun 10am–4pm; March–Dec daily 10am–4/6pm; car park £2; ⓣ 01877 382383).

ACCOMMODATION AND EATING

Lake of Menteith Hotel Port of Menteith ⓣ 01877 385258, ⓦ lake-hotel.com. The Lake of Menteith (see opposite) is a beautiful place to stay: the hotel enjoys a lovely waterfront setting next to Port of Menteith's Victorian Gothic parish church, and also has a classy restaurant. **£130**

Loch Katrine

Heading down the northern side of the Duke's Pass you come first to **Loch Achray**, tucked under Ben A'an. At the head of the loch, a road leads the short distance to the southern end of **Loch Katrine** at the foot of Ben Venue (2370ft).

Cruises on Loch Katrine

April–Oct daily • £8 return; shorter 45min cruises with no stops £12 • ⓣ 01877 376315, ⓦ lochkatrine.co.uk

An elegant Victorian passenger **steamer**, the SS *Sir Walter Scott*, has been plying the waters of Loch Katrine since 1900, chugging up to the wild country of Glengyle. It makes various cruises each day, but only the first (departing at 10.30am) stops off at Stronachlachar every day; on Wednesdays and weekends there's a second trip to Stronachlachar departing at 2.30pm. A popular combination is to **rent a bike** from the Katrinewheelz hut by the pier (ⓣ 01877 376366, ⓦ katrinewheelz.co.uk), take the steamer up to Stronachlachar, then cycle back around the north side of the loch.

HIKING AND BIKING IN THE TROSSACHS

The Trossachs is ideal for exploring **on foot** or on a **mountain bike**. This is partly because the terrain is slightly more benign than the Highlands proper, but much is due to the excellent management of the **Queen Elizabeth Forest Park**, a huge chunk of the national park between Loch Lomond and Loch Lubnaig. The main visitor centre for the area, David Marshall Lodge, is just outside Aberfoyle (see above).

For **hill-walkers**, the prize peak is Ben Lomond (3192ft), best accessed from Rowardennan on Loch Lomond's east shore. Other highlights include Ben Venue (2370ft) and Ben A'an (1520ft) on the shores of Loch Katrine, as well as Ben Ledi (2857ft), just northwest of Callander, which all offer relatively straightforward but very rewarding climbs and, on clear days, stunning views. Walkers can also choose from any number of waymarked routes through the forests and along lochsides; pick up a map of these at the visitor centre.

The area is also a popular spot for **mountain biking**, with a number of useful rental shops (see p.810), a network of forest paths and one of the more impressive stretches of the National Cycle Network cutting through the region from Loch Lomond to Killin.

EATING AND DRINKING — LOCH KATRINE

Byre Inn Brig O'Turk 01877 376292, byreinn.co.uk. A tiny country pub and classy restaurant set in an old stone barn with wooden pews and a welcoming open fire; it's the starting point for waymarked walks to lochs Achray, Drunkie and Venachar. Mon–Sat 11am–11pm, Sun noon–11pm.

Callander

CALLANDER, on the eastern edge of the Trossachs, sits on the banks of the River Teith at the southern end of the **Pass of Leny**, one of the key routes into the Highlands. Significantly larger than Aberfoyle, eleven miles west, it is a popular summer holiday base and suffers in high season for being on the main tourist trail from Stirling through to the west Highlands. There are no attractions as such in the town itself.

ARRIVAL AND DEPARTURE — CALLANDER

Callander has **bus** connections with Katrine (late June to mid-Oct 4 daily Thurs–Tues; 55min).

GETTING AROUND

Mounter Bikes Handily located in the centre of Callander, offering rental, sales, repairs and accessories (01877 331052, mounterbikes.co.uk).

Wheels Cycling Centre Next to Trossachs Tryst (see below) 1.5 miles southwest of Callander. The best rental place in the area, with front- or full-suspension models available, as well as baby seats and children's cycles (01877 331100, scottish-cycling.co.uk).

20

ACCOMMODATION

Arden House Bracklinn Rd 01877 330235, ardenhouse.org.uk. A grand Victorian guesthouse in its own gardens with good views and woodland walks from the back door. Closed Nov–March. £75

Roman Camp Country House Hotel Main St 01877 330003, romancamphotel.co.uk. The town's most upmarket option is this romantic, turreted seventeenth-century hunting lodge situated in twenty-acre gardens on the River Teith. £150

★ **Trossachs Tryst** Invertrossachs Rd 01877 331200, scottish-hostel.com. A friendly, well-equipped and comfortable 32-bed hostel and activity centre with self-catering dorms and family rooms. It's located a mile southwest of town, down a turn-off from the A81 to Port of Monteith. Bike rental available. Dorm £20, double £50

EATING AND DRINKING

Lade Inn Kilmahog, a mile west of Callander 01877 330152, theladeinn.com. Pub food can be had at this convivial inn where the owners are particularly keen on real ales; an on-site shop sells bottled beers from all over Scotland. Mon–Fri noon–2.30pm & 5.30pm–9pm, Sat noon–9pm, Sun 12.30–8pm.

★ **Mhor Fish** 75–77 Main St 01877 330213, mhor.net. One of a new breed of fish and chip shops; it has a sustainable fish policy, daily specials and everything from snacks to bistro-style seafood dishes – and you can get fish suppers, burgers, pies and haggis to take away. Daily 10am–10pm.

Fife

The ancient Kingdom of **Fife** is a small area, barely fifty miles at its widest point, but one which has a definite identity, inextricably linked with the waters that surround it on three sides – the Tay to the north, the Forth to the south, and the cold North Sea to the east. Despite its small size, Fife encompasses several different regions, with a marked difference between the rural north and the semi-industrial south. Fishing still has a role, but ultimately it is to **St Andrews**, the home of the world-famous Royal and Ancient Golf Club, that most visitors are drawn. South of St Andrews, the tiny stone harbours of the **East Neuk** fishing villages are an appealing extension to any visit to this part of Fife.

Inland from St Andrews is the absorbing village of **Falkland** with its impressive ruined palace. To the **south**, the perfectly preserved town of **Culross** is the most obvious draw with its cobbled streets and collection of historic buildings.

St Andrews

Confident, poised and well groomed, if a little snooty, **ST ANDREWS**, Scotland's oldest **university town** and a pilgrimage centre for **golfers** from all over the world, is situated on a wide bay on the northeastern coast of Fife. Of all Scotland's universities, St Andrews is the most often compared to Oxford or Cambridge, both for the dominance of gown over town, and for the intimate, collegiate feel of the place. In fact, the university attracts a significant proportion of English undergraduates, among them Prince William, who spent four years studying here, where he met fellow student and future wife Kate Middleton.

According to legend, the town was founded, pretty much by accident, in the fourth century. **St Rule** – or Regulus – a custodian of the bones of St Andrew in Patras in southern Greece, had a vision in which an angel ordered him to carry five of the saint's bones to the western edge of the world, where he was to build a city in his honour. The conscientious courier set off, but was shipwrecked on the rocks close to the present harbour. Struggling ashore with his precious burden, he built a shrine to the saint on what subsequently became the site of the **cathedral**; St Andrew became Scotland's patron saint and the town its ecclesiastical capital.

On the three main thoroughfares, **North Street**, **Market Street** and **South Street** – which run west to east towards the ruined Gothic cathedral – are several of the original university buildings from the fifteenth century. Narrow alleys connect the cobbled streets, and attic windows and gable ends shape the rooftops, and here and there you'll see the old wooden doors with heavy knockers and black iron hinges.

20

St Andrews Cathedral

Visitor centre Daily: April–Sept 9.30am–5.30pm; Oct–March 9.30am–4.30pm • HS • £4.50, with castle £7.60 **Grounds** Daily 9am–5.30pm • HS • Free • ⓣ 01334 472563

The ruin of the great **St Andrews Cathedral**, at the east end of town, gives only an idea of the importance of what was once Scotland's largest cathedral. Founded in 1160, the cathedral was plundered and left to ruin during the Reformation by supporters of John Knox, fresh from a rousing meeting.

In front of the cathedral window a slab is all that remains of the high altar, where the relics of St Andrew were once enshrined. Previously, it is believed that they were kept in **St Rule's Tower**, the austere Romanesque monolith next to the cathedral, which was built as part of an abbey in 1130. From the top of the tower (a climb of 157 steps) there's a good view of the town and surroundings, and of the remains of the monastic buildings that made up the priory. Around the entire complex is a sturdy wall dating from the sixteenth century, more than half a mile long and with three gateways.

St Andrews Castle

Daily: April–Sept 9.30am–5.30pm; Oct–March 9.30am–4.30pm • HS • £5.50, with cathedral £7.60 • ⓣ 01334 477196

Not far north of the cathedral, the rocky coastline curves inland to the ruined **castle**, with a drop to the sea on two sides and a moat on its inland side. Founded around 1200 and extended over the centuries, it was built as part of the Palace of the Bishops and Archbishops of St Andrews. There's not a great deal left of the castle, since it fell into ruin in the seventeenth century, and most of what can be seen dates from the sixteenth century, apart from the fourteenth-century Fore Tower.

The beaches

St Andrews has two great **beaches**: the West Sands, which stretch for two miles from just below the R&A Clubhouse, and the shorter, more compact, East Sands that curve round from the harbour beyond the cathedral. The West Sands are best known from the opening sequences of the Oscar-winning film *Chariots of Fire*. The blustery winds, which are the scourge of golfers and walkers alike, do at least make the beach a great place to **fly kites**.

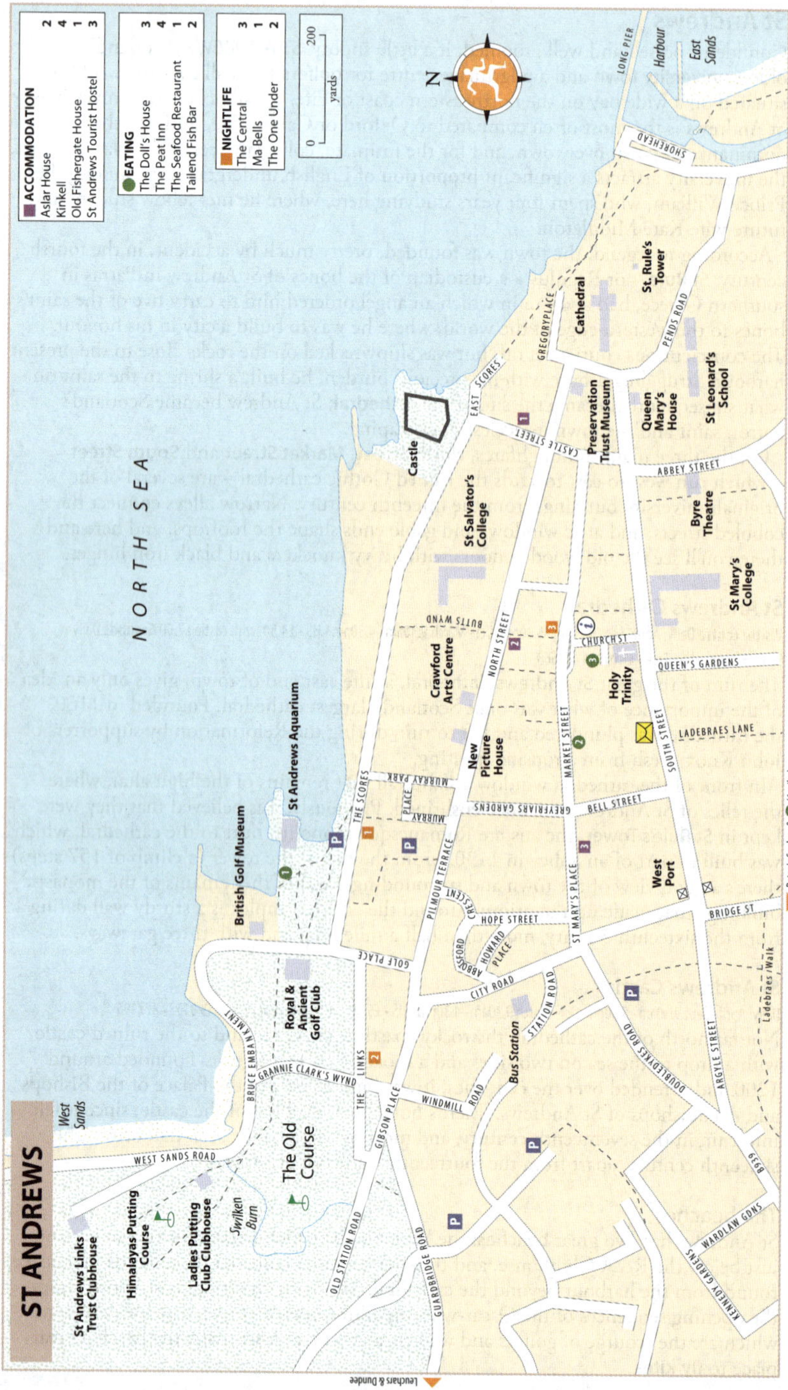
ST ANDREWS
ACCOMMODATION
Aslar House 2
Kinkell 4
Old Fishergate House 1
St Andrews Tourist Hostel 3
EATING
The Doll's House 3
The Peat Inn 4
The Seafood Restaurant 1
Tailend Fish Bar 2
NIGHTLIFE
The Central 3
Ma Bells 1
The One Under 2
0
200
yards
N
NORTH SEA
Long Pier
Harbour
East Sands
Shorehead
Castle
Cathedral
St. Rule's Tower
Preservation Trust Museum
Queen Mary's House
St Leonard's School
St Salvator's College
Byre Theatre
St Mary's College
Crawford Arts Centre
Holy Trinity
New Picture House
West Port
St Andrews Aquarium
British Golf Museum
Royal & Ancient Golf Club
Bus Station
The Old Course
Swilken Burn
Himalayas Putting Course
Ladies Putting Club Clubhouse
St Andrews Links Trust Clubhouse
West Sands
East Scores
Gregory Place
Pends Road
Castle Street
Abbey Street
North Street
Butts Wynd
Market Street
Church St
Queen's Gardens
South Street
Ladebraes Lane
Murray Park
Murray Place
The Scores
Greyfriars Gardens
Bell Street
St Mary's Place
Pilmour Terrace
Hope Street
Howard Place
Abbotsford Crescent
Bridge St
Golf Place
City Road
Station Road
Doubledykes Road
Argyle Street
Ladebraes Walk
Bruce Embankment
Grannie Clark's Wynd
The Links
Windmill Road
Gibson Place
West Sands Road
Old Station Road
Guardbridge Road
Wardlaw Gdns
Kennedy Gardens
B939
Crail, Kinkell & 4
Botanic Gardens & 4 (6 miles)
Leuchars & Dundee

GOLF IN ST ANDREWS

St Andrews **Royal and Ancient Golf Club** (or "R&A") has been the international governing body for golf since 1754, when a meeting of 22 of the local gentry founded the Society of St Andrews Golfers, being "admirers of the ancient and healthful exercise of golf". The game itself has been played here since the fifteenth century. Those early days were instrumental in establishing Scotland as the home of golf, for the rules were distinguished from those of the French game by the fact that participants had to manoeuvre the ball into a hole, rather than hit an above-ground target. It was not without its opponents, however – particularly James II who, in 1457, banned his subjects from playing since it was distracting them from archery practice.

The approach to St Andrews from the west runs adjacent to the famous **Old Course**, the oldest course in the world, and just one of seven in the immediate vicinity of the town. The R&A's strictly private **clubhouse**, a stolid, square building dating from 1854, is at the eastern end of the Old Course overlooking both the 18th green and the long strand of the West Sands. The British Open Championship was first held here in 1873, having been inaugurated in 1860 at Prestwick in Ayrshire, and since then it has been held at St Andrews regularly, pulling in enormous crowds.

PLAYING GOLF

St Andrews Links Trust Alongside the fairway of the first hole of the Old Course ⓦ standrews.org.uk. It is possible to play on St Andrew's courses, including the venerated Old Course itself (for this you'll need a valid handicap certificate and must enter a daily ballot for tee times; the green fees, for those who are successful, are £130 in summer). For full details contact the St Andrews Links Trust, the organization that looks after all the courses in town.

Himalayas Arguably the best golfing experience in St Andrews, even if you can't tell a birdie from a bogey, this fantastically lumpy eighteen-hole putting course is in an ideal setting next to the Old Course and the sea. Officially the Ladies Putting Club, founded in 1867, with its own clubhouse, it has grass as perfectly manicured as the championship course, and you can have all the thrill of sinking a six-footer in golf's most famous location, at a bargain price. April–Sept Mon–Sat 10.30am–6.30pm, Sun noon–6.30pm. £1.50

British Golf Museum

Bruce Embankment • April–Oct Mon–Sat 9.30am–5.30pm, Sun 10am–5pm; Nov–March Mon–Sat 10am–4.30pm • £6 • ⓣ 01334 460046, ⓦ www.britishgolfmuseum.co.uk

Pictures of golfing greats from Tom Morris to Tiger Woods, along with clubs and a variety of memorabilia donated by famous players, are displayed in the admirable **British Golf Museum**, on the waterfront below the Royal and Ancient Golf Club clubhouse, which tells the story of British golf from its beginnings to the present day.

ARRIVAL AND INFORMATION — ST ANDREWS

By train St Andrews' nearest train station (on the Edinburgh–Dundee line) is 5 miles northwest at Leuchars, across the River Eden, from where regular buses make the 15min trip into town. When you buy your rail ticket to Leuchars, ask for a St Andrews rail-bus ticket, which includes the bus fare.

Destinations Aberdeen (every 1–2hr; 1hr 30min); Dundee (every 1–2hr; 15min); Edinburgh (every 1–2hr; 1hr).

By bus The station is on Station Rd, just off City Rd and near the town centre.

Destinations Dundee (every 15min; 35min); Dunfermline (hourly; 1hr 15min); Edinburgh (every 30min; 1hr 50min); Glasgow (every 30min; 2hr 25min); Glenrothes (hourly; 40min); Kirkcaldy (every 30min; 1hr); Stirling (every 2hr; 1hr 55min).

Tourist office 70 Market St (April–June Mon–Sat 9.30am–5.30pm, Sun 11am–4pm; July & Aug Mon–Sat 9.30am–7pm, Sun 10am–5pm; Sept & Oct Mon–Sat 9.30am–6pm, Sun 11am–4pm; Nov–March Mon–Sat 9.30am–5pm; ⓣ 01334 472021).

ACCOMMODATION

There's no shortage of accommodation both in town and around, although average **prices** in all categories vie with Edinburgh's as the highest in Scotland. There are plenty of **guesthouses**, though rooms often fill up in summer, when you should definitely book in advance.

Aslar House 120 North St 01334 473460, aslar.com. A smart guesthouse in a three-storey townhouse with an unusual round tower at the back. £90

★ **Kinkell** 01334 472003, kinkell.com. Countryside B&B in a lovely family farmhouse near the beach, about 2 miles south of town off the A917. £45

Old Fishergate House North Castle St 01334 470874, oldfishergatehouse.co.uk. Seventeenth-century townhouse in the oldest part of St Andews, with two spacious twin rooms brimming with period features. £90

St Andrews Tourist Hostel St Mary's Place 01334 479911, hostelsaccommodation.com/hostels. Superbly located backpacker hostel in a converted townhouse above *The Grill House* restaurant, with plenty of dorm beds, but no doubles. The cheapest option in town, and not the quietest. £18

University of St Andrews 01334 462000. Rooms for rent in various student residences between June and Sept, all on a B&B basis. Self-catering houses also available. Closed Oct–May. £50

EATING

The Doll's House 3 Church Square 01334 477422, dolls-house.co.uk. Stylish modern dishes based around top Scottish produce, with a continental feel to the outdoor tables. Mains £10–18 at dinner, with good-value lunch menus. Daily noon–2.30pm 5–9.30pm.

The Peat Inn Cupar, 6 miles southwest of town 01334 840206, thepeatinn.co.uk. Maintaining its reputation as one of Scotland's gourmet hot spots after 25 years, *The Peat Inn* offers fine dining using top local produce – roast loin of lamb in a pistachio crust with roast apricots, for example – in an intimate room. Menus range from a three-course set lunch (£18) to a six-course tasting menu (£60). They also have eight plush, if pricey, suites. Tues–Sat 12.30–1.30pm & 7–9pm.

20

★ **The Seafood Restaurant** The Scores 01334 479475, theseafoodrestaurant.com. The venue has as much of a wow-factor as the fish-dominated menu (three courses £45; try the sea trout with citrus mash): an amazing location in a custom-built glass building on the beach between the Aquarium and the Old Course. Mon–Sat noon–2.30pm & 6.30–9pm, Sun noon–3pm & 6.30–9pm.

Tailend Fish Bar 130 Market St 01334 474070, tailendfishbar.co.uk. A terrific and popular takeway – a modern twist on the trad chippy, dishing up locally sourced fresh fish. There are reasonably priced fish suppers with crisp batter and excellent chips, plus specials such as sea bass, swordfish or skate. A simple café adjoins the takeaway. Daily 11.30am–10pm.

DRINKING AND ENTERTAINMENT

Byre Theatre Abbey St 01334 475000, byretheatre.com. Occupies a stylish modern building, with a pleasant bar and bistro. Productions range from important Scottish drama to populist musicals.

The Central Market St 01334 478296. Prominent, popular old pub right in the heart of town serving real ales and pub grub. Mon–Thurs 11am–11.45pm, Fri & Sat 11am–midnight, Sun 12.30–11.45pm.

Ma Bells 40 The Scores 01334 472611, standrews-golf.co.uk. In the basement of the *St Andrews Golf Hotel*, this is a lively pub serving cheap food and often thronged with students. Tues–Sat 11am–1am, Sun 12.30pm–midnight, Mon 11am–midnight.

The One Under 16 Pilmour Links 01334 473393, roccagrill.com/oneunderhome.php. Hotel bar with views of the Old Course and gastro pub food. Open daily.

The East Neuk

Extending south of St Andrews as far as Largo Bay, the **East Neuk** is famous for its quaint fishing villages replete with crow-stepped gables and red pan-tiled roofs, the Flemish influence indicating a history of strong trading links with the Low Countries. The area is dotted with blustery **golf courses**, and there are plenty of bracing coastal paths, including the waymarked **Fife Coastal Path**: tracing the shoreline between St Andrews and the Forth Rail Bridge, it's at its most scenic in the East Neuk stretch.

GETTING AROUND — THE EAST NEUK

From St Andrews, **bus** #95 runs along the East Neuk coast to Leven.

Crail

CRAIL is the archetypally charming East Neuk fishing village, its maze of rough cobbled streets leading steeply down to a tiny stone-built harbour surrounded by piles of lobster creels, and with fishermen's cottages tucked into every nook and cranny in the cliff. Though often populated by artists at their easels and camera-toting tourists, it is still a working harbour, and if the boats have been out you can buy fresh lobster and crab cooked to order from a small wooden shack on the harbour edge (see below). You can trace the history of the town at the **Crail Museum and Heritage Centre**, 62 Marketgate (April Sat 10am–5pm, Sun noon–5pm; May–Sept Mon–Sat 10am–5pm, Sun noon–5pm; free), while the **Crail Pottery**, 75 Nethergate (Mon–Fri 9am–5pm, Sat & Sun 10am–5pm), is worth a visit for its wide range of locally made pottery.

INFORMATION — CRAIL

Tourist office Crail Museum and Heritage Centre, 62 Marketgate (April Sat 10am–5pm, Sun noon–5pm; May–Sept Mon–Sat 10am–5pm, Sun noon–5pm; T 01333 450869).

EATING

Crail Harbour Gallery and Tearoom Shoregate T 01333 451896, W crailharbourgallery.co.uk. Tucked into a wee cottage on the way down to the harbour, with a terrace overlooking the Isle of May. They serve Fairtrade coffees, hot chocolate and paninis, plus local crab, smoked salmon and herring. Daily 11am–5pm.

★ **Mrs Riley's** The harbour. This tiny lobster and crab shack offers fresh seafood with sea views, and is the best place in town for a snack. Mid-April to early Oct Tues–Sun noon–4pm.

Anstruther

ANSTRUTHER is the largest of the East Neuk fishing harbours; with an attractively old-fashioned air and no shortage of character in its houses and narrow streets, it's also home to the wonderfully unpretentious **Scottish Fisheries Museum**.

Scottish Fisheries Museum

Harbourhead • April–Oct Mon–Sat 10am–5.30pm, Sun 11am–5pm; Nov–March Mon–Sat 10am–4.30pm, Sun noon–4.30pm • £5 • T 01333 310628, W scotfishmuseum.org

Set in an atmospheric complex of sixteenth- to nineteenth-century buildings with timber ceilings and wooden floors, the **Scottish Fisheries Museum** chronicles the history of the fishing and whaling industries with ingenious displays, including a series of exquisite ships' models built on site by a resident model-maker.

20

Isle of May

Offshore from Anstruther • **Boats from Anstruther** May–Sept 1 daily; May & June no sailing on Tues; check departure times, 4–5hr for a round trip • £19 • T 01333 310103, W isleofmayferry.com

Located on the rugged **Isle of May**, several miles offshore from Anstruther, is a lighthouse erected in 1816 by Robert Louis Stevenson's grandfather, as well as the remains of Scotland's first lighthouse, built in 1636. The island is now a **nature reserve** and bird sanctuary, and can be reached by boat from Anstruther.

INFORMATION — ANSTRUTHER

Tourist office Scottish Fisheries Museum, Harbourhead (April–Sept Mon–Sat 10am–5pm, Sun 11am–4pm; Oct Mon–Sat 10am–4pm, Sun noon–4pm; T 01333 311073).

EATING

★ **The Cellar** 24 East Green T 01333 310378, W cellaranstruther.co.uk. Tucked in beside the museum in one of the village's oldest buildings, once a cooperage and smokehouse, this fantastic fish restaurant serves classy dishes including a delicious appetizer of marinated herring. Two courses lunch £19.50, dinner £34.95; three courses £24.50/£39.95. Lunch Fri & Sat, Tues–Sat from 6.30pm.

Central Fife

The main A92 road cuts right through **Central Fife**, ultimately connecting the Forth Road Bridge on the southern coast of Fife with the Tay Road Bridge on the northern coast. The main settlement of this inland region is **Glenrothes**, a new town created after

World War II in old coal-mining territory. Generally, the scenery in this part of the county is pleasant rather than startling, though it's worth making a detour to **Falkland** and its magnificent ruined palace.

Falkland

The **Howe of Fife**, north of Glenrothes, is a low-lying stretch of ground (or "howe") at the foot of the twin peaks of the heather-swathed **Lomond Hills** – West Lomond (1696ft) and East Lomond (1378ft). Nestling in the lower slopes of East Lomond, the narrow streets of **FALKLAND** are lined with fine and well-preserved seventeenth- and eighteenth-century buildings.

Falkland Palace

March–Oct Mon–Sat 10am–5pm, Sun 1–5pm • NTS • £11 • ⓣ 0844 4932186

The village grew up around **Falkland Palace**, which stands on the site of an earlier castle, home to the Macduffs, the earls of Fife. James IV began the construction of the present palace in 1500; it was completed and embellished by James V, and became a favoured country retreat for the royal court. The palace was completely restored by the third Marquess of Bute, and today it is a stunning piece of architecture, complete with parapets, mullioned windows, round towers and massive walls. Free audioguides lead you round a cross section of public and private rooms in the south and east wings. Outside, the **gardens** are also worth a look, their well-stocked herbaceous borders lining a pristine lawn. Don't miss the high walls of the oldest real (or Royal) tennis court in Britain – built in 1539 for James V and still used.

ACCOMMODATION AND EATING — FALKLAND

Ladywell House B&B Half a mile from Falkland ⓣ 01337 858414, ⓦ ladywellhousefife.co.uk. A fine Georgian country house set in walled gardens. Meals are served in the spacious conservatory, and there's a smart drawing room. £70

★ **Pillars of Hercules Organic Farm** Just outside Falkland on the A912 ⓣ 01337 857749, ⓦ pillars.co.uk. A great little farm shop and café; you can camp here, and there's a bothy available to hire. They also host monthly restaurant nights with live music. Daily 9am–6pm

Southern Fife

Although the coast of **southern Fife** is predominantly industrial – with everything from cottage industries to the refitting of nuclear submarines – mercifully, only a small part has been blighted by insensitive development. Thanks to its proximity to the early coal mines, the charming village of **Culross** was once a lively port which enjoyed a thriving trade with Holland, the Dutch influence obvious in its lovely gabled houses. It was from nearby **Dunfermline** that Queen Margaret ousted the Celtic Church from Scotland in the eleventh century; her son, David I, founded an abbey here in the twelfth century. Southern Fife is linked to Edinburgh by the two **Forth bridges**, the red-painted girders of the Rail Bridge representing one of Britain's great engineering spectacles.

Culross

CULROSS (pronounced "Coorus") is one of Scotland's most picturesque settlements, owing to the work of the National Trust for Scotland, which has been renovating its whitewashed, pan-tiled buildings since 1932. For an excellent introduction to the burgh's history, head to the **National Trust Visitor Centre** (April, May & Sept Thurs–Mon noon–5pm; June–Aug daily noon–5pm; Oct Thurs–Mon noon–4pm; NTS; joint ticket for Town House, Palace and Study £9), located in the **Town House** facing Sandhaven, where goods were once unloaded from ships.

The charm of Culross is revealed simply by wandering through its narrow streets looking for old inscriptions above windows and investigating crooked passageways. Leading uphill from the Town House, a cobbled alleyway known as **Back Causeway** leads up to the **Study** (same hours as visitor centre), a restored house that takes its name from the small room at the top of the corbelled projecting tower, reached by a turnpike stair. Further up the hill from the Study lie the remains of **Culross Abbey**, founded by Cistercian monks on land given to the church in 1217 by the Earl of Fife.

Culross Palace

April, May & Sept Thurs–Mon noon–5pm; June–Aug daily noon–5pm; Oct Thurs–Mon noon–4pm • NTS • Joint ticket for Town House, Palace and Study £9 • T 0844 4932189

The most impressive building in the village is the ochre-coloured **Culross Palace** (same hours), built by wealthy coal merchant George Bruce in the late sixteenth century; it's not a palace at all but a grand and impressive house, with lots of small rooms and connecting passageways. Inside, well-informed staff point out the wonderful painted ceilings, pine panelling, antique furniture and curios; outside, dormer windows and crow-stepped gables dominate the walled court in which the house stands.

Dunfermline

Scotland's capital until the Union of the Crowns in 1603, **DUNFERMLINE** lies inland seven miles east of Culross, north of the Forth bridges.

Dunfermline Abbey

April–Sept daily 9.30am–5.30pm; Oct–March Mon–Wed & Sat 9.30am–4.30pm, Thurs 9.30am–12.30pm, Sun 2–4.30pm • HS • £3.70 • T 01383 724586

The oldest part of **Dunfermline Abbey** is attributable to Queen Margaret, who began building a Benedictine priory in 1072, the remains of which can still be seen beneath the nave of the present church; her son, **David I**, raised the priory to the rank of abbey in the following century. In 1303, during the first of the **Wars of Independence**, the English king Edward I occupied the palace and ordered the destruction of most of the monastery buildings. **Robert the Bruce** helped rebuild the abbey, and when he died of leprosy 25 years later he was buried here, although his body went undiscovered until building began on a new parish church in 1821. Inside, the stained glass is impressive, and the columns are artfully carved into chevrons, spirals and arrowheads.

20

ARRIVAL AND DEPARTURE — DUNFERMLINE

By train The station is on the south side of the centre, with its main entrance off St Margaret's Drive.

Destinations Edinburgh (every 30min; 35min); Kirkcaldy (hourly; 40min).

By bus Buses stop at Queen Anne St, between Carnegie Drive and High St.

Destinations Culross (hourly; 20min); Edinburgh (every 30min; 40min); Glasgow (every 30min; 1hr 10min); Kirkcaldy (hourly; 30min); Stirling (every 2hr; 1hr 15min).

North Queensferry

The highlight of Fife's **south coast** is one of Scotland's largest man-made structures, the impressive Forth Rail Bridge, which joins Fife at **NORTH QUEENSFERRY.** Until the opening of the road bridge, this small fishing village was the northern landing point of the ferry from South Queensferry (see p.747), but today everything in the village is quite literally overshadowed by the two great bridges, each about a mile and a half in length, which traverse the Firth of Forth at its narrowest point.

Forth Rail Bridge

The cantilevered **Forth Rail Bridge**, built from 1883 to 1890 by Sir John Fowler and Benjamin Baker, ranks among the supreme achievements of Victorian engineering, with some 50,000 tons of steel used in the construction of a design that manages to express grace as well as might. The only way to cross the rail bridge is on a train heading to or from Edinburgh, though this doesn't allow much of a perspective of the spectacle itself. For the best **panorama**, use the pedestrian and cycle lanes on the east side of the road bridge.

Forth Road Bridge

Derived from American models, the suspension format chosen for the **Forth Road Bridge** alongside the rail bridge makes an interesting modern complement to the older structure. Erected between 1958 and 1964, it finally killed off the 900-year-old ferry, and now attracts such a heavy volume of traffic that a second road crossing is being considered.

Deep Sea World

Battery Quarry • Mon–Fri 10am–5pm, Sat & Sun 10am–6pm • £12 • ⓣ 01383 411880, ⓦ deepseaworld.com

Tucked beneath the mighty rail bridge is **Deep Sea World**, one of Scotland's most popular family attractions. Full of weird and wonderful creatures from sea horses to piranhas, the highlight is a huge aquarium that boasts the world's largest underwater viewing tunnel, through which you glide on a moving walkway while sharks, conger eels and all manner of fish from the deep swim nonchalantly past.

Perthshire

20

Genteel, attractive **Perthshire** is, in many ways, the epitome of well-groomed rural Scotland. An area of gentle glens, mature woodland, rushing rivers and peaceful lochs, it's the long-established domain of Scotland's well-to-do country set. First settled more than eight thousand years ago, it was ruled by the Romans and then the Picts before Celtic missionaries established themselves.

The ancient town of **Perth** occupies a strategic position at the mouth of the River Tay; salmon, wool and, by the sixteenth century, whisky, were exported, while a major import was Bordeaux claret. At nearby **Scone**, Kenneth MacAlpine established the capital of the kingdom of the Scots and the Picts in 846. When this settlement was washed away by floods in 1210, William the Lion founded Perth as a royal burgh.

North and west of Perth, **Highland Perthshire** is made up of gorgeous and mighty woodlands, particularly along the banks of the River Tay. The area is dotted with neat, confident towns and villages like **Dunkeld** and **Birnam**, with its mature trees and lovely ruined cathedral, and **Aberfeldy** set deep amongst farmland east of Loch Tay. Further north, the countryside becomes more sparsely populated and spectacular, with some wonderful walking country, especially around **Pitlochry**, **Blair Atholl** and the wild expanses of **Rannoch Moor** to the west.

OUTDOOR ACTIVITIES IN PERTHSHIRE

In Perthshire, outdoor activities range from gentle strolls through ancient oak forests to white-knuckle rides down frothing waterfalls. The variety of landscapes and relative accessibility from the central belt has led to a significant number of **outdoor operators** being based in the area: the tourist board's **Activity Line** (ⓣ 01577 861186, ⓦ www.adventureperthshire.co.uk) can give advice and contacts for more than thirty companies who comply with the Adventure Perthshire Operators' Charter.

Highland Adventure Safaris Aberfeldy ⓣ 01887 820071, ⓦ highlandadventuresafaris.co.uk. An inspiring introduction to wild Scotland in which you're taken by 4WD to search for golden eagle eyries, stags and pine martens.

Nae Limits Dunkeld and Ballinluig ⓣ 01796 482600, ⓦ naelimits.co.uk. Canyoning, cliff-jumping, bungee jumping and sphere-ing (which involves tumbling down a hillside inside a giant plastic ball) for adrenalin junkies.

National Kayak School Aberfeldy ⓦ nationalkayakschool.com. Everything from whitewater kayaking courses to sea-kayaking holidays.

Splash Aberfeldy ⓣ 01887 829706, ⓦ rafting.co.uk. Rafting on larger craft through the best rapids on the Tay at Grandtully.

Perth and around

Surrounded by fertile agricultural land and beautiful scenery, the bustling market town of **PERTH** was Scotland's capital in the fifteenth century, and expanded in the eighteenth. Today, with the whisky and insurance trades employing significant numbers, it remains an important town.

Two large areas of green parkland, known as the North and South Inch, flank the **centre**; the city's main shopping areas are **High Street** and **South Street**, as well as St John's shopping centre on King Edward Street. Perth is at its most attractive along **Tay Street**, with a succession of grander buildings along one side and the attractively landscaped riverside embankment on the other.

Fergusson Gallery

Corner of Tay St and Marshall Place • Sept–April Mon–Sat 10am–5pm; May–Aug Mon–Sat 10am–5pm, Sun 1–4.30pm • Free • Ⓣ 01738 783425, Ⓦ pkc.gov.uk

Perth's highlight is the **Fergusson Gallery**, occupying a striking round Victorian sandstone water tower, and home to an extensive collection of work by J.D. Fergusson, foremost artist of the Scottish Colourist movement (see p.783). Greatly influenced by Impressionist and Post-Impressionist artists, he created a distinctive approach that marries both movements' freedom of style with bold use of colour and lighting – shown, for example, in his portrait of Elizabeth Dryden, *The Hat with the Pink Scarf*. As well as oils, the collection includes sketches, notebooks and sculpture: among the latter, look out for *Eastre: Hymn to the Sun*, an exotic and radiant brass head inspired by his dancer wife and collaborator Margaret Morris.

20

Scone Palace

A couple of miles north of Perth on the A93 • April–Oct daily 9.30am–5.30pm • £9.60, grounds only £5.50 • Ⓣ 01738 552300, Ⓦ scone-palace.co.uk • Bus #3 or #58 from Perth

Scone Palace (pronounced "skoon") is one of Scotland's finest historical country homes. Owned and occupied by the Earl and Countess of Mansfield, the two-storey building on the eastern side of the Tay is stately but not overpowering, more a home than an untouchable monument. The rooms, although full of priceless antiques and lavish furnishings, feel lived-in.

The abbey that stood here in the sixteenth century was where all Scottish kings until James IV were crowned. Long before that, Scone was the capital of Pictavia, and it was here that Kenneth MacAlpine brought the famous Coronation **Stone of Destiny**, or Stone of Scone, now to be found in Edinburgh Castle, and where he ruled as the first king of a united Scotland. A replica of the (surprisingly small) stone can be found on Moot Hill, opposite the palace.

In the **grounds** you'll also find a beech-hedge maze in the pattern of the heraldic family crest and avenues of venerable trees. Scone was the birthplace of botanist and plant collector **David Douglas**, and following the trail named after him brings you to a fragrant pinetum planted in 1848 with many of the exotics he discovered in California and elsewhere.

ARRIVAL AND INFORMATION — PERTH

By train The station is in the southwest of town on Leonard St.

Destinations Aberdeen (hourly; 1hr 40min); Blair Atholl (3–7 daily; 45min); Dundee (hourly; 25min); Dunkeld (3–7 daily; 20min); Edinburgh (every 1–2hr; 1hr 25min); Glasgow Queen St (hourly; 1hr); Inverness (4–9 daily; 2hr); Pitlochry (4–9 daily; 30min); Stirling (hourly; 30min).

By bus The bus station is opposite the train station on Leonard St.

Destinations Aberfeldy (10 daily; 1hr 15min); Crieff (hourly; 45min); Dundee (hourly; 45min); Dunkeld (hourly; 30min); Edinburgh (hourly; 1hr 20min); Glasgow (hourly; 1hr 35min); Gleneagles (hourly; 25min); Inverness (hourly; 2hr 45min); Pitlochry (hourly; 45min); Stirling (hourly; 50min).

Tourist office West Mill St (April–June, Sept & Oct Mon–Sat 9am–5pm, Sun 11am–4pm; July & Aug Mon–Sat 9am–6.30pm, Sun 10am–5pm; Nov–March Tues–Sat 10am–4pm; Ⓣ 01738 450600, Ⓦ perthshire.co.uk).

ACCOMMODATION

Kinnaird House 5 Marshall Place ⓣ01738 628021, ⓦkinnaird-guesthouse.co.uk. A warm welcome in a lovely townhouse overlooking South Inch Park, with six well-equipped double/twin en-suite rooms and lots of organic options on the breakfast menu. £70

Parklands Hotel 2 St Leonards Bank ⓣ01738 622451, ⓦtheparklandshotel.com. Of the numerous central hotels, aim for the fourteen-bedroom *Parklands* close to the train station, which has a dash of contemporary styling and touches of luxury; there's a good restaurant and bistro on site. £100

EATING AND DRINKING

63, Tay Street 63 Tay St ⓣ01738 441451, ⓦ63taystreet.co.uk. At the top end of the market in Perth – and indeed the country – serving classy and expensive modern Scottish food with Mediterranean influences. Mains from £13 at lunch; three-course dinner menu £35.Tues–Sat noon–2pm & 6.30–9pm.

Café Tabou 4 St John's Place ⓣ01738 446698, ⓦcafetabou.co.uk. For moderately priced food try *Café Tabou* with its menu of French classics and outdoor seating. There are lots of seafood options, including oyster, langoustines and mussels, with set lunch menus (£11–15), pre-theatre menus, and dinner mains from £14. Sun noon–3pm, Mon 10am–3pm, Tues–Thurs 10am–9.30pm, Fri & Sat 10am–10pm.

Kerachers 168 South St ⓣ01738 449777, ⓦkerachers-restaurant.co.uk. Homely upstairs restaurant, located in a restored Wesleyan chapel, and best known for its elegant fish dishes. Tues–Thurs from 6pm, Fri & Sat from noon & from 6pm.

Strath Tay

20

North of Perth, both the railway and main A9 trunk road speed through some of Perthshire's most attractive countryside before heading into the bleaker Highlands. Magnificent woodland spreads around the valley – or "strath" – of the River Tay, as it heads towards the sea from attractive **Loch Tay**. On the eastern side of the loch, the Tay calmly glides past the attractive country town of **Aberfeldy**. The loch itself, meanwhile, is set up among the high Breadalbane mountains, which include the striking peak of **Ben Lawers**, Perthshire's highest, and the hills that enclose the long, enchanting **Glen Lyon**.

Dunkeld

Twelve miles north of Perth, **DUNKELD** was proclaimed Scotland's ecclesiastical capital by Kenneth MacAlpine in 850. The town is one of the area's most pleasant communities, with handsome whitewashed houses, appealing arts and crafts shops and a charming cathedral.

Dunkeld Cathedral

Daily: May–Sept 9.30am–6.30pm; Oct–April 9.30am–4pm • Free • ⓦdunkeldcathedral.org.uk

Dunkeld's partly ruined **cathedral** is on the northern side of town, in an idyllic setting amid lawns and trees on the east bank of the Tay. The present structure consists of the fourteenth-century choir and the fifteenth-century nave; the choir, restored in 1600 (and several times since), now serves as the parish church, while the nave remains roofless apart from the clocktower.

Loch of the Lowes

Two miles east of Dunkeld off the A923 • **Visitor centre** April–Sept 10am–5pm • £3 • ⓣ01350 727337, ⓦscottishwildlifetrust.org.uk

The **Loch of the Lowes** nature reserve, covering 95 hectares, offers a rare chance to see breeding ospreys, as well as other wildfowl, woodland birds and red squirrels; the **visitor centre** has video relay screens and will point you in the direction of the best vantage points.

INFORMATION — DUNKELD

Tourist office The Cross, town centre (April–June, Sept & Oct Mon–Sat 10am–4.30pm, Sun 10.30am–3.30pm; July & Aug Mon–Sat 9.30am–6.30pm, Sun 10am–4pm; ⓣ01350 727688).

EATING AND DRINKING

Robert Menzies Deli 1 Atholl St, Dunkeld 01350 728028, scottish-deli.com. Pick up snacks, sandwiches, Scottish beers and fresh fruit; they also have a tiny café. There's been a deli here for more than fifty years, and the shop retains its original fittings. Mon–Fri 9.30am–5.30pm, Sat 9am–5.30pm, Sun 10am–4.30pm.

★ **Taybank Hotel** Tay Terrace 01350 727340, thetaybank.com. A characterful beacon for music fans, who come for the regular live sessions in the convivial bar. Decent bar meals, too (the stovies are a speciality). Mon–Fri & Sun 11am–11pm, Sat 11am–11.30pm.

Birnam

Dunkeld is linked to its sister community, **BIRNAM**, by Thomas Telford's seven-arched bridge of 1809. This little village has a place in history thanks to Shakespeare, for it was on Dunsinane Hill, to the southeast of the village, that Macbeth declared: "I will not be afraid of death and bane Till Birnam Forest come to Dunsinane", only to be told later by a messenger "I look'd toward Birnam, and anon me thought The Wood began to move…".

The **Birnam Oak**, a gnarly old character propped up by crutches on the waymarked riverside walk, is inevitably claimed to be a survivor of the infamous mobile forest. Several centuries after Shakespeare, another literary personality, Beatrix Potter, drew inspiration from the area: there's a Potter-themed exhibition and garden, aimed at both children and adults, on the main road in the impressive barrel-fronted **Birnam Institute** (daily 10am–5pm; birnaminstitute.com; free), a modern theatre, arts and community centre.

A mile and a half from Birnam is **The Hermitage**, set in a grandly wooded gorge of the plunging River Braan. Here you'll find a pretty eighteenth-century folly, known as Ossian's Hall, which neatly frames a dramatic waterfall. Nearby, you can see a Douglas fir, claimed to be the tallest tree in Britain.

ACCOMMODATION — BIRNAM

Waterbury Guest House Murthly Terrace 01350 727324, waterbury-guesthouse.co.uk. Set in a turreted end-of-terrace Victorian villa. Breakfasts are excellent: the honey comes from Bee Cottage at Inver, and meat is provided by an award-winning local butcher. **£65**

Aberfeldy

From Dunkeld the A9 runs north alongside the Tay for eight miles to Ballinluig, and the turn-off along the A827 to **ABERFELDY**. A prosperous settlement of large stone houses and 4WDs, Aberfeldy acts as a service centre for the wider Loch Tay area.

The town's main attraction is **Dewar's World of Whisky** at the Aberfeldy Distillery (April–Oct Mon–Sat 10am–6pm, Sun noon–4pm; Nov–March Mon–Sat 10am–4pm; dewarswow.com; £6.50), which puts on an impressive show of describing the making of whisky. The rest of the small town centre is a busy mixture of craft and tourist shops, the most interesting being **The Watermill** on Mill Street (Mon–Sat 10am–5pm, Sun 11am–5pm; aberfeldywatermill.com), an inspiring bookshop and art gallery in a restored early nineteenth-century mill.

ARRIVAL AND INFORMATION — ABERFELDY

By bus Buses connect Aberfeldy with Perth (6 daily; 1hr 20min).

Tourist office The Square (April–June, Sept & Oct Mon–Sat 9.30am–5pm, Sun 11am–3pm; July & Aug Mon–Sat 9.30am–6.30pm, Sun 10am–4pm; Nov–March Mon–Sat 10am–4pm; 01887 820276). They're an enthusiastic bunch here, providing advice on local accommodation and details of nearby walking trails.

EATING

The Watermill Mill St 01887 822896, aberfeldywatermill.com. Your best bet for a good coffee or a light lunch. There are comfy sofas, and the excellent soups, sandwiches and cakes are made locally, mainly with organic ingredients. Mon–Sat 10am–5pm, Sun 11am–5pm.

Loch Tay

Aberfeldy grew up around a crossing point on the River Tay, which leaves it, oddly, six miles adrift of **Loch Tay**, a fourteen-mile-long stretch of fresh water that virtually hooks together the western and eastern Highlands. Guarding the northern end of the loch is **KENMORE**, a cluster of whitewashed estate houses and well-tended gardens. The main attraction here is the fantastic heritage museum, **Scottish Crannog Centre**.

Scottish Crannog Centre

Daily: April–Oct 10am–5.30pm; Nov 10am–4pm • £7 • ⓣ 01887 830583, ⓦ crannog.co.uk

Crannogs are Iron Age loch dwellings built on stilts over the water. Originally they would have had a gangway to the shore; upon the approach of hostile intruders, whether animal or human, the gangway would quickly be raised. At the **Scottish Crannog Centre** visitors can walk out over the loch to a superbly reconstructed, thatched, wooden crannog. The whole place is set up to look as it would have 2500 years ago, complete with sheepskin rugs and wooden bowls.

Ben Lawers

Dominating the northern side of Loch Tay is moody **Ben Lawers** (3984ft), Perthshire's highest mountain; from the top there are incredible views towards both the Atlantic and the North Sea. The ascent – which should not be tackled unless you're properly equipped for Scottish hillwalking – takes around three hours from the **NTS visitor centre** (April–Sept daily 10am–5pm), located at 1300ft and reached by a winding hill road off the A827.

Glen Lyon

North of Breadalbane, the mountains tumble down into **Glen Lyon** – at 34 miles long, the longest enclosed glen in Scotland. The narrow singletrack road through the glen starts at **Keltneyburn**, near Kenmore at the northern end of the loch; a few miles on, the village of **FORTINGALL** is little more than a handful of pretty thatched cottages, although locals make much of their 5000-year-old yew tree, believed (by them at least) to be the oldest living thing in Europe. The venerable tree can be found in the churchyard, showing its age a little but well looked after, with a timeline nearby listing some of the events the yew has lived through. One of these, bizarrely, is the birth of Pontius Pilate, reputedly the son of a Roman officer stationed near Fortingall in the last years BC.

Highland Perthshire

North of the Tay valley, Perthshire doesn't discard its lush richness immediately, but there are clear indications of the more rugged, barren influences of the Highlands proper. The principal settlements of **Pitlochry** and **Blair Atholl**, both just off the A9, are separated by the narrow gorge of Killiecrankie, a crucial strategic spot in times past for anyone seeking to control movement of cattle or armies from the Highlands to the Lowlands. Greater rewards, however, are to be found further from the main drag, most notably in the winding westward road along the shores of **Loch Tummel** and **Loch Rannoch** past the distinctive peak of **Schiehallion**, which eventually leads to the remote wilderness of **Rannoch Moor**.

Pitlochry

PITLOCHRY has, on the face of it, a lot going for it, not least the backdrop of Ben Vrackie and the River Tummel slipping by. However, there's little charm to be found on the main street, filled with crawling traffic and endless shops selling cut-price woollens, knobbly walking sticks and glass baubles.

Edradour Distillery

A couple of miles east of Pitlochry on the A924 • March & April, Nov & Dec Mon–Sat 10am–4pm, Sun noon–4pm; May & Oct Mon–Sat 10am–5pm, Sun noon–5pm; June–Sept 9.30am–5pm, Sun noon–5pm; Jan & Feb Mon–Sat 10am–4pm • £5 • ⓦ edradour.co.uk

The one attraction with some distinction in Pitlochry is the **Edradour Distillery**, Scotland's smallest, in an idyllic position tucked into the hills. Although the tour of the distillery itself isn't out of the ordinary, the lack of industralization and the fact that the whole traditional process is done on site gives Edradour more personality than many of its rivals.

INFORMATION — PITLOCHRY

Tourist office 22 Atholl Rd (April–June & Oct Mon–Sat 9am–5pm, Sun 10am–5pm; July–Sept Mon–Sat 9am–6pm, Sun 10am–6pm; Nov–March Mon–Sat 10am–4pm; ⓣ01796 472215).

Cycling info Escape Route at 3 Atholl Rd (ⓣ01796 473859, ⓦescape-route.biz). Advice on local cycling routes, bike rental and general outdoor gear.

ACCOMMODATION

Craigatin House and Courtyard 165 Atholl Rd ⓣ01796 472478, ⓦcraigatinhouse.co.uk. On the northern section of the main road through town, this attractive, contemporary B&B has large beds, soothing decor and a pleasant garden. **£80**

Pitlochry Backpackers Hotel 134 Atholl Rd ⓣ01796 470044, ⓦpitlochrybackpackershotel.com. This central hostel is based in a former hotel and offers dorms along with around ten twin and double rooms. Closed Nov–April. Dorm **£18**, Double **£52**

EATING AND DRINKING

Pitlochry is the domain of the tearoom, and you have to hunt to find decent places for a full **meal**.

Moulin Inn Moulin, on the outskirts along the A924 ⓣ01796 472196, ⓦmoulininn.co.uk. The best bet for traditional pub grub, this award-winning inn is handily placed at the foot of Ben Vrackie. The original building dates back to 1695. Open daily.

Port-na-craig Inn ⓣ01796 472777, ⓦportnacraig.com. This ancient stone-built inn has a beautiful riverside location near Pitlochry's theatre, and a light-filled conservatory. The food uses fresh local ingredients, some of them home grown, for dishes such as Buckie haddock in beer batter (£9.95). Daily 10am till late.

20

ENTERTAINMENT

Pitlochry Festival Theatre Port Na Craig ⓣ01796 484626, ⓦpitlochry.org.uk. On the western edge of town, just across the river, Scotland's renowned "Theatre in the Hills" stages a variety of productions – mostly mainstream theatre from the resident repertoire company, along with regular music events – during the summer season (May–Oct) and on ad hoc dates the rest of the year.

RANNOCH MOOR

Rannoch Moor occupies roughly 150 square miles of uninhabited and uninhabitable peat bogs, lochs, heather hillocks, strewn lumps of granite and a few gnarled Caledonian pine, all of it more than 1000ft above sea level. Perhaps the most striking thing about the moor is its inaccessibility: one road, between Crianlarich and Glen Coe, skirts its western side, while another struggles west from Pitlochry to reach its eastern edge at Rannoch Station. The only regular form of transport is the **West Highland railway**, which stops at Rannoch and, a little to the north, Corrour Station, which has no road access at all. From Rannoch Station it's possible to catch the train to Corrour and walk the nine miles back; it's a longer slog west to the eastern end of Glen Coe (see p.891), the dramatic peaks of which poke up above the moor's western horizon. Determined hillwalkers will find a clutch of Munros around Corrour, including remote Ben Alder (3765ft), high above the forbidding shores of Loch Ericht.

SYHA Loch Ossian A mile from Corrour train station on the shores of Loch Ossian ⓣ0870 004 1139, ⓦsyha.org.uk. This comfortable, cosy – and remote – eco-hostel is a great place for hikers seeking somewhere genuinely off the beaten track. Good wildlife-watching opportunities, too. Closed Nov–March. **£18**

Loch Tummel

West of Pitlochry, the B8019/B846 makes a memorably scenic, if tortuous, traverse of the shores of **Loch Tummel** and then **Loch Rannoch**. These two lochs and their adjoining rivers were much changed by massive hydroelectric schemes built in the 1940s and 1950s, yet this is still a spectacular stretch of countryside and one which deserves leisurely exploration. **Queen's View** at the eastern end of Loch Tummel is an obvious vantage point, looking down the loch to the misty peak of **Schiehallion** (3520ft), whose name comes from the Gaelic meaning "Fairy Mountain". One of Scotland's few freestanding hills, it's a popular, fairly easy and inspiring climb, with views on a good day to both sides of the country and north to the massed ranks of Highland peaks. The path up starts at Braes of Foss, just off the B846, which links Aberfeldy with Kinloch Rannoch: allow three to four hours to the top and back.

Loch Rannoch

Beyond Loch Tummel, at the eastern end of Loch Rannoch, the small community of **KINLOCH RANNOCH** doesn't see a lot of passing trade other than fishermen and hillwalkers. Otherwise, the only real destination here is **Rannoch Station**, a lonely outpost on the Glasgow–Fort William West Highland train line, sixteen miles further on at the end of the road.

ARRIVAL AND DEPARTURE — LOCH RANNOCH

20

By train Rannoch Station sees trains to Corrour (3–4 daily; 12min); Fort William (3–4 daily; 1hr); Glasgow Queen St (3–4 daily; 2hr 45min); London Euston (sleeper service; Sun–Fri daily; 11hr).

By bus Buses run to Kinloch Rannoch from Pitlochry (3 daily; 50min), with local buses from Kinloch Rannoch (Broons Bus #85; 4 daily; 40min) and a postbus from Pitlochry (#223; departs 8am, Mon–Sat) providing connections to Rannoch Station.

ACCCOMMODATION

Moor of Rannoch Rannoch Station ⓣ01882 633238, ⓦmoorofrannoch.co.uk. Pleasant small hotel in a handsome whitewashed building. Despite a friendly welcome, there's still a feeling of isolation in this empty landscape. Closed Nov to mid-Feb. **£90**

Pass of Killiecrankie

Four miles north of Pitlochry, the A9 cuts through the **Pass of Killiecrankie**, a breath-taking wooded gorge which falls away to the River Garry below. This dramatic setting was the site of the **Battle of Killiecrankie** in 1689, when the Jacobites quashed the forces of General Mackay. Legend has it that one soldier of the Crown, fleeing for his life, made a miraculous jump across the 18-foot **Soldier's Leap**, an impossibly wide chasm halfway up the gorge. Exhibits at the slick **NTS visitor centre** recall the battle and examine the gorge in detail. **Guided walks** from the centre take you through thick, mature forest, full of interesting plants and creatures.

INFORMATION — PASS OF KILLIECRANKIE

Killiecrankie NTS visitor centre East side of the Pass of Killiecrankie (April–Oct daily 10am–5.30pm; parking £2; ⓣ0844 493 2194, ⓦnts.org.uk).

Blair Atholl

Three miles north of Killiecrankie, the village of **BLAIR ATHOLL** makes for a much quieter and more idiosyncratic stop than Pitlochry. You can wander round the **Water Mill** on Ford Road (April–Oct daily 10.30am–5.30pm; ⓦblairathollwatermill.co.uk), which dates from 1613, and witness flour being milled. The mill also has a nice tearoom – see opposite.

Blair Castle

April–Oct daily 9.30am–4.30pm (last admission); Nov–March Tues & Sat 9.30am–12.30pm • £9.25, grounds only £5.10 • ⓣ 01796 481207, ⓦ blair-castle.co.uk

By far the most important and eye-catching building in these parts is **Blair Castle**, seat of the Atholl dukedom. This whitewashed, turreted castle looks particularly impressive as you sweep along the driveway leading from the centre of Blair Atholl village, especially if a piper is playing. The pipers belong to the Atholl Highlanders, a select group retained by the duke as his private army – a unique privilege afforded to him by Queen Victoria, who stayed here in 1844. Highlights are the soaring **entrance hall**, with every spare inch of wood panelling covered in weapons of some description, and the vast **ballroom**, with its timber roof, antlers, and mixture of portraits.

INFORMATION — BLAIR ATHOLL

Atholl Estates Information Centre Opposite the Blair Castle Caravan Park, just off the A9 (April–Oct daily 9am–4.45pm; ⓣ 01796 481646, ⓦ athollestatesrangerservice.co.uk). They provide details of the extensive network of local walks and bike rides and information on surrounding flora and fauna.

EATING

Blair Atholl Water Mill Ford Rd ⓣ 01796 481321 ⓦ blairathollwatermill.co.uk. Lovely little working mill where you can enjoy home-baked scones and light lunches in its timber-beamed tearoom. April–Oct daily 10.30am–5.30pm.

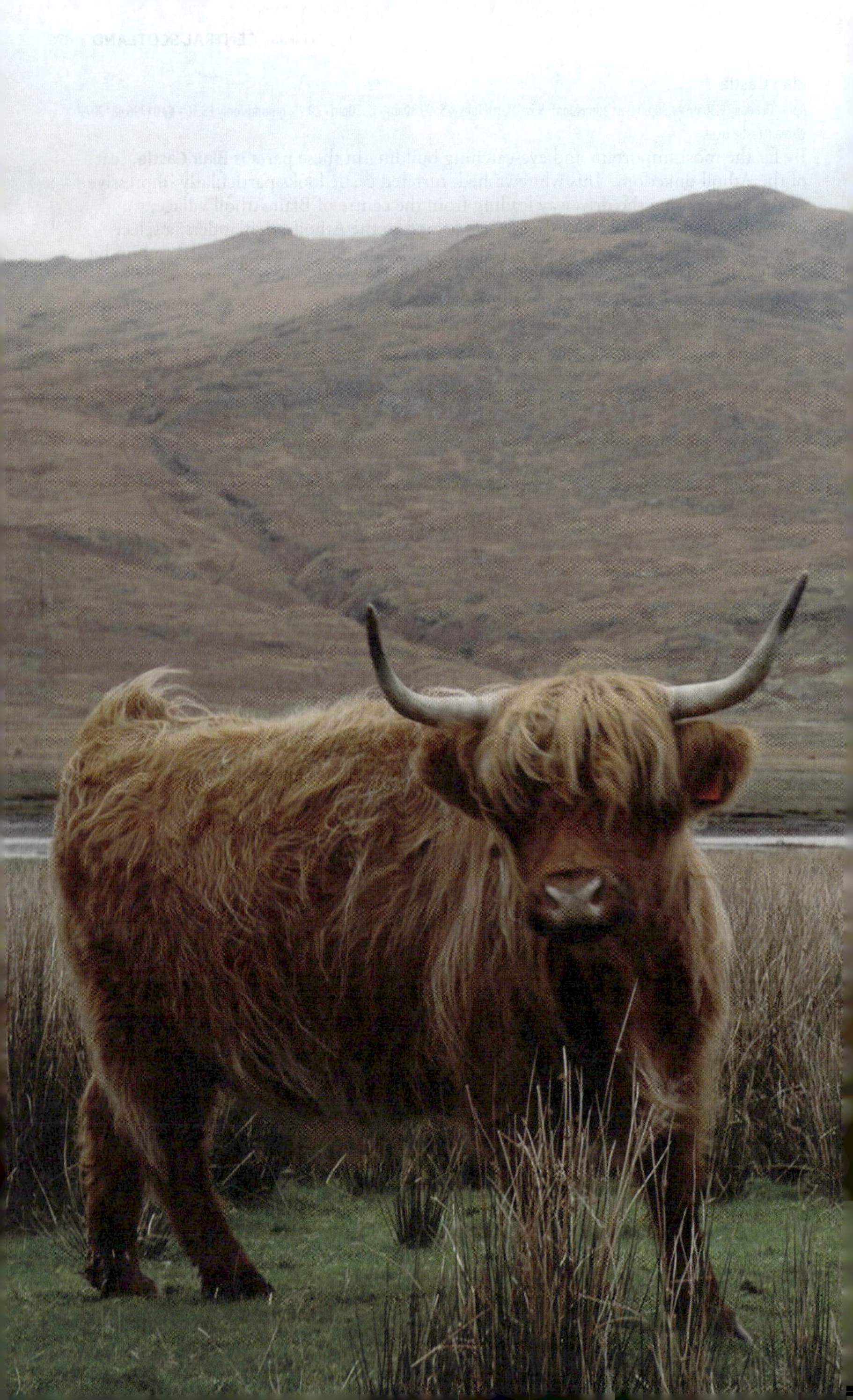

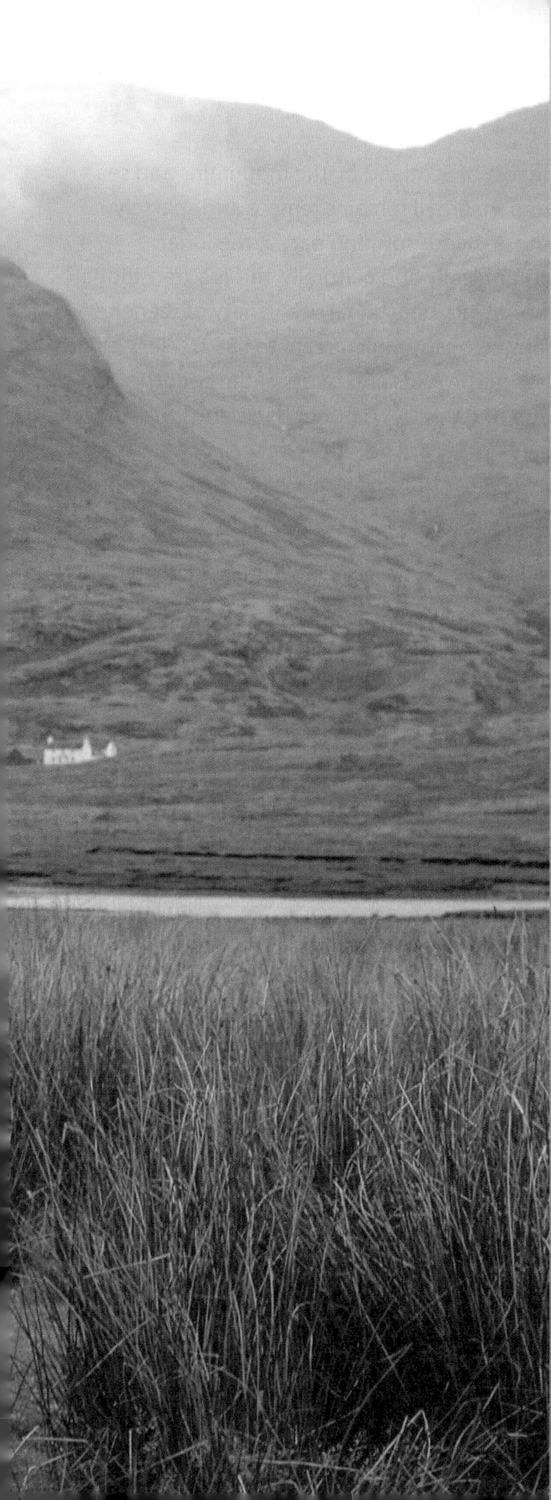

Argyll

828 Isle of Bute

832 Inveraray

834 Oban

834 Isle of Mull

837 Isle of Iona

838 Isle of Coll

839 Isle of Tiree

840 Mid-Argyll

841 Kintyre

843 Isle of Arran

845 Isle of Islay

848 Isle of Jura

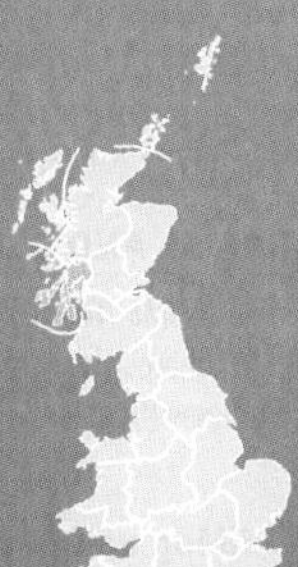

HIGHLAND CATTLE, MULL

Argyll

Cut off for centuries from the rest of Scotland by the mountains and sea lochs that characterize the region, Argyll remains remote and sparsely populated, its scatter of offshore islands forming part of the Inner Hebridean archipelago. Geographically and culturally, this is a transitional area between Highland and Lowland, boasting a rich variety of scenery from subtropical gardens warmed by the Gulf Stream to flat, treeless islands on the edge of the Atlantic. It's in the folds and twists of the countryside, the interplay of land and water and the views out to the islands that the strengths and beauties of mainland Argyll lie – the one area of man-made sights you shouldn't miss, however, is the cluster of Celtic and prehistoric sites near Kilmartin.

The eastern duo of **Bute** and **Arran** are the most popular of Scotland's more southerly islands, the latter – now, strictly, part of Ayrshire – justifiably so, with spectacular scenery ranging from the granite peaks of the north to the Lowland pasture of the south. Of the Hebridean islands covered in this chapter, mountainous **Mull** is the most visited, and is large enough to absorb the crowds, many of whom are only passing through en route to the tiny isle of **Iona**, a place of spiritual pilgrimage for centuries. **Islay**, best known for its malt whiskies, is fairly quiet even in the height of summer, as is neighbouring **Jura**, which offers excellent walking. And, for those seeking further solitude, there are the more remote islands of **Tiree** and **Coll**, which, although swept with fierce winds, have more sunny days than anywhere else in Scotland.

GETTING AROUND — ARGYLL

Argyll's **public transport** options are minimal, though buses do serve most major settlements, and the train line reaches Oban. In the remoter parts and on the islands, you'll have to rely on walking, shared taxis and the postbus. If you're planning to take a **vehicle** across to one of the islands, make sure to reserve both your outward and return journeys as early as possible, as the ferries get very booked up.

Isle of Bute

The island of **BUTE** is, in many ways, simply an extension of the Cowal peninsula, from which it is separated by the narrow Kyles of Bute. Thanks to its consistently mild climate and a **ferry link** with Wemyss Bay, Bute (Ⓦ isle-of-bute.com) has been a popular holiday and convalescence spot for Clydesiders – particularly the elderly – for over a century.

ARRIVAL AND DEPARTURE — ISLE OF BUTE

Regular CalMac **ferries** (Ⓦ calmac.co.uk) run from Wemyss Bay, 30 miles west of Glasgow, to Rothesay (every 45min; 30min). There's also a small CalMac ferry crossing from Colintraive, 25 miles south of Inveraray, to Rhubodach, 6 miles north of Rothesay (frequently; 5min).

Hiking up Goat Fell p.844
Islay whisky p.846
Geese on Islay p.847
George Orwell on Jura p.848

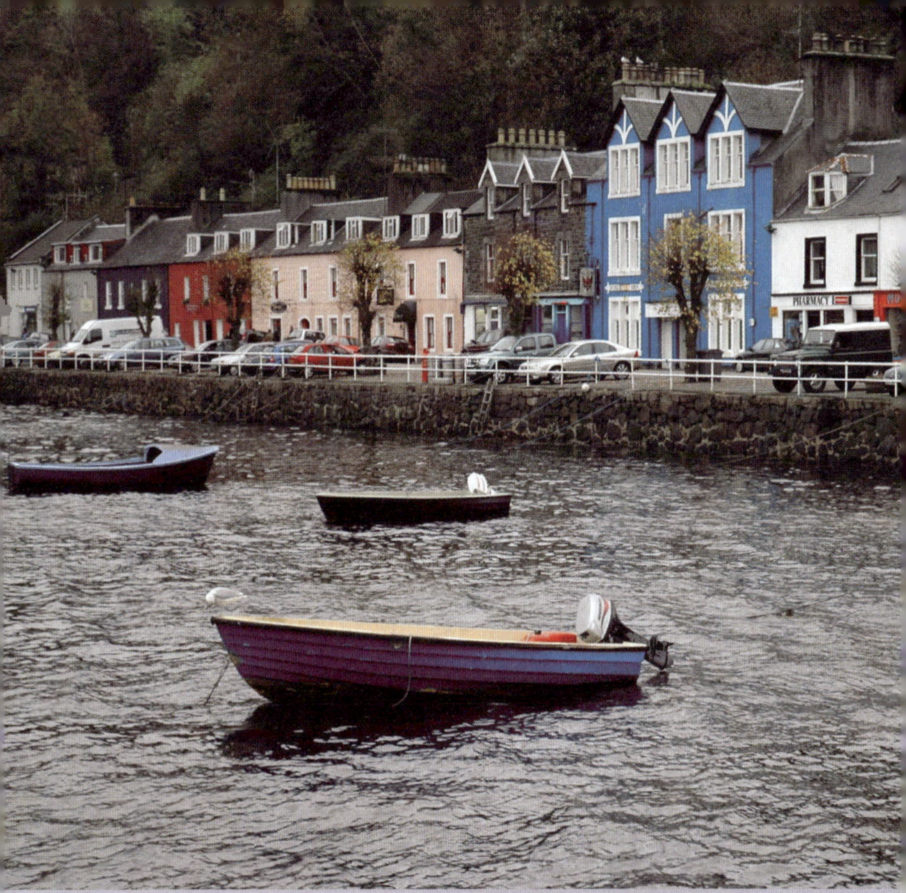

TOBERMORY

Highlights

❶ **Mount Stuart, Bute** Architecturally overblown aristocratic mansion, set in the most beautiful grounds in the region. **See p.832**

❷ **Tobermory, Mull** The archetypal picturesque fishing village, ranged around a sheltered harbour and backed by steep hills. **See p.835**

❸ **Isle of Iona** A centre of Christian culture since the sixth century, Iona is, despite the crowds, a very special place. **See p.837**

❹ **Golden beaches** Argyll abounds in stunning sandy beaches, with lovely stretches at Islay, Coll and Tiree. **See p.838, p.839 & p.846**

❺ **Isle of Gigha** The ideal island-scape: sandy beaches, friendly folk and the azaleas of Achamore Gardens – you can even stay at the laird's house. **See p.842**

❻ **Goat Fell, Arran** Spectacular views over north Arran's craggy mountain range and the Firth of Clyde. **See p.844**

❼ **Whisky distilleries, Islay** With eight, often beautifully situated, distilleries to choose from, Islay is the ultimate whisky-lover's destination. **See p.846**

HIGHLIGHTS ARE MARKED ON THE MAP ON PP.830–831

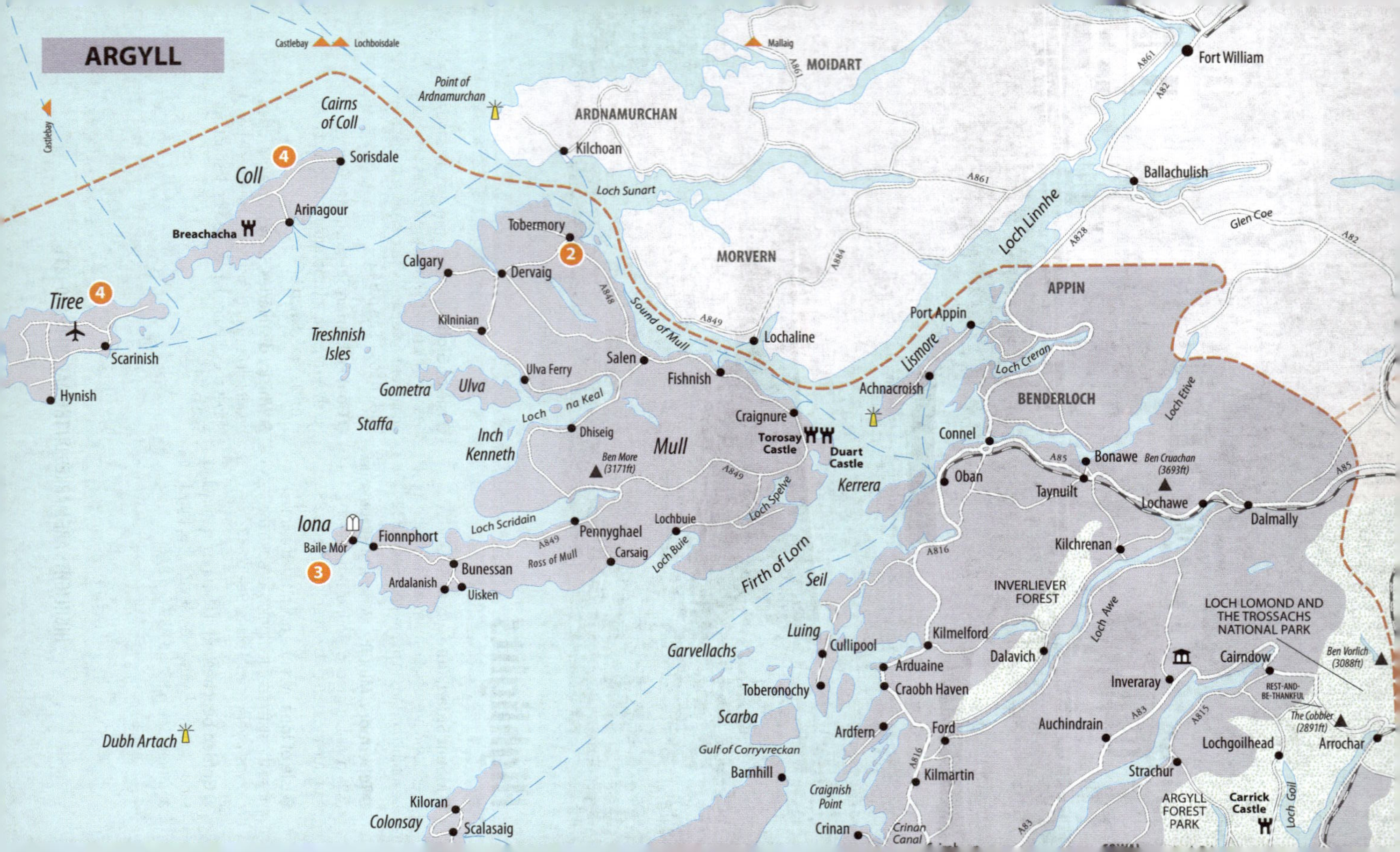
ARGYLL
Castlebay
Lochboisdale
Mallaig
MOIDART
Fort William
Point of Ardnamurchan
Cairns of Coll
ARDNAMURCHAN
Kilchoan
Coll
Sorisdale
Arinagour
Breachacha
Loch Sunart
Ballachulish
Loch Linnhe
Glen Coe
MORVERN
Tobermory
Calgary
Dervaig
Tiree
Scarinish
Hynish
Kilninian
Treshnish Isles
Sound of Mull
Lochaline
Port Appin
APPIN
Lismore
Salen
Fishnish
Ulva Ferry
Gometra
Ulva
Loch na Keal
Achnacroish
Loch Creran
BENDERLOCH
Loch Etive
Staffa
Dhiseig
Craignure
Torosay Castle
Duart Castle
Connel
Inch Kenneth
Mull
Ben More (3171ft)
Bonawe
Ben Cruachan (3693ft)
Oban
Taynuilt
Lochawe
Dalmally
Kerrera
Loch Spelve
Iona
Baile Mór
Fionnphort
Loch Scridain
Pennyghael
Lochbuie
Loch Buie
Carsaig
Ross of Mull
Bunessan
Ardalanish
Uisken
Kilchrenan
Firth of Lorn
Seil
INVERLIEVER FOREST
Loch Awe
LOCH LOMOND AND THE TROSSACHS NATIONAL PARK
Luing
Cullipool
Kilmelford
Arduaine
Dalavich
Inveraray
Cairndow
Ben Vorlich (3088ft)
Garvellachs
Toberonochy
Craobh Haven
REST-AND-BE-THANKFUL
The Cobbler (2891ft)
Scarba
Ardfern
Ford
Auchindrain
Lochgoilhead
Arrochar
Dubh Artach
Gulf of Corryvreckan
Barnhill
Kilmartin
Strachur
Craignish Point
ARGYLL FOREST PARK
Carrick Castle
Loch Goil
Kiloran
Colonsay
Scalasaig
Crinan
Crinan Canal

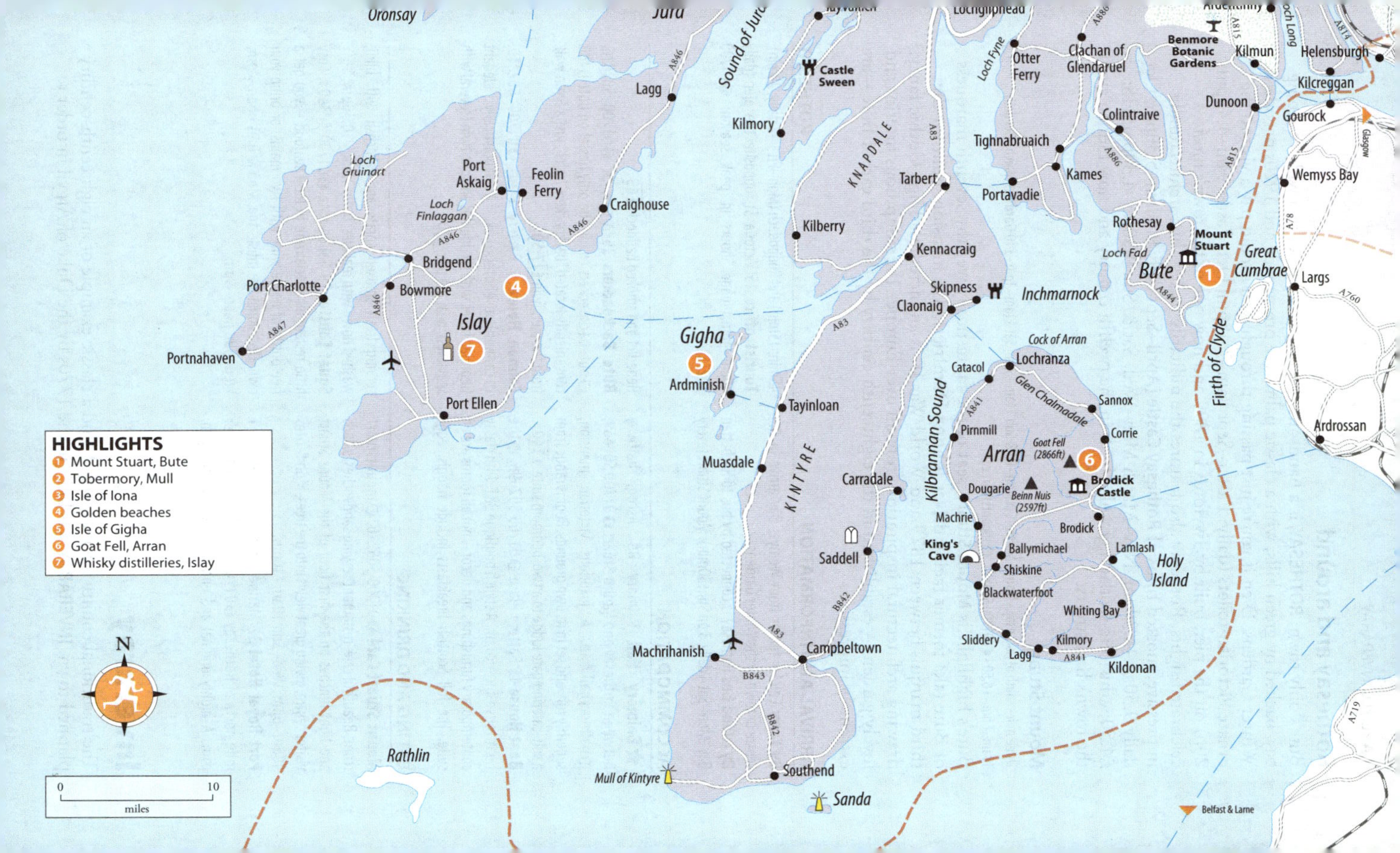

HIGHLIGHTS
1 Mount Stuart, Bute
2 Tobermory, Mull
3 Isle of Iona
4 Golden beaches
5 Isle of Gigha
6 Goat Fell, Arran
7 Whisky distilleries, Islay
Oronsay
Jura
Sound of Jura
Islay
Gigha
Arran
Bute
Inchmarnock
Great Cumbrae
Holy Island
Rathlin
Sanda
KNAPDALE
KINTYRE
Firth of Clyde
Kilbrannan Sound
Loch Fyne
Loch Long
Loch Gruinart
Loch Finlaggan
Loch Fad
Port Askaig
Feolin Ferry
Craighouse
Lagg
Bridgend
Bowmore
Port Charlotte
Portnahaven
Port Ellen
Ardminish
Tayinloan
Muasdale
Carradale
Saddell
Machrihanish
Campbeltown
Southend
Mull of Kintyre
Castle Sween
Kilmory
Kilberry
Tarbert
Kennacraig
Skipness
Claonaig
Portavadie
Tighnabruaich
Kames
Otter Ferry
Clachan of Glendaruel
Colintraive
Rothesay
Mount Stuart
Benmore Botanic Gardens
Kilmun
Dunoon
Helensburgh
Kilcreggan
Gourock
Glasgow
Wemyss Bay
Largs
Ardrossan
Cock of Arran
Lochranza
Catacol
Glen Chalmadale
Sannox
Corrie
Pirnmill
Goat Fell (2866ft)
Beinn Nuis (2597ft)
Brodick Castle
Dougarie
Machrie
Brodick
King's Cave
Ballymichael
Shiskine
Lamlash
Blackwaterfoot
Whiting Bay
Sliddery
Lagg
Kilmory
Kildonan
Belfast & Larne
N
0
10
miles
A846
A847
A83
B842
B843
A841
A844
A886
A815
A814
A78
A760
A719

21

Rothesay and around

Bute's only town, **ROTHESAY,** is a handsome Victorian resort set in a wide sweeping bay, backed by green hills, with a classic palm-tree promenade and 1920s pagoda-style Winter Gardens. Even if you're just passing through, you should pay a visit to the ornate **Victorian toilets** (daily: Easter–Sept 8am–7.45pm; Oct–Easter 9am–4.45pm; 20p) on the pier, built by Twyfords in 1899 and now one of the town's most celebrated sights. Rothesay also features the militarily useless, but architecturally impressive, moated ruins of **Rothesay Castle** (April–Sept daily 9.30am–5.30pm; Oct daily 9.30am–4.30pm; Nov–March Mon–Wed, Sat & Sun 9.30am–4.30pm; HS; £4.50; historic-scotland.gov.uk), built in the twelfth century and now hidden amid the town's backstreets.

Mount Stuart

Three miles south of Rothesay • **House** March–Oct Mon–Fri & Sun 11am–5pm, Sat 11am–1pm • £10 **Gardens** March–Oct daily 10am–6pm • £6.50 • 01700 503877, mountstuart.com

Bute's highlight is **Mount Stuart**, seat of the fantastically wealthy seventh marquess of Bute (aka former racing driver Johnny Dumfries). The mansion, built for the third marquis between 1879 and World War II, is an incredible High Gothic fancy, drawing architectural inspiration from all over Europe. The sumptuous interior and lovely gardens – established in the eighteenth century by the third earl of Bute – are extremely impressive.

ARRIVAL AND INFORMATION — ROTHESAY

By ferry CalMac ferries from Wemyss Bay arrive in the centre of town by the Winter Gardens.

By island bus Rothesay is connected by bus to Kilchattan Bay (Mon–Sat 4 daily, 3 on Sun; 30min); Mount Stuart (every 45min; 15min) and Rhubodach (Mon–Fri 1–2 daily; 20min).

Tourist office 15 Victoria St, opposite the pier (daily 10am–4pm; longer hours in peak season; 01700 502151).

ACCOMMODATION

★ **Balmory Hall** Balmory Rd, Ascog, halfway between Rothesay and Mount Stuart 01700 500669, balmoryhall.com. A luxurious Victorian mansion, superbly run, and set in its own grounds. Rooms range from a self-catering gate lodge to a two-bedroom suite. **£140**

Boat House 15 Battery Place 01700 502696, theboathouse-bute.co.uk. A stylish boutique B&B with classy contemporary furnishings and decor – not all rooms are en suite. The full Scottish breakfasts include haggis, eggs Benedict and smoked haddock. **£65**

Bute Backpackers 36 Argyle St 01700 501876, butebackpackers.co.uk. The only hostel on Bute is this conveniently located "backpackers' hotel", just a 5min walk from the pier. Twin **£17.50**

Cannon House 5 Battery Place 01700 502819, cannonhousehotel.co.uk. A fantastically elegant Georgian hotel, with six doubles and one twin (several with seaviews), near the pier. **£70**

EATING AND DRINKING

Mount Stuart Café 01700 505276, mountstuart.com. Beautiful café-restaurant serving sandwiches, salads and light lunches on the first floor of the Mount Stuart visitor centre, giving great views into the trees. Mon & Tues 10am–6pm, Wed–Sun 10am–10pm.

Port Royal Hotel 37 Marine Rd, Port Bannatyne, 1 mile north of Rothesay 01700 505073, butehotel.com. A highly original and engaging, Russian-run pub, serving fresh smoked sprats and razorfish with blini, washed down with real ales. Daily 12.30–10.30pm.

Squat Lobster 29 Gallowgate 01700 503603. Cosy little restaurant specializing in local seafood – you get a free bottle of house wine with two mains, or bring your own. Occasional live music, too. Mon & Tues noon–4pm, Wed–Sun noon–9pm.

Inveraray

The traditional county town of Argyll, and a classic example of an eighteenth-century planned town, **INVERARAY** was built in the 1770s by the Duke of Argyll in order to distance his newly rebuilt castle from the hoi polloi in the town and to establish a commercial and legal centre for the region. Inveraray has changed very little since and remains an absolute set piece of Scottish Georgian architecture, with a truly memorable setting, the brilliant white arches of Front Street reflected in the still waters of Loch Fyne.

Squeezed onto a promontory some distance from the duke's new castle, Inveraray's "New Town" has a distinctive **Main Street** (set at a right angle to Front Street), flanked by whitewashed terraces, whose window casements are picked out in black. At the top of the street, the road divides to circumnavigate the town's Neoclassical church, originally built in two parts: the southern half served the Gaelic-speaking community, while the northern half served those who spoke English.

Inveraray Jail

East of the church • Daily: April–Oct 9.30am–6pm; Nov–March 10am–5pm • £8.75 • T 01499 302381, W inverarayjail.co.uk

Inveraray Jail, whose attractive Georgian courthouse and grim prison blocks ceased to function in the 1930s, is now an enjoyable museum graphically recounting prison conditions from medieval times to the modern day. You can try out the minute "Airing Yards" where the prisoners got to exercise for an hour a day, and sit in the semicircular courthouse with its great views over the loch, and listen to a re-enactment of a trial of the period.

Inveraray Castle

A 10min walk north of Main St • April–Oct daily 10am–5.45pm • £9.20 • T 01499 302203, W inveraray-castle.com

Around half a mile north of Main Street, **Inveraray Castle** remains the family home of the Duke of Argyll. Built in 1745, it was given a touch of the Loire in the nineteenth century with the addition of dormer windows and conical corner spires. Inside, the most startling feature is the armoury hall, where the displays of weaponry – supplied to the Campbells by the British government to put down the Jacobites – rise through several storeys. Otherwise, the interior is pretty unremarkable, though it is worth looking out for Rob Roy's rather sad-looking sporran and dirk handle.

ARRIVAL AND INFORMATION — INVERARAY

By bus Buses pick up and drop off on Front St.

Destinations Glasgow (4–6 daily; 1hr 45min); Oban (Mon–Sat 4 daily, 2 on Sun; 1hr 5min); Tarbert (2–3 daily; 1hr 30min).

Tourist office Front St (April–Oct Mon–Sat 9am–5pm, Sun noon–5pm; Nov–March Mon–Fri 10am–3pm, Sat & Sun 11am–3pm; T 01499 302263), by the town's landmark *Argyll Hotel*.

ACCOMMODATION

Newton Hall Shore Rd T 01499 302484, W newtonhallinveraray.co.uk. A former church, built in 1895, and now a guesthouse just a 5min walk from the centre of town. The views over the loch are lovely, and each of the seven rooms is luxurious and individually styled. Closed Dec & Jan. **£70**

Rudha-Na-Craige T 01499 302668, W rudha-na-craige.f2s.com. A beautifully restored Scottish Baronial house on the southern edge of town next to the golf course. Free wi-fi and a baby grand piano that guests are welcome to play. **£95**

SYHA hostel Dalmally Rd T 01499 302454, W syha.org.uk. Simple, low-key wooden hut of a hostel, a short way north up the A819 Dalmally road. Closed Nov–March. **£14**

EATING AND DRINKING

★ **Cairndow Oyster Bar & Restaurant** 6 miles up the A83 towards Glasgow T 01499 600482, W lochfyne.com. The best place to sample Loch Fyne's delicious fresh fish and seafood. *Cairndow* sells more oysters than anywhere else in the country, plus lots of other fishy treats; you can stock up on provisions and take away, or sit down and eat at the restaurant. Daily 9am–9pm.

21

Oban

The solidly Victorian resort of **OBAN** (@oban.org.uk) enjoys a superb setting distinguished by a bizarre granite amphitheatre, dramatically lit at night, on the hilltop above the town. Despite a small population, it's by far the largest port in northwest Scotland, and the main departure point for ferries to the Hebrides. If you arrive late, or are catching an early boat, you may have to spend the night here; if you're staying elsewhere, it's a useful base for wet-weather activities and shopping.

McCaig's Tower

The town's landmark, **McCaig's Tower**, is a stiff ten-minute climb from the quayside. Built in imitation of Rome's Colosseum, it was the brainchild of a local businessman a century ago, who had the twin aims of alleviating off-season unemployment among the local stonemasons and creating a museum, art gallery and chapel. In his will, McCaig gave instructions for the lancet windows to be filled with bronze statues of the family, though no such work was ever undertaken. Instead, the folly has been turned into a sort of walled garden, and provides a wonderful seaward panorama, particularly at sunset.

ARRIVAL AND INFORMATION — OBAN

By ferry The CalMac ferry terminal (T 01631 566688) for the islands is on Railway Pier, near the train station.

By train Trains from Glasgow Queen Street (Mon–Sat 3–4 daily, Sun 1–3 daily; 3hr) pull up on Station Square.

By bus Oban's bus station (Glasgow Mon–Sat 4 daily, Sun 2 daily; 3hr; Mallaig 1 daily; 2hr 30min) is right next door to the train station.

Tourist office In a converted church on Argyll Square (April–Oct daily 10am–5pm, longer hours in peak season; Nov–March Mon–Sat 10am–5pm, Sun noon–5pm; T 01631 563122).

ACCOMMODATION

Alt na Craig House Glenmore Rd T 01631 564524, W guesthouseinoban.com. A handsome Victorian house just south of town, with a woodland garden, beautifully furnished rooms and views of the bay. **£120**

Kilchrenan House Corran Esplanade T 01631 562663, W kilchrenanhouse.co.uk. A tasteful, hospitable place in a grand Victorian villa – rooms are spacious and many have sea views. **£60**

Oban Backpackers Breadalbane St T 01631 562107, W hostel-scotland.co.uk. The friendliest, cheapest and most central of the three hostels. Closed Nov–Feb. **£12**

EATING AND DRINKING

Coast 104 George St T 01631 569900, W coastoban.com. A stylish option serving acclaimed and original fish, game and meat dishes. Daily noon–2pm (no lunch Sun) & 5.30–9pm.

The Lorne Stevenson St T 01631 570020, W thelornebar.co.uk. An attractive and popular pub that serves real ales, forty malts and local seafood as well as light snacks at lunch time. Mon–Thurs noon–1am, Fri & Sat noon–2am, Sun 12.30pm–2am.

Waterfront On the waterfront, near the station T 01631 563110, W waterfrontoban.co.uk. Upstairs in the old Fishermen's Mission, and enjoying lovely views over the bay, this restaurant uses the best of the daily catch: oysters, scallops, halibut and salmon. Daily noon–2.15pm & 5.30–9.30pm.

Isle of Mull

Just forty minutes from Oban by ferry, **Mull** (W holidaymull.co.uk) is by far the most accessible of the Hebrides. As so often, first impressions largely depend on the weather – it's the wettest of the Hebrides (and that's saying something) – as without the sun the large tracts of moorland, particularly around the island's highest peak, Ben More (3196ft), can appear bleak and unwelcoming. There are, however, areas of more gentle pastoral scenery around **Dervaig** in the north and the indented west coast varies from the sandy beaches around **Calgary** to the cliffs of Loch na Keal. The most common mistake is to try and "do" the island in a day or two: slogging up the main road to the picturesque capital of **Tobermory**, then covering the fifty-odd miles between there and Fionnphort, in order to visit **Iona**. Mull is a place that will grow on you only if you have the time and patience to explore.

ARRIVAL AND DEPARTURE — ISLE OF MULL

There are frequent daily **car ferries** from Oban to Craigmore (booking ahead advisable), plus a smaller and less expensive daily car ferry from Lochaline on the Morvern peninsula (see p.892) to Fishnish, 6 miles northwest of Craignure. Another even smaller car ferry connects Kilchoan on the Ardnamurchan peninsula (see p.894) with Tobermory, Mull's capital.

Craignure

CRAIGNURE is little more than a scattering of cottages with a small shop, a bar, toilets and a CalMac and **tourist office**, but two **castles** lie immediately southeast.

At the time of writing **Torosay Castle**, a full-blown Scots Baronial creation with magnificent **gardens** was for sale; to see if it is open, contact the tourist office.

Duart Castle

Lochdon • April Mon–Thurs & Sun 11am–4pm; May–Oct daily 10.30am–5.30pm • £5.50 • ☎ 01680 812309, 🌐 duartcastle.com

On a picturesque spit of rock, **Duart Castle** is clearly visible from the Oban–Craignure ferry. Headquarters of the once-powerful MacLean clan from the thirteenth century, it was burnt down by the Campbells and confiscated after the 1745 rebellion. Finally in 1911, the 26th clan chief, Fitzroy MacLean (1835–1936), managed to buy it back and restore it. You can peek at the dungeons, climb up to the ramparts, study the family photos, and learn about the world scout movement – the 27th clan chief became Chief Scout in 1959. After your visit, you can enjoy home-made cakes and tea at the castle's excellent tearoom (May–Sept).

ARRIVAL AND INFORMATION — CRAIGNURE

By ferry Car ferries travel from Oban to Craignure (summer Mon–Sat 6–7 daily, Sun 4–5 daily; 45min).

By bus Buses run to Craignure from Fionnphort (Mon–Sat 3–4 daily, Sun 1 daily; 1hr 10min), Fishnish (3 daily; 10min) and Tobermory (4–6 daily; 45min).

Tourist office Opposite the pier (April to mid-Oct Mon–Fri 8.30am–5.15pm, Sat 9am–5pm, Sun 10.30am–5.15pm, longer hours in summer; mid-Oct to March Mon–Sat 9am–5pm, Sun 10.30am–noon & 3.30–5pm); ☎ 01680 812 377, 🌐 visitscottishheartlands.com.

ACCOMMODATION AND EATING

Craignure Inn ☎ 01680 812305, 🌐 craignure-inn.co.uk. A snug pub to hole up in, just a minute's stroll up the road towards Fionnphort. They serve dinner nightly, with an emphasis on local food (mains from £13). **£78**

Shieling campsite ☎ 01680 812496, 🌐 www.shielingholidays.co.uk. Quiet and very appealing family-run campsite on the south side of Craignure Bay, behind the village hall, with views across to Ben Nevis. Closed Nov–March. Pitch **£15**

Tobermory

Mull's chief town, **TOBERMORY**, at the northern tip of the island, is easily the most attractive fishing port on the west coast of Scotland, its clusters of brightly coloured houses and boats sheltering in a bay backed by a steep bluff. Apart from the beauty of the setting, the harbour's shops are good for browsing, and you could pay a visit to the **Mull Museum,** on Main Street (Easter to mid-Oct Mon–Fri 10am–4pm, Sat 10am–1pm; £1), which packs in a great deal of information as well as artefacts – including a few objects salvaged from the sixteenth-century wreck of the *San Juan*, a Spanish Armada ship that sank in the bay. A stiff climb up Back Brae will bring you to the island's main arts centre, **An Tobar** (March–Dec Mon–Sat 10am–5pm; May–Sept also Sun 1–4pm; free; antobar.co.uk), which hosts exhibitions and live events, and has a café with comfy sofas set before a real fire.

ARRIVAL AND INFORMATION — TOBERMORY

By ferry Car ferries run from Kilchoan (summer Mon–Sat 7 daily; June–Aug also Sun every 2hr; 35min).

By bus Buses run to Tobermory from Calgary (Mon–Sat 2 daily; 45min), Dervaig (Mon–Fri 3 daily, Sat 2 daily; 30min) and Fishnish (2–4 daily; 40min).

Tourist office Main St (April–Oct Mon–Fri 9am–5pm, Sat & Sun noon–5pm; longer hours in summer; 01680 812377, tobermory.co.uk).

ACCOMMODATION AND EATING

There are several **accommodation** options on **Main Street**, which is also the place to go for places to eat, including a highly rated fish-and-chip van (which also serves scallops) on the old pier.

Glassbarn Tearooms Glengorm Rd glassbarn tearooms.blogspot.com. The prettiest eating option on Mull: a spacious glasshouse with sofas and wooden furniture serving good coffee, snacks and cakes. They also make and sell Isle of Mull cheese: you can see the cows being milked at 4pm. Tues–Sun 10am–4.30pm.

Highland Cottage Breadalbane St 01688 302030, highlandcottage.co.uk. A luxurious B&B run by a very welcoming couple in a quiet street high above the harbour; the outstanding four-course Scottish menu in the restaurant costs around £40 a head. £150

Mishnish Main St 01688 302009, mishnish.co.uk. Very popular, lively local pub with live music at the weekend and a music festival in April. Daily 11am–1am.

SYHA hostel Main St 0870 004 1151, syha.org.uk. Small, friendly hostel in a great central position. Closed Nov–Feb. Dorm £16.75

The Water's Edge Tobermory Hotel, Main St 01688 302091, thetobermoryhotel.com. Scottish seafood, venison and cheese are served in this upmarket hotel restaurant: they charge £27 for two courses. Daily 6–9pm.

Isle of Staffa

Seven miles off the west coast of Mull, **Staffa** is the most romantic and dramatic of Scotland's many uninhabited islands. On its south side, the perpendicular rock face features an imposing series of black basalt columns, known as the Colonnade, which have been cut by the sea into cathedralesque caverns, most notably **Fingal's Cave**. The Vikings knew about the island – the name derives from their word for "Island of Pillars" – but it wasn't until 1772 that it was "discovered" by the world. Turner painted it, Wordsworth explored it, but Mendelssohn's *Die Fingalshöhle*, inspired by the sounds of the sea-wracked caves he heard on a visit here in 1829, did most to popularize the place – after which Queen Victoria gave her blessing, too. The geological explanation for these polygonal basalt organ-pipes is that they were created by a massive subterranean explosion some sixty million years ago. A huge mass of molten basalt burst forth onto land and, as it cooled, solidified into what are, essentially, crystals.

ARRIVAL AND DEPARTURE — ISLE OF STAFFA

From April to October several operators offer **boat trips to Staffa**: long-established Turus Mara (0800 085 8786, www.turusmara.com) sets out from Ulva Ferry and charges around £50 return, as does Gordon Grant Marine (01681 700338, staffatours.com), departing from Fionnphort. Iolaire (01681 700358, www.staffatrips.co.uk), charge £25 for passage from Fionnphort.

Ben More and the Ross of Mull

From the southern shores of Loch na Keal, which almost splits Mull in two, rise the terraced slopes of **Ben More** (3169ft) – literally "big mountain" – a mighty extinct volcano. Stretching for twenty miles west of Ben More as far as Iona is Mull's rocky southernmost peninsula, the **Ross of Mull**, which, like much of Scotland, appears blissfully tranquil in good weather, and desolate and bleak in bad.

Fionnphort

The road ends at **FIONNPHORT**, facing Iona. This is probably the least attractive place to stay on the Ross, though it has a nice sandy bay backed by pink, granite rocks. Partly to ease congestion on Iona, and to give their neighbours a slice of the tourist pound, Fionnphort was chosen as the site for the little-visited **St Columba Centre** (Easter–Sept daily 10.30am–1pm & 2–5.30pm; free); inside, a small exhibition outlines Iona's history, tells a little of Columba's life, and has a few facsimiles of the illuminated manuscripts produced by the island's monks. In reality, though, the major reason to come here is to get to Iona.

ARRIVAL AND DEPARTURE **FIONNPHORT**

Passenger-only **ferries** run from Fionnphort to Iona (summer Mon–Sat frequently, Sun hourly; 5min).

Isle of Iona

Less than a mile off the southwest tip of Mull, **IONA** (ⓦisle-of-iona.com), just three miles long and not much more than a mile wide – has been a place of pilgrimage for several centuries, and a place of Christian worship for more than 1400 years. It was to this flat Hebridean island that **St Columba** fled from Ireland in 563 and established a monastery, compiling a vast library of illuminated manuscripts and converting more or less all of pagan Scotland as well as much of northern England. This history and the island's splendid isolation have lent it a peculiar religiosity; in the much-quoted words of Dr Johnson, who visited in 1773, "That man is little to be envied … whose piety would not grow warmer among the ruins of Iona." Today, however, the island can barely cope with the constant flood of day-trippers, and charges for entry to its abbey, so, in order to appreciate the special atmosphere and to have time to see the whole island, including the often-overlooked west coast, you should stay at least one night.

Baile Mór

The passenger ferry from Fionnphort drops you off at the island's main village, **BAILE MÓR** (literally "large village"), which is in fact little more than a single terrace of cottages facing the sea. Just inland lie the extensive pink-granite ruins of the **Augustinian nunnery**, built around 1200 but disused since the Reformation – if nothing else, it gives you an idea of the state of the present-day abbey before it was restored. Just south of the manse and church, stands the fifteenth-century **MacLean's Cross**, a fine, late medieval example of the distinctive, flowing, three-leaved foliage of the Iona school.

Iona Heritage Centre

Easter–Oct Mon–Sat 10.30am–4.30pm • £3 • ⓣ01681 700576

Across the road to the north of MacLean's Cross is the Iona Heritage Centre, with displays on the social history of the island over the last two hundred years, including the Clearances, which nearly halved the island's population of five hundred in the mid-nineteenth century.

There's a simple **tearoom** in the garden next door.

Iona Abbey

Daily: April–Sept 9.30am–5.30pm; Oct–March 9.30am–4.30pm • HS • £4.70 • ⓣ01681 700512

No buildings remain from Columba's time: the present **Iona Abbey** dates from the arrival of the Benedictines in around 1200, was extensively rebuilt in the fifteenth and

21 sixteenth centuries, and restored virtually wholesale early last century. Adjoining the facade is a small steep-roofed chamber, believed to be St Columba's grave, now a small chapel. The three high crosses in front of the abbey date from the eighth to tenth centuries, and are decorated with the Pictish serpent and boss and Celtic spirals for which Iona's early Christian masons were renowned. For reasons of sanitation, the cloisters were placed, contrary to the norm, on the north side of the church (where running water was available); entirely reconstructed in the late 1950s, they now shelter a useful historical account of the abbey's development.

Oran's Cemetery

South of Iona Abbey

Iona's oldest building, the plain-looking **St Oran's Chapel**, has an eleventh-century door. It stands at the centre of Iona's sacred burial ground, **Reilig Odhráin** (Oran's Cemetery), which is said to contain the graves of sixty kings of Norway, Ireland, France and Scotland, including Duncan and Macbeth. The best of the early Christian gravestones and medieval effigies that lay in the Reilig Odhráin have been removed to the **Infirmary Museum** behind the abbey (Ⓦ ionahistory.org.uk/infirmary).

ARRIVAL AND DEPARTURE — ISLE OF IONA

Passenger-only **ferries** run from Fionnphort to Iona (summer Mon–Sat frequently, Sun hourly; 5min).

ACCOMMODATION AND EATING

As demand far exceeds supply you should book **acccommodation** well in advance. If you want to stay with the **Iona Community**, contact the MacLeod Centre (Ⓣ 01681 700404, Ⓦ iona.org.uk), popularly known as the "Mac".

Argyll Ⓣ 01681 700334, Ⓦ argyllhoteliona.co.uk. By far the nicer of the island's two hotels, housed in a terrace of stone-built cottages overlooking the Sound of Iona. They grow much of the organic produce used in the restaurant, as well as making use of local fish and meat. Closed Dec & Jan. £70

Clachan Corrach Ⓣ 01681 700323. B&B in a working croft in the middle of the island and offering great views. Dinner available. Closed Nov–April. £50

★ **Iona Hostel** Ⓣ 01681 700781, Ⓦ ionahostel.co.uk. In the north of the island, this simple, very attractive hostel sleeps 22 in 5 bedrooms. There's an open-plan kitchen and a living room with wood-burning stove, windows on three sides and sweeping views out to the Treshnish Isles. To reach the hostel, follow the road past the abbey for half a mile. £19.50

Martyrs' Bay Restaurant By the jetty Ⓣ 01681 700382, Ⓦ martyrsbay.co.uk. Good seafood dishes served in the restaurant and in the convivial attached pub, the only one on the island. Daily 11am–11pm.

Isle of Coll

The fish-shaped rocky island of **Coll** (Ⓦ visitcoll.co.uk), with a population of around a hundred, lies less than seven miles off the coast of Mull. The CalMac ferry drops off at Coll's only real village, **ARINAGOUR**, whose whitewashed cottages dot the western shore of Loch Eatharna. Half the island's population lives here, where you'll find the hotel and pub, post office, churches and a couple of shops.

On the southwest coast there are two edifices, both confusingly known as **Breachacha Castle**. The older is a restored fifteenth-century tower house, and now a training centre for overseas aid volunteers. The less attractive "new castle", to the northwest, is made up of a central block built around 1750 and two side pavilions added a century later, and has been converted into holiday homes. Much of the area around the castles is now owned by the RSPB, with the aim of protecting the island's small corncrake population. A vast area of **giant sand dunes** lies to the west of the castles, with two glorious golden sandy bays stretching for more than a mile on either side.

ARRIVAL AND DEPARTURE — ISLE OF COLL

Car **ferries** link Coll with Oban (summer 1 daily; 2hr 40min).

ACCOMMODATION

Coll Hotel Arinagour ☎ 01879 230334, 🌐 collhotel.com. Small, family-run hotel offering decent accommodation and delicious meals, and doubling as the island's social centre. £100

Garden House In the west of the island, near Breachacha beach ☎ 01879 230374. Campsite in the shelter of an old walled garden surrounded by an RSPB reserve and five minutes from Breachacha beach. Closed Oct–March. £6 per adult.

Tigh-na-Mara Arinagour ☎ 01879 230354, 🌐 tighnamara.info. Purpose-built modern guesthouse near the pier with seven bedrooms, two of them family rooms. You can seal-spot from the dining room. £62

EATING AND DRINKING

First Port of Coll In the old harbour stores ☎ 01879 230488, 🌐 firstportofcoll.com. Simple café in the stores overlooking the bay, offering hot meals all day and lots of home-made puds, using as much local produce as possible. Take out also available. Summer Thurs–Tues 11am–2pm & 5–7.30pm, Sun lunch until 6.30pm.

Isle of Tiree

Tiree (🌐 isleoftiree.com) as its Gaelic name *tir-iodh* ("land of corn") suggests, was once known as the breadbasket of the Inner Hebrides, thanks to its acres of rich machair (sandy, grassy, lime-rich land). Nowadays crofting and tourism are the main sources of income for the small resident population. One of the most distinctive features of the island is its architecture, in particular the large numbers of "pudding" or "spotty" houses, where only the mortar is painted white. The sandy beaches attract large numbers of windsurfers for the **Tiree Wave Classic** every October. The **ferry** calls at Gott Bay Pier, now best known for **An Turas** (The Journey), Tiree's award-winning artistic "shelter".

Scarinish

Just up the road from Gott Bay Pier is the village of **SCARINISH**, home to a post office, public toilets, a supermarket, a butcher's and a bank, with a petrol pump back at the pier. Also here you'll find **An Iodhlann** (June–Sept Tues–Fri noon–5pm; Oct–May Mon–Fri 10.30am–3.30pm; £3) – meaning "haystack" in Gaelic – the island's two-roomed archive, which puts on occasional exhibitions.

Hynish

The most intriguing sights lie in the bulging western half of the island, where Tiree's two landmark hills rise up. Below the higher of the two is **HYNISH**, with its restored **harbour**, designed by Alan Stevenson in the 1830s to transport building materials for the magnificent 140ft-tall **Skerryvore Lighthouse**, which lies on a sea-swept reef some twelve miles southwest of Tiree. Up on the hill behind the harbour, a stumpy granite signal tower, whose signals used to be the only contact the lighthouse keepers had with civilization, now houses a **museum** telling the history of the Herculean effort required to erect the lighthouse, which, weather permitting, you can see from a viewing platform.

ARRIVAL AND DEPARTURE — ISLE OF TIREE

By plane Flights connect Tiree with Glasgow (1 daily Mon–Sat; 45min).

By ferry Car ferries arrive from Barra (summer Wed 1 daily; 3hr 5min) and Oban (summer daily; 3hr 40min).

Ring'n'Ride A useful minibus service that will take you anywhere on the island (Mon–Sat 7am–6pm, Tues until 10pm; ☎ 01879 220419).

21

ACCOMMODATION

Cèabhar Sandaig ⓣ01879 220684, ⓦceabhar.com. A very welcoming guesthouse and restaurant with five bedrooms, a communal lounge, and games cupboard. The proximity to the beach makes it popular with surfers. £70

Millhouse Drumaglea, Cornaigmore ⓣ01879 220435, ⓦtireemillhouse.co.uk. Great hostel in a snugly converted barn dating from the early 1900s, near Loch Bhasapol, in the northwest of the island. £15

Wild Diamond Watersports Loch Bhasapol ⓣ01879 220399, ⓦwilddiamond.co.uk. Campsite in the southwest of the island, with watersport activities around the loch. £12 per adult.

EATING

Elephant's End Gott Bay ⓣ01879 220694, ⓦelephantsend.com. Local goodies such as crab, lobster and langoustine (all around £12) served in a homely little restaurant. Mon–Sat 10am–4pm & 7pm–late, Sun 12.30pm–2.30pm & 7pm–late.

Mid-Argyll

Mid-Argyll is a vague term that loosely describes the central wedge of land south of Oban and north of Kintyre. The highlights of this gently undulating scenery lie along the sharply indented west coast, in particular the rich Bronze Age and Neolithic remains in the **Kilmartin** valley.

Kilmartin Glen

The **Kilmartin Glen** is the most important prehistoric site on the Scottish mainland, whose most remarkable relic is the **linear cemetery**, where several cairns are aligned for more than two miles, to the south of the village of Kilmartin. These are thought to represent the successive burials of a ruling family or chieftains, but nobody can be sure. The best view of the cemetery's configuration is from the Bronze Age **Mid-Cairn**, but the Neolithic **South Cairn**, dating from around 3000 BC, is by far the oldest and the most impressive, with its large chambered tomb roofed by giant slabs. Close to the Mid-Cairn, the two **Temple Wood stone circles** appear to have been the architectural focus of burials in the area from Neolithic times to the Bronze Age. Visible to the south are the impressively cup-marked **Nether Largie standing stones** (no public access), the largest of which stands more than 10ft high.

Kilmartin House Museum

Kilmartin • March–Oct daily 10am–5.30pm • £5 • ⓣ01546 510278, ⓦkilmartin.org

On high ground to the north of the cairns, in the tiny village of Kilmartin, **Kilmartin House Museum** is an enlightening and entertaining exhibition on the area's prehistory, set within the old manse next to the village church. The church is also worth a look, as it shelters the badly damaged and weathered **Kilmartin crosses**, while a separate enclosure in the graveyard houses a large collection of medieval grave slabs of the Malcolms of Poltalloch.

Dunadd

South of Kilmartin, beyond the linear cemetery, lies the raised peat bog of Mòine Mhór (Great Moss), best known as home to the Iron Age fort of **Dunadd**, one of Scotland's most important Celtic sites, occupying a distinctive 176ft-high rocky knoll once surrounded by the sea but currently stranded beside the winding River Add. It was here that Fergus, the first king of Dalriada, established his royal seat, having arrived from Ireland in around 500 AD. Its strategic position, the craggy defences and the view from the top are all impressive, but it's the **stone carvings** (albeit now fibreglass copies) between the twin summits which make Dunadd so remarkable: several lines of Pictish inscription in *ogam* (an ancient alphabet of Irish origin), the faint outline of a boar, a hollowed-out footprint and a small basin. The footprint and basin have been interpreted as being part of the royal coronation rituals of the kings of Dalriada. It's thought that the Stone of Destiny was used at Dunadd before being moved to Scone Palace (see p.819).

ACCOMMODATION **KILMARTIN GLEN**

★ **Dunchraigaig House** A mile or so south of Kilmartin ⓣ01546 605300, ⓦdunchraigaig.co.uk. A large detached Victorian house opposite the Ballymeanoch standing stones, where you can have home-made clootie dumpling for breakfast. £75

EATING

Glebe Cairn Café Kilmartin House Museum, Kilmartin ⓣ01546 510278, ⓦkilmartin.org. Lovely stone-built licensed café with a green oak conservatory. Home-made soup, snacky lunches and cakes during the day, with a more sophisticated menu in the evening. Mon–Wed & Sun 10am–5pm, Thurs–Sat 6–9pm.

Crinan Canal

In 1801 the nine-mile-long **Crinan Canal** opened, linking Loch Fyne, at Ardrishaig south of Lochgilphead, with the Sound of Jura, thus cutting out the long and treacherous journey around the Mull of Kintyre. The canal runs parallel to the sea for quite some way before hitting a flight of locks either side of **CAIRNBAAN** (there are fifteen in total); a walk along the towpath is both picturesque and pleasantly unstrenuous. There are usually one or two yachts passing through the locks, but the most relaxing place from which to view the canal in action is **CRINAN**, a pretty little fishing port at its western end.

ACCOMMODATION **CRINAN CANAL**

Bellanoch House 1 mile outside Crinan ⓣ01546 830149, ⓦbellanochhouse.co.uk. A grand old schoolhouse with stripped pine floors and lots of character, right on the canal. £90

The Stables Achnamara, 5 miles south of Crinan ⓣ01546 850276, ⓦthestablesbandb.co.uk. An old hunting lodge in beaver country, with beautiful oakwood floors, and two cosy loft rooms. £70

EATING AND DRINKING

Cairnbaan Hotel Cairnbaan ⓣ01546 603668, ⓦcairnbaan.com. An eighteenth-century coaching inn overlooking the canal at Lock 5, with a decent restaurant and bar meals featuring locally caught seafood. Free wi-fi. Food served daily noon–2.30pm & 6–9.30pm.

Crinan Hotel Crinan ⓣ01546 830261, ⓦcrinanhotel.com. It's worth having a pint or one of the excellent bar meals at the hotel's Crinan Seafood Bar, which has lovely views out to sea and an outdoor terrace. Food served daily noon–2.30pm & 6–8.30pm.

Kintyre

But for the mile-long isthmus between West Loch Tarbert and the much smaller East Loch Tarbert, the little-visited peninsula of **KINTYRE** (ⓦkintyre.org) – from the Gaelic *Ceann Tire*, "land's end" – would be an island. Despite its relative proximity to Scotland's Central Belt, Kintyre remains quiet and unfashionable; its main towns, **Tarbert** and **Campbeltown**, have few obvious attractions, but that's part of their appeal. In many ways, it's a peninsula in a time warp, where you can hole up in perfect solitude.

Tarbert

A distinctive rocket-like church steeple heralds the fishing village of **TARBERT** (in Gaelic *An Tairbeart*, meaning "isthmus"), sheltering an attractive little bay backed by rugged hills. Tarbert's harbourfront is pretty, and is best appreciated from the rubble of Robert the Bruce's fourteenth-century **castle** above the town to the south.

ARRIVAL AND INFORMATION — TARBERT

By ferry Regular ferries connect Tarbert with Portavadie (hourly; 25min).

By bus Tarbert is met by buses from Campbeltown (Mon–Sat 4 daily, 2 on Sun; 1hr 15min); Claonaig (Mon–Sat 3 daily; 30min); Glasgow (3 daily; 3hr 15min); Kennacraig (3–6 daily; 15min) and Tayinloan (3–6 daily; 30min).

Tourist office Harbour St (April–Oct Mon–Fri 11am–5pm, Sat & Sun 11am–5pm; ⓣ01880 820429).

ACCOMMODATION AND EATING

Victoria Hotel Barmore Rd ⓣ01880 820263, ⓦvictoriahoteltarbert.co.uk. Behind its garish yellow exterior, this is a comfortable old hotel overlooking the harbour. Its real strength is the food served in the conservatory restaurant and the back bar, cooked by an award-winning French chef. Food served noon–2pm & 6–9pm. **£70**

Isle of Gigha

Gigha (ⓦgigha.org.uk) – pronounced "geeya" – is a low-lying, fertile island three miles off the west coast of Kintyre, reputedly occupied for 5000 years. Like many of the smaller Hebrides, Gigha was bought and sold numerous times after its original lairds, the MacNeils, sold up in 1865, and was finally bought by the islanders themselves in 2002. The island is so small – six miles by one – that most visitors come here just for the day. The real draw, apart from the peace and quiet, is the white sandy **beaches**.

The ferry from Tayinloan, 23 miles south of Tarbert, deposits you at Gigha's only village, **ARDMINISH**, where you'll find the post office and shop, and a lovely beach. A mile and a half south, the **Achamore Gardens** (daily 9am–dusk; £4) were established by the first postwar owner, Sir James Horlick (of hot-drink fame). Their spectacularly colourful display of azaleas is best seen in early summer.

ARRIVAL AND DEPARTURE — ISLE OF GIGHA

Regular CalMac **ferries** connect Gigha with Tayinloan (hourly; 20min). The island post office offers **bike** rental.

ACCOMMODATION

Achamore House Achamore Gardens ⓣ01583 505400, ⓦwww.achamorehouse.com. You can stay in the style of a laird by booking into one of the grand rooms in the whitewashed Scots Baronial mansion in the midst of these beautiful gardens. Not all rooms are en- suite. **£90**

EATING

The Boathouse Ardminish ⓣ01583 505123, ⓦboathouse-bar.com. This licensed, converted boathouse by the CalMac pier is the place to go for delicious local food and, occasionally, live music and quiz nights. April–Oct daily 11am–4pm & 6–11pm.

Campbeltown

CAMPBELTOWN's best feature is its setting, in a deep bay sheltered by Davaar Island and the surrounding hills. With a population of around 5000, it's Kintyre's largest town and its shops are by far the best place to stock up on supplies. Campbeltown's heyday was the Victorian era, when shipbuilding was going strong, coal was shipped by canal from Drumlemble, the fishing fleet was vast and Campbeltown had no fewer than 34 whisky distilleries – today only a few remain.

Whisky tours

If you're interested in visiting one of the distilleries, pop into **Cadenhead's** whisky shop at 7 Bolgam St (ⓣ01586 551710), which runs parallel with Longrow. Here you can sign up for a guided tour (ⓦspringbankwhisky.com; Mon–Fri 10am & 2pm,

Sat & Sun by appointment; £6–20) of **Springbank**, the deeply traditional, family-owned distillery that does absolutely everything – from malting to bottling – on its own premises.

ARRIVAL AND DEPARTURE — CAMPBELTOWN

By plane Flights from Glasgow connect with Campbeltown (Mon–Fri 2 daily; 35min).
By bus Campbeltown is served by buses from Glasgow (2–3 daily; 4hr 25min) and Tarbert Mon–Sat 4 daily, 2 on Sun; 1hr 15min).
Tourist office Old Quay (Mon–Fri 10am–4pm; ⊕01586 552056).

ACCOMMODATION AND EATING

Ardshiel Hotel Kilkerran Rd ⊕01586 552133, ⊛ardshiel.co.uk. Well-run hotel in a former whisky distiller's Victorian mansion on a lovely leafy square. The bar meals are excellent too. **£70**
Oatfield House Just under 3 miles from the town centre down the A842 to Southend ⊕01586 551551, ⊛oatfield.org. A beautifully renovated, whitewashed laird's house set in its own grounds. Free wi-fi, Shetland ponies, a walled garden and a pond. **£80**

ENTERTAINMENT

Wee Pictures Hall St ⊕01586 533657, ⊛www.weepictures.co.uk. On the town's palm-tree-dotted waterfront you'll find this little Art Deco cinema, built in 1913 and still going strong. Daily except Fri.

Mull of Kintyre

The bulbous, hilly end of Kintyre, south of Campbeltown, features some of the most spectacular scenery on the whole peninsula, mixed with large swathes of Lowland-style farmland. Most people venture west of Campbeltown to make a pilgrimage to the **Mull of Kintyre**, made famous by the mawkish number-one hit by Paul McCartney with the help of the Campbeltown Pipe Band. The nearest Britain gets to Ireland – whose coastline, just twelve miles away, appears remarkably close on fine days – this storm-wracked spot offers nothing specifically to see other than the view and a memorial to the 29 military personnel who died in 1994 when an RAF helicopter crashed into the hillside. The roads up to the "**Gap**" (1150ft) – where you must leave your car – and particularly down to the lighthouse, itself 300ft above the ocean waves, are terrifyingly tortuous.

Isle of Arran

Shaped like a kidney bean and occupying centre stage in the Firth of Clyde, **Arran** (⊛visitarran.net) is the most southerly (and therefore the most accessible) of all the Scottish islands. The Highland–Lowland dividing line passes right through its centre – hence the cliché about it being like "Scotland in miniature" – leaving the northern half sparsely populated, mountainous and bleak, while the lush southern half enjoys a much milder climate. The population of around 5000 – many of whom are incomers – tend to stick to the southeastern quarter of the island, leaving the west and the north relatively undisturbed.

ARRIVAL AND DEPARTURE — ISLE OF ARRAN

CalMac **ferries** run from Ardrossan, 14 miles north of Ayr, to Brodick (4–6 daily; 55min), and, in summer only, a small ferry runs from Claonaig, 8 miles south of Tarbert, to Lochranza (8–9 daily; 30min).

Brodick

As the island's capital and main communication hub, **BRODICK** (from the Norse *breidr vik*, "broad bay") is the busiest town on Arran. Although the resort is a place of only

HIKING UP GOAT FELL

The desolate north half of Arran – effectively the Highland part – features bare granite peaks, the occasional golden eagle and miles of unspoilt scenery, within reach only to those prepared to do some serious hiking. Arran's most accessible peak is also the island's highest, **Goat Fell** (2866ft), which can be ascended in just three hours from Brodick, though it's a strenuous hike. You can also hike up Goat Fell from Corrie, Arran's prettiest little seaside village, six miles north of Brodick, where a procession of pristine cottages lines the road to Lochranza and wraps itself around an exquisite little harbour and pier.

moderate charm, it does at least have a grand setting in a wide, sandy bay set against a backdrop of granite mountains.

Brodick Castle

North side of the bay • **Castle** Daily: April–Sept 11am–4pm; Oct 11am–3pm • NTS • £11 **Walled garden** April–Oct daily 10am–4.30pm; Nov & Dec Sat & Sun 10am–3.30pm **Country park** Daily 9.30am to sunset • NTS • £6 • ⓣ 0844 493 2152

The local dukes of Hamilton used to rule the town from **Brodick Castle**, on a steep bank on the north side of the bay. The interior is comfortable if undistinguished, but the **walled garden** and extensive **country park** contain a treasury of exotic plants and trees and command a superb view across the bay. Hidden in the grounds is a bizarre Bavarian-style summerhouse lined entirely with pine cones, one of three built by the eleventh duke to make his wife, Princess Marie of Baden, feel at home.

ARRIVAL AND INFORMATION — BRODICK

By ferry Ferries arrive on the south side of Brodick Bay, a short walk from the town centre.

By bus Island buses connect Brodick with Blackwaterfoot (Mon–Sat 8–10 daily, 4 on Sun; 30min); Corrie (3–5 daily; 20min); Lamlash (Mon–Sat hourly, 4 on Sun; 10–15min) and Lochranza (3–5 daily; 45min). An Arran Rural Rover day-ticket costs around £5.

Tourist office By the CalMac pier (June–Sept daily 9am–5pm; Oct–May Mon–Sat 9am–5pm; ⓣ 01770 303776).

ACCOMMODATION

The Barn Southwest edge of Brodick in Glencloy ⓣ 01770 303615, ⓦ arranbarn.co.uk. A charming early nineteenth-century B&B with real style. Breakfast includes eggs from the barn's chickens. Free wi-fi. Closed Nov–Feb. **£60**

Dunvegan Guest House Shore Rd ⓣ 01770 302811, ⓦ dunveganguesthouse.co.uk. An attractive stone-built Victorian B&B with a traditional feel but tastefully modernized en-suite rooms. The best choice if you need to stay close to the ferry terminal. **£50**

Glen Rosa Campsite 2 miles from the town centre off the B880 to Blackwaterfoot ⓣ 01770 302380, ⓦ arrancamping.co.uk. A lovely, but very basic, farm site (cold water only and no showers, but campfires permitted). **£5** per person.

Lamlash and around

The southern half of Arran is less spectacular and less forbidding than the north; it's more heavily forested and the land is more fertile, and the vast majority of the population lives here. With its distinctive Edwardian architecture and mild climate, **LAMLASH** epitomizes the sedate charm of southeast Arran.

Holy Island

Ferries run more or less hourly • £8 return • ⓣ 01770 600998

You can take a boat out from Lamlash to the slug-shaped hump of **Holy Island**, which shelters the bay, and where a group of Tibetan Buddhists have established a retreat – providing you don't dawdle, it's possible to scramble up to the top of **Mullach Mór** (1030ft), the island's highest point, and still catch the last ferry back. Otherwise, consider staying at the Buddhist centre (see opposite).

ACCOMMODATION AND EATING — **LAMLASH AND AROUND**

Glenisle Hotel & Restaurant Lamlash ⊕01770 600559, ⊕glenislehotel.com. A cut above your average Lamlash B&B: every room of this Victorian hotel overlooking the bay has been tastefully refurbished, and the restaurant serves tasty dishes from beetroot gravadlax to home-made burgers with gruyère and onion chutney. **£105**

Peace Centre Holy Island ⊕01770 601100, ⊕holyisland.org. The Buddhist centre on Holy Island welcomes visitors. Guests are welcome to join in the daily meditation sessions. Smoking, alcohol and sex are prohibited. All room rates include veggie full board. Dorm **£28**, twin **£72**

Lochranza

The ruined castle which occupies the mud flats of the bay, and the brooding north-facing slopes of the mountains which frame it, provide **LOCHRANZA** with one of the most spectacular settings on the island. Despite being the only place of any size in this sparsely populated area, Lochranza attracts far fewer visitors than other Arran resorts. The castle is worth a brief look inside, but Lochranza's main tourist attraction is the island's modern **distillery** (mid-March to Oct Mon–Sat 10am–6pm, Sun 11am–6pm; Nov–Feb daily 11am–4pm; ⊕01770 830264, ⊕arranwhisky.com; £3.50), distinguished by its pagoda-style roofs.

ARRIVAL AND DEPARTURE — **LOCHRANZA**

CalMac **ferries** arrive and depart from the pier, a 10min walk north of Lochranza distillery.

ACCOMMODATION

Castlekirk ⊕01770 830229, ⊕castlekirk.co.uk. A converted church (with an art gallery attached) that retains lots of original features, including a rose window in the breakfast room with views out over the castle. The four rooms all have unusual, pitched ceilings, and only the double is en suite. **£65**

Lochranza Caravan & Camping Site ⊕01770 830273, ⊕arran-campsite.com. Beautifully placed by the golf course on the Brodick road, where red deer come to graze in the early evening. The well-equipped campsite has a friendly tearoom serving all-day breakfasts and light snacks. Closed Nov–Feb. **£14** for two people, car and a small tent.

SYHA hostel ⊕01700 830631, ⊕syha.org.uk. Popular hostel halfway between the distillery and the castle, with views over the bay. Closed Nov to mid-Feb. **£15**

Isle of Islay

The fertile, largely treeless island of **ISLAY** (⊕isle-of-islay.com) is famous for one thing – single malt **whisky**. The smoky, peaty, pungent quality of Islay whisky is unique, recognizable even to the untutored palate, and most of the island's distilleries offer fascinating guided tours, ending with the customary complimentary dram. In medieval times, Islay was the political centre of the Hebrides, with **Finlaggan**, near **Port Askaig**, the seat of the MacDonalds, lords of the Isles. The picturesque, whitewashed villages you see on Islay today, however, date from the planned settlements founded by the Campbells in the late eighteenth and early nineteenth centuries. Apart from whisky and solitude, the other great draw is the **bird life** – there's a real possibility of spotting a golden eagle, or the rare, crow-like chough, and no possibility at all of missing the scores of white-fronted and barnacle geese who winter here in their thousands.

ARRIVAL AND DEPARTURE — **ISLE OF ISLAY**

By ferry CalMac ferries from Kennacraig, 12 miles south of Tarbert, go either to Port Ellen or Port Askaig (3–4 daily; 2hr 5min/2hr 20min). On Wednesdays, the ferry also makes a day-trip to Colonsay from Port Askaig (1 on Wed; 1hr 10min). There's also a small ferry that runs between Port Askaig and Feolin Ferry on Jura (Mon–Sat hourly, Sun 7–8 daily; 10min).

By plane Islay's airport, 6 miles north of Port Ellen in Glenegedale, has regular flights from Glasgow (Mon–Fri 2 daily, 1 on Sat; 40min).

ISLAY WHISKY

Islay has woken up to the fact that its **whisky distilleries** are a major tourist attraction. Nowadays, just about every distillery offers guided tours, traditionally ending with a generous dram, and a refund (or discount) for your entrance fee if you buy a bottle in the shop. Phone ahead to make sure there's a tour running, as times do change.

Ardbeg 01496 302244, ardbeg.com. Ardbeg is traditionally considered the saltiest, peatiest malt on Islay (and that's saying something). The distillery has been thoroughly restored, yet it still has bags of character inside. The Old Kiln Café is excellent (June–Aug daily 10am–5pm; Sept–May Mon–Fri 10am–4pm). Guided tours regularly 10.30am, noon & 3pm; £5.

Bowmore 01496 810671, bowmore.co.uk. Bowmore is the most touristy of the Islay distilleries, and by far the most central (with unrivalled disabled access). Daily guided tours Easter–June Mon–Sat 9am–5pm; July to mid-Sept Mon–Sat 9am–5pm, Sun noon–4pm; mid-Sept to Easter Mon–Fri 9am–5pm, Sat 9am–noon; £5.

Bruichladdich 01496 850190, bruichladdich.com. Rescued in 2001 by a group of whisky fanatics, this independent distillery is building a new distillery in Port Charlotte. Guided tours Easter–Oct Mon–Fri 10.30am, 11.30am & 2.30pm, Sat 11.30am & 2.30pm; Nov–Easter Mon–Fri 11.30am & 2.30pm, Sat 11.30am; £5.

Bunnahabhainn 01496 840646, bunnahabhain.com. A visit to Bunnahabhain (pronounced "Bunna-have-in") is really only for whisky obsessives. The whisky is the least characteristically Islay and the distillery is only in production for a few months each year. Guided tours April–Oct Mon–Fri 10.30am, 1.30pm & 3.15pm; Nov to mid-Dec by appointment; £4.

Kilchoman 01496 850011, kilchomandistillery.com. Established in 2005, Kilchoman is a very welcoming, tiny, farm-based enterprise that grows its own barley, as well as distilling, maturing and bottling its whisky on site. The café serves good coffee, plus home-made soup and baking (Mon–Sat 10am–5pm; Nov–March Mon–Fri only). Guided tours April–Oct Mon–Sat 11am & 3pm; Nov–March Mon–Fri 11am & 3pm; £5.

Lagavulin 01496 302730, discovering-distilleries.com. Lagavulin is the classic, all-round Islay malt, with lots of smoke and peat and the distillery enjoys a fabulous setting. Guided tours April–Oct Mon–Fri 9.30 & 11.15am, 2.30 & 3.45pm, Sat 9.30 & 11.15am; Nov–March Mon–Fri 9.30 & 11.15am; £6.

Laphroaig 01496 302418, laphroaig.com. Another classic smoky, peaty Islay malt, and another great setting – you also get to see the malting and see and smell the peat kilns. Guided tours March–Oct Mon–Fri 10am & 11.30am & 2pm & 3.30pm, Sat & Sun 10am, noon & 2pm; Nov–Feb daily 10am & 2pm; £3.

Port Ellen and around

Laid out as a planned village in 1821 by Walter Frederick Campbell, and named after his wife, **PORT ELLEN** is the chief port on Islay, with the island's largest fishing fleet, and main CalMac ferry terminal. The neat whitewashed terraces that overlook the town's bay of golden sand are pretty enough, but the view is dominated by the village's modern maltings, whose powerful odours waft across the town.

The only reason to pause in this part of the island is to head off east along a dead-end road that passes three **distilleries** in as many miles (see above). Another six miles down the track and you eventually come to the simple thirteenth-century **Kildalton Chapel**, which has an eighth-century Celtic ringed cross made from the local "bluestone". The exceptional quality of the scenes matches any to be found on the crosses carved by the monks in Iona.

ARRIVAL AND DEPARTURE PORT ELLEN

By ferry CalMac ferries arrive in the centre of town, on the west side of the bay.

By bus Island buses connect Port Ellen with Bowmore (Mon–Sat 10 daily, Sun 4 daily; 20–30min).

ACCOMMODATION

Glenegedale House Hotel Glenegedale 01496 300400, glenegedalehouse.co.uk. This whitewashed nineteenth-century guesthouse, opposite the airport, offers luxurious rooms, full of character, plus delicious home cooking and fantastic breakfasts. **£110**

Kintra Farm Kintra, 3 miles west of Port Ellen 01496 302051, kintrafarm.co.uk. Lovely set of farm buildings at the southern tip of sandy Laggan Bay. The Victorian farmhouse has three rooms (two en-suite) and offers B&B, or you can camp in the nearby dunes – book ahead for Gaelic lessons. Closed Oct–March. **£70**

Bowmore

On the north side of the monotonous peat bog of Duich Moss, on the southern shores of the tidal Loch Indaal, lies **BOWMORE**, Islay's administrative capital. It's a striking place, laid out in 1768 on a grid plan rather like Inveraray, with the whitewashed terraces of Main Street climbing up the hill in a straight line from the pier on Loch Indaal to the town's crowning landmark, the **Round Church**. Built in the round, so that the devil would have no corners in which to hide, it has a plain, wood-panelled interior, with a lovely tiered balcony and a big central mushroom pillar.

ARRIVAL AND INFORMATION — BOWMORE

By bus Bowmore is connected by island buses to Port Askaig (Mon–Sat 6–8 daily, Sun 4 daily; 25min), Port Charlotte (Mon–Sat 5–6 daily, Sun 3 daily; 25min) and Port Ellen (Mon–Sat 10 daily, Sun 4 daily; 20–30min).

Tourist office Islay's only tourist office is on The Square (April–Oct Mon–Sat 10am–5pm, Sun noon–3pm; Nov–March Mon–Fri 10am–3pm; T 01496 810254).

ACCOMMODATION

Lambeth House Jamieson St T 01496 810597, E lambethguesthouse@tiscali.co.uk. Newly modernized B&B run by a welcoming couple who offer three-course evening meals as well as breakfast. All rooms are en-suite and there's free wi-fi. **£90**

EATING AND DRINKING

Harbour Inn Main St T 01496 810330, W harbour-inn.com. You can warm yourself by a peat fire in the cosy pub, where they also do bar food, or sidle next door to the restaurant (booking advisable) – the seafood specials are super-fresh. Daily noon–2.30pm & 6–9.30pm.

Port Charlotte

PORT CHARLOTTE is Islay's prettiest village, its immaculate whitewashed cottages clustered around a sandy cove overlooking Loch Indaal. On the northern fringe of the village, in a whitewashed former chapel, the imaginative **Museum of Islay Life** (April–Oct Mon–Sat 10.30am–4.30pm; Nov–March Mon–Sat 10am–4pm; £3), has a children's corner, quizzes, a good library of books about the island, and tantalizing snippets about eighteenth-century illegal whisky distillers. The **Wildlife Information Centre** (Easter–Oct daily except Sat 10am–4pm; June–Aug daily 10am–4pm; £2.50), housed in the former distillery warehouse, is also worth a visit for anyone interested in the island's fauna and flora.

ARRIVAL AND DEPARTURE — PORT CHARLOTTE

Island **buses** run from Bowmore to Port Charlotte (Mon–Sat 5–6 daily, Sun 3 daily; 25min).

GEESE ON ISLAY

If you're visiting Islay between mid-September and the third week of April, it's impossible to miss the island's staggeringly large wintering population of **barnacle and white-fronted geese**. During this period, the geese dominate the landscape, feeding incessantly off the rich pasture, strolling by the shores, and flying in formation across the winter skies. You can see the geese just about anywhere on the island – there are an estimated 15,000 white-fronted and 40,000 barnacles here (and rising) – though in the evening, they tend to congregate in the tidal mud flats and fields around **Loch Gruinart**.

ACCOMMODATION AND EATING

The Monachs Nerabus, 3 miles along the road to Portnahaven ☎ 01496 850094, ⓦ islayguesthouse.co.uk. A spacious, luxury new-build B&B villa with stupendous sea views. Free wi-fi. £100

Port Charlotte Hotel ☎ 01496 850360, ⓦ portcharlottehotel.co.uk. You'll receive a welcome here, one of Islay's most comfortable, relaxing places to stay – the seafood lunches served in the bar are very popular, and there's a good, more expensive restaurant. £170

Port Mòr Campsite Just outside on the village on the road to Portnahaven ☎ 01496 850441, ⓦ islandofislay.co.uk. Community-run campsite, with sea views and tip-top modern facilities (and a café). £8 per person.

SYHA hostel ☎ 0870 004 1128, ⓦ syha.org.uk. Capacious modern hostel in an old bonded warehouse by the sea, next door to the Wildlife Information Centre. Closed Nov–March. £16

Loch Finlaggan

Just beyond Ballygrant, on the road from Bowmolre to Port Askaig, a narrow road leads north to **Loch Finlaggan**, site of a number of prehistoric crannogs (artificial islands) and, for 400 years from the twelfth century, headquarters of the Lords of the Isles, semi-autonomous rulers over the Hebrides and Kintyre. You can happily skip the **information centre** (Easter & Oct Tues, Thurs & Sun 2–4pm; May–Sept daily except Sat 2.30–5pm; £2), to the northeast of the loch, and simply head on down to the site itself (access at any time), which is dotted with interpretive panels. Duckboards allow you to walk out across the reed beds of the loch and explore the main crannog, **Eilean Mor**, where several carved gravestones are displayed under cover in the chapel, which seem to support the theory that the Lords of the Isles buried their wives and children there, while having themselves interred on Iona.

ACCOMMODATION — LOCH FINLAGGAN

★ **Kilmeny Farmhouse** Just southwest of Ballygrant ☎ 01496 840668, ⓦ kilmeny.co.uk. This whitewashed farmhouse richly deserves all the superlatives it regularly receives, its rooms furnished with antiques and its dinners (Tues & Thurs only) worth the extra £35 or so a head. £115

Isle of Jura

The long, whale-shaped island of **Jura** is one of the wildest and most mountainous of the Inner Hebrides, its entire west coast uninhabited and inaccessible except to the dedicated walker. Jura's distinctive Paps – so called because of their smooth breast-like shape, though there are in fact three of them – seem to dominate every view off the west coast of Argyll, their glacial rounded tops covered in a light dusting of quartzite scree. The island's name is commonly thought to derive from the Norse *dyr-oe* (deer island) and, appropriately enough, the current deer population of 6000 far outnumbers the 180 humans. With just one road, which sticks to the more sheltered eastern coast, and only one hotel and a smattering of B&Bs, Jura is an ideal place to go for peace and quiet and some great walking.

GEORGE ORWELL ON JURA

In April 1946, Eric Blair (better known by his pen name of **George Orwell**), suffering badly from TB and intending to give himself "six months' quiet" in which to write his new novel *The Last Man in Europe* (later to become 1984), moved to a remote farmhouse called Barnhill, on the northern tip of Jura. He lived out a spartan existence there for two years but was forced to return to London shortly before his death. The house, 23 miles north of Craighouse up an increasingly poor road, is as remote today as it was in Orwell's day, and is now let out as a **self-catering cottage** (☎ 01786 850274).

Anything that happens on Jura happens in the island's only real village, **CRAIGHOUSE**, eight miles up the road from Feolin Ferry. The village enjoys a sheltered setting, overlooking Knapdale on the mainland – so sheltered, in fact, that there are even a few palm trees thriving on the seafront. There's a shop, a post office, the island hotel and a tearoom, plus the tiny **Isle of Jura distillery** (T 01496 820240, W isleofjura.com), which is very welcoming to visitors.

ARRIVAL AND DEPARTURE — ISLE OF JURA

The main car **ferry** departs from Port Askaig on Islay to Feolin Ferry (Mon–Sat hourly, Sun 3 daily; 10min; T 01496 840681), 8 miles from Craighouse. There's also a passenger ferry service from Tayvallich, on the Argyll mainland, to Craighouse (Mon, Fri & Sat 2 daily, 1 on Sun; 1hr; T 07768 450000, W jurapassengerferry.com).

ACCOMMODATION AND EATING

Jura Hotel Craighouse T 01496 820243, W jurahotel.co.uk. Not much to look at from the outside, but warm and friendly within, and centre of the island's social scene. The cheaper rooms are not en-suite. The hotel does moderately expensive bar meals, and has a shower block and laundry facilities round the back for those who wish to camp in the hotel gardens. £78

Sealladh na Mara Knockrome, T 01496 820349, W isleofjura.net. A modern croft house B&B, 4 miles north of Craighouse, with two pristine all-white first-floor rooms with wooden floors and lovely views over the island. £74

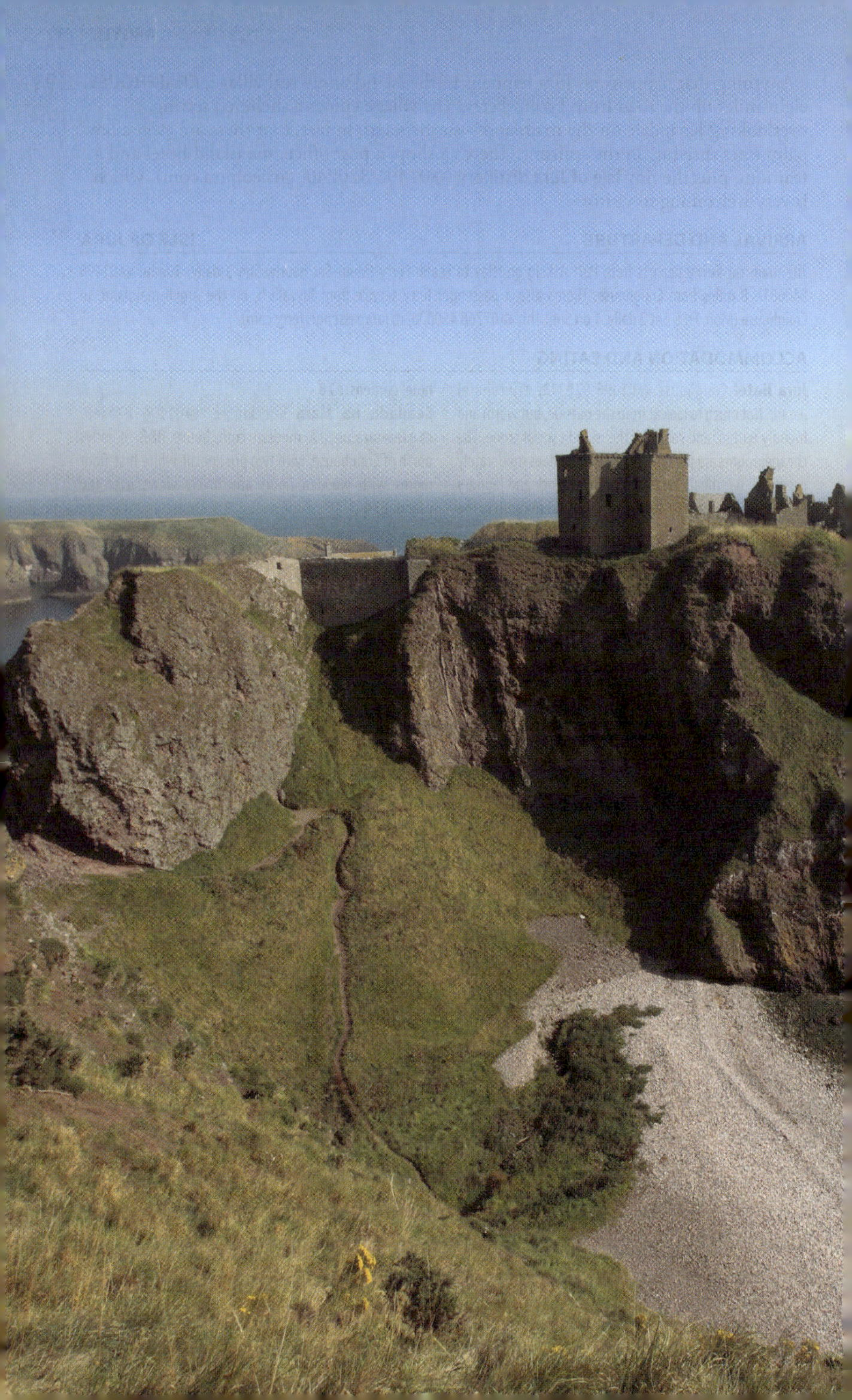

Northeast Scotland

852 Angus

863 Aberdeenshire and Moray

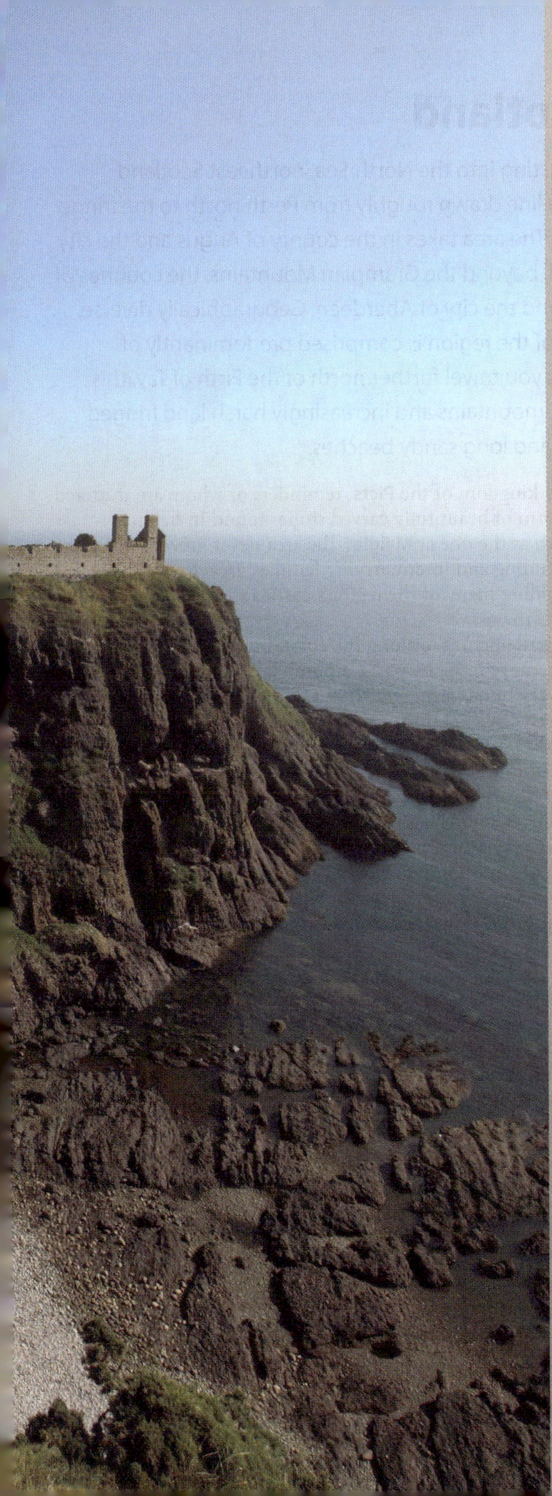

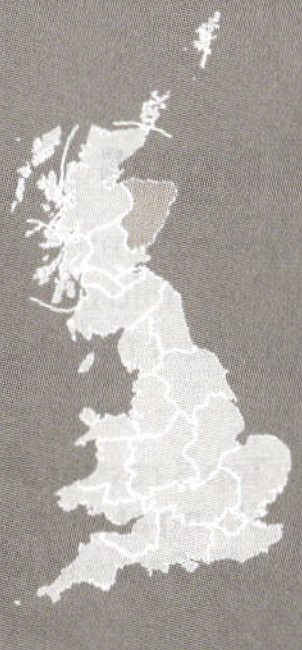

DUNNOTTAR CASTLE

Northeast Scotland

A large triangle of land thrusting into the North Sea, northeast Scotland comprises the area east of a line drawn roughly from Perth north to the fringe of the Moray Firth at Forres. The area takes in the county of Angus and the city of Dundee to the south and, beyond the Grampian Mountains, the counties of Aberdeenshire and Moray and the city of Aberdeen. Geographically diverse, the landscape in the south of the region is comprised predominantly of undulating farmland, but as you travel further north of the Firth of Tay, this gives way to wooded glens, mountains and increasingly harsh land fringed by a dramatic coast of cliffs and long sandy beaches.

The northeast was the southern kingdom of the **Picts**, reminders of whom are scattered throughout the region in the form of beautifully carved stones found in fields, churchyards and museums, such as the one at **Meigle**. The area never grew particularly prosperous, and a handful of feuding and intermarrying families grew to wield disproportionate influence, building many of the region's **castles** and religious buildings and developing and planning its towns.

Many of the most appealing settlements are along the coast, but while the fishing industry is but a fondly held memory in many parts, a number of the northeast's ports were transformed by the discovery of **oil** in the North Sea in the 1960s – particularly **Aberdeen**, Scotland's third-largest city. The northeast's next-largest metropolis, **Dundee**, is valiantly shedding its depressed post-industrial image with a reinvigorated cultural scene and some heavily marketed tourist attractions.

North of the glens and west of Aberdeen is **Deeside**, a fertile, ruggedly attractive area made famous by the Royal Family: **Balmoral** has been a royal residence since Victoria's time. Beyond are the eastern sections of the **Cairngorm National Park**, and travelling north into Moray brings you to Scotland's most productive whisky-making area, **Speyside**. The northeast coast, meanwhile, offers yet another aspect of a diverse region, with rugged cliffs, empty beaches and historic fishing villages tucked into coves and bays.

GETTING AROUND **NORTHEAST SCOTLAND**

Northeast Scotland is well served by an extensive **road** network, with fast links between Dundee and Aberdeen, and the area north and west of Aberdeen dissected by a series of efficient routes. **Trains** from Edinburgh and Glasgow connect with Dundee, Aberdeen and other coastal towns, while an inland line from Aberdeen heads northwest to Elgin and on to Inverness. A reasonably comprehensive scheduled **bus service** is complemented by a network of **postbuses** in the Angus glens: only in the most remote and mountainous parts does public transport disappear altogether.

Angus

The predominantly agricultural county of **Angus**, east of the A9 and north of the Firth of Tay, holds some of the northeast's greatest scenery and is relatively free of tourists, who tend to head further west for the Highlands proper. The coast from **Montrose** to

Top 5 castles and abbeys p.859
Skiing at Glen Shee p.861
J.M. Barrie in Kirrie p.862
The Malt Whisky Trail p.869
The Findhorn Foundation p.873

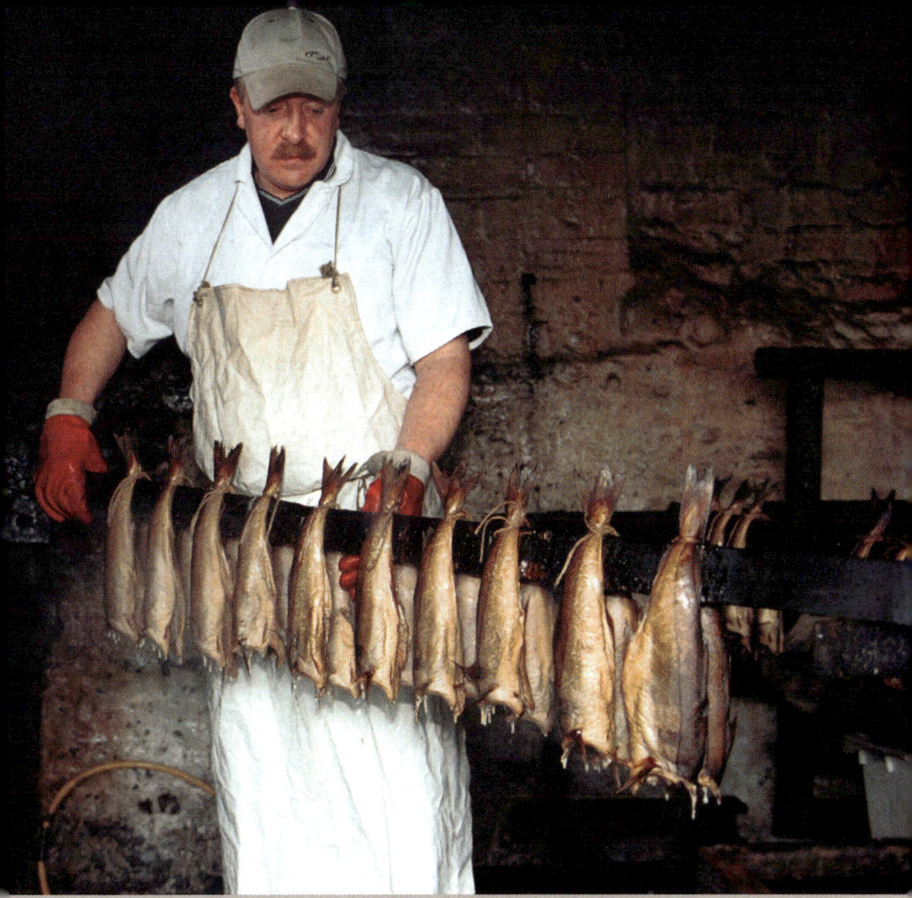

ARBROATH SMOKIES

Highlights

❶ **DCA, Dundee** Buzzing arts centre with a cinema and a café at the hip heart of Dundee's up-and-coming cultural scene. **See p.857**

❷ **Arbroath smokies** A true Scottish delicacy: succulent haddock eaten while still warm from the oak smoker. **See p.859**

❸ **Meigle Pictish stones** These fascinating carved relics of a lost culture can be seen standing eerily alone in remote fields, but to learn a bit more about them, head to a museum. The museum at Meigle displays a very good variety. **See p.861**

❹ **Dunnottar Castle** The moodiest cliff-top ruin in the country, built in the ninth century and surrounded by crashing seas. **See p.865**

❺ **Speyside's whiskies** See the distilleries and landscapes of places such as Glenfiddich, Glenlivet and Glen Grant – visits give you a splendid opportunity to taste their whiskies too. **See p.869**

❻ **Museum of Scottish Lighthouses, Fraserburgh** Lights, lenses and legends at one of the quirkiest and most intriguing small museums in the country. **See p.871**

HIGHLIGHTS ARE MARKED ON THE MAP ON PP.854–855

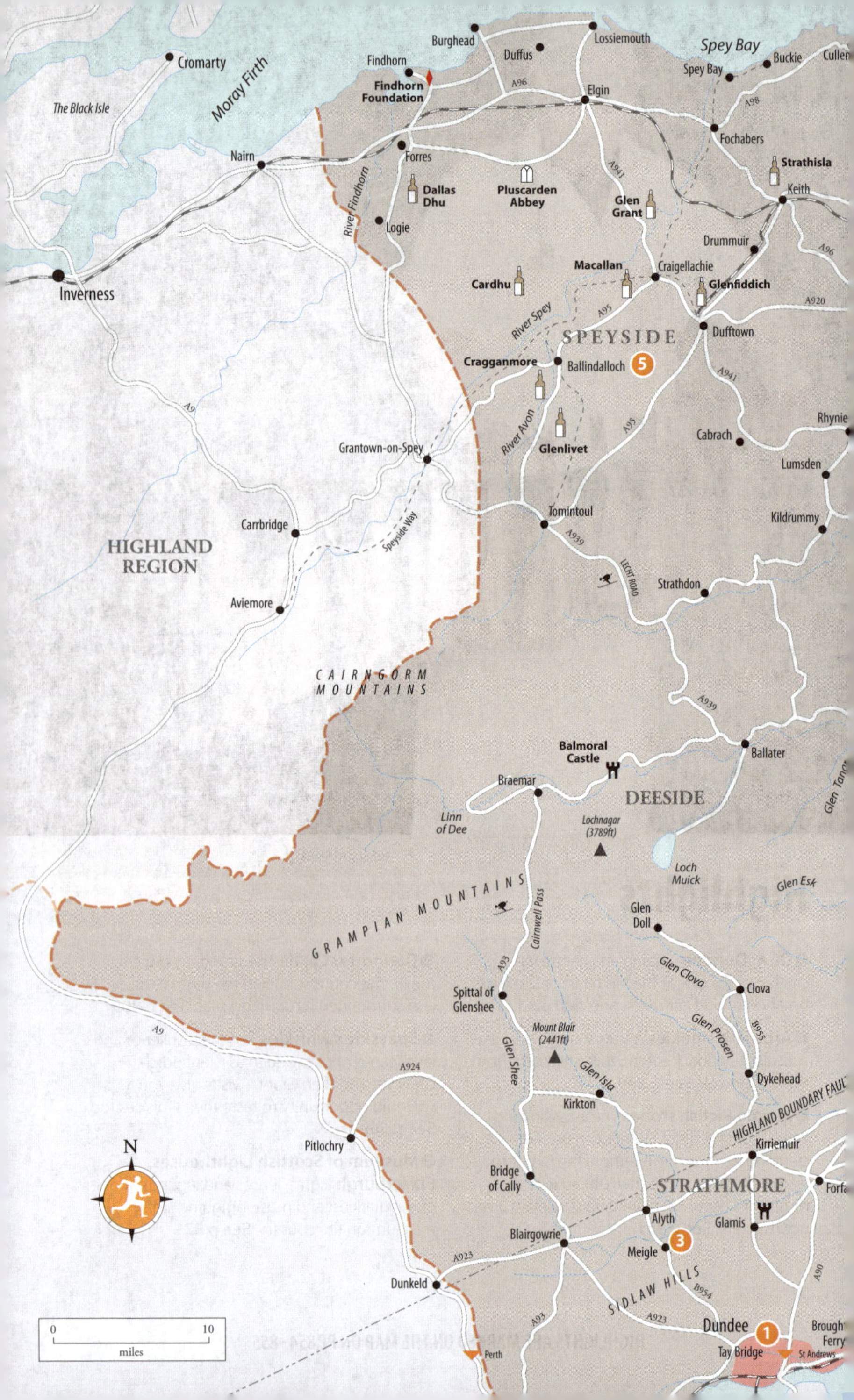
Cromarty
Moray Firth
The Black Isle
Inverness
Nairn
Burghead
Findhorn
Findhorn Foundation
Duffus
Lossiemouth
Spey Bay
Spey Bay
Buckie
Cullen
A96
Elgin
A98
Fochabers
Forres
Dallas Dhu
Pluscarden Abbey
Strathisla
Keith
A941
Glen Grant
River Findhorn
Logie
Drummuir
A96
Macallan
Craigellachie
Glenfiddich
Cardhu
A920
A95
River Spey
SPEYSIDE
Dufftown
Cragganmore
Ballindalloch
5
A941
A9
Rhynie
A95
River Avon
Glenlivet
Cabrach
Grantown-on-Spey
Lumsden
Tomintoul
Carrbridge
Speyside Way
Kildrummy
A939
HIGHLAND REGION
LECHT ROAD
Strathdon
Aviemore
CAIRNGORM MOUNTAINS
A939
Balmoral Castle
Ballater
Braemar
DEESIDE
Glen Tanar
Linn of Dee
Lochnagar (3789ft)
Loch Muick
GRAMPIAN MOUNTAINS
Glen Esk
Cairnwell Pass
Glen Doll
Glen Clova
A93
Clova
Spittal of Glenshee
Glen Prosen
B955
Mount Blair (2441ft)
A9
Glen Shee
A924
Glen Isla
Dykehead
Kirkton
HIGHLAND BOUNDARY FAULT
Pitlochry
Kirriemuir
N
Bridge of Cally
STRATHMORE
Forfar
Alyth
Glamis
Blairgowrie
3
Meigle
A923
SIDLAW HILLS
B954
A90
Dunkeld
A923
A93
Dundee
1
Broughty Ferry
0
10
miles
Perth
Tay Bridge
St Andrews

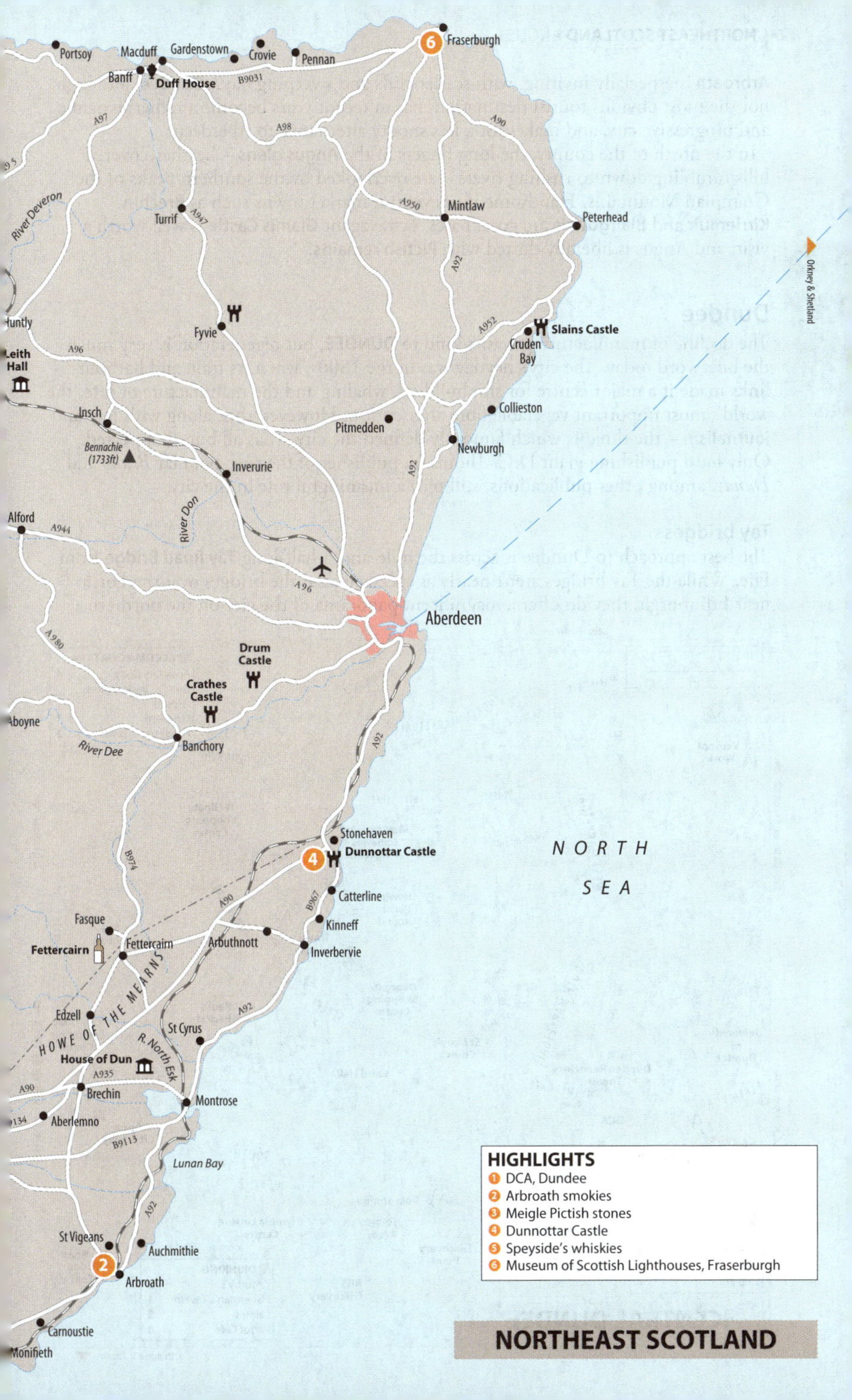
Fraserburgh
Portsoy
Macduff
Gardenstown
Crovie
Pennan
Banff
Duff House
B9031
A97
A98
A90
River Deveron
Turrif
A947
A950
Mintlaw
Peterhead
A92
Orkney & Shetland
Huntly
Fyvie
A952
Slains Castle
Cruden Bay
Leith Hall
A96
Collieston
Insch
Pitmedden
Newburgh
Bennachie (1733ft)
Inverurie
River Don
Alford
A944
A96
Aberdeen
A980
Drum Castle
Crathes Castle
Aboyne
River Dee
Banchory
Stonehaven
Dunnottar Castle
NORTH SEA
B974
Catterline
B967
A90
Fasque
Kinneff
Fettercairn
Fettercairn
Arbuthnott
Inverbervie
HOWE OF THE MEARNS
Edzell
A92
St Cyrus
R. North Esk
House of Dun
A935
A90
Brechin
Montrose
Aberlemno
B9113
Lunan Bay
A92
St Vigeans
Auchmithie
Arbroath
Carnoustie
Monifieth
HIGHLIGHTS
1 DCA, Dundee
2 Arbroath smokies
3 Meigle Pictish stones
4 Dunnottar Castle
5 Speyside's whiskies
6 Museum of Scottish Lighthouses, Fraserburgh
NORTHEAST SCOTLAND

Arbroath is especially inviting, with scarlet cliffs and sweeping bays. **Dundee**, although not the most obvious tourist destination, has in recent years become a rather dynamic and progressive city, and makes for a less snooty alternative to Aberdeen.

In the north of the county, the long fingers of the **Angus glens** – heather-covered hills tumbling down to rushing rivers – are overlooked by the southern peaks of the Grampian Mountains. Handsome if uneventful market towns such as **Brechin**, **Kirriemuir** and **Blairgowrie** are good bases, extravagant **Glamis Castle** is well worth a visit, and Angus is liberally dotted with **Pictish remains**.

Dundee

The decline of manufacturing wasn't kind to **DUNDEE**, but regeneration is very much the buzzword today. The city's heyday was in the 1800s, when its train and harbour links made it a major centre for shipbuilding, whaling and the manufacture of **jute**, the world's most important vegetable fibre after cotton. However, this, along with jam and **journalism** – the three Js which famously defined the city – has all but disappeared. Only local publishing giant D.C. Thomson, publisher of the ever-popular *Beano* and *Dandy*, among other publications, still play a meaningful role in the city.

Tay bridges

The best approach to Dundee is across the mile-and-a-half-long **Tay Road Bridge** from Fife. While the Tay bridges aren't nearly as spectacular as the bridges over the Forth near Edinburgh, they do offer a magnificent panorama of the city on the northern

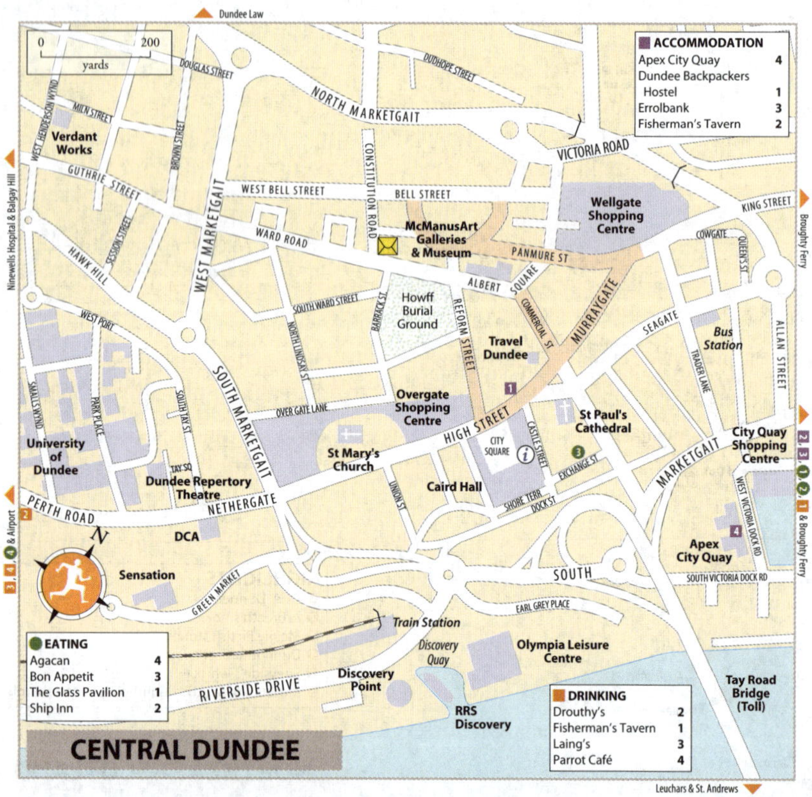

bank of the firth. The bridge, opened in 1966, has a central walkway for pedestrians and a £1 toll for cars. Running parallel half a mile upstream is the **Tay Rail Bridge**, opened in 1887 to replace the spindly structure that collapsed in a storm in December 1879 just eighteen months after it was built, killing the crew and 75 passengers on a train passing over the bridge at the time.

City centre

Dundee's city centre, dominated by large shopping malls filled with chain stores, is focused on attractive, pedestrianized **City Square**, a couple of hundred yards north of the Tay. Where Reform Street meets City Square, look out for a couple of statues to Dundee heroes: **Desperate Dan** and **Minnie the Minx**, both from the *Dandy* comic, which is produced a few hundred yards away in the D.C. Thomson building on Albert Square.

McManus Art Galleries and Museum

Albert Square • Mon–Sat 10am–5pm, Sun 12.30–4.30pm • Free • Ⓣ 01382 307200, Ⓦ www.mcmanus.co.uk

The **McManus Art Galleries and Museum**, Dundee's most impressive Victorian structure, is in the heart of the city. Recently reopened after a major restoration, this is an unmissable stop for art lovers. The ground-floor rooms explore the nature of museums, the surrounding natural landscape and the making of modern Dundee, while upstairs an impressive collection by masters including Rossetti and Henry Raeburn cover the curved red walls of the splendid Victoria gallery. The rest of this floor is equally engrossing, holding an eclectic ethnographic collection, work by the Scottish Colourists, historic and modern ceramics, and a number of fine art acquisitions including contemporary photography. The museum's bright **café** is a good pit-stop, especially on a sunny day when you can sit on the terrace outside.

Verdant Works

West Henderson Wynd, Blackness • April–Oct Mon–Sat 10am–6pm, Sun 11am–6pm; Nov–March Wed–Sat 10.30am–4.30pm, Sun 11am–4.30pm • £7.25, joint ticket with Discovery Point £12 • Ⓣ 01382 309060, Ⓦ www.rrsdiscovery.com

Ten minutes' walk west of the McManus, the award-winning **Verdant Works** tells the story of jute from its harvesting in India to its arrival in Dundee on clipper ships. The museum, set in an old jute mill, makes a lively attempt to re-create the turn-of-the-century factory floor, the highlight being the chance to watch jute being processed on fully operational quarter-size machines originally used for training workers.

The Cultural Quarter

Immediately west of the city centre, High Street becomes Nethergate and passes into what has been dubbed, with some justification, Dundee's "**Cultural Quarter**". As well as the university and the highly respected **Rep Theatre**, the area is also home to the best concentration of pubs and cafés in the city.

DCA

152 Nethergate • Mon–Sat 10.30am–midnight, Sun noon–midnight **Galleries** Tues–Sat 10.30am–5.30pm, until 8.30pm Thurs, Sun noon–5.30pm • Ⓣ 01382 909900, Ⓦ dca.org.uk

The hip and exciting **DCA**, or Dundee Contemporary Arts, is a stunningly designed five-floor complex which incorporates galleries, a print studio, a classy design shop and an airy café-bar. The centre, opened in 1999, was designed by Richard Murphy, who converted an old brick garage and car showroom into an inspiring new space, given energy and confidence by its bright, sleek interior and distinctive ship-like exterior. It's worth visiting for the stimulating temporary and touring exhibitions of contemporary art, as well as an eclectic programme of art-house films and cult classics.

Discovery Point

Discovery Quay • April–Oct Mon–Sat 10am–6pm, Sun 11am–6pm; Nov–March Mon–Sat 10am–5pm, Sun 11am–5pm • £6.95, joint ticket with Verdant Works £11.25 • ☎ 01382 309060, Ⓦ rrsdiscovery.com

Just south of the city centre, at the water's edge alongside the Tay Road Bridge, the domed **Discovery Point** is an impressive development centring on the Royal Research Ship *Discovery*. Something of an icon for Dundee's renaissance, *Discovery* is a three-mast steam-assisted vessel built in Dundee in 1901 to take Captain Robert Falcon Scott on his polar expeditions. A combination of brute strength and elegance, she has been beautifully restored, with polished wood panels and brass trimmings giving scant indication of the privations suffered by the crew.

ARRIVAL AND INFORMATION — DUNDEE

By plane Dundee Airport is just west of the city centre, with flights from London City (Mon–Fri 4 daily, Sat 1 daily, Sun 2 daily; 1hr 25min), Birmingham, Belfast and Jersey.

By train Taybridge Station (☎ 0845 748 4950) is on South Union St about 300yds south of the city centre near the river.

Destinations Aberdeen (every 30min; 1hr 15min); Arbroath (every 30min; 20min); Edinburgh (every 30min–1hr; 1hr 15min); Glasgow (every 30min–1hr; 1hr 30min); Montrose (every 30min–1hr; 30min).

By bus Long-distance buses arrive at the Seagate bus station, a couple of hundred yards east of the centre. Local buses leave from High St or nearby Union St (☎ 01382 201121).

Destinations Aberdeen (hourly; 1hr 20min); Arbroath (hourly; 50min); Blairgowrie (7 daily; 50min); Forfar (hourly; 30min); Glamis (5 daily; 35min); Kirriemuir (5 daily; 55min); Meigle (hourly; 40min); Montrose (hourly; 1hr 10min).

Travel information Travel Dundee Travel Centre, in the Forum Centre, 92 Commercial St (Ⓦ traveldundee.co.uk).

Tourist office 21 Castle St (June–Aug daily; Sept–May Mon–Sat; ☎ 01382 527527, Ⓦ angusanddundee.co.uk).

ACCOMMODATION

Dundee accommodation isn't plentiful, but it is comparatively inexpensive and there's a decent backpacker hostel. You'll find plenty of rooms out by the suburb of **Broughty Ferry**, a 20min bus ride away.

Apex City Quay Hotel West Victoria Dock Rd ☎ 01382 202404, Ⓦ apexhotels.co.uk. Large, sleek and modern hotel that stands out among the new developments of the dockland area, incorporating a spa, swimming pool and restaurant. £100

Dundee Backpackers Hostel 71 High St ☎ 01382 224646, Ⓦ hoppo.com. Dundee's only hostel, with ninety beds in a building dating back to 1560. £15

Errolbank 9 Dalgleish Rd ☎ 01382 462118, Ⓦ errolbank-guesthouse.com. Friendly Victorian villa with clean bright rooms and good views of the Tay. Hearty Scottish breakfast. £50

Fisherman's Tavern 10–16 Fort St, Broughty Ferry ☎ 01382 775941, Ⓦ fishermanstavern.co.uk. Just off the shore in a busy traditional cottage, with neat contemporary rooms, mostly en suite, above a cosy and popular traditional pub with a roaring fire. Seafood and real ales a speciality – try the Arbroath Smokie Pie. £74

EATING

The **west end** of Dundee, around the main university campus and Perth Road, is the best area for eating and drinking. The suburb of **Broughty Ferry** is a pleasant alternative, with a good selection of pubs and restaurants that get particularly busy on summer evenings.

Agacan 113 Perth Rd ☎ 01382 644227. Tiny Turkish restaurant with a colourful exterior and rough-hewn walls; they serve up decent and cheap kebabs and stuffed pittas, and also do takeaways. Mon–Thurs & Sun 12.30–10.30pm, Fri & Sat 12.30–11pm.

Bon Appetit 22–26 Exchange St ☎ 01382 809000, Ⓦ bonappetit-dundee.com. Probably Dundee's most reliable (if not necessarily glamorous) spot for well-sourced, confidently cooked food. Friendly service and tasty, good-value French cuisine; mains around £16. Mon–Thurs noon–2pm & 5.30–9.30pm, Fri & Sat noon–2pm & 6–10.30pm.

The Glass Pavilion The Esplanade, Broughty Ferry ☎ 01382 732738, Ⓦ theglasspavilion.co.uk. Dramatic, glass-fronted former (1930s) bathing shelter with Art Deco styling serving delicious home baking, healthy light meals (mains around £15) and a sumptuous traditional high tea (5–7pm; £12.95). Tues–Sun 9am–10pm; Mon closes after lunch.

Parrot Café 91 Perth Rd ☎ 01382 206277. Art on the walls, and inexpensive home-made soups, sarnies and cakes on the tables in this traditional wee café. Tues–Fri 10am–5pm, Sat 10am–4.30pm.

DRINKING

Drouthy's 142 Perth Rd 01382 202187, fullerthomson.com/eating-and-drinking/drouthy-neebors. Revamped and glamourized studenty pub with regular live music: rock, jazz and Scottish. Daily noon–late.

Laing's 8 Roseangle, off Perth Rd 01382 228250, laingsbar.co.uk. Packed on warm summer nights, thanks to its beer garden and great river views. Lively student haunt, with regular footie screenings. Daily noon–late.

Ship Inn 121 Fisher St, Broughty Ferry 01382 779176, theshipinn-broughtyferry.co.uk. A narrow pub with a warm atmosphere and nautical feel right on the waterfront with good views over the Tay. Good seafood dishes with fine selection of beers. Mon–Sat 11am–midnight, Sun 12.30pm–midnight.

ENTERTAINMENT

DCA 152 Nethergate 01382 909900, dca.org.uk. The DCA has two comfy auditoriums showing a range of foreign and art-house movies alongside more challenging mainstream releases.

Dundee Repertory Theatre Tay Square 01382 223530, dundeereptheatre.co.uk. Right at the heart of the Cultural Quarter on Tay Square, north of Nethergate, is the prodigious rep, home to an indigenously produced contemporary theatre and the only permanent repertory company in Scotland.

DIRECTORY

Hospital Ninewells Hospital in the west of the city has an Accident and Emergency department (01382 660111).

Police Tayside Police HQ, West Bell St (01382 223200).

Post office 4 Meadowside (Mon–Fri 9am–5.30pm, Sat 9am–12.30pm).

The Angus coast

Two roads link Dundee to Aberdeen and the northeast coast of Scotland. By far the more pleasant option is the slightly longer A92 coast road, which joins the inland A90 at Stonehaven, just south of Aberdeen. Intercity **buses** follow both roads, while the coast-hugging train line from Dundee is one of the most picturesque in Scotland, passing attractive beaches and impressive cliffs, and stopping in the old seaports of **Arbroath** and **Montrose**.

Arbroath

Since it was settled in the twelfth century, local fishermen have been landing their catches at **ARBROATH**, about fifteen miles northeast of Dundee. The town's most famous product is the **Arbroath smokie** – line-caught haddock, smoke-cured over smouldering oak chips and still made here in a number of family-run smokehouses tucked in around the harbour. One of the most approachable and atmospheric is **M&M Spink's** tiny whitewashed premises at 10 Marketgate (01241 875287, arbroathsmokies.co.uk); chef and cookery writer Rick Stein described the fish here, warm from the smoke, as "a world-class delicacy".

Arbroath Abbey

Abbey St • Daily: April–Sept 9.30am–5.30pm; Oct–March 9.30am–4.30pm • HS • £4.50 • 01241 878756

The town's real glory days came with the completion in 1233 of **Arbroath Abbey**, whose rose-pink sandstone ruins were described by Dr Johnson as "fragments of magnificence". Founded in 1178 but not granted abbey status until 1285, it was the scene of one of the most significant events in Scotland's history when, on April 6, 1320,

TOP 5 CASTLES AND ABBEYS

Arbroath Abbey See p.859
Crathes Castle See p.867
Dunnottar Castle See p.865
Glamis Castle See p.862
Pluscarden Abbey See p.872

a group of Scottish barons drew up the **Declaration of Arbroath**, asking the pope to reverse his excommunication of Robert the Bruce and recognize him as king of a Scottish nation independent from England. The wonderfully resonant language of the document still makes for a stirring expression of Scottish nationhood: "For so long as one hundred of us remain alive, we will never in any degree be subject to the dominion of the English, since it is not for glory, riches or honour that we do fight, but for freedom alone, which no honest man loses but with his life." It was duly dispatched to Pope John XXII in Avignon, who in 1324 agreed to Robert's claim. The **visitor centre** at the Abbey Street entrance offers in-depth background on these events and other aspects of the history of the building.

ARRIVAL AND INFORMATION — ARBROATH

By train The train station is on Keptie St in the centre of town.

By bus Buses stop on Catherine St, near the train station.

Tourist office Fishmarket Quay in the revamped harbour area (April, May & Sept Mon–Fri 9am–5pm, Sat 10am–5pm; June–Aug Mon–Sat 9.30am–5.30pm, July–Aug also Sun 10am–3pm; Oct–March Mon–Fri 9am–5pm, Sat 10am–3pm; T 01241 872609).

ACCOMMODATION

★ **Old Vicarage** 2 Seaton Rd T 01241 430475, W theoldvicaragebandb.co.uk. The central and friendly Old Vicarage offers chintzy en-suite rooms and a breakfast table that includes smokies, a freshly baked loaf and home-made preserves. **£80**

Montrose and around

A seaport and market town since the thirteenth century, **MONTROSE** sits on the edge of a virtually landlocked two-mile-square lagoon of mud known as the Basin. It's a great little town to visit, with a pleasant old centre and an interesting **museum**.

Montrose Basin Wildlife Centre

A mile west of Montrose along the A92 • Mid-March to mid-Nov daily 10.30am–5pm; mid-Nov to mid-March Fri–Sun 10.30am–4pm • £3 • W montrosebasin.org.uk

On the south side of the Basin, the **Montrose Basin Wildlife Centre** has binoculars, high-powered telescopes, bird hides and remote-control video cameras. In addition, the centre's resident ranger leads regular guided walks around the reserve where you can spot geese, swans and wading birds.

The House of Dun

Four miles west of Montrose • April–June & Sept–Oct Wed–Sun 12.30–5.30pm; July & Aug daily 11.30am–5.30pm • NTS • £8 • Accessible on the hourly Montrose–Brechin Strathtay Scottish bus #30; ask the driver to let you off outside

Across the Basin, west of Montrose, the Palladian **House of Dun,** crammed full of period furniture and objets d'art was built in 1730 for David Erskine, Laird of Dun, to designs by William Adam. Inside, the ornate relief plasterwork is the most impressive feature, extravagantly emblazoned with Jacobite symbolism. The buildings in the courtyard – a hen house, gamekeeper's workshop and potting shed – have been renovated, and include a tearoom and a craft shop. Bikes can be hired from the shop.

ARRIVAL AND DEPARTURE — MONTROSE

Most **buses** stop on High St, while the **train** station lies a block back on Western Rd.

ACCOMMODATION

Lunan Lodge Lunan T 01241 830679, W lunanlodge.co.uk. This Angus gem is just south of Montrose by Inverkeilor near the sweep of Lunan Bay. The friendly owners of the house, which is part eighteenth-century, will pick you up from Montrose or Arbroath train stations. In addition to a gargantuan breakfast they can rustle up a picnic lunch or hearty dinner. **£70**

The Angus Glens and around

Immediately north of Dundee, the low-lying Sidlaw Hills divide the city from the rich agricultural region of **Strathmore**, whose string of tidy market towns lies on a fertile strip along the southernmost edge of the heather-covered lower slopes of the Grampian Mountains. These towns act as gateways to the **Angus glens** (Ⓦangusglens.co.uk), a series of tranquil valleys penetrated by singletrack roads and offering some of the most rugged and majestic landscapes in northeast Scotland. It's a rain-swept, wind-blown, sparsely populated area, whose roads become impassable with the first snows, sometimes as early as October, and where the summers see clouds of ferocious midges. The most useful road through the glens is the A93, which cuts through **Glen Shee**, linking Blairgowrie to Braemar on Deeside (see p.868). It's pretty dramatic stuff, threading its way over Britain's highest main road, the **Cairnwell Pass** (2199ft).

Blairgowrie

The upper reaches of **Glen Shee**, the most dramatic and best known of the Angus glens, are dominated by its **ski fields**, ranged over four mountains above the Cairnwell mountain pass. To get to Glen Shee from the south you'll pass through the well-heeled little town of **BLAIRGOWRIE**, set among raspberry fields on the glen's southernmost tip and a good place to pick up information and plan your activities.

INFORMATION — BLAIRGOWRIE

Tourist office On the high side of Wellmeadow (April–June & Sept–Oct Mon–Sat 10am–4pm, Sun 10am–2pm; July & Aug Mon–Sat 9.30am–5.30pm, Sun 10.30am–3.30pm; Nov–March Tues–Sat 10am–3pm; Ⓣ01250 872960, Ⓦperthshire.co.uk).

ACCOMMODATION AND EATING

Cargills Lower Mill St Ⓣ01250 876735, Ⓦcargillsbistro.com. Family-run café serving inexpensive formal meals and civilized coffee and cakes, plus breakfast from 10.30am. There are menus for vegetarians and kids. Daily 10.30am–9pm.

Heathpark House Coupar Angus Rd Ⓣ01250 870700, Ⓦheathparkhouse.com. One of a number of Blairgowrie's grand houses offering B&B: the impressive Victorian villa has spacious gardens. **£75**

West Freuchies Kirkton of Glenisla Ⓣ01575 582716, Ⓦglenisla-westfreuchies.co.uk. Airy and comfortable rooms, with hiking, horse-riding, birdwatching, angling and cycling, all on the doorstep. **£64**

Meigle Museum

Fifteen miles north of Dundee on the B954 • April–Sept daily 9.30am–6.30pm • HS • £2.20 • Ⓣ01828 640612

The tiny settlement of **MEIGLE** is home to Scotland's most important collection of early Christian and **Pictish inscribed stones**. The exact meaning and purpose of the stones and their enigmatic symbols is obscure, as is the reason why so many of them were found here. The most likely theory is that Meigle was once an important ecclesiastical centre that attracted secular burials of prominent Picts. Housed in a modest former

SKIING AT GLEN SHEE

Scotland's **ski resorts** make for a fun day out for anyone from beginners to experienced skiers and, given that **Glen Shee** is both the most extensive and the most accessible of Scotland's ski areas, just over two hours from both Glasgow and Edinburgh, it's as good an introduction as any to the sport in Scotland.

For information, contact Ski Glenshee (Ⓣ013397 41320, Ⓦski-glenshee.co.uk), which also offers ski rental and lessons. **Ski rental** starts at around £16 a day, and a 90min lesson is around £15. **Lift passes** cost £24 per day or £96 for a five-day (Mon–Fri) ticket. For the latest snow and **weather conditions**, phone the centre itself or check out the Ski Scotland website (Ⓦski.visitscotland.com). For **cross-country** skiing, there are some good touring areas in the vicinity; contact Braemar Mountain Sports (Ⓣ013397 41242, Ⓦbraemarmountainsports.com) for information and equipment rental.

schoolhouse, the **Meigle Museum** displays some thirty pieces dating from the seventh to the tenth centuries, all found in and around the nearby churchyard. The majority are either gravestones that would have lain flat, or cross slabs inscribed with the sign of the cross, usually standing. Most impressive is the 7ft-tall great cross slab, said to be the gravestone of Guinevere, wife of King Arthur.

Glen Isla

Three miles north of Meigle is **Alyth**, near which, legend has it, Guinevere was held captive by Mordred. The sleepy village lies at the south end of **Glen Isla**, which runs parallel to Glen Shee and is linked to it by the A926. Ten miles or so up the glen is the tiny hamlet of **KIRKTON OF GLENISLA**.

ACCOMMODATION AND EATING — GLEN ISLA

Glenisla Hotel Kirkton of Glenisla ⓣ01575 582223, ⓦglenisla-hotel.com. Cosy hotel that's great for classy home-made bar food and convivial drinking. Rooms are comfy, though on the small side; they advise on which ones get noisy when the pub is full. **£60**

Glamis Castle

Daily: Mid-March to Oct 10am–6pm; Nov & Dec 11am–5pm • £7.50, grounds only £3.70 • ⓣ01307 840393, ⓦglamis-castle.co.uk

The wondrously over-the-top, five-storey pink-sandstone **Glamis Castle** is set in an extensive landscaped park complete with highland cattle and pheasants beside the picturesque village of **GLAMIS** (pronounced "glahms"). One of Scotland's most famous castles, featuring in *Macbeth* and with **royal connections** (as the childhood home of the late Queen Mother and birthplace of the late Princess Margaret), it's an essential stop on every bus tour of Scotland.

Obligatory guided tours take in the fifteenth-century **crypt**, where the 12ft-thick walls enclose a haunted "lost" room, the family **chapel** and **Duncan's Hall**, a fifteenth-century guardroom, the – inaccurate – setting for Duncan's murder by Macbeth. Glamis' **grounds,** including the Italian Gardens, are worth a few hours in their own right, with verdant walks out to Earl John's Bridge and through the woodland.

Kirriemuir

The sandstone town of **KIRRIEMUIR**, known locally as Kirrie, is set on a hill six miles northwest of Forfar on the cusp of **glens Clova** and **Prosen**. The main cluster of streets have all the appeal of an old film set, with their old-fashioned bars, tiled butcher's shop, tartan outlets and haberdasheries somehow managing to avoid being contrived and quaint – although the re-cobbling of the town centre around a twee statue of Peter Pan undermines this somewhat.

ACCOMMODATION — KIRRIEMUIR

Airlie Arms St Malcolm's Wynd ⓣ01575 572847, ⓦtheairliearms.co.uk. A reasonably priced and attractive small hotel. Rooms are modern and spacious and there's even a small gym. **£75**

J.M. BARRIE IN KIRRIE

The presence of a statue of Peter Pan in Kirrie is justified, since the town was the birthplace of his creator, **J.M. Barrie (1860–1937)**. A local handloom-weaver's son, Barrie first came to notice with his series of novels about "Thrums", a village based on his home town, and he wrote the story of *Peter Pan*, the little boy who never grew up, in 1904 – some say as a response to an upbringing dominated by the memory of his older brother, who died as a child. **Barrie's birthplace**, a plain little whitewashed cottage at 9 Brechin Rd (April–June & Sept Mon–Wed & Sat noon–5pm, Sun 1–5pm; July & Aug Mon–Sat 11am–5pm, Sun 1–5pm; £5; NTS), has been opened up as a visitor attraction, with a series of small rooms decorated as they would have been during the author's childhood, as well as displays about his life and works.

Glen Clova/Glen Doll

With its stunning cliffs, heather slopes and valley meadows, **Glen Clova** – which in the north becomes **Glen Doll** – is one of the loveliest of the Angus glens. Although it can get unpleasantly congested in peak season, the area is still remote enough to enable you to lose the crowds with little effort. Wildlife is abundant, with deer on the mountains, wild hare and even grouse and the occasional buzzard. The meadow flowers on the valley floor and arctic plants (including great splashes of white and purple saxifrage) on the rocks also make it something of a botanist's paradise.

ACCOMMODATION AND EATING — GLEN CLOVA

Glen Clova Hotel Glen Clova ⓣ 01575 550350, ⓦ clova.com. The hamlet of Clova consists of little more than this hearty place, which also runs a bunkhouse (rates include B&B) and a private fishing loch. The restaurant serves up traditional Scottish food, such as venison casserole and haggis. Dorm £18, double £90

Aberdeenshire and Moray

Aberdeenshire and Moray cover a large chunk of northern Scotland – some 3500 square miles, much of it open and varied country dotted with historic and archeological sights, from neat NTS properties and eerie prehistoric standing stones to quiet kirkyards and a rash of dramatic castles. Geographically, the counties break down into two distinct areas: the **hinterland**, once barren and now a patchwork of fertile farms, rising towards high mountains, sparkling rivers and gentle valleys; and the **coast**, a classic stretch of rocky cliffs, remote fishing villages and long, sandy beaches.

For visitors, the large city of **Aberdeen** is the obvious focal point of the region, and while it's not a place to keep you engrossed for long, it does have some intriguing architecture, attractive museums and a lively social scene. From here, it's a short hop west to **Deeside**, visited annually by the Royal Family, where the trim villages of **Ballater** and **Braemar** act as a gateway to the spectacular Cairngorms National Park, which covers much of the upland areas in the west of this region. Further north, the "Malt Whisky Country" of **Speyside** has less impressive scenery but numerous whisky distilleries, while the **coast** beyond features dramatic cliffs and long beaches punctuated by picturesque fishing villages.

Aberdeen and around

The third-largest city in Scotland, **ABERDEEN,** commonly known as the "Granite City", lies 120 miles northeast of Edinburgh on the banks of the rivers Dee and Don, smack in the middle of the northeast coast. Based around a working harbour, it's a place that people either love or hate. Certainly, while some extol the many tones and colours of Aberdeen's **granite** buildings, others see only uniform grey and find the city grim and cold. The weather doesn't help: Aberdeen lies on a latitude north of Moscow and the cutting wind and driving rain (even if it does transform the buildings into sparkling silver) can be tiresome.

In the twelfth century, Alexander I noted "Aberdon" as one of his principal towns, and by the thirteenth century it had become a centre for **trade and fishing**. A century or so later Bishop Elphinstone founded the Catholic university in the area north of town known today as **Old Aberdeen**, while the rest of the city developed as a mercantile centre and important port. By the mid-twentieth century, Aberdeen's traditional industries were in decline, but the discovery of **oil** in the North Sea transformed the place from a depressed port into a boom town. Since the 1970s, oil has made Aberdeen a hugely wealthy and self-confident place. Despite (or perhaps because of) this, it can sometimes feel like a soulless city, existing mainly as a departure point for the transient population who live on the oil platforms out to sea.

22

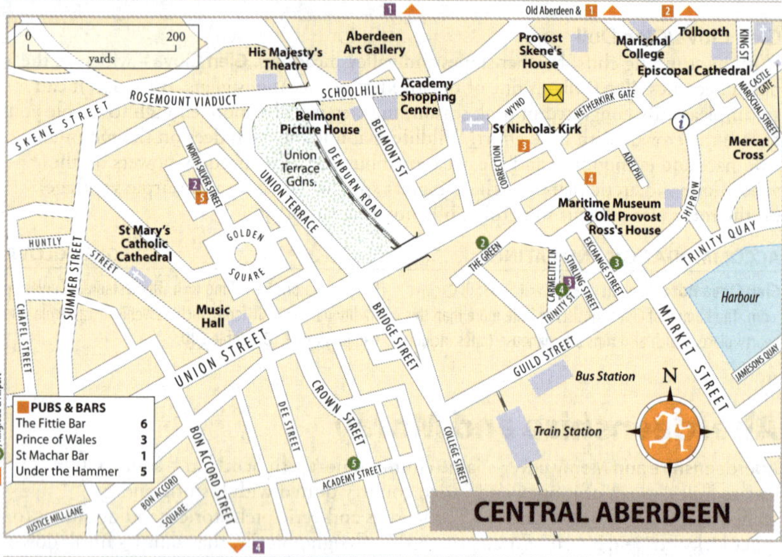

CAFÉS & RESTAURANTS

Ashvale	6	Foyer	5
Café 52	2	Musa	3
Carmelite	4	Silver Darling	1

ACCOMMODATION

Carmelite	3	Ferryhill House	4
Crombie Johnston Halls	1	Globe Inn	2

CLUBS AND LIVE MUSIC

Lemon Tree	2
The Tunnels	4

Castlegate

Any exploration of the **city centre** should begin at the open, cobbled **Castlegate**, where Aberdeen's long-gone castle once stood. At its centre is the late seventeenth-century **Mercat Cross**, carved with a unique gallery of Stewart sovereigns alongside some fierce gargoyles. The view up gently rising Union Street – a jumble of grey spires, turrets and jostling double-decker buses – is quintessential Aberdeen.

The Aberdeen Art Gallery

Schoolhill • Tues–Sat 10am–5pm, Sun 2–5pm • Free • T 01224 52370, W aagm.co.uk

Aberdeen's engrossing **Art Gallery**, purpose-built in 1884, is entered via the airy **Centre Court**. Barbara Hepworth's central fountain dominates, while nearby are a number of pieces of contemporary art, with British work to the fore. The **Memorial Court**, a white-walled circular room beneath a skylit dome, serves as the city's principal war memorial and houses the Lord Provost's book of condolence for the 167 people who died in the 1988 Piper Alpha oil rig disaster. The **upstairs** rooms house the main body of the gallery's painting collection. This includes a superb collection of Victorian narrative art, some decent twentieth-century British painting and a collection of Impressionist art, including works by Boudin, Courbet, Sisley, Monet, Pissarro and Renoir.

Maritime Museum

Shiprow • Mon–Sat 10am–5pm, Sun noon–3pm • Free • T 01224 337700, W aagm.co.uk

Just off cobbled Shiprow, peering towards the harbour through a striking glass facade, the engrossing **Maritime Museum** combines a modern, airy museum with the aged, labyrinthine corridors of **Provost Ross's House**. Just inside the entrance you'll see a blackboard updated daily with the price of a barrel of crude oil, and suspended above the foyer, visible from five different levels, is a spectacular 27ft-high model of an oil rig. The older industries of herring fishing, whaling, shipbuilding and lighthouses also have their place, with well-designed displays, many drawing heavily on personal reminiscences.

Old Aberdeen

An independent burgh until 1891, tranquil **Old Aberdeen**, a ten-minute ride north of the city centre on bus #20 from Marischal College, has maintained a village-like identity. Dominated by **King's College** and **St Machar's Cathedral**, its medieval cobbled streets, wynds and little lanes are beautifully preserved.

King's College Chapel

High St • Mon–Fri 8am–4pm • Free • ⓦ abdn.ac.uk/chaplaincy/chapel/

King's College Chapel, the first and finest of the college buildings was completed in 1495, with a chunky Renaissance spire. The highlights of the interior, which, unusually, has no central aisle, are the ribbed arched wooden ceiling and the rare and lovely examples of medieval Scottish woodcarving in the screen and the stalls.

St Machar's Cathedral

18 Chanonry • Daily 9am–5pm, except during services • Free • ⓣ 01224 485988, ⓦ stmachar.com

From King's College, High Street leads a short way north to **St Machar's Cathedral** on the leafy Chanonry, overlooking Seaton Park and the River Don. The site was reputedly founded in 580 AD by Machar, a follower of Columba, when he was sent by the latter to find a grassy platform near the sea, overlooking a river shaped like the crook on a bishop's crozier. This setting fitted the bill perfectly, and the cathedral, a huge fifteenth-century fortified building, became one of the city's first great granite edifices.

The beach

Aberdeen can surely claim to have the best sandy **beach** of all Britain's large cities. Less than a mile east of Union Street is a great two-mile sweep of clean sand, broken by groynes and lined all along with an esplanade, where most of the city's population seems to gather on sunny days. The massive **Beach Leisure Centre** includes flumes and a wave machine, and a ten-minute walk south will take you to sprawling **Codona's amusement park** complete with its new roller coaster, slides and restaurant areas. Further north, most of the beach's hinterland is devoted to golf links.

Dunnottar Castle

Fifteen miles south of Aberdeen, 2 miles south of Stonehaven • Easter–Oct Mon–Sat 9am–6pm, Sun 2–5pm; Oct–Easter Fri–Mon 9am–sunset • £5 • ⓣ 01569 762173, ⓦ dunnottarcastle.co.uk

South of Aberdeen, the A92 and the main train line follow the coast to the pretty little harbour town of **STONEHAVEN**. Two miles south, the stunningly capricious **Dunnottar Castle** is one of Scotland's finest ruined castles, a huge ninth-century fortress set on a three-sided sheer cliff jutting into the sea – a setting striking enough to be chosen as the backdrop for Zeffirelli's movie version of *Hamlet*. Once the principal fortress of the northeast, the ruins are worth a good root around, and there are many dramatic views out to the crashing sea. Bloodstained drama splatters the castle's past – not least in 1297, when the entire English Plantaganet garrison was burned alive here by William Wallace.

ARRIVAL AND INFORMATION — ABERDEEN

By plane Aberdeen's Dyce Airport lies 7 miles northwest of town.

Destinations Kirkwall, Orkney (1 daily; 55min); London Gatwick (min 3 daily; 1hr 35min); London Heathrow (Mon–Fri min 7 daily, Sat–Sun min 2; 1hr 30min); Sumburgh, Shetland (Mon–Fri 5 daily, Sat & Sun 2 daily; 1hr).

By train The main station is on Guild St, in the centre of the city.

22

Destinations Arbroath (every 30min; 1hr); Dundee (every 30min; 1hr 15min); Edinburgh (every 30min–1hr; 2hr 35min); Elgin (Mon–Sat 10 daily, Sun 5 daily; 1hr 30min); Glasgow (hourly; 2hr 35min); Inverness (Mon–Sat 10 daily, Sun 5 daily; 2hr 15min); London (Sun–Fri sleeper service; 10hr); Montrose (every 30min; 45min); Nairn (Mon–Sat 10 daily, Sun 5 daily; 1hr 50min); Stonehaven (every 30min; 15min).

By bus The terminal is beside the train station.

Destinations Ballater (hourly; 1hr 45min); Banff (hourly; 1hr 55min); Braemar (min every 2hr; 2hr 10min); Cullen (hourly; 2hr 30min); Dundee (hourly; 2hr); Elgin (hourly; 3hr 20min); Fraserburgh (hourly; 1hr 30min); Macduff (hourly; 1hr 50min); Stonehaven (every 15min; 50min).

By ferry Aberdeen has links to Lerwick in Shetland and Kirkwall in Orkney, with regular crossings from Jamieson's Quay in the harbour (T 0845 6000449, W northlinkferries .co.uk).

Destinations Kirkwall, Orkney (Thurs, Sat & Sun plus Tues in summer; 6hr); Lerwick, Shetland (daily; 10–12hr overnight).

Tourist office 23 Union St (July & Aug daily; Sept–June Mon–Sat; T 01224 288828).

ACCOMMODATION

Carmelite Stirling St T 01224 589101, W carmelite hotels.com. A boutique hotel fusing trad and modern in a revamped 1820s building. The stylish restaurant serves simple, tasty Scottish-influenced cuisine. **£98**

Crombie Johnston Halls College Bounds, Old Aberdeen T 01224 273444, W abdn.ac.uk/summer _accommodation. Private rooms in the city's best student halls, in one of the most interesting parts of town. Mostly available from early July to Sept, though some year-round accommodation is also available. From **£50**

Ferryhill House 169 Bon Accord St T 01224 590867, W ferryhillhousehotel.co.uk. A mansion set in its own grounds within walking distance of Union St. They serve good-value lunches; there's also a beer garden and a great Malt Room for guests to sample real ales and whisky by a roaring fire. **£70**

Globe Inn 13–15 North Silver St T 01224 624258, W the-globe-inn.co.uk. Easy-going city-centre inn with seven en-suite rooms above a bar that hosts live jazz and blues Fri & Sat. Continental breakfast included. **£75**

EATING

Most of Aberdeen's cafés and restaurants are clustered around **Union** and **Belmont** streets; you'll find them pricier than elsewhere in northeast Scotland.

Ashvale 42–48 Great Western Rd T 01224 596981 W theashvale.co.uk. Diners who finish the "Ashvale Whale", a 1lb cod fillet (£12.45) receive another for free at this renowned chippy and family-oriented restaurant. Daily 11.45am–11pm.

★ **Café 52** 52 The Green T 01224 590094, W cafe52 .net. Cosy, bohemian hangout by day that turns into a hip restaurant by night with Cullen Skink soup, game and vegetarian meals (around £12) among the tasty options. Great seating outside, screened by bamboo, on an attractive quiet street. Mon–Sat noon–midnight, Sun noon–6pm.

Foyer 82a Crown St T 01224 582277, W foyer restaurant.com. A light, bright and stylish restaurant and contemporary art gallery. There are set-menu deals; otherwise mains such as North Sea gurnard with tomato and fennel fondue are around £16. Tues–Sat 11am–11.30pm.

★ **Musa** Exchange St T 01224 571771, W www .musaaberdeen.com/food. Based in an old church and banana warehouse, this good-value café, gallery and music venue has a terrific vibe, with live music and mouthwatering dining: produce for their risottos, fish and meat dishes (from £12) is supplied by small Scottish suppliers. Tues–Sat noon till late.

Silver Darling Pocra Quay, North Pier T 01224 576229, W silverdarling.co.uk. The French owner specializes in delicious, freshly caught seafood at this attractively located restaurant at the harbour in Footdee. Mains from £18.50. Mon–Fri noon–1.30pm & 6.30–9.30pm, Sat 6.30–9.30pm.

DRINKING

The Fittie Bar 18 Wellington St T 01224 582911. You'll find good-value lunches, bearded mariners and a sense of history in this atmospheric pub close to the harbour. Mon–Sat 11am–11pm, Sun 11am–12.30pm.

Prince of Wales 7 St Nicholas Lane T 01224 640597. Opened in 1850, the quintessential Aberdeen pub has a 19ft-long bar and flagstone floor. With fine pub grub, renowned real ales and folk sessions on Sunday evenings, it's often crowded. Daily.

St Machar Bar 97 High St, Old Aberdeen T 01224 483079, W themachar.com. The medieval quarter's only pub, a poky, old-fashioned bar attracting an intriguing mix of King's College students and workers. Mon–Sat 11am–11pm, Sun 12.30–6pm.

Under the Hammer 11 North Silver St ⓣ01224 640253. This snug little basement wine bar has a continental, convivial vibe and is a popular refuge when icy winter winds hit the city. Daily.

NIGHTLIFE AND ENTERTAINMENT

Belmont Picture House 9 Belmont St ⓣ01224 343536, ⓦpicturehouses.co.uk. Art-house cinema showing the more cerebral new releases alongside classic, cult and foreign-language films. There's a comfortable café-bar and some good places nearby on Belmont St for a bite before or after.

His Majesty's Theatre Rosemount Viaduct ⓣ01224 641122, ⓦboxofficeaberdeen.com. The city's main theatre resides in a beautiful Edwardian building, with an extensive programme ranging from serious drama and opera to panto.

Lemon Tree 5 West North St ⓣ01224 642230, ⓦboxofficeaberdeen.com. The fulcrum of the city's arts scene, with a great buzz and regular live music, club nights and comedy, as well as decent theatre.

The Tunnels Carnegies Brae ⓣ01224 211121, ⓦthetunnels.co.uk. One of Aberdeen's most popular live music venues, in the old tunnels beneath Union St. Live bands and a different musical genre every evening, including reggae, hip-hop, ska and Northern Soul.

22

DIRECTORY

Hospital The Royal Infirmary, on Foresterhill, northeast of the town centre, has a 24hr casualty department (ⓣ01224 681818).

Police The main station is on Queen St (ⓣ0845 600 5700); it includes the lost property office.

Post office The central office is in the St Nicholas Centre, between Union St and Upperkirkgate (Mon–Sat 9am–5.30pm).

Deeside

More commonly known as **Royal Deeside**, the land stretching west from Aberdeen along the River Dee revels in its connections with the Royal Family, who have regularly holidayed here, at **Balmoral**, since Queen Victoria bought the estate. Eighty thousand Scots turned out to welcome her on her first visit in 1848, but some weren't so charmed: one local journalist remarked that the area was about to be "desolated by cockneys and other horrible reptiles". Today, most locals are fiercely protective of the royal connection.

Deeside is undoubtedly handsome in a fierce, craggy way, and the royal presence has helped keep a lid on unattractive mass development. The villages strung along the A93, the main route through the area, are well-heeled, with an old-fashioned air, and visitor facilities are first-class. It's an excellent area for **outdoor activities**, too, with hiking routes into the Grampian and Cairngorm mountains, good mountain biking, horseriding and skiing.

Crathes Castle

Fourteen miles west of Aberdeen • Daily: April–Sept 10.30am–5.30pm; Oct 10.30am–4.30pm; Nov–March Wed–Sun 10.30am–3.45pm • NTS • £10

Crathes Castle is a splendid sixteenth-century granite tower house adorned with flourishes such as overhanging turrets, gargoyles and conical roofs. Its thick walls, narrow windows and tiny rooms loaded with heavy old furniture make it all rather claustrophobic, but well worth visiting for some wonderful painted ceilings, either still in their original form or sensitively restored; the earliest dates from 1602. The grounds include an impressive walled garden complete with yew hedges subjected to a spot of topiary.

Aboyne

A dozen or so miles west of Crathes Castle on the A93, **ABOYNE** is a typically well-mannered Deeside village at the mouth of **Glen Tanar**, which runs southwest from here for around ten miles deep into the Grampian hills. The glen, with few steep gradients and some glorious stands of mature Caledonian pine, is ideal for walking, mountain biking or horseriding; the ranger information point two miles into the glen off the B976 has details of suitable routes, while the Glen Tanar Equestrian Centre (T 01339 886448) offers one- and two-hour **horse rides**.

Ballater

22 Ten miles west of Aboyne, the neat and ordered town of **BALLATER** stands attractively hemmed in by the river and fir-covered mountains. It was here that Queen Victoria first arrived in Deeside by train from Aberdeen back in 1848; she wouldn't allow a station to be built any closer to Balmoral, eight miles further west. Although the line has long been closed, the town's rather self-important royalism is much in evidence with oversized "By Appointment" crests sported above the doorways of most businesses.

Ballater is an excellent base for local **walks** and **outdoor activities**. There are numerous hikes from Loch Muik (pronounced "mick"), including the well-worn but strenuous all-day trek up and around Lochnagar (3789ft), the mountain much painted and written about by Prince Charles.

Balmoral Estate

April–July daily 10am–5pm • £9 • T 013397 42534, W balmoralcastle.com

Originally a sixteenth-century tower house built for the powerful Gordon family, **Balmoral Castle** has been a royal residence since 1852. The Royal Family traditionally spend their summer holidays here each August, but despite its fame it can be something of a disappointment even for a dedicated royalist – only the ballroom, an exhibition room and the grounds are open to the public.

INFORMATION — BALLATER

Ballater's **tourist office** is in the renovated (disused) train station (daily: July & Aug 9am–6pm; rest of year 10am–5pm; T 013397 55306).

ACCOMMODATION AND EATING

The Auld Kirk Braemar Rd T 01339 755762, W theauldkirk.co.uk. A restaurant with rooms, serving excellent fresh local produce (2 courses for £28.50) and offering six smart bedrooms. **£110**

Green Inn Restaurant 9 Victoria Rd T 013397 55701, W green-inn.com. This pricey but very good restaurant features locally sourced game; comfortable en-suite rooms are attached. **£80**

Habitat@Ballater Bridge Square T 013397 53752, W habitat-at-ballater.com. Excellent, well-equipped hostel with bunkrooms, family rooms and twins. There's a kitchen/dining room with a wood-burning stove. Dorm **£17**, twin **£45**

Schoolhouse Anderson Rd T 013397 56333, W school-house.eu. Good-quality bunkhouse accommodation and breakfast at this restored Victorian schoolhouse, plus ghost walks and storytelling. **£76**

Braemar

Continuing westwards for another few miles, the road rises to 1100ft above sea level in the upper part of Deeside and the village of **BRAEMAR**, situated where three passes meet. It's an invigorating, outdoor kind of place, well patronized by committed hikers, but probably best known for its Highland Games, the annual **Braemar Gathering**, on the first Saturday of September (W braemargathering.org). Since Queen Victoria's day, successive generations of royals have attended and the world's most famous Highland Games have become rather an overcrowded, overblown event. You're not guaranteed to get in if you just turn up; the website has details of how to book tickets in advance.

INFORMATION — BRAEMAR

Tourist office The Mews, in the middle of the village on Mar Rd (June & Sept daily 9am–5pm; July & Aug daily 9am–6pm; Oct Mon–Sat 9am–5pm, Sun 1–5pm; Nov–May Mon–Sat 10.30am–1.30pm & 2–5pm, Sun 1–4pm; T 013397 41600).

ACCOMMODATION

Clunie Lodge Guest House Clunie Bank Road ⓣ013397 41330, ⓦclunielodge.com. A good B&B in a former manse on the outskirts of town, with lovely views up Clunie Glen. **£60**

Corrie Feragie 21 Glenshee Rd ⓣ01339 741659, ⓦsyha.org.uk. This large SYHA hostel is set in a former shooting lodge, and features a pool table and BBQ area. Closed Nov & Dec. **£16**

Rucksacks 15 Mar Rd ⓣ013397 41517. An easy-going bunkhouse, well-equipped for walkers and backpackers, just behind the Mews complex. Rooms sleep 2 to 10, and there's a sauna, drying room and log fires. From **£12**

EATING AND DRINKING

The Gathering Place Invercauld Rd ⓣ013397 41234, ⓦthe-gathering-place.co.uk. In the heart of the village, *The Gathering Place* is a splendid place for mouthwatering, if pricey, freshly prepared Scottish-based cuisine. Tues–Sat 6–9pm.

Taste Airlie House ⓣ013397 41425, ⓦtaste-braemar.co.uk. A coffee shop and moderately priced contemporary restaurant on the road out to the Linn of Dee – preferable to the large hotels, which tend to be filled with coach parties. Mon & Thurs–Sun 10am–5pm.

Speyside

Strictly speaking, the term **Speyside** refers to the entire region surrounding the River Spey, but to most people the name is synonymous with the **whisky triangle**, stretching from just north of Craigellachie, down towards Tomintoul in the south and east to Huntly. There are more whisky distilleries and famous brands (including Glenfiddich and Glenlivet) concentrated in this small area than in any other part of the country. Running through the heart of the region is the River Spey, whose clean, clear,

THE MALT WHISKY TRAIL

There are eight distilleries on the official **Malt Whisky Trail** (ⓦmaltwhiskytrail.com), a clearly signposted seventy-mile meander around Speyside. All offer a guided tour (some are free, others charge but then give you a voucher that is redeemable against a bottle of whisky from the distillery shop), with a tasting to round it off; if you're driving you'll often be offered a miniature to take away. You could cycle or walk parts of the route, using the Speyside Way (see p.872). The following are selected highlights.

Cardhu B9102 at Knockando. Established more than a century ago, when the founder's wife would raise a red flag to warn crofters if the authorities were on the lookout for their illegal stills. With attractive, pagoda-topped buildings, it sells rich, full-bodied whisky with distinctive peaty flavours. April–June Mon–Fri 10am–5pm; July–Sept Mon–Sat 10am–5pm, Sun noon–4pm; Oct–April Mon–Fri 11am–3pm tours 11am, 1pm & 2pm; £4 including voucher.

Glen Grant Rothes. Well-known, floral whisky aggressively marketed to the younger customer. The highlight here is the attractive Victorian garden, with well-tended lawns, mixed, mature trees, a tumbling waterfall and a hidden whisky safe. Mid-Jan to mid-Dec Mon–Sat 9.30am–5pm, Sun noon–5pm; £3.50 including voucher.

Glenfiddich A941 just north of Dufftown. The biggest and slickest of all the Speyside distilleries, still owned by the same family who founded it in 1887. It's a light, sweet whisky packaged in triangular bottles – unusually, the bottling is still done on the premises and can be seen as part of the tours. Jan to mid-Dec Mon–Sat 9.30am–4.30pm, Sun noon–4.30pm; free.

Glenlivet B9008. A famous name in a lonely hillside setting; the Glenlivet twelve-year-old malt is a floral, fragrant, medium-bodied whisky. This was the first licensed distillery in the Highlands, and the Speyside Way passes through the grounds. April–Oct Mon–Sat 9.30am–4pm, Sun noon–4pm; free.

Speyside Cooperage Craigellachie. An unusual alternative to a distillery tour, but part of the official trail, demonstrating the ancient and skilled art of cooperage. Mon–Fri 9.30am–4pm; £3.30.

Strathisla Keith. A small, old-fashioned distillery claiming to be Scotland's oldest (1786); it's certainly one of the most attractive, with pagoda-shaped buildings and the River Isla rushing by. The malt itself has a rich, almost fruity taste and is pretty rare, but is used as the heart of the better-known Chivas Regal blend. You can get here on the restored Keith & Dufftown Railway (see p.870). April–Oct Mon–Sat 9.30am–4pm, Sun noon–4pm; £5.

fast-flowing waters not only play such a vital part in the whisky industry, but also make it one of Scotland's finest angling locations. At the centre of Speyside, the quiet market town of **Dufftown** and the well-kept nearby villages of **Craigellachie** and **Aberlour** make good bases for a tour of whisky country.

Dufftown and around

The cheery community of **DUFFTOWN**, founded in 1817 by James Duff, the fourth Earl of Fife, proudly proclaims itself "Malt Whisky Capital of the World" with good reason – it produces more of the stuff than any other town in Britain. There are nine distilleries around Dufftown (not all of them still working), as well as a cooperage and a coppersmith; an extended stroll around the outskirts gives a good idea of the density of whisky distilling going on, with glimpses of giant warehouses filled with barrels of the heady liquid, and whiffs of fermenting barley or peat smoke lingering on the breeze.

On the edge of town along the A941 is the town's largest working distillery, **Glenfiddich** (see p.869), as well as the old Dufftown train station, which has been restored by enthusiasts and is now the departure point for the **Keith & Dufftown Railway** (April–Sept Sat & Sun 3 trips daily, June–Aug also runs Fri; 40min; T 01340 821181, W keith-dufftown-railway.co.uk; £9.50 return), which uses restored diesel locomotives to chug through whisky country to Keith, home of the Strathisla distillery (see p.869).

Craigellachie

Four miles north of Dufftown, the small settlement of **CRAIGELLACHIE** (pronounced "Craig-*ell*-ach-ee") sits above the confluence of the sparkling waters of the Fiddich and the Spey, spanned by a beautiful iron bridge built by Thomas Telford in 1815. The main sight here is the **Speyside Cooperage**, which is on Speyside's official Malt Whisky Trail (see p.869).

ARRIVAL AND INFORMATION — DUFFTOWN AND AROUND

By bus Buses connect Dufftown with Aberlour (Mon–Sat hourly; 15min; Sun every 2hr) and Elgin (Mon–Sat hourly; Sun every 2hr; 50min).

Tourist office Dufftown's official tourist office is in the handsome clocktower at the centre of the square (Mon–Sat 10am–1pm & 2–5/5.30pm, Sun 11am–3pm; T 01340 820501); there's also an information and accommodation booking service at The Whisky Shop (T 01340 821097) across the road.

ACCOMMODATION AND EATING

Archiestown Hotel Archiestown by Aberlour, a few miles west of Craigellachie T 01340 810218, W archiestownhotel.co.uk. This pleasant, traditional hotel caters for anglers and outdoor types, and serves good evening meals. **£80**

★ **Green Hall Gallery** 2 Victoria St, Craigellachie T 01340 871010, W aboutscotland.com/greenhall. An extremely welcoming and tasteful B&B attached to a gallery selling woollen goods and crafts. **£70**

Tannochbrae 22 Fife St, Dufftown T 01340 820541, W tannochbrae.co.uk. A pleasant, enthusiastically run B&B in a fine stone terrace with a small restaurant on the ground floor. They offer bike rental. **£70**

The Moray coast

The **coast** of northeast Scotland from Aberdeen to Inverness has a rugged, sometimes bleak fringe with pleasant if undramatic farmland rolling inland. Still, if the weather is good, it's well worth spending a couple of days meandering through the various little fishing villages and along the miles of deserted, unspoilt beaches.

The largest coastal towns are **Peterhead** and **Fraserburgh**, both dominated by sizeable fishing fleets; the latter's **Museum of Scottish Lighthouses** is one of the most attractive small museums in Scotland. Most visitors, however, are more drawn to the quieter spots along the Moray coast, including the charming villages of **Pennan**, **Gardenstown**, **Portsoy** and nearby **Cullen**. The other main attractions are **Duff House** in Banff, a branch of the National Gallery of Scotland; the working abbey at **Pluscarden** by Elgin; and the **Findhorn Foundation**, near Forres.

Museum of Scottish Lighthouses

Kinnaird Head, Stevenson Rd, Fraserburgh • April–June, Sept & Oct Mon–Sat 11am–5pm, Sun noon–5pm; July & Aug Mon–Sat 10am–6pm, Sun 11am–6pm; Nov–March Mon–Sat 11am–4pm, Sun noon–4pm • £5 • T 01346 511022, W lighthousemuseum .org.uk

Large and severe-looking **FRASERBURGH** is home to the excellent **Museum of Scottish Lighthouses.** Here you can see a collection of huge lenses and prisms gathered from decommissioned lighthouses, and a display on various members of the famous "Lighthouse" Stevenson family (including the father and grandfather of author Robert Louis Stevenson), who designed many of them. The highlight is the tour of Kinnaird Head lighthouse itself, preserved as it was when the last keeper left in 1991, with its century-old equipment still in perfect working order.

Pennan

PENNAN, twelve miles west of Fraserburgh, is a tiny fishing hamlet consisting of little more than a single row of whitewashed stone cottages tucked between a cliff and the sea. The movie *Local Hero* was filmed here in 1982; one of the landmarks from the film, the *Pennan Inn*, offers rooms and a pub/restaurant.

ACCOMMODATION AND EATING — PENNAN

Pennan Inn Pennan Harbour T 01346 561201, W thepennaninn.co.uk. This cosy and clean whitewashed inn had a starring role in *Local Hero*. The two en-suite rooms have been recently refurbished, and the restaurant menu features fresh haddock with chips, Cullen Skink, steaks and Thai curries. **£75**

Banff

Heading west along the coast from Pennan brings you, after ten miles, to **Macduff** and its neighbour **BANFF**, separated by the beautiful seven-arch bridge over the River Deveron. Banff's mix of characterful old buildings and boarded-up shops give little clue to the extravagance of **Duff House**, the town's main attraction.

Duff House

Generally April–Oct daily 11am–5pm; Nov–March Thurs–Sun 11am–4pm • HS • £6.55 • T 01261 818181, W duffhouse.org.uk

Built to William Adam's design in 1730, this elegant four-floor Georgian Baroque house has been painstakingly restored and reopened as an outpost of the **National Gallery of Scotland**. While the emphasis is on displaying period artwork rather than any broader selection of the Gallery's paintings, temporary exhibitions of work from the collections are mounted regularly.

ARRIVAL AND INFORMATION — BANFF

By bus Regular buses run from Fraserburgh to Banff (2 daily; 55min).

Tourist office In the gatehouse of Duff House, St Mary Square (April–Oct Mon–Sat 10am–1pm & 2–5pm; T 01261 812419).

Cullen to Spey Bay

Twelve miles west of Banff is **CULLEN**, strikingly situated beneath a superb series of arched viaducts. The town is made up of two sections: Seatown, by the harbour, and the new town on the hillside. The local delicacy, **Cullen Skink** – a soup made from milk (or cream), potato and smoked haddock – is available at local hotels and bars.

West of Cullen, the scruffy working fishing town of **BUCKIE** marks one end of the **Speyside Way** long-distance footpath which follows the coast west for five miles to windy **Spey Bay**, at the mouth of the river of the same name (which can also be reached by a small coastal road from Buckie). It's a remote spot bounded by sea, river and sky; there's a small **wildlife centre** (April–Oct daily 10.30am–5pm; Nov–March Sat & Sun 10.30am–5pm; Ⓦwdcs.org/wildlifecentre; free), whose main mission is researching the Moray Firth dolphin population (see p.885).

Elgin and around

The lively market town of **ELGIN**, just inland about fifteen miles west of Cullen, grew up around the River Lossie in the thirteenth century.

Elgin Cathedral

North College St • April–Sept daily 9.30am–5.30pm; Oct–March Mon–Wed, Sat & Sun 9.30am–4.30pm • HS • £4.70 • Ⓣ01343 547171

The lovely ruin of **Elgin Cathedral**, once considered Scotland's most beautiful cathedral, is little more than a shell today. Founded in 1224, the three-towered building stood as the region's highest religious house until 1390 when the inimical Wolf of Badenoch (Alexander Stewart, Earl of Buchan and illegitimate son of Robert II) burned the place down, along with the rest of the town, in retaliation for having been excommunicated by the bishop of Moray when he left his wife.

Pluscarden Abbey

Seven miles southwest of Elgin • Daily 9am–5pm • Free • Ⓦwww.pluscardenabbey.org

Pluscarden Abbey looms impressively large in a peaceful clearing off an unmarked road southwest of Elgin. One of just two abbeys in Scotland with a permanent community of monks, it was founded in 1230 for a French order. In 1948 a small group of Benedictine monks from Gloucester established the present community. They are very active, running stained-glass workshops, making honey and even recording Gregorian chants on CD, all of which is detailed on the website. The abbey itself is airy and tranquil, with the monks' songs often eerily floating through from the connecting chapel.

ARRIVAL AND INFORMATION — ELGIN AND AROUND

By bus Elgin is connected by bus to Aberdeen (hourly; 3hr 30min), Forres (hourly; 25min), Nairn (hourly; 45min) and Pluscarden (1 daily schooldays only; 20min).

Tourist office 17 High St, Elgin (daily April–Sept; Oct–March Mon–Sat; Ⓣ01343 542666).

ACCOMMODATION

Old Church of Urquhart Dyke by Forres Ⓣ01343 843063, Ⓦoldkirk.co.uk. Five miles east of Elgin, this is the most appealing place to stay in the area, an unusual and comfortable B&B in an imaginatively converted church. **£70**

Findhorn

Northwest of Elgin, at one end of a wide sweep of sandy beach, **FINDHORN** is a tidy village with some neat fishermen's cottages and a delightful harbour dotted with moored yachts. Findhorn is best known, however, for the controversial **Findhorn Foundation**, based beside the town's caravan park about a mile before you reach the village itself.

Moray Art Centre

The Park • Tues–Fri 10am–5pm, Sat 10am–4pm, Sun 1–5pm • Free • Ⓣ01309 692426, Ⓦmorayartcentre.org

It's worth taking a look at the **Moray Art Centre**, on the edge of the foundation but not officially a part of it. The centre, in a terracotta-hued eco-friendly building, hosts eclectic and imaginative temporary exhibitions and regular art classes.

THE FINDHORN FOUNDATION

In 1962, with little money and no employment, Eileen and Peter Caddy, their three children and friend Dorothy Maclean, settled on a caravan site at Findhorn. Dorothy believed she had a special relationship with what she called the "devas … the archetypal formative forces of light or energy that underlie all forms in nature – plants, trees, rivers", and from the uncompromising sandy soil they built a remarkable garden filled with plants and vegetables, far larger than had ever been seen in the area. A few of those who came to see the phenomenon stayed to help out and tune into the spiritual aspect of the daily life of the nascent community. With its emphasis on inner discovery and development, but unattached to any particular doctrine or creed, the **Findhorn Foundation** has blossomed into a permanent community of a couple of hundred people, with a well-developed series of courses and retreats drawing another eight thousand or so visitors each year. The original caravan still stands, surrounded by other caravans, a host of newer timber buildings and a group of round houses made from huge reclaimed whisky distillery barrels; all employ green initiatives including solar power and earth roofs. Elsewhere you can see an ecological sewage treatment centre, a huge wind generator and various community businesses including a café, pottery and weaving studio.

The foundation is not without controversy: a community leader once declared that "behind the front lies a hard core of New Agers experimenting with hallucinatory techniques marketed as spirituality". Whether that is true or not Findhorn can certainly be accused of being overly well-heeled, as betrayed by a glance into the shop or a tally of the smart cars parked outside the well-appointed eco-houses. However, there's little doubt that the community continues to prosper, and its worldwide reputation attracts visitors both sympathetic and sceptical.

Visitors are generally free to stroll around, but the **guided tour** is worthwhile; you can also guide yourself via a booklet (£3) available from the shop or visitor centre (see below), which also has information on staying within the community.

ARRIVAL AND INFORMATION — FINDHORN

By bus Findhorn sees regular buses from Elgin (hourly; 25min) and Foress (hourly; 20min).

Findhorn visitor centre The Park, Findhorn (Mon–Fri 10am–5pm, also Sat & Sun 1–4pm in summer; guided tours April–Nov Mon, Wed & Fri–Sun 2pm; no Sun tour in April, Oct & Nov; £3; T 01309 690311, W findhorn.org).

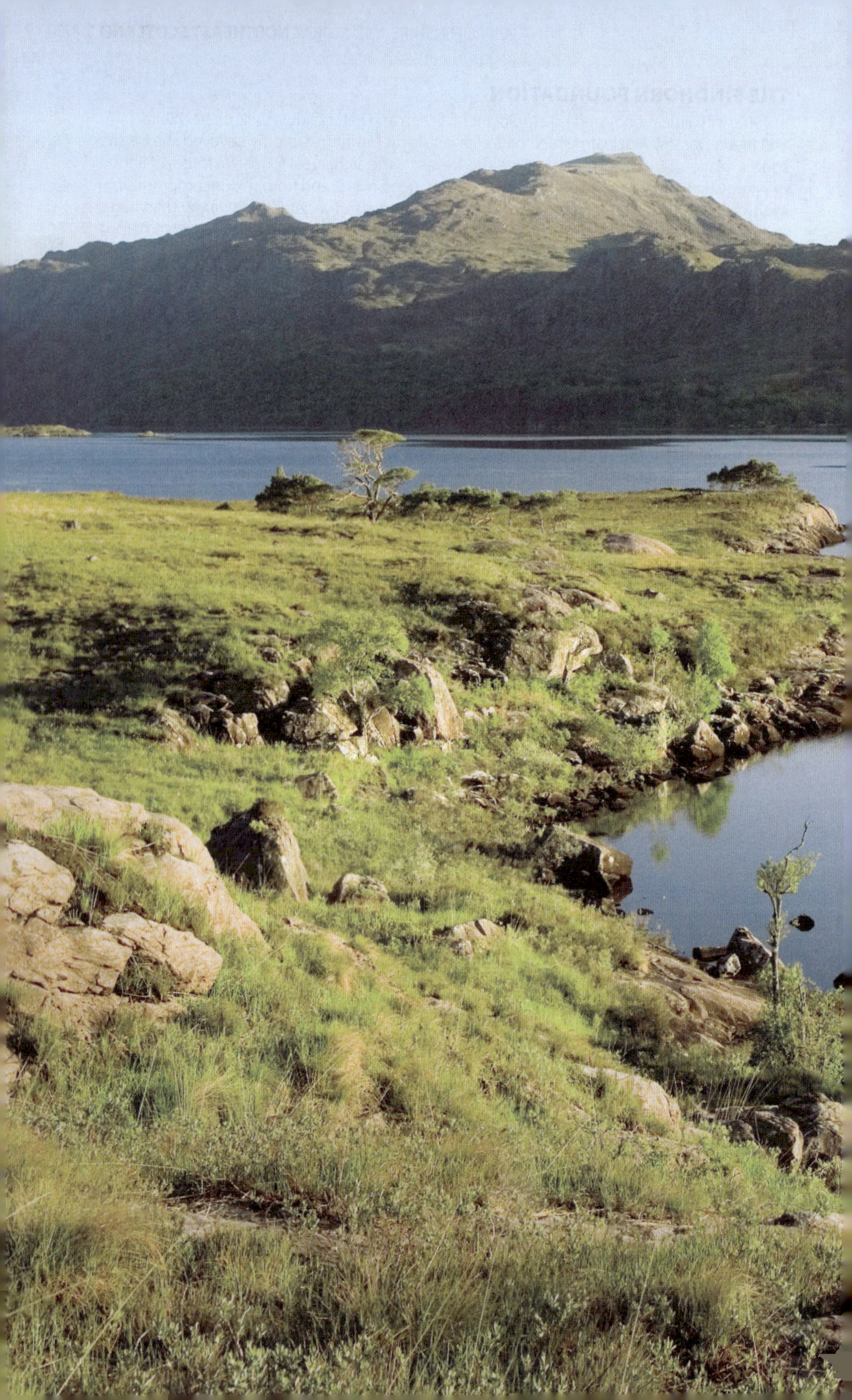

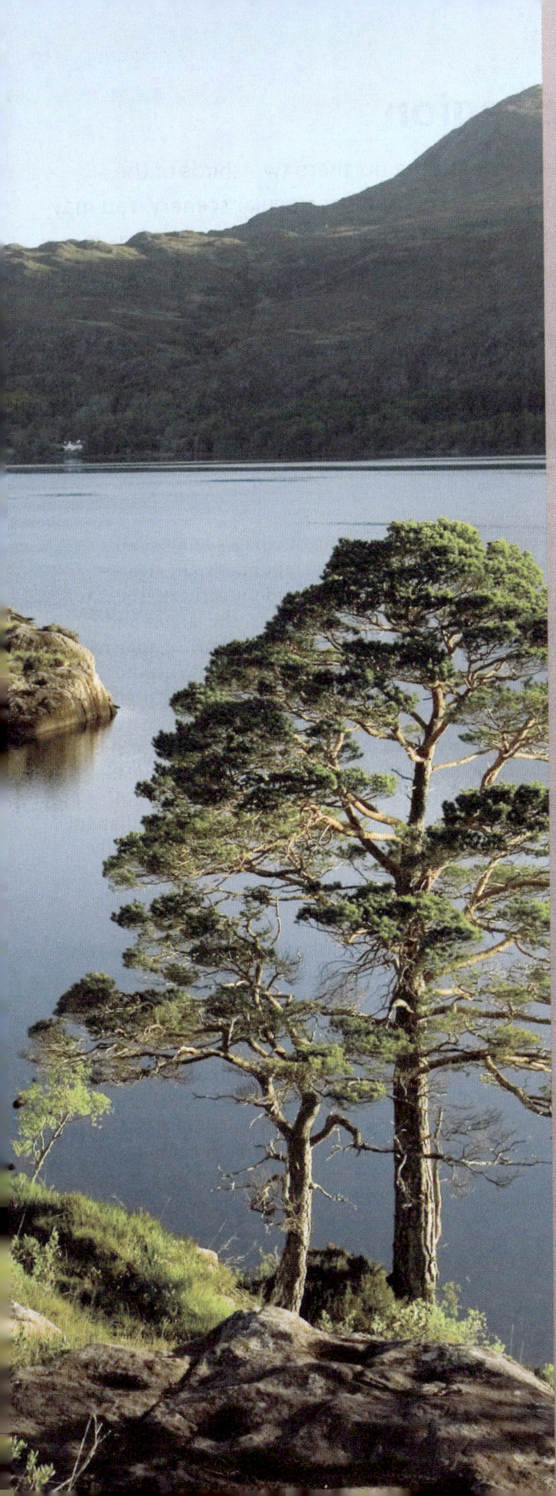

The Highland region

880 Inverness and around

883 The Cairngorms and Strathspey

886 The Great Glen

892 The west coast

904 The north coast

907 The east coast

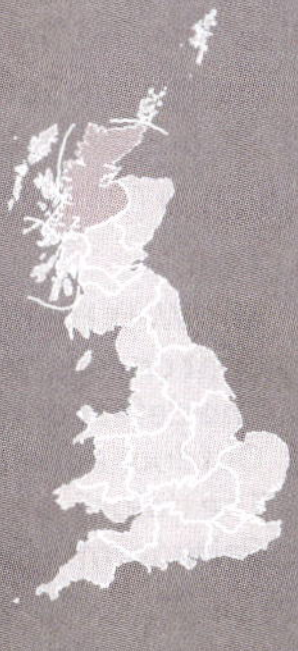

LOCH MAREE, WESTER ROSS

The Highland region

Scotland's Highland region, covering the northern two-thirds of the country, holds much of the mainland's most spectacular scenery. You may be surprised at just how remote much of it still is: the vast peat bogs in the north, for example, are among the most extensive and unspoilt wilderness areas in Europe, while a handful of the west coast's isolated crofting villages can still be reached only by boat. The only major city, Inverness, is best used as a springboard for more remote areas where you can soak in the Highlands' classic combination of mountains, glens, lochs and rivers, surrounded on three sides by a magnificently pitted and rugged coastline.

South of Inverness, the **Strathspey** region, with a string of villages lying along the River Spey, is dominated by the dramatic **Cairngorm mountains**, an area brimming with attractive scenery and opportunities for outdoor activity. The Monadhliath mountains lie between Strathspey and **Loch Ness**, the largest and most famous of the necklace of lochs which make up the **Great Glen**, an ancient geological fault line which cuts southwest across the region from Inverness to the town of **Fort William**. From Fort William, located beneath Scotland's highest peak, Ben Nevis, it's possible to branch out to some fine scenery – most conveniently the beautiful expanses of **Glen Coe**, but also in the direction of the appealing **west coast**, notably the remote and tranquil **Ardnamurchan peninsula**, the "Road to the Isles" to **Mallaig**, and the lochs and glens that lead to **Kyle of Lochalsh** on the most direct route to Skye. Between Kyle of Lochalsh and **Ullapool**, the main settlement in the northwest, lies **Wester Ross**, home to quintessentially west-coast scenes of sparkling sea lochs, rocky headlands and sandy beaches set against some of Scotland's most dramatic mountains, with Skye and the Western Isles on the horizon.

The little-visited **north coast** stretching from wind-lashed **Cape Wrath**, at the very northwest tip of the mainland, east to **John O'Groats** is even more rugged, with sheer cliffs and sand-filled bays bearing the brunt of frequently fierce Atlantic storms. The main settlement on this coast is **Thurso**, jumping-off point for the main ferry service to Orkney.

On the fertile **east coast**, stretching north from Inverness to the old herring port of **Wick**, green fields and woodland run down to the sweeping sandy beaches of the **Black Isle** and the **Cromarty** and **Dornoch firths**. This region is rich with historical sites, including the **Sutherland Monument** by Golspie, **Dornoch**'s fourteenth-century sandstone cathedral, and a number of places linked to the Clearances, a poignantly remembered chapter in the Highland story.

The West Highland Railway p.880
Boat cruises from Inverness p.882
The defeat of the Jacobites p.883
Outdoor activities at Aviemore p.884
The dolphins of the Moray Firth p.885
Cairngorms National Park p.886
Nessie p.887
The Nevis Range p.890
Walks around Glen Coe p.891
Top 5 Highland hostels p.897
Walks around Torridon p.899
Carbisdale Castle p.909

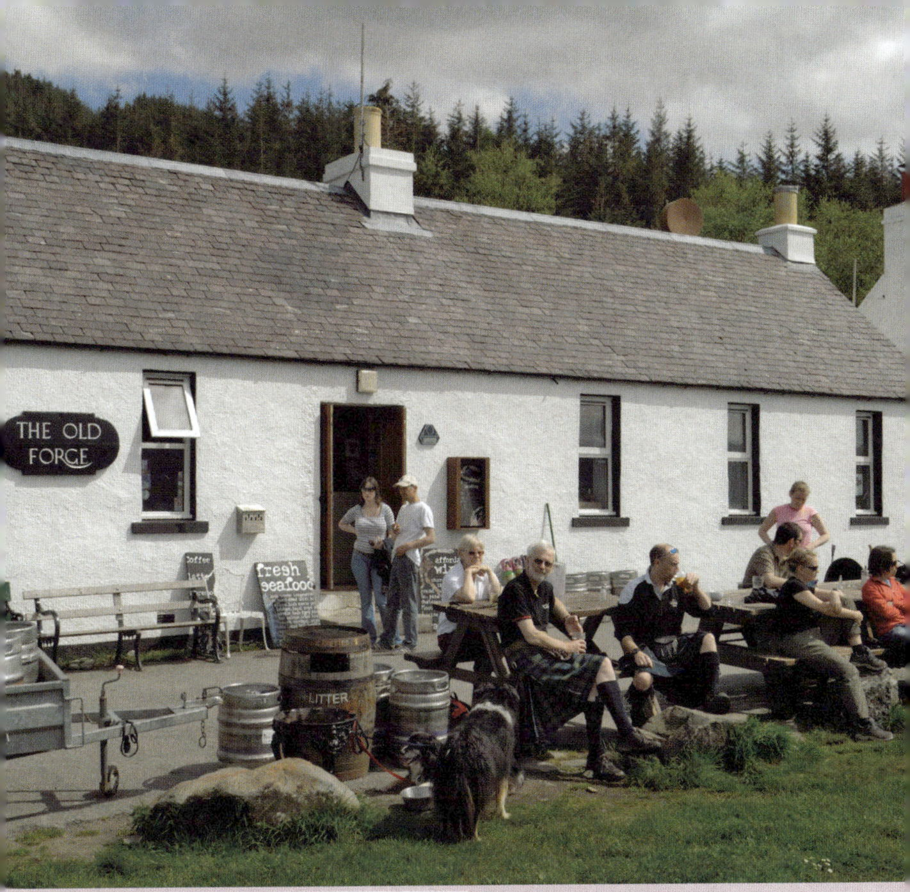

OLD FORGE PUB, KNOYDART

Highlights

❶ **West Highland Railway** From Glasgow to Mallaig via Fort William: the further north you travel, the more spectacular it gets. **See p.880**

❷ **The Cairngorms** Scotland's grandest mountain massif, a place of rare plants, wild animals, inspiring vistas and challenging outdoor activities. **See p.883**

❸ **Glen Coe** Stunning, moody, poignant and full of history – a glorious place for hiking or simple admiration. **See p.891**

❹ **Loch Shiel** This romantic, unspoilt loch is where Bonnie Prince Charlie first raised an army. **See p.895**

❺ **Knoydart** Only accessible by boat or a two-day hike over the mountains, this peninsula also boasts mainland Britain's most isolated pub, the welcoming *Old Forge*. **See p.896**

❻ **Wester Ross** Scotland's finest scenery – a heady mix of high mountains, rugged sea lochs, sweeping bays and scattered islands. **See p.898**

❼ **Ceilidh Place, Ullapool** The best venue for modern Highland culture, with evenings of music, song and dance. **See p.902**

❽ **Cromarty** Set on the fertile Black Isle, this charming small town boasts beautiful vernacular architecture and dramatic east-coast scenery. **See p.908**

HIGHLIGHTS ARE MARKED ON THE MAP ON PP.878–879

THE HIGHLAND REGION

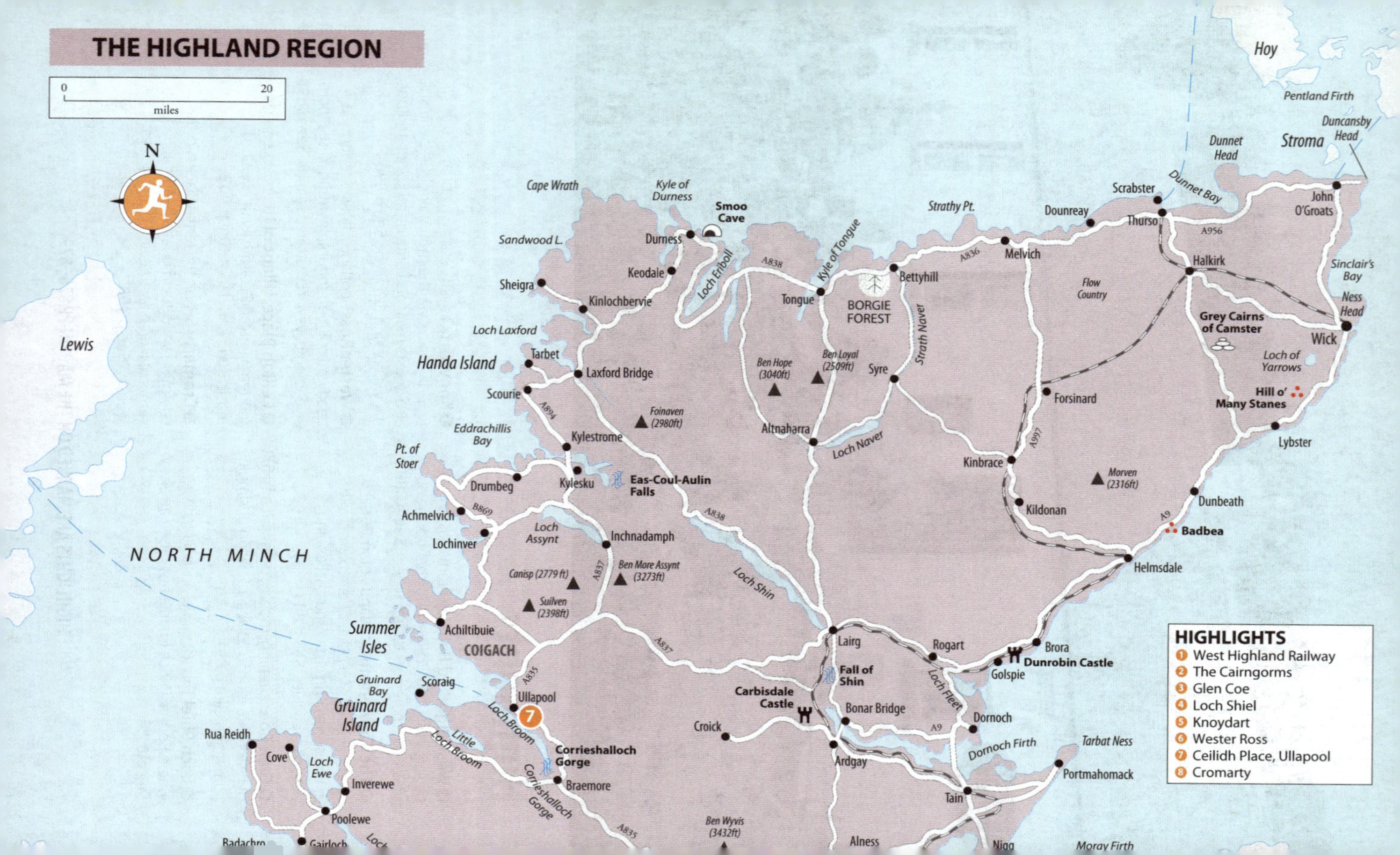

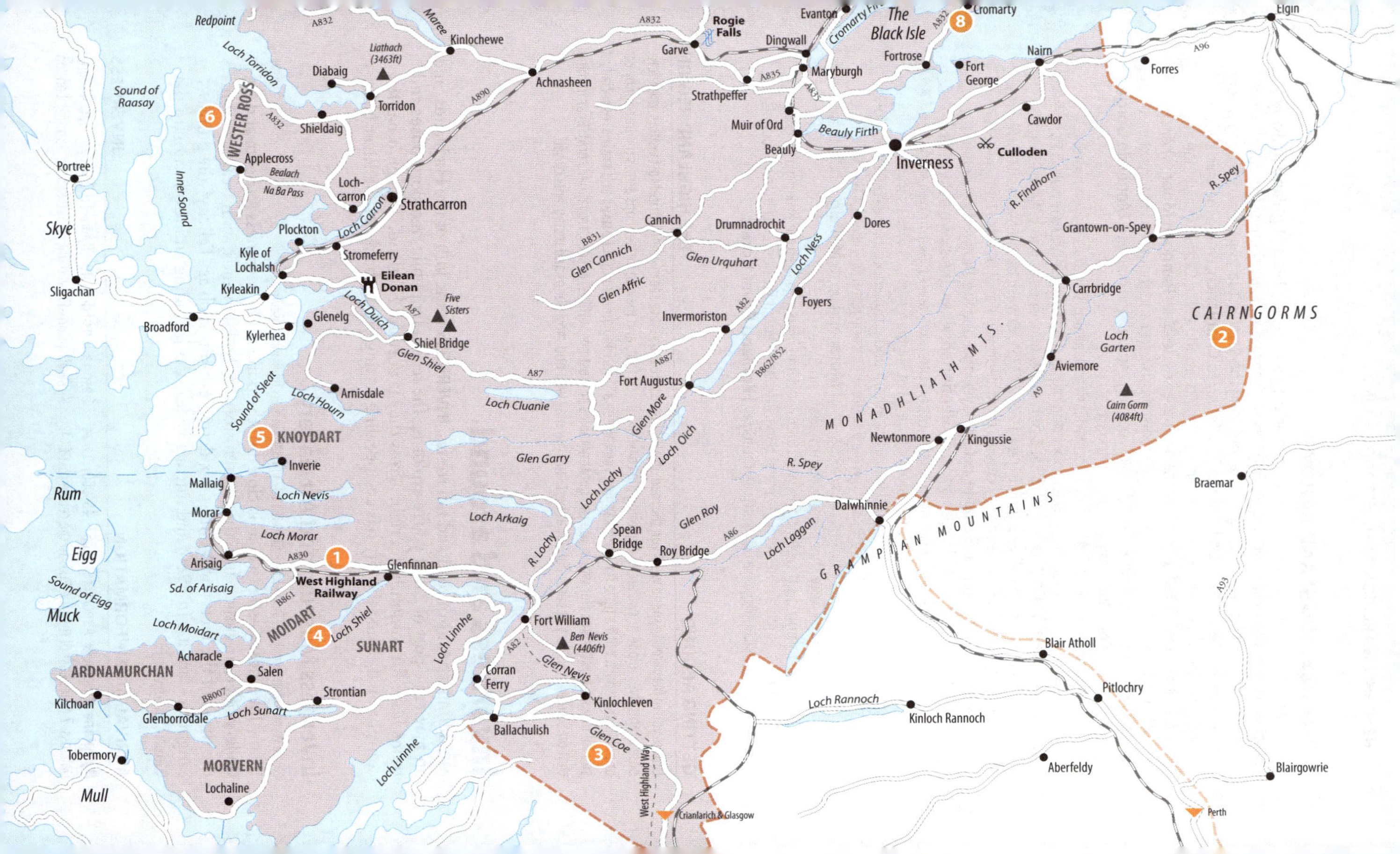

CAIRNGORMS
MONADHLIATH MTS.
GRAMPIAN MOUNTAINS
The Black Isle
WESTER ROSS
KNOYDART
MOIDART
SUNART
ARDNAMURCHAN
MORVERN
Skye
Rum
Eigg
Muck
Mull
Elgin
Forres
Nairn
Cawdor
Culloden
Fort George
Fortrose
Cromarty
Evanton
Cromarty Firth
Dingwall
Maryburgh
Strathpeffer
Muir of Ord
Beauly
Beauly Firth
Inverness
Rogie Falls
Garve
Kinlochewe
Maree
Achnasheen
Redpoint
Loch Torridon
Liathach (3463ft)
Diabaig
Torridon
Shieldaig
Applecross
Bealach
Na Ba Pass
Lochcarron
Strathcarron
Loch Carron
Plockton
Stromeferry
Kyle of Lochalsh
Kyleakin
Eilean Donan
Loch Duich
Five Sisters
Shiel Bridge
Glen Shiel
Glenelg
Kylerhea
Broadford
Sligachan
Portree
Sound of Raasay
Inner Sound
Sound of Sleat
Arnisdale
Loch Hourn
Inverie
Loch Nevis
Mallaig
Morar
Loch Morar
Arisaig
Sd. of Arisaig
Sound of Eigg
Loch Moidart
Acharacle
Salen
Strontian
Loch Sunart
Kilchoan
Glenborrodale
Tobermory
Lochaline
Glenfinnan
West Highland Railway
Loch Shiel
Loch Linnhe
Fort William
Ben Nevis (4406ft)
Glen Nevis
Corran Ferry
Ballachulish
Kinlochleven
Glen Coe
West Highland Way
Crianlarich & Glasgow
Loch Arkaig
R. Lochy
Loch Lochy
Spean Bridge
Roy Bridge
Glen Roy
Loch Laggan
Glen Garry
Loch Cluanie
Glen More
Loch Oich
Fort Augustus
Invermoriston
Loch Ness
Foyers
Dores
Drumnadrochit
Glen Urquhart
Cannich
Glen Cannich
Glen Affric
Dalwhinnie
Newtonmore
Kingussie
R. Spey
Aviemore
Carrbridge
Grantown-on-Spey
R. Findhorn
Loch Garten
Cairn Gorm (4084ft)
Braemar
Blair Atholl
Pitlochry
Aberfeldy
Blairgowrie
Perth
Loch Rannoch
Kinloch Rannoch
A96
A832
A835
A890
A87
A887
A82
B862/852
B831
A9
A86
A93
A830
B861
B8007

THE WEST HIGHLAND RAILWAY

Scotland's most famous railway line is the brilliantly engineered **West Highland Railway**, running from Glasgow to Mallaig via Fort William. The line is in two sections: the southern part travels from **Glasgow** Queen Street station along the Clyde estuary and up Loch Long before switching to the banks of Loch Lomond on its way to **Crianlarich**, where the train divides with one section heading for Oban. After climbing around Beinn Odhar on a unique horseshoe-shaped loop of viaducts, the line traverses desolate **Rannoch Moor**, where the track had to be laid on a mattress of tree roots, brushwood and thousands of tons of earth and ashes. The train then swings into Glen Roy, passing through the dramatic **Monessie Gorge** and entering **Fort William** from the northeast.

The second leg of the journey, from Fort William to Mallaig, is arguably even more spectacular, and from June to mid-October one of the scheduled services is pulled by the **Jacobite Steam Train** (Mon–Fri, also Sat & Sun July & Aug; departs Fort William 10.20am, departs Mallaig 2.10pm; day-return £31; ⓣ01524 737751, ⓦwestcoastrailways.co.uk). Shortly after leaving Fort William the railway crosses the Caledonian Canal beside Neptune's Staircase by way of a swing bridge at **Benavie**, before travelling along the shores of Locheil and crossing the magnificent 21-arch viaduct at **Glenfinnan**, where the steam train, in its "Hogwarts Express" livery, was filmed for the *Harry Potter* movies. At Glenfinnan station there's a small **museum** dedicated to the history of the West Highland line, as well as two old railway carriages that have been converted into a restaurant and a bunkhouse (see p.895). Not long afterwards the line reaches the coast, where there are unforgettable views of the Small Isles and Skye as it runs past the famous silver sands of **Morar** and up to **Mallaig**, where there are connections to the ferry that crosses to Armadale on Skye.

If you're planning on travelling the West Highland line, and in particular linking it to other train journeys (such as the similarly attractive route between Inverness and Kyle of Lochalsh), it's worth considering one of ScotRail's multiday **Highland Rover tickets**.

GETTING AROUND — THE HIGHLAND REGION

Unless you're prepared to spend weeks on the road, the Highlands are too vast to see in a single trip. Most visitors, therefore, base themselves in one or two areas, exploring the coast or hills on foot, and making longer hops across the interior by car or public transport. With a little forward planning you can see a surprising amount using **buses** and **trains**, especially if you fill in with **postbuses** (for which you can get timetables at most post offices, or see ⓦroyalmail.com). Bear in mind that on Sundays bus services are sporadic at best, and you may well find most shops and restaurants closed.

Inverness and around

Straddling a nexus of road and rail routes, **INVERNESS** is the hub of the Highlands, and an inevitable port of call if you're exploring the region by public transport: **buses** and **trains** leave for communities right across the far north of Scotland. Though it has few conventional sights, the city has an appealing setting on the banks of the River Ness.

Inverness Museum and Art Gallery

Castle Wynd • Mon–Sat 9am–5pm • Free • ⓣ01463 237114, ⓦinverness.highland.museum

Below **Inverness Castle** (which is closed to the public), the **Inverness Museum and Art Gallery** offers an insight into the social history of the Highlands, with treasures from the times of the Picts and Vikings, taxidermy exhibits such as "Felicity" the puma, caught in Cannich in 1980, and interactive features including an introduction to the Gaelic language.

ARRIVAL AND INFORMATION — INVERNESS

By plane Inverness Airport (ⓣ01667 464000) is at Dalcross, 7 miles east of the city. Taxis to the centre cost £14.

Destinations Edinburgh (Mon–Fri 2 daily, 1 Sat; 45min); Kirkwall (Mon–Fri 2 daily, 1 Sat & Sun; 45min); London

(Gatwick 4 daily Mon–Fri; 3 Sat & Sun; Heathrow 1 daily; Luton (Mon–Fri 1 daily; 2 daily Sat & Sun; 1hr 30min); Shetland (Mon–Fri 2 daily; 1 daily Sat & Sun; 1hr 40min); Stornoway (Mon–Fri 4 daily, Sat 2 daily, Sun 1 daily; 40min).

By train The station lies just off Academy St northeast of the centre.

Destinations Aberdeen (Mon–Sat 10 daily; 5 Sun; 2hr 15min); Aviemore (Mon–Sat 9 daily, 5 Sun; 40min); Edinburgh (Mon–Sat 5 daily, 3 Sun; 3hr 30min); Glasgow (Mon–Sat 3 daily; 3 Sun; 3hr 20min); Kyle of Lochalsh (Mon–Sat 2–3 daily, 2 Sun; 3hr); London (Mon–Fri & Sun 1 nightly; 11hr); Thurso (Mon–Sat 2 daily, 1 Sun; 3hr 25min); Wick (Mon–Sat 2 daily, 1 Sun; 3hr 45min).

By bus The bus station (Ⓣ01463 233371) is next to the train station, just off Academy St, northeast of the centre.

Destinations Aberdeen (hourly; 3hr 40min); Aviemore (6 Mon–Sat, 5 Sun; 45min); Drumnadrochit (8 daily; 25min); Durness (Mon–Sat 1 daily; 2hr 40min; also bike bus, May–Sept Mon–Sat 1 daily, also July–Aug Sun 1 daily); Fort Augustus (5 daily; 1hr); Fort William (6 daily; 2hr); Glasgow (6 daily direct; 3hr 35min–4hr 25min); Kyle of Lochalsh (3 daily; 2hr 10min); Nairn (hourly; 50min); Perth (10 daily; 2hr 35min); Portree (3 daily; 3hr); Thurso (Mon–Sat 5 daily, Sun 2 daily; 3hr 30min); Ullapool (2 Mon, Tues, Thurs & Sat; 3 Wed & Fri; 2hr 25min); Wick (Mon–Sat 3 daily, Sun 2 daily; 3hr).

Tourist office Castle Wynd (March–April & Sept–Nov Mon–Sat 9am–5pm, Sun 10am–4pm; June–Aug Mon–Sat 9am–6pm, Sun 10am–4pm, Dec–Feb Mon–Sat 9am–5pm; Ⓣ01463 234353, Ⓦvisithighlands.com).

ACCOMMODATION

Inverness is one of the few places in the Highlands where you're unlikely to have problems finding accommodation, although you should **book ahead** in July and August.

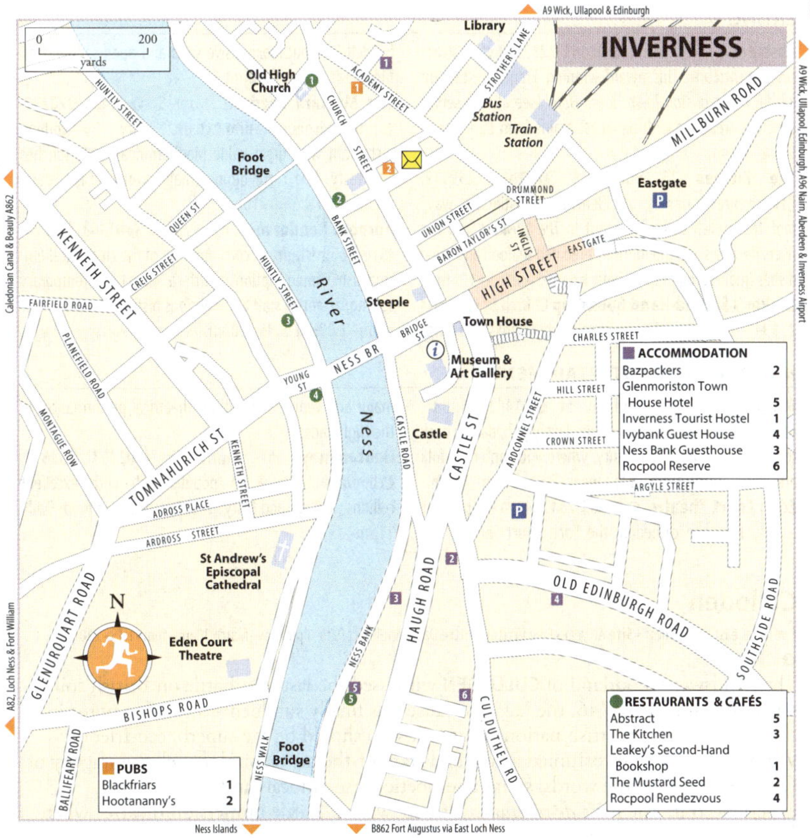

BOAT CRUISES FROM INVERNESS

Inverness is the departure point for a range of **day-tours** and **cruises** to nearby attractions, including Loch Ness and the Moray Firth. **Loch Ness cruises** typically incorporate a visit to a monster exhibition at **Drumnadrochit** and **Urquhart Castle** – try Jacobite Cruises (from £11.50; ⓣ01463 233999, ⓦjacobite.co.uk) or **Cruise Loch Ness** (ⓣ01320 366277, ⓦcruiselochness.com).

Bazpackers Castle St ⓣ01463 717663, ⓦbazpackershostel.co.uk. The cosiest and most relaxed of the city's hostels, with more than thirty beds including two doubles and a twin (£36); some dorms are mixed. Good location, great views and a garden that's used for barbecues. Dorm £15, double £44

Glenmoriston Town House Hotel 20 Ness Bank ⓣ01463 223777, ⓦglenmoristontownhouse.com. An upmarket, contemporary hotel by the riverside just a few minutes' walk from the town centre. Muted decor and a good restaurant, *Abstract*. £110

Inverness Tourist Hostel 24 Rose St ⓣ01463 241962, ⓦinvernesshostel.com. A central, clean, well-equipped sixty-bed hostel where top-notch amenities include wide-screen TVs and internet. £9

Ivybank Guest House 28 Old Edinburgh Rd ⓣ01463 232796, ⓦivybankguesthouse.com. A grand Georgian home just up the hill from the castle, with open fires and a lovely homely interior. £60

Ness Bank Guesthouse 7 Ness Bank ⓣ01463 232939, ⓦnessbankguesthouse.co.uk. Five lovely tasteful rooms in a Grade II-listed Victorian house on the river. £60

★ **Rocpool Reserve** Culduthel Rd ⓣ01463 240089, ⓦrocpool.com. Just a 10min walk south from the castle, this acclaimed boutique hotel and restaurant offers hip, chic and decadent rooms and upmarket modern dining. £210

EATING

Abstract 20 Ness Bank ⓣ01463 223777, ⓦabstractrestaurant.com. This award-winning French restaurant within *Glenmoriston Town House Hotel* (see above) serves delicious creations with panache: mains from £20. Tues–Sat 6–10pm.

The Kitchen 15 Huntly St ⓣ01463 259119, ⓦkitchenrestaurant.co.uk. Beneath a distinctive wavy roof, this stylish sister restaurant to *The Mustard Seed* has riverside views and thoughtfully prepared seafood and meat dishes (mains around £16). Daily noon–3pm & 5–10pm.

Leakey's Second-Hand Bookshop Church St ⓣ01463 239947. Tear yourself away from the old books and maps for delicious but inexpensive soup and open sandwiches. Mon–Sat 10am–5.30pm.

The Mustard Seed 16 Fraser St ⓣ01463 220220, ⓦmustardseedrestaurant.co.uk. Airy, welcoming restaurant with great-value Mediterranean-style lunches and tasty, à la carte dining (mains around £16). Daily noon–3pm & 5.30–10pm.

Rocpool Rendezvous 1 Ness Walk ⓣ01463 717274, ⓦrocpoolrestaurant.com. Another of the city's excellent, smartish dining options, with a smart contemporary setting, attentive staff and delicious bistro food. Mon–Sat noon–2.30pm, 5.45–10pm.

NIGHTLIFE AND ENTERTAINMENT

Blackfriars 93–95 Acadamy St ⓣ01463 233881, ⓦblackfriarshighlandpub.co.uk. Lively pub, dating back to the late eighteenth-century, where you can enjoy folk and ceilidh music five nights a week. Daily 11am–11pm.

Eden Court Theatre ⓣ01463 234234, ⓦeden-court.co.uk. Near the cathedral, the Eden Court Theatre is a major arts venue, and hub for theatrical performances in the Highlands.

Hootananny's 67 Church St ⓣ01463 233651, ⓦhootananny.co.uk. A popular pub with excellent ceilidhs, real ale and tasty "Thai Tananny" bar food. Daily 11am–11pm.

Culloden

Five miles east of Inverness • **Site** All year • Free **Visitor centre** Daily: April–Oct 9am–6pm; Nov–March 10am–4pm • NTS • £10 • ⓣ0844 493 2159

The windswept moorland of **CULLODEN** witnessed the last-ever battle on British soil when, on April 16, 1746, the Jacobite cause was finally subdued – a turning point in the history of the Scottish nation. Your first stop should be the superb, eco-friendly **visitor centre**, where costumed actors and state-of-the-art technology tell the tragedy of Culloden through the words, songs and poetic verse of locals and soldiers who experienced it. The *pièce de résistance* is the powerful "battle immersion theatre" where

THE DEFEAT OF THE JACOBITES

The second Jacobite rebellion had begun on August 19, 1745, with the raising of the Stuarts' standard at **Glenfinnan** on the west coast (see p.895). Shortly after, Edinburgh fell into Jacobite hands, and Bonnie Prince Charlie began his march on London. The English had appointed the ambitious young Duke of Cumberland to command their forces, and his pursuit, together with bad weather and lack of funds, eventually forced the Jacobites to retreat north. They ended up at **Culloden**, where, ill-fed and exhausted, they were hopelessly outnumbered by the English. After the battle, in which 1500 Highlanders were slaughtered (many of them as they lay wounded on the battlefield), Bonnie Prince Charlie fled west to the hills and islands. He eventually escaped to France, leaving his erstwhile supporters to their fate – the clans were disarmed, the wearing of tartan and playing of bagpipes forbidden, and the chiefs became landlords greedy for higher and higher rents. Within a century, the Highland way of life had changed out of all recognition.

visitors are surrounded on all sides by lifelike cinematography and the sounds of the raging, bloody scenes of the fight. Go up to the rooftop platform to enjoy the elevated view across the actual battlefield before walking around the battle site armed with a nifty audioguide. Flags mark out the positions of the two armies while simple headstones mark the **clan graves**.

Fort George

Eighteen miles northwest of Inverness • Daily: April–Sept 9.30am–5.30pm; Oct–March 9.30am–4.30pm • HS • £6.90 • ⓣ 01667 460232

Eight miles or so of undulating coastal farmland separate Culloden from **Fort George**, an old Hanoverian bastion with walls a mile long, considered by military architectural historians to be one of the finest fortifications in Europe. Crowning a sandy spit that juts into the middle of the Moray Firth, it was built between 1747 and 1769 as a base for George II's army, in case the Highlanders should attempt to rekindle the Jacobite flame. Apart from the sweeping panoramic views across the Firth from its ramparts, the main incentive to visit Fort George is the **Regimental Museum** of the Queen's Own Highlanders. Displayed in polished glass cases is a predictable array of regimental silver, coins, moth-eaten uniforms and medals, along with some macabre war trophies, ranging from blood-stained nineteenth-century Sudanese battle robes to Iraqi gas masks gleaned in the First Gulf War.

The Cairngorms and Strathspey

Rising high in the heather-clad hills above remote Loch Laggan, forty miles south of Inverness, the **River Spey**, Scotland's second longest river, drains northeast towards the Moray Firth through one of the Highlands' most spellbinding valleys. Famous for its ancient forests, salmon fishing and ospreys, the area around the upper section of the river, known as **Strathspey**, is dominated by the sculpted **Cairngorms**, Britain's most extensive mountain massif, unique in supporting subarctic tundra on its high plateau. Outdoor enthusiasts flock to the area to take advantage of the superb hiking, water sports and winter snows, aided by the fact that the area is easily accessible by road and rail from both central Scotland and Inverness. A string of villages along the river provide useful bases for setting out into the wilder country, principal among them **Aviemore**.

Aviemore and around

AVIEMORE was first developed as a ski and tourism resort in the mid-1960s and, over the years, fell victim to profiteering developers with scant regard for the needs of the local

OUTDOOR ACTIVITIES AT AVIEMORE

While Aviemore is best known as a winter resort, it has a number of excellent summer activities, from gentle walking to canyoning.

SKIING

Scottish **skiing** on a commercial level first really took off in Aviemore. By continental European and North American standards it's on a tiny scale, but occasionally snow, sun and lack of crowds coincide and you can have a great day. February and March are usually the best times, but there's a chance of decent snow at any time between mid-November and April. Lots of places – not just in Aviemore itself – sell or rent equipment; for a rundown of ski schools and rental facilities in the area, visit Ⓦ ski.visitscotland.com.

The **Cairngorm Ski Area** (Ⓦ cairngormmountain.com), nine miles southeast of Aviemore, above Loch Morlich in Glenmore Forest Park, is well served in winter by buses from Aviemore. Facilities include a ski school and a separate terrain park for skiers and boarders. If there's lots of snow, the area around **Loch Morlich** and into the **Rothiemurchus Estate** provides enjoyable cross-country skiing through lovely woods, beside rushing burns and even over frozen lochs.

WALKING

Walking is a highlight of the Aviemore area, though you should heed the usual safety guidelines. These are particularly important if you want to climb to the high tops, which include a number of Scotland's loftiest peaks. There are some lovely and well-signposted **low-level walks** in the area, too. It takes an hour or so to complete the gentle circular walk around pretty **Loch an Eilean** (with its ruined castle) in the Rothiemurchus Estate, beginning at the end of the back road that turns east off the B970 a mile south of Inverdruie. The helpful estate **visitor centres** at the lochside and at Inverdruie provide more information on the many woodland trails that crisscross this area.

Another good shortish (half-day) walk leads along a well-surfaced forestry track from *Glenmore Lodge* up towards the **Ryvoan Pass**, taking in An Lochan Uaine, known as the "Green Loch" because of its amazing colours that range from turquoise to slate grey depending on the weather. The **Glenmore Forest Park Visitor Centre** by the road at the turn-off to the lodge has information on other trails in this section of the forest.

A pleasant day-trip involves walking along the Speyside Way from Aviemore to Boat of Garten, on to the RSPB osprey sanctuary at Loch Garten, and then returning on the **Strathspey Steam Railway** (June–Sept 4 daily; less regular service at other times; Ⓣ 01479 810725, Ⓦ strathspeyrailway.co.uk for details).

Ordnance Survey Explorer Maps nos. 402 & 403 or *OS Outdoor Leisure Map* no. 3 are the best maps to use.

MOUNTAIN BIKING

The area around Aviemore is great for mountain biking. Both Rothiemurchus and Glenmore estates provide waymarked **routes**; the Rothiemurchus Visitor Centre at Inverdruie has maps.

WATERSPORTS

Full On Adventure Ⓣ 07885 835838, Ⓦ fullonadventure.com. Whitewater rafting trips on the Findhorn River.

G2 Outdoor Ⓣ 01479 811008, Ⓦ g2outdoor.co.uk. Guided kayaking and canyoning.

Loch Insh Watersports Centre 6 miles up-valley near Kincraig Ⓣ 01540 651272, Ⓦ lochinsh.com. Sailing, windsurfing and canoeing in beautiful surroundings; rental and tuition available.

Loch Morlich Watersports Centre 5 miles east of Aviemore on the way to Cairn Gorm Mountain Ⓣ 01479 861221, Ⓦ lochmorlich.com. Sailing, windsurfing and canoeing in a lovely setting with a sandy beach. Rental and tuition available.

community. Although a face-lift has removed some of the architectural eyesores of that era, the settlement remains dominated by a string of soulless shopping centres and sprawling housing estates surrounding a Victorian railway station. That said, Aviemore is well equipped with visitor facilities, and is the most convenient base for the Cairngorms.

THE DOLPHINS OF THE MORAY FIRTH

The **Moray Firth**, a great wedge-shaped bay forming the eastern coastline of the Highlands, is one of only three areas of UK waters that support a resident population of **dolphins**. More than a hundred of these beautiful, intelligent marine mammals live in the estuary, the most northerly breeding-ground in Europe for this particular species – the bottle-nosed dolphin (*Tursiops truncatus*) – and you stand a good chance of spotting a few, either from the shore or a boat.

One of the best places in Scotland, if not in Europe, to look for them is **Chanonry Point**, on the Black Isle (see p.908) – a spit of sand protruding into a narrow, deep channel, where converging currents bring fish close to the surface, and thus the dolphins close to shore; a rising tide is the most likely time to see them. **Kessock Bridge**, a mile north of Inverness, is another prime dolphin-spotting location. You can go all the way down to the beach at the small village of North Kessock, underneath the road bridge or stop above the village in a car park just off the A9 at the **Dolphin and Seal Visitor Centre** and listening post (June–Sept daily 9.30am–12.30pm & 1–4.30pm; free), run by the Whale and Dolphin Conservation Society (WDCS), where hydrophones allow you to eavesdrop on the clicks and whistles of underwater conversations.

Several companies run dolphin-spotting **boat trips** around the Moray Firth. However, researchers claim that the increased traffic is causing the dolphins unnecessary stress, particularly during the all-important breeding period when passing vessels are thought to force calves underwater for uncomfortably long periods, so if you decide to go on a cruise to see the dolphins – and perhaps minke whales, porpoises, seals and otters – make sure the operator is a member of the Dolphin Space Programme's **accreditation scheme** (see ⓦdolphinspace.org for a list). Trips (April–Oct; from £10/hr) are very popular, so book well in advance.

23

ARRIVAL AND INFORMATION — AVIEMORE

By train The station on Grampian Rd sees good connections with Edinburgh (Mon–Sat 9 daily, 5 on Sun; 2hr 30min), Glasgow (9 daily, 5 on Sun; 2hr 30min) and Inverness (Mon–Sat 9 daily, 5 on Sun; 1hr).

By bus Buses link Aviemore's town centre with the Cairngorm ski area (hourly; 30min), Edinburgh (5 daily; 2hr 30min–3hr 30min), Glasgow (7 daily; 3hr 30min), Grantown-on-Spey (Mon–Sat every 30min; 35min) and Inverness (Mon–Sat 6 daily, 5 on Sun; 45min).

Tourist office 7 The Parade, Grampian Rd (April–Oct Mon–Sat 9am–5pm, Sun 10am–4pm; Nov–March Mon–Fri 9am–5pm, Sat 10am–4pm; ⓣ01479 810930, ⓦvisitscotland.com).

ACCOMMODATION

Aviemore Bunkhouse Dalfaber Rd ⓣ01479 811181, ⓦaviemore-bunkhouse.com. A large modern place within walking distance from the train station. They have a double and a family room. Dorm £17, double £55

Aviemore SYHA 25 Grampian Rd ⓣ0870 004 1104, ⓦsyha.org.uk. Aviemore's sizeable, well-equipped SYHA hostel is within walking distance of the centre of the village. £17

★ **Corrour House Hotel** Inverdruie, 2 miles southeast of Aviemore ⓣ01479 810220, ⓦcorrourhousehotel.co.uk. Secluded small hotel with a distinctly upmarket atmosphere. £80

Glenmore Lodge 8 miles east of Aviemore ⓣ01479 861256, ⓦglenmorelodge.org.uk. Excellent accommodation in twin rooms (with shared facilities) and self-catering lodges – superb facilities include a pool, weights room, sauna and indoor climbing wall. £50

Ravenscraig Guest House Grampian Rd ⓣ01479 810278, ⓦaviemoreonline.com. This welcoming, twelve-bedroom guesthouse has a handy central location and is very family-friendly. Self catering is also available. £100

EATING AND DRINKING

★ **Mountain Café** 111 Grampian Rd ⓣ01479 812473, ⓦmountaincafe-aviemore.co.uk. Aviemore's main drag is lined with bistros and takeaways serving predictable, run-of-the-mill food. One exception is the reasonably priced *Mountain Café*, above Cairngorm Mountain Sports, which serves an all-day menu of wholesome snacks and freshly prepared meals. Mon, Sat & Sun 8.30am–5.30pm, Tues–Fri 8.30am–5pm.

The Old Bridge Inn East side of the railway on Dalfaber Rd ⓣ01479 811137, ⓦoldbridgeinn.co.uk. Decent pub grub and real ales in a mellow, cosy setting. Most of the ingredients come from local farmers and suppliers. Mon–Thurs 11am–midnight, Fri & Sat 11am–1am, Sun 12.30pm–midnight.

CAIRNGORMS NATIONAL PARK

The **Cairngorms National Park** (cairngorms.co.uk) covers some 1500 square miles and incorporates the **Cairngorms massif**, the UK's largest mountainscape and only sizeable plateau over 2500ft. While Aviemore and the surrounding area is the main point of entry, particularly for those planning outdoor activities, it's also possible to access the eastern side of the park from both Deeside and Donside in Aberdeenshire. There are 52 summits higher than 2953ft in the park, as well as a quarter of Scotland's native woodland, and a quarter of the UK's threatened wildlife species. Vegetation ranges from one of the largest tracts of ancient **Caledonian pine and birch forest** remaining in Scotland, at Rothiemurchus, to subarctic tundra on the high plateau, where **alpine flora** such as starry saxifrage and the star-shaped pink flowers of moss campion peek out of the pink granite in the few months of summer that the ground is free of snow. **Birds of prey** you're most likely to see are the **osprey**, especially at Loch Garten's osprey observation centre (see below), or fishing on the lochs around Aviemore.

Cairn Gorm Mountain

From Aviemore, a road leads past Rothiemurchus and Loch Morlich and winds its way up into the Cairngorms, reaching the Coire Cas car park at a height of 2150ft. Here is the base station for the ski area with a **ranger office** (daily: April–Oct 9am–5pm; Nov–March 8.30am–4.30pm) where you can find out about the area's various trails. It's also the departure point for the **Cairn Gorm Mountain Railway** (daily every 20min 10am–5pm; last train up 4.20pm; £9.75; cairngormmountain.com), a two-car funicular railway that whisks skiers in winter, and tourists at any time of year, along a mile and a half of track to the top station at an altitude of 3600ft, not far from the summit of Cairn Gorm Mountain.

Abernethy Forest RSPB Reserve

Loch Garten, 7 miles northeast of Aviemore and 8 miles south of Grantown-on-Spey • **Observation centre** April–Aug daily 10am–6pm; guided walks Wed 9.30am • £3 • 01479 831476

The **Abernethy Forest RSPB Reserve**, on the shore of **Loch Garten**, is famous as the nesting site of the **osprey**. Having completely disappeared from the British Isles, a single pair of these exquisite white-and-brown raptors mysteriously reappeared in 1954 and built a nest in a tree half a mile or so from the loch; the birds are now well established here and elsewhere across the Highlands. The best time to visit is between April and August, when the RSPB opens an **observation centre**, complete with telescopes and CCTV monitoring of the nest. The reserve is also home to other rare birds and animals, including the Scottish crossbill, capercaillie, whooper swan and red squirrel.

The Great Glen

The **Great Glen**, a major geological fault line cutting diagonally across the Highlands from Fort William to Inverness, is the defining geographic feature of the north of Scotland. A huge rift valley was formed when the northwestern and southeastern sides of the fault slid in opposite directions for more than sixty miles, while the present landscape was shaped by glaciers that retreated only around 8000 BC. The glen is impressive more for its sheer scale than its beauty, but the imposing barrier of loch and mountain means that no one can travel into the northern Highlands without passing through it. With the two major service centres of the Highlands at either end it makes an obvious and rewarding route between the west and east coasts.

Of the Great Glen's four elongated lochs, the most famous is **Loch Ness**, home to the mythical monster; lochs **Oich**, **Lochy** and **Linnhe** (the last of these a sea loch) are less renowned, though no less attractive. All four are linked by the Caledonian Canal. The southwestern end of the Great Glen is dominated by **Fort William**, the second-largest town in the Highland region. Situated at the heart of the Lochaber area, it's a useful base and an excellent hub for outdoor activities. Dominating the scene to the south is **Ben Nevis**, Britain's highest peak, best approached from scenic Glen Nevis. The most famous glen of all, **Glen Coe**, lies on the main A82 road half an hour's drive south of Fort William. Nowadays the whole area is unashamedly given over to tourism, and Fort William is swamped by bus tours throughout the summer, but, as ever in the Highlands, within a thirty-minute drive you can be totally alone.

Loch Ness

Twenty-three miles long, unfathomably deep, cold and often moody, **Loch Ness** is bounded by rugged heather-clad mountains rising steeply from a wooded shoreline with attractive glens opening up on either side. Its fame, however, is based overwhelmingly on its legendary inhabitant Nessie, the "Loch Ness monster", who ensures a steady flow of hopeful visitors to the settlements dotted along the loch, in particular **Drumnadrochit**. Nearby, the impressive ruins of **Castle Urquhart** – a favourite monster-spotting location – perch atop a rock on the lochside and attract a deluge of bus parties in summer. Almost as busy in high season is the village of **Fort Augustus**, at the more scenic southwest tip of Loch Ness, where you can watch queues of boats tackling one of the Caledonian Canal's longest flights of locks.

Drumnadrochit

Situated above a verdant, sheltered bay of Loch Ness fifteen miles southwest of Inverness, **DRUMNADROCHIT** is the southern gateway to remote Glen Affric and the

NESSIE

The world-famous **Loch Ness monster**, affectionately known as **Nessie** (and by aficionados as *Nessiteras rhombopteryx*), has been a local celebrity for some time. The first mention of a mystery creature crops up in St Adamnan's seventh-century biography of **St Columba**, who allegedly calmed an aquatic animal that had attacked one of his monks. In 1934, the *Daily Mail* published London surgeon R.K. Wilson's sensational photograph of the head and neck of the monster peering up out of the loch, and the hype has hardly diminished since. Encounters range from glimpses of ripples by anglers to the famous occasion in 1961 when thirty hotel guests saw a pair of humps break the water's surface and cruise for about half a mile before submerging.

Photographic evidence is showcased in the two "Monster Exhibitions" at Drumnadrochit, but the most impressive of these exhibits – including the famous black-and-white movie footage of Nessie's humps moving across the water, and Wilson's original head and shoulders shot – have now been exposed as fakes. Indeed, in few other places on earth has watching a rather lifeless and often grey expanse of water seemed so compelling, or have floating logs, otters and boat wakes been photographed so often and with such excitement. Yet while even high-tech sonar surveys carried out over the past two decades have failed to come up with conclusive evidence, it's hard to dismiss Nessie as pure myth. After all, no one yet knows where the unknown layers of silt and mud at the bottom of the loch begin and end: best estimates say the loch is more than 750ft deep, deeper than much of the North Sea, while others point to the possibilities of underwater caves and undiscovered channels connected to the sea. Technological advances have also expanded the scope for Nessie-watching: Ⓦ lochness.co.uk offers round-the-clock **webcams** for views across the loch, while Ⓦ lochnessinvestigation.org is packed with research information. The local tourist industry's worst fear – dwindling interest – is about as unlikely as an appearance of the mysterious monster herself.

epicentre of Nessie-hype. Of two rival monster exhibitions, the **Loch Ness Centre & Exhibition** (daily: Easter–May 9.30am–5pm; June & Sept 9am–6pm; July & Aug 9am–8pm; Oct 9.30am–5.30pm; Nov–Easter 10am–3.30pm; £6.50) is the better bet, offering an in-depth rundown of eyewitness accounts and information on various research projects that have attempted to shed further light on the mysteries of the loch.

Cruises on the loch aboard *Deep Scan Cruises* run from the Loch Ness 2000 Exhibition (hourly; Easter–Sept 10am–6pm; 1hr; £10; T 01456 450218); the *Nessie Hunter* (hourly: Easter–Dec 9am–6pm; 50min; £10; T 01456 450395, W loch-ness-cruises.com) can be booked at the Nessieland Monster Centre.

Castle Urquhart

Two miles east of Drumnadrochit • Daily: April–Sept 9.30am–5.30pm; Oct–March 9.30am–4.30pm • HS • £7.20 • T 01456 450551

Most photographs allegedly showing the monster have been taken a couple of miles east of Drumnadrochit, around the thirteenth-century ruined lochside **Castle Urquhart**.

It's one of Scotland's classic picture-postcard ruins, crawling with tourists by day but particularly splendid when floodlit at night after the crowds have gone.

INFORMATION — DRUMNADROCHIT

Tourist office In the main car park (April, May, Sept & Oct Mon–Sat 9am–5pm, Sun 10am–4pm; June–Aug Mon–Sat 9am–6pm, Sun 10am–4pm; T 01456 459086).

ACCOMMODATION

Benleva Lewiston, 0.5 miles from Drumnadrochit T 01456 450080, W benleva.co.uk. A friendly and simply furnished hotel/pub with several real ales on tap and locally sourced game on the menu. £80

Gillyflowers Lewiston, 0.5 miles from Drumnadrochit T 01456 450641, W cali.co.uk/freeway/gillyflowers. A very welcoming B&B in a renovated 1780s farmhouse on a country lane in Lewiston. £54

Loch Ness Backpackers Lodge Coiltie Farmhouse, Lewiston; follow the signs to the left when coming from Drumnadrochit T 01456 450807, W lochness-backpackers.com. Immaculate and friendly hostel where accommodation is spread through an eighteenth-century farm cottage and barns. £16

EATING AND DRINKING

Fiddlers' Café Bar The Green T 01456 450678, W fiddledrum.co.uk. Local steaks, salmon and hearty lunches (starting around £12), along with bottled beers from local independent brewers.

Glen Café The Green T 01456 450282. Less upmarket than the neighbouring *Fiddlers'*, offering a short and simple menu of basic grilled food.

Glen Affric

West of Drumnadrochit is a vast area of high peaks, remote glens and few roads, including **Glen Affric**, generally held as one of Scotland's most beautiful landscapes and heaven for walkers, climbers and mountain bikers. The approach is through the small settlement of **CANNICH**, fourteen miles west of Drumnadrochit on the A831.

Hemmed in by a string of Munros, Glen Affric is great for picnics and pottering, particularly on a calm and sunny day, when the still water reflects the islands and surrounding hills. From the car park at the head of the single-track road along the glen, ten miles southwest of Cannich, there's a selection of **walks**: the trip around Loch Affric will take you a good five hours but captures the glen, its wildlife and Caledonian pine and birch woods in all their remote splendour.

ACCOMMODATION AND EATING — GLEN AFFRIC

Cannich Campsite Cannich T 01456 415364, W btinternet.com/~highlandcamping/. An excellent campsite where mountain bikes can be rented. Their chalet-like *Bog Cotton Café* is the best option for food in these parts. Food served daily 9am–3pm. £6 per adult

Fort Augustus

FORT AUGUSTUS, a tiny, busy village at the scenic southwestern tip of Loch Ness, was named after George II's son, the chubby lad who later became the "Butcher" Duke of Cumberland of Culloden fame; today, the village is dominated by comings and goings along the Caledonian Canal, which leaves Loch Ness here. From its berth by the Clansman Centre, *Cruise Loch Ness* (March–Oct; 1hr; £11.50; T 01320 366277, W cruiselochness.com) sails five miles up Loch Ness, using sonar technology to provide impressive live 3D imagery of the deep.

INFORMATION — FORT AUGUSTUS

Tourist office The Fort Augustus office has useful free walking leaflets (May–Sept daily 9.30am–5pm; Oct–Dec & mid-Feb to March Sat & Sun 11am–3pm; T 01320 366779).

ACCOMMODATION

Abbey Cottage Main St T 0845 471 8332, W abbeycottagelochness.co.uk. A nicely renovated B&B with a breakfast room overlooking the Caledonian Canal. **£60**

Morag's Lodge Bunoich Brae on the Loch Ness side of town T 01320 366289, W moragslodge.com. Quality budget accommodation in a bright and colourful hostel; the atmosphere livens up with the daily arrival of backpackers' minibus tours. Family rooms available. Dorm **£18**, double **£46**

23

Fort William

With its stunning position on Loch Linnhe, tucked in below the snow-streaked bulk of Ben Nevis, the important regional centre of **FORT WILLIAM** (often known as "Fort Bill"), should be a gem. Sadly, the same lack of taste that nearly saw the town renamed "Abernevis" in the 1950s is evident in the ribbon bungalow development and dual carriageway – complete with grubby pedestrian underpass – which have wrecked the waterfront. The main street and the little squares off it are more appealing, though occupied by some decidedly tacky tourist gift shops.

ARRIVAL AND INFORMATION — FORT WILLIAM

By train Trains arrive at Station Square near the town centre.

Destinations Arisaig (Mon–Sat 3–4 daily, Sun 1–2 daily; 1hr 10min); Crianlarich (Mon–Sat 5 daily, 2 on Sun; 1hr 50min); Glasgow (Mon–Sat 4 daily, 2 on Sun; 3hr 45min); Glenfinnan (Mon–Sat 3–4 daily, Sun 2–4 daily; 35min); London (Sun–Fri 1 nightly; 12hr); Mallaig (Mon–Sat 3–4 daily, Sun 2–4 daily; 1hr 25min).

By bus The bus station is by the train station near the centre of town.

Destinations Acharacle (Mon–Sat 1–2 daily; 1hr 30min); Drumnadrochit (8 daily; 1hr 30min); Edinburgh (4 daily; 4hr); Fort Augustus (5 daily; 1hr); Glasgow (4 daily; 3hr); Inverness (5 daily; 2hr 15min); Kilchoan (1–2 daily on request only from Acharacle; 3hr 35min); Kyle of Lochalsh (3 daily; 4hr 20min–5hr); Mallaig (Mon–Fri 3 daily; 1hr 20min); Oban (Mon–Sat 4 daily; 1hr 30min); Portree, Skye (2 daily; 3hr).

Tourist office Cameron Square, just off High St (April, May & Sept Mon–Sat 9am–5pm, Sun 10am–4pm; July & Aug Mon–Sat 9am–6pm, Sun 10am–5pm; Oct Mon–Sat 10am–5pm; Nov–March Mon–Sat 10am–4pm; T 01397 701801, W visithighlands.com).

Mountain guides Local guides include Alan Kimber of *Calluna* (see below), or contact the Snowgoose Mountain Centre (T 01397 772467, W highland-mountain-guides.co.uk), which also offers instruction and residential courses on activities such as mountaineering.

Mountain biking information Off Beat Bikes, 117 High St (T 01397 704008, W offbeatbikes.co.uk) know the best routes, issue free maps and have a branch at the Nevis Range gondola base station (June–Sept; T 01397 705825), with forest rides and a world-championship-standard downhill track.

ACCOMMODATION

Calluna Heathercroft, Connachie Rd T 01397 700451, W fortwilliamholiday.co.uk. Well-run self-catering and hostel accommodation just a 10min walk from the centre of town. Free pick-up available, along with on-site laundry and mountain-guiding services (W westcoast-mountainguides.co.uk). Dorm **£15**

Fort William Backpackers Alma Rd T 01397 700711, W fortwilliambackpackers.com. A rambling, busy, archetypal backpacker hostel with 38 beds, a 5min walk uphill from town, with great views and large communal areas. Dorm **£18**, twin **£47**

The Grange Grange Rd 01397 705516, thegrange-scotland.co.uk. Top-grade accommodation in a striking old stone house, with log fires, views towards Loch Linnhe and luxurious en-suite doubles. Vegetarian breakfasts on request. Closed Nov–March. **£58**

★ **Lime Tree** Achintore Rd 01397 701806, limetreefortwilliam.co.uk. A stylish and relaxing option in an old manse, with a great modern restaurant and an excellent gallery; they've got the practicalities covered with a drying room, map room and bike storage. **£110**

Rhu Mhor Alma Rd 01397 702213, rhumhor.co.uk. Congenial and characterful B&B, a 10min walk from the centre, offering good breakfasts; vegetarians and vegans catered for on request. **£68**

EATING AND DRINKING

Crannog at the Waterfront Town Pier 01397 705589, crannog.net. Lochside views and fresh seafood, including lobster, oak-smoked salmon and langoustines, alongside a reasonable wine list. Daily noon–2.30pm & 6–9pm.

23

Grog and Gruel 66 High St 01397 705078, grogandgruel.co.uk. Loud and friendly pub that's a good bet for Scottish real ales and malts, traditional pub grub and live music. Mon–Wed noon–11.30pm, Thurs–Sat noon–12.30am, Sun 12.30–11.30pm.

Lime Tree Restaurant Achintore Rd 01397 701806, limetreefortwilliam.co.uk. Located in a hotel (see above), the *Lime Tree* serves excellent contemporary Scottish food, with a five-course menu starting at £30. Daily 6–10pm.

Glen Nevis

A ten-minute drive south of Fort William, **GLEN NEVIS** is among the Highlands' most impressive glens: a U-shaped glacial valley hemmed in by steep bracken-covered slopes and swaths of blue-grey scree. Herds of shaggy Highland cattle graze the valley floor, where a sparkling river gushes through glades of trees.

A great **low-level walk** (six miles round-trip) runs from the end of the road at the top of Glen Nevis. The rocky path leads through a dramatic gorge with impressive falls and rapids, then opens out into a secret hanging valley, carpeted with wild flowers, with a high waterfall at the far end. Of all the walks in and around Glen Nevis, however, the **ascent of Ben Nevis** (4406ft), Britain's highest summit, inevitably attracts the most attention. Despite the fact that it's quite a slog up to the summit, and it's by no means the most attractive mountain in Scotland, in high summer the trail is teeming with hikers, whatever the weather. It can snow round the summit any day of the year, so take the necessary precautions; in winter, of course, the mountain should be left to

THE NEVIS RANGE

Seven miles northeast of Fort William by the A82, on the slopes of **Aonach Mhor**, one of the high mountains abutting Ben Nevis, the **Nevis Range** (01397 705825, nevis-range.co.uk) is Scotland's highest winter ski area. Highland Country bus #42 runs from Fort William (Mon–Sat 5 daily, 3 on Sun) to the base station of the country's only **gondola** system (daily: 10am–5pm; July & Aug 9.30am–6pm; closed mid-Nov to mid-Dec; £8.50 return). The 1.5-mile gondola trip (15min), rising 2000ft, gives an easy approach to some high-level walking as well as spectacular views from the terrace of the self-service restaurant at the top station. From the top of the gondola station, you can experience Britain's only World-Cup-standard **downhill mountain-bike course** (mid-May to mid-Sept 11am–3pm; £10.25 includes gondola one way; £19 multitrip), a hair-raising 3km route that's not for the faint-hearted. There are also 25 miles of waymarked off-road bike routes, known as the Witch's Trails, on the mountainside and in the Leanachan Forest, ranging from gentle paths to cross-country scrambles. Alpine Bikes (Mon–Sat 9am–5.30pm, Sun 10am–5pm; half-day £10, full day £15; 01397 704008, alpinebikes.co.uk) rents mountain bikes as well as full-suspension bikes for the downhill course from their shops in Fort William and at the gondola base station (mid-May to mid-Sept). The base station area also has a café and there's a play area and nature trail nearby.

the experts. The most obvious **route** to the summit, a Victorian pony path up the whaleback south side of the mountain, built to service the observatory that once stood on the top, starts from the helpful **Glen Nevis visitor centre** (see below): allow a full day for the climb (8hr).

ARRIVAL AND INFORMATION — GLEN NEVIS

By bus Highland Country bus #42 (May–Sept; every 1hr 20min) runs from Fort William bus station via the SYHA hostel to the Lower Falls car park almost 5 miles up the Glen Nevis road.

Glen Nevis visitor centre 1.5 miles along the Glen Nevis road (daily: Easter to mid-May & Oct 9am–5pm; mid-May to end Sept 9am–6pm; T 01397 705922.

ACCOMMODATION AND EATING

Achintee Farm Guest House Achintee, Glen Nevis T 01397 702240, W achinteefarm.com. Friendly B&B with adjoining hostel and self-catering cottage, located right by the *Ben Nevis Inn* at the start of the Ben Nevis footpath. **£70**

★ **Ben Nevis Inn** Achintee, Glen Nevis T 01397 701227, W ben-nevis-inn.co.uk. A basic, twenty-bed bunkhouse in the basement of a lively 250-year-old pub. Terrific pub grub and atmosphere. **£15.50**

23

Glen Coe

Sixteen miles south of Fort William on the A82, breathtakingly beautiful **Glen Coe** (literally "Valley of Weeping") is the best known of the Highland glens: a spectacular mountain valley between velvety-green conical peaks, their tops often wreathed in cloud, their flanks streaked by cascades of rock and scree. In 1692 it was the site of a notorious massacre, in which the MacDonalds were victims of a long-standing government desire to suppress the clans. When clan chief **Alastair MacDonald** missed the deadline of January 1, 1692, to sign an oath of allegiance to William III, a plot was hatched to make an example of "that damnable sept". **Campbell of Glenlyon** was ordered to billet his soldiers in the homes of the MacDonalds, who for ten days entertained them with traditional Highland hospitality. In the early morning of February 13, the soldiers turned on their hosts, slaying between 38 and 45, and causing more than three hundred to flee.

Glencoe

Beyond the small village of **GLENCOE** at the western end of the glen, the glen itself (a property of the National Trust for Scotland since the 1930s) is virtually uninhabited,

WALKS AROUND GLEN COE

A good introduction to the splendours of Glen Coe is the half-day hike over the **Devil's Staircase**, which follows part of the old military road that once ran between Fort William and Stirling. The trail, part of the West Highland Way (see p.880), starts at the village of **Kinlochleven** and is marked by thistle signs, which lead uphill to the 1804ft pass and down the other side into Glen Coe.

Set right in the heart of the glen, the half-day **Allt Coire Gabhail** hike starts at the car park opposite the distinctive Three Sisters massif on the main A82. This explores the so-called "Lost Valley" where the Clan MacDonald fled and hid their cattle when attacked. Once in the valley, there are superb views of the upper slopes of Bidean nan Bian, Gearr Aonach and Beinn Fhada, which improve as you continue on to its head, another twenty- to thirty-minute walk.

One of the finest walks in the Glen Coe area that doesn't entail the ascent of a Munro is the **Buachaille Etive Beag** circuit, which follows the textbook glacial valleys of Lairig Eilde and Lairig Gartain, ascending 1968ft in only nine miles of rough trail. Park near the waterfall at **The Study** – the gorge part of the A82 through Glen Coe – and walk up the road until you see a sign pointing south to "Loch Etiveside". Refer to the *Ordnance Survey Explorer Map* no. 384.

and provides outstanding climbing and walking. Enlightening ranger-led **guided walks** (Easter & June–Sept) leave from the centre a mile south of the village (see below), which also has an exhibition with a balanced account of the massacre alongside some entertaining material on rock and hill-climbing down the years. A cabin area provides information on the local weather and wildlife, and a café sells good cakes.

INFORMATION — GLEN COE

NTS visitor centre A mile south of Glencoe village (March daily 10am–4pm; April–Aug daily 9.30am–5.30pm; Sept & Oct daily 10am–5pm; Nov to mid-Dec, Jan & Feb Thurs–Sun 10am–4pm; NTS; £6).

ACCOMMODATION AND EATING

23

★ **Clachaig Inn** Glencoe ⓣ 01855 811252, ⓦ clachaig.com. The lively inn is a great place to swap stories with fellow climbers and to reward your exertions with cask-conditioned ales and heaped platefuls of food; it's 3 miles south of Glencoe village on the minor road off the A82.

Glencoe hostel Between Glencoe village and the Clachaig Inn ⓣ 01855 811906, ⓦ glencoehostel.co.uk. Occupying rustic whitewashed buildings, this attractive hostel is cheaper than the SYHA alternative, with a drying room, internet access and laundry. From £13

Red Squirrel campsite Between Glencoe village and the Clachaig Inn ⓣ 01855 811256, ⓦ redsquirrelcampsite.co.uk. This sylvan year-round site needs to be booked well in advance at holiday times. There's woodland, a swimming hole and permit fishing. Campfires permitted. Adults £7.50

The west coast

The Highlands' starkly beautiful **west coast** – stretching from the **Morvern peninsula** (opposite Mull) in the south to wind-lashed **Cape Wrath** in the far north – is arguably the finest part of Scotland. Serrated by fjord-like sea lochs, the long coastline is scattered with windswept white-sand beaches, cliff-girt headlands, and rugged mountains sweeping up from the shoreline. When the sun shines, the sparkle of the sea, the richness of colour and the clarity of the views out to the scattered Hebrides are simply irresistible. This is the least populated part of Britain, with just two small towns, and yawning tracts of moorland and desolate peat bog between crofting settlements.

Lying within easy reach of Inverness, the popular stretch of the coast between Kyle of Lochalsh and Ullapool features the region's more obvious highlights: the awesome mountainscape of **Torridon**, **Gairloch**'s sandy beaches, the famous botanic gardens at **Inverewe**, and **Ullapool** itself, a picturesque and bustling fishing town from where ferries leave for the Outer Hebrides. However, press on further north, or south, and you'll get a truer sense of the isolation that makes the west coast so special. Traversed by few roads, the remote northwest corner of Scotland is wild and bleak, receiving the full force of the North Atlantic's frequently ferocious weather. The scattered settlements of the far southwest, meanwhile, tend to be more sheltered, but they are separated by some of the most extensive wilderness areas in Britain – lonely peninsulas with evocative Gaelic names like **Ardnamurchan**, **Knoydart** and **Glenelg**.

GETTING AROUND — THE WEST COAST

Without your own vehicle, transport can be a problem. There's a reasonable **train** service from Inverness to Kyle of Lochalsh and from Fort William to Mallaig, and a useful **summer bus** service connects Inverness to Ullapool, Lochinver, Scourie and Durness. **Driving** is a much simpler option: the roads aren't busy, though they are frequently singletrack and scattered with sheep.

The "Rough Bounds"

The remote and sparsely populated southwest corner of the Highlands, from the empty district of **Morvern** to the isolated peninsula of **Knoydart**, is a dramatic,

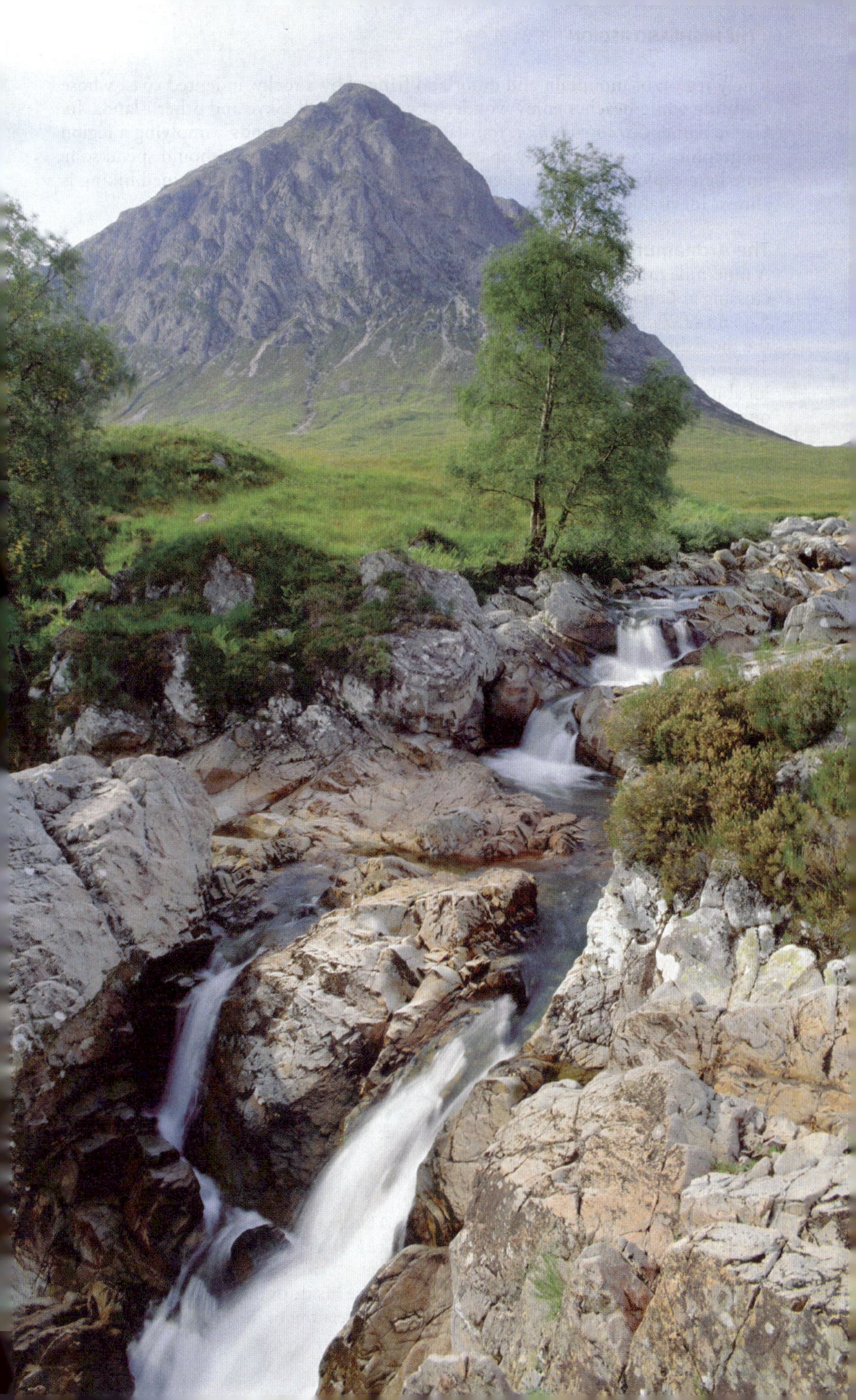

lonely region of mountain and moorland fringed by a rocky, indented coast whose stunning white beaches enjoy wonderful views to Mull, Skye and other islands. Its Gaelic name, *Garbh-chiochan*, translates as the "**Rough Bounds**", implying a region geographically and spiritually apart. Even if you have a car, you should spend some time here exploring on foot; there are so few roads that some determined hiking is almost inevitable.

The Ardnamurchan peninsula

A nine-mile drive south of Fort William down Loch Linnhe, the five-minute ferry crossing at **Corran Ferry** (every 20–30min; Mon–Sat 6.30am–9.20pm, Sun 8.45am–9.20pm; car and passengers £5.20; foot passengers and bicycles free) provides the most direct point of entry for Morvern and the rugged **Ardnamurchan peninsula**. The most westerly point on the British mainland, the peninsula lost most of its inhabitants during the infamous Clearances and is now sparsely populated with only a handful of tiny crofting settlements clinging to its jagged coastline. It boasts some beautiful, pristine, empty beaches – especially about three miles north of the Ardnamurchan lighthouse at **Sanna Bay**, a shell-strewn strand and series of dunes that offers truly unforgettable vistas of the Small Isles to the north, circled by gulls, terns and guillemots. The coastal hamlet of **SALEN** marks the turn-off for Ardnamurchan Point: from here it's a further 25 miles of slow, scenic driving along the singletrack road which follows the northern shore of Loch Sunart.

Nàdurra Centre

Glenmore, Arachle • April–Oct Mon–Sat 10.30am–5.30pm, Sun 11.30am–5.30pm; Nov–March Mon–Fri 10.30am–4pm, Sun 11.30am–4pm • £4 • T 01972 500209, W nadurracentre.co.uk

Just west of the hamlet of **GLENBORRODALE**, look out for the engaging **Nàdurra Centre**, which provides an inspiring introduction to the diverse flora, fauna and geology of Ardnamurchan: CCTV cameras relay pictures of the comings and goings of heron, a pine marten's nest and sea and golden eagles feeding nearby. The *Antler Tearoom* provides light refreshments.

Kilchoan

Nine miles west of the Glenmore Centre, **KILCHOAN** is Ardnamurchan's main village – an appealing crofting township overlooking the Sound of Mull.

ARRIVAL AND INFORMATION — KILCHOAN

By ferry A car ferry runs from Kilchoan to Tobermory on Mull (Mon–Sat 8am–6.40pm 7 daily; May–Aug also Sun 10.15am–4.45pm 5 daily; 35min).

Tourist office In the village community centre (Easter–Oct daily 9am–5pm; T 01972 510222, W ardnamurchan.com); the community centre itself offers advice year round.

ACCOMMODATION

Ardnamurchan campsite T 07787 812084, W ardnamurchanstudycentre.co.uk. This site, with lovely coastal views, is located by the Ardnamurchan Study Centre, about half a mile beyond the Ferry Stores. Closed Oct–Easter. Tent and 1 person **£7**

Torrsolais T 01972 510389, W ardnamurchan-holidays.co.uk. Two-bedroom guesthouse enjoying lovely views over the bay and Sound of Mull. Rooms are bright and modern. **£60**

Ardnamurchan Point Lighthouse

Ardnamurchan Point • April–Oct daily 10am–5pm • £5 • T 01972 510210, book ahead at peak times

The road continues beyond Kilchoan to the rocky, windy **Ardnamurchan Point** and its famous **lighthouse.** The lighthouse buildings house a small café and an absorbing **exhibition**. Best of all is the chance to climb up the inside of the Egyptian-style lighthouse tower; at the top, a guide tells tall tales relating to the lighthouse and shows you around the lighting mechanism.

The Road to the Isles

The "**Road to the Isles**" (road-to-the-isles.org.uk) from Fort William to Mallaig, followed by the West Highland Railway and the narrow, winding A830, traverses the mountains and glens of the Rough Bounds before breaking out onto a spectacularly scenic coast of sheltered inlets, white beaches and wonderful views to the islands of Rùm, Eigg, Muck and Skye. This is country associated with **Bonnie Prince Charlie**, whose adventures of 1745–46 began and ended on this stretch of coast, with his first, defiant gathering of the clans at **Glenfinnan**, nineteen miles west of Fort William at the head of lovely **Loch Shiel**. The spot is marked by a column (now a little lopsided), crowned with a clansman in full battle dress, erected in 1815.

Glenfinnan

GLENFINNAN is a poignant place, a beautiful stage for the opening scene in a brutal drama that was to change the Highlands for ever. The **visitor centre** and café (daily: April, May, June, Sept & Oct 10am–5pm; July & Aug 9.30am–5.30pm; NTS; £3.50), opposite the monument, gives an account of the '45 uprising through to the rout at **Culloden** eight months later (see p.882). Loch Shiel Cruises (01687 470322, highlandcruises.co.uk) run a number of **boat trips** on the loch, all offering a worthwhile opportunity to view the remote, captivating scenery and occasionally a golden eagle.

This area is the most spectacular section of the **West Highland Railway** line (see p.880), offering glimpses of the graceful Loch Shiel. There's a **Glenfinnan Station Museum** (June–Sept Mon–Fri 9.30am–5pm, Sat & Sun 10am–5pm; 50p) in the old booking office of the station.

23

ACCOMMODATION AND EATING — GLENFINNAN

The Dining Car Station Cottage 01397 722300, glenfinnanstationmuseum.co.uk/dining_car.asp. A quirky restaurant in a railway carriage next to the station museum, where you can tuck into light lunches and home baking (phone ahead for evening meals). June–Sept daily 10am–5pm.

Sleeping Car Station Cottage 01397 722295, glenfinnanstationmuseum.co.uk/sleeping_car.asp. Adjoining the *Dining Car*, this converted railway carriage sleep ten in bunk beds. Year-round. **£14**

Arisaig and around

West of Glenfinnan, the A830 runs alongside captivating Loch Eilt and onto a coast marked by acres of white sands, turquoise seas and rocky islets draped with orange seaweed. **ARISAIG**, scattered round a sandy bay at the west end of the Morar peninsula, makes a good base for exploring the vicinity. A **bypass** whizzes cars (and, more importantly, fish lorries) on their way to Mallaig, but you shouldn't miss the slower coast road, which enjoys the best of the scenery.

Stretching north of Arisaig is a string of stunning **beaches** backed by flowery machair, with barren granite hills and moorland rising up behind, and wonderful seaward views of Eigg and Rùm.

Mallaig

A cluttered, noisy port whose pebble-dashed houses struggle for space with great lumps of exposed granite strewn over the hillsides sloping down to the sea, **MALLAIG**, 47 miles west of Fort William, isn't pretty. As the main ferry stop for Skye, the Small Isles and Knoydart, it's always full of visitors, though the continuing source of the village's wealth is its **fishing** industry. When the fleet is in, trawlers encircled by flocks of raucous gulls choke the harbour, and the pubs, among the liveliest on the west coast, host bouts of serious drinking.

ARRIVAL AND INFORMATION — MALLAIG

By ferry The CalMac ticket office (01687 462403), serving passengers for Skye and the Small Isles, is near the tourist office on the harbour.

Destinations Armadale on Skye (Mon–Sat 8 daily; also

mid-May to mid-Sept Sun at least 4 daily; 30min); and, on the Small Isles: Canna (Mon, Wed, Fri & Sat 1 daily; 2hr 30min); Eigg (Mon, Thurs, Sat 1 daily; 1hr 15min); Muck (Tues, Thurs, Fri, Sat 1 daily; 2hr 5min); Rùm (Mon, Wed, Fri, Sat 1 daily; 1hr 20min). For Knoydart, Bruce Watt Cruises (T 01687 462320, W knoydart-ferry.co.uk) sails to Inverie, on the Knoydart peninsula (2 daily: mid-May to mid-Sept Mon–Fri; mid-Sept to mid-May Mon, Wed & Fri).

Tourist office Main St, by the harbour (April–Oct Mon–Sat 10am–5pm; variable winter hours; T 01687 462064).

ACCOMMODATION

Sheena's Backpackers' Lodge Station Rd T 01687 462764, W mallaigbackpackers.co.uk. A refreshingly laidback independent hostel overlooking the harbour, which has mixed dorms and the (licensed) *Tea Garden Restaurant* (see below). **£15**

Western Isles Guest House East Bay T 01687 462320, W road-to-the-isles.org.uk/western-isles.html. Cheery and modern B&B. **£64**

EATING AND DRINKING

Cornerstone Main St, opposite the tourist office T 01687 462306, W seafoodrestaurantmallaig.com. Fresh fish and chips – or scallops and chips if you're feeling decadent – plus langoustines, prawns, haddock, monkfish, sole and mussels (mains from £12). Daily noon–9pm.

Tea Garden Restaurant Station Rd T 01687 462764, W mallaigbackpackers.co.uk. A great place to watch the world go by while you tuck into a bowl of Cullen Skink, a pint of prawns or home-made scones; from 6pm they serve bistro-style meals (from £10). Daily 9am–9pm.

The Knoydart peninsula

Flanked by **Loch Nevis** ("Loch of Heaven") in the south and the fjord-like inlet of **Loch Hourn** ("Loch of Hell") to the north, **Knoydart peninsula**'s knobbly green peaks – three of them Munros – sweep straight out of the sea, shrouded for much of the time in a pall of grey mist. To get to the heart of the peninsula, you must catch a **boat** from Mallaig or Glenelg, or else **hike** for a couple of days across rugged moorland and mountains and sleep rough in old stone bothies (most of which are marked on Ordnance Survey maps).

At the end of the eighteenth century, around a thousand people eked out a living from this inhospitable terrain through crofting and fishing. These days the peninsula supports around seventy, most of whom live in the hamlet of **INVERIE.** Nestled beside a sheltered bay on the south side of the peninsula, it has a pint-sized post office, a shop, and mainland Britain's most remote pub.

INFORMATION — THE KNOYDART PENINSULA

Your best source of information for walking and wildlife in the area (including guided walks) is from the **ranger post** (T 01687 462242) beside the *Old Forge* in Inverie.

ACCOMMODATION AND EATING

★ **Doune Stone Lodges** Doune T 01687 462667, W doune-knoydart.co.uk. Rebuilt from ruined crofts and offering pine-fitted en-suite doubles right on the shore, this place provides isolation and creature comforts. They serve delicious meals, and owner Martin is a great source of walking info. It's not easy to get to by land, but they'll pick you up by boat from Mallaig (£20pp). Minimum stay three nights. Full board. **£75**

Knoydart Foundation Bunkhouse Inverie T 01687 462242, W knoydart-foundation.com. A simple and straightforward option, with adequate facilities in old steadings a 10min walk from the pub. **£15**

★ **Old Forge** Inverie T 01687 462267, W theoldforge.co.uk. The *Old Forge* is one of Scotland's finer pubs, with a convivial atmosphere where visitors and locals mix happily. Generous bar meals (from £8) often feature freshly caught seafood, real ales, an open fire, and a good chance of live music of an evening. Daily 12.30–3pm & 6.30–9.30pm.

Kyle of Lochalsh and around

As the main gateway to Skye, **KYLE OF LOCHALSH** used to be an important transit point for tourists, locals and services. However, with the building of the **Skye Bridge** in 1995, Kyle was left as merely the terminus for the train route from Inverness, with little else to offer. Of more interest is nearby **Eilean Donan Castle**, perched at the end of a stone causeway on the shores of **Loch Duich**. A few miles north of Kyle of Lochalsh is the delightful village of **Plockton**, a refreshing alternative to its utilitarian neighbour, with cottages grouped around a yacht-filled bay and Highland cattle wandering the streets.

ARRIVAL AND INFORMATION — KYLE OF LOCHALSH

By train Trains connect Kyle of Lochalsh with Dingwall (Mon–Sat 3–4 daily, 1–2 on Sun; 2hr), Inverness (Mon–Sat 3–4 daily, 1–2 on Sun; 2hr 40min) and Plockton (Mon–Sat 3–4 daily, 1–2 on Sun; 15min).

By bus Buses run to Kyle of Lochalsh from Glasgow (3 daily; 5hr) via Fort William (1hr 50min) and Invergarry, and from Inverness (3 daily; 2hr) via Invermoriston, and all continue at least as far as Portree on Skye: book in advance for all of them (T 0870 550 5050, W citylink.co.uk). Buses also shuttle across the bridge to Kyleakin on Skye every 30min or so.

Tourist office On the small hill near the old ferry jetty (April–Oct Mon–Fri 9.30am–5pm, Sat & Sun 10am–4pm).

ACCOMMODATION AND EATING

Ardenlea Church St T 01599 534630. Spacious and comfortable, this is a good central B&B. The "master suite" has a sitting room and en-suite bedroom. **£60**

Cúchulainn's Station Rd T 01599 534492. A simple bunkhouse above a pub across the main street from the tourist office. There are twelve beds in three rooms, plus a kitchen and launderette. **£9.50**

Waverley Restaurant Main St T 01599 534337. Sample the inexpensive fresh fish dishes and delicious home-made puddings in this tiny restaurant on the main street. Fri–Wed 5.30–9.30pm.

23

Eilean Donan Castle

Ten miles north of Shiel Bridge on the A87 • Daily: April–June, Sept & Oct 10am–5pm; July & Aug 9am–5pm • £6 • T 01599 555202, W eileandonancastle.com

Eilean Donan Castle is one of Scotland's most photographed monuments. The forbidding crenellated tower rises from the water's edge, joined to the shore by a narrow stone bridge and with sheer mountains as a backdrop. The original castle was established in 1230 by Alexander II to protect the area from the Vikings. Later, during a Jacobite uprising in 1719, it was occupied by troops dispatched by the king of Spain to help the "**Old Pretender**", James Stuart. However, when King George heard of their whereabouts, he sent frigates to take the Spaniards out, and the castle was blown up with their stocks of gunpowder. Thereafter, it lay in ruins until John Macrae-Gilstrap had it rebuilt between 1912 and 1932. Eilean Donan has since featured in several major **films**, including *Highlander*, *Entrapment*, and the James Bond adventure *The World is Not Enough*. Three floors, including the banqueting hall, the bedrooms and the troops' quarters, are open to the public, with various Jacobite and clan relics also on display, though like many of the region's most popular castles, the large numbers of people passing through make it hard to appreciate the real charm of the place.

Plockton

A fifteen-minute train ride north of Kyle at the seaward end of islet-studded Loch Carron lies the unbelievably picturesque village of **PLOCKTON**: a chocolate-box row of neatly painted cottages ranged around the curve of a tiny harbour and backed by a craggy landscape of heather and pine. The unique brilliance of Plockton's light has also made it something of an artists' hang-out, and during the summer the waterfront, with its row of shaggy palm trees, even shaggier Highland cattle, flower gardens and pleasure boats, is invariably dotted with painters dabbing at their easels.

TOP 5 HIGHLAND HOSTELS

Carbisdale Castle SYHA Near Bonar Bridge. See p.909

Carn Dearg SYHA Gairloch coast. See p.900

Glencoe hostel See p.892

Lazy Crofter Bunkhouse Durness. See p.904

Station Bunkhouse Plockton. See p.898

ACCOMMODATION AND EATING — PLOCKTON

Heron's Flight 01599 544220, heronsflight.org. Beyond the tiny post office, *Heron's Flight* is perched on a little crag and enjoys loch views from its two upstairs bedrooms. Closed Dec–Feb. **£50**

Plockton Hotel 41 Harbour St 01599 544274, plocktonhotel.co.uk. Comfortable and atmospheric, with live music in summer and terrific harbour and loch views. They serve local real ales and fresh seafood is a staple on the evening menu. **£65**

★ **Station Bunkhouse** On the outskirts of Plockton, opposite the train station 01599 544235. Attractive and unusual hostel with four- and six-bed dorms and an open-plan kitchen and living area. The owners also do B&B (£45). **£13**

Wester Ross

23 The western seaboard of the old county of Ross-shire, **Wester Ross**, blends all the classic elements of Scotland's **coastal scenery** – dramatic mountains, sandy beaches, whitewashed crofting cottages and shimmering island views – in spectacular fashion. Though popular with generations of adventurous Scottish holiday-makers, only one or two places feel blighted by tourist numbers, with places such as **Applecross** and the peninsulas north and south of **Gairloch** maintaining an endearing simplicity and sense of isolation. There's some tough but wonderful **hiking** to be enjoyed in the mountains around **Torridon** and **Coigach**, while **boat trips** out among the islands and the prolific sea- and birdlife of the coast are another draw. The main settlement is the attractive fishing town of **Ullapool**, port for ferry services to Stornoway in the Western Isles, but a pleasant enough place to use as a base, not least for its active social and cultural scene.

The Applecross peninsula

The most dramatic approach to the **Applecross peninsula** (the English-sounding name is a corruption of the Gaelic *Apor Crosan*, meaning "estuary") is from the south, up a glacial U-shaped valley and over the infamous **Bealach na Bà** (literally "Pass of the Cattle"). Crossing the forbidding hills behind Kishorn and rising to 2053ft, with a gradient and switchback bends worthy of the Alps, this route – a popular cycling piste – is hair-raising in places, and the panoramic views across the Minch to Raasay and Skye augment the experience.

Applecross

The sheltered, fertile coast around **APPLECROSS** village (applecross.info), where the Irish missionary monk Maelrhuba founded a monastery in 673 AD, comes as a surprise after the bleakness of the moorland approach. Maybe it's the journey, but Applecross feels like an idyllic place: you can wander along lanes banked with wild iris and orchids, and explore beaches and rock pools on the shore. There's a small **Heritage Centre** (April–Oct Mon–Sat noon–4pm; applecrossheritage.org.uk) overlooking Clachan church and graveyard, and a number of short **waymarked trails** along the shore – great for walking off a pub lunch.

ACCOMMODATION AND EATING — APPLECROSS

Applecross Inn 01520 744262, applecross.uk.com. The old, family-run inn right beside the sea is the focal point of the community, with rooms upstairs, and a lively bar that serves delicious local seafood and produce. Food served noon–9pm. **£60**

★ **Littlehill of My Heart** Meall mo Chridhe, Camusterrach 01520 744432, applecrossaccommodation.com. This excellent village B&B has classy spacious rooms and delicious breakfasts, including a full Scottish. **£70**

★ **Potting Shed Café and Restaurant** 01520 744440, applecrossgarden.co.uk. A mile down the road from the village, this is a culinary and visual delight, where the walled Victorian garden, woods and sea provide fresh, rich pickings for the chefs, who serve delicious dishes in a laidback atmosphere. Fairly inexpensive in its daytime incarnation as a café, it's pricier in the evening; they operate a rickshaw service to take you to and from the village. March–Oct Mon–Sat 11am–8.30pm, Sun 11am–4pm.

Loch Torridon

Loch Torridon marks the northern boundary of the Applecross peninsula, its awe-inspiring setting enhanced by the appealingly rugged mountains of **Liathach** and **Beinn Eighe**, hulks of reddish 750-million-year-old Torridonian sandstone tipped by streaks of white quartzite. Some 15,000 acres of the massif are under the protection of the National Trust for Scotland, which runs a **Countryside Centre**, by Torridon Village by the head of the loch (Easter–Sept Mon–Sat 10am–5pm; £3), where you can learn about the local geology, flora and fauna.

ACCOMMODATION AND EATING — LOCH TORRIDON

Torridon By Achnasheen ⓣ01445 791242, ⓦthetorridon.com. On the south side of the loch stands one of the area's grandest hotels, a smart, rambling Victorian building set amid well-tended lochside grounds. **£215**

Torridon Inn By Achnasheen ⓣ01445 791242, ⓦthetorridon.com. A cheaper option next to and run by the hotel, this is a cyclist- and walker-friendly modern farmstead conversion with neat twins and doubles and a moderately priced bar/bistro serving real ales, boar sausage and the like. Closed Nov–Feb. **£95**

23

Loch Maree

About eight miles north of Loch Torridon, **Loch Maree**, dotted with Caledonian pine-covered islands, is one of the west's scenic highlights, best viewed from the A832 road that skirts the loch's southern shore, passing the **Beinn Eighe Nature Reserve**, the UK's oldest wildlife sanctuary. Parts of the reserve are forested with Caledonian pinewood, which once covered the whole of the country, and it is home to pine marten, wildcat, buzzards and golden eagles.

A mile north of Kinlochewe, the well-run **Beinn Eighe Visitor Centre** (Easter & May–Oct daily 10am–5pm) on the A832, offers excellent information on the area's rare species. Outside, "talking trails" provide an easy walk through the vicinity, while several longer **walks** start from the car park, a mile north of the visitor centre.

Gairloch

GAIRLOCH spreads itself around the northeastern corner of the wide sheltered bay of Loch Gairloch. During the summer, Gairloch thrives as a low-key holiday resort with several tempting sandy beaches and some excellent coastal walks within easy reach. The main supermarket and **tourist office** (see p.900) are in Achtercairn, right by the **Gairloch Heritage Museum** (March–Sept daily 10am–5pm; Oct Mon–Sat 10am–1.30pm; £4), which has eclectic, appealing displays covering geology, archeology, fishing and farming.

WALKS AROUND TORRIDON

There can be difficult conditions on virtually all hiking routes around Torridon, and the weather can change rapidly. If you're relatively inexperienced but want to do the magnificent ridge walk along the **Liathach** (pronounced "lee-ach") massif, or the strenuous traverse of **Beinn Eighe** (pronounced "ben ay"), join a National Trust Ranger Service guided hike (July & Aug; Torridon Countryside Centre; ⓣ01445 791221).

For those confident to go it alone, one of many possible routes takes you behind Liathach and down the pass, **Coire Dubh**, to the main road in Glen Torridon. This is a great, straightforward, full-day walk, covering thirteen miles and taking in superb landscapes. Another rewarding walk, even in rough weather, is the seven-mile hike up the coast from **Lower Diabaig**, ten miles northwest of Torridon village, to **Redpoint**. On a clear day, the views across to Raasay and Applecross from this gentle path are superlative, but you'll have to return along the same trail, or else make your way back via Loch Maree on the A832. The *Ordnance Survey Explorer Map* no. 433 is particularly useful for Torridon.

ARRIVAL AND INFORMATION — GAIRLOCH

By bus For Redpoint and Melvaig only, you can use the local Dial-a-Bus service (☎ 01445 712255).
Destinations Inverness (Mon–Sat 1 daily; also ScotBus June–Sept 1 daily Mon–Sat; 2hr 45min); Ullapool (1 daily Mon, Wed, Thurs & Sat).

Tourist office Achtercairn (June–Sept daily 9am–5.30pm; Oct Mon–Sat 9am–5.30pm; Nov–May Mon–Sat 10am–4pm; ☎ 01445 712071).

ACCOMMODATION AND EATING

Gairloch has a good choice of accommodation, but you might prefer to stay out along the road north to **Melvaig** or south to **Redpoint** (see below).

Duisary 24 Strath ☎ 01445 712252, Ⓦ duisary.freeserve.co.uk. Child-friendly B&B in a restored croft with Torridon mountain views. Closed Nov–March. £40

Kerrysdale House Flowerdale Glen ☎ 01445 712292, Ⓦ kerrysdalehouse.co.uk. At the southern edge of Gairloch, just before the turn-off to Badachro, this atmospheric and tastefully furnished place is set back in its own lovely gardens. £62

23

The Old Inn The harbour ☎ 01445 712006, Ⓦ theoldinn.net. Upmarket accommodation, with moderately priced seafood on its bar menu, a very good range of Scottish real ales and snug rooms. £104

The Gairloch coast

The area's main attraction is its beautiful coastline, easily explored on a wildlife-spotting **cruise**: several operators, including Gairloch Marine Life Centre & Cruises (Easter–Oct; ☎ 01445 712636; Ⓦ porpoise-gairloch.co.uk; from £20), run informative and enjoyable boat trips across the bay in search of dolphins, seals and even the odd whale. One of the most impressive stretches of **coastline** is around the north side of the bay, along the singletrack B8021, at **BIG SAND**, which has a cleaner and quieter beach than Gairloch. Three miles beyond is the **Rubha Reidh lighthouse** (see below).

Three miles south of Gairloch, a narrow singletrack lane winds west to **BADACHRO**, a sleepy former fishing village in a very attractive setting with a wonderful **pub**. Beyond Badachro, the road winds for five more miles along the shore to **REDPOINT**, a straggling hamlet with beautiful beaches of peach-coloured sand and great views to Raasay, Skye and the Western Isles.

ACCOMMODATION AND EATING — THE GAIRLOCH COAST

Badachro Inn Badachro ☎ 01445 741255, Ⓦ badachroinn.com. Right by the water's edge: you can sit in the beer garden watching the boats come and go and tuck into quite pricey fresh seafood with a real ale. Daily 11am–11pm.

Rua Reidh Lighthouse Rubha Reidh ☎ 01445 771263, Ⓦ ruareidh.co.uk. Three miles beyond Big Sand at Rubha Reidh (pronounced "roo-a-ray"), you can stay at the headland's operational lighthouse, which looks out to the Outer Hebrides. Comfortable accommodation includes a bunkhouse, doubles and family rooms; breakfast (£6.50) and a pre-booked evening meal (£15.50) can be provided, and they offer guided walking and climbing courses. Dorm £13, double £42

★ **SYHA hostel** Carn Dearg, just outside Big Sand ☎ 01445 712219, Ⓦ syha.org.uk. A former hunting lodge converted into an SYHA hostel, spectacularly set on the edge of a cliff with views to Skye. Closed Oct–March. £17

Inverewe Gardens

Half a mile across the bay from Poolewe on the A832 • Daily: April–Oct 9.30am–9pm or dusk; Nov–March 9.30am–4pm **Visitor centre** April–Sept daily 9.30am–5pm • NTS • £9

It's a fifteen-minute hop by bus over the headland from Gairloch to the trim little village of **Poolewe**, which sits by a small bay at the sheltered southern end of Loch Ewe. Across the bay, **Inverewe Gardens**, a verdant oasis of foliage and riotously colourful flower collections, forms a vivid contrast to the wild, heathery crags of the adjoining coast. Taking advantage of the area's famously temperate climate (a consequence of the Gulf Stream, which draws a warm sea current from Mexico to within a stone's throw of these shores), plants from all over the world grow here, flourishing on rich soil brought over as ballast on Irish ships to overlay the previously infertile beach gravel and sea grass. The **visitor centre** houses an informative display on the history of the garden and is the starting point for **guided walks**.

Ullapool

ULLAPOOL (ullapool.co.uk), northwest Scotland's principal centre of population, was founded at the height of the herring boom in 1788 by the British Fisheries Society, on a sheltered arm of land jutting into Loch Broom. The grid-plan town is still an important fishing centre, though the **ferry** link to Stornoway on Lewis (see p.927) ensures that in high season it's swamped with visitors. Though busy, Ullapool remains a hugely appealing place and a good base for exploring the northwest Highlands.

By day, Ullapool's attention focuses on the comings and goings of the ferry, fishing boats and smaller craft, while in the evening, yachts swing on the current, shops stay open late, and drinkers at the *Ferry Boat Inn* line the sea wall. In summer, trips head to the **Summer Isles** – a cluster of uninhabited islets a couple of miles offshore – to view seabird colonies, dolphins and porpoises.

The only formal attraction in town is the award-winning **museum**, in the old parish church on West Argyle Street (April–Oct Mon–Sat 10am–5pm; 01854 612987; £3), which provides an insight into life in a Highland community, including crofting, fishing, local religion and emigration.

ARRIVAL AND INFORMATION — ULLAPOOL

By bus Regular buses run from Ullapool to Durness (May–Sept Mon–Sat 1 daily; also July & Aug 1 on Sun; 3hr) and Inverness (Mon–Sat 2 daily; 1hr 30min), and there's an early-morning run to the remote train station at Lairg.

By ferry Day-trips to Lewis (Mon–Sat 2 daily; 2hr 45min) by ferry and bus can be organized through CalMac (0870 565 0000).

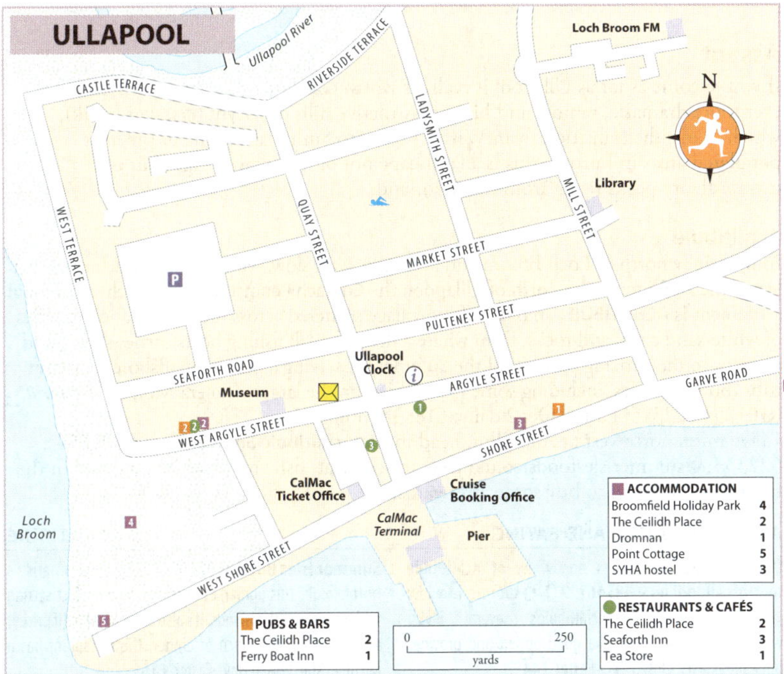

Tourist office Argyle St (April–May Mon–Sat 9am–4.30pm; June–Aug Mon–Sat 9am–5pm, Sun 10am–4pm; Oct Mon–Fri 10am–5pm; call ⓣ01854 612486 for winter opening hours).

ACCOMMODATION

Broomfield Holiday Park West Shore St ⓣ01854 612020. Large, good-value campsite, a 5min walk from town. It's exposed to the wind off Loch Broom, but offers great views and warm showers. From **£13** for a pitch

★ **The Ceilidh Place** 14 West Argyle St ⓣ01854 612103, ⓦtheceilidhplace.com. The tastefully furnished interior of this charismatic place, renowned for its live music and ceilidhs, includes thirteen en-suite bedrooms, an excellent café-bar and a bookshop specializing in Scottish literature, history and art. You can also reserve a bed in its small bunkhouse across the road. Bunkhouse from **£17**, double from **£53**

23

★ **Dromnan** Garve Rd ⓣ01854 612333, ⓦdromnan.co.uk. Excellent B&B run by welcoming hosts, who serve up a hearty breakfast. Lovely sea views, and from the dining area you can walk onto the patio or down to the shore. **£75**

Point Cottage 22 West Shore St ⓣ01854 612494, ⓦpointcottage.co.uk. Rustic, very well-equipped B&B at the quieter end of the seafront. Guests can borrow bikes and there's free wi-fi. **£60**

SYHA Hostel Shore St ⓣ01854 612254, ⓦsyha.org.uk. Busy hostel on the front, with internet access, laundry and lots of good information about local walks. Closed Nov–Feb. **£17.50**

EATING, DRINKING AND ENTERTAINMENT

The Ceilidh Place 14 West Argyle St ⓣ01854 612103, ⓦtheceilidhplace.com. A popular spot for lunch, snacks and dinners (mains around £15) in a pleasant bistro. They also hold regular ceilidhs and music nights.

Ferry Boat Inn Shore St ⓣ01854 612366, ⓦferryboat-inn.com. You can enjoy a pint of real ale at the "FBI" at the lochside – midges permitting – as well as live Scottish folk music.

Seaforth Inn Quay St ⓣ01854 612122, ⓦtheseaforth.com. Though the interior is hardly intimate, this busy bar/restaurant serves terrific-value mains and starters, including a scrumptious fish pie. They also host regular live music performances.

Tea Store Argyle St ⓣ01854 612995, ⓦtheteastore.co.uk. For a no-frills option, locals' favourite the tiny *Tea Store* serves up hearty, inexpensive breakfasts, home baking and a refreshing cuppa.

Assynt

If you've come as far as Ullapool it really is worth continuing further north into the ever more dramatic, remote and highly distinctive hills of **Assynt** (ⓦassynt.co.uk), which marks the transition from Wester Ross into Sutherland. One of the least populated areas in Europe, this is a landscape not of mountain ranges but of extraordinary peaks rising from the moorland.

Achiltibuie

Immediately north of Loch Broom and accessible via a slow, winding singletrack road that leaves the A835 ten miles north of Ullapool, the **Coigach Peninsula's** (ⓦcoigach.com) main settlement is **ACHILTIBUIE**, an old crofting village scattered across the hillside above a series of white-sand coves and rocks, from where a fleet of small fishing boats carries sheep, and tourists, to the enticing pastures of the **Summer Isles**, lying a little way offshore. For **boat** trips round the isles, including some time ashore on the largest, Tanera Mor, try *Hectoria* (ⓣ01854 622315; Easter–Oct 2 daily; £18; 3hr 30min).

Five miles northwest at Altandhu, head to the **Achiltibuie Smokehouse** (ⓣ01854 622353; ⓦsummerislesfoods.co.uk; free) to see meat, fish and game being cured in the traditional way and to buy some afterwards.

ACCOMMODATION AND EATING — ACHILTIBUIE

Dornie House 2.5 miles northwest of Achiltibuie towards Altandhu ⓣ01854 622271, ⓔsummerisleview@btinternet.com. Of Achiltibuie's several B&Bs, welcoming *Dornie House* is a good option and provides huge breakfasts. Closed Dec–Easter. **£44**

Summer Isles Hotel ⓣ01854 622282, ⓦsummerisleshotel.co.uk. This upmarket hotel enjoys a perfect setting with views over the islands. It's also a memorable (if pricey) spot for a seafood lunch or dinner; the restaurant has a Michelin star. Closed Nov–Easter. **£155**

Lochinver and around

The potholed and narrow road north from Achiltibuie through Inverkirkaig is unremittingly spectacular, threading its way through a tumultuous landscape of heaving valleys, moorland and bare rock, past the distinctive sugar-loaf **Suilven** (2398ft). Sixteen miles north of Ullapool (although more than thirty by road), **LOCHINVER** is one of the busiest fishing harbours in Scotland, from where large trucks head off for the continent. The **Assynt Visitor Centre** (April–Oct Mon–Sat 10am–5pm, June–Sept also Sun 10am–4pm) gives an interesting rundown on the area's geology, wildlife and history and has a CCTV link to a nearby heronry.

The first village worthy of a detour on the road north is **ACHMELVICH**, three miles northwest of Lochinver, where a tiny bay cradles a stunning white-sand beach lapped by startlingly turquoise water. However, for total peace and quiet, head to other, equally seductive beaches beyond the headlands.

ARRIVAL AND INFORMATION — LOCHINVER AND AROUND

By bus Lochinver has connections with Inverness (May–Sept 1 daily; plus July–Aug 1 on Sun; 3hr 10min) and Ullapool (Mon–Sat 2 daily;1hr).

Tourist office Inside the Assynt Visitor Centre (April–Oct Mon–Sat 10am–5pm, June–Sept also Sun 10am–4pm; ⓦ assynt.info). They have a handy leaflet, *Walks around Assynt*, outlining 31 walks.

23

Kylesku and around

At **KYLESKU**, 33 miles north of Ullapool on the main A894 road, a long, curving road bridge sweeps over the mouth of lochs Glencoul and Glendhu. Statesman Cruises runs entertaining **boat trips** (March–Oct 2 daily Sun–Fri; round trip 2hr; £15; ⓣ 01971 502345) from the jetty below the *Kylesku Hotel* to the 650ft **Eas-Coul-Aulin**, Britain's highest waterfall, at the head of Loch Glencoul; otters, seals, porpoises and minke whales can occasionally be spotted along the way. The boat also makes regular trips out to **Kerracher Gardens** (mid-May to mid-Sept Tues, Thurs & Sun 1pm; £15), which are only accessible from the sea; this remarkable plot created on a disused croft harnesses the Gulf Stream weather to create a riot of colour and exotic vegetation in the rugged Highland scenery.

ACCOMMODATION — KYLESKU

★ **Kylesku Hotel** Kylesku ⓣ 01971 502231, ⓦ kyleskuhotel.co.uk. The congenial *Kylesku Hotel*, by the water's edge above the old ferry slipway, has a welcoming bar with real ales where you can feast on reasonably priced dishes including fresh seafood. Closed Nov–Feb. **£99**

The far northwest coast

The Sutherland coastline north of Kylesku is a bridge too far for some, yet for others the stark, elemental beauty of the Highlands is to be found on the **far northwest coast** as nowhere else. Here, the peaks become more widely spaced and settlements smaller and fewer, linked by twisting singletrack roads and shoreside footpaths that make excellent hiking trails. Places to stay and eat can be thin on the ground, particularly out of season.

Scourie and around

Ten miles north of Kylesku, the widely scattered crofting community of **SCOURIE**, on a bluff above the main road, surrounds a beautiful sandy beach.

Handa Island Wildlife Reserve

Weather permitting, boats (ⓣ 01971 502347) leave for Handa throughout the day (Easter–Sept Mon–Sat 9.30am–2pm outbound; £10) from the tiny cove of Tarbet, 3 miles northwest of the main road and accessible by postbus from Scourie

Visible just offshore north of Scourie is **HANDA ISLAND**, a huge chunk of red Torridon sandstone surrounded by sheer cliffs, carpeted with machair and purple-tinged moorland,

and teeming with seabirds. A **wildlife reserve** administered by the Scottish Wildlife Trust (swt.org.uk), Handa Island supports one of the largest seabird colonies in northwest Europe. It's a real treat for ornithologists, with razorbills and guillemots breeding on its guano-covered cliffs during summer. From late May to mid-July, large numbers of puffins waddle comically over the turf-covered cliff-tops where they dig their burrows. You'll need about three hours to follow the **footpath** around the island. Camping is not allowed.

ACCOMMODATION **SCOURIE**

Scourie Lodge North side of the bay 01971 502248, scourielodge.co.uk. Scourie has some good accommodation, including this charming place: an old three-bedroomed shooting retreat surrounded by trees. **£80**

The north coast

23

Though a constant stream of sponsored walkers, caravans and tour groups makes it to the dull town of **John O'Groats**, surprisingly few visitors travel the whole length of the Highlands' wild **north coast**. Those that do, however, rarely return disappointed. Pounded by one of the world's most ferocious seaways, Scotland's rugged northern shore is backed by barren mountains in the west, and in the east by lochs and open rolling grasslands. Between its far ends, miles of crumbling cliffs and sheer rocky headlands shelter bays whose perfect white beaches are nearly always deserted, even in the height of summer – though, somewhat incongruously, they're also home to Scotland's best **surfing** waves.

Durness is a good jumping-off point for nearby **Balnakiel beach**, one of the area's most beautiful sandy strands, and for rugged **Cape Wrath**, the windswept promontory at Scotland's northwest tip. **Thurso**, the largest town on the north coast, is really only visited by those en route to Orkney. More enticing are the huge seabird colonies clustered in clefts and on remote stacks at **Dunnet Head** and **Duncansby Head**, to the east of Thurso.

Durness and around

Scattered around a string of sheltered sandy coves and grassy cliff-tops, **DURNESS** (durness.org) is the most northwesterly village on the British mainland. It straddles the turning point on the main A838 road as it swings east from the inland peat bogs of the interior to the north coast's fertile strip of limestone machair. Durness village sits above its own sandy bay, Sango Sands, while half a mile to the east is **SMOO**, formerly a RAF station. In between Durness and Smoo is the village hall, whose windblown and rather forlorn community garden harbours a memorial commemorating the Beatle **John Lennon**, who used to come to Durness on family holidays as a child (and revisited the place in the 1960s with Yoko). It's worth pausing at Smoo to see the 200ft-long **Smoo Cave**, a gaping hole in a sheer limestone cliff formed partly by the action of the sea and partly by the small burn that flows through it.

ARRIVAL AND INFORMATION **DURNESS**

By bus Public transport to Durness is sparse; the key service is the Dearman Coaches link (May–Sept Mon–Sat 1 daily; also Sun in July & Aug) from Inverness via Ullapool and Lochinver. Postbuses provide a more complicated year-round alternative and meet trains at Lairg; check schedules at the post office or tourist office.

Tourist office The helpful Durness office in the centre of the village features excellent interpretive panels detailing the area's history, geology, flora, fauna and community life (March–April & Oct Mon–Sat 10am–5pm; May–Sept Mon–Sat 10am–5pm, Sun 10am–4pm; Nov–Feb Mon–Fri 10am–1.30pm).

ACCOMMODATION

★ **Lazy Crofter Bunkhouse** 01971 511202, durnesshostel.com. Run by the proprietors of *Mackays* next door, this congenial and attractive bunkhouse is brightly furnished and colourful with a living room and well-equipped kitchen. **£14**

★ **Mackays Room and Restaurant** At the western edge of the village ⊤01971 511202, ⓦvisitmackays.com. This stylish place stands out for its welcoming personal touches and its pricey restaurant with daily-changing menus (from 7pm) featuring locally sourced seafood, lamb and beef. Book ahead at busy times. **£100**

Seafood Platter On the eastern fringe of the village opposite the SYHA hostel ⊤01971 511215. This basic place has simple, tasty and moderately priced food; they also do takeway snacks. Closed Oct–April.

Cape Wrath

An excellent day-trip begins two miles southwest of Durness at **KEOLDALE**, where (tides and MOD permitting) a foot-passenger **ferry** (daily: May, June & Sept 11am & 1.30pm; July & Aug 4 trips 9.30am–6.30pm; ⊤01971 511376 for ferry; £5.50 return) crosses the spectacular Kyle of Durness estuary to link with a **minibus** (⊤01971 511343; May–Sept; £7.50 return) that runs the eleven miles out to **Cape Wrath**, mainland Britain's most northwesterly point. Note that Garvie Island (An Garbh-eilean) is an air bombing range, and the military regularly close the road to Cape Wrath. The headland takes its name not from the stormy seas that crash against it for most of the year, but from the Norse word *hvarf*, meaning "turning place" – a throwback to the days when Viking warships used it as a navigation point during raids on the Scottish coast.

23

Tongue and around

The road takes a wonderfully slow and circuituous route around Loch Eriboll and east over the top of A' Mhoine moor to the pretty crofting village of **TONGUE**. Dominated by the ruins of **Castle Varrich** (Caisteal Bharraich), a medieval stronghold of the Mackays (three-mile return walk), the village is strewn above the east shore of the **Kyle of Tongue**, which you can either cross via a new causeway, or by following the longer and more scenic singletrack road around its southern side. When the tide recedes, this shallow estuary becomes a mass of golden sand flats, superb on sunny days, with the sharp profiles of **Ben Hope** (3040ft), the most northerly Munro, and **Ben Loyal** (2509ft) looming like twin sentinels to the south.

ACCOMMODATION AND EATING — TONGUE AND AROUND

Cloisters Church Holme, Talmine ⊤01847 601286, ⓦcloistertal.demon.co.uk. On the western side of the Kyle at Talmine, this popular B&B occupies a converted nineteenth-century church with great views towards the Orkney Islands. **£55**

SYHA hostel Beside the causeway a mile north of the village centre on the Kyle's eastern shore ⊤0870 155 3255, ⓦsyha.org.uk. Well-kitted-out stone lodge with some double rooms. Dorm **£17**

Tongue Hotel ⊤01847 611206, ⓦtonguehotel.co.uk. The best accommodation in Tongue is this nineteen-bedroom hotel, the plush former hunting lodge of the Duke of Sutherland. They also serve delicious food and have a cosy downstairs bar. Closed Nov–March. **£110**

Bettyhill and around

Twelve miles east of Tongue, **BETTYHILL** is a major crofting village, set among rocky green hills. The village's splendid, sheltered **Farr beach** forms an unbroken arc of pure white sand between the Naver and Borgie rivers. Even more visually impressive is the River Naver's narrow tidal estuary, to the west of Bettyhill, and **Torrisdale beach**, which ends in a smooth white spit that forms part of the **Invernaver Nature Reserve**.

The Flow Country

At a junction six miles before Dounreay, you can head forty miles or so south towards Helmsdale on the A897, through the fascinating blanket bog of the **Flow Country**, whose name comes from *flói*, an Old Norse word meaning "marshy ground". At the train station at **FORSINARD**, fourteen miles south of Melvich and easily accessible from Thurso, Wick and the south, there is an RSPB **visitor centre** (April–Oct daily 9am–6pm; ⊤01641 571225), with CCTV coverage of hen harriers nesting, as well as a **Peatland Centre**, which explains the wonders of peat. To get to grips with the whole concept of blanket bog, take a leaflet and follow the short **Dubh Lochan Trail** through peat banks to some nearby black lochans.

Thurso

Approached from the isolation of the west, **THURSO** feels like a metropolis. In reality, it's a relatively small service centre visited mostly by people passing through to the adjoining port of **Scrabster** to catch the ferry to Orkney, or by increasing numbers of surfers attracted to the waves on the north coast. There's little to see, but the grid-plan streets have some rather handsome Victorian architecture in the local, greyish sandstone. If you're coming to **surf**, want a lesson, need to hire a board (£10/day) or simply fancy a coffee and home-made cake before hitting the waves, head for Tempest Surf on Riverside Road by Thurso harbour (T 01847 892500).

23

Caithness Horizons

High St • Mon–Sat 10am–6pm, Sun 11am–6pm • T 01847 896508, W caithnesshorizons.co.uk

Caithness Horizons, in the revamped Victorian town hall, comprises a museum, tourist office and café. The museum uses interactive technology and evocative old photos to explore local geology, history, farming and fishing, with treasures including a Bronze Age beaker and a Viking brooch. There's also a display on the decommissioning of Dounreay.

ARRIVAL AND INFORMATION — THURSO

By train Thurso station is near the town centre on Princes St. Destinations Dingwall (Mon–Sat 4 daily, 2 on Sun; 3hr); Inverness (Mon–Sat 4 daily, 2 on Sun; 3hr 20min); Lairg (Mon–Sat 4 daily, 2 on Sun; 1hr 50min); Wick (Mon–Sat 3 daily, 2 on Sun; 35min).

By bus Buses pull in next to the train station. Destinations Inverness (4–5 daily; 3hr 30min); John O'Groats (Mon–Fri 4 daily, 3 on Sat; 1hr); Wick (4 daily; 35min).

By ferry Regular buses from the train station in the morning, and from Olrig St in the afternoon, run to the Scrabster ferry terminal, a mile or so northwest of town. Ferries head to Stromness on Orkney Mainland (2–3 daily; 90min).

Tourist office Caithness Horizons (April–June, Sept & Oct Mon–Sat 10am–5pm; July & Aug Mon–Sat 9.30am–5.30pm, Sun 10am–4pm; T 01847 896508).

ACCOMMODATION

Murray House 1 Campbell St T 01847 895759, W murrayhousebb.com. Central, comfortable and friendly guesthouse that will rustle up a tasty three-course dinner for £15 per person. **£50**

Sandra's 24–26 Princes St T 01847 894575, W sandras-backpackers.ukf.net. This refurbished, clean and well-run place is affiliated to the SYHA and owned by the popular chippie downstairs. All rooms (some family options) are en-suite and guests have free use of bikes and internet. Dorm **£16**, double **£38**

Tigh na Abhainn 21 Millers Lane T 01847 893443. B&B in an old whitewashed house – one of the oldest in town – serving kippers and suchlike for breakfast. **£60**

EATING AND DRINKING

Captain's Galley The Harbour, Scrabster T 01847 894999, W captainsgalley.co.uk. A former ice-house and salmon bothy which serves the best seafood in the area; each day the menu details the boats the fish have come in on (mains from £12). Tues–Sat 7–9pm.

Gallery Café Caithness Horizons, High St W caithnesshorizons.wordpress.com/cafe/. The museum's cheerful daytime café serves sandwiches, soup and home-baking, and has a kids' menu. Mon–Sat 10am–6pm, Sun 11am–6pm.

Tempest Surf Café Riverside Rd T 01847 892500. Inexpensive snacks by the harbour, and the place to warm up after a play in the waves. Daytime only.

Dunnet Head

Thurso doesn't have much of a beach, so if you want to sink your toes into sand, head five miles east along the A836 to **Dunnet Bay**, a vast golden beach backed by huge dunes. The bay is enormously popular with surfers – even in the winter you can usually spot intrepid figures far out in the Pentland Firth's breakers. At the northeast end of the bay, there's a **Ranger Centre** (Sun–Fri: April, May & Sept 2–5.30pm; July & Aug 10.30am–5.30pm; free) beside the excellent campsite, where you can pick up information on local history and nature walks.

Despite the publicity that John O'Groats customarily receives, mainland Britain's most northerly point is in fact **Dunnet Head**, north of Dunnet along the B855, which runs for four miles over bleak heather and bog to the tip of the headland, crowned with a Stevenson lighthouse, at 344ft above sea level. On a clear day you can see the whole northern coastline from Cape Wrath to Duncansby Head, and across the treacherous Pentland Firth to Orkney.

The Castle of Mey

Fifteen miles east of Thurso • May–July & mid-Aug to Sept daily 10.30am–4pm • £9.75 • ⓦ castleofmey.org.uk

Roughly fifteen miles east of Thurso, just off the A836, lies the Queen Mother's former Scottish home and the most northerly castle on the UK mainland, the **Castle of Mey**. It's a modest little place, hidden behind high flagstone walls, with great views north to Orkney, and a herd of the Queen Mother's beloved Aberdeen Angus grazing out front. She used to spend every August here, and unusually for a royal palace, it's remarkably unstuffy inside, the walls hung with works by local amateur artists (and watercolours by Prince Charles).

John O'Groats and around

Romantics expecting to find a magical meeting of land and water at **JOHN O'GROATS** (ⓦvisitjohnogroats.com) are invariably disenchanted – sadly it remains an uninspiring tourist trap. The views north to Orkney are fine enough, but the village offers little more than a string of souvenir shops and cafés thronged with coach parties. A number of **boat trips** set off from here, with some operators offering whitewater rafting and others heading out to Duncansby head and local seal colonies. The village gets its name from the Dutchman Jan de Groot, who obtained the ferry contract for the hazardous crossing to Orkney in 1496. The eight-sided house he built for his eight quarrelling sons (so that each one could enter by his own door) is echoed in the octagonal tower of the much-photographed but now vacant *John O'Groats Hotel*.

Duncansby Head

If you're disappointed by John O'Groats, press on a couple of miles further east to **Duncansby Head**, which, with its lighthouse, dramatic cliffs and well-worn coastal path, is much more stimulating. The birdlife here is prolific, and south of the headland lie some spectacular 200ft cliffs, cut by sheer-sided clefts known locally as *geos*, and several impressive sea stacks.

The east coast

The **east coast** of the Highlands, between Inverness and Wick, is nowhere near as spectacular as the west, with gently undulating moors, grassland and low cliffs where you might otherwise expect to find sea lochs and mountains. While many visitors speed up the main A9 road through this region in a headlong rush to the Orkneys' prehistoric sites, those who choose to dally will find a wealth of brochs, cairns and standing stones, many in remarkable condition. The area around the Black Isle and the Tain was a Pictish heartland, and has yielded many important finds. Further north, from around the ninth century AD onwards the **Norse** influence was more keenly felt than in any other part of mainland Britain, and dozens of Scandinavian-sounding names recall the era when this was a Viking kingdom.

The fishing heritage is a recurring theme along this coast, though there are only a handful of working boats scattered around the harbours today; the area remains one of the country's poorest, reliant on relatively thin pickings from sheep farming, fishing and tourism. The one stretch of the east coast that's always been relatively rich, however, is the **Black Isle** just over the Kessock Bridge heading north out of Inverness, whose main village, **Cromarty**, is the region's undisputed highlight. Beyond the golfing resort of **Dornoch**, the ersatz-Loire chateau **Dunrobin Castle** is the main tourist attraction, a monument as much to the iniquities of the Clearances as to the eccentricities of Victorian taste. **Wick**, the largest town in these parts, has an interesting past entwined with the fishing industry, but is otherwise uninspiring.

The Black Isle

Sandwiched between the Cromarty Firth to the north and, to the south, the Moray and Beauly firths which separate it from Inverness, the **Black Isle** is not an island at all, but a fertile peninsula whose rolling hills, prosperous farms and stands of deciduous woodland make it more reminiscent of Dorset or Sussex than the Highlands. It probably gained its name because of its mild climate: there's rarely frost, which leaves the fields "black" all winter; another explanation is that the name derives from the Gaelic word for black, *dubh* – a possible corruption of St Duthus. On the south side of the Black Isle, near Fortrose, **Chanonry Point** juts into a narrow channel in the Moray Firth and is an excellent place to look for **dolphins** (see p.885).

Cromarty

An ancient legend recalls that the twin headlands flanking the entrance to the **Cromarty Firth**, known as The Sutors (from the Gaelic word for shoemaker), were once a pair of giant cobblers who used to protect the Black Isle from pirates. Nowadays, however, the only giants in the area are the colossal oil rigs marooned in the estuary off Nigg and Invergordon like metal monsters marching out to sea. They form a surreal counterpoint to the web of tiny streets and charming workers' cottages of **CROMARTY**. The Black Isle's main settlement, Cromarty was an ancient ferry-crossing point on the pilgrimage trail to St Duthus's shrine in Tain, but lost much of its trade during the nineteenth century to places served by the railway; a branch line to the town was begun but never completed. Cromarty became a prominent port in 1772 when an entrepreneurial local landlord, George Ross, founded a hemp mill here, fuelling a period of prosperity during which Cromarty acquired some of Scotland's finest Georgian houses: these, together with the terraced fishers' cottages of the nineteenth-century herring boom, have left the town with a wonderfully well-preserved concentration of Scottish domestic architecture.

The **museum**, housed in the old **Courthouse** on Church Street (daily: April–Oct 10am–5pm; £5), tells the history of the town using audiovisuals and animated figures. Dolphin- and other wildlife-spotting trips (£22; 2hr) are offered locally by EcoVentures (T 01381 600323, W ecoventures.co.uk), who travel out through the Sutors to the Moray Firth in a powerful RIB.

ARRIVAL AND DEPARTURE — CROMARTY

The tiny two-car Nigg–Cromarty **ferry** (daily, every 30min: June & Sept 8am–6.15pm; July & Aug 8am–7.15pm; £2.50) is Scotland's smallest. Embark from the jetty near the lighthouse.

ACCOMMODATION

Gisborne B&B Marine Terrace T 01381 600376, W go-bedandbreakfast.co.uk/Gisborne/. Once the cottage hospital, this is now a pleasant little B&B, offering full Scottish breakfast and wi-fi, and packed lunches on request. **£55**

Sydney House High St T 01381 600451, W sydneyhouse.co.uk. A grand red-brick place that once had the distinction of being a temperance hotel. They offer locally sourced Scottish breakfasts and haggis. **£60**

EATING AND DRINKING

Cromarty Bakery 8 Bank St ⓣ01381 600388. The excellent village bakery provides tasty home-baked breads including spinach and walnut, and whisky cake. Closed Sun.

★ **Sutor Creek** 21 Bank St ⓣ01381 600855, ⓦsutorcreek.co.uk. There are few more down-to-earth but satisfying restaurants in the Highlands than this. It serves organic wines, delicious seafood and fresh pizza cooked in a wood-fired oven; the imaginative toppings (and the daily blackboard specials) are local and seasonal rather than conventionally Italian. Mains £10–23. Wed–Sun 11am–late.

The Dornoch Firth and around

North of the Cromarty Firth, the hammer-shaped **Fearn peninsula** can still be approached from the south by the ancient ferry crossing from Cromarty to Nigg, though to the north the link is a causeway over the **Dornoch Firth**, the inlet that marks the northern boundary of the peninsula. On the southern edge of the Dornoch Firth the A9 bypasses the quiet town of **TAIN**, an attractive, old-fashioned small town of grand whisky-coloured sandstone buildings that was the birthplace of **St Duthus**, an eleventh-century missionary who inspired great devotion in the Middle Ages. Tain's main attraction is the **Glenmorangie whisky distillery** where the highly rated malt is produced (ⓣ01862 892477; tours Mon–Fri 10.30am–3.30pm, Sat 10.30am–2.30pm, Sun 12.30–2.30pm; £2.50 including discount voucher); it lies beside the A9 on the north side of town. Booking is recommended for the tours; there is also a shop.

23

Dornoch

DORNOCH, a genteel and appealing town eight miles north of Tain, lies on a flattish headland overlooking the **Dornoch Firth**. A middle-class holiday resort, with trees and flowers in profusion, solid Edwardian hotels, and miles of sandy beaches giving good views across the estuary to the Fearn peninsula, the town is renowned for its championship **golf course**, Scotland's most northerly first-class course. Nearby Skibo Castle was where Madonna married Guy Ritchie; she also had her son baptized in Dornoch **cathedral**.

INFORMATION — DORNOCH

Tourist offfice Court St, next to the *Dornoch Castle Hotel* (Easter–May Mon–Fri 9am–5pm; June & Sept Mon–Fri 9am–5pm, Sat 9.30am–5pm; July & Aug Sun Mon–Fri 9am–5pm, Sat 9.30am–5pm, Sun 10am–4pm; ⓣ01862 810594).

CARBISDALE CASTLE

Towering high above the River Shin, twenty miles northwest of Tain, the daunting neo-Gothic profile of **Carbisdale Castle** overlooks the Kyle of Sutherland, as well as the battlefield where the gallant Marquess of Montrose was defeated in 1650, finally forcing Charles II to accede to the Scots' demand for Presbyterianism. The castle was erected between 1906 and 1917 for the dowager Duchess of Sutherland, following a protracted family feud. Designed in three distinct styles (to give the impression that it was added to over a long period of time), Carbisdale was eventually acquired by a Norwegian shipping magnate in 1933, and finally gifted, along with its entire contents and estate, to the SYHA, which has turned it into what must be one of the most opulent **hostels** in the world. Bring a bike to take advantage of the several miles of **mountain-biking trails** in the nearby Balblair and Carbisdale woods.

Carbisdale hostel Three miles northwest of Bonar Bridge ⓣ01549 421232, ⓦsyha.org.uk. Thirty dorms and some family rooms in this opulent castle hostel, full of white Italian-marble sculptures, huge gilt-framed portraits, sweeping staircases and magnificent drawing rooms alongside standard facilities such as self-catering kitchens, games and TV rooms. You can tuck into a hearty three-course dinner (£11.50) at the restaurant before wandering the supposedly haunted corridors in search of ghosts. The best way to get here by public transport is to take a train from Inverness to nearby Culrain station. Closed Nov–Feb. Dorm £23, twin £64

ACCOMMODATION AND EATING

2 Quail Castle St ⊕01862 811811, ⊕2quail.com. Expensive gourmet meals are available in this classy restaurant with rooms. Food served May–Sept Tues–Sat; Oct–April Fri & Sat. £100

Caravan Park ⊕01862 810423, ⊕www.dornochcaravans.co.uk. Attractively set between the manicured golf course and the uncombed vegetation of the sand dunes that fringe the beach. It also offers camping; the site gets busy with caravans in July and Aug. Closed Nov–March. Tents from £11

Dornoch Castle Hotel Castle St ⊕01862 810216, ⊕dornochcastlehotel.com. This fifteenth-century hotel, in the Bishop's Palace on the Square, has a decent restaurant and a cosy old-fashioned bar with a roaring, 11ft-wide log fire. Sadly, the revamped interior doesn't live up to the buttressed, turreted facade. From £166

Luigi's Castle St ⊕01862 810893, ⊕luigidornoch.com. Familiar but decent Italian-style snacks and meals, making use of local seafood (mains from £12). It's also a popular spot for a weekend brunch. Daily 10am–9pm.

Tordarroch B&B Castle St ⊕01862 810855. Extremely welcoming, good value B&B in a stone-built house opposite the cathedral. There's a pretty garden. Closed Nov–Feb. £60

Golspie

23

Ten miles north of Dornoch on the A9 lies the straggling red sandstone town of **GOLSPIE**, whose status as an administrative centre does little to relieve its dullness. It is, however, the jumping-off point for some brilliant **mountain biking**: the fabulous Highland Wildcat Trails (⊕highlandwildcat.com) are within the forested hills just half a mile to the west. The easy to severe (colour-coded) trails include a huge descent from the summit of Ben Bhraggie to sea level and a ride past the **Sutherland monument**, erected in memory of the landowner who oversaw the eviction of thousands of his tenants in a process known as the **Clearances**.

Dunrobin Castle

A mile north of Golspie • April, May, Sept & early Oct Mon–Sat 10.30am–4.30pm, Sun noon–4.30pm; June–Aug daily 10.30am–5.30pm • £8.50 • ⊕01408 633177, ⊕dunrobincastle.co.uk

Mountain bikers aside, the main reason to stop at Golspie is to look around **Dunrobin Castle**, overlooking the sea north of town. This fairy-tale confection of turrets and pointed roofs – modelled by the architect Sir Charles Barry (designer of the Houses of Parliament) on a Loire chateau – is the seat of the infamous Sutherland family, at one time Europe's biggest landowners, with a staggering 1.3 million acres, and the principal driving force behind the Clearances in this area. The castle boasts 189 furnished rooms; the tour takes in only seventeen. Staring up at the pile from its elaborate **formal gardens**, it's worth remembering that such extravagance was paid for by uprooting literally thousands of crofters from the surrounding glens.

Sutherland Monument

Immediately behind Golspie, you can't miss the 100ft **monument** to the first Duke of Sutherland, which peers proprietorially down from the summit of the 1293ft **Beinn a'Bhragaidh** (Ben Bhraggie). An inscription cut into its base recalls that the statue was erected in 1834 by "a mourning and grateful tenantry [to] a judicious, kind and liberal landlord [who would] open his hands to the distress of the widow, the sick and the traveller". Unsurprisingly, there's no reference to the fact that the duke, widely regarded as Scotland's own Josef Stalin, forcibly evicted 15,000 crofters from his million-acre estate. It's worth the stiff **climb** to the top of the hill (round trip 1hr 30min) for the wonderful views south along the coast past Dornoch to the Moray Firth and west towards Lairg and Loch Shin. The path is steep and strenuous in places, however, and there's no view until you're out of the trees, about twenty minutes from the top.

Helmsdale

Eleven scenic miles north along the A9 from Golspie, **HELMSDALE** is an old herring port, founded in the nineteenth century to house the evicted inhabitants of Strath

Kildonan, which lies behind it. The Strath was the unlikely location of a gold rush in the 1860s, and a few determined prospectors still pan the Kildonan Burn. The story of the area's gold hunters is told in the **Timespan Heritage Centre**, beside the river (Easter–Oct Mon–Sat 10am–5pm, Sun noon–5pm; £3), along with tales of Viking raids, witch-burning, Clearances and fishing. The centre also has an art gallery, café and garden.

Just north of Helmsdale, the A9 begins its long haul up the **Ord of Caithness**. Once over the pass, the landscape changes dramatically as heather-clad moors give way to miles of treeless green grazing lands, peppered with derelict crofts and latticed by long dry-stone walls. As you come over the pass, look out for signs to the ruined village of **Badbea**, a ten-minute walk from the car park at the side of the A9. Built by tenants cleared from nearby Ousdale, the settlement is now deserted, its ruined hovels showing what hardship the crofters had to endure: the cottages stood so near the windy cliff edge that children had to be tethered to prevent them from being blown into the sea.

Lybster

The planned village of **LYBSTER** (pronounced "libe-ster"), nineteen miles north of the Ord of Caithness, was established at the height of the nineteenth-century herring boom, when 200-odd boats worked out of its harbour; now there are just one or two. The **Water Lines** heritage centre by the harbour (May to mid-Oct daily 11am–5pm; £2.50) is an attractive modern display about the "silver darlings" and the fishermen that pursued them; there's a snug café downstairs. There's not much else to see here beyond the harbour area.

Wick

Originally a Viking settlement named *Vik* (meaning "bay"), **WICK** has been a royal burgh since 1589. It's actually two towns: Wick proper, and **Pultneytown**, south across the river, a messy, rather run-down community planned by Thomas Telford in 1806 to encourage evicted crofters to take up fishing. Wick's heyday was in the mid-nineteenth century, when it was the busiest herring port in Europe, with a fleet of more than 1100 boats exporting tons of fish to Russia, Scandinavia and the West Indian slave plantations. Though redevelopment of the harbour is underway, the town still has a down-at-heel air. The area around the harbour in Pultneytown, lined with rows of fishermen's cottages, is most worth a wander, with acres of largely derelict net-mending sheds, stores and cooperages around the harbour giving some idea of the former scale of the fishing trade. The town's story is told in the **Wick Heritage Centre** in Bank Row, Pultneytown (Easter–Oct Mon–Sat 10am–5pm; £3). The only other visitor attraction is the fairly simple **Pulteney Distillery** (Mon–Fri 10am–1pm & 2–4pm; tours 11am & 2pm or by arrangement ⊤01955 602371; £4) on nearby Huddart Street, a few blocks from the sea.

ARRIVAL AND DEPARTURE — WICK

By plane The airport, just north of town, sees flights from Edinburgh (Mon–Fri 1 daily; 1hr 10min) and Aberdeen (Mon–Fri 4 daily; 35min).

By train The train station is just north of the town centre.

Destinations Dingwall (Mon–Sat 4 daily, Sun 2 daily; 3hr 30min); Inverness (Mon–Sat 4 daily, Sun 2 daily; 4hr); Lairg (Mon–Sat 4 daily, Sun 2 daily; 2hr 20min).

By bus Buses connect Wick's town centre with John O'Groats (4 daily Mon–Sat; 50min).

ACCOMMODATION AND EATING

Bilbster House 5 miles beyond Wick towards Thurso ⊤01955 621212, ⓦbedandbreakfastnationwide.com/wick-bilbster-house-1.html. A lovely eighteenth-century manor house with walled gardens. April–Oct, in winter by prior arrangement. **£54**

Bord de l'Eau 2 Market St ⊤01955 604400. This moderately priced *bistro* offers a reasonable menu of classic French standards. Closed Mon.

Mackay's South side of the river in the centre ⊤01955 602323, ⓦmackayshotel.co.uk. The best of the hotels. Decor is a little bland, but it's clean and comfortable. **£99**

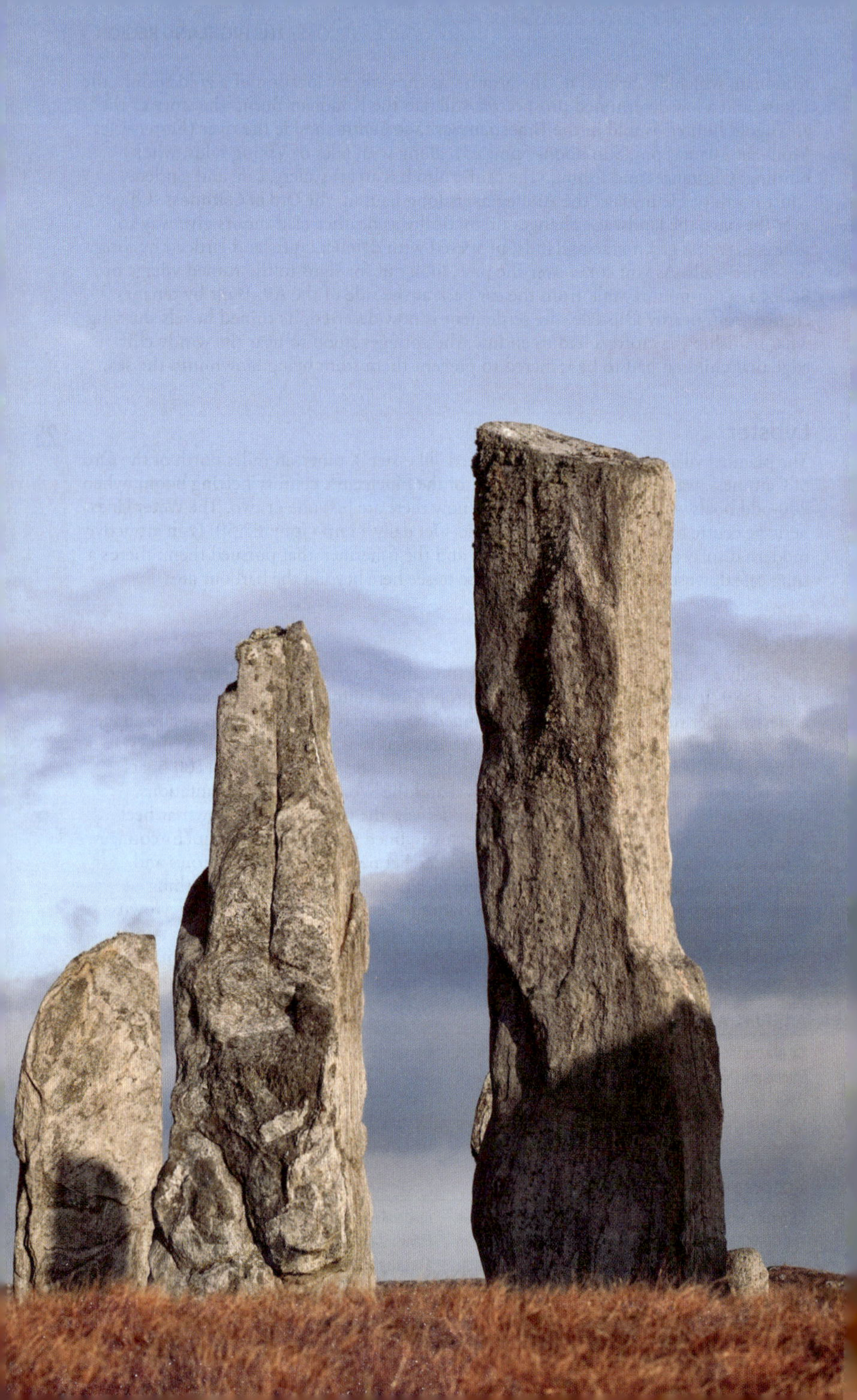

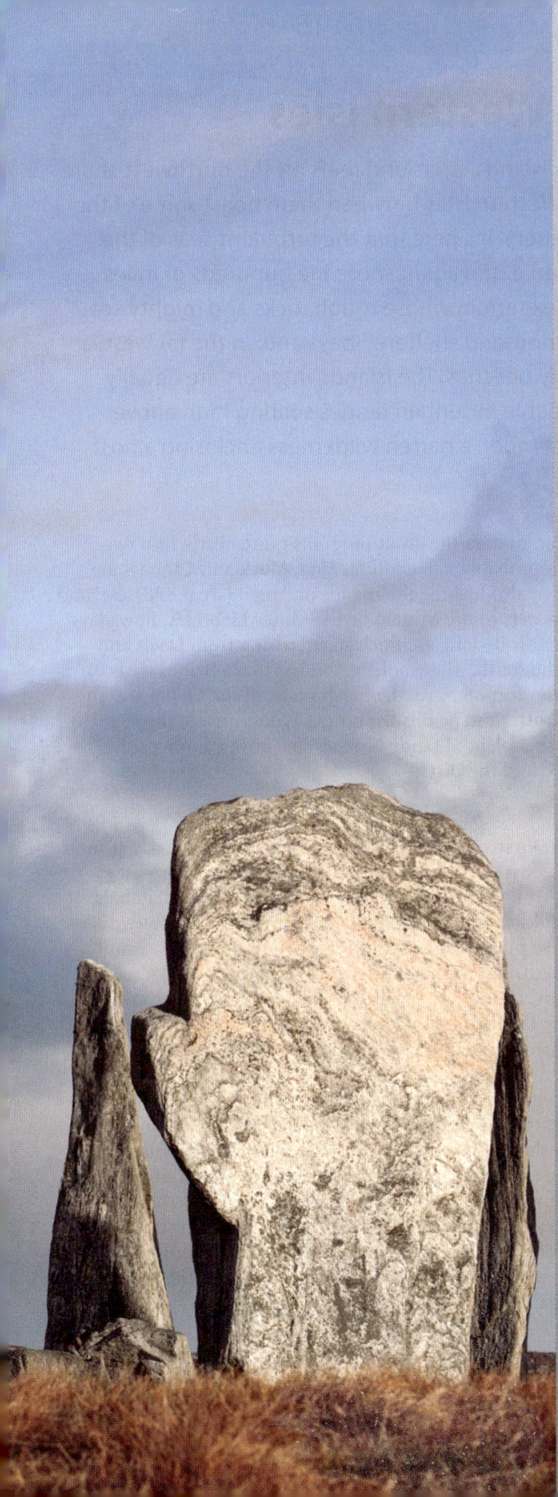

Skye and the Western Isles

917 Skye

923 The Small Isles

926 The Western Isles

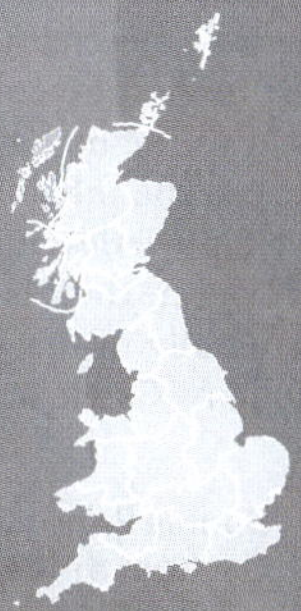

CALANAIS STANDING STONES, LEWIS

Skye and the Western Isles

A procession of Hebridean islands, islets and reefs off the northwest shore of Scotland, Skye and the Western Isles between them boast some of the country's most alluring scenery. It's here that the turbulent seas of the Atlantic smash up against an extravagant shoreline hundreds of miles long, a geologically complex terrain whose rough rocks and mighty sea cliffs are interrupted by a thousand sheltered bays and, in the far west, a long line of sweeping sandy beaches. The islands' interiors are equally dramatic, a series of formidable mountain ranges soaring high above great chunks of boggy peat moor, a barren wilderness enclosing a host of lochans, or tiny lakes.

Each island has its own character, though the grouping splits quite neatly into two. **Skye** and the **Small Isles** – the improbably named **Rùm**, **Eigg**, **Muck** and **Canna** – are part of the Inner Hebrides, which also include the islands of Argyll (see p.828). Beyond Skye, across the unpredictable waters of the Minch, lie the Outer Hebrides, nowadays known as the **Western Isles**, a 130-mile-long archipelago stretching from **Lewis** and **Harris** in the north to **Barra** in the south. The whole region has four obvious areas of outstanding natural beauty to aim for: on Skye, the harsh peaks of the **Cuillin** and the bizarre rock formations of the **Trotternish** peninsula; on the Western Isles, the mountains of **North Harris** and the splendid sandy beaches that string along the Atlantic seaboard of **South Harris** and the **Uists**.

Brief history

Skye and the Western Isles were first settled by Neolithic farming peoples in around 4000 BC. They lived along the coast, where they are remembered by scores of remains, from passage graves through to stone circles, most famously at **Calanais** (Callanish) on Lewis. Viking colonization gathered pace from 700 AD onwards – on Lewis four out of every five place names is of Norse origin – and it was only in 1266 that the islands were returned to the Scottish crown. James VI (James I of England), a Stuart and a Scot, though no Gaelic-speaker, was the first to put forward the idea of clearing the Hebrides. However, it wasn't until after the Jacobite uprisings, in which many Highland clans backed the losing side, that the **Clearances** began in earnest.

The isolation of the Hebrides exposed them to the whims and fancies of the various merchants and aristocrats who bought them up. Time and again, from the mid-eighteenth century to the present day, both the land and its people were sold to the highest bidder. Some proprietors were well-meaning, others simply forced the inhabitants onto ships bound for North America. Always the islanders were powerless and almost everywhere they were driven from their ancestral homes. However, their language survived, ensuring a degree of cultural continuity, especially in the Western Isles, where even today the first language of the majority remains **Gaelic** (pronounced "gallic").

Bonnie Prince Charlie p.922
Gaelic in the Western Isles p.927
Whisky Galore! p.934

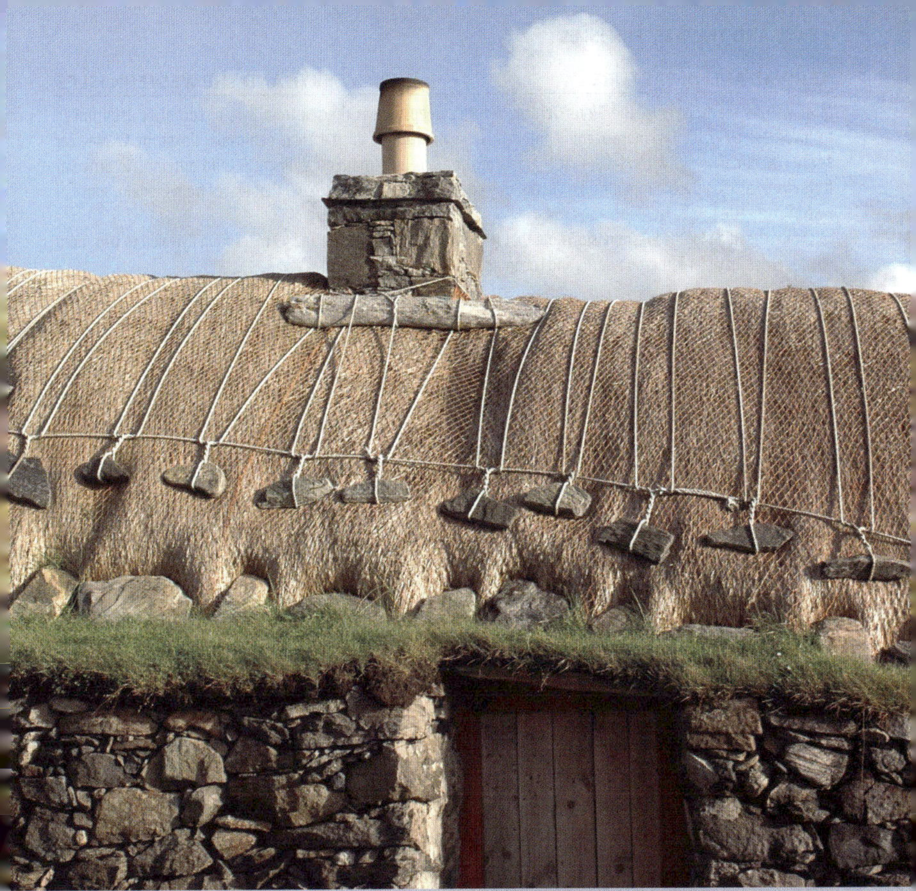

GEARRANNAN

Highlights

❶ **Skye Cuillin** These jagged peaks dominate and define Skye's landscape – and provide splendid opportunities for climbing. **See p.919**

❷ **Loch Coruisk boat trip, Skye** Take the boat from Elgol to the beautiful, remote, glacial Loch Coruisk in the midst of the Skye Cuillin, and then walk back. **See p.919**

❸ **Kinloch Castle, Rùm** The most outrageous Edwardian pile in the Hebrides – and one where you can spend the night. **See p.924**

❹ **Gearrannan (Garenin), Lewis** A painstakingly restored crofting village of thatched blackhouses. **See p.929**

❺ **Calanais (Callanish), Lewis** Scotland's finest standing stones are set in a serene lochside setting. **See p.929**

❻ **Golden sandy beaches** Harris and the Uists have some stunning, mostly deserted, golden beaches, backed by flower-strewn machair. **See pp.930–932**

❼ **Roghadal (Rodel) Church, Harris** The pre-Reformation St Clement's Church has the most ornate sculptural decoration in the Outer Hebrides. **See p.931**

HIGHLIGHTS ARE MARKED ON THE MAP ON P.916

ARRIVAL AND DEPARTURE

SKYE AND THE WESTERN ISLES

Most visitors reach Skye via the **Skye Bridge**, which sweeps across the sea from Kyle of Lochalsh, itself linked to Inverness by train. The more scenic approach is via **Armadale** on the Sleat peninsula, linked by CalMac car **ferry** (ⓦcalmac.co.uk) with Mallaig, at the end of the train line from Fort William. A third option is to arrive at **Kylerhea,** also on the Sleat peninsula, via the tiny **car ferry** (ⓦskyeferry.co.uk) that leaves from Glenelg, south of Kyle of Lochalsh.

If you're heading for the Western Isles, note that it's 57 miles from Armadale and 49 miles from Kyleakin to **Uig**, from where ferries leave for Tarbert on Harris and Lochmaddy on North Uist.

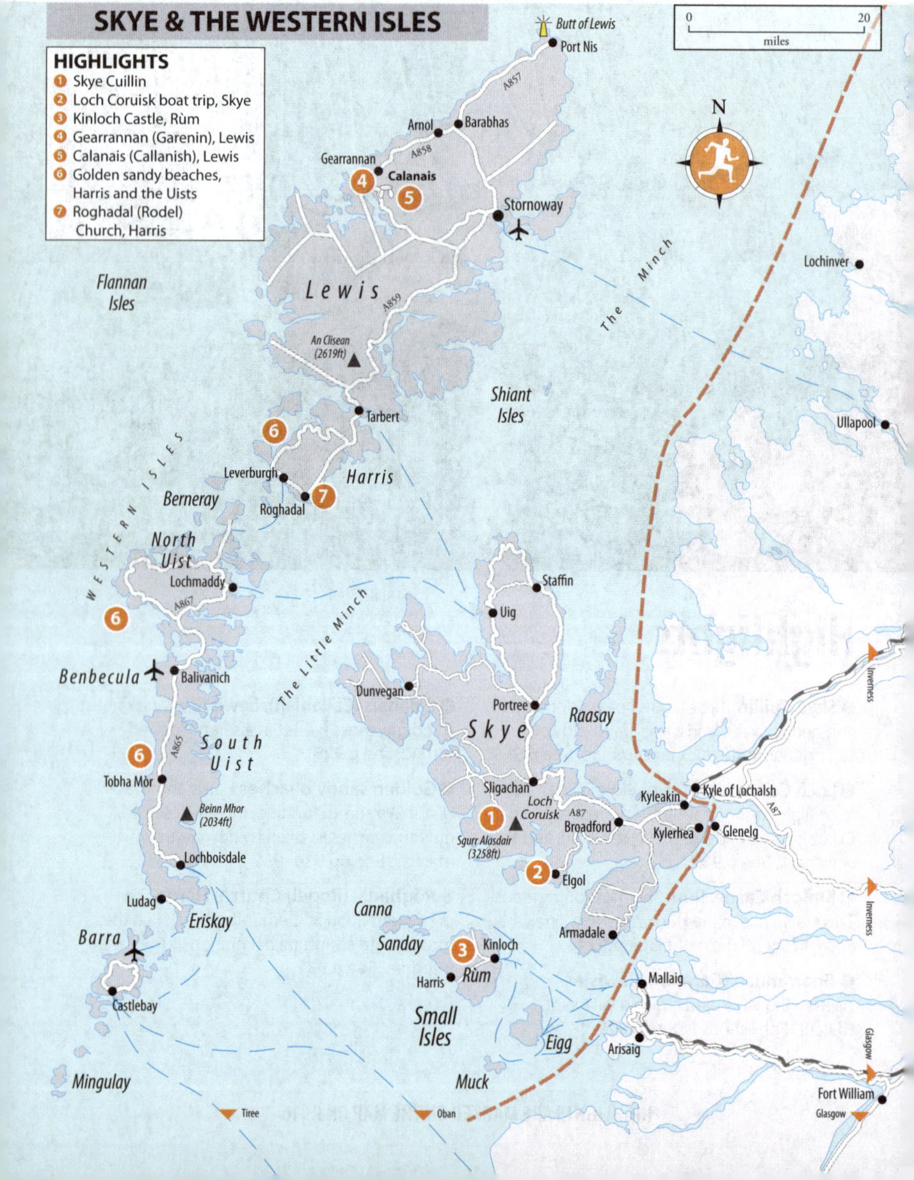

Skye

Jutting out from the mainland like a giant butterfly, the bare and bony promontories of **Skye** fringe a deeply indented coastline. The island's most popular destination is the **Cuillin** ridge, whose jagged peaks dominate the island during clear weather. More accessible and equally dramatic in their own way are the rock formations of the **Trotternish** peninsula, in the north, from which there are inspirational views across to the Western Isles. Of the two main settlements, **Portree** is the only one with any charm, and a useful base for exploring the Trotternish.

GETTING AROUND — SKYE

Getting around Skye by **bus** is tricky. Services peter out in the more remote areas, and many close down on Sundays. If you are depending on buses, however, it may be worth buying a Skye dayrider ticket (£7/day). Check isleofskye.co.uk for details of local transportation along with features on the island's attractions and history.

Sleat

Ferries from Mallaig connect with **ARMADALE** (Armadal), on the **Sleat** (pronounced "Slate") **peninsula**, Skye's southern tip, an uncharacteristically fertile area known as "The Garden of Skye".

Armadale Castle Gardens

On the A851 • April–Oct daily 9.30am–5.30pm • £7 • 01471 844305, clandonald.com

One of the best tourist attractions on the island, the handsome forty-acre **Armadale Castle Gardens** include the shell of the MacDonalds' neo-Gothic castle, a café and a library for those who want to chase up their ancestral Donald connections. The gardens' slick, purpose-built **Museum of the Isles** has a good section on the Jacobite period and its aftermath and one or two top-notch works of art by Angelika Kaufmann and Henry Raeburn.

ARRIVAL AND DEPARTURE — SLEAT

By ferry Car ferries run from Glenelg to Kylerhea (daily, frequently; 15min), and CalMac ferries travel from Mallaig to Armadale (Mon–Sat 8 daily, 4–6 on Sun; 30min).

By bus Services run from Armadale to Broadford (Mon–Sat 5 daily, 2 on Sun; 35min); Portree (Mon–Sat 5 daily, 2 on Sun; 1hr 20min) and Sligachan (Mon–Sat 5 daily, 2 on Sun; 1hr).

ACCOMMODATION AND EATING

Ardvasar Hotel Ardvasar, 1 mile southwest of Armadale 01471 844223, ardvasarhotel.com. Old-fashioned inn with a good restaurant serving Speyside beef and lamb, venison, duck and local seafood – you can eat the same dishes (or simpler bar food) in the lounge bar. Food served daily noon–2.30pm & 6–9pm.

Flora MacDonald Hostel Kilmore, 3 miles north of Armadale 01471 844272, skye-hostel.co.uk. Bright, modern, well-run hostel that's definitely not a party destination – Old McDonald and his wife have Eriskay ponies on their farm. Last check-in 8pm; curfew midnight. Dorm £14, double £35

Morar Kilmore, 3 miles north of Armadale 01471 844378, accommodation-on-skye.co.uk. A modern croft-house B&B, just beyond the Ardvasar Hotel, with superb views, a heated indoor pool and (weather permitting) a sun terrace. Breakfast includes eggs from their hens and home-made bread. £75

Kyleakin

The **Skye Bridge** links the tidy hamlet of **KYLEAKIN** (Caol Acain – pronounced "Kalakin") – now a favourite with backpackers – with the Kyle of Lochalsh on the mainland. Strictly speaking there are, in fact, two bridges, with an island in the middle, **Eilean Bàn**, whose lighthouse cottages were once the home of author and naturalist Gavin Maxwell. One of the houses is now a museum and can be visited, along with the lighthouse, on a guided tour (£6); numbers are limited and must be booked in advance through the **Bright Water Visitor Centre** (phone for times; ⓣ01599 530040, ⓦeileanban.org) in Kyleakin.

ARRIVAL AND DEPARTURE — KYLEAKIN

There are **buses** to and from Broadford (Mon–Sat hourly, 2 on Sun; 15min), Kyle of Lochalsh (Mon–Sat hourly, 2 on Sun; 10min), Portree (Mon–Sat 5 daily, 2 on Sun; 1hr), and Uig (Mon–Sat 2 daily; 1hr 20min).

ACCOMMODATION

Dun Caan Hostel Kyleakin ⓣ01599 534087, ⓦskyerover.co.uk. This is a cosy hostel, and although there's no curfew, you're supposed to be quiet after 11pm. Good kitchen, laundry and drying room. No under-12s. Dorm £16, double £38

Saucy Mary's Lodge Kyleakin ⓣ01599 534845, ⓦsaucymarys.com. If you're looking for a party atmosphere, this is the hostel to head for: it has a bar with Sky Sports, pool and occasional live music. Dorm £17, double £50

Broadford

Skye's second-largest village is the charmless **BROADFORD** (An t-Ath Leathann), which, while it holds little of appeal, does have some useful facilities, including a **tourist office** as well as a laundry, small shop and bureau de change.

ARRIVAL AND INFORMATION — BROADFORD

24

By bus Services run to and from Elgol (Mon–Fri 4 daily, 2 on Sat; 45min); Glasgow (3 daily; 5hr 30min); Inverness (2 daily; 2hr 50min); Kyle of Lochalsh (Mon–Sat hourly; 25min) and Portree (Mon–Sat 5–10 daily; 40min).

Tourist office By the 24hr garage on the main road (Easter–Oct Mon–Fri 9am–6pm; Sat 9am–5pm; ⓣ0845 225 5121).

ACCOMMODATION AND EATING

Creelers South end of Broadford Bay ⓣ01471 822281, ⓦskye-seafood-restaurant.co.uk. Popular restaurant serving traditional French (and occasionally Cajun) takes on local seafood, including a superb two-course bouillabaisse (£30 a head). March–Nov Mon–Sat noon–9.30pm.

★ **Tigh an Dochais** 13 Harrapool ⓣ01471 820022, ⓦskyebedbreakfast.co.uk. A striking piece of contemporary architecture as well as a very comfortable guesthouse, with stunning views across Broadford Bay (binoculars provided), and locally sourced food for breakfast. £80

Isle of Raasay

Despite lying less than a mile offshore, the long, hilly island of **Raasay** (Ratharsair) sees surprisingly few visitors. The population stands at around 200, many of them members of the Free Presbyterian Church – the most obvious manifestation of this for visitors is the island's strict observance of the Sabbath. The ferry docks in Churchton Bay, near **INVERARISH**, the island's tiny village set within thick woods on the southwest coast. The grand Georgian mansion of **Raasay House**, built by the MacLeods in the late 1740s, stands on the western edge of the village; it was run as an **outdoor centre** until a fire gutted it in 2009, and the centre is currently based at nearby Borodale House (see opposite). Activities include everything from sailing and kayaking to climbing and hillwalking.

The most obvious spot to head for in the island's interior is the curiously truncated basalt cap on top of **Dun Caan** (1456ft) – the trail to the top of the peak is fairly easy to follow, a splendid five-mile trek up through the forest and along the burn behind Inverarish.

ARRIVAL AND DEPARTURE — ISLE OF RAASAY

CalMac **ferries** from Sconser arrive at Churchton Bay (Mon–Sat 8–10 daily, 2 on Sun; 25min).

ACCOMMODATION AND EATING

Raasay Outdoor Centre ⊕01478 660266, ⊕raasay-house.co.uk. The outdoor centre offers twelve en-suite rooms, a restaurant and a café serving good local food. **£85**

SYHA hostel ⊕0478 660240, ⊕syha.org.uk. Isolated but beautifully placed hostel with a total of 20 beds in simple, comfortable dorms. Closed mid-Sept to mid-May. **£17**

The Cuillin and the Red Hills

For many people, the **Cuillin** (An Cuiltheann), whose sharp peaks rise mirage-like from the flatness of the surrounding terrain, are Skye's *raison d'être*. When the clouds finally disperse, they are the dominating feature of the island, visible from every other peninsula.

There are three **approaches** to the Cuillin: from the south, by foot or by boat from **Elgol**; from the **Sligachan Hotel** to the north; or from **Glen Brittle** to the west of the mountains. The second route, down Glen Sligachan, divides the granite of the round-topped **Red Hills** (sometimes known as the Red Cuillin) to the east from the dark, coarse-grained jagged-edged gabbro of the real Cuillin (also known as the Black Cuillin) to the west. With some twenty Munros between them, these are mountains to be taken seriously, and many routes through the Cuillin are for experienced climbers only.

Elgol and around

The road to **ELGOL** (Ealaghol), fourteen miles southwest of Broadford at the tip of the Strathaird peninsula, is one of the most dramatic on the island, with a stunning view from the top down to Elgol pier. Weather permitting (April–Oct), you can take a **boat** from Elgol across Loch Scavaig, past a seal colony, to a jetty near the entrance of the glacial loch **Loch Coruisk**.

24

Loch Coruisk

Loch Coruisk, a needle-like shaft of water nearly two miles long but only a couple of hundred yards wide, lies in the shadow of the highest peaks of the Black Cuillin, a wonderfully overpowering landscape. The journey from Elgol takes about an hour and passengers are dropped to spend time ashore. **Walkers** can hike amidst the Red Hills, or over the pass into **Glen Sligachan**.

ACCOMMODATION AND EATING — ELGOL AND AROUND

Coruisk House Elgol ⊕01471 866330, ⊕coruiskhouse.com. A real find at the end of a long and winding road, this restaurant with rooms – two beautiful, bright, cheerful rooms – offers scrumptious seafood caught at Elgol, fish from Mallaig and chicken stuffed with haggis. Closed Nov–March. Restaurant April–Oct daily 7pm–late. **£85**

Sligachan Hotel, Bar, Bunkhouse & Campsite Northern end of Glen Sligachan ⊕01478 650204, ⊕sligachan.co.uk. The *Sligachan*, the only place for miles and with a stunning location, doesn't have to try very hard. For walkers and climbers, the roadside campsite (April–Oct) and the secluded bunkhouse make good bases, and there's nothing better than piling into *Seamus Bar* after a day on the hills. There's hearty bar food, real ales from the hotel's own microbrewery and more than 250 single malt whiskies, plus the occasional live band. But if you're looking for a decent hotel, you could do better elsewhere. Bar daily noon–11pm. Bunkhouse dorm **£15**

Glen Brittle

Six miles along the A863 to Dunvegan from the *Sligachan Hotel*, a turning signed "Carbost and Portnalong" quickly leads to the entrance to stony **Glen Brittle**, edging the most spectacular peaks of the Cuillin; at the end of the glen, idyllically situated by the sea, is the village of **GLENBRITTLE**. Climbers and serious walkers tend to congregate at the SYHA **hostel** or the beautifully situated **campsite,** both of which have the only grocery stores for miles.

From the valley a score of difficult and strenuous trails lead east into the **Black Cuillin**, a rough semicircle of peaks, rising to about 3000ft, which surround Loch Coruisk. One of the easiest walks is the five-mile round-trip (3hr) from the campsite up **Coire Làgan**, to a crystal-cold lochan squeezed in among the sternest of rock faces. Above the lochan is Skye's highest peak, **Sgùrr Alasdair** (3258ft), one of the more difficult Munros, while Sgurr na Banachdich (3166ft), to the northwest, is considered the most easily accessible Munro in the Cuillin.

ARRIVAL AND ACCOMMODATION — GLEN BRITTLE

Glenbrittle is connected to Portree by **bus** (Mon–Fri 2 daily; 50min).

SYHA hostel ⓣ 01478 640404, ⓦ syha.org.uk. A simple hostel with friendly staff and an absolutely spectacular location at the foot of the Cuillin. Closed Oct–March. **£16**

Dunvegan

After the Portnalong and Glen Brittle turning, the A863 slips north across bare rounded hills to skirt the bony sea cliffs and stacks of the west coast. Twenty miles on, it reaches **DUNVEGAN** (Dùn Bheagain), an unimpressive place, but a good base for exploring the interesting Duirinish peninsula.

Dunvegan Castle

April to mid-Oct daily 10am–5.30pm • £9, gardens only £7 • ⓣ 01470 521206, ⓦ dunvegancastle.com

Dunvegan's chief tourist-trap is **Dunvegan Castle**, which sprawls on top of a rocky outcrop, sandwiched between the sea and several acres of beautifully maintained gardens. Seat of the Clan MacLeod since the thirteenth century, the present greying, rectangular fortress dates from the 1840s. Inside, you don't get a lot of castle for your money, and the contents are far from stunning; most intriguing are the battered remnants of the **Fairy Flag** which was allegedly carried back to Skye by Norwegian king Harald Hardrada's Gaelic boatmen after the Battle of Stamford Bridge in 1066.

24

ARRIVAL AND INFORMATION — DUNVEGAN

By bus Dunvegan sees regular buses from Portree (Mon–Sat 3–4 daily; 45min).

Tourist office On the road to the castle (April & May Mon–Fri 10am–5pm; June–Oct Mon–Sat 10am–5pm; July & Aug also Sun 10am–4pm; Nov–March Mon–Fri 10am–1.30pm; ⓣ 0845 225 5121).

ACCOMMODATION

Carter's Rest Glendale, 8 miles west of Dunvegan ⓣ 01470 511272, ⓦ cartersrestskye.co.uk. A spotless, high-quality modern B&B that serves excellent food. All three rooms have laptops with free wi-fi and flatscreen TVs, two have sleigh beds and one has a jacuzzi bath. **£160**

Roskhill House Ose, 6 miles from Dunvegan ⓣ 01470 521317, ⓦ roskhillhouse.co.uk. This guesthouse – once the village post office – is now a lovely place to stay, with exposed stone walls and a log fire in the lounge and five simply decorated rooms with free wi-fi. **£80**

EATING AND DRINKING

★ **Stein Inn** Stein, 8 miles north of Dunvegan ⓣ 01470 592362, ⓦ steininn.co.uk. An atmospheric old pub, down by the pier in Stein. Snuggle up by the welcoming fires and enjoy real ales and malt whiskies. The food is good, too. Easter–Oct daily 12.30–4pm & 6.30–9.30pm; Nov–Easter daily noon–2.30pm & 5.30–8.30pm.

Three Chimneys 5 miles west of Dunvegan ⓣ 01470 511258, ⓦ threechimneys.co.uk. Skye's most famous restaurant, on the road to Colbost, serves sublime three-course meals at just under £50 a head (lunch around £30). April–Oct Mon–Sat 12.15–1.45pm & 6.15pm till late, Sun 6.15pm till late; Nov, Dec, Feb & March daily 6.15pm till late.

Portree

PORTREE is the only real town on Skye. It's also one of the most attractive fishing ports in northwest Scotland, its deep, cliff-edged harbour filled with fishing boats and circled by multicoloured restaurants and guesthouses. Above the harbour is the spick-and-span town centre, spreading out from **Somerled Square**, which was built in the late eighteenth century and now houses the bus station and car park. The **Royal Hotel** on Bank Street occupies the site of *McNab's Inn* where Bonnie Prince Charlie took leave of Flora MacDonald (see p.922), and where, 27 years later, Boswell and Johnson had "a very good dinner, porter, port and punch".

Aros Centre

A mile from Portree on the Sligachan road • Daily 9am–5.30pm • ⓣ 01478 613750, ⓦ aros.co.uk

Despite being little more than an enormous souvenir shop, the **Aros Centre,** a mile beyond "the village", is one of Skye's most successful tourist attractions. You can watch a live RSPB webcam centred on sea eagles' nests and take an audiovisual roam around the island (£4). The centre also hosts gigs and contains a **cinema**, a modern exhibition space, a licensed bar and a popular café, and even a special play area for small children.

ARRIVAL AND INFORMATION — PORTREE

By bus Buses pick up and drop off at Somerled Square. Destinations Duntulm (Mon–Sat 4–5 daily; 55min); Dunvegan (Mon–Sat 3–4 daily; 45min); Glenbrittle (Mon–Fri 2 daily; 50min); Staffin (Mon–Sat 4–5 daily; 35min); Uig (Mon–Sat 7–8 daily, 3 on Sun; 30min).

Tourist office Just off Bridge St (April–Oct Mon–Sat 9am–6pm, Sun 10am–4pm; Nov–March Mon–Fri 9am–5pm, Sat 10am–4pm; ⓣ 0845 225 5121).

ACCOMMODATION

Ben Tianavaig 5 Bosville Terrace ⓣ 01478 612152, ⓦ ben-tianavaig.co.uk. The best B&B in the centre of town, with charming hosts, views over the harbour, and free wi-fi. **£70**

Torvaig campsite 1.5 miles north of town off the A855 Staffin road ⓣ 01478 611849, ⓦ portreecampsite.co.uk. Well-maintained campsite, with a friendly owner, free hot showers and laundry facilities. Closed Nov–March.

★ **Viewfield House** ⓣ 01478 612217, ⓦ viewfieldhouse.com. For old-school Scots Baronial style, it's hard to beat this hotel on the southern outskirts of town, which has been in the hands of the MacDonalds for more than two hundred years, and has a real Victorian air, with stuffed polecats and antiques. Closed mid-Oct to mid-April. **£140**

EATING AND DRINKING

★ **Café Arriba** Quay Brae ⓣ 01478 611830, ⓦ cafearriba.co.uk. This relaxed, licensed café does great coffee, breakfast until 4.30pm, flatbread melts, and an array of dishes, from kedgeree to veggie lasagne, for under £10. Summer daily 7am–10pm; winter Mon–Sat 9am–5pm, Sun 10am–4pm.

Isles Inn Somerled Square ⓣ 01478 612129, ⓦ accommodationskye.co.uk. A proper old pub and a popular evening venue, with excellent bar meals (including local scallops) and live music. Mon–Sat 8am–10pm.

24

Trotternish

Protruding twenty miles north from Portree, the **Trotternish peninsula** boasts some of the island's most bizarre scenery, particularly on the east coast, where volcanic basalt has pressed down on the softer sandstone and limestone underneath, causing massive landslides. These, in turn, have created pinnacles and pillars that are at their most eccentric in the **Quiraing**, above **Staffin Bay**, on the east coast. Most people visit the **west coast** to catch the ferry to the Western Isles from **Uig**, or the **folk museum**, further up the coast.

The east coast

The first geological eccentricity on the peninsula, six miles north of Portree along the A855, is the **Old Man of Storr**, a distinctive 165ft column of rock, shaped like a willow leaf, which, along with its neighbours, is part of a massive landslip. Huge blocks of stone still occasionally break off the cliff face of the Storr (2358ft) above and slide downhill. It's a half-hour trek up a footpath to the foot of the column from the woods beside the car park.

Further north, **Staffin Bay** is spread out before you, dotted with whitewashed and "spotty" houses. A singletrack road cuts across the peninsula from the north end of

BONNIE PRINCE CHARLIE

Prince Charles Edward Stewart – better known as **Bonnie Prince Charlie** or "The Young Pretender" – was born in Rome in 1720, where his father, "The Old Pretender", claimant to the British throne, was living in exile. At the age of 25, having little military experience, no knowledge of Gaelic, an imperfect grasp of English and a strong attachment to the Catholic faith, the prince set out for Scotland with two French ships. He arrived on the Hebridean island of **Eriskay** on July 23, 1745, and went on to raise the royal standard at Glenfinnan, gather a Highland army, win the Battle of Prestonpans, march south into England and reach Derby before finally (and foolishly) agreeing to retreat. Back in Scotland, he won one last victory, at Falkirk, before the final disaster at **Culloden** in April 1746.

The prince spent the following five months in hiding, with a price of £30,000 on his head. He endured his share of cold and hunger whilst on the run, but the real price was paid by the Highlanders who risked, and sometimes lost, their lives by aiding and abetting him. The most famous of these was 23-year-old **Flora MacDonald**, whom Charles met on South Uist in June 1746. Flora was persuaded – either by his beauty or her relatives, depending on which account you believe – to convey Charles "over the sea to Skye", disguised as a servant. She was arrested later in Portree, and held in the Tower of London until July 1747. She went on to marry a local man, had seven children, and in 1774 emigrated to America, where her husband was taken prisoner during the American War of Independence. Flora returned to Scotland and was reunited with her husband on his release; they resettled in Skye and she died aged 68.

Charles eventually boarded a ship back to France in September 1746, but never returned to Scotland; nor did he see Flora again. After mistreating a string of mistresses, he eventually got married at the age of 52 to the 19-year-old Princess of Stolberg, in an effort to produce a Stewart heir. They had no children, and she eventually fled from his violent drunkenness; in 1788, a none-too-"bonnie" Prince Charles died in the arms of his illegitimate daughter in Rome.

the bay, allowing access to the **Quiraing**, a spectacular forest of mighty pinnacles and savage rock formations. There are two car parks: from the first, beside a cemetery, it's a steep half-hour climb to the rocks; from the second, on the saddle, it's a longer but more gentle traverse.

Behind (and now part of) the *Flodigarry Country House Hotel*, three miles up the coast from Staffin, is the cottage where local heroine **Flora MacDonald** (see above) lived, and had six of her seven children, from 1751 to 1759.

Skye Museum of Island Life

Easter–Oct Mon–Sat 9.30am–5pm • £2.50 • ⓦ skyemuseum.co.uk

The **Skye Museum of Island Life** is an impressive cluster of thatched blackhouses on an exposed hill overlooking the Western Isles. The museum, run by locals, gives a fascinating insight into a way of life that was commonplace on Skye a hundred years ago. Behind the museum, in the cemetery up the hill, are the graves of **Flora MacDonald** and her husband. Thousands turned out for her funeral in 1790, creating a procession a mile long – so widespread was her fame that the original family mausoleum fell victim to souvenir hunters and had to be replaced.

Uig

Skye's chief ferry port for the Western Isles is **UIG** (Uige), which curves its way round a dramatic, horseshoe-shaped bay on the west coast of the Trotternish peninsula. Most folk are just passing through, but if you've time to kill, there's a lovely, gentle **walk** up Glen Uig, better known as the **Faerie Glen**, at the east end of the bay.

ARRIVAL AND DEPARTURE — TROTTERNISH

By bus Uig sees services to and from Glasgow (2 daily; 6hr 50min); Portree (Mon–Sat 7–8 daily, 3 on Sun; 30min). The Flodigarry Circular bus service #57A and #57C gives access to almost all the coast.

By ferry Uig has connections to Lochmaddy (1–2 daily; 1hr 40min) and Tarbert (Mon–Sat 1–2 daily; 1hr 45min).

ACCOMMODATION AND EATING

Dun Flodigarry hostel Flodigarry ⓣ01470 552212, ⓦhostelflodigarry.co.uk. Neat and attractive east coast hostel a couple of minutes' walk away from the very posh *Flodigarry Country House Hotel*. Excellent kitchen facilities and spectacular views out to sea. Dorm £13, double £35

Flodigarry Country House Hotel Flodigarry ⓣ01470 552203, ⓦflodigarry.co.uk. Delicious, pricey bar snacks – from haddock and chips to venison stew – served on the castellated terrace of this stylish hotel. Food served noon–2.30pm & 7–9.30pm.

The Glenview Culnaknock, near Staffin ⓣ01470 562248, ⓦglenviewskye.co.uk. This solidly built Victorian croft house and former village shop on the east coast is now a very welcoming, beautifully renovated, hotel with five en-suite rooms and free wi-fi. It also has a small, excellent restaurant – the short menu is strictly seasonal, and all food is locally sourced (three courses for just over £30). Booking essential. Dinner daily 7–8.30pm. £110

SYHA hostel Uig ⓣ01470 542746, ⓦsyha.org.uk. The hostel is a 15min walk away from Uig, high up on the south side of the village, with exhilarating views over the bay. Closed Nov–March. £16

Woodbine House Uig ⓣ01470 542243, ⓦskyeactivities.co.uk. A luxurious Victorian house just under a mile from the pier, tastefully furnished by a couple who also run boat trips from Uig. Closed Nov–Feb. £65

The Small Isles

The history of the **Small Isles**, to the south of Skye, is typical of the Hebrides: early Christianization, followed by Norwegian rule ending in 1266 when the islands fell into Scottish hands. Their support for the Jacobites resulted in hard times after the failed 1745 rebellion, but the biggest problems came with the introduction of the **potato** in the mid-eighteenth century, which prompted a population explosion. At first, the problem of overcrowding was lessened by the **kelp** boom, but the economic bubble burst with the end of the Napoleonic Wars and most owners eventually resorted to forced Clearances.

Since then, each of the islands has been bought and sold several times, though only **Muck** is now privately owned by the benevolent laird, Lawrence MacEwen. **Eigg** was bought by the islanders themselves in 1997. The other islands were bequeathed to national agencies: **Rùm**, by far the largest and most-visited of the group, possessing a cluster of formidable volcanic peaks and the architecturally remarkable Kinloch Castle, belongs to Scottish Natural Heritage; while **Canna**, with its high basalt cliffs, is owned by the National Trust for Scotland.

24

ARRIVAL AND ACCOMMODATION — THE SMALL ISLES

CalMac **ferries** run to the Small Isles from Mallaig (Mon–Sat; ⓣ01687 462403), and the **Sheerwater** boat (ⓣ01687 450224, ⓦarisaig.co.uk; April–Sept), has services from Arisaig to Rùm, Eigg and Muck. **Accommodation** on the Small Isles is limited and every establishment requires booking, whatever the time of year.

Rùm

Like Skye, **Rùm** (ⓦisleofrum.com) is dominated by its Cuillin, which, though only reaching a height of 2663ft at the summit of Askival, rises up with comparable drama straight up from the sea in the south of the island. The majority of the island's twenty or so inhabitants now live in **KINLOCH**, the only village, overlooking the large bay on the sheltered east coast, and most are employed by Scottish Natural Heritage (SNH), which runs the island as a National Nature Reserve. Two gentle waymarked **heritage trails** start from Kinloch, both taking around two hours.

The island's best beach is at **KILMORY**, to the north, though check with the reserve manager about public access (ⓣ01687 462026). The hamlet of **HARRIS** on the southwest coast once housed a large crofting community; all that remains now are several ruined blackhouses and the extravagant **Bullough Mausoleum**, which was built in the style of a Greek Doric temple by Sir George to house the remains of his father, and overlooks the sea.

Kinloch Castle

Kinloch • March–Oct guided tours daily 1pm or 2pm to coincide with the ferry • £6 • ⓣ 01687 462037, ⓦ isleofrum.com

Rùm's chief formal attraction is **Kinloch Castle**, a squat red sandstone edifice fronted by colonnades and topped by crenellations and turrets, that overshadows the village of Kinloch. From the galleried hall, with its tiger rugs, stags' heads and giant Japanese incense-burners, to the "Extra Low Fast Cushion" of the Soho snooker table in the Billiard Room, the interior is packed with knick-knacks and technical gizmos accumulated by **Sir George Bullough** (1870–1939), the spendthrift son of self-made

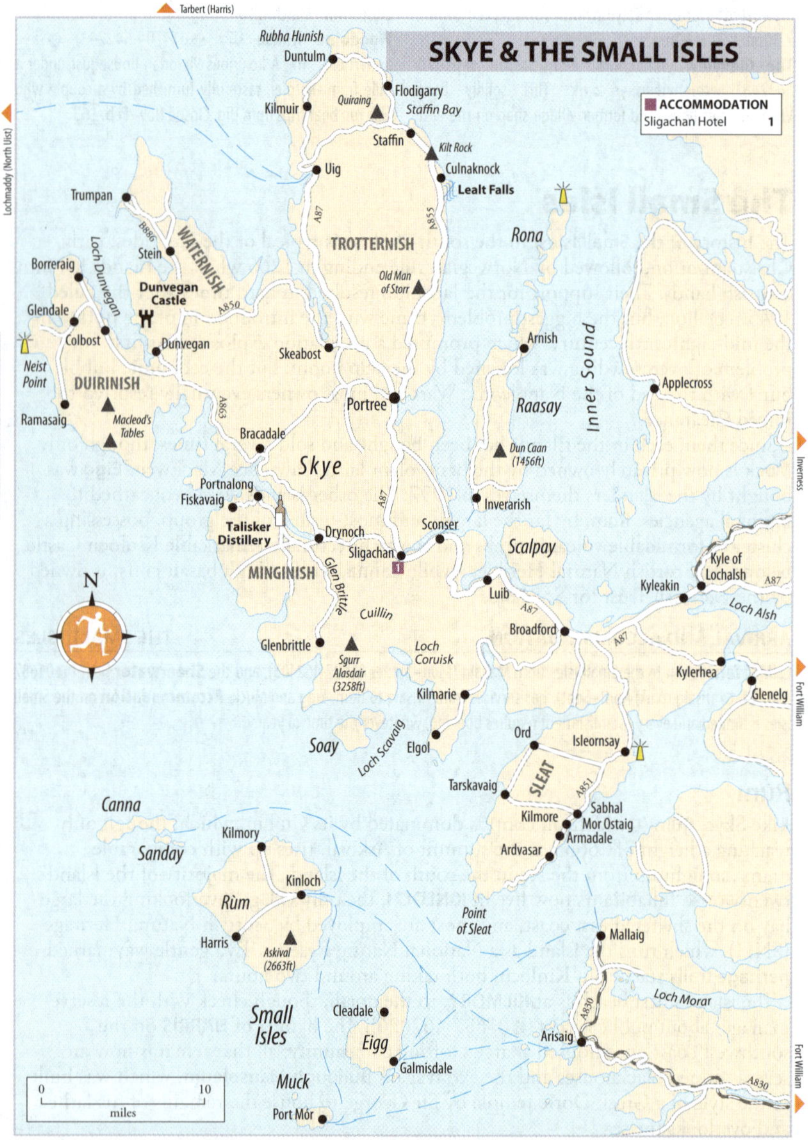

millionaire Sir John Bullough, who bought the island as a sporting estate in 1888. Look out for the orchestrion, an electrically driven barrel organ (originally destined for Balmoral) crammed in under the stairs. You can also **spend the night** here, and there's a bistro and a bar; see below.

ARRIVAL AND DEPARTURE — RÙM

CalMac **ferries** run to Rùm from Mallaig (Mon, Wed, Fri & Sat; 1hr 20min–2hr 30min); Eigg (Mon & Sat; 1hr–3hr 30min); Muck (Sat; 1hr 10min) and Canna (Mon, Wed, Fri & Sat; 55min). The **Sheerwater** boat runs from Arisaig (April–Sept Tues & Thurs; June–Aug also Sat).

ACCOMMODATION AND EATING

In addition to a community campsite at Kinloch, **wild camping** is permitted on Rùm – it's not for the faint-hearted, however, given Rùm's notoriety for midges – and there are two mountain **bothies** (maximum stay 3 nights), in Dibidil and Guirdil.

★ **Kinloch Castle** Kinloch ⓣ 01687 462037. The castle lets a few of its (non en-suite) four-poster rooms, but it's basically run as a hostel, with dorms in the old servants' quarters and a kitchen that anyone staying on the island can use. The licensed bistro serves breakfasts, offers packed lunches and charges around £15 a head for an unpretentious three-course evening meal for residents and non-residents; you can also have a drink in the mock-Gothic hostel bar, which has a stag's head above the open fire. Restaurant daily, bar daily 5–11pm. Dorm £16, double £45

Eigg

Eigg (ⓦ isleofeigg.net) is the most easily distinguishable of the Small Isles from a distance, since the island is mostly made up of a basalt plateau 1000ft above sea level, and a great stump of columnar pitchstone lava, known as **An Sgurr**, rising out of the plateau another 290ft. It's also the most vibrant, populous and welcoming of the Small Isles, with a strong sense of community. Ferries arrive at the causeway, which juts out into **Galmisdale Bay** at the southeast corner of the island where **An Laimhrig** (The Anchorage), the island's community centre, stands, housing a shop, post office, tearoom and information centre. With the island's great landmark, **An Sgurr** (1292ft), watching over you wherever you go, many folk feel duty-bound to climb it, and enjoy the wonderful views over to Muck and Rùm (3–4hr return).

24

ARRIVAL AND DEPARTURE — EIGG

CalMac **ferries** run to Eigg from Mallaig (Mon, Tues & Thurs–Sat; 1hr 15min–2hr 25min); Muck (Tues & Thurs–Sat; 35min); Rùm (Mon & Sat; 1hr–3hr 30min) and Canna (Mon & Sat; 2hr 15min). The **Sheerwater** boat also runs from Arisaig (April–Sept Fri–Wed).

ACCOMMODATION AND EATING

Cleadale Camping ⓣ 01687 482480, ⓦ eiggyurtingandcamping.co.uk. At Sue Hollands' organic croft in the north of the island, you can pitch your own tent, hire the family tent or stay in the yurt (sleeps 3). Yurt £30

Glebe Barn A mile from the pier ⓣ 01687 482417, ⓦ glebebarn.co.uk. A very comfortable bunkhouse, with an open fire in the lounge, in a substantial converted nineteenth-century barn. £17

★ **Kildonan House** North side of Galmisdale Bay ⓣ 01687 482446, ⓦ kildonanhouseeigg.co.uk. A beautifully situated eighteenth-century wood-panelled house, offering good rooms and tasty home cooking. £120

Lageorna Cleadale, on the north of the island ⓣ 01687 482405, ⓦ lageorna.com. This attractively designed modern house offers superb views from both of the bright white en-suite doubles over to Rùm. Rates include breakfast and dinner. Free wi-fi. They also offer good lunches and dinner to non-residents (call for times and to book). £120

Muck

Smallest and most southerly of the Small Isles, **Muck** (ⓦ isleofmuck.com) is low-lying, mostly treeless and extremely fertile. You'll arrive at **PORT MÓR**, the village on the southeast corner of the island. A road, a little more than a mile long, connects Port Mór with the island's main farm, **Gallanach**, which overlooks the rocky seal-strewn skerries on the north side of the island; to the east lies the nicest sandy beach, **Camas na Cairidh**. In the southwest corner of the island, it's worth climbing **Beinn Airein** (452ft) for the 360-degree panoramic view; the return journey from Port Mór takes around two hours.

ARRIVAL AND INFORMATION — MUCK

By ferry CalMac ferries run to Muck from Mallaig (Tues, Thurs, Fri & Sat; 1hr 40min–4hr 20min); Eigg (Tues, Thurs & Sat; 35min) and Rùm (Tues & Sat; 2hr 45min). The *Sheerwater* boat also sails to Muck from Arisaig (April–Sept Mon, Wed & Fri; June–Aug also Sun).

Tourist information The craft shop in Port Mór (April–Sept), which springs into life when day-trippers arrive, is a de facto information centre.

ACCOMMODATION AND EATING

You can **camp** rough on Muck – ask at the craft shop in Port Mór (April–Sept), which also serves evening **meals** on request – and there's an island yurt.

Bunkhouse T 01687 462042, W isleofmuck.com. Despite the name, the island's characterful, wood-panelled bunkhouse has beds not bunks – two twins and a double – and is heated by a oil-fired Raeburn stove. **£24**

Port Mór House T 01687 462365, W isleofmuck.com. It's possible to stay with one of the MacEwen family, who have owned the island since 1896; the rooms are pine-clad and enjoy great views, and the food is delicious. Rates include a three-course dinner and B&B. **£120**

Canna

24

Measuring just over four miles by one, and with a population of around twenty, **Canna** is run as a single farm and bird sanctuary by the National Trust for Scotland. For visitors, the chief pastime is walking: from the dock it's about a mile across a grassy basalt plateau to the bony sea cliffs of the north shore, which rise to a peak around **Compass Hill** (458ft) – so called because its high metal content distorts compasses – in the northeastern corner of the island, from where you get great views across to Rùm and Skye. The cliffs of the buffeted western half of the island are a breeding ground for Manx shearwater, razorbill and puffin.

ARRIVAL AND DEPARTURE — CANNA

CalMac **ferries** arrive in Canna from Mallaig (Mon, Wed, Fri & Sat; 2hr 30min–3hr 50min), Eigg (Mon & Sat; 2hr 30min) and Muck (Sat; 1hr 35min).

ACCOMMODATION AND EATING

It is possible to **camp rough** on Canna, though you need to bring your own supplies, as there's no shop to speak of. You can also hire a traditional bell tent which sleeps five (W cannafolk.co.uk).

Gille Brighde (Oystercatcher) T 01687 460164, W cannarestaurant.com. The island restaurant overlooks the harbour and offers light lunches and dinner featuring local beef and lamb and lots of fish and seafood. March–Oct Tues–Fri 11am–3pm & 6–10pm, Sat 10am–9pm.

Tighard Half a mile from the jetty T 01687 462474, W peaceofcanna.co.uk. This substantial, red sandstone, Victorian house is the island's only guesthouse; its spacious rooms have glorious views, and they'll cook guests dinner when the *Oystercatcher* restaurant's not open (bring your own bottle). **£80**

The Western Isles

Beyond Skye, across the unpredictable waters of the Minch, lie the wild and windy Outer Hebrides or Outer Isles, also known as the **Western Isles** (W visithebrides.com), a 130-mile-long archipelago stretching from Lewis and Harris in the north to the Uists and Barra in the south. An elemental beauty pervades the more than 200 islands that

GAELIC IN THE WESTERN ISLES

The Outer Hebrides remain the heartland of **Gaelic** culture, with the language spoken by the majority of islanders, though its everyday usage remains under constant threat from the dominance of English. Except in Stornoway, and Balivanich on North Uist, **road signs** in the Western Isles are almost exclusively in Gaelic; the English names can often provide a rough pronunciation guide. Particularly if you're driving, it's a good idea to buy the bilingual Western Isles **map**, available at most tourist offices.

make up the Long Isle, as it's sometimes known; only a handful are inhabited, by a total population of just under 27,000 people.

The interior of the northernmost island, **Lewis**, is mostly peat moor, a barren and marshy tract that gives way abruptly to the bare peaks of **North Harris**. Across a narrow isthmus lies **South Harris**, presenting some of the finest scenery in Scotland, with wide beaches of golden sand trimming the Atlantic in full view of a rough boulder-strewn interior. Across the Sound of Harris, to the south, a string of tiny, flatter isles – **North Uist**, **Benbecula**, **South Uist** – linked by causeways, offer breezy beaches, whose fine sands front a narrow band of boggy farmland, which, in turn, is mostly bordered by a lower range of hills to the east. Finally, tiny **Barra** contains all these landscapes in one small Hebridean package, and is a great introduction to the region.

In direct contrast to their wonderful landscapes, villages in the Western Isles are rarely very picturesque. **Stornoway**, the only real town in the Outer Hebrides, rarely impresses. Many visitors, walkers and nature-watchers forsake the settlements altogether and retreat to secluded cottages and B&Bs.

GETTING AROUND — THE WESTERN ISLES

A series of causeways makes it possible to travel by road from one end of the Western Isles to the other with just two interruptions – the **ferry** from Harris to Berneray, and from Eriskay to Barra. The islands have a decent **bus** service, though there are no buses on Sundays. **Bike rental** is also available, but the wind makes cycling something of a challenge – head south to north to catch the prevailing wind.

Lewis (Leodhas)

The northernmost island in the Hebridean archipelago, **Lewis** is the largest and most populous of the Western Isles. **Stornoway**, on the east coast, is the only substantial town in the islands, but it's really only useful for stocking up on provisions or catching the bus. Most of Lewis's 20,000 inhabitants live in the crofting and fishing villages strung out along the northwest coast, where you'll find the islands' best-preserved **prehistoric remains** – including the Calanais standing stones. The landscape is mostly flat peat bog, but the shoreline is more dramatic, as is the south of the island. Here, where Lewis is physically joined with Harris, the land rises to just over 1800ft, providing an exhilarating backdrop for the excellent beaches that pepper the isolated west coast.

Stornoway (Steornabhagh)

In these parts, **STORNOWAY** is a buzzing metropolis, with more than six thousand inhabitants. For the visitor, however, the town is unlikely to win any great praise – aesthetics are not its strong point, and the urban pleasures on offer are limited. Stornoway's best-looking building is the old **Town Hall** on South Beach, a splendid Scots Baronial pile, its rooftop interspersed with conical towers, above which a central clocktower rises. One block east along South Beach, you'll find **An Lanntair** (Mon–Sat 10am–10pm; free; ⓦlanntair.com) – Gaelic for "lantern" – Stornoway's state-of-the-art cultural centre, which houses a 250-seat auditorium and cinema, and gallery space for temporary exhibitions, plus a decent café-bar. Continuing up the pedestrian precinct into Francis Street, you'll eventually reach the **Museum nan Eilean** (April–Sept Mon–Sat 10am–5.30pm; Oct–March

Tues–Fri 10am–5pm, Sat 10am–1pm; free; cne-siar.gov.uk), with lots of information about the island's history and its herring and weaving industries.

Lews Castle

Woodland Centre Mon–Sat 10am–5pm • Free • lews-castle.com

Northwest of the town centre, across the bay, stands **Lews Castle,** a castellated Gothic pomposity built by Sir James Matheson in 1863 after resettling the crofters who used to live there. As the former laird's pad, the castle is seen as a symbol of old oppression by many and it's currently in a state of some disrepair awaiting renovation. The mature wooded grounds, however, are a unique sight on the Western Isles, and the **Woodland Centre** has a straightforward exhibition on the history of the castle and the island upstairs, and a **café** downstairs.

ARRIVAL AND INFORMATION — STORNOWAY

By plane The island's airport (01851 707400, hial.co.uk) is 4 miles east of the town centre: the hourly bus takes 15min, and it's £5 by taxi.

Destinations Benbecula (Mon–Fri 2 daily; 30min); Edinburgh (Mon–Fri 2 daily, Sat & Sun 1 daily; 1hr 5min); Glasgow (Mon–Fri 3–4 daily, Sat & Sun 1–2 daily; 1hr 10min); Inverness (Mon–Fri 3 daily, Sat & Sun 1 daily; 40min).

24

By ferry CalMac ferries run between Ullapool and Stornoway (Mon–Sat 2–3 daily, 1 on Sun; 2hr 45min).

By bus Buses stop by the ferry terminal.

Destinations Calanais (Mon–Sat 4–6 daily; 40min); Carlabhagh (Mon–Sat 5–6 daily; 45min); Gearrannan (Mon–Sat 3–4 daily; 1hr); Leverburgh (Mon–Sat 4–5 daily; 2hr); Port Nis (Mon–Sat 6–8 daily; 1hr); Tarbert (Mon–Sat 5 daily; 1hr); Uig (Mon–Sat 4 daily; 1hr–1hr 30min).

Tourist office 26 Cromwell St (April to mid-Oct Mon–Fri 9am–6pm, Sat 9am–5pm, plus open to meet the evening ferry; mid-Oct to March Mon–Fri 9am–5pm; 01851 703088).

ACCOMMODATION

Heb Hostel 25 Kenneth St 01851 709889, hebhostel.co.uk. Stornoway's clean, central hostel offers B&B in a terrace house with a cosy peat fire and a friendly owner. **£16**

Jannel 5 Stewart Drive 0800 634 3270, jannel-stornoway.co.uk. A short walk from the town centre, this B&B is run by a delightful landlady, and offers five spacious, immaculate en-suite rooms. Free wi-fi. **£75**

EATING AND DRINKING

★ **An Lanntair** Kenneth St 01851 703307, lanntair.com. Stylish café-restaurant in the arts centre with views over the harbour and ferry terminal – sandwiches, pasta, burgers and fish and chips for lunch; local scallops with black pudding and squash and sage risotto in the evening. Free wi-fi. Mon–Sat noon–2.30pm & 5.30–9pm.

Digby Chick 5 Bank St 01851 700026, digbychick.co.uk. Smart, modern little bistro with an emphasis on local produce. Sandwiches available at lunchtimes or two courses for around £10; three-course dinners are under £25. Mon–Sat noon–2pm & 5.30–9pm.

Thai Café 27 Church St 01851 701811. Despite the name, this is a restaurant, serving authentic Thai food. Bring your own bottle. Mon–Sat noon–2.30pm & 5–11pm.

The road to Port Nis (Port of Ness)

Northwest of Stornoway, the A857 crosses the vast, barren **peat bog** of the interior, an empty undulating wilderness riddled with stretchmarks formed by peat cuttings and pockmarked with freshwater lochans. For the people of Lewis the peat continues to serve as a valuable energy resource, its pungent smoke one of the most characteristic smells of the Western Isles.

Twelve miles across the peat bog, near Barabhas (Barvas), the road divides, heading southwest towards Calanais (see p.929), or northeast through a string of scattered settlements to the fishing village of **PORT NIS** (Port of Ness). Shortly before Port Nis, a minor road heads two miles northwest to the hamlet of **EOROPAIDH** (Europie) – pronounced "yor-erpee". Here, by the road junction that leads to the Butt of Lewis, stands the simple stone structure of **Teampull Mholuaidh** (St Moluag's Church), thought to date from the twelfth century. From Eoropaidh, a narrow road twists to the blustery northern tip of the island, Rubha Robhanais – known to devotees of the BBC shipping forecast as the **Butt of Lewis** – where a lighthouse sticks up above a series of sheer cliffs and stacks, alive with seabirds and a great place for marine mammal-spotting.

ARRIVAL AND DEPARTURE — PORT NIS

Regular **buses** run from Stornoway to Port Nis (Mon–Sat 6–8 daily; 1hr).

ACCOMMODATION AND EATING

Galson Farm Gabhsann Bho Dheas (South Galson) ⓣ 01851 850492, ⓦ galsonfarm.co.uk. An attractive converted eighteenth-century farmhouse, 7 miles before Port Nis, which offers dinner, bed and breakfast, and runs a six-bunk bunkhouse close by. Dorm £15, double £80

Port Beach House Port Nis ⓣ 01851 810000. The best place to eat in Port Nis, with great views out to sea, and locally caught fish and seafood on the menu. April–Oct Tues–Sat 10.30am–5pm.

Westside

Heading southwest from the crossroads near Barabhas brings you to the **Westside** (An Toabh Siar), an area where several villages meander down towards the sea, and which is home to the **Calanais** stone circle.

Arnol Blackhouse

Arnol • Mon–Sat: April–Sept 9.30am–5.30pm; Oct–March 9.30am–4.30pm • HS • £4 • ⓣ 01851 710395

In **Arnol**, the remains of numerous blackhouses lie abandoned by the roadside; at the north end of the village, no. 42 has been preserved as the **Arnol Blackhouse**, which shows exactly how a true blackhouse (*taigh dubh*) would have been. The dark interior is lit and heated by a small peat fire, which is kept alight in the central hearth of bare earth, and is usually fairly smoky as there's no chimney; instead, smoke drifts through the thatch, helping to kill any creepy-crawlies, keep out the midges and turn the heathery sods and oat-straw thatch itself into next year's fertilizer.

24

Gearrannan

May–Sept Mon–Sat 9.30am–5.30pm • £2.50

At Carlabhagh a mile-long road leads off north to the beautifully remote coastal settlement of **GEARRANNAN** (Garenin). Here, rather than re-create a single museum-piece blackhouse as at Arnol, a whole cluster of nine thatched crofters' houses – the last of which was abandoned in 1974 – have been restored and put to a variety of uses. As an ensemble, they also give a great impression of what a blackhouse village must have been like.

Dùn Charlabhaigh

Just beyond Carlabhagh village, **Dùn Charlabhaigh** perches on top of a conspicuous rocky outcrop overlooking the sea. This is one of Scotland's best-preserved brochs (a circular, prehistoric stone fort), its dry-stone circular walls reaching a height of more than 30ft on one side. The broch consists of two concentric walls, the inner one perpendicular, the outer one slanting inwards, the two originally fastened together by roughly hewn flagstones, which also served as lookout galleries reached via a narrow stairwell.

Calanais (Callanish)

Overlooking the sheltered, islet-studded waters of Loch Ròg, on the west coast, are the islands' most dramatic prehistoric ruins, the **Calanais standing stones**, which occupy a serene lochside setting. These monoliths – nearly fifty slabs of gnarled and finely grained gneiss up to 15ft high – were transported here between 3000 and 1500 BC, but their exact function remains a mystery. No one knows for certain why the ground plan resembles a colossal Celtic cross, nor why there's a central burial chamber. It's likely that such a massive endeavour was prompted by the desire to predict the seasonal cycle upon which these early farmers were entirely dependent, and indeed many of the stones are aligned with the positions of the sun and the stars. Whatever the reason for their existence, there's certainly no denying the powerful primeval presence, not to mention sheer beauty, of the stones.

ACCOMMODATION AND EATING — CALANAIS

Leumadair ⊕01851 612706, ⊕leumadair.co.uk. A comfortable, new-build guesthouse near the Calanais stones, owned by a very friendly Lewis couple, who cure and smoke their own bacon, keep hens and have a pet hawk. For an extra £20, you can have dinner, too. **£70**

Harris (Na Hearadh)

Harris, south of Lewis, is much hillier, more dramatic and much more appealing than its neighbour, its boulder-strewn slopes descending to aquamarine bays of dazzling, white sand. The "island" is clearly divided by a minuscule isthmus into the wild, inhospitable mountains of **North Harris** and the gentler landscape and sandy shores of **South Harris.**

Tarbert (An Tairbeart)

Sheltered in a green valley on the narrow isthmus, **TARBERT** is the largest place on Harris; views of its impressive mountain backdrop and steeply terraced houses makes it a wonderful place to arrive by boat.

ARRIVAL AND INFORMATION — TARBERT

24

By ferry CalMac ferries run from Uig to Tarbert (Mon–Sat 1–2 daily; 1hr 45min).

By bus There are buses from Leverburgh (Mon–Sat 5–7 daily; 45min–1hr) and Stornoway (Mon–Sat 5 daily; 1hr)

Tourist office Tarbert boasts Harris's only tourist office (April–Oct Mon–Sat 9am–5pm; also open to greet the evening ferry; ⊕0845 225 5121), close to the ferry terminal.

ACCOMMODATION AND EATING

Isle of Harris Inn ⊕01859 502566, ⊕isleofharrisinn.co.uk. Next door to (and not to be confused with) the *Harris Hotel*, this pub has a short menu of seafood specials worth perusing. Food served Mon–Sat 10.30am–9pm.

Rockview Bunkhouse Main St ⊕01859 502081. Simple, clean hostel, with a real fire, in the centre of Tarbert, run by a lovely couple – they don't live on site, though, so it's best to book ahead. **£12**

Tigh na Mara Scalpay Rd ⊕01859 502270, ⊕tigh-na-mara.co.uk. Traditional croft-house B&B, just up the Scalpay road, with a single, a twin and an en-suite double, and fabulous views over East Loch Tarbert from the conservatory. **£56**

North Harris (Ceann a Tuath na Hearadh)

If you're coming from Stornoway on the A859, mountainous **North Harris** is a spectacular introduction to Harris, its bulging, pyramidal mountains of gneiss looming over the dramatic, fjord-like **Loch Shìphoirt** (Loch Seaforth). You weave your way over a boulder-strewn saddle between mighty **Sgaoth Aird** (1829ft) and An Cliseam or the **Clisham** (2619ft), the highest peak in the Western Isles. This bitter terrain, littered with debris left behind by retreating glaciers, offers but the barest of vegetation, with an occasional cluster of crofters' houses sitting in the shadow of a host of pointed peaks, anywhere between 1000ft and 2500ft high.

ACCOMMODATION — NORTH HARRIS

GHHT hostel Reinigeadal (Rhenigdale) ⊕gatliff.org.uk. Simple hostel in a lonely coastal hamlet. To walk there from Tarbert, take the hiking route from Caolas Scalpaigh (Kyles Scalpay) – it will take 2–3hr one-way. Camping permitted. No advance booking. **£10**

South Harris (Ceann a Deas na Hearadh)

The mountains of **South Harris** are less dramatic than in the north, but the scenery is equally breathtaking. There's a choice of routes from Tarbert to the ferry port of

Leverburgh, which connects with North Uist: the east coast, known as Na Baigh (The Bays), is rugged and seemingly inhospitable, while the **west coast** is endowed with some of the finest stretches of golden sand **beaches** in the whole of the archipelago, buffeted by the Atlantic winds. Most stunning of all is the vast golden strand of **Tràigh Losgaintir**, with the islet-studded turquoise sea to the west, and even on the dullest day the sand glowing beneath the waves. Paradoxically, most people on South Harris live along the harsh eastern coastline of **Bays** rather than the more fertile west side. But not by choice – they were evicted from their original crofts to make way for sheep-grazing.

ACCOMMODATION AND EATING — SOUTH HARRIS

Beul-na-Mara Seiilebost ⓣ01859 550205, ⓦbeulnamara.co.uk. A very good modern B&B with a conservatory overlooking the sands of Tràigh Losgaintir. Evening meals are available for just under £30 a head. **£80**

Pairc an t-Srath Na Buirgh (Borve) ⓣ01859 550386, ⓦpaircant-srath.co.uk. This lovely, tastefully converted Victorian croft house also serves excellent three-course dinners (also available to non-guests) for £35 a head. Free wi-fi. **£100**

Leverburgh

The west coast road veers to the southeast to trim the island's south shore, eventually reaching the sprawling settlement of **LEVERBURGH** (An t-Ob), named after Lord Leverhulme, who planned to turn the place into the largest fishing port on the west coast of Scotland. The main reason to come here is to catch the CalMac **car ferry** service to Berneray and the Uists.

24

ARRIVAL AND DEPARTURE — LEVERBURGH

CalMac **ferries** run from Berneray to Leverburgh (3–4 daily; 1hr).

ACCOMMODATION AND EATING

★ **Am Bothan** Ferry Rd ⓣ01859 520251, ⓦambothan.com. Quirky, luxurious and welcoming timber-clad bunkhouse just a few minutes' walk from the ferry. **£20**

The Anchorage By the ferry slipway ⓣ01859 520225. For local langoustines, home-made cakes and the usual comfort food – along with great views and the occasional night of live music – head over to this lively bar and restaurant. Mon–Sat noon–9pm.

Roghadal

A mile or so from Rubha Reanais (Renish Point), the southern tip of Harris, is the old port of **ROGHADAL** (Rodel), where a smattering of ancient stone houses lies among the hillocks. On top of one of these grassy humps is **St Clement's Church** (Tur Chliamainn), burial place of the MacLeods of Harris and Dunvegan in Skye. Dating from the 1520s, the church's bare interior is distinguished by its wall tombs; look out, too, for the *Sheela-na-gig* (a naked pre-Christian fertility goddess) halfway up the south side of the tower. Unusually, she has a brother displaying his genitalia too, below a carving of St Clement on the west face.

North Uist (Uibhist a Tuath)

Compared to the mountainous scenery of Harris, **North Uist** – seventeen miles long and thirteen miles wide – is much flatter and for some comes as something of an anticlimax. More than half the surface area is covered by water, creating a distinctive peaty-brown lochan-studded "drowned landscape". Most visitors are here for the trout and salmon **fishing** and the deerstalking, both of which (along with poaching) are critical to the island's economy. Others come for the smattering of **prehistoric sites**, the **birds**, or the sheer peace of this windy isle, and the solitude of North Uist's vast sandy **beaches**, which extend – almost without interruption – along the north and west coasts.

Lochmaddy

Despite being situated on the east coast, some distance away from any beach, the ferry port of **LOCHMADDY** (Loch nam Madadh, or "Loch of the Dogs") makes a good base for exploring the island. The village itself, occupying a narrow, bumpy promontory, is nothing special, but it does have a tourist office, and the nearby **Taigh Chearsabhagh**, a converted eighteenth-century merchant's house, now home to a community arts centre.

Taigh Chearsabhagh

Mon–Sat 10am–5pm • Free • ⓣ 01876 500293, ⓦ taigh-chearsabhagh.org

A converted eighteenth-century merchant's house, **Taigh Chearsabhagh** is now home to a vibrant community arts centre that houses a café, post office, shop and an excellent museum, which puts on some seriously innovative exhibitions. The arts centre was one of the prime movers behind the commissioning of a series of seven **sculptures** dotted about the Uists – ask for directions to those in and around Lochmaddy, the most interesting of which is the **Both nam Faileas** (Hut of the Shadow), 1km north of town.

Berneray (Bhearnaraigh)

The ferry connection with Harris leaves from the southeasternmost point of **Berneray** (ⓦ isleofberneray.com), a low-lying island immediately north of North Uist and connected to the latter via a causeway. Two miles by three, with a population of around 140, the island has a superb three-mile-long sandy beach on the west and north coast, backed by rabbit-free dunes and machair.

Balranald RSPB Reserve

North Uist's other main draw is the **Balranald RSPB Reserve**, on the western tip of the island and best known for its population of corncrakes: there are usually one or two making a loud noise right outside the RSPB **visitor centre**, from which you can pick up a leaflet outlining a two-hour walk along the headland, marked by posts. A wonderful carpet of flowers covers the machair in summer, and there are usually corn buntings and arctic terns inland, and gannets, Manx shearwater and skuas out to sea.

ARRIVAL AND INFORMATION — NORTH UIST

By ferry CalMac car ferries run from Uig on Skye to Lochmaddy (1–2 daily; 1hr 40min) and from Leverburgh on Harris to Berneray (3–4 daily; 1hr).

By bus There are services between Lochmaddy and Balivanich (Mon–Sat 6 daily; 45min–2hr), Balranald (Mon–Sat 3 daily; 50min), Bernerary (Mon–Sat 6–7 daily; 20–30min) and Lochboisdale (Mon–Sat 6 daily; 1hr 30min).

Tourist office Pier Rd, Lochmaddy (April–Oct Mon–Sat 9am–5pm; also open to greet the evening ferry; ⓣ 01876 500321).

ACCOMMODATION AND EATING

GHHT hostel Berneray ⓦ gatliff.org.uk. A wonderful hostel occupying a pair of thatched blackhouses in a lovely beachside spot beyond Loch a Bhàigh. **£10**

Moorcroft Holidays Carinis ⓣ 01876 580305. An exposed, but very well-equipped campsite (and bunkhouse), overlooking the sea just south of Carinis (Carinish). Dorm **£10**

Redburn House Lochmaddy ⓣ 01876 500301, ⓦ redburnhouse.com. Nicely renovated Victorian house, with four en-suite rooms, plus a stunning studio and a boat house available for anyone staying more than one night. **£70**

Tigh Dearg Lochmaddy ⓣ 01876 500700, ⓦ tighdearghotel.co.uk. Cherry-red, purpose-built hotel whose stylish modern rooms are pretty much unique on the Uists; guests get free use of the gym, sauna and steam room, and the bar and restaurant (open to non-guests) serve delicious food. Free wi-fi. **£170**

Benbecula (Beinn na Faoghla)

Blink and you could miss the pancake-flat island of **Benbecula** (stress on the second syllable), sandwiched between Protestant North Uist and Catholic South Uist. Most visitors simply trundle along the main road that cuts across the middle of the island in less than five miles – not such a bad idea, since the island is scarred from the postwar presence of the Royal Artillery who until recently made up half the local population.

The legacy of Benbecula's military past is only too evident in barracks-like **BALIVANICH** (Baile a Mhanaich), the grim, grey island capital. The only reason to come here at all is if you happen to be flying into or out of **Benbecula airport**, need an ATM, the laundrette (behind the bank) or a supermarket.

ARRIVAL AND DEPARTURE — BENBECULA

By plane Benbecula has flight connections with Barra (Mon–Fri 1 daily; 20min); Glasgow (Mon–Fri 2 daily, Sat & Sun 1 daily; 55min) and Stornoway (Mon–Fri 2 daily; 30min).

By bus Buses run from Balivanich to Berneray (Mon–Sat 5–7 daily; 1hr 15min); Eriskay (Mon–Sat 5–7 daily; 1hr 30min); Lochboisdale (Mon–Sat 7–9 daily; 1hr) and Lochmaddy (Mon–Sat 6 daily; 45min–2hr).

South Uist (Uibhist a Deas)

South Uist (Ⓦsouthuist.com) is arguably the most appealing of the southern chain of islands. The west coast is blessed with some of the region's finest machair and **beaches** – a necklace of gold and grey sand strung twenty miles from one end to the other – while the east coast features a ridge of high mountains rising to 2034ft at the summit of Beinn Mhor. However, the chief settlement and ferry port, **LOCHBOISDALE**, occupying a narrow, bumpy promontory on the southeast coast, is only worth visiting to catch the ferry.

Tobha Mòr

One of the best places to gain access to the sandy shoreline is at **TOBHA MÒR** (Howmore), a pretty little crofting settlement with a fair number of restored houses, many still thatched, including one distinctively roofed in brown heather. Close by are the shattered, lichen-encrusted remains of no fewer than four medieval churches and chapels, and a burial ground now harbouring just a few scattered graves. From the village church, it's an easy walk across the flower-infested machair to the gorgeous **beach**.

Kildonan Museum (Taigh-tasgaidh Chill Donnain)

Five miles south of Tobha Mòr • April–Oct Mon–Sat 10am–5pm, Sun 2–5pm • £2 • Ⓦkildonanmuseum.co.uk

The **Kildonan Museum** includes mock-ups of Hebridean kitchens through the ages, two lovely box beds and an impressive selection of old photos. Pride of place goes to the sixteenth-century **Clanranald Stone**, carved with the arms of the clan who ruled over South Uist from 1370 to 1839, which used to lie in the church at Tobha Mòr. The museum also has a café.

ARRIVAL AND INFORMATION — SOUTH UIST

By ferry CalMac ferries run to Lochboisdale from Castlebay (Mon, Wed, Fri & Sun; 1hr 40min) and Oban (Tues, Thurs, Sat & Sun; 5hr 20min–6hr 30min).

By bus There are buses between Lochboisdale and Eriskay (Mon–Sat 6–7 daily; 35min).

Tourist office Pier Rd, Lochboisdeale (April–Oct Mon–Sat 9am–5pm; open to meet the ferry; Ⓣ01878 700286).

ACCOMMODATION AND EATING

GHHT hostel Tobha Mòr (Howmore) Ⓦgatliff.org.uk. This hostel occupies a house near the village church, and is a short distance from the machair and the beach. £10

Polochar Inn Polochar Ⓣ01878 700215, Ⓦpolocharinn.com. Somewhere you could happily hole up, right on the south coast overlooking the Sound of Barra, and with its own sandy beach close by; all rooms have sea views and free wi-fi. The pub has a real fire and decent bar meals, with live music on Saturday nights. £70

Uist Bunkhouse Dalabrog (Daliburgh), three miles west of Lochboisdale Ⓣ01878 700566, Ⓦuistbunkhouse.co.uk. Clean, modern hostel offering singles, doubles and family rooms as well as bunks. Dorm £17, double £34

WHISKY GALORE!

In addition to jerseys, ponies and Bonnie Prince Charlie, Eriskay's other claim to fame came in 1941 when the 8000-ton **SS Politician** or *Polly* as it's fondly known, sank on its way from Liverpool to Jamaica, along with its cargo of bicycle parts, £3 million in Jamaican currency and 264,000 bottles of whisky, inspiring Compton MacKenzie's book – and the Ealing comedy (filmed here in 1948) – **Whisky Galore!** (released in the US as *Tight Little Island*). The real story was somewhat less romantic, especially for the nineteen islanders imprisoned in Inverness for helping themselves to the whisky. The ship's stern can still be seen to the northwest of Calvey Island at low tide, and one of the original bottles (and lots of other related memorabilia) is on show in the island's modern pub, *Am Politician*, on the west coast.

Eriskay (Eiriosgaigh)

Famous for its patterned jerseys and a diminutive breed of pony, the barren, hilly island of **Eriskay** is connected to the south of South Uist by a causeway. The island, which measures just over two miles by one, and shelters a population of about 150, makes a great day-trip from South Uist; look out for the ponies, who roam free on the hills but tend to graze around Loch Crakavaig, the island's freshwater source. The island's main beach on the west coast, Coilleag a Phrionnsa (Prince's Cockle Strand), was where **Bonnie Prince Charlie** landed on Scottish soil on July 23, 1745 – the sea bindweed that grows there to this day is said to have sprung from the seeds Charles brought with him from France.

ARRIVAL AND DEPARTURE — ERISKAY

CalMac runs a car **ferry** between Barra and the southwest coast of Eriskay (4–5 daily; 40min).

Barra (Barraigh)

Four miles wide and eight miles long, **Barra** (@isleofbarra.com) is like the Western Isles in miniature. It has sandy beaches backed by machair, glacial mountains, prehistoric ruins, Gaelic culture, and a welcoming Catholic population of around 1300.

Castlebay

The only settlement of any size is **CASTLEBAY** (Bàgh a Chaisteil), which curves around the barren rocky hills of a wide bay on the south side of the island. Barra's religious allegiance is immediately announced by the large Catholic church, Our Lady, Star of the Sea, which overlooks the bay; to underline the point, there's a Madonna and Child on the slopes of **Sheabhal** (1260ft), the largest peak on Barra, and a fairly straightforward hike from the bay.

Kisimul Castle

April–Sept daily 9.30am–5.30pm • HS • £5 • ❶ 01871 810313

As its name suggests, Castlebay has a castle in its bay, the medieval islet-fortress of Caisteal Chiosmuil or **Kisimul Castle**, ancestral home of the MacNeil clan. The castle burned down in the eighteenth century, but in 1937 the 45th MacNeil chief bought the island back and set about restoring Kisimul. There's nothing much to see inside, but the whole experience is fun – head down to the slipway at the bottom of Main Street, where the ferryman will take you over (weather permitting).

Cockle Strand

Oddly enough, one of Barra's most interesting sights is its **airport**, on the north side of the island, where planes land and take off from the crunchy shell sands of Tràigh Mhór, better known as **Cockle Strand**; the exact timing of the flights depends on the tides, since at high tide the beach (and therefore the runway) is covered in water.

ARRIVAL AND INFORMATION

BARRA

By plane Barra has flights to Benbecula (Mon–Fri 1 daily; 20min) and Glasgow (Mon–Sat 2–3 daily; 1hr 10min).

By ferry There are two ferry terminals on Barra: from Eriskay (5 daily; 40min), you arrive in the northeast of the island; from Oban (1 daily; 4hr 50min), Lochboisdale (Mon & Tues; 1hr 30min) and Tiree (Thurs; 3hr), you arrive in Castlebay.

By bus Buses run between Castlebay, the airport, and the Eriskay ferry dock (Mon–Sat 4–6 daily; 35–45min).

Tourist office Main St, Castlebay just round from the pier (April–Oct Mon–Sat 9am–5pm; also open to greet the Oban ferry; T 01871 810336).

ACCOMMODATION AND EATING

CASTLEBAY

Café Kisimul Main St T 01871 810645, W cafekisimul.co.uk. A lovely little café by the harbour, serving all-day breakfasts, cheap-and-cheerful Scottish fry-ups and Indian and Italian comfort food. Daily till late.

Castlebay Hotel T 01871 810223, W castlebay-hotel.co.uk. The more welcoming of the town's two hotels, this place has been going since 1880. All rooms are en suite, have free wi-fi, and either have views of the hills or (for slightly more) the sea. The cosy bar regularly has cockles, crabs and scallops on its menu, and good views out over the bay. **£100**

Dunard Hostel T 01871 810443, W dunardhostel.co.uk. Relaxed, family-run place just west of the ferry terminal, with hot showers, a large kitchen and a living room with an open fire. They also offer sea kayaking. Dorm **£16**, double **£38**

Heritage Café Dualchas, west of Castlebay W barraheritage.com. The café of this interesting heritage centre is a useful stop-off for a light lunch, with soups, paninis, and home-made cakes. April–Oct Mon–Sat 10.30am–4.30pm.

Tigh-na-Mara T 01871 810304, W tighnamara-barra.co.uk. Long-established B&B in a Victorian "spotty house" a couple of minutes' walk from the pier, overlooking the sea, with three small, clean and bright en-suite rooms. Closed Nov–March. **£60**

BAGH A TUATH (NORTHBAY)

Heathbank Hotel T 01871 890266, W barrahotel.co.uk. This former church is both a comfortable hotel and a popular local watering hole, serving filling three-course meals for under £20 a head. **£88**

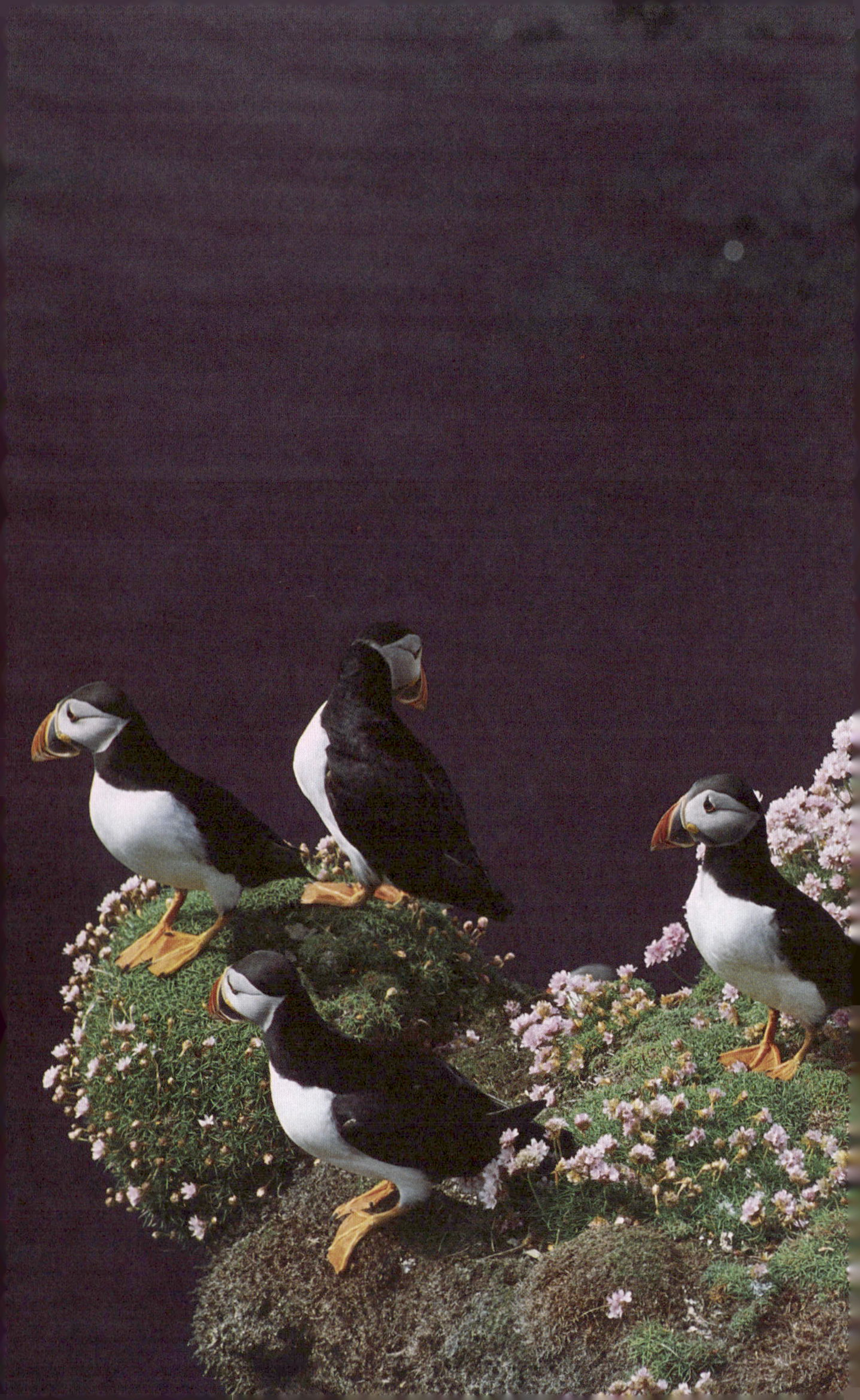

Orkney and Shetland

938 Orkney

950 Shetland

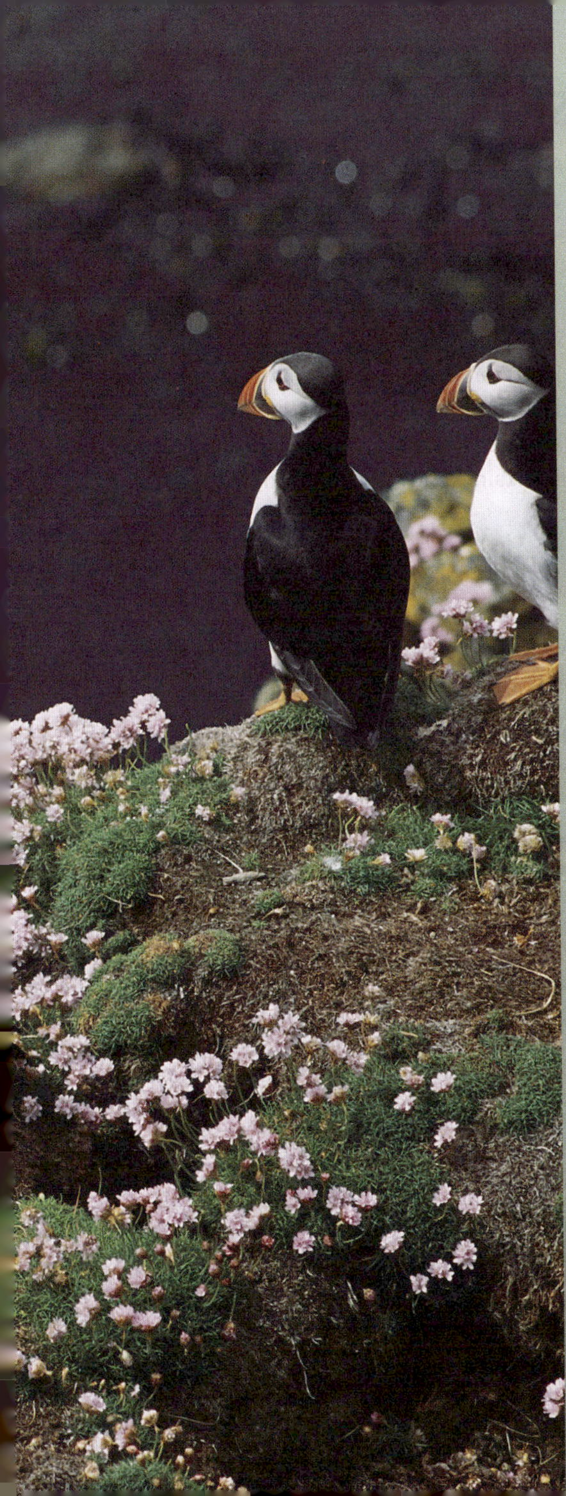

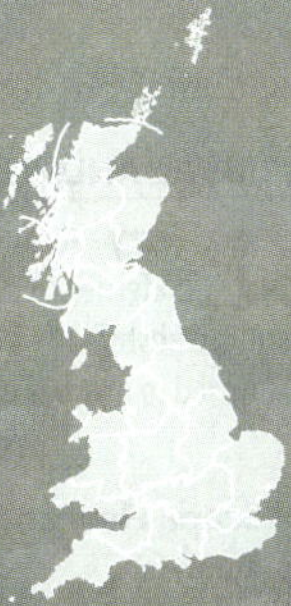

PUFFINS AT SUMBURGH HEAD

25

Orkney and Shetland

Reaching up towards the Arctic Circle, and totally exposed to turbulent Atlantic weather systems, the Orkney and Shetland islands gather into two distinct and very different clusters. The Orkney archipelago lies just a short step north of the Scottish mainland. With the exception of Hoy, which is high and rugged, these islands are mostly low-lying, gently sloping and richly fertile. Sixty miles further north, Shetland is a complete contrast. Ice-sculpted sea inlets cut deep into the land that rises straight out of the water to rugged, heather-coated hills. With little fertile ground, Shetlanders have traditionally been crofters rather than farmers, often looking to the sea for an uncertain living in fishing and whaling or the naval and merchant services.

Orkney, in particular, boasts a well-preserved treasury of Stone Age settlements, such as **Skara Brae**, standing stones and chambered cairns. The Norse heritage is equally apparent in Shetland, where there are many well-preserved prehistoric sites, such as **Mousa Broch** and **Jarlshof**. It's impossible to underestimate the influence of the **weather** up here. More often than not, it will be windy and rainy, though you can have all four seasons in one day. The wind-chill factor is not to be taken lightly, and there's frequently a dampness or drizzle in the air, even when it's not raining.

Orkney

A short way from John O'Groats, **Orkney** is a unique and fiercely independent archipelago. For an Orcadian, the **Mainland** means the largest island in Orkney rather than the rest of Scotland, and their history is inextricably linked with Scandinavia. Orkney Mainland has two chief settlements: the old port of **Stromness**, an attractive old fishing town on the far southwestern shore, and the central capital of **Kirkwall**.

Mainland is relatively heavily populated and farmed throughout, and is joined by causeways to a string of southern islands, the largest of which is **South Ronaldsay**. **Hoy**, the second largest island in the archipelago, south of Mainland, presents a superbly dramatic landscape, with some of the highest sea cliffs in the country. Hoy, however, is atypical: Orkney's smaller, much quieter **northern islands** are low-lying, elemental but fertile outcrops of rock and sand, scattered across the ocean.

ARRIVAL AND DEPARTURE — ORKNEY

By car ferry Northlink Ferries (T 0845 600 0449, W northlinkferries.co.uk) have services to Stromness from Scrabster (2–3 daily; 1hr 30min), which is connected to nearby Thurso by shuttle bus, and ferries to Kirkwall from Aberdeen (4 weekly; 6hr) and from Lerwick in Shetland (3 weekly; 5hr 30min). Pentland Ferries (T 01856 831226, W pentlandferries.co.uk) runs catamarans from Gills Bay, near John O'Groats (linked by

Scapa Flow and the Churchill Barriers p.946

Noss p.953

Mousa Broch p.954

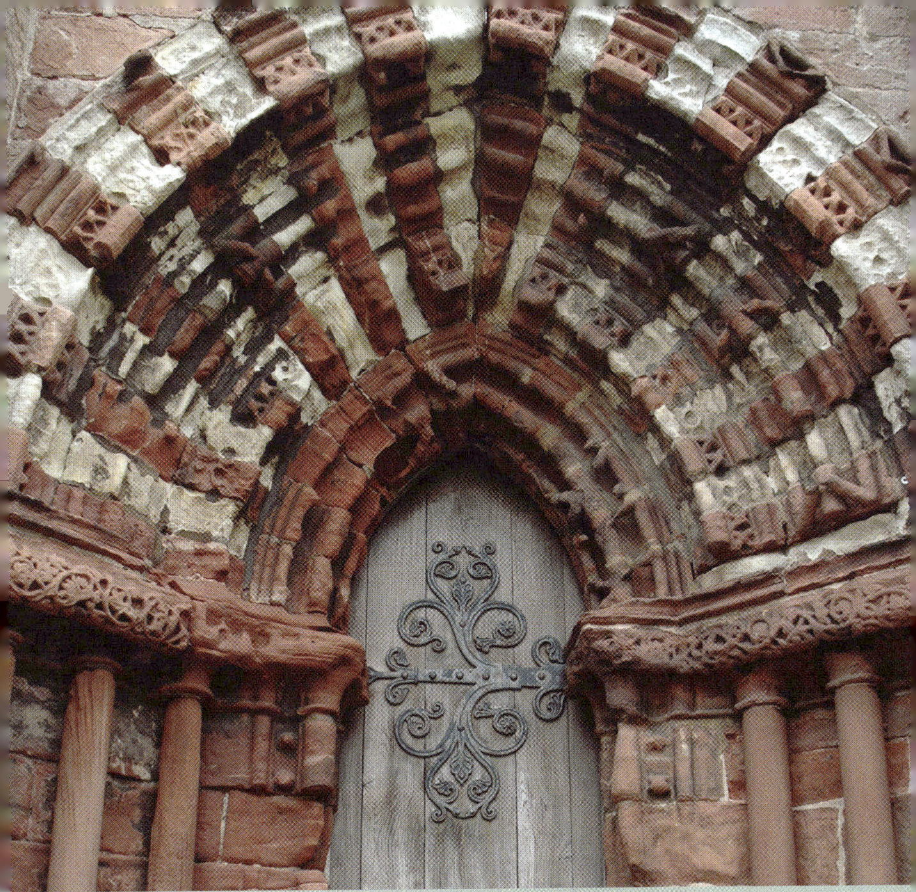

ST MAGNUS CATHEDRAL

Highlights

❶ **Maes Howe, Orkney** Orkney's, and Europe's, finest Neolithic chambered tomb. **See p.942**

❷ **Skara Brae, Orkney** Neolithic village giving a fascinating insight into prehistoric life. **See p.942**

❸ **St Magnus Cathedral, Kirkwall, Orkney** Beautiful red-stone cathedral built by the Vikings. **See p.943**

❹ **Rackwick, Orkney** Experience splendid isolation, rumbling rocky beach and the famous Old Man of Hoy. **See p.945**

❺ **Scapa Flow Visitor Centre & Museum, Lyness, Orkney** Learn about the wartime history of Orkney's great natural harbour and the scuttling of the German Fleet. **See p.946**

❻ **Westray, Orkney** Thriving Orkney island with seabird colonies, sandy beaches and a ruined castle. **See p.947**

❼ **Isle of Noss, Shetland** Guaranteed seals, puffins and dive-bombing "bonxies". **See p.953**

❽ **Mousa, Shetland** Remote Shetland islet with a 2000-year-old broch and nesting storm petrels. **See p.954**

❾ **Jarlshof, Shetland** Site mingling Iron Age, Bronze Age, Pictish, Viking and medieval settlements. **See p.955**

HIGHLIGHTS ARE MARKED ON THE MAPS ON P.940 AND P.951

25 bus to Wick and Thurso) to St Margaret's Hope on South Ronaldsay (3 daily; 1hr).

By passenger ferry John O'Groats Ferries (T 01955 611353, W jogferry.co.uk) runs a passenger ferry from John O'Groats to Burwick on South Ronaldsay (May & Sept 2 daily; June–Aug 4 daily; 40min); departures are timed to connect with the arrival of the Orkney Bus from Inverness, and there's also a free shuttle service from Thurso train station for certain sailings. The ferry is small and, except in fine weather, is really only recommended for travellers with strong stomachs.

By plane Flybe (W flybe.com) offers direct flights to Kirkwall airport from Sumburgh in Shetland, Inverness, Aberdeen, Edinburgh and Glasgow.

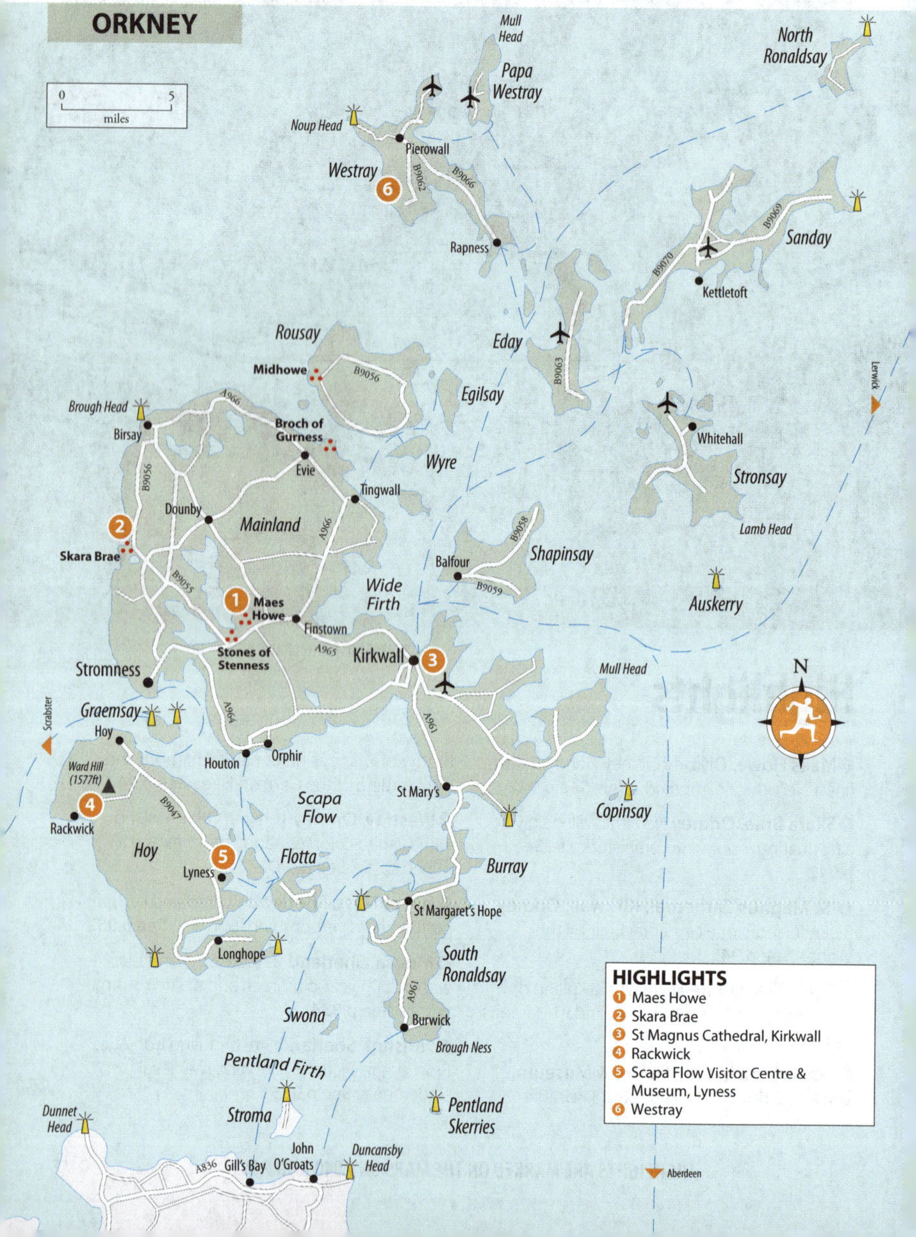

GETTING AROUND

INTER-ISLAND TRANSPORT

Getting to the other islands from the Orkney Mainland isn't difficult, though it's expensive. Travel between individual islands by sea or air is less straightforward, but careful planning may reduce the need to travel via Kirkwall on the Mainland.

By ferry Orkney Ferries (T 01856 872044, W orkneyferries.co.uk) operates all the ferries; it's essential to book well in advance. It's worth asking about their additional Sunday sailings in summer, which often make useful inter-island connections.

By plane Flights from Kirkwall to most of the outer isles are operated by Loganair (T 01856 872494, W loganair.co.uk), using an eight-seater plane, with discounted fares to North Ronaldsay and Papa Westray and between the islands if you stay over.

GETTING AROUND THE ISLANDS

By bus Bus services (W stagecoachbus.com) on Mainland are infrequent, and skeletal on Sundays – a free timetable is available from the tourist office. On the smaller islands, a minibus usually meets the ferry and will take you to your destination.

By bike Cycling is not a bad option if the weather holds, since there are few steep hills and the distances you'll be covering are modest, though the wind can make it hard going.

Stromness

STROMNESS has to be one of the most enchanting ports at which to arrive by boat, its picturesque waterfront a procession of tiny sandstone jetties and slate roofs. An important harbour town since the eighteenth century, it is well worth a day's exploration, and in many ways is a better base than Kirkwall, especially during the popular four-day **Orkney Folk Festival** (W orkneyfolkfestival.com) in May.

Pier Arts Centre

Victoria St • Mon–Sat 10.30am–5pm • Free • T 01856 850209, W pierartscentre.com

The warehouse on the first of the old jetties on the main street now forms half of the **Pier Arts Centre**; the other half is a modern glass-and-steel structure which offers views of the harbour framed like pictures. The galley features a remarkable collection of twentieth-century British art, including work by Eduardo Paolozzi as well as by members of the Cornish school such as Barbara Hepworth, Ben Nicholson, and the self-taught Alfred Wallis. In addition, there are contemporary works, many by northern and Scandinavian artists, which continue the marine themes of the original collection.

Stromness Museum

52 Alfred St • May–Sept daily 10am–5pm; Oct–April Mon–Sat 11am–3.30pm • £3.50 • T 01856 850025

The intriguing **Stromness Museum**, built in 1858, has a wonderfully old-fashioned natural-history collection – don't miss the pull-out drawers of birds' eggs, butterflies and moths – and an early inflatable like the one used by John Rae, the Stromness-born Arctic explorer, whose fiddle, octant and shotgun are also on display. Look out, too, for the barnacle-encrusted crockery from the German High Seas Fleet that was sunk in Scapa Flow in 1919.

ARRIVAL AND INFORMATION — STROMNESS

By bus Stromness is connected by bus to Kirkwall (Mon–Sat hourly, 6 on Sun; 30min), Skara Brae (Mon–Fri & Sun 3–4 daily; 20min) and Tingwall (Wed & Fri 2 daily; 1hr).

By ferry Car ferries travel to Stromness from Scrabster on the Scottish mainland (2–3 daily; 1hr 30min).

Tourist office In the ferry terminal (March–Oct daily 9am–5pm; T 01856 850716, W visitorkney.com).

ACCOMMODATION AND EATING

45 John Street 45 John St T 01856 850949, W 45johnstreet.co.uk. Cheery, family-run B&B in a former harbourmaster's house (later a pub) near the ferry terminal on the edge of the old town. Breakfasts are excellent and they can make packed lunches. £60

Hamnavoe 35 Graham Place T 01856 850606. The town's most ambitious cooking, concentrating on local produce such as grilled sole or peppered monkfish – mains start at around £15. Booking essential. April–Sept Tues–Sun 7–10pm; Nov–March Sat & Sun 7–10pm.

25

Hamnavoe Hostel 10a North End Rd 01856 851202, hamnavoehostel.co.uk. No beauty from the outside, this hostel is spotless and well-equipped. Rooms have coin-operated heaters, and the kitchen has great views over the harbour. Free wi-fi. Dorm £17, single £20

Julia's Café and Bistro Ferry Rd 01856 850904. Bustling bistro opposite the ferry terminal with a sunny conservatory, offering imaginative meals and delicious cakes for under £10. Daily 9am–5pm; June–Aug also open in the evenings Wed–Sun.

Point of Ness Campsite A mile south of the ferry terminal 01856 873535. The local campsite enjoys a superb (though extremely exposed) setting, with views over to Hoy. Laundry and lounge area. Closed Oct–March. £10 per pitch

West Mainland

The great bulk of the **West Mainland** is fertile, productive farmland, fenced off into a patchwork of fields. It's fringed by some spectacular coastline, particularly in the west, and littered with some of the island's most impressive prehistoric sites, such as the village of **Skara Brae**, the **Stones of Stenness** and the chambered tomb of **Maes Howe**.

Stenness

The twin lochs of Stenness and Harray lie at the heart of Orkney's most important Neolithic ceremonial complex. The most visible part is the **Stones of Stenness**, originally a circle of twelve rock slabs, now just four, the tallest of which is more than 16ft high and remarkable for its incredible thinness. A broken table-top lies within the circle, surrounded by a much-diminished henge (a circular bank of earth and a ditch) with a couple of entrance causeways. Less than a mile to the northwest, you reach the **Ring of Brodgar**, a much wider circle dramatically sited on raised ground. Here there were originally sixty stones, 27 of which now stand; of the henge, only the ditch survives.

Maes Howe

Daily: April–Sept 9.30am–5pm; Oct–March 9.30am–4.30pm; guided tours every 45min; timed tickets in summer • HS • £5.50 • 01856 761606

Less than a mile northeast of the Stones of Stenness is **Maes Howe**, the most impressive Neolithic burial chamber complex in Europe. Dating from around 3000 BC, its excellent state of preservation is partly due to the massive slabs of sandstone it was constructed from, the largest of which weighs more than thirty tons. Perhaps its most extraordinary aspect is that the tomb is aligned so that the rays of the winter solstice sun reach right down the passage to the ledge of one of the three cells built into the walls of the tomb. The Vikings entered in the twelfth century, leaving large amounts of runic graffiti, cut into the walls of the main chamber and still clearly visible today.

Skara Brae

Daily: April–Sept 9.30am–5.30pm; Oct–March 9.30am–4.30pm • HS • £5.90–6.90 • 01856 841815

North of Stromness is the best known of Orkney's prehistoric monuments, **Skara Brae**, beautifully situated beside the white curve of the Bay of Skaill. Here, the extensive remains of a small Neolithic fishing and farming village, dating back to 3000 BC, were discovered in 1850 after a fierce storm. The village is amazingly well preserved, its houses huddled together and connected by narrow passages which would originally have been covered over with turf. The houses themselves consist of a single, spacious living room, filled with domestic detail, including fireplaces, cupboards, beds and boxes, all ingeniously constructed from slabs of stone. Unfortunately, visitor numbers mean that you can only look down from the outer walls. However, before you reach the site you can view a full-scale replica of the best-preserved house; it's all a tad neat and tidy, but it'll give you the general idea.

Birsay

The parish of **BIRSAY**, in the northwest corner of Mainland, was the centre of Norse power in Orkney for several centuries before the earls moved to Kirkwall. Today a tiny cluster of homes is gathered around the sandstone ruins of the **Earl's Palace**, built in the sixteenth century by Robert Stewart, Earl of Orkney, using the forced labour of the islanders. The palace appears to have lasted barely a century before falling into rack and ruin, though the crumbling walls and turrets retain much of their grandeur.

Brough of Birsay

Mid-June to Sept daily 9.30am–5.30pm • £4

Just over half a mile northwest of the palace is the **Brough of Birsay**, a substantial Pictish settlement on a small tidal island only accessible during the two hours each side of low tide. The focus of the village was – and still is – the sandstone-built twelfth-century **St Peter's Church**. Close by is a large complex of Viking-era buildings, including several houses, a sauna and some sophisticated stone drains.

Broch of Gurness

Evie • April–Oct daily 9.30am–5.30pm • HS • £5 • T 01856 751414

The **Broch of Gurness** is the best-preserved broch on an archipelago replete with them, and still surrounded by a remarkable complex of later buildings. As at Birsay, the sea has eaten away half the site, but the broch itself, dating from 100 BC, still stands, its walls up to 12ft in places, its inner cells still intact. The compact group of homes huddled around the broch have also survived amazingly well, with much of their original and ingenious stone shelving and fireplaces still in place.

ACCOMMODATION **WEST MAINLAND**

★ **Mill of Eyrland** Stenness, off the A964 to Orphir T 01856 850136, W millofeyrland.com. The best B&B in the West Mainland is a lovingly converted water mill, set in a delightful spot by a trout-filled stream. Rooms are beautifully furnished – one has a four-poster bed – and the guest lounge is set around the old mill equipment. Free wi-fi. £80

Woodwick House Evie T 01856 751330, W woodwickhouse.co.uk. Old house in a beautiful, secluded position southeast of Evie, providing excellent breakfasts; some rooms have shared, slightly ancient bathrooms, but the lounge has a real fire and the wooded grounds are delightful. £70

Kirkwall

KIRKWALL, Orkney's capital, has one great redeeming feature – its sandstone **cathedral**, without doubt the finest medieval building in the north of Scotland. Nowadays, the town is divided into two main focal points: the old **harbour**, at the north end of the town, where inter-island ferries come and go all year round, and the flagstoned **main street**, which changes its name four times as it twists its way south from the harbour past the cathedral. Kirkwall's chief cultural bash is the week-long **St Magnus Festival** (W stmagnusfestival.com), a superb arts festival held in the middle of June.

St Magnus Cathedral

April–Sept Mon–Sat 9am–6pm, Sun 2–5pm; Oct–March daily 9am–1pm & 2–5pm • Free • W stmagnus.org

Standing at the very heart of Kirkwall, **St Magnus Cathedral** is the town's most compelling sight. This beautiful red sandstone building was begun in 1137 by the Viking Earl Rognvald, who built the cathedral in honour of his uncle Magnus, killed on the orders of his cousin Håkon in 1117. Today much of the detail in the soft sandstone has worn away – the capitals around the main doors are reduced to gnarled stumps – but it's still immensely impressive, its shape and style echoing the great cathedrals of Europe. Inside, the atmosphere is surprisingly intimate, the bulky sandstone columns drawing your eye up to the exposed brickwork arches, while around

25 the walls is a series of mostly seventeenth-century tombstones, many carved with a skull and crossbones and other emblems of mortality.

Bishop's and Earl's Palaces

Watergate • April–Oct daily 9.30am–5.30pm • HS • £4.50 • ⓣ 01856 871918

To the south of the cathedral are the ruined remains of the **Bishop's Palace**, residence of the Bishop of Orkney since the twelfth century. Most of what you see now, however, dates from the time of Bishop Robert Reid, sixteenth-century founder of Edinburgh University. A narrow spiral staircase takes you to the top for a good view over the cathedral and Kirkwall's rooftops.

The **Earl's Palace**, on the other side of Watergate, was built by the infamous Earl Patrick Stewart around 1600, using forced labour. With its grand entrance, fancy oriel windows, dank dungeons, massive fireplaces and magnificent central hall, it is reckoned to be one of the finest examples of Renaissance architecture in Scotland. The roof may be missing, but many domestic details remain, including a set of toilets and the stone shelves used by the clerk.

Orkney Museum

Broad St • May–Sept Mon–Sat 10.30am–5pm; Oct–April Mon–Sat 10.30am–12.30pm & 1.30–5pm • Free • ⓣ 01856 873191

Opposite the cathedral stands the sixteenth-century Tankerness House, a former home for the clergy, now home to the **Orkney Museum**. Among the more unusual artefacts to look out for are a witch's spell box, and a lovely whalebone plaque from a Viking boat grave discovered on Sanday.

ARRIVAL AND INFORMATION — KIRKWALL

By plane Kirkwall airport is about 3 miles southeast of town on the A960.

By bus The bus station is a few minutes' walk west of the centre on West Castle St.

Destinations Birsay (Mon–Fri 2 daily; 45min); Burwick (5 daily; 40–55min); Evie (Mon–Sat 4–5 daily; 30min); Houton (Mon–Fri 5 daily, 3 on Sat; 20–40min); Kirkwall airport (Mon–Sat every 30min–hourly, 9 on Sun; 15min); Skara Brae (June–Aug Mon–Fri 2 daily; 1hr 15min); St Margaret's Hope (Mon–Sat hourly; 30min); Stromness (Mon–Sat hourly, 6 on Sun; 30min); Tingwall (Mon–Fri 4 daily, 2 on Sat; 30–40min).

By ferry NorthLink ferries from Shetland and Aberdeen (and all cruise ships) dock at the Hatston terminal, a mile or so northwest of town; buses will take you into Kirkwall. Orkney Ferries to Eday, North Ronaldsay, Sanday, Shapinsay, Stronsay and Westray leave from Kirkwall harbour in the centre of town.

Destinations Aberdeen (4 weekly; 6hr); Eday (2–3 daily; 1hr 15min–2hr); Lerwick (3 weekly; 5hr 30min); North Ronaldsay (Fri; 2hr 40min); Sanday (2 daily; 1hr 25min); Shapinsay (4–5 daily; 45min); Stronsay (2 daily; 1hr 40min–2hr); Westray (2–3 daily; 1hr 25min).

Tourist office In the travel centre by the bus station, West Castle St (Mon–Sat 9am–5pm, Sun 10am–4pm; ⓣ 01856 872856, ⓦ visitorkney.com).

ACCOMMODATION

Berstane House Berstane Rd ⓣ 01856 876277, ⓦ berstane.co.uk. The B&B rooms and self-catering flats are a steal at this handsome Victorian pile, set in its own wooded grounds with sea views – it's a mile and a half southeast of town. £50

Peedie Hostel 1 Ayre Houses ⓣ 01856 875477, ⓦ peediehostel.yolasite.com. Overlooking the old harbour and out to sea, this is a clean and comfortable hostel with just eleven beds. Dorm £15, twin £30

Pickaquoy Campsite Ayre Rd ⓣ 01856 879900, ⓦ pickaquoy.net. Central, and well-equipped and maintained, Kirkwall's site is behind (and run by) the local leisure centre, but it's not the prettiest of spots. Closed Nov–March. £11.50 for two people, tent and car

EATING AND DRINKING

Helgi's 14 Harbour St ⓣ 01856 879293. A popular pub on the harbourfront, which serves filling comfort food: from baked tatties to catch of the day and Sunday roast. Food served Mon–Sat noon–2pm & 6–9pm, Sun 12.30–2.30pm & 6–9pm.

★ **Lucano** 31–33 Victoria Rd ⓣ 01856 875687, ⓦ lucanokirkwall.com. Swish modern café bringing a startling slice of Italian sophistication to Kirkwall: all-day frittate, tostate and ciabatte, plus pizza, pasta and Italian standards. Daily 7am–10pm.

The Reel 6 Broad St ⓣ01856 871000, ⓦwrigleyandthereel.com. Near the cathedral, this laidback café is run by Orkney's musical Wrigley Sisters, serves great coffee, sandwiches and cakes, and offers free wi-fi and occasional live music. Mon–Fri 8.30am–6pm, Sat 8.30am–1am, Sun 10am–5pm.

South Ronaldsay

At the southern end of the Churchill Barriers (see p.946) is low-lying **South Ronaldsay**, the largest of the islands linked to the Mainland. Its main settlement is **ST MARGARET'S HOPE** – or "The Hope" – a pleasing little gathering of stone-built houses overlooking a sheltered bay. The Hope was once a thriving port, but nowadays, despite the presence of the **Pentland Ferries terminal**, it remains a peaceful place.

Tomb of the Eagles

Liddle • Daily: March 10am–noon; April–Oct 9.30am–5.30pm; Nov–March by appointment • £6.80 • ⓣ01856 831339, ⓦtomboftheeagles.co.uk

One of the most enjoyable archeological sights on Orkney is the Isbister chambered burial cairn at the southeastern corner of South Ronaldsay, known as the **Tomb of the Eagles**. Discovered, excavated and still owned by local farmer, Ronald Simpson, the tomb makes a refreshing change from the usual interpretative centre. First, you get to look round the family's private museum of prehistoric artefacts; then, you get a brief guided tour of a nearby Bronze Age **burnt mound**, which is basically a Neolithic rubbish dump; and finally you can walk out to the **chambered cairn**, by the cliff's edge, where human remains were found alongside talons and carcasses of sea eagles. To enter the cairn, you must lie on a trolley and pull yourself in using an overhead rope.

ARRIVAL AND DEPARTURE — SOUTH RONALDSAY

Catamarans run from Gills Bay, near John O'Groats, to St Margaret's Hope (3 daily; 1hr), while passenger **ferries** run from John O'Groats to Burwick, 7 miles from St Margaret's Hope (2–4 daily; 40min).

ACCOMMODATION AND EATING

Backpackers Hostel Back Rd, St Margaret's Hope ⓣ01856 831225, ⓦorkneybackpackers.com. This hostel lies off a lovely courtyard behind *Jim Freds* café, with singles, doubles and family rooms. Dorm £13, double £26

The Creel Front Rd, St Margaret's Hope ⓣ01856 831311, ⓦthecreel.co.uk. The luxury option: a harbourfront B&B above one of Orkney's finest restaurants, a cosy little place offering superb three-course dinners for around £30. Food served April–Oct daily 7–9pm. £110

Wheems On the eastern side of South Ronaldsay, a mile and a half from the war memorial on the main road outside The Hope ⓣ01856 831537, ⓦwheemsorganic.co.uk. An organic farm with a field for camping, with great sea views and plenty of wind. Closed Nov–March. £10 for two people, tent and car

Hoy

Hoy, Orkney's second-largest island, rises sharply out of the sea to the southwest of the Mainland. Its dramatic landscape is made up of great glacial valleys and mountainous moorland rising to more than 1500ft, dropping into the sea off the red sandstone cliffs of St John's Head. The passenger ferry from Stromness arrives at **Moaness Pier**, near the tiny village of **Hoy**.

Rackwick

RACKWICK, four miles west of Hoy village, is an old crofting and fishing settlement squeezed between towering sandstone cliffs on the west coast. A small farm building beside the hostel (see p.946) serves as a tiny **museum** (open any time; free), with a few old photos and a brief rundown of Rackwick's rough history. Despite its isolation, Rackwick has a steady stream of walkers and climbers passing through en route to the **Old Man of Hoy**, a great sandstone column some 450ft high, perched on an old lava

25 flow which protects it from the erosive power of the sea. The well-trodden footpath from Rackwick is an easy three-mile walk (3hr return). Halfway along the road between Hoy village and Rackwick, duckboards head across the heather to the **Dwarfie Stane**, Orkney's most unusual chambered tomb, cut from a solid block of sandstone and dating back to 3000 BC.

Scapa Flow Visitor Centre & Museum

Lyness, opposite the ferry terminal • March, April & Oct Mon–Fri 9am–4.30pm; May–Sept Mon–Sat 9am–4.30pm, Sun from first ferry to last • Free • T 01856 791300, W scapaflow.co.uk

Hoy played a major role for the Royal Navy during both world wars and the harbour and hills around Lyness are still scarred with the scattered remains of concrete structures that once served as hangars and storehouses during World War II. The old oil pump house has been turned into the **Scapa Flow Visitor Centre & Museum**, a fascinating insight into wartime Orkney. The pump house itself retains much of its old equipment – you can ask for a working demo of one of the oil-fired boilers – used to pump oil off tankers moored at Lyness into sixteen tanks, and from there into underground reservoirs cut into the neighbouring hillside. Even the café has an old NAAFI feel about it.

ARRIVAL AND DEPARTURE — HOY

A passenger **ferry** runs from Stromness to Moaness pier, by Hoy village (Mon–Fri 4–5 daily, Sat & Sun 2 daily; 25min; T 01856 850624), and a car ferry runs from Houton on the Mainland to Lyness (Mon–Fri 6–8 daily, Sat & Sun 2–4 daily; 35min–1hr; T 01856 811397). There's a seasonal Hoy Hopper **bus** service (mid-May to mid-Sept Wed–Fri only), which departs from Kirkwall Travel Centre and drives onto the ferries.

ACCOMMODATION AND EATING

Beneth'hill Café A short walk from Moaness Pier T 01856 851116. A friendly, simple café serving Cullen Skink, fresh local crab, home-made puddings and proper coffee – they'll even do you a packed lunch and an evening meal on a Friday. May–Sept Mon–Fri 10.30am–4.45pm, Sat & Sun 10am–6pm.

Rackwick Hostel Rackwick T 01856 873535 ext 2415, W hostelsorkney.co.uk. Simple hostel with just eight beds. You can camp behind the hostel, or beside the basic heather-thatched Burnside Bothy (T 01856 791316) by the beach. Be warned, though, North Hoy is probably the worst place on Orkney for midges. Closed Oct–March. Dorm **£13**

Wild Heather Lyness T 01856 791098, W wildheatherbandb.co.uk. B&B in a converted mill, near the naval cemetery, with just two en-suite rooms, both with sea views and a lovely breakfast conservatory – they'll offer dinners, too, if required. **£60**

SCAPA FLOW AND THE CHURCHILL BARRIERS

The presence of a huge naval base in **Scapa Flow** during both world wars presented an irresistible target to the Germans, and protecting the fleet was always a nagging problem for the Allies. During World War I, blockships were sunk to guard the eastern approaches, but just weeks after the outbreak of World War II, a German U-boat managed to manoeuvre past the blockships and torpedo the battleship HMS *Royal Oak*, which sank with the loss of 833 lives.

The sinking of the *Royal Oak* convinced the First Lord of the Admiralty, Winston Churchill, that Scapa Flow needed better protection, and in 1940 work began on a series of barriers – known as the **Churchill Barriers** – to seal the waters between the Mainland and the string of islands to the south. Special camps were built to accommodate the 1700 men involved in the project; their numbers were boosted by the surrender of Italy in 1942, when Italian POWs were sent to work here.

Besides the barriers, the Italians also left behind the beautiful **Italian Chapel** (daily dawn–dusk; free) on the first of the islands, Lamb Holm. This, the so-called "miracle of Camp 60", must be one of the greatest adaptations ever, made from two Nissen huts, concrete, barbed wire and parts of a rusting blockship. It has a great false facade, and colourful trompe l'oeil decor, lovingly restored by the chapel's principal architect, Domenico Chiocchetti.

Rousay

Just over half a mile from the Mainland's northern shore and an easy day-trip, the hilly island of **Rousay** is home to a number of intriguing prehistoric sites. A trio of cairns is spread out across a couple of miles on and off the road that leads west from the ferry terminal, and after four miles, the road passes the most significant and impressive of the island's archeological remains. If you're approaching from the east, **Midhowe Cairn** comes as something of a surprise, both for its immense size – it's known as "the great ship of death" and is nearly 100ft long – and for the fact that it's now entirely surrounded by a stone-walled barn with a corrugated roof. Unfortunately, you can't actually explore the roofless communal burial chamber, dating back to 3500 BC, but only look down from the overhead walkway. A couple of hundred yards beyond is Rousay's finest archeological site, **Midhowe Broch**, whose compact layout suggests that it was originally built as a sort of fortified family house, surrounded by a complex series of ditches and ramparts. The interior is divided into two separate rooms, each with their own hearth, water tank and quernstone, all of which date from the final phase of occupation around the second century AD.

ARRIVAL AND GETTING AROUND — ROUSAY

Rousay is connected by **ferry** with Tingwall on the Mainland (5–6 daily; 30min; ⓣ 01856 751360). A **bus** service runs (on request ⓣ 01856 821360) every Thursday, and, in season, there are minibus tours available on demand (ⓣ 01856 821234, ⓦ rousaytours.co.uk; £16.50; 5–7hr), which connect with ferries.

ACCOMMODATION AND EATING

The Pier Overlooking the ferry terminal ⓣ 01856 821359. The island pub serves Orkney ales and standard bar meals and will prepare fresh crab sandwiches if you phone in advance. Mon, Tues, Thurs & Fri 11am–9pm or later, Wed 11am–6.30pm, Sun noon–6.30pm.

The Taversoe Two miles west of the ferry terminal ⓣ 01856 821325, ⓦ taversoehotel.co.uk. No beauty from the outside, but inside it offers surprisingly pleasant accommodation and does unpretentious, filling bar meals (phone to check that they're serving food). **£70**

Trumland Farm Half a mile west of the terminal ⓣ 01856 821252. If you want to be near the ancient sites, your best bet is this hostel, on a working organic farm. As well as a couple of dorms, you can also camp, and they offer bike rental. Dorm **£10**

Westray

Although exposed to the full force of the Atlantic weather in the far northwest of Orkney, **Westray** shelters one of the most tightly knit and prosperous island communities. The main village and harbour is **PIEROWALL** set around a wide bay in the north. The village's **Westray Heritage Centre** (May–Sept Mon 11.30am–5pm, Tues–Sat 10am–noon & 2–5pm, Sun 1.30–5.30pm; £2.50) is a great place to gen up on (and with any luck catch a glimpse of) the Westray Wife or **Orkney Venus**, a remarkable, miniature Neolithic female figurine found in 2009 in the nearby dunes. Above the village to the west is the sandstone hulk of **Noltland Castle**, begun around 1560 by Gilbert Balfour, Master of the Household to Mary, Queen of Scots, who was implicated in the murder of her husband Lord Darnley. To explore, pick up the key at the nearby farm.

The northwestern tip of Westray rises up sharply, culminating in the dramatic sea cliffs of **Noup Head**. In early summer, the guano-covered rock ledges are packed with more than 100,000 nesting seabirds, primarily guillemots, razorbills, kittiwakes and fulmars, with puffins as well – an awesome sight, sound and smell. For a closer view of puffins, head for **Castle o' Burrian**, a sea stack in the southeast of the island.

ARRIVAL AND GETTING AROUND — WESTRAY

There are **flights** to and from Kirkwall (Mon–Sat 2 daily, 1 on Sun; 12min). **Ferries** from Kirkwall (2–3 daily; 1hr 25min; ⓣ 01856 872044) arrive at Rapness on the island's southernmost tip, 8 miles from Pierowall. A **minibus** meets the ferry

25 and heads for Pierowall (May–Sept; at other times phone 01857 677758); you can book your seat while on the ferry. Minibus **tours** can be arranged with Westraak (01857 677777, westraak.co.uk), who will meet you at the ferry, and also offer bike rental.

ACCOMMODATION AND EATING

★ **The Barn** Pierowall 01857 677214, thebarnwestray.co.uk. This hostel and campsite, in an old farm at the southern edge of Pierowall, is run by friendly hosts; the facilities are luxurious, with family rooms and twins available, a games room and a well-equipped kitchen. Dorm £16, twin £32

No. 1 Broughton Pierowall 01857 677726, no1broughton.co.uk. Good-value B&B in a renovated mid-nineteenth-century house on the south shore of the bay, with a lovely conservatory and a sauna. £60

Pierowall Hotel Pierowall 01857 677472, pierowallhotel.co.uk. An unpretentious and welcoming family-run hotel – the cheaper rooms have shared facilities – whose bar, the social hub of the village, serves excellent fish and chips made with the catch from the local fleet. Food served daily noon–2pm & 5–8.45pm. £65

Papa Westray

Across the short Papa Sound from Westray is the island of **Papa Westray**, known locally as "Papay". With a population hovering around seventy, Papay has had to fight hard to keep itself viable over the last couple of decades, helped by a hefty influx of outsiders. With one of Orkney's best-preserved Neolithic settlements, and a large nesting seabird population, the island is worthy of a stay in its own right or makes an easy day-trip from its neighbour.

A road leads down from Holland House, in the high central point of the island, to the western shore, where the **Knap of Howar** stands. Dating from around 3500 BC, this Neolithic farm building makes a fair claim to being the oldest standing house in Europe. Half a mile north along the coast is **St Boniface Kirk**, a restored pre-Reformation church, with a bare flagstone floor, dry-stone walls, a little wooden gallery and just a couple of surviving box pews.

ARRIVAL AND DEPARTURE — PAPA WESTRAY

By plane Papay is connected to Westray by the world's shortest scheduled flight – just 2min, or less with a following wind. You can also fly direct from Kirkwall (Mon–Sat 2–3 daily, 1 on Sun; 12–19min) for a return fare of £20 if you stay overnight.

By ferry The daily passenger ferry from Pierowall (3–6 daily; 25min) makes Papay an easy day-trip from Westray. The car ferry from Kirkwall to Westray continues on to Papa Westray on Fri (2hr 15min); at other times, a bus (which accepts a limited number of bicycles) from Rapness on Westray, connects with the Pierowall passenger ferry.

GETTING AROUND

Papay's Community Co-operative **minibus** (01857 644321) will take you from the pier to wherever you want; they also do a "Peedie Package" guided tour (£20–25).

ACCOMMODATION

Beltane House 01857 644321, papawestray.co.uk. Papay's Community Co-operative runs a sixteen-bed SYHA-affiliated hostel, and B&B with four en-suite rooms, in the old estate-workers' cottages east of Holland House. Dorm £13, double £70

Eday

A long, thin island at the centre of Orkney's northern isles, **Eday** is dominated by a great block of heather-covered upland, with farmland confined to a narrow strip of coastal ground. The chief points of interest are all in the northern half of the island, beyond the community shop on the main road. First of all, there's a bird hide by the road, looking south over **Mill Loch**, where several pairs of red-throated divers regularly breed. Clearly visible on the other side of the road is the 15ft **Stone of Setter**, Orkney's most distinctive standing stone, weathered into three thick, lichen-encrusted fingers. From here, you can climb the hill to the **Vinquoy Chambered Cairn**, which has a similar structure to that of Maes Howe. You can crawl into the tomb through the narrow entrance: a skylight inside lets light into the main, beehive chamber, now home to some lovely ferns, but not into the four side cells.

ARRIVAL AND DEPARTURE — EDAY

By plane It's possible to do a day-trip flight (Wed) from Kirkwall to Eday (T 01856 872494 or 873457).

By ferry Ferries from Kirkwall (2–3 daily; 1hr 15min–2hr) pull into the terminal at Backaland pier in the south (T 01856 872044).

GETTING AROUND

Car rental and **taxis** can be organized through J&J by the pier (T 01857 622206); they also run **minibus tours** (May–Aug Mon, Wed & Fri; £12).

ACCOMMODATION AND EATING

Eday Youth Hostel T 01857 622283, W syha.org.uk. SYHA-affiliated, community-run barn of a hostel (camping also), in an exposed spot just north of the airport – phone ahead, as there's no resident warden. £12

Roadside Public House T 01857 622303, E anne.cant@hotmail.co.uk. The island's evening-only pub overlooks the ferry terminal and offers B&B in two en-suite rooms – if you want to eat, you'll need to give them advance warning. £60

Stronsay

A wonderful combination of green pastures, white sands and clear turquoise bays, **Stronsay** was a centre for the curing of herring from the 1840s to the 1930s. **WHITEHALL** is the island's only real village, made up of rows of stone-built fishermen's cottages set between two large piers. Wandering along the tranquil, rather forlorn harbourfront today, it's hard to believe that the village once supported 5000 people in the fishing industry during the summer season, as well as a small army of coopers, coal merchants, butchers, bakers, several Italian ice-cream parlours and a cinema. The old fish market by the pier displays a few photos and artefacts from the herring days; ask at the adjacent café. **Papa Stronsay**, the tiny island that shelters Whitehall from the north, is home to a new multimillion-pound **Golgotha Monastery** belonging to the The Sons of the Most Holy Redeemer – they're happy to take visitors across to (and around) the island by boat, by prior arrangement (T 01857 616389).

ARRIVAL AND GETTING AROUND — STRONSAY

The airport, 2 miles west of Whitehall, sees regular **flights** from Kirkwall (Mon–Sat 2 daily; 25min); **ferries** from Kirkwall pull in to Whitehall harbour (2 daily; 1hr 40min–2hr). There's no bus service, but D.S. Peace (T 01857 616335) operates **taxis** and rents cars.

ACCOMMODATION AND EATING

Stronsay Fish Mart Hostel Whitehall T 01857 616263. Hostel in the old fish market by the pier, with a well-equipped kitchen, washing machine and three comfortable bunk-bedded rooms. £10

Stronsay Hotel Whitehall T 01857 616213, W stronsayhotelorkney.co.uk. Nicely refurbished old hotel, which once boasted the longest bar in the north of Scotland. It's also the island's only restaurant, which serves good pub food – try the seafood taster. £70

Sanday

Sanday, though the largest of the northern isles, is also the most insubstantial, a great low-lying, drifting dune strung out between several rocky points. The island's sweeping aquamarine bays and vast stretches of clean white sand are the finest in Orkney, and in

25 dry, clear weather it's a superb place to spend a day or two. The entire coastline presents the opportunity for superb walks, with particularly spectacular sand dunes to the south of Cata Sand. The most impressive archeological sight is **Quoyness Chambered Cairn**, on the fertile farmland of Els Ness peninsula, dating from before 2000 BC, and partially reconstructed to a height of around 13ft.

ARRIVAL AND DEPARTURE — SANDAY

The airfield is in the centre of the island, with regular **flights** to Kirkwall (Mon–Sat 2 daily; 10min). **Ferries** from Kirkwall (2 daily; 1hr 25min) arrive at Loth Pier at the southern tip of the island and are met by a minibus (book on ⓣ01857 600284).

ACCOMMODATION AND EATING

The hotels in the fishing port of **Kettletoft** both serve pub food.

Ayre's Rock ⓣ01857 600410, ⓦayres-rock-sanday-orkney.co.uk. Well-equipped hostel and campsite overlooking the bay, with washing and laundry facilities, a chip shop (Tues & Sat) and bike rental. £13.50

Marygarth Manse ⓣ01857 600467, ⓦbedandbreakfast-orkney.co.uk. A nicely modernized nineteenth-century former manse near the Bay of Brough. £50

North Ronaldsay

North Ronaldsay is Orkney's most northerly island. Measuring just three miles by one and rising only 66ft above sea level, the island is almost overwhelmed by the enormity of the sky, the strength of wind and the ferocity of the sea. The island's **sheep** are a unique, tough, goat-like breed, who feed mostly on seaweed, giving their flesh a dark tone and a rich, gamey taste, and making their thick wool highly prized. A high **dry-stone dyke**, completed in the mid-nineteenth century and running the thirteen miles around the edge of the island, keeps the sheep off the farmland, except during lambing season. The most frequent visitors to the island are ornithologists, who come to catch a glimpse of the rare migrants who land here briefly on their spring and autumn migrations. The only features to interrupt the island's flat horizon are two **lighthouses**.

ARRIVAL AND DEPARTURE — NORTH RONALDSAY

By plane If you stay the night on the island, you're eligible for a £20 return fare for a flight from Kirkwall (2–3 daily; 15min).

By ferry There's a weekly ferry from Kirkwall (Fri; 2hr 40min), and day-trips are possible on occasional summer Sundays (ⓣ01856 872044).

ACCOMMODATION AND EATING

Bird Observatory ⓣ01857 633200, ⓦnrbo.co.uk. The eco-friendly NRBO offers accommodation in an en-suite room or a hostel bunk, and you can camp outside; the *Obscafé* serves decent meals. You don't have to be mad (on birds) to stay there, but it helps. Dorm £15, double £70

Burrian Inn Southeast of the war memorial ⓣ01856 633221. The island's small pub does hot food. Irregular opening hours; phone to check.

Shetland

Many maps plonk the **Shetland** islands in a box somewhere off Aberdeen, but in fact they're a lot closer to Bergen in Norway than they are to Edinburgh. Shetland endures the most violent weather experienced in the British Isles. There are some good spells of dry, sunny weather from May to September, but it's the "**simmer dim**", the twilight which lingers through the small hours at this latitude, that makes Shetland summers so memorable.

The islands' capital, **Lerwick**, is a busy little port and the only town of any size. Many parts of Shetland can be reached from here on a day-trip. **South Mainland** is a narrow finger of land that runs some 25 miles from Lerwick to **Sumburgh Head**, an area particularly rich in archeological remains, including the Iron Age **Mousa Broch** and the ancient settlement of **Jarlshof**. A further 25 miles south of Sumburgh Head is the remote but thriving **Fair Isle**, synonymous with knitwear and exceptional birdlife. Even more remote are the distinctive peaks and precipitous cliffs of the island of **Foula**,

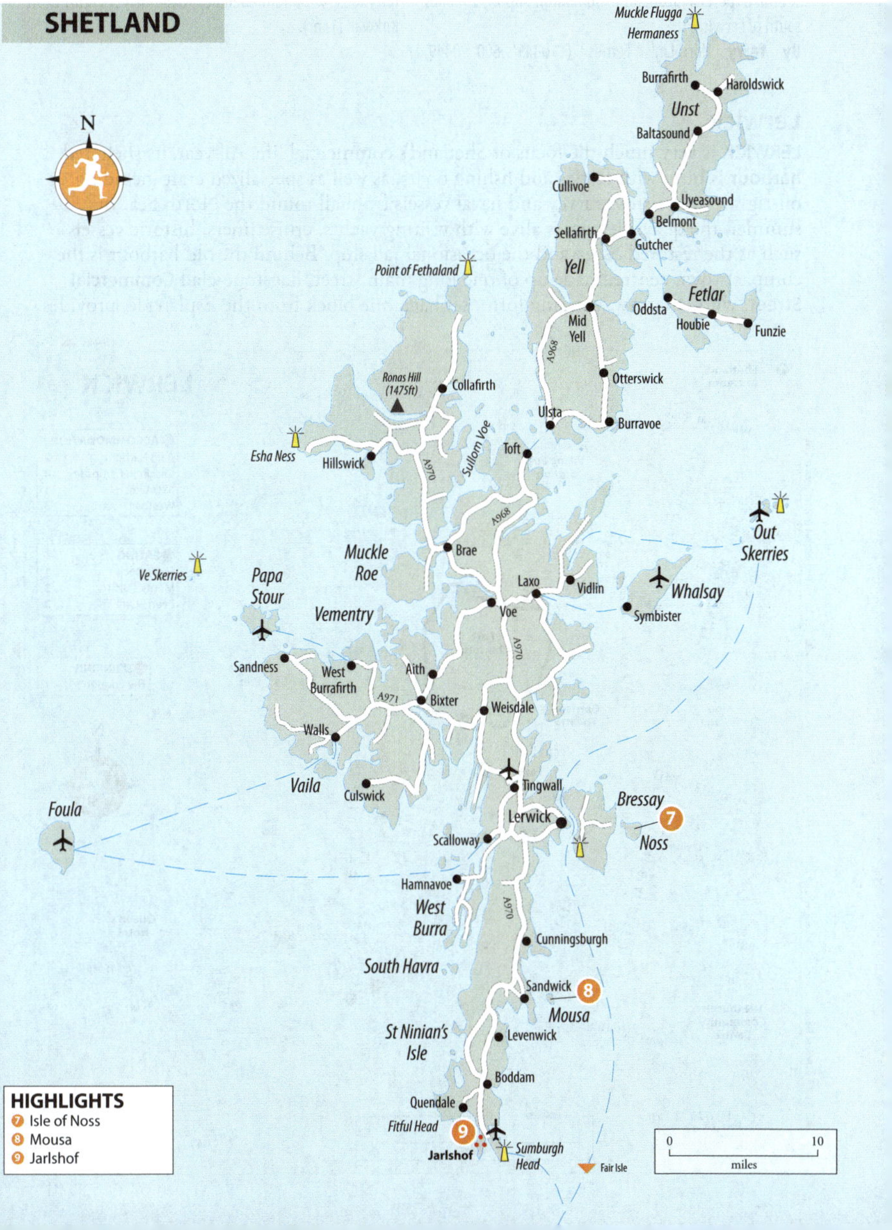

fourteen miles west of Mainland. Shetland's three **North Isles** bring Britain to a dramatic, windswept end: **Yell** has the largest population of otters in the UK; **Fetlar** is home to the rare red-necked phalarope; north of **Unst**, there's nothing until you reach the North Pole.

ARRIVAL AND DEPARTURE — SHETLAND

By plane Flybe (T 0870 850 9850) runs direct flights from several airports in Scotland to Sumburgh airport, 25 miles south of Lerwick.

By ferry NorthLink Ferries (T 0845 600 0449, W northlinkferries.co.uk) operates a daily overnight car ferry to Lerwick from Aberdeen, either direct (12hr) or via Kirkwall (14hr).

Lerwick

LERWICK is very much the focus of Shetland's commercial life. All year, its sheltered **harbour** is busy with ferries and fishing boats, as well as specialized craft including oil-rig supply, seismic survey and naval vessels from all round the North Sea. In summer, the quayside comes alive with visiting yachts, cruise liners, historic vessels such as the restored *Swan* and the occasional tall ship. Behind the old harbour is the compact town centre, made up of one long main street, flagstone-clad **Commercial Street**, whose narrow, winding form, set back one block from the Esplanade, provides

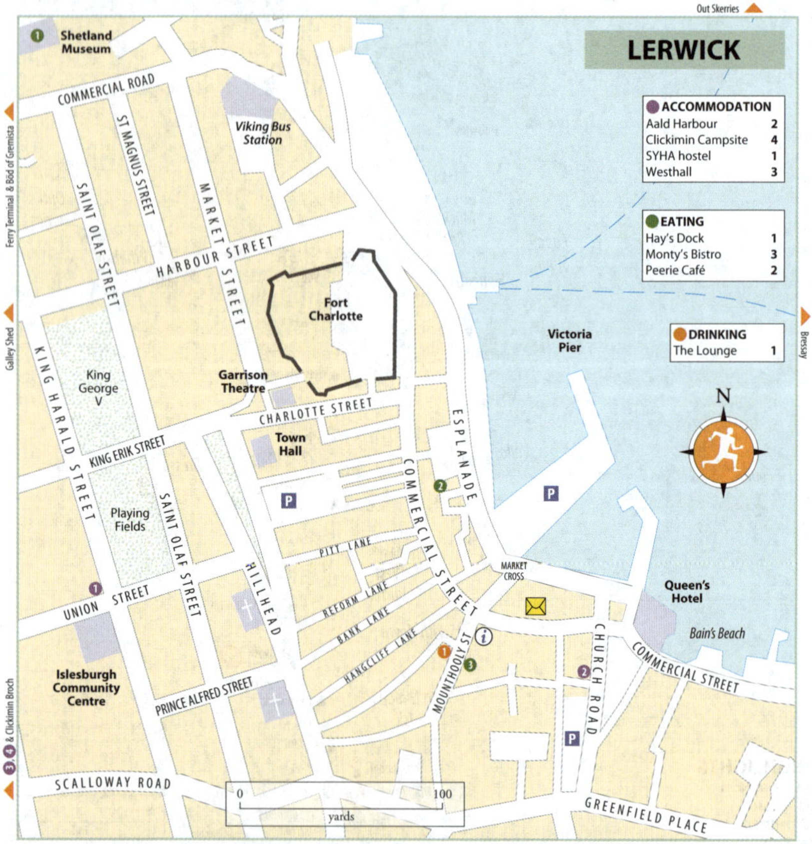

shelter from the elements even on the worst days. From here, narrow lanes, known as **closses**, rise westwards to the late Victorian new town.

The northern end of Commercial Street is marked by the towering walls of **Fort Charlotte** (daily: June–Sept 9am–10pm; Oct–May 9am–4pm; free), begun for Charles II in 1665, burnt down by the Dutch fleet in August 1673, and repaired and named in honour of George III's queen in the 1780s.

Shetland Museum

Hay's Dock, off Commercial Rd • Mon–Wed, Fri & Sat 10am–5pm, Thurs 10am–7pm, Sun noon–5pm • Free • ⓣ 01595 695057, ⓦ shetland-museum.org.uk

Exhibits at the **Shetland Museum**, in a wonderful purpose-built waterfront building, include replicas of a hoard of Pictish silver found locally, the Monks Stone, thought to show the arrival of Christianity in Shetland, and a block of butter, tax payment for the King of Norway, found preserved in a peat bog.

Among the boats artistically suspended in the Boat Hall is a sixareen, used, amazingly enough, as a mailboat to Foula. The Upper Gallery concentrates on the last two centuries of the islands' social history from knitting and whaling to the oil industry.

ARRIVAL AND INFORMATION — LERWICK

By bus Buses stop on the Esplanade, very close to the old harbour, or at the Viking bus station on Commercial Rd, north of the town centre.

Destinations Brae (Mon–Sat 4–6 daily; 45min); Hillswick (Mon–Sat 1 daily; 1hr 40min); Scalloway (Mon–Sat hourly; 15min); Sumburgh (Mon–Sat 6–8 daily, 4 on Sun; 45min); Toft (Mon–Sat 3–5 daily; 50min); Voe (Mon–Sat 5–6 daily; 35min); Walls (Mon–Sat 1–3 daily; 45min).

By ferry The main ferry terminal lies in the north harbour, about a mile from the town centre.

Destinations Aberdeen (daily; 12hr); Kirkwall (Orkney; 3–4 weekly; 6hr).

Tourist office Market Cross, Commercial St (April–Oct Mon–Fri 9am–5pm, Sat & Sun 10am–4pm; Nov–March Mon–Fri 9am–5pm; ⓣ 01595 6693434, ⓦ visitshetland .com).

ACCOMMODATION

Aald Harbour 7 Church Rd ⓣ 01595 690870. A minute's stroll from the harbour, this is a well-run B&B with modern furnishings and very welcoming hosts. £70

Clickimin Campsite ⓣ 01595 741000. Though it enjoys the excellent facilities of the neighbouring Leisure Complex, its sheltered suburban location, west of the town centre, is far from idyllic. Closed Oct–April. £8.30

SYHA hostel King Harald St ⓣ 01595 692114. Islesburgh House offers unusually comfortable surroundings and has family rooms, a café and laundry facilities. £17

Westhall Lower Sound ⓣ 01595 694247, ⓦ bedand breakfastlerwick.co.uk. A splendid Victorian mansion, known locally as the "Sheriff's Hoose", set in its own grounds a mile or so southwest of town overlooking a bay. Rooms are spacious, the breakfasts are immense and there's free wi-fi. £90

NOSS

Inhabited until World War II, and now a National Nature Reserve, **Noss** is a popular day-trip from Lerwick. Sloping gently into the sea at its western end, and plunging vertically for more than 500ft at its eastern end, the island has the dramatic outline of a half-sunk ocean liner. The cliffed coastline is home to vast colonies of gannets, puffins, guillemots, shags, razorbills and fulmars. As Noss is only one mile wide, it's easy enough to do an entire circumference in one day. If you do, keep close to the coast, since otherwise you're likely to be dive-bombed by the great skuas (locally known as "bonxies"). **Boat trips** from Lerwick to Noss include those run by Seabirds and Seals (mid-April to mid-Sept; 3hr return; £40; ⓣ 07595 540224, ⓦ www.seabirds-and-seals.com). It's also possible to take a ferry to Maryfield on **Bressay**; from here it's a two-mile walk to the landing stage where a Scottish Natural Heritage RIB can take you to Noss (May–Aug Tues, Wed & Fri–Sun 11am–5pm; £3 return; phone ⓣ 0800 107 7818 before setting off).

25

EATING AND DRINKING

★ **Hay's Dock** Shetland Museum, Hay's Dock ⊕01595 741569, ⊕haysdock.co.uk. Bright, modern, licensed café-restaurant with a great view over the north bay, and a short, imaginative menu of local dishes, filled bannocks and cakes. Mon 10.30am–4.30pm, Tues–Sat 10.30am–4.30pm & 6.30–11pm, Sun noon–4.30pm.

The Lounge 4 Mounthooly St ⊕01595 692231. The friendliest pub in town is the upstairs bar in the *Lounge*, where local musicians often play informal sessions. Daily 11am–1am.

Monty's Bistro 5 Mounthooly St ⊕01595 696555, ⊕montys-shetland.co.uk. Unpretentious place serving snacky meals like smoked haddock fishcake for under £10 at lunchtimes, and more accomplished cooking, such as crispy duck, in the evening. Mon 5–9pm, Tues–Sat noon–2pm & 5–9pm.

Peerie Café Esplanade ⊕01595 692816, ⊕peerieshopcafe.com. A really nice café, on two floors, serving cakes, soup and sandwiches. Mon–Sat 9am–6pm.

Scalloway

Once the capital of Shetland, **SCALLOWAY** waned in importance throughout the eighteenth century as Lerwick grew. Nowadays, Scalloway is fairly sleepy, though its harbour is busy enough. The town is dominated by the imposing shell of **Scalloway Castle**, a classic fortified tower house built with forced labour in 1600 by the infamous Earl Patrick Stewart, who held court in the castle and gained a reputation for cruelty and corruption. On Main Street, the small **Scalloway Museum** (May–Sept Mon–Sat 10am–noon & 2–4.30pm; free) tells the story of the Shetland Bus, the link between Shetland and Norway which helped to sustain the Norwegian resistance in World War II.

ARRIVAL AND DEPARTURE — SCALLOWAY

There are regular **buses** from Lerwick (Mon–Sat hourly; 15min).

ACCOMMODATION AND EATING

Scalloway Hotel Main St ⊕01595 880444, ⊕scallowayhotel.com. Hotel on the harbourfront, with simple, modern rooms. Its bar acts as the local pub, and serves delicious bar food. **£65**

South Mainland

Shetland's **South Mainland** is a long, thin finger of land, just three or four miles wide, but 25 miles long, ending in the cliffs of **Sumburgh Head** (262ft), which rises sharply out of the land only to drop vertically into the sea. The road up to Sumburgh lighthouse is the perfect site for watching nesting kittiwakes, fulmars, shags, razorbills,

MOUSA BROCH

The island of **Mousa** boasts the most amazingly well-preserved broch in Scotland. Rising to more than 40ft, and looking rather like a Stone Age cooling tower, **Mousa Broch** has a remarkable presence, and even makes an appearance in the Norse sagas. The low entrance-passage leads through two concentric walls to a central courtyard, divided into separate beehive chambers. Between the walls, a rough (very dark) staircase leads to the top parapet; a torch is provided for visitors. Mousa is only a mile wide, but if the weather's not too bad it's easy enough to spend the whole day here. From late May to late July, thousands of **storm petrels** breed in and around the broch walls, fishing out at sea during the day, and returning to the nests after dark.

A small **passenger ferry** runs to Mousa from Sandwick (April to mid-Sept; £13 return; ⊕01950 431367, ⊕mousaboattrips.co.uk). The ferry runs special late-night trips (late May to mid-July Wed & Sat weather permitting), setting off in the "simmer dim" twilight around 11pm.

guillemots, gannets and puffins (May to early Aug). South Mainland also harbours some of Shetland's most impressive archeological treasures – in particular, **Jarlshof** and **Mousa Broch**.

Old Scatness Broch and Iron Age Village

June–Aug Mon–Thurs & Sun 10am–5pm • £4 • ⓣ01950 461869, ⓦshetland-heritage.co.uk

Extending Sumburgh airport revealed a vast Iron Age archaeological site known as **Old Scatness Broch and Iron Age Village**. At the centre of the site are the remains of an Iron Age broch, surrounded by a settlement of interlocking wheelhouses – so called because of their circular groundplan. Tours are led by costumed guides, who will take you around the ongoing dig and inside two of the wheelhouses that have been either partially or wholly reconstructed.

Jarlshof

South of Sumburgh airport • April–Sept daily 9.30am–5.30pm • HS • £5.50 • ⓣ01950 460112

Jarlshof is the largest and most impressive of Shetland's archeological sites. Only half of the original broch survives, and its courtyard is now an Iron Age aisled roundhouse, with stone piers. It's difficult to distinguish the original broch from the later Pictish **wheelhouses** that now surround it, but it's great fun to explore, as you're free to roam around the cells, checking out the in-built stone shelving, water tanks, beds and so on. Inland lies the maze of grass-topped foundations marking out the **Viking longhouses**, and towering over the whole complex are the ruins of the laird's house, built by Robert Stewart, Earl of Orkney and Lord of Shetland, in the late sixteenth century, and the **Old House of Sumburgh**, built by his son, Earl Patrick.

ARRIVAL AND DEPARTURE — SOUTH MAINLAND

There are **buses** from Lerwick to Sumburgh (Mon–Sat 6–8 daily, 4 on Sun; 45min).

ACCOMMODATION AND EATING

Levenwick Campsite Levenwick,18 miles south of Lerwick ⓣ01950 422207. Simple campsite run by the local community, with hot showers, a tennis court, friendly Shetland ponies and a superb view over the east coast. Closed Oct–April. £6 per tent

★ **Mucklehus** Levenwick, 18 miles south of Lerwick ⓣ01950 422370, ⓦmucklehus.co.uk. A lovely B&B in a former Master Mariner's house built in 1890 near the beach. Rooms are small but stylish, and there's free wi-fi. £70

Spiggie Hotel Seven miles north of Sumburgh ⓣ01950 460409, ⓦthespiggiehotel.co.uk. The Spiggie has a lively bar serving real ales and a restaurant with great views over the Loch of Spiggie and out to Foula; both serve very reasonably priced and well-presented dishes. £100

Fair Isle

Tiny **Fair Isle** is marooned in the sea halfway between Shetland and Orkney. By the 1950s, the population had shrunk to just 44, at which point George Waterston set up a bird observatory in 1948 and rejuvenation began. The croft land and the island's scattered houses are concentrated in the south, but the focus for many visitors is the **Bird Observatory**, recently rebuilt just above the sandy bay of North Haven where the ferry from Shetland Mainland arrives. It's one of Europe's major centres for ornithology and its work in watching, trapping, recording and ringing resident and migrant birds goes on all year. Fair Isle is even better known for its **knitting** patterns, still produced with great skill by the local knitwear cooperative. There are a few samples on display at the island's **museum** (Mon 2–4pm, Wed 10.30am–noon, Fri 2–3.30pm; free; ⓣ01595 760244), next door to the Methodist chapel.

ARRIVAL AND DEPARTURE — FAIR ISLE

By plane Flights arrive from Tingwall (Mon, Wed, Fri & Sat 2 daily; 25min) and Sumburgh (Sat; 15min).

By ferry The passenger ferry connects Fair Isle with either Lerwick (alternate Thurs; 4–5hr) or Grutness in Sumburgh (Tues, alternate Thurs & Sat; 3hr); it's advisable to book in advance (T 01595 760363).

ACCOMMODATION AND EATING

Fair Isle Lodge & Bird Observatory T 01595 760258, W fairislebirdobs.co.uk. New en-suite doubles, twins and singles. The observatory also serves tea, coffee and good home-cooking, available to residents and non-residents alike. £50 per person full board

South Light House T 01595 760355, W www.southlightfairisle.co.uk. This is a comfortable B&B in the newly refurbished keepers' cottages next to the lighthouse. Free collection from the ferry/airport and free wi-fi. £40 per person full board

Foula

Foula is without a doubt the most isolated inhabited island in Britain, separated from the nearest point on Mainland Shetland by about fourteen miles of often turbulent ocean. Its western **cliffs**, the second highest in Britain after those of St Kilda, rise at **The Kame** to some 1220ft above sea level; a clear day at The Kame offers a magnificent panorama stretching from Unst to Fair Isle. On a bad day, the exposure is complete and the cliffs generate blasts of wind known as "flans", which rip through the hills with tremendous force. In addition to its forty human inhabitants, the island is home for a quarter of a million **birds**, including a colony of **great skuas** or "bonxies" which you can't fail to notice in the breeding season.

ARRIVAL AND DEPARTURE — FOULA

By plane There are flights from Tingwall to Foula (Mon & Tues 1 daily, Wed & Fri 2 daily; 15min; around £50 return).

By ferry Ferries from Scalloway (Sat & alternate Thurs; 3hr 30min) and Walls (Tues & alternate Thurs; 2hr) arrive at Ham, in the middle of Foula's east coast. Be sure to book and reconfirm your journey (T 07881 823732, W atlanticferries.co.uk). Day-trips are not possible on the regular ferry, but Cycharters (T 01595 696598, W cycharters.co.uk) do boat trips on Wednesdays.

ACCOMMODATION

Leraback T 01595 753226, W originart.eu/leraback/leraback.html. Foula's only accommodation, unless you camp, is a modern croft-house bungalow near Ham, which does full board; they will collect you from the airstrip or pier. £75 per double full board

North Mainland

The **North Mainland**, stretching more than thirty miles north from Lerwick, is wild even for Shetland. The tiny, picturesque fishing port of **VOE** is well worth visiting – not so **BRAE**, built hastily during the 1970s oil boom. **HILLSWICK,** the main settlement in the northwest peninsula of **Northmavine**, was once a centre for deep-sea or haaf fishing, and later a herring station. By the harbour is **Da Böd**, founded by a Hanseatic merchant in 1684, which later became Shetland's oldest pub and is now a seal and wildlife sanctuary (T 01806 503348).

A side road leads west to the exposed headland of **Esha Ness** (pronounced "Aysha Ness"), celebrated for its red sandstone cliffs, stacks, blowholes and its lighthouse. A mile or so south off the main road is the **Tangwick Haa Museum** (Easter–Sept daily 11am–5pm; free), which tells the moving story of this remote corner of Shetland and its role in the dangerous trade of deep-sea fishing and whaling.

ARRIVAL AND DEPARTURE — NORTH MAINLAND

From Lerwick there are **buses** to Brae (Mon–Sat 4–6 daily; 45min), Hamnavoe (Mon–Sat 2 daily; 30min), Hillswick (Mon–Sat 1 daily; 1hr 40min), Vidlin (Mon–Sat 2 daily; 45min) and Voe (Mon–Sat 5–6 daily; 35min).

ACCOMMODATION AND EATING

Busta House Brae ⓣ01806 522506, ⓦbustahouse.com. One of Shetland's finest hotels, a lovely laird's house with stepped gables that has been tastefully enlarged over the last four hundred years and which sits across the bay from the modern sprawl of Brae. Even if you're not staying, it's worth coming for afternoon tea in the Long Room or for a drink and a bar meal in the pub-like bar. £115

★ **Lunna House** Vidlin, 8 miles northeast of Voe down the B9071 ⓣ01806 577311, ⓦlunnahouse.co.uk. Built in 1660, *Lunna House* is a wonderful place to stay, with spacious bedrooms, lovely views and top-class breakfasts. £60

The Pierhead Restaurant & Bar Voe ⓣ01806 588332. This cosy wood-panelled pub (a former butcher's) has a real fire and offers a good bar menu; a longer version is on offer in the upstairs restaurant, featuring local scallops and the odd catch from the fishing boats. Occasional live music. Mon–Sat noon–11pm, Sun 12.30–10.30pm.

Voe House ⓣ01595 693434, ⓦcamping-bods.co.uk. The largest camping böd on Shetland, in a nicely restored eighteenth-century manse with its own peat fire. Mattresses provided, but bring your own bedding. Closed Nov–March. From £8

The North Isles

Many visitors never make it out to Shetland's trio of remote **North Isles**, which is a shame, as the ferry links are frequent and inexpensive, the roads fast, and with Lerwick that much further away, the spirit of independence and self-sufficiency is much more keenly felt. **Yell**, the largest of the three, is best known for its otter population. **Fetlar**, the smallest, is home to the rare red-necked phalarope. **Unst**, though, probably has the widest appeal, partly as the most northerly landmass in the British Isles, but also for its nesting seabirds.

Yell

The interior of **Yell** features a lot of peat moorland, but the coastline is gentler and greener and provides an ideal habitat for a large population of **otters**. The only sight as such is at **BURRAVOE**, in the island's southeastern corner. Here, there's a lovely whitewashed laird's house dating from 1672, with crow-stepped gables, which now houses the **Old Haa Museum** (April–Sept Tues–Thurs & Sat 10am–4pm, Sun 2–5pm; free). Stuffed with artefacts, the museum has lots of material on the history of the local herring and whaling industry and there's a pleasant wood-panelled café on the ground floor.

ARRIVAL AND DEPARTURE YELL

By ferry Frequent ferries run to Ulsta on Yell from Toft, 30 miles north of Lerwick, on the Mainland (every 30–45min; 20min).

By bus Buses run from Lerwick to Toft (Mon–Sat 3–5 daily; 50min) for the ferry to Yell; there are also buses from Lerwick that go onto the ferry and drive up to Gutcher (Mon–Sat 1–2 daily; 2hr 10min). On Yell, buses run from Mid Yell to Gutcher for the Unst ferry terminal (Mon–Sat 1–5 daily, 1 on Sun in school term; 20min).

ACCOMMODATION

Wind Dog Café By the Yell–Unst ferry terminal at Gutcher ⓣ01957 744321, ⓦwinddogcafe.co.uk. Funky café with a simple menu of snacks, soups and cakes, a library, internet access, plus the odd event. Mon–Fri 9am–5pm, Sat & Sun 10am–4.30pm.

Windhouse Lodge ⓣ01595 694688, ⓦcamping-bods.co.uk. This camping böd, in the gatehouse of a much larger abaondoned house on the main road just outside Mid Yell, is currently the only place to stay on Yell. It has a wood- and peat-fired heater and hot showers. Closed Oct–March. Dorm £8

Fetlar

Fetlar (ⓦfetlar.org) is the most fertile of the North Isles, much of it covered by grassy moorland and lush green meadows with masses of summer flowers. At the main settlement, **HOUBIE**, you can learn more about the island from the welcoming **Fetlar Interpretive Centre** (May–Sept Mon–Fri 11am–3pm, Sat & Sun 1–4pm; £2; ⓦfetlar.com).

25

Fetlar is also one of the very few places in the UK where you'll see graceful **red-necked phalarope** (late May to early Aug): a hide has been provided overlooking the marshes (or mires) to the east of the **Loch of Funzie** (pronounced "finny").

ARRIVAL AND DEPARTURE — FETLAR

By ferry Ferries depart daily from both Yell (Gutcher) and Unst (Belmont), docking at Hamar's Ness, 3 miles northwest of Houbie (Mon–Sat 7–9 daily, 5 on Sun; 25–40min).

ACCOMMODATION

Aithbank T01595 693434, W camping-bod.co.uk. Cosy wood-panelled camping böd, a mile east of Houbie. Closed Oct–March. Dorm £8

Gord Houbie T01957 733227, E nicboxall@gord.shetland.co.uk. A warm, comfortable, modern, family-run B&B attached to the island shop. £50 per person full board

Unst

Much of **Unst** (W unst.org) is rolling grassland but the coast is more dramatic: a fringe of cliffs relieved by some beautiful sandy beaches. As Britain's most northerly inhabited island, there is a surfeit of "most northerly" sights, which is fair enough, given that many visitors only come here in order to head straight for **Hermaness**, to see the seabirds and look out over Muckle Flugga and the northernmost tip of Britain, to the North Pole beyond.

On the south coast of the island, not far from Uyeasound, lie the ruins of **Muness Castle**, a diminutive defensive structure, with matching bulging bastions and corbelled turrets at opposite corners. The castle was built in 1598 by the Scots incomer, Laurence Bruce, stepbrother and chief bullyboy of the infamous Earl Robert Stewart. Unst's main settlement, **BALTASOUND** boasts Britain's most northerly brewery, the Valhalla Brewery (by appointment; T01957 711658, W valhallabrewery.co.uk). As you leave Baltasound, heading north, be sure to look at **Bobby's bus shelter** (W unstbusshelter.shetland.co.uk), an eccentric, fully furnished, award-winning bus shelter on the edge of the town. The **Keen of Hamar**, east of Baltasound, and signposted from the main road, is one of the largest expanses of serpentine debris in Europe, home to an extraordinary array of plant life.

Haroldswick

Beyond the Keen of Hamar, the road drops down into **HAROLDSWICK**, where near the shore you'll find the **Unst Boat Haven** (May–Sept daily 11am–5pm; free), displaying a beautifully presented collection of historic boats with many tools of the trade and information on Unst's former herring industry. If you want to learn about other aspects of Unst's history, head for the nearby **Unst Heritage Centre** (May–Sept daily 11am–5pm; £2), housed in the old school building by the main crossroads. Less than a mile north is the ugly former **Saxa Vord RAF base**, now containing a restaurant, bar, hostel, chocolate factory (Mon–Sat 11.30am–5pm, Sun 1–4pm; free), and an exhibition on the history of the RAF on Unst.

A road heads off northwest from Haroldswick to the bleak headland of **Hermaness**, home to more than 100,000 nesting seabirds (May–Aug). There's an excellent **visitor centre** in the former lighthouse-keeper's shore station, where you can pick up a leaflet showing the marked routes across the heather to the view over to **Muckle Flugga** lighthouse and **Out Stack**, the most northerly bit of Britain. The views from here are marvellous, as is the birdlife; there's a huge gannetry on one of the stacks, and puffins burrow all along the cliff-tops.

ARRIVAL AND DEPARTURE — UNST

By ferry Ferries shuttle regularly from Gutcher on Yell to Belmont on Unst (T01957 722259; 10min).

By bus Lerwick–Baltasound (Mon–Sat 1–2 daily; 2hr 40min); Baltasound–Haroldswick (Mon–Sat 3–4 daily; 10min); Belmont–Baltasound (Mon–Sat 2–3 daily; 20min); Belmont–Uyeasound (Mon–Sat 1–2 daily; 5min).

ACCOMMODATION

Buness House Baltasound ⓣ01957 711315, ⓦusers.zetnet.co.uk/buness-house. A seventeenth-century "Haa", still owned and run by the eccentric Edmondstons (of chickweed fame). The decor is eclectic: the decoupage in the nursery dates from 1899, while the south-facing conservatory is modern. **£120**

Gardiesfauld Hostel Uyeasound ⓣ01957 755240, ⓦgardiesfauld.shetland.co.uk. A clean and modern hostel (no resident warden) near the pier; dorms mostly, plus one twin. You can also camp. Closed Oct–March. Dorm **£13**, twin **£26**

Prestegaard Uyeasound ⓣ01957 755234, ⓦprestegaard@postmaster.co.uk. Lovely spacious whitewashed Victorian B&B in Uyeasound, with just a couple of rooms. Evening meals available on request. **£60**

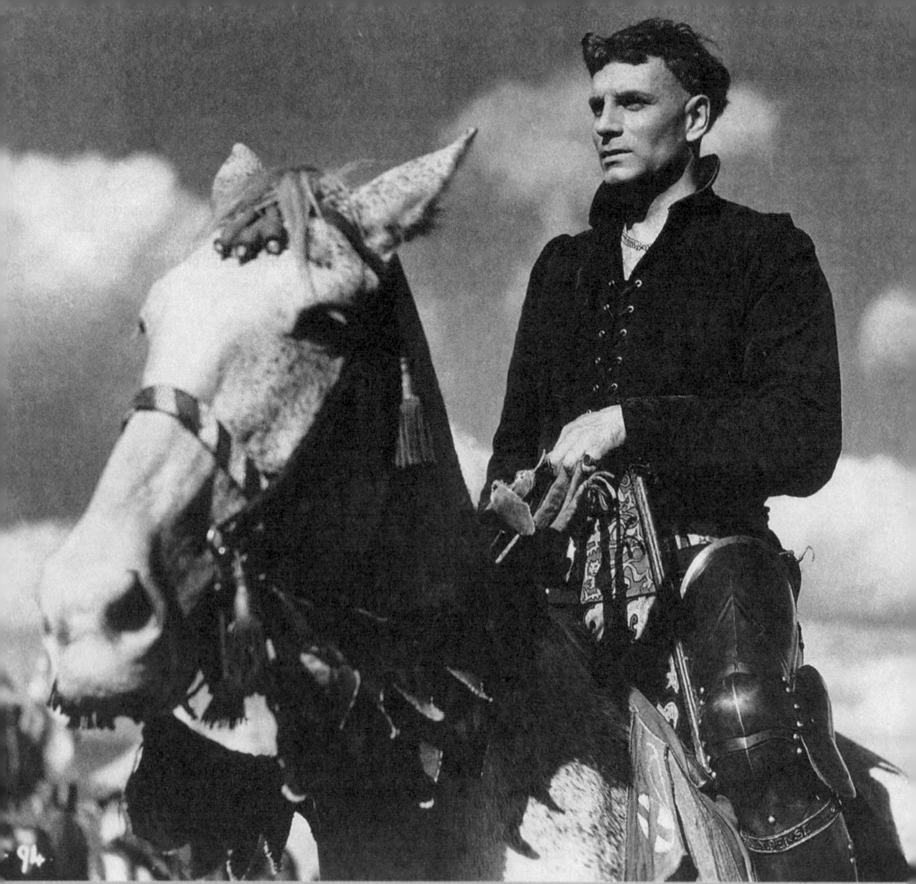

LAURENCE OLIVIER IN SHAKESPEARE'S *HENRY V* (1944)

Contexts

961 History

978 Books

983 Film

History

Britain's history is long and densely woven, its protagonists influential in western Europe from Anglo-Saxon times, and as leaders of the global British Empire from the eighteenth century onwards. What follows is a necessarily brief introduction.

From the Stone Age to the Iron Age

Britain has been inhabited for over half a million years. The earliest archeological evidence is scant, but **Old Stone Age (Palaeolithic)** bones and flint tools have been found in several different parts of the country. The comings and goings of these migrant peoples were dictated by successive **Ice Ages**, the most recent of which lasted for the ten thousand years up to 5000 BC. Although its final thawing caused the British Isles to separate from the European mainland, the **sea barrier** did little to hinder further influxes of nomadic hunters, drawn by the game that inhabited Britain's forests.

Around 3500 BC, a new wave of colonists reached Britain, probably via Ireland, bringing a **New Stone Age** (**Neolithic**) culture based on farming and livestock. These tribes were the first to impact upon the environment, clearing forests, enclosing fields and scouring the land for flint for their tools and weapons. Their most profuse relics are **graves**, usually stone-chambered, turf-covered mounds called long barrows, cairns or cromlechs, such as those at Belas Knap in Gloucestershire, Barclodiad y Gawres in Anglesey, and Maes Howe on Orkney.

The next transition, to the **Bronze Age**, began around 2500 BC, with the importation from northern Europe of artefacts attributed to the **Beaker Culture** – named after the distinctive cups found at many burial sites. Spreading along established trade routes, this stimulated the development of a well-organized social structure with an established aristocracy. Many of Britain's **stone and timber circles** were completed at the tail end of the Neolithic period, including **Stonehenge** in Wiltshire and Calanais on the Isle of Lewis, while others belong entirely to the Bronze Age, including Norfolk's Seahenge and the Hurlers and the Nine Maidens on Cornwall's Bodmin Moor.

From 700 BC onwards, the British **Iron Age** saw the consolidation of a sophisticated farming economy with a social hierarchy dominated by a druidic priesthood. Most farmers grew wheat and barley, and kept cattle, sheep and pigs; chickens arrived later, with the Romans. These early Britons gradually developed better methods of **metal-working**, favouring iron and gold rather than bronze, from which they forged not just weapons but also coins and ornamental works, thus creating the first recognizable indigenous art. A network of **hill forts** or brochs and other defensive works now stretched over the entire country, the greatest being at **Maiden Castle** in Dorset and **Mousa** in the Shetland Islands. These earthworks suggest endemic tribal warfare, a situation further complicated by the appearance of bands of **Celts**, who arrived from central Europe around 600 BC, though some historians dispute the notion of a Celtic "invasion", arguing that change and conflict were triggered by trade rather than conquest.

5000 BC

As the ice sheets retreat, the sea floods in, separating Britain from continental Europe.

3952 BC

The date of the Creation – as determined by the careful calculations of the Venerable Bede (673–735).

2500 BC

The start of the Bronze Age – and the construction of dozens of stone and timber circles.

55 BC

Chickens reach Britain for the first time – courtesy of Julius Caesar.

The Romans

The **Roman** invasion of Britain began hesitantly, when **Julius Caesar** led small cross-Channel incursions in 55 and 54 BC. While Britain's rumoured mineral wealth was a primary motive, the immediate spur to the eventual conquest a century later was anti-Roman collaboration between the Britons of southern England and their Celtic cousins in Gaul (France). The subtext was that the **Emperor Claudius**, who led the invasion, owed his power to the army and needed a military triumph. The death of the British king Cunobelin (the original of Shakespeare's Cymbeline), ruler of southeast England, offered the opportunity Claudius required. In 43 AD, a substantial force landed in Kent, then fanned out to establish a base along the Thames estuary. Joined by elephants and camels for major battles, the Romans soon reached Camulodunum (Colchester), and within four years were dug in on the frontier of south Wales.

By 80 AD the Roman governor, **Agricola**, felt secure enough in the south of Britain to begin an invasion of the **north**, stringing forts across the Clyde–Forth line and defeating the Scottish tribes at Mons Graupius. The long-term effect, however, was slight. In 123 AD the emperor Hadrian sealed the frontier against the northern tribes by building **Hadrian's Wall** from the Solway Firth to the Tyne. Twenty years later, the Romans again ventured north and built the **Antonine Wall** between the Clyde and the Forth. Forty years later, however, the Romans, frustrated by the inhospitable terrain of the Highlands, gave up their attempt to subjugate the north, opting instead for containment.

The written history of Britain begins with the Romans, whose rule lasted nigh on four centuries. For the first time, most of England was absorbed into a unified political structure, in which commerce flourished and cities prospered, and **Londinium** assumed a pivotal role in commercial and administrative life. Although Latin became the language of the Romano-British ruling elite, local traditions were allowed to coexist, so that British gods were often worshipped at the same time as Rome's. **Christianity** was introduced during the third century, and became entrenched after its official recognition across the Roman Empire in 313.

The Anglo-Saxons

By the middle of the third century AD, the **Roman Empire** was plagued by frequent collapses of central authority that encouraged its military commanders to act independently. In Britain, the Germanic **Saxons** had begun to raid England's eastern shore. By the end of the fourth century, with Britain irrevocably detached from what remained of the Roman Empire, the **Saxons** – and the **Angles**, also from northern Germany – were settling England and parts of Scotland. Romano-British resistance was led by such semi-mythical figures as **King Arthur**, said to have held court at Caerleon in Wales, but crumbled after the **Battle of Dyrham** (near Bath) in 577. By the end of the sixth century, Romano-British culture was all but eliminated in England, which was divided into the **Anglo-Saxon kingdoms** of Northumbria, Mercia, East Anglia, Kent and Wessex. Even today, some ninety percent of English place names have an Anglo-Saxon derivation. Meanwhile, those native Britons who had not been absorbed by the invaders were dispersed into Wales, the far southwest of England, and Scotland, which was a real mix, with Angles on the east coast, Irish-Celtic **Scotti** on the west, the Picts, descended from Iron Age tribes, to the north, and Romano-Britons in between. The

43 AD	60 AD	313	c. 500
The Roman Emperor Claudius invades Britain – and he means business.	An affronted and enraged Boudicca and her Iceni sack Roman Colchester.	The Emperor Constantine makes Christianity the official religion of the Roman Empire.	St David, the patron saint of Wales, is born on a cliff-top during a violent storm.

Scotti spoke **Goidelic** (or Q-Celtic), the precursor of modern Gaelic, while **Brythonic** (P-Celtic) was spoken in Wales and Cornwall.

In England, the revival of Christianity was driven by **St Augustine**, who landed in Kent in 597 at the behest of the pope, accompanied by forty monks. His mission to convert the pagan Anglo-Saxons went smoothly and was continued by a long succession of monkish missionaries; the last part of England to become Christian was Sussex in 680. On what might be called the Celtic fringe, a Christian church had survived from Roman times, winning new converts and promoting a hermetical vision of holiness exemplified by St David, ultimately Wales's patron saint, and **St Columba**, who founded several Christian outposts in Scotland, including on the island of Iona. Liturgical differences between this "Ionan Church" and the "Roman Church" of St Augustine were resolved when the **Synod of Whitby** determined in 663 that the English church should follow the rule of Rome.

In the eighth century, the kingdom of **Mercia**, occupying what is today the Midlands, became the dominant power in England. Its most talented ruler, Offa, was responsible for **Offa's Dyke**, an earthwork stretching from the River Dee to the Severn, marking the border with Wales. After Offa's death, **Wessex** gained the upper hand; by 825, its King Egbert had conquered or taken allegiance from all the other English kingdoms. Meanwhile, in Scotland, **Kenneth MacAlpine** united the Scotti and the Picts into one kingdom in 843. His successors extended their fiefdoms by marriage and force of arms until, by 1034, almost all of modern Scotland was under their rule.

The supremacy of Wessex coincided with the first large-scale **Viking** (or Norse) invasions, which began with coastal raids, like the one that destroyed the great monastery of Lindisfarne in 793, but grew into a migration. By 871, a substantial **Danish army** had conquered Northumbria, Mercia and East Anglia. The new king of Wessex, however, **Alfred the Great** (reigned 871–99), successfully resisted the Danes, and signed a truce that fixed an uneasy border between Wessex and Danish territory – the **Danelaw** – to the north and east. While the Danes soon succumbed to Christianity and internal warfare, Alfred modernized his kingdom and strengthened its defences. His successor, **Edward the Elder**, established Saxon supremacy over the Danelaw to become the de facto overlord of all England. The relative calm continued under Edward's son, **Athelstan** (925–40), who extended his sway over much of Scotland and Wales, and his son, **Edgar** (959–75), crowned as the first **king of England** in 973. However, this was but a lull in the Viking storm. Returning in force, the Vikings milked Edgar's son **Ethelred the Unready** (978–1016) for all the money they could, but the ransom (the Danegeld) paid brought only temporary relief and Ethelred hot-footed it to Normandy, leaving the Danes in command.

The first Danish king of England, the shrewd **Canute** (1016–35), constructed an Anglo-Scandinavian empire, but the Saxons regained the initiative from his two disreputable sons, and placed Ethelred's son, **Edward the Confessor** (1042–66), on the throne. It was a poor choice. More suited to be a priest than a king, Edward allowed power to drift into the hands of his most powerful subject, Godwin, Earl of Wessex, and his son Harold. On Edward's death, the Witan – a sort of council of elders – confirmed **Harold** (1066) as king, ignoring several rival claims. That of **William, Duke of Normandy**, was a curious affair, but he always insisted that the childless Edward the Confessor had promised him his crown. Unluckily for Harold, his two main rivals struck at the same time. First to do so was his alienated brother Tostig and his ally King Harald of Norway, reliably reckoned to be seven feet tall. They landed with a Viking

597	**793**	**796**	**1066**
St Augustine lands in Kent with instructions to convert Britain to Christianity.	In a surprise attack, Viking raiders destroy the monastery at Lindisfarne.	Death of King Offa, the most powerful king in England and long-time ruler of Mercia.	King Harold, the last Saxon king of England, catches an arrow in the eye at the Battle of Hastings.

army in Yorkshire and Harold hurriedly marched north to meet them. Harold won a crushing victory at Stamford Bridge, but then heard that William of Normandy had invaded the south. Rashly, Harold dashed south without mustering more men. William famously routed the Saxons – and killed Harold – at the **Battle of Hastings** in 1066. On Christmas Day, William the Conqueror was installed as king in Westminster Abbey.

England: Normans and Plantagenets (1066–1399)

William I (1066–87) imposed a Norman aristocracy on his new subjects, bolstering his rule by constructing such strongholds as the Tower of London. His most effective measure, however, was the compilation of the **Domesday Book** in 1086. Recording land ownership, type of cultivation, the number of inhabitants and their social status, it afforded William an unprecedented body of information, providing the framework for taxation, the judicial structure and feudal obligations.

William was succeeded by his son **William Rufus** (1087–1100), an ineffectual ruler who died in mysterious circumstances, killed by an unknown assailant's arrow while hunting in the New Forest. The throne then passed to **Henry I** (1100–35), William I's youngest son, who spent much of his time struggling with his unruly barons, but at least proved conciliatory in his dealings with the Saxons, even marrying into one of their leading families.

A long-winded civil war followed the death of Henry I, ending when **Henry II** (1154–89), the first of the **Plantagenets**, secured the throne. Energetic and far-sighted, Henry kept his barons in check and instigated profound administrative reforms, including the introduction of trial by jury. England was not Henry's only concern, as his inheritance had bequeathed him great chunks of France. His attempt to subordinate Church to Crown went terribly awry in 1170, when he sanctioned the murder in Canterbury Cathedral of his erstwhile drinking companion **Thomas à Becket**, whose canonization three years later created an enduring Europe-wide cult. Henry II was succeeded by his eldest son, **Richard I** (or Lionheart; 1189–99), who spent most of his reign crusading in the Holy Land. Neglected, England fell prey to Richard's scheming but inept brother **John** (1199–1216), the villain of the Robin Hood tales, who became king in his own right after Richard's death. John's failure to hold on to his French possessions alienated the English barons, who in 1215 forced him to sign a charter guaranteeing their rights and privileges, the **Magna Carta**, at Runnymede, on the Thames.

Although the power struggle between king and barons continued under **Henry III** (1216–72), Henry's successor, **Edward I** (1272–1307), was much more in control. Also a great law-maker, Edward became obsessed by military matters, spending years subduing Wales and imposing English jurisdiction over Scotland. Fortunately for the Scots, the next king of England, **Edward II** (1307–27), proved completely hopeless. After Robert the Bruce inflicted a huge defeat on his guileless army at the Battle of Bannockburn in 1314 (see p.804), Edward ended up murdered by his wife Isabella and her lover Roger Mortimer in 1327.

After sorting out the Scottish imbroglio, **Edward III** (1327–77) turned his attention to his (essentially specious) claim to the throne of France. Starting in 1337, the ensuing **Hundred Years War** began with several English victories, principally Crécy in 1346 and Poitiers in 1356, but was interrupted by the outbreak of the **Black Death** in 1349. The

1085	**1102**	**1190**	**1220**
The Normans start work on the Domesday Book, detailing who owns what, does what and lives where.	By the terms of the Synod of Westminster, clergy are forbidden to marry.	King Richard complains that in England it is "cold and always raining," and joins the Third Crusade.	Work begins on York Minster and Salisbury Cathedral – heady days for stone masons.

plague claimed one and a half million English souls – a third of the population – and the resultant scarcity of labour gave the peasantry great economic clout. Predictably, the landowners attempted to restrict the concomitant rise in wages, provoking widespread rioting that culminated in the **Peasants' Revolt** of 1381. The rebels marched on London hoping to appeal to the king – **Richard II** (1377–99) – for fair treatment. The monarch agreed to meet their spokesman, **Wat Tyler**, but his bodyguards killed **Tyler** instead and dispersed his followers amid mass slaughter.

The conquest of Wales (1272–1415)

Rather than attempting to subdue Wales, William the Conqueror installed a retinue of barons, the **Lords Marcher**, along the border. At the end of the thirteenth century, **Edward I** decided to conquer Wales instead, provoked in part by a Welsh chief, **Llywelyn the Last**, who failed to attend his coronation and refused to pay him homage. Aided by the skilful use of sea power, Edward had little trouble in forcing Llywelyn into Snowdonia. The 1277 **Treaty of Aberconwy** robbed Llywelyn of almost all his land, but left him with the hollow title of "Prince of Wales". Five years later, Llywelyn's brother **Dafydd** rose against Edward and Llywelyn felt obliged to help. It was a disaster: Edward crushed the revolt with relative ease and both brothers were killed. The **Treaty of Rhuddlan** in 1284 set down the terms by which the English king was to rule Wales: those parts of the country not given to the Lords Marcher were divided into administrative and legal districts similar to those in England. Often seen as a symbol of English subjugation, the treaty in fact respected much of Welsh law and provided a basis for civil rights and privileges. Many Welsh accepted Edward's rule, but after he brutally crushed a 1294 rebellion led by **Madog ap Llywelyn**, many of those privileges were rescinded.

Although the Anglo-Welsh aristocracy then took firm hold of Wales, one of their number, the charismatic Welsh hero **Owain Glyndŵr**, rose in revolt in 1400, declaring himself "Prince of Wales" in defiance of his English overlord, **Henry IV**. The key fortress of Conwy Castle was captured in 1401 and three years later Glyndŵr summoned a parliament in Machynlleth, and had himself crowned Prince of Wales. He then demanded independence for the Welsh Church from Canterbury and set about securing alliances with disaffected English noblemen. However, Glyndŵr's allies deserted him, and the rebellion fizzled out, though Glyndŵr was never captured and disappeared into the mountains, where he died in 1415 or 1416.

Medieval Scotland (1040–1320)

In 1040, **Macbeth** famously killed King Duncan and usurped the Scottish throne. In 1057, however, Duncan's son, **Malcolm III**, returned to Scotland and defeated Macbeth. His long reign was to transform Scottish society. Malcolm established a secure dynasty – the **Canmores** ("Bigheads") – based on succession through the male line, and replaced the old Gaelic system of blood ties with **feudalism**: the followers of a Gaelic king were his kindred, whereas those of a feudal king were his vassals. While the Canmores successfully feudalized much of southern and eastern Scotland by making grants to their Norman, Breton and Flemish followers, traditional clan-based social relations persisted to the north and west, a division which was to define much of Scotland's later history.

1237

The Treaty of York, signed by Henry III of England and Scotland's Alexander II, sets the Anglo-Scottish border.

1256

The calendar is getting out of sync, so in England a decree installs a leap year – one leap day every four years.

1266

Alexander III, the king of Scotland, buys the Western Isles from the Norwegians.

1277

Well armed and well organized, Edward I of England embarks upon the conquest of Wales.

The Canmores also set about reforming the Church. Malcolm III's English wife **Margaret** brought Scottish religious practices into line with the rest of Europe, while **David I** (1124–53) imported monks to found monasteries, principally in the Borders at Kelso, Melrose, Jedburgh and Dryburgh. By 1200 the country was covered by eleven bishoprics, although church organization remained weak within the Highlands. Similarly, the dynasty founded **royal burghs**, recognizing towns such as Edinburgh, Stirling and Berwick as centres of trade. Their charters usually granted a measure of self-government, which the monarchy hoped would encourage loyalty and increase prosperity. Scotland's Gaelic-speaking clans had little influence within the burghs, and by 1550 Scots – a northern version of Anglo-Saxon – had become the main language throughout the Lowlands.

Scotland's progress as an independent nation was threatened by the hotly contested succession that followed the death of **Alexander III** in 1286. Edward I, king of England, muscled in, presiding over a conference in which the rival claimants to the Scottish throne presented their cases. Edward chose John Balliol, in preference to **Robert the Bruce**, and obliged John to pay him homage, thus turning Scotland into a vassal kingdom. Bruce's refusal to accept this decision prolonged the conflict, and in 1295 Balliol switched his allegiance from England to **France** – the start of what is known as the "Auld Alliance". In the warfare that followed, Balliol was defeated and imprisoned, and Edward seized control of almost all of Scotland.

Edward's cruelty provoked a truly national resistance that focused on **William Wallace**, a man of relatively lowly origins who forged a proto-nationalist army of peasants, lesser knights and townsmen that was determined to expel the English. Wallace never received the support of the nobility, however, and after ten bitter years he was betrayed, captured and executed in London.

Feudal intrigue now resumed. In 1306 **Robert the Bruce** defied Edward and had himself crowned king of Scotland. Edward died the following year, but the turbulence dragged on until 1314, when Bruce decisively defeated an English army under Edward II at the battle of **Bannockburn**. At last Bruce was firmly in control, and in 1320 the Scots asserted their right to independence in a successful petition to the pope, now known as the **Arbroath Declaration**.

England: the houses of Lancaster and York (1399–1485)

In 1399, **Henry IV** (1399–1413), the first **Lancastrian** king, supplanted the weak and indecisive Richard II. His son and successor, the bellicose **Henry V** (1413–22), promptly renewed the Hundred Years War. A comprehensive victory at **Agincourt** forced the French king to acknowledge Henry as his heir in the Treaty of Troyes of 1420. However, Henry died just two years later and his son, **Henry VI** (1422–61 & 1470–1471) – or rather his regents – all too easily succumbed to a French counterattack inspired by **Joan of Arc**; by 1454, only Calais was left in English hands.

When it became obvious that Henry VI was mentally unstable, two aristocratic factions fought for the throne – the **Yorkists**, whose emblem was the white rose, and the **Lancastrians**, represented by the red rose. At first, in the **Wars of the Roses**, the Lancastrians had the better of things, but the Yorkist **Edward IV** seized the crown in 1461. When he imprudently tried to shrug off his most powerful backer, Richard Neville, Earl of Warwick, "Warwick the Kingmaker" returned the favour by switching sides. Edward was driven into

1290
Edward I of England expels the Jews from his kingdom, one of several medieval pogroms.

1295
France and Scotland sign a treaty of mutual assistance – the start of the "Auld Alliance".

1314
At the Battle of Bannockburn, Robert the Bruce's Scots destroy an English army.

1349
The Black Death reaches England and moves on into Scotland the year after.

exile and **Henry VI** came back for a second term as king – but not for long. In 1471, Edward IV returned, Warwick was killed and Henry captured – and dispatched – when the Yorkists crushed the Lancastrians at the Battle of Tewkesbury.

Edward IV (1461–70 & 1471–83) proved to be a precursor of the great Tudor princes – licentious, cruel and despotic, but also a patron of Renaissance learning. In 1483, his 12-year-old son succeeded as **Edward V** (1483), but his reign was cut short after only two months, when he and his younger brother were murdered in the Tower of London – probably by their uncle, the Duke of Gloucester, who was crowned **Richard III** (1483–85). Richard was himself killed at the battle of Bosworth Field in 1485 and Henry Tudor, Earl of Richmond, took the throne as **Henry VII.**

England: the Tudors (1485–1603)

The start of the **Tudor** period brought radical transformations. A Lancastrian through his mother's line, **Henry VII** (1485–1509) promptly reconciled the Yorkists by marrying Edward IV's daughter Elizabeth, a shrewd gambit that ended the Wars of the Roses at a stroke. By marrying his daughter off to James IV of Scotland and his son to Catherine, the daughter of Ferdinand and Isabella of Spain, Henry began to establish England as a major European power.

Henry's son, **Henry VIII** (1509–47) is best remembered for separating of the English Church from Rome and setting up the independent Protestant **Church of England.** His schism with the pope was triggered not by doctrinal issues but by the failure of his wife **Catherine of Aragon** – his elder brother's widow – to produce male offspring. When Pope Clement VII refused to grant a decree of nullity, Henry dismissed his chancellor Thomas Wolsey and turned to **Thomas Cromwell**, who helped make the English Church recognize Henry as its head. One consequence, the **Dissolution of the Monasteries**, enabled both king and nobles to get their hands on valuable monastic property. In his later years Henry became a corpulent, syphilitic wreck, six times married but at last furnished with an heir, **Edward VI** (1547–53), who was only nine years old when he ascended the throne. His short reign saw Protestantism established on a firm footing, with churches stripped of their images and Catholic services banned.

Despite the spread of Protestantism, most of the country accepted **Mary** (1553–58), daughter of Catherine of Aragon and a fervent Catholic, as queen upon Edward's death. Returning England to the papacy, Mary married the future Philip II of Spain, forging an alliance that provoked war with France and the loss of Calais, England's last French possession. The marriage was unpopular and so was Mary's persecution of Protestants: the leading lights of the English Reformation, Hugh Latimer, Nicholas Ridley and Thomas Cranmer, the archbishop of Canterbury, were all executed.

When she came to the throne on the death of her half-sister, **Elizabeth I** (1558–1603) looked vulnerable. The country was divided by religion and threatened from abroad by Philip II of Spain, the most powerful man in Europe. Famously, Elizabeth eschewed marriage and, although a Protestant herself, steered a delicate course in relations with the Catholic Church. Her prudence rested well with the burgeoning English merchant class, who were mostly opposed to foreign military entanglements. An exception was, however, made for the piratical activities of English seafarers like Walter Raleigh, Martin Frobisher, John Hawkins and Francis Drake, who made a fortune raiding

1380s	**1485**	**1559**	**1567**
Geoffrey Chaucer begins work on *The Canterbury Tales* and changes the face of English literature forever.	Battle of Bosworth Field: Richard III deposed and killed, ending the Wars of the Roses.	Religious reformer John Knox returns to Scotland, where he leads the Protestant Reformation.	Mary, Queen of Scots implicated in the murder of her second husband – pandemonium ensues.

Spain's American colonies. Inevitably, Philip II's irritation took a warlike turn, but his **Spanish Armada** was defeated in 1588. Elizabeth's reign also saw the efflorescence of a specifically English Renaissance, especially in the field of literature, with **William Shakespeare** (1564–1616) pre-eminent.

Wales under the Tudors

Welsh allegiance during the Wars of the Roses lay broadly with the Lancastrians, who had the support of the ascendant **Tewdwr** (or Tudor) family of north Wales. Welsh expectations of the first Tudor monarch, Henry VII, were high, but control remained shared between the Crown and the largely independent Marcher lords until a uniform administrative structure was implemented under Henry VIII, who also passed two **Acts of Union**, in 1536 and 1543, formalizing English sovereignty. As for the **Church**, Protestantism made rapid headway in Wales, supplanting Catholicism during Henry VIII's reign, and the Bible was translated into Welsh.

With new landownership laws, the stimulus provided by the Dissolution of the Monasteries hastened the emergence of the **Anglo-Welsh gentry**, eager to claim a Welsh pedigree while promoting the English language and the legal system. Meanwhile, landless peasants remained poor, only gaining slightly from the increase in cattle trade with England and the development of mining and ore smelting.

Bruces and Stewarts in Scotland (1320–1603)

Following the death of Robert the Bruce in 1329, the Scottish monarchy declined. The last of the Bruce dynasty died in 1371, to be succeeded by the "Stewards", hence **Stewarts** (known as Stuarts in England). Several, however, came to the throne as children, and the power vacuum was filled by key members of the nobility acting as **regents**. Although **James IV** (1488–1513), the most talented of the early Stewarts, might have restored the authority of the Crown, his invasion of England ended in a terrible defeat – and his own death – at the **Battle of Flodden Field**.

The reign of **Mary, Queen of Scots** (1542–87) typified the problems of the Scottish monarchy. Just one week old when she came to the throne, Mary immediately caught the attention of the English king, Henry VIII, who sought, first by persuasion and then by force of arms, to secure her hand in marriage for his 5-year-old son, Edward. Faced with devastating English attacks from 1544 onwards, the Scots turned to the "**Auld Alliance**". The French king promised military assistance in return for marriage between Mary and the Dauphin Francis. The 6-year-old queen sailed for France in 1548, leaving her loyal nobles and their French allies in control. A temporary truce between England and Scotland was agreed in 1551; and when Mary returned in 1561, following the death of Francis, she had to deal with a very different set of problems.

The **Scottish Reformation** was a complex social process, whose threads are hard to unravel. By the middle of the sixteenth century the established Church was held in general contempt. Protestantism benefited from its association with anti-French feeling, stirred to boiling point by **Mary of Guise**, the French mother of the absent Queen Mary, who became regent of Scotland in 1554. In 1557, a group of Scottish nobles banded together to form the **Lords of the Congregation**, and deposed Mary of

c. 1592	**1603**	**1605**	**1642**
First performance of Shakespeare's *Henry VI, Pt 1*, at the Rose Theatre, Bankside, London.	King James unites the crowns of Scotland and England.	Gunpowder Plot: Guy Fawkes et al plan to blow up the Houses of Parliament, but fail.	The Civil War begins when Charles I raises his standard in Nottingham.

Guise with English military backing in 1559. When the Scottish Parliament assembled shortly afterwards, it asserted the primacy of Protestantism.

After her return from France, Queen Mary tried to avoid an open breach with her Protestant subjects, but her difficulties were exacerbated by a disastrous second marriage to **Lord Darnley**. A cruel man, his jealousy led to his involvement in the murder of Mary's favourite, **David Rizzio**, who was dragged from the queen's chambers and stabbed 56 times. Perturbed Scottish Protestants were even more horrified when Darnley himself was murdered in 1567, and Mary married the **Earl of Bothwell**, widely believed to be the murderer. The Scots rose in rebellion, driving Mary into exile in England at the age of just 25. The queen's illegitimate half-brother, the **Earl of Moray**, became regent and her son, the infant **James**, was left behind to be raised a Protestant prince. Mary, meanwhile, was such a threat to the English throne that Queen Elizabeth I had little choice but to imprison and ultimately execute her.

With Mary gone, Protestant reformer **John Knox** concentrated on the organization of the reformed Church, or **Kirk**, which he envisaged as a body empowered to intervene in the daily lives of the people. **Andrew Melville** proposed the abolition of all traces of episcopacy – the rule of the bishops in the Church – and suggested instead a **presbyterian** structure, administered by a hierarchy of assemblies, part elected and part appointed. In 1592, the Melvillian party achieved a measure of success when presbyteries and synods were accepted as legal church courts and the office of bishop was suspended.

United Kingdom:1603–60

James VI of Scotland, the son of Mary, Queen of Scots, succeeded Elizabeth as **James I of England** (1603–25), thereby **uniting** the English and Scottish crowns. James quickly moved to end hostilities with Spain and adopted a policy of toleration to the country's Catholics. Both initiatives offended many Protestants, whose fears were confirmed in 1605 when **Guy Fawkes** and his Catholic co-conspirators, led by Robert Catesby, were discovered preparing to blow up the Houses of Parliament in the **Gunpowder Plot**: Fawkes was hung, drawn and quartered. **Puritan** sentiment and commercial interests converged with the founding of the first permanent **colony in North America**, Virginia, in 1608. Twelve years later, the **Pilgrim Fathers** landed in New England, establishing a colony that absorbed a hundred thousand Puritan immigrants by the middle of the century.

Meanwhile, James restored the Scottish bishops, much to the chagrin of the Presbyterians and assorted Protestants, and alienated his landed gentry in England. His absolutist vision of the monarchy – the **divine right of kings** – was totally out of step with the Protestant leanings of his subjects, and he also relied heavily on court favourites, especially the reviled George Villiers, Duke of Buckingham. It was a recipe for disaster, but it was his successor, **Charles I** (1625–49), who reaped the whirlwind.

Inheriting James's dislike of Protestants and approval of absolutism, Charles I ruled without Parliament from 1629 to 1640, but overreached himself by trying to impose a new Anglican prayer book on the Kirk. Denouncing these changes as "popery", Scottish reformers organized the **National Covenant**, a pledge to "Labour by all means lawful to recover the purity and liberty of the Gospel as it was established and professed." Backed by his Scottish bishops, Charles declared the "**Covenanters**" to be rebels. Consequently, when the king backed down from military action and called a General Assembly of the

1660	**1669**	**1678**	**1684**
The Restoration: Charles II takes the throne – and digs up the body of Oliver Cromwell to hammer home his point.	Samuel Pepys gives up his diary, after nine years of detailed jottings.	John Bunyan, the Protestant preacher and reformer, writes his *Pilgrim's Progress*.	Isaac Newton observes gravity – but is probably not hit on the head by an apple.

Kirk, it promptly abolished the episcopacy. Lack of finance stopped Charles from responding with an effective military campaign, whereas the Covenanters, well financed by the Kirk, assembled a proficient army under Alexander Leslie. In desperation, Charles summoned the English Parliament hoping it would pay for an army, but they refused their support. Indeed, the **Long Parliament**, as it became known, impeached several of Charles's allies, and compiled its grievances in the Grand Remonstrance of 1641.

Confronted by this concerted hostility, the king withdrew to Nottingham where, in 1642, he raised his standard, the opening act of the **Civil War**. The Royalist forces ("Cavaliers") were initially successful, winning the Battle of Edgehill, but in response, **Oliver Cromwell** overhauled part of the Parliamentary army ("Roundheads"), to create the formidable **New Model Army**, which helped win the battles of Naseby and Marston Moor. In defeat, Charles surrendered to the Scots, who handed him over to the English Parliament, by whom he was ultimately executed in 1649. The following year, Charles's son, the future Charles II, returned from exile to Scotland. To secure Scottish support, he was obliged to sign the Covenant, a bitter pill indeed. However, the New Model Army proved too good for the Royalists and, after several defeats, Charles had to flee into exile yet again.

For the next eleven years the whole of Britain was a **Commonwealth** – at first a true republic, then, after 1653, a **Protectorate** with **Oliver Cromwell** as Lord Protector and commander-in-chief. He reformed the government, secured commercial treaties with foreign nations and put the fear of God into his enemies. The turmoil of the Civil War and the pre-eminence of the army spawned a host of leftist sects, including the **Levellers**, who demanded wholesale constitutional reform. **Nonconformist** religious groups also flourished – such as the **Quakers**, led by George Fox (1624–91), and the **Baptists** – garnering the support of the most famous writers of the day, John Milton (1608–74) and John Bunyan (1628–88). After Cromwell died in 1658, his son **Richard Cromwell** ruled briefly and ineffectually until 1660, when **Charles II** (1660–85) regained the throne: the aristocracy and much of the gentry were relieved if not delighted.

The Restoration and the later Stuarts (1660–1714)

To facilitate his **Restoration**, Charles II offered an amnesty to all who had fought against the Stuarts, except the regicides who had signed Charles I's death warrant. This period saw a new exuberance in art, literature and theatre, and the foundation of the **Royal Society**, whose scientific endeavours were furthered by **Isaac Newton** (1642–1727), but also the **Great Plague** of 1665 and the **Great Fire of London** (1666). Politically, underlying tensions persisted between the monarchy and Parliament, though the latter was more concerned with the struggle between the **Whigs** and **Tories**, factions representing, respectively, the low-church gentry and the high-church aristocracy. There was a degree of religious toleration too, but its brittleness was all too apparent in the anti-Catholic riots of 1678.

The succession of the Catholic **James II** (1685–88), brother of Charles II, provoked much opposition, though the response was indifferent when the Protestant **Duke of Monmouth**, the favourite among Charles II's illegitimate sons, raised a rebellion in the West Country. Monmouth was defeated at Sedgemoor, in Somerset, in July 1685; nine days later he was beheaded at Tower Hill, and in the subsequent **Bloody Assizes** of Judge Jeffreys, hundreds of rebels and suspected sympathizers were executed or deported.

1703	**1707**	**1715**	**1745**
"The Great Storm", a week-long hurricane, blasts through southern England.	The Act of Union merges the Scottish Parliament into the English Parliament.	First Jacobite Rebellion: James Stuart ("The Old Pretender") raises a Scottish army, but is defeated.	Second Jacobite Rebellion: Charles Stuart (Bonnie Prince Charlie) invades England with a Scots army, but is defeated at Culloden.

James's unpopularity increased when his **Declaration of Indulgence** removed anti-Catholic restrictions, and the birth of his son secured a Catholic succession. Alarmed, powerful Protestants sent for **William of Orange**, the Dutch husband of Mary, the Protestant daughter of James II, to save them from "popery". William landed in Devon and, as James's forces simply melted away, speedily took control of London in the **Glorious Revolution** of 1688. This was the final postscript to the Civil War – although it was another three years before James and his Jacobite forces were finally defeated in Ireland.

William and Mary (1688–94) became joint sovereigns after they agreed to a **Bill of Rights** defining the limitations of the monarch's powers and the rights of subjects, thereby making Britain a **constitutional monarchy**, in which the roles of legislature and executive were separate and interdependent. The model was broadly consistent with that outlined by the philosopher and political thinker **John Locke** (1632–1704), whose essentially Whig doctrines of toleration and social contract were gradually embraced as the new orthodoxy.

After Mary's death, **William** (1694–1702) ruled alone; during his reign the **Act of Settlement of 1701** barred Catholics, or anyone married to one, from succession to the English throne. This Act did not, however, apply in Scotland, and the English feared that the Scots would invite James II's son, **James Edward Stuart**, back from France to be their king. These fears were allayed when Scotland passed the **Act of Union** uniting the English and Scottish parliaments in 1707, though neither the Scottish legal system nor the Presbyterian Kirk were merged with their English equivalents.

After William's death the crown passed to Mary's sister **Anne** (1702–14). A string of British victories on the continent now began with the Duke of Marlborough's triumph at Blenheim in 1704, followed the next year by the capture of Gibraltar, establishing a British presence in the Mediterranean. These military escapades were part of the Europe-wide **War of the Spanish Succession**, a long-winded dynastic squabble that rumbled on until the **Treaty of Utrecht** in 1713 all but settled the European balance of power for the rest of the century.

The Hanoverians (1714–1815)

On Anne's death, the crown passed to the Protestant Elector of Hanover, who became **George I** (1714–27). During his lacklustre reign, power leached into the hands of a Whig oligarchy led by a chief minister – or prime minister – the longest serving of whom was **Robert Walpole** (1676–1745). In the meantime, plans were being hatched for a **Jacobite Rebellion** in support of **James Edward Stuart**, the "Old Pretender". Its timing appeared perfect: Scottish opinion was moving against the Union, which had failed to bring Scotland tangible economic benefits, and many English Catholics supported the Jacobite cause too, toasting the "king across the water". In 1715, the Earl of Mar raised the Stuart standard at Braemar Castle, and just eight days later he captured Perth, where he gathered an army of more than 10,000 men. Mar's rebellion took the government by surprise. They had only 4000 soldiers in Scotland, but Mar dithered until he lost the military advantage. There was an indecisive battle at Sheriffmuir, but by the time the Old Pretender landed in Scotland in December 1715, 6000 veteran Dutch troops had reinforced the government forces. The rebellion disintegrated rapidly and James slunk back to exile in France.

1781	**1783**	**1814**	**1819**
Opening of the Iron Bridge – the first iron bridge the world has ever seen – over the River Severn.	End of the American War of Independence – the American colonies break from Britain.	Walter Scott publishes his first novel, *Waverley*, a sympathetic account of the Jacobite Rebellion of 1745.	Peterloo Massacre: in Manchester, the cavalry wade into a huge crowd who are demanding parliamentary reform. Many are killed.

Under **George II** (1727–60), England became embroiled in yet another dynastic squabble, the War of the Austrian Succession (1740–48), but this played second fiddle to the **Jacobite rebellion** of 1745, when the **Young Pretender**, **Charles Stuart** (Bonnie Prince Charlie) and his Highland army reached Derby, just 100 miles from London. There was panic in the capital, but Charlie's army proved too small – he had failed to rally the Lowland Scots, never mind the English – and his supply lines too over-extended to press home his advantage, and the Jacobites retreated north. A Hanoverian army under the Duke of Cumberland caught up with them at **Culloden Moor** near Inverness in April 1746, and hacked them to pieces. The prince lived out the rest of his life in drunken exile, while wearing tartan, bearing arms and playing bagpipes were all banned. Most significantly, the government prohibited the private armies of the chiefs, thereby destroying the clan system.

At the tail end of George II's reign, the **Seven Years War** (1756–63) harvested England yet more overseas territory in India and Canada at the expense of France; and, in 1768, with **George III** (1760–1820) now on the throne, **Captain James Cook** stumbled upon New Zealand and Australia, the extending Britain's empire still further.

Political tussles between king and Parliament, enlivened by **John Wilkes**, the first of an increasingly vociferous line of parliamentary radicals, revived during the early years of George II's long reign. The contest was exacerbated when the deteriorating relationship with the thirteen colonies of North America came to a head with the **American Declaration of Independence** and Britain's subsequent defeat in the **Revolutionary War** (1775–83). The British government was not, however, directly involved in the momentous events across the Channel, where the **French Revolution** convulsed Britain's most consistent foe. Out of the turmoil emerged one of Britain's most daunting enemies, **Napoleon** (1769–1821), whose stunning military progress was interrupted by Nelson at **Trafalgar** in 1805 and finally halted ten years later by the Duke of Wellington at **Waterloo**.

The Industrial Revolution

Britain's triumph over Napoleon was fuelled by its financial strength, born out of the **Industrial Revolution**. This switch from an agricultural to a manufacturing economy transformed Britain within a century. The earliest mechanized production lines were in the Lancashire **cotton mills**, where cotton spinning progressed from a cottage industry to a highly productive factory-based system. Initially, the cotton mills were powered by water, but in 1781 James Watt patented his **steam engine**. As Watt's engines needed **coal**, the population shifted towards the Midlands, central Scotland and the north of England, where the great coal reserves were mined. The industrial economy boomed and diversified, and regional towns mushroomed at an extraordinary rate. Sheffield was a steel town, Manchester possessed huge cotton warehouses, and Liverpool had the docks, where raw materials from India and the Americas flowed in and manufactured goods went out. Commerce and industry were also served by improving transport facilities, such as the construction of **canals**. A second major leap forward arrived with the **railway**, heralded by the Stockton–Darlington line in 1825, followed five years later by the Liverpool–Manchester railway, where George Stephenson's *Rocket* made its first outing.

1824

Charles Dickens' father is imprisoned as a debtor; his son never forgets.

1834

Tolpuddle Martyrs: agricultural workers from Dorset are transported to Australia for daring to organize.

1841

Thomas Cook organizes his first package tour, taking several hundred temperance campaigners from Leicester to Loughborough. More exciting excursions are promised.

Boosted by a vast influx of Jewish, Irish, French and Dutch workers, the country's **population** rose from eight and a half million to more than fifteen million during George III's reign. As the factories and their attendant towns expanded, so the rural settlements of England declined, inspiring the elegiac pastoral yearnings of Samuel Taylor Coleridge and William Wordsworth, the first great names of the **Romantic movement**. Later Romantics such as Percy Bysshe Shelley and Lord Byron adopted a more socially engaged position.

The Chartists – and social reform

Workers in both the cities and the countryside, whose livelihoods were threatened by mechanization, joined the **Chartist movement**, which demanded parliamentary reform – the most important industrial boom towns remained unrepresented in Parliament – and the repeal of the **Corn Laws**, which kept the price of bread artificially high. In 1819, during a mass demonstration in support of parliamentary reform in Manchester, protestors were hacked down by troops in the so-called **Peterloo Massacre**.

Social tensions ran high throughout the 1820s, but judicious parliamentary acts helped quieten things down: the **Reform Act** of 1832 established the principle (if not always the practice) of popular representation; the **Poor Law** of 1834 improved the condition of the most destitute; and the **Corn Laws** were repealed in 1846. Significant sections of the middle class supported progressive reform, as evidenced by the immense popularity of **Charles Dickens** (1812–70), whose novels railed against poverty and injustice. **John Wesley** (1703–91) and his **Methodists** had pre-empted these social concerns by leading the anti-slavery campaign. As a result of their efforts, **slavery** was banned in Britain in 1772 and throughout the British Empire in 1833.

Victorian Britain

In 1820, a blind and insane George III died. His two sons, **George IV** (1820–30) and **William IV** (1830–37), were succeeded in turn by his niece, **Victoria** (1837–1901), whose long reign witnessed the zenith of British power. The economy boomed, and the British trading fleet was easily the mightiest in the world. Victoria became the symbol of both the nation's success and the imperial ideal. There were extraordinary intellectual achievements too – as typified by the publication of **Charles Darwin**'s *On the Origin of Species* in 1859. Britain's industrial and commercial prowess was embodied by the engineering feats of **Isambard Kingdom Brunel** (1806–1859) and by the **Great Exhibition** of 1851, a display of manufacturing achievements without compare.

During the last third of the century, Parliament was dominated by the duel between **Disraeli** and the Liberal leader **Gladstone**. While Disraeli eventually passed the Second Reform Bill in 1867, further extending the electoral franchise, Gladstone's first ministry of 1868–74 created such far-reaching legislation as compulsory education, and the full legalization of trade unions.

As for foreign entanglements, troops were sent in 1854 to protect the Ottoman Empire against the Russians in the **Crimea**, an inglorious debacle whose horrors reached the public via the first-ever press coverage of a military campaign, and the revelations of **Florence Nightingale** (1820–1910), who was appalled by the lack of medical care for the soldiers. The **Indian Mutiny** of 1857 exposed the fragility of

1858	**1865**	**1871**	**1888**
English engineer Isambard Kingdom Brunel builds the iron-hulled S.S *Great Eastern*, the largest ship in the world.	William Booth from Nottingham founds the Salvation Army, in the East End of London.	The explorer Stanley "finds" the missionary Dr David Livingstone in Africa.	First football game between Celtic and Rangers in Glasgow.

Britain's hold over the Asian subcontinent, though the imperial status quo was restored and Victoria took the title Empress of India after 1876. Thereafter, the British army fought various minor wars against poorly armed Asian and African opponents, but came unstuck when it faced the better armed Dutch settlers of South Africa in the **Boer War** (1899–1902). The British ultimately fought their way to a sort of victory, but the discreditable conduct of the war prompted a military shake-up at home that proved significant in the coming European war.

The two World Wars (1914–45)

Victoria was succeeded by her son, **Edward VII** (1901–10), whose leisurely lifestyle epitomized the complacent era to which he gave his name. This came to an end under his successor, **George V** (1910–36), when the Liberal government, honouring the Entente Cordiale signed with France in 1904, declared war on Germany on August 4, 1914. Hundreds of thousands volunteered for the army, but their enthusiastic nationalism could not ensure a quick victory, and **World War I** dragged on for four miserable years. Britain and her allies eventually prevailed, but the number of dead beggared belief, undermining respect for the ruling class, whose generals had displayed a startling combination of incompetence and indifference to the plight of their men. Many Britons looked admiringly towards the Soviet Union, where Communists had rid themselves of the Tsar and seized control in 1917.

After the war ended in 1918, the sheer weight of public opinion pushed Parliament into extending the **vote** to all men over 21 and to women over 30. The liberalization of women's rights owed much to the efforts of the radical **Suffragettes**, led by Emmeline Pankhurst and her daughters Sylvia and Christabel, but the process was only completed in 1929 when women were at last granted the vote at 21.

During this period, the **Labour Party** supplanted the Liberals as the main force on the left of British politics, its strength founded on an alliance between the working-class trade unions and middle-class radicals. Labour formed its first government in 1923 under **Ramsay MacDonald**, but the publication of the Zinoviev Letter, a forgery in which the Soviets supposedly urged British leftists to promote revolution, undermined his position and the Conservatives were returned with a large parliamentary majority in 1924. Two years later, a bitter dispute between coal miners and mine-owners escalated into a **General Strike**, which quickly spread to the railways, the newspapers and the iron and steel industries. Involving half a million workers, the strike lasted nine days before it was broken when the government called in the army. The economic situation deteriorated further after the **crash** of the New York Stock Exchange in 1929, precipitating a worldwide depression. Unemployment topped 2.8 million in 1931, generating mass demonstrations that peaked with the 1936 **Jarrow March** from the Northeast of England to London.

Abroad, the structure of the **British Empire** was undergoing profound changes. The status of **Ireland** had been partly resolved following the electoral gains of the nationalist Sinn Féin in 1918 and the establishment of the Irish Free State in 1922, though the six counties of the mainly Protestant North (two-thirds of the ancient province of **Ulster**) chose to stay part of the United Kingdom. Four years later, the **Imperial Conference** recognized the autonomy of the British dominions, comprising all the major countries

1909	**1912**	**1926**	**1946**	**1950**
Lord Baden-Powell forms the "British Boy Scouts".	Bad news: the *Titanic* sinks and Captain Scott and his men die on the ice in the Antarctic.	Britain's first-ever General Strike: a nine-day walkout in support of the coal miners. The workers lose (again).	Death of John Maynard Keynes, one of the most influential economists of all time.	Soap rationing ends in Britain – a general clean-up follows.

that had previously been part of the Empire. This agreement was formalized in the 1931 Statute of Westminster: each dominion was given an equal footing in a **Commonwealth of Nations**, though each still recognized the British monarch. The royal family itself was shaken in 1936 by the **abdication of Edward VIII** (1936), following his decision to marry a twice-divorced American, Wallis Simpson. In the event, the succession passed smoothly to his brother **George VI** (1936–52).

When Hitler set about rearming Germany in the mid-1930s, the British government adopted a policy of appeasement. When Britain declared war on Germany following Hitler's invasion of Poland in September 1939, therefore, she was poorly prepared. After embarrassing military failures during the first months of **World War II**, the discredited government was replaced in May 1940 by a national coalition headed by the charismatic **Winston Churchill** (1874–1965). Partly through Churchill's manoeuvrings, the United States started supplying food and munitions to Britain, then broke trade links with Japan in protest at its attacks on China. In response to the Japanese bombing of Pearl Harbour in December, 1941, the US joined the war, and its intervention, combined with the stirring efforts of the Soviet Red Army, swung the military balance. In terms of casualties, World War II was not as calamitous as World War I, but its impact upon British civilians was much greater. In its first wave of **bombing** on the UK, the Luftwaffe caused massive damage to industrial and supply centres such as London, Glasgow, Swansea, Coventry, Manchester, Liverpool, Southampton and Plymouth. Later raids, intended to shatter morale rather than factories and docks, battered the cathedral cities of Canterbury, Exeter, Bath, Norwich and York.

Postwar Britain: from Attlee to Major (1945–97)

Hungry for change (and demobilization), voters in 1945's immediate postwar election replaced Churchill with the Labour Party under **Clement Attlee**, who set about a radical programme to **nationalize** the coal, gas, electricity, iron and steel industries, as well as the inland transport services. The early passage of the **National Insurance Act** and the **National Health Service Act** gave birth to what became known as the **welfare state**. Despite substantial American aid, the huge problems of rebuilding the economy made austerity the keynote, and food and fuel rationing endured for many years.

Meanwhile, Britain, the US, Canada, France and the Benelux countries defined their postwar international commitments in 1949's **North Atlantic Treaty**, a counterbalance to Soviet power in Eastern Europe. Continuing confusion over Britain's imperial – or rather post-imperial – role, however, bubbled to the surface in the **Suez Crisis** of 1956, when Anglo-French and Israeli forces invaded Egypt to secure control of the Suez Canal, only to be hastily recalled following international (American) condemnation. After this shoddy fiasco laid bare severe limitations on Britain's capacity for independent action, the Conservative prime minister, **Anthony Eden**, resigned. His replacement, the pragmatic, silk-tongued **Harold Macmillan,** accepted the end of empire, but was still eager for Britain to play a leading international role – and the country kept its nuclear arms, despite the best efforts of the Campaign for Nuclear Disarmament (CND).

1951	**1955**	**1962**	**1967**	**1970**
Britain's first supermarket opens in south London. Shopping trolleys become a new traffic hazard.	Fashion designer Mary Quant opens her first shop in London. Skirt hems are about to rise.	The Beatles hit the big time with their first single, *Love Me Do*.	First withdrawal from a cash dispenser (ATM) in Britain – at a branch of Barclays.	First Glastonbury Festival held – music lovers get used to mud.

The dominant political figure in the 1960s was **Harold Wilson,** a witty speaker and skilled tactician who was Labour prime minister from 1964 to 1970. The 1960s saw a boom in consumer spending, pioneering social legislation (primarily on homosexuality and abortion), and a corresponding cultural upswing, with London becoming the hippest city on the planet. But the good times lasted barely a decade: the Conservatives returned to office in 1970 and although the new prime minister, the ungainly **Edward Heath**, led Britain into the brave new world of the **European Economic Community (ECC)**, the 1970s were a decade of recession and industrial strife. In 1975, with Labour back in power, Heath was usurped by **Margaret Thatcher.** Four years later, to the amazement of many pundits, Thatcher won the general election primed and ready to break the unions and anyone else who crossed her path.

Thatcher pushed the UK towards sharp social polarization. While taxation policies and easy credit fuelled a consumer boom for the professional classes, the erosion of manufacturing industry and the weakening of the welfare state impoverished a great swathe of the population. With the enthusiastic backing of most of the national press, Thatcher won a second term of office in 1983, largely thanks to the recapture of the **Falkland Islands**, a remote British dependency in the south Atlantic, retrieved from Argentine occupiers in 1982.

Social and political tensions surfaced in sporadic urban rioting and the year-long **miners' strike** (1984–85) against colliery closures, a bitter dispute in which the police were given unprecedented powers to restrict the movement of citizens. Violence in Northern Ireland also intensified, and in 1984 IRA bombers almost blew up the entire Cabinet, who were staying in a Brighton hotel during the Conservatives' annual conference.

The divisive politics of Thatcherism reached their apogee when the desperately unpopular **Poll Tax** led to her overthrow by Conservative colleagues who feared defeat if she led them into another election. Her uninspiring successor, **John Major**, somehow managed to win the Conservatives a fourth term of office in 1992, with a much reduced majority. While his government presided over steady economic growth, they gained little credit amid allegations of mismanagement, incompetence, corruption and feckless leadership. The Conservatives were also divided over Europe, with the pro-European Union (formerly EEC) faction pitted against the vocal right-wing Eurosceptics.

The return of Labour

Wracked by factionalism in the 1980s, the **Labour Party** regrouped under Neil Kinnock and then John Smith. The political rewards, however, dropped into the lap of a new and dynamic young leader, **Tony Blair**, who moved the party away from traditional left-wing socialism. Blair's mantle of idealistic, media-friendly populism swept Labour to power in 1997, on a wave of genuine popular optimism. There were immediate rewards in enhanced relations with Europe and progress in the Irish peace talks, and Blair's electoral touch was soon repeated in Labour-sponsored **devolution referenda**, whose results semi-detached Scotland and Wales from their larger neighbour. The Scots got a Parliament, the Welsh an Assembly, reflecting different levels of devolution. Despite Labourite tub-thumping about the need to improve **public services**, Blair only set about the task after being re-elected with another parliamentary landslide in 2001.

1975	1985	1994	1999	2005
First North Sea oil comes ashore.	The bitter, year-long miners' strike is crushed by Margaret Thatcher.	The Channel Tunnel opens to traffic.	The Scottish Parliament and the National Assemblies for Wales and Northern Ireland take on devolved powers.	The Civil Partnership Act comes into effect, allowing couples of the same sex to have legal recognition of their relationships.

This second victory was, however, accompanied by little of the previous optimism. Few voters fully trusted Blair, and his administration had by then developed a reputation for "**spin**" – laundering events to present the government in the best possible light.

At a stroke, the terrorist attacks of **September 11, 2001**, downgraded Blair's domestic agenda in favour of a rush to support President Bush in his assaults on Afghanistan and then **Iraq**, in 2003, thereby alienating a large section of Labour's support. In the event, Saddam Hussein was deposed with relative ease, but neither Bush nor Blair had a coherent exit strategy, and back home Blair was widely seen as having "spun" Britain into the war by exaggerating the danger presented by Saddam. Even so, Blair's political opponents failed to deliver the *coup de grâce* and he managed to win a third general election in 2005, though not before he had promised to step down before the next election – by any standard, a rather odd way to secure victory. After subsequently teasing and tormenting his many political enemies with promises of his imminent departure, Blair finally did move on in June 2007, and was succeeded uncontested by his arch-rival, the Chancellor of the Exchequer, **Gordon Brown**.

The obsessive Brown proved to be a clumsy prime minister with a tin ear for the public mood. Failing to create a coherent narrative for either himself or his government, he even failed to secure credit for his one major achievement, staving off a banking collapse during the worldwide **financial crisis** that hit the UK hard in the autumn of 2007. Brown's bold decision to keep public investment high by borrowing vast sums of money almost certainly prevented an economic collapse in 2008 and 2009 – though his failure to regulate the banks had helped to create the crisis in the first place.

Back to the future – Britain today

In the build up to the **general election of 2010**, all three main political parties – the Liberals, Conservatives and Labour – spoke of the need to cut public spending more or less drastically, manoeuvring the electorate away from blaming the bankers, if not indeed capitalism per se. Although no party managed to secure a majority, an impasse was avoided when the Liberals swapped principles for power to join a **Conservative–Liberal coalition**, which took office in May 2010 with the Conservative **David Cameron** as prime minister. An old Etonian with a PR background, Cameron made a confident and sure-footed start, keeping his ideological cards well hidden (if indeed he has any), while his government limbered up in the background for a savage attack on the public sector under the guise of reducing the national debt. All seemed set fair, with the Liberals suitably supine, but key policy initiatives soon began to run aground and the coalition zigzagged between decision and revision, for example in its plans to transform (that is, part privatise) the Health Service.

In the longer term, it's hard to say how much opposition the coalition's attempt to turn back the clock by slashing public expenditure will encounter, either on the streets or in Parliament. Whatever happens, the wily **Alex Salmond**, leader of the **Scottish Nationalists** and Scotland's First Minister, is likely to benefit. Salmond knows full well that Cameron has little electoral interest in Scotland, whereas Labour needs its Scottish MPs to stand any chance of winning a majority in Westminster again. Salmond wants greater devolution as a stepping stone towards independence for Scotland – and he's in a great position to get it.

2006	2007	2009	2011	2012
Smoking banned in enclosed public places in Scotland.	Smoking banned in enclosed public places in England and Wales.	Economic crisis prompts the Bank of England to reduce interest rates to a record low of 0.5%: misery for savers; pleasure for spenders.	Murdoch media empire in crisis over illegal phone-hacking: *News of the World* newspaper closed.	London hosts the Olympic Games.

Books

The bibliography we've given here is necessarily selective, and entirely subjective. Most of the books reviewed are currently in print, though if local bookshops can't help, then Amazon almost certainly can (@amazon.co.uk; @amazon.com). The ★ symbol indicates titles that are especially recommended.

TRAVEL AND JOURNALS

★ **Bill Bryson** *Notes from a Small Island.* Bryson's best-selling and highly amusing account of an extended journey around Britain in the 1990s.

William Cobbett *Rural Rides.* First published in 1830, Cobbett's account of his various fact-finding tours bemoaned the death of the old rural England and its customs, while decrying both the growth of cities and the iniquities suffered by the exploited urban poor.

David Craig *On the Crofter's Trail.* Using anecdotes and interviews with descendants, Craig conveys the hardship and tragedy of the Highland Clearances without being mawkish.

Daniel Defoe *Tour through the Whole Island of Great Britain.* Defoe, the son of a London butcher, was a novelist, pamphleteer, journalist and sometime spy. This classic travelogue opens a fascinating window onto 1720s Britain.

Jan Morris *The Matter of Wales.* Prolific half-Welsh travel writer Jan Morris immerses herself in the country that she evidently loves. Highly partisan and fiercely nationalistic, the book combs over the origins of the Welsh character, and describes the people and places of Wales with precision and affection. Published in the mid-1980s.

J.B. Priestley *English Journey.* Quirky account of the Bradford-born author's travels around England in the 1930s.

Dorothy Wordsworth *Journals.* The engaging diaries of William's sister, with whom he shared Dove Cottage in the Lake District, provide a vivid account of walks and visits, and reflect Dorothy's fascination with the natural world.

HISTORY, SOCIETY AND POLITICS

Catherine Bailey *Black Diamonds – the Rise and Fall of an English Dynasty.* Thoroughly researched book telling the tale of the feuding, coal-owning Fitzwilliam family, powerful aristocrats who were holed up in Wentworth, their lavish Yorkshire mansion, for generations.

★ **Beatrix Campbell** *Diana, Princess of Wales: How sexual politics shook the monarchy.* A little hastily written perhaps, but still the most penetrating insight into the life and times of the much put-upon Diana.

Linda Colley *Britons: Forging the Nation 1707–1837.* Successful and immaculately researched book that offers fresh insights into eighteenth-century Britain and the evolution of a national identity.

★ **David Daiches (ed)** *The New Companion to Scottish Culture.* More than 300 articles interpreting Scottish culture in its widest sense, from eating to marriage customs, the Scottish Enlightenment to children's street games. Published in 1993.

Friedrich Engels *The Conditions of the Working Class in England.* Portrait of life in England's hellish industrial towns, written in 1844 when Engels was just 24.

Mark Girouard *Life in the English Country House.* Fascinating documentation of the day-to-day existence of the landed gentry; packed with the sort of facts that get left out by tour guides.

Christopher Hill *The English Revolution* and *The World Turned Upside-Down.* Britain's foremost Marxist historian, Hill was without doubt the most interesting writer on the Civil War and Commonwealth period.

★ **Eric Hobsbawm** *Industry and Empire.* Ostensibly an economic history of Britain from 1750 to the late 1960s, charting Britain's decline and fall as a world power, this book's great skill lies in its detailed analysis of the effects on ordinary people. By the same author, *Captain Swing* focuses on the labourers' uprisings of nineteenth-century England, while his magnificent trilogy, *The Age of Revolution 1789–1848*, *The Age of Capital 1848–1875* and *The Age of Extremes 1914–1991* simply can't be bettered.

Philip Jenkins *A History of Modern Wales 1536–1990.* Splendidly thorough book, placing Welsh history in its British and European contexts. Unbiased and rational appraisal of events and the struggle to preserve Welsh consciousness.

★ **David Kynaston** *Austerity Britain 1945–51.* Superbly researched volume on everything and anything important in postwar Britain, with oodles of vox pop. Also see the comparable *Family Britain 1951–57.*

Michael Lynch (ed) *The Oxford Companion to Scottish History.* Printed in 2001, this copious collection covers two thousand years and subjects as varied as climate, archeology, folklore and national identity.

★ **A.J.P. Taylor** *The First World War: An Illustrated History.* Penetrating analysis of how the war started and why it went on for so long; first published in 1963, but still unsurpassed. Similarly unrivalled is *The Origins of the Second World War*, also published in the 1960s; both sets of research are incorporated within the same writer's *English History 1914–1945*.

★ **E.P. Thompson** *The Making of the English Working Class*. A seminal text – essential reading for anyone who wants to understand the fabric of English society.

Wynford Vaughan-Thomas *Wales – a History*. Working chronologically from the pre-Celtic dawn to the aftermath of the 1979 devolution vote, this masterpiece is a warm and spirited history of Wales, offering perhaps the clearest explanation of the evolution of Welsh culture.

REGIONAL GUIDES

★ **Simon Jenkins** *England's Thousand Best Churches* and *England's Thousand Best Houses*. These two superb books from a well-known UK journalist describe the pick of England's churches and houses in lucid detail. Wittily written, they're divided into counties with a star system to indicate the best.

Pathfinder Walks Series of practical guides with maps and route descriptions to popular outdoor spots such as the Yorkshire Dales, the Brecon Beacons, Cornwall and the Cairngorms. Produced by the Ordnance Survey.

★ **A. Wainwright** *A Coast to Coast Walk*. Beautiful palm-sized guide by acclaimed English hiker and Lake District expert. Printed from his handwritten notes and sketched maps. Also in the series are seven authoritative books covering a variety of walks and climbs in the Lake District.

★ **Ben Weinreb and Christopher Hibbert** *The London Encyclopaedia*. More than a thousand pages of concisely presented and well-illustrated information on London past and present – the most fascinating single book on the capital.

ART, ARCHITECTURE AND ARCHEOLOGY

John Betjeman *Ghastly Good Taste, Or, A Depressing Story of the Rise and Fall of English Architecture*. Classy – and classic – one-hundred page account of England's architecture written by one of the country's shrewdest poet-commentators. First published in 1970.

David Dimbleby (ed) *Seven Ages of Britain*. Based on a popular TV series, this lavishly illustrated book picks some of Britain's most significant art pieces – from Pictish carvings to YBA works – to explore its history.

William Gaunt *English Painting*. This succinct and excellently illustrated book provides a useful introduction to its subject, covering the Middle Ages to the twentieth century in just 260 pages.

★ **Duncan MacMillan** *Scottish Art 1460–2000* and *Scottish Art in the Twentieth Century*. The former is a lavish overview of Scottish painting with good sections on landscape, portraiture and the Glasgow Boys, while the latter covers the last hundred years in splendid detail.

Thomas Pakenham *Meetings With Remarkable Trees*. Unusual and intriguing picture book about the author's favourite sixty trees, delving into their character as much as the botany.

FICTION BEFORE 1900

★ **Jane Austen** *Pride and Prejudice*; *Sense and Sensibility*; *Emma*; *Persuasion*. All-time classics on manners, society and provincial life; laced with bathos and ever-so-subtle twists of plot.

R.D. Blackmore *Lorna Doone*. Blackmore's swashbuckling, melodramatic romance, set on Exmoor, has done more for West Country tourism than any other book.

James Boswell *The Life of Samuel Johnson*. England's most famous man of letters and pioneer dictionary-maker displayed – warts and all – by his engagingly low-life Scottish biographer.

★ **Emily Brontë** *Wuthering Heights*. Set on the Yorkshire Moors, this is the ultimate English melodrama, complete with volcanic passions, craggy landscapes, ghostly presences and gloomy Yorkshire villagers.

John Bunyan *Pilgrim's Progress*. Simple, allegorical tale of hero Christian's struggle to achieve salvation. Prepare to feel guilty.

Thomas De Quincey *Confessions of an English Opium-Eater*. Tripping out with the most famous literary drug-taker after Coleridge – *Fear and Loathing in Las Vegas* it isn't, but neither is this a simple cautionary tale.

Charles Dickens *Bleak House*; *David Copperfield*; *Little Dorrit*; *Oliver Twist*; *Hard Times*. Many of Dickens' novels are set in London, including *Bleak House*, *Oliver Twist* and *Little Dorrit*, and these contain some of his most trenchant pieces of social analysis; *Hard Times*, however, is set in a Lancashire mill town, while *David Copperfield* draws on Dickens' own unhappy experiences as a boy, with much of the action taking place in Kent and Norfolk.

George Eliot *Scenes of Clerical Life*; *Middlemarch*; *Mill on the Floss*. Eliot (real name Mary Ann Evans) wrote mostly about the county of her birth, Warwickshire, the setting for the three searing tales that comprise her fictional debut, *Scenes of Clerical Life*. *Middlemarch* is a gargantuan portrayal of English provincial life prior to the Reform Act of 1832, while the exquisite *Mill on the Floss* is based on her own childhood experiences.

Thomas Hardy *Far from the Madding Crowd*; *The Mayor of Casterbridge*; *Tess of the D'Urbervilles*; *Jude the Obscure*. Hardy's novels contain some famously evocative descriptions of his native Dorset, but at the time of their publication it was Hardy's defiance of conventional pieties that attracted most attention: *Tess*, in which the heroine has a baby out of wedlock and commits murder, shocked his contemporaries, while his bleakest novel, the Oxford-set *Jude the Obscure*, provoked such a violent response that Hardy gave up novel-writing altogether.

Walter Scott *Waverley*. Swirl the tartan, blow the pipes, this is the first of the books by Scott that did much to create a highly romanticized version of Scottish life and history. Others include *Rob Roy*, a rich and ripping yarn that transformed the diminutive brigand into a national hero.

Lawrence Sterne *Tristram Shandy*. Anarchic, picaresque eighteenth-century ramblings based on life in a small English village; full of bizarre textual devices – like an all-black page in mourning for one of the characters.

★ **Robert Louis Stevenson** *Dr Jekyll and Mr Hyde*; *Kidnapped*; *The Master of Ballantrae*; *Treasure Island*; *Weir of Hermiston*. Superbly imagined and pacily written nineteenth-century tales of intrigue and derring-do.

Anthony Trollope *Barchester Towers*. Trollope was an astonishingly prolific novelist who also, in his capacity as a postal surveyor, found time to invent the letterbox. The "Barsetshire" novels, of which *Barchester Towers* is the best known, are set in and around a fictional version of Salisbury.

CONTEMPORARY FICTION

Peter Ackroyd *English Music*. A typical Ackroyd novel, constructing parallels between interwar London and distant epochs to conjure a kaleidoscopic vision of English culture. His other novels, such as *Chatterton*, *Hawksmoor* and *The House of Doctor Dee*, are variations on his preoccupation with the English psyche's darker depths.

Julian Barnes *England, England*; *Metroland; The Sense of an Ending*. One of the UK's most versatile writers, Barnes seems to be able to turn his hand to just about anything. His controversial *England, England* is a satire on the role of tourism in England with the country being re-created as a theme park on the Isle of Wight, while *Metroland* tells the story of two boys growing up in London's suburbs. His latest novel, *The Sense of an Ending*, touches on themes of sex and inhibition, regret and false recollection.

George Mackay Brown *Beside the Ocean of Time*. A child's journey through the history of an Orkney island, and an adult's effort to make sense of the place's secrets in the late twentieth century.

John Buchan *The Complete Richard Hannay*. This one volume includes *The 39 Steps*, *Greenmantle*, *Mr Standfast*, *The Three Hostages* and *The Island of Sheep*. Good gung-ho stories with a great feel for Scottish landscape.

Joseph Conrad *The Secret Agent*. Spy story based on the 1906 anarchist bombing of Greenwich Observatory, exposing the hypocrisies of both the police and anarchists.

Daphne du Maurier *Rebecca*. Long derided in many quarters as a popular piece of fluff, this darkly romantic novel has come to be appreciated as a Gothic meditation on sexual inequality and obsession, focused around the brooding mansion of Manderley, on du Maurier's beloved Cornish coast. See also the same author's *Frenchman's Creek* and *Jamaica Inn*.

E.M. Forster *Howards End*. Bourgeois angst in Hertfordshire and Shropshire, by one of the country's best-loved modern novelists.

John Fowles *The Collector*; *The French Lieutenant's Woman*; *Daniel Martin*. *The Collector*, Fowles' first novel, is a psychological thriller in which the heroine is kidnapped by a psychotic pools-winner, the story being told once by each protagonist. *The French Lieutenant's Woman*, set in Lyme Regis on the Dorset coast, is a tricksy neo-Victorian novel with a famous DIY ending, while *Daniel Martin* is a dense, realistic novel set in postwar Britain.

Lewis Grassic Gibbon *A Scots Quair*. A landmark trilogy, set in northeast Scotland during and after World War I, the events are seen through the eyes of Chris Guthrie, "torn between her love for the land and her desire to escape a peasant culture". Strong, seminal work.

★ **William Golding** *The Spire*. Atmospheric novel centred on the building of a cathedral spire, taking place in a thinly disguised medieval Salisbury. Also, if you ever wondered what it was like to be at sea in an early nineteenth-century British ship, try the splendid *Rites of Passage* trilogy.

Robert Graves *Goodbye to All That*. Horrific and humorous memoirs of public school and World War I trenches, followed by postwar trauma and life in Wales, Oxford and Egypt.

Alasdair Gray *Lanark*. Gray's first novel was twenty-five years in the writing and remains his most influential, leading Anthony Burgess to hail him as "the most important Scottish writer since Sir Walter Scott". This challenging, loosely autobiographical work – part science fiction, part *bildungsroman* – relates, in sometimes hallucinatory style, the journey of a man who hankers to create great art.

Alan Hollinghurst *The Stranger's Child.* Hollinghurst excels in pin-sharp and often very funny observations of British society. His latest work starts with a pre-World War I encounter in a country house, by turns bucolic, edgy and romantic. The focus of attention is a young poet who is killed in the war, and the narrative that follows develops into a satire on the uncertain art of biography.

James Kelman *The Busconductor Hines*; *How Late It Was, how late*. The first is a wildly funny story of a young Glasgow bus conductor with an intensely boring job and a limitless imagination. *How Late It Was* is Kelman's award-winning and controversial look at life from the perspective of a blind Glaswegian drunk. A disturbing study of personal and political violence, with language to match.

D.H. Lawrence *Sons and Lovers*; *Lady Chatterley's Lover*. Lawrence's less-than-flattering take on working-class life in a Nottinghamshire pit village never went down well with the locals. His *Sons and Lovers*, a fraught, autobiographical novel, contains some of his finest writing, as does the infamous *Lady Chatterley's Lover*, which pushes sex and class hard together.

Laurie Lee *Cider with Rosie*. Beautifully written reminiscences of adolescent frolics in the rural Cotswolds of the 1920s.

Richard Llewellyn *How Green Was My Valley*; *Up into the Singing Mountain*; *Down Where the Moon is Small*; *Green, Green My Valley Now*. Vital tetralogy in eloquent and passionate prose, following the life of Huw Morgan from his youth in a South Wales mining valley through emigration to the Welsh community in Patagonia and back to 1970s Wales. A bestseller during World War II and still the best introduction to the vast canon of "valleys novels", *How Green Was My Valley* captured a longing for a simple if tough life, and steered clear of cloying sentimentality.

★ **Ian McEwan** *Atonement*; *On Chesil Beach*. One of Britain's finest contemporary novelists, McEwan's dark and brooding works are punctuated by the unforeseen and the accidental. *Atonement* is possibly his most masterful book, tracing the course of three lives from a sweltering country garden in 1935 to absolution in the new century, while *On Chesil Beach* is a tale of innocence and loss, misunderstanding and tenderness between two newlyweds in a hotel on the Dorset coast in the early 1960s.

Alan Sillitoe *Saturday Night and Sunday Morning*. Gritty account of factory life and sexual shenanigans in Nottingham in the late 1950s.

★ **Dylan Thomas** *Under Milk Wood*; *Collected Stories*; *Collected Poems: 1934–1953*. *Under Milk Wood* is Thomas's most popular play, telling the story of a microcosmic Welsh seaside town over a 24-hour period. *Collected Stories* contains all of Thomas's classic prose pieces: *Quite Early One Morning*, which metamorphosed into *Under Milk Wood*, the magical *A Child's Christmas in Wales* and the compulsive, crackling autobiography, *Portrait of the Artist as a Young Dog*. Thomas's beautifully wrought and inventive poems carry a deep, pained concern with mortality and the nature of humanity.

Sarah Waters Waters is a consummate storyteller, specializing in subtly psychological and sexually charged historical novels that have a very strong sense of place – that is, London and Southeast England. *Tipping the Velvet*, *Affinity* and *Fingersmith* are set in Victorian times; *The Night Watch* in World War II, and *The Little Stranger*, an eerie ghost story, takes place in the postwar period.

Evelyn Waugh The *Sword of Honour* trilogy. A brilliant satire of the World War I officer class laced with some of Waugh's funniest set pieces. The best-selling *Brideshead Revisited* is possibly his worst book, rank with snobbery, nostalgia and love of money.

PG Wodehouse *Thank You, Jeeves*; *A Damsel in Distress*. For many, Wodehouse (1881–1975) is the quintessential English humorist and his deftly crafted tales – with their familiar cast of characters, primarily Bertie Wooster and Jeeves – have remained popular for decades.

CONTEMPORARY CRIME FICTION

PD James *Original Sin*. James writes skilful tales of murder and mystery; of her fourteen novels featuring Police Commander/poet Adam Dalgliesh, this is one of the best. The novels *An Unsuitable Job for a Woman* and *The Skull Beneath the Skin* are also worth reading, featuring London Private Detective Cordelia Gray.

Ian Rankin *Knots and Crosses*; *The Falls*. Britain's best-selling crime author introduced John Rebus in 1987 and since then the hard-drinking, anti-authoritarian, emotionally scarred detective has featured in almost twenty novels. He inhabits the mean streets of Edinburgh – streets the tourists rarely see – though visitors can rub shoulders with him in cherished locations like the *Oxford Bar* pub.

Ruth Rendell/Barbara Vine *From Doon With Death*; *Gallowglass*; *King Solomon's Carpet*; *Grasshopper*; *The Birthday Present*. Rendell writes brilliantly and disturbingly of contemporary dysfunction in all its guises. Her long-standing Inspector Wexford series is set in the fictional West Sussex town of Kingsmarkham, but it's when writing as Barbara Vine that Rendell excels in creating a sense of place, namely London, producing serious, memorable fictions from unsung locales like Kilburn and Cricklewood, the London tube, and the streets and rooftops of Maida Vale.

Peter Robinson *Gallows View*; *A Piece of My Heart*. Robinson's lauded Inspector Banks series has used the bleak corners and beauty spots of the Yorkshire Dales to dramatic effect. His gritty novels, featuring the troubled, music-loving detective, show a sophistication gleaned from studying creative writing under Joyce Carol Oates.

POETRY BEFORE 1900

★ **Robert Burns** *Selected Poems*. Comprises the best-known work of Scotland's greatest poet, who employed vigorous vernacular language. Immensely popular all over the world, his famous early poems include *Auld Lang Syne* and *My Love Is Like A Red, Red Rose*.

★ **Samuel Taylor Coleridge** Coleridge wrote little, but to the highest quality. *Kubla Khan* and *The Rime of the Ancient Mariner* are among the strangest products of the

Romantic period, but equally noteworthy are the quieter "conversation" poems such as *Frost at Midnight*.

★ **John Keats** *Selected Poems*. Keats died when he was only 25, but there's still little argument that he was one of Britain's greatest writers. His achievements in poems such as the *Ode to Autumn* are simply extraordinary.

Alfred Tennyson *Selected Poems*. Tennyson wrote the most purely musical poetry in English, filled with sensuous detail and dreamy evocations of natural beauty and the past. *In Memoriam* shows him to be the great poet of Victorian doubt and faith.

★ **William Wordsworth** *Selected Poetry*. It's impossible to exaggerate Wordsworth's originality and his influence on the future direction of English culture; his presence is clearly felt in the novels of Dickens and George Eliot as well as in the work of later poets.

TWENTIETH-CENTURY POETRY

W.H. Auden *Collected Poems*. Auden combines the themes of history, politics and love in poems that are definitive expressions of his times. The politically committed work of the 1930s gives way to a later religious commitment, but all his work is marked by stylistic virtuosity.

John Betjeman *Collected Poems*. Betjeman's humorous and often nostalgic work dissected England and the English in satirical light verse, homing in on provincial and suburban manners.

T.S. Eliot *The Waste Land*. Published in 1922, this is considered one of the cornerstones of Modernist writing, offering a revolutionary vision of Western civilization imbued with resonant images of contemporary and ancient London.

Ted Hughes *Collected Poems*. Best known for his brooding, sometimes brutal portrayals of nature, Hughes set much of his verse in his native Yorkshire.

Philip Larkin *Collected Poems*. Larkin used plain language in his work, the subject of which is often the insignificance of human life. Many of the poems achieve an apparently unstudied beauty, though in fact Larkin published very little, preferring to refine his verse to its basic elements.

Hugh MacDiarmid *Selected Poems*. A poet and nationalist who sought, through his fine lyrical verse, to reinvigorate the use of Scottish literary language.

Roger McGough *Blazing Fruit: Selected Poems*. A contemporary Liverpool poet, whose witty rhetorical verse is instantly recognizable. Some of McGough's earlier work, alongside that of Adrien Henri and Brian Patten, can be found in the influential 1960s collection *The Mersey Sound*.

Wilfred Owen *The Poems of Wilfred Owen*. Owen's striking and deeply unsettling World War I poetry is at its best in works such as *Strange Meeting*, with its original use of half-rhymes.

Film

Britain has produced a wealth of great films as well as some of the world's finest actors, producers and directors. Those reviewed below all depict a particular aspect of British life, whether reflecting the experience of immigrant communities, investigating its rippling class tensions or just having a self-deprecatory laugh. The ★ symbol indicates films that are especially recommended.

THE 1930S AND 1940S

★ **Brief Encounter** (David Lean, 1945). Wonderful weepie in which Trevor Howard and Celia Johnson teeter on the edge of adultery after a chance encounter at a railway station. Noël Coward wrote the clipped dialogue; the flushed, dreamy sountrack features Rachmaninov's *Piano Concerto No.2*.

Brighton Rock (John Boulting, 1947). A fine adaptation of Graham Greene's novel, featuring a young, scary Richard Attenborough as the psychopathic Pinkie, who marries a witness to one of his crimes to ensure her silence. Beautiful cinematography and good performances, with a real sense of film noir menace.

Fires Were Started (Humphrey Jennings, 1943). This outstanding wartime documentary relates the experiences of a group of firemen through one night of the Blitz. The use of real firemen rather than professional actors, and the avoidance of formulaic heroics, gives the film great power as an account of the courage of ordinary people who fought, often uncelebrated, on the home front.

★ **Great Expectations** (David Lean, 1946). An early film by one of Britain's finest directors – also responsible for *Lawrence of Arabia* and *Bridge on the River Kwai* – this superb rendition of the Dickens novel features magnificent performances by John Mills (as Pip) and Finlay Currie (as Abel Magwitch). The scene in the graveyard will (should) make your hair stand on end.

Henry V (Laurence Olivier, 1944). With dreamlike Technicolor backdrops, this rousing piece of wartime propaganda is emphatically cinematic rather than "theatrical", the action spiralling out from the Globe Theatre itself. Olivier is a brilliantly charismatic king, and the atmospheric pre-battle scene where he goes disguised amongst his men is heartachingly muted.

★ **I Know Where I'm Going!** (Michael Powell and Emeric Pressburger, 1945). Powell and Pressburger made some of the finest British films of all time (see also *A Matter of Life and Death*, *The Life and Death of Colonel Blimp*, *Black Narcissus*, *The Red Shoes* and *A Canterbury Tale*), all of which expose the peculiarities of the British character and reveal hidden depths and longings. In this delightful romance, Wendy Hiller's modern young woman, who knows what she wants and how to get it, is stymied in her goals by the mysterious romanticism of the Scottish islands and their inhabitants.

Jane Eyre (Robert Stevenson, 1943). Joan Fontaine does a fine job of portraying Jane, and Orson Welles is a suavely sardonic Rochester – the scene where he is thrown from his horse in the mist hits the perfect melodramatic pitch. With the unlikely tagline "A Love Story Every Woman Would Die a Thousand Deaths to Live!", it briefly features a young Elizabeth Taylor as a dying Helen Burns.

Kind Hearts and Coronets (Robert Hamer, 1949). As with the best of the Ealing movies, this is a savage comedy on the cruel absurdities of the British class system. With increasing ingenuity, Dennis Price's suave and ruthless anti-hero murders his way through the d'Ascoyne clan (all brilliantly played by Alec Guinness) to claim the family title.

Rebecca (Alfred Hitchcock, 1940). Hitchcock does Du Maurier: Laurence Olivier is wonderfully enigmatic as Maxim de Winter, and Joan Fontaine glows as his meek second wife, living in the shadow of her mysterious predecessor.

The Thirty-Nine Steps (Alfred Hitchcock, 1935). Hitchcock's best-loved British movie, full of wit and bold acts of derring-do. Robert Donat stars as innocent Richard Hannay, inadvertently caught up in a mysterious spy ring and forced to flee both the spies and Scotland Yard. In a typically perverse Hitchcock touch, he spends a generous amount of time handcuffed to Madeleine Carroll, fleeing across the Scottish countryside, before the action returns to London for the film's great music-hall conclusion.

★ **The Wicked Lady** (Leslie Arliss, 1945). One of the best of Gainsborough Studios' series of escapist romances, this features a magnificently amoral and headstrong Margaret Lockwood, wooed into a criminal double life by James Mason's dashing highwayman. Its opulent re-creation of eighteenth-century England is appealing, as are the tempestuous entanglements of its two wayward stars.

★ **Wuthering Heights** (William Wyler, 1939). The version of Emily Brontë's novel that everyone remembers, with Laurence Olivier as the dysfunctional Heathcliff and Merle Oberon as Cathy. It's tense, passionate and wild, and lays proper emphasis on the Yorkshire landscape, the best of all possible places for doomed lovers.

1950 TO 1970

Billy Liar! (John Schlesinger, 1963). Tom Courtenay is Billy, stuck in a dire job as an undertaker's clerk in a northern town, spending his time creating extravagant fantasies. His life is lit up by the appearance of Julie Christie, who holds out the glamour and promise of swinging London.

Carry On Screaming (Gerald Thomas, 1966). One of the best from the Carry On crew, with many of the usual suspects (Kenneth Williams, Charles Hawtrey, Joan Sims) hamming it up with the usual nudge-nudge merriment in a Hammer Horror spoof.

Far From the Madding Crowd (John Schlesinger, 1967). An imaginative adaptation of Hardy's doom-laden tale of the desires and ambitions of wilful/wishful Bathsheba Everdene. Julie Christie is a radiant and spirited Bathsheba, Terence Stamp flashes his blade to dynamic effect, Alan Bates is quietly charismatic as dependable Gabriel Oak, and the West Country setting is sparsely beautiful.

★ **Kes** (Kenneth Loach, 1969). The unforgettable story of a neglected Yorkshire schoolboy who finds solace and liberation in training his kestrel. As a still-pertinent commentary on poverty and an impoverished school system, it's bleak but idealistic. Pale and pinched David Bradley, who plays Billy Casper, is hugely affecting.

★ **The Ladykillers** (Alexander Mackendrick, 1955). Alec Guinness is fabulously toothy and malevolent as "Professor Marcus", a murderous con man who lodges with a sweet little old lady, Mrs Wilberforce, in this skewed Ealing comedy.

A Man for All Seasons (Fred Zinnemann, 1966). Sir Thomas More takes on Henry VIII in one of British history's great moral confrontations. Robert Bolt's wry screenplay, muted visuals and a heavenly host of theatrical talent (including Orson Welles as Cardinal Wolsey) add to the spectacle if not the tension, which is where the film dithers.

★ **Night and the City** (Jules Dassin, 1950). Great film noir, with Richard Widmark as an anxious nightclub hustler on the run. It's gripping and convincingly sleazy, and the London streetscapes have an Expressionist edge of horror.

Saturday Night and Sunday Morning (Karel Reisz, 1960). Reisz's monochrome captures all the grit and dead-end grind of Albert Finney's life working in a Nottingham bicycle factory – and then his attempts to find excitement in the city's pubs and on its canal banks.

This Sporting Life (Lindsay Anderson, 1963). One of the key British films of the 1960s, and a classic of the gritty "kitchen sink" genre. In the story of a Northern miner turned star player for his local rugby league team, the young Richard Harris gives a great performance as the inarticulate anti-hero, able only to express himself through physical violence.

Zulu (Cy Endfield, 1964). This lively portrayal of a Welsh Regiment's heroic final stand against the Zulu Nation in 1879 may not stick to the facts – the real regiment wasn't entirely Welsh, and the tear-jerking round of *Men of Harlech* never happened – but this is one of the best war movies ever made, with a young Michael Caine in his first starring role.

THE 1970S AND 1980S

★ **Babylon** (Franco Rosso, 1980). A moving account of black working-class London life. We follow the experiences of young Blue through a series of encounters that reveal the nation's insidious racism. Good performances and a great reggae soundtrack: an all too rare example of Black Britain taking centre stage in a British movie.

Comrades (Bill Douglas, 1986). In 1830s England, a group of farm workers decide to stand up to the exploitative tactics of the local landowner, and find themselves prosecuted and transported to Australia. Based on the true story of the Tolpuddle Martyrs, this combines political education with a visually stunning celebration of working lives – but it does ramble.

★ **Distant Voices, Still Lives** (Terence Davies, 1988). Beautifully realized autobiographical tale of growing up in Liverpool in the 1940s and 1950s. The mesmeric pace is punctuated by astonishing moments of drama, and the whole is a very moving account of how a family survives and triumphs, in small ways, against the odds.

Get Carter (Mike Hodges, 1971). Vivid British gangster movie, featuring a hard-nosed Michael Caine as the eponymous hero-villain, returning to his native Newcastle to avenge his brother's death. Great use of its Northeastern locations and a fine turn by playwright John Osborne as the local godfather.

Hope and Glory (John Boorman, 1987). A glorious autobiographical feature about the Blitz seen through the eyes of 9-year-old Bill, who revels in the liberating chaos of bomb-site playgrounds, tumbling barrage balloons and shrapnel collections.

The Last of England (Derek Jarman, 1987). Jarman was a genuine maverick in Eighties Britain and this is his most abstract account of the state of the nation. Composed of apparently unrelated shots of decaying London landscapes, rent boys, and references to emblematic national events such as the Falklands War, this may not be to all tastes, but it is a fitting testament to Jarman's unique talent.

Monty Python and the Holy Grail (The Monty Python team, 1974). You can't get much more British than the surreal Monty Python crew, and this daft movie, loosely based on the stories of King Arthur and the Holy Grail, remains fresh and funny today with its exuberant combination of histrionics, slick slapstick and clever wordplay.

★ **My Beautiful Laundrette** (Stephen Frears, 1985). A slice of Thatcher's Britain, with a young, on-the-make Asian, Omar, opening a ritzy laundrette in London. His lover, Johnny (Daniel Day-Lewis), is an ex-National Front glamour boy, angry and inarticulate when forced by the acquisitive Omar into a menial role in the laundrette. The racial, sexual and class dynamics of their relationship mirror the tensions in the city itself.

Withnail and I (Bruce Robinson, 1986). Richard E. Grant is superb as the raddled, drunken Withnail, a "resting" actor with a penchant for drinking lighter fluid. Paul McGann is the "I" of the title – a bemused spectator of Withnail's wild excesses, as they abandon their grotty London flat for a remote country cottage, and the attentions of Withnail's randy Uncle Monty.

THE 1990S

★ **Bhaji on the Beach** (Gurinder Chadha, 1993). An Asian women's group takes a day-trip to Blackpool in this issue-laden but enjoyable picture. A lot of fun is had contrasting the seamier side of British life with the mores of the Asian aunties, though the male characters are cartoon villains all.

Braveheart (Mel Gibson, 1995). Enjoyable cod-Highland camp, with a shaggy-haired Mel Gibson wielding his claymore as thirteenth-century Scottish nationalist William Wallace. The English are thieving effete scum, the Scots all warm-blooded noble savages, and history takes a back seat. Filmed largely in Ireland.

Breaking the Waves (Lars von Trier, 1996). A lyrical, moving drama set in a devout community in the north of Scotland. An innocent young woman, Bess (Emily Watson), falls in love with Danish oil-rig worker Jan (Stellan Skarsgaard). Blaming herself for the injury that cripples him, she embarks on a masochistic sexual odyssey, which rapidly takes her into uncharted waters.

East Is East (Damien O'Donnell, 1999). Seventies Salford is the setting for this lively tragi-comedy, with a Pakistani chip-shop owner struggling to keep control of his seven children as they rail against the strictures of Islam and arranged marriages. Inventively made, and with some pleasing performances.

Elizabeth (Shekhar Kapur, 1998). Cate Blanchett is stunning in this visually beautiful, Gothic production, where the young, innocent Elizabeth slowly adapts to the role of the "Virgin Queen" in order to survive. It's better than its sequel *Elizabeth: The Golden Age* (2007), which also stars Blanchett, and focuses on the defeat of the Spanish Armada.

The Full Monty (Peter Cattaneo, 1997). Set in Sheffield, where six unemployed former steel workers throw caution to the wind and become male strippers, their boast being that all will be revealed in the "full monty". Unpromising physical specimens all, they score an unlikely hit with the local lasses. The film was itself an unlikely hit worldwide and the long-awaited striptease is a joy to behold.

The Madness of King George (Nicholas Hytner, 1994). Adapted from a witty Alan Bennett play, this royal romp is handsomely staged, with the king's loopy antics (a wonderfully nuanced performance from Nigel Hawthorne) played out against a cartoon-like court and its acolytes. Rupert Everett is superb as the effete Prince Regent.

Nil by Mouth (Gary Oldman, 1997). With strong performances by Ray Winstone as a brutish south Londoner and Kathy Burke as his battered wife, this brave and bleak picture delves deep into domestic violence and drug/drink addiction. Brace yourself.

★ **Orlando** (Sally Potter, 1993). An exhilaratingly ambitious rendition of Virginia Woolf's novel, with time, space and gender in constant flux as Tilda Swinton's picaresque nobleman romps through various historical eras. Look out for Quentin Crisp as Queen Elizabeth I.

Ratcatcher (Lynne Ramsay, 1999). Set in 1970s Glasgow during a refuse-workers' strike, Ramsay's striking first feature follows 12-year-old James, who is implicated in the accidental drowning of his friend as the rubbish around the tenement blocks mounts. Weaving rich humour into the gloomy narrative, Ramsay layers poetic images of the city, rejecting realism in favour of a lyrical, symbolic approach.

The Remains of the Day (James Ivory, 1993). Kazuo Ishiguro's masterly novel of social and personal repression translates beautifully to the big screen. Anthony Hopkins is the overly decorous butler who gradually becomes aware of his master's fascist connections, Emma Thompson the housekeeper who struggles to bring his real, deeply suppressed feelings to the surface.

Richard III (Richard Loncraine, 1995). A splendid film version of a renowned National Theatre production, which brilliantly transposed the action to a fascist state in the 1930s. The infernal political machinations of a snarling Ian McKellen as Richard are heightened by Nazi associations, and the style of the period imbues the film with the requisite glamour, as does languorously drugged Kristin Scott-Thomas as Lady Anne.

Small Faces (Gillies MacKinnon, 1995). A moving little saga about the lives of three brothers growing up in 1960s Glasgow amid feuding gangs of local teenagers. We follow the rough education of young Lex, torn between the excitement and real danger of a life of fighting, and the alternative artistic ambitions of his older brother.

★ **Trainspotting** (Danny Boyle, 1996). High-octane dip into the heroin-scarred world of a group of young Scotsmen, including what might be the best cinematic representation of a heroin fix ever.

Wonderland (Michael Winterbottom, 1999). One Bonfire Night in London as experienced by three unhappy sisters. Winterbottom's use of real locations, natural light and 16mm film gives it a naturalistic air that's also dreamlike, an effect heightened by Michael Nyman's haunting score.

2000S

24 Hour Party People (Michael Winterbottom, 2002). Steve Coogan plays the entrepreneurial/inspirational Tony Wilson in this fast-moving recreation of the early days of Manchester's Factory Records. Stunning soundtrack too.

Atonement (Joe Wright, 2007). This adaptation of Ian McEwan's highly literary novel of misunderstanding and regret benefits from strong performances from Keira Knightley and James McAvoy and fluent plotting, though the set-piece one-take Dunkirk scene, while clever, comes across as a tad showy.

Bend It Like Beckham (Gurinder Chadha, 2003). Immensely successful film focusing on the coming of age of a football-loving Punjabi girl in a suburb of London. Both socially acute and comic.

Bridget Jones's Diary (Sharon Maguire, 2001). American Renée Zellweger put on a plummy English accent and several pounds to play the lead in this *Pride and Prejudice* for the new millennium. Ably assisted by deliciously nasty love-interest Hugh Grant, the film stands out as one of the better British romcoms of recent years.

★ **Bronson** (Nicolas Winding Refn, 2009). The subject matter may seem unappetizing – Welsh criminal Bronson (Tom Hardy) is reputed to be the most violent man ever locked up in a British prison – and it's not easy viewing, but Refn's take on this unusual anti-hero is inventive, creative and insightful.

Control (Anton Corbijn, 2007). Ian Curtis, the lead singer of Joy Division, committed suicide in 1980 at the age of 23. This biopic tracks his life in and around Manchester, based on the account provided by his wife, Deborah. Some have raved over Sam Riley's portrayal of Curtis, others have been less convinced, but as an evocation of the early days of Factory Records it's hard to beat.

Dirty Pretty Things (Stephen Frears, 2003). A tumbling mix of melodrama, social criticism and black comedy, this forceful, thought-provoking film explores the world of Britain's illegal migrants.

Gosford Park (Robert Altman, 2001). Astutely observed upstairs-downstairs murder mystery set in class-ridden 1930s England. The multi-layered plot is typical of the director, the script, from Julian Fellowes, is more nuanced than some of his later TV work, and the who's who of great British actors is led by the superb Maggie Smith.

Harry Potter and the Philosopher's Stone (Chris Columbus, 2001). The first film in a series about hero Harry Potter's life at wizard school did wonders for the English tourist industry with its use of places such as Alnwick Castle as locations. The subsequent films are also darkly enjoyable, with excellent ensemble casts – Spall, Gambon, Rickman et al.

In the Loop (Armando Iannucci, 2009). Look what we have to put up with from our politicians, screams Iannucci, in this satire on the opaque and corrupt meanderings of our leaders and their assorted advisors.

The King's Speech (Tom Hooper, 2010). This massive, Oscar-scooping hit hints at the rotten core at the heart of the monarchy without demonizing the royals. Colin Firth is suitably repressed as the vocally challenged King George VI who is given the confidence to become king by Geoffrey Rush's exuberant Australian speech therapist, and there are superb performances from Helena Bonham Carter as his imperious wife (later to become the Queen Mother) and Guy Pearce as the spoiled, tormented Edward VIII.

London to Brighton (Paul Andrew Williams, 2006). Shot on a minimal budget by an unknown writer/director and unknown actors, this thriller follows a prostitute and a 12-year-old runaway fleeing from the criminal underworld. The sordid storyline and bleak settings are quintessentially British, making even Brighton look like hell, but the film has a raw charm that is all its own.

Made in Dagenham (Nigel Cole, 2010). Good-hearted, good-natured film about the struggle for equal pay in the car industry in 1960s Britain.

The Queen (Stephen Frears, 2006). Dame Helen Mirren became an official national treasure after taking on the royal of Her Majesty in this PR movie for the palace, which covers the crisis in the monarchy after the death of Princess Diana. Michael Sheen does a great Tony Blair impression, while Sylvia Sims brings a dash of humour to the role of Queen Mum.

Sexy Beast (Jonathan Glazer, 2000). Gangster thriller distinguished by the performances of Ray Winstone and more especially Ben Kingsley, who plays one of the hardest, meanest criminals ever.

★ **This is England** (Shane Meadows, 2007). British cinema rarely ventures into the East Midlands, but this is where Shane Meadows is at home. Set in the early 1980s, this thoughtful film deals with a young working-class lad who falls in with skinheads – the good-hearted ones to begin with, the racists thereafter. If it gives you a taste for Meadows, see also his *Dead Man's Shoes* (2004), a searing tale of revenge for the cruel murder of the protagonist's brother; again, there's a Midlands setting.

★ **Vera Drake** (Mike Leigh, 2004). Moving story of a 1950s working-class woman, who performs illegal abortions from the goodness of her heart and without thought for either money or the legal consequences, which eventually threaten to destroy her and her close-knit family. A powerful counterblast to the anti-abortion lobby.

Wuthering Heights (Andrea Arnold, 2011). Arnold, whose previous movies were set in urban council estates – *Red Road*, which used CCTV to tell a story of obsession in Glasgow, and *Fish Tank*, a searing coming of age tale – demonstrates a lyrical eye for the natural world in her arty, elemental reworking of Emily Brontë's romantic tragedy, in which Heathcliff is a black boy and the emotions are bruisingly raw.

Small print and index

988 Small print
989 About the authors
991 Index
1006 Map symbols

A ROUGH GUIDE TO ROUGH GUIDES

Published in 1982, the first Rough Guide – to Greece – was a student scheme that became a publishing phenomenon. Mark Ellingham, a recent graduate in English from Bristol University, had been travelling in Greece the previous summer and couldn't find the right guidebook. With a small group of friends he wrote his own guide, combining a highly contemporary, journalistic style with a thoroughly practical approach to travellers' needs.

The immediate success of the book spawned a series that rapidly covered dozens of destinations. And, in addition to impecunious backpackers, Rough Guides soon acquired a much broader readership that relished the guides' wit and inquisitiveness as much as their enthusiastic, critical approach and value-for-money ethos.

These days, Rough Guides include recommendations from budget to luxury and cover more than 200 destinations around the globe, as well as producing an ever-growing range of eBooks and apps.

Visit **roughguides.com** to see our latest publications.

Rough Guide credits

Editor: Samantha Cook
Layout: Nikhil Agarwal
Cartography: Ashutosh Bharti
Picture editor: Rhiannon Furbear
Proofreader: Susanne Hillen
Managing editor: Alice Park
Assistant editor: Dipika Dasgupta
Production: Rebecca Short
Cover design: Rhiannon Furbear, Nikhil Agarwal
Editorial assistant: Lorna North, Eleanor Aldridge
Senior pre-press designer: Dan May
Design director: Scott Stickland
Travel publisher: Joanna Kirby
Digital travel publisher: Peter Buckley
Reference director: Andrew Lockett
Operations coordinator: Becky Doyle
Operations assistant: Johanna Wurm
Publishing director (Travel): Clare Currie
Commercial manager: Gino Magnotta
Managing director: John Duhigg

Publishing information

This eighth edition published March 2012 by
Rough Guides Ltd,
80 Strand, London WC2R 0RL
11, Community Centre, Panchsheel Park,
New Delhi 110017, India
Distributed by the Penguin Group
Penguin Books Ltd,
80 Strand, London WC2R 0RL
Penguin Group (USA)
375 Hudson Street, NY 10014, USA
Penguin Group (Australia)
250 Camberwell Road, Camberwell,
Victoria 3124, Australia
Penguin Group (NZ)
67 Apollo Drive, Mairangi Bay, Auckland 1310,
New Zealand
Rough Guides is represented in Canada by Tourmaline Editions Inc. 662 King Street West, Suite 304, Toronto, Ontario M5V 1M7
Printed in Singapore
© Rough Guides 2012
Maps © Rough Guides

No part of this book may be reproduced in any form without permission from the publisher except for the quotation of brief passages in reviews.
1008pp includes index
A catalogue record for this book is available from the British Library
Trade edition: ISBN: 978-1-84836-679-4
UK promotional edition only: ISBN: 978-1-40936-028-5
The publishers and authors have done their best to ensure the accuracy and currency of all the information in **The Rough Guide to Britain**, however, they can accept no responsibility for any loss, injury, or inconvenience sustained by any traveller as a result of information or advice contained in the guide.
1 3 5 7 9 8 6 4 2

FSC www.fsc.org MIX Paper from responsible sources FSC™ C018179

Help us update

We've gone to a lot of effort to ensure that the eighth edition of **The Rough Guide to Britain** is accurate and up-to-date. However, things change – places get "discovered", opening hours are notoriously fickle, restaurants and rooms raise prices or lower standards. If you feel we've got it wrong or left something out, we'd like to know, and if you can remember the address, the price, the hours, the phone number, so much the better.

Please send your comments with the subject line "**Rough Guide Britain Update**" to Ⓔ mail@uk.roughguides.com. We'll credit all contributions and send a copy of the next edition (or any other Rough Guide if you prefer) for the very best emails.

Find more travel information, connect with fellow travellers and book your trip on Ⓦ roughguides.com

ABOUT THE AUTHORS

Rob Andrews has written Rough Guides to Devon & Cornwall and Somerset, as well as various parts of Italy.

Jules Brown is the author of the *Rough Guide to the Lake District* and co-author of the *Rough Guide to England*.

Tim Burford After two decades of writing about Eastern Europe, Latin America and even Alaska, the arrival of a Welsh girlfriend and her friends has led me to explore at least one corner of my home island. Diolch– it's been great!

Dan Hodgkinson Despite a career travelling to remote corners of Africa, Dan Hodgkinson remains a loving son of Manchester – his family home and the subject of a forthcoming intellectual history that he is co-authoring.

Rob Humphreys has lived in London for over twenty years. He recently qualified as a City of London Tour Guide and spends his spare time directing shows on the Puppet Theatre Barge.

Phil Lee has been writing for Rough Guides for well over twenty years. He lives in Nottingham, where he was born and watered.

Norm Longley is a regular visitor to Wales from his home in Bath, and has a particular fondness for the Brecons and the Gower. He is also the author of Rough Guides to Slovenia, Montenegro, Hungary and Romania.

Donald Reid is the author or co-author of four Rough Guides covering Scotland and South Africa. Based in Edinburgh, he works as a freelance editor and writer, mainly in the realm of Scottish food and drink.

Claire Saunders worked for Rough Guides as an editor and then Managing Editor for nine years before moving to Lewes in East Sussex, where she now lives and works.

Jos Simon was raised on the Llŷn Peninsula in North Wales and, after teaching here and there, settled in Yorkshire. Having come late to travel writing, and after authoring several guidebooks, he satisfied a long-held ambition to describe his adopted county, first by writing the *Rough Guide to Yorkshire*, then by updating the relevant chapters of the Rough Guides to England and Britain.

Helena Smith is a travel writer and photographer. She blogs about food and her community at eathackney.com.

Gavin Thomas has written and contributed to numerous Rough Guides over the past decade. A reformed ex-Londoner, he now lives in a small town in the Chilterns, from where he covered Oxford and the Cotswolds for this edition of the guide.

Amanda Tomlin and Matthew Hancock are authors of the *Rough Guide to Hampshire, Dorset and the Isle of Wight*. Matthew Hancock is also author of the Rough Guides to Portugal, Madeira, Lisbon and the Algarve.

Lucy White During normal waking hours, Lucy is an editor at Rough Guides, but has also found time to contribute to a few books as an author, including the Rough Guides to France and England. A Yorkshire girl at heart, she nevertheless has a very soft spot for the Northeast and rates its beautiful beaches as the best in Britain.

Paul Whitfield's earliest memory of Wales is burying his plastic boat on the beach at Rhos and being unable to find it again. Since then he's tried to be less forgetful when researching the *Rough Guide to Wales*. He now lives in New Zealand.

Acknowledgements

Robert Andrews I'd like to acknowledge the Queen of Belfast City.

Tim Burford Thanks above all to Freddie and Robbie in Haverfordwest, and to Ceri Jones and Jane Harris at Visit Wales, Susan Owen at Carmarthenshire Tourism, Mike and Jill at the *Drovers Inn*, Llandovery, and Sylvia at the *New White Lion*, Llandovery. Also to Katy, Norm, Paul and all at Rough Guides.

Dan Hodgkinson Thanks to Lorna Richardson, Ian Little, Tom Raines, Tim Archer and Saoirse Townshend.

Phil Lee would like to thank his editor, Sam Cook, for her diligent attention to detail during the preparation of this new edition of the guide. Special thanks also to Kate Eccles at Marketing Birmingham; Ellen at the *Adelphi Guest House*; Michelle Marriott-Lodge at the *Castle Hotel*; Pat and Joan Chapman at Grosvenor House; Melanie Cook of VisitNorwich; Pat Edgar; Martyn Livermore for bags of tips; Kathryn McGarr; Pam Farrell; Jeanette Goodrich; Paul Dickson; Rebecca Scott for her comments and commentary; Squeak of *Kiwi Inns*; Regis Crepy at the *Great House*, Lavenham; Pat Edgar of PR Matters; and Emma Rees for the chance to eat a squirrel.

Norm Longley would like to offer special thanks to Ceri Jones and Jane Harris at Visit Wales.

Claire Saunders would like to thank Sam for perfect project management, Ian for the long weekends of solo parenting, Pauline for putting me up in Whitstable, and mum for her company on the long drives around Kent.

Jos Simon would like to thank Andrew Denton at Welcome to Yorkshire for lots of practical support, Catherine and Matt for invaluable help with research, and Samantha Cook for highly sympathetic editing.

Helena Smith Thanks to editor Sam for her care and patience, and Colin Campbell for the sneak peek at the Riverside Museum in Glasgow.

Gavin Thomas At Rough Guides, thanks to Ed Aves for giving me the job, and Sam Cook, for helping to knock it all into shape with her customary aplomb. In Oxford and the Cotswolds thanks to Jean-Marie and Clare Lauzier, Chris Dee, Judith Diment, Heather Armitage, Melissa Jones, Mhairi Smith, and all the many unpaid and under-appreciated staff at tourist offices and other attractions around the region who provided me with reams of invaluable information en route.

Lucy White would like to thank all those who helped on her wet and windy trip round the Northeast, including a long-suffering Caroline, Robin and Inca. Thanks, too, to Sam for being a great editor as usual, and to Christopher for general support and patience.

Paul Whitfield Thanks a heap to Ceri Jones at Visit Wales, Jim for showing me the coast of Anglesey and Mike for pointers, inspiration and a good roast.

Photo credits

All photos © Rough Guides except the following:
(Key: t-top; c-centre; b-bottom; l-left; r-right)

p.1 4Corners: Colin Dutton
p.2 AWL Images: David Bank
p.4 Corbis: Jane Sweeney (tl). Dorling Kindersley (tc)
p.5 AWL Images: Travel Pix Collection
p.9 Corbis: Gavin Hellier (tl). AWL Images: David Bank (b)
p.10 Alamy: Ian Dagnall
p.11 Alamy: BANANA PANCAKE (tr); Vanda Ralevska (br); Hazlitt's hotel (c)
p.12 Getty Images: Duncan Shaw
p.13 Corbis: Frank Krahmer
p.15 Corbis: Robbie Jack (bl)
p.16 Photolibrary
p.17 Alamy: Tim Gartside (t); Getty Images: Shirlaine Forrest/WireImage (c); AWL Images: Travel Pix Collection (b)
p.18 Alamy: Arch White (t). NHPA/Photoshot: Karen van der Zijden (c). AWL Images: Travel Pix Collection (b)
p.19 Alamy: Neil Setchfield (tr); Getty Images: Jeff J Mitchell (br)
p.20 Alamy: Tony Wright/earthscapes (tr); Corbis: Eric Nathan/Loop Images (br)
p.21 Alamy: David Pick (t); Imagestate Media Partners Limited – Impact Photos (c); John Morrison (b)
p.22 Corbis: Robert Harding World Imagery (t); AWL Images: Travel Pix Collection (b)
p.23 Alamy: Michael Jenner (tr); Tim E White (tl); Getty Images: Matt Cardy (br)
p.24 AWL Images: Travel Pix Collection (t); Corbis: Chris Warren/Loop Images (c); Alamy: Mike Sivyer (b)
p.25 Alamy: Premier (bl); travelib europe (br)
p.28 Corbis: David Tipling/Robert Harding World Imagery
p.55 Getty Images: EIGHTFISH
p.132 Corbis: John Miller/Robert Harding World Imagery
p.151 Alamy: TTL Images (tr)
p.197 Corbis: Jason Hawkes (t)
p.284 Corbis: Roy Rainford/Robert Harding World Imagery
p.313 Corbis: Frank Krahmer (tl)
p.374 Corbis: Neale Clarke/Robert Harding World Imagery
p.395 Corbis: Robbie Jack (t); Getty Images: Neale Clarke/Robert Harding World Imagery (b)
p.414 Photolibrary
p.442 Getty Images: Steve Allen
p.445 Alamy: eye35.com
p.461 AWL Images: Carlos Sanchez Pereyra (tr); Photolibrary (b)
p.482 Corbis: John Short/Design Pics
p.508 Corbis: Wig Worland
p.511 Alamy: Wildscape
p.561 Corbis: Roy Rainford/Robert Harding World Imagery
p.579 Corbis: Neale Clark/Robert Harding World Imagery (t); Ocean (b)
p.598 Corbis: Chris Warren/Loop Images
p.644 Superstock: Chris Warren/Purestock
p.681 Alamy: ImageState
p.695 Superstock: Chris Warren (c)
p.748 Superstock: Travel Library Limited
p.751 Alamy: Stephen Miller
p.770 Getty Images: Jeff J Mitchell
p.799 Corbis: Peter Adams/JAI
p.850 Corbis: Jan Holm/Loop Images
p.853 Alamy: Louisa Macdonell
p.874 Superstock: Alan Majchrowicz
p.877 Alamy: Gary Cook
p.893 Corbis: Kathy Collins/Robert Harding World Imagery
p.912 Superstock: Cody Duncan
p.936 Superstock: Minden Pictures
p.960 Corbis: Bettmann

Front cover St Agnes, Cornwall © Gary Eastwood/Loop Images/Photolibrary
Back cover Sycamore Gap, Hadrian's Wall © Superstock/Lee Frost (t). Southwold beach huts © Rough Guides/Diana Jarvis (cl); Beefeaters © Rough Guides/Tim Draper (cr)

Index

Maps are marked in **grey**

7 Stanes.....758

A

A La Ronde.....292
Abbotsbury.....209
Abbotsford.....753
Aberaeron.....668
Aberconwy House.....706
Abercynon.....609
Aberdare.....610
Aberdaron.....698
Aberdeen.....863–867
Aberdeen, Central.....864
Aberdeenshire.....863
Aberdyfi.....674
Abereiddi.....641
Aberfan (disaster).....609
Aberfeldy.....818, 821
Aberfoyle.....808, 809
Abergavenny.....654
Aberglaslyn Gorge.....692
Aberglasney.....630
Abergwesyn.....658
Abergwili.....629
Abergynolwyn.....674
Aberlour.....870
Abernethy Forest RSPB Reserve.....886
Abersoch.....697
Aberystwyth.....669–671
Aberystwyth.....669
Aboyne.....867
accommodation.....34–36
Achamore Gardens.....842
Achiltibuie.....902
Achmelvich.....903
Achnasheen.....899
Achtercairn.....900
Act of Union.....971
adventure tour operators.....31
Ailsa Craig.....769
Aira Force.....504
Aisholt.....279
Aldeburgh.....347
Alfred the Great, King.....189, 963
Alloway.....767
Allt Coire Gabhail.....891
Allt Dinas.....688
Alnmouth.....592
Alnwick.....592
Alresford.....191
Altarnun.....334
Alternative Technology, Centre for.....673
Althorp.....432
Alton.....191
Alum Bay.....187
Alveston.....382
Alyth.....862
Amberley.....171
Ambleside.....491
An Tairbeart.....930
An Turas.....839
Angel of the North.....578
Anglesey.....700–703
Anglo-Saxons.....962
Angus.....852–863
Anne of Cleves House.....163
Anstruther.....815
Antonine Wall.....962
Aonach Mhor.....890
Applecross peninsula.....898
Appledore.....310
Arbroath.....859
Archiestown.....870
Arden, Mary.....381
Ardminish.....842
Ardnamurchan peninsula.....894
Ardrossan.....843
Ardvasar.....917
Argyll.....826–849
Argyll.....830–831
Arinagour.....838
Arisaig.....895
Armadale.....916
Arnol.....929
Arran, Isle of.....843–845
Arthur, King.....274, 330, 331
Arundel.....170–172
Ascog.....832
Ashby-de-la-Zouch.....429
Askrigg.....531
Assynt.....902
ATMs.....49
Auckland Castle.....569
Austen, Jane.....190, 192, 210, 268
Avalon, Isle of.....275
Avebury.....216
Aviemore.....883–885
Awful Hand Range.....764
Ayr.....766
Ayrshire.....766–769
Aysgarth.....531

B

B&Bs.....35
Badachro.....900
Badbea.....911
Baile Mór.....837
Bakewell.....412
Bala.....685
Balivanich.....933
Ballater.....868
Ballinluig.....818
Balloch.....806
Ballygrant.....848
Balmaha.....807
Balmoral.....868
Balnakiel.....904
Balranald RSPB Reserve.....932
Baltasound.....958
Bamburgh.....594
Banff.....871
Bangor.....703
bank holidays.....50
Bannockburn, Battle of.....804, 966
Barabhas.....928
Barafundle Bay.....635
Barden Bridge.....526
Barden Tower.....526
Bardsey Island.....698
Barnard Castle.....569
Barnstaple.....307
Barra.....934
Barraigh.....934
Barrasford.....586
Barricane Beach.....308
Barrie, J.M., birthplace.....862
bars.....38
Baslow.....413
Bass Rock.....744
Bateman's.....158
Bath.....265–271
Bath.....266
Bath, Somerset and Bristol.....258
Bathampton.....270
Battle.....157
Bayard's Cove.....298
Beachy Head.....160
Beadnell.....593
Bealach na Bà.....898
Beamish Museum.....568
Beatles, The.....466
Beau Nash, Richard.....267
Beaulieu.....194
Beaumaris.....700, 701
Becket, Thomas à.....964
Beddgelert.....691
Bede, Venerable.....584
Bedruthan Steps.....330
beer.....38

Beer....293
Beinn a'Bhragaidh....910
Beinn Eighe....899
Beinn na Faoghla....932
Belas Knap....247
Bellever Forest....304
Bellever Tor....304
Bellingham....588
Bempton....546
Ben Alder....823
Ben Hope....905
Ben Lawers....822
Ben Lomond....809
Ben Loyal....905
Ben More....836
Ben Nevis....889
Benavie....880
Benbecula....932
Berneray....932
Berwick-upon-Tweed....596
Bess of Hardwick....425
Bettyhill....905
Betws-y-Coed....686–689
Beverley....545
Bhearnaraigh....932
Biddenden....155
Bideford....310
Big Pit National Mining Museum....608
Big Sand....900
Biggin Dale....408
Bignor Roman Villa....171
Binchester Roman Fort....569
Birdoswald Fort....507
Birmingham....399–405
Birmingham....400
Birnam....821
Birsay....943
Bishop Auckland....569
Bishops Lydeard....278
Black Cuillin, The....919
Black Isle, The....908
Black Mountains, The....653
Blackpool....470–473
Blackpool....470
Blackpool Sands (Devon)....298
Blackwall (Lake District)....490
Blackwaterfoot....844
Blaenafon....607
Blaenau Ffestiniog....692
Blair Atholl....824
Blair Castle....825
Blairgowrie....861
Blakeney....360
Blakeney Point....359
Blenheim Palace....238
Blisland....333
Blists Hill....394
Bloomsbury Group, The....163
Blue John (fluorspar)....411
Bodelwyddan Castle....709
Bodiam Castle....158
Bodleian Library....232
Bodmin....333
Bodmin Moor....332–335
Bodnant Garden....706
Boggle Hole....553
Bolton Abbey....526
Bolton Castle....532
Bolventor....334
Bonchurch....186
Bonfire Societies, Lewes....162
Bonnie Prince Charlie....883, 895, 922, 934, 972
books....978–982
Boot....501
Borders, The Scottish....750–759
Borrowdale....499
Boscastle....331
Boscombe....196
Bosherton....635
Boswinger....317
Bosworth Field, Battle of....429
bothies....36
Bournemouth....196
Bourton-on-the-Water....245
Bowhill House....756
Bowland, Forest of....474
Bowmore....847
Bowness-on-Windermere....490
Bradford....523
Brading....185
Brae....956
Braemar....868
Brancaster Staithe....362
Brantwood....495
Bray....224
Breachacha....839
Brecon....650
Brecon....650
Brecon Beacons National Park....650–654
Breedon-on-the-Hill....430
Brent Tor....305
Bressay....953
Bridge of Allan....805
Bridges Long Mynd....397
Bridgwater....278
Bridlington....546
Bridport....210
Brig o'Turk....810
Brighton....164–170
Brighton....165
Bristol, Bath and Somerset....254–283
Bristol, Bath and Somerset....258
Bristol....256–265
Bristol....260
British embassies....47
British Golf Museum....813
Britten, Benjamin....347
Brixham....295
Broad Haven....635
Broadford....918
Broads, The Norfolk....357
Broadstairs....141
Broadway....247
Broch of Gurness....943
Brockenhurst....196
Brockhole....489
Brodgar, Ring of....942
Brodick....843
Brontës, The....524
Broughton House....764
Broughty Ferry....858
Brown Willy....334
Brownsea Island....200
Bruce, Robert the....817, 966
Brunel, Isambard Kingdom....256, 262
Brynrefail....691
Buachaille Etive Beag....891
Buckie....872
Buckland Abbey....301
Buckland-in-the-Moor....304
Buckler's Hard....195
Bude....332
Bull Ring, Birmingham....401
bunkhouses....36
Burford....241
Burghley House....441
Burnham Deepdale....362
Burnham Market....362
Burns, Robert....761, 767, 768
Burravoe....957
Burry Holms....627
Burton Bradstock....210
Burwash....158
buses
to Britain....30
within Britain....33
Bute, Isle of....828
Butetown....616
Butt of Lewis....929
Buttermere....501
Butteryhaugh....589
Buxton....408–410
Buxton....409
Bwlch Nant yr Arian....672

C

Cadair Idris....675
CADW Welsh Historic Monuments....46
Caerfai Bay....641
Caerhays Castle....316
Caerlaverock Castle....761
Caerlaverock Wildfowl and Wetlands Centre....762
Caernarfon....699
Caernarfon....699
Caerphilly....617

Cairn Gorm Mountain 886
Cairnbaan 841
Cairngorms, The 883
Cairngorms National Park 886
Cairnryan 766
Cairnwell Pass 861
Calanais 929
Caldey Island 633
Caledonian Canal 889
Calf of Man 479
Callander 809
Callanish 929
Camber Sands 159
Cambrian coast, The.... 666–677
Cambridge 366–373
Cambridge 367
Camelford 331, 334
Campbeltown 842
camping 36
CAMRA 39
Camusterrach 898
Canna 926
Cannich 888
Canterbury 142–147
Canterbury 143
Canute 963
Cape Cornwall 324
Cape Wrath 905
Capel Curig 688
Captain Cook 555, 557
car rental 34
Carbisdale Castle 909
Cardiff 611–620
Cardiff Bay 615
Cardiff, Central 612
- accommodation 618
- arrival 617
- Butetown 616
- Cardiff Arcades 613
- Cardiff Bay 614
- Cardiff Bay Barrage 616
- Cardiff Castle 613
- Cardiff Story, The 613
- Cathays Park 613
- drinking 619
- eating 618
- information 618
- Mermaid Quay 615
- Millennium Stadium 611
- National Assembly for Wales 615
- National Museum and Gallery 614
- nightlife 620
- Norwegian church 615
- performing arts 620
- Pierhead Building 615
- transport 618
- Wales Millennium Centre 615

Cardigan 666
Carew 637
Carisbrooke Castle 189
Carlisle 505–507
Carlisle 506
Carlisle to Settle Railway 529
Carmarthen 629
Carmarthenshire 628–634
Carn Ingli 643
Carreg Cennan Castle 631
Cartmel 488
Castell Coch 616
Castell Dinas Brân 684
Castell-y-Bere 674
Castle Douglas 763
Castle Drogo 304
Castle Howard 541
Castle O'Burrian 947
Castle Rushen 480
Castle Urquhart 888
Castlebay 934
Castlerigg Stone Circle 498
Castleton 410
Castletown 480
Cat Bells 499
Cecil, William 439
cell phones 50
Celtic Football Club 786
Celtic languages 963
Celts, The 961
Central Scotland 796–825
Central Scotland 800–801
Cerne Abbas 205
Chagford 304
Channel Ports, The 148
Chanonry Point 885, 908
Charleston Farmhouse 163
Charlestown 315
Charmouth 211
Chartists, The 605, 973
Chartwell 154
Chatham 138
Chatsworth House 413
Chawton 192
Cheddar caves 274
Cheddar Gorge 273
Cheesewring 335
Cheltenham 248
Cheltenham 248
chemists 48
Chepstow 603
Chesil Beach 209
Chester 458–462
Chester 459
Chesters Roman Fort 584
Cheviot Hills, The 588
Chichester 172
Chigford 306
children, travellers with 51
Chillingham Castle 590
Chiltern Hills, The 223
Chipping Campden 246
choirs, Welsh male voice 610
Christchurch 199
Christie, Agatha 296
Church Stretton 397
Churchill Barriers 946
Churchill, Winston 154, 238, 975
Chysauster 324
Cilborth Beach 667
Cilgerran 666
cinema 983–986
Cinque Ports, The 148
Cirencester 241
Civil War, The 970
Claerwen Reservoir 659
Clatteringshaws Loch 764
Cleveland Way, The 547–549
Cley-next-the-Sea 359
Clifton, Bristol 262
climate 45
Clitheroe 474
Clouds Hill 202
Clova 863
Clovelly 310
Clyde, The 792–795
Clyde, Glasgow and the 770–795
Clyde, Glasgow and the 774
Clydeside 784
coal mining, South Wales 608
Coalbrookdale 393
Coalport 394
Cockermouth 503
Cockle Strand 934
Coed-y-Brenin 675
Coigach peninsula 902
Coire Dubh 899
Coire Làgan 919
Colchester 340–342
Coleridge Way 278
Coleridge, Samuel Taylor 278, 494
Coll, Isle of 838
Colvend coast, The 762
Combe Florey 278
Compton Acres 200
Compton Bay 187
concessionary rates 47
congestion charge (London) 111
Coniston village 495
Coniston Water 494–496
Constable, John 343
Constantine Bay 329
Conwy 705–707
Conwy 705
Conwy Falls 687
Cookham 224
Corfe Castle 202
Corn Du 651
Cornaigmore 840
Cornwall 311–335
Cornwall, Devon and 284–335
Cornwall, Devon and 288
Corran Ferry 894
Corrie 844
Corris Mine 673
Corrour 823
costs 45–47

Cotswolds, The 240–248
Cotswolds, Oxfordshire and the 218–253
Cotswolds, Oxfordshire and the 222
cottages, rental 36
Covenanters, The 969
Coventry Cathedral 385
Coverack 320
Cowes 188
Coxwold 549
Crackington Haven 332
Crag Lough 585
Cragside 589
Craig Goch 659
Craig y Deryn 674
Craigellachie 870
Craighouse 849
Craignure 835
Crail 814
Crannog Centre, Scottish 822
Crantock Beach 328
Craster 593
Crathes Castle 867
credit cards 49
Cregneash 480
Crianlarich 880
Criccieth 696
cricket 43
Crickhowell 653
crime 47
Crinan 841
Croft-on-Tees 573
Cromarty 908
Cromarty Firth 908
Cromer 357
Cromwell, Oliver 365, 970
Crook O' Lune 473
Crooklets 332
Crosby Beach 467
Crowcombe 278
Crown Jewels 85
Croyde Bay 309
Cuillin, The 919
cuisine 37
Cullen 871
Culloden 882
Culnaknock 923
Culross 816
Culzean Castle 768
Cumbria and the Lakes 482–507
Cumbria and the Lakes 486
Cupar 814
currency 49
Cwm Idwal 689
cycling 34, 43
Cynon Valley, The 608

D

Dalabrog 933
Dale 638
Dalemain 505
Dales Way, The 526
Daliburgh 933
Danelaw 963
Dan-yr-ogof showcaves 652
Darlington 573
Dartmeet 304
Dartmoor 302–307
Dartmoor 303
Dartmouth 297
Dartmouth Steam Railway 295
Daymer Bay 329
Deal 149
Dedham 343
Dee Valley, The 680
Deeside 863
Dent 530
Dentdale 530
Derwent Water 498
Destiny, The Stone of 718, 819
Devil's Bowling Green 764
Devil's Bridge 671
Devil's Staircase (Glen Coe) 891
Devil's Staircase (Mid-Wales) 658
Devon 289–311
Devon and Cornwall 284–335
Devon and Cornwall 288
Devorgilla Bridge 759
Dickens, Charles 137, 141, 181
Dimbola Lodge 187
Dinefwr Castle 630
disabilities, travellers with 51
Dissolution of the Monasteries 967
distances, weights and measures 49
Dodman Point 316
Dolgellau 674
Dolgoch 658
Dolgoch Falls 674
dolphins (Moray Firth) 885
Dolydd 700
Domesday Book 964
Dorchester 204–206
Dornoch 909
Dorset, Wiltshire and Hampshire 174–217
Dorset, Wiltshire and Hampshire 178
Douglas 476
Doune 804
Dounreay 906
Dove Cottage 494
Dover 150
Dozmary Pool 331, 334
Dracula 554
Dragon Hill 225
Drewsteignton 304
drinking 38
driving
from Europe 30
in Britain 33
Drumkinnon Tower 806
Drumlanrig Castle 761
Drumnadrochit 887, 882
Dryburgh Abbey 753
Dualchas 935
Duart Castle 835
Dubh Lochan Trail 906
Duckpool 332
Duff House 871
Dufftown 870
Duke's Pass 808
Dulverton 280
Dumbarton 793
Dumfries 759
Dumfries 760
Dumfries and Galloway 759–766
Dumfries House 769
Dun Caan 918
Dùn Charlabhaigh Broch 929
Dun, House of 860
Dunadd 840
Dunblane 804
Duncansby Head 907
Dundee 856–859
Dundee, Central 856
Dunderhole Point 331
Dunfermline 817
Dungeness 152
Dunkeld 820
Dunkery Beacon 280
Dunnet 907
Dunnottar Castle 865
Dunrobin Castle 910
Dunstanburgh Castle 593
Dunster 280
Dunvegan 920
Dunwich 350
Durdle Door 204
Durham 564–568
Durham 564
Durlston Country Park 203
Durness 904
Duxford Imperial War Museum 371
Dwarfie Stane 946
Dysynni Valley, The 674

E

Easby Abbey 532
Eas-Coul-Aulin 903
East Anglia 336–373
East Anglia 340

East Bergholt.....343
East Kilbride.....794
East Lothian..... 743–745
East Lulworth.....203
East Midlands, The..... 414–441
East Midlands, The..... 418
East Neuk, The.....814
Eastbourne..... 160–162
Easton Grey.....244
Edale.....412
Eday.....948
Eden Project, The.....316
Edinburgh and the Lothians..... 710–747
Edinburgh and the Lothians..... 714
Edinburgh..... 712–743
Edinburgh, Central..... 716–717
- accommodation.....736–738
- arrival.....732
- art, contemporary.....729
- Arthur's Seat.....725
- bars.....741
- bistros.....738–741
- Botanic Garden, Royal.....731
- *Britannia, The*.....732
- cafés.....738–741
- Calton Hill.....730
- Canongate.....722
- Castle.....718
- Charlotte Square.....729
- cinema.....743
- clubs.....742
- Crown Jewels.....719
- Crown Square.....719
- dance.....742
- Dance Base.....727
- Dean Gallery, The.....731
- Edinburgh Festival.....734
- gay scene.....742
- George Street.....729
- Georgian House.....729
- Gladstone's Land.....720
- Grassmarket.....727
- Greyfriars.....726
- High Kirk of St Giles.....721
- history.....712
- Hogmanay.....743
- Holyrood.....723
- Holyrood Park.....725
- Hub, The.....720
- information.....735
- Leith.....732
- Mansfield Place Church.....730
- Mary King's Close.....721
- Museum of Edinburgh.....722
- music, live.....742
- National Gallery of Scotland.....728
- National Monument.....730
- National Museum of Scotland.....726
- National War Museum of Scotland.....719
- Nelson Monument.....730
- New Town, The.....727
- Newhaven.....740
- nightlife.....742
- Old Royal High School.....730
- Old Town, The.....718
- Our Dynamic Earth.....725
- performing arts.....742
- Princes Street.....727
- Princes Street Gardens.....728
- pubs.....741
- Queen's Gallery.....724
- restaurants.....738–741
- Royal Botanic Garden.....731
- Royal Mile, The.....720
- Royal Scottish Academy.....728
- St Margaret's Chapel.....719
- Scotch Whisky Experience.....720
- Scott Monument.....728
- Scottish National Gallery of Modern Art.....731
- Scottish National Portrait Gallery.....730
- Scottish Parliament.....724
- Scottish Poetry Library.....723
- Scottish Storytelling Centre.....722
- shopping.....742
- Stevenson, Robert Louis.....721
- Stone of Destiny, The.....718
- Surgeons' Hall Museum.....725
- Talbot Rice Art Gallery.....725
- theatre.....742
- tours.....736
- transport.....736
- University of Edinburgh.....725
- Writers' Museum.....720
- Zoo.....732

Edradour Distillery.....823
Egglestone Abbey.....570
Eigg.....925
Eilean Bàn.....917
Eilean Donan Castle.....897
Eilean Mor.....848
Eiriosgaigh.....934
Eisteddfod, International Music.....683
Elan Valley.....659
electricity.....47
Elgin.....872
Elgol.....919
Elterwater.....493
Ely..... 364–366
embassies, British.....47
emergencies.....48
English Heritage (EH).....46
entry requirements.....47
Erddig Hall.....684
Eriskay.....922, 934
Esha Ness.....956
Eskdale.....501
Eton.....107
Europaidh.....928
Europie.....928
Eurostar.....30
Eurotunnel.....30
Evie.....943
Ewyas, Vale of.....655
exchange rate.....49
Exeter..... 289–292
Exeter..... 290
Exford.....280
Exmoor..... 279–283

F

Faerie Glen.....922
Fair Isle.....955
Fairy Flag.....920
Fairy Rock.....769
Falkirk.....805
Falkland.....816
Falls of the Clyde.....795
Falmouth.....318
farmers' markets.....51
farmshops.....51
Farne Islands.....594
Farr beach.....905
Fearn peninsula.....909
Felinfach.....652
ferries to Britain.....30
festivals..... 40–42
Fetlar.....957
Ffestiniog Railway.....694
Fforest Fawr.....652
Fiddington.....279
Fife..... 810–818
Fife Coast Path, The.....814
Filey.....547
film..... 983–986
Findhorn.....872
Findhorn Foundation.....873
Fingal's Cave.....836
Fingle Bridge.....304
Finlaggan.....845
Fionnphort.....836
Firth of Clyde.....793
Fishbourne Roman Palace.....173
Fishguard.....642
Fistral Bay.....328
Flamborough Head.....546
Flatford Mill.....343
flights
- from Australia.....29
- from Canada.....29
- from Ireland.....29
- from New Zealand.....29
- from South Africa.....29
- from the US.....29
- within Britain.....31

Flodigarry.....923
Floors Castle.....755
Flow Country, The.....905
food..... 36–38
football.....42
Forest of Bowland.....474
Forsinard.....905
Fort Augustus.....889
Fort George.....883
Fort William.....807, 880, 889
Forth Rail Bridge.....817
Forth Road Bridge.....818
Fortingall.....822
Fotheringhay.....433
Foula.....956
Fountains Abbey.....534

Fowey...314
Fraserburgh...871
Frenchman's Creek...320

G

Gainsborough, Thomas...344
Gairloch...899
Gallanach...925
Galloway Forest Park...764
Galloway, Dumfries and ... 759–766
Galmpton...296
Gardenstown...871
Garenin...929
Garreg Du...659
gastropubs...37
Gateshead...576
gay travellers...47
Gearrannan...929
Gedney...439
Georgeham...307
Gibraltar Point National Nature Reserve...438
Gigha, Isle of...842
Gigrin Farm...659
Glamis...862
Glasgow and the Clyde ... 770–795
Glasgow and the Clyde ... 774
Glasgow ... 772–792
Glasgow ... 776–777
Glasgow City Centre ... 778
Glasgow Boys, The...783
Glasgow Colourists...783
Glastonbury ... 274–276
Glen Affric...888
Glen Brittle...919
Glen Clova...863
Glen Coe...807, 823, 891
Glen Doll...863
Glen Isla...862
Glen Lyn Gorge...282
Glen Lyon...822
Glen Nevis...890
Glen Shee...861
Glen Sligachan...919
Glen Tanar...867
Glenborrodale...894
Glenbrittle...919
Glencloy...844
Glencoe village...891
Glendale...920
Glenelg...916
Glenfinnan...880, 895
Glengedale...846
Glenmore...894
Glenmore Forest Park...884
Glenridding...504
Glenrothes...815
Glentress Forest...758
Glentrool...764
Glorious Revolution...971
Gloucester...251
Gloucester ... 251
Glyderau...689
Glyndebourne...164
Glyndŵr, Owain...672, 965
GMT...51, 103
Goat Fell...844
Goddess of the North...578
Golden Cap...211
golf in St Andrews...813
Golf Museum, British...813
Golitha Falls...335
Golspie...910
Goodrich...391
Goodrington Sands...295
Gordale Scar...528
Gormley, Antony...467, 578
Gosport...179
Gott Bay...840
Gourock...793
Gowbarrow Park...504
Gower Peninsula, The ... 626–628
Grail, Holy...275
Grasmere...493
Grassholm Island...638
Grassington...527
Great British Heritage Pass...46
Great Glen ... 886–892
Great Langdale...493
Great Malvern...387
Great Tosson...590
Greenhaugh...589
Greenway...296
Grimspound...304
Grizedale Forest...497
Grosmont...551
Grosmont Castle...607
guest houses...35
Gurness, Broch of...943
Gwydyr Castle...687
Gwydyr Forest Park...687
Gyllyngvase Beach...318

H

Hadrian's Wall ... 584–587, 962
Hadrian's Wall ... 585
Hadrian's Wall Path...568, 584
Haltwistle...584
Hampshire, Dorset and Wiltshire ... 174–217
Hampshire, Dorset and Wiltshire ... 178
Hampton Court...107
Handa Island...903
Hardknott Roman Fort...501
Hardwick Hall...425
Hardy, Thomas...204
Harewood House...519
Harlech...676
Harlyn Bay...329
Harman's Cross...202
Harnham...212
Haroldswick...958
Harris (Rùm)...923
Harris...930
Harrogate...534
Hartington...408
Hartland...311
Hartlepool...573
Hastings ... 155–157
Hastings, Battle of...157, 964
Hathaway, Anne...381
Haverfordwest...637
Hawes...530
Hawk's Tor...334
Hawkcombe...282
Hawkshead...496, 497
Haworth...524
Hay-on-Wye...656
Haystacks...501
health...48
Hebrides, Outer ... 926–935
Helensburgh...794
Helford...320
Heligan, Lost Gardens of...316
Helmsdale...910
Helmsley...549
Helston...319
Helvellyn...504
Hemmick Beach...316
Henley-on-Thames...223
Henley Royal Regatta...223
Hepworth Gallery...520
Hepworth Museum, Barbara...325
Hereford...389
Herefordshire ... 388–391
Hereward the Wake...364
Heritage Pass, Great British...46
Hermaness...958
Hermitage, The...821
Herriott, James...530, 547
Hever Castle...154
Hexham...587
Heydon Bridge...586
Heysham...475
high commissions...47
High Force...571
Highland Games (Braemar)...868
Highland Region, The ... 874–911
Highland Region, The ... 878–879
hiking...43, 49
Hill House...794
Hill Top...497
Hillswick...956

Historic Scotland (HS) 46
history 961–977
HMS Victory 179
Hockney, David 523
Hogmanay 743
holidays, public 50
Holker Hall 488
Holkham Bay 361
Holmes, Sherlock 304
Holne 304
Holst, Gustav 249
Holy Grail 275
Holy Island (Arran) 844
Holy Island (Northumberland) 595
Holyhead 702
Holyrood 723
Holywell Bay 328
Honister Pass 500
Hood, Robin 419, 424
Hope 411
Hopetoun House 747
Horton in Ribblesdale 529
hostels 35
hotels 34
Houbie 957
Hound Tor 304
House of Dun 860
Housesteads Roman Fort 585
Howe of Fife 816
Howmore 933
Hoy 945
Hoy village 945
Hull 543–545
Humshaugh 586
Hunkin, Tim 351
Hunstanton 362
Hurlers, The 335
Hurworth 573
Hutton le Hole 550
Hynish 839

I

Idwal Slabs 689
Ilfracombe 308
imperial system 49
Imperial War Museum North 452
Inchailloch 808
Inchcolm 747
Inchmahome 809
Industrial Revolution, The 972
information, tourist 51
Ingleton 529
insurance, travel 48
Inveraray 832
Inverarish 918
Inverdruie 885
Inverewe Gardens 900
Inverie 896
Invernaver 905
Inverness 880–882
Inverness 881
Iona, Isle of 837
Ipswich 345
Ireshopeburn 572
Ironbridge Gorge 392–396
Ironbridge Gorge 392
Irvine 769
Islawrdref 675
Islay, Isle of 845–848
Isle of Man 475–481
Isle of Whithorn 765
Isle of Wight 184–189
Isles of Scilly 326

J

Jackfield 393, 394
Jacob's Ladder 273
Jacobites 883, 971, 972
Jamaica Inn 334
Jarlshof 955
Jarrow 584
Jarrow March, The 974
Jedburgh 758
John O'Groats 907
Judge Jeffreys 204
Jura, Isle of 848
Jurassic Coast 211

K

Kame cliffs 956
Keen of Hamar 958
Keith & Dufftown Railway 870
Kelso 755
Keltneyburn 822
Kendal 484–488
Kenmore 822
Kennack Sands 320
Kent Weald, The 152–155
Keoldale 905
Kerracher Gardens 903
Kessock Bridge 885
Keswick 498–500
Keswick 498
Kettletoft 950
Kettlewell 527
Kidwelly 628
Kielder Forest 588
Kielder village 589
Kielder Water 588
Kilburn 548
Kilchoan 836, 894
Killhope Lead Mining Museum 572
Killiecrankie 824
Killin 809
Kilmahog 810
Kilmar 335
Kilmartin 840
Kilmore 917
Kilmory 923
Kimmeridge Bay 201
Kincraig 884
Kinder Scout 411
King Arthur 274, 330, 331
King's Lynn 363
Kingsbridge 298
Kingston Lacy 199
Kingswear 295
Kinloch 923
Kinloch Rannoch 824
Kinlochleven 891
Kintra 846
Kintyre 841
Kintyre, Mull of 843
Kipling, Rudyard 158
Kippford 762
Kirk Yetholm 411
Kirkcudbright 763–765
Kirkstall Abbey 522
Kirkton of Glenisla 861
Kirkwall 943–945
Kirriemuir 862
Kirroughtree 764
Kisimul Castle 934
Kittochside 794
Knap of Howar 948
Knighton 660
Knightwood Oak 193
Knole 155
Knoydart peninsula 896
Kyle of Lochalsh 896, 916
Kyle of Tongue 905
Kyleakin 917
Kylerhea 916
Kylesku 903
Kynance Cove 320

L

Lacock 216
Lairg 910
Lake District, The 484–504
Lake of Menteith 808
Lake Vyrnwy 665
Lake Windermere 490
Lakes, Cumbria and the 482–507
Lakes, Cumbria and the 486
Lamlash 844
Lamphey 636
Lanark 794
Lancaster 473
Land's End 323

Langdale Pikes....493
Langland Bay....626
Langton Matravers....203
Lanhydrock....333
Laugharne....631
Lavenham....344
Lawrence D. H.....324, 422
Lawrence, T.E. (of Arabia)....202
Laxey....477
Leanachan Forest....890
Leaplish Waterside Park....588
Leeds....517–523
Leeds....518
Leeds Castle....154
Leicester....425–428
Leith....732
Lerwick....952–954
Lerwick....952
lesbian travellers....47
Levellers, The....241
Levens Hall....487
Levenwick....955
Leverburgh....931
Lewes....162–164
Lewis, Butt of....929
Lewis....927–930
Lewiston....888
Lews Castle....928
Liathach....899
Lincoln....434–437
Lincoln....435
Lincolnshire....434–441
Lindisfarne....595
Linlithgow....746
Littlehempston....297
Liverpool....462–470
Liverpool....463
Lizard peninsula, The....319–321
Llaethdy....641
Llanberis....689
Llancaiach Fawr....609
Llandaff Cathedral....616
Llandeilo....630
Llandrillo....685
Llandrindod Wells....658
Llandudno....707
Llanerchaeron....668
Llanfair Caereinion....664
Llanfairpwll....702
Llanfihangel-y-Pennant....674
Llanfyllin....665
Llangennith....627
Llangollen....683–685
Llangranog....667
Llanidloes....662
Llanllawen Fawr....698
Llanrhaedr-ym-Mochnant....665
Llanthony Priory....655
Llanwrtyd Wells....657
Llechwedd Slate Caverns....693
Llugwy Valley, The....687
Llwyndafydd....668
Llŷn Idwal....689
Llŷn, The....694–700
Llŷn Ogwen....689
Llŷn Tegid....685
Loch Achray....809
Loch an Eilean....884
Loch Bhasapol....840
Loch Coruisk....919
Loch Duich....896
Loch Eriboll....905
Loch Ericht....823
Loch Finlaggan....848
Loch Fyne....833
Loch Gairloch....899
Loch Garten....886
Loch Gruinart....847
Loch Hourn....896
Loch Katrine....809
Loch Lomond....806–808
Loch of the Lowes....820
Loch Maree....899
Loch Morlich....884
Loch Ness....882, 887
Loch Nevis....896
Loch Ossian....823
Loch Rannoch....824
Loch Seaforth....930
Loch Shiel....895
Loch Shiphoirt....930
Loch Tay....822
Loch Torridon....899
Loch Tummel....824
Lochboisdale....933
Lochinver....903
Lochmaddy....932
Lochranza....845
Loe Bar....320
Loe Pool....320
Logan Rock....323
Lomond Hills....816
LONDON....52–131
Bankside and Southwark....90–91
Bloomsbury and around....75
Central London....60–61
Chelsea to Notting Hill....94–95
City and around....80–81
Greater London....56–57
South Bank....87
West End and Westminster....64–65
accommodation....111–115
airports....108
Albert Memorial....93
Apsley House....93
arrival....108
ballet....130
Bank....83
Bank of England....83
Banqueting House....63
Barbican....82
bars....121–124
Bevis Marks Synagogue....83
Big Ben....66
bike rental....110
Bloomsbury....74
boats, River Thames....104
Bond Street....70
Borough Market....90
Brick Lane market....131
British Library....77
British Museum....76
Buckingham Palace....68
bus stations....109
Butler's Wharf....92
Cabinet War Rooms....63
cabs....110
cafés....115–117
Camden market....131
Camden Town....100
Canary Wharf....86
Cenotaph....63
Changing of the Guard....63
Charing Cross....59
Charles Dickens Museum....76
Cheesegrater, The....84
Chelsea....97
Chelsea, Kensington &....92
Childhood, V&A Museum of....86
Chinatown....72
Chiswick House....105
Churchill War Rooms....63
cinema....128
City Hall....92
City, The....78
Clarence House....69
Clerkenwell....78
Clockmakers' Museum....83
clubs....125
comedy clubs....128
congestion charge....111
Courtauld Gallery....74
Covent Garden....72
Crown Jewels....85
Cutty Sark....102
cycle rental....110
Dennis Severs' House....86
Design Museum....92
Dickens Museum, Charles....76
Docklands....86
Dulwich Picture Gallery....104
East End, The....85
Fleet Street....79
Freud Museum....101
gay scene....126
Gherkin, The....84
Globe, Shakespeare's....89
Golden Hinde....89
Greenwich....102
Guildhall....82
Guildhall Art Gallery....83
Ham House....106
Hampstead....100
Hampstead Heath....101
Hampton Court....107
Harrods....130
Hendon RAF Museum....102
Heron Tower....84
Highgate Cemetery....101
HMS Belfast....92
Holborn....77
Holocaust Exhibition....88
Horniman Museum....104

Horse Guards 63
Household Cavalry museum 63
Houses of Parliament 66
Hoxton 78
Hunterian Museum 78
Hyde Park 93
Imperial War Museum 88
information 111
Jewish Museum 100
John Soane's Museum, Sir 78
Keats' House 100
Kensington and Chelsea 92
Kensington Gardens 93
Kensington Palace 96
Kenwood House 101
Kew Bridge Steam Museum 105
Kew Gardens 106
Kew Palace 106
Leicester Square 71
Leighton House 96
lesbian scene 126
Lloyd's Building 84
London Aquarium 88
London Bridge 83
London Bridge Experience 91
London Dungeon 91
London Eye 88
London Film Museum 88
London Transport Museum 72
London Zoo 100
Madame Tussauds 71
Mall, The 68
Marble Arch 93
Maritime Museum, National 103
markets 131
Marylebone 71
Mayfair 69
Millennium Bridge 89
Monument 84
Mosque, Central 98
Museum of London 82
Museum of London Docklands 86
music, classical 129
music, live 124
National Army Museum 98
National Gallery 59
National Maritime Museum 103
National Portrait Gallery 62
Natural History Museum 97
NatWest Tower 84
Nelson's Column 59
nightlife 124
Notting Hill Carnival 125
Number 10 Downing Street 63
Old Compton Street 72
Old Operating Theatre & Herb Garret 91
Old Royal Naval College 103
Olympic Park 86
opera 129
Orientation 58
Osterley House 105
Oxford Street 70
oyster card 110
Piccadilly 70
Piccadilly Circus 69
Pinnacle, The 84
Portobello market 131
postcodes 112
Proms, the 129
pubs 121–124
RAF Museum, Hendon 102
Regent Street 70
Regent's Canal 100
Regent's Park 98
restaurants 118–121
Richmond 106
Royal Academy of Arts 70
Royal Ballet 130
Royal Collection 68
Royal Hospital 98
Royal Mews 69
Royal Observatory 103
Royal Opera House 74, 130
Saatchi Gallery 98
Sadler's Wells Theatre 130
St Bartholomew-the-Great 79
St Bride's Church 79
St James's 67
St James's Palace 69
St James's Park 68
St Martin-in-the-Fields 59
St Mary Abchurch 79
St Mary Aldermary 79
St Mary Woolnoth 79
St Paul's Cathedral 79
St Stephen Walbrook 79
Science Museum 97
Serpentine Gallery 93
Severs' House, Dennis 86
Shakespeare's Globe 89
Shard, The 90
shopping 130
Shoreditch 78
Shri Swaminarayan Mandir 102
Sir John Soane's Museum 78
skyscrapers 84
Soho 71
Somerset House 74
South Bank, The 87
Southbank Centre 87
Southwark 89
Southwark Cathedral 90
Spitalfields 85
Strand, The 74
Strawberry Hill 107
Syon House 105
Tate Britain 67
Tate Modern 89
taxis 110
Temple 77
theatre 127
tourist offices 111
Tower Bridge 85
Tower of London 84
Trafalgar Square 59
train stations 109
transport 109
travelcards 110
tube, the 109
underground trains 109
V&A 96
V&A Museum of Childhood 86
Velodrome 86
Walkie Talkie 84
Wallace Collection 71
Wellcome Collection 77
Wellington Arch 93
Westminster 58
Westminster Abbey 66
Westminster Cathedral 67
Whispering Gallery 82
Whitehall 62
Windsor 107
Zoo, London 100
Long Mynd 397
Long Sutton 439
Longframlington 590
Longleat 217
Looe 312
Lothians, Edinburgh and the 710–747
Lothians, Edinburgh and the 714
Low Force 571
Lower Diabaig 899
Lowry, L.S. 452
Ludham 357
Ludlow 398
Lulworth Cove 203
Lunan 860
Lundy Island 309
Lybster 911
Lydford 305
Lydstep Haven 634
Lyke Wake Walk 548
Lyme Regis 210
Lymington 195
Lyndhurst 194
Lyness 946
Lynmouth 282
Lynton 281

M

Macbeth 862, 965
Macduff 871
Machynlleth 672
Mackintosh, Charles Rennie 779, 780, 794
MacLellan's Castle 764
Maenporth 318
Maes Howe 942
magazines 39
Magna Carta 964
Maiden Castle 205, 961
mail 48
Malham 528
Malhamdale 528
Mallaig 880, 895, 916
Malmsebury 243
Malt Whisky Trail 869
Malvern Hills 387
Man, Isle of 475–481
Manaton 306
Manchester 446–458
Manchester, Central 448
Manorbier 634
Mappa Mundi 389
maps 49
Margate 140
Market Bosworth 428

markets 51
Marloes 639
Marlow 224
Marston Moor, Battle of 538
Martin's Haven 638
Mary, Queen of Scots 968
Mary Rose 179
Masham 531
Matfen 587
Maughold 478
Maumbury Rings 204
May, Isle of 815
media, The 39
medical treatment 48
Meigle 861
Melkridge 586
Mellerstain House 755
Melrose 753
Melvaig 900
Menabilly House 314
Mendips, The 273
Menteith, Lake of 808
Menteith, Port of 809
Mersey Ferry, Liverpool 465
metric system 49
Mevagissey 316
Mey Castle 907
Middlesborough 574
Middleton-in-Teesdale 571
Mid-Hants Watercress Line Railway 191
Mid-Wales 644–677
Mid-Wales 648–649
Midhowe Broch 947
Midhowe Cairn 947
Midlands and the Peak District, The West 374–413
Midlands and the Peak District, The West 378
Midlands, The East 414–441
Midlands, The East 418
Midlothian 745
Millendreath 312
MIMA 574
Minehead 280
Minffordd 694
Minions 335
Minismere RSPB Nature Reserve 350
Minster of St Cuthberga 199
Miralles, Enric 724
Moaness Pier 945
mobile phones 50
Modern Art Wales, Museum of 672
Monessie Gorge 880
money 49
Monmouth 605
Monmouth Rebellion 204, 277
Monsal Trail 413
Montgomery 662
Montrose 860
Morar 880
Moray 863
Moray Coast, The 870
Moray Firth 882, 885
Morecambe 475
Moretonhampstead 304
Morgan, William 709
Morston 360
Morte Point 308
Mortehoe 309
Morvern peninsula 892
Mount Edgcumbe 301
Mount Grace Priory 548
Mount Snowdon 689
Mount Stuart 832
Mousa 954, 961
Mousehole 322
Muck 925
Muckle Flugga 958
Muddiford 308
Mull, Isle of 834
Mull of Galloway 766
Mull of Kintyre 843
Mullion 320
Mullion Cove 320
Mumbles 626
Muncaster Castle 502
Muness Castle 958
Mynach Falls 672

N

Na Baigh 931
Na Hearadh 930–931
Nàdurra Centre 894
Nant Peris 691
Nantyderry 655
National Army Museum 98
National Assembly, Wales 615
National Botanic Garden of Wales 630
National Coal Mining Museum 520
National Football Museum 451
National Gallery 59
National Gallery of Modern Art, Scottish 731
National Gallery of Scotland (Banff) 871
National Gallery of Scotland (Edinburgh) 728
National History Museum, Wales 617
National Library of Wales 670
National Maritime Museum 103
National Media Museum 523
National Mining Museum, The Big Pit 608
National Museum and Gallery of Wales 614
National Museum of Flight 744
National Museum of Scotland 726
National Museum of Scottish Rural Life 794
national parks 44
National Portrait Gallery 62
National Portrait Gallery, Scottish 730
National Portrait Gallery, Welsh 709
National Railway Museum (Shildon) 569
National Railway Museum (York) 540
National Slate Museum, Welsh 691
National Trust (NT) 46
National Trust for Scotland (NTS) 46
National War Museum of Scotland 719
Needles, The 187
Neidpath Castle 757
Nelson 609
Nene Way, The 433
Nerabus 848
Nether Booth 412
Nether Largie standing stones 840
Nether Stowey 278
Nevis Range, The 890
New Abbey 762
New Forest, The 193–196
New Lanark 794
New Quay 667
Newcastle upon Tyne 574–583
Newcastle upon Tyne 575
Newhaven 740
Newport (Isle of Wight) 189
Newport (Pembrokeshire) 643
Newquay 327–329
Newquay 327
newspapers 39
Newstead Abbey 424
Newton Ferrers 302
Newton House 630
Newton-on-Sea 593
Newton Stewart 764
NHS Direct 48
Niton 187
Noltland Castle 947
Norfolk Broads, The 357
Norfolk Coast Path 338
North Berwick 744
North Kessock 885
North Queensferrry 817
North Ronaldsay 950
North Uist 931
North Wales 678–709
North Wales 682

North York Moors 547–551
North Yorkshire Moors Railway 551
Northampton 431
Northeast England 558–597
Northeast England 562–563
Northeast Scotland 850–873
Northeast Scotland ... 854–855
Northleach 244
Northmavine 956
Northumberland Coast 591–597
Northumberland National Park 588–591
Northwest England 442–481
Northwest England 446
Norwich 352–356
Norwich 353
Noss 953
Nottingham 419–423
Nottingham 420
Noup Head 947

O

Oakham 430
Oban 834
Obby Oss 329
Offa's Dyke 660, 963
Offham 172
Ogham Cross 633
Ogwen Valley, The 689
Okehampton 305
Old Laxey 478
Old Man of Coniston 495
Old Man of Hoy 945
Old Man of Storr 921
Old Sarum 214
Old Scatness Broch 955
Old Trafford 453
Olympic Games (London 2012) 86
Once Brewed 585
opening hours 49
operators, tour 30
Ord of Caithness 911
Ordnance Survey maps 49
Orford 347
Orkney and Shetland 936–959
Orkney 938–950
Orkney 940
Orwell, George 351, 848
OS maps 49
Osborne House 188
Ose 920
Osmotherley 548
Ouseburn Valley 576
Out Stack 958
Outer Hebrides 926–935
Over Stowey 279
Oxfordshire and the Cotswolds 218–253
Oxfordshire and the Cotswolds 222
Oxford 226–237
Oxford 228–229
Oystermouth 626

P

package tours 30
Padarn Country Park 690
Padstow 329
Paignton 295
Painswick 243
Paisley 793
Pallant House Gallery 172
Papa Stronsay 949
Papa Westray 948
parking 33
Parrog 643
Pass of Killiecrankie 824
Pass of Leny 810
passes, tourist 46
passport control 47
Pattinson 584
Peak Cavern 410
Peak District, The West Midlands and the 374–413
Peak District, The West Midlands and the 378
Peak District, The 406–413
Peak District, The 407
Peddars Way 338
Peebles 757
Peel 478
Pembroke 635
Pembrokeshire 634–643
Pen Cerrig-calch 653
Pen y Fan 651
Penally 634
Pendennis Castle 318
Pendrift Common 333
Penmaenpool 675
Pennan 871
Pennine Way, The 411
Penrhyn Castle 704
Penrith 504
Penshurst 154
Pentewan 316
Pentre Ifan 643
Penwith peninsula, The 321–326
Penygadair 675
Pen-y-garreg 659
Pen-y-ghent 529
Pen-y-Pass 691
Penzance 321
Perran Beach 328
Perth 819
Perthshire 818–825
Petworth House 171
Peveril Castle 410
pharmacies 48
phones 50
Pickering 550
Pictish stones 861
Picts, The 852
Pierowall 947
Pistyll Rhaeadr 665
Pitlochry 822
Plas Mawr 706
Plas Newydd (Llangollen) 683
Plas Newydd (Anglesey) 702
Plas-y-Brenin 687
Plen-an-Gwary 324
Plockton 897
Pluscarden Abbey 872
Plymouth 299–302
Plymouth 300
Poldhu 320
police 47
Polochar 933
Polperro 312
Polridmouth 314
Polurrian 320
Polzeath 329
Pontcysyllte Aqueduct 684
Pont-y-Pair Falls 686
Pontypridd 608
Poole 200
Poole's Cavern 409
Poolewe 900
Porlock 281
Port Askaig 845
Port Bannatyne 832
Port Charlotte 847
Port Ellen 846
Port Erin 479
Port Eynon 628
Port Lympne Wild Animal Park 152
Port Mór 925
Port Nis 928
Port of Menteith 809
Port of Ness 928
Port St Mary 479
Portavadie 842
Portchester Castle 182
Porth Beach 328
Porth Clais 641
Porth Neigwl 697
Porthcurno 323
Porthgwidden 325
Porthleven 320
Porthluney Cove 316
Porthmadog 694
Porthmeor Beach 325
Porthminster Beach 325
Portland, Isle of 209
Portmeirion 696
Portpatrick 766

Portree....920
Portsmouth.... 176–182
Portsmouth.... 180
post....48
Postbridge....303
Potter, Beatrix....490, 496
Powis Castle....664
Praa Sands....320
Prestwick, Glasgow airport....767
Prideaux Place....329
Princetown....303
public holidays....50
pubs....38
Puffin Island....701
Pultneytown....911
Punch Bowl....671
Purbeck, Isle of....201
Putsborough Sands....309
Pwllheli....697

Q

Quantock Hills....277
Queen Elizabeth Forest Park....809
Quincey, Thomas De....494
Quiraing....922
Quoyness Chambered Cairn....950

R

Raasay, Isle of....918
Raby Castle....571
Rackwick....945
radio....40
Radnorshire....646
Raglan....606
Ramsey Island....642
Ramsgate....142
Rangers Football Club....786
Rannoch Moor....807, 823, 880
Rannoch Station....823
Ratlinghope....397
Ravenglass....501
Reading....225
Real Ale....39
Red Cuillin, The....919
Redpoint....899
Reeth....532
Reinigeadal....930
restaurants....38
Restoration, The....970
Rhaeadr Valley....665
Rheged....505
Rheidol, Vale of....671
Rhenigdale....930
Rhinns of Galloway, The....766
Rhondda, The....610
Rhondda Fawr....610
Rhossili....627
Rhyader....659
Rhyd Ddu....692
Rhydlewis....667
Ribblesdale....528
Richmond....532
Ridgeway National Trail, The....223, 225
Rievaulx Abbey....549
Rievaulx Terrace....549
Rinsey Head....320
Ripon....533
Road to the Isles, The....895
Rob Roy....808
Robert the Bruce....817, 966
Robin Hood....419, 424
Robin Hood's Bay....553
Rochester.... 137–139
Rock (Cornwall)....329
Rockliffe....762
Rodel....931
Roghadal....931
Romaldkirk....571
Roman Army Museum....585
Roman Baths (Bath)....267
Romans, The....962
Romney and Denge marshes....152
Romney, Hythe & Dymchurch Railway....152
Roslin....745
Ross of Mull....836
Rosslyn Chapel....745
Ross-on-Wye....390
Rosthwaite....499
Rothbury....589
Rotherham....516
Rothesay....832
Rothiemurchus Estate....884
Rough Bounds, The....892
Rough Island....762
Rough Tor....334
Rousay....947
Rowardennan....808
Royal and Ancient Golf Club....813
Royal Deeside....867
Royal Mail....48
Royal Scottish Academy....728
Royal Shakespeare Company....381, 383
Royal Tunbridge Wells....153
Rubha Reidh....900
rugby....42
Rùm.... 923–925
Rushen Abbey....480
Ruskin, John....495, 515
Rutland....430
Rydal Mount....494
Ryde....184
Rye.... 158–160
Ryvoan Pass....884

S

safety....47
sailing....44
St Andrews.... 811–814
St Andrews.... 812
St Asaph....709
St Austell....315
St Bees....503
St Catherine's Point....187
St Columba....837, 887
St Cuthberga, Minster of....199
St Cuthbert....565
St Davids.... 639–641
St Davids.... 639
St Davids peninsula....641
St Dogmael's....667
St Enodoc....329
St Fagans....617
St Ives....325
St John's....478
St Justinians....641
St Just-in-Penwith....324
St Keverne....320
St Lawrence....186
St Margaret's Hope....945
St Mary's....326
St Mawes....319
St Michael's Mount....322
St Neot....334
St Non's Bay....641
St Oswald's Bay....204
Salcombe....298
Salen....894
Salford Quays....452
Salisbury.... 212–214
Salisbury.... 212
Salisbury Plain....214
Saltaire....523
Salthouse....358
Saltram House....301
Sandaig....840
Sanday, Isle of....949
Sandown....185
Sandwich....147
Sandy Mouth....332
Sanna Bay....894
Saunton Sands....309
Saxons, The....962
Scafell Pike....499
Scalloway....954
Scapa Flow....946
Scarborough....552
Scarinish....839
Schiehallion....824
Scilly Isles....326
Scone Palace....819

Scone, Stone of 718, 819
Scotland, Central 796–825
Scotland, Central 800–801
Scotland, Northeast 850–873
Scotland, Northeast 854–855
Scotland, Southern 748–769
Scotland, Southern 752
Scott, Sir Walter 753, 754, 756
Scottish Academy, Royal 728
Scottish Borders, The 750–759
Scottish Crannog Centre 822
Scottish Fisheries Museum 815
Scottish Football Museum 786
Scottish Lighthouses, Museum of 871
Scottish Maritime Museum 769
Scottish Parliament, The 724
Scottish Seabird Centre 744
Scottish Storytelling Centre 722
Scourie 903
Scrabster 906
scrumpy 38
Sculpture Park, Yorkshire 520
Seahouses 594
Seathwaite 499
Seaview 185
Segedunum 583
self-catering 36
Selkirk 756
Senedd, The 615
Sennen Cove 323
Setter, Stone of 948
Settle 528
Settle to Carlisle Railway 529
Seven Sisters Country Park 160
Sevenoaks 155
Sgùrr Alasdair 920
Shaftesbury 207
Shakespeare, William 379–383
Shandy Hall 549
Shanklin 186
Sheffield 514–517
Sheffield 514
Shell Bay 203
Sherborne 206
Sheringham 356
Sherwood Forest 424, 425
Shetland, Orkney and 936–959
Shetland 950–959
Shetland 951
Shildon 569
Showery Tor 334
Shrewsbury 396
Shropshire 391–399
Sidmouth 292
Silbury Hill 216
Simonsbath 280
Simonside Hills 589
Sissinghurst 153
Sizergh Castle 487
Skara Brae 942
Skegness 438
Skenfrith Castle 607
Skerryvore Lighthouse 839
Skipton 526
Skirrid Mountain 654
Skokholm Island 638
Skomer Island 638
Skye 917–923
Skye and the Western Isles 912–935
Skye and the Western Isles 916
Skye and the Small Isles 924
Skye Bridge 896, 916, 917
Slaidburn 474
Slate Museum, Welsh National 691
Sleat 917
Small Isles, The 923–926
Small Isles, Skye and the 924
smoking 51
Smoo 904
Snaefell 478
Snape 348
Snowdon, Mount 689
Snowdonia 685–693
Snowdonia, Central 686
Soar-y-Mynydd 658
Somerset, Bristol and Bath 254–283
Somerset, Bristol and Bath 258
South Devon Railway 297
South Downs National Park 161
South Downs Way, The 161
South Hams, The 298
South Queensferry 747
South Ronaldsay 945
South Stack, Anglesey 702
South Uist 933
South Wales 598–643
South Wales 602–603
South Wales Valleys 607–611
South West Coast Path, The 281, 289
Southampton 183
Southeast England 132–173
Southeast England 136–137
Southern Scotland 748–769
Southern Scotland 752
Southsea 181
Southwold 351
Sparrowpit 411
Spencer, Stanley 224
Spey Bay 872
Spey, River 883
Speyside 869
Speyside Way 872
sports 42–45
Stackpole Quay 635
Stackpole Warren 635
Staffa, Isle of 836
Staffin Bay 921
Staffordshire Hoard, The 401
Staithes 557
Stamford 439–441
Stamford Bridge, Battle of 538
Stanhope 571
Stannersburn 589
Steel Rigg 585
Steeple Point 332
Stein 920
Stenness 942
Stepper Point 329
Sterne, Laurence 549
Stevenson, Robert Louis 721
Steyning 161
Stickle Ghyll 493
Stickle Tarn 493
Stiperstones 397
Stirling 798–806
Stirling, Central 803
Stoke 311
Stoke Bruerne 433
Stoke Fleming 298
Stoker, Bram 554
Stone of Destiny, The 718, 819
Stonehaven 865
Stonehenge 215
Stornoway 927
Stour River Valley 342
Stourhead 217
Stowe's Hill 335
Stow-on-the-Wold 245
Stranraer 766
Stratford-upon-Avon 379–383
Stratford-upon-Avon 380
Strath Tay 820
Strathmore 861
Strathspey 883
Strathspey Steam Railway 884
Strid 526
Stripple Stones 334
Stromness 941
Stronsay 949
Strumble Head 642
student discounts 47
student rooms 36
Studland 203
Studley Royal 534
Sudbury 344
Suffolk coast, The 346–352
Sugar Loaf Mountain 654
Suilven 903
Sumburgh Head 954
Summer Isles, The 901
surfing 44, 310, 627
Surrey 134
Sustrans 43
Sutherland Monument 910
Sutherland, Graham 385
Sutton Bank 548
Swaledale 532
Swallow Falls 687
Swanage 202

Swanpool Beach 318
Swansea 621–626
Swansea 621
Sware Trail 757
Sweetheart Abbey 762

T

Table Mountain 653
Taff Valley, The 608
Tain 909
Talmine 905
Talyllyn Valley, The 674
Tantallon Castle 744
Tarbert (Isle of Harris) 930
Tarbert (Kintyre) 841
Tarka Line 307
Taunton 277
Tavistock 305
Tay Rail Bridge 857
Tay Road Bridge 856
tearooms 37
Tees Valley, The 573
Teesdale 570
Teifi Marshes 666
Teifi Pools 659
Teifi River 666
telephones 50
television 39
Telscombe 164
Temple Newsam 519
Temple Wood stone circles 840
Tenby 632–634
tennis 43
Tennyson Down 187
Tenterden 155
Thanet, Isle of 134
Thirsk 547
Thomas, Dylan 621, 622, 623, 631, 632
Thompson, Robert 549
Threave Castle 763
Three Castles, The 606
Three Peaks Walk 529
Thurso 906
Tiger Bay, Cardiff 614
time zones 51
Tintagel 330
Tintern Abbey 604
tipping 47
Tiree, Isle of 839
Titchwell 362
Tobermory 835
Tobha Mòr 933
Tolcarne Beach 329
Tolethorpe Hall 441
Tolpuddle 205
Tomb of the Eagles 945
Tongue 905
Torosay Castle 835
Torquay 294
Torrisdale beach 905
Totnes 296
tour operators 30
tourist information 51
tourist passes 46
Towan Beach 328
Tower Knowe 588
Traethmawr beach 643
Tràigh Losgaintir 931
trains 30–32
Traquair House 757
travel insurance 48
travellers' cheques 49
Treak Cliff Cavern 411
Trehafod 610
Tremadog 697
Treryn Dinas 323
Tresaith 667
Tresco Abbey Gardens 326
Trethevy Quoit 335
Treyarnon Bay 330
Triscombe 279
Trossachs, The 808–810
Trotternish 921
Trough of Bowland 474
Truro 317
Tryfan 689
Tunbridge Wells, Royal 153
Tweed Valley 753
Tŷ Siamas 675
Tyncornel 658
Tyne Bridge 576
Tynwald 478
Tywi Valley, The 629
Tywyn 674

U

Uffington Castle 225
Uibhist a Deas 933
Uibhist a Tuath 931
Uig 922
Ullapool 901
Ullapool 901
Ullswater 504
Ulva Ferry 836
Unst 958
Upper Wharfedale 527
Urquhart Castle 882
Uyeasound 958

V

Vale of Eywas 655
Vale of Rheidol 671
Vale of White Horse 225
Valle Crucis Abbey 684
Varrich Castle 905
Venerable Bede 584
Ventnor 186
Veryan Bay 316
Via Ferrata, Honister 500
Vidlin 957
Vindolanda Roman Fort 585
Vinquoy Chambered Cairn 949
visas 47
Voe 956
Vyrnwy, Lake 665

W

Wainwright, Alfred 486
Wales, Centre for Alternative Technology 673
Wales, Mid- 644–677
Wales, Mid- 648–649
Wales, Museum of Modern Art 672
Wales, North 678–709
Wales, North 682
Wales, South 598–643
Wales, South 602–603
walking 43
walking maps 49
Wallington 589
Wallsend 583
Walmer Castle 149
Wantage 225
Wareham 202
Wark-on-Tyne 586
Warkworth 591
Wars of the Roses 966
Warwick 383
Wash, The 439
water sports 44
Watercress Line Railway 191
Watergate Bay 328
Wayland's Smithy 225
Weald, The Kent 152–155
Weardale 571
Wells 271–273
Wells-next-the-Sea 360
Welsh Bicknor 391
Welsh Highland Railway 692
Welsh male voice choirs 610
Welsh Wildlife Centre 666
Welshpool 663
Wemyss Bay 793
Wensleydale 530
West Bagborough 279
West Bay 210
West Highland Railway 880
West Highland Way, The 807
West Kennet Long Barrow 216
West Lothian 745
West Lulworth 203
West Mersea 342

West Midlands and the Peak District, The 374–413
West Midlands and the Peak District, The 378
West Somerset Railway 278
Wester Ross 898
Western Isles, Skye and the 912–935
Western Isles, Skye and the 916
Western Isles, The 926–935
Weston Mouth 293
Westray 947
Weymouth 208
Wharfedale 526
whisky 39
Whisky Trail, Malt 869
Whistler, Rex 702
Whitby 554–557
Whitby 555
White Castle 606
White Horse Hill 225
White Horse, Vale of 225
White Scar Caves 530
Whitehall 949
Whitehaven 502
Whitesand Bay 323
Whitesands Bay 641
Whithorn, Isle of 765
Whitsand Bay 301
Whitstable 139
Wick 911
Widecombe 306
Widecombe-in-the-Moor 304
Widemouth Bay 332
Wigtown 765
Wilberforce, William 544
Williamson, Henry 307
Wills Neck 278
Wilton House 214
Wiltshire, Hampshire and Dorset 174–217
Wiltshire, Hampshire and Dorset 178
Wimborne Minster 199
Winchcombe 247
Winchelsea 159
Winchester 189–192
Winchester 190
Windermere town 488–490
Windermere, Lake 490
Windsor Castle 108
windsurfing 44
wine, English 155
Winnats Pass 411
Winsford 280
Winterbourne Steepleton 206
Wistman's Wood 304
Wiveton Hall 359
Wolvesey Castle 191
Woodstock 237
Wookey Hole 273
Woolacombe 309
Wooler 590
Woolstone 226
Worcester 385–387
Worcestershire 385
Wordsworth, William 493, 503
Worms Head 627
Wrekin, The 396
Wroxham 357
Wye River Valley, The (Shropshire) 391
Wye Valley, The (Monmouthshire) 602

Y

Yarmouth (Isle of Wight) 188
Yell 957
Yns-hir Nature Reserve 673
Ynys Enlli 698
Ynys Lochtyn 667
Ynysangharad Park 608
York 536–543
York 537
Yorkshire 508–557
Yorkshire 512–513
Yorkshire Dales, The 525–533
Yorkshire Moors, North 547–551
Yorkshire Moors Railway, North 551
Yorkshire Sculpture Park 520
youth discounts 47
youth hostels 35
Yr Wyddfa 690
Ystradfellte 652

Z

Zennor 324

Map symbols

The symbols below are used on maps throughout the book.

- Metro station
- Bus stop
- Ferry stop
- General point of interest
- Post office
- Internet access
- Hospital
- Tourist office
- Parking
- Campsite
- Battle site
- Golf course
- Ski area
- Whisky distillery
- Abbey
- Ruins
- Museum
- Public gardens
- Statue
- Gate
- Mountain peak
- Hill
- Waterfall
- Gorge
- Cave
- Standing stones
- Marshland
- Lighthouse
- Swimming pool
- Building
- Stadium
- Park
- Cemetery
- Beach
- Wall
- Ferry
- Funicular railway

Listings key

- Accommodation
- Restaurant/café
- Pub/club/live music venue/nightlife
- Shop

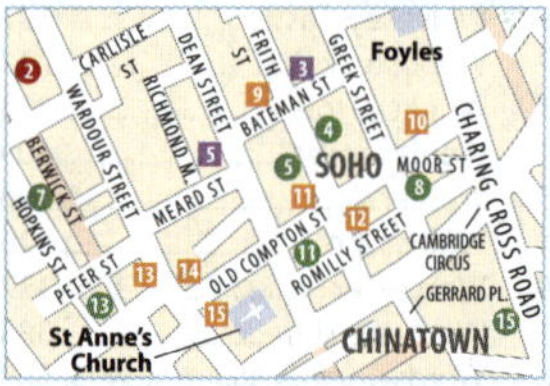

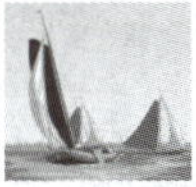

The Perch

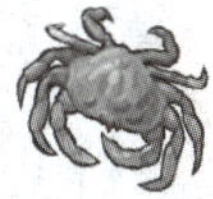

A lovely 1860s stone built town house to rent in the Victorian seaside resort of Ventnor on the Isle of Wight.

Just a five-minute walk to the town centre, seafront and coastal path, The Perch has three comfortable double bedrooms, bathroom with separate shower room, kitchen, lounge and conservatory and garden with spectacular views of Ventnor Downs and the sea.

Ventnor is at the most southern tip of the island, thirty minutes from the ferry port and has an excellent bus service. The climate in Ventnor is mild throughout the year, and has a reputation for being sub-tropical in the summer months.

Whether you want the beach, a walking holiday or just to relax, The Perch is a perfect place to base yourself.

The house is available throughout the year at very competitive prices.

For all details and prices see www.holidaylettings.co.uk/27734 or contact Viv on 01159263872 or 07891455213; viv.mccrossen@hotmail.co.uk

SO NOW WE'VE TOLD YOU HOW TO MAKE THE MOST OF YOUR TIME, WE WANT YOU TO STAY SAFE AND COVERED WITH OUR FAVOURITE TRAVEL INSURER

WorldNomads.com

keep travelling safely

RECOMMENDED BY ROUGH GUIDES

GET AN ONLINE QUOTE

roughguides.com/insurance

MAKE THE MOST OF YOUR TIME ON EARTH™

ROUGH GUIDES

MAKE THE MOST OF YOUR CITY BREAK

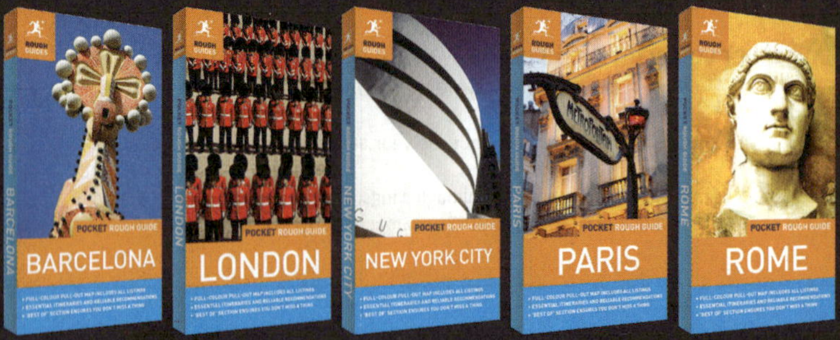

FREE PULL OUT MAP WITH EVERY SIGHT AND LISTING FROM THE GUIDE

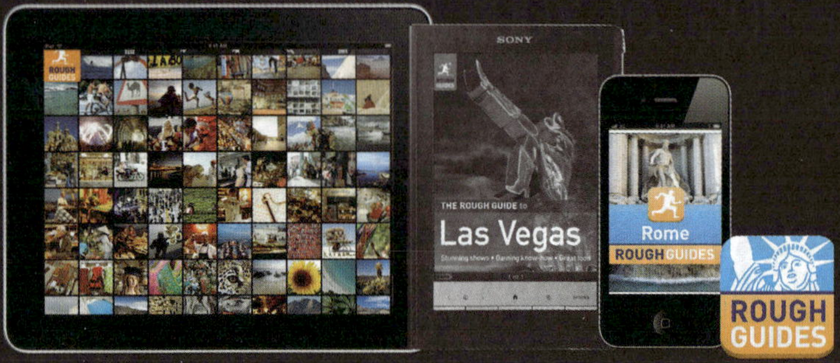

ESSENTIAL ITINERARIES AND RELIABLE RECOMMENDATIONS

BOOKS | EBOOKS | APPS

Start your journey at **roughguides.com**

MAKE THE MOST OF YOUR TIME ON EARTH™